THE UNIVERSAL ALMANAC 1990

Edited by
JOHN W. WRIGHT

ANDREWS AND McMEEL
A Universal Press Syndicate Company
Kansas City • New York

General Editor, John W. Wright
Senior Editor, Lincoln P. Paine

Executive Editor for Science
Bryan H. Bunch, Pace University; President, Scientific Publishing

Consulting and Contributing Editors
Economics: Peter Cappelli, The Wharton School, University of Pennsylvania; Contributing Editor, Allison Paxton Paine
History (U.S.): Stanley Kutler, University of Wisconsin; Contributing Editor, Glen Gendzel
The Media: James Monaco and the staff of Baseline II (Electronic); Mary Quigley, New York University (Print); Contributing Editor, James Pallot, Baseline II
Nations of the World: John L. Connelly, Regis H.S. (Europe); James Malloy, University of Pittsburgh (Latin America); John Major, Historian (Nations of Asia, Africa, and the Middle East); Patricia Szczerba (Statistics)
Sports: David Klatell, Institute for Broadcast Sports, Boston University

Data Entry
Dorothy C. Green, Diane Cavanaugh (DMC Lexicon), Gerri Stanton, Natasha Fried, Tim Gray

Maps
David Lindroth, West Milford, New Jersey

Section Editors
Curtis Church (The Fifty States); Edward J. Dwyer (U.S. Cities and Counties); Sherwood Harris (Education); Lawrence Lorimer (Religion); Sarah Myers (World Geography); Patricia Szczerba, (The United Nations; International Organizations; World Population); Jenny Tesar (Health and Medicine)

Senior Writers
David Brownstone, Irene Franck, Thomas S. Kane, Thomas LaRosa, Stephen Lichtman, Leonard Peters, John Rosenthal

Staff Writers
Charles Epstein, Jerold Kappes, Benedict Leerburger, David Lippman, Eugene McCaffrey, Barbara Mujica, William Mullaney, Charles Myers, Lisa Renaud, Eric Rosenthal, Peggy Rosenthal, Bruce Wetterau, Robert White

Researchers
Richard Carlin, John Donovan, Ben Fischler, William Hubbard, Evelyn Jones, Ralph A. Lee, Paul Miller, David Myers, Dee Shedd

Fact Checkers and Proofreaders
Gretchen Brown, Maureen Chiofalo, Frederica Harvey, Jerold Kappes, David Lichtman

Editorial Director, Donna Martin
Designers, Barrie Maguire, Cameron Poulter

Production Manager
Lisa Shadid

Production Editor
Jean Lowe

Editorial Coordinator/Word Processing
Patty Donnelly Dingus

Word Processors
Kathy Holder, Susan Kyle, Kimberly Ross, Kristen Theus, Connie Turner

Chief Copyeditor
Sharon Boast Wirt

Copyeditors
Leslee Anderson, Barb Glessner, Jane Guthrie

Proofreaders
Elizabeth Andersen, Brooke Fredericksen, Sue Grieser, Jake Morrissey

The manuscript for this book was prepared in electronic form.
Typography by Connell-Zeko Type & Graphics, Kansas City, Missouri.
Printing and binding by The Banta Company/Harrisonburg, Virginia.

ISBN: 0-8362-7977-8 (hd)
ISBN: 0-8362-7949-2 (ppb)
ISSN: 1045-9820

Contents

1992

SEPTEMBER
S M T W T F S

OCTOBER
S M T W T F S

NOVEMBER
S M T W T F S

DECEMBER
S M T W T F S

MAY
S M T W T F S

JUNE
S M T W T F S

JULY
S M T W T F S

AUGUST
S M T W T F S

JANUARY
S M T W T F S

FEBRUARY
S M T W T F S

MARCH
S M T W T F S

APRIL
S M T W T F S

1995

SEPTEMBER
OCTOBER
NOVEMBER
DECEMBER
MAY
JUNE
JULY
AUGUST
JANUARY
FEBRUARY
MARCH
APRIL

1991

SEPTEMBER
OCTOBER
NOVEMBER
DECEMBER
MAY
JUNE
JULY
AUGUST
JANUARY
FEBRUARY
MARCH
APRIL

1994

SEPTEMBER
OCTOBER
NOVEMBER
DECEMBER
MAY
JUNE
JULY
AUGUST
JANUARY
FEBRUARY
MARCH
APRIL

1990

SEPTEMBER
OCTOBER
NOVEMBER
DECEMBER
MAY
JUNE
JULY
AUGUST
JANUARY
FEBRUARY
MARCH
APRIL

1993

SEPTEMBER
OCTOBER
NOVEMBER
DECEMBER
MAY
JUNE
JULY
AUGUST
JANUARY
FEBRUARY
MARCH
APRIL

Obituaries

November 1, 1988–October 10, 1989

Abubakar III, 85, Nigerian potentate and religious leader; sultan of Sokoto, in northern Nigeria, and spiritual leader of the majority of Muslims in sub-Saharan Africa; knighted in 1954. Sokoto, Nigeria, Nov. 1, 1988.

Aflaq, Michel, 79, Syrian Christian who with Salah Baytar founded the Arab Socialist Renaissance (Ba'ath) party in 1934. Paris, June 23, 1989.

Allison, Fran, 81, U.S. singer, who in 1948 became the "Fran" of television's *Kukla, Fran, and Ollie.* Sherman Oaks, Calif., June 13, 1989.

Alsop, Joseph, 78, U.S. journalist, well-known syndicated newspaper columnist whose strong opinions (including his unswerving support of the Vietnam War), made him controversial and widely read. Washington, D.C., Aug. 28, 1989.

Anderson, Forrest, 76, U.S. politician and former Democratic governor of Montana (1969–73) who reformed the state government. By his own hand, Helena, Mont., July 22, 1989.

Anderson, Robert B., 79, U.S. businessman and politician who served as secretary of the navy (1953–54) and secretary of the treasury (1957–61). His otherwise distinguished career was marred by his conviction for tax evasion in 1987, for which he served one month in prison. New York City, Aug. 15, 1989.

Armstrong, Henry (Henry Jackson), 75, U.S. boxer. World featherweight, welterweight, and lightweight champion in 1938, only man to hold three titles simultaneously. Los Angeles, Oct. 24, 1988.

Ayer, A.J. (Alfred J.), 78, British philosopher and author, whose work with the Vienna Circle in the mid-1930s led to his first book, *Language, Truth, and Logic* (1936), his English-language introduction to logical positivism. London, June 27, 1989.

Backus, Jim (James Gilmore Backus), 76, U.S. actor, from 1949 the voice of Mr. Magoo. He also appeared in several television series, including *Gilligan's Island,* and in films. Los Angeles, July 3, 1989.

Ball, Lucille, 77, U.S. actress. After a film career in the 1930s and 1940s, in 1951 she and her husband, Desi Arnaz, began their long-running comedy series, *I Love Lucy,* one of the most successful shows in television history. Los Angeles, Apr. 26, 1989.

Barthelme, Donald, 58, U.S. writer. A leading modern short-story writer and novelist; author of *Unspeakable Practices, Unnatural Acts* (1968) and *City Life* (1978). Won a 1972 National Book Award for a children's book, *The Slightly Irregular Fire Engine.* Houston, July 23, 1989.

Beadle, George Wells, 85, U.S. geneticist. Shared the 1958 Nobel Prize in medicine and physiology for his contribution to understanding the role played by chemical factors in the development of mutations. President of the University of Chicago 1961–68. Pomona, Calif., June 9, 1989.

Berlin, Irving, 101, Russian-American songwriter. Composed over 1,500 songs, including *God Bless America, Always, Blue Skies, Alexander's Ragtime Band, White Christmas,* and *Oh! How I Hate to Get Up in the Morning.* Honored with a congressional medal and presidential proclamation in 1952. Charter member of the American Society of Composers, Arrangers, and Performers (ASCAP); donated copyright—and royalties—of songs to funds in support of Boy Scouts, Girl Scouts, and other charitable organizations. New York City, Sept. 22, 1989.

Blake, Amanda (Beverly Louise Nell), 60, U.S. actress best known for her role as Miss Kitty in the television series *Gunsmoke.* Sacramento, Calif., Aug. 16, 1989.

Blanc, Mel (Melvin Jerome Blanc), 81, U.S. actor, who became the voice of approximately 400 cartoon characters, including Bugs Bunny, Porky Pig, and Woody Woodpecker. Los Angeles, July 10, 1989.

Bolger, William F., 66, American postman, the second career-postal-worker to hold office of postmaster general. As the 65th U.S. postmaster general (1978–84), he led the service to a budget surplus for first time in more than 30 years. Arlington, Va., Aug. 21, 1989.

Branton, Wiley, 65, U.S. lawyer and civil rights leader. Successfully argued the 1957 Little Rock, Ark., school desegregation case; dean of Howard University Law School 1978–83. Washington, D.C., Dec. 15, 1988.

Brickwedde, Ferdinand Graft, 86, U.S. physicist. In 1931, worked with Harold Urey in the earliest measurement of deuterium, a basic element in the development of atomic physics. Bellefont, Pa., Apr. 18, 1989.

Busch, August A., Jr., ("Gussie"), 90, U.S. brewer and businessman who turned a family operation into the world's largest brewing company (Anheuser Busch) and Budweiser into the most popular brand of beer in the world. Bought for the company the St. Louis Cardinals baseball team and several amusement parks. St. Louis County, Mo., Sept. 29, 1989.

Bustamente, José Luis, 94, Peruvian lawyer and politician. President of Peru 1945–48; deposed in a military coup and forced into exile for eight years. Headed the International Court of Justice 1967–70. Peru, Jan. 11, 1989.

Carradine, John (Richmond Reed Carradine), 82, U.S. actor. Shakespearean stage actor but best known for film roles, especially in *The Grapes of Wrath* (1940), and for his scores of villainous roles in Hollywood films. Milan, Italy, Nov. 27, 1988.

Cassavetes, John, 59, U.S. actor and director. Appeared in *Edge of the City* (1957), *Rosemary's Baby* (1968); directed *Shadows* (1960), *Faces* (1968), *Minnie and Moscowitz* (1971), and *Gloria* (1980). Los Angeles, Feb. 3, 1989.

Chapman, Graham, 48, British comic actor; a founding member of the Monty Python group, he was also a Cambridge-educated physician. London, Oct. 4, 1989.

Clubb, Oliver Edmund, 88, U.S. diplomat, teacher, and author. A leading American foreign-service officer in China, 1928–50; became a victim of McCarthyism in the early 1950s; though cleared of all charges, his career was destroyed. Later taught at Columbia University's East Asian Institute. New York City, May 9, 1989.

Collins, Joe, 66, U.S. baseball player. Played first base for the New York Yankees (1948–57) and was a member of six World Series champion teams. Union, N.J., Aug. 30, 1989.

Cowley, Malcolm, 90, U.S. editor, poet, translator. Influenced American literature as literary editor of the *New Republic* 1929–44 and as an adviser to Viking Press from 1948; author of *Exile's Return* (1934). New Milford, Conn., Mar. 27, 1989.

Cyrankiewicz, Josef, 77, Polish politician. Became a Communist while in Nazi concentration camps during World War II; premier of Poland 1947–52, 1954–70. Poland, Jan. 20, 1989.

Dali, Salvador, 84, Spanish artist. Surrealist painter whose hallucinatory style and portrayal of the bizarre, coupled with his genius for self-promotion, made him one of the most controversial figures in modern art. Figueres, Spain, Jan. 23, 1989.

Daniel, Yuli, 63, Soviet poet. Imprisonment, 1966–70, with fellow intellectual Andrei Sinyavsky, generated an international campaign for their release. Moscow, Dec. 29, 1988.

Daniels, Billy, 73, U.S. popular singer. His career began in Harlem in the 1920s; famous for his rendition of "That Old Black Magic" (introduced in 1943). Los Angeles, Oct. 7, 1988.

Dart, Raymond Arthur, 95, Australian–South African physical anthropologist and anatomist. In 1925, discovered 3-million-year-old fossil skull he named *Australopithecus africanus,* calling the species a "missing link" between humans and apes. Johannesburg, South Africa, Nov. 22, 1988.

Davis, Bette, 82, U.S. actress who appeared in almost 100 films. Nominated for an Academy Award a record 10 times (she won twice, for *Dangerous* and *Jezebel);* her most famous films include *Dark Victory, All about Eve,* and *Whatever Happened to Baby Jane?.* Her many honors include the Lifetime Achievement Award of the American Film Institute. Outside of Paris, Oct. 6, 1989.

Dempsey, John Meel, 74, U.S. politician; liberal Democratic governor of Connecticut 1961–71. Kellingly, Conn., July 16, 1989.

Diori, Hamani, 72, nationalist leader in former French West Africa, who became the first president of Niger (1960–74), then being deposed by a military coup and held for 13 years. Rabat, Morocco, Apr. 23, 1989.

du Maurier, Daphne, 81, British novelist. Author of *Rebecca* (1931), made into the classic Laurence Olivier–Joan Fontaine film in 1940, *Jamaica Run,* and *Frenchman's Creek.* Par, Cornwall, England, Apr. 19, 1989.

Furillo, Carl "Skoonj," 66, U.S. baseball player. Star right fielder for Brooklyn and then for the Los Angeles Dodgers 1946–60. Stony Creek Mills, Pa., Jan. 21, 1989.

Giamatti, A. Bartlett, 51, American humanist. Professor of literature; later, president of Yale (1978–86). A lifelong Red Sox fan—"All I ever wanted to be was president of the American League"—was president of the National League (1986–89) and, at his death, commissioner of baseball. Wrote widely on Renaissance literature, the role of the university, and baseball. Martha's Vineyard, Mass., Sept. 1, 1989.

Glushko, Valentin, 80, Soviet engineer. Rocket scientist from the late 1920s; created the rockets that put *Sputnik* into orbit and launched the first intercontinental ballistic missile in 1957. Had primary responsibility for the first manned space station, *Mir.* Moscow, Feb. 1989.

Goldman, Eric Frederick, 73, U.S. historian

and author. Adviser to President Lyndon B. Johnson in the 1960s and author of *Rendezvous with Destiny* (1960) and *The Tragedy of Lyndon Johnson* (1969). Princeton, N.J., Feb. 19, 1989.

Gomez, Vernon "Lefty," 80, U.S. baseball player. Pitcher for the New York Yankees, 1931–42; inducted into the Baseball Hall of Fame 1972. Larkspur, Calif., Feb. 17, 1989.

Graham, Sheila (Lily Shiel), 84, British-American journalist and author. Influential Hollywood gossip columnist. Her highly publicized liaison with F. Scott Fitzgerald was memorialized in her book *Beloved Infidel* (1958). Palm Beach, Fla., Nov. 17, 1988.

Gromyko, Andrei, 79, Soviet political leader. Economist who became a leading diplomat after the Soviet purge trials of the late 1930s; as ambassador to the U.S., he was present at Yalta and a key figure in the founding of the UN. As chief Soviet foreign minister (1957–85), he played a vital role in establishing the policy of détente. Moscow, July 2, 1989.

Harrington, Michael, 61, U.S. socialist and prolific writer on matters of social justice; author of best-selling *The Other America,* which first exposed the depth of poverty in the U.S. and led directly to the federal programs of the sixties. Cochairman of the Democratic Socialists of America. Larchmont, N.Y., July 31, 1989.

Hicks, Sir John, 85, British economist and teacher. Made major contributions to mathematics-based aspects of modern economic theory, especially value theory, public finance, and taxation; was awarded the Nobel Prize for Economics, 1972. England, May 20, 1989.

Hirohito, 87, emperor of Japan (1926–88). Emperor during the rise of Japanese fascism and militarism; functioned as a symbol and figurehead rather than as a ruler, doing little to oppose those who led Japan to invade China and into World War II. Tokyo, Jan. 6, 1989.

Hoffman, Abbie, 52, Yippie leader and anti–Vietnam War activist. Convicted and later acquitted as one of the Chicago Seven after the Chicago Democratic Convention disorders of 1968. In 1980, came out of hiding to face a 1973 drug charge. By his own hand. New Hope, Pa., Apr. 12, 1989.

Hook, Sidney, 86, prominent and influential philosopher; politically active in conservative causes for over 50 years. An expert on Karl Marx, Hook was one of the earliest opponents of Stalin. Although a militant anticommunist whose organization was funded by the CIA, he strongly opposed Sen. Joseph McCarthy. Stanford, Calif., July 12, 1989.

Houseman, John (Jacques Haussman), 86, Anglo-American producer and actor. Partner with Orson Welles in the Mercury Theatre company, and after World War II, a director and producer in Hollywood and the New York theater. In 1960s, returned to acting in film and television; best known for *The Paper Chase.* Malibu, Calif., Oct. 30, 1988.

Hu Yaobang, 73, Chinese politician. Communist from the 1920s, ally of Deng Xiaoping, and reform-minded chairman of the Chinese Communist party; fell from power in the conservative backlash of 1986. His death sparked the huge student demonstrations of 1989. (See "The Year in Review.") China, Apr. 15, 1989.

Hubbell, Carl Owen, 85, U.S. baseball player. Hall of Fame pitcher with New York Giants

(1928–43). In the 1934 All-Star game struck out five Hall of Famers in a row: Babe Ruth, Lou Gehrig, Jimmie Foxx, Al Simmons, and Joe Cronin. Scottsdale, Ariz., Nov. 21, 1988.

Hufnagel, Charles A., 72, U.S. heart surgeon. Invented and successfully implanted the first artificial heart valve (1952) and later helped develop the heart-lung machine. Washington, D.C., May 31, 1989.

Jorgenson, Christine, 62, transsexual. George Jorgenson completed his pioneering sexual transformation by means of surgery in Copenhagen in 1952. She later worked as an entertainer. San Clemente, Calif., May 10, 1989.

Kádár, János, 77, Hungarian political leader, who joined the reformers in 1956, changed sides to join the Soviet invaders, and was premier of Hungary until 1988. Hungary, July 6, 1989.

Karajan, Herbert von, 81, German conductor and a leading figure in German music from 1937. A Nazi party member, he resumed, in 1947, a career that included 30 years of leadership of the Berlin Philharmonic Orchestra. Salzburg, Austria, July 16, 1989.

Khomeini, Ruhollah (Ayatollah Ruhollah Kendi), 86, Iranian religious and political leader. From 1963, led Islamic fundamentalists from exile, returning as the undisputed leader of his country on Feb. 1, 1979, to reverse the course of Westernization pursued by the Pahlevi shahs. Instituted reign of terror that destroyed internal opposition and promoted anti-Western (especially anti-American) terrorism and Islamic fundamentalism. Supported the hostage-taking at the U.S. embassy in Tehran in 1979, encouraged hostage-taking in Lebanon, and pursued the long Iran-Iraq war. In 1989, openly called for the murder of heretical author Salman Rushdie. (See "The Year in Review.") Tehran, June 3, 1989.

Laing, R.D., 62, British psychiatrist whose book, *The Divided Self* (1960) rocked the psychiatric establishment by attributing most psychological torment to the treatment given by psychiatrists. London, Aug. 24, 1989.

Lattimore, Owen, 88, U.S. diplomat, author, and authority on Asia. Editor of *Pacific Affairs* 1934–41 and adviser in China during World War II; in 1950 Sen. Joseph McCarthy destroyed his diplomatic career by falsely accusing him of being a Soviet spy; he was later cleared by a Senate committee. In 1952, indicted for perjury; charges withdrawn in 1955. Wrote of his experiences as a witch-hunt victim in *Ordeal by Slander.* Providence, R.I., May 31, 1989.

Lee, Jennie, 84, British politician. With her husband, Aneurin Bevan, a leader of the Left in the Labour party during the postwar period. Member of Parliament 1928–31 and 1945–70; arts minister, 1964; Labour party chair 1970. London, Nov. 16, 1988.

Leland, George Thomas "Mickey," 44, U.S. congressman from Houston who established the House Select Committee on World Hunger. One of the most prominent black politicians in the House of Representatives, Leland was killed, along with others, when their plane crashed en route to a refugee camp in western Ethiopia Aug. 14, 1989.

Lemnitzer, Lyman Louis, 89, U.S. army officer. Commander of American Mediterranean forces

at the end of World War II; divisional commander during the Korean War; chairman of the Joint Chiefs of Staff 1960–62; Supreme Allied Commander, Europe 1963–69. Washington, D.C., Nov. 12, 1988.

Lillie, Beatrice Gladys, 94, Canadian-British actress. Film, radio, and television comedienne in Britain and the U.S. from the 1920s, best known for her rendition of Noel Coward's "Mad Dogs and Englishmen." One of the best known and appreciated theatrical personalities of her time. Henley-on-Thames, England, Jan. 20, 1988.

Lorenz, Konrad Zacharias, 85, Austrian zoologist and psychiatrist. With Nicholas Tinbergen, developed ethology, the scientific study of animal behavior. Lorenz, Tinbergen, and Karl von Freisch were co-recipients of the 1973 Nobel Prize for Physiology and Medicine. Author of *On Aggression* (1966). Altenburg, Austria, Feb. 7, 1989.

Magnuson, Warren Grant, 84, U.S. politician. Representative (D-Washington) 1937–45, and senator 1945–81. Longtime head of the Senate Appropriations Committee; especially close to presidents Truman and Johnson. Seattle, May 20, 1989.

Mapplethorpe, Robert, 42, U.S. photographer and filmmaker. A major figure in photography. Boston, Mar. 9, 1989.

Marcos, Ferdinand E., 72, Filipino political leader who was president of the Philippines from 1965 until deposed in 1986. Staunch American ally, especially during the Vietnam War; received hundreds of millions of dollars in U.S. aid despite his authoritative regime—including a nine-year period of martial law (1972–81). Widespread government corruption and the assassination of opposition leader Benigno Aquino in 1983 led to large public demonstrations against Marcos, and in Feb. 1986, he and his family fled to Hawaii after a military coup put Corazon Aquino—Benigno's wife—in power. During the last few years, the Filipino and U.S. governments filed lawsuits alleging that Marcos had stolen or embezzled millions on the way to accumulating a personal fortune estimated at $5 billion. Honolulu, Sept. 28, 1989.

Miki, Takeo, 81, Japanese politician. As a member of parliament from 1937, he opposed the growth of Japanese militarism. During the postwar period, held many cabinet posts; deputy prime minister 1972–74; prime minister 1974–76. Japan, Nov. 14, 1988.

Mills, Herbert, 77, U.S. singer. For 50 years, one of the Mills Brothers, a popular vocal group known for their renditions of *Paper Doll, Tiger Rag,* and *You Always Hurt the One You Love;* made more than 2,000 recordings. Las Vegas, Apr. 12, 1989.

Mitchell, John Newton, 75, lawyer. U.S. attorney-general (1969–72) and head of the Nixon reelection campaign involved in illegal wiretapping, harassment of antiwar and civil rights activists, the "dirty tricks" campaign, and the Watergate cover-up. Convicted on Watergate-related charges in 1975; served 19 months in prison. Washington, D.C., Nov. 9, 1988.

Newton, Huey Percy, 47, U.S. political leader; vital figure in the black power movement of the late 1960s and early 1970s. Cofounder (with

Bobby Seale) and defense minister of the Black Panther party; shot to death. Oakland, Calif., Aug. 23, 1989.

Noguchi, Isamu, 84, Japanese-American sculptor and designer. A student of Brancusi; his diverse body of work included major stone sculptures, urban gardens such as those at the Paris headquarters of UNESCO, and theater sets. New York City, Jan. 3, 1989.

Norris, Clarence, 76. Last surviving member of the "Scottsboro Boys," nine blacks falsely accused of rape in Alabama in 1931, generating one of the most notable civil rights cases in American history. After several trials, all nine were imprisoned. Paroled in 1946, Norris moved north, and ultimately gained his pardon in 1976. His autobiography, *The Last of the Scottsboro Boys,* was published in 1979. New York City, Jan. 23, 1989.

Olivier, Laurence, 82, British actor, producer, and director. Considered by most the greatest actor of the century, he was also the first director of Great Britain's National Theatre and an accomplished film director as well. Among his most memorable film roles were Shakespeare's Hamlet and Henry V, Heathcliff in *Wuthering Heights,* and Archie Rice in *The Entertainer,* among a great many more. Steyning, England, July 11, 1989.

Onassis, Christina, 37, daughter of Aristotle Onassis, stepdaughter of Jacqueline Bouvier Kennedy Onassis. Engaged in some philanthropic activities following the settlement of her father's estate in the mid-1970s. Buenos Aires, Argentina, Nov. 19, 1988.

Orbison, Roy, 52, U.S. country music singer. Popular performer and recording artist of the 1950s and 1960s (*Pretty Woman, Crying*); made a comeback in the 1980s. Hendersonville, Tenn., Dec. 6, 1988.

Pepper, Claude Denson, 88, U.S. politician. Senator (D-Fla.), 1936–51, and representative, 1963–89. In the Senate, an outspoken New Deal liberal; as head of the House Select Committee on Aging from 1979, spokesperson for social security and other issues affecting the elderly; from 1983, headed the Rules Committee. Washington, D.C., May 30, 1989.

Philips, Judson, 85, U.S. mystery writer. Under his own name and as Hugh Pentecost, wrote more than 100 mystery novels over seven decades. Sharon, Conn., Mar. 7, 1989.

Radner, Gilda, 42, U.S. actress. In television, theater, and films; created memorable roles for television's "Saturday Night Live." Los Angeles, May 20, 1989.

Richter, Curt Paul, 94, U.S. psychobiologist. Pioneered the study of biorhythms and helped lay the basis of much of modern biomedicine; he introduced the concept of the "biological clock" in 1927. Baltimore, Dec. 21, 1988.

Robinson, Max, 49, U.S. television newsman, who in 1978 became a co-anchor of ABC's World News Tonight, and the first black anchor in network television. Washington, D.C., Dec. 20, 1988.

Robinson, Sugar Ray (Walker Smith Robinson), 67, U.S. boxer—considered by many the greatest of the century. Five-time world middleweight champion and one-time world welterweight champion. Culver City, Calif., Apr. 12, 1989.

Said al-Mufti, 93, Jordanian politician. A leader of Jordan's Circassian community since 1947, he was prime minister four times during the 1950s; thereafter, held a series of positions in government. Jordan, Mar. 25, 1989.

Schiff, Dorothy, 86, newspaper publisher who acquired the *New York Post* in 1939 and served as publisher 1942–76. Credited with keeping the paper afloat by concentrating on human-interest stories, gossip, and scandal. New York City, Aug. 30, 1989.

Scott, Charles S., Sr., 67, U.S. lawyer, who with his brother, John, and Charles Bledsoe in 1951 initiated the landmark school desegregation suit, *Brown* vs. *the Board of Education of Topeka, Kansas.* Topeka, Mar. 3, 1989.

Segrè, Emilio, 84, Italian-American physicist. A Jewish refugee from Italian fascism in 1938, he worked with Enrico Fermi in neutron physics at Palermo University 1928–35; at Los Alamos, codiscoverer of plutonium; with Owen Chamberlain, shared the 1959 Nobel Prize for physics for creating the antiproton concept, confirming the existence of antimatter. Lafayette, Calif., Apr. 22, 1989.

Sendic, Raul, 64, Uruguayan politician, known as "Rufo." Socialist founder of the Tuparemos guerrilla movement in the 1960s; captured in 1970 and imprisoned until the general amnesty of 1985. Went on to lead the Tuparemos as a legal political party. Paris, Apr. 17, 1989.

Shockley, William B., 79, British-born U.S. physicist who shared a Nobel Prize for his work in the development of the transistor. His career was later marred by his controversial theories on race and the genetic transmission of intelligence. Palo Alto, Calif., Aug., 14, 1989.

Simenon, Georges, 86, Belgian writer. Author of over 84 novels featuring the charming Inspector Maigret, 136 other novels, and more than 1,000 novellas, short stories, and essays. His works were translated into 47 languages and collectively sold more than 600 million copies. Paris, Sept. 6, 1989.

Stone, I.F. (Isadore Feinstein Stone), 81, U.S. liberal journalist and author. Washington newsletter, *I.F. Stone's Weekly*—initiated in 1953 at the height of the McCarthy period—became a leading source of investigative journalism for the next 19 years, gaining national prominence as an influential opponent of the Vietnam War. Boston, June 18, 1989.

Symington, William Stuart, 87, industrialist and politician. Held several administrative posts during the Truman years. Senator (D-Missouri) 1953–77; ran unsuccessfully for the Democratic presidential nomination in 1980. New Canaan, Conn., Dec. 14, 1988.

Terry, Bill, 90, U.S. baseball player. First baseman and, later, manager of the New York Giants; hit .401 in 1930; had a lifetime batting average of .341. Member of the Baseball Hall of Fame. Jacksonville, Fla., Jan. 9, 1989.

Thompson, Frank, Jr., 71, U.S. politician and influential member of the House (D-N.J.) for 26 years until he was convicted in 1980 of bribery and conspiracy charges in connection with the Abscam investigation. Baltimore, Md., July 22, 1989.

Thomson, Virgil, 92, U.S. composer and music critic. Best known for two operas (with libretti by Gertrude Stein), *Four Saints in Three Acts* (1934), and *The Mother of Us All* (1947), he received the Pulitzer Prize for his film score to *Louisiana Story* (1948). An influential intellectual figure for over 50 years, Thomson was music critic of the *New York Herald Tribune* 1940–54 and the author of several books, including an autobiography and the *Virgil Thomson Reader,* the latter winning the National Book Award in 1981. Among his many awards and honors were membership in the National Institute of Arts and in the French Legion of Honor; he also received the Kennedy Center Award for Lifetime Achievement. New York City, Sept. 30, 1989.

Tinbergen, Nikolaas, 81, Anglo-Dutch zoologist. With Konrad Lorenz, developed ethology, the scientific study of animal behavior. He, Lorenz, and Karl von Freisch were co-recipients of the 1973 Nobel Prize for Physiology and Medicine. Oxford, England, Dec. 21, 1988.

Truong Chinh (Dang Xuan Khu), 81, Vietnamese politician. Colleague of Ho Chi Minh; a founder of the Communist party of Indochina 1929, and secretary-general in 1941–56 and 1986; a longtime North Vietnamese government official. Hanoi, Oct. 1, 1988.

Tuchman, Barbara, 77, historian and writer. Works include *The Guns of August* (1962), *Stillwell and the American Experience in China, 1911–1945* (1971)—for each she received the Pulitzer Prize—and *A Distant Mirror* (1978). Greenwich, Conn., Feb. 6, 1989.

Vreeland, Diana, née Dalziel, age unknown; American, born Paris, around the turn of the century. A moving force in the fashion world for more than half a century; fashion editor of *Harper's Bazaar* (1937–62) and editor in chief of *Vogue* (1962–71). New York City, Aug. 22, 1989.

Warner, John Christian, 91, U.S. chemist. With the Manhattan Project team, helped develop plutonium. Associated with the Carnegie Institute of Technology for almost four decades; president 1950–65. Pittsburgh, Pa., Apr. 12, 1989.

Warren, Robert Penn "Red", 84, American writer and teacher. Won three Pulitzer Prizes, in fiction for *All the King's Men* (1947), about a populist politician based on Gov. Huey Long; and in poetry, *Promises: 1954–56* (1957) and *Now and Then Poems* (1979). Cofounder and editor of *The Southern Review,* he was the first official U.S. poet laureate (1986–88). Sept. 1989.

Whitley, Keith, 33, U.S. country singer. On stage from the age of 9, and an internationally popular recording artist from 1985. Goodlettsville, Tenn., May 9, 1989.

Williams, Guy, 65, U.S. actor. Starred in the television series *The Mark of Zorro* and *Lost in Space.* Buenos Aires, Argentina, May 15, 1989.

Wilson, Lois Burnham, 97, founder of Al-Anon Family Groups, an organization for relatives of alcoholics. Al-Anon complements the work of Alcoholics Anonymous, founded by her husband, Bill Wilson. Mt. Kisco, N.Y., Oct. 5, 1988.

Yakovlev, Aleksandr, 84, Soviet aeronautical engineer whose YAK-1 and YAK-9 were the mainstays of the Soviet Air Force in World War II. Moscow, Aug. 22, 1989.

Zita of Bourbon-Parma, 96, Habsburg empress. Wife of Charles I, emperor of Austria-Hungary 1916–18. After Charles abdicated, she spent much of the rest of her life attempting to regain her lost throne. Zizers, Switzerland, Mar. 14, 1989.

Late-Breaking News

October

3 A group of Panamanian military officers with the support of about 200 troops attempted to kidnap dictator Gen. Antonio Manuel Noriega, with the intention of turning him over to the United States for prosecution on drug-smuggling charges. After a day of heavy fighting, troops loyal to Noriega succeeded in ending the coup. Pres. Bush denied any U.S. involvement in the incident.

4 As 11,000 more East Germans swarmed into Prague seeking refuge at the West German embassy, the East German government temporarily suspended passport- and visa-free travel to Czechoslovakia. Since May about 37,000 people had left East Germany.

5 The Bush administration acknowledged that U.S. troops had played a role in the attempt to kidnap Gen. Noriega in Panama. At the request of the rebels, the United States blocked two routes thought to be useful to the loyalist forces. (It was later revealed that the U.S. commanding officer in Panama had the president's permission to take Noriega captive if the circumstances were right.)

In Charlotte, N.C., Jim Bakker was convicted on all 24 fraud and conspiracy charges brought by the federal government in connection with the PTL scandal. He could spend the rest of his life in jail and pay $5 million in fines.

7 An estimated 250,000 people marched in Washington, D.C., to protest the plight of the homeless and to demand affordable housing (see the section "The Homeless" on p. 246).

In an extraordinary meeting in Budapest, the Hungarian Communist party voted to change its name to the Hungarian Socialist party and to introduce more democratic procedures for choosing its leadership and formulating policy. In East Berlin, at the end of the 40th anniversary celebration of East Germany's founding, an estimated 5,000 demonstrators marched through the center of the city shouting "Freedom," "We want to stay," and "New Forum" (a new reform group); similar protests had taken place in Leipzig and Dresden earlier in the week, and all were broken up violently by the police.

8 Protesters again marched and demonstrated peacefully in the major cities of East Germany and were again met by violent police attacks. These demonstrations, the largest antigovernment protests since 1953, prompted the government to close its borders to foreign journalists.

In Seoul, South Korea, an estimated 650,000 people attended a mass conducted by Pope John Paul II on the first day of his journey through East Asia.

9 In contrast to the weekend of violence, East German authorities allowed approximately 50,000 people to march peacefully through Leipzig, giving some indication that the gov-

ernment might accept some of the protesters' demands.

10 The Florida state legislature vetoed 10 measures that would have sharply curtailed abortion rights, one of the first major political tests following the Supreme Court's decision to grant states more authority over abortion laws.

South African Pres. F.W. de Klerk announced that the government would release from prison Walter Sisulu and several other leaders of the banned African National Congress. The 77-year-old Sisulu is a longtime friend of Nelson Mandela, with whom he was incarcerated in 1963. De Klerk said he hoped this action would "contribute to the spirit of reconciliation that is presently evident in our country."

11 The U.S. Congress voted to extend Medicaid coverage for abortions to victims of rape or incest, and in a separate judgment, Pres. Bush promised to veto the congressional measures.

12 Scientists at the Stanford Linear Accelerator Center in California and at the European Laboratory for Particle Physics in Geneva announced separately that they had demonstrated with certainty, independently of each other, that the universe contains no more than three fundamental types of matter. This is of great importance to astrophysicists seeking to confirm the theories about the origins of the universe and about its future.

13 Prices on the New York Stock Exchange plunged on a wave of late selling that sent the Dow Jones Industrial Average (see pp. 307–8) to its second largest decline in history, 190.58 points. The largest—508 points—occurred almost exactly two years before, on Oct. 19, 1987.

14 Seeking to assure stability in the nation's financial markets, the Federal Reserve Board announced that it would make money freely available when trading resumed on Monday. In the 1987 crash the lack of cash needed to meet selling demand led to an even deeper decline in stock prices.

Throughout the major cities of South Africa an estimated 150,000 marched to protest apartheid, the single largest protest in the nation's history. The largest—40,000 people—took place in Port Elizabeth.

17 At 5:04 p.m. Pacific time, the second most powerful earthquake in U.S. history devastated the San Francisco Bay Area killing nearly 100 people and injuring more than 2,000. Measuring 6.9 on the Richter Scale, the quake leveled numerous older buildings, buckled highways, split open gas mains starting several significant fires, and caused a 30–foot section of the Bay Bridge's upper level to cave in on the level below. The worst disaster occurred on Interstate 880 (part of the Nimitz Freeway) when the top level of the highway crashed down onto the road below, killing an estimated 50 people. The quake was centered near Hollister, 80 miles southeast of San Francisco. Major damage occurred throughout a seven-county area affecting highly populated centers such as Santa Cruz and San Jose. Shocks from the quake were felt as far away as Sacramento and Los Angeles.

18 On the day following the massive earthquake the Bay Area remained in shock as all businesses and schools were ordered to close so rescue crews and official personnel could continue to search for possible survivors and to as-

sess the full extent of the damage. Fortunately sewer lines and water supply lines were not severely affected and the airport was able to resume service during the day.

NASA launched the Galileo space probe on a six-year journey to Jupiter. Equipped with much more advanced television cameras than Voyager II, the 2.5-ton spacecraft will be the first to probe the atmosphere of one of the outer planets.

NOBEL PRIZES, 1989

Chemistry Thomas R. Cech, Univ. of Colorado, and Sidney Altman, Yale Univ., for discovering (independently) that the substance RNA was not just a passive carrier of genetic information, but could actively aid chemical reaction in cells.

Economic Science Trygve Haavelmo, 77, professor emeritus, Oslo Univ., for his work in the 1940s on the development of econometric models used to prove the validity of economic theories.

Literature Camilo José Cela, 73, of Spain, whose novels, especially *The Family of Pascual Duarte* (1942) portrayed life realistically.

Peace The Dalai Lama, exiled religious and political leader of Tibet, in recognition of his nonviolent campaign to end China's domination of Tibet.

Physics Norman F. Ramsey, Harvard Univ., for the development during the late 1940s and the 1950s of the cesium atomic clock now commonly used to measure the vibrations of atoms.

Hans G. Demelt, Univ. of Washington, and Wolfgang Paul, Univ. of Bonn, for the development of methods to isolate atoms and subatomic particles for detailed study.

Physiology or Medicine Drs. J. Michael Bishop and Harold E. Varmus, Univ. of California Medical School in San Francisco, for their discovery that normal genes can cause cancer when they malfunction through mutation or changes caused by chemical carcinogens.

MAJOR LEAGUE BASEBALL

THE LEAGUE CHAMPIONSHIP SERIES

NATIONAL LEAGUE
S.F. Giants defeat Chicago Cubs
4 games to 1

Game 1	San Francisco 11	Chicago 9
Game 2	Chicago 9	San Francisco 5
Game 3	San Francisco 5	Chicago 4
Game 4	San Francisco 6	Chicago 4
Game 5	San Francisco 3	Chicago 2

AMERICAN LEAGUE
Oakland A's defeat Toronto Blue Jays
4 games to 1

Game 1	Oakland 7	Toronto 3
Game 2	Oakland 6	Toronto 3
Game 3	Toronto 7	Oakland 3
Game 4	Oakland 6	Toronto 5
Game 5	Oakland 4	Toronto 3

Note: See the section "The World Series" on p. 556.

THE YEAR IN REVIEW

Chronology of the Year's Key Events
November 1988

1 Israel's Likud party, led by prime minister Yitzhak Shamir, won a narrow victory in parliamentary elections, beginning a period of negotiations with Israel's far Right and ultraorthodox parties, in an attempt to form a government. Shamir finally reached an accord on Dec. 19 with Labor party leader Shimon Peres, who would serve as finance minister.

2 A computer virus (a set of instructions, hidden in a computer system, that wipes out stored information) designed by Robert Morris, Jr., a Cornell University graduate student, closed down over 6,000 computers and affected many others, such as the Defense Department's Milnet and Arpanet (Advanced Research Projects Agency Network), in the major U.S. computer network Internet.

3 Between 150 and 200 foreign mercenaries made a coup attempt in the Maldives, a chain of small islands in the Indian Ocean approximately 400 miles southwest of India. The attempt succeeded until 1,500 Indian troops, with air and naval support, were flown in to put down the coup on the night of Nov. 3 and the following morning. The mercenaries fled by ship on Nov. 4, taking hostages with them; on Nov. 6, Indian commandos stormed and took the ship. Four hostages were found aboard dead.

Financier Robert Maxwell won his fight to take over the Macmillan Publishing Co.

6 An estimated 1,000 people died when a massive earthquake measuring 7.6 on the Richter scale hit China's Yunnan province.

7 The U.S. Supreme Court, in *Town of Huntington, New York* vs. *National Association for the Advancement of Colored People*, struck down as discriminatory a local ordinance limiting public housing to areas where minorities already resided in large numbers.

8 George Bush won the U.S. presidency (see the section "Presidential Elections") and immediately nominated James A. Baker III as secretary of state.

15 Angola-Namibia Peace Accords. (See "Major News Stories of the Year.")

Palestinian state formed by the PLO. (See "Major News Stories of the Year.")

16 The Pakistani People's party, led by Benazir Bhutto, won a plurality in free Pakistani elections, the first since the August 1988 death of dictator Zia-ul-Haq. Mrs. Bhutto is the daughter of Zulkifar Ali Bhutto, the founder of the People's party, who won the last free parliamentary elections in 1977 but was overthrown later the same year in a military coup engineered by Zia-ul-Haq, and was executed in 1979.

17 Ethnic unrest grew in Yugoslavia; large ethnic Albanian protest demonstrations in Kosovo province, beginning on Nov. 17, generated a counterdemonstration by hundreds of thousands of Serbs in Belgrade on Nov. 19.

18 Former New York congressman Mario Biaggi was sentenced to eight years in prison and fined $242,000 for his involvement in an influence-peddling scheme on behalf of the Wedtech Corp.

21 Canada's Progressive Conservative party, led by Brian Mulroney, swept the Canadian parliamentary elections, winning 160 of 195 seats and ensuring passage of the Canadian-U.S. trade agreement that had been the major issue of the campaign.

Bronx Congressman Robert Garcia, his wife, Jane Lee Garcia, and lawyer Ralph Vallone, Jr., were indicted on charges stemming from the Wedtech scandal.

22 The U.S. Department of Energy, in a trailblazing agreement with the State of Ohio, agreed to clean up environmental contamination at the Portsmouth Uranium Enrichment Complex.

South African Pres. P.W. Botha commuted the death sentences of the Sharpeville Six, a group of five men and one woman who were sentenced to death for circumstantial involvement in the lynching of a black township official, Jacob Dlamini.

Ethnic clashes escalated in Armenia and Azerbaijan; three soldiers were killed, and hundreds of demonstrators injured, while many Armenians fled Azerbaijan. On Nov. 25 the cities of Yerevan and Baku were placed under army rule.

Brent Scowcroft, the former cochairman of the Center for Strategic and International Studies, was nominated U.S. national security adviser by president-elect George Bush.

26 Palestine Liberation Organization leader Yasir Arafat, seeking to visit New York to speak to the United Nations, was denied a visa by the U.S. government.

29 A major cyclone off the Bay of Bengal struck Bangladesh and the Indian coast, killing at least 1,000 and leaving tens of thousands homeless.

Democrat George J. Mitchell of Maine was chosen Senate majority leader.

The reopening of South Carolina's Savannah River nuclear plant, the nation's sole source of tritium, a radioactive form of hydrogen used in nuclear warheads, was delayed because of continuing safety problems. The 36-year-old plant was the subject of an Energy Department project to overhaul operating and safety procedures when unexplained marks and abnormalities were found on two reactors, similar to those on another Savannah River reactor which was shut down permanently in 1984.

The U.S. Supreme Court, in *Arizona* vs. *Youngblood,* ruled that negligent or careless mishandling of evidence by police does not void a conviction, in the absence of police bad faith.

30 The RJR Nabisco takeover battle was won by Kohlberg, Kravis, Roberts, and Co., after a long, bitter contest with its management group; the $25.07-billion company purchase price was the largest in American history.

December 1988

1 Massive structural political changes begin in the Soviet Union. (See "Major News Stories of the Year.")

Benazir Bhutto became prime minister of Pakistan.

Pres. Carlos Salinas de Gortari, at his inaugural, called for renegotiation of Mexico's $104-billion external debt.

2 Five Soviet hijackers seized a bus carrying 30 Soviet schoolchildren at Ordzhonikidze, in the Caucasus; exchanged the children for a cargo plane and $3 million; and were flown to Israel, who let the plane land and then arrested the hijackers, returning them to the USSR on Dec. 3, in an unprecedented display of Israeli-Soviet cooperation.

The U.S. space shuttle *Atlantis,* carrying five astronauts, made a trouble-free lift-off from Cape Canaveral, Florida, at 9:30 a.m., on a military mission that successfully launched an all-weather spy satellite. It returned safely on Dec. 6.

In Argentina 400 soldiers stationed at an infantry school outside Buenos Aires revolted and tried to free several right-wing officers from a military prison nearby. Prodemocracy, progovernment civilian demonstrations followed. The main bulk of the armed forces supported the government, and by Dec. 4, loyal troops had attacked and disarmed the insurgents.

5 The Rev. Jim Bakker, the Assembly of God minister who ran the PTL (Praise the Lord) Corp., and former aide Richard Dortch were indicted on 24 PTL-connected federal criminal counts by a grand jury in Charlotte, North Carolina. Two other former aides, David A. Taggart and James H. Taggart, were also indicted on PTL-connected charges. PTL concerns include a daily talk-show syndicated over hundreds of stations nationwide through the PTL network and a 2,300-acre religious theme-park, Heritage, U.S.A. In 1986 PTL revenues equaled $129 million.

A federal jury convicted the Long Island Lighting Co. of fraudulent rate increase applications because of false statements regarding the opening schedule of the Shoreham nuclear plant, awarding Suffolk County, New York, $22.8 million in damages.

The Rocky Flats, Colorado, nuclear plant reopening was delayed, while a plutonium dust cleanup went on. The plant, operated by Rockwell International Corp., was closed in October 1988 after three persons were exposed to radioactive contamination during an inspection tour.

6 Soviet premier Mikhail Gorbachev began a New York visit with an address at the UN General Assembly, pledging Soviet military cuts; he then met with Pres. Ronald Reagan and president-elect George Bush. He would cut his visit short because of the Armenian earthquake disaster.

7 Armenian earthquake. (See "Major News Stories of the Year.")

11 A Soviet cargo plane carrying rescue workers and supplies to Armenia crashed at Leninikan airport, Armenia, killing 78.

12 Two commuter trains collided in south London, killing 36 and injuring 133.

13 Yasir Arafat addressed a special meeting of the UN General Assembly in Geneva; the meeting was convened after the United States refused to grant Arafat a visa to address the United Nations in New York.

14 The United States agreed to begin talks with the PLO in Tunisia. (See "Major News Stories of the Year.")

In Spain 7–8 million workers mounted a one-day general strike to protest government wage and price policies.

16 John Tower was nominated by president-elect Bush as secretary of defense. (See "Major News Stories of the Year.")

Lyndon H. LaRouche, Jr., an ultraright-wing political organizer who ran for president in the last three national elections, and six associates were convicted on 47 counts of mail fraud and conspiracy by a federal jury in Alexandria, Virginia. On Jan. 27, 1989, LaRouche was sentenced to 15 years in prison; his associates received sentences ranging from 3 to 5 years, plus fines.

18 After 10 weeks of blocking a purchase offer by Grand Metropolitan, a British company, Pillsbury accepted a $66 per share tender offer and was acquired by Grand Met for $5.7 billion. With $6 billion in sales, Pillsbury's leading brands are Green Giant, Jeno's, VandeKamp, Bumble Bee, and Häagen-Dazs, as well as restaurant chains Burger King, Bennigan's, and Steak & Ale.

19 After 50 days without a government, the Israeli Likud and Labor parties agreed once again to form a coalition government, led by prime minister Yitzhak Shamir. Earlier Shamir had tried and failed to form a conservative coalition with the minor religious parties, when their religious demands, especially as to redefinition of *Jewishness*, proved entirely unacceptable to large and influential Jewish groups in the United States, as well as to some in Israel.

In the first Sri Lankan presidential election since 1982, prime minister Ranasinghe Premadasa was elected president. The ballot followed three months of campaign-related violence between Tamils (18% of the population) and Sinhalese (75%). An estimated 700–900 were killed and thousands more injured.

Jack Kemp, formerly a Republican congressman and 1988 presidential candidate, was nominated to head the Department of Housing and Urban Development by president-elect George Bush.

21 Drexel, Burnham, Lambert settlement. (See "Major News Stories of the Year.")

Lockerbie aircraft bombing. (See "Major News Stories of the Year.")

22 After a two-and-a-half-month trial, Bess Myerson, her boyfriend Carl A. Capasso, and former judge Hortense S. Gabel were acquitted of all charges. Myerson had been accused of attempting to use her position as New York City Cultural Affairs commissioner to influence Judge Gabel in a divorce case involving Capasso and had been forced to resign her position because of the accusations.

24 Elizabeth Hanford Dole, wife of Republican senator (Kansas)/Senate Minority Leader Robert Dole, was nominated secretary of labor by president-elect George Bush.

29 Eight sailors died when the freighter *Lloyd Bermuda* sank in a gale off the New Jersey coast.

January 1989

1 The Canadian-U.S. trade agreement reached in 1988 became operational. The pact eliminated most bilateral tariffs over a period of 10 years and some were immediately voided, such as duties on computers, animal feed, leather, whiskey, fur, vending machines, and skis.

A major U.S.–European Community dispute began, over an EC ban on U.S. hormone-treated meat; the U.S. retaliated by placing 100% duties on some European food products.

4 Two U.S. F-14 carrier-based fighters shot down two Libyan MIG-23s in the Mediterranean off Libya. The United States claims their fighters acted in self-defense during a routine flight patrol when the Libyan fighters displayed hostile intent. Libya claims the United States was going to bomb a newly built chemical arms plant.

5 Iran-Contra special prosecutor Lawrence E. Walsh moved to dismiss the main government charges against Oliver L. North, after the White House refused to supply requested documents for trial use. Judge Gerhard A. Gesell dismissed the charges on Jan. 13. (See "Major News Stories of the Year.")

6 The first group of grand jury indictments, against Teledyne Industries and several individuals, occurred in the Pentagon procurement scandal, while Hazeltine Corp. pleaded guilty to procurement-related charges and was penalized a total of $1.9 million.

8 A British Midland Boeing 737 crashed while trying to make an emergency landing near Kegworth, England, about 100 miles north of London; 32 died and over 80 were injured.

10 Cuban troop withdrawals from Angola began. (See "Major News Stories of the Year.")

11 Pres. Ronald Reagan delivered his farewell address.

In a record-breaking antidiscrimination settlement, the Harris Trust and Savings Bank (Chicago) agreed to pay $14 million to settle federal racial and sexual discrimination charges.

13 Bernhard Goetz was sentenced to one year in prison for illegal possession of an unlicensed gun, in the aftermath of his Dec. 22, 1984, shooting of four on a New York subway; in 1987 he had been acquitted of all major charges in the case.

15 Over 1,000 were injured and 170 died in a railway collision of an express train carrying Islamic pilgrims and a mail train at Tongi, north of Dhaka, in Bangladesh.

The Vienna meeting of the 35-nation Conference on Security and Cooperation, consisting of all the European nations but Albania, plus Canada and the United States, signed a major new agreement on human rights to ensure their citizens, among other things, fundamental freedom, equal treatment of men and women, and privacy and integrity of postal and phone communications.

16 Blacks in the Overtown section of Miami began what became three days of rioting, after a Miami police officer shot and killed a black motorcyclist.

17 Five children, all of them Southeast Asian refugees, were murdered in a Stockton, California, schoolyard by Patrick West, using an AK-47 semiautomatic assault rifle; 30 more children and adults were injured in the attack. West then committed suicide.

The Justice Department issued a highly critical report, alleging major violations of federal ethics codes by Edwin Meese III while he was attorney general.

20 George Bush was inaugurated 41st U.S. president.

23 An earthquake in Tadzhikistan, in Soviet central Asia, caused a landslide that killed 274. The U.S. Supreme Court, in *City of Richmond* vs. *J.A. Croson Co.*, invalidated Richmond's affirmative action law, which required that 30% of public works expenditures be with minority-owned companies; it called such programs reverse discrimination unless remedying specific, identifiable acts of discrimination.

24 Serial killer Theodore Bundy was executed in Florida.

30 Disbarred New York lawyer Joel B. Steinberg was convicted of manslaughter in the death of 6-year-old Lisa Steinberg, his illegally adopted daughter, in a child abuse case that had attracted major attention. On Mar. 24 he was sentenced to 8–25 years in prison.

February 1989

2 After 34 years in power, Paraguayan dictator Alfredo Stroessner was deposed in a military coup led by his longtime associate Gen. Andrés Rodriguez, who on Feb. 3 replaced Stroessner as president and commander in chief.

8 A U.S. chartered jet crashed in the Azores killing all 144 aboard, including 137 Italian vacationers and an American crew of seven.

10 Washington lawyer Ronald H. Brown became the chairman of the Democratic National Committee, and the first black to lead a major U.S. political party.

A major Catholic church policy statement issued by the Vatican condemned apartheid, anti-Semitism, and all other forms of racism.

11 In Boston, Episcopal minister Barbara Clementine Harris became the first woman bishop of the Episcopal church and of the worldwide Anglican communion.

14 Ayatollah Ruhollah Khomeini pronounced a "death sentence" on author Salman Rushdie and the publishers of his novel *The Satanic Verses*. (See "Major News Stories of the Year.")

Five Central American presidents, meeting at Tesoro Beach, El Salvador, reached agreement on a draft plan providing for the disarming and dispersal of the Nicaraguan Contras, to be followed by free Nicaraguan elections. Those involved were Oscar Arias Sanchez of Costa Rica, Daniel Ortega Saavedra of Nicaragua, Vinicio Cerezo of Guatemala, José Napoleon Duarte of El Salvador, and José Azcona Hayo of Honduras.

Union Carbide settled the Indian government's Bhopal-related claims for $470 million, ending four years of negotiation and litigation concerning the Dec. 3, 1984, methyl isocyanate gas leak at a pesticide plant that killed between 2,000 and 3,329 and injured 20,000.

15 The last Soviet troops left Afghanistan. (See "Major News Stories of the Year.")

16 The main organizations of the South African antiapartheid movement distanced themselves from Winnie Mandela, after strongly supported allegations that she and her bodyguards had been involved in the murder of a Soweto teenager. She was also publicly criticized by the African National Congress.

18 Former grand wizard of the Knights of the Ku Klux Klan David Dukes was elected a Republican member of the Louisiana state legislature.

21 Dissident Czech playwright Vaclav Havel was sentenced to nine months imprisonment on charges that he participated in a series of banned prodemocracy demonstrations in January. Trials and sentences of other dissidents followed.

23 The Tower nomination was rejected by the Senate Armed Services Committee. (See "Major News Stories of the Year.")

24 Emperor Hirohito of Japan received an elaborate state funeral in Tokyo, attended by scores of major world leaders, including Pres. George Bush. After ruling Japan for 62 years, Emperor Hirohito died on Jan. 7, 1989, of cancer at age 87.

Nine died and 24 were injured when part of the fuselage of a United Airlines Boeing 747 tore off in midair near Hawaii; the pilot, David M. Cronin, succeeded in returning the damaged plane safely to Honolulu.

27 In Venezuela, government-imposed austerity measures aimed to facilitate IMF loan negotiations generated massive riots and a declaration of martial law; 300–600 died and over 1,000 were injured in a week of demonstrations over 30–50% price increases and shortages of basic commodities.

Federal authorities and the state of Washington agreed on a plan to clean up some of the most contaminated areas at the Hanford nuclear plant, near Richland, which has been closed for safety repairs since January 1987.

March 1989

2 In an attempt to preserve the ozone layer, European Community nations agreed to ban production of chlorofluorocarbons by the year 2000.

3 Former National Security Adviser Robert C. McFarlane was sentenced to two years probation and fined $20,000 on charges stemming from the Iran-Contra scandal.

4 Machinists at Eastern Airlines began a strike, shutting down most airline operations. Eastern filed for bankruptcy, but the federal government refused to intervene.

Time Inc. and Warner Communications announced merger plans that would create the world's largest communications and entertainment company, with annual revenues of $10 billion. Time- and Warner-owned enterprises include Scott, Foresman & Co., Home Box Office (HBO), Cinemax, American Television & Communications Corp. (82% ownership), Paragon Communications (50% ownership), Lorimar Telepictures Corp., Warner Cable Communications, Warner Bros. Records, Atlantic Records, Elektra Entertainment, Warner/Chappel Music, Warner Books, DC Comics, and Mad Magazine.

5 Large proindependence demonstrations began in Tibet; the Chinese government imposed martial law on Nov. 7 and sent thousands of troops into Lhasa. An estimated 50–100 were killed and hundreds injured.

6 New East-West arms reduction talks began in Vienna, with conventional arms reduction put forward by both sides.

Afghan rebels began a long-awaited assault on Jalalabad. (See "Major News Stories of the Year.")

Rockwell International was fined $5.5 million after pleading guilty to criminal fraud in connection with its defense contracts.

8 Japanese supertanker *Nissei Maru* accidentally struck and sank a small craft carrying Vietnamese refugees in the South China Sea, killing an estimated 130 refugees.

9 The full Senate rejected the John Tower nomination, 53–47. (See "Major News Stories of the Year.")

13 The space shuttle *Discovery*, carrying five U.S. astronauts, took off from Cape Canaveral, Florida. The shuttle set out to deploy a tracking and data-relay satellite to provide improved contact between orbiting spacecraft and the New Mexico ground station, and to conduct diverse technical and scientific experiments. On Mar. 18, after a successful flight, it landed at Edwards Air Force Base, California.

Federal racketeering charges against the Teamsters Union were settled by an agreement that provided for several union reforms, including direct election of national officers and formation of a permanent board to continuously review union affairs. The case, begun in June 1988, aimed to oust the union's 18-member board and replace it with a government-appointed trustee in order to eliminate Mafia control and influence.

After cyanide was found to have been injected into two Chilean seedless grapes shipped into the United States, the federal government quarantined and forced inspection of all Chilean fruit imports. The ban was lifted on Mar. 17.

California's state assembly voted a ban on the sale, manufacture, or possession of semiautomatic assault rifles; public pressure for the ban had grown after the Jan. 17 Stockton schoolyard murders.

14 Heavy fighting began again between Christian and Muslim forces in Beirut; it would grow into an intensified Lebanon war.

In a major policy change, the federal government indefinitely banned imports of semiautomatic assault rifles.

17 Representative Richard Cheney was swiftly confirmed as secretary of defense by a 92–0 Senate vote, in a process that took only one week. He had been nominated by Pres. George Bush on Mar. 10, the day after the Senate had rejected John Tower.

19 Hard-line rightist Alfredo Cristiani won El Salvador's presidential elections; insurgent groups did not participate in the elections, instead escalating the level of armed violence in the country.

21 The U.S. Supreme Court, in *Skinner* vs. *Railway Labor Executives' Association* and in *National Treasury Employees Union* vs. *Von Raab*, upheld federal compulsory drug testing following railway accidents and for prospective employees of the Customs Service.

23 Ethnic Albanians rioted in Yugoslavia's Kosovo province, beginning a weeklong series of clashes with riot police that left at least 21 dead and hundreds injured.

24 *Exxon Valdez* oil spill. (See "Major News Stories of the Year.")

A Soviet government investigatory commission stated that mass graves near Kiev contained the remains of tens of thousands and perhaps even hundreds of thousands purged during the Stalin period.

26 After a mass escape failed, inmates seized El Pavon prison, near Guatemala City, Guatemala, taking hostages. Seven died and scores were injured during the seizure, which ended on Mar. 30, after negotiation.

Soviet election held. (See "Major News Stories of the Year.")

29 A federal grand jury indicted Drexel, Burnham, Lambert executive Michael Milken and two associates on 98 counts of racketeering, securities fraud, mail fraud, insider trading, and market manipulation, among other crimes. (See "Major News Stories of the Year.")

April 1989

1 SWAPO (South West Africa People's Organization) incursions from Angola were met by South African forces in Namibia, threatening the Namibia peace accords. (See "Major News Stories of the Year.")

2 Mikhail Gorbachev completed the state visits he had been forced to cancel owing to the Armenian earthquake. He visited Cuba Apr. 2–5, reaching only partial agreement with Fidel Castro on substantive issues and no agreement on internal reforms, and visited Great Britain Apr. 5–7.

An attempted military coup began in Haiti, which by Apr. 9 had been defeated by the government forces of Pres. Prosper Avril.

3 Richard M. Daley, Jr., was elected mayor of Chicago, in a vote largely along racial lines.

5 Solidarity and the Polish government reached agreement on Polish reforms, including the legalization of Solidarity and the holding of the first free elections in over four decades.

7 A Soviet nuclear submarine caught fire and sank off Norway; 42 died. No nuclear environmental contamination was reported.

Islamic fundamentalists who favor an Islamic state in Egypt and the implementation of Sharia, or Islamic law, rioted in Fayoum, Egypt; throughout April the Egyptian government responded by arresting at least 1,500 Muslim activists.

9 Washington, D.C., saw a massive demonstration by proabortion forces, as the abortion rights debate grew; estimates ranged from 300,000 to 600,000.

Soviet troops suppressed nationalist demonstrations in Georgia, a southwest Soviet republic; at least 20 died and hundreds were injured. Soviet authorities later affirmed that the troops had made unauthorized use of poison gas against the demonstrators.

Austrian police charged four nurses with the murders of at least 49 elderly patients at Lainz General Hospital in Vienna.

11 To protect the country's fast-dwindling elephant population, and in a policy reversal, Kenya called for a worldwide ban on ivory trading.

12 In the search for missing Texas college student, Mark Kilroy, 12 bodies (including Kilroy's) were found in a mass grave near Matamoros, Mexico; they were allegedly the victims of drug dealers who were also cultist Satan worshipers.

13 The Drexel, Burnham, Lambert case was settled; Drexel would pay $350 million into a fund for those injured by its securities law violations, as well as a $15-million fine. (See "Major News Stories of the Year.")

Two former Teledyne Electronics executives were found guilty on federal criminal charges, in the first criminal convictions to spring from the Pentagon procurement scandal.

15 The beginning of Chinese student demonstrations in Beijing in support of democratic reforms. (See "Major News Stories of the Year.")

At Hillsborough, Sheffield, England, a penned-in soccer stadium crowd stampeded in panic; in the resultant crush, 95 died and hundreds were injured.

17 Speaker of the House James C. Wright, Jr., was charged with ethics violations by the House Ethics Committee. (See "Major News Stories of the Year.")

19 A gun turret explosion on the U.S.S. *Iowa* killed 47. A navy report issued on Sept. 7 called the explosion a deliberate act on the part of a navy gunner, who died in the explosion.

21 A white female jogger in Central Park in New York City was severely beaten and raped by a group of black teenagers, who had earlier attacked others in the park, in a case that attracted a great deal of national media attention.

U.S. Lt. Col. James N. Rowe was murdered by terrorists in Quezon City, near Manila, in the Philippines, while on his way to work; the Communist New Peoples Army claimed credit for the murder.

25 Japanese premier Noboru Takeshita announced his coming resignation, because of his involvement in the Recruit scandal. (See "Major News Stories of the Year.")

Because of pressure from reform forces led by premier Mikhail Gorbachev, 110 members of the Soviet Communist party Central Committee and Central Auditing Commission resigned.

Reports of attacks killing at least 450 Senegalese living in Nouakchott, the capital of Mauritania, triggered reprisals against Mauritanians living in Senegal, where mounting violence caused at least 50 lynchings of Mauritanians.

26 An enormous scandal in the U.S. Department of Housing and Urban Development began to unfold, with release of an internal audit showing abusive practices involving many former Reagan administration figures.

Tornadoes in Bangladesh killed an estimated 1,000, injuring at least 10,000 more, and leaving scores of thousands homeless.

27 The three-astronaut crew of the Soviet space station *Mir* returned to Earth after eight months in space.

28 Fourteen British soccer fans were found guilty of manslaughter in a Belgian court, on charges stemming from the deaths of 39 in the 1985 Heysel stadium riots.

Mobil Oil Co. announced plans to sell its South African operations because of economic considerations stemming from the 1987 U.S. tax law prohibiting Mobil from taking tax credit for taxes paid to South Africa, thus causing Mobil to pay 72% of its profits in taxes.

May 1989

2 Hungary began taking down the 150-mile-long barbed wire fence that stretched along its Austrian border since 1949. Later in the year, a flood of emigrants from the more repressive nations of Eastern Europe, especially from East Germany, poured into Hungary.

An 80-nation UN environmental meeting in Helsinki, Finland, called for a ban on chlorofluorocarbons by the year 2000 and on all ozone-damaging substances as soon as possible.

3 Six South Korean riot police were killed in Pusan when they attempted to rescue five colleagues being held hostage by student protesters at a Pusan university. The students were protesting the arrest of students after police-student clashes.

4 Oliver North was convicted. (See "Major News Stories of the Year.")

The Magellan Venus probe was launched by the space shuttle *Atlantis*.

The 22-mile-long Rogers Pass railroad tunnel through the Canadian Rockies, the longest tunnel in the Western Hemisphere, was officially opened.

7 Elections in Panama resulted in a sweeping majority for democratic forces, led by presidential candidate Guillermo Endarra, as attested to by the Catholic church and a group of international observers that included former U.S. president Jimmy Carter. The forces of Gen. Manuel Antonio Noriega then stole the election, falsifying returns and declaring Carlos Duque president-elect. Facing widespread condemnation for fraud, on May 10 Noriega annulled the election; on that day, opposition candidates were physically assaulted, as well. Although U.S. Pres. George Bush and other world leaders condemned the Panamanian regime and attempted to isolate Noriega, he continued to rule Panama.

9 Reversing a long-held position, the executive committee of the British Labour party favored multilateral rather than unilateral disarmament.

In Guatemala a coup attempt by elements of the air force was suppressed by the army.

14 Carlos Saul Menem was elected president of Argentina, succeeding Raúl Alfonsín.

15 The apple industry announced that it would stop using the chemical alar entirely by the autumn of 1989, after consumers, reacting to adverse publicity about apple growers' use of alar, sharply cut back their purchases of apples and apple-based products.

16 An attempted army coup in Ethiopia failed, as the forces of Pres. Mengistu Haile Mariam successfully attacked the insurgents, who were led by most of the army's general staff. The uprising was precipitated by the army's demoralization and battlefield defeats at the hands of the Eritrean and Tigrean rebels and Mengistu's refusal to consider a negotiated peace.

17 The government of Poland legally recognized the Roman Catholic church.

20 Ethnic Turks rioted against Bulgarian assimilationist policies; an estimated 50–100 died; mass emigration of Turks out of Bulgaria into Turkey followed.

24 Paul Tuvier, a long-sought French World War II war criminal, was captured at the St. Francis Priory, in Nice; he allegedly had been harbored by right-wing French clerics.

25 The Soviet Congress opened; Mikhail Gorbachev was elected Soviet president. (See "Major News Stories of the Year.")

26 House Majority Whip Tony Coelho announced that he would resign as whip and from Congress in order to avoid facing an expected probe into his personal finances.

29 Pres. George Bush proposed cuts in conventional forces at a 40th anniversary summit meeting of the NATO powers in Brussels.

Food riots and looting spread throughout Argentina as inflation worsened; outgoing president Raoúl Alfonsín declared a state of siege.

30 The Warsaw Pact nations proposed conventional forces cuts at continuing East-West arms controls talks in Vienna.

31 House Speaker James C. Wright, Jr., announced his planned resignation as Speaker and from Congress. (See "Major News Stories of the Year.")

June 1989

3 Tienanmen Square Massacre. (See "Major News Stories of the Year.")

Ayatollah Ruhollah Khomeini died; his death was immediately followed by a leadership struggle in Iran. His funeral, on June 5, was attended by an estimated 3 million Iranians, some of whom for a time made it impossible to bury him. The second try at bringing the body to the grave site by helicopter worked, the mourners being driven far enough back for the burial to be completed.

A gas pipeline exploded just as two Soviet trains were passing nearby, on the Trans-Siberian railroad near the town of Ufa, in the Urals, killing an estimated 500 and injuring hundreds more.

In Uzbekistan, a southern Soviet republic, Sunni Muslim fundamentalists began a series of violent attacks on the Meskheian Shiite Muslim minority, which fought back. Soviet troops brought order after nine days of rioting, but an estimated 100–200 were killed and over 1,000 injured.

4 Solidarity swept the first free Polish elections in four decades. (See "Major News Stories of the Year.")

5 The U.S. Supreme Court, in *Wards Cove Packing Co.* vs. *Atonio,* ruled that the burden of specifically proving job-related discrimination rested on the worker alleging discrimination, making it far more difficult to successfully bring such cases against employers.

6 Thomas S. Foley of Washington was elected Democratic Speaker of the House of Representatives, succeeding James C. Wright, Jr.

Paramount Communications launched an attempt to take over Time Inc., upsetting the planned Time-Warner merger, announced on Mar. 4, 1989.

7 A Suriname Airways DC-8 flight from Amsterdam crashed while trying to land in heavy fog near Paramaribo, Suriname, killing 169 of 182 aboard.

10 The Rev. Jerry Falwell announced the dissolution of the Moral Majority, stating that the organization was no longer needed because it had accomplished its goal of getting conservative Christians involved in politics.

12 The U.S. Supreme Court, in *Martin* vs. *Wilks,* ruled that whites claiming reverse discrimination, who had not been parties to affirmative action dispute settlements, could legally attack such settlements as violations of their civil rights, thereby reopening many previously settled discrimination disputes.

13 A minimum wage bill to raise the minimum wage to $4.55 in three years was vetoed by Pres. George Bush; the veto was sustained by the House of Representatives on June 14.

16 Ferenc Nagy, premier of Hungary during the 1956 Hungarian Revolution, and four of his associates, were reburied with honor in Budapest; hundreds of thousands of Hungarians attended, many returning from abroad for the occasion.

20 Former Congressman Patrick J. Swindall was found guilty of perjury by a federal jury in Atlanta in connection with his involvement in a drug-money-laundering scheme in 1987.

The Soviet passenger ship *Maxim Gorky,* with 1,000 aboard, struck an iceberg in the Arctic Sea, north of Norway. A Norwegian coast guard ship rescued all, without serious injury.

21 The U.S. Supreme Court, in *Texas* vs. *Johnson,* ruled that flag burning was protected by the First Amendment, invalidating existing flag desecration laws throughout the United States and generating a storm of protest, which included a June 27 call by Pres. George Bush for an amendment to the Constitution banning desecration of the flag.

22 The UNITA-MPLA truce in Angola. (See "Major News Stories of the Year.")

24 Reformist Zhao Ziyang was removed as general secretary of the Chinese Communist party and denounced; he was succeeded by hardliner Jiang Zemin, the former mayor of Shanghai.

Many other reformist and moderate leaders were also purged.

27 The 1988 illegal lobbying conviction of former White House aide Lynn Nofziger was reversed by the U.S. Court of Appeals for the District of Columbia.

30 The federal government agreed to settle thousands of claims arising from the nuclear contamination caused by the operations of the Fernald, Ohio, nuclear installation that produces nuclear weapons and reactor fuel assemblies, pledging $73 million for these purposes.

In the Sudan a military coup led by army officer Omar Hassan Ahmed al-Bashir overthrew the civilian government of Premier Sahdi al-Mahdi; no casualties were reported.

July 1989

1 Greek conservatives and Communists joined to form a coalition government, led by Premier Tzannis Tzannetakis, and which replaced the eight-year-long socialist government of Andreas Papandreou.

2 An estimated 5,000 Hong Kong citizens, frightened by China's violent suppression of the student democratic movement, and angered by the British refusal to grant them British passports while facing Chinese takeover of the colony in 1997, demonstrated during the visit of British foreign secretary Geoffrey Howe.

3 The U.S. Supreme Court upheld abortion rights limitations. (See "Major News Stories of the Year.")

5 Nelson Mandela and P.W. Botha held a secret meeting in Cape Town, South Africa.

7 Cuban Gen. Arnaldo Ochoa Sanchez and three other Cuban officers were sentenced to death for drug trafficking and related crimes; they were executed on July 13.

8 Pres. Carlos Saul Menem was inaugurated in Argentina, five months earlier than previously scheduled. Former president Raúl Alfonsín had resigned early, finding himself virtually unable to govern as a lame duck in the face of mounting economic problems that had generated mass demonstrations and forced him to declare a state of siege.

9 Pres. George Bush began a four-day visit to Poland and Hungary. In Poland he addressed the parliament, proposing a relatively modest assistance program. The $100-million program, the Polish-American Enterprise Fund, includes broad rescheduling of foreign debt, U.S. support for a $325-million World Bank loan, $15 million for pollution cleanup, and cultural information centers for each country.

10 Soviet coal miners in Siberia mounted a major wildcat strike for improved wages, working conditions, living conditions, and industrial democracy. They were joined by Ukrainian coal miners on July 17. A series of agreements granting better pay and improved living conditions for the miners and full economic and legal independence for the mines ended the crisis in late July, with the Siberian miners beginning to return to work on July 19.

14 The Group of Seven (Canada, France, Great Britain, Japan, the United States, West Germany, and Italy) held its annual economic summit meeting in Paris, coincident with the 200th anniversary of the French Revolution.

19 The tail engine of a Denver-Chicago

United Airlines DC-10 exploded, destroying all three of the plane's hydraulic systems. The pilot attempted an emergency landing at the Sioux City, Iowa, airport and nearly succeeded, but the plane turned over after touchdown, split open, and burned; 111 of the 296 aboard died, and many others were injured.

Gen. Wojciech Jaruzelski was voted president of Poland by the Polish parliament.

24 Premier Sosuke Uno of Japan, embroiled in a sex scandal, resigned after his party lost the elections to the upper house of the diet for the first time in 44 years. (See "Major News Stories of the Year.")

After defeating a Paramount Communications takeover attempt, Time Inc. and Warner Communications were joined, but as a purchase of Warner by Time, rather than as the merger originally planned.

28 Ali Akbar Hashemi Rafsanjani, the speaker of the Iranian Majlis (parliament) and acting armed forces commander, was elected president of Iran.

The Lebanon hostage crisis intensified once again, with the Israeli kidnapping of Sheik Abdul Karim Obeid and the reported murder of U.S. Lt. Col. William R. Higgins. (See "Major News Stories of the Year.")

August 1989

1 The nomination of William C. Lucas—a black Detroit lawyer, former FBI agent, sheriff, and county executive of Wayne County, Michigan—as assistant attorney general for civil rights was rejected by the Senate Judiciary Committee. The committee cited his lack of experience in litigation and civil rights as the reason for the rejection. The NAACP also opposed the nomination.

2 Indictments of 46 Chicago-based commodities traders were announced by the U.S. Justice Department, after a federal investigation lasting two-and-a-half years, in which federal agents often posed as traders and exchange employees. The criminal charges covered a wide range of alleged violations, including several kinds of fraud, tax law violations, and racketeering.

In the days before the Aug. 6 all-white South African parliamentary elections, antiapartheid activists, including Anglican Archbishop Desmond Tutu, began a nationwide civil disobedience campaign, which was met by South African police using whips, dogs, tear gas, and gunfire.

3 Public awareness of the extent of the massive Housing and Urban Development scandal, which had unfolded during the course of U.S. congressional hearings that began on May 11, developed even further with the release of documents showing the extent of the political favoritism involved. Meanwhile, federal investigations and grand jury consideration of 500–1,000 specific potential criminal cases continued.

7 The presidents of Costa Rica, El Salvador, Guatemala, Honduras, and Nicaragua, meeting in Honduras, agreed on a schedule for the dispersal of the Nicaraguan Contras and destruction of their base camps. Their previous meeting was held on Feb. 14, in El Salvador.

Texas Democratic congressman Mickey Leland

and 15 others were killed in a plane crash in Ethiopia, while flying to a Sudanese refugee camp on a famine relief mission.

9 Toshiki Kaifu became premier of Japan, replacing Sosuke Uno, who had been forced to resign because of his sex scandal involvement.

Pres. Bush signed the savings and loan bailout bill into law. (See "Major News Stories of the Year.")

Approximately 150 died and 200 were injured when a train in northern Mexico derailed and fell into a flooding river.

14 South African Pres. P.W. Botha resigned. He was succeeded on Aug. 15 by National party leader Frederik W. de Klerk.

16 Some of the drugs produced by a substantial number of U.S. generic-drug makers were found to be defective by the Food and Drug Administration; the information came as a major scandal developed, involving many generic-drug makers.

17 AZT (azidothymidine) was formally reported by the U.S. Department of Health and Human Services to be capable of delaying the onset of AIDS, for those carrying the virus but not yet afflicted with the disease.

18 Colombian Liberal party presidential candidate Luis Carlos Galan was assassinated, precipitating a hot war between the Colombian government and the drug cartels. (See "Major News Stories of the Year.")

19 George Adamson, the British conservationist who was a main figure in the book *Born Free*, was murdered by Somali bandits at Kora game preserve, in Kenya.

20 A nighttime collision between a barge and a smaller party boat in the Thames, near Southwark Bridge in London, killed an estimated 56 partygoers, injuring many more.

23 Massive nationalist demonstrations in Latvia, Lithuania, and Estonia marked the 50th anniversary of the 1939 Nazi-Soviet pact, which had cleared the way for Soviet annexation of the Baltic countries.

Yusef Hawkins, a 16-year-old black teenager, was shot to death during an unprovoked assault on himself and three friends by a mob of young whites in Bensonhurst, Brooklyn. Five murder indictments quickly followed. The murder touched off a series of demonstrations in which interracial groups marched through Bensonhurst on several occasions, and also became a major factor in the New York mayoralty campaign.

24 Solidarity leader Tadeusz Mazowiecki became premier of Poland. (See "Major News Stories of the Year.")

Cincinnati Reds manager and former playing great Pete Rose was barred from baseball by Major League commissioner A. Bartlett Giamatti, after a long investigation of alleged gambling activities.

25 Voyager 2 reached Neptune, climaxing a history-making flight to the outer planets. During the next three days, before moving on into the regions beyond Pluto, the craft sent back photos and other data that greatly added to existing knowledge of the outer planets. (See "Major News Stories of the Year.")

28 Josef Cardinal Glemp, the Catholic primate of Poland, publicly and sharply attacked

Jewish protesters who during the previous two months had demonstrated against his decision not to honor a 1987 agreement providing for withdrawal of a Catholic convent on the site of Auschwitz, one of the worst Nazi death camps. His remarks, widely viewed as anti-Semitic, were publicly disclaimed by many Polish and Polish-American leaders and were criticized by the Solidarity newspaper. He later canceled a planned trip to the United States.

30 A federal jury in New York City convicted hotel magnate Leona Helmsley (known as the "Queen") on 33 counts of tax fraud, conspiracy, tax evasion, and filing false tax returns.

September 1989

2 Labor Day weekend riots erupted at Virginia Beach, Virginia, as black college students attending the annual fraternity and sorority Greekfest, an event that drew an estimated 100,000, clashed with police and the National Guard. Scores were injured and hundreds arrested.

4 Liberal novelist Wang Meng was dismissed as Chinese cultural minister, in a further indication that the Chinese government was determined to pursue hard-line antidemocratic policies.

A Cuban Airlines crash near Havana claimed 125 lives, most of them Italian tourists.

A Brazilian plane crashed in the Amazonian rain forest, killing eight of the 54 people aboard.

5 Pres. George Bush proposed his promised antidrug program, in a nationally televised address.

6 South African whites returned the National party to power, but with reduced parliamentary representation, as the liberal Democratic party and the right-wing Conservative party both made substantial gains. The segregated elections drew nationwide protests, which were met by police violence; at least 23 demonstrators were killed in and around Capetown alone on Sept. 6 and 7, and hundreds more were injured.

Alleged Colombian drug cartel money-launderer Eduardo Martinez Romero was extradited to the United States. (See "Major News Stories of the Year.")

In Beirut the United States closed its embassy, after Christian demonstrators, encouraged by Gen. Michel Aoun, the leader of the pro-Western Christian army, surrounded the embassy compound.

The trial of TV evangelist Jim Bakker continued, after he had been declared competent to continue with the trial. The proceedings had been halted on Aug. 31, after Bakker suffered a temporary breakdown.

8 Physicians at the Mayo Clinic performed brain surgery on former president Ronald Reagan, who had a buildup of fluid in the brain as a result of a fall from a horse on July 4.

10 An estimated 10,000 East Germans were allowed to leave Hungary across the open Austrian border, despite bitter protests from the conservative East German government. During the days that followed, at least 5,000 more East Germans followed.

12 Manhattan borough president David Dinkins defeated incumbent mayor Edward I. Koch and two other candidates in the New York City

Democratic primary, while former U.S. attorney Rudolph Giuliani defeated Ronald S. Lauder in the Republican primary. Dinkins, if elected, would become New York's first black mayor.

The U.S. House of Representatives passed a bill that would outlaw flag burning.

13 In the first such instance in three years, the South African government of F.W. de Klerk gave official permission for an antiapartheid demonstration; an estimated 20,000 peaceful marchers, led by Archbishop Desmond Tutu, demonstrated in Capetown. On Sept. 15, an equally large and peaceful march took place in Johannesburg.

14 Sam Nujoma, head of the South West Africa People's Organization (SWAPO) returned to Namibia, after 29 years in exile. (See "Major News Stories of the Year.")

18 The world's largest bank, the Dai-Ichi Kangyo Bank of Tokyo, announced plans to pay $1.4 billion for controlling interest in the Manufacturers Hanover unit, the CIT Group, and for 4.9% of Manufacturers Hanover stock. This was the largest investment to date by a Japanese bank in a U.S. financial company.

India agreed to withdraw its 43,000 troops from Sri Lanka by Dec. 31, 1989, thus ending India's involvement in the violent struggle with the Tamil insurgent group. Troops had arrived in 1987 to help control the guerrilla forces of the predominantly Hindu Tamil minority who had been fighting since 1983 for more power from the Buddhist-dominated Sinhalese majority.

19 The Vatican urged removal of the Carmelite convent from the site of Auschwitz, Poland. On Sept. 21 Jozef Cardinal Glemp withdrew his opposition to the move, ending the dispute.

A bomb destroyed a French DC-10 en route from Chad to Paris, in the air over Niger, killing all 170 aboard; Muslim extremists later claimed responsibility for the bombing.

20 At a meeting of the Communist party leadership in Moscow, Pres. Gorbachev ousted five members of the politburo who were believed to be hard-line opponents of his reforms.

22 Hurricane Hugo, carrying 138-mile-per-hour winds, struck Charleston, South Carolina, and adjacent areas, causing enormous damage; tens of thousands were left homeless, power and water were cut in large areas, and an estimated $2–3 billion in damages resulted. The storm had previously struck sections of the Caribbean equally hard, causing tremendous damage and over 30 deaths. Montserrat, Guadaloupe, the Virgin Islands, and Puerto Rico were especially hard-hit; U.S. troops were flown in to St. Croix to suppress looting and restore public order.

In Alton, Texas, a school bus fell into a chasm after being struck by a truck; 19 students were killed and 50 injured.

The Irish Republican Army claimed responsibility for the bombing of a British barracks housing military-band personnel; 10 were killed, 22 wounded.

23 In the deepening HUD scandal, former secretary of Housing and Urban Development Samuel R. Pierce took the constitutional shield of the Fifth and Sixth Amendments in refusing to testify before a House of Representatives subcommittee.

A Christian-Muslim truce arranged by the Arab League brought at least temporary peace to Lebanon.

25 In a speech to the United Nations, Pres. Bush pledged to cut the U.S. supply of chemical weapons by 80% if the Soviets would do the same. The Soviet Union quickly agreed and added proposals of their own.

26 Vietnamese troops completed their final pullout from Cambodia, which braced for renewed civil war between government forces and those of the Khmer Rouge.

27 A sightseeing plane crashed at the Grand Canyon, killing 10 and injuring 11.

(See page viii for late-breaking news.)

Major News Stories of the Year
(Nov. 1, 1988–Oct. 1, 1989)
International

Angola-Namibia Peace Accords On Nov. 15, 1988, Angolan, South African, and Cuban representatives, at meetings in Geneva mediated by the United States and supported by the Soviet Union, reached a series of agreements aimed at ending the 13-year-old Angolan civil war, ending the 22-year-old Namibian war of independence, and withdrawing Cuban and South African troops from the region. Signed by Angola, South Africa, and Cuba at Brazzaville, Congo, on Dec. 13, 1988, the agreement provided for a staged withdrawal of the estimated 50,000 Cuban troops in Angola over a 27-month period, a UN-supervised Namibian transition to independence beginning Apr. 1, 1989, and withdrawal of the estimated 60,000 South African troops in Namibia before scheduled Nov. 1, 1989, elections in that country. It did not provide for a truce between the Angolan government forces of the Popular Movement for the Liberation of Angola (MPLA) and the forces of the National Union for the Total Independence of Angola (UNITA), led by Jonas Savimbi, who vowed to fight on.

The Namibian agreement held, although it was greatly threatened by the movement of South West Africa People's Organization (SWAPO) forces into Namibia on Apr. 1, in violation of the agreements. South African forces quickly struck at the SWAPO groups, decimating them; but the fighting was soon contained, and the independence process continued.

Fighting did not end in Angola until the UNITA-MPLA truce of June 22, 1989, signed by Pres. de Santos of Angola and Jonas Savimbi at Gbadolite, Zaire, under the auspices of the Organization of African Unity and directly mediated by Pres. Mobuto of Zaire and several other African heads of state.

Lockerbie Aircraft Bombing On Dec. 21, 1988, Pan Am Flight 103, a Boeing 747 jetliner carrying 244 passengers and a crew of 15, took off from Heathrow Airport, London, en route to New York's Kennedy Airport. Shortly afterward, while passing over Lockerbie, Scotland, it was blown up in midair by a bomb planted in its luggage compartment by Islamic terrorists.

Part of the resulting debris smashed into the town of Lockerbie, killing 11 on the ground. All 259 of those on the plane were killed. No direct American or British retaliation followed, as the precise identity and location of the terrorists were never determined, even though the PLO offered assistance in finding them. Security measures in international airports were once again declared tightened by the U.S. Federal Aircraft Administration as a result of the bombing. Considerable criticism of the FAA was also voiced for not alerting travelers to the possible risks involved, as telephoned threats and warnings regarding the Frankfurt–London–New York route had been received as recently as Dec. 5, and some U.S. embassies in Europe had allegedly warned their personnel of the threats, while not informing the public.

Ayatollah Khomeini Calls for Murder of Indian Author Beginning in late 1988, Islamic fundamentalists throughout the world battled to ban *The Satanic Verses*, a novel by Salman Rushdie, for its alleged insults to Muhammad and the Muslim religion, beginning one of the most notable censorship controversies of the century. The Indian government responded in October 1988, banning the book, while the campaign against it continued to develop. The campaign soon included public book burning, most notably by Muslims in Bradford, England, in January 1989, a practice abhorrent to most in the West for its identification with Nazi book-burning and Adolf Hitler. On Feb. 12 and 13, police in Pakistan and India fired on anti-Rushdie Muslim rioters; at least nine died.

On Feb. 14 the matter escalated even further, for on that day, Iran's Ayatollah Ruhollah Khomeini pronounced death sentences on Rushdie and the publishers of the book and offered a $1-million reward to Rushdie's murderers. His call to murder was echoed by Islamic terrorist groups in several countries, while the book itself was banned throughout the Islamic world and in South Africa. Bookstores were bombed in London, Los Angeles, Berkeley, Karachi, and several other cities, and demonstrations erupted in New York, London, and many other cities throughout the world.

Initially, some American and British bookstore chains were intimidated by the campaign. But an enraged writing and publishing community, and the powerful movement for freedom to publish and against censorship that very quickly grew throughout the world, forced them to reverse course. The publisher, Viking Penguin, refused to give way, providing security for its people and continuing to reprint and promote the book as it became a worldwide bestseller, despite the fundamentalist campaign. The British government broke relations with Iran over Khomeini's death threat and provided security for Rushdie. Khomeini and his terrorist associates were also condemned by the whole European Community, which also broke relations with Iran, as well as by Canada and many other countries. There were those who, like U.S. Vice Pres. Dan Quayle, called the book offensive, although he also stated that he had not read it; but very few supported the death threats and book burning. Even in the Islamic

world, which had banned the book, there was little support for the fundamentalist death threats. The furor over *The Satanic Verses* had died down by midyear; however, the "death sentence" remained and was restated by Iranian leader Hashemi Rafsanjani on June 22. Rushdie stayed in hiding, while death threats and bookstore bombings continued.

Gorbachev Continues to Make Dramatic Changes in the Soviet Union During 1989 major political changes were introduced in the Soviet Union, following the decisive political victories of Mikhail Gorbachev and his reformers during 1988. On Dec. 1, 1988, the Supreme Soviet, formerly a rubber-stamp body that automatically and unanimously endorsed all party decisions, essentially voted itself out of existence, to be replaced by a body consisting of 2,250 delegates, 1,500 of them directly elected by district and 750 elected by existing Communist party and other organizations, most of them previously dominated by that party. This upper house of the Soviet legislature would in turn elect what were ultimately 542 members of the lower house, which would be the actual working body of the legislature, and would also elect the Soviet president, who would be limited to two five-year terms. Unique in the history of the Soviet Union, elections were to be multicandidate, though not multiparty; however, a loose dissident coalition seeming very much like a nascent second party did later emerge in the new legislature.

All this did come to pass, with the continuing encouragement of the Gorbachev-led Soviet government, which ensured that the new steps toward democracy were carried by Soviet television into every community in the country. The election campaign began in January, with such dissidents as former Moscow Communist party chairman Boris Yeltsin and physicist and human-rights activist Andrei Sakharov both nominated and later elected. The elections, held on Mar. 26, brought many reformers and dissidents into office, and even forced April runoffs in those districts in which unpopular Communist party leaders, often running unopposed, had failed to gain the required 50 percent of the votes cast, many voters simply crossing off their names.

The new Congress predictably elected Gorbachev president, but began a lengthy, spirited criticism of the Communist party leadership, past and present, including Gorbachev. Yeltsin, at first excluded from the lower house (the Supreme Soviet), was ultimately included and emerged as an opposition leader. And the Supreme Soviet, which convened on June 7, was far from a rubber stamp. During its first month of life, it witnessed a walkout by Baltic deputies, several sharp public debates unprecedented in Soviet history, and even more notably, it refused to approve six of the 71 cabinet appointments made by premier Nikolai I. Rhzhkov.

The Baltic deputies' walkout was more than an isolated incident, for Gorbachev's new democracy had encouraged several ethnic groups to voice long-existing concerns and to make new demands. In Latvia, Lithuania, and Estonia, illegally annexed by the Soviet Union before World War II, a powerful independence movement developed and, during the summer and autumn of 1989, moved on a conflict course with the Soviet government, which explicitly stated that it would not consider independence for the Baltic nations. Ethnic unrest also caused demonstrations and in some instances violence in Soviet Armenia, Azerbaijan, Uzbekistan, Moldavia, and Georgia.

Armenian Earthquake On Dec. 7, 1988, while Soviet premier Mikhail Gorbachev was visiting New York to address the United Nations and meet with Pres. Ronald Reagan and president-elect George Bush, a huge earthquake struck Soviet Armenia, killing at least 55,000 people, injuring scores of thousands more, and leaving an estimated 500,000 people homeless. Many villages and towns were almost completely destroyed, including the substantial city of Leninikan, with its population of 290,000. As reported by the Soviet media, many of the worst-hit structures in the region were also the most recently built, attesting to the shoddiness of much recent construction in the area, a fact affirmed by Premier Gorbachev while touring the area after cutting short his New York visit.

For the first time since before World War II, the Soviet Union accepted proffered foreign aid to meet the crisis, further demonstrating the will of its leaders to bring the country into the international community. Emergency aid came from many nations and private sources and in a wide variety of forms, including disaster relief teams, aircraft, medical supplies, food, clothing, cash, and equipment.

Solidarity Triumphs in Poland Political change in Poland began in earnest on Jan. 18, 1989, with a highly conditional government offer to legalize Solidarity. Then followed months of negotiations, ending with the historic Apr. 5 agreements to restructure the Polish political system along democratic lines, hold free elections, legalize Solidarity, create free organs of expression, and develop a more independent judiciary. These agreements generated the free elections of June 4 and the runoff elections of June 18 from which Solidarity emerged the majority party, which as of Aug. 24 officially led Poland.

Climaxing this extraordinary reversal of fortunes, on Aug. 24, 1989, Catholic Solidarity leader and journalist Tadeusz Mazowiecki became premier of Poland. The triumph of the previously outlawed Solidarity movement came within the new communist world atmosphere generated by the coming of Mikhail Gorbachev's *glasnost* and *perestroika* to the Soviet Union. It also included a direct Gorbachev assist, in the form of an 11th-hour, 40-minute telephone call from Gorbachev to Polish Communist leader Mieczyslaw Rakowski, followed by a United Workers party agreement to participate in the new government. The new Solidarity-led Polish government became the first fully democratic Eastern European government in four decades.

Soviet Troops Leave Afghanistan; Civil War Continues The last contingent of Soviet troops left Afghanistan on Feb. 15, 1989, ending over nine years of involvement in what began as a civil war, became largely a war between Soviet forces and Mujaheddin guerrilla forces, and was now once again a civil war.

When the Soviets left, most observers did not expect Afghan government forces to survive for very long. Mujaheddin forces surrounded both Kabul and Jalalabad and were within striking distance of other major cities, while government forces were thought to be demoralized and ineffective. As it turned out, insurgent forces besieged Jalalabad for five months but could not take the city, while the forces around Kabul erratically bombarded but did not even attack the city. Mujaheddin forces were divided, with both regional rivalries and fundamentalist-moderate splits making it very difficult to unite and win against well-equipped government forces. As the war dragged on in its 10th year, the government still controlled the major cities, and the Mujaheddin the countryside.

Lebanese War Intensifies On Mar. 14 the Lebanese army, led by Gen. Michel Aoun, began a direct attempt to end the 14-year-old Lebanese civil war by interdicting the flow of arms and supplies to Muslim forces through the Muslim-controlled ports and with the announced intention of driving Syrian forces from Lebanon. Syrian and other Muslim forces responded with a powerful, months-long bombardment of the Christian-held portions of Beirut, which generated counterbombardment by Christian forces. By late August the constant shelling, broken only by a three-week truce in May and early June, had driven out an estimated 1 million of the 1.5 million left in the city and turned much of what was left of Beirut into rubble. In mid-August, Syrian troops and their Muslim allies for the first time also mounted ground attacks on Christian forces entrenched in mountain positions near Beirut. By early autumn at least 1,000 more were dead and thousands more injured, as the civil war moved into its 15th year.

Chinese Student Demonstrations End in Bloodbath On Apr. 15, 1989, following the death of democratic reformer Hu Yaobang, Chinese students began memorial demonstrations in his honor. These soon swelled into more general, entirely peaceful prodemocracy meetings, marches, and demonstrations in Shanghai, Beijing, and many other cities. By Apr. 18 the demonstrations in Beijing had centered on Tienanmen Square and were swelling in size. On Apr. 20 the government publicly demanded an end to the demonstrations, threatening police action, whereupon Chinese and, to a lesser extent, worldwide media began to pay attention to the developing crisis.

During the next several days, the demonstrations grew, fueled by increasing government threats, coupled with inaction, and by the growing perception that deep divisions over how to handle the protests were immobilizing the Chinese Communist leadership; two factions emerged, led respectively by Li Peng and Zhao Zhiang. The students, from Apr. 24 boycotting Beijing University classes, were now supported by teachers, journalists, workers, and large sections of the population of Beijing and were holding demonstrations and marches involving hundreds of thousands.

On the anniversary of the May 4th Movement, hundreds of thousands of demonstrators appeared in many cities. The government agreed to talk with the students, later broadcasting the meeting on Chinese television, but it remained intransigent regarding the students' demands for a more open democractic government.

On May 13 prodemocracy students began a hunger strike in Tienanmen Square. On May 15 Soviet Premier Mikhail Gorbachev arrived in Beijing for a state visit aimed at normalizing previously bitter Chinese-Soviet relations, the first such Soviet visit in 30 years. With him came a major portion of the international press corps. Greeting Gorbachev and the press were an estimated 150,000–200,000 still entirely peaceful prodemocracy demonstrators in Tienanmen Square, most of them from Beijing but many from other cities as well. For the international press, the demonstrations immediately became one of the major stories of the decade; for the Chinese government, the demonstrations became a tremendous international embarrassment, while the foreign media's beaming of reports back into China spread the story throughout much of the country, stimulating other, smaller protests, some of them turning violent.

On May 17 an estimated 1 million Chinese peacefully demonstrated for democratic reform in Tienanmen Square, while the whole world watched and kept on watching. On May 18 they were visited by the leader of the prodemocratic group in the Chinese leadership, Zhao Zhiang. On the night of May 20, Li Peng declared martial law and attempted to move troops into the city. The troops proved less than willing to move against the more than 1 million residents of Beijing who peacefully blocked their way. Massive protests developed in many other Chinese cities, and even in Hong Kong.

The Tienanmen Square demonstrations continued but diminished during the next two weeks, while the Communist leadership struggle dragged on and was finally resolved in favor of the hard-line faction, led by Li Peng and with the full support of Deng Xiaoping. On May 29 the students in the square erected a statue symbolizing democracy and much resembling the American Statue of Liberty.

On the night of June 4, after earlier unsuccessful government efforts to clear the square with minimal violence, People's Liberation Army units, numbering in the thousands and including columns of tanks, attacked some tens of thousands of demonstrators in Tienanmen Square, in many instances firing point-blank into crowds of unarmed demonstrators attempting to leave the square. At least many hundreds and in all probability 3,000–5,000 demonstrators were killed and many thousands more injured. Some demonstrators fought back with sticks and paving stones; a small number of soldiers were killed or wounded, a few of them lynched by the demonstrators. The Chinese government later denied that anyone had been killed that night, then claimed that a few had been killed, most of them soldiers.

China then took an enormous leap backward in an attempt to destroy all traces of the prodemocracy movement and without regard for the international condemnation that followed the Tienanmen Square massacre. Zhao Zhiang was entirely discredited; widespread arrests were followed by quick sentences and in some instances by summary executions. The government officially announced several dozen executions in the months that followed; Amnesty International and other observers indicated that many secret trials and executions had also taken place. The foreign press was banned, the Chinese media became purely an instrument of government propaganda, and China, at least in the months following the massacre, became once again a hard-line totalitarian state.

Japan's Recruit Stock Scandal Topples Government On Apr. 25, 1989, Japanese Premier Noboru Takeshita resigned after a series of revelations linking him to the Recruit stock scandal, which had involved leading circles in the long-ruling Liberal Democratic party with the activities of the Recruit Cosmos Realty Co. in such matters as the acceptance of direct payments, loans, insider stock, and massive direct campaign contributions. The Recruit scandal became public in July 1988; by the time of Takeshita's resignation announcement, it had forced three cabinet-level resignations and generated what ultimately became a score of arrests. On Apr. 26, after Takeshita's resignation, an aide, Ihei Aoki, who had been implicated in several Recruit-Takeshita financial arrangements, committed suicide. Former premier Yasuhiro Nakasone was also involved, on May 28 announcing his resignation from the Liberal Democratic party as an act of atonement.

In a factually unrelated scandal, but one that may have surfaced largely because of the atmosphere created by the Recruit affair, Takeshita's successor, Sosuke Uno, who had become premier on June 2, was forced to resign after only two months in office, after a sex scandal. He was replaced on Aug. 9 by Toshiki Kaifu.

Lebanon Hostage Crisis Continues; Col. Higgins Murdered The smoldering Lebanon hostage situation suddenly became a major crisis once again in late July after Israeli commandos kidnapped Hezbollah leader Sheikh Abdul Karim Obeid from his home in Lebanon in an attempt to barter him for three Israeli military prisoners held in Lebanon since 1986. In response the Hezbollah terrorist organization holding UN observer U.S. Marine Lt. Col. William R. Higgins threatened to immediately murder him if Obeid was not immediately released.

Although initial American and British reaction to the Israeli kidnapping was sharply negative, no resolution of the situation was immediately effected. On July 31 the Hezbollah terrorists released a videotape purporting to show Higgins hanged, while the terrorists

holding American hostage Joseph James Cicippio threatened to murder him on Aug. 1 if Obeid was not released.

Intense diplomatic activity followed, led by Pres. Bush, who personally spoke with a substantial number of world leaders, while preparing military action should Cicippio be murdered. Obeid remained an Israeli captive. Higgins was thought dead; it was not clear whether he had been previously murdered or was murdered because of the Obeid kidnapping. The Cicippio murder did not take place. Amid a flurry of public Israeli, American, Iranian, and Hezbollah offers, counteroffers, and threats, negotiations continued on the hostage crisis.

Intifada Continues; Palestine State Proclaimed The Intifada (Uprising) in the West Bank and Gaza Israeli-occupied territories continued into its second year, with the region's 1.7 million Arab inhabitants continuing their defiance of the occupying Israelis. Violence continued as Palestinian demonstrators, most of them rock-throwing but otherwise unarmed children and teenagers, continued to confront the heavily armed but thoroughly frustrated Israeli army, which proved unable to suppress the uprising, even though by midyear over 500 Palestinians had been killed since the Intifada began, with thousands more injured and at least 20,000 arrested, many of them detained without charge or trial for long periods. The occupying Israelis had by then suffered at least 20 dead and hundreds of injured.

On Nov. 15 the Palestine National Council, meeting in Algiers, reversed a long-held, centrally important position and specifically accepted UN resolutions 242 and 338, together forming a basis for negotiations leading to a two-nation resolution of the long Arab-Israeli dispute. Simultaneously, the council proclaimed the formation of a Palestinian state, led by Yasir Arafat, constituting itself as the leading body of the Palestinian government-in-exile. By late 1989 over 50 nations had recognized the new Palestinian state. Although Israel refused to talk directly with the PLO, the U.S. ambassador in Tunisia in December 1988 began what became a long series of direct talks with the PLO, while pressing Israel to take positive steps toward peace in the area. On May 23, 1989, Secretary of State James A. Baker publicly advised Israel to give up any territorial designs it might have had regarding the West Bank and the Gaza Strip and to begin serious peace talks with the Palestinians. In February Israeli Premier Shamir responded to PLO and American pressure by proposing elections leading to a measure of future autonomy for the occupied territories, then continuing to push his plan against criticism from hard-liners in his own Likud party, while the Palestinians called it inadequate but seemed willing to use it as a partial basis for negotiation. In early July, however, his internal opponents forced a major revision of the plan, ending for a time the possibility of its acceptance by the Palestinians or by the United States. The Intifada continued.

Drexel, Burnham, Lambert Settles Charges; Milken Case Remains On Dec. 21, 1988, Drexel, Burnham, Lambert, Inc. agreed to pay $650 million in penalties in settlement of six securities law felony charges, most of them relating to its dealings with convicted financier Ivan Boesky, who had helped the government make its case against Drexel. The settlement, conditional upon subsequent settlement of massive Securities Exchange Commission (SEC) civil charges, was by far the largest such in American history. Drexel also agreed to fire Michael R. Milken, head of its junk bond department, should he later be indicted, as was expected.

On Apr. 13, 1989, Drexel did settle the SEC civil charges, made a series of staff and procedural changes, was placed under administrative surveillance by the SEC, and named former SEC chairman John S. Shad chairman of the firm.

Michael Milken left Drexel to form his own firm on June 15, 1989, having been on leave since his Mar. 29 federal grand jury indictment, with two other Drexel employees, on 98 criminal counts. The indictment was followed by a prosecution assertion that it would seek forfeitures totaling $1.8 billion in connection with the charges.

Exxon Valdez Oil Spill It was the worst oil spill in American history. On the night of Mar. 24, 1989, at 12:04 a.m., the supertanker *Exxon Valdez*, carrying 1,260,000 barrels of oil, grounded on Bligh Reef in Prince William Sound, off the coast of Alaska. The ship was then 25 miles from Valdez, a pipeline terminus. At the time of the accident, the vessel was in shallow water and off course. Capt. Joseph Hazelwood had left the bridge, leaving the vessel on automatic pilot and in the hands of a third mate unauthorized to navigate in those waters. The damaged tanker spilled 260,000 barrels of oil (over 11 million gallons) into the cold waters of the sound; within a week a 50-mile-long oil slick had been created, which ultimately reached Katmai National Park, 150 miles away, and contaminated over 350 miles of Alaska's shoreline. The remaining million barrels of oil in the tanker were later pumped into other vessels.

Neither Exxon nor the Alyeska Pipeline were at all able to cope with the spill, making so little headway in controlling it that the state of Alaska and local fishing people were forced to take over the effort after several days. By then, much of the damage was irretrievable; the environmental disaster that resulted was in process, although some vital salmon hatcheries were saved. During the course of the next several months, Exxon claimed to have spent $115 million on cleanup efforts; however, state and Coast Guard officials reported that the results of Exxon's cleanup efforts had been negligible, with only several miles of shoreline cleaned, and those ineffectively. Exxon promised continuing cleanup efforts, the Coast Guard promised renewed vigilance, supertankers continued to load at Valdez, and environmentalists continued to warn that the situation was, as before, an environmental disaster waiting to happen—again.

Tower Nomination Rejected The first major defeat of the new Bush administration came with the Senate's Mar. 9, 1989, refusal to confirm the nomination of ex-senator John Goodwin Tower to become secretary of defense. The final vote was 53–47, almost completely along party lines, with one Republican voting against Tower and three Democrats for him. The Senate Armed Services Committee had recommended against confirmation of the nomination

Tower had been nominated by president-elect Bush on Dec. 16, 1988. The committee hearings, conducted Jan. 25–Feb. 1, were relatively uneventful, rather friendly, and nonpartisan—until Jan. 31, when conservative lobbyist Paul M. Weyrich raised questions about Tower's alleged drinking and womanizing problems. New allegations then emerged, and further FBI checks were demanded by the committee. On Feb. 1 Tower denied having a drinking problem when directly asked about it by the committee. On Feb. 2 the committee deferred a confirmation vote and deferred it again on Feb. 8, while Pres. Bush publicly reaffirmed his support for Tower, and the committee began to split along party lines. On Feb. 23 the adverse committee vote came, and on Feb. 26 Tower appeared on three national television shows, denied having a drinking problem, and read an extraordinary pledge of sobriety. On Mar. 2 the Senate floor debate began, becoming increasingly bitter until finally resolved by the Mar. 9 rejection vote.

Savings and Loan Bailout Biggest in U.S. History Faced with large-scale and accelerating savings and loan association insolvencies and determined to make good on depression-era federal deposit guarantees in order to preserve the integrity of the U.S. financial system, the federal government in 1989 finally undertook its long-awaited savings and loan bailout. On Aug. 9, 1989, Pres. George Bush signed into law a plan providing $166 billion for the bailout and restructuring of the ailing savings and loan industry, which had long been crippled by bad loans, high proffered rates to depositors, inept administration, inadequate regulation, and massive fraud. The bill provided for $20 billion in immediate bailout funds, with $30 billion more to be quickly raised by bond issues, though this was expected to be only part of the estimated $250–300 billion—or more—that would eventually be needed. In a Democratic-Republican political-purposes compromise, only the first $20 billion was to be figured as part of current expenditure for budget (and therefore deficit-figuring) purposes; the remaining $30 billion was to be "off-budget" and therefore not regarded as part of the federal deficit. The new law also provided tighter capital and investment regulations for thrift institutions and specifically prohibited junk bond investments.

North Convicted in Iran-Contra Aftermath On May 4, 1989, after 12 days of deliberation fol-lowing a three-month-long trial, the jury in the Iran-Contra-connected case found former White House aide Lt. Col. Oliver L. North guilty on three felony counts and acquitted him on nine other counts; four counts had previously been dismissed by Judge Gerhard A. Gesell. In this first major case growing out of the Iran-Contra scandal, North was found guilty of destroying relevant National Security Council documents, aiding and abetting the obstruction of congressional Iran-Contra inquiries, and receiving an illegal gratuity.

On July 6 Judge Gesell sentenced North to 1,200 hours of community service, suspended a three-year jail sentence, placed him on probation for two years beyond that, and fined him $150,000. Gesell justified the lightness of the sentence by characterizing North as a "low-ranking subordinate" rather than as a prime mover in the Iran-Contra scandal, blaming a "few cynical superiors" for the scandal. North's supporters expressed pleasure at the lightness of the sentence; special prosecutor Lawrence E. Walsh made no public comment on the matter.

House Speaker Wright Resigns On May 31, 1989, Speaker of the House James C. Wright, Jr., who had for almost a year faced charges of unethical conduct while in office, announced that he would resign his Speakership and his House seat after 35 years as a Texas Democratic representative, 10 of them as majority leader. He did so on June 30, becoming the first Speaker to resign in office while so charged.

Wright had been elected Speaker in 1987; in 1988, during the barrage of charges and countercharges that had characterized the 1988 presidential election, he had been accused of unethical conduct while in office. Formal charges were filed by Republican Newt Gingrich, and a House Ethics Committee investigation was voted on June 10, 1988. The question of alleged ethical lapses continued to haunt both political parties after the election in the aftermath of the Iran-Contra scandal and the intense bitterness generated by the rejection of the Tower secretary of defense nomination. Although Wright vigorously defended himself, the House Ethics Committee on Apr. 17, 1989, unanimously voted out five counts of unethical conduct, containing 69 specific alleged violations, which Wright ultimately chose not to formally defend, instead resigning.

In a factually unrelated development, but very much as a result of the Washington atmosphere of the time, Democratic House majority whip Tony Coelho on May 26 announced his resignation as whip and from the House, rather than defending threatened personal financial disclosure omissions charges. He resigned on June 15.

Supreme Court Upholds Abortion Right Limitations On July 3, 1989, the U.S. Supreme Court, in the case of *Webster* vs. *Reproductive Health Services*, declared constitutional a Missouri law sharply restricting the right to abortion in that state, especially for those of limited means. The law made it illegal for public employees to perform abortions or for public facilities to be used in the performance of abortions, unless the mother's life was in danger. The law also required doctors to test fetuses believed to be at least 20 weeks old for probable viability outside the womb. The 5–4 decision, made by a bitterly divided court, went far to dismantle the landmark 1973 *Roe* vs. *Wade* decision, which had for 16 years governed American abortion law, returning to the states the right to legislate in much of that area of the law. The court majority made it clear that it would continue to reevaluate the law in this area by taking three more abortion-related cases for its next term.

Abortion foes were delighted; prochoice proponents were enraged. The stage was set for a series of extensive political fights between the Pro-Choice movement and the Right-to-Life movement throughout the country, as the abortion issue was fought out state by state and on the national level.

Colombian Drug War In the summer of 1989, the long-simmering war between the Colombian government and the drug cartels became a major conflict, which quickly drew in the United States.

As pressure against the cartels intensified, antigovernment terrorist activities escalated. On Aug. 16 Carlos Ernesto Valencia joined a long list of murdered judges, generating a national judges strike. On Aug. 17 a provincial police chief was murdered. On Aug. 18 leading Liberal party presidential candidate Luis Carlos Galan was murdered—and that was too much for the Colombian government and people.

On Aug. 19, in a nationally televised address, Pres. Juan Virgilio Barco declared war on the drug cartels, sending army and police units against the cartels, seizing over 160 aircraft, boats, estates, and other assets and reinstating a law allowing extradition to the United States. Four days later accused drug-money launderer Eduardo Martinez Romero was captured and soon after extradited, as were several lower-level cartel figures. The cartels responded with an intensified bombing and assassination campaign—over 80 people were wounded when a bomb ripped though the office of a leading Bogotá newspaper on Sept. 2.

Pres. George Bush quickly offered Colombia material help amounting to $65 million, including aircraft and military advisers; later he expanded that offer to include more advisers but declared that he would not send troops; nor did the Colombian government ask for them.

As part of an expanded U.S. antidrug program, the United States later also offered military equipment and advisers to Peru and Bolivia and attempted to enhance its own internal war on the drug trade, an effort formally initiated by Pres. Bush on Sept. 5 in a nationally televised address.

The drug cartel responded with renewed violence on Sept. 15, Colombia's annual "Day of Love and Friendship." Several banks were bombed, and random shootings left two policemen dead and five wounded. On Sept. 20 Colombia's justice minister resigned (the eighth to do so in the last three years) out of fear for her family's safety. Since 1980 the cartel has assassinated 50 judges and 170 judicial employees. As September came to a close, word spread that Pres. Bush's grandchildren had been threatened, and extra security was employed.

The Year in Science

Pulsar Found in Supernova 1987A Remnants

Astronomers observing the gas cloud formed by supernova 1987A observed a pulsar shining through a gap in the cloud for about seven hours on Jan. 18. Then the gases moved, the pulsar was hidden, and it has not been seen since. Nevertheless, most astronomers think the evidence for the pulsar is quite strong. (Supernovae and pulsars are discussed in "The Universe," pp. 322-324.)

Supernova 1987A was once a blue giant star named Sanduleak -69°202 in the nearby miniature galaxy known as the Large Magellanic Cloud. Because the star became the nearest supernova to Earth in modern times when it exploded some 170,000 years ago, it has been intensely observed ever since the explosion was detected on Earth on Feb. 23, 1987. A supernova is a rare event, but the explosions are so enormous that astronomers often detect them in other galaxies, much farther from Earth than the Large Magellanic Cloud. The last one seen in our own galaxy was observed in 1604, and there have been only six or seven observations, mostly by Chinese astronomers, of supernovae earlier.

One of the exciting things about the discovery of the pulsar in 1987A is that it is spinning faster by far than any previously known pulsar. It is spinning 1,968.629 times each second. Another unusual circumstance is that the signal seemed to reveal another part of the original star, perhaps about the size of Jupiter, that is in orbit about the pulsar.

The Large Magellanic Cloud can only be observed from the Southern Hemisphere. The team of 14 researchers, working at the Cerro Tololo Inter-American Observatory in Chile, was led by Carl Pennypacker of the Lawrence Berkeley Laboratory, Jerome Kristian of the Carnegie Institution of Washington, and John Middleditch of Los Alamos National Laboratory.

Cold Fusion?

On Mar. 23, 1989, electrochemists B. Stanley Pons of the University of Utah at Salt Lake City and Martin Fleischmann of the University of Southampton in England announced that they had discovered a way to make nuclear fusion occur using simple equipment. Most previous efforts to achieve nuclear fusion involved giant magnets, powerful lasers, or other very expensive, high-tech devices. The Pons-Fleischmann experiment used a jar filled with heavy water (water in which some of the ordinary hydrogen has been replaced with deuterium, a form of hydrogen that contains a neutron), a platinum electron, a palladium electrode, and a source of electric current. Some nicknamed it "fusion in a jar."

Since heavy water is abundant and cheap—the technology for making it has been known for about 50 years, and it is used in certain types of nuclear reactors—and indications are that less-expensive metals, such as titanium, could be substituted for palladium if necessary, cold fusion would be an important energy boon if it indeed works. Pons and Fleischmann claim to have produced four times the energy that was put into their device. No one else, however, has consistently succeeded in such a result. Furthermore, most physicists who study fusion think that the reaction Pons and Fleischmann are supposed to be obtaining is not likely to occur in a sufficient amount to be a useful energy source.

All nuclear fusion, whether cold or hot, involves the blending of two atomic nuclei into one, which release energy because the amount of energy necessary to hold the single new nucleus together is less than the sum of the amounts needed to hold the two previous nuclei together. Fusion is the process that produces most of the energy released by the sun and stars. It is also the source of most of the energy in a thermonuclear device, more familiarly called a hydrogen bomb.

If cold fusion occurs, the process would be similar in some ways to the fusion process in young stars and in hydrogen bombs. In stars, gravity pushes nuclei of hydrogen together, forming either heavier types of hydrogen (with additional neutrons) or forms of helium (with one more proton and perhaps additional neutrons). This process is accelerated by heat, which causes nuclei to move faster and collide more often. In a hydrogen bomb, heat is the principal cause of the collisions, but pressure is also a factor. What Pons and Fleischmann think is happening in their palladium electrode is that the palladium is absorbing hydrogen from the heavy water. When the concentration of hydrogen builds up to great enough degree in the palladium, the hydrogen is squeezed close enough for fusion to occur. It is not necessary for the hydrogen to be moving very fast—which is the same as saying that the hydrogen does not have to be hot. The result would be cold fusion.

There are several different pathways by which hydrogen and heavy hydrogen can fuse. All the likely ones produce a great many neutrons. These neutrons are dangerous to life and destructive to materials. They also create radioactive elements. Pons and Fleischmann reported that their experiments produced a few neutrons, but only about a billionth as many as known fusion pathways make. As with the other results reported by Pons and Fleischmann, this relative absence of neutrons would make cold fusion a more attractive energy source.

Most experiments that seemed to confirm Pons and Fleischmann were later withdrawn by the researchers because of flaws they discovered later. An exception is a series of experiments that had been started independently and were concurrent with the original Pons and Fleischmann research. These experiments, conducted by Steven E. Jones of Brigham Young University in Provo, Utah, show that cold fusion can take place, but only at levels of energy so small as to have no practical value. Unlike the Pons-Fleischmann results, which most scientists feel are not valid, the Jones experiments are generally accepted.

Nevertheless, the University of Utah is proceeding to invest millions of dollars in a Center for Cold-Fusion Research, to be headed by Pons, and a cold-fusion newsletter is being marketed for $345 for 12 annual issues.

Phobos 2 Fails

The Soviet Union launched two missions to Mars on July 7 and 12, 1988, Phobos 1 and Phobos 2. On Aug. 29, 1988, an error in a computer command sent from Earth put Phobos 1 into a tumble that caused it to lose all power, leaving it completely out of touch with Earth. All did not seem to be lost, however, for Phobos 2 carried many of the same observational tools and could conduct similar experiments. On Mar. 27, 1989, just as Phobos 2 was reaching its destination, the Martian moon Phobos, where it was to deploy two surface landers, contact with the spacecraft was suddenly lost.

Once again the computer turned out to be the problem. Its sudden "crash" put a premature end to the mission. All was not completely lost, as 17 minutes of garbled, but decipherable, data were returned before the shutdown. The Soviet Union plans future trips to Mars, but the next generation of spacecraft will rely upon instructions from Earth, not on the spacecraft's own computers.

Laczkovich Squares Circle

Every mathematician knows that the ancient Greek problem of constructing a square that has the same area as a circle ("squaring the circle") using only a ruler and compass cannot be solved. This result was not established until 1882, but no mathematician doubts it. If you remove the restriction that only a ruler and compass be used, however, all bets are off.

In 1925 the mathematician Alfred Tarski proposed a different version of the circle-squaring problem. In essence, he asked if it was possible to cut up a circle and its interior and rearrange the pieces to form a square with the same area. Area and volume are not nearly so well understood by mathematicians as length; some of the results they have proved about area and volume still seem paradoxical to most observers. Nevertheless, by 1963 mathematicians showed that any squaring of the circle in the Tarski sense would require cutting out pieces with very strange boundaries, but they still could not show that it was possible even with the strange pieces.

In April 1989 Miklós Laczkovich of Eötvös Loránd University in Budapest showed that it was possible to square the circle in the Tarski sense using just a finite number of pieces. The finite number, however, is very large—approximately 1 followed by 50 zeros.

Premature Baby Breathes Liquid

On May 10, 1989, Thomas H. Shaffer and coworkers replaced the air in a dying premature infant with an oxygen-saturated liquid known as a perfluorocarbon. Although successful experiments with animals made it seem likely that the procedure would help the baby breathe, the team held their collective (ordinary) breath until it was clear that the perfluorocarbon worked. The baby breathed the liquid for 15 minutes before returning to breathing air. Further damage to the lungs stopped, and the baby lived for another 19 hours, finally succumbing to lung damage that had resisted (and been caused in part by) conventional treatment.

A problem that premature infants often face is that they are born before a natural chemical called a surfactant forms in the lungs. The surfactant is necessary to keep the tiny air pockets in the lungs from collapsing as a result of surface tension. A perfluorocarbon eliminates that problem since there is no liquid-air interface to cause surface tension. After giving time for the perfluorocarbon to suffuse all of the air pockets, it can be removed, since enough will stick to the tissues to defeat the surface tension.

Shaffer and his team will test the procedure several more times on premature infants after conventional therapy has failed. If all the tests suggest success, they will apply for permission to use the new treatment on babies before lung damage can occur. Later, the same treatment might also be used on adults with various forms of lung injury, such as fluid in the lungs (that does not carry oxygen the way perfluorocarbons do), damage from smoke or fire, or accidental breathing in of foreign substances of any kind. In the last two types of injury, the perfluorocarbon would be used essentially to wash the lungs while maintaining oxygen flow to the blood.

Can Sperm Carry Engineered Genes to Eggs?

On June 2, 1989, *Cell* carried a report of research by a team led by Corrado Spadafora of the Institute of Biomedical Technology in Rome that claimed success in using mouse sperm to transfer foreign genes into mouse eggs, resulting in mice born with the foreign gene. If confirmed by other laboratories, this technique would be a major breakthrough in genetic engineering of mammals. The current technique for gene implantation, which involves using microtools to insert the gene into embryos, requires great skill and expensive equipment. The Italian team, on the other hand, simply mixed the sperm and the DNA that carried the gene. After incubating the mixture for an hour, the DNA and the sperm became associated in some way that is not clearly understood. About 30 percent of mice eggs fertilized with the sperm went on to produce offspring with the foreign gene, which was also transferred according to the rules of genetics by ordinary breeding to a successive generation.

Other researchers have not been able to duplicate these results, but many are still hopeful that they will find the key to the Italian's success. Unlike the controversy over cold fusion, the Italian sperm experiment has not roused much opposition, even though efforts to duplicate it have all failed.

Largest Known Prime Found

On Aug. 6, 1989, a team of computer scientists at the Amdahl Corporation announced that they had found the largest known prime number. A prime number is one that has no factors other than 1 and itself; for example, 37 is prime, but 39 is not since it is equal to 3 x 13. The Amdahl prime is best indicated as

$$(391{,}581 \times 2^{216{,}193}) - 1$$

If it were written out in the ordinary way, in the Hindu-Arabic numeration system it would have 65,087 digits, taking a couple of pages in this almanac.

Euclid proved that there was no *largest* prime. While a specific large prime is not of any practical value, large primes are important in some codes used both by business and government. Furthermore, finding them has improved ways computers can calculate and suggested new results in mathematics.

Gene for Cystic Fibrosis Located

On Aug. 6, 1989, teams of researchers led by Francis S. Collins of the University of Michigan and Lap-Chee Tsui and Jack R. Riordan of the University of Toronto submitted three research papers describing the location and characteristics of the gene for cystic fibrosis. They announced their results to the public on Aug. 24, shortly before publication of the papers on Sept. 8 and two days after Reuters News Service had broken the story.

Cystic fibrosis is the most common genetic disease affecting people of European descent in the United States. It is a devastating disease that begins in childhood. Even with the best modern treatments, it usually kills by the age of 30. The principal cause of death is that thick mucus builds up in the lungs and air passageways, leaving the victim prone to various lung diseases. Up till now the most useful treatment has been to use physical therapy to clear away mucus and antibiotics to ward off infection by bacteria.

One out of 20 white Americans carries one defective cystic fibrosis gene. When two people with the same defect produce children, one in four will have the disease. The new results show that the defect is the same small change in the gene in about 70 percent of the cases of the disease, while other gene defects account for the rest. A genetic disease is caused when errors in genes cause the gene to fail to produce a specific protein correctly. Knowledge of the nature of the gene is enough to determine the protein, which previously had been one of the mysteries of cystic fibrosis.

Knowledge of the gene can have many practical benefits. First of all, prospective parents with known cystic fibrosis in the family can find out whether or not they are carriers. Using the techniques for examining fetal cells, carriers can learn early in pregnancy whether or not the fetus has the disease. In the long run, knowing the protein involved may result in better treatments or even cures for people with the disease—although that is far from certain. Lastly, if gene therapy ever becomes practical, it may be possible to provide the true gene to people who have two defective copies.

Voyager 2 Flies by Neptune

Voyager 2 (see "The Voyager Mission" on p. 320) made its last visit in the solar system on Aug. 24, 1989, then took a sharp turn toward the stars. The spaceprobe sent back immense amounts of information about Neptune, currently the planet farthest from the Sun (Pluto is farthest most of the time), its rings, and its moons. The Neptune encounter was the latest success of the spacecraft, which had previously visited Jupiter, Saturn, and Uranus, returning

5 trillion bits of data, among them 115,000 images, to Earth on its 12-year mission. Radio communication with Voyager 2 should continue for at least the next 30 years, so scientists continue to expect to reap dividends from "the little spacecraft that could" as it heads on its way toward becoming the farthest artificial object from Earth, a distinction now held by the slower-traveling Pioneer 11.

Neptune. Like Earth, Neptune is blue—although for a different reason. Neptune's blue comes from methane in its atmosphere, not from water on its surface. Because Neptune is so far from Earth, its blue color was about all that was known for sure about the planet, which was not discovered until 1846. From its size and density it was clear that Neptune was, like Jupiter, Saturn, and Uranus, a gas giant—a very large body of gas, perhaps liquefied to form a surface beneath the atmosphere, with a comparatively small rocky core, about the size of Earth. Two moons were known, the large moon Triton that seemed to many scientists to resemble ancient Earth before life appeared, and the much smaller Nereid, first observed in 1949. One of the Neptunian mysteries is that Triton is the only moon in the solar system known to revolve in a direction opposite its planet's rotation. Another mystery concerned the possibility that from Earth Neptune seemed to have partial rings—dubbed ring arcs—unlike the complete rings known to encircle the three other gas giants.

Voyager's dramatic images of the planet quickly resolved the mystery of the partial rings. Although the rings of Neptune are clumpy, they are complete. It is thought that the clumpiness, the way that parts of the outer ring seem to contain more material than other parts, caused the illusion of ring arcs. The rest of the outer ring and all the inner rings are tenuous, and not even easily seen from Voyager's close-up look from 50,000 miles. It is not even clear how many rings there are, with some scientists counting three, while others see five. The outermost ring is about 39,000 miles from Neptune's center, while another thin ring is about 33,000 miles from the center, although this may be the most visible part of a wider ring. Further in is where the confusion really reigns, for it is not clear that the inner ring is actually separated from the planet's upper atmosphere.

A question of interest about any planet is whether or not it has a magnetic field—a question that can only be answered by visiting the planet. Some do, and some do not, with a pattern that is not yet clear. Neptune turns out to be one that does have such a field. Like Earth's magnetic field, that of Neptune channels the solar wind to the magnetic poles where it interacts with the atmosphere, causing a faint aurora. Since the moon Triton also has an atmosphere and is within Neptune's magnetic field, it also has a fair aurora—although Triton has no magnetic field of its own.

A surprise concerning Neptune's field is that it, like the magnetic field of Uranus, is far out of line with the planet's rotation. The north magnetic pole is about 50° away from Neptune's north pole, compared with 11.7° currently for

Earth. It is known that Earth's magnetic field has both wandered and reversed in the past. While something like that might account for Neptune's situation, many scientists think it more likely that a collision with another body caused the field to be displaced. So far, however, no one knows for certain why the field is tipped so far.

Knowing the magnetic poles gave scientists the first accurate measurement of Neptune's rate of rotation, which turned out to be about 16 hours, 3 minutes, give or take 4 minutes.

Voyager 2 also found some totally unexpected features of Neptune. Neptune has a storm system similar to Jupiter's Great Red Spot, a giant storm, 180,000 miles long, that has been in existence for at least the last 300 years. Dubbed the Great Dark Spot, Neptune's storm is about 10° south of the equator and only 7,900 miles long. Near it are several smaller storms, all in the southern hemisphere. The smallest, called the Scooter, is moving around the planet at 390 miles an hour.

Much of the data from the mission will be analyzed and reanalyzed for months or even years to to come. Gradually, more of the mysteries of Neptune will be resolved.

Triton. Although Voyager 2 discovered six new moons—all very small—most of the interest in Neptune's satellites was focused on Triton. Indeed, when Voyager turned its cameras on Triton, near the end of the flyby, it soon became clear that discoveries at Triton would eclipse those at Neptune itself.

For one thing, it appears that Triton is the third body in the universe that is volcanically active, along with Earth and Jupiter's moon Io (the jury is still out on whether Venus is volcanically active). The evidence for volcanoes consists of streaks 30 miles wide and 45 miles long that are difficult to explain in any other way. One idea is that the volcanoes, if that is what they are, are powered by nitrogen that thaws from a solid into a gas, expanding immensely in the process. The volcanoes of Io are powered by a similar mechanism, with sulfur dioxide the solid that is heated to a gas by tidal forces caused by Jupiter's gravitational pull.

Nitrogen appears to be a dynamic part of Triton in other ways. Voyager found a bright polar cap at the south pole of the moon. One theory is that the cap forms when the north pole is warmed by the sun. Frozen nitrogen evaporates at the north pole, and nitrogen gas streams to the dark south pole, where it refreezes. As the distribution of sunlight on the moon changes, the nitrogen ice melts at the south pole, and a new cap forms at the north pole.

Cloud Forming into Galaxy Discovered?

In September 1989 Martha P. Haynes of Cornell University and Riccardo Giovanelli announced their observations of a large cloud of gas with the radiotelescope at Arecibo Observatory in Puerto Rico. The previously unknown gas cloud is 10 times the diameter of the Milky Way galaxy (which implies the volume might be a thousand times the Milky Way) and only—as astronomers say—65 million light years from here.

Haynes and Giovanelli think that the gas cloud is a galaxy in formation. This would be a major discovery if confirmed, since most theories of the formation of the universe have all the galaxies forming 10 to 15 billion years ago. Other astronomers, however, have found existing stars in the same region as the gas cloud, which might be a small galaxy that just happens to have a great deal of gas around it. Further observations are needed to determine the full story, but the giant cloud of gas is a major discovery even if it is not a galaxy in formation.

Pi to a Billion Digits

Using new computer techniques, Gregory V. and David D. Chudnovsky of Columbia University computed π to 480,000,000 digits in June 1989, a new record. In July the previous record holder, Yasumasa Manada of the University of Tokyo, took back the record, reaching 536,870,000 digits. The Chudnovskys struck back in September with 1,011,196,691 digits.

Pi is an irrational number whose digits continue infinitely with no discernible pattern when written as an ordinary Hindu-Arabic numeral. Although there is no need for closer and closer approximations to π (most people are satisfied with just three digits, 3.14), computer scientists have found computing the digits to be a good way to test a computer's speed and accuracy, while mathematicians have developed new means of computation working on the problem.

A New Form of Hot Fusion

In the Sept. 18, 1989, *Physical Review Letters,* Robert J. Beuhler, Lewis Friedman, and Gerhart Friedlander of Brookhaven National Laboratory announced yet another route to fusion. Like the Pons-Fleischmann experiments (see "Cold Fusion?" above), the Brookhaven method uses heavy water and a metal that absorbs hydrogen. There the resemblance stops.

In the Brookhaven experiments, the heavy water is in the form of tiny droplets that carry electric charges. Because of the electric charges, an electric field can be used to speed the droplets through a vacuum chamber, at the end of which is a target consisting of titanium that has absorbed heavy hydrogen. When the droplets hit the target at several hundred thousand miles an hour, the pressure and temperature at the target both become very great. This classic combination of high pressure and temperature is enough to cause fusion.

The Brookhaven evidence is much more convincing than that of Pons and Fleischmann. The fusion route is a likely one, with two heavy hydrogen atoms joining to form the even heavier form of hydrogen called tritium, releasing protons in the process. Both the tritium and the protons, which quickly capture an electron to become ordinary hydrogen, have been observed. Changing the recipe by substituting ordinary hydrogen produces no evidence of fusion—which is another sign that the Brookhaven process really works.

The Brookhaven investigators will now use larger accelerators to see if they can get even more definite evidence of the reaction. Any practical application would seem to be far in the future at this time.

CALENDAR OF THE YEAR

Understanding Calendars

The Day Earth turns at a fairly steady pace about the imaginary line that defines the North and South poles. This line through the poles is called Earth's axis. Each turn about the axis, called a rotation, takes slightly less than 24 hours. Since Earth is also traveling around the Sun, however, the time it takes for one rotation to noon is longer than the time it takes for one rotation—about 3 minutes and 56 seconds longer, or almost exactly 24 hours. The time from noon to noon changes slightly during the year, depending on where Earth is in its path. If you average all the days in a year, the average time from noon to noon is exactly 24 hours.

The Year All the nine planets of the solar system travel in nearly circular paths, called orbits, around the Sun. Each trip around the Sun is called a revolution. The planets all revolve in the same direction, which can be observed from Earth by noting the position the Sun has among the background stars. (Since you can't see the Sun and stars at the same time, you can observe where the Sun rises or sets each day and then note the stars that appear in the same region). The apparent trip of the Sun through 12 different constellations, which is actually the trip of Earth around the Sun, is the annual path of the Sun through the zodiac. The zodiac consists of the 12 constellations in which the Sun is seen each year.

Earth's trip around the Sun, reflected in the sun's trip through the zodiac, takes about 365.25 days. It varies slightly from time to time, so careful astronomers add or delete a second in some years to keep their records in tune with Earth's motion. (See also "Precession of the Equinoxes" below.)

The Seasons Most of us have learned that the seasons change on the 21st of March, June, September, and December. It is therefore surprising to discover that in some years the dates in these months may swing from the 20th to the 23d and that the climate does not seem to behave in accord with the starts and ends of the official seasons.

The seasons do *not* coincide with climate changes. In the northeastern United States, it still snows after Mar. 21, it gets quite hot before June 21, and there is not much winter until sometime in January. What the seasons mark is the length of daylight.

Because the Earth is tilted with respect to its path around the Sun, different parts receive different amounts of sunlight during Earth's annual orbit, the time we know as a year. Between late September (around the 21st) and late March, Earth's Northern Hemisphere is tilted away from the Sun. It is winter in the north, but below the equator, it is summer. This is defined, not by weather, but by the longer amount of daylight in summer and the shorter amount in winter. The rest of the year, the Northern Hemisphere is tilted toward the Sun, while the Southern Hemisphere is tilted away from it. Northerners have long days, while on the other side of the world, the hours of daylight are short. Around the times of change from long days to short days and vice versa, daylight hours are equal to nighttime hours. These are called the *equinoxes*, the times when days and nights are equal. In the spring, about Mar. 21, we have the *vernal equinox*. The *autumnal equinox* occurs in the fall. Officially, summer begins on the day of the longest daytime during the year, about June 21 in the Northern Hemisphere, called the *summer solstice*. The word *solstice* means "standing-still sun." It is so called because the apparent movement of where the Sun rises or sets reaches its extreme positions on the solstices and then reverses direction. The winter solstice, about Dec. 21, has the shortest amount of daylight and the longest night of the year.

Precession of the Equinoxes Ancient Greek astronomers determined that the direction Earth's axis points is constantly, but very slowly, changing in a regular pattern. The kind of change is similar to the way a spinning top slowly leans first one way than another as its axis changes direction, which is called *precession*. The precession of both the Earth and the top is a result of neither being perfect spheres. Earth's diameter is about 27 miles greater from one side of the equator to the other than it is from one pole to the other. (Earth is oblate, or fat around the middle, which is caused by Earth's rotation.)

Picture Earth without considering its revolution. Keep Earth's center in the same place mentally, and think about how the axis changes position during precession. Any point on Earth's axis (except the center of the planet) moves in a slow circle as a result of precession. This movement is so slow that it takes 26,000 years for a point to return to its original spot. In the meantime the axis gradually moves from pointing at the North Star, as it does today, to pointing at different stars. In A.D. 14,980, for example, the star Vega will be directly above the North Pole. By A.D. 27,990 the present North Star (officially known as Polaris) will have returned to its present position.

As the precession continues, one of its effects is to change the times of the year that seasons occur. Instead of the vernal equinox being around Mar. 21, 13,000 years from now, it will occur around Sept. 21, the date at which the autumnal equinox is now. For this reason, the precession of Earth is generally known as the precession of the equinoxes.

Although the precession of the equinoxes is slow, it can be easily observed. The year of about 365.25 days is the time it takes from one vernal equinox to the next. Because of the precession of the equinoxes, however, the time it takes the Sun to appear in the same position with respect to the stars is 20 minutes 24 seconds longer than the period from one equinox to the next. For this reason, very accurate star

---

THE SEASONS 1990

In 1990 the seasons begin as follows:
Vernal equinox (spring): Mar. 20, 4:19 p.m. EST
Summer solstice: June 21, 11:33 a.m. EDT
Autumnal equinox (fall): Sept. 23, 2:55 a.m. EDT
Winter solstice: Dec. 21, 10:07 p.m. EST
Add one hour to times for Atlantic time. Subtract one hour for central time, two hours for mountain, three hours for Pacific, four hours for Yukon, five hours for Alaska-Hawaii, and six hours for Bering time.

---

maps have to specify both the date and year for which they are intended.

Lunar Calendar

There is some evidence that very early humans (c. 25,000 B.C.) used marks on bone to indicate the passage of time, which they may have measured by the Moon's phases. A calendar for the year can be based upon the Moon's phases, which gives a year of 12 periods from new moon to new moon (hence the word *month*) that is about 354 days. This is short by about 11 days of the time it takes Earth to revolve around the Sun. The Chinese, who still use a version of this calendar, resolve this by inserting extra months at fixed intervals to bring the lunar and solar years into alignment. The Chinese year is separated into months that are either 29 or 30 days long, since the time from new moon to new moon is approximately 29.5 days. (The Moon takes about 27.33 days to orbit Earth, but Earth is moving with respect to the Sun during that time, so the combined movement produces the period of about 29.5 days.) The New Year begins at the first new moon over China between Jan. 21 and Feb. 19, and is celebrated for a four-day period. Each year has both a number and a name. The year 1990 is the Year of the Horse, or 4627, and begins Jan. 27.

Solar Calendar

The ancient Egyptians were the first people known to have instituted a solar calendar. In actuality their calendar might be called a stellar calendar, since the year began with the

---

rising of Sirius—the brightest star in the sky—at the same place the Sun rises, which generally happened at the same time the Nile flooded. The Egyptians determined that a year was 365 days and set their year at that number. This number is about 0.25 day short of the true solar year, so gradually the Egyptian calendar no longer coincided with the seasons. Historical records reveal when the Egyptian calendar and the rising of Sirius coincided, from which astronomers inferred that the Egyptian calendar must have been instituted in either 4241 B.C. or 2773 B.C. The Egyptian calendar had 12 30-day months and five days of festival, a system adopted by various early cultures, although some continued to use lunar calendars.

Julian Calendar

In 46 B.C. Julius Caesar was in control of what was about to become the Roman Empire. He realized that various parts of the land controlled by Rome used different calendars, so he asked the astronomer Sosigenes to develop a uniform calendar. Sosigenes proposed that since the year was 365.25 days long (which is not exact), a 365-day calendar be kept with one day added (a "leap day") every fourth year. When Caesar introduced the new system, he also added days to the year 46 B.C., bringing it to a total of 445 days, so as to bring the seasons in line with the calendar. As a result 46 is the longest calendar year on record. A year at that time began in March, and the months were numbered. *September, October, November,* and *December* derive from this system, and mean "seventh, eighth, ninth," and "tenth" months, respectively.

There was a little further adjustment of the calendar, however, by Augustus Caesar, the first Roman emperor. The fifth month (starting with March) had been renamed July (instead of *Quintilis*) to honor Julius Caesar. Not to be left out, Augustus renamed the sixth month after himself, August. So that August, which originally had only 30 days, would not be shorter than 31-day July, Augustus also borrowed a day from Feb. to add to August.

Because of the Roman Empire's great sphere of influence, the Julian calendar became the ordinary calendar of Western nations.

Gregorian Calendar

From at least A.D. 730, it was known that the solar year—measured from vernal equinox to vernal equinox—was somewhat short of 365.25 days. Each century the solar year gets

---

CHINESE YEARS

Rat	Ox	Tiger	Hare (Rabbit)	Dragon	Snake	Horse	Sheep (Goat)	Monkey	Rooster	Dog	Pig
1900	1901	1902	1903	1904	1905	1906	1907	1908	1909	1910	1911
1912	1913	1914	1915	1916	1917	1918	1919	1920	1921	1922	1923
1924	1925	1926	1927	1928	1929	1930	1931	1932	1933	1934	1935
1936	1937	1938	1939	1940	1941	1942	1943	1944	1945	1946	1947
1948	1949	1950	1951	1952	1953	1954	1955	1956	1957	1958	1959
1960	1961	1962	1963	1964	1965	1966	1967	1968	1969	1970	1971
1972	1973	1974	1975	1976	1977	1978	1979	1980	1981	1982	1983
1984	1985	1986	1987	1988	1989	1990	1991	1992	1993	1994	1995

about half a second shorter. In 1990 the solar year is calculated at 365 days 5 hours 48 minutes 45.5 seconds long, not 365 days 6 hours, which is what the Julian calendar assumes. Because the date of Easter (determined on the basis of the Sunday following the first full Moon after the vernal equinox) was slipping, Pope Gregory XIII instituted calendrical reform in 1582. He proclaimed that the day following Oct. 4 would be Oct. 15, which dropped 10 days from the year. Furthermore, on the advice of astronomer Christoph Clavius, the new calendar would be kept in line by omitting the leap year in century years unless they were divisible by 400. Thus 1900 was not a leap year in the Gregorian calendar, as it came to be called, but 2000 would be.

Most Roman Catholic countries and some other Western countries adopted the new system, but England did not. Finally, in 1752, England and its colonies adopted the Gregorian calendar, but they had to drop 11 days to fit common Western practice. It was at this time that New Year's Day in England was moved from Mar. 25 to Jan. 1, changing the number of the year for the almost three months affected. Thus, George Washington was born according to the Julian calendar on Feb. 11, 1731, but came to celebrate his birth as Feb. 22, 1732, on the Gregorian calendar.

Because the solar year is shortening, astronomers today keep the Gregorian calendar in line by making a 1-second adjustment as needed, usually on Dec. 31 at midnight, whenever the error's accumulation nears one second.

HOLIDAYS AND HOLY DAYS

Federal Holidays in the United States

Congress and the president have designated 10 days as federal holidays. Although these are so widely observed as to be considered "national" holidays, they technically apply only to federal employees and the District of Columbia. It is up to the individual states to designate their own holidays. When a federal holiday falls on a Saturday or a Sunday, it is observed on the preceding Friday or the following Monday.

New Year's Day (Jan. 1) The observance of the New Year dates back to pre-Christian times when rites were performed to ensure the return of spring.

Martin Luther King, Jr., Day (Third Monday in January) Before his assassination in 1968, Martin Luther King, Jr., was the foremost civil rights leader of the 1950s and 1960s, and in 1964 he won the Nobel Peace Prize. In 1983 Congress set aside this day to celebrate his life and accomplishments.

Presidents' Day (Third Monday in February) Presidents' Day combines the observance of George Washington's birthday (Feb. 22), first observed in 1782, and Abraham Lincoln's birthday (Feb. 12), which became a federal holiday in 1892.

Memorial Day (Last Monday in May) Memorial Day (also known as Decoration Day) honors soldiers fallen in battle. Dating from the Civil War, it is traditionally marked with parades and memorial services.

Independence Day (Fourth of July) The most important U.S. holiday, Independence Day commemorates the signing of the Declaration of Independence on July 4, 1776, an event that marked America's birth as a free nation. The holiday was first observed in 1777 and is celebrated with fireworks, parades, and oratory.

Labor Day (First Monday in September) The idea of Peter J. McGuire, president of the United Brotherhood of Carpenters and Joiners of America, the official observance of a day celebrating the American worker was signed into law on June 28, 1894.

Columbus Day (Second Monday in October) On Oct. 12, 1492, Christopher Columbus and his crew landed in the Bahama Islands after sailing across the Atlantic. First celebrated in 1792, Columbus Day was not officially recognized until 1909. Its observance is of special national pride to Italian-Americans who claim the Genoese Columbus for their own.

Veterans' Day (Nov. 11) Armistice Day, which marked the end of World War I on Nov. 11, 1918, was made a legal holiday in 1938. The name was changed to Veterans' Day in 1954 to honor all of America's veterans.

Thanksgiving Day (Fourth Thursday in November) Thanksgiving Day was first observed in Plymouth Colony (Mass.) in 1621, the year in which the Pilgrims landed in the New World and gave thanks for their first harvest and for the new land they had colonized. President Lincoln proclaimed Thanksgiving a national holiday in 1863.

Christmas Day is celebrated on Dec. 25. (See above, "Christian Holy Days.")

U.S. Minor Holidays and Occasions

April Fool's Day (Apr. 1) A day for practical jokes; the origin of April's Fool Day is obscure, but it bears some resemblance to an ancient Roman festival honoring the goddess of nature.

Arbor Day (Last Friday in April) Dedicated to trees and their preservation; its observance is meant to encourage preservation of the environment. Internationally, it is observed on Dec. 22.

IMPORTANT DATES IN THE U.S. AND CANADA, 1990–95

Event	1990	1991	1992[1]	1993	1994	1995
New Year's Day[2]	Jan. 1	Jan. 1	Jan. 1	Jan. 1	Jan. 1	Jan. 1
Martin Luther King, Jr., Day[2]	Jan. 15	Jan. 21	Jan. 20	Jan. 18	Jan. 17	Jan. 16
Groundhog Day	Feb. 2	Feb. 2	Feb. 2	Feb. 2	Feb. 2	Feb. 2
St. Valentine's Day	Feb. 14	Feb. 14	Feb. 14	Feb. 14	Feb. 14	Feb. 14
Susan B. Anthony Day	Feb. 15	Feb. 15	Feb. 15	Feb. 15	Feb. 15	Feb. 15
Presidents' Day[2]	Feb. 19	Feb. 18	Feb. 17	Feb. 15	Feb. 21	Feb. 20
Mardi Gras	Feb. 27	Feb. 12	Mar. 3	Feb. 23	Feb. 15	Feb. 28
St. Patrick's Day	Mar. 17	Mar. 17	Mar. 17	Mar. 17	Mar. 17	Mar. 17
April Fool's Day	Apr. 1	Apr. 1	Apr. 1	Apr. 1	Apr. 1	Apr. 1
Daylight Saving begins	Apr. 1	Apr. 7	Apr. 5	Apr. 4	Apr. 3	Apr. 2
Arbor Day	Apr. 27	Apr. 26	Apr. 24	Apr. 30	Apr. 29	Apr. 28
National Teacher Day	May 8	May 7	May 5	May 4	May 3	May 8
Mother's Day	May 13	May 12	May 10	May 9	May 8	May 14
Armed Forces Day	May 19	May 18	May 16	May 15	May 21	May 20
Victoria Day[3]	May 21	May 20	May 18	May 24	May 23	May 22
National Maritime Day	May 22	May 22	May 22	May 22	May 22	May 22
Memorial Day[2]	May 28	May 27	May 25	May 31	May 30	May 29
Flag Day	June 14	June 14	June 14	June 14	June 14	June 14
Father's Day	June 17	June 16	June 21	June 20	June 19	June 18
Canada Day[3]	July 1	July 1	July 1	July 1	July 1	July 1
Independence Day[2]	July 4	July 4	July 4	July 4	July 4	July 4
Labor Day[2, 3]	Sept. 3	Sept. 2	Sept. 7	Sept. 6	Sept. 5	Sept. 4
Citizenship Day	Sept. 17	Sept. 17	Sept. 17	Sept. 17	Sept. 17	Sept. 17
Columbus Day[2]	Oct. 8	Oct. 14	Oct. 12	Oct. 11	Oct. 10	Oct. 9
Thanksgiving Day[3]	Oct. 8	Oct. 14	Oct. 12	Oct. 11	Oct. 10	Oct. 9
United Nations Day	Oct. 24	Oct. 24	Oct. 24	Oct. 24	Oct. 24	Oct. 24
Daylight Savings ends	Oct. 28	Oct 27	Oct. 25	Oct. 31	Oct. 30	Oct. 29
Halloween	Oct. 31	Oct. 31	Oct. 31	Oct. 31	Oct. 31	Oct. 31
Election Day (U.S.)	Nov. 6	Nov. 5	Nov. 3	Nov. 2	Nov. 8	Nov. 7
Veterans' Day[2]	Nov. 11	Nov. 11	Nov. 11	Nov. 11	Nov. 11	Nov. 11
Remembrance Day[3]	Nov. 11	Nov. 11	Nov. 11	Nov. 11	Nov. 11	Nov. 11
Thanksgiving Day[2]	Nov. 29	Nov. 28	Nov. 26	Nov. 25	Nov. 24	Nov. 23
Christmas Day[2, 3]	Dec. 25	Dec. 25	Dec. 25	Dec. 25	Dec. 25	Dec. 25
Boxing Day[3]	Dec. 26	Dec. 26	Dec. 26	Dec. 26	Dec. 26	Dec. 26
New Year's Eve	Dec. 31	Dec. 31	Dec. 31	Dec. 31	Dec. 31	Dec. 31

Note: For dates of Jewish, Christian, and Muslim holy days 1990–95, see above.   1. Leap year; February has 29 days.   2. Federal holiday in the United States.   3. Federal holiday in Canada.

Armed Forces Day (Third Saturday in May) A day to honor members of the U.S. Armed Forces.

Citizenship Day (Sept. 17) First observed by presidential proclamation in 1952, Citizenship Day falls on the same day as the old Constitution Day, which it replaces, but the name of which is still in use.

Daylight Saving Time During this period, clocks are set one hour ahead of standard time; daylight saving time lasts from the first Sunday in April to the last Sunday in October, when clocks are turned back one hour—"Spring ahead, fall back."

Election Day (the Tuesday after the first Monday in November) In years evenly divisible by four, presidential elections are held; in years evenly divisible by two, elections for all members of the House of Representatives and for one-third of the members of the Senate are held.

Father's Day (Third Sunday in June) Father's Day was first observed in West Virginia in 1908, but it was not until 1972 that the president signed a congressional resolution designating its official observance. Father's Day is a uniquely American institution.

Flag Day (June 14) The first observance of Flag Day was in 1877, the centenary of the adoption of the Flag Resolution, which adopted the design of the American flag flown today. President Harry Truman signed the Flag Day Bill in 1949.

Groundhog Day (Feb. 2) On this day, as legend has it, the groundhog peeks out of his burrow to look for his shadow, and if he sees his shadow, six weeks of winter will follow; if he doesn't, spring is just around the corner.

Halloween (Oct. 31) All Hallow's Eve began as a pagan custom honoring the dead and as a celebration of autumn. The wearing of costumes can be traced back to medieval religious practice in which parishioners dressed as saints and angels and paraded through the churchyard. The modern practice of "trick or treating" is of American origin with no apparent historical basis.

Mother's Day (Second Sunday in May) Conceived by Anne M. Jarvis of Philadelphia, Pennsylvania, where it was first observed, as a day for children to pay tribute to their mothers, this was declared a national holiday by presidential proclamation in 1914.

National Maritime Day (May 22) Designated by presidential proclamation in 1935, this commemorates the anniversary of the departure of the SS *Savannah* on the first successful transoceanic voyage of a steam-powered vessel, in 1819. It is also a day of remembrance of merchant mariners who died in defense of their country.

National Teacher Day (Tuesday of the first full week in May) The day when students and communities around the country honor their teachers and the teaching profession.

Susan B. Anthony Day (Feb. 15) Anthony (1820–1906) was one of the first women's rights advocates, working especially for equal suffrage. She was a cofounder and later president of the National Woman Suffrage Association.

St. Patrick's Day (Mar. 17) A day in honor of Ireland's patron saint, St. Patrick's Day is a religious, political, and social event rolled into one. In Ireland St. Patrick is honored by church ceremonies and a three-day period of devotion. In the United States, Mar. 17 is celebrated with parades and the "wearing of the green."

St. Valentine's Day (Feb. 14) Originally, an occasion to honor two Christian saints martyred by the Roman Emperor Claudius (214–270). Since the Middle Ages, the day has been dedicated to lovers, probably because it is believed to be the day birds choose their mates.

United Nations Day (Oct. 24) Commemorates the ratification of the UN Charter on this date in 1945 by the five permanent members of the Security Council and a majority of the other charter signatories.

Christian Holy Days

Christmas is the celebration of Christ's birth. The exact date of his birth is unknown, but the date of Dec. 25 was probably chosen because it coincided with the ancient midwinter celebrations honoring pagan deities. The 12 days of Christmas fall between Christmas and Epiphany (Jan. 6), the day the Wise Men visited the Christ child.

Easter is the most important holy day in the Christian religion. It is the celebration of Christ's Resurrection from the dead, which gave Christians the hope of salvation and eternal life. Although Easter is only one day, the full observance of the holy day spans from Septuagesima Sunday (70 days before Easter Sunday), which may fall as early as January, to Pentecost, which can occur as late as June.

SHROVE TUESDAY (MARDI GRAS; FAT TUESDAY) Originally a day of penance, the last day before the beginning of Lent is now celebrated with feasting and merrymaking.

ASH WEDNESDAY derives its name from the rite of burning the palms carried on the Palm Sunday of the year before and using the ashes to mark worshipers' foreheads with a cross.

LENT, a 40-day period of fasting and penitence beginning on Ash Wednesday and ending on Easter Sunday, is traditionally observed by fasting, performing acts of charity, and by giving up certain pleasures and amusements.

PALM SUNDAY, the Sunday before Easter, celebrates Jesus's triumphant entry into Jerusalem, where palm branches were spread before him to honor his path.

HOLY (MAUNDY) THURSDAY is the anniversary of the Last Supper. The traditional services mark three events that occurred during the week before Jesus was crucified: he washed the feet of his 12 disciples; he instituted the Eucharist (the sacrament of Holy Communion); and he was arrested and imprisoned.

GOOD FRIDAY marks the day of Christ's Crucifixion. The holy day is observed with fasting, mourning, and penitence.

HOLY SATURDAY is the day that anticipates the Resurrection. In the Catholic church, special vigils are held on Holy Saturday evening.

EASTER SUNDAY marks the day of Christ's Resurrection. Many worshipers celebrate the holy day with sunrise services, a custom believed to be inspired by the example of Mary Magdalene, who went to Christ's tomb "early, while it was yet dark."

PENTECOST (literally, 50th day) is the end of the full ecclesiastical observance of Easter. It takes place on the seventh Sunday after Easter Sunday and commemorates the descent of the Holy Spirit upon the Apostles.

The Annunciation This holy day marks the archangel Gabriel's announcement to Mary that she would conceive and give birth to Jesus. It is celebrated by Roman Catholics on Mar. 25; it is not observed by Protestant denominations.

Trinity Sunday The Sunday after Pentecost, this occasion honors the Father, Son, and Holy Ghost. It was declared a part of the church calendar in 1334 by Pope John XXII and is observed by Roman Catholics and by some Protestant denominations.

Corpus Christi This feast celebrates the presence of the body (corpus) of Christ in the Eucharist. At one time this was the principal feast of the church year, but today it is observed only by Catholic churches. Corpus Christi is celebrated on the Thursday following Trinity Sunday.

All Saints' Day, celebrated on Nov. 1, honors all of the Christian saints. In America many churches mark the Sunday nearest Nov. 1 as a day to pay tribute to those who have died during the year. All Saints' Day is observed primarily by Roman Catholics.

Advent, a religious season that begins on the Sunday closest to Nov. 30 and lasts until Christmas, both celebrates the birth of Jesus and anticipates his second coming. At one time Advent was a solemn season observed by fasting, but this is no longer the case.

Holy Days of Obligation are feast days in the Catholic calendar, observed by attendance at Mass and rest from unnecessary work. Six holy days of obligation are observed in the United States:

  1. Solemnity of Mary, Jan. 1
  2. Ascension Thursday (of Jesus to Heaven), 40 days after Easter

CALENDAR OF CHRISTIAN HOLY DAYS

Year A.D.	Ash Wednesday	Easter Sunday	Pentecost	Trinity Sunday	Advent
1990	Feb. 28	Apr. 15	June 3	June 10	Dec. 2
1991	Feb. 13	Mar. 31	May 19	May 26	Dec. 1
1992	Mar. 4	Apr. 19	June 7	June 14	Nov. 29
1993	Feb. 24	Apr. 11	May 30	June 6	Nov. 28
1994	Feb. 16	Apr. 3	May 22	May 29	Nov. 27
1995	Mar. 1	Apr. 16	June 4	June 11	Dec. 3

3. Assumption of the Blessed Virgin into Heaven, Aug. 15

4. All Saints' Day, Nov. 1

5. Mary's Immaculate Conception (honoring the Mother of God as the only person conceived without original sin), Dec. 8

6. Christmas, Dec. 25

The Jewish Calendar

The months of the Jewish year are Tishri, Heshvan, Kislev, Tebet, Shebat, Adar, Nisan, Iyar, Sivan, Tammuz, Ab, and Elul. The Jewish era dates from the year of the creation (*anno mundi*, or A.M.), which is equal to 3761 B.C.E. (before the Christian era); thus 1990 in the Gregorian calendar is A.M. 5750/51. (Tishri, the first month of the Jewish year, falls in either September or October of the Gregorian calendar.)

Because the Jewish calendar is a blend of solar and lunar calendars, there are intercalated months to keep the lunar and solar years in alignment. (Intercalation is the insertion of an extra day, month, or other unit—Feb. 29 in a leap year, for example—into a calendar. The intercalated month here is called Adar Sheni, or Veadar—"Second Adar." The year 5749 was a leap year).

Jewish Holy Days

Sabbath is the first and most important Jewish holiday, occurring each week from sundown Friday to sundown Saturday. It is a day of rest and spiritual growth, given to men and women so they will remember the sweetness of freedom and keep it. Sabbath takes precedence over all other observances.

Rosh Hashanah (New Year), held to be the birthday of the world, is also called the Day of Judgment and Remembrance, and the day of the shofar—a ram's horn—which is blown to remind Jews of Abraham's willingness to sacrifice his son Isaac. The holiday takes place on the first and second days of Tishri (September or October).

Yom Kippur (Day of Atonement) concludes the 10 days of repentance that Rosh Hashanah begins and takes place from sundown on the ninth day of Tishri until sundown on the 10th. The observance begins with the recitation of the most famous passage in the Jewish liturgy—the *Kol Nidre*—which nullifies unfulfilled vows made in the past year. The entire day is spent praying and fasting.

Sukkoth (Tabernacles) is a harvest festival celebrated from the 15th through the 22d of Tishri. Sukkoth also commemorates the journey of the Jewish people through the wilderness to the land of Israel. Jewish families take their meals this week in a roughly constructed *sukkah* (booth)—a reminder of an agricultural society, of the Exodus, and of how precarious and fragile life can be. On the Simchath Torah, the 23d of Tishri, a congregation finishes reading the last book of the Torah and immediately starts again with the first.

Hanukkah (Feast of Dedication; Festival of Lights) The importance of the eight-day feast, which begins on the 25th day day of Kislev, is its commemoration of the first war in human

CALENDAR OF JEWISH HOLY DAYS

Year A.M. (A.D.)	Rosh Hashanah	Yom Kippur	Sukkoth	Hanukkah	Purim	Pesach	Shavuoth
5751 (1990–91)	Sept. 20	Sept. 29	Oct. 4	Dec. 12	Feb. 28	Mar. 30	May 19
5752 (1991–92)	Sept. 9	Sept. 18	Sept. 23	Dec. 2	Mar. 19	Apr. 18	June 7
5753 (1992–93)	Sept. 28	Oct. 7	Oct. 12	Dec. 20	Mar. 7	Apr. 6	May 26
5754 (1993–94)	Sept. 16	Sept. 25	Sept. 30	Dec. 9	Feb. 25	Mar. 27	May 16
5755 (1994–95)	Sept. 6	Sept. 15	Sept. 20	Nov. 28	Mar. 16	Apr. 15	June 4
5756 (1995–96)	Sept. 25	Oct. 4	Oct. 9	Dec. 18	Mar. 5	Apr. 4	May 24

CALENDAR OF MUSLIM HOLY DAYS

Year A.H. (A.D.)	1st day of Ramadan	1st day of Shawwal, Id al-Fitr	10th day of Dhu al-Hijja, Id al-Adha
1410 (1990–91)	Mar. 28	Apr. 27	July 3
1411 (1991–92)	Mar. 17	Apr. 16	June 23
1412 (1992–93)	Mar. 6	Apr. 4	June 11
1413 (1993–94)	Feb. 23	Mar. 25	June 1
1414 (1994–95)	Feb. 12	Mar. 14	May 21
1415 (1995–96)	Feb. 1	Mar. 3	May 10

history fought in the cause of religious freedom. The Maccabees vanquished not just the military threat to Judaism but also the internal forces for assimilation into the Hellenistic culture of Israel's rulers. Jews light candles for eight nights to mark a miracle: a day's supply of oil, found in the recaptured Temple, that burned for eight days.

Purim (Feast of Lots), set on the 14th day of Adar, is another celebration of survival, noting the events described in the Book of Esther. At Purim Jews rejoice at Queen Esther's and her cousin Mordecai's defeat of Haman, the Persian King Ahaseurus's adviser who plotted to slaughter all the Persian Jews. Ahaserus ruled around 400 B.C.

Pesach (Passover), beginning on the 15th day of Nissan and lasting seven days, commemorates the exodus of the Hebrews from Egypt in about 1300 B.C. The name Passover also recalls God's sparing (passing over) of Jewish first-born during the plagues upon the land brought by God through Moses. The holiday is marked by eating only unleavened foods and participating in a seder, or special meal.

Shavuoth (Feast of Weeks) is observed on the sixth or seventh day of Sivan. Originally an agricultural festival, Shavuoth is a celebration of the revelation of the Torah at Mt. Sinai, by which God established his covenant with the Jewish people.

The Islamic Calendar

The 12 months of the Islamic year are: Muharram, Safar, Rabi I, Rabi II, Jumada I, Jumada II, Rajab, Sha'ban, Ramadan, Shawwal, Dhu'l-Qa'dah, Dhu'l-Hijja. The Islamic calendar is based on a lunar year of 12 months of 30 and 29 days (alternating every month), and the year is equal to 354 days. It runs in cycles of 30 years, of which the second, fifth, seventh, 10th, 13th, 16th, 18th, 21st, 24th,

26th, and 29th are leap years. Leap years have 355 days, the extra day being added to the last month, Dhu'l-Hijja. The year A.H. 1410 (*anno hegirae*, in the year of the hejira) is the 30th year in the cycle. There are no intercalated months or leap years, so the Islamic year does not keep a constant relationship to the solar year—which dictates the seasons—and months occur about 10 or 11 days earlier than in the year before.

The caliph Abu Bakr adopted A.D. 622—the year of the hejira (Muhammad's migration from Mecca to Medina)—as the first year of Islam. However, dating of the Muslim era varies throughout the Islamic world. In some countries the year of the Muslim era is obtained by subtracting 622 from the Gregorian year; A.D. 1990 equals A.H. 1368.

Other countries (Saudi Arabia, Yemen, and the principalities of the Persian Gulf) continue to use a purely lunar year. To approximate the Muslim era equivalent of the Gregorian year, subtract 622 (the year of hejira in the Gregorian calendar) from the current year and multiply the result by 1.031 (days in the year of the Gregorian calendar divided by days in the lunar year): A.D. 1990 = (1990 − 622) × 1.031 = A.H. 1410.

Muslim Holy Days

Ramadan, the ninth month of the Islamic calendar, is the Islamic faith's holiest period. To honor the month in which the Koran was revealed, all adult Muslims of sound body and mind observe fasting—eschewing food, water, or even a kiss between the hours of sunrise and sunset. Exempted from the fast are women in menstruation or childbirth bleeding, the chronically ill, or people on a journey, all of whom must make up the fast days at a later date.

Id al-Fitr This day of feasting is celebrated at the end of Ramadan. To mark the fast's break, worshipers also attend an early morning service, Salat-ul-'Id, at which they give alms in staple foodstuffs or their monetary value.

Id al-Adha The Feast of Sacrifice takes place on the 10th day of Dhu'l-Hijja, the last month of the year and the season of the *haj,* or pilgrimage. The day begins with a service in the mosques or other places of gathering, and for those who are not pilgrims continues with the ritual slaughter of a sheep in commemoration of God's ransom of Abraham's son from sacrifice. At least a third of the meat of the animal is to be set aside for charity.

Fridays At noontime Muslims attend mosque or comparable gathering places to say the congregational Friday prayer that ends the week. While Friday is the holy day of the weekly Muslim calendar, it is not a Sabbath comparable to Christian Sundays or Jewish Saturdays, and there are no restrictions on work or other worldly enterprises.

The Hindu Year

The Hindu year consists of 12 months: Caitra, Vaisakha, Jyaistha, Asadha, Sravana, Bhadrapada, Asvina, Karttika, Margasivsa, Pansa, Magha, and Phalguna. Calendrically, holidays are of two types, lunar and solar. Solar holidays in the Hindu calendar include the following:

Mesasamkranti is the beginning of the new astrological year, when the sun enters the constellation Aries.

Makaraj-Samkranti, the winter solstice, occurs when the sun enters the constellation Capricorn.

Mahavisuva Day is New Year's Eve.

Principal holidays determined by the lunar year are these:

Ramanavami (Caitra 9) celebrates the birth of Rama, in Hindu folklore the epitome of chivalry, courage, and obedience to sacred law. Rama is considered an incarnation of Vishnu, and his name is synonymous with God.

Rathayatra (Asadha 2) is the pilgrimage of the chariot festival of Orissa.

Janmastami (Sravana 8) is the birthday of Krishna, an incarnation of the supreme deity, Vishnu, celebrated as a philosopher-king and hero.

Dasahra (Asvina 7–10) commemorates Rama's victory over the demon Ravana.

Laksmipuja (Asvina 15) honors Laksmi, goddess of good fortune.

Dipavali (Karttika 15) occasions the festival of lights and exchanging of presents.

Mahasivaratri (Magha 13) honors the god Shiva, one of the three supreme Hindu gods. Shiva, whose name means "Auspicious One," is a god of both reproduction and destruction.

THE MONTHS OF THE YEAR

Gregorian	Hebrew	Hindu	Muslim
January	Shebat	Magha	*Muharram*
February	Adar	Phalguna	Safar
March	Nisan	*Caitra*	Rabi I
April	Iyar	Vaisakha	Rabi II
May	Sivan	Jyaistha	Jumada I
June	Tammuz	Asadha	Jumada II
July	Ab	Sravana	Rajab
August	Elul	Bhadrapada	Sha'ban
September	*Tishri*	Asvina	Ramadan
October	Heshvan	Karttika	Shawwal
November	Kislev	Margasivsa	Dhu'l-Qa'dah
December	Tebet	Pansa	Dhu'l-Hijja

Note: The months of the Gregorian, Hebrew, Hindu, and reformed Muslim calendars occur at roughly the same time of year, while those of the traditional (lunar) Muslim calendar occur at different times every year. Months in italics indicate the first month of the year in the respective calendars.

Key Astronomical Events of 1990

The main astronomical events include when the Moon is closest to Earth (perigee) or farthest (apogee); when the Earth is closest to the Sun (Sun's perigee, or perihelion); visits from periodic comets; occultation (passing in front) of bright stars or planets by the Moon; eclipses of the Sun and Moon; the start of each season; and the phases of the Moon.

Although one would think that the phase of the Moon halfway between a new moon and full moon, when we see half a disk, would be called a half moon, modern usage is to call this phase a quarter moon. Also, the quarter moon between the full moon and the new moon is called, rather ungrammatically, the last quarter (the second of two in English is usually the latter, while last is reserved to the final one of a list of three or more). The harvest moon is the full moon that occurs nearest the autumnal equinox, while the hunter's moon is the full moon that follows the harvest moon.

Often the Moon is not close enough to Earth to cover the Sun completely. In that case, the eclipse is called annular (ring-shaped), since,

where the eclipse is at its maximum, a ring of sunlight surrounds the Moon's shadow. Chances of an eclipse being annular are about equal to chances of its being total, so there are as many annular eclipses in the 1990s as there are total eclipses. Of most interest to people in the United States is the annular eclipse of May 10, 1994, which will be visible from Texas to Maine. No total eclipse will be visible in any state except Hawaii and Alaska during the 1990s.

SOLAR, LUNAR, AND COMET PHENOMENA, 1990

Entries that have no comment are repeats of previous entries for which the first such entry will have a comment that applies to all others of the same type. A time given as 2 p.m. is to the nearest hour, while a time given as 2:00 p.m. is to the nearest minute.

Date	Time (E.S.T.)	Event	Comments
Jan. 4	5:40 a.m.	Moon's first quarter	We see half a disk.
Jan. 4	noon	Sun's perigee	Closest approach of Earth to Sun (91,400,000 mi.).
Jan. 7	2 p.m.	Moon's perigee	Closest approach of Moon to Earth (221,463 mi.).
Jan. 10	11:57 p.m.	Full moon	A complete disk.
Jan. 18	4:17 p.m.	Moon's last quarter	The other half disk.
Jan. 19	11 a.m.	Moon's apogee	Farthest distance of Moon from Earth (238,857 mi.).
Jan. 20	N.A.	Comet Kopff	Is 147,870,000 mi. from Sun; period of revolution 6.5 years.
Jan. 22	3 a.m.	Moon occults Antares	Moon passes in front of the bright star Antares, visible in parts of Southern Hemisphere.
Jan. 26	N.A.	Annular eclipse of Sun	Visible in Antarctica, South America.
Jan. 26	2:20 p.m.	New moon	Moon completely in shadow of Earth.
Feb. 2	1:32 p.m.	Moon's first quarter	
Feb. 2	2 p.m.	Moon's perigee	
Feb. 8	N.A.	Comet Tuttle-Giacobini-Kresak	Is 99,510,000 mi. from Sun; period of revolution 5.5 years.

Date	Time (E.S.T.)	Event	Comments
Feb. 8	2:16 p.m.	Full moon	
Feb. 9	N.A.	Total eclipse of Moon	Visible in arctic regions, Australia, Europe.
Feb. 16	8 a.m.	Moon's apogee	
Feb. 17	1:48 p.m.	Moon's last quarter	
Feb. 18	11 a.m.	Moon occults Antares	Visible in Southern Hemisphere and west of Central America.
Feb. 25	3:54 a.m.	New moon	
Feb. 28	3 a.m.	Moon at perigee	
Mar. 4	9:05 p.m.	Moon's first quarter	
Mar. 11	5:58 p.m.	Full moon	Harvest moon in Southern Hemisphere.
Mar. 16	3 a.m.	Moon at apogee	
Mar. 18	7 p.m.	Moon occults Antares	Visible in Southern Hemisphere.
Mar. 19	9:30 a.m.	Moon's last quarter	
Mar. 20	4:19 p.m.	Vernal equinox	Marks official start of spring.
Mar. 22	5:18 p.m.	Moon occults Mars	Moon passes in front of planet Mars; visible in central Pacific, North America.
Mar. 26	2:48 p.m.	New moon	
Mar. 28	3 a.m.	Moon at perigee	

Date	Time (E.S.T.)	Event	Comments
Apr. 1	N.A.	Comet Sanguin	Is 168,300.000 mi. from Sun; period of revolution 12.5 years.
Apr. 2	5:24 a.m.	Moon's first quarter	
Apr. 10	10:18 p.m.	Full moon	Hunter's moon in Southern Hemisphere.
Apr. 12	3 p.m.	Moon at apogee	
Apr. 14	2 a.m.	Moon occults Antares	Visible in Southern Hemisphere.
Apr. 18	2:02 a.m.	Moon's last quarter	
Apr. 24	11:27 a.m.	New moon.	
Apr. 25	noon	Moon at perigee	
May 1	3:18 p.m.	Moon's first quarter	
May 9	2:31 p.m.	Full moon	
May 10	9 p.m.	Moon at apogee	
May 11	1 p.m.	Moon occults Antares	Visible in Southern Hemisphere.
May 17	2:45 p.m.	Moon's last quarter	
May 18	N.A.	Comet Russel 3	Is 234,360,000 mi. from Sun; period of revolution 7.5 years.
May 18	N.A.	Comet Schwassmann-Wachmann 3	Is 87,420,000 mi. from Sun; period of revolution 5.4 years.
May 24	6:47 a.m.	New moon	
May 24	3 p.m.	Moon at apogee	
May 31	3:11 a.m.	Moon's first quarter	
June 6	11 p.m.	Moon at apogee	
June 7	2 p.m.	Moon occults Antares	Visible in Southern Hemisphere.
June 8	6:01 a.m.	Full moon	
June 16	11:48 p.m.	Moon's last quarter	
June 21	10:33 a.m.	Summer solstice	Sun reaches highest point; marks official beginning of summer.
June 21	6 a.m.	Moon at perigee	
June 22	1:55 p.m.	New moon	
June 25	N.A.	Comet Peters-Hartley	Is 151,590,000 mi. from Sun; period of revolution 8.1 years.
June 29	9:01 a.m.	Moon's first quarter	
July 3	11 a.m.	Moon at apogee	
July 3	11:05 p.m.	Sun's apogee	Farthest distance from Earth to Sun (94,533,000 mi.).
July 5	9 p.m.	Moon occults Antares	Visible in Mexico, Central America, and parts of Southern Hemisphere.
July 7	N.A.	Comet Russel 4	Is 206,460,000 mi. from Sun; period of revolution 6.6 years.
July 7	N.A.	Comet Tritton	Is 133,920,000 mi. from Sun; period of revolution 6.3 years.
July 8	8:23 p.m.	Full moon	
July 15	6:04 a.m.	Moon's last quarter	
July 19	6 a.m.	Moon at perigee	
July 22	N.A.	Total eclipse of Sun	Visible in northeastern Europe, arctic regions, northwest of North America.
July 22	9:54 p.m.	New moon	
July 29	9:01 a.m.	Moon's first quarter	
July 31	3 a.m.	Moon at apogee	
Aug. 1	4 a.m.	Moon eclipses Antares	Visible in Southern Hemisphere.
Aug. 6	9:10 a.m.	Full moon	
Aug. 6	N.A.	Partial eclipse of Moon	Visible over southwestern Alaska, Pacific Ocean, Antarctica, Australia, eastern Asia.
Aug. 13	10:54 a.m.	Moon's last quarter	
Aug. 15	5 a.m.	Moon at perigee	
Aug. 18	8:00 a.m.	Moon occults Jupiter	Visible in central North America, southern Greenland, southwestern Europe, northern Africa.
Aug. 18	7 p.m.	Moon occults Venus	Visible in Southern Hemisphere.

Date	Time (E.S.T.)	Event	Comments
Aug. 20	7:39 a.m.	New moon	
Aug. 22	7 a.m.	Moon occults Mercury	Visible in northeast Atlantic, Africa, Indian Ocean.
Aug. 27	10 p.m.	Moon at apogee	
Aug. 28	2:34 a.m.	Moon's first quarter	
Aug. 28	noon	Moon occults Antares	Visible in Southern Hemisphere.
Sept. 4	8:46 p.m.	Full moon	
Sept. 9	6 a.m.	Moon at perigee	
Sept. 11	3:53 p.m.	Moon's last quarter	
Sept. 12	N.A.	Comet Honda-Mrkos-Pajdusakova	Is 50,220,000 mi. from Sun; period of revolution 5.3 years.
Sept. 15	1 a.m.	Moon occults Jupiter	Visible in southern Africa, Saudi Arabia, Indian Ocean.
Sept. 18	7:46 p.m.	New moon	
Sept. 23	1:55 a.m.	Autumnal equinox	Marks official start of fall.
Sept. 24	5 p.m.	Moon at apogee	
Sept. 24	9 p.m.	Moon occults Antares	Visible in Mexico, Central America, Cuba, northern South America.
Sept. 26	9:06 p.m.	Moon's first quarter	
Oct. 4	7:02 a.m.	Full moon	Harvest moon in Northern Hemisphere.
Oct. 6	1 p.m.	Moon at perigee	
Oct. 10	10:31 p.m.	Moon's last quarter	
Oct. 12	3 p.m.	Moon occults Jupiter	Moon passes in front of planet Jupiter; visible in Australia, southern oceans.
Oct. 18	10:37 a.m.	New moon	
Oct. 22	3 a.m.	Moon occults Antares	Visible in southern Asia and Indonesia.
Oct. 22	11 a.m.	Moon at apogee	
Oct. 25	noon	Moon occults Saturn	Moon passes in front of planet Saturn; visible in Antarctica.
Oct. 26	3:26 p.m.	Moon's first quarter	
Oct. 28	N.A.	Comet Enke	Is 30,690,000 mi. from Sun; period of revolution 3.3 years.
Nov. 2	4:48 p.m.	Full moon	Hunter's moon in Northern Hemisphere.
Nov. 3	6 p.m.	Moon at perigee	
Nov. 9	8:02 a.m.	Moon's last quarter	
Nov. 17	4:05 a.m.	New moon	
Nov. 18	N.A.	Comet Johnson	Is 214,830,000 mi. from Sun; period of revolution 7.0 years.
Nov. 18	10 p.m.	Moon at apogee	
Nov. 21	11 p.m.	Moon occults Saturn	Visible in Antarctica and southern oceans.
Nov. 22	N.A.	Comet Kearns-Kwee	Is 206,460,000 mi. from Sun; period of revolution 9.0 years.
Nov. 25	8:11 a.m.	Moon's first quarter	
Dec. 2	2:50 a.m.	Full moon	
Dec. 2	6 a.m.	Moon at perigee	
Dec. 8	7:04 p.m.	Moon's last quarter	
Dec. 15	4 p.m.	Moon occults Antares	Visble in northeastern Asia, Alaska, western North America.
Dec. 15	11 p.m.	Moon at apogee	
Dec. 16	N.A.	Comet Wild 2	Is 146,940,000 mi. from Sun; period of revolution 6.4 years.
Dec. 16	11:22 p.m.	New moon	
Dec. 19	10 a.m.	Moon occults Saturn	Moon passes in front of planet Saturn; visible in east Pacific, South America, south Atlantic, central Africa.
Dec. 21	10:07 p.m.	Winter solstice	Official start of winter.
Dec. 24	10:16 p.m.	Full moon	
Dec. 28	N.A.	Comet Taylor	Is 181,350,000 mi. from Sun; period of revolution 7.0 years.
Dec. 30	7 p.m.	Moon at perigee	
Dec. 31	12:35 p.m.	Full moon	

Source: The Nautical Almanac Office, U.S. Naval Observatory, and Her Majesty's Nautical Almanac Office, Royal Greenwich Observatory, *Astronomical Phenomena for the Year 1990* (1988).

TOTAL SOLAR ECLIPSES IN THE 1990s

A total eclipse is one of nature's most spectacular sights, and many people will travel halfway around the world to see one. A total eclipse occurs when the Moon is close enough to Earth to cover the entire Sun. As the Earth turns below, the shadow of the Moon races roughly from west to east in a long curving path. People not near the midline of that path see only a partial eclipse. Since the period of totality is only a few minutes, weather along the path is especially important. The viewing notes here are based on historical records of cloud cover at the time of the eclipse for places along the path.

Date	Path	Remarks	Date	Path	Remarks
July 22, 1990	Near Helsinki, Finland, along USSR's Arctic Coast, to Aleutian Islands	View at dawn in Finland, where weather is most likely to be best; cloud cover 99% of time in Aleutians	Oct. 24, 1995	From Iran; across Afghanistan, Pakistan, India, Southeast Asia; and into western Pacific	Shortest eclipse of decade, lasting little over 2 minutes over China Sea; best viewing in Great Indian Desert near Calcutta, India
July 11, 1991	Island of Hawaii, over the Pacific to Baja California, through Mexico and Central America, into South America to Brazil's rain forest	Best eclipse of decade because of 3 excellent viewing sites: Hawaii, Baja California, and Brazil; longest total-eclipse period until 2137	Mar. 9, 1997	From Mongolia, across Siberia, almost to North Pole	If you can stand the cold of March in Siberia, best viewing is between Magadan and Yakutsk on banks of frozen Lena
June 30, 1992	From coast of South America to tip of South Africa, almost entirely in Atlantic Ocean	Over 5 min. long in mid-Atlantic; best seen from ship	Feb. 26, 1998	From eastern Pacific; past Galapagos; across Panama, Columbia, and Venezuela; into Caribbean	North of Marcaibo, Venezuela, should provide good viewing, or vicinity of Leeward Islands in Caribbean
Nov. 3, 1994	Starts in eastern Pacific but reaches land near Arequipa, Peru; crosses Chile, Bolivia, Paraguay, Brazil; and heads into Atlantic	Best viewing in inland Peru in terms of chance of clouds, but total-eclipse longest in Atlantic	Aug. 11, 1999	From western Atlantic off Nova Scotia to Isles of Scilly and the southwest tip of Great Britain; through central Europe, Middle East, India and Pakistan, to Bay of Bengal	First total eclipse for central Europe since 1961, but best viewing should be in Iran and Iraq; southeastern Europe and Turkey also should be good

Source: Jay Anderson, "Eclipse Prospects for the 1990s," *Astronomy* (Feb. 1989).

ANNULAR SOLAR ECLIPSES IN THE 1990s

Date	Region where visible
Jan. 26, 1990	Antarctica, South America
Jan. 15, 1991	Australia, New Zealand
Jan. 4, 1992	Pacific Ocean
May 10, 1994	Pacific Ocean, Mexico, U.S., Canada, Atlantic Ocean
Apr. 29, 1995	South Pacific, South America
Aug. 22, 1998	Indonesia, Malaysia, New Guinea
Feb. 16, 1999	Indian Ocean, Australia

Source: Jay Anderson, "Eclipse Prospects for the 1990s," *Astronomy* (Feb. 1989).

LUNAR ECLIPSES

There will be two lunar eclipses in 1990 (Feb. 9 and Aug. 6), neither visible in most of the United States. A lunar eclipse occurs when Earth's shadow falls on the Moon. If the shadow completely covers the Moon, the eclipse is total; if the shadow covers only part of the Moon, the eclipse is partial. Whether a lunar eclipse is visible from a particular place on Earth depends on the time of day. If it is daylight, the eclipse is not visible. Even so, lunar eclipses can be seen over a wider range of places than can solar eclipses. Since a lunar eclipse takes an appreciable amount of time from beginning to end (about six hours, or a quarter of a day, for a total eclipse), the end of an eclipse can be seen by people living in different regions than those who saw the beginning. (See table "Solar, Lunar, and Comet Phenomena, 1990," on pages 18–19, for more information.)

STANDARD WEIGHTS & MEASURES

SYSTEMS OF MEASUREMENT

There are two measurement systems that are widely used. Most of the world uses a system known as the metric system, or the International System. The United States continues to use a system called U.S. customary measure. From time to time, our government has taken steps to change from the customary system to the International System (abbreviated SI from Système internationale, its name in French), but these efforts have failed. Metric measure is legal in the United States, but nearly everyone continues to use the customary system. One result is a need in the country to be able to convert back and forth from one system to another.

Customary measure in the United States is derived from English measure, but in some details, the American system is different from the English as well as from Canadian customary measures, also derived from the English.

Today both the United Kingdom and Canada officially use the International System. The International System is also generally used in scientific pursuits and increasingly in international trade.

The following tables show first the U.S. customary system, then the International System, and finally some important conversion factors between the two.

Length or Distance

U.S. CUSTOMARY

1 foot (ft.) = 12 inches (in.)
1 yard (yd.) = 3 feet = 36 inches
1 rod (rd.) = 5½ yards = 16½ feet
1 furlong (fur.) = 40 rods = 220 yards = 660 feet
1 mile (mi.) = 8 furlongs = 1,760 yards = 5,280 feet

An International nautical mile has been defined as 6,076.1155 feet.

INTERNATIONAL SYSTEM

The basic unit for length is the meter, which is slightly longer than the customary yard. Other units of length are decimal subdivisions or multiples of the meter.

decimeter (dm) = 10 centimeters = 0.1 meter
centimeter (cm) = 0.01 meter
millimeter (mm) = 0.1 centimeter = 0.001 meter
micron (μ) = 0.001 millimeter = 0.0001 centimeter = 0.000001 meter
angstrom (Å) = 0.0001 micron = 0.0000001 millimeter
dekameter (dam) = 10 meters

hectometer (hm) = 10 dekameters =
100 meters
kilometer (km) = 10 hectometers =
100 dekameters =
1,000 meters

In 1959 the relationship between customary and international measures of length was officially defined as follows:

0.0254 meter (exactly) = 1 inch
0.0254 meter × 12 = 0.3048 meter =
1 international foot.

This definition, which makes many conversions simple, defines a foot that is shorter (by about 6 parts in 10,000,000) than the survey foot, which had earlier been defined as exactly 1200/3937, or 0.3048006 meter.

Following the international foot standard, the major equivalents are as listed below:

1 inch = 2.54 centimeters = 0.0254 meter
1 foot = 30.48 centimeters = 0.3048 meter
1 yard = 91.44 centimeters = 0.9144 meter
1 mile = 1,609.344 meters =
1.609344 kilometers

1 centimeter = 0.3937 inch
1 meter = 1.093613 yards =
3.28084 feet =
0.00062137 mile.

Area

CUSTOMARY

Areas are derived from lengths as follows:

1 square foot = 144 square inches
(sq. ft. or ft²) (sq. in.)
1 square yard = 9 square feet
(sq. yd. or yd²)
1 square rod = 30¼ square yards =
(sq. rd.) 272½ sq. ft.
1 acre = 160 square rods =
4,840 sq. yd. =
43,560 sq. ft.
1 square mile = 640 acres =
1 section = 1 mile square
1 township = 6 miles square =
36 square miles

INTERNATIONAL SYSTEM

1 sq. millimeter (mm²) = 1,000,000
sq. microns
1 sq. centimeter (cm²) = 100 sq.
millimeters
1 sq. meter (m²) = 10,000 sq.
centimeters
1 are (a) = 100 square meters
1 hectare (ha) = 100 ares =
10,000 sq. meters
1 sq. kilometer (km²) = 100 hectares =
1,000,000 sq.
meters

CONVERSIONS

1 sq. inch = 6.4516 cm²
1 sq. foot = 929.0304 cm² =
0.09290304 m²
1 sq. yard = 8,361.2736 cm² =
0.83612736 m²
1 acre = 4,046.8564 m² =
0.40468564 ha
1 sq. mile = 2,589,988.11 m² =
258.998811 ha =
2.58998811 km²

1 cm² = 0.1550003 sq. in.
1 m² = 1,550.003 sq. in. =
10.76391 sq. ft. =
1.195990 sq. yd.
1 hectare = 107,639.1 sq. ft. =
11,959.90 sq. yd. =
2.4710538 acres =
0.003861006 sq. mi.
1 km² = 247.10538 acres =
0.3861006 sq. mi.

Cubic Measure

CUSTOMARY

1 cubic foot (ft³) = 1,728 cubic inches (in³)
1 cubic yard (yd³) = 27 cubic feet

INTERNATIONAL SYSTEM

1 cubic centimeter = 1,000 cubic millimeters
(cm³) (mm³)
1 cubic decimeter = 1,000 cubic centimeters
(dm³)
1 cubic meter (m³) = 1,000 cubic
decimeters =
1,000,000 cubic
centimeters

Cubic centimeter is sometimes abbreviated *cc* and is used in fluid measure interchangeably with milliliter (ml).

CONVERSIONS

1 in³ = 16.387064 cm³
1 ft³ = 28,316.846592 cm³ =
0.0028316847 m³
1 yd³ = 764,554.857984 cm³ =
0.764554858 m³
1 cm³ = 0.06102374 in³
1 m³ = 61,023.74 in³ =
35.31467 ft³ =
1.307951 yd³

Fluid volume

CUSTOMARY MEASURE

A gallon is equal to 231 cubic inches of liquid or capacity.

1 tablespoon (tbs.) = 3 teaspoons (tsp.) =
0.5 fluid ounce (fl. oz.)
1 cup = 8 fluid ounces
1 pint (pt.) = 2 cups = 16 fl. oz.
1 quart (qt.) = 2 pt. = 4 cups =
32 fl. oz.
1 gallon (gal.) = 4 qt. = 8 pt. = 16 cups
1 bushel (bu.) = 8 gallon = 32 quarts

INTERNATIONAL SYSTEM

Fluid-volume measurements are directly tied to cubic measure. One milliliter of fluid occupies a volume of 1 cubic centimeter (cm³ or cc). A liter of fluid (slightly more than the customary quart) occupies a volume of 1 cubic decimeter, or 1,000 cubic centimeters.

1 centiliter (cl) = 10 milliliters (ml)
1 deciliter (dl) = 10 centiliters =
100 milliliters
1 liter (L) = 10 deciliters =
1,000 milliliters
1 dekaliter (dal) = 10 liters
1 hectoliter (hl) = 10 dekaliters =
100 liters
1 kiloliter (kl) = 100 hectoliters =
1,000 liters

CONVERSIONS

1 fluid ounce = 29.573528 ml = 0.02957 L
1 cup = 236.588 ml = 0.236588 L
1 pint = 473.176 ml = 0.473176 L
1 quart = 946.3529 ml =
0.9463529 L
1 gallon = 3,785.41 ml = 3.78541 L

1 mililiter = 0.0338 fluid ounce
1 liter = 33.814 fluid ounces =
4.2268 cups = 2.113 pints =
1.0567 quarts = 0.264 gallon

Dry Volume

CONVERSIONS

1 pint, dry = 33.600 cu. in. = 0.551 L
1 quart, dry = 67.201 cu. in. = 1.101 L

MASS AND WEIGHT

Mass and weight are often confused. Mass is a measure of the quantity of matter in an object and does not vary with changes in altitude or in gravitational force (as on the moon or another planet). Weight, on the other hand, is a measure of the force of gravity on an object and so does change with altitude or gravitational force.

CUSTOMARY

In customary measure it is more common to measure weight than mass. The most common customary system of weight is avoirdupois:

1 pound (lb.) = 16 ounces (oz.)
1 (short) hundred-
weight (cwt.) = 100 lb.
1 (short) ton = 20 hundredweights =
2,000 lb.
1 long hundred-
weight = 112 lb.
1 long ton = 20 long hundredweights = 2,240 lb.

A different system called troy weight is used to weigh precious metals. In troy weight the ounce is slightly larger than in avoirdupois, but there are only 12 ounces to the troy pound.

INTERNATIONAL SYSTEM

Instead of weight, the International System generally is used to measure mass. The International System's basic unit for measurement of mass is the gram, which was originally defined as the mass of 1 milliliter (= 1 cc) of water at 4 degrees Celsius (about 39°F). Today the official standard of measure is the kilogram (1,000 g).

1 centigram (cg) = 10 milligrams (mg)
1 decigram (dg) = 10 centigrams =
100 milligrams
1 gram (g) = 10 decigrams =
100 centigrams =
1,000 milligrams
1 kilogram (kg) = 10 hectograms (hg) =
100 dekagrams (dag) =
1,000 grams
1 metric ton (t) = 1,000 kilograms

CONVERSIONS

Since mass and weight are identical at standard conditions (sea level on earth), grams and other International System units of mass are often used as measures of weight or converted into customary units of weight. Under standard conditions

$$1 \text{ ounce} = 28.3495 \text{ grams}$$
$$1 \text{ pound} = 453.59 \text{ grams} =$$
$$0.45359 \text{ kilogram}$$
$$1 \text{ short ton} = 907.18 \text{ kilograms} =$$
$$0.907 \text{ metric ton}$$
$$1 \text{ milligram} = 0.000035 \text{ ounce}$$
$$1 \text{ gram} = 0.03527 \text{ ounce}$$
$$1 \text{ kilogram} = 35.27 \text{ ounces} =$$
$$2.2046 \text{ pounds}$$
$$1 \text{ metric ton} = 2,204.6 \text{ pounds} =$$
$$1.1023 \text{ short ton}.$$

Time

CUSTOMARY AND INTERNATIONAL SYSTEM

The International System in 1967 adopted a second that is based on the microwaves emitted by the vibrations of hot cesium atoms. A second is the time it takes the atoms to vibrate exactly 9,192,631,770 times. In the customary measure of time, the day is divided into 24 hours, the hour into 60 minutes, and the minute into 60 seconds. Since the Earth's rotation is gradually slowing, scientists must periodically add a second to a day to keep the year in sequence with their clocks (most recently done on Dec. 31, 1987). The change is so small that for almost all practical purposes an International System second and a customary second are the same.

Decimal fractions of time are used to measure smaller time intervals:

millisecond (ms) = 0.001 second (10^{-3})
microsecond (μs) = 0.000001 second (10^{-6})
nanosecond (ns) = 0.000000001 second (10^{-9})
picosecond (ps) = 0.000000000001 second (10^{-12})

Temperature

CUSTOMARY

Customary measure is often said to include the Fahrenheit scale of temperature measurement (abbreviated F). In this system, water freezes at 32 degrees F and boils at 212 degrees F. Absolute zero is –459.7 degrees F.

INTERNATIONAL SYSTEM

For the common range of temperature, the International System measures in the Celsius (formerly called centigrade) scale denoted by the abbreviation C. In this scale, water freezes at 0 degrees C and boils at 100 degrees C.

For very low temperatures, measurement is made on the Kelvin scale (abbreviated K), or as it is sometimes called, the absolute scale. One degree Kelvin is exactly the same as one degree Celsius, but zero Kelvin is set at 273.15 degrees below zero Celsius. Zero Kelvin is the temperature absolute zero, which is as cold as anything can become. Thus the equivalencies between Fahrenheit, Kelvin, and Celsius are the following:

	F	C	K
Absolute zero	–459.7	–273.15	0
Freezing point, water	32	0	273.15
Normal human body temperature	98.6	37	310.15
Boiling point, water	212	100	373.15

In measuring very high temperatures, the difference between the Kelvin and Celsius scales becomes insignificant.

CUSTOMARY

The simplest means of converting is by formula: *To convert a Fahrenheit temperature to Celsius* on a calculator, subtract 32 from the temperature and multiply the difference by 5; then divide the product by 9. The formula is

$$C = \tfrac{5}{9} (F - 32).$$

To convert a Celsius temperature to Fahrenheit on a calculator, multiply the temperature by 1.8, then add 32; the formula is often given with the fraction 9/5 instead of the equivalent decimal, 1.8.

$$F = \tfrac{9}{5} (C + 32)$$

To convert to Kelvin, find the temperature in Celsius and add 273.15.

$$K = C + 273.15$$

Force, Work/Energy, Power

CUSTOMARY SYSTEM

The foot/pound/second system of reckoning includes the following units:

slug = the mass to which a force of 1 poundal will give an acceleration of 1 foot per second (= approximately 32.17 lbs.)
poundal = fundamental unit of force
foot-pound = the work done when a force of 1 poundal produces a movement of 1 foot
foot-pound/second = the unit of power equal to 1 foot/pound per second.

Another common unit of power is horsepower, which is equal to 550 foot-pounds per second.

Thermal work or energy is often measured in British thermal units (Btu), which are defined as the energy required to increase the temperature of 1 pound of water by 1 degree Fahrenheit. The Btu is equal to 0.778^+ foot-pound.

INTERNATIONAL SYSTEM

In physics, compound measurements of force, work or energy, and power are essential. There are two parallel systems using International System units: the centimeter/gram/second system (cgs) is used for small measurements, and the meter/kilogram/second system (mks) is used for larger measurements. They are described below.

Measurement of Force

cm/g unit	dyne (dy)	The force required to accelerate a mass of 1 g 1 cm/s²
m/kg unit	newton (new)	The force required to accelerate a mass of 1 kg 1 m/s²

Measurement of Work or Energy

cm/g unit	erg	The dyne-centimeter, i.e., the work done when a force of 1 dy produces a movement of 1 cm
m/kg unit	joule (j)	The newton-meter, i.e., the work done when a force of 1 newton produces a movement of 1 m (= 10,000,000 ergs)

Measurement of Power

cm/g unit	erg/second	A rate of 1 erg per second
m/kg unit	watt (w)	The joule/second, i.e., a rate of 1 joule per second (= 10,000,000 erg-seconds)

Heat energy is also measured using the calorie (cal), which is defined as the energy required to increase the temperature of 1 cubic centimeter (1 ml) of water by 1 degree C. One calorie is equal to about 4.184 joules. The kilocalorie (Kcal or Cal) is equal to 1,000 calories and is the unit in which the energy values of food are measured. This more familiar unit, also commonly referred to as a Calorie, is equal to about 4,184 joules.

CONVERSIONS

Measurement of Force
$$1 \text{ poundal} = 13,889 \text{ dynes} =$$
$$0.13889 \text{ newtons}$$
$$1 \text{ dyne} = 0.000072 \text{ poundals}$$
$$1 \text{ newton} = 7.2 \text{ poundals}$$

Measurement of Work/Energy
$$1 \text{ foot-pound} = 1,356 \text{ joules}$$
$$\text{British thermal unit} = 1,055 \text{ joules} =$$
$$252 \text{ gram calories}$$
$$1 \text{ joule} = 0.0007374$$
$$\text{foot-pounds}$$
$$1 \text{ (gram) calorie} = 0.003968 \text{ Btu}$$
$$1 \text{ (kilo) Calorie} = 3.968 \text{ Btu}$$

Measurement of Power
$$1 \text{ foot-pound/second} = 1.3564 \text{ watts}$$
$$1 \text{ horsepower} = 746 \text{ watts} =$$
$$0.746 \text{ kilowatts}$$
$$1 \text{ watt} = 0.73725 \text{ foot-}$$
$$\text{pound/second} =$$
$$0.00134 \text{ horse-}$$
$$\text{power}$$
$$1 \text{ kilowatt} = 737.25 \text{ ft.-lb./sec.} =$$
$$1.34 \text{ horsepower}$$

Electrical Measure

Measures for electricity form a separate system of their own.

The basic unit of quantity in electricity is the coulomb. A coulomb is equal to the passage of 6.25×10^{18} electrons past a given point in an electrical system.

The unit of electrical flow is the ampere, which is equal to a coulomb-second, i.e., the flow of 1 coulomb per second. The ampere is analogous in electrical measure to a unit of flow such as gallons-per-minute in physical measure.

The unit for measuring electrical potential energy is the volt, which is defined as 1 joule/coulomb, i.e., 1 joule of energy per coulomb of electricity. The volt is analogous to a measure of pressure in a water system.

The unit for measuring electrical power is the watt as defined in the previous section. Power in watts is the product of the electrical flow in amperes and the potential electrical energy in volts.

P (in watts) = I (electrical current in amperes) × V (potential energy in volts)

Since the watt is such a small unit for practical applications, the kilowatt (= 1,000 watts) is often used. A kilowatt-hour is the power of 1,000 watts over an hour's time.

The unit for measuring electrical resistance is the ohm, which is the resistance offered by a circuit to the flow of 1 ampere being driven by the force of 1 volt. It is derived from Ohm's law, which defines the relationship between flow or current (amperes), potential energy (volts), and resistance (ohms). It states that the current in amperes (I) is proportional to potential energy in volts (E) and inversely proportional to resistance in ohms (R). Thus, when voltage and resistance are known, amperage can be calculated by the simple formula

$$I \text{ (in amperes)} = \frac{E \text{ (in volts)}}{R \text{ (in ohms)}}.$$

Astronomical Distances

One very large measure of distance useful in astronomy is the light-year. It is defined as the distance light travels through a vacuum in a year (approximately 365¼ days). Light travels though a vacuum at the rate of about 186,250 miles an hour (exactly 299,792,458 m/sec.—exact because the meter is defined in terms of the speed of light in a vacuum). It is approximately equivalent to 5,880 billion miles (9,460 billion km).

Astronomers also use a measure even larger than the light-year, the parsec, equal to 3.258 light-years, or about 19,180 billion miles (30,820 billion km).

A smaller unit, for measurements within the solar system, is the astronomical unit, which is the average distance between the earth and the sun, or about 93 million miles (150 million km).

SIMPLIFIED CONVERSION TABLE
(alphabetical order)

To convert	into	multiply by
centimeters	feet	0.03281
centimeters	inches	0.3937
cubic cm	cubic in.	0.06102
cubic ft.	cubic m	0.02832
degrees	radians	0.01745
feet	cm	30.48
feet	meters	0.3048
gallons	liters	3.785
gal. water	lb. water	8.3453
grams	ounces	0.03527
grams	pounds	0.002205
inches	cm	2.54
kilograms	pounds	2.205
kilometers	feet	3,280.8
kilometers	miles	0.6214
knots	mi./hr.	1.151
liters	gallons	0.2642
liters	pints	2.113
meters	feet	3.281
miles	km	1.609
ounces	grams	28.3495
ounces	pounds	0.0625
pounds	kg	0.4536

Measure of Angles and Arcs

Angles are measured by systems that are not part of either the customary or International systems, although degree measure might be described as the customary system for most people most of the time. Arcs of a circle can be measured by length, but they are also often measured by angles. In the latter case, the measure of the arc is the same as the measure of an angle whose vertex is at the center of the circle and whose sides pass through the ends of the arc. Such an angle is said to be subtended by the arc.

The most commonly used angle measure is degree measure. One degree is the angle subtended by an arc that is 1/360 of a circle. This is an ancient system of measurement probably originally developed by Sumerian astronomers. These astronomers used a numeration system based on 60 (60 x 6 = 360), as well as a 360-day year. They divided the day into 12 equal periods of 30 smaller periods each (12 × 30 = 360) and used roughly the same system for dividing the circle. Even when different years and numeration systems were adopted by later societies, astronomers continued to use a variation of the Sumerian system.

$$1 \text{ degree } (1°) = 60 \text{ minutes } (60') = $$
$$3,600 \text{ seconds } (3,600'')$$
$$1 \text{ minute } = 60 \text{ seconds}$$

When two lines are perpendicular to each other, they form four angles of the same size, which are called right angles. Two right angles make up a line, which in this context is considered a straight angle.

$$1 \text{ right angle } = 90°$$
$$1 \text{ straight angle } = 180°$$

While this system is workable for most purposes, it is artificial. Mathematicians discovered that using a natural system of angle measurement produces results that make better sense in mathematical and many scientific applications. This system is called radian measure. One radian is the measure of the angle subtended by an arc of a circle that is exactly as long as the radius of the circle.

$$1 \text{ radian } = \text{ about } 57° \, 17' \, 45''$$

The circumference, C, of a circle is given by the formula $C = 2\pi r$, where π is a number (approximately 3.14159) and r is the radius. Therefore, a semicircle whose radius is 1 is π units long, which implies that there are π radians in a straight angle. Many of the angles commonly encountered are measured in multiples of π radians:

$$0° = 0 \text{ radians}$$
$$30° = \pi/6 \text{ radians}$$
$$45° = \pi/4 \text{ radians}$$
$$60° = \pi/3 \text{ radians}$$
$$90° = \pi/2 \text{ radians}$$
$$180° = \pi \text{ radians}$$
$$270° = 3\pi/2 \text{ radians}$$
$$360° = 2\pi \text{ radians}$$

To convert from radians to degrees, use the formula $t \text{ radians} = (180/\pi) \, t°$. To convert from degrees to radians, use the formula
$$\theta° = (\pi/180)\theta \text{ radians}.$$

The U.S. artillery uses the mil to measure angles. A mil is the angle subtended by an arc that is 1/6400 of a circle.

$$1 \text{ mil} = 0.05625° = 3' \, 22.5''$$
$$1 \text{ mil} = \text{almost } 0.001 \text{ radian}$$

TEMPERATURE CONVERSIONS

Often you need to know only the approximate values to convert a weather report or temperature in a recipe from Celsius to Fahrenheit. The following table can be used to get an approximate conversion between the two scales for temperatures frequently encountered.

Because a Celsius degree is larger than a Fahrenheit degree, the two scales necessarily cross; that is, there is one temperature given as the same in both scales, –40°F is the same temperature as –40°C.

Celsius	Fahrenheit	Fahrenheit	Celsius
–45.0 =	–49.0	–45.0 =	–42.8
–40.0 =	–40.0	–40.0 =	–40.0
–35.0 =	–31.0	–35.0 =	–37.2
–30.0 =	–22.0	–30.0 =	–34.4
–25.0 =	–13.0	–25.0 =	–31.7
–20.0 =	–4.0	–20.0 =	–28.9
–15.0 =	5.0	–15.0 =	–26.1
–10.0 =	14.0	–10.0 =	–23.3
–5.0 =	23.0	–5.0 =	–20.6
0.0 =	32.0	0.0 =	–17.8
5.0 =	41.0	5.0 =	–15.0
10.0 =	50.0	10.0 =	–12.2
15.0 =	59.0	15.0 =	–9.4
20.0 =	68.0	20.0 =	–6.7
25.0 =	77.0	25.0 =	–3.9
30.0 =	86.0	30.0 =	–1.1
35.0 =	95.0	35.0 =	1.7
40.0 =	104.0	40.0 =	4.4
45.0 =	113.0	45.0 =	7.2
50.0 =	122.0	50.0 =	10.0
55.0 =	131.0	55.0 =	12.8
60.0 =	140.0	60.0 =	15.6
65.0 =	149.0	65.0 =	18.3
70.0 =	158.0	70.0 =	21.1
75.0 =	167.0	75.0 =	23.9
80.0 =	176.0	80.0 =	26.7
85.0 =	185.0	85.0 =	29.4
90.0 =	194.0	90.0 =	32.2
95.0 =	203.0	95.0 =	35.0
100.0 =	212.0	100.0 =	37.8
105.0 =	221.0	105.0 =	40.6
110.0 =	230.0	110.0 =	43.3
115.0 =	239.0	115.0 =	46.1
120.0 =	248.0	120.0 =	48.9
125.0 =	257.0	125.0 =	51.7
130.0 =	266.0	130.0 =	54.4
135.0 =	275.0	135.0 =	57.2
140.0 =	284.0	140.0 =	60.0
145.0 =	293.0	145.0 =	62.8
150.0 =	302.0	150.0 =	65.6
155.0 =	311.0	155.0 =	68.3
160.0 =	320.0	160.0 =	71.1
165.0 =	329.0	165.0 =	73.9
170.0 =	338.0	170.0 =	76.7
175.0 =	347.0	175.0 =	79.4

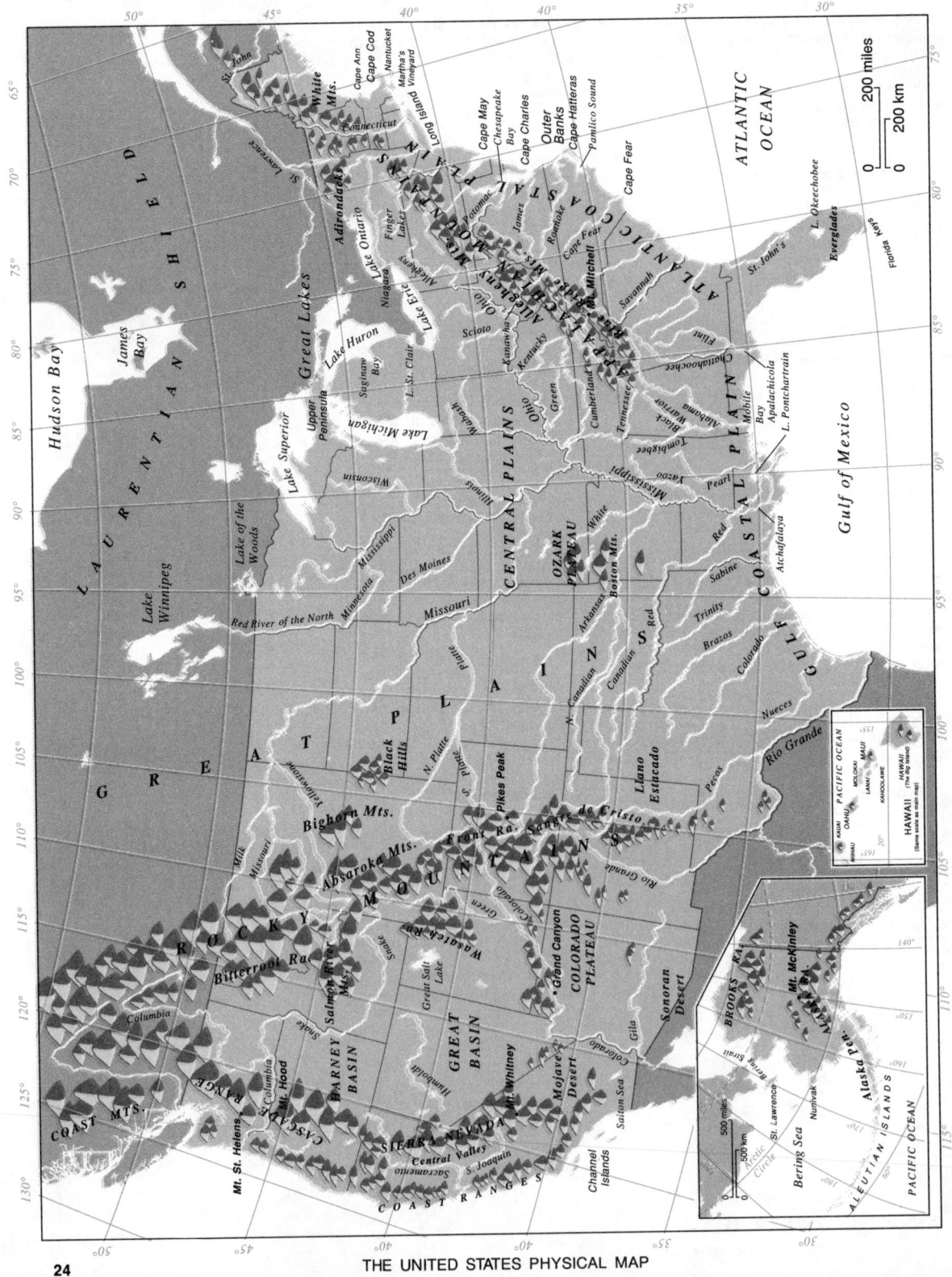

THE UNITED STATES PHYSICAL MAP

UNITED STATES GEOGRAPHY

Location The United States of America shares the North American continent with Canada, Mexico, and the Central American nations. The 48 conterminous states lie in a broad landmass from approximately latitude 24° N to 49° N (south to north), and longitude 67° W to 124° W (east to west). It is bordered on the north by Canada, on the south by Mexico and the Gulf of Mexico, on the east by the Atlantic Ocean, and on the West by the Pacific Ocean. The state of Alaska is located to the northwest on the North American continent; Hawaii is in the Pacific Ocean Basin approximately 2,100 miles southwest of the state of California.

Political-Geographic Divisions

The U.S. Bureau of the Census groups the states into divisions and subdivisions.

Northeast New England Maine, N.H., Vt., Mass., R.I., Conn.
Middle Atlantic N.Y., N.J., Pa.

Midwest East North-Central Ohio, Ind., Ill., Mich., Wis.
West North-Central Minn., Iowa, Mo., N.Dak., S.Dak., Nebr., Kans.

South South Atlantic Del., Md., D.C., Va., W.Va., N.C., S.C., Ga., Fla.
East South-Central Ky., Tenn., Ala., Miss.
West South-Central Ark., La., Okla., Tex.

Pacific Mountain Mont., Idaho, Wyo., Colo., N.Mex., Ariz., Utah, Nev.
Pacific Wash., Oreg., Calif., Alaska, Hawaii.

Physiographic Regions of the United States

The physiographic regions, that is the primary geological features and landforms, of the United States are as follows:

Atlantic and Gulf Coast Plains Run from the islands of southern New England, Cape Cod, and Long Island, through N.J., Del., Md., Va., N.C., S.C., Ga., Fla., Ala., Miss., La., Tex.; including lower Mississippi valley in Ark., Mo., Tenn.

Appalachian System Divided into five parts: NEW ENGLAND White mountains (N.H.), Green mountains (Vt.), Champlain Lowland and Hudson Valley (Vt., N.Y.), Catskill mountains (N.Y.). THE PIEDMONT Pa., Va., N.C., S.C., Ga., Ala. GREAT SMOKY AND BLUE RIDGE MOUNTAINS Pa. (Poconos), [discontinuous], Va., N.C., Ga. RIDGE AND VALLEY Pa., W.Va., Va., Ky., Tenn., Ala. APPALACHIAN PLATEAU Pa., Ohio, W.Va., Ky., Tenn., Ala.

Canadian (or Laurentian) Shield Covers much of eastern Canada and extends into the U.S. in two places:

ADIRONDACK MOUNTAINS N.Y. SUPERIOR UPLAND Upper Mich., Wis., Minn.
Central Lowland Includes most of the U.S. interior and is divided into four parts: INTERIOR LOWLANDS Ohio, Ky., Tenn. MISSISSIPPI GREAT LAKES BASIN Ohio, Ind., Ill., Mich., Wis., Iowa, N.Dak., S.Dak. INTERIOR HIGHLANDS Ozark Mountains: Mo., Ark., Okla.; Ouachita Mountains: Ark., Okla. GREAT PLAINS N.Dak., S.Dak., Nebr., Kans., Okla., Tex., Mont., Wyo., Colo., N.Mex.
Cordilleran Province Rocky Mountains N.Mex., Colo., Wyo., Mont.
Intermontane Range Divided into four sections: COLORADO PLATEAU Colo., Utah, N.Mex., Ariz. (including the Grand Canyon). BASIN AND RANGE PLATEAU Nev., Utah (including Wasatch Range). DESERT BASIN AND RANGE Calif. (including Death Valley), Ariz. SNAKE AND COLUMBIA RIVER BASINS Idaho, Wash., Oreg.
Pacific Coastlands Divided into four sections, three oriented north-south, the other east-west: CASCADE MOUNTAINS AND SIERRA NEVADA Wash., Oreg., Calif. PUGET SOUND, WILLAMETTE VALLEY, AND CENTRAL VALLEY Wash., Oreg., Calif. COAST RANGES Wash., Oreg., Calif. LOS ANGELES EXTENSION Tehachapi Mountains (east-west), San Gabriel Mountains, and San Bernardino Mountains.

Source: J.H. Paterson, *North America*, 8th ed. (New York: Oxford University Press, 1989).

SELECTED NATIONAL PARK SERVICE AREAS—ACREAGE, 1987, AND VISITS AND OVERNIGHT STAYS, 1985–87

Area	FEDERAL ACRES (thousands) 1987	RECREATION VISITS (millions) 1985	RECREATION VISITS (millions) 1987	OVERNIGHT STAYS[1] (thousands) 1985	OVERNIGHT STAYS[1] (thousands) 1987
Total, all areas[2]	76,056	263.4	287.2	15,780	17,123
Acadia National Park, Maine	41	3.7	4.3	208	212
Big Bend National Park, Texas	708	0.2	0.2	238	225
Blue Ridge Parkway, N.C.-Va.	79	17.2	18.6	230	246
Cape Cod National Seashore, Mass.	27	4.4	4.9	17	16
Chesapeake and Ohio National Historical Park, Md.-D.C.-W.Va.	14	6.2	5.9	62	9
Death Valley National Monument, Calif.-Nev.	2,049	0.6	0.7	337	314
Gateway National Recreation Area, N.Y.-N.J.	20	8.6	9.4	10	6
George Washington Memorial Parkway, Va.-Md.	7	8.8	9.6	—	—
Glacier National Park, Mont.	1,013	1.6	1.7	266	307
Glen Canyon National Recreation Area, Ariz.-Utah	1,194	2.1	2.9	1,628	2,062
Golden Gate National Recreation Area, Calif.	28	18.3	21.8	99	112
Grand Canyon National Park, Ariz.	1,179	2.7	3.5	733	866
Grand Teton National Park, Wyo.	307	1.3	1.5	452	453
Great Smoky Mountain National Park, N.C.-Tenn.	520	9.3	10.2	479	495
Gulf Island National Seashore, Miss.-Fla.	99	9.9	4.8	153	174
Kings Canyon National Park, Calif.	462	0.8	1.1	269	284
Lake Mead National Recreation Area, Ariz.-Nev.	1,469	7.0	8.1	1,304	1,302
Mesa Verde National Park, Colo.	52	0.7	0.7	187	217
Natchez Trace Parkway, Miss.-Tenn.-Ala.	50	12.9	9.9	17	23
Olympic National Park, Wash.	911	2.5	2.8	375	372
Rocky Mountain National Park, Colo.	264	2.2	2.5	201	205
Sequoia National Park, Calif.	402	0.9	1.1	375	442
Shenandoah National Park, Va.	195	1.9	1.8	430	354
Valley Forge National Historical Park, Pa.	3	4.2	4.3	—	—
Virgin Island National Park, V.I.	13	0.7	0.8	196	203
Yellowstone National Park, Idaho-Mont.-Wyo	2,220	2.2	2.6	1,270	1,398
Yosemite National Park, Calif.	759	2.8	3.2	2,068	2,199
Zion National Park, Utah	143	1.5	1.8	208	263

Notes: As of Dec. 31. Area selection based on minimum of 4 million visits or 200,000 overnight stays in 1987. Dash (—) represents zero. 1. The passing of one night by a visitor within a park, and occurs each night a visitor remains in the park. 2. Includes areas not shown separately. **Sources:** U.S. National Park Service, *National Park Statistical Abstract* (annual) and unpublished data.

LAND USE

National Parks

The National Park Service manages 340 large national parks and other recreational locations. It is estimated that more than 290 million people visited its facilities in 1989.

On this page are the state parks and recreation areas, the parks that have been most visited, and a list of organizations that can provide information on how to become more involved in the national heritage we all share.

10 MOST VISITED NATIONAL PARK SERVICE AREAS, 1987

Rank	Area	Visitors
1.	Golden Gate National Recreation Area, Calif.	21,759,271
2.	Blue Ridge Parkway, N.C.-Va.	20,002,975
3.	Natchez Trace Parkway, Ala.-Miss.-Tenn.	11,685,584
4.	George Washington Memorial Parkway, Va.-Md.	9,537,694
5.	National Capital Parks, D.C.-Md.	8,986,712
6.	Great Smoky Mountains National Park, N.C.-Tenn.	8,770,781
7.	Lake Mead National Recreation Area, Ariz.-Nev.	8,327,850
8.	Gateway National Recreation Area, N.J.-N.Y.	6,215,162
9.	Cape Cod National Seashore, Mass.	5,180,070
10.	Acadia National Park, Maine	4,502,283

Source: U.S. National Park Service.

Associations

Camping

American Alpine Club, 113 E. 90th St., New York, NY 10128. (212) 722-1628. Members have made mountain ascents. Conducts scientific studies and explorations. Estab. 1902. Mem. 1,600.

American Camping Association, 5000 State Rd., 67N, Martinsville, IN 46151. (317) 342-8456. People interested in organized camping. Estab. 1910. Mem. 5,500.

American Hiking Society, 1015 31st St., N.W., Washington, D.C. 20007. (703) 385-3252. Educates public in appreciation of walking and use of foot trails; promotes hikers' interests. Estab. 1977. Mem. 1,500.

Appalachian Mountain Club, 5 Joy St., Boston, MA 02108. (617) 523-0636. Promotes knowledge and enjoyment of the outdoors throughout northeastern U.S. Estab. 1876. Mem. 30,000.

Appalachian Trail Conference, P.O. Box 807, Harpers Ferry, WV 25425. (304) 535-6331. Trail and hiking clubs and individuals interested in walking. Estab. 1925. Mem. 20,000.

Explorers Club, 46 E. 70th St., New York, NY 10021. (212) 628-8383. Promotes exploration and disseminates information about scientific exploration. Estab. 1904. Mem. 3,200.

National Campers and Hikers Association, 4808 Transit Rd., Bldg. 2, Depew, NY 14043. (716) 668-6242. Family campers and hikers interested in outdoor activities and conservation. Estab. 1949. Mem. 120,000.

National Camping Association, 353 W. 56th St., New York, NY 10019. (212) 246-10052. Cooperative organization of camp owners and directors. Estab. 1947. Mem. N.A.

Environment

National Audubon Society, 950 Third Ave., New York, NY 10022. (212) 832-3200. Local groups (500) interested in ecology and conservation of natural resources, emphasizing wildlife and their habitats. Estab. 1905. Mem. 550,000.

National Wildlife Federation, 1412 16th St., N.W., Washington, D.C. 20036. (202) 637-3700. Estab. 1936. Mem. 4,800,000.

Natural Resources Council of America, 1412 16th St., N.W., Washington, D.C. 20036. (202) 639-8596. Federation of organizations and scientific societies interested in conservation of natural resources. Estab. 1946. Mem. 50.

Nature Conservancy, 1800 N. Kent St., Ste. 800, Arlington, VA 22209. (703) 841-5736. Dedicated to the preservation of ecological diversity through the protection of natural areas. Estab. 1917. Mem. 365,000.

Sierra Club, 730 Polk St., San Francisco, CA 94109. (415) 776-2211. Undertakes and publishes scientific studies concerning the protection and conservation of the world's ecosystem. Estab. 1892. Mem. 416,000.

World Wildlife Fund, 1250 24th St., N.W., Washington, D.C. 20037. (202) 293-4800. Estab. 1961. Mem. 312,000.

STATE PARKS AND RECREATION AREAS, 1987

State	ACREAGE (thousands)	VISITORS Total[1]	VISITORS Day	REVENUE Total (thousands)	REVENUE % of operating budget
Total U.S.	13,752	694,432	634,531	$309,626	36.5%
Alabama	48	6,099	5,186	8,799	57.0
Alaska	3,110	5,920	2,222	55	1.1
Arizona	37	2,088	1,800	1,395	25.8
Arkansas	44	7,148	6,360	8,799	53.7
California	1,269	72,857	65,941	32,255	23.9
Colorado	287	7,924	7,497	8,635	110.2
Connecticut	181	7,706	7,261	2,282	22.8
Delaware	11	2,738	2,390	2,916	72.4
Florida	278	14,290	13,098	10,459	49.7
Georgia	61	13,310	10,056	8,569	48.2
Hawaii	25	20,200	20,068	1,193	25.5
Idaho	47	2,281	2,069	815	32.2
Illinois	363	35,190	34,711	2,123	9.3
Indiana	54	9,885	8,279	7,434	74.8
Iowa	52	10,024	9,412	2,162	43.0
Kansas	37	4,452	3,246	1,929	44.0
Kentucky	42	24,210	23,140	31,858	62.3
Louisiana	38	740	525	990	23.8
Maine	72	2,072	1,872	1,266	32.5
Maryland	216	6,890	6,339	5,535	36.3
Massachusetts	266	12,240	11,409	6,050	32.3
Michigan	253	22,845	17,575	13,951	71.1
Minnesota	3,441	6,001	5,267	4,596	39.9
Mississippi	22	4,434	4,046	4,246	103.7
Missouri	107	12,442	11,457	2,324	14.1
Montana	52	4,195	3,636	467	16.3
Nebraska	148	8,413	7,319	3,957	52.9
Nevada	144	3,104	2,856	757	23.5
New Hampshire	30	3,906	3,726	6,819	99.5
New Jersey	300	9,599	9,063	5,213	26.0
New Mexico	119	6,791	4,597	2,231	38.1
New York	258	37,514	34,767	22,632	22.6
North Carolina	125	7,152	6,815	1,182	16.4
North Dakota	16	950	837	640	40.3
Ohio	193	68,164	65,568	10,000	27.7
Oklahoma	95	15,656	13,632	5,606	30.8
Oregon	89	37,156	35,312	6,223	33.9
Pennsylvania	276	36,303	34,824	5,475	16.4
Rhode Island	9	5,807	5,711	1,465	26.7
South Carolina	79	7,803	6,854	8,360	61.6
South Dakota	113	5,579	5,231	2,532	51.8
Tennessee	120	24,343	23,307	15,662	50.7
Texas	225	19,925	17,821	11,107	40.6
Utah	95	5,350	3,691	2,322	23.5
Vermont	171	786	486	2,801	91.0
Virginia	54	3,635	3,177	1,558	24.8
Washington	234	46,686	44,536	5,323	24.0
West Virginia	206	9,129	8,215	10,462	53.4
Wisconsin	119	11,275	9,927	6,097	59.8
Wyoming	119	1,856	1,397	101	4.2

1. Includes overnight visitors.   **Source:** National Association of State Park Directors, Austin, Tex., *Annual Information Exchange* (1988).

LAND COVER AND USE, BY STATE, 1982 (in thousands of acres)

STATE	TOTAL SURFACE AREA[1]	FEDERAL SURFACE AREA	Urban and built-up land[2]	Rural transportation[3]	NONFEDERAL LAND AREAS Cropland	Pastureland	Rangeland	Forestland
UNITED STATES[4]	1,937,725	404,063	46,416	26,914	420,994	132,356	405,914	393,197
Alabama	33,091	904	906	639	4,510	3,817	—	20,633
Arizona	72,960	32,056	711	291	1,206	79	30,948	4,760
Arkansas	34,040	3,114	636	540	8,102	5,794	162	14,340
California	101,572	45,552	3,265	1,037	10,518	1,393	18,125	15,218
Colorado	66,618	23,611	672	609	10,603	1,260	24,233	4,030
Connecticut	3,212	9	603	55	245	114	—	1,828
Delaware	1,309	33	128	26	519	35	—	348
Florida	37,545	3,129	2,770	601	3,557	4,273	3,804	12,430
Georgia	37,702	2,068	1,632	504	6,568	2,977	—	21,884
Hawaii	4,141	342	126	23	333	974	—	1,474
Idaho	53,481	33,445	189	255	6,390	1,274	6,733	3,977
Illinois	36,061	493	1,846	870	24,727	3,157	—	3,429
Indiana	23,159	489	1,102	517	13,781	2,212	—	3,640
Iowa	36,016	172	623	1,061	26,441	4,536	—	1,756
Kansas	52,658	585	721	1,104	29,118	2,241	16,909	626
Kentucky	25,862	1,125	636	570	5,934	5,880	—	10,158
Louisiana	30,561	1,104	823	546	6,409	2,369	241	12,895
Maine	21,290	135	212	270	953	569	—	16,770
Maryland	6,695	158	763	114	1,794	534	—	2,425
Massachusetts	5,302	89	883	128	297	202	—	2,970
Michigan	37,457	3,087	1,966	873	9,443	2,911	—	15,360
Minnesota	54,017	3,373	904	1,154	23,024	3,590	199	13,956
Mississippi	30,521	1,618	582	539	7,415	3,975	—	15,243
Missouri	44,606	2,094	1,117	977	14,998	12,573	168	10,986
Montana	94,109	27,107	197	784	17,197	3,036	37,837	5,228
Nebraska	49,507	639	415	826	20,277	2,125	23,096	732
Nevada	70,759	60,189	199	152	860	304	7,908	357
New Hampshire	5,938	727	236	109	158	125	—	4,085
New Jersey	4,984	145	1,163	69	809	240	—	1,848
New Mexico	77,819	26,420	267	382	2,413	163	40,982	4,734
New York	31,429	237	1,811	594	5,912	3,872	—	16,517
North Carolina	33,708	2,116	1,622	727	6,695	1,980	—	16,729
North Dakota	45,250	1,879	198	1,036	27,039	1,272	10,948	438
Ohio	26,451	346	2,187	645	12,447	2,714	—	6,380
Oklahoma	44,772	1,192	851	789	11,568	7,138	15,060	6,539
Oregon	62,127	32,122	526	365	4,356	1,966	9,392	11,889
Pennsylvania	28,997	668	2,073	613	5,896	2,593	—	15,300
Rhode Island	776	4	140	14	27	36	—	406
South Carolina	19,912	1,150	839	475	3,579	1,208	—	11,026
South Dakota	49,354	2,824	231	833	16,947	2,703	22,784	562
Tennessee	26,972	1,343	1,000	588	51,592	5,356	—	11,529
Texas	170,756	2,998	4,388	2,234	33,320	17,043	95,353	9,324
Utah	54,336	35,819	274	152	2,039	490	8,489	3,235
Vermont	6,153	315	97	101	648	501	—	4,087
Virginia	26,091	2,347	1,219	329	3,397	3,392	—	13,625
Washington	43,609	12,474	990	492	7,793	1,345	5,637	12,690
West Virginia	15,508	1,104	312	205	1,093	1,869	—	10,423
Wisconsin	35,938	1,800	1,125	770	11,457	3,394	—	13,393
Wyoming	62,598	29,315	148	330	2,587	755	26,915	987

1. Includes 107.9 million acres of water area and minor land cover and uses that are not shown separately. 2. In urbanized areas and places of 2,500 or more population outside of urbanized areas. 3. Rural highway, road, and railroad rights-of-way, and airports. 4. Does not include Alaska. **Source:** U.S. Dept. of Agriculture, Soil Conservation Service, and Iowa State University, Statistical Laboratory, Basic Statistics—1982, National Resources Inventory (1987).

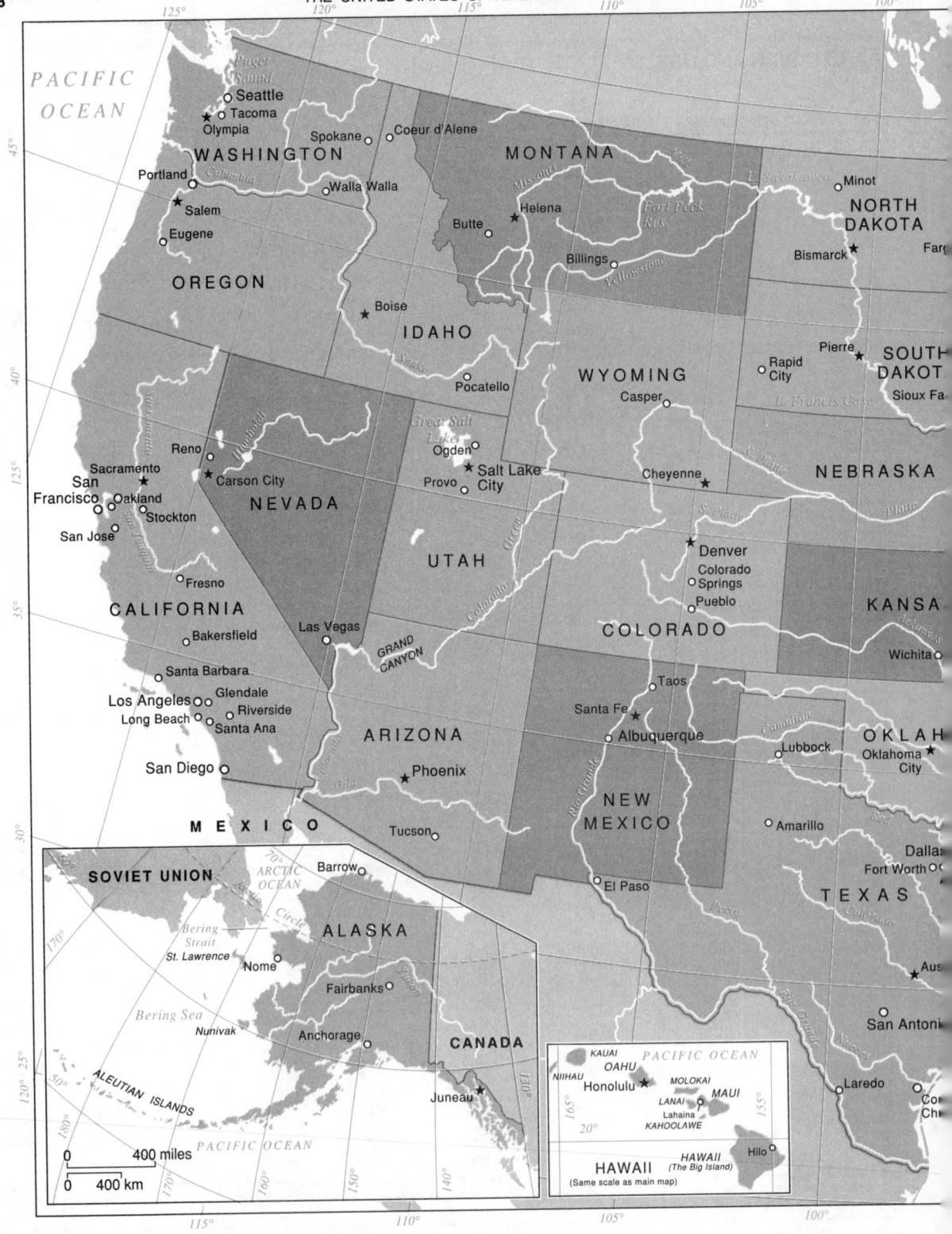

PACIFIC OCEAN

Puget Sound

○ Seattle
★ ○ Tacoma
Olympia

WASHINGTON

○ Spokane
○ Coeur d'Alene

MONTANA

Portland ○
Columbia
○ Walla Walla
★ Salem
Eugene ○

★ Helena
○ Butte

○ Minot

NORTH DAKOTA

○ Billings
Yellowstone

Bismarck ★
Farg

OREGON

★ Boise

IDAHO

WYOMING

○ Rapid City

Pierre ★
SOUTH DAKOT

○ Pocatello

○ Casper

Sioux Fa

○ Reno

Sacramento ★
San ○
Francisco ○ Oakland
○ Stockton
San Jose ○

★ Carson City

NEVADA

Great Salt Lake
○ Ogden
★ Salt Lake City
Provo ○

Cheyenne ★

NEBRASKA

Platte

Denver ★
Colorado ○ Springs
Pueblo ○

KANSA

○ Fresno

UTAH

Colorado

CALIFORNIA

○ Bakersfield

Las Vegas ○

GRAND CANYON

COLORADO

○ Wichita

Santa Barbara ○
Glendale ○
Los Angeles ○○ ○ Riverside
Long Beach ○ ○ Santa Ana

Taos ○

Santa Fe ○ ★ Albuquerque

OKLAH

○ Lubbock

Oklahoma ★ City

San Diego ○

ARIZONA

★ Phoenix

NEW MEXICO

○ Amarillo

Dalla
Fort Worth

MEXICO

○ Tucson

Rio Grande

○ El Paso

TEXAS

Aus ★

SOVIET UNION

ARCTIC OCEAN

○ Barrow

Circle

ALASKA

Bering Strait
St. Lawrence

○ Nome

○ Fairbanks

Nunivak

Bering Sea

○ Anchorage

CANADA

San Antoni ○

ALEUTIAN ISLANDS

PACIFIC OCEAN

★ Juneau

0   400 miles
0   400 km

KAUAI
NIIHAU   OAHU
Honolulu ★   MOLOKAI
LANAI   MAUI
Lahaina
KAHOOLAWE

PACIFIC OCEAN

Laredo ○

Co
Chr

HAWAII   *HAWAII (The Big Island)*
(Same scale as main map)

Hilo ○

95° 90° 85° 80° 75° 70° 50° 65°

65°

C A N A D A

Lake of the Woods

L. Superior

MAINE

Duluth

MINNESOTA

St. Paul

Minneapolis

MICHIGAN

WISCONSIN

Green Bay

Milwaukee

Madison

Grand Rapids

Lansing

Warren

Detroit

IOWA

Cedar Rapids

Chicago

Des Moines

Omaha

Lincoln

ILLINOIS

INDIANA

Fort Wayne

Springfield

Indianapolis

St. Louis

Kansas City

Kansas City

Topeka

Jefferson City

MISSOURI

Tulsa

ARKANSAS

Fort Smith

Little Rock

OHIO

Columbus

Dayton

Cincinnati

Louisville

Frankfort

Lexington

Charleston

KENTUCKY

WEST VIRGINIA

Toledo

Cleveland

L. Huron

L. Michigan

L. Erie

L. Ontario

Rochester

Buffalo

Syracuse

Albany

NEW YORK

Scranton

PENNSYLVANIA

Harrisburg

Pittsburgh

Baltimore

WASHINGTON, D.C.

Annapolis

MARYLAND

Newark

New York

NEW JERSEY

Trenton

Philadelphia

Wilmington

Dover

DELAWARE

St. Lawrence

Lake Champlain

Burlington

Montpelier

VERMONT

Concord

NEW HAMPSHIRE

Augusta

Portland

Portsmouth

MASSACHUSETTS

Boston

Worcester

Providence

Hartford

New Haven

Long Island

RHODE ISLAND

CONNECTICUT

Cape Cod

Nantucket

VIRGINIA

Richmond

Norfolk

Virginia Beach

Chesapeake Bay

James

Roanoke

Greensboro

Raleigh

NORTH CAROLINA

Knoxville

Asheville

Charlotte

Outer Banks

Nashville

TENNESSEE

Chattanooga

Huntsville

Memphis

Birmingham

ALABAMA

MISSISSIPPI

Jackson

Montgomery

Mobile

Pensacola

Columbus

Macon

GEORGIA

Atlanta

Greenville

Columbia

SOUTH CAROLINA

Charleston

Savannah

Wilmington

Cape Fear

A T L A N T I C

O C E A N

70°

35°

40°

45°

Shreveport

Baton Rouge

New Orleans

Houston

LOUISIANA

Apalachicola

Tallahassee

Jacksonville

F L O R I D A

Cape Canaveral

Tampa

St. Petersburg

L. Okeechobee

Fort Myers

Naples

Miami

Hialeah

West Palm Beach

Fort Lauderdale

Miami Beach

Key West

KEYS

Gulf of Mexico

30°

25°

0 ——— 200 miles

0 ——— 200 km

95° 90° 85° 80° 75°

EXTREME AND MEAN ELEVATIONS, STATES AND OUTLYING AREAS

State	HIGHEST POINT Name	Elevation Feet	Elevation Meters	LOWEST POINT Name	Elevation Feet	Elevation Meters	APPROXIMATE MEAN ELEVATION Feet	APPROXIMATE MEAN ELEVATION Meters
United States	**Mt. McKinley (Alaska)**	**20,320**	**6,198**	**Death Valley (Calif.)**	**−282**	**−86**	**2,500**	**763**
Ala.	Cheaha Mountain	2,407	734	Gulf of Mexico		Sea level	500	153
Alaska	Mount McKinley	20,320	6,198	Pacific Ocean		Sea level	1,900	580
Ariz.	Humphreys Peak	12,633	3,853	Colorado River	70	21	4,100	1,251
Ark.	Magazine Mountain	2,753	840	Ouachita River	55	17	650	198
Calif.	Mount Whitney	14,494	4,421	Death Valley	−282	−86	2,900	885
Colo.	Mount Elbert	14,433	4,402	Arkansas River	3,350	1,022	6,800	2,074
Conn.	Mount Frissell, on south slope	2,380	726	Long Island Sound		Sea level	500	153
D.C.	Tenleytown	410	125	Potomac River	1	(Z)	150	46
Del.	Elbright Rd., New Castle Co.	442	135	Atlantic Ocean		Sea level	60	18
Fla.	Sec. 30, T6N, R20W, Walton Co.	345	105	Atlantic Ocean		Sea level	100	31
Ga.	Brasstown Bald	4,784	1,459	Atlantic Ocean		Sea level	600	183
Hawaii	Mauna Kea	13,796	4,208	Pacific Ocean		Sea level	3,030	924
Idaho	Borah Peak	12,662	3,862	Snake River	710	217	5,000	1,525
Ill.	Charles Mound	1,235	377	Mississippi River	279	85	600	183
Ind.	Franklin Township, Wayne Co.	1,257	383	Ohio River	320	98	700	214
Iowa	Sec. 29, T100N, R41W, Osceola Co.	1,670	509	Mississippi River	480	146	1,100	336
Kans.	Mount Sunflower	4,039	1,232	Verdigris River	680	207	2,000	610
Ky.	Black Mountain	4,145	1,264	Mississippi River	257	78	750	229
La.	Driskill Mountain	535	163	New Orleans	−5	−2	100	31
Maine	Mount Katahdin	5,268	1,607	Atlantic Ocean		Sea level	600	183
Mass.	Mount Greylock	3,491	1,065	Atlantic Ocean		Sea level	500	153
Md.	Backbone Mountain	3,360	1,025	Atlantic Ocean		Sea level	350	107
Mich.	Mount Arvon	1,979	604	Lake Erie	572	174	900	275
Minn.	Eagle Mountain, Cook Co.	2,301	702	Lake Superior	602	184	1,200	366
Miss.	Woodall Mountain	806	246	Gulf of Mexico		Sea level	300	92
Mo.	Taum Sauk Mountain	1,772	540	St. Francis River	230	70	800	244
Mont.	Granite Peak	12,799	3,904	Kootenai River	1,800	549	3,400	1,037
N.C.	Mount Mitchell	6,684	2,039	Atlantic Ocean		Sea level	700	214
N.Dak.	White Butte, Slope Co.	3,506	1,069	Red River	750	229	1,900	580
Nebr.	Johnson Township, Kimball Co.	5,426	1,655	Southeast corner of state	840	256	2,600	793
Nev.	Boundary Peak	13,143	4,009	Colorado River	470	143	5,500	1,678
N.Y.	Mount Marcy	5,344	1,630	Atlantic Ocean		Sea level	1,000	305
N.H.	Mount Washington	6,288	1,918	Atlantic Ocean		Sea level	1,000	305
N.J.	High Point	1,803	550	Atlantic Ocean		Sea level	250	76
N.Mex.	Wheeler Peak	13,161	4,014	Red Bluff Reservoir	2,817	859	5,700	1,739
Ohio	Campbell Hill	1,550	473	Ohio River	433	132	850	259
Okla.	Black Mesa	4,973	1,517	Little River	287	88	1,300	397
Oreg.	Mount Hood	11,239	3,428	Pacific Ocean		Sea level	3,300	1,007
Pa.	Mount Davis	3,213	980	Delaware River		Sea level	1,100	336
R.I.	Jerimoth Hill	812	248	Atlantic Ocean		Sea level	200	61
S.C.	Sassafras Mountain	3,560	1,086	Atlantic Ocean		Sea level	350	107
S.Dak.	Harney Peak	7,242	2,209	Big Stone Lake	962	293	2,200	671
Tenn.	Clingmans Dome	6,643	2,026	Mississippi River	182	56	900	275
Tex.	Guadalupe Peak	8,749	2,668	Gulf of Mexico		Sea level	1,700	519
Utah	Kings Peak	13,528	4,126	Beaverdam Creek	2,000	610	6,100	1,861
Va.	Mount Rogers	5,729	1,747	Atlantic Ocean		Sea level	950	290
Vt.	Mount Mansfield	4,393	1,340	Lake Champlain	95	29	1,000	305
Wash.	Mount Rainier	14,410	4,395	Pacific Ocean		Sea level	1,700	519
Wis.	Timms Hill	1,951	595	Lake Michigan	581	177	1,050	320
W.Va.	Spruce Knob	4,863	1,483	Potomac River	240	73	1,500	458
Wyo.	Gannett Peak	13,804	4,210	Belle Fourche River	3,100	946	6,700	2,044
Amer. Samoa	Lata Mountain	3,160	964	Pacific Ocean		Sea level	1,300	397
Guam	Mount Lamlam	1,329	405	Pacific Ocean		Sea level	330	101
P.R.	Cerro de Punta	4,389	1,339	Atlantic Ocean		Sea level	1,800	549
V.I.	Crown Mountain	1,556	475	Atlantic Ocean		Sea level	750	229

Note: Z = less than 0.5 meter. Sec. denotes section; T, township; R, range; N, north; W, west. **Source:** U.S. Geological Survey, *Elevations and Distances in the United States* (1980).

CHIEF CROPS BY STATE, 1987

State	Crops, in order of value
U.S. total[1]	**Corn, soybeans, hay, wheat**
Alabama	Cotton lint, peanuts, hay, soybeans
Arizona	Cotton lint, lettuce, hay, cottonseed
Arkansas	Soybeans, rice, cotton lint, hay
California	Grapes, cotton lint, hay, tomatoes
Colorado	Hay, wheat, corn, potatoes
Connecticut	Hay, mushrooms, apples, sweet corn
Delaware	Soybeans, corn, potatoes, hay
Florida	Oranges, tomatoes, grapefruit, potatoes
Georgia	Peanuts, tobacco, corn, cotton lint
Hawaii	Sugarcane, pineapples, macadamia nuts, papayas
Idaho	Potatoes, hay, wheat, barley
Illinois	Corn, soybeans, hay, wheat
Indiana	Corn, soybeans, hay, wheat
Iowa	Corn, soybeans, hay, oats
Kansas	Wheat, sorghum, soybeans, hay
Kentucky	Tobacco, hay, corn, soybeans
Louisiana	Cotton lint, soybeans, rice, hay
Maine	Potatoes, hay, apples, oats
Maryland	Corn, hay, soybeans, tobacco
Massachusetts	Cranberries, hay, apples, sweet corn
Michigan	Corn, hay, soybeans, apples
Minnesota	Soybeans, corn, hay, wheat
Mississippi	Cotton lint, soybeans, rice, hay
Missouri	Soybeans, corn, hay, cotton lint
Montana	Wheat, hay, barley, oats
Nebraska	Corn, soybeans, hay, wheat
Nevada	Hay, potatoes, barley, wheat
New Hampshire	Hay, apples
New Jersey	Hay, corn, peaches, soybeans
New Mexico	Hay, cotton lint, onions, wheat
New York	Hay, corn, apples, potatoes
North Carolina	Tobacco, soybeans, corn, peanuts
North Dakota	Wheat, hay, sunflower, potatoes
Ohio	Soybeans, corn, hay, wheat
Oklahoma	Wheat, hay, cotton lint, peanuts
Oregon	Hay, wheat, potatoes, pears
Pennsylvania	Hay, corn, mushrooms, apples
Rhode Island	Hay, potatoes, apples
South Carolina	Tobacco, soybeans, corn, peaches
South Dakota	Corn, hay, soybeans, wheat
Tennessee	Cotton lint, soybeans, hay, tobacco
Texas	Cotton lint, hay, sorghum, corn
Utah	Hay, corn, wheat, potatoes
Vermont	Hay, apples
Virginia	Hay, tobacco, soybeans, peanuts
Washington	Wheat, potatoes, hay, barley
West Virginia	Hay, apples, corn, tobacco
Wisconsin	Corn, hay, potatoes, cranberries
Wyoming	Hay, barley, wheat, corn

1. Excludes Alaska. **Source:** U.S. Dept. of Agriculture, National Agricultural Statistics Service, *Crop Production* (annual) and *Crop Values* (annual).

FARMS: NUMBER AND ACREAGE, BY STATE, 1980-88

State	Farms (thousands) 1980	Farms (thousands) 1988	Acreage (millions) 1980	Acreage (millions) 1988	Acreage per farm 1980	Acreage per farm 1988
U.S. TOTAL	**2,433**	**2,159**	**1,039**	**999**	**427**	**463**
Alabama	59	49	12	11	207	224
Alaska	(Z)	1	2	1	3,378	2,123
Arizona	8	8	38	37	5,080	4,506
Arkansas	59	47	17	15	280	319
California	81	78	34	33	417	417
Colorado	27	27	36	34	1,358	1,234
Connecticut	4	4	(Z)	(Z)	117	119
Delaware	4	3	1	1	186	197
Florida	39	40	13	13	344	325
Georgia	59	49	15	13	254	265
Hawaii	4	4	2	2	458	443
Idaho	24	23	15	14	623	609
Illinois	107	83	29	29	269	345
Indiana	87	72	17	16	193	228
Iowa	119	107	34	34	284	313
Kansas	75	69	48	48	644	694
Kentucky	102	99	15	15	143	146
Louisiana	37	35	10	10	273	271
Maine	8	8	2	2	195	192
Maryland	18	16	3	2	157	147
Massachusetts	6	6	1	1	116	111
Michigan	65	58	11	11	175	193
Minnesota	104	94	30	30	291	319
Mississippi	55	43	15	14	265	314
Missouri	120	113	31	30	261	9
Montana	24	23	62	61	2,601	2,605
Nebraska	65	55	48	47	734	856
Nevada	3	2	9	9	3,100	3,667
New Hampshire	3	3	1	1	160	158
New Jersey	9	7	1	1	109	112
New Mexico	14	14	47	45	3,467	3,333
New York	47	40	9	9	200	213
North Carolina	93	70	12	11	126	150
North Dakota	40	33	42	40	1,043	1,243
Ohio	95	84	16	16	171	186
Oklahoma	72	69	35	33	481	478
Oregon	35	37	18	18	517	488
Pennsylvania	62	56	9	8	145	150
Rhode Island	1	1	(Z)	(Z)	87	96
South Carolina	34	27	6	5	188	200
South Dakota	39	35	45	44	1,169	1,278
Tennessee	96	94	14	13	142	136
Texas	189	156	138	132	731	846
Utah	14	13	12	11	919	850
Vermont	8	7	2	2	226	223
Virginia	58	49	10	10	169	196
Washington	38	38	16	16	429	421
West Virginia	22	21	4	4	191	176
Wisconsin	93	82	19	18	200	215
Wyoming	9	9	35	35	3,846	4,000

Note: Z = less than 500 farms or 500,000 acres. **Source:** U.S. Dept. of Agriculture, National Agriculture Statistics Service, *Crop Production* (Aug. 1988).

U.S. FARMLAND

Year	Number of farms (thousands)	Acres (thousands)	Average acreage
1850	1,449	293,561	203
1860	2,044	407,213	199
1870	2,660	407,735	153
1880	4,009	536,082	134
1890	4,565	623,219	137
1900	5,740[1]	841,202	147
1910	6,366	881,431	139
1920	6,454	958,677	149
1930	6,295	990,112	157
1940	6,102	1,065,114	175
1950	5,388	1,161,420	216
1960	3,962	1,176,946	297
1970	2,954	1,102,769	373
1980	2,432	1,038,885	427
1985	2,275	1,014,000	446
1986	2,212	1,008,000	456
1987	2,173	1,002,000	461

1. Beginning with 1900 the figures include Alaska and Hawaii.
Sources: For 1850 to 1970, U.S. Bureau of Census, *Historical Statistics of the United States: Colonial Times to 1970* (1975). For 1971–87, reports of the Census of Agriculture, U.S. Dept. of Commerce.

LUMBER PRODUCTION, BY KIND OF WOOD, 1960–87
(millions of board feet)

Item	1960	1970	1980	1985	1987
TOTAL PRODUCTION	**32,926**	**34,668**	**35,354**	**36,445**	**44,893**
SOFTWOODS[1,2]	26,672	27,530	28,239	30,479	37,422
Cedar	N.A.	633	722	759	920
Douglas fir	8,832	7,727	6,853	7,751	10,406
Hemlock	2,032	1,980	1,855	N.A.	N.A.
Ponderosa pine	3,169	3,429	3,269	3,773	4,123
Redwood	1,000	1,078	770	1,155	1,157
Southern yellow pine[2]	5,660	7,063	8,217	10,230	12,068
White fir	2,224	2,063	1,643	2,272	2,891
White pine	675	898	N.A.	N.A.	N.A.
HARDWOODS[1,2]	6,254	7,138	7,115	5,966	7,471
Ash	125	159	N.A.	218	265
Beech	195	188	183	89	116
Cottonwood and aspen	206	229	303	216	239
Elm	195	155	149	N.A.	N.A.
Maple	602	742	225[3]	532	635
Oak	2,789	3,250	3,356	2,793	3,667
Sweet gum[4]	331	376	371	293	329
Tupelo and black gum	292	335	N.A.	N.A.	N.A.
Yellow poplar	592	606	661	544	800

Notes: Figures for 1960 do not include Alaska and Hawaii. 1. Includes types not shown separately. 2. Beginning in 1986, data are not directly comparable to previous years due to the inclusion of 200 sawmills in the survey for the first time. 3. Excludes hard maple. 4. Red and sap.
Source: U.S. Bureau of the Census, *Current Industrial Reports* (annual).

U.S. FARM POPULATION

Year	Total (thousands)	% of total population
1880	21,973	43.8%
1890	24,771	42.3
1900	29,875	41.9
1910	32,077	34.9
1920	31,974	30.1
1930	30,529	24.9
1940	30,547	23.2
1950	23,048	15.3
1960	15,635[1]	8.7
1970	9,712	4.8
1980	6,051	2.7
1985	5,355	2.4
1986	5,226	2.2

1. Beginning with 1960 the figures include Alaska and Hawaii.
Sources: For 1880–1970, U.S. Bureau of Census, *Historical Statistics of the United States: Colonial Times to 1970* (1975). For 1970 on, U.S. Bureau of Census, *Statistical Abstract of the United States, 1987* (Washington, D.C., 1987).

LAND LOST IN FOREST FIRES, 1980–88
(millions of acres)

Year	Acreage	Year	Acreage
1980	5.3	1985	5.3
1981	4.8	1986	3.2
1982	2.3	1987	4.4
1983	5.1	1988	6.0
1984	3.0		

Source: U.S. Forest Service.

FORESTLAND AND TIMBERLAND (thousands of acres)

Region/state	Total forestland	Total timberland[1]
NORTH	**169.790**	**158,304**
NORTHEAST	85,251	80,103
Connecticut	1,815	1,777
Delaware	398	388
Maine	17,713	17,174
Maryland	2,632	2,462
Massachusetts	3,097	3,010
New Hampshire	5,021	4,803
New Jersey	1,985	1,914
New York	18,775	15,798
Pennsylvania	16,997	16,186
Rhode Island	399	368
Vermont	4,479	4,424
West Virginia	11,942	11,799
NORTH CENTRAL	80,310	74,672
Illinois	4,265	4,030
Indiana	4,439	4,296
Iowa	1,562	1,460
Michigan	18,220	17,364
Minnesota	16,583	13,572
Missouri	12,523	11,995
Ohio	7,397	7,229
Wisconsin	15,319	14,726
GREAT PLAINS	4,229	3,529
Kansas	1,358	1,207
Nebraska	722	537
North Dakota	460	338
South Dakota	1,690	1,447
SOUTH	**199,943**	**195,384**
SOUTHEAST	87,744	84,594
Florida	16,721	15,238
Georgia	23,907	23,384
North Carolina	18,891	18,354
South Carolina	12,257	12,179
Virginia	15,968	15,435
SOUTH CENTRAL	112,199	110,790
Alabama	21,725	21,659
Arkansas	16,987	16,673
Kentucky	12,256	11,909
Louisiana	13,883	13,872
Mississippi	16,693	16,674
Oklahoma	4,838	4,749
Tennessee	13,258	12,840
Texas	12,559	12,414
WEST	**358,189**	**129,384**
PACIFIC NORTHWEST	178,956	54,361
Alaska	129,045	15,763
Oregon	28,055	21,749
Washington	21,856	16,849
PACIFIC SOUTHWEST	41,129	17,412
California	39,381	16,712
Hawaii	1,748	700
ROCKY MOUNTAINS	138,104	57,611
Arizona	19,384	3,789
Colorado	21,338	11,740
Idaho	21,818	14,534
Montana	21,910	14,737
Nevada	8,928	221
New Mexico	18,526	5,180
Utah	16,234	3,078
Wyoming	9,966	4,332
U.S. TOTAL	**727,921**	**483,072**

1. Timberland is forestland that is producing or is capable of producing crops of industrial wood and not withdrawn from timber utilization by statute or administrative regulations. Areas qualifying as timberland have the capability of producing in excess of 20 cubic feet per acre per year of industrial wood in natural stands. Currently inaccessible and inoperable areas and timberland under federal ownership or management and under state, county, or municipal ownership as well as privately owned timberland are included. **Source:** U.S. Forest Service, *Past, Present, and Future Trends in U.S. Timber Sector: 1952–2040* (forthcoming).

RIVERS AND LAKES

Major Navigable Rivers of the United States

The U.S. inland and intracoastal waterway system handles over 500 million tons of traffic each year, carried by a fleet of more than 3,000 towboats and 28,000 barges on over 11,000 miles of primary channels. Ninety percent of these channels have depths of between 9 and 14 feet. Maintenance and improvement of the waterways—including channel dredging, bridge and levee maintenance, and the construction of canals and locks—are in large measure the responsibility of the U.S. Army Corps of Engineers. The 522-mile New York State Barge Canal System is the only major nonfederal waterway in the country.

The major inland river transportation network is the Mississippi River and its tributaries. This north-south-oriented system includes the Mississippi River, the Ohio River System, the Illinois Waterway, and the Arkansas and Missouri rivers, among others. In this system there are about 7,000 miles of heavily used, improved navigable channels, 85% of which have at least 9-foot navigable channel depths.

At its mouth the Mississippi River is intersected by the Gulf Intracoastal Waterway (GIWW), which parallels the Gulf Coast for 1,180 miles from St. Marks River, Florida, to Brownsville, Texas, at the Mexican border. The GIWW is intersected by a number of river systems in addition to the Mississippi, including the Mobile River, the Apalachicola, and the Houston Ship Channel.

This network of major inland and coastal waterways connects some of the largest Gulf Coast ports—New Orleans, Louisiana; Houston, Beaumont, and Corpus Christi, Texas; and Mobile, Alabama—with some of the largest inland ports—St. Louis, Missouri; Pittsburgh, Pennsylvania; Huntington, West Virginia; Cincinnati, Ohio; Memphis, Tennessee; and Chicago, Illinois. The 40-foot controlling depth of the Mississippi River between the Gulf of Mexico and Baton Rouge allows ocean shipping to join the barge traffic, making this segment especially vital to both the domestic and foreign commerce of the United States.

The Atlantic Intracoastal Waterway provides 1,329 miles of protected channels for commercial and recreational navigation along the Atlantic Coast from Key West, Florida, to Norfolk, Virginia. Partially protected segments of the waterway continue north from Norfolk along the Delmarva Peninsula, the New Jersey coast, and Long Island. Among the major Atlantic Coast ports located along this waterway are Miami, Florida; Savannah, Georgia; Baltimore, Maryland; Philadelphia, Pennsylvania; and the Port of New York and New Jersey.

In comparison with the Mississippi River system and the intracoastal waterways of the Atlantic and Gulf coasts, the inland and coastal waterways of the Pacific are few. Shallow draft waterways include the Columbia-Snake Waterway and the Willamette River above Portland, Oregon; the Sacramento River above Sacramento, California; the San Joaquin River above Stockton, California; and a few short navigable rivers stretching along the Washington and Oregon coasts.

The table on p. 34 shows the major navigable rivers in the United States, their total length, the distance commercially navigable, the body of water they flow into and the head of navigation—the upriver point beyond which commercial ships cannot pass—and the states through or by which the rivers pass, from source to mouth.

The Great Lakes and St. Lawrence Seaway

The Great Lakes were crucial to the development of the United States and Canada. They were the highways along which people and finished goods moved West, and along which raw materials such as lumber, minerals, and grains were transported to eastern markets. Later the cities of the Great Lakes, such as Chicago, Duluth, Detroit, and Buffalo, became important centers of finance, industry, and trade in their own right. So important was the maritime trade of the Great Lakes that in the 1890s, Chicago was the fourth-largest port in the world, despite being closed by ice for as many as five months a year.

An early obstacle to Great Lakes navigation was the fact that the lakes are not all at the same elevation: there is a difference of 354 feet between the level of the westernmost Lake Superior and easternmost Lake Ontario, and there is another 246 feet descent from Lake Ontario down the St. Lawrence River to where it empties into the Atlantic Ocean.

The first canal (1799) was built on the St. Marys River between Lake Superior and Lake Huron. (Today there are two Sault Sainte Marie [or Soo] Canals—one U.S. and one Canadian—along the 70-mile river.) In 1825 the United States opened the way between the upper Lakes (all but Lake Ontario) and the Atlantic via the 353-mile Erie Canal between Buffalo, on Lake Erie, and Albany, on the Hudson River north of New York City. Canada followed with the 27-mile Welland Canal (1833) connecting Welland on Lake Erie and St. Catherine's on Lake Ontario.

The most ambitious undertaking was the construction of the St. Lawrence Seaway, a joint Canadian-American effort to open the entire length of the St. Lawrence and the Great Lakes to oceangoing navigation. Started in 1955 and opened to navigation in 1959, the seaway's system of canals and locks allows ships of up to 730 feet in length and 27 feet draft to sail the entire 2,342 miles from the mouth of the St. Lawrence to Duluth, Minnesota, at the western end of Lake Superior. The seaway also provides hydroelectric power for Canada and the United States.

THE GREAT LAKES

Lake	Area Sq. mi.	Area Sq km	Depth Feet	Depth Meters	Height above sea level Feet	Height above sea level Meters
Ontario	7,540	19,529	802	244	246	75
Erie	9,940	25,745	210	64	571	174
Michigan	22,400	58,016	923	281	577	176
Huron	23,010	59,596	750	229	577	176
Superior	31,820	82,414	1,333	406	600	183

Source: U.S. Environmental Protection Agency and Environment Canada, *The Great Lakes: An Environmental Atlas and Resource Book* (1987).

FISHERIES: QUANTITY OF CATCH, BY STATE, 1980–87
(in millions of pounds, live weight)

Area and state	1980	1985	1987
U.S. TOTAL	**6,482**	**6,258**	**6,896**
NEW ENGLAND	788	590	545
Maine	245	175	170
New Hampshire	19	8	8
Massachusetts	438	296	258
Rhode Island	81	104	100
Connecticut	5	7	9
MIDDLE ATLANTIC	244	151	163
New York	39	39	41
New Jersey	201	108	116
Delaware	4	5	6
CHESAPEAKE BAY	717	815	791
Maryland	80	92	81
Virginia	637	723	710
SOUTH ATLANTIC	473	311	235
North Carolina	356	215	157
South Carolina	21	13	15
Georgia	19	17	15
Florida (east coast)	77	66	48
GULF STATES	1,979	2,412	2,501
Florida (west coast)	115	117	124
Alabama	25	30	24
Mississippi	232	471	436
Louisiana	1,412	1,693	1,804
Texas	94	103	111
PACIFIC COAST	2,140	1,816	2,493
Washington	156	167	205
Oregon	126	101	139
California	804	363	452
Alaska	1,054	1,185	1,697
Hawaii	11	17	16
MISSISSIPPI RIVER AND TRIBUTARIES	85	92	110
GREAT LAKES[1]	44	54	42

1. Includes, in addition to the Great Lakes, small amounts for Lake St. Clair (Mich.), Lake of the Woods, Namakan Lake, and Rainy Lake (Minn.). **Source:** U.S. National Oceanic and Atmospheric Administration, National Marine Fisheries Service, *Fishery Statistics of the United States* (annual) and *Fisheries of the United States* (annual).

MAJOR NAVIGABLE RIVERS AND CANALS IN THE U.S.

Ultimate outflow/river	Length	Navigable length	Mouth to head of navigation	States (from source to mouth)
ATLANTIC OCEAN				
St. Lawrence	760	760	Gulf of St. Lawrence to Lake Ontario	N.Y.; Ontario, Quebec (Can.)
Cape Cod Canal	17	17	Sandwich to Buzzards Bay, Mass.	Mass.
Connecticut	407	52	Long Island Sound to Hartford, Conn.	N.H., Vt., Mass., Conn.
Hudson	306	134	New York Bay to Troy, N.Y., New York State Barge Canal (522 mi.) links to Lake Erie (353 mi. Troy to Buffalo) and to Lakes Champlain, Ontario, Cayuga, Seneca	N.Y.
Delaware	367	77	Delaware Bay to Trenton, N.J.	N.Y., Pa., N.J., Del.
Chesapeake and Delaware Canal	14	14	Delaware Bay to Chesapeake Bay	Del., Md.
Potomac	287	101	Chesapeake Bay to Washington, D.C.	Va., Md., D.C.
James	340	87	Chesapeake Bay to Richmond, Va.	Va.
Roanoke	410	112	Atlantic Ocean to Altavista, N.C.	Va., N.C.
Cape Fear	202	111	Atlantic Ocean to Fayetteville, N.C.	N.C.
Savannah	314	181	Atlantic Ocean to Augusta, Ga.	S.C., Ga.
Saint Johns	285	160	Atlantic Ocean to Lake Harney, Fla.	Fla.
GULF OF MEXICO				
Chattahoochee	436	194	Apalachicola River to Columbus, Ga.	Ga., Ala.
Apalachicola	90	90	Gulf of Mexico to Chattahoochee, Fla.	Fla.
Mobile	45	45	Mobile Bay to confluence of Alabama and Tombigbee rivers	Ala.
Alabama	318	305	Mobile River to Montgomery, Ala.	Ala.
Tombigbee	362	362	Mobile River to Amory, Miss. Linked to Tennessee River by Tennessee-Tombigbee Waterway (253 mi.)	Miss., Ala.
Black Warrior	217	217	Tombigbee River to Birmingham, Ala.	Ala.
Houston Ship Channel	57	57	Galveston Bay to Houston, Tex.	Tex.
Rio Grande[1]	1,885	13	Gulf of Mexico to Brownsville, Tex.	Colo., N. Mex., Mexico, Tex.
MISSISSIPPI RIVER SYSTEM				
Mississippi	2,348	1,807	Gulf of Mexico to Minneapolis, Minn.	Minn., Wis., Iowa, Ill., Mo., Ky., Tenn., Ark., Miss., La.
EASTERN TRIBUTARIES				
Illinois	273	271	Mississippi River to Joliet, Ill. Also linked to Mississippi by Illinois and Mississippi Canal; to Lake Michigan (at Chicago, Calumet, East Chicago, Gary) by Illinois Waterway	Ill.
Ohio	981	981	Mississippi River to Pittsburgh, Pa.	Pa., Ohio, W.Va., Ind., Ky., Ill.
Monongahela	129	129	Ohio River to Fairmont, W.Va.	W.Va., Pa.
Allegheny	325	72	Ohio River to East Brady, Pa.	N.Y., Pa.
Kanawha	97	91	Ohio River to Charleston, W.Va.	W.Va.
Kentucky	259	82	Ohio River to Beattyville, Ky.	Ky.
Green	360	103	Ohio River to Bowling Green, Ky.	Ky.
Cumberland	694	387	Ohio River to Burnside, Ky.	Ky., Tenn.
Tennessee	652	648	Ohio River to Knoxville, Tenn.	Tenn., Ala., Miss., Ky.
Yazoo	169	165	Mississippi River to Greenwood, Miss.	Miss.
WESTERN TRIBUTARIES				
Missouri	2,315	753	Mississippi River to Ponca, Nebr.	Mont., N.Dak., S.Dak., Nebr., Iowa, Kans., Mo.
Arkansas	1,396	448	McClellan-Kerr Arkansas River system from Mississippi River to Catoosa, Okla.; incorporates sections of White, Arkansas, Verdigris rivers	Colo., Kans., Okla., Ark.
Ouachita[2]	605	351	Mississippi River to Camden, Ark.	Ark., La.
Red	1,018	236	Mississippi River to Shreveport, La.	N.Mex., Tex., Okla., Ark., La.
Atchafalaya[3]	220	220	Atchafalaya Bay to Mississippi River	La.
PACIFIC OCEAN AND ARCTIC OCEAN				
San Joaquin	340	103	Sacramento River to Hills Ferry, Calif.	Calif.
Sacramento	374	163	San Francisco Bay to Chico Landing, Calif.	Calif.
Snake	1,083	192	Columbia River to Johnson Bar Landing, Idaho	Wyo., Idaho, Oreg., Wash.
Willamette	294	133	Columbia River to Harrisburg, Oreg.	Oreg.
Columbia	1,210	285	Pacific Ocean to Pasco, Wash.	B.C., Can.; Wash., Oreg.
Yukon	1,979	1,197	Arctic Ocean to Dawson, Yukon	Yukon (Can.); Alaska

Note: All distances in nautical miles except for the Mississippi River system. One nautical mile = 1.151 statute miles.   1. In Mexico, known as the Río Bravo del Norte from the Mississippi River to the Gulf of Mexico.   **Source:** National Oceanic and Atmospheric Administration, *Distances between United States Ports, 1987* (1987).   2. Lower 57 miles known as the Black River.   3. Flows

FISHERIES: DOMESTIC CATCH AT SELECTED U.S. PORTS, 1987 (millions of pounds)

Port	1987
Cameron, La.	672.4
Pascagoula–Moss Point, Miss.	391.6
Empire-Venice, La.	357.4
Dulac-Chauvin, La.	331.7
Intercoastal City, La.	314.3
Kodiak, Alaska	204.1
Los Angeles, Calif.	203.1
Dutch Harbor–Unalaska, Alaska	128.2
Gloucester, Mass.	93.0
Beaufort–Morehead City, N.C.	85.7
New Bedford, Mass.	78.7
Cordova, Alaska	69.6
Cape May–Wildwood, N.J.	56.8
Bellingham, Wash.	47.5
Astoria, Oreg.	46.6
Point Judith, R.I.	46.6
Portland, Maine	43.8
Petersburg, Alaska	42.4
Port Hueneme–Osnard–Ventura, Calif.	42.3
Rockland, Maine	38.7

Source: U.S. National Oceanic and Atmospheric Administration, National Marine Fisheries Service, *Fishery Statistics of the United States* (annual) and *Fisheries of the United States* (annual).

The Panama Canal

One of the great engineering feats of the world, the 44-mile Panama Canal bisects the continents of North and South America, making it possible for ships to sail between the Atlantic and Pacific Oceans without rounding the treacherous Cape Horn at the tip of South America. The U.S. government began construction of the canal in 1904, and it was opened to commercial navigation Aug. 15, 1914. For interocean shippers the savings in distance and time afforded by the canal are enormous. A ship sailing from New York to San Francisco via the Panama Canal travels a distance of 5,263 miles, a savings of more than 7,800 miles—or about 20 days—over the 13,100-mile route around Cape Horn. The minimum depth of the canal is 41 feet, the minimum width 300 feet, and the highest elevation above sea level 85 feet.

The Canal Zone, a 10-mile-wide strip of land around the canal in the Republic of Panama, was acquired in 1903 by the United States, who governed it until 1979. The Panama Canal Treaty of 1977 abolished the Canal Zone as an independent political entity, but the canal's maintenance and operation remain the responsibility of the U.S. Panama Canal Commission until 1999, when the Republic of Panama assumes full responsibility.

Commerce in Major U.S. Ports

In 1986, the latest year for which figures are available, 46 ports in the United States handled in excess of 10 million tons of cargo—three million more than in 1985. Of these, four handled more than 100 million tons: New York, 157.8 million; New Orleans, 149.1 million; Houston, 101.7 million; and Valdez, Alaska, 101.1 million (virtually all of it oil). Twenty-four of the nation's largest ports were located on the Atlantic and Gulf coasts, nine on the Pacific, seven on the Mississippi and Ohio rivers, and six on the Great Lakes.

TONNAGE HANDLED BY PRINCIPAL U.S. PORTS, 1985–86 (in thousands of short tons)

Rank 1986	Port	Tonnage 1986	1985	Rank 1985
1.	New York, N.Y.	157,801	152,054	1
2.	New Orleans, La.	149,082	146,678	2
3.	Houston, Tex.	101,659	90,669	4
4.	Valdez, Alaska	101,118	99,624	3
5.	Baton Rouge, La.	77,184	70,716	5
6.	Corpus Christi, Tex.	50,105	42,682	9
7.	Norfolk, Va.	44,069	47,181	6
8.	Long Beach, Calif.	42,718	43,977	8
9.	Tampa, Fla.	39,909	46,905	7
10.	Los Angeles, Calif.	38,859	36,374	12
11.	Mobile, Ala.	37,576	37,749	10
12.	Philadelphia, Pa.	35,661	32,690	14
13.	Texas City, Tex.	35,480	33,441	13
14.	Baltimore, Md.	35,432	36,425	11
15.	Lake Charles, La.	30,921	25,494	20
16.	Marcus Hook, Pa.	30,554	27,418	17
17.	Duluth-Superior, Minn.-Wis.	29,155	28,817	15
18.	St. Louis, Mo.	28,003	26,620	19
19.	Beaumont, Tex.	27,454	26,842	18
20.	Pittsburgh, Pa.	26,709	28,552	16
21.	Portland, Oreg.	25,590	21,845	22
22.	Chicago, Ill.	24,330	22,574	21
23.	Pascagoula, Miss.	23,700	20,006	23
24.	Boston, Mass.	21,036	17,269	27
25.	Huntington, W.Va.	20,852	19,644	24
26.	Port Arthur, Tex.	18,880	15,755	33
27.	Richmond, Calif.	18,833	17,178	26
28.	Newport News, Va.	18,531	19,169	25
29.	Paulsboro, N.J.	18,529	16,101	31
30.	Toledo, Ohio	17,819	18,400	26
31.	Seattle, Wash.	17,098	16,230	29
32.	Tacoma, Wash.	16,173	15,795	32
33.	Detroit, Mich.	15,219	15,612	34
34.	Indianapolis, Ind.	14,014	13,549	36
35.	Freeport, Tex.	13,370	12,918	37
36.	Anacortes, Wash.	12,747	10,208	43
37.	Jacksonville, Fla.	12,442	11,332	40
38.	San Juan, P.R.	12,361	11,642	39
39.	Cincinnati, Ohio	12,276	16,215	30
40.	Cleveland, Ohio	12,188	13,767	35
41.	Savannah, Ga.	12,041	11,327	41
42.	Port Everglades, Fla.	11,536	11,649	38
43.	Lorain, Ohio	11,427	9,426	44
44.	Memphis, Tenn.	10,985	10,375	42
45.	Longview, Wash.	10,313	N.A.	N.A.
46.	New Haven, Conn.	10,065	9,349	45

Source: Dept. of the Army, Corps of Engineers, unpublished data, 1989.

FREIGHT CARRIED ON U.S. INLAND WATERWAYS, 1960–86 (billions of ton-miles)

System	1960	1970	1980	1985	1986
Total	**220.3**	**318.6**	**406.9**	**381.7**	**392.6**
Atlantic Coast waterways	28.6	28.6	30.4	24.8	25.6
Gulf Coast waterways	16.9	28.6	36.6	36.5	39.0
Pacific Coast waterways[1]	6.0	8.4	14.9	19.9	20.8
Mississippi River system[2]	69.3	138.5	228.9	224.7	239.3
Great Lakes system[3]	99.5	114.5	96.0	75.8	67.9

Notes: Excludes Alaska and Hawaii except as noted. Includes waterways, canals, and connecting channels. 1. Includes Alaskan waterways. 2. Main channels and all tributaries of the Mississippi, Illinois, Missouri, and Ohio rivers. 3. Does not include traffic between foreign ports. **Source:** Dept. of the Army, Corps of Engineers, *Waterborne Commerce of the United States* (annual).

U.S. ENERGY

Energy is often measured in millions or larger quantities of Btu, or British thermal units. One Btu is approximately the energy released in burning a wooden match. A million Btu of energy is released when an engine burns eight gallons of gasoline. A quadrillion Btu is a billion millions Btu, equivalent to the energy in eight billion gallons of gasoline.

Between 1960 and 1980, energy consumption in the United States increased 77 percent, from 43 quadrillion Btu to 76 quadrillion. Throughout the 1980s, however, energy consumption remained steady, even though population continued to increase.

U.S. END-USE ENERGY CONSUMPTION PER CAPITA, 1950–87

Year	End-Use consumption (quadrillion Btu)	Population (millions)	Consumption per capita (million Btu)
1950	20.37	151.3	194
1955	34.02	165.1	206
1960	37.96	179.3	212
1965	44.93	193.5	232
1970	54.91	203.2	270
1975	56.16	215.5	261
1980	58.60	226.5	259
1985	55.40	238.7	232
1986	55.62	241.1	231
1987	56.84	243.4	234

Source: U.S. Dept. of Energy, *Annual Energy Review, 1987* (1988).

U.S. ENERGY PRODUCTION AND CONSUMPTION BY ENERGY SOURCE, 1960–87 (quadrillion Btu)

	1960	1965	1970	1975	1980	1985	1986	1987
PETROLEUM PRODUCTS								
Domestic production	16.39	18.40	22.91	20.10	20.50	21.23	20.53	19.82
Imports	4.00	5.40	7.47	12.95	14.65	10.61	13.20	13.88
Exports	−0.43	−0.39	−0.55	−0.44	−1.16	−1.66	−1.67	−1.66
NET CONSUMPTION	19.96	23.41	29.83	32.61	33.99	30.18	32.06	32.04
NATURAL GAS								
Domestic production	12.66	15.78	21.67	19.64	19.91	16.91	16.47	16.84
Imports	0.16	0.47	0.85	0.98	1.01	0.95	0.75	0.99
Exports[1]	−0.03	−0.09	−0.18	−0.16	−0.14	−0.14	−0.14	−0.13
NET CONSUMPTION	12.79	16.16	22.34	20.46	20.78	17.72	17.08	17.70
COAL								
Domestic production	10.82	13.06	14.61	14.99	18.60	19.33	19.51	20.12
Imports[1]	0.07	0.04	0.07	0.19	0.31	0.54	0.48	0.55
Exports	−1.02	−1.38	−1.94	−1.76	−2.42	−2.44	−2.25	−2.10
NET CONSUMPTION	9.87	11.72	12.74	13.42	16.49	17.43	17.74	18.57
Nuclear power production	0.01	0.04	0.24	1.90	2.74	4.15	4.47	4.92
Hydroelectric production	1.61	2.06	2.63	3.15	2.90	2.94	3.03	2.61
Other production[2]	—	0.01	0.02	0.07	0.11	0.21	0.23	0.24
Adjustments[3]	−0.43	−0.72	−1.37	−1.07	−1.05	1.31	−0.36	−0.07
TOTAL CONSUMPTION	**43.81**	**52.68**	**66.43**	**70.54**	**75.96**	**73.94**	**74.25**	**76.01**

1. Categories contain small amounts of other materials exported or imported. 2. Primarily generation of electricity from geothermal or other renewable energy sources. 3. Losses, unaccounted for, reductions in stocks, etc.

ENERGY CONSUMPTION BY SOURCE AS PERCENTAGE OF TOTAL CONSUMPTION

	1960	1965	1970	1975	1980	1985	1986	1987
Petroleum products	45.6%	44.4%	44.9%	46.2%	44.7%	40.8%	43.2%	42.2%
Natural gas	29.2	30.7	33.6	29.0	27.4	24.0	23.0	23.3
Coal	22.5	22.2	19.2	19.0	21.7	23.6	23.9	24.4
Nuclear power	—	0.1	0.4	2.7	3.6	5.6	6.0	6.5
Hydroelectric power	3.7	3.9	4.0	4.5	3.8	4.0	4.1	3.4
Other	—	—	—	0.1	0.1	0.3	0.3	0.3
Adjustments	−1.0	−1.4	−2.1	−1.5	−1.4	1.8	−0.5	−0.1
TOTAL	100.0%	100.0%	100.0%	100.0%	100.0%	100.0%	100.0%	100.0%

Source: U.S. Dept. of Energy, *Annual Energy Review, 1987* (1988).

Per Capita Energy Consumption

End-use consumption of energy (total consumption less losses incurred in electricity generation, transmission, and distribution, and less electricity used by power plants) increased about 6 percent between 1982 and 1987. Since population was increasing, however, per capita consumption of energy increased by only 1.3 percent, from 231 million to 234 million Btu.

Each individual each day consumes, on average, 855,000 Btu of energy. This is equivalent to about 6.8 gallons of gasoline for every man, woman, and child—the equivalent of more than 1.6 billion gallons in the United States each day!

PER CAPITA DAILY CONSUMPTION OF ENERGY BY SOURCE, 1987

IN COMMON MEASURES

Petroleum products	2.9 gallons
Natural gas	184.0 cubic feet
Coal	18.8 pounds
Electricity	28.0 kilowatt-hours

IN Btu

Nonindustrial energy use	549,000.0 Btu
Industrial energy use	306,000.0 Btu
Total per capita daily energy use	**855,000.0 Btu**

CLIMATE AND WEATHER

WEATHER WORDS

Air mass A large body of air that, at a given elevation, has about the same temperature and humidity throughout.

Barometric pressure The weight of the column of air at a particular place is determined by measuring the height of mercury in a thermometer. At sea level the average barometric pressure measured this way is 29.53 inches (75 cm). In the International System, air pressure is measured in bars or in kiloPascals. A bar is slightly more than the standard air pressure at sea level, and a kiloPascal is one hundredth of a bar. At any location, however, barometric pressure is affected by changes in temperature, humidity, or elevation. When the "barometer is falling," the air pressure is decreasing, often a sign of a storm.

Cold front The place where cold air that is advancing meets warm air that is retreating before it. This kind of weather not only lowers temperature as it passes but also causes high winds and may cause thunderstorms.

Degree-days A degree-day is one degree of deviation of the daily mean temperature from a given norm, usually 75°F. Cooling degree-days are the number of degrees Fahrenheit by which the mean temperature exceeds 65°F, while heating degree-days are the number of degrees the mean temperature is below 65°F. During a year, keeping track of the total number of degree-days (adding the ones for each day) is used to keep track of cooling or heating needs. For example, oil companies use heating degree-days to estimate how much oil their customers have used and when they might need a refill.

Depression Any region of low air pressure. In temperate regions over land, the typical depression is a low in contrast with the often more powerful depression occurring over tropical waters, called a tropical depression, which can become a tropical storm or a hurricane.

Dew point The temperature at which dew (drops of water) begins to form as water vapor in the air condenses. Air can hold only a certain amount of water vapor at a given temperature. When the temperature falls, excess water vapor must turn into a liquid.

El Niño A change in the circulation and temperature of the waters off the west coast of South America that occurs every few years. Water that is normally cold is replaced by warmer water, disrupting the local environment in many ways (e.g., moving fish away from the surface, which results in less food for water fowl, and causing rain in normally dry regions). Because El Niño is linked to other weather systems, a strong El Niño can affect weather worldwide.

Front The boundary between two different air masses.

High An air mass characterized hy higher-than-normal air pressure; usually this is a fair-weather system. Some highs are typically found in the same place each year, such as one that occurs over Bermuda in most summers.

Jet stream A strong river or two of high winds in the upper atmosphere (but below the stratosphere) that meanders partway or all the way around the globe, most often in the middle latitudes. Discovered by American bomber pilots attacking Japan in World War II, it is now known to have significant effects on weather. The position of the jet stream is responsible for most cold spells and heat waves.

Low An air mass characterized by lower-than-normal air pressure; usually this is the heart of a storm system. Some lows are found in the same region most of the year, such as the low in the Pacific just off the coast of Alaska.

Mean temperature Technically, this should be the average of all temperatures during the day; sometimes it is the average of 24 temperatures taken once each hour; but most often the mean temperature is simply the average of the high and low for the day.

Occluded front When a cold front overtakes a warm front, the denser cold air flows under the less dense warm air.

Prevailing winds Throughout the world, winds follow regular patterns. In some places winds are so light and infrequent as to scarcely exist, such as in the doldrums along the equator and in the horse latitudes near latitude 30° north and south. In other places the winds tend to come from a particular direction and are called prevailing winds.

Relative humidity The amount of moisture (water vapor) in the air compared with the total amount it can hold expressed as a percent. Warm air can hold more water vapor than cold air, so a relative humidity of 75% on a warm summer day is moister than a relative humidity of 75% on a cool winter day. However, because evaporation is greater on warm days, the relative humidity in summer is generally higher than in winter.

Secondary cold front A cold front that sometimes forms behind another cold front and that is often even colder than the first front.

Secondary depression A low that forms to the south or east of a low that is a storm center.

Squall line A line of instability that often precedes a cold front, marked by wind gusts and often by heavy rain.

Stationary front A front that stays in the same place.

Storm surge The rise in water levels in the ocean or a large lake that comes from a combination of wind and low pressure during a storm, especially pronounced during a hurricane.

Temperature-humidity index A number derived from a formula relating temperature and humidity to discomfort. When it is 75, many are uncomfortable, while at 80 or above, almost everyone is uncomfortable. Temperatures are

CLIMATE OF SELECTED WORLD CITIES

Highest and lowest average temperatures for selected months in degrees Fahrenheit. Precipitation is the average monthly amount in inches of rainfall equivalent.

City	JANUARY Temp. Max.	Min.	Avg. precip.	APRIL Temp. Max.	Min.	Avg. precip.	JULY Temp. Max.	Min.	Avg. precip.	OCTOBER Temp. Max.	Min.	Avg. precip.
Accra, Ghana	87	73	0.6	88	76	3.2	81	73	1.8	85	74	2.5
Amsterdam, Netherlands	40	34	2.0	52	43	1.6	69	59	2.6	56	48	2.8
Athens, Greece	54	42	2.2	67	52	0.8	90	72	0.2	74	60	1.7
Baghdad, Iraq	60	39	0.9	85	57	0.5	110	76	trace	92	61	0.1
Bangkok, Thailand	89	67	0.2	95	78	2.3	90	76	6.9	88	76	9.9
Beirut, Lebanon	62	51	7.5	72	58	2.2	87	73	trace	81	69	2.0
Belfast, United Kingdom	42	34	4.2	53	38	2.4	65	52	3.5	55	44	3.8
Berlin, West Germany	35	26	1.9	55	38	1.7	74	55	3.1	55	41	1.7
Bombay, India	88	62	0.1	93	74	trace	88	75	24.3	93	73	2.5
Budapest, Hungary	35	26	1.5	62	44	2.0	82	61	2.0	61	45	2.1
Buenos Aires, Argentina	85	63	3.1	72	54	3.5	57	42	2.2	69	50	3.4
Cairo, Egypt	65	47	0.2	83	57	0.1	96	70	0.0	86	65	trace
Calcutta, India	80	55	0.4	97	76	1.7	90	79	12.8	89	74	4.5
Canton, China	65	49	0.9	77	65	6.8	91	77	8.1	85	67	3.4
Capetown, South Africa	78	60	0.6	72	53	1.9	63	45	3.5	70	52	1.2
Casablanca, Morocco	63	24	2.1	69	52	1.4	79	65	0.0	76	58	1.5
Christchurch, New Zealand	70	53	2.2	62	45	1.9	50	35	2.7	62	44	1.7
Colombo, Sri Lanka	86	72	3.5	88	76	9.1	85	77	5.3	85	75	13.7
Copenhagen, Denmark	36	29	1.6	50	37	1.7	72	55	2.2	53	42	2.1
Dakha, Bangladesh	77	56	0.3	92	74	5.4	88	77	5.3	85	75	13.7
Dakar, Senegal	79	64	trace	81	65	trace	88	76	3.5	89	76	1.5
Dublin, Ireland	47	35	2.7	54	38	1.9	67	51	2.8	57	43	2.7
Edinburgh, United Kingdom	43	35	2.5	50	39	1.6	65	52	3.1	53	44	2.9
Geneva, Switzerland	39	29	1.9	58	41	2.5	77	58	2.9	58	44	3.8
Hanoi, Vietnam	68	58	0.8	80	79	3.6	92	79	11.9	94	72	3.5
Hong Kong	64	56	1.3	75	67	5.4	87	78	15.0	81	73	4.5
Istanbul, Turkey	45	36	3.7	61	45	1.9	81	65	1.7	67	54	3.8
Jakarta, Indonesia	84	74	11.8	87	75	5.8	87	73	2.5	87	74	4.4
Jerusalem, Israel	55	41	5.1	73	50	0.9	87	63	0.0	81	59	0.3
Kabul, Afghanistan	36	18	1.3	66	43	3.3	92	61	0.1	73	64	0.4
Karachi, Pakistan	77	55	0.5	90	73	0.1	91	81	3.2	91	72	0.1
Kinshasa, Zaire	87	70	5.3	89	71	7.7	81	64	0.1	88	70	4.7
Lagos, Nigeria	88	74	1.1	89	77	5.9	83	74	11.0	85	74	8.1
Leningrad, USSR	23	12	1.0	45	31	1.0	71	57	2.5	45	37	1.8
Lima, Peru	82	66	0.1	80	63	trace	67	57	0.3	71	58	0.1
Lisbon, Portugal	56	46	3.3	64	52	2.4	79	63	0.2	69	57	3.1
London, United Kingdom	44	35	2.0	56	40	1.8	73	55	2.0	58	44	2.3
Madrid, Spain	47	33	1.1	64	44	1.7	87	62	0.4	66	48	1.9
Manila, Philippines	87	72	4.8	91	73	5.8	88	73	6.5	89	73	7.9
Melbourne, Australia	78	57	1.9	68	51	2.3	56	42	1.9	67	48	2.6
Mexico City, Mexico	66	42	0.2	78	52	0.7	74	54	4.5	70	50	1.6
Montreal, Canada	21	6	3.8	50	34	2.6	78	61	3.7	54	40	3.4
Moscow, USSR	21	9	1.5	47	31	1.9	76	55	3.0	46	34	2.7
Nairobi, Kenya	77	54	1.5	75	58	8.3	69	51	0.6	76	55	2.1
Oslo, Norway	30	20	1.7	50	34	1.6	73	56	2.9	49	37	2.9
Paris, France	42	32	1.5	60	41	1.7	76	55	2.1	59	44	2.2
Prague, Czechoslovakia	34	25	0.9	55	40	1.5	74	58	2.6	54	44	1.2
Reykjavik, Iceland	36	28	4.0	43	33	2.1	58	48	2.0	44	36	3.4
Rio de Janiero, Brazil	84	73	4.9	80	69	4.2	75	63	1.6	77	66	3.1
Riyadh, Saudi Arabia	70	46	0.1	89	64	1.0	107	78	0.0	94	61	0.0
Rome, Italy	54	39	3.3	68	46	2.0	88	64	0.4	73	53	4.3
Santiago, Chile	85	53	0.1	74	45	0.5	59	37	3.0	72	45	0.6
Seoul, South Korea	32	15	1.2	62	41	3.0	84	70	14.8	67	45	1.6
Shanghai, China	47	32	1.9	67	49	3.6	91	75	5.8	75	56	2.9
Singapore, Malaya Fed.	86	73	9.9	88	75	7.4	88	75	6.7	87	74	8.2
Stockholm, Sweden	31	23	1.5	45	32	1.5	70	55	2.8	48	39	2.1
Sydney, Australia	78	65	3.5	71	58	5.3	50	46	4.6	71	56	2.8
Tahiti, Society Islands	89	72	13.2	89	72	6.8	86	68	2.6	87	70	3.4
Taipei, Taiwan	66	53	3.8	77	64	5.3	92	76	8.8	80	68	5.5
Tehran, Iran	45	27	1.8	71	49	1.4	99	72	0.1	76	53	0.3
Tokyo, Japan	47	29	1.9	63	46	5.3	83	70	5.6	69	55	8.2
Toronto, Canada	30	16	2.7	50	34	2.5	79	59	3.0	56	40	2.4
Warsaw, Poland	30	21	1.2	54	38	1.5	75	56	3.0	54	41	1.7
Wellington, New Zealand	69	56	3.2	63	51	3.8	53	42	5.4	60	48	4.0

Source: U.S. Dept. of Commerce, *Climates of the World* (1972).

less comfortable at high humidities because cooling by sweating is less efficient.

Tropical storm A storm that forms over the ocean in the tropics and often moves onto land, where it loses strength. Technically, a storm is designated a tropical storm only when winds are between 39 and 74 miles per hour. If winds become greater, a tropical storm becomes a hurricane.

Trough A low that is long, rather than nearly circular.

Warm front The boundary of a moving warm-air mass.

Wind-chill factor A number that represents the effective chilling caused by a combination of wind and low temperature (see below).

Wind-Chill Factor

Sometimes called a wind-chill index, this is a measure of the cooling power of air movement and low temperature on the human body. Because heat passes directly from a warm body to the cooler air surrounding it—a process known as convection—wind produces a continuing source of cooler air and a chilling effect that is equivalent to a lower temperature. The effect of wind on a warm day is pleasant, but as temperatures approach freezing, wind chill is not only unpleasant but can be dangerous. As the table below shows, a temperature of 5°F combined with a breeze of 10 miles per hour produces a wind-chill temperature of –15°F—a temperature at which frostbite occurs much sooner than at 5°F. Wind speeds above 45 miles per hour have little additional cooling effect.

BEAUFORT SCALE OF WIND STRENGTH

The Beaufort Scale is commonly used by sailors to describe winds and is one basis for classification of a strong wind as a storm or a hurricane. When the numbers are used, they are referred to with the word *force*; a "force 7" wind is a moderate gale, for instance.

Beaufort number	Type of wind	Wind speed	Description and effect
0	Calm	less than 1.6 km/hr. less than 1 mi./hr.	Still; smoke rises vertically.
1	Light air	1.6–8.0 km/hr. 1–5 mi./hr.	Wind direction shown by smoke drift; weather vanes inactive.
2	Light breeze	9–18 km/hr. 6–11 mi./hr.	Wind felt on face; leaves rustle; weather vanes active.
3	Gentle breeze	19–31 km/hr. 12–19 mi./hr.	Leaves and small twigs move constantly; wind extends lightweight flags.
4	Moderate breeze	32–46 km/hr. 20–28mi./hr.	Raises dust and loose paper; moves twigs and thin branches.
5	Fresh breeze	47–62 km/hr. 29–38 mi./hr.	Small trees in leaf begin to sway.
6	Strong breeze	63–80 km/hr. 39–49 mi./hr.	Large branches move; telephone wires whistle; umbrella difficult to control.
7	Moderate gale	81–99 km/hr. 50–61 mi./hr.	Whole trees sway; somewhat difficult to walk.
8	Fresh gale	100–120 km/hr. 62–74 mi./hr.	Twigs broken off trees; walking against wind very difficult.
9	Strong gale	121–143 km/hr. 75–88 mi./hr.	Slight damage to buildings, shingles blown off roof.
10	Whole gale	144–165 km/hr. 89–102 mi./hr.	Trees uprooted; considerable damage to buildings.
11	Storm	166–190 km/hr. 103–117 mi./hr.	Widespread damage; rarely occurs inland.
12–17	Hurricane	greater than 190 km/hr. greater than 117 mi./hr.	Extreme destruction.

DETERMINING THE WIND-CHILL FACTOR

Wind speed	Actual temperature																	Wind speed
	35°F	30°F	25°F	20°F	15°F	10°F	5°F	0°F	–5°F	–10°F	–15°F	–20°F	–25°F	–30°F	–35°F	–40°F	–45°F	
5 mph	33°	27°	21°	16°	12°	7°	0°	–5°	–10°	–15°	–21°	–26°	–31°	–36°	–42°	–47°	–52°	5 mph
10 mph	22	16	10	3	–3	–9	–15	–22	–27	–34	–40	–46	–52	–58	–64	–71	–77	10 mph
15 mph	16	9	2	–5	–11	–18	–25	–31	–38	–45	–51	–58	–65	–72	–78	–85	–92	15 mph
20 mph	12	4	–3	–10	–17	–24	–31	–39	–46	–53	–60	–67	–74	–81	–88	–95	–102	20 mph
25 mph	8	1	–7	–15	–22	–29	–36	–44	–51	–59	–66	–74	–81	–88	–96	–103	–110	25 mph
30 mph	6	–2	–10	–18	–25	–33	–41	–49	–56	–64	–71	–79	–86	–93	–101	–109	–116	30 mph
35 mph	4	–4	–12	–20	–27	–35	–43	–52	–58	–67	–74	–82	–89	–97	–105	–113	–120	35 mph
40 mph	3	–5	–13	–21	–29	–37	–45	–53	–60	–69	–76	–84	–92	–100	–107	–115	–123	40 mph
45 mph	2	–6	–14	–22	–30	–38	–46	–54	–62	–70	–78	–85	–93	–102	–109	–117	–125	45 mph

TORNADOES, FLOODS, AND TROPICAL CYCLONES, 1980–87

Item	1980	1981	1982	1983	1984	1985	1986	1987
Tornadoes, number	866	783	1,046	931	907	684	764	656
Lives lost, total	28	24	64	34	122	94	15	59
Most in a single tornado	5	5	10	3	16	18	3	30
Floods: lives lost	97	90	155	200	126	304	80	N.A.
Property loss (mil.)	$1,500	$1,000	$3,500	$4,100	$4,000	$3,000	$4,000	N.A.
North Atlantic tropical cyclones and hurricanes:								
Number reaching U.S. coast	2	2	1	2	2	11	6	7
Hurricanes only	1	—	—	1	1	7	4	3
Lives lost in U.S.	2	—	—	22	4	30	9	

Note: A tornado is a violent, rotating column of air descending from a cumulonimbus cloud in the form of a tubular or funnel-shaped cloud, usually characterized by movements along a narrow path and wind speeds from 100 to 300 miles per hour; also known as a twister or waterspout. Tropical cyclones have maximum winds of 39 to 73 miles per hour; hurricanes have maximum winds of 74 miles per hour or higher. **Source:** U.S. National Oceanic and Atmospheric Administration, data for 1980, *Climatological Data: National Summary* (monthly with annual summary); thereafter, *Storm Data* (monthly).

CLIMATES OF SELECTED U.S. CITIES

If you plan to travel or move to a different city, it is helpful to know the normal daily high temperature for each month (given here in degrees Fahrenheit and shown with a degree sign) and the normal monthly rain or snow (precipitation—given here in inches and indicated with the symbol for *inches: "*). Precipitation data are based on rain and melted snow or ice. The third line is snow and ice pellets where applicable. *T* means "trace," and a blank in the third line means no snow or ice pellets fell.

	Jan.	Feb.	Mar.	Apr.	May	June	July	Aug.	Sept.	Oct.	Nov.	Dec.
Baltimore, Md.	41°	44°	53°	65°	74°	83°	87°	86°	79°	68°	56°	45°
	3.0"	3.0"	3.7"	3.4"	3.4"	3.8"	3.9"	4.6"	3.5"	3.1"	3.1"	3.4"
	6.1"	7.2"	3.9"	0.1"	T						1.1"	3.5"
Boston, Mass.	36°	38°	45°	57°	67°	77°	82°	80°	72°	63°	52°	40°
	4.0"	3.7"	4.1"	3.7"	3.5"	2.9"	2.7"	3.7"	3.4"	3.4"	4.2"	4.5"
	12.5"	11.4"	7.6"	1.0"							1.4"	7.6"
Chicago, Ill.	29°	34°	44°	59°	70°	79°	83°	82°	76°	64°	48°	35°
	1.6"	1.3"	2.6"	3.7"	3.2"	4.1"	3.6"	3.5"	3.4"	2.3"	2.1"	2.1"
	11.4"	7.8"	7.1"	1.9"	0.1"				T	0.3"	2.1"	9.1"
Cleveland, Ohio	33°	35°	45°	58°	69°	78°	82°	80°	74°	63°	49°	38°
	2.5"	2.2"	3.0"	3.3"	3.3"	3.5"	3.4"	3.4"	2.9"	2.5"	2.8"	2.8"
	12.6"	11.5"	10.2"	2.3"	0.1"				T	0.7"	5.1"	11.6"
Columbus, Ohio	35°	38°	49°	62°	73°	81°	84°	83°	77°	65°	51°	39°
	2.8"	2.2"	3.2"	3.4"	3.8"	4.0"	4.0"	3.7"	2.8"	1.9"	2.6"	2.6"
	8.6"	6.3"	4.5"	1.0"	T				T		2.5"	5.6"
Dallas–Ft. Worth, Tex.	54°	59°	67°	77°	84°	93°	98°	97°	90°	80°	66°	58°
	1.7"	1.9"	2.4"	3.6"	4.3"	2.6"	2.0"	1.8"	3.3"	2.5"	1.8"	1.7"
	1.4"	1.0"	0.2"								0.1"	0.3"
Denver, Colo.	43°	47°	51°	61°	71°	82°	88°	86°	78°	67°	52°	46°
	0.5"	0.7"	1.2"	1.8"	2.5"	1.6"	1.9"	1.5"	1.2"	1.0"	0.8"	0.6"
	7.8"	7.5"	12.8"	9.3"	1.8"				1.7"	3.7"	8.4"	7.3"
Detroit, Mich.	31°	34°	43°	58°	69°	79°	83°	82°	74°	63°	48°	35°
	1.9"	1.7"	2.5"	3.2"	2.8"	3.4"	3.1"	3.2"	2.3"	2.1"	2.3"	2.5"
	10.4"	8.7"	7.0"	1.8"	T					0.1"	3.3"	10.7"
El Paso, Tex.	58°	63°	70°	79°	87°	96°	95°	93°	88°	79°	66°	58°
	0.4"	0.5"	0.3"	0.2"	0.2"	0.6"	1.6"	1.2"	1.4"	0.7"	0.3"	0.4"
	1.4"	0.8"	0.4"	0.4"							1.0"	1.8"
Houston, Tex.	62°	66°	72°	79°	85°	91°	94°	93°	89°	82°	72°	65°
	3.2"	2.3"	3.3"	2.7"	4.2"	4.7"	4.1"	3.3"	3.7"	4.9"	3.4"	3.7"
	0.2"	0.2"									T	T
Indianapolis, Ind.	34°	39°	49°	63°	73°	82°	85°	84°	78°	66°	51°	39°
	2.7"	2.5"	3.6"	3.7"	3.7"	4.0"	4.3"	3.5"	2.7"	2.5"	3.0"	3.0"
	6.3"	5.9"	3.5"	0.5"	T						1.9"	4.8"
Jacksonville, Fla.	65°	67°	73°	80°	85°	89°	91°	90°	87°	80°	72°	66°
	1.7"	1.9"	1.3"	1.5"	3.2"	5.0"	3.7"	4.8"	6.5"	4.3"	3.2"	1.7"
	T											T
Los Angeles, Calif.	67°	69°	69°	71°	73°	78°	84°	84°	83°	79°	73°	68°
	3.7"	3.0"	2.4"	1.2"	0.2"	0.0"	0.0"	0.1"	0.3"	0.2"	1.9"	2.0
			T									
Memphis, Tenn.	48°	53°	61°	73°	81°	88°	92°	90°	84°	75°	61°	52°
	4.6"	4.3"	5.4"	5.8"	5.1"	3.4"	4.0"	3.7"	3.6"	2.4"	4.2"	4.9"
	2.5"	1.5"	0.9"	T							0.1"	0.7"
Milwaukee, Wis.	26°	30°	39°	54°	65°	75°	80°	78°	71°	60°	45°	32°
	1.7"	1.3"	2.6"	3.4"	2.7"	3.6"	3.5"	3.1"	2.9"	2.3"	2.0"	2.0"
	13.1"	9.3"	8.9"	1.8"					T	0.1"	2.8"	10.7"
New Orleans, La.	62°	65°	71°	79°	85°	90°	91°	90°	87°	79°	79°	64°
	5.0"	5.2"	4.7"	4.5"	5.1"	4.6"	6.7"	6.0"	5.9"	2.7"	4.1"	5.3"
	0.1"	T									T	0.1"
New York, N.Y.	38°	40°	49°	61°	72°	80°	85°	84°	76°	66°	54°	42°
	3.2"	3.1"	4.2"	3.8"	3.8"	3.2"	3.8"	4.0"	3.7"	3.4"	4.1"	3.8"
	7.6"	8.7"	5.0"	0.9"	T						0.9"	5.5"
Phoenix, Ariz.	65°	70°	75°	83°	92°	102°	105°	102°	98°	88°	74°	66°
	0.7"	0.6"	0.8"	0.3"	0.1"	0.2"	0.7"	1.0"	0.6"	0.6"	0.5"	0.8"
			T	T								
Philadelphia, Pa.	39°	41°	51°	63°	73°	82°	86°	85°	79°	67°	55°	43°
	3.2"	2.8"	3.9"	3.5"	3.2"	3.9"	3.9"	4.1"	3.4"	2.8"	3.3"	3.5"
	6.6"	6.9"	3.8"	0.3"	T						0.6"	3.6"
San Antonio, Tex.	62°	66°	74°	80°	86°	92°	95°	95°	89°	82°	71°	65°
	1.6"	1.9"	1.3"	2.7"	3.7"	3.0"	1.9"	2.7"	3.8"	2.9"	2.3"	1.4"
	1.6"	0.7"	0.2"	T							0.5"	0.2"
San Diego, Calif.	65°	66°	66°	68°	69°	71°	76°	78°	77°	75°	70°	66°
	2.1"	1.4"	1.6"	0.8"	0.2"	0.1"	0.0"	0.1"	0.2"	0.3"	1.1"	1.4"
	T		T								T	T
San Francisco, Calif.	56°	59°	60°	61°	63°	64°	64°	65°	69°	68°	63°	57°
	4.5"	2.8"	2.6"	1.5"	0.4"	0.2"	0.0"	0.1"	0.2"	1.1"	2.5"	3.5"
	T	T	T	T							T	T
Seattle, Wash.	45°	50°	53°	58°	65°	69°	75°	74°	69°	60°	51°	47°
	5.9"	4.2"	3.7"	2.5"	1.7"	1.5"	0.9"	1.4"	2.0"	3.4"	5.4"	6.3"
	3.3"	0.8"	0.6"		T						0.8"	1.9"
Washington, D.C.	43°	46°	55°	67°	76°	84°	88°	86°	80°	69°	57°	47°
	2.8"	2.6"	3.5"	2.9"	3.5"	3.4"	3.9"	4.4"	3.2"	2.9"	2.8"	3.2"
	5.5"	5.8"	2.1"		T						0.9"	3.1"

Source: NOAA, *Comparative Climactic Data for the United States through 1967* (no date).

Area Codes of the United States and Selected Countries

AREA CODES OF THE UNITED STATES AND CANADA, BY STATE AND PROVINCE, AND OF THE CARIBBEAN ISLANDS

Alabama	205
Alaska	907
Alberta, Canada	403
Arizona	602
Arkansas	501
Bermuda	809
British Columbia, Canada	604
California (Fresno)	209
California (Long Beach, Los Angeles)	213
California (San Jose)	408
California (San Francisco, Oakland)	415
California (San Diego)	619
California (Santa Rosa, Eureka)	707
California (Anaheim, Orange)	714
California (Bakersfield)	805
California (Burbank)	818
California (Sacramento)	916
Caribbean islands[1]	809
Colorado (Aspen, Denver)	303
Colorado (Colorado Springs, Pueblo)	719
Connecticut	203
Delaware	302
Florida (Ft. Lauderdale, Miami)	305
Florida (Melbourne, Orlando)	407
Florida (Ft. Myers, Tampa)	813
Florida (Jacksonville, Tallahassee)	904

Georgia (Atlanta, Columbus)	404
Georgia (Macon, Savannah)	912
Hawaii	808
Idaho	208
Illinois (Decatur, Springfield)	217
Illinois (Moline, Peoria)	309
Illinois (Aurora, Chicago)	312
Illinois (Centralia, East St. Louis)	618
Illinois (Joliet, Rockford)	815
Indiana (Ft. Wayne, Gary)	219
Indiana (Indianapolis, Muncie)	317
Indiana (Evansville, Terre Haute)	812
Iowa (Cedar Rapids, Dubuque)	319
Iowa (Ames, Des Moines)	515
Iowa (Council Bluffs, Sioux City)	712
Kansas (Emporia, Wichita)	316
Kansas (Kansas City, Salina, Topeka)	913
Kentucky (Bowling Green, Louisville)	502
Kentucky (Covington, Lexington)	606
Louisiana (Lafayette, Shreveport)	318
Louisiana (Baton Rouge, New Orleans)	504
Maine	207
Manitoba, Canada	204
Maryland	301

Massachusetts (Amherst, Springfield)	413
Massachusetts (Cape Cod, Lowell, New Bedford)	508
Massachusetts (Boston, Worcester)	617
Michigan (Ann Arbor, Detroit, Flint)	313
Michigan (Lansing, Midland, Saginaw)	517
Michigan (Grand Rapids, Kalamazoo)	616
Michigan (Escanaba, Upper Peninsula)	906
Minnesota (Duluth)	218
Minnesota (Rochester, Winona)	507
Minnesota (Minneapolis–St. Paul, Minnetonka)	612
Mississippi	601
Missouri (Jefferson City, St. Louis)	314
Missouri (Joplin, Springfield)	417
Missouri (Kansas City, St. Joseph)	816
Montana	406
Nebraska (Grand Island, North Platte)	308
Nebraska (Lincoln, Omaha)	402
Nevada	702
New Brunswick, Canada	506
New Hampshire	603

New Jersey (Jersey City, Newark)	201
New Jersey (Atlantic City, Trenton)	609
New Mexico	505
New York City (Bronx, Manhattan)	212
New York (Syracuse, Utica)	315
New York (Hempstead, Long Island)	516
New York (Albany, Schenectady)	518
New York (Binghampton, Elmira)	607
New York (Buffalo, Rochester)	716
New York City (Brooklyn, Queens, Staten Island)	718
New York (White Plains, Yonkers)	914
Newfoundland, Canada	709
North Carolina (Asheville, Charlotte)	704
North Carolina (Raleigh, Winston-Salem)	919
North Dakota	701
Northwest Territories, Canada	403
Nova Scotia, Canada	902
Ohio (Akron, Cleveland)	216
Ohio (Sandusky, Toledo)	419
Ohio (Cincinnati, Dayton)	513
Ohio (Columbus, Steubenville)	614
Oklahoma (Lawton, Oklahoma City)	405
Oklahoma (Muskogee, Tulsa)	918
Ontario, Canada (Toronto)	416
Ontario, Canada (London)	519

Ontario, Canada (Ottawa)	613	Puerto Rico	809	Tennessee (Jackson, Memphis)	901	Virginia (Richmond, Virginia Beach) 804
Ontario, Canada (North Bay)	705			Texas (Dallas)	214	Virgin Islands 809
Ontario, Canada (Ft. William, Thunder		Quebec, Canada (Quebec City)	418	Texas (Galveston)	409	
Bay)	807	Quebec, Canada (Montreal)	514	Texas (Austin, San Antonio)	512	Washington (Seattle, Vancouver) 206
Oregon	503	Quebec, Canada (Sherbrooke)	819	Texas (Houston)	713	Washington (Spokane, Yakima) 509
				Texas (Amarillo)	806	Washington, D.C. 202
Pennsylvania (Allentown,		Rhode Island	401	Texas (Arlington, Ft. Worth)	817	West Virginia 304
Philadelphia)	215	Saskatchewan, Canada	306	Texas (Abilene, El Paso)	915	Wisconsin (Green Bay, Milwaukee) 414
Pennsylvania (Pittsburgh)	412	South Carolina	803			Wisconsin (La Crosse, Madison) 608
Pennsylvania (Harrisburg, Scranton)	717	South Dakota	605	Utah	801	Wisconsin (Eau Claire, Wausau) 715
Pennsylvania (Altoona, Erie)	814					Wyoming 307
Prince Edward Island, Canada	902	Tennessee (Chattanooga, Knoxville,		Vermont	802	
		Nashville)	615	Virginia (Alexandria, Roanoke)	703	Yukon, Canada 403

Note: When no cities are listed, the area code is for the entire state or province. 1. Includes Anguilla, Antigua, the Bahamas, Barbados, Bequia, Bermuda, Cayman Islands, Dominica, Dominican Republic, Jamaica, Montserrat, Mustique, Nevis, Puerto Rico, St. Kitts, St. Lucia, St. Vincent, Trinidad and Tobago, Virgin Islands.

AREA CODES OF THE UNITED STATES AND CANADA, BY NUMBER CODE

201 New Jersey (Jersey City, Newark)
202 Washington, D.C.
203 Connecticut
204 Manitoba, Canada
205 Alabama
206 Washington (Seattle, Vancouver)
207 Maine
208 Idaho
209 California (Fresno)
212 New York City (Bronx, Manhattan)
213 California (Long Beach, Los Angeles)
214 Texas (Dallas)
215 Pennsylvania (Allentown, Philadelphia)
216 Ohio (Akron, Cleveland)
217 Illinois (Decatur, Springfield)
218 Minnesota (Duluth)
219 Indiana (Ft. Wayne, Gary)

301 Maryland
302 Delaware
303 Colorado (Aspen, Denver)
304 West Virginia
305 Florida (Ft. Lauderdale, Miami)
306 Saskatchewan, Canada
307 Wyoming
308 Nebraska (Grand Island, North Platte)
309 Illinois (Moline, Peoria)
312 Illinois (Aurora, Chicago)
313 Michigan (Ann Arbor, Detroit, Flint)
314 Missouri (Jefferson City, St. Louis)
315 New York (Syracuse, Utica)
316 Kansas (Emporia, Wichita)
317 Indiana (Indianapolis, Muncie)
318 Louisiana (Lafayette, Shreveport)
319 Iowa (Cedar Rapids, Dubuque)

401 Rhode Island
402 Nebraska (Lincoln, Omaha)
403 Alberta, Northwest Territories, Canada
404 Georgia (Atlanta, Columbus)
405 Oklahoma (Lawton, Oklahoma City)
406 Montana
407 Florida (Melbourne, Orlando)
408 California (San Jose)
409 Texas (Galveston)
412 Pennsylvania (Pittsburgh)
413 Massachusetts (Amherst, Springfield)
414 Wisconsin (Green Bay, Milwaukee)
415 California (Oakland, San Francisco)
416 Ontario, Canada (Toronto)
417 Missouri (Joplin, Springfield)
418 Quebec, Canada (Quebec City)
419 Ohio (Sandusky, Toledo)

501 Arkansas
502 Kentucky (Bowling Green, Louisville)
503 Oregon
504 Louisiana (Baton Rouge, New Orleans)
505 New Mexico
506 New Brunswick, Canada
507 Minnesota (Rochester, Winona)
508 Massachusetts (Cape Cod, Lowell, New Bedford)
509 Washington (Spokane, Yakima)
512 Texas (Austin, San Antonio)
513 Ohio (Cincinnati, Dayton)
514 Quebec, Canada (Montreal)
515 Iowa (Ames, Des Moines)
516 New York (Hempstead, Long Island)
517 Michigan (Lansing, Midland, Saginaw)
518 New York (Albany, Schenectady)

519 Ontario, Canada (London)

601 Mississippi
602 Arizona
603 New Hampshire
604 British Columbia, Canada
605 South Dakota
606 Kentucky (Covington, Lexington)
607 New York (Binghampton, Elmira)
608 Wisconsin (La Crosse, Madison)
609 New Jersey (Atlantic City, Trenton)
612 Minnesota (Minneapolis–St. Paul, Minnetonka)
613 Ontario, Canada (Ottawa)
614 Ohio (Columbus, Steubenville)
615 Tennessee (Chattanooga, Knoxville, Nashville)
616 Michigan (Grand Rapids, Kalamazoo)
617 Massachusetts (Boston, Worcester)
618 Illinois (Centralia, East St. Louis)
619 California (San Diego)
701 North Dakota
702 Nevada
703 Virginia (Alexandria, Roanoke)
704 North Carolina (Asheville, Charlotte)
705 Ontario, Canada (North Bay)
707 California (Santa Rosa, Eureka)
709 Newfoundland, Canada
712 Iowa (Council Bluffs, Sioux City)
713 Texas (Houston)
714 California (Anaheim, Orange)
715 Wisconsin (Eau Claire, Wausau)
716 New York (Buffalo, Rochester)
717 Pennsylvania (Harrisburg, Scranton)

718 New York City (Brooklyn, Queens, Staten Island)
719 Colorado (Colorado Springs, Pueblo)

801 Utah
802 Vermont
803 South Carolina
804 Virginia (Richmond, Virginia Beach)
805 California (Bakersfield)
806 Texas (Amarillo)
807 Ontario, Canada (Ft. William, Thunder Bay)
808 Hawaii
809 Caribbean islands[1]
812 Indiana (Evansville, Terre Haute)
813 Florida (Fort Myers, Tampa)
814 Pennsylvania (Altoona, Erie)
815 Illinois (Joliet, Rockford)
816 Missouri (Kansas City, St. Joseph)
817 Texas (Arlington, Ft. Worth)
818 California (Burbank)
819 Quebec, Canada (Sherbrooke)

901 Tennessee (Jackson, Memphis)
902 Nova Scotia, Prince Edward Island, Canada
904 Florida (Jacksonville, Tallahassee)
906 Michigan (Escanaba, Upper Peninsula)
907 Alaska
912 Georgia (Macon, Savannah)
913 Kansas (Kansas City, Salina, Topeka)
914 New York (White Plains, Yonkers)
915 Texas (Abilene, El Paso)
916 California (Sacramento)
918 Oklahoma (Muskogee, Tulsa)
919 North Carolina (Raleigh, Winston-Salem)

Note: When no cities are listed, the area code is for the entire state or province. 1. Includes Anguilla, Antigua, the Bahamas, Barbados, Bequia, Bermuda, Cayman Islands, Dominica, Dominican Republic, Jamaica, Montserrat, Mustique, Nevis, Puerto Rico, St. Kitts, St. Lucia, St. Vincent, Trinidad and Tobago, Virgin Islands.

Essential Documents in U.S. History

The Declaration of Independence (July 4, 1776)

After a year of war with Britain, American patriots were driven to make the final break in 1776. On June 7, before the Continental Congress in Philadelphia, Richard Henry Lee of Virginia proposed a declaration that the colonies "are, and of right ought to be, free and independent States." A committee of five, headed by Thomas Jefferson, was appointed to draw up the formal Declaration of Independence on June 10. The committee brought its version, mainly the work of Jefferson, back to Congress on June 28. Congress voted unanimously to declare independence on July 2, and after making several changes in the Jefferson committee's draft, they unanimously adopted the Declaration of Independence on July 4. Copies of the declaration were dispatched to the states for approval. The original document is on display today at the National Archives in Washington, D.C.

The Declaration of Independence

July 4, 1776

In Congress, July 4, 1776,
THE UNANIMOUS DECLARATION OF THE THIRTEEN UNITED STATES OF AMERICA,

When in the Course of human events, it becomes necessary for one people to dissolve the political bands which have connected them with another, and to assume among the Powers of the earth, the separate and equal station to which the Laws of Nature and of Nature's God entitle them, a decent respect to the opinions of mankind requires that they should declare the causes which impel them to the separation.

We hold these truths to be self-evident, that all men are created equal, that they are endowed by their Creator with certain unalienable Rights, that among these are Life, Liberty and the pursuit of Happiness. That to secure these rights, Governments are instituted among Men, deriving their just powers from the consent of the governed. That whenever any Form of Government becomes destructive of these ends, it is the Right of the People to alter or to abolish it, and to institute new Government, laying its foundation on such principles and organizing its powers in such form, as to them shall seem most likely to effect their Safety and Happiness. Prudence, indeed, will dictate that governments long established should not be changed for light and transient causes; and accordingly all experience hath shown, that mankind are more disposed to suffer, while evils are sufferable, than to right themselves by abolishing the forms to which they are accustomed. But when a long train of abuses and usurpations, pursuing invariably the same Object evinces a design to reduce them under absolute Despotism, it is their right, it is their duty, to throw off such Government, and to provide new Guards for their future security. Such has been the patient sufferance of these Colonies; and such is now the necessity which constrains them to alter their former Systems of Government. The history of the present King of Great Britain is a history of repeated injuries and usurpations, all having in direct object the establishment of an absolute Tyranny over these States. To prove this, let Facts be submitted to a candid world.

He has refused his Assent to Laws, the most wholesome and necessary for the public good.

He has forbidden his Governors to pass Laws of immediate and pressing importance, unless suspended in their operation till his Assent should be obtained; and when so suspended, he has utterly neglected to attend to them.

He has refused to pass other Laws for the accommodation of large districts of people, unless those people would relinquish the right of Representation in the Legislature, a right inestimable to them and formidable to tyrants only.

He has called together legislative bodies at places unusual, uncomfortable, and distant from the depository of their Public Records, for the sole purpose of fatiguing them into compliance with his measures.

He has dissolved Representative Houses repeatedly, for opposing with manly firmness his invasions on the rights of the people.

He has refused for a long time, after such dissolutions, to cause others to be elected; whereby the Legislative Powers, incapable of Annihilation, have returned to the People at large for their exercise; the State remaining in the mean time exposed to all the dangers of invasion from without, and convulsions within.

He has endeavoured to prevent the population of these States; for that purpose obstructing the Laws of Naturalization of Foreigners; refusing to pass others to encourage their migration hither, and raising the conditions of new Appropriations of Lands.

He has obstructed the Administration of Justice, by refusing his Assent to Laws for establishing Judiciary Powers.

He has made Judges dependent on his Will alone, for the tenure of their offices, and the amount and payment of their salaries.

He has erected a multitude of New Offices, and sent hither swarms of Officers to harass our People, and eat out their substance.

He has kept among us, in times of peace, Standing Armies without the Consent of our legislature.

He has affected to render the Military independent of and superior to the Civil Power.

He has combined with others to subject us to a jurisdiction foreign to our constitution, and unacknowledged by our laws; giving his Assent to their acts of pretended legislation:

For quartering large bodies of armed troops among us:

For protecting them, by a mock Trial, from Punishment for any Murders which they should commit on the Inhabitants of these States:

For cutting off our Trade with all parts of the world:

For imposing taxes on us without our consent:

For depriving us in many cases, of the benefits of Trial by Jury:

For transporting us beyond Seas to be tried for pretended offences:

For abolishing the free System of English Laws in a neighbouring Province, establishing therein an Arbitrary government, and enlarging its Boundaries so as to render it at once an example and fit instrument for introducing the same absolute rule into these Colonies:

For taking away our Charters, abolishing our most valuable Laws, and altering fundamentally the forms of our Government:

For suspending our own legislature, and declaring themselves invested with Power to legislate for us in all cases whatsoever.

He has abdicated Government here, by declaring us out of his Protection and waging War against us.

He has plundered our seas, ravaged our Coasts, burnt our towns, and destroyed the lives of our people.

He is at this time transporting large armies of foreign mercenaries to compleat the works of death, desolation and tyranny, already begun with circumstances of Cruelty & perfidy scarcely paralleled in the most barbarous ages, and totally unworthy of the Head of a civilized nation.

He has constrained our fellow Citizens taken Captive on the high Seas to bear Arms against their Country, to become the executioners of their friends and Brethren, or to fall themselves by their Hands.

He has excited domestic insurrections amongst us, and has endeavoured to bring on the inhabitants of our frontiers, the merciless

Indian Savages, whose known rule of warfare, is an undistinguished destruction of all ages, sexes and conditions.

In every stage of these Oppressions We have Petitioned for Redress in the most humble terms: Our repeated Petitions have been answered only by repeated injury. A prince, whose character is thus marked by every act which may define a Tyrant, is unfit to be the ruler of a free People.

Signers of the Declaration of Independence

Name of Delegate	Colony	Born/Died
Adams, John	Massachusetts	1735–1826
Adams, Samuel	Massachusetts	1722–1803
Bartlett, Josiah	New Hampshire	1729–95
Braxton, Carter	Virginia	1736–97
Carroll, Charles	Maryland	1737–1832
Chase, Samuel	Maryland	1741–1811
Clark, Abraham	New Jersey	1726–94
Clymer, George	Pennsylvania	1739–1813
Ellery, William	Rhode Island	1727–1820
Floyd, William	New York	1734–1821
Franklin, Benjamin	Pennsylvania	1706–90
Gerry, Elbridge	Massachusetts	1744–1814
Gwinnett, Button	Georgia	1732–77
Hall, Lyman	Georgia	1724–90
Hancock, John	Massachusetts	1737–93
Harrison, Benjamin	Virginia	1726–91
Hart, John	New Jersey	?–1779
Hewes, Joseph	North Carolina	1730–79
Heyward, Thomas, Jr.	South Carolina	1746–1809
Hooper, William	North Carolina	1742–90
Hopkins, Stephen	Rhode Island	1707–85
Hopkinson, Francis	New Jersey	1737–91
Huntington, Samuel	Connecticut	1731–96
Jefferson, Thomas	Virginia	1743–1826
Lee, Francis Lightfoot	Virginia	1734–97
Lee, Richard Henry	Virginia	1732–94
Lewis, Francis	New York	1713–1803
Livingston, Philip	New York	1716–78
Lynch, Thomas, Jr.	South Carolina	1749–79
McKean, Thomas	Delaware	1734–1817
Middleton, Arthur	South Carolina	1742–87
Morris, Lewis	New York	1726–98
Morris, Robert	Pennsylvania	1734–1806
Morton, John	Pennsylvania	1724–77
Nelson, Thomas, Jr.	Virginia	1738–89
Paca, William	Maryland	1740–99
Paine, Robert Treat	Massachusetts	1731–1814
Penn, John	North Carolina	1741–88
Read, George	Delaware	1733–98
Rodney, Caesar	Delaware	1728–84
Ross, George	Pennsylvania	1730–79
Rush, Benjamin	Pennsylvania	1745–1813
Rutledge, Edward	South Carolina	1749–1800
Sherman, Roger	Connecticut	1721–93
Smith, James	Pennsylvania	1713–1806
Stockton, Richard	New Jersey	1730–81
Stone, Thomas	Maryland	1743–87
Taylor, George	Pennsylvania	1716–81
Thornton, Matthew	New Hampshire	1714–1803
Walton, George	Georgia	1741–1804
Whipple, William	New Hampshire	1730–85
Williams, William	Connecticut	1731–1811
Wilson, James	Pennsylvania	1742–98
Witherspoon, John	New Jersey	1723–94
Wolcott, Oliver	Connecticut	1726–97
Wythe, George	Virginia	1726–1806

Nor have We been wanting in attention to our British brethren. We have warned them from time to time of attempts by their legislature to extend an unwarrantable jurisdiction over us. We have reminded them of the circumstances of our emigration and settlement here. We have appealed to their native justice and magnanimity, and we have conjured them by the ties of our common kindred to disavow these usurpations, which would inevitably interrupt our connections and correspondence. They too have been deaf to the voice of justice and of consanguinity. We must, therefore, acquiesce in the necessity, which denounces our Separation and hold them, as we hold the rest of mankind, Enemies in War, in Peace Friends.

We, therefore, the Representatives of the United States of America, in General Congress, Assembled, appealing to the Supreme Judge of the world for the rectitude of our intentions, do, in the Name, and by Authority of the good People of these Colonies, solemnly publish and declare, That these United Colonies are, and of Right ought to be Free and Independent States; that they are Absolved from all Allegiance to the British Crown, and that all political connection between them and the State of Great Britain, is and ought to be totally dissolved; and that as Free and Independent States, they have full Power to levy War, conclude Peace, contract Alliances, establish Commerce, and to do all other Acts and Things which Independent States may of right do. And for the support of this Declaration, with a firm reliance on the Protection of Divine Providence, we mutually pledge to each other our Lives, our Fortunes and our sacred Honor.

JOHN HANCOCK

The Emancipation Proclamation

(Jan. 1, 1863)

On July 22, 1862, Lincoln read to his cabinet a preliminary draft of an emancipation proclamation. Secretary of State William Seward suggested that the proclamation not be issued until a military victory had been won. The battle of Antietam gave Lincoln his desired opportunity, and on Sept. 22, he read to his cabinet a second draft of the proclamation. After some changes this was issued as a preliminary proclamation; the formal and definite proclamation came Jan. 1, 1863.

THE PRESIDENT OF THE UNITED STATES OF AMERICA: *A Proclamation.*

Whereas on the 22nd day of September, A.D. 1862, a proclamation was issued by the President of the United States, containing among other things, the following, to wit:

"That on the 1st day of January, A.D. 1863, all persons held as slaves within any State or designated part of a State the people whereof shall then be in rebellion against the United States shall be then, thenceforward, and forever free; and the executive government of the United States, including the military and naval

authority thereof, will recognize and maintain the freedom of such persons, and will do no act or acts to repress such persons, or any of them, in any efforts they may make for their actual freedom.

"That the executive will on the 1st day of January aforesaid, by proclamation, designate the States and parts of States, if any, in which the people thereof, respectively, shall then be in rebellion against the United States; and the fact that any State or the people thereof shall on that day be in good faith represented in the Congress of the United States by members chosen thereto at elections wherein a majority of the qualified voters of such States shall have participated shall, in the absence of strong countervailing testimony, be deemed conclusive evidence that such State and the people thereof are not then in rebellion against the United States."

Now, therefore, I, Abraham Lincoln, President of the United States, by virtue of the power in me vested as Commander-in-Chief of the Army and Navy of the United States in time of actual armed rebellion against the authority and government of the United States, and as a fit and necessary war measure for suppressing said rebellion, do, on this 1st day of January, A.D. 1863, and in accordance with my purpose so to do, publicly proclaimed for the full period of one hundred days from the first day above mentioned, order and designate as the States and parts of States wherein the people thereof, respectively, are this day in rebellion against the United States the following, to wit:

Arkansas, Texas, Louisiana (except the parishes of St. Bernard, Plaquemines, Jefferson, St. John, St. Charles, St. James, Ascension, Assumption, Terrebonne, Lafourche, St. Mary, St. Martin, and Orleans, including the city of New Orleans), Mississippi, Alabama, Florida, Georgia, South Carolina, North Carolina, and Virginia (except the forty-eight counties designated as West Virginia, and also the counties of Berkeley, Accomac, Northhampton, Elizabeth City, York, Princess Anne, and Norfolk, including the cities of Norfolk and Portsmouth), and which excepted parts are for the present left precisely as if this proclamation were not issued.

And by virtue of the power and for the purpose aforesaid, I do order and declare that all persons held as slaves within said designated States and parts of States are, and henceforward shall be, free; and that the Executive Government of the United States, including the military and naval authorities thereof, will recognize and maintain the freedom of said persons.

And I hereby enjoin upon the people so declared to be free to abstain from all violence, unless in necessary self-defense; and I recommend to them that, in all cases when allowed, they labor faithfully for reasonable wages.

And I further declare and make known that such persons of suitable condition will be received into the armed service of the United States to garrison forts, positions, stations, and other places, and to man vessels of all sorts in said service.

And upon this act, sincerely believed to be an

act of justice, warranted by the Constitution upon military necessity, I invoke the considerate judgment of mankind and the gracious favor of Almighty God.

The Gettysburg Address

(Nov. 19, 1863)

Abraham Lincoln's most famous and most eloquent words were delivered at the dedication of the cemetery that held the remains of the 45,000 soldiers who fell at the Battle of Gettysburg, a significant Union victory. A powerful summation of Lincoln's war aims as well as a moving tribute to those who died for a just cause, the Gettysburg Address has become justly famous as a rhetorical masterpiece as well as a stirring example of Lincoln's statesmanship.

Four score and seven years ago our fathers brought forth on this continent, a new nation, conceived in Liberty, and dedicated to the proposition that all men are created equal.

Now we are engaged in a great civil war, testing whether that nation or any nation so conceived and so dedicated, can long endure. We are met on a great battlefield of that war. We have come to dedicate a portion of that field, as a final resting place for those who here gave their lives that that nation might live. It is altogether fitting and proper that we should do this.

But, in a larger sense, we can not dedicate—we can not consecrate—we can not hallow—this ground. The brave men, living and dead, who struggled here, have consecrated it, far above our poor power to add or detract. The world will little note, nor long remember what we say here, but it can never forget what they did here. It is for us the living, rather, to be dedicated here to the unfinished work which they who fought here have thus far so nobly advanced. It is rather for us to be here dedicated to the great task remaining before us—that from these honored dead we take increased devotion to that cause for which they gave the last full measure of devotion—that we here highly resolve that these dead shall not have died in vain—that this nation, under God, shall have a new birth of freedom—and that government of the people, by the people, for the people, shall not perish from the earth.

The Pledge of Allegiance

(1892)

The original version of the Pledge of Allegiance appeared in the Sept. 8, 1892, issue of *Youth's Companion* magazine. Authorship was in dispute between magazine staffers Francis Bellamy and James B. Upham until 1939, when the United States Flag Association declared Bellamy the author; the Library of Congress concurred in 1957. Congress mandated two wording changes in the original version by substituting "the flag of the United States of America" for "my flag" in 1923 and adding "under

God" in 1954. Public schools throughout the United States made the daily Pledge of Allegiance obligatory, and students who refused were punished, until the Supreme Court ruled in *West Virginia Board of Education* vs. *Barnette* (1943) that the First Amendment protected the "right of silence" as well as freedom of speech.

I pledge allegiance to the flag of the United States of America, and to the Republic for which it stands, one nation, under God, indivisible, with liberty and justice for all.

The U.S. Constitution (1787)

(Ratified March 4, 1789)

During and after the Revolution, the United States was governed by the Continental Congress under the Articles of Confederation, which delegated very limited powers to the national government and reserved the rest to the states. Economic chaos, political confusion, and widespread dissatisfaction with the lack of central authority peaked after Shays's Rebellion in 1786. George Washington lent his prestige to the call for a convention to consider a new form of government. Congress endorsed the plan on Feb. 21, 1787, "for the sole and express purpose of revising the Articles of Confederation." All states but Rhode Island sent delegates to the convention, which opened in Philadelphia on May 14. The delegates moved at once to discard the articles, draw up a new Constitution, and conduct their meetings in secrecy, while Washington presided and James Madison took notes. A long summer of debate and compromise finally produced the document that most of the delegates signed on Sept. 17. Congress ordered the Constitution sent to the states for ratification on Sept. 28, requiring approval by at least nine of them to validate the new charter. Whether the Constitution would be adopted was in doubt until June 21, 1788, when New Hampshire became the ninth state to ratify it. The Constitution went into effect on Mar. 4, 1789. All of the original 13 states eventually ratified the Constitution, ending with Rhode Island on May 29, 1790. The U.S. Constitution remains the world's oldest written constitution.

THE CONSTITUTION OF THE UNITED STATES OF AMERICA
Preamble

WE, THE PEOPLE OF THE UNITED STATES, in order to form a more perfect union, establish justice, insure domestic tranquillity, provide for the common defense, promote the general welfare, and secure the blessing of liberty to ourselves and our posterity, do ordain and establish this Constitution for the United States of America.

ARTICLE I

SECTION 1 All legislative powers herein granted shall be vested in a Congress of the United States, which shall consist of a Senate and House of Representatives.

SECTION 2 [1] The House of Representatives shall be composed of members chosen every second year by the people of the several States, and the electors in each State shall have the qualifications requisite for electors of the most numerous branch of the State legislature.

[2] No person shall be a Representative who shall not have attained to the age of twenty-five years, and been seven years a citizen of the United States, and who shall not, when elected, be an inhabitant of that State in which he shall be chosen.

[3] Representatives and direct taxes shall be apportioned among the several States which may be included within this Union, according to their respective numbers, which shall be determined by adding to the whole number of free persons, including those bound to service for a term of years, and excluding Indians not taxed, three-fifths of all other persons. The actual enumeration shall be made within three years after the first meeting of the Congress of the United States, and within every subsequent term of ten years, in such manner as they shall by law direct. The number of Representatives shall not exceed one for every thirty thousand, but each State shall have at least one Representative; and until such enumeration shall be made, the State of New Hampshire shall be entitled to choose three; Massachusetts, eight; Rhode Island and Providence Plantations, one; Connecticut, five; New York, six; New Jersey, four; Pennsylvania, eight; Delaware, one; Maryland, six; Virginia, ten; North Carolina, five; South Carolina, five; and Georgia, three.

[4] When vacancies happen in the representation from any State, the executive authority thereof shall issue writs of election to fill such vacancies.

[5] The House of Representatives shall choose their Speaker and other officers, and shall have the sole power of impeachment.

SECTION 3 [1] The Senate of the United States shall be composed of two Senators from each State, chosen by the legislature thereof for six years; and each Senator shall have one vote.

[2] Immediately after they shall be assembled in consequence of the first election, they shall be divided as equally as may be into three classes. The seats of the Senators of the first class shall be vacated at the expiration of the second year, of the second class at the expiration of the fourth year, and of the third class at the expiration of the sixth year, so that one-third may be chosen every second year; and if vacancies happen by resignation or otherwise during the recess of the legislature of any State, the executive thereof may make temporary appointments until the next meeting of the legislature, which shall then fill such vacancies.

[3] No person shall be a Senator who shall not have attained to the age of thirty years, and been nine years a citizen of the United States, and who shall not, when elected, be an inhabitant of that State for which he shall be chosen.

[4] The Vice-President of the United States shall be President of the Senate, but shall have no vote, unless they be equally divided.

[5] The Senate shall choose their other

officers and also a President *pro tempore* in the absence of the Vice-President, or when he shall exercise the office of President of the United States.

[6] The Senate shall have the sole power to try all impeachments. When sitting for that purpose, they shall be on oath or affirmation. When the President of the United States is tried, the Chief Justice shall preside; and no person shall be convicted without the concurrence of two-thirds of the members present.

[7] Judgment in cases of impeachment shall not extend further than to removal from office, and disqualification to hold and enjoy any office of honor, trust, or profit under the United States; but the party convicted shall, nevertheless, be liable and subject to indictment, trial, judgment, and punishment, according to law.

SECTION 4 [1] The times, places, and manner of holding elections for Senators and Representatives shall be prescribed in each State by the legislature thereof; but the Congress may at any time by law make or alter such regulations, except as to the places of choosing Senators.

[2] The Congress shall assemble at least once in every year, and such meeting shall be on the first Monday in December, unless they shall by law appoint a different day.

SECTION 5 [1] Each House shall be the judge of the elections, returns, and qualification of its own members, and a majority of each shall constitute a quorum to do business; but a smaller number may adjourn from day to day, and may be authorized to compel the attendance of absent members, in such manner, and under such penalties, as each House may provide.

[2] Each House may determine the rules of its proceedings, punish its members for disorderly behavior, and with the concurrence of two-thirds, expel a member.

[3] Each House shall keep a journal of its proceedings, and from time to time publish the same, excepting such parts as may in their judgment require secrecy, and the yeas and nays of the members of either House on any question shall, at the desire of one-fifth of those present, be entered on the journal.

[4] Neither House, during the session of Congress, shall, without the consent of the other, adjourn for more than three days, nor to any other place than that in which the two Houses shall be sitting.

SECTION 6 [1] The Senators and Representatives shall receive a compensation for their services, to be ascertained by law and paid out of the Treasury of the United States. They shall, in all cases except treason, felony, and breach of the peace, be privileged from arrest during their attendance at the session of their respective Houses, and in going to and returning from the same; and for any speech or debate in either House they shall not be questioned in any other place.

[2] No Senator or Representative shall, during the time for which he was elected, be appointed to any civil office under the authority of the United States, which shall have been created, or the emoluments whereof shall have

been increased during such time; and no person holding any office under the United States shall be a member of either House during his continuance in office.

SECTION 7 [1] All bills for raising revenue shall originate in the House of Representatives; but the Senate may propose or concur with amendments as on other bills.

[2] Every bill which shall have passed the House of Representatives and the Senate shall, before it becomes a law, be presented to the President of the United States; if he approves he shall sign it, but if not he shall return it, with his objections, to that House in which it shall have originated, who shall enter the objections at large on their journal and proceed to reconsider it. If after such reconsideration two-thirds of that House shall agree to pass the bill, it shall be sent, together with the objections, to the other House, by which it shall likewise be reconsidered, and if approved by two-thirds of that House it shall become a law. But in all such cases the vote of both Houses shall be determined by yeas and nays, and the names of the persons voting for and against the bill shall be entered on the journal of each House respectively. If any bill shall not be returned by the President within ten days (Sundays excepted) after it shall have been presented to him, the same shall be a law, in like manner as if he had signed it, unless the Congress by their adjournment prevent its return, in which case it shall not be a law.

[3] Every order, resolution or vote to which the concurrence of the Senate and House of Representatives may be necessary (except on a question of adjournment) shall be presented to the President of the United States; and before the same shall take effect shall be approved by him, or being disapproved by him, shall be repassed by two-thirds of the Senate and House of Representatives, according to the rules and limitations prescribed in the case of a bill.

SECTION 8 [1] The Congress shall have power to lay and collect taxes, duties, imposts and excises, to pay the debts and provide for the common defense and general welfare of the United States; but all duties, imposts and excises shall be uniform throughout the United States;

[2] To borrow money on the credit of the United States;

[3] To regulate commerce with foreign nations, and among the several States, and with the Indian tribes;

[4] To establish an uniform rule of naturalization, and uniform laws on the subject of bankruptcies throughout the United States;

[5] To coin money, regulate the value thereof, and of foreign coin, and fix the standard of weights and measures;

[6] To provide for the punishment of counterfeiting the securities and current coin of the United States;

[7] To establish post offices and post roads;

[8] To promote the progress of science and useful arts by securing for limited times to authors and inventors the exclusive right to their respective writings and discoveries;

[9] To constitute tribunals inferior to the

Supreme Court;

[10] To define and punish piracies and felonies committed on the high seas and offenses against the law of nations.

[11] To declare war, grant letters of marque and reprisal, and make rules concerning captures on land and water;

[12] To raise and support armies, but no appropriation of money to that use shall be for a longer term than two years;

[13] To provide and maintain a navy;

[14] To make rules for the government and regulation of the land and naval forces;

[15] To provide for calling forth the militia to execute the laws of the Union, suppress insurrections, and repel invasions;

[16] To provide for organizing, arming and disciplining the militia, and for governing such part of them as may be employed in the service of the United States, reserving to the States respectively the appointment of the officers, and the authority of training the militia according to the discipline prescribed by Congress;

[17] To exercise exclusive legislation in all cases whatsoever over such district (not exceeding ten miles square) as may, by cession of particular States and the acceptance of Congress, become the seat of the Government of the United States, and to exercise like authority over all places purchased by the consent of the legislature of the State in which the same shall be, for the erection of forts, magazines, arsenals, dockyards, and other needful buildings;

[18] To make all laws which shall be necessary and proper for carrying into execution the foregoing powers, and all other powers vested by this Constitution in the Government of the United States, or in any department or officer thereof.

SECTION 9 [1] The migration or importation of such persons as any of the States now existing shall think proper to admit shall not be prohibited by the Congress prior to the year one thousand eight hundred and eight, but a tax or duty may be imposed on such importation, not exceeding ten dollars for each person.

[2] The privilege of the writ of habeas corpus shall not be suspended, unless when in cases of rebellion or invasion the public safety may require it.

[3] No bill of attainder or ex post facto law shall be passed.

[4] No capitation or other direct tax shall be laid, unless in proportion to the census or enumeration hereinbefore directed to be taken.

[5] No tax or duty shall be laid on articles exported from any State.

[6] No preference shall be given by any regulation of commerce or revenue to the ports of one State over those of another; nor shall vessels bound to or from one State be obliged to enter, clear or pay duties in another.

[7] No money shall be drawn from the Treasury but in consequence of appropriations made by law; and a regular statement and account of the receipts and expenditures of all public money shall be published from time to time.

[8] No title of nobility shall be granted by the United States; and no person holding any office of profit or trust under them shall, without the

consent of the Congress, accept of any present, emolument, office, or title of any kind whatever from any king, prince, or foreign state.

SECTION 10 [1] No State shall enter into any treaty, alliance, or confederation; grant letters of marque and reprisal; coin money, emit bills of credit, make anything but gold and silver coin a tender in payment of debts; pass any bill of attainder, ex post facto law or law impairing the obligation of contracts, or grant any title of nobility.

[2] No State shall, without the consent of the Congress, lay any imports or duties on imports or exports, except what may be absolutely necessary for executing its inspection laws; and the net produce of all duties and imposts, laid by any State on imports or exports, shall be for the use of the Treasury of the United States; and all such laws shall be subject to the revision and control of the Congress.

[3] No State shall, without the consent of Congress, lay any duty of tonnage, keep troops and ships of war in time of peace, enter into any agreement or compact with another State or with a foreign power, or engage in war, unless actually invaded or in such imminent danger as will not admit of delay.

ARTICLE II

SECTION 1 [1] The executive power shall be vested in a President of the United States of America. He shall hold his office during the term of four years, and together with the Vice-President, chosen for the same term, be elected as follows:

[2] Each State shall appoint, in such manner as the legislature thereof may direct, a number of Electors, equal to the whole number of Senators and Representatives to which the State may be entitled in the Congress; but no Senator or Representative, or person holding an office of trust or profit under the United States shall be appointed an Elector.

[3] The Electors shall meet in their respective States and vote by ballot for two persons, of whom one at least shall not be an inhabitant of the same State with themselves. And they shall make a list of all the persons voted for, and of the number of votes for each; which list they shall sign and certify, and transmit sealed to the seat of government of the United States, directed to the President of the Senate. The President of the Senate shall, in the presence of the Senate and House of Representatives, open all the certificates, and the votes shall then be counted. The person having the greatest number of votes shall be the President, if such number be a majority of the whole number of Electors appointed; and if there be more than one who have such majority, and have an equal number of votes, then the House of Representatives shall immediately choose by ballot one of them for President; and if no person have a majority, then from the five highest on the list the said House shall in like manner choose the President. But in choosing the President the votes shall be taken by States, the representation from each State having one vote; a quorum for this purpose shall consist of a member or members from two-thirds of the States, and a majority of all the States shall be necessary to

a choice. In every case, after the choice of the President, the person having the greatest number of votes of the Electors shall be the Vice-President. But if there should remain two or more who have equal votes, the Senate shall choose from them by ballot the Vice-President.

[4] The Congress may determine the time of choosing the Electors and the day on which they shall give their votes, which day shall be the same throughout the United States.

[5] No person except a natural-born citizen, or citizen of the United States at the time of the adoption of this Constitution, shall be eligible to the office of President; neither shall any person be eligible to that office who shall not have attained to the age of thirty-five years, and been fourteen years a resident within the United States.

[6] In case of the removal of the President from office, or of his death, resignation, or inability to discharge the powers and duties of the said office, the same shall devolve on the Vice-President, and the Congress may by law provide for the case of removal, death, resignation, or inability, both of the President and Vice-President, declaring what officer shall then act as President, and such officer shall act accordingly until the disability be removed or a President shall be elected.

[7] The President shall, at stated times, receive for his services a compensation, which shall neither be increased nor diminished during the period for which he shall have been elected, and he shall not receive within that period any other emolument from the United States or any of them.

[8] Before he enter on the execution of his office he shall take the following oath or affirmation:

"I do solemnly swear (or affirm) that I will faithfully execute the office of President of the United States, and will to the best of my ability preserve, protect, and defend the Constitution of the United States."

SECTION 2 [1] The President shall be Commander-in-Chief of the Army and Navy of the United States, and of the militia of the several States when called into the actual service of the United States; he may require the opinion, in writing, of the principal officer in each of the executive departments, upon any subject relating to the duties of their respective offices, and he shall have power to grant reprieves and pardons for offenses against the United States, except in cases of impeachment.

[2] He shall have power, by and with the advice and consent of the Senate, to make treaties, provided two-thirds of the Senators present concur; and he shall nominate, and, by and with the advice and consent of the Senate, shall appoint ambassadors, other public ministers and consuls, judges of the Supreme Court, and all other officers of the United States whose appointments are not herein otherwise provided for, and which shall be established by law; but the Congress may by law vest the appointment of such inferior officers, as they think proper, in the President alone, in the courts of law, or in the heads of departments.

[3] The President shall have power to fill up

all vacancies that may happen during the recess of the Senate, by granting commissions which shall expire at the end of their next session.

SECTION 3 He shall from time to time give to the Congress information of the state of the Union, and recommend to their consideration such measures as he shall judge necessary and expedient; he may, on extraordinary occasions, convene both Houses, or either of them, and in case of disagreement between them with respect to the time of adjournment, he may adjourn them to such time as he shall think proper; he shall receive ambassadors and other public ministers; he shall take care that the laws be faithfully executed, and shall commission all the officers of the United States.

SECTION 4 The President, Vice-President and all civil officers of the United States shall be removed from office on impeachment for and conviction of treason, bribery, or other high crimes and misdemeanors.

ARTICLE III

SECTION 1 The judicial power of the United States shall be vested in one Supreme Court, and in such inferior courts as the Congress may from time to time ordain and establish. The judges, both of the Supreme and inferior courts, shall hold their offices during good behavior, and shall, at stated times, receive for their services a compensation which shall not be diminished during their continuance in office.

SECTION 2 [1] The judicial power shall extend to all cases, in law and equity, arising under this Constitution, the laws of the United States, and treaties made, or which shall be made, under their authority; to all cases affecting ambassadors, other public ministers, and consuls; to all cases of admiralty and maritime jurisdiction; to controversies to which the United States shall be a party; to controversies between two or more States; between a State and citizens of another State; between citizens of different States; between citizens of the same State claiming lands under grants of different States, and between a State, or the citizens thereof, and foreign states, citizens, or subjects.

[2] In all cases affecting ambassadors, other public ministers and consuls, and those in which a State shall be party, the Supreme Court shall have original jurisdiction. In all the other cases before mentioned the Supreme Court shall have appellate jurisdiction, both as to law and fact, with such exceptions and under such regulations as the Congress shall make.

[3] The trial of all crimes, except in cases of impeachment, shall be by jury; and such trial shall be held in the State where the said crimes shall have been committed; but when not committed within any State, the trial shall be at such place or places as the Congress may by law have directed.

SECTION 3 [1] Treason against the United States shall consist only in levying war against them, or in adhering to their enemies, giving them aid and comfort. No person shall be convicted of treason unless on the testimony of two witnesses to the same overt act, or on confession in open court.

[2] The Congress shall have power to declare the punishment of treason, but no attainder of treason shall work corruption of blood or forfeiture except during the life of the person attained.

ARTICLE IV

SECTION 1 Full faith and credit shall be given in each State to the public acts, records, and judicial proceedings of every other State. And the Congress may by general laws prescribe the manner in which such acts, records, and proceedings shall be proved, and the effect thereof.

SECTION 2 [1] The citizens of each State shall be entitled to all privileges and immunities of citizens in the several States.

[2] A person charged in any State with treason, felony, or other crime, who shall flee from justice, and be found in another State, shall, on demand of the executive authority of the State from which he fled, be delivered up, to be removed to the State having jurisdiction of the crime.

[3] No person held to service or labor in one State, under the laws thereof, escaping into another, shall, in consequence of any law or regulation therein, be discharged from such service or labor, but shall be delivered up on claim to the party to whom such service or labor may be due.

SECTION 3 [1] New States may be admitted by the Congress into this Union; but no new State shall be formed or erected within the jurisdiction of any other State; nor any State be formed by the junction of two or more States or parts of States, without the consent of the legislatures of the States concerned as well as of the Congress.

[2] The Congress shall have power to dispose of and make all needful rules and regulations respecting the territory or other property belonging to the United States; and nothing in this Constitution shall be so construed as to prejudice any claims of the United States or of any particular State.

SECTION 4 The United States shall guarantee to every State in this Union a republican form of government, and shall protect each of them against invasion, and on application of the legislature, or of the executive (when the legislature cannot be convened), against domestic violence.

ARTICLE V

The Congress, whenever two-thirds of both Houses shall deem it necessary, shall propose amendments to this Constitution, or, on the application of the legislatures of two-thirds of the several States, shall call a convention for proposing amendments, which in either case shall be valid to all intents and purposes as part of this Constitution, when ratified by the legislatures of three-fourths of the several States, or by conventions in three-fourths thereof, as the one or the other mode of ratification may be proposed by the Congress; provided that no amendment which may be made prior to the year one thousand eight hundred and eight shall in any manner affect the first and fourth clauses in the Ninth Section of the First Article; and that no State, without its consent shall be deprived of its equal suffrage in the State.

ARTICLE VI

[1] All debts contracted and engagements entered into, before the adoption of this Constitution, shall be as valid against the United States under this Constitution as under the Confederation.

[2] This Constitution, and the laws of the United States which shall be made in pursuance thereof, and all treaties made, or which shall be made, under the authority of the United States, shall be the supreme law of the land; and the judges in every State shall be bound thereby, anything in the Constitution or laws of any State to the contrary notwithstanding.

[3] The Senators and Representatives before mentioned and the members of the several State legislatures, and all executive and judicial officers both of the United States and of the several States, shall be bound by oath or affirmation to support this Constitution; but no religious test shall ever be required as a qualification to any office or public trust under the United States.

ARTICLE VII

The ratification of the conventions of nine States shall be sufficient for the establishment of this Constitution between the States so ratifying the same.

Amendments to the Constitution

The first 10 amendments, known collectively as The Bill of Rights, were all adopted in 1791.

AMENDMENT I

Congress shall make no law respecting an establishment or religion, or prohibiting the free exercise thereof; or abridging the freedom of speech or of the press; or the right of the people peaceably to assemble, and to petition the government for a redress of grievances.

AMENDMENT II

A well-regulated militia being necessary to the security of a free State, the right of the people to keep and bear arms shall not be infringed.

AMENDMENT III

No soldier shall, in time of peace, be quartered in any house without the consent of the owner, nor in time of war, but in a manner to be prescribed by law.

AMENDMENT IV

The right of the people to be secure in their persons, houses, papers, and effects, against unreasonable searches and seizures, shall not be violated, and no warrants shall issue but upon probable cause, supported by oath or affirmation, and particularly describing the place to be searched, and the persons or things to be seized.

AMENDMENT V

No person shall be held to answer for a capital, or otherwise infamous crime, unless on a presentment or indictment of a grand jury, except in cases arising in the land or naval forces, or in the militia, when in actual service in time of war or public danger; nor shall any person be subject for the same offense to be twice put in jeopardy of life or limb; nor shall be compelled in any criminal case to be a witness against himself, nor be deprived of life, liberty or property, without due process of law; nor shall private property be taken for public use without just compensation.

AMENDMENT VI

In all criminal prosecutions, the accused shall enjoy the right to a speedy and public trial, by an impartial jury of the State and district wherein the crime shall have been committed, which district shall have been previously ascertained by law, and to be informed of the nature and cause of the accusation; to be confronted with the witnesses against him; to have compulsory process for obtaining witnesses in his favor, and to have the assistance of counsel for his defense.

AMENDMENT VII

In suits at common law, where the value in controversy shall exceed twenty dollars, the right of trial by jury shall be preserved, and no fact tried by a jury shall be otherwise re-examined in any court of the United States, than according to the rules of the common law.

AMENDMENT VIII

Excessive bail shall not be required, nor excessive fines imposed, nor cruel and unusual punishments inflicted.

AMENDMENT IX

The enumeration in the Constitution of certain rights shall not be construed to deny or disparage others retained by the people.

AMENDMENT X

The powers not delegated to the United States by the Constitution, nor prohibited by it to the States, are reserved to the States respectively, or to the people.

AMENDMENT XI
[Adopted January 8, 1798]

The judicial power of the United States shall not be construed to extend to any suit in law or equity, commenced or prosecuted against one of the United States by citizens of another State, or by citizens or subjects of any foreign state.

AMENDMENT XII
[Adopted September 25, 1804]

[1] The Electors shall meet in their respective States and vote by ballot for President and Vice-President, one of whom, at least, shall not be an inhabitant of the same State with themselves; they shall name in their ballots the person voted for as President, and in distinct ballots the person voted for as Vice-President, and they shall make distinct lists of all persons voted for as President and of all persons voted for as Vice-President, and of the number of votes for each; which lists they shall sign and

certify, and transmit sealed to the seat of the government of the United States, directed to the President of the Senate. The President of the Senate shall, in the presence of the Senate and House of Representatives, open all the certificates and the votes shall then be counted. The person having the greatest number of votes for President shall be the President, if such number be a majority of the whole number of Electors appointed; and if no person have such majority, then from the persons having the highest numbers not exceeding three on the list of those voted for as President, the House of Representatives shall choose immediately, by ballot, the President. But in choosing the President the votes shall be taken by States, the representation from each State having one vote; a quorum for this purpose shall consist of a member or members from two-thirds of the States, and a majority of all the States shall be necessary to a choice. And if the House of Representatives shall not choose a President whenever the right of choice shall devolve upon them, before the fourth day of March next following, then the Vice-President shall act as President, as in the case of the death or other constitutional disability of the President.

[2] The person having the greatest number of votes as Vice-President shall be the Vice-President, if such number be a majority of the whole number of Electors appointed; and if no person have a majority, then from the two highest numbers on the list the Senate shall choose the Vice-President; a quorum for the purpose shall consist of two-thirds of the whole number of Senators, and a majority of the whole number shall be necessary to a choice. But no person constitutionally ineligible to the office of President shall be eligible to that of Vice-President of the United States.

AMENDMENT XIII
[Adopted Dec. 18, 1865]

SECTION 1 Neither slavery nor involuntary servitude, except as a punishment for crime whereof the party shall have been duly convicted, shall exist within the United States, or any place subject to their jurisdiction.

SECTION 2 Congress shall have power to enforce this article by appropriate legislation.

AMENDMENT XIV
[Adopted July 28, 1868]

SECTION 1 All persons born or naturalized in the United States, and subject to the jurisdiction thereof, are citizens of the United States and of the State wherein they reside. No State shall make or enforce any law which shall abridge the privileges or immunities of citizens of the United States; nor shall any State deprive any person of life, liberty or property, without due process of law; nor deny to any person within its jurisdiction the equal protection of the laws.

SECTION 2 Representatives shall be apportioned among the several States according to their respective numbers, counting the whole number of persons in each State, excluding Indians not taxed. But when the right to vote at any election for the choice of Electors for President and Vice-President of the United States,

Representatives in Congress, the executive and judicial officers of a State, or the members of the legislature thereof, is denied to any of the male inhabitants of such State, being twenty-one years of age, and citizens of the United States, or in any way abridged except for participation in rebellion or other crime, the basis of representation therein shall be reduced in the proportion which the number of such male citizens shall bear to the whole number of male citizens twenty-one years of age in such State.

SECTION 3 No person shall be a Senator or Representative in Congress, or elector of President and Vice-President, or hold any office, civil or military, under the United States or under any State, who, having previously taken an oath as a member of Congress, or as an officer of the United States, or as a member of any State legislature, or as an executive or judicial officer of any State, to support the Constitution of the United States, shall have engaged in insurrection or rebellion against the same, or given aid or comfort to the enemies thereof. But Congress may, by a vote of two-thirds of each House, remove such disability.

SECTION 4 The validity of the public debt of the United States, authorized by law, including debts incurred for payment of pensions and bounties for services in suppressing insurrection or rebellion, shall not be questioned. But neither the United States nor any State shall assume or pay any debt or obligation incurred in aid of insurrection or rebellion against the United States, or any claim for the loss or emancipation of any slave; but all such debts, obligations, and claims shall be held illegal and void.

SECTION 5 The Congress shall have power to enforce, by appropriate legislation, the provisions of this article.

AMENDMENT XV
[Adopted March 30, 1870]

SECTION 1 The right of citizens of the United States to vote shall not be denied or abridged by the United States or by any State on account of race, color, or previous condition of servitude.

SECTION 2 The Congress shall have power to enforce this article by appropriate legislation.

AMENDMENT XVI
[Adopted February 25, 1913]

The Congress shall have power to lay and collect taxes on incomes, from whatever source derived, without apportionment among the several States, and without regard to any census or enumeration.

AMENDMENT XVII
[Adopted May 31, 1913]

SECTION 1 The Senate of the United States shall be composed of two Senators from each State, elected by the people thereof, for six years; and each Senator shall have one vote. The electors in each State shall have the qualifications requisite for electors of the most numerous branch of the State legislatures.

SECTION 2 When vacancies happen in the representation of any State in the Senate, the executive authority of such State shall issue

writs of election to fill such vacancies: Provided, that the legislature of any State may empower the executive thereof to make temporary appointments until the people fill the vacancies by election as the legislature may direct.

SECTION 3 This amendment shall not be so construed as to affect the election or term of any Senator chosen before it becomes valid as part of the Constitution.

AMENDMENT XVIII
[Adopted January 29, 1919]

SECTION 1 After one year from the ratification of this article the manufacture, sale or transportation of intoxicating liquors within, the importation thereof into, or the exportation thereof from the United States and all territory subject to the jurisdiction thereof, for beverage purposes, is hereby prohibited.

SECTION 2 The Congress and the several States shall have concurrent power to enforce this article by appropriate legislation.

SECTION 3 This article shall be inoperative unless it shall have been ratified as an amendment to the Constitution by the legislatures of the several States, as provided in the Constitution, within seven years from the date of the submission hereof to the States by the Congress.

AMENDMENT XIX
[Adopted August 26, 1920]

SECTION 1 The right of citizens of the United States to vote shall not be denied or abridged by the United States or by any State on account of sex.

SECTION 2 Congress shall have power to enforce this article by appropriate legislation.

AMENDMENT XX
[Adopted February 6, 1933]

SECTION 1 The terms of the President and Vice-President shall end at noon on the 20th day of January, and the terms of Senators and Representatives at noon on the 3d day of January, of the years in which such terms would have ended if this article had not been ratified; and the terms of their successors shall then begin.

SECTION 2 The Congress shall assemble at least once in every year, and such meeting shall begin at noon on the 3d day of January, unless they shall by law appoint a different day.

SECTION 3 If, at the time fixed for the beginning of the term of the President, the President-elect shall have died, the Vice-President-elect shall become President. If a President shall not have been chosen before the time fixed for the beginning of his term or if the President-elect shall have failed to qualify, then the Vice-President-elect shall act as President until a President shall have qualified; and the Congress may by law provide for the case wherein neither a President-elect nor a Vice-President-elect shall have qualified, declaring who shall then act as President, or the manner in which one who is to act shall be selected, and such person shall act accordingly until a President or Vice-President shall have qualified.

SECTION 4 The Congress may by law provide for the case of the death of any of the persons from whom the House of Representatives may choose a President whenever the right of choice shall have devolved upon them, and for the case of death of any of the persons from whom the Senate may choose a Vice-President whenever the right of choice shall have devolved upon them.

SECTION 5 Sections 1 and 2 shall take effect on the 15th day of October following the ratification of this article.

SECTION 6 This article shall be inoperative unless it shall have been ratified as an amendment to the Constitution by the legislatures of three-fourths of the several States within seven years from the date of its submission.

AMENDMENT XXI
[Adopted December 5, 1933]

SECTION 1 The eighteenth article of amendment to the Constitution of the United States is hereby repealed.

SECTION 2 The transportation or importation into any State, territory, or possession of the United States for delivery or use therein of intoxicating liquors, in violation of the laws thereof, is hereby prohibited.

SECTION 3 This article shall be inoperative unless it shall have been ratified as an amendment to the Constitution by conventions in the several States, as provided in the Constitution, within seven years from the date of the submission hereof to the States by the Congress.

AMENDMENT XXII
[Adopted February 26, 1951]

SECTION 1 No person shall be elected to the office of President more than twice, and no person who has held the office of President, or acted as President, for more than two years of a term to which some other person was elected President shall be elected to the office of President more than once. But this Article shall not apply to any person holding the office of President when this Article was proposed by the Congress, and shall not prevent any person who may be holding the office of President, or acting as President, during the term within which this Article becomes operative from holding the office of President or acting as President during the remainder of such term.

SECTION 2 This article shall be inoperative unless it shall have been ratified as an amendment to the Constitution by the legislatures of three-fourths of the several States within seven years from the date of its submission to the States by the Congress.

AMENDMENT XXIII
[Adopted Apr. 3, 1961]

SECTION 1 The District constituting the seat of Government of the United States shall appoint in such manner as the Congress may direct:

A number of electors of President and Vice-President equal to the whole number of Senators and Representatives in Congress to which the District would be entitled if it were a State, but in no event more than the least popu-lous State; they shall be in addition to those appointed by the States, but they shall be considered, for the purposes of the election of President and Vice-President, to be electors appointed by a State; and they shall meet in the District and perform such duties as provided by the twelfth article of amendment.

SECTION 2 The Congress shall have power to enforce this article by appropriate legislation.

AMENDMENT XXIV
[Adopted January 23, 1964]

SECTION 1 The right of citizens of the United States to vote in any primary or other election for President or Vice-President, for electors for President or Vice-President, or for Senator or Representative in Congress, shall not be denied or abridged by the United States or any State by reason of failure to pay any poll tax or other tax.

SECTION 2 The Congress shall have power to enforce this article by appropriate legislation.

AMENDMENT XXV
[Adopted February 10, 1967]

SECTION 1 In case of the removal of the President from office or of his death or resignation, the Vice-President shall become President.

SECTION 2 Whenever there is a vacancy in the office of the Vice-President, the President shall nominate a Vice-President who shall take office upon confirmation by a majority vote of both Houses of Congress.

SECTION 3 Whenever the President transmits to the President pro tempore of the Senate and the Speaker of the House of Representatives his written declaration that he is unable to discharge the powers and duties of his office, and until he transmits to them a written declaration to the contrary, such powers and duties shall be discharged by the Vice-President as Acting President.

SECTION 4 Whenever the Vice-President and a majority of either the principal officers of the executive departments or of such other body as Congress may by law provide, transmit to the President pro tempore of the Senate and the Speaker of the House of Representatives their written declaration that the President is unable to discharge the powers and duties of his office, the Vice-President shall immediately assume the powers and duties of the office as Acting President.

Thereafter, when the President transmits to the President pro tempore of the Senate and the Speaker of the House of Representatives his written declaration that no inability exists, he shall resume the powers and duties of his office unless the Vice-President and a majority of either the principal officers of the executive department or of such other body as Congress may by law provide, transmit within four days to the President pro tempore of the Senate and the Speaker of the House of Representatives their written declaration that the President is unable to discharge the powers and duties of his office. Thereupon Congress shall decide the issue, assembling within forty-eight hours for that purpose if not in session. If the Congress, within twenty-one days after receipt of the latter written declaration, or, if Congress is not in session, within twenty-one days after Congress is required to assemble, determines by two-thirds vote of both Houses that the President is unable to discharge the powers and duties of his office, the Vice-President shall continue to discharge the same as Acting President; otherwise the President shall resume the powers and duties of his office.

AMENDMENT XXVI
[Adopted June 30, 1971]

SECTION 1 The right of citizens of the United States, who are eighteen years of age or older, to vote shall not be denied or abridged by the United States or by any State on account of age.

SECTION 2 The Congress shall have power to enforce this article by appropriate legislation.

Popular American Songs and Hymns

The Star Spangled Banner

Words: Francis Scott Key (1814)
Melody: John Stafford Smith (1775)

Inspired by his experience as a prisoner aboard a British ship during the bombardment of Fort McHenry in 1814, Francis Scott Key penned the poem that he then adapted to the tune of the "Anacreontic Song," written by the English composer John Stafford Smith. It was officially adopted as the national anthem in 1931.

> Oh say! can you see,
> by the dawn's early light,
> What so proudly we hailed
> at the twilight's last gleaming?
> Whose broad stripes and bright stars
> thro' the perilous fight,
> O'er the ramparts we watch'd,
> were so gallantly streaming?
> And the rockets' red glare,
> the bombs bursting in air,
> Gave proof thro' the night
> that our flag was still there.
> Oh, say, does that
> Star spangled Banner yet wave
> O'er the land of the free
> and the home of the brave!
>
> On the shore, dimly seen
> thro' the mists of the deep,
> Where the foe's haughty host
> in dread silence reposes,
> What is that which the breeze,
> o'er the towering steep,
> As it fitfully blows,

half conceals half discloses?
Now it catches the gleam
of the morning's first beam
In full glory reflected
now shines on the stream;
'Tis the Star Spangled Banner,
Oh, long may it wave
O'er the land of the free
and the home of the brave!

Oh, thus be it ever
when free men shall stand
Between their lov'd homes
and the war's desolation!
Blest with vict'ry and peace,
may the heav'n rescued land
Praise the Pow'r that hath made
and preserved us a nation!
Then conquer we must,
    when our cause it is just,
And this be our motto:
"In God is our trust!"
And the Star Spangled Banner
in triumph shall wave
O'er the land of the free
and the home of the brave!

Dixie

Melody and Words:
Daniel Decatur Emmett
Date of Composition: Unknown

Although written by a Northerner and popular among Union troops, "Dixie" was the great inspirational song of the Confederacy and was played at the inauguration of Jefferson Davis and before Pickett's charge at Gettysburg.

I wish I was in the land of cotton,
Old times there are not forgotten,
Look away, look away, look away
    Dixie land.

Then I wish I was in Dixie,
Hooray! Hooray!
In Dixie land I'll take my stand
To live and die in Dixie,
Away, away, away down South in Dixie.
Away, away, away down South in Dixie.

In Dixie land where I was born in
Early on a frosty mornin',
Look away, look away, look away,
    Dixie Land.

Then I wish I was in Dixie,
Hooray! Hooray!
In Dixie land I'll take my stand
To live and die in Dixie,
Away, away, away down South in Dixie.
Away, away, away down South in Dixie.

There's buckwheat cake and Indian batter,
Makes you fat or a little fatter,
Look away, look away, look away,
    Dixie Land.

Then I wish I was in Dixie,
Hooray! Hooray!
In Dixie land I'll take my stand
To live and die in Dixie,
Away, away, away down South in Dixie.
Away, away, away down South in Dixie.

Then hoe it down and scratch your gravel,
To Dixie's land I'm bound to travel,
Look away, look away, look away,
    Dixie land.

Then I wish I was in Dixie,
Hooray! Hooray!
In Dixie land I'll take my stand
To live and die in Dixie,
Away, away, away down South in Dixie.
Away, away, away down South in Dixie.

Battle Hymn of the Republic

Words: Julia Ward Howe (1861)
Melody: A popular Sunday-school hymn on which "John Brown's Body" was based.

This most famous of Civil War songs first appeared in the *Atlantic Monthly*. Mrs. Howe, a well-known author and suffragist, had heard the melody sung by the Union soldiers during her visit to Washington in 1861.

Mine eyes have seen the glory of the
    coming of the Lord;
He is trampling out the vintage
    where the grapes of wrath are stored;
He hath loosed the fateful lightning
    of His terrible swift sword.
His truth is marching on.

Glory! glory hallelujah!
Glory! glory hallelujah!
Glory! glory hallelujah!
His truth is marching on.

I have seen Him in the watch-fires
    of a hundred circling camps;
They have builded Him an altar in
    the evening dews and damps;
I can read His righteous sentence
    by the dim and flaring lamps.
His day is marching on.
Glory! glory hallelujah!
Glory! glory hallelujah!
Glory! glory hallelujah!
His truth is marching on.

He has sounded forth the trumpet
    that shall never call retreat;
He is sifting out the hearts of men
    before His judgment seat;
Oh, be swift, my soul, to answer Him!
    be jubilant, my feet!
Our God is marching on.
Glory! glory hallelujah!
Glory! glory hallelujah!
Glory! glory hallelujah!
His truth is marching on.

In the beauty of the lilies Christ
    was born across the sea;
With a glory in His bosom that
    transfigures you and me;
As He died to make men holy, let us
    die to make men free,
While God is marching on.
Glory! glory hallelujah!
Glory! glory hallelujah!
Glory! glory hallelujah!
His truth is marching on.

America, the Beautiful

Words: Katherine Lee Bates (1893)
Melody: Samuel A. Word (to the tune of "Materna") (1892)

Katherine Bates, a professor of English at Wellesley College, wrote this shortly after taking in the view from the summit of Pike's Peak in 1893.

O beautiful for spacious skies,
For amber waves of grain,
For purple mountain majesties
Above the fruited plain.
America! America!
God shed His grace on thee,
And crown thy good with brotherhood
From sea to shining sea.

O beautiful for pilgrim feet
Whose stern impassion'd stress
A thorough-fare for freedom beat
Across the wilderness.
America! America!
God mend thine ev'ry flaw,
Confirm thy soul in self control,
Thy liberty in law.

O beautiful for heroes prov'd
In liberating strife,
Who more than self their country lov'd
And mercy more than life.
America! America!
May God thy gold refine
Till all success be nobleness,
And ev'ry gain divine.

O beautiful for patriot dream
That sees beyond the years,
Thine alabaster cities gleam,
Undimmed by human tears.
America! America!
God shed His grace on thee,
And crown thy good with brotherhood
From sea to shining sea.

Rock of Ages

Words: Augustus M. Toplady (1774)
Melody: Thomas Hastings (1832)

A passionate expression of evangelical faith, "Rock of Ages" remains one of the most popular hymns in English.

Rock of Ages, cleft for me,
Let me hide myself in Thee;
Let the water and the blood,
From thy wounded side that flow'd,
Be of sin, the perfect cure;
Save me, Lord, and make me pure.

Could my zeal no respite know,
Could my tears forever flow,
All for sin could not atone,
Thou must save, and Thou alone;
Nothing in my hand I bring,
Simply to Thy cross I cling.

While I draw this fleeting breath,
When my eyelids close in death,
When I soar to worlds unknown,
And behold Thee on Thy throne,
Rock of ages, cleft for me,
Let me hide myself in Thee.

America
(My Country 'Tis of Thee)

Words: Samuel Francis Smith (1831)
Melody: Uncertain origin (based on the British National Anthem)

Samuel Smith, a Boston minister, wrote the words for a service at the Park Street Church, later setting them to a melody he found in a German songbook, unaware that it was "God Save the Queen."

My country, 'tis of thee,
Sweet land of liberty, Of thee I sing.
Land where my fathers died!
Land of the Pilgrims' pride!
From ev'ry mountainside,
Let freedom ring!

My native country, thee,
Land of the noble free,
Thy name I love.
I love thy rocks and rills,
Thy woods and templed hills;
My heart with rapture thrills
Like that above.

Let music swell the breeze,
And ring from all the trees
Sweet freedom's song.
Let mortal tongues awake;
Let all that breathe partake;
Let rocks their silence break,
The sound prolong.

Our fathers' God, to Thee,
Author of liberty,
To Thee we sing.
Long may our land be bright
With freedom's holy light;
Protect us by Thy might,
Great God, our King!

Swing Low, Sweet Chariot

Words and Melody: Negro folk origins
Date of composition: Unknown

Structured on a five-tone scale often used in songs of the American Indians, the so-called Negro spiritual, a moving cry for spiritual and physical salvation, gained wide attention when the Fisk Jubilee Singers toured London in 1875.

Swing low, sweet chariot,
Comin' for to carry me home,
O swing low sweet chariot,
Comin' for to carry me home.

I looked over Jordan and what did I see
Comin' for to carry me home,
A band of angels comin' after me,
Comin' for to carry me home.

Swing low, sweet chariot,
Comin' for to carry me home,
O swing low sweet chariot,
Comin' for to carry me home.

If you get a there before I do
Comin for to carry me home,
Tell all of my friends I'm comin' too,
Comin' for to carry me home.

Yankee Doodle

The date of composition and name of the author are unknown (the earliest reference was in the libretto of *The Disappointment*, an American comic opera published in 1767). Historians believe that "Yankee Doodle" originated as an instrumental tune, arriving in this country from England, Scotland, and Ireland, with various texts added to it over time.

Yankee Doodle went to town
Riding on a pony,
Stuck a feather in his crown,
And called it macaroni.
Yankee Doodle, keep it up,
Yankee Doodle dandy;
Mind the music and the step,
And with the girls be handy.

Yankee Doodle went to town,
To buy a pair of trousers,
He swore he could not see the town
Because of all the houses.
Yankee Doodle, keep it up,
Yankee Doodle dandy;
Mind the music and the step,
And with the girls be handy.

Fath'r and I went down to camp,
Along with Captain Goodwin,
And there we saw the men and boys
As thick as hasty puddin'.
Yankee Doodle, keep it up,
Yankee Doodle dandy;
Mind the music and the step,
And with the girls be handy.

And there we saw a thousand men,
As rich as Squire David,
And what they wasted ev'ry day,
I wish it could be saved.
Yankee Doodle, keep it up,
Yankee Doodle dandy;
Mind the music and the step,
And with the girls be handy.

And there was Captain Washington
Upon a slapping stallion,
A-giving orders to his men;
I guess there was a million.
Yankee Doodle, keep it up,
Yankee Doodle dandy;
Mind the music and the step,
And with the girls be handy.

Auld Lang Syne

Words: Robert Burns
Melody: William Shield
Date of Composition: Brought to America in the 1790s

The standard song of New Year's Eve, "Auld Lang Syne," was originally a dance from the region of Spey in Scotland. It was adapted by Robert Burns (from the original words) and was popularized by William Shield in one of his operas.

Should auld acquaintance be forgot,
And never brought to min'?
Should auld acquaintance be forgot,
And auld lang syne?

For auld lang syne, my dear,
For auld lang syne,
We'll tak a cup o' kindness yet
For auld lang syne.

We twa hae paid l't i' the burn,
From mornin' sun to dine;
But seas between us braid hae roar'd
Sin' auld lang syne.

For auld lang syne, my dear,
For auld lang syne,
We'll tak a cup o' kindness yet
For auld lang syne.

And there's a hand, my trusty fier,
And gie's a hand o' thine;
And we'll tak a right guid willie waught
For auld lang syne.

For auld lang syne, my dear,
For auld lang syne,
We'll tak a cup o' kindness yet
For auld lang syne.

Jeanie, with the
Light Brown Hair

Words and Melody: Stephen C. Foster
Date of Composition: 1850

Although it was commonly assumed Foster wrote this, one of his most popular songs, with his wife in mind, it is now thought that it may have been inspired during one of their periodic separations.

I dream of Jeanie with the light brown hair,
Borne like a vapor, on the summer air;
I see her tripping where the bright
streams play,
Happy as the daisies that dance on her way.
Many were the wild notes her merry
voice would pour,
Many were the blithe birds that warbled
them o'er;
Ah! I dream of Jeanie with the light
brown hair,
Floating like a vapor, on the soft
summer air.

I long for Jeanie with the day-dawn smile,
Radiant in gladness, warm with
winning guile;
I hear her melodies, like joys gone by,
Sighing round my heart o'er the fond
hopes that die;
Sighing like the night wind and
sobbing like the rain,
Wailing for the lost one that comes
not again;
Ah! I dream of Jeanie with the
light brown hair,
Floating like a vapor, on the soft
summer air.

Oh! Susanna

Words and Music: Stephen Foster
Date of Composition: 1848

Although he literally gave the song away upon its completion, "Oh! Susanna" established Stephen C. Foster (1826–1864) as the most important songwriter of his time. Over a period of 20 years, he produced some 200 songs, many of them now regarded as part of the American folk tradition. In addition to those printed below, Foster also wrote "My Old Kentucky Home," "Camptown Races," and "Old Black Joe." He died at the age of 38, probably from alcoholism, alone and broke in a New York hotel room.

I come from Alabama with my banjo
   on my knee;
I'm going to Louisiana my true love
   for to see.
It rained all night the day I left,
   the weather it was dry;
The sun so hot I froze to death,
Susanna don't you cry.

Oh! Susanna,
don't you cry for me;
I come from Alabama,
with my banjo on my knee.

I had a dream the other night,
When everything was still;
I thought I saw Susanna dear,
A-coming down the hill.
The buckwheat cake was in her mouth,
The tear was in her eye,
Said I, I'm coming from the south,
Susanna don't you cry.

Oh! Susanna,
don't you cry for me;
I come from Alabama,
with my banjo on my knee.

I soon will be in New Orleans,
And then I'll look all 'round,
and when I find Susanna,
I'll fall upon the ground.
But if I do not find her,
This darkey'll surely die,
And when I'm dead and buried,
Susanna don't you cry.

Oh! Susanna,
don't you cry for me;
I come from Alabama,
with my banjo on my knee.

Amazing Grace

Words: Rev. John Newton
Date of Composition: Unknown
Melody: Folk origins

A deserter from the British navy and a merciless captain of a slave ship, John Newton wrote this most enduring of hymns after a storm at sea nearly destroyed his ship and inspired his conversion.

Amazing grace, how sweet the sound,
That saved a wretch like me;
I once was lost but now I'm found,
Was blind, but now I see.

'Twas grace that taught my heart to fear,
And grace my fears relieved;
How precious did that grace appear,
The hour I first believed.

Through many dangers, toils and snares,
I have already come.
'Tis grace hath brought me safe thus far,
And grace will lead me home.

How sweet the name of Jesus sounds
In a believer's ear.
It soothes his sorrows, heals his wounds,
And drives away his fear.

Must Jesus bear the cross alone
And all the world go free?
No, there's a cross for everyone
And there's a cross for me.

Beautiful Dreamer

Words and Melody: Stephen C. Foster
Date of Composition: 1862

Although it was billed as the last song he ever wrote (supposedly only two days before his death), "Beautiful Dreamer," considered the finest effort of Foster's undistinguished later period, was actually written two years earlier.

Beautiful dreamer, wake unto me,
Starlight and dew-drops are waiting
   for thee,
Sounds of the rude world,
   heard in the day,
Lull'd by the moon-light
   have all passed away.
Beautiful dreamer,
Queen of my song,
List while I woo thee,
   with soft melody;
Gone are the cares of life's busy throng,
Beautiful dreamer, awake unto me!
Beautiful dreamer, awake unto me!

The Old Folks at Home
(Swanee River)

Words and Melody: Stephen C. Foster
Date of Composition: 1851

After Foster and his brother consulted an atlas for a two-syllable name for a southern river to complement a nostalgic tune, they arrived at *Swanee*, making the little Florida river (spelled *Suwanee*) famous the world-over.

'Way down upon the Swanee River,
Far, far away,
There's where my heart is turning ever,
There's where the old folks stay.
All up and down the whole creation,
Sadly I roam,
Still longing for the old plantation,
And for the old folks at home.
All the world is sad and dreary,
Ev'rywhere I roam;
Oh! ladies, how my heart grows weary,
Far from the old folks at home.

All 'round the little farm I wandered,
When I was young;
Then many happy days I squandered,
Many the songs I sung.
When I was playing with my brother,
Happy was I;
Oh, take me to my kind old mother,
There let me live and die.
All the world is sad and dreary,
Ev'rywhere I roam;
Oh! ladies, how my heart grows weary,
Far from the old folks at home.

One little hut among the bushes,
One that I love,
Still sadly to my mem'ry rushes,
No matter where I rove.
When will I see the bees a-humming
All 'round the comb?
When will I hear the banjo tumming,
Down in my good old home?
All the world is sad and dreary,
Ev'rywhere I roam;
Oh! ladies, how my heart grows weary,
Far from the old folks at home.

Home, Sweet Home

Words: John Howard Payne (1823)
Melody: Henry R. Bishop (1823)

Ironically, the lyricist of one of the most popular sentimental ballads of all time spent a good part of his life as a vagabond.

Mid pleasures and palaces though we
   may roam,
Be it ever so humble, there's no place
   like home!
A charm from the skies seems to
   hallow us there,
Which, seek through the world, is
   ne'er met with elsewhere.

Home! home! sweet, sweet home!
There's no place like home!
There's no place like home.

I gaze on the moon as I tread the
   drear wild,
And feel that my mother now thinks
   of her child;
As she looks on that moon from
   our own cottage door,
Through the woodbine whose fragrance
   shall cheer me no more.

Home! home! sweet, sweet home!
There's no place like home!
There's no place like home.

An exile from home, splendor dazzles
   in vain;
Oh, give me my lowly thatched cottage
   again;
The birds singing gaily, that came
   at my call;
Give me them, and that peace of mind,
   dearer than all.

Home! home! sweet, sweet home!
There's no place like home!
There's no place like home.

Chronology of American History

c. 1000 Viking explorer Leif Ericson explores North American coast and founds temporary colony called Vinland.

1492 On first voyage to America, Christopher Columbus lands at San Salvador island in Bahamas.

1493 Pope Alexander VI divides New World between Spain and Portugal.

1497 John Cabot claims Newfoundland for King Henry VII of England.

1499 Florentine merchant Amerigo Vespucci visits New World and begins writing popular accounts of his voyages.

1506 Columbus dies poor and embittered, convinced he found new route to Asia and refusing to believe he discovered new continent.

1507 German mapmaker Martin Waldseemüller, after reading Amerigo Vespucci's descriptions of New World, names it America after him.

1513 Juan Ponce de León discovers Florida. Vasco Nuñez de Balboa crosses Panama and sights Pacific Ocean.

1519 Hernán Cortés lands in Mexico.

1520 Ferdinand Magellan, first to sail around world, discovers South American straits, named after him.

1522 Cortés captures Mexico City and conquers Aztec empire.

1524 Giovanni de Verrazano, commissioned by King Francis I of France, discovers New York harbor and Hudson River.

1534 Jacques Cartier of France explores coast of Newfoundland and Gulf of St. Lawrence.

1536 Traveling overland from Gulf of Mexico, Alvar Núñez Cabeza de Vaca reaches Gulf of California.

1539 Fernando de Soto conquers Florida and begins three-year trek across Southeast.

1540 Francisco Vásquez de Coronado explores Southwest, discovering Grand Canyon and introducing horses to North America.

1541 Coronado discovers Mississippi River.

1542 João Rodrígues Cabrilho (Cabrillo) explores coast of California, missing San Francisco Bay.

1565 Don Pedro Menéndez de Aviles founds first permanent European settlement in North America, at St. Augustine, Florida.

1572 Sir Francis Drake of England makes first voyage to America, landing in Panama.

1576 English explorer Martin Frobisher searches for Northwest Passage.

1577 Drake begins voyage of plunder around world.

1579 Drake lands north of San Francisco Bay and claims region for Queen Elizabeth I.

1584 Sir Walter Raleigh discovers Roanoke Island and names land Virginia, after Queen Elizabeth.

1585 Raleigh establishes England's first American colony at Roanoke.

1586 Drake evacuates surviving Roanoke settlers.

1587 Raleigh resettles Roanoke with 150 new colonists. Virginia Dare first child of English parents born in America.

1591 Relief expedition returns to Roanoke colony; all settlers have disappeared without trace.

1602 Capt. Bartholomew Gosnold, first Englishman to set foot in New England, explores Cape Cod and Martha's Vineyard.

1603 Samuel de Champlain of France explores St. Lawrence Seaway; later founds Quebec.

1607 First permanent English settlement in America established at Jamestown, Va. Only 32 of original 105 colonists survive first winter.

1608 Capt. John Smith imprisoned by Indians and saved by Pocahontas, daughter of Chief Powhatan.

1609 Henry Hudson sets out in search of Northwest Passage. Champlain sails into Great Lakes.

1611 Hudson cast adrift by mutinous crewmen to die in bay later named for him.

1612 First Dutch trading post appears on Manhattan Island.

1616 Smallpox epidemic decimates Indian tribes from Maine to Rhode Island.

1619 Dutch traders bring first African slaves to Virginia for sale. Americans hold first election when Virginia planters vote for House of Burgesses.

1620 Pilgrims and others arrive in Plymouth, Mass., aboard *Mayflower*. They draw up Mayflower Compact.

1622 Most of Virginia colony wiped out in Indian attack.

1624 King James I revokes Virginia's charter and makes it royal colony.

1626 Dutch colony of New Amsterdam founded on Manhattan Island, bought from Indian people for about $24.

1630 John Winthrop sets sail for Massachusetts with 900 Puritans and others, beginning Great Migration to New England.

1632 King Charles I of England grants Lord Baltimore charter to establish colony in Maryland.

1634 Massachusetts adopts representative government. Jean Nicolet of France begins trading with Indians in Wisconsin.

1635 Roger Williams, banished from Massachusetts, founds dissident colony of Rhode Island.

1636 New Englanders massacre hundreds of Indians in Pequot War. Harvard College established.

1638 First Swedish colony founded in Delaware.

1639 "Oath of a Free Man" the first English document printed in America. First public school appears in Dorchester, first post office in Boston, and Connecticut writes first colonial constitution.

1644 Indians make last, unsuccessful attempt to expel English settlers from Virginia. First American ship built in Boston.

1647 Margaret Brent of Maryland first American woman to demand right to vote. Massachusetts passes first compulsory education law. First witchcraft execution takes place in Hartford, Conn.

1648 Boston shoemakers and coopers establish first American labor unions.

1651 British Parliament passes first Navigation Act regulating colonial trade.

1652 Rhode Island first colony to outlaw slavery. First American coins minted in Boston.

1654 Jacob Barsimon, first American Jew, arrives in New Amsterdam, followed by 23 more Jews from Brazil.

1655 Dutch colonists capture Swedish colony in Delaware. Lady Deborah Moody of Long Island first American woman to vote.

1656 First Quakers arrive in America; imprisoned in Boston, beaten, and deported.

1659 Massachusetts hangs two Quakers on Boston Common.

1660 British Parliament forbids Americans to export goods to countries other than England. Massachusetts outlaws celebration of Christmas.

1661 Virginia first colony to recognize slavery as legal.

1662 Connecticut granted royal charter. Massachusetts appoints official press censors and institutes "half-way" covenant.

1663 British Parliament requires colonial imports from Europe to pass first through England. King Charles II grants charters to Carolina and Rhode Island.

1664 New Amsterdam captured by Richard Nicolls, who renames it New York. New Jersey established.

1670 Charles Town, later called Charleston, first permanent settlement in Carolina.

1672 British Parliament tightens trade restrictions on colonies and appoints American customs collectors.

1673 French explorers Jacques Marquette and Louis Jolliet paddle down Mississippi River to Arkansas. Regular mail service begins between Boston and New York. Dutch forces recapture New York.

1674 Treaty of Westminster restores New York to England. King Louis XIV of France sends Sieur de La Salle to explore Mississippi River.

1675 Thousands die in King Philip's War between New Englanders and five Indian tribes.

1676 Bacon's Rebellion overthrows government of Virginia and burns down Jamestown.

1680 New Hampshire separated from Massachusetts and made royal colony.

1681 King Charles II names William Penn proprietor of Pennsylvania.

1682 Penn founds Philadelphia. Sieur de La Salle claims North American interior for France, naming it Louisiana.

1683 First German-Americans, a group of Mennonites, arrive in Philadelphia.

1684 King Charles II revokes Massachusetts charter.

1686 King James II appoints Sir Edmund Andros governor-general of Dominion of New England, dissolving colonial governments.

1688 Quakers publish first antislavery tracts in Pennsylvania.

1689 Andros surrenders to Boston mobs, and colonial self-government is reestablished. Jacob Leisler seizes power in New York uprising. King William's War begins in America.

1690 Massachusetts issues first colonial paper money. American campaigns against French Canada fail. French and Indians burn Schenectady, N.Y.

1691 Jacob Leisler surrenders and is hanged. Massachusetts rechartered with religious freedom.

1692 Witchcraft hysteria breaks out in Salem, Mass., leading to 20 executions.

1693 College of William and Mary chartered, the second college in America.

1695 New York City organizes public relief for poor and homeless.

1696 British Parliament places more commercial restrictions on colonies. American merchants join slave trade.

1697 Treaty of Ryswick ends King William's War.

1701 Antoine de la Mothe Cadillac establishes French outpost at Detroit, Mich. Yale College founded. Delaware separated from Pennsylvania.

1702 Queen Anne's War breaks out.

1704 *Boston News-Letter* first regularly published newspaper in America.

1710 German Migration to America begins. British and American forces capture Port Royal, Nova Scotia.

1711 Anglo-American attack on Quebec fails. Tuscarora Indian War breaks out in North Carolina.

1712 Militia quell slave rebellion in New York City. Pennsylvania prohibits importing slaves.

1713 Treaty of Utrecht ends Queen Anne's War.

1714 Americans begin drinking tea. *Androborus*, a political satire, first play written in America.

1716 First theater in America built in Williamsburg, Va. Slavery introduced to

French Louisiana.

1718 Jean Baptiste Le Moyne founds French city of New Orleans.

1721 Sir Robert Walpole loosens colonial trade restrictions with policy of "salutary neglect."

1722 France declares New Orleans capital of Louisiana.

1723 America's first business corporation chartered in Connecticut.

1724 France expels all Jews from Louisiana.

1728 First American synagogue built in New York City.

1729 North and South Carolina receive royal charters.

1731 Benjamin Franklin founds first American library in Philadelphia.

1732 King George II grants charter to Georgia. Only Catholic church in colonial America opens in Philadelphia. Benjamin Franklin begins publishing *Poor Richard's Almanack.* George Washington born in Virginia.

1733 British Parliament passes Molasses Act, taxing imports from non-British sugar islands.

1734 Beginning of Great Awakening, widespread religious revival.

1735 French begin settling in Illinois.

1737 Boston holds its first public celebration of St. Patrick's Day.

1739 War of Jenkin's Ear begins. South Carolina slaves mount Stono Rebellion. French explorers Pierre and Paul Mallet discover Rocky Mountains.

1741 Danish navigator Vitus Bering, hired by Peter the Great of Russia, explores coast of Alaska. *American Magazine,* the first in colonies, begins publishing in Philadelphia. Slave insurrection panic sweeps New York City.

1742 First sugarcane planted in Louisiana.

1744 King George's War breaks out.

1745 British and Americans capture Ft. Louisbourg on Cape Breton Island. French and Indians raid Maine.

1748 Ft. Louisbourg restored to France by Treaty of Aix-la-Chapelle, ending King George's War.

1751 British Parliament forbids New England colonies to issue paper money.

1752 Benjamin Franklin conducts famous kite experiment. Liberty bell is cracked in Philadelphia.

1753 Governor Robert Dinwiddie of Virginia sends George Washington into Ohio country to demand withdrawal of French. First steam engine arrives in America.

1754 Washington skirmishes with French patrol, touching off French and Indian War. Franklin presents Albany Plan of Union for colonies.

1755 Quakers withdraw from Pennsylvania assembly rather than vote for military spending. Washington leads retreat from Battle of the Wilderness.

1758 British and American forces lose Battle of Ticonderoga but capture Louisbourg and Ft. Duquesne. New Jersey sets aside first Indian reservation for

Onami tribe.

1759 General Wolfe defeats General Montcalm as British capture Quebec. Both generals fall in battle.

1760 After fall of Montreal, all of New France surrenders to Britain. King George III crowned in England.

1762 King Louis XV of France secretly cedes Louisiana to Spain.

1763 Treaty of Paris ends French and Indian War. France cedes Canada to Britain. King George III prohibits Americans to settle in West. Conspiracy of Pontiac threatens frontier.

1764 British Parliament passes Sugar Act and forbids all colonies to issue paper money. French settlers found St. Louis. "Paxton Boys" march on Philadelphia. In Boston James Otis protests, "No taxation without representation."

1765 Parliament passes Stamp Act (tax on newspapers, legal documents, etc.) and Quartering Act (requiring housing of British soldiers in homes). Sons of Liberty organize resistance and nonimportation throughout colonies. Stamp Act Congress meets in New York.

1766 Parliament repeals Stamp Act but passes Declaratory Act, affirming its right to pass laws binding on colonies. Chief Pontiac makes peace.

1767 Parliament enacts Townshend Duties and suspends New York assembly for resisting Quartering Act.

1768 "Regulators" rebel in North Carolina. Boston riots against Townshend Duties.

1769 Daniel Boone explores Kentucky. Father Junipero Serra founds San Diego, the first Spanish mission in California. Gaspar de Portola sails into San Francisco Bay.

1770 Five Americans perish in Boston Massacre (Mar. 5). British Parliament repeals Townshend Duties, except tax on tea.

1771 North Carolina "Regulators" defeated by militia.

1772 Rhode Island mob burns British revenue ship *Gaspee.* Boston appoints first Committee of Correspondence.

1773 British Parliament passes Tea Act, leading to Boston Tea Party (Dec. 16).

1774 Parliament passes "Intolerable Acts," punishing colonists for Tea Party. Boston is occupied by British forces under Gen. Thomas Gage. First Continental Congress meets in Philadelphia.

1775 American Revolution begins with Battle of Lexington and Concord (Apr. 19). Second Continental Congress appoints George Washington as commander of Continental Army. British win Battle of Bunker Hill. First abolition society organized in Pennsylvania.

1776 Tom Paine's *Common Sense* published. Declaration of Independence signed. Congress adopts name United States of America. British occupy New York

City. George Washington crosses Delaware to win Battle of Trenton, N.J.

1777 Americans win battles at Princeton and Saratoga. British occupy Philadelphia. Congress adopts Stars and Stripes flag and endorses Articles of Confederation. Washington's army spends winter at Valley Forge, Pa.

1778 France makes alliance with U.S. and declares war on Britain. When French fleet arrives, British evacuate Philadelphia.

1779 Congress offers to make peace in exchange for independence. British withdraw from New York City.

1780 Pennsylvania first state to abolish slavery. British occupy Charleston, S.C. Washington quells Continental Army mutiny. Benedict Arnold defects to British.

1781 French and American victory at Battle of Yorktown ends American Revolution. Articles of Confederation take effect. Los Angeles founded by Spanish missionaries.

1782 British Parliament votes for peace with U.S. Negotiations in Paris lead to provisional Anglo-American peace treaty. Virginia permits owners to free their slaves. First English Bible printed in America.

1783 Massachusetts, Connecticut, and Rhode Island abolish slavery. Treaty of Paris signed (Sept. 3), officially ending American Revolution. Washington retires to Mount Vernon, Va.

1784 Congress ratifies Treaty of Paris. Spain closes Mississippi River to American trade. First bale of American cotton shipped to Britain.

1785 First state university chartered in Georgia.

1786 Virginia proclaims religious freedom. Shays's Rebellion put down in Massachusetts. Annapolis Convention calls for revising Articles of Confederation. New Jersey abolishes slavery.

1787 Convention in Philadelphia writes Constitution. Congress passes Northwest Ordinance and submits Constitution for states' approval.

1788 Constitution ratified and takes effect.

1789 First presidential election results in victory for George Washington. Federal government begins meeting in New York City. Congress enacts first federal tariff.

1790 First antislavery petitions are submitted to Congress. Temporary capital moved to Philadelphia. Pope Pius VI appoints John Carroll first Catholic bishop in U.S. First U.S. census lists population at 3,929,625.

1791 Congress sets up First Bank of the United States and first internal revenue law, a tax on whiskey. Vermont enters Union as 14th state. Bill of Rights takes effect. Pres. Washington selects site of new U.S. capital on Potomac River.

1792 New York stock traders begin meeting under a tree on Wall Street. Pres. Washington unanimously reelected. Construction begins on White House.

1793 Eli Whitney invents cotton gin. Congress passes first Fugitive Slave Act. Pres. Washington holds first official cabinet meeting and lays cornerstone for Capitol. Britain begins confiscating American ships trading with France.

1794 Pres. Washington defeats Whiskey Rebellion in Pennsylvania. U.S. and Britain sign Jay's Treaty. Ohio Indians defeated at Battle of Fallen Timbers.

1795 Georgia stung by scandal of Yazoo land frauds. Senate ratifies Jay's Treaty with Britain.

1796 Pres. Washington delivers "Farewell Address." France begins to confiscate ships trading with Britain.

1797 France insults American diplomats in XYZ affair. Spanish begin building Mission San Juan Capistrano in California.

1798 Georgia last state to abolish slave trade. Congress passes Alien and Sedition Acts. U.S. renounces alliance with France as unofficial naval war breaks out.

1799 Russian-American trading company set up in Alaska. New York abolishes slavery. George Washington dies.

1800 Library of Congress founded. Convention of 1800 signed, ending quasi-war between U.S. and France. Spain secretly cedes Louisiana to France. Congress begins meeting in Washington, D.C.

1801 Election of Thomas Jefferson results in first transfer of executive power between rival parties. Congress takes jurisdiction over District of Columbia. Tripoli pirates declare war on U.S. for not paying tribute.

1802 U.S. Military Academy established at West Point, N.Y.

1803 Louisiana Purchase from France doubles size of U.S. federal outpost founded at Ft. Dearborn, Ill., future site of Chicago.

1804 Lewis and Clark expedition sets out from St. Louis. New Jersey begins gradual emancipation. Alexander Hamilton killed in duel with Aaron Burr.

1805 Barbary War with Tripoli ends.

1806 Congress authorizes construction of Cumberland Road. Noah Webster's first dictionary published. Aaron Burr conspires to create private frontier empire.

1807 Britain and France enact blockades in Europe, confiscating American trading ships. British attack USS *Chesapeake*. Embargo Act forbids all American exports.

1808 Congress declares end to African slave trade.

1809 Embargo Act replaced with Non-Intercourse Act, outlawing exports to Britain and France. Henry Clay of Kentucky enters U.S. Senate. First steamboat sea voyage made from New York

City to Philadelphia.

1810 Pres. James Madison annexes West Florida.

1811 Worst earthquake in U.S. history rocks Ohio-Mississippi valleys. Russians settle at Ft. Ross, Calif. First Bank of the United States fails to obtain recharter. Gen. William Henry Harrison defeats Indians at Battle of Tippecanoe.

1812 War of 1812 begins by close vote in Congress. New England resists war. Daniel Webster of Massachusetts elected to Congress. British clamp blockade on U.S. ports, capture Detroit, and repel American attack on Canada at Queenstown.

1813 Americans regain Detroit, attack Toronto and Ft. George in Canada, but surrender to British at Beaver Dams, Ontario. Capt. Oliver H. Perry wins control of Great Lakes. British and Indians burn Buffalo, N.Y.

1814 British destroy Ft. Oswego, N.Y., and set fire to Washington, D.C. Francis Scott Key writes "The Star Spangled Banner." New Englanders opposed to war meet secretly at Hartford Convention. First textile mill established at Waltham, Mass. Treaty of Ghent ends War of 1812.

1815 Gen. Andrew Jackson routs British at Battle of New Orleans, before news arrives that War of 1812 is over.

1816 Congress charters Second Bank of the United States.

1817 Rush-Bagot Treaty between Britain and U.S. demilitarizes Great Lakes. Harvard Law School founded. New York Stock and Exchange Board organized. Work begins on Erie Canal. Indian attack touches off first Seminole War in Florida.

1818 Cumberland Road opened. Congress adopts present format for American flag. Canadian boundary dispute with Britain settled.

1819 Panic of 1819 plunges South and West into depression. U.S. obtains Florida from Spain in Adams-Onís Treaty, settling border of Louisiana. *Savannah* makes first successful transatlantic crossing under steam power.

1820 Missouri Compromise solves crisis over admission of Missouri as slave state. Abolitionists begin colonizing freed slaves in Africa.

1821 First Catholic cathedral in U.S. built in Baltimore.

1822 Denmark Vesey and 36 others executed for organizing rebel slave conspiracy in Charleston, S.C.

1823 Monroe Doctrine, masterminded by Sec. of State John Quincy Adams, announced by Pres. James Monroe.

1824 Russia and U.S. sign treaty settling territorial disputes in Pacific Northwest. First presidential nominating convention held in Utica, N.Y.

1825 John Quincy Adams chosen president in infamous "Corrupt Bargain" with

Henry Clay, who becomes secretary of state. Erie Canal opened. Mexico invites Americans to settle in Texas.

1826 Anti-Mason party organized. John Adams and Thomas Jefferson die on 50th anniversary of Declaration of Independence. Jedediah Smith leads first overland expedition to California.

1827 Joseph Smith has visions of Book of Mormon. U.S. and Britain agree to joint occupation of Pacific Northwest.

1828 Congress passes protectionist "Tariff of Abominations" over southern protests.

1829 Mexico refuses Pres. Andrew Jackson's offer to buy Texas.

1830 Webster-Hayne Debate in U.S. Senate reveals sectional tension. Church of Latter-day Saints (the Mormons) founded by Joseph Smith in Fayette, N.Y. Mexico forbids further American immigration to Texas.

1831 Nat Turner leads bloodiest of all slave rebellions, killing 57 whites in Virginia. Abolitionists petition Congress for end to slavery.

1832 Black Hawk War fought in Illinois and Wisconsin. First nationwide Democratic party convention held in Baltimore. Pres. Jackson vetoes bill to recharter national bank. South Carolina nullifies "Tariff of Abominations."

1833 Massachusetts last state to end tax support for churches. Congress lowers tariff and passes "Force Bill" to pressure South Carolina, which rescinds nullification. American Anti-Slavery Society organized. Oberlin College becomes first coeducational college.

1834 Whig party organized by Senators Henry Clay and Daniel Webster in opposition to Pres. Jackson. Antiabolitionist riots break out in New York and Philadelphia.

1835 Samuel Morse invents telegraph. National debt completely paid off. Pres. Jackson survives first attempt to assassinate a president. Second Seminole War begins in Florida.

1836 Samuel Colt invents revolver. Texas declares independence from Mexico and requests U.S. annexation. Mexican army captures Alamo, but Texans are victorious at San Jacinto.

1837 Panic of 1837 begins lengthy economic depression.

1838 Joshua Giddings of Ohio is first abolitionist elected to Congress. Transatlantic steamship service established. Congress blocks abolitionist petitions with "Gag Rule."

1839 Abner Doubleday of Cooperstown, N.Y., codifies rules of baseball. Congress outlaws dueling in Washington, D.C.

1840 "Log Cabin Campaign" between William Henry Harrison and Martin Van Buren begins era of mass political participation. Liberty party founded by abolitionists in Albany, N.Y.

1841 First emigrant train of 48 covered wagons arrives in California. Pres. William Henry Harrison dies after month in office. First Japanese immigrant arrives in New Bedford, Mass.

1842 Webster-Ashburton Treaty settles Canada boundary disputes between U.S. and Britain. U.S. accidentally seizes California, then returns it with apology to Mexico.

1843 End of Second Seminole War. B'Nai B'rith founded in New York. Mormons begin practicing polygamy.

1844 Baptist is first church to split North and South over slavery. Samuel Morse sends first telegraph message. James K. Polk, first dark horse candidate, elected president.

1845 Potato Famine begins massive Irish immigration. U.S. annexes Texas, over Mexican protests. U.S. Naval Academy opens at Annapolis, Md.

1846 Mexican War begins when U.S. troops are attacked in disputed Texas territory. American settlers in California stage Bear Flag Revolt. Oregon Treaty gives U.S. sole possession of Pacific Northwest up to 49th parallel. First recorded baseball game played in Hoboken, N.J.

1847 Wilmot Proviso, forbidding slavery expansion, passes House and sets off wave of panic in South. Gen. Winfield Scott conquers Mexico City. Brigham Young leads Mormons to Utah. Abraham Lincoln of Illinois arrives in Congress.

1848 Treaty of Guadalupe-Hidalgo ends Mexican War, ceding Southwest to U.S. Revolution of 1848 begins wave of German immigration. New York–Chicago telegraph line completed. Chicago Board of Trade established. Free Soil party organized. Gold discovered in California. First Chinese immigrants arrive in San Francisco. Lucretia Mott and Elizabeth Cady Stanton hold first Women's Rights Convention in Seneca Falls, N.Y.

1849 Gold Rush brings hundreds of thousands to California. Over 20 killed in New York City riot between fans of rival actors. Elizabeth Blackwell first American woman to receive medical degree.

1850 Sen. Henry Clay's Compromise of 1850 solves crisis over slavery expansion. Clayton-Bulwer Treaty pledges Anglo-American cooperation in building any Central American canal. John C. Calhoun of South Carolina delivers last address to Senate.

1851 Young Men's Christian Association (YMCA) established. Northern mobs resist Fugitive Slave Act. Maine is first state to pass prohibition laws. Hungarian patriot Louis Kossuth draws huge crowds touring country. *New York Times* founded. Herman Melville's *Moby Dick* published.

1852 Harriet Beecher Stowe's *Uncle Tom's Cabin* published.

1853 U.S. buys Gila River valley from Mexico in Gadsden Purchase. Native American, or "Know-Nothing," party founded. Commodore Matthew C. Perry opens trade with Japan.

1854 Congress passes Kansas-Nebraska Act, setting off mass protests across North. Republican party founded. U.S. threatens to seize Cuba from Spain in Ostend Manifesto.

1855 "Bleeding Kansas" fighting begins as proslavery and antislavery settlers hold rival state conventions. First railroad train crosses Mississippi River at Rock Island, Ill., into Davenport, Iowa.

1856 Congressman Preston Brooks of South Carolina beats Sen. Charles Sumner of Massachusetts unconscious on Senate floor for insulting another senator. John Brown leads Pottawatomie massacre in Kansas. First Republican national convention nominates John C. Frémont for president in Pittsburgh, Pa.

1857 New York–St. Louis railroad completed. Supreme Court hands down controversial *Dred Scott* decision protecting slavery. Panic of 1857 sends North into depression.

1858 Lincoln-Douglas Debates dramatize issue of slavery expansion in Illinois race for Senate. First transatlantic telegraph cable laid.

1859 John Brown's raid on Harper's Ferry arsenal to launch abolitionist war against slavery ends in his capture and execution. Slave insurrection panic sweeps South. Comstock Lode discovered in Nevada. First-producing oil well in U.S. flows in Titusville, Pa.

1860 Democratic party splits into northern and southern wings. South Carolina is first Southern state to secede from Union after victory of Abraham Lincoln. Crittenden Compromise fails to preserve Union. Pony Express begins mail delivery between California and Missouri.

1861 Civil War begins with attack on Ft. Sumter in South Carolina (Apr. 12). Pres. Abraham Lincoln calls for 75,000 volunteers to put down rebellion. Jefferson Davis of Mississippi elected president of Confederate States of America. New York–San Francisco telegraph link completed. Yale awards first American Ph.D. Congress enacts first federal income tax.

1862 Congress issues "greenbacks," subsidizes transcontinental railroad, abolishes slavery in District of Columbia, and passes Homestead Act. Pres. Lincoln issues Emancipation Proclamation after Battle of Antietam, bloodiest fight of Civil War.

1863 Emancipation Proclamation takes effect (Jan. 1). Union victories at Vicksburg, Miss., and Gettysburg, Pa., signal turning point of Civil War. West

Virginia secedes from Virginia and rejoins Union. Hundreds killed in New York City draft riot. Pres. Lincoln proclaims Thanksgiving national holiday.

1864 Pres. Lincoln names Gen. Ulysses S. Grant as commander of Union armies. Gen. William T. Sherman destroys Atlanta and conducts "March to the Sea." Confederate army of Gen. Robert E. Lee crippled in Wilderness Campaign. Cheyenne and Arapaho slaughtered in Sand Creek Massacre in Colorado.

1865 Gen. Lee surrenders to Gen. Grant at Appomattox Court House, Virginia (Apr. 9). Pres. Lincoln assassinated by John Wilkes Booth in Washington, D.C. (Apr. 14). Confederacy dissolved, ending Civil War. Pres. Andrew Johnson proclaims amnesty for most rebels. Slavery outlawed by adoption of 13th Amendment. Ku Klux Klan founded in Pulaski, Tenn.

1866 In the struggle over Reconstruction policy, Congress overrides Pres. Johnson's vetoes of Civil Rights Act and New Freedmen's Bureau Bill. Whites riot in New Orleans to protest black suffrage. Grand Army of the Republic organized by Union veterans. Young Women's Christian Association (YWCA) founded in Boston.

1867 Congress takes control of Reconstruction in South by passing First Reconstruction Act over Pres. Johnson's veto and Tenure of Office Act. U.S. purchases Alaska from Russia for $7.2 million (2¢ an acre). Farmers organize Patrons of Husbandry, beginning Granger movement. Cigarettes appear on American market. First elevated trains begin running in New York City.

1868 For violating Tenure of Office Act of 1867, Pres. Johnson is impeached in the House (Feb. 24), but acquitted in the Senate by a single vote (May 16). U.S. and China sign Burlingame Treaty to allow immigration. Fourteenth Amendment grants equal citizenship and protection to freedmen (July 28). Half a million black votes help elect Gen. Ulysses S. Grant to presidency. Typewriter invented. University of California chartered.

1869 "Hard Money" prevails when Congress passes Public Credit Act, promising repayment of government debts in gold. Transcontinental railroad completed when Union Pacific and Central Pacific lines meet at Promontory Point, Utah (May 10). Jay Gould and James Fisk cause financial panic by trying to corner gold market on "Black Friday" (Sept. 24). Knights of Labor national union organized. National Women's Suffrage Association formed in New York. Wyoming Territory grants first U.S. women's suffrage.

1870 Fifteenth Amendment guarantees right to vote for all U.S. citizens,

though only Wyoming and Utah territories allow women's suffrage (Mar. 30). Congress passes first Ku Klux Act to enforce 15th Amendment. First black senator and black congressman elected. Yale and Harvard initiate first graduate studies programs in U.S. All states represented in Congress for first time since 1860.

1871 Congress passes second Ku Klux Act to enforce 14th Amendment in South. U.S. and Britain resolve Civil War disputes with Treaty of Washington. Tammany Hall ring overthrown in New York City when *New York Times* begins publishing exposé of William Marcy "Boss" Tweed. Most of Chicago destroyed in Great Fire (Oct. 8–11). Anti-Chinese race riots in Los Angeles. Illinois enacts first railroad regulations.

1872 Liberal Republicans bolt from Pres. Grant and nominate newspaperman Horace Greeley for president. Crédit Mobilier scandal implicates Vice Pres. Schuyler Colfax and embarrasses Grant administration. Yellowstone National Park created. Susan B. Anthony arrested for leading suffragists to the polls. Jehovah's Witnesses, originally called Russellites, founded by Charles Taze Russell. Montgomery Ward opens for business in Chicago.

1873 Silver withdrawn from money supply in "Crime of '73." Congressmen raise their own salaries 50%, retroactive for two years, and double president's pay in "Salary Grab" Act. Panic of 1873, triggered by failure of Jay Cooke's banking house, begins depression of 1870s. New York Stock Exchange forced to close for 10 days. Great Bonanza silver lode discovered in Nevada. San Francisco installs first cable cars.

1874 Granger movement begins passing railroad regulations in midwestern states. Women's Christian Temperance Union founded in Cleveland, Ohio. Young Men's Hebrew Association organized in New York. Democrats recapture Congress for first time since Civil War. Greenback party formed in Indianapolis, Ind. Black rioters attack courthouse in Vicksburg, Miss. Chautauqua movement begins bringing educational speakers to rural communities across the country.

1875 Congress passes Specie Resumption Act to reduce money supply by redeeming greenbacks for gold, and Civil Rights Act to guarantee equal rights for freedmen. Whiskey Ring scandal casts further pall on Grant administration. Archbishop John McCloskey of New York first American bishop. *Aristides* wins first Kentucky Derby at Churchill Downs, Ky.

1876 U.S. awards patent to Alexander Graham Bell for telephone. Gen. George A. Custer and 265 men massacred by Sioux Indians at Little Big Horn,

Mont. (June 25). Centennial of U.S. celebrated. Democrat Samuel Tilden outpolls Republican candidate Rutherford B. Hayes as presidential election is thrown into the House (Nov. 7). Professional baseball's National League established. Kappa Alpha opens first college fraternity house at Williams College. Central Park in New York completed.

1877 Congress appoints Electoral Commission to solve impasse over disputed 1876 election (Jan. 29). House votes 185 to 184 to declare Rutherford B. Hayes president-elect, three days before his inauguration (Mar. 2). Reconstruction officially ends with withdrawal of federal troops from South (Apr. 24). Pres. Hayes sends in troops as Great Railroad Strike paralyzes much of nation (July 17). Anti-Chinese riots break out in San Francisco. Colorado silver rush begins.

1878 Sen. A.A. Sargent introduces Women's Suffrage Amendment in Congress (Jan. 10). Greenback-Labor party formed in Toledo, Ohio. Limited coinage of silver resumes with Bland-Allison Act. Democrats win control of both houses of Congress for first time since 1858. American Bar Association organized in Saratoga, N.Y. Edison Electric begins operating in New York City. New Haven, Conn., sets up first commercial telephone network.

1879 U.S. resumes specie payments for greenbacks. Pres. Hayes battles with Congress over use of federal troops in elections. F.W. Woolworth opens his first store in Utica, N.Y. First Church of Christ, Scientist, founded in Boston. Thomas Edison invents light bulb. California adopts state constitution forbidding employment of Chinese labor. Henry George's radical social critique, *Progress and Poverty*, becomes national best-seller.

1880 Pres. Hayes declares U.S. must control any Isthmian canal. Ex-pres. Grant fails in attempt to regain Republican nomination. U.S. and China agree to Chinese Exclusion Treaty (Nov. 17). National Farmers' Alliance organized in Chicago. American branch of Salvation Army founded in Philadelphia, Pa. Census lists U.S. population over 50 million for first time (50,155,783).

1881 Pres. James Garfield assassinated by Charles Guiteau in Washington, D.C. (July 2; dies Sept. 19). Chester A. Arthur becomes president (Sept. 20). Clara Barton creates American Red Cross. Booker T. Washington founds Tuskegee Institute for black education in Alabama. First summer camp for children opens in Squam Lake, N.H. Russian Jews begin immigrating to U.S. to escape pogroms.

1882 John D. Rockefeller organizes Standard Oil trust, first such combination. Congress passes first Chinese Exclusion Act (May 10), which would be renewed for decades, and legislates first immigration restrictions: no paupers, convicts, or mental defectives (Aug. 3). Polygamists forbidden to vote or hold office. Knights of Columbus founded with permission from Roman Catholic church.

1883 Congress passes Pendleton Act, requiring civil service competition for federal jobs. Brooklyn Bridge opened in New York. Supreme Court strikes down Civil Rights Act of 1875 (Oct. 15). New York–Chicago telephone service begins. Ohio River floods devastate Cincinnati. U.S. Navy builds its first steel ships. Railroads agree on standard time zones for North America.

1884 "Mugwumps" bolt Republican party. Statue of Liberty cornerstone laid (Aug. 5). Belva A. Lockwood of Equal Rights party first woman candidate for president. Grover Cleveland of New York first Democrat elected president since Civil War. Home Insurance building of Chicago first skyscraper in world. Moses Fleetwood Walker first black professional baseball player.

1885 Washington Monument completed after 36 years of construction. U.S. Post Office begins Special Delivery service. U.S. Marines land in Panama (Apr. 24). Senate refuses to ratify treaty for building canal across Nicaragua. Congress outlaws building fences on public lands in West. Stanford University founded in Palo Alto, Calif. Josiah Strong's best-seller *Our Country* argues for American imperialism.

1886 Knights of Labor rail strike sets off national wave of strikes for eight-hour day. Haymarket Riot in Chicago leads to execution of seven anarchists. Pres. Cleveland has first White House wedding (June 2). Statue of Liberty in New York Harbor dedicated (Oct. 28). American Federation of Labor (AFL) founded in Columbus, Ohio. Indian wars end with capture of Geronimo. U.S. Treasury begins accumulating large revenue surplus.

1887 Congress creates Interstate Commerce Commission, the first federal regulatory agency, but with weak enforcement powers. Pres. Cleveland orders Confederate battle flags returned to South, provoking outcry (June 7). Congress distributes reservation land to Indians; also bans opium imports. First electric trolley line built in Richmond, Va. U.S. Navy leases base at Pearl Harbor, Hawaii. First American golf club founded in Foxburg, Pa.

1888 Snow falls for 36 hours in New York, killing 400 people in Great Blizzard of '88 (Mar. 12). First secret-ballot election held in Louisville, Ky. George Eastman brings first Kodak camera onto market. National Geographic Society founded in Washington, D.C. Ed-

ward Bellamy's utopian novel, *Looking Backward*, becomes sensational bestseller.

1889 Four new states—N.Dak., S.Dak., Mont., Wash.—all admitted in one day (Feb. 22). Oklahoma Land Rush results when former Indian territory opened for settlement (Apr. 22). Johnstown Flood claims thousands of lives in Pennsylvania (May 31). Kansas passes first antitrust law. Jane Addams founds Hull House in Chicago. First all-American college football players chosen. Tower Building, the first New York skyscraper, completed.

1890 Congress passes Sherman Antitrust Act (July 2) and Sherman Silver Purchase Act. Wyoming admitted as first state with women's suffrage (July 10). Sioux uprising ends at Battle of Wounded Knee (Dec. 29). Yosemite National Park created. Mormons renounce polygamy. Mississippi leads South in disfranchising black voters. Jacob Riis's *How the Other Half Lives* awakens Americans to problem of urban poverty. First army-navy football game played—navy 24, army 0.

1891 Pres. Grover Cleveland denounces "dangerous and reckless experiment" of silver coinage. New Orleans mob lynches 11 Italian immigrants. People's, or Populist, party organized in Cincinnati. U.S. and Chile nearly go to war over death of two American sailors in Valparaiso (Oct. 16). Dr. James A. Naismith invents basketball in Springfield, Mass. Thomas Edison patents first American-made motion picture camera.

1892 Immigrants begin landing at Ellis Island in New York (Jan. 1). Populist candidate James B. Weaver of Iowa receives over million votes for president. Violent strikes break out among steel workers in Homestead, Pa., and among silver miners in Coeur d'Alene, Idaho. Chinese immigrants forced to register with federal government. George W.G. Ferris invents Ferris Wheel. First gasoline-powered American automobile built in Chicopee, Mass. Boll weevil first appears in Texas.

1893 U.S. gold reserve falls below $100 million (Apr. 21). Panic of 1893, touched off by New York stock market crash (June 27), begins second-worst depression in U.S. history. Congress repeals Sherman Silver Purchase Act (Oct. 30). Hawaii requests U.S. annexation. Mormon Temple dedicated in Salt Lake City, Utah. Thousands perish in Louisiana cyclone. Frank Lloyd Wright completes first solo project, the Winslow home in Chicago.

1894 Coxey's Army of unemployed march on Washington, D.C. (Apr. 30). U.S. Treasury issues two $50-million bond offerings to shore up dwindling gold reserves. Congress enacts first peace-

time federal income tax, denounced as "socialism, communism, devilism" (Aug. 27). Pullman strike paralyzes railroads across nation. Senate refuses to annex Hawaii. Thomas Edison exhibits his kinetoscope.

1895 Billionaire banker J.P. Morgan bails out U.S. Treasury, faced with gold drain. "Silver Democrats" appeal for unlimited silver coinage as way out of depression. Supreme Court rules income tax unconstitutional (May 20). Venezuelan boundary dispute brings U.S. and Britain close to war. Cuban insurrection against Spanish rule begins, winning American sympathy. National Association of Manufacturers formed in Cincinnati. First professional football game played in Latrobe, Pa.

1896 Supreme Court approves segregation (*Plessy* vs. *Ferguson*). William Jennings Bryan, "Silver Democrat" of Nebraska, wins nomination with "Cross of Gold" speech (July 7). Gold discovered in Klondike, Alaska, defusing money question (Aug. 16). American athletes sweep nine of 12 events at first International Olympics. Henry Ford builds his first automobile. First American motion pictures appear in theaters. "The Yellow Kid," first comic strip, begins running in New York World. First American hockey league organized in New York.

1897 U.S. and Britain consent to arbitration of boundary disputes in Olney-Pauncefote Convention (Jan. 11). Venezuelan boundary dispute ends with Britain accepting arbitration. Klondike gold rush to Alaska moves into full swing. Senate again refuses to annex Hawaii. U.S. offers to mediate Cuban rebellion; lodges official complaint against Spanish brutality. "Yellow press" newspapers keep up constant assault on Spain. First American subway completed in Boston.

1898 After mysterious explosion of battleship *Maine* in Havana harbor (Feb. 15), Spanish-American War breaks out (Apr. 21). Commodore George Dewey destroys Spanish fleet at Manila Bay (May 1), and U.S. takes Manila (Aug. 13). After Battle of San Juan Hill (July 1), Spanish garrison at Santiago, Cuba, surrenders (July 17). U.S. takes Cuba, Puerto Rico, Guam, Wake Island, and Philippines from Spain in Treaty of Paris (Dec. 10). Senate finally agrees to annex Hawaii.

1899 Philippine Revolt against U.S. rule erupts. Sec. of State John Hay issues Open Door notes to European powers and Japan, requesting no spheres of influence in China (Sept. 6). U.S. and Germany agree to partition Samoan Islands (Dec. 2). Congress investigates incompetence in War Department, revealed during Spanish-American War. William McKinley first president to ride in an automobile.

1900 "Hard Money" triumphs as U.S. returns to single gold standard (Mar. 14). Puerto Rico and Hawaii become U.S. territories by acts of Congress (Apr. 12 and 30). U.S. troops relieve foreign legations under siege in Peking, China, during Boxer Rebellion (Aug. 14). Olds Co. opens first Detroit, Mich., auto factory. Carrie Nation leads hatchet-wielding women into Kansas saloons to smash liquor barrels. Professional baseball's American League organized. Census lists U.S. population above 75 million for first time (75,994,575).

1901 J.P. Morgan creates U.S. Steel, first billion-dollar corporation. U.S. retains control over Cuba with Platt Amendment. Pres. McKinley shot by anarchist Leon Czolgosz in Buffalo, N.Y. (Sept. 6; dies Sept. 14). Hay-Pauncefote Treaty secures British approval for U.S.-built canal in Panama (Nov. 18). First great Texas oil strike made near Beaumont, Tex. Army War College opens in Washington, D.C. Pres. Theodore Roosevelt promises to "speak softly and carry a big stick."

1902 End of Philippine Insurrection. Reclamation Act initiates federal policy of conservation of natural resources (June 17). Congress declares Philippines an unorganized territory and its inhabitants non-U.S. citizens (July 1). Pres. Roosevelt escapes injury in trolley car accident near Pittsfield, Mass. First Tournament of Roses football game (later known as Rose Bowl) played—Michigan 49, Stanford 0. Pres. Roosevelt helps mediate Pennsylvania coal strike.

1903 U.S. prevails over Canada in Alaskan boundary dispute. Pres. Roosevelt helps Panama gain independence from Colombia, then negotiates treaty to build Panama Canal (Nov. 2–18). Orville and Wilbur Wright conduct first powered-flight near Kitty Hawk, N.C. (Dec. 17). *The Great Train Robbery*, first feature-length motion picture, appears in theaters. Wisconsin holds first primary elections. Ford Motor Co. formed. Boston defeats Pittsburgh in first baseball World Series.

1904 Supreme Court upholds antitrust dissolution of Northern Securities company (Mar. 14). Pres. Roosevelt wins reelection and says he will not run again (Nov. 8). "Roosevelt Corollary" to Monroe Doctrine justifies U.S. intervention to keep other powers out of Western hemisphere (Dec. 6). First New York City subway opened. New York State enacts first speed limit: 20 mph on open roads. Publication of Lincoln Steffens's *The Shame of the Cities*, well-known muckraking book. Deaf, dumb, and blind, Helen Keller graduates with honors from Radcliffe College.

1905 Supreme Court disallows limits on length of working day. Industrial Workers of the World, a radical labor union, formed in Chicago. Pres. Roosevelt mediates Treaty of Portsmouth, ending Russo-Japanese War (Sept. 5). U.S. takes control of Santo Domingo trade. Black leaders hold Niagara Falls Conference, calling for equal rights. Winslow's Soothing Syrup for babies found to contain morphine and poison.

1906 San Francisco destroyed by earthquake and fire (Apr. 18–19). Responding to consumer pressure, Congress passes Pure Food and Drug Act and Meat Inspection Act (June 30). Race riot breaks out in Atlanta (Sept. 22). Japan protests segregation of Asian students in California schools (Oct. 25). Pres. Roosevelt first American to win Nobel Peace Prize and first sitting president to leave U.S. on visit to Panama.

1907 Panic of 1907 triggers crash on Wall Street (Mar. 13) and run on banks across nation. Pres. Roosevelt orders exclusion of Japanese laborers (Mar. 14). U.S. Navy's Great White Fleet embarks on tour around world (Dec. 16). Congress outlaws corporate contributions to political campaigns. Hundreds killed in coal mine explosions in Monongah, W.Va., and Jacobs Creek, Pa. All-time-record 1,285,349 immigrants arrive in one year.

1908 U.S. and Japan conclude "Gentleman's Agreement" limiting immigration. Ford Model T appears on market (Oct. 1). Root-Takahira Agreement promises U.S. and Japan will respect each other's interests in Pacific. Pres. Roosevelt appoints National Conservation Commission. Federal Bureau of Investigation established. New York City outlaws women smoking in public. Lt. Thomas W. Selfridge, U.S. Army, first American air crash fatality. Gideons place their first Bible in hotel in Iron Mountain, Mont.

1909 Robert E. Peary plants American flag at North Pole (Apr. 6). Pres. William Howard Taft opens 700,000 acres for settlement in West. W.E.B. DuBois founds National Association for the Advancement of Colored People (NAACP), advocating racial equality. U.S. Mint issues first Lincoln-head pennies. U.S. troops land in Nicaragua.

1910 Theodore Roosevelt calls for "New Nationalism" in speech at Osawatomie, Kans. (Aug. 31). *Los Angeles Times* building destroyed by terrorist bomb (Oct. 1). Glacier National Park created. Mann Act cracks down on "white slave" trade. Milwaukee, Wis., elects socialist mayor and congressman. Boy Scouts of America chartered. Ballinger-Pinchot controversy reveals major differences over conservation policy in Taft administration.

Barney Oldfield sets land speed record (133 mph) in Daytona Beach, Fla.

1911 Sen. Robert M. LaFollette of Wisconsin founds National Progressive Republican League to promote reform (Jan. 21). Pres. Taft orders U.S. troops to border during Mexican Revolution. Supreme Court upholds antitrust breakups of Standard Oil (May 15) and American Tobacco (May 29). Calbraith P. Rodgers makes first transcontinental airplane flight. U.S. bankers take control of Nicaragua's finances. Steel magnate Andrew Carnegie donates $125 million for philanthropic purposes.

1912 *Titanic* sinks on maiden voyage from England (Apr. 15). Congress approves free-trade tariff reciprocity with Canada (July 22), rejected by Canadian Parliament (Sept. 21). Progressive, or "Bull Moose," party founded by Theodore Roosevelt, who survives assassination attempt by John Schrank in Milwaukee, Wisc. (Oct. 14). Massachusetts adopts first minimum wage law. U.S. Marines land in Honduras, Cuba, Nicaragua, and Santo Domingo. Textile strike in Lawrence, Mass.

1913 Sixteenth Amendment empowers federal government to collect income taxes (Feb. 25), and 17th Amendment allows for popular election of U.S. senators (May 31). Congress creates Federal Reserve system. Ford Motor Co. introduces assembly line. John D. Rockefeller donates $100 million to philanthropic Rockefeller Foundation. Civil War veterans hold 50th anniversary reunion at Gettysburg. Grand Central Station opens in New York City.

1914 Pres. Woodrow Wilson nearly goes to war with Mexico over arrests of American sailors in Tampico (Apr. 14). U.S. Navy shells Vera Cruz and lands marines in retaliation (Apr. 21). U.S. declares neutrality in World War I (Aug. 4). Congress passes Clayton Act, toughening antitrust standards. Yale Bowl, the first full-size football stadium, opened in New Haven, Conn. Congress proclaims Mother's Day.

1915 *Birth of a Nation* first movie blockbuster. Panama-Pacific International Exposition opens in miraculously rebuilt San Francisco. Pres. Wilson strongly protests German sinking of *Lusitania* with 128 Americans aboard (May 7). U.S. Marines land in Haiti (July 28). J.P. Morgan arranges $500-million war loan to France and Britain. Ku Klux Klan revived in Atlanta, Ga. Coast-to-coast long-distance telephone service begins.

1916 House-Grey Memorandum warns Germany that refusal to negotiate may bring U.S. into World War I. Gen. John Pershing chases Pancho Villa into Mexico after border raid on Columbus, N.Mex. (Mar. 15). Britain blacklists

U.S. firms doing business with Germany. U.S. acquires Virgin Islands from Denmark for $25 million (Aug. 4). Pres. Wilson wins reelection with slogan He Kept Us out of War (Nov. 7). Jeanette Rankin of Montana first woman elected to Congress. Louis D. Brandeis first Jewish member of Supreme Court. Margaret Sanger opens first birth-control clinic in Brooklyn, N.Y. National Park Service created.

1917 Germany resumes unrestricted submarine warfare, leading U.S. to sever diplomatic relations (Feb. 3). Gen. John Pershing withdraws from Mexico. Zimmerman Telegram, intercepted by British intelligence and made public, reveals German overtures to Mexico in case of war (Feb. 24). U.S. merchant ships armed for self-defense against German submarines (Mar. 13). After Pres. Wilson proclaims "world must be made safe for democracy," Congress declares war on Germany (Apr. 6) and Austria-Hungary (Dec. 7), bringing U.S. into World War I. Prohibition begins as wartime conservation measure (Aug. 10). Race riot breaks out in East St. Louis, Mo. American soldiers begin fighting in Europe.

1918 Pres. Wilson announces U.S. war aims in "Fourteen Points" speech (Jan. 8). U.S. troops join Allied intervention in Russian Revolution (Aug. 2). Congress passes Sedition Act. Over million U.S. troops participate in monthlong Meuse-Argonne campaign (Sept. 26–Nov. 11). Republicans win control of Congress, a rebuke to Pres. Wilson (Nov. 5). Armistice Day ends World War I (Nov. 11); mass celebrations break out across country. Pres. Wilson goes to Europe for peace conference (Dec. 4). Supreme Court approves draft laws and strikes down child labor laws. Influenza epidemic takes hundreds of thousands of American lives.

1919 Eighteenth Amendment establishes Prohibition (Jan. 29). Strike wave sweeps country, triggering Red Scare. American Communist party organized in Chicago. Race riots in Washington, D.C., and Chicago (July 19 and 27). Pres. Wilson suffers incapacitating stroke during nationwide speaking tour (Sept. 26). Volstead Act implements national Prohibition enforcement. Versailles Treaty, including League of Nations, rejected by Senate (Nov. 19). Grand Canyon National Park created. New York–Chicago daily airmail service begins.

1920 Atty. Gen. A. Mitchell Palmer stages "Palmer Raids," arresting and deporting thousands of radicals and immigrants. Sacco and Vanzetti arrested for murder in Braintree, Mass. (May 5). Supreme Court upholds Prohibition. Nineteenth Amendment establishes women's suffrage (Aug. 26). National League of Women Voters

organized. Wall Street rocked by terrorist bomb, killing 30 bystanders (Sept. 16). First regular radio broadcasts begin in East Pittsburgh, Pa. Pres. Wilson receives Nobel Peace Prize. U.S. population, more urban than rural for first time, tops 100 million (105,710,620).

1921 Pres. Warren G. Harding, promising "return to normalcy," takes office. U.S. agrees to compensate Colombia for supporting Panama revolution and seizing Panama Canal. Former Pres. William Howard Taft receives job he wants most, chief justice of U.S. (June 30). U.S. negotiates separate peace with Germany, Austria, and Hungary. Ku Klux Klan spreads terror in South. International disarmament conference meets in Washington, D.C. Jack Dempsey defeats Georges Carpentier in first million-dollar prize fight.

1922 Washington Conference concludes with nine international treaties to limit naval arms race, relax tensions in Pacific, and protect China. Supreme Court upholds women's suffrage. Lincoln Memorial dedicated in Washington, D.C. (May 30). Pres. Harding vetoes "Bonus Bill" for World War I veterans. Congress passes joint resolution in favor of Jewish homeland in Palestine (Sept. 21). Narcotics Control Board established. First commercial radio show broadcast in New York.

1923 Last U.S. occupation troops leave Germany (Jan. 10). Senate begins investigating corruption in Veterans Bureau and Teapot Dome oil leases (Oct. 25). Pres. Harding dies mysteriously of "apoplexy" in San Francisco (Aug. 2). Pres. Calvin Coolidge's address to Congress, calling for economy in government, first radio broadcast of a presidential speech (Dec. 6). Oklahoma declares martial law to crack down on Ku Klux Klan. Yankee Stadium opens in New York .

1924 Congress provides bonuses for World War I veterans over Pres. Coolidge's veto. Congress passes Immigration Act, imposing strict national quota system. European powers accept Dawes Plan for repayment of war debts and reparations. U.S. Marines withdraw from Santo Domingo. Coast-to-coast airmail service begins. Tornados wreak havoc in Midwest. Ford Motor Co. turns out its 10-millionth automobile.

1925 Tennessee outlaws teaching evolution in school, leading to Scopes Trial in Dayton, Tenn. (July 10–21). Ku Klux Klan marches on Washington, D.C. (Aug. 8) Nellie Tayloe Ross of Wyoming first woman governor. Florida land boom draws hordes of speculators. Col. Billy Mitchell suspended from U.S. Army for advocating stronger air force. Chicago gang wars break out as Al Capone consolidates bootlegging operations.

1926 Sec. of Treasury Andrew Mellon's drastic tax cuts approved. Adm. Richard E. Byrd and Floyd Bennett first to fly over North Pole (May 9). Henry Ford institutes 8-hour day and 5-day work week at Ford Motor Co. factories (Sept. 25). Hurricane sweeps Florida, killing 372 people. Book of the Month Club founded. California evangelist Aimee Semple MacPherson fakes her own kidnapping to draw publicity. U.S. Marines return to Nicaragua.

1927 Charles Lindbergh completes nonstop solo flight from New York to Paris (May 20–21); returns home to huge welcoming crowds. Sacco and Vanzetti executed in Massachusetts, despite international protests (Aug. 23). *The Jazz Singer* with Al Jolson becomes first "talkie" motion picture (Oct. 6). Holland Tunnel in New York opened. Mississippi River floods causes $300-million damage. Ford Model A unveiled. Mechanical cotton picker invented. New York–London commercial telephone service begins.

1928 U.S. joins 14 countries in signing Kellogg-Briand Pact for "outlawry of war" (Aug. 27). Clark Memorandum disavows future U.S. interventions in Latin America. Pres. Coolidge refuses to aid American farmers mired in agricultural depression. Walt Disney creates "Steamboat Willie," first Mickey Mouse cartoon. George Eastman demonstrates color motion-picture technology. Republicans promise a "chicken in every pot, a car in every garage."

1929 St. Valentine's Day Massacre claims six lives in Chicago gang wars. Young Plan replaces Dawes Plan for payment of war debts and reparations. Ramsay MacDonald first prime minister of Great Britain to address Congress (Oct. 7). Albert B. Fall, former secretary of interior, found guilty in Teapot Dome scandal (Oct. 25). Stock market crash on "Black Friday" (Oct. 29) ushers in Great Depression. Supreme Court upholds "pocket veto." Pres. Hoover insists business confidence is intact.

1930 Wave of bank failures sweeps U.S., wiping out millions of savings accounts and leading to private hoarding of gold. Chicago bootlegging outfit worth $50 million broken up. U.S., Britain, and Japan sign London Naval Treaty limiting naval arms race (Apr. 22). Hawley-Smoot Tariff raises barriers to world trade, worsening depression (June 17). Congress creates Veteran's Administration (July 3). Hoover Dam begun near Las Vegas, Nev. The planet Pluto discovered.

1931 World War I veterans offered "Bonus Loans" to combat Great Depression. "Star Spangled Banner" becomes national anthem. "Scottsboro Boys" arrested for rape in Alabama. Empire

State building, tallest building in world, opened in New York City. Pres. Herbert Hoover declares moratorium on international debt and reparations payments. George Washington Bridge over Hudson River completed.

1932 Stimson Doctrine announces U.S. disapproval of Japanese invasion of China. Congress approves Reconstruction Finance Corporation to help recovery. Norris-LaGuardia Act restricts use of injunctions against labor strikes. Franklin D. Roosevelt, promising "New Deal" for Americans, elected president in Democratic landslide. Stock market drops to 10% of its 1929 value; national income cut in half. "Bonus Army" of poor veterans marches on Washington, D.C. Amelia Earhart first woman to fly solo across Atlantic.

1933 Giuseppe Zangara kills Chicago Mayor Anton J. Cermak in Miami, Fla., motorcade, narrowly missing president-elect Franklin D. Roosevelt (Feb. 15). Banks closed for four days by presidential order (Mar. 5). During "Hundred Days" (Mar. 9-June 16), Pres. Roosevelt pushes New Deal through Congress, conducts first "fireside chat" on radio, and takes U.S. off gold standard. Beer and wine made legal again (Mar. 22). Congress passes National Industrial Recovery Act (June 16). U.S. recognizes Soviet Union (Nov. 16). U.S. Marines withdraw from Nicaragua. Frances Perkins, secretary of labor, becomes first woman cabinet member.

1934 Dust storms inundate Southwest, driving "Okies" and "Arkies" to California. General strike paralyzes San Francisco (July 16). John Dillinger, public enemy number one, killed by FBI agents (July 22). Upton Sinclair mounts unsuccessful EPIC (End Poverty in California) campaign for governor. Sen. Gerald P. Nye of North Dakota begins investigating role of U.S. munitions manufacturers in World War I. U.S. releases Cuba from Platt Amendment. U.S. troops withdrawn from Haiti. Roman Catholic Legion of Decency begins censoring motion pictures.

1935 Supreme Court invalidates National Industrial Recovery Act. Pres. Roosevelt pushes more "Second New Deal" legislation through Congress, notably, Wagner Act protecting unions (July 5), Social Security Act (Aug. 14), and "soak-the-rich" Wealth Tax Act (Aug. 30). Sen. Huey P. Long of Louisiana assassinated (Sept. 8). Congress of Industrial Organization (CIO) formed (Nov. 9). Congress passes first Neutrality Act. Alcoholics Anonymous founded.

1936 Congress passes second Neutrality Act. France, Britain, and U.S. sign New London Naval Treaty (Mar. 25). U.S. declares neutrality in Spanish

Civil War (Aug. 7). Congress of Industrial Organizations auto workers begin sit-down strikes in Flint, Mich. (Dec. 30). *Life* magazine begins publishing. William "Liberty Bell" Lemke, Republican of North Dakota, runs for president on Union party ticket endorsed by radio demagogue Father Charles E. Coughlin. Jesse Owens wins four gold medals at "Nazi Olympics" in Berlin.

1937 Congress passes third Neutrality Act. Pres. Roosevelt proposes controversial "court-packing" plan. German dirigible *Hindenburg* explodes and burns in Lakehurst, N.J. (May 6). Pres. Roosevelt angers isolationists with "Quarantine Speech" (Oct. 5). Japanese planes sink U.S. Navy gunboat *Panay* in China (Dec. 12). Golden Gate Bridge completed in San Francisco. Slow recovery ends abruptly as economic depression worsens.

1938 Republican gains in Congress signal end of New Deal. Pres. Roosevelt calls for military buildup (Jan. 28). Mexico seizes U.S.-owned oil wells (Mar. 18). Rep. Martin Dies of Texas begins House Un-American Activities Committee (HUAC) investigations of Communists and Fascists. Howard Hughes sets record for around-the-world flight in less than four days (July 14). "Invasion from Mars" radio broadcast by Orson Welles causes widespread panic (Oct. 30). Hurricane devastates Atlantic Coast, killing 700 people.

1939 Supreme Court upholds Tennessee Valley Authority. First food stamp program begins in Rochester, N.Y. (May 16). Pan Am begins first regular transatlantic passenger service from New York to Lisbon, Portugal (June 28). U.S. declares neutrality in World War II (Sept. 5). Congress passes fourth Neutrality Act, approving Pres. Roosevelt's request for "cash-and-carry" arms sales to belligerents. Nylon stockings appear on market.

1940 As World War II engulfs Europe, Pres. Roosevelt announces U.S. has moved from "neutrality" to "non-belligerency" (June 10). U.S. and Britain conclude Destroyers-for-Bases deal (Sept. 2). Congress enacts a peacetime draft (Sept. 16) and massive increases in military spending. Over 16 million men register for draft as Pres. Roosevelt's embargo on strategic exports takes effect. Roosevelt, reelected to unprecedented third term, calls for U.S. to become "arsenal of democracy" (Dec. 20). Both the Committee to Defend America by Aiding the Allies and the isolationist America First Committee organized.

1941 Congress appropriates $7 billion in Lend-Lease aid to Britain. German submarine sinks merchant ship *Robin Moor*, first U.S. casualty of war (May 21). Roosevelt responds by declaring

"unlimited national emergency" (May 27), freezing German and Italian assets in U.S. (June 14) and promising aid to USSR (June 24). Roosevelt freezes Japanese assets in retaliation for invasion of Indochina (July 25). Pres. Roosevelt and Prime Minister Winston Churchill issue Atlantic Charter (Aug. 12). U.S. Navy is ordered to "shoot on sight" at German warships (Sept. 11). "America has been attacked, the shooting has started," Pres. Roosevelt informs nation (Oct. 27). Japanese planes attack Pearl Harbor, Hawaii, killing 2,400 U.S. servicemen and civilians (Dec. 7). U.S. declares war on Japan (Dec. 10). Germany and Italy declare war on U.S. (Dec. 11). U.S. declares war on Germany and Italy (Dec. 11).

1942 Roosevelt creates War Production Board, calls for mass mobilization, and puts New Deal on hold. U.S. troops land in North Ireland, first to arrive in Europe (Jan. 26). Pres. Roosevelt approves internment of Japanese-Americans for duration of war (Feb. 20). Japanese submarine shells an oil refinery in Santa Barbara, Calif. (Feb. 23). Maj. James H. Doolittle stages carrier-launched bombing raid on Tokyo (Apr. 18). U.S. forces surrender in Philippines (May 6) but win major naval victories over Japan in Coral Sea (May 4–8) and at Midway (June 3–6). U.S. offensive begins in Pacific with invasion of Guadalcanal Island (Aug. 7). First all-U.S. bombing attack launched against German forces at Rouen, France (Aug. 17). Congress approves "Victory Tax" on wartime incomes (Oct. 21). Allies land 400,000 men in North Africa (Nov. 7–8). Eight German saboteurs apprehended in New York; six executed. Cocoanut Grove nightclub fire in Boston claims lives of 492 patrons.

1943 Congress appropriates $100 billion for war effort. Roosevelt and Prime Minister Winston Churchill demand "unconditional surrender" at Casablanca conference in Morocco (Jan. 24). U.S. Marines drive last Japanese from Guadalcanal (Feb. 9). U.S. troops defeated in first battle with Germans at Kasserine Pass, Tunisia (Feb. 20). Pres. Roosevelt declares wage-and-price freeze to stem inflation (Apr. 8). U.S. and Britain invade Sicily (July 10) and Italy proper (Sept. 3). Roosevelt and Churchill meet with Chiang Kai-Shek of China in Cairo, Egypt (Nov. 22), and with Josef Stalin of Soviet Union in Tehran, Iran (Dec. 4–6). Gen. Dwight D. Eisenhower named Supreme Commander of Allied Forces in Europe. Congress approves federal income tax withholding. Race riots in Detroit and Harlem leave 40 dead. Chicago opens its first subway.

1944 U.S. and British planes begin around-the-clock bombing of Berlin. Allied forces land at Anzio, Italy (Jan. 22). Congress approves $1.35 billion for UN Relief and Reconstruction Agency, first U.S. foreign aid (Mar. 29). Allied forces enter Rome (June 5) as reconquest of Europe begins with D-Day invasion of Normandy (June 6). Allied breakout from Normandy sends German forces reeling across France (July 25). Postwar financial arrangements made at international conference in Bretton Woods, N.H. (July 1–22). Plans for UN made at Dumbarton Oaks conference (Aug. 21–Oct. 7). Gen. Douglas MacArthur begins reconquest of Philippines with landings at Leyte Gulf (Oct. 20). Congress passes Servicemen's Readjustment Act, known as "GI Bill of Rights." Roosevelt wins fourth term.

1945 Roosevelt, Churchill, and Stalin meet for last time at Yalta in Soviet Crimea to begin postwar planning (Feb. 4–11). Allied forces cross Rhine River and drive into heart of Germany (Mar. 7). U.S. air raids destroy Tokyo (Mar. 10–11). Pres. Roosevelt dies suddenly of cerebral hemorrhage in Warm Springs, Ga. (Apr. 12). UN Conference begins meeting in San Francisco (Apr. 24). Germany surrenders, ending war in Europe (May 7). Fifty nations sign UN Charter (June 26). First atomic explosion occurs in test at Alamagordo, N. Mex. (July 16). Pres. Harry S Truman meets with Churchill and Stalin at Potsdam, Germany (July 17–Aug. 2). Atomic bombs dropped on Hiroshima (Aug. 6) and Nagasaki (Aug. 9); Japan surrenders (Aug. 14), ending World War II. Council of Allied Foreign Ministers meets in London, unable to agree on peace treaty (Dec. 16–27). Television channels are allotted for commercial use. Empire State building hit by B-25 bomber in heavy fog.

1946 Strike wave sweeps U.S., idling 4.6 million U.S. workers. Congress passes Employment Act, committing federal government to postwar economic management. Winston Churchill warns Americans about Communist expansion with "Iron Curtain" speech at Westminster College in Fulton, Mo. (Mar. 5). Pres. Truman seizes control of railroads and coal mines during strikes. Paris Peace Conference ends in failure (July 29–Oct. 15). U.S. presents Baruch Plan for international control of atomic energy, grants independence to Philippines (July 4), and agrees to loan Britain $3.5 billion for postwar reconstruction. Congress creates Atomic Energy Commission. UN General Assembly begins meeting in New York. John D. Rockefeller, Jr., donates $8.5 million for UN Headquarters. Most wartime wage and price controls lifted. Dr. Benjamin Spock

publishes influential guidebook on baby care.

1947 Council of Foreign Ministers meets in Moscow, again unable to agree on peace treaty (Mar. 10–Apr. 24). Pres. Truman announces Truman Doctrine, promising aid to countries threatened by subversion (May 12). Sec. of State George C. Marshall announces Marshall Plan for postwar reconstruction of Europe (June 5). Republican-dominated Congress restricts union organizing with Taft-Hartley Act. House Committee on Un-American Activities (HUAC) begins investigating communism in Hollywood (Oct. 20). Council of Foreign Ministers meets for last time in London (Nov. 25–Dec. 16). Texas City, Tex., wiped out when munitions ship explodes, killing over 500 people. Jackie Robinson of Brooklyn Dodgers breaks color line in baseball.

1948 Postwar inflation keeps prices rising fast. Congress approves $5.3 billion for Marshall Plan aid to Europe with Foreign Assistance Act. U.S. recognizes new state of Israel (May 14) and admits 205,000 war refugees from Europe. Britain and U.S. begin airlifting supplies into West Berlin after Soviets cut off all traffic into city (June 26). Pres. Truman orders peacetime draft and desegregation of U.S. armed forces. HUAC charges Alger Hiss with spying for Soviet Union. Pres. Truman wins upset reelection victory over Republican candidate Thomas E. Dewey of New York, despite Progressive and Dixiecrat walkouts from Democratic party. Idlewild International Airport, largest in world, opens in New York.

1949 Pres. Truman calls for "Fair Deal" domestic programs and "Point Four" foreign aid programs. U.S., Canada, and 10 Western European nations sign treaty that will lead to North Atlantic Treaty Organization (NATO). Berlin Airlift ends when Soviets finally lift blockade (May 12). State Department issues "white paper" disclaiming responsibility for Communist takeover in China. Pres. Truman announces Soviet atomic bomb test (Sept. 23). Eleven U.S. Communist leaders convicted of conspiring to overthrow government. UN Headquarters on East River dedicated in New York City (Oct. 24). Steel strike idles half a million workers nationwide (Oct. 1–Nov. 11). *Lucky Lady II* of U.S. Air Force completes first nonstop around-the-world flight.

1950 Sen. Joseph R. McCarthy of Wisconsin issues his first accusations of Communists in government at speech in Wheeling, W.Va. North Korea invades South Korea, beginning Korean War (June 25). Pres. Truman orders U.S. intervention (June 27), obtains UN support (July 7), asks Congress for a

$10-billion rearmament program (July 20), and calls up reserves (Aug. 4). Inchon landing begins rout of North Korean invaders (Sept. 15). Congress passes Internal Security Act, requiring registration of Communist organizations, over Pres. Truman's veto (Sept. 23). UN troops recapture Seoul (Sept. 26) and invade North Korea (Oct. 7). Puerto Rican nationalists nearly assassinate Pres. Truman in Washington (Nov. 11). After China intervenes in Korean War, Pres. Truman proclaims national emergency (Dec. 16). U.S. population tops 150 million (150,697,361).

1951 Gen. Dwight D. Eisenhower comes out of retirement to accept command of Allied forces in Europe (Apr. 4). Julius and Ethel Rosenberg sentenced to death for spying (atom bomb secrets) for Soviets (Apr. 5). Pres. Truman removes Gen. Douglas MacArthur from command in Korea for insubordination (Apr. 11). MacArthur returns to U.S., greeted by exultant crowds, to deliver address to Congress. Missouri River floods devastate Kansas City, causing over $1 billion in damages (July 11–25). U.S. concludes a mutual defense pact with Australia and New Zealand and signs a peace treaty with Japan (Sept. 8). Congress passes Mutual Security Act, providing $7 billion for foreign aid and military cooperation with pro-U.S. nations. Sen. Estes Kefauver of Tennessee investigates gambling and organized crime. CBS transmits first color television broadcast from New York.

1952 Pres. Truman seizes steel mills paralyzed by strikes (Apr. 8). U.S., Britain, and France sign peace treaty with West Germany (May 26). GI Bill extended to Korean War veterans. Construction begins on USS *Nautilus*, first atomic submarine. Supreme Court upholds barring subversives from teaching in schools. Sen. Richard M. Nixon of California, Republican candidate for vice president, delivers "Checkers Speech" on national television to explain his "secret slush fund." Republicans win control of White House and both houses of Congress for first time since 1928. Supreme Court rejects appeal of Julius and Ethel Rosenberg. U.S. announces first successful hydrogen bomb test at Eniwetok Atoll in Marshall Islands (Nov. 16). Pres.-elect Dwight D. Eisenhower visits U.S. troops in Korea.

1953 Sen. John W. Bricker of Ohio proposes sharp limits on presidential powers to make treaties. Thirteen more Communist leaders convicted of conspiring to overthrow government. Julius and Ethel Rosenberg executed in Ossining, N.Y. (June 19). Pres. Eisenhower lifts wage and price controls, increases U.S. support for French war effort in

Indochina, negotiates armistice ending Korean War (June 27). Congress creates Department of Health, Education, and Welfare (Apr. 1). U.S. pledges aid to Spain in exchange for military bases (Sept. 26). First "atomic cannon" tested in Nevada. Maj. Chuck Yeager of U.S. Air Force sets new air speed record in rocket-powered X-1 jet plane. *The Robe* first motion picture in CinemaScope.

1954 Sec. of State John Foster Dulles vows "massive retaliation" against Soviet aggression (Jan. 12). Foreign Ministers Conference in Berlin fails to achieve reunification of Germany (Jan. 25-Feb. 18). Puerto Rican nationalists shoot five Congressmen on floor of House of Representatives (Mar. 1). U.S. negotiates the Southeast Asia Treaty Organization (SEATO) security pact (Sept. 8). Army-McCarthy hearings discredit Sen. Joseph McCarthy and his methods. Supreme Court orders school desegregation in *Brown* decision (May 17). CIA helps overthrow Arbenz government in Guatemala (June 29). Congress passes Communist Control Act. Senate censures Sen. McCarthy. France announces that U.S. has paid for most of Indochina war. New York Stock Exchange prices finally reattain 1929 levels.

1955 Pres. Eisenhower promises to use atomic weapons in case of war and conducts first televised press conference. U.S., Soviet Union, and Allies agree on Austrian peace treaty to end occupation. Summit conference of U.S., British, French, and Soviet leaders in Switzerland produces "spirit of Geneva." Supreme Court orders school desegregation to proceed "with all deliberate speed." Pres. Eisenhower hospitalized for three weeks following heart attack. Interstate Commerce Commission orders desegregation on interstate trains and buses. AFL and CIO labor federations merge to form AFL-CIO, with 15 million members (Dec. 5). Dr. Jonas Salk perfects polio vaccine. Civil rights leader Dr. Martin Luther King, Jr., leads bus boycott in Montgomery, Ala.

1956 Pres. Eisenhower refuses to intervene against Soviet invasion of Hungary and exerts pressure on Allies to withdraw from Suez. Congressmen signing Southern Manifesto promise "massive resistance" to school desegregation. Atomic Energy Commission approves commercial nuclear power plants. Congress passes Highway Act, appropriating $32 billion for construction of vast nationwide road system. TWA and United airliners collide in midair and crash in Grand Canyon, killing 128 people (June 30). *Peyton Place* blockbuster best-seller of year. First transatlantic telephone cable begins operating. Albert Woolson, last Union

veteran of Civil War, dies at age 109. American actress Grace Kelly marries Prince Rainier III of Monaco.

1957 Pres. Eisenhower announces Eisenhower Doctrine, promising aid to any Middle Eastern country threatened by communism. McClellan Committee begins investigating corruption and racketeering in International Brotherhood of Teamsters union. Sen. J. Strom Thurmond of South Carolina sets all- time filibuster record (24 hrs., 27 min.) with speech against civil rights (Aug. 30). Congress eventually approves first Civil Rights Act since Reconstruction (Sept. 9). Pres. Eisenhower sends troops to Little Rock, Ark., to enforce federal desegregation order (Sept. 24). First underground atomic test conducted in Nevada (Sept. 19). Sen. John F. Kennedy of Massachusetts wins Pulitzer Prize for *Profiles in Courage.*

1958 In response to Soviet launch of Sputnik, U.S. launches Explorer I, first American satellite; Congress creates National Aeronautics and Space Administration (NASA) and passes National Defense Education Act. Vice Pres. Richard M. Nixon nearly killed by angry mob in Caracas, Venezuela. At request of weak government in Beirut, Pres. Eisenhower orders U.S. Marines to land in Lebanon (July 15). Nuclear submarine *Nautilus* performs first undersea crossing of North Pole (Aug. 5). Presidential assistant Sherman Adams forced to resign in scandal over accepting favors (Sept. 22). Dr. Linus Pauling predicts 5 million birth defects from radioactivity already released into atmosphere by atomic tests.

1959 Fidel Castro's takeover of Cuba begins rapid deterioration of U.S.-Cuba relations (Jan. 1). Alaska becomes 49th state (Jan. 3), and Hawaii 50th (Aug. 21). Joint U.S.-Canada St. Lawrence Seaway project completed. Congress passes Landrum-Griffin Act to suppress racketeering in labor unions. Vice Pres. Nixon holds impromptu "kitchen debate" in Moscow with Soviet Premier Nikita Khrushchev, who later visits U.S. USS *George Washington*, the first U.S. Navy ballistic-missile submarine, launched. Charles Van Doren testifies that his victory on "$64,000 Question" TV game show was fixed. Walter Williams, last surviving Civil War veteran, dies at age 117.

1960 U.S. and Japan conclude new security treaty (Jan. 19). Black students stage first sit-in at Woolworth's lunch counter in Greensboro, N.C. (Feb. 1). U-2 spy plane, with American pilot Francis Gary Powers, shot down over Soviet Union (May 1). Congress passes second Civil Rights Act since Reconstruction. Congress investigates "payola"

in radio industry, leading to arrest of Alan Freed, "father of rock 'n' roll." After Cuba rejects American protests over confiscated property, Pres. Eisenhower imposes trade embargo. John F. Kennedy and Richard M. Nixon hold first televised presidential campaign debates. Kennedy wins by 0.3% of popular vote, closest presidential election since 1884 (Nov. 8).

1961 Pres. Eisenhower breaks diplomatic relations with Cuba, warns Americans to beware of "military-industrial complex." CIA-backed Bay of Pigs invasion fails to overthrow Castro regime in Cuba (Apr. 17). Commander Alan B. Shephard, Jr., U.S. Navy, first American in space on Mercury rocket (May 5). Soviet construction of Berlin Wall creates temporary crisis (Aug. 13). Pres. Kennedy creates Peace Corps and Alliance for Progress. American families advised to build nuclear fallout shelters. "Freedom Rides" civil rights protests broken up by riots in Anniston and Birmingham, Ala. American Medical Association reports link between smoking and heart disease. National Council of Churches endorses birth control for families.

1962 Lt. Col. John H. Glenn, Jr., first American to orbit Earth. Stock market has worst day since 1929 (May 28). Pres. Kennedy convinces steel companies to rescind price increases. U.S. conducts first successful test of sea- launched long-range ballistic missile with nuclear warhead. Pres. Kennedy sends U.S. marshals to protect James H. Meredith, a black student at University of Mississippi. U.S. extends $100-million emergency loan to the UN. Threat of nuclear war during Cuban Missile Crisis averted when Soviet Union agrees to withdraw missiles from Cuba (Oct. 22–28). Rachel Carson's *Silent Spring* draws attention to environmental crisis. U.S. Military Assistance Command set up in South Vietnam.

1963 Pres. Kennedy proposes Medicare program. U.S., Great Britain, and Soviet Union conclude Nuclear Test-Ban Treaty outlawing atmospheric testing (July 25). "Hot line" between Washington and Moscow put in place. Civil rights movement reaches climax with mass demonstrations in Birmingham, Ala., and epic March on Washington, where Martin Luther King delivers his "I Have a Dream" speech (Aug. 28). Pres. Kennedy assassinated in Dallas, Tex., by Lee Harvey Oswald (Nov. 22), who is murdered by Jack Ruby (Nov. 24). Joseph Valachi testifies before Congress about extent of organized crime in U.S. Arnold Palmer first pro golfer to earn over $100,000 in one year.

1964 Pres. Lyndon B. Johnson, taking up Pres. Kennedy's cause, calls for "War on Poverty." Supreme Court orders states to redraw Congressional boundaries to ensure fair representation. Alaska declared disaster area after major earthquake rocks Anchorage (Mar. 28). Mississippi "Freedom Summer" begins with murder of three civil rights workers (June 22). Pres. Johnson pushes landmark Civil Rights and Economic Opportunity acts through Congress. After alleged North Vietnamese attack on U.S. Navy destroyers, Congress passes Tonkin Gulf Resolution, giving Pres. Johnson free hand in Vietnam (Aug. 7). Warren Commission reports there was no conspiracy to assassinate Pres. Kennedy (Sept. 27). Martin Luther King wins Noble Peace Prize. Verrazano Narrows Bridge, the longest suspension bridge in world, opened in New York.

1965 Pres. Johnson calls for "Great Society." Black nationalist Malcolm X assassinated in New York City (Feb. 21). Pres. Johnson orders U.S. Marines into South Vietnam (Mar. 8) and into Santo Domingo (Apr. 38). U.S. troops authorized to undertake offensive operations in South Vietnam (June 8). Martin Luther King leads civil rights marches from Selma to Montgomery, Ala., and in white neighborhoods of Chicago. Congress approves Medicare (July 30) and Voting Rights Act (Aug. 6). Watts Riot in Los Angeles leaves 34 dead and over $200 million in damage (Aug. 11–16), accelerating wave of ghetto riots. Tornadoes sweep Midwest, killing 271 and injuring 5,000. East Coast power blackout affects over 30 million Americans and Canadians (Nov. 9–10).

1966 East Coast blizzard results in 165 deaths (Jan. 29–31). Pres. Johnson orders first B-52 strategic bombing raids on North Vietnam (Apr. 12). Supreme Court rules police must advise suspects of their rights (June 13). Cesar Chavez leads United Farm Workers strike and boycott against California grape growers. Stokeley Carmichael of Student Non-Violent Coordinating Committee demands "Black Power." Congress enacts safety standards for automobiles. Edward W. Brooke of Massachusetts is first black senator since Reconstruction. National Football League and American Football League agree to play Super Bowl championship game. Number of blacks voting in South nearly doubles in one year. U.S. troops in Vietnam increases from 215,000 to over 400,000.

1967 The 500th U.S. plane shot down over North Vietnam (Apr. 4). Hundreds of thousands of antiwar protesters march on Washington (Apr. 15 and Oct. 21–22). Pres. Johnson announces U.S. troop level will reach 525,000 by end of 1968. Worst race riot in U.S. history erupts in Detroit, Mich. (July

23), leaving 43 dead, while riot in Newark, N.J. (July 12), kills another 26. Sen. Eugene McCarthy of Minnesota announces antiwar candidacy for president (Nov. 30). U.S. agrees to refrain from placing nuclear weapons in space and joins General Agreement on Tariffs and Trade (GATT). Albert DeSalvo, the "Boston Strangler," sentenced to life in prison. Stalin's daughter Svetlana Aliluyeva defects to U.S. Thurgood Marshall becomes first black justice on Supreme Court.

1968 North Korea seizes USS *Pueblo*, holding 82 crewmen hostage (Jan. 23). North Vietnam and Viet Cong launch massive Tet Offensive (Jan. 30). Pres. Johnson makes surprise announcement that he will not seek reelection (Mar. 31). Martin Luther King murdered by James Earl Ray in Memphis, Tenn. (Apr. 4). Student protesters take over Columbia University (Apr. 23). Washington-Hanoi peace talks begin in Paris (May 10). After winning California primary, Sen. Robert F. Kennedy of New York murdered by Sirhan Sirhan in Los Angeles (June 5). U.S. signs Nuclear Non-Proliferation Treaty. Democratic Convention in Chicago marred by riots and police violence against antiwar demonstrators. Shirley Chisholm of New York is first black woman elected to Congress. Apollo VIII completes first moon orbit.

1969 Oil spill off Santa Barbara, Calif., draws attention to need for environmental protection (Feb. 5). Pres. Richard Nixon asks Congress to fund Anti-Ballistic Missile program (ABM) as "safeguard" for strategic defense. U.S. losses in Vietnam exceed losses in Korean War. U.S. troop withdrawals from Vietnam begin (July 8). Sen. Edward M. Kennedy of Massachusetts drives off bridge at Chappaquiddick, Mass., killing Mary Jo Kopechne (July 18). After $25 billion spent on U.S. space program, Neil Armstrong and Buzz Aldrin of Apollo XI are first men to walk on moon (July 20). Hurricane Camille claims over 300 victims in South. Trial of Chicago Eight (later Chicago Seven, after Bobby Seale tried separately) begins. Woodstock music festival near Bethel, N.Y., draws 400,000 young fans (Aug. 15–18). Vietnam Moratorium and "March against Death" antiwar demonstrations draw hundreds of thousands to Washington. U.S. and the USSR begin Strategic Arms Limitation Talks (SALT) in Helsinki, Finland.

1970 Pres. Nixon calls for "Vietnamization" to decrease U.S. involvement in war. U.S. bombing of North Vietnam escalates dramatically; nationwide protests break out when U.S. invades Cambodia (Apr. 29). Four students killed and nine wounded by National Guard units at Kent State University

in Ohio (May 4). SALT negotiations reopen in Vienna, Austria. Lt. William L. Calley court-martialed for massacre of 102 civilians in My Lai, South Vietnam (Nov. 12). Supreme Court upholds new 18-year-old voting age (Dec. 21). Congress passes Water Quality Improvement Act, Air Quality Control Act, and Occupational Safety and Health Act. U.S. troops in Vietnam down to 340,000 at year's end. U.S. population tops 200 million (203,235,000).

1971 Pres. Nixon proposes federal revenue sharing with states. Charles Manson and three women followers convicted for Tate-LaBianca murders in Los Angeles (Jan. 25). Major earthquake rocks Southern California, killing 64 and injuring over 1,000 (Feb. 9). U.S. Ping-Pong team visits China, relaxing Cold War tensions. Supreme Court approves of busing to achieve school integration. Indian occupation of Alcatraz Island in San Francisco Bay comes to end. Prison riot in Attica, N.Y., kills 43 inmates and guards. *New York Times* begins publishing "Pentagon Papers," top-secret history of Vietnam War (June 13). U.S. devalues dollar (Dec. 18). U.S. troops in Vietnam reach 139,000; U.S. air attacks are heaviest since 1968. Billie Jean King first woman athlete to earn over $100,000 in one year.

1972 Nixon first president to visit China (Feb. 21–28) and Soviet Union (May 22–30). Airlines begin screening passengers to prevent hijackings. Congress passes Equal Rights Amendment and submits it to states for ratification. Gov. George Wallace of Alabama shot and seriously wounded by Arthur Bremer while campaigning for president in Laurel, Md. (May 15). Five men arrested for breaking into Democratic National Committee headquarters at Watergate complex in Washington, D.C. (June 17). Federal grand jury indicts five burglars and two former White House aides in Watergate trial (Sept. 15). Pres. Nixon angers farmers with "Great Grain Robbery," a secret deal to sell wheat at discount to Soviet Union. National Security adviser Henry Kissinger announces "peace is at hand" in Vietnam in time for Pres. Nixon to carry 49 states in election. U.S. troops in Vietnam fall to 69,000 as Nixon orders resumption of heavy bombing of North Vietnam (Dec. 18).

1973 Supreme Court disallows state restrictions on abortions (*Roe* vs. *Wade*). U.S. signs Paris peace accords ending Vietnam War (Jan. 27). North Vietnam releases U.S. prisoners of war. Trial of Watergate burglars reveals conspiracy to conceal White House involvement. Top presidential aides H.R. Haldeman, John Ehrlichman, John Dean, and

Atty. Gen. Richard Kleindienst resign amid charges of White House cover-up (Apr. 30). Sen. Sam Ervin of North Carolina chairs Senate investigation of Watergate scandal on national television (May 17–Nov. 15). Vice Pres. Spiro Agnew resigns after threat of indictment for tax evasion (Oct. 10). Gasoline prices skyrocket after Arab nations embargo oil exports to U.S. in retaliation for U.S. aid to Israel in Yom Kippur War (Oct. 17). Pres. Nixon fires Watergate Special Prosecutor Archibald Cox and others in "Saturday Night Massacre" (Oct. 20). Pres. Nixon turns over first White House tapes, which include mysterious 18½-minute gap (Nov. 26). Gerald R. Ford of Michigan sworn in as first vice president chosen under 25th Amendment (Dec. 6). Indians defy federal authority in Wounded Knee, S.D.

1974 Arab oil embargo of U.S. lifted (Mar. 18). Pres. Nixon admits owing nearly $500,000 in back taxes (Apr. 3). Supreme Court rules that Pres. Nixon must submit all White House tapes to Special Prosecutor Leon Jaworski (July 24). House Judiciary Committee votes three articles of impeachment (July 24–30). Pres. Nixon releases transcripts of tapes that show he ordered cover-up (Aug. 5). Citing "political" difficulties, Pres. Nixon announces resignation (Aug. 8), elevating Vice Pres. Ford to presidency (Aug. 9). Pres. Ford shocks nation by pardoning Nixon for all crimes he may have committed in office (Sept. 8). Democrats make major gains in midterm elections. Pres. Ford meets with Soviet Premier Leonid Brezhnev in Vladivostock to approve SALT treaty (Nov. 23–24). FBI and CIA efforts to disrupt civil rights and antiwar movements in 1960s revealed. Newspaper heiress Patty Hearst kidnapped in Berkeley, Calif., by radical Symbionese Liberation Army, which extorts $2-million food giveaway for needy.

1975 Nixon aides convicted of obstructing justice in Watergate investigation (Jan. 1). Senate committee chaired by Frank Church begins investigation into illegal CIA and FBI activities. Last Americans evacuate Saigon as South Vietnam falls to North Vietnamese invasion (Apr. 30). Cambodia seizes USS *Mayaguez* (May 12), and Pres. Ford orders rescue operation (May 14). Apollo-Soyuz, joint Soviet-American space mission, achieves linkup in space (July 17). Lynette "Squeaky" Fromme and Sarah Jane Moore attempt to assassinate Pres. Ford in separate California incidents (Sept. 5 and 22). Congress votes to admit women to army, navy, and air force academies. President's Commission on Civil Rights reports southern schools more integrated than northern schools.

Democrats in House of Representatives dismantle seniority system. Church Committee discovers CIA helped overthrow Salvador Allende of Chile and plotted to assassinate Fidel Castro of Cuba.

1976 Congress repeatedly overrides Pres. Ford's vetoes of bills providing for jobs, health, education, and welfare programs. Senate investigators find Lockheed Corp. paid $22 million in bribes to foreign officials. Supreme Court upholds death penalty (July 3). Bicentennial of U.S. celebrated coast to coast. Congressman Wayne Hays of Ohio, chairman of House Ways and Means Committee, resigns over sex scandal. Sec. of Agriculture Earl Butz forced to resign for telling racist joke. Pres. Ford, in campaign debate with Democratic candidate James E. "Jimmy" Carter, insists there is "no Soviet domination of Eastern Europe" (Oct. 7). Justice Department begins probing South Korean bribery of congressmen and other officials. NASA's Viking I and Viking II space probes land on Mars and transmit scientific data, along with color photographs, back to Earth. "Legionnaire's Disease" breaks out at American Legion convention in Philadelphia, eventually claiming 29 victims. Patty Hearst convicted of armed robbery in California. Hundreds of West Point cadets found to have cheated on exams.

1977 Cold winter and heavy snows hit eastern states. Pres. Carter pardons Vietnam War draft evaders, threatens to reduce foreign aid to countries violating human rights, calls for "moral equivalent of war" in energy conservation, and signs Panama Canal treaty (Sept. 7). U.S. declares 200-mi. sovereignty zone in Atlantic and Pacific oceans to exclude foreign fishing vessels. Power blackout sets off arson and looting spree in New York City (July 13–14). Oil begins flowing through Alaska pipeline. Pres. Carter accuses oil industry of "biggest rip-off in history" (Oct. 13). National Women's Conference held in Houston, Tex. Severe drought leads to water rationing on West Coast. ABC's weeklong TV series *Roots,* based on Alex Haley's best-seller about his slave ancestors, draws about 130 million viewers.

1978 Pres. Carter postpones production of neutron bomb. California voters approve Proposition 13, reducing property taxes and setting off nationwide "taxpayers' revolt." Supreme Court gives limited approval to affirmative action programs but disallows quotas for college admissions (June 28). In private talks with Anwar Sadat and Menachem Begin, Pres. Carter mediates peace between Egypt and Israel with landmark Camp David Accords (Sept. 17). Nearly 1,000 American

followers of the Rev. Jim Jones commit mass suicide in Jonestown, Guyana, after cult members murder Congressman Leo Ryan of California and others (Nov. 18). House investigations of John F. Kennedy and Martin Luther King assassinations conclude that conspiracies were probable in both cases (Dec. 30). Congress extends deadline for ratifying Equal Rights Amendment. Federal loan guarantees rescue New York City from financial crisis.

1979 U.S. resumes diplomatic relations with China (Jan 1). Pres. Carter commutes Patty Hearst's sentence, releasing her from jail. Farmers drive thousands of tractors into Washington to dramatize grievances. Worst nuclear accident in U.S. history takes place at Three Mile Island power plant near Harrisburg, Pa., releasing giant clouds of radioactive steam (Mar. 28) Pres. Carter and Premier Brezhnev sign SALT II treaty in Vienna (June 18). Shah of Iran and Anastasio Somoza of Nicaragua, both U.S.-supported dictators, flee revolutions in their countries. Iranian militants seize U.S. embassy in Tehran, taking 66 American hostages and demanding return of shah from U.S. (Nov. 4). Iranians release 13 American hostages, all blacks or women. Pres. Carter deports illegal Iranian students, freezes Iranian assets, and bars oil imports from Iran. Pope John Paul II visits U.S. Inflation reaches highest level in 33 years as Organization of Petroleum Exporting Countries (OPEC) doubles price of oil.

1980 Canadian embassy officials help six Americans escape from Iran (Jan. 29). In response to Soviet invasion of Afghanistan, Pres. Carter embargoes grain and high-tech exports to Soviet Union, approves arms sales to China, and secures U.S. boycott of Olympics in Moscow. Congress grants Pres. Carter's request for Crude Oil Windfall Profits Tax and for resumption of Selective Service draft registration. Pres. Carter's secret rescue mission for American hostages in Iran fails when U.S. Navy helicopter crashes in desert, killing eight servicemen (Apr. 24). Race riot breaks out in Miami, protesting police brutality (May 17). Mt. St. Helens erupts in Washington State, killing 26 people and causing $2.7 billion in damage (May 18). Banking and trucking industries deregulated. FBI's "Abscam" operation implicates over 30 public officials, including a senator and seven congressmen, for accepting bribes. Republicans capture control of Senate for only second time in 50 years.

1981 Minutes after Pres. Ronald Reagan is sworn in, Iran releases 52 American hostages after 444 days in captivity. Pres. Reagan shot by John Hinckley in Washington, D.C. (Mar. 30); undergoes surgery and makes full recovery. *Columbia* completes first successful space shuttle mission (Apr. 12–14). Gov. Jerry Brown of California orders aerial spraying to combat Mediterranean fruit fly. Federal air-traffic controllers go on strike and lose jobs when Pres. Reagan fires all 13,000 of them. Senate votes 99 to 0 to confirm Sandra Day O'Connor as first woman justice of Supreme Court. Pres. Reagan lifts grain embargo against Soviet Union but imposes new sanctions after Poland declares martial law. Congress accepts Pres. Reagan's plans for tax cuts, lower domestic spending, and major defense buildup. U.S. sends military advisers and aid to El Salvador. Professional baseball players stage two-month strike.

1982 Ending 13-year antitrust suit, American Telephone and Telegraph agrees to surrender control of local Bell System phone companies in return for expansion into new business pursuits (Jan. 8). Pres. Reagan calls for "New Federalism," transferring programs to state and local control. Half a million Americans demonstrate in New York City in favor of nuclear freeze (June 12). Congress rejects nuclear freeze (Aug. 5). Democratic gains in midterm elections fail to dislodge Republican control of Senate. U.S. supports Great Britain in Falklands War with Argentina. Professional football players stage 57-day strike. Unemployment exceeds 10% for first time since Great Depression, and federal budget deficit exceeds $100 billion a year for first time ever. After a decade, Equal Rights Amendment fails, falling three states short of ratification.

1983 Inflation slows as oil prices decline sharply. Congress admits internment of Japanese-Americans during World War II was unjust and agrees to bail out Social Security system. National Commission on Excellence in Education reports U.S. is "nation at risk" because of inferior elementary and secondary schools. Sally Ride, aboard space shuttle *Challenger*, is first American woman astronaut. Klaus Barbie, Nazi war criminal, revealed to be living in U.S. with government protection. Pres. Reagan strongly condemns Soviet Union for shooting down Korean airliner with 269 people aboard (Sept. 1). U.S. Marines join multinational peacekeeping force in Beirut, Lebanon, where Muslim terrorists kill 240 of them in suicide bombing (Oct. 23). With several Caribbean nations, U.S. invades Grenada to overthrow Cuban-backed regime (Oct. 25). Pres. Reagan calls for large-scale funding of Strategic Defense Initiative, or "Star Wars."

1984 Reagan recovery under way as unemployment falls, inflation rate declines, economic growth accelerates, and U.S. dollar soars on international markets. Lt. Robert C. Goodman, Jr., U.S. Navy pilot downed over Lebanon during air raid against Muslim positions; freed by Syrian intercession (Jan. 3). Pres. Reagan orders U.S. Marines out of Lebanon (Feb. 7). Congress censures Pres. Reagan for misusing funds to mine Nicaraguan harbors, later condemned by World Court. Pres. Reagan visits China (Apr. 26–May 1). Rep. Geraldine Ferraro, Democrat of New York, first woman to receive major party nomination for vice president. Soviet bloc countries boycott Olympics in Los Angeles. Jesse Jackson, Democrat of Illinois, mounts first major challenge by black candidate for major party nomination. Walter Mondale, Democratic candidate for president, carries only his home state of Minnesota.

1985 Pres. Reagan calls for more tax and budget cuts to sustain economic growth (Feb. 4–6). Despite worldwide protests from Jewish organizations, Pres. Reagan visits West Germany to deliver address at Bitburg cemetery, where Nazi SS troops are buried (May 5). Muslim terrorists hijack TWA airliner (June 14), kill one American hostage, then release rest in Beirut (June 30). Palestinian terrorists kill an American hostage aboard hijacked Italian cruise ship *Achille Lauro* (Oct. 9). Pres. Reagan and Soviet Premier Mikhail Gorbachev hold their first summit meeting in Geneva (Nov. 19–21). Pres. Reagan signs Gramm-Rudman Act, requiring automatic spending cuts if Congress cannot reduce burgeoning federal deficit. Plane crash in Gander, Newfoundland, kills 248 U.S. troops coming home for Christmas (Dec. 12).

1986 Pres. Reagan, blaming Libya for supporting terrorism, freezes Libyan assets in U.S. Space shuttle *Challenger* explodes in midair over Florida, killing six astronauts and civilian passenger (Jan. 28); investigations reveal NASA relaxed safety regulations to speed up launch date. U.S. Navy repels attack by Libyan forces during maneuvers in Gulf of Sidra (Mar. 24). Pres. Reagan blames Libya for death of two Americans in terrorist bombing of West Berlin disco, then orders retaliatory air raids on Tripoli and Benghazi (Apr. 14). Jonathan Jay Pollard found guilty of spying for Israel (June 4). Congress overrides Pres. Reagan's veto of trade sanctions against South Africa (Oct. 2). Second Reagan-Gorbachev summit in Reykjavík, Iceland, reaches impasse over arms control and "Star Wars" (Oct. 12). Congress approves sweeping revision of U.S. tax structure. Democrats regain control of Senate. Pres. Reagan denies trading arms for hostages as Iran-Contra scandal breaks (Nov. 19). Wall Street financier Ivan Boesky fined $100 million for illegal insider-trading on stock market. Acquired immune deficiency syndrome (AIDS) has killed well over 10,000 Americans.

1987 Pres. Reagan submits first trillion-dollar U.S. budget to Congress as national debt mounts steadily. Stock market closes above 2,000 for first time in U.S. history. Tower Commission inquiry into Iran-Contra affair criticizes White House staff and Pres. Reagan's "management style," prompting Chief of Staff Donald Regan to resign. TV evangelist Jim Bakker resigns after admitting his extramarital affair with Jessica Hahn. U.S.–Japan trade war erupts. After Pres. Reagan orders U.S. Navy into Persian Gulf to escort Kuwaiti oil tankers, an Iraqi warplane accidentally attacks USS *Stark*, killing 37 sailors (May 27). Bernhard Goetz acquitted of major charges in New York City "Subway Vigilante" shootings. Congressional hearings on Iran-Contra affair bestow fame on former White House aide Lt. Col. Oliver North. Stock market crashes 508 points in one day, an all-time record, jolting markets around world (Oct. 16). Third Reagan-Gorbachev summit in Washington, D.C. produces agreement to dismantle medium-range missiles in Europe (Dec. 8).

1988 Vice Pres. George Bush denies involvement in Iran-Contra scandal. Congress rejects Pres. Reagan's request for aid to Contras. U.S. pressure on ruler Manuel Noriega to step down plunges Panama into economic turmoil. After Iran lays mines in Persian Gulf, U.S. Navy warships and planes destroy two Iranian oil platforms and repel Iranian counterattacks (Apr. 18–19). Pres. Reagan visits Moscow to meet with Premier Gorbachev (May 29–June 2). In Persian Gulf, USS *Vincennes* accidentally shoots down Iranian passenger plane carrying 290 people (July 3). Atty. Gen. Edwin Meese resigns amid accusations of financial misdealings. *Discovery* completes first space shuttle mission since *Challenger* disaster (Oct. 3). George Bush becomes first sitting vice president elected president since 1836. Almost 1.4 million illegal immigrants, most from Mexico, apply for amnesty under one-time offer from U.S. government. Pentagon procurement scandal reveals "influence peddling" and other irregularities are commonplace. Summer drought afflicts North America, helping to spread fires that destroy 4 million acres of forest. President's Commission on AIDS calls for increased federal spending and curbs on discrimination against AIDS victims, whose numbers exceed 60,000.

Biographies of U.S. Presidents

1. George Washington
(1789–1797)

Born in Westmoreland County, Virginia, on Feb. 22, 1732, the first president, with a love for the land, trained as a surveyor in his teens. At age 16 he went to live with his brother Lawrence, who built Mount Vernon. Lawrence died only four years later, leaving his property to George, who went on to become one of Virginia's foremost landowners, ultimately acquiring more than 100,000 acres in Virginia and what is now West Virginia. In 1753 Washington joined the French and Indian War as an officer in the Virginia militia and fought bravely if poorly. The war provided Washington with the beginnings of his anti-British sentiments, exposing him to the arrogance of his British commanders. Upon returning to plantation life, and marrying Martha Custis, in 1759, Washington's resentment of the British was further fueled by their commercial restrictions. With the passage of the Stamp Act of 1765, Washington joined opposition to imperial rule in the Virginia House of Burgesses, becoming ever more active in resisting the British. He went as a delegate to the Continental Congress, which chose him to command the Continental Army when war with Britain broke out in 1775. Washington proved an uncommonly resourceful general, keeping his ragtag army together through years of defeat, retreat, and hard winters to outlast the British and finally prevail at Yorktown in 1781. Here, as in all his life, Washington earned respect for his judgment, dignity, and bearing. Retiring to Mount Vernon after the war, the general quashed suggestions that he assume military dictatorship of the fledgling republic, not wanting to subvert the very principles for which the Americans had fought. But because of his belief in a strong central government, Washington felt compelled to return to public life to salvage his country from the chaotic Articles of Confederation. In 1787 he presided over the Constitutional Convention in Philadelphia, which framed the presidency with him in mind, the only president ever elected unanimously in the electoral college (twice).

Washington's renowned judgment equaled the task of setting presidential precedent, for, as he wrote, "It is devoutly wished on my part, that these precedents may be fixed on true principles." His first act as president was to urge adoption of the Bill of Rights. Other notable achievements included national unity, quelling the Whiskey Rebellion, bolstering the treasury with a national bank, settling Jay's Treaty of commerce with Britain, and maintaining neutrality in the French Revolution.

Washington successfully implemented executive power and quieted fears and suspicions of executive tyranny. But he regretted the rivalry between Thomas Jefferson and Alexander Hamilton, which led to the birth of political parties in his own cabinet; Washington feared that allegiance to "factions" would someday eclipse the guiding light of patriotism. After refusing a third term in 1796, Washington in his Farewell Address warned against party spirit, sectionalism, and "entangling alliances" with other nations. He died on Dec. 14, 1799, "first in war, first in peace, and first in the hearts of his countrymen," as his friend Henry Lee eulogized him.

2. John Adams
(1797–1801)

A fifth-generation American directly descended from a Mayflower passenger, John Adams was born on Oct. 30, 1735, in Braintree, Massachusetts. At Harvard Adams considered the ministry but turned to law. He joined his cousin Sam Adams as an early opponent of the Stamp Act of 1765, organizing the Sons of Liberty and defending Americans accused of smuggling. Yet he also defended the British soldiers brought to trial for the Boston Massacre in 1770. In the Revolution, Adams persuaded the Continental Congress to commission George Washington as commander in chief, declare independence, and put stars and stripes on the flag. He wrote the Massachusetts state constitution in 1779 and negotiated peace with Britain in 1782. The first vice president, Adams called that position the "most insignificant office that ever the invention of man contrived or his imagination conceived."

Elected president as a Federalist in 1796, Adams retained Washington's cabinet, but Alexander Hamilton turned the party against him for refusing to make war on France. Adams built up the navy and kept the peace, but disaffecting the Federalists and signing the Alien and Sedition Acts (1798) politically weakened "His Rotundity." Adams lost the 1800 election to the increasingly popular Thomas Jefferson. The first president to reside in the White House, Adams lived to be 90, able to see his son John Quincy Adams elected the sixth president in 1824. John Adams died on the same day that Thomas Jefferson did: July 4, 1826, the 50th anniversary of the Declaration of Independence they both signed.

3. Thomas Jefferson
(1801–1809)

Thomas Jefferson was born on Apr. 13, 1743, in Albemarle County, Virginia, son of a self-made Virginian who died when Jefferson was 14. Jefferson graduated from William and Mary in 1762, began practicing law in 1767, and joined the Virginia House of Burgesses in 1769. With his pen Jefferson sharply criticized British rule, winning a place on Virginia's Committee of Correspondence to keep in touch with patriots in other colonies. His writings amassed great respect, earning him the right, as a delegate to the Continental Congress in 1776, to draft the Declaration of Independence. He then returned to Virginia as wartime governor, narrowly escaping capture when British

troops destroyed his home. Congress sent Jefferson to Europe in 1784; he was minister to France during the Constitutional Convention and the early French Revolution, an event that affected him profoundly. As secretary of state under Washington, Jefferson's faith in democracy and states' rights clashed repeatedly with Alexander Hamilton's pursuit of central executive power. Jefferson resigned in 1793 and led opposition to the Federalists, whom Jefferson called "monarchists in principle." As vice president after 1796, Jefferson speeded the Federalists' downfall by secretly authoring the Kentucky Resolutions, critical of the Alien and Sedition Acts.

The House of Representatives chose Jefferson (ironically, with Hamilton's support) over Aaron Burr, whose electoral votes for president equaled his in 1800. "We are all Republicans—we are all Federalists," appealed Jefferson in his inaugural address, easing the transfer of power. In his first term, Jefferson slashed the budget, lowered taxes, reduced the national debt, and sent marines to fight Barbary pirates. Despite some concern over his constitutional authority to make the acquisition, Jefferson's greatest feat was the Louisiana Purchase from France in 1803, which doubled the size of the United States. "The less said about the constitutional difficulties, the better," wrote Jefferson, sending Lewis and Clark to explore the new lands. In his second term, Jefferson's unpopular Embargo Act (1807) was an attempt to avoid war with Britain or France, but it ruined American merchants. Retiring to Monticello in 1809, Jefferson busied himself with inventions and designing the University of Virginia. He died on the 50th anniversary of the Declaration of Independence, July 4, 1826. His amazingly broad interests spanned music, science, architecture, agronomy, and the classics, as well as politics and government.

4. James Madison
(1809–1817)

James Madison was born to a wealthy family on Mar. 16, 1751, in Port Conway, Virginia. A Princeton graduate, Madison attended the first Virginia state convention in 1776, drafting a bill that guaranteed religious liberty. As the youngest member of the Continental Congress in 1780, he led the movement to revise the Articles of Confederation. At the Constitutional Convention in Philadelphia in 1787, Madison's Virginia Plan became the pivot of discussion. Madison, dubbed the Father of the Constitution, tirelessly directed debate and applied his political wisdom. His voluminous notes provide the best record of the convention. Madison helped ratify the Constitution by coauthoring The Federalist (1787–88) with John Jay and Alexander Hamilton. A four-term congressman, Madison drafted the Bill of Rights and cofounded the Democratic-Republican party. In 1794 he married a young and ebullient widow, Dolley Payne Todd, an especially popular first lady. Madison led the opposition to the Federalists' Alien and Sedition Acts with the Virginia Resolutions, arguing the acts were unconstitutional attacks on liberty. Jefferson chose Madison as his secretary of state and later as his successor. Madison easily won the election of 1808. Britain and France preyed on American shipping throughout Madison's first term. Pushed by war hawks in Congress, Madison asked for a declaration of war to defend American rights against British outrages. Reelected despite numerous American defeats in the War of 1812, Madison barely escaped Washington as the British burned the White House. Yet he persisted in "Mr. Madison's War" until the Peace of Ghent (1814) and belated victory at New Orleans (1815) vindicated him. War expenses forced Madison to recharter the national bank and raise the tariff, contrary to his Jeffersonian principles. But by 1817 Madison could retire confident of secure independence, surging nationalism, and the total collapse of his Federalist opponents who had opposed the war. He died on June 28, 1836, having outlived all the founding fathers. Madison's presidency pales beside his greatest contributions—the Constitution and the Bill of Rights.

5. James Monroe
(1817–1825)

The last Revolutionary hero and member of the "Virginia Dynasty" to become president, James Monroe was born on Apr. 28, 1758, in Westmoreland County, Virginia. He left the College of William and Mary to answer the call to arms in 1775. Wounded at Trenton, Monroe fought courageously and rose to lieutenant colonel under Gen. Washington. He learned law as an aide to Thomas Jefferson, who helped Monroe into Congress and the Senate. Much diplomatic experience followed Monroe's appointment as minister to France in 1794. Governor of Virginia from 1799 to 1802, Monroe returned to Europe to negotiate the Louisiana Purchase and later served in Britain and Spain. James Madison appointed him secretary of state in 1811 and secretary of war in 1814. Chosen to succeed Madison, Monroe won the 1816 election and presided over the Era of Good Feeling, a period marked by minimal sectional or partisan discord. Monroe bought Florida from Spain in 1819, and his popularity survived the Panic of 1819 as well as rancorous debates over the admission of Missouri as a slave state. Monroe toured the nation to jubilant crowds, winning reelection with all but one electoral vote in 1820. John Quincy Adams, his secretary of state, suggested Monroe proclaim American opposition to European encroachment in the Western Hemisphere, which he did in 1823; decades later this became known as the Monroe Doctrine. After retiring, Monroe became a regent of the University of Virginia (1826) and a member of the Virginia constitutional convention of 1829. Because of lack of attention over the years, his private affairs had suffered greatly, and Monroe discovered he was lapsing into bankruptcy. He sold his plantation and died all but penniless on Independence Day, July 4, 1831.

6. John Quincy Adams
(1825–1829)

The only president's son to become president, John Quincy Adams was born on July 11, 1767, in Braintree, Massachusetts. A true child of the Revolution, Adams watched the Battle of Bunker Hill while holding his mother's hand, and he spent his teens in Europe with his father, John Adams, on diplomatic missions for the new nation. He entered Harvard in 1785, already an experienced diplomat fluent in seven languages. After a brief career as a Boston lawyer, Adams was minister to Holland in 1794 and to Prussia in 1797. As a Federalist, Adams was elected to the Senate in 1803, but after supporting Thomas Jefferson, he had to resign. James Madison made Adams minister to Russia in 1809, in time to witness Napoleon's invasion. Then Adams helped negotiate the Peace of Ghent (1814) before serving as ambassador to England, the second of three Adams generations to hold that post. James Monroe recalled Adams from Europe—where he had spent most of his life—to appoint him secretary of state in 1817, and in that post, Adams purchased Florida from Spain, patched relations with Britain, and conceived the Monroe Doctrine.

Running for president in 1824, Adams was beaten by Andrew Jackson in both popular and electoral votes; but with Henry Clay's support, the House of Representatives made Adams president. No one ever became president with less than Adams's 31.9 percent of the vote, yet he refused to conciliate his foes or even act like a politician. Adams posed above politics and made no effort to deal with Congress or use patronage. Consequently, elaborate plans for internal improvements and national academies came to naught. Adams, like his father, could not win a second term, as Jackson gained revenge at the polls in 1828. Massachusetts rescued Adams from despair by sending him to Congress in 1830, and "Old Man Eloquent" remained a powerful antislavery leader until he collapsed on the floor of the House at age 80; he died in the Speaker's Room on Feb. 23, 1848. John Quincy Adams, who considered himself a failure as president, worked for the first 11 presidents and numbers among the most important architects of early American foreign policy.

7. Andrew Jackson
(1829–1837)

Born to Scotch-Irish immigrants in Waxhaw, South Carolina, on Mar. 15, 1767, Andrew Jackson was the first first-generation American to become president, as well as the first president from the western frontier and the first of seven to be born in a log cabin. Orphaned at 15, he was by then already a revolutionary veteran, a former prisoner of war, and scarred by the saber of a British officer whose boots he refused to clean. Jackson read law and made his way to the Tennessee frontier, marrying Rachel Donelson Robards in 1791. She neglected to divorce her first husband, but Jackson challenged to a duel anyone who questioned his marriage, once even killing a man on the field of honor. Jackson's frontier law practice prospered, and Tennessee elected him its first congressman in 1796. He served only briefly in the Senate; Washington so disgusted the rough-hewn Jackson that he resigned. Back in Tennessee, Jackson became a respected judge and honorary major general of the militia. In the War of 1812, Jackson led troops to victory at the Battle of New Orleans (1815), his men routing British invaders twice their number.

"Old Hickory" was now a national icon, reentering the Senate in 1823 and running for president as a hero above party. Jackson won more popular and electoral votes than anyone in 1824 but lost when the election was thrown into the House and Henry Clay supported John Quincy Adams. Vowing revenge against the politicians, Jackson swept to victory in 1828 as the "people's choice" reform candidate. Jackson's wife died on the eve of his inauguration. As president, Jackson aggrandized the power of his office on behalf of the common man by expanding suffrage, rotating officeholders (the "spoils system"), and economizing in government. Under Jackson the federal government completely paid off the national debt. Jackson vetoed federal road-building and banking—yet he asserted federal authority by ordering troops to South Carolina in the Nullification Crisis of 1832–33. The Whig party arose in opposition to "King Andrew I," especially to his high-handed veto of the national bank, but voters endorsed Jackson's war on privilege by reelecting him in 1832. In his second term, Jackson seized land from the Native Americans, ignoring the Supreme Court, and he recognized Texas in hopes of taking more land from Mexico. He became the first president to ride a train (1833) and to survive an assassination attempt (1835). After placing his friend Martin Van Buren in the White House, Jackson retired to the Hermitage, his plantation in Tennessee. He remained quite influential behind the scenes, persuading the Democrats to discard Van Buren and nominate James K. Polk in 1844. Andrew Jackson finally succumbed to dropsy and old wounds on June 8, 1845.

8. Martin Van Buren
(1837–1841)

The first president to have played no part in the Revolution, Martin Van Buren was born to a Dutch family in Kinderhook, New York, on Dec. 5, 1782. Apprenticed to a lawyer at 14, Van Buren took to law and politics—so well, in fact, that he came to be called the Little Magician. By 1821 staunch party loyalty elevated him to the Senate, where Van Buren led northern supporters of Andrew Jackson and guided his victory in 1828. Brief service as New York governor ended when Jackson appointed him secretary of state in 1829. Van Buren helped build the Democratic party, and Jackson made him vice president in 1832. As Jackson's heir apparent, Van Buren won the 1836 election, but two months after he took office, the Panic of 1837 launched a severe depression that spoiled his presidency. "Martin Van Ruin" responded by creating the independent treasury system, but his lack of popularity was beyond repair. He made enemies in the North by protecting slavery and in the South by refusing to annex Texas. Though the self-made son of an innkeeper, Van Buren was cast by his opponents as an aristocrat; William Henry

Harrison's "Hard Cider" campaign of 1840 (touting that Van Buren sipped champagne while Harrison preferred hard cider) washed him out of office. In 1844 Van Buren lost the Democratic nomination when Jackson abandoned him over the Texas issue. But in 1848 Van Buren guaranteed a Democratic defeat by founding the Free Soil party and running for president, which split the decisive New York vote. Van Buren died a Unionist on July 24, 1862, the only president whose life touched both the Revolution and the Civil War.

9. William Henry Harrison
(1841)

Son of a signatory of the Declaration of Independence and grandfather of a president, William Henry Harrison was born in Charles City County, Virginia, on Feb. 9, 1773. Campaign legend held that his birthplace was a log cabin, but in fact it was a plantation mansion. Harrison left medical school to join the army and fight Native Americans in the Northwest in 1791. After an illustrious military career, he served in Congress (1816–19), the U.S. Senate (1825–28), and as ambassador to Colombia (1828–29) before falling victim to Andrew Jackson's spoils system. Harrison fit Whig designs of defeating Jacksonians with a war hero of their own and received the Whig nomination to face Martin Van Buren in 1840. Harrison's campaign sidestepped issues to cast him as a plain frontiersman who guzzled hard cider while Van Buren sipped champagne. In the first modern election full of hoopla and hype, "Tippecanoe and Tyler Too"—the Whig slogan—linked Harrison's most famous victory with his obscure running mate. A huge turnout gave Harrison the victory at age 67, the oldest president before Ronald Reagan. Harrison delivered a record 8,500-word inaugural address hatless and coatless on a drizzly winter day. He caught a cold that never left and succumbed to pneumonia on Apr, 4, 1841, the first president to die in the White House—where he lived for only 31 days. His grandson, Benjamin Harrison, was the 23d president.

10. John Tyler
(1841–1845)

The first vice president to become president by succession, the first president to see impeachment proposed against him, and the only president to change parties in office, John Tyler was born on Mar. 29, 1790, in Charles City County, Virginia. He was a Virginia legislator, congressman, senator, and governor before the Whigs chose him as William Henry Harrison's running mate in 1840. Though a strict constructionist and states' rights advocate, Tyler earned the Whigs' favor by opposing Andrew Jackson. But as president after Harrison's death, "His Accidency" earned their ire by vetoing, in mid-1842, two tariff bills vital to the Whig party. Eventually, his cabinet resigned and his party expelled him. Outraged members of Congress called for his impeachment. On July 10, 1842, John Minor Botts, a Whig representative from Richmond, Virginia, proposed the appointment of a special committee to investigate Tyler's conduct in office with an eye toward impeachment. The

proposal was defeated on Jan. 10, 1843, by a vote of 127 to 83. This was the first time presidential impeachment proceedings were introduced in Congress. Tyler concluded the Webster-Ashburton Treaty (1842), which adjusted the northeastern boundary of the United States, and the Texas annexation (1845), but without popular or partisan support, he was powerless and decided against running for reelection. A veto on his last day in office became the first ever to be overridden. Tyler died on Jan. 18, 1862, awaiting his seat in the Confederate Congress.

11. James Knox Polk
(1845–1849)

The first dark-horse president, James Knox Polk was born in Mecklenburg County, North Carolina, on Nov. 2, 1795. A star orator in Tennessee politics, Polk idolized Andrew Jackson. "Young Hickory" took Jackson's old seat in Congress in 1825 and was reelected seven times. Polk was speaker of the house from 1835 to 1839 and governor of Tennessee until 1841. He lost two bids for reelection, and his political career seemed over when the Democrats nominated him for president in 1844. Polk's name had not even appeared on the first seven ballots, but the deadlocked convention latched onto Polk as a proexpansion dark horse. In the election he defeated Henry Clay by 1.5 percent of the vote on a platform that ignored slavery. From his inaugural address onward, Polk pursued expansion in the West. In 1846, he bluffed the British into believing the United States would go to war over Oregon, extracting a treaty for it. When Mexico attacked U.S. troops in disputed Texas territory, Polk called it an invasion and got a declaration of war. The ensuing Mexican War (1846–48) won California and the Southwest for the United States in the Treaty of Guadalupe-Hidalgo. Polk declined a second term, having fulfilled the nation's "Manifest Destiny" to span the continent. The last strong president before Abraham Lincoln, Polk added a million square miles to the United States. But the issue of slavery in the new territories split the Democrats and soon the whole country. "The presidency is not a bed of roses," complained Polk, who left the White House totally exhausted and died three months later, on June 15, 1849.

12. Zachary Taylor
(1849–1850)

Zachary Taylor, the first president to have no previous political experience, was born on Nov. 24, 1784, in Montebello, Virginia. His father was a colonel in the Revolutionary War, and Taylor—along with four brothers—served as a professional soldier for nearly 40 years. After distinguished service against the British and Native Americans, Gen. Taylor's finest hour came during the Mexican War, when he captured Monterrey and smashed Gen. Santa Ana's much larger army at the Battle of Buena Vista (1847). Though Taylor had never held office or even voted, the Whigs eagerly nominated "Old Rough and Ready" for president in 1848; Taylor, like William Henry Harrison, was an apolitical war hero above the slavery

controversy. He won the election when the new Free Soil party siphoned off Democratic votes, but Taylor took office with Congress in chaos over the admission of California as a free state. Taylor opposed the Compromise of 1850 and probably would have vetoed it, but he died suddenly of acute indigestion on July 9, 1850. (A long, hot Fourth of July at Washington Monument ceremonies had no doubt contributed to his weakened state.) Backers of the compromise rejoiced that Taylor's death saved the Union. Taylor was both the last of eight slave owners and the last Whig to be elected president.

13. Millard Fillmore
(1850–1853)

Born in a log cabin on Jan. 7, 1800, Millard Fillmore was the son of a poor farmer in Locke Township, New York. Apprenticed to a cloth maker in his youth, Fillmore struggled for an education and got a job teaching even though he never attended college. Clerking for a judge taught Fillmore enough law to join the bar at age 23, allowing him to become a prosperous New York attorney. Fillmore entered politics as an Anti-Mason and was a four-term congressman when the Whigs made him Zachary Taylor's vice president in 1848. Dignified good looks were Fillmore's main political asset; he was quite unprepared for the presidency when Taylor died suddenly in 1850. Fillmore delayed civil war another decade by signing the Compromise of 1850, but he lost the nomination in 1852 when the Whigs turned to Gen. Winfield Scott, yet another genial war hero and their last candidate. In 1856 Fillmore ran again for president as candidate of the American, or "Know-Nothing," party. Fillmore hoped to unite the country behind anti-Catholicism and nativism, submerging the slavery issue, but he carried only Maryland. Though a Unionist in the Civil War, Fillmore denounced Abraham Lincoln and remained sharply critical of Republicans until his death on Mar. 8, 1874.

14. Franklin Pierce
(1853–1857)

Son of a Revolutionary War hero, Franklin Pierce was born in Hillsboro, New Hampshire, on Nov. 23, 1804—the first president born in the 19th century. A leader of Jacksonian Democrats in Congress in the 1830s, Pierce had been absent from national politics for a decade when the deadlocked Democratic convention nominated him for president on the 49th ballot in 1852. A dark horse candidate, Pierce won enough southern votes to defeat Gen. Winfield Scott, his Mexican War commander, becoming the youngest president as of that date. Pierce greatly hastened the coming of the Civil War by signing the Kansas-Nebraska Act (1854), which repealed the Missouri Compromise and reopened the dangerous issue of slavery expansion. He continually appeased the South by backing proslavery ruffians in "Bleeding Kansas," encouraging slavery expansionists who coveted Cuba, and buying the land known as the Gadsden Purchase from Mexico for a southern railroad. As a result Pierce's party lost elections to Republicans who charged that "slave power" controlled the White House. In

1856 Pierce became the only elected president to be denied his own party's renomination. During the Civil War, Pierce criticized the Emancipation Proclamation and was nearly lynched by angry New Englanders. He died a forgotten, depressed alcoholic, in Concord, New Hampshire, on Oct. 8, 1869, the only president from New Hampshire.

15. James Buchanan
(1857–1861)

Considered one of the worst presidents because of his lack of good judgment and moral courage, and also the only bachelor president, James Buchanan was born in Mercersburg, Pennsylvania, on Apr. 23, 1791. A lawyer and veteran of the War of 1812, Buchanan compiled more than 40 years of public service as legislator and diplomat. The Democrats nominated Buchanan in 1856 largely because he was in England during the Kansas-Nebraska debate and thus remained untainted by either side of the issue. Millard Fillmore's "Know-Nothing" candidacy helped Buchanan defeat John C. Frémont, the first Republican candidate for president. Buchanan favored "popular sovereignty" over slavery in the territories and was the last of the Doughfaces, or northern politicians submissive to the South. Few Americans shared Buchanan's faith that the Supreme Court's *Dred Scott* decision (1857) would end conflict over slavery expansion "speedily and finally." When it did not, Buchanan tried to close the issue himself by urging that Kansas be admitted as a slave state—an even worse miscalculation. Democrats deserted him, and Republicans won the House in 1858, but Buchanan's vetoes and southern votes in the Senate stalemated the government. He inadvertently helped Abraham Lincoln win in 1860 by refusing to conciliate his own party. The secession crisis paralyzed Buchanan, who denied both the southern right to secede and the federal government's right to do anything about it; he was relieved to hand Lincoln the reins. Buchanan died on June 1, 1868. On the day before, he predicted that "history will vindicate my memory," but historians continue mainly to denigrate him.

16. Abraham Lincoln
(1861–1865)

A largely unpopular president until he was assassinated (the first assassinated president), Abraham Lincoln was born in a log cabin in Hodgenville, Kentucky, on Feb. 12, 1809. He accumulated barely a year's total education while growing up, though he did learn to write and developed a fondness for reading. Family moves took him to Indiana and then to Illinois by the time he was 21. At age 19 Lincoln had worked his way down the Mississippi and came away appalled at slavery. He served in the Black Hawk War (1832) before losing an election for the state legislature. A failed storekeeper, Lincoln worked odd jobs while he taught himself law, sometimes walking 20 miles to borrow books. He finally made the state legislature in 1834 as a Whig, and in 1842 married Mary Todd, having canceled their engagement once previously.

Elected to Congress in 1846, Lincoln denounced James K. Polk for precipitating the Mexican War. He returned to his Springfield, Illinois, law practice after only one term. But the repeal of the Missouri Compromise shocked Lincoln back into politics, and he helped organize the Illinois Republicans. An unsuccessful candidate for the Senate in 1858, Lincoln drew national attention in debates with Stephen A. Douglas, the nation's leading Democrat. Lincoln was rewarded with his party's nomination for president in 1860, the least objectionable candidate among several more prominent Republicans. He defeated three opponents in the election, though his name did not even appear on the ballot in the South. As Southern states left the Union, Lincoln preached conciliation and promised no harm to slavery—but he vowed to crush secession and forced the issue at Ft. Sumter. After early reverses in the Civil War, Lincoln decided slavery had to be abolished altogether to restore the Union, and he issued the Emancipation Proclamation (1862). Lincoln's management of the war was thwarted by incompetent generals, feuding politicians, and his own inexperience, which matched that of his troops. Yet, like them, Lincoln learned on the job, settling on Ulysses S. Grant as his top general by 1864. The powers of the presidency expanded dramatically under Lincoln, who stretched the Constitution on behalf of the war effort. Lincoln defeated Gen. George McClellan for reelection in 1864, vowing to "bind up the nation's wounds." Before he had the chance, Lincoln was shot on Good Friday, five days after the war's end, by John Wilkes Booth, an arch-Confederate. Lincoln died the next morning, on Apr. 15, 1865. His martyrdom spurred the vengefulness of Reconstruction, ironically against Lincoln's own wishes. Millions of Americans lined the 1,700-mile route of Lincoln's funeral train, their mournful cries resounding all the way back to Illinois. Lincoln's prestige has grown with time, until many have come to regard him as the greatest president.

17. Andrew Johnson
(1865–1869)

The only president ever impeached, Andrew Johnson was born in Raleigh, North Carolina, on Dec. 29, 1808, the son of a poor laborer. No president could claim humbler origins: Johnson's father died when he was three, his mother worked as a washerwoman, and he never attended a day of school in his life. As a teenager he ran away to Tennessee, opened a successful tailor's shop, and got elected mayor of Greeneville by age 21. A fiery Democratic stump speaker, Johnson's attacks on Whigs and rich planters won him a seat in the state legislature in 1835 and in Congress in 1843, made him governor in 1853, and took him to the Senate in 1857. Alone among 22 Southern senators, Johnson stayed loyal to the Union in 1861, though a mob of Virginians nearly lynched him for it. Lincoln appointed Johnson military governor of Tennessee, and he was nominated for vice president on the "National Union" ticket in 1864. Suddenly made president by Lincoln's assassination, Johnson

vowed to carry on Lincoln's policy of leniency toward the South, but radical Republican opposition and his own coarse ineptitude led to serious clashes with Congress. Johnson vetoed 29 bills and was overridden 15 times, more than any other president to that time. A former slave owner, Johnson resisted Republican efforts to aid the freedmen. His only victory was the unpopular purchase of Alaska in 1867. Congress systematically stripped him of power until Johnson fought back by removing his disloyal secretary of war, Edwin M. Stanton. Impeached in the House for defying the Tenure of Office Act, Johnson was tried in the Senate and acquitted by a single vote on May 26, 1868. Few presidents were so stymied in office. Tennessee helped vindicate Johnson by making him the only former president elected to the Senate, but he died a few months later, on July 31, 1875.

18. Ulysses S. Grant
(1869–1877)

A better general than president, Ulysses Simpson Grant was born in Point Pleasant, Ohio, on Apr. 27, 1822. Having barely passed West Point's height requirement for entrance, Grant attended the academy and graduated in the middle of his class in 1843. Fifty of Grant's classmates fought with or against him as Civil War generals. He served under Gen. Zachary Taylor in the Mexican War before marrying his sweetheart, Julia Dent, in 1848. Assigned to isolated posts after 1852, Grant grew bored away from his family and reportedly turned to heavy drinking. Finally resigning from the army in 1854, he went to Missouri, only to fail in farming and real estate. When the Civil War began, Grant was working in his younger brother's leather shop in Galena, Illinois. He received a commission and rose rapidly to brigadier general. U.S. Grant acquired the nickname Unconditional Surrender for his string of western victories, notably at Vicksburg and Chattanooga in 1863. Once Abraham Lincoln made him supreme commander in 1864, Grant opened a relentless offensive that quickly ended the war. He personally accepted Gen. Robert E. Lee's surrender at Appomattox in 1865. After feuding with Andrew Johnson, Grant joined the Republicans and was elected president in 1868. Grant pressed radical Reconstruction in the South with mixed results. Corruption—notably the Jay Gould (1869), Crédit Mobilier (1872), and Whiskey Ring (1875) scandals—marred Grant's presidency; nevertheless, he easily won reelection in 1872. The Panic of 1873 triggered a deep economic depression that dissuaded Grant from a third term in 1876. Reconsidering in 1880, he sought the Republican nomination again and nearly succeeded. Afterward Grant retired and went bankrupt. To provide for his family, he began writing his memoirs. Developing cancer, Grant valiantly hung on to finish the project, which would earn him some literary fame and his family half a million dollars. He died on July 23, 1885, just four days after completing his autobiography.

19. Rutherford B. Hayes
(1877–1881)

Rutherford Birchard Hayes was born a frail child on Oct. 4, 1822, in Delaware, Ohio, where he was raised by his mother. After attending Harvard Law School, he set up a successful Cincinnati law practice in 1849. Hayes defended fugitive slaves and helped found the Ohio Republicans. In 1852 he married Lucy Ware Webb, the first college graduate First Lady. A decorated Civil War veteran, Hayes was wounded five times and promoted to general. From 1868–76 he served as governor of Ohio. Republicans turned to Hayes as a scandal-free hero in 1876 and nominated him for president. He lost the election to Samuel Tilden of the Democrats, but Republicans in Congress disputed enough state vote totals to connive "Rutherfraud" into office with the support of southern Democrats. Hayes's first acts were to appoint an ex-Confederate to his cabinet and to withdraw federal troops from the South. He never overcame the resulting stigma of political bargain, and facing a Democratic Congress, Hayes seemed destined for a weak presidency. Yet he put the nation back on the gold standard, put down railroad strikes, reformed the civil service, and banished liquor from the White House before keeping his promise to serve only one term. Hayes viewed the return of prosperity and Republican majorities in Congress as personal triumphs. He worked quietly for charitable causes until his death on Jan. 17, 1893.

20. James A. Garfield
(1881)

The last log cabin president, James Abram Garfield was born near Orange, Ohio, on Nov. 19, 1831, and like Rutherford B. Hayes, Garfield was raised by his mother. Garfield graduated from Williams College in 1856, became a classics professor, president of Hiram College, a lawyer, and at age 30 the youngest Union general in the Civil War. Garfield left the battlefield in 1864 to enter Congress, where he remained until the Republicans nominated him for president in 1880, a dark-horse compromise between Grant and James G. Blaine. Garfield defeated Gen. Winfield Scott Hancock of the Democrats by 0.1 percent of the vote in a campaign stressing tariffs. Republicans immediately swarmed to Garfield, demanding patronage for their rival "Stalwart" and "Half-Breed" factions. After only four months in office, Garfield was shot in a train station by Charles J. Guiteau, a disappointed Stalwart office-seeker. Garfield died 80 days later, on Sept. 19, 1881, the second presidential assassination ending the second-shortest presidency. When hordes of Republican hopefuls had besieged the White House begging for jobs, Garfield had exclaimed: "My God! What is there in this place that a man should ever want to get in it?"

21. Chester A. Arthur
(1881–1885)

The only president never elected to any office, including the presidency, Chester Alan Arthur was born a preacher's son on Oct. 5, 1829, in Fairfield, Vermont. He grew up in Vermont and in New York to become an ardent abolitionist like his father. A true machine politician, Arthur worked for Republican candidates in New York and enjoyed several patronage jobs during the Civil War. Ulysses S. Grant appointed him collector of the port of New York in 1871, and Arthur prospered there until 1879, when Rutherford B. Hayes removed him in the name of reform. In 1880 "Half-Breed" Republicans nominated Arthur for vice president in a conciliatory gesture to his "Stalwart" faction. "The office of Vice President is a greater honor than I ever dreamed of attaining," he said. But Arthur acceded to the presidency on Sept. 19, 1881, when another Stalwart assassinated James A. Garfield. Perhaps shamed into supporting civil service reform, Arthur signed the Pendleton Act (1883) and rooted out post office graft. Democrats in Congress thwarted the rest of Arthur's initiatives; Republicans, whose calls for spoils Arthur ignored, denied him renomination in 1884. He lost a Senate race in New York and died two years later, on Nov. 18, 1886. Arthur was the last of three presidents in the single year 1881.

22., 24. Grover Cleveland
(1885–1889; 1893–1897)

The only president to serve two nonconsecutive terms, Stephen Grover Cleveland was a minister's son, born in Caldwell, New Jersey, on Mar. 18, 1837. The family moved to New York, where Cleveland's uncle made him a lawyer. He showed scant interest in politics until Buffalo elected him mayor in 1881, and the next year Cleveland became governor. His war on corrupt Tammany Hall made Cleveland the perfect Democratic reform candidate for president in 1884. During the election campaign, backers of James G. Blaine, the Republican candidate, accused Cleveland of fathering an illegitimate child. He admitted it and won anyway—by 0.3 percent of the vote—but not before the Republicans came up with the immortal campaign chant "Ma! Ma! Where's my Pa?/Gone to the White House,/Ha! Ha! Ha!" The first Democratic president after the Civil War, Cleveland pushed for civil-service reform and lower tariffs. In the first White House wedding, Cleveland married Frances Folsom in 1886. Cleveland cast over 300 vetoes—more than twice the combined total of all previous presidents. He cut Civil War pensions, seized 81 million acres of unused land from railroads, and signed the Interstate Commerce Act (1887). Defeated in the 1888 election, Cleveland claimed there was "no happier man in the United States"; yet four years later he won a rematch with Benjamin Harrison. Back in the White House, Cleveland underwent a secret operation to remove his cancerous upper jaw. His tight-money policies did nothing to help the depression after the Panic of 1893. Cleveland sent federal troops to break up the Pullman strike (1894) and supported William McKinley, a Republican, for president in 1896. "I have tried so hard to do right," Cleveland said on his deathbed on June 24, 1908.

23. Benjamin Harrison
(1889–1893)

Benjamin Harrison was born on Aug. 20, 1833, at the North Bend, Ohio, farm of his grandfather William Henry Harrison, the ninth president. He took up the law in Indiana before joining the Union Army in 1862. Harrison finished the Civil War a brigadier general and returned to Indiana, where he was a prominent Republican, defeated for governor in 1876 but elected senator in 1881. A colorless compromise candidate for president, Harrison won the 1888 election despite receiving fewer popular votes than Grover Cleveland. Harrison bowed to the "Billion Dollar Congress" of free-spending Republicans who escalated Civil War pensions, transportation subsidies, naval construction, and spoils patronage. The McKinley Tariff, the Sherman Anti-Trust Act, the Sherman Silver Purchase Act (all 1890), and Secretary of State James G. Blaine's vigorous foreign policy were hallmarks of Harrison's administration, which oversaw the admission of six new states. Democrats won back Congress in 1890 and the White House in 1892, when Harrison lost to Cleveland in their rematch. A legal expert, Harrison taught at Stanford University and defended Venezuela in a boundary dispute with Britain before his death, on Mar. 13, 1901. Harrison referred to the White House as "my jail."

25. William McKinley
(1897–1901)

The last Civil War veteran to become president, William McKinley was born in Niles, Ohio, on Jan. 29, 1843, son of an iron founder. A college dropout, McKinley was a post office clerk when the Civil War began. He volunteered as a private and mustered out as a 22-year-old major. McKinley studied law and was elected to Congress in 1876. A longtime Republican floor leader, he authored the record-high McKinley Tariff of 1890, before losing his seat that same year. Ohio millionaire Marcus Hanna, McKinley's political manager, engineered two governor's terms for him and funded McKinley's run for the presidency in 1896. William Jennings Bryan opposed him on a free-silver platform, but McKinley's dignified front porch campaign stressed sound money, tariffs, and the "full dinner pail." He won the election with the first popular majority since Grant's reelection. Strongly probusiness, McKinley raised the tariff still higher and reluctantly led the country into the Spanish-American War (1898). By acquiring the Philippines and other islands, the country became a world power under McKinley, who went on to proclaim the open-door policy in China. McKinley defeated Bryan by an even larger margin in 1900 and was enjoying great popularity when anarchist Leon Czolgosz shot him in Buffalo, New York. McKinley died two weeks later, on Sept. 14, 1901.

26. Theodore Roosevelt
(1901–1909)

Theodore Roosevelt was born in New York City on Oct. 27, 1858, the only president born there. A small, sickly child plagued by asthma, Roosevelt overcame a pampered youth to live the "strenuous life": he boxed, hiked, hunted, rode horses, and climbed the Matterhorn. After graduating Phi Beta Kappa from Harvard in 1880, he attended Columbia Law School and became the youngest member of New York's legislature. Rich men of his day did not consider politics a suitable avocation, but Roosevelt desperately wanted "to be of the governing class." His first wife, Alice Hathaway Lee, died on the same day his mother died in 1884. Roosevelt wrote books and ran a cattle ranch in North Dakota until he married Edith Kermit Carow in 1886 and they moved to Oyster Bay, New York. During the Spanish-American War, Roosevelt left a job at the Navy Department in 1898 to lead the Rough Riders volunteer regiment in Cuba, achieving glory in the Battle of San Juan Hill. Elected governor of New York immediately upon returning home, Roosevelt soon thereafter was named William McKinley's vice-presidential running mate, in 1900. Roosevelt learned of McKinley's death while on a mountain-climbing expedition.

The youngest president at 42, "T.R." promised a Square Deal to close the gap between capital and labor. He mounted well-publicized campaigns against big business and successfully arbitrated major strikes. "Teddy's" popularity soared when he humbled billionaire J. P. Morgan in the Northern Securities case, and a record plurality reelected him in 1904. Roosevelt signed progressive laws to regulate railroads, inspect food and drugs, and create more than 150 million acres of national parks and forests. No less vigorous in foreign policy, Roosevelt's corollary to the Monroe Doctrine asserted the country would intervene to prevent European involvement in Latin America. For helping to end the Russo-Japanese War, Roosevelt became the first American to win the Nobel Prize, but he considered the Panama Canal his greatest achievement. Roosevelt kept his pledge not to seek a third term in 1908—but in 1912 he ran against his chosen successor, William Howard Taft. Denied his party's nomination, Roosevelt survived an assassination attempt and won more than 4 million votes as the Progressive, or Bull Moose, candidate. During World War I, Roosevelt bitterly denounced the neutrality policy of Woodrow Wilson, who then denied Roosevelt's request to lead troops in France. Roosevelt's four sons fought there; Quentin, the youngest, was killed in action. While laying plans for another run at the White House, Roosevelt died suddenly of a cardiac embolism on Jan. 6, 1919. "No President has ever enjoyed himself as much as I have enjoyed myself," he said.

27. William Howard Taft
(1909–1913)

By far the largest president at over 330 pounds, William Howard Taft was born in Cincinnati, Ohio, on Sept. 15, 1857. He graduated from Yale in 1878, then followed his father into law and Republican politics: "I always had my plate right side up when offices were falling," Taft wrote. William McKinley sent him to govern the Philippines in 1900, and Theodore Roosevelt appointed him secretary of war in 1904. Taft traveled around the world as Roosevelt's personal emissary, becoming T.R.'s chosen successor in 1908. As president, Taft tried to carry on Roosevelt's policies, but he wrecked the Republican party by alienating progressives from conservative "Stand-Patters" over tariff and conservation issues. Taft initiated the income tax and pursued antitrust suits against big business—but generally he sided with wealthy interests. An infuriated Roosevelt challenged Taft unsuccessfully for the Republican nomination in 1912, then outpolled him in the election, giving Woodrow Wilson the victory. With eight electoral votes, Taft suffered the worst-ever defeat for an incumbent president. But the better part of his career lay ahead: Taft, always more comfortable as a jurist, taught law at Yale until he was appointed chief justice of the United States in 1921. He served with distinction, alternating a liberal nationalism in economic affairs with political and social conservatism. Taft died on Mar. 8, 1930. Never nostalgic for the White House, Taft once said, "I don't remember that I ever was President."

28. Woodrow Wilson
(1913–1921)

Born on Dec. 28, 1856, in Staunton, Virginia, the son of a Presbyterian minister, Thomas Woodrow Wilson grew up in Virginia, Georgia, South Carolina, and North Carolina—the first southern president since Andrew Jackson. Probably dyslexic, Wilson was slow to read; yet he became the most highly educated president. Graduated from Princeton in 1879, Wilson studied law before taking a Ph.D. in political science at Johns Hopkins in 1886. He taught at Bryn Mawr and Wesleyan University before Princeton appointed him professor in 1890. Wilson attracted the attention of Democratic bosses after he was elected Princeton's president in 1902, and they persuaded him to run for New Jersey governor in 1910. A strong progressive, Wilson won easily—and then turned on party bosses by sponsoring anti-machine reforms. In 1912 the Democrats nominated Wilson for president on the 46th ballot, and he won, with Theodore Roosevelt and William Howard Taft splitting the Republican vote.

Wilson's expert knowledge of government and strong party leadership pushed the Underwood Tariff, the Federal Reserve Act, the Federal Trade Commission, and the Clayton Antitrust Act through Congress by 1914. Restoring competition to the monopoly-plagued economy was the goal of Wilson's "New Freedom," until war in Europe made neutrality his top priority. German attacks on Allied ships carrying Americans strained Wilson's commitment, but he was narrowly reelected in 1916 on the slogan He Kept Us out of War. After Germany spurned Wilson's mediation and resumed attacks on Allied shipping, Congress declared war at Wilson's behest in April 1917. World War I would "make the world safe for democracy," Wilson vowed, and he issued "Fourteen Points" for a just peace. After the armistice in November 1918, Wilson became the first president to visit Europe when he attended the Paris peace conference that produced the Versailles Treaty. Wilson's dream of "peace without vengeance" was frustrated at Versailles, where he compromised away his Fourteen Points to obtain the League of Nations for collective security. In July 1919, Wilson returned home to face hostile Republicans in the Senate, where his treaty languished. On a nationwide speaking tour, Wilson collapsed from exhaustion in Colorado and suffered a paralytic stroke in October 1919. Wilson, all but incapacitated, refused to compromise as the Senate rejected the Versailles Treaty. Wilson's second wife, Edith Bolling Galt, whom he married in 1915, shielded the disabled president from the press and politicians until the end of his term in 1921. Woodrow Wilson died in his sleep on Feb. 3, 1924, frustrated by his own country's refusal to join the League of Nations.

29. Warren G. Harding
(1921–1923)

The first president born after the Civil War, Warren Gamaliel Harding was born in Blooming Grove, Ohio, which earlier had been named Corsica, on Nov. 2, 1865. He taught, studied law, and sold insurance before following his father into the newspaper business. Marriage to Florence DeWolfe, a wealthy widow, in 1891 helped finance Harding's paper, the *Marion Star*. A staunch Republican, Harding's pro-business editorials got him elected state senator and lieutenant governor. Although defeated for governor in 1910, Harding was elected senator four years later. Republicans turned to him in 1920 as a compromise candidate for president, the "best of the second-raters"; his good looks were expected to win over women first-time voters. Elected by an unprecedented 61 percent majority, Harding promised a return to "normalcy" for Americans tired of war and Woodrow Wilson. Harding's administration featured higher tariffs, lower taxes, and immigration restriction—but perhaps most notably, pervasive corruption and incompetence by Harding's crooked appointees. Harding was disturbed by the dishonesty of "my God-damn friends," two of whom committed suicide to avoid prosecution. While visiting San Francisco, Harding died suddenly of mysterious causes on Aug. 2, 1923. Scandals involving secret love affairs, official graft, and the vast Teapot Dome swindle erupted soon thereafter. Mrs. Harding zealously tracked down Harding's letters and destroyed them, leaving him the most enigmatic president, and certainly one of the worst.

30. Calvin Coolidge
(1923–1929)

The only president to share the nation's birthday, John Calvin Coolidge was born in Plymouth, Vermont, on July 4, 1872. Descended from a long line of New Englanders, he graduated from Amherst in 1895, practiced law in Massachusetts, and entered Republican politics in 1899. Coolidge rose slowly through a succession of state offices until he was elected governor of Massachusetts in 1918. Acclaimed for crushing the Boston police strike in 1919, Coolidge became the unexpected Republican vice-presidential nominee in 1920. After Warren G. Harding's death while still in office, Coolidge's own father swore him in as the new president. "Silent Cal" was the butt of jokes for his laconic utterances, but his minimalist approach to government fit the public mood, and he restored respectability to the White House, tainted by Harding's corrupt appointees and all-night poker parties. Instead of the whiskey that once flowed freely there, ice water in paper cups was served to visitors. Coolidge, untouched by leftover scandals, won the election in his own right in 1924. Pronouncing that the "business of America is business," he ushered in the heady years of Coolidge Prosperity, as the stock market soared higher and higher. Coolidge ignored foreign affairs and made frugality his trademark, slashing the budget at the expense of farmers and veterans, even driving out a White House cook who could not abide Coolidge's cost cutting. "It's a pretty good idea to get out when they still want you," Coolidge said, surprising the nation at the peak of his success by declining to run again in 1928. A popular president, Coolidge was safely out of politics when the Great Depression arrived. He died on Jan. 5, 1933, on the eve of the New Deal.

31. Herbert Hoover
(1929-1933)

Born in West Branch, Iowa, on Aug. 10, 1874, Herbert Clark Hoover was the first president from west of the Mississippi. Orphaned at eight and raised by Quaker relatives in Iowa and Oregon, Hoover joined the first graduating class of Stanford University in 1895. He became a world-famous mining engineer and a multimillionaire by age 40. In World War I, Hoover helped rescue Americans stranded in Europe, distributed food supplies to occupied Belgium, and convinced the nation to save food ("Hooverize") for the war effort. Hoover was Woodrow Wilson's economic adviser at Versailles, and he organized relief for famine-struck Russia during the revolution. Joining the Republicans in 1919, Hoover earned prominence as the secretary of commerce in the 1920s and was elected president in 1928—the only electoral victory of his life. He promised a "chicken in every pot," but a few months later, the Wall Street crash brought on the Great Depression. Paralyzed by his conservative instincts, Hoover could not halt the spread of bank failures, bankruptcy, unemployment, and despair. Government should not get involved, he believed, and public relief would ruin American morals—so Hoover called for a balanced budget while promising the return of prosperity. He sent tanks to disperse veterans begging for pensions, and shanty towns across the country were dubbed Hoovervilles. Massively defeated by Franklin D. Roosevelt in 1932, Hoover called the New Deal "socialistic, collectivistic, fascistic and communistic." For decades Americans blamed Hoover for the depression and criticized his hard-hearted refusal to help the needy. Hoover lived another 31 years, the longest postpresidential lifespan, and he salvaged his reputation with more relief work after World War II. In retirement Hoover chaired two bipartisan commissions on government reorganization, issuing many important recommendations for federal reform. Boulder Dam on the Colorado River was renamed to honor Hoover before he died, at age 90, on Oct. 20, 1964.

32. Franklin D. Roosevelt
(1933-1945)

The only president elected more than twice, Franklin Delano Roosevelt was born to a wealthy Hyde Park, New York, family on Jan. 30, 1882. He followed his cousin, Theodore Roosevelt, into Harvard and Columbia Law School—but not into the Republican party. F.D.R. was a Democratic state senator, assistant secretary of the navy, and nominee for vice president in 1920. Paralyzed by polio in 1921, Roosevelt learned to walk with braces and canes. As governor of New York after 1928, he pioneered unemployment relief in the Great Depression, earning him the Democratic nomination for president in 1932. Herbert Hoover, brooding and baffled by the depression, posed little challenge to the beaming, magnetic Roosevelt, who won the election by 23 million to 16 million votes. F.D.R. promised vague but bold experimentation ("above all, try something"), and as he took office in the worst inaugural crisis since Abraham Lincoln's, he assured Americans they had "nothing to fear but fear itself." F.D.R.'s first 100 days set a breakneck pace as compliant congressmen approved his New Deal for relief and recovery. Major landmarks were the National Industrial Recovery Act, the Agricultural Adjustment Act, the Tennessee Valley Authority, the Works Progress Administration, the National Labor Relations Act (Wagner Act), and the Social Security Act (1933-35). Though often contradictory and ineffective, the New Deal established the federal government's responsibility for protecting farmers, workers, and the unemployed while actively regulating the economy to prevent another crash. F.D.R.'s high-profile "fireside chats," public works projects, and Social Security programs overcame despair and restored public confidence in the economy and government.

Reelected by a huge margin in 1936, Roosevelt proved incapable of ending the depression, as he ran afoul of the "nine old men" on the Supreme Court. Almost as many Americans called Roosevelt a Communist as praised him for rescuing the common man. Despite alienating many voters with his court-packing plan and "soak the rich" taxes, F.D.R. won an unprecedented third term in 1940. As war loomed in Europe, F.D.R. used his mastery of public opinion to lead Americans away from isolation, helping Britain with the destroyers-for-bases deal (1940) and Lend-Lease Act (1941) even before Pearl Harbor. World War II then occupied F.D.R.'s full attention as he shelved the New Deal and orchestrated the mammoth war effort. Roosevelt crisscrossed the globe to meet with Allied leaders and kept close personal control of diplomacy and grand strategy. He rallied a powerful sense of national purpose in the war, winning his fourth election in 1944. Together with Winston Churchill and Josef Stalin, F.D.R. planned a postwar peace of UN cooperation. Just after the Yalta Conference, Roosevelt died suddenly of a cerebral hemorrhage on Apr. 12, 1945, days before the war's end. His wife of 40 years, Eleanor Roosevelt, easily the most influential First Lady, led her husband's campaign on behalf of disadvantaged Americans and continued it long after his death.

33. Harry S Truman
(1945-1953)

A plain midwestern farmer and World War I artilleryman, Harry S Truman (the S does not stand for a middle name) was born on May 8, 1884, in Lamar, Missouri. After his Kansas City haberdashery failed, Truman entered politics as a Democrat in the 1920s, and the local Pendergast machine arranged his election to the Senate as a New Dealer in 1934. National attention came to Truman when he headed a congressional committee investigating government waste during World War II. When Franklin D. Roosevelt needed a new vice president in 1944, he chose Truman. After only a few weeks in office, Truman had the presidency thrust upon him by Roosevelt's sudden death in April 1945. "Pray for me boys," he told his first press conference. Utterly unprepared, Truman did not even know about the atomic bomb project, but he vowed to carry on Roosevelt's policies. Truman proved a remarkably capable chief executive, educating himself in foreign affairs and dispatching crucial decisions rapidly. In his first four months, Truman approved the United Nations, accepted the German surrender, met with Allied leaders at Potsdam, and ordered atomic bombs dropped on Japan. As the Cold War commenced, Truman talked tough with the Soviets, accusing them of breaking agreements and intimidating helpless neighbors. In 1947 he proclaimed the Truman Doctrine, promising U.S. aid to threatened countries, and the Marshall Plan to aid European recovery and contain communism. The next year Truman ordered the Berlin airlift when the Soviets cut off West Berlin, and he promised to help Third World countries with the Point Four program. No less assertive at home, Truman made progress on civil rights, subdued restive unions, and prevented the Republican-controlled Congress from dismantling the New Deal—a specter that he effectively raised to win surprise reelection in 1948. Truman committed the country to the NATO alliance in 1949 and sent troops to South Korea when Communist armies invaded in 1950. But as Congress rejected Truman's ambitious Fair Deal domestic program and the Korean War bogged down, Truman's last years were barren. He had more vetoes overridden than all presidents but Andrew Johnson, and his poll ratings were lower than all but Jimmy Carter's. Truman, who initially raised fears of subversion with his loyalty program, could not quell the Red Scare that swept his party from power in 1952, as Republicans hammered away on the theme that Democrats were "soft on communism." Truman was convinced that he saved the world from communism, prevented World War III, and could have won another term if he chose to run in 1952. "He did his damndest" was the only eulogy Harry Truman desired on his death, on Dec. 26, 1972. Out of favor when he left office, Truman has gained rising respect since his death.

34. Dwight D. Eisenhower
(1953–1961)

The last war hero president, Dwight David Eisenhower was born in Denison, Texas, on Oct. 14, 1890, and grew up poor in Kansas. A military history buff, Eisenhower graduated with the 1915 class of West Point that produced 59 generals. He married Mamie Doud, his wife of 52 years, and spent World War I as a tank-training instructor. Eisenhower, only a major at age 40, rose rapidly during World War II, promoted past 350 senior officers to become commander of U.S. forces in Europe in 1942. By the end of 1944, he was the first U.S. five-star general and Supreme Allied Commander, taking the German surrender in May 1945. By that point a global celebrity, Eisenhower was army chief of staff until 1948, when he resigned to become president of Columbia University. Harry S Truman named him to command NATO forces in 1950, but two years later Eisenhower retired again to take the Republican nomination and run for president against Adlai E. Stevenson.

"Ike" became perhaps the most popular president in U.S. history, though many questioned his lax work habits, detached management style, and baffling speeches. Prominent millionaires in Eisenhower's cabinet and arch-conservatives such as Secretary of State John Foster Dulles seemed to have free rein, and Eisenhower acquiesced in Sen. Joe McCarthy's wild charges of subversion. His administration stockpiled atomic weapons and promised "massive retaliation" against Soviet aggression—yet did nothing when the Red Army rolled into Hungary in 1956. Eisenhower did end the Korean War, concluded several alliance agreements, and cut the defense budget. The "Eisenhower Doctrine" promised U.S. aid to Middle Eastern countries fighting communism. When Britain, France, and Israel invaded the Suez Canal in 1956, Eisenhower led UN condemnation and forced them to withdraw, though he sent U.S. marines into Lebanon two years later. He began heavy U.S. involvement in Vietnam by backing the French and then the puppet Diem regime. At home Eisenhower promised to scale back the government—yet he expanded Social Security; created the Department of Health, Education, and Welfare; and spent billions on public housing and freeways. He pointedly stressed religious devotion. The Supreme Court's *Brown* decision (1954), which Eisenhower deeply regretted, inaugurated the civil rights movement. Eisenhower defeated Stevenson again in 1956, but Soviet domination of space, revolution in Cuba, embarrassment over the Soviets' shooting down of a U.S. spy plane, and his own ill health marred his second term. Eisenhower reluctantly sent paratroopers to enforce desegregation in Little Rock, Arkansas, in 1957. Democrats controlled Congress for all but two years of Eisenhower's presidency, and they called for more active leadership when he ended his term as the oldest

president before Ronald Reagan. In retirement Eisenhower approved of U.S. intervention in Vietnam and counseled presidents until his death, on Mar. 28, 1969.

35. John F. Kennedy
(1961–1963)

The youngest man elected president, the only Roman Catholic, and the first born in the 20th century, John Fitzgerald Kennedy was born in Brookline, Massachusetts, on May 29, 1917, to a family of Irish politicos. His father, Joseph P. Kennedy, was ambassador to England and one of the richest men in America. Kennedy attended Dexter and Choate academies, the London School of Economics, and Princeton before graduating from Harvard in 1940. A patrol boat commander in World War II, Kennedy was decorated for bravery in saving the lives of wounded crew members. Kennedy's father arranged his election to Congress, where he served three undistinguished terms before entering the Senate in 1952. After 1953, the year he married wealthy socialite Jacqueline Bouvier, Kennedy's health deteriorated from Addison's disease and agonizing back ailments. He won the Pulitzer Prize for *Profiles in Courage* (1957), a study of principled politicians supposedly written from his hospital bed. Kennedy positioned himself for a presidential run by lambasting Republicans for insufficient anticommunism and "vigor." In 1960, Kennedy prevailed over three prominent opponents for the Democratic nomination, then scraped past Richard M. Nixon in the election by 118,000 votes out of 69 million cast. The campaign featured the first televised presidential debates, capitalizing on Kennedy's exceptional poise and polish.

In accepting the Democratic nomination, Kennedy had pledged a New Frontier, but his social programs languished in Congress. Undaunted, Kennedy plunged into foreign affairs, his primary interest. Just after taking office, he approved the disastrous Bay of Pigs invasion, and a year later he terrified the world by confronting the Soviets over the presence of their missiles in Cuba. He visited the Berlin Wall and expressed solidarity with Germans under the Russian gun. Kennedy's bellicosity eventually subsided as he set up the Washington-Moscow hotline and signed the Nuclear Test Ban Treaty (1963). Thousands of U.S. troops went to Vietnam as Kennedy escalated the commitment to containing communism. Kennedy vastly increased spending for defense and space programs, vowing to put a man on the moon. He also engineered a $10-billion tax cut that eventually brought prosperity and increased revenues. As racial unrest spread, Kennedy cautiously supported the civil rights movement, introducing sweeping legislation that would not pass in his lifetime—nor would his plans for aid to education and medical care for the elderly reach fruition before his death. Gearing up for reelection, Kennedy embarked on a speaking tour across the South, where he was least popular. In a Dallas, Texas, motorcade on Nov. 22, 1963, he was fatally shot. Kennedy's alleged assassin, Lee Harvey Oswald, a left-wing ex-marine, was in turn

murdered by Jack Ruby two days later. While doubts persisted that Oswald acted alone, Kennedy's martyrdom helped realize his legislative legacy, and subsequent revelation of his many peccadilloes have not tarnished the "Kennedy myth."

36. Lyndon B. Johnson
(1963–1969)

The eighth vice president to succeed by death of a president, Lyndon Baines Johnson was born on his father's Texas ranch near Stonewall on Aug. 27, 1908. He worked his way through Southwest Texas State Teachers College, taught briefly, then took a job in Washington—where he would live for all but two years until he left the White House. Government fascinated Johnson, and he reveled in making connections, marrying heiress Claudia Alta "Lady Bird" Taylor after a two-month courtship in 1934. An ardent New Dealer, Johnson won election to Congress as a Democrat in 1937. Reelected three times without opposition, Johnson became the first congressman to volunteer for combat in World War II, winning a Silver Star before returning to Washington. In 1948, on his second try, "Landslide Lyndon" was elected to the Senate by just 87 votes. Hard work and Texas oil money made Johnson the youngest Senate majority leader by 1955. A huge and hearty man, Johnson's powers of persuasion were legendary, but he failed in his bid for the Democratic nomination for president in 1960. Johnson accepted John F. Kennedy's offer of the vice presidency and campaigned hard in the South to aid their narrow victory. Made president a thousand days later by the tragedy in Dallas, Johnson vowed to continue Kennedy's programs, pushing them through Congress with surprising ease. Notable were the Civil Rights Act outlawing segregation and the Equal Opportunity Act, which declared "war on poverty." After less than a year in office, Johnson defeated Barry Goldwater by the biggest plurality in history.

Now president in his own right, Johnson unveiled plans for a Great Society free from poverty and discrimination and passed the Education Act, Medical Care Act, and the Voting Rights Act in 1965. But Johnson came to grief in Vietnam, where he broke his 1964 campaign promise not to send "American boys to fight Asian wars." Earlier administrations committed the U.S. to defending South Vietnam, but Johnson intervened massively to prove American credibility to allies and enemies alike. No doubt he also feared resurgent McCarthyism if another nation were "lost" to communism. Following the Tonkin Gulf incident (1964), Johnson steadily expanded American power and lives in Vietnam, but victory, or a means to achieve it, never came within reach—despite the presence of over half-a-million U.S. troops by 1968. Johnson's presidency unraveled as American losses mounted, antiwar protests grew strident, race riots exploded in inner cities across the nation, and the government developed a credibility gap. Virtually a prisoner of the White House, Johnson faced a war he could neither win nor leave behind and a nation more deeply divided than at any time since the Civil War. In March 1968 Johnson effectively resigned by announcing he would not seek another term. He retired to his sprawling Texas ranch and stayed out of politics until his death, on Jan. 22, 1973. Johnson left a domestic reform legacy second only to the New Deal; but he squandered it in Vietnam by raising expectations he could not meet at home and abroad. The day after he died, diplomats signed the Paris peace agreement, formally ending the war.

37. Richard M. Nixon
(1969–1974)

The only president to resign from office, Richard Milhous Nixon was born in Yorba Linda, California, to a poor Quaker family on Jan. 9, 1913. A graduate of Whittier College and Duke University Law School, Nixon married Thelma "Pat" Ryan in 1940, saw noncombat service in World War II, and rode into Congress on the Republican wave of 1946. He gained fame in the anti-Communist trial of Alger Hiss before entering the Senate in 1950. Dwight D. Eisenhower made Nixon his running mate in 1952, but Nixon was nearly forced to resign for accepting questionable contributions. He appealed for national exoneration in the televised "Checkers" speech. A well-traveled vice president, Nixon almost lost his life to hostile Latin American mobs in 1958, and he waged an impromptu debate in Moscow with Soviet premier Nikita Khrushchev in 1959. Eisenhower's obvious successor in 1960, Nixon narrowly lost the election to John F. Kennedy, and when he lost a California gubernatorial race in 1962, Nixon's career seemed over. Yet he practiced law in New York until the Republicans nominated him again in 1968. To a nation riven by the Vietnam War, Nixon promised "law and order," appealing to calm and unity against a background of riots, assassinations, and protest. Nixon defeated Hubert H. Humphrey with the smallest victor's share of the vote since 1912—the first former vice president in 132 years to be elected president.

Vowing to "bring us together," Nixon tried to thwart the bureaucracy and Democrats in Congress by centralizing executive power. To control inflation, he ordered wage-price controls and devalued the dollar for the first time since the depression. Seeking "peace with honor" in Vietnam, Nixon built up the South Vietnamese army and withdrew U.S. troops—while massively escalating bombing of North Vietnam. Antiwar protests reached fever pitch when the United States invaded Cambodia in 1970. Nixon responded with appeals to the "silent majority," attacks on press freedom, and clandestine harassment of administration critics. High points of his first administration were the Apollo moon landing in 1969, Nixon's path-breaking visit to China in 1972, and the first Strategic Arms Limitation Treaty with the Soviet Union. Twelve days after announcing "peace is at hand" in Vietnam, Nixon was reelected by a landslide, carrying an unprecedented 49 states. During the campaign five burglars were arrested in the Democratic party headquarters, and by early 1973, they were linked to the White House. The ensuing "Watergate" scandal exposed the Nixon administration's rampant corruption, illegality, and deceit. Nixon himself downplayed the scandal as mere politics, but when his aides resigned in disgrace, Nixon's role in ordering an illegal cover-up came to light in the press, courts, and congressional investigations. Nixon evaded taxes, accepted illicit campaign contributions, ordered secret bombings, and harassed opponents with executive agencies, wiretaps, and break-ins. Vice President Spiro T. Agnew resigned in October 1973 for accepting bribes, but Nixon hung on to power, claiming, "I am not a crook," as the House began impeachment proceedings. Subpoenas and Supreme Court orders forced Nixon to release tapes of his White House conversations authorizing the Watergate cover-up. Ultimately, he resigned to avoid impeachment for obstruction of justice, abuse of power, and contempt of Congress. Claiming to have lost his "political base," Nixon announced his resignation on national television on Aug. 9, 1974. He never admitted wrongdoing, though he later conceded errors of judgment. Saved by a blanket pardon from Gerald R. Ford, his second vice president and successor as president, Nixon retired to his California mansion, later moving to New York and then New Jersey.

38. Gerald R. Ford
(1974–1977)

The only vice president and president never elected to either office, Gerald Rudolph Ford was born in Omaha, Nebraska, on July 14, 1913. An Eagle Scout, he grew up in Michigan and attended the University of Michigan on a football scholarship, playing on the national championship teams of 1932 and 1933. After graduating in 1935, Ford coached football and boxing at Yale while attending law school; he received his degree in 1941. In the navy he earned 10 battle stars in the Pacific during World War II. Ford ran for Congress in 1948 as a Republican, marrying divorcée Betty Bloomer during the campaign, which he won. Thereafter he would be reelected 12 times, never by less than 60 percent of the vote. In Congress Ford's solid conservative record elevated him to House Republican minority leader by 1965. For supporting Richard M. Nixon in Congress, Ford was rewarded with the vice presidency in December 1973, replacing Spiro T. Agnew under the 25th Amendment. "I do not think the public would stand for it," Ford said at his confirmation hearings, when asked if he would ever pardon Nixon. For eight months Ford stayed loyal to Nixon, until his resignation made Ford the new president on Aug. 9, 1974. Ford announced "our long national nightmare is over," but a month later he shocked the nation by giving Nixon a blanket pardon. Ford denied any deal had been made, but his public standing never recovered. He struggled with huge Democratic majorities in Congress to stem soaring inflation and unemployment, casting 66 vetoes in all. Ford asked for tax increases in 1974, tax rebates in 1975, and in 1976 his budget contained the largest peacetime deficit to that date. Congress refused Ford's request for aid to South Vietnam and intervention in the Angolan civil war. In the *Mayaguez* incident, Ford sent the marines to rescue 39 Americans captured by Cambodia, and 41 of the servicemen died in the effort.

Breaking a 1973 pledge, Ford decided to seek reelection, and while campaigning, he survived two assassination attempts by California women. Fending off Ronald Reagan's bid for the Republican nomination in 1976, Ford was far behind Jimmy Carter in the polls, but he carried four more states than Carter in the election—which Ford lost by 57 electoral votes. It was the first defeat of an incumbent president since Herbert Hoover's. Gerald Ford reminded Americans after Watergate that not all politicians were dishonest, and Congress passed a resolution commending his "openness and honesty that have done much to restore confidence in our government." Of himself, he said, "I'm a Ford, not a Lincoln."

39. Jimmy Carter
(1977–1981)

James Earl Carter, the first deep-southerner elected president in 128 years, was born in Plains, Georgia, on Oct. 1, 1924. He grew up on a farm with no plumbing or electricity but realized his dream of attending the U.S. Naval Academy. Carter graduated in 1946 and married Rosalynn Smith, his sister's best friend. He joined the submarine fleet and studied nuclear physics, leaving the navy in 1953 to run the family peanut business. He was elected to the Georgia state senate in 1962. Defeated for governor in 1966, Carter campaigned constantly for the next four years, winning on his second try in 1970. Carter reorganized the government and hired more blacks, declaring that the "time for racial discrimination is over." A month before leaving office in 1974, Carter was the first Democrat to announce his candidacy for president in 1976, again campaigning constantly. "Jimmy Who?" burst into headlines by winning narrow pluralities over nine rivals in early primaries. Carter's grinning, homespun style and earnest vows of honesty ("I will never lie to you") struck a chord with voters after Watergate. Carter won the nomination and defeated incumbent Gerald R. Ford by 2 percent of the vote. Lack of Washington connections helped his candidacy but not his presidency, for Carter never shook his image as the provincial amateur. Democratic majorities in Congress ignored Carter's pleas for tax reform and energy policy. Transportation deregulation, environmental protection, and new departments of energy and education were Carter's main domestic achievements.

But as federal spending mounted and oil prices doubled, most Americans blamed Carter for runaway inflation. His 20 percent approval rating in August 1979 was the lowest ever recorded in opinion polls. In foreign affairs Carter obtained a Panama Canal treaty, normalized relations with China, and mediated the Camp David peace accords between Israel and Egypt. He moved toward closer relations with the Soviet Union, signing the SALT II treaty in 1979, but the Soviet invasion of Afghanistan led Carter to embargo grain sales to the USSR and to order a boycott of the 1980 Moscow Olympics. The Carter Doctrine announced the United States would defend the Persian Gulf, where ironically, Carter soon met his downfall in the Iran hostage crisis. Early public support for Carter's restraint gradually withered under the glare of relentless media coverage that kept tensions high throughout 1980. Carter himself became a hostage of Iran, trapped in the White House as Edward Kennedy nearly deprived him of the Democratic nomination. In April 1980, Carter approved a military rescue mission, its tragic failure reinforcing his image of incompetence and weakness, which Republican candidate Ronald Reagan flayed. Carter's patience paid off with the safe return of all American hostages in January 1981—but by then he had lost the election in a Reagan landslide. Carter left the White House thoroughly discredited, his informal style ridiculed as inappropriate, his platitudes betraying lack of vision, his appeals for support seen as poor leadership. Yet Carter was a hard-working president wrecked by a hostile press, extortionate oil exporters, military miscues, Iranians, and other forces beyond his control. Carter, a born-again Christian, has resumed low-profile charity work and Sunday-school teaching.

40. Ronald Reagan
(1981–1989)

At 69 the oldest elected president, only to be reelected at 73, Ronald Wilson Reagan was born in Tampico, Illinois, on Feb. 6, 1911. He excelled at acting and campus politics in high school and at Eureka College. Reagan was a radio sports announcer when he made his first movie in 1937. Over 50 more films would follow in Reagan's prolific Hollywood career. In 1940 he married actress Jane Wyman, who divorced him in 1948. During World War II, Reagan made training films, and after the war he was president of the Screen Actors Guild. Then a Democrat, Reagan assailed Communists in Hollywood. He married Nancy Davis, another actress, in 1952. As his movie career waned, Reagan hosted television shows and espoused conservative causes, switching to the Republican party in 1960. Reagan made a dramatic speech at the end of the 1964 campaign and despite his total lack of experience, was elected governor of California in 1966 by a million votes. As governor, Reagan broke all promises by raising taxes, increasing spending, and expanding the state government—yet he easily won reelection in 1970. Reagan made a stab at the Republican presidential nomination in 1968, then bided his time until 1976, when he almost took the nomination from Gerald R. Ford. A close defeat at the Republican convention left Reagan waiting another four years until 1980, when he won the Republican nomi-

nation at last. Then he swept past Jimmy Carter in the crushing "Reagan Revolution" of 1980, carrying 44 states and making huge Republican gains in Congress.

"Reaganomics" promised to cut taxes and social spending while vastly increasing the defense budget and somehow balancing the budget. Congress was unmoved until Mar. 20, 1981, when a crazed youth named John Hinckley shot Reagan twice in the chest. Reagan's good humor and rapid recovery charmed Americans—especially the press, which had questioned his age and health. Reagan then prevailed over Congress to pass mammoth tax cuts. The national debt began its meteoric rise under Reagan as defense spending outweighed cuts in social programs. By 1986 the country had become a net borrower for the first time since World War I, but falling oil prices slowed inflation and rekindled economic growth, for which Reagan took credit. Calling the Soviet Union an evil empire, Reagan built up the armed forces, deployed U.S. nuclear missiles in Europe, and began the Strategic Defense Initiative. He sent U.S. marines to Lebanon, where 240 of them died in a terrorist attack. To halt the spread of communism, Reagan ordered the invasion of Grenada and isolated the Sandinista government of Nicaragua. Reelected by another landslide in 1984, with the economy booming and his public esteem high, Reagan seemed headed for an even more successful second term. He ordered bombing raids on Libya and met with Soviet leader Mikhail Gorbachev, eventually producing historic arms control agreements. But in 1987 Reagan's invincible popularity finally succumbed to the Iran-Contra scandal: White House staff secretly sold arms to Iran in hopes of freeing American hostages held in Lebanon, using the profits illegally to fund Contra fighters in Nicaragua. Many top Reagan aides had to resign, but more damaging was the president's evident lack of control over his own administration. By 1988 Reagan was reduced to "lame duck" status but regained enough popularity to successfully bestow his mantle on Vice President George Bush.

41. George Bush
(1989–   )

The first sitting vice president elected president in over 150 years, George Herbert Walker Bush was born in Milton, Massachusetts, on June 12, 1924. His father was Prescott Sheldon Bush, Wall Street banker and U.S. senator from Connecticut from 1952 to 1963. Bush grew up in Greenwich, Connecticut, and he was elected senior class president at Phillips Academy, Andover, Massachusetts. One of the navy's youngest pilots during World War II, he was shot down over the Pacific and rescued at sea. For bravery in combat, Bush received the Distinguished Flying Cross and three Air Medals. He married Barbara Pierce, a Smith

College student, on Jan. 6, 1945. After the war he went to Yale University, graduating Phi Beta Kappa in economics in 1948. Bush spurned an offer from his father's Wall Street firm, instead pursuing a career in the Texas oil fields, which eventually made him a millionaire in his own right. He cofounded Zapata Petroleum Corporation in 1953 and served as president of its offshore subsidiary before entering politics in the early 1960s.

Bush won the Republican nomination for Senate in 1964, mounting a conservative anti-Communist and anticivil rights campaign in support of Barry Goldwater. For a Republican in Texas, Bush captured a record share of the vote but lost anyway. Two years later he was elected to Congress from a wealthy suburban Houston district, which reelected him in 1968. Despite strong backing from President Richard Nixon and the oil industry, Bush lost another Senate race in 1970, this time to Lloyd Bentsen, Jr. Nixon compensated Bush by appointing him U.S. ambassador to the United Nations, though Bush had no diplomatic experience at the time. In 1973, as the Watergate scandal unfolded, Nixon appointed him chairman of the Republican National Committee, and Bush firmly supported the president to the end. His reward was an appointment as chief of the U.S. Liaison Office in China in 1974. Bush returned home when President Gerald R. Ford appointed him director of the Central Intelligence Agency in 1976, but President James E. "Jimmy" Carter removed him in 1977. Bush campaigned hard for the Republican presidential nomination in 1980, defeating heavily favored Ronald Reagan in some early primaries before he withdrew and accepted Reagan's offer to join him on the winning ticket.

As vice president, Bush traveled the globe, chaired various presidential task forces, and participated in national-security policy decisions—though he denied any involvement in the Iran-Contra affair. Reagan formally designated Bush as acting president (under the 25th Amendment) when Reagan was incapacitated by surgery in 1985. Bush carefully maintained a low profile in office and avoided any appearance of disagreement with the president. By 1988 he was the obvious choice as Reagan's successor, besting Robert Dole in a brief contest for the Republican nomination. With Reagan's endorsement, Bush handily defeated Michael S. Dukakis, largely by renewing the Reagan pledge of no tax increases. His new Republican administration brought back to power many eastern moderates locked out by Reagan's Sunbelt conservatives, but Bush vowed to uphold the Reagan legacy of less government, strong defense, and family values. The Bushes, who have four sons and one daughter, maintain a family estate at Kennebunkport, Maine.

Presidential Elections 1796–1988

Notes: The vote totals reported in this almanac were gathered from *Presidential Elections Since 1789*, 3d ed. (Congressional Quarterly, Inc., 1983). Most scholars consider CQ to be the best source for vote totals. The CQ volumes contain the names and popular and electoral vote totals for all major and minor candidates. The vote totals for the 1984 and 1988 elections are those reported by the Associated Press based on official numbers supplied to the AP by the states' secretaries of state several weeks after the elections.

For a comprehensive discussion of every presidential election, readers are encouraged to examine the four-volume *History of American Presidential Elections, 1789–1968*, ed. Arthur M. Schlesinger, Jr. (1971). A supplement to the series brings the set up to the 1984 election.

N.A. in tables is used to mean not applicable. For an explanation of voting procedures through 1820, see "The Electoral College."

1789 and 1792

George Washington of Virginia ran unopposed for president in 1789 and 1792. He received 69 and 132 electoral votes, respectively, in those years. John Adams of Massachusetts was elected vice president in both years, receiving 34 and 77 electoral votes, respectively.

1796

Party	Candidate	Popular vote	%	Electoral vote
Federalist	John Adams (Mass.)	N.A.	N.A.	71
	and Thomas Pinckney (S.C.)	N.A.	N.A.	59
Democratic-Republican	Thomas Jefferson (Va.)	N.A.	N.A.	68
	and Aaron Burr (N.Y.)	N.A.	N.A.	30

Key Issues Washington set a precedent by refusing to run for a third term. Though the Founders hoped to avoid parties, factions developed around Hamilton and Jefferson during Washington's first term. Hamilton's Federalists supported a strong central government that would play a major role in the national economy and represent the commercial interests of the North. Jefferson's Republicans advocated states' rights and the agrarian interests of the South.

Regional Influences Though led by Hamilton, the Federalists nominated the more moderate Adams. Jefferson's strength in the South was balanced by Adams's power in the North. Eleven Federalist electors in New Hampshire failed to vote for Pinckney, their party's vice-presidential nominee, giving the position to Jefferson.

1800

Party	Candidate	Popular vote	%	Electoral vote
Democratic-Republican	Thomas Jefferson (Va.)	N.A.	N.A.	73
	and Aaron Burr (N.Y.)	N.A.	N.A.	73
Federalist	John Adams (Mass.)	N.A.	N.A.	65
	and Charles C. Pinckney (S.C.)	N.A.	N.A.	64
Federalist	John Jay (N.Y.)	N.A.	N.A.	1

Key Issues Adams divided the Federalists by keeping the United States out of war with France over seizures of American ships. In the meantime the Republicans under Jefferson organized nationally. They accused the Federalists of aristocratic and monarchial leanings, citing large taxes levied to maintain a standing army and navy, the Alien and Sedition Acts seeking to silence the administration's critics, and suppression of the Whiskey Rebellion.

Regional Influences The Republicans again carried the South but also won New York through the efforts of vice-presidential nominee Burr. The election was thrown into the House when Jefferson and Burr received an equal number of electoral votes. With Hamilton's support, Jefferson won the election in the Federalist-dominated House.

1804

Party	Candidate	Popular vote	%	Electoral vote
Democratic-Republican	Thomas Jefferson (Va.)	N.A.	N.A.	162
	and George Clinton (N.Y.)	N.A.	N.A.	162
Federalist	Charles C. Pinckney (S.C.)	N.A.	N.A.	14
	and Rufus King (N.Y.)	N.A.	N.A.	14

Key Issues In 1804 Vice President Burr, a northern Republican, joined with a group of northeastern Federalists in a plot to unite New York and New England in a separate nation. The plot was exposed, discrediting the Federalists. Jefferson, already popular for his personal qualities as well as the Louisiana Purchase, swept to an easy victory.

Regional Influences Jefferson lost only three states and even swept all of New England with the exception of Connecticut.

1808

Party	Candidate	Popular vote	%	Electoral vote
Democratic-Republican	James Madison (Va.)	N.A.	N.A.	122
	and George Clinton (N.Y.)	N.A.	N.A.	113
Federalist	Charles C. Pinckney (S.C.)	N.A.	N.A.	47
	and Rufus King (N.Y.)	N.A.	N.A.	47

Note: Clinton received six electoral votes for president. Madison and James Monroe of Virginia both received three electoral votes for vice president.

Key Issues Jefferson reinforced the two-term precedent by refusing to run for a third term. Madison, his chosen successor, easily won the Republican nomination and the presidency.

Regional Influences Pinckney and the Federalists regained most of the New England votes lost four years earlier and increased their strength in Congress as a result of commercial opposition to the embargo imposed by Jefferson on the export of American goods to warring European nations.

1812

Party	Candidate	Popular vote	%	Electoral vote
Democratic-Republican	James Madison (Va.)	N.A.	N.A.	128
	and Elbridge Gerry (Mass.)	N.A.	N.A.	131
Federalist	DeWitt Clinton (N.Y.)	N.A.	N.A.	89
	and Jared Ingersoll (Pa.)	N.A.	N.A.	86

Regional Influences Commercial interests in the Northeast were opposed to war with Great Britain. The original 13 states were evenly split in the election, favoring Madison 90–89. New England, except Vermont, voted for Clinton, as did a majority of the Middle Atlantic states. The South voted unanimously for Madison. But all of the western states voted for Madison and thus for war.

Key Issues The election was a referendum on Madison's bid for a declaration of war against Great Britain in response to Britain's attempts to block the sale of southern raw materials in European markets. A vote for Madison was a vote for war; a vote for Clinton a vote for peace.

1816

Party	Candidate	Popular vote	%	Electoral vote
Democratic-Republican	James Monroe (Va.)	N.A.	N.A.	183
	and D.D. Tompkins (N.Y.)	N.A.	N.A.	183
Federalist	Rufus King (N.Y.)	N.A.	N.A.	34
	and John E. Howard (Md.)	N.A.	N.A.	22

Regional Influences Monroe, Madison's chosen successor, won a landslide victory that seemed to validate Madison's nationalistic program, which called for a stronger standing army, a protective tariff, uniform currency, and a nationwide system of roads and canals, including the Cumberland Road. The Federalists won only three states, all in New England.

Key Issues Nationalism triumphed after the war with Britain, a time of national and economic growth that saw establishment of an expanded standing army, central bank, federal tariff, and large internal improvements despite opposition from northeastern Federalists.

1820

Party	Candidate	Popular vote	%	Electoral vote
Democratic-Republican	James Monroe (Va.)	N.A.	N.A.	231
	and D.D. Tompkins (N.Y.)	N.A.	N.A.	218
Democratic-Republican	John Q. Adams (Mass.)	N.A.	N.A.	1

Regional Influences Monroe ran unopposed for reelection. One elector from New Hampshire voted for Adams so that only Washington would hold the honor of being elected to the presidency by a unanimous vote.

Key Issues The election was held at the height of the Era of Good Feelings, though sectional differences over slavery earlier in the year led to the Missouri Compromise, which in its final version resulted in the admittance of Missouri as a slave state with the provision that it allow free blacks of other states to retain their freedom while in Missouri. The Federalists ceased to exist as a functioning party by the time of the election and failed to run a candidate against Monroe.

1824

Party	Candidate	Popular vote	%	Electoral vote
Democratic-Republican	John Q. Adams (Mass.)	113,122	30.92	84
Democratic-Republican	Andrew Jackson (Tenn.)	151,271	41.34	99
Democratic-Republican	William H. Crawford (Ga.)	40,876	11.17	41
Democratic-Republican	Henry Clay (Ky.)	47,531	12.99	37
Other		13,053	3.57	—
	Total vote	365,833		
	Jackson plurality	38,149		

Regional Influences Each candidate represented his region: Adams the commercial Northeast, Crawford the cotton South, Clay and Jackson the agrarian West. Jackson, a hero of the War of 1812 and battles against Indians, won a clear plurality of the popular vote, and was the only candidate with support outside his home region. But no candidate won a majority of the electoral vote and the election was decided in the House, where Speaker Clay's support gave the victory to Adams.

Key Issues Personalities dominated an election in which all four candidates ran as Democratic-Republicans. Crawford, Monroe's treasury secretary, won the nomination of the party's congressional caucus. But few attended the caucus and most electors were chosen by state legislatures. Crawford later suffered a stroke and was not a serious candidate. John C. Calhoun of South Carolina ran unopposed for vice president.

"I cannot believe that the killing of 2,000 Englishmen at New Orleans qualifies a person for . . . the presidency."

—Henry Clay

1828

Party	Candidate	Popular vote	%	Electoral vote
Democratic-Republican	Andrew Jackson (Tenn.)	642,553	55.97	178
	and John C. Calhoun (S.C.)			171
National-Republican	John Q. Adams (Mass.)	500,987	43.63	83
	and Richard Rush (Pa.)			83
Other		4,568	0.40	—
	Total vote	1,148,018		
	Jackson plurality	141,656		

Regional Influences Jackson won the South and West easily and appealed to discontented laborers in the North. Adams carried only New England, New Jersey, Maryland, and Delaware.

Key Issues Personalities again overshadowed issues. The Jackson campaign catered to popular prejudices, portraying the contest as one between democracy and aristocracy. The Jackson coalition was a forerunner of the modern Democratic party and reestablished two-party politics in the country.

1832

Party	Candidate	Popular vote	%	Electoral vote
Democrat	Andrew Jackson (Tenn.)	701,780	54.23	219
	and Martin Van Buren (N.Y.)			189
National-Republican	Henry Clay (Ky.)	484,205	37.42	49
	and John Sergeant (Pa.)			49
Anti-Masonic	William Wirt (Md.)	100,715	7.78	7
	and Amos Ellmaker (Pa.)			7
Independent	John Floyd (Va.)	N.A.	N.A.	11
	and Henry Lee (Mass.)			11
Other		7,273	0.56	—
	Total vote	1,293,973		
	Jackson plurality	217,575		

Regional Influences Anti-Masonic strength was concentrated in rural sections of New England and the Middle Atlantic states. In those states, National-Republicans and Anti-Masons supported the same ticket. With the forces against him divided, Jackson won easily. Clay won only half of the New England states, Wirt only Vermont. Jackson captured Maine and New Hampshire. In South Carolina, where electors still were chosen by the legislature, nullificationists cast their ballots for Floyd.

Key Issues The Anti-Masons, the first third-party in American politics, began in opposition to secret societies in particular and privileged groups in general but were at heart an anti-Jackson party. The two established parties followed the Anti-Masons' lead by holding national nominating conventions to select a presidential nominee. While Jackson's opposition to the Bank of the United States was made an issue by the two major parties, the election was more a referendum on Jackson himself.

1836

Party	Candidate	Popular vote	%	Electoral vote
Democrat	Martin Van Buren (N.Y.)	764,716	50.83	170
	and Richard M. Johnson (Ky.)			147
Whig	William Henry Harrison (Ohio)	550,816	36.63	73
Whig	Hugh L. White (Tenn.)	146,107	9.72	26
Whig	Daniel Webster (Mass.)	41,201	2.74	14
	Willie P. Mangum (N.C.)	N.A.	N.A.	11
Other		1,234	0.08	—
	Total vote	1,503,534		
	Van Buren plurality	213,360		

Regional Influences Whig strategy was to throw the election into the House, where they could unite around a single candidate. Webster was to win New England, Harrison the West, and White the South. Van Buren, forced on the Democrats by Jackson, foiled the plan by picking up enough states throughout the nation to win by a slim majority. Johnson fell one electoral vote short of a majority for vice president and was selected by the Senate. The South Carolina legislature cast its votes for Mangum.

Key Issues Jackson's heavy-handed tactics, especially in his successful battle against the national bank, led the National-Republicans to rename themselves Whigs, after the 18th-century British party that tried to lessen the power of the Crown. But lacking effective national leadership and divided along sectional lines, the anti-Jackson forces could not agree on a single candidate or platform and instead ran three regional candidates.

"Van Buren is a demagogue with a tincture of aristocracy— an amalgamated metal of lead and copper."

—John Quincy Adams to his diary

1840

Party	Candidate	Popular vote	%	Electoral vote
Whig	William Henry Harrison (Ohio) and John Tyler (Va.)	1,275,390	52.88	234
Democrat	Martin Van Buren (N.Y.)	1,128,854	46.81	60
Liberty	James G. Birney (N.Y.)	6,797	0.28	—
Other		767	0.03	—
	Total vote	2,411,808		
	Harrison plurality	146,536		

Regional Influences Van Buren won only seven states, just one outside of the South or West. Harrison was long associated with the West, and Tyler was a conservative southerner and friend of Henry Clay. For the first time, active two-party politics was established across the nation. The 68-year-old Harrison caught a severe cold after delivering a lengthy inaugural address in the rain and died one month into his term.

Key Issues With the country still reeling from the Panic of 1837, the Democrats were on the defensive. Though differences prevented them from writing a platform, the Whigs rallied around Harrison. In a campaign notable for its absence of issues, the Whigs turned the tables on Jackson's party. Harrison, despite his wealthy origins, was portrayed as the "log-cabin, hard-cider candidate" opposing the allegedly aristocratic Van Buren. The Democrats left the selection of a vice-presidential candidate to each state.

"Tippecanoe and Tyler, too."
—Harrison campaign slogan

"Log cabin and hard cider."
—Tyler campaign slogan

1844

Party	Candidate	Popular vote	%	Electoral vote
Democrat	James K. Polk (Tenn.) and George M. Dallas (Pa.)	1,339,494	49.54	170
Whig	Henry Clay (Ky.) and Theodore Frelinghuysen (N.J.)	1,300,004	48.08	105
Abolitionist	James G. Birney (N.Y.)	62,103	2.30	—
Other		2,058	0.08	—
	Total vote	2,703,659		
	Polk plurality	39,490		

Regional Influences Expansionism was immensely popular, especially in the South and West, where memories of the depression following 1837 added to the attraction of new, vast, and open public lands. Support for Manifest Destiny more than made up for antislavery sentiment elsewhere, and Polk won a narrow plurality but a clear victory.

Key Issues Manifest Destiny, the goal of a nation stretching from the Atlantic to the Pacific, was the central issue because of the question of the annexation of Texas. With the election approaching, opponents of slavery led the Senate to reject a treaty between Texas and the Tyler Administration that would have preserved slavery in Texas and made the state a U.S. territory. The two leading presidential candidates, Clay and Van Buren, sought to smother the Texas issue by ignoring it. But Polk snatched the Democratic nomination with his clear and vocal advocacy of annexation of Texas and general territorial expansion.

"Fifty-four forty or fight."
—Polk campaign slogan

1848

Party	Candidate	Popular vote	%	Electoral vote
Whig	Zachary Taylor (La.) and Millard Fillmore (N.Y.)	1,361,393	47.28	163
Democrat	Lewis Cass (Mich.) and William O. Butler (Ky.)	1,223,460	42.49	127
Free Soil	Martin Van Buren (N.Y.) and Charles Francis Adams (Mass.)	291,501	10.12	—
Other		2,830	0.10	—
	Total vote	2,879,184		
	Taylor plurality	137,933		

Regional Influences Both major parties balanced their tickets with a northerner and southerner. Free Soilers were mostly northern Democrats, antislavery Whigs and abolitionists. There was no distinct pattern in the Electoral College following a lackluster campaign. Free Soil strength in New York gave the state and the election to the Whigs.

Key Issues The Wilmot Proviso, calling for a ban on extension of slavery into territories acquired in the Mexican War, dominated the election. But both major parties evaded the issue. Slavery foes banded together to form the Free Soil party, which won no electoral votes but drew enough popular support away from the Democrats to throw the election to Old Rough and Ready, Zachary Taylor, a slave holder. Taylor died in July 1850.

1852

Party	Candidate	Popular vote	%	Electoral vote
Democrat	Franklin Pierce (N.H.) and William R.D. King (Ala.)	1,607,510	50.84	254
Whig	Winfield Scott (Va.) and William A. Graham (N.C.)	1,386,942	43.87	42
Free Soil	John P. Hale (N.H.) and George Washington Julian (Ind.)	155,210	4.91	—
Other		12,168	0.38	—
	Total vote	3,161,830		
	Pierce plurality	220,568		

Regional Influences The Democrats won a resounding electoral victory, capturing 27 states to the four taken by the Whigs: Massachusetts, Vermont, Kentucky, and Tennessee. Free Soilers returned to the Democrats and the Whigs never again were a political force in a nation that believed the slave question was behind it.

Key Issues The election was a referendum on the Compromise of 1850, in which Congress voted to admit California as a free state, create the territories of New Mexico and Utah with no restriction on slavery, abolish the slave trade in the District of Columbia, purchase disputed land from Texas on behalf of New Mexico, and toughen the Fugitive Slave Act. The Democrats strongly endorsed the Compromise, but the bitterly divided Whigs only vaguely accepted it.

*"We Polked you in '44;
We shall Pierce you in '52."*
—Campaign slogan

1856

Party	Candidate	Popular vote	%	Electoral vote
Democrat	James Buchanan (Pa.) and John C. Breckinridge (Ky.)	1,836,072	45.28	174
Republican	John C. Fremont (Calif.) and William L. Dayton (N.J.)	1,342,345	33.11	114
Whig	Millard Fillmore (N.Y.) and Andrew J. Donelson (Tenn.)	873,053	21.53	8
Other		3,177	0.08	—
	Total vote	4,054,647		
	Buchanan plurality	493,727		

Regional Influences Fremont carried all but five of the free states. But Buchanan won all of the South in addition to the five northern states and was elected. Fillmore, supported by the "Know-Nothings" and Whig remnants, won only Maryland but strongly challenged the Democrats in the South.

Key Issues The Democrats firmly endorsed "popular sovereignty," even though it led to great turmoil in the territory of Kansas. But they chose as their nominee Buchanan, largely because he had been out of the country and was untainted by the "Bleeding Kansas" battle, which pitted supporters and foes of slavery trying to organize the territory into a slave or free state. The Republicans, a new party of northern Whigs and Democrats committed to the containment of slavery, ran Fremont, a popular general and explorer.

*"Peace at any price;
peace and union."*
—Fillmore campaign slogan

1860

Party	Candidate	Popular vote	%	Electoral vote
Republican	Abraham Lincoln (Ill.) and Hannibal Hamlin (Maine)	1,865,908	39.82	180
Democrat	Stephen A. Douglas (Ill.) and Herschel V. Johnson (Ga.)	1,380,202	29.46	12
Democrat	John C. Breckinridge (Ky.) and Joseph Lane (Oreg.)	848,019	18.09	72
Constitutional Union	John Bell (Tenn.) and Edward Everett (Mass.)	590,901	12.61	39
Other		531	0.01	—
	Total vote	4,685,561		
	Lincoln plurality	485,706		

Key Issues Sectional differences over slavery came to a head in 1860. The Democrats could not agree on a candidate and split into northern and southern factions. The northern faction backed Douglas and popular sovereignty, the southern faction Breckinridge and federal protection of slavery in the territories. The Republicans, virtually all northerners, were a protariff, nationalistic party that opposed the extension of slavery but did not seek to overturn it where it already existed. Bell, the candidate of Whigs and Know-Nothings who backed Fillmore in 1856, ran for the Constitutional Union, a compromise party expressing support for preservation of the Union.

Regional Influences In effect there were two separate contests in 1860: Lincoln versus Douglas in the North, Breckinridge versus Bell in the South. Free states outnumbered slave states and cast half again as many electoral votes. Lincoln won every northern state except New Jersey and, though not even on the ballot in 10 southern states, was elected president. Breckinridge captured 11 of the 15 southern states. The four southern states won by Douglas and Bell were in the upper South.

1864

Party	Candidate	Popular vote	%	Electoral vote
Republican	Abraham Lincoln (Ill.) and Andrew Johnson (Tenn.)	2,218,388	55.02	212
Democrat	George B. McClellan (N.Y.) and George H. Pendleton (Ohio)	1,812,807	44.96	21
	Total vote	4,031,887		
	Lincoln plurality	405,581		

Regional Influences Military victories around election time helped the embattled incumbent. Lincoln won a convincing popular and electoral victory with the support of middle-class professionals, farmers, laborers and the strongly pro-Union voters who voted for Bell four years earlier. McClellan was strongest in areas carried by Breckinridge four years before. Eleven Confederate states did not participate in the election.

Key Issues Lincoln's renomination was not assured. Radical Republicans thought he was not aggressive enough in his conduct of the war or plans for the eventual peace, but moderation ultimately prevailed. The Republicans ran as the Union party and nominated Johnson, a pro-Union Democrat, for vice president. The Democrats ran a peace campaign, calling the war a failure. But McClellan, a popular general, broke with his party's platform and denied the war was a failure, denouncing members of his party who seemed to advocate peace at any price. He opposed emancipation as a goal of the war.

"With malice toward none, with charity for all, with firmness in the right as God gives us to see the right, let us strive on to finish the work we are in."

—Abraham Lincoln

1868

Party	Candidate	Popular vote	%	Electoral vote
Republican	Ulysses S. Grant (Ohio) and Schuyler Colfax (Ind.)	3,013,650	52.66	214
Democrat	Horatio S. Seymour (N.Y.) and Francis P. Blair (Mo.)	2,708,744	47.34	80
Other		46	—	—
	Total vote	5,722,440		
	Grant plurality	304,906		

Regional Influences Despite Grant's popularity, the Republicans were just able to win the election. Seymour carried only eight states, though he did well in the states won by Grant. Without black votes in the South, Grant would not have received a majority of the popular vote. The votes of the "unreconstructed" states of Mississippi, Texas, and Virginia were not counted.

Key Issues The Republicans waved the "bloody shirt" of the war and ran on their program of Radical Reconstruction. While calling for Negro suffrage in the South, the Republicans asserted it was a matter for individual northern states to decide for themselves. Democrats ran against Reconstruction, declaring that the question of Negro suffrage should be decided by individual southern states as well.

1872

Party	Candidate	Popular vote	%	Electoral vote
Republican	Ulysses S. Grant (Ohio) and Henry Wilson (Mass.)	3,598,235	55.63	286
Liberal Republican/Democrat	Horace Greeley (N.Y.) and Benjamin Gratz Brown (Mo.)	2,834,761	43.83	—
Straight Democrat	Charles O'Conor (N.Y.)	18,602	—	—
Other		16,081	—	—
	Total vote	6,467,679		
	Grant plurality	763,474		

Regional Influences Greeley carried only two states in the lower South and four border states. He died after the election, and his electoral votes went to other candidates: Thomas Hendricks, Indiana, 42; Benjamin Gratz Brown, Missouri, 18; Charles J. Jenkins, Georgia, 2; and David Davis, Illinois, 1.

Key Issues Liberal Republicans broke with Grant over corruption in his administration, high tariffs and continued Radical Reconstruction. They nominated Greeley, editor of the *New York Tribune*. The Democrats endorsed Greeley and the Liberal platform. But the great scandals of the Grant administration were not yet revealed, and the Republicans again waved the bloody shirt to victory.

1876

Party	Candidate	Popular vote	%	Electoral vote
Republican	Rutherford B. Hayes (Ohio) and William A. Wheeler (N.Y.)	4,034,311	47.95	185
Democrat	Samuel J. Tilden (N.Y.) and Thomas A. Hendricks (Ind.)	4,288,546	50.97	184
Greenback	Peter Cooper (N.Y.)	75,973	0.90	—
Other		14,271	0.17	—
	Total vote	8,413,101		
	Tilden plurality	254,235		

Regional Influences As election day approached, Tilden could count on winning all of the South except for the three states still controlled by Republican carpetbaggers: South Carolina, Louisiana, and Florida. He seemed assured of victory when those states appeared to vote for him, along with several northern states, including New York and New Jersey. But Republicans claimed South Carolina, Louisiana, and Florida for Hayes, arguing that thousands of blacks who would have voted for Hayes were barred from voting there. Election boards in those Republican-controlled states gave Hayes the needed majority, and thus the election. In the uproar that followed, Congress set up an Election Commission to validate the returns. The commission voted strictly along party lines, eight to seven, to give the election

Key Issues The Republicans were in trouble as 1876 approached, due to rampant corruption in the Grant administration and the economic depression that followed the Panic of 1873. Hayes, a three-term Ohio governor known for his unassailable integrity, was nominated to run against the favored Democrat, Tilden, a New York reform governor whose reputation was made in opposition to the Tweed political machine. Both men espoused conservative economics. Cooper and the Greenbacks advocated currency expansion.

to Hayes. Despite charges that Republicans stole the election, Hayes was later inaugurated peaceably after he let it be known that as president he would end military reconstruction by withdrawing federal troops from the South and would restore "efficient local government" there.

1880

Party	Candidate	Popular vote	%	Electoral vote
Republican	James A. Garfield (Ohio) and Chester A. Arthur (N.Y.)	4,461,158	48.27	214
Democrat	Winfield S. Hancock (Pa.) and William H. English (Ind.)	4,444,260	48.25	155
Greenback	James B. Weaver (Iowa) and Benjamin J. Chambers (Tex.)	305,997	3.32	—
Other		14,005	0.15	—
	Total vote	9,210,420		
	Garfield plurality	16,898		

Regional Influences The balance between Republican strength in the Midwest and West and Democratic strength in the South resulted in a plurality of less than 17,000 for Garfield out of more than 9 million votes cast. Four months into his term, Garfield was shot by a disappointed office-seeker.

Key Issues With the war and Reconstruction behind, no major issues arose over which the major parties disagreed. The Democrats, the party of secession 20 year earlier, nominated Gen. Hancock to help combat the stigma of treason. Garfield made a protectionist tariff central to his campaign.

1884

Party	Candidate	Popular vote	%	Electoral vote
Democrat	Grover Cleveland (N.Y.) and Thomas A. Hendricks (Ind.)	4,874,621	48.50	219
Republican	James G. Blaine (Maine) and John A. Logan (Ill.)	4,848,936	48.25	182
Greenback	Benjamin F. Butler (Mass.)	175,096	1.74	—
Prohibitionist	John P. St. John (Kans.)	147,482	1.47	—
Other		3,619	0.04	
	Total votes	10,049,754		
	Cleveland plurality	25,685		

Regional Influences Cleveland carried all of the southern states as well as the key swing states of Indiana, New Jersey, Connecticut, and New York, becoming the first Democrat elected president since the Civil War. Cleveland carried his home state of New York and its 36 electoral votes by less than 1,200 votes.

Key Issues The private lives and morals of the candidates were the focus of a campaign notable for mudslinging. Blaine was accused of accepting bribes from a railroad company for whom he obtained a federal grant, and Republicans taunted Cleveland for fathering a son out of wedlock. Still, Cleveland, known for his independence and integrity in public life, attracted the votes of many liberal Republicans and reformers unable to stomach Blaine, a Radical Republican leader.

1888

Party	Candidate	Popular vote	%	Electoral vote
Republican	Benjamin Harrison (Ind.) and Levi P. Morton (N.Y.)	5,443,892	47.82	233
Democrat	Grover Cleveland (N.Y.) and Allen G. Thurman (Ohio)	5,534,488	48.62	168
Prohibitionist	Clinton B. Fisk (N.J.)	249,813	2.19	—
Union Labor	Alson J. Streeter (Ill.)	146,602	1.29	—
Other		8,519	0.07	—
	Total vote	11,383,320		
	Cleveland plurality	90,596		

Regional Influences Despite the emphasis on the tariff, Cleveland still carried manufacturing states such as New Jersey and Connecticut as well as most of the South. But though Cleveland won 90,000 more popular votes than Harrison, the Republican carried the protariff swing states of Indiana and New York by slight margins to win the election in the electoral college in one of the most corrupt campaigns in history.

Key Issues Cleveland made tariff reform central to his administration, seeking to lower existing high tariffs. The Republicans campaigned on the need to maintain high wages by keeping a high tariff on imported goods.

> *"We Americans have no permission from God to police the world."*
>
> —Benjamin Harrison

1892

Party	Candidate	Popular vote	%	Electoral vote
Democrat	Grover Cleveland (N.Y.) and Adlai E. Stevenson (Ill.)	5,551,883	46.05	277
Republican	Benjamin Harrison (Ind.) and Whitelaw Reid (N.Y.)	5,179,244	42.96	145
Populist	James B. Weaver (Iowa) and James G. Field (Va.)	1,024,280	8.50	22
Prohibitionist	John Bidwell (Calif.)	270,770	2.25	—
Other		29,920	0.25	—
	Total votes	12,056,097		
	Cleveland plurality	372,639		

Regional Influences Cleveland improved on his 1884 and 1888 showings to win the most decisive presidential victory in 20 years. This time he carried the swing states of New York, New Jersey, Connecticut, and Indiana as well as the traditionally Republican states of Illinois, California, and Wisconsin.

Key Issues Cleveland and Harrison again fought a battle over the tariff, which the Republicans drastically raised in 1890. Both men were out of touch with the growing agrarian and populist discontent. Weaver, campaigning for free silver, became the first third-party candidate to gain electoral votes since the war.

> *"Ma, Ma, where's my Pa? Gone to the White House, ha, ha, ha."*
>
> —Chant poking fun at Cleveland, who admitted siring an illegitimate child

1896

Party	Candidate	Popular vote	%	Electoral vote
Republican	William McKinley (Ohio) and Garret A. Hobart (N.J.)	7,108,480	51.01	271
Democrat/Populist	William J. Bryan (Nebr.) and Democrat Arthur Sewall (Maine) and Populist Thomas E. Watson (Ga.)	6,511,495	46.73	176 149
National Democrat	John M. Palmer (Ill.)	133,435	0.96	—
Prohibition	Joshua Levering (Md.)	125,072	0.90	—
Other		57,256	0.41	—
	Total vote	13,935,738		
	McKinley plurality	596,985		

Regional Influences Bryan did not carry a single state north of Virginia or east of Missouri. His hold on the agricultural South and West was broken by Republican victories in Maryland, Delaware, West Virginia, Kentucky, California, and Oregon. Bryan, failing to appeal to labor, carried no industrial or urban states.

Key Issues The Democrats absorbed Populist energies and abandoned the conservatism of Cleveland by nominating Bryan and adopting key elements of the Populist program, especially the call for free silver. The protariff and progold Republicans led by McKinley and Mark Hanna outspent the Democrats by almost 12 to 1. In losing, Bryan amassed more votes than any victorious candidate before him.

> *"You shall not press down upon the brow of labor this crown of thorns. You shall not crucify mankind upon a cross of gold."*
>
> —William Jennings Bryan

1900

Party	Candidate	Popular vote	%	Electoral vote
Republican	William McKinley (Ohio) and Theodore Roosevelt (N.Y.)	7,218,039	51.67	292
Democrat	William J. Bryan (Nebr.) and Adlai E. Stevenson (Ill.)	6,358,345	45.51	155
Prohibition	John C. Woolley (Ill.)	209,004	1.50	—
Social Democrat	Eugene V. Debs (Ind.)	86,935	0.62	—
Other		98,147	0.70	—
	Total vote	13,970,470		
	McKinley plurality	859,694		

Regional Influences Bryan carried only the solid South and four silver states in the West and was defeated in the silver states of Kansas, South Dakota, Utah, and Wyoming as well as his home state of Nebraska. Both houses of Congress were led by significant Republican majorities.

Key Issues Imperialism in the Philippines joined free silver and the tariff as the key issues in a replay of the 1896 election. Bryan tried to unite the silver interests in the West and South with supporters of the gold standard in a coalition against imperialism, which the Democratic platform called the "paramount issue" of the campaign. But voters did not desert McKinley in a time of prosperity.

> *"McKinley drinks soda water,*
> *Bryan drinks rum;*
> *McKinley is a gentleman,*
> *Bryan is a bum."*
>
> —Campaign song

1904

Party	Candidate	Popular vote	%	Electoral vote
Republican	Theodore Roosevelt (N.Y.) and Charles W. Fairbanks (Ind.)	7,626,593	56.41	336
Democrat	Alton B. Parker (N.Y.) and Henry G. Davis (W. Va.)	5,082,898	37.60	140
Socialist	Eugene V. Debs (Ind.)	402,489	2.98	—
Prohibition	Silas C. Swallow (Pa.)	258,596	1.91	—
Other		148,388	1.10	—
	Total votes	13,518,964		
	Roosevelt plurality	2,543,695		

Regional Influences Roosevelt won a landslide victory based largely on his own personality and popularity. The Democrats won only 13 states, none outside the South.

Key Issues Roosevelt stole the mantle of reform from the Democrats with his campaigns against the "malefactors of great wealth." The Democrats turned to the right by nominating the lackluster Parker, a judge with close ties to Wall Street. Parker turned his back on Bryan Democrats by renouncing free silver.

1908

Party	Candidate	Popular vote	%	Electoral vote
Republican	William H. Taft (Ohio) and James S. Sherman (N.Y.)	7,662,258	51.58	321
Democrat	William J. Bryan (Nebr.) and John W. Kern (Ind.)	6,406,801	43.05	162
Socialist	Eugene V. Debs (Ind.)	420,380	2.82	—
Prohibition	Eugene W. Chafin (Ill.)	252,821	1.70	—
Other		126,474	0.85	—
	Total vote	14,882,734		
	Taft plurality	1,269,457		

Regional Influences Bryan again carried the South. But the appeal of Roosevelt's reform programs helped the Republicans do well in the West, and Taft's background as a Yale graduate and federal jurist enabled him to carry the East as well.

Key Issues The immensely popular Roosevelt declined to run. Taft, his secretary of war and handpicked successor, debated Bryan over who was better qualified to complete TR's progressive program. Bryan abandoned silver and courted labor but ran a lackluster, losing campaign.

1912

Party	Candidate	Popular vote	%	Electoral vote
Democrat	Woodrow Wilson (N.J.) and Thomas Marshall (Ind.)	6,293,152	41.84	435
Progressive	Theodore Roosevelt (N.Y.) and Hiram Johnson (Calif.)	4,119,207	27.39	88
Republican	William H. Taft (Ohio) and James S. Sherman (N.Y.)	3,486,333	23.18	8
Socialist	Eugene V. Debs (Ind.)	900,369	5.99	—
Other		241,902	1.61	—
	Total vote	15,040,963		
	Wilson plurality	2,173,945		

Regional Influences Though he amassed fewer votes than did Bryan in 1908, Wilson took advantage of the split in the Republican ranks to win a decisive plurality of the vote. He did best in traditional Democratic states but was able to win most traditionally Republican states as well. Roosevelt won only six states, including California, which he carried by fewer than 200 votes. Taft carried Utah and Vermont. The Democrats also won control of both houses of Congress, their best overall performance since the Civil War.

Key Issues Taft's conservatism and political ineptitude led Roosevelt to challenge him within the party from the left. Unable to wrest the nomination from Taft, Roosevelt ran a third-party campaign. The election boiled down to a contest between Roosevelt and Wilson and their respective conceptions of progressivism. Roosevelt's "New Nationalism" called for strong federal regulations to control the trusts and big businesses. Wilson's "New Freedom" sought instead to revive competition through vigorous application of antitrust laws. The Progressives advocated a broad array of social reforms to be implemented by the federal government, while the Democrats emphasized the primacy of the states in such matters.

"My hat is in the ring."
—Theodore Roosevelt

1916

Party	Candidate	Popular vote	%	Electoral vote
Democrat	Woodrow Wilson (Va.) and Thomas Marshall (Ind.)	9,126,300	49.24	277
Republican	Charles Evans Hughes (N.Y.) and Charles W. Fairbanks (Ind.)	8,546,789	46.11	254
Socialist	Allen L. Benson (N.Y.)	589,924	3.18	—
Prohibitionist	James F. Hanly (Ind.)	221,030	1.19	—
Other		50,979	0.28	—
	Total vote	18,535,022		
	Wilson plurality	579,511		

Regional Influences Hughes, a former reform governor of New York who left the Supreme Court to challenge Wilson, carried all of the East except New Hampshire and all of the Old Northwest, except Ohio. But the South was again solid for the Democrats as was every state west of the Mississippi except Minnesota, Iowa, South Dakota, and Oregon, which Wilson lost by close margins. The electoral vote was the closest since 1876.

Key Issues The campaign was a referendum on Wilson's first term: his program of domestic reform and his policy toward the war in Europe. He ran a peace campaign with the slogan He Kept Us Out of War and attracted the votes of many Bull Moosers. Voters who felt Wilson was either too harsh or too lenient toward Germany tended to vote Republican. Irish-American and German-American extremists, virulently opposed to aiding Great Britain, embarrassed Hughes with their vocal support. A coalition of labor, farmers, reformers, and intellectuals won the election for Wilson.

"He kept us out of war."
—Wilson campaign slogan

1920

Party	Candidate	Popular vote	%	Electoral vote
Republican	Warren G. Harding (Ohio) and Calvin Coolidge (Mass.)	16,133,314	60.30	404
Democrat	James M. Cox (Ohio) and Franklin D. Roosevelt (N.Y.)	9,140,884	34.17	127
Socialist	Eugene V. Debs (Ind.)	913,664	3.42	—
Farmer-Labor	Parley P. Christensen (Utah)	264,540	0.99	—
Other		301,384	1.13	—
	Total Vote	26,753,786		
	Harding Plurality	6,992,430		

Regional Influences Harding carried every state outside of the South, except Tennessee. The Republicans added to their majorities in both houses of Congress, regained in 1918.

Key Issues The voters turned against Wilsonian progressivism and internationalism by electing Harding, a vacuous party hack who promised a "return to normalcy" after the turbulent years of domestic reform and world war. The undistinguished Cox ran in support of the League of Nations and little else.

"Cox and cocktails."

"Back to normalcy."
—Cox and Harding campaign slogans

1924

Party	Candidate	Popular vote	%	Electoral vote
Republican	Calvin Coolidge (Mass.) and Charles G. Dawes (Ohio)	15,717,553	54.00	382
Democrat	John W. Davis (N.Y.) and Charles W. Bryan (Nebr.)	8,386,169	28.84	136
Progressive Socialist	Robert M. LaFollette (Wis.) and Burton K. Wheeler (Mont.)	4,814,050	16.56	13
Other		158,187	0.55	—
	Total vote	29,075,959		
	Coolidge plurality	7,331,384		

Regional Influences All 12 of the Democratic states were from the South. LaFollette's 13 electoral votes came from his home state of Wisconsin.

Key Issues The country "kept cool with Coolidge," since the Democrats could not overcome prosperity or themselves. Davis, a conservative Wall Street lawyer, was a compromise nominee selected by a bitterly divided party after 103 ballots. Reformers, laborers, and farmers flocked to the LaFollette candidacy.

"Keep cool with Coolidge."

—Campaign slogan

1928

Party	Candidate	Popular vote	%	Electoral vote
Republican	Herbert C. Hoover (Calif.) and Charles E. Curtis (Kans.)	21,411,911	58.20	444
Democrat	Alfred E. Smith (N.Y.) and Joseph T. Robinson (Ark.)	15,000,185	40.77	87
Socialist	Norman Thomas (N.Y.)	266,453	0.72	—
Worker's	William Z. Foster (Ill.)	48,170	0.13	—
Other		63,565	0.17	—
	Total vote	36,790,364		
	Hoover plurality	6,411,806		

Regional Influences The solid South was shattered as Hoover Democrats gave Republicans the states of Virginia, North Carolina, Tennessee, Florida, and Texas for the first time since Reconstruction. Smith lost his own state and every western and border state. But Smith set the stage for the New Deal coalition: with the votes of urban ethnics, he carried the nation's 12 largest cities, all of which had been won by the Republicans four years earlier. The Democrats also won votes in the traditionally Republican West among farmers uncertain about prosperity.

Key Issues Booze, bigotry, Tammany, and prosperity did in the Democrats. Rural America would not vote for an anti-Prohibition, big-city, Catholic machine-politician, despite Smith's success as governor of New York, especially while the Republicans could convincingly cite the success of their economic leadership.

"I have no fears for the future of our country. It is bright with hope."

—Hoover's inaugural address

1932

Party	Candidate	Popular vote	%	Electoral vote
Democrat	Franklin D. Roosevelt (N.Y.) and John Nance Garner (Tex.)	22,825,016	57.42	472
Republican	Herbert C. Hoover (Calif.) and Charles E. Curtis (Kans.)	15,758,397	39.64	59
Socialist	Norman Thomas (N.Y.)	883,990	2.22	—
Communist	William Z. Foster (Ill.)	102,221	0.26	—
Other		179,758	0.45	—
	Total vote	39,749,382		
	Roosevelt plurality	7,066,619		

Regional Influences Roosevelt lost only six states—Maine, New Hampshire, Vermont, Connecticut, Delaware, and Pennsylvania—carrying all of the agricultural West and South. He put the finishing touches on the New Deal coalition by improving on Smith's margins of victory in the nation's big cities.

Key Issues The Democrats won by blaming the Republicans for the Great Depression. Roosevelt was the first presidential nominee of a major party to address his nominating convention, pledging to help the "forgotten man at the bottom of the economic pyramid." In a vague and contradictory platform, the Democrats promised to balance the federal budget by drastically reducing expenses and vowed to spend federal dollars to attack the nation's economic woes.

1936

Party	Candidate	Popular vote	%	Electoral vote
Democrat	Franklin D. Roosevelt(N.Y.) and John Nance Garner (Tex.)	27,747,636	60.79	523
Republican	Alfred M. Landon (Kans.) and Frank Knox (Ill.)	16,679,543	36.54	8
Union	William Lemke (N.Dak.)	892,492	1.96	—
Socialist	Norman Thomas (N.Y.)	187,785	0.41	—
Other		134,847	0.30	—
	Total vote	45,642,303		
	Roosevelt plurality	11,068,093		

Regional Influences Roosevelt carried every state except Maine and Vermont. The New Deal coalition was at its height, with every large city voting overwhelmingly for FDR. The middle class, farmers in the West and South, big-city ethnics, laborers, and reform intellectuals flocked to the Democrats. Northern blacks also began to vote heavily Democratic for the first time.

Key Issues Despite intense opposition to the New Deal, its great public appeal was confirmed in the most one-sided election since 1820 and sweeping victories for the Democrats in Congress. The populist forces of the late Huey Long coalesced around Lemke but failed to gather widespread support.

> *"In the place of the palace of privilege we seek to build a temple out of faith and hope and charity."*
>
> —Franklin D. Roosevelt

1940

Party	Candidate	Popular vote	%	Electoral vote
Democrat	Franklin D. Roosevelt (N.Y.) and Henry A. Wallace (Iowa)	27,263,448	54.70	449
Republican	Wendell L. Willkie (Ind.) and Charles L. McNary (Ore.)	22,336,260	44.82	82
Socialist	Norman Thomas (N.Y.)	116,827	0.23	—
Prohibitionist	Roger W. Babson (Mass.)	58,685	0.12	—
Other		65,223	0.13	—
	Total vote	49,840,443		
	Roosevelt plurality	4,927,188		

Regional Influences Willkie carried only 10 states, mostly in the Midwest. But Roosevelt's percentage of the popular vote was markedly down from 1936.

Key Issues With war raging in Europe, the electorate turned its attention from domestic to foreign affairs. The international scene led the Democrats to break with tradition and renominate FDR for a third term. The Republicans turned to businessman and political neophyte Willkie, a charismatic former Democrat. Willkie's internationalism and the pledge of both candidates to keep the country out of the war minimized the role of foreign policy in the campaign.

1944

Party	Candidate	Popular vote	%	Electoral vote
Democrat	Franklin D. Roosevelt (N.Y.) and Harry S Truman (Mo.)	25,611,936	53.39	432
Republican	Thomas E. Dewey (N.Y.) and John W. Bricker (Ohio)	22,013,372	45.89	99
Socialist	Norman Thomas (N.Y.)	79,100	0.16	—
Prohibitionist	Claude A. Watson (Calif.)	74,733	0.16	—
Other		195,778	0.41	—
	Total vote	47,974,819		
	Roosevelt plurality	3,598,564		

Regional Influences Roosevelt won 36 states, and the Democrats improved their control over Congress and the nation's statehouses. The Republicans won only a handful of western and New England states.

Key Issues With both candidates supporting New Deal social legislation and an international organization to maintain peace after the war, the nation chose to let FDR lead America into the postwar era. Big-city bosses and southern conservatives, with FDR's private support, ousted Henry Wallace from the ticket in favor of Truman.

1948

Party	Candidate	Popular vote	%	Electoral vote
Democrat	Harry S Truman (Mo.) and Alben W. Barkley (Ky.)	24,105,587	49.51	303
Republican	Thomas E. Dewey (N.Y.) and Earl Warren (Calif.)	21,970,017	45.12	189
States' Rights	Strom Thurmond (S.C.) and Fielding L. Wright (Miss.)	1,169,134	2.40	—
Progressive	Henry A. Wallace (Iowa) and Glen H. Taylor (Idaho)	1,157,057	2.38	—
Other		290,647	0.60	—
	Total vote	48,692,442		
	Truman plurality	2,135,570		

Regional Influences Dewey captured all of the Middle Atlantic and New England states, except Massachusetts and Connecticut, along with the Dakotas, Nebraska, and Kansas in the Midwest and Oregon in the Northwest. Thurmond won South Carolina, Mississippi, Alabama, and Louisiana in the Deep South.

Key Issues The Republicans were sure of victory after 16 years of Democratic rule and the desertion of the Democrats by conservative southern Dixiecrats and the ultraliberal Wallace faction. But Dewey's dour personality and Truman's intense whistle-stop campaign against the "do-nothing, good-for-nothing" Republican 80th Congress resulted in one of the biggest upsets in presidential history.

"To err is Truman."
—Popular joke

1952

Party	Candidate	Popular vote	%	Electoral vote
Republican	Dwight D. Eisenhower (Kans.) and Richard M. Nixon (Calif.)	33,936,137	55.13	442
Democrat	Adlai E. Stevenson (Ill.) and John J. Sparkman (Ala.)	27,314,649	44.38	89
Progressive	Vincent W. Hallinan (Calif.)	140,416	0.23	—
Prohibition	Stuart Hamblen (Calif.)	73,413	0.12	—
Other		86,503	0.14	—
	Total vote	61,551,118		
	Eisenhower plurality	6,621,485		

Regional influences Stevenson, who appealed to northern liberals as well as southern states' rights Democrats, carried only nine states in the South. The Republicans also won slight majorities in both houses of Congress and were in control of the national government for the first time in 20 years.

Key Issues Popular war-hero Eisenhower swept to victory after uniting the internationalist and isolationist factions of the Republican party. He routed the Democrats by promising to kick out alleged crooks and Communists in Washington, wage a more aggressive fight against Communists worldwide, and "go to Korea," implying that he had a plan to end the war there.

"I like Ike."

"We need Adlai badly."
—Campaign slogans

1956

Party	Candidate	Popular vote	%	Electoral vote
Republican	Dwight D. Eisenhower (Kans.) and Richard M. Nixon (Calif.)	35,585,247	57.37	457
Democrat	Adlai E. Stevenson (Ill.) and Estes Kefauver (Tenn.)	26,030,172	41.97	73
Constitution/States' Rights	T. Coleman Andrews (Va.)	108,055	0.17	—
Socialist-Labor	Eric Hass (New York)	44,300	0.07	—
Other		257,600	0.42	—
	Total vote	62,025,372		
	Eisenhower plurality	9,555,073		

Regional Influences Winning even more handsomely than he did in 1952, Eisenhower lost only seven southern states.

Key Issues Eisenhower won an easy victory in a rematch of the 1952 election. His popularity did not translate into victories for his party elsewhere, as Democrats increased their control of Congress—regained in 1954—and their hold on the nation's governorships.

1960

Party	Candidate	Popular vote	%	Electoral vote
Democrat	John F. Kennedy (Mass.) and Lyndon B. Johnson (Tex.)	34,221,344	49.72	303
Republican	Richard M. Nixon (Calif.) and Henry Cabot Lodge (Mass.)	34,106,671	49.55	219
Socialist-Labor	Eric Hass (N.Y.)	47,522	0.07	—
Other		337,175	0.48	—
Unpledged (Miss.)		116,248	0.17	—
	Total vote	68,828,960		
	Kennedy plurality	114,673		

Note: Harry F. Byrd of Virginia received 15 electoral votes, including all eight of Mississippi's, six of Alabama's 11 and one of Oklahoma's eight.

Regional Influences The Democrats won a thin victory by narrowly defeating the Republicans in the Middle Atlantic states, the Deep South, Illinois, and Texas. Nixon carried most of the Midwest, border, and western states.

Key Issues Kennedy called for the government to play a larger role in stimulating the national economy in order to fund domestic social programs as well as to sustain a defense buildup and keep ahead militarily of the USSR. The election was the first in which there were nationally televised debates between the two candidates. Kennedy's slick television performance played a role in his narrow triumph.

"And so, my fellow Americans, ask not what your country can do for you; ask what you can do for your country."

—John F. Kennedy

1964

Party	Candidate	Popular vote	%	Electoral vote
Democrat	Lyndon B. Johnson (Tex.) and Hubert H. Humphrey (Minn.)	43,126,584	61.05	486
Republican	Barry M. Goldwater (Ariz.) and William E. Miller (N.Y.)	27,177,838	38.47	52
Socialist-Labor	Eric Hass (N.Y.)	45,187	0.06	—
Socialist Workers	Clifton DeBerry (N.Y.)	32,701	0.05	—
Other		258,794	0.37	—
	Total vote	70,641,104		
	Johnson plurality	15,948,746		

Regional Influences Johnson won all but six states—Goldwater's home state of Arizona and five states in the Deep South—in the biggest popular and electoral landslide since 1936. Forty new northern Democrats were elected to the House on LBJ's coattails.

Key Issues Johnson ran for election in his own right on the basis of his "Great Society" domestic programs. The reactionary Goldwater campaigned against the New Deal and for the bombing of North Vietnam.

"So here is the Great Society. It's the time— and it's going to be soon— when nobody in this country is poor."

—Lyndon B. Johnson

1968

Party	Candidate	Popular vote	%	Electoral vote
Republican	Richard M. Nixon (Calif.) and Spiro T. Agnew (Md.)	31,785,148	43.42	301
Democrat	Hubert H. Humphrey (Minn.) and Edmund S. Muskie (Maine)	31,274,503	42.72	191
American Independent	George C. Wallace (Ala.) and Curtis LeMay (Ohio)	901,151	13.53	46
Socialist-Labor	Henning A. Blomen (Mass.)	52,591	0.07	—
Other		189,977	0.20	—
	Total vote	73,203,370		
	Nixon plurality	510,645		

Regional Influences Barely more than 500,-000 votes separated Nixon and Humphrey, but the Republican edge in the Electoral College was comfortable, and the combined anti-Democratic vote amounted to a repudiation of the Johnson-Humphrey administration. Humphrey's strength was in the eastern seaboard states. Wallace won five states in the Deep South.

Key Issues With the country divided over Vietnam, Humphrey failed to emerge from the shadow of the unpopular Johnson, while the previously hawkish Nixon pledged to end the war there and hinted he had a secret plan to do so. Wallace attacked desegregation, "pointy-headed" intellectuals, the administration's timidity in Vietnam amd federal encroachment on states' rights, in an effort to capture blue-collar votes in the North as well as in his southern base.

"Hey, hey, L.B.J.! How many kids did you kill today?"

—Antiwar slogan

1972

Party	Candidate	Popular vote	%	Electoral vote
Republican	Richard M. Nixon (Calif.) and Spiro T. Agnew (Md.)	47,170,179	60.69	520
Democrat	George S. McGovern (S.Dak.) and R. Sargent Shriver (Md.)	29,171,791	37.53	17
American Independent	John G. Schmitz (Calif.)	1,090,673	1.40	—
People's	Benjamin Spock	78,751	0.10	—
Other		216,196	0.28	—
	Total vote	77,727,590		
	Nixon plurality	17,998,388		

Regional Influences The GOP's effort to gain southern Democratic votes was aided by an assassination attempt on Wallace that knocked him out of the race. Nixon lost only Massachusetts and the District of Columbia, but Democrats added to their majority in the Senate and maintained control of the House.

Key Issues Seeking to create a Republican majority by converting Wallace Democrats, Nixon pursued a "Southern strategy" of denouncing busing, the welfare state, the media, and intellectuals. McGovern was unable to overcome an image of radicalism furthered by Republican charges that he was the candidate of "acid, abortion, and amnesty."

"Nixon. Now more than ever."

—Nixon campaign slogan

1976

Party	Candidate	Popular vote	%	Electoral vote
Democrat	Jimmy Carter (Ga.) and Walter F. Mondale (Minn.)	40,830,763	50.06	297
Republican	Gerald R. Ford (Mich.) and Robert Dole (Kans.)	39,147,793	48.00	241
Independent	Eugene J. McCarthy (Minn.)	756,691	0.93	—
Libertarian	Roger MacBride (Va.)	173,011	0.21	—
Other		647,631	0.79	—
	Total vote	81,555,889		
	Carter plurality	1,682,970		

Regional Influences Despite an unimpressive campaign filled with miscues, Ford nearly overcame a huge early deficit in the polls. But Carter's background as a southern moderate enabled him to eke out a victory through wins in a combination of northern, southern, and border states.

Key Issues In the wake of Watergate, Carter ran a moralistic campaign as a political outsider. Vague on issues, he railed against the Washington bureaucracy and vowed to lead a "government that is as good and honest and decent . . . as filled with love as are the American people." He also promised Americans that he would never lie to them.

"Gritz and Fritz."

—Carter-Mondale

1980

Party	Candidate	Popular vote	%	Electoral vote
Republican	Ronald Reagan (Calif.) and George Bush (Tex.)	43,901,812	50.75	489
Democrat	Jimmy Carter (Ga.) and Walter F. Mondale (Minn.)	35,483,820	41.02	49
Independent	John B. Anderson (Ill.) and Patrick J. Lucey (Wis.)	5,719,722	6.61	—
Libertarian	Edward E. Clark (Calif.)	921,188	1.06	—
Other		486,754	0.56	—
	Total vote	86,513,296		
	Reagan plurality	8,417,992		

Regional Influences Reagan swept to a landslide win in the Electoral College, with Carter carrying only six states and the District of Columbia.

Key Issues Inflation, an energy shortage, the taking of American hostages by Iran, and a strong primary challenge from Edward Kennedy of Massachusetts weakened Carter. Reagan, promising to get government "off the backs of the American people," pledged to cut taxes, increase defense spending, and balance the federal budget. Anderson, a Republican, ran as an independent to the left of both Carter and Reagan.

"We have to move ahead, but we are not going to leave anyone behind."

—Ronald Reagan

1984

Party	Candidate	Popular vote	%	Electoral vote
Republican	Ronald Reagan (Calif.) and George Bush (Tex.)	54,450,603	58.78	525
Democrat	Walter F. Mondale (Minn.) and Geraldine Ferraro (N.Y.)	37,573,671	40.56	13
Libertarian	David Bergland (Calif.)	227,949	0.25	—
Other		570,343	0.61	—
	Total vote	92,628,458		
	Reagan plurality	16,876,932		

Key Issues The economy was flying after emerging in late 1983 from the worst economic downturn since the Great Depression. Reagan, whose commercials proclaimed it was "morning in America," ridiculed Mondale as an old-fashioned "tax-and-spend, gloom-and-doom" Democrat. Controversy over her husband's finances blunted Ferraro's appeal as the first woman on a major party ticket.

Regional Influences Mondale carried only his home state of Minnesota and the District of Columbia, while Reagan won the greatest electoral victory in American history and the fifth-highest share of the popular vote.

The 1988 Presidential Vote

Vice President George Bush defeated Massachusetts Gov. Michael S. Dukakis in every major section of the country and among most segments of the electorate in the 1988 presidential election. The result was a comfortable win for Bush in the popular vote, 48,881,278 to 41,805,374, and an easy victory in the Electoral College, 426 to 111. (One Democratic elector from West Virginia voted for the Democratic vice-presidential nominee, Texas Sen. Lloyd Bentsen, instead of Dukakis.)

Bush eked out a victory in the East, Dukakis's home region, won easily in the Midwest and West and crushed Dukakis in the South, where he amassed 4.4 million of his national plurality of more than 7 million votes. The only significant gaps in the Republican victory, according to a *New York Times*/CBS News poll, were among minorities—especially blacks and Hispanics—Jewish voters, union households, low-income voters and, of course, voters identifying themselves as Democrats or liberals. In percentages the vote broke down as follows:

• Men voted 57–41 for Bush, while women went for the Republican 50–49.

• Dukakis swept the black vote (86–12) and won handily among Hispanics (69–30).

• Bush overwhelmed Dukakis in the South, 58–41. The Republican also won in the East (50–49), the Midwest (52–47) and the West (52–46).

• Bush won in all age categories surveyed: 18–29 years old, 30–44, 45–59, and 60+.

• Bush trounced Dukakis among white Protestants (66–33) and won the Catholic vote (52–47). White fundamentalists and evangelical Christians voted overwhelmingly for the GOP (81–18). Jews were the only religious group in the Democratic column (64–35).

• The only economic group to vote Democratic were the lowest-income voters. Those from families with an income under $12,500 voted for Dukakis 66–33, while voters with family incomes between $12,500 and $24,999 narrowly voted for the Massachusetts governor. A comfortable majority of voters from every other income category voted for Bush.

• Students, teachers and the unemployed were the only groups classified by occupation to vote Democratic. The GOP won large victories among professionals, white-collar workers, and farmers.

• Blacks once again were by far the most reliable Democratic voters, despite widely reported tensions between the Dukakis campaign and supporters of the Rev. Jesse L. Jackson. But while nearly 90% of black voters voted Democratic, studies indicate that black voters showed up at the polls in smaller numbers than in other recent presidential elections.

• While white Democrats were four times as likely as black Democrats to desert the party and vote for Bush, Dukakis did surprisingly well in garnering the votes of so-called Reagan Democrats. Dukakis captured 51% of the votes of Democrats who voted for Reagan in 1984. Jimmy Carter received the votes of only 23% of these voters in 1980.

• Bush's top state was Utah, where he received nearly two-thirds of the vote. He collected at least 60% of the vote in eight states. Dukakis's strongest tally was in the District of Columbia, where he received 82.6% of the vote. In no other state did he even approach 60% of the vote.

1988

Party	Candidate	Popular vote	%	Electoral vote
Republican	George Bush (Tex.) and Dan Quayle (Ind.)	48,881,011	53.37	426
Democrat	Michael S. Dukakis (Mass.) and Lloyd Bentsen (Tex.)	41,828,350	45.67	112
Libertarian	Ron Paul (Tex.)	431,499	0.47	—
New Alliance	Leonora Fulani (N.Y.)	218,159	0.24	—
Populist	David Duke	48,267	0.05	—
Consumer	Eugene J. McCarthy	30,510	0.03	—
American Independent	James Griffin	27,818	0.03	—
National Economic Recovery	Lyndon H. LaRouche, Jr.	25,082	0.03	—
Right-to-Life	William Mara	20,497	0.02	—
Worker's League	Ed Winn	18,579	0.02	—
Socialist Workers	James Warren	13,338	0.01	—
Peace Freedom	Herbert Lewin	10,312	0.01	—
Prohibition	Earl F. Dodge	7,984	0.01	—
Worker's World	Larry Holmes	7,719	0.01	—
Socialist	Willa Kenoyer	3,800	—	—
American	Delmar Dennis	3,456	—	—
Grassroots	Jack Herer	1,949	—	—
Independent	Louie Youngkite	372	—	—
Third World Assembly	John Martin	235	—	—
Other		6,934	—	—
	Total vote	91,585,871		
	Bush plurality	7,052,661		

Key Issues Bush fought back from an early-summer 17-point Dukakis lead with a relentless attack on his opponent's "liberalism." Bush accused Dukakis of coddling up to criminals and made a household name out of Willie Horton, a Massachusetts prison inmate who raped a Maryland woman while out of jail on a furlough. He also attacked Dukakis for the pollution in Boston Harbor. Dukakis said early in the campaign that the election was about "competence, not ideology." Bush responded that the values of the Massachusetts governor were not those of the American people.

Dukakis failed to respond to the charges made by the Bush campaign and ran away from the "liberal" label until late in the campaign. He hammered unsuccessfully at Bush's links to the Iran-Contra scandal, Panama's drug-running leader, Gen. Manuel Noriega, and mocked

VOTER TURNOUT BY STATE, 1988, COMPARED WITH 1984 VOTER PERCENTAGE

State	Voting-age population	1988 total turnout	Total voted	1984 voted	Change 88–84
Alabama	3,010,000	1,378,476	45.80%	49.85%	–4.06%
Alaska	385,000	200,116	51.98	59.15	–7.17
Arizona	2,805,000	1,171,875	44.99	45.23	–0.25
Arkansas	1,761,000	827,738	47.00	51.84	–4.84
California	20,875,000	9,887,065	47.36	49.56	–2.19
Colorado	2,489,000	1,372,393	55.14	55.05	+0.09
Connecticut	2,492,000	1,443,394	57.92	61.10	–3.17
Delaware	490,000	249,891	51.00	55.46	–4.46
District of Columbia	489,000	192,877	39.44	43.21	–3.77
Florida	9,814,000	4,302,313	44.75	48.24	–3.49
Georgia	4,665,000	1,809,657	38.79	41.98	–3.19
Hawaii	824,000	354,461	43.02	44.31	–1.29
Idaho	701,000	408,968	58.34	59.93	–1.59
Illinois	8,550,000	4,559,120	52.32	57.11	–3.79
Indiana	4,068,000	2,168,621	53.31	55.92	–2.62
Iowa	2,068,000	1,225,612	59.27	62.25	–2.99
Kansas	1,829,000	993,044	54.29	55.84	–2.55
Kentucky	2,746,000	1,322,517	48.16	50.77	–2.61
Louisiana	3,175,000	1,628,202	51.28	54.55	–3.27
Maine	893,000	555,025	62.15	64.77	–2.62
Maryland	3,491,000	1,714,358	49.11	51.41	–2.30
Massachusetts	4,535,000	2,632,801	58.06	57.60	+0.45
Michigan	6,791,000	3,669,163	54.03	57.90	–3.87
Minnesota	3,161,000	2,096,790	66.33	68.16	–1.83
Mississippi	1,867,000	952,527	51.02	52.23	–1.21
Missouri	3,821,000	2,093,778	54.80	57.25	–2.45
Montana	586,000	365,594	62.41	65.04	–2.63
Nebraska	1,167,000	661,465	56.68	55.64	+1.04
Nevada	780,000	350,067	44.88	41.49	+3.39
New Hampshire	823,000	450,525	54.74	52.98	+1.76
New Jersey	5,943,000	3,094,139	52.06	56.58	–4.52
New Mexico	1,101,000	521,287	47.35	51.33	–3.99
New York	13,480,000	6,485,683	48.11	51.18	–3.06
North Carolina	4,913,000	2,134,370	43.44	47.36	–3.92
North Dakota	483,000	297,261	61.54	62.67	–1.13
Ohio	7,970,000	4,393,585	55.13	58.20	–3.07
Oklahoma	2,404,000	1,171,036	48.71	52.15	–3.43
Oregon	2,051,000	1,201,603	58.59	61.62	–3.23
Pennsylvania	9,060,000	4,536,251	50.07	53.98	–3.91
Rhode Island	764,000	404,569	52.95	55.85	–2.89
South Carolina	2,534,000	986,009	38.91	40.66%	–1.75%
South Dakota	509,000	312,991	61.49	62.57	–1.08
Tennessee	3,661,000	1,636,250	44.69	49.05	–4.36
Texas	12,270,000	5,427,410	44.23	47.20	–2.96
Utah	1,078,000	647,016	60.02	61.55	–1.53
Vermont	412,000	243,328	59.06	59.84	–0.78
Virginia	4,554,000	2,191,609	48.23	50.69	–2.46
Washington	3,417,000	1,865,253	54.59	58.09	–3.51
West Virginia	1,398,000	653,311	46.73	51.74	–5.01
Wisconsin	3,536,000	2,191,618	61.98	63.46	–1.48
Wyoming	351,000	176,000	50.30	53.38	–3.08
Total	**182,628,000**	**91,609,673**	**50.16**	**53.11**	**–2.95**

Source: Committee for the Study of the American Electorate, *Non-Voter Study* (1989).

VOTER TURNOUT IN PRESIDENTIAL ELECTIONS, 1928–88

Year	Total vote	Voting-age population (VAP)	% of VAP voting	Est. no. of registered voters	% of registered voters voting
1928	36,879,414	71,185,000	51.8%	N.A.	N.A.
1932	39,816,522	75,768,000	52.6	N.A.	N.A.
1936	45,646,817	80,354,000	56.8	N.A.	N.A.
1940	49,815,312	84,728,000	58.8	N.A.	N.A.
1944	48,025,684	95,573,000	56.1	N.A.	N.A.
1948	48,833,680	95,573,000	51.1	N.A.	N.A.
1952	61,551,919	99,929,000	61.6	N.A.	N.A.
1956	62,033,908	104,515,000	59.4	N.A.	N.A.
1960	68,838,000	109,672,000	62.8	82,500,000	75.4%
1964	70,645,000	114,090,000	61.9	87,000,000	76.7
1968	73,212,000	120,285,000	60.9	90,000,000	74.8
1972	77,625,000	140,777,000	55.2	103,000,000	73.0
1976	81,603,000	152,308,000	53.5	106,500,000	70.0
1980	86,497,000	164,595,000	52.6	115,000,000	69.9
1984	92,653,000	174,467,000	53.1	127,500,000	73.1
1988	91,609,673	182,628,000	50.2	129,483,000	70.9

Source: Committee for the Study of the American Electorate, *Non-Voter Study* (1989).

Bush's running mate, Sen. Dan Quayle. Ultimately, the voters decided to stay with the Republicans in a time of peace, prosperity, and continued popularity for the GOP incumbent, Ronald Reagan.

Regional Influences Dukakis won only 10 states and the District of Columbia. Pockets of Democratic strength were found on the West Coast and in the northern Midwest: Dukakis won in Washington, Oregon, and Hawaii in the West and in Minnesota, Wisconsin, and Iowa in the Midwest. The Democrat also captured New York, West Virginia, Rhode Island, and his home state of Massachusetts. Bush swept the rest of the country easily and did especially well in the formerly Democratic "solid South."

Nonvoter Study

Voter turnout hit a 64-year low in 1988, with 50.16% of the voting age population turning up at the presidential polls. The total number of voters also declined in absolute terms by more than a million, despite an increase of nearly 8 million people in the eligible voting pool. Turnout of registered voters also fell, from 72.6% in 1984 to 70.5% in 1988.

The decrease continues a trend that began in 1960, when 62.8% of eligible voters cast presidential ballots. The only increase in voter turnout during that period came in 1984, when 53.1% of the voting-age population voted, compared to 52.8% in 1980. The 3% decline from 1984 was the third largest since 1920. Only the Dewey-Truman race of 1948 and the Nixon-McGovern race of 1972 had bigger drop-offs from the previous election. Additionally, voter-turnout figures for the 1972 race were exaggerated by the enfranchisement of voters in the low-voting 18–20 age range.

Minnesota ranked highest in voter turnout, with 66.33% of its voting population casting ballots. Georgia ranked lowest with only 38.79% of its eligible voters going to the polls. In 12 states (Maine, Minn., Miss., Mont., Nebr., Nev., N.C., N. Dak., Utah, Vt., Wash., and Wyo.), turnout for the presidential race was lower than for Senate and governor races.

The Federal Election Campaign Act

In 1971 Congress passed the Federal Election Campaign Act to deal with various aspects of campaign financing. The law was amended and strengthened in 1974 and 1976, and the Federal Election Commission (FEC) was established to administer the law, which affects candidates for the U.S. House of Representatives, the U.S. Senate, the presidency, and the political committees that support them. The act requires disclosure of sources and uses of funds for federal elections, provides public financing for presidential elections, and sets limits on campaign contributions. The specific requirements of each of these three parts of the act are detailed below.

Public Disclosure Candidates for federal office and the political committees that support them must register and file periodic disclosures of their campaign finance activities with the clerk of the House, the secretary of the Senate, or the FEC. These reports are available to the public within 48 hours of their disclosure. A candidate

OFFICIAL 1988 PRESIDENTIAL ELECTION RESULTS

State	Total votes	George H.W. Bush, Republican Votes	%	Michael S. Dukakis, Democrat Votes	%	Ron Paul, Libertarian Votes	%	Lenora B. Fulani, New Alliance Votes	%	Other Votes	%	Plurality Votes/party
Alabama	1,378,476	815,576	59.2%	549,506	39.9%	8,460	0.6%	3,311	0.2%	1,623	0.1%	266,070 R
Alaska	199,108	118,817	59.7	72,105	36.2	5,459	2.7	1,015	0.5	1,712	0.9	46,712 R
Arizona	1,171,875	702,541	60.0	454,029	38.8	13,351	1.1	1,662	0.1	292	N.A.	248,512 R
Arkansas	827,738	466,578	56.4	349,237	42.2	3,297	0.4	2,161	0.2	6,465	0.8	117,341 R
California	9,887,065	5,054,917	51.1	4,702,233	47.6	70,105	0.7	31,181	0.3	28,629	0.3	352,684 R
Colorado	1,372,393	728,177	53.1	621,453	45.3	15,483	1.1	2,539	0.2	4,741	0.3	106,724 R
Connecticut	1,443,394	750,241	52.0	676,584	46.9	14,071	1.0	2,491	0.1	7	N.A.	73,657 R
Delaware	249,891	139,639	55.9	108,647	43.5	1,162	0.4	443	0.2	N.A.	N.A.	30,992 R
District of Columbia	192,877	27,590	14.3	159,407	82.6	554	0.3	2,901	1.5	2,425	1.3	131,817 D
Florida	4,299,149	2,616,597	60.9	1,655,851	38.5	19,781	0.4	6,644	0.2	276	N.A.	960,746 R
Georgia	1,809,672	1,081,331	59.7	714,792	39.5	8,435	0.5	5,099	0.3	15	N.A.	366,539 R
Hawaii	354,461	158,625	44.7	192,364	54.3	1,999	0.6	1,003	0.3	470	0.1	33,739 D
Idaho	408,968	253,881	62.1	147,272	36.0	5,313	1.3	2,502	0.6	N.A.	N.A.	106,609 R
Illinois	4,559,120	2,310,939	50.7	2,215,940	48.6	14,944	0.3	10,276	0.2	7,021	0.2	94,999 R
Indiana	2,168,621	1,297,763	59.8	860,643	39.7	N.A.	N.A.	10,215	0.5	N.A.	N.A.	437,120 R
Iowa	1,225,612	545,355	44.5	670,557	54.7	2,494	0.2	539	0.1	6,667	0.5	125,202 D
Kansas	993,024	554,049	55.8	422,636	42.5	12,533	1.3	3,806	0.4	N.A.	N.A.	131,413 R
Kentucky	1,322,517	734,281	55.5	580,368	43.9	2,118	0.2	1,256	0.1	4,494	0.3	153,913 R
Louisiana	1,628,202	883,702	54.3	717,460	44.1	4,115	0.2	2,355	0.1	20,570	1.3	166,242 R
Maine	555,035	307,131	55.3	243,569	43.9	2,700	0.5	1,405	0.3	230	N.A.	63,562 R
Maryland	1,714,335	876,167	51.1	826,304	48.2	6,748	0.4	5,115	0.3	1	N.A.	49,863 R
Massachusetts	2,632,801	1,194,635	45.4	1,401,415	53.2	24,251	0.9	9,561	0.4	2,939	0.1	206,780 D
Michigan	3,669,163	1,965,486	53.5	1,675,783	45.7	18,336	0.5	2,513	0.1	7,045	0.2	289,703 R
Minnesota	2,096,790	962,337	45.9	1,109,471	52.9	5,109	0.2	1,734	0.1	18,139	0.9	147,134 D
Mississippi	931,527	557,890	59.9	363,921	39.1	3,329	0.4	2,155	0.2	4,232	0.4	193,969 R
Missouri	2,093,228	1,084,953	51.8	1,001,619	47.9	N.A.	N.A.	6,656	0.3	N.A.	N.A.	83,334 R
Montana	365,694	190,412	52.1	168,956	46.2	5,047	1.4	1,279	0.3	N.A.	N.A.	21,456 R
Nebraska	662,372	398,447	60.1	259,646	39.2	2,536	0.4	1,743	0.3	N.A.	N.A.	138,801 R
Nevada	350,067	206,040	58.9	132,738	37.9	3,520	1.0	835	0.2	6,934	2.0	73,302 R
New Hampshire	450,525	281,537	62.5	163,696	36.3	4,502	1.0	790	0.2	N.A.	N.A.	117,841 R
New Jersey	3,094,139	1,740,604	56.2	1,317,541	42.6	8,413	0.3	5,138	0.2	22,443	0.7	423,063 R
New Mexico	521,287	270,341	51.9	244,497	46.9	3,268	0.6	2,237	0.4	944	0.2	25,844 R
New York	6,485,683	3,081,871	47.5	3,347,882	51.6	12,109	0.2	15,845	0.3	27,976	0.4	266,011 D
North Carolina	2,134,370	1,237,258	58.0	890,167	41.7	1,263	N.A.	5,682	0.3	N.A.	N.A.	347,091 R
North Dakota	297,261	166,559	56.0	127,739	43.0	1,315	0.5	396	0.1	1,252	0.4	38,820 R
Ohio	4,393,585	2,416,549	55.0	1,939,629	44.1	11,926	0.3	12,017	0.3	13,464	0.3	476,920 R
Oklahoma	1,171,036	678,367	57.9	483,423	41.3	6,261	0.5	2,985	0.3	N.A.	N.A.	194,944 R
Oregon	1,201,603	560,126	46.6	616,206	51.3	14,811	1.2	6,487	0.6	3,973	0.3	56,080 D
Pennsylvania	4,536,251	2,300,087	50.7	2,194,944	48.4	12,051	0.3	4,379	0.1	24,790	0.5	105,143 R
Rhode Island	404,569	177,761	43.9	225,123	55.7	825	0.2	280	0.1	580	0.1	47,362 D
South Carolina	986,009	606,443	61.5	370,554	37.6	4,935	0.5	4,077	0.4	N.A.	N.A.	235,889 R
South Dakota	312,991	165,415	52.9	145,560	46.5	1,060	0.3	730	0.2	226	0.1	19,855 R
Tennessee	1,636,250	947,233	57.9	679,794	41.5	2,041	0.1	1,334	0.1	5,848	0.4	267,439 R
Texas	5,427,410	3,036,829	56.0	2,352,748	43.3	30,355	0.6	7,208	0.1	270	N.A.	684,081 R
Utah	647,016	428,442	66.2	207,352	32.0	7,472	1.2	455	0.1	3,295	0.5	221,090 R
Vermont	243,328	124,331	51.1	115,775	47.6	1,000	0.4	205	0.1	2,017	0.8	8,556 R
Virginia	2,191,609	1,309,162	59.7	859,799	39.2	8,336	0.4	14,312	0.7	N.A.	N.A.	449,363 R
Washington	1,865,253	903,835	48.5	933,516	50.0	17,240	0.9	3,520	0.2	7,142	0.4	29,681 D
West Virginia	653,311	310,065	47.5	341,016	52.2	N.A.	N.A.	2,230	0.3	N.A.	N.A.	30,951 D
Wisconsin	2,191,608	1,047,499	47.8	1,126,794	51.4	5,157	0.2	1,953	0.1	10,205	0.5	79,295 D
Wyoming	176,551	106,867	60.5	67,113	38.0	2,026	1.2	545	0.3	N.A.	N.A.	39,754 R
Totals	91,584,820	48,881,278	53.4	41,805,374	45.6	431,616	0.5	217,200	0.2	249,352	0.3	7,075,904 R

Source: The Congressional Quarterly, Jan. 1989.

is defined as one who has raised or spent more than $5,000 in any given year in campaigning for federal office. A political committee is defined as a club, committee, association, or organization that receives contributions or makes expenditures of more than $1,000 to a federal candidate in any calendar year. In recent years they have come to be called PACs, for Political Action Committee.

Public Financing Public financing is provided for eligible presidential candidates in primary and general elections, and for national party committees for the nominating conventions. Financing is given in the form of matching payments to primary candidates, public grants to nominees in the general elections, and public grants to the national party committees for the conventions. The money for public financing is raised by the Presidential Election Campaign Fund, which collects one dollar from the tax payment of every taxpayer who checks off this box on his or her federal income-tax return.

Contribution Limits and Prohibitions In federal elections the act prohibits contributions from the treasuries of national banks, corporations, and labor organizations; contributions from government contractors; contributions from foreign nationals (green-card holders); cash contributions in excess of $100 per person; contributions supplied by one person in the name of another person.

Additionally, the act sets contribution limits according to the following table.

CONTRIBUTION LIMITS TO CANDIDATES AND POLITICAL COMMITTEES

| | CONTRIBUTOR | | |
Recipient	Individual contributor	Multi-candidate committee	Other political committee
Each candidate or candidate committee[1]	$1,000	$5,000	$1,000
National party committee[1]	20,000	15,000	20,000
Other political committee[2]	5,000	5,000	5,000
Total per calendar year	**25,000**	**no limit**	**no limit**

1. Per election year. 2. Per calendar year.
Source: Federal Election Committee.

THE GIVERS
Top 25 PACs: Jan. 1, 1987– June 30, 1988

Rank	PAC	Disbursements
1.	Democratic Republican Independent Voter Education Committee	$4,041,306
2.	Campaign America	3,295,280
3.	National Congressional Club	3,186,321
4.	American Citizens for Political Action	2,888,123
5.	American Medical Association PAC	2,856,907
6.	Realtors Political Action Committee	2,684,349
7.	National Security Political Action Committee	2,634,593
8.	League of Conservative Voters	2,570,452
9.	National Conservative Political Action Committee	2,127,446
10.	American Telephone & Telegraph Company Inc. PAC	2,046,357
11.	National Association of Retired Federal Employees PAC	1,843,134
12.	The Fund for America's Future Inc.	1,579,236
13.	Human Rights Campaign Fund	1,569,438
14.	National Committee for an Effective Congress	1,558,447
15.	UAW-V-CAP (UAW Volunteer Community Action Program)	1,556,926
16.	Machinists Non-Partisan Political League	1,551,148
17.	National PAC	1,546,120
18.	National Education Association Political Action Committee	1,525,427
19.	Association of Trial Lawyers of America PAC	1,464,913
20.	National Committee to Preserve Social Security PAC	1,402,727
21.	American Federation of State, County and Municipal Employees	1,377,491
22.	International Brotherhood of Electrical Workers	1,347,514
23.	Ruff Political Action Committee	1,316,079
24.	Committee on Letter Carriers Political Education	1,304,802
25.	National Association of Life Underwriters PAC	1,299,945

Source: Federal Election Commission.

PORTRAIT OF THE ELECTORATE, 1980–88:

NEW YORK TIMES/CBS NEWS POLLS

The New York Times/CBS News exit polls were conducted on election day in 1980, 1984, and 1988. The data for 1980 are based on polls of 15,201 voters, for 1984 on polls of 9,174 voters, and for 1988 on polls of 11,645 voters. Respondents who gave no answers are not shown.

Respondents	Percent of 1988 total	VOTE IN 1988 Bush	Dukakis	VOTE IN 1984 Reagan	Mondale	VOTE IN 1980 Reagan	Carter	Anderson
Total	—	**53%**	**45%**	**59%**	**40%**	**51%**	**41%**	**7%**
Men	48%	57	41	62	37	55	36	7
Women	52	50	49	56	44	47	45	7
Whites	85	59	40	64	35	55	36	7
Blacks	10	12	86	9	89	11	85	3
Hispanics	3	30	69	37	61	35	56	8
Married	69	57	42	62	38	N.A.	N.A.	N.A.
Not married	31	46	53	52	46	N.A.	N.A.	N.A.
18–29 years old	20	52	47	59	40	43	44	11
30–44 years old	35	54	45	57	42	54	36	8
45–59 years old	22	57	42	59	39	55	39	5
60 and older	22	50	49	60	39	54	41	4
Not high school graduate	8	43	56	49	50	46	51	2
High school graduate	27	50	49	60	39	51	43	4
Some college education	30	57	42	61	37	55	35	8
College graduate or more	35	56	43	58	41	52	35	11
College graduate	19	62	37	N.A.	N.A.	N.A.	N.A.	N.A.
Postgraduate education	16	50	48	N.A.	N.A.	N.A.	N.A.	N.A.
White Protestant	48	66	33	72	27	63	31	6
Catholic	28	52	47	54	45	49	42	7
Jewish	4	35	64	31	67	39	45	15
White fundamentalist or evangelical Christian[1]	9	81	18	78	22	63	33	3
Union household	25	42	57	46	53	43	48	6
Family income under[2]								
$12,500	12	37	62	45	54	42	51	6
$12,500–24,999	20	49	50	57	42	44	46	7
$25,000–34,999	20	56	44	59	40	52	39	7
$35,000–49,999	20	56	42	66	33	59	32	8
$50,000 and over	24	62	37	69	30	63	26	9
$50,000–100,000	19	61	38	N.A.	N.A.	N.A.	N.A.	N.A.
Over $100,000	5	65	32	N.A.	N.A.	N.A.	N.A.	N.A.
From the East	25	50	49	52	47	47	42	9
From the Midwest	28	52	47	58	40	51	40	7
From the South	28	58	41	64	36	52	44	3
From the West	19	52	46	61	38	53	34	10
Republicans	35	91	8	93	6	86	8	4
Democrats	37	17	82	24	75	26	67	6
Independents	26	55	43	63	35	55	30	12
Liberals	18	18	81	28	70	25	60	11
Moderates	45	49	50	53	47	48	42	8
Conservatives	33	80	19	82	17	72	23	4
Professional or manager	31	59	40	62	37	57	32	9
White-collar worker	11	57	42	59	40	50	41	8
Blue-collar worker	13	49	50	54	45	47	46	5
Full-time student	4	44	54	52	47	N.A.	N.A.	N.A.
Teacher	5	47	51	51	48	46	42	10
Unemployed	5	37	62	32	67	39	51	8
Homemaker	10	58	41	61	38	N.A.	N.A.	N.A.
Agricultural worker	2	55	44	N.A.	N.A.	36	59	4
Retired	16	50	49	60	40	N.A.	N.A.	N.A.
1984 Reagan voters	56	80	19	100	0	75	9	2
1984 Democratic Reagan voters	9	48	51	100	0	57	23	2
1984 Mondale voters	28	7	92	0	100	14	63	8
Democratic primary voters	23	21	78	N.A.	N.A.	N.A.	N.A.	N.A.

PORTRAIT OF THE ELECTORATE, 1980–88:

Respondents	Percent of 1988 total	VOTE IN 1988 Bush	Dukakis	VOTE IN 1984 Reagan	Mondale	VOTE IN 1980 Reagan	Carter	Anderson
Republican primary voters	18	87	11	N.A.	N.A.	N.A.	N.A.	N.A.
First-time voters	7	51	47	61	38	N.A.	N.A.	N.A.
White men	41	63	36	67	32	59	32	7
White women	44	56	43	62	38	52	39	8
Black men	5	15	81	12	84	14	82	3
Black women	5	9	90	7	93	9	88	3
Men, 18–29 years old	10	55	43	63	36	47	39	11
Women, 18–29 years old	11	49	50	55	44	39	49	10
Men, 30–44 years old	17	58	40	61	38	59	31	8
Women, 30–44 years old	19	50	49	54	45	50	41	8
Men, 45–59 years old	11	62	36	62	36	60	34	5
Women, 45–59 years old	12	52	48	57	42	50	44	5
Men, 60 and older	11	53	46	62	37	56	40	3
Women, 60 and older	11	48	52	58	42	52	43	4
Whites, 18–29 years old	16	60	39	68	31	48	38	12
Blacks, 18–29 years old	3	12	86	6	94	7	89	3
Whites, 30–44 years old	30	60	39	63	36	59	31	8
Blacks, 30–44 years old	4	13	85	10	89	12	84	3
Whites, 45–59 years old	19	63	36	65	34	59	34	5
Blacks, 45–59 years old	2	10	86	10	86	13	84	3
Whites, 60 and older	20	54	45	63	37	56	39	4
Blacks, 60 and older	2	9	90	15	81	20	77	3
Married men	34	60	39	64	35	N.A.	N.A.	N.A.
Married women	35	54	46	59	41	N.A.	N.A.	N.A.
Unmarried men	14	51	47	55	42	N.A.	N.A.	N.A.
Unmarried women	17	42	57	49	50	N.A.	N.A.	N.A.
Republican men	18	91	8	94	5	87	8	4
Republican women	17	90	9	93	7	85	10	5
Democratic men	16	18	80	27	72	29	63	6
Democratic women	21	16	84	21	78	23	71	5
Independent men	13	58	40	66	32	60	27	10
Independent women	13	52	46	59	39	49	34	13
White Democrats	27	21	79	29	70	30	62	6
Black Democrats	7	4	95	3	96	4	94	2
Men with less than high school education	4	49	50	52	47	51	47	2
Women with less than high school education	4	38	62	46	52	41	55	2
Male high school grads.	12	50	49	62	37	53	42	3
Female high school grads.	15	50	50	58	41	50	44	5
Men with some college	13	60	38	65	33	59	31	8
Women with some college	17	54	45	58	41	52	39	8
Male college graduates[3]	19	63	36	63	36	58	28	11
Female college graduates[3]	16	49	51	52	47	42	44	12
Whites in the East	21	54	45	57	42	51	38	10
Blacks in the East	2	12	85	7	90	12	85	3
Whites in the Midwest	25	57	42	64	35	55	37	7
Blacks in the Midwest	2	8	91	6	92	11	84	4
Whites in the South	23	67	32	71	28	61	35	3
Blacks in the South	42	12	86	10	89	9	89	2
Whites in the West	15	58	41	66	33	55	32	10
Blacks in the West	2	13	83		Insufficient data available			

Note: N.A. indicates that a question was not asked in a particular year.   1. Fundamentalist or evangelical Christian was labeled born-again Christian in 1980 and 1984.   2. Family income categories in 1980 were: these: less than $10,000; $10,000–14,999; $15,000–24,999; $25,000–49,999; and $50,000 and over.   3. Male and female college graduates include postgraduate education.   **Source:** New York Times.

PACS: A HISTORY OF THEIR GROWTH

Year[1]	Corporate PACs	Labor PACs	Noncon- nected[2]	Total PACs
1974	89	201	N.A.	608
1975	139	226	N.A.	722
1976	433	224	N.A.	1,146
1977	550	234	110	1,360
1978	785	217	162	1,653
1979	950	240	247	2,000
1980	1,206	297	374	2,551
1981	1,329	318	531	2,902
1982	1,469	380	723	3,371
1983	1,538	378	793	3,525
1984	1,682	394	1,053	4,009
1985	1,710	388	1,003	3,992
1986	1,744	384	1,007	4,157
1987	1,775	364	957	4,165
1988	1,816	354	1,115	4,268

1. All figures as of Dec. 31 of the given year, except for 1975, when PAC totals were counted on Nov. 24.   2. Includes trade, membership, and health PACs.   **Source:** Federal Election Commission.

TOP 10 LABOR PACS: Jan. 1, 1987–June 30, 1988

Rank PAC	Disbursements
1. Democratic Republican Independent Voter Education Committee	$4,041,306
2. UAW-V-CAP (UAW Voluntary Community Action Program)	1,556,926
3. Machinists Non-Partisan Political League	1,551,148
4. National Education Association PAC	1,525,427
5. American Federation of State, County, and Municipal Employees	1,377,491
6. International Brotherhood of Electrical Workers	1,347,514
7. Committee on Letter Carriers Political Education	1,304,802
8. CWA-COPE Political Contributions Committee	1,235,563
9. Air Line Pilots Association PAC	1,228,584
10. Transportation Political Education League	1,082,279

Source: Federal Election Commission.

TOP 10 CORPORATE PACS: Jan. 1, 1987–June 30, 1988

Rank PAC	Disbursements
1. American Telephone and Telegraph Company Inc. PAC	$2,046,357
2. Federal Express Corporation PAC	684,393
3. Philip Morris PAC (PHIL-PAC)	664,697
4. UPS-PAC	616,544
5. Non-Partisan Political Support Committee for GE Employees	501,243
6. Citicorp Voluntary Political Federal Fund	466,325
7. Waster Management Inc. Employees Better Government Fund	430,994
8. Lockheed Employees PAC	400,573
9. Barnett People for Better Government Inc (Barnett Banks)	397,958
10. American Family Political Action Committee	389,412

Source: Federal Election Commission.

The Receivers

Spending by Senate candidates in the 1988 election increased by 3% over 1986 levels and by 7% for House candidates. In the House the proportion of contributions coming from PACs increased from 35% in 1986 to over 40% in 1988. Overall, 978 House candidates raised $202.3 million: $99.0 million from individuals and $81.4 million from PACs. They spent a total of $166.2 million.

PAC contributions constituted 24% of Senate contributions in both 1986 and 1988, while roughly two-thirds of all Senate contributions came from individuals. Overall, 100 Senate candidates raised $156.5 million: $105 million from individuals and $38.2 million from PACs. They spent a total of $143.8 million.

TOP 10 PAC RECIPIENTS, 1987–88

HOUSE

Rank	Congressman	Receipts
1.	Robert Michel (R-Ill.)	$523,466
2.	Jim Moody (D-Wisc.)	482,403
3.	Thomas Foley (D-Wash.)	456,248
4.	James Jontz (D-Ind.)	440,604
5.	Robert Matsui (D-Calif.)	435,191
6.	Byron Dorgan (D-N.Dak.)	430,796
7.	John Dingell (D-Mich.)	425,642
8.	David Price (D-N.C.)	403,195
9.	Ronnie Flippo (D.-Ala.)	392,410
10.	Dan Rostenkowski (D-Ill.)	382,048

SENATE

Rank	Senator	Receipts
1.	Lloyd Bentsen (D-Tex.)	$2,144,016
2.	Pete Wilson (R-Calif.)	1,598,290
3.	James Sasser (D-Tenn.)	1,287,027
4.	Frank Lautenberg (D-N.J.)	1,272,471
5.	Dave Durenberger (R-Minn.)	1,239,932
6.	John Heinz (R.-Pa.)	1,213,513
7.	Donald Riegle, Jr. (D-Mich.)	1,191,791
8.	Orrin Hatch (R-Utah)	1,054,213
9.	John C. Danforth (R-Mo.)	1,051,557
10.	Jeff Bingaman (D-N.Mex.)	1,007,630

Note: Gary Hart raised $408,248 in his bid to unseat California Congressman Robert Lagomarsino (19th District), and George V. Voinovich raised $1,151,016 in his bid for the Ohio Senate seat of Howard Metzenbaum, but they are omitted from the list because they lost.
Source: Federal Election Commission.

The Electoral College

The Electoral College is the body of electors chosen by all of the states that ultimately is responsible for selecting the president of the United States. The Constitution's framers did not want the nation's chief executive chosen by either the national legislature or the people directly. Instead they set up what came to be known as the Electoral College—probably based on the Sacred College of Cardinals responsible for electing the pope—under Article II, sections 2 and 3, of the Constitution to provide for indirect election of the president: "Each State shall appoint, in such manner as the legislature thereof may direct, a number of Electors, equal to the whole number of Senators and Representatives to which the State may be entitled in the Congress; but no Senator or Representative, or person holding an office of trust of profit under the United States, shall be appointed an Elector."

Electors were supposed to be distinguished, enlightened citizens who would cast a disinterested vote for president. From the start, though, electors have been instruments of partisan passions. At first most state legislatures were responsible for choosing electors. By 1828, however, all states except South Carolina allowed electors to be chosen by direct popular election. (In South Carolina the legislature continued to select electors until the Civil War.) When electors began being selected by popular vote, parties presented slates of candidates for presidential electors who were tacitly pledged to support the party's nominees for president and vice president. This is how the practice began of state's voting as a unit. Subsequently, many states passed laws requiring their electors to vote as a bloc. Where it is not required by law, it is customary for all of a state's electors to vote for the candidate receiving a plurality of the popular vote in that state. The names of the candidates for electors may or may not appear on the ballot alongside the names of the candidates to whom they are pledged. Voters really vote for presidential electors, though, even when they seem to be casting a ballot for a presidential candidate.

The presidential electors chosen by the voters in November meet in their state capitals on the first Monday after the second Wednesday in December to cast their vote for president and vice president. The results of this balloting are sent to the president of the U.S. Senate, the directors of the U.S. General Services Administration, the state's secretary of state, and to the judge of the federal district court of the district in which the electors gathered. Sealed state ballots are opened and counted at a joint session of Congress on Jan. 6 following the election year.

Originally, electors voted for two individuals for president on a single ballot. The winner of a majority of the vote was elected president; the runner-up, vice-president. The framers fully expected there to be many elections in which no candidate would gain a majority of the vote, and the president would have to be selected by the House of Representatives, where each state delegation would cast a single vote. But in 1789 and 1792, every elector voted for George Washington. In both years John Adams was the runner-up and thus vice president.

Problems inherent in this system became apparent once Washington no longer was a candidate. In 1796 Adams and Thomas Jefferson finished first and second in the balloting and were elected president and vice president, respectively, despite their being fierce foes. By 1800 two formal parties had evolved that nominated a single candidate for both president and vice president. A Federalist elector purposely failed to vote for the party's vice-presidential nominee, Thomas Pinckney, in order to assure a potential majority for John Adams. But overzealous Republican electors all voted for both Jefferson and the party's vice-presidential nominee, Aaron Burr. Both men received the same majority of the electoral vote, and the election had to be decided by the House, where Jefferson won. This led to adoption of the 12th Amendment to the Constitution, implemented in 1804, which required that electors cast separate ballots for president and vice president. If no candidate achieves a majority of the electoral vote for vice president, the position is determined by the Senate, with each senator casting a single ballot. This has happened only once, when the Senate selected Richard M. Johnson after he fell one electoral vote short of a majority for vice president in 1836.

Currently, 270 votes are needed to reach a majority in the Electoral College. There have been two elections in which no candidate received a majority of the electoral vote—in 1824 and in 1876, when disputed results in several states prevented either Rutherford B. Hayes or Samuel J. Tilden from achieving a majority. (John Quincy Adams and Hayes won those contests, respectively.) A candidate also can be elected president despite losing the popular vote. This occurred, again in 1824 and 1876, when the House selected Adams and Hayes, though they lost the popular vote to Andrew Jackson and Tilden, respectively, and in 1888, when Benjamin Harrison was elected over Grover Cleveland despite receiving a minority of the popular vote.

Critics of the Electoral College throughout the years have sought to diminish the power of the states in the selection of presidents. It is said to be unfair for all of a state's electoral votes to go to a candidate who merely achieved a plurality of the vote in that state. The many proposals offered to bypass the states and provide for the direct, popular election of the president have foundered, however, on the fear that while such a system might encourage third-and fourth-party candidates to run for office, it would make it even more likely for a candidate to be elected president with a minority of the total popular vote.

> *"My country has in its wisdom contrived for me the most insignificant office that ever the invention of man contrived or his imagination conceived; and as I can do neither good nor evil, I must be borne away by others and meet the common fate."*
>
> —John Adams, vice president
> Letter to Abigail Adams, 1793

Political Office Holders 1789–1989

The Vice Presidency

Unlike the office of president, that of vice president has sometimes been left vacant after the death of the vice president or the latter's assumption of higher office on the death of the president. Until adoption of the 25th Amendment to the Constitution in 1967, there was no provision to fill a vacancy in the vice presidency. Under the amendment the president must name a vice president when the office is vacant, and the nominee must pass a majority vote of approval in both houses of Congress. Gerald Ford, Richard Nixon's choice to replace Spiro Agnew after the latter's resignation in 1973, was the first vice president to gain the office under the amendment. The second was Nelson Rockefeller, whom Ford nominated to the position after he became president upon Nixon's resignation the following year. While the 25th Amendment does not supersede the presidential order of succession, it decreases the likelihood of the office's ever falling to the Speaker of the House or a sitting cabinet member.

Presidential Order of Succession

Article II of the Constitution gives to Congress the power to determine the presidential order of succession should both the president and vice president die, become incapacitated, or be disqualified from office. The present law, passed in 1947, puts the Speaker of the House first in line to the presidency, followed by the president pro tempore of the Senate. The order of succession then goes through the members of the cabinet, in the order in which the executive departments were established: (1) Secretary of State, (2) Secretary of the Treasury, (3) Secretary of Defense, (4) Attorney General, (5) Secretary of the Interior, (6) Secretary of Agriculture, (7) Secretary of Commerce, (8) Secretary of Labor, (9) Secretary of Health and Human Services, (10) Secretary of Housing and Urban Development, (11) Secretary of Transportation, (12) Secretary of Energy, (13) Secretary of Education, (14) Secretary of Veterans Affairs.

Until the 1970 legislation removing the postmaster general from the cabinet and establishing an independent postal service, the postmaster general was fifth in line to the presidency. The heads of new departments are automatically added to the line of succession as the new departments are created.

A cabinet member must be a U.S. citizen and at least 35 years old in order to become acting president. If a cabinet member next in line to fill a presidential vacancy is not yet 35, the presidency passes to the next cabinet member in the order of succession who has attained that age.

VICE PRESIDENTS OF THE UNITED STATES

	Name	Party	Dates in office	State, birth–death
1.	John Adams	Fed.	1789–97	Mass., 1735–1826
2.	Thomas Jefferson	D-R	1797–1801	Va., 1743–1826
3.	Aaron Burr	D-R	1801–05	N.Y., 1756–1836
4.	George Clinton	D-R	1805–12	N.Y., 1739–1812
5.	Elbridge Gerry	D-R	1813–14	Mass., 1744–1814
6.	Daniel D. Tompkins	D-R	1817–25	N.Y., 1774–1825
7.	John C. Calhoun	D-R	1825–32	S.C., 1782–1850
8.	Martin Van Buren	D	1833–37	N.Y., 1782–1862
9.	Richard M. Johnson	D	1837–41	Ky., 1780–1850
10.	John Tyler	Whig	1841[1]	Va., 1790–1862
11.	George M. Dallas	D	1845–49	Pa., 1792–1864
12.	Millard Fillmore	Whig	1849–50[2]	N.Y., 1800–74
13.	William R. King	D	1853	Ala., 1786–1853
14.	John C. Breckenridge	D	1857–61	Ky., 1821–75
15.	Hannibal Hamlin	R	1861–65	Maine, 1809–91
16.	Andrew Johnson	D	1865[3]	Tenn., 1808–75
17.	Schuyler Colfax	R	1869–73	Ind., 1823–85
18.	Henry Wilson	R	1873–75	Mass., 1812–75
19.	William A. Wheeler	R	1877–81	N.Y., 1819–87
20.	Chester A. Arthur	R	1881[4]	N.Y., 1829–86
21.	Thomas A. Hendricks	D	1885[5]	Ind., 1819–85
22.	Levi P. Morton	R	1889–93	N.Y., 1824–1920
23.	Adlai E. Stevenson	D	1893–97	Ill., 1835–1914
24.	Garret A. Hobart	R	1897–99	N.J., 1844–99
25.	Theodore Roosevelt	R	1901[6]	N.Y., 1858–1919
26.	Charles W. Fairbanks	R	1905–09	Ind., 1852–1918
27.	James S. Sherman	R	1909–12	N.Y., 1855–1912
28.	Thomas R. Marshall	D	1913–21	Ind., 1854–1925
29.	Calvin Coolidge	R	1921–23[7]	Mass., 1872–1933
30.	Charles G. Dawes	R	1925–29	Ill., 1865–1951
31.	Charles Curtis	R	1929–33	Kans., 1860–1936
32.	John Nance Garner	D	1933–41	Tex., 1868–1967
33.	Henry A. Wallace	D	1941–45	Iowa, 1888–1965
34.	Harry S Truman	D	1945[8]	Mo., 1884–1972
35.	Alben W. Barkley	D	1949–53	Ky., 1877–1956
36.	Richard M. Nixon	R	1953–61	Calif., 1913–
37.	Lyndon B. Johnson	D	1961–63[9]	Tex., 1908–73
38.	Hubert H. Humphrey	D	1965–69	Minn., 1911–78
39.	Spiro T. Agnew	R	1969–73[10]	Md., 1918–
40.	Gerald R. Ford	R	1973–74[11]	Mich., 1913–
41.	Nelson A. Rockefeller	D	1974–77	N.Y., 1908–79
42.	Walter F. Mondale	D	1977–81	Minn., 1928–
43.	George Bush	R	1981–89	Tex., 1924–
44.	J. Danforth Quayle	R	1989–	Ind., 1947–

Note: Fed. = Federalist, D = Democrat, D-R = Democratic-Republican, R = Republican.   1. Tyler became president after the death of Harrison four months into his term.   2. Fillmore became president after the death of John Tyler.   3. Andrew Johnson was a Democrat nominated by the Republicans to run with Abraham Lincoln on the Union ticket in 1864. He became president after Lincoln's assassination.   4. Arthur became president after Garfield's assassination.   5. Hendricks died after eight months in office.   6. Roosevelt became president after McKinley's assassination.   7. Coolidge became president after Harding's death.   8. Truman became president after Roosevelt's death.   9. Johnson became president after Kennedy's assassination in 1963. There was no vice president until Johnson was elected president in his own right in 1964.   10. Agnew resigned from office after revealing he was under investigation for receiving kickbacks while governor of Maryland.   11. Ford assumed the presidency after Nixon resigned under threat of impeachment, and named Rockefeller vice president.

SPEAKERS OF THE U.S. HOUSE OF REPRESENTATIVES

	Name	Party	State	Dates in office
1.	Frederick A.C. Muhlenberg	D-R	Pa.	1789–91
2.	Jonathan Trumbull	Fed.	Conn.	1791–93
3.	Frederick A.C. Muhlenberg	D-R	Pa.	1793–95
4.	Jonathan Dayton	Fed.	N.J.	1795–97
5.	George Dent	Fed.	Md.	1797–99
6.	Theodore Sedgwick	Fed.	Mass.	1799–1801
7.	Nathaniel Macon	D-R	N.C.	1801–07
8.	Joseph B. Varnum	D-R	Mass.	1807–11
9.	Henry Clay	D-R	Ky.	1811–14
10.	Langdon Cheves	D-R	S.C.	1814–15
11.	Henry Clay	D-R	Ky.	1815–20
12.	John W. Taylor	D-R	N.Y.	1820–21
13.	Philip Barbour	D-R	Va.	1821–23
14.	Henry Clay	D-R	Ky.	1822–24
15.	John W. Taylor	D-R	N.Y.	1825–27
16.	Andrew Stevenson	D	Va.	1827–34
17.	John Bell	D	Tenn.	1834–35
18.	James K. Polk	D	Tenn.	1835–39
19.	Robert M.T. Hunter	Whig	Va.	1839–41
20.	John White	Whig	Ky.	1841–43
21.	John W. Jones	D	Va.	1843–45
22.	John W. Davis	D	Ind.	1845–47
23.	Robert C. Winthrop	Whig	Mass.	1847–49
24.	Howell Cobb	D	Ga.	1849–51
25.	Linn Boyd	D	Ky.	1851–55
26.	Nathaniel Banks	R	Mass.	1855–57
27.	James L. Orr	D	S.C.	1857–59
28.	William Pennington	Whig	N.J.	1859–61
29.	Galusha A. Grow	R	Pa.	1861–63
30.	Schuyler Colfax	R	Ind.	1863–69
31.	James G. Blaine	R	Maine	1869–75
32.	Michael C. Kerr	D	Ind.	1875–76
33.	Samuel J. Randall	D	Pa.	1876–81
34.	J. Warren Keifer	R	Ohio	1881–83
35.	John G. Carlisle	D	Ky.	1883–89
36.	Thomas B. Reed	R	Maine	1889–91
37.	Charles F. Crisp	D	Ga.	1891–95
38.	Thomas B. Reed	R	Maine	1895–99
39.	David B. Henderson	R	Iowa	1899–1903
40.	Joseph G. Cannon	R	Ill.	1903–11
41.	Champ Clark	D	Mo.	1911–19
42.	Frederick H. Gillett	R	Mass.	1919–25
43.	Nicholas Longworth	R	Ohio	1925–31
44.	John N. Garner	D	Tex.	1931–33
45.	Henry T. Rainey	D	Ill.	1933–34
46.	Joseph W. Byrns	D	Tenn.	1935–36
47.	William B. Bankhead	D	Ala.	1936–39
48.	Sam Rayburn	D	Tex.	1940–46
49.	Joseph W. Martin, Jr.	R	Mass.	1947–49
50.	Sam Rayburn	D	Tex.	1949–52
51.	Joseph W. Martin, Jr.	R	Mass.	1953–54
52.	Sam Rayburn	D	Tex.	1955–61
53.	John W. McCormack	D	Mass.	1962–71
54.	Carl B. Albert	D	Okla.	1971–76
55.	Thomas P. O'Neill, Jr.	D	Mass.	1977–87
56.	James C. Wright, Jr.	D	Tex.	1987–

Note: D = Democrat, D-R = Democratic-Republican, Fed. = Federalist, R = Republican.

CABINET MEMBERS

Washington Administration (1789–97)

Secretary of State	Thomas Jefferson	1789–93
	Edmund Randolph	1794–95
	Timothy Pickering	1795–97
Secretary of Treasury	Alexander Hamilton	1789–95
	Oliver Wolcott	1795–97
Secretary of War	Henry Knox	1789–94
	Timothy Pickering	1795–96
	James McHenry	1796–97
Attorney General	Edmund Randolph	1789–93
	William Bradford	1794–95
	Charles Lee	1795–97
Postmaster General	Samuel Osgood	1789–91
	Timothy Pickering	1791–94
	Joseph Habersham	1795–97

John Adams Administration (1797–1801)

Secretary of State	Timothy Pickering	1797–1800
	John Marshall	1800–01
Secretary of Treasury	Oliver Wolcott	1797–1800
	Samuel Dexter	1800–01
Secretary of War	James McHenry	1797–1800
	Samuel Dexter	1800–01
Attorney General	Charles Lee	1797–1801
Postmaster General	Joseph Habersham	1797–1801
Secretary of Navy	Benjamin Stoddert	1798–1801

Jefferson Administration (1801–09)

Secretary of State	James Madison	1801–09
Secretary of Treasury	Samuel Dexter	1801
	Albert Gallatin	1801–09
Secretary of War	Henry Dearborn	1801–09
Attorney General	Levi Lincoln	1801–05
	Robert Smith	1805
	John Breckinridge	1805–06
	Caesar Rodney	1807–09
Postmaster General	Joseph Habersham	1801
	Gideon Granger	1801–09
Secretary of Navy	Robert Smith	1801–09

Madison Administration (1809–17)

Secretary of State	Robert Smith	1809–11
	James Monroe	1811–17
Secretary of Treasury	Albert Gallatin	1809–13
	George Campbell	1814
	Alexander Dallas	1814–16
	William Crawford	1816–17
Secretary of War	William Eustis	1809–12
	John Armstrong	1813–14
	James Monroe	1814–15
	William Crawford	1815–17
Attorney General	Caesar Rodney	1809–11
	William Pinckney	1811–14
	Richard Rush	1814–17
Postmaster General	Gideon Granger	1809–14
	Return Meigs	1814–17
Secretary of Navy	Paul Hamilton	1809–13
	William Jones	1813–14
	Benjamin Crowninshield	1814–17

Monroe Administration (1817–25)

Secretary of State	John Quincy Adams	1817–25
Secretary of Treasury	William Crawford	1817–25

Monroe Administration (1817–25)

Secretary of War	George Graham	1817
	John C. Calhoun	1817–25
Attorney General	Richard Rush	1817
	William Wirt	1817–25
Postmaster General	Return Meigs	1817–23
	John McLean	1823–25
Secretary of Navy	Benjamin Crowninshield	1817–18
	Smith Thompson	1818–23
	Samuel Southard	1823–25

John Quincy Adams Administration (1825–29)

Secretary of State	Henry Clay	1825–29
Secretary of Treasury	Richard Rush	1825–29
Secretary of War	James Barbour	1825–28
	Peter Porter	1828–29
Attorney General	William Wirt	1825–29
Postmaster General	John McLean	1825–29
Secretary of Navy	Samuel Southard	1825–29

Jackson Administration (1829–37)

Secretary of State	Martin Van Buren	1829–33
	Edward Livingston	1831–33
	Louis McLane	1833–34
	John Forsyth	1834–37
Secretary of Treasury	Samuel Ingham	1829–31
	Louis McLane	1831–33
	William Duane	1833
	Roger B. Taney	1833–34
	Levi Woodbury	1834–37
Secretary of War	John H. Eaton	1829–31
	Lewis Cass	1831–37
	Benjamin Butler	1837
Attorney General	John M. Berrien	1829–31
	Roger B. Taney	1831–33
	Benjamin Butler	1833–37
Postmaster General	William Barry	1829–35
	Amos Kendall	1835–37
Secretary of Navy	John Branch	1829–31
	Levi Woodbury	1831–34
	Mahlon Dickerson	1834–37

Van Buren Administration (1837–41)

Secretary of State	John Forsyth	1837–41
Secretary of Treasury	Levi Woodbury	1837–41
Secretary of War	Joel Poinsett	1837–41
Attorney General	Benjamin Butler	1837–38
	Felix Grundy	1838–40
	Henry D. Gilpin	1840–41
Postmaster General	Amos Kendall	1837–40
	John M. Niles	1840–41
Secretary of Navy	Mahlon Dickerson	1837–38
	James Paulding	1838–41

William Harrison Administration (1841)

Secretary of State	Daniel Webster	1841
Secretary of Treasury	Thomas Ewing	1841
Secretary of War	John Bell	1841
Attorney General	John J. Crittenden	1841
Postmaster General	Francis Granger	1841
Secretary of Navy	George Badger	1841

Tyler Administration (1841–45)

Secretary of State	Daniel Webster	1841–43
	Hugh S. Legaré	1843
	Abel P. Upshur	1843–44
	John C. Calhoun	1844–45

Tyler Administration (1841–45)

Secretary of Treasury	Thomas Ewing	1841
	Walter Forward	1841–43
	John C. Spencer	1843–44
	George Bibb	1844–45
Secretary of War	John Bell	1841
	John C. Spencer	1841–43
	James M. Porter	1843–44
	William Wilkins	1844–45
Attorney General	John J. Crittenden	1841
	Hugh S. Legaré	1841–43
	John Nelson	1843–45
Postmaster General	Francis Granger	1841
	Charles Wickliffe	1841
Secretary of Navy	George Badger	1841
	Abel P. Upshur	1841
	David Henshaw	1843–44
	Thomas Gilmer	1844
	John Y. Mason	1844–45

Polk Administration (1845–49)

Secretary of State	James Buchanan	1845–49
Secretary of Treasury	Robert J. Walker	1845–49
Secretary of War	William L. Marcy	1845–49
Attorney General	John Y. Mason	1845–46
	Nathan Clifford	1846–48
	Isaac Toucey	1848–49
Postmaster General	Cave Johnson	1845–49
Secretary of Navy	George Bancroft	1845–46
	John Y. Mason	1846–49

Taylor Administration (1849–50)

Secretary of State	John M. Clayton	1849–50
Secretary of Treasury	William Meredith	1849–50
Secretary of War	George Crawford	1849–50
Attorney General	Reverdy Johnson	1849–50
Postmaster General	Jacob Collamer	1849–50
Secretary of Navy	William Preston	1849–50
Secretary of Interior	Thomas Ewing	1849–50

Fillmore Administration (1850–53)

Secretary of State	Daniel Webster	1850–52
	Edward Everett	1852–53
Secretary of Treasury	Thomas Corwin	1850–53
Secretary of War	Charles Conrad	1850–53
Attorney General	John J. Crittenden	1850–53
Postmaster General	Nathan Hall	1850–52
	Sam D. Hubbard	1852–53
Secretary of Navy	William A. Graham	1852–53
	John P. Kennedy	1852–53
Secretary of Interior	Thomas McKennan	1850
	Alexander Stuart	1850–53

Pierce Administration (1853–57)

Secretary of State	William L. Marcy	1853–57
Secretary of Treasury	James Guthrie	1853–57
Secretary of War	Jefferson Davis	1853–57
Attorney General	Caleb Cushing	1853–57
Postmaster General	James Campbell	1853–57
Secretary of Navy	James C. Dobbin	1853–57
Secretary of Interior	Robert McClelland	1853–57

Buchanan Administration (1857–61)

Secretary of State	Lewis Cass	1857–60
	Jeremiah S. Black	1860–61
Secretary of Treasury	Howell Cobb	1857–60
	Philip Thomas	1860–61
	John A. Dix	1861

Buchanan Administration (1857–61)

Secretary of War	John B. Floyd	1857–61
	Joseph Holt	1861
Attorney General	Jeremiah S. Black	1857–60
	Edwin M. Stanton	1860–61
Postmaster General	Aaron W. Brown	1857–59
	Joseph Holt	1859–61
	Horatio King	1861
Secretary of Navy	Isaac Toucey	1857–61
Secretary of Interior	Jacob Thompson	1857–61

Lincoln Administration (1861–65)

Secretary of State	William H. Seward	1861–65
Secretary of Treasury	Samuel P. Chase	1861–64
	William P. Fessenden	1864–65
	Hugh McCulloch	1865
Secretary of War	Simon Cameron	1861–62
	Edwin M. Stanton	1862–65
Attorney General	Edward Bates	1861–64
	James Speed	1864–65
Postmaster General	Horatio King	1861
	Montgomery Blair	1861–64
	William Dennison	1864–65
Secretary of Navy	Gideon Welles	1861–65
Secretary of Interior	Caleb B. Smith	1861–63
	John P. Usher	1863–65

Andrew Johnson Administration (1865–69)

Secretary of State	William H. Seward	1865–69
Secretary of Treasury	Hugh McCulloch	1865–69
Secretary of War	Edwin M. Stanton	1865–67
	Ulysses S. Grant	1867–68
	John M. Schofield	1868–69
Attorney General	James Speed	1865–66
	Henry Stanbery	1866–68
	William M. Evarts	1868–69
Postmaster General	William Dennison	1865–66
	Alexander Randall	1866–69
Secretary of Navy	Gideon Welles	1865–69
Secretary of Interior	John P. Usher	1865
	James Harlan	1865–66
	Orville H. Browning	1866–69

Grant Administration (1869–77)

Secretary of State	Elihu B. Washburne	1869
	Hamilton Fish	1869–77
Secretary of Treasury	George S. Boutwell	1869–73
	William Richardson	1873–74
	Benjamin Bristow	1874–76
	Lot M. Morrill	1876–77
Secretary of War	John A. Rawlins	1869
	William T. Sherman	1869
	William W. Belknap	1869–76
	Alphonso Taft	1876
	James D. Cameron	1876–77
Attorney General	Ebenezer Hoar	1869–70
	Amos T. Ackerman	1870–71
	G.H. Williams	1871–75
	Edwards Pierrepont	1875–76
	Alphonso Taft	1876–77
Postmaster General	John A. J. Creswell	1869–74
	James W. Marshall	1874
	Marshall Jewell	1874–76
	James N. Tyner	1876–77
Secretary of Navy	Adolph E. Borie	1869
	George M. Robeson	1869–77
Secretary of Interior	Jacob D. Cox	1869–70
	Columbus Delano	1870–75
	Zachariah Chandler	1875–77

Hayes Administration (1877–81)

Secretary of State	William M. Evarts	1877–81
Secretary of Treasury	John Sherman	1877–81
Secretary of War	George W. McCrary	1877–79
	Alex Ramsey	1879–81
Attorney General	Charles Devens	1877–81
Postmaster General	David M. Key	1877–80
	Horace Maynard	1880–81
Secretary of Navy	Richard W. Thompson	1877–80
	Nathan Goff, Jr.	1881
Secretary of Interior	Carl Schurz	1877–81

Garfield Administration (1881)

Secretary of State	James G. Blaine	1881
Secretary of Treasury	William Windom	1881
Secretary of War	Robert T. Lincoln	1881
Attorney General	Wayne MacVeagh	1881
Postmaster General	Thomas L. James	1881
Secretary of Navy	William H. Hunt	1881
Secretary of Interior	Samuel J. Kirkwood	1881

Arthur Administration (1881–85)

Secretary of State	James G. Blaine	1881
	F.T. Frelinghuysen	1881–85
Secretary of Treasury	William Windom	1881
	Charles J. Folger	1881–84
	Walter Q. Gresham	1884
	Hugh McCulloch	1884–85
Secretary of War	Robert T. Lincoln	1881–85
Attorney General	Wayne MacVeagh	1881
	Benjamin H. Brewster	1881–85
	Thomas L. James	1881
Postmaster General	Timothy O. Howe	1881–83
	Walter Q. Gresham	1883–84
	Frank Hatton	1884–85
Secretary of Navy	William H. Hunt	1881–82
	William E. Chandler	1882–85
Secretary of Interior	Samuel J. Kirkwood	1881–82
	Henry M. Teller	1882–85

Cleveland Administration (1885–89)

Secretary of State	Thomas F. Bayard	1885–89
Secretary of Treasury	Daniel Manning	1885–87
	Charles S. Fairchild	1887–89
Secretary of War	William C. Endicott	1885–89
Attorney General	Augustus H. Garland	1885–89
Postmaster General	William F. Vilas	1885–88
	Don M. Dickinson	1888–89
Secretary of Navy	William C. Whitney	1885–89
Secretary of Interior	Lucius Q.C. Lamar	1885–88
	William F. Vilas	1888–89
Secretary of Agriculture	Norman J. Colman	1889

Benjamin Harrison Administration (1889–93)

Secretary of State	James G. Blaine	1889–92
	John W. Foster	1892–93
Secretary of Treasury	William Windom	1889–91
	Charles Foster	1891–93
Secretary of War	Redfield Proctor	1889–91
	Stephen B. Elkins	1891–93
Attorney General	William H. H. Miller	1889–93
Postmaster General	John Wanamaker	1889–93
Secretary of Navy	Benjamin F. Tracy	1889–93
Secretary of Interior	John W. Noble	1889–93

Benjamin Harrison Administration (1889–93)

Secretary of Agriculture	Jeremiah M. Rusk	1889–93

Cleveland Administration (1893–97)

Secretary of State	Walter Q. Gresham	1893–95
	Richard Olney	1895–97
Secretary of Treasury	John G. Carlisle	1893–97
Secretary of War	Daniel S. Lamont	1893–97
Attorney General	Richard Olney	1893–95
	James Harmon	1895–97
Postmaster General	Wilson S. Bissell	1893–95
	William L. Wilson	1895–97
Secretary of Navy	Hilary A. Herbert	1893–97
Secretary of Interior	Hoke Smith	1893–96
	David R. Francis	1896–97
Secretary of Agriculture	Julius S. Morton	1893–97

McKinley Administration (1897–1901)

Secretary of State	John Sherman	1897–98
	William R. Day	1898
	John Hay	1898–1901
Secretary of Treasury	Lyman J. Gage	1897–1901
Secretary of War	Russell A. Alger	1897–99
	Elihu Root	1899–1901
Attorney General	Joseph McKenna	1897–98
	John W. Griggs	1898–1901
	Philander C. Knox	1901
Postmaster General	James A. Gary	1897–98
	Charles E. Smith	1898–1901
Secretary of Navy	John D. Long	1897–1901
Secretary of Interior	Cornelius N. Bliss	1897–99
	Ethan A. Hitchcock	1899–1901
Secretary of Agriculture	James Wilson	1897–1901

Theodore Roosevelt Administration (1901–09)

Secretary of State	John Hay	1901–05
	Elihu Root	1905–09
	Robert Bacon	1909
Secretary of Treasury	Lyman J. Gage	1901–02
	Leslie M. Shaw	1902–07
	George B. Cortelyou	1907–09
Secretary of War	Elihu Root	1901–04
	William H. Taft	1904–08
	Luke E. Wright	1908–09
Attorney General	Philander C. Knox	1901–04
	William H. Moody	1904–06
	Charles J. Bonaparte	1906–09
Postmaster General	Charles E. Smith	1901–02
	Henry C. Payne	1902–04
	Robert J. Wynne	1904–05
	George B. Cortelyou	1905–07
	George von L. Meyer	1907–09
Secretary of Navy	John D. Long	1901–02
	William H. Moody	1902–04
	Paul Morton	1904–05
	Charles J. Bonaparte	1905–06
	Victor H. Metcalf	1906–08
	Truman H. Newberry	1908–09
Secretary of Interior	Ethan A. Hitchcock	1901–07
	James R. Garfield	1907–09
Secretary of Agriculture	James Wilson	1901–09
Secretary of Labor and Commerce	George B. Cortelyou	1903–04
	Victor H. Metcalf	1904–06
	Oscar S. Straus	1906–09

Taft Administration (1909–13)

Secretary of State	Philander C. Knox	1909–13
Secretary of Treasury	Franklin MacVeagh	1909–13
Secretary of War	Jacob M. Dickinson	1909–11
	Henry L. Stimson	1911–13
Attorney General	George W. Wickersham	1909–13
Postmaster General	Frank H. Hitchcock	1909–13
Secretary of Navy	George von L. Meyer	1909–13
Secretary of Interior	Richard A. Ballinger	1909–11
	Walter Fisher	1911–13
Secretary of Agriculture	James Wilson	1909–13
Secretary of Labor and Commerce	Charles Nagel	1909–13

Wilson Administration (1913–21)

Secretary of State	William J. Bryan	1913–15
	Robert Lansing	1915–20
	Bainbridge Colby	1920–21
Secretary of Treasury	William G. McAdoo	1913–18
	Carter Glass	1918–20
	David F. Houston	1920–21
Secretary of War	Lindley M. Garrison	1913–16
	Newton D. Baker	1916–21
Attorney General	James C. McReynolds	1913–14
	Thomas W. Gregory	1914–19
	A. Mitchell Palmer	1919–21
Postmaster General	Albert S. Burleson	1913–21
Secretary of Navy	Josephus Daniels	1913–21
Secretary of Interior	Franklin K. Lane	1913–20
	John B. Payne	1920–21
Secretary of Agriculture	David F. Houston	1913–20
	Edwin T. Meredith	1920–21
Secretary of Commerce	William C. Redfield	1913–19
	Joshua W. Alexander	1919
Secretary of Labor	William B. Wilson	1913–21

Harding Administration (1921–23)

Secretary of State	Charles E. Hughes	1921–23
Secretary of Treasury	Andrew Mellon	1921–23
Secretary of War	John W. Weeks	1921–23
Attorney General	Harry M. Daugherty	1921–23
Postmaster General	Will H. Hays	1921–22
	Hubert Work	1922–23
	Harry S. New	1923
Secretary of Navy	Edwin Denby	1921–23
Secretary of Interior	Albert B. Fall	1921–23
	Hubert Work	1923
Secretary of Agriculture	Henry C. Wallace	1921–23
Secretary of Commerce	Herbert C. Hoover	1921–23
Secretary of Labor	James J. Davis	1921–23

Coolidge Administration (1923–29)

Secretary of State	Charles E. Hughes	1923–25
	Frank B. Kellogg	1925–29
Secretary of Treasury	John W. Weeks	1923–25
	Dwight F. Davis	1925–29
Attorney General	Harry M. Daugherty	1923–24
	Harlan F. Stone	1924–25
	John G. Sargent	1925–29
Postmaster General	Harry S. New	1923–29
Secretary of Navy	Edwin Denby	1923–24
	Curtis D. Wilbur	1924–29
Secretary of Interior	Hubert Work	1923–28
	Roy O. West	1928–29
Secretary of Agriculture	Henry C. Wallace	1923–24
	Howard M. Gore	1924–25
	William M. Jardine	1925–29

Coolidge Administration (1923–29)

Secretary of Commerce	Herbert C. Hoover	1923–28
	William F. Whiting	1928–29
Secretary of Labor	James J. Davis	1923–29

Hoover Administration (1929–33)

Secretary of State	Henry L. Stimson	1929–33
Secretary of Treasury	Andrew Mellon	1929–32
	Ogden L. Mills	1932–33
Secretary of War	James W. Good	1929
	Patrick J. Hurley	1929–33
Attorney General	William D. Mitchell	1929–33
Postmaster General	Walter F. Brown	1929–33
Secretary of Navy	Charles F. Adams	1929–33
Secretary of Interior	Ray L. Wilbur	1929–33
Secretary of Agriculture	Arthur M. Hyde	1929–33
Secretary of Commerce	Robert P. Lamont	1929–32
	Roy D. Chapin	1932–33
Secretary of Labor	James J. Davis	1929–30
	William N. Doak	1930–33

Franklin D. Roosevelt Administration (1933–45)

Secretary of State	Cordell Hull	1933–44
	Edward R. Stettinius, Jr.	1944–45
Secretary of Treasury	William H. Woodin	1933–34
	Henry Morgenthau, Jr.	1934–45
Secretary of War	George H. Dern	1933–36
	Henry A. Woodring	1936–40
	Henry L. Stimson	1940–45
Attorney General	Homer S. Cummings	1933–39
	Frank Murphy	1939–40
	Robert H. Jackson	1940–41
	Francis Biddle	1941–45
Postmaster General	James A. Farley	1933–40
	Frank C. Walker	1940–45
Secretary of Navy	Claude A. Swanson	1933–40
	Charles Edison	1940
	Frank Knox	1940–44
	James V. Forrestal	1944–45
Secretary of Interior	Harold L. Ickes	1933–45
Secretary of Agriculture	Henry A. Wallace	1933–40
	Claude R. Wickard	1940–45
Secretary of Commerce	Daniel C. Roper	1933–39
	Harry L. Hopkins	1939–40
	Jesse Jones	1940–45
	Henry A. Wallace	1945
Secretary of Labor	Frances Perkins	1933–45

Truman Administration (1945–53)

Secretary of State	Edward R. Stettinius, Jr.	1945
	James F. Byrnes	1945–47
	George C. Marshall	1947–49
	Dean G. Acheson	1949–53
Secretary of Treasury	Fred M. Vinson	1945–46
	John W. Snyder	1946–53
Secretary of War[1]	Robert P. Patterson	1945–47
	Kenneth C. Royall	1947
Attorney General	Tom C. Clark	1945–49
	J. Howard McGrath	1949–52
	James P. McGranery	1952–53
Postmaster General	Frank C. Walker	1945
	Robert E. Hannegan	1945–47
	Jesse M. Donaldson	1947–53
Secretary of Navy[1]	James V. Forrestal	1945–47
Secretary of Interior	Harold L. Ickes	1945–46
	Julius A. Krug	1946–49
	Oscar L. Chapman	1949–53

Truman Administration (1945–53)

Secretary of Agriculture	Clinton P. Anderson	1945–48
	Charles F. Brannan	1948–53
Secretary of Commerce	Henry A. Wallace	1945–46
	W. Averell Harriman	1946–48
	Charles W. Sawyer	1948–53
Secretary of Labor	Lewis B. Schwellenbach	1945–48
	Maurice J. Tobin	1948–53
Secretary of Defense	James V. Forrestal	1947–49
	Louis A. Johnson	1949–50
	George C. Marshall	1950–51
	Robert A. Lovett	1951–53

1. On July 26, 1947, the Dept. of War and the Dept. of the Navy were consolidated under the Dept. of Defense.

Eisenhower Administration (1953–61)

Secretary of State	John Foster Dulles	1953–59
	Christian A. Herter	1959–61
Secretary of Treasury	George M. Humphrey	1953–57
	Robert B. Anderson	1957–61
Secretary of Defense	Charles E. Wilson	1953–57
	Neil H. McElroy	1957–59
	Thomas S. Gates, Jr.	1959–61
Attorney General	Herbert Brownell, Jr.	1953–58
	William P. Rogers	1958–61
Postmaster General	Arthur E. Summerfield	1953–61
Secretary of Interior	Douglas McKay	1953–56
	Fred A. Seaton	1956–61
Secretary of Agriculture	Ezra T. Benson	1953–61
Secretary of Commerce	Sinclair Weeks	1953–58
	Lewis L. Strauss[2]	1958–59
	Frederick H. Mueller	1959–1961
Secretary of Labor	Martin P. Durkin	1953
	James P. Mitchell	1953–61
Secretary of Health, Education, and Welfare	Oveta Culp Hobby	1953–55
	Marion B. Folsom	1955–58
	Arthur S. Flemming	1958–61

2. Apppointed Oct. 1958 but not confirmed.

Kennedy Administration (1961–63)

Secretary of State	Dean Rusk	1961–63
Secretary of Treasury	C. Douglas Dillon	1961–63
Secretary of Defense	Robert S. McNamara	1961–63
Attorney General	Robert F. Kennedy	1961–63
Postmaster General	J. Edward Day	1961–63
	John A. Gronouski	1963
Secretary of Interior	Stewart L. Udall	1961–63
Secretary of Agriculture	Orville L. Freeman	1961–63
Secretary of Commerce	Luther H. Hodges	1961–63
Secretary of Labor	Arthur J. Goldberg	1961–62
	W. Willard Wirtz	1962–63
Secretary of Health, Education, and Welfare	Abraham A. Ribicoff	1961–62
	Anthony J. Celebrezze	1962–63

Lyndon Johnson Administration (1963–69)

Secretary of State	Dean Rusk	1963–69
Secretary of Treasury	C. Douglas Dillon	1963–65
	Henry H. Fowler	1965–69
Secretary of Defense	Robert F. McNamara	1963–68
	Clark Clifford	1968–69
Attorney General	Robert F. Kennedy	1963–64
	Nicholas Katzenbach	1965–66
	Ramsey Clark	1967–69
Postmaster General	John A. Gronouski	1963–65
	Lawrence F. O'Brien	1965–68
	Marvin Watson	1968–69
Secretary of Interior	Stewart L. Udall	1963–69
Secretary of Agriculture	Orville L. Freeman	1963–69

Lyndon Johnson Administration (1963–69)

Secretary of Commerce	Luther H. Hodges	1963–64
	John T. Connor	1964–67
	Alexander B. Trowbridge	1967–68
	Cyrus R. Smith	1968–69
Secretary of Labor	W. Willard Wirtz	1963–69
Secretary of Health,	Anthony J. Celebrezze	1963–65
Education, and Welfare	John W. Gardner	1965–68
	Wilbur J. Cohen	1968–69
Secretary of Housing and	Robert C. Weaver	1966–69
Urban Development	Robert C. Wood	1969
Secretary of Transportation	Alan S. Boyd	1967–69

Nixon Administration (1969–74)

Secretary of State	William P. Rogers	1969–73
	Henry A. Kissinger	1973–74
Secretary of Treasury	David M. Kennedy	1969–70
	John B. Connally	1971–72
	George P. Shultz	1972–74
	William E. Simon	1974
Attorney General	John N. Mitchell	1969–72
	Richard G. Kleindienst	1972–73
	Elliot L. Richardson	1973
	William B. Saxbe	1973–74
Postmaster General	Winton M. Blount	1969–71
Secretary of Interior	Walter J. Hickel	1969–70
	Rogers Morton	1971–74
Secretary of Agriculture	Clifford M. Hardin	1969–71
	Earl L. Butz	1971–74
Secretary of Commerce	Maurice H. Stans	1969–72
	Peter G. Peterson	1972–73
	Frederick B. Dent	1973–74
Secretary of Labor	George P. Shultz	1969–70
	James D. Hodgson	1970–73
	Peter J. Brennan	1973–74
Secretary of Defense	Melvin R. Laird	1969–73
	Elliot L. Richardson	1973
	James R. Schlesinger	1973–74
Secretary of Health,	Robert H. Finch	1969–70
Education, and Welfare	Elliot L. Richardson	1970–73
	Caspar W. Weinberger	1973–74
Secretary of Housing and	George Romney	1969–73
Urban Development	James T. Lyon	1973–74
Secretary of Transportation	John A. Volpe	1969–73
	Claude S. Brinegar	1973–74

Ford Administration (1974–77)

Secretary of State	Henry A. Kissinger	1974–77
Secretary of Treasury	William E. Simon	1974–77
Secretary of Defense	James R. Schlesinger	1974–75
	Donald Rumsfeld	1975–77
Attorney General	William Saxbe	1974–75
	Edward Levi	1975–77
Secretary of Interior	Rogers Morton	1974–75
	Stanley K. Hathaway	1975
	Thomas Kleppe	1975–77
Secretary of Agriculture	Earl L. Butz	1974–76
	John A. Knebel	1976–77
Secretary of Commerce	Frederick B. Dent	1974–75
	Rogers Morton	1975–76
	Elliot L. Richardson	1976–77
Secretary of Labor	Peter J. Brennan	1974–75
	John T. Dunlop	1975–76
	W.J. Usery	1976–77
Secretary of Health,	Caspar Weinberger	1974–75
Education, and Welfare	Forrest D. Mathews	1975–77
Secretary of Housing and	James T. Lynn	1974–75
Urban Development	Carla A. Hills	1975–77
Secretary of Transportation	William T. Coleman	1975–77

Carter Administration (1977–81)

Secretary of State	Cyrus R. Vance	1977–80
	Edmund Muskie	1980–81
Secretary of Treasury	W. Michael Blumenthal	1977–79
	G. William Miller	1979–81
Secretary of Defense	Harold Brown	1977–81
Attorney General	Griffin Bell	1977–79
	Benjamin R. Civiletti	1979–81
Secretary of Interior	Cecil D. Andrus	1977–81
Secretary of Agriculture	Robert Bergland	1977–81
Secretary of Commerce	Juanita M. Kreps	1977–79
	Philip M. Klutznick	1979–81
Secretary of Labor	F. Ray Marshall	1977–81
Secretary of Health,	Joseph A. Califano	1977–79
Education, and Welfare	Patricia R. Harris	1979
Secretary of Health and	Patricia R. Harris	1979–81
Human Services		
Secretary of Education	Shirley M. Hufstedler	1979–81
Secretary of Housing and	Patricia R. Harris	1977–79
Urban Development	Moon Landrieu	1979–81
Secretary of Transportation	Brock Adams	1977–79
	Neil E. Goldschmidt	1979–81
Secretary of Energy	James R. Schlesinger	1977–79
	Charles W. Duncan	1979–81

Reagan Administration (1981–89)

Secretary of State	Alexander M. Haig	1981–82
	George P. Shultz	1982–89
Secretary of Treasury	Donald Regan	1981–85
	James A. Baker III	1985–88
	Nicholas F. Brady	1988–89
Attorney General	William F. Smith	1981–85
	Edwin A. Meese III	1985–88
	Dick Thornburgh	1988–89
Secretary of Interior	James Watt	1981–83
	William P. Clark, Jr.	1983–85
	Donald P. Hodel	1985–89
Secretary of Agriculture	John Block	1981–86
	Richard E. Lyng	1986–89
Secretary of Commerce	Malcolm Baldrige	1981–87
	C. William Verity, Jr.	1987–89
Secretary of Labor	Raymond Donovan	1981–85
	William E. Brock	1985–87
	Ann McLaughlin	1987–89
Secretary of Defense	Caspar Weinberger	1981–87
	Frank Carlucci	1987–89
Secretary of Health and	Richard Schweiker	1981–83
Human Services	Margaret Heckler	1983–85
	Otis R. Bowen	1985–89
Secretary of Education	Terrel H. Bell	1981–85
	William J. Bennett	1985–89
	Lauro Cavazos	1988–89
Secretary of Housing and	Samuel Pierce	1981–89
Urban Development		
Secretary of Transportation	Drew Lewis	1981–83
	Elizabeth Dole	1983–87
	James H. Burney	1987–89
Secretary of Energy	James Edwards	1981–82
	Donald P. Hodel	1982–85
	John S. Herrington	1985–89

Bush Administration (1989–   )

Secretary of State	James Addison Baker III	1989–
Secretary of Treasury	Nicholas Brady	1989–
Secretary of Defense	Richard B. Cheney	1989–
Attorney General	Richard Thornburgh	1989–
Secretary of Interior	Manuel Lujan, Jr.	1989–
Secretary of Agriculture	Clayton K. Yeutter	1989–

Bush Administration (1989–   )

Secretary of Commerce	Robert Adam Mossbacher	1989–
Secretary of Labor	Elizabeth Hanford Dole	1989–
Secretary of Health and		
Human Services	Louis W. Sullivan	1989–
Secretary of Housing and		
Urban Development	Jack F. Kemp	1989–
Secretary of Transportation	Samuel Knox Skinner	1989–
Secretary of Energy	James D. Watkins	1989–
Secretary of Education	Lauro D. Cavazos	1989–
Secretary of Veterans		
Affairs	Edward J. Derwinski	1989–

The Supreme Court in U.S. History

CHIEF JUSTICES OF THE UNITED STATES

Chief Justice	Dates	Appointed by
John Jay	1789–95	George Washington
John Rutledge	1795–95	George Washington
Oliver Ellsworth	1796–1800	George Washington
John Marshall	1801–35	John Adams
Roger B. Taney	1836–64	Andrew Jackson
Salmon P. Chase	1864–73	Abraham Lincoln
Morrison R. Waite	1874–88	Ulysses S. Grant
Melville W. Fuller	1888–1910	Grover Cleveland
Edward D. White	1910–21	William Howard Taft
William Howard Taft	1921–30	Warren G. Harding
Charles Evans Hughes	1930–41	Herbert Hoover
Harlan F. Stone	1941–46	Franklin D. Roosevelt
Fred M. Vinson	1946–53	Harry S Truman
Earl Warren	1953–69	Dwight D. Eisenhower
Warren E. Burger	1969–87	Richard M. Nixon
William H. Rehnquist	1987–	Ronald Reagan

Important Supreme Court Decisions

Marbury vs. Madison (1803) The Court struck down a law "repugnant to the constitution" for the first time and set the precedent for judicial review of acts of Congress. In a politically ingenious ruling on the Judiciary Act of 1789, Chief Justice John Marshall asserted the Supreme Court's power to "say what the law is," while avoiding a confrontation with Pres. Thomas Jefferson. Not until the *Dred Scott* case of 1857 would another federal law be ruled unconstitutional.

Fletcher vs. Peck (1810) The Court ruled that Georgia could not deprive land speculators of their title, even though the previous owners had obtained the land from the state through fraud and bribery. Arising from the infamous Yazoo land frauds of 1795, this decision followed the Constitution's obligation of contracts clause and was the first time the Court invalidated a state law.

Dartmouth College vs. Woodward (1819) The Court encouraged business investment with this decision by treating corporate charters as fully protected contracts. Not even the state legislatures that originally granted them could tamper with charters to private corporations, unless they retained the power to do so. Dartmouth College remained a private institution despite New Hampshire's attempt to take it over. This decision, which opened the way for abuse of corporate priv-

SUPREME COURT JUSTICES

Name	Tenure	Appointed by
Baldwin, Henry	1830–44	Andrew Jackson
Barbour, Philip P.	1836–41	Andrew Jackson
Black, Hugo L.	1937–71	Franklin D. Roosevelt
Blackmun, Harry A.	1970–	Richard M. Nixon
Blair, John	1789–1796	George Washington
Blatchford, Samuel	1882–93	Chester A. Arthur
Bradley, Joseph P.	1870–92	Ulysses S. Grant
Brandeis, Louis D.	1916–39	Woodrow Wilson
Brennan, William J., Jr.	1956–	Dwight D. Eisenhower
Brewer, David J.	1889–1910	Benjamin Harrison
Brown, Henry B.	1890–1906	Benjamin Harrison
Burton, Harold H.	1945–58	Harry S Truman
Butler, Pierce	1922–39	Warren G. Harding
Byrnes, James F.	1941–42	Franklin D. Roosevelt
Campbell, John A.	1853–61	Franklin Pierce
Cardozo, Benjamin N.	1932–38	Herbert Hoover
Catron, John	1837–65	Martin Van Buren
Chase, Samuel	1796–1811	George Washington
Clark, Tom C.	1949–67	Harry S Truman
Clarke, John H.	1916–22	Woodrow Wilson
Clifford, Nathan	1858–81	James J. Buchanan
Curtis, Benjamin R.	1851–57	Millard Fillmore
Cushing, William	1789–1810	George Washington
Daniel, Peter V.	1841–60	Martin Van Buren
Davis, David	1862–77	Abraham Lincoln
Day, William R.	1903–22	Theodore Roosevelt
Douglas, William O.	1939–75	Franklin D. Roosevelt
Duval, Gabriel	1811–36	James Madison
Field, Stephen J.	1863–97	Abraham Lincoln
Fortas, Abe	1965–69	Lyndon B. Johnson
Frankfurter, Felix	1939–62	Franklin D. Roosevelt
Goldberg, Arthur J.	1962–65	John F. Kennedy
Gray, Horace	1881–1902	Chester A. Arthur
Grier, Robert C.	1846–70	James K. Polk
Harlan, John Marshall	1877–1911	Rutherford B. Hayes
Harlan, John Marshall	1955–71	Dwight D. Eisenhower
Harrison, Robert H.	1789–1790	George Washington
Holmes, Oliver Wendell	1902–32	Theodore Roosevelt
Hughes, Charles Evans[1]	1910–16	William Howard Taft
Hunt, Ward	1872–82	Ulysses S. Grant
Iredell, James	1790–1799	George Washington
Jackson, Howell E.	1893–95	Benjamin Harrison
Jackson, Robert H.	1941–54	Franklin D. Roosevelt
Johnson, Thomas	1791–1793	George Washington
Johnson, William	1804–34	Thomas Jefferson
Kennedy, Anthony M.	1987–	Ronald Reagan

Name	Tenure	Appointed by
Lamar, Joseph R.	1911–16	William Howard Taft
Lamar, Lucius Q.C.	1888–93	Grover Cleveland
Livingston, H. Brockholst	1806–23	Thomas Jefferson
Lurton, Horace H.	1910–14	William Howard Taft
Marshall, Thurgood	1967–	Lyndon B. Johnson
Matthews, Stanley	1881–89	James A. Garfield
McKenna, Joseph	1898–1925	William McKinley
McKinley, John	1837–52	Martin Van Buren
McLean, John	1829–61	Andrew Jackson
McReynolds, James C.	1914–41	Woodrow Wilson
Miller, Samuel F.	1862–90	Abraham Lincoln
Minton, Sherman	1949–56	Harry S Truman
Moody, William H.	1906–10	Theodore Roosevelt
Moore, Alfred	1799–1804	John Adams
Murphy, Frank	1940–49	Franklin D. Roosevelt
Nelson, Samuel	1845–72	John Tyler
O'Connor, Sandra Day	1981–	Ronald Reagan
Paterson, William	1793–1806	George Washington
Peckham, Rufus W.	1895–1910	Grover Cleveland
Pitney, Mahlon	1912–22	William Howard Taft
Powell, Lewis F., Jr.	1972–87	Richard M. Nixon
Reed, Stanley F.	1938–57	Franklin D. Roosevelt
Rehnquist, William H.[1]	1972–86	Richard M. Nixon
Roberts, Owen J.	1930–45	Herbert Hoover
Rutledge, John[1]	1789–1791	George Washington
Rutledge, Wiley B.	1943–49	Franklin D. Roosevelt
Sanford, Edward T.	1923–30	Warren G. Harding
Scalia, Antonin	1986–	Ronald Reagan
Shiras, George	1892–1903	Benjamin Harrison
Stevens, John Paul	1975–	Gerald R. Ford
Stewart, Potter	1959–81	Dwight D. Eisenhower
Stone, Harlan F.[1]	1925–41	Calvin Coolidge
Story, Joseph	1811–45	James Madison
Strong, William	1870–80	Ulysses S. Grant
Sutherland, George	1922–38	Warren G. Harding
Swayne, Noah H.	1862–81	Abraham Lincoln
Thompson, Smith	1823–43	James Monroe
Todd, Thomas	1807–26	Thomas Jefferson
Trimble, Robert	1826–28	John Quincy Adams
Van Devanter, Willis	1910–37	William Howard Taft
Washington, Bushrod	1798–1829	John Adams
Wayne, James M.	1835–67	Andrew Jackson
White, Byron R.	1962–88	John F. Kennedy
White, Edward D.[1]	1894–1910	Grover Cleveland
Whittaker, Charles E.	1957–62	Dwight D. Eisenhower
Wilson, James	1789–1798	George Washington
Woodbury, Levi	1845–51	James K. Polk
Woods, William B.	1880–87	Rutherford B. Hayes

1. Chief Justice.

ileges, would later be modified in the *Charles River Bridge (1837)* and *Munn* vs. *Illinois* (1877) cases.

McCulloch vs. Maryland (1819) "Broad," as opposed to "strict," construction of the Constitution received high-court approval in Chief Justice John Marshall's opinion upholding the constitutionality of the national bank against a Maryland challenge. This ruling enhanced federal governmental authority by liberally interpreting the power of Congress to make laws "necessary and proper" for its specified powers. At a time when states were trying to tax the Bank of the United States out of existence, this decision also forbade such state interference with the federal government. "The power to tax," Marshall wrote, "involves the power to destroy."

Cohens vs. Virginia (1821) With this ruling, the Court reiterated its power to hear appeals from state courts, and affirmed the national supremacy of federal judicial power. Virginia's conviction of the Cohens for selling lottery tickets in violation of state law was upheld, but so too was the Cohens' right to appeal to the Court, which Virginia had challenged. Critics of judicial "consolidationalism" were reminded of the Court's comprehensive powers as the ultimate appellate court for all Americans.

Gibbons vs. Ogden (1824) In a dispute arising from a New York ferry monopoly, the Court ruled that states could not restrain interstate commerce in any way, and that congressional power to regulate interstate commerce "does not stop at the jurisdictional lines of the several states." The decision helped prevent interstate trade wars, quite common under the Articles of Confederation, from breaking out under the Constitution. Chief Justice Marshall's opinion also confirmed the broad potential power of the Constitution's commerce clause.

Charles River Bridge vs. Warren Bridge (1837)
A key decision for economic development, this case arose when state-chartered proprietors of a Boston toll bridge objected that a new state-chartered bridge across the Charles River would put them out of business. Chief Justice Roger B. Taney, in his first constitutional ruling, held that state charters implied no vested rights and that ambiguities must be construed in favor of the public, who would benefit from the new toll-free bridge. This decision balanced private property rights against the public welfare.

Dred Scott vs. Sanford (1857)
Dred Scott, a Missouri slave, sued for his liberty after his owner took him into free territory. The Court ruled that Congress could not bar slavery in the territories. Scott remained a slave because the Missouri Compromise of 1820, prohibiting slavery from part of the Louisiana Purchase, violated the Fifth Amendment by depriving slave owners of their right to enjoy property without due process of law. Scott himself could not even sue, for he was held to be property, not a citizen. This decision sharpened sectional conflict by sweeping away legal barriers to the expansion of slavery.

Ex Parte Milligan (1866)
Pres. Abraham Lincoln's suspension of some civil liberties during the Civil War was attacked in this decision, which upheld the right of habeus corpus. The Court ruled that the president could not hold military tribunals in areas remote from battle and where civil courts were open and functioning. Milligan's conviction by such a Civil War tribunal in Indianapolis, Indiana, was overturned. The Constitution, admonished the Court, applies "at all times, and under all circumstances."

Slaughter-House Cases (1873)
In its first ruling on the 14th Amendment, the Court held that Louisiana's grant of a butcher monopoly did not violate the privileges and immunities of competitors, nor deny them equal protection of the laws, nor deprive them of property without due process. Only a few rights deriving from "federal citizenship" were subject to federal protection, while states still protected most civil and property rights. Federal protection of civil rights, even for former slaves, was very narrowly interpreted in this ruling. But this decision broadly upheld business regulation by states until *Santa Clara Co.* vs. *Southern Pacific Railroad Co.* (1886) applied the 14th Amendment to defense of corporate property rights.

Munn vs. Illinois (1877)
This decision, in one of the "Granger Cases," enabled states to regulate private property in the public interest when the public had an interest in that property. The Court held that Illinois laws setting maximum rates for grain storage did not violate the 14th Amendment's ban on deprivation of property without due process of law and did not restrain interstate commerce. But for the next half-century, the Court imposed the burden of proof on the states for their regulatory laws.

Civil Rights Cases (1993)
Racial equality was postponed 80 years by this decision, which struck down the Civil Rights Act of 1875 and allowed for private segregation. The 14th Amendment's guarantee of equal protection, the Court ruled, applied against state action—but not against private individuals, whose discrimination unaided by the states was beyond federal control. Segregation of public facilities was approved soon afterward in *Plessy* vs. *Ferguson* (1896).

United States vs. E.C. Knight Co. (1895)
The first ruling on the Sherman Antitrust Act of 1890, this decision curtailed federal regulation of monopolies by placing national manufacturers beyond the reach of the Constitution's commerce clause. Only the actual interstate commerce of monopolies, not their production activities, was subject to federal control. The Court's distinction between production and commerce impeded federal regulation of manufacturing until *National Labor Relations Board* vs. *Jones & Laughlin Steel Corp.* (1937).

Plessy vs. Ferguson (1896)
The "separate but equal" doctrine supporting public segregation by law received the Court's approval in this ruling, which originated with segregated railroad cars in Louisiana. The Court held that as long as equal accommodations were provided, segregation was not discrimination and did not deprive blacks of equal protection of the laws under the 14th Amendment. This decision was overturned in *Brown* vs. *Board of Education* (1954).

Lochner vs. New York (1905)
This decision struck down a New York law placing limits on maximum working hours for bakers. The law violated the 14th Amendment by restricting individual "freedom of contract" to buy and sell labor and was an excessive use of state police power, the Court held. The ruling was soon modified in *Muller* vs. *Oregon* (1908), which approved state-regulated limits on women's labor after the Court utilized sociological and economic data to consider the health and morals of women workers.

Standard Oil Co. of New Jersey vs. United States (1911)
Federal efforts to break up monopolies under the Sherman Antitrust Act had to follow the "rule of reason," according to this ruling. Only those combinations in restraint of trade that were contrary to the public interest, and therefore unreasonable, were illegal. Although the Taft administration's prosecution of Standard Oil was upheld, breaking up one of the nation's leading monopolies, further antitrust suits were impaired by this decision, which facilitated the 1920s' merger movement.

Schenk vs. United States (1919)
The Court unanimously upheld that World War I limits on freedom of speech did not violate the First Amendment—if the speech in question represented a "clear and present danger." That famous doctrine of Justice Oliver Wendell Holmes, which approved the arrest of a draft resister for handing out pamphlets to soldiers in wartime, became an important standard for interpreting the First Amendment. But in subsequent cases of this period, the Court added that the mere "bad tendency" of speech to cause danger could be grounds for censorship.

Schechter Poultry Corp. vs. United States (1935)
At the height of its assault on the New Deal, the Court struck down the National Industrial Recovery Act in the famous "Sick Chicken Case." The NIRA was found to delegate excessive legislative regulatory powers to the executive without constitutional authority, and to regulate commerce within states in violation of the commerce clause. Schechter's kosher chicken supply house in New York did not have to abide by the NIRA's rigid industry codes, the Court ruled.

National Labor Relations Board vs. Jones & Laughlin Steel Corp. (1937)
Under pressure from public opinion and Pres. Franklin D. Roosevelt, the Court made an abrupt about-face and began approving New Deal legislation. In this case, laws protecting unions and barring "unfair labor practices" were upheld by the "stream of commerce" doctrine, holding that employers who sold their goods and obtained their raw materials through interstate commerce were subject to federal regulation. This ruling overturned *United States* vs. *E.C. Knight Co.* (1895) and became the basis for the modern, expansive understanding of commerce power.

West Virginia Board of Education vs. Barnette (1943)
The Court reversed its earlier ruling in *Minersville School District* vs. *Gobitis* (1940), which had required Jehovah's Witnesses to salute the flag in school. In this case, also brought against a Jehovah's Witness, the Court recognized that refusing to salute the flag did not violate anyone's rights, and that the First Amendment protected the "right of silence" as well as freedom of speech.

Korematsu vs. United States (1944)
Pres. Franklin D. Roosevelt's Executive Order No. 9066, which approved the West Coast evacuation and internment of 120,000 Japanese-Americans during World War II, was upheld on the grounds of "military necessity" in this ruling. The Court was reluctant to interfere with executive authority in time of national emergency. But in *Ex parte Endo* (1944), the Court held that persons of proven loyalty should not be interned. In August 1988 Congress made a formal apology to former internees and appropriated $1.25 billion in compensation for the 60,000 survivors.

Dennis vs. United States (1951)
At the height of the postwar "Red Scare," the Court upheld the conviction of 11 American Communist leaders under the Smith Act of

1940, which made it a crime to belong to organizations teaching or advocating the violent overthrow of the government. The "clear and present danger" doctrine could be disregarded, the Court held, if "the gravity of the 'evil,' discounted by its improbability, justifies such invasion of free speech as is necessary to avoid the evil." Over 100 Communists were indicted as a result, effectively destroying the Communist party as a political force.

Youngstown Sheet and Tube Co. vs. Sawyer (1952)
During the Korean War, when Pres. Harry S Truman seized steel plants to keep them operating despite a strike, the Court held that his action was an unconstitutional usurpation of legislative authority. Only an act of Congress, not the president's inherent executive powers or military powers as commander in chief, could justify such a sizable confiscation of property, despite the wartime emergency.

Brown vs. Board of Education of Topeka (1954)
Chief Justice Earl Warren led the Court unanimously to decide that segregated schools violated the equal protection clause of the 14th Amendment. The "separate but equal" doctrine of *Plessy* vs. *Ferguson* (1896) was overruled after a series of cases dating back to *Missouri ex. rel. Gaines* vs. *Canada* (1938) had already limited it. "Separate educational facilities are inherently unequal," held the Court. Efforts to desegregate southern schools after the *Brown* decision met with massive resistance for many years.

Baker vs. Carr (1962)
Overrepresentation of rural districts in state legislatures, which effectively disfranchised millions of voters, led the Court to abandon its traditional noninterference in drawing legislative boundaries. Tennessee citizens deprived of full representation by "arbitrary and capricious" malapportionment were denied equal protection under the 14th Amendment, ruled the Court. All states eventually reapportioned their legislatures in conformance with the "one man, one vote" doctrine of *Reynolds* vs. *Sims* (1964).

Gideon vs. Wainwright (1963)
Reversing an earlier ruling in *Betts* vs. *Brady* (1942), the Court held that the Sixth Amendment guaranteed access to qualified counsel, which was "fundamental to a fair trial." Gideon was entitled to a retrial because Florida failed to provide him with an attorney. After this decision, states were required to furnish public defenders for indigent defendants in felony cases. In *Argersinger* vs. *Hamlin* (1972), the ruling was extended to all cases that might result in imprisonment.

Heart of Atlanta Motel, Inc. vs. United States (1964)
The Court upheld Title II of the Civil Rights Act of 1964, outlawing private discrimination in public accommodations, as a legitimate exertion of federal power over interstate commerce. Congress had "ample power" to forbid racial discrimination in facilities that affected commerce by serving interstate travelers. The Heart of Atlanta Motel was located on two interstate highways,

so the Court could sidestep the *Civil Rights Cases* (1883) protection of private discrimination to overrule it.

South Carolina vs. Katzenbach (1966)
Federal intervention on behalf of voting rights was upheld in this decision. South Carolina sued the attorney general, contending that the 1965 Voting Rights Act encroached on the reserved powers of the states, treated the states unequally, and violated separation of powers. Chief Justice Warren ruled that the 15th Amendment gave Congress broad powers to "use any rational means to effectuate the constitutional prohibition of racial discrimination in voting." After this decision blacks registered and voted in massive numbers in the South.

Miranda vs. Arizona (1966)
Expanding on *Gideon* vs. *Wainwright* (1963) and *Escobedo* vs. *Illinois* (1964), the Court set forth stringent interrogation procedures for criminal suspects, to protect their Fifth Amendment freedom from self-incrimination. Miranda's confession to kidnapping and rape was obtained without counsel and without his having been advised of his right to silence, so it was ruled inadmissable as evidence. This decision obliged police to advise suspects of their rights upon taking them into custody.

New York Times Co. vs. United States (1971)
When the *New York Times* and the *Washington Post* published the top-secret "Pentagon Papers" in 1971, revealing government duplicity in the Vietnam War, the Nixon administration obtained an injunction against the *Times* on grounds of national security. But in a brief *per curiam* opinion, the Court observed that in this case the government had not met the "heavy burden of showing justification" for "prior restraint" on freedom of the press.

Roe vs. Wade (1973)
In a controversial ruling, the Court held that state laws restricting abortion were an unconstitutional invasion of a woman's right to privacy. Only in the last trimester of pregnancy, when the fetus achieved viability outside the womb, might states regulate abortion—except when the life or health of the mother was at stake. Feelings ran high on both sides in the aftermath of this decision. In *Planned Parenthood of Central Missouri* vs. *Danforth* (1976), the Court added further that wives did not need their husbands' consent to obtain abortions.

United States vs. Nixon (1974)
In a unanimous ruling, the Court held that the secret White House recordings of Pres. Richard M. Nixon's conversations with aides were subject to subpoena in the Watergate cover-up trial. Nixon's claim to "executive privilege" was rejected as invalid because military and national security issues were not at stake, and Chief Justice Warren Burger cited *Marbury* vs. *Madison* (1803) to assert the Court's primacy in constitutional issues. Once the tapes were released, documenting Nixon's obstruction of justice, the president resigned to avoid impeachment.

University of California Regents vs. Bakke (1978)
Twice refused admission to medical school, Bakke sued the University of California for giving "affirmative action" preference to less-qualified black applicants. In an ambiguous 5–4 ruling, the Court agreed that Bakke's right to equal protection was denied, that he should be admitted, and that affirmative action quotas should be discarded. But at the same time, the Court recognized race as a "factor" in admissions and hiring decisions. Affirmative action could continue as long as rigid quotas did not constitute, in effect, "reverse discrimination."

Immigration and Naturalization Service vs. Chadha (1983)
The legislative veto, contained in hundreds of federal statutes since 1932, was disallowed in this decision. Congress exceeded its constitutional powers when it blocked the attorney general's suspension of a deportation order for Jagdish Rai Chadha, a Kenyan student who overstayed his visa. The Court held that the Immigration and Nationality Act's legislative veto provision violated the constitutional separation of powers. Chief Justice Warren Burger recognized that Congress would prefer to delegate authority to the executive branch and reserve the right to veto administrative regulations, but "we have not found a better way to preserve freedom" than the separation of powers.

> *"Our Constitution is color-blind and neither knows nor tolerates classes among citizens. In respect of civil rights, all citizens are equal before the law. The humblest is the peer of the most powerful."*
> —Justice John Marshall Harlan, sole dissent in *Plessy* vs. *Ferguson*, 1896

In their desire to create a government based on an elaborate system of "checks and balances," the Founding Fathers divided the sources of power into three separate and distinct branches of government—the legislative, the judicial, and the executive. Despite the passing of more than two centuries, the creation of dozens of departments and agencies and commissions, the ongoing employment of over 2½ million civilian workers, and the creation of a standing peacetime military force of over 2 million, this structure remains essentially unchanged.

Below is a full listing of every major body within the federal government, including the entire Congress and the federal judiciary. Every entry mentions the date each entity was founded and summarizes its official function. These are followed by charts outlining the number of employees and the estimated budget outlays for the most well known departments and agencies. (Unless otherwise noted, the sources of this information are the *United States Government Manual 1988–89* and the *Budget of the U.S. Government, Fiscal Year 1989.*)

HOW A BILL BECOMES LAW

Usually bills are raised in any of the various committees of the Senate or House of Representatives. If the bill is supported by a majority of the committee, it is brought to the floor of the house in which it originated, and voted on. If it gains majority support in the full Senate or House, the other house of Congress votes on it. If the bill is passed in both the Senate and House, it is sent to the president, who may either sign it, veto it, or not act on it. If the president signs it or refuses to act within 10 days and the Congress is still in session, the bill becomes law. If the president vetoes it, it is returned to the Senate and the House for another vote; a two-thirds majority in each house is then required to overturn the veto. However, if the president refuses to act on a bill and Congress adjourns before the end of the 10-day period, the legislation is dead. This is known as a pocket veto.

Occasionally bills are raised on the floor of the Senate or the House, in which case the first step of committee voting is avoided, and the legislation process begins with the full Senate or House vote. All other processes remain the same.

The Legislative Branch

Architect of the Capitol U.S. Capitol Building, Washington, D.C. 20515. (202) 225-1200. First Architect appointed in 1793 by president. Permanent authority for care of Capitol established by act of Aug. 15, 1876. Responsible for care and maintenance of Capitol building and grounds, Library of Congress buildings, and U.S. Supreme Court building. Operates Senate and House restaurants. Maintains, operates, and cares for House and Senate office buildings. Plans future construction, renovation, reconstruction, and alterations to existing buildings.

United States Botanic Garden Director's Office: 245 First St. S.W., Washington, D.C. 20024. (202) 225-8333. Conservatory: Maryland Avenue–First to Second Sts. S.W., Washington, D.C. 20024. (202) 225-6646. Nursery: Poplar Point, 700 Howard Road S.E., Anacostia, D.C. 20020. (202) 225-6420. Created in 1820. Collects, cultivates, and grows vegetable and plant matter of U.S. and other countries for exhibition and display. Provides study materials on vegetable and plant matter for students, botanists, horticulturists, floriculturists, and garden clubs.

General Accounting Office (GAO) 441 G St. N.W., Washington, D.C. 20548. (202) 275-5067. Created in 1921 by Budget and Accounting Act. Provides legal, accounting, auditing, and claims-settlement services for Congress. Facilitates more efficient and effective government operations.

Government Printing Office (GPO) North Capitol and H Sts. N.W., Washington, D.C. 20401. (202) 275-2051. Created June 23, 1860, by Congressional Joint Resolution 25. Provides printing and binding services for Congress and departments and establishments of federal government. Furnishes blank paper, ink, and supplies to all agencies. Prepares and distributes catalogs and government publications.

Library of Congress 101 Independence Ave. S.E., Washington, D.C. 20540. (202) 287-5000. Created by law of Apr. 24, 1800. Librarian appointed by president. Buys books necessary for use by Congress and/or other governmental agencies. National library of U.S. Develops and maintains national book classification-systems such as Library of Congress and Dewey Decimal systems. Maintains and publishes *The National Union Catalogs.*

Office of Technology Assessment (OTA) 600 Pennsylvania Ave. S.E., Washington, D.C. 20510. (202) 224-8713. Created by Technology Assessment Act of 1972. Provides objective analyses and evaluations of scientific and technological public-policy issues.

Congressional Budget Office (CBO) Second and D Sts. S.W., Washington, D.C. 20515. (202) 226-2600. Created by Congressional Budget Act of 1974. Provides Congress with basic budget data. Analyzes and evaluates alternative fiscal and budgetary policy options and programs and makes recommendations to Congress. Publishes annual report on budget.

Copyright Royalty Tribunal Suite 450, 1111 20th St. N.W., Washington, D.C. 20036. (202) 653-5175. Created by act of Oct. 19, 1976. Establishes and monitors copyright royalty rates for various recorded and published materials.

United States Tax Court 400 Second Street N.W., Washington, D.C. 20217. (202) 376-2751. Created by Article I of Constitution. Independent judicial body in legislative branch. Tries and adjudicates controversies involving deficiencies or overpayments of income, estate, and gift taxes.

THE 101ST CONGRESS OF THE UNITED STATES

On the following pages are the names, states, districts, and party affiliations of all members of the current House and Senate. In addition, for all members who voted during the previous congressional session, there are ratings given by three prominent political groups of differing viewpoints.

The Americans for Democratic Action (ADA), a liberal group founded in 1947, rates members of Congress on a wide variety of issues, but they stand basically for slowing defense spending, preventing violations of civil rights, and for government activity to end inequality. The American Conservative Union (ACU) rates members for their votes on budgetary, social, and foreign-policy issues from a conservative perspective. The American Security Council's rating, called the National Security Index (NSI), has been measuring congressional votes on defense since 1965; a high rating indicates support for developing large weapons systems and support of the peace-through-strength approach to foreign policy.

THE 101ST CONGRESS OF THE UNITED STATES

Senate Offices

President	Dan Quayle (R)
Majority leader	George J. Mitchell (D)
Majority whip	Alan Cranston (D)
Minority leader	Robert Dole (R)
Minority whip	Alan K. Simpson (R)

House Offices

Speaker	Thomas S. Foley (D)
Majority leader	Richard A. Gephardt (D)
Majority whip	William A. Gray III (D)
Minority leader	Robert H. Michel (R)
Minority whip	Newt Gingrich (R)

THE SENATE

State	Senator	ADA[1]	ACU[2]	NSI[3]	State	Senator	ADA[1]	ACU[2]	NSI[3]
Alabama	Howell Heflin (D)	30	58	100	Montana	Max Baucus (D)	80	8	0
	Richard C. Shelby (D)	35	60	100		Conrad Burns (R)	75	N.A.	N.A.
Alaska	Ted Stevens (R)	25	64	100	Nebraska	J. James Exon (D)	35	48	90
	Frank H. Murkowski (R)	15	79	100		Bob Kerrey (D)	N.A.	83	N.A.
Arizona	Dennis DeConcini (D)	55	33	40	Nevada	Harry Reid (D)	55	28	50
	John McCain (R)	10	80	100		Richard H. Bryan (D)	N.A.	N.A.	N.A.
Arkansas	Dale Bumpers (D)	80	12	0	New Hampshire	Gordon J. Humphrey (R)	5	100	100
	David Pryor (D)	75	16	10		Warren Rudman (R)	15	68	100
California	Alan Cranston (D)	95	0	0	New Jersey	Bill Bradley (D)	75	9	20
	Pete Wilson (R)	15	75	100		Frank R. Lautenberg (D)	90	0	0
Colorado	William L. Armstrong (R)	5	96	100	New Mexico	Peter V. Domenici (R)	15	72	100
	Timothy E. Wirth (D)	95	0	0		Jeff Bingaman (D)	70	20	50
Connecticut	Christopher J. Dodd (D)	85	8	10	New York	Daniel Patrick Moynihan (D)	90	8	20
	Joseph L. Lieberman (D)	N.A.	N.A.	N.A.		Alfonse M. D'Amato (R)	15	80	100
Delaware	William V. Roth, Jr. (R)	20	60	100	North Carolina	Jesse A. Helms (R)	5	100	100
	Joseph R. Biden, Jr. (D)	15	0	0		Terry Sanford (D)	90	4	11
Florida	Robert Graham (D)	55	28	90	North Dakota	Quentin N. Burdick (D)	85	16	20
	Connie Mack III (R)	N.A.	N.A.	N.A.		Kent Conrad (D)	80	24	10
Georgia	Sam Nunn (D)	40	42	100	Ohio	John H. Glenn, Jr. (D)	80	9	70
	Wyche Fowler, Jr. (D)	75	8	10		Howard M. Metzenbaum (D)	80	4	0
Hawaii	Daniel K. Inouye (D)	85	4	10	Oklahoma	David Lyle Boren (D)	25	48	90
	Spark M. Matsunaga (D)	90	0	0		Don Nickles (R)	0	92	100
Idaho	James A. McClure (R)	5	91	90	Oregon	Mark O. Hatfield (R)	70	30	0
	Steven D. Symms (R)	0	100	100		Robert W. Packwood (R)	55	40	67
Illinois	Alan J. Dixon (D)	45	44	70	Pennsylvania	H. John Heinz III (R)	55	41	60
	Paul Simon (D)	85	0	0		Arlen Specter (R)	60	33	30
Indiana	Richard G. Lugar (R)	10	88	90	Rhode Island	Claiborne Pell (D)	100	0	0
	Daniel R. Coats (R)	N.A.	N.A.	N.A.		John H. Chafee (R)	90	4	10
Iowa	Charles E. Grassley (R)	5	88	70	South Carolina	Strom Thurmond (R)	0	92	100
	Tom Harkin (D)	95	0	0		Ernest F. Hollings (D)	55	48	100
Kansas	Robert Dole (R)	15	91	100	South Dakota	Larry Pressler (R)	0	96	100
	Nancy L. Kassebaum (R)	30	61	80		Thomas A. Daschle (D)	85	13	0
Kentucky	Wendell H. Ford (D)	65	24	20	Tennessee	James R. Sasser (D)	75	9	10
	Mitch McConnell (R)	5	92	100		Albert Gore, Jr. (D)	60	9	38
Louisiana	J. Bennett Johnston, Jr. (D)	50	36	60	Texas	Lloyd Bentsen (D)	40	42	70
	John B. Breaux (D)	55	44	60		Phil Gramm (R)	0	95	100
Maine	William S. Cohen (R)	35	46	100	Utah	Edwin Jacob Garn (R)	0	96	100
	George J. Mitchell (D)	95	0	10		Orrin G. Hatch (R)	5	96	100
Maryland	Paul S. Sarbanes (D)	90	4	0	Vermont	Patrick J. Leahy (D)	100	0	0
	Barbara A. Mikulski (D)	95	0	0		James M. Jeffords (R)	N.A.	N.A.	N.A.
Massachusetts	Edward M. Kennedy (D)	95	0	0	Virginia	John William Warner (R)	5	87	100
	John F. Kerry (D)	90	0	0		Charles S. Robb (D)	N.A.	N.A.	N.A.
Michigan	Donald W. Riegle, Jr. (D)	90	4	10	Washington	Brock Adams (D)	90	0	0
	Carl Levin (D)	80	0	10		Slade Gorton (R)	N.A.	N.A.	N.A.
Minnesota	David Durenberger (IR)	60	26	30	West Virginia	Robert C. Byrd (D)	55	36	60
	Rudy Boschwitz (IR)	20	70	90		John D. (Jay) Rockefeller IV (D)	70	16	10
Mississippi	Thad Cochran (R)	5	96	100	Wisconsin	Robert W. Kasten, Jr. (R)	10	84	100
	Trent Lott (R)	N.A.	N.A.	N.A.		Herbert H. Kohl (D)	N.A.	N.A.	N.A.
Missouri	John C. Danforth (R)	20	72	80	Wyoming	Malcolm Wallop (R)	0	100	100
	Christopher S. Bond (R)	0	88	100		Alan K. Simpson (R)	15	92	100

Note: (D)=Democrat, (DFL)=Democratic-Farmer-Labor (Minnesota), (IR)=Independent Republican (Minnesota), (R)=Republican. 1. Americans for Democratic Action: based on 20 House or Senate votes in the 100th Congress. 2. The American Conservative Union: based on 22 House or Senate votes in the 100th Congress. 3. National Security Index of the American Security Council: based on 10 House or Senate votes in the 100th Congress.

THE HOUSE OF REPRESENTATIVES

State/Dist. (city)	Representative	ADA[1]	ACU[2]	NSI[3]
ALABAMA				
1st Dist. (Mobile)	H.L. ("Sonny") Callahan (R)	10	96	100
2d Dist. (Montgomery)	William L. Dickinson (R)	20	92	100
3d Dist. (Anniston)	Glen Browder (D)	N.A.	N.A.	N.A.
4th Dist. (Jasper)	Tom Bevill (D)	45	50	100
5th Dist. (Huntsville)	Ronnie G. Flippo (D)	45	60	100
6th Dist. (Birmingham)	Ben Erdreich (D)	50	60	100
7th Dist. (Tuscaloosa)	Claude Harris, Jr. (D)	45	68	100
ALASKA				
1st Dist. (at large)	Don Young (R)	30	63	100
ARIZONA				
1st Dist. (Tempe)	John J. Rhodes III (R)	10	96	100
2d Dist. (Phoenix)	Morris K. Udall (D)	75	13	0
3d Dist. (Flagstaff)	Bob Stump (R)	0	100	100
4th Dist. (Scottsdale)	Jon L. Kyl (R)	0	100	100
5th Dist. (Tucson)	Jim Kolbe (R)	20	80	100
ARKANSAS				
1st Dist. (Jonesboro)	Bill Alexander (D)	80	5	44
2d Dist. (Little Rock)	Tommy F. Robinson (D)	55	52	100
3d Dist. (Fort Smith)	John Paul Hammerschmidt (R)	10	96	100
4th Dist. (Pine Bluff)	Beryl F. Anthony, Jr. (D)	80	16	11
CALIFORNIA				
1st Dist. (Santa Rosa)	Douglas H. Bosco (D)	80	8	20
2d Dist. (Chico)	Wally Herger (R)	0	92	100
3d Dist. (Sacramento)	Robert T. Matsui (D)	90	4	0
4th Dist. (Sacramento)	Vic Fazio (D)	85	0	20
5th Dist. (San Francisco)	Nancy Pelosi (D)	100	0	0
6th Dist. (Marin County)	Barbara Boxer (D)	80	5	0
7th Dist. (Richmond)	George Miller (D)	95	4	0
8th Dist. (Oakland)	Ronald V. Dellums (D)	100	0	0
9th Dist. (Hayward)	Fortney H. (Pete) Stark (D)	90	0	0
10th Dist. (San Jose)	Don Edwards (D)	100	0	0
11th Dist. (San Mateo Co.)	Tom Lantos (D)	85	8	20
12th Dist. (Sunnyvale)	Tom Campbell (R)	N.A.	N.A.	N.A.
13th Dist. (San Jose)	Norman Y. Mineta (D)	95	4	0
14th Dist. (Stockton)	Norman D. Shumway (R)	0	100	100
15th Dist. (Modesto)	Tony L. Coelho (D)[4]	90	12	0
16th Dist. (Monterey)	Leon E. Panetta (D)	90	4	0
17th Dist. (Fresno)	Charles Pashayan, Jr. (R)	35	64	100
18th Dist. (Fresno)	Richard H. Lehman (D)	85	9	0
19th Dist. (Santa Barbara)	Robert J. Lagomarsino (R)	35	80	100
20th Dist. (Bakersfield)	William M. Thomas (R)	25	78	100
21st Dist. (Thousand Oaks)	Elton Gallegly (R)	15	96	100
22d Dist. (Pasadena)	Carlos J. Moorhead (R)	10	96	100
23d Dist. (Beverly Hills)	Anthony C. Beilenson (D)	95	8	0
24th Dist. (Hollywood)	Henry A. Waxman (D)	90	0	0
25th Dist. (Los Angeles)	Edward R. Roybal (D)	95	0	0
26th Dist. (Van Nuys)	Howard L. Berman (D)	95	4	0
27th Dist. (Santa Monica)	Mel Levine (D)	95	4	0
28th Dist. (Culver City)	Julian C. Dixon (D)	85	0	0
29th Dist. (Los Angeles)	Augustus F. Hawkins (D)	85	0	10
30th Dist. (El Monte)	Matthew G. Martinez (D)	90	0	20
31st Dist. (Compton)	Mervyn M. Dymally (D)	90	0	0
32d Dist. (Long Beach)	Glenn M. Anderson (D)	70	10	22
33d Dist. (Pomona)	David Dreier (R)	5	100	100
34th Dist. (West Covina)	Esteban Edward Torres (D)	90	0	0
35th Dist. (Redlands)	Jerry Lewis (R)	5	90	100
36th Dist. (Riverside)	George E. Brown, Jr. (D)	80	5	20
37th Dist. (Palm Springs)	Alfred A. McCandless (R)	10	95	100
38th Dist. (Santa Ana)	Robert K. Dornan (R)	0	100	100
39th Dist. (Anaheim)	William E. Dannemeyer (R)	0	100	100
40th Dist. (Newport Beach)	Christopher Cox (R)	N.A.	N.A.	N.A.
41st Dist. (San Diego)	William Lowery (R)	15	92	100
42d Dist. (Long Beach)	Dana Rohrabacher (R)	N.A.	N.A.	N.A.
43d Dist. (Carlsbad)	Ronald C. Packard (R)	5	100	100
44th Dist. (San Diego)	Jim Bates (D)	95	8	0
45th Dist. (Coronado)	Duncan L. Hunter (R)	0	100	100
COLORADO				
1st Dist. (Denver)	Patricia Schroeder (D)	95	0	0
2d Dist. (Boulder)	David E. Skaggs (D)	95	16	0
3d Dist. (Pueblo)	Ben Nighthorse Campbell (D)	65	21	40
4th Dist. (Greeley)	Hank Brown (R)	30	72	80
5th Dist. (Colorado Springs)	Joel Hefley (R)	5	100	100
6th Dist. (Lakewood)	Dan Schaefer (R)	15	83	100
CONNECTICUT				
1st Dist. (Hartford)	Barbara B. Kennelly (D)	90	8	10
2d Dist. (New London)	Samuel Gejdenson (D)	95	0	0
3d Dist. (New Haven)	Bruce A. Morrison (D)	100	4	0
4th Dist. (Stamford)	Christopher Shays (R)	90	24	40
5th Dist. (Waterbury)	John G. Rowland (R)	45	60	100
6th Dist. (New Britain)	Nancy L. Johnson (R)	50	56	90
DELAWARE				
1st Dist. (at large)	Thomas R. Carper (D)	75	24	30
FLORIDA				
1st Dist. (Pensacola)	Earl Dewitt Hutto (D)	20	76	100
2d Dist. (Tallahassee)	William Grant (D)	50	54	67
3d Dist. (Jacksonville)	Charles E. Bennett (D)	65	28	60
4th Dist. (Daytona Beach)	Craig T. James (R)	40	46	100
5th Dist. (Orlando)	Bill McCollum (R)	0	100	100
6th Dist. (Ocala)	Clifford B. Stearns (R)	N.A.	N.A.	N.A.
7th Dist. (Tampa)	Sam M. Gibbons (D)	60	13	40
8th Dist. (St. Petersburg)	C.W. (Bill) Young (R)	10	35	100
9th Dist. (Clearwater)	Michael Bilirakis (R)	10	88	100
10th Dist. (Winter Haven)	Andy Ireland (R)	5	96	100
11th Dist. (Melbourne)	Bill Nelson (D)	0	100	100
12th Dist. (N. Palm Beach)	Tom Lewis (R)	25	56	100
13th Dist. (Ft. Myers)	Porter J. Goss (R)	N.A.	N.A.	N.A.
14th Dist. (W. Palm Beach)	Harry A. Johnston (D)	N.A.	N.A.	N.A.
15th Dist. (Ft. Lauderdale)	E. Clay Shaw Jr. (R)	5	96	100
16th Dist. (Hollywood)	Lawrence J. Smith (D)	85	17	30
17th Dist. (N. Miami Beach)	William Lehman (D)	100	8	0
18th Dist. (Miami)	Claude Pepper (D)[5]	65	18	50
19th Dist. (Coral Gables)	Dante B. Fascell (D)	75	17	30
GEORGIA				
1st Dist. (Savannah)	Robert Lindsay Thomas (D)	50	48	90
2d Dist. (Albany)	Charles F. Hatcher (D)	50	43	80
3d Dist. (Columbus)	Richard B. Ray (D)	20	53	100
4th Dist. (Dunwoody)	Ben Jones (D)	N.A.	N.A.	N.A.
5th Dist. (Atlanta)	John Lewis (D)	100	0	0
6th Dist. (Carrollton)	Newt Gingrich (R)	5	100	100
7th Dist. (Marietta)	George (Buddy) Darden (D)	45	50	100
8th Dist. (Macon)	J. Roy Rowland (D)	55	46	80
9th Dist. (Dalton)	Ed Jenkins (D)	45	54	90
10th Dist. (Augusta)	Doug Barnard, Jr. (D)	25	64	100
HAWAII				
1st Dist. (Honolulu)	Patricia F. Saiki (R)	50	39	100
2d Dist. (outer islands)	Daniel K. Akaka (D)	85	0	20
IDAHO				
1st Dist. (Boise)	Larry E. Craig (R)	5	100	100
2d Dist. (Pocatello)	Richard H. Stallings (D)	55	48	50

State/Dist. (city)	Representative	ADA[1]	ACU[2]	NSI[3]
ILLINOIS				
1st Dist. (Chicago)	Charles A. Hayes (D)	95	0	0
2d Dist. (S. Chicago)	Gus Savage (D)	100	0	10
3d Dist. (Oak Lawn)	Martin A. Russo (D)	80	28	0
4th Dist. (Joliet)	George E. Sangmeister (D)	N.A.	N.A.	N.A.
5th Dist. (Chicago)	William O. Lipinski (D)	55	35	78
6th Dist. (Wheaton)	Henry J. Hyde (R)	15	92	100
7th Dist. (Chicago)	Cardiss Collins (D)	90	0	0
8th Dist. (Chicago)	Dan Rostenkowski (D)	65	19	22
9th Dist. (Chicago)	Sidney R. Yates (D)	80	5	0
10th Dist. (Evanston)	John Edward Porter (R)	30	68	56
11th Dist. (Chicago)	Frank Annunzio (D)	75	17	0
12th Dist. (Palatine)	Philip M. Crane (R)	0	100	100
13th Dist. (Oak Brook)	Harris W. Fawell (R)	40	64	90
14th Dist. (Elgin)	J. Dennis Hastert (R)	10	92	100
15th Dist. (Bloomington)	Edward R. Madigan (R)	15	77	100
16th Dist. (Rockford)	Lynn Martin (R)	30	76	90
17th Dist. (Moline)	Lane Evans (D)	100	0	0
18th Dist. (Peoria)	Robert H. Michel (R)	10	92	100
19th Dist. (Danville)	Terry L. Bruce (D)	75	24	0
20th Dist. (Springfield)	Richard J. Durbin (D)	90	16	0
21st Dist. (East St. Louis)	Jerry F. Costello (D)	N.A.	N.A.	N.A.
22d Dist. (Carbondale)	Glenn Poshard (D)	N.A.	N.A.	N.A.
INDIANA				
1st Dist. (Gary)	Peter J. Visclosky (D)	100	0	0
2d Dist. (Muncie)	Philip R. Sharp (D)	75	20	10
3d Dist. (South Bend)	John P. Hiler (R)	5	100	100
4th Dist. (Fort Wayne)	Jill Long (D)	N.A.	N.A.	N.A.
5th Dist. (Kokomo)	James Jontz (D)	95	4	0
6th Dist. (Indianapolis)	Dan Burton (R)	0	100	100
7th Dist. (Terre Haute)	John T. Myers (R)	15	83	100
8th Dist. (Evansville)	Francis X. McCloskey (D)	75	16	0
9th Dist. (Bloomington)	Lee H. Hamilton (D)	85	8	10
10th Dist. (Indianapolis)	Andrew Jacobs, Jr. (D)	95	12	0
IOWA				
1st Dist. (Davenport)	James A.S. Leach (R)	75	32	0
2d Dist. (Cedar Rapids)	Thomas J. Tauke (R)	45	67	50
3d Dist. (Waterloo)	David R. Nagle (D)	80	8	10
4th Dist. (Des Moines)	Neal Smith (D)	80	16	30
5th Dist. (Council Bluffs)	Jim Ross Lightfoot (R)	10	90	78
6th Dist. (Sioux City)	Fred Grandy (R)	40	64	80
KANSAS				
1st Dist. (Dodge City)	Pat Roberts (R)	10	79	90
2d Dist. (Topeka)	James Slattery (D)	55	33	60
3d Dist. (Kansas City)	Jan Meyers (R)	35	58	80
4th Dist. (Wichita)	Dan Glickman (D)	80	16	30
5th Dist. (Emporia)	Robert Whittaker (R)	10	88	100
KENTUCKY				
1st Dist. (Paducah)	Carroll Hubbard, Jr. (D)	50	54	80
2d Dist. (Owensboro)	William H. Natcher (D)	75	16	50
3d Dist. (Louisville)	Romano L. Mazzoli (D)	75	21	40
4th Dist. (Covington)	Jim Bunning (R)	0	100	100
5th Dist. (Somerset)	Harold Rogers (R)	5	96	100
6th Dist. (Lexington)	Larry J. Hopkins (R)	20	76	90
7th Dist. (Ashland)	Carl C. Perkins (D)	85	12	0
LOUISIANA				
1st Dist. (New Orleans)	Robert L. Livingston (R)	5	100	100
2d Dist. (New Orleans)	Lindy (Mrs. Hale) Boggs (D)	80	5	22
3d Dist. (New Iberia)	W.J. ("Billy") Tauzin (D)	45	64	100
4th Dist. (Shreveport)	Jim McCrery (R)	12	94	100
5th Dist. (Monroe)	Thomas J. Huckaby (D)	40	65	100
6th Dist. (Baton Rouge)	Richard H. Baker (R)	5	100	100
7th Dist. (Lafayette)	James A. Hayes (D)	55	52	50
8th Dist. (Alexandria)	Clyde C. Holloway (R)	0	96	100

State/Dist. (city)	Representative	ADA[1]	ACU[2]	NSI[3]
MAINE				
1st Dist. (Portland)	Joseph E. Brennan (D)	90	12	0
2d Dist. (Bangor)	Olympia J. Snowe (R)	60	40	60
MARYLAND				
1st Dist. (Eastern Shore)	Roy Dyson (D)	55	50	88
2d Dist. (Towson)	Helen Delich Bentley (R)	10	86	100
3d Dist. (Baltimore)	Benjamin L. Cardin (D)	90	4	0
4th Dist. (Annapolis)	C. Thomas McMillen (D)	75	12	50
5th Dist. (Landover)	Steny H. Hoyer (D)	95	0	10
6th Dist. (Hagerstown)	Beverly B. Byron (D)	30	68	89
7th Dist. (Baltimore)	Kweisi Mfume (D)	95	4	0
8th Dist. (Montgomery Co.)	Constance A. Morella (R)	90	8	22
MASSACHUSETTS				
1st Dist. (Pittsfield)	Silvio O. Conte (R)	90	8	10
2d Dist. (Springfield)	Richard E. Neal (D)	N.A.	N.A.	N.A.
3d Dist. (Worcester)	Joseph D. Early (D)	85	8	0
4th Dist. (Newton)	Barney Frank (D)	100	0	0
5th Dist. (Lowell)	Chester G. Atkins (D)	100	0	0
6th Dist. (Lynn)	Nicholas Mavroules (D)	90	8	10
7th Dist. (Malden)	Edward J. Markey (D)	90	0	0
8th Dist. (Cambridge)	Joseph P. Kennedy II (D)	95	4	0
9th Dist. (Boston)	John Joseph Moakley (D)	90	8	0
10th Dist. (Cape Cod)	Gerry E. Studds (D)	100	0	0
11th Dist. (Boston)	Brian J. Donnelly (D)	80	8	0
MICHIGAN				
1st Dist. (Detroit)	John Conyers, Jr. (D)	90	0	0
2d Dist. (Ann Arbor)	Carl D. Pursell (R)	45	46	60
3d Dist. (Lansing)	Howard E. Wolpe (D)	100	0	0
4th Dist. (Benton Harbor)	Frederick S. Upton (R)	30	64	100
5th Dist. (Grand Rapids)	Paul B. Henry (R)	50	52	60
6th Dist. (Pontiac)	Robert Carr (D)	80	21	0
7th Dist. (Flint)	Dale E. Kildee (D)	95	4	0
8th Dist. (Bay City)	Bob Traxler (D)	80	14	0
9th Dist. (Traverse City)	Guy Vander Jagt (R)	15	91	100
10th Dist. (Midland)	Bill Schuette (R)	40	63	100
11th Dist. (Upper Peninsula)	Robert W. Davis (R)	60	42	100
12th Dist. (Port Huron)	David E. Bonior (D)	95	4	0
13th Dist. (Detroit)	George W. Crockett, Jr. (D)	85	0	0
14th Dist. (Warren)	Dennis M. Hertel (D)	95	4	0
15th Dist. (Wayne)	William D. Ford (D)	100	0	0
16th Dist. (Dearborn)	John D. Dingell (D)	80	13	11
17th Dist. (Southfield)	Sander M. Levin (D)	100	0	10
18th Dist. (Birmingham)	William S. Broomfield (R)	30	84	100
MINNESOTA				
1st Dist. (Rochester)	Timothy J. Penny (DFL)	60	36	30
2d Dist. (Willmar)	Vin Weber (IR)	15	96	90
3d Dist. (Bloomington)	Bill Frenzel (IR)	35	57	100
4th Dist. (St. Paul)	Bruce F. Vento (DFL)	90	4	0
5th Dist. (Minneapolis)	Martin Olav Sabo (DFL)	100	0	10
6th Dist. (Stillwater)	Gerry Sikorski (DFL)	90	12	0
7th Dist. (St. Cloud)	Arlan Stangeland (IR)	5	92	100
8th Dist. (Duluth)	James L. Oberstar (DFL)	90	12	0
MISSISSIPPI				
1st Dist. (Oxford)	Jamie L. Whitten (D)	65	20	40
2d Dist. (Vicksburg)	Mike Espy (D)	85	12	10
3d Dist. (Meridian)	G.V. ("Sonny") Montgomery (R)	25	71	100
4th Dist. (Jackson)	Mike Parker (D)	N.A.	N.A.	N.A.
5th Dist. (Pascagoula)	Larkin I. Smith (R)	N.A.	N.A.	N.A.
MISSOURI				
1st Dist. (St. Louis)	William Clay (D)	90	0	0
2d Dist. (Kirkwood)	Jack Buechner (R)	15	88	100
3d Dist. (St. Louis)	Richard A. Gephardt (D)	75	10	0

State/Dist. (city)	Representative	ADA[1]	ACU[2]	NSI[3]
MISSOURI				
4th Dist. (Jefferson City)	Ike Skelton (D)	40	58	100
5th Dist. (Kansas City)	Alan Wheat (D)	100	0	0
6th Dist. (St. Joseph)	E. Thomas Coleman (R)	25	76	100
7th Dist. (Springfield)	Melton D. Hancock (R)	N.A.	N.A.	N.A.
8th Dist. (Cape Girardeau)	Bill Emerson (R)	10	90	100
9th Dist. (Hannibal)	Harold L. Volkmer (D)	60	35	56
MONTANA				
1st Dist. (Helena)	Pat Williams (D)	85	0	0
2d Dist. (Billings)	Ron Marlenee (R)	0	96	100
NEBRASKA				
1st Dist. (Lincoln)	Douglas K. Bereuter (R)	20	76	90
2d Dist. (Omaha)	Peter Hoagland (D)	15	94	100
3d Dist. (Grand Island)	Virginia Smith (R)	25	80	80
NEVADA				
1st Dist. (Las Vegas)	James H. Bilbray (D)	60	44	44
2d Dist. (Reno)	Barbara F. Vucanovich (R)	10	92	100
NEW HAMPSHIRE				
1st Dist. (Manchester)	Robert C. Smith (R)	5	100	100
2d Dist. (Concord)	Chuck Douglas (R)	N.A.	N.A.	N.A.
NEW JERSEY				
1st Dist. (Pine Hill)	James J. Florio (D)	80	9	0
2d Dist. (Ocean City)	William J. Hughes (D)	70	16	30
3d Dist. (Toms River)	Frank Pallone, Jr. (D)	N.A.	N.A.	N.A.
4th Dist. (Trenton)	Christopher H. Smith (R)	60	48	60
5th Dist. (Ridgewood)	Margaret S. Roukema (R)	40	50	80
6th Dist. (Edison)	Bernard J. Dwyer (D)	85	4	0
7th Dist. (Union)	Matthew J. Rinaldo (R)	45	54	90
8th Dist. (Paterson)	Robert A. Roe (D)	70	13	10
9th Dist. (Hackensack)	Robert G. Torricelli (D)	85	4	10
10th Dist. (Newark)	Donald M. Payne (D)	95	0	N.A.
11th Dist. (Parsippany)	Dean A. Gallo (R)	30	72	100
12th Dist. (Hackettstown)	James A. Courter (R)	25	74	100
13th Dist. (Bordentown)	H. James Saxton (R)	30	72	100
14th Dist. (Jersey City)	Frank J. Guarini (D)	70	14	20
NEW MEXICO				
1st Dist. (Albuquerque)	Steven Schiff (R)	N.A.	N.A.	N.A.
2d Dist. (Picacho)	Joseph R. Skeen (R)	5	100	100
3d Dist. (Santa Fe)	Bill Richardson (D)	75	21	30
NEW YORK				
1st Dist. (E. Long Island)	George Hochbrueckner (D)	80	12	20
2d Dist. (Babylon)	Thomas J. Downey (D)	100	0	10
3d Dist. (Huntington)	Robert J. Mrazek (D)	95	4	0
4th Dist. (E. Rockaway)	Norman F. Lent (R)	25	68	100
5th Dist. (Valley Stream)	Raymond J. McGrath (R)	25	55	80
6th Dist. (Jamaica)	Floyd H. Flake (D)	95	0	0
7th Dist. (Flushing)	Gary L. Ackerman (D)	95	0	0
8th Dist. (Queens)	James H. Scheuer (D)	85	5	0
9th Dist. (Astoria)	Thomas J. Manton (D)	60	18	25
10th Dist. (Flatbush)	Charles E. Schumer (D)	100	4	0
11th Dist. (Brooklyn)	Edolphus Towns (D)	90	0	0
12th Dist. (Brooklyn)	Major R. Owens (D)	95	0	0
13th Dist. (Brooklyn)	Stephen J. Solarz (D)	95	4	10
14th Dist. (Staten Island)	Guy V. Molinari (R)	30	63	90
15th Dist. (Manhattan)	Bill Green (R)	75	25	20
16th Dist. (Harlem)	Charles B. Rangel (D)	85	0	0
17th Dist. (Manhattan)	Theodore S. Weiss (D)	75	0	0
18th Dist. (Bronx)	Robert Garcia (D)	85	4	0
19th Dist. (Bronx)	Eliot L. Engel (D)	N.A.	N.A.	N.A.
20th Dist. (Westchester)	Nita M. Lowey (D)	N.A.	N.A.	N.A.
21st Dist. (Poughkeepsie)	Hamilton Fish, Jr. (R)	60	32	60

State/Dist. (city)	Representative	ADA[1]	ACU[2]	NSI[3]
NEW YORK				
22d Dist. (Middletown)	Benjamin A. Gilman (R)	55	42	90
23d Dist. (Albany)	Michael R. McNulty (D)	45	N.A.	N.A.
24th Dist. (Saratoga Springs)	Gerald B.H. Solomon (R)	15	88	100
25th Dist. (Utica)	Sherwood Boehlert (R)	65	24	70
26th Dist. (Watertown)	David O'B. Martin (R)	25	68	100
27th Dist. (Syracuse)	James T. Walsh (R)	10	N.A.	N.A.
28th Dist. (Binghamton)	Matthew F. McHugh (D)	95	4	0
29th Dist. (Rochester)	Frank J. Horton (R)	65	22	40
30th Dist. (Rochester)	Louise M. Slaughter (D)	85	8	0
31st Dist. (Buffalo)	L. William Paxon (R)	N.A.	N.A.	N.A.
32d Dist. (Niagara Falls)	John J. LaFalce (D)	80	8	10
33d Dist. (Buffalo)	Henry J. Nowak (D)	90	12	10
34th Dist. (Corning)	Amory Houghton, Jr. (R)	45	56	90
NORTH CAROLINA				
1st Dist. (Greenville)	Walter B. Jones (D)	80	13	0
2d Dist. (Durham)	Tim Valentine (D)	45	48	70
3d Dist. (Goldsboro)	H. Martin Lancaster (D)	60	40	80
4th Dist. (Raleigh)	David E. Price (D)	75	24	20
5th Dist. (Winston-Salem)	Stephen L. Neal (D)	70	21	33
6th Dist. (Greensboro)	Howard Coble (R)	10	92	80
7th Dist. (Wilmington)	Charles G. Rose (D)	60	11	25
8th Dist. (Salisbury)	W.G. ("Bill") Hefner (D)	65	25	50
9th Dist. (Charlotte)	J. Alex McMillan III (R)	15	88	100
10th Dist. (Hickory)	Cass Ballenger (R)	10	92	100
11th Dist. (Asheville)	James McClure Clarke (D)	60	29	20
NORTH DAKOTA				
1st Dist. (at large)	Byron L. Dorgan (D)	75	17	20
OHIO				
1st Dist. (Cincinnati)	Thomas A. Luken (D)	70	14	30
2d Dist. (Cincinnati)	Willis D. ("Bill") Gradison, Jr. (R)	35	62	100
3d Dist. (Dayton)	Tony P. Hall (D)	75	17	10
4th Dist. (Findlay)	Michael G. Oxley (R)	20	88	100
5th Dist. (Bowling Green)	Paul E. Gillmor (R)	N.A.	N.A.	N.A.
6th Dist. (Portsmouth)	Bob McEwen (R)	5	96	100
7th Dist. (Springfield)	Michael DeWine (R)	5	100	100
8th Dist. (Hamilton)	Donald E. ("Buz") Lukens (R)	0	96	100
9th Dist. (Toledo)	Marcy Kaptur (D)	75	13	10
10th Dist. (Lancaster)	Clarence E. Miller (R)	15	92	100
11th Dist. (Cleveland)	Dennis E. Eckart (D)	90	8	10
12th Dist. (Columbus)	John R. Kasich (R)	15	92	100
13th Dist. (Oberlin)	Donald J. Pease (D)	90	8	10
14th Dist. (Akron)	Thomas C. Sawyer (D)	95	4	10
15th Dist. (Columbus)	Chalmers P. Wylie (R)	30	80	90
16th Dist. (Canton)	Ralph S. Regula (R)	30	76	90
17th Dist. (Youngstown)	James A. Traficant, Jr. (D)	95	8	10
18th Dist. (Steubenville)	Douglas Applegate (D)	70	24	50
19th Dist. (Cleveland)	Edward F. Feighan (D)	95	0	10
20th Dist. (Cleveland)	Mary Rose Oakar (D)	90	8	10
21st Dist. (Cleveland)	Louis Stokes (D)	70	0	0
OKLAHOMA				
1st Dist. (Tulsa)	James M. Inhofe (R)	10	92	100
2d Dist. (Muskogee)	Michael L. Synar (D)	100	0	10
3d Dist. (Ada)	Wes Watkins (D)	50	46	60
4th Dist. (Norman)	Dave McCurdy (D)	60	30	70
5th Dist. (Bartlesville)	Mickey Edwards (R)	10	92	100
6th Dist. (Oklahoma City)	Glenn English (D)	40	60	90
OREGON				
1st Dist. (Portland)	Les AuCoin (D)	95	8	0
2d Dist. (Medford)	Robert F. ("Bob") Smith (R)	5	92	80
3d Dist. (Portland)	Ron Wyden (R)	90	16	0
4th Dist. (Eugene)	Peter A. DeFazio (D)	80	13	0
5th Dist. (Salem)	Denny Smith (R)	5	96	100

State/Dist. (city)	Representative	ADA[1]	ACU[2]	NSI[3]
PENNSYLVANIA				
1st Dist. (Philadelphia)	Thomas M. Foglietta (D)	90	4	0
2d Dist. (Philadelphia)	William H. Gray III (D)	95	0	0
3d Dist. (Philadelphia)	Robert A. Borski (R)	80	12	10
4th Dist. (New Castle)	Joseph P. Kolter (D)	60	22	60
5th Dist. (Chester)	Richard T. Schulze (R)	30	76	100
6th Dist. (Reading)	Gus Yatron (D)	65	24	33
7th Dist. (Swarthmore)	Curt Weldon (R)	30	59	90
8th Dist. (Bucks County)	Peter H. Kostmayer (D)	85	4	10
9th Dist. (Altoona)	E.G. ("Bud") Shuster (R)	5	100	100
10th Dist. (Scranton)	Joseph M. McDade (R)	40	54	100
11th Dist. (Wilkes-Barre)	Paul E. Kanjorski (D)	70	20	40
12th Dist. (Johnstown)	John P. Murtha (D)	55	46	100
13th Dist. (Villanova)	Lawrence Coughlin (R)	50	48	60
14th Dist. (Pittsburgh)	William J. Coyne (D)	95	0	0
15th Dist. (Allentown)	Donald L. Ritter (R)	10	84	100
16th Dist. (Lancaster)	Robert S. Walker (R)	5	100	100
17th Dist. (Harrisburg)	George W. Gekas (R)	10	92	100
18th Dist. (Pittsburgh)	Douglas Walgren (D)	90	4	0
9th Dist. (York)	William F. Goodling (R)	30	63	80
20th Dist. (McKeesport)	Joseph M. Gaydos (D)	65	24	60
21st Dist. (Erie)	Thomas J. Ridge (R)	50	36	50
22d Dist. (Monangahela)	Austin J. Murphy (D)	60	24	50
23d Dist. (Warren)	William F. Clinger, Jr. (R)	25	63	100
RHODE ISLAND				
1st Dist. (Providence)	Ronald K. Machtley (R)	N.A.	N.A.	N.A.
2d Dist. (Warwick)	Claudine Schneider (R)	80	17	10
SOUTH CAROLINA				
1st Dist. (Charleston)	Arthur Ravenel, Jr. (R)	25	76	100
2d Dist. (Columbia)	Floyd D. Spence (R)	10	85	100
3d Dist. (Aiken)	Butler Derrick (D)	70	36	60
4th Dist. (Spartanburg)	Elizabeth J. Patterson (D)	45	48	60
5th Dist. (Rock Hill)	John M. Spratt, Jr. (D)	55	29	33
6th Dist. (Florence)	Robin M. Tallon, Jr. (D)	40	60	90
SOUTH DAKOTA				
1st Dist. (at large)	Tim Johnson (D)	70	28	10
TENNESSEE				
1st Dist. (Kingsport)	James H. Quillen (R)	15	91	100
2d Dist. (Knoxville)	John J. Duncan (R)	N.A.	N.A.	N.A.
3d Dist. (Chattanooga)	Marilyn Lloyd (D)	50	54	89
4th Dist. (Shelbyville)	Jim Cooper (D)	70	28	30
5th Dist. (Nashville)	Bob Clement (D)	75	20	40
6th Dist. (Murfreesboro)	Bart Gordon (D)	80	12	30
7th Dist. (Memphis)	Don Sundquist (R)	10	96	100
8th Dist. (Jackson)	John S. Tanner (D)	N.A.	N.A.	N.A.
9th Dist. (Memphis)	Harold E. Ford (D)	85	0	0
TEXAS				
1st Dist. (Texarkana)	Jim Chapman, Jr. (D)	50	52	80
2d Dist. (Lufkin)	Charles Wilson (D)	35	55	100
3d Dist. (Dallas)	Steve Bartlett (R)	10	96	100
4th Dist. (Tyler)	Ralph M. Hall (D)	15	92	100
5th Dist. (Dallas)	John Bryant (D)	85	9	30
6th Dist. (Ennis)	Joe L. Barton (R)	5	96	100
7th Dist. (Houston)	Bill Archer (R)	0	100	100
8th Dist. (Humble)	Jack Fields (R)	0	100	100
9th Dist. (Beaumont)	Jack Brooks (D)	75	9	13
10th Dist. (Austin)	J.J. ("Jake") Pickle (D)	80	16	40
11th Dist. (Waco)	J. Marvin Leath (D)	15	71	90
12th Dist. (Fort Worth)	Jim Wright (D)[4]	speaker rarely votes		

State/Dist. (city)	Representative	ADA[1]	ACU[2]	NSI[3]
13th Dist. (Amarillo)	Bill Sarpalius (D)	N.A.	N.A.	N.A.
14th Dist. (Victoria)	Greg Laughlin (D)	N.A.	N.A.	N.A.
15th Dist. (McAllen)	E. (Kika) de la Garza (D)	50	20	63
16th Dist. (El Paso)	Ronald D. Coleman (D)	80	17	50
17th Dist. (Abilene)	Charles W. Stenholm (D)	20	78	100
18th Dist. (Houston)	Mickey Leland (D)	100	0	0
19th Dist. (Lubbock)	Larry Combest (R)	0	92	100
20th Dist. (San Antonio)	Henry B. Gonzalez (D)	100	0	0
21st Dist. (Midland)	Lamar S. Smith (R)	5	100	100
22d Dist. (Houston)	Thomas D. DeLay (R)	0	100	100
23d Dist. (San Antonio)	Albert G. Bustamante (D)	70	8	40
24th Dist. (Dallas)	Martin Frost (D)	70	9	40
25th Dist. (Houston)	Michael A. Andrews (D)	75	29	70
26th Dist. (Arlington)	Richard K. Armey (R)	0	100	100
27th Dist. (Corpus Christi)	Solomon P. Ortiz (D)	55	26	70
UTAH				
1st Dist. (Ogden)	James V. Hansen (R)	0	100	100
2d Dist. (Salt Lake City)	Wayne Owens (D)	75	16	0
3d Dist. (Provo)	Howard C. Nielson (R)	5	92	100
VERMONT				
1st Dist. (at large)	Peter Smith (R)	N.A.	N.A.	N.A.
VIRGINIA				
1st Dist. (Newport News)	Herbert H. Bateman (R)	20	84	100
2d Dist. (Norfolk)	Owen B. Pickett (D)	50	40	60
3d Dist. (Richmond)	Thomas J. Bliley, Jr. (R)	10	96	100
4th Dist. (Portsmouth)	Norman Sisisky (D)	55	40	90
5th Dist. (Danville)	Lewis F. Payne (D)	N.A.	50	N.A.
6th Dist. (Roanoke)	James R. Olin (D)	70	28	10
7th Dist. (Charlottesville)	D. French Slaughter, Jr. (R)	10	92	100
8th Dist. (Alexandria)	Stanford E. Parris (R)	15	96	100
9th Dist. (Blacksburg)	Rick Boucher (D)	75	9	10
10th Dist. (Arlington)	Frank R. Wolf (R)	25	88	100
WASHINGTON				
1st Dist. (Seattle)	John R. Miller (R)	60	38	90
2d Dist. (Everett)	Al Swift (D)	90	0	10
3d Dist. (Olympia)	Jolene Unsoeld (D)	N.A.	N.A.	N.A.
4th Dist. (Yakima)	Sid Morrison (R)	55	64	100
5th Dist. (Spokane)	Thomas S. Foley (D)	85	4	11
6th Dist. (Tacoma)	Norman D. Dicks (D)	85	9	40
7th Dist. (Seattle)	James A. McDermott (D)	N.A.	N.A.	N.A.
8th Dist. (Seattle)	Rodney Chandler (R)	45	56	80
WEST VIRGINIA				
1st Dist. (Wheeling)	Alan B. Mollohan (D)	50	42	90
2d Dist. (Morgantown)	Harley O. Staggers, Jr. (D)	80	12	0
3d Dist. (Charleston)	Robert E. Wise, Jr. (D)	75	12	20
4th Dist. (Huntington)	Nick Joe Rahall II (D)	70	22	0
WISCONSIN				
1st Dist. (Kenosha)	Les Aspin (D)	75	4	20
2d Dist. (Madison)	Robert W. Kastenmeier (R)	100	4	0
3d Dist. (Eau Claire)	Steve Gunderson (R)	45	54	90
4th Dist. (Milwaukee)	Gerald D. Kleczka (D)	95	4	0
5th Dist. (Wauwatosa)	Jim Moody (D)	80	5	0
6th Dist. (Oshkosh)	Thomas E. Petri (R)	35	75	90
7th Dist. (Wausau)	David R. Obey (D)	90	4	0
8th Dist. (Green Bay)	Toby Roth (R)	10	83	90
9th Dist. (Sheboygan)	F. James Sensenbrenner, Jr. (R)	15	88	70
WYOMING				
1st Dist. (at large)	Craig Thomas	N.A.	N.A.	N.A.

NONVOTING REPRESENTATIVES

AMERICAN SAMOA	(Delegate) Eni F. H. Faleomavaega (D)	PUERTO RICO	(Resident commissioner) Jaime B. Fuster (D)
GUAM	(Delegate) Ben Blaz (R)	VIRGIN ISLANDS	(Delegate) Ron de Lugo (D)
DISTRICT OF COLUMBIA	(Delegate) Walter E. Fauntroy (D)		

Note: (D) = Democrat, (DFL) = Democratic-Farmer-Labor (Minnesota), (IR) = Independent Republican (Minnesota), (R) = Republican. 1. Americans for Democratic Action: based on 20 House or Senate votes in the 100th Congress. 2. The American Conservative Union: based on 22 House or Senate votes in the 100th Congress. 3. National Security Index of the American Security Council: based on 10 House or Senate votes in the 100th Congress. 4. Resigned, June 1989. 5. Deceased, June 1989.

Judicial Branch

THE SUPREME COURT, 1989

Name	Appointment	Born	State	Law school
William J. Brennan, Jr.	Eisennhower, 1956	1906	New Jersey	Harvard
Byron R. White	Kennedy, 1962	1917	Colorado	Yale
Thurgood Marshall	Johnson, 1967	1908	New York	Howard
Harry A. Blackmun	Nixon, 1970	1908	Minnesota	Harvard
William H. Rehnquist	Nixon, 1972 (justice) Reagan, 1986 (chief justice)	1924	Arizona	Stanford
John Paul Stevens	Ford, 1975	1920	Illinois	Northwestern
Sandra Day O'Connor	Reagan, 1981	1930	Arizona	Stanford
Antonin Scalia	Reagan, 1986	1936	Virginia	Harvard
Anthony M. Kennedy	Reagan, 1987	1936	California	Harvard

SUPREME COURT OF THE UNITED STATES

United States Supreme Court Building; 1 First St. N.E.; Washington, D.C. 20543. (202) 479-3000. Created by Judiciary Act of Sept. 24, 1789, in accordance with Article III, Section 1 of Constitution. Composed of chief justice and a number of associate justices to be fixed by Congress. Justices (including the chief justice) are chosen by president with advice and consent of Senate and have lifetime tenure. Court terms begin first Monday of October and usually last until end of June. The court deals with approximately 5,000 cases a year.

Jurisdiction of Supreme Court is outlined by Constitution in Article III, Section 2. In general, Supreme Court has original jurisdiction in cases in which a state or an ambassador is party; it has appellate jurisdiction in other federal cases involving the various states or in which U.S. is party.

UNITED STATES COURTS OF APPEALS

These intermediate appellate courts were created by act of Mar. 3, 1981, to relieve Supreme Court of having to reconsider all trials originally decided by federal courts. Decisions of these courts are final except when law provides for direct review by the Supreme Court. Each of the 50 states is assigned to one of 12 judicial circuits that compose court of appeals system.

Circuit District of Columbia
Circuit Justice William H. Rehnquist
Circuit Judges Patricia M. Wald (chief judge); Spottswood M. Robinson II, Abner J. Mikva, Harry T. Edwards, Ruth B. Ginsburg, Kenneth W. Starr, Laurence H. Silberman, James L. Buckley, Stephen F. Williams, Douglas Ginsburg, David Bryan Sentelle, (vacancy).

First Circuit Districts of Maine, New Hampshire, Massachusetts, Rhode Island, and Puerto Rico
Circuit Justice William J. Brennan, Jr.
Circuit Judges Levin H. Campbell (chief judge); Frank M. Coffin, Hugh H. Bownes, Stephen G. Breyer, Juan R. Torruella, Bruce M. Selya.

Second Circuit Districts of Vermont, northern New York, southern New York, eastern New York, and western New York
Circuit Justice Thurgood Marshall
Circuit Judges Wilfred Fienberg (chief judge), James L. Oakes, Thomas J. Meskill, Jon O. Newman, Amalya Lyle Kearse, Richard J. Cardamone, Lawrence W. Pierce, Ralph K. Winter, Jr., George C. Pratt, Roger J. Miner, Frank S. Altimari, J. Daniel Mahoney

Third Circuit Districts of New Jersey, eastern Pennsylvania, western Pennsylvania, Delaware, and the Virgin Islands
Circuit Justice William J. Brennan, Jr.
Circuit Judges John J. Gibbons (chief judge); Collins J. Seitz, Joseph F. Weis, Jr., A. Leon Higginbotham, Jr., Dolores Korman Sloviter, Edward R. Becker, Walter K. Stapleton, Carol Los Mansmann, William D. Hutchinson, Robert E. Cowen, Morton I. Greenberg, Anthony J. Sirica

Fourth Circuit Districts of Maryland, northern West Virginia, eastern Virginia, western Virginia, eastern North Carolina, western North Carolina, and South Carolina
Circuit Justice William H. Rehnquist
Circuit Judges Harrison L. Winter (chief judge), Donald S. Russell, H. Emory Widener, Jr., Kenneth K. Hall, James Dickson Phillips, Jr., Francis D. Murnaghan, Jr., James M. Sprouse, Sam J. Ervin III, William W. Wilkins, Jr.

Fifth Circuit Districts of northern Mississippi, southern Mississippi, eastern Louisiana, middle Louisiana, western Louisiana, northern Texas, southern Texas, eastern Texas, and western Texas
Circuit Justice Byron R. White
Circuit Judges Carlos Clark (chief judge), Thomas G. Gee, Alvin B. Rubin, Thomas M. Reavley, Henry A. Pollitz, Carolyn Dineen Randall, Samuel D. Johnson, Jr., Jerre S. Williams, William L. Garwood, E. Grady Jolly, Patrick E. Higginbotham, W. Eugene Davis, Edith H. Jones, Jerry Edwin Smith

Sixth Circuit Districts of northern Ohio, southern Ohio, eastern Michigan, western Michigan, eastern Kentucky, western Kentucky, eastern Tennessee, middle Tennessee, and western Tennessee
Circuit Justice Antonin Scalia
Circuit Judges Albert J. Engel (chief judge), Pierce Lively, Damon J. Keith, Gilbert S. Merritt, Boyce R. Martin, Jr., Nathaniel T. Jones, Robert B. Krupansky, Harry W. Wellford, H. Ted Milburn, Ralph B. Guy, Jr., James L. Ryan, David A. Nelson, Danny J. Boggs, Alan E. Norris

Seventh Circuit Districts of northern Indiana, southern Indiana, northern Illinois, southern Illinois, eastern Illinois, western Illinois, eastern Wisconsin, and western Wisconsin
Circuit Justice John Paul Stevens
Circuit Judges William J. Bauer (chief judge), Walter J. Cummings, Harlington Wood, Jr., Richard D. Cudahy, Richard A. Posher, John L. Coffey, Joel M. Flaum, Kenneth F. Ripple, Frank H. Easterbrook, Daniel A. Manion, Michael S. Kanne

Eighth Circuit Districts of Minnesota, northern Iowa, southern Iowa, eastern Missouri,

HOW A CASE GETS TO THE SUPREME COURT

In both civil and criminal law, the United States Supreme Court is the ultimate court of appeal. All other remedies must be exhausted before petitioning the Court for appeal or review of a lower court decision. Cases originating in state courts can be appealed to the Court directly from state supreme courts; cases originating in federal court must go through the United States District Court and the United States Court of Appeals first. The Constitution limits the Court to original jurisdiction only in cases involving the United States or citizens of different states or foreign ambassadors or a state against a state. The Court itself decides whether to hear a case or let a decision stand. When the Court accepts a case, it grants a *writ of appeal*—or more often, a *writ of certiorari*—which announces the Court's intention to review a decision. Very rarely, the Court grants a *writ of certification* in response to a lower court's direct request for the Court's opinion. But in all cases, the Court will decline to review decisions lacking a "substantial federal question" at issue, which is what happens to the vast majority of cases brought before it. Yet the mounting backlog of cases awaiting the Court's attention periodically raises calls for easing the Court's work load by changing its review and appeal procedures, or even by adding another layer of appellate courts.

western Missouri, eastern Arkansas, western Arkansas, North Dakota, and South Dakota
Circuit Justice Harry A. Blackmun
Circuit Judges Donald P. Lay (chief judge), Gerald W. Heaney, Theodore McMillan, Richard S. Arnold, John R. Gibson, George B. Fagg, Pasco M. Bowman II, Roger L. Wollman, Frank J. Magill, Clarence Arlen Beam.

Ninth Circuit Districts of northern California, eastern California, central California, southern California, Oregon, Nevada, Montana, eastern Washington, western Washington, Idaho, Arizona, Alaska, Hawaii, Territory of Guam, and District Court for the Northern Mariana Islands
Circuit Justice Sandra Day O'Connor
Circuit Judges Alfred T. Goodwin (chief judge), James R. Browning, J. Clifford Wallace, J. Blaine Anderson, Proctor Hug, Jr., Thomas Tang, Mary M. Schroeder, Betty B. Fletcher, Jerome Farris, Harry Pregerson, Arthur L. Alarcon, Cecil F. Poole, Dorothy W. Nelson, William C. Canby, Jr., William A. Norris, Stephen A. Reinhardt, Robert B. Beezer, Cynthia Holcomb Hall, Charles E. Wiggins, Melvin Brunetti, Alex Kozinski, David R. Thompson, John T. Noonan, Jr., Diarmuid F. O'Scannlain, Edward Leavy, Stephen S. Trott.

Tenth Circuit Districts of Colorado, eastern Oklahoma, western Oklahoma, northern Oklahoma, and New Mexico
Circuit Justice Byron R. White
Circuit Judges William J. Holloway, Jr. (chief judge), Monroe G. McKay, James K. Logan, Stephanie K. Seymour, John P. Moore, Stephen H. Anderson, Deanell Reece Tacha, Bobby R. Baldock, Wade Brorby.

Eleventh Circuit Districts of northern Georgia, middle Georgia, southern Georgia, northern Florida, middle Florida, southern Florida, northern Alabama, middle Alabama, and southern Alabama
Circuit Justice Anthony M. Kennedy
Circuit Judges Paul H. Roney (chief judge), Gerald B. Tjoflat, James C. Hill, Peter T. Fay, Robert S. Vance, Phyllis A. Kravitch, Frank M. Johnson, Jr., Joseph Woodrow Hatchett, R. Lanier Anderson III, Thomas A. Clark, J.L. Edmondson

UNITED STATES COURT OF APPEALS FOR THE FEDERAL CIRCUIT

Established under Article III of Constitution pursuant to Federal Courts Improvement Act of 1982 to replace U.S. Court of Customs and Patent Appeals and Court of Claims. Has nationwide jurisdiction over patent, trademark, and copyright cases. Hears appeals from district and territorial courts in contract, internal revenue, and other cases in which U.S. is a defendant.
Circuit Justice Chief Justice William H. Rehnquist
Circuit Judges Howard T. Markey (chief judge), Daniel M. Friedman, Giles S. Rich, Oscar H. Davis, Glenn L. Archer, Jr., Edward S.

ANNUAL NUMBER OF CASES COMMENCED IN MAJOR FEDERAL COURTS, 1983–88

	1983	1985	1988
Court of appeals	29,630	33,360	37,524
Total District courts	180,576	273,670	239,634
Social Security cases	20,315	19,771	15,152
Total Bankruptcy courts[1]	374,734	364,536	594,567
Business	69,818	66,651	68,501

1. Figures are for petitions filed only, not terminated. **Source:** Administrative Office of the U.S. Courts.

U.S. SUPREME COURT: CASES FILED AND DISPOSITION, 1970–87

	1970	1980	1985	1987
TOTAL CASES ON DOCKET	4,212	5,144	5,158	5,268
Cases acted upon	3,415	4,351[1]	4,374	2,224
Cases not acted upon	777	769	974	353
TOTAL CASES AVAILABLE FOR ARGUMENT	267	264	276	280
Cases argued	151	154	171	167
Cases dismissed or remanded without explanation	9	8	4	8
Cases decided by signed opinions	126	144	161	151

1. Includes cases granted review but carried over to next term.
Source: Office of the Clerk of the Supreme Court of the U.S.

Smith, Helen W. Nies, Pauline Newman, Jean Galloway Bissell, Haldane Robert Mayer, Paul R. Michel.

UNITED STATES DISTRICT COURTS

These are trial courts of general federal jurisdiction. There are 89 courts in the 50 states, including at least one in each state and District of Columbia. Each court has from two to 27 federal district judgeships, depending on amount of work in territory, totaling 541 overall. Usually one judge is required to decide case, but often three-judge panel is employed.

Special Courts Power to create special courts is vested in Congress in part by Article III of Constitution and in part by Supreme Court decree. Appeals from these special courts may be taken to U.S. Court of Appeals for the Federal Circuit.
United States Claims Court Estab. Oct. 1, 1982, to replace Court of Claims. Composed of 16 judges appointed for 15-year terms by president with advice and consent of Senate. President designates chief judge. Has jurisdiction over monetary claims against U.S. based on Constitution or acts of Congress.
United States Court of International Trade Estab. June 10, 1890, as Board of United States General Appraisers. Has jurisdiction over civil actions against U.S. involving federal laws governing imports.
United States Court of Military Appeals Estab. May 5, 1950, to be part of Article I of Constitution. Exclusively appellate criminal court. Serves as final court of appeal for court-martial

convictions for all armed services.
Temporary Emergency Court of Appeals Estab. by Economic Stabilization Act Amendments of 1971. Has exclusive jurisdiction over all appeals from district courts arising from economic stabilization and energy conservation laws.

Administrative Office of the United States Courts Washington, D.C. 20544. (Various telephones.) Created by act of Aug. 7, 1939. Handles all nonjudicial, clerical, and administrative work of U.S. courts. Maintains transcripts, files, and records. Disburses funds necessary to operate and maintain U.S. judicial system. Its areas of primary concern are administering courts, supervising probation offices, and overseeing administration of bankruptcy courts, magistrate offices, and public defender's offices.

Federal Judicial Center Dolley Madison House, 1520 H St. N.W., Washington, D.C. 20005. (202) 633–6011. Created by act of Dec. 20, 1967. Conducts research, develops improvement of personnel and data systems, and recommends improvements in administration and management for and about judicial branch.

Executive Branch

EXECUTIVE OFFICE OF THE PRESIDENT

White House Office 1600 Pennsylvania Ave. N.W., Washington, D.C. 20500. (202) 456-1414. Serves president in performance of duties incident to his or her office. Maintains communication with Congress, individual members of Congress, heads of executive agencies, media, and public.

Office of Management and Budget (OMB) Executive Office Building, Washington, D.C. 20503. (202) 395-3080. Created July 1, 1970, by Reorganization Plan No. 2 of 1970. Assists president in reviewing and assessing efficiency of structure and management of executive branch. Expands interagency cooperation. Assists president in preparing government's budget and fiscal program. Supervises, controls, and administers budget. Coordinates departmental advice and makes recommendations to president based on this advice. Plans, conducts, and promotes evaluation efforts to help president assess program objectives, performance, and efficiency. Keeps president informed of work planned and performed by the various government agencies.

Council of Economic Advisers Old Executive Office Building, Washington, D.C. 20500. (202) 395-5084. Created by Employment Act of 1946. Council's three members—appointed by president—analyze the various segments of the economy, appraise and assess existing economic programs, recommend new economic programs, and assist in preparation of president's economic reports to Congress.

National Security Council (NSC) Old Executive Office Building, Washington, D.C. 20506. (202) 395-4974. Created by National Security Act of 1947. Chaired by president. Members include vice president and secretaries of state and defense. Chairman of Joint Chiefs of Staff is statutory military adviser; CIA director is intelligence adviser. Advises president on integration of domestic, foreign, and military policies relating to national security.

Office of Policy Development (OPD) 1600 Pennsylvania Ave. N.W., Washington, D.C. 20500. (202) 456-1414. Created in 1981 to replace Domestic Policy Staff (estab. Mar. 26, 1978). Advises and assists president in formulating, evaluating, and coordinating long-range economic and domestic public policy.

Office of the United States Trade Representative 600 17th St. N.W., Washington, D.C. 20506. (202) 395-3230. Created as Office of the Special Representative for Trade Negotiations by Executive Order

PRESIDENT GEORGE BUSH'S CABINET

President Reagan's decision in 1988 to name a cabinet-level Department of Veterans Affairs brings to 14 the number of cabinet-level departments. William Bennett was appointed by President Bush to the cabinet-level role of "drug czar," though he supervises no cabinet department. The cabinet departments and their secretaries, in rank of importance, are the following:

State	James Addison Baker III	**Labor**	Elizabeth Hanford Dole
Treasury	Nicholas Brady	**Health and Human Services (HHS)**	Louis W. Sullivan
Defense	Richard B. Cheney	**Housing and Urban Development (HUD)**	Jack F. Kemp
Justice	Atty. Gen. Richard Thornburgh	**Transportation**	Samuel Knox Skinner
Interior	Manuel Lujan Jr.	**Energy**	Adm. James D. Watkins
Agriculture	Clayton K. Yeutter	**Education**	Lauro D. Cavazos
Commerce	Robert Adam Mosbacher	**Veterans Affairs (VA)**	Edward J. Derwinski

11075 of Jan. 15, 1963. Congress made it agency of executive office under Trade Act of 1974. Administers trade agreements program of Tariff Act of 1930, Trade Expansion Act of 1962, and Trade Act of 1974. Sets and administers overall trade policy. Representative is chief representative of U.S. for all activities of General Agreement on Tariffs and Trade (GATT) and at discussions, meetings, and negotiations in most conferences in which trade and commodity are issues.

Council on Environmental Quality 722 Jackson Place N.W., Washington, D.C. 20503. (202) 395-5750. Created by National Environmental Policy Act of 1969. Recommends national policies to improve quality of environment. Analyzes environmental changes and trends. Assesses and evaluates existing environmental programs. Assists President in compiling annual environmental quality report to Congress.

Office of Science and Technology Policy Old Executive Office Building, Washington, D.C. 20506. (202) 395-4692. Created May 11, 1976, by National Science and Technology Policy, Organization, and Priorities Act of 1976. Serves as source of scientific, engineering, and technological analysis and expertise for president with respect to public policy in areas of economy, national security, health, foreign relations, and environment. Appraises sale, quality, and effectiveness of U.S. efforts in science and technology.

Office of Administration Old Executive Office Building, Washington, D.C. 20500. (202) 456-7050. Created Dec. 12, 1977, by Reorganization Plan No. 1. Provides administrative services to all units within executive office except those in direct support of president.

EXECUTIVE DEPARTMENTS

Department of Agriculture (USDA) 14th St. and Independence Ave. S.W., Washington, D.C. 20250. (202) 447-2791. Created by act of May 15, 1862. Works to improve farms and farm income, expand foreign markets for U.S. agriculture, and curb poverty, hunger, and malnutrition. Helps maintain natural resources such as soil, water, and forests. Maintains food quality standards through inspection and grading. USDA is divided into seven major administrations.

Small Community and Rural Development Provides loans and economic aid to Americans in rural areas and communities. Loans granted for farm ownerships and operations; youth projects (e.g., 4-H clubs); soil, water, and other conservation projects; Native American tribes; rural housing projects; business and industry; community facilities; improvement of rural telephone and electric service; and emergencies resulting from natural disasters.

Marketing and Inspection Services Helps farmers organize protective cooperatives to sell farm products and buy farm supplies. Standardizes, grades, classifies, tests, and inspects more than 300 agricultural products, most notably, grain, meat, and poultry. Ensures food quality for buyers. Regulates plant and animal health. Regulates packing and transportation of agricultural products.

Food and Consumer Services Regulates and improves America's nutrition through Food Stamp programs, food distribution programs, and nutritional information and education.

International Affairs and Commodity Programs Stabilizes production of many different agricultural products through loans and land grants, commodity and price stabilization programs, and establishment of international agricultural cooperation.

Science and Education Performs research to improve animal and plant protection and production; conservation and improvement of soil, water, air, and other natural resources; processing, storage, and distribution of agricultural products. Provides grants for independent research. Shares research nationwide through cooperation among the states and through National Agricultural Library.

Natural Resources and Environment Operates U.S. Forest Service to protect and maintain U.S. forests. Conserves, protects, and helps recycle renewable natural resources such as soil, water, air, and trees.

Economics Performs economic evaluations of the agricultural and food sectors. Provides economic information about agricultural sector to aid public policy.

Department of Commerce 14th St. between Constitution Ave. and E St. N.W.,

Washington, D.C. 20230. (202) 377-2000. Created Febr. 14, 1903, as part of Department of Commerce and Labor. Redesignated Department of Commerce by act of Mar. 4, 1913. Promotes international trade, economic growth, and technological advancement through encouragement of competitive free-enterprise system, prevention of unfair trade, granting of patents, economic promotion of domestic development, research in telecommunications, promotion of tourism, and assistance in growth of minority businesses. Department is divided into 12 administrations.

National Technical Information Service (NTIS) Clearinghouse for sale of government-sponsored research, development, and engineering reports. Its library exceeds 1.5 million titles.

Bureau of the Census Estab. Mar. 6, 1902, by act of Congress. Collects, tabulates, and publishes census statistics about America, its people and its economy. Statistics are used by Congress, president, and public to aid development and evaluation of public policy. Population and housing censuses are performed every 10 years. Censuses of agriculture, state and local governments, manufacturers, mineral industries, distributive trades, and construction and transportation industries are performed every five years. Special censuses are performed on demand from state and local governments.

Bureau of Economic Analysis (BEA) Estab. Dec. 1, 1953, by secretary of commerce. Prepares diagnoses of health of economy through compilation and assessment of economic indicators.

Bureau of Export Administration (BXA) Estab. Oct. 1, 1987, by secretary of commerce. Licenses exporters, advises on matters of economic export regulations, and enforces U.S. export control laws.

Economic Development Administration (EDA) Estab. by Public Works and Economic Development Act of 1965. Promotes new jobs, protects existing jobs, and stimulates job growth in areas where unemployment is high or incomes are low. Programs are carried out through sponsorship of industrial parks, water and sewer lines, and airport developments; loan guarantees to industrial and commercial firms; planning grants to states, cities, districts, and Indian reservations; technical assistance for existing firms; planning grants; and emergency aid to communities to avoid long-term economic deterioration.

International Trade Administration (ITA) Estab. Jan. 2, 1980. Promotes world trade and strengthens U.S. position in relation to world trade and investment.

Minority Business Development Agency (MBDA) Estab. Nov. 1, 1979. Promotes minority business. Ensures effective, equitable, and competitive participation by minority business in free enterprise system.

National Bureau of Standards (NBS) Estab. by act of Mar. 3, 1901. Nonregulatory agency. Performs scientific research for specific purpose of aiding U.S. industry and science. Its four areas of primary research are engineering, physical and chemical measurements, materials science, and computer sciences. Through this research, NBS increases U.S. productivity and innovation in world scientific market.

National Oceanic and Atmospheric Administration (NOAA) Estab. Oct. 3, 1970. Investigates and maps oceans of world. Discovers, utilizes, and conserves living resources of oceans. Monitors and predicts conditions of atmosphere, sun, and oceans; warns against deterioration of these conditions arising from natural and manmade events and circumstances. Provides weather reports and forecasts. Forecasts floods, hurricanes, and other weather-related natural disasters.

National Telecommunications and Information Administration (NTIA) Estab. Mar. 27, 1978. Fosters development and use of telecommunication and information services.

Patent and Trademark Office (PTO) Estab. by Congress in Article I, Section 8 of Constitution. Promotes incentives to invent and make inventions public through granting of exclusive patents. Issues more than 75,000 patents and 55,000 trademarks every year. Patents are of three kinds: design, plant, and utility.

United States Travel and Tourism Administration (USTTA) Estab. 1981 by National Tourism Policy Act of 1981. Ensures fullest utilization of U.S. tourism resources. Expands tourism where possible. Stimulates demand abroad for tourism in U.S.

Department of Defense (DOD) The Pentagon, Washington, D.C. 20301-1155. (202) 545-6700. Created by National Security Act Amendments of 1949. Provides necessary military forces to deter war and protect security of the country. Advises president on matters of war and military security. More than 2 million men and women serve in the four branches of armed services. Additional 1.7 million serve in reserve forces, and 1.2 million employees work for civilian defense department.

Organization of the Joint Chiefs of Staff Consists of chairman of Joint Chiefs of Staff; chief of staff of U.S. Army; chief of naval operations; chief of staff of U.S. Air Force; and commandant of Marine Corps. Advises and assists president and secretary of defense on most military issues. Assists president and secretary of defense in planning, direction, and allocation of strategic resources. Compares strengths and capabilities of American forces with those of potential adversaries.

Department of the Air Force Estab. Sept. 18, 1947, by National Security Act of 1947. Works in conjunction with other armed forces to protect peace and security of the U.S. Focuses on air missions and protecting American interests from invasion by air.

Department of the Army U.S. Army estab. June 14, 1775, by Continental Congress. Dept. of the Army estab. 1947 by National Security Act of 1947. Organizes, trains, and equips active and reserve forces to protect peace, security, welfare, and defense of U.S. Works in conjunction with other armed forces. Its mission focuses on land operations and maneuvers.

Department of the Navy U.S. Navy estab. Oct. 13, 1775, by Continental Congress. Dept. of the Navy estab. by act of April 30, 1798. Protects U.S. from attack by sea. Encompasses Marine Corps. Maintains freedom of the seas. Seizes or defends naval bases. Supports and works together with other armed forces. Its mission focuses on marine operations and sea-to-air maneuvers (through the Marine Corps).

Department of Education 400 Maryland Ave. S.W., Washington, D.C. 20202. (202) 245-3192. Created Oct. 17, 1979, by Department of Education Organization Act. Establishes policy for, administers, and coordinates almost all federal assistance to education. Department's budget includes funding for following four corporations: *American Printing House for the Blind:* Distributes Braille books, books on tape and educational aids for the blind. *Gallaudet University:* Provides college education for deaf who need special facilities. Encourages further education and study by its students. *Howard University:* Has special responsibility for admission and education of black students. *National Technical Institute for the Deaf (NTID), Rochester Institute of Technology:* Educates large numbers of deaf students within university designed for hearing students. Helps deaf students adapt to and join mainstream American hearing society.

Department of Energy 1000 Independence Ave. S.W., Washington, D.C. 20585. (202) 586-5000. Created Aug. 4, 1977, by Department of Energy Organization Act. Coordinates and administrates energy functions of federal government, including research and development of energy technology, marketing federal power, energy conservation, nuclear weapons, and energy regulation. Three administrations are included under its aegis.

Energy Information Administration (EIA) Collects, processes, and publishes statistics and information regarding energy resources, energy production, consumption, demand, distribution, and technology. Performs analyses of these data to help users understand energy trends and their impact.

Economic Regulatory Administration (ERA) Administers all regulatory programs not administered by Federal Energy Regulatory Commission (see below).

Federal Economic Regulatory Commission Sets rates for sale and transport of oil, natural gas, and electricity. Sets rates for and licenses hydroelectric power plants.

Department of Health and Human Services (HHS) 200 Independence Ave. S.W., Washington, D.C. 20201. (202) 245-6296. Created Apr. 11, 1953, as Department of Health, Education, and Welfare. Redesignated Department of Health and Human Services Oct. 17, 1979, by Department of Education Organization Act. Advises president in formulation of public policy regarding health, welfare, and income and security programs. Department is divided into five administrations.

Office of Human Development Services (HDS) Advises secretary of HHS on human-development services and human-service programs. Provides leadership in planning and developing HDS programs. Supervises use of research funds. Controls equal employment opportunity and civil rights policies and programs.

Public Health Service (PHS) Estab. by Public Health Service Act of July 1, 1944. Promotes national physical and mental health. Coordinates national health policy between and among the states. Conducts medical research. Sponsors research for improved health care, disease prevention and control, and alcohol and drug abuse prevention. Enforces laws to assure safety and efficiency of foods, drugs, cosmetics, and medical devices. Encompasses National Institute of Mental Health, Centers for Disease Control, Food and Drug Administration, and National Institutes of Health, among others.

Health Care Financing Administration (HCFA) Estab. Mar. 8, 1977. Oversees Medicare and Medicaid health insurance and grant programs.

Social Security Administration (SSA) Estab. July 16, 1946, by Federal Security Agency Reorganization Plan II of 1946. Administers national social insurance program known as Social Security. Employers and employees pay contributions to Social Security Fund. When employee retires, monthly cash benefits are paid to replace the lost earnings.

Family Support Administration (FSA) Advises secretary of HHS on programs to aid children and low-income families. Coordinates Work Incentive Program (WIN) with Department of Labor and directs Office of Child Support Enforcement.

Department of Housing and Urban Development (HUD) 451 Seventh St. S.W., Washington, D.C. 20410. (202) 755–5111. Created Nov. 9, 1965, by Department of Housing and Urban Development Act. Administers mortgage programs to help families become home owners. Fosters construction of new housing and renovation of existing rental housing. Provides aid for low-income families who cannot afford their rent. Enacts programs to prevent housing discrimination. Encourages strong private-sector housing industry. Department's program areas are considered neither bureaus nor administrations. They include Community Planning and Development, Fair Housing and Equal Opportunity Housing, Public and Indian Housing, Government National Mortgage Association, and Policy Development and Research. Each program area is responsible for enforcing legislation under its aegis.

Department of the Interior 1800 C St. N.W., Washington, D.C. 20240. (202) 343–3171. Created by act of Mar. 3, 1849. Principal U.S. conservation agency. Directs use and conservation of public lands and natural resources. Prescribes use of land and water resources, fish and wildlife, national parks and historic places, and mineral resources. Aids in preservation of American Indian reservation communities. The department supervises programs of nine service bureaus.

United States Fish and Wildlife Service Conserves and protects fish and wildlife and their habitats. Encourages understanding of preservation of these resources. Sponsors research to promote fish and wildlife conservation. Assesses environmental impact of pesticides, thermal pollution, hydroelectric dams, and nuclear power sites.

National Park Service Estab. by act of Aug. 25, 1916. Administers, protects, and maintains diverse system of national parks, monuments, historic areas, and recreation areas. Protects natural environment of these areas. Encourages understanding of the historic value of these sites through lectures, tours, exhibits, and films. Operates campgrounds, concessions, and transportation services on these sites.

Bureau of Mines Estab. July 1, 1910, by Organic Act of May 16, 1910. Research agency. Ensures that U.S. has enough nonfuel minerals for security. Attempts to replace imported minerals with domestic ones. Seeks to suppress pollution, increase mine safety, and encourage recycling.

Office of Surface Mining Reclamation and Enforcement (OSMRE) Estab. by Surface Mining Control and Reclamation Act of 1977. Protects society from adverse effects of coal mining. Ensures continuing surface coal mining without permanent damage to land and water resources.

Geological Survey Estab. by act of Mar. 3, 1879. Identifies and classifies land, water, energy, and mineral resources. Investigates potential hazards such as earthquakes and volcanoes. Conducts topographic mapping.

Bureau of Indian Affairs Estab. 1824 as part of Department of War. Transferred to Department of Interior in 1849. Trains American Indian and Alaska native peoples to manage their own affairs under trust relationship to federal government. Facilitates public and private aid to advancement of these peoples.

Minerals Management Service (MMS) Estab. Jan. 19, 1982, by Secretarial Order No. 3071. Assesses nature, extent, value, and recoverability of leasable minerals on outer continental shelf. Collects royalties on use of these minerals.

Bureau of Land Management (BLM) Estab. July 16, 1946, by consolidation of the General Land Office and the Grazing Service. Manages 270 million acres of public lands primarily in Far West and in Alaska. Resources in these lands include timber, oil, gas, hard minerals, and wildlife habitats.

Bureau of Reclamation Estab. 1902 as Reclamation Service, within U.S. Geological Survey, by Reclamation Act of 1902. Renamed Bureau of Reclamation in 1923. Provides year-round water and irrigation supply for towns, farms, and industries in western states. Generates hydroelectric power, regulates rivers and flood control, and enhances fish and wildlife habitats.

Department of Justice Constitution Avenue and 10th St. N.W., Washington, D.C. 20530. (202) 633–2000. Created by act of June 22, 1870. Enforces the law in the public interest. Nation's largest law firm. Ensures fair competition in free enterprise system. Enforces drug, immigration, and naturalization laws. Aids in law enforcement, crime prevention, crime detection, and prosecution and rehabilitation of criminals. Conducts all Supreme Court suits in which U.S. is party or is concerned. Advises president on legal matters. Supervises all U.S. attorneys and marshals in judicial districts throughout country. Encompassed in department's authority are seven bureaus.

Federal Bureau of Investigation (FBI) Estab. 1908. Principal investigative bureau of Justice Department. Investigates violations of federal law. Areas of primary concern are organized crime (including drug-trafficking), terrorism, white-collar crime, and foreign counterintelligence. Gathers and reports facts, locates witnesses, and compiles evidence in federal cases.

Bureau of Prisons Imprisons and rehabilitates criminals convicted of federal crimes and sentenced to serve time in federal prison.

United States Marshals Service Provides security and support to federal court system. Apprehends federal fugitives. Ensures safety of federal witnesses. Protects and transports federal prisoners. Executes court orders and arrest warrants. Maintains custody, manages, and sells property seized from criminals.

International Criminal Police Organization (INTERPOL) Estab. in 1923. Promotes international cooperation in prevention and suppression of international crime.

Immigration and Naturalization Service (INS) Estab. by act of Mar. 3, 1891. Controls immigration into U.S. by facilitating entry to qualified persons and denying admission to unqualified aliens. Deports illegal aliens already in U.S. Encourages and facilitates naturalization and citizenship.

Drug Enforcement Administration (DEA) Estab. July, 1973. Investigates interstate drug-trafficking. Enforces government regulations regarding manufacture, distribution, sale, and dispensing of controlled substances. Manages a national narcotics intelligence system. Performs research, training, and information exchange to foster drug traffic prevention and control.

Office of Justice Programs (OJP) Estab. by Justice Assistance Act of 1984. Fosters cooperation and coordination among the various arms of criminal justice system to create more effective justice.

Department of Labor 200 Constitution Ave. N.W., Washington, D.C. 20210. (202) 523–8165. Created by act of Mar. 4, 1913. Improves welfare of wage earners. Improves working conditions. Guarantees minimum wages and overtime pay. Prevents employment discrimination. Guarantees unemployment insurance and workers' compensation. Protects pension rights. Provides for job training programs. Strengthens collective bargaining. Helps workers find jobs. Pays special attention to labor-related needs of minority workers, old and young, women, and disabled people. Department has nine administrations and bureaus.

Employment and Training Administration (ETA) Provides employment security through unemployment insurance, worker dislocation programs, and federal-state employment service system. Trains or retrains and finds employment for disadvantaged workers through Job Training Partnership Act (JTPA).

Office of Labor-Management Standards (OLMS) Estab. May 3, 1984. Regulates union procedures. Protects rights of members in 48,000 unions. Areas of concern include handling of union funds, reporting of unions' financial transactions and administrative practices, and election of union officers.

Pension and Welfare Benefits Administration (PWBA) Estab. Sept. 2, 1974, by Employment Retirement Income Security Act of 1974. Requires private pension and welfare plan administrators to give participants summaries of pension and welfare plans. Keeps summaries on file. Regulates financial operations of pension and welfare plans.

Labor-Management Relations and Cooperative Programs (BLMRCP) Provides information and technical assistance to employers, unions, and other organizations for purpose of improving labor relations. This goal is achieved through sponsoring conferences, publishing special reports, preparing training materials, and reviewing economic efficiency of and adherence to collective-bargaining relationships.

Employment Standards Administration Administers and directs programs dealing with minimum wage and overtime requirements, wages for government-sponsored work, affirmative action, and workers' compensation.

Occupational Safety and Health Administration (OSHA) Estab. 1970 by Occupational Safety and Health Act. Promotes safety and health standards in work place. Issues regulations, conducts investigations, issues citations, and proposes penalties for violations of health standards and regulations.

Mine Safety and Health Administration (MSHA) Estab. 1977 by Federal Mine Safety and Health Amendments Act of 1977. Responsible for all mine safety and health regulations. Issues regulations, investigates violations, assesses penalties for noncompliance, and in coordination with Department of Health and Human Services, improves mine safety and health research.

Bureau of Labor Statistics (BLS) Data-gathering agency. Collects, processes, interprets, and distributes data involving employment, unemployment, wages, family income and expenditures, workers' compensation, industrial relations, productivity, and technological change.

Veterans' Employment and Training Service (VETS) Maximizes training and employment opportunities for veterans and disabled. Ensures that legislation involving veterans is carried out by local public employment services and by private enterprise.

Department of State 2201 C St. N.W., Washington, D.C. 20520. (202) 647-4000. Created by act of July 27, 1789, as Department of Foreign Affairs. Renamed Department of State by act of Sept. 15, 1789. Advises president on foreign policy. Formulates and executes policy to protect and defend American interests overseas. Negotiates treaties and agreements with foreign countries. Speaks for U.S. in United Nations. Both United States Mission to the UN and Foreign Service are under authority of State Department.

United States Mission to the United Nations Represents U.S. at U.N. Carries out U.S. foreign policy as it relates to U.N.

Foreign Service Maintains relations with more than 140 nations around world. Reports to State Department on developments relating to safety and welfare of U.S., its citizens, and their interests. Ambassadors to each country are personal representatives of the president and have full responsibility for carrying out U.S. foreign policy within the country. Ambassadors negotiate agreements between host country and U.S., explain and administer U.S. foreign policy, and maintain relations with government and public of host country.

Department of Transportation (DOT) 400 Seventh St. SW; Washington, D.C. 20590. (202) 366-4000. Created by act of October 15, 1966. Establishes nation's comprehensive transportation policy. Its nine umbrella administrations are responsible for highway planning, development, and construction; urban mass transit; railroads; aviation; and the safety of waterways, ports, highways, and oil and gas pipelines. Decisions made in conjunction with state and local authorities have strong bearing on land planning, energy conservation, and resource utilization policies. The Department is divided into nine administrations and agencies.

United States Coast Guard Estab. by act of Jan. 28, 1915. Included in Dept. of Transportation Apr. 1, 1967. Coast Guard is at all times a branch of armed forces and a service with Dept. of Transportation except when operating as part of navy during war. Primary maritime law enforcement agency for U.S. Suppresses drug smuggling and trafficking. Licenses marine vessels. Administers and inspects violations of safety standards for design, construction, equipment, and maintenance of commercial marine vessels and offshore structures in U.S. waters. Provides search and rescue functions for saving lives and property in U.S. waters. Provides flood relief and removes hazards to navigation. Enforces rules ensuring safe and orderly navigation through ports, waterways, and bridges. Operates ice-breaking vessels to facilitate marine transportation. Provides military and reserve training.

Federal Aviation Administration (FAA) Estab. 1958 by Federal Aviation Act. Included in Dept. of Transportation in 1967 by Dept. of Transportation Act. Regulates air commerce in effort to promote safety and secure national defense interests. Directs use of navigable U.S. airspace. Promotes and encourages civil aeronautics. Installs and operates air-navigation facilities. Develops and operates system of air traffic control for both civil and military aircraft. Regulates aircraft noise and other environmental effects of civil aviation.

Federal Highway Administration (FHWA) Included in Dept. of Transportation in 1967 by Dept. of Transportation Act. Promotes highway safety. Provides aid for construction and maintenance of state and federal highway systems. Facilitates and provides aid for safety improvements to state and federal highway systems. Helps states formulate agreed-upon size and weight regulations for trucks and commercial traffic. Administers highway planning and beautification programs.

Federal Railroad Administration (FRA) Estab. 1966 by section 3(e)(1) of Dept. of Transportation Act of 1966. Administers and enforces railroad safety regulations such as track maintenance, inspection and equipment standards, and operating practices. Maintains research and development programs and Transportation Test Center to foster further safety and efficiency of rail travel.

National Highway Traffic Safety Administration Estab. 1970 by Highway Safety Act of 1970. Promotes highway safety through various programs. These include enforcing a uniform and nationwide speed limit, administering laws to prevent odometer tampering, issuing theft prevention standards, setting average fuel-economy and air-pollution standards for motor vehicles, and enforcing inspection standards. Research and development programs are aimed at reducing number of highway collisions, reducing severity of injuries and economic loss involved in highway accidents, and reducing fatalities resulting from highway crashes.

Urban Mass Transportation Administration (UMTA) Estab. July 1, 1968, by Reorganization Plan No. 2 of 1968, Section 3. Improves equipment and methods used in urban mass transit. Encourages planning of cost-effective mass transit systems. Provides economic and technical assistance for mass transit programs. Encourages private sector involvement in local mass-transit systems.

Maritime Administration Estab. May 24, 1950, by Reorganization Plan No. 21 of 1950. Included in Dept. of Transportation Aug. 6, 1981, by Maritime Act of 1981. Constructs or supervises construction of U.S.-flag merchant ships for federal government. Generates business for U.S. ships. Develops ports and facilities for maritime transport. Promotes domestic shipping. Provides economic and technical aid to private shipbuilding. Regulates sales of ships.

Saint Lawrence Seaway Development Corporation Estab. by act of May 13, 1954. Owns, develops, maintains, and operates St. Lawrence Seaway between Montreal and Lake Erie within territorial limits of U.S. Provides safe and efficient waterway for maritime commerce. Charges user tolls and encourages traffic. Operates in coordination with Canadian owners, St. Lawrence Seaway Authority of Canada.

Research and Special Programs Administration (RSPA) Estab. Sept. 23, 1977; reorganized 1985. Its six umbrella organizations regulate transportation of hazardous materials; enforce safety standards for pipeline transportation of liquid and gaseous materials involved in or affecting interstate commerce; maintain information and research offices devoted to transportation, safety, and economics of aviation; and prepare emergency transportation programs.

Department of the Treasury 1500 Pennsylvania Ave. N.W., Washington, D.C. 20220. (202) 566-2000. Created by act of Sept. 2, 1789. Formulates and recommends economic, financial, tax, and fiscal policies. Acts as financial agent for U.S. government. Enforces the law. Manufactures coins and currency. Department is divided into 11 bureaus, offices, and administrations.

Bureau of Alcohol, Tobacco and Firearms Estab. July 1, 1972, by Treasury Dept. Order

No. 221. Enforces and administers laws regulating production, use, distribution, and sale of alcohol and tobacco products, firearms, and explosives. Bureau's objectives are to eliminate illegal trafficking, possession, and use of firearms and explosives, to suppress illegal alcohol and tobacco trafficking, and to ensure safety of storage facilities for explosives.

Office of the Comptroller of the Currency Estab. by act of Feb. 25, 1863. Issues and executes laws regulating national banks. Inspects, examines, and issues official approvals of national banks, their operations, and their financial soundness.

United States Customs Service Estab. Mar. 3, 1927, as Bureau of Customs. Redesignated Customs Service Apr. 4, 1973, by Treasury Dept. Order 165–23. Collects revenue from imports. Enforces customs treaties. Assesses and collects customs duties, excise taxes, fees, and penalties on imported merchandise. Seizes contraband including narcotics and illegal drugs. Processes people, mail, carriers, and cargo in and out of U.S. Apprehends violators of U.S. customs regulations and related laws including copyright, patent, and trademark, and import quotas. Intercepts high-technology exports to Soviet-bloc countries. Suppresses traffic of illegal narcotics, pornography, counterfeit monetary instruments, and quarantined animals, plants, and foods.

Bureau of Engraving and Printing Estab. by act of July 11, 1862. Designs, prints, and finishes Federal Reserve notes, U.S. postage stamps, identification cards, and Treasury securities. Inhibits counterfeiting of these documents.

Federal Law Enforcement Training Center Estab. Mar. 2, 1970, by Treasury Dept. Order. 217. Teaches basic law-enforcement skills to police and investigators. Also teaches courses in white-collar crime, computer crime, law-enforcement photography, contract fraud, and marine law enforcement.

Financial Management Service Manages money of federal government. Improves cash management, credit management, and debt collection and payment programs. Invests social security and other trust funds. Serves as government's central accounting system. Publishes daily, monthly, and quarterly reports of government's financial operations and status.

Internal Revenue Service (IRS) Estab. by act of July 1, 1862. Administers and enforces internal revenue laws except those relating to alcohol, tobacco, firearms, and explosives. Determines, assesses, and collects federal tax revenues from public. Encourages, assesses, and enforces compliance with tax laws.

United States Mint Mint of the United States estab. by act of April 2, 1792. Bureau of the Mint estab. Feb. 12, 1873. Renamed United States Mint Jan. 9, 1984, by Secretarial Order. Manufactures and distributes coins for circulation through Federal Reserve Banks. Produces foreign coins. Processes gold and silver bullion. Manufactures national medals, proof coin sets, and commemorative coins for sale to public.

Bureau of the Public Debt Estab. June 30, 1940, by Reorganization Act of 1939. Manages public debt. Offers public-debt securities. Audits retired securities and interest coupons.

Maintains accounting control over public-debt receipts and expenditures, securities, and interest costs. Adjudicates claims of lost, stolen, or destroyed securities.

United States Savings Bonds Division Estab. Dec. 26, 1945, by Treasury Order. Promotes sale and retention of U.S. Savings Bonds. Encourages support and understanding of Savings Bonds program.

United States Secret Service Protects president and vice president (and president-elect and vice president-elect) of U.S. and their families. Protects former presidents and their wives until their death. Protects distinguished foreign visitors and U.S. officials abroad at direction of president. Detects and apprehends counterfeiters. Suppresses forgery of government securities and documents. Provides security at White House complex, vice president's residence, and various foreign diplomatic missions or embassies as directed by president.

Department of Veterans Affairs (VA)

810 Vermont Ave. N.W., Washington, D.C. 20420. (202) 233–2300. Created July 21, 1930, by Executive Order 5398. Administers benefit programs for veterans and their families—e.g., military-related death or disability compensation, education and rehabilitation, home loan guaranty and medical care programs. Operates VA hospitals, medical centers, clinics, and nursing homes. Made cabinet-level post in 1988.

INDEPENDENT ESTABLISHMENTS AND CORPORATIONS

ACTION 806 Connecticut Ave. N.W., Washington, D.C. 20525. (202) 634–9380. Created July 1, 1971, by Reorganization Plan No. 1 of 1971. Encourages and mobilizes Americans to perform voluntary services and programs for low-income individuals and communities. Identifies and appraises new volunteer grants and programs. Develops volunteer service opportunities for widest possible range of Americans. Included in its programs are Volunteers In Service to America (VISTA), Foster Grandparents Program (FGP) and Retired Senior Volunteer Program (RSVP).

Administrative Conference of the United States 2120 L Street N.W., Washington, D.C. 20037. (202) 254–7020. Created in 1964 by Administrative Conference Act. Develops improvements in federal administration of government programs. Agency heads meet with lawyers, university professors, and other experts to exchange ideas, share experiences and judgments, and conduct studies at this forum.

African Development Foundation Suite 600, 1625 Massachusetts Ave. N.W., Washington, D.C. 20036. (202) 673–3916. Created in 1984 by African Development Foundation Act. Nonprofit government corporation. Through grants, loans, and loan guarantees, aids self-help efforts by poor people in African countries. Fosters stronger bonds between Africa and U.S. Stimulates and assists expansion and development by Africans in their respective nations.

American Battle Monuments Commission 20 Massachusetts Ave. N.W., Washington, D.C. 20314. (202) 272–0533. Created by act of Mar. 4, 1923. Designs, constructs, and maintains federal military cemeteries and memorial sites here and abroad. Regulates erection of memorials, monuments, and markers by Americans or American organizations abroad.

Appalachian Regional Commission (ARC) 1666 Connecticut Ave. N.W., Washington, D.C. 20235. (202) 673–7893. Created by Appalachian Regional Development Act of 1965. Federal-state government agency concerned with economic, physical, and social development of 13-state Appalachian region (includes parts of Ala., Ga., Ky., Md., Miss., N.Y., N.C., Ohio, Pa., S.C., Tenn., and Va., and all of W.Va.). Constructs Appalachian Development Highway System and local access roads to stimulate industrial and commercial growth and to provide access to schools, health clinics and hospitals, and other community facilities. Strengthens local governments to create jobs and industry in region. Provides aid to the 88 poorest counties by providing safe drinking water and waste disposal.

Board for International Broadcasting Suite 400, 1201 Connecticut Ave. N.W., Washington, D.C. 20036. (202) 254–8040. Created by Board for International Broadcasting Act of 1973. Oversees broadcast operations of Radio Liberty (RL) to Soviet Union and of Radio Free Europe (RFE) to Poland, Romania, Czechoslovakia, Hungary, Bulgaria, and Baltic States. Appraises broadcast content within context of U.S. policy objectives.

Central Intelligence Agency (CIA) Washington, D.C. 20505. (703) 482–1100. Created by National Security Act of 1947. Under direction of president and National Security Council. Advises NSC on intelligence matters of national security. Collects, evaluates, and disseminates intelligence information relating to national security and to drug production and trafficking. Collects, produces, and disseminates counterintelligence and foreign intelligence here (in conjunction with FBI) and abroad. Conducts special activities as directed by president. Protects security of its activities, information, and personnel by necessary and appropriate means.

Commission on the Bicentennial of the United States Constitution 736 Jackson Place N.W., Washington, D.C. 20503. (202) USA-1787. Created Sept. 29, 1983, by act of Congress. Continues through 1991. Promotes, coordinates, and develops events and activities commemorating the 200th anniversary of adoption of Constitution on Sept. 17, 1787.

Commission on Civil Rights (CCR) 1121 Vermont Ave. N.W., Washington, D.C. 20425. (202) 376–8177. Created by Civil Rights Act of 1957. Holds public hearings and collects and studies information on discrimination or denial of equal protection based on race, color, religion, sex, age, handicap, or national origin. Studies in particular fair enforcement of civil rights laws and guarantee of voting rights and equal opportunity in education, employment, and housing.

Commission of Fine Arts 708 Jackson Place

N.W., Washington, D.C. 20006. (202) 566-1066. Created May 17, 1910, by act of Congress. Advises president, members of Congress, and other governmental agencies on matters pertaining to plans for public buildings, parks, and other architectural elements of Washington, D.C.

Commodity Futures Trading Commission (CFTC) 2033 K St. N.W., Washington, D.C. 20581. (202) 254-6387. Created May 14, 1973, by Commodity Futures Act of 1973. Regulates trading on the 11 U.S. futures exchanges. Regulates activities of commodity exchange members, public brokerage houses, commodity trading advisers, and other related employees. Ensures fair futures trading. Protects rights of customers and financial integrity of marketplace.

Consumer Product Safety Commission (CPSC) 5401 Westbard Ave., Bethesda, MD 20207. (301) 492-5500. Created May 14, 1973, by Consumer Product Safety Act. Protects public from unreasonable risk of injury from consumer products. Develops, enforces, and evaluates safety standards for consumer products.

Environmental Protection Agency (EPA) 401 M St. S.W., Washington, D.C. 20460. (202) 382-2090. Created Dec. 2, 1970, by Reorganization Plan No. 3 of 1970. Protects and enhances environment. Controls and reduces pollution of air and water. Regulates solid-waste disposal and use of pesticides, radiation, and toxic substances.

Equal Employment Opportunity Commission (EEOC) 2401 E Street N.W., Washington, D.C. 20507. (202) 634-6036. (800) USA-EEOC. Created July 2, 1965, by Title VII of Civil Rights Act of 1964. Protects against discrimination based on race, color, handicap, religion, sex, age, and national origin in hiring, promoting, firing, wages, testing, training, apprenticeship, and all other terms and conditions of employment.

Export-Import Bank of the United States 811 Vermont Ave. N.W., Washington, D.C. 20571. (202) 566-8990. Created Feb. 2, 1934, by Executive Order 6581. Facilitates and aids exports of U.S. goods and services through loans, loan guarantees, and insurance to exporters and private banks.

Farm Credit Administration 1501 Farm Credit Drive, McLean, VA 22102. (703) 883-4000. Created by Farm Credit Act of 1971. Regulates and examines programs, banks, associations, organizations of the Farm Credit System, which provides credit to farmers, ranchers, producers of farm products, rural home-owners, and associations and organizations of farmers, ranchers, and farm-equipment producers.

Federal Communications Commission (FCC) 1919 M Street N.W., Washington, D.C. 20554. (202) 632-7000. Created by Communications Act of 1934. Regulates interstate and foreign communications by radio, television, wire, and cable. Oversees development of broadcast services and rapid and efficient provision of telephone and telegraph services nationwide.

Federal Deposit Insurance Corporation (FDIC) 550 17th St. N.W., Washington, D.C. 20429. (202) 393-8400. Created June 16, 1933, by Federal Reserve Act. Fosters public confidence in banks and protects money supply by insuring deposits in and reviewing operations of state-chartered banks that are not members of Federal Reserve System.

Federal Election Commission (FEC) 999 E St. N.W., Washington, D.C. 20463. (202) 376-3120; (800) 424-9530. Created by Federal Election Campaign Act of 1971. Provides public funding for presidential elections. Ensures public disclosure of campaign finance activities. Administers and enforces contribution and spending limits for federal elections. (See also discussion of FEC Act and Political Action Committees—PACs—under "U.S. Presidential Elections," above.)

Federal Emergency Management Agency (FEMA) 500 C St. S.W., Washington, D.C. 20472. (202) 646-4600. Created Mar. 31, 1979, by Reorganization Plan No. 3 of 1978. Provides single point of accountability for all federal emergency preparedness, mitigation, and response activities. Facilitates most efficient use of resources in cases of natural or man-made emergencies.

Federal Home Loan Bank Board 1700 G St. N.W., Washington, D.C. 20552. (202) 377-6000. Created July 22, 1932, by Federal Home Loan Bank Act. Encourages economically efficient home-ownership. Supervises and regulates savings institutions that finance purchase and construction of homes and residential real estate. Operates Federal Savings and Loan Insurance Corporation (FSLIC), which insures savings of more than 84 million Americans with savings accounts in savings and loan associations insured by the corporation.

Federal Labor Relations Authority (FLRA) 500 C St. S.W., Washington, D.C. 20424. (202) 382-0711. Created Jan. 1, 1979, by Reorganization Plan No. 2 of 1978. Protects rights of federal employees to organize, bargain collectively, and participate in labor organizations. Oversees rights and obligations of federal employees and labor organizations that represent them.

Federal Maritime Commission 1100 L St. N.W., Washington, D.C. 20573. (202) 523-5773. Created Aug. 12, 1961, by Reorganization Plan No. 7 of 1961. Regulates foreign and domestic maritime offshore commerce. Keeps U.S. international trade open and fair to all nations. Protects against unauthorized activity in U.S. waterborne commerce.

Federal Mediation and Conciliation Service 2100 K St. N.W., Washington, D.C. 20427. (202) 653-5290. Created in 1947 by Labor Management Relations Act. Promotes development of stable labor-management relations. Prevents or minimizes work stoppages by helping to settle disputes and by advocating collective bargaining, mediation, and arbitration.

Federal Reserve System Board of Governors of Federal Reserve System. 20th St. and Constitution Ave. N.W., Washington, D.C. 20551. (202) 452-3000. Created Dec. 23, 1913, by Federal Reserve Act. Central bank of U.S. Administers and creates national credit and monetary policy. Regulates money supply. Maintains soundness of banking industry.

Federal Retirement Thrift Investment Board 805 15th St. N.W., Washington, D.C. 20005. (202) 523-4511. Created by Federal Employees' Retirement System Act of 1986. Administers Thrift Savings Plan for federal employees.

Federal Trade Commission (FTC) Pennsylvania Ave. at Sixth St. N.W., Washington, D.C. 20580. (202) 326-2222. Created in 1914 by Federal Trade Commission Act and Clayton Act. Maintains free and fair competition in free enterprise system. Breaks up monopolies. Seeks to prevent corruption, restraints on trade, and unfair trade practices.

General Services Administration (GSA) General Services Building, 18th and F Sts. N.W., Washington, D.C. 20405. (202) 472-1082; (202) 566-0705. Created July 1, 1949, by Federal Property and Administrative Services Act of 1949. Establishes policy for, maintains and manages government property and records, construction of buildings, distribution of supplies, and other government services. Its services are divided among four service agencies.
INFORMATION RESOURCES MANAGEMENT SERVICES (IRMS) Coordinates and manages government's information distribution systems and programs. Facilitates use of automated data-processing and telecommunications equipment, improves federal records and information, and manages and operates Federal Information Centers.
FEDERAL SUPPLY SERVICE (FSS) Contracts and distributes supplies, services, and property to federal agencies worldwide.
PUBLIC BUILDINGS SERVICE (PBS) Oversees design, building, appraisal, repair, operation, and maintenance of most federally controlled buildings.
FEDERAL PROPERTY RESOURCES SERVICE (FPRS) Utilizes and disposes of government-owned real estate. Acquires, sells, and manages National Defense Stockpile of strategic and critical materials.

Inter-American Foundation 1515 Wilson Boulevard, Rosslyn, VA 22209. (703) 841-3800. Created by Congress in 1969. Supports social and economic development in Latin America and Caribbean. Makes grants to self-help organizations for the poor.

Interstate Commerce Commission (ICC) 12th St. and Constitution Ave. N.W., Washington, D.C. 20423. (202) 275-7119. Created by act of Feb. 4, 1887. Regulates interstate transportation involved in commerce. Certifies interstate carriers. Ensures fair rates and services to public.

Merit Systems Protection Board (MSPB) 1120 Vermont Ave. N.W., Washington, D.C. 20419. (202) 653-7124. Created Jan. 1, 1979, to succeed United States Civil Service Commission (estab. Jan. 16, 1883). Oversees personnel practices of government. Hears and decides charges of wrongdoing and orders corrective and disciplinary action against agencies when necessary.

National Aeronautics and Space Administration (NASA) 600 Independence Ave. S.W., Washington, D.C. 20546. (202) 453-1000. Created by National Aeronautics and Space Act of 1958. Develops, constructs, tests, and operates vehicles for in-flight research within and outside earth's atmosphere. Disseminates information about space exploration and agency's activities.

National Archives and Records Administration (NARA) Seventh St. and Pennsylvania Ave. N.W., Washington, D.C. 20408. (202) 523-3220. Created by act of Oct. 19, 1984. Establishes policy for managing records of U.S. government. Helps government document, store, and maintain its records. Makes records available to public.

National Capital Planning Commission (NCPC) 1325 G St. N.W., Washington, D.C. 20576. (202) 724-0174. Created by National Capital Planning Act of 1952. Coordinates planning and development activities in National Capital region, which includes Washington D.C., Montgomery and Prince Georges counties in Maryland, and Fairfax, Loudon, Prince William, and Arlington counties in Virginia.

National Credit Union Administration (NCUA) 1776 G St. N.W., Washington, D.C. 20456. (202) 357-1100. Created by act of Mar. 10, 1970. Charters, insures, supervises, and examines federal credit unions. Administers National Credit Union Share Insurance Fund. Supplies emergency loans to credit unions through Central Liquidity Facility. Credit unions are financial cooperatives that encourage thrift and provide credit at reasonable rates to their members.

National Foundation on the Arts and the Humanities 1100 Pennsylvania Ave. N.W., Washington, D.C. 20506. Created by National Foundation on the Arts and the Humanities Act of 1965. Its three divisions encourage and support national progress in humanities and arts.
NATIONAL ENDOWMENT FOR THE ARTS (NEA)1100 Pennsylvania Ave. N.W., Washington, D.C. 20506. (202) 682-5400. Fosters professional excellence in arts. Creates climate for arts to flourish and be appreciated, experienced, and enjoyed by public.
NATIONAL ENDOWMENT FOR THE HUMANITIES (NEH)1100 Pennsylvania Ave. N.W., Washington, D.C. 20506. (202) 786-0438. Independent grant-making agency supports research, education, and public programs in humanities.
INSTITUTE OF MUSEUM SERVICES (IMS) Room 510, 1100 Pennsylvania Ave. N.W., Washington, D.C. 20506. (202) 786-0539. Independent grant-making agency assists museums in maintaining, increasing, and improving services to public.

National Labor Relations Board (NLRB) 1717 Pennsylvania Ave. N.W., Washington, D.C. 20570. (202) 655-4000. Created by National Labor Relations Act of 1935 (also known as Wagner Act). Administers federal labor law. Safeguards employees' rights to organize, conducts elections to determine whether workers want unions as their bargaining representative, and prevents or remedies unfair labor practices.

National Mediation Board 1425 K St. N.W., Washington, D.C. 20572. (202) 523-5920. Created June 21, 1934, by amendment to Railway Labor Act. Resolves and investigates representation disputes in railroad and airline industries that could interrupt flow of commerce and endanger national economy. These disputes include grievances over wages, hours, and working conditions. Supervises representation disputes in the two industries.

National Science Foundation (NSF) 1800 G St. N.W., Washington, D.C. 20550. (202) 357-5000. Created by National Science Foundation Act of 1950. Promotes progress of science and engineering through support of research and education programs. Educational programs are designed to facilitate increased understanding of science and engineering and to ensure adequate supply of scientists for country's needs.

National Transportation Safety Board (NTSB) 800 Independence Ave. S.W., Washington, D.C. 20594. (202) 382-6600. Created Apr. 1, 1975, by Independent Safety Board Act of 1974. Ensures safe operation of all types of transportation in U.S. Investigates accidents, conducts studies, and makes policy recommendations to government agencies, transportation industry, and others on ways to implement and improve safety measures and programs.

Nuclear Regulatory Commission (NRC) 1717 H St. N.W., Washington, D.C. 20555. (202) 492-7000. Created by Energy Reorganization Act of 1974. Licenses and regulates uses of civilian nuclear energy to protect public health and environment. Sets licensing regulations, issues licenses for, and inspects construction, ownership, and operation of nuclear reactors and other nuclear materials.

Occupational Safety and Health Review Commission (OSHRC) 1825 K St. N.W., Washington, D.C. 20006. (202) 634-7943. Created by Occupational Safety and Health Act of 1970. Adjudicates disputes forwarded by Department of Labor over results of safety and health inspections performed by Occupational Safety and Health Administration (OSHA). Serves as court of both first and last resort for health and safety violations in workplace.

Office of Personnel Management (OPM) 1900 E St. N.W., Washington, D.C. 20415. (202) 632-5491. Created Jan. 1, 1979, by Reorganization Plan No. 2 of 1978. Recruits, examines, trains, and promotes people for government jobs, regardless of race, religion, sex, political influence, and other nonmerit factors. Provides direct benefits to employees and to retired employees and their survivors.

Office of the Special Counsel 1120 Vermont Ave. N.W., Washington, D.C. 20005. (202) 653-7188; (800) 872-9855. Investigates allegations of personnel practice violations by federal, state, and local employees and other personnel wrongdoings before the Merit Systems Protection Board.

Panama Canal Commission Room 560, 2000 L St. N.W., Washington, D.C. 20036. (202) 634-6441. Created by Panama Canal Act of 1979. Operates, maintains, and improves the Panama Canal to provide safe and economical transit for world shipping.

Peace Corps 806 Connecticut Ave. N.W., Washington, D.C. 20526. (202) 254-6886 (locator); (202) 254-5010 (public information). Created by Peace Corps Act of 1961. Promotes world peace and friendship. Helps people of other countries develop manpower. Promotes understanding of American people by people abroad and vice versa. Special emphasis placed on helping poorest areas of countries served by the Peace Corps.

Pennsylvania Avenue Development Corporation (PADC) Suite 1220 North, 1331 Pennsylvania Ave. N.W., Washington, D.C. 20004-1703. (202) 724-9091. Created by act of Oct. 27, 1972. Guides and oversees development and revitalization of Pennsylvania Avenue between White House and Capitol and adjacent blocks north of the avenue.

Pension Benefit Guaranty Corporation (PBGC) 2020 K St. N.W., Washington, D.C. 20006. (202) 778-8800. Created Sept. 2, 1974, by Title IV of Employee Retirement Income Security Act of 1974. Guarantees payment of nonforfeitable pension benefits in covered private-sector defined benefit pension plans.

Postal Rate Commission 1333 H St. N.W., Washington, D.C. 20268-0001. (202) 789-6800. Created Aug. 12, 1970, by Postal Reorganization Act. Recommends changes in postal rates, fees, services, programs, studies, and mail classification schedules. Hears complaints about postal rates, services, and fees.

Railroad Retirement Board 844 Rush St., Chicago, IL 60611. (312) 751-4776. Washington Legislative/Liaison Office: 2000 L St. N.W., Washington, D.C. 20036. (202) 653-9540. Created by Railroad Retirement Act of 1935. Administers comprehensive retirement-survivor and unemployment-sickness benefit programs for railroad workers and their families under Railroad Retirement and Railroad Unemployment Insurance Acts. Assists in administration of employee protection measures provided by other federal railroad legislation.

Securities and Exchange Commission (SEC) 450 Fifth St. N.W., Washington, D.C. 20549. (202) 272-3100. Created July 2, 1934, by Securities Exchange Act of 1934. Provides fullest possible disclosure to the public of securities sales, operations, and registrations. Protects public against malpractice in securities and financial markets.

Selective Service System National Headquarters, Washington, D.C. 20435. (202) 724-0820. Created June 24, 1948, by Military Selective Service Act. Requires registration, and maintains list of males age 18-26 eligible to serve in armed forces in case of national security emergency.

Small Business Administration (SBA) Imperial Building, 1441 L St. N.W., Washington, D.C. 20416. (202) 653-6554 (personnel locator); (202) 653-7561 (answer desk); (800) 368-5855 (toll-free); (202) 653-7557 (fraud-waste). Created by Small Business Act of 1953. Aids, counsels, makes loans to, and protects interests of small businesses. Ensures that small businesses receive fair amount of government purchases and contracts and sales of government property.

Tennessee Valley Authority (TVA) 400 West Summit Hill Drive, Knoxville, TN 37902. (615) 632-2101. Capitol Hill Office Building, 412 First St. S.E., Washington, D.C. 20444. (202) 245-0101. Created by act of May 18, 1933. Government-owned corporation. Conducts resource development programs for advancement of growth in Tennessee Valley region. Controls floods, develops navigation, produces electric power, develops fertilizer, improves recreation, and develops forestry and wildlife.

United States Arms Control and Disarmament Agency (ACDA) 320 21st St. N.W., Washington, D.C. 20451. (202) 647–4000. Created by act of Sept. 26, 1961. Formulates and implements arms control and disarmament policies to promote security and foreign relations. Prepares and participates in negotiations with Soviet Union and other countries on issues such as strategic arms limitations, mutual force reductions in central Europe, chemical weapons, and worldwide arms trade.

United States Information Agency (USIA) 301 Fourth St. S.W., Washington, D.C. 20547. (202) 485–7700. Created by United States Information and Educational Exchange Act of 1948 and Mutual Educational and Cultural Exchange Act of 1961. Oversees and administers overseas information and cultural programs, including Voice of America and Fulbright scholarship program. Strengthens foreign understanding of American society and tries to obtain support abroad for U.S. foreign policies. Advises president and National Security Council on worldwide opinion of U.S. policies.

United States International Development Cooperation Agency (IDCA) 320 21st St. N.W., Washington, D.C. 20523. (202) 647–1850. Created Oct. 1, 1979, by Reorganization Plan No. 2 of 1979. Plans, sets, and coordinates policy relevant to international economic issues affecting developing countries. Ensures that development goals are considered in all executive-branch policies regarding trade, financing and monetary affairs, technology, and other economic issues. It is divided into three umbrella agencies.

AGENCY FOR INTERNATIONAL DEVELOPMENT (AID) Carries out economic assistance and self-help programs for people in developing countries. Improves human and natural resources, quality of life, and political and economic stability.

OVERSEAS PRIVATE INVESTMENT CORPORATION (OPIC) Facilitates, fosters, and encourages U.S. investments in more than 100 foreign countries that both reap profits for investors and help social and economic development of the countries.

TRADE AND DEVELOPMENT PROGRAM (TDP) Created July 1, 1980. Promotes economic development. Exports U.S. goods and services to Third World countries. Finances studies for development projects for Third-World countries.

United States International Trade Commission 701 E St. N.W., Washington, D.C. 20436. (202) 523–0161. Created by act of Sept. 8, 1916. Furnishes studies, reports, and recommendations regarding international trade and tariffs to president, Congress, and other government agencies. Conducts investigations, public hearings, and research projects pertaining to U.S. international economic policies.

United States Postal Service 475 L'Enfant Plaza S.W., Washington, D.C. 20260–0010. (202) 268–2000. Created Aug. 12, 1970, by Postal Reorganization Act. Provides mail-processing and delivery service to individuals and businesses in U.S. Protects mail from loss or theft and apprehends violators of postal laws.

Quasi-Official Agencies

Legal Services Corporation 400 Virginia Ave. S.W., Washington, D.C. 20024–2751. (202) 863–1820. Created by Legal Services Act of 1974. Provides financial assistance to individuals, firms, corporations, and programs engaged in furnishing legal assistance to people who cannot afford legal services. Establishes maximum income-levels for eligibility.

National Railroad Passenger Corporation (AMTRAK) 400 North Capitol St. N.W., Washington, D.C. 20001. (202) 383–3000. Created by Rail Passenger Service Act of 1970. Develops, operates, and improves intercity rail passenger service to create national rail transportation system.

Smithsonian Institution 1000 Jefferson Drive S.W., Washington, D.C. 20560. (202) 357–1300. Created by act of Aug. 10, 1846. Performs fundamental research; publishes results of studies, explorations, and investigations; preserves for study and research more than 100 million items of scientific, cultural, and historical interest. Maintains exhibits representative of arts, American history, technology, aeronautics, and natural history. Many institutions and museums are under direction of Smithsonian. Most prominent are Arthur M. Sackler Gallery (in Cambridge, Mass.), Cooper-Hewitt Museum of Design (in New York City), National Air and Space Museum, National Zoological Park, Smithsonian Astrophysical Laboratories, National Gallery of Art, and John F. Kennedy Center for the Performing Arts (all in Washington, D.C.).

State Justice Institute 120 South Fairfax St., Alexandria, Va. 22314. (703) 684–6100. Created by State Justice Institute Act of 1984. Directs and ensures protection of fair and effective judicial system, fosters cooperation with federal judiciary, and disseminates information regarding state judicial systems.

United States Institute of Peace 1550 M St. N.W., Washington, D.C. 20005–1708. (202) 457–1700. Created by act of Oct. 19, 1984. Develops and disseminates knowledge about peaceful resolution of international conflicts. Provides grants to other institutions promoting peace through development and dissemination of information.

> *"You must not complicate your government beyond the capacity of its electorate to understand it. If you do . . . it will lose the public confidence."*
> —H. L. Mencken

Federal Employees and Budget Outlays by Agency 1989

Federal Jobs and Salaries

The U.S government employs more than 3 million civilian employees, or roughly 3% of the entire civilian work-force. Members of the federal civil service represent more than 900 occupations, from parachute packing (65 employees), instrument dial painting (8), door systems mechanic (4), to funeral directing (41), clothing design (45), and nuclear material courier (220). Over 100 agencies direct their efforts, though three—the Department of Defense, the Postal Service, and the Veterans Administration—account for 75% of all federal workers.

In the decade 1977–87, federal employment grew 7%, though this growth owes much to the growth of the Department of Defense and the Postal Service (14% combined), and the Veterans Administration (9%). Employment in most other departments fell, owing to a variety of factors. The Department of Health and Human Services, one of the hardest hit, experienced the close of underused public-health facilities, the computerization of operations at the Social Security Administration, and lowered employment ceilings.

In 1987, 80% of all nonpostal worker federal employees were classified as white-collar work-

FEDERAL CIVILIAN EMPLOYMENT, U.S. CIVILIAN POPULATION, AND U.S. CIVILIAN EMPLOYMENT, 1977–87

Year	Federal civilian employment (thousands)	Civilian population (millions)	U.S. civilian employment (millions)
1977	2,854	217	79
1981	2,910	227	88
1983	2,878	232	87
1985	3,001	236	94
1987[1]	3,050	241	98
Change 1977–87			
Number	196	23	20
Percent	7%	11%	25%

Note: Includes all agencies except the CIA and other intelligence organizations. 1. October 1986 through May 1987. **Source:** Congressional Budget Office, *Federal Civilian Employment* (1987).

ers, and 20% were blue collar. Within the former category, the tendency has been toward more skilled professional and administrative jobs—an increase from 35% to 42% in the last decade—and the number of employees holding a bachelor's degree or better rose from 25% to 31%. In addition to being well educated, federal employees are well entrenched: their average tenure is 13.5 years, down from 14.1 in 1976. In recent years there has been an increase in retirements, especially from the Senior Executive Service (SES), the top echelon of government managers. From 1981 to 1987, retirements from the SES rose from 3.8% to 6.1%, raising concern about the government's ability to retain and attract experienced executives.

Roughly three dozen pay systems, determined by acts of Congress or delegated by Congress to the directors of specific agencies,

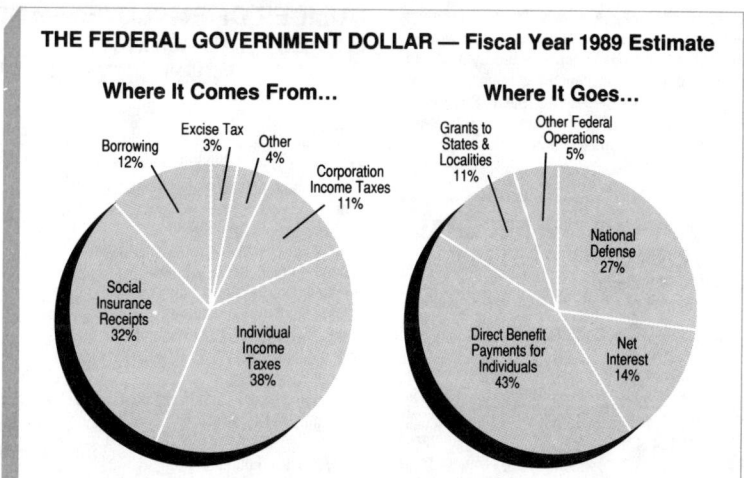

THE FEDERAL GOVERNMENT DOLLAR — Fiscal Year 1989 Estimate

Where It Comes From...

- Borrowing 12%
- Excise Tax 3%
- Other 4%
- Corporation Income Taxes 11%
- Social Insurance Receipts 32%
- Individual Income Taxes 38%

Where It Goes...

- Grants to States & Localities 11%
- Other Federal Operations 5%
- National Defense 27%
- Direct Benefit Payments for Individuals 43%
- Net Interest 14%

TOP 20 GOVERNMENT-SCHEDULE WHITE-COLLAR OCCUPATIONS, BY NUMBER EMPLOYED, 1987

	Number employed	Average salary
Secretary	101,096	$18,437
Miscellaneous clerk and assistant	62,096	17,250
Clerk typist	59,714	13,888
Computer specialist	44,033	35,101
Nurse	38,920	29,031
Miscellaneous administration and programs	36,941	38,458
Supply clerical and technician	29,274	31,837
Criminal investigating	27,466	38,226
Electronics engineering	27,136	40,916
Engineering technician	26,193	28,084
Mail and file clerk	23,674	14,705
Air traffic control	23,486	38,869
Accounting technician	22,350	18,481
Tax examining	21,420	17,716
Electronics technician	20,911	32,958
General engineering	20,296	47,190
Social insurance administrator	20,079	31,798
General attorney	18,698	50,188
Program analysis	18,026	38,935

TOP 5 GOVERNMENT-SCHEDULE BLUE-COLLAR OCCUPATIONS, BY NUMBER EMPLOYED, 1987

Occupation	Number employed	Average salary
Warehouse working	24,896	$21,310
Aircraft mechanic	15,601	26,810
Heavy mobile equipment mechanic	13,070	25,279
Food service working	12,351	17,902
Sheet metal mechanic	12,241	25,728

Note: As of Sept. 30, 1987. **Source:** U.S. Office of Personnel Management, *Occupations of Federal White-Collar and Blue-Collar Workers* (1987).

NUMBER OF EMPLOYEES AND BUDGET OUTLAYS BY FEDERAL AGENCIES

EXECUTIVE DEPARTMENTS OF THE WHITE HOUSE

Department	Employees[1]	Outlays '87[2] (thousands)	Outlays '88[3] (thousands)	Outlays '89[4] (thousands)
Agriculture	116,372	$ 52,518	$ 59,874	$ 55,493
Commerce	53,037	2,155	2,420	2,413
Defense (civil functions only)	31,765	35,137	36,887	38,460
Education	4,546	19,608	20,257	24,213
Energy	16,987	10,125	10,756	12,530
Health & Human Services	122,257	159,715	176,731	191,417
HHS (Social Security only)	—	221,992	251,468	273,336
Housing & Urban Development	13,359	14,657	15,410	16,510
Interior	73,946	5,279	5,436	4,794
Justice	77,731	5,210	5,382	6,155
Labor	18,294	30,252	31,472	31,712
State	25,231	3,765	3,740	3,837
Transportation	64,137	26,122	27,079	26,088
Treasury	161,570	181,857	198,968	215,752
Veterans Affairs	244,921	27,363	28,129	30,097
TOTAL Executive depts.	**1,024,153**	**$795,755**	**$874,009**	**$932,807**

INDEPENDENT AGENCIES AND CORPORATIONS

Agency	Employees	Outlays '87 (thousands)	Outlays '88 (thousands)	Outlays '89 (thousands)
ACTION	446	$ 156	$ 163.1	$ 166.0
Administrative Conference of the U.S.	24	1.5	1.9	1.9
African Development Foundation	33	6.6	7.0	7.1
Agency for International Development	4,725[5]	1,444.6	1,527.6	1,501.4
American Battle Monuments Commission	393	14.8	12.4	15.1
Appalachian Regional Commission	5	105.0	107.0	N.A.
Board for International Broadcasting	15	173.2	219.0	227.1
Central Intelligence Agency	N.A.	125.8	134.7	144.5
Commission on Bicentennial of Constitution	65	13.2	21.0	11.4
Commission on Civil Rights	99	7.5	5.7	13.4
Commission of Fine Arts	7	4.5	4.9	0.5
Commodities Futures Trading Commission	545	29.8	32.8	35.6
Consumer Product Safety Commission	530	24.6	32.7	32.9
Environmental Protection Agency	15,381	5,343.5	4,963.7	4,680.2
Equal Employment Opportunity Commission	3,069	169.5	179.8	194.6
Export-Import Bank of U.S.	327	78.1	110.0	336.0

govern the wages and salaries of federal employees. The majority of blue-collar workers are covered by the Federal Wage System, and white-collar workers by three major statutory pay systems: the General Schedule, the Foreign Service, and one affecting certain employees of the Veterans Administration.

GROWTH OF THE FEDERAL GOVERNMENT, 1901–88
(millions of dollars)

Year	Number of employees[1]	Receipts	Outlays	Surplus or deficit (–)
1901	239,476	$ 588	$ 525	$ 63
1910	388,708	676	694	–18
1920	655,265	6,649	6,358	291
1930	601,319	4,058	3,320	738
1940	1,042,420	6,548	9,468	–2,920
1945	3,816,310	45,159	92,712	–47,553
1950	1,960,708	39,443	42,562	–3,119
1960	2,398,704	92,492	92,191	301
1970	2,984,574	192,807	195,649	–2,842
1980	2,875,866	517,112	590,920	–73,808
1984	2,966,426	666,457	851,781	–185,324
1986	3,045,683	769,091	990,258	–221,167
1988	3,126,697	909,163[2]	1,055,904[2]	–146,741[2]

1. Paid civilians only.   2. Estimate.   **Sources:** U.S. Bureau of the Census, *The Statistical History of the U.S.* (1976); U.S. Office of Personnel Management; Office of Management and Budget, *Budget of the U.S. Government, FY 1989.*

SALARIES OF THE PRESIDENT AND VICE PRESIDENT, CONGRESS, AND JUDGES

EXECUTIVE
President	$250,000
Expense allowances	90,000
Vice president	115,000
Expense allowances	10,000

LEGISLATIVE
Speaker of the House	$115,000
Expense allowances	10,000
President pro tem. of the senate and majority and minority leaders in the House and Senate	99,500
Congressmen	89,500

JUDICIAL
Chief Justice	$115,000
Associate justices	110,000
Circuit judges	95,000
District and other judges	89,500

NUMBER OF EMPLOYEES AND BUDGET OUTLAYS BY FEDERAL AGENCIES
INDEPENDENT AGENCIES AND CORPORATIONS

Agency	Employees	Outlays '87 (thousands)	Outlays '88 (thousands)	Outlays '89 (thousands)
Farm Credit Administration	574	N.A.	N.A.	N.A.
Federal Communications Commission	1,859	87.5	75.0	72.2
Federal Deposit Insurance Corporation	8,111	1,099.3	903.0	27.0
Federal Election Commission	268	12.9	14.2	15.4
Federal Emergency Management Agency	2,563	644.2	649.2	714.7
Federal Home Loan Bank Board	1,289	1,600.0	3,986.0	2,000.0
Federal Labor Relations Authority	254	16.6	17.6	17.6
Federal Maritime Commission	217	11.9	13.6	15.2
Federal Mediation & Conciliation Service	319	23.9	24.5	24.9
Federal Mine Safety/Health Review Commission	49	3.8	3.9	4.1
Federal Reserve System	1,514	N.A.	N.A.	N.A.
Federal Retirement Thrift Investment Board	71	154.8	N.A.	N.A.
Federal Trade Commission	998	65.0	66.2	68.0
General Services Administration	19,989	280.9	–1.2	32.4
Inter-American Foundation	71	11.8	13.0	13.9
Interstate Commerce Commission	714	46.8	44.3	14.4
Merit Systems Protection Board	367	23.9	25.6	25.2
NASA	22,297	10,923.1	8,926.5	11,488.0
National Archives & Records Administration	2,971	101.7	116.3	117.9
National Capital Planning Commission	40	2.7	2.9	2.9
National Credit Union Administration	808	N.A.	N.A.	N.A.
National Foundation/Arts & Humanities	599	325.4	330.1	330.1
National Labor Relations Board	2,378	132.2	133.1	138.6
National Mediation Board	54	6.5	7.0	6.6
National Science Foundation	1,221	1,622.8	1,717.0	2,050.0
National Transportation Safety Board	350	22.2	24.0	24.6
Nuclear Regulatory Commission	3,343	401.0	392.8	450.0
Occupational Safety & Health Review Commission	70	5.8	5.9	6.0
Office of Personnel Management	6,740	44,775.3	47,678.8	50,455.7
Office of the Special Counsel	N.A.	N.A.	N.A.	N.A.
Overseas Private Investment Corporation	N.A.	N.A.	N.A.	25.4
Panama Canal Commission	8,610	5.0	176.9	N.A.
Peace Corps	1,193	138.0	146.2	150.0
Pennsylvania Avenue Development Corporation	37	6.3	5.5	5.4
Pension Benefit Guaranty Corporation	557	N.A.	N.A.	N.A.
Postal Service[6]	839,319	2,944.0	1,699.1	2,412.1
Railroad Retirement Board	1,678	4,858.1	4,961.1	4,581.1
Securities and Exchange Commission	2,189	114.5	135.2	159.8
Selective Service System	268	26.1	25.5	26.1
Small Business Administration	4,609	603.7	475.0	778.1
Smithsonian Institution	5,027	251.9	271.2	296.2
Tennessee Valley Authority	27,655	1,342.5	1,371.9	888.6
U.S. Information Agency	8,797	847.6	820.9	881.2
U.S. Institute of Peace	40	1.0	N.A.	N.A.
U.S. International Development Cooperation Agency	4,875	N.A.	N.A.	N.A.
U.S. International Trade Commission	496	33.9	34.8	37.1
Miscellaneous	2,843	N.A.	N.A.	N.A.
TOTAL ind. agencies & corps.	**1,013,955**	**$81,273.1**	**$82,815.9**	**$85,724.2**

JUDICIAL BRANCH

Agency	Employees	Outlays '87 (thousands)	Outlays '88 (thousands)	Outlays '89 (thousands)
Supreme Court	339	$ 17.8	$ 17.4	$ 18.4
Ct. of Appeals, Dist. Courts, etc.	20,955	1,180.0	1,250.5	1,626.8
Administrative offices	N.A.	30.2	31.2	42.0
Miscellaneous	N.A.	25.9	25.7	29.4
TOTAL Judicial	**21,294**	**$1,253.9**	**$1,324.8**	**$1,716.6**

NUMBER OF EMPLOYEES AND BUDGET OUTLAYS BY FEDERAL AGENCIES

LEGISLATIVE BRANCH

Agency	Employees	Outlays '87 (thousands)	Outlays '88 (thousands)	Outlays '89 (thousands)
U.S. Senate	7,185	$ 338.2	$ 348.1	$ 386.4
House of Representatives	11,950	564.0	567.4	628.3
Architect of the Capitol	2,152	10.3	11.3	12.1
U.S. Botanic Garden	55	2.1	12.2	2.5
General Accounting Office	5,359	311.0	329.8	393.9
Government Printing Office	5,129	95.1	89.5	104.5
Library of Congress	4,848	289.5	306.4	332.6
Office of Technology Assessment	208	16.6	16.9	18.3
Congressional Budget Office	211	17.8	17.9	18.9
Copyright Royalty Tribunal	7	0.1	0.1	0.1
United States Tax Court	335	25.6	27.8	29.4
Miscellaneous	54	202.0	178.3	195.4
TOTAL Legislative	**37,493**	**$1,872.3**	**$1,905.7**	**$2,122.4**

EXECUTIVE BRANCH

Agency	Employees	Outlays '87 (thousand)	Outlays '88 (thousand)	Outlays '89 (thousand)
White House Office	368	$ 24.8	$ 26.4	$ 28.0
Office of Vice President	27	0.2	0.3	0.3
Office of Management & Budget	561	39.0	41.3	42.1
Council of Economic Advisers	33	2.4	2.5	2.8
National Security Council	58	4.6	5.0	5.1
Office of Policy Development	36	2.7	3.0	3.0
Office of U.S. Trade Rep.	158	13.5	15.2	15.4
Council on Environ. Quality	12	0.8	0.8	0.9
Office of Sci. & Technol. Policy	11	1.9	1.9	1.8
Office of Administration	222	15.9	16.0	16.9
Miscellaneous	90	12.2	13.0	8.2
TOTAL Executive	**1,576**	**$118.0**	**$125.4**	**$124.5**
Funds appropriated to president		$13,002.2	$10,474.4	$10,627.9
TOTAL (as detailed above)		**893,372.3**	**970,680.5**	**1,033,094.7**
SUBTOTAL (according to OMB)[7]		**892,724.1**	**970,227.3**	**1,032,266.7**
Undistributed offsetting receipts		−72,300.0	−77,700.0	−89,900.0
TOTAL Civilian	**2,098,471**	**820,424.1**	**892,527.3**	**942,366.7**
Defense (military)[8]	1,022,124	279,469.2	283,159.1	290,784.0
TOTAL	**3,120,595**	**$1,099,893.3**	**$1,175,686.4**	**$1,233,150.7**

Note: Excludes some part-time workers under special programs. 1. Figures for November 1988. 2. Actual. 3. Estimate. 4. Estimate. 5. Estimate for 1988. November 1988 figures not available. 6. Includes Postal Rate Commission. 7. Disparity between detailed total and subtotal due to rounding. 8. By law, military functions of the Department of Defense are exempt from full-time equivalent employment controls. **Sources:** Budget figures: Office of Management and Budget, *Budget of the U.S. Government 1989* (1988); personnel figures: Office of Personnel Management.

BUDGET RECEIPTS BY SOURCE, 1980–89
(millions of dollars)

Source	ACTUAL 1980	ACTUAL 1985	ACTUAL 1987	ESTIMATE 1988	ESTIMATE 1989
Individual income tax	$244,069	$334,531	$392,557	$393,395	$412,353
Corporation income tax	64,600	61,331	83,926	105,567	117,704
Social insurance taxes and contributions[1]	157,803	265,163	303,318	331,513	354,565
Excise taxes[2]	24,329	35,992	32,457	35,342	35,213
Estate and gift taxes	6,389	6,422	7,493	7,567	7,795
Customs duties	7,174	12,079	15,085	16,399	17,244
Miscellaneous receipts[3]	12,748	18,539	19,307	19,380	19,819
Total	**$517,112**	**$734,057**	**$854,143**	**$909,163**	**$964,674**

1. Includes old age, survivors, disability, and hospital insurance (OASDHI), railroad retirement, unemployment insurance, federal employees retirement employee contributions, and contributions for nonfederal employees. 2. Includes federal funds and trust funds. 3. Includes deposits of earnings by federal reserve system. **Source:** Office of Management and Budget *Budget of the U.S. Govt., FY 1989.*

The General Schedule (GS) Covers almost half of all federal employees (1,480,150 people as of Mar. 31, 1988). There are 18 grades broadly defined in terms of responsibility, difficulty, and qualifications. Within each grade are steps (10 each for GS-1–15, nine for GS-16, five for GS-17, and one for GS-18). Within-grade advancement occurs on a fixed schedule, though employees demonstrating "high quality performance" can receive "quality step increases."

THE GENERAL SCHEDULE

Grade	Employees	Mean salary
GS-1	1,544	$10,039
GS-2	11,908	11,568
GS-3	57,764	13,153
GS-4	153,645	15,120
GS-5	200,208	17,181
GS-6	95,678	19,425
GS-7	145,391	21,193
GS-8	30,505	24,116
GS-9	156,344	25,747
GS-10	28,984	29,378
GS-11	185,479	31,400
GS-12	189,892	37,995
GS-13	125,807	45,580
GS-14	65,352	54,270
GS-15	30,829	65,067
GS-16	652	71,786
GS-17	106	72,500
GS-18	62	72,500

Note: As of March 31, 1988. Salaries paid under the General Schedule increased 4% as of Jan. 1, 1989. **Source:** U.S. Office of Personnel Management, *Pay Structure of the Federal Civil Service* (1988).

The Executive Schedule (ES) Five grades cover senior-level employees in the executive branch. Broadly speaking, the levels cover the following job descriptions: level I—cabinet members; level II—deputy secretaries of major departments; level III—presidential advisers, chief administrators of major independent agencies, undersecretaries; level IV—assistant secretaries, deputy undersecretaries, and general counsels in executive departments; level V—deputy assistant secretaries, administrators, commissioners, and directors.

THE EXECUTIVE SCHEDULE, 1988

Level	Salary
I	$99,500
II	89,500
III	82,500
III	82,500
IV	77,500
V	72,500

Note: As of Jan. 1, 1988. **Source:** U.S. Office of Personnel Management, *Pay Structure of the Federal Civil Service* (1988).

Key Government Functions

FEDERAL SOCIAL INSURANCE PROGRAMS

In order to provide a safety net for disadvantaged, elderly, and disabled persons, the federal government administers a range of social insurance and social assistance programs, including Medicare, unemployment insurance, workers' compensation, and temporary disability insurance. Also included are an array of "income support programs" such as supplemental security income, aid to families with dependent children, Medicaid, food stamps, low-income home-energy assistance, public housing, special nutritional programs, and general assistance. Three additional programs provide for veterans, public employees, and railroad employees.

Social insurance programs were not developed all at once to fulfill a specific agenda of national need. Rather, they are a hodgepodge of legislation passed (and often altered) over the years to meet the needs of particular groups of citizens at particular times. In what the government calls social insurance programs, certain risks—injury, disability, unemployment, old age, and death—are lumped together. "Premiums," usually in the form of a payroll tax, are paid by employees and/or their employers. The benefit is paid, regardless of other financial resources (other than earnings), when one of those "risks" occurs.

Social Security

The Great Depression proved that the traditional support systems—the family, private charities, and local government—failed in nationwide economic hard times. Many old people had exhausted their savings and were destitute; in fact, during the depression less than 10% of the aged left estates large enough to be probated. This led to the enactment of one of the most comprehensive pieces of legislation ever passed by Congress, the Social Security Act.

Signed into law by Franklin Roosevelt on Aug. 14, 1935, the act established two social insurance programs: a federal system of old-age benefits for retired workers in commerce and industry and a federal-state system of unemployment insurance. The law also provided for federal matching grants-in-aid to states to help them assist the needy aged, blind persons, and children. Today, in the words of former Social Security Commissioner Dorcas R. Hardy, it is the "most complex government program that God and Congress ever created."

THE SOCIAL SECURITY SYSTEM: WHO PAYS, HOW MUCH

Year	Top wage base	Tax rate for retirement survivors and disability insurance	Tax rate for hospital insurance (Medicare)	Total for employee and employer (each)
EMPLOYEE WORKERS				
1988	$45,000	6.06%	1.45%	7.51%
1989	48,000	6.06	1.45	7.51
1990 on	50,100	6.20	1.45	7.65
SELF-EMPLOYED WORKERS				
1988	$45,000	12.12%	2.90%	15.02%
1989	48,000	12.12	2.90	15.02
1990 on	50,000	12.40	2.90	15.30

WHO RECEIVES, HOW MUCH

Program	People covered	Total cost (billions)
Old-Age, Survivors and Disability Insurance (OASDI)	38.6 million (61% retired, 7% disabled, 32% spouses or children of disabled, deceased, or retired workers)	$217.0 (1988)
Medicare	28.2 million age 65 and over 2.9 million disabled under 65	70.7 (1985)
Medicaid	21.8 million	41.3 (1985)
Food Stamps	19.4 million	10.6 (1985)
Aid to Families with Dependent Children (AFDC)	11.03 million children and adults in 3.7 million families	16.3 (1985)
Supplemental Security Income (SSI)	4.3 million (2 million age 65 or older)	11.7 (1986)

APPROXIMATE MONTHLY RETIREMENT BENEFITS FOR WORKERS RETIRING AT NORMAL RETIREMENT AGE

Worker's age in 1989	Worker's family	Retired worker's earnings in 1989			
		$15,000	$25,000	$35,000	$45,000 +
55	Retired worker only	626	897	994	1,063
	Worker and spouse[1]	939	1,147	1,429	1,594
65	Retired worker only	563	800	865	899
	Worker and spouse[1]	844	1,032	1,261	1,348

Note: To estimate your retirement benefit, find your age and the figure closest to your earnings in 1987. The accuracy of these estimates depends on the pattern of actual past and future earnings. 1. Spouse is assumed to be the same age as the worker. Spouse may qualify for a higher retirement benefit based on his or her own work record. **Source:** Dept. of Health and Human Services, Social Security Administration publication, *Retirement* (1989).

The first payments of monthly benefits were made in 1940. Major changes in the scope of Social Security were made in 1956, when the program was broadened through the addition of disability insurance; in 1965, through the addition of Medicare and Medicaid; in 1970, when the "black lung" program was developed to provide benefits to coal miners (and their survivors) who suffer from pneumoconiosis (black lung disease); and in 1974, when Social Security insurance was taken over by the Social Security Administration. Since the first check went out half a century ago, $22 trillion in cash benefits have been paid.

In 1990 the Social Security program will spend almost $200 billion per year. Bankrupt just five years ago, the system today is paying its own way, and huge surpluses are projected. Through a system of quick increases in both the tax rate and the amount of taxable income, the program quickly began building reserves because there were millions more workers paying into the system than there were retirees and others receiving benefits. In 1987 the government was collecting $110 million a day more than needed for current payouts. Thanks to the baby boomers in the work force, projections show annual surpluses reaching $500 million a day or close to $200 billion a year by the start of the next century.

Workers and their employers each contribute an equal amount to the Social Security program to pay for retirement, disability, and Medicare benefits. The amount deducted from paychecks has increased steadily since 1983, and will level off in 1990 at 7.65% on earnings up to an estimated $50,000 (depending on inflation). Employers must contribute the same amount. Self-employed workers pay twice the employee rate. The elderly benefit more than any other group. They pay about 10% of the total income and payroll taxes and receive more than 68% of Social Security benefits, including Medicare, food stamps, and housing subsidies.

Old-Age, Survivors and Disability Insurance (OASDI) The program's basic principles are that benefits are related to earnings in covered work, benefits are paid regardless of income from savings, pensions, etc., and universal compulsory coverage is to assure a base of economic security. Monthly benefits are payable at age 65 to workers who are eligible, and lump sum payments are made to the estates of workers who die before reaching 65. The addition of disability insurance in 1956 broadened the program's scope, and in 1972 Congress authorized provisions for cost-of-living increases. The 1983 amendments improved the program's financial footing with tax rate increases, permanent increases in self-employment tax rates, and taxing up to one-half of benefits for certain upper-income beneficiaries. (The latter applies to single retirees with adjusted gross income above $25,000 and married couples above $32,000.)

Eligibility Insured status: A worker must have a specific amount of work-covered employment (about 95% of all jobs today are covered by the program, compared with 60% in 1937). Persons reaching age 62 in 1991 or later will need credit for 10 years of work in covered jobs to qualify for retirement benefits. If a worker dies before achieving fully insured status, survivor benefits may be paid to his or her spouse.

Annual Earnings Test Monthly benefits are paid to a worker and to his or her family members and survivors only when they do not have substantial earnings from work. A retiree under 65 may earn up to $6,480. A retiree age 65 to 69 may earn $8,800 in income before benefits are reduced. Retirees over age 70 receive benefits regardless of income.

Disability Requirement For monthly benefits, the impairment must prohibit the individual from engaging in any kind of substantial gainful work (up to $300 a month). Work is encouraged by referrals to state vocational rehabilitation agencies, and the individual is allowed a

AVERAGE MONTHLY BENEFITS FOR OASDI PROGRAMS, 1989

All retired workers	$ 537
Aged couple, both receiving benefits	921
Widowed mother and two children	1,112
Aged widow alone	492
Disabled worker, wife and children	943
All disabled workers	529

Source: Social Security Administration.

NUMBER OF PERSONS RECEIVING OASDI BENEFITS, 1940–86, AND AVERAGE MONTHLY PAYMENT, 1986

Type of Beneficiary	1940	1960	1980	1986	Average monthly payment
All beneficiaries	222,488	14,844,589	35,618,840	37,708,225	$438.56
Retired workers	112,331	8,061,469	16,582,625	222,986,678	488.44
Disabled workers	N.A.	455,371	2,861,253	2,727,386	487.86
Spouses of retired and disabled workers	29,749	2,345,983	3,480,212	3,388,435	241.06
Widow(er)s	4,437	1,543,843	4,287,930	4,825,443	444.09
Widowed mothers and fathers	20,499	401,358	562,798	349,982	338.41
Disabled widow(er)s	N.A.	N.A.	126,659	106,039	319.78
Children[1]	56,648	2,000,451	4,609,813	3,290,772	261.44
Parents	824	36,114	14,796	8,699	386.80
Special age-72 beneficiaries	N.A.	N.A.	92,754	24,791	139.65

Note: Figures are for December of each year.   1. Includes children of retired, deceased, and disabled workers, as well as disabled adult children age 18 or older whose disabilities developed before age 22.   **Source:** Social Security Administration, Social Security Bulletin 50:4 (1987).

APPROXIMATE MONTHLY DISABILITY BENEFITS IF THE WORKER BECAME DISABLED IN 1989 AND HAD STEADY EARNINGS

Worker's age	Worker's family	Disabled worker's earnings in 1988			
		$15,000	$25,000	$35,000	$45,000 +
25	Disabled worker only	$585	$ 845	$ 969	$1,100
	Disabled, with dependents[1]	878	1,267	1,454	1,650
35	Disabled worker only	581	838	962	1,055
	Disabled, with dependents[1]	872	1,257	1,443	1,583
45	Disabled worker only	580	837	933	986
	Disabled, with dependents[1]	871	1,256	1,399	1,480
55	Disabled worker only	580	823	898	934
	Disabled, with dependents[1]	871	1,235	1,347	1,401
64	Disabled worker only	577	818	885	919
	Disabled, with dependents[1]	866	1,227	1,328	1,378

1. Includes spouse and child, the maximum family benefit.   **Source:** Social Security Administration publication Disability, 1989.

trial period of work during which benefits continue.

Administration The Social Security Administration, part of the Department of Health and Human Services, manages the OASDI program. The OASI and DI programs are financed from taxes collected on earnings in covered jobs from employees and employers and which are deposited in two separate trust funds. The money received by the trust funds can be used only to pay benefits and operating expenses.

Benefit Amounts A worker's Social Security benefit is based on his or her average "covered" earning computed over the period of time he or she could have been expected to work. Workers become eligible for benefits at age 62. However, a worker who retires at 62 receives only 80% of the full amount that would have been payable at age 65. The normal retirement age will be increased gradually from 65 to 67, beginning in 2003. The highest basic monthly payment for workers who retired at age 65 in 1989 and who consistently had earnings at or above the maximum amount was $899.

Medicare The Social Security Amendments of 1965 established two contributory

health-insurance programs designed to provide assistance for medical expenses. The first is a compulsory program of hospital insurance (HI)

MEDICARE: RECIPIENTS, AND BENEFITS PAID
(thousands of persons)

RECIPIENTS

Medicare program	Total enrolled[1]	Total served	Rate served per 1,000 enrolled	Average benefits paid per enrollee[2]
AGED				
Total[3]	28,791	21,066	732	$2,332
HI	28,257	6,002	212	1,562
SMI	27,863	20,919	751	826
DISABLED				
Total[3]	2,959	2,015	681	$2,938
HI	2,959	668	226	1,849
SMI	2,727	1,988	729	1,182

1. As of July 1, 1986.   2. Based on total number of enrollees as of July 1, 1986.   3. Unduplicated counts of persons enrolled under one or both parts of the program.   **Source:** Dept. of Health and Human Services, Fast Facts & Figures about Social Security (1988).

that provides basic protection against the costs of inpatient hospital services and related post-hospital care, including home health services, part-time nursing care, and physical therapy. The average hospital payment made by Medicare in 1989 was $4,700. The 1972 amendments provided that persons reaching age 65 without qualifying for HI may voluntarily enroll by paying a monthly premium. Beginning in 1989, people who were eligible for Medicare and who had taxable income were required to pay a supplemental premium for catastrophic Medicare coverage. The premium rate for 1989 was $22.50 for each $150 of taxable income, with a maximum annual premium of $800 per person.

The second program is supplementary medical insurance (SMI) coverage, a voluntary program of supplemental medical insurance in which enrolled individuals pay a monthly premium of $27.90. The program's coverage includes physician's and surgeon's services, outpatient services and laboratory tests, ambulance services, surgical dressings, home health services, and comprehensive outpatient services.

Administration In March 1977, management of Medicare was transferred from the Social Security Administration to the Health Care Financing Administration. Hospital insurance is financed by tax on earnings. (In 1989, for example, the 7.51% payroll tax was divided, with 6.06% going to OASDI and 1.45% to HI.)

Effectiveness of Social Security

According to the government, the Social Security system has achieved its basic goal of helping elderly people maintain a basic standard of living. It has dramatically reduced the poverty rate for the elderly from 35% in 1959 to 12.6% in 1985. The benefits are the primary source of cash income for most elderly Americans, providing at least 50% of total income for 62% of retirees age 65 and over. For another 24% of the elderly, it constitutes 90% or more of total income. And for another 14% of the elderly, Social Security is the only source of income. For all people receiving Social Security benefits—not just the elderly—the payouts lifted 15.1 million out of poverty, reducing the number of poor to 35.5 million in 1986.

Other Social Insurance Programs

Unemployment Insurance The Social Security Act provided an inducement to states to enact unemployment insurance laws, and by 1937 all 48 states, the 10 territories of Alaska and Hawaii, and the District of Columbia had passed such laws. All contributions collected under state laws are deposited in the unemployment trust fund of the U.S. Treasury, but each state maintains a separate account. A state may withdraw money from its account only to pay benefits. Each state has the major responsibility for the content and development of its unemployment insurance law. About 97% of all wage and salary workers were covered in 1986.

Eligibility Workers must be ready, able, and willing to work and must be registered for work

APPROXIMATE MONTHLY SURVIVORS-BENEFITS IF THE WORKER DIED IN 1989 AND HAD STEADY EARNINGS

Worker's age	Worker's family	Disabled worker's earnings in 1988			
		$15,000	$25,000	$35,000	$45,000 +
25	Spouse and 1 child[1]	$ 882	$1,274	$1,458	$1,656
	Spouse and 2 children[2]	1,071	1,488	1,703	1,933
	1 child only	441	637	729	828
	Spouse at age 60	420	607	695	789
35	Spouse and 1 child[1]	872	1,258	1,448	1,622
	Spouse and 2 children[2]	1,055	1,470	1,691	1,893
	1 child only	436	629	724	811
	Spouse at age 60	416	600	690	773
45	Spouse and 1 child[1]	870	1,256	1,406	1,490
	Spouse and 2 children[2]	1,052	1,466	1,642	1,741
	1 child only	435	628	703	745
	Spouse at age 60	415	598	670	710
55	Spouse and 1 child[1]	870	1,234	1,346	1,400
	Spouse and 2 children[2]	1,051	1,442	1,572	1,636
	1 child only	435	617	673	700
	Spouse at age 60	415	588	642	668
65	Spouse and 1 child[1]	844	1,200	1,296	1,348
	Spouse and 2 children[1]	1,023	1,402	1,515	1,575
	1 child only	422	600	648	674
	Spouse at age 60	402	572	618	643

1. Amounts shown also equal the benefits paid to two children, if no parent survives or if surviving parent has substantial earnings.   2. Equals the maximum family benefit.   **Source:** Social Security Administration publication *Survivors*, 1989.

at a state public employment office. A worker's benefit is based on his or her employment in covered work over a prior performance period. No state can deny benefit to a claimant if he or she refuses to accept a new job under substandard labor conditions or where he or she would be required to join a company union. In 1986 the average weekly benefit was $135 and the average duration of benefit was 14.6 weeks. The weekly benefit varies from state to state, but the general formula is designed to compensate for a fraction of the weekly wage, normally 50%. All but three states provide a statutory minimum of 26 weeks of benefits in a benefit year.

Administration All covered employers are charged a tax of 6.2% on the first $7,000 of each worker's covered wages annually. The federal functions of the program are the responsibility of the Employment and Training Administration's Federal Unemployment Insurance Service in the U.S. Department of Labor.

Workers' Compensation Social insurance began in the United States with workers' compensation. A law covering federal civilian employees engaged in hazardous jobs was enacted in 1908, and the first state compensation law to be held constitutional was enacted in 1911. These laws made industry responsible for the compensation of workers (or their survivors) injured or killed while on the job, and were designed to provide cash benefits and medical care when workers were injured in connection with their jobs. A worker incurring an occupational injury is compensated regardless of fault or blame in the accident. A federal program enacted in 1969 protects coal miners suffering from black lung disease. In 1984, $19,529,000 was paid in disability benefits.

Eligibility The cash benefits for temporary

total disability, permanent, total, or partial disability, or death of a breadwinner is usually about 66.6% of weekly earnings at the time of the accident. Most state laws pay temporary disability benefits for as long as the disability lasts and the condition has not been stabilized to the point where no further improvement can result from medical treatment. Maximum weekly benefits range from $140 to $1,114. In 1986 about 87 million employees were covered by compensation laws. The most usual exempted workers are domestic, agricultural, and casual laborers.

Permanent partial disability Compensation for specific, or "schedule," injuries (for clearly measurable matters) is generally subject to different (usually lower) dollar maximums and is determined without regard to loss of earning power. Compensation for "nonschedule" injuries (injuries to head, back, nervous system) is the difference between wages before and after impairment.

Death benefits Compensation is related to earnings and is graduated by the number of dependents.

Medical benefits Furnished without limit as to time or amount for accidental injuries.

Administration of federal provisions are handled by the Employment Standards Administration's Office of Workers' Compensation Programs in the U.S. Department of Labor. Almost exclusively financed by employers, on the principle that the cost of work-related accidents is part of the expense of production. Employers can use private insurance companies or can qualify as self-insurers.

Black Lung Program Established by the Federal Coal Mine Health and Safety Act of 1969, this provides monthly cash benefits to coal miners who are totally disabled because of black lung disease (pneumoconiosis) and to survivors of miners who die from this disease. As of 1985, 450,000 disabled workers, dependents, and survivors were receiving cash benefits. The monthly benefit payable to a disabled miner is a flat amount equal to 37.5% of the monthly pay rate for a federal government employee in the first step of Grade GS-2. As of January 1987, this amounted to $338. The benefit is increased based on the number of dependents, up to $676 for three or more.

Administration is handled by the Employment Standards Administration's Office of Workers' Compensation in the U.S. Department of Labor in conjunction with the Social Security Administration. Most of the benefits are paid out of a trust fund financed by an excise tax on coal.

Temporary Disability Insurance provides coverage against the risk of lost wages due to short-term nonoccupational disability. The Federal Unemployment Tax Act permits states where employees make contributions under the unemployment insurance program to use some or all of those contributions for disability benefits. It is estimated that in 1984 about two-thirds of the nation's wage and salary earners had some protection through various voluntary and governmental group arrangements. In general the benefit amount for a week is intended to replace at least half the weekly wage loss for a maximum of 26 to 39 weeks per year.

Administration Five of the seven temporary disability insurance programs are administered by the Employment and Training Administration in the U.S. Department of Labor. In general there is no government contribution.

Programs for Special Groups

Veterans' Benefits The tradition of veterans' benefits dates back to the 18th century when the Continental Congress provided disability pensions for veterans of the Revolutionary War. World War I triggered the establishment of several veterans' programs including disability compensation, insurance, and vocational rehabilitation. The final significant features of the veterans' benefit system were added in 1944 through the G.I. Bill. Major new features included extensive education benefits and a home loan program.

Compensation Veterans have two major cash benefit programs. The first provides compensation to veterans with service-connected disabilities, and upon the veteran's death, to the spouse, parents, and children. These benefits are paid regardless of the veteran's other income. The amount of monthly compensation depends on the degree of disability. Payments range from $71 a month for 10% disability to $1,411 a month for total disability. In addition specific rates of up to $4,031 a month are paid for veterans suffering certain severe disabilities. Veterans who have at least a 30% service-connected disability are entitled to an additional allowance for dependents.

Pension The second major cash benefit program is a pension for veterans with nonservice-connected disabilities. Monthly cash payments are provided to wartime veterans on limited income who are totally or permanently disabled, or over age 65 and not working. To qualify, a veteran discharged under other than dishonorable conditions must have served at least 90 days during the Mexican border period (1916–17), World War I, World War II, the Korean conflict, or the Vietnam era. The maximum annual benefit ranges from $6,214 for a veteran without dependents to $11,866 a month for a veteran who is in need of regular aid and assistance and who has one dependent. The pension is increased by $1,055 annually for each additional dependent.

Administration All veterans' benefits are administered by the Veterans Administration.

Public Employee Programs In September 1986, 2.2 million federal workers were covered by the Civil Service Retirement System (CSRS), and 500,000 by the Federal Employees' Retirement System (FERS). Under the CSRS, regular benefits are based on the average of a worker's three highest-salaried years, with cost-of-living adjustments made.

Armed Forces Since 1957 all members have been covered by the Social Security system. Those with 20 or more years of service are eligible for retirement benefits under the military retirement system.

State and Local Government The majority of employees are covered by retirement systems maintained by states or localities, whose provisions vary.

Railroad Retirement The Railroad Retirement Act of 1974 (amended in 1981 and 1983) provides individuals with a retirement annuity (and in some cases disability annuities) for 10 years of creditable service. Annuities are also awarded to qualified spouses, children, and parents of deceased career-employees. Additional benefits are also provided under the Railroad Unemployment Insurance Act. Payments are coordinated by the Social Security Administration and the Railroad Retirement Board.

Income Support Programs

To be eligible for these programs, a person must have income and assets below a certain level and often must meet other eligibility criteria. Today Supplemental Security Income (SSI) and Aid to Families with Dependent Children (AFDC) are the two major cash assistance programs. A number of other programs, including Medicaid and food stamps, provide benefits for special needs and purposes.

Poverty Income Guidelines The Poverty Income Guidelines are used to determine whether a person or family is eligible for assistance under a particular federal program. Since 1973 the poverty income guidelines have been computed from the official poverty-threshold by increasing the weighted average poverty-thresholds by the percentage change in the Consumer Price Index during the preced-

VETERANS' COMPENSATION AND BENEFITS, BY PERIOD OF SERVICE AND STATUS, 1980–87

Period of service and veteran status	Veterans on rolls (thousands)			Average payment (annual basis[1])		
	1980	1985	1987	1980	1985	1987
LIVING VETERANS	3,195	2,931	2,844	$2,600	$3,666	$3,821
Service connected	2,273	2,240	2,212	2,669	3,692	3,808
Nonservice connected	922	690	631	2,428	3,581	3,865
DECEASED VETERANS	1,451	1,075	964	1,863	3,066	3,504
Service connected	358	336	328	3,801	5,836	6,296
Nonservice connected	1,093	739	636	1,228	1,809	2,066
PRIOR TO WORLD WAR I	14	7	5	1,432	1,855	2,068
Living	(z)	(z)	(z)	2,634	4,436	5,420
Deceased	14	7	5	1,403	1,822	2,025
WORLD WAR I	692	381	295	1,683	2,461	2,817
Living	198	68	42	2,669	4,439	5,243
Deceased	494	313	253	1,288	2,029	2,415
WORLD WAR II	2,520	2,097	1,943	2,307	3,317	3,513
Living	1,849	1,575	1,464	2,462	3,460	3,621
Deceased	671	522	479	1,880	2,888	3,182
KOREAN CONFLICT[2]	446	399	393	2,691	4,114	4,389
Living	317	309	308	2,977	4,260	4,457
Deceased	129	90	86	1,990	3,615	4,147
PEACETIME	312	404	433	3,080	3,973	3,965
Living	262	352	382	2,828	3,589	3,563
Deceased	50	52	52	4,399	6,577	6,937
VIETNAM ERA[3]	662	716	738	2,795	4,021	4,244
Living	569	626	649	2,709	3,849	4,029
Deceased	93	90	89	3,324	5,220	5,818
Total	**4,646**	**4,006**	**3,808**	**$2,370**	**$3,505**	**$3,741**

Notes: (z) = fewer than 500.   1. Averages calculated by multiplying average monthly payment by 12.   2. Service during period June 27, 1950, to Jan. 31, 1955.   3. Service from Aug. 5, 1964, to May 7, 1975.   **Source:** U.S. Bureau of the Census, *Statistical Abstract of the United States, 1989.*

ing year and rounding the value for a family of four up to the next higher $50. All family sizes above and below four are computed by adding or subtracting equal dollar amounts derived from the average difference between poverty lines, for families with one to eight persons, rounded to the nearest multiple of $20.

Supplemental Security Income (SSI) In 1972 Congress replaced the federal-state programs for the needy aged, blind, and disabled people with the federal supplementary security income program of the Social Security Administration, making eligibility requirements uniform. Monthly cash payments are made to eligible persons whose "countable" income is less than $4,416 per year. Individual assets are limited to $2,000. The qualifying standards for disability benefits are the same as those used for the Social Security disability insurance program. The basic SSI payment is $368 for eligible individuals and $558 for eligible couples. To encourage SSI recipients to work, $85 of earned income in any month is excluded from countable income.
Administration Financing derives from federal government general revenues. Applications are taken at SSA district offices.

Aid to Families with Dependent Children (AFDC) The Social Security Act of 1935 included a provision authorizing a federal-state program to help needy families with children. To qualify for grants, the states must comply with federal guidelines. States may choose whom they will assist, how the assistance will be given, and how much it will be. The states compute "needs standards," taking into account allowances for food, clothing, shelter, utilities, and other necessities. The family's need is theoretically equal to the difference between the amount of the "needs standard" and the family's income. However, states are not required to provide the full amount of the difference. In 1987 the needs standard for a family of three was $497 in New York, $368 in Mississippi, and $421 in Colorado. The average benefit nationwide was $347.19 per family or $118.33 per recipient, ranging from $114.91 per family in Alabama to $602.76 per family in Alaska. To qualify, children generally have to be under the age of 18. AFDC recipients who are employable must register for work in the work incentive program (WIN) and must work a specific number of hours to receive aid.
Administration Cost of the program is shared by federal, state, and local governments. Federal administration is the responsibility of the Family Support Administration in the Department of Health and Human Services.

Medicaid Enacted jointly with Medicare in 1965, Medicaid provides federal matching funds to states to help pay the cost of medical care and services for low-income persons. Payments are made to suppliers of the care and service. To be eligible for matching funds, a state Medicaid program must cover all persons who receive assistance under AFDC. (Most SSI recipients are also covered.) In 1985, 21.8 million aged, blind, disabled, or poor persons with families received Medicaid benefits. Medicaid

POVERTY INCOME GUIDELINES

Family size	Contiguous 48 states	Alaska	Hawaii
1 person	$ 5,500	$ 6,680	$ 6,310
2 people	7,400	9,240	8,500
3 people	9,300	11,620	10,690
4 people	11,200	14,000	12,880
5 people	13,100	16,380	15,070
6 people	15,000	18,760	17,260
7 people	16,900	21,140	19,450
8 people	18,800	23,520	21,640
Increment	1,900	2,380	2,190

Note: As of February 1987. **Source:** Social Security Bulletin 50:4 (1987).

PERSONS RECEIVING SSI PAYMENTS AND AVERAGE BENEFIT AMOUNT, 1987
(thousands of persons)

	Total[1]	Aged	Blind	Disabled
TYPE OF PAYMENT				
Total	**4,303**	**1,509**	**83**	**2,711**
Federal SSI payments	3,887	1,295	74	2,517
Federal SSI payments only	2,528	896	44	1,589
Federal SSI and federally administered state supplements	1,358	400	30	929
State supplements	345	181	8	155
State-administered supplements only	72[2]	32	0.4	38
AMOUNT OF PAYMENT				
Total	**$243**	**$177**	**$289**	**$277**
Federal SSI payments	212	147	235	244
Federally administered supplements only	114	113	160	113
State-administered state supplements	103	99	117	109

1. Figures may not add to total owing to rounding.   2. Includes persons for whom reason for eligibility was not available.   **Source:** Social Security Administration, Social Security Bulletin 50:4 (1987).

FEDERALLY ADMINISTERED SSI PAYMENTS, 1987
(numbers in thousands)

Type of payment	Number	Percent
All recipients	4,385	100%
Federal SSI	4,019	92
Federal SSI only	2,578	59
Federal SSI and state supplementation	1,441	33
State supplementation only	366	8

SSI RECIPIENTS, BY BASIS FOR ELIGIBILITY AND BY AGE, 1987 (numbers in thousands)

Recipients	Number	Percent	Percent over age 65
Total	**4,385**	**100%**	**46%**
Aged	1,455	33	100
Blind	83	2	28
Disabled	2,846	65	19

Source: Dept. of Health and Human Services, Fast Facts & Figures about Social Security (1988).

SSI RECIPIENTS—AVERAGE MONTHLY PAYMENTS, 1987

Basis for eligibility	Total	Federal SSI payments	Federally administered state supplements
AGED			
Individual	$182	$153	$113
Couple	350	255	323
BLIND			
Individual	296	239	171
Couple	471	330	428
DISABLED			
Individual	288	250	126
Couple	391	306	319

Source: Dept. of Health and Human Services, Fast Facts & Figures about Social Security (1988).

AID TO FAMILIES WITH DEPENDENT CHILDREN (AFDC), RECIPIENTS AND PAYMENTS, 1960–87

Year	Recipients (thousands)			Payments (in 1987 dollars)		
	Total	Families	Children	Total[1]	Family[2]	Recipient[2]
1960	3,005	787	2,314	$ 3,913	$414	$108
1970	8,466	2,208	6,214	14,472	547	142
1980	10,774	3,712	7,419	17,531	394	136
1987	10,873	3,727	7,176	16,300	365	125

1. In millions of dollars.   2. Monthly average.   **Source:** Dept. of Health and Human Services, Fast Facts & Figures about Social Security (1988).

may also pay the premiums for supplementary medical insurance and the deductible and coinsurance cost of hospital insurance. Medicaid also covers some medical services that Medicare does not.
Administration is handled jointly by the states

and the Health Care Financing Administration in the Department of Health and Human Services. Total 1985 expenditures were $14.3 billion.

MEDICAID: RECIPIENTS AND PAYMENTS, 1986

	Recipients	Payments
Total	22,405,000	$40.9 billion
Aged	14%	37%
Blind	—	1
Disabled	14	36
Dependent children under 21	44	12
Adults in families with dependent children	25	12
Other	6	2

Note: Dash (—) indicates less than 0.5%. **Source:** Dept. of Health and Human Services, *Fast Facts & Figures about Social Security* (1988).

Food Stamp Program By providing eligible applicants with coupons to buy food, the program enables families in need to purchase a nutritionally adequate diet. In general a household is considered eligible if it has less than $2,000 in disposable assets and if 30% of its countable cash income is insufficient to purchase an adequate low-cost diet, as defined by the U.S. Department of Agriculture's (USDA) "Thrifty Food Plan."

The Food Stamp Act of 1964 set eligibility requirements for food stamp program participants, and provides coupons through state and local agencies that are used to buy food in approved retail stores. The program involved 18.8 million participants as of May 1988, with each participant receiving an average of $50 in monthly coupons. States delegate varying degrees of authority to counties and cities, but the federal government finances 100% of the state-issued food benefits and part of the state's administrative costs. In fiscal year 1987, benefits totaled $10.4 billion, and administrative expenses amounted to about $1.1 billion. Local offices consider applicants for benefits. The Omnibus Budget Reconciliation Act of 1982 tightens eligibility and authorizes pilot projects in which recipients lose their stamps if they don't work at least 20 hours a week.

Although the objective of the Food Stamp Program is to provide benefits equitably to similarly qualified applicants, because of the different state methods of calculating monthly incomes—average or actual—households with monthly incomes close to the eligibility limit ($1,192 for a four-person household) can obtain food stamps in some states but not in others. The Government Accounting Office has recommended that the USDA determine whether it would be beneficial to adopt a uniform policy for calculating monthly income.
Administration Handled at the federal level by the Food and Nutrition Service in the Department of Agriculture.

Special Nutrition Programs The government provides a number of related programs designed to help safeguard the health and well-being of the nation's children by assisting the states in providing adequate meals to all children at a moderate cost. The programs include the National School Lunch Program,

the School Breakfast Program, the Summer Food Service Program, the Child Care Food Program, the Special Milk Program, and the Special Supplemental Food Program for Women, Infants, and Children (WIC) Program. The nutrition program for the elderly requires no income test, but preference is given to those with the greatest need.
Administration Handled by Food and Nutrition Service in the Department of Agriculture.

Housing Subsidies The Department of Housing and Urban Development (HUD) provides direct assistance to low- and very low-income families (those with income below 50% of the median income for the community) and to the homeless to find decent, safe, and sanitary housing in private accommodations.

Housing Voucher Program Authorized by Section 8(o) of the Housing Act of 1937, this program enables families to rent units that are beyond the fair market rent. Monthly payments are based on the difference between a payment standard for the area—not the actual rent—and 30% of the family's monthly income. In 1987 the program assisted more than 108,000 families and elderly households. Section 8 of the same act enables families certified as eligible by the Public Housing Administration (PHA) to negotiate directly with landlords for appropriate rental housing. Eligible tenants must pay the highest of either 30% of their adjusted income, 10% of their gross income, or the portion of their welfare assistance designated for housing. In 1987 the program assisted more than 800,000 families.

Housing for the Homeless In 1987 HUD awarded $94.2 million for housing and related services for the homeless, including transitional housing, permanent housing for disabled homeless, and rental assistance to homeless individuals needing single-occupancy accommodations. Specific grants made under the Stewart B. McKinney Homeless Assistance Act of 1987 included $19.2 million for 34 projects for the chronically mentally ill, and $20.2 million for 47 projects for families with children.
Administration Handled by the Federal Housing Administration in the Department of Housing and Urban Development.

Future of Social Security

Originally funded on a "pay-as-you-go" basis, the system was overhauled in 1988 to keep it fiscally sound into the future. In 1988 the program's funds were running down because of an interval in the 1970s when prices outpaced wages and cost-of-living adjustments were not being offset by increased payments into the funds. To bolster the fund and protect today's young generation from large tax hikes when the baby-boom generation retires, the government ordered incremental increases in the Social Security tax rate, leveling off in 1990 at 12.4% on earnings up to $50,000 (depending on inflation). The Social Security Trust Funds are increasing at the rate of $110 million a day, and projections indicate annual surpluses reaching $500 million a day or close

to $200 billion a year by the start of the next century. Only well into the next century, when the baby boom retires, do forecasts show the surpluses diminishing. However, the Hospital Insurance Fund (Medicare) will start to run a deficit because of the aging population by the year 2000 unless it receives additional funding. Estimates are that the "nest egg" for retire-

SOCIAL SECURITY RESERVES AND THE FEDERAL DEFICIT, 1989–94
(billions of dollars)

Employee and other payments to Social Security are kept in trust funds and are intended solely to pay benefits to those who have made contributions to the fund—hence the word *trust*. However, the federal government currently lists the reserves in the various Social Security Trust Funds among its total assets. This allows the government to deduct Social Security reserves from the total national debt, and to project deficit figures that are lower than they actually are.

Year	Real deficit	Minus	Social Security reserve	Equals	Projected Deficit
1989	$200	–	$ 52	=	$148
1990	200	–	63	=	137
1991	206	–	74	=	132
1992	213	–	86	=	127
1993	219	–	99	=	120
1994	229	–	113	=	116

Source: Dept. of Health and Human Services, *Fast Facts & Figures about Social Security* (1988).

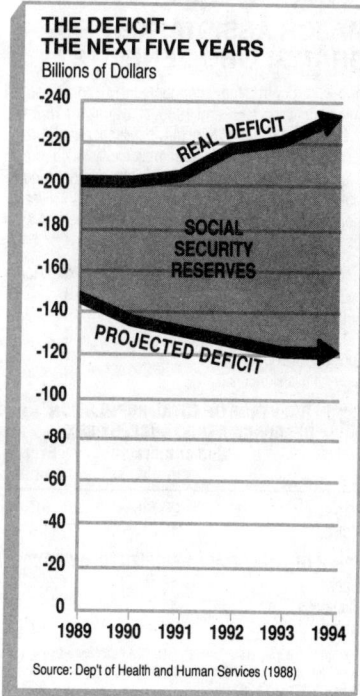

THE DEFICIT— THE NEXT FIVE YEARS
Billions of Dollars

REAL DEFICIT

SOCIAL SECURITY RESERVES

PROJECTED DEFICIT

1989 1990 1991 1992 1993 1994

Source: Dep't of Health and Human Services (1988)

ment benefits will have disappeared by 2050, eaten away by generations of baby boomers who will have started to retire in 2010.

The annual surpluses collected by government (difference between payroll taxes collected and payments disbursed) were integrated into the federal budget by President Lyndon Johnson during the Vietnam War to argue against a tax increase. According to the Congressional Budget Office, the projected 1993 budget deficit would almost double to $219 billion if the surplus were not included in the unified budget. Whether the surpluses should continue to be combined with the federal government's general account (persuading the markets to let interest rates decline) or be separated (thereby imposing discipline on spending) is the subject of ongoing controversy.

SOCIAL SECURITY TRUST FUND OPERATIONS, 1987–88 (billions of dollars)

Trust fund	Income 1987	1988	Outgo 1987	1988	End-of-year reserve 1987	1988
OASI	$210.7	$787.0	$2,314.0	$3,913.0	$414.0	$108.0
DI	20.3	22.8	21.4	22.4	62.1	7.0
HI	64.1	68.9	50.3	53.1	53.7	69.6
SMI	31.8	35.3	31.7	36.1	8.4	7.6

Source: Dept. of Health and Human Services, *Fast Facts & Figures about Social Security* (1988).

MAJOR ASSISTANCE PROGRAMS: WHO BENEFITS?

In a 32–month study conducted by the Census Bureau between 1983 and 1986, an estimated 18.3% of the general population (44.2 million people) received benefits from federal major-assistance programs for one or more months. In the same period, 7.5% (18.1 million people) received benefits every month. The average number of recipients, per month for major programs included the following.

Medicaid	22.6 million
Food stamps	20.9
AFDC	11.0
SSI	4.4
Low-income housing	2.1
General-assistance aid	1.3

PERCENTAGE OF TOTAL POPULATION RECEIVING ASSISTANCE, BY SEX

	One or more months	Every month
Females	20.5%	6.7%
Males	15.2	11.8

PROPORTION OF ALL RECIPIENTS, BY RACE

Blacks	48.5%	24.0%
Hispanics	34.2	15.8
Whites	13.9	4.7

Source: U.S. Bureau of the Census, *Statistical Abstract of the United States 1988* and *Characteristics of Persons Receiving Benefits from Major Assistance Programs, 1989.*

THE NATIONAL DEFENSE

Throughout history the primary goal of every central government has been the protection of its citizens from hostile attacks of foreign enemies. Today the United States spends over $290 billion to keep 2.2 million people in active military service and to build and maintain the greatest arsenal of weapons ever known.

Since the end of World War II, a large percentage of people and materiel has been committed to regions around the world that the government has determined are vital to U.S. interests. Between 1961 and 1980, the defense budget averaged around $200 billion (1982 constant dollars), even during the Vietnam War. In 1981, however, the Reagan administration began a massive defense buildup that not only swelled the defense budgets to unprecedented numbers but also helped quadruple the annual federal deficit in less than five years.

The figures and charts below are divided into three sections: personnel, weapons, and defense spending.

Organization of U.S. Military Forces

U.S. Air Force For administrative and military purposes, the Air Force is organized into a number of commands. Within commands concerned with the strategic or tactical operation of aircraft, the primary subdivisions are indicated by the term *air force* prefaced by a number, as the Third Air Force. Such an air force is composed of wings; a wing consists of two or more groups; a group, of two or more squadrons; and a squadron, of two or more flights. A flight is the basic tactical unit and consists of four or more planes.

MAIN COMMANDS

Strategic Air Command (SAC) Headquarters: Offutt AFB, Bellevue, Nebr. Eighteen bomber bases in SAC: 17 in continental U.S. and one in Marianas Islands. Administered by Eighth Air Force, Barksdale, AFB, Bossier City, La.; 15th Air Force, March AFB, Moreno Valley, Calif.

Tactical Air Command (TAC) Forty-three tactical air wings: 28 in continental U.S., two in Alaska, two in South Korea, two in Japan, one in Philippines, four in West Germany, three in England, and one in Spain (scheduled for deactivation). Twelfth Air Force, Bergstrom AFB, Austin, Tex.

U.S. Air Forces in Europe Third Air Force, Mildenhall, United Kingdom; 16th Air Force, Torrejon, Spain; 17th Air Force, Sembach, West Germany.

Pacific Air Forces Fifth Air Force, Yokata AFB, Japan; Seventh Air Force, Osan Air Base, Korea; 13th Air Force, Clark AFB, Philippines.

Alaskan Air Command.

Space Command (SPACECOM).

Military Airlift Command (MAC).

Air Training Command (ATC).

Pacific Air Forces (PACAF) Alaskan Air Command.

SUPPORTING COMMANDS
Air Force Communication Command (AFCC).
Air Force Logistics Command (AFLC).
Air Force Systems Command (AFSC).
Electronic Security Command (ESC).
Air University (AU).

SEPARATE OPERATING AGENCIES (SOA) and DIRECT REPORTING UNITS (DRU) A number of these provide additional support.

U.S. Army The largest unit is a numbered army, such as the Fifth Army. In time of war, two or three armies may be brought under a single command in an army group. An army comprises two or more corps plus a headquarters unit; a corps, of two or more divisions (and a headquarters); a division, of several regiments and/or brigades (and headquarters); a brigade, of two or more regiments and/or battalions (and headquarters); a regiment, of two battalions; a battalion, of several companies; a company, of several platoons; and a platoon, of four squads. A squad consists of about 10 soldiers commanded by a sergeant. This organization, however, is very flexible.

ARMIES
First U.S. Army Ft. Meade, Md.
Third U.S. Army Ft. McPherson, Ga.
Fifth U.S. Army Ft. Sam Houston, Tex.
Sixth U.S. Army Presidio of San Francisco, Calif.
Seventh U.S. Army Heidelberg, Germany.
Eighth U.S. Army Youngsan, South Korea.
U.S. Army Europe Heidelberg, Germany.
U.S. Army Camp Zama, Japan.

DIVISIONS Eighteen active and 10 reserve divisions in U.S. Army combat forces. Usually a division fights as part of corps, two to five divisions making up corps. Division is, however, self-sufficient force. Typical division consists of three brigades (each comprising 3 to 5 battalions) plus various combat support elements such as engineers, artillery, air defense, military intelligence, quartermasters, transportation unit, medical units, military police.

Air Assault Divisions 101st, Ft. Campbell, Ky.
Airborne Divisions 82d, Ft. Bragg, N.C.
Armored Divisions First, West Germany; First Cavalry (Armored), Ft. Hood, Tex.; Second, Ft. Hood, Tex.; Third, West Germany.
Infantry Divisions Second, Korea; Sixth, Alaska Seventh Light Infantry, Ft. Ord, Calif.; Ninth, Ft. Lewis, Wash.; 10th, Ft. Drum, N.Y.; 25th, Hawaii.
Mechanized Infantry Divisions First, Ft. Riley, Kans.; Third, Würzburg, West Germany; Fourth, Ft. Carson, Colo.; Fifth, Ft. Polk, La.; Eighth, Bad Kreuznach, West Germany; 24th, Ft. Stewart, Ga.

NONDIVISIONAL UNITS In addition to divisions, Army combat forces include special-purpose units such as Ranger Battalions and Special Operations Forces.

U.S. Marine Corps There are four regular combat divisions and one reserve, three regular air wings and one reserve, and three regular and one reserve force service-support groups. These units are divided between the Fleet Marine Force Pacific and Fleet Marine Force Atlantic.

FLEET MARINE FORCE PACIFIC First Marine Division, Third Marine Division, First

Marine Aircraft Wing, Third Marine Aircraft Wing.

FLEET MARINE FORCE PACIFIC Second Marine Division, Second Marine Aircraft Wing. ORGANIZATION OF A MARINE DIVISION 3 Infantry regiments, 1 Artillery regiment, 1 Headquarters battalion, 1 Tank battalion, 1 Engineer battalion, 1 Reconnaissance battalion, 1 Light armored assault battalion, and 1 battalion each for service, shore party, medical, and motor transport.

ORGANIZATION OF A MARINE AIR WING 3 Fighter/attack groups, 1 Helicopter group, 1 Support group, 1 Air Control group, 1 Headquarters squadron, 1 Reconnaissance squadron, 1 Electronic warfare squadron, 1 aerial refueler/transport squadron.

U.S. Navy The ships of the U.S. Navy are organized into the Pacific Fleet, the Atlantic Fleet, and U.S. Naval Forces Europe. These are composed of numbered fleets. A numbered fleet consists of two to four carrier battle groups, one or more battleship surface action groups, and one or more underway replenishment groups. A division is a tactical unit of four or so ships. A squadron consists of two or more divisions; and a flotilla, of two or more squadrons. The phrase *naval task force* designates a collection of ships under a single command designed to accomplish a particular tactical or strategic purpose. An amphibious squadron consists of amphibious assault ships, amphibious transport docks, dock landing ships, and tank landing ships, and transports troops and equipment necessary for an assault landing from the sea.

PACIFIC FLEET *Third Fleet* (Eastern Pacific) 2 Carrier battle groups, 1 Underway replenishment group.

Seventh Fleet (Western Pacific) 5 Carrier battle groups, 2 battleship surface action groups, 4 underway replenishment groups.

ATLANTIC FLEET *Second Fleet* 4 Carrier battle groups, 1 Battleship surface action group, 3 Underway replenishment groups.

U.S. NAVAL FORCES EUROPE *Sixth Fleet* (Mediterranean) 4 Carrier battle groups, 1 Battleship surface action group, 2 Underway replenishment groups.

SEA-BASED STRATEGIC NUCLEAR FORCE Fleet of 28 Poseidon and eight Trident ballistic missile submarines divided among four bases: Bangor, Wash., on U.S. West Coast; Charleston, S.C., and King's Bay, Ga., on East Coast; and Holy Loch, Scotland.

U.S. Special Operations Command Intended to achieve particular military objectives of a limited and specific nature (e.g., the attempted rescue of the hostages in Iran, for example), it includes the army: U.S. Army Special Forces, Rangers, Psychological Operations, Civil Affairs, and Special Operations Aviation units; the navy: SEAL and SEAL delivery vehicle teams; and the air force: 23d Air Force Special Operations Force.

The U.S. Coast Guard The Coast Guard is a branch of the U.S. armed forces on duty at all times. What distinguishes it from the other services is that it is part of the Department of Transportation—not Defense—except during wartime, when it operates as part of the navy, or at the direction of the president. A successor

to the Revenue Marine established in 1790, it primarily serves to enforce federal maritime law. In 1987 the Coast Guard's budget was $1.8 billion, and the active duty force consisted of 38,576 personnel.

ACTIVE-DUTY MILITARY PERSONNEL, BY SERVICE, 1988

Service	Ashore	Afloat	Total
All Services	1,890,503	247,710	2,138,213
Army	771,847	—	771,847
Navy	351,020	241,550	592,570
Marine Corps	191,190	6,160	197,350
Air Force	576,446	—	576,446

Source: Dept. of Defense.

MILITARY PERSONNEL ON ACTIVE DUTY: SELECTED YEARS 1801–1988

Year/War	Total[1]	Year/War	Total[1]
1801	7,108	1918	2,897,167
1810	11,554	1919	1,172,602
WAR OF 1812		1920	343,302
1813	25,152	1930	255,648
1814	46,858	1940	458,365
1815	40,885	1941	1,801,101
1820	15,113		
1830	11,942	WORLD WAR II	
1840	21,616	1942	3,858,791
MEXICAN WAR		1943	9,044,745
1846	39,165	1944	11,451,719
1847	57,761	1945	12,123,455
1848	60,308	1946	3,030,088
1850	20,824	1950	1,460,261
1860	27,958		
CIVIL WAR		KOREAN CONFLICT	
1861	217,112	1951	3,249,455
1862	673,124	1952	3,635,912
1863	960,061	1953	3,555,067
1864	1,031,724	1960	2,476,435
1865	1,062,848		
1870	50,348	VIETNAM CONFLICT	
1880	37,894	1966	3,094,058
1890	38,666	1967	3,376,880
SPANISH-AMERICAN WAR		1968	3,547,902
1898	235,785	1969	3,460,162
1900	139,344	1970	3,066,294
1915	174,112	1975	2,128,000[2]
WORLD WAR I		1980	2,051,000[2]
1917	643,833	1986	2,169,000[2]
		1987	2,174,000[2]
		1988	2,247,000[2]

1. Excludes the Coast Guard. 2. Figures rounded after 1970.
Source: Bureau of the Census, *Statistical History of the U.S.* (1976) and *Statistical Abstract of the United States, 1989.*

SUBSISTENCE ALLOWANCE FOR MILITARY PERSONNEL

OFFICERS $119.61/month

ENLISTED MEMBERS	E-1, less than four months	All other enlisted
When on leave or authorized to mess separately	$5.27/day	$5.70/day
When rations in-kind are not available	5.95/day	6.44/day
When assigned to duty under emergency conditions where no mess facilities of the U.S. are available	7.89/day	8.53/day

Note: In addition, military personnel not living on base are provided a basic allowance for quarters, which ranges from approximately $250–600 a month for enlisted members. Officers with dependents receive approximately $400–700 a month, enlisted members $280–500 a month.   1. Basic pay is limited to $6,291.00 per month, to correspond to Level V of the Executive Schedule (as of Apr. 1989). 2. Less than four months' service.   **Source:** Dept. of Defense.

U.S. NAVY FLEET DISPOSITIONS, 1988–89

Fleet	Location	Force structure
Second	Atlantic	4 Carrier battle groups 1 Battleship surface action group 3 Underway replenishment groups
Third	Eastern Pacific	2 Carrier battle groups 1 Underway replenishment group
Sixth	Mediterranean	4 Carrier battle groups 1 Battleship surface action group 2 Underway replenishment groups
Seventh	Western Pacific and Indian Ocean	5 Carrier battle groups 2 Battleship surface action groups 4 Underway replenishment groups

Source: Dept. of Defense, *Report of the Sec. of Defense to the Congress* (1988).

MILITARY PERSONNEL IN THE U.S.

State	Personnel
Alabama	20,588
Alaska	22,490
Arizona	24,829
Arkansas	9,144
California	204,791
Colorado	38,326
Connecticut	7,423
Delaware	4,587
District of Columbia	12,642
Florida	77,039
Georgia	62,057
Hawaii	43,953
Idaho	5,558
Illinois	37,873
Indiana	5,790
Iowa	397
Kansas	23,172
Kentucky	38,420
Louisiana	22,772
Maine	5,500
Maryland	34,326
Massachusetts	8,725
Michigan	8,929
Minnesota	928
Mississippi	14,382
Missouri	15,236
Montana	4,210
Nebraska	13,129
Nevada	9,237
New Hampshire	3,922
New Jersey	18,626
New Mexico	15,179
New York	28,321
North Carolina	89,880
North Dakota	10,872
Ohio	11,452
Oklahoma	33,971
Oregon	659
Pennsylvania	6,124
Rhode Island	3,703
South Carolina	41,820
South Dakota	6,710
Tennessee	10,041
Texas	126,356
Utah	5,832
Vermont	77
Virginia	100,844
Washington	42,026
West Virginia	436
Wisconsin	882
Wyoming	3,922
UNDISTRIBUTED	
Air Force	5,463
Army	19,377
Navy	13,233

Source: Dept. of Defense, *Distribution of Personnel by State and by Selected Lcoations . . . (1988).*

ACTIVE DUTY, MONTHLY BASIC PAY TABLE EFFECTIVE JAN. 1, 1989

Pay grade	Rank	Years of service 2	10	20	26
COMMISSIONED OFFICERS:					
O–10	General / Admiral	$5,911.80	$6,138.30	$7,115.10[1]	$7,558.50[1]
O–9	Lt. General / Vice-Admiral	5,193.90	5,439.30	6,478.80[1]	6,875.10[1]
O–8	Maj. General / Rear Admiral	4,721.40	5,193.90	6,138.30	6,289.50
O–7	Brig. General / Commodore	4,068.00	4,496.70	5,551.20	5,551.20
O–6	Colonel / Captain	3,102.00	3,305.10	4,250.40	4,877.10
O–5	Lt. Colonel / Commander	2,651.40	2,920.50	3,845.10	3,979.20
O–4	Major / Lt. Commander	2,317.80	2,808.60	3,327.60	3,327.60
O–3	Captain / Lieutenant	1,977.60	2,676.30	2,877.90	2,877.90
O–2	1st Lieutenant / Lieut. (J.G.)	1,684.50	2,135.40	2,135.40	2,135.40
O–1	2d Lieutenant / Ensign	1,394.10	1,684.50	1,684.50	1,685.40
WARRANT OFFICERS:					
W-4	Chief Warrant / Comm. Warrant	$1,933.20	$2,249.10	$2,762.70	$3,077.40
W-3	Chief Warrant / Comm. Warrant	1,776.60	2,067.30	2,430.00	2,606.40
W-2	Chief Warrant / Comm. Warrant	1,551.90	1,844.10	2,180.70	2,268.60
W-1	Warrant Officer / Warrant Officer	1,370.40	1,684.50	2,023.50	2,023.50
ENLISTED MEMBERS:					
E-9	Sgt. Major / Master C.P.O.	N.A.	$2,096.10	$2,337.00	$2,698.80
E-8	Master Sgt. / Senior C.P.O.	N.A.	1,808.10	2,048.40	2,410.20
E-7	Sgt. 1st Class / Chief Petty Officer	$1,324.80	1,566.00	1,807.20	2,168.70
E-6	Staff Sgt. / Petty Officer, 1st Class	1,150.80	1,392.90	1,583.10	1,583.10
E-5	Sergeant / Petty Officer, 2d Class	1,008.60	1,272.60	1,343.40	1,343.40
E-4	Corporal / Petty Officer, 3d Class	912.60	1,082.40	1,082.40	1,082.40
E-3	Private 1st / Seaman	858.90	928.80	928.80	928.80
E-2	Private / Seaman Apprentice	783.60	783.60	783.60	783.60
E-1	Recruit[2] / Seaman Recruit[2]	646.20	646.20	646.20	646.20

Note: In addition, military personnel not living on base are provided a basic allowance for quarters, which ranges from approximately $250–600 a month for enlisted members. Officers with dependents receive approximately $400–700 a month, enlisted members $280–500 a month.   1. Basic pay is limited to $6,291.60 per month, to correspond to Level V of the Executive Schedule (as of Apr. 1989).   2. Less than four months' service.
Source: Dept. of Defense.

SUMMARY OF U.S. FORCES WORLDWIDE, 1988

Region	No. of military personnel
U.S. territory (includes continental U.S., Alaska, and Hawaii) and special locations	1,597,625
Western and southern Europe	356,251
Eastern Europe	203
East Asia and Pacific	140,967
Africa, Near East, and South Asia	18,373
Western Hemisphere (excluding U.S. and territories)	24,496
Antarctica	141
Undistributed	157
Total worldwide	**2,138,213**

Source: Dept. of Defense.

MAJOR U.S. MILITARY CONTINGENTS IN FOREIGN COUNTRIES, 1988

Nation/territory (installations)	No. of military personnel
West Germany (33 army bases, 7 air bases)	249,411
Japan (incl. Okinawa) (3 naval bases, 3 air bases, 1 army base)	49,680
South Korea (7 army bases, 4 air bases)	45,401
England (8 Royal Air Force bases)	28,497
Philippines (1 air base, 1 naval station)	16,655
Italy (3 naval bases, 2 army bases, 2 air bases)	14,829[1]
Panama (2 air bases)	11,000
Spain (2 air bases, 1 naval base)	8,724
Guam (1 air base, 1 naval base)	8,519
Turkey (1 air base)	5,034

Nation/territory (installations)	No. of military personnel
Puerto Rico (1 army base, 1 naval base)	3,361
Belgium (NATO headquarters)	3,317
Greece (2 air bases, 1 naval station)	3,284
Iceland (1 naval station)	3,234
Netherlands (1 air force base)	2,872
Cuba (1 naval base)	2,337
Bermuda (1 naval air station)	1,844
Portugal (Azores) (1 air force base)	1,700
British Ocean Territory[2] (1 naval base)	1,001

1. Not including the 22,000 members of the Sixth Fleet. 2. Including Diego Garcia. **Source:** Dept. of Defense.

THE DEFENSE BUDGET

U.S. DEFENSE BUDGET, 1988–91 (millions of dollars)

	ACTUAL 1988	ESTIMATED 1989	ESTIMATED 1990	1991
Department of Defense				
Military personnel	$76,584	$78,566	$79,845	$82,060
Operation and maintenance	81,629	85,939	91,725	95,518
Procurement	80,053	79,232	84,115	91,894
Research, development, test, and evaluation	36,521	37,542	41,024	41,252
Military construction	5,349	5,703	5,280	5,937
Family housing	3,199	3,266	3,280	3,671
Revolving funds and others	1,274	749	853	968
Offsetting receipts	−855	−811	−786	−749
Allowance: other legislation (proposed)	N.A.	N.A.	309	358
Defense department subtotal	**$283,755**	**$290,186**	**$305,645**	**$320,909**
Atomic energy defense activities	7,749	8,100	9,027	9,389
Defense-related activities	504	519	521	525
Total national defense budget	**$292,008**	**$298,805**	**$315,193**	**$330,823**

Source: Office of Management and Budget, Budget of the U.S. Govt., FY 1990.

DEFENSE BUDGET, BY MISSION CATEGORIES, 1988–91 (billions of dollars)

Major missions and programs	ACTUAL 1988	ESTIMATED 1989	ESTIMATED 1990	1991
Strategic forces	$ 19.8	$ 21.2	$ 23.4	$ 27.6
General purpose forces[1]	114.9	112.8	117.8	122.8
Intelligence and communication	28.3	29.6	31.7	32.8
Airlift and sealift	4.4	5.4	6.3	7.1
Guard and reserve	16.9	17.2	17.2	17.8
Research and develop.[2]	28.4	29.1	32.1	32.6
Central supply and maintenance	24.3	325.3	27.0	28.1
Trng., medical, & other gen. personnel activities	37.3	38.5	40.0	42.1
Administration and associated activities	6.7	6.9	5.9	6.3
Support of other nations	0.8	1.0	1.1	1.1
Spec. operations forces	2.0	3.2	3.1	2.6
Totals	**$283.8**	**$290.2**	**$305.6**	**$320.9**

Note: Preliminary data subject to revision. 1. Excludes strategic systems development, which is included in research and development. 2. Excludes research and development in other program areas on systems approved for production. **Source:** Office of Management and Budget, Budget of the U.S. Govt., FY 1989.

> *"To be prepared for war is one of the most effectual means of preserving peace."*
> —George Washington,
> first annual address (Jan. 8, 1790)

DEFENSE BUDGET AUTHORITY, BY COMPONENT, 1985–89
(millions of dollars)

Component	1985	1986[1]	1987	1988	1989
Dept. of the Army[2]	$ 84,570	$ 81,105	$ 79,797	$ 78,345	$ 77,806
Dept. of the Navy[2]	112,313	106,571	100,812	103,471	96,437
Dept. of the Air Force[2]	112,264	105,108	98,883	103,471	96,437
Defense Agencies/ OSD/JCS[3]	15,215	17,489	20,829	17,626	18,611
Defense-wide	1,106	1,590	1,254	2,138	706
Totals[4]	**$325,467**	**$311,864**	**$301,575**	**$292,758**	**$290,784**

Note: Fiscal years, in constant fiscal-year 1989 dollars. 1. Lower budget authority in military personnel accounts in fiscal year 1986 reflects the congressional direction to finance $4.5 billion for the military pay raise and retirement accrual from prior year unobligated balances. 2. Includes retired pay accrual. 3. Office of the Secretary of Defense, Joint Chiefs of Staff. 4. Numbers may not add exactly because of rounding. **Source:** Dept. of Defense, Report of the Sec. of Defense . . . to the Congress (1988).

STRATEGIC DEFENSE FORCES BUDGET, 1987–89
(millions of dollars)

Program	1987 Actual	1988 Planned	1989 Proposed
Strategic Defense Initiative ("Star Wars")	$3,279.7	$3,551.0	$4,545.9
Air Defense Initiative	35.6	49.2	213.6
Space Control Development	208.3	203.6	74.5
Totals	**$3,526.6**	**$3,803.8**	**$4,834.0**

Source: Dept. of Defense, Report of the Sec. of Defense . . . to the Congress (1988).

WEAPONS

SUMMARY OF MAJOR MILITARY FORCES, 1980–88

Category	1980	1985	1988
STRATEGIC FORCES			
Land-based ICBMs	1,054	1,028	1,000
Sea-launched BMs	576	648	674
Strategic bombers	413	328	423
Strategic interceptors	292	264	252
GENERAL PURPOSE FORCES (active)			
Army divisions	16	17	18
Marine Corps divisions	3	3	3
Air Force tactical aircraft	3,813	4,406	4,470
Navy/Marine Corps tactical aircraft	2,013	1,970	1,962
NAVAL FORCES			
Aircraft carriers	13	13	14
Battleships	—	3	3
Nuclear attack submarines	74	96	96
Other warships	180	204	195
Amphibious assault ships	63	60	62
AIRLIFT AND SEALIFT FORCES			
C-5 aircraft (PAA)	70	70	102
Other Air Force aircraft (PAA)	820	787	781
Navy/Marine Corps tactical support aircraft (PAA)	88	88	87
Ships (NDRF)	164	214	209

Note: ICBM = intercontinental ballistic missile; BM = ballistic missile. **Source:** U.S. Bureau of the Census, *Statistical Abstract of the United States, 1989.*

NUMBERS OF MILITARY WEAPONS, 1980–88

Service	1980	1988	Change
ARMY			
Tanks	10,985	16,316	5,331
AIR FORCE[1]			
Fighters, attack aircraft (including reserves)	2,472	254	72
Bombers	376	275	–101
Interceptors	384	258	–126
Airlift aircraft	890	873	–17
NAVY			
Nuclear submarines	36	35	–1
Cruisers, destroyers, frigates	180	221	41
Carriers	12	14	2
Battleships		3	3
Attack submarines	82	100	18
STRATEGIC NUCLEAR LAUNCHERS			
ICBMs	1,052	1,000	–52
SLBMs	576	624	48
Bombers	316	360	44
Total nuclear warheads	9,566	12,978	3,412

Note: ICBM = intercontinental ballistic missile; SLBM = submarine launched ballistic missile. 1. Figures for U.S. Air Force include projections for fiscal 1990. **Source:** Center for Defense Information, Congressional Research Service, Dept. of Defense, International Institute for Strategic Studies.

U.S. NAVY FORCE STRUCTURE, 1980–89

	1980[1]	1987	1989	Goal
SSBNs	40	37	37	20–40
Deployable aircraft carriers	13	14	14	15
Battleships	—	3	4	4
AAW cruisers/destroyers	63	73	77	100
ASW destroyers	44	32	32	37
Frigates	71	115	100	10
Attack submarines	79	102	103	100
Mine countermeasures ships	3	4	9	14
Amphibious ships (MAF and MAB)	66	63	67	75
Patrol combatants	3	6	6	6
Combat logistics ships	48	56	60	65
Support ships and auxiliaries	49	63	71	60–65
Totals	**479**	**568**	**580**	**600[2]**

Note: AAW = anti-air warfare; ASW = antisubmarine warfare; MAB = Marine amphibious brigade; MAF = Marine amphibious force; SSBN = ballistic missile submarine, nuclear-powered. 1. Years are fiscal years. 2. Approximate. **Source:** Dept. of Defense, *Report of the Sec. of Defense . . . to the Congress* (1988).

GOVERNMENT SPENDING ON RESEARCH AND DEVELOPMENT (billions of dollars)

Fiscal year	Defense	Nondefense
1981	$24.2	$20.8
1982	28.0	18.1
1983	29.8	16.9
1984	33.2	17.5
1985	38.0	18.3
1986	40.3	17.8
1987	41.3	19.1
1988	41.8	20.4

Source: Office of Management and Budget, *Special Analysis of the U.S. Govt., FY 1989.*

DEFENSE BUDGET YEARLY AVERAGE, 1961–88 (billions of dollars)

Administration	Current dollars	Constant 1982 dollars	% of GNP
Kennedy/Johnson (1961–68)	$59.0	$207.8	8.9%
Nixon/Ford (1969–76)	81.8	189.3	6.8
Carter (1977–80)	113.0	158.1	4.9
Reagan (1981–88)	234.2	216.9	6.1

Source: Office of Management and Budget.

MILITARY PRIME CONTRACT AWARDS, BY PROGRAM, 1975–87 (billions of dollars)

Department of Defense procurement program	1975[1]	1980[1]	1985[1]	1987[1]
INTRAGOVERNMENTAL[2]	$ 5.0	$ 10.2	$ 12.4	$ 8.8
WORK OUTSIDE U.S.	2.4	5.4	8.6	8.9
EDUCATIONAL AND NONPROFIT ORGS.	0.8	1.5	3.1	3.5
FOR FIRMS IN U.S.[3]	37.1	66.7	139.6	135.3
Major hard goods	22.2	41.0	98.1	93.0
Aircraft	6.7	12.5	34.6	27.7
Electronics and communications	4.7	9.6	22.0	22.6
Missiles and space sys.	4.6	7.9	18.7	19.8
Ships	3.5	6.0	10.4	11.5
Tank-automotive	0.9	2.1	5.2	4.9
Ammunition	1.3	1.9	4.7	4.6
Weapons	0.4	1.1	2.6	2.1
SERVICES	3.1	5.9	9.1	11.0
ALL OTHER	11.9	19.8	32.3	31.3
Totals	**$45.3**	**$83.8**	**$163.7**	**$156.5**

1. Fiscal years. 2. Covers only purchases from other federal agencies and reimbursable purchases on behalf of foreign governments. 3. Includes Defense Department contracts awarded for work in U.S. possessions, Puerto Rico, Trust Territories, and other areas subject to complete sovereignty of the U.S.; contracts in a classified location; and any intragovernmental contracts entered into overseas. **Sources:** Dept. of Defense, *Military Prime Contract Awards* (1988); U.S. Bureau of the Census, *Statistical Abstract of the United States, 1989* (1989).

MILITARY EXPENDITURES: U.S. AND ITS ALLIES, 1987

	Spending (billions)	As percent of GDP	Spending per person	GDP per person
U.S.	$281.10	6.8%	$1,164	$17,174
France	28.46	3.9	514	13,077
West Germany	27.69	3.1	454	14,664
Britain	27.33	5.1	481	9,616
Japan	19.84	1.0	163	16,159
Italy	13.46	2.2	235	10,484
Canada	7.90	2.2	308	14,162
Spain	6.01	3.1	156	5,928
Netherlands	5.32	3.1	365	11,925
Belgium	3.40	3.0	345	11.436
Turkey	2.73	4.8	54	1,140
Greece	2.42	6.1	243	3,987
Norway	2.17	3.1	520	16,562
Denmark	1.65	2.0	322	16,118
Portugal	0.94	3.2	91	2,857
Luxembourg	0.05	1.1	145	13,439

Note: GDP = gross domestic product. **Source:** Dept. of Defense.

THE BUSINESS OF ARMS

STATES RANKED BY DEFENSE DEPARTMENT CONTRACTS AWARDED, PERCENT OF TOTAL, 1988

State	Dollar amount	% of total	Rank
Alabama	$ 1,825,552	1.5%	18
Alaska	421,943	0.3	38
Arizona	2,652,075	2.1	14
Arkansas	742,423	0.6	29
California	23,457,695	18.7	1
Colorado	2,890,570	2.3	13
Connecticut	4,911,301	3.9	9
Delaware	233,314	0.2	41
District of Columbia	1,664,582	1.3	—
Florida	5,327,773	4.2	7
Georgia	1,616,361	1.3	19
Hawaii	540,991	0.4	33
Idaho	61,531	—	48
Illinois	1,499,700	1.2	20
Indiana	1,518,076	1.2	21
Iowa	560,905	0.4	34
Kansas	950,128	0.8	26
Kentucky	397,344	0.3	39
Louisiana	1,438,736	1.1	22
Maine	517,879	0.4	35
Maryland	4,270,989	3.4	10
Massachusetts	7,212,149	5.7	5
Michigan	1,270,454	1.0	23
Minnesota	2,082,759	1.7	17
Mississippi	2,421,981	1.9	16
Missouri	5,507,801	4.4	6
Montana	80,113	0.1	45
Nebraska	258,548	0.2	42
Nevada	206,732	0.2	43
New Hampshire	480,822	0.4	36
New Jersey	3,358,094	2.7	11
New Mexico	663,286	0.5	30
New York	7,705,717	6.1	4
North Carolina	1,241,399	1.0	24
North Dakota	117,297	0.1	46
Ohio	5,060,402	4.0	8
Oklahoma	540,760	0.4	32
Oregon	452,853	0.4	37
Pennsylvania	3,309,472	2.6	12
Rhode Island	428,961	0.3	40
South Carolina	566,225	0.5	31
South Dakota	53,605	—	49
Tennessee	1,206,912	1.0	25
Texas	9,001,310	7.2	4
Utah	870,485	0.7	27
Vermont	121,705	0.1	47
Virginia	10,238,011	8.1	2
Washington	2,625,078	2.1	15
West Virginia	218,461	0.2	44
Wisconsin	911,489	0.7	28
Wyoming	54,613	—	50
State totals	$125,767,432	N.A.	N.A.
Not distributed by state	$ 16,386,942	N.A.	N.A.
Total U.S.	$142,154,374	100.0%	N.A.

Notes: Fiscal year, 1988. Dash (—) indicates less than 0.5%. N.A. = Not applicable. **Source:** Dept. of Defense, *Prime Contract Awards by State, FY 1988.*

DEFENSE PAYROLL, AND CIVILIAN AND MILITARY PERSONNEL, BY STATE, 1987

State	Payroll (millions of dollars)	Civilian employees (thousands)	Military personnel (thousands)
Alabama	$1,301	27.4	23.8
Alaska	604	5.5	22.1
Arizona	793	10.7	24.9
Arkansas	322	5.0	9.8
California	9,568	137.7	206.5
Colorado	1,090	14.5	42.7
Connecticut	419	4.9	7.2
Delaware	132	1.9	4.8
District of Columbia	924	17.2	13.0
Florida	3,623	33.3	75.7
Georgia	2,245	40.2	62.9
Hawaii	1,757	20.7	45.4
Idaho	140	1.4	5.9
Illinois	1,340	22.1	37.3
Indiana	565	15.2	6.5
Iowa	54	1.5	0.4
Kansas	691	7.3	23.1
Kentucky	1,083	14.3	39.2
Louisiana	730	9.1	25.2
Maine	433	10.6	5.8
Maryland	2,103	43.5	35.7
Massachusetts	541	12.1	9.4
Michigan	550	12.9	9.3
Minnesota	102	2.9	0.9
Mississippi	690	11.5	17.5
Missouri	962	20.9	15.7
Montana	105	1.3	4.0
Nebraska	411	4.0	13.5
Nevada	244	2.2	10.0
New Hampshire	133	1.5	4.1
New Jersey	1,185	28.7	19.7
New Mexico	635	10.1	16.6
New York	993	19.5	27.0
North Carolina	2,311	16.2	94.8
North Dakota	246	1.9	11.2
Ohio	1,292	34.3	11.8
Oklahoma	1,305	26.1	30.8
Oregon	118	3.2	0.8
Pennsylvania	1,694	57.3	6.6
Rhode Island	269	4.6	3.9
South Carolina	1,690	20.7	44.6
South Dakota	164	1.5	6.7
Tennessee	389	7.7	10.5
Texas	4,381	67.0	135.1
Utah	721	22.3	6.0
Vermont	19	0.6	0.1
Virginia	7,216	108.6	100.0
Washington	1,880	29.8	43.3
West Virginia	58	1.6	0.4
Wisconsin	107	3.3	0.9
Wyoming	103	1.2	4.1

Notes: Comprises military awards for supplies, services, and construction. Value is net value of contracts of over $25,000 for work in each state. Figures reflect the impact of prime contracting on state distribution of defense work. Often the state in which the prime contractor was located was not the state in which the subcontracted work was done. **Source:** U.S. Bureau of the Census, *Statistical Abstract of the United States, (1989).*

THE 10 LARGEST DEFENSE CONTRACTORS, 1987

In 1987 the Dept. of Defense awarded approximately $142.5 billion in prime defense contracts (excluding small awards of less than $25,000). The top 100 companies received $95.4 billion, or 66.9%, of the total. Of these 100, the top 10, listed below, were awarded about $48.1 billion, or 33.85% of the total.

Company	Awards (thousands)	Percent of total
McDonnell Douglas Corp.	$8,002,741	5.83%
General Dynamics Corp.	6,522,124	4.75
General Electric Co.	5,700,635	4.15
Tenneco Inc.	5,057,922	3.69
Raytheon	4,055,346	2.95
Martin Marietta Corp.	3,715,106	2.71
General Motors Corp.	3,550,180	2.59
Lockheed Corp.	3,537,658	2.58
United Technologies Corp.	3,508,055	2.55
Boeing Co.	3,017,839	2.20

Source: Dept. of Defense, *100 Companies Receiving the Largest Dollar Volume of Prime Contract Awards, FY 1987* (1988).

"In the councils of government, we must guard against the acquisition of unwarranted influence, whether sought or unsought, by the military-industrial complex. The potential for the disastrous rise of misplaced power exists and will persist."

—Dwight D. Eisenhower, from his farewell address

GOVERNMENT AND BIG BUSINESS

According to the Government Services Administration, in 1988 five of America's largest corporations received more than 50% of their total sales from the federal government: Lockheed (86%), General Dynamics (85%), Martin Marietta (85%), McDonnell Douglas (65%), and Raytheon (55%). All together these five have sold the government more than $26 billion worth of goods and services, almost all of it related to defense and space.

U.S. Military Aid

An important aspect of U.S. defense strategy has been the development of a military aid program that provides assistance to allied nations. Aid can be in the form of cash loans or grants that the recipients use to purchase arms, or it can be in actual arms or in training programs. The basic intention is to provide for their defense (Israel, for example) or to allow the United States to establish bases of its own in strategic areas (as in Spain and Turkey).

Since 1946 the United States has provided almost $350 billion (in constant 1989 dollars) in military aid, 36% of the total foreign aid program. Since 1977 over half of all aid has gone to the Middle East, with Israel receiving a total of $28.5 billion (39% of the total) and Egypt $14 billion.

THE ARMS BAZAAR: ARMS SUPPLIERS' SHARE OF DELIVERIES TO IRAN AND IRAQ, BY REGION AND ALLIANCE

Between 1980 and 1987, military spending by Iran averaged about 7% of GNP, and 12% of its imports were military in nature. By contrast, military spending by Iraq constituted 35% of GNP, and arms comprised 46% of all imports.

Who benefited? The outcome of the war was militarily inconclusive and the human toll staggering—450,000 dead (some estimates put the toll at more than 1 million), and 800,000 wounded. But arms dealers had a field day: 41 countries supplied the two belligerents with more than $55 billion in arms; of these, 28 supplied both sides.

Supplier	Iran	Iraq
Warsaw Pact	16%	57%
NATO	20	22
Other Europe	12	5
East Asia	43	11
All other	9	5
Total suppliers	**35**	**34**
Exclusive suppliers	7	6
Total value of deliveries	**$11,828 bil.**	**$43,225 bil.**

Source: Arms Control and Disarmament Agency, *World Military Expenditures and Arms Transfers 1988.*

U.S. MILITARY SALES DELIVERIES TO FOREIGN GOVERNMENTS, 1950–87 (millions of dollars)

Country	1950–82[1]	MILITARY SALES DELIVERIES 1985	1986	1987	Percent change 1986–87
Australia	$ 2,111.4	$ 428.3	$ 370.1	$ 619.4	67.4%
Belgium	1,189.8	119.4	27.8	27.0	−2.9
Canada	1,588.9	73.3	114.4	128.7	12.5
China: Taiwan	1,964.9	339.5	249.0	387.1	55.5
Denmark	794.7	47.4	25.2	62.8	149.2
Egypt	1,621.0	580.3	619.5	1,141.9	84.3
El Salvador	22.9	114.8	108.3	80.3	−25.9
France	404.0	45.5	142.7	100.5	−29.6
Greece	1,590.8	119.1	73.7	86.8	17.8
Indonesia	220.2	17.8	12.8	24.3	89.8
Israel	8,020.8	483.1	195.8	1,374.3	601.9
Italy	802.0	54.9	65.7	89.6	36.4
Japan	1,175.8	389.7	151.3	306.2	102.4
Jordan	964.7	122.8	62.8	64.8	3.2
Kuwait	668.8	34.0	71.9	83.1	15.6
Morocco	537.5	49.5	37.1	43.3	16.7
Netherlands	1,468.1	339.4	319.6	459.8	43.9
Norway	1,021.9	30.0	43.2	92.3	113.7
Pakistan	545.7	358.0	148.2	135.2	−8.8
Philippines	176.2	16.0	37.3	33.8	−9.4
Portugal	29.2	97.5	26.5	27.8	4.9
Saudi Arabia	17,956.6	2,270.7	2,789.6	3,497.0	25.4
Singapore	219.3	22.4	134.9	163.2	21.0
South Korea	2,036.2	258.3	387.5	403.9	4.2
Spain	891.0	92.8	236.0	753.0	219.1
Sudan	155.1	25.3	27.7	27.1	−2.2
Thailand	861.4	118.9	118.5	100.7	−15.0
Tunisia	96.2	154.8	26.0	44.3	70.4
Turkey	978.3	389.7	290.3	296.1	2.0
United Kingdom	3,119.9	386.4	363.8	228.4	−37.2
Venezuela	264.4	243.2	80.3	51.1	−36.4
West Germany	7,144.0	222.2	206.3	344.3	66.9
Totals[2]	**$75,286.9[3]**	**$8,476.9**	**$7,979.6**	**$12,010.3**	**50.5%**

1. Includes military construction sales deliveries. 2. Includes countries not shown individually. 3. Between 1950 and 1987, the United States had military sales to Iran of $10.7 billion. **Source:** U.S. Bureau of the Census, *Statistical Abstract of the United States (1989).*

U.S. FOREIGN AID BY MAJOR PROGRAMS, 1946–89 (billions of constant 1989 dollars)

Year	Development assistance	Food aid	Other economic aid	Multilateral development banks	Economic support fund	Military aid	Total
1950	$19.3	N.A.	$6.0	N.A.	N.A.	$6.3	**$31.6**
1955	2.8	$2.5	0.1	N.A.	$6.0	7.9	**19.3**
1960	4.4	4.0	0.1	$0.3	3.4	9.2	**21.4**
1965	6.4	5.1	1.0	1.2	1.8	4.9	**20.4**
1970	4.2	3.5	0.5	1.5	1.5	8.9	**20.1**
1975	2.9	2.9	0.6	1.7	2.7	4.4	**15.2**
1980	2.8	2.2	0.9	2.2	3.3	3.2	**14.6**
1985	3.2	2.3	0.7	1.8	6.0	6.6	**20.6**
1986	2.9	1.8	0.6	1.3	5.4	6.4	**18.4**
1987	2.7	1.6	0.7	1.3	4.2	5.5	**16.0**
1988 (est.)	2.6	1.6	0.7	1.3	3.4	5.6	**15.2**
1989 (est.)	2.4	1.4	0.6	1.3	3.3	5.7	**14.7**

Source: House Committee on Foreign Affairs.

SELECTED U.S. MILITARY AID, BY REGION AND SELECTED NATIONS, 1979–88 (millions of dollars)

	1979		1985		1986		1988	
	Loan	Grant	Loan	Grant	Loan	Grant	Loan	Grant
AFRICA								
Chad	N.A.	N.A.	N.A.	$5.3	N.A.	$6.0	N.A.	$5.7
Kenya	$10.0	$0.4	N.A.	21.7	N.A.	20.6	N.A.	6.2
Liberia	1.2	0.3	N.A.	13.2	N.A.	5.6	N.A.	0.5
Zaire	8.0	1.8	N.A.	8.3	N.A.	7.9	N.A.	4.0
Total[1]	$21.2	$3.0	$10.0	$71.2	N.A.	$62.9	N.A.	$18.1
ASIA								
Indonesia	$32.0	$2.8	$32.5	$1.7	$19.1	$1.9	$4.0	$1.8
S. Korea	225.0	13.4	230.0	2.0	162.7	1.8	N.A.	1.7
Pakistan	N.A.	0.5	325.0	1.0	31.0	0.9	230.0	30.8
Philippines	15.6	16.1	15.0	27.2	14.3	90.6	N.A.	127.6
Thailand	30.0	2.1	95.0	7.3	80.5	7.0	23.5	22.2
Total[1]	$310.1	$36.2	$701.5	$41.5	$589.2	$104.7	$257.5	$186.1
LATIN AMERICA								
Colombia	$12.5	$0.5	N.A.	$0.8	N.A.	$5.2	N.A.	$1.0
Dominican Republic	0.5	0.5	$3.0	5.7	N.A.	4.5	N.A.	N.A.
Ecuador	N.A.	0.4	4.0	2.7	$3.8	0.7	N.A.	0.7
El Salvador	N.A.	N.A.	10.0	125.5	N.A.	121.1	N.A.	86.5
Guatemala	N.A.	N.A.	N.A.	0.5	N.A.	5.3	N.A.	7.9
Honduras	2.0	0.3	N.A.	67.4	N.A.	61.2	N.A.	41.2
Peru	5.0	0.5	8.0	0.5	N.A.	0.5	N.A.	0.4
Total[1]	$27.5	$3.0	$25.0	$243.8	$7.6	$226.3	N.A.	$142.1
MIDDLE EAST								
Egypt	$1,500.0	$0.4	N.A.	1,176.4	N.A.	$1,245.8	N.A.	$1,301.5
Israel	2,700.0	1,300.0	N.A.	1,400.0	N.A.	1,722.6	N.A.	1,800.0
Jordan	67.0	42.6	$90.0	1.8	$81.3	1.7	N.A.	28.5
Lebanon	42.5	0.6	N.A.	0.7	N.A.	0.5	N.A.	0.4
Morocco	45.0	1.1	8.0	41.5	1.0	35.0	$12.0	41.0
Oman	N.A.	N.A.	40.0	0.1	9.1	N.A.	N.A.	0.2
Somalia	N.A.	N.A.	N.A.	34.0	N.A.	20.2	N.A.	6.5
Sudan	5.0	0.3	N.A.	46.4	N.A.	17.0	N.A.	0.9
Tunisia	20.0	1.1	50.0	16.5	25.8	39.8	N.A.	28.4
Total[1]	$4,379.5	$1,346.7	$188.0	$2,725.3	$117.3	$3,088.5	$12.0	$3,210.4
Greece	140.0	31.0	500.0	1.4	430.7	1.2	313.0	81.1
Portugal	N.A.	30.7	55.0	73.0	43.1	69.2	2.5	82.5
Spain	120.0	44.7	400.0	2.9	382.8	2.4	N.A.	2.4
Turkey	175.0	6.5	485.0	218.0	409.5	208.9	178.0	159.3
Total[1]	$435.0	$113.0	$1,440.0	$295.3	$1,266.0	$281.7	$649.5	$275.4
World Totals[1]	$5,173.3	$1,501.9	$2,364.5	$3,377.1	$1,980.1	$3,764.1	$919.0	$3,832.1

1. Totals are for the whole region and so include aid to countries not listed individually.   **Source:** Dept. of Defense.

THE U.S. POSTAL SERVICE

At first glance the most compelling facts about today's Postal Service are the sheer size and scope of the operation. With over 800,000 employees moving more than 160 billion pieces of mail annually (656 per capita, and 40% of the world's total), this is surely one of the most vital services the government performs for business and the citizenry alike. What most people don't realize is that it's done at a cost to the consumer significantly less than in any other industrial nation, and that for first-class mail, the on-time delivery rate is still over 95% for local mail and 90% for cross-country.

First established by the Continental Congress in 1775, the Postal Service was made part of the federal system in the Constitution, and the office of postmaster general was established in George Washington's very first cabinet. In 1969, however, in response to vociferous complaints of mismanagement, waste, unreliable service, and staggering financial losses, the Nixon administration reorganized the service as an independent establishment within the executive branch. The Postal Service Act of 1969 removed the postmaster general from the cabinet and created a self-supporting postal corporation owned by the federal government and vested power in an 11-member board of governors, nine of whom are appointed by the president with the consent of the Senate; these in turn appoint the postmaster general, who serves as the CEO of the Postal Service; the 11th member of the board is chosen by the other 10 and serves as deputy postmaster general.

Finally, the 1969 law established an independent Postal Rate Commission of five members, appointed by the president, to recommend postal rates and classifications for adoption by the board of governors.

Just how well this new arrangement has worked is hard to judge. In the years 1979 to 1988, the Postal Service has had five years of losses and five years in the black. In terms of service, a poll conducted by the service indicates that between 1984 and 1988, some 80% of those surveyed said they perceived the Postal Service as "very or somewhat favorable."

" 'Tis our true policy to steer clear of permanent alliances with any portion of the foreign world . . . There can be no greater error than to expect or calculate upon real favors from nation to nation."

—George Washington
Farewell Address, 1776

NUMBER OF POSTAL EMPLOYEES AND POST OFFICES, 1988

CAREER EMPLOYEES
Headquarters
Washington, D.C.	2,311
Field support-units	5,677

FIELD CAREER-EMPLOYEES
Postmasters	27,774
Supervisors	44,170
Clerks	296,712
City delivery carriers	236,160
Mail handlers	49,937
Rural delivery carriers	39,095
Building and equipment maintenance	32,418
Professional admin. technical personnel	10,532
Motor vehicle operators	7,117
Vehicle maintenance	4,828
Inspection service	4,146
Special delivery messengers	2,146
Regional offices	437
Nurses	321
Total career employees	**763,781**

NONCAREER EMPLOYEES[1]
Casuals, temporaries, substitutes, etc.	69,702

OFFICES, STATIONS, AND BRANCHES
Post offices	29,203
Stations, branches, community post offices	10,914
Total	**40,117**

1. Includes substitutes on vacant routes. **Source:** U.S. Postal Service.

VOLUME OF MAIL HANDLED, 1988 (billions of pieces)

First class	82.30
Second class	10.45
Third class	61.97
Fourth class	0.65
Penalty and franked	3.88
International	0.72
Total	**160.49**

Source: U.S. Postal Service, *Postage, Rates, Fees, and Information* (1988).

10 CITIES THAT GET MOST MAIL, 1988

City	Total pieces (in billions)
New York, N.Y.	5.69
Los Angeles, Calif.	3.77
Philadelphia, Pa.	2.53
Chicago, Ill.	2.51
San Francisco, Calif.	2.49
Boston, Mass.	2.40
Atlanta, Ga.	2.34
Dallas, Tx.	2.19
Houston, Tx.	2.03
Detroit, Mich.	1.94

DOMESTIC POSTAGE RATES

FIRST CLASS
1st ounce	**$0.25**
Each additional ounce	**0.20**
POSTCARDS	**$0.15**

THIRD CLASS Regular and bulk third-class mail rates apply to circulars, books, catalogs, and other printed matter; merchandise; and seeds, cuttings, bulbs, roots, scions, and plants. The maximum weight is 16 oz.

Weight	Rate	Weight	Rate
1 oz.	**$0.25**	8 oz.	**$1.10**
2 oz.	**0.45**	10 oz.	**1.20**
3 oz.	**0.65**	12 oz.	**1.30**
4 oz.	**0.85**	14 oz.	**1.40**
6 oz.	**1.00**	over 14–16 oz.	**1.50**

Note: For information on second- and fourth-class rates, consult your postmaster.

INTERNATIONAL POSTAGE RATES

POSTCARDS
Canada	**$0.21**
Mexico	**0.15**
All other countries	
Surface	**0.28**
Airmail	**0.36**
AEROGRAMMES	**$0.39**

LETTERS AND LETTER PACKAGES

Weight	Canada	Mexico	All other countries Surface	All other countries Airmail
0.5 oz.	N.A.	N.A.	N.A.	$0.45
1.0	$0.30	$0.25	$0.40	0.90
1.5	N.A.	N.A.	N.A.	1.35
2.0	0.52	0.45	0.86	1.80

10 CITIES THAT GET MOST MAIL PER PERSON, 1988

City	Pieces of mail per person	Total mail
Hartford, Conn.	8,383	1.16 bil.
Orlando, Fla.	7,764	1.13 bil.
Fort Lauderdale, Fla.	5,998	894.0 mil.
Atlanta, Ga.	5,554	2.34 bil.
Tampa, Fla.	5,273	1.47 bil.
Minneapolis, Minn.	4,976	1.78 bil.
Richmond, Va.	4,473	975.0 mil.
Des Moines, Iowa	4,436	852.0 mil.
St. Louis, Mo.	4,223	1.80 bil.
Oakland, Calif.	4,197	1.50 bil.

Source: U.S. Postal Service.

SPECIAL SERVICES FOR DOMESTIC MAIL
(fees in addition to postage)

INSURANCE
(for coverage against loss or damage)

Liability	Fee
$0.01 to $50.00	$0.70
50.01 to 100.00	1.50
100.01 to 150.00	1.90
150.01 to 200.00	2.20
200.01 to 300.00	3.15
300.01 to 400.00	4.30
400.01 to 500.00	5.00

REGISTERED MAIL
(for maximum protection and security)

Value	Articles covered by postal insurance	Articles not covered by postal insurance
$ 0.01 to 100	$4.50	$4.40
100.01 to 500.00	4.85	4.70
500.01 to 1,000.00[1]	5.25	5.05

Other Services	Fee
CERTIFIED MAIL	$ 0.85
CERTIFICATE OF MAILING	0.45

EXPRESS MAIL
Letter rate (up to 8 oz.)	8.75
Less than 2 lbs.	12.00
More than 2 lbs., less than 5 lbs.	15.25
More than 5 lbs., less than 70 lbs., consult postmaster.	

MONEY ORDERS
$0.01 to $35.00	0.75
$35.01 to $700.00	1.00
International money orders	3.00

RESTRICTED DELIVERY (for insured, certified, and registered mail)	2.00

RETURN RECEIPT (with insured, certified, and registered mail)
Requested before delivery:
Showing to whom and when delivered	0.90
Showing to whom, when, and where delivered	1.20
Requested after delivery:	
Showing to whom and when addressed	5.00

RETURN RECEIPT (for merchandise; without another special service)
Showing to whom and when addressed	1.00
Showing to whom, when, and where delivered	1.35

SPECIAL HANDLING (3d- and 4th-class mail only)
10 lbs. and less	1.55
More than 10 lbs.	2.25

1. Consult postmaster for articles valued more than $1,000.
Source: U.S. Postal Service, *Postage, Rates, Fees, and Information* (1988).

SELECTED FOREIGN POSTAL RATES, AND U.S. RATE, BY RANK
(rate for first unit of domestic postage)

Country	National currency	Postage in U.S. cents
Italy	650.00 Lire	50.9
Japan	60.00 Yen	49.5
Germany	0.80 Mark	46.3
Norway	2.90 Kroner	44.5
Austria	5.00 Schilling	41.1
Netherlands	0.75 Guilder/florin[1]	38.5
Sweden	2.30 Kronor	38.3
France	2.20 Francs	37.2
Belgium	13.00 Belg. francs	35.8
U.K.	0.19 Pound	35.2
Switzerland	0.50 Swiss francs	34.5
Australia	0.39 $A	34.0
Canada	0.38 $C[1]	32.1
U.S.	0.25 $U.S.	25.0

Note: Foreign exchange rates prevailing on Dec. 1, 1988. 1. Effective January 1989. **Source:** U.S. Postal Service.

THE INTERNAL REVENUE SERVICE

Founded in 1862, the Internal Revenue Service (IRS) is the office of the Department of the Treasury charged with collecting federal taxes. The Constitution empowers Congress to levy excise taxes and—in emergencies—to raise direct taxes. Congress's right to levy taxes on the income of individuals and corporations was contested throughout the 19th century, but that authority was written into the Constitution with the passage of the 16th Amendment in 1913. Today the source of most of the federal government's revenues are the individual income tax, corporate income tax, excise taxes, estate taxes, and gift taxes. The IRS is responsible for these taxes as well as for collecting employee and employer payments for social insurance and retirement insurance (see "Social Insurance"); since 1986, taxes on alcohol, tobacco, firearms, and explosives have been collected by the Bureau of Alcohol, Tobacco, and Firearms. In 1988 the IRS processed 194 million tax returns totaling $935 billion. Individual returns made up 55% of the number of returns, and revenues from individual income taxes constituted 51% of total revenues.

TAX RETURNS PROCESSED, 1988

Individual tax returns	106,993,675
Corporate income tax	3,986,259
Individual estimated-tax returns	35,488,541
Other (e.g., estate, gift, etc.)	47,836,950
Total returns	**194,305,425**

Source: IRS, *Annual Report 1988*.

CURRENT TAX RATE SCHEDULES

The following tables show the current tax rate schedules as of November 1989. Although there are only two stated tax rates—15% and 28%—a surtax on higher-earning taxpayers creates a third rate of 33%.

MARRIED INDIVIDUALS FILING JOINT RETURNS, AND SURVIVING SPOUSES

Taxable income	What you pay
$0.00–30,950	15% of sum over $0.00
$30,950–74,850	$4,642.50 + 28% of sum over $30,950
$74,850–155,320	16,934.50 + 33% of sum over $74,850
$155,320 +	43,489.60 + 28% of sum over $155,320

HEADS OF HOUSEHOLDS

Taxable income	What you pay
$0.00–24,850	15% of sum over $0.00
$24,850–64,200	$3,727.50 + 28% of sum over $24,850
$64,200–128,810	14,745.50 + 33% of sum over $64,200
$128,810 +	36,066.80 + 28% of sum over $128,810

SINGLE INDIVIDUALS

Taxable income	What you pay
$0.00–18,550	15% of sum over $0.00
$18,550–44,900	$2,782.50 + 28% of sum over $18,550
$44,900–93,130	10,160.50 + 33% of sum over $44,900
$93,130 +	26,076.40 + 28% of sum over $93,130

FILING SEPARATE RETURNS

Taxable income	What you pay
$0.00–15,475	15% of sum over $0.00
$15,475–37,425	$2,321.25 + 28% of sum over $15,475
$37,425–117,895	8,467.25 + 33% of sum over $37,425
$117,895 +	35,022.35 + 28% of sum over $117,895

"The income tax has made liars out of more Americans than golf."
—Will Rogers

REVENUES FOR TAX YEARS 1958 AND 1988

Source	1988	1958
Individuals	$ 473,666,566[1]	$ 38,568,559
Employment taxes	318,038,990[2]	8,644,386
Corporate taxes	109,682,554	20,533,316
Other taxes	33,718,484	12,232,215
Gross tax revenues	**935,106,594**	**79,978,476**

1. Includes $33,421,709 to the presidential election campaign fund. 2. OASDHI, railroad retirement, and unemployment insurance. **Source:** IRS, *Annual Report 1988*.

NET INTERNAL REVENUE COLLECTIONS, 1988
(thousands of dollars)

	Gross Collections	Refunds[1]	NET COLLECTIONS Amount	NET COLLECTIONS Percent of total
Grand total	**$935,106,594**	**$92,760,500**	**$842,346,094**	**100.0%**
Corporation income taxes	109,682,554	15,536,227	94,146,327	11.2
Individual income taxes	473,666,566	75,134,813[2]	398,531,753	47.3
Employment taxes, total	318,038,990	996,914	317,042,075	37.6
OSDHI[3]	307,594,215	707,750	306,886,465	36.4
Railroad retirement	4,266,775	30,318	4,236,457	0.5
Unemployment insurance	6,178,000	258,846	5,919,154	0.7
Estate and gift taxes	7,784,445	190,189	7,594,256	0.9
Excise taxes	25,934,040	902,357	25,031,683	3.0

1. Does not include interest paid on refunds totaling $1.7 billion. 2. Refunds with forms 1040, 1040–A, and 1040–EZ, including withheld taxes minus FICA. 3. Old-age, survivor's, disability, and hospital insurance. **Source:** IRS, *Annual Report 1988*.

RETURNS FILED, AND EXAMINED, AND RECOMMENDED ADDITIONAL TAXES AND PENALTIES, 1988

	Total filed	Total examined	Percent examined	Recommended changes (millions)[1]	Addl. tax per return examined
Total individual returns	103,251,000	1,060,807	1.03%	$ 5,343	$ 5,036
1040–A, TPI less than $10,000	20,198,000	91,350	0.45	375	4,105
Non 1040–A, TPI less than $10,000	10,050,000	35,632	0.35	74	2,076
TPI $10,000–25,000, simple	21,599,000	131,628	0.61	146	1,109
TPI $10,000–25,000, complex	10,044,000	125,429	1.25	147	1,171
TPI $25,000–50,000	24,951,000	302,670	1.21	537	1,774
TPI $50,000+	10,177,000	236,480	2.32	2,673	11,303
Schedule C, TGR less than $25,000	1,931,000	28,076	1.45	83	2,956
Schedule C, TGR $25,000–100,000	2,156,000	45,732	2.12	228	4,985
Schedule C, TGR $100,000+	1,216,000	51,059	4.20	996	19,506
Schedule F, TGR less than $25,000	244,000	1,904	0.78	3	1,575
Schedule F, TGR $25,000–100,000	443,000	4,224	0.95	9	2,130
Schedule F, TGR $100,000+	242,000	6,623	2.74	72	10,871
Fiduciary	2,336,000	4,201	0.18	198	47,131
Partnerships	1,702,786	15,789	0.93	N.A.	N.A.
Corporations	2,868,500	38,078	1.33	11,676	306,633
Small business corporations (1120-S)	892,000	8,848	0.99	156	17,631
All other[2]	29,283,970	77,503	0.20	2,586	33,366

Notes: Totals may not add owing to rounding. TGR = total gross income. TPI = total positive income.   1. Includes additional taxes and penalties.   2. Includes Form 1120–DISC, estates, gifts, excise, employment, windfall profit, and miscellaneous taxes.
Source: IRS, *Annual Report 1988.*

Principal Deductions

Personal Exemptions In filing income tax, taxpayers are allowed to claim personal exemptions for themselves and each dependent. Congress determines the amount allowable for deductions on personal and other exemptions. For income earned in 1989, the amount was $2,000. Starting in 1990, the exemption is pegged to the inflation rate.
Interest Expenses Nonbusiness interest expense falls into four categories: consumer interest (on loans used for personal reasons, such as auto loans, school loans, and insurance); mortgage interest; investment interest; and passive activity interest. In 1989 taxpayers can deduct 20% of interest expense on consumer loans. The allowable deduction falls to 10% in 1990 and is thereafter phased out.
Medical Expenses Although almost all medical expenses are deductible, it is difficult to take a deduction because your combined expenses for the year must total 7.5% of your adjusted gross income. So, for someone with an adjusted gross income of $25,000, medical expenses would have to exceed $1,875.

THE IRS AND YOU

Examination and Enforcement: The Odds of Being Audited

Over 83% of all taxpayers pay their taxes voluntarily; but to ensure that appropriate taxes are paid, and to locate delinquent taxpayers, the IRS has a number of examination and enforcement procedures. The most broad-reaching of the IRS's examination systems is the matching document program, formally known as the Information Returns Program (IRP). This matches third-party information on wages, interest, dividends, and certain deductions with the amounts reported by taxpayers on their returns and identifies people who are reported to have received income but did not file returns. When information does not agree with filed documents, taxpayers are asked to explain the discrepancy. In 1988 the IRS received 913 million information forms and through the IRP found 3.8 million discrepancies, and identified 3 million people who failed to file tax returns.

In 1988 the IRS examined 1.25% of all federal returns filed (not including returns for tax-exempt organizations and alcohol, tobacco, and firearms taxes). Field and office audits examined 1.03 million returns, resulting in $19.2 billion recommended additional taxes and penalties. Correspondence by tax service centers also corrected 18 million returns for $737 million in recommended additional taxes and penalties. The IRS's most sophisticated program is the Coordinated Examination Program, which tackles the largest and most complex domestic and foreign-controlled corporations. In 1988 the IRS conducted 1,461 examinations by Coordinated Examination Program specialists, which resulted in recommended additional taxes and penalties of $9.58 billion, approximately $6.6 million per corporation examined.

AVERAGE ITEMIZED DEDUCTIONS

Adjusted gross income	Medical expenses	Average deduction for		
		Taxes	Contributions	Interest
Under $5 thousand	$ 3,469	$ 839	$ 428	$ 2,834
$5m–10m	3,269	1,113	583	2,583
$10m–15m	2,611	1,391	663	2,979
$15m–20m	2,012	1,629	720	3,137
$20m–25m	1,795	1,855	767	3,298
$25m–30m	1,548	2,331	815	3,636
$30m–40m	1,817	2,817	885	4,369
$40m–50m	2,201	3,590	1,077	5,305
$50m–75m	3,330	4,869	1,499	6,910
$75m–100m	4,887	7,241	2,468	10,151
$100m–200m	12,603	11,063	4,308	13,939
$200m–500m	28,636	23,737	16,393	22,761
$500m–1 million	31,738	48,283	31,983	41,593
Over $1 million	62,000	151,897	199,875	97,161

Note: m = thousand.   **Source:** IRS.

IRS PERSONNEL SUMMARY, 1988

National office	7,964
Regional offices	115,234
Data-processing operations	38,225
Collection	19,481
Taxpayer service	8,041
Examination	32,863
Employee plans/exempt organizations	2,753
Appeals	2,984
Tax fraud	4,634
Executive direction	140
Management services	2,850
Resources management	6,298
Counsel	3,059
Inspection	1,158
International	712
Total	**123,198**

Source: IRS, *Annual Report 1988.*

INTERNAL REVENUE COLLECTIONS, COSTS, EMPLOYEES, AND U.S. POPULATION, 1960–88

Fiscal year	Collections	Cost of collecting $100	Population (thousands)	Tax per capita
1960	$ 91,774,802,823	$0.40	180,671	$ 507.96
1965	114,434,633,721	0.52	194,303	588.95
1970	195,722,096,497	0.45	204,878	955.31
1975	293,822,725,772	0.54	213,559	1,375.84
1980	519,375,273,361	0.44	228,231	2,275.66
1985	742,871,541,283	0.48	239,714	3,098.99
1986	782,251,812,225	0.49	241,995	3,232.51
1987	886,290,589,996	0.49	244,344	3,627.22
1988	935,106,594,222	0.54	246,590	3,792.15

Source: IRS, *Annual Report 1988.*

Tax Freedom Day

To gauge the extent of the total tax burden on individual taxpayers, experts have devised a formula to calculate how long a person has to work to pay all his or her obligations to the state. Suppose you began paying your taxes for the year on Jan. 1 and spent no money until these were paid off. The day you started paying for food, rent, schools, and other necessities is called tax freedom day. In 1929, the beginning of the Great Depression, tax freedom day fell on Feb. 9; in 1988 it was May 4. Looked at another way, while you would have spent 52 minutes out of each day to earn enough money for a day's worth of taxes, you now spend 2 hours and 43 minutes. In other words, you spend 3.1 times more of your annual income on taxes now than you would have 60 years ago.

TAX FREEDOM DAY, 1929–1988

		Tax bite in the 8-hour day (hours:minutes)		
Year	Tax free-dom day	Total	Federal	State & local
1929	Feb. 9	0:52	0:19	0:33
1940	Mar. 8	1:29	0:45	0:44
1950	Apr. 3	2:02	1:30	0:32
1960	Apr. 17	2:22	1:40	0:42
1970	Apr. 28	2:34	1:40	0:54
1980	May 1	2:39	1:48	0:51
1988	May 4	2:43	1:46	0:57

Source: Tax Foundation, *Facts and Figures on Government Finance 1988–89.*

A FRIEND INDEED

In 1988 taxpayers in eight states suffered losses because of floods, hurricanes, tornadoes, and other emergencies and disasters. The IRS provided on-site help to the victims in preparing amended returns for casualty loss claims and expediting refunds to the affected taxpayers.
Source: *IRS Annual Report 1988.*

STATES, TERRITORIES, AND POSSESSIONS

This section, a compilation of history and statistics about the 50 United States, the District of Columbia, and U.S. territories and possessions, includes a brief history of each state and territory; its official motto and other emblems; a summary of geographic, demographic, and economic facts; as well as a list of prominent natives, places, and dates.

Statistical sources include the U.S. Census Bureau's *1980 Census of Population and Housing, General Social and Economic Characteristics, The County and City Data Book 1988, The Statistical Abstract 1988,* and *Projections of the Population of States by Age, Sex, and Race;* the Council of State Governments' *Book of the States 1988–89* and *State Elective Officials and the Legislatures 1989–90;* and the Bureau of Economic Analysis's *Survey of Current Business,* "Gross State Product by Industry 1963–86" (1988).

The headings for demographic statistics in the paragraphs on People and Language conform to U.S. Census Bureau usage, although "Indian" is used as a short form for American Indian, Eskimo, and Aleut, "American Indian langs." is used for American Indian and Alaska native languages, and "Asian" is used for Asian and Pacific Islander.

Alabama

In the cradle of the Confederacy, cotton culture and the rural way of life are shrinking. But the state's populist roots still show in swings toward and away from progressivism. White candidates who court black votes, yet Alabama still ranks near last in taxes and most services. Increasingly urban—50 years ago 70 percent of the population lived in rural areas, compared with less than 40 percent today—and increasingly dependent on heavy industry, Alabama's economy is progressing slowly.

NAME Probably after Alabama tribe. NICKNAME Heart of Dixie. CAPITAL Montgomery. ENTERED UNION Dec. 14, 1819 (22d). MOTTO "We dare defend our rights."
Emblems BIRD Yellowhammer. DANCE Square dance. GAME BIRD Wild turkey. FISH Tarpon. FOSSIL *Basilosaurus oetoides.* MINERAL Hematite. NUT Pecan. SONG "Alabama." STONE Marble. TREE Southern (longleaf) pine.
Land TOTAL AREA 51,705 sq. mi. (29th), incl. 938 sq. mi. inland water. BORDERS Tenn., Ga.,

Fla., Gulf of Mexico, Miss. RIVERS Alabama, Chattahoochee, Mobile, Tennessee, Tennessee-Tombigbee Waterway, Tensaw, Tombigbee. LAKES Guntersville, Pickwick, Wheeler, Wilson (all formed by Tennessee Valley Authority [TVA]); Dannelly Res., Martin, Lewis Smith, Weiss. MOUNTAINS Cumberland, Lookout, Raccoon, Sand.
Elected officials Gov. Harold Guy Hunt (R). Lt. Gov. Jim Folsom, Jr. (D). Sec. State Perry Hand (R). Atty. Gen. Don Siegelman (D).
People (1988 est.) 4,127,000 (22d). RACE/NATIONAL ORIGIN (1980): White 73.79%. Black 25.59%. Indian 0.24%. Asian 0.27%. Hispanic 0.87%. Foreign-born 1.00%. LANGUAGES (1980): English 98.14%. French 0.29%. German 0.29%. Spanish 0.10%. Italian 0.05%.
Cities (1986) Birmingham 277,510. Mobile 203,260. Montgomery 194,290. Huntsville 163,420. Tuscaloosa 73,830. Dothan 53,310. Gadsden 45,180.
Business GROSS STATE PRODUCT (GSP, 1986) $55 bil. (24th). Sectors of GSP: Farms 2.06%. Agricultural services, forestry, & fisheries 0.36%. Mining 2.53%. Construction 3.19%. Manufacturing 23.48%. Transportation & public utilities 10.12%. Wholesale 6.56%. Retail 9.54%. Finance, insurance, & real estate 13.16%. Services 13.45%. Federal government 4.62%. Federal military 2.00%. State & local government 8.93%. FORTUNE 500 COMPANIES (1988): 4: Intergraph, Russell, SCI Systems, Vulcan Materials.
Famous natives Hank Aaron, baseball player. Tallulah Bankhead, actress. William B. Bankhead, politician. Hugo L. Black, jurist. Wernher von Braun (b. Germany), rocket scientist. Nat ("King") Cole, singer. Red Eagle (William Weatherfield), Creek leader. W.C. Handy, musician. Frank M. Johnson, Jr., jurist. Helen Keller, author. Coretta Scott (Mrs. Martin Luther) King, reformer. Harper Lee, author. Joe Louis, boxer. Jesse Owens, runner. Leroy Robert ("Satchell") Paige, baseball player. Walker Percy, author. George Wallace, politician. Hank Williams, singer.
Noteworthy places Alabama Deep Sea Fishing Rodeo, Dauphin Island. Alabama Space and Rocket Center, U.S. Space Camp, Huntsville. Battleship USS *Alabama,* Mobile. Birmingham Museum of Art. First White House of the Confederacy, Montgomery. Horseshoe Bend Natl. Military Park. Mound State Monument Archaeological Museum, Moundville. Museum of Natural History, Univ. Alabama, Tuscaloosa. Point Clear (resort). Russell Cave Natl. Monument. Tuskegee Institute.
Memorable events Humans first inhabit Russell Cave c. 6000 B.C. First Europeans in Mobile Bay 1519. Hernando de Soto's battle with Tuscaloosa possibly bloodiest encounter ever between Europeans and Native Americans in U.S. 1540. Spanish at Mobile Bay 1599. Pierre Le Moyne, sieur d'Iberville, establishes first permanent colony at Mobile 1711. Treaty of Paris gives Mobile to Britain 1763. U.S. control recognized 1783. Chickasaws, Choctaws, and Cherokees cede lands to U.S. 1805. First Baptist Church established 1808. Gen. Andrew Jackson defeats Creek Indian Confederacy at Horseshoe Bend 1814. Cotton

principal cash crop 1820s. Beginnings of coal and iron mining and steel manufacturing 1850s. Alabama secedes from Union; first capital of Confederate States of America at Montgomery 1861. Battle of Mobile Bay 1864. Readmitted to Union 1868. Booker T. Washington founds Tuskegee Institute 1881. Destruction of cotton crops by boll weevils leads to diversification of rural economy 1915. Tennessee Valley Authority enacted by Congress 1933. Montgomery bus boycott 1955. Freedom march from Selma to Montgomery 1965.

Tourist information 1–800–ALABAMA or 1–205–261–4169.

Alaska

Here the struggle between economic development and conservation is played out on a grand scale. A majority of Alaskans voted in 1980 to reconsider statehood after President James E. Carter sequestered millions of acres from development. Yet they have also voted against removing special fishing privileges for Native Americans. A place of extremes, Alaska is one of the least populated areas of the human sphere.

NAME From Aleut *alaska* and Eskimo *alakshak*, both meaning "mainland." NICKNAME None. CAPITAL Juneau. ENTERED UNION Jan. 3, 1959 (49th). MOTTO "North to the future."

Emblems BIRD Willow ptarmigan. FISH King salmon. FLOWER Forget-me-not. GEM Jade. MARINE MAMMAL Bowhead whale. MINERAL Gold. SONG "Alaska's Flag." SPORT Mushing (dog-team racing). TREE Sitka spruce.

Land TOTAL AREA 591,004 sq. mi. (1st), incl. 20,171 sq. mi. inland water. BORDERS Arctic Ocean (Chukchi Sea, Beaufort Sea), Yukon, British Columbia, Pacific Ocean, and Bering Strait. RIVERS Colville, Porcupine, Noatak, Yukon, Susitna, Copper, Kobuk, Koyukuk, Kuskokwim, Tanana. MOUNTAINS Alaska Range (Mt. McKinley 20,320 ft., highest in North America), Aleutian Range, Brooks Range, Kuskokwim, St. Elias. OTHER NOTABLE FEATURES Aleutian Islands, Alexander Archipelago, Kodiak Island, Nunivak Island, Point Barrow (71° 23′N), Pribilof Islands, Seward Peninsula, St. Lawrence Island.

Elected officials Gov. Steve Cowper (D). Lt. Gov. Stephen McAlpine (D). Sec. State, none. Atty. Gen. Doug Baily (R).

People (1988 est.) 513,000 (49th). RACE/ NATIONAL ORIGIN (1980): White 77.76%. Black 3.42%. Indian 16.02% (American Indian 5.63%, Eskimo 8.42%, Aleut 1.97%). Asian 2.07%. Hispanic 2.25%. Foreign-born 4.00%. LANGUAGES (1980): English 87.5%. American Indian langs. 7.06%. Spanish 1.46%. German 0.77%. Philippine langs. 0.57%.

Cities (1986) Anchorage 235,000. Fairbanks 27,610. Juneau 25,000. Sitka 7,700. Ketchikan 7,400. Kodiak 7,140. Kenai 6,370. Bethel 3,900.

Business GROSS STATE PRODUCT (GSP, 1986) $19.6 bil. (38th). SECTORS OF GSP: Farms 0.12%. Agricultural services, forestry, & fish-

eries 1.50%. Mining 33.36%. Construction 10.12%. Manufacturing 4.99%. Transportation & public utilities 7.64%. Wholesale 2.50%. Retail 5.66%. Finance, insurance, & real estate 9.22%. Services 8.42%. Federal government 3.27%. Federal military 3.63%. State & local government 9.57%. *FORTUNE* 500 COMPANIES (1988): 0.

Famous natives Aleksandr Baranov (b. Russia), 1st governor of Russian America. Vitus Bering (b. Denmark), explorer. Ernest Gruening (b. N.Y.), governor. Carl Ben Eielson, bush pilot. Walter Hickel (b. Kans.), governor.

Noteworthy places Aniakchak Natl. Monument. Cape Krusenstern Natl. Monument. Denali Natl. Park (formerly Mt. McKinley Natl. Park). Gates of the Arctic Natl. Park. Glacier Bay Natl. Park. Katmai Natl. Park (Valley of Ten Thousand Smokes). Kenai Fjords Natl. Park. Klondike Gold Rush Natl. Hist. Park. Kobuk Valley Natl. Park. Lake Clark Natl. Park. Little Diomede Island—2.5 mi. from Big Diomede Island (USSR). Sitka Natl. Hist. Park. St. Michael's Cathedral, Sitka. Wrangell–St. Elias Natl. Park.

Memorable events Earliest migration from Asia to Americas across Bering Sea land bridge, c. 15,000 years ago. Alaska inhabited by Tlingits, Tinnehs, Aleuts, and Eskimos. Peter the Great sponsors expedition to find land opposite Siberia 1728. Bering expedition lands near Mt. Elias; begins Pacific Northwest fur trade with Europe and Asia 1741. Russians establish first European settlement at Three Saints Bay 1784. Russian-American Company chartered 1799. Baranov's massacre of Tlingits at Sitka 1802. Gold discovered at Stikine Creek (1861), Juneau (1880), Fortymile Creek (1886), Nome (1898), Fairbanks (1903). Russians sell Alaska to U.S. for $7.2 million 1867. First salmon cannery established 1878. Japanese occupy Agattu, Attu, and Kiska islands 1942–43. Alaskans vote for statehood 1946. Statehood 1959. Earthquake destroys Anchorage, Northwest Panhandle, and Cook Inlet; tsunami wipes out Valdez; coast sinks 32 ft. at Kodiak and Seward and rises 16 ft. at Cordova 1964. Oil discovered on North Slope 1968. Completion of 789-mi. pipeline to Valdez 1977. Population growth of 32.8% highest in U.S. 1980–86.

Tourist information 1–800–642–0066.

Arizona

The Hopi village of Oraibi is the oldest continuously inhabited town in the United States, but in Arizona's growth-oriented oasis cities—made livable by air-conditioning—recently arrived retirees and manufacturing employees are altering the voting base. The Arizona growth rate is exceeded only by Alaska, Nevada, and Florida, although, because of air pollution, doctors are no longer so quick to recommend Phoenix for asthma sufferers. Mexican-Americans are now an important political force; ex-governor Bruce Babbitt campaigned actively in Spanish with a greater awareness of America's southern neighbor. As in most western states, water rights are a major struggle.

NAME Probably from the Pima or Papago for "place of small springs." NICKNAME Grand Canyon State. CAPITAL Phoenix. ENTERED UNION Feb. 14, 1912 (48th). MOTTO *Ditat deus* (God enriches).

Emblems BIRD Cactus wren. FLOWER Blossom of the saguaro cactus. GEMSTONE Turquoise. OFFICIAL NECK WEAR Bola tie. SONGS "Arizona March Song," "Arizona." TREE Palo verde.

Land TOTAL AREA 114,000 sq. mi. (6th), incl. 492 sq. mi. inland water. BORDERS Utah, Colo., N.Mex., Sonora, Baja California Norte, Calif., Nev. RIVERS Colorado, Gila, Little Colorado, Salt, Zuni. LAKES Havasu, Mead, Mohave, Powell, Roosevelt, San Carlos. MOUNTAINS Black, Gila, Hualpai, Mohawk, San Francisco Peaks (Humphreys Peak 12,633 ft.). OTHER NOTABLE FEATURES Grand Canyon, Kaibab Plateau, Painted Desert, Petrified Forest, Sonoran Desert.

Elected officials Gov. Rose Mofford (D). Lt. Gov., none. Sec. State Jim Shumway (D). Atty. Gen. Robert K. Corbin (R).

People (1988 est.) 3,466,000 (25th). RACE/ NATIONAL ORIGIN (1980): White 85.15%. Black 2.73%. Indian 5.67%. Asian 0.10%. Hispanic 16.34%. Foreign-born 6.00%. LANGUAGES (1980): English 79.88%. Spanish 13.21%. American Indian langs. 3.87%. German 0.65%. French 0.38%. Italian 0.31%.

Cities (1986) Phoenix 894,070. Tucson 358,850. Mesa 251,430. Tempe 136,480. Glendale 125,820. Scottsdale 114,500.

Business GROSS STATE PRODUCT (GSP, 1986) $53.3 bil. (25th). SECTORS OF GSP: Farms 1.53%. Agricultural services, forestry, & fisheries 0.58%. Mining 1.28%. Construction 10.01%. Manufacturing 13.47%. Transportation & public utilities 8.72%. Wholesale 5.26%. Retail 11.51%. Finance, insurance, & real estate 16.73%. Services 16.99%. Federal government 2.52%. Federal military 1.58%. State & local government 9.83%. *FORTUNE* 500 COMPANIES (1988): 1: Phelps Dodge.

Famous natives Bruce Babbitt, politician. Cesar Chavez, labor leader. Cochise, Apache chief. Andrew Ellicott Douglass (b. Vt.), dendrochronologist. Wyatt Earp (b. Ill.), lawman. Barry Goldwater, politician. Goyathlay (Geronimo), Apache chieftain. Carl T. Hayden, congressman. Eusebio Kino (b. Italy), missionary. Sandra Day O'Connor, jurist. William H. Rehnquist, jurist. Linda Ronstadt, singer. Morris Udall, politician.

Noteworthy places Canyon de Chelly Natl. Monument. Casa Grande Ruins Natl. Monument. Chiricahua Natl. Monument. Ft. Bowie. Grand Canyon Natl. Park. Heard Museum, Phoenix. London Bridge, Lake Havasu City. Montezuma Castle Natl. Monument. Navajo Natl. Monument. Organ Pipe Cactus Natl. Monument. Painted Desert. Petrified Forest Natl. Park. Pipe Spring Natl. Monument. Saguaro Natl. Monument. Sunset Crater Natl. Monument. Taliesin West, near Scottsdale. Tonto Natl. Monument. Tumacacori Natl. Monument. Tuzigoot Natl. Monument. Walnut Canyon Natl. Monument. Wupatki Natl. Monument.

Memorable events Apaches and Navajos absorb Pueblos C. A.D. 1000. Alvar Núñez

Cabeza de Vaca, first Spanish explorer 1536. Marcos de Niza 1539. Ruled as part of New Spain 1598–1821. First missionaries among Hopis 1638. Tubac first European settlement 1752. Tucson founded 1776. Apaches wipe out settlements under Mexican control, except Tucson 1821. Northern part ceded to U.S. following Mexican War 1848. Area south of Gila River to U.S. after Gadsden Purchase 1853. Territory 1863. Southern Pacific Railroad reaches Tucson 1880. Apaches subjugated 1886. Congress refuses to grant statehood 1906. Roosevelt Dam and Reservoir built on Salt River 1911. Native Americans given right to vote 1948. New Cornelia Tailings Dam, world's largest, completed 1973. Population growth of 22.1% highest in continental U.S. 1980–86.
Tourist information 1–602–542–3618.

Arkansas

Midway between the South and the West, Arkansas has one of the highest rural populations among the 50 states. In 1957 Gov. Orvil Faubus defied a Supreme Court order to admit black students to Little Rock public schools by ordering the National Guard to block their entry. Since his 1966 retirement, Arkansas has become generally progressive. Racial relations have improved, and manufacturing is increasing, though services rank low, as do levels of income and education.

Name For term for Quapaw tribe given by other Indians. NICKNAME Land of Opportunity. CAPITAL Little Rock. ENTERED UNION June 15, 1836 (25th). MOTTO *Regnat populus* (Let the people rule).
Emblems BIRD Mockingbird. FLOWER Apple blossom. GEM Diamond. SONG "Arkansas." TREE Pine.
Land TOTAL AREA 53,187 sq. mi. (27th), incl. 1,109 sq. mi. inland water. BORDERS Mo., Tenn., Miss., La., Tex., Okla. RIVERS Arkansas, Mississippi, Ouachita, Red, St. Francis, White. LAKES Beaver, Bull Shoals, Chicot, Dardanelle, Greers Ferry, Greeson, Norfolk, Ouachita. OTHER NOTABLE FEATURES Ozark Mts.
Elected officials Gov. Bill Clinton (D). Lt. Gov. Winston Bryant (D). Sec. State W.J. ("Bill") McCuen (D). Atty. Gen. Steve Clark (D).
People (1988 est.) 2,422,000 (33d). RACE/ NATIONAL ORIGIN (1980): White 82.66%. Black 16.32%. Indian 0.56%. Asian 0.32%. Hispanic 0.74%. Foreign-born 1.00%. LANGUAGES (1980): English 98.15%. Spanish 0.63%. German 0.26%. French 0.23%. Vietnamese 0.05%.
Cities (1986) Little Rock 181,030. Fort Smith 74,320. North Little Rock 63,540. Pine Bluff 61,320. Fayetteville 40,110. Hot Springs 36,950. Jonesboro 30,050. Jacksonville 29,650.
Business GROSS STATE PRODUCT (GSP, 1986) $31.6 bil. (33d). SECTORS OF GSP: Farms 5.56%. Agricultural services, forestry, & fisheries 0.41%. Mining 1.61%. Construction 4.91%. Manufacturing 24.60%. Transportation & public utilities 10.42%. Wholesale 5.43%. Retail 10.43%. Finance, insurance, & real estate 14.16%. Services 12.10%. Federal

government 1.44%. Federal military 1.27%. State & local government 7.69%. *FORTUNE* 500 COMPANIES (1988): 3: Murphy Oil, Riceland Foods, Tyson Foods.
Famous natives Maya Angelou, author. Glen Campbell, singer. Hattie W. Caraway, first woman senator. Johnny Cash, singer. Eldridge Cleaver, author. William Fulbright (b. Mo.), politician. Alan Ladd, actor. Douglas MacArthur, general. Dick Powell, actor. Brooks Robinson, baseball. Winthrop Rockefeller (b. N.Y.), politician/philanthropist. Edward Durrell Stone, architect. C. Vann Woodward, historian.
Noteworthy places Arkansas Post Natl. Monument (1st permanent French settlement in lower Mississippi Valley). Buffalo Natl. River. Crater of Diamonds State Park, Murfreesboro. Eureka Springs. Ft. Smith Natl. Hist. Site. Hot Springs Natl. Park. Pea Ridge Natl. Military Park.
Memorable events Bluff-dwellers present c. A.D. 500, followed by mound-building cultures. Hernando de Soto explores for Spain 1541. Jacques Marquette and Louis Jolliet explore for France 1673. René-Robert de La Salle meets Quapaws 1682. Henri de Tonti founds Arkansas Post on Arkansas River 1686. Ceded from France to Spain 1782; to France 1800; to U.S. 1803. Territory 1819. Admitted to Union as slave state, under terms of 1820 Missouri Compromise, 1836. Secedes from Union 1861. Fall of Little Rock to Union army 1863. Readmitted to Union 1868. Bauxite discovered 1887. Oil production begins 1920s. Federal troops called to Little Rock to ensure high school desegregation 1957. McClellan-Kerr Arkansas River Navigation System links Arkansas and Oklahoma to Mississippi River system 1971.
Tourist information 1–800–643–8383 or 1–800–482–8999.

California

Some demographers expect that within 50 years, more than 40 percent of California's population will be Hispanic, a higher proportion than at any time since the days of the 1849 Gold Rush. At the same time, the trend toward a two-tier society increases, with Caucasians and Asians on top and blacks and Latins on the bottom. Multiculturalism dates from the earliest human settlement here. Before the Europeans arrived, no area of comparable size contained a greater variety of languages and cultures. Among the 50 states, California is the one that could most easily survive as an independent nation. Yet, like an independent nation, it has many complex elements. In 1982 one referendum endorsed a bilateral nuclear freeze with the USSR; another rejected handgun registration and restrictions. The bloom is partly off the California rose as some recent immigrants—from both overseas and the rest of the U.S.—have moved on to neighboring states, especially Oregon and Washington.

Name Probably from mythical island in García Ordoñez de Montalvo's 16th-century romance, *The Deeds of Esplandián*. NICKNAME Golden State. CAPITAL Sacramento. ENTERED

UNION Sept. 9, 1850 (31st). MOTTO "Eureka" (I have found it).
Emblems ANIMAL California grizzly bear (extinct). BIRD California valley quail. FISH California golden trout. FLOWER Golden poppy. FOSSIL California saber-toothed cat. GEMSTONE Benitoite. INSECT California dog-face butterfly. MARINE MAMMAL California gray whale. MINERAL Gold. REPTILE California desert tortoise. ROCK Serpentine. SONG "I Love You, California." TREE California redwood.
Land TOTAL AREA 158,706 sq. mi. (3d), incl. 2,407 sq. mi. inland water. BORDERS Oreg., Nev., Ariz., Baja California Norte, Pacific Ocean. RIVERS American, Colorado, Colorado River Aqueduct, Eel, Friant-Kern Canal, Klamath, Russian, Sacramento, Salinas, San Joaquin. LAKES Clear, Goose, Honey, Mono, Owens, Salton Sea, Shasta, Tahoe. MOUNTAINS Coast Ranges, Klamath, Lassen Peak, Sierra Nevada (Mt. Whitney 14,494 ft.). OTHER NOTABLE FEATURES Catalina Islands, Death Valley (282 ft. below sea level), San Francisco Bay, San Joaquin Valley.
Elected officials Gov. George Deukmejian (R). Lt. Gov. Leo T. McCarthy (D). Sec. State March Fong Eu (D). Atty. Gen. John Van de Kamp (D).
People (1988 est.) 28,168,000 (1st). RACE/ NATIONAL ORIGIN (1980): White 66.97%. Black 7.54%. Indian 0.08%. Asian 5.25% (Japanese 1.14%, Chinese 1.38%, Filipino 1.51%, Korean 0.43%, Asian Indian 0.25%, Vietnamese 0.36%). Hispanic 19.19%. Foreign-born 15.10%. LANGUAGES (1980): English 77.40%. Spanish 14.26%. Chinese 1.17%. Philippine langs. 1.05%. German 0.77%. Italian 0.60%. Japanese 0.58%. French 0.51%.
Cities (1986) Los Angeles 3,259,340. San Diego 1,015,190. San Francisco 749,000. San Jose 712,080. Long Beach 396,280. Oakland 356,960. Sacramento 323,550. Fresno 284,660. Anaheim 240,730.
Business GROSS STATE PRODUCT (GSP, 1986) $533.8 bil. (1st). SECTORS OF GSP: Farms 1.49%. Agricultural services, forestry, & fisheries 0.62%. Mining 1.11%. Construction 4.47%. Manufacturing 18.30%. Transportation & public utilities 7.85%. Wholesale 7.25%.

Retail 10.34%. Finance, insurance, & real estate 17.57%. Services 19.37%. Federal government 2.01%. Federal military 1.76%. State & local government 7.85%. *FORTUNE* 500 COMPANIES (1988): 42: incl. Apple Computer, Atari, Atlantic Richfield, Chevron, Clorox, Hewlett-Packard, Homestake Mining, Lockheed, Mattel, Northrop, Occidental Petroleum, Sun-Diamond Growers, Tandem Computer, Teledyne, Times Mirror, Unocal.

Famous natives Ansel Adams, photographer. Dave Brubeck, musician. Luther Burbank (b. Mass.), horticulturist. John Cage, composer. Joe DiMaggio, baseball player. Robert Frost, poet. Ernest and Julio Gallo (b. Italy), vintners. Pancho Gonzales, tennis. Samuel Ichiye Hayakawa, politician/educator. William Randolph Hearst, publisher. Steve Jobs, computer scientist. Billie Jean King, athlete. Allen Lockheed, aviator. Jack London, author. Paul Masson (b. France), vintner. Marilyn Monroe, actress. John Muir (b. Scotland), naturalist. Richard M. Nixon, U.S. president. John Northrop, aviator. Adlai Stevenson, politician. John Steinbeck, author. Levi Strauss (b. Germany), clothier. Edward Teller (b. Hungary), nuclear physicist. Shirley Temple, actress. Earl Warren, politician/jurist.

Noteworthy places Big Sur, Monterey. Cabrillo Natl. Monument. California Academy of Sciences, San Francisco. California Palace of the Legion of Honor, San Francisco. Channel Islands Natl. Park. Devils Postpile Natl. Monument. Death Valley Natl. Monument. Disneyland. Fine Arts Museum of San Francisco. Fishermen's Wharf, San Francisco. Hollywood. Huntington Library and Botanical Gardens, San Marino. J. Paul Getty Museum, Malibu. Joshua Tree Natl. Monument. Kings Canyon Natl. Park. Lassen Volcanic Natl. Park. Lava Beds Natl. Monument. Los Angeles Co. Museum of Art. Muir Woods Natl. Monument. Mt. Palomar Observatory. Natl. Maritime Museum, San Francisco. Natural History Museum, Los Angeles. Natural History Museum of San Diego. Norton Simon Museum of Art at Pasadena. Pinnacles Natl. Monument. Redwood Natl. Park. Rosicrucian Egyptian Museum, San José. San Diego Museum of Art. San Diego Museum of Man. San Diego Zoo. San Francisco Museum of Modern Art. Sequoia Natl. Park. Southwest Museum (Casa de Adobe), Los Angeles. Yosemite Natl. Park.

Memorable events João Rodrigues Cabrilho lands at San Diego Bay 1542. Francis Drake lands north of San Francisco Bay 1579. Junípero Serra founds missions at San Diego (1769), Monterey (1770), San Luis Obispo (1772), and San Juan Capistrano (1776). California declares allegiance to independent Mexico 1821. First wagon train from Missouri 1841. Gold discovered north of Los Angeles 1842. California declares itself independent republic 1846. Gold found at John Sutter's mill; nine days later, by Treaty of Guadalupe Hidalgo, Mexico cedes California to U.S. 1848. Announcement of gold discovery brings 80,000 'Forty-niners. Gold rush peaks 1852. Transcontinental telegraph completed 1861. Transcontinental railway completed 1869. U.S. Congress enacts Chinese Exclusion Act, pro-

hibiting immigration of Chinese laborers 1882, 1892, and 1902; Act repealed 1943. San Francisco earthquake kills 452, destroys 28,000 buildings 1906. Webb Alien Land Law prohibits Japanese from holding land 1913. Los Angeles has one car for every three people, twice national average, 1925. Dust Bowl immigrants 1930. Hollywood produces bulk of movies for U.S. theaters, which number more than banks 1940. Most populous state 1963. Proposition 13 limits property tax 1978. California sixth-strongest economic power in world 1988.

Tourist information 1–800–862–2543 or 1–916–322–1397.

Colorado

The native peoples of Colorado were the Plains Indians (Arapahoe and Cheyenne) to the east and the Great Basin Indians (Utes) to the west. This pre-Columbian division of the land is reflected today in Colorado's economy, which is a mix of agriculture and technology in the east and mining and ski tourism in the mountains. Despite a lack of natural sources of water on the Plains, sugar-beet processing has for years been a staple of the agricultural sector. During the oil price shocks of the 1970s, shale-oil production on the Western Slope created a boom comparable to the silver and lead boom in the late 19th century. Colorado's love of the outdoors is increasingly in conflict with its tradition of unhindered growth. Colorado's cities east of the Rockies sprawl without effective plans for land use. While a state of great natural beauty, it must cope with a high altitude that almost doubles the effect of auto emissions. Economic development means in large part resource extraction and requires more and more water, whose limited supply poses a great question for the future.

NAME Spanish for the *color red*. NICKNAME Centennial State. CAPITAL Denver. ENTERED UNION Aug. 1, 1876 (38th). MOTTO *Nil sine numine* (Nothing without providence).

Emblems ANIMAL Rocky Mountain bighorn sheep. BIRD Lark bunting. FLOWER Rocky Mountain Columbine. GEM Aquamarine. SONG "Where the Columbines Grow." TREE Colorado blue spruce.

Land TOTAL AREA 104,091 sq. mi. (8th), incl. 496 sq. mi. inland water. BORDERS Wyo., Nebr., Kans., N.Mex., Ariz., Utah. RIVERS Arkansas, Colorado, Green, Platte, Rio Grande. LAKES Blue Mesa, Dillon, Granby. MOUNTAINS Front Range, Laramie, Sangre de Cristo, San Juan, Sawatch Range (Mt. Elbert 14,443 ft.).

Elected officials Gov. Roy Romer (D). Lt. Gov. Michael Callihan (D). Sec. State Natalie Meyer (R). Atty. Gen. Duane Woodard (D).

People (1988 est.) 3,290,000 (26th). RACE/NATIONAL ORIGIN (1980): White 89.66%. Black 3.16%. Indian 0.73%. Asian 1.19%. Hispanic 11.82%. Foreign-born 3.90%. LANGUAGES (1980): English 89.41%. Spanish 6.72%. German 1.21%. French 0.42%. Italian 0.27%.

Cities (1986) Denver 505,000. Colorado Springs 272,660. Aurora 217,990. Lakewood 122,140. Pueblo 101,240. Arvada 91,310.

Boulder 76,480.

Business GROSS STATE PRODUCT (GSP, 1986) $59.2 bil. (23d). SECTORS OF GSP: Farms 2.15%. Agricultural services, forestry, & fisheries 0.41%. Mining 2.88%. Construction 5.93%. Manufacturing 12.90%. Transportation & public utilities 11.09%. Wholesale 6.39%. Retail 10.62%. Finance, insurance, & real estate 16.37%. Services 17.27%. Federal government 2.97%. Federal military 2.22%. State & local government 8.79%. *FORTUNE* 500 COMPANIES (1988): 3: Adolph Coors, Cyprus Minerals, Manville.

Famous natives Charlie Bent (b. Va.), trapper. "Unsinkable" Molly Brown, *Titanic* survivor. Scott Carpenter, astronaut. Lon Chaney, actor. Jack Dempsey, boxer. Mamie Eisenhower, First Lady. Douglas Fairbanks, actor. Anne Parrish, novelist. Lowell Thomas, journalist. Byron R. White, jurist. Paul Whiteman, conductor.

Noteworthy Places Black Canyon of the Gunnison Natl. Monument. Buffalo Bill grave site, Evergreen. Central City Opera House. Colorado Springs Fine Arts Center. Denver Art Museum. Denver Mint. Denver Museum of Natural History. Dinosaur Natl. Monument. Florissant Fossil Beds Natl. Monument. Garden of the Gods, Colorado Springs. Great Sand Dunes Natl. Monument. Hovenweep Natl. Monument. Mesa Verde Natl. Park. Molly Brown House, Denver. Pikes Peak. Red Rocks Amphitheater. Rocky Mountain Natl. Park, Aspen. U.S. Air Force Academy, Colorado Springs. U.S. Olympic Headquarters, Colorado Springs. Yucca House Natl. Monument.

Memorable events Pueblos build cliff dwellings near Mesa Verde through 1200s. Arapahos and Cheyennes settle area after 13th century. France abandons claims 1763. Juan de Uribarri explores area 1786. Spain restores area to France 1801. To U.S. as part of Louisiana Purchase 1803. Zebulon Pike explores for U.S. 1806. Kit Carson and other scouts explore and trade with Native Americans 1810s–20s. Native Americans form alliance at Brent's Fork 1840. John Frémont's explorations 1842–53. Present territorial limits after Mexican War 1848. First permanent settlement at San Luis 1851. Gold found west of Denver—"Pike's Peak or Bust"—1858. Mineral springs bring first tourists 1861. Homestead Act encourages farming 1862. U.S. Army kills 400 Cheyenne at Sand Creek Massacre 1864. Utes and Cheyennes fight white settlement through 1870s. Railroad link to Denver 1870. Silver and lead discoveries 1875. Uranium discovered near Grand Junction 1946. U.S. Air Force Academy founded Denver 1954; to Colorado Springs 1958. Shale oil boom on Western Slope 1974 and 1979. Accumulation of nuclear waste threatens suspension of operations at Rocky Flats 1988.

Tourist information 1–800–433–2656 or 1–303–592–5410.

Connecticut

Called the "arsenal of the nation" during the Revolution, Connecticut today leads the 50 states in defense-contract dollars per capita, although population ebb and flow continue to test its manufacturing wealth. Hartford has been the insurance capital of the world since before 1800, and Connecticut's quarries provided much of the red sandstone that became known as "brownstone" after it lined New York City streets. With conditions favorable for affluent business, Connecticut, without a state income tax, now resorts for revenue to the lottery and jai alai. Corporate relocation and booming housing prices are changing the relation of Connecticut to its larger neighbor, New York, and turning suburbia into megalopolis.

NAME From Mahican word meaning "beside the long tidal river." NICKNAMES Constitution State, Nutmeg State. CAPITAL Hartford. ENTERED UNION Jan. 9, 1788 (5th). MOTTO *Qui transtulit sustinet* (He who transplanted still sustains).

Emblems ANIMAL Sperm whale. BIRD American robin. FLOWER Mountain laurel. HERO Nathan Hale. INSECT European praying mantis. MINERAL Garnet. SHIP USS *Nautilus*. SONG "Yankee Doodle." TREE White oak.

Land TOTAL AREA 5,018 sq. mi. (48th), incl. 146 sq. mi. inland water. BORDERS Mass., R.I., Long Island Sound, N.Y. RIVERS Connecticut, Housatonic, Mianus, Naugatuck, Thames. LAKES Bantam, Barkhamstead, Candlewood, Waramaug. OTHER NOTABLE FEATURES Berkshire Hills, Long Island Sound.

Elected officials Gov. William A. O'Neill (D). Lt. Gov. Joseph J. Fauliso (D). Sec. State Julia H. Tashjian (D). Atty. Gen. Clarine Nordi Riddle (D).

Population (1988 est.) 3,241,000 (28th). RACE/NATIONAL ORIGIN (1980): White 90.50%. Black 6.97%. Indian 0.16%. Asian 0.68%. Hispanic 4.03%. Foreign-born 8.60%. LANGUAGES (1980): English 85.67%. Spanish 3.52%. Italian 3.12%. French 2.05%. Polish 1.45%. Portuguese 0.72%. German 0.69%. Greek 0.34%.

Cities (1986) Bridgeport 141,860. Hartford 137,980. New Haven 123,450. Waterbury 102,300. Stamford 101,080. Norwalk 77,220. New Britain 72,040. Danbury 64,530.

Business GROSS STATE PRODUCT (GSP, 1986) $70.6 bil. (22d). SECTORS OF GSP: Farms 0.40%. Agricultural services, forestry, & fisheries 0.29%. Mining 0.11%. Construction 4.18%. Manufacturing 24.32%. Transportation & public utilities 7.62%. Wholesale 7.12%. Retail 9.65%. Finance, insurance, & real estate 19.91%. Services 16.66%. Federal government 2.48%. Federal military 0.74%. State & local government 6.53%. FORTUNE 500 COMPANIES (1988): 31: incl. American Brands, Coleco Industries, General Electric, Insilco, Olin, Pitney Bowes, Singer, Union Carbide, United Technologies, Xerox.

Famous natives Benedict Arnold, traitor. P.T. Barnum, showman. Lyman Beecher, theologian. John Brown, abolitionist. Samuel Colt, inventor. Jonathan Edwards, theologian. Charles Goodyear, inventor. Nathan Hale, patriot. Katharine Hepburn, actress. Charles Ives, composer. J.P. Morgan, financier. Ralph Nader, consumer advocate. Frederick Law Olmsted, landscape architect. Harriet Beecher Stowe, author. John Trumbell, artist. Noah

Webster, lexicographer. Eli Whitney, inventor.

Noteworthy places Charles Ives Center, Danbury. Eugene O'Neill Memorial Theater Center, Waterford. Gilette Castle. Housatonic State Park. Mark Twain House, Hartford. Mystic Marinelife Aquarium. Mystic Seaport. Norwalk Maritime Center. U.S. Coast Guard Academy. USS *Nautilus*, New London. Wadsworth Atheneum, Hartford. Whitney Museum of Modern Art, Stamford. Yale Center for British Art, New Haven. Yale University, New Haven.

Memorable events Adriaen Block claims for Dutch 1614. First English settlement in Windsor 1633. Royal charter of 1662 hidden in Charter Oak 1687. *Hartford Courant*, oldest continuously published newspaper in U.S., first published 1764. Samuel Colt develops six-shooter 1835. Horace Wells uses first anesthesia 1844. Elias Howe invents sewing machine 1845. U.S. Coast Guard Academy founded New London 1876. First woman governor elected in her own right, Ella T. Grasso, 1974.

Tourist information 1–800–243–1685 or 1–203–566–3385.

Delaware

The du Pont family has enjoyed a political and economic prominence in Delaware unmatched in the history of the other 49 states. Seven generations ago E.I. du Pont de Nemours and Co. was founded as a gunpowder mill, then grew into a monopoly, and in the wake of World War I, diversified into today's giant, with interests in banking, media, and real estate. Only half the size of Los Angeles County, Delaware was called the corporate state by Ralph Nader's "raiders" in 1973. Its liberal incorporation laws have led more than half the *Fortune* 500 companies to incorporate there. It was one of the few states to prosper even during the recession of the early 1980s.

NAME For Thomas West, Lord De La Warre, colonial governor of Virginia. NICKNAMES First State, Diamond State. CAPITAL Dover. ENTERED UNION Dec. 7, 1787 (1st). MOTTO "Liberty and Independence."

Emblems BIRD Blue hen chicken. FISH Weakfish. FLOWER Peach blossom. INSECT Ladybug. ROCK Sillimanite. SONG "Our Delaware." TREE American holly.

Land TOTAL AREA 2,044 sq. mi. (49th), incl. 112 sq. mi. inland water. BORDERS Pa., N.J., Atlantic Ocean, Md. RIVERS Chesapeake and Delaware Canal, Delaware, Nanticoke.

Elected officials Gov. Michael N. Castle (R). Lt. Gov., Dale E. Wolf (R). Sec. State Michael Harkins (R). Atty. Gen. Charles M. Oberly III (D).

People (1988 est.) 660,000 (47th). RACE/NATIONAL ORIGIN (1980): White 82.10%. Black 16.12%. Indian 0.23%. Asian 0.40%. Hispanic 1.61%. Foreign-born 3.20%. LANGUAGES (1980): English 94.51%. Spanish 1.42%. Italian 0.75%. Polish 0.68%. German 0.52%. French 0.42%. Greek 0.19%.

Cities (1986) Wilmington 69,690. Newark 24,180. Dover 22,660. Elsmere 6,330. Milford 5,680. Seaford 5,320.

Business GROSS STATE PRODUCT (GSP, 1986) $11.7 bil. (46th). SECTORS OF GSP: Farms 1.86%. Agricultural services, forestry, & fisheries 0.28%. Mining 0.02%. Construction 4.83%. Manufacturing 28.40%. Transportation & public utilities 7.79%. Wholesale 5.61%. Retail 8.41%. Finance, insurance, & real estate 18.19%. Services 13.81%. Federal government 1.41%. Federal military 1.47%. State & local government 7.92%. FORTUNE 500 COMPANIES (1988): 3: E.I. du Pont de Nemours, Hercules, Himont.

Famous natives Valerie Bertinelli, actress. John Dickinson (b. Md.), Penman of the Revolution. Eleuthère I. du Pont, manufacturer. Pierre S. ("Pete") du Pont, politician. Morgan Edwards, founder of Brown University (R.I.). Thomas Macdonough, navy officer. Howard Pyle, illustrator. Edward R. Squibb, physician/manufacturer. Christopher Ward, historian.

Noteworthy places Brandywine Zoo, Wilmington. Delaware Art Museum, Wilmington. Delaware State Museum, Dover. Dover Downs International Speedway. Grand Opera House, Wilmington. Hagley Museum, Wilmington. Rehoboth Beach.

Memorable events Dutch arrive 1631. Swedes establish first permanent settlement at Wilmington 1638. Captured by Dutch 1655. To England 1664. Part of territory granted to William Penn 1682. Breaks off from Pennsylvania; first to ratify Constitution 1776. E.I. du Pont de Nemours Co. founded 1802. Railroad connects Wilmington to Philadelphia and Baltimore 1838. Though slave state, sides with Union during Civil War 1861–65. Delaware last state to abolish whipping post (last used 1952) 1972.

Tourist information 1–800–441–8846 or 1–404–736–4271.

District of Columbia

Chosen as the site for the nation's capital by George Washington, Washington, D.C., was carved out of land ceded by Maryland and Virginia. Although under federal jurisdiction, the District has petitioned for statehood as New Columbia. In 1961 Congress enacted the 23d Amendment granting citizens of D.C. the right to vote in presidential elections for the first time, and ten years later gave the District a nonvoting delegate to the House of Representatives. The District's largest employer is the federal government, and printing is the largest industry. President John F. Kennedy called it a city of "Southern efficiency and Northern charm," but since his time, the city has become a leading patron of the arts. The problems of any large city are made worse by the city's largely transient population of government workers. The city, as the seat of the U.S. government, is a mecca for tourists from around the world, and more than 17 million people visit it each year.

NAME After Christopher Columbus; Columbia was commonly used for the U.S. before 1800. NICKNAME None. CAPITAL Washington. BECAME CAPITAL Dec. 1, 1800. MOTTO *Justitia omnibus* (Justice for all).

Emblems BIRD Wood thrush. FLOWER American beauty rose. TREE Scarlet oak.
Land TOTAL AREA 69 sq. mi., incl. 6 sq. mi. inland water. BORDERS Md., and Va. RIVERS Anacostia, Potomac.
Elected officials Mayor Marion S. Barry, Jr. (D).
People (1988 est.) 620,000. RACE/NATIONAL ORIGIN (1980): White 27.37%. Black 70.24%. Indian 0.16%. Asian 1.08%. Hispanic 2.76%. Foreign-born 6.40%. LANGUAGES (1980): English 92.12%. Spanish 3.11%. French 1.45%. Chinese 0.34%. Italian 0.28%.
Business GROSS STATE PRODUCT (GSP, 1986) $28.8 bil. SECTORS OF GSP: Farms 0.00%. Agricultural services, forestry, & fisheries 0.02%. Mining 0.02%. Construction 6.87%. Manufacturing 3.62%. Transportation & public utilities 6.23%. Wholesale 1.84%. Retail 4.40%. Finance, insurance, & real estate 9.23%. Services 28.48%. Federal government 32.33%. Federal military 2.43%. State & local government 3.90%. *FORTUNE* 500 COMPANIES (1988): 2: Danaher, Washington Post.
Famous natives Edward Albee, playwright. Carl Bernstein, journalist. John Foster Dulles, politician. Duke Ellington, composer. J. Edgar Hoover, FBI director. Marjorie Kinnan Rawlings, novelist. John Philip Sousa, composer.
Noteworthy places The Capitol. Chesapeake & Ohio Canal Natl. Hist. Park. Corcoran Gallery of Art. Dumbarton Oaks. Folger Shakespeare Library. Freer Gallery of Art. Hirshhorn Museum. Jefferson Memorial. Kennedy Center. Library of Congress. Lincoln Memorial. Natl. Air and Space Museum. Natl. Gallery of Art. Natl. Museum of African Art. Natl. Museum of American Art. Natl. Museum of American History. Natl. Museum of Natural History. Natl. Portrait Gallery. Naval Observatory. Navy Memorial Museum. Renwick Gallery. Smithsonian Institution. Vietnam Veterans Memorial. Washington Monument. Washington Zoo. White House.
Memorable events Originally part of Maryland. Congress approves plan to secure land for seat of federal government, no more than 10 miles square, on land in Virginia and Maryland 1787. George Washington commissions Pierre Charles l'Enfant to lay out city 1791. Government moves 1800. British sail up the Potomac and burn capital 1814. Virginia reclaims its half of District 1846. President Abraham Lincoln assassinated 1865. Coxey's Army marches on Washington 1894. The Bonus Army—17,000 veterans—marches on Washington 1932. Led by Martin Luther King, Jr., 200,000 march for Civil Rights 1963. One hundred thousand protest Vietnam War 1971. Democratic party headquarters at Watergate burglarized by men linked to President Richard M. Nixon's reelection effort 1972. Congress grants limited self-rule; mayor and city council elected 1975.
Tourist information 1–202–789–7000.

Florida

A vast network of swamps, rivers, and lakes, much of Florida is barely above sea level.

Home to Disney World, Cypress Gardens, the wealth-laden resort of Palm Beach, the *National Enquirer*, and the Okefenokee Swamp, the pleasant climate and proximity to the Caribbean and Latin America have attracted large populations of the elderly and of immigrants, as well as millions of tourists. One of the fastest-growing states, Florida has been plagued by drug trafficking and racial disturbances, as well as environmental damage to such wildlife as the crocodile, alligator, and the Florida panther.
NAME By Juan Ponce de León for Pascua Florida (Easter festival of the flowers). NICKNAME Sunshine State. CAPITAL Tallahassee. ENTERED UNION Mar. 3, 1845 (27th). MOTTO "In God We Trust." POET LAUREATE Dr. Edmund Skellings.
Emblems ANIMAL Florida panther. BEVERAGE Orange juice. BIRD Mockingbird. FLOWER Orange blossom. FRESHWATER FISH Florida largemouth bass. GEM Moonstone. MARINE MAMMALS Dolphin, manatee. SALTWATER FISH Atlantic sailfish. SHELL Horse conch. SONG "Old Folks at Home" ("Swanee River"). STONE Agatized coral. TREE Sabal palmetto palm.
Land TOTAL AREA 58,664 sq. mi. (22d), incl. 4,511 sq. mi. inland water. BORDERS Ga., Atlantic Ocean, Gulf of Mexico, Ala. RIVERS Apalachicola, Caloosahatchee, Indian, Kissimmee, Perdido, St. Johns, St. Mary's, Suwanee, Withlacoochee. LAKES Apopka, George, Okeechobee, Seminole. OTHER NOTABLE FEATURES Everglades, Florida Keys, Okefenokee Swamp.
Elected officials Gov. Bob Martinez (R). Lt. Gov. Bobby Brantley (R). Sec. State Jim Smith (R). Atty. Gen. Robert A. Butterworth (D).
People (1988 est.) 12,377,000 (4th). RACE/NATIONAL ORIGIN (1980): White 84.0%. Black 13.78%. Indian 0.23%. Asian 0.64%. Hispanic 8.08%. Foreign-born 10.90%. LANGUAGES (1980): English 86.82%. Spanish 8.56%. French 0.78%. German 0.74%. Italian 0.65%. Greek 0.17%. Polish 0.22%. Hungarian 0.01%.
Cities (1986) Jacksonville 609,860. Miami 373,940. Tampa 277,580. St. Petersburg 239,410. Hialeah 161,760. Ft. Lauderdale 148,620. Orlando 145,900. Hollywood 120,910. Tallahassee 119,450. Clearwater 97,520. Miami Beach 95,000.
Business GROSS STATE PRODUCT (GSP, 1986) $177.7 bil. (6th). SECTORS OF GSP: Farms 1.81%. Agricultural services, forestry, & fisheries 0.69%. Mining 0.87%. Construction 7.25%. Manufacturing 10.80%. Transportation & public utilities 9.29%. Wholesale 7.08%. Retail 12.08%. Finance, insurance, & real estate 18.77%. Services 19.46%. Federal government 1.97%. Federal military 1.93%. State & local government 7.99%. *FORTUNE* 500 COMPANIES (1988): 8: incl. DWG, Harris, Harcourt Brace Jovanovich, Knight-Ridder.
Famous natives Mary Bethune, educator/reformer. Faye Dunaway, actress. Zora Neale Hurston, writer. James Weldon Johnson, lawyer/novelist. Osceola, Seminole chief. Sidney Poitier, actor. A. Philip Randolph, labor leader. Edmund Kirby Smith, Confederate general. Joseph Warren ("Vinegar Joe") Stillwell, army officer. Ben Vereen, actor/singer.

Noteworthy places Biscayne Natl. Park. Castillo de San Marcos, St. Augustine. Everglades Natl. Park. Florida State Museum, Gainesville. Ft. Jefferson Natl. Monument. Ft. Matanzas Natl. Monument. Kennedy Space Center, Cape Canaveral. Ringling Museum, Sarasota. St. Augustine. Walt Disney World/Epcot Center, Orlando.
Memorable events Juan Ponce de León claims Florida for Spain 1513. French stake claim for Florida 1562; build Ft. Caroline 1564. Pedro Menéndez de Avilés founds St. Augustine, first permanent European settlement in U.S. 1565. Spain cedes Florida to U.S. 1819. Seminole War 1835–42. State secedes from Union 1861. Readmitted 1868. Carl Fisher begins to develop Miami Beach as resort 1912. Florida's first paper mill opens expanding forest industry 1931. More than 100,000 Cuban refugees enter U.S., most through Florida, during Mariel boat lift 1980.
Tourist information 1–904–487–1462.

Georgia

The largest state east of the Mississippi River, Georgia is diverse in its terrain, embracing the woods of the Blue Ridge Mountains to the north and the alligators of the Okefenokee Swamp in the south. Though two-thirds of the population are urban dwellers, Georgia's farms rank first in poultry production and are leading producers of pecans, cattle, hogs, and peanuts. Up from a past of slavery and separate-but-equal facilities, in the early 1970s Atlanta elected Andrew Young the first black member of the U.S. Congress and Maynard Jackson the first black mayor from the South since Reconstruction. Today divisions linger in Georgia, the cities favoring a progressive stance and the rural areas clinging to some of the ways of the Old South.
NAME For King George II of England 1732. NICKNAMES Empire State of the South, Peach State. CAPITAL Atlanta. ENTERED UNION Jan. 2, 1788 (4th). MOTTO "Wisdom, justice, moderation."
Emblems BIRD Brown thrasher. FISH Largemouth bass. FLOWER Cherokee rose. FOSSIL Shark tooth. GEM Quartz. INSECT Honeybee. SONGS "Georgia," "Georgia on My Mind." TREE Live oak. WILDFLOWER Azalea.
Land TOTAL AREA 58,910 sq. mi. (21st), incl. 854 sq. mi. inland water. BORDERS Tenn., N.C., S.C., Atlantic Ocean, Fla., Ala. RIVERS Altamaha, Apalachicola, Chattahoochee, Flint, Ocmulgee, Oconee, Savannah, Suwanee. LAKES Clark Hill, Harding, Hartwell, Seminole, Sidney Lanier, Sinclair, Walter F. George, West Point Lake. OTHER NOTABLE FEATURES Blue Ridge Mountains (Mt. Enotah 4,784 ft.), Okefenokee Swamp.
Elected officials Gov. Joe Frank Harris (D). Lt. Gov. Zell Miller (D). Sec. State Max Cleland (D). Atty. Gen. Michael J. Bowers (D).
People (1988 est.) 6,401,000 (11th). RACE/NATIONAL ORIGIN (1980): White 72.30%. Black 26.81%. Indian 0.18%. Asian 0.47%. Hispanic 1.12%. Foreign-born 1.70%. LANGUAGES (1980): English 97.35%. Spanish 0.94%. Ger-

man 0.38%. French 0.37%. Korean 0.10%. Chinese 0.07%.

Cities (1986) Atlanta 421,910. Columbus 180,180. Savannah 146,800. Macon 118,420. Albany 84,950. Warner Robins 45,620. Augusta 45,440. Athens 43,100.

Business GROSS STATE PRODUCT (GSP, 1986) $102.9 bil. (12th). SECTORS OF GSP: Farms 1.75%. Agricultural services, forestry, & fisheries 0.33%. Mining 0.56%. Construction 5.38%. Manufacturing 20.92%. Transportation & public utilities 10.98%. Wholesale 9.56%. Retail 10.04%. Finance, insurance, & real estate 13.76%. Services 14.17%. Federal government 2.96%. Federal military 2.05%. State & local government 7.55%. FORTUNE 500 COMPANIES (1988): 16: incl. Coca-Cola, Georgia Gulf, Georgia-Pacific, RJR Nabisco, West Point Pepperell.

Famous natives James Brown, singer. Erskine Caldwell, author. James Earl ("Jimmy") Carter, U.S. president. Ray Charles, musician. Ty Cobb, baseball player. James Dickey, poet. W.E.B. DuBois, educator/reformer. Martin Luther King, Jr., minister/reformer. Sidney Lanier, author. Little Richard, musician. Carson McCullers, author. Alexander McGillivray, Creek chief. Margaret Mitchell, author. Elijah Muhammad, religious leader. Flannery O'Connor, author. Burt Reynolds, actor. Jackie Robinson, baseball player. Tomochichi, Yamacraw chief. Joanne Woodward, actress.

Noteworthy places Chickamauga and Chattanooga Natl. Military Park. Confederate Memorial, Stone Mountain. Ft. Frederica Natl. Monument. Ft. Pulaski Natl. Monument. High Museum of Art, Atlanta. Martin Luther King Natl. Hist. Site., Atlanta. Ocmulgee Natl. Monument. Okefenokee Swamp. Savannah Historic District.

Memorable events Hernando de Soto explores region 1540. Cotton gin invented 1793. Georgia expels Cherokee Indian tribes on Trail of Tears 1832–38. Secedes from Union 1860. Gen. William T. Sherman's 60,000 troops cut 60-mi. swath in their "march to the sea" 1864. Formula for Coca-Cola developed by chemist in search of cure for hangover 1886. Cyclone kills 1,000 in Charleston, S.C., and Savannah 1893. Franklin D. Roosevelt dies at the Little White House, Warm Springs 1945. First state to give vote to 18-year-olds 1948. Emory University designated to receive $100-million philanthropic gift from Robert W. Woodruff 1979.

Tourist information 1–800–VISIT–GA or 1–404–656–3590.

Hawaii

What the air conditioner did for the Sunbelt, the jetliner has done for Hawaii. Because of the jet, Hawaii is a possible vacation spot for millions and welcomes 20 times the air travelers of 25 years ago. Thousands of miles from both California and mainland Asia, Hawaii was originally peopled by Polynesian seafarers around A.D. 500 and has the richest ethnic mix of any state, with the lowest percentage of whites and high percentages of Asians. It was partly fear of this diversity that stalled its statehood. A

link bewteen the United States and Asia, Hawaii is the center of U.S. defense in the Pacific and is home to 100,000 veterans, three-quarters of them veterans of Vietnam. Hawaii produces large quantities of pineapples and sugar cane, and efforts are under way to harness thermal electric power from Mauna Loa volcano.

NAME Of unknown origin, perhaps from Hawaii Loa, traditional discoverer of islands, or from Hawaiki, the traditional Polynesian homeland. NICKNAMES Aloha State, Paradise of the Pacific. CAPITAL Honolulu. ENTERED UNION Aug. 21, 1959 (50th). MOTTO *Ua mau ke ea o ka aina i ke pono* (The life of the land is perpetuated in righteousness).

Emblems BIRD Nene (Hawaiian goose). FISH Humuhumunukunukuapuaa. FLOWER Pua aloalo (hibiscus). SONG "Hawaii Ponoi." TREE Kukui (candlenut).

Land TOTAL AREA 6,470 sq. mi. (47th), incl. 45 sq. mi. inland water. Surrounded by Pacific Ocean. RIVERS Kaukonahua Stream, Wailuku Stream. LAKES Halulu, Kolekole, Salt Lake, Waiia Res. OTHER NOTABLE FEATURES Pearl Harbor. Hualalai, Kilauea, Mauna Kea (13,796 ft.), and Mauna Loa volcanoes. MAIN ISLANDS Hawaii, Kauai, Maui, Molokai, Oahu.

Elected officials Gov. John D. Waihee III (D). Lt. Gov. Benjamin J. Cayetano (D). Sec. State, none. Atty. Gen. Warren Price (D).

People (1988 est.) 1,093,000 (40th). RACE/ NATIONAL ORIGIN (1980): White 32.24%. Black 1.76%. Indian 0.002%. Asian 57.62% (Japanese 24.85%, Filipino 13.69%, Hawaiian 12.26%, Chinese 5.80%, Korean 1.81%, Samoan 1.49%, Other 1.33%). Hispanic 7.40%. Foreign-born 14.20%. LANGUAGES (1980): English 74.20%. Japanese 9.04%. Philippine langs. 7.51%. Chinese 2.26%. Spanish 1.34%. Korean 1.04%. German 0.37%. French 0.33%. Vietnamese 0.31%. Thai 0.24%.

Cities (1986) Honolulu 372,300; (1980) Pearl City 42,575. Kailua 35,812. Hilo 35,269. Aiea 32,879. Kaneohe 29,919. Waipahu 29,139.

Business GROSS STATE PRODUCT (GSP, 1986) $19.3 bil. (40th). SECTORS OF GSP: Farms 2.00%. Agricultural services, forestry, & fisheries 0.35%. Mining 0.01%. Construction 6.12%. Manufacturing 5.18%. Transportation & public utilities 9.89%. Wholesale 4.35%. Retail 11.13%. Finance, insurance, & real estate 17.59%. Services 19.79%. Federal government 6.12%. Federal military 9.57%. State & local government 7.90%. FORTUNE 500 COMPANIES (1988): 1: Pacific Resources.

Famous natives Bernice P. Bishop, philanthropist. Sanford B. Dole, statehood advocate. Charlotte (b. Ohio) and Luther Halsey Gulick, Camp Fire Girls founders. Don Ho, singer. Daniel J. Inouye, politician. Duke Kahanamoku, swimmer. Victoria Kaiulani, last heiress presumptive to Hawaiian throne. Kamehameha I, king. Kamehameha III, king. Liliuokalani, queen. Bette Midler, singer.

Noteworthy places Bernice P. Bishop Museum, Honolulu. Diamond Head. Haleakala Natl. Park, Maui. Hawaii Volcanoes Natl. Park (Kilauea and Mauna Loa), Hawaii. Iolani Palace, Honolulu. Kaloko-Honokohau Natl. Hist. Park, Molokai. Natl. Cemetery of the Pacific

Hawaii:

"The loveliest fleet of islands that lies anchored in any ocean."

—**Mark Twain**

and USS *Arizona* Memorial. Polynesian Cultural Center, Laiea. Pu'uhonua o Honaunau Natl. Hist. Park, Hawaii.

Memorable events Polynesians first arrive 6th century. Second wave of Polynesians arrive 10th century. Captain James Cook first European to visit islands 1778; killed on Hawaii 1779. Sugar production begins 1835. Land reform ends feudal system 1848. Monarchy rule ends in revolution 1893. Becomes U.S. Territory 1900. Japanese attack Pearl Harbor 1941. Statehood 1959.

Tourist information 1–808–923–1811.

Idaho

Idaho is 25 percent Morman, and the Latter-day Saints here have their greatest influence outside Utah. The northern Panhandle, where people tend to look west to Washington, and the south, where Mormons look to Utah, are connected by a single highway. The health of Boise's economy, with its large share of home-grown industrial success, unites the two other areas. Home to some of the most isolated and rugged country in the United States, Idaho's diversified economy has traditionally been based on lumber, potatoes, and mining, lately improved by small high-tech industries fleeing the high cost of business in California.

NAME Means "gem of the mountains." NICKNAME Gem State. CAPITAL Boise. ENTERED UNION July 3, 1890 (43d). MOTTO *Esto perpetua* (May it last forever).

Emblems BIRD Mountain bluebird. FLOWER Syringa. GEM Star garnet. HORSE Appaloosa. SONG "Here We Have Idaho." TREE Western white pine.

Land TOTAL AREA 83,564 sq. mi. (13th), incl. 1,152 sq. mi. inland water. BORDERS British Columbia, Mont., Wyo., Utah, Nev., Oreg., Wash. RIVERS Bear, Clearwater, Payette, Salmon, Snake. LAKES American Falls Res., Coeur d'Alene, Pend Oreille. MOUNTAINS Bitterroot Range, Centennial, Clearwater, Salmon River, Sawtooth Range (Castle Peak 11,820 ft.), Wasatch Range. OTHER NOTABLE FEATURES

Grand Canyon of the Snake River.

Elected officials Gov. Cecil D. Andrus (D). Lt. Gov. C.L. Otter (R). Sec. State Pete T. Conarussa (R). Atty. Gen. James Jones (R).

People (1988 est.) 999,000 (42d). RACE/NATIONAL ORIGIN (1980): White 95.77%. Black 0.29%. Indian 1.12%. Asian 0.71%. Hispanic 3.87%. Foreign-born 2.50%. LANGUAGES (1980): English 94.41%. Spanish 3.19%. German 0.62%. American Indian langs. 0.30%. French 0.29%. Japanese 0.14%.

Cities (1986) Boise 108,390. Pocatello 44,420. Idaho Falls 42,830. Nampa 28,250. Twin Falls 27,750. Lewiston 27,730.

Business GROSS STATE PRODUCT (GSP, 1986) $13.2 bil. (44th). SECTORS OF GSP: Farms 8.17%. Agricultural services, forestry, & fisheries 0.90%. Mining 1.29%. Construction 3.31%. Manufacturing 16.34%. Transportation & public utilities 10.48%. Wholesale 5.84%. Retail 10.36%. Finance, insurance, & real estate 15.79%. Services 15.03%. Federal government 2.35%. Federal military 1.57%. State & local government 8.54%. *FORTUNE* 500 COMPANIES (1988): 1: Boise Cascade.

Famous natives Joseph, Nez Percé chief. Ezra Taft Benson, politician. Gutzon Borglum, sculptor. Frank Church, politician. Ezra Pound, poet. Harmon Killebrew, baseball player. Jerry Kramer, football player. Sacagawea (Bird Woman), Shoshone interpreter. Lana Turner, actress.

Noteworthy places Craters of the Moons Natl. Monument. Hell's Canyon Natl. Recreation Area. Nez Percé Natl. Hist. Park. Sawtooth Natl. Recreation Area. Sun Valley ski resort.

Memorable events Lewis and Clark expedition 1805. Becomes part of U.S. when Idaho Treaty concluded with Britain 1846. Gold Rush 1860. Nez Percé War 1877. Statehood 1890. World's first breeder reactor built at Idaho Falls, 1951. Snake River opened to navigation, linking Lewiston to Pacific Ocean at Astoria, Oregon, 1975. New Teton River Dam collapses as it is being filled for first time; 10 dead, $400 million in damage 1976.

Tourist information 1-800-635-7820 or 1-208-334-2470.

Illinois

The Illinois economy is enormously productive and diverse. While Chicago is a leader in world finance and trade, the southern part of the state has rich farmlands (the state is second to Iowa in corn and soybean exports) and mineral deposits (both coal and gas). There are also rich coal deposits, especially in the southeast region around Cairo, known as Little Egypt. Manufacturing centers around Chicago, Rockford—the state's second-largest city—and Springfield, the capital. Chicago is also a major transportation hub with extensive rail networks, an international port serving ships from both the Atlantic and Gulf of Mexico, and the largest airport in the country. Another leading industry in Illinois is political patronage, infecting both the Chicago-based Democrats and the downstate Republicans. Reform of the system, which boasted 12,000 patronage

positions for the governor and cabinet officials in the 1970s, seems a remote possibility and would take the bite out of the state's tradition of muckraking journalism.

NAME Corruption of *iliniwek* ("tribe of the superior men"), natives of region at time of earliest French explorations. NICKNAME Prairie State. CAPITAL Springfield. ENTERED UNION Dec. 3, 1818 (21st). MOTTO "State sovereignty—national unity." SLOGAN "Land of Lincoln."

Emblems ANIMAL White-tailed deer. BIRD Cardinal. FLOWER Violet. INSECT Monarch butterfly. MINERAL Fluorite. SONG "Illinois." TREE White oak.

Land TOTAL AREA 56,345 sq. mi. (24th), incl. 700 sq. mi. inland water. BORDERS Wis., Lake Michigan, Ind., Ky., Mo., Iowa. RIVERS Fox, Illinois, Illinois Waterway, Kankakee, Kaskaskia, Mississippi, Ohio, Rock, Vermillion, Wabash. LAKES Carlyle, Crab Orchard. OTHER NOTABLE FEATURES Charles Mound (1,235 ft.), Little Egypt.

Elected officials Gov. James R. Thompson (R). Lt. Gov. George H. Ryan (R). Sec. State James Edgar (R). Atty. Gen. Neil F. Hartigan (D).

People (1988 est.) 11,544,000 (6th). RACE/NATIONAL ORIGIN (1980): White 81.11%. Black 14.65%. Indian 0.17%. Asian 1.51%. Hispanic 5.55%. Foreign-born 7.20%. LANGUAGES (1980): English 88.46%. Spanish 4.72%. Polish 1.30%. German 0.92%. Italian 0.80%. Greek 0.43%.

Cities (1986) Chicago 3,009,530. Rockford 135,760. Peoria 110,290. Springfield 100,290. Decatur 90,360. Aurora 85,350. Joliet 76,010. Waukegan 74,480. Elgin 72,110.

Business GROSS STATE PRODUCT (GSP, 1986) $209.7 bil. (4th). SECTORS OF GSP: Farms 1.61%. Agricultural services, forestry, & fisheries 0.27%. Mining 0.76%. Construction 4.12%. Manufacturing 20.16%. Transportation & public utilities 10.80%. Wholesale 8.48%. Retail 9.39%. Finance, insurance, & real estate 17.52%. Services 17.48%. Federal government 1.73%. Federal military 0.70%. State & local government 6.97%. *FORTUNE* 500 COMPANIES (1988): 50: incl. Amoco, Beatrice, Caterpillar, Firestone Tire, Fruit of the Loom, Kraft, Morton Thiokol, Motorola, Quaker Oats, Sara Lee, Tribune, Wm. Wrigley, Jr., Zenith.

Famous natives Jane Addams, reformer (Nobel Peace Prize, 1930). Ernie Banks, baseball player. Saul Bellow, author (Nobel Prize, 1976). Harry A. Blackmun, jurist. Ray Bradbury, author. Gwendolyn Brooks, poet. William Jennings Bryan, politician. Edgar Rice Burroughs, novelist. St. Frances Xavier Cabrini (b. Italy). Clarence Darrow, lawyer. Miles Davis, musician. John Dos Passos, novelist. Enrico Fermi (b. Italy), nuclear physicist (Nobel Prize, 1938). Robert Louis ("Bob") Fosse, choreographer. Milton Friedman, economist (Nobel Prize, 1976). Benny Goodman, musician. Ernest Hemingway, novelist. Charlton Heston, actor. William Holden, actor. Vachel Lindsay, poet. Archibald MacLeish, poet. Ludwig Mies van der Rohe (b. Germany), architect. Charles W. Post, cereal manufacturer. Ronald Reagan, U.S. president. Carl Sandburg, poet. Albert G. Spalding, merchant. John Paul

Stevens, jurist. Gloria Swanson, actress.

Noteworthy places Art Institute of Chicago. Crab Orchard Wildlife Refuge. Dickson Mounds Museum, Lewistown. Field Museum of Natural History, Chicago. Ft. Chartres. Ft. Kaskaskia. Ft. Massac. Frank Lloyd Wright Historic District, Oak Park. Illinois State Museum, Springfield. Lincoln Home Natl. Hist. Park, Springfield. Mormon Settlement, Nauvoo. Morton Arboretum, Lisle. Museum of Science and Industry, Chicago. Shawnee Natl. Forest. Starved Rock State Park.

Memorable events French missionary explorers Jacques Marquette and Louis Jolliet in Illinois 1673. Cahokia first European settlement 1699. Territory to England after French and Indian War 1763. Chicago founded by Jean-Baptiste Point du Sable 1779. Illinois and Michigan Canal links Lake Michigan and Mississippi River 1848. Lincoln-Douglas Debates at Springfield 1860. Half of Chicago destroyed by great fire 1871. Terrorist bombing leaves nine dead and 130 wounded in Haymarket affair, Chicago 1886. Columbia Exposition, Chicago 1893. First successful nuclear chain reaction created at University of Chicago 1942. Riots at Democratic National Convention in Chicago 1968. Sears Tower, world's tallest building (1,454 ft.), completed in Chicago 1973.

Tourist information 1-800-223-0121, 1-217-782-7137, or 1-800-252-8987.

Indiana

Indiana is strong in both farms and manufacturing. Its southern half has large coal deposits and produces most of the limestone quarried in the U.S. To the north the fertile land helps make Indiana one of the primary farm-belt states. Indiana is also very much a part of the industrial Midwest, where unemployment is always a threat, especially in the heavily industrial areas of Gary and Indianapolis. These geographic divisions have parallels in the political history of the state, which during the Civil War was Union in the north and Confederate in the south. In 1966 the state's patronage politics were upset by reapportionment, and urban counties increased representation. George Bush recognized the importance of Indiana's votes and value as a home of traditional values when he chose J. Danforth Quayle as his running mate.

NAME For the land of Indians by early settlers, who found many distinct tribes living in region. NICKNAME Hoosier State. CAPITAL Indianapolis. ENTERED UNION Dec. 11, 1816 (19th). MOTTO "The Crossroads of America."

Emblems BIRD Cardinal. FLOWER Peony. POEM "Indiana." SONG "On the Banks of the Wabash, Far Away." STONE Indiana limestone. TREE Tulip tree.

Land TOTAL AREA 36,185 sq. mi. (38th), incl. 253 sq. mi. inland water. BORDERS Lake Michigan, Mich., Ohio, Ky., Ill. RIVERS Kankakee, Ohio, Tippecanoe, Wabash, White, Whitewater. LAKES Freeman, Shafer.

Elected officials Gov. Evan Bayh (D). Lt. Gov. Frank L. O'Bannon (D). Sec. State Joseph H. Hogsett (D). Atty. Gen. Linley E. Pearson (R).

People (1988 est.) 5,575,000 (14th). RACE/
NATIONAL ORIGIN (1980): White 91.23%. Black
7.55%. Indian 0.18%. Asian 0.44%. Hispanic
1.58%. Foreign-born 1.9%. LANGUAGES (1980):
English 95.86%. Spanish 1.36%. German
0.79%. Polish 0.31%. French 0.26%. Serbo-
Croatian 0.13%.
Cities (1986) Indianapolis 719,820. Ft. Wayne
172,900. Gary 136,790. Evansville 129,480.
South Bend 107,190. Hammond 86,380. Muncie 72,600. Anderson 61,020.
Business GROSS STATE PRODUCT (GSP, 1986)
$84.9 (14th). SECTORS OF GSP: Farms 2.43%.
Agricultural services, forestry, & fisheries
0.24%. Mining 0.66%. Construction 4.58%.
Manufacturing 29.80%. Transportation &
public utilities 9.64%. Wholesale 5.87%. Retail
10.05%. Finance, insurance, & real estate
14.48%. Services 12.90%. Federal government 1.58%. Federal military 0.53%. State &
local government 7.25%. FORTUNE 500
COMPANIES (1988): 9: incl. Arvin, Ball, Cummins Engine, Eli Lilly, Great Lakes Chemical.
Famous natives Hoagy Carmichael, composer.
Eugene V. Debs, politician/organizer. Theodore
Dreiser, author. Benjamin Harrison, U.S. presi-
dent. Jimmy Hoffa, union leader. Michael Jack-
son, singer. Carole Lombard, actress. Cole
Porter, composer. Ernie Pyle, journalist.
Knute Rockne (b. Norway), football player.
Paul Samuelson, economist (Nobel Prize,
1960). Booth Tarkington, author. Kurt Von-
negut, author. Wendell L. Willkie, politician.
Wilbur Wright, aviation pioneer.
Noteworthy places Ernie Pyle birthplace,
Dana. George Rogers Clark Natl. Hist. Park,
Vincennes. Benjamin Harrison home, Indi-
anapolis. Hoosier Natl. Forest. Indiana Dunes
Natl. Lakeshore. Indianapolis Motor Speedway
and Museum. Indianapolis Museum of Art.
New Harmony village. Old state capital, Cory-
don. Wilbur Wright State Memorial, Millville.
Wyandotte Cave. Tippecanoe sites.
Memorable events Mound Builders present c.
A.D. 1000. René-Robert Cavelier de La Salle
explores for French 1679–87. French near Vin-
cennes from c. 1700. French cede territory to
British 1763. Gen. Ambrose Clark captures Ft.
Vincennes 1779. Territory ceded to U.S. 1783;
included in Northwest Territory 1787. Miamis
defeat U.S. twice in 1790. Gen. Anthony
Wayne defeats Miamis at Battle of Fallen Timbers 1794. Territory included in Indiana Territory 1800. Gen. William Henry Harrison
defeats Tecumseh's Indian Confederation at
Tippecanoe 1811. Statehood 1816. Studebaker
wagon company founded in South Bend 1852.
U.S. Steel establishes mill at company-built
town of Gary 1906. First Indianapolis 500 run
1911. Only a dozen car companies producing
cars, down from a pre-World War I peak of
375, 1920. Studebaker, last Indiana-based car
manufacturer, closes 1963.
Tourist information 1-800-2-WANDER or
1-317-232-8860.

Iowa

Iowa lies between the two great rivers of the
central United States, the Mississippi and the
Missouri, with a quarter of the nation's richest
and deepest topsoil. Iowa's farmers lead the
country in the production of corn, and Iowa is
also a big producer of hogs, cattle, and other
livestock. With about 75 percent of Iowans
employed in agriculture-related industries and
90 percent of the land farmed, Iowa is deeply
affected by natural disasters such as the 1988
drought. Yet more than 120 FORTUNE 500
COMPANIES have production facilities in this
farm state. Industrial production has risen
since World War II, though in the early 1980s,
many workers were laid off in the Mississippi
River cities of Dubuque and Davenport. Iowans
send abroad a quarter of the food they produce.
As a result they are better attuned to world
developments than their election-year notori-
ety from holding the country's earliest presidential caucus would lead one to believe of this
traditionally Republican state.
NAME For Iowa tribe. NICKNAME Hawkeye
State. CAPITAL Des Moines. ENTERED UNION
Dec. 28, 1846 (29th). MOTTO "Our liberties we
prize and our rights we will defend."
Emblems BIRD Eastern goldfinch. FLOWER
Wild rose. SONG "The Song of Iowa." STONE
Geode. TREE Oak.
Land TOTAL AREA 56,275 sq. mi. (25th), incl.
310 sq. mi. inland water. BORDERS Minn., Wis.,
Ill., Mo., Nebr., S.Dak. RIVERS Big Sioux, Des
Moines, Mississippi, Missouri. LAKES Okoboji,
Rathburn Res., Red Rock, Saylorville Res.,
Spirit, Storm. OTHER NOTABLE FEATURES
Ocheyedan Mound 1,675 ft.
Elected officials Gov. Terry E. Branstad (R).
Lt. Gov. Jo Ann Zimmerman (D). Sec. State
Elaine Baxter (D). Atty. Gen. Thomas J. Miller
(D).
People (1988 est.) 2,834,000 (29th). RACE/
NATIONAL ORIGIN (1980): White 97.51%. Black
1.45%. Indian 0.22%. Asian 0.48%. Hispanic
0.90%. Foreign-born 1.60%. LANGUAGES
(1980): English 96.58%. German 0.95%. Span-
ish 0.77%. French 0.20%. Dutch 0.16%. Czech
0.15%.
Cities (1986) Des Moines 192,060. Cedar
Rapids 108,370. Davenport 98,750. Sioux City
79,590. Waterloo 70,010. Dubuque 59,700.
Council Bluffs 56,900.
Business GROSS STATE PRODUCT (GSP, 1986)
$43.8 bil. (29th). SECTORS OF GSP: Farms
10.43%. Agricultural services, forestry, &
fisheries 0.58%. Mining 0.21%. Construction
3.19%. Manufacturing 21.05%. Transportation & public utilities 8.11%. Wholesale
6.75%. Retail 9.01%. Finance, insurance, &
real estate 17.87%. Services 13.40%. Federal
government 0.40%. Federal military 0.23%.
State & local government 8.77%. FORTUNE 500
COMPANIES (1988): 3: Hon Industries, Maytag,
Meredith.
Famous natives Norman E. Borlaug, agron-
omist (Nobel Peace Prize, 1970). William F.
("Buffalo Bill") Cody, scout/showman. George
Gallup, pollster. Josiah B. Grinnell (b. Vt.), abo-
litionist. Herbert Hoover, U.S. president.
Harry L. Hopkins, politician. John L. Lewis,
labor leader. John R. Mott, religious leader.
Billy Sunday, baseball player/evangelist. John
Wayne, actor. Meredith Wilson, composer.
Grant Wood, painter.
Noteworthy places Amana Colonies. Daven-
port Art Gallery. Des Moines Art Center.
Effigy Mounds Natl. Monument, Marquette.
Ft. Dodge Hist. Museum. Herbert Hoover birth-
place and library, West Branch. Natl. Rivers
Hall of Fame, Dubuque. Putnam Museum,
Davenport.
Memorable events Mound Builders present c.
A.D. 1000. Jacques Marquette and Louis Jolliet
claim land for France 1673. Part of Louisiana
Purchase 1803. Part of Missouri Territory
1812–21. Black Hawk Wars 1832, 1834–37.
First permanent settlement at Dubuque 1833.
Organized as Iowa Territory (incl. parts of Min-
nesota, North Dakota, and South Dakota)
1838. Statehood 1846. Capital moved from
Iowa City to Des Moines 1857. Fifty percent of
Iowa's farms foreclosed during depression
1929–35. Urban population exceeds rural for
first time 1960. Population loss of 2.2% greater
than any other state 1980–86.
Tourist information 1-800-345-IOWA.

Kansas

Kansas burst on the American scene as the
territory called Bleeding Kansas, seething with
conflict over slavery, though its myth today
includes being the home, this side of the rainbow, of *Wizard of Oz* heroine Dorothy Gale. Victorious New England abolitionists imprinted
the state with the Puritan ethic. They were
early supporters of prohibition, partly to discourage foreign newcomers. The geographic
center of the continental United States is near
Lebanon. Kansas has suffered postwar decline
with other Plains states, but it is a primary producer of wheat, cattle, and other agricultural
products. Its manufacturing base also includes
extensive aircraft industries, and it leads the
states in the production of helium.
NAME For Kansa or Kaw, "people of the
south wind." NICKNAME Sunflower State. CAPI-
TAL Topeka. ENTERED UNION Jan. 29, 1861
(34th). MOTTO *Ad astra per aspera* (To the stars
through adversity).
Emblems ANIMAL American buffalo. BIRD
Western meadowlark. FLOWER Wild native
sunflower. MARCH "The Kansas March." SONG
"Home on the Range." TREE Cottonwood.
Land TOTAL AREA 82,277 sq. mi. (14th), incl.
499 sq. mi. inland water. BORDERS Nebr., Mo.,
Okla., Colo. RIVERS Arkansas, Kansas, Mis-
souri, Republican, Saline, Smoky Hill, Sol-
omon. LAKES Kanapolis, Malvern, Perry,
Pomona, Tuttle Creek, Waconda. OTHER NOTA-
BLE FEATURES Flint Hills.
Elected officials Gov. Mike Hayden (R). Lt.
Gov. Jack D. Walker (R). Sec. State Bill Graves
(R). Atty. Gen. Robert T. Stephan (R).
People (1988 est.) 2,487,000 (32d). RACE/
NATIONAL ORIGIN (1980): White 91.81%. Black
5.35%. Indian 0.76%. Asian 0.75%. Hispanic
2.65%. Foreign-born 2.00%. LANGUAGES
(1980): English 95.28%. German 1.86%. Span-
ish 0.86%. French 0.26%. Vietnamese 0.12%.
Cities (1986) Wichita 288,870. Kansas City
162,070. Topeka 118,580. Overland Park
96,510. Lawrence 56,490. Olathe 52,180.
Salina 42,830.

Business GROSS STATE PRODUCT (GSP, 1986) $42.5 bil. (30th). SECTORS OF GSP: Farms 6.65%. Agricultural services, forestry, & fisheries 0.33%. Mining 2.07%. Construction 4.05%. Manufacturing 18.65%. Transportation & public utilities 11.98%. Wholesale 6.94%. Retail 9.00%. Finance, insurance, & real estate 15.47%. Services 13.27%. Federal government 1.23%. Federal military 2.07%. State & local government 8.29%. FORTUNE 500 COMPANIES (1988): 2: Coleman, National Coop. Refinery.

Famous natives Walter Chrysler, car maker. Robert Dole, politician. Amelia Earhart, aviator. Dwight David Eisenhower (b. Tex.), general/U.S. president. Nancy Landon Kassebaum, politician. Alf Landon, politician. Edgar Lee Masters, poet. Carry Nation (b. Ky.), prohibitionist. Charlie ("Bird") Parker, musician. Damon Runyon, writer. Gale Sayers, football player. William Allen White, the Sage of Emporia, editor.

Noteworthy places Agricultural Hall of Fame, Kansas City. Dodge City. Eisenhower Center, Abilene. Ft. Larned. Ft. Leavenworth. Ft. Riley. Ft. Scott. John Brown's Cabin, Osawatomie. Kansas Cosmosphere and Space Discovery Center, Hutchinson. Kansas State Historical Society Museum, Topeka. Wichita Art Museum.

Memorable events First major expedition to region under Francisco Vásquez de Coronado 1540–41. La Salle claims territory including Kansas for France 1682. Part of Louisiana Purchase 1803. Area visited by Meriwether Lewis and George Rogers Clark (1803), Zebulon Pike (1806), and Stephen H. Long (1819). Santa Fe Trail crosses Kansas 1821. Fts. Leavenworth (1827), Scott (1842), and Riley (1853) established to protect pioneers on Santa Fe and Oregon trails. Organized as Territory by Kansas-Nebraska Act 1854, which repealed Missouri Compromise of 1820. "Bleeding Kansas" scene of free vs. slave rivalry 1854–56. Statehood 1861. Introduction of winter wheat makes Kansas leading U.S. wheat producer 1870. Airplane manufacturing starts in Wichita 1919. "Dust Bowl" drought drives thousands of farmers off the land, especially in western Kansas, 1934–35. Murder of Clutter family by Richard E. Hickock and Perry E. Smith at Holcomb (later the subject of Truman Capote's *In Cold Blood*) 1959.

Tourist information 1–913–296–2009 or 1–800–252–6727.

Kentucky, Commonwealth of

Pioneered by English immigrants in the mid-17th century, Kentucky had a golden age as a choice frontier destination in the early 1800s, which the Civil War brought to an end. During the Civil War, the Bluegrass gentry supported the Confederacy, while the Appalachian backwoods men enlisted in the Union Army. Many took advantage of their uniforms to settle old accounts, and the social order was often threatened before the turn of the century. Though the state is known today for its bourbon and horse breeding, many Kentuckians make their living from the land as tobacco farmers or coal miners. The Appalachian part of the state in the east delivers about 20 percent of the nation's coal, but its economic problems remain acute, despite vast expenditures during the "war on poverty."

NAME Corruption of Iroquois *kenta-ke* (meadowland) or Wyandot *kah-ten-tah-teh* (land of tomorrow). **NICKNAME** Bluegrass State. **CAPITAL** Frankfort. **ENTERED UNION** June 1, 1792 (15th). **MOTTO** "United we stand, divided we fall."

Emblems BIRD Cardinal. COLORS Blue and gold. FISH Bass. FLOWER Goldenrod. SONG "My Old Kentucky Home." TREE Kentucky coffee tree. WILD ANIMAL Gray squirrel.

Land TOTAL AREA 40,409 sq. mi. (37th), incl. 740 sq. mi. inland water. BORDERS Ind., Ohio, W.Va., Va., Tenn., Mo., Ill. RIVERS Cumberland, Kentucky, Licking, Ohio, Tennessee. LAKES Barkley, Barren River Res., Dewey, Grayson Res., Laurel Res., Nolin Res., Rough Res. MOUNTAINS Appalachian (Black Mt. 4,145 ft.), Cumberland. OTHER NOTABLE FEATURES Tennessee Valley.

Elected officials Gov. Wallace G. Wilkinson (D). Lt. Gov. Brereton C. Jones (D). Sec. of the Commonwealth Bremer Ehrler (D). Atty. Gen. Fredric J. Cowan (D).

People (1988 est.) 3,721,000 (23d). RACE/NATIONAL ORIGIN (1980): White 92.34%. Black 7.08%. Indian 0.13%. Asian 0.32%. Hispanic 0.74%. Foreign-born 0.90%. LANGUAGES (1980): English 98.21%. Spanish 0.53%. German 0.32%. French 0.27%. Korean 0.06%.

Cities (1986) Louisville 286,470. Lexington-Fayette 212,900. Owensboro 56,280. Covington 45,670. Bowling Green 41,300. Hopkinsville 29,100. Frankfort 26,920.

Business GROSS STATE PRODUCT (GSP, 1986) $53.1 bil. (26th). SECTORS OF GSP: Farms 3.21%. Agricultural services, forestry, & fisheries 0.39%. Mining 5.66%. Construction 4.93%. Manufacturing 24.02%. Transportation & public utilities 8.73%. Wholesale 4.97%. Retail 9.65%. Finance, insurance, & real estate 14.89%. Services 11.96%. Federal government 2.44%. Federal military 2.10%. State & local government 7.04%. FORTUNE 500 COMPANIES (1988): 3: Ashland Oil, Brown-Forman, Storage Technology.

Famous natives Muhammad Ali, boxer. Alben W. Barkley, politician. Daniel Boone (b. Pa.), frontiersman. Louis D. Brandeis, jurist. Kit Carson, frontiersman. Henry Clay, politician. Jefferson Davis, president of Confederate States of America. D.W. Griffith, director. John Marshall Harlan, jurist. Abraham Lincoln, U.S. president. Col. Harland Sanders, entrepreneur. Frederick M. Vinson, jurist. Robert Penn Warren, author.

Noteworthy places Abraham Lincoln birthplace, Hodgenville. Churchill Downs, Louisville. George S. Patton, Jr. Military Museum, Fort Knox. J.B. Speed Art Museum, Louisville. Land Between the Lakes Natl. Rec. Area. Mammoth Cave Natl. Park. My Old Kentucky Home, Bardstown. Old Ft. Harrod State Park.

Memorable events English enter territory through Cumberland Gap 1750. Territory included in area ceded by French 1763. Daniel Boone leads expeditions into region 1769. First settlement Harrodsburg 1774. Daniel Boone blazes Wilderness Trail through Cumberland Gap, establishes Ft. Boonesborough 1775. Organized as a county of Virginia 1776. British support Indian resistance ("Dark and Bloody Wars") until George Rogers Clark captures British forts in Indiana and Illinois 1778. Included as part of U.S. after Revolution 1783. Virginia approves separate statehood, achieved 1792. First steamboat reaches Louisville from New Orleans 1815. Invaded by Confederate armies 1862. Kentucky Derby first run at Louisville 1875. State has highest per capita income of southern states 1900; ranks last among all 48 states in per capita income 1940. Farm population decreases by 76%, and total number of farms by 53%, 1945–80.

Tourist information 1–800–225–TRIP or 1–800–255–PARK.

Louisiana

European influences and ethnic diversity have set Louisiana apart from the nation and the rest of the South. When Louisiana entered the Union in 1812, it brought with it a French legal system and a bilingualism that still survive. Blacks, Cajuns, and Creoles have contributed to the fame of its music and its cuisine. The state has rich farmland, more oil and gas reserves than any other state but Texas, and in New Orleans an international port that serves the most extensive river system in North America. Although its natural resources have allowed many to enjoy prosperity, other factors—high unemployment, widespread poverty, and an inability to absorb shocks in the oil industry—make its successes fragile, and pollution remains a serious problem. Hurricanes periodically pose a threat because of Louisiana's prevailing south and southeast winds.

NAME For King Louis XIV. **NICKNAME** Pelican State. **CAPITAL** Baton Rouge. **ENTERED UNION** Apr. 30, 1812 (18th). **MOTTO** "Union, justice, confidence."

Emblems BIRD Eastern brown pelican. COLORS Gold, white, and blue. CRUSTACEAN Crawfish. DOG Catahoula leopard. FLOWER Magnolia. FOSSIL Petrified palmwood. GEM Agate. INSECT Honeybee. SONGS "Give Me Louisiana," "You Are My Sunshine." TREE Bald cypress.

Land TOTAL AREA 47,751 sq. mi. (31st), incl. 3,230 sq. mi. inland water. BORDERS Ark., Miss., Gulf of Mexico, Tex. RIVERS Atchafalaya, Mississippi, Ouachita, Pearl, Red, Sabine. LAKES Bistineau, Borgne, Caddo, Catahoula, Grand, Maurepas, Pontchartrain, Salvador, White. OTHER NOTABLE FEATURES Bayou Barataria, Bayou Bodcau, Bayou D'Arbonne, Driskill Mt. (535 ft.).

Elected officials Gov. Charles E. ("Buddy") Roemer (D). Lt. Gov. Paul Hardy (R). Sec. State Walter McKeithen (D). Atty. Gen. William J. Guste, Jr. (D).

People (1988 est.) 4,420,000 (20th). RACE/NATIONAL ORIGIN (1980): White 69.32%. Black 29.45%. Indian 0.31%. Asian 0.60%. Hispanic 2.37%. Foreign-born 2.00%. LANGUAGES (1980): English 90.00%. French 6.85%. Span-

ish 1.32%. Vietnamese 0.23%. Italian 0.20%. German 0.20%.
Cities (1986) New Orleans 554,500. Baton Rouge 241,130. Shreveport 220,380. Lafayette 89,830. Kenner 75,710. Lake Charles 73,400. Monroe 56,210. Bossier City 57,060.
Business GROSS STATE PRODUCT (GSP, 1986) $74.4 bil. (20th). SECTORS OF GSP: Farms 0.90%. Agricultural services, forestry, & fisheries 0.31%. Mining 16.82%. Construction 5.25%. Manufacturing 12.99%. Transportation & public utilities 11.15%. Wholesale 5.73%. Retail 8.86%. Finance, insurance, & real estate 14.82%. Services 13.11%. Federal government 1.37%. Federal military 1.25%. State & local government 7.45%. FORTUNE 500 COMPANIES (1988): 2: Freeport-McMoran, Louisiana Land and Exploration.
Famous natives Louis Armstrong ("Satchmo"), jazz musician. Pierre Beauregard, Confederate general. Braxton Bragg, Confederate general. Truman Capote, author. Clyde Cessna, aviator. Michael DeBakey, surgeon. Fats Domino, singer. Lillian Hellman, author. Mahalia Jackson, singer. Jean Baptiste Le Moyne, sieur de Bienville (b. Canada), founded New Orleans. Jerry Lee Lewis, singer. Huey P. Long, senator. Ferdinand Joseph La Menthe ("Jelly Roll") Morton, musician. Leonidas K. Polk, clergyman/Confederate general. Henry Miller Shreve (b. N.J.), riverboat captain. Edward D. White, Jr., jurist.
Noteworthy places Avery Island. Cabildo, New Orleans. French Quarter, New Orleans. Garden District, New Orleans. Hodges Gardens, Natchitoches. Jean Lafitte Natl. Hist. Park, Chalmette. Kent House Museum, Alexandria. Longfellow-Evangeline State Commemorative Area, St. Martinsville. Louisiana Maritime Museum, Baton Rouge. New Orleans Museum of Art.
Memorable events Area first visited by Alonso Alvarez de Piñeda 1519. Claimed by René-Robert Cavelier de La Salle for France 1682. New Orleans founded 1718. French crown colony 1731. Four thousand Acadians (Cajuns) from Nova Scotia forcibly transported by British to Louisiana and settled in Bayou Teche 1755. Lands west of Mississippi given to Spain for help in French and Indian War 1763. Lands east of Mississippi ceded to Britain 1763. Same lands retroceded to France 1800. Jefferson negotiates Louisiana Purchase; U.S. acquires 885,000 sq. mi. for $15 million 1803. Statehood 1812. Andrew Jackson beats British at Battle of New Orleans 1815. State secedes 1861. Surrenders to Union forces 1862. Readmitted to Union 1868. Petroleum discovered 1901. Huey "The Kingfish" Long elected to senate 1928; assassinated 1935. Racial designation law of 1970 repealed 1983.
Tourist information 1-800-33-GUMBO.

Maine

Down-Easters—the original Puritans as well as the later French Canadians—are distinct from the New Englanders of Maine's economically more vital sister states. Their land, especially the coast, is rugged, and the living everywhere is hard. Maine touches only one other state, and it has an end-of-the-line feel to it. Lumbering, fishing, and potato farming were the traditional industries. More than half of the state is still unorganized territory largely owned by paper companies. In the 18th century, canneries, textiles, and shoe factories developed. Recently Maine's economy has combined light industry and tourism that is moving it into the mainstream. The modern Maine entrepreneur, often an out-of-stater, seeks an economy based on small industries and more in keeping with Maine's independent temperament.
NAME Either for Maine in France or to distinguish mainland from islands in Gulf of Maine. NICKNAME Pine Tree State. CAPITAL Augusta. ENTERED UNION Mar. 15, 1820 (23d). MOTTO *Dirigo* (I direct).
Emblems ANIMAL Moose. BIRD Chickadee. FISH Landlocked salmon. FLOWER White pinecone and tassel. INSECT Honeybee. MINERAL Tourmaline. SONG "State of Maine Song." TREE Eastern white pine.
Land TOTAL AREA 33,265 sq. mi. (39th), incl. 2,270 sq. mi. inland water. BORDERS Quebec, New Brunswick, Atlantic Ocean, N.H. RIVERS Alagash, Androscoggin, Aroostock, Kennebec, Machias, Penobscot, Piscataqua, Salmon Falls, St. John. LAKES Chamberlain, Chesuncook, Grand, Moosehead, Rangeley, Sebago. OTHER NOTABLE FEATURES Longfellow Mts. (Mt. Katahadin 5,268 ft.), Mt. Desert Island, Penobscot Bay.
Elected officials Gov. John R. McKernan, Jr. (R). Lt. Gov., none. Sec. State G. William Diamond (D). Atty. Gen. James E. Tierney (D).
People (1988 est.) 1,206,000 (38th). RACE/ NATIONAL ORIGIN (1980): White 99.96%. Black 0.30%. Indian 0.39%. Asian 0.27%. Hispanic 0.47%. Foreign-born 3.90%. LANGUAGES (1980): English 89.21%. French 9.01%. Spanish 0.28%. German 0.25%. Greek 0.25%. Italian 0.11%. American Indian langs. 0.09%.
Cities (1986) Portland 62,670. Lewiston 38,890. Bangor 30,160. Auburn 22,870. South Portland 21,620. Biddeford 20,700. Augusta 20,640.
Business GROSS STATE PRODUCT (GSP, 1986) $17.3 bil. (42d). SECTORS OF GSP: Farms 1.09%. Agricultural services, forestry, & fisheries 1.20%. Mining 0.04%. Construction 6.29%. Manufacturing 21.14%. Transportation & public utilities 9.34%. Wholesale 5.95%. Retail 11.48%. Finance, insurance, & real estate 16.31%. Services 14.46%. Federal government 3.09%. Federal military 1.95%. State & local government 7.71%. FORTUNE 500 COMPANIES (1988): 0.
Famous natives Cyrus H.K. Curtis, publisher. Hannibal Hamlin, politician. Sarah Orne Jewett, novelist. Henry Wadsworth Longfellow, poet. Sir Hiram and Hudson Maxim, inventors. Edna St. Vincent Millay, poet. Edmund S. Muskie, politician. John Knowles Paine, composer. Kenneth Roberts, novelist. Edward Arlington Robinson, poet. Nelson Rockefeller, politician. Marguerite Yourcenar (b. France), author.
Noteworthy places Acadia Natl. Park, Mt. Desert Island. Allagash Natl. Wilderness Waterway. Boothbay Railway Museum Cam-pobello-Longfellow House, Portland. Maine Maritime Museum, Bath. Portland Art Museum Roosevelt-Campobello Intl. Park, Campobello Island. St. Croix Island Natl. Monument.
Memorable events Vikings explore coast c. A.D. 1000. Bartholomew Gosnold sails along coast 1602. French settlers at St. Croix River 1604. Included in grant to Plymouth Company 1606. Monhegan Island and Saco settled 1622. Annexed to Massachusetts Colony 1652. French attack northern territory intermittently through 1713. Statehood 1820. Border with Canada settled 1842. First state prohibition law enacted 1851. Penobscot and Passamaquoddy tribes file claim against state for $300-million compensation for land seized in violation of 1790 Indian Non-Intercourse Act, 1972; settled for $81.5 million 1980. First state to allow inheritance taxes to be paid with works of art 1979.
Tourist information 1-207-289-2423 or 1-800-533-9595.

Maryland

Maryland wraps like a fishhook from the Atlantic Ocean around the fish-rich Chesapeake Bay and into the Cumberland Mountains in the northwest. Baltimore—full of urban problems but newly redeveloped with urban homesteading and shopsteading—holds the center. The suburbs of Baltimore and Washington seem far removed from the Delmarva (DELaware, MARyland, VirginiA) peninsula with its watermen hanging on to an older way of life. Terrain, cultures, and history are a border state's mix of North and South. Founded as a haven for Catholics, Maryland's population is still 20 percent Catholic.
NAME For Henrietta Maria, queen consort of Charles I. NICKNAMES Old Line State, Free State. CAPITAL Annapolis. ENTERED UNION Apr. 28, 1788 (7th). MOTTO *Fatti maschii, parole femine* (Manly deeds, womanly words).
Emblems BIRD Baltimore oriole. DOG Chesapeake Bay retriever. FISH Rockfish. FLOWER Black-eyed Susan. FOSSIL *Ecphora quadricostata* (extinct snail). INSECT Baltimore checkerspot butterfly. SONG "Maryland, My Maryland." SPORT Jousting. TREE White oak.
Land TOTAL AREA 10,460 sq. mi. (42d), incl. 623 sq. mi. inland water. BORDERS Pa., Del., Atlantic Ocean, Va., D.C., W.Va. RIVERS Chester, Choptank, Nanticoke, Patapsco, Patuxent, Pocomoke, Potomac, Susquehanna. OTHER NOTABLE FEATURES Allegheny Mts., Blue Ridge Mts., Chesapeake Bay.
Elected officials Gov. William Donald Schaefer (D). Lt. Gov. Melvin A. Steinberg (D). Sec. State Winfield M. Kelly, Jr. (D). Atty. Gen. J. Joseph Curran, Jr. (D).
People (1988 est.) 4,644,000 (18th). RACE/ NATIONAL ORIGIN (1980): White 75.08%. Black 22.70%. Indian 0.22%. Asian 1.61%. Hispanic 1.50%. Foreign-born 4.60%. LANGUAGES (1980): English 93.84%. Spanish 1.40%. French 0.66. German 0.62%. Italian 0.43%. Polish 0.30%. Korean 0.30%. Chinese 0.30%.
Cities (1986) Baltimore 752,800. Rockville

46,900. Bowie 35,740. Frederick 33,800. Hagerstown 33,670. Annapolis 33,360. Gathersburg 32,350. Cumberland 23,230.
Business GROSS STATE PRODUCT (GSP, 1986) $76.5 bil. (18th). SECTORS OF GSP: Farms 0.81%. Agricultural services, forestry, & fisheries 0.40%. Mining 0.15%. Construction 5.24%. Manufacturing 11.90%. Transportation & public utilities 8.61%. Wholesale 7.15%. Retail 11.46%. Finance, insurance, & real estate 16.76%. Services 20.05%. Federal government 7.06%. Federal military 1.87%. State & local government 8.52%. *FORTUNE* 500 COMPANIES (1988): 5: incl. Black & Decker, Crown Central Petroleum, McCormick, Martin Marietta, Noxell.
Famous natives Russell Baker, journalist. Benjamin Banneker, surveyor. Eubie Blake, pianist. Rachel Carson, biologist/author. Stephen Decatur, navy officer. Frederick Douglass, abolitionist. Billie Holiday, singer. Johns Hopkins, financier/philanthropist. Francis Scott Key, lawyer/poet. Thurgood Marshall, jurist. H.L. Mencken, writer. Charles Willson Peale, artist. William Pinckney, statesman. James Rouse, urban planner. Babe Ruth, baseball player. Upton Sinclair, author. Roger B. Taney, jurist. Harriet Tubman, abolitionist.
Noteworthy places Aberdeen Proving Ground. Antietam Natl. Battlefield, Sharpsburg. Assateague Island Natl. Seashore. Baltimore Aquarium. Baltimore Museum of Art. Baltimore Museum of Industry. Calvert Marine Museum, Solomons. Chesapeake & Ohio Canal Natl. Hist. Park. Chesapeake Bay Maritime Museum, St. Michaels. Ft. McHenry Natl. Monument, Baltimore. Harpers Ferry Natl. Hist. Park. Liberty ship *John W. Brown*, Baltimore. St. Marys City. State House, Annapolis. U.S. Naval Academy, Annapolis. USS *Constellation*, Baltimore. Walters Art Gallery, Baltimore.
Memorable events John Smith explores area 1608. William Claiborne sets up trading post on Kent Island 1631. Land granted to Cecilius Calvert, Lord Baltimore, 1632. Leonard Calvert and 200 Roman Catholic settlers land on Blakistone Island 1634. Mason Dixon Line establishes northern boundary of state 1763–67; later identified as boundary between slave and nonslave states. Francis Scott Key composes "The Star Spangled Banner" after British fail to take Ft. McHenry 1814. U.S. Naval Academy founded Annapolis 1845. State under federal military control during Civil War 1861–65. First state to adopt income tax 1938. Alabama Gov. George C. Wallace shot while campaigning in Democratic presidential primary 1972.
Tourist information 1–800–331–1750.

Massachusetts, Commonwealth of

Massachusetts is rich in the history of the early American republic. The Boston Tea Party, the "shot heard 'round the world" from Lexington and Concord, and the Battle of Bunker Hill are American folklore. So is the feast of Thanksgiving, first celebrated by the Puritans at Plymouth. Fishing, trade, textiles, and leather industries were the backbone of Massachusetts's 19th-century economy. Today Boston's Route 128 is the East Coast's counterpart to California's Silicon Valley, with some of the nation's most advanced computer and electronic research and manufacturing. Another staple of the Massachusetts scene is education, in which the state is a national leader. Boston alone boasts such institutions as Harvard University (founded 1636), M.I.T., Northeastern, Brandeis, Boston University, Boston College, Wellesley, and Tufts. To the west are the University of Massachusetts, Amherst, Williams, Smith, and Mt. Holyoke.
NAME For Massachuset tribe, whose name means "at or about the great hill." NICKNAME Bay State. CAPITAL Boston. ENTERED UNION Feb. 6, 1788 (6th). MOTTO *Ense petit placidam sub libertate quietem* (By the sword we seek peace, but peace only under liberty).
Emblems BEVERAGE Cranberry juice. BIRD Chickadee. BUILDING & MONUMENT STONE Granite. DOG Boston terrier. EXPLORER ROCK Dighton Rock. FISH Cod. FLOWER Mayflower. FOLK SONG "Massachusetts." GEM Rhodonite. HEROINE Deborah Samson. HISTORICAL ROCK Plymouth Rock. HORSE Morgan. INSECT Ladybug. MARINE MAMMAL Right whale. MINERAL Babingtonite. POEM "Blue Hills of Massachusetts." ROCK Roxbury pudding stone. SONG "All Hail to Massachusetts." STONE Granite. TREE American elm.
Land TOTAL AREA 8,284 sq. mi. (45th), incl. 460 sq. mi. inland water. BORDERS Vt., N.H., Atlantic Ocean, R.I., Conn., N.Y. RIVERS Cape Cod Canal, Connecticut, Merrimack, Taunton. OTHER NOTABLE FEATURES Buzzard's Bay, Cape Ann, Cape Cod, Cape Cod Bay, Connecticut Valley, Elizabeth Islands, Martha's Vineyard, Monomoy Island, Nantucket Island.
Elected officials Gov. Michael S. Dukakis (D). Lt. Gov. Evelyn F. Murphy (D). Sec. of Commonwealth Michael Joseph Connolly (D). Atty. Gen. James M. Shannon (D).
People (1988 est.) 5,871,000 (13th). RACE/NATIONAL ORIGIN (1980): White 93.75%. Black 3.85%. Indian 0.16%. Asian 0.92%. Hispanic 2.46%. Foreign-born 8.7%. LANGUAGES (1980): English 86.95%. French 2.50%. Portuguese 2.21%. Spanish 2.01%. Italian 1.98%. Polish 0.92%. Greek 0.66%.
Cities (1986) Boston 573,600. Worcester 157,770. Springfield 149,410. New Bedford 96,450. Brockton 93,870. Lowell 92,880. Cambridge 91,260. Fall River 90,420.
Business GROSS STATE PRODUCT (GSP, 1986) $115.5 bil. (10th). SECTORS OF GSP: Farms 0.31%. Agricultural services, forestry, & fisheries 0.42%. Mining 0.06%. Construction 4.71%. Manufacturing 21.73%. Transportation & public utilities 7.14%. Wholesale 4.41%. Retail 9.94%. Finance, insurance, & real estate 17.08%. Services 22.11%. Federal government 1.54%. Federal military 0.56%. State & local government 7.09%. *FORTUNE* 500 COMPANIES (1988): 19: incl. Dennison Manufacturing, Digital Equipment, Gillette, Ocean Spray Cranberries, Polaroid, Raytheon, Wang Laboratories.
Famous natives John Adams, U.S. president. John Quincy Adams, U.S. president. Samuel Adams, patriot. Horatio Alger, clergyman/author. Susan B. Anthony, suffragette. Clara Barton, nurse. Leonard Bernstein, composer. George Herbert Walker Bush, U.S. president. John ("Johnny Appleseed") Chapman, pioneer. Richard Cardinal Cushing, prelate. Bette Davis, actress. Emily Dickinson, poet. Ralph Waldo Emerson, author. Marshall Field, merchant. R. Buckminster Fuller, inventor/engineer. John Hancock, patriot. Oliver Wendell Holmes, jurist. Winslow Homer, painter. Elias Howe, inventor. John F. Kennedy, U.S. president. Jack Kerouac, author. Cotton Mather, theologian. Samuel Eliot Morison, historian. Samuel Morse, inventor. Thomas P. ("Tip") O'Neill, congressman. Edgar Allan Poe, poet/author. Paul Revere, patriot/silversmith. Louis Sullivan, architect. Henry David Thoreau, author.
Noteworthy places Addison Gallery of American Art, Andover. Arnold Arboretum, Boston. Arthur M. Sackler Museum, Cambridge. Berkshires Museum, Pittsfield. Boston Museum of Fine Arts. Boston Natl. Hist. Park (incl. Bunker Hill, Charlestown Navy Yard, Old North Church). Busch-Reisinger Museum, Cambridge. Cape Cod Natl. Seashore. Clark Art Institute, Williamsburg. Fogg Art Museum, Boston. Gardner Art Museum, Boston. Lowell Natl. Hist. Park. Minute Man Natl. Hist. Park, Lexington and Concord. Nantucket Hist. Society. Old Sturbridge. Peabody Museum, Salem. Plimoth Plantation, Plymouth. Shaker Village. Tanglewood Music Festival, Lenox. USS *Constitution* ("Old Ironsides"), Charlestown. Walden Pond. Woods Hole Oceanographic Institute. Worcester Art Museum.
Memorable events Pilgrims land at Plymouth 1620. First Thanksgiving celebrated 1621. Harvard College founded 1636. Region acquires province of Maine 1652. Colonists battle Wampanoags in King Philip's War 1655–56. Boston Massacre 1770. Boston Tea Party protests taxation 1773. Battles at Lexington, Concord, and Bunker Hill 1775. Shays's Rebellion 1785–86. Maine becomes a separate state 1820. Massachusetts receives influx of Irish immigrants fleeing famine 1845. Textile workers' strike at Lawrence brings International Workers of the World (IWW) to prominence in East 1912. Cape Cod Canal completed 1914. International protest follows trial and execution of anarchists Nicola Sacco and Bartolomeo Vanzetti for robbery and murder 1920; names cleared by governor's proclamation 1970. Eleven robbers steal $2.7 million from Brink's North Terminal Garage 1950. Martha's Vineyard and Nantucket symbolically vote to secede from state 1973.
Tourist information 1–617–536–4100 or 1–800–858–0200.

Michigan

The automobile is the single commodity with which Michigan is most identified, and it is the home of the big three automakers, General Motors, Ford, and Chrysler. More than 50 percent of Michiganders live in the southeastern corner of the state, where the car industry flourishes. In the Upper Peninsula, across the Straits of Mackinac, lumber and copper have been the principal commodities from the 19th century, and the northern part of the Lower Peninsula boasts rich farmland. Michigan's boundaries include parts of four of the five Great Lakes, and it has more coastline than any state except Alaska. Michigan has had an outstanding reputation in higher education, and the University of Michigan at Ann Arbor and Michigan State are helping to foster the state's high-tech industries. But the state's heavy reliance on auto manufacturing makes it vulnerable to economic downturns, as was witnessed in the early 1980s when the state's unemployment was among the very highest in the nation.

Name From Fox *mesikami*, "large lake." **Nicknames** Wolverine State, Lake State. **Capital** Lansing. **Entered Union** Jan. 26, 1837 (26th). **Motto** *Si quaeris peninsulam amoenam circumspice* (If you are looking for a beautiful peninsula, look around you).

Emblems **Bird** Robin. **Fish** Trout. **Flower** Apple blossom. **Gem** Chlorastrolite. **Insect** Dragonfly. **Song** "Michigan, My Michigan." **Stone** Petoskey stone. **Tree** White pine.

Land **Total area** 58,527 sq. mi. (23d), incl. 1,573 sq. mi. inland water. **Borders** Lake Superior, Ontario, Lake Huron, Lake Erie, Ohio, Ind., Lake Michigan, Wis. **Rivers** Brule, Detroit, Kalamazoo, Menominee, Montreal, Muskegon, St. Joseph, St. Mary's. **Lakes** Burt, Higgins, Houghton, Huron, Manistique, Michigan, Mullett, St. Clair, Superior. **Other notable features** Isle Royale, Mt. Curwood (1,980 ft.), Saginaw Bay, Traverse Bay, Whitefish Bay.

Elected officials Gov. James J. Blanchard (D). Lt. Gov. Martha W. Griffiths (D). Sec. State Richard H. Austin (D). Atty. Gen. Frank J. Kelley (D).

People (1988 est.) 9,300,000 (8th). **Race/national origin** (1980): White 85.22%. Black 12.93%. Indian 0.49%. Asian 4.5%. Hispanic 1.70%. Foreign-born 4.50%. **Languages** (1980): English 93.46%. Spanish 1.21%. Polish 1.05%. German 0.69%. Italian 0.55%. French 0.39%. Arab 0.35%.

Cities (1986) Detroit 1,086,220. Grand Rapids 186,530. Warren 149,800. Flint 145,590. Lansing 128,980. Sterling Heights 111,960. Ann Arbor 107,810. Livonia 100,540.

Business **Gross state product** (GSP, 1986) $153.2 bil. (9th). **Sectors of GSP:** Farms 1.07%. Agricultural services, forestry, & fisheries 0.23%. Mining 0.66%. Construction 3.18%. Manufacturing 31.02%. Transportation & public utilities 7.41%. Wholesale 6.19%. Retail 9.26%. Finance, insurance, & real estate 15.78%. Services 15.13%. Federal government 1.10%. Federal military 0.33%. State & local government 8.65%. *Fortune* 500 **companies** (1988): 17: incl. Chrysler, Dow Corning, Ford Motor, General Motors, Gerber Products, Kellogg, Thorn Apple Valley, Upjohn, Whirlpool.

Famous natives Ralph J. Bunche, statesman (Nobel Peace Prize, 1950). Paul de Kruif, bacteriologist. Thomas Dewey, politician. Herbert H. Dow (b. Canada), chemical manufacturer. Edna Ferber, author. Henry Ford, industrialist. Edgar Guest, journalist/poet. Robert Ingersoll, industrialist. Will Kellogg, businessman/philanthropist. Charles A. Lindbergh, aviator. Antoine de La Mothe, sieur de Cadillac (b. France), founded Detroit. Pontiac, Ottawa chief. William Upjohn, drug manufacturer.

Noteworthy places Detroit Historical Society. Detroit Institute of Arts. Dossin Great Lakes Museum, Detroit. Great Lakes Indian Interpretive Museum, Detroit. Greenfield Village, Dearborn. Historic Ft. Wayne, Detroit. Isle Royale Natl. Park. Mackinac Island. Pictured Rocks Natl. Lakeshore, Lake Superior. Sleeping Bear Dunes Natl. Lakeshore, Lake Superior.

Memorable events French explorers in region 1634. Jacques Marquette settles Sault Ste. Marie 1668. Detroit founded as French military post 1701. Region ceded to England 1763; to U.S. 1783. Included in Northwest Territory but British maintain control until 1796. Michigan Territory 1805. First steamboat on Great Lakes reaches Detroit 1818. Statehood 1837. First state to outlaw capital punishment 1846. Republican party organized at Jackson 1854. Canals at Sault Ste. Marie link Lakes Superior and Huron 1855. Ransom E. Olds and Henry Ford, working independently, develop gas-powered car 1896. United Auto Workers first to use sit-down strike successfully in contract negotiations 1935. Worst race riot in U.S. history leaves 43 dead and $200 million in damages in Detroit 1967. Congress authorizes $1.5 billion in federal loan guarantees to bail out Chrysler Corporation 1979.

Tourist information 1-800-543-2YES or 1-517-373-1195.

Minnesota

A land of at least 10,000 lakes, Minnesota is a magnet for outdoorsmen, canoers, and fishermen. It is also home to the largest Scandinavian populations in the United States. Originally exploited for its wealth of lumber and iron—the Mesabi Range still produces 60 percent of the nation's iron ore—Minnesota also has highly developed agribusinesses (especially dairy products), manufacturing, and transportation industries. Minneapolis and St. Paul are at the north end of the Mississippi River system, and Duluth at the westernmost point of Lake Superior is the largest U.S. inland port. Both self-sufficient and politically liberal, Minnesota has one of the best state school systems.

Name From the Sioux *minisota*, "sky-tinted waters." **Nicknames** North Star State, Gopher State. **Capital** St. Paul. **Entered Union** May 11, 1858 (32d). **Motto** *L'étoile du nord* (Star of the north).

Emblems **Bird** Common loon. **Drink** Milk. **Fish** Walleye. **Flower** Pink and white lady's slipper. **Gem** Lake Superior agate. **Grain** Wild rice. **Mushroom** Morel, or sponge mushroom. **Song** "Hail, Minnesota!." **Tree** Red pine.

Land **Total area** 84,402 sq. mi. (12th), incl. 4,854 sq. mi. inland water. **Borders** Manitoba, Ontario, Lake Superior, Wis., Iowa, S.Dak., N.Dak. **Rivers** Minnesota, Mississippi, Red River of the North, St. Croix. **Lakes** Itasca, Lake of the Woods, Leech, Mille Lacs, Red, Winnibigoshish. **Other notable features** Mesabi Range.

Elected officials Gov. Rudy Perpich (Democratic-Farmer-Labor). Lt. Gov. Marlene Johnson (DFL). Sec. State Joan Anderson Growe (DFL). Atty. Gen. Hubert H. Humphrey III (DFL).

People (1988 est.) 4,306,000 (21st). **Race/national origin** (1980): White 96.71%. Black 1.28%. Indian 0.90%. Asian 0.79%. Hispanic 0.79%. Foreign-born 2.60%. **Languages** (1980): English 94.41%. German 1.44%. Norwegian 0.69%. Spanish 0.59%. Swedish 0.38%. Finnish 0.34%. French 0.27%.

Cities (1986) Minneapolis 356,840. St. Paul 263,680. Bloomington 85,740. Duluth 82,380. Rochester 58,130. Brooklyn Park 53,550. Plymouth 46,590. Minnetonka 44,330.

Business **Gross state product** (GSP, 1986) $75.6 bil. (19th). **Sectors of GSP:** Farms 4.40%. Agricultural services, forestry, & fisheries 0.33%. Mining 0.54%. Construction 3.65%. Manufacturing 20.91%. Transportation & public utilities 9.06%. Wholesale 7.96%. Retail 9.63%. Finance, insurance, & real estate 18.29%. Services 15.43%. Federal government 1.14%. Federal military 0.24%. State & local government 8.43%. *Fortune* 500 **companies** (1988): 19: incl. Deluxe Check Printers, General Mills, Geo. A. Hormel, Honeywell, Land O'Lakes, Minnesota Mining & Manufacturing (3M), Pillsbury.

Famous natives Warren Burger, jurist. Bob Dylan, musician. F. Scott Fitzgerald, novelist. Judy Garland, actress. J. Paul Getty, businessman. Sinclair Lewis, author (Nobel Prize, 1930). Paul Manship, sculptor. William and Charles Mayo, surgeons. Eugene McCarthy, politician. Walter F. Mondale, politician. Charles Schulz, cartoonist. Ole Edvart Rölvaag (b. Norway), novelist. Richard W. Sears, merchant.

Noteworthy places Boundary Waters Canoe Area. Grand Portage Natl. Monument. International Falls. Lake Itasca State Park (headwaters of Mississippi). Mayo Clinic, Rochester. Minneapolis Institute of Arts. Minnehaha Falls, Minneapolis. Minnesota Zoological Gardens. Pipestone Natl. Monument. Tyrone Guthrie Theater, Minneapolis. Voyageurs Natl. Park. Walker Art Center, Minneapolis.

Memorable events Pierre Esprit Radisson and Médard Chouart des Groseilliers visit area 1654-60. René-Robert de La Salle and Louis Hennepin explore upper Mississippi 1680. Daniel Greysolon, sieur Duluth, claims region for France 1679. Area east of Mississippi to Britain 1763; to U.S. 1783. Western region of state as part of Louisiana Purchase 1803. Britain cedes northern strip to U.S. 1818. Ft. Snelling built 1820. Northern border settled by Ashburton Treaty 1842. Minnesota Territory created 1849. Statehood 1858. Sioux driven from state after uprising led by Chief Little Crow 1862. Iron ore deposits discovered in Mesabi Range 1890. Democratic party merges with Farmer-Labor party 1944.

Tourist information 1-800-328-1461, 1-612-296-5029 or 1-800-652-9747.

Mississippi

Mississippi's rank as the poorest state in the nation can be traced to the Civil War. Before the Civil War, Mississippi was the fifth-wealthiest state in the nation. The war cost the state 30,000 men (65% of the Southerners who died). Plantation owners who survived the war were virtually bankrupted by the emancipation of the slaves, and Union troops under Sherman and others left widespread destruction in their wake. The increasingly harsh race-laws passed around 1900 also cost the state in the emigration of almost half a million (75% blacks, 25% whites) in the 1940s. Compounding all this was the fact that until World War II, Mississippi had virtually no urban center such as Jackson to attract or sustain major industry. In race relations particularly, Mississippi has made vast improvements, and there have been substantial gains in education and the attraction of out-of-state companies, especially light industry.

NAME From Ojibwa *misi sipi*, "great river." NICKNAME Magnolia State. CAPITAL Jackson. ENTERED UNION Dec. 10, 1817 (20th). MOTTO *Virtue et armis* (By virtue and arms).

Emblems BEVERAGE Milk. BIRD Mockingbird. FISH Largemouth or black bass. FLOWER Magnolia. FOSSIL Prehistoric whale. INSECT Honeybee. MAMMAL White-tailed deer. SONG "Go, Mississippi." STONE Petrified wood. TREE Magnolia. WATERFOWL Wood duck. WATER MAMMAL Porpoise.

Land TOTAL AREA 47,689 sq. mi. (32d), incl. 456 sq. mi. inland water. BORDERS Tenn., Ala., Gulf of Mexico, La., Ark. RIVERS Big Black, Mississippi, Pearl, Tennessee, Yazoo. LAKES Arkabutla, Grenada, Ross Barnett Res., Sardis. OTHER NOTABLE FEATURES Pontotoc Ridge.

Elected officials Gov. Ray Mabus (D). Lt. Gov. Brad Dye (D). Sec. State Dick Molpus (D). Atty. Gen. Mike Moore (D).

People (1988 est.) 2,627,000 (31st). RACE/NATIONAL ORIGIN (1980): White 64.10%. Black 35.19%. Indian 0.27%. Asian 0.31%. Hispanic 0.96%. Foreign-born 0.90%. LANGUAGES (1980): English 98.08%. Spanish 0.63%. French 0.35%. American Indian langs. 0.16%. German 0.16%. Italian 0.06%. Vietnamese 0.05%. Chinese 0.05%.

Cities (1986) Jackson 208,420. Biloxi 47,750. Gulfport 43,410. Meridian 42,970. Hattiesburg 40,740. Greenville 40,000.

Business GROSS STATE PRODUCT (GSP, 1986) $31.8 bil. (32d). SECTORS OF GSP: Farms 2.98%. Agricultural services, forestry, & fisheries 0.44%. Mining 2.60%. Construction 4.49%. Manufacturing 27.24%. Transportation & public utilities 8.55%. Wholesale 5.15%. Retail 10.67%. Finance, insurance, & real estate 13.41%. Services 11.24%. Federal government 2.24%. Federal military 2.40%. State & local government 8.58%. FORTUNE 500 COMPANIES (1988): 0.

Famous natives Medgar Evers, reformer. William Faulkner, novelist. Shelby Foote, historian. B.B. King, musician. Elvis Presley, singer. Leontyne Price, opera singer. John C. Stennis, politician. Strom Thurmond, politician. Conway Twitty, singer. Muddy Waters, musician. Eudora Welty, novelist. Ben Ames Williams, novelist. Tennessee Williams, playwright. Richard Wright, author.

Noteworthy places Delta Blues Museum, Clarksdale. Natchez Trace Natl. Parkway. Seafood Industry Museum, Biloxi. Tupelo Natl. Battlefield. Vicksburg Natl. Military Park.

Memorable events Hernando de Soto's expedition travels through Mississippi 1540–41. René-Robert Cavelier de La Salle claims Mississippi Valley for France 1682. Pierre Le Moyne, sieur d'Iberville builds Ft. Maurepas on Biloxi Bay 1699. Natchez (Ft. Rosalie) established 1716. France cedes territory to Britain 1763. Mississippi Territory (including present-day Alabama) created 1798. Statehood (Natchez first capital) 1817. Secedes from Union; Jefferson Davis becomes president of Confederacy 1861. Siege of Vicksburg 1863. Petroleum discovered 1939. Gov. Ross R. Barnett found guilty of contempt in preventing desegregation of University of Mississippi; James H. Meredith first black enrolled at University of Mississippi 1962. Civil rights leader Medgar Evers assassinated in Jackson and buried in Arlington National Cemetery 1963. White civil rights workers James Cheney, Andrew Goodman, and Michael Schwerner killed 1964.

Tourist information 1-800-647-2290 or 1-601-359-3414.

Missouri

Missouri is remarkable for the number and variety of its neighbors—southern states (Arkansas, Kentucky, and Tennessee), midwestern states (Illinois and Iowa), and Plains states (Oklahoma, Nebraska, and Kansas). For Missouri, geography was destiny. Still one of the country's most important inland ports, St. Louis was founded at the confluence of the Missouri and Mississippi rivers and became the gateway to the West; and Independence (now part of metropolitan Kansas City) got its start provisioning wagons for the Oregon and Santa Fe trails. The Pony Express from St. Joseph to Sacramento began in 1860, and the first attempt at airmail service was tried in St. Louis in 1911. While farming and livestock are still important to the state's economy, manufacturing and banking are now the biggest sectors.

NAME From Iliniwek *missouri*, "owner of big canoes." NICKNAME Show Me State. CAPITAL Jefferson City. ENTERED UNION Aug. 10, 1821 (24th). MOTTO *Salus populi suprema lex esto* (The welfare of the people shall be the supreme law).

Emblems BIRD Bluebird. FLOWER Hawthorne. INSECT Honeybee. MINERAL Galena. ROCK Mozarkite. SONG "Missouri Waltz." TREE Dogwood.

Land TOTAL AREA 69,697 sq. mi. (19th), incl. 752 sq. mi. inland water. BORDERS Iowa, Ill., Ky., Tenn., Ark., Okla., Kans., Nebr. RIVERS Des Moines, Mississippi, Missouri, Osage, St.

> *"A Missourian gets used to Southerners thinking him a Yankee, a Northerner considering him a cracker, a Westerner sneering at his effete Easternness, and the Easterner taking him for a cowhand."*
>
> —**William Least Heat Moon,** *Blue Highways,* 1982

Francis. LAKES Bull Shoals, Clearwater, Lake of the Ozarks, Lake of the Woods, Tablerock, Wappapella. OTHER NOTABLE FEATURES Ozark Mts. (Taum Sauk Mt. 1,772 ft.).

Elected officials Gov. John Ashcroft (R). Lt. Gov. Mel Carahan (D). Sec. State Roy D. Blunt (R). Atty. Gen. William L. Webster (R).

People (1988 est.) 5,139,000 (15th). RACE/NATIONAL ORIGIN (1980): White 88.44%. Black 10.44%. Indian 0.30%. Asian 0.51%. Hispanic 1.06%. Foreign-born 1.70%. LANGUAGES (1980): English 96.94%. Spanish 0.81%. German 0.68%. French 0.28%. Italian 0.23%.

Cities (1986) Kansas City 441,170. St. Louis 426,300. Springfield 139,360. Independence 112,950. St. Joseph 74,070. Columbia 63,140. Florissant 59,040. University City 42,270.

Business GROSS STATE PRODUCT (GSP, 1986) $83.5 bil. (15th). SECTORS OF GSP: Farms 2.33%. Agricultural services, forestry, & fisheries 0.30%. Mining 0.35%. Construction 4.14%. Manufacturing 22.64%. Transportation & public utilities 10.96%. Wholesale 7.03%. Retail 10.42%. Finance, insurance, & real estate 15.61%. Services 16.14%. Federal government 2.61%. Federal military 0.83%. State & local government 6.63%. FORTUNE 500 COMPANIES (1988): 16: incl. Anheuser-Busch, Emerson Electric, General Dynamics, McDonnell Douglas, Monsanto, Ralston Purina.

Famous natives Thomas Hart Benton, painter. Yogi Berra, baseball player. George Caleb Bingham (b. Va.), painter. Omar Bradley, general. Adophus Busch (b. Germany), brewer. George Washington Carver, botanist. Walter Cronkite, journalist. Walt Disney, film producer. T.S. Eliot, author. Walker Evans, photographer. Langston Hughes, poet. Jesse James, outlaw. Marianne Moore, poet. Reinhold Niebuhr, theologian. J.C. Penny, businessman. John J. ("Black Jack") Pershing, soldier. Joseph Pulitzer (b. Hungary), publisher. Ginger Rogers, dancer. Casey Stengel, baseball player. Virgil Thompson, composer. Harry S Truman, U.S. president. Mark Twain, writer. Tom Watson, golfer. Shelley Winters, actress.

Noteworthy places Churchill Memorial, St. Aldermanbury Church, Fulton. Gateway Arch, St. Louis. George Washington Carver Natl. Monument. Harry S Truman Library, Independence. Mark Twain Area, Hannibal. Nelson-Atkins Museum of Art, Kansas City. Pony Express Museum, St. Joseph. St. Louis Art Museum. Wilson's Creek Natl. Battlefield.

Memorable events French miners and hunters settle at Ste. Genevieve 1735. Pierre Laclade settles St. Louis 1765. Statehood 1821. Missouri legislature split over secesssion: minority party adopts secession ordinance; Missouri admitted to Confederacy; majority party remains loyal to Union 1861. Jesse James killed by fellow gang member at St. Joseph 1882. Lake of the Ozarks formed after completion of Bagnell Dam on Missouri River 1931. Winston Churchill delivers "iron curtain" speech at Fulton 1952. Gateway Arch, 630 ft. high, opened at St. Louis 1964. St. Louis population declines 47% 1950–80.

Tourist information 1–314–751–4133.

Montana

Mountains account for only the western two-fifths of the state, where copper mining, lumbering, and tourism are the chief industries. The eastern portion of the state is part of the Great Plains. There the "Big Sky Country" is devoted to agriculture and especially ranching. For many years Montana was in the grip of the Anaconda Copper Mining Company, which virtually owned the state government and took most of the company's profits out of the state. After Anaconda's demise in the 1970s, Montana developed some of the most stringent environmental laws in the West. Although the copper mining damage is done, these laws will have a beneficial impact on the southeastern corner of the state, which is now being exploited for its enormous reserves of low-sulphur coal.

NAME From Spanish *montaña*, "mountainous." NICKNAMES Treasure State, Big Sky Country. CAPITAL Helena. ENTERED UNION Nov. 8, 1889 (41st). MOTTO *Oro y plata* (Gold and silver).

Emblems BIRD Western meadowlark. FISH Blackspotted cutthroat trout. FLOWER Bitterroot. GEMS Yogo sapphire, Montana agate. GRASS Bluebunch wheatgrass. SONG "Montana." STATE BALLAD "Montana Melody." TREE Ponderosa pine.

Land TOTAL AREA 147,046 sq. mi. (4th), incl. 1,658 sq. mi. inland water. BORDERS British Columbia, Alberta, Saskatchewan, N.Dak., S.Dak., Wyo., Idaho. RIVERS Kootenai, Milk, Missouri, Musselshell, Powder, Yellowstone. LAKES Bighorn, Canyon Ferry, Elwell, Flathead, Ft. Peck. MOUNTAINS Absaroka Range, Beartooth Range (Granite Peak 12,799 ft.), Big Belt, Bitterroot Range, Centennial, Crazy, Lewis Range, Little Belt. OTHER NOTA-

BLE FEATURES Continental Divide, Missoula Valley.

Elected officials Gov. Stan Stephens (R). Lt. Gov. Allen Kolstad (R). Sec. State Mike Cooney (D). Atty. Gen. Marc Racicot (R).

People (1988 est.) 804,000 (44th). RACE/NATIONAL ORIGIN (1980): White 94.18%. Black 0.22%. Indian 4.79%. Asian 0.29%. Hispanic 1.28%. Foreign-born 2.30%. LANGUAGES (1980): English 94.82%. German 1.41%. American Indian langs. 1.07%. Spanish 0.76%. French 0.33%. Norwegian 0.30%.

Cities (1986) Billings 80,310. Great Falls 57,310. Missoula 33,960. Butte-Silver Bow 33,380. Helena 24,670. Bozeman 23,490.

Business GROSS STATE PRODUCT (GSP, 1986) $12.2 bil. (45th). SECTORS OF GSP: Farms 7.79%. Agricultural services, forestry, & fisheries 0.50%. Mining 7.30%. Construction 8.40%. Manufacturing 7.24%. Transportation & public utilities 12.23%. Wholesale 5.45%. Retail 8.6%. Finance, insurance, & real estate 16.51%. Services 13.21%. Federal government 2.65%. Federal military 1.22%. State & local government 8.89%. *FORTUNE* 500 COMPANIES (1988): 0.

Famous natives Gary Cooper, actor. Marcus Daly (b. Ireland), mine owner. Chet Huntley, journalist. Myrna Loy, actress. Mike Mansfield (b. N.Y.), politician/diplomat. Jeanette Rankin, politician/reformer. Charles M. Russell, artist.

Noteworthy places Big Hole Natl. Battlefield. Bob Marshall Wilderness. Charles M. Russell Museum, Great Falls. Custer Battlefield Natl. Monument. Ft. Union Trading Post Natl. Hist. Site. Lewis and Clark Caverns State Park. Museum of the Plains Indian, Browning. Natl. Bison Range. Waterton-Glacier International Peace Park. World Museum of Mining, Butte. Yellowstone Natl. Park.

Memorable events French explorers and trappers visit region 1740s. Large part of state in Louisiana Purchase 1803. Lewis and Clark expedition 1805–06. Ft. Benton first permanent settlement 1846. Western part of state included in Washington Territory 1853 and 1859; eastern part in Nebraska (1854) and Dakota (1861) territories. Gold discovered at Bannack (1862) and Alder Gulch (1863). Organized as Montana Territory 1864. Dakota and Cheyenne defeat U.S. troops under Gen. William Armstrong Custer at Battle of Little Bighorn 1876. Under Chief Joseph, Nez Percé beat U.S. Army at Big Hole Basin 1877. Marcus Daly discovers copper near Butte 1880s. Statehood 1889. Homesteaders enter state 1909. Ft. Peck Dam completed 1940. Anaconda Copper Mining, dominant in Montana industry and politics since 1915, closes mining operations at Butte 1983.

Tourist information 1–800–548–3390 or 1–406–444–2654.

Nebraska

Although set aside as Indian territory in 1834 and made off-limits to white settlement, thousands of whites crossed the region along the Independence, Mormon, and Oregon trails.

Eventually Congress opened the land to settlement, which accelerated after the Homestead Act of 1862 and the coming of the railroads. The newcomers took up ranching and farming under hard conditions. The winter of 1886–87 killed thousands of cattle and drove many large-scale ranchers into bankruptcy, while the dust bowl of the 1930s spurred a mass exodus. Significant industry did not develop until World War II, when many war-related industries and army airfields moved to the center of the country. Nearly half of the work force of the state—among the leading agricultural states, especially in the production of corn for grain and livestock—is in agriculture. A state constitutional amendment passed in 1982 prevents the sale of farmlands and ranch lands to anyone other than a Nebraska family farm corporation.

NAME From Oto *nebrathka*, "flat water." NICKNAME Cornhusker State. CAPITAL Lincoln. ENTERED UNION Mar. 1, 1867 (37th). MOTTO "Equality before the law."

Emblems BIRD Western meadowlark. FLOWER Goldenrod. FOSSIL Mammoth. GEM Blue agate. GRASS Little blue stem. INSECT Honeybee. MAMMAL White-tailed deer. ROCK Prairie agate. SOIL Soils of the Holdrege series. SONG "Beautiful Nebraska." TREE Western cottonwood.

Land TOTAL AREA 77,355 sq. mi. (15th), incl. 711 sq. mi. inland water. BORDERS S.Dak., Iowa, Mo., Kans., Colo., Wyo. RIVERS Missouri, North Platte, Republican, South Platte. LAKES Harlan Co. Res., Lewis and Clark Lake. OTHER NOTABLE FEATURES Pine Ridge, Sand Hills.

Elected officials Gov. Kay A. Orr (R). Lt. Gov. William E. Nichol (R). Sec. State Allen J. Beermann (R). Atty. Gen. Robert M. Spire (R).

People (1988 est.) 1,601,000 (36th). RACE/NATIONAL ORIGIN (1980): White 95.06%. Black 3.05%. Indian 0.58%. Asian 0.52%. Hispanic 1.80%. Foreign-born 2.00%. LANGUAGES (1980): English 92.44%. German 1.23% Spanish 1.21%. Czechoslovakian 0.62%. Polish 0.23%. French 0.21%.

Cities (1986) Omaha 349,270. Lincoln 183,050. Grand Island 39,100. Bellevue 32,200. Fremont 23,780. Hastings 22,990. Kearney 22,770.

Business GROSS STATE PRODUCT (GSP, 1986) $26.5 bil. (34th). SECTORS OF GSP: Farms 12.03%. Agricultural services, forestry, & fisheries 0.50%. Mining 0.26%. Construction 3.61%. Manufacturing 13.76%. Transportation & public utilities 11.27%. Wholesale 7.06%. Retail 8.91%. Finance, insurance, & real estate 17.29%. Services 13.45%. Federal government 0.23%. Federal military 2.01%. State & local government 9.62%. *FORTUNE* 500 COMPANIES (1988): 2: AG Processing, Conagra.

Famous natives Fred Astaire, dancer. Marlon Brando, actor. Willa Cather (b. Va.), author. Loren Eiseley, anthropologist. The Rev. Edward J. Flanagan (b. Ireland), reformer. Henry Fonda, actor. Gerald Ford, U.S. president. Rollin Kirby, cartoonist. Melvin Laird, politician. Harold Lloyd, actor. Mahpiua Luta (Red Cloud), Oglala Sioux chief. Malcolm X, religious leader. Roscoe Pound, educator.

Noteworthy places Agate Fossil Beds Natl. Monument. Arbor Lodge State Park, Nebraska City. Boys Town, Omaha. Buffalo Bill Ranch State Hist. Park. Chimney Rock Hist. Site. Homestead Natl. Monument, Beatrice. Oregon Trail. Pioneer Village, Minden. Scotts Bluff Natl. Monument. Stuhr Museum of the Prairie Pioneer, Grand Island.

Memorable events Acquired as part of Louisiana Purchase 1803. Separate territory created by Kansas-Nebraska Act 1854. Size reduced after creation of Colorado and Dakota territories 1861. Statehood 1867. To encourage tree planting, becomes first state to observe Arbor Day 1872. Adopts unicameral legislature 1937. Oil discovered 1939. Population peaks at 1,605,000 1984–85.

Tourist information 1–800–228–4307 or 1–800–742–7595.

Nevada

Set in the Great Basin desert, Nevada is one of the most barren places in North America, and the state receives less rainfall than any other. First explored by Europeans in 1776, it was 75 years before anyone thought of establishing a town in the area, and it did not last a decade. Miners came to Nevada early, but the discovery of the Comstock Lode in 1859 brought thousands. To add free-state congressional votes, Nevada was hustled into the Union in 1864, three years before its boundaries were settled. That boom was over by the 1870s, and it took more gold and silver strikes in the early 1900s, as well as the discovery of copper, to get the economy rolling again. The mainstay of the economy since World War II has been the gambling industry, which generates virtually half of all tax revenues; Las Vegas alone can accommodate as many as 150,000 conventioneers and tourists at one time. In 1980 31 percent had lived in the state for no longer than five years.

NAME From Spanish, meaning "snow-covered sierra." NICKNAMES Sagebrush State, Silver State. CAPITAL Carson City. ENTERED UNION Oct. 31, 1864 (36th). MOTTO "All for our country."

Emblems ANIMAL Desert bighorn sheep. BIRD Mountain bluebird. FLOWER Sagebrush. FOSSIL Icthyosaur. GRASS Indian ricegrass. METAL Silver. SONG "Home Means Nevada." TREE Single-leaf piñon.

Land TOTAL AREA 110,561 sq. mi. (7th), incl. 667 sq. mi. inland water. BORDERS Oreg., Idaho, Utah, Ariz., Calif. RIVERS Colorado, Humboldt. LAKES Pyramid, Walker, Winnemucca. OTHER NOTABLE FEATURES Black Rock Desert, Carson Sink, Humboldt Salt Marsh, Mojave Desert.

Elected officials Gov. Robert J. Miller (D). Lt. Gov. vacant. Sec. State Frankie Sue Del Papa (D). Atty. Gen. Brian McKay (R).

People (1988 est.) 1,060,000 (41). RACE/ NATIONAL ORIGIN (1980): White 97.82%. Black 0.06%. Indian 0.02%. Asian 0.02%. Hispanic 0.07%. Foreign-born 6.70%. LANGUAGES (1980): English 90.32%. Spanish 4.67%. German 0.78%. Italian 0.68%. French 0.47%.

American Indian langs. 0.35%.

Cities (1986) Las Vegas 191,510. Reno 110,430. Sparks 51,980. North Las Vegas 50,290. Henderson 46,950. Carson City 36,900. Elko 11,660.

Business GROSS STATE PRODUCT (GSP, 1986) $19.4 bil. (39th). SECTORS OF GSP: Farms 0.57%. Agricultural services, forestry, & fisheries 0.30%. Mining 2.82%. Construction 7.75%. Manufacturing 4.80%. Transportation & public utilities 9.44%. Wholesale 4.07%. Retail 9.82%. Finance, insurance, & real estate 14.14%. Services 35.53%. Federal government 1.85%. Federal military 1.59%. State & local government 7.34%. FORTUNE 500 COMPANIES (1988): 0.

Famous natives Walter Van Tilburg Clark (b. Me.), author. Sarah Winnemucca Hopkins, interpreter/teacher. John William MacKay, miner. William Morris Stewart (b. N.Y.), lawyer/senator.

Noteworthy places Death Valley Natl. Monument. Lehman Caves Natl. Monument. Valley of the Fire State Park, Overton.

Memorable events Francisco Tomás Garcés explores area 1775–76. Jedediah Smith, trader, crosses region 1826–27. Old Spanish Trail (1830) and California Trail (1833) cross region. John Frémont explores area 1843–45. To U.S. after Mexican War 1846. Genoa, first settlement in Nevada, founded as Mormon Station 1849. Gold of Comstock Lode discovered 1859. Organized as separate territory 1861. Statehood 1864. Nevada legalizes gambling 1931. Hoover Dam completed 1931. Nuclear tests begun at Yucca Flats 1951. Population grows more than 550% 1950–88.

Tourist information 1–800–NEVADA8.

New Hampshire

New Hampshire has a disproportionate influence on presidential elections because by state law its primary must fall at least one week before any other state's (though Iowa's caucuses can come earlier). Through independence the mainstays of the economy were fishing, trade, and farming. Boston proved more suitable for trade, and New Hampshire's stubborn land was outproduced by the more fertile valleys to the south and west. The state's economy receded until the beginning of the Industrial Revolution, when there was tremendous growth in textile-producing mill towns in the Merrimack River Valley. The mills began to close after World War I, and the economy faltered again. Lately improvement has come as high-tech firms from Boston have sought refuge in New Hampshire's favorable tax climate. Expansion here, too, has threatened New Hampshire's natural spaces.

NAME For English county of Hampshire. NICKNAME Granite State. CAPITAL Concord. ENTERED UNION June 21, 1788 (9th). MOTTO "Live free or die."

Emblems AMPHIBEAN Spotted newt. BIRD Purple finch. FLOWER Purple lilac. GEM Smoke quartz. INSECT Ladybug. MINERAL Beryl. SONG "Old New Hampshire." TREE White birch.

Land TOTAL AREA 9,279 sq. mi. (44th), incl.

286 sq. mi. inland water. BORDERS Quebec, Maine, Atlantic Ocean, Mass., Vt. RIVERS Connecticut, Merrimack, Piscataqua, Saco, Salmon Falls. LAKES First Connecticut, Francis, Newfound, Ossipee, Sunapee, Winnipesaukee. OTHER NOTABLE FEATURES Isles of Shoals, White Mts. (Mt. Washington 6,288 ft., highest peak in Northeast).

Elected officials Gov. Judd Gregg (R). Lt. Gov., none. Sec. State William Gardner (D). Atty. Gen. John P. Arnold (R).

People (1988 est.) 1,097,000 (39th). RACE/ NATIONAL ORIGIN (1980): White 98.91%. Black 0.47%. Indian 0.15%. Asian 0.37%. Hispanic 0.57%. Foreign-born 4.40%. LANGUAGES (1980): English 89.59%. French 7.21%. Greek 0.51%. Spanish 0.46%. German 0.42%. Polish 0.40%.

Cities (1986) Manchester 97,280. Nashua 76,510. Concord 32,770. Portsmouth 25,970. Dover 23,770. Rochester 23,370. Keene 22,370.

Business GROSS STATE PRODUCT (GSP, 1986) $18.5 bil. (41st). SECTORS OF GSP: Farms 0.46%. Agricultural services, forestry, & fisheries 0.35%. Mining 0.14%. Construction 7.29%. Manufacturing 25.99%. Transportation & public utilities 6.31%. Wholesale 5.67%. Retail 10.64%. Finance, insurance, & real estate 18.70%. Services 15.94%. Federal government 1.42%. Federal military 0.86%. State & local government 6.26%. FORTUNE 500 COMPANIES (1988): 2: Tyco Laboratories, Henley Manufacturing.

Famous natives Salmon P. Chase, jurist. Ralph Adams Cram, architect. Mary Baker Eddy, founder, Church of Christ, Scientist. Daniel Chester French, sculptor. Horace Greeley, journalist. Sarah Buell Hale, author. Franklin Pierce, U.S. president. Augustus Saint-Gaudens (b. Ireland), sculptor. Alan Shepard, astronaut. Daniel Webster, politician. Eleazar Wheelock (b. Conn.), Dartmouth founder.

Noteworthy places Currier Gallery of Art, Manchester. The Flume (gorge). Franconia Notch. Isles of Shoals. Lake Winnipesaukee. Mt. Washington. Shaker Village, Canterbury. St. Gaudens Natl. Hist. Site. Strawberry Bank. White Mountains Natl. Forest.

Memorable events Martin Pring sails along coast 1603. Champlain explores area 1604. John Smith visits Isles of Shoals 1614. Included in king's grant to John Mason and Sir Ferdinando Gorges 1622. First settlers at Little Harbor, near Portsmouth 1623. Made separate royal province 1679, though under Massachusetts governor 1699–1741. Rogers's Rangers halt Indian raids 1759. New Hampshire patriots seize British fort at Portsmouth and drive out Royal governor 1775. Province relinquishes claims to New Connecticut (Vermont) 1782. First textile mill built 1803. Treaty of Portsmouth ends Sino-Russian War 1905. Bretton Woods conference leads to establishment of International Monetary Fund 1944. First state to adopt lottery to support public education 1963.

Tourist information 1–603–271–2666.

New Jersey

With the entire state population classified as living in metro areas, New Jersey is the most densely populated state, 15 times the national average. The image survives of New Jersey as a chemical-industrial wasteland south of New York Harbor. Pharmaceuticals and chemicals are in fact New Jersey's leading products, but the next most important industry is tourism, because of the money tourists spend at the gaming tables of Atlantic City. What earns New Jersey its nickname Garden State is its extensive small-scale agriculture that produces tomatoes, dairy products, asparagus, blueberries, corn, and poultry. New Jersey lies on a plain between Philadelphia and New York City, two larger neighbors that have overshadowed New Jersey on the national scene since colonial days. Yet during the Revolution, more than 100 battles were fought on New Jersey soil, and today the overwhelming majority of containerized shipping in the Port of New York and New Jersey is shipped from New Jersey terminals. Per capita income is always among the top five in the nation.

NAME After English Channel Island of Jersey. NICKNAME Garden State. CAPITAL Trenton. ENTERED UNION Dec. 18, 1787 (3d). MOTTO "Liberty and prosperity."
Emblems ANIMAL Horse. BIRD Eastern goldfinch. FLOWER Violet. INSECT Honeybee. MEMORIAL TREE Dogwood. TREE Red oak.
Land TOTAL AREA 7,787 sq. mi. (46th), incl. 319 sq. mi. inland water. BORDERS N.Y., Atlantic Ocean, Del., Pa. RIVERS Delaware, Hackensack, Hudson, Passaic. LAKES Greenwood, Hopatcong, Round Valley Res., Spruce Run. OTHER NOTABLE FEATURES Delaware Water Gap, Kittatinny Mts., Palisades, Pine Barrens, Ramapo Mts.
Elected officials Gov. Thomas H. Kean (R). Lt. Gov., none. Sec. State Jane Burgio (R). Atty. Gen. Peter N. Perretti (R).
People (1988 est.) 7,720,000 (9th). RACE/ NATIONAL ORIGIN (1980): White 83.57%. Black 12.56%. Indian 0.14%. Asian 1.49%. Hispanic 6.71%. Foreign-born 10.30%. LANGUAGES (1980): English 84.12%. Spanish 6.00%. Italian 2.80%. Polish 1.12%. German 1.05%. Portuguese 0.54%. French 0.47%. Greek 0.40%.
Cities (1986) Newark 316,240. Jersey City 219,480. Paterson 139,130. Elizabeth 106,540. Trenton 91,160. Camden 82,810. East Orange 77,420. Clifton 76,040.
Business GROSS STATE PRODUCT (GSP, 1986) $154.8 bil. (8th). SECTORS OF GSP: Farms 0.32%. Agricultural services, forestry, & fisheries 0.30%. Mining 0.06%. Construction 4.90%. Manufacturing 19.73%. Transportation & public utilities 10.50%. Wholesale 8.71%. Retail 8.96%. Finance, insurance, & real estate 18.55%. Services 18.01%. Federal government 1.81%. Federal military 0.52%. State & local government 7.65%. FORTUNE 500 COMPANIES (1988): 25: incl. BASF, Campbell Soup, Ingersoll-Rand, Johnson & Johnson, Lipton, Liz Claiborne, Squibb.
Famous natives Count Basie, jazz musician.

William J. Brennan, jurist. Aaron Burr, politician. Grover Cleveland, U.S. president. James Fenimore Cooper, novelist/historian. Stephen Crane, author. Albert Einstein (b. Germany), nuclear physicist. Waldo Frank, author. Joyce Kilmer, poet. Jerry Lewis, actor. Jack Nicholson, actor. Zebulon Pike, explorer. Molly Pitcher, Revolutionary War heroine. Paul Robeson, actor/singer. Walter Schirra, astronaut. Frank Sinatra, singer. Alfred Stieglitz, photographer. Meryl Streep, actress. Aaron Montgomery Ward, merchant. Walt Whitman, poet. William Carlos Williams, poet.
Noteworthy places Cape May Historic District. Edison Natl. Hist. Site, West Orange. Lakehurst Naval Air Station. Liberty State Park, Jersey City. Morristown Natl. Hist. Park. Newark Museum. Palisades Interstate Park. Pine Barrens wilderness area. Princeton University. Walt Whitman House, Camden.
Memorable events Giovanni de Verrazano explores 1524. Hudson explores up Hudson River 1609. Dutch settlers establish Ft. Nassau 1623. New Jersey taken over by British and organized as colony under Sir George Carteret 1665. Major battles of Revolution at Trenton (1776), Princeton (1777), and Monmouth (1778). Women given vote at Elizabethtown 1800. Voting rights restricted to men 1807. Adopts state constitution 1844. Passenger ship *Morro Castle* burns off Asbury Park; 134 die 1934. Dirigible *Hindenburg* explodes while mooring at Lakehurst; 36 die 1937. New Jersey Turnpike linking New York City and Philadelphia opens 1952. Five days of race riots in Newark leave 26 dead 1967. Gambling legalized in Atlantic City 1978.
Tourist information 1–800–JERSEY7 or 1–609–292–2470.

New Mexico

The development problem of the western states is shared by New Mexico, which of all states has the smallest percentage of its area covered by water. Rich in other resources, it is the uranium capital of the world. The state mineral tax brings in 28 percent of state revenues, some of which goes into permanent endowments. Distribution of wealth in New Mexico remains uneven, but Hispanics, who tend to register as Democrats, vote in roughly the same ways as Anglos. A higher percentage of Native Americans lives in New Mexico than in any other state. Today mining is the biggest industry, though manufacturing is growing. Despite the enormous governmental investment in research at Los Alamos, where the atom bomb was born, the highly classified nature of this work limits the development of related industry.

NAME By Spanish explorers after Mexico. NICKNAME Land of Enchantment. CAPITAL Santa Fe. ENTERED UNION Jan. 6, 1912 (47th). MOTTO *Crescit eundo* (It grows as it goes).
Emblems ANIMAL Black bear. BIRD Roadrunner (chaparral bird). FISH Cutthroat trout. FLOWER Yucca. FOSSIL *Coelphysis* dinosaur. GEM Turquoise. SONGS "O, Fair New Mexico," "Así es Nuevo Mejico." TREE Piñon. VEGETA-

BLES Frijole, chili.
Land TOTAL AREA 121,593 sq. mi. (5th), incl. 258 sq. mi. inland water. BORDERS Colo., Okla., Tex., Chihuahua, Ariz. RIVERS Gila, Pecos, Rio Grande, Zuni. LAKES Conchas Res., Eagle Nest, Elephant Butte Res., Navajo Res., Ute Res. MOUNTAINS Chuska, Guadalupe, Sacramento, San Andres, Sangre de Cristo. OTHER NOTABLE FEATURES Carlsbad Caverns, Continental Divide, Staked Plain.
Elected officials Gov. Garrey E. Carruthers (R). Lt. Gov. Jack L. Stahl (R). Sec. State Rebecca D. Vigil-Giron (D). Atty. Gen. Hal Stratton (R).
People (1988 est.) 1,510,000 (37th). RACE/ NATIONAL ORIGIN (1980): White 62.22%. Black 1.77%. Indian 8.19%. Asian 0.59%. Hispanic 36.62%. Foreign-born 4.00%. LANGUAGES (1980): English 62.22%. Spanish 29.66%. American Indian langs. 6.21%. German 0.46%. French 0.27%. Italian 0.16%
Cities (1986) Albuquerque 366,750. Santa Fe 55,980. Las Cruces 54,090. Roswell 44,110. Farmington 39,050. Hobbs 34,870. Clovis 33,780. Carlsbad 27,850.
Business GROSS STATE PRODUCT (GSP, 1986) $23.6 bil. (37th). SECTORS OF GSP: Farms 1.90%. Agricultural services, forestry, & fisheries 0.27%. Mining 13.48%. Construction 6.68%. Manufacturing 7.97%. Transportation & public utilities 10.29%. Wholesale 4.06%. Retail 9.38%. Finance, insurance, & real estate 14.36%. Services 14.84%. Federal government 3.98%. Federal military 2.49%. State & local government 10.31%. FORTUNE 500 COMPANIES (1988): 0.
Famous natives William ("Billy the Kid") Bonney (b. N.Y.), outlaw. Peter Hurd, artist. Archbishop Jean Baptiste Lamy (b. France), missionary. Georgia O'Keeffe (b. Wis.), artist. Popé, Tewa Pueblo chief.
Noteworthy places Aztec Ruins Natl. Monument. Bandelier Natl. Monument. Capulin Mt. Natl. Monument. Carlsbad Caverns Natl. Park. Chaco Culture Natl. Hist. Park. El Morro Natl. Monument. Ft. Union Natl. Monument. Gila Cliff Dwellings Natl. Monument. Museum of New Mexico, Santa Fe. Pecos Mission. Salinas Mission. Santa Fe Opera. Wheelwright Museum of the American Indian, Santa Fe. White Sands Natl. Monument.
Memorable events Marcos de Niza enters Zuni country 1539. Juan de Oñate establishes first Spanish settlement on Rio Grande near Espanola 1598. Santa Fe founded; becomes capital of New Mexico 1710. Santa Fe Trail from Independence, Missouri, completed; Mexico secedes from Spain 1821. Manuel Armijo suppresses revolt against Mexican rule (1837); defeats invasion from Republic of Texas (1841). Land annexed by U.S. after Mexican-American War 1848. Organized as territory with Arizona and part of Colorado 1850. Lincoln County War pits cattlemen against merchants 1878–81. Statehood; 17 killed in raid by Pancho Villa 1912. Los Alamos selected as first research and development facility for nuclear weapons 1942. First atom bomb exploded at Alamagordo 1945.
Tourist information 1–800–545–2040 or 1–505–827–0291.

New York

New York's greatest and most inviting asset has always been its strategic location and long arteries into the hinterland. New York Bay is one of the great natural harbors of the world, and the broad Hudson River is one of the most fortunately placed. After the opening of the Erie Canal in 1825, New York City became the trading center for the Midwest as well as the Hudson Valley and the Atlantic Coast. Buffalo also experienced a boom, becoming a major Great Lakes industrial port. New York is still the first state in number of manufacturing establishments and employees. Wall Street alone employs half a million people. Yet Nelson Rockefeller, the most important politician in postwar New York, failed three times to get the Republican nomination for president—an indication of the change in the state's political clout. As its place among the 50 states has fallen by some measures, New York City's worldwide importance in business, culture, and communications has risen.

NAME For Duke of York, later James II, of England. NICKNAME Empire State. CAPITAL Albany. ENTERED UNION 26 July, 1788 (11th). MOTTO *Excelsior* (Higher).
Emblems ANIMAL Beaver. BEVERAGE Milk. BIRD Bluebird. FISH Brook or speckled trout. FLOWER Rose. FOSSIL Prehistoric crab *(Eurypterus remipes)*. FRUIT Apple. GEM Garnet. SONG "I Love New York." TREE Sugar maple.
Land TOTAL AREA 49,108 sq. mi. (30th), incl. 1,731 sq. mi. inland water. BORDERS Lake Ontario, Ontario, Quebec, Vt., Mass., Conn., Atlantic Ocean, N.J., Pa., Lake Erie. RIVERS Allegheny, Delaware, Genesee, Hudson, Mohawk, New York State Barge Canal, Niagara, St. Lawrence, Susquehanna. LAKES Cayuga, Champlain, Chautauqua, Erie, George, Oneida, Ontario, Seneca. MOUNTAINS Adirondack (Mt. Marcy 5,344 ft.), Allegheny, Berkshire Hills, Catskill, Kittatinny, Ramapo. OTHER NOTABLE FEATURES Hudson Valley, Mohawk Valley, Niagara Falls, Palisades, Thousand Islands.
Elected officials Gov. Mario M. Cuomo (D). Lt. Gov. Stan Lundine (D). Sec. State Gail S. Schaffer (D). Atty. Gen. Robert Abrams (D).
People (1988 est.) 17,898,000 (2d). RACE/NATIONAL ORIGIN (1980): White 79.92%. Black 13.70%. Indian 0.25%. Asian 1.89%. Hispanic 9.46%. Foreign-born 13.60%. LANGUAGES (1980): English 79.93%. Spanish 8.52%. Italian 3.22%. German 1.02%. French 1.01%. Yiddish 0.94%. Polish 0.87%. Chinese 0.77%. Greek 0.58%.
Cities (1986) New York 7,262,750. Buffalo 324,820. Rochester 235,970. Yonkers 186,080. Syracuse 160,750. Albany 97,020. Utica 69,440. New Rochelle 69,170. Mount Vernon 68,400. Schenectady 67,210. Niagara Falls 64,550.
Business GROSS STATE PRODUCT (GSP, 1986) $362.7 bil. (2d). SECTORS OF GSP: Farms 0.41%. Agricultural services, forestry, & fisheries 0.18%. Mining 0.14%. Construction 4.11%. Manufacturing 16.51%. Transportation & public utilities 9.18%. Wholesale 8.44%. Retail 8.03%. Finance, insurance, & real estate 22.17%. Services 21.10%. Federal government 1.42%. Federal military 0.30%. State & local government 9.01%. *FORTUNE* 500 COMPANIES (1988): 60: incl. AT&T, Avon Products, Colgate-Palmolive, Colt Industries, Dow Jones, Eastman Kodak, Exxon, Grumman, IBM, International Paper, Macmillan, McGraw-Hill, Mobil, New York Times, Pepsico, Pfizer, Philip Morris, Revlon Group, Texaco.
Famous natives Woody Allen, director. John Jacob Astor (b. Germany), merchant. Humphrey Bogart, actor. George Burns, actor. Aaron Copland, composer. Agnes De Mille, choreographer. George Eastman, camera inventor. Millard Fillmore, U.S. president. Lou Gehrig, baseball player. George Gershwin, composer. Julia Ward Howe, reformer. Washington Irving, author. Henry James, author. Vince Lombardi, football coach. Groucho Marx, comedian. Herman Melville, author. Ogden Nash, poet/humorist. Eugene O'Neill, playwright. Otetiani (Red Jacket), Seneca chief. Channing E. Phillips, minister/reformer. John D. Rockefeller, industrialist. Norman Rockwell, illustrator. Richard Rodgers, composer. Franklin Delano Roosevelt, U.S. president. Theodore Roosevelt, U.S. president. Jonas Salk, physician. St. Elizabeth Ann Seton. Elizabeth Cady Stanton, suffragette. James Johnson Sweeney, art critic. Martin Van Buren, U.S. president. Mae West, actress. E.B. White, author. Walt Whitman, poet.
Noteworthy places Albright-Knox Gallery of American Art, Buffalo. American Merchant Marine Museum, Kings Point. Baseball Hall of Fame, Cooperstown. Bear Mt. State Park. Buffalo Museum of Science. Corning Glass Center, Corning. Erie Canal Museum, Syracuse. Farmers' Museum, Cooperstown. Fenimore House, Cooperstown. Franklin D. Roosevelt Natl. Hist. Site, Hyde Park. Ft. Stanwix Natl. Monument, Rome. Ft. Ticonderoga. Hudson Valley. Mohawk Valley. Niagara Falls. Palisades Interstate Park. Saratoga Natl. Hist. Park. Vanderbilt Museum. U.S. Military Academy, West Point. Women's Rights Natl. Hist. Park, Seneca Falls. NEW YORK CITY American Academy of Arts & Sciences. American Museum of Natural History. Bronx Zoo. Brooklyn Botanical Garden. Brooklyn Museum. Cathedral of St. John the Divine. Cooper-Hewitt Museum. Federal Hall. Fraunces Tavern. Frick Collection. Guggenheim Museum. Hispanic Society of America. Jewish Museum. Lincoln Center for the Performing Arts. Metropolitan Museum of Art. Museum of Modern Art. Museum of the American Indian. N.Y. Public Library. N.Y. Stock Exchange. Rockefeller Center. South Street Seaport Museum. Statue of Liberty. United Nations.
Memorable events Giovanni de Verrazano sails into New York Bay 1524. Samuel de Champlain sails down the St. Lawrence River 1603. Henry Hudson sails up Hudson River 1609. Dutch establish Ft. Orange (Albany) 1614. Peter Minuit buys Manhattan Island and founds colony of New Amsterdam 1625. British take New Amsterdam and name it New York 1664. Ethan Allen takes Ft. Ticonderoga 1775. George Washington inaugurated president New York City 1789. U.S. Military Academy founded West Point 1802. Erie Canal opened 1825. Statue of Liberty dedicated 1886. New York City includes Manhattan, Bronx, Queens, Brooklyn, and Staten Island 1898. President William McKinley assassinated in Buffalo 1901. UN headquarters established at New York City 1945. St. Lawrence Seaway opened 1959.
Tourist information 1-800-225-5697 or 1-518-474-4116.

North Carolina

At the time of the Revolution, tobacco and rice plantations dominated the economy of the eastern part of the state, which in turn dominated the legislature. Last to ratify the Constitution, North Carolina was also the last Southern state to secede from the Union. The Civil War cost North Carolina dearly; reconstruction was short-lived, and blacks were effectively disenfranchised again by the turn of the century. Since World War II, the state has grown increasingly prosperous, especially in the "academic triangle" that encloses the University of North Carolina at Chapel Hill, Duke, and North Carolina State. The traditional industries of textiles, furniture, and tobacco still lead, partly because of diversification within them. Although North Carolina benefits from the general Sunbelt boom and from an influx of foreign capital, the state is still burdened by low-skilled jobs and has the lowest industrial index in the United States.

NAME For King Charles I (Carolus is Latin for Charles). NICKNAMES Tarheel State, Old North State. CAPITAL Raleigh. ENTERED UNION Nov. 21, 1789 (12th). MOTTO *Esse quam videri* (To be rather than to seem).
Emblems BIRD Cardinal. FISH Channel bass. FLOWER Dogwood. INSECT Honeybee. PRECIOUS STONE Emerald. REPTILE Eastern box turtle. ROCK Granite. SHELL Scotch bonnet. SONG "The Old North State." TREE Pine.
Land TOTAL AREA 52, 669 sq. mi. (28th), incl. 3,826 sq. mi. inland water. BORDERS Va., Atlantic Ocean, S.C., Tenn. RIVERS Albemarle, Pee Dee, Roanoke, Yadkin. LAKES Buggs Island, High Rock, Mattamuskeet, Norman, Waccamaw. MOUNTAINS Black, Blue Ridge, Great Smoky, Unaka. OTHER NOTABLE FEATURES Great Dismal Swamp, Outer Banks, Pamlico Sound.
Elected officials Gov. James G. Martin (R). Lt. Gov. Jim Gardner (R). Sec. State Rufus L. Edmisten (D). Atty. Gen. Lacy H. Thornburg (D).
People (1988 est.) 6,526,000 (10th). RACE/NATIONAL ORIGIN (1980): White 77.84%. Black 22.43%. Indian 1.12%. Asian 0.39%. Hispanic 0.95%. Foreign-born 1.30%. LANGUAGES (1980): English 97.64%. Spanish 0.79%. French 0.43%. German 0.28%. Greek 0.09%. Italian 0.06%.
Cities (1986) Charlotte 352,070. Raleigh 180,430. Greensboro 176,650. Winston-Salem 148,080. Durham 113,890. Fayetteville 75,770. High Point 66,560.
Business GROSS STATE PRODUCT (GSP, 1986)

$101 bil. (13th). SECTORS OF GSP: Farms 2.05%. Agricultural services, forestry, & fisheries 0.35%. Mining 0.28%. Construction 3.98%. Manufacturing 31.37%. Transportation & public utilities 8.63%. Wholesale 6.38%. Retail 10.14%. Finance, insurance, & real estate 12.66%. Services 11.74%. Federal government 1.64%. Federal military 2.78%. State & local government 8.00%. *FORTUNE* 500 COMPANIES (1988): 3: Fieldcrest Cannon, Guilford Mills, Nucor.

Famous natives Virginia Dare, first English colonist born in North America (1587). Benjamin Newton Duke and James Buchanan Duke, industrialists/philanthropists. Richard J. Gatling, inventor. Billy Graham, minister. O. Henry, writer. Jesse Jackson, minister/reformer. Andrew Johnson, U.S. president. William Rufus King, politician. Meadow Lark Lemon, athlete. Dolley Madison, First Lady. Thelonius Monk, musician. Edward R. Murrow, journalist. James Knox Polk, U.S. president. Moses Waddell, Confederate general.

Noteworthy places Bennett Place. Blue Ridge Natl. Parkway. Cape Hatteras and Cape Lookout Natl. Seashore. Carl Sandburg home, Hendersonville. Ft. Raleigh. Great Smoky Mountains Natl. Hist. Park. Guilford Courthouse Natl. Military Park. Mint Museum, Charlotte. Moores Creek Natl. Battlefield. North Carolina Maritime Museum, Beaufort. North Carolina Museum of Art, Raleigh. Roanoke Island. Wright Brothers Natl. Memorial, Kitty Hawk.

Memorable events Part of Carolina grant given to eight noblemen by Charles II 1663. Culpepper's Rebellion in reaction to unfair tax collection policies 1677. Tuscarora lose war against European immigrants 1713. Proprietors sell rights to Crown; becomes royal province 1729. Mecklenburg Declaration (1775), forerunner of Declaration of Independence. Becomes first colony to sanction explicitly declaration of independence from Britain in Apr. 1776. Gen. Charles Cornwallis wins Battle of Guilford Courthouse, but British lose control of colony 1781. Ratifies Constitution 1789. Gives up claims to western territories, now part of Tennessee 1790. Establishes first state university system in U.S. 1829. Cherokees driven out of North Carolina to Oklahoma 1838. Secedes 1861. Readmitted to Union 1868. American Tobacco Company founded 1890. Wright brothers launch first successful airplane at Kitty Hawk 1903. Confrontation between Ku Klux Klan and anti-Klan demonstrators leaves five dead; 12 Klansmen charged with first-degree murder 1979.

Tourist information 1-800-VISITNC.

North Dakota

The first permanent settlers in North Dakota were Scots-Canadians who settled at Pembina on the Red River near the Canadian border, and who traded primarily with Winnipeg and St. Paul. The arrival of the Northern Pacific Railway in 1872 created a surge of huge farms, many of which were wiped out by drought and harsh winters in the 1880s. There followed a huge influx of Norwegians and Germans whose influence is still very apparent today. North Dakota's economy is heavily agricultural and leads the nation in production of wheat. Farming is centered in the fertile Red River of the North Valley, with livestock throughout the rest of the state. In recent years this has been augmented by mining—North Dakota has the greatest lignite coal reserves of any state in the United States and some natural gas reserves.

NAME For northern section of Dakota territory; *dakota* is Sioux word for "allies." **NICKNAMES** Sioux State, Peace Garden State, Flickertail State. **CAPITAL** Bismarck. **ENTERED UNION** Nov. 2, 1889 (39th). **MOTTO** "Liberty and union, now and forever, one and inseparable."

Emblems BEVERAGE Milk. BIRD Western meadowlark. FISH Northern pike. FLOWER Wild prairie rose. GRASS Western wheatgrass. MARCH "Spirit of North Dakota." SONG "North Dakota Hymn." STONE Teredo petrified wood. TREE American elm.

Land TOTAL AREA 70,703 sq. mi. (17th), incl. 1,403 sq. mi. inland water. BORDERS Saskatchewan, Manitoba, Minn., S.Dak., Mont. RIVERS Missouri, Red River of the North. LAKES Ashtabula, Devils, Oahe, Sakakawea. OTHER NOTABLE FEATURES Geographical center of North America, Missouri Plateau, Red River Valley, Rolling Drift Prairie.

Elected officials Gov. George A. Sinner (D). Lt. Gov. Lloyd Omdahl (D). Sec. State Jim Kusler (D). Atty. Gen. Nicholas Spaeth (D).

People (1988 est.) 663,000 (46th). RACE/NATIONAL ORIGIN (1980): White 95.96%. Black 0.38%. Indian 3.06%. Asian 0.35%. Hispanic 0.53%. Foreign-born 2.30%. LANGUAGES (1980): English 88.70%. German 6.21%. Norwegian 2.08%. Spanish 0.56%. American Indian langs. 0.45%. Czechoslovakian 0.38%. **Cities** (1986) Fargo 68,020. Bismarck 48,040. Grand Forks 45,090. Minot 35,850. Dickinson 17,320. Mandan 15,770.

Business GROSS STATE PRODUCT (GSP, 1986) $10.7 bil. (48th). SECTORS OF GSP: Farms 14.39%. Agricultural services, forestry, & fisheries 0.40%. Mining 6.33%. Construction 5.52%. Manufacturing 5.80%. Transportation & public utilities 10.53%. Wholesale 7.84%. Retail 8.32%. Finance, insurance, & real estate 16.89%. Services 12.59%. Federal government 0.08%. Federal military 3.24%. State & local government 8.24%. *FORTUNE* 500 COMPANIES (1988): 0.

Famous natives Angie Dickinson, actress. John Bernard Flannagan, sculptor. Louis L'Amour, novelist. Peggy Lee, singer. Eric Sevareid, broadcaster. Vihjalmur Stefansson (b. Canada), ethnologist. Lawrence Welk, entertainer.

Noteworthy places Ft. Abraham Lincoln State Park. Ft. Union Trading Post Natl. Hist. Site. International Peace Garden. Knife River Indian Villages Natl. Hist. Site. Theodore Roosevelt Natl. Park, the Badlands.

Memorable events Pierre Gaultier de Varennes, sieur de Vérendrye first European to visit area 1738. U.S. acquires half of territory in Louisiana Purchase 1803. Meriwether Lewis and George Rogers Clark expedition builds Ft. Mandan 1804–05. First peramanent settlement at Pembina 1812. Britain cedes western half of state to U.S. 1818. Missouri River steamboats reach territory 1838. First railroad arrives 1873. Statehood 1889. First state to hold presidential primary 1912. Garrison Dam completed, forming Lake Sakakawea; gambling (blackjack) legalized 1981.

Tourist information 1-800-437-2077, 1-701-224-2525, or 1-800-472-2100; 1-800-537-8879 (from Canada).

Ohio

The first settlements in Ohio were Marietta, in 1788, and Cincinnati in 1789, on the Ohio River, but significant migration into the state didn't occur until after the War of 1812. Shipping flourished in the 1820s and 1830s thanks to a network of canals connecting the Ohio and Lake Erie. Since 1959 the St. Lawrence Seaway has helped keep Ohio among the top five exporting states. Heavy industry also flourished in the northern cities that had access to coal and iron ore from the Lake Superior region. The 1870s saw the development of a manufacturing base that later became an integral part of the automotive industry. Although Ohio's economy has traditionally been well balanced between agriculture, industry, mining, and trade, the recession of the early 1980s weakened manufacturing, triggered flight from the industrial cities, and saw a dramatic shift to a service economy.

NAME From Iroquois *oheo*, "beautiful." **NICKNAME** Buckeye State. **CAPITAL** Columbus. **ENTERED UNION** Mar. 1, 1803 (17th). **MOTTO** "With God, all things are possible."

Emblems BEVERAGE Tomato juice. BIRD Cardinal. FLOWER Scarlet carnation. GEM Ohio flint. INSECT Ladybug. SONG "Beautiful Ohio." TREE Buckeye.

Land TOTAL AREA 41,330 sq. mi. (35th), incl. 326 sq. mi. inland water. BORDERS Mich., Lake Erie, Pa., W.Va., Ky., Ind. RIVERS Cuyahoga, Maumee, Miami, Muskingum, Ohio, Sandusky, Scioto. LAKES Berlin Res., Dillon Res., Erie, Mosquito Res., St. Mary's. OTHER NOTABLE FEATURES Allegheny Mts.

Elected officials Gov. Richard F. Celeste (D). Lt. Gov. Paul R. Leonard (D). Sec. State Sherrod Brown (D). Atty. Gen. Anthony J. Celebrezze, Jr. (D).

People (1988 est.) 10,872,000 (7th). RACE/NATIONAL ORIGIN (1980): White 88.97%. Black 9.97%. Indian 0.14%. Asian 0.49%. Hispanic 1.11%. Foreign-born 2.80%. LANGUAGES (1980): English 94.81%. Spanish 0.97%. German 0.83%. Italian 0.53%. Polish 0.38%. French 0.33%. Hungarian 0.26%

Cities (1986) Columbus 566,030. Cleveland 535,830. Cincinnati 369,750. Toledo 340,680. Akron 222,060. Dayton 178,920. Youngstown 104,690. Parma 89,460.

Business GROSS STATE PRODUCT (GSP, 1986) $176.1 bil. (7th). SECTORS OF GSP: Farms 1.08%. Agricultural services, forestry, & fisheries 0.25%. Mining 0.82%. Construction 3.16%. Manufacturing 29.20%. Transportation & public utilities 9.26%. Wholesale 6.50%. Retail 9.80%. Finance, insurance, & real estate 15.37%. Services 15.18%. Federal government 1.72%. Federal military 0.41%. State & local government 7.26%. *FORTUNE* 500 COMPANIES (1988): 37: incl. American Greetings, B.F. Goodrich, BP America, Champion Spark Plugs, Eaton, Goodyear Tire & Rubber, MCR, Mead, Ohio Mattress, Penn Central, Procter & Gamble, Rubbermaid, Sherwin-Williams, United Brands.

Famous natives Sherwood Anderson, writer. Neil Armstrong, astronaut. George Bellows, artist. Ambrose Bierce, author. George Armstrong Custer, army officer. Paul Laurence Dunbar, poet. Thomas A. Edison, inventor. James A. Garfield, U.S. president. John Glenn, astronaut/politician. Ulysses S. Grant, U.S. president. Zane Grey, author. Warren G. Harding, U.S. president. Benjamin Harrison, U.S. president. Rutherford B. Hayes, U.S. president. Bob Hope, entertainer. William McKinley, U.S. president. Annie Oakley, markswoman. Ransom Eli Olds, carmaker. Eddie Rickenbacker, pilot. William Sherman, army officer. William Howard Taft, U.S. president/chief justice. Art Tatum, pianist. Tecumseh, Shawnee chief. James Thurber, humorist. Orville Wright, airplane inventor.

Noteworthy places Air Force Musem, Dayton. Cleveland Museum of Art. Cleveland Museum of Natural History. Columbus Museum of Art. Great Lakes Historical Society Museum, Vermilion. Mound City Group Natl. Monument, Chillicothe. Neil Armstrong Air and Space Museum, Wapakoneta. Ohio River Museum, Marietta. Pro Football Hall of Fame, Canton. Toledo Museum of Art.

Memorable events Hopewell Mound-Builders present throughout state prior to arrival of Miamis, Shawnees, Wyandots, and Delawares. Conflicting claims by France, Virginia, Connecticut, and New York 1609–1786. René-Roger Cavelier de La Salle visits region 1669–70. To Britain 1763. To U.S. after 1783. Becomes part of Northwest Territory 1787. First settlement at Marietta 1788. Gen. "Mad" Anthony Wayne beats Tecumseh at Battle of Fallen Timbers 1794. Enters Union 1803. Harrison beats Tecumseh at Battle of Tippecanoe 1811. Oliver Hazard Perry beats British fleet at Battle of Put-in-Bay 1813. Ohio and Erie Canal completed 1832. Dayton flood kills 400 in Miami River Valley; damage put at $100 million 1913. Carl B. Stokes elected mayor of Cleveland, first black mayor of major U.S. city 1967. Four students protesting Vietnam War killed by National Guard at Kent State University 1970.

Tourist information 1–800–BUCKEYE.

Oklahoma

French trappers began ascending the rivers running through the Oklahoma area in the 1700s. This was the geographic end of the Trail of Tears, for a time called Indian Territory, where the Indian Removal Act of 1830 deported Indians from the southeast. They fared well until the Civil War, when they sup-ported the Confederacy. In 1869 Col. George Armstrong Custer led a massacre of Cheyenne at the Battle of the Washita. Twenty years later the territory was opened to settlement, and statehood came in 1907. Oklahoma's fuel resources are considerable, and the first major oil strike was in 1897. The state led the country in oil and gas production through the 1920s. Agriculture was hit heavily by the dust bowl of the 1930s, and thousands of "Okies" fled. While agriculture and the petroleum industry are still vital to the state economy, manufacturing is increasingly important. Tulsa is a significant inland port with access to the Gulf of Mexico via the Arkansas-Mississippi River system.

NAME From Choctaw *okla humma*, "land of the red people." NICKNAME Sooner State. CAPITAL Oklahoma City. ENTERED UNION Nov. 16, 1907 (46th). MOTTO *Labor omnia vincit* (Work overcomes all obstacles).

Emblems ANIMAL American buffalo. BIRD Scissor-tailed flycatcher. COLORS Green and white. FISH White bass. FLORAL EMBLEM Mistletoe. GRASS Indian grass. POEM "Howdy Folks." REPTILE Collared lizard (mountain boomer). SONG "Oklahoma!" STONE Barite rose (rose rock). TREE Redbud. WALTZ "Oklahoma Wind."

Land TOTAL AREA 69,956 sq. mi. (18th), incl. 1,301 sq. mi. inland water. BORDERS Kans., Mo., Ark., Tex., N.Mex. RIVERS Arkansas, Canadian, Cimarron, Red. LAKES Canton, Lake o' the Cherokees, Oologah, Texoma. OTHER NOTABLE FEATURES Ouachita Mts., Ozark Plateau, Staked Plain, Wichita Mts.

Elected officials Gov. Henry Bellmon (R). Lt. Gov. Robert S. Kerr III (D). Sec. State Hannah D. Atkins (D). Atty. Gen. Robert Henry (D).

People (1988 est.) 3,263,000 (27th). RACE/ NATIONAL ORIGIN (1980): White 86.04%. Black 6.77%. Indian 5.66%. Asian 0.65%. Hispanic 1.91%. Foreign-born 1.90%. LANGUAGES (1980): English 95.96%. Spanish 1.46%. American Indian langs. 0.74%. German 0.44%. French 0.25%. Vietnamese 0.12%.

Cities (1986) Oklahoma City 446,120. Tulsa 373,750. Lawton 82,830. Norman 78,390. Midwest City 53,470. Broken Arrow 51,470. Edmond 50,980.

Business GROSS STATE PRODUCT (GSP, 1986) $49.8 bil. (27th). SECTORS OF GSP: Farms 3.39%. Agricultural services, forestry, & fisheries 0.27%. Mining 10.40%. Construction 4.28%. Manufacturing 14.27%. Transportation & public utilities 10.52%. Wholesale 6.12%. Retail 9.87%. Finance, insurance, & real estate 13.54%. Services 13.07%. Federal government 3.68%. Federal military 2.04%. State & local government 8.54%. *FORTUNE* 500 COMPANIES (1988): 5: Kerr McGee, Mapco, Phillips Petroleum, Telex, Wilson Foods.

Famous natives Ralph Ellison, author. Woody Guthrie, reformer/musician. Patrick J. Hurley, diplomat. Karl Jansky, electrical engineer. Mickey Mantle, baseball player. Wiley Post, aviator. Tony Randall, actor. Oral Roberts, evangelist. Will Rogers, humorist. Maria Tallchief, ballerina. Jim Thorpe, athlete.

Noteworthy places American Indian Hall of Fame, Anadarko. Chisholm Trail Museum, Kingfisher. Ft. Gibson Stockade, Muskogee. Natl. Cowboy Hall of Fame, Oklahoma City. Ouachita Natl. Forest. Pioneer Woman Museum, Ponca City. Will Rogers Memorial, Claremore.

Memorable events Francisco Vásquez de Coronado expedition in territory 1541. Except for panhandle, becomes part of Louisiana purchase 1803. Region made Indian Territory (not organized) in 1830 and becomes home of "Five Civilized Tribes"—Cherokee, Choctaw, Chickasaw, Creek, and Seminole— after they left the southeast on Trail of Tears 1828–46. U.S. acquires panhandle with annexation of Texas 1845. Territory opened to homesteaders 1889. Commercial oil well at Bartlesville 1897. Indian Territory and Oklahoma Territory merged and granted statehood 1907. Gov. John C. Walton impeached after declaring martial law to quell violence 1923. McClellan-Kerr Arkansas River Navigation System links Oklahoma to Mississippi, making Catoosa (Tulsa) major inland port 1971.

Tourist information 1–800–652–6552 or 1–800–522–8565.

Oregon

Although the Lewis and Clark expedition reached the mouth of the Columbia River in 1805, interest in the area was kindled by the Hudson's Bay Company and later by Jason Lee, a Methodist minister who settled near Salem in 1834. After the decline of the fur trade, lumbering became the most important industry in Oregon. Though lumbering and related industries are still leading employers, Oregon has benefited from the arrival of smaller computer and electronics firms leaving California in search of a more favorable business climate. Traditionally progressive, it is one of most active states in the environmental protection movement. Only one-third of the population is affiliated with an organized religion.

NAME Unknown origin, first applied to Columbia River. NICKNAME Beaver State. CAPITAL Salem. ENTERED UNION Feb. 14, 1859 (33d). MOTTO "The Union." POET LAUREATE William E. Stafford.

Emblems ANIMAL Beaver. BIRD Western meadowlark. DANCE Square dance. FISH Chinook salmon. FLOWER Oregon grape. INSECT Swallowtail butterfly. SONG "Oregon, My Oregon." STONE Thunderegg. TREE Douglas fir.

Land TOTAL AREA 97,073 sq. mi. (10th), incl. 889 sq. mi. inland water. BORDERS Wash., Idaho, Nev., Calif., Pacific Ocean. RIVERS Columbia, Snake, Willamette. MOUNTAINS Cascade Range, Coast Range, Klamath. OTHER NOTABLE FEATURES Willamette Valley.

Elected officials Gov. Neil Goldschmidt (D). Lt. Gov., none. Sec. State Barbara Roberts (D). Atty. Gen. Dave Frohnmayer (R).

People (1988 est.) 2,741,000 (30th). RACE/ NATIONAL ORIGIN (1980): White 94.81%. Black 1.42%. Indian 1.16%. Asian 1.56%. Hispanic 2.51%. Foreign-born 4.10%. LANGUAGES (1980): English 94.65%. Spanish 1.72%. German 0.81%. French 0.35%. Chinese 0.24%. Vietnamese 0.18%.

Cities (1986) Portland 387,870. Eugene 105,410. Salem 93,920. Medford 43,580. Corvallis 39,880. Gresham 38,850. Springfield 38,400.

Business GROSS STATE PRODUCT (GSP, 1986) $41.3 bil. (31st). SECTORS OF GSP: Farms 3.04%. Agricultural services, forestry, & fisheries 0.91%. Mining 0.14%. Construction 3.28%. Manufacturing 19.82%. Transportation & public utilities 10.03%. Wholesale 7.78%. Retail 9.48%. Finance, insurance, & real estate 17.84%. Services 15.46%. Federal government 2.52%. Federal military 0.39%. State & local government 9.31%. *FORTUNE* 500 COMPANIES (1988): 4: Louisiana Pacific, Nerco, Tektronix, Willamette Industries.

Famous natives In-mut-too-yah-lat-lat (Joseph), Nez Percé chief. Edwin Markham, poet. Dr. John McLoughlin, fur trader ("Father of Oregon"). Linus Pauling, chemist. John Reed, author. William Simon U'Ren (b. Wis.), lawyer/reformer.

Noteworthy places Bonneville Dam, Columbia River. Columbia River Gorge. Columbia River Museum, Astoria. Crater Lakes Natl. Park. Ft. Clatsop Natl. Monument. Hells Canyon. High Desert Museum, Bend. John Day Fossil Beds Natl. Monument. Mt. Hood. Oregon Caves Natl. Monument. Oregon Dunes Natl. Recreation Area. Point Perpetua. Timberline Lodge.

Memorable events Sir Francis Drake turns away from fogbound coast of Pacific Northwest 1578. Capt. James Cook visits 1778. Mouth of Columbia River explored by Capt. Robert Gray, who claims region for U.S. 1792. Meriwether Lewis and George Rogers Clark expedition arrives at mouth of Columbia 1805. Claims to Oregon Territory, from California border to Alaska and east to Montana and Wyoming, relinquished by Spain (1819), Russia (1825), and Britain (1846). First settlers arrive Willamette Valley 1843. Organized as territory 1848. Statehood 1859. Railroad arrives 1883. Bonneville Dam completed 1937. Following severe rain and snow that claim 40 lives, Oregon declared disaster area 1964. First state to enact "bottle law" 1972. Snake River opened to navigation, linking Astoria to Lewiston, Idaho, 1975.

Tourist information 1-800-547-7842 or 1-800-543-8838.

Pennsylvania, Commonwealth of

William Penn and his Quakers encouraged settlement and religious tolerance, and Pennsylvania was the first state to abolish slavery. In the late colonial period, Philadelphia was the cultural capital of the colonies. The first Continental Congress convened there in 1774, and it was for some 15 years the U.S. capital. With access to both the Great Lakes and to the Atlantic, Pennsylvanians took a lead in opening up the Midwest. Its resources include large coal deposits—which contribute to its iron-making capabilities— lumber, textiles, and leather. Leadership in these sectors lasted well into the 20th century, when Pennsylvania lost

ground to Sunbelt states. As in many states, there has been growth in tourist and service industries, though machinery production and trade continue to expand significantly.

NAME For Adm. William Penn, father of William Penn, founder of commonwealth. NICKNAME Keystone State. CAPITAL Harrisburg. ENTERED UNION Dec. 12, 1787 (2d). MOTTO "Virtue, liberty and independence."

Emblems ANIMAL White-tailed deer. BEAUTIFICATION AND CONSERVATION PLANT Penngift crown vetch. BEVERAGE Milk. BIRD Ruffled goose. DOG Great dane. FISH Brook trout. FLOWER Mountain laurel. INSECT Firefly. SONG "Pennsylvania." TREE Hemlock.

Land TOTAL AREA 45,308 sq. mi. (33d), incl. 420 sq. mi. inland water. BORDERS N.Y., N.J., Del., Md., W.Va., Ohio, Lake Erie. RIVERS Allegheny, Delaware, Juniata, Monongahela, Ohio, Schuylkill, Susquehanna. LAKES Allegheny Res., Erie, Pymatuning Res., Shenango Res. MOUNTAINS Allegheny, Kittatinny, Laurel Hills, Pocono.

Elected officials Gov. Robert P. Casey (D). Lt. Gov. Mark Singel (D). Sec. State James J. Haggerty (D). Atty. Gen. Ernie Preate (R).

People (1988 est.) 12,027,000 (5th). RACE/NATIONAL ORIGIN (1980): White 89.92%. Black 8.81%. Indian 0.09%. Asian 0.59%. Hispanic 1.29%. Foreign-born 3.40%. LANGUAGES (1980): English 93.14%. Italian 1.27%. Spanish 1.21%. German 0.75%. Polish 0.69%. French 0.31%. Slovak 0.26%. Ukranian 0.19%.

Cities (1986) Philadelphia 1,642,900. Pittsburgh 387,490. Erie 115,270. Allentown 104,360. Scranton 82,260. Reading 77,620. Bethlehem 70,340.

Business GROSS STATE PRODUCT (GSP, 1986) $183.6 bil. (5th). SECTORS OF GSP: Farms 1.03%. Agricultural services, forestry, & fisheries 0.28%. Mining 1.02%. Construction 4.06%. Manufacturing 22.14%. Transportation & public utilities 10.50%. Wholesale 6.70%. Retail 9.51%. Finance, insurance, & real estate 16.23%. Services 18.49%. Federal government 2.52%. Federal military 0.49%. State & local government 7.02%. *FORTUNE* 500 COMPANIES (1988): 37: incl. Alcoa, Bethlehem Steel, Hershey Foods, H.J. Heinz, Mack Trucks, Quaker State, Rockwell International, Scott Paper, Sun, Unisys, Westinghouse Electric, Wheeling-Pittsburgh Steel.

Famous natives Louisa May Alcott, author. Maxwell Anderson, playwright. James Buchanan, U.S. president. Alexander Calder, sculptor. Andrew Carnegie (b. Scotland), industrialist/philanthropist. Mary Cassatt, painter. Wilt Chamberlain, basketball player. Bill Cosby, comedian/philanthropist. Stephen Foster, songwriter. Benjamin Franklin, inventor/statesman. Robert Fulton, inventor. Milton S. Hershey, chocolatier. George C. Marshall, statesman. Andrew W. Mellon, financier/philanthropist. Robert E. Peary, explorer. Betsy Ross, patriot. Andy Warhol, artist. Johnny Weismuller, swimmer/actor. Benjamin West, painter.

Noteworthy places Academy of Natural Sciences, Philadelphia. Carnegie Institute, Pittsburgh. Delaware Water Gap Natl. Recreation

Area. Ft. Necessity Natl. Battlefield. Franklin Institute, Philadelphia. Gettysburg Battlefield. Hugh Moore Hist. Park and Museums, Easton. Independence Natl. Hist. Park, Philadelphia. Liberty Bell, Carpenters Hall, Philadelphia. Pennsylvania Academy of Fine Arts, Philadelphia. Pennsylvania Dutch Country. Philadelphia Museum of Art. Pine Creek Gorge. Valley Forge Natl. Hist. Park.

Memorable events Cornelis Jacobssen sails into Delaware Bay 1614. Swedes settle at Tinicum Island 1643. Charles II grants proprietary charter to William Penn 1681. First U.S. hospital established, in Philadelphia, 1751. Mason-Dixon Line establishes southern boundary of state 1763-67—later, boundary between slave and nonslave states. Declaration of Independence (1776) and Constitution (1787) signed in Philadelphia. Becomes first state to abolish slavery 1780. Bank of North America becomes first bank chartered in U.S. 1781. Philadelphia capital of U.S. 1790-1800. First iron furnace in U.S. 1792. Battle of Gettysburg turning point in Civil War; Lincoln's Gettysburg Address 1863. Centennial Exhibition at Philadelphia 1876. Johnstown flood—worst in U.S. history—kills 2,200 people 1889. Twenty coal miners killed during strike for eight-hour day and other concessions 1897. More than 500 injured during three-day race riot in Philadelphia 1964. Partial meltdown at Three Mile Island forces closure of nuclear reactor 1979. Storage tank spills 713,000 gallons diesel fuel into Monongahela River disrupting water supplies in Pennsylvania, West Virginia, and Ohio 1988.

Tourist information 1-800-VISITPA.

Rhode Island, Commonwealth of, and Providence Plantations

Giovanni de Verrazano was the first European to record visiting the area of Narragansett Bay, the prominent inlet that almost splits the eastern third of the state from the rest. The first settlers were followers of Roger Williams, who left the restrictive religious atmosphere of the Puritan Massachusetts Bay Colony to found Providence in 1636. Rhode Island is the site of the first U.S. Baptist church, at Providence, and at Newport the first Quaker meetinghouse and the first synagogue. It was the last of the 13 original colonies to ratify the Constitution, the centralized federalism to which many Rhode Islanders objected. The development of 19th-century Rhode Island was influenced by immigration and the Industrial Revolution; the state's leading manufacturers are still silver, jewelry, and textiles.

NAME For Rhode Island in Narragansett Bay, named in turn for Mediterranean island of Rhodes. NICKNAMES Ocean State, Little Rhody. CAPITAL Providence. ENTERED UNION May 29, 1790 (13th). MOTTO "Hope."

Emblems BIRD Rhode Island red. FLOWER Violet. MINERAL Bowenite. ROCK Cumberlandite. SONG "Rhode Island." TREE Red maple.

Land TOTAL AREA 1,212 sq. mi. (50th), incl.

157 sq. mi. inland water. BORDERS Mass., Atlantic Ocean, Conn. RIVERS Blackstone, Pawcatuck, Providence, Sakonnet. OTHER NOTABLE FEATURES Block Island, Narragansett Bay, Rhode Island (Aquidneck Island).
Elected officials Gov. Edward D. DiPrete (R). Lt. Gov. Roger N. Begin (D). Sec. State Kathleen S. Connell (D). Atty. Gen. James E. O'Neal (D).
People (1988 est.) 995,000 (43d). RACE/NATIONAL ORIGIN (1980): White 95.07%. Black 2.89%. Indian 0.34%. Asian 0.70%. Hispanic 2.00%. Foreign-born 8.90%. LANGUAGES (1980): English 83.90%. French 4.55%. Portuguese 4.32%. Italian 3.16%. Spanish 1.35%. Polish 0.66%.
Cities (1986) Providence 157,200. Warwick 86,960. Cranston 73,760. Pawtucket 72,640. East Providence 50,440.
Business GROSS STATE PRODUCT (GSP, 1986) $15.2 bil. (43d). SECTORS OF GSP: Farms 0.42%. Agricultural services, forestry, & fisheries 0.70%. Mining 0.06%. Construction 2.65%. Manufacturing 24.31%. Transportation & public utilities 6.76%. Wholesale 6.39%. Retail 10.64%. Finance, insurance, & real estate 17.86%. Services 18.22%. Federal government 2.19%. Federal military 1.75%. State & local government 8.06%. *FORTUNE* 500 COMPANIES (1988): 3: Hasbro, Nortek, Textron.
Famous natives George M. Cohan, actor/producer. Nathanael Greene, army officer. Metacomet (King Philip), Wampanoag chief. Oliver H. Perry and Matthew C. Perry, naval officers. Gilbert Stuart, portraitist.
Noteworthy places John Carter Brown Library, Providence. First Baptist Church in North America (1638), Providence. Ft. Adams State Park, Newport. Nathanael Greene homestead, Coventry. Hoffenreffer Museum of Anthropology, Bristol. Museum of Art of the Rhode Island School of Design, Providence. Naval War College Museum, Newport. Newport mansions. Museum of Yachting, Newport. Tennis Hall of Fame, Newport. Trouro Synagogue (1763, oldest extant in North America), Newport.
Memorable events Roger Williams, expelled from Massachusetts Bay Colony, settles in Providence 1636. Other religious exiles settle in Portsmouth (1638), Newport (1639), and Warwick (1642). King Philip's War 1675–76. First Quaker meetinghouse in North America founded 1699. First colony to renounce allegiance to Britain 1776. Last colony to ratify Constitution 1790. Dorr's Rebellion achieves liberalization of state constitution, which had remained unchanged since 1663, 1842. America's Cup Race held in Newport for first time 1930. Newport Bridge across Narragansett Bay completed 1969. *Australia II* first non-U.S. boat to win America's Cup in 132 years 1983.
Tourist information 1–401–277–2601 or 1–800–556–2484.

South Carolina

South Carolina's early economy was based on rice—its plantations worked by slaves—though tobacco later played a major role. As was true in North Carolina, many settlers made their way into the back country where they eked out a living as tenant farmers. During the Revolution, Ft. Charlotte was the first British installation to fall to Colonial troops, and at the outbreak of the Civil War, Ft. Sumter was the first Union installation to fall to Confederate forces. While agriculture remained a staple of the state's economy through the close of the 19th century, textile manufacture took over in the early 20th century. The postwar era has seen the rapid expansion of the chemical and paper industries, as well as large-scale development of the Atlantic Coast ports of Charleston, Georgetown, and Port Royal.

NAME For King Charles II (Carolus is Latin for Charles). NICKNAME Palmetto State. CAPITAL Columbia. ENTERED UNION May 23, 1788 (8th). MOTTO *Animis opibusque parati* (Prepared in mind and deed); *Dum spiro spero* (While I breathe I hope). POET LAUREATE Helen von Kolnitz Hyer.
Emblems ANIMAL White-tailed deer. BEVERAGE Milk. BIRD Carolina wren. DANCE Shag. DOG Boykin spaniel. FISH Striped bass. FLOWER Yellow jessamine. FRUIT Peach. SHELL Lettered olive. SONG "Carolina." STONE Blue granite. TREE Palmetto. WILD GAME BIRD Wild turkey.
Land TOTAL AREA 31,113 sq. mi. (40th), incl. 910 sq. mi. inland water. BORDERS N.C., Atlantic Ocean, Ga. RIVERS Congaree, Edisto, Pee Dee, Savannah, Tugalos, Wateree. LAKES Greenwood, Hartwell, Keowee, Marion, Murray, Santee Res., Wylie. OTHER NOTABLE FEATURES Blue Ridge Mts., Congaree Swamp, Sea Islands.
Elected officials Gov. Carroll A. Campbell, Jr. (R). Lt. Gov. Nick A. Theodore (D). Sec. State John T. Campbell (D). Atty. Gen. Travis Medlock (D).
People (1988 est.) 3,493,000 (24th). RACE/NATIONAL ORIGIN (1980): White 68.80%. Black 30.37%. Indian 0.22%. Asian 0.43%. Hispanic 1.08%. Foreign-born 1.50%. LANGUAGES (1980): English 97.53%. Spanish 0.76%. French 0.53%. German 0.30%. Philippine langs 0.08%. Greek 0.08%.
Cities (1986) Columbia 93,020. Charleston 68,900. North Charleston 61,430. Greenville 58,370. Spartanburg 44,210.
Business GROSS STATE PRODUCT (GSP, 1986) $44.7 bil. (28th). SECTORS OF GSP: Farms 0.97%. Agricultural services, forestry, & fisheries 0.40%. Mining 0.23%. Construction 4.00%. Manufacturing 26.72%. Transportation & public utilities 8.45%. Wholesale 5.80%. Retail 1.10%. Finance, insurance, & real estate 12.94%. Services 12.46%. Federal government 2.52%. Federal military 4.42%. State & local government 9.99%. *FORTUNE* 500 COMPANIES (1988): 2: Spring Industries, Sonoco Products.
Famous natives James F. Byrnes, politician/jurist. John C. Calhoun, politician. Dizzy Gillespie, musician. Althea Gibson, athlete. DuBose Heyward, author. Andrew Jackson, U.S. president. Eartha Kitt, singer. James Longstreet, army officer. Francis Marion, army officer/politician. Charles C. Pinckney

and Thomas Pinckney, diplomats. Edward Rutledge and John Rutledge, politicians. Strom Thurmond, politician.
Noteworthy places Charleston Museum (1773, oldest in U.S.). Congaree Swamp Natl. Monument. Cowpens Natl. Battlefield. Ft. Moultrie, Ft. Johnson, and Ft. Sumter Natl. Monument, Charleston. Hilton Head Island. Kings Mountain Natl. Military Park. Ninety-Six Natl. Hist. Site, Greenwood. Patriots Point Maritime Museum, Charleston. Sea Islands. Spoleto Music Festival, Charleston.
Memorable events Spanish visit 1521. French Huguenots at Port Royal 1562. Included in Carolina grant by Charles II 1663. Charleston founded 1680. Becomes royal province 1729. Ratifies Constitution 1787. *Best Friend of Charleston*, first American steam locomotive built for passenger use 1833. First state to secede from Union Dec. 20, 1860. Confederate forces attack Ft. Sumter Apr. 12, 1861. Secession repealed 1865. Readmitted to Union 1868. Cyclone kills 1,000 in Savannah, Ga., and Charleston 1893. Savannah River nuclear plant begins production near Aiken 1951; closed for safety reasons 1988.
Tourist information 1–803–734–0122.

South Dakota

The United States did not organize the Dakota Territory until 1861, and even then interest in the region was scant until gold was discovered in 1874. The majority of those who remained after the gold rush turned to cattle ranching, which was a mainstay of the economy through the first half of the 20th century. A manufacturing base was developed after four major dams were built on the Missouri River in the 1930s. They provided hydroelectric power and increased irrigation along the Missouri, which cuts the state in half. Concerned especially over the abrogation of 19th-century treaties, the American Indian Movement (AIM) took over the courthouse at Wounded Knee for 10 weeks in 1973. While U.S. courts have found in favor of the Sioux in several cases concerning the earlier treaties, many maintain that the settlements are insufficient, and the disparity in living conditions between whites and Native Americans remains pronounced.

NAME For southern section of Dakota territory; *dakota* is Sioux word for "allies." NICKNAMES Coyote State, Sunshine State. CAPITAL Pierre. ENTERED UNION Nov. 2, 1889 (40th). MOTTO "Under God the people rule."
Emblems ANIMAL Coyote. BIRD Chinese ring-necked pheasant. FISH Walleye. FLOWER Pasque flower. GEM Fairburn agate. GRASS Western wheatgrass. INSECT Honeybee. MINERAL Rose quartz. SONG "Hail, South Dakota." TREE Black Hills spruce.
Land TOTAL AREA 77,116 sq. mi. (16th), incl. 1,164 sq. mi. inland water. BORDERS N.Dak., Minn., Iowa, Nebr., Wyo., Mont. RIVERS Cheyenne, James, Missouri, Moreau, White. LAKES Belle Fourche Res., Big Stone, Traverse. OTHER NOTABLE FEATURES Badlands, Black Hills (Harney Peak 7,242 ft.).
Elected officials Gov. George S. Mickelson (R).

Lt. Gov. Walter D. Miller (R). Sec. State Joyce Hazeltine (R). Atty. Gen. Roger Tellinghuisen (R).
People (1988 est.) 715,000 (45th). RACE/NATIONAL ORIGIN (1980): White 92.63%. Black 0.31%. Indian 6.60%. Asian 0.28%. Hispanic 0.55%. Foreign-born 1.40%. LANGUAGES (1980): English 92.19%. German 3.47%. American Indian langs. 2.07%. Spanish 0.47%. Norwegian 0.43%. Czechoslovakian 0.29%. French 0.17%.
Cities (1986) Sioux Falls 97,550. Rapid City 52,480. Aberdeen 25,670. Watertown 16,670. Brookings 14,800.
Business GROSS STATE PRODUCT (GSP, 1986) $9.8 bil. (49th). SECTORS OF GSP: Farms 15.32%. Agricultural services, forestry, & fisheries 0.56%. Mining 1.19%. Construction 3.83%. Manufacturing 9.97%. Transportation & public utilities 9.51%. Wholesale 6.27%. Retail 10.37%. Finance, insurance, & real estate 17.53%. Services 13.53%. Federal government 1.79%. Federal military 2.13%. State & local government 7.99%. *FORTUNE* 500 COMPANIES (1988): 0.
Famous natives Tom Brokaw, journalist. Martha ("Calamity") Jane Burk (b. Mo.) frontierswoman. Alvin Hansen, economist. Hubert H. Humphrey, politician. Ernest O. Lawrence, physicist (Nobel Prize, 1939). George McGovern, politician. Ta-sunko-witko (Crazy Horse), Oglala Sioux chief. Tatanka Iyotake (Sitting Bull), Sioux chief.
Noteworthy places Badlands Natl. Park. Crazy Horse State Memorial, Custer. Custer State Park. Ft. Sisseton. Geographical center of the United States. Jewel Cave Natl. Monument. Mount Rushmore Natl. Memorial. Wind Cave Natl. Park. Yellowstone Natl. Park.
Memorable events French visit region 1742-43. Region to U.S. in Louisiana Purchase 1803. Ft. Pierre first permanent settlement 1817. Part of Dakota Territory 1861. Gold discovered in Black Hills 1874. Divided from North Dakota; statehood 1889. U.S. troops massacre Sioux at Battle of Wounded Knee 1890.
Tourist information 1-800-843-1930 or 1-800-952-2217.

Tennessee

At first claimed by Virginia and later by North Carolina, the first great pioneer was Daniel Boone, who traversed the region in the 1760s. Political attitudes in the 18th century were shaped by the land, with the cotton and tobacco growers in the fertile western part of the state favoring slavery and the backwoods people of the eastern hills opposed to it. The Cherokees were removed to Oklahoma by the federal government in the 1830s. The state was captured by Union troops in 1862 and put under the governorship of Andrew Johnson, later a U.S. president. Its economy of the last 50 years has been radically altered by the creation of the Tennessee Valley Authority, which provided abundant energy for industry, and to a lesser extent by the location of the government's first uranium enrichment facility at

Oak Ridge during World War II. The state's leading industries are textiles, food processing, and chemicals, and there is considerable lead and coal mining in the east.
NAME For Tenase, principal village of Cherokees. **NICKNAME** Volunteer State. **CAPITAL** Nashville. **ENTERED UNION** June 1, 1796. **MOTTO** "Agriculture and commerce." **SLOGAN** Tennessee—America at its best. **POET LAUREATE** Richard M. ("Pek") Gunn.
Emblems ANIMAL Raccoon. BIRD Mockingbird. FOLK DANCE Square dance. CULTIVATED FLOWER Iris. GEM Tennessee pearl. INSECTS Ladybug, firefly. POEM "Oh Tennessee, My Tennessee." PUBLIC SCHOOL SONG "My Tennessee." ROCK Limestone agate. SONGS "When It's Iris Time in Tennessee," "The Tennessee Waltz," "My Homeland, Tennessee," "Rocky Top." TREE Tulip poplar. WILDFLOWER Passion flower.
Land TOTAL AREA 42,144 sq. mi. (34th), incl. 989 sq. mi. inland water. BORDERS Ky., Va., N.C., Ga., Ala., Miss., Ark., Mo. RIVERS Clinch, Cumberland, Mississippi, Tennessee. LAKES Boone, Center Hill, Cherokee, Dale Hollow, Douglass, J. Percy Priest, Watauga. OTHER NOTABLE FEATURES Cumberland Mts., Great Smoky Mts., Tennessee Valley, Unaka Mts.
Elected officials Gov. Ned Ray McWherter (D). Lt. Gov. John S. Wilder (D). Sec. State Gentry Crowell (D). Atty. Gen. Charles W. Burson (D).
People (1988 est.) 4,919,000 (16th). RACE/NATIONAL ORIGIN (1980): White 83.60%. Black 15.79%. Indian 0.15%. Asian 0.33%. Hispanic 0.74%. Foreign-born 1.10%. LANGUAGES (1980): English 98.07%. Spanish 0.62%. German 0.28%. French 0.28%. Chinese 0.06%. Italian 0.06%.
Cities (1986) Memphis 652,640. Nashville 473,670. Knoxville 173,210. Chattanooga 162,170. Jackson 52,810.
Business GROSS STATE PRODUCT (GSP, 1986) $72.3 bil. (21st). SECTORS OF GSP: Farms 1.64%. Agricultural services, forestry, & fisheries 0.28%. Mining 0.49%. Construction 4.41%. Manufacturing 25.02%. Transportation & public utilities 7.76%. Wholesale 7.29%. Retail 11.32%. Finance, insurance, & real estate 14.28%. Services 15.40%. Federal government 4.06%. Federal military 0.63%. State & local government 7.44%. *FORTUNE* 500 COMPANIES (1988): 2: Dixie Yarns, Holly Farms.
Famous natives James Agee, author. Davy Crockett, frontiersman. David Farragut, naval officer. Aretha Franklin, singer. Cordell Hull, statesman (Nobel Peace Prize, 1945). Dolly Parton, singer. Sikawyi (Sequoya), Cherokee scholar. Alvin York, soldier.
Noteworthy places American Museum of Science and Energy, Oak Ridge. Andrew Johnson Natl. Hist. Site, Greenville. Chickamauga and Chattanooga Natl. Military Park. Cumberland Natl. Hist. Park. Ft. Donelson Natl. Military Park. Grand Old Opry, Nashville. Great Smoky Mountains Natl. Park. The Hermitage (Andrew Jackson home), Nashville. Lookout Mountain, Chattanooga. The Parthenon, Nashville. Shiloh Natl. Military Park, Pittsburg Landing. Stones River Natl. Battlefield, Murfreesboro.
Memorable events De Soto expedition passes

through region 1540. French claim territory as part of Louisiana; English claim territory as part of Carolina grant 1663. French claim given up after French and Indian War 1763. State of Franklin established in what is now eastern Tennessee 1784-87. Organized as Territory South of the Ohio 1790. Statehood 1796. Secedes from Union 1861. Battles of Shiloh (1862), Chattanooga (1863), Stones River (1863), and Nashville (1864). Readmitted to Union 1866. Clarence Darrow defends John T. Scopes for violating ban on teaching evolution in public schools; loses case 1925. Congress creates Tennessee Valley Authority 1933. First operational nuclear reactor at Oak Ridge 1943. Martin Luther King assassinated at Memphis 1968.
Tourist information 1-615-741-2158.

Texas

The land that is Texas today was originally part of Spain's holdings in Mexico. After Mexico won independence, the new government invited U.S. citizens to settle there. After many clashes between the Mexican and Anglo cultures, Texas broke away and for 10 years was an independent country before becoming a state in 1845. Modern Texas was made by oil, discovered at Spindletop in 1901, and the state's economy has been tied to the oil market ever since. After World War II, the Texas economy soared, bringing both prosperity and an unprecedented population boom. With the oil glut of the early 1980s, growth came to a halt, causing a drastic realignment of economic priorities. Since 1985, energy's share of Texas's economic output has fallen almost 50 percent. Texas has enormous resources ranging from cotton, cattle, and timber to aerospace, computers, and electronics. The largest of the 48 contiguous states, Texas's image as a state of wide-open spaces is understandable, but fully 80 percent of its people live in metropolitan areas, and Dallas, Houston, and San Antonio are among the nation's 10 largest cities. Twenty-five percent of the population is Hispanic, and the majority of those are Mexican-American.
NAME From Caddo *tavshas*, "friends." **NICKNAME** Lone Star State. **CAPITAL** Austin. **ENTERED UNION** Dec. 29, 1845 (28th). **MOTTO** "Friendship."
Emblems BIRD Mockingbird. DISH Chili. FLOWER Bluebonnet. GEM Topaz. GRASS Sideoats grama. SONGS "Texas, Our Texas," "The Eyes of Texas." STONE Palmwood. TREE Pecan.
Land TOTAL AREA 266,807 sq. mi. (2d), incl. 4,790 sq. mi. inland water. BORDERS Okla., Ark., La., Gulf of Mexico, Tamaulipas, Coahuila, Chihuahua, N.Mex. RIVERS Brazos, Colorado, Red, Rio Grande, Trinity. LAKES Sam Rayburn Res., Texoma, Toledo Bend Res. OTHER NOTABLE FEATURES Balcomes Escarpment, Diablo Sierra, Edwards Plateau, Guadalupe Mts., Staked Plain, Stockton Plateau.
Elected officials Gov. William P. Clements, Jr. (R). Lt. Gov. William P. Hobby (D). Sec. State Jack Rains (R). Atty. Gen. Jim Mattox (D).
People (1988 est.) 16,780,000 (3d). RACE/

> *"Texas is a state of mind. Texas is an obsession. Above all, Texas is a nation in every sense of the word."*
>
> —John Steinbeck

NATIONAL ORIGIN (1980): White 79.44%. Black 11.98%. Indian 0.36%. Asian 0.95%. Hispanic 20.96%. Foreign-born 6.00%. **LANGUAGES** (1980): English 78.24%. Spanish 19.01%. German 0.65%. French 0.36%. Czechoslovakian 0.20%. Vietnamese 0.18%.
Cities (1986) Houston 1,728,910. Dallas 1,003,520. San Antonio 914,350. El Paso 491,800. Austin 466,550. Ft. Worth 429,550. Corpus Christi 263,900. Arlington 249,770.
Business GROSS STATE PRODUCT (GSP, 1986) $303.5 bil. (3d). SECTORS OF GSP: Farms 1.60%. Agricultural services, forestry, & fisheries 0.33%. Mining 10.25%. Construction 5.35%. Manufacturing 16.05%. Transportation & public utilities 10.96%. Wholesale 7.64%. Retail 9.31%. Finance, insurance, & real estate 13.64%. Services 14.23%. Federal government 1.95%. Federal military 1.42%. State & local government 7.26%. FORTUNE 500 COMPANIES (1988): 28: incl. American Petrofina, Kimberly-Clark, Texas Instruments, Temple-Inland, Compaq Computer, Pennzoil, Shell Oil, Tenneco, Vista Chemical.
Famous natives Stephen Austin (b. Va.), pioneer. James ("Jim") Bowie (b. Ky.), army officer. Carol Burnett, comedian. J. Frank Dobie, folklorist. Dwight D. Eisenhower, U.S. president/general. Samuel Houston (b. Va.), president Republic of Texas/governor state of Texas. Howard Hughes, industrialist/aviator. Lyndon Baines Johnson, U.S. president. Janis Joplin, singer. Barbara Jordan, politician. Audie Murphy, soldier/actor. Chester Nimitz, navy officer. Katherine Anne Porter, author. Samuel T. Rayburn, politician. Mildred ("Babe") Didrikson Zaharias, athlete.
Noteworthy places The Alamo, San Antonio. Alibates Flint Quarries Natl. Monument. Big Bend Natl. Park. Ft. Davis. Galveston Historical Foundation. Guadalupe Mountains Natl. Park. Houston Museum of Fine Arts. Lyndon B. Johnson Natl. Hist. Park, Johnson City. Lyndon B. Johnson Space Center, Houston. Old Stone Ft., Nacogdoches. Padre Island Natl. Seashore. San Antonio Missions Natl. Hist.

Park. Texas Ranger Museum, Waco.
Memorable events Alonso Alvarez de Piñeda sails along coast 1519. Estevanico blazes trail through West Texas 1539. Spanish establish settlement at Ysleta near El Paso 1682. René-Robert Cavelier de La Salle attempts to found colony on Matagorda Bay, establishing claim to region for France 1685. Effective Spanish occupation 1715. U.S. acquires French claim to region with Louisiana Purchase 1803. U.S. relinquishes claim to Spain 1819. Americans move into region in early 19th century. Mexico, of which Texas is a province, wins independence from Spain 1821. Declaration of Independence from Mexico; Santa Anna victor at Battle of the Alamo; Sam Houston victor at Battle of San Jacinto; founding of Republic of Texas 1836. Texas granted statehood by U.S. 1845. Secedes from Union 1861; readmitted 1870. Hurricane kills 6,000 at Galveston 1900. NASA Space Center opens at Houston 1962. President John F. Kennedy assassinated at Dallas 1963.
Tourist information 1-800-888-8TEX.

Utah

In the middle of the Great Basin between the Rocky Mountains and the Sierra Nevada, Utah was an arid and uninviting region. After Joseph Smith, the founder of the Church of Jesus Christ of Latter-day Saints (Mormons), was lynched in Illinois, Brigham Young led his people west, ultimately to the Salt Lake Valley in 1847. The chief obstacle to statehood was polygamy, which the church eventually renounced. There was an influx of non-Mormons after the discovery of silver in 1863, but Mormons still comprise two-thirds of the state's population, and the state remains conservative in outlook. Although the federal government is a major employer, government policy has lately been challenged by increased concern over the issues of chemical weapons testing, the MX missile, and disposal of nuclear waste from the Rocky Mountain Arsenal in neighboring Colorado.

NAME For Ute Indians. NICKNAMES Beehive State, Mormon State. CAPITAL Salt Lake City. ENTERED UNION Jan. 4, 1896 (45th). MOTTO "Industry."
Emblems ANIMAL Elk. BIRD Seagull. EMBLEM Beehive. FISH Rainbow trout. FLOWER Sego lily. GEM Topaz. SONG "Utah, We Love Thee." TREE Blue spruce.
Land TOTAL AREA 84,899 sq. mi. (11th), incl. 2,826 sq. mi. inland water. BORDERS Idaho, Wyo., Colo., Ariz., Nev. RIVERS Bear, Colorado, Green, Sevier. LAKES Bear, Great Salt, Utah. MOUNTAINS La Sal, Uinta (Kings Peak 13,528 ft.), Wasatch Range. OTHER NOTABLE FEATURES Great Salt Lake Desert (Bonneville Salt Flats), Kaibab Plateau.
Elected officials Gov. Norman H. Bangerter (R). Lt. Gov. W. Val Oveson (R). Sec. State, none. Atty. Gen. R. Paul Van Dam (D).
People (1988 est.) 1,691,000 (35th). RACE/NATIONAL ORIGIN (1980): White 94.73%. Black 0.66%. Indian 1.38%. Asian 1.38%. Hispanic 4.11%. Foreign-born 3.50%. LANGUAGES

(1980): English 92.59%. Spanish 2.84%. German 0.90%. American Indian langs. 0.77%. French 0.39%. Dutch 0.26%.
Cities (1986) Salt Lake City 158,440. Provo 77,480. Ogden 67,490. Sandy City 67,430. Orem 61,590.
Business GROSS STATE PRODUCT (GSP, 1986) $24 bil. (36th). SECTORS OF GSP: Farms 1.45%. Agricultural services, forestry, & fisheries 0.21%. Mining 2.60%. Construction 5.08%. Manufacturing 16.62%. Transportation & public utilities 12.64%. Wholesale 6.56%. Retail 10.01%. Finance, insurance, & real estate 14.89%. Services 14.58%. Federal government 5.18%. Federal military 1.18%. State & local government 9.01%. FORTUNE 500 COMPANIES (1988): 0.
Famous natives Maude Adams, actress. John Moses Browning, inventor. Philo Farnsworth, engineer. Merlin Olsen, football player/actor. Ivy Baker Priest, U.S. treasurer. Brigham Young (b. Vt.), religious leader. Loretta Young, actress.
Noteworthy places Arches Natl. Park. Bryce Canyon Natl. Park. Canyonlands Natl. Park. Capitol Reef Natl. Park. Cedar Breaks Natl. Monument. Dinosaur Natl. Monument. Flaming Gorge Dam Natl. Monument. Great Salt Lake. Lake Powell Natl. Monument. Monument Valley. Mormon Tabernacle, Salt Lake City. Natural Bridges Natl. Monument. Promontory Point. Rainbow Bridge Natl. Monument. Temple Square, Salt Lake City. Timpanogas Cave Natl. Monument. Zion Natl. Park.
Memorable events First visited probably by explorers from Coronado expedition 1540. Silvestre Vélez de Escalante and Francisco Atanasio Dominguez explore for Spain 1776. James Bridger discovers Great Salt Lake 1824. Led by Brigham Young, Mormons reach Great Salt Lake 1847. U.S. acquires Utah region from Mexico 1848. Mormons organize state of Deseret 1849; Congress refuses to recognize and instead organizes Territory of Utah 1850. Silver discovered at Little Cottonfield Canyon 1868. First transcontinental railroad completed with driving of golden spike at Promontory Point 1869. Mormon church renounces polygamy 1890, paving way to statehood 1896. Uranium discovered near Moab 1952.
Tourist information 1-801-538-1030.

Vermont

Originally claimed by both New Hampshire and New York, Vermont's independence was asserted by Ethan Allen. His Green Mountain Boys rid the state of New Yorkers in 1770, fought well against the British in the Revolution, and declared the independent republic of New Connecticut in 1777. Allen was eventually overthrown, and Vermont joined the Union. Vermont traditionally has strong ties to Canada, and there was an influx of French-Canadians as Vermont began to develop its manufacturing base in the mid-19th century. Vermont's politics have always been characterized by tolerance and progressivism. As New Connecticut, it abolished slavery and allowed universal male suffrage. More recently Bernard Sanders was the Socialist mayor of Burlington, from 1981 to 1989. Vermont's environmental concerns focus on acid rain and the degree to which development (especially by the tourist industry) should infringe on the state's remaining unspoiled land.

Name From French *vert mont*, "green mountain." **Nickname** Green Mountain State. **Capital** Montpelier. **Entered Union** Mar. 4, 1791 (14th). **Motto** "Freedom and unity."
Emblems **Animal** Morgan horse. **Beverage** Milk. **Bird** Hermit thrush. **Cold-water fish** Brook trout. **Flower** Red clover. **Insect** Honeybee. **Song** "Hail, Vermont!." **Tree** Sugar maple. **Warm-water fish** Walleye pike.
Land **Total area** 9,614 sq. mi. (43d), incl. 341 sq. mi. inland water. **Borders** Quebec, N.H., Mass., N.Y. **Rivers** Connecticut, Lamoille, Otter Creek, Poultney, White, Winooski. **Lakes** Bomoseen, Champlain, Memphremagog, Willoughby. **Other notable features** Grand Isle, Green Mts. (Mt. Mansfield 4,393 ft.), Taconic Mts.
Elected officials Gov. Madeleine M. Kunin (D). Lt. Gov. Howard Dean (D). Sec. State James H. Douglas (R). Atty. Gen. Jeffrey L. Amestoy (R).
People (1988 est.) 556,000 (48th). **Race/national origin** (1980): White 99.14%. Black 0.23%. Indian 0.21%. Asian 0.32%. Hispanic 0.66%. Foreign-born 8.79%. **Languages** (1980): English 93.40%. French 4.19%. German 0.48%. Spanish 0.46%. Italian 0.37. Polish 0.27%.
Cities (1986) Burlington 38,310. Rutland 18,080. South Burlington 11,420. Barre 10,070. Montpelier 8,120.
Business **Gross state product** (GSP, 1986) $8.6 bil. (50th) **Sectors of GSP:** Farms 2.73%. Agricultural services, forestry, & fisheries 0.44%. Mining 0.27%. Construction 6.23%. Manufacturing 22.94%. Transportation & public utilities 8.00%. Wholesale 5.54%. Retail 10.11%. Finance, insurance, & real estate 18.20%. Services 15.90%. Federal government 1.83%. Federal military 0.38%. State & local government 7.45%. *Fortune* 500 companies (1988): 0.
Famous natives Ethan Allen (b. Conn.), army officer. Chester Arthur, U.S. president. Calvin Coolidge, U.S. president. John Deere, industrialist. George Dewey, naval officer. John Dewey, philosopher. Stephen Douglas, politician. James Fisk, financier. Rudy Vallee, singer.
Noteworthy places Bennington Battleground/Monument. Calvin Coolidge Homestead, Plymouth. Maple Grove Maple Museum, Rock of Ages Tourist Center, Graniteville. Shelburne Museum. St. Johnsbury. Vermont Marble Exhibit, Proctor.
Memorable events Samuel de Champlain explores for France 1609. First French settlement at Ste. Anne 1666. First English settlers build Ft. Drummer near Brattleboro 1724. Bennington settled 1761. Ethan Allen organizes Green Mountain Boys 1764. Green Mountain Boys capture Ft. Ticonderoga and Ft. Crown Point 1775. Gen. John Stark defeats British Gen. John Burgoyne near Bennington; constitution abolishes slavery and grants universal male suffrage 1777. Claims to area relinquished by Massachusetts (1781), New

"I love Vermont because of her hills and valleys, her scenery, and invigorating climate, but most of all, because of her indomitable people."

—Calvin Coolidge, 1928

Hampshire (1782), and New York (1790). First state admitted after original 13 1791. MacDonough defeats British Lake Champlain fleet 1814. Canal between Hudson River and Lake Champlain gives Vermont direct access to port of New York 1823. Confederate soldiers steal $400,000 from St. Albans bank 1864. Blue law repealed, allowing stores to open on Sundays 1982.
Tourist information 1–802–828–3236.

Virginia, Commonwealth of

The first successful English settlement in America was at Jamestown in 1607. The differences between the Virginia colonists and those of Massachusetts were pronounced, and the commercial southern planter class shared little of their New England counterparts' religious zeal. Virginia bred its own strain of independence, and it was the fiery Patrick Henry who heralded the American Revolution with the cry "Give me liberty or give me death." Seven of the first 12 presidents were from Virginia. With an economy very dependent on labor-intensive tobacco in the mid-19th century, Virginia seceded from the Union over the slavery issue, despite the misgivings of many, including Robert E. Lee. After the war Virginia developed an increasingly diversified industrial and manufacturing base that survives today, with food products, tobacco, and chemicals leading the way. Despite the dramatic decline of the American merchant marine, Virginia's shipbuilding industry in Newport News flourishes, thanks to the Pentagon's commitment to a 600-ship navy. Norfolk is also one of the country's leading commercial ports.

Name For Elizabeth I, called Virgin Queen. **Nicknames** Old Dominion, Mother of Presidents, Mother of States. **Capital** Richmond. **Entered Union** June 25, 1788 (10th). **Motto** *Sic semper tyrannis* (Thus always to tyrants).

Emblems **Beverage** Milk. **Bird** Cardinal. **Dog** Foxhound. **Flower** Dogwood. **Shell** Oyster. **Song** "Carry Me Back to Old Virginia." **Tree** Dogwood.
Land **Total area** 40,767 sq. mi. (36th), incl. 1,063 sq. mi. inland water. **Borders** Md., D.C., Atlantic Ocean, N.C., Tenn., Ky., W.Va. **Rivers** James, Potomac, Rappahannock, Roanoke, Shenandoah, York. **Lakes** Buggs Island, Claytor, Gaston, Leesville. **Mountains** Allegheny, Blue Ridge, Cumberland, Unaka. **Other notable features** Great Dismal Swamp, Shenandoah Valley.
Elected officials Gov. Gerald Lee Baliles (D). Lt. Gov. L. Douglas Wilder (D). Sec. of the Commonwealth Sandra D. Bowen (D). Atty. Gen. Mary Sue Terry (D).
People (1988 est.) 5,996,000 (12th). **Race/national origin** (1980): White 79.23%. Black 18.87%. Indian 0.19%. Asian 1.32%. Hispanic 1.49%. Foreign-born 3.30%. **Languages** (1980): English 95.57%. Spanish 1.29%. French 0.56%. German 0.48%. Philippine langs. 0.23%. Korean 0.20%.
Cities (1986) Virginia Beach 333,400. Norfolk 274,800. Richmond 217,700. Newport News 161,700. Chesapeake 134,400. Hampton 126,000. Portsmouth 111,000.
Business **Gross state product** (GSP 1986) $104.2 (11th). **Sectors of GSP:** Farms 0.93%. Agricultural services, forestry, & fisheries 0.33%. Mining 1.07%. Construction 5.77%. Manufacturing 17.86%. Transportation & public utilities 9.20%. Wholesale 5.47%. Retail 9.41%. Finance, insurance, & real estate 14.74%. Services 15.74%. Federal government 6.04%. Federal military 5.96%. State & local government 7.49%. *Fortune* 500 companies (1988): 14: incl. A.H. Robins, Fairchild Industries, Gannett, Media General, Smithfield Foods, Universal.
Famous natives Richard E. Byrd, explorer/aviator. William Clark, explorer. Jerry Falwell, evangelist. William Henry Harrison, U.S. president. Patrick Henry, Revolutionary patriot. Thomas Jefferson, U.S. president. Joseph E. Johnston, Confederate general. John Paul Jones (b. Scotland), navy officer. Robert E. Lee, Confederate general. Meriwether Lewis, explorer. James Madison, U.S. president. John Marshall, jurist. Cyrus Hall McCormick, inventor. James Monroe, U.S. president. Walter Reed, doctor. Pat Robertson, evangelist/politician. Bill ("Bojangles") Robinson, dancer. George C. Scott, actor. Thomas Sumter, army officer. Zachary Taylor, U.S. president. John Tyler, U.S. president. Booker T. Washington, educator. George Washington, U.S. president. Woodrow Wilson, U.S. president.
Noteworthy places Appomattox Courthouse Natl. Hist Park. Arlington Natl. Cemetery. Booker T. Washington Natl. Monument, Roanoke. Colonial Natl. Hist. Park (incl. Jamestown, Yorktown, and Williamsburg). Fredericksburg and Spotsylvania Natl. Military Park. George Washington birthplace, Frederick Co. Harpers Ferry Natl. Hist. Site. The Mariners' Museum, Newport News. Monticello, Charlottesville. Mount Vernon. Petersburg Natl. Battlefield. Robert E. Lee Memorial, Lexington. Shenandoah Natl. Park.

Virginia Beach. Virginia Museum of Fine Arts. Wolf Trap Farm for the Performing Arts, Reston.

Memorable events John Smith founds Jamestown, first permanent settlement in North America, 1607. John Rolfe marries Pocahontas, daughter of Powhatan, leader of so-called Powhatan Confederacy 1614. First English women arrive at Jamestown; House of Burgesses established 1619. Northampton Declaration first resistance to taxation without representation 1653. College of William and Mary founded 1693. First state to establish Committee of Correspondence 1773. American Revolution ends with Charles Cornwallis's surrender to George Washington at Yorktown 1781. Nat Turner's slave revolt 1831. State secedes from Union 1861. Civil War ends with Robert E. Lee's surrender to Ulysses S. Grant at Appomattox Courthouse 1865. Readmitted to Union 1870. Norfolk Naval Base founded 1917. John D. Rockefeller, Jr. undertakes restoration of Colonial Williamsburg 1926. E. Claiborne Robins donates $50 million to University of Richmond 1969.

Tourist information 1-800-VISITVA.

Washington

Boston merchant Captain Robert Gray began a trade in sea otter pelts, which soon attracted others, both British and American, to the region. The first settlers in the region were led by the missionary Marcus Whitman, who established a town near Walla Walla in 1836. The primary occupations of the region were agriculture and lumbering, which remain economic staples. After World War I, Puget Sound became a heavily industrialized shipbuilding center. Today Boeing maintains one of the country's largest airplane-manufacturing plants in Tacoma. The industrial work force was open to progressive and sometimes radical unionism, and the International Workers of the World (Wobblies) had their national headquarters at Seattle. Before statehood the territorial government pioneered women's suffrage, but Congress declared the women's right to vote unconstitutional.

NAME For George Washington. NICKNAME Evergreen State. CAPITAL Olympia. ENTERED UNION Nov. 11, 1889 (42d). MOTTO *Alki* (By and by).

Emblems BIRD Willow goldfinch. FISH Steelhead trout. FLOWER Western rhododendron. GEM Petrified wood. SONG "Washington, My Home." TREE Western hemlock.

Land TOTAL AREA 68,138 sq. mi. (20th), incl. 1,627 sq. mi. inland water. BORDERS British Columbia, Idaho, Oreg., Pacific Ocean. RIVERS Chehalis, Columbia, Pend Oreille, Snake, Yakima. LAKES Baker, Bank, Chelan, Franklin D. Roosevelt, Ross, Rufus Woods. MOUNTAINS Cascade Range, Coast Range, Kettle River Range, Olympic. OTHER NOTABLE FEATURES Puget Sound, San Juan Islands, Strait of Juan de Fuca.

Elected officials Gov. Booth Gardner (D). Lt. Gov. Joel Pritchard (R). Sec. State Ralph Munro (R). Atty. Gen. Kenneth O. Eikenberry (R).

People (1988 est.) 4,619,000 (19th). RACE/ NATIONAL ORIGIN (1980): White 91.74%. Black 2.56%. Indian 1.54%. Asian 2.70%. Hispanic 2.94%. Foreign-born 5.80%. LANGUAGES (1980): English 93.07%. Spanish 2.05%. German 0.97%. French 0.40%. Philippine langs. 0.39%. Chinese 0.37%. Japanese 0.34%.

Cities (1986) Seattle 486,200. Spokane 172,890. Tacoma 158,950. Bellevue 80,940. Everett 60,380. Yakima 49,370. Bellingham 44,960.

Business GROSS STATE PRODUCT (GSP, 1986) $77.7 bil. (16th). SECTORS OF GSP: Farms 2.61%. Agricultural services, forestry, & fisheries 1.05%. Mining 0.22%. Construction 5.75%. Manufacturing 17.27%. Transportation & public utilities 8.58%. Wholesale 8.04%. Retail 10.72%. Finance, insurance, & real estate 15.66%. Services 15.04%. Federal government 2.96%. Federal military 2.25%. State & local government 9.85%. *FORTUNE* 500 COMPANIES (1988): 4: Boeing, Longview Fibre, Paccar, Weyerhaeuser.

Famous natives Harry L. ("Bing") Crosby, singer. Merce Cunningham, choreographer. Jimi Hendrix, guitarist. Henry M. ("Scoop") Jackson, politician. Robert Joffrey, choreographer. Marcus Whitman (b. N.Y.), missionary/ pioneer.

Noteworthy places Klondike Gold Rush Natl. Hist. Park, Seattle. Mount Rainier Natl. Park. Mount Saint Helens Natl. Monument. North Cascades Natl. Park. Olympic Natl. Park. San Juan Islands Natl. Hist. Park. Seattle Art Museum.

Memorable events Sir Francis Drake skirts coast of Pacific Northwest 1579. Juan de Fuca sails into straits now bearing his name. Bruno de Heceta lands at Hoh River 1775. Capt. James Cook arrives 1778. Capt. Robert Gray discovers mouth of Columbia River, which he names for his ship; George Vancouver explores Puget Sound 1792. Lewis and Clark expedition winters at Columbia River 1805. Marcus Whitman, Protestant Mission Board, settles near Walla Walla 1836. Territorial status 1853. Northern Pacific railroad reaches Puget Sound 1883. Alaska-Yukon-Pacific Exposition at Seattle 1909. Grand Coulee Dam, largest concrete hydroelectric dam in U.S., completed 1941. Hanford Works atomic energy plant opens 1943. Mt. Saint Helens erupts, killing 60 1980.

Tourist information 1-800-544-1800.

West Virginia

When Virginia seceded in 1861, its western counties reorganized and in 1863 were admitted to the Union as a separate state. Despite the rugged terrain, through which transportation has always been difficult, farming remained the backbone of the economy until the close of the 19th century, when coal mining and other extractive industries developed. After World War II, the manufacturing base developed to include steel and chemical manufacturing. The Monongahela, Kanawha, and Little Kanawha rivers are all navigable tributaries of the Ohio River, which forms West Virginia's western border, but the state's internal transportation needs have not been met. Even with vast natural resources, West Virginia has long been one of the poorest states in the union. Population losses in the 1950s and 1960s were the worst of any state in U.S. history, and today there is low participation in the work force by women, and educational achievements are well below the national average.

NAME For western part of Virginia. NICKNAME Mountain State. CAPITAL Charleston. ENTERED UNION June 20, 1863 (35th). MOTTO *Montani semper liberi* (Mountaineers are always free).

Emblems ANIMAL Black bear. BIRD Cardinal. COLORS Old gold and blue. FISH Brook trout. FLOWER *Rhododendron maximum* (big laurel). FRUIT Apple. SONGS "The West Virginia Hills," "West Virginia, My Home Sweet Home," "This Is My West Virginia." TREE Sugar maple.

Land TOTAL AREA 24,231 sq. mi. (41st), incl. 112 sq. mi. inland water. BORDERS Ohio, Pa., Md., Va., Ky. RIVERS Big Sandy, Guayandotte, Kanawha, Little Kanawha, Monongahela, Ohio, Potomac. LAKES Summersville Dam. MOUNTAINS Allegheny, Blue Ridge, Cumberland.

Elected officials Gov. Gaston Caperton (D). Lt. Gov., none. Sec. State Ken Hechler (D). Atty. Gen. Charlie Brown (D).

People (1988 est.) 1,884,000 (34th). RACE/ NATIONAL ORIGIN (1980): White 96.15%. Black 3.34%. Indian 0.12%. Asian 0.30%. Hispanic 0.67%. Foreign-born 1.10%. LANGUAGES (1980): English 97.86%. Spanish 0.44%. Italian 0.31%. French 0.27%. German 0.24%. Polish 0.10%.

Cities (1986) Huntington 59,310. Charleston 57,920. Wheeling 39,980. Parkersburg 38,540. Morgantown 26,840. Weirton 23,640.

Business GROSS STATE PRODUCT (GSP, 1986) $24.1 bil. (35th). SECTORS OF GSP: Farms 0.77%. Agricultural services, forestry, & fisheries 0.16%. Mining 13.19%. Construction 4.79%. Manufacturing 14.46%. Transportation & public utilities 13.64%. Wholesale 5.11%. Retail 9.36%. Finance, insurance, & real estate 14.56%. Services 12.48%. Federal government 1.75%. Federal military 0.29%. State & local government 9.45%. *FORTUNE* 500 COMPANIES (1988): 1: Weirton Steel.

Famous natives Newton D. Baker, politician. Pearl Buck, novelist (Nobel Prize, 1938). John W. Davis, politician. Thomas ("Stonewall") Jackson, Confederate general. Dwight Whitney Morrow, lawyer/diplomat. Michael Owens, manufacturer. Walter Reuther, labor leader. Cyrus Vance, statesman. Charles ("Chuck") Yeager, pilot.

Noteworthy places Cass Scenic Railroad. Harpers Ferry Natl. Hist. Park. Monongahela Natl. Forest. New River Gorge Bridge. Science and Cultural Center, Charleston.

Memorable events First permanent settlement by Morgan Morgan at Mill Creek 1731. Coal discovered on Coal River 1742. Wheeling Convention repudiates act of secession; forms new state of Kanawha 1861. Enters Union as West Virginia 1863. Population peaks at 2.5 million 1950. Unemployment jumps 8.6% to 18.0%, highest in nation, 1980-83.

Tourist information 1-800-CALLWVA.

Wisconsin

The indigenous people of the region had a largely agricultural economy, but the fur trade drew Europeans into the region. Native resistance to white settlement was strong and not overcome until the Black Hawk Wars of 1832. In the early 19th century, German, Scandinavian, and Dutch farmers immigrated to the region in large numbers. Many social welfare policies now common to the nation as a whole—including aid to dependent children, workmen's compensation, and old-age assistance—were pioneered in Wisconsin. Although manufacturing accounts for the lion's share of Wisconsin's profits, agriculture is extremely important, and the state is the nation's leading producer of dairy products. There are major shipping facilities at Superior, Green Bay, and Milwaukee.

NAME From Ojibwa *wishkonsing*, "place of the bearer." NICKNAME Badger State. CAPITAL Madison. ENTERED UNION May 29, 1848 (30th). MOTTO "Forward."

Emblems ANIMAL Badger. BIRD Robin. DOMESTIC ANIMAL Dairy cow. FISH Muskellunge. FLOWER Wood violet. INSECT Honeybee. MINERAL Galena. ROCK Red granite. SOIL Antigo silt loam. SONG "Oh, Wisconsin!" SYMBOL OF PEACE Mourning dove. TREE Sugar maple. WILDLIFE ANIMAL White-tailed deer.

Land TOTAL AREA 56,153 sq. mi. (26th), incl. 1,727 sq. mi. inland water. BORDERS Minn., Lake Superior, Mich., Lake Michigan, Ill., Iowa. RIVERS Black, Chippewa, Menominee, Mississippi, St. Croix, Wisconsin. LAKES Chippewa, Du Bay, Mendota, Michigan, Superior, Winnebago. OTHER NOTABLE FEATURES Apostle Islands, Door Peninsula, Green Bay.

Elected officials Gov. Tommy G. Thompson (R). Lt. Gov. Scott McCallum (R). Sec. State Douglas La Follette (D). Atty. Gen. Donald J. Hanaway (R).

People (1988 est.) 4,858,000 (17th). RACE/NATIONAL ORIGIN (1980): White 94.48%. Black 3.89%. Indian 0.65%. Asian 0.47%. Hispanic 1.33%. Foreign-born 2.70%. LANGUAGES (1980): English 94.24%. German 1.79%. Spanish 1.09%. Polish 0.68. Norwegian 0.24%. French 0.24%. Italian 0.24%.

Cities (1986) Milwaukee 605,090. Madison 175,830. Green Bay 93,470. Racine 82,440. Kenosha 74,960. Appleton 64,190.

Business GROSS STATE PRODUCT (GSP, 1986) $76.9 bil. (17th). SECTORS OF GSP: Farms 4.02%. Agricultural services, forestry, & fisheries 0.38%. Mining 0.11%. Construction 3.05%. Manufacturing 27.69%. Transportation & public utilities 7.90%. Wholesale 5.98%. Retail 9.19%. Finance, insurance, & real estate 17.57%. Services 13.85%. Federal government 1.09%. Federal military 0.39%. State & local government 8.79%. FORTUNE 500 COMPANIES (1988): 10: incl. Allis-Chalmers, Harley-Davidson, Harnischfeger Industries, Snap-on Tools, Universal Foods.

Famous natives King Camp Gillette, inventor/businessman. Harry Houdini (b. Hungary), magician. Robert La Follette, politician. Liberace (Wladziu Valentino), pianist. Alfred Lunt, actor. Joseph R. McCarthy, politician. Spencer Tracy, actor. Thorstein Veblen, economist. Orson Welles, director. Laura Ingalls Wilder, novelist. Thornton Wilder, author. Frank Lloyd Wright, architect.

Noteworthy places Apostle Island Natl. Lakeshore. Chequamegon Natl. Forest. Circus World Museum, Baraboo. Door County Peninsula. Ice Age Natl. Scientific Reserve. Manitowoc Maritime Museum. Milwaukee Art Museum. Milwaukee Public Museum. Nicolet Natl. Forest. Old Wade House and Carriage Museum, Greenbush. Old World Wisconsin, Eagle. Villa Louis, Prairie du Chien. Wisconsin Dells.

Memorable events Jean Nicolet lands at Green Bay 1634. French establish mission and trading post near Ashland 1634. British take control of region 1763. Land ceded to U.S. 1787, but U.S. control not established until after War of 1812. Becomes independent Territory 1836. Statehood 1848. More than 800 die in forest fire near Peshtigo 1871. First hydroelectric plant completed at Appleton 1882. Ringling Brothers circus formed at Baraboo 1884. First state to enact income tax 1911.

Tourist information 1-608-266-2161 or 1-800-372-2737.

Wyoming

Tens of thousands of migrants traveled through the region along the Oregon Trail, which was pioneered in 1812–13, but few settled the land until Ft. Laramie was built in 1834. Territorial status came in 1869. Wyoming was the first state to give the vote to women, and in 1925 Nellie Tayloe Ross became the first woman governor following the death of her husband. Cattle ranching is the traditional mainstay of the economy. The state ranks second in uranium output and has 35 percent of the country's deposits. In the last 20 years, petroleum and coal production have become increasingly important. Wyoming is best known for its natural wonders. Yellowstone National Park—the site of Old Faithful—is the oldest and largest national park in the country. Following a decade-long mining boom in the 1970s and 1980s, Wyoming's population declined, and it has fallen behind even Alaska in total population.

NAME From Delaware *maugh-wau-wa-ma*, "large plains" or "mountains and valleys alternating." NICKNAME Equality State. CAPITAL Cheyenne. ENTERED UNION July 10, 1890 (44th). MOTTO "Equal rights."

Emblems BIRD Meadowlark. FLOWER Indian paintbrush. GEM Jade. SONG "Wyoming." TREE Cottonwood.

Land TOTAL AREA 97,809 sq. mi. (9th), incl. 820 sq. mi. inland water. BORDERS Mont., S.Dak., Nebr., Colo., Utah, Idaho. RIVERS Bighorn, Green, North Platte, Powder, Snake, Yellowstone. LAKES Bighorn, Yellowstone. MOUNTAINS Absaroka, Bighorn, Black Hills, Laramie, Owl Creek, Teton Range, Wind River Range, Wyoming Range.

Elected officials Gov. Michael J. Sullivan (D). Lt. Gov., none. Sec. State Kathy Karpan (D). Atty. Gen. Joe Meyer (D).

People (1988 est.) 471,000 (50th). RACE/NATIONAL ORIGIN (1980): White 95.09%. Black 0.70%. Indian 1.76%. Asian 0.44%. Hispanic 5.23%. Foreign-born 2.00%. LANGUAGES (1980): English 93.66%. Spanish 3.41%. German 0.89%. French 0.37%. American Indian langs. 0.32%. Italian 0.18%.

Cities (1986) Cheyenne 53,960. Casper 47,310. Laramie 24,930. Gillette 23,280. Rock Springs 21,970.

Business GROSS STATE PRODUCT (GSP, 1986) $11.7 bil. (47th). SECTORS OF GSP: Farms 1.61%. Agricultural services, forestry, & fisheries 0.27%. Mining 26.38%. Construction 11.8%. Manufacturing 2.84%. Transportation & public utilities 13.57%. Wholesale 3.45%. Retail 6.56%. Finance, insurance, & real estate 13.89%. Services 7.77%. Federal government 1.83%. Federal military 1.15%. State & local government 8.88%. FORTUNE 500 COMPANIES (1988): 0.

Famous natives James Bridger (b. Va.), pioneer. Jackson Pollock, painter. Nellie Tayloe Ross (b. Mo.), politician.

Noteworthy places Buffalo Bill Museum, Cody. Devil's Tower Natl. Monument. Ft. Bridger State Park. Ft. Laramie Natl. Hist. Site. Fossil Butte Natl. Monument. Grand Teton Natl. Park. Natl. Elk Refuge. Yellowstone Natl. Park (Old Faithful).

Memorable events Part of Louisiana Territory claimed for France 1682. Pierre Gaultier de Varennes, sieur de Vérendrye explores region for France 1743. Region to U.S. with Louisiana Purchase 1803. John Colter crosses area of Yellowstone 1807–08. Part of region under joint Anglo-American occupation 1818–46. Indian Wars follow massacre of army detachments 1854 and 1866. Wyoming Territory organized 1868. Women's suffrage adopted permanently (first instance in U.S.); Union Pacific railroad crosses state 1869. Yellowstone, world's first national park, opens 1872. White mob kills 50 Chinese miners and burns Chinatown in Rock Springs 1885. Statehood 1890. Nellie Tayloe Ross first woman governor 1925. First Intercontinental Ballistic Missile (ICBM) base opens near Cheyenne 1951.

Tourist information 1-800-CALLWYO.

SHIFTING STATE POPULATIONS

Twenty states had more people move out than move in between 1980 and 1988. Those with the largest net losses:

Michigan	−524,000
Illinois	−469,000
Ohio	−466,000
New York	−343,000

Those with the largest gains:

California	2.5 million
Florida	1.3 million
Texas	1.1 million

Source: U.S. Bureau of the Census

POPULATION GROWTH AND DECLINE

Population Change Due to Migration

In the 1980s the nation's population increased by 16.9 million; together the West and South accounted for 15 million—almost 90%. Nearly half of the increase—7.4 million—in the two regions was due to net inmigration, while the Northeast and Midwest experienced net outmigration of 2.5 million. In the period 1980–88, the five states with the highest growth due to migration were Nevada, Florida, Arizona, New Hampshire (the only Northeast state with a gain greater than 3.5%), and California. The only state in the Midwest with a population gain due to migration was Missouri, with an increase of 0.1%. The five states with the greatest population decline due to migration were Wyoming, Iowa, West Virginia, Michigan, and North Dakota.

NET MIGRATION BY STATE, 1980–88

State	Total (thousands)	Percent change	Percent rank
Alabama	14	0.3%	25
Alaska	42	10.6	6
Arizona	501	18.4	3
Arkansas	12	0.5	24
California	2,516	10.6	5
Colorado	133	4.6	13
Connecticut	—	—	27
Delaware	31	5.3	12
District of Columbia	-44	-6.9	—
Florida	2,270	23.3	2
Georgia	488	8.9	7
Hawaii	26	2.7	19
Idaho	-31	-3.3	38
Illinois	-469	-4.1	43
Indiana	-211	-3.9	41
Iowa	-204	-7.0	49
Kansas	-17	-0.7	29
Kentucky	-101	-2.8	37
Louisiana	-162	-3.9	42
Maine	33	3.0	18
Maryland	155	3.7	16
Massachussetts	-46	-0.8	30
Michigan	-524	-5.7	47
Minnesota	-40	-1.0	31
Mississippi	-66	-2.6	36
Missouri	7	0.1	26
Montana	-39	-5.0	45
Nebraska	-59	-3.8	40
Nevada	187	23.4	1
New Hampshire	109	11.8	4
New Jersey	80	1.1	22
New Mexico	57	4.4	15
New York	-343	-2.0	34
North Carolina	311	5.3	11
North Dakota	-37	-5.6	46
Ohio	-466	-4.3	44
Oklahoma	19	0.6	23
Oregon	-10	-0.4	28
Pennsylvania	-172	-1.5	33
Rhode Island	17	1.8	21
South Carolina	142	4.5	14
South Dakota	-25	-3.6	39
Tennessee	103	2.3	20
Texas	1,117	7.8	8
Utah	-18	-1.3	32
Vermont	18	3.5	17
Virginia	345	6.4	9
Washington	219	5.3	10
West Virginia	-122	-6.3	48
Wisconsin	-113	-2.4	35
Wyoming	-43	-9.2	50

Source: U.S. Bureau of the Census press release, 1989.

COMPOSITION OF STATE LEGISLATURES, 1989

State	Body	Dem.	Rep.
Alabama	Senate[1]	28	6
	House[2]	85	17
Alaska	Senate	8	12
	House	23	17
Arizona	Senate	13	17
	House	26	34
Arkansas	Senate	31	4
	House[3]	88	11
California	Senate[3]	24	15
	House[1]	46	33
Colorado	Senate	11	24
	House	26	39
Connecticut	Senate	23	13
	House	88	63
Delaware	Senate	13	8
	House	18	23
Florida	Senate	23	17
	House	73	47
Georgia	Senate	45	11
	House	144	36
Hawaii	Senate	22	3
	House	45	6
Idaho	Senate	19	23
	House	20	64
Illinois	Senate	31	28
	House	67	51
Indiana	Senate	24	26
	House	50	50
Iowa	Senate	30	20
	House	61	39
Kansas	Senate	18	22
	House	58	67
Kentucky	Senate	30	8
	House	72	28
Louisiana	Senate	34	5
	House[4]	86	17
Maine	Senate	20	15
	House	97	54
Maryland	Senate	40	7
	House	125	16
Massachussetts	Senate	32	8
	House	128	32
Michigan	Senate	18	20
	House	61	49
Minnesota	Senate	44[5]	23[6]
	House[1]	80[5]	53[6]
Mississippi	Senate	44	8
	House[7]	112	9
Missouri	Senate	22	15
	House[1]	104	58
Montana	Senate	23	27
	House	52	48
Nebraska (non partisan)	49 Unicameral legislature		
Nevada	Senate	8	13
	House	30	12
New Hampshire	Senate	8	16
	House	119	281
New Jersey	Senate	24	16
	House	39	41
New Mexico	Senate	26	16
	House	45	25
New York	Senate	27	34
	House	92	58
North Carolina	Senate	37	13
	House	74	46
North Dakota	Senate	32	21
	House	45	61
Ohio	Senate	14	19
	House	59	40
Oklahoma	Senate	33	15
	House[1]	68	32
Oregon	Senate	19	11
	House	32	28
Pennsylvania	Senate	23	27
	House	104	99
Rhode Island	Senate	41	9
	House	83	17
South Carolina	Senate	35	11
	House	87	37
South Dakota	Senate	15	20
	House	24	46
Tennessee	Senate	22	11
	House	59	40
Texas	Senate	23	8
	House	93	57
Utah	Senate	7	22
	House	28	47
Vermont	Senate	16	14
	House	74	76
Virginia	Senate	30[5]	10
	House	64	35
Washington	Senate	24	25
	House	63	35
West Virginia	Senate	29	5
	House	79	21

State	Body	Dem.	Rep.
Wisconsin	Senate	20	13
	House	56	43
Wyoming	Senate	11	19
	House	23	41
All states	**Senate[8]**	**1,194**	**750**
	House[9]	**3,275**	**2,179**
American Samoa (non partisan)	4 Senate		
	1 House[1]		
District of Columbia	Unicameral council	12	0
Guam	Unicameral legislature	13	8
N. Mariana Islands	Senate	2	7
	House	8	7
Puerto Rico	Senate[10]	18[11]	8[12]
	House[10]	36[11]	14[12]
Virgin Islands	Unicameral legislature[13]	9	3

As of January, 1989.   1. One vacancy.   2. Three vacancies.
3. Also, one Independent.   4. Two vacancies.   5. Democrat-
Farmer-Labor.   6. Independent-Republican.   7. Also, one
Independent-Democrat.   8. Also, one Independent; one vacancy.
9. Also, two Independents and one Independent-Democrat; nine
vacancies.   10. Also, one Puerto Rican Independent party.
11. Popular Democratic party.   12. New Progressive party.
13. Also, two Independents and one Independent Citizens Movement.
Source: Council of State Governments, *State Elective Officials and the Legislatures 1989–90* (1989).

State	Governor	Lieutenant Governor	Secretary State	Attorney General
N.Dak.	$ 60,856	$ 49,992	$46,000	$ 52,000
Ohio.	65,000	42,536	50,000	50,000
Okla.	70,000	40,000	37,500	55,000
Oreg.	73,500	none	55,000	60,996
Pa.	85,000	67,500	58,000	65,000
R.I.	69,900	52,000	52,000	55,000
S.C.	81,600	35,700	69,360	69,360
S.D.	57,324	50,003	38,937	48,672
Tenn.	85,000	24,200	65,000	65,650
Tex.	91,600	7,200	64,890	73,233
Utah	60,000	50,000	none	49,000
Vt.	63,600	26,500	40,000	48,000
Va.	85,000	20,000	53,085	75,000
Wash.	83,800	45,000	46,300	63,800
W.Va.	72,000	none	43,200	50,400
Wis.	86,149	46,360	42,089	73,930
Wyo.	70,000	none	52,500	61,088
D.C.	83,010[2]	none	69,556	69,556
Amer. Samoa	50,000	45,000	NONE	40,000
Guam	50,000	45,000	NONE	40,838
Northern Marianas	50,000	45,000	NONE	42,000
Puerto Rico	45,000	NONE	50,000	50,000
Virgin Islands	60,000	57,600	N.A.	55,000

Source: 1. Based on a salary range of $37,245–44,776.
2. Mayor.   **Source:** Council of State Governments, *The Book of the States 1987–88* (1987).

SALARIES OF MAJOR STATE ELECTED OFFICIALS

State	Governor	Lieutenant Governor	Secretary State	Attorney General
Ala.	$ 70,223	$ 46,260	$36,234	$ 77,000
Alaska	81,648	76,188	none	77,304
Ariz.	75,000	none	50,000	70,000
Ark.	35,000	22,500	22,500	26,500
Calif.	85,000	72,500	72,500	77,500
Colo.	70,000	48,500	48,500	60,000
Conn.	78,000	55,000	50,000	60,000
Del.	70,000	32,400	53,100	70,000
Fla.	96,646	85,656	85,656	85,656
Ga.	84,594	51,328	64,494	66,092
Hawaii	80,000	76,000	none	68,400
Idaho	55,000	15,000	45,000	48,000
Ill.	93,266	65,835	82,294	82,294
Ind.	77,200	64,000	46,000	59,200
Iowa	70,000	23,900	50,000	62,500
Kans.	65,693	19,128	52,530	60,417
Ky.	68,364	58,101	58,101	58,101
La.	73,400	63,367	60,169	66,566
Maine	70,000	none	47,154	56,366
Md.	85,000	72,500	45,000	72,500
Mass.	85,000	70,000	70,000	75,000
Mich.	100,077	67,377	89,000	89,000
Minn.	94,204	51,814	51,814	73,594
Miss.	63,000	34,000	45,000	51,000
Mo.	81,000	50,058	66,744	72,300
Mont.	50,452	36,140	33,342	46,015
Nebr.	58,000	40,000	40,000	57,500
Nev.	77,500	11,494	50,500	57,471
N.H.	68,005	none	41,010[1]	60,708
N.J.	85,000	none	90,000	90,000
N.Mex.	63,000	40,425	40,425	46,200
N.Y.	130,000	110,000	83,179	110,000
N.C.	105,000	64,092	64,092	64,092

SUMMARY OF STATE GOVERNMENT FINANCES, 1986–87

Item	Amount (millions)
REVENUE	
Revenue, total	**$516,941**
General revenue	419,487
Intergovernmental revenue	102,381
From federal government	95,463
From local governments	6,918
General revenue from own sources	317,106
Taxes	246,933
Property	4,609
Sales, gross receipts, and customs	119,838
Individual income	75,965
Corporation net income	20,724
Other taxes	25,797
Charges and miscellaneous general revenue	70,173
Utility and liquor store revenue	5,776
Insurance trust revenue	91,678
Unemployment compensation	18,839
Employee retirement	64,405
Other insurance trust revenue	8,434
EXPENDITURE	
Expenditure, total	**$455,696**
By function:	
General expenditure	403,939
Current expenditure	368,853
Capital outlay	35,086
Education services:	
Education	149,901
Libraries	585
Social services and income maintenance:	
Public welfare	78,454
Hospitals	18,048
Health	14,083
Social insurance administration	2,741

Item	Amount (millions)
REVENUE	
Veterans' services	129
Transportation:	
Highways	38,273
Air transportation	697
Water transport and terminals	561
Other transportation	2,171
Public safety:	
Police protection	4,048
Fire protection	—
Correction	11,704
Protective inspection and regulation	2,925
Environment and housing:	
Natural resources	7,816
Parks and recreation	2,135
Housing and community development	2,129
Sewerage	970
Sanitation other than sewerage	—
Governmental administration:	
Financial administration	6,459
Judicial and legal	4,287
General public buildings	1,106
Other governmental administration	1,904
Interest on general debt	18,583
General expenditure	34,230
Utility and liquor store expenditure	8,442
Insurance trust expenditure	43,316
Unemployment compensation	15,174
Employee retirement	22,189
Other insurance trust expenditure	5,953
Indebtedness—total debt outstanding at end of fiscal year	$265,677

Source: U.S. Bureau of the Census, *Government Finances in 1986–87* (1988).

STATE GOVERNMENT INDIVIDUAL INCOME TAXES, 1987

State	TAXABLE INCOME RATES (range in percent)	TAXABLE INCOME BRACKETS Lowest: amount under	TAXABLE INCOME BRACKETS Highest: amount over
Alabama[1]	2.0–5.0%	$ 500[2]	$ 3,000[2]
Arizona[3]	2.0–8.0	1,155	6,930
Arkansas	1.0–7.0	2,999	25,000
California[3]	1.0–11	1,710	28,790
Colorado	5% of federal income tax liability		
Connecticut	Very limited income tax		
Delaware[1]	1.0–8.8	1,000	40,000
District of Columbia	2.0–11.0	1,000	25,000
Georgia	1.0–6.0	750	7,000
Hawaii	2.25–10	1,000	20,000
Idaho	2.0–8.2	1,000	20,000
Illinois	2.5	Flat rate	
Indiana[1]	3.4	Flat rate	
Iowa[1,3]	0.5–13.0	1,023[4]	76,725[4]
Kansas	2.0–9.0	2,000	25,000
Kentucky[1]	2.0–6.0	3,000	8,000
Louisiana	2.0–6.0	10,000	50,000
Maine[3]	1.0–10.0	2,000	25,000
Maryland[1]	2.0–5.0	1,000	3,000
Massachusetts	5.0	Flat rate	
Michigan	4.6	Flat rate	
Minnesota[1,3]	1.0–9.9	310	16,800
Mississippi	3.0–5.0	5,000	10,000

State	TAXABLE INCOME RATES (range in percent)	TAXABLE INCOME BRACKETS Lowest: amount under	TAXABLE INCOME BRACKETS Highest: amount over
Missouri[1]	1.5–6.0	1,000[5]	9,000[5]
Montana[3]	2.0–11.0	1,300	46,400
Nebraska	2.0–5.9	1,800	27,000
New Hampshire	Very limited income tax		
New Jersey	2.0–3.5	20,000	50,000
New Mexico	1.8–8.5	5,200	41,600
New York[1]	2.0–8.5	1,000	14,000
North Carolina	3.0–7.0	2,000	10,000
North Dakota	2.67–12[7]	3,000[7]	50,000[7]
Ohio[1]	0.751–6.9	5,000	100,000
Oklahoma	0.5–6.0[8]	1,000[8]	7,500[8]
Oregon[3]	5.0–9.0	2,000	5,000
Pennsylvania[1]	2.1	Flat rate	
Rhode Island	23.46% of federal income tax liability		
South Carolina	3.0–7.0	4,000	10,000
Tennessee	Very limited income tax		
Utah	2.75–7.75	750	3,750
Vermont	25.8% of federal income tax liability		
Virginia	2.0–5.75	3,000	14,000
West Virginia	3.0–6.5	10,000	60,000
Wisconsin[3]	5.0–7.9	7,500	30,000

Note: Alaska, Florida, Nevada, South Dakota, Texas, Washington, and Wyoming have no state income tax. 1. States in which one or more local governments levy a local income tax. 2. Social Security (FICA) taxes are deducted from taxable income. 3. Indexed by an inflation factor. Income brackets shown are for 1986. Oregon and Wisconsin are scheduled to begin indexing in 1987. 4. Tax cannot reduce after-tax income of taxpayer to below $5,000. 5. FICA Taxes deductible when itemizing deductions. 6. No taxpayer is subject to tax if gross income is $3,000 or less ($1,500 married, filing separately). 7. Taxpayers have the option of paying a tax of 14% of the taxpayer's adjusted federal income tax liability or using the long form with a separate schedule; taxpayers using the long form may deduct federal income tax paid; a 10% surtax was also imposed in 1987. 8. These tax rates and brackets apply to single persons not deducting federal income tax. For individuals deducting federal income tax, rates range from 0.5% of the first $1,000 to 17% on income over $49,000. **Source:** U.S. Bureau of the Census, *Statistical Abstract of the United States 1989* (1989).

> *"In this world, nothing can be said to be certain, except death and taxes."*
>
> —Ben Franklin

FEDERAL EXPENDITURES BY STATE, PER CAPITA, AND RANK, 1988

State	Total (millions)	Per capita	Per capita rank
Alabama	$ 14,354	$ 3,478.05	20
Alaska	2,664	5,193.29	3
Arizona	12,248	3,533.83	19
Arkansas	7,485	3,090.32	37
California	102,366	3,634.14	16
Colorado	12,973	3,943.09	11
Connecticut	13,770	4,248.59	8
Delaware	2,088	3,163.38	33
District of Columbia	15,257	24,607.95	—
Florida	42,997	3,473.95	21
Georgia	18,451	2,882.46	42
Hawaii	4,957	4,535.16	5
Idaho	3,407	3,410.25	24
Illinois	31,962	2,768.68	46
Indiana	14,807	2,655.99	49
Iowa	9,697	3,421.56	23
Kansas	8,995	3,616.69	17
Kentucky	10,686	2,871.82	43
Louisiana	12,682	2,869.28	44
Maine	4,025	3,337.50	27
Maryland	23,745	5,113.00	4
Massachusetts	25,079	4,271.64	7
Michigan	23,651	2,543.17	50
Minnesota	13,840	3,214.21	31
Mississippi	9,895	3,766.58	12
Missouri	21,559	4,195.18	9
Montana	2,929	3,643.16	15
Nebraska	5,935	3,707.09	14
Nevada	3,429	3,235.29	30
New Hampshire	3,198	2,915.56	41
New Jersey	23,984	3,106.74	36
New Mexico	8,685	5,751.54	2
New York	60,677	3,390.17	26
North Carolina	17,743	2,718.82	47
North Dakota	2,881	4,344.84	6
Ohio	33,521	3,083.27	38
Oklahoma	10,762	3,298.33	28
Oregon	8,237	3,005.08	39
Pennsylvania	39,569	3,289.98	29
Rhode Island	3,567	3,584.77	18
South Carolina	10,934	3,130.28	34
South Dakota	2,691	3,763.94	13
Tennessee	15,705	3,192.81	32
Texas	49,485	2,949.05	40
Utah	5,750	3,400.39	25
Vermont	1,550	2,787.83	45
Virginia	35,698	5,953.71	1
Washington	18,306	3,963.30	10
West Virginia	5,861	3,110.86	35
Wisconsin	13,127	2,702.19	48
Wyoming	1,626	3,452.84	22
American Samoa	62	1,629.92	—
Guam	685	5,266.84	—
Northern Mariana Islands	61	3,059.90	—
Puerto Rico	6,231	1,892.77	—
Virgin Islands	239	2,253.27	—
Undistributed	27,361	—	—
U.S. Total	**$884,131**	**$3,545.13**	**—**

Source: U.S. Bureau of the Census, *Federal Expenditures by State for Fiscal Year 1988* (1989).

EXCISE TAXES, BY STATE, 1987

State	General sales and gross receipts (%)	Cigarettes (cents per package)	Gasoline (cents per gallon)
Alabama	4.0%[1,2]	16.5¢	11.0¢
Alaska	N.A.	16.0	8.0
Arizona	5.0[1]	15.0	16.0
Arkansas	4.0[1,2]	21.0	13.5
California	4.75[1]	10.0	9.0
Colorado	3.0[1]	20.0	18.0
Connecticut	7.5	26.0	19.0
Delaware	N.A.	14.0	16.0
District of Columbia	6.0	17.0	15.5
Florida	5.0	24.0	4.0
Georgia	3.0[1,2]	12.0	7.5[3]
Hawaii	4.0[2]	(4)	11.0[5]
Idaho	5.0[2]	18.0	14.5
Illinois	5.0	20.0	13.0
Indiana	5.0	15.5	14.0
Iowa	4.0[1]	26.0	16.0
Kansas	4.0[1,2]	24.0	11.0
Kentucky	5.0[1]	3.0	15.0
Louisiana	4.0	16.0	16.0
Maine	5.0	28.0	14.0
Maryland	5.0	13.0	18.5
Massachusetts	5.0	26.0	11.0
Michigan	4.0	21.0	15.0
Minnesota	6.0[1]	38.0	17.0
Mississippi	6.0[2]	18.0	15.0
Missouri	4.225[1,2]	13.0	11.0
Montana	N.A.	16.0	20.0
Nebraska	4.0[1]	27.0	17.6
Nevada	5.75[1]	20.0	14.25
New Hampshire	N.A.	17.0	14.0
New Jersey	6.0	27.0	8.0
New Mexico	4.75[1]	15.0	14.0
New York	4.0[1]	21.0	8.0
North Carolina	3.0[1,2]	2.0	15.5
North Dakota	5.5	27.0	17.0
Ohio	5.0[1]	18.0	14.7
Oklahoma	4.0[1,2]	23.0	16.0
Oregon	N.A.	27.0	12.0
Pennsylvania	6.0	18.0	12.0
Rhode Island	6.0	25.0	15.0
South Carolina	5.0[2]	7.0	15.0
South Dakota	5.0[1,2]	23.0	13.0
Tennessee	5.5[1,2]	13.0	17.0
Texas	5.25[1]	20.5	15.0
Utah	5.094[1]	23.0	19.0
Vermont	4.0	17.0	13.0
Virginia	3.5[1,2]	2.5	17.5
Washington	6.5[2]	31.0	18.0
West Virginia	5.0	17.0	10.5
Wisconsin	5.0[1]	30.0	20.0
Wyoming	3.0[1,2]	8.0	8.0

Notes: N.A. = not applicable. Both food and prescription drugs are exempt from sales tax unless otherwise noted. 1. Local sales tax rates are additional. 2. Only prescription drugs are exempt from sales tax. 3. An additional tax is levied at the rate of 3% of the retail sales price, less the current 7.5 per gallon. 4. Tax is 40% of the wholesale price. 5. Combined state and county rates are: Hawaii 16.0, Honolulu 22.5, Kauai 15.0, and Maui 19.0. **Source:** Advisory Commission on Intergovernmental Relations, *Significant Features of Fiscal Federalism, 1988 Edition.*

STATES RANKED ACCORDING TO SELECTED TAX AMOUNTS, 1987

State	Total tax collections (thousands)	Total tax	PER CAPITA General sales tax	Personal income tax	State	Total tax collections (thousands)	Total tax	PER CAPITA General sales tax	Personal income tax
Ala.	$ 3,222,201 (26)	$ 789.17 (40)	$216.45 (42)	$217.44 (35)	Mont.	591,001 (46)	730.53 (47)	N.A. (—)	240.64 (30)
Alaska	1,062,391 (41)	2,023.60 (1)	N.A. (—)	0.81 (44)	N.C.	6,235,163 (11)	972.27 (22)	227.04 (40)	400.11 (11)
Ariz.	3,469,477 (23)	1,024.65 (19)	299.68 (25)	225.08 (33)	N.Dak.	573,465 (47)	853.37 (33)	288.36 (32)	119.27 (40)
Ark.	1,889,066 (33)	791.07 (39)	457.01 (6)	224.17 (34)	Nebr.	1,203,344 (39)	754.92 (44)	245.01 (38)	225.72 (32)
Calif.	35,790,750 (1)	1,293.81 (8)	395.28 (12)	501.54 (6)	Nev.	1,118,326 (40)	1,110.55 (14)	549.15 (4)	N.A. (—)
Colo.	2,561,477 (29)	777.15 (41)	218.04 (41)	313.92 (19)	N.H.	562,712 (48)	532.37 (50)	N.A. (—)	8.21 (43)
Conn.	4,359,175 (19)	1,357.58 (6)	567.74 (3)	145.12 (38)	N.J.	9,491,417 (9)	1,237.15 (11)	379.53 (14)	339.33 (16)
Del.	989,298 (43)	1,536.18 (3)	N.A. (—)	670.32 (3)	N.Mex.	1,574,692 (36)	1,049.79 (18)	466.38 (5)	161.75 (37)
Fla.	9,846,189 (7)	818.95 (37)	455.65 (7)	N.A. (—)	N.Y.	24,676,346 (2)	1,384.37 (5)	285.99 (34)	699.97 (1)
Ga.	5,323,689 (16)	855.62 (32)	279.54 (35)	345.41 (15)	Ohio	9,717,146 (8)	901.07 (28)	313.70 (22)	298.40 (20)
Hawaii	1,697,424 (35)	1,567.34 (2)	754.87 (1)	501.47 (7)	Okla.	2,669,188 (27)	815.77 (38)	187.58 (44)	207.47 (36)
Idaho	829,698 (44)	831.36 (35)	298.49 (27)	265.87 (24)	Oreg.	2,235,073 (30)	820.51 (36)	N.A. (—)	536.57 (5)
Ill.	10,429,524 (5)	900.49 (29)	294.02 (28)	267.24 (23)	Pa.	11,378,764 (3)	953.31 (24)	299.00 (26)	230.38 (31)
Ind.	4,774,190 (18)	863.17 (30)	407.17 (10)	263.04 (25)	R.I.	1,050,144 (42)	1,065.05 (17)	355.79 (16)	364.10 (12)
Iowa	2,662,110 (28)	939.35 (26)	291.50 (30)	337.06 (17)	S.C.	3,339,515 (25)	975.04 (21)	396.05 (11)	294.58 (22)
Kans.	2,085,490 (31)	842.28 (34)	293.55 (29)	256.25 (26)	S.Dak.	416,386 (50)	587.29 (49)	289.82 (31)	N.A. (—)
Ky.	3,520,409 (22)	944.57 (25)	239.35 (39)	247.11 (28)	Tenn.	3,603,331 (21)	742.19 (45)	410.78 (9)	14.03 (42)
La.	3,448,641 (24)	773.06 (42)	266.69 (37)	98.33 (41)	Tex.	11,227,796 (4)	668.76 (48)	274.07 (36)	N.A. (—)
Maine	1,288,480 (38)	1,085.49 (15)	370.18 (15)	356.54 (13)	Utah	1,438,325 (37)	856.15 (31)	332.86 (19)	316.47 (18)
Mass.	8,463,874 (10)	1,445.58 (4)	318.83 (20)	679.59 (2)	Va.	5,526,557 (15)	936.07 (27)	186.77 (45)	414.26 (10)
Md.	5,204,499 (17)	1,147.63 (13)	287.20 (33)	480.94 (8)	Vt.	537,905 (49)	981.58 (20)	199.73 (43)	295.57 (21)
Mich.	9,857,122 (6)	1,071.43 (16)	307.45 (24)	348.75 (14)	Wash.	5,639,369 (13)	1,242.70 (10)	723.75 (2)	N.A. (—)
Minn.	5,546,422 (14)	1,306.27 (7)	345.88 (17)	544.52 (4)	Wis.	5,673,577 (12)	1,180.27 (12)	343.65 (18)	462.67 (9)
Miss.	1,943,388 (32)	740.34 (46)	386.82 (13)	120.17 (39)	W.Va.	1,830,168 (34)	964.77 (23)	416.66 (8)	254.19 (27)
Mo.	3,942,295 (20)	772.54 (43)	318.25 (21)	244.47 (29)	Wyo.	631,669 (45)	1,289.12 (9)	307.51 (23)	N.A. (—)
					All states	$247,148,658 (—)	$1,018.00 (—)	$328.77 (—)	$313.20 (—)

Note: N.A. = not applicable.   **Source:** U.S. Dept. of Commerce press release, 1988.

STATE GOVERNMENT TAX COLLECTIONS, 1987 (millions of dollars)

State	Total[1]	General sales and gross receipts	Motor fuels	Alcohol and tobacco	Individual income	Corporation net income	Motor vehicle and operators' licenses
Alabama	$ 3,222	$ 884	$ 263	$ 169	$ 888	$ 162	$ 113
Alaska	1,062	N.A.	32	22	N.A.	141	18
Arizona	3,469	1,547	310	92	762	199	187
Arkansas	1,889	716	206	87	535	116	77
California	35,791	10,935	1,248	400	13,874	4,759	1,019
Colorado	2,561	719	292	103	1,035	124	82
Connecticut	4,359	1,823	254	122	466	680	197
Delaware	989	N.A.	33	17	432	121	44
District of Columbia	1,915	379	25	17	507	169	20
Florida	9,846	5,478	716	776	N.A.	596	422
Georgia	5,324	1,739	386	208	2,149	449	87
Hawaii	1,697	818	48	54	543	77	18
Idaho	830	298	82	22	265	47	36
Illinois	10,430	3,405	741	319	3,095	862	614
Indiana	4,774	2,252	397	110	1,455	236	89
Iowa	2,662	826	252	91	955	150	188
Kansas	2,085	727	157	107	634	137	80
Kentucky	3,520	892	294	66	921	267	147
Louisiana	3,449	1,190	357	131	439	191	85
Maine	1,288	439	97	73	423	68	53
Maryland	5,204	1,302	328	95	2,181	270	94
Massachusetts	8,464	1,867	310	252	3,979	1,204	179
Michigan	9,857	2,829	718	360	3,208	1,645	354
Minnesota	5,546	1,469	357	135	2,312	423	274
Mississippi	1,943	1,015	128	91	315	103	64
Missouri	3,942	1,624	215	108	1,248	235	197
Montana	591	N.A.	85	26	195	35	32
Nebraska	1,203	391	162	51	360	67	54
Nevada	1,118	553	98	34	N.A.	N.A.	53
New Hampshire	563	N.A.	84	43	9	152	48
New Jersey	9,491	2,912	344	269	2,603	1,088	350
New Mexico	1,575	700	108	36	243	99	40
New York	24,676	5,098	496	563	12,477	2,143	480
North Carolina	6,235	1,456	554	148	2,566	566	238
North Dakota	573	194	55	17	80	33	33
Ohio	9,717	3,383	642	251	3,218	475	352
Oklahoma	2,669	614	205	127	679	84	228
Oregon	2,235	N.A.	150	89	1,462	136	183
Pennsylvania	11,379	3,569	651	368	2,750	1,016	446
Rhode Island	1,050	351	53	37	359	88	27
South Carolina	3,340	1,356	262	137	1,009	190	80
South Dakota	416	205	57	22	N.A.	24	35
Tennessee	3,603	1,994	489	145	68	299	145
Texas	11,228	4,601	1,273	697	N.A.	N.A.	746
Utah	1,438	559	127	33	532	61	45
Vermont	538	109	40	27	162	38	34
Virginia	5,527	1,103	439	112	2,446	321	249
Washington	5,639	3,284	449	235	N.A.	N.A.	154
West Virginia	1,830	790	162	42	482	90	68
Wisconsin	5,674	1,652	419	174	2,224	471	163
Wyoming	632	151	35	6	N.A.	N.A.	37
Total U.S.	**$247,149**	**$79,819**	**$15,661**	**$7,696**	**$76,038**	**$20,740**	**$9,037**

Note: N.A. = not applicable.   1. Includes amount for types of taxes not shown separately.   **Source:** U.S. Bureau of the Census, *Statistical Abstract of the United States 1989* (1989).

ESTIMATED STATE AND LOCAL TAXES PAID BY A FAMILY OF FOUR IN SELECTED LARGE CITIES, BY INCOME LEVEL, 1987

City	TOTAL TAXES PAID, BY GROSS FAMILY-INCOME LEVEL					City	TOTAL TAXES PAID, BY GROSS FAMILY-INCOME LEVEL				
	$20,000	$35,000	$50,000	$75,000	$100,000		$20,000	$35,000	$50,000	$75,000	$100,000
Albuquerque, N.Mex.	$1,504	$2,594	$4,056	$ 6,448	$ 8,996	Louisville, Ky.	1,800	3,104	4,610	6,733	8,652
Atlanta, Ga.	1,897	3,388	5,263	7,946	10,365	Memphis, Tenn.	1,601	2,366	3,222	4,536	5,788
Baltimore, Md.	2,148	3,767	5,669	8,525	11,236	Milwaukee, Wis.	2,542	4,671	7,009	10,620	13,946
Bridgeport, Conn.	2,742	4,374	6,514	9,566	12,019	Newark, N.J.	2,706	4,711	6,906	10,474	13,707
Burlington, Vt.	1,570	2,709	4,225	7,035	9,895	New York City, N.Y.	1,913	3,932	6,462	10,199	13,950
Charleston, W.Va.	1,560	2,695	4,393	7,043	9,565	Norfolk, Va.	1,619	2,757	4,283	7,051	8,542
Charlotte, N.C.	1,663	2,887	4,562	6,920	9,198	Omaha, Nebr.	1,642	2,714	4,237	6,648	8,977
Chicago, Ill.	1,707	2,821	4,150	6,008	7,748	Philadelphia, Pa.	2,527	4,173	5,799	8,446	10,924
Cleveland, Ohio	1,832	3,260	4,940	7,682	10,567	Portland, Maine	1,570	3,055	5,140	8,625	12,903
Columbia, S.C.	1,568	2,918	4,739	7,262	9,620	Portland, Oreg.	2,281	4,008	6,163	9,558	12,643
Des Moines, Iowa	2,027	3,586	5,569	8,410	11,041	Providence, R.I.	2,297	3,865	6,168	9,840	13,224
Detroit, Mich.	2,400	4,102	6,139	9,280	12,262	St. Louis, Mo.	1,557	2,607	3,998	5,816	7,213
Honolulu, Hawaii	1,905	3,380	5,240	8,012	10,700	Salt Lake City, Utah	1,866	3,304	5,168	7,766	10,279
Indianapolis, Ind.	1,648	2,672	3,936	5,831	7,441	Sioux Falls, S.Dak.	1,912	2,903	3,991	5,558	6,950
Jackson, Miss.	1,508	2,685	4,300	6,546	8,529	Washington, D.C.	2,086	3,797	5,623	8,726	11,935

Notes: Data based on an average family of four—two wage earners and two school-age children—owning their own house and living in a city where taxes apply. Comprises state and local sales, income, auto, and real estate taxes.
Source: Government of the District of Columbia, Dept. of Finance and Revenue, *Tax Rates and Tax Burdens in the District of Columbia: A Nationwide Comparison,* (1988).

UNITED STATES TERRITORIES AND POSSESSIONS

The provisions of the Northwest Ordinance of 1787 established the system under which U.S. territories can achieve statehood. In order to elect a territorial legislature and send a nonvoting delegate to Congress, a territory must contain 5,000 inhabitants of voting age; it is eligible for statehood when the population numbers 60,000. Today the United States administers a number of overseas territories and commonwealth states under a variety of circumstances.

In 1947 the United Nations created the Trust Territory of the Pacific Islands—comprising what are known today as the Federated States of Micronesia (FSM), the Republic of the Marshall Islands, the Commonwealth of the Marshall Islands, and the Republic of Palau. Only Palau is still administered as a Trust Territory; a compact of free association with the United States has failed to win a 75 percent majority plebiscite. The Marshall Islands and FSM are now self-governing states with close ties to the United States defined by a compact of free association. Under the compact their defense is the responsibility of the United States, they receive extensive U.S. economic assistance, and their conduct of foreign affairs must be consistent with the terms of the compact. The Northern Marianas are subject to provisions of U.S. law, except regarding customs, minimum wages, immigration, and taxation. Its people are, as a rule, U.S. citizens.

American Samoa came under U.S. control in 1889, and Guam and Puerto Rico were ceded to the United States by Spain after the Spanish-American War in 1899. American Samoa is an unorganized, unincorporated territory with its own government but under the plenary authority of the Department of the Interior. Guam is an unincorporated, organized territory; the Guam Commonwealth Act has been approved by the people of Guam and is currently before Congress. Puerto Rico is a U.S. commonwealth. The Virgin Islands of the United States (USVI), is an unincorporated, organized territory. American Samoa, Guam, and the USVI have nonvoting representatives in Congress, and Puerto Rico is represented by a nonvoting resident commissioner. Residents of American Samoa are U.S. nationals, and those of Guam, Puerto Rico, and the USVI, U.S. citizens.

In addition to these territories, the United States has a number of possessions whose population is too small to make local government practicable, or which are uninhabited altogether.

American Samoa
Territory of American Samoa
Geography Location: seven islands (Tutuila, Tau, Olosega, Ofu, Aunun, Rose, Swain's) in southern central Pacific Ocean. **Boundaries:** Hawaii about 2,300 mi. (3,700 km) to NE, Cook Islands to E, Tonga to SW, Western Samoa to W. **Total land area:** 75.2 sq. mi. (194.8 sq km). **Coastline:** 72 mi. (116 km). **Comparative area:** slightly larger than Washington, D.C. **Land use:** 10% arable land; 10% permanent crops; 0% meadows and pastures; 70% forest and woodland; 10% other. **Major cities:** (1980 census) Pago Pago (capital) 3,075.

People Population: 39,254 (1988). **Nationality:** noun—American Samoan(s); adjective—American Samoan. **Ethnic groups:** mostly Samoan (Polynesian). **Languages:** Samoan (closely related to Hawaiian and other Polynesian languages) and English; most people are bilingual. **Religions:** 50% Christian Congregationalist, 20% Roman Catholic, 30% mostly Protestant denominations and other.

Government Type: unincorporated and unorganized territory of U.S. **Constitution:** ratified 1966. **National holiday:** Flag Day, Apr.

17. **Heads of government:** A. P. Lutai, governor (since Nov. 1984). **Structure:** executive—governor is popularly elected to four-year term and exercises authority under direction of U.S. secretary of the interior; legislative—bicameral legislature (Fono) with 18-member Senate chosen by county councils to serve four-year terms and House of Representatives with 20 members popularly elected to serve two-year terms, plus nonvoting delegate from Swain's Island; judicial—high court with chief justice and associate justices appointed by U.S. secretary of the interior.

Economy Monetary unit: U.S. dollar. **Budget:** (1986 est.) *income:* $62.9 mil.; *expend.:* $67.6 mil. **GNP:** $55.8 mil., $1,845 per capita (1982). **Chief crops:** bananas, coconuts, vegetables, taro, breadfruit. **Livestock:** pigs. **Natural resources:** pumice and pumicite. **Major industries:** tuna canneries (largely dependent on foreign supplies of raw tuna), tourism. **Labor force:** 10,000 (1986 est.); 45% government, 20% tuna canneries, 35% other; 13% unemployment. **Exports:** $253.6 mil. (f.o.b., 1986); 96% canned tuna, 3% pet food, 1% fish meal, shark fins, other. **Imports:** $313.2 mil. (c.i.f., 1986); 45% petroleum products, 17% food, 8% jewelry, 7% machines and motor vehicles, 5% building materials, 18% other. **Major trading partners:** (1981) *exports:* 99.6% U.S.; *imports:* 74% U.S., 12% Japan, 6% New Zealand, 8% other.

American Samoa consists of seven islands between 14° and 15° south, and 168° and 171° west. First peopled by Polynesians in the first millennium B.C., the islands had as their first European visitor Louis Antoine de Bougainville, who visited in 1768 and called them the "Islands of the Navigators," in recognition of the islanders' seamanship. American whalers and missionaries began arriving in the 1830s, and the United States secured trading privileges by treaty in 1878. In 1889 the United States, Britain, and Germany established tripartite control of the islands. After 10 years of warring among the islanders, the British withdrew their claim, and Germany and the United States divided responsibility for the islands along longitude 171° west. The high chiefs of Tutuila ceded the islands of Tutuila and Aunun to the United States in 1900, and the high chiefs of the Manu'a islands ceded those of Tau, Ofu, Olosega, and Rose in 1904. Swain's Island became part of American Samoa in 1925.

Administered by the U.S. Department of the Interior since 1904, American Samoa is an unincorporated and unorganized territory, and there is no congressional intent to grant statehood to the island. American Samoans will reconsider their relationship with the United States in 1994. The people have their own Constitution and elect their own governor and representatives to the Fono, the bicameral legislature; but the Justices of the high court are appointed by the secretary of the interior. The population is more than 80 percent rural.

Baker and Howland Islands

About 1,900 miles south-southwest of Hawaii and 1,000 miles west of Jarvis Island are Baker and Howland islands (0°48′N, 176°38′W) and Howland Island (0°14′N, 176°28′W, 40 mi. north of Baker). Discovered in 1842, the two coral atolls were worked for guano until about 1890. Great Britain claimed them in 1889, but the United States made them territories in 1935 and sent colonists to them. With an area of about 1 square mile each, neither is inhabited today.

Guam
Territory of Guam

Geography Location: southernmost and largest of Mariana Islands in western North Pacific Ocean. **Boundaries:** Tokyo, Japan, about 1,350 mi. (2,170 km) to N; Honolulu, Hawaii 3,300 mi. (5,300 km) to E; Federated States of Micronesia to S; Philippines to W across Philippine Sea. **Total land area:** 209 sq. mi. (541 sq km). **Coastline:** undetermined. **Comparative area:** slightly more than 3 times size of Washington, D.C. **Land use:** 11% arable land; 11% permanent crops; 15% meadows and pastures; 18% forest and woodland; 45% other. **Major cities:** Agaña (capital), 881 (1980).

People Population: 130,266 (1988). **Nationality:** noun—Guamanian(s); adjective—Guamanian. **Ethnic groups:** 50% Chamorro, 25% Filipino, 10% Caucasian, 15% Chinese, Japanese, Korean, other. **Languages:** English and Chamorro; most people bilingual; Japanese also widely spoken. **Religions:** 98% Roman Catholic, 2% other.

Government Type: organized, unincorporated territory of U.S. **Constitution:** Organic Act of Aug. 1, 1950. **National holiday:** Guam Discovery Day, first Monday in March. **Heads of government:** Peter Ada, governor (since 1986). **Structure:** executive—governor elected to four-year term; legislative—Senate has 21 members elected for two-year terms; judicial—U.S. District Court, Guam Superior Court.

Economy Monetary unit: U.S. dollar. **Bud-**

get: (1982) *income:* $277.0 mil.; *expend.:* $450.6 mil. **GNP:** undetermined. **Chief crops:** fruits, vegetables, eggs, copra; relatively undeveloped with most food imported. **Livestock:** poultry, pigs, cattle. **Natural resources:** fishing (largely undeveloped), tourism (especially from Japan). **Major industries:** U.S. military, tourism, petroleum refining. **Labor force:** 42,000 (1986); 45% government, 55% other; 6.1% unemployment. **Exports:** $39 mil. (f.o.b., 1983); mostly transshipments to U.S., Northern Mariana Islands, and Federated States of Micronesia; refined petroleum and petroleum products, copra, fish. **Imports:** $61 mil. (c.i.f., 1983); mostly crude petroleum and petroleum products, food, manufactured goods. **Major trading partners: exports:** 60% U.S., 40% other; *imports:* 75% U.S., 25% other.

Guam was inhabited by Chamorros from the Malay Peninsula as early as 1500 B.C.; the first European to stop at Guam was Ferdinand Magellan in 1521. Spanish colonization began with the arrival of Jesuit missionaries in 1668. By 1700 pestilence and insurrection had reduced the Chamorro population from 50,000 to about 2,000. Guam was ceded to the United States in 1899. In 1941 it was occupied by Japan—the only inhabited U.S. territory to be seized by enemy forces during World War II. It was retaken by the Americans in 1944, and in 1950 it received its first nonmilitary administration in more than 200 years. Though Guam is unincorporated, the congressionally approved Guam Organic Act provides for a republican form of government with executive, legislative, and judicial branches. The Guam Commonwealth Act has been approved by plebiscite and is awaiting congressional ratification. Although Chamorros represent a significant portion of the population, Guam is a multiethnic state.

Jarvis, Kingman, and Palmyra

Jarvis Island (0°23′S, 160°02′W; about 1,510 mi. S of Hawaii), Kingman Reef (6°24′N, 162°22′W; about 1,070 mi. SSW of Hawaii), and Palmyra Atoll (5°52′N, 162°05′W; about 1,100 mi. SSW of Hawaii) are in the Line Island group. Discovered in 1798, Kingman Reef was annexed by the United States in 1922 and used as an aviation station during the 1930s. Discovered in 1802, Palmyra Atoll consists of about 50 islets with a combined area of 4 square miles. It was annexed by the Kingdom of Hawaii in 1862, by Great Britain in 1889, and claimed by the United States in 1912. Privately owned, it is administered by the Department of the Navy, as is Kingman Reef. Jarvis Island was claimed by the United States in 1857, annexed by Great Britain in 1889, and reclaimed by the United States in 1935. Its rich guano deposits were worked by U.S. and British companies in the late 19th century.

Johnston Atoll

Geography Location: Johnston Island and Sand Island (uninhabited) in central Pacific Ocean. **Boundaries:** Honolulu, Hawaii, about 700 mi. (1,130 km) to NE; Marshall Islands to

SW. **Total land area:** 1.1 sq. mi. (2.8 sq km). **Coastline:** 6.21 mi. (10 km). **Comparative area:** about 4.7 times size of the Mall in Washington, D.C. **Land use:** 0% arable land; 0% permanent crops; 0% meadows and pastures; 0% forest and woodland; 100% other. **Major cities:** none.

People Population: 1,000 (1987); all U.S. government personnel and contractors.

Government Type unincorporated territory of U.S.

Johnston Atoll (16°45′N, 169°32′W; 820 mi. SW of Hawaii) includes Johnston and Sand islands, with a total area of 1.5 square miles. Claimed by the United States in 1858, they are manned and administered by the Department of the Air Force.

Midway Islands

Geography Location: Sand Island and Eastern Island in northern Pacific Ocean. **Boundaries:** Hawaii about 1,150 mi. (1,850 km) to SE, Marshall Islands to SW. **Total land area:** 2.0 sq. mi. (5.2 sq km). **Coastline:** 9.3 mi. (15 km). **Comparative area:** about nine times size of the Mall in Washington, D.C. **Land use:** 0% arable land; 0% permanent crops; 0% meadows and pastures; 0% forest and woodland; 100% other. **Major cities:** none.

People Population: 1,500 (1987). **Nationality:** noun—Midway Islander(s); adjective—Midway Island. **Languages:** English. **Religions:** Christianity.

Government Type: unincorporated territory of U.S.

Economy Monetary unit: U.S. dollar. **Major industries:** support of U.S. naval air facility. **Labor force:** 200 (1980).

Midway (28°13′N, 177°26′W) consists of Midway Atoll, Eastern Island, and Sand Island. Although they are part of the Leeward Islands—the westernmost islands of the Hawaiian chain—they are not part of the state of Hawaii. They were the site of the Battle of Midway, June 1942, a turning point in the Pacific theater of World War II. Today they are administered by the Department of the Navy, and there is a naval air station on Midway.

Navassa

Located in the Caribbean between the islands of Jamaica and Haiti, Navassa was claimed by the U.S. in 1856. It is uninhabited except for a lighthouse under U.S. Coast Guard administration.

Northern Mariana Islands
Commonwealth of the Northern Mariana Islands

Geography Location: 16 islands in western central Pacific Ocean. **Boundaries:** Japan to N; Honolulu, Hawaii, about 3,300 mi. (5,300 km) to E; Guam to S; Philippines to W across Philippine Sea. **Total land area:** 293 sq. mi. (759 sq km). **Coastline:** undetermined. **Comparative area:** slightly more than 2.5 times size of Washington, D.C. **Land use:** 1% arable land;

N.A. % permanent crops; 19% meadows and pastures; N.A. % forest and woodland; N.A. % other. **Major cities:** (1985) Saipan (capital) 17,182.

People Population: 20,591 (1988). **Nationality:** undetermined. **Ethnic groups:** Chamorro majority, Carolinians, other Micronesians; Spanish, German, Japanese admixtures. **Languages:** English, Chamorro, Carolinian. **Religions:** Christian with Roman Catholic majority; some traditional beliefs.

Government Type: commonwealth. **Constitution:** Covenant Agreement effective Nov. 3, 1986. **National holiday:** Commonwealth Day, Jan. 8. **Heads of government:** Pedro P. Tenorio, governor (since 1978). **Structure:** executive—governor elected by popular vote; legislative—bicameral legislature (nine-member Senate elected for four-year term, 15-member House of Representatives elected for two-year term); judiciary—U.S. District Court, Commonwealth Trial Court, Commonwealth Appeals Court.

Economy Monetary unit: U.S. dollar. **Budget:** undetermined. **GNP:** $165 mil., $9,170 per capita (1982). **Chief crops:** coffee, coconuts, fruits, tobacco. **Livestock:** cattle, pigs. **Natural resources:** N.A. **Major industries:** tourism, construction, light industry, handicrafts. **Labor force:** 8,700 (1982 est.). **Exports:** vegetables, beef, pork. **Imports:** undetermined. **Major trading partners:** undetermined.

Running north from the island of Guam across a 600-mile-long archipelago in the Pacific Island group known as Micronesia, the 14 islands of the Marianas (CNMI) were originally settled by Pacific argonauts as early as 1500 B.C. Ferdinand Magellan landed at Saipan in 1521, introducing Western culture to the region. The Spanish took control of the archipelago in 1565 and ruled until 1898, when Germany took over the islands. After World War I, the League of Nations mandated the Marianas to Japan, which developed extensive sugar-processing works on Saipan. Allied forces took the Marianas in 1944. In 1947 the islands were included in the UN Trust Territory of the Pacific and placed under U.S. administration. In 1976 the CNMI adopted its own Constitution. A mutually approved *Covenant to Establish a Commonwealth* was implemented by the Marianas and the United States in 1986.

The CNMI benefits substantially from U.S. assistance. A seven-year agreement to end in 1992 allocates $288 million for development, government operations, and other programs, and the CNMI is also eligible for other federal programs provided to the 50 states. Tourism—which has registered a yearly increase of 7.5 percent since 1980—accounts for approximately 37 percent of the island's gross product. The government is the largest employer.

Trust Territory of the Pacific Islands
(Republic of Palau)
Geography Location: more than 200 islands, in a chain about 400 mi. (650 km) long, in western central Pacific Ocean. **Boundaries:** Japan to N, Guam 720 mi. (1,160 km) to NE, Federated States of Micronesia to E, island of New Guinea to S, Philippines to W across Philippine Sea. **Total land area:** 177 sq. mi. (458 sq km). **Coastline:** undetermined. **Comparative area:** slightly more than 2.5 times size of Washington, D.C. **Land use:** N.A. **Major cities:** Koror (capital—pop. N.A.).

People Population: 14,106 (1988). **Nationality:** noun—Palauan(s); adjective—Palauan. **Ethnic groups:** composite of Polynesian, Malayan, and Melanesian races. **Languages:** Palauan (official), English, Trukese dialect. **Religions:** predominantly Christian, mainly Roman Catholic.

Government Type: constitutional government, which signed Compact of Free Association with U.S. Jan. 10, 1986. **Constitution:** Jan. 11, 1981. **National holiday:** N.A. **Heads of government:** Lazarus Salii, president (since 1984). **Structure:** executive—president and vice president popularly elected; legislative—bicameral legislature (Olbiil Era Kelalu); judicial—Supreme Court headed by chief justice.

Economy Monetary unit: U.S. dollar. **Budget:** (1986 est.) $26 mil. **GDP:** $31.6 mil., $2,257 per capita (1986). **Chief crops:** subsistence-level production of coconut, copra, cassava, sweet potatoes. **Livestock:** N.A. **Natural resources:** forests, minerals (especially gold), marine products, deep seabed minerals. **Major industries:** tourism; craft items in shell, wood, and pearl; some commercial fishing and agriculture. **Labor force:** about 20.2% unemployment (1986). **Exports:** $0.5 mil. (f.o.b.,1986). **Imports:** $27.2 mil. (c.i.f., 1986). **Major trading partners:** *exports:* U.S., Japan; *imports:* U.S.

The first inhabitants of Palau (or Belau) probably arrived from Indonesia and the Philippines about 1500 B.C. The first European to visit the area was Ferdinand Magellan, in 1521. However, it was the British who dominated trade to Palau until 1885, when Pope Leo XIII acknowledged Spain's claims to the Carolines. Spain controlled Palau from 1885 to 1899, when Palau was sold to Germany. The Germans introduced coconut planting and phosphate mining, and introduced sanitary measures that arrested the deadly epidemics of dysentery and influenza, which in 120 years reduced the population from 40,000 to 4,000.

Japan occupied Palau in 1914 and over the next 30 years, increased the mining, agriculture and fishing industries; in 1938 Palau became a closed military area and was the site of heavy fighting during World War II. Although Palau has had its own government and Constitution since 1980, because Palauans have not approved a Compact of Free Associa-

tion with the United States by the requisite 75 percent majority, Palau continues to be administered by the United States under the auspices of the UN Trusteeship Council. The most remote of U.S. Pacific dependencies, Palau is about 4,600 west-southwest of Hawaii, and 1,000 miles southeast of Manila.

Fisheries and tourism are the main industries, and Palau realizes substantial receipts from granting fishing rights to companies and associations from Japan, Taiwan, the Philippines, and the United States. In 1988 the United States provided $14.7 million in funds for government operations and a further $5.4 million for capital development.

Puerto Rico
Commonwealth of Puerto Rico
Geography Location: large island of Puerto Rico, together with Vieques, Culebra, and many smaller islands, in northeastern Caribbean Sea. **Boundaries:** Atlantic Ocean to N, Virgin Islands to E, Caribbean Sea to S, Dominican Republic 50 mi. (80 km) to W. **Total land area:** 3,459 sq. mi. (8,959 sq km). **Coastline:** undetermined. **Comparative area:** slightly less than three times size of Rhode Island. **Land use:** 8% arable land; 7% permanent crops; 38% meadows and pastures; 21% forest and woodland; 28% other; includes 4% irrigated. **Major cities:** (1980) San Juan (capital) 434,849; Bayamón 196,206; Ponce 189,046; Carolina 165,954; Caguas 117,959.

People Population: 3,358,879 (1988). **Nationality:** noun—Puerto Rican(s); adjective—Puerto Rican. **Ethnic groups:** almost entirely Hispanic. **Languages:** Spanish (official), English. **Religions:** mostly Christian, 85% Roman Catholic, 15% Protestant and other.

Government Type: commonwealth associated with U.S. **Constitution:** effective July 25, 1952. **National holiday:** Constitution Day, July 25. **Heads of government:** Rafael Hernandez Colón. **Structure:** executive—governor elected by direct vote to four-year term; legislative—bicameral legislature (Senate with 27 members, House of Representatives with 51 members, all elected by popular vote to four-year terms); judiciary—Supreme Court appointed by governor.

Economy Monetary unit: U.S. dollar. **Budget:** (1984) *income:* $3.8 bil.; *expend.:* $3.7 bil. **GNP:** $14.8 bil., $4,520 per capita (1985). **Chief crops:** sugarcane, coffee, bananas, yams, pineapples; more than 50% of food requirements are imported. **Livestock:** chickens, cattle, pigs. **Natural resources:** some copper and nickel; potential for onshore and offshore crude oil. **Major industries:** manufacturing, pharmaceuticals, chemicals. **Labor force:** 964,000 (1985); 19% government, 15% trade, 14% manufacturing, 4% agriculture, 27% other; 21% unemployment. **Exports:** $11.6 bil. (f.o.b., 1986). **Imports:** $10.1 bil. (c.i.f., 1986); chemicals, apparel, fish products, electronic products. **Major trading partners:** (1986) *exports:* 87% U.S.; *imports:* 60% U.S.

Initially peopled by Igneris and Taínos, Puerto Rico had as its first European visitor Christopher Columbus, in 1493. In 1508 Juan Ponce de Léon led the first European settlers to San Juan, and by 1514 the Taíno population had dropped from an estimated 30,000 to 4,000. In the 17th and 18th centuries, Puerto Rico was invaded by both English and Danish forces, and though San Juan was captured or burned several times, the Spanish maintained their control of the island.

The Spanish Constitution granted Puerto Ricans citizenship in 1812, but a revolution was put down in 1868. Spain granted Puerto Rico self-government in 1897, but this was repealed when sovereignty was transferred to the United States after the Spanish–American War. Despite early attempts to Americanize Puerto Rico, including an effort to make English the official language and granting citizenship in 1917, the Popular Democratic party, founded in 1938, brought about a change in political status from that of a U.S. colony to an autonomous commonwealth in 1952.

Governed under the Puerto Rican Federal Relations Act and a Constitution modeled on that of the United States, Puerto Rico is nonetheless an autonomous political entity in voluntary association with the United States. Despite dramatic increases in industrial development since the 1950s, Puerto Rico suffered from net outward migration until 1988.

Puerto Ricans remain divided between those who favor statehood and those who favor maintaining commonwealth status. (Those seeking independence are a vocal but small minority). How evenly divided islanders are on the issue can be seen in the results of the November 1988 election, in which pro-commonwealth Pres. Hernández Colón won only 48.7 percent of the vote, against the prostatehood Baltasar Corrada del Rio's 45.8 percent.

Virgin Islands
Virgin Islands of the United States
Geography **Location:** three main inhabited islands (St. Croix, St. Thomas, and St. John) and about 50 smaller islands, mostly uninhabited, in northeastern Caribbean Sea. **Boundaries:** British Virgin Islands to N, Netherlands Antilles to E, Caribbean Sea to S, Puerto Rico about 40 mi. (64 km) to W. **Total land area:** 137 sq. mi. (355 sq km). **Coastline:** undetermined. **Comparative area:** slightly less than twice size of Washington, D.C. **Land use:** 15% arable land; 6% permanent crops; 26% meadows and pastures; 6% forest and woodland; 47% other. **Major cities:** (1980 census) Charlotte Amalie (capital) 11,842.

People Population: 112,636 (1988). **Nationality:** noun—Virgin Islander(s); adjective—Virgin Islander. **Ethnic groups:** 74% West Indian (45% born in Virgin Islands, 29% born elsewhere in West Indies), 13% U.S. mainland, 5% Puerto Rican, 8% other; 80% black, 15% white, 5% other; 14% of Hispanic origin. **Languages:** English (official), Spanish, Creole. **Religions:** 42% Baptist, 34% Roman Catholic, 17% Episcopalian, 7% other.

Government Type: organized, unincorporated territory of U.S. **Constitution:** Revised Organic Act of July 22, 1954, serves as constitution. **National holiday:** Transfer Day (from Denmark to U.S.), Mar. 31. **Heads of government:** Alexander Farrelly, governor. **Structure:** executive—governor elected to four-year term; legislative—unicameral legislature (senate with 15 members elected to two-year terms); judiciary—two U.S. district courts.

Economy **Monetary unit:** U.S. dollar. **Budget:** (1986) *income:* $245 mil.; *expend.:* $280 mil. **GNP:** $1.0 bil., $9,030 per capita (1985). **Chief crops:** truck gardens, fruit, sorghum. **Livestock:** chickens, cattle, goats, sheep, pigs. **Natural resources:** sun, sand, sea, surf. **Major industries:** tourism, government service, petroleum refining. **Labor force:** 45,000 (1987); 3.5% unemployment. **Exports:** $3.4 bil. (f.o.b., 1985); 94% refined petroleum products to U.S. **Imports:** $3.7 bil. (c.i.f., 1985); 82% crude petroleum for refining. **Major trading partners:** *exports:* U.S.; *imports:* undetermined.

The Virgin Islands of the United States (USVI) consists of more than 50 islands located about 40 miles east of Puerto Rico and about 1,730 miles east-southeast of Miami. Excavations have revealed evidence of human habitation in the Virgin Islands (both British and U.S.) from as early as A.D. 100. By 1493, when Christopher Columbus landed on the islands—which he named Virgin Islands for the virgin martyr St. Ursula—they were inhabited by Carib Indians who were driven out by the Spanish in 1555.

In 1672 St. Thomas was settled by the Danish West India Company. The Danes laid claim to St. John in 1683 and purchased St. Croix from the French in 1773. The United States purchased the Virgin Islands from Denmark for $25 million in 1917, making them a territory under the jurisdiction of the navy. U.S. citizenship was granted in 1927, and the Department of the Interior assumed administration of the islands in 1931. The first governor elected by popular vote was installed in 1970, and an independent constitution was voted down by the electorate in 1979.

The primary industry is tourism, with annual receipts put at more than $135 million. The USVI has no known natural resources, and agriculture is restricted by the limited land space available and generally hilly terrain. Most food and other goods are imported, chiefly from the United States.

Wake Island
Geography **Location:** island in western Pacific Ocean. **Boundaries:** Hawaii to E, Marshall Islands to S, Guam about 1,280 mi. (2,060 km) to W. **Total land area:** 2.5 sq. mi. (6.5 sq km). **Coastline:** undetermined. **Comparative area:** about 11 times size of Washington, D.C. **Land use:** 0% arable land; 0% permanent crops; 0% meadows and pastures; 0% forest and woodland; 100% other. **Major cities:** none.

People Population: 302 (1988); no indigenous inhabitants; temporary population consists of U.S. Air Force personnel and about 225 U.S. and Thai contractors.

Government Type: unincorporated territory of U.S.

The Wake Island group (19°17′N, 166°36′E) includes Wake, Peale, and Wilkes islands. Acquired by the United States in 1898, Wake became a civil aviation station in the 1930s and was captured by the Japanese shortly after Pearl Harbor. It was retaken in 1944.

TERRITORIAL EXPANSION OF THE UNITED STATES AND ACQUISITIONS OF OTHER AREAS

Accession	Acquisition date	Gross area (land and water) Sq. mi.	Sq km
The 50 states	(X)	3,618,770	9,372,614
Territory in 1790[1]	(X)	891,364	2,308,623
Louisiana Purchase	1803	831,321	2,153,121
Purchase of Florida	1819	69,866	180,953
Texas	1845	384,958	997,041
Oregon	1846	283,439	734,107
Mexican Cession	1848	530,706	1,374,529
Gadsden Purchase	1853	29,640	76,768
Alaska	1867	591,004	1,530,700
Hawaii	1898	6,471	16,760
Other areas			
Puerto Rico	1898	3,515	9,104
Guam	1898	209	541
American Samoa	1899	77	199
Virgin Islands, U.S.	1917	132	342
Trust Territory of the Pacific Islands	1947	533[2]	1,380
Northern Mariana Is.	1947	184	477
All other	(X)	14	36
Total U.S. territory		**3,623,434**	**9,384,694**

Note: Boundaries of all U.S. territories listed here were indefinite, at least in part, at the time of acquisition. Area figures shown here represent precise determinations of specific territories that have been marked on maps, based on interpretations of the several treaties of cession, which are necessarily debatable. These determinations were made by a committee of representatives of various governmental agencies in 1912. Subsequently, these figures were adjusted to bring them into agreement with remeasurements made in 1980.   1. Includes that part of the drainage basin of the Red River of the North, south of the 49th parallel, sometimes considered part of the Louisiana Purchase.   2. Land area area only.
Source: U.S. Bureau of the Census; *Statistical Abstract of the United States 1989* (1989).

CITIES AND COUNTIES IN THE U.S.

Included here is basic information about population change, health, consumer prices, and government finances in major U.S. cities, metropolitan statistical areas, and counties. In addition there are brief descriptions and statistics for each of the 50 largest cities—from Albuquerque to Virginia Beach. Statistical sources include the U.S. Census Bureau's *City Government Finances in 1986–87*, *County and City Data Book 1988*, and the *Statistical Abstract of the United States 1989*, along with the Commerce Clearing House.

Cities in America

Since 1960 the growth of the urban population has occurred primarily in cities of under 250,000. In that year there were five cities of a million or more people; in 1986 there were eight. Over the same time period, the number of cities of between 500,000 and one million inhabitants declined from 16 to 15, while the number of cities of 250,000 to 500,000 inhabitants grew 23%, from 30 to 37. The number of cities with populations between 10,000 and 250,000 increased from 1,603 to 2,273, or 42%

More significant is the larger cities' dwindling share of the total urban population, which for cities of one million or more has declined from 19% in 1960 to 17% in 1986. Even though the number of cities above 250,000 has increased, their total share of population has fallen from 43% to 36%.

POPULATION CHANGE IN THE 50 LARGEST U.S. CITIES, 1980–86

Rank 1986	City	Population 1986	Population 1980	Rank 1980	Percent change	Rank 1986	City	Population 1986	Population 1980	Rank 1980	Percent change
1	New York, N.Y.	7,262,700	7,071,639	1	2.7%	26	Nashville, Tenn.	473,670	455,651	25	4.0
2	Los Angeles, Calif.	3,259,300	2,968,528	3	9.8	27	Austin, Tex.	466,550	372,564	35	25.2
3	Chicago, Ill.	3,009,530	3,005,072	2	0.2	28	Oklahoma City, Okla.	446,210	404,014	31	10.4
4	Houston, Tex.	1,728,910	1,611,382	5	7.3	29	Kansas City, Mo.	441,170	448,028	27	-1.5
5	Philadelphia, Pa.	1,642,900	1,688,210	4	-2.3	30	Fort Worth, Tex.	429,550	305,164	34	11.5
6	Detroit, Mich.	1,086,220	1,203,369	6	-9.7	31	St. Louis, Mo.	426,300	452,804	26	-5.9
7	San Diego, Calif.	1,015,190	875,538	8	16.0	32	Atlanta, Ga.	421,910	425,022	29	-0.7
8	Dallas, Tex.	1,003,520	904,599	7	10.9	33	Long Beach, Calif.	396,280	361,496	38	9.6
9	San Antonio, Tex.	914,350	810,353	9	12.8	34	Portland, Oreg.	387,870	396,666	32	-2.2
10	Phoenix, Ariz.	894,070	790,183	10	13.1	35	Pittsburgh, Pa.	387,490	423,960	30	-8.6
11	Baltimore, Md.	752,800	786,741	11	-4.3	36	Miami, Fla.	373,940	346,681	42	7.9
12	San Francisco, Calif.	749,000	678,974	13	10.3	37	Tulsa, Okla.	373,750	360,919	39	3.6
13	Indianapolis, Ind.	719,820	700,807	12	2.7	38	Honolulu, Hawaii	372,330	367,878	37	1.2
14	San Jose, Calif.	712,080	629,402	17	13.1	39	Cincinnati, Ohio	369,750	385,410	33	-4.0
15	Memphis, Tenn.	652,640	646,170	14	1.0	40	Albuquerque, N.Mex.	366,750	332,336	46	10.4
16	Washington, D.C.	626,000	638,432	15	-1.9	41	Tucson, Ariz.	358,850	338,636	45	6.0
17	Jacksonville, Fla.	610,030	540,920	22	12.8	42	Oakland, Calif.	356,960	339,337	44	5.2
18	Milwaukee, Wis.	605,090	636,298	16	-4.9	43	Minneapolis, Minn.	356,840	370,951	36	-3.8
19	Boston, Mass.	573,600	562,994	20	1.9	44	Charlotte, N.C.	352,070	326,330	48	7.9
20	Columbus, Ohio	566,030	565,032	19	0.2	45	Omaha, Nebr.	349,270	342,786	43	1.9
21	New Orleans, La.	554,500	557,927	21	-0.6	46	Toledo, Ohio	340,680	354,635	41	-3.9
22	Cleveland, Ohio	535,830	573,822	18	-6.6	47	Virginia Beach, Va.	333,400	262,199	56	27.2
23	Denver, Colo.	505,000	492,694	24	2.5	48	Buffalo, N.Y.	324,820	357,870	40	-9.2
24	El Paso, Tex.	491,800	425,259	28	15.6	49	Sacramento, Calif.	323,550	275,741	52	17.3
25	Seattle, Wash.	486,200	493,846	23	-1.5	50	Newark, N.J.	316,300	329,248	47	-3.9

Source: U.S. Bureau of the Census, *County and City Data Book 1988* (1988).

CITIES, BY POPULATION SIZE, 1960–86

Population size	NUMBER OF CITIES 1960	1970	1986	POPULATION (million) 1960	1970	1986	PERCENT OF TOTAL 1960	1970	1986
Total	**1,654**	**1,967**	**2,333**	**91.0**	**105.7**	**120.5**	**100.0%**	**100.0%**	**100.0%**
1 million +	5	6	8	17.5	18.8	20.0	19.2	17.8	16.6
500,000–1 million	16	20	15	11.1	13.0	10.0	12.2	12.3	8.3
250,000–500,000	30	30	37	10.8	10.5	13.3	11.8	9.9	11.0
100,000–250,000	79	97	122	11.4	13.9	17.9	12.5	13.1	14.9
50,000–100,000	180	232	286	12.5	16.2	19.6	13.7	15.3	16.3
25,000–50,000	366	455	563	12.7	15.7	19.4	14.0	14.9	16.1
10,000–25,000	978	1,127	1,302	15.1	17.6	20.4	16.5	16.7	16.9

Source: U.S. Bureau of the Census, *Statistical Abstract of the United States 1989* (1989).

25 FASTEST-GROWING MAJOR CITIES IN THE U.S., 1980–86, RANKED BY PERCENTAGE GROWTH

Rank	City	Population 1980	Population 1986	Percent growth	Rank	City	Population 1980	Population 1986	Percent growth
1	Mesa, Ariz.	162,011	251,430	55.2%	13	Scottsdale, Ariz.	88,622	111,140	25.4
2	Arlington, Tex.	161,872	249,770	54.3	14	Austin, Tex.	372,564	466,550	25.2
3	Portsmouth, Va.	72,331	111,000	53.5	15	Pomona, Calif.	92,742	115,540	24.6
4	Aurora, Colo.	158,588	217,990	37.5	16	Modesto, Calif.	106,963	132,940	24.3
5	Anchorage, Alaska	174,431	235,000	34.7	17	Stockton, Calif.	149,554	183,430	22.7
6	Bakersfield, Calif.	113,193	150,400	32.9	18	Laredo, Tex.	96,453	117,060	21.4
7	Glendale, Ariz.	97,172	125,800	29.5	19	Brownsville, Tex.	84,997	102,110	20.1
8	Ontario, Calif.	88,820	114,310	28.7	20	Oxnard, Calif.	110,710	130,800	18.1
9	Tempe, Ariz.	106,919	136,480	27.6	21	Sacramento, Calif.	275,740	303,550	17.5
10	Virginia Beach, Va.	262,199	333,400	27.2	22	Chesapeake, Va.	114,486	134,400	17.4
11	Garland, Tex.	138,857	176,510	27.1	23	Las Vegas, Nev.	164,730	193,240	17.3
12	Colorado Springs, Colo.	215,105	272,000	26.4	24	Irving, Tex.	109,943	128,530	16.9
					25	Fremont, Calif.	131,945	153,580	16.4

Note: Major cities with population of 100,000 or more (182 total). **Source:** U.S. Bureau of the Census, 1987.

25 MAJOR U.S. CITIES WITH LARGEST DECLINES IN POPULATION, 1980–86, RANKED BY PERCENT DECLINE

Rank	City	Population 1980	Population 1986	Percent decline	Rank	City	Population 1980	Population 1986	Percent decline
1	Peoria, Ill.	124,160	110,290	–11.17%	13	Syracuse, N.Y.	170,105	160,750	–5.52
2	Gary, Ind.	151,968	136,790	–9.99	14	Milwaukee, Wis.	636,298	605,090	–4.90
3	Detroit, Mich.	1,203,369	1,086,220	–9.74	15	Yonkers, N.Y.	195,351	186,080	–4.75
4	Youngstown, Ohio	115,510	104,690	–9.37	16	Chattanooga, Tenn.	169,520	162,710	–4.34
5	Buffalo, N.Y.	357,870	324,820	–9.24	17	Baltimore, Md.	786,741	752,800	–4.31
6	Flint, Mich.	159,611	145,590	–8.78	18	Livonia, Mich.	104,814	100,540	–4.08
7	Pittsburgh, Pa.	423,960	387,490	–8.60	19	Cincinnati, Ohio	385,410	369,750	–4.06
8	Dayton, Ohio	193,549	178,920	–7.56	20	Toledo, Ohio	354,635	340,680	–3.94
9	Warren, Mich.	161,134	149,800	–7.03	21	Newark, N.J.	329,248	316,300	–3.93
10	Cleveland, Ohio	573,822	535,830	–6.62	22	Minneapolis, Minn.	370,951	356,840	–3.80
11	Akron, Ohio	237,177	222,060	–6.37	23	Louisville, Ky.	298,694	287,460	–3.76
12	St. Louis, Mo.	452,804	426,300	–5.85	24	Birmingham, Ala.	286,799	277,510	–3.24
					25	Erie, Pa.	119,123	115,270	–3.23

Note: Major cities with population of 100,000 or more (182 total). **Source:** U.S. Bureau of the Census, 1987.

CITIES WITH 100,000 INHABITANTS OR MORE IN 1986—POPULATION, 1970–86, AND LAND AREA, 1985

City	TOTAL POPULATION (in thousands) 1970	1980	1986	Rank 1986	Percent change 1980–86	Per sq. mi. 1986	Land area (sq. mi.) 1985	City	TOTAL POPULATION (in thousands) 1970	1980	1986	Rank 1986	Percent change 1980–86	Per sq. mi. 1986	Land area (sq. mi.) 1985
Abilene, Tex.	90	98	112	151	14.4%	1,219	92.2	Birmingham, Ala.	301	284	278	55	–2.4	2,781	99.8
Akron, Ohio	275	237	222	68	–6.4	3,576	62.1	Boise City, Idaho	75	102	108	160	6.0	2,562	42.3
Albuquerque, N.Mex.	245	332	367	40	10.4	2,883	127.2	Boston, Mass.	641	563	574	19	1.9	12,153	47.2
Alexandria, Va.	111	103	108	162	4.5	7,187	15.0	Bridgeport, Conn.	157	143	142	117	–0.5	9,650	14.7
Allentown, Pa.	110	104	104	170	0.6	5,963	17.5	Brownsville, Tex.	53	85	102	174	20.1	3,533	28.9
Amarillo, Tex.	127	149	166	96	11.1	1,915	86.6	Buffalo, N.Y.	463	358	325	48	–9.2	7,771	41.8
Anaheim, Calif.	166	219	241	63	9.7	5,398	44.6	Cedar Rapids, Iowa	111	110	108	161	–1.7	1,963	55.2
Anchorage, Alaska	48	174	235	67	34.7	136	1,732.0	Charlotte, N.C.	241	315	352	44	11.6	2,315	152.1
Ann Arbor, Mich.	100	108	108	163	–0.2	4,295	25.1	Chattanooga, Tenn.	120	170	162	98	–4.3	1,310	123.8
Arlington, Tex.	90	160	250	61	56.0	2,739	91.2	Chesapeake, Va.	90	114	134	127	17.4	395	340.0
Atlanta, Ga.	495	425	422	32	–0.7	3,216	131.2	Chicago, Ill.	3,369	3,005	3,010	3	0.1	13,194	228.1
Aurora, Colo.	75	159	218	71	37.5	3,293	66.2	Chula Vista, Calif.	68	84	119	141	41.6	4,485	26.5
Austin, Tex.	254	346	467	27	34.9	2,011	232.0	Cincinnati, Ohio	454	385	370	39	–4.1	4,740	78.0
Bakersfield, Calif.	70	106	150	109	42.4	1,921	78.3	Cleveland, Ohio	751	574	536	22	–6.6	6,783	79.0
Baltimore, Md.	905	787	753	11	–4.3	9,375	80.3	Colorado Springs, Colo.	136	215	273	57	26.8	1,973	138.2
Baton Rouge, La.	166	220	241	62	9.4	3,308	72.9	Columbus, Ga.	155	169	180	88	6.3	828	217.5
Beaumont, Tex.	118	118	120	139	1.5	1,622	73.9	Columbus, Ohio	540	565	566	20	0.2	3,030	186.8
Berkeley, Calif.	114	103	104	171	0.8	9,551	10.9								

City	TOTAL POPULATION (in thousands) 1970	1980	1986	Rank 1986	POPULATION Percent change 1980–86	Per sq. mi. 1986	Land area (sq. mi.) 1985
Concord, Calif.	85	104	106	166	2.1	3,617	29.3
Corpus Christi, Tex.	205	232	264	58	13.7	2,248	117.4
Dallas, Tex.	844	905	1,004	6	10.9	3,028	331.4
Dayton, Ohio	243	194	179	89	-7.6	3,289	54.4
Denver, Colo.	515	493	505	23	2.5	4,728	106.8
Des Moines, Iowa	201	191	192	78	0.6	2,901	66.2
Detroit, Mich.	1,514	1,203	1,086	6	-9.7	8,010	135.6
Durham, N.C.	95	101	114	149	12.6	2,182	52.2
Elizabeth, N.J.	113	106	107	165	0.3	9,106	11.7
El Paso, Tex.	322	425	492	24	15.6	2,052	239.7
Erie, Pa.	129	119	115	147	-3.2	5,312	21.7
Eugene, Oreg.	79	106	105	167	-0.2	2,978	35.4
Evansville, Ind.	139	130	129	130	-0.8	3,444	37.6
Flint, Mich.	193	160	146	116	-8.8	4,452	32.7
Fort Lauderdale, Fla.	140	153	149	112	-3.0	5,021	29.6
Fort Wayne, Ind.	178	172	173	94	0.3	2,921	59.2
Fort Worth, Tex.	393	385	430	30	11.5	1,662	258.5
Fremont, Calif.	101	132	154	108	16.4	1,959	78.4
Fresno, Calif.	166	217	285	53	30.9	3,015	94.4
Fullerton, Calif.	86	102	109	159	6.4	4,899	22.2
Garden Grove, Calif.	121	123	135	126	9.4	7,619	17.7
Garland, Tex.	81	139	177	91	27.1	3,146	56.1
Gary, Ind.	175	152	137	122	-10.0	3,472	39.4
Glendale, Ariz.	36	97	126	135	29.5	2,501	50.3
Glendale, Calif.	133	139	154	107	10.5	5,022	30.6
Grand Rapids, Mich.	198	182	187	80	2.6	4,298	43.4
Greensboro, N.C.	144	156	177	90	13.5	2,427	72.8
Hampton, Va.	121	123	126	134	2.8	2,456	51.3
Hartford, Conn.	158	136	138	121	1.2	7,752	17.8
Hayward, Calif.	93	94	102	176	8.5	2,286	44.4
Hialeah, Fla.	102	145	162	100	11.4	8,338	19.4
Hollywood, Fla.	107	121	121	138	-0.3	4,779	25.3
Honolulu, Hawaii	325	365	372	38	2.0	4,280	87.0
Houston, Tex.	1,234	1,595	1,729	4	8.4	3,019	572.2
Huntington Beach, Calif.	116	171	184	83	7.7	6,751	27.2
Huntsville, Ala.	139	143	163	97	14.7	1,406	116.2
Independence, Mo.	112	112	113	150	1.0	1,401	80.6
Indianapolis, Ind.	737	701	720	13	2.7	2,045	352.0
Inglewood, Calif.	90	94	103	172	8.9	11,522	8.9
Irving, Tex.	97	110	129	132	16.9	1,907	67.4
Jackson, Miss.	154	203	208	74	2.7	1,963	106.2
Jacksonville, Fla.	504	541	610	17	12.7	803	759.7
Jersey City, N.J.	260	224	219	70	-1.8	16,627	13.2
Kansas City, Kans.	168	161	162	99	0.6	1,509	107.4
Kansas City, Mo.	507	448	441	29	-1.5	1,394	316.4
Knoxville, Tenn.	175	175	173	93	-1.0	2,209	78.4
Lakewood, Colo.	93	114	122	137	7.3	3,008	40.6
Lansing, Mich.	131	130	129	131	-1.1	3,654	35.1
Laredo, Tex.	69	91	117	145	28.0	4,320	27.1
Las Vegas, Nev.	126	165	192	79	16.3	2,850	67.2
Lexington-Fayette, Ky.	108	204	213	73	4.3	748	284.7
Lincoln, Nebr.	150	172	183	85	6.5	3,006	60.9
Little Rock, Ark.	132	159	181	86	13.7	1,866	97.0
Livonia, Mich.	110	105	101	181	-4.1	2,889	34.8
Long Beach, Calif.	359	361	396	33	9.6	7,957	49.8
Los Angeles, Calif.	2,812	2,969	3,259	2	9.8	6,996	465.9
Louisville, Ky.	362	299	286	52	-4.0	4,689	61.1
Lubbock, Tex.	149	174	186	81	7.2	1,754	106.3
Macon, Ga.	122	117	118	143	1.3	2,383	49.7
Madison, Wis.	172	171	176	92	3.1	3,157	55.7
Memphis, Tenn.	624	646	653	15	1.0	2,471	264.1
Mesa, Ariz.	63	152	251	60	65.0	2,647	95.0
Miami, Fla.	335	347	374	36	7.9	10,902	34.3
Milwaukee, Wis.	717	636	605	18	-4.9	6,316	95.8
Minneapolis, Minn.	434	371	357	43	-3.8	6,476	55.1
Mobile, Ala.	190	200	203	75	1.4	1,486	136.8
Modesto, Calif.	62	107	133	128	24.3	4,888	27.2
Montgomery, Ala.	133	178	194	77	9.2	1,462	132.9
Nashville-Davidson, Tenn.	426	456	474	26	4.0	988	479.5
Newark, N.J.	382	329	316	50	-3.9	13,122	24.1
New Haven, Conn.	138	126	123	136	-2.1	6,532	18.9
New Orleans, La.	593	558	554	21	-0.6	2,781	199.4
Newport News, Va.	138	145	162	101	11.6	2,476	65.3
New York, N.Y.	7,896	7,072	7,263	1	2.7	24,089	301.5
Bronx	1,472	1,169	1,194	—	2.1	28,633	41.7
Brooklyn	2,602	2,231	2,293	—	1.0	32,664	70.2
Manhattan	1,539	1,428	1,478	—	3.5	66,577	22.2
Queens	1,987	1,891	1,923	—	1.7	17,707	108.6
Staten Island	295	352	375	—	6.5	6,388	58.7
Norfolk, Va.	308	267	275	56	2.9	5,185	53.0
Oakland, Calif.	362	339	357	42	5.2	6,623	53.9
Odessa, Tex.	78	90	101	178	12.4	2,892	35.0
Oklahoma City, Okla.	368	404	446	28	10.4	739	604.0
Omaha, Nebr.	347	314	349	45	11.3	3,517	99.3
Ontario, Calif.	64	89	114	148	28.7	3,149	36.3
Orange, Calif.	77	91	101	180	10.2	4,458	22.6
Orlando, Fla.	99	128	146	115	13.7	2,416	60.4
Oxnard, Calif.	71	108	127	133	17.4	5,162	24.6
Pasadena, Calif.	113	118	130	129	10.0	5,599	23.2
Pasadena, Tex.	90	113	118	144	4.9	3,090	38.2
Paterson, N.J.	145	138	139	119	0.8	16,763	8.3
Peoria, Ill.	127	124	110	158	-11.2	2,614	42.2
Philadelphia, Pa.	1,949	1,688	1,643	5	-2.7	12,080	136.0
Phoenix, Ariz.	584	790	894	10	13.1	2,384	375.0
Pittsburgh, Pa.	520	424	387	35	-8.6	6,994	55.4
Plano, Tex.	18	72	111	155	53.3	1,788	62.1
Pomona, Calif.	87	93	116	146	24.6	5,045	22.9
Portland, Oreg.	380	368	388	34	5.4	3,405	113.9
Portsmouth, Va.	111	105	111	157	6.1	3,712	29.9
Providence, R.I.	179	157	157	106	0.3	8,317	18.9
Pueblo, Colo.	97	102	101	177	-0.4	3,040	33.3
Raleigh, N.C.	123	150	180	87	20.1	2,325	77.6
Reno, Nev.	73	101	110	154	9.6	3,051	36.2
Richmond, Va.	249	219	218	72	-0.7	3,622	60.1
Riverside, Calif.	140	171	197	76	15.3	2,659	74.0
Roanoke, Va.	92	100	102	175	1.7	2,364	43.1
Rochester, N.Y.	295	242	236	66	-2.4	6,900	34.2
Rockford, Ill.	147	140	136	124	-2.8	3,311	41.0
Sacramento, Calif.	257	276	324	49	17.3	3,325	97.3
Salt Lake City, Utah	176	163	158	104	-2.8	1,577	100.5
San Antonio, Tex.	654	786	914	9	16.3	3,003	304.5
San Bernardino, Calif.	107	119	139	120	16.7	2,507	55.3
San Diego, Calif.	697	876	1,015	7	16.0	3,086	329.0
San Francisco, Calif.	716	679	749	12	10.3	16,142	46.4
San Jose, Calif.	460	629	712	14	13.1	4,209	169.2
Santa Ana, Calif.	156	204	237	65	16.1	8,642	27.4
Savannah, Ga.	118	142	147	114	3.6	2,585	56.8
Scottsdale, Ariz.	68	89	111	154	25.4	610	182.1
Seattle, Wash.	531	494	486	25	-1.5	5,816	83.6
Shreveport, La.	182	206	220	69	7.1	2,443	90.2
South Bend, Ind.	126	110	107	164	-2.3	2,945	36.4
Spokane, Wash.	171	171	173	95	0.9	3,104	55.7
Springfield, Ill.	92	100	100	182	0.3	2,428	41.3
Springfield, Mass.	164	152	149	111	-1.9	4,713	31.7
Springfield, Mo.	120	133	139	118	4.7	2,074	67.2
St. Louis, Mo.	622	453	426	31	-5.9	6,943	61.4
St. Paul, Minn.	310	270	264	59	-2.4	5,032	52.4
St. Petersburg, Fla.	216	239	239	64	0.3	4,283	55.9
Stamford, Conn.	109	102	101	179	-1.4	2,653	38.1
Sterling Heights, Mich.	61	109	112	153	2.7	3,059	36.6

City	TOTAL POPULATION (in thousands) 1970	1980	1986	Rank 1986	Percent change 1980–86	Per sq. mi. 1986	Land area (sq. mi.) 1985
Stockton, Calif.	110	150	183	84	22.7	4,276	42.9
Sunnyvale, Calif.	96	107	112	152	5.2	4,792	23.4
Syracuse, N.Y.	197	170	161	102	–5.5	6,754	23.8
Tacoma, Wash.	154	159	159	103	0.3	3,325	47.8
Tallahassee, Fla.	73	82	119	140	46.5	2,042	58.5
Tampa, Fla.	278	272	278	54	2.2	2,664	104.2
Tempe, Ariz.	64	107	136	123	27.6	3,527	38.7
Toledo, Ohio	383	355	341	46	–3.9	4,046	84.2
Topeka, Kans.	125	119	119	142	–0.1	2,259	52.5
Torrance, Calif.	135	130	136	125	4.4	6,613	20.5
Tucson, Ariz.	263	331	359	41	8.6	2,862	125.4

City	TOTAL POPULATION (in thousands) 1970	1980	1986	Rank 1986	Percent change 1980–86	Per sq. mi. 1986	Land area (sq. mi.) 1985
Tulsa, Okla.	330	361	374	37	3.6	2,008	186.1
Virginia Beach, Va.	172	262	333	47	27.2	1,476	225.9
Waco, Tex.	95	101	105	168	3.9	1,388	75.8
Warren, Mich.	179	161	150	110	–7.0	4,355	34.4
Washington, D.C.	757	638	626	16	–1.9	9.984	62.7
Waterbury, Conn.	108	103	102	173	–0.9	3,577	28.6
Wichita, Kans.	277	280	289	51	3.2	2,575	112.2
Winston–Salem, N.C.	134	132	148	113	12.3	2,134	69.4
Worcester, Mass.	177	162	158	105	–2.5	4,218	37.4
Yonkers, N.Y.	204	195	186	82	–4.7	10,168	18.3
Youngstown, Ohio	141	116	105	169	–9.4	3,034	34.5

Source: U.S. Bureau of the Census, *Statistical Abstract of the United States 1989* (1989).

SUMMARY OF CITY GOVERNMENT FINANCES, 1986–87 (millions of dollars)

Item	Amount 1986–87	% distribution 1986–87	% change over 1985–86
Revenue, total	**$169,814**	**(X)**	**6.9%**
GENERAL REVENUE, TOTAL	130,217	100.0%	6.6
Intergovernmental revenue	37,740	29.0	1.6
From state governments	26,384	20.3	7.1
General local government support	7,537	5.8	6.4
From federal government	8,420	6.5	–14.2
From local governments	2,937	2.3	9.1
General revenue from own sources	92,476	71.0	8.8
Taxes	55,366	42.5	8.9
Property	27,163	20.9	8.4
General Sales	9,567	7.3	6.1
Selective sales	6,031	4.6	7.3
Income	8,059	6.2	13.9
Other	4,547	3.5	11.4
Charges and miscellaneous	37,110	28.5	8.8
Current charges	19,318	14.8	6.9
Sewerage	6,093	4.7	9.0
Education	3,330	2.6	–0.4
Interest earnings	7,398	5.7	0.1
Special assessments	1,197	0.9	10.2
Sale of property	440	0.3	–15.7
Other and unallocable	8,756	6.7	24.3
UTILITY REVENUE	28,833	100.0	4.6
Electric power	14,929	51.8	5.1
Water supply	9,883	34.3	7.4
Transit system	1,743	6.0	10.5
Gas supply	2,278	7.9	–11.4
LIQUOR STORE REVENUE	270	(X)	1.1
INSURANCE TRUST REVENUE	10,494	100.0	17.1
Expenditure, total	**$164,146**	**100.0%**	**7.4%**
EXPENDITURE BY FUNCTION			
General expenditure	124,614	100.0	8.5
Intergovernmental expenditure	4,903	3.9	16.2
Direct general expenditure	119,711	96.1	8.2
Capital outlay	19,428	15.6	9.1
Other	110,283	80.5	8.0
GENERAL EXPENDITURE BY FUNCTION			
Education services:			
Education	13,417	10.8	8.5
Capital outlay	573	0.5	–8.5
Libraries	1,607	1.3	11.1
Social services and income maintenance:			
Public welfare	6,395	5.1	2.3

Item	Amount 1986–87	% distribution 1986–87	% change over 1985–86
Cash assistance payments	2,108	1.7	0.7
Medical vendor payments	337	0.3	5.0
Other	3,950	3.2	2.9
Hospitals	5,461	4.4	2.7
Own	4,977	4.0	2.5
Capital outlay	248	0.2	–12.7
Other	484	0.4	5.2
Health	1,922	1.5	10.5
Transportation			
Highways	10,086	8.1	8.0
Capital outlay	4,091	3.3	14.3
Air transportation	2,205	1.8	11.6
Parking facilities	653	0.5	7.9
Water transport	434	0.3	–3.6
Transit subsidies	1,300	1.0	39.6
Public safety			
Police protection	14,835	11.9	8.8
Fire protection	7,893	6.3	8.1
Correction	1,335	1.1	15.5
Protective inspection and regulation	1,144	0.9	12.9
Environment and housing			
Sewerage	9,082	7.3	11.4
Capital outlay	4,202	3.4	11.7
Sanitation other than sewerage	4,433	3.6	5.3
Parks and recreation	5,975	4.8	10.0
Capital outlay	1,520	1.2	19.9
Housing and community development	5,589	4.5	0.6
Capital outlay	2,142	1.7	–3.7
Natural resources	89	0.1	27.1
Government administration:			
Financial administration	3,308	2.7	8.1
Judicial and legal	1,480	1.2	9.3
General public buildings	1,657	1.3	15.6
Other	2,555	2.1	6.3
Interest on general debt	9,300	7.5	14.9
General expenditure not elsewhere classified	12,458	10.0	7.6
UTILITY EXPENDITURE	33,464	100.0	4.9
LIQUOR STORE EXPENDITURE	246	(X)	1.2
INSURANCE TRUST EXPENDITURE	5,822	100.0	12.5
EXHIBIT: SALARIES AND WAGES	55,476	33.8	7.0
Debt outstanding at end of fiscal year	**$179,860**	**100.0%**	**9.1%**
Cash and security holdings	**$177,313**	**100.0%**	**12.5%**

Source: U.S. Bureau of the Census, *City Government Finances in 1986–87* (1989).

50 LARGEST CITIES

Albuquerque, New Mexico

Seventy million years ago, earthquakes and volcanoes pushed the land that is now Albuquerque above the sea, forming the Rio Grande valley and a ring of mountain ranges. Even today the 10,000-foot-high Sandia Mountains are rising slowly, and the Rio Grande Valley continues gradually to deepen. During the Ice Age, Sandia Man roamed the area hunting mastodon and buffalo, and some 3,000 years ago, the Anasazi built stone and adobe cities, which still stand. The 1530s marked the arrival of Spanish conquistadors and missionaries.

Founded as a Spanish villa in 1706, when 35 families moved to the land along the Rio Grande, Albuquerque was named by Don Francisco Cuervo y Valdez in honor of the duke of Albuquerque, King Phillip's viceroy of New Spain. Indian raids arrested the villa's expansion, and 100 years after its founding, its population numbered a mere 2,200. Benefiting from their proximity to the Santa Fe trail, the people farmed; raised cattle; marketed adobe, for building, and wool; and ran trading posts, military supply depots, saloons, hotels, and mer-

cantile businesses. The introduction of the railroad in 1880 spurred Albuquerque's growth, and the 1940 population of 35,000 has since grown more than tenfold.

Today Albuquerque's thriving high-tech economy draws strength from such major installations as Sandia National Laboratories, GTE Communications Systems, Unisys, General Electric, DEC, and many others. The city occupies a central position along the Rio Grande Research Corridor, which stretches from Los Alamos to Las Cruces, and is home to the University of New Mexico, which is part of a statewide science and engineering research network that includes Sandia National Laboratories, Los Alamos National Laboratory, the Air Force Weapons Laboratory, and numerous other facilities.

Population 366,750 (1986). Rank: 40. Pop. density: 2,883/sq. mi. (1,113/sq km). County: Bernalillo.

Terrain and climate Elev.: 5,300 ft. Area: 127.2 sq. mi. (329.4 sq km). Avg. daily min. temp.: Jan.: 22.3°F/–5.3°C; avg. daily max.: July: 92.8°F/33.7°C. Avg. annual rainfall: 8.12"; snowfall: 11"; clear days: 71; precipitation days: 135.

Government Form: mayor and council. Mayor: Ken Schultz. Municipal tel. number: (505)

768–3000.

City finances (1987) Total revenues: $433.9 mil. Total genl. expend.: $400.2 mil. Gross debt outstanding: $1,086.7 mil.

Major employers BDM Corp., DEC, General Electric, GTE Communications Systems, Gulton Industries, Honeywell, Intel, Johnson & Johnson Ethicon Div., Motorola, Sandia National Laboratories, Signetics, Unisys.

Atlanta, Georgia

Atlanta, the capital and largest city of Georgia, lies at the base of the Blue Ridge Mountains near the Chattahoochee River. First settled in 1836, the area became the terminus for the Georgia Railroad in 1845 and took the name Atlanta. Population had grown to 15,000 by 1861, and during the Civil War, it became a strategic Confederate depot and collection point for recruits, establishing it as one of the most important cities of the Confederacy, and making it a vital objective during Gen. William Tecumseh Sherman's infamous march to the sea in 1864. After two months of bitter battle, Sherman took the city on Sept. 1. After the war the ravaged city was rebuilt, and it became the state capital in 1878.

THE COST OF LIVING INDEX IN SELECTED U.S. CITIES, 1988

The cost of living index, compiled by the American Chamber of Commerce Researchers Association, measures relative price levels for consumer goods and services. The nationwide average equals 100, and each area's index is read as a percentage of the nationwide average. (Notice that New York City is significantly above the national average in every category, while Indianapolis is below the average in all but one category.) The index reflects differentials for a middle-manager standard of living by its weighting structure. Home ownership costs, for example, are more heavily weighted than they would be if the index were structured to reflect average costs for all urban consumers.

Urban area	Composite index	Grocery items	Housing	Utilities	Transportation	Health care	Misc. goods and services
Albuquerque, N.Mex.	100.8	95.4	108.7	93.7	107.2	103.5	97.4
Atlanta, Ga.	108.9	101.8	116.6	116.8	99.3	121.4	105.5
Baltimore, Md.	103.8	102.4	105.6	102.8	108.0	110.0	100.3
Boston, Mass.	164.8	111.5	332.2	128.5	106.8	145.9	115.0
Buffalo, N.Y.	100.5	101.5	90.1	115.0	107.1	97.0	100.4
Charlotte, N.C.	101.2	96.4	108.6	95.4	91.7	105.3	103.8
Chicago, Ill.	122.3	110.3	161.6	120.4	108.1	122.4	107.2
Cincinnati, Ohio	102.0	102.5	98.2	107.2	103.4	95.5	103.6
Cleveland, Ohio	100.2	98.2	95.7	96.0	106.6	108.0	101.4
Columbus, Ohio	102.7	95.0	107.4	107.4	104.3	95.5	102.8
Dallas, Tex.	104.1	105.9	101.7	110.1	112.8	107.4	98.2
Denver, Colo.	103.9	91.0	119.7	90.4	108.1	117.3	99.5
El Paso, Tex.	99.2	105.1	96.2	87.6	104.3	98.7	100.4
Houston, Tex.	101.3	106.8	80.2	117.1	112.8	105.5	102.0
Indianapolis, Ind.	97.0	95.5	97.0	98.5	106.0	96.3	93.5
Kansas City, Mo.	95.2	102.9	92.7	94.5	92.7	90.5	95.1
Memphis, Tenn.	100.1	104.6	93.3	103.3	100.4	102.7	100.6
Miami, Fla.	108.8	102.2	114.1	131.2	103.1	110.4	102.5
New Orleans, La.	96.3	96.8	92.5	110.7	91.9	96.1	95.5
New York, N.Y.	154.5	111.1	249.9	189.3	108.0	140.0	120.0
Oklahoma City, Okla.	97.7	105.2	79.9	97.8	94.4	109.1	105.3
Omaha, Nebr.	92.5	92.2	92.0	83.5	104.7	91.8	91.1
Philadelphia, Pa.	125.7	113.9	136.9	163.8	109.9	138.1	114.3
Phoenix, Ariz.	105.0	104.6	105.7	93.3	101.3	120.5	106.9
Portland, Oreg.	101.2	99.1	99.6	73.0	107.8	131.9	103.8
Sacramento, Calif.	107.0	102.5	106.5	106.6	113.1	133.7	101.2
San Antonio, Tex.	99.7	105.1	91.2	106.4	105.5	97.7	98.3
San Diego, Calif.	124.0	105.5	179.7	78.5	134.7	120.9	106.4
San Jose, Calif.	120.7	103.7	177.2	70.3	114.1	133.9	107.1
St. Louis, Mo.	97.9	99.6	95.0	104.4	97.2	100.7	96.5

Source: American Chamber of Commerce Researchers Association, *Cost of Living Index: Comparative Data for 246 Urban Areas*, (2d quarter 1988).

The chief commercial, industrial, insurance, telecommunications, and distributing center of the Southeast, Atlanta includes among its wide cross-section of industries railroad shops, large printing and publishing operations, automobile assembly plants, telecommunications equipment manufacturing, and numerous factories producing items ranging from foods and beverages to furniture.

An important educational and cultural center, the city boasts more than 20 institutions of higher learning, including Georgia Tech, Emory University, and Ogelthorpe University, and is the site of the Atlanta Historical Society Library and exhibition, the Cyclorama (a three-dimension painting re-creating the battle of Atlanta during the Civil War), and the Ferbank Science Center, featuring the nation's third-largest planetarium.

Population 421,910 (1986). Rank: 32. Pop. density: 3,216/sq. mi. (1,241.69/sq km). County: Fulton.

Terrain and climate Elev.: 1,034 ft. Area: 131.2 sq. mi. (339.80 sq km). Avg. daily min. temp.: Jan.: 32.6°F/0.3°C; avg. daily max.: July: 87.9°F/31°C. Avg. annual rainfall: 48.61"; snowfall: 2"; clear days: 108; precipitation days: 116.

Government Form: mayor and council. Mayor: Andrew Young. Municipal tel. number: (404) 330-6100.

City finances (1987) Total revenues: $641.7 mil. Total genl. expend.: $586.7 mil. Gross debt outstanding: $1,234.2 mil.

Major employers AT&T, Bell South, Coca-Cola, Georgia Pacific, RJR Nabisco, State of Georgia.

Austin, Texas

Austin, the capital of Texas, lies about 80 miles northeast of San Antonio on the banks of the Colorado River. First inhabited by nomadic Indian tribes, the area had as its first permanent European settler Jacob Harrell, in 1835, who, with the three families who joined him a few years later, established the town of Waterloo. In 1838 it was chosen as the site of the Texas Republic's capital and was renamed Austin after Stephen F. Austin, who brought the first Anglo settlers to Texas in the 1820s. After 1845, when Texas gained admission into the Union, Austin began to flourish, and by 1930 it had grown into a major regional center with a population of 75,000.

Austin was originally a business and distribution center serving the farmers of the Blackland Prairies to the east; its farmers now produce cotton, maize, corn, livestock, and poultry. Traditional industries such as meat packing, canning, and furniture manufacturing have been outstripped by the high-tech companies that have helped to nearly double the population since 1970. The University of Texas, founded in 1881 in Austin, boasts the highest endowment of any U.S. university—a legacy of the Texas oil fields. As the university developed into a first-class institution feeding the city's cultural and economic life, and with the influx of electronics and computer companies, Austin has prospered into a metropolis of national, even worldwide, scope.

Population 466,550 (1986). Rank: 27. Pop.

density: 2,011/sq. mi. (776.4/sq km). County: Travis.

Terrain and climate Elev.: 570 ft. Area: 232 sq. mi. (600.9 sq km). Avg. daily min. temp.: Jan.: 38.8°F/3.8°C; avg. daily max.: July: 95.4°F/35.2°C. Avg. annual rainfall: 31.50"; snowfall: 1"; clear days: 115; precipitation days: 82.

Government Form: council and manager. Mayor: Lee Cooke. Municipal tel. number: (512) 499-2000.

City finances (1987) Total revenues: $1,100.6 mil. Total genl. expend.: $1,156.7 mil. Gross debt outstanding: $2,242.6 mil.

Major employers IBM 7,000; Motorola 5,100; Texas Instruments 2,300; Tracor Inc. 2,300; Lockheed 2,256; Abbott Laboratories 1,750; Southwestern Bell 1,750; Advanced Micro Devices 1,700.

Baltimore, Maryland

Baltimore, one of America's most active seaports since Colonial days and chartered in 1729 as a major conduit of tobacco exportation, was named after the founder of the colony of Maryland, George Calvert, Lord Baltimore. By the time of the Revolutionary War, it earned fame as an important commercial and maritime center, and ships sailing from Baltimore plied their trade with northern Europe, the Mediterranean, and the Caribbean. Chartered as a city in 1797, Baltimore saw its commercial activity begin to surge with the burgeoning of its iron and copper industries, its proximity to the nation's capital, and the arrival of the Baltimore and Ohio Railroad, which developed links to the Midwest. However, the deep, divisive passions of the Civil War stunted growth, and it would take years before the city recovered.

A fire in 1904 destroyed almost every building in the downtown area, providing impetus for needed revitalization. The approach of World War I renewed demands for Baltimore's port facilities and fostered development of a solid heavy-industrial base. Similarly, World War II brought the city's maritime structure into prominence. Following the war, however, the city's infrastructure aged and decayed. Today Baltimore remains a large port and industrial city with one of the largest steel plants in the world (Bethlehem Steel's Sparrow Point works). Much of the city has been rebuilt through urban renewal efforts, and its population seems to have stabilized after a loss of almost 20% in 1960.

Among the city's historic sites is Fort McHenry, where Francis Scott Key wrote "The Star-Spangled Banner." Baltimore is home to St. Mary's Seminary and University (1791), Johns Hopkins University (1876), and the University of Baltimore (1925), among other noted institutions of higher learning.

Population 752,800 (1986). Rank: 11. Pop. density: 9,375/sq. mi. (3,619.7/sq km). County: Baltimore.

Terrain and climate Elev.: 155 ft. Area: 80.3 sq. mi. (208 sq km). Avg. daily min. temp.: Jan.: 24.3°F/-4.2°C; avg. daily max.: July: 87.1°F/30.6°C. Avg. annual rainfall: 43.39"; snowfall: 22"; clear days: 106; precipitation days: 112.

Government Form: mayor and council. Mayor: Kurt L. Schmoke. Municipal tel. number: (301) 396-3100.

City finances (1987) Total revenues: $1,771.9 mil. Total genl. expend.: $1,400.3 mil. Gross debt outstanding: $1,315.3 mil.

Major employers AT&T Technologies, Baltimore Gas & Electric, Bethlehem Steel, C&P Telephone Co., General Motors, Johns Hopkins Univ., Montgomery Ward & Co., Social Security Administration, Univ. of Maryland, Westinghouse Corp.

Boston, Massachusetts

Named for the English port from which many Puritan immigrants to America came, Boston was first settled in 1630 under the leadership of John Winthrop. As the capital of the Massachusetts Bay Colony, it quickly became the cultural and mercantile capital of the New England colonies. Bostonians never wholly embraced British authority, and they provided the earliest challenges to British rule in their reaction to the Stamp Act (1765) and through the Boston Tea Party (1783). The colonists killed in the Boston Massacre (1770) were the first to fall in the years immediately preceding the American Revolution.

With the end of the Revolution, Boston merchants found themselves shut out of English ports by prohibitive tariffs, and in their quest for new markets for American goods, opened American trade to the Orient and India. In the 19th century, Boston benefited early from the Industrial Revolution and from several waves of immigration, particularly blacks from the Southern states, and Irish and Italians from Europe.

Although Boston's preeminence in trade and industry did not survive the 19th century, the city continues to be a major center for banking and financial services. Since World War II, its suburbs have flourished as centers of research and development and of the computer industry—Route 128 is the East Coast's answer to California's "Silicon Valley"—spurring investment in downtown Boston. As the gateway to New England and the birthplace of the Revolution, Boston is also a center for tourism.

Perhaps most important to its identity is Boston's wealth of educational, cultural, and religious tolerance. Harvard (across the Charles River in Cambridge, 1636) is the country's oldest college, and Roxbury Latin (1645) the country's oldest privately endowed secondary school. Today Boston embraces more than 20 colleges and universities, as well as some of the finest cultural institutions in the country, including the American Academy of Arts and Sciences (1780), the Massachusetts Historical Society (1791), the Boston Athenaeum (1807), the Boston Public Library (the nation's first, 1854), the Boston Museum of Fine Arts (1870), and the Boston Symphony (1881). The *Boston Globe* is one of the nation's oldest and most distinguished daily and Sunday newspapers.

Population 573,600 (1986). Rank: 19. Pop. density: 12,153/sq. mi. (4,692.3/sq km). County: Suffolk.

Terrain and climate Elev.: 10 ft. Area: 47.2 sq. mi. (122.2 sq km). Avg. daily min. temp.: Jan.:

22.8°F/–5.1°C; avg. daily max.: July: 81.8°F/27.6°C. Avg. annual rainfall: 43.81"; snowfall: 42"; clear days: 99; precipitation days: 128.

Government Form: mayor and council. Mayor: Raymond L. Flynn. Municipal tel. number: (617) 725–4000.

City finances (1987) Total revenues: $1,455.8 mil. Total genl. expend.: $1,308.9 mil. Gross debt outstanding: $782.0 mil.

Major employers AT&T; Boston Univ.; Digital Equipment Corp.; General Electric; Harvard Univ.; John Hancock Mutual Life Insurance; Jordan Marsh; Massachusetts General Hospital; MIT; New England Telephone; Polaroid; Raytheon; Sears, Roebuck & Co.

Buffalo, New York

Bordering Lake Erie and located on the Niagara River where the Peace Bridge connects the United States to Canada, Buffalo, the second-largest city in New York State, offers a wide variety of commercial activity. An international inland port via the St. Lawrence Seaway and the Erie Canal, one of the busiest railroad systems in the country, and its position as the western terminus for the New York State Thruway—all make Buffalo an important transportation center. While the city's manufacturing base declined from 32 percent of total commerce in 1971 to 19 percent in 1987, the emergence of service businesses and financial organizations, particularly banks, has bolstered the local economy. The proximity to Niagara Falls lures thousands of tourists to the city every year.

The Erie Canal made Buffalo a strategic gateway to the West. The town dates back to the 1700s when the Holland Land Company acquired tracts of land in western New York, and after a plan was drawn up in 1800, the residents chose the name Buffalo, probably after the Indians' mispronunciation of the French *beau fleuve* (beautiful river)—the Niagara. After completion of the Erie Canal in 1825, the city evolved into a heavy manufacturing center, the biggest ship-to-rail grain-transfer point in the country, and in 1932 the "Queen City of the Great Lakes" was incorporated.

Buffalo was the birthplace of Presidents Millard Fillmore and Grover Cleveland; the Wilcox Mansion, where Theodore Roosevelt was sworn in as president after the assassination of William McKinley, stands as a national historic site.

Population 324,820 (1986). Rank: 48. Pop. density: 7,771/sq. mi. (3,000.4/sq km). County: Erie.

Terrain and climate Elev.: 706 ft. Area: 41.8 sq. mi. (108.3 sq km). Avg. daily min. temp.: Jan.: 17°F/–8°C; avg. daily max.: July: 80.2°F/26.7°C. Avg. annual rainfall: 37.52"; snowfall: 90"; clear days: 55; precipitation days: 168.

Government Form: mayor and council. Mayor: James D. Griffin. Municipal tel. number: (716) 851–4841.

City finances (1987) Total revenues: $548.1 mil. Total genl. expend.: $550.0 mil. Gross debt outstanding: $306.8 mil.

Major employers General Motors 15,333; New York State 13,500; State Univ. of New York 12,466; Niagara Frontier Services 11,300;

U.S. government 10,000; Erie County 9,222; City of Buffalo 7,674; Marine Midland Bank 4,961; Moog Inc. 3,897; Buffalo General Hospital Corp. 3,739.

Charlotte, North Carolina

An area of lush green foothills lying at the southernmost tip of the Carolina Piedmont, Charlotte has long been a crossroads city and an important distribution point for the surrounding farmlands. About 250 years ago, Scottish and Irish settlers retracing old Catawba Indian trading routes established a settlement where the paths crossed, and in 1762 it was named Charlotte, after the new bride of King George III. Remembering Gen. Cornwallis's reference to Charlotte as a "hornet's nest" while his army briefly occupied it during the American Revolution, the city adopted the symbol as its emblem. The discovery of a 17–pound gold nugget in 1799 triggered a gold rush, and although the mines dotting the landscape boosted business, the California gold rush in the mid-1800s lured away prospectors, putting Charlotte on its future course as a top cotton producer. A leading city of the Confederacy in the Civil War, Charlotte hosted the last full meeting of the Confederate cabinet in 1865.

Recently, the city's economic base has diversified beyond the production of chemicals, foodstuffs, machinery, metals, and textiles. The city has matured into a major center of world trade and technology, with more than 160 multinational companies engaging in such businesses as microelectronics, insurance, machining, and biomedical supplies. Located equidistant from the Northwestern, Midwestern, and southern Florida markets, with an inland port of entry for goods and a foreign trade zone where items may be held without duty, Charlotte remains a key distribution conduit. A mid-size city at the heart of a rapidly expanding metropolitan region, Charlotte ranks as the nation's fifth-largest urban area with a population of more than 5 million living within a 100–mile radius of the city. The Charlotte Motor Speedway, a large, gleaming, stock car stadium with 52 VIP suites and 40 condominiums overlooking the first turn, and the Charlotte Hornets, one of the expansion teams added to the NBA in 1988, are sources of civic pride.

Population 352,070 (1986). Rank: 44. Pop. density: 2,315/sq. mi. (893.8/sq km). County: Mecklenburg.

Terrain and climate Elev.: 665 ft. Area: 152.1 sq. mi. (393.9 sq km). Avg. daily min. temp.: Jan.: 30.7°F/–0.7°C; avg. daily max.: July: 88.3°F/31.2°C. Avg. annual rainfall: 43.16"; snowfall: 6"; clear days: 111; precipitation days: 111.

Government Form: council and manager. Mayor: Sue Myrick. Municipal tel. number: (704) 336–2040.

City finances (1987) Total revenues: $308.5 mil. Total genl. expend.: $351.1 mil. Gross debt outstanding: $606.3 mil.

Major employers Duke Power 9,500; Charlotte/Mecklenburg Schools 8,000; Charlotte/Mecklenburg Authority 5,700; IBM Informa-

tion Products Div. 5,500; State of North Carolina 4,756; City of Charlotte 4,000; First Union Corp. 3,974; NCNB Corp. 3,300; U.S. government 3,121.

> *"Chicago likes audacity and is willing to have anybody try anything once; no matter who you are, where you came from, or what you set out to do, Chicago will give you a chance."*
> —Lincoln Steffens, 1931

Chicago, Illinois

Chicago extends roughly 26 miles along the southwestern shoreline of Lake Michigan. The city has historically been a major transportation hub and gateway to the Great Plains and continues to be one today, with major air, rail, and highway hubs. Nineteen trunk-line railroad routes converge at Chicago, linking it with every major U.S. and Canadian city. The city has three major airports, including O'Hare, the busiest in the nation. It is also the terminus for major interstate highways running east–west and north–south.

Historically, Chicago's rise parallels the growth of the American republic to the west. Chicago was first settled in 1779, when Jean Baptiste Point de Sable built a house on the site. In 1803 federal troops built a stockade named Fort Dearborn, but by 1830 only 12 families had settled in the area. In the 1830s, however, the population grew rapidly as Americans spread westward, and the city of Chicago was incorporated in 1837 with a population of 4,170. Chicago then began to grow into a bustling Great Lakes port, connected to the Mississippi via a system of rivers and canals.

Chicago has maintained its strategic importance despite changes in transportation technology and remains today a prosperous city. Over the years Chicago has been noted as a hotbed of labor reform, the center of violent organized-crime gang wars during the Prohibition era, and a prime example of the good and the bad of American city machine-politics. Despite its checkered past, however, it has grown into the wealthiest and most vibrant city in the Midwest, with hardly a sign of the rust-belt malaise plaguing many of its sister cities. Chicago ranks first among American cities in the number of employed chemists and second in engineers. It has grown into a financial center with three of the nation's four largest futures exchanges and the world's largest listed-stock-options exchange.

Chicago also far outstrips other Midwestern cities in cultural, entertainment, recreational, and commercial facilities. Major attractions include the Museum of Science and Industry, the Field Museum of Natural History, the Chicago Historical Society, the Lincoln Park Zoo, the Chicago Lyric Opera Company, the Chicago Symphony Orchestra, and the Chicago Art Institute. Downtown Chicago currently has three of the five tallest man-made structures in the world—the Sears Tower (110 stories, 1,454 ft. high), the Amoco building (1,136 ft.), and the John Hancock building (1,127 ft.). It is also home to the world's tallest apartment complex, the 70-story Lake Point Tower, and the world's largest commercial building, the Merchandise Mart.

Population 3,009,530 (1986). Rank: 3. Pop. density: 13,194/sq. mi. (5,094.2/sq km). County: Cook.

Terrain and climate Elev.: 623 ft. Area: 228.1 sq. mi. (590.8 sq km). Avg. daily min. temp.: Jan.: 13.6°F/–10.2°C; avg. daily max.: July: 83.3°F/28.5° Avg. annual rainfall: 33.34"; snowfall: 40"; clear days: 94; precipitation days: 123.

Government Form: mayor and council. Mayor: Richard M. Daley. Municipal tel. number: (312) 744–4000.

City finances (1987) Total revenues: $3,102.8 mil. Total genl. expend.: $3,078.5 mil. Gross debt outstanding: $3,137.2 mil.

Major employers Abbott Laboratories, Amoco, Beatrice, Borg-Warner, IC Industries, Illinois Bell, Inland Steel, Navistar International, Quaker Oats, Sara Lee.

Cincinnati, Ohio

Cincinnati's origins can be traced to 1788, when the town of Columbia was founded between the Little Maumee and Great Maumee rivers where they meet the Ohio. In 1790 it was renamed Cincinnati, after the Society of the Cincinnati, an organization of Revolutionary War veterans. Settlement of the city increased after the Battle of Fallen Timbers (1794) put down Miami resistance to European-settler control of the region.

In 1811 the *New Orleans*, the first steamboat on the Western rivers, arrived from Pittsburgh, and thereafter Cincinnati became a major inland port. The city's commercial status was consolidated in the 1840s after the opening of the Miami and Erie Canal, which joined the Ohio River at Cincinnati with Lake Erie at Toledo, and the arrival of the first railroads in 1843. Large numbers of German immigrants gave the city a European flavor. By mid-century Cincinnati had reached its zenith as a commercial and manufacturing center, well deserving of Longfellow's epithet, "Queen City of the West." Cincinnati continued to prosper after the Civil War, though it was beset by problems ranging from perennial flooding to extensive government corruption. By 1910 its population had reached 360,000, about what it is today.

Cincinnati continues to be a hub of transportation and industry, particularly strong in the manufacture of transportation equipment and industrial machinery, food and beverage prod-

ucts, and steel and in printing. It is one of the nation's largest inland coal ports and a regional center for wholesaling, retailing, insurance, and finance.

Among its many colleges and universities are the University of Cincinnati, Cincinnati Technical College, the Athenaeum of Ohio, Hebrew Union College-Jewish Institute of Religion (founded in 1875 and the oldest rabbinic college in the U.S.), and Cincinnati Bible Seminary. It is the home of the William Howard Taft birthplace, the Harriet Beecher Stowe House State Memorial, Tyler-Davidson Fountain, and the Cincinnati Zoo, the second-oldest zoo in the country. Cincinnati is also the home port of the restored historic riverboats *Delta Queen* and *Mississippi Queen*.

Population 369,750 (1986). Rank: 39. Pop. density: 4,740/sq. mi. (1,830.1/sq km). County: Hamilton.

Terrain and climate Elev.: 540 ft. Area: 78 sq. mi. (202 sq km). Avg. daily min. temp.: 20.4°F/–6.4°C; avg. daily max.: July: 85.8°F/29.8°C. Avg. annual rainfall: 40.10"; snowfall: 19"; clear days: 80; precipitation days: 131.

Government Form: council and manager. Mayor: Charles J. Luken. Municipal tel. number: (513) 352–3000.

City finances (1987) Total revenues: $668.0 mil. Total genl. expend.: $454.1 mil. Gross debt outstanding: $190.0 mil.

Major employers General Electric Aircraft Engine Group 19,000; Procter & Gamble 13,000; Univ. of Cincinnati 10,748; Kroger Co. 10,000; U.S. government 8,967; ARMCO Inc. 6,000; Cincinnati Public Schools 5,998; City of Cincinnati 5,450.

Cleveland, Ohio

The largest city in Ohio, Cleveland was founded in 1795 and named after Moses Cleaveland, a surveyor with the Connecticut Land Company, which administered the state of Connecticut's lingering claim on 3.5 million acres of what is now Ohio (the Western Reserve). A frontier village at the mouth of the Cuyahoga River on Lake Erie, Cleveland was transformed into the business and manufacturing center of northern Ohio by the opening of the Erie Canal in 1825, and the Ohio and Erie Canal, which linked Cleveland with Portsmouth on the Ohio River. When the Soo Locks opened Lake Superior to trade with the Lower Lakes in 1855, Cleveland became a major shipping center for ore, lumber, copper, coal, and farm produce.

During the Civil War, the city's iron ore and coal deposits were mined for steel production, and commercial activity increased to meet the Union's increased demands for heavy machinery, railroad equipment, and ships. In the postwar years, Cleveland's mills and factories expanded even further to satisfy the increased needs of new cities and farms springing up in the wake of westward migration.

Although heavy manufacturing employs 22.5 percent of the city's work force (more than the national average), the national trend toward a service economy has had a severe impact on the local economy, the population of the Cleveland metropolitan area declining from

a high of 2.8 million in 1970 to only 2.4 today. Nonetheless, heavy industry is a cornerstone of the city's economy, with many large industrial companies located there. In addition, there are many medical and industrial research firms, most notably the world-famous Cleveland Clinic and NASA's Lewis Research Center.

Cleveland's industrial strength manifests itself in its flourishing cultural institutions. University Circle, a nearly 500-acre site near Case Western Reserve University (a merger of Western Reserve University and Case Institute of Technology), is home to the Cleveland Play House, the nation's oldest repertory theater; the world-famous Cleveland Orchestra; the Cleveland Museum of Natural History; Western Reserve Historical Society; the Cleveland Health Museum; Allen Memorial Medical Library, and the Cleveland Zoo. In the revitalized downtown area, centered on the Mall are the Cleveland Institute of Art, the Cleveland Institute of Music, the Cleveland Play House,; and the Karamu Center for interracial cultural events.

Population 535,830 (1986). Rank: 22. Pop. density: 6,783/sq. mi. (2,618.9/sq km). County: Cuyahoga.

Terrain and climate Elev.: 805 ft. Area: 79 sq. mi. (204.6 sq km). Avg. daily min. temp.: Jan.: 18.5°F/–7.5°C; avg. daily max.: July: 81.7°F/27.6°C. Avg. annual rainfall: 35.40"; snowfall: 52"; clear days: 70; precipitation days: 156.

Government Form: mayor and council. Mayor: George V. Voinovich. Municipal tel. number: (216) 664–2000.

City finances (1987) Total revenues: $558.7 mil. Total genl. expend.: $674.1 mil. Gross debt outstanding: $504.8 mil.

Major employers U.S. government 20,100; Cleveland Board of Education 9,932; Cleveland Clinic Foundation 9,400; Cuyahoga County government 9,200; Durkee International Foods 8,500; City of Cleveland 8,226; Goodyear Tire and Rubber 7,300; Little Tikes Inc. 7,244; Ohio Bell Telephone 7,000.

Columbus, Ohio

The Ohio legislature designated a site along the banks of the Scioto River in the center of the state as the capital in 1812 and named it Columbus in honor of the famous explorer of the New World. From the first, the city exploited its status as the seat of government and its prime location in the middle of the nation's growing network of roads, canals, and highways. Incorporated in 1834, Columbus became a thriving hub of agricultural trade.

Between 1850 and 1900, its population grew from 17,800 to more than 100,000. Because of the many carriage factories, in the 19th century, Columbus was known as the Buggy Capital of the World. Five railroads passed through the city, so banks soon began to spring up, making Columbus a financial center for the surrounding farm counties.

As in the 19th century, Columbus's modern economy is built on government, agriculture, local finance, and education. In 1950, to counter the trend of suburbanization, the city developed a policy of annexation of surrounding communities. Because it is less reliant on heavy industry than other Midwestern cities, it has weathered the decline of the rust belt better than most, remaining a bustling metropolis. In the 1980s the city realized the creation of more than $780 million in new development and 97,550 new jobs.

Ohio State University, one of the nation's large state universities, opened as the Ohio Agricultural and Mechanical College in 1870, and the city today has a rich academic community that includes the Ohio Dominican College (whose origins date to 1868), the Columbus College of Art and Design, and the Ohio Institute of Technology. Business leaders and politicians have joined in an effort to make the city a center for the arts, refurbishing three theaters and building a complex of three more.

Population 566,030 (1986). Rank: 20. Pop. density: 3,030/sq. mi. (1,169.9/sq km). County: Franklin.

Terrain and climate Elev.: 833 ft. Area: 186.8 sq. mi. (483.8 sq km). Avg. daily min. temp.: Jan.: 19.4°F/–7°C; avg. daily max.: July: 84.4°F/29.1°C. Avg. annual rainfall: 36.97"; snowfall: 28"; clear days: 75; precipitation days: 136.

Government Form: mayor and council. Mayor: Dana G. Rinehart. Municipal tel. number: (614) 645–8100.

City finances (1987) Total revenues: $465.7 mil. Total genl. expend.: $498.2 mil. Gross debt outstanding: $504.8 mil.

Major employers State of Ohio 19,968; Ohio State Univ. 15,200; Columbus Public Schools 7,639; AT&T 7,500; City of Columbus 6,500; Rockwell International 6,500; Nationwide Insurance Co. 6,000.

Dallas, Texas

First settled in 1841 by John Neely Bryan, a Tennessee trader and lawyer, Dallas stretches about 30 miles east of Fort Worth on the Trinity River. Named in 1846 after James K. Polk's vice president, George Mifflin Dallas, it was chartered as a city in 1871. Though it grew substantially with the arrival of railroads in 1872, the population numbered a mere 92,000 in 1910.

Located in the heart of the northern Texas oil belt, Dallas today thrives on a diverse economic base, which, in addition to oil and natural gas, includes production of brick clay and the raw materials for Portland cement, and cotton, grains, fruits, beef, dairy cattle, hogs, sheep, and poultry from surrounding farms. One of the largest inland cotton markets, and a leading distributor of farm goods and machinery, Dallas also serves as the Southwest's banking center with major banks, insurance companies, and the Federal Reserve Bank for the 11th District. Key manufacturing industries include aerospace, electronics, transportation equipment, machinery, food and related products, and apparel.

Some of Dallas's distinguished universities are Southern Methodist, Southwestern Medical School of the University of Texas, Dallas Theological Seminary and Graduate School of Theology, and the Baylor University Schools of Dentistry and Nursing. The Dallas Symphony Orchestra, Dallas Theater Center, Dallas Civic Opera, Dallas Historical Society Museum in the Texas Hall of State, and the Dallas Garden Center contribute to the city's rich cultural life. Fair Park, the site of the annual State Fair of Texas, remains the most widely attended state fair in the country.

Population 1,003,520 (1986). Rank: 8. Pop. density: 3,028/sq. mi. (1,169.1/sq km). County: Dallas.

Terrain and climate Elev.: 596 ft. Area: 331.4 sq. mi. (858.3 sq km). Avg. daily min. temp.: Jan.: 33.9°F/1°C; avg. daily max.: July: 97.8°F/ 36.5°C. Avg. annual rainfall: 34.16"; snowfall: 3"; clear days: 138; precipitation days: 79.

Government Form: council and manager. Mayor: Annette Strauss. Municipal tel. number: (214) 670–4054.

City finances (1987) Total revenues: $1,011.6 mil. Total genl. expend.: $1,040.3 mil. Gross debt outstanding: $1,360.5 mil.

Major employers Texas Instruments 33,000; AMR Corp. 16,000; LTV Corp. 14,975; Dallas Independent School District 14,538; City of Dallas, 14,224; Southwestern Bell 11,367; Pepsico Inc. 9,111; Sears Roebuck & Co. 8,809; Cullum Cos. 8,750; E-Systems Inc. 8,299; U.S. Postal Service 8,248.

Denver, Colorado

Denver was born during the great "Pike's Peak or Bust" gold rush of 1859, when small flakes of placer gold were found where the South Platte River meets Cherry Creek. In its first few years, the city survived a flood, several major fires, Indian attacks, and an invasion by Confederate soldiers during the Civil War. With the discovery of more gold in the Rocky Mountains, Denver became a boom town. Saloons, gambling halls, and wagon trains lined the mud-filled streets, and just about every outlaw, desperado, and lawman in the West made at least one visit to the city. The turn of the century brought respectability, and the wealth of the mountains was poured into parks, fountains, tree-lined streets, and elaborate mansions.

During the oil crisis of the late 1970s and early 1980s, Denver experienced a second boom when it became a corporate center for oil-from-shale companies working the Western Slope of the Rockies. Then one of the fastest-growing cities in the United States, in 1983 it doubled its office space as part of a five-year building campaign that added 16 skyscrapers, a $76–million pedestrian mall, and an $80–million performing arts center. Although expansion was slowed by the energy glut of the mid-1980s, the city is planning the construction of a new airport, convention center, and billion-dollar light-rail system.

Denver's population is among the youngest in the nation: The median age is 29.5 (as compared to the U.S. median of 32.2), and 35 percent of the residents are between 18 and 35. The youthful flavor of the city is very evident; Denver leads the nation in movie attendance and has more sporting goods stores per resident than any city in the world. The city's 205 parks are so active that a speed limit was recently instituted—for bicycles.

Population 505,000 (1986). Rank: 23. Pop.

density: 4,728/sq. mi. (1,825.5/sq km). County: Denver.

Terrain and climate Elev.: 5,280 ft. Area: 106.8 sq. mi. (276.6 sq km). Avg. daily min. temp.: Jan.: 15.9°F/–8.9°C; avg. daily max.: July: 88°F/31°C. Avg. annual rainfall: 15.31"; snowfall: 60"; clear days: 115; precipitation days: 88.

Government Form: mayor and council. Mayor: Federica Pena. Municipal tel. number: (303) 575–2721.

City finances (1987) Total revenues: $955.6 mil. Total genl. expend.: $977.0 mil. Gross debt outstanding: $1,165.5 mil.

Major employers Martin Marietta 14,700; US West 12,840; Adolph Coors Co. 9,000; AT&T 7,600; Continental Airlines 7,186.

Detroit, Michigan

Founded in 1701 by Antoine de La Mothe, sieur de Cadillac, Detroit lies on the Detroit River between Lake Erie and Lake Huron. Named Fort Pontchartrain-du-Détroit (of the strait), the oldest permanent settlement on the Great Lakes flourished as a trading post for trappers, under French control (to 1760), then British (to 1796), and then American.

The first steamboat reached Detroit from Buffalo in 1818, but it was the easy access to Eastern markets via the Erie Canal in 1825 that allowed Detroit to exploit the abundant natural resources in the Michigan peninsula and fostered its emergence as a modern industrial giant in the post–Civil War years. Tenth among cities in the value of its manufactures by 1899, Detroit's main exports included iron ore, copper, lead, salt, and fish. The development of the automotive industry, which eventually became centered in Detroit, propelled Detroit to number three by the 1920s. While Detroit is the home of General Motors, Chrysler, and Ford, recently the automotive industry has been as much a curse as a blessing, for every setback to any of the "Big Three" is felt throughout the Motor City.

Despite the fact that it remains third in industrial manufacturing in the country, Detroit has been plagued by urban decline. The relatively low standard of living among the predominantly black inhabitants ignited riots in the 1940s and 1960s, and the city's crime rate is today among the highest in the nation. However, it was Detroit blacks who gave rise to one of the most sensational expressions of popular culture in the 1960s. Founded in 1960, the Tamla Motown label propelled the Jackson 5, the Supremes, and Stevie Wonder—among others—to world renown, and in the process created the largest black-owned business in the country.

The city's rich and diverse cultural institutions include the Detroit Institute of Arts, which houses one of the largest collections of American art in the world, in addition to extensive European holdings; the Detroit Symphony; the Cranbrook Academy of Art, and the 1,000-acre Belle Isle Park, situated on an island in the Detroit River and including beaches, a yacht basin, a zoo, an aquarium, and a botanical garden.

Population 1,086,220 (1986). Rank: 6. Pop.

density: 8,010/sq. mi. (3,092.7/sq km). County: Wayne.

Terrain and climate Elev.: 581 ft. Area: 135.6 sq. mi. (351.2 sq km). Avg. daily min. temp.: Jan.: 16.1°F/−8.8°C; avg. daily max.: July: 83.1°F/28.3°C. Avg. annual rainfall: 30.97"; snowfall: 39"; clear days: 75; precipitation days: 133.

Government Form: mayor and council. Mayor: Coleman A. Young. Municipal tel. number: (313) 224-3400.

City finances (1987) Total revenues: $1,932.2 mil. Total genl. expend.: $1,801.2 mil. Gross debt outstanding: $1,083.2 mil.

Major employers Chrysler Corp., City of Detroit, Detroit Board of Education, Detroit Edison, Detroit Medical Center, U.S. government, Ford Motor Co., General Motors Corp., Henry Ford Hospital, NBD Bank Corp., State of Michigan, Wayne County.

El Paso, Texas

The largest Texas city bordering Mexico, El Paso sits in the western part of the state on the northern bank of the Rio Grande across from Juarez. A major port of entry, with the biggest commercial and manufacturing base in the area, the city encompasses a region of mines, oil fields, livestock ranches, and farms (principal crops: pecans, fruit, cotton, alfalfa, onions, lettuce, chilies). Important industries include metals smelting and refining, oil and gas refining, textiles, meat packing, and food processing. The city is also home to the University of Texas, at El Paso.

In 1536 Alvar Núñez Cabeza de Vaca crossed the Rio Grande, becoming the first European to step foot in the area, but settlement did not follow until 1659, with the establishment of both El Paso del Norte on the southern bank of the Rio Grande, and the Mission of Guadalupe. In 1682 settlers from New Mexico founded Yselta, an area within the current city limits of El Paso, but permanent settlement did not begin until the arrival of Juan Maria Ponce de Léon in 1827. Incorporated as a city in 1873, El Paso grew into a major industrial center with the introduction of the railroads in 1881.

El Paso's access to sources of cheap labor complemented its mining, refining, and agricultural activities and helped build the city's manufacturing base. Its proximity to Juarez, Mexico, makes it a vibrant tourist haven, and its pleasant climate, combined with its position on the immigration route from Latin America, have made El Paso one of the fastest-growing cities in the country. El Paso also has the highest percentage of citizens with Hispanic ancestry of any American city.

Population 491,800 (1986). Rank: 24. Pop. density: 2,052/sq. mi. (792.3/sq km). County: El Paso.

Terrain and climate Elev.: 3,700 ft. Area: 239.7 sq. mi. (620.8 sq km). Avg. daily min. temp.: Jan.: 30.4°F/−0.8°C; avg. daily max.: July: 95.3°F/35.1°C. Avg. annual rainfall: 7.82"; snowfall: 5"; clear days: 194; precipitation days: 45.

Government Form: mayor and council. Mayor: Suzanne F. Azar. Municipal tel. number: (915) 541-4145.

City finances (1987) Total revenues: $266.7 mil. Total genl. expend.: $230.8 mil. Gross debt outstanding: $430.6 mil.

Major employers Bank El Paso; BTK Industries; El Paso Electric Co.; El Paso Natural Gas Co.; Farah Inc.; N.A., Southwestern Bell; Sun Drugs; Texas Commerce Bank.

Fort Worth, Texas

Named in 1849 after Gen. William J. Worth, commander of the U.S. Army in Texas, Fort Worth originally served to protect settlers from Indian attacks. It grew slowly, mainly as a stopover on the cattle drives along the Chisolm Trail, until the Texas and Pacific Railroad reached the city in 1871. Stockyards sprang up, making Fort Worth a conduit of cattle shipping, and with the building of a grain elevator, it developed into a milling center as well. By the turn of the century, it had also emerged as a successful meat-packing market. Oil was discovered in 1917, bringing prosperity and transforming the city into a major refining center with a dozen operating facilities. The two world wars introduced military installations (particularly airfields) to the area, and having added 200,000 jobs in 1987, Forth Worth is the sixth-largest city in Texas, boasting the state's three finest art museums and a network of parks with total acreage second only to Chicago's.

Population 429,550 (1986). Rank: 30. Pop. density: 1,662/sq. mi. (641.7/sq km). County: Fort Worth.

Terrain and climate Elev.: 670 ft. Area: 258.5 sq. mi. (670.3 sq km). Avg. daily min. temp.: Jan.: 33.9°F/1°C; avg. daily max.: July: 97.8°F/36.5°C. Avg. annual rainfall: 29.45"; snowfall: 1.4"; clear days: 137; precipitation days: 78.

Government Form: council and manager. Mayor: Bob Bolen. Municipal tel. number: (817) 870-6117.

City finances (1987) Total revenues: $438.8 mil. Total genl. expend.: $408.4 mil. Gross debt outstanding: $871.6 mil.

Major employers General Dynamics 25,000; U.S. Air Force Base 8,791; Bell Helicopter 8,000; City of Fort Worth 6,008; Tandy Corp. 5,200; Winn-Dixie Texas Inc. 3,500; Harris Methodist Health System 3,300.

Honolulu, Hawaii

Discovered by Europeans in 1794, Honolulu, meaning "sheltered harbor," has attracted droves of visitors ever since. Situated on Oahu Island, it benefits from a large bay fully protected by coral reefs and its large port facilities. Because of its hospitable climate, the beaches of Waikiki, its majestic mountains, and exotic locale, tourism is Honolulu's major industry; several million visitors come annually, mainly from the U.S. mainland and the Far East, particularly from Japan.

The defense industry is the second mainstay of Honolulu's economy; the United States has long maintained major installations around the island, including the naval base at Pearl Harbor, Hickam Air Force Base, and the U.S. Army's Schofield Barracks and Fort Shafter. Honolulu also serves as the center for Hawaii's export crops—sugar, pineapple, and molasses—

and is the principal port for the import of much of the island-state's necessities.

Population 372,300 (1986). Rank: 38. Pop. density: 4,779/sq. mi. (1,845.2/sq km). County: Honolulu.

Terrain and climate Elev.: 15 ft. Area: 25.3 sq. mi. (65.52 sq km). Avg. daily min. temp.: Jan.: 65.3°F/18.5°C; avg. daily max.: July: 87.1°F/30.6°C. Avg. annual rainfall: 23.47"; snowfall: 0"; clear days: 90; precipitation days: 102.

Government Form: mayor and council. Mayor: Frank F. Fasi. Municipal tel. number: (808) 523-4141.

City finances (1987) Total revenues: $575.5 mil. Total genl. expend.: $656.1 mil. Gross debt outstanding: $871.6 mil.

Major employers Alexander & Baldwin Inc., Aloha Airlines, Amerloo Corp., AMFAC Inc., C. Brewer & Co. Inc., Castle & Cooke Inc., Crown Corp., Dillingham Corp., Hawaiian Airlines, Hawaiian Electric Co., Hawaiian Telephone, Interisland Resorts, Maui Land & Pineapple, Pacific Resources Inc.

Houston, Texas

On Aug. 30, 1836, brothers August C. and John K. Allen founded this city, naming it after Sam Houston, the first president of the Republic of Texas. The Allens paid just over $1.40 per share for 6,642 acres of land near the headwaters of Buffalo Bayou about 50 miles inland from the Gulf of Mexico. Houston's proximity to Stephen Austin's central Texas colonies gave it great potential as a marketing and distribution site. Incorporated in 1837, the city served as capital of the Republic of Texas until 1840. When the first railroad in Texas began operating out of Houston in 1853, the city developed into a major agricultural center, while the discovery of oil in southeast Texas at Spindletop in 1901 and the opening of the manmade Houston Ship Channel in 1914 stimulated petroleum refining and metal fabricating. During World War II, petrochemical production began on a large scale, and with the building of NASA's $761–million complex in the early 1960s (now known as the Johnson Space Center), Houston took center stage as the main player in manned spacecraft.

A major corporate and international business center—13 *Fortune*-500 companies are based there—present-day Houston has successfully limited its dependence on the energy economy. Ranked third nationally in number of trade offices, fifth in foreign consulates, sixth in international air passengers, and with more than half the Port of Houston's cargo in foreign trade in 1987, Houston ranked second among U.S. ports in foreign tonnage.

The presence of the Texas Medical Center also makes Houston a vital U.S. center for the practice and progress of modern high-tech medicine. The Center's 39 institutions occupy in excess of 550 acres and as of 1987, employed over 522,000 workers, with a student enrollment exceeding 10,000.

Population 1,728,910 (1986). Rank: 4. Pop. density: 3,019/sq. mi. (1,165.6/sq km). County: Harris.

Terrain and climate Elev.: 49 ft. Area: 572.7 sq. mi. (1,483.3 sq km). Avg. daily min. temp.:

Jan.: 40.8°F/4.8°C; avg. daily max.: July: 93.6°F/34.2°C. Avg. annual rainfall: 44.77"; snowfall: 0"; clear days, 94; precipitation days: 107.

Government Form: mayor and council. Mayor: Katherine J. Whitemore. Municipal tel. number: (713) 247–2200.

City finances (1987) Total revenues: $1,581.7 mil. Total genl. expend.: $1,791.1 mil. Gross debt outstanding: $3,135.7 mil.

Major employers American General, Coastal, Tenneco, Texas Air, Texas Medical Center.

Indianapolis, Indiana

Indianapolis, the capital of Indiana and a major commercial center in the country's heartland, is intersected by more highways than any other in the nation, earning it the name, the Crossroads of America. Fifty percent of America's population is within a day's drive of the city, a geographic asset that makes it a focal point of transportation and manufacturing.

The Euramerican settlement, established in 1820 where Fall Creek meets the White River, was chosen as the location of Indiana's capital in 1825. The state government created jobs triggering an expanding population that further swelled with the routing of the National Road (U.S. 40) in 1830. Development mushroomed in 1839 with the building of the Central Canal on the White River, providing a vital transportation link and the necessary water power to run factories, sawmills, and paper mills. Maintenance of the canal, however, proved impossible, and the town declined until the introduction of the railroad. By 1853 railroad lines fed into Indianapolis from every corner of the nation, and at one point, nearly 200 trains passed through daily. At the turn of the century, Indianapolis had emerged as a sophisticated city with sidewalks and streetcars. The city's economy prospered during early stages of the automotive industry, producing more than 50 types of cars—including the Dusenberg, the Marmon, and the Stutz—before Detroit gained ascendancy.

Having survived the decline in heavy industry and the flight of the affluent to the suburbs, Indianapolis remains a hub of manufacturing and transportation, with a bustling wheat, soybean, and livestock market. Key industries include electronics, metal fabrication, pharmaceuticals, and transportation equipment. Downtown Indianapolis has enjoyed a renaissance with the construction of a convention center, the Hoosier Dome, Market Square Arena, and the refurbishment of Union Station. The city also built a number of amateur sports arenas and in 1987 hosted the Pan Am Games.

Population 719,820 (1986). Rank: 13. Pop. density: 2,045/sq. mi. (789.6/sq km). County: Marion.

Terrain and climate Elev.: 808 ft. Area: 352 sq. mi. (911.7 sq km). Avg. daily min. temp.: Jan.: 17.8°F/–7.8°C; avg. daily max.: July: 85.2°F/29.5°C. Avg. annual rainfall: 39.12"; snowfall: 21"; clear days: 90; precipitation days: 122.

Government Form: mayor and council. Mayor: William H. Hudnut III. Municipal tel. number: (317) 236–3600.

City finances (1987) Total revenues: $669.1 mil. Total genl. expend.: $691.1 mil. Gross debt outstanding: $547.8 mil.

Major employers General Motors Allison Gas Turbine Div. 7,500; Methodist Hospital of Indiana 5,000; Indiana Bell Telephone 4,500; Fort Benjamin Harrison Finance Center 4,200; General Motors Truck & Bus Manufacturing Div. 3,750; Community Hospital of Indianapolis 3,400; Naval Avionics 3,100; St. Vincent Hospital 3,050; Ford Motor Co. 3,000; Blue Cross & Blue Shield of Indiana 3,000.

Jacksonville, Florida

The first Europeans to visit the area were French Huguenots, who in 1564 established a colony at Fort Caroline on the Saint Johns River in northeast Florida. The Spanish destroyed the fort in the following year. Permanent settlement began in 1816, and in 1822 Jacksonville was laid out and named for then Maj. Gen. Andrew Jackson, who had lead the U.S. campaign to take Florida from the Spanish. Growth was slow until after the Civil War, but by 1960 the population was more than 200,000. In 1968 the population jumped to more than 500,000 when it was consolidated with Duval County, and Jacksonville became the largest city by area in the nation.

Presently Florida's largest city, Jacksonville is a major regional center for commerce, industry, finance, and medicine. After years of improvements on its harbor, 25 miles west from the mouth of the Saint Johns, it has grown into a major port of entry and is the primary distribution center for the region. Jacksonville has also emerged as a leading resort with extensive recreational and convention facilities. Among its amenities are the Haydon Burns Library, Cummer Gallery of Art, Jacksonville Art Museum, Jacksonville Zoological Park, Saint Johns River Park, and Fort Caroline National Memorial, site of the first European colony in Florida. Among its leading educational institutions are Jacksonville University and the University of Northern Florida.

Population 609,860 (1986). Rank: 17. Pop. density: 803/sq. mi. (310/sq km). County: Duval.

Terrain and climate Elev.: 31 ft. Area: 759.7 sq. mi. (1,967.6 sq km). Avg. daily min. temp.: Jan.: 41.7°F/5°C; avg. daily max.: July: 90.7°F/29.5°C. Avg. annual rainfall: 52.77"; snowfall: 0"; clear days: 98; precipitation days: 116.

Government Form: mayor and council. Mayor: Thomas L. Hazouri. Municipal tel. number: (904) 630–1776.

City finances (1987) Total revenues: $1,261.0 mil. Total genl. expend.: $1,361.7 mil. Gross debt outstanding: $3,135.0 mil.

Major employers Publix Supermarkets 6,675; Southern Bell 4,174; CSX Transportation 3,500; Blue Cross/Blue Shield 2,726; Prudential Insurance Co. 2,700.

Kansas City, Missouri

Kansas City's Euramerican beginnings were as a trading outpost established by the French fur trader François Chouteau in 1821. In 1833 the town of Westport was founded nearby, and in 1850 the City of Kansas received its first charter. (Its name was changed to Kansas City in 1889.)

Situated at the confluence of the Kansas and Missouri rivers, Kansas City prospered early on as a river port and as the terminus of the Santa Fe and Oregon trails. With the arrival of the railroad in 1866, Kansas City's status as a major commercial hub was assured. Thanks to its central location and the development of excellent and diversified transportation and storage facilities, Kansas City is one of the nation's key markets for agricultural and livestock products, as well as for the distribution of heavy agricultural machinery. The Kansas City Board of Trade is one of the largest grain and commodities trading markets in the world. Other major industries are greeting card publishing, telecommunications, and high-tech manufacturing, especially instrument-landing systems for airplanes. Kansas City is also home to the 10th Federal Reserve Bank.

An early oasis of culture in the midst of an unsettled (by Euramericans), "untamed" prairie (the city once boasted two opera houses), Kansas City remains a mecca of the arts, with such cultural offerings as the Kansas City Art Institute, the Nelson-Atkins Museum of Art, the Kansas City Symphony, the Lyric Opera, and the Missouri Repertory Theatre. The city's beginnings are preserved in the Lone Jack Civil War Museum and in Missouri Town 1855, and it is the site of the annual American Royal Livestock, Horse Show, and Rodeo, held as part of the annual convention of the Future Farmers of America. Among its institutes of higher learning are Rockhurst College (1916), the University of Missouri-Kansas City, and the DeVry Institute of Technology.

Population 441,170 (1986). Rank: 29. Pop. density: 1,394/sq. mi. (538.2/sq km). Counties: Clay, Jackson, and Platte.

Terrain and climate Elev.: 744 ft. Area: 316.4 sq. mi. (819.5 sq km). Avg. daily min. temp.: Jan.: 17.2°F/–8.2°C; avg. daily max.: July: 88.5°F/31.3°C. Avg. annual rainfall: 29.27"; snowfall: 5.9"; clear days: 132; precipitation days: 97.

Government Form: council and manager. Mayor: Richard L. Berkley. Municipal tel. number: (816) 274–2595.

City finances (1987) Total revenues: $560.6 mil. Total genl. expend.: $516.9 mil. Gross debt outstanding: $499.1 mil.

Major employers Allied-Signal Aerospace Co., Hallmark Cards, Marion Laboratories Inc., Trans World Airlines, U.S. Sprint.

Long Beach, California

Originally the site of an Indian trading camp, by the end of the 18th century, the area that is now Long Beach was part of the Spanish Ranchos Los Alamitos and Cerritos. In 1881 William E. Willmore began development of the land as a resort (which he named for himself). When first incorporated in 1888, it was named Long Beach after its 8.5 miles of Pacific beachfront. Content to remain a resort community, Long Beach had its fortunes rewritten in 1921 when extensive petroleum deposits were first discovered at Signal Hill. Today industry is a major presence in Long Beach—especially ship repair, transportation, oil refining, and marine research; in addition the Navy maintains a large base with dry dock facilities.

Among its cultural and recreational attractions are Long Beach's own Museum of Art; the Terrace Theater, home of the Long Beach Symphony Orchestra; and the Long Beach Community Playhouse. Popular tourist attractions include Los Cerritos, a Spanish adobe house dating to 1844; the magnificent ocean liner *Queen Mary*, which today serves as a floating maritime museum, convention center, and hotel; and the *Spruce Goose*, Howard Hughes's unflyable plane of gigantic proportions. Long Beach is also the site of a Formula 1 Grand Prix every spring. Disneyland is in nearby Anaheim.

Population 396,280 (1986). Rank: 33. Pop. density: 7,957/sq. mi. (3,072.2/sq km). County: Los Angeles.
Terrain and climate Elev.: 35 ft. Area: 49.8 sq. mi. (129 sq km). Avg. daily min. temp.: Jan.: 44.3°F/6.8°C; avg. daily max.: July: 83°F/28.3°C. Avg. annual rainfall: 12"; snowfall: 0"; clear days, 143; precipitation days: 35.
Government Form: council and manager. Mayor: Ernie Kell. Municipal tel. number: (213) 590–6505.
City finances (1987) Total revenues: $571.4 mil. Total genl. expend.: $601.1 mil. Gross debt outstanding: $545.9 mil.
Major employers City of Long Beach, Earth Technology Corp., Petrolane Inc., U.S. Navy.

Los Angeles, California

In pre-Spanish days, the area of Los Angeles was inhabited by approximately 4,000 Indian peoples, representing some 30 different groups. The Uto-Aztecan village of Yang-na, with a population of 300, was located in what is now downtown Los Angeles, in the vicinity of Alameda and Commercial streets. In October 1542 Joao Rodrigues Cabrilho, a Portuguese explorer in the employ of Spain, became the first European to set foot on Los Angeles soil, but 200 years passed before a land expedition under the command of Gaspar de Portola crossed the territory on the way from Monterey to San Diego, in 1769.

The establishment of the Mission of San Gabriel (destined to become the largest of the Franciscan Missions) followed, and in 1781 Spanish Gov. Felipe Neve founded the city of El Pueblo de Nuestra Señora de los Angeles de Porciuncula (The Village of Our Lady of the Angels) as part of a plan to colonize California. Spanish rule continued until 1822, when Spain relinquished her holdings in western America, prompting California to pledge her allegiance to the Mexican empire. With the Treaty of Guadalupe Hidalgo (1848), the United States acquired all of California from Mexico, and in 1850 Los Angeles was incorporated as a city. Introduction of the Southern Pacific Railroad in 1876 sparked a 12-year land boom, promoting the city's growth. By 1892 Los Angeles thrived as a center of oil production, and in 1899 work began on the largest man-made deep-water facility in the world. Emerging as the motion picture capital of the world by 1910, industry accelerated in the 1920s, and today

L.A. ranks as one of the three great industrial cities in the country.

A thriving metropolis, Los Angeles boasts one of the finest highway systems in the world, handling over 5.6 million cars registered in its five-county area—a car for every two people, the highest ratio in the world. Three transcontinental railway systems terminate in L.A., 37 certified air carriers fly to all parts of the world, its harbors have 46 miles of waterfront, and the city has the largest trucking center in the West. L.A. remains the world's movie mecca, teeming with studios, stars, and the starstruck.

> *Los Angeles: "Nineteen suburbs in search of a metropolis."*
>
> —H.L. Mencken, 1925

Los Angelinos live with daily problems of smog, traffic jams, spectacular traffic accidents, and the everpresent threats of mud slides, fires, floods, high winds, and earthquakes. But the year-round sunshine, and the number of beaches and mountain areas, all within an easy drive, tend to ameliorate one's anxiety.

Population 3,259,340 (1986). Rank: 2. Pop. density: 6,996/sq. mi. (2,701.2/sq km). County: Los Angeles.
Terrain and climate Elev.: 104 ft. Area: 465.9 sq. mi. (1,206.7 sq km). Avg. daily min. temp.: Jan.: 47.3°F/8.5°C; avg. daily max.: July: 75.3°F/24°C. Avg. annual rainfall: 14.85"; snowfall: 0"; clear days: 143; precipitation days: 35.
Government Form: mayor and council. Mayor: Tom Bradley. Municipal tel. number: (213) 485–2121.
City finances (1987) Total revenues: $5,087.1 mil. Total genl. expend.: $4,450.4 mil. Gross debt outstanding: $5,056.2 mil.
Major employers City of Los Angeles, Pacific Bell, Security Pacific Bank Corp., Southern California Edison, State of California, Trans-America Corp.

Memphis, Tennessee

The first settlers in the area of Memphis, the Chickasaw, arrived on the bluffs overlooking the Mississippi River more than a thousand years ago. The Chickasaw forcibly displaced these people and lived there for eight centuries until 1838, when the U.S. government scattered the entire tribe to Oklahoma and parts further west so that Euramericans could develop the land. The Spanish explorer Hernando de Soto first set eyes on the bluffs in 1541. Other explorers passed through over the next century, and in 1739 the French built Fort Assumption. The French, Spanish, and Chickasaw fought over the land for the balance

of the 18th century until it became a part of the United States in 1797. The area's original American owners, Gen. James Winchester, Judge John Overton, and Gen. Andrew Jackson (who later sold his share and went on to become president), established the town in 1819 and named it Memphis, after the ancient Egyptian city on the Nile.

River boatmen gave young Memphis a reputation for brawls and bawdiness, while mosquitoes gave it a history of yellow fever epidemics, which in the 1880s, claimed more than half the city's population and jeopardized its charter. A sewage system, the first of its kind, finally helped conquer the epidemic. Between the river traffic and cotton crops, the city prospered, attracting Irish and German immigrants, and by the 20th century, was on its way to becoming the unofficial capital of the mid-South. Elvis Presley, who lived and died in Memphis, remains the city's most enduring contribution to popular culture.

Population 652,640 (1986). Rank: 15. Pop. density: 2,471/sq. mi. (954.1/sq km). County: Shelby.
Terrain and climate Elev.: 307 ft. Area: 264.1 sq. mi. (684 sq km). Avg. daily min. temp.: Jan.: 30.9°F/-0.6°C; avg. daily max.: July: 91.5°F/33°C. Avg. annual rainfall: 51.57"; snowfall: 6"; clear days: 118; precipitation days: 106.
Government Form: mayor and council. Mayor: Richard C. Hackett. Municipal tel. number: (901) 576–6000.
City finances (1987) Total revenues: $1,537.9 mil. Total genl. expend.: $1,410.6 mil. Gross debt outstanding: $842.2 mil.
Major employers U.S. government 15,036; Federal Express Corp. 14,757; Memphis City Schools 14,402; U.S. Navy 14,160; Malone & Hyde Inc. 8,500; City of Memphis 7,659; Baptist Memorial Hospital 6,035; Shelby County Government 5,206.

Miami, Florida

Miami, the most southerly major city in the continental United States, sits about two degrees north of the Tropic of Cancer, a location that has made it a long-standing resort haven. Miami in the 1980s also thrived as a major hub of commerce and as a population center for Latin American immigrants, particularly those arriving from Cuba, whose ambition and business acumen contributed to the city's prosperity. While tourists still generate over 60 percent of the area's economic activity, many other areas of enterprise, such as construction, light industry, and agriculture (limes, tomatoes, avocados, mangoes, and beans) have flourished.

Miami (whose name is thought to derive from the Indian *mayami*, meaning "big water"), dates back to the 16th century when Native Americans occupied the southern part of Florida. Fort Dallas, built near the mouth of the Miami River in 1836 as a base of war against the Seminoles, became the first permanent Euramerican settlement. The building of the Florida East Coast Railroad, coinciding with Miami's incorporation as a city in 1896 (population 343), offered ready access to the area. Resort hotels quickly cropped up, and Miami, along with the rest of Florida, enjoyed great success. In 1926 a severe hurricane submerged much of its land under water, abruptly ending Miami's prosperity, but the city managed to grow steadily by draining and developing swampland. After World War II, new resorts rose up, and Miami thrived.

The relative success of the large influx of Cubans in the 1960s and early 1980s is reportedly a source of ill feelings, especially to many in the black community, and twice in the 1980s, the city has been wracked by rioting—most recently, just prior to Super Bowl XXIII, in 1989.

Population 373,940 (1986). Rank: 36. Pop. density: 10,902/sq. mi. (4,209.3/sq km). County: Dade.

Terrain and climate Elev.: 12 ft. Area: 34.3 sq. mi. (88.8 sq km). Avg. daily min. temp.: Jan.: 59.2°F/15.1°C; avg. daily max.: July: 88.7°F/31.5°C. Avg. annual rainfall: 57.55"; snowfall: 0"; clear days: 76; precipitation days: 129.

Government Form: council and manager. Mayor: Xavier L. Suarez. Municipal tel. number: (305) 579–6010.

City finances (1987) Total revenues: $327.3 mil. Total genl. expend.: $292.3 mil. Gross debt outstanding: $338.9 mil.

Major employers Burdines Stores, Dade County Public Schools, Eastern Airlines, Florida Power and Light, Jackson Memorial Hospital, Metro-Dade County, Pan-American World Airways, Southeast Bank Corp., Southern Bell, State of Florida, Univ. of Miami, U.S. government.

Milwaukee, Wisconsin

During the 1670s the French explorers Jacques Marquette and Louis Jolliet were the first Europeans to visit the site of present-day Milwaukee, an area on the western shore of Lake Michigan at the confluence of the Menomonee and Kinnickinnic rivers. In 1795 Jacques Vicau of the North West Company established a trading post, and in 1818 Solomon Laurent Juneau, the first permanent Euramerican settler, founded Milwaukee (from the Indian term *millioke*, meaning "beautiful land"). From the 1840s on, large numbers of German immigrants came to the city, making up more than 60 percent of the 1850 population; today an estimated one-third of the city's residents are of German descent.

A flourishing agricultural center, Milwaukee had by the Civil War become the largest wheat market in the world. Its industrial base expanded after the war, and by 1940 the city ranked fourth in manufacturing among U.S. cities. Still one of the most vigorous producers of durable goods—especially automotive parts, construction and road-building equipment, diesel and gasoline engines, tractors, and outboard motors—Milwaukee has also emerged as a major meat-packing center. Reflecting its German heritage, the city developed a successful brewing industry, with two of the largest beer-producing companies in the country—Schlitz and Pabst. A major Great Lakes and, since the opening of the St. Lawrence Seaway, international port, Milwaukee handles 12 international steamship lines.

Population 605,090 (1986). Rank: 18. Pop. density: 6,316/sq. mi. (2,438.6/sq km). County: Milwaukee.

Terrain and climate Elev.: 581 ft. Area: 95.8 sq. mi. (248.1 sq km). Avg. daily min. temp.: Jan.: 11.3°F/–11.5°C; avg. daily max.: July: 79.8°F/26.5°C. Avg. annual rainfall: 30.94"; snowfall: 45"; clear days: 96; precipitation days: 122.

Government Form: mayor and council. Mayor: John Norquist. Municipal tel. number: (414) 278–3200.

City finances (1987) Total revenues: $739.7 mil. Total genl. expend.: $550.0 mil. Gross debt outstanding: $576.5 mil.

Major employers Allis Chalmers, A.O. Smith, Briggs & Stratton, Bucyrus-Erie, Clark Oil & Refining Corp., Congoleum, Harnischfeger, Johnson Controls, Joseph Schlitz Brewing, Koehring, Pabst Brewing, Rexnord.

> *"Where I come from, when a Catholic marries a Lutheran it is considered the first step on the road to Minneapolis."*
> —Garrison Keillor

Minneapolis, Minnesota

Despite its arctic winters, Minneapolis is one of the most desirable cities in the United States. It sits astride the Mississippi River, near the headwaters of the Minnesota River, about 350 miles northwest of Chicago. While it is the largest commercial metropolis in the north between Milwaukee and Seattle, no single industry dominates, although many large computer and electronics companies make Minneapolis their home. A regional banking center and the site of the Federal Reserve Bank for the Ninth District, Minneapolis has the world's largest cash grain exchange and the world's four largest wheat-flour-milling companies, and provides the upper Midwest with truck, barge, and air transport.

In 1682 Father Louis Hennepin, the French priest who explored the Mississippi, was the first European to set eyes on the Falls of St. Anthony, the future site of Minneapolis. Unsettled until Fort Snelling was built in 1819 to protect the fur traders from the Sioux and Chippewa, the town of St. Anthony began growing up on one side of the Mississippi and Minnesota on the other, until the two were consolidated in 1872. Named for the Indian word *minne*, meaning "water," and the Greek word for "city," *polis*, Minneapolis blossomed on the basis of its flour and lumber milling. By century's end, the forests to the north had been depleted, but flour milling continues as a thriving industry to this day.

Long considered a center of progressive political and social thinking, it is a mecca of education and culture. Minneapolis is the site of the main campus of the University of Minnesota, the Minnesota Orchestra, and the Minneapolis Institute of the Arts. A haven for outdoor enthusiasts, the park system numbers 153 parks encompassing 6,000 acres, and with 10 percent of its surface covered by water, Minneapolis has 12 lakes within its city limits.

Population 356,840 (1986). Rank: 43. Pop. density: 6,476/sq. mi. (2,500.4/sq km). County: Hennepin.

Terrain and climate Elev.: 828 ft. Area: 55.1 sq. mi. (142.7 sq km). Avg. daily min. temp.: Jan.: 2.4°F/–16.4°C; avg. daily max.: July: 83.4°F/28.5°C. Avg. annual rainfall: 26.36"; snowfall: 46"; clear days: 100; precipitation days: 113.

Government Form: mayor and council. Mayor: Donald McKay Fraser. Municipal tel. number: (612) 348–2100.

City finances (1987) Total revenues: $790.8 mil. Total genl. expend.: $566.7 mil. Gross debt outstanding: $1,977.2 mil.

Major employers City of Minneapolis, Control Data Corp., General Mills, Honeywell Inc., IDS, Land O'Lakes, Minneapolis Public School, Northwest Airlines, State of Minnesota, 3-M Corp., West Publishing Co., Unisys.

Nashville, Tennessee

In the winter of 1779–80, settlers from North Carolina, led by James Robertson, arrived at a place on the Cumberland River called Big Salt Lick, and built forts on both sides of the river, one of which they named Nashborough, after Gen. Francis Nash of the Revolutionary Army. Adopting the name Nashville in 1784, the settlement was chartered as a city in 1806, became state capital in 1843, and prospered until the Civil War as the northern terminus of the Natchez Trace, a 500-mile road to Natchez, Mississippi. The site of one of the war's last major battles in December 1864, the city underwent a long period of rebuilding, and by the end of the century, the population reached 81,000. The city continued to grow, doubling in population by World War II, and has experienced even greater expansion since that time.

While best known as a major center of both the recording and music-publishing industries, Nashville enjoys a widely diversified economic foundation and serves as a distribution and marketing point for the upper southern region of the country. Several religious organizations and their publishing operations are headquartered there, and the city comprises more than a dozen institutions of higher learning, including Vanderbilt University, Fisk University, and Tennessee State University. With a growing base of manufacturing, insurance, and banking, Nashville, as home of the Grand Ole Opry, has also developed into a regional tourist and convention attraction. A full-scale replica of the Greek temple the Parthenon is a noted site.

Population 473,670 (1986). Rank: 26. Pop. density: 988/sq. mi. (381.5/sq km). County: Davidson.

Terrain and climate Elev.: 605 ft. Area: 479.5 sq. mi. (1,241.9 sq km). Avg. daily min. temp.: Jan.: 27.8°F/–2.3°C; avg. daily max.: July: 89.8°F/32.1°C. Avg. annual rainfall: 48.49";

snowfall: 10.7"; clear days: 103; precipitation days: 119.

Government Form: mayor and council. Mayor: Bill Boner. Municipal tel. number: (615) 259–6047.

City finances (1987) Total revenues: $1,316.2 mil. Total genl. expend.: $1,321.1 mil. Gross debt outstanding: $2,460.8 mil.

Major employers Hospital Corp. of America, Ingram Industries Inc., Mid-South Industries Inc., Northern Telecom Inc., Service Merchandise Co. Inc., Shoney's Inc.

Newark, New Jersey

First called Pesayak Towne, and later New Milford, Newark was first settled by Connecticut Puritans in 1666. It takes its present name from the English Newark-on-Trent. Situated on Newark Bay at the mouth of the Passaic River about eight miles west of New York City, Newark was made the seat of Essex County in 1682, received its first charter in 1683, and was incorporated as a city in 1836. Home to Princeton University from 1747 to 1756, and the site of many important battles during the American Revolution, Newark today is the largest city in New Jersey.

Newark's first industry was tanning and leather-goods manufacture. The city's inability to accommodate the great influx of immigrants who began arriving in 1880 gave rise to the squalid tenements that mark the city even now. Although the insurance industry took root, Newark did not capitalize on its access to the Atlantic until the Port of Newark—now integrated with the Port of New York and New Jersey—was established in 1914. Extensive container port facilities in neighboring Elizabeth and the huge Newark International Airport make Newark a major international trading center. It is also a leader in the petrochemical industry and printing.

For all its promise, Newark has never lived up to its potential. Its better-off residents have habitually fled to the suburbs, leaving poverty and an eroded tax base behind: it was the lack of adequate housing that sparked severe riots in the inner city in the late 1960s. Newark has received more federal housing aid than any other city. Newark is the site of the New Jersey Institute of Technology, a campus of Rutgers University, and the well-respected Newark Museum.

Population 316,240 (1986). Rank: 50. Pop. density: 13,122/sq. mi. (5,066.4/sq km). County: Essex.

Terrain and climate Elev.: 146 ft. Area: 24.1 sq. mi. (62.4 sq km). Avg. daily min. temp.: Jan.: 24.2°F/–4.3°C; avg. daily max.: July: 85.6°F/29.7°C. Avg. annual rainfall: 42.34"; snowfall: N.A.; clear days: 95; precipitation days: 122.

Government Form: mayor and council. Mayor: Sharpe James. Municipal tel. number: (201) 733–6400.

City finances (1987) Total revenues: $339.4 mil. Total genl. expend.: $318.2 mil. Gross debt outstanding: $163.4 mil.

Major employers Bambergers, First Fidelity Bancorp, New Jersey Bell, Prudential Insurance Co. of America, Public Service Gas and Electric.

New Orleans, Louisiana

Founded in 1718 by Jean Baptiste le Moyne and named Ville d'Orléans after the regent of France, the city of New Orleans is one of the nation's most distinctive cities. Situated only 110 miles from the mouth of the Mississippi River, it has long been a major international port (it ranks second in the nation today), and thanks to overlapping waves of French, Spanish, African-American, and Anglo-American immigrants, it has one of the most richly textured cultures of any city in North America. It is geographically distinct, too, in that much of it is below sea level; the almost constant threat of flooding is mitigated by an intricate network of canals and levees.

After half a century under French rule, New Orleans became the capital of Spanish Louisiana in 1763. It was briefly under French rule again (1800–03) before being acquired by the United States as part of the Louisiana Purchase. Although Louisiana was admitted as a state in 1815, New Orleans continues to reflect its Spanish and French heritage in its architecture, cuisine, and its flamboyant Mardi Gras celebration at the beginning of Lent. African-American traditions are strong here, too, and Dixieland jazz—long heralded as a uniquely American music—is a fusion of African and European styles.

In addition to being a major port for the export of cotton, rice, petroleum products, iron, steel, and corn and the importing of sugar, bananas, coffee, bauxite, and molasses, New Orleans is a major center for offshore drilling in the Gulf of Mexico. In recent years its industrial sector, with an emphasis on aerospace research and technology, petroleum refinement, and shipbuilding, has been strong.

A major tourist attraction in its own right, the city includes among its special points of interest St. Louis Cathedral, the French Market, Preservation Hall and Dixieland Hall, and the Presbytère—all in the French Quarter—the celebrated residential architecture of the Garden District, the New Orleans Museum of Art, the Confederate Museum, and Audubon Park Zoo. Among its educational institutions are Tulane University, Sophie Newcomb College, and Dillard University.

Population 554,500 (1986). Rank: 21. Pop. density: 2,781/sq. mi. (1,073.7/sq km). Parish: Orleans.

Terrain and climate Elev.: 30 ft. Area: 199.4 sq. mi. (516.4 sq km). Avg. daily min. temp.: Jan.: 43°F/6.1°C; avg. daily max.: July: 90.7°F/32.6°C. Avg. annual rainfall: 59.74"; snowfall: 0.2"; clear days: 109; precipitation days: 113.

Government Form: mayor and council. Mayor: Sidney J. Barthelemy. Municipal tel. number: (504) 586–4000.

City finances (1987) Total revenues: $631.9 mil. Total genl. expend.: $601.1 mil. Gross debt outstanding: $902.3 mil.

Major employers Avondale Industries, D.H. Holmes Co., Martin Marietta Corp., National Supermarkets of Louisiana, Ochsner Foundation Hospital and Clinic, Popeye's Famous Fried Chicken, Schwegmann Bros. Giant Supermarkets, Shell Oil Co., South Central Bell, Tulane Univ., Winn Dixie of Louisiana.

> *"Mammon, noun. The god of the world's leading religion. His chief temple is in the holy city of New York."*
>
> —Ambrose Bierce,
> *The Devil's Dictionary*, 1906

New York City, New York

Even before the arrival of Europeans in North America, the waters that today make New York one of the world's foremost ports—and the foremost city in the United States—were the scene of lively trade between the predominant Algonquian tribes in the region. The city's modern history dates to 1524, when the Florentine explorer Giovanni de Verrazano sailed into New York Bay. In 1609 Henry Hudson, an English navigator sailing for the Dutch East India Company, explored the river that bears his name today. In 1625 the Dutch West India Company purchased Manhattan and established Nieuw Amsterdam, which quickly became a profitable trading post. Dutch settlers soon expanded beyond the original colony, settling Breukelen, Nieuw Harlem, Bronx, and Staaten Eylandt. Taken by the British in 1664 (the Dutch briefly regained control in 1673–74), and renamed for the duke of York, the town continued to prosper.

As resentment of British authority grew, New York became a seat of colonial discontent, participating in actions against the Stamp Act (1763) and tea tax (1773). But after the Battle of Long Island and Washington's retreat in August 1776, the British held New York through the end of the war. Yet Washington was inaugurated president at Federal Hall (today the site of the second Federal Reserve Bank) on Wall Street, and from 1789–90 New York was the nation's capital.

Industry and trade expanded dramatically after the opening of the Erie Canal from Troy (150 miles up the Hudson River) and Buffalo (350 miles west of Troy) gave New York direct access to raw materials and markets of the Great Lakes states. In the mid-19th century, New York became the country's primary port of immigration, and many of the millions of immigrants who came to America carved out distinctly ethnic neighborhoods throughout the city in a patchwork that survives to the present.

In 1898 an act of the state legislature created "Greater New York," and today New

York's population is greater than that of Los Angeles and Chicago (the second- and third-largest cities in the country) combined. Even if they were separate cities, four of New York boroughs would rank in the top 10—Brooklyn fourth (2.3 million), Queens fifth (1.9 million), Manhattan eighth (1.5 million), and Bronx ninth (1.2 million). In March 1989 the Supreme Court declared unconstitutional the city's Board of Estimate—which had final say over the administration of the city's $28-billion budget and much else besides—because it violated the constitutional concept of one-man, one-vote. Whatever changes are made in the city's charter, the way New York is governed will soon undergo sweeping change.

New York's attractions are almost innumerable—enough to draw 17.8 million visitors in 1987—but they include 150 museums, 400 art galleries, 38 Broadway theaters, and scores of concert halls, clubs, and dance halls. In addition there are 780 landmark buildings, 50 landmark interiors, and 51 historic districts. (A list of attractions can be found under "New York State.") The city leads the nation in the arts, fashion, advertising, banking and financial services, publishing, broadcasting, and certain of the service industries; it is the home of the UN General Assembly; and there are 87 colleges and universities, including Columbia University, New York University, Long Island University, Brooklyn College, St. Johns University, the Pratt Institute of Technology, the Juilliard School, and the School of Visual Arts. Manufactured products comprise apparel, chemicals, metal products, and printing.

And if all this has whetted your appetite, you can nosh at one of the 25,000 eateries in the "Big Apple."

Population 7,262,700 (1986). Rank: 1. Pop. density: 24,089/sq. mi. (9,300.8/sq km). Counties: Bronx, Kings, New York, Queens, and Richmond.

Terrain and climate Elev.: 87 ft. Area: 301.5 sq. mi. (780.9 sq km). Avg. daily min. temp.: Jan.: 25.6°F/–3.5°C; avg. daily max.: July: 85.3°F/29.6°C. Avg. annual rainfall: 44.12"; snowfall: 29"; clear days: 107; precipitation days, 121.

Government Form: mayor and council. Mayor: Edward I. Koch. Municipal tel. number: (212) 566-5700.

City finances (1987) Total revenues: $31,967.6 mil. Total genl. expend.: $29,622.3 mil. Gross debt outstanding: $17,577.0 mil.

Major employers American Express, Chase Manhattan Bank, Citicorp, City of New York, U.S. government, Merrill Lynch, Metropolitan Life Insurance, New York Telephone, Philip Morris, State of New York.

Oakland, California

The first Euramerican to settle present-day Oakland was Dom Luis Maria Peralta, in 1820, who established the 44,000-acre settlement called Rancho San Antonio in 1820. Its first real growth began with the establishment of ferry service to San Francisco in 1852, though the ferry was dramatically superceded by Oakland's selection as the western terminus of the first transcontinental railroad in 1869. The city remained in the economic shadow of its

more sophisticated neighbor across the Bay until the San Francisco earthquake of 1906 drove 100,000–150,000 thousand people to Oakland for shelter. An estimated 65,000 of these are thought to have settled there permanently, providing an impetus for Oakland's long period of growth as an international port and industrial center.

A major commercial and cultural center with a container port ranked 10th in the world, Oakland is also the major northern hub of the California freeway system, which is integrated with the Bay Area Rapid Transit (BART) System. It has also become the premier biotechnology center in the region, and regional and international headquarters for firms in finance, medicine, telecommunications, international trade, and heavy industry are headquarted there.

Long a primarily industrial urban center, Oakland is undergoing a thorough revamping of its downtown area with $500 million of new development, and the Jack London waterfront—named for the author who spent his youth on the Oakland docks—is the site of a further $100 million expansion. With more than 50 percent of its population between the ages of 25 and 49, Oakland thrives as a youthful, vibrant metropolis. Almost 35 percent live in households with incomes of $34,000 or more, and nearly half the population either attended college or received four-year degrees. More artists reside in Oakland than anywhere else in the country with the exception of New York's Greenwich Village. Although Oakland embraces a racially and culturally diverse populace, a 1980 University of Wisconsin study found it the most integrated city in the nation.

Population 356,960 (1986). Rank: 42. Pop. density: 6,623/sq. mi. (2,557.1/sq km). County: Alameda.

Terrain and climate Elev.: 42 ft. Area: 53.9 sq. mi. (139.6 sq km). Avg. daily min. temp.: Jan.: 43.4°F/6.3°C; avg. daily max.: July: 70.6°F/29.6°C. Avg. annual rainfall: 18.03"; snowfall: N.A.; clear days: N.A.; precipitation days: N.A.

Government Form: council and manager. Mayor: Lionel J. Wilson. Municipal tel. number: (415) 273-3141.

City finances (1987) Total revenues: $433.5 mil. Total genl. expend.: $436.0 mil. Gross debt outstanding: $1,018.7 mil.

Major employers Kaiser Foundation Health Plan 18,970; Alameda County 9,200; Oakland Public Schools 6,065; Pacific Bell 5,376; City of Oakland 3,770; U.S. Army 3,376.

Oklahoma City, Oklahoma

Oklahoma City quite literally sprang up during the Great Land Rush of 1889 and, by presidential proclamation, opened for Euramerican settlement officially on April 22 of that year. At day's end approximately 10,000 settlers had moved in—the greatest one-day nonannexation population increase in the history of cities. Oklahoma became a state in 1907 and Oklahoma City its capital in 1910, by which time the population had swelled to about 64,000. Since then, it has become Oklahoma's largest city, its leading commercial center, and home to the National Cowboy Hall of Fame.

Oklahoma City's economy, based on oil and livestock, thrives on petroleum production, meat processing, and the breeding of stocker and feeder cattle. The city hosts a flourishing printing and publishing industry and manufactures a diversity of products, including automobiles, electronics equipment, computers, communications switches, and oil well supplies. As a vital banking center serving the central and western regions of the state, Oklahoma City boasts a Federal Reserve branch bank. On a somewhat less positive note, Oklahoma City reportedly sparked the "go-go" banking syndrome that characterized the 1970s oil boom, when the Penn Square Bank's ill-advised oil patch loans nearly devastated the U.S. banking system.

Population 446,120 (1986). Rank: 28. Pop. density: 739/sq. mi. (285.3/sq km). County: Oklahoma.

Terrain and climate Elev.: 1,304 ft. Area: 604 sq. mi. (1,564.4 sq km). Avg. daily min. temp.: Jan.: 25.2°F/–3.7°C; avg. daily max.: July: 93.5°F/34.1°C. Avg. annual rainfall: 30.89"; snowfall: 9"; clear days: 141; precipitation days: 81.

Government Form: council and manager. Mayor: Ronald D. Nordick. Municipal tel. number: (405) 231-2424.

City finances (1987) Total revenues: $337.6 mil. Total genl. expend.: $316.6 mil. Gross debt outstanding: $483.1 mil.

Major employers U.S. Air Force 17,636; General Motors 6,000; AT&T Technologies 5,778; Southwestern Bell Telephone Co. 3,534; Oklahoma Gas & Electric Co. 3,460; Oklahoma Memorial Hospital 3,100; Federal Aviation Administration 3,000; Baptist Medical Center of Oklahoma 2,600; Univ. of Oklahoma Health Sciences Center 2,271; Kerr-McGee Corp. 2,000; Firestone Tire & Rubber Co. 1,700.

Omaha, Nebraska

Euramerican settlement in what is now Omaha began with a fur-trading post established shortly after the Lewis and Clark expedition passed through the area in 1804. In 1820 the U.S. government built Ft. Atkinson, and the surrounding community became a major stop on both the Mormon and the Lewis and Clark trails, and was incorporated as a city in 1854. After strong lobbying by citizens of Council Bluffs, Iowa, just across the Missouri River to the east, Omaha (the name means "above all others on the stream") became the eastern terminus of the Union-Pacific transcontinental railroad, the country's first railroad, in 1869. Within six years the population grew to 39,000 and by the turn of the century had passed the 100,000 mark.

As a major transportation hub of the Midwest—Omaha today boasts seven major railroads, and the recently expanded Port of Omaha services a dozen barge lines—the city became a major distribution center for meat and grain, living up to its motto We Feed the World. Its major food products include pasta, potato chips, coffee, pancake mixes, frozen dinners, and Omaha steaks. With 44 *Fortune*-500 manufacturing operations and a healthy publishing industry (roughly one out of every four manufacturers is either a publisher or printer), Omaha's diversified economy also has strong roots in insurance; communications; sophisticated medical facilities, centered around the medical schools of Creighton University and the University of Nebraska; and in Offutt Air Force Base, headquarters of the Strategic Air Command.

Among its performing arts institutions are the Omaha Symphony, Opera/Omaha, the Omaha Ballet, the Orpheum Theater, and the Omaha Community Playhouse. Museums and historic sites include the Boys Town Hall of Fame, the Henry Doorly Zoo and Aquarium, the Great Plains Black Museum, the historic ships USS *Hazard* and USS *Marlin,* and the Old Market, a mixed-use National Historic District on the Missouri River.

Population 349,270 (1986). Rank: 45. Pop. density: 3,517/sq. mi. (1,357.9/sq km). County: Douglas.

Terrain and climate Elev.: 982 ft. Area: 99.3 sq. mi. (257.2 sq km). Avg. daily min. temp.: Jan.: 10.2°F/–12.1°C; avg. daily max.: July: 88.5°F/31.3°C. Avg. annual rainfall: 30.34"; snowfall: 32"; clear days: 113; precipitation days: 99.

Government Form: mayor and council. Mayor: P.J. Morgan. Municipal tel. number: (402) 444-5000.

City finances (1987) Total revenues: $232.5 mil. Total genl. expend.: $189.1 mil. Gross debt outstanding: $184.3 mil.

Major employers AT&T Network Systems, City of Omaha, First Data Resources, Mutual of Omaha/United of Omaha, Northwestern Bell Telephone, Omaha Public Schools, St. Joseph Hospital, Union Pacific Railroad, Univ. of Nebraska Medical Center, U.S. Air Force.

"In Boston they ask, How much does he know? In New York, How much is he worth? In Philadelphia, Who were his parents?"

—*What Paul Bourget Thinks of Us* (1899)

Philadelphia, Pennsylvania

In 1632 a small contingent of Swedes and Finns came to the land where the Schuylkill River meets the Delaware and founded New Sweden. In 1655 Peter Stuyvesant seized New Sweden for the Dutch, inciting conflict with the British until the Dutch relinquished their rights to the territory in 1673. Nine years later William Penn established a town between the Schuylkill and the Delaware rivers, naming it Philadelphia, the "city of brotherly love," and in two years it evolved into an active settlement of about 2,500 people, most of them Quakers.

In the mid-1700s, Benjamin Franklin began shaping the destiny of Philadelphia by presiding over the founding of the University of Pennsylvania (America's first university), Pennsylvania Hospital, and a fire insurance company (both also firsts). Under his guidance Philadelphia became the premier colonial city for the arts and the home of many famous educators, scientists, mathematicians, authors, and painters. In addition a total of 17 libraries were founded at this time. The meeting place of the Continental Congress and the site of the signing of the Declaration of Independence, Philadelphia was the nation's first capital, from 1790 to 1800, the year the federal government moved permanently to Washington, D.C.

Throughout the 19th century, the influx first of Irish and German, then Jewish, Italian, Polish, and Slavic immigrants from Europe, and blacks from the South, helped build the city's industrial base. Today Philadelphia ranks second among U.S. cities in oil refining, and its principal industries are electrical machinery, automobile and truck bodies, petrochemicals, metalworking, and scientific instruments. The city's extensive military installations include the Philadelphia Naval Base, the Naval Air Engineering Center, the Frankford Arsenal, the Navy Supply Depot, the Defense Support Center, and the U.S. Marine Corps Supply Activity.

Population 1,642,900 (1986). Rank: 5. Pop. density: 12,080/sq. mi. (4,664.1/sq km). County: Philadelphia.

Terrain and climate Elev.: 28 ft. Area: 136 sq. mi. (352.2 sq km). Avg. daily min. temp.: Jan.: 23.8°F/–4.5°C; avg. daily max.: July: 86.1°F/30°C. Avg. annual rainfall: 41.42"; snowfall: 20"; clear days: 92; precipitation days: 116.

Government Form: mayor and council. Mayor: M. Wilson Goode. Municipal tel. number: (215) 686-7116.

City finances (1987) Total revenues: $2,815.6 mil. Total genl. expend.: $2,843.1 mil. Gross debt outstanding: $3,875.6 mil.

Major employers Acme Markets, Bell of Pennsylvania, Budd Co., CIGNA, Conrail, General Electric, Philadelphia Electric Co., Sears Roebuck & Co., Smithkline Beckman Corp., Strawbridge & Clothier, Temple Univ., Univ. of Pennsylvania, Westinghouse Electric Co.

Phoenix, Arizona

Phoenix, the capital of Arizona and its largest city, sits in the Salt River valley in a former desert that has become a prosperous agricultural area because of a network of irrigated dams located northeast of the city. Long a resort area owing to its mild climate, Phoenix has recently emerged as a lively commercial and agricultural center as well. A prospering high-tech haven attracting businesses engaged in electronics, communications, and research and development, the city also has a strong manufacturing base, which includes airport parts, electronic equipment, agricultural chemicals, radios, air conditioners, and leather goods. Among its agricultural products are lettuce, melons, vegetables, grapefruit, oranges, lemons, and olives.

While Phoenix benefits from modern irriga-

tion efforts, the Hohokam Indian people dug the area's first irrigation ditches in the third century B.C., and developed an extensive network of canals during their culture's decline in A.D. 1400. The area was not resettled until 1864, when a hay camp was established to supply Camp McDowell 30 miles away. Jack Weilling and "Lord Darrell" Dupa rebuilt the old Indian irrigation ditches in 1867 and named the site Phoenix, after the mythical bird that rose from its own ashes. The settlement grew as a trading post, was incorporated as a city in 1881, and became capital of the territory in 1889 and state capital when Arizona was admitted to the Union in 1912.

With the westward exodus from the snow-belt states, and the perfecting of air conditioning to make the summer heat bearable, the small 1950s resort city of 106,818 people has since swelled almost ninefold.

Population 894,070 (1986). Rank: 10. Pop. density: 2,384/sq. mi. (920.5/sq km). County: Maricopa.

Terrain and climate Elev.: 1,107 ft. Area: 375 sq. mi. (971.3 sq km). Avg. daily min. temp.: Jan.: 39.4°F/4.1°C; avg. daily max.: July: 105°F/40.5°C. Avg. annual rainfall: 7.11"; snowfall: 0"; clear days: 214; precipitation days: 34.

Government Form: council and manager. Mayor: Terry Goddard. Municipal tel. number: (602) 262-7116.

City finances (1987) Total revenues: $955.7 mil. Total genl. expend.: $886.0 mil. Gross debt outstanding: $1,765.3 mil.

Major employers State of Arizona 30,706; Motorola 22,000; Samaritan Health Service 14,243; Maricopa County 14,243; Arizona Public Service Co. 10,500; City of Phoenix 10,340; Valley National Bank 7,100; U.S. West Communications 7,000; Smitty's Super Valu Inc. 6,850; Garrett Engine Div. 6,700; Honeywell (number N.A.); Sperry Aerospace Group 6,399.

Pittsburgh, Pennsylvania

Long one of the leading urban industrial areas in the country, Pittsburgh sits at the confluence of the Allegheny and Monongahela rivers, which join to form the Ohio River. In 1754 the British chose the site for its access to this extensive river network (which reaches to the Gulf of Mexico, the Great Lakes, and up the Missouri River) and began building Fort Pitt, named for Prime Minister William Pitt. Pittsburgh is also situated in the midst of extensive deposits of oil, coal, and natural gas; the production of steel and iron began in the 1790s. In the 19th century, Pittsburgh was one of the nation's largest producers of steel and iron, and in 1881 its industrial workers formed the American Federation of Labor (AFL).

After the boom years of the 1940s and 1950s, the city's fortunes began to shrivel with the decline of heavy industry, a dwindling population—it is the only city in the top 50 with a higher death rate than birth rate—and high unemployment in the 1980s. Yet with 40 miles of riverfront, Pittsburgh remains the country's largest inland port, and is still a leader in the manufacture of petrochemicals and glass products, as well as the home of more than 150 industrial research companies.

Moreover, Pittsburgh's industrial past has left a rich cultural legacy, which contributed to its recent ranking as number one in the country by *Places Rated Almanac*. Its cultural institutions include Phipps Conservatory, Buhl Planetarium, Carnegie Institute, Carnegie Music Hall, and Carnegie Museum of Natural History (the latter three named for the Scots-born industrialist and philanthropist Andrew Carnegie), as well as the Pittsburgh Symphony Orchestra, the Pittsburgh Public Theater, and Pittsburgh Dance Theater. Its universities include the University of Pittsburgh, Pittsburgh Theological Seminary, Duquesne University, and Carnegie-Mellon University.

Population 387,490 (1986). Rank: 35. Pop. density: 6,994/sq. mi. (2,700.4/sq km). County: Allegheny.

Terrain and climate Elev.: 1,223 ft. Area: 55.4 sq. mi. (143.5 sq km). Avg. daily min. temp.: Jan.: 19.2°F/−7.1°C; avg. daily max.: July: 86.1°F/30°C. Avg. annual rainfall: 36.29″; snowfall: 45″; clear days: 59; precipitation days: 152.

Government Form: mayor and council. Mayor: Sophie Masloff. Municipal tel. number: (412) 255–2100.

City finances (1987) Total revenues: $366.3 mil. Total genl. expend.: $346.1 mil. Gross debt outstanding: $551.7 mil.

Major employers Alcoa, Consolidated Natural Gas, Dravo, Equimark, H.J. Heinz, Mellon National Corp., PPG Industries, Rockwell International, USX Corp., Westinghouse Electric.

Portland, Oregon

Portland's renowned beauty is a result of its unique natural setting, which offers a view of the Cascade Mountains and Mt. Hood to the east, Mt. Adams to the northeast, and Mt. St. Helens and Mt. Rainier to the north. Eleven bridges span the Willamette River, which divides the city into east and west sections.

Indian traders traveling between Oregon City and Vancouver carved out an acre of land by the Willamette River 12 miles north of Oregon City, which became known as The Clearing. In 1884 William Overton claimed the 640 acres surrounding the area, which he then sold to Asa Lovejoy and Francis W. Pettygrove, who set out to build a city. Winning a coin toss, Pettygrove named the city-to-be after his hometown.

As a vital port of entry (the coast's only freshwater port) with a large inland harbor, Portland is a leader in the shipping of lumber, flour, and grain and has blossomed into Oregon's largest city. Main industries also include paper and pulp, mining, high-tech equipment, and aerospace. Portland enjoys an active arts community, and its residents partake of the beaches and ski slopes within easy driving distance.

Population 387,870 (1986). Rank: 34. Pop. density: 3,405/sq. mi. (1,314.7/sq km). County: Multnomah.

Terrain and climate Elev.: 39 ft. Area: 113.9 sq. mi. (295 sq km). Avg. daily min. temp.: Jan.: 33.5°F/0.8°C; avg. daily max.: July: 79.5°F/

26.3°C. Avg. annual rainfall: 37.39″; snowfall: 7″; clear days: 69; precipitation days: 152.

Government Form: commission. Mayor: J.E. "Bud" Clark. Municipal tel. number: (503) 248–4120.

City finances (1987) Total revenues: $343.0 mil. Total genl. expend.: $392.2 mil. Gross debt outstanding: $554.5 mil.

Major employers Boeing, Frito-Lay, Intel, Louisiana-Pacific, NERCO, NIKE, Pacificorp, Tektronix, U.S. Bancorp, Willamette Industries.

Sacramento, California

The capital of California and its seventh-largest city, Sacramento sits 75 miles northwest of San Francisco at the confluence of the American and Sacramento rivers. A wholesale and retail center for the surrounding rich farmland, the city includes among its main commercial enterprises food processing and canning and one of the world's largest almond-shelling plants.

Receiving a land grant from the Mexican government in 1839, Swiss-American John Augustus Sutter founded a colony called New Helvetia, and when Fort Sutter was constructed in 1844, it became one of California's chief trading posts. Established soon after the discovery of gold in 1848, Sacramento grew to 7,000 residents by 1850, became state capital in 1854, and in 1863 was incorporated as a city.

The "Gateway to the Goldfields," "Old Sacramento" became a pivotal point of commerce in the 1860s, connected to the mining towns by the American River and transporting produce from the farms and orchards lining the banks of the Sacramento River. Sailors stopping in San Francisco visited Sacramento to replenish their stocks of fresh produce and to entertain themselves in the saloons and gambling halls. The wealthy lived in great mansions by the river, and cobblestone streets, gaslights, and wood sidewalks imbued the town with a touch of civility. Today's Sacramento, appreciated for its subtle, quiet charms, embraces 120 parks; hiking and biking trails along the American River Parkway; a large collection of art galleries; two symphony orchestras; ballet, theater and opera companies; and a number of jazz clubs and coffeehouses.

Population 323,550 (1986). Rank: 49. Pop. density: 3,325/sq. mi. (1,283.8/sq km). County: Sacramento.

Terrain and climate Elev.: 25 ft. Area: 97.3 sq. mi. (252 sq km). Avg. daily min. temp.: Jan.: 37.9°F/3.2°C; avg. daily max.: July: 93.3°F/34°C. Avg. annual rainfall: 17.87″; snowfall: 0.1″; clear days: 193; precipitation days: 57.

Government Form: council and manager. Mayor: Anne Rudin. Municipal tel. number: (916) 449–5706.

City finances (1987) Total revenues: $263.8 mil. Total genl. expend.: $232.4 mil. Gross debt outstanding: $191.3 mil.

Major employers Pacific Bell 4,633; Aerojet General 4,200; Sutter Health 3,635; Mercy Healthcare Sacramento 2,772; Raley's Inc. 2,700.

St. Louis, Missouri

St. Louis is one of the nation's major centers of transportation, manufacturing, commerce, and education. With abundant water and electric power, with a work force of over a million people in the metropolitan area, and in an area rich in mineral resources, St. Louis ranks as one of the top 10 industrial areas in the country. It is also one of the nation's busiest river ports, the third-largest rail center, and the eighth-largest trucking center, and has the sixth-busiest airport. Aircraft, automobiles, printing, beer, and chemicals are among the principal products. The metropolitan area boasts five universities, 23 colleges, and seven junior colleges. St. Louis University, the oldest university west of the Mississippi, founded in 1818, and Washington University are world famous for their medical schools and research programs and their Nobel Prize winners.

For the 40 years after its founding in 1764 by Pierre Laclede, St. Louis was a French settlement and trading post, outfitting fur trading expeditions up the Missouri River. With the Louisiana Purchase in 1803, St. Louis came under American control. The city was incorporated in 1823 with a population of almost 5,000 people. The first steamboat docked at St. Louis in 1817, and steamboats then became a vital part of the city's growth. Fueled by settlers from the east and by waves of Irish and German immigrants attracted by the prosperity of the river trade, the city's population grew rapidly. In 1870 St. Louis had a population of 311,000, and it was the country's third-largest city after New York and Philadelphia. The population continued to grow to a peak of 856,800 in 1950, but the post–World War II flight to the suburbs hit St. Louis hard, reducing its population by almost half.

The downtown St. Louis area has many landmarks and historic buildings. The Old Cathedral, completed in 1834, and the Old Courthouse, where the Dred Scott case was first tried, have been preserved as part of the Jefferson National Expansion Memorial. Atop of the famous Gateway Arch, the observation room provides a panoramic view of St. Louis. Kiel Auditorium contains a 3,500–seat opera house and a 10,000–seat convention hall. Forest Park, site of the 1904 Louisiana Purchase Exposition (also known as the St. Louis World's Fair), comprises the St. Louis Zoo, McDonnell Planetarium, and the Jewel Box, an all-glass floral display house. St. Louis is also the home of the Missouri Botanical Gardens, which features the Climatron—a geodesic dome with rare orchids and other tropical plants—and the nation's largest Japanese garden. The St. Louis Symphony (founded in 1880) is the country's second oldest and is housed in Powell Symphony Hall.

Population 426,300 (1986). Rank: 31. Pop. density: 6,943/sq. mi. (2,680.7/sq. km). County: independent.

Terrain and climate Elev.: 564 ft. Area: 61.4 sq. mi. (159 sq km). Avg. daily min. temp.: Jan.: 19.9°F/−6.7°C; avg. daily max.: July: 89°F/31°C. Avg. annual rainfall: 33.91″; snowfall: 18″; clear days: 105; precipitation days: 108.

Government Form: mayor and council. Mayor:

Vincent C. Shoemehl, Jr. Municipal tel. number: (314) 622–3201.
City finances (1987) Total revenues: $595.7 mil. Total genl. expend.: $531.3 mil. Gross debt outstanding: $653.7 mil.
Major employers Anheuser-Busch, Emerson Electric, General Dynamics, McDonnell-Douglas, Ralston Purina, Southwestern Bell.

REMEMBER THE ALAMO
In 1836, to give General Sam Houston time to organize his forces against Mexican General Santa Ana's army of thousands, a band of 163 Texans attempted to hold off the invaders. The siege began on February 23 and ammunition ran out on March 6. Every defender at the Alamo lost his life. The heroic defense gave Houston the time he needed and so saved the independence of Texas.

San Antonio, Texas
San Antonio, the third-largest city in Texas, lies in the state's south-central region at the edge of the Gulf Coastal Plain 140 miles from the Gulf of Mexico. One of the fastest-growing cities in the nation with a projected population of 1 million by or before the 1990 census, its economy thrives on agriculture, livestock, and the activity of wholesale traders who dominate the commerce of southwestern Texas and northern Mexico. Adding further stimulus to the economy are five major military installations—Fort Sam Houston, Randolph Air Force Base, Kelly Air Force Base, Lackland Air Force Base, and Brooks Air Force Base.

The founding of the mission of San Antonio de Valero (later known as the Alamo) and the Presidio of San Antonio in 1718 represented the area's first permanent Euramerican settlement. When 56 settlers from the Canary Islands joined the original coterie of ranchers, missionaries, and soldiers, they formed the first municipal organization in Texas, called the villa of San Fernando de Bexar, which became a city in 1809; and they suffered under Mexican rule until the battle of San Jacinto in 1836. With the influx of American pioneers and German immigrants, the population grew to more than 96,000 by 1910, and has since increased nearly tenfold.

Today San Antonio is a popular haven for vacationers, with over 10 million visitors in 1987. San Antonio's attractions include the Alamo and its four sister missions; the Riverwalk along the San Antonio River; Breckenridge Park, home of one of America's largest zoos; Sea World of Texas; La Villita; the Tower of the Americas; and the Spanish Governor's Palace.
Population 914,350 (1986). Rank: 9. Pop. density: 3,003/q. mi. (1,159.5/sq km). County: Bexar.
Terrain and climate Elev.: 701 ft. Area: 304.5 sq. mi. (788.7 sq km). Avg. daily min. temp.: Jan.: 39°F/3.8°C; avg. daily max.: July: 96.3°F/35.7°C. Avg. annual rainfall: 29.13"; snowfall: 0.5"; clear days: 110; precipitation days: 81.
Government Form: council and manager. Mayor: Lila Cockrell. Municipal tel. number: (512) 299–7060.

City finances (1987) Total revenues: $1,425.5 mil. Total genl. expend.: $1,771.3 mil. Gross debt outstanding: $3,193.0 mil.
Major employers Baptist Memorial System, H.E. Butt Grocery Co., Santa Rosa Medical Center, Southwest Research Institute, Southwestern Bell Telephone Co., United Services Automobile Association.

San Diego, California
Sixty years after João Rodrigues Cabrilho first sailed into San Diego Bay, Sebastian Vizcaino embarked from Spain with three ships to explore the coast of California and in November 1602, anchored on the lee of what is now known as Point Loma. When he finished charting the bay two days later, he changed its original name, San Miguel, to San Diego, in honor of the saint San Diego de Alcalal de Henares. In 1769 Father Junipero Serra established California's first mission, the Mission San Diego de Alcala.

Compared to its sister cities to the north— Los Angeles and San Francisco—San Diego developed slowly, despite its large and hospitable harbor. In 1887 the city became the southern terminus for the Santa Fe Railroad, but floods soon washed out the tracks and track beds, and the railroad was rebuilt to terminate in L.A. This, along with L.A.'s man-made harbor, put San Diego at an almost insurmountable disadvantage. With its industrial development stunted, San Diego welcomed the establishment of a U.S. Navy base during World War I; since then, about a quarter of the Navy's seagoing vessels and roughly 20 percent of the Marine Corps' forces have located there. Jonas Salk's work on polio and the emergence of the University of California at San Diego has earned the city the reputation as a premier biomedical research center, luring billions of dollars in development and research grants.

San Diego, a picturesque city with many tourist attractions, enjoys an average of 350 days of sunshine, enticing both residents and visitors to its 70 beaches and the parks, resorts, and health spas lining its great bay. Balboa Island is the site of both Balboa Park, host to international expositions in 1915 and 1935, and the San Diego Zoo, one of the finest in the nation. The pleasure boats berthed at the city's numerous yacht clubs offer a curious contrast to the naval warships moored nearby.
Population 1,015,190 (1986). Rank: 7. Pop. density: 3,086/sq. mi. (1,191.5/sq km). County: San Diego.
Terrain and climate Elev.: 13 ft. Area: 329 sq. mi. (852.1 sq km). Avg. daily min. temp.: Jan.: 48.4°F/9.1°C; avg. daily max.: July: 75.6°F/24.2°C. Avg. annual rainfall: 9.32"; snowfall: 0"; clear days: 150; precipitation days: 41.
Government Form: council and manager. Mayor: Maureen O'Connor. Municipal tel. number: (619) 236–6363.
City finances (1987) Total revenues: $990.9 mil. Total genl. expend.: $837.5 mil. Gross debt outstanding: $1,561.8 mil.
Major employers Hybritech, San Diego Gas & Electric, Univ. of California, U.S. Marine Corps, U.S. Navy.

San Francisco, California
Located near the Golden Gate, the strait between San Francisco Bay and the Pacific Ocean, fog-bound San Francisco hid from some of the greatest European navigators to explore the West Coast. João Rodrigues Cabrilho discovered the Farrallon Islands just off the coast in 1542, and Sir Francis Drake landed a few miles north of the Golden Gate in 1579. Yet it was another 200 years before Don Gasper de Portola sailed into the bay, followed six years later by Don Juan Manuel Ayala, who established a town and mission.

Neither the Spanish nor (after 1821) the Mexican governments were very keen on capitalizing on San Francisco's temperate and strategic location, and when Capt. John Montgomery raised the American flag there on July 9, 1846, the community consisted of only 840 people. The discovery of gold at Sutter's mill in 1848, and the gold rush of 1849— which brought 40,000 of the hopeful to California, most by ship—catapulted San Francisco onto the world map, and the following year it was incorporated as a city.

San Francisco continued to prosper as a major transportation and industrial center, but in 1906 an earthquake registering 8.6 on the Richter scale claimed 452 lives, 28,000 buildings, and losses totaling approximately $350 million. San Francisco rose from the ashes to become a thriving, multifaceted, cosmopolitan city and one of the country's leaders in world trade. It is a port of call for more than 40 steamship lines, which import approximately $25 billion worth of goods from more than 300 ports around the world. A major international financial center, it is the headquarters of three of the nation's largest banks, the 12th Federal Reserve District, and the Pacific Stock Exchange. There are also more than 650 insurance companies, and the city is a haven for venture capitalists and entrepreneurs: More than 90 percent of its businesses have fewer than 25 employees. Several U.S. military installations are based in the area.

Well known for its spirit of individualism, San Francisco was a haven for the beat movement of the 1950s, and the capital of the 1960s hippie movement was the Haight-Ashbury district. The city's more traditional arts institutions include the San Francisco Ballet, the San Francisco Opera, the San Francisco Symphony, and the American Conservatory Theater. Among its leading educational institutions are the University of San Francisco, the Heald Institute of Technology, the University of California, the San Francisco Art Institute, the San Francisco Conservatory of Music, and the San Francisco College of Mortuary Science. Among its many museums are the National Maritime Historic Park, the Fine Arts Museum, and the California Palace of the Legion of Honor. Other attractions include its historic cable cars (first used in 1873), Chinatown, and Fisherman's Wharf.

Population 749,000 (1986). Rank: 12. Pop. density: 16,142/sq. mi. (6,232.4/sq km). County: San Francisco.
Terrain and climate Elev.: 155 ft. Area: 46.4

sq. mi. (120.2 sq km). Avg. daily min. temp.: Jan.: 41.5°F/5.2°C; avg. daily max.: July: 71°F/21°C. Avg. annual rainfall: 19.71"; snowfall: 0"; clear days: 162; precipitation days: 67.

Government Form: mayor and council. Mayor: Art Agnos. Municipal tel. number: (415) 554-6141.

City finances (1987) Total revenues: $2,497.5 mil. Total genl. expend.: $2,059.2 mil. Gross debt outstanding: $1,744.4 mil.

Major employers Bank America Corp., Bechtel, Chevron, McKesson, Pacific Bell, Pacific Gas & Electric, Transamerica Corp., Wells Fargo.

San Jose, California

Located at the southern end of San Francisco Bay, about 45 miles south of San Francisco, San Jose was the first nonreligious community founded in California. Pueblo de San Jose de Guadalupe was settled in 1777 by enterprising farmers who sought to make themselves and the region independent of Mexico and the Spanish-mission network for their supplies. Fruit and olive trees, hides, tallow, livestock, grain, and lively retail activity all contributed to San Jose's early prosperity, and it was the first state capital (1849-52).

San Jose remained an agricultural center until World War II, when industry and technology began to expand. The rapid growth of innovative industry over the last 20 years, taking its lead from research and development begun at nearby Stanford University in the 1930s, changed the area dramatically. With the revolution in high technology, Santa Clara County became known as Silicon Valley, excelling in the production of information systems, personal computers, peripherals, instruments, and an array of defense contractors keeping pace with the burgeoning semiconductor industry. At the same time, financial services, real estate, construction, and retail industries all flourished.

The rate of change did not slow in the 1980s, and San Jose was the third-fastest growing of the 25 largest cities in America. From 1980 to 1986, population expanded 13 percent, from 629,400 to 712,000. More than 2,600 high-tech companies employing 250,000 people are located in San Jose, and one-third of the labor force works in manufacturing, a very high proportion in postindustrial America. Santa Clara County has the highest median family income in California, and according to a 1987 survey of buying power by *Sales and Marketing* magazine, the San Jose metropolitan area is third in the nation in median household "effective buying power." The same survey ranks it second in California, and fifth in the nation, in manufacturing as measured by value of shipments—$30.5 billion in 1986.

Population 712,080 (1986). Rank: 14. Pop. density: 4,209/sq. mi. (1,625.1/sq km). County: Santa Clara.

Terrain and climate Elev.: 65 ft. Area: 169.2 sq. mi. (438.2 sq km). Avg. daily min. temp.: Jan.: 41.1°F/5°C; avg. daily max.: July: 81.5°F/27.5°C. Avg. annual rainfall: 13.86"; snowfall: 0"; clear days: N.A.; precipitation days: N.A.

Government Form: council and manager. Mayor: Thomas McEnery. Municipal tel. number: (408) 277-4237.

City finances (1987) Total revenues: $611.9 mil. Total genl. expend.: $594.9 mil. Gross debt outstanding: $1,744.4 mil.

Major employers Lockheed 30,907; IBM 17,500; Hewlett-Packard 17,000; National Semiconductor 8,000; Xidex Corp. 7,000; Pacific Bell 6,700; Apple Computers 5,800; Amdahl Corp. 5,207; FMC Corp. 5,165; Advanced Micro Devices 5,039.

Seattle, Washington

Located on the protected waters of Puget Sound, Seattle was the first Euramerican settlement established in the Pacific Northwest north of the Columbia River. Starting out at Alki Point in 1851, the settlers moved to what is now known as Pioneer Square. Befriended by the Suquamish chief Sealth (Seattle is a loose approximation of his name), the people turned to lumber harvesting and log milling, which formed the backbone of the city's economy.

With the completion of the Great Northern Railway in 1893 and with the Alaska gold rush of 1897, when Seattle became the "Gateway to the Klondike," the city was transformed into a metropolis of merchants and entrepreneurs. Even as gold fever abated, and despite a devastating fire in 1899, the city prospered as a major port to the Orient and as an industrial center. In 1909 Seattle was the site of the Alaska-Yukon-Pacific Exposition. The completion of the Panama Canal in 1914 brought even more business to the already bustling port. Two years later a small company began building two-seater biplanes, marking the start of Seattle's enduring link with the aerospace industry. In time the little company became Boeing, the world's largest producer of commercial planes, employing more than 85,000 people in the Seattle area.

Endowed with spectacular natural beauty, with the broad expanse of Puget Sound before it, and the snow-capped peaks of the Cascade Mountains and Mt. Rainier visible to the south and east, the Seattle area offers a wide variety of outdoor activities, from skiing and hiking to fishing and boating. A second international exposition, the Seattle World's Fair in 1962, helped establish the city's reputation as a center of technology, trade, industry, and tourism. The leading cultural programs are put on by the Seattle Symphony Orchestra, the Seattle Opera Association, and the Seattle Repertory Theater. Other attractions include the Seattle Art Museum, Pioneer Square, Pike Place Market, the historic ships on Lake Union, and Woodland Park and Zoo, as well as the many events at the 74-acre Seattle Convention Center, whose buildings, and parklike grounds and fountains are legacies of the World's Fair. Among the 20 universities and colleges in the area are the University of Washington and Seattle Pacific University.

Population 486,200 (1986). Rank: 25. Pop. density: 5,816/sq. mi. (2,245.6/sq km). County: King.

Terrain and climate Elev.: 450 ft. Area: 83.6 sq. mi. (216.5 sq km). Avg. daily min. temp.: Jan.: 34.3°F/1.2°C; avg. daily max.: July:

75.2°F/24°C. Avg. annual rainfall: 38.85"; snowfall: 15"; clear days: 57; precipitation days: 160.

Government Form: mayor and council. Mayor: Donald T. Walley. Municipal tel. number: (206) 855-1661.

City finances (1987) Total revenues: $815.6 mil. Total genl. expend.: $849.7 mil. Gross debt outstanding: $774.3 mil.

Major employers Boeing, City of Seattle, Safeway Stores, Sears, Roebuck & Co., State of Washington, Univ. of Washington, U.S. government, U.S. West Communications.

Toledo, Ohio

Toledo's origins can be traced to late 18th-century speculators who purchased tracts of land on either side of the Maumee River near its mouth, at the western end of Lake Erie. Although the smaller upriver towns of Perrysburg and Maumee were settled earlier, the twin towns of Port Lawrence and Vistula, laid out in 1832, were right on the lake. When it was found that steamers could navigate the river, the newer towns merged, adopting an anonymous suggestion to name it for the city in Spain.

Toledo's early history and prosperity was tied to plans for the Miami and Erie Canal, which when completed in 1845, linked the Ohio River and Lake Erie. The border between Ohio (statehood, 1803) and Michigan (1837) was ill-defined. In the Toledo War (1835-36), Michigan held that Toledo was theirs. But Toledans opted for Ohio, figuring that the state would not finance a canal to the benefit of another state. Toledo and Ohio won the day, though in exchange Michigan received the Upper Peninsula and admission to the Union the following year.

Though the canal was only moderately successful, Toledo benefited from the railroads that superceded it, and by the Civil War, it was a major rail center. Served by six railroads today, and shipping 23 tons of coal, grain, iron ore, and general cargo annually, Toledo is the second-largest port on the Great Lakes. The city's manufactures include automotive components, plastics, and glass. In 1887, Edward Libbey relocated his New England Glass Company in Toledo, and the present-day offspring of Libbey-Owens-Ford, Owens-Illinois, and Owens-Corning are mainstays of the economy—Toledo's nickname is "Glass Capital of the World." In the 1890s, Toledo was the nation's leading producer of bicycles, but that gave way to car parts, and in World War II, the Willys-Overland Company developed and manufactured the jeep there. Although unemployment reached a high of 11.9 percent in 1982, it has dropped considerably as new companies have been taking root, especially medical research companies drawn by the Medical College of Ohio's development of the Health Technology Park (which will include the Northwest Ohio Technology Center).

Toledo's cultural attractions include the Toledo Opera, Toledo Symphony Orchestra, Toledo Ballet, and the Toledo Repertoire Theatre. In addition there is the excellent Toledo Museum of Art as well as the Glass Apple, which exhibits glass pieces by local and inter-

national artists. Toledo's major educational institutions include the University of Toledo, Bowling Green State University, and the Medical College of Ohio.
Population 340,680 (1986). Rank: 46. Pop. density: 4,046/sq. mi. (1,562.2/sq km). County: Lucas.
Terrain and climate Elev.: 692 ft. Area: 84.2 sq. mi. (218.1 sq km). Avg. daily min. temp.: Jan.: 15.5°F/-9.1°C; avg. daily max.: 83.4°F/28.5°C. Avg. annual rainfall: 31.77"; snowfall: 37"; clear days: 71; precipitation days: 136.
Government Form: council and manager. Mayor: Donna Owens. Municipal tel. number: (419) 245-1010.
City finances (1987) Total revenues: $251.4 mil. Total genl. expend.: $205.2 mil. Gross debt outstanding: $185.5 mil.
Major employers Jeep Corp. 5,600; General Motors Hydra-matic Div. 4,750; Owens-Illinois 2,700; Toledo Edison 2,396; Libbey-Owens-Ford 2,000.

Tucson, Arizona

The first European to travel through the area that is now Tucson was the Jesuit missionary Eusebio Kino, in 1692. In 1700 the mission of San Xavier del Bac was established among the Papago Indians nearby. It was not until 1776, however, that the Spanish established a permanent settlement, taking its name from the Papago *Stjukshon* (or *Chuk Shon*), meaning "village of the dark spring at the foot of the mountain." Tucson remained under Spanish and Mexican control until it was acquired by the U.S. government as part of the Gadsden Purchase in 1853. During the Civil War, it was under Confederate control, but from 1867 to 1877, it was the territorial capital.

Despite the arrival of the Southern Pacific railroad in 1880 and the discovery of extensive copper deposits in southern Arizona, neither its location nor its natural resources much stimulated its economy. It was best known as a winter and health resort and as a commercial hub for the surrounding agricultural and mining industries. In 1950 the population was only 45,500.

The last 40 years have seen a dramatic change. One of the many beneficiaries of the exodus from the industrial states to the Sunbelt, Tucson has seen its population grow almost tenfold in that period, and in the last decade, Tucson added 20,000 manufacturing jobs. In 1986 alone, 11 corporations moved there, and with them, an estimated 1,660 people per month. Surrounded by a wealth of natural beauty, the city is still appealing to retirees and tourists, as is reflected in the many golf courses, ranches, and resorts in and around Tucson. It is surrounded by four mountain ranges: the Rincon, Santa Catalina, Tucson, and Santa Rita. Other natural wonders include Sabino Canyon (which has the only year-round stream in the region), the Saguaro National Monument (a preserve for Saguaro cacti), and Tucson Mountain Park, site of the Arizona-Sonora Desert Museum. The University of Arizona is located in Tucson, and the Davis-Mothan Air Force Base and Kitts Peak Observatory are nearby.

Population 358,850 (1986). Rank: 41. Pop. density: 2,862/sq. mi. (1,105/sq km). County: Pima.
Terrain and climate Elev.: 2,584 ft. Area: sq. mi. (324.8 sq km). Avg. daily min. temp.: Jan.: 38.1°F/3.3°C; avg. daily max.: July: 98.5°F/3.3°C. Avg. annual rainfall: 11.14"; snowfall: 2"; clear days: 198; precipitation days: 50.
Government Form: council and manager. Mayor: Tom Volgy. Municipal tel. number: (602) 791-4201.
City finances (1987) Total revenues: $401.5 mil. Total genl. expend.: $403.4 mil. Gross debt outstanding: $185.5 mil.
Major employers Univ. of Arizona 9,148; U.S. Air Force 7,830; Hughes Aircraft 7,500; Tucson Unified School District 7,052; State of Arizona 6,322; IBM 5,100.

Tulsa, Oklahoma

Tulsa was first settled by Indian nations forced out of the South Atlantic states by the Indian Removal Act of 1830. The name they chose for their new home was Tulsey Town, a corruption of *Tullahassee*, meaning "Old Town." The name Tulsa was made official with the establishment of a post office in 1879. In 1900, Tulsa's population numbered less than 2,000, but the discovery of extensive oil fields at the turn of the century, beginning with the Glenn Pool and Red Ford strikes, started Tulsa on its way from a small Indian settlement to a sizable metropolis. By 1907 its population had increased to 7,298, and by 1920 it was 10 times that. Soon Tulsa was "Oil Capital of the World."

While still heavily involved in the oil and gas industry—it remains the home of about 500 oil-related companies—modern Tulsa is a far more diverse city than its oil patch origins. Among Tulsa's top employees are regional, national, and international firms involved in aviation and aerospace, energy, computer technology, insurance, telecommunications, health care, and electronic equipment. The Port of Catoosa, which opened in 1971 after completion of the 445-mile Arkansas-Mississippi Waterway, is a major inland port, providing Tulsa with a direct link to the Mississippi River system and the Gulf of Mexico.

While growing in business, Tulsa has preserved the cultural heritage of its early oil barons and workers as well as that of its original Indian settlers. Thomas Gilcrease, a Creek Indian, became a millionaire with the Glenn Pool oil strike, and founded the Thomas Gilcrease Institute of American History and Art, devoted to American Indian heritage. The Tulsa Opera Company was founded in the early 1900s, and along with the city's philharmonic, ballet, and theaters, it gives Tulsa just cause to lay claim to being the cultural capital of Oklahoma. Tulsans also honor their roots through rodeos and regional music festivals. In addition representatives of the state's 65 Indian tribes gather in Tulsa each summer for their annual powwow. Among Tulsa's eight colleges and universities are the University of Tulsa, Oral Roberts University, and University Center at Tulsa, a consortium of Langston Uni-

versity, Northeastern State University, Oklahoma State University, and the University of Oklahoma.
Population 373,750 (1986). Rank: 37. Pop. density: 2,008/sq. mi. (775.3/sq km). County: Tulsa.
Terrain and climate Elev.: 676 ft. Area: 186.1 sq. mi. (482 sq km). Avg. daily min. temp.: Jan.: 24.8°F/-4°C; avg. daily max.: July: 93.9°F/34.3°C. Avg. annual rainfall: 38.77"; snowfall: 9"; clear days: 127; precipitation days: 90.
Government Form: commission. Mayor: Roger Randle. Municipal tel. number: (918) 596-7411.
City finances (1987) Total revenues: $432.6 mil. Total genl. expend.: $439.7 mil. Gross debt outstanding: $1,142.9 mil.
Major employers American Airlines 8,000; Tulsa Public Schools 4,500; City of Tulsa 4,000; McDonnell-Douglas 3,139; St. Francis Hospital 3,000; St. John Medical Center 2,400; Rockwell International 2,000.

Virginia Beach, Virginia

Throughout much of its history—which dates to the landing of the Jamestown colonists at Point Henry in 1607–Virginia Beach was overshadowed by its northern neighbor, Norfolk, which with its magnificent harbor, was long the home of many shipping and naval enterprises at the mouth of Chesapeake Bay. But Virginia Beach has seen remarkable change in the last two decades.

In 1970 Virginia Beach's population was 172,000, only slightly more than half that of Norfolk. By 1986 it had grown 93 percent, to 330,000, and in the period 1980–86, it experienced the fastest growth of any of the country's 50 largest cities. Local initiative accounts for most of this growth; in the same period, Norfolk's population fell 11 percent. A dominant presence is the U.S. Navy, which has three bases—Oceana Naval Air Station, Little Creek Naval Amphibious Base, and the Dam Neck Fleet Training Center—and which together with the U.S. Army's Fort Story, employ 36,000 military and civilian personnel.

With 38 miles of Atlantic shoreline, 28 miles of public beaches, and the Seashore State Park—2,700 acres of shady upland woods, cypress swamps, and Spanish moss—tourism remains a major factor in the city's economy, attracting 2.5 million visitors a year. The city's main industries, which include marine and engineering services, construction, communications, and electronics, occupy 10 industrial/business parks, including four built by the Virginia Beach Development Authority.

Among Virginia Beach's outstanding historic and recreational attractions are the Virginia Marine Science Museum; the Adam Thoroughgood House (c. 1680, one of the oldest brick houses in North America); the Old Cape Henry Lighthouse, authorized by the first Congress in 1790; and the statue of Adm. Compte de Grasse, whose defeat of the British at the Battle of the Virginia Capes brought about the defeat of Gen. Cornwallis at Yorktown and the end of the American Revolution in 1781.
Population 333,400 (1986). Rank: 47. Pop.

density: 1,476/sq. mi. (569.9/sq km). County: independent.

Terrain and climate Elev.: 12 ft. Area: 225.9 sq. mi. (585.1 sq km). Avg. daily min. temp.: Jan.: 31.7°F/–0.1°C; avg. daily max.: July: 86.9°F/30.5°C. Avg. annual rainfall: 45.22"; snowfall: 7"; clear days: 110; precipitation days: 115.

Government Form: council and manager. Mayor: Meyera E. Oberndorf. Municipal tel. number: (804) 427–4581.

City finances (1987) Total revenues: $466.5 mil. Total genl. expend.: $458.7 mil. Gross debt outstanding: $372.8 mil.

Major employers U.S. Navy 33,360; Computer Dynamics Corp. 600; Lillian Vernon Corp. 550; QED Systems Inc. 500.

Washington, D.C.

Chosen as the site for the nation's capital by George Washington, Washington, D.C., was carved out of land ceded by Maryland and Vir-

ginia. Although under federal jurisdiction, the District has petitioned for statehood as New Columbia. In 1961 Congress enacted the 23d Amendment granting citizens of D.C. the right to vote in presidential elections for the first time, and ten years later gave the District a nonvoting delegate to the House of Representatives. The District's largest employer is the federal government, and printing is the largest industry. President John F. Kennedy called it a city of "Southern efficiency and Northern charm," but since his time, the city has become a leading patron of the arts. The problems of any large city are made worse by the city's largely transient population of government workers. The city, as the seat of the U.S. government, is a mecca for tourists from around the world, and more than 17 million people visit it each year.

Population 626,000 (1986). Rank: 16. Pop. density: 9,984/sq. mi. (3,854.8/sq km). County:

independent.

Terrain and climate Elev.: 30 ft. Area: 62.7 sq. mi. (162.4 sq km). Avg. daily min. temp.: Jan.: 27.5°F/–2.5°C; avg. daily max.: July: 87.9°F/31°C. Avg. annual rainfall: 39"; snowfall: 16"; clear days: 101; precipitation days: 111.

Government Form: mayor and council. Mayor: Marion Barry, Jr. Municipal tel. number: (202) 727–2980.

City finances (1987) Total revenues: $3,684.3 mil. Total genl. expend.: $3,665.5 mil. Gross debt outstanding: $2,709.2 mil.

Major employers Georgetown Univ., IBM Corp., Marriott Corp., US Air, U.S. government, Washington Metropolitan Area Transit Authority.

Metropolitan Statistical Areas

The Office of Management and Budget divides the population of the United States into metropolitan and nonmetropolitan populations. Although the 282 metropolitan areas of the United States make up only 16% of the country's land area, they are home to 77% of all Americans. The metropolitan population was 56% of the total in 1950 and only 63% in 1960. For statistical purposes the OMB distinguishes

between metropolitan statistical areas (MSAs), consolidated metropolitan statistical areas (CMSAs), primary metropolitan statistical areas (PMSAs), and in the Northeast, New England county metropolitan areas (NECMAs).

An MSA is either one city of 50,000 or more inhabitants, or an urbanized area (as defined by the Census Bureau) of at least 50,000 inhabitants and a total MSA population of at least 100,000 (in New England, 75,000). An MSA includes the county in which the central city is

located plus any adjacent counties in which at least 50% of the population lives in the urbanized area. Within metropolitan complexes of one million or more population, separate component areas—PMSAs—are defined if specified criteria are met; and any area containing PMSAs is designated a CMSA. As of June 30, 1988, there were 266 MSAs (17 of which had a population of at least one million), and 21 CMSAs made up of a total of 73 PMSAs.

THE 50 LARGEST METROPOLITAN STATISTICAL AREAS BY POPULATION, AND POPULATION CHANGE, 1980–87

Rank	Metropolitan statistical area	Population 1980	1987 est.	Growth Number	Percent
1.	N.Y.–N.J.–Conn. (CMSA)	17,539,532	18,053,800	514,300	2.9%
2.	Los Angeles–Anaheim–Riverside, Calif. (CMSA)	11,497,549	13,470,900	1,973,400	17.2
3.	Chicago–Gary–Lake City, Ill.–Ind.–Wis. (CMSA)	7,937,290	8,146,900	209,600	2.6
4.	San Francisco–Oakland–San Jose, Calif. (CMSA)	5,367,900	5,953,100	585,200	10.9
5.	Philadelphia–Wilmington–Trenton, Pa.–N.J.–Del.–Md. (CMSA)	5,680,509	5,890,600	210,100	3.7
6.	Detroit–Ann Arbor, Mich. (CMSA)	4,752,764	4,629,400	–123,400	–2.6
7.	Boston–Lawrence–Salem, Mass.–N.H. (CMSA)	3,971,792	4,092,900	121,100	3.0
8.	Dallas–Fort Worth, Tex. (CMSA)	2,930,568	3,724,900	794,300	27.1
9.	Washington, D.C.–Md.–Va. (MSA)	3,250,921	3,646,000	395,100	12.2
10.	Houston–Galveston–Brazoria, Tex. (CMSA)	3,099,942	3,626,300	526,400	17.0
11.	Miami–Fort Lauderdale, Fla. (CMSA)	2,643,766	2,954,100	310,400	11.7
12.	Cleveland–Akron–Lorain, Ohio (CMSA)	2,834,062	2,766,900	–67,100	–2.4
13.	Atlanta, Ga. (MSA)	2,138,136	2,656,800	518,600	24.3
14.	St. Louis, Mo.–Ill. (MSA)	2,376,968	2,458,100	81,100	3.4
15.	Seattle–Tacoma, Wash. (CMSA)	2,093,285	2,340,600	247,300	11.8
16.	Minneapolis–St. Paul, Minn.–Wis. (MSA)	2,137,133	2,335,600	198,400	9.3
17.	Baltimore, Md. (MSA)	2,199,497	2,302,900	103,400	4.7
18.	Pittsburgh–Beaver Valley, Pa. (CMSA)	2,423,311	2,296,400	–126,900	–5.2
19.	San Diego, Calif. (MSA)	1,861,846	2,285,900	424,000	22.8
20.	Tampa–St. Petersburg–Clearwater, Fla. (MSA)	1,613,600	1,965,100	351,500	21.8
21.	Phoenix, Ariz. (MSA)	1,509,175	1,959,600	450,400	29.8
22.	Denver–Boulder, Colo. (CMSA)	1,618,461	1,861,300	242,800	15.0
23.	Cincinnati–Hamilton, Ohio–Ky.–Ind. (CMSA)	1,660,257	1,714,600	54,300	3.3
24.	Milwaukee–Racine, Wis. (CMSA)	1,570,152	1,562,100	–8,000	–0.5
25.	Kansas City, Mo.–Kans. (MSA)	1,433,464	1,546,400	113,000	7.9
26.	Portland–Vancouver, Oreg.–Wash. (CMSA)	1,297,977	1,383,400	85,400	6.6
27.	Norfolk–Virginia Beach–Newport News, Va. (MSA)	1,160,311	1,346,100	185,800	16.0
28.	Sacramento, Calif. (MSA)	1,099,814	1,336,500	236,700	21.5
29.	New Orleans, La. (MSA)	1,256,668	1,321,000	64,300	5.1
30.	Columbus, Ohio (MSA)	1,243,827	1,320,100	76,300	6.1
31.	San Antonio, Tex. (MSA)	1,072,125	1,306,700	234,600	21.9
32.	Indianapolis, Ind. (MSA)	1,166,575	1,228,600	62,100	5.3
33.	Buffalo–Niagara Falls, N.Y. (CMSA)	1,242,826	1,174,500	–68,300	–5.5
34.	Providence–Pawtucket–Fall River, R.I.–Mass. (CMSA)	1,083,139	1,117,700	34,600	3.2
35.	Charlotte–Gastonia–Rock Hill, N.C.–S.C. (MSA)	971,447	1,091,000	119,500	12.3
36.	Hartford–New Britain–Middletown, Conn. (CMSA)	1,013,508	1,057,500	43,900	4.3
37.	Salt Lake City–Ogden, Utah (MSA)	910,222	1,054,500	144,300	15.9
38.	Rochester, N.Y. (MSA)	971,230	979,100	7,800	0.8
39.	Oklahoma City, Okla. (MSA)	860,969	975,000	114,100	13.2
40.	Memphis, Tenn.–Ark.–Miss. (MSA)	913,472	971,900	58,500	6.4
41.	Louisville, Ky.–Ind. (MSA)	956,426	966,500	10,100	1.1
42.	Nashville, Tenn. (MSA)	850,505	956,200	105,700	12.4
43.	Dayton–Springfield, Ohio (MSA)	942,083	938,800	–3,300	–0.4

Rank	Metropolitan statistical area	Population 1980	1987 est.	Growth Number	Percent		Rank	Metropolitan statistical area	Population 1980	1987 est.	Growth Number	Percent
44.	Orlando, Fla. (MSA)	699,904	934,700	234,800	33.5		47.	Jacksonville, Fla. (MSA)	722,252	878,200	156,200	21.6
45.	Birmingham, Ala. (MSA)	883,993	916,900	32,900	3.7		48.	Albany–Schenectady–Troy, N.Y. (MSA)	835,880	846,400	10,500	1.3
46.	Greensboro–Winston Salem–High Point, N.C. (MSA)	851,444	915,700	64,200	7.5		49.	Honolulu, Hawaii (MSA)	762,565	830,600	68,000	8.9
							50.	Richmond–Petersburg, Va. (MSA)	761,311	825.300	64,000	8.4

Note: CMSA = consolidated metropolitan statistical area. MSA = metropolitan statistical area. **Source:** U.S. Bureau of the Census, 1988.

POPULATIONS OF METROPOLITAN STATISTICAL AREAS WITH 250,000 AND OVER, 1970, 1980, 1987, AND PERCENT CHANGE AND RANK

Metropolitan statistical area	POPULATION (in thousands) 1970	1980	1987	RANK 1980	1987	Average annual % change 1970–80	1980–87
Albany–Schenectady–Troy, N.Y. (MSA)	811	836	846	46	48	0.3%	0.2%
Albuquerque, N.Mex. (MSA)	316	420	486	80	75	2.8	2.0
Allentown–Bethlehem, Pa.—N.J. (MSA)	594	635	666	54	55	0.7	0.6
Appleton–Oshkosh–Neenah, Wis. (MSA)	277	291	309	107	113	0.5	0.8
Atlanta, Ga. (MSA)	1,684	2,138	2,657	16	13	2.4	3.0
Atlantic City, N.J. (MSA)	235	276	303	113	114	1.6	1.3
Augusta, Ga.—S.C. (MSA)	291	346	392	95	90	1.7	1.7
Austin, Tex. (MSA)	360	537	738	63	52	4.0	4.4
Bakersfield, Calif. (MSA)	330	403	505	84	72	2.0	3.1
Baltimore, Md. (MSA)	2,089	2,200	2,303	15	17	0.5	0.6
Baton Rouge, La. (MSA)	376	494	538	69	68	2.7	1.2
Beaumont–Port Arthur, Tex. (MSA)	348	375	371	88	96	0.8	-0.1
Binghamton, N.Y. (MSA)	268	263	260	123	126	-0.2	-0.2
Birmingham, Ala. (MSA)	794	884	917	42	45	1.1	0.5
Boston–Lawrence–Salem, Mass.—N.H. (CMSA)	3,939	3,972	4,093	7	7	0.1	0.4
Boston, Mass. (PMSA)	2,887	2,806	2,842	N.A.	N.A.	-0.3	0.2
Brockton, Mass. (PMSA)	163	183	185	N.A.	N.A.	1.2	0.2
Lawrence–Haverhill, Mass.—N.H. (PMSA)	301	339	375	N.A.	N.A.	1.2	1.4
Lowell, Mass.—N.H. (PMSA)	225	243	260	N.A.	N.A.	0.8	0.9
Nashua, N.H. (PMSA)	100	143	172	N.A.	N.A.	3.5	2.6
Salem–Gloucester, Mass. (PMSA)	263	258	258	N.A.	N.A.	-0.2	(Z)
Brownsville–Harlingen, Tex. (MSA)	140	210	264	138	124	4.1	3.2
Buffalo–Niagara Falls, N.Y. (CMSA)	1,349	1,243	1,175	29	33	-0.8	-0.8
Buffalo (PMSA)	1,113	1,015	958	N.A.	N.A.	-0.9	-0.8
Niagara Falls (PMSA)	236	227	216	N.A.	N.A.	-0.4	-0.7
Canton, Ohio (MSA)	394	404	397	83	88	0.3	-0.3
Charleston, S.C. (MSA)	336	430	502	77	74	2.5	2.1
Charleston, W. Va. (MSA)	257	270	261	118	125	0.5	-0.4
Charlotte–Gastonia–Rock Hill, N.C.—S.C. (MSA)	840	971	1,091	36	35	1.4	1.6
Chattanooga, Tenn.—Ga. (MSA)	371	427	432	78	82	1.4	0.2
Chicago–Gary–Lake Co. (Ill.), Ill.–Ind.–Wis. (CMSA)	7,779	7,937	8.147	3	3	0.2	0.4
Aurora–Elgin, Ill. (PMSA)	277	316	352	N.A.	N.A.	1.3	1.5
Chicago, Ill. (PMSA)	6,093	6,060	6,199	N.A.	N.A.	-0.1	0.3
Gary–Hammond, Ind. (PMSA)	633	643	604	N.A.	N.A.	0.1	-0.9
Joliet, Ill. (PMSA)	274	355	377	N.A.	N.A.	2.6	0.8
Kenosha, Wis. (PMSA)	118	123	120	N.A.	N.A.	0.4	-0.4
Lake Co., Ill. (PMSA)	383	440	494	N.A.	N.A.	1.4	1.6
Cincinnati–Hamilton, Ohio–Ky.–Ind. (CMSA)	1,613	1,660	1,715	20	23	0.3	0.4
Cincinnati, Ohio–Ky.–Ind. (PMSA)	1,387	1,401	1,438	N.A.	N.A.	0.1	0.4
Hamilton–Middletown, Ohio (PMSA)	226	259	276	N.A.	N.A.	1.3	0.9
Cleveland–Akron–Lorain, Ohio (CMSA)	3,000	2,834	2,767	11	12	-0.6	-0.3
Akron (PMSA)	679	660	647	N.A.	N.A.	-0.3	-0.3
Cleveland (PMSA)	2,064	1,899	1,851	N.A.	N.A.	-0.8	-0.3
Lorain–Elyria (PMSA)	257	275	268	N.A.	N.A.	0.7	-0.3
Colorado Springs, Colo. (MSA)	236	309	390	105	91	2.7	3.2
Columbia, S.C. (MSA)	323	410	451	82	78	2.4	1.3

Metropolitan statistical area	POPULATION (in thousands) 1970	1980	1987	RANK 1980	1987	Average annual % change 1970–80	1980–87
Columbus, Ohio (MSA)	1,149	1,244	1,320	28	30	0.8	0.8
Corpus Christi, Tex. (MSA)	285	326	360	99	100	1.4	1.4
Dallas–Fort Worth, Tex. (CMSA)	2,352	2,931	3,725	10	8	2.2	3.3
Dallas (PMSA)	1,556	1,957	2,456	N.A.	N.A.	2.3	3.1
Fort Worth–Arlington (PMSA)	795	973	1,269	N.A.	N.A.	2.0	3.7
Davenport–Rock Island–Moline, Iowa—Ill. (MSA)	363	384	367	86	97	0.6	-0.7
Dayton–Springfield, Ohio (MSA)	975	942	939	39	43	-0.3	(–Z)
Daytona Beach, Fla. (MSA)	169	259	332	124	108	4.2	3.4
Denver–Boulder, Colo. (CMSA)	1,238	1,618	1,861	21	22	2.7	1.9
Boulder–Longmont (PMSA)	132	190	217	N.A.	N.A.	3.6	1.8
Denver (PMSA)	1,106	1,429	1,645	N.A.	N.A.	2.6	1.9
Des Moines, Iowa (MSA)	340	368	385	89	93	0.8	0.6
Detroit–Ann Arbor, Mich. (CMSA)	4,788	4,753	4,629	6	6	-0.1	-0.4
Ann Arbor (PMSA)	234	265	268	N.A.	N.A.	1.2	0.2
Detroit (PMSA)	4,554	4,488	4,362	N.A.	N.A.	-0.1	-0.4
El Paso, Tex. (MSA)	359	480	573	70	67	2.9	2.4
Erie, Pa. (MSA)	264	280	279	111	121	0.6	-0.1
Eugene–Springfield, Oreg. (MSA)	215	275	265	115	123	2.5	-0.5
Evansville, Ind.—Ky. (MSA)	255	276	281	114	120	0.8	0.2
Fayetteville, N.C. (MSA)	212	247	259	127	128	1.5	0.6
Flint, Mich. (MSA)	446	450	435	73	81	0.1	-0.5
Fort Myers–Cape Coral, Fla. (MSA)	105	205	295	140	116	6.7	5.0
Fort Wayne, Ind. (MSA)	335	354	364	93	98	0.6	0.4
Fresno, Calif. (MSA)	413	515	597	67	64	2.2	2.1
Grand Rapids, Mich. (MSA)	539	602	657	56	57	1.1	1.2
Greensboro–Winston–Salem–High Point, N.C. (MSA)	743	852	916	44	46	1.4	1.0
Greenville–Spartanburg, S.C. (MSA)	473	569	612	59	61	1.8	1.0
Harrisburg–Lebanon–Carlisle, Pa. (MSA)	510	555	584	62	66	0.8	0.7
Hartford–New Britain–Middletown, Conn. (CMSA)	1,000	1,014	1,057	35	36	0.1	0.6
Bristol (PMSA)	70	74	78	N.A.	N.A.	0.5	0.8
Hartford (PMSA)	711	716	748	N.A.	N.A.	0.1	0.6
Middletown (PMSA)	74	82	85	N.A.	N.A.	1.0	0.6
New Britain (PMSA)	145	142	147	N.A.	N.A.	-0.2	0.4
Honolulu, Hawaii (MSA)	631	763	831	47	49	1.9	1.2
Houston–Galveston–Brazoria, Tex. (CMSA)	2,169	3,101	3,626	9	10	3.6	2.2
Brazoria (PMSA)	108	170	187	N.A.	N.A.	4.5	1.3
Galveston–Texas City (PMSA)	170	196	211	N.A.	N.A.	1.4	1.1
Houston (PMSA)	1,891	2,736	3,228	N.A.	N.A.	3.7	2.3
Huntington–Ashland, W. Va.—Ky.—Ohio (MSA)	307	336	323	97	111	0.9	-0.5
Indianapolis, Ind. (MSA)	1,111	1,167	1,229	30	32	0.5	0.7
Jackson, Miss. (MSA)	289	362	396	92	89	2.3	1.2
Jacksonville, Fla. (MSA)	613	722	878	50	47	1.6	2.7
Johnson City–Kingsport–Bristol, Tenn.—Va. (MSA)	374	434	443	76	80	1.5	0.3
Johnstown, Pa. (MSA)	263	265	252	121	131	0.1	-0.7
Kansas City, Mo.—Kans. (MSA)	1,373	1,433	1,546	25	25	0.4	1.0

Metropolitan statistical area	POPULATION (in thousands)			RANK		Average annual % change	
	1970	1980	1987	1980	1987	1970–80	1980–87
Knoxville, Tenn. (MSA)	477	566	594	60	65	1.7	0.7
Lakeland–Winter Haven, Fla. (MSA)	229	322	387	101	92	3.4	2.6
Lancaster, Pa. (MSA)	320	362	404	91	86	1.2	1.5
Lansing–East Lansing, Mich. (MSA)	378	420	428	81	83	1.0	0.3
Las Vegas, Nev. (MSA)	273	463	600	72	63	5.3	3.6
Lexington–Fayette, Ky. (MSA)	267	318	342	103	105	1.7	1.0
Little Rock–North Little Rock, Ark. (MSA)	381	474	512	71	71	2.2	1.0
Los Angeles–Anaheim–Riverside, Calif. (CMSA)	9,981	11,498	13,471	2	2	1.4	2.2
Anaheim–Santa Ana (PMSA)	1,421	1,933	2,219	N.A.	N.A.	3.1	1.9
Los Angeles–Long Beach (PMSA)	7,042	7,478	8,505	N.A.	N.A.	0.6	1.8
Oxnard–Ventura (PMSA)	378	529	628	N.A.	N.A.	3.4	2.4
Riverside–San Bernardino (PMSA)	1,139	1,558	2,119	N.A.	N.A.	3.1	4.2
Louisville, Ky.–Ind. (MSA)	907	957	967	38	41	0.5	0.1
Macon–Warner Robins, Ga. (MSA)	235	264	283	122	118	1.2	1.0
Madison, Wis. (MSA)	290	324	347	100	102	1.1	1.0
McAllen–Edinburg–Mission, Tex. (MSA)	182	283	379	110	94	4.4	4.0
Melbourne–Titusville–Palm Bay, Fla. (MSA)	230	273	375	116	95	1.7	4.4
Memphis, Tenn.–Ark.–Miss. (MSA)	834	913	972	40	40	0.9	0.9
Miami–Fort Lauderdale, Fla. (CMSA)	1,888	2,644	2,954	12	11	3.4	1.5
Fort Lauderdale–Hollywood–Pompano Beach (PMSA)	620	1,018	1,163	N.A.	N.A.	5.0	1.8
Miami–Hialeah (PMSA)	1,268	1,626	1,791	N.A.	N.A.	2.5	1.3
Milwaukee–Racine, Wis. (CMSA)	1,575	1,570	1,562	23	24	(–Z)	–0.1
Milwaukee (PMSA)	1,404	1,397	1,389	N.A.	N.A.	–0.1	–0.1
Racine (PMSA)	171	173	173	N.A.	N.A.	0.1	(Z)
Minneapolis–St. Paul, Minn.–Wis. (MSA)	1,982	2,137	2,336	17	16	0.8	1.2
Mobile, Ala. (MSA)	377	444	483	74	76	1.6	1.2
Modesto, Calif. (MSA)	195	266	327	120	109	3.1	2.9
Montgomery, Ala. (MSA)	226	273	297	117	115	1.9	1.2
Nashville, Tenn. (MSA)	699	851	956	45	42	2.0	1.6
New Haven–Meriden, Conn. (MSA)	489	500	519	68	69	0.2	0.5
New London–Norwich, Conn.–R.I. (MSA)	243	251	259	125	127	0.3	0.4
New Orleans, La. (MSA)	1,100	1,256	1,321	27	29	1.3	0.7
New York–Northern New Jersey–Long Island, N.Y.–N.J.–Conn. (CMSA)	18,193	17,539	18,054	1	1	–0.4	0.4
Bergen–Passaic, N.J. (PMSA)	1,358	1,293	1,294	N.A.	N.A.	–0.5	(Z)
Bridgeport–Milford, Conn. (PMSA)	444	439	444	N.A.	N.A.	–0.1	0.2
Danbury, Conn. (PMSA)	136	170	189	N.A.	N.A.	2.2	1.4
Jersey City, N.J. (PMSA)	608	557	547	N.A.	N.A.	–0.9	–0.2
Middlesex–Somerset–Hunterdon, N.J. (PMSA)	852	886	966	N.A.	N.A.	0.4	1.2
Monmouth–Ocean, N.J. (PMSA)	670	849	957	N.A.	N.A.	2.4	1.6
Nassau–Suffolk, N.Y. (PMSA)	2,556	2,606	2,631	N.A.	N.A.	0.2	0.1
Newark, N.J. (PMSA)	1,937	1,879	1,891	N.A.	N.A.	–0.3	0.1
New York, N.Y. (PMSA)	9,077	8,275	8,529	N.A.	N.A.	–0.9	0.4
Norwalk, Conn. (PMSA)	128	127	126	N.A.	N.A.	–0.1	–0.1
Orange County, N.Y. (PMSA)	222	260	288	N.A.	N.A.	1.6	1.4
Stamford, Conn. (PMSA)	206	199	193	N.A.	N.A.	–0.4	–0.4
Norfolk–Virginia Beach–Newport News, Va. (MSA)	1,059	1,160	1,346	31	27	0.9	2.0
Oklahoma City, Okla. (MSA)	719	861	975	43	39	1.8	1.7
Omaha, Nebr.–Iowa (MSA)	556	585	616	57	60	0.5	0.7
Orlando, Fla. (MSA)	453	700	935	51	44	4.3	4.0
Pensacola, Fla. (MSA)	243	290	344	109	103	1.8	2.4
Peoria, Ill. (MSA)	342	366	339	90	107	0.7	–1.1
Philadelphia–Wilmington–Trenton, Pa.–N.J.–Del.–Md. (CMSA)	5,749	5,681	5,891	4	5	–0.1	0.5
Philadelphia, Pa.–N.J. (PMSA)	4,824	4,717	4,866	N.A.	N.A.	–0.2	0.4
Trenton, N.J. (PMSA)	304	308	327	N.A.	N.A.	0.1	0.8
Vineland–Millville–Bridgeton, N.J. (PMSA)	121	133	138	N.A.	N.A.	0.9	0.5
Wilmington, Del.–N.J.–Md. (PMSA)	499	523	559	N.A.	N.A.	0.5	0.9
Phoenix, Ariz. (MSA)	971	1,509	1,960	24	21	4.4	3.6
Pittsburgh–Beaver Valley, Pa. (CMSA)	2,556	2,423	2,296	13	18	–0.5	–0.7
Beaver Co., Pa. (PMSA)	208	204	191	N.A.	N.A.	–0.2	–0.9
Pittsburgh, Pa. (PMSA)	2,348	2,219	2,105	N.A.	N.A.	–0.6	–0.7
Portland–Vancouver, Oreg.–Wash. (CMSA)	1,047	1,298	1,383	26	26	2.1	0.9
Portland, Oreg. (PMSA)	919	1,106	1,168	N.A.	N.A.	1.9	0.8
Vancouver, Wash. (PMSA)	128	192	216	N.A.	N.A.	4.0	1.6
Poughkeepsie, N.Y. (MSA)	222	245	258	129	129	1.0	0.7
Providence–Pawtucket–Fall River, R.I.–Mass. (CMSA)	1,065	1,083	1,118	33	34	0.2	0.4
Fall River, Mass.–R.I. (PMSA)	152	157	153	N.A.	N.A.	0.3	–0.4
Pawtucket–Woonsocket–Attleboro, R.I.–Mass. (PMSA)	301	307	322	N.A.	N.A.	0.2	0.6
Providence, R.I. (PMSA)	612	619	643	N.A.	N.A.	0.1	0.5
Raleigh–Durham, N.C. (MSA)	446	561	665	61	56	2.3	2.4
Reading, Pa. (MSA)	296	313	324	104	110	0.5	0.5
Richmond–Petersburg, Va. (MSA)	676	761	825	48	50	1.2	1.1
Rochester, N.Y. (MSA)	962	971	979	37	38	0.1	0.1
Rockford, Ill. (MSA)	272	280	281	112	119	0.3	0.1
Sacramento, Calif. (MSA)	848	1,100	1,336	32	28	2.6	2.7
Saginaw–Bay, Bay City–Midland, Mich. (MSA)	401	422	404	79	85	0.5	–0.6
St. Louis, Mo.–Ill. (MSA)	2,429	2,377	2,458	14	14	–0.2	0.5
Salem, Oreg. (MSA)	187	250	266	126	122	2.9	0.9
Salinas–Seaside–Monterey, Calif. (MSA)	247	290	343	108	104	1.6	2.3
Salt Lake City–Ogden, Utah (MSA)	684	910	1,055	41	37	2.9	2.0
San Antonio, Tex. (MSA)	888	1,072	1,307	34	31	1.9	2.7
San Diego, Calif. (MSA)	1,358	1,862	2,286	19	19	3.2	2.8
San Francisco–Oakland–San Jose, Calif. (CMSA)	4,754	5,368	5,953	5	4	1.2	1.4
Oakland (PMSA)	1,628	1,762	1,968	N.A.	N.A.	0.8	1.5
San Francisco (PMSA)	1,482	1,489	1,590	N.A.	N.A.	(Z)	0.9
San Jose (PMSA)	1,065	1,295	1,415	N.A.	N.A.	2.0	1.2
Santa Cruz (PMSA)	124	188	222	N.A.	N.A.	4.2	2.3
Santa Rosa–Petaluma (PMSA)	205	300	354	N.A.	N.A.	3.8	2.3
Vallejo–Fairfield–Napa (PMSA)	251	334	404	N.A.	N.A.	2.9	2.6
Santa Barbara–Santa Maria–Lompoc, Calif. (MSA)	264	299	341	106	106	1.2	1.8
Sarasota, Fla. (MSA)	120	202	256	143	130	5.3	3.2
Scranton–Wilkes-Barre, Pa. (MSA)	696	729	731	49	54	0.5	(Z)
Seattle–Tacoma, Wash. (CMSA)	1,837	2,093	2,341	18	15	1.3	1.5
Seattle (PMSA)	1,425	1,607	1,796	N.A.	N.A.	1.2	1.5
Tacoma (PMSA)	412	486	545	N.A.	N.A.	1.6	1.6
Shreveport, La. (MSA)	296	333	364	98	99	1.2	1.2
Spokane, Wash. (MSA)	287	342	355	96	101	1.7	0.5
Springfield, Mass. (MSA)	528	515	517	66	70	–0.2	(Z)
Stockton, Calif. (MSA)	291	347	443	94	79	1.8	3.4
Syracuse, N.Y. (MSA)	637	643	647	53	58	0.1	0.1
Tampa–St. Petersburg–Clearwater, Fla. (MSA)	1,106	1,614	1,965	22	20	3.8	2.7
Toledo, Ohio (MSA)	606	617	611	55	62	0.2	–0.1
Tucson, Ariz. (MSA)	352	531	619	64	59	4.1	2.1
Tulsa, Okla. (MSA)	526	657	733	52	53	2.2	1.5
Utica–Rome, N.Y. (MSA)	340	320	314	102	112	–0.6	–0.3
Visalia–Tulare–Porterville, Calif. (MSA)	188	246	292	128	117	2.7	2.4
Washington, D.C.–Md.–Va. (MSA)	3,040	3,251	3,646	8	9	0.7	1.6
West Palm Beach–Boca Raton–Delray Beach, Fla. (MSA)	349	577	790	58	51	5.0	4.3
Wichita, Kans. (MSA)	417	442	475	75	77	0.6	1.0
Worcester, Mass. (MSA)	400	403	410	85	84	0.1	0.2
York, Pa. (MSA)	330	381	404	87	87	1.5	0.8
Youngstown–Warren, Ohio (MSA)	537	531	503	65	73	–0.1	–0.8

Note: N.A. = not applicable. Z = less than 0.05 percent. **Source:** U.S. Bureau of the Census, *Statistical Abstract of the United States 1989* (1989).

25 FASTEST-GROWING U.S. METROPOLITAN STATISTICAL AREAS, 1980–87

Rank	Metropolitan statistical area	Population 1980	Population 1987	Growth Number	Growth Percent
1.	Naples, Fla. (MSA)	85,971	127,900	42,000	48.8%
2.	Ocala, Fla. (MSA)	122,488	181,300	58,900	48.1
3.	Fort Myers–Cape Coral, Fla. (MSA)	205,266	294,600	89,300	43.5
4.	Fort Pierce, Fla. (MSA)	151,196	215,400	64,200	42.5
5.	Austin, Tex. (MSA)	536,688	738,000	201,300	37.5
6.	Melbourne–Titusville–Palm Bay, Fla. (MSA)	272,959	374,900	101,900	37.3
7.	West Palm Beach–Boca Raton–Delray Beach, Fla. (MSA)	576,758	790,100	213,300	37.0
8.	Riverside–San Bernardino, Calif. (PMSA)	1,555,215	2,119,000	560,800	36.0
9.	Las Cruces, N.Mex. (MSA)	96,340	128,800	32,500	33.7
10.	McAllen–Edinburg–Mission, Tex. (MSA)	283,323	378,600	95,100	33.6
11.	Orlando, Fla. (MSA)	699,904	934,700	234,800	33.5
12.	Fort Walton Beach, Fla. (MSA)	109,920	145,300	35,400	32.2
13.	Fort Worth–Arlington, Tex. (PMSA)	973,138	1,268,900	295,700	30.4
14.	Midland, Tex. (MSA)	82,636	107,700	25,100	30.3
15.	Phoenix, Ariz. (MSA)	1,509,175	1,959,600	450,400	29.8
16.	Las Vegas, Nev. (MSA)	463,087	599,900	136,800	29.5
17.	Daytona Beach, Fla. (MSA)	258,762	331,900	73,000	28.3
18.	Stockton, Calif. (MSA)	347,342	443,500	96,100	27.7
19.	Anchorage, Alaska (MSA)	174,431	222,600	48,200	27.6
20.	Sarasota, Fla. (MSA)	202,251	255,600	53,300	26.4
21.	Colorado Springs, Colo. (MSA)	309,424	389,900	80,500	26.0
22.	Bryan–College Station, Tex. (MSA)	93,588	117,800	24,300	25.9
23.	Brownsville–Harlingen, Tex. (MSA)	209,727	263,600	53,900	25.7
24.	Dallas, Tex. (PMSA)	1,957,430	2,456,000	498,600	25.5
25.	Panama City, Fla. (MSA)	97,740	122,300	24,600	25.2

Note: MSA = metropolitan statistical area. PMSA = primary metropolitan statistical area. **Source:** U.S. Bureau of the Census, 1988.

THE 25 U.S. METROPOLITAN STATISTICAL AREAS WITH THE LARGEST PERCENTAGE DECLINE IN POPULATION, RANKED BY PERCENT DECLINE, 1980–87

Rank	Metropolitan statistical area	Population 1980	Population 1987	Decline Number	Decline Percent
1.	Duluth, Minn.–Wis. (MSA)	266,650	241,700	−25,000	−9.4%
2.	Steubenville–Weirton, Ohio–W.Va. (MSA)	163,734	149,000	−14,800	−9.0
3.	Waterloo–Cedar Rapids, Iowa (MSA)	162,781	149,300	−13,500	−8.3
4.	Elmira, N.Y. (MSA)	97,656	90,400	−7,300	−7.5
5.	Peoria, Ill. (MSA)	365,864	338,500	−27,300	−7.5
6.	Casper, Wyo. (MSA)	71,856	66,600	−5,300	−7.4
7.	Wheeling, W.Va.–Ohio (MSA)	185,566	172,800	−12,800	−6.9
8.	Beaver County, Pa. (PMSA)	204,441	191,000	−13,400	−6.6
9.	Muncie, Ind. (MSA)	128,587	120,500	−8,100	−6.3
10.	Gary–Hammond, Ind. (PMSA)	642,733	604,300	−38,400	−6.0
11.	Buffalo, N.Y. (PMSA)	1,015,472	958,300	−57,200	−5.6
12.	Cumberland, Md.–W.Va. (MSA)	107,782	101,900	−5,900	−5.5
13.	Youngstown–Warren, Ohio (MSA)	531,350	502,500	−28,800	−5.4
14.	Decatur, Ill. (MSA)	131,375	124,600	−6,800	−5.1
15.	Pittsburgh, Pa. (PMSA)	2,218,870	2,105,400	−113,500	−5.1
16.	Kankakee, Ill. (MSA)	102,926	97,800	−5,100	−4.9
17.	Niagara Falls, N.Y. (PMSA)	227,354	216,200	−11,100	−4.9
18.	Enid, Okla. (MSA)	621,820	591,800	−3,000	−4.8
19.	Johnstown, Pa. (MSA)	264,506	252,200	−12,300	−4.7
20.	Davenport–Rock Island–Moline, Iowa–Ill. (MSA)	384,749	366,600	−18,100	−4.7
21.	Anderson, Ind. (MSA)	139,336	132,800	−6,600	−4.7
22.	Pittsfield, Mass. (MSA)	83,490	79,900	−3,600	−4.3
23.	Saginaw Bay–Bay City–Midland, Mich. (MSA)	421,518	404,400	−17,100	−4.1
24.	Huntington–Ashland, W.Va.–Ky.–Ohio (MSA)	336,410	323,400	−13,000	−3.9
25.	Benton Harbor, Mich. (MSA)	171,276	164,800	−6,400	−3.8

MSA = metropolitan statistical area. PMSA = primary metropolitan statistical area. **Source:** U.S. Bureau of the Census, 1988.

COUNTIES IN AMERICA

In 1986 there were 3,139 counties in the United States. While 50 percent of Americans live in cities, almost every American lives in a county. Counties were originally the creation of state governments, which saw them as the local arm of state authority, with special responsibility for rural areas. Counties were intended more for the administrative convenience of the state than to meet the immediate needs of county residents and were not designed to have the intimate relationship with or understanding of the needs of localities theoretically characteristic of municipalities. But most states have loosened the reins on county governments in recent years, giving them more authority to meet the needs of population centers that have pushed beyond municipal limits.

(Note that in Louisiana, counties are called parishes, and in Alaska they are known as boroughs. The five boroughs of New York City are counties.)

Expenditures County governments spent $103 billion on revenues of $105.8 billion in fiscal year 1986–87, the most recent year for which such figures are available. Among the major programs counties spent their money on were public welfare, education, health, and transportation. Counties also have responsibilities involving law enforcement, jails and detention facilities, electoral and judicial administration, public-record-keeping, tax assessment and collection, issuance of licenses, building and upkeep of roads and highways, and programs to promote agriculture and rural areas, public health, and welfare. Many counties also run community colleges.

Revenues The primary source of funds for counties in 1986–87 was intergovernmental aid, monies received from other governments mostly in the form of grants or shared revenues. Intergovernmental aid accounted for $37.2 billion, or 35.2% of all county revenues. The second-largest source of county funds were property taxes, which made up $27.4 billion, or 25.9% of the total. Utility and other charges contributed 15.3% to county revenue, while sales, income, and other taxes contributed 9.3% to county coffers.

Most of the intergovernmental aid received by counties was contributed by state governments, which accounted for $32.1 billion, or 86.3% of all intergovernmental aid. In 1986 the Reagan administration ended the Federal General Revenue Sharing program, established in 1972 to distribute funds directly to county governments to meet locally identified needs. The end of federal revenue sharing and cutbacks in other federal programs aiding local governments have forced state governments to find new sources of funds for local governments to continue providing needed services. This has been done mostly through increases in direct financial assistance to the counties by the states and by the states granting counties more authority to raise local taxes.

Although property taxes remain by far the greatest source of locally generated revenue—$27 billion, or 73.4% of all county taxes—growth rates in property taxes have been slow compared with increases in other revenue sources. From 1984 to 1987, revenue from

selective and general sales taxes each rose more than 50%, revenue from income taxes and state governments more than 30%, and revenue from property taxes and current charges 28%. Revenue from the federal government declined 9.5%.

In fiscal year 1987, property taxes rose 8% to $4 billion. There were increases of 16% in selective sales taxes, 12% in general sales taxes, 10% in local income taxes, 9% in fees and charges, and 9% in revenues from state governments. Only revenue from the federal government decreased during the year, down 7% from $4 billion to $3.7 billion.

COUNTY EXPENDITURES, 1986–87

In 1986–87, counties spent
- $29.8 billion on social services;
- $14.8 billion on education and libraries;
- $11.3 billion on public safety;
- $9.8 billion on transportation programs, of which $8.2 billion was spent on highways;
- $7.2 billion on environment and housing.

SUMMARY OF COUNTY GOVERNMENT FINANCES, 1986–87 (millions of dollars)

Item	Amount 1986–87	% distribution 1986–87	% change 1985–86
Revenue, total	**$105,803**	(X)	9.3%
GENERAL REVENUE, TOTAL	101,229	100.0%	9.0
Intergovernmental revenue	37,240	36.8	7.0
From state governments	32,132	31.7	9.0
General local government support	3,791	3.7	9.8
From federal government	3,670	3.6	−7.2
From local governments	1,438	1.4	6.8
General revenue from own sources	63,989	63.2	10.2
Taxes	37,240	36.8	9.3
Property	27,362	27.0	7.9
General sales	5,794	5.7	12.0
Selective sales	1,211	1.2	15.7
Income	1,002	1.0	10.4
Other	1,872	1.8	19.2
Charges and miscellaneous	26,748	26.4	11.5
Current charges	15,008	14.8	8.8
Sewerage	932	0.9	9.4
Hospitals	6,982	6.9	4.1
Education	753	0.7	4.0
Interest earnings	4,469	4.4	2.2
Special assessments	532	0.5	17.2
Sale of property	165	0.2	11.5
Other and unallocable	6,574	6.5	25.7
UTILITY REVENUE	1,161	100.0	11.3
Electric power	99	8.5	62.3
Water supply	936	80.6	8.7
Transit system	111	9.5	6.7
Gas supply	16	1.3	—
LIQUOR STORE REVENUE	252	(X)	5.4
EMPLOYEE RETIREMENT	3,162	(X)	18.5
Expenditure, total	**$102,982**	**100.0%**	**11.1%**
EXPENDITURE BY FUNCTION			
General expenditure	99,358	100.0	11.3
Intergovernmental expenditure	5,054	5.1	19.4
Direct general expenditure	94,303	94.9	10.9
Capital outlay	10,663	10.7	22.1
Other	83,641	84.2	9.6
GENERAL EXPENDITURE BY FUNCTION			
Education services:			
Education	14,001	14.1	9.6
Capital outlay	939	0.9	45.8
Libraries	844	0.8	7.0

Item	Amount 1986–87	% distribution 1986–87	% change 1985–86
Social services and income maintenance:			
Public welfare	14,338	14.4	8.3
Cash assistance payments	6,789	6.8	7.4
Medical vendor payments	566	0.6	−0.4
Other	6,983	7.0	10.1
Hospitals	9,854	9.9	6.6
Own	9,338	9.4	6.9
Capital outlay	514	0.5	28.2
Other	516	0.5	1.0
Health	5,655	5.7	4.8
Transportation:			
Highways	8,175	8.2	8.0
Capital outlay	2,524	2.5	11.1
Air transportation	975	1.0	18.3
Parking facilities	27	—	50.0
Water transport	83	0.1	69.4
Transit subsidies	506	0.5	24.6
Public safety:			
Police protection	5,254	5.3	9.2
Fire protection	1,119	1.1	11.0
Correction	4,643	4.7	14.8
Protective inspection and regulation	308	0.3	10.4
Environment and housing:			
Sewerage	1,952	2.0	20.9
Capital outlay	987	1.0	20.1
Sanitation other than sewerage	1,355	1.4	24.0
Parks and recreation	1,782	1.8	0.4
Capital outlay	413	0.4	−19.8
Housing and community development	859	0.9	5.8
Capital outlay	216	0.2	2.9
Natural resources	1,205	1.2	11.9
Government administration:			
Financial administration	2,826	2.8	7.9
Judicial and legal	4,588	4.6	9.5
General public buildings	1,856	1.9	21.9
Other	2,150	2.2	7.3
Interest on general debt	6,671	6.7	21.8
General expenditure not elsewhere classified	8,333	8.4	25.5
UTILITY EXPENDITURE	2,234	(X)	9.8
EMPLOYEE RETIREMENT	1,171	(X)	10.4
LIQUOR STORE EXPENDITURE	214	(X)	4.4
Exhibit: salaries and wages	37,008	35.9	3.9
Debt outstanding at end of fiscal year	**$99,154**	**100.0%**	**15.4%**
Cash and security holdings	**$78,872**	**100.0%**	**12.2%**

Source: U.S. Bureau of the Census, *County Government Finances in 1986–87* (1989).

COUNTY RANKINGS BY SELECTED SUBJECTS

25 LARGEST COUNTIES, BY POPULATION, 1986

County	Number
Los Angeles, Calif.	8,295,900
Cook, Ill.	5,297,900
Harris, Tex.	2,798,300
Kings, N.Y.	2,293,200
San Diego, Calif.	2,201,300
Orange, Calif.	2,166,800
Wayne, Mich.	2,164,300
Queens, N.Y.	1,923,300
Maricopa, Ariz.	1,900,200
Dallas, Tex.	1,833,100
Dade, Fla.	1,769,500
Philadelphia, Pa.	1,642,900
New York, N.Y.	1,478,000
Cuyahoga, Ohio	1,445,400
Santa Clara, Calif.	1,401,600
Allegheny, Pa.	1,373,600
Middlesex, Mass.	1,367,000
Kings, Wash.	1,362,300
Nassau, N.Y.	1,323,000
Suffolk, N.Y.	1,312,000
Alameda, Calif.	1,208,700
Bronx, N.Y.	1,193,600
Bexar, Tex.	1,170,000
Broward, Fla.	1,142,400
San Bernardino, Calif.	1,139,100
Total U.S.	**241,078,000**

Source: U.S. Bureau of the Census, *City and County Data Book 1988* (1988)

25 COUNTIES WITH LARGEST POPULATION DECLINE, 1980–86

County	Number
Wayne, Mich.	−173,500
Allegheny, Pa.	−76,600
Cuyahoga, Ohio	−53,000
Erie, N.Y.	−50,700
Philadelphia, Pa.	−45,400
Baltimore City, Md.	−33,900
Milwaukee, Wis.	−32,600
Lake, Ind.	−31,200
St. Louis City, Mo.	−26,500
St. Louis, Minn.	−20,300
Peoria, Ill.	−17,100
Summit, Ohio	−16,700
Genesee, Mich.	−15,600
Mahoning, Ohio	−12,900
Washington, D.C.	−12,400
Luzerne, Pa.	−12,000
Lane, Oreg.	−12,000
Saginaw, Mich.	−11,700
Beaver, Pa.	−11,200
Westmoreland Pa.	−11,100
Niagara, N.Y.	−10,500
Black Hawk, Iowa	−10,400
Cambria, Pa.	−10,000
Lucas, Ohio	−9,600
Essex, N.J.	−9,400

Source: U.S. Bureau of the Census, *City and County Data Book 1988* (1988).

TOP 25 COUNTIES BY FEDERAL FUNDS AND GRANTS, 1986
(millions of dollars)

County	Dollars
Los Angeles, Calif.	$ 32,766.4
Kings, N.Y.	23,320.1
Washington, D.C.	14,598.2
Cook, Ill.	13,574.5
San Diego, Calif.	10,864.8
Philadelphia, Pa.	7,752.8
Santa Clara, Calif.	7,601.4
St. Louis City, Mo.	7,461.2
Orange, Calif.	7,265.5
Middlesex, Mass.	6,801.2
Tarrant, Tex.	6,672.1
Nassau, N.Y.	6,577.9
Wayne, Mich.	6,233.2
King, Wash.	5,619.6
Maricopa, Ariz.	5,604.6
Harris, Tex.	5,492.9
Hamilton, Ohio	5,263.9
Montgomery, Md.	5,240.4
Alameda, Calif.	5,100.6
Allegheny, Pa.	4,995.4
Sacramento, Calif.	4,990.0
Essex, Mass.	4,704.2
Dallas, Tex.	4,673.4
Cuyahoga, Ohio	4,634.5
Bexar, Tex.	4,613.3
U.S. Total	**822,618.7**

Source: U.S. Bureau of the Census, *City and County Data Book 1988* (1988).

25 FASTEST-GROWING COUNTIES, 1980–86

County	Number
Los Angeles, Calif.	818,700
Maricopa, Ariz.	391,000
Harris, Tex.	388,800
San Diego, Calif.	339,500
Dallas, Tex.	276,700
San Bernardino, Calif.	244,100
Tarrant, Tex.	240,700
Orange, Calif.	233,900
Riverside, Calif.	198,800
Bexar, Tex.	181,100
Palm Beach, Fla.	178,800
Dade, Fla.	144,000
Travis, Tex.	131,400
Sacramento, Calif.	131,300
Hillsborough, Fla.	128,900
Broward, Fla.	124,200
Fairfax, Va.	114,800
Gwinnett, Ga.	110,000
Santa Clara, Calif.	106,600
Clark, Nev.	106,400
Orange, Fla.	104,400
Alameda, Calif.	103,300
Cobb, Ga.	94,700
Kings, Wash.	92,400
Kern, Calif.	91,100
Total U.S.	**14,532,000**

Source: U.S. Bureau of the Census, *City and County Data Book 1988* (1988).

TOP 25 COUNTIES BY POPULATION GROWTH RATE, 1980–86

County	Rate
Matanuska-Susitna, Alaska	119.0%
Hernando, Fla.	74.8
Kenai Peninsula, Alaska	70.7
Osceola, Fla.	68.7
Flagler, Fla.	66.5
Gwinnett, Ga.	65.9
Esmeralda, Nev.	65.1
Uinta, Wyo.	63.5
Fayette, Ga.	62.9
Nye, Nev.	61.1
Rockwall, Tex.	59.7
Millard, Utah	58.6
Hood, Tex.	58.1
Douglas, Colo.	54.2
Campbell, Wyo.	50.7
Hays, Tex.	49.8
Williamson, Tex.	49.8
Custer, Idaho	49.7
Fort Bend, Tex.	48.7
Washington, Utah	48.2
Bastrop, Tex.	47.5
Mercer, N.Dak.	47.0
Citrus, Fla.	46.5
Collin, Tex.	45.7
Camden, Ga.	45.1
Total U.S.	**6.4%**

Source: U.S. Bureau of the Census, *City and County Data Book 1988* (1988).

25 COUNTIES WITH HIGHEST POPULATION DENSITY, 1986

County	No. per sq. mi.
New York, N.Y.	67,181.8/sq. mi.
Kings, N.Y.	32,760.0
Bronx, N.Y.	28,419.0
Queens, N.Y.	17,645.0
San Francisco, Calif.	16,282.6
Philadelphia, Pa.	12,080.1
Hudson, N.J.	12,023.9
Suffolk, Mass.	11,603.5
Washington, D.C.	9,938.1
Baltimore City, Md.	9,410.0
Alexandria, Va. (IC)	7,186.7
St. Louis City, Mo.	6,988.5
Essex, N.J.	6,629.1
Richmond, N.Y.	6,349.2
Arlington, Va.	6,103.8
Cook, Ill.	5,530.2
Norfolk, Va.	5,184.9
Union, N.J.	4,893.2
Falls Church, Va.	4,850.0
Nassau, N.Y.	4,609.8
Denver, Colo.	4,549.6
Harrisonburg, Va. (IC)	4,500.0
Charlottesville, Va. (IC)	4,110.0
Milwaukee, Wis.	3,868.9
Portsmouth, Va. (IC)	3,700.0
Total U.S.	**68.1/sq. mi.**

Note: IC = independent city, i.e., a city located outside of any county area and administering functions elsewhere commonly performed by counties. **Source:** U.S. Bureau of the Census, *City and County Data Book 1988* (1988).

CRIME AND PUNISHMENT

National crime statistics are maintained by the Federal Bureau of Investigation (FBI) and the Bureau of Justice Statistics, two divisions of the U.S. Department of Justice. The FBI compiles annual figures from law enforcement agencies around the country that it publishes in *Uniform Crime Reports*. The most serious crimes—called crime index offenses—are divided into violent crimes (murder and non-negligent manslaughter, forcible rape, robbery, and aggravated assault) and property crimes (burglary, larceny and theft, motor vehicle theft, and arson).

Between 1978 and 1987, the number of crime index offenses committed grew 21 percent. After a high of 13.4 million crime index offenses in 1981, there was a steady decline until 1984, when there were only 11.8 million. From 1985 to 1987, however, crime grew at a fast rate, with 13.5 million crime index offenses reported in 1987. The rate of crime per 100,000 inhabitants followed similar trends, the year of living most dangerously being 1980, when there were 5,950 crime index offenses per 100,000, as against only 5,031 in 1984. In 1987 the rate was 5,550. Both the number and rate of murders nationwide declined slightly in the period 1986-87, but this probably does not signal the beginning of a long-term trend, as unofficial figures for 1988 and early 1989 apparently show a sharp rise.

Cities with populations of more than 50,000 had the highest crime rates—6,294.5 per 100,000—followed by other cities and rural counties. This ranking was the same for all offenses except murder; rural counties had 5.7 murders per 100,000, and cities of less than 50,000 inhabitants only 4.5.

NATIONAL CRIME, RATE, AND PERCENT CHANGE, BY OFFENSE, 1978–87

Serious crimes	Crime 1987		Change over 1986		Change over 1978	
	Number	Rate per 100,000	%	Rate per 100,000	%	Rate per 100,000
VIOLENT CRIME TOTAL	**1,484,000**	**609.7**	**-0.3%**	**-1.3%**	**36.7%**	**22.5%**
Murder	20,100	8.3	-2.5	-3.5	2.8	-7.8
Forcible rape	91,110	37.4	-0.4	-1.3	34.8	20.6
Robbery	517,700	212.7	-4.6	-5.5	21.3	8.6
Aggravated assault	855,090	351.3	2.5	1.5	49.6	34.0
PROPERTY CRIME TOTAL	**12,024,700**	**4,940.3**	**2.6**	**1.6**	**18.8**	**6.4**
Burglary	3,236,200	1,329.6	-0.2	-1.1	3.4	-7.3
Larceny/theft	7,499,900	3,081.3	3.3	2.4	25.2	12.2
Motor vehicle theft	1,288,700	529.4	5.3	4.3	28.3	15.0
TOTAL serious crimes	**13,508,700**	**5,550.0**	**2.2%**	**1.4%**	**20.5%**	**8.1%**

Source: FBI, *Uniform Crime Reports 1987* (1988).

counted for 58% of all corrections spending. Federal law-enforcement expenditures ranked last in absolute dollars and accounted for only 0.6% of all federal spending. By way of comparison, the federal government spent $24 million more on space exploration and 43 times more on national defense and international relations than on law enforcement.

GOVERNMENTAL EXPENDITURE ON POLICE, CORRECTIONS, AND JUDICIAL AND LEGAL, BY LEVEL OF GOVERNMENT, 1986–87

TOTAL GOVERNMENT EXPENDITURES = $1,810,006

	Law enforcement expenditures (in millions)	Percentage of total law enforcement	Percentage of all govt. expenditure by level of govt.
TOTAL U.S.	**$60,603**	**100.0%**	**3.3%**
Police	29,332	48.4	1.6
Corrections	18,549	30.6	1.0
Judicial/legal	12,722	21.0	0.7
Federal	**$ 7,426**	**12.2%**	**0.4%**
Police	4,231	7.0	0.2
Corrections	924	1.5	0.1
Judicial/legal	2,271	3.7	0.1
State	**$20,039**	**33.1%**	**1.0%**
Police	4,048	6.7	0.2
Corrections	11,704	19.3	0.6
Judicial/legal	4,287	7.1	0.2
Local	**$33,138**	**54.7%**	**1.8%**
Police	21,053	34.7	1.2
Corrections	5,921	9.8	0.3
Judicial/legal	6,164	10.2	0.3

Source: Bureau of the Census, *Governmental Finances in 1986-1987* (1988).

Value of stolen property While the taxpayer cost of fighting crime, which is easily calculated, is high, the overall burden to society is greater still, especially in the inestimable emotional cost to victims and their families. The most immediate cost is to the crime victim in value of property or goods stolen. In 1987 this amounted to $11.8 billion, of which only $4.3 billion, or 37%, was recovered. By type of crime, motor vehicle thefts had the highest cumulative value of $5.9 billion, an average value per incident of $4,964, even higher than that for bank robberies. The average value of property stolen during the course of murders and rapes was $107 and $30, respectively. Of property recovered, motor vehicles ranked first by value—$3.9 billion—and as a percentage of property stolen—65.2%; televisions, radios, and stereos ranked last at 5%.

VALUE OF PROPERTY STOLEN, BY TYPE, 1987
(millions of dollars)

Type of Property	Value of property		% recovered
	Stolen	Recovered	
Currency, notes, etc.	$ 719,659	$ 41,962	5.8%
Jewelry and precious metals	1,143,415	61,146	5.3
Clothing and furs	268,144	39,448	14.7
Motor vehicles	5,907,293	3,854,165	65.2
Office equipment	177,884	15,758	8.9
Television, stereos, etc.	1,056,844	52,850	5.0
Firearms	115,139	11,867	10.3
Household goods	209,044	14,137	6.8
Consumable goods	79,492	11,975	15.1
Livestock	19,553	3,105	15.9
Miscellaneous	2,087,748	207,129	9.9
TOTAL	**11,784,215**	**4,313,542**	**36.6%**

Note: Based on a survey of 13,149 law enforcement agencies representing 225,052,000 inhabitants. **Source:** FBI, *Uniform Crime Reports 1987* (1988).

HIGH COST OF CRIME

Government expenditures In fiscal year 1986-87, local, state, and federal governments spent a combined total of $60.6 billion on law enforcement, an amount equal to 3.3% of all government spending. Police protection accounted for $29.3 billion, or 48% of the total. Expenditures for corrections and judicial and legal administration came to $18.5 billion (31%) and $12.7 billion (21%), respectively.

Spending on law enforcement was highest at the local level both in absolute dollars—$33.1 billion—and as a percentage of spending by level of government—14%. Local government spending on legal and judicial administration was almost equal that of state and federal government combined, while local government expenditures on police protection were 2.5 times that of state and federal government combined.

Overall, state government spending ranked second, but state outlays on corrections ac-

CRIME RATES PER 100,000 POPULATION FOR MAJOR OFFENSES, BY STATE, 1987

State	All serious crimes	Murder	Violent crime Forcible rape	Robbery	Aggra-vated assault	Property crime Burglary	Larceny/theft	Motor vehicle theft
Ala.	4,451.4	9.3	27.8	112.2	409.9	1,198.3	2,431.1	262.8
Alaska	5,377.5	10.1	65.0	73.1	307.2	970.1	3,465.7	486.3
Ariz.	7,188.6	7.5	41.2	138.4	425.5	1,626.1	4,527.3	422.6
Ark.	4,245.2	7.6	32.6	79.1	292.6	1,078.0	2,548.7	206.5
Calif.	6,506.4	10.6	43.8	301.3	562.4	1,518.2	3,240.2	830.1
Colo.	6,451.3	5.8	40.8	118.8	302.1	1,534.6	4,012.9	436.3
Conn.	4,995.7	4.9	24.9	178.1	211.1	1,218.3	2,829.4	529.0
D.C.	8,451.6	36.2	39.4	717.4	817.4	1,807.7	4,021.2	1,012.4
Del.	4,938.8	5.1	68.5	122.5	234.6	1,020.5	3,175.9	311.6
Fla.	8,503.2	11.4	50.2	356.6	606.3	2,256.9	4,545.2	676.7
Ga.	5,792.0	11.8	43.1	209.2	312.4	1,552.1	3,171.0	492.4
Hawaii	5,817.9	4.8	36.3	98.0	124.2	1,155.6	4,033.1	366.0
Idaho	4,156.3	3.1	17.5	24.2	169.3	976.8	2,797.9	167.4
Ill.	5,416.5	8.3	38.4	314.3	435.2	1,123.7	2,957.1	539.5
Ind.	4,119.8	5.6	29.1	88.6	205.2	946.7	2,490.0	354.5
Iowa	4,140.2	2.1	11.9	36.2	181.1	917.8	2,840.1	151.1
Kans.	4,903.9	4.4	32.6	82.1	241.6	1,138.0	3,152.0	253.2
Ky.	3,270.0	7.5	21.0	90.2	219.1	847.1	1,892.5	192.7
La.	5,873.3	11.1	35.9	179.0	467.0	1,444.5	3,323.2	412.5
Maine	3,532.3	2.5	15.7	25.6	108.3	770.7	2,436.1	173.4
Mass.	4,733.8	3.0	31.9	177.3	352.5	1,059.9	2,185.1	924.2
Md.	5,477.6	9.6	39.6	290.3	428.3	1,162.5	2,965.5	581.8
Mich.	6,456.8	12.2	67.2	276.5	424.2	1,452.2	3,472.5	752.0
Minn.	4,615.8	2.6	33.9	102.5	146.3	1,068.9	2,960.1	301.4
Miss.	3,438.6	10.2	29.2	57.0	173.3	1,201.4	1,807.0	160.5
Mo.	4,707.5	8.3	28.9	164.1	343.3	1,111.3	2,625.2	426.3
Mont.	4,599.4	4.1	19.8	24.2	103.1	806.1	3,404.3	237.8
Nebr.	4,131.6	3.5	21.6	47.1	179.0	847.9	2,866.5	165.9
Nev.	6,371.4	8.4	61.8	272.5	353.0	1,629.4	3,491.3	555.0
N.C.	4,649.9	8.1	29.1	93.9	352.9	1,356.1	2,586.0	223.8
N.Dak.	2,833.0	1.5	9.4	7.6	38.4	455.4	2,197.6	123.2
N.H.	3,371.7	3.0	26.6	26.5	93.5	694.8	2,310.9	216.5
N.J.	5,261.5	4.6	33.4	232.8	270.3	1,008.8	2,866.3	845.4
N.Mex.	6,546.8	10.1	43.1	108.3	466.9	1,787.7	3,785.1	345.5
N.Y.	5,952.4	11.3	31.1	503.3	462.4	1,216.4	3,024.8	703.1
Ohio	4,575.3	5.8	39.9	153.1	222.5	1,062.5	2,708.6	382.9
Okla.	6,025.6	7.5	35.8	109.5	264.8	1,782.8	3,220.3	604.9
Oreg.	6,969.0	5.6	45.8	196.0	292.2	1,782.7	4,181.6	465.1
Pa.	3,163.2	5.4	26.2	144.4	193.3	722.0	1,722.7	349.2
R.I.	5,285.5	3.5	24.4	107.7	224.0	1,441.0	2,701.3	783.5
S.C.	5,161.9	9.3	43.7	101.1	510.8	1,358.0	2,858.2	280.8
S.Dak.	2,678.0	1.8	20.6	12.3	85.0	534.1	1,928.5	95.6
Tenn.	4,665.6	9.1	43.9	193.8	286.6	1,351.8	2,213.4	566.9
Tex.	7,722.4	11.7	48.1	226.7	344.8	2,118.0	4,238.5	734.8
Utah	5,618.6	3.3	21.7	52.8	152.0	950.9	4,228.5	209.5
Va.	3,959.5	7.4	26.0	105.8	155.8	806.9	2,603.2	254.4
Vt.	4,271.2	2.7	22.4	16.8	94.5	1,110.4	2,825.7	198.5
Wash.	7,017.1	5.6	52.2	141.4	240.2	1,904.5	4,277.9	395.2
Wis.	4,169.4	3.5	19.8	66.4	160.2	842.6	2,830.4	246.5
W.Va.	2,190.7	4.8	22.6	31.2	78.7	603.6	1,288.1	161.7
Wyo.	4,031.2	2.0	31.4	20.0	229.6	717.6	2,892.0	138.6
TOTAL U.S.	**5,550.0**	**8.3**	**37.4**	**212.7**	**351.3**	**1,329.6**	**3,081.3**	**529.4**

Source: FBI, *Uniform Crime Reports, Crime in the United States 1987* (1988).

SERIOUS CRIME IN THE 50 LARGEST CITIES, 1987 (by crime rate per 1,000 inhabitants)

City	Crime index offenses	Rate per 1,000[1]	Murder	Violent Crime Forcible rape	Robbery	Aggra-vated assault	All property crimes
Fort Worth	77,997	180.4	135	476	3,270	3,810	70,306
Portland, Oreg.	65,281	167.0	66	407	3,667	4,623	56,518
Dallas	165,395	163.8	323	1,260	9,091	9,412	145,309
Atlanta	67,171	156.2	207	636	5,100	6,950	54,278
Miami	58,981	153.2	128	202	5,594	5,385	47,672
Seattle	73,369	148.4	54	465	2,959	3,618	66,273
San Antonio	119,812	130.2	174	849	3,253	1,816	113,720
Detroit	139,978	128.2	686	1,417	15,093	10,582	112,200
Newark	40,761	128.0	81	577	4,230	4,038	31,835
St. Louis	54,971	128.0	153	332	3,296	5,997	45,193
Oklahoma City	56,462	127.9	48	381	1,322	2,047	52,664
Minneapolis	45,621	126.9	38	520	2,866	2,114	40,083
Oakland	44,995	122.9	114	538	3,176	2,657	38,510
Kansas City, Mo.	53,330	120.0	131	486	3,279	4,527	44,907
Jacksonville	74,718	118.6	147	609	3,876	4,945	65,141
Boston	67,590	117.4	76	550	5,408	5,920	55,636
Tucson	42,562	113.6	23	281	911	2,308	39,039
Charlotte	39,943	112.0	52	308	1,486	4,146	33,951
Sacramento	34,624	104.4	78	241	1,841	1,676	30,788
Albuquerque	37,199	100.1	48	211	987	2,599	33,354
Tulsa	36,736	99.3	35	234	1,074	1,786	33,607
Memphis	64,555	97.9	143	831	4,696	3,163	55,722
Austin	44,579	94.9	39	284	985	1,005	42,266
Houston	165,181	94.9	323	1,172	9,692	7,784	146,210
New Orleans	51,280	93.3	205	359	3,786	3,328	43,602
Columbus	52,772	92.9	85	534	2,864	1,898	47,391
Chicago[2]	277,338	91.9	691	—	29,879	34,194	212,574
Denver	46,630	91.5	79	401	1,612	1,749	42,789
New York	662,954	91.0	1,672	3,507	78,890	64,244	514,641
Phoenix	84,434	90.7	111	503	2,287	5,280	76,253
Nashville[3]	43,001	88.3	99	509	2,350	2,295	37,748
Los Angeles	294,083	88.0	811	2,169	26,192	34,661	230,250
Baltimore	66,229	86.6	226	595	7,466	6,008	51,934
Toledo	29,756	86.3	33	360	1,299	1,075	26,989
El Paso	42,219	85.3	25	219	969	3,119	37,887
San Diego	88,562	85.1	96	410	3,452	5,154	79,450
Washington, D.C.	52,826	84.9	225	245	4,462	5,084	42,810
Cleveland	46,365	84.6	145	750	3,541	2,528	39,401
Milwaukee	50,670	83.4	92	437	1,984	3,495	44,662
Pittsburgh	31,251	80.3	37	263	2,834	1,184	26,933
Buffalo	25,611	78.6	35	268	1,552	1,700	22,056
Long Beach	31,519	77.6	62	221	2,467	1,910	26,859
San Francisco	58,213	75.8	103	452	4,654	4,089	48,915
Cincinnati	27,751	74.7	69	344	1,183	1,571	24,584
Omaha	24,450	65.2	28	189	570	1,749	21,914
Indianapolis	30,588	63.9	57	432	1,334	2,720	26,045
Honolulu	49,371	59.3	36	322	985	915	47,113
Philadelphia	95,931	58.2	338	1,102	9,302	6,656	78,533
Virginia Beach	18,855	55.4	11	124	322	261	18,137
San Jose	36,904	50.5	24	393	944	3,017	32,526

1. Rates per 1,000 inhabitants were computed by the editors on the basis of figures supplied by the FBI. 2. Forcible rape figures supplied by the Illinois Department of State police are not in accordance with the FBI's Uniform Crime Report guidelines. The number for crime index offenses does not include any rape figures. The editors believe that the rate-per-1,000 figure would not change significantly with the addition of rape figures. 3. Arson is not included in the figures for either property crimes or crime index offenses.
Source: FBI, *Uniform Crime Reports 1987* (1988).

NUMBER OF MURDERS BY STATE, 1987

State	Murder 1987 Total	Rate per 100,000	Change over 1986 %	Rate per 100,000
Alabama	380	9.3	−7.1%	−7.9
Alaska	53	10.1	15.2	17.4
Arizona	253	7.5	−17.6	−19.4
Arkansas	182	7.6	−4.7	−6.2
California	2,924	10.6	−3.8	−6.2
Colorado	191	5.8	−17.0	−17.1
Connecticut	156	4.9	5.4	6.5
Delaware	33	5.1	6.5	4.1
District of Columbia	225	36.2	16.0	16.8
Florida	1,371	11.4	0.0	−2.6
Georgia	735	11.8	7.1	5.4
Hawaii	52	4.8	2.0	0.0
Idaho	31	3.1	3.1	−3.1
Illinois	967	8.3	−5.5	−6.7
Indiana	307	5.6	−6.7	−6.7
Iowa	59	2.1	15.7	16.7
Kansas	110	4.4	1.9	0.0
Kentucky	280	7.5	12.9	11.9
Louisiana	496	11.1	−13.7	−13.3
Maine	30	2.5	30.4	25.0
Maryland	436	9.6	8.7	6.7
Massachusetts	173	3.0	−16.8	−16.7
Michigan	1,124	12.2	8.9	8.0
Minnesota	112	2.6	6.7	4.0
Mississippi	269	10.2	−8.8	−8.9
Missouri	423	8.3	−8.8	−9.8
Montana	33	4.1	37.5	41.4
Nebraska	55	3.5	10.0	12.9
Nevada	85	8.4	−29.8	−33.3
New Hampshire	32	3.0	39.1	36.4
New Jersey	351	4.6	−12.0	−11.5
New Mexico	152	10.1	−10.6	−12.2
New York	2,016	11.3	5.7	5.6
North Carolina	519	8.1	0.8	0.0
North Dakota	10	1.5	42.9	50.0
Ohio	630	5.8	5.9	5.5
Oklahoma	244	7.5	−9.3	−7.4
Oregon	153	5.6	−14.0	−15.2
Pennsylvania	642	5.4	−2.6	−1.8
Rhode Island	35	3.5	2.9	0.0
South Carolina	318	9.3	9.3	8.1
South Dakota	13	1.8	−53.6	−55.0
Tennessee	444	9.1	−11.4	−12.5
Texas	1,959	11.7	−13.2	−13.3
Utah	55	3.3	3.8	3.1
Vermont	15	2.7	36.4	35.0
Virginia	437	7.4	6.3	4.2
Washington	256	5.6	14.8	12.0
West Virginia	92	4.8	−19.3	−18.6
Wisconsin	168	3.5	12.8	12.9
Wyoming	10	2.0	−63.0	−62.3
TOTAL U.S.	20,096	8.3	−2.5	−3.5

Source: FBI, *Uniform Crime Reports 1987* (1988).

PRISONERS

Jails are locally administered facilities that house inmates after arraignment, prisoners serving terms of less than one year, and prisoners who cannot be housed in state prisons owing to overcrowding. Jail population calculations are based on a daily population. As of June 30, 1987, the adult population of 294,092 included 139,394 convicted and 150,101 unconvicted inmates.

Prison Inmates In the decade from 1977 to 1986, the number of prisoners in state and federal facilities skyrocketed both in absolute numbers—84%, from 285,456 to 523,922—and in rate per 100,000 population—67%, from 129 to 216. Overall, the ratio of men to women behind bars is about 20:1, and the rate of prisoners per 100,000 by sex is 423 for men, as against only 20 for women.

Prisoners are demographically distinct from the general population. They are younger, less educated, and they are more than two-and-a-half times as likely never to have married.

STATE AND FEDERAL PRISON POPULATION, 1987

	Number	Rate/100,000 population
Federal prisoners	48,300	16
State prisoners	533,309[1]	212
TOTAL	581,609	228
Of which:		
Male	552,770	445
Female	28,839	21

Note: As of Dec. 31. 1. Owing to overcrowding, there were also 12,220 state prisoners held in local jails. **Source:** BJS Bulletin, *Prisoners in 1987* (1988).

ADMISSIONS TO AND RELEASES FROM JAILS, 1986–87

Admissions	1987	1986	% change 1986–87
Adults	8,529,983	8,261,176	3.3%
Male	7,670,765	7,410,057	3.5
Female	859,218	851,119	1.0
Juveniles	97,217	92,856	4.7
Male	74,970	72,046	4.1
Female	22,247	20,810	6.9
TOTAL Admissions	8,627,200	8,354,032	3.3
Releases			
Adults	8,314,491	8,193,124	1.5
Male	7,469,188	7,342,940	1.7
Female	845,303	850,184	−0.6
Juveniles	94,423	91,552	3.1
Male	72,567	70,442	3.0
Female	21,856	21,110	3.5
TOTAL Releases	8,408,914	8,284,676	1.5%

Source: BJS Bulletin, *Jail Inmates 1987* (1988).

AVERAGE DAILY POPULATION OF JAILS AND RATED CAPACITY, 1987

Average daily population	Number of jail inmates 1987	1986	% change 1986–87
All inmates	290,300	265,517	9%
Adults	288,725	264,113	9
Male	264,113	143,143	9
Female	23,796	20,970	13
Juveniles	1,575	1,404	12
Rated capacity of jails	301,198	285,726	6
Percent of rated capacity occupied	98%	96%	3

Source: BJS Bulletin, *Jail Inmates 1987* (1988).

CHARACTERISTICS OF STATE PRISON INMATES AND THE GENERAL POPULATION COMPARED, 1986

Characteristic	Prisoners	General population
SEX		
Male	95.6%	48.7%
Female	4.4	51.3
RACE		
White	49.7%	84.7%
Black	46.9	12.2
Other	3.4	3.1
ETHNICITY		
Non-Hispanic	87.4%	92.5%
Hispanic	12.6	7.5
MARITAL STATUS		
Married	20.3%	62.9%[1]
Widowed	1.9	7.7
Divorced	18.1	7.8
Separated	6.0	N.A.
Never married	53.7	21.6
AGE		
Median age	28.0 years	31.8 years
Less than 18	0.5%	26.2%[2]
18–24	26.7	11.6
25–34	45.7	17.8
35–44	19.4	13.7
45–54	5.2	9.4
55–64	1.8	9.2
Over 65	0.6	12.1
EDUCATION		
Median years of education	10.0 years	12.3 years[3]
Less than 12	61.6%	33.5%
12 or more	38.4	66.5
PRE-ARREST EMPLOYMENT		
Employed	69.0%	61.1%
Looking	18.0	4.5[4]
Not looking	13.0	34.4[5]

1. Persons 18 and older. 2. Includes total population under 18. 3. Persons 25 and older. 4. Percent of labor force looking for work. Official unemployment for 1987 was 7%. 5. Percentage not in labor force. **Note:** N.A. = not available. **Sources:** BJS, *Sourcebook of Criminal Justice Statistics 1987* (1988); U.S. Bureau of the Census, *Statistical Abstract of the United States 1988.*

PRISON CAPACITY, 1986–87

	1987 prison pop. as % of:		1986–87 net change in:	
	Lowest capacity	Highest capacity	Highest capacity	Lowest capacity
Federal	137%	173%	386	–84[1]
State[2]	105	120	37,884	30,045
TOTAL U.S.	107	124	38,270	29,961

1. Net decline in lowest capacity of the federal prison system attributed to the loss of 1,300 beds after disturbances at Oakdale (La.) Detention Center and Atlanta Penitentiary. 2. Not including state-sentenced inmates held in local jails owing to overcrowding. **Source:** BJS Bulletin, *Prisoners in 1987* (1988).

Probation and Parole In the five years of 1983–87, nationwide the number of people under "correctional supervision"—that is, in prison, on parole, or on probation—jumped almost 40 percent, from 2.47 million to 3.46 million. The strain has been felt at every level of the criminal justice system. When an offender is convicted, the primary sentencing alternatives are incarceration or probation. Once imprisoned, the offender may become eligible for parole, a form of conditional release. As prison space has decreased in proportion to the number of criminal offenders, the number of these conditional releases has increased to alleviate overcrowding. Of the offenders under correctional supervision in 1987, 2.2 million—65%—were on probation, and 362,192—10%—were on parole from prison.

Prison Capacity is measured by the number of beds a corrections rating authority assigns it, by the number of prisoners the staff can accommodate, and by the number of prisoners the facility was built to house. In 1987 the highest and lowest of these three capacity figures exceeded 100% nationwide.

Recidivism In 1986, 82% of all state and federal prisoners were recidivists—inmates who had committed crimes after serving a previous prison term or after being on probation or parole. Of all inmates, 60% had been imprisoned two or more times, 45% three or more, and 20% six or more.

CRIMINAL HISTORIES OF STATE PRISON INMATES, 1986

	First-timers			Recidivists			
	Total	Non-violent	Violent	Non-violent	Prior violent only	Current violent only	Current & prior violent
NUMBER of inmates	447,185	23,808	58,983	129,465	49,827	98,946	86,155
PERCENT of all inmates	100.0%	5.3%	13.2%	29.0%	11.1%	22.1%	19.3%
SEX (%)							
Male	95.6%	91.2%	93.3%	93.6%	97.5%	97.4%	98.3%
Female	4.4	8.8	6.7	6.4	2.5	2.6	1.7
RACE (%)							
White	49.7%	63.2%	50.7%	56.9%	44.9%	47.1%	40.2%
Black	46.9	33.3	45.6	40.5	51.6	48.9	56.2
Other	3.4	3.5	3.7	2.6	3.5	4.0	3.6
MEDIAN AGE							
All prisoners	28	29	28	27	29	28	30
1st arrest	17	23	22	17	16	16	15
1st confinement	19	25	24	19	17	19	18
AVERAGE TERM of current confinement (months)	27.3	21.0	30.6	19.6	20.7	32.1	32.0

Source: BJS, *Sourcebook of Criminal Justice Statistics 1987* (1988).

ADULT PRISONERS UNDER CORRECTIONAL SUPERVISION, 1983–87

Correctional population	Number	1987 % of prison pop.	Number	1983 % of prison pop.	% change
Probation	2,242,053	64.8%	1,582,947	64.0%	41.6%
Jail	294,092	8.5	221,815	9.0	32.6
Prison	562,623	16.3	423,898	17.1	32.7
Parole	362,192	10.5	246,440	10.0	47.0
TOTAL[1]	3,460,960	100.0%	2,475,100	100.0%	39.8%

1. Percentages may not add to total owing to rounding. **Source:** BJS Bulletin, *Probation and Parole 1987* (1988).

ARRESTS

In 1987, males constituted 82%, and adults 84%, of all arrests for serious crimes. While juveniles accounted for a third of all property crime arrests, 15% of violent crime arrests, and 13% of other crimes, juvenile males were arrested for 14% of all violent crimes—more than females of all age groups. Yet juvenile and young adult males, those under 25, account for 48% of all those charged with crimes; 17% are juveniles under age 18, and 31% are between the ages of 18 and 24. Although involvement in property crime is highest at age 16 for both sexes, violent crime manifests itself at different ages in men and women.

INCIDENCE OF ARRESTS FOR VIOLENT CRIMES, 1987

	Male		Female	
	Age	No. of arrests	Age	No. of arrests
Murder	18	819	24	98
Rape	24	1,369	15	25
Robbery	17	7,619	23	561
Aggravated assault	24	11,424	24	1,828

Source: FBI, *Uniform Crime Reports 1987* (1988).

CAPITAL PUNISHMENT

In the period 1930-87, 3,952 executions were carried out under state or federal authority. Overall, the number of prisoners executed each year declined steadily between 1930 and 1968. There were 1,667 executions in the 1930s, 1,284 in the 1940s, 717 in the 1950s, and 191 between 1960 and 1967. There were none between 1968 and 1978—the Supreme Court ruled the death penalty unconstitutional in 1972, and reinstated it in 1976. But between 1977 and 1987, 93 executions were carried out, all but one for murder, and all but one, male.

Fourteen states have carried out 100 or more executions since 1930; but as of 1987, 13 states and the District of Columbia did not authorize the death penalty for any crime. In Maine, Minnesota, and Wisconsin, there has been no death penalty statute in force since at least 1930, and Alaska and Hawaii have had no death penalty statute since 1960. The death penalty was either abolished or declared unconstitutional in Michigan (1963), Iowa and West Virginia (1965), Kansas (1973), the District of Columbia (1973), Rhode Island (1979), Oregon (1981), and Massachusetts and New York (1984). South Dakota abolished the death penalty in 1915, restored it in 1939, abolished it again in 1977, and restored it again in 1979. In California the death penalty was found "partially unconstitutional" in 1984.

NUMBER OF PRISONERS EXECUTED, BY STATE, 1930-87

State	No. executed Since 1930	Since 1977	In 1987	On death row 1987
Georgia	378	12	5	116
New York	329	—	N.A.	N.A.
Texas	323	26	6	256
California	292	—	—	200
North Carolina	266	3	—	76
Florida	187	17	1	277
Ohio	172	—	—	80
South Carolina	164	2	—	45
Mississippi	157	13	2	50
Pennsylvania	152	—	—	80
Louisiana	148	15	8	42
Alabama	138	3	1	90
Arkansas	118	—	—	28
Kentucky	103	—	—	32
Virginia	98	6	1	38
Tennessee	93	—	—	62
Illinois	90	—	—	108
New Jersey	74	—	—	28
Maryland	68	—	—	17
Missouri	62	—	—	52
Oklahoma	60	—	—	86
Washington	47	—	—	8
Colorado	47	—	—	3
Indiana	43	2	—	44
West Virginia	40	N.A.	N.A.	N.A.
District of Columbia	40	N.A.	N.A.	N.A.
Arizona	38	—	—	73
Nevada	31	2	—	38
Massachusetts	27	—	N.A.	N.A.
Connecticut	21	—	—	1
Oregon	19	—	—	5
Iowa	18	—	N.A.	N.A.
Kansas	15	N.A.	N.A.	N.A.
Utah	15	2	1	7
Delaware	12	—	—	6
New Mexico	8	—	—	2
Wyoming	7	—	—	2
Montana	6	—	—	6
Vermont	4	—	—	—
Nebraska	4	—	—	13
Idaho	3	—	—	13
South Dakota	1	—	—	—
New Hampshire	1	—	—	—
Wisconsin	N.A.	N.A.	N.A.	N.A.
Rhode Island	—	—	N.A.	N.A.
North Dakota	—	N.A.	N.A.	N.A.
Minnesota	N.A.	N.A.	N.A.	N.A.
Michigan	—	N.A.	N.A.	N.A.
Maine	N.A.	N.A.	N.A.	N.A.
Hawaii	N.A.	N.A.	N.A.	N.A.
Alaska	N.A.	N.A.	N.A.	N.A.
FEDERAL SYSTEM	33	—	—	—
TOTAL U.S.	**3,952**	**93**	**25**	**1,984**

Notes: As of Dec. 31. N.A. indicates that no death penalty statute was in force during the period in question. **Source:** BJS Bulletin, *Capital Punishment 1987* (1988).

Race and Capital Punishment Apart from the broad question of whether it is right for the state to take the life of an individual, the major issues of concern to those opposed to capital punishment are whether it is a deterrent to crime, whether it is in violation of the Eighth Amendment prohibiting "cruel and unusual punishment," and whether it is used fairly with respect to race.

Historically, blacks have been more likely to be executed than whites in proportion both to the general population and to the prison population. Blacks represent 53% of prisoners executed between 1930 and 1987, as against 46% whites, and 1 percent classified as other. It is worth noting, however, that of the 33 women executed in the same period, 21 (64%) were white and 12 (36%) black. In the decade 1977-87, 61% of those executed were white, and 39% black.

PRISONERS EXECUTED, TOTAL AND BY RACE, 1977-87

	Total	White	Black
1977	1	1	—
1978	—	—	—
1979	2	2	—
1980	—	—	—
1981	1	1	—
1982	2	1	1
1983	5	4	1
1984	21	13	8
1985	18	11	7
1986	18	11	7
1987	25	13	12
1977–87	**93**	**57**	**36**

Sources: BJS, *Sourcebook of Criminal Justice Statistics 1987* (1988); BJS Bulletin, *Capital Punishment 1987* (1988).

PRISONERS EXECUTED, BY RACE, 1930-87

	1930–87 Number	%	1930–67 Number	%	1967–87[1] Number	%
White	1,808	45.7%	1,751	45.4%	57	61.3%
Black	2,102	53.2	2,066	53.5	36	38.7
Other	42	1.1	42	1.1	0	0.0
TOTAL[2]	3,952	100.0%	3,859	100.0%	93	100.0%

1. No executions were carried out between 1968 and 1976.
2. Total includes 42 prisoners classified as "Other" 1930-67.
Sources: BJS, *Sourcebook of Criminal Justice Statistics 1987* (1988); BJS Bulletin, *Capital Punishment 1987* (1988).

EDUCATION

The American people's unwavering commitment to public education dates back more than 150 years. Fueled by a demand for literacy from two different creeds, one described in the Bible, the other in the Declaration of Independence, the American system of education grew to be an essential element in Americans' faith that their nation was uniquely the land of opportunity.

Today that belief has evolved into what is called equality of opportunity, and this vital idea has helped create a school system whose size and scope is unrivaled by any Western democracy.

Over 58 million students and almost 7 million teachers, administrators, and support staff are directly involved in education. The cost of this undertaking is, of course, staggering: over $300 billion annually—about $5,000 per student—or 6.8 percent of the gross national product, virtually all of it for public education. And while some may complain bitterly about the quality of the results, or about overt waste, mismanagement, and even fraud, no one any longer questions the essential role of education in American life today.

Expenditures in Public Elementary and Secondary Schools

Between 1978 and 1982, expenditures per student remained stable after adjustment for inflation. Prior to 1978 and after 1982, they increased faster than inflation. Annual expenditures per student in public elementary and secondary schools rose to a record high of $4,810 in 1988-89.

Total expenditures on education now account for almost 7 percent of the U.S. gross national product (GNP). After rising rapidly from 1959 to 1969, the proportion of GNP spent on education declined as enrollment in elementary and secondary schools declined.

NUMBER OF CATHOLIC SCHOOLS, PUPILS, AND TEACHERS, 1960-87

	1960	1970	1980	1987
ELEMENTARY				
Number	10,501	9,362	8,043	7,601
Pupils enrolled	4,373,000	3,359,000	2,269,000	1,942,000
Teachers, total	108,000	112,000	97,000	93,000
Religious	79,000	52,000	25,000	15,000
Lay	29,000	60,000	72,000	78,000
SECONDARY				
Number	2,392	1,981	1,516	1,391
Pupils enrolled	880,000	1,008,000	837,000	681,000
Teachers, total	44,000	54,000	49,000	47,000
Religious	33,000	28,000	14,000	10,000
Lay	11,000	26,000	35,000	37,000

Sources: National Catholic Education Assn.; U.S. Bureau of the Census, 1989.

PUBLIC EDUCATION EXPENDITURE: TOTAL, PER STUDENT, AND AS PERCENTAGE AGE OF GNP, 1939–88

School year ending	Expenditures (billions)	Expenditure per student	As percentage of GNP
1940	$ 3.3	$ 106	3.6%
1950	8.9	259	3.5
1960	23.9	472	4.8
1970	68.5	955	7.1
1980	165.6	2,491	6.6
1981	182.8	2,761	6.7
1982	197.8	2,997	6.5
1983	212.1	3,230	6.7
1984	228.6	3,500	6.7
1985	247.7	3,760	6.6
1986	269.5	4,070	6.7
1987	290.9[1]	4,300	6.9
1988	310.0[2]	4,570	6.8

1. Preliminary. figure. 2. Estimated. **Source:** National Center for Education Statistics, *American Education at a Glance* (1989).

NUMBER OF SCHOOLS IN THE U.S., 1987–88

ELEMENTARY AND SECONDARY	Public	Private[1]
Elementary	59,311	15,303
Secondary	20,758	2,438
Combined	2,179	4,949
Other schools[2]	1,000	2,926
Total	**83,248**	**25,616**

COLLEGES AND UNIVERSITIES	Total	Public	Private
4-year colleges	2,135	599	1,536
2-year colleges	1,452	992	460
Total	**3,587**	**1,591**	**1,996**

1. 1985–86. 2. Includes special, alternative schools and others not reported by grade span. **Source:** National Center for Education Statistics, *American Education at a Glance* (1989).

PRIVATE SCHOOLS

Data concerning private elementary and secondary schools are obviously not as readily available as for public institutions. According to the Department of Education:

- there are 25,616 private schools, 15,303 elementary, 2,438 secondary, and 4,949 combined, and 2,926 other types.
- 9,911, or almost 40%, are affiliated with the Roman Catholic church, 10,771 with all other religious groups, and 4,934 have no religious affiliation.
- Private schools employ 404,000 teachers (92,000 in nonreligious schools), who are paid average base salaries of $13,600 to $16,500.
- Overall, 76% of the students are female, but only 51.5% are in secondary schools; 39% of the schools enroll less than 5% minority students, 72% less than 24%.

Source: U.S. Dept. of Education, 1986.

REVENUES FOR PUBLIC ELEMENTARY AND SECONDARY SCHOOLS

In 1979 a historic shift occurred in the source of money to operate the American public school system. That was the year the state share of revenues rose above the local share for the first time. The federal share for elementary and secondary schools has always been relatively small.

School year ending	Total revenues (billions)	Source by percent		
		Federal	State	Local
1920	$ 1.0	0.3%	16.5%	83.2%
1930	2.1	0.4	16.9	82.7
1940	2.3	1.8	30.3	68.0
1950	5.4	2.9	39.8	57.3
1960	14.7	4.4	39.1	56.5
1970	40.3	8.0	39.9	52.1
1975	64.4	9.0	42.2	48.8
1979	88.0	9.8	45.6	44.6
1980	96.9	9.8	46.8	43.4
1981	105.9	9.2	47.4	43.4
1982	110.2	7.4	47.6	45.0
1983	117.5	7.1	47.9	45.0
1984	126.1	6.8	47.8	45.4
1985	137.3	6.6	48.9	44.4
1986	149.1	6.7	49.4	43.9
1987	158.8	6.4	49.8	43.9

Source: National Center for Education Statistics, *American Education at a Glance* (1989).

SCHOOL ENROLLMENT, KINDERGARTEN THROUGH UNIVERSITY LEVEL

Public elementary and public secondary school enrollment declined between 1975 and 1984 as the number of young people decreased, but it began rising again in 1985. Higher-education enrollment has increased during the past two decades despite a drop, which began in 1981, in the traditional college-age population.

	Fall enrollment (students in millions)				
	1970	1975	1980	1985	1990[1]
ELEMENTARY (K–8)					
Public	32.6	30.5	27.7	27.0	29.4
Private	4.1	3.7[2]	4.0	4.2	4.2
SECONDARY (9–12)					
Public	13.3	14.3	13.3	12.5	11.4
Private	1.3	1.3[2]	1.3	1.4	1.2
HIGHER EDUCATION					
Public	6.4	8.8	9.5	9.5	10.2
Private	2.2	2.4	2.6	2.8	2.9
Total	**59.9**	**61.0**	**58.4**	**57.4**	**59.3**

1. Projected. 2. Estimated. **Source:** National Center for Education Statistics, *American Education at a Glance* (1989).

HOW THE STATES RANK IN PUBLIC EDUCATION, 1986–87

	Enrollment (rank)	Expenditures per pupil (rank)	Average teacher salary (rank)	High school graduation rate (rank)
U.S.	**39,881,460**	**$3,983**	**$26,551**	**71.5%**
Ala.	733,735 (20)	$2,610 (48)	$23,500 (31)	67.3 (39)
Alaska	110,418 (47)	8,842 (1)	43,970 (1)	68.3 (36)
Ariz.	614,565 (24)	2,784 (46)	25,972 (24)	63.0 (47)
Ark.	437,438 (32)	2,772 (42)	19,904 (49)	78.0 (15)
Calif.	4,377,989 (1)	3,887 (23)	31,219 (5)	66.7 (41)
Colo.	558,415 (27)	4,107 (18)	27,387 (18)	73.1 (28)
Conn.	471,916 (30)	5,552 (5)	28,902 (7)	89.8 (2)
D.C.	86,405 (51)	5,349 (6)	33,797 (2)	56.8 (51)
Del.	94,410 (49)	4,776 (8)	27,467 (16)	70.7 (33)
Fla.	1,607,320 (8)	4,056 (20)	23,785 (29)	62.0 (50)
Ga.	1,096,372 (10)	3,167 (40)	24,200 (27)	62.7 (48)
Hawaii	164,336 (40)	4,372 (15)	26,315 (20)	70.8 (32)
Idaho	211,360 (38)	2,555 (49)	21,480 (44)	79.0 (13)
Ill.	1,825,185 (4)	3,980 (21)	28,238 (12)	75.8 (21)
Ind.	964,761 (13)	3,310 (37)	26,083 (23)	71.4 (30)
Iowa	481,346 (29)	3,270 (27)	22,603 (39)	87.5 (5)
Kans.	461,091 (33)	4,150 (17)	23,427 (33)	81.5 (8)
Ky.	642,778 (23)	3,107 (41)	22,612 (38)	68.6 (35)
La.	793,400 (17)	3,008 (44)	20,054 (48)	62.7 (48)
Maine	207,349 (39)	3,650 (29)	21,257 (47)	76.5 (20)
Mass.	841,250 (14)	4,856 (7)	28,410 (10)	76.7 (18)
Md.	675,747 (22)	4,660 (10)	28,893 (8)	76.6 (19)
Mich.	1,671,500 (7)	3,967 (22)	31,500 (4)	67.8 (37)
Minn.	693,134 (21)	4,329 (16)	28,340 (11)	91.4 (1)
Miss.	498,649 (26)	2,534 (50)	19,447 (50)	63.3 (46)
Mo.	800,606 (16)	3,345 (36)	23,468 (32)	75.6 (22)
Mont.	153,121 (43)	4,070 (19)	23,206 (34)	87.2 (6)
Nebr.	366,604 (37)	3,437 (35)	22,063 (40)	88.1 (4)
Nev.	161,200 (42)	3,548 (32)	26,960 (19)	65.2 (42)
N.H.	163,717 (41)	3,682 (28)	22,011 (42)	73.3 (27)
N.J.	1,107,467 (9)	6,177 (4)	28,718 (9)	77.6 (16)
N.Mex.	268,765 (36)	3,537 (33)	23,977 (28)	72.3 (29)
N.C.	1,091,552 (11)	3,473 (34)	23,775 (30)	70.0 (34)
N.Dak.	118,094 (46)	3,174 (39)	21,284 (46)	89.7 (3)
N.Y.	2,588,936 (3)	6,224 (3)	32,000 (3)	64.2 (45)
Ohio	1,793,500 (5)	3,764 (26)	26,288 (22)	80.4 (11)
Okla.	603,132 (26)	3,082 (43)	22,060 (41)	71.6 (31)
Oreg.	449,300 (31)	4,383 (14)	26,690 (21)	74.1 (25)
Pa.	1,674,161 (6)	4,691 (9)	27,422 (17)	78.5 (14)
R.I.	134,147 (44)	4,574 (12)	31,079 (6)	67.3 (39)
S.C.	610,700 (25)	3,096 (42)	23,190 (35)	64.5 (43)
S.Dak.	124,607 (45)	3,190 (38)	18,781 (51)	81.5 (8)
Tenn.	823,283 (15)	2,842 (45)	22,627 (37)	67.4 (38)
Tex.	3,209,515 (2)	3,551 (31)	24,588 (26)	64.3 (44)
Utah	415,994 (34)	2,455 (51)	23,035 (36)	80.3 (12)
Va.	974,754 (12)	3,809 (24)	25,473 (25)	73.9 (26)
Vt.	90,200 (50)	4,459 (13)	21,835 (43)	77.6 (16)
Wash.	761,771 (19)	3,808 (25)	27,527 (15)	75.2 (23)
Wisc.	767,819 (18)	4,607 (11)	27,976 (14)	86.3 (7)
W.Va.	351,691 (35)	3,619 (30)	21,446 (45)	75.5 (24)
Wyo.	100,955 (48)	6,253 (2)	28,103 (13)	81.2 (10)

1. Enrollment figures are as of fall 1986, graduation as of June 1986; expenditures and average salary are for 1986–87 school year. **Sources:** National Education Association, *Rankings of the States, 1987*; U.S. Dept. of Education, Office of Planning, Budget, and Evaluation, 1988.

EDUCATIONAL ATTAINMENT OF THE POPULATION, AGES 25 AND OVER, 1987

	Number of persons (in thousands)	4 years of high school or more	1 or more years of college	4 or more years of college
All persons	**149,144**	**75.6%**	**37.0%**	**19.9%**
SEX				
Male	70,677	76.0	40.6	23.6
Female	78,467	75.3	33.6	16.5
RACE				
White	129,170	77.0	37.8	20.5
Black	15,580	63.4	26.4	10.7
Other[1]	4,394	78.4	50.9	33.4
Hispanic origin	9,449	50.9	21.9	8.6
REGION				
Northeast	32,030	76.5	36.8	22.2
Midwest	36,332	77.4	33.7	17.6
South	50,848	70.8	34.1	18.3
West	29,943	80.6	45.9	22.8
RESIDENCE				
Metropolitan area	115,614	77.6	40.0	22.1
Nonmetropolitan area	33,529	68.7	26.5	12.6
AGE GROUPS				
25 to 34	42,635	86.5	45.4	23.9
35 to 44	33,632	85.9	46.8	26.5
45 to 54	23,018	77.6	35.6	19.5
55 to 64	21,882	67.8	28.0	14.9
65 to 74	17,232	56.9	21.9	10.6
75 or older	10,743	42.0	18.0	8.9

1. Includes Orientals and Native Americans.   **Source:** U.S. Bureau of the Census, *Educational Attainment in the U.S., March 1987 and 1986* (1988).

EDUCATIONAL ATTAINMENT BY PERCENTAGE OF POPULATION 25 YEARS AND OLDER AND BY SEX, 1940–87

Across all categories the percentage of the nation completing high school and college has risen steadily.

	COMPLETED 4 YEARS OF HIGH SCHOOL OR MORE			COMPLETED 4 YEARS OF COLLEGE OR MORE		
	Both sexes	Male	Female	Both sexes	Male	Female
1940	24.5%	22.7%	26.3%	4.6%	5.5%	3.8%
1950	34.3	32.6	36.0	6.2	7.3	5.2
1959	43.7	42.2	45.2	8.1	10.3	6.0
1970	55.2	55.0	55.4	11.0	14.1	8.2
1980	68.6	69.1	68.1	17.0	20.8	13.5
1987	75.6	76.0	75.3	19.9	23.6	16.5

Source: U.S. Bureau of the Census, *Educational Attainment in the U.S.: March 1987 and 1986* (1988).

NUMBER OF DEGREES CONFERRED BY TYPE IN U.S., 1950–90

Year	All degrees[1]	Bachelor's	First professional[2]	Master's[3]	Doctorates
1949–50	498,373	433,734[4]		58,219	6,420
1959–60	479,215	394,889[4]		74,497	9,829
1965–66	714,624	524,117	31,496	140,772	18,239
1970–71	1,147,985	846,110	38,276	231,486	32,113
1975–76	1,344,581	934,443	63,061	313,001	34,076
1980–81	1,335,793	935,140	71,956	295,739	32,958
1985–86	1,383,953	987,823	73,910	288,567	33,653
1989–90[5]	1,382,000	984,000	74,300	290,000	33,700

1. Does not include associate of arts (A.A.) or associate of science (A.S.) degrees; more than 400,000 of these have been given each year since 1980.   2. Degrees are medical doctor, law, dentistry, optometry, podiatry, pharmacy, theology, chiropractic, and veterinary medicine.   3. Until 1965–66 some master's degrees (e.g., library science and social work) were listed in first-professional category.   4. Prior to 1961 bachelor's and first-professional degrees were listed together.   5. Figures for this year are estimates.   **Source:** U.S. Dept. of Education.

EDUCATIONAL ATTAINMENT TODAY

The Census Bureau's latest report shows that in 1987
- 76% of U.S. adults over 25 had completed at least four years of high school.
- 20% had completed four or more years of college.
- 24% of adult men and 17% of adult women had completed four or more years of college.
- Among men and women over 65, slightly less than 10% had four or more years of college; of those between 45 and 64, slightly more than 17% did; and of those 25–44, just over 25%.
- Among black Americans the proportions were significantly smaller than for whites: of those age 25 or over, 63% had completed high school, and 11% had four or more years of college (as compared with 77% and 21%, respectively, for whites).
- Among Hispanics the proportions were smaller still: of those over 25, 51% had completed high school, and 9% had four or more years of college.

Source: U.S. Bureau of the Census, 1989

Higher Education: Growth and Change, 1950–90

The figures below give a startling picture of just how the coming of age of the Baby Boom generation transformed U.S. higher education. In just one decade (the 1960s), the number of undergraduate degrees conferred more than doubled, while the number of doctorates actually tripled. These extraordinary changes were matched in kind by dramatic shifts in what students wanted to study: during the late 1960s, for example, the number of degrees in sociology and psychology jumped by more than 15,000 each in just a few years (1966–70), while interest in business soared during the 1980s.

"Human history becomes more and more a race between education and catastrophe."

—H.G. Wells

MOST POPULAR MAJORS AMONG INCOMING FRESHMEN, FALL 1988

Major	Percent
1. Business administration	7.3%
2. Accounting	6.1
3. Elementary education	4.9
4. Management	4.9
5. Psychology	4.1
6. Political science	3.2
7. Communications	2.9
8. Electrical engineering	2.9
9. Marketing	2.9
10. Premedicine, predental, preveterinary	2.8
11. Nursing	2.5
12. Arts	2.1
13. Finance	2.0
14. Therapy	2.0
15. General biology	1.8
16. Mechanical engineering	1.8
17. Aeronautical engineering	1.7
18. Computer science	1.7
19. Secondary education	1.7
20. Law enforcement	1.6

Source: Higher Education Research Institute, University of California, Los Angeles, *The American Freshman: National Norms for Fall, 1988.*

College Entrance Examination Scores

SATs (Scholastic Aptitude Tests) measure verbal and mathematical reasoning abilities. These tests are developed and administered by the Educational Testing Service, Princeton, N.J., for the College Board, headquartered in New York City. The College Board is a non-profit organization that provides tests and many other educational services for students, schools, and colleges.

ACTs are administered by the American College Testing Program, a nonprofit educational organization, which has its national headquarters in Iowa City, Iowa. The ACT composite score is the average of four tests that measure academic abilities in English, mathematics, social studies, and natural sciences.

Little change has occurred over the last 10 years in national average scores for all groups on college entrance examinations given by the College Board (SAT) and the American College Testing Program (ACT). Men continue to score higher than women. And, despite steady improvement by minority test-takers, white students still score higher than other racial/ethnic groups by a substantial margin.

AVERAGE SAT SCORES BY GROUPS

	Combined verbal and math			Total test-takers
	1978	1983	1988	Class of 1988
White	931	927	935	813,116
Mexican-American	772	792	810	22,722
Black	686	708	737	97,483
National average, all groups	897	893	904	1,134,364
Men	927	923	933	544,065
Women	869	865	877	590,299

AVERAGE ACT SCORES BY GROUPS

	Composite scores			Total test-takers
	1978	1983	1988	Class of 1988
White	19.6	19.2	19.6	640,027
Mexican-American	14.3	14.3	15.7	19,454
Black	12.5	12.3	13.6	68,781
National average, all groups	18.6	18.3	18.7	842,322
Men	19.3	19.1	19.6	385,475
Women	17.8	17.6	18.1	456,847

Sources: College Entrance Examination Board; The American College Testing Program.

PROFILES OF SAT SCORE, BY GENDER, 1988

In 1988 exactly 1,134,364 students took the SATs. The mean score of the combined math and verbal tests was 926. Because males consistently outscore females on these tests, some groups have raised the issue of gender bias, i.e., that the tests are inherently unfair to women students.

VERBAL

Male			Female	
Number	Percent	Score	Number	Percent
621	—	750–800	365	—
5,500	1%	700–749	3,986	1%
14,674	3	650–699	11,346	2
25,139	5	600–649	21,404	4
44,932	8	550–599	41,513	7
68,284	13	500–549	67,544	11
85,904	16	450–499	89,576	15
97,269	18	400–449	108,582	18
83,187	15	350–399	97,328	16
61,662	11	300–349	76,402	13
35,900	7	250–299	45,677	8
20,993	4	200–249	26,576	5
Total: 544,065			**Total: 590,299**	
Mean score: 435			**Mean score: 422**	

MATH

Male			Female	
Number	Percent	Score	Number	Percent
8,547	2%	750–800	1,761	—
23,861	4	700–749	8,691	1%
40,669	7	650–699	21,537	4
55,505	10	600–649	39,117	7
72,227	13	550–599	63,342	11
75,104	14	500–549	77,734	13
74,485	14	450–499	88,878	15
71,156	13	400–449	96,078	16
56,729	10	350–399	84,452	14
40,574	7	300–349	65,012	11
21,454	4	250–299	37,024	6
3,754	1	200–249	6,673	1
Total: 544,065			**Total: 590,299**	
Mean score: 498			**Mean score: 455**	

Note: Dash (—) indicates less than 0.5%.   **Source:** College Board.

AVERAGE COST OF 4-YEAR COLLEGES, 1978–89 (tuition and fees, per year)

	Public	Private
1977–78	$ 621	$2,476
1978–79	651	2,647
1979–80	680	2,923
1980–81	706	3,279
1981–82	819	3,709
1982–83	979	4,021
1983–84	1,105	4,627
1984–85	1,126	5,016
1985–86	1,242	5,418
1986–87	1,337	5,793
1987–88	1,359	7,110
1988–89	1,566	7,693

Source: College Board.

Foreign Students in U.S. Colleges and Universities

A total of 356,187 foreign students attended U.S. colleges and universities in the 1987–88 school year. This was an increase of 6,578 over the preceding year—the largest increase since 1982–83. For the first time, Asian students constituted more than 50 percent of the total foreign student enrollments in the United States. Eight of the 10 leading homelands are now in South and East Asia. Taiwan heads the list with 26,660 students. China, the second-leading country of origin, has had the fastest-growing foreign student population in the nation for five consecutive years. The number of Chinese students grew a remarkable 25.7 percent in 1987–88 to bring their total to 25,170 in that school year.

LEADING COUNTRIES OF ORIGIN OF FOREIGN STUDENTS

Country	1986–87	1987–88	Percent change
1. Taiwan	25,660	26,660	3.9%
2. China	20,030	25,170	25.7
3. India	18,350	21,010	14.5
4. South Korea	19,940	20,520	2.9
5. Malaysia	21,640	19,480	–10.0
6. Japan	15,070	18,050	19.8
7. Canada	15,700	15,690	–0.1
8. Hong Kong	11,010	10,550	–3.3
9. Iran	12,230	10,420	–14.8
10. Indonesia	9,240	9,010	–2.5
11. Nigeria	11,700	8,340	–28.7
12. United Kingdom	6,240	6,600	5.8
13. Pakistan	5,950	6,570	10.4
14. Thailand	6,480	6,430	–0.8
15. Mexico	5,330	6,170	15.8
16. Lebanon	6,450	5,820	–9.8
17. West Germany	5,090	5,730	12.6
18. Saudi Arabia	5,840	5,490	–6.0
19. Jordan	5,650	5,140	–9.0
20. Singapore	4,530	4,870	7.5

INSTITUTIONS WITH THE MOST FOREIGN STUDENTS

Institution	1987–88
1. Miami-Dade Community College	5,148
2. University of Southern California	3,767
3. University of Texas, Austin	3,135
4. University of Wisconsin, Madison	2,825
5. University of California, Los Angeles	2,765
6. Ohio State University, Columbus	2,756
7. Boston University	2,641
8. University of Arizona	2,599
9. University of Minnesota, Twin Cities	2,514
10. Columbia University[1]	2,474

1. Figures don't include include Barnard and Teachers colleges.
Source: Institute of International Education, *Open Doors: 1987/88.*

RELIGION IN AMERICA

As of 1987, the most recent year for which figures are available, 147.5 million Americans claimed affiliation with a religious group. This represents about 61 percent of the population. The following table shows that 94 percent of the religiously affiliated were members of Christian or quasi-Christian denominations. Non-Christian religions—primarily Judaism and Islam—account for the other 6 percent.

Christians in the United States are members of a bewildering variety of denominations, each independent of the next. The *Yearbook of American and Canadian Churches* lists about 220 Christian denominations, and other sources list more than 1,000. For simplicity's sake the following table groups the denominations into 20 major families. Denominations listed in the same family nearly always share common historical roots and some principal doctrines. They may disagree violently about other doctrines and issues, however. Following the table are brief descriptions of each of the Christian denominational families and of major non-Christian faiths. See also information in "World Religion."

Roman Catholic Church

The Roman Catholic church is at once the largest "family" and the largest single Christian denomination in the United States. It claims nearly 36 percent of all religiously affiliated people—22 percent of the total population. Worldwide, there are nearly 900 million Roman Catholics (see "World Religion").

Many U.S. Catholics—descendants of immigrants from Ireland, Germany, Poland, Italy, and France—are concentrated in the Northeast and the industrial Midwest. Hispanic-Americans in Florida and the Southwest are also predominantly Catholic.

The church is hierarchically organized. Bishops, who administer church affairs in a given region, are appointed by higher authority. The world leader of the Roman church is the pope, who directs the church from Vatican City in Rome.

Priests are male and in most parts of the church must be and remain unmarried. Orders of nuns and monks provide many educational and charitable services. Many local churches operate parochial elementary schools. Regional bodies and religious orders operate high schools and help administer many seminaries and church-related colleges. In recent years the number of applicants for the priesthood and for religious orders has sharply decreased, even as membership in the church has continued to increase.

Catholic leaders have taken strong stands on many contemporary issues. The National Conference of Catholic Bishops has taken relatively liberal positions on efforts to bring about world peace and economic justice. In areas of personal conduct, the church is more conservative. It leads the campaign to outlaw abortion and opposes mechanical means of birth control.

Baptist Churches

The Baptist family of churches is the largest Protestant family in the United States. Baptists trace their theological roots back to radical reformers in Europe in the 1500s, but the number of Baptists in the world was tiny until the 1800s, when Baptist faith and practice became predominant in the American South (both for whites and for blacks). Baptists are still most heavily represented in the southern and border states.

Local Baptist congregations have great independence, determining many of their own policies. At the same time, these churches share many practices. They agree that the rite of baptism should be administered only to those who have reached an age of independent judgment. Consequently, children are baptized no earlier than the age of 6 or 7, often by total immersion in the baptismal water. A Baptist child is not counted as a member until after baptism, which means that small children are not included in the membership totals reported above.

Most Baptists take a strong stand on the authority of the Bible, and many (though not all) believe that it should be interpreted literally. Baptists have traditionally been strong supporters of separation of church and state. Many Baptist denominations have mounted energetic missionary campaigns to bring the Christian message to people around the world.

The Southern Baptist Convention, a predominantly white church, is the largest Protestant denomination in the United States. The two National Baptist Conventions and the Progressive National Baptist Convention are predominantly black churches. Together they account for the religious affiliation of more blacks than any other family of churches.

Methodist Churches

Methodist churches trace their origins to John Wesley (1703–91), a minister in the Church of England who sought to bring a new sense of warmth and commitment to individuals' religious life. He urged his followers to set aside regular times to study the Bible and pray together. Wesley's opponents laughingly called his followers Methodists because of their discipline and seriousness. Wesley himself remained in the Church of England his whole life, but his followers began to develop independent organizations, both in England and the United States.

On the American frontier, Methodist "circuit riders" traveled from settlement to settlement, preaching and marrying, baptizing and burying members of pioneer families. Methodism grew with astonishing swiftness. By 1820 it was the largest religious family in the United States, and it remained the largest Protestant family until the 1920s.

The United Methodist Church accounts for more than two-thirds of the Methodist family's total membership. This denomination is made up of not only traditional Methodists but also several churches of German origin whose beliefs and spirit accorded well with methodism. The two "African" churches and the Christian Methodist Church are predominantly black churches, and they account for nearly all of the remaining third of the Methodist group.

Lutheran Churches

Lutherans trace their churches back to the German reformer Martin Luther (1483–1546). Luther sought to reform the doctrine and practice of the Roman Christian Church in Europe. He complained about corruption among the clergy and advocated worship in the language of the people rather than in Latin. He also came to favor a married, rather than a celibate, clergy. The Church of Rome considered Luther disloyal and eventually drove him out. He then helped establish independent churches in northern Germany.

Immigrants from Germany and Scandinavia brought the Lutheran faith to North America, concentrating first in Pennsylvania. Later immigrants settled in the upper Midwest. By 1900 scores of small Lutheran Church bodies were divided from one another by language, theology, and degree of assimilation into American society. The Evangelical Lutheran Church in America represents a uniting of many of those earlier churches. The Lutheran Church—Missouri Synod, a national church despite its name, is more conservative theologically.

Pentecostal Churches

The Pentecostal churches share a belief that God grants believers special spiritual gifts—especially the experience called "speaking in tongues," a common feature of Pentecostal services.

Pentecostal churches trace their origin to the day of Pentecost, described in the biblical book of Acts, when early Christians received ecstatic or mystical powers. Modern Pentecostalism began in the early 1900s, when members of some Holiness churches received the gift of tongues (see "Holiness Churches" following).

Pentecostal congregations tend to be small. They may meet in storefronts or in rented quarters on upper floors. Yet the Pentecostal faith, with its immediacy and emotional power, is perhaps the fastest-growing in the nation, attracting thousands of new adherents each year. In addition Pentecostal beliefs have had an impact on Roman Catholic, Lutheran, Episcopal, and other denominations. These denominations report a growth among adherents of "charismatic renewal," a movement based on spiritual gifts.

The two Churches of God in Christ and the United Pentecostal Church are predominantly black denominations. The Assemblies of God is the largest predominantly white denomination. Many Pentecostal organizations are regional or purely local. Because of this loose organization, there are likely to be thousands of Pentecostal believers not counted here because their local congregations are not affiliated with a regional or national group.

RELIGIOUS AFFILIATIONS IN THE UNITED STATES

FAMILY/Denomination	Local congregations	Total clergy	Total membership	% of total affiliated
ALL RELIGIOUSLY AFFILIATED	346,092	532,697	147,499,662	100.0%
CHRISTIAN CHURCHES	342,576	526,082	138,585,662	94.0%
ROMAN CATHOLIC CHURCH	23,561	53,382	52,893,217	35.9%
BAPTIST CHURCHES	97,004	146,818	28,224,395	19.1%
Southern Baptist Convention	37,072	63,200	14,613,618	
National Baptist Convention, USA, Inc.	26,000	27,500	5,500,000	
National Baptist Convention of America	11,398	28,574	2,668,799	
American Baptist Churches in the USA	5,864	7,678	1,576,483	
Baptist Bible Fellowship International	3,449	4,500	1,405,900	
Progressive Natl. Baptist Convention, Inc.	655	863	521,692	
General Assoc. of Regular Baptist Churches	1,571	2,045	300,839	
American Baptist Association	1,705	1,760	250,000	
National Primitive Baptist Convention, Inc.	606	636	250,000	
Baptist Missionary Association of America	1,359	2,450	228,125	
Conservative Baptist Assoc. of America	1,140	—	225,000	
Free Will Baptists, Natational Assoc. of	2,483	2,895	205,546	
Baptist General Conference	762	1,700	131,480	
Liberty Baptist Fellowship	267	374	130,000	
Others (10 denominations)	2,673	2,643	216,913	
METHODIST CHURCHES	52,704	53,554	13,343,996	9.0%
United Methodist Church	37,876	37,808	9,192,172	
African Methodist Episcopal Church	6,200	6,550	2,210,000	
African Methodist Episcopal Zion Church	6,057	6,396	1,195,173	
Christian Methodist Episcopal Church	2,340	2,650	718,922	
Others (4 denominations)	231	150	27,729	
LUTHERAN CHURCHES	18,739	27,153	8,455,747	5.7%
Evangelical Lutheran Church in America	11,041	16,929	5,318,844	
Lutheran Church—Missouri Synod	5,897	8,044	2,630,588	
Wisconsin Evangelical Lutheran Synod	1,180	1,497	416,493	
Others (9 denominations)	621	683	89,822	
PENTECOSTAL CHURCHES	41,501	80,431	7,901,625	5.4%
Church of God in Christ	9,982	10,425	3,709,661	
Assemblies of God	10,886	26,837	2,135,104	
Church of God (Cleveland, Tenn.)	5,346	9,638	505,775	
United Pentecostal Church International	3,410	6,984	500,000	
Church of God in Christ, International	300	1,600	200,000	
International Church of the Foursquare Gospel	1,250	3,482	186,213	
Pentecostal Holiness Church, International	1,461	3,422	113,000	
Others (24 denominations)	8,866	18,043	551,872	
REFORMED CHURCHES	22,513	36,527	5,733,828	3.9%
Presbyterian Church (USA)	11,531	19,514	3,007,322	
United Church of Christ	6,406	10,071	1,676,105	
Reformed Church in America	928	1,636	340,359	
Christian Reformed Church in North America	650	1,077	219,988	
Presbyterian Church in America	913	1,702	188,083	
Others (12 denominations)	2,085	2,527	301,971	
ORTHODOX CHURCHES	1,746	2,236	4,459,177	3.0%
Greek Orthodox Archdiocese of North and South America	535	655	1,950,000	
Orthodox Church in America	440	531	1,000,000	
Armenian Church of Amer., Diocese of the	66	61	450,000	
Antiochan Orthodox Christian Archdiocese of North America	120	180	280,000	
Coptic Orthodox Church	28	28	115,000	
American Carpatho-Russian Orthodox Greek Catholic Church	70	66	100,000	
Others (14 denominations)	487	715	564,177	
LATTER-DAY SAINTS CHURCHES	9,575	45,614	4,057,131	2.8%
Church of Jesus Christ of Latter-day Saints	8,396	28,598	3,860,000	
Reorganized Church of Jesus Christ of Latter-Day Saints	1,094	16,585	192,077	
Others (2 denominations)	85	431	5,054	
CHRISTIAN CHURCHES AND CHURCHES OF CHRIST	23,151	12,282	3,793,915	2.6%
Churches of Christ	13,364	—	1,623,754	
Christian Church (Disciples of Christ)	4,221	6,806	1,106,692	
Christian Churches and Churches of Christ	5,566	5,476	1,063,469	
EPISCOPAL CHURCHES	7,175	14,235	2,516,240	1.7%
Episcopal Church	7,054	14,111	2,504,507	
Others (2 denominations)	121	124	11,733	
HOLINESS CHURCHES	14,843	22,395	1,398,557	0.9%
Church of the Nazarene	5,018	8,667	530,912	
Christian and Missionary Alliance	1,691	2,154	238,734	
Church of God (Anderson, Ind.)	2,296	3,313	188,662	
Wesleyan Church	1,704	2,596	109,196	
Christian Congregation, Inc.	1,450	1,455	105,478	
Others (13 denominations)	2,684	4,210	225,575	
JEHOVAH'S WITNESSES	8,336	—	752,404	0.5%
CHURCH OF CHRIST, SCIENTIST	—	—	700,000[1]	0.5%
ADVENTIST CHURCHES	4,641	6,236	698,521	0.5%
Seventh-Day Adventists	4,055	5,481	666,199	
Others (4 denominations)	586	755	32,322	
SALVATION ARMY	1,092	5,195	432,893	0.3%
ROMAN RITE CHURCHES	308	316	347,092	0.2%
Polish National Catholic Church of Amer.	162	141	282,411	
North American Old Roman Catholic Church	133	150	62,611	
Others (2 denominations)	13	25	2,070	
MENNONITE CHURCHES	2,365	3,168	239,681	0.2%
Mennonite Church	989	2,399	91,167	
Old Order Amish Church	696	—	62,640	
Others (9 denominations)	680	769	85,874	
BRETHREN CHURCHES	1,545	2,718	216,217	0.1%
Church of the Brethren	1,059	1,963	155,967	
Others (3 denominations)	486	755	60,250	
UNITARIAN UNIVERSALIST ASSOCIATION	956	1,069	173,167	0.1%
FRIENDS (QUAKER) CHURCHES (5 denominations)	1,395	1,095	120,320	0.1%
MISCELLANEOUS CHURCHES	9,426	11,658	1,127,539	0.8%
Community Churches, International Confederation of	350	350	200,000	
Independent Fundamental Churches of America	1,019	1,366	120,446	
Congregational Christian Churches, National Association of	464	826	108,115	
Christian Brethren (also known as The Plymouth Brethren)	1,150	500	98,000	
Evangelical Free Church of America	880	1,484	95,722	
Evangelical Covenant Church	570	930	86,079	
Others (37 denominations)	4,993	6,202	419,177	
OTHER CHRISTIANS (UNREPORTED)	—	—	1,000,000[1]	0.7%
OTHER RELIGIONS	3,516	6,615	8,914,000	6.0%
JEWS	3,416	6,500	5,814,000	3.9%
MUSLIMS	—	—	2,500,000[1]	1.7%
BUDDHIST CHURCHES OF AMERICA	100	115	100,000	0.1%
OTHER NON-CHRISTIANS (UNREPORTED)	—	—	500,000[1]	0.3%

1. Estimates—denominations/organizations do not report membership. **Sources:** Christianity—*Yearbook of American and Canadian Churches 1988.* An estimated 1 million people are members of very small denominations or independent congregations not accounted for in the *YACC.* Judaism—*Yearbook of American and Canadian Churches 1988.* Number represents the total of all who are considered members of the Jewish cultural community. Islam—based on *The World Christian Encyclopedia,* 1985 estimate for North America. Number represents the total of all who are considered members of the Islamic cultural community. Other—*Universal Almanac* estimate. Number includes 100,000 in the Buddhist Church of America and members of other non-Christian religious organizations.

Reformed Churches

The Reformed churches are those that trace their descent to the French-Swiss reformer John Calvin (1509–64). These churches were especially significant in the early settlement of the present-day United States. The Pilgrims and Puritans who settled in New England established the Congregational Church, which is a main component of today's United Church of Christ. New York was settled by the Dutch, who established the present-day Reformed Church in America. Later, immigrants of Scottish and Scotch-Irish descent established a strong Presbyterian Church. Presbyterians differed from Congregationalists in matters of church governance but shared many points of theology and practice.

Reformed church buildings are generally simple and sparsely adorned. Similarly, worship in these churches is austere and simple. Reformed churches generally value a well-educated clergy. In the past they helped found Harvard, Yale, and Princeton. Direct ties to these universities have ended, but Reformed organizations still support many colleges.

The Presbyterian Church (USA) is the result of several mergers between smaller Presbyterian churches that had been separated by regional and doctrinal differences. The United Church of Christ includes, in addition to Congregational churches, descendants of German Reformed churches and of the Evangelical and Reformed Church (also of German descent). The Reformed Church in America and the Christian Reformed Church are both of Dutch descent.

Orthodox Churches

The first great schism in the Christian church occurred in A.D. 1054 between the Western church, centered at Rome, and the Eastern church, centered at Constantinople (present-day Istanbul). In 1054 Eastern Christianity was predominant in Greece and the Middle East, and missionaries had already introduced the faith in Russia. The Russian church celebrated its 1,000th anniversary in 1988. Immigrants from these countries brought Orthodox churches to the United States.

The two largest Orthodox churches in the United States today are Greek and Russian, respectively. The next largest represent Armenians (whose homeland straddles the border between Iran and the Soviet Union) and Syrians. Together these four churches have more than 80 percent of the Orthodox membership.

Orthodox churches are organized hierarchically. Archbishops and bishops possess special spiritual authority and administer church affairs. Religious observances tend to be solemn and elaborate. Ancient liturgies in the ancient languages have been carefully preserved. Orthodox clergy are male, and in most churches, they are allowed to marry. Because of differences in calculating feast days, Easter and other movable feasts may occur on different dates in the Orthodox church than in the Western churches.

In the United States, many Orthodox churches have served as cultural centers for immigrants seeking to preserve their own ethnic heritage. At the same time, however, many denominations are active members of ecumenical groups such as the National Council of Churches.

Latter-day Saints (Mormons)

The churches of the Latter-day Saints, known popularly as Mormon churches, were founded by a 19th-century American prophet named Joseph Smith (1805–44). Smith, who grew up in western New York State, reported direct revelations from God. His religious vision included both traditional Christian elements and new accounts of God's visitations to pre-Columbian America.

Smith assembled a community of believers that settled first in western New York and later in Ohio, Missouri, and Illinois. Wherever it went, it aroused the antagonism of neighboring non-Mormons. Persecution came to a climax with the murder of Smith himself in 1844.

The next great leader of the church was Brigham Young (1801–77), who led the majority of Mormons westward to settle in the then-uninhabited basin by the Great Salt Lake. There the church grew and prospered. Even today the majority of religiously affiliated people in Utah belong to the Church of the Latter-day Saints. There are also many adherents in surrounding states, and the Mormons pursue a worldwide campaign of proselytizing.

The Reorganized Church is the largest of the groups that did not make the trek to the Great Salt Lake. Their headquarters are in Independence, Missouri, which Smith had designated as the site of a great future temple.

Christian Churches and Churches of Christ

This family of churches traces its origins to a great religious awakening in 1800 on the Pennsylvania and Kentucky frontiers. Discouraged by sectarian competition among Methodists, Presbyterians, and others, leaders of the revival did not seek to form a denomination but to reestablish a single nondenominational Christian church. In time they became a denomination themselves.

In the 1870s the Churches of Christ and the Christian Church (Disciples) split over questions of using musical instruments in worship and over the issue of centralizing some church functions. The Churches of Christ opposed both instrumental music and national organization. The Disciples allowed instrumental music and established a central missionary board to coordinate mission work. They are ecumenically minded and have a long history of cooperation and discussion with other denominations.

The third group, the Christian Churches and Churches of Christ, split from the Disciples in the 1920s and 1930s. They do allow instrumental music but are theologically more conservative than the Disciples.

Episcopal Family of Churches

The Episcopal churches are descendants of the Church of England, which was established as a separate church by King Henry VIII in 1534. Churches descending from the English church make up the worldwide Anglican Communion. The American church takes its name from the word *bishop*, which suggests its hierarchical organization.

In colonial times the Church of England was established in the southern colonies and had some influence in the middle colonies, but it was not welcome in New England, where Reformed churches were predominant. During the American Revolution, most Church of England members and clergy remained loyal to England. Thousands emigrated to Canada. Those who remained were under suspicion, and some were persecuted. The church almost ceased to function.

After the revolution, a small group of Anglicans loyal to the United States gradually revived the church. It never grew as rapidly as the Methodist and Baptist families, but it did gain considerable influence. Especially in eastern cities, many families of wealth and power were Episcopalian.

The Episcopal Church accommodates a wide spectrum of belief and practice. It is usually considered Protestant and shares much with other Protestant denominations, yet its worship services retain much of pre-Reformation Catholic tradition. One wing of the church retains a strong emphasis on the church's Catholic heritage.

Holiness Churches

The Holiness churches grew from a religious revival in the late 1800s, primarily in Methodist congregations. The originators of the movement objected to the excessive bureaucracy of established denominations and sought to refocus attention on the need for deep personal change. They placed great emphasis on the teachings of Methodism's founder, John Wesley, that those who are saved may aspire to the gift of complete sanctification, or holiness.

Around 1900, groups of especially intense Holiness worshipers began experiencing further "gifts of the Spirit." From these experiences grew the first Pentecostal churches with their emphasis on speaking in tongues. Many who began as adherents of Holiness churches became Pentecostalists. The Holiness churches rejected what they considered the extremism of Pentecostal worship.

Jehovah's Witnesses

Jehovah's Witnesses are a remarkably active and dynamic sect, visible to most from street-corner or door-to-door encounters. They were founded by Charles Taze Russell (1852–1916) in western Pennsylvania in the 1870s. The Witnesses preach a slightly unorthodox form of the Christian message and look intently for the end of the present world. They claim 3 million members worldwide, of whom about a quarter live in the United States.

Church of Christ, Scientist

Christian Scientists, as adherents are often known, follow the teachings of Mary Baker Eddy (1821–1910), who founded the church in 1879 in Boston and wrote *Science and Health with a Key to the Scriptures*, which remains a major sourcebook for the church. Christian Science asserts that sickness and other adversities exist only in the mind and that disciplined spiritual thinking can correct them. Thus, Christian Scientists avoid most or all medical treatment. Christian Science practitioners help adherents deal with illness but do not serve as clergy. The church operates many reading rooms open to the public.

The Adventist Family of Churches

Adventist churches sprang up in the United States in the 1840s with a wave of concern about prophecies of the end of the world. Adventists anticipate and prepare for the world's end and the second coming of Jesus Christ. The largest Adventist group, the Seventh-Day Adventists, is one of the most dynamic religious groups in the world today, claiming a worldwide membership of 5 million and a growth rate of more than 7 percent annually. As their name suggests, they worship on Saturday rather than Sunday. They operate parochial schools, colleges, medical schools, and hospitals.

The Salvation Army

The Salvation Army is familiar to outsiders through its work among the homeless and the poor and its fund-raising on the streets, especially before Christmas. The church, which originated in England in 1865, is organized in quasi-military style, and many of its members devote their lives to its service.

Roman Rite Churches

The Roman Rite churches are those that have split from the Roman Catholic church in recent times but have maintained many of its rituals and doctrines. The Polish church was established in Scranton, Pennsylvania, in the 1890s by church leaders of Polish descent. The Old Catholic churches had their origin in Europe after 1870.

Mennonite Churches

Mennonites trace their roots to a small group of Christians after 1530 who sought a reformation even more radical than those advocated by Lutherans and Calvinists. They were called Mennonites after Menno Simons (1469–1561), one of their early leaders. Their most distinctive practice is adult baptism, offered only to those who have made a decision to follow Christ's teachings.

Because they would not swear oaths and would not bear arms in the service of their temporal leaders, Mennonites were severely persecuted. Small bands were scattered to many corners of the world. Some settled in Pennsylvania beginning in the late 1600s. In the 1870s other groups arrived from Russia. Today more than 40 percent of the world's Mennonites live in the United States. The next-largest group (estimated to be 150,000) lives in the Soviet Union. In recent times Mennonites have become well known for their world relief work.

The Amish are groups with Mennonite beliefs who seek to remain quite aloof from the surrounding culture. The Old Order Amish, centered in Pennsylvania, wear "plain" clothing and still drive horses and buggies rather than automobiles.

Churches of the Brethren

The Brethren, founded as a dissenting group in Germany in the early 1700s, immigrated to Pennsylvania in the 1720s to escape persecution. There they have remained. Brethren share many doctrinal points with their neighbors, the Mennonites. They practice adult baptism, refuse to swear oaths, and will not serve as combatants in war. The various Brethren denominations agree in basic theology but differ on less significant matters of interpretation.

Unitarian Universalist Association

Unitarianism was an outgrowth of New England Congregationalism in the late 1700s and early 1800s. Unitarians asserted God's unity and repudiated the doctrine of the Trinity. They also interpreted other Christian beliefs in a liberal, figurative manner. Universalism was a separate movement emphasizing the availability of God's care to all people, not only to a small chosen group. In 1961 Unitarian and Universalist organizations merged.

Religion	Members	Percent of affiliated
Christianity	138,585,662	94.0%
Judaism	5,814,000	3.9
Islam	2,500,000	1.7
Other	600,000	0.4
Total affiliated	147,499,662	100.0%

Friends (Quaker) Churches

Known popularly as Quakers, the Friends were established by the English religious mystic George Fox (1624–91), in the mid-1600s. They were presecuted in England for refusing to take oaths or to serve as combatants in war. Under the protection of William Penn (1644–1718), many settled in Pennsylvania. According to Fox, they were called Quakers because they were admonished to "tremble at the word of the Lord." In Pennsylvania the Quakers set themselves apart, dressing plainly and avoiding worldly amusements. In Philadelphia they became influential business people.

The most distinctive doctrine of the Friends is that of the Inner Light, the spark of God in each individual. Friends have avoided setting up formal church structures, and many groups have no clergy. Friends have organized remarkable world relief and peace organizations, by which they are perhaps best known to outsiders.

Other Christian Churches

Among the other denominations reported by the *Yearbook of American and Canadian Churches*, there is a wide variety of religious belief and practice. Many of the groups are radically congregational, making generalizations

risky. Other groups are heterodox offshoots from the Pentecostal family. In many cases they depend on a single strong leader. The smallest denominations listed may actually be a single local congregation that reports as a separate church body.

Among the miscellaneous groups are spiritualist and other "New Age" groups. Some of these mix spiritualism with Christianity; others may not consider themselves Christian in any sense.

The estimated one million adherents of unlisted organizations are primarily members of independent Christian congregations. These may be Baptist, Methodist, Holiness, or Pentecostal in belief or practice; they may be unaffiliated because of disputes with a regional or national body or simply by long-standing tradition. Many such congregations are remote and isolated.

Others in this category are Christian or quasi-Christian sects that may revolve around a broadcast ministry, an itinerant revival ministry, or a single powerful individual. One such group, on which reliable information is lacking, is the Reunification Church of the Rev. Sun Myung Moon.

OTHER RELIGIONS

Judaism

Judaism is the largest non-Christian religious family in the United States. As descendants of the Jews of biblical times, Jews worship one God and follow the religious precepts in the Hebrew scriptures, the writings called the Old Testament by Christians. Jews recognize Jesus as a religious teacher but do not acknowledge him as the Messiah or Son of God. Jews still await the coming of the Messiah as foretold by the prophets.

A handful of Jews arrived in North America in the 1600s. In the 1800s, Jews from Germany arrived with other immigrants. Then between 1890 and 1920, several million Jews arrived from eastern Europe, fleeing persecution and hard times in Russia and Poland. In the 1930s and 1940s, Jews reached America as refugees from the Nazi extermination campaigns. The slaughter of some 6 million Jews by the Germans, called the Holocaust, is one of two central facts of modern Jewish experience. The second is the establishment of Israel as an independent state in 1948. Today more Jews live in Israel than in any other country except the United States.

Jewish organizations report that there are 5.8 million Americans Jews. Of these, perhaps 3.8 million are religiously affiliated or observant. The remaining 2 million consider their Judaism to be more ethnic or cultural than religious.

There are three main branches of religious Judaism—Reform, Conservative, and Orthodox. Reform Judaism flowered in the United States in the late 1800s, especially among immigrants from Germany. In some respects it resembles liberal Protestantism in the spectrum of Christian churches. Reform temples may have stained glass windows and large pipe organs. A Sabbath service may include choral music and a sermon. About 1.4 million Jews are affiliated with Reform temples.

Conservative Judaism rose in response to Reform. It sought to preserve more of the ancient observances of old orthodoxy but without losing touch with American culture and behavior. As a middle road between Reform and Orthodox Judaism, Conservative Judaism has gained numerical superiority. About 2 million Jews are affiliated with Conservative institutions.

Orthodox Judaism is by far the smallest of the three branches, with an estimated 400,000 adherents. However, Orthodox Jews are more visible by their distinctive dress and by their tendency to remain aloof from the larger community. The majority of Orthodox Jews live in New York City in small self-contained communities. Orthodox Judaism consists of scores of small groups, each with its own history and slightly differing patterns of belief and ritual.

Muslims

The Islamic faith, whose followers are called Muslims, is the third of the great theistic world religions, along with Judaism and Christianity. Each of these religions worships the same God (for whom the Muslim name is Allah), and each has its holiest places in the Middle East. Jerusalem is a holy city for all three faiths. (see "World Religions.")

The first sizable group of Muslims arrived in the United States from Lebanon in the early 1900s. Later waves of immigration have brought Pakistanis, Indians, Arabs, and Iranians, among others. Some have been refugees from political or religious persecution. Some came as students and remained. Perhaps one million engage in at least some religious observance during the year. Many of the rest consider themselves loyal supporters of Islam even if they do not participate regularly.

There are about 600 Islamic centers in the United States, many of which include a mosque for worship. The largest concentrations of Muslims are in cities in the Northeast and industrial Midwest. Observances may vary from one center to another, depending on the nationality of its adherents and their length of residence in the United States. In general, recent immigrants are more conservative and follow Islamic ritual and custom more closely.

Buddhist Churches of America

The Buddhist Churches of America is the oldest and largest U.S. Buddhist group. It represents the Jodo Shinshu sect of Buddhism, and many of its members are of Japanese descent.

There are many other Buddhist organizations in the United States and may be as many as 100,000 additional Americans who subscribe to Buddhist tenets. They are included under the heading "not separately listed."

Other Non-Christians (Unreported)

This category includes other Buddhists (not members of Buddhist Churches of America), Hindus, followers of tribal religions, and adherents of recent quasi-religious sects such as est and Scientology.

HEALTH AND MEDICINE

MILESTONES IN THE HISTORY OF MEDICINE

B.C.

c. 2700 Chinese emperor Shen Nung develops principles of herbal medicine and acupuncture.

c. 1900 The Code of Hammurabi, king of Babylon, comprises regulations concerning physicians, including what they may treat and what their fees should be.

c. 1500 The Ebers Papyrus describes many remedies used in Ancient Egypt to treat dental ailments.

c. 400 Hippocrates (Greek), teacher and medical practitioner known as Father of Medicine, writes Hippocratic Oath, which sets ethical standards still followed by physicians throughout the world.

c. 300 Herophilus (Greek) pioneers dissection of human body and founds first school of anatomy.

A.D.

c. 20 Cornelius Celsus (Roman) writes first-known medical textbook.

c. 100 Romans develop a public medical service and appoint physicians to provide medical help to poor.

c. 180 Claudius Galen (Greek) writes *Methodus Medando*, which summarizes medical knowledge of ancient times. Galen's views on human physiology and disease would influence medical thought for more than 1500 years.

c. 450 Susruta (India) notes relationship of malaria to mosquitoes and of bubonic plague to rats.

c. 900 Rhazes (Persian) is first to describe smallpox and establish criteria for diagnosing and treating it.

1030 Ibn Sina (Persian), also known as Avicenna, publishes *Canon of Medicine*, which becomes leading medical encyclopedia for centuries.

c. 1270 Spectacles are introduced by Venetian –80 glassmakers.

1403 Venice imposes world's first quarantine of infected areas as safeguard against Black Death (bubonic plague).

1530 First book devoted to dentistry published anonymously in Germany.

1543 Andreas Vesalius (Flemish) publishes first accurate anatomy text and establishes foundations of modern anatomy.

1597 Gasparo Tapliacossi (Italian) publishes first textbook of plastic surgery and revives operation of rhinoplasty (nose surgery).

1601 James Lancaster (English) writes that lemon juice helps prevent scurvy.

1628 William Harvey (English) describes functions of the heart and how blood circulates throughout the body.

1658 Jan Swammerdam (Dutch) discerns red blood cells.

1670 Thomas Willis (English) rediscovers connection between sugar in urine and diabetes (known in antiquity by Greeks, Chinese, and Indians).

1761 Leopold Auenbrugger (Styrian-Viennese) discovers that fluid in chest cavity and other health problems can be detected by tapping gently on the chest.

Giovanni Morgagni (Italian) establishes modern pathological anatomy with publication of *On the Seats and Causes of Disease.*

1796 Edward Jenner (English) develops smallpox vaccine from cowpox serum.

1816 Rene T.H. Laennec (French) invents stethoscope and introduces practice of auscultation (monitoring sounds made by internal organs).

1818 James Blundel (English) performs first successful human blood transfusion.

1831 Samuel Guthrie (American) discovers chloroform.

1833 William Beaumont (American) provides first clear insight into nature of gastric digestion.

1839 Horace Hayden and Chapin Harris (Americans) found world's first dental school, Baltimore College of Dental Surgery.

1842 Crawford Long (American) removes tumor from patient inhaling ether—first known operation under general anesthesia; publishes his findings in 1849, three years after William Morton (American) demonstrates effectiveness of ether as anesthetic.

1850 Hermann Helmholtz (German) invents ophthalmoscope, instrument used to examine interior of the eye.

1855 Manuel Garcia (Spanish) invents modern laryngoscope, device used to inspect the throat, especially the larynx and vocal cords.

1863 International Red Cross established at

Geneva, Switzerland.

1865 Joseph Lister (English) revolutionizes surgery when he introduces use of disinfectants to reduce infection.

Gregor Mendel (Austrian) discovers laws of heredity.

Louis Pasteur (French) shows that spoilage of wine can be prevented by partial heat-sterilization; process, called pasteurization, soon applied to milk and other foods.

1866 Thomas Allbutt (English) invents clinical thermometer.

1868 Carl Wunderlich (German) establishes that fever is a symptom, not a disease, and introduces use of thermometer for taking body temperature.

1876 Robert Koch (German) demonstrates that anthrax is caused by rod-shaped bacterium—the first time a microorganism is proved cause of a disease.

1881 Louis Pasteur (French) produces vaccine that successfully prevents anthrax—first disease prevented by vaccine.

1890 Emil von Behring (German) and Shibasaburo Kitasato (Japanese) independently discover antitoxins.

1892 Dmitri Ivanovski (Russian) discovers filterable viruses (viruses tiny enough to pass through fine filters previously believed to trap all living organisms).

1893 Felix Hofmann (German) develops a process for production of acetylsalicylic acid, the form of aspirin used today.

1895 Wilhelm Roentgen (German) discovers X rays, which soon leads to their use as diagnostic tools for medicine and surgery.

1900 Sigmund Freud (Austrian), founder of psychoanalysis, publishes his most important work, *The Interpretation of Dreams*.

Karl Landsteiner (Austrian) discovers three blood groups, later named A, B, and O; fourth group, to be named AB, discovered in 1902.

Walter Reed (American) establishes that yellow fever virus is transmitted by mosquitoes.

1901 Jokichi Takamine (Japanese-American) isolates adrenalin, first hormone to be isolated.

1902 Eugene Opie (American) establishes that diabetes results from destruction of specific portions of pancreatic tissue—the islets of Langerhans.

1905 Albert Einhorn (American) synthesizes procaine (Novocain), which becomes the most widely used dental anesthetic.

1906 August von Wassermann (German) develops blood test for syphilis.

1910 Marie Curie (French) isolates pure radium metal, which came to be used to treat cancer.

1913 Elmer McCollum and Marguerite Davis (Americans) discover fat-soluble factor in butterfat, later named vitamin A.

Bela Schick (Hungarian-American) perfects test for determining susceptibility to diphtheria.

1915 Death certificates come into general use in U.S.

1918 Francis Benedict (American) devises basal metabolism test for measuring rate at which metabolism (total of all chemical reactions) occurs in the body.

1921 Frederick G. Banting and Charles H. Best (Canadians) extract insulin from the pancreas.

1928 Alexander Fleming (Scottish) discovers penicillin, a substance in green mold *Penicillium notatum* that destroys certain bacteria.

1937 Bernard Fantus (American) establishes first blood bank, in Chicago.

Alton Ochsner and Michael DeBakey (Americans) suggest that cigarette smoking is cause of lung cancer.

1943 Selman Waksman (American) isolates streptomycin, an antibiotic effective against bacterium that causes tuberculosis.

1944 Willem Kolff (Dutch) develops first kidney dialysis machine.

Oswald Avery, Colin MacLeod, and Maclyn McCarty (Americans) prove that DNA (deoxyribonucleic acid) is blueprint of heredity that determines how an organism develops.

1945 Alfred Blalock (American) introduces first operation to enable blue, or cyanotic, babies to survive. (Cyanosis, which is caused by poor circulatory flow or other problems, results in diminished oxygen in blood, causing bluish discoloration of the skin.)

1947 Eugene Payne (American) uses chloromycetin, developed by Parke-Davis researchers, to treat typhus patients—first use of "broad-spectrum" antibiotic.

1948 Philip S. Hench and Edward C. Kendall (Americans) synthesize cortisone and use it to treat arthritis victims.

1952 Jonas Salk (American) develops first vaccine against polio.

James Watson (American) and Francis Crick (English) discover double-helical structure of DNA (deoxyribonucleic acid).

1953 John Gibbon (American) uses heart-lung machine he invented in successful open-heart operation.

1954 Surgeons led by Joseph Murray (American) perform first successful kidney transplant.

E. Cuyler Hammond and Daniel Horn (Americans) present dramatic evidence of dangers in smoking.

1957 Alick Isaacs and Jean Lindenmann (English) discover interferon, a protein that interferes with viral reproduction.

1961 Scientists at Bell Laboratories (U.S.) announce first continuously operating laser, a tool having many surgical uses.

1963 Thomas Starzl (American) performs

first human liver transplant operation.

1964 James Hardy (American) performs first human lung transplant.

1966 Paul Parkman and Harry Myer (Americans) develop vaccine for rubella (German measles).

Insulin synthesized independently by Michael Katsoyannis (American) and scientists in the People's Republic of China—first hormone to be synthesized.

1967 Christiaan Barnard (South African) performs world's first heart transplant.

Rene Favaloro (Argentinian) performs first successful coronary bypass operation.

1969 Denton Cooley (American) implants first temporary artificial heart in human being.

1970 Hars Khorana (American) synthesizes first artificial gene.

1972 Computerized axial tomography (CAT scan) is introduced in Great Britain.

1975 First cases of what comes to be known as Lyme disease are reported in Lyme, Connecticut.

1977 Scientists at Genentech Corporation (U.S.) induce bacteria to make human-brain hormone somatostatin—first human chemical produced by recombinant-DNA techniques.

1978 First "test-tube baby" (person conceived outside human body) is born, in England.

1981 Scientists identify previously unknown disease, acquired immune deficiency syndrome (AIDS).

Surgeons at University of California at San Francisco perform first successful operation on a fetus.

1982 William DeVries (American) performs first complete replacement of human heart with artificial heart on Dr. Barney B. Clark at University of Utah.

1984 First baby produced from frozen embryo is born, in Melbourne, Australia.

French and U.S. scientists isolate first viruses believed to cause AIDS.

1989 Steven A. Rosenberg (American) and other researchers at National Institutes of Health introduce foreign gene into human patient for first time.

HEALTH CARE EXPENDITURES

Health care costs are soaring, increasing much faster than the inflation rate. They are expected to continue to rise into the 1990s, to the point where health care expenditures may account for 15 percent of the gross national product (GNP). The increases reflect higher prices for medical services plus greater use of these services. Many factors contribute: the rapidly increasing elderly population, who use medical care more intensely than younger people; more sophisticated, higher-priced medical equipment; specialization and labor intensiveness in the health care industry; an absence of appropriate and less expensive alternatives to hospital care; costly treatments for cancer, AIDS, and other ailments; abuses of Medicare and Medicaid programs; services needed by victims of crime, drugs, and accidents; and so on.

There is increasing pressure to curb spending. The federal government and private insurers have set limits on the fees paid for treatment of various illnesses and have helped reduce the amount of time patients spend in hospitals. But as changes have been made in how physicians and hospitals are paid, concerns have been raised that providers facing restricted budgets and low payment rates might skimp on services, to the detriment of patients' health, and that third-party payers will seek low-cost providers without sufficient attention to the quality of care.

Who Pays the Bills?

Medical care is generally paid for in one of three ways:

1. Out of a patient's current income; 29% of the nation's medical costs are paid by individual patients.

2. By an insurance plan; 31% of all medical costs are paid by private insurers; much of this in turn is paid by employer health plans. General Motors Corp. spent $2.9 billion for employee health benefits in 1987; AT&T spent about $1 billion.

3. As a public charge, which means that the government—and, ultimately, the taxpayer—pays the bill; 39% of medical costs are paid by the government. In some instances the percentage is even greater. For example, injuries caused by firearms cost an estimated $429 million annually in hospital expenses alone; 85.6% of this is borne by taxpayers, according to a University of California study published in 1988. The cost would top $1 billion if expenses such as ambulance services, doctors' fees, follow-up care, and rehabilitation were included.

Health Insurance Americans spend more than 3 percent of their disposable income for health insurance premiums. There are five basic types of insurance:

1. Hospital expense insurance—pays costs of hospital room, X rays, medicines, etc.

2. Surgical expense insurance—pays costs of an operation.

3. Medical expense insurance—pays for visits to a physician's office.

4. Major medical expense insurance—pays costs associated with extended sickness or injury.

5. Disability income insurance—pays a benefit when the person is unable to work because of illness or injury.

Federal Insurance Plans Two government health programs, Medicare and Medicaid, pay approximately 29 percent of U.S. health costs. (The remaining federal health spending covers military and veterans' health care.)

Medicare is a federal health insurance plan for people age 65 and older and for people under age 65 who are severely disabled. Created by Title XVIII of the Social Security Act in 1966, it pays hospitals, physicians, and other medical

---

NATIONAL EXPENDITURES FOR HEALTH CARE, 1970–2000

National health expenditures topped $500 billion in 1987, continuing to consume an increasing share of the GNP. Spending for health claimed 11.1 percent of the GNP in 1987, up from 10.7 percent in 1986 and 9.1 percent in 1980.

	Amount in billions of dollars					
	1970	1975	1980	1985	1987	2000[1]
TOTAL expenditures	$75.0	$132.7	$248.1	$419.0	$500.3	$1,529.3
PRIVATE	47.2	76.4	142.9	244.0	293.0	879.4
PUBLIC	27.8	56.3	105.2	175.0	207.3	649.9
Federal	17.7	37.0	71.0	123.0	144.7	498.6
State and local	10.1	19.3	34.2	52.0	62.6	151.3
Per capita amount						
TOTAL expenditures	$349	$591	$1,055	$1,596	$1,987	$5,551
PRIVATE	220	340	608	888	1,163	3,192
PUBLIC	129	251	447	708	824	2,359
Federal	82	165	302	498	575	1,810
State and local	47	86	145	210	249	549
Percent distribution						
TOTAL expenditures	100.0%	100.0%	100.0%	100.0%	100.0%	100.0%
PRIVATE	63.0	57.5	57.6	58.2	58.6	57.5
PUBLIC	37.0	42.5	42.4	41.8	41.4	42.5
Federal	23.5	27.9	28.6	29.4	28.9	32.6
State and local	13.5	14.6	13.8	12.4	12.5	9.9

1. Projected.   **Source:** Dept. of Health and Human Services, Health Care Financing Administration.

---

providers. More than 30 million people are enrolled in Medicare. The program spent more than $97 billion in 1988.

Medicaid, established in 1965 by an amendment to the Social Security Act, is a health care program for poor people. It is funded jointly by federal and state agencies. In 1988, Medicaid costs totaled about $51 billion to provide health care for 22 million people.

Health Maintenance Organizations (HMOs) An HMO is a prepaid health care plan that provides comprehensive health care services to enrolled members on a prepaid basis. In other words, it integrates insurance and health care delivery within one organization. Between 1976 and 1985, the number of HMOs increased from 174 to 478, and enrollment rose from 6 million to 21 million. Enrollment has been highest in the West and lowest in the South.

There are three basic types of HMOs:

1. Staff HMOs, which provide medical services at one or more central locations through physicians employed by the HMO;

2. Group practices, which contract with a group of physicians to provide medical services at one or more sites;

3. Individual practice associations, which contract with an association of physicians from various settings (a mixture of solo and group practices) to provide health care in their own offices. These associations account for an increasingly large proportion of HMO enrollees, growing from 7 percent in 1976 to 30 percent in 1985.

HOW THE MONEY IS SPENT

Total	Amt. in billions	Percent
Total	**$500.3**	**100.0%**
Hospital care	194.7	38.9
Physicians' services	102.7	20.5
Dentists' services	32.8	6.6
Other professional services	16.2	3.2
Drugs, other aids, and supplies	43.5	8.7
Nursing-home care	40.6	8.1
Other personal health care	12.0	2.4
Administration and net cost of private health insurance	25.9	5.2
Government public health activities	14.7	2.9
Research	8.8	1.8
Construction	8.3	1.7

Note: 1987 data.   **Source:** Health Care Financing Administration.

FEDERAL EXPENDITURES FOR HEALTH CARE

(billions of dollars)

	1980	1985	1987	2000[1]
MEDICARE				
Personal health care	$35.7	$70.5	$78.9	320.8
Hospital care	25.9	48.9	50.9	207.3
Nursing-home care	0.4	0.6	0.6	1.8
MEDICAID				
Personal health care	25.2	40.1	47.5	138.0
Hospital care	9.6	14.9	16.9	41.1
Nursing home care	9.8	14.8	17.3	45.0

1. Projected.   **Source:** Health Care Financing Administration.

The Uninsured Some 37 million Americans—one person in six—do not have health insurance. The number is growing by a million a year. Most of these people are working poor—their employers do not offer insurance, and they earn too little to be able to buy insurance on their own. A Census Bureau study based on 1983 data found that whites were much more likely to have health insurance, especially private insurance, than blacks or Hispanics. They also were more likely to have health insurance through their employer.

International Comparisons

According to data compiled from statistics of the Organization for Economic Cooperation and Development, the United States spends more than any other developed nation on health care relative to its economy.

HEALTH EXPENDITURES AS PERCENTAGE OF GNP, 1986

Nation	%
United States	11.1
Sweden	9.1
Canada	8.5
France	8.5
Netherlands	8.3
Germany	8.1
Switzerland	8.0
Italy	6.7
Japan	6.7
United Kingdom	6.2
Spain	6.0

Source: "International Health Care Spending and Utilization Trends," *Health Affairs* (Fall 1988).

Nursing-Home Care

People who reach age 65 have a 30 to 50 percent chance of spending some time in a nursing home before they die. The cost for such care is high . . . and rising rapidly. According to the Brookings Institution, it currently averages about $22,000 a year. Thirty years from now the projected cost will be $55,000 a year.

In total, Americans spent $35.2 billion on nursing-home care in 1985. The majority of this cost—51.4 percent—was paid for by individual and family savings. Medicaid paid 41.8 percent, Medicare paid 1.7 percent, and private insurance paid 1 percent. Other sources were responsible for the remaining costs.

The average stay in a nursing home is 408 days. Most patients, however, stay for comparatively short periods: 31 percent for one month or less and 21 percent for one to three months.

THE BOOMING COST OF HOSPITAL CARE

Hospital care has long claimed the biggest share of health care dollars—and the percentage is growing. In 1950 hospital care accounted for 30.4 percent of personal health care costs. By 1987 the percentage had reached 43.9 percent.

Costs vary markedly depending on the care required and the locale. For example, thoracic surgery cost $7,508 per hospital admission in the Southeast in 1986, while the same surgery averaged $5,462 in the Southwest. A vaginal delivery of a normal infant in 1986 involved hospital charges averaging $1,270 in Utah and $1,890 in Florida (physician fees brought the costs up to $2,220 and $3,490, respectively). The estimated average annual malpractice-insurance cost per bed in California hospitals was $3,160 in 1985 but only $474 in Arizona.

State	Average daily room charge 1980	1985	1987	Average cost per day 1980	1985	1987	Average cost per stay 1980	1985	1987
U.S. Total	**$127**	**$213**	**$233**	**$245**	**$460**	**$537**	**$1,851**	**$3,245**	**$3,849**
Alabama	96	162	188	209	389	461	1,459	2,653	3,222
Alaska	189	274	372	408	693	892	2,276	3,742	5,057
Arizona	106	193	259	290	591	710	2,013	3,547	4,167
Arkansas	86	141	154	185	381	414	1,172	2,292	2,738
California	161	281	327	362	654	742	2,395	4,050	4,755
Colorado	124	212	243	247	486	592	1,760	3,221	4,040
Connecticut	127	206	247	271	502	612	2,039	3,610	4,446
Delaware	125	214	279	238	474	563	1,937	3,357	3,878
District of Columbia	170	274	374	358	612	722	3,189	4,962	5,636
Florida	109	182	208	247	494	583	1,803	3,381	4,083
Georgia	92	151	160	218	386	456	1,380	2,501	3,116
Hawaii	127	231	267	245	420	512	1,868	3,522	4,106
Idaho	110	199	223	208	373	444	1,251	2,402	2,898
Illinois	144	247	279	277	498	575	2,183	3,607	4,228
Indiana	107	184	208	214	446	531	1,620	2,942	3,435
Iowa	107	179	194	199	359	402	1,465	2,735	3,290
Kansas	104	184	213	207	401	422	1,592	2,954	3,276
Kentucky	92	176	199	189	367	448	1,268	2,323	2,834
Louisiana	89	156	188	233	475	566	1,492	2,842	3,518
Maine	124	209	222	217	394	436	1,707	2,870	3,426
Maryland	119	187	219	251	443	516	2,136	3,237	3,677
Massachusetts	151	229	262	294	500	605	2,578	4,194	4,624
Michigan	151	270	296	267	507	607	2,087	3,666	4,376
Minnesota	105	188	228	203	369	427	1,818	3,302	3,834
Mississippi	67	114	125	174	319	354	1,178	2,037	2,423
Missouri	107	185	209	230	457	546	1,848	3,383	4,089
Montana	113	203	221	160	312	331	1,321	2,658	3,095
Nebraska	100	155	174	194	347	370	1,526	2,892	3,539
Nevada	125	241	227	343	677	766	2,201	3,953	4,635
New Hampshire	125	199	219	203	422	496	1,432	2,644	3,137
New Jersey	146	183	215	212	400	452	1,850	2,914	3,373
New Mexico	115	192	227	263	501	578	1,549	2,837	3,236
New York	157	224	262	257	419	494	2,469	3,930	4,520
North Carolina	87	139	151	187	356	442	1,397	2,416	3,168
North Dakota	93	176	186	177	322	367	1,528	2,918	3,596
Ohio	139	229	253	241	493	572	1,907	3,428	3,897
Oklahoma	101	165	177	239	455	518	1,527	2,814	3,465
Oregon	133	230	263	277	549	655	1,671	2,879	3,451
Pennsylvania	132	256	294	234	468	544	1,947	3,412	4,060
Rhode Island	138	205	248	260	447	502	2,162	3,432	4,009
South Carolina	80	140	156	186	358	434	1,367	2,508	3,060
South Dakota	96	162	174	189	282	318	1,265	2,442	2,887
Tennessee	91	142	170	204	397	469	1,427	2,709	3,247
Texas	91	159	184	226	461	565	1,491	2,799	3,496
Utah	112	169	244	271	556	647	1,462	2,799	3,453
Vermont	116	211	257	183	343	445	1,472	2,705	3,274
Virginia	101	164	180	211	399	476	1,647	2,862	3,358
Washington	125	229	266	262	546	630	1,502	3,062	3,602
West Virginia	110	164	184	195	399	463	1,393	2,520	3,103
Wisconsin	104	167	174	218	392	446	1,765	2,974	3,327
Wyoming	98	166	179	242	360	403	1,189	2,357	2,848

Sources: Health Insurance Association of America, *Source Book of Health Insurance Data, 1985,* and *Survey of Semi-Private Room Charges* (semiannual); American Hospital Association, *Hospital Statistics* (annual, 1988).

SURGERY

Increases in the number of surgical operations during the past decade have been accompanied by dramatic changes in the rates of some procedures. An excellent example is the growing incidence of Cesarean sections—surgical incisions through the abdomen and uterus for removal of a baby, performed when normal vaginal delivery is deemed hazardous for the mother or child. Cesareans accounted for 10.4 percent of all live births in 1975, 16.5 percent in 1980, and 22.7 percent in 1985, and 24.4 percent in 1987.

The frequency of certain procedures varies according to age but, surprisingly, there may also be variations from one geographical region to another. For example, 32 percent of the 1985 births in New Orleans covered by Blue Cross and other commercial insurers were Caesareans—10 percent higher than the national average. Hysterectomies are performed on fewer than 5 out of 1,000 women per year in the Northeast but on more than 8 per 1,000 in the South.

Eliminating the Need for Exploratory Surgery

Technological advances are creating new milestones in the art of medicine. Nowhere is this more apparent—or welcome—than in the diagnosis of people's health. Thanks to sophisticated electronics and other tools, physicians can obtain highly detailed views of internal organs without surgery. This often can be done on an outpatient basis, thereby lowering costs and avoiding risks associated with exploratory surgery. Furthermore, the techniques enable physicians to detect cancers and other problems in their earliest stages, allowing them to take preventive action that will decrease chances of severe damage or death.

New imaging techniques include the following:

CAT Computerized Axial Tomography—Uses X rays to take pictures, or tomograms, of the patient's body. The pictures are reconstructed by a computer to produce a crisp, 3-D image. CAT scans are particularly helpful in locating tumors, including ones deep in the brain.

PET Positron-Emission Tomography—Small amounts of positron-emitting isotopes are injected into the blood to study the flow of blood and its distribution to heart muscles or other tissues.

SPECT Single Photo Emission Computer Tomography—Uses radioisotopes to measure blood flow in small vessels. SPECT is particularly well suited to imaging the brain and is used to study such disorders as epilepsy, schizophrenia, Parkinson's disease, and strokes.

MRI Magnetic Resonance Imaging—Uses a combination of a strong magnetic field and radio waves to measure the distribution and chemical bonds of the protons in the body's hydrogen atoms. A computer translates measurements into 3-D images. MRI is frequently used to view the brain and other soft tissues.

DSA Digital Subtraction Angiography—An

HOSPITAL FACILITIES AND THEIR USE

Year	Number of hospitals	Number of beds (thousands)	Admissions (thousands)	Occupancy rate (%)	Outpatient visits (thousands)
1946	6,125	1,436	15,675	79.5%	N.A.
1950	6,788	1,456	18,483	86.0	N.A.
1955	6,956	1,604	21,073	85.0	N.A.
1960	6,876	1,658	25,027	84.6	N.A.
1965	7,123	1,704	28,812	82.3	125,793
1970	7,123	1,616	31,759	80.3	181,370
1975	7,156	1,466	36,157	76.7	254,844
1980	6,965	1,365	38,892	77.7	262,951
1985	6,872	1,318	36,304	69.0	282,140
1987	6,821	1,267	34,439	68.9	310,707

Note: N.A. = not available.   **Source:** American Hospital Association.

MOST COMMON OPERATIONS

	Operations (thousands) 1979	1982	1984	Operations per 1,000 population 1979	1982	1984
MALES, ALL AGES[1]	8,505	8,805	9,073	78.1	76.3	76.4
Cardiac catheterization	228	439	533	2.2	3.9	4.7
Prostatectomy	335	367	410	3.1	3.2	3.4
Reduction of fracture (excluding skull, nose, and jaw)	325	339	367	2.9	2.8	3.0
Repair of inguinal hernia	483	370	290	4.6	3.3	2.5
Tonsillectomy	195	135	115	2.0	1.3	1.2
	1979	1982	1984	1979	1982	1984
FEMALES, ALL AGES[1]	15,989	15,994	16,583	126.1	117.2	118.3
Procedures to assist delivery	2,391	2,494	2,938	18.4	18.4	20.7
Cesarean section	619	877	953	4.8	6.3	6.7
Hysterectomy	649	670	655	5.2	5.0	4.8
Repair of lacerations due to giving birth	355	548	660	2.8	3.9	4.7
Removal of one or both ovaries	483	525	490	3.9	4.0	3.7
Destruction or closing off of fallopian tubes	641	466	415	4.9	3.3	2.9
Diagnostic dilation and curettage of uterus	923	349	206	7.3	2.6	1.5

Notes: Data are for inpatients discharged from nonfederal, short-stay hospitals, based on a sample of hospital records. Includes operations not listed. Rates are age adjusted.   1. Excludes those performed incidental to other abdominal surgery.   **Source:** National Center for Health Statistics.

iodine-containing substance that is opaque to X rays is injected into blood vessels. Before and after X-ray images create a sharp picture of the vessels and the flow of blood.

Ultrasound imaging, or sonography High-frequency sound waves are beamed at the body's organs. The echoes that bounce back are translated into computer images. Because it doesn't use X rays, sonography is recommended for use on pregnant women. It also is well suited for examining the gall bladder, liver, heart, and prostate gland.

Thermographic imaging Data on the body's heat gathered by an infrared camera is converted by a computer into a temperature map, which is useful in detecting cancers and studying blood flow into limbs.

Organ Transplantation

Transplant surgery is more successful than ever, thanks to improved surgical techniques, a better understanding of the body's immune system, and the development of drugs that combat rejection of implanted organs. Kidney transplants, for instance, enjoy a high rate of success and are much less expensive—and much more convenient—than maintaining a patient on dialysis.

Unfortunately, a scarcity of donor organs keeps thousands of patients waiting, sometimes in vain. According to the American Council on Transplantation, on any given day, some 15,000 Americans wait for donor organs, including 13,000 for kidneys, 900 for hearts, and 500 for livers.

In 1986 states began enacting laws requiring hospitals to solicit organ donations from families of dead or dying patients. Dramatic increases in donations were reported. In New York, corneal donations to the Eye Bank jumped 60 percent in the first four months after the state's law took effect, from 295 eyes in 1985 to 474 eyes in 1986.

There are approximately 70 organ procurement programs in the country. Many have toll-free telephone numbers. Two national procurement programs with toll-free numbers are the United Network for Organ Sharing (1-800-446-2726) and the American Council on Transplantation (1-800-ACT-GIVE).

Leading Transplant Centers To perform transplants, hospitals must be licensed. Of the 6,281 hospitals reporting to the American Hospital Association's 1987 Annual Survey, 319 (5.1%) had facilities for performing organ transplants. The largest percentage of these (29.2%) were hospitals with 500 or more beds. California (28) and Texas (26) led the states with the most organ-transplant facilities.

The following medical centers are leading transplant facilities that perform all or most of the proceduress listed above.

ALABAMA The University of Alabama Hospital, 619 South 19 St., Birmingham, AL 35233; (205) 934-4011.

CALIFORNIA University of California Medical Center, 10833 Le Conte Ave., Los Angeles, CA 90024; (213) 825-9111.

FLORIDA Shands Hospital, University of Florida, Gainesville, FL 32610; (904) 395-0111.

ILLINOIS University of Chicago Medical Center, 5841 Maryland Ave., Chicago, IL 60637; (312) 702-1000.

MARYLAND Johns Hopkins Medical Institutions, 600 North Wolfe St., Baltimore, MD 21205; (301) 955-5000.

MASSACHUSETTS Massachusetts General Hospital, 32 Fruit St., Boston, MA 02114; (617) 726-2000.

MINNESOTA The Mayo Clinic and Hospitals, 220 First St., S.W., Rochester, MN 55901; (507) 284-2511. The University of Minnesota Hospital and Clinics, Harvard Street at East River Road, Minneapolis, MN 55455; (612) 626-3000.

MISSOURI Barnes Hospital, Barnes Hospital Plaza, St. Louis, MO 63110; (314) 362-5000.

NEW YORK The Presbyterian Hospital, Columbia-Presbyterian Medical Center, New York, NY 10032-3784; (212) 305-5156.

NORTH CAROLINA Duke University Medical Center, Durham, NC 27710; (919) 684-8111.

OHIO The Cleveland Clinic Foundation, 9500 Euclid Avenue, Cleveland, OH 44106; (216) 444-2200.

PENNSYLVANIA Presbyterian-University Hospital, DeSoto at O'Hara St., Pittsburgh, PA 15213; (412) 647-2345.

TEXAS The Texas Medical Center, 6565 Fannin, Houston, TX 77030; (713) 790-3311.

UTAH University Hospital and Clinics, The University of Utah Health Sciences Center, 50 N. Medical Drive, Salt Lake City, UT 84132; (801) 581-2121.

VIRGINIA Medical College of Virginia Hospitals, 401 North 12 St., Richmond, VA 23298; (804) 786-4682.

WISCONSIN University of Wisconsin Hospital and Clinics, 600 Highland Ave., Madison, WI 53792; (608) 263-6400.

NUMBER AND COST OF TRANSPLANT OPERATIONS

Organ	First performed	Number of transplants			Average cost (1987)	Success rate, % (1987)
		1982	1984	1987		
Bone marrow	1963	N.A.	N.A.	1,659	$80,000–111,000	N.A.
Cornea	1905	—	24,000	35,000	3,500–7,000	90–95
Heart	1967	103	346	1,512	80,000–140,000	82
Heart-lung	1981	—	30	43	130,000–200,000	68–70
Kidney	1954	5,358	6,968	8,967	30,000–40,000	80–89
Liver	1963	62	308	1,182	135,000–338,000	77
Pancreas	1966	—	87	129	30,000–40,000	44

Source: American Council on Transplantation.

Abortion

The deliberate termination of a pregnancy before the fetus is capable of living outside the womb has generally been legal in the country since 1973, when the U.S. Supreme Court ruled (in *Roe vs. Wade*) that abortion cannot be prohibited during the first three months. In 1985 women under 25 years of age constituted 61 percent of those who had abortions that were reported to the Centers for Disease Control; 67 percent were white, 81 percent were single, and 57 percent had never given birth to a live child. Not all abortions are reported to the Centers for Disease Control, however; the actual totals are believed to be significantly higher.

The rate of abortion among American women is greater than among women in many other industrialized nations. The Alan Guttmacher Institute of New York projects, based on current abortion rates, that among every 100 women in the U.S., there will be 76 abortions, with some women having more than one. In contrast, in Canada there will be 36 abortions among every 100 women.

The Guttmacher Institute also estimates

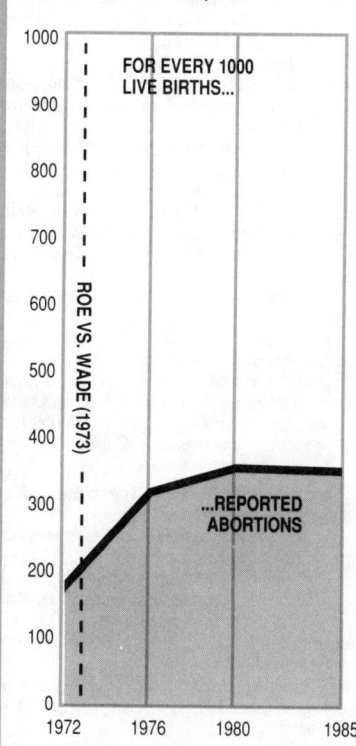

REPORTED ABORTIONS PER 1000 LIVE BIRTHS, 1972-85

FOR EVERY 1000 LIVE BIRTHS...

ROE VS. WADE (1973)

...REPORTED ABORTIONS

1972   1976   1980   1985

Source: Centers for Disease Control.

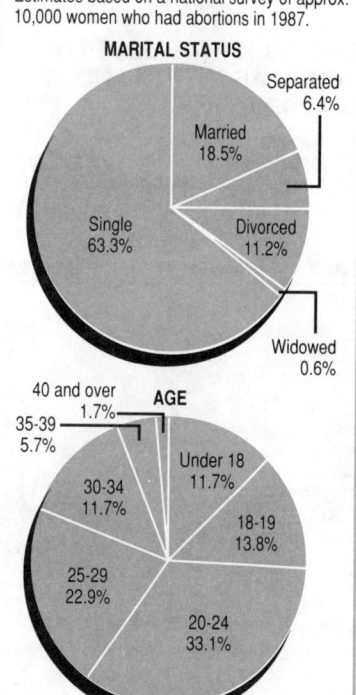

WHO HAS ABORTIONS?
Estimates based on a national survey of approx. 10,000 women who had abortions in 1987.

MARITAL STATUS

Single 63.3%
Married 18.5%
Separated 6.4%
Divorced 11.2%
Widowed 0.6%

AGE

Under 18 11.7%
18-19 13.8%
20-24 33.1%
25-29 22.9%
30-34 11.7%
35-39 5.7%
40 and over 1.7%

Source: Alan Guttmacher Institute.
Published in "Family Planning Perspectives" and *New York Times*.

that American women have more unplanned pregnancies than women in other nations, possibly because in the other nations, a wider variety of contraceptives are available and are easy to obtain. In 1983 51.2 percent of pregancies in the United States were unplanned, versus 31.8 percent in Great Britain and 17 percent in the Netherlands.

REPORTED ABORTIONS

	Number of abortions			
	1972	1976	1980	1985
Reported abortions	586,760	988,267	1,297,606	1,328,570
Number per 1,000 live births	180.1	312.0	359.2	353.8
	Percent of total number			
RACE				
White	77.0%	66.6%	69.9%	66.6%
Other	23.0	33.4	30.1	33.4
MARITAL STATUS				
Married	29.7	24.6	23.1	19.3
Unmarried	70.3	75.4	76.9	80.7
AGE				
Under 20	32.6	32.1	29.2	26.3
20-24	32.5	33.3	35.5	34.7
25 or older	34.9	34.6	35.3	39.0

Source: Centers for Disease Control.

MORTALITY RATES FROM LEGAL ABORTION AND CHILDBIRTH

The death rate among women from legal abortions has dropped sharply since 1970. At the same time, women's death rate from childbirth has also dropped, though less rapidly.

	MORTALITY RATES	
Year	Abortion[1]	Childbirth[2]
1970	19.0	16.0
1971	11.0	14.9
1972	4.1	15.2
1973	3.4	12.5
1974	2.9	12.4
1975	2.8	10.3
1976	0.9	10.2
1977	1.3	9.8
1978	0.6	9.7
1979	1.2	8.0
1980	0.6	7.5
1981	0.4	7.2
1982	0.8	7.9
1983	0.7	8.0

1. Per 100,000 abortions. 2. Per 100,000 live births.
Sources: Centers for Disease Control; Alan Guttmacher Institute.

DISEASE

Causes of disease are many, five of the most common categories of disease being the following:

1. Hereditary diseases—transferred from parent to child by genes. Examples: hemophilia, Down's syndrome, cystic fibrosis, sickle cell anemia.

2. Deficiency diseases—caused by lack of vitamins or other essential nutrients. Examples: scurvy, pellagra.

3. Infectious diseases—caused by viruses, bacteria, fungi, and other organisms and transferred from person to person. Examples: common cold, influenza, chicken pox, measles.

4. Diseases caused by chemical and physical agents such as radiation, smoke, drugs, and poisons. Examples: allergies, asbestosis, byssinosis, lead poisoning.

5. Degenerative diseases—resulting from natural aging processes. In some cases, cancer and high blood pressure are degenerative diseases.

Heart Disease

Cardiovascular diseases (diseases of the heart and blood vessels) are America's number one killer. During 1987 an estimated 966,000 people died from these diseases. This represented approximately 45 percent of all deaths.

Death rates vary according to age, sex, race, even geographical location. Rates increase with age and are about 77 percent higher among men than among women. For both sexes, death rates are significantly higher among blacks than among whites, though the disparity has narrowed substantially in the past 20 years.

A study that divided the nation into nine geographic areas found that, on the average, people in the Mountain states have the lowest death rates from cardiovascular diseases, while those in the east south-central states (Kentucky, Tennessee, Alabama, and Mississippi) have the highest.

The good news is that death rates from heart disease have declined. This is due in part to improved drug treatments and other medical advancements. Another factor has been improved personal health habits: people have stopped smoking, decreased the amount of fat in their diets, and taken other steps that reduce their risks of cardiovascular disease.

Major risk factors for heart disease are the following:

1. High blood pressure. Have your blood pressure checked once a year.

2. High blood cholesterol levels. Adopt a balanced diet that derives a maximum of 30% of its calories from fat, with no more than 10% from saturated fat and a maximum of 300 milligrams of cholesterol a day.

3. Smoking. Don't.

4. Sedentary life-style. Exercise regularly and sensibly.

DEATH RATES FROM HEART DISEASE (per 100,000 population)

	MALE			
	1960	1970	1980	1985
Total under age 25	439.5	422.5	368.6	342.8
25-34 years	20.1	15.2	11.4	11.5
35-44 years	112.7	103.2	68.7	58.4
45-54 years	420.4	376.4	282.6	236.9
55-64 years	1,066.9	987.2	746.8	651.9
65-74 years	2,291.3	2,170.3	1,728.0	1,508.4
75-84 years	4,742.4	4,534.8	3,834.3	3,498.0
85 and over	9,788.9	8,426.2	8,752.7	8,123.7

	FEMALE			
	1960	1970	1980	1985
Total under age 25	300.6	304.5	305.1	304.3
25-34 years	11.3	7.7	5.3	5.0
35-44 years	38.2	32.2	21.4	18.3
45-54 years	127.5	109.9	84.5	73.8
55-64 years	429.4	351.6	272.1	250.3
65-74 years	1,261.3	1,082.7	828.6	745.3
75-84 years	3,582.7	3,120.8	2,497.0	2,245.2
85 and over	9,016.8	7,591.8	7,350.5	6,935.7

Source: National Center for Health Statistics.

Heart Attacks A heart attack occurs when the blood supply to the heart muscles is blocked. An uncomfortable pressure, fullness, squeezing, or pain in the center of the chest that lasts for two minutes or more may be a sign of a heart attack. Sweating, dizziness, nausea, fainting, or shortness of breath may also occur. Some 1,500,000 people suffer heart attacks annually. One-third of these people do not survive. Of the survivors, 100,000 will have a second heart attack within two years.

Strokes and Bypass Surgery A stroke occurs when the blood supply to the brain is blocked, usually by a clot. The primary signal of a stroke is a sudden, temporary weakness or numbness of the face, arm, or leg on one side of the body. Other signals include temporary loss of speech, difficulty in speaking or understanding speech, temporary vision problems (particularly in one eye), unsteadiness, or unexplained dizziness.

Some 230,000 bypass operations at an estimated cost of $6 billion are performed annually in the country, more than double the number performed in 1980. In this operation a blood vessel from elsewhere in the body is used to reroute blood around a blocked coronary artery. The purpose: to reduce the person's risk of a stroke. Studies have indicated, however, that for a significant percentage of patients such surgery does not significantly improve their chances of survival over the following six years. Other research found that up to 44 percent of bypass operations are unnecessary or inappropriate.

ESTIMATED CANCER DEATHS BY SITE AND SEX, 1988

Lung cancer is the leading cause of cancer deaths, killing an estimated 93,000 men and 46,000 women in 1988. Among women, breast cancer is the second most common, though if detected early and treated properly, it has a very high cure rate. Among men, prostate cancer causes the second greater number of deaths. It, too, has a high survival rate if discovered while still localized within the general region of the prostate.

Site	New cases Total	Male	Female	Deaths Total	Male	Female
Skin	27,300[1]	14,600[1]	12,700[1]	7,800	4,800	3,000
Oral	30,200	20,500	9,700	9,050	6,000	3,050
Lung, bronchus, and other respiratory	168,300	112,800	55,500	144,250	97,000	47,250
Breast	135,900[2]	900[2]	135,000[2]	42,300	300	42,000
Esophagus	9,800	6,900	2,900	9,100	6,600	2,500
Stomach	24,800	15,000	9,800	14,400	8,500	5,900
Liver and bile passages	14,000	7,100	6,900	10,900	5,500	5,400
Pancreas	27,000	13,000	14,000	24,500	12,000	12,500
Colon and Rectum	147,000	71,000	76,000	61,500	29,600	31,900
Other plus unspecified digestive	4,900	2,500	2,400	1,950	950	1,000
Urinary (bladder, kidney, etc.)	68,900	48,100	20,800	20,000	12,800	7,200
Leukemias	26,900	15,000	11,900	18,100	9,800	8,300
Other blood plus lymph tissues	50,700	26,400	24,300	26,200	13,500	12,700
Bone	2,100	1,200	900	1,300	700	600
Connective tissue	5,500	3,000	2,500	2,900	1,400	1,500
Endocrine glands	12,100	3,600	8,500	1,850	800	1,050
Eye	1,900	1,000	900	300	150	150
Brain and central nervous system	14,700	8,100	6,600	10,900	6,000	4,900
Ovary	19,000	—	19,000	12,000	—	12,000
Uterus	46,900	—	46,900	10,000	—	10,000
Other genital, female	4,800	—	4,800	1,100	—	1,100
Prostate	99,000	99,000	—	28,000	28,000	—
Testis	5,600	5,600	—	350	350	—
Other genital, male	1,200	1,200	—	250	250	—
All other plus unspecified sites	36,500	18,500	18,000	35,000	18,000	17,000

1. Melanoma only. 2. Invasive cancer only. **Source:** American Cancer Society.

Cancer The nation's second leading cause of death is a group of diseases characterized by the unrestrained growth of cells. It afflicts people of all ages and races, and it varies greatly in cause, symptoms, response to treatment, and possibility of cure.

Overall, cancer incidence and mortality rates have increased steadily. In part this is due to an increasingly aging population. Also, some cancers, particularly lung cancer, have a long latency period, developing after years of exposure to tobacco smoke or other cancer-causing agents.

Warning Signs Early detection is the key in fighting cancer. See your doctor if one of the following symptoms lasts longer than two weeks.

1. Unusual bleeding or discharge.
2. A sore that does not heal.
3. A change in a wart or mole.
4. A lump or thickening in the breast or elsewhere.
5. A change in bowel or bladder habits.
6. Nagging cough or hoarseness.
7. Indigestion or difficulty in swallowing.

CHANGES IN CANCER DEATH RATES

Since the 1950s, cancer death rates have fallen dramatically for children and young adults. Slighter declines have occurred among adults age 45–55, while death rates for older adults have increased slightly. Much of this increase is due to lung cancer. For example, if lung cancer deaths are excluded, the death rates per 100,000 people ages 75-84 would have been 1,092.4 in 1950, falling to 1,004.2 in 1985. Instead, the rate rose from 1,147.5 to 1,290.2 during that time.

Age	Rates per 100,000 people 1950	1975	1985	% change 1950–85
ALL AGES	157.0	162.2	171.3	9.1%
0–4 years	11.0	5.2	3.6	−67.3
5–14 years	6.6	4.7	3.5	−47.0
15–24 years	8.5	6.6	5.3	−37.6
25–34 years	19.6	14.6	12.8	−34.7
35–44 years	63.9	53.9	48.2	−24.6
45–54 years	174.7	179.2	169.3	−3.1
55–64 years	392.0	423.2	441.3	12.6
65–74 years	695.0	769.7	848.0	22.0
75–84 years	1147.5	1155.8	1290.2	12.4
85 and older	1444.8	1437.6	1596.2	10.5

Source: National Cancer Institute.

Cancer Survival Rates According to the American Cancer Society, more than 5 million Americans are alive who have a history of cancer, 3 million of them with the diagnosis made five or more years ago. Chances of surviving cancer have steadily improved. In the 1930s fewer than two out of 10 American cancer patients survived at least five years after diagnosis. In contrast, four out of 10 who get cancer this year will be alive five years after diagnosis. Survival depends on many factors. Two of the most important are the site of the tumor and how much the cancer spread before treatment was begun. The American Cancer Society estimated that about 174,000 people with cancer who died in 1988 might have been saved by earlier diagnosis and prompt treatment.

5-YEAR SURVIVAL RATES FOR CASES DIAGNOSED IN 1960–63, 1970–73, 1979–84 (in percent)

Cancer site	Whites 1960–63	1970–73	1979–84
All sites	39%	43%	50%
Bladder	53	61	77
Breast (females)	63	68	75
Cervix	58	64	67
Colon	43	49	54
Leukemia	14	22	32
Liver	2	3	3
Lung and bronchus	8	10	13
Ovary	32	36	37
Pancreas	1	2	3
Prostate	50	63	73
Rectum	38	45	52
Stomach	11	13	16
Thyroid	83	86	93

Cancer site	Blacks 1960–63	1970–73	1979–84
All sites	27%	31%	37%
Bladder	24	36	57
Breast (females)	46	51	62
Cervix	47	61	59
Colon	34	37	49
Leukemia	N.A.	N.A.	27
Liver	N.A.	N.A.	5
Lung and bronchus	5	7	11
Ovary	32	32	36
Pancreas	1	2	5
Prostate	35	55	60
Rectum	27	30	34
Stomach	8	13	17
Thyroid	N.A.	N.A.	95

Source: National Cancer Institute.

AIDS

Acquired immune deficiency syndrome (AIDS) has been called the "most alarming disease of our times." An estimated 1.5 million Americans are infected. By mid-1989, the disease had claimed more than 52,000 lives just in the United States. Tens of thousands more will die within the next few years. Yet this devastating disease was unknown until 1981.

AIDS is caused by the human immunodeficiency virus (HIV), which is spread through contact with infected body fluids such as blood and semen. Infected people may harbor the virus within their bodies for several years or even longer before developing any symptoms. Though symptomless, they can still infect others.

The illness suppresses the body's immune system, making patients very susceptible to deadly "opportunistic diseases" that strike when body defenses are down. Among these are Kaposi's Sarcoma, a rare form of skin cancer, and pneumocystis, a parasitic lung infection.

AIDS is apparently fatal: no one has recovered from the disease. No cure has yet been developed—nor do researchers anticipate development in the near future of a vaccine to prevent infection. Numerous drugs to combat AIDS are being tested, and several are being used to suppress the AIDS virus and combat the infections that afflict AIDS patients. Only azidothymidine (AZT) has thus far been demonstrated to extend life.

Who Are the Patients? In the United States, homosexual and bisexual males make up approximately 62 percent of the total patients. The other major group afflicted with AIDS are intravenous drug abusers—both men and women—who constitute 20 percent of the total. New infections are increasing at a much higher rate among drug users than among homosexuals.

Cases are not limited to these high-risk groups. Anyone may become infected by having sex with someone who is infected with the AIDS virus. Babies of infected women may be born with the disease because it can be transmitted from the mother to the baby before or during birth. Also, prior to blood screening that began in 1985, some hemophiliacs and other people were infected when they received blood contaminated with the HIV virus.

AIDS CASES CLUSTERED IN LARGE CITIES

Most cases of AIDS have occurred in metropolitan areas. As of Jan. 1, 1989, 15 cities had reported more than 1,000 cases.

City	Number of cases
New York, N.Y.	18,035
San Francisco, Calif.	6,642
Los Angeles, Calif.	6,049
Houston, Tex.	2,580
Newark, N.J.	2,479
Washington, D.C.	2,399
Miami, Fla.	2,162
Chicago, Ill.	2,128
Dallas, Tex.	1,755
Philadelphia, Pa.	1,674
Atlanta, Ga.	1,417
Boston, Mass.	1,249
San Diego, Calif.	1,132
Jersey City, N.J.	1,071
Ft. Lauderdale, Fla.	1,018

Source: Centers for Disease Control.

AIDS: 1981–92

By the end of 1992, 360,000 Americans will have developed AIDS.

By the end of 1992, an estimated 260,000 Americans will have died from AIDS.

NEW CASES OF AIDS 1981–92

- 1981: 293
- 1984: 5,845
- 1988: 27,975
- 1992: 80,000

1992

Source: Centers for Disease Control.

NUMBER OF REPORTED AIDS CASES AND DEATHS

	1981	1982	1983	1984	1985	1986	1987	1988[2]
Number of reported cases	293	1,053	2,899	5,845	10,765	17,175	23,109	27,975
Total cases to date	293	1,346	4,245	10,090	20,855	38,030	61,139	87,545[2]
Number of known deaths[1]	268	941	2,617	4,886	8,664	11,891	11,851	9,657
Total deaths to date	268	1,209	3,826	8,712	17,386	29,277	41,128	50,785[2]

1. Reporting of deaths is incomplete.   2. As of Nov. 30, 1988. In addition, there were 85 cases diagnosed prior to 1981. Of these, 71 are known to have died.   **Source:** Centers for Disease Control.

ADULTS AND ADOLESCENTS WITH AIDS, 1981–87

	Males	%	Females	%	Both sexes	%
Homosexual/bisexual males	50,325	68%		0%	50,325	62%
Intravenous (IV) drug abusers	12,529	17	3,622	52	16,151	20
Homosexual male and IV drug abusers	5,874	8			5,874	7
Hemophilia/coagulation disorder	751	1	22	0	773	1
Heterosexuals	1,516	2	2,073	30	3,589	4
Blood transfusion	1,297	2	747	11	2,044	3
Undetermined[1]	2,143	3	519	7	2,662	3
Total	**74,435**	**91**	**6,983**	**9**	**81,418**	**100**

Note: Provisional data. Cases with more than one risk factor other than the combinations listed are tabulated only in the category listed first.   1. Includes patients on whom risk information is incomplete, patients still under investigation, men reported only to have had heterosexual contact with a prostitute, and patients for whom no specific risk was identified; also includes one health care worker who developed AIDS after a documented needle-stick to blood.   **Source:** Centers for Disease Control.

CHILDREN WITH AIDS, 1981–87

	Males	%	Females	%	Both sexes	%
Hemophilia/coagulation disorder	81	11%	2	0%	83	6%
Parents with/at risk of AIDS[1]	524	71	520	86	1,044	78
Blood transfusion	106	14	63	10	169	13
Undetermined[2]	27	4	23	4	50	4
Total	**738**	**55**	**608**	**45**	**1,346**	**100**

Note: Provisional data. Includes all patients under 13 years of age at time of diagnosis. Cases with more than one risk factor other than the combinations listed are tabulated only in the category listed first.   1. Data suggest transmission from an infected mother to her fetus or infant during the perinatal period.   2. Includes patients on whom risk information is incomplete and patients still under investigation.   **Source:** Centers for Disease Control.

A Worldwide Problem By the beginning of 1989, approximately 140 nations had reported cases of AIDS to the World Health Organization (WHO). Reported cases are the tip of the iceberg, however. Though 132,976 cases were reported to WHO as of Dec. 31, 1988, the number of actual adult cases was estimated to be about 350,000. The shortfall results from less than complete case detection and reporting, as well as from delay in reporting cases to WHO. Some experts estimate underreporting to be as high as 90 percent in Africa, compared to about 20 percent underreporting in the U.S.

Furthermore, WHO experts believe that, worldwide, 5 million to 10 million people are infected with the AIDS virus. This will result in 500,000 to 3 million cases of AIDS by 1993—just among people now carrying the virus.

AIDS cases and infections have been reported from all continents, but there are significant differences in incidence and patterns of infection. Incidence has been lowest in Asia, while Africa, particularly Central and East Africa, has been hardest hit.

There are three patterns of AIDS spread. In Africa, parts of Latin America, and the Caribbean, AIDS spread has been predominantly among heterosexuals, and the disease affects both sexes fairly equally. In the United States and Western Europe, the disease appeared first in homosexuals and bisexuals, though heterosexual transmission is growing in those areas. The remainder of the world—Eastern Europe, the Middle East, North Africa, and most countries in Asia and the Pacific—is experiencing a "delayed" spread, having only about 1 percent of the AIDS cases reported to WHO.

AIDS CASES REPORTED TO WHO THROUGH DEC. 31, 1988, BY REGION AND SELECTED COUNTRIES

Region	Country	Number of Cases
AFRICAN REGION		20,905
	Angola	85
	Burundi	1,408
	Ghana	227
	Kenya	2,732
	Malawi	2,586
	Mozambique	19
	Nigeria	13
	Senegal	149
	South Africa	150
	Tanzania	3,055
	Uganda	5,508
	Zambia	1,056
AMERICAN REGION		93,723
	Argentina	197
	Bahamas	236
	Barbados	67
	Bermuda	92
	Brazil	4,436
	Canada	2,181
	Chile	100
	Colombia	308
	Costa Rica	79
	Cuba	34
	Dominican Republic	566
	Guatemala	46
	Haiti	1,661
	Jamaica	72
	Mexico	1,642
	Nicaragua	1
	Panama	64
	Peru	122
	United States	**80,538**
	Venezuela	263
EASTERN MEDITERRANEAN REGION		178
	Afghanistan	0
	Bahrain	0
	Cyprus	5
	Egypt	6
	Jordan	3
	Morocco	18
	Pakistan	6
	Sudan	81
	Syria	4
	Tunisia	21
EUROPEAN REGION		16,883
	Austria	220
	Belgium	408
	Czechoslovakia	12
	Denmark	345
	France	4,874
	Germany, East	6
	Germany, West	2,580
	Greece	151
	Ireland	64
	Israel	67
	Italy	2,556
	Netherlands	676
	Norway	95
	Poland	4
	Spain	1,850
	Sweden	235
	Switzerland	605
	United Kingdom	1,862
	USSR	4
SOUTHEAST ASIA REGION		21
	Bangladesh	0
	India	9
	Indonesia	3
	Mongolia	0
	Nepal	0
	Sri Lanka	1
	Thailand	8
WESTERN PACIFIC REGION		1,316
	Australia	1,079
	China	3
	Hong Kong	13
	Japan	90
	Malaysia	4
	New Zealand	93
	Philippines	17
	Samoa	0
	Singapore	4

Source: World Health Organization.

Hepatitis: A Growing Cause of Liver Disease

One of today's most serious health problems caused by viruses is viral hepatitis, a disease that attacks the liver. Of particular concern is hepatitis B, which is generally transmitted via contact with the blood of an infected person during sex, during birth, or through contaminated needles and syringes. People at high risk are intravenous drug users who share needles, homosexual men, and heterosexuals with multiple partners.

According to the Centers for Disease Control, new infections increased from about 200,000 cases in 1978 to 300,000 in 1988. Some of those infected become chronic carriers. An estimated one million Americans are believed to be chronic carriers, capable of transmitting the virus to other people. Furthermore, chronic carriers are at high risk of developing cirrhosis or liver cancer. Each year in the United States, about 4,000 hepatitis B patients die of cirrhosis and 1,000 die of liver cancer. The toll is much higher in developing countries, where the virus often is passed from mothers to their newborn infants. Even in the United States, some 3,500 infants become infected each year.

A vaccine for hepatitis B was licensed in 1981. But few people have been vaccinated, partly because of the high cost—about $100—of vaccination.

Sexually Transmitted Diseases

The most common sexually transmitted diseases (STDs) include genital warts, herpes, chlamydia, gonorrhea, and syphilis. STDs have been around at least since the beginning of recorded history, and while the prevalence of some have declined, rates for others have exploded. Today, millions of people suffer from STDs. The ubiquity of these diseases can be attributed in part to the fact that more people have been engaging in sex . . . and with multiple partners, which increases the likelihood of infection. Also, there was a decline in safe-sex activities, including the use of condoms and other "barrier" contraceptives—a trend that shows signs of changing because of the fear of AIDS.

Many STDs have similar symptoms. Some have no symptoms at all, particularly in women. The following may indicate the presence of an STD: vaginal or penile discharge; inflammation, itching or pain in the genital or anal area; pain during intercourse; burning during urination; sores, blisters, bumps, or rashes; fever or swollen glands; lower abdominal or testicular pain.

Immediate, proper treatment is urged for all STDs. Failure to do so can have serious consequences, resulting in infertility, blindness, cancer, and death. Children born to women afflicted with STDs may suffer brain damage and other disorders.

OCCUPATIONAL DISEASE

A recent study of heart patients suggests that jobs that require vigilance over others' well-being cause the most stress. Some examples: bus driver, preschool teacher, forester, physician, airline stewardess, locomotive engineer, biological scientist, restaurant manager, sheriff.

Source: National Institute for Occupational Safety and Health.

DEATHS

During 1987 an estimated 2,127,000 deaths occurred in the United States—approximately 20,000 more than in 1986 and the greatest number ever recorded. The National Center for Health Statistics points out that the record number of deaths in 1987 was consistent with a general increase in the size of the population, especially for people age 65 and over.

Deaths and Death Rates

Males experience a greater number of deaths and higher death rates than do females, with black males having significantly higher numbers and rates than white males.

LEADING CAUSES OF DEATH

For the purpose of national mortality statistics, every death is attributed to one underlying condition.

Cause of death	Total deaths 1986	% of total 1986	Death rate per 100,000 1979	Death rate per 100,000 1986
All causes	2,105,361[1]	100.0%	852.2	873.2
Heart diseases	765,490	36.4	326.5	317.5
Cancer	469,376	22.3	179.6	194.7
Cerebrovascular diseases	149,643	7.1	75.5	62.1
Accidents	95,277	4.6	46.9	39.5
Pulmonary diseases	76,559	3.6	22.2	31.8
Pneumonia and influenza	69,812	3.3	20.1	29.0
Diabetes mellitus	37,184	1.8	14.8	15.4
Suicide	30,904	1.5	12.1	12.8
Liver disease and cirrhosis	26,159	1.2	13.2	10.9
Atherosclerosis	22,706	1.1	12.8	9.4
Kidney diseases	21,767	1.0	7.0	9.0
Homicide and legal intervention	21,731	1.0	10.0	9.0
Septicemia	18,795	0.9	3.6	7.8
Perinatal-related conditions	18,391	0.9	10.4	7.6
Congenital anomalies	12,638	0.6	6.0	5.2

1. Includes causes not listed separately. **Source:** National Center for Health Statistics.

NUMBER OF CASES OF VENEREAL DISEASES

Only cases of syphilis and gonorrhea are currently reported to the Centers for Disease Control. Even with these, the actual number of cases is believed to be significantly higher than reported. Estimates for new cases of gonorrhea approach 2 million annually; for syphilis the estimates are approximately 100,000.

It is estimated that as many as 40 million Americans suffer from genital warts, with some 500,000 to 750,000 new cases annually. Herpes is believed to afflict up to 20 million people, with 200,000 to 500,000 new cases each year. And each year there may be more than 5 million new cases of chlamydia, a disease caused by the bacterium *Chlamydia trachomatis* and perhaps the fastest-spreading STD in the country today.

Disease	1970	1974	Reported cases[1] 1980	1984	1988
Syphilis	91,382	83,771	68,832	69,886	40,430
Gonorrhea	600,072	906,121	1,004,029	879,587	699,587

1. Includes both civilian and military cases. **Source:** Centers for Disease Control.

NUMBER OF REPORTED CASES OF COMMON INFECTIOUS DISEASES, 1950–88

Disease	1950	1960	1970	1980	1985	1988
Aseptic meningitis	N.A.	1,593	6,480	8,028	10,619	6,927
Brucellosis (undulant fever)	3,510	751	213	183	153	78
Diphtheria	5,796	918	435	3	3	1
Encephalitis	1,135	2,341	1,950	1,402	1,537	920
Leprosy	44	54	129	223	361	178
Malaria	2,184	72	3,051	2,062	1,049	985
Meningococcal infections	3,788	2,259	2,505	2,840	2,479	2,747
Mumps (thousands)	N.A.	N.A.	105	8.6	3	4.7
Pertussis (whooping cough) (thousands)	120.7	14.8	4.2	1.7	3.6	3.0
Plague[1]	N.A.	2.0	13.0	18.0	17.0	14.0
Poliomyelitis	33,300	3,190	33	9	7	2
Rabies, in animals	7,901	3,567	3,224	6,421	5,565	4,220
Rubella (German measles) (thousands)	N.A.	N.A.	56.6	3.9	0.6	0.2
Tetanus	486	368	148	95	83	49
Trichinosis	327	160	109	131	61	46
Tularemia[1]	927	390	172	234	177	179
Typhoid fever	2,484	816	346	510	402	397
Typhus fever, tick-borne	464	204	380	1,163	714	615
Venereal disease[2]						
Gonorrhea (thousands)	286.7	258.9	600.1	1,004	911	688.1
Syphilis (thousands)	217.6	122	91.4	69	68	40.3

1. Plague: disease caused by the bite of fleas infected with the bacterium *Yersinia pestis.* Tularemia: disease caused by the bacterium *Pasturella tularensis,* transmitted to humans by insects or direct contact with infected animals. 2. Civilian cases only. **Sources:** National Center for Health Statistics, Centers for Disease Control.

DEATHS AND DEATH RATES, 1986 (per 100,000 population)

Age	Total deaths	Rates Both sexes	Rates Male	Rates Female
ALL AGES	2,105,361	873.2	940.7	809.3
under 1 year	38,891	1,032.1	1,152.7	905.8
1–4 years	7,480	52.0	57.9	45.8
5–9 years	4,082	23.6	27.5	19.5
10–14 years	4,706	28.4	36.1	20.3
15–19 years	16,224	87.2	124.3	48.6
20–24 years	23,705	116.1	176.5	55.6
25–29 years	26,474	120.3	177.8	62.6
30–34 years	30,056	144.7	208.7	81.0
35–39 years	33,496	178.9	248.8	110.6
40–44 years	36,897	257.2	339.9	177.7
45–49 years	46,415	389.2	504.8	279.1
50–54 years	68,746	631.3	816.9	457.9
55–59 years	110,323	978.8	1,291.0	695.7
60–64 years	168,706	1,539.1	2,023.8	1,118.0
65–69 years	218,649	2,263.0	2,984.1	1,665.8
70–74 years	266,890	3,479.7	4,661.6	2,601.3
75–79 years	293,520	5,206.1	7,012.9	4,049.9
80–84 years	281,629	8,230.0	10,838.7	6,846.2
85 and older	427,473	15,398.9	18,187.4	14,297.5
Not stated	999[1]			

1. Not distributed among rates. **Source:** National Center for Health Statistics.

CHANGES IN THE LEADING CAUSES OF DEATH, 1900–87

Over the years the leading causes of death have changed significantly. In 1900, infectious diseases took many lives, a fact reflected in the five leading causes of death: (1) pneumonia and influenza, (2) tuberculosis, (3) gastritis, (4) heart disease, and (5) cerebrovascular diseases. Today none of the top five are infectious diseases.

Cause of death	Percent of deaths					
	1900	1920	1940	1960	1980	1987[1]
NATURAL CAUSES						
Ischemic heart disease; other myocardial insufficiencies	7.9%	12.2%	26.5%	28.9%	28.8%	24.1%
Hypertensive heart disease and hypertension	[2]	[2]	[2]	[2]	1.5	1.4
Other heart diseases	[2]	[2]	[2]	7.8	8.2	10.6
Cerebrovascular disease	4.7	6.6	7.4	11.3	8.6	7.0
Diseases of the arteries, arterioles, capillaries	0.3	1.8	1.8	2.1	2.5	2.2
Cancer	3.8	6.6	11.5	15.6	20.9	22.4
Diabetes	0.6	1.2	2.5	1.7	1.8	1.8
Influenza and pneumonia	10.4	11.7	6.5	3.9	2.7	3.2
Chronic liver disease and cirrhosis	1.3	0.8	0.9	1.2	1.5	1.2
Other diseases	65.9	52.3	34.1	20.4	15.3	19.3
Total natural causes	**94.9%**	**93.2%**	**91.2%**	**92.9%**	**91.9%**	**93.2%**
EXTERNAL CAUSES						
Motor vehicle accidents	—	0.8%	2.4%	2.2%	2.7%	2.2%
Other accidents	4.4	4.7	4.4	3.3	2.8	2.3
Suicide	0.6	0.8	1.4	1.1	1.4	1.4
Homicide	0.1	0.5	0.6	0.5	1.2	0.9
Total external causes	5.1%	6.8%	8.8%	7.1%	8.1%	6.8%

1. Preliminary figures.   2. Included with "Other Diseases."   **Source:** National Center for Health Statistics.

Life Expectancy

Life expectancy figures represent the average number of years people are expected to live. Life expectancy has improved steadily over the years, largely owing to a decline in deaths during childhood. The development of drugs to combat infectious diseases, plus improved nutrition and better environmental sanitation have played major roles in combating early deaths.

But significant differences in life expectancy remain, depending on people's sex and race. White females have the highest life expectancy at birth (78.8 years), followed by black females (73.5), white males (72.0), and black males (65.2).

LIFE EXPECTANCY IN 1900 AND TODAY

Since 1900, life expectancy at birth has increased by a hefty 26 years. For people age 20, it has increased by fully 13 years. But at age 65, life expectancy has grown by only five years, and at age 85 by just over one year.

In 1900 only 41 out of 100 people lived to age 65. Today 79 out of 100 live that long—almost double the proportion. That's because in 1900 nearly 1 in 4 people died before the age of 20, compared with only 1 in 50 today. In 1900 about half of 20-year-olds lived to age 65. Today 80 percent of 20-year-olds will live that long.

Source: American Demographics.

LIFE EXPECTANCY AT BIRTH

The difference in life expectancy between the sexes widened from 1920 to 1972. Females born in the year 1920 had an average life expectancy one year longer than males. During the 1970s the difference was 7.7 years. Since 1979 the difference has narrowed. The difference was 7 years in 1985 and 1986.

The difference in life expectancy between white and black populations narrowed from 7.6 years in 1970 (the first year such data became available) to 5.6 years in 1983 and 1984, then increased to 5.8 years in 1985 and 6 years in 1986. Increases in death rates from homicides, killings in police confrontations, auto accidents, AIDS, and tuberculosis had a disproportionate impact on the races in the latest years, affecting blacks more than whites.

	All races		Whites		Blacks	
Year[1]	Male	Female	Male	Female	Male	Female
1920[2]	53.6	54.6	54.4	55.6	45.5	45.2
1930[2]	58.1	61.6	59.7	63.5	47.3	49.2
1940[2]	60.8	65.2	62.1	66.6	51.5	54.9
1950[2]	65.6	71.1	66.5	72.2	59.1	62.9
1960[2]	66.6	73.1	67.4	74.1	61.1	66.3
1970	67.1	74.7	68.0	75.6	60.0	68.3
1980	70.0	77.4	70.7	78.1	63.8	72.5
1986	71.3	78.3	72.0	78.8	65.2	73.5

1. Data prior to 1960 exclude Alaska and Hawaii. Data prior to 1940 is for death-registration states only.   2. Data for blacks include all racial groups other than whites.   **Source:** National Center for Health Statistics.

AVERAGE REMAINING LIFE EXPECTANCY (in years)

Based on individuals' age in 1986, their average remaining life expectancy for years between birth and age 85 can be calculated. For example, white females who were 40 years old in 1985 could expect to live an average of 40.4 more years; black males age 75 in 1986 can expect to live another 9.2 years.

Age in 1986	All races		Whites		Other Races	
	M	F	M	F	M	F
At birth	71.3	78.3	72.0	78.8	67.2	75.1
1	71.1	78.0	71.7	78.4	67.4	75.1
2	70.2	77.0	70.8	77.5	66.4	74.2
3	69.2	76.1	69.8	76.5	65.5	73.2
4	68.2	75.1	68.8	75.5	64.5	72.3
5	67.3	74.1	67.8	74.6	63.6	71.3
6	66.3	73.1	66.9	73.6	62.6	70.3
7	65.3	72.2	65.9	72.6	61.6	69.4
8	64.3	71.2	64.9	71.6	60.6	68.4
9	63.3	70.2	63.9	70.6	59.7	67.4
10	62.4	69.2	62.9	69.6	58.7	66.4
11	61.4	68.2	61.9	68.6	57.7	65.4
12	60.4	67.2	61.0	67.7	56.7	64.4
13	59.4	66.2	60.0	66.7	55.7	63.4
14	58.4	65.2	59.0	65.7	54.8	62.5
15	57.5	64.3	58.0	64.7	53.8	61.5
16	56.5	63.3	57.1	63.7	52.8	60.5
17	55.6	62.3	56.1	62.8	51.9	59.5
18	54.6	61.3	55.2	61.8	51.0	58.6
19	53.7	60.4	54.3	60.8	50.0	57.6
20	52.8	59.4	53.4	59.9	49.1	56.6
21	51.9	58.4	52.5	58.9	48.2	55.7
22	51.0	57.5	51.5	57.9	47.3	54.7
23	50.1	56.5	50.6	56.9	46.4	53.7
24	49.2	55.5	49.7	56.0	45.5	52.8
25	48.2	54.6	48.8	55.0	44.7	51.8
26	47.3	53.6	47.9	54.0	43.8	50.9
27	46.4	52.6	47.0	53.1	42.9	49.9
28	45.5	51.7	46.0	52.1	42.0	49.0
29	44.6	50.7	45.1	51.1	41.1	48.0
30	43.7	49.7	44.2	50.1	40.3	47.1
31	42.7	48.8	43.2	49.2	39.4	46.1
32	41.8	47.8	42.3	48.2	38.5	45.2
33	40.9	46.8	41.4	47.2	37.7	44.3
34	40.0	45.9	40.5	46.3	36.8	43.3
35	39.1	44.9	39.5	45.3	36.0	42.4
36	38.2	44.0	38.6	44.3	35.1	41.5
37	37.3	43.0	37.7	43.4	34.3	40.6
38	36.4	42.1	36.8	42.4	33.5	39.7
39	35.5	41.1	35.9	41.5	32.6	38.7
40	34.5	40.2	34.9	40.5	31.8	37.8
41	33.6	39.2	34.0	39.6	31.0	36.9
42	32.8	38.3	33.1	38.6	30.2	36.0
43	31.9	37.3	32.2	37.7	29.4	35.1
44	31.0	36.4	31.3	36.7	28.6	34.3
45	30.1	35.5	30.4	35.8	27.8	33.4
46	29.2	34.6	29.5	34.9	27.0	32.5
47	28.4	33.7	28.7	33.9	26.2	31.6
48	27.5	32.8	27.8	33.0	25.4	30.8
49	26.6	31.8	26.9	32.1	24.6	29.9
50	25.8	31.0	26.1	31.2	23.9	29.1
51	25.0	30.1	25.2	30.3	23.1	28.2
52	24.1	29.2	24.4	29.4	22.4	27.4

Age in 1986	All races M	F	Whites M	F	Other Races M	F
53	23.3	28.3	23.6	28.6	21.7	26.6
54	22.5	27.5	22.7	27.7	21.0	25.8
55	21.8	26.6	21.9	26.8	20.3	25.0
56	21.0	25.8	21.2	26.0	19.6	24.2
57	20.2	24.9	20.4	25.1	19.0	23.4
58	19.5	24.1	19.6	24.3	18.3	22.7
59	18.8	23.3	18.9	23.4	17.7	21.9
60	18.0	22.5	18.2	22.6	17.0	21.2
61	17.3	21.7	17.5	21.8	16.4	20.5
62	16.7	20.9	16.8	21.0	15.8	19.8
63	16.0	20.1	16.1	20.2	15.3	19.1
64	15.3	19.4	15.4	19.5	14.7	18.4
65	14.7	18.6	14.8	18.7	14.1	17.7
66	14.1	17.9	14.1	18.0	13.6	17.1
67	13.4	17.1	13.5	17.2	13.1	16.4
68	12.8	16.4	12.9	16.5	12.5	15.7
69	12.2	15.7	12.3	15.8	12.0	15.1
70	11.7	15.0	11.7	15.1	11.5	14.5
71	11.1	14.3	11.1	14.4	11.0	13.8
72	10.6	13.7	10.6	13.7	10.5	13.2
73	10.1	13.0	10.1	13.0	10.1	12.7
74	9.6	12.4	9.6	12.4	9.6	12.1
75	9.1	11.7	9.1	11.8	9.2	11.5
76	8.6	11.1	8.6	11.1	8.7	11.0
77	8.2	10.5	8.1	10.5	8.3	10.4
78	7.7	9.9	7.7	9.9	7.9	9.9
79	7.3	9.4	7.3	9.4	7.5	9.4
80	6.9	8.8	6.9	8.8	7.1	8.9
81	6.5	8.3	6.5	8.3	6.8	8.4
82	6.1	7.8	6.1	7.8	6.5	7.9
83	5.8	7.3	5.7	7.3	6.2	7.5
84	5.5	6.8	5.4	6.8	5.9	7.1
85	5.2	6.4	5.1	6.4	5.7	6.8

Source: National Center for Health Statistics.

Infant Mortality

In 1986 there were 38,891 deaths of infants age 1 year or less. The most commonly used index for measuring the risk of dying during the first year of life are infant mortality rates, which are calculated by dividing the number of infant deaths by the number of live births registered for the same period. The 1986 rate of 10.4 infant deaths per 1,000 live births was the lowest ever recorded for the United States.

The rate among white infants is less than half that of black infants. The reasons for this are not understood, although an important factor is believed to be the quality of medical care received by people of different socioeconomic groups. For example, several studies of infant deaths have shown that adequate prenatal care is strongly associated with higher infant birth weight and survival. Many black mothers, who are far more likely to be poor than white mothers, do not have access to proper prenatal care. Poor nutrition, alcohol and drug abuse, and other social factors also play significant roles.

Disproportionate poverty among minority groups is not the whole story, however. Studies have shown that even black infants born to college-educated mothers had nearly twice the mortality rate of comparable white infants.

INFANT MORTALITY RATE
(per 1,000 live births)

	1940	1950	1960	1970	1980	1986	1987[1]
ALL RACES	47.0	29.2	26.0	20.0	12.6	10.4	10.0
White	43.2	26.8	22.9	17.8	11.0	8.9	N.A.
Black	72.9	43.9	44.3	32.6	21.4	18.0	N.A.

1. Provisional figures.   **Source:** National Center for Health Statistics.

COMPARISON OF INFANT MORTALITY RATES IN INDUSTRIALIZED NATIONS

Data from the UN Department of International Economic and Social Affairs indicate that the United States has the highest infant-mortality record among 20 industrialized nations.

Nation	Infant deaths per 1,000 births[1]
United States	10.4
Austria	9.9
Australia	9.8
Belgium	9.7
East Germany	9.2
United Kingdom	9.1
Ireland	8.7
West Germany	8.6
Spain	8.5
Norway	8.5
Denmark	8.2
Canada	7.9
France	7.6
Netherlands	7.6
Hong Kong	7.5
Singapore	7.4
Switzerland	6.8
Finland	6.3
Sweden	5.7
Japan	5.2

1. Babies who die before one year of age. Figures are the last available from each country; they are from 1985, 1986, or 1987.   **Source:** UN Dept. of International Economic and Social Affairs.

Suicide

Each year some 30,000 Americans kill themselves—about one person every 20 minutes. In addition an estimated 400,000 unsuccessful attempts are made. Although most attempts are made by women, most completed suicides are by men.

Particularly troublesome is the suicide rate for people ages 15 to 23, which has almost tripled since 1950. The causes of youth suicide are not yet known, although some evidence suggests that suicide is not as frequently associated with depression in young people as it is in adults. Many young suicide victims had a history of impulsive, aggressive, or antisocial behavior, often complicated by drug abuse. Having a parent who committed suicide also seems to increase a person's vulnerability.

Significant differences in suicide rates exist among the states. For 1986 the highest rates were reported for Nevada (24.1), Montana (21.7), New Mexico (19.4), Arizona (19.3), and Wyoming (19.1). The lowest were for New York (7.6), New Jersey (7.6), Massachusetts (9.2), Connecticut (9.6), and Rhode Island (10.2).

Most Americans who commit suicide shoot themselves, usually with handguns. Other common methods, in decreasing order of frequency, include drug overdose (primarily drugs prescribed by physicians), cutting and stabbing, jumping from high places, inhaling poisonous gas, hanging, and drowning.

Many experts believe that suicide statistics are grimmer than reported. They contend that numerous suicides are categorized as accidents or other deaths to spare families.

NUMBER AND RATE OF SUICIDES IN U.S.

	Total 1986	Rate per 100,000 population 1950	1986
All ages	30,904	11.4	12.8
0–4 years	—	—	—
5–years	255	0.2	0.8
15–24 years	5,120	4.5	13.1
25–34 years	6,711	9.1	15.7
35–44 years	5,013	14.3	15.2
45–54 years	3,736	20.9	16.4
55–64 years	3,782	27.0	17.0
65–74 years	3,414	29.3	19.7
75–84 years	2,283	31.1	25.2
85 and older	578	28.8	20.8

Sources: National Center for Health Statistics; Public Health Service.

ACCIDENTS

Every 10 minutes two people are killed and about 170 are disabled in accidents in the United States. Accidents are the nation's fourth most common cause of death. But for people between the ages of 1 and 44, accidents are the leading cause of death. And among youths ages 15 to 24, accidents claim more lives than all other causes combined. More than three out of four accident victims in this age group are males.

Injuries also cause significantly more problems and deaths among the poor, many of whom belong to minority groups. In 1984, blacks, who constitute 12 percent of the U.S. population, accounted for 15.3 percent of all deaths due to injury. The rate ratios of black-white deaths were highest for homicides (5.2:1) and residential fires (3.2:1).

The costs incurred from accidents top $130 billion annually—for medical care, wage loss, insurance administration, property damage, etc.

Around the House

More than 22 million home injuries occurred in 1986. Over 3 million of these disabled people for one or more days. About 80,000 resulted in permanent impairment.

TYPES OF ACCIDENTAL DEATHS, 1987

Type	Number of deaths	0–4	5–14	15–24	25–44	45–64	65–74	75+
All accidents	**94,000**	**3,700**	**4,200**	**19,300**	**26,900**	**14,300**	**8,700**	**16,900**
Motor vehicle	48,700	1,100	2,400	15,200	16,200	6,800	3,200	3,800
Falls	11,300	100	60	290	1,050	1,400	1,500	6,900
Drowning	5,300	750	550	1,300	1,600	650	280	170
Fires and burns	4,800	859	499	399	1,050	800	600	800
Poisoning by solids and liquids[1]	4,400	50	40	500	2,650	600	260	300
Suffocation	3,200	180	50	70	250	600	550	1,500
Firearms	1,400	30	250	400	450	180	50	40
Poisoning by gases	1,000	40	50	140	350	270	60	90
All other[2]	13,900	600	400	1,100	3,300	3,000	2,200	3,300

1. Deaths from poisons, drugs, medicines, mushrooms, and shellfish. Excludes poisonings from spoiled foods, salmonella, etc., which are classified as disease deaths. 2. Medical complications, air and water transport, machinery, excessive cold, etc. **Source:** National Safety Council, *Accident Facts* (1988 ed.).

ACCIDENTS, 1987

	Deaths	Disabling injuries	Cost
Total[1]	**94,000**	**8,800,000**	**$133.2 billion**
Motor vehicle	48,700	1,800,000	64.7 billion
Home	20,500	3,100,000	16.7 billion
Work	11,100	1,800,000	42.4 billion
Other	18,000	2,300,000	11.5 billion

1. Deaths and injuries for the four separate classes total more than national figures owing to rounding and because some deaths and injuries are included in more than one class. For example, 4,200 work-related deaths involved motor vehicles and are in both the work and motor vehicle totals. **Source:** National Safety Council, *Accident Facts* (1988 ed.).

ESTIMATED NUMBER OF INJURIES BY PRODUCT, 1987

Product	Estimated injuries	Product	Estimated injuries
Chain saws	36,248	Lawn mowers	57,019
Hammers	42,881	Gasoline	15,528
Ladders, stools	121,496	Nails, screws, tacks	231,650
Stairs, steps	801,461	Carpets, rugs	69,019
Sinks, toilets	38,112	Bathtubs, showers	116,454
Bunk beds	31,200	Television sets	30,731
Glass bottles, jars	70,738	Drinking glasses	117,596
Cooking ranges, ovens	38,367	Refrigerators	24,105
Vacuum cleaners	11,701	Irons	14,805
Scissors	19,753	Pens, pencils	28,386
Jewelry	35,002	Paper money, coins	22,936
Footwear	68,615	Pins, needles	24,002
Contact lenses	29,168	Drugs, medications	138,754
Skateboards	91,664	Swings, swing sets	77,458
Sleds	32,183	Baby strollers	11,817
Exercise equipment	63,289	Toys	130,873

Notes: These national estimates are based on injuries treated in hospital emergency rooms participating in the National Electronic Injury Surveillance System. Patients said their injuries were related to the products; this does not necessarily mean the injuries were caused by the products. **Source:** Consumer Product Safety Commission, National Electronic Injury Surveillance System, 1987.

Motor Vehicle Deaths

Overall, death rates (number of deaths per 100,000 population) declined 52 percent between 1912 and 1987, from 82 to 39. The reduction would have been even greater had it not been for a sevenfold increase in the motor-vehicle death rate, from three to 20. Here's how people died in motor vehicle accidents during 1987:

20,500 deaths—collisions between two or more motor vehicles;

14,200 deaths—noncollision accidents;

8,500 deaths—pedestrians struck by motor vehicles;

3,400 deaths—collisions with guardrails and other fixed objects;

1,400 deaths—cyclists who collided with motor vehicles;

600 deaths—collisions with railroad trains;

100 deaths—other types of collisions, usually ones involving animals or animal-drawn vehicles.

NOBEL PRIZES in Physiology or Medicine

1901 Emil A. von Behring (Germany) Marburg Univ. "for his work on serum therapy, especially its application against diphtheria, by which he has opened a new road in the domain of medical science and thereby placed in the hands of the physician a victorious weapon against illness and deaths."

1902 Sir Ronald Ross (Great Britain) University College "for his work on malaria, by which he has shown how it enters the organism and thereby has laid the foundation for successful research on this disease and methods of combating it."

1903 Niels R. Finsen (Denmark) Finsen Medical Light Institute "in recognition of his contribution to the treatment of diseases, especially lupus vulgaris, which concentrated light radiation, whereby he has opened a new avenue for medical science."

ACCIDENTAL DEATHS AND DEATH RATES BY NATION

Internationally, accidental deaths are classified on the basis of a World Health Organization standard. However, differences in reporting among nations affect comparisons.

Nation	Year reported	No. of deaths	Rate per 100,000 pop.
Hong Kong	1986	740	13.4
Syrian Arab Republic	1985	1,388	13.5
Singapore	1986	488	18.9
Japan	1986	28,610	23.7
England, Wales	1985	12,482	25.0
Netherlands	1986	3,730	25.6
Iceland	1985	64	26.5
Chile	1985	3,314	27.5
Sweden	1986	2,828	33.8
Kuwait	1986	615	34.3
West Germany	1986	21,078	34.5
Israel	1985	1,479	34.9
Australia	1985	5,570	35.3
Canada	1985	9,245	36.5
Uruguay	1985	1,154	38.3
United States	1985	93,457	39.1
Bulgaria	1986	2,068	40.4
Greece	1985	4,310	43.4
New Zealand	1985	1,483	45.2
Portugal	1986	4,923	48.2
Ecuador	1986	4,712	48.8
Poland	1986	18,695	49.9
Switzerland	1986	3,308	50.9
Austria	1986	3,892	51.4
France	1985	34,399	62.4
Hungary	1986	7,823	73.6

Source: World Health Organization, except for U.S.; U.S. deaths: National Center for Health Statistics; U.S. rate: National Safety Council.

1904 Ivan P. Pavlov (Russia) Military Medical Academy "in recognition of his work on the physiology of digestion, through which knowledge on vital aspects of the subject has been transformed and enlarged."

1905 Robert Koch (Germany) Institute for Infectious Diseases "for his investigations and discoveries in relation to tuberculosis."

1906 Camillo Golgi (Italy) Pavia Univ., and **Santiago Ramon Y Cajal** (Spain) Madrid Univ. "in recognition of their work on the structure of the nervous system."

1907 Charles L.A. Laveran (France) Institut Pasteur "in recognition of his work on the role played by protozoa in causing diseases."

1908 Il'ja I. Mečnikov (Russia) Institut Pasteur (Paris), and **Paul Ehrlich** (Germany) Goettingen Univ. and Royal Institute for Experimental Therapy "in recognition of their work on immunity."

1909 Emil T. Kocher (Switzerland) Berne Univ. "for his work on the physiology, pathology, and surgery of the thyroid gland."

1910 Albrecht Kossel (Germany) Heidelberg Univ. "in recognition of the contributions to our knowledge of cell chemistry made through his work on proteins, including the nucleic substances."

1911 **Allvar Gullstrand** (Sweden) Uppsala Univ. "for his work on the dioptrics of the eye."

1912 **Alexis Carrel** (France) Rockefeller Institute for Medical Research (New York) "in recognition of his work on vascular suture and the transplantation of blood-vessels and organs."

1913 **Charles R. Richet** (France) Sorbonne Univ. "in recognition of his work on anaphylaxis."

1914 **Robert Bárány** (Austria) Vienna Univ. "for his work on the physiology and patholcgy of the vestibular apparatus."

1915 No award.

1916 No award.

1917 No award.

1918 No award.

1919 **Jules Bordet** (Belgium) Brussels Univ. "for his discoveries relating to immunity."

1920 **Schack A.S. Krough** (Denmark) Copenhagen Univ. "for his discovery of the capillary motor regulating mechanism."

1921 No award.

1922 **Sir Archibald V. Hill** (Great Britain) London Univ. "for his discovery relating to the production of heat in the muscle"; **Otto F. Meyerhof** (Germany) Kiel Univ. "for his discovery of the fixed relationship between the consumption of oxygen and the metabolism of lactic acid in the muscle."

1923 **Sir Frederick B. Banting** (Canada) Toronto Univ., and **John J.R. Macleod** (Canada) Toronto Univ. "for the discovery of insulin."

1924 **Willem Einthoven** (Netherlands) Leyden Univ. "for his discovery of the mechanism of the electrocardiogram."

1925 No award.

1926 **Johannes A.G. Fibiger** (Denmark) Copenhagen Univ. "for his discovery of the Spiroptera carcinoma."

1927 **Julius Wagner-Jauregg** (Austria) Vienna Univ. "for his discovery of the therapeutic value of malaria inoculation in the treatment of dementia paralytica."

1928 **Charles J.H. Nicolle** (France) Institut Pasteur "for his work on typhus."

1929 **Christiaan Eijkman** (Netherlands) Utrecht Univ."for his discovery of the antineuritic vitamin"; **Sir Frederick G. Hopkins** (Great Britain) Cambridge Univ. "for his discovery of the growth-stimulating vitamins."

1930 **Karl Landsteiner** (Austria) Rockefeller Inst. for Medical Research (New York) "for his discovery of human blood groups."

1931 **Otto H. Warburg** (Germany) Kaiser-Wilhelm-Institut (now Max-Planck-Institut) "for his discovery of the nature and mode of action of the respiratory enzyme."

1932 **Sir Charles S. Sherrington** (Great Britain) Oxford Univ., and **Lord Edgar D. Adrian** (Great Britain) Cambridge Univ. "for their discoveries regarding the functions of neurons."

1933 **Thomas H. Morgan** (U.S.) California Institute of Technology "for his discoveries concerning the role played by the chromosome in heredity."

1934 **George H. Whipple** (U.S.) Rochester Univ., and **George R. Minot** (U.S.) Harvard Univ., and **William P. Murphy** (U.S.) Harvard Univ. "for their discoveries concerning liver therapy in cases of anaemia."

1935 **Hans Spemann** (Germany) Univ. of Freiburg im Breisgau "for his discovery of the organizer effect in embryonic development."

1936 **Sir Henry H. Dale** (Great Britain) National Institute for Medical Research, and **Otto Loewi** (Austria) Graz Univ. "for their discoveries relating to chemical transmission of nerve impulses."

1937 **Albert Szent-Györgyi von Nagyrapolt** (Hungary) Szeged Univ. "for his discoveries in connection with the biological combustion processes, with special reference to vitamin C and the catalysis of fumaric acid."

1938 **Corneille J.F. Heymans** (Belgium) Ghent Univ. "for the discovery of the role played by the sinus and aortic mechanisms in the regulation of respiration."

1939 **Gerhard Domagk** (Germany) Munster Univ. "for the discovery of the antibacterial effects of prontosil."

1940 No award.

1941 No award.

1942 No award.

1943 **Henrik C.P. Dam** (Denmark) Polytechnic Institute "for his discovery of vitamin K"; **Edward A. Doisy** (U.S.) St. Louis Univ. "for his discovery of the chemical nature of vitamin K."

1944 **Joseph Erlanger** (U.S.) Washington Univ., and **Herbert S. Gasser** (U.S.) Rockefeller Institute for Medical Research "for their discoveries relating to the highly differentiated functions of single nerve fibres."

1945 **Sir Alexander Fleming** (Great Britain) London Univ., **Sir Ernst B. Chain** (Great Britain) Oxford Univ., and **Lord Howard W. Florey** (Great Britain) Oxford Univ. "for the discovery of penicillin and its curative effect in various infectious diseases."

1946 **Hermann J. Muller** (U.S.) Indiana Univ. "for the discovery of the production of mutations by means of X-ray irradiation."

1947 **Carl F. Cori** (U.S.) Washington Univ., and his wife **Gerty T. Cori** (U.S.) Washington Univ. "for their discovery of the course of the catalytic conversion of glycogen"; **Bernardo A. Houssay** (Argentina) Institute for Biology and Experimental Medicine "for his discovery of the part played by the hormone of the anterior pituitary lobe in the metabolism of sugar."

1948 **Paul H. Müller** (Switzerland) Laboratory of the J.R. Geigy Dye-Factory Co. "for his discovery of the high efficiency of DDT as a contact poison against several arthropods."

1949 **Walter R. Hess** (Switzerland) Zurich Univ. "for his discovery of the functional organization of the interbrain as a co-ordinator of the activities of the internal organs; and **Antonio Caetano de Abreu F.E. Moniz** (Portugal) Univ. of Lisbon "for his discovery of the therapeutic value of leucotomy in certain psychoses."

1950 **Edward C. Kendall** (U.S.) Mayo Clinic, **Tadeus Reichstein** (Switzerland) Basel Univ.; and **Philip S. Hench** (U.S.) Mayo Clinic "for their discoveries relating to the hormones of the adrenal cortex, their structure, and biological effects."

1951 **Max Theiler** (Union of South Africa) Laboratories Division of Medicine and Public Health, Rockefeller Foundation (New York) "for his discoveries concerning yellow fever and how to combat it."

1952 **Selman A. Waksman** (U.S.) Rutgers Univ. "for his discovery of streptomycin, the first antibiotic effective against tuberculosis."

1953 **Sir Hans A. Krebs** (Great Britain) Sheffield Univ. "for his discovery of the citric acid cycle"; **Fritz A. Lipmann** (U.S.) Harvard Medical School and Massachusetts General Hospital "for his discovery of co-enzyme A and its importance for intermediary metabolism."

1954 **John F. Enders** (U.S.) Harvard Medical School; Research Division of Infectious Diseases, Children's Medical Center; **Thomas H. Weller** (U.S.) Research Division of Infectious Diseases, Children's Medical Center; and **Frederick C. Robbins** (U.S.) Western Reserve Univ. "for their discovery of the ability of poliomyelitis viruses to grow in cultures of various types of tissue."

1955 **Axel H.T. Theorell** (Sweden) Nobel Medical Institute "for his discoveries concerning the nature and mode of action of oxidation enzymes."

1956 **Andre F. Cournand** (U.S.) Cardio-Pulmonary Laboratory, Columbia Univ. Division, Bellevue Hospital; **Werner Forssmann** (Germany) Mainz Univ. and Bad Kreuznach; and **Dickinson W. Richards** (U.S.) Columbia Univ. "for their discoveries concerning heart catheterization and pathological changes in the circulatory system."

1957 **Daniel Bovet** (Italy) Chief Institute of Public Health "for his discoveries relating to synthetic compounds that inhibit the action of certain body substances, and especially their action on the vascular system and the skeletal muscles."

1958 **George W. Beadle** (U.S.) California Institute of Technology, and **Edward L. Tatum** (U.S.) Rockefeller Institute for Medical Research "for their discovery that genes act by regulating definite chemical events"; **Joshua Lederberg**

(U.S.) Wisconsin Univ. "for his discoveries concerning genetic recombination and the organization of the genetic material of bacteria."

1959 Severo Ochoa (U.S.) New York Univ., College of Medicine, and **Arthur Kornberg** (U.S.) Stanford Univ. "for their discovery of the mechanisms in the biological synthesis of ribonucleic acid and deoxyribonucleic acid."

1960 Sir Frank M. Burnet (Australia) Water and Eliza Hall Institute for Medical Research, and **Sir Peter B. Medawar** (Great Britain) University College "for discovery of acquired immunological tolerance."

1961 Georg von Békésy (U.S.) Harvard Univ. "for his discoveries of the physical mechanism of stimulation within the cochlea."

1962 Francis H.C. Crick (Great Britain) Institute of Molecular Biology, **James D. Watson** (U.S.) Harvard Univ., and **Maurice H.F. Wilkins** (Great Britain) University of London "for their discoveries concerning the molecular structure of nuclear acids and its significance for information transfer in living material."

1963 Sir John C. Eccles (Australia) Australian National Univ., **Sir Alan L. Hodgkin** (Great Britain) Cambridge Univ., and **Sir Andrew F. Huxley** (Great Britain) London Univ. "for their discoveries concerning the ionic mechanisms involved in excitation and inhibition in the peripheral and central portions of the nerve cell membrane."

1964 Konrad Bloch (U.S.) Harvard Univ., and **Feodor Lynen** (Germany) Max-Planck-Institut fur Zellchemie "for their discoveries concerning the mechanism and regulation of the cholesterol and fatty acid metabolism."

1965 François Jacob (France) Institut Pasteur, **André Lwoff** (France) Institut Pasteur; and **Jacques Monod** (France) Institut Pasteur "for their discoveries concerning genetic control of enzyme and virus synthesis."

1966 Peyton Rous (U.S.) Rockefeller Univ. "for his discovery of tumor-inducing viruses"; **Charles B. Huggins** (U.S.) Ben May Laboratory for Cancer Research, Univ. of Chicago "for his discoveries concerning hormonal treatment of prostatic cancer."

1967 Ragnar Granit (Sweden) Karolinska Institutet, **Haldan K. Hartline** (U.S.) The Rockefeller Univ. and **George Wald** (U.S.) Harvard Univ. "for their discoveries concerning the primary physiological and chemical visual processes in the eye."

1968 Robert W. Holley (U.S.) Cornell Univ., **Har G. Khorana** (U.S.) Univ. of Wisconsin, and **Marshall W. Nirenberg** (U.S.) National Institutes of Health "for their interpretation of the genetic code and its functions in protein synthesis."

1969 Max Delbrück (U.S.) California Institute of Technology, **Alfred D.**

Hershey (U.S.) Carnegie Institution of Washington, and **Salvador Luria** (U.S.) M.I.T. "for their discoveries concerning the replication mechanism and the genetic structure of viruses."

1970 Sir Bernard Katz (Great Britain) University College, **Ulf von Euler** (Sweden) Karolinska Institutet, and **Julius Axelrod** (U.S.) National Institutes of Health "for their discoveries concerning the humoral transmittors in the nerve terminals and the mechanism for their storage, release, and inactivation."

1971 Earl W. Sutherland, Jr. (U.S.) Vanderbilt Univ. "for his discoveries concerning the mechanisms of the action of hormones."

1972 Gerald M. Edelman (U.S.) Rockefeller Univ., and **Rodney R. Porter** (Great Britain) University of Oxford "for their discoveries concerning the chemical structure of antibodies."

1973 Karl von Frisch (W. Germany) Zoologisches Institut der Universitat Munchen; **Konrad Lorenz** (Austria) Osterreichische Akademie der Wissenschaften, Institut fur vergleichende Verhaltensforschung; and **Nikolaas Tinbergen** (Great Britain) Dept. of Zoology, University Museum "for their discoveries concerning organization and elicitation of individual and social behavior patterns."

1974 Albert Claude (Belgium) Université Catholique de Louvain, **Christian de Duve** (Belgium) The Rockefeller Univ. (New York), and **George E. Palade** (U.S.) Yale Univ. School of Medicine "for their discoveries concerning the structural and functional organization of the cell."

1975 David Baltimore (U.S.) M.I.T., and **Renato Dulbecco** (U.S.) Imperial Cancer Research Fund Laboratory (London), and **Howard M. Temin** (U.S.) Univ. of Wisconsin "for their discoveries concerning the interaction between tumour viruses and the genetic material of the cell."

1976 Baruch S. Blumberg (U.S.) The Institute for Cancer Research, and **D. Carleton Gajdusek** (U.S.) National Institutes of Health "for their discoveries concerning new mechanisms for the origin and dissemination of infectious diseases."

1977 Roger Guillemin (U.S.) The Salk Institute, and **Andrew V. Schally** (U.S.) Veterans Administration Hospital, New Orleans "for their discoveries concerning the peptide hormone production of the brain"; **Rosalyn Yalow** (U.S.) Veterans Administration Hospital, Bronx "for the development of radioimmunoassays of peptide hormones."

1978 Werner Arber (Switzerland) Biozentrum der Universitat, **Daniel Nathans** (U.S.) Johns Hopkins Univ. School of Medicine, and **Hamilton O. Smith** (U.S.) Johns Hopkins Univ. School of Medicine "for the discovery of restriction enzymes

and their application to problems of molecular genetics."

1979 Allan M. Cormack (U.S.) Tufts Univ., and **Sir Godfrey N. Hounsfield** (Great Britain) "for the development of computer assisted tomography."

1980 Baruj Benacerraf (U.S.) Harvard Medical School; **Jean Dausset** (France) Université de Paris, Laboratoire Immuno-Hemetologie; and **George D. Snell** (U.S.) Jackson Laboratory "for their discoveries concerning genetically determined structures on the cell surface that regulate immunological reactions."

1981 Roger W. Sperry (U.S.) California Institute of Technology "for his discoveries concerning the functional specialization of the cerebral hemispheres; **David H. Hubel** (U.S.) Harvard Medical School, and **Torsten N. Wiesel** (Sweden) Harvard Medical School "for their discoveries concerning information processing in the visual system."

1982 Sune K. Bergström (Sweden) Karolinska Institutet, **Bengt I. Samuelsson** (Sweden) Karolinska Institute, and **Sir John R. Vane** (Great Britain) The Wellcome Research Laboratories "for their discoveries concerning prostaglandins and related biologically active substances."

1983 Barbara McClintock (U.S.) Cold Spring Harbor Laboratory "for her discovery of mobile genetic elements."

1984 Niels K. Jerne (Denmark) Basel Institute for Immunology (Basel, Switzerland), **Georges J.F. Köhler** (W. Germany) Basel Institute for Immunology, and **César Milstein** (Great Britain and Argentina) Medical Research Council Laboratory of Molecular Biology (Cambridge) "for theories concerning the specificity in development and control of the immune system and the discovery of the principle for production of monoclonal antibodies."

1985 Michael S. Brown (U.S.) Univ. of Texas Health Science Center at Dallas, and **Joseph L. Goldstein** (U.S.) Univ. of Texas Health Science Center at Dallas "for their discoveries concerning the regulation of cholesterol metabolism."

1986 Stanley Cohen (U.S.) Vanderbilt Univ. School of Medicine, and **Rita Levi-Montalcini** (Italy and U.S.) Institute of Cell Biology of the C.N.R. (Rome) "for their discoveries of growth factors."

1987 Susumu Tonegawa (U.S.) M.I.T. "for discovery of the genetic principle for generation of antibody diversity."

1988 Sir James W. Black (United Kingdom) King's College Hospital Medical School, **Gertrude B. Elion** (U.S.) Wellcome Research Laboratories, and **George H. Hitchings** (U.S.) Wellcome Research Laboratories "for their discoveries of Important Principles for Drug Treatment."

Sources: *Nobel Foundation Directory* (1987–88); Mission of Sweden.

THE AMERICAN PEOPLE TODAY

POPULATION GROWTH, BY REGION, 1790–2000
(numbers in thousands)

	Northeast	Midwest[1]	South[2]	West
1790	1,968	N.A.	1,961	N.A.
1800	2,636	51	2,622	N.A.
1810	3,487	292	3,461	N.A.
1820	4,360	859	4,419	N.A.
1830	5,542	1,610	5,708	N.A.
1840	6,761	3,352	6,951	N.A.
1850	8,627	5,404	8,983	179
1860	10,594	9,097	11,133	619
1870	12,299	12,981	12,288	991
1880	14,507	17,364	16,517	1,801
1890	17,407	22,410	20,028	3,134
1900	21,047	26,333	24,524	4,309
1910	25,869	29,889	29,389	7,082
1920	29,662	34,020	33,126	9,214
1930	34,427	38,594	37,858	12,324
1940	35,977	40,143	41,666	14,379
1950	39,478	44,461	47,197	20,190
1960	44,678	51,619	54,973	28,053
1970	49,041	56,572	62,795	34,804
1980[3]	49,100	58,900	75,400	43,200
1987[3]	50,300	59,500	83,900	49,700
1990[4]	50,600	59,800	87,300	52,300
2000[4]	51,800	59,600	96,900	59,400

1. Called North Central prior to 1980.   2. Includes black slave population through 1860.   3. Figures rounded.   4. Projections.
Sources: U.S. Bureau of the Census, *The Statistical History of the U.S.* (1976) and *Statistical Abstract of the United States 1989* (1989).

U.S. POPULATION

STATE	1790	1800	1810	1820
TOTAL U.S. POP.	3,929,214	5,308,483	7,239,881	9,638,453
Alabama	–	1,250	9,046	127,901
Alaska	–	–	–	–
Arizona	–	–	–	–
Arkansas	–	–	1,062	14,273
California	–	–	–	–
Colorado	–	–	–	–
Connecticut	237,946	251,002	261,942	275,248
Delaware	59,096	64,273	72,674	72,749
District of Columbia	–	8,144	15,471	23,336
Florida	–	–	–	–
Georgia	82,548	162,686	252,433	340,989
Hawaii	–	–	–	–
Idaho	–	–	–	–
Illinois	–	–	12,282	55,211
Indiana	–	5,641	24,520	147,178
Iowa	–	–	–	–
Kansas	–	–	–	–
Kentucky	73,677	220,955	406,511	564,317
Louisiana	–	–	76,556	153,407
Maine	96,540	151,719	228,705	298,335
Maryland	319,728	341,548	380,546	407,350
Massachusetts	378,787	422,845	472,040	523,287
Michigan	–	–	4,762	8,896
Minnesota	–	–	–	–
Mississippi	–	7,600	31,306	75,448
Missouri	–	–	19,783	66,586
Montana	–	–	–	–
Nebraska	–	–	–	–
Nevada	–	–	–	–
New Hampshire	141,885	183,858	214,460	244,161
New Jersey	184,139	211,149	245,562	277,575
New Mexico	–	–	–	–
New York	340,120	589,051	959,049	1,372,812
North Carolina	393,751	478,103	555,500	638,829
North Dakota	–	–	–	–
Ohio	–	45,365	230,760	581,434
Oklahoma	–	–	–	–
Oregon	–	–	–	–
Pennsylvania	434,373	602,365	810,091	1,049,458
Rhode Island	68,825	69,122	76,931	83,059
South Carolina	249,073	345,591	415,115	502,741
South Dakota	–	–	–	–
Tennessee	35,691	105,602	261,727	422,832
Texas	–	–	–	–
Utah	–	–	–	–
Vermont	85,425	154,465	217,895	235,981
Virginia[3]	747,610	880,200	974,600	1,065,366
Washington	–	–	–	–
West Virginia	–	–	–	–
Wisconsin	–	–	–	–
Wyoming	–	–	–	–

1. Excludes military and overseas population. Populations of regions, areas, and territories prior to statehood are wherever possible that of 1980 area of state.

The United States is the fourth most populous nation in the world, ranking behind only China, India, and the Soviet Union. According to the U.S. Census Bureau, on May 1, 1989, the resident population of the United States was 247,818,000, more than three times the 1900 figure of 76 million, about double what it was in 1930, and almost 100 million more than the 1950 total. The Census Bureau predicts that this kind of rapid growth, based mainly as it was on high birth rates and, during the first two decades of the century, extraordinarily high immigration rates, cannot occur during the next century. In fact the underlying shifts in social behavior that will cause dramatic changes in the nature of the population have been in place for 20 years or so, just at the end of a most prolific period of population expansion.

Between 1946 and 1964, just over 75 million babies were born in America, a demographic achievement so noteworthy that those born during this time have their own collective designation, the "Baby Boom generation." During these years the crude birth rate soared to as high as 24 live births (per 1,000 population) in some years, compared to 20 or so in the years before the war; fertility rates, too, reached exceptional levels, ranging from 101 to 121 (per 1,000 women ages 15–44), as compared with an average of about 75 in earlier years. As a result the population grew at an annual rate of between 1.4% and 1.8%.

Quite remarkably, however, this population burst came to a sudden unexpected halt, so sudden that by 1968 the population growth had sunk to 1%, the birth rate to under 18, and fertility rates to about 85, levels that have sunk much farther since. As a result projected population growth over the next few decades is extremely low: 7.1% for the 1990s and 5.3% for the first decade of the new century. By way of comparison, between 1950 and 1960, the population grew 19%.

Of course it is that period of unparalleled growth that has affected so many aspects of daily life and will continue to do so for another 50 years. Demographers sometimes refer to the Baby Boomers, somewhat inelegantly perhaps, as the "Pig in the Python" in order to explain how this group has continued to distort the normal contours of the general body of the population. During the fifties their numbers required great capital outlays for new schools and later for expanding colleges and universities. In the seventies they jammed the labor market, causing higher unemployment rates, but helped the economy by increasing consumption and expanding the housing market. After the turn of the century, the Baby Boom generation will begin to enter the retirement years, and even here they will cause a strain on existing structures. What will happen is that the ratio of people working—those born during the 1970s and 1980s, now being called the Baby Bust—to those retired will shrink dramatically. Today that ratio is 5–1, but by 2020 or so, it will be 2.5–1.

If the Baby Boomers and those in much smaller numbers who followed them represent, demographically speaking, the most significant group among the American people, it is the immigrant group that has caused the most interest in recent years. Because their numbers have increased greatly since the 1960s, many see them as the key to preventing future population decline, as current U.S. birth and fertility rates stabilize at a very low level. In 1987 immigration accounted for 26% of the nation's growth. Over the last 20 years, the origins of most immigrants have been Asian and Latin American nations, so the ethnic composition of the American people is clearly going to change and become even more diverse than today.

In the pages that follow, all of these matters are taken up—fertility, race, immigration—to create a statistical portrait of the population both past and present, with a glimpse at the future as well.

BY STATE, 1790–1980

1830	1840	1850	1860	1870	1880	1890	1900	1910	1920	1930	1940	1950	1960	1970	1980[2]
12,860,702	17,063,353	23,191,876	31,443,321	38,558,371	50,189,209	62,979,766	76,212,168	92,228,496	106,021,537	123,202,624	132,164,569	151,325,798	179,323,175	203,302,031	226,542,203
309,527	590,756	771,623	964,201	996,992	1,262,505	1,513,401	1,828,697	2,138,093	2,348,174	2,646,248	2,832,961	3,061,743	3,266,740	3,444,354	3,894,025
—	—	—	—	—	33,426	32,052	63,592	64,356	55,036	59,278	72,524	128,643	226,167	302,583	401,851
—	—	—	—	9,658	40,440	88,243	122,931	204,354	334,162	435,573	499,261	749,587	1,302,161	1,775,399	2,716,546
30,388	97,574	209,897	435,450	484,471	802,525	1,128,211	1,311,564	1,574,449	1,752,204	1,854,482	1,949,387	1,909,511	1,786,272	1,923,322	2,286,357
—	—	92,597	379,994	560,247	864,694	1,213,396	1,485,053	2,377,549	3,426,861	5,677,251	6,907,387	10,586,223	15,717,204	19,971,069	23,667,764
—	—	—	34,277	39,864	194,327	413,249	539,700	799,024	939,629	1,035,791	1,123,296	1,325,089	1,753,947	2,209,596	2,889,735
297,675	309,978	370,792	460,147	537,454	622,700	746,258	908,420	1,114,756	1,380,631	1,606,903	1,709,242	2,007,280	2,535,234	3,032,217	3,107,564
76,748	78,085	91,532	112,216	125,015	146,608	168,493	184,735	202,322	223,003	238,380	266,505	318,085	446,292	548,104	594,338
30,261	33,745	51,687	75,080	131,700	177,624	230,392	278,718	331,069	437,571	486,869	663,091	802,178	763,956	756,668	638,432
34,730	54,477	87,445	140,424	187,748	269,493	391,422	528,542	752,619	968,470	1,468,211	1,897,414	2,771,305	4,951,560	6,791,418	9,746,961
516,823	691,392	906,185	1,057,286	1,184,109	1,542,180	1,837,353	2,216,331	2,609,121	2,895,832	2,908,506	3,123,723	3,444,578	3,943,116	4,587,930	5,462,982
—	—	—	—	—	—	—	154,001	191,874	255,881	368,300	422,770	499,794	632,772	769,913	964,691
—	—	—	—	14,999	32,610	88,548	161,772	325,594	431,866	445,032	524,873	588,637	667,191	713,015	944,127
157,445	476,183	851,470	1,711,951	2,539,891	3,077,871	3,826,352	4,821,550	5,638,591	6,485,280	7,630,654	7,897,241	8,712,176	10,081,158	11,110,285	11,427,409
343,031	685,866	988,416	1,350,428	1,680,637	1,978,301	2,192,404	2,516,462	2,700,876	2,930,390	3,238,503	3,427,796	3,934,224	4,662,498	5,195,392	5,490,214
—	43,112	192,214	674,913	1,194,020	1,624,615	1,912,297	2,231,853	2,224,771	2,404,021	2,470,939	2,538,268	2,621,073	2,757,537	2,825,368	2,913,808
—	—	—	107,206	364,399	996,096	1,428,108	1,470,495	1,690,949	1,769,257	1,880,999	1,801,028	1,905,299	2,178,611	2,249,071	2,364,236
687,917	779,828	982,405	1,155,684	1,321,011	1,648,690	1,858,635	2,147,174	2,289,905	2,416,630	2,614,589	2,845,627	2,944,806	3,038,156	3,220,711	3,660,324
215,739	352,411	517,762	708,002	726,915	939,946	1,118,588	1,381,625	1,656,388	1,798,509	2,101,593	2,363,880	2,683,516	3,257,022	3,644,637	4,206,116
399,455	501,793	583,169	628,279	626,915	648,936	661,086	694,466	742,371	768,014	797,423	847,226	913,774	969,265	993,722	1,125,043
447,040	470,019	583,034	687,049	780,894	934,943	1,042,390	1,188,044	1,295,346	1,449,661	1,631,526	1,821,244	2,343,001	3,100,689	3,923,897	4,216,933
610,408	737,699	994,514	1,231,066	1,457,351	1,783,085	2,238,947	2,805,346	3,366,416	3,852,356	4,249,614	4,316,721	4,690,514	5,148,578	5,689,170	5,737,093
31,369	212,267	397,654	749,113	1,184,059	1,636,937	2,093,890	2,420,982	2,810,173	3,668,412	4,842,325	5,256,106	6,371,766	7,823,194	8,881,826	9,262,044
—	—	6,077	172,023	439,706	780,773	1,310,283	1,751,394	2,075,708	2,387,125	2,563,953	2,792,300	2,982,483	3,413,864	3,806,103	4,075,970
136,621	375,651	606,526	791,305	827,922	1,131,597	1,289,600	1,551,270	1,797,114	1,790,618	2,009,821	2,183,796	2,178,914	2,178,141	2,216,994	2,520,770
140,455	383,702	682,044	1,182,012	1,721,295	2,168,380	2,679,185	3,106,665	3,293,335	3,404,055	3,629,367	3,784,664	3,954,653	4,319,813	4,677,623	4,916,762
—	—	—	—	20,595	39,159	142,924	243,329	376,053	548,889	537,606	559,456	591,024	674,767	694,409	786,690
—	—	—	28,841	122,993	452,402	1,062,656	1,066,300	1,192,214	1,296,372	1,377,963	1,315,834	1,325,510	1,411,330	1,485,333	1,569,825
—	—	—	6,857	42,491	62,266	47,355	42,335	81,875	77,407	91,058	110,247	160,083	285,278	488,738	800,508
269,328	284,574	317,976	326,073	318,300	346,991	376,530	411,588	430,572	443,083	465,293	491,524	533,242	606,921	737,681	920,610
320,823	373,306	489,555	672,035	906,096	1,131,116	1,444,933	1,883,669	2,537,167	3,155,900	4,041,334	4,160,165	4,835,329	6,066,782	7,171,112	7,365,011
—	—	61,547	93,516	91,874	119,565	160,282	195,310	327,301	360,350	423,317	531,818	681,187	951,023	1,017,055	1,303,302
1,918,608	2,428,921	3,097,394	3,880,735	4,382,759	5,082,871	6,003,174	7,268,894	9,113,614	10,385,227	12,588,066	13,479,142	14,830,192	16,782,304	18,241,391	17,558,165
737,987	753,419	869,039	992,622	1,071,361	1,399,750	1,617,949	1,893,810	2,206,287	2,559,123	3,170,276	3,571,623	4,061,929	4,556,155	5,084,411	5,880,095
—	—	—	—	2,405[1]	36,909	190,983	319,146	577,056	646,872	680,845	641,935	619,636	632,446	617,792	652,717
937,903	1,519,467	1,980,329	2,339,511	2,665,260	3,198,062	3,672,329	4,157,545	4,767,121	5,759,394	6,646,697	6,907,612	7,946,627	9,706,397	10,657,423	10,797,603
—	—	—	—	—	—	258,657	790,371	1,657,155	2,028,283	2,396,040	2,336,434	2,233,351	2,328,284	2,559,463	3,025,487
—	—	12,093	52,465	90,923	174,768	317,704	413,536	672,765	783,389	953,786	1,089,684	1,521,341	1,768,687	2,091,533	2,633,156
1,348,233	1,724,033	2,311,786	2,906,215	3,521,951	4,282,891	5,258,113	6,302,115	7,665,111	8,720,017	9,631,350	9,900,180	10,498,012	11,319,366	11,800,766	11,864,720
97,199	108,830	147,545	174,620	217,353	276,531	345,506	428,556	542,610	604,397	687,497	713,346	791,896	859,488	949,723	947,154
581,185	594,398	668,507	703,708	705,606	995,577	1,151,149	1,340,316	1,515,400	1,683,724	1,738,765	1,899,804	2,117,027	2,382,594	2,590,713	3,120,729
—	—	—	4,837	11,776[1]	98,268	348,600	401,570	583,888	636,547	692,849	642,961	652,740	680,514	666,257	690,768
681,904	829,210	1,002,717	1,109,801	1,258,520	1,542,359	1,767,518	2,020,616	2,184,789	2,337,885	2,616,556	2,915,841	3,291,718	3,567,089	3,926,018	4,591,023
—	—	212,592	604,215	818,579	1,591,749	2,235,527	3,048,710	3,896,542	4,663,228	5,824,715	6,414,824	7,711,194	9,579,677	11,198,655	14,225,513
—	—	11,380	40,273	86,786	143,963	210,779	276,749	373,351	449,396	507,847	550,310	688,862	890,627	1,059,273	1,461,037
280,652	291,948	314,120	315,098	330,551	332,286	332,422	343,641	355,956	352,428	359,611	359,231	377,747	389,881	444,732	511,456
1,211,405	1,239,797	1,421,661	1,596,318	1,225,163	1,512,565	1,655,980	1,854,184	2,061,612	2,309,187	2,421,851	2,677,773	3,318,680	3,966,949	4,651,448	5,346,797
—	—	1,201	11,594	23,955	75,116	357,232	518,103	1,141,990	1,356,621	1,563,396	1,736,191	2,378,963	2,853,214	3,413,244	4,132,353
—	—	—	—	442,014	618,457	762,794	958,800	1,221,119	1,463,701	1,729,205	1,901,974	2,005,552	1,860,421	1,744,237	1,950,186
—	30,945	305,391	775,881	1,054,670	1,315,497	1,693,330	2,069,042	2,333,860	2,632,067	2,939,006	3,137,587	3,434,575	3,951,777	4,417,821	4,705,642
—	—	—	—	9,118	20,789	62,555	92,531	145,965	194,402	225,565	250,742	290,529	330,066	332,416	469,557

2. 1980 figures are revised estimates issued by the Census Bureau in 1987. 3. The figures for Virginia through 1860 are from the 1960 census; in the 1980 summary, the Census Bureau gave separate figures for West Virginia between 1790 and 1860, even though it did not become a state until 1863. Since the result diminishes Virginia's population by over 300,000 in 1850 and 1860, a crucial period, we decided to keep the earlier breakdowns.
Source: U.S. Bureau of the Census, *1980 Census of Population: U.S. Summary, Number of Inhabitants* (1981).

U.S. POPULATION, POPULATION DENSITY, AND AREA OF RESIDENCE, 1790–1985

Year	Total population	% increase	Pop. per sq. mi.	% urban	% rural
1790	3,929,214	N.A.	4.5	5.1%	94.9%
1800	5,308,483	35.1%	6.1	6.1	93.9
1810	7,239,881	36.4	4.3	7.3	92.7
1820	9,638,453	33.1	5.5	7.2	92.8
1830	12,866,020	33.5	7.4	8.8	91.2
1840	17,069,453	32.7	9.8	10.8	89.2
1850	23,191,876	35.9	7.9	15.3	84.7
1860	31,443,321	35.6	10.6	19.8	80.2
1870	39,818,449	26.6	13.4	25.7	74.3
1880	50,155,783	26.0	16.9	28.2	71.8
1890	62,947,714	25.5	21.2	35.1	64.9
1900	75,994,575	20.7	25.6	39.6	60.4
1910	91,972,266	21.0	31.0	45.6	54.4
1920	105,710,620	14.9	35.6	51.2	48.8
1930	122,775,046	16.1	41.2	56.1	43.9
1940	131,669,275	7.2	44.2	56.5	43.5
1950	150,697,361	14.5	50.7	64.0	36.0
1960	179,323,175	18.5	50.6	69.9	30.1
1970	203,302,031	13.4	57.4	73.5	26.5
1980	226,545,805	11.4	64.0	73.7	26.3
1985	237,839,000[1]	5.0	64.0	N.A.	N.A.

1. Figures are rounded. **Sources:** U.S. Bureau of the Census, *The Statistical History of the U.S.* (1976) and *Statistical Abstract of the United States 1989* (1989).

FASTEST-GROWING STATES, 1990–2010

1990–2000 % change		2000–2010 % change	
Arizona	23.1%	Hawaii	15.9%
Nevada	21.1	Arizona	15.2
New Mexico	20.6	New Mexico	14.2
Florida	20.3	Nevada	13.9
Georgia	19.4	Florida	13.7
Alaska	19.3	Georgia	13.7
Hawaii	17.9	California	11.5
New Hampshire	16.7	Alaska	11.4
California	15.0	Texas	10.2
Texas	14.1	New Hampshire	9.2

STATES WITH THE GREATEST PERCENTAGE DECLINES, 1990–2010

1990–2000 % change		2000–2010 % change	
Iowa	-7.6%	Iowa	-6.6%
West Virginia	-7.2	West Virginia	-6.1
North Dakota	-4.7	Pennsylvania	-3.2
Pennsylvania	-2.7	North Dakota	-2.9
Wyoming	-2.6	Ohio	-2.2

Source: U.S. Bureau of the Census, *Projections of the Populations of States by Age, Sex, and Race, 1988 to 2010* (1989).

PROJECTED STATE POPULATION CHANGES IN NUMBERS, RANK, AND PERCENT, 1986–2010 (numbers in thousands)

State	1986 (rank)	1990 (rank)	2000 (rank)	2010 (rank)	% change 1986–2010
Alabama	4,052 (22)	4,181 (22)	4,410 (23)	4,609 (21)	13.2%
Alaska	534 (49)	576 (48)	687 (47)	765 (46)	38.7
Arizona	3,319 (25)	3,752 (23)	4,618 (20)	5,319 (18)	51.4
Arkansas	2,372 (33)	2,427 (33)	2,529 (32)	2,624 (31)	10.3
California	26,981 (1)	29,126 (1)	33,500 (1)	37,347 (1)	34.4
Colorado	3,267 (27)	3,434 (26)	3,813 (25)	4,098 (25)	23.6
Connecticut	3,189 (28)	3,279 (28)	3,445 (27)	3,532 (27)	10.4
Delaware	633 (47)	666 (46)	734 (45)	790 (45)	23.3
Florida	11,675 (5)	12,818 (4)	15,415 (4)	17,530 (4)	43.8
Georgia	6,104 (11)	6,663 (11)	7,957 (10)	9,045 (9)	42.3
Hawaii	1,062 (39)	1,141 (40)	1,345 (38)	1,559 (37)	41.2
Idaho	1,002 (41)	1,017 (42)	1,047 (43)	1,079 (43)	7.4
Illinois	11,552 (6)	11,612 (6)	11,580 (5)	11,495 (5)	-0.5
Indiana	5,504 (14)	5,550 (14)	5,502 (14)	5,409 (17)	-1.8
Iowa	2,851 (29)	2,758 (30)	2,549 (31)	2,382 (33)	-17.4
Kansas	2,460 (32)	2,492 (32)	2,529 (33)	2,564 (32)	4.2
Kentucky	3,729 (23)	3,745 (24)	3,733 (26)	3,710 (26)	-0.5
Louisiana	4,501 (18)	4,513 (20)	4,516 (21)	4,545 (23)	1.0
Maine	1,173 (38)	1,212 (38)	1,271 (41)	1,308 (41)	11.1
Maryland	4,463 (19)	4,729 (18)	5,274 (16)	5,688 (14)	25.2
Massachusetts	5,832 (12)	5,880 (13)	6,087 (13)	6,255 (13)	7.1
Michigan	9,145 (8)	9,293 (8)	9,250 (8)	9,097 (8)	-0.6
Minnesota	4,214 (21)	4,324 (21)	4,490 (22)	4,578 (22)	8.4
Mississippi	2,625 (31)	2,699 (31)	2,877 (30)	3,028 (29)	14.6
Missouri	5,066 (15)	5,192 (15)	5,383 (15)	5,521 (15)	8.6
Montana	819 (44)	805 (44)	794 (44)	794 (44)	-3.1
Nebraska	1,598 (36)	1,588 (37)	1,556 (37)	1,529 (37)	-4.3
Nevada	963 (43)	1,076 (41)	1,303 (40)	1,484 (39)	46.7
New Hampshire	1,027 (40)	1,142 (39)	1,333 (39)	1,529 (38)	37.5
New Jersey	7,619 (9)	7,899 (9)	8,546 (9)	8,980 (10)	16.0
New Mexico	1,479 (37)	1,632 (36)	1,968 (35)	2,248 (34)	45.2
New York	17,772 (2)	17,773 (2)	17,986 (3)	18,139 (3)	2.1
North Carolina	6,333 (10)	6,690 (10)	7,483 (11)	8,154 (11)	26.5
North Dakota	679 (46)	660 (47)	629 (48)	611 (48)	-10.4
Ohio	10,752 (7)	10,791 (7)	10,629 (7)	10,397 (7)	-3.3
Oklahoma	3,305 (26)	3,285 (27)	3,376 (28)	3,511 (28)	6.2
Oregon	2,698 (30)	2,766 (29)	2,877 (29)	2,991 (29)	10.5
Pennsylvania	11,888 (4)	11,827 (5)	11,503 (6)	11,134 (6)	-6.4
Rhode Island	975 (42)	1,002 (43)	1,049 (42)	1,085 (42)	10.9
South Carolina	3,377 (24)	3,549 (25)	3,906 (24)	4,205 (24)	22.9
South Dakota	708 (45)	708 (45)	714 (46)	722 (47)	1.9
Tennessee	4,803 (16)	4,972 (16)	5,266 (17)	5,500 (16)	13.8
Texas	16,685 (3)	17,712 (3)	20,211 (2)	22,281 (2)	30.3
Utah	1,665 (35)	1,776 (35)	1,991 (34)	2,171 (35)	27.8
Vermont	541 (48)	562 (49)	591 (49)	608 (49)	12.0
Virginia	5,787 (13)	6,157 (12)	6,877 (12)	7,410 (12)	25.9
Washington	4,462 (20)	4,657 (19)	4,991 (18)	5,282 (19)	17.4
West Virginia	1,918 (34)	1,856 (34)	1,722 (36)	1,617 (36)	-16.5
Wisconsin	4,785 (17)	4,808 (17)	4,784 (19)	4,713 (20)	-1.5
Wyoming	507 (50)	502 (50)	489 (50)	487 (50)	-4.1

Source: U.S. Bureau of the Census, *Projections of the Populations of States by Age, Sex, and Race 1988 to 2010* (1989).

U.S. POPULATION ABROAD BY SELECTED COUNTRY, 1988

Country	Number of resident U.S. citizens (thousands)	Country	Number of resident U.S. citizens (thousands)
Australia	68.7	Jerusalem	30.4
Belgium	13.9	Mexico	396.0
Brazil	40.4	Netherlands	34.5
Canada	235.1	Panama	11.3
Colombia	19.9	Philippines	156.3
Costa Rica	17.1	Portugal	15.7
Dominican Republic	63.2	Saudi Arabia	21.6
France	43.5	South Africa	9.4
Greece	54.4	South Korea	10.0
Hong Kong	14.5	Spain	60.1
Ireland	30.0	Switzerland	24.1
Israel	60.9	United Kingdom	158.8
Italy	86.4	Venezuela	20.6
Japan	41.7	West Germany	134.1
Total[1] U.S. citizens, resident abroad:			2,174,600

Note: Includes U.S. government employees (nonmilitary) and dependents of both U.S. military and civilian employees.   1. Includes other countries not shown here.   **Source:** U.S. Bureau of the Census, *Statistical Abstract of the United States 1989* (1989) from unpublished data of U.S. Dept. of State.

THE POPULATION, BY RACE AND HISPANIC ORIGIN

It is important to note that the Census Bureau's classification of the population by race, in its words, "reflects common usage, not an attempt to define biological stock." Only since 1960, however, have the Census Bureau's race figures been based on self-identification.

The people of the United States are predominantly white, accounting for an estimated 84.1% of the total population in 1990. This dominance has been true since colonial days, although even then the indigenous peoples and the African slaves were significant racial minorities. In fact, as slave labor became essen-

PROJECTIONS OF THE POPULATION, BY RACE AND HISPANIC ORIGIN, 1990–2000

Although total U.S. population growth will be below 1% a year throughout the 1990s, all of the minority groups will experience very strong increases.

	1990	1995	2000	% change 1990–2000
Total pop.	252,293	264,077	274,479	8.8%
White	191,594	195,347	197,634	3.2
Black	30,915	33,237	35,440	14.6
Hispanic origin	21,854	25,991	30,295	38.6
Other races (incl. Asians)	7,930	9,502	11,110	40.1

Source: U.S. Bureau of the Census, *Projections of the Population of the U.S. by Age, Sex, and Race 1983–2080* (1989).

tial to the southern economy, so many slaves were brought here that just before the Civil War, blacks constituted 15% of the population.

After the war, however, the proportion of whites rapidly increased as millions of immigrants from northern Europe settled throughout the country. The relentless movement of the population westward deprived the Native Americans of their lands and—with the assistance of several bloody wars—helped to reduce their numbers to a small fraction (less than 100,000 perhaps) of what they were estimated to have been only a century before.

The black population, with 9–10% of the total, remained the only significant minority group until the 1960s, when a surge of new immigrants from Puerto Rico, Mexico, and Cuba made the Hispanic presence felt in very short order. So rapid and strong an impression did these groups make that the Census Bureau created a new population category, "Hispanic Origin"; since some Hispanics are black, some white, and still others Indian, this designation has nothing to do with race.

During the 1970s and 1980s, the arrival of hundreds of thousands of Asians again caused a noticeable change in the composition of the population. Unfortunately, the Census Bureau already had a category called "Other Races" that included not only peoples from Asia but also those from the Pacific Islands, as well as Eskimos, Aleuts, and American Indians. As a result of the sizable increase in the number of Asians, the "Other Races" category has suddenly swollen in size but is now overwhelmingly made up of people from Asia.

The Black Population

(Note that the statistics presented in this introduction are based on estimates for the year 1988, while some of the information in the charts below is for 1985; the latter are taken from the Census Bureau's first attempt to produce race statistics independent of the decennial census.)

Ever since the Founding Fathers reached their "famous compromise" declaring a slave the equivalent of three-fifths of a person, the black population has had a less-than-equal standing in relation to the majority of Americans. Over the last two centuries, the struggle for equality, even in a nation pledged to that ideal, has proven long, hard, and in many cases intractable, as so many contemporary facts and figures in this book make all too evident. From higher infant mortality rates and poverty rates to lower life expectancy and family income levels, the black population continues to reap the effects of two centuries of slavery and one of institutionalized segregation.

In 1988 the black population numbered 29.3 million, an estimated 12.2% of all Americans, by far the nation's largest minority group. Since 1980 the black population has grown 12.7%, more than twice the rate of growth for whites (6.2%); the Census Bureau projections indicate that this trend will continue through the 1990s. So too will the age differences between the races. In 1988 the median age for blacks was 27.3, about six years below the

BLACK POPULATION OF THE U.S., 1790–1988

Year	Number (thousands)	% of total pop.	Year	Number (thousands)	% of total pop.
1790	757	19.3%	1920	10,463	9.9%
1800	1,002	18.9	1930	11,891	9.7
1850	3,639	15.7	1940	12,866	9.8
1860	4,442	14.1	1950	15,042	10.0
1870	4,880	12.7	1960[1]	18,872	10.5
1880	6,581	13.1	1970	22,581	11.1
1890	7,489	11.9	1980	26,683	11.8
1900	8,834	11.6	1985	28,900[2]	12.1
1910	9,828	10.7	1988 (est.): 29,300		12.7

1. Includes Alaska and Hawaii for first time.   2. Figure is rounded.
Sources: U.S. Bureau of the Census, *Statistical Abstract of the United States 1989* (1989) and *Population Profile of the U.S. 1989* (1989).

TOTAL BLACK POPULATION OF THE U.S., BY REGION AND PERCENT, 1985–2010
(numbers in thousands)

Region	1985 (%)[1]	1990 (%)[2]	2000 (%)[2]	2010 (%)[2]
Northeast	5,405 (10.8)	5,705 (11.3)	6,363 (12.3)	6,941 (13.2)
Midwest	5,644 (9.5)	5,995 (10.0)	6,542 (11.0)	7,013 (11.9)
South	15,253 (18.7)	16,379 (18.8)	18,546 (19.1)	20,630 (19.7)
West	2,601 (5.4)	3,947 (5.6)	3,555 (6.0)	4,126 (6.3)
Total U.S.	28,902 (12.1)	31,026 (12.4)	35,006 (13.1)	38,710 (13.7)

1. Estimates.   2. Projections.   **Sources:** U.S. Bureau of the Census, *Population Estimates by Race and Hispanic Origin for States, Metropolitan Areas, and Selected Counties: 1980 to 1985* (1989) and *Projections of the Population of States by Age, Sex, and Race: 1988 to 2010* (1989).

white population's 33.1. Other indications of the youthful nature of the black population are the proportion over 65 (only 8% compared with 13% for whites) and the percentage under 18 (33% to 25%).

Most black people (56%) continue to live in the South where they made up 20% of the population in 1988; in the Northeast, blacks were 10% of the population, 9% of the Midwest's, and only 5% of the West's. In 1988 the majority of blacks (57%) lived in central cities of metropolitan areas more than twice the proportion for whites (27%); the ratios in the suburban parts of metropolitan areas were just the opposite with 50% of the white population living there and only 25% of blacks.

Significant differences between the races also exist in other demographic categories, most notably in the high divorce rates for blacks and the related numbers of married-couple families and households run by women. Between 1970 and 1988, in the category "female householder, no spouse present," the percentage for blacks rose from 28.3% to 42.8% while the percentage of black married-couple families declined to 51.3% from 68.1% in 1970.

BLACK POPULATION AND PERCENT OF TOTAL IN THE 50 LARGEST METROPOLITAN AREAS, 1980–85

Metropolitan area	Number of blacks 1980	1985	Percent black 1980	1985	Metropolitan area	Number of blacks 1980	1985	Percent black 1980	1985
Albany-Schenectady-Troy, N.Y.	30,700	50,800	3.7%	3.9%	Miami-Ft. Lauderdale, Fla.	399,300	492,500	15.1%	17.1%
Atlanta, Ga.	526,100	608,300	24.6	24.9	Milwaukee-Racine, Wis.	165,300	181,500	10.5	11.5
Baltimore, Md.	560,800	592,200	25.5	26.0	Minneapolis-St. Paul, Minn.-Wis.	49,800	60,400	2.3	2.7
Birmingham, Ala.	240,300	252,800	27.2	27.9	Nashville, Tenn.	137,200	145,400	16.1	16.1
Boston-Lawrence-Salem-Lowell, Mass.	181,500	202,800	5.0	5.5	New Orleans, La.	409,700	445,900	32.6	33.6
Buffalo-Niagara Falls, N.Y.	116,100	119,800	9.3	10.0	New York, New Jersey–Long Island–Ct.	2,941,200	3,201,200	16.9	18.1
Charlotte–Gastonia–Rock Hill, N.C.-S.C.	194,400	211,100	20.0	20.2	Norfolk–Virginia Beach–Newport News, Va.	326,800	362,600	28.2	28.1
Chicago–Gary–Lake County, Ill.-Ind.	1,564,100	1,645,300	19.7	20.3	Oklahoma City, Okla.	78,900	92,200	9.2	9.5
Cincinnati-Hamilton, Ohio-Ky.	186,100	195,900	11.2	11.6	Orlando, Fla.	90,900	106,400	13.0	12.8
Cleveland-Akron-Lorain, Ohio	427,200	444,300	15.1	16.0	Philadelphia-Wilmington-Trenton	1,044,400	1,108,800	18.4	19.2
Columbus, Ohio	137,800	148,300	11.1	11.5	Phoenix, Ariz.	48,100	60,200	3.2	3.3
Dallas–Ft. Worth, Tex.	417,000	485,400	14.2	13.9	Pittsburgh–Beaver Valley, Pa.	182,000	185,600	7.5	7.9
Dayton-Springfield, Ohio	118,900	126,100	12.6	13.5	Portland-Vancouver	34,100	37,400	2.6	2.7
Denver-Boulder, Colo.	78,500	91,100	4.8	5.0	Providence-Pawtucket-Woonsocket, R.I.	25,600	30,100	3.0	3.4
Detroit–Ann Arbor, Mich.	921,200	949,300	19.4	20.4	Richmond-Petersburg, Va.	221,900	237,200	29.1	29.5
Greensboro–Winston-Salem, High Point, N.C.	161,900	172,000	19.0	19.4	Rochester, N.Y.	78,700	86,100	8.1	8.7
Hartford–New Britain–Middletown, Conn.	75,000	83,500	7.1	7.8	Sacramento, Calif.	61,900	79,600	5.6	6.3
Honolulu, Hawaii	17,800	22,300	2.3	2.7	St. Louis, Mo.-Ill.	407,600	430,800	17.1	17.8
Houston-Galveston-Brazoria, Tex.	564,300	641,300	18.2	18.0	Salt Lake City-Ogden, Utah	9,100	10,400	1.0	1.0
Indianapolis, Ind.	157,700	168,100	13.5	14.1	San Antonio, Tex.	72,600	83,400	6.8	6.8
Jacksonville, Fla.	156,000	178,200	21.6	21.6	San Diego, Calif.	105,500	124,900	5.7	5.8
Kansas City, Mo.-Kans.	179,900	193,900	12.5	13.0	San Francisco–Oakland–San Jose, Calif.	471,000	523,900	8.8	8.9
Los Angeles–Anaheim–Riverside, Calif.	1,065,100	1,194,500	9.3	9.2	Seattle-Tacoma, Wash.	88,800	101,400	4.2	4.5
Louisville, Ky.	121,100	126,900	12.7	13.3	Tampa–St. Petersburg–Clearwater, Fla.	148,400	169,700	9.2	9.1
Memphis, Tenn.-Ark.-Miss.	364,100	389,300	39.9	41.4	Washington, D.C.-Md.-Va.	874,300	964,600	26.9	27.3

Note: Largest in 1987; most are consolidated metropolitan statistical areas (CMSAs—see the description in the section "Cities and Counties in America").
Source: U.S. Bureau of the Census, *Population Estimates by Race and Hispanic Origin for States, Metropolitan Areas, and Selected Counties: 1980 to 1985* (1989).

BLACK POPULATION AND PERCENT OF TOTAL FOR THE STATES, 1985, 1990, 2000
(numbers in thousands)

State	1985 (%)	1990 (%)	2000 (%)	State	1985 (%)	1990 (%)	2000 (%)
Alabama	1,055 (26.2)	1,071 (25.6)	1,136 (25.8)	Nevada	61 (6.6)	74 (6.9)	94 (7.2)
Alaska	18 (3.4)	20 (3.4)	23 (3.4)	New Hampshire	5 (N.A.)	7 (0.6)	10 (0.8)
Arizona	92 (2.9)	99 (2.7)	123 (2.7)	New Jersey	1,025 (13.6)	1,134 (14.4)	1,349 (15.8)
Arkansas	392 (16.6)	387 (15.9)	398 (15.7)	New Mexico	29 (2.0)	29 (1.7)	34 (1.7)
California	2,074 (7.8)	2,392 (8.2)	2,909 (8.7)	New York	2,733 (15.4)	2,858 (16.1)	3,180 (17.7)
Colorado	120 (3.7)	133 (3.9)	156 (4.1)	North Carolina	1,392 (22.5)	1,480 (22.1)	1,641 (21.9)
Connecticut	244 (7.7)	269 (8.2)	313 (9.1)	North Dakota	3 (N.A.)	3 (0.5)	4 (0.6)
Delaware	106 (17.1)	126 (18.9)	155 (21.1)	Ohio	1,136 (10.6)	1,188 (11.0)	1,274 (12.0)
Florida	1,565 (13.9)	1,823 (14.2)	2,279 (14.8)	Oklahoma	228 (6.9)	223 (6.8)	231 (6.8)
Georgia	1,600 (27.0)	1,789 (26.9)	2,151 (27.0)	Oregon	41 (1.5)	44 (1.6)	50 (1.7)
Hawaii	23 (2.2)	21 (1.8)	24 (1.8)	Pennsylvania	1,102 (9.3)	1,108 (9.4)	1,131 (9.8)
Idaho	3 (N.A.)	4 (0.4)	6 (0.5)	Rhode Island	34 (3.5)	38 (3.8)	45 (4.3)
Illinois	1,775 (15.4)	1,869 (16.1)	2,029 (17.5)	South Carolina	1,012 (30.5)	1,067 (30.1)	1,170 (30.0)
Indiana	436 (8.0)	469 (8.4)	513 (9.3)	South Dakota	2 (N.A.)	2 (0.3)	2 (0.3)
Iowa	45 (1.6)	52 (1.9)	58 (2.3)	Tennessee	766 (16.2)	810 (16.3)	877 (16.8)
Kansas	137 (5.6)	145 (5.8)	158 (6.2)	Texas	1,910 (11.8)	2,104 (11.9)	2,439 (12.1)
Kentucky	264 (7.1)	280 (7.5)	294 (7.9)	Utah	12 (N.A.)	12 (0.7)	13 (0.7)
Louisiana	1,348 (30.0)	1,380 (30.6)	1,452 (32.1)	Vermont	2 (N.A.)	2 (0.4)	3 (0.5)
Maine	4 (N.A.)	4 (0.3)	4 (0.4)	Virginia	1,091 (19.0)	1,171 (19.0)	1,332 (19.4)
Maryland	1,076 (24.2)	1,233 (26.1)	1,469 (27.9)	Washington	122 (2.8)	114 (2.4)	116 (2.3)
Massachussetts	258 (4.4)	284 (4.8)	327 (5.4)	West Virginia	64 (3.3)	54 (2.9)	45 (2.6)
Michigan	1,243 (13.5)	1,355 (14.6)	1,497 (16.2)	Wisconsin	204 (4.3)	231 (4.8)	273 (5.7)
Minnesota	64 (1.5)	67 (1.6)	77 (1.7)	Wyoming	4 (N.A.)	4 (0.4)	6 (0.5)
Mississippi	949 (36.3)	962 (35.6)	1,037 (36.1)				
Missouri	545 (10.9)	559 (10.8)	600 (11.2)				
Montana	2 (N.A.)	2 (0.2)	2 (0.2)				
Nebraska	53 (3.3)	54 (3.4)	58 (3.7)				

Note: Figures for 1985 are estimates, those for 1990 and 2000 are projections. **Sources:** U.S. Bureau of the Census, *Population Estimates by Race and Hispanic Origin for States, Metropolitan Areas, and Selected Counties: 1980 to 1985* (1989) and *Projections of the Population of States by Age, Sex, and Race: 1988 to 2010* (1989).

The Hispanic Population

Between 1980 and 1987, the U.S. population grew by 6%, but the number of Hispanics increased by 30% (4.2 million), making them one of the fastest growing segments of the U.S. population. In late 1988 the Census Bureau estimated the total number of Hispanics in the United States at 19.4 million, but this figure does not include illegal immigrants who number between 1.4 and 2.4 million, according to a study by the National Academy of Sciences.

A look at earlier population statistics reveals a pattern of tremendous growth among U.S. Hispanics. In 1970 there were approximately 9 million Hispanics in the United States. By 1980 the number had increased to 14.6 million, and by 1987 it had reached 18.8 million. Prior to 1970, Census Bureau surveys were conducted differently from the way they are now. Spanish-surnamed Americans and people who were born, or whose parents were born, in a Hispanic country were identified, but non-Spanish-surnamed Hispanics and third- or fourth-generation Hispanics were not. Therefore, government data on Hispanics compiled before 1970 are highly inaccurate.

The rapid growth of the Hispanic population is due to immigration and a higher fertility rate than that of the non-Hispanic population. According to the National Center for Health Statistics, between 1983 and 1985 the birth rate among Hispanic women rose 11% as compared with 3% for non-Hispanics. In 1985 Hispanic births accounted for 17% of all births in the United States, although Hispanics only composed about 7% of the population.

Within the next 25 years, the Hispanic population will become the largest minority in the United States, surpassing blacks. As of mid-1990 the number of Hispanics is likely to exceed 22.0 million and may number 31.2 million by the year 2000. If these projections prove correct, Hispanics will make up 11.6% of the total U.S. population, while blacks will constitute 13.3%. The Census Bureau forecasts that by 2025 the number of Hispanics could reach 60.9 million, or 20.2% of the population, although these figures may prove high if fertility and immigration rates decrease. A more conservative estimate places the Hispanic population at 39.3 million by 2025.

Geographical Distribution Arizona, California, Colorado, Florida, Illinois, New Jersey, New Mexico, New York, and Texas. Over half of all U.S. Hispanics live in California or Texas. In 1987, 6.2 million (23%) of the residents of California and 4.2 million (25%) of the residents of Texas were Hispanic. The great majority of the Hispanics in these two states are of Mexican origin. New York, with 2.2 million, is the state with the third-largest number of Hispanics, the majority of whom are Puerto Rican. Florida, where 1.3 million Hispanics reside, has the fourth-largest Hispanic population; the majority are of Cuban background.

In order of rank, the following 20 cities have the largest Hispanic populations: Los Angeles; New York; San Antonio, Tex.; Chicago; San Francisco; Miami; Houston; McAllen, Tex.; Albuquerque; El Paso, Tex.; Fresno, Calif.; San Diego; Phoenix; Dallas–Fort Worth; Sacramento; Corpus Christi, Tex.; Denver; Philadelphia; Tucson; Salinas-Monterey, Calif. Two U.S. cities had more than two million Hispanic residents in 1980: Los Angeles, with 2,838,694, and New York, with 2,063,007. By 1985 the Hispanic population of Los Angeles had grown to over 4 million and that of New York to 2.4 million. By 1990 Los Angeles will have an estimated Hispanic population of over 6 million and New York, 2.7 million. Los Angeles has more Mexicans than any other city except metropolitan Mexico City and nearly half as many Salvadorans (300,000) as San Salvador. By 1990 Chicago, San Francisco, Miami, and Houston are all expected to have over a million Hispanics, and Austin, Tex., will become one of the top 20 Hispanic cities.

Who Is Hispanic? Broadly understood, the term Hispanic refers to people of Spanish or Spanish-American origin. American Hispanics are of diverse backgrounds. The majority trace their roots to Mexico, Puerto Rico or Cuba; however, every Spanish-speaking country is represented in the U.S. Hispanic population. (People of Brazilian origin are not included because Brazil is a Portuguese-speaking country.) In recent years extreme poverty and upheaval have led political Salvadorans and other Central Americans to emigrate to the United States in increasing numbers.

Contrary to popular opinion, Spanish-speaking countries are not culturally homogeneous but varied and complex, incorporating Spanish and other European influences as well as Indian and African traits. In the Caribbean area, Panama, and the coasts of Venezuela, Colombia, Ecuador, and sections of Peru, African culture has left a strong legacy. In Mexico, most of Central America, and the Andean countries, diverse Indian cultures have had a major impact. Latin American society varies greatly according to social class, and vast differences exist between urban and rural areas. Since American Hispanics come from different countries and social backgrounds, they do not compose a uniform, cohesive population group.

U.S. Hispanics are of many races, since every race is represented in Spanish America. In some areas intermingling has made it impossible to distinguish one race from another, but in others, races are clearly defined. In Argentina, for example, there is a white majority of 99.6%—mostly of Italian, German, or English extraction. Cuba, the Dominican Republic, Panama, Venezuela, and the coastal areas of Colombia, Ecuador, and Peru all have significant black populations. In Bolivia about one-half of the population is Indian and a third is mestizo (of mixed white and Indian ancestry). Both Peru and Cuba have concentrations of persons of Chinese ancestry, and Peru has a growing Japanese population. About 63% of U.S. Hispanics trace their roots to Mexico, where about 55% of the population is mestizo, 30% Indian, and 15% white.

Despite their diversity there are many factors that unite the Hispanic peoples, among them language, religion, customs, and attitudes toward self, family, and society. In the United States, these factors vary in importance according to the degree to which an individual has assimilated into the mainstream. For example, although language has traditionally been an important unifying factor, large numbers of second-generation Hispanics are English-dominant. About 85% of U.S. Hispanics speak English. According to the 1980 census, about 5.3% of the total U.S. population speaks Spanish at home, although only about 1.3% is monolingual in Spanish. It is possible that the influx of immigrants from Central America will alter this situation. Although the Spanish language continues to exert a strong emotional pull among U.S. Hispanics, it is difficult to assess to what extent Spanish will remain a unifying force among future generations.

Origins of U.S. Hispanics The majority of U.S. Hispanics are of Mexican origin. Mexicans and Mexican-Americans compose 63% of the total U.S. Hispanic population. The number of people of Mexican background living in the United States grew from about 8.4 million in 1980 to over 12 million in 1988.

About 12.2% of U.S. Hispanics are Puerto Rican. This group has shown a less dramatic gain during the 1980s, increasing from about 2 million to 2.3 million between 1980 and 1988. (These figures do not include Puerto Ricans living in Puerto Rico, which is a U.S. territory but for which a separate census report is issued.) In recent years the flow of Puerto Ricans to U.S. cities has been reversed, with more Puerto Ricans emigrating from the mainland to the island than the other way around.

The U.S. Central and South American populations showed the highest growth rate between 1980 and 1987. At the beginning of the decade, the number of Central Americans living in the United States was small. In census data Central Americans were included in the general category "Other," which was composed of persons of Spanish or South American origin, as well as Hispanics who did not specify their origin on census surveys. By 1982 the U.S. Central American population had increased so significantly that the Census Bureau created a new category: Central and South American. In the 1990 census, Central and South American Hispanics will be asked to specify their country of origin, thereby enabling the government to compile more accurate figures on Salvadorans and other groups. In 1982 there were approximately 1.5 million persons in the Central and South American category; by 1987 there were over 2.1 million, an increase of 40%. Central and South Americans now make up 11.4% of the total U.S. Hispanic population.

Most Central American immigrants are from Nicaragua and El Salvador, although a significant number are from Guatemala. Statistical data on Salvadorans is uncertain, since the 1980 census did not break down the Central American category according to country or origin, and since many Salvadorans arrived here illegally after 1980 and do not figure in any subsequent census update. During the latter part of the 1980s, large numbers of Nicaraguans entered the country as political refugees. In Miami, where between 150 and 200 Central American immigrants arrive every week, Central Americans compose nearly 17% of the entire Hispanic population; in 1970, they composed less than 1%. There are an estimated 150,000 Nicaraguans presently living in the United States, and 100,000 more are expected to arrive in 1989.

Cubans and Cuban-Americans make up 5.4% of the total number of Hispanics in the United States. Large numbers of Cubans arrived in 1961 during the Cuban airlift and again in 1980 during the Mariel boat lift. Between 1980 and 1987, the number of Americans of Cuban origin increased from 800,000 to one million. Since 1985 the Cuban population has shown little fluctuation or perhaps a very slight decrease.

The remaining 8.4% of the U.S. Hispanic population is of "Other Spanish" origin. This group grew from approximately 1.2 million in 1982 to 1.6 million in 1988.

A Brief History Hispanics are among the oldest residents of the American Southwest. The viceroyalty of New Spain, formed by the Spanish crown in 1535, included the territory that is now Mexico and the southwestern United States. The majority of the inhabitants were Spaniards, Indians, and mestizos. The first churches, schools, and hospitals in the Southwest were founded by Spanish priests who came to the New World to teach Roman Catholic doctrine to the Indians.

After the War of Mexican Independence in 1810, the Southwest became part of Mexico. It was not until the Mexican-American War

STATES WITH LARGEST HISPANIC POPULATIONS

State	Number of Hispanics (millions)	% of U.S. Hispanics	% of state's population
California	6.6	34%	23%
Texas	4.1	21	24
New York	2.1	11	12
Florida	1.5	8	12
Illinois	0.8	4	7
Arizona	0.6	3	18
New Jersey	0.6	3	8
New Mexico	0.5	3	35
Colorado	0.4	2	11

Note: Of all U.S. Hispanics, 89% live in only nine states.
Source: U.S. Bureau of the Census, *The Hispanic Population in the U.S., March 1986 and 1987* (1989).

SELECTED CHARACTERISTICS OF PERSONS OF HISPANIC AND NON-HISPANIC ORIGIN IN THE U.S., 1987

	Total non-Hispanic origin	Total Hispanic origin	HISPANIC ORIGIN				
			Mexican	Puerto Rican	Cuban	Central and S. America	Other Spanish
Number (thousands)	219,999	18,790	11,762	2,284	1,017	2,139	1,588
Percent of total	—	100.0%	62.6%	12.2%	5.4%	11.4%	8.4%
Percent male	48.5%	50.1%	51.6%	46.4%	50.3%	47.0%	48.4%
ALL AGES:							
Percent under 15	21.1%	30.3%	33.0%	32.9%	16.5%	24.5%	22.4%
15–24	15.3	19.4	20.3	18.7	15.6	19.9	16.3
25–34	17.8	19.2	18.9	18.1	16.9	22.5	19.8
35–44	14.2	13.0	11.9	14.5	12.4	16.8	14.2
45–54	9.8	7.7	6.9	6.9	13.3	9.0	9.9
55–64	9.5	5.5	4.8	5.3	13.2	4.5	7.8
65 and over	12.3	4.9	4.2	3.6	12.1	2.8	9.6
MEDIAN AGE	32.6	25.1	23.5	24.3	35.8	27.3	30.9
MARITAL STATUS:[1]							
Never married	26.0%	31.5%	31.8%	35.3%	22.5%	33.5%	28.7%
Married	59.4	57.5	57.9	51.6	59.9	59.2	58.0
Widowed	7.3	3.9	3.7	3.8	7.5	2.9	4.2
Divorced	7.3	7.1	6.6	9.3	10.1	4.4	9.1
TYPE OF FAMILY:							
Married couple–families	80.5%	70.9%	74.8%	53.0%	77.5%	66.8%	72.0%
Female householder, no husband present	15.7	23.4	19.2	43.3	17.7	25.5	22.8
Male householder, no wife present	3.8	5.7	6.0	3.7	4.8	7.7	5.2

1. Age 15 and over. **Source:** U.S. Bureau of the Census, *The Hispanic Population in the U.S., March 1986 and 1987* (1989).

(1846–48) that this area officially became part of the United States, although many Americans had already settled there. The territory was ceded to the United States by the Treaty of Guadalupe-Hidalgo, which specified that the inhabitants would have all the same rights and immunities as other American citizens. Even after the war, Hispanics continued to dominate the social, cultural, and political life of many areas of the Southwest.

The situation changed radically at the beginning of this century. When the Mexican Revolution broke out in 1910, waves of working-class Mexicans crossed the border, fleeing the violence and hardship caused by the war. During World War I, the working-class Mexican population increased as the United States, plagued by a labor shortage at home, opened its doors to foreign workers. The influx continued until 1929, when the depression led the nation to deport Mexicans in order to provide jobs for Americans. World War II produced a new labor shortage, especially in agriculture. Through the Bracero program, the United States imported thousands of farmhands to harvest crops throughout the Southwest. The Bracero program was designed as a temporary measure, but it lasted until 1964. Mexican immigration has continued until the present, although owing to the growth of industry in cities, new immigrants tend to settle in urban rather than rural areas.

Although some Mexican-American families are descended from the early Spanish and Mexican settlers, most arrived in the 20th century. The availability of jobs continues to be the single most important reason why Mexicans emigrate to the United States.

Compared with Mexican-Americans, Puerto Ricans have been in the United States only a short time. Puerto Rico was a Spanish territory until 1898, when U.S. troops occupied the island during the Spanish-American War. Puerto Rico became an American territory with an American governor, and in 1917 Puerto Ricans became American citizens. In 1952 Puerto Rico became a Free Associated State with its own domestic government, an elected governor, and a representative to the U.S. Congress, who has no vote. As American citizens, Puerto Ricans may enter the United States and travel freely throughout the country. This, combined with overpopulation and harsh economic conditions on the island, contributed to a strong influx of Puerto Ricans to the mainland in the decades following World War II.

A third large group of Hispanics arrived after 1959, when Fidel Castro came to power in Cuba. Although these immigrants were of varied backgrounds, many were professionals or businessmen who reestablished themselves in Florida. Cubans are widely credited with rebuilding the Miami area and turning it into a thriving, attractive metropolis. In 1980 Castro permitted another 125,000 Cubans to leave. Less educated and well-off than their predecessors, many in this group have met with an unenthusiastic reception not only from non-Hispanic Americans but from Cubans from the earlier wave as well.

The newest group of Hispanic immigrants comes from Central America. The economic crisis in Marxist Nicaragua and the continued violence and poverty in El Salvador have spurred an exodus from these countries. An estimated 100,000 Nicaraguans have settled in Miami during the past decade or so, and Salvadorans are the fastest-growing minority in Washington, D.C.

The Asian and Pacific Islander Population

In 1970 the Census Bureau counted about 1.5 million Asians and Pacific Islanders living in the United States. By the 1980 census, that figure had more than doubled to 3.4 million, thanks in large part to the more than 400,000 Southeast Asian refugees who came to America during 1975–80 under the Refugee Resettlement Program. Between 1980 and 1985, 1.1 million Asian immigrants entered the United States, leading the Census Bureau and others to project a total population of about 6 million in 1988. Some demographers project a total population of 6.53 million for the 1990 census, the largest groups being the Chinese at 1.26 million (there were 812,000 in the 1980 census), Filipinos 1.41 million (782,000 in 1980), Vietnamese 860,000 (245,000 in 1980), Koreans 810,000 (357,000), Japanese 800,000 (716,000), and Asian Indians 680,000 (387,000).

In 1985, the most recent year for which estimates are available, one-half of the Asian and Pacific Islander population lived in four states: California (2.3 million), Hawaii (692,000), New York (516,000), and Texas (315,000); during 1980–85 the Asian population in Texas grew by 67%, by far the largest increase in the nation. The five metropolitan areas with the largest Asian and Pacific Islander populations in 1985 were Los Angeles (1.1 million), San Francisco (752,000), New York (604,000), Honolulu (539,000), and Chicago (234,000). The two metropolitan areas with the fastest-growing Asian populations were Dallas and Houston, with projected increases of over 80%. (Note: These figures are taken from the U.S. Bureau of the Census, *Population Estimates by Race and Hispanic Origin for States, Metropolitan Areas, and Selected Counties: 1980 to 1985* [1989]. Note that the Census Bureau's official designation is "Other Races," a category referring to the population that is neither white nor black; in addition to Asians and Pacific Islanders, the other major group is American Indian, which includes Eskimos and Aleuts. Since population increase among the latter groups has been negligible, it is safe to assume that most of the growth in "Other Races" is due to Asian immigration.)

The Native American Population

There are currently 1.5 million American Indians and 64,000 Alaska Natives (Eskimos and Aleuts) living in the United States. This represents a significant increase since the 1960 census, when only 524,000 (42,500 Alaska Natives) were counted. About 50% of Native Americans live in the West, 27% in the South, 17% in the Midwest, and only 0.6% in the Northeast. According to the 1980 census, four states had over 100,000 Native Americans: California (198,275), Oklahoma (169,292), Arizona (152,498), and New Mexico (105,976).

The federal government's Bureau of Indian Affairs recognizes 503 distinct Native American communities including numerous Alaska Native villages; 278 reservations, where about 25% of the population (340,000) still resides; and the so-called historic areas of Oklahoma, former reservations whose boundaries were legally established during the 1900–1907 period (9% of the total population, or 116,000, lived there in 1980).

For many observers the reservation system today stands as a symbol of the profound failure of U.S. policy toward Native Americans for more than two centuries. Despite annual federal expenditures exceeding $1 billion, the social and economic well-being of those living on reservations remains significantly substandard. In 1985, for example, unemployment on reservations averaged 34%, with many of the larger ones having even higher rates; educational attainment is characteristically lower as well: in 1980 only 43% of those over 25 on the 10 largest reservations were high school graduates. The poverty rate not surprisingly was an extraordinary 45% in 1980 (not including noncash benefits such as housing, food, or medical assistance.)

For the more than 65% of Native Americans who live off-reservation (mainly in urban areas), income and educational levels were significantly higher in 1980, although they were still below that of the general population: fifty-six percent had completed four or more years of high school (as against 67% for the general population); median family income was about 30% less than the general population, as compared with almost 60% for those living on reservations.

The 1990 census is expected to show many changes in the Native American situation. One that has been written about only slightly may have more profound effects than expected. Throughout the country Native Americans have begun to recognize the economic and political potential of their vast, untapped wealth in land and minerals. Native American property within U.S. boundaries, including original treaty lands and land won in legal battles, currently amounts to 53 million acres, about 2.5% of total U.S. acreage. At 16 million acres, the Navajo nation alone is about the size of West Virginia.

These lands include some of the most beautiful areas in the country, as well as some of the most valuable. Sixty percent of the U.S. uranium resources, a third of the strippable coal west of the Mississippi, a third of the U.S. reserves of low-sulphur coal, 15% of the total U.S. coal reserves, and 15% of the total U.S. natural gas reserves are under Native American lands.

For many reasons—including legal complexities, federal bureaucracy, fragile tribal governments—the vast majority of Native American communities have yet to translate this raw wealth into better lives for themselves. A few enterprising Native groups, however, have made enormous economic strides, among them a Choctaw group in Mississippi, whose auto-parts assembly plants and other enterprises make them the state's 15th-largest employer; the Warm Springs tribe of Oregon, who control a substantial fishing industry, a major resort, and a hydroelectric plant; and the Passamaquoddy and Penobscot tribes of Maine, who have parlayed a 1980 land claims settlement into more than $100 million in business investments and land holdings.

While it is too soon to tell just what kind of impact the ventures will have on the well-being of these tribes, it clearly cannot be measured in financial terms alone. For the first time in centuries, the destiny of some Native Americans is actually in their own hands, and that is the true revolution in their status.

The U.S. Population by Age

With birth rates and fertility rates declining rapidly since 1965, it should come as no surprise that the median age of the U.S. population has been rising almost as quickly. It will continue to rise for the foreseeable future in part because of, ironically enough, the aging of the Baby Boom generation.

During the Baby Boom years of the 1950s and 1960s, the median age of the population actually declined, the only time in U.S. history it has done so. Since then, however, the steady decline in the number of young people, especially those under 18 years of age (from 34.1% in 1970 to 25.6% in 1990), combined with the increase of those between 25 and 44 (23.6% of the population in 1970 and 32.6% in 1990) has driven the median age from 28 in 1970 to 33 in 1990. A five-year increase in 20 years is unprecedented in our history, but what's more remarkable is that we will most likely duplicate

that feat over the next 20 years.

The other major factor in the so-called "graying of America" is the increased life expectancy for older people. The Census Bureau estimates that in 1990 there will be 31.7 million Americans (12.3% of the population) over the age of 65; this represents a 24.1% increase since 1980. By the year 2000, the bureau projects another increase of 10.2%, or 34.9 million people over the age of 65. Over the first decade of the 21st century, the over-65 population will grow at about the same rate—from 10–12%—but between 2010 and 2020, the projected increase jumps to 31.2%, and to 25.6% between 2020 and 2030, as the members of the Baby Boom generation finally become senior citizens. In the year 2030, 21% of the population, or 65 million Americans, will be 65 years old or older. That's only 40 years from now, a demographic stone's throw away. By way of comparison, bear in mind that 40 years ago today, in 1950, the over-65 population totaled 7% of all Americans and numbered 9 million.

THE MEDIAN AGE OF THE U.S. POPULATION, 1820–2030

Year	age	Year	age	Year	age
1820	16.7	1900	22.9	1980	30.0
1830	17.2	1910	24.1	1985	31.3
1840	17.8	1920	25.3	1987	32.1
1850	18.9	1930	26.4	1990[1]	33.0
1860	19.4	1940	29.0	2000	36.4
1870	20.2	1950	30.2	2010	38.9
1880	20.9	1960	29.5	2020	40.2
1890	22.0	1970	28.0	2030	41.8

1. Figures for 1990 and after are projections the Census Bureau refers to as its "most likely" series. **Sources:** The U.S. Bureau of the Census, *The Statistical History of the U.S.* (1976) and *Projections of the Population of the U.S by Age, Sex, and Race 1988 to 2040* (1989).

The U.S. Population by Sex

According to census records, males always outnumbered females in the United States until 1950. Since then, however, the ratio of males to females has been declining every decade, especially in the older age brackets. Because women live so much longer on average than men do, there are currently over 30% more women in the over-65 category. In the crucial mating and marrying years (14–44), however, the numbers are not significantly different.

U.S. POPULATION BY SEX:
Totals and Ratio of Males to Females

Year	Male (thousands)	Female (thousands)	No. of males per 100 females All ages	14–24	25–44	65 +
1920	53,900	51,810	104.0	97.3	105.1	101.3
1930	62,137	60,638	102.5	98.4	101.8	100.5
1940	66,062	65,608	100.7	98.9	98.5	95.5
1950	74,833	75,864	98.6	98.2	96.4	89.6
1960	88,331	90,992	97.1	98.7	95.7	82.8
1970	98,926	104,309	94.8	98.7	95.5	72.1
1980	110,053	116,493	94.5	101.9	97.4	67.6
1987[1]	118,531	124,869	94.9	102.4	98.8	68.4

1. Estimated figures. **Source:** U.S. Bureau of the Census, *Statistical Abstract of the United States 1989* (1989).

NUMBER OF PERSONS AND PERCENT OF TOTAL POPULATION, BY AGE GROUP, 1960–2020
(numbers in thousands)

Age in years	1960	1970	1980	1990	2000	2010	2020
Under 5	20,341	17,166	16,458	18,408	16,898	16,899	17,095
	11.3%	8.4%	7.2%	7.4%	6.3%	6.0%	5.8%
5–13	32,965	36,672	31,095	32,393	33,483	31,001	31,697
	18.2%	17.9%	13.7%	12.9%	12.5%	11.0%	10.8%
14–17	11,219	15,924	16,142	13,237	15,332	14,746	14,074
	6.2%	7.8%	7.1%	5.3%	5.7%	5.2%	4.8%
18–24	16,128	24,712	30,350	26,140	25,231	27,155	25,018
	8.9%	12.1%	13.3%	10.4%	9.4%	9.6%	8.5%
25–34	22,919	25,323	37,626	43,925	37,149	37,572	39,100
	12.7%	12.3%	16.5%	17.5%	13.8%	13.3%	13.3%
35–44	24,221	23,150	25,868	37,897	43,911	37,202	37,591
	13.4%	11.3%	11.4%	15.1%	16.4%	13.2%	12.8%
45–64	36,203	41,999	44,515	46,851	61,381	78,637	77,722
	20.0%	20.5%	19.5%	18.7%	22.9%	27.8%	26.4%
65+	16,675	20,107	25,704	31,559	34,882	39,362	52,067
	9.2%	9.8%	11.3%	12.6%	13.0%	13.9%	17.7%
85+	940	1,430	2,269	3,254	4,622	6,115	6,651
	0.5%	0.7%	1.0%	1.3%	1.7%	2.2%	2.3%
100+	3	5	15	56	100	171	266
	—	—	—	—	—	—	0.1%
Total U.S. pop.	**180,671**	**205,052**	**227,757**	**250,410**	**268,266**	**282,575**	**294,364**
Median age	**29.4**	**27.9**	**30.0**	**33.0**	**36.4**	**38.9**	**40.2**

Note: Figures for 1990 and after are the projections the Census Bureau calls the "middle" or "most likely" series. **Sources:** U.S. Bureau of the Census, *Projections of the Population of the U.S. by Age, Sex, and Race 1988 to 2040* (1989) and *Statistical Abstract of the United States 1989* (1989).

GROWTH OF THE POPULATION 65 AND OVER, BY NUMBER AND PERCENT, 1900–2030

Year	Population 65 and over (thousands)	Percent increase by decade	Percent of population 65 and over
1900	3,099	N.A.	4.1%
1910	3,986	28.6%	4.3
1920	4,929	23.7	4.7
1930	6,705	36.0	5.5
1940	9,031	34.7	6.9
1950	12,397	37.3	8.1
1960	16,675	34.5	9.2
1970	20,107	20.6	9.8
1980	25,549	27.1	11.3
1990	29,835	24.1	12.7
2000	31,697	10.2	13.0
2010	34,921	12.2	13.8
2020	39,195	31.2	17.3
2030	51,422	25.6	21.2

Note: Figures for 1990 through 2030 are Census Bureau projections based on their "most likely" series of estimates. **Source:** Population Reference Bureau, Beth J. Soldo and Emily Agree, *America's Elderly* (1988). Based on U.S. Bureau of the Census data.

VITAL STATISTICS: BIRTHS, DEATHS, MARRIAGES, DIVORCES

The National Center for Health Statistics does a month-by-month tracking of four sets of numbers that both it and the Census Bureau refer to as "vital": births, deaths, marriages, and divorces.

Births An estimated 3.91 million babies were born in the United States in 1988, 2% more than the provisional number reported in 1987. While this is the largest number of live births reported since 1964, the crude birth rate—the number of live births per 1,000 total population—of 15.9 remained substantially smaller than at any time before 1970. The Census Bureau attributes the slight increase in the absolute number of births since 1975 to the increased number of women of childbearing age, i.e., the women of the Baby Boom era. In 1987 and 1988, the increase was the result, in part, of that same group having babies at a much later age than women of previous generations.

Deaths An estimated 2.17 million deaths occurred in 1988, also the largest number ever recorded. The death rate of 8.8 per 1,000 population was slightly higher than in previous years due to the increasing proportion of older persons in the population and a serious influenza outbreak during the first four months of the year. (For infant mortality figures and for more specific information about death rates by cause, see "Health and Medicine.")

In 1988 there were 1,742,000 more births

BIRTHS AND DEATHS IN THE U.S., 1910–88 (numbers in thousands)

Year	Live births	Birth rate[1]	Deaths[2]	Death rate[1]
1910	2,777	30.1	N.A.	14.7
1920	2,950	27.7	N.A.	13.0
1930	2,618	21.3	N.A.	11.3
1935	2,377	18.7	1,393	10.9
1940	2,559	19.4	1,417	10.8
1945	2,858	20.4	1,402	10.6
1950	3,632	24.1	1,452	9.6
1955	4,097	25.0	1,529	9.3
1960	4,258	23.7	1,712	9.5
1965	3,760	19.5	1,828	9.4
1970	3,731	18.4	1,921	9.5
1975	3,144	14.6	1,893	8.8
1980	3,612	15.9	1,990	8.8
1981	3,629	15.8	1,978	8.6
1982	3,681	15.9	1,975	8.5
1983	3,639	15.5	2,019	8.6
1984	3,669	15.5	2,039	8.6
1985	3,761	15.8	2,086	8.7
1986	3,757	15.6	2,105	8.7
1987	3,829	15.7	2,127	8.7
1988	3,913	15.9	2,171	8.8

1. Per 1,000 total population. 2. Excludes fetal deaths.
Sources: U.S. Bureau of the Census, *The Statistical History of the U.S.* (1976); U.S. National Center for Health Statistics, *Vital Statistics of the United States 1987* (1988) and *Monthly Vital Statistics Report, March 1989* (1989).

than deaths; this figure is called the *natural increase*, meaning the growth in population without immigration (which has accounted for another 600,000 people per year in recent years).

BIRTH RATES AND DEATH RATES IN THE U.S., 1910–88
(annual births and deaths per 1,000 population)

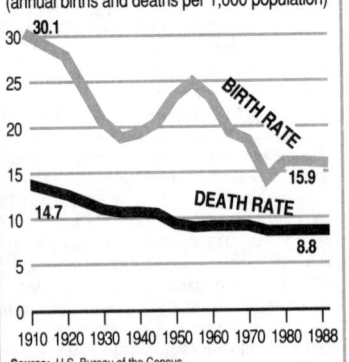

BIRTH RATE 30.1 ... 15.9
DEATH RATE 14.7 ... 8.8

Source: U.S. Bureau of the Census.

BIRTHS

By month, most babies were born in July (336,381), September (334,058), and August (331,351) in 1988. By day of the week, more babies were born on a Tuesday (an average of 11,422) than on any other day. Fortuitously, fewer babies were born on a Sunday (an average of 8,546).

Source: National Center for Health Statistics.

MARITAL STATUS OF THE POPULATION, BY SEX AND AGE, 1988

| | MALE | | | | | | | FEMALE | | | | | |
| | | Percent distribution by marital status | | | | | | | Percent distribution by marital status | | | | |
Age	Total number (thousands)	Single never married	Married spouse present	Married spouse absent	Widowed	Divorced	Age	Total number (thousands)	Single never married	Married spouse present	Married spouse absent	Widowed	Divorced
18–19	3,581	96.6%	2.2%	0.5%	0.1%	0.7%	18–19	3,640	89.3%	8.0%	1.4%[1]	0.1%	1.3%
20–24	9,254	77.7	19.2	1.6	0.1	1.4	20–24	9,586	61.1	32.5	3.2	0.2	3.0
25–29	10,669	43.3	48.6	2.8	0.2	5.2	25–29	10,854	29.5	57.4	4.9	0.5	7.8
30–34	10,651	25.0	62.3	3.9	0.2	8.6	30–34	10,795	16.1	67.2	5.2	0.6	10.9
35–39	9,321	14.0	70.3	4.3	0.5	10.9	35–39	9,533	9.0	70.9	5.1	1.4	13.6
40–44	7,755	7.5	77.6	4.1	0.4	10.5	40–44	8,073	6.2	71.1	5.4	2.4	14.8
45–54	11,520	5.6	79.5	3.7	1.3	9.8	45–54	12,275	5.1	71.6	4.6	5.9	12.9
55–64	10,186	4.9	81.6	2.8	3.7	6.9	55–64	11,456	4.0	67.3	3.3	16.7	8.6
65–74	7,736	4.8	79.5	2.3	8.7	4.7	65–74	9,736	4.6	51.5	1.9	36.3	5.8
75+	4,101	4.2	66.8	2.9	23.7	2.4	75+	6,955	6.2	23.6	1.3	66.1	2.7

1. Includes separated and husband in armed forces for all age groups.   **Source:** U.S. Bureau of the Census, *Marital Status and Living Arrangements: March 1988* (1989).

MARRIAGES AND DIVORCES IN THE U.S., 1920–88
(numbers in thousands)

Year	Marriages	Rate per 1,000 of population	Divorces	Rate per 1,000 of population
1920	1,274	12.0	171	1.6
1925	1,188	10.3	175	1.5
1930	1,127	9.2	196	1.6
1935	1,327	10.4	218	1.7
1940	1,596	12.1	264	2.0
1945	1,613	12.2	485	3.5
1950	1,667	11.1	385	2.6
1955	1,531	9.3	377	2.3
1960	1,523	8.5	393	2.2
1965	1,800	9.3	479	2.5
1970	2,163	10.6	708	3.5
1975	2,153	10.0	1,036	4.8
1980	2,390	10.6	1,189	5.2
1981	2,422	10.6	1,213	5.3
1982	2,456	10.6	1,170	5.0
1983	2,446	10.5	1,158	4.9
1984	2,477	10.5	1,169	5.0
1985	2,413	10.1	1,190	5.0
1986	2,400	10.0	1,159	4.8
1987	2,421	9.9	1,157	4.8
1988[1]	2,389	9.7	1,183	4.8

1. Estimated figures.   **Sources:** U.S. Bureau of the Census, *The Statistical History of the U.S.* (1976); U.S. National Center for Health Statistics, *Vital Statistics of the United States 1987* (1988) and *Monthly Vital Statistics Report, March 1989* (1989).

Marriages An estimated 2.38 million couples married during 1988, a decrease of 1% from 1987; the marriage rate also fell from 9.9 to 9.7 per 1,000 population. Until 1987 the rate had not fallen below 10 during the 1970s or the 1980s. Whether or not this represents any kind of trend is difficult to determine, since so many people are postponing marriage until they are much older than what was once the norm. In 1960, for example, about 40% of all 19-year-old women were married, but by 1988 only 14% were. Also in 1960, 90% of all women were married before they reached age 30, but by 1988 only 70% were. For men the figures are just as startling: in 1970 only 21% of men were still unmarried before the age of 30, but by 1988 the figure was 43%.

Divorces An estimated 1.18 million divorces were granted in 1988, a 2% increase over 1987; the divorce rate per 1,000 population remained at 4.8, where it has been since 1986, down from its peak of 5.3 in 1979. (In that year the divorce rate per 1,000 married women reached 22.8, up from 9.2 in 1960.)

In 1985, the most recent year for which final divorce statistics (as opposed to estimates) are available, there were 5.4 million divorced men and 7.9 million divorced women. Divorce rates were highest for teenage wives (48 per 1,000 married teenagers), about twice the rate of wives ages 35–39.

Divorce is generally more prevalent among the young. In 1985, 40% of men and 50% of women divorcing for the first time were under 30, figures that reflect the early demise of a sizable portion of all marriages: 12% had lasted one year or less, 30%, three years or less.

MARRIAGE RATES AND DIVORCE RATES IN THE U.S. 1960–88 (per 1,000 population)

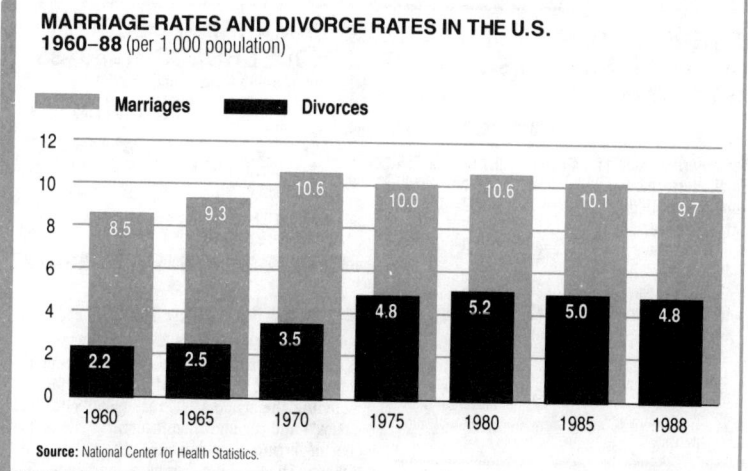

Source: National Center for Health Statistics.

MEDIAN AGE AT FIRST MARRIAGE, BY SEX, 1890–1988

Year	Male	Female
1890	26.1	22.0
1900	25.9	21.9
1910	25.1	21.6
1920	24.6	21.2
1930	24.3	21.3
1940	24.3	21.5
1950	22.8	20.3
1960	22.8	20.3
1970	23.2	20.8
1980	24.7	22.0
1985	25.5	23.3
1988	25.9	23.6

Sources: U.S. Bureau of the Census, *The Statistical History of the U.S.* (1976) and *Marital Status and Living Arrangements: March 1988* (1989).

PERCENT OF POPULATION NEVER MARRIED, BY AGE AND SEX, 1960–88

Sex and age	1960	1970	1980	1988
MEN				
Total: 15 and over	**23.2%**	**28.1%**	**29.6%**	**29.9%**
15–17	98.8	99.4	99.4	99.3
18	94.6	95.1	97.4	98.0
19	87.1	89.9	90.9	95.1
20–24	53.1	54.7	68.8	77.7
25–29	20.8	19.1	33.1	43.3
30–34	11.9	9.4	15.9	25.0
35–39	8.8	7.2	7.8	14.0
40–44	7.3	6.3	7.1	7.5
45–54	7.4	7.5	6.1	5.6
55–64	8.0	7.8	5.3	4.9
65+	7.7	7.5	4.9	4.6

Sex and age	1960	1970	1980	1988
WOMEN				
Total: 15 and over	**17.3%**	**22.1%**	**22.5%**	**22.9%**
15–17	93.2	97.3	97.0	97.7
18	75.6	82.0	88.0	92.4
19	59.7	68.8	77.6	86.0
20–24	28.4	35.8	50.2	61.1
25–29	10.5	10.5	20.9	29.5
30–34	6.9	6.2	9.5	16.1
35–39	6.1	5.4	6.2	9.0
40–44	6.1	4.9	4.8	6.2
45–54	7.0	4.9	4.7	5.1
55–64	8.0	6.8	4.5	4.0
65+	8.5	7.7	5.9	5.3

Source: U.S. Bureau of the Census, *Marital Status and Living Arrangements: March 1988* (1989).

INTERRACIAL MARRIED COUPLES IN THE U.S., 1970–87 (in thousands)

	1970	1980	1987
Total married couples	44,597	49,714	52,286
Total interracial	310	651	799
Total black–white	65	167	177
Husband black, wife white	41	122	121
Wife black, husband white	24	45	56
Total other interracial	245	484	622
Husband black	8	20	33
Wife black	4	14	8
Husband white	139	287	358
Wife white	94	163	223

Source: U.S. Bureau of the Census, *Statistical Abstract of the United States 1989* (1989).

DIVORCED PERSONS PER 1,000 MARRIED PERSONS, BY SEX AND RACE, 1960–88

	1960	1970	1980	1988
BOTH SEXES				
All races	35	47	100	133
White	33	44	92	124
Black	62	83	203	263
Hispanic[2]	N.A.	61	98	137
MALE				
All races	28	35	79	110
White	27	32	74	102
Black	45	62	149	216
Hispanic	N.A.	40	64	106
FEMALE				
All races	42	60	120	156
White	38	56	110	146
Black	78	104	258	311
Hispanic	N.A.	81	132	167

Note: With spouse present.   2. Persons of Hispanic origin may be of any race.   **Source:** U.S. Bureau of the Census, *Marital Status and Living Arrangements: March 1988* (1989).

UNMARRIED COUPLE HOUSEHOLDS, 1960–88
(numbers in thousands)

	1960	1970	1980	1988
Total	439	523	1,589	2,588
Without children under 15	242	327	1,159	1,786
With children under 15	197	196	431	802

Source: U.S. Bureau of the Census, *Marital Status and Living Arrangements: March 1988* (1989).

The Fertility Rates of American Women

Population experts predict future trends in population growth by studying many factors, including the crude birth rate (see "Vital Statistics") and the significant fertility rates. The *general fertility rate* measures the ratio of live births to the total number of women ages 15 to 44. The *total fertility rate* is the number of births 1,000 women ages 10 to 50 would have in their lifetimes if at each year of age they experienced the birth rates occurring to women of that age in the specified calendar year. The total fertility rate is sometimes defined in the popular media as the number of *likely* births one woman will have in her lifetime. In 1988, for example, the official total fertility rate was 1,930 per 1,000 women, but it often appeared in the media as 1.9 per woman.

The total fertility rate is most helpful in measuring long-term trends, especially in determining whether or not the nation is sustaining a level of reproduction necessary for maintaining current population levels. That level, generally regarded as 2,100 per 1,000 women, has not been achieved in the United States since 1971. Since 1980 the figure has hovered around 1,800, and despite sudden upward bursts such as occurred in 1987 and 1988, the Census Bureau predicts that the rates will not reach 2,100 again in the foreseeable future. It is this fact that has made the topic of immigration policy such a crucial one for the future. (See also the section "Immigration.")

FERTILITY RATES OF U.S. WOMEN, 1930–88

Year	General fertility rate	Total fertility rate
1930	89.2	2,600
1931	84.6	2,467
1932	81.7	2,383
1933	76.3	2,235
1934	78.5	2,294
1935	77.2	2,250
1936	75.8	2,207
1937	77.1	2,236
1938	79.1	2,288
1939	77.6	2,238
1940	79.9	2,301
1941	83.4	2,399
1942	91.5	2,628
1943	94.3	2,718
1944	88.8	2,568
1945	85.9	2,491
1946	101.9	2,943
1947	113.3	3,274
1948	107.3	3,109
1949	107.1	3,110
1950	106.2	3,091
1951	111.4	3,267
1952	113.8	3,355
1953	115.0	3,418
1954	117.9	3,537
1955	118.3	3,574
1956	121.0	3,682
1957	122.7	3,760
1958	120.0	3,693
1959	119.9	3,705
1960	118.0	3,654
1961	117.2	3,629
1962	112.2	3,474
1963	108.5	3,333
1964	105.0	3,208
1965	96.6	2,928
1966	91.3	2,736
1967	87.6	2,573
1968	85.7	2,477
1969	86.5	2,465
1970	87.9	2,480
1971	81.6	2,267
1972	73.1	2,010
1973	68.8	1,879
1974	67.8	1,835
1975	66.0	1,774
1976	65.0	1,738
1977	66.8	1,790
1978	65.5	1,760
1979	67.2	1,808
1980	68.4	1,840
1981	67.4	1,815
1982	67.3	1,829
1983	65.8	1,803
1984	65.4	1,806
1985	66.2	1,843
1986	64.9	1,823[1]
1987	65.7	1,871[1]
1988	67.3	1,930[1]

1. Estimated.   **Source:** U.S. Bureau of the Census, *U.S. Population Estimates and Components of Change 1970–87* (1988).

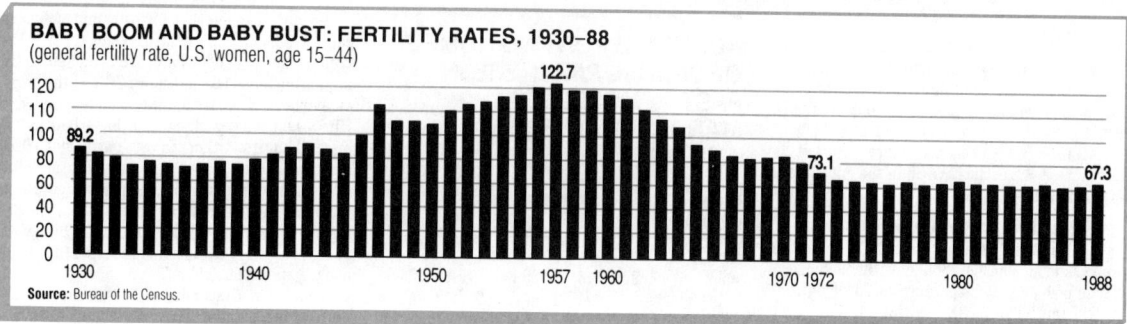

BABY BOOM AND BABY BUST: FERTILITY RATES, 1930–88
(general fertility rate, U.S. women, age 15–44)

Source: Bureau of the Census.

Women and Childbearing: Current Trends

According to the Census Bureau's Current Population Survey, there were 52,586,000 women in the Unitd States ages 18 to 44; 3.7 million of them reported having a birth in the preceding 12 months, resulting in an estimated fertility rate of 69.7 births per 1,000 women ages 18 to 44 (it was 67.3 for women ages 15–44). These figures have not fluctuated a great deal over the last decade, despite the increased number of women of childbearing age in the population. This means that more women today are not having children (38.0% in 1988, as compared with 35.1% in 1976), and all the predictions are that this trend will continue.

Minorities Significantly higher fertility rates were reported among minorities: 94 per 1,000 Hispanic women and 87 for black women, as compared with 66 for white women. It should be noted, however, that there were no significant differences between black and white fertility rates among women over 24; only in the 18–24 category do black women have significantly more births per 1,000 women (151.2 as against 76.3 for white women).

Hispanic women ages 18 to 44 accounted for 11% of all births in the Census Bureau survey, although they represented only 8% of all women in the United States. The fertility rate among Hispanic women was 94.0 births per 1,000 women ages 18–44, as compared with 67.5 per 1,000 for all women. Only 33.6% of Hispanic women ages 18–44 were childless, as compared with 38.4% for non-Hispanic women. Not surprisingly, Hispanic women ages 18–44 have an average of 1.6 children each, as compared with 1.3 for non-Hispanic women.

Women over 29 The Census Bureau noted again, as it had in previous reports, that a significant number of women in their thirties were having children or were planning to. In 1976 only 19% of the children born in the United States were born to women in their thirties, but in the 12 months ending June 1988, 33% were; the birth rate for women ages 30–34 was 81.6 in 1988, as compared with 60.0 in 1980 and 56.4 in 1976; for women 35–39 the birth rate was 33.8 in 1988, as against 22.6 the decade before. (There has also been a relatively sharp increase in the birth rate for women ages 40–44, from 6.5 per 1,000 in 1976 to 9.2 in the 1988 survey).

For a variety of economic and social reasons, many women of the Baby Boom generation have been postponing childbirth, but they are not planning to remain childless. In the 1988 survey, 15% of all married women ages 30–34 were childless, much higher than the 1975 figure of 7.9%; but in 1988 over 54% of childless wives 30–34 said they were expecting a future birth, a significant increase over the 33% who gave the same answer in the 1975 survey.

Work Force Directly related to women's postponing childbirth is the increase in their labor force participation rates and in their levels of education attainment. In 1976, 31% of all women ages 18–44 were in the labor force, but in the 1988 survey, 50.9% were. Among college-educated women this figure soared to just under 60%, and for older women (30–44) to over 68%. Only among Hispanic women did labor force participation remain relatively low (36.6%) in the year they had a birth.

Pregnancies of Unmarried Women Finally, the Census Bureau reports that the number of out-of-wedlock and premaritally conceived births continued to increase. Between 1985 and 1988, 40% of all first births to women ages 15–29 fell into these categories, an increase of over 7 percentage points for 1970–74 when the figure was 32.8%. Among black women the proportion of first births in these categories was 78.8%, as compared with 32.8% for whites and 42.7% for Hispanics.

BIRTH RATES PER 1,000 WOMEN, BY AGE GROUP, 1960–86

Age of mother (years)	1960	1970	1980	1986
10–14	0.8	1.2	1.1	1.3
15–19	89.1	68.3	53.0	50.6
20–24	258.1	167.8	115.1	108.2
25–29	197.4	145.1	112.9	109.2
30–34	112.7	73.3	61.9	69.3
35–39	56.2	31.7	19.8	24.3
40–44	15.5	8.1	3.9	4.1
Live births (thousands)	**4,258**	**3,731**	**3,612**	**3,757**

Source: U.S. National Center for Health Statistics, *Vital Statistics of the United States 1986* (1988).

PERCENTAGE OF FIRST BIRTHS, BY AGE OF MOTHER, 1970–87

Age	1970	1987
Under 20	35.6%	23.3%
20–24	45.6	33.0
25–29	14.8	27.8
30–34	3.0	12.4
35+	1.0	3.5

Source: U.S. National Center for Health Statistics.

SEX IN AMERICA

Pollsters scrutinize every angle of American life, including what goes on beyond closed bedroom doors. The research ranges from the statistical—like the survey done by the National Center for Health Statistics—to the anecdotal, such as reader polls taken by popular "women's" magazines.

The National Survey of Family Growth is conducted periodically by the National Center for Health Statistics, with a national sample of women ages 15 to 44 years old. The most recent report, issued in July 1987, used data compiled in 1982. Questions concerned marriage and sexual activity. Some findings from the report:

• By age 25, 97% of women have had sexual intercourse.

• Of women ages 15 to 19, 47% have had intercourse.

• Nearly 70% of all married women had premarital intercourse.

• Women in their early 20s began having intercourse earlier than women who are presently in their early 30s.

• Patterns of first intercourse were affected by educational level and family life-style. College-educated women were likely to begin having intercourse later (and to marry later) than high school dropouts. Women who came from single-parent families were more likely to begin having intercourse (and to marry) at earlier ages than women who had lived with both parents.

Among women who had intercourse in the three months before the National Survey of Family Growth interview, more than two-thirds reported having intercourse once a week or more, and over two-fifths said they had intercourse at least several times a week. Women ages 25–29 were more likely than either older or younger women to have intercourse several times a week. The data suggest a pattern in which intercourse becomes more frequent as age increases, reaches a peak in the mid-to-late 20s, and then declines.

Number of Sexual Partners

The National Opinion Research Center at the University of Chicago looked at the sexual behavior of 1,481 adults (a representative nationwide sample) in 1988 and found that most adults were either monogamous or abstained from sex. The survey's findings:

- 60% of men and women claimed only one sexual partner.
- 22% claimed no sexual partner.
- 11% claimed two to four.
- 2% five or more.
- 6% didn't respond.

In reference to gender of partners, 91.3% of the male respondents said their partners were exclusively female; 3% said partners were exclusively male; 0.4% said they were bisexual; and 5.3% did not answer the question. Of the female respondents, 95.4% said their partners were exclusively male; 0.2% said their partners were exclusively female; and 4.4% did not answer the question.

In addition, 6% of the men and 1% of the women indicated that at least one partner was a casual date or a "pickup."

Similar results were obtained from a *Los Angeles Times* telephone survey of 2,095 adults in July 1987. In that survey 15% said they had no sexual partners in the last year; 70% said they had only one; 8% two to four partners, 3% five or more partners, and 4% refused to answer or were not sure.

What Americans Believe about Sex: A Summary of Some Recent Surveys

Government agencies and university research centers are not alone in their efforts to find out what men and women think about sex and related topics. Magazines survey their readers, and the results mirror the magazine's image, whether traditional *Redbook* or "liberated" *Cosmopolitan*. A sampling of several recent surveys:

Redbook This magazine, aimed at the woman who "juggles" home, husband, and work, received 26,000 replies to a questionnaire distributed in 1987. The results were compared to a similar *Redbook* survey in 1974. The findings: more than half the respondents had their first sexual encounter when 17 or younger, compared with 39% in 1974. In 1974, 33% said they were satisfied with their sex lives compared with 43% in 1987. However, *Redbook* readers reported having sex less often in 1987, with 41% of the readers reporting sex once a week or less, compared with 28% in 1974. "Lack of time" and "too tired" were reasons commonly cited. The majority (85%) have seen at least one X-rated movie, compared with 60% in the earlier survey. Fewer readers report extramarital af-

ADULTS REPORTING NUMBER OF SEXUAL PARTNERS IN THE PAST 12 MONTHS, BY MARITAL STATUS, SEX, AND AGE, 1988

Number of sex partners	Age of respondents 18–29	30–44	45–60	+61	Total
ALL MEN:					
0	9.7%	8.2%	16.4%	30.3%	14.6%
1	46.1	71.0	64.6	60.6	61.3
2	9.1	5.6	6.4	0.8	5.6
3	9.7	3.9	1.8	2.3	4.7
4	6.1	2.6	0.9	2.3	3.1
5–10	8.5	1.3	0.9	–	2.8
10+	3.0	0.9	1.8	–	1.4
No answer	7.9	6.5	7.3	3.8	6.4
ALL WOMEN:					
0	7.3%	7.1%	28.5%	60.8%	26.7%
1	66.0	77.8	62.9	29.8	58.2
2	13.1	5.2	2.6	0.8	5.2
3	4.2	4.8	0.7	–	2.6
4	2.1	0.8	–	–	0.7
5–10	1.0	0.4	–	0.4	0.5
10+	–	0.4	0.7	–	0.2
No answer	6.3	3.6	4.6	8.2	5.9
MARRIED MEN, SPOUSE IN HOUSEHOLD:					
0	0%	3.8%	8.9%	20.4%	8.5%
1	80.0	87.2	78.5	74.2	81.2
2	2.0	2.6	3.8	–	2.1
3	4.0	–	1.3	1.1	1.1
4	2.0	–	–	1.1	0.5
5–10	–	0.6	1.3	–	0.5
10	–	–	1.3	–	0.3
No answer	12.0	5.8	5.1	3.2	5.8
MARRIED WOMEN, SPOUSE IN HOUSEHOLD:					
0	0%	3.5%	7.3%	24.5%	8.8%
1	89.3	91.6	85.4	65.3	82.9
2	3.6	–	–	1.0	1.0
3	2.4	–	–	–	0.5
4	–	–	–	–	–
5–10	–	–	–	1.0	0.2
10+	–	–	1.2	–	0.2

Note: Dash (–) indicates zero. **Source:** National Opinion Research Center, *General Social Survey, 1988* (1988).

fairs—26%—versus 29% in 1974.

Cosmopolitan Aimed at the liberated 1980s woman, this magazine polled 100 women between the ages of 19 and 45 in late 1987. They found that 49% had only one sex partner in 1987, over 25% had two partners, and 9% had more than three partners. The number of women who were celibate was 9%. Most of the women (47%) had sexual relations with a new partner by the third or fourth date, 37% waited longer, and about 1% did so on the first date.

Glamour This magazine for the college and young working woman wanted to see if fear of contracting AIDS had changed readers' lives. A 1988 survey, based on interviews with 1,800 women, found that among single women, 67% had become more selective about partners, 22% had become monogamous, 21% had the man use a condom to prevent the spread of AIDS, and 11% had become celibate.

Several other surveys have examined Americans' sex lives. Some, like the ones reported by popular author Shere Hite, are attacked as using highly biased data. (About 70% of the women married five years or more who responded to Hite's last survey claimed to have had extramarital affairs.) Other surveys, while not 100% statistically representative samples of adult Americans, are believed to be fairly accurate in their findings. (The 1950 Kinsey Report is still regarded as the most reliable report in the last 40 years.) One such survey was reported in a 1982 book, *American Couples*. To compile information for this book, University of Washington sociologists Philip Blumstein and Pepper Schwartz used information from 12,000 questionnaires, filled out by heterosexual, gay, and lesbian couples. Their findings on two much-discussed topics are as follows:

Sexual Frequency The study found that although married men are less monogamous than women and have more sexual partners, they do not have as many emotional attachments. Women who are nonmonogamous are much more likely to be involved in an affair rather than a strictly sexual relationship.

In 1985 advice columnist Ann Landers asked her readers whether they would rather cuddle or couple. An astonishing 72% of almost

"DEAR ABBY" ON MARITAL FIDELITY

One of the most widely read columns in the history of newspapers, "Dear Abby" appears in 1,200 publications worldwide and is read by 90 million people a week. So, what "Abby"—Abigail Van Buren—says about our mores and morals is worth listing.

In her fidelity survey of June 1987, which brought over 210,000 responses, Abby said she was both astonished and reassured to learn that the marriage vow—to forsake all others—is still honored by 85% of the females and 74% of the males who responded. The most surprising revelation in this survey was the number of male bisexuals that surfaced. Although mental health professionals in the past have estimated that 10% of the population is either gay or bisexual, Dear Abby's survey indicated that there are possibly twice that number. However, the number of faithful older lovers was heartening to Abby. Letter after letter described enduring, true-blue marriages, from couples in their 60s, 70s, and 80s who have been faithful for 40 or more years. One such couple summed it up succinctly when they told Dear Abby: "We're writing because we want to add to the number of couples who have never cheated. I'm 92 and my wife is 88. We've been married for 71 years, still have all our marbles and enjoy every aspect of married life, though we have slowed up some in recent years (arthritis)."

100,000 women respondents said they would rather hug than have sexual intercourse. Forty percent of the women who would rather cuddle were under 40 years old.

Homosexuality in the United States

Despite all the attention focused on AIDS, there has not been a generally accepted tally of the number of homosexuals in the country. A group of scientists in 1989 called for a new national survey of sexual preferences because of the lack of reliable data. The last major national survey was done 40 years ago by Alfred Kinsey. The Kinsey team found in their 1950 study that 37% of the male sample had had at least one homosexual experience, and that 4% identified their primary sexual orientation as homosexual. However, many sociologists question the 37% because Kinsey's sample included a disproportionate number of prison inmates, a group much more likely to engage in homosexual activity. With respect to lesbians, Kinsey found that 13% of women claimed to have had a same-sex experience, while 3% defined their sexual orientation as lesbian.

A more recent survey, presented in a paper at the 1988 American Sociological Association by Professor Joseph Harry of Northern Illinois University, found that 3.7% of the 663 respondents to a phone survey said they were primarily homosexual or bisexual. And 42% of those men were currently married. The survey was designed to be as accurate as possible using a weighted sample.

Birth Control

Sterilization is the leading method of contraception, with almost a third of all married women choosing this method for birth control. The percentage of married males and females opting for sterilization has increased markedly in the last 15 years. In 1973, 11.2% of married males were sterilized, and of married females, 12.3%. Use of the pill has declined sharply among married women from a high of 36.1% in 1973, although it is still by far the number one choice among unmarried women. One reason for the difference is that many physicians discourage use of the pill after age 35, so a sizable number of women, having married and had children, turn to sterilization after years of birth control pill use while they were single. Use of condoms has gone up from 1982, when 9% of single women used this method. The reason may be an increased use to prevent sexually transmitted diseases.

Birth Control Devices

Barrier Methods (Foams, Jellies, Suppositories) Failure rates of 10% to 25%; available without prescription.
Cervical Cap Failure rate of 4% to 25%; can be worn for several days prior to intercourse; some difficulty in fitting properly.
Condom Failure rate of 3% to 15% because of incorrect use; protects against sexually transmitted diseases; available without prescrip-

tion; inconvenient to use.
Diaphragm Failure rate of 4% to 25% because of improper or inconsistent use; no side effects; may provide protection against some sexually transmitted diseases; must be fitted by a doctor; must be worn for a certain length of time before and after intercourse to be effective.
Intrauterine Device (IUD) Failure rate of 1% to 5%; requires insertion by a physician; may cause some pelvic diseases.
Pill Failure rate is from 1% to 5%, usually because women forget to take it; highly effective and convenient; reduces risk of some types of ovarian and uterine cancers; nearly triples the risk of heart attack or stroke (very uncommon in young women); some studies found pill can double risk of breast cancer.
Sponge Failure rates of 10% to 25%; available without prescription.
Sterilization Close to 100% effective; safe, highly effective, and convenient; usually not reversible.

The Pornography Industry

Regardless of one's definition of *pornography*—whether it is the narrow category of hardcore "smut" or the broader one including all "sexually explicit material"—it is a huge industry, with sales of between $2 billion to $10 billion a year. With the advent of X-rated videocassettes, Dial-A-Porn phone lines, and computer subscription services, the industry has moved out of seedy movie theaters into big business.

Since most porn producers do not issue annual reports, it is difficult to arrive at accurate figures. The most widely accepted industry report was completed in 1986 by the U.S. Attorney General's Commission on Pornography. The 11-member commission issued a two-volume, 1,900-page report after listening to testimony from witnesses around the country and reviewing 2,375 magazines, 725 books, and 2,370 films. Although the report's recommendations came under attack from civil libertarians, its findings on the pornography industry provide a comprehensive look at how money is made. Some findings from the report:

Motion Pictures

The average cost of producing a feature-length pornographic movie is $75,000. A current trend is for the producer (who is also the writer and director) to do a takeoff on a general-release film (*On Golden Blonde*, *The Wizard of Ahs*). It is not uncommon for producers to use the same script for more than one movie. Films are shot in motel rooms, private homes, or on sound stages. On average, female performers earn between $350 and $500 a day, men between $250 and $450 per day. Some porn "stars" earn as much as $1,000 to $2,500 per day. Actors are also paid on the basis of the number and type of sex acts they perform; some receive as much as $250 per sex act. In 1985 about 100 full-length, sexually explicit films were distributed to nearly 700 "adult" theaters. With estimated sales of about 2 million tickets per week, these theaters generated an estimated $500 million annually in box-office receipts.

Videotape Cassettes

After VCRs were first marketed in 1975, X-rated videotapes constituted more than half of videocassette sales. Though the increase in sales of legitimate videos has slashed the porn video's market share, porn videos are still an important part of the market. Nearly 40% of all VCR owners polled in a 1985 *Newsweek* survey said they bought or rented an X-rated videotape within the previous year. About 1,600 adult videos were released in 1986, according to *Adult Video News*, a trade publication. One reason for the large number of releases is that videos are cheap to make and extremely profitable. A 60-minute video can be produced in two days at a cost of between $4,000 and $8,000. A 90-minute video takes three days at a cost of between $10,000 and $20,000. The producer often sells his video at 100% profit to a distributor, who in turn markets it to stores nationwide. Even the most successful X-rated tape sells no more than 10,000 copies.

Dial-A-Porn

This "dirty talk"—prerecorded descriptions of sex acts and live conversations with paid performers—began in 1982 when the FCC deregulated Dial-it services. Phone companies held lotteries to select Dial-it providers. Telephone-porn lines are a $2.4 billion industry, making profits for both the provider and the phone companies. In the first type of call—an explicit conversation between the caller and the performer—the charge of $15 to $30 is billed directly to the caller's credit card. The cost of the second type of call—a prerecorded message—is charged to the caller's monthly phone bill. Many Dial-it providers can transmit messages to as many as 50,000 callers per hour. The message provider and the telephone company generally split the call charge according to local regulations. The telephone company earns from two cents to 19 cents for a one-minute call, with the remainder going to the porn provider. Pacific Bell estimated that in the year ending in October 1985, it earned $12 million from Dial-A-Porn calls. A major criticism of these services is that anyone, including children, can dial these openly advertised numbers.

Computers

Instead of calling up a database, some computer operators punch up a conversation with a sex service. A computer operator can subscribe to a service for an initial cost of $35 to $100 and a user fee of $15 to $25 per hour. SEXTEX is one computer network that offers several services from "dirty talk" conference calls via computer to a bulletin board for personal messages.

Magazines

While many people do not consider magazines such as *Playboy* pornography, these publications do fall under the general heading of sexually explicit material. Beginning in 1980 the circulation of *Penthouse*, *Playboy*, *Gallery*, *Oui*, and other men's "skin" magazines has fallen off. Between 1980 and 1987, *Playboy* and *Penthouse* each dropped about 2 million copies in circulation. *Playboy* went from an average monthly circulation of 5 million in 1980 to 3.4

million in 1987, and *Penthouse* from 4.2 million to 2.2 million. Two reasons are cited for the decrease: one is the increased availability of X-rated videocassettes (and the corresponding increase in VCRs), and the other is the reluctance of many convenience stores (the primary source of sales) to sell or openly display men's magazines, due to pressures from conservatives, women's groups, and the government. To make up for lost profits, *Playboy* and *Penthouse* have ventured into producing videocassettes. *Playboy* also runs a cable channel, which has met with mixed results.

HOUSEHOLDS AND FAMILIES

Since the very first census in 1790, the federal government has not only attempted to count every individual, it has also tried to determine where those individuals live and with whom. While the definition of *household* has changed somewhat over the years, it has remained a central element in understanding the basic structure of American society. Since 1970 the size and composition of the household unit has revealed the extent of social change more clearly than any other measure.

Virtually all Americans are part of a household. As of March 1988, the Census Bureau determined that 240.1 million persons—out of a total population of 245.1 million—belonged to some form of household unit (the remainder were in institutions or other kinds of group living arrangements). According to the official Census Bureau definition, a household consists of "all persons who occupy a housing unit. A house, an apartment or other group of rooms, or a single room is regarded as a housing unit when it is occupied or intended for occupancy as separate living quarters; that is, when the occupants do not live and eat with any other persons in the structure, and there is direct access from the outside or through a common hall."

FAMILIES: NUMBER, AVERAGE SIZE, AND PERCENT DISTRIBUTION, BY NUMBER OF CHILDREN, 1970–88

			PERCENT DISTRIBUTION by number of own children under 18				
Year	No. of families (thousands)	Avg. size of family	None	1	2	3	4 or more
1970	51,586	3.58	44.1%	18.2%	17.4%	10.6%	9.8%
1975	55,712	3.42	46.0	19.7	18.0	9.3	6.9
1980	59,550	3.29	47.9	20.9	19.3	7.8	4.1
1985	62,706	3.23	50.4	20.9	18.6	7.2	3.0
1987	64,491	3.19	50.5	21.3	18.5	6.9	2.8
1988	65,133	3.17	51.0	21.0	18.2	7.0	2.8

Sources: U.S. Bureau of the Census, *Household and Family Characteristics: March 1988* (1989) and *Statistical Abstract of the United States 1989* (1989).

HOUSEHOLDS AND FAMILIES: GROWTH AND CHANGE, 1960–88 (numbers in thousands)

Type of unit	1960	1970	1980	1985	1988	Percent change 1970–80	Percent change 1980–88
HOUSEHOLDS	**52,799**	**63,401**	**80,776**	**86,789**	**91,061**	**27.4%**	**12.7%**
Average size	3.33	3.14	2.76	2.69	2.64	N.A.	N.A.
Family households	44,905	51,456	59,550	62,706	65,133	15.7	9.4
Married couple	39,254	44,728	49,112	50,350	51,809	9.8	5.5
Male householder[1]	1,228	1,228	1,733	2,228	2,715	41.1	56.7
Female householder[1]	4,422	5,500	8,705	10,129	10,608	58.3	21.9
Nonfamily households	7,895	11,945	21,226	24,082	25,929	77.7	22.2
Male householder	2,716	4,063	8,807	10,114	11,305	116.8	28.4
Female householder	5,179	7,882	12,419	13,968	14,623	57.6	17.7
One person	6,896	10,851	18,296	20,602	21,884	68.6	19.6
FAMILIES	**45,111**	**51,586**	**59,550**	**62,706**	**65,133**	**15.4%**	**9.4%**
Average size	3.67	3.58	3.29	3.23	3.17	N.A.	N.A.
Married couple	39,329	44,755	49,112	50,350	51,809	9.7	5.5
Male householder[1]	1,275	1,239	1,733	2,228	2,715	39.9	56.7
Female householder[1]	4,507	5,591	8,705	10,129	10,608	55.7	21.9
UNRELATED SUBFAMILIES	**207**	**130**	**360**	**526**	**537**	**176.9%**	**49.2%**
Married couple	75	27	20	46	38	N.A.[2]	N.A.[2]
Male reference persons[1]	47	11	36	85	46	N.A.[2]	N.A.[2]
Female reference persons[1]	85	91	304	395	452	234.1	48.7
RELATED SUBFAMILIES	**1,514**	**1,150**	**1,150**	**2,228**	**2,396**	**0%**	**108.3%**
Married couple	871	617	582	719	765	-5.7	31.4
Father-child[1]	115	48	54	116	152	N.A.[2]	N.A.[2]
Mother-child[1]	528	484	512	1,392	1,479	5.8	188.9

1. No spouse present. 2. Not shown; base less than 75,000. **Sources:** U.S. Bureau of the Census. *Household and Family characteristics: March 1988* (1989), *The Statistical History of the U.S.* (1976), and *Statistical Abstract of the United States* (1989).

There are two major categories of households identified by the Census Bureau: family and nonfamily. A family or family household requires the presence of at least two persons, the householder (i.e., the person in whose name the housing unit is owned or rented) and one or more additional family members related to the householder through birth, adoption or marriage. A nonfamily household consists of a householder who either lives alone or exclusively with persons who are not related to the householder. Since 1970 the rapid growth of nonfamily households has led to a continuous increase in the number of households and a fall in the average number of persons in each.

As of March 1988, there was a total of 91.1 million households in the United States, the largest number ever, with an average of 2.64 persons in each, the lowest number ever. While the U.S. population grew by 8.5% between 1980 and 1988, the number of households increased 13.9%, or 11.1 million units. This continues a trend begun during the 1970s when the number of households increased by more than 20%, or over 17.3 million units, nearly double the 1940s and 1950s growth and over 60% more than the relatively explosive 1960s. The most significant change helping to ignite this surge was the unprecedented increase in the number of nonfamily households, which grew by 53.4% in the 1970s and 45.7% during the 1980s.

Several factors help to account for this sudden boom, including the rapid rise in the divorce rate and an increase in the number of young single people living on their own and deciding to postpone marriage. The demo-graphic results can be found in the increasing number of people living alone (up 54% in the 1970s and 20% in the 1980s); in 1988 some 22 million people lived alone, a total of 84% of the 25.9 million nonfamily households.

An additional 2.6 million unmarried-couple households make up the largest proportion of the remaining number; while they compose only 5% of the 54.4 million couples in the United States who maintain their own households, their sudden appearance on the American social landscape during the 1970s—they increased by about 120% during that decade—made them the subject of widespread media coverage. As currently defined by the Census Bureau, an unmarried-couple household is two persons of the opposite sex who share living quarters; although a close personal relationship is implied, other types—including tenancy—are included. But no more than two unrelated adults are present in an unmarried-couple household, although children under age 15 may be present (31%, or about 806,000, did contain such children in 1988).

Despite all the attention given to the growth of nonfamily households, the fact remains that the overwhelming majority of Americans—206.7 million in 1988–live in some kind of family situation. This is not to say that the size and structure of the family hasn't undergone major revamping in recent decades, but rather to emphasize its inherent strength as the basic social unit despite the presence of powerful forces for change.

In 1988 there were 65.1 million families in the United States; almost 80% (51.8 million) were married couples, and almost half of those

NUMBER OF U.S. HOUSEHOLDS AND AVERAGE NUMBER OF PERSONS PER HOUSEHOLD, 1940–88

Year	Number of households (thousands)	Average number per household All ages	Under 18	18 yrs. and older
1940	34,949	3.67	1.14	2.53
1950	43,544	3.37	1.06	2.31
1955	47,874	3.33	1.14	2.19
1960	52,799[1]	3.33	1.21	2.12
1965	57,436	3.29	1.21	2.09
1970	63,401	3.14	1.09	2.05
1975	71,120	2.94	0.93	2.01
1980	80,776	2.76	0.79	1.97
1985	86,789	2.69	0.72	1.97
1988	91,066	2.64	0.70	1.94

1. Alaska and Hawaii included for first time. **Sources:** U.S. Bureau of the Census, *The Statistical History of the U.S.* (1976) and *Households, Families, Marital Status and Living Arrangements (Advance Report) 1988* (1989).

NUMBER OF U.S. FAMILIES AND AVERAGE NUMBER OF PERSONS PER FAMILY HOUSEHOLD, 1940–88

Year	Number of families (thousands)	Average number per family families All ages	Under 18	Over 18
1940	31,491	3.76	1.24	2.52
1950	38,838	3.54	1.17	2.37
1955	41,732	3.59	1.30	2.29
1960[1]	44,905	3.67	1.41	2.26
1965	47,838	3.70	1.44	2.26
1970	51,456	3.58	1.34	2.25
1975	55,563	3.42	1.18	2.23
1980	59,550	3.29	1.05	2.23
1985	62,706	3.23	0.98	2.24
1988	65,133	3.17	0.96	2.21

1. Alaska and Hawaii included for first time. **Sources:** U.S. Bureau of the Census, *The Statistical History of the U.S.* (1976) and *Households, Families, Marital Status and Living Arrangements (Advance Report) 1988* (1989).

HOUSING UNITS, POPULATION, AND ROOMS, 1940–85
(figures in millions, except estimates)

Year	Year-round housing units	Resident population	Rooms	Estimated[1] rooms per unit	Estimated[1] rooms per person
1940	37	132	180	4.86	1.36
1950	46	151	217	4.71	1.44
1960	58	179	285	4.91	1.59
1970	68	203	342	5.03	1.68
1980	85	227	454	5.34	2.00
1985	97	239	523	5.39	2.19

1. Estimates are *Universal Almanac* calculations. **Source:** U.S. Bureau of the Census, *Housing in America 1985/86* (1989).

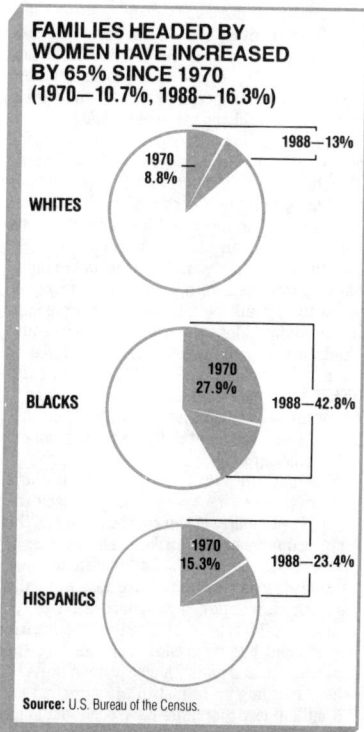

FAMILIES HEADED BY WOMEN HAVE INCREASED BY 65% SINCE 1970
(1970—10.7%, 1988—16.3%)

WHITES — 1970 8.8%, 1988—13%

BLACKS — 1970 27.9%, 1988—42.8%

HISPANICS — 1970 15.3%, 1988—23.4%

Source: U.S. Bureau of the Census.

(24.6 million) had children of their own under age 18. Because of the growth in nonfamily households and the postponement of marriage and childbearing, these figures represent very slow growth during the 1970s and 1980s. During these years, too, the number of female householders grew from 5.5 million to 10.6 million. All of these factors have contributed to two of the most significant social changes of the last 20 years: the lowering of average family size from 3.58 in 1970 to 3.17 in 1988 and the decline in the number of families without children under 18, of from 55.8% in 1970 to 49.0% in 1988.

Another important, though less vital, sign of change is the growth in the number of so-called subfamilies. These are families who live in a household and are either related to or not related to the householder. The Census Bureau describes a *related subfamily* as a married couple with or without children, or one parent with one or more of his or her own single (never married) children under 18 living in a household and related to the person who maintains the household. Related subfamilies have grown dramatically since 1980 (108%) to 2.4 million, and almost all of them are made up of mothers with children. They are not counted in the total number of families. An *unrelated subfamily* is a group of two persons or more who are related to each other by birth, marriage, or adoption, but who are not related to the householder. Unrelated subfamilies currently number 537,000, a more than 200% increase since 1970; often they are guests or boarders or resident employees.

HOUSING

According to a U.S. Bureau of the Census survey, there were about 88 million housing units occupied by home owners and renters in 1985, the latest year for which compete data are available. Home owners occupied 56 million units, and renters 32 million. The 11.5 million vacant housing units were either empty year-round (8 million) or on a seasonal basis (3 million).

Who Owns Homes? In 1987 about 64% of house holders owned their own homes, down from the record 68% in 1980. (About 78% of all married couples and about 73% of senior citizens owned homes.) White households had the highest home ownership at 66.8%, followed by blacks at 43.5%, and Hispanics at 39.6%.

The profile of owners and renters by age reflects the passage of adults through various stages of their lives. A majority of adults begin their householder life cycles as renters, become married, then take on ownership and mortgage payments. In 1985 most householders under 35 were renters, most householders 35 and older were owners. In terms of five-year age groups, however, ownership dominance began with the 30–34 age group.

Where Is the Housing Located? Overall, about 43% of all housing is located in suburbs, about 33% in cities, and about 24% in rural areas. About 49% of the owner-occupied units are in the suburbs; the other 51% is about equally divided between urban and rural. As for rental units, 47% were in cities, 36% in suburbs and, 17% in rural areas.

What Do They Cost? The median price of a new one-family house in the Northeast was $125,000 in 1986. In other areas of the country, the median prices for new houses in 1985 were $92,600 in the West, $80,300 in the Midwest, and $75,000 in the South. The high cost of houses is pricing many young couples out of the market. In the mid-1980s, fewer than half of young married renters had the income needed to buy a first home, as contrasted with the mid-1970s when three-fourths of such couples could afford a first home.

What Are the Monthly payments? The median monthly cost for owners of mortgaged homes—including taxes, fuel and utilities—was $566. The median cost of a nonmortaged home was $191. The median gross rent was $365 for all renters in 1985.

Condominiums and Cooperatives There were 3.7 million condos in 1985, with almost one-half in the South and one-fourth in the West. One million condos, half located in the South, were built from 1980 to 1985. About 700,000 condos are used seasonally, with the South again accounting for about three-fourths of all such units.

How Big Are the Houses? The median size of

single, detached homes and mobile homes was 1,583 square feet in 1985. Home-owner units were a median 1,712 square feet, about 38% larger than renter units at 1,245 square feet. The median size for one-unit family homes and mobile homes was 0.37 acre for home-owner lots and 0.30 acre for renter lots.

The average size of new houses built in 1986 was 1,825 square feet; about one-third were 2,000 square feet or more. This represents an increase of about 300 square feet, or 20%, over new houses built in 1966. Housing units in multifamily buildings built during the 1970s and 1980s averaged between 900 and 1,000 square feet, and in 1986 the average was 911 square feet.

The total number of rooms in housing units indicated growth in the amount of housing space available. In 1985 there were more than 500 million rooms in approximately 97 million year-round housing units. With a resident population of 240 million, this was an average of more than two rooms per person. About 46% of total rooms were bedrooms.

THE HOMELESS

Although homeless people have become a common sight in almost every community, their plight is always surrounded by some kind of controversy, one that is fueled by a wide range of opinions, some based on fact and others on stereotypes. The often shrill debate about just who the homeless are and what can or should be done for them has been hampered by a lack of reliable information on everything from the causes of homelessness to the actual number of people living on the streets or in shelters.

The Number of Homeless Estimates of the total number of homeless vary depending on the group doing the counting. The total ranges from about 50,000 (the U.S. Department of Housing and Urban Development) to three million (homeless advocacy groups).

A 1988 study by the National Alliance to End Homelessness calculated that on a given night, there are about 735,000 homeless in the United States, and that during the course of the year, between 1.3 and 2 million people will be homeless for one or more nights. Another study, released in 1988 by the Urban Institute, concluded that there were about 600,000 Americans living in shelters or on the streets on a given night.

The first comprehensive federal effort to count the homeless will be done as part of the 1990 census count. The Census Bureau plans to hire thousands of people who, armed with flashlights and survey questionnaires, will attempt to locate every homeless person they can find between 6 p.m. and 4 a.m. They plan to seek out homeless people in shelters, as well as those living on the streets and in cars and abandoned buildings. The Census Bureau has attempted to count the homeless before but not with such a wide-scale effort.

Who Are the Homeless? While a 1988 study of 27 major cities by the U.S. Conference of Mayors did not give a figure for the total number of homeless, the study did pinpoint a number of characteristics. Contrary to common belief, not all homeless are single men. The number of middle-age men has been shrinking, while families with young children are the fastest growing group. And, the demographics of the homeless differ dramatically from city to city.

The composition of the cities' homeless population, on average, was 49% single men; 34% members of families; 13% single women; and 5% runaway and so-called throwaway youth. Children—both in families and runaways—account for about 25% of the population. Persons considered mentally ill account for about 25% of the population; substance abusers account for 34%. The survey also found that 21% of homeless people are employed in full- or part-time jobs; 26% are veterans.

Another study found that the average age of single homeless men and women was between 34 and 37, which is much lower than found in previous decades. Homeless adults are likely to have never been married; they also usually don't have strong family ties.

The Institute of Medicine (part of the National Academy of Sciences) looked at a number of surveys and found that minorities composed the largest number of homeless in major cities like New York, Detroit, Chicago, Baltimore, and St. Louis. Whites accounted for the highest percentage in cities such as Milwaukee, Phoenix, Portland, and the state of Ohio.

Cities in which single men accounted for 60% or more of the homeless population included Charleston, Minneapolis, Nashville, Phoenix, Saint Paul, Salt Lake City, San Francisco, and San Juan. Cities where single men accounted for 30% or less of the population included Detroit, Kansas City, Mo., Norfolk, and Portland.

Unaccompanied youths, which are runaways and "throwaways" (children rejected by parents), account for 10% or more of the population in Denver, Los Angeles, New Orleans, Providence, San Antonio, San Francisco, and San Juan.

Thirty percent or more of the homeless were considered severely mentally ill in Boston, Charleston, Cleveland, Denver, Kansas City, Los Angeles, Nashville, Providence, San Francisco, San Juan, and Seattle. A survey funded by the Robert Wood Johnson Foundation estimated that a third of homeless adults are mentally ill.

Forty percent or more of the homeless were considered to be substance abusers in Cleveland, Hartford, Minneapolis, Providence, San Juan, Seattle, and Trenton.

A number of surveys have found that homeless elderly people make up less than 10% of the total. Several reasons for the low numbers are cited, including the availability of social welfare and medical programs to people over age 65, as well as the possibility that homeless people, in general, do not live to old age.

Homeless Families Families with chil-

dren account for more than half the homeless population in Detroit, New York City, Norfolk, Portland, and Trenton. They compose one-fifth or less in Charleston, Minneapolis, New Orleans, Phoenix, Saint Paul, San Francisco, and San Juan. Among homeless families 23% were headed by two parents; the rest by single parents, usually a woman with two to three children under the age of 5. Several studies cited by the Institute of Medicine found that two-parent homeless families are more common in the West and in rural, as opposed to urban, areas. Many homeless families face a wide variety of difficulties, including economic, educational, vocational, and social problems. A 1988 U.S. Department of Education survey estimated that there were 220,000 homeless school-age children; of those children, more than 65,000 do not attend school regularly.

Causes of Homelessness Every city surveyed by the Conference of Mayors cited lack of affordable housing for low-income people as the main cause of homelessness. Other causes frequently cited were unemployment, mental illness, substance abuse, poverty, teen pregnancy, and domestic violence.

A 1988 Institute of Medicine review of data on the causes of homelessness found three patterns: temporary, episodic, and chronic. In the first category fell people displaced from their homes by natural and man-made disasters, like hurricanes and fires. Once a low-income or poor person or family is temporarily homeless, it often becomes difficult to resettle in permanent housing because of other problems like loss of possessions, family breakup and substance abuse. Episodically homeless people are frequently welfare recipients who run out of funds halfway into the month, as well as runaway or throwaway youths who move in and out of family situations. They are also abused wives and children who may move in with relatives or friends from time to time. The chronically homeless—who live on the streets for long periods of time—are more likely to suffer from substance abuse and mental illness than members of the other groups.

The institute study also found that there appears to be a direct correlation between the reduced availability of low-cost housing and the increased number of homeless. The number of low-cost housing units has decreased, because as many as half a million are lost annually through conversion, abandonment, fire, or demolition. Moreover, since 1980 the federal government has reduced its subsidies for the construction and maintenance of such units by 60%. According to the institute, approximately 2.5 million low-cost units have been lost since 1980.

The institute also points to the jump in the number of poor Americans, about 10 million over the last decade, as a reason for the growing number of homeless.

The institute also noted that in several studies there was general agreement that deinstitutionalization from large mental facilities contributed to the increased number of homeless in the 1980s. They cited the lack of local community mental health services, such as group homes, as one of the primary reasons mentally ill people end up homeless.

Housing Today The average wait for assisted housing in the mayors' survey cities was 21 months. During 1988 the request for emergency shelter increased by an average of 13% across the survey cities. A 1989 HUD survey found that the private sector has shouldered a great deal of the burden in providing shelter. In 1988 the HUD survey found that 9 out of 10 shelters for the homeless were operated by community groups and churches, and that nearly 80,000 volunteers worked in shelters.

Federal Funding The various federal government programs to assist the homeless are grouped under the Stewart B. McKinney Homeless Assistance Act, which became law in July 1987. The act includes nearly 20 different provisions for emergency shelter, food, health care, mental health care, housing, educational programs, job training, and other community services. Federal agencies providing services include HUD, Health and Human Resources, the Federal Emergency Management Agency, and the Labor, Education, and Veterans' departments. Although the bill authorized $634 million in payments in fiscal 1989, Congress appropriated only $388 million. President George Bush's proposed 1990 budget included full funding for the McKinney program at $676 million. However, states and cities still pick up the major part of the bill for caring for the homeless. New York City, for example, budgeted $475 million to help the homeless in fiscal 1989.

IMMIGRATION

Over the last two centuries, the mingling of peoples from all parts of the world has been a vital element in the formation of the United States, both as a land of opportunity and in its emergence as a world power. In one relatively brief period, between 1880 and 1920, the massive influx of more than 20 million European immigrants provided the inexhaustible and indefatigable labor supply necessary to transform the nation from an agricultural society to an industrialized one with unparalleled rapidity.

NATIONS SENDING LARGEST PERCENTAGE OF TOTAL U.S. IMMIGRANTS, 1820–1987

Germany	13.0%
Italy	10.0
United Kingdom	9.4
Ireland	8.8
Canada	7.9
USSR	6.3
Austria-Hungary[1]	6.0
Mexico	5.0

1. All between 1860 and 1910.   **Source:** U.S. Immigration and Naturalization Service, *1987 Statistical Yearbook*, (1988).

ESTIMATED TOTAL NUMBER OF U.S. IMMIGRANTS, BY REGION AND SELECTED COUNTRY OF LAST RESIDENCE 1820–1988

Region/country	Total 1820–1988[1]	1988
EUROPE	**36,882,696**	**71,854**
Austria-Hungary	4,334,463	3,200
Austria	1,822,327[2]	2,493
Hungary	1,666,060[2]	707
Belgium	209,024	706
Czechoslovakia[3]	144,697	744
Denmark	369,121	581
France	779,221	3,637
Germany	7,060,894	9,748
Greece	695,429	4,690
Ireland[4]	4,708,410	5,121
Italy	5,345,773	5,332
Netherlands	371,464	1,152
Norway-Sweden	2,142,215	1,669
Norway	752,611[5]	446
Sweden	1,244,177[5]	1,223
Poland	574,693	7,298
Portugal	493,334	3,290
Romania[6]	197,810	2,915
Spain	280,225	1,972
Switzerland	357,079	920
USSR	3,424,357	1,408
United Kingdom[7]	5,083,135	14,667
Yugoslavia[8]	131,029	2,039
Other Europe	180,323	785

Region/country	Total 1820–1988[1]	1988
ASIA	**5,400,881**	**254,745**
China[9]	834,453	34,300
Hong Kong	272,606	11,817
India	398,308	25,312
Iran	148,919	9,846
Israel	126,140	4,444
Japan	450,359	5,085
Korea	578,268	34,151
Philippines	889,255	61,017
Turkey	406,584	2,200
Vietnam	430,348	12,856
Other Asia	865,641	66,093
AMERICA	**11,344,382**	**294,906**
Canada	4,252,649	15,821
Mexico	2,802,883	95,170
CARIBBEAN	**2,502,945**	**110,949**
Cuba	729,751	16,610
Dominican Republic	441,256	27,195
Haiti	201,547	34,858
Jamaica	382,261[10]	20,474
Other Caribbean	748,130	11,812
CENTRAL AMERICA	**572,112**	**31,311**
El Salvador	137,438	12,043
SOUTH AMERICA	**1,103,670**	**41,646**
Argentina	121,399	2,556
Colombia	256,652	10,153
Ecuador	135,706	4,736
Other South America	589,913	24,201
Other America	110,123	9
AFRICA	**278,863**	**17,124**
OCEANIA	**192,862**	**4,324**
Not specified	266,923	72
TOTAL ALL COUNTRIES	**54,666,007**	**643,025**

1. Because of changes in boundaries, changes in lists of countries, and lack of data for specified countries for various periods, data for certain countries are not comparable throughout. Data for specified countries are included with countries to which they belonged prior to World War I.   2. Data for Austria and Hungary not reported until 1861 and are not reported separately for all years.   3. Data begin in 1920.   4. Prior to 1926, data for Northern Ireland included in Ireland.   5. Data for Norway and Sweden not reported separately until 1871.   6. Data begin in 1880.   7. Since 1925, data for UK refer to England, Wales, Scotland, and Northern Ireland.   8. Since 1922 the Serb, Croat, and Slovene Kingdom recorded as Yugoslavia.   9. Beginning in 1957 China includes Taiwan. 10. Data not collected until 1953; in prior years, consolidated under British West Indies (included in "Other Caribbean").   **Source:** U.S. Immigration and Naturalization Service, *1988 Statistical Yearbook* (forthcoming).

Over the next 40 years, however, the flow of immigration was reduced dramatically by a governmental decision to close the doors to most foreign groups. Motivated at first by a disconcerting kind of nativism, the anti-immigration sentiments were later bolstered by the Great Depression and the need to provide work for those already living here. World War II and 'he subsequent national readjustment limited immigration for several decades.

Since 1960 a steadily increasing number of immigrants—both legal and illegal—has had a very noticeable impact on both the size and ethnic composition of the American population. The startling upsurge in the number of Asians and Hispanic immigrants during the 1970s and 1980s has been caused by a variety of factors, from wars and political upheaval to the mundane fact of geographical proximity in the case of Mexico. Currently, over half a million new legal immigrants are arriving annually, and well over half are from those two ethnic backgrounds.

While immigration is higher today than in the recent past, it is hard to predict what the future holds. Many demographers argue that if the

THE STATUE OF LIBERTY

The Statue of Liberty was conceived and designed by Frédéric Auguste Bartholdi (with Gustave Eiffel's help) and given to the United States by the French government in honor of the centennial of American independence in 1876. Funded by subscriptions from the French people, it was dedicated by President Grover Cleveland in 1886 and became a national monument in 1924.

Measuring 151 feet (46 m) to the top of her torch, Miss Liberty still stands guard over the entrance to New York harbor, the inscription on her base a poignant reminder of the vision Americans once had of their country:

Give me your tired, your poor
Your huddled masses yearning to breathe free,
The wretched refuse of your teeming shore,
Send these, the homeless, tempest-tost to me:
I lift my lamp beside the golden door.

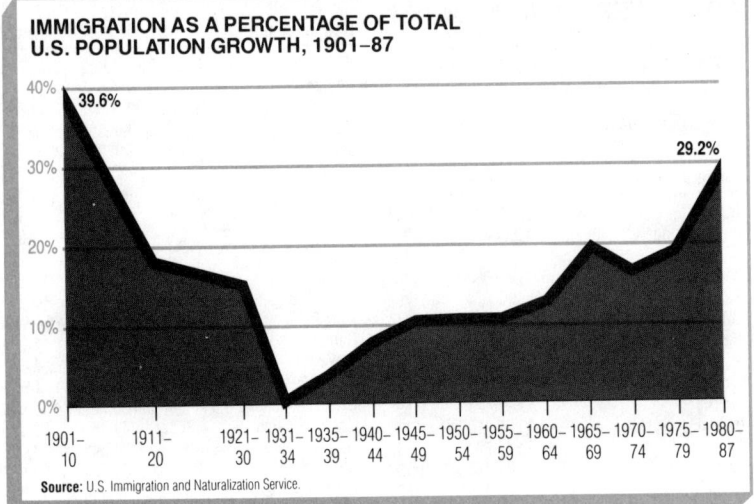

IMMIGRATION AS A PERCENTAGE OF TOTAL U.S. POPULATION GROWTH, 1901–87

39.6%

29.2%

40%

30%

20%

10%

0%

1901–10 1911–20 1921–30 1931–34 1935–39 1940–44 1945–49 1950–54 1955–59 1960–64 1965–69 1970–74 1975–79 1980–87

Source: U.S. Immigration and Naturalization Service.

RECENT TRENDS: IMMIGRANTS TO U.S., BY COUNTRY OF BIRTH, 1961–87 (numbers in thousands)

Region and Country	1961–70	1971–80	1981–86	1987
ALL COUNTRIES	3,321.7	4,493.3	3,466.1	601.5
EUROPE[1]	1,238.6	801.3	384.3	61.2
Austria	13.7	4.7	2.4	0.5
Belgium	8.5	4.0	3.2	0.6
Czechoslovakia	21.4	10.2	6.2	1.4
Denmark	11.8	4.5	3.1	0.5
Finland	5.8	3.4	1.9	0.3
France	34.3	17.8	12.6	2.5
Germany	200.0	66.0	41.6	7.3
Greece	90.2	93.7	18.8	2.7
Hungary	17.3	11.6	4.7	1.0
Ireland	42.4	14.1	7.4	3.1
Italy	206.7	130.1	20.9	2.8
Netherlands	27.8	10.7	6.9	1.2
Norway	16.4	4.0	2.3	0.3
Poland	73.3	43.6	44.8	7.5
Portugal	79.3	104.5	25.2	3.9
Romania	14.9	17.5	22.0	3.8
Soviet Union[2]	15.7	43.2	42.1	2.4
Spain	30.5	30.0	9.2	1.6
Sweden	16.7	6.3	5.8	1.1
Switzerland	16.3	6.6	3.9	0.8
United Kingdom	230.5	123.5	85.4	13.5
Yugoslavia	46.2	42.1	10.1	1.8
ASIA[1]	445.3	1,633.8	1,644.5	257.7
Cambodia	1.2	8.4	83.6	12.5
China (mainland and Taiwan)	96.7	202.5	219.4	37.7[3]
Hong Kong	25.6	47.5	30.7	4.7
India	31.2	176.8	145.9	27.8
Iran	10.4	46.2	79.0	14.4
Iraq	6.4	23.4	14.2	1.1
Israel	12.9	26.6	20.1	3.7
Japan	38.5	47.9	24.0	4.2
Jordan	14.0	29.6	18.0	3.1
Korea	35.8	272.0	201.8	35.8
Laos	0.1	22.6	105.2	6.8
Lebanon	7.5	33.8	21.0	4.4
Pakistan	4.9	31.2	31.8	6.3
Philippines	101.5	360.2	273.8	50.1
Thailand	5.0	44.1	32.5	6.7
Turkey	6.8	18.6	13.2	1.6
Vietnam	4.6	179.7	264.8	24.2
NORTH AMERICA[1]	1,351.1	1,645.0	1,093.4	216.6
Canada	286.7	114.8	66.6	11.9
Mexico	443.3	637.2	401.7	72.4
CARIBBEAN[1]	519.5	759.8	473.2	102.9
Barbados	9.4	20.9	11.0	1.7
Cuba	256.8	276.8	92.0	28.9
Dominican Republic	94.1	148.0	130.8	24.9
Haiti	37.5	58.7	56.6	14.8
Jamaica	71.0	142.0	120.1	23.1
Trinidad and Tobago	24.6	61.8	19.9	3.5
CENTRAL AMERICA[1]	97.7	132.4	151.5	29.3
El Salvador	15.0	34.4	53.8	10.7
Guatemala	15.4	25.6	25.1	5.7
Nicaragua	10.1	13.0	17.1	3.3
Panama	18.4	22.7	17.6	2.1

immigration rate falls much below current levels, the effect on American population growth could be severe. With the dramatic decline in its birth rates and fertility rates, the United States might very well begin to experience negative population growth by the year 2030; by 2020, immigration will add more population than natural increase will. According to the Office of Population Research at Princeton University, the United States will need 464,000 immigrants each year over the next century just to keep total population in 2100 at the same size as in 1980.

IMMIGRATION AS A PERCENTAGE OF TOTAL POPULATION GROWTH, 1901–87

Period	Percent	Period	Percent
1901–10	39.6%	1950–54	10.6%
1911–20	17.7	1955–59	10.7
1921–30	15.0	1960–64	12.5
1930–34	–0.1	1965–69	19.7
1935–39	3.2	1970–74	16.2
1940–44	7.4	1975–79	19.5
1945–49	10.2	1980–87	29.2

Sources: U.S. Immigration and Naturalization Service, Population Reference Bureau, Population Bulletin, "Immigration to the U.S.: The Unfinished Story" (1986); U.S. Bureau of the Census, Estimates of the U.S. Population and Components of Change 1970–87 (1989).

THE U.S. IMMIGRATION RATE BY DECADE, 1820–1987

Period	Total number (thousands)	Rate per 1,000 U.S. pop.
1820–30	152	1.2
1831–40	599	3.9
1841–50	1,713	8.4
1851–60	2,598	9.3
1861–70	2,315	6.4
1871–80	2,812	6.2
1881–90	5,247	9.2
1891–1900	3,688	5.3
1901–10	8,795	10.4
1911–20	5,736	5.7
1921–30	4,107	3.5
1931–40	528	0.4
1941–50	1,035	0.7
1951–60	2,515	1.5
1961–70	3,322	1.7
1971–80	4,493	2.1
1981–87	4,068	2.5
Total, 1820–1987	**53,784**	**3.4**

Source: U.S. Immigration and Naturalization Service, 1987 Statistical Yearbook (1988).

IMMIGRATION TO THE U.S. IN THE 1980s

The following 10 nations sent the most legal immigrants to the U.S. between 1981 and 1988:

Mexico	569,997
Philippines	411,366
South Korea	269,766
China (mainland and Taiwan)	266,824
Vietnam	252,853
India	193,378
Dominican Republic	183,155
Jamaica	160,909
Cuba	125,619
Haiti	105,169

Source: U.S. Immigration and Naturalization Service.

Region and Country	1961–70	1971–80	1981–86	1987
SOUTH AMERICA[1]	228.3	284.4	225.9	44.4
Argentina	42.1	25.1	12.4	2.1
Brazil	20.5	13.7	11.0	2.5
Colombia	70.3	77.6	63.0	11.7
Ecuador	37.0	50.2	26.7	4.6
Guyana	7.1	47.5	53.1	11.4
Peru	18.6	29.1	26.7	5.9
AFRICA[1]	39.3	91.5	94.5	17.7
Egypt	17.2	25.5	17.2	3.4
AUSTRALIA	9.9	14.3	8.0	1.3
NEW ZEALAND	3.7	5.3	3.8	0.6
OTHER COUNTRIES	5.5	17.7	11.7	2.0

1. Includes countries not shown separately. 2. Europe and Asia.
3. From mainland China figure is 25.8 thousand. **Sources:** U.S. Immigration and Naturalization Service, *Statistical Yearbook* (annual) and releases.

Illegal Immigrants

By the very nature of how they enter the United States, it is impossible to know with any accuracy just how many illegal immigrants reside here (estimates range from 4–12 million). Many illegals cross the border from Mexico for only a brief period to find temporary work (usually in agriculture) and then return. Mexico remains the primary source of illegal immigrants, with perhaps 55–60% of the total.

During the 1980s the federal government stepped up its efforts to seal off the 2,000-mile U.S.-Mexican border. Apprehensions of illegals rose from about one million a year in 1980 to almost 2 million by 1987. But, obviously, the government can't incarcerate such large numbers of people for any protracted period of time, so many illegals just keep trying until they are successful.

Both the cost and the futility of trying to stop the flow of illegal immigration with force led Congress to pass the Immigration Reform and Control Act of 1986. This bill proposed to curb illegal immigration by imposing severe fines and possible prison terms on any employer who knowingly hires someone not authorized to work in the United States. Without the incentive of available jobs, supporters of the bill believe illegals will cease their efforts to come here.

The law also recognized that the government can't deport millions of illegals as it did in the 1930s and 1950s, so the bill provided for amnesty for all aliens who entered the United States before Jan. 1, 1982; they also received temporary resident status, with the right to apply for permanent resident alien status, and in five years, for citizenship status. Aliens who worked at least 90 days in U.S. agriculture for three years qualified for permanent resident status after one year; those who worked at least 90 days between May 1985 and May 1986 were given temporary resident status, and they could become permanent residents after two years. An estimated 3.1 million illegal aliens were able to gain legal status.

In May 1989 the U.S. General Accounting Office, making its first public assessment of the 1986 act, determined that the INS had provided 1.7 million employers with information

about the law, issued warnings to over 4,000, and fined 1,700. There is little or no indication that the flow of illegal immigrants has slowed down. Some experts believe that those granted amnesty are encouraging relatives to enter illegally, since they now have someone who can provide for them legally.

AMERICAN PUBLIC OPINION

In an effort to discover what Americans think about different subjects, polling organizations conduct surveys, sampling a cross section of Americans. The most accurate surveys are conducted on the phone or in person. According to statistical theory, a careful sampling of between 1,200 and 2,000 people is sufficient to measure the opinions of most American adults.

Abortion Many surveys have been done on this controversial issue. The National Opinion Research Center has been asking the same questions about abortion since 1965. Its results show that a majority of Americans (ranging from 75% to 90%) consistently supports legalized abortion when a woman's health is seriously endangered, when the woman has been raped, or when the baby is likely to be born with serious birth defects. However, when the woman wants an abortion because she is unmarried or does not want more children for emotional or financial reasons, the surveys have found that less than half of all Americans think legal abortion should be available.

A *New York Times*/CBS News poll of 1,533 adults conducted in January 1989 found that opinions on abortion varied according to the wording of the question. One question in the poll asked, "If a woman wants to have an abortion and her doctor agrees to it, should she be allowed to have an abortion or not?" The findings: 61% said "yes," 25% said "no," and 11% said it depended on the circumstances. But far fewer respondents had an absolute yes or no to the more pointed question in the same poll that asked, "Should abortion be legal as it is now, or legal only in such cases as rape, incest, or to save the life of the mother, or should it not be permitted at all?" The findings: 46% said it should be completely legal as it is now; 41% said it should be legal only in such cases as rape, incest, or to save the life of the mother, and 9% said it should not be legal at all.

The day after the July 1989 Supreme Court decision to allow states to limit abortion, the *Los Angeles Times* conducted a telephone poll of 792 Americans nationwide. The findings: 49% approved of the decision, 40% disapproved, and 11% were not sure. However, the poll has a margin of error of 5 percentage points. On the question of whether they intended to take some political action because of the decision, 25% said they intend to take political action, and 35% said the abortion issue would prompt them to switch their vote to a candidate who agreed with their position. Asked whether they favored or opposed abortion, 41% of the respondents said they were opposed, 38% favored abortion, and 21% said they had no

opinion. Finally, on the question of when life begins, 47% said at conception, 25% said at the first signs of life, and 13% said at birth.

Whom Do You Trust? The Gallup Poll asked adults in late 1988 to rate the honesty and ethical standards of people in different fields. Pharmacists and clergymen were rated highest; advertising people and car salesmen were rated lowest.

Profession	Percent ranked "very high"
MOST RESPECTED	
Druggist, pharmacist	66%
Clergymen	60
College teachers	54
Medical doctors	53
Dentists	51
Engineers	48
Policemen	47
Bankers	26
Funeral directors	24
Journalists	23
LEAST RESPECTED	
Business executives	16%
Congressmen	16
Local office-holders	14
Labor union leaders	14
Real estate agents	13
Stockbrokers	13
State office-holders	11
Insurance salesmen	10
Advertising practitioners	7
Car salesmen	6

Our Country's Problems Gallup polled adults in May 1989, asking them what they thought was the most important problem facing the country today. The findings:

Problems	Percent ranked number 1
Economic problems (net)	34%
Economy	8
Federal budget deficit	7
Unemployment	7
Cost of living, inflation	3
Trade deficit	3
Other economic	8
Drug abuse	27
Poverty	10
Crime	6
Moral decline	5
Environment, pollution	4
International, foreign aid	4
Education	3
Fear of war	2
Dissatisfaction with government	2
AIDS	1
Other noneconomic	8
None, don't know	7

Note: These figures add to more than 100% because of multiple responses.

Environment One of the notable findings of the poll was the number of people who ranked the environment as the nation's most important problem. While only 4% of those polled cited the environment as the major problem in 1988, throughout most of the 1980s, 1%

or less had rated it number one.

In the same poll, 76% of Americans identified themselves as environmentalists. Large majorities say they worry a great deal about the pollution of lakes, rivers, and reservoirs (72%), contamination of soil and water by toxic wastes (69%), air pollution (63%), and ocean and beach pollution (60%).

Most Americans say they are making some effort to protect the environment by taking various measures such as recycling newspapers and other household waste (78%); reducing energy consumption by improving home insulation or changing heating or air-conditioning systems (76%); replacing a "gas-guzzling" automobile with one that is more fuel efficient (66%); cutting household use of water (65%); or contributing to an environmental or conservation group (49%).

Most Americans (79%) would also favor a ban on chlorofluorocarbons (CFCs) and other chemicals that damage the ozone layer even if it meant higher prices for air conditioners, refrigerators, and other consumer products.

Protectionism Another Gallup poll found that the public believes America's ability to compete in world markets over the last 10 years has worsened (47%) rather than improved (21%) or stayed the same (27%). Americans now regard Japan (58%), not the United States (29%), as the leading economic power. Many people blame American business practices for causing this economic decline. Among the major reasons cited are perceptions that U. S. businesses put too much emphasis on short-term profits (61%), the proliferation of corporate takeovers (52%), currency imbalances (52%), a stronger work ethic in Japan (48%), and poor management (40%).

Worries about the Future Gallup asked Americans what worries them most about the future. The poll found that 42% worried about an increase in taxes, 24% about an increase in prices, 14% about job loss, 11% about an increase in interest rates; 5% expressed no worries, and 4% didn't know.

Self-Identification Gallup interviewed 4,244 Americans for a poll completed in September 1987 for the *Times Mirror*. Americans were asked the extent to which they strongly identify politically with the following terms.

Term of self-identification	% with strong identification
Anticommunist	70%
Religious person	49
Supporter of civil rights	47
Supporter of peace movement	46
Environmentalist	39
Supporter of antiabortion movement	32
Democrat	31
Supporter of women's movement	29
Supporter of business interests	28
Conservative	27
Supporter of the National Rifle Association	27
Union supporter	27
Pro-Israel	20
Republican	20
Liberal	19
Supporter of gay rights	8

Note: These figures add to more than 100% because of multiple responses.

AWARDS IN THE ARTS AND ENTERTAINMENT

THE ACADEMY AWARDS

The "Oscars" are officially known as the Academy of Motion Picture Arts and Sciences Awards; they were inaugurated in 1928 as part of Hollywood's drive to improve its less-than-respectable image. (The stated aim of the academy, founded in 1927, was to raise the "cultural, educational, and scientific standards" of the motion picture industry.) Membership in the academy (currently over 3,000) is by invitation only, with members divided into 13 branches. Each branch selects up to five nominees for awards in its own area of expertise, with the entire membership making "Best Film" nominations, and then voting on all the categories. Major awards are shown in the chart. The year 1934 marked a growing number of award categories. "Best Foreign Film" awards, which began in 1956, are listed in a separate table at the end of this section. "Best Directors" are named for films winning "Best Picture" except where indicated.

Year	Best Picture	Best Director	Best Actor	Best Actress	Best Cinematographer
1928	*Wings*	Frank Borzage *Seventh Heaven* Lewis Milestone *2 Arabian Knights*	Emil Jannings *The Way of All Flesh, The Last Command*	Janet Gaynor *Seventh Heaven, Sunrise, Street Angel*	Charles Rosher, Karl Struss *Sunrise*
1929	*Broadway Melody*	Frank Lloyd *The Divine Lady*	Warner Baxter *In Old Arizona*	Mary Pickford *Coquette*	Clyde DeVinna *White Shadows, In the South Seas*
1930	*All Quiet on the Western Front*	Lewis Milestone	George Arliss *Disraeli*	Norma Shearer *The Divorcee*	Joseph T. Rucker, Willard Van Der Veer *With Byrd at the South Pole*
1931	*Cimarron*	Norman Taurog *Skippy*	Lionel Barrymore *A Free Soul*	Marie Dressler *Min and Bill*	Floyd Crosby *Tabu*
1932	*Grand Hotel*	Frank Borzage *Bad Girl*	Wallace Beery *The Champ* Fredric March *Dr. Jekyll and Mr. Hyde*	Helen Hayes *The Sin of Madelon Claudet*	Lee Garmes *Shanghai Express*
1933	*Cavalcade*	Frank Lloyd	Charles Laughton *The Private Life of Henry VIII*	Katharine Hepburn *Morning Glory*	Charles Bryant Lang, Jr. *A Farewell to Arms*

Year	Best Picture	Director	Best Actor	Best Actress	Best Supporting Actor	Best Supporting Actress	Best Song (from film)	Original Score	Best Cinematographer
1934	It Happened One Night	Frank Capra	Clark Gable It Happened One Night	Claudette Colbert It Happened One Night	—	—	"The Continental" The Gay Divorcee	Louis Silvers[1] One Night of Love	Victor Milner Cleopatra
1935	Mutiny on the Bounty	John Ford The Informer	Victor McLaglen The Informer	Bette Davis Dangerous	—	—	"Lullaby of Broadway" Lullaby of Broadway	Max Steiner[1] The Informer	Hal Mohr A Midsummer Night's Dream
1936	The Great Ziegfeld	Frank Capra Mr. Deeds Goes to Town	Paul Muni The Story of Louis Pasteur	Luise Rainer The Great Ziegfeld	Walter Brennan Come and Get It	Gale Sondergaard Anthony Adverse	"The Way You Look Tonight" Swing Time	Leo Forbstein[1] Anthony Adverse	Gaetano Gaudio Anthony Adverse
1937	The Life of Emile Zola	Leo McCarey The Awful Truth	Spencer Tracy Captains Courageous	Luise Rainer The Good Earth	Joseph Schildkraut The Life of Emile Zola	Alice Brady In Old Chicago	"Sweet Leilani" Waikiki Wedding	Charles Previn[1] 100 Men and a Girl	Karl Freund The Good Earth
1938	You Can't Take It with You	Frank Capra	Spencer Tracy Boys Town	Bette Davis Jezebel	Walter Brennan Kentucky	Fay Bainter Jezebel	"Thanks for the Memory" Big Broadcast of 1938	Alfred Newman Alexander's Ragtime Band Erich Wolfgang Korngold The Adventures of Robin Hood	Joseph Ruttenberg The Great Waltz
1939	Gone with the Wind	Victor Fleming	Robert Donat Goodbye, Mr. Chips	Vivien Leigh Gone with the Wind	Thomas Mitchell Stagecoach	Hattie McDaniel Gone with the Wind	"Over the Rainbow" The Wizard of Oz	Herbert Stothart The Wizard of Oz Richard Hageman, Frank Harling, John Leipold, Leo Shuken Stagecoach	Gregg Toland Wuthering Heights Ernest Haller, Ray Rennahan Gone with the Wind
1940	Rebecca	John Ford The Grapes of Wrath	James Stewart The Philadelphia Story	Ginger Rogers Kitty Foyle	Walter Brennan The Westerner	Jane Darwell The Grapes of Wrath	"When You Wish upon a Star" Pinocchio	Alfred Newman Tin Pan Alley Leigh Harline, Paul J. Smith, Ned Washington Pinocchio	George Barnes Rebecca George Perinal Thief of Bagdad
1941	How Green Was My Valley	John Ford	Gary Cooper Sergeant York	Joan Fontaine Suspicion	Donald Crisp How Green Was My Valley	Mary Astor The Great Lie	"The Last Time I Saw Paris" Lady Be Good	Bernard Herrmann All That Money Can Buy Frank Churchill, Oliver Wallace Dumbo	Arthur Miller How Green Was My Valley Ernest Palmer, Ray Rennahan Blood and Sand
1942	Mrs. Miniver	William Wyler	James Cagney Yankee Doodle Dandy	Greer Garson Mrs. Miniver	Van Heflin Johnny Eager	Teresa Wright Mrs. Miniver	"White Christmas" Holiday Inn	Max Steiner Now, Voyager Ray Heindorf, Heinz Roemheld Yankee Doodle Dandy	Joseph Ruttenberg Mrs. Miniver Leon Shamroy The Black Swan
1943	Casablanca	Michael Curtiz	Paul Lukas Watch on the Rhine	Jennifer Jones The Song of Bernadette	Charles Coburn The More the Merrier	Katina Paxinou For Whom the Bell Tolls	"You'll Never Know" Hello, Frisco, Hello	Alfred Newman The Song of Bernadette Ray Heindorf This Is the Army	Arthur Miller The Song of Bernadette Hal Mohr, W. Howard Greene The Phantom of the Opera
1944	Going My Way	Leo McCarey	Bing Crosby Going My Way	Ingrid Bergman Gaslight	Barry Fitzgerald Going My Way	Ethel Barrymore None But the Lonely Heart	"Swinging on a Star" Going My Way	Max Steiner Since You Went Away Carmen Dragon, Morris Stoloff Cover Girl	Joseph LaShelle Laura Leon Shamroy Wilson
1945	The Lost Weekend	Billy Wilder	Ray Milland The Lost Weekend	Joan Crawford Mildred Pierce	James Dunn A Tree Grows in Brooklyn	Anne Revere National Velvet	"It Might As Well Be Spring" State Fair	Miklos Rozsa Spellbound Georgie Stoll Anchors Aweigh	Harry Stradling The Picture of Dorian Gray Leon Shamroy Leave Her to Heaven

Year	Best Picture	Director	Best Actor	Best Actress	Best Supporting Actor	Best Supporting Actress	Best Song (from film)	Original Score	Best Cinematographer
1946	*The Best Years of Our Lives*	William Wyler	Fredric March *The Best Years of Our Lives*	Olivia DeHavilland *To Each His Own*	Harold Russell *The Best Years of Our Lives*	Anne Baxter *The Razor's Edge*	"On the Atchison, Topeka and Santa Fe" *The Harvey Girls*	Hugo Friedhofer *The Best Years of Our Lives* Morris Stoloff *The Jolson Story*	Arthur Miller *Anna and the King of Siam* Charles Rosher, Leonard Smith, Arthur Arling *The Yearling*
1947	*Gentleman's Agreement*	Elia Kazan	Ronald Colman *A Double Life*	Loretta Young *The Farmer's Daughter*	Edmund Gwenn *Miracle on 34th Street*	Celeste Holm *Gentleman's Agreement*	"Zip-A-Dee-Doo-Dah" *Song of the South*	Miklos Rozsa *A Double Life* Alfred Newman *Mother Wore Tights*	Guy Green *Great Expectations* Jack Cardiff *Black Narcissus*
1948	*Hamlet*	John Huston *Treasure of the Sierra Madre*	Laurence Olivier *Hamlet*	Jane Wyman *Johnny Belinda*	Walter Huston *Treasure of the Sierra Madre*	Claire Trevor *Key Largo*	"Buttons and Bows" *The Paleface*	Brian Easdale *The Red Shoes* Johnny Green, Roger Edens *Easter Parade*	William Daniels *The Naked City* Joseph Valentine, William V. Skall, Winton Hoch *Joan of Arc*
1949	*All the King's Men*	Joseph L. Mankiewicz *A Letter to Three Wives*	Broderick Crawford *All the King's Men*	Olivia DeHavilland *The Heiress*	Dean Jagger *Twelve O'Clock High*	Mercedes McCambridge *All the King's Men*	"Baby, It's Cold Outside" *Neptune's Daughter*	Aaron Copeland *The Heiress* Roger Edens, Lenny Hayton *On the Town*	Paul C. Vogel *Battleground* Winton Hoch *She Wore a Yellow Ribbon*
1950	*All About Eve*	Joseph L. Mankiewicz	Jose Ferrer *Cyrano de Bergerac*	Judy Holliday *Born Yesterday*	George Sanders *All About Eve*	Josephine Hull *Harvey*	"Mona Lisa" *Captain Carey, US*	Franz Waxman *Sunset Boulevard* Adolph Deutsch, Roger Edens *Annie Get Your Gun*	Robert Krasker *The Third Man* Robert Surtees *King Solomon's Mines*
1951	*An American in Paris*	George Stevens *A Place in the Sun*	Humphrey Bogart *The African Queen*	Vivien Leigh *A Streetcar Named Desire*	Karl Malden *A Streetcar Named Desire*	Kim Hunter *A Streetcar Named Desire*	"In the Cool, Cool, Cool of the Evening" *Here Comes the Groom*	Franz Waxman *A Place in the Sun* Saul Chaplin, Johnny Green *An American in Paris*	William C. Mellor *A Place in the Sun* Alfred Gilks, John Alton (ballet) *An American in Paris*
1952	*The Greatest Show on Earth*	John Ford *The Quiet Man*	Gary Cooper *High Noon*	Shirley Booth *Come Back, Little Sheba*	Anthony Quinn *Viva Zapata!*	Gloria Grahame *The Bad and the Beautiful*	"High Noon (Do Not Forsake Me, Oh My Darlin')" *High Noon*	Dimitri Tiomkin *High Noon* Alfred Newman *With a Song in My Heart*	Robert Surtees *The Bad and the Beautiful* Winton Hoch, Archie Stout *The Quiet Man*
1953	*From Here to Eternity*	Fred Zinnemann	William Holden *Stalag 17*	Audrey Hepburn *Roman Holiday*	Frank Sinatra *From Here to Eternity*	Donna Reed *From Here to Eternity*	"Secret Love" *Calamity Jane*	Bronislau Kaper *Lili* Alfred Newman *Call Me Madam*	Burnett Guffey *From Here to Eternity* Loyal Griggs *Shane*
1954	*On the Waterfront*	Elia Kazan	Marlon Brando *On the Waterfront*	Grace Kelly *The Country Girl*	Edmond O'Brien *The Barefoot Contessa*	Eva Marie Saint *On the Waterfront*	"Three Coins in the Fountain" *Three Coins in the Fountain*	Dimitri Tiomkin *The High and the Mighty* Saul Chaplin, Adolph Deutsch *Seven Brides for Seven Brothers*	Boris Kaufman *On the Waterfront* Milton Krasner *Three Coins in the Fountain*
1955	*Marty*	Delbert Mann	Ernest Borgnine *Marty*	Anna Magnani *The Rose Tattoo*	Jack Lemmon *Mister Roberts*	Jo Van Fleet *East of Eden*	"Love Is a Many Splendored Thing" *Love Is a Many Splendored Thing*	Alfred Newman *Love Is a Many Splendored Thing* Robert Russell Bennett, Jay Blackton, Adolph Deutsch *Oklahoma!*	James Wong Howe *The Rose Tattoo* Robert Burks *To Catch a Thief*
1956	*Around the World in 80 Days*	George Stevens *Giant*	Yul Brynner *The King and I*	Ingrid Bergman *Anastasia*	Anthony Quinn *Lust for Life*	Dorothy Malone *Written on the Wind*	"Whatever Will Be, Will Be (Que Sera, Sera)" *The Man Who Knew Too Much*	Victor Young *Around the World in 80 Days* Alfred Newman, Ken Darby *The King and I*	Boris Kaufman *Baby Doll* Lionel Lindon *Around the World in 80 Days*

Year	Best Picture	Director	Best Actor	Best Actress	Best Supporting Actor	Best Supporting Actress	Best Song (from film)	Original Score	Best Cinematographer
1957	The Bridge on the River Kwai	David Lean	Alec Guinness *The Bridge on the River Kwai*	Joanne Woodward *The Three Faces of Eve*	Red Buttons *Sayonara*	Miyoshi Umeki *Sayonara*	"All the Way" *The Joker Is Wild*	Malcolm Arnold *The Bridge on the River Kwai*	Jack Hildyard *The Bridge on the River Kwai*
1958	Gigi	Vincente Minnelli	David Niven *Separate Tables*	Susan Hayward *I Want to Live!*	Burl Ives *The Big Country*	Wendy Hiller *Separate Tables*	"Gigi" *Gigi*	Dimitri Tiomkin *The Old Man and the Sea* Andre Previn *Gigi*	Sam Leavitt *The Defiant Ones* Joseph Ruttenberg *Gigi*
1959	Ben Hur	William Wyler	Charlton Heston *Ben Hur*	Simone Signoret *Room at the Top*	Hugh Griffith *Ben Hur*	Shelley Winters *The Diary of Anne Frank*	"High Hopes" *A Hole in the Head*	Miklos Rosza *Ben Hur* Andre Previn, Ken Darby *All That Jazz*	William C. Mellor *The Diary of Anne Frank* Robert L. Surtees *Ben Hur*
1960	The Apartment	Billy Wilder	Burt Lancaster *Elmer Gantry*	Elizabeth Taylor *Butterfield 8*	Peter Ustinov *Spartacus*	Shirley Jones *Elmer Gantry*	"Never on Sunday" *Never on Sunday*	Ernest Gold *Exodus* Morris Stoloff, Harry Sukman *Song without End*	Freddie Francis *Sons and Lovers* Russell Metty *Spartacus*
1961	West Side Story	Jerome Robbins, Robert Wise	Maximilian Schell *Judgment at Nuremberg*	Sophia Loren *Two Women*	George Chakiris *West Side Story*	Rita Moreno *West Side Story*	"Moon River" *Breakfast at Tiffany's*	Henry Mancini *Breakfast at Tiffany's* Saul Chaplin, Johnny Green, Sid Ramin, Irwin Kostal *West Side Story*	Eugen Shuftan *The Hustler* Daniel L. Fapp *West Side Story*
1962	Lawrence of Arabia	David Lean	Gregory Peck *To Kill a Mockingbird*	Anne Bancroft *The Miracle Worker*	Ed Begley *Sweet Bird of Youth*	Patty Duke *The Miracle Worker*	"Days of Wine and Roses" *Days of Wine and Roses*	Maurice Jarre *Lawrence of Arabia*	Jean Bourgoin, Walter Wottitz *The Longest Day* Fred A. Young *Lawrence of Arabia*
1963	Tom Jones	Tony Richardson	Sidney Poitier *Lilies of the Field*	Patricia Neal *Hud*	Melvyn Douglas *Hud*	Margaret Rutherford *The V.I.P.s*	"Call Me Irresponsible" *Papa's Delicate Condition*	John Addison *Tom Jones*	James Wong Howe *Hud* Leon Shamroy *Cleopatra*
1964	My Fair Lady	George Cukor	Rex Harrison *My Fair Lady*	Julie Andrews *Mary Poppins*	Peter Ustinov *Topkapi*	Lila Kedrova *Zorba the Greek*	"Chim Chim Cher-ee" *Mary Poppins*	Richard M. Sherman, Robert B. Sherman *Mary Poppins*	Walter Lassally *Zorba the Greek* Harry Stradling *My Fair Lady*
1965	The Sound of Music	Robert Wise	Lee Marvin *Cat Ballou*	Julie Christie *Darling*	Martin Balsam *A Thousand Clowns*	Shelley Winters *A Patch of Blue*	"The Shadow of Your Smile" *The Sandpiper*	Maurice Jarre *Dr. Zhivago*	Ernest Laszlo *Ship of Fools* Freddie Young *Dr. Zhivago*
1966	A Man for All Seasons	Fred Zinnemann	Paul Scofield *A Man for All Seasons*	Elizabeth Taylor *Who's Afraid of Virginia Woolf?*	Walter Matthau *The Fortune Cookie*	Sandy Dennis *Who's Afraid of Virginia Woolf?*	"Born Free" *Born Free*	John Barry *Born Free*	Haskell Wexler *Who's Afraid of Virginia Woolf?* Ted Moore *A Man for All Seasons*
1967	In the Heat of the Night	Mike Nichols *The Graduate*	Rod Steiger *In the Heat of the Night*	Katharine Hepburn *Guess Who's Coming to Dinner*	George Kennedy *Cool Hand Luke*	Estelle Parsons *Bonnie and Clyde*	"Talk to the Animals" *Doctor Dolittle*	Elmer Bernstein *Thoroughly Modern Millie*	Burnett Guffey *Bonnie and Clyde*
1968	Oliver!	Carol Reed	Cliff Robertson *Charly*	Katharine Hepburn *The Lion in Winter* Barbra Streisand *Funny Girl*	Jack Albertson *The Subject Was Roses*	Ruth Gordon *Rosemary's Baby*	"The Windmills of Your Mind" *The Thomas Crown Affair*	John Barry *The Lion in Winter*	Pasqualino DeSantis *Romeo and Juliet*
1969	Midnight Cowboy	John Schlesinger	John Wayne *True Grit*	Maggie Smith *The Prime of Miss Jean Brodie*	Gig Young *They Shoot Horses Don't They?*	Goldie Hawn *Cactus Flower*	"Raindrops Keep Fallin' on My Head" *Butch Cassidy and the Sundance Kid*	Burt Bacharach *Butch Cassidy and the Sundance Kid*	Conrad Hall *Butch Cassidy and the Sundance Kid*
1970	Patton	Franklin Schaffner	George C. Scott *Patton*	Glenda Jackson *Women in Love*	John Mills *Ryan's Daughter*	Helen Hayes *Airport*	"For All We Know" *Lovers and Other Strangers*	Francis Lai *Love Story* The Beatles (music, lyrics) *Let It Be*	Freddie Young *Ryan's Daughter*

Year	Best Picture	Director	Best Actor	Best Actress	Best Supporting Actor	Best Supporting Actress	Best Song (from film)	Original Score	Best Cinematographer
1971	The French Connection	William Friedkin	Gene Hackman The French Connection	Jane Fonda Klute	Ben Johnson The Last Picture Show	Cloris Leachman The Last Picture Show	"Theme from Shaft" Shaft	Michel Legrand The Summer of '42	Oswald Morris Fiddler on the Roof
1972	The Godfather	Bob Fosse Cabaret	Marlon Brando The Godfather	Liza Minnelli Cabaret	Joel Grey Cabaret	Eileen Heckart Butterflies Are Free	"The Morning After" The Poseidon Adventure	Charles Chaplin, Raymond Rasch, Larry Russell Limelight	Geoffrey Unsworth Cabaret
1973	The Sting	George Roy Hill	Jack Lemmon Save the Tiger	Glenda Jackson A Touch of Class	John Houseman The Paper Chase	Tatum O'Neal Paper Moon	"The Way We Were" The Way We Were	Marvin Hamlisch The Way We Were	Sven Nykvist Cries and Whispers
1974	The Godfather Part II	Francis Ford Coppola	Art Carney Harry and Tonto	Ellen Burstyn Alice Doesn't Live Here Anymore	Robert DeNiro The Godfather Pt. II	Ingrid Bergman Murder on the Orient Express	"We May Never Love Like This Again" The Towering Inferno	Nino Rota, Carmine Coppola The Godfather Pt. II	Fred Koenekamp, Joseph Biroc The Towering Inferno
1975	One Flew over the Cuckoo's Nest	Miloš Forman	Jack Nicholson One Flew over the Cuckoo's Nest	Louise Fletcher One Flew over the Cuckoo's Nest	George Burns The Sunshine Boys	Lee Grant Shampoo	"I'm Easy" Nashville	John Williams Jaws	John Alcott Barry Lyndon
1976	Rocky	John G. Avildsen	Peter Finch Network	Faye Dunaway Network	Jason Robards All the President's Men	Beatrice Straight Network	"Evergreen" (love theme) A Star Is Born	Jerry Goldsmith The Omen Leonard Rosenman Bound for Glory	Haskell Wexler Bound for Glory
1977	Annie Hall	Woody Allen	Richard Dreyfuss The Goodbye Girl	Diane Keaton Annie Hall	Jason Robards Julia	Vanessa Redgrave Julia	"You Light Up My Life" You Light Up My Life	John Williams Star Wars	Vilmos Zsigmond Close Encounters of the Third Kind
1978	The Deer Hunter	Michael Cimino	Jon Voight Coming Home	Jane Fonda Coming Home	Christopher Walken The Deer Hunter	Maggie Smith California Suite	"Last Dance" Thank God It's Friday	Giorgio Moroder Midnight Express	Nestor Almendros Days of Heaven
1979	Kramer vs. Kramer	Robert Benton	Dustin Hoffman Kramer vs. Kramer	Sally Field Norma Rae	Melvyn Douglas Being There	Meryl Streep Kramer vs. Kramer	"It Goes Like It Goes" Norma Rae	Georges Delerue A Little Romance	Vittorio Storaro Apocalypse Now
1980	Ordinary People	Robert Redford	Robert DeNiro Raging Bull	Sissy Spacek Coal Miner's Daughter	Timothy Hutton Ordinary People	Mary Steenburgen Melvin and Howard	"Fame" Fame	Michael Gore Fame	Geoffrey Unsworth, Ghislain Cloquet Tess
1981	Chariots of Fire	Warren Beatty Reds	Henry Fonda On Golden Pond	Katharine Hepburn On Golden Pond	John Gielgud Arthur	Maureen Stapleton Reds	"Arthur's Theme" (Best That You Can Do) Arthur	Vangelis Chariots of Fire	Vittorio Storaro Reds
1982	Gandhi	Richard Attenborough	Ben Kingsley Gandhi	Meryl Streep Sophie's Choice	Lou Gossett, Jr. An Officer and a Gentleman	Jessica Lange Tootsie	"Up Where We Belong" An Officer and a Gentleman	John Williams E.T.	Billy Williams, Ronnie Taylor Gandhi
1983	Terms of Endearment	James L. Brooks	Robert Duvall Tender Mercies	Shirley MacLaine Terms of Endearment	Jack Nicholson Terms of Endearment	Linda Hunt The Year of Living Dangerously	"Flashdance . . . What a Feeling" Flashdance	Bill Conti The Right Stuff	Sven Nykvist Fanny and Alexander
1984	Amadeus	Miloš Forman	F. Murray Abraham Amadeus	Sally Field Places in the Heart	Haing S. Ngor The Killing Fields	Peggy Ashcroft A Passage to India	"I Just Called to Say I Love You" The Woman in Red	Maurice Jarre A Passage to India Prince Purple Rain	Chris Menges The Killing Fields
1985	Out of Africa	Sydney Pollack	William Hurt Kiss of the Spider Woman	Geraldine Page The Trip to Bountiful	Don Ameche Cocoon	Anjelica Huston Prizzi's Honor	"Say You, Say Me" White Nights	John Barry Out of Africa	David Watkin Out of Africa
1986	Platoon	Oliver Stone	Paul Newman The Color of Money	Marlee Matlin Children of a Lesser God	Michael Caine Hannah and Her Sisters	Dianne Wiest Hannah and Her Sisters	"Take My Breath Away" Top Gun	Herbie Hancock 'Round Midnight	Chris Menges The Mission
1987	The Last Emperor	Bernardo Bertolucci	Michael Douglas Wall Street	Cher Moonstruck	Sean Connery The Untouchables	Olympia Dukakis Moonstruck	"(I've Had) The Time of My Life" Dirty Dancing	Ryuichi Sakamoto, David Byrne, Cong Su The Last Emperor	Vittorio Storaro The Last Emperor
1988	Rain Man	Barry Levinson	Dustin Hoffman Rain Man	Jodie Foster The Accused	Kevin Kline A Fish Called Wanda	Geena Davis The Accidental Tourist	"Let the River Run" Working Girl	Dave Grusin "The Milagro Beanfield War"	Peter Biziou Mississippi Burning

1. From 1934 to 1937, the "Best Original Score" award was presented to the head of the music department of the relevant studio, and not necessarily to the composer of the score.   **Source:** BASELINE II, INC.

BEST FOREIGN LANGUAGE FILM

Year	Film	Country	Director
1956	La Strada	Italy	Federico Fellini
1957	The Nights of Cabiria	Italy	Federico Fellini
1958	Mon Oncle	France	Jacques Tati
1959	Black Orpheus	France/Italy/Brazil	Marcel Camus
1960	The Virgin Spring	Sweden	Ingmar Bergman
1961	Through a Glass Darkly	Sweden	Ingmar Bergman
1962	Sundays and Cybele	France	Serge Bourguignon
1963	8½	Italy	Federico Fellini
1964	Yesterday, Today and Tomorrow	Italy/France	Vittorio de Sica
1965	The Shop on Main Street	Czechoslovakia	Jan Kadar
1966	A Man and a Woman	France	Claude Lelouch
1967	Closely Watched Trains	Czechoslovakia	Jirí Menzel
1968	War and Peace	USSR	Sergei Bondarchuk
1969	Z	France/Algeria	Costa-Gavras
1970	Investigation of a Citizen above Suspicion	Italy	Elio Petri
1971	The Garden of the Finzi-Continis	Italy	Vittorio de Sica
1972	The Discreet Charm of the Bourgeoisie	France	Luis Buñuel

Year	Film	Country	Director
1973	Day for Night	France/Italy	François Truffaut
1974	Amarcord	Italy/France	Federico Fellini
1975	Dersu Uzala	USSR/Japan	Akira Kurosawa
1976	Black and White in Color	France/Switzerland/Ivory Coast	Jean-Jacques Annaud
1977	Madame Rosa	France	Moshe Mizrahi
1978	Get Out Your Handkerchiefs	France	Bertrand Blier
1979	The Tin Drum	Germany	Volker Scholondorff
1980	Moscow Does Not Believe in Tears	USSR	Vladimir Menshov
1981	Mephisto	Austria/Germany/Hungary	Istvan Szabo
1982	To Begin Again	Spain	Jose Luis Garci
1983	Fanny and Alexander	Sweden	Ingmar Bergman
1984	Dangerous Moves	France	Richard Dembo
1985	The Official Story	Argentina	Luis Puenzo
1986	The Assault	Netherlands	Fons Rademakers
1987	Babette's Feast	Denmark	Gabriel Axel
1988	Pelle the Conqueror	Denmark	Bille August

THE EMMYS

The "Emmy's" National Academy of Television Arts and Sciences Awards—The academy was formed in 1946 and the first awards presented in 1949. Only a selection is printed here; not only has the number of awards changed from year to year (peaking in 1978 with a total of 75 categories), but the categories themselves have fluctuated to reflect change in the industry.

1948

Outstanding TV Personality: Shirley Dinsdale (and her puppet Judy Splinters) (KTLA)
Most Popular TV Program: *Pantomime Quiz Time* (KTLA)
Best Film Made for Television: "The Necklace," *Your Show Time* (NBC)
Special Award: Louis McManus, for his original design of the Emmy.

1949

Best Live Show: *The Ed Wynn Show* (CBS)
Best Kinescope[1] Show: *Texaco Star Theater* (NBC)
Outstanding Live Personality: Ed Wynn (CBS)
Outstanding Kinescope Personality: Milton Berle (NBC)
Best Film Made for TV: *The Life of Riley* (NBC)

1950

Best Actor: Alan Young (CBS)
Best Actress: Gertrude Berg (CBS)
Outstanding Personality: Groucho Marx (NBC)
Best Variety Show: *The Alan Young Show* (CBS)
Best Dramatic Show: *Pulitzer Prize Playhouse* (ABC)
Best Game Show: *Truth or Consequences* (CBS)

1951

Best Dramatic Show: *Studio One* (CBS)

1. Kinescope was an early method of recording TV shows, before the advent of videotape. A movie camera was placed in front of a monitor in the TV studio and would "film" the show directly from the screen. The finished program could then be broadcast at a later date.

Best Comedy Show: *The Red Skelton Show* (CBS)
Best Variety Show: *Your Show of Shows* (NBC)
Best Actor: Sid Caesar (NBC)
Best Actress: Imogene Coca (NBC)
Best Comedian or Comedienne: Red Skelton (NBC)

1952

Best Dramatic Program: *Robert Montgomery Presents* (NBC)
Best Variety Program: *Your Show of Shows* (NBC)
Best Mystery, Action, or Adventure Program: *Dragnet* (NBC)
Best Situation Comedy: *I Love Lucy* (CBS)
Best Actor: Thomas Mitchell
Best Actress: Helen Hayes

1953

Best Dramatic Program: *The U.S. Steel Hour* (ABC)
Best Situation Comedy: *I Love Lucy* (CBS)
Best Variety Program: *Omnibus* (CBS)
Best Male Star of Regular Series: Donald O'Connor, *Colgate Comedy Hour* (NBC)
Best Female Star of Regular Series: Eve Arden, *Our Miss Brooks* (CBS)
Best Mystery, Action, or Adventure Program: *Dragnet* (NBC)

1954

Best Actor Starring in a Regular Series: Danny Thomas, *Make Room for Daddy* (ABC)
Best Actress Starring in a Regular Series: Loretta Young, *The Loretta Young Show* (NBC)
Best Mystery or Intrigue Series: *Dragnet* (NBC)
Best Variety Series Including Musical Varieties: *Disneyland* (ABC)
Best Situation Comedy Series: *Make Room for Daddy* (ABC)
Best Dramatic Series: *The U.S. Steel Hour* (ABC)

1955

Best Action or Adventure Series: *Disneyland* (ABC)
Best Comedy Series: *The Phil Silvers Show* (CBS)
Best Variety Series: *The Ed Sullivan Show* (CBS)
Best Dramatic Series: *Producers' Showcase* (NBC)
Best Actor (Continuing Performance): Phil Silvers, *The Phil Silvers Show* (CBS)
Best Actress (Continuing Performance): Lucille Ball, *I Love Lucy* (CBS)

1956

Best Single Program of the Year: "Requiem for

AMERICAN FILM INSTITUTE LIFE ACHIEVEMENT AWARDS

Awarded to individuals whose "talent has fundamentally advanced the art of American film or television . . . and whose work has withstood the test of time."

1973	John Ford
1974	James Cagney
1975	Orson Welles
1976	William Wyler
1977	Henry Fonda
1978	Bette Davis
1979	Alfred Hitchcock
1980	James Stewart
1981	Fred Astaire
1982	Frank Capra
1983	John Huston
1984	Lillian Gish
1985	Gene Kelly
1986	Billy Wilder
1987	Barbara Stanwyck
1988	Jack Lemmon
1989	Gregory Peck

Source: American Film Institute.

a Heavyweight," *Playhouse 90* (CBS)

Best Series (Half Hour or Less): *The Phil Silvers Show* (CBS)

Best Series (One Hour or More): *Caesar's Hour* (NBC)

Best Continuing Performance by an Actor in a Dramatic Series: Robert Young, *Father Knows Best* (NBC)

Best Continuing Performance by an Actress in a Dramatic Series: Loretta Young, *The Loretta Young Show* (NBC)

1957

Best Single Program of the Year: "The Comedian," *Playhouse 90* (CBS)

Best Dramatic Series with Continuing Characters: *Gunsmoke* (CBS)

Best Comedy Series: *The Phil Silvers Show* (CBS)

Best Musical, Variety, Audience Participation, or Quiz Series: *The Dinah Shore Chevy Show* (NBC)

Best Continuing Performance by an Actor in a Leading Role in a Dramatic or Comedy Series: Robert Young, *Father Knows Best* (NBC)

Best Continuing Performance by an Actress in a Leading Role in a Dramatic or Comedy Series: Jane Wyatt, *Father Knows Best* (NBC)

1958–59

Most Outstanding Single Program of the Year: "An Evening with Fred Astaire" (NBC)

Best Dramatic Series (One Hour or Longer): *Playhouse 90* (CBS)

Best Dramatic Series (Less Than One Hour): *Alcoa-Goodyear Theatre* (NBC)

Best Comedy Series: *The Jack Benny Show* (CBS)

Best Musical or Variety Series: *The Dinah Shore Chevy Show* (NBC)

Best Western Series: *Maverick* (ABC)

Best Actor in a Leading Role (Continuing Character) in a Dramatic Series: Raymond Burr, *Perry Mason* (CBS)

Best Actress in a Leading Role (Continuing Character) in a Dramatic Series: Loretta Young, *The Loretta Young Show* (NBC)

Best Actor in a Leading Role (Continuing Character) in a Comedy Series: Jack Benny, *The Jack Benny Show* (CBS)

Best Actress in a Leading Role (Continuing Character) in a Comedy Series: Jane Wyatt, *Father Knows Best* (CBS and NBC)

1959–60

Outstanding Program Achievement in the Field of Humor: "The Art Carney Special" (NBC)

Outstanding Program Achievement in the Field of Drama: *Playhouse 90* (CBS)

Outstanding Program Achievement in the Field of Variety: "The Fabulous Fifties" (CBS)

Outstanding Performance by an Actor in a Series (Lead or Support): Robert Stack, *The Untouchables* (ABC)

Outstanding Performance by an Actress in a Series (Lead or Support): Jane Wyatt, *Father Knows Best* (CBS)

Outstanding Performance in a Variety or Musical Program or Series: Harry Belafonte, "Tonight with Belafonte," *The Revlon Revue* (CBS)

1960–61

The Program of the Year: "Macbeth," *Hallmark Hall of Fame* (NBC)

Outstanding Program Achievement in the Field of Humor: *The Jack Benny Show* (CBS)

Outstanding Program Achievement in the Field of Drama: "Macbeth," *Hallmark Hall of Fame* (NBC)

Outstanding Program Achievement in the Field of Variety: "Astaire Time" (NBC)

Outstanding Performance by an Actor in a Series (Lead): Raymond Burr, *Perry Mason* (CBS)

Outstanding Performance by an Actress in a Series (Lead): Barbara Stanwyck, *The Barbara Stanwyck Show* (NBC)

Outstanding Performance in a Variety or Musical Program or Series: Fred Astaire, "Astaire Time" (NBC)

1961–62

Program of the Year: "Victoria Regina," *Hallmark Hall of Fame* (NBC)

Outstanding Program Achievement in the Field of Humor: *The Bob Newhart Show* (NBC)

Outstanding Program Achievement in the Field of Drama: *The Defenders* (CBS)

Outstanding Program Achievement in the Field of Variety: *The Garry Moore Show* (CBS)

Outstanding Continued Performance by an Actor in a Series (Lead): E.G. Marshall, *The Defenders* (CBS)

Outstanding Continued Performance by an Actress in a Series (Lead): Shirley Booth, *Hazel* (NBC)

Outstanding Performance in a Variety or Musical Program or Series: Carol Burnett, *The Garry Moore Show* (CBS)

1962–63

Program of the Year: "The Tunnel" (NBC)

Outstanding Program Achievement in the Field of Humor: *The Dick Van Dyke Show* (CBS)

Outstanding Program Achievement in the Field of Drama: *The Defenders* (CBS)

Outstanding Program Achievement in the Field of Music: "Julie and Carol at Carnegie Hall" (CBS)

Outstanding Program Achievement in the Field of Variety: *The Andy Williams Show* (NBC)

Outstanding Continued Performance by an Actor in a Series (Lead): E.G. Marshall, *The Defenders* (CBS)

Outstanding Continued Performance by an Actress in a Series (Lead): Shirley Booth, *Hazel* (NBC)

Outstanding Performance in a Variety or Musical Program or Series: Carol Burnett, "Julie and Carol at Carnegie Hall" (CBS) and "Carol and Company" (CBS)

1963–64

Program of the Year: "The Making of the President 1960" (ABC)

Outstanding Program Achievement in the Field of Comedy: *The Dick Van Dyke Show* (CBS)

Outstanding Program Achievement in the Field of Drama: *The Defenders* (CBS)

Outstanding Program Achievement in the Field of Variety: *The Danny Kaye Show* (CBS)

Outstanding Continued Performance by an Actor in a Series (Lead): Dick Van Dyke, *The Dick Van Dyke Show* (CBS)

Outstanding Continued Performance by an Actress in a Series (Lead): Mary Tyler Moore, *The Dick Van Dyke Show* (CBS)

Outstanding Performance in a Variety or Musical Program or Series: Danny Kaye, *The Danny Kaye Show* (CBS)

1964–65

Outstanding Achievements in Entertainment: *The Dick Van Dyke Show* (CBS); "The Magnificent Yankee," *Hallmark Hall of Fame* (NBC); "My Name Is Barbra" (CBS)

Outstanding Individual Achievements in Entertainment (Actors and Performers): Lynn Fontanne, "The Magnificent Yankee," *Hallmark Hall of Fame* (NBC); Barbra Streisand, "My Name Is Barbra" (CBS); Dick Van Dyke, *The Dick Van Dyke Show* (CBS)

1965–66

Outstanding Comedy Series: *The Dick Van Dyke Show* (CBS)

Outstanding Variety Series: *The Andy Williams Show* (NBC)

Outstanding Dramatic Series: *The Fugitive* (ABC)

Outstanding Continued Performance by an Actor in a Leading Role in a Dramatic Series: Bill Cosby, *I Spy* (NBC)

Outstanding Continued Performance by an Actress in a Leading Role in a Dramatic Series: Barbara Stanwyck, *The Big Valley* (ABC)

Outstanding Continued Performance by an Actor in a Leading Role in a Comedy Series: Dick Van Dyke, *The Dick Van Dyke Show* (CBS)

Outstanding Continued Performance by an Actress in a Leading Role in a Comedy Series: Mary Tyler Moore, *The Dick Van Dyke Show* (CBS)

1966–67

Outstanding Comedy Series: *The Monkees* (NBC)

Outstanding Variety Series: *The Andy Williams Show* (NBC)

Outstanding Dramatic Series: *Mission: Impossible* (CBS)

Outstanding Continued Performance by an Actor in a Leading Role in a Dramatic Series: Bill Cosby, *I Spy* (NBC)

Outstanding Continued Performance by an Actress in a Leading Role in a Dramatic Series: Barbara Bain, *Mission: Impossible* (CBS)

Outstanding Continued Performance by an Actor in a Leading Role in a Comedy Series: Don Adams, *Get Smart* (NBC)

Outstanding Continued Performance by an Actress in a Leading Role in a Comedy Series: Lucille Ball, *The Lucy Show* (CBS)

1967–68

Outstanding Comedy Series: *Get Smart* (NBC)

Outstanding Dramatic Series: *Mission: Impossible* (CBS)

Outstanding Continued Performance by an Actor in a Leading Role in a Dramatic Series: Bill Cosby, *I Spy* (NBC)

Outstanding Continued Performance by an Actress in a Leading Role in a Dramatic Series: Barbara Bain, *Mission: Impossible* (CBS)

Outstanding Continued Performance by an Actor in a Leading Role in a Comedy Series: Don Adams, *Get Smart* (NBC)

Outstanding Continued Performance by an Actress in a Leading Role in a Comedy Series: Lucille Ball, *The Lucy Show* (CBS)

1968–69

Outstanding Comedy Series: *Get Smart* (NBC)

Outstanding Dramatic Series: *NET Playhouse* (NET)

Outstanding Musical or Variety Series: *Rowan and Martin's Laugh-In* (NBC)

Outstanding Continued Performance by an Actor in a Leading Role in a Dramatic Series: Carl Betz, *Judd, for the Defense* (ABC)

Outstanding Continued Performance by an Actress in a Leading Role in a Dramatic Series: Barbara Bain, *Mission: Impossible* (CBS)

Outstanding Continued Performance by an Actor in a Leading Role in a Comedy Series: Don Adams, *Get Smart* (NBC)

Outstanding Continued Performance by an Actress in a Leading Role in a Comedy Series: Hope Lange, *The Ghost and Mrs. Muir* (NBC)

1969–70

Outstanding Comedy Series: *My World and Welcome to It* (NBC)

Outstanding Dramatic Series: *Marcus Welby, M.D.* (ABC)

Outstanding Variety or Musical Series: *The David Frost Show* (syndicated)

Outstanding Continued Performance by an Actor in a Leading Role in a Dramatic Series: Robert Young, *Marcus Welby, M.D.* (ABC)

Outstanding Continued Performance by an Actress in a Leading Role in a Dramatic Series: Susan Hampshire, *The Forsythe Saga* (NET)

Outstanding Continued Performance by an Actor in a Leading Role in a Comedy Series: William Windom, *My World and Welcome to It* (NBC)

Outstanding Continued Performance by an Actress in a Leading Role in a Comedy Series: Hope Lange, *The Ghost and Mrs. Muir* (ABC)

1970–71

Outstanding Series—Comedy: *All in the Family* (CBS)

Outstanding Series—Drama: *The Senator* (NBC)

Outstanding Variety Series—Musical: *The Flip Wilson Show* (NBC)

Outstanding Continued Performance by an Actor in a Leading Role in a Dramatic Series: Hal Holbrook, *The Senator* (NBC)

Outstanding Continued Performance by an Actress in a Leading Role in a Dramatic Series: Susan Hampshire, *The First Churchills (Masterpiece Theatre)* (PBS)

Outstanding Continued Performance by an Actor in a Leading Role in a Comedy Series: Jack Klugman, *The Odd Couple* (CBS)

Outstanding Continued Performance by an Actress in a Leading Role in a Comedy Series: Jean Stapleton, *All in the Family* (CBS)

1971–72

Outstanding Series—Comedy: *All in the Family* (CBS)

Outstanding Series—Drama: *Elizabeth R (Masterpiece Theatre)* (PBS)

Outstanding Variety Series—Musical: *The Carol Burnett Show* (CBS)

Outstanding Variety Series—Talk: *The Dick Cavett Show* (ABC)

Outstanding Continued Performance by an Actor in a Leading Role in a Dramatic Series: Peter Falk, *Columbo* (NBC)

Outstanding Continued Performance by an Actor in a Leading Role in a Comedy Series: Carroll O'Connor, *All in the Family* (CBS)

Outstanding Continued Performance by an Actress in a Leading Role in a Comedy Series: Jean Stapleton, *All in the Family* (CBS)

1972–73

Outstanding Comedy Series: *All in the Family* (CBS)

Outstanding Drama Series: *The Waltons* (CBS)

Outstanding Variety Musical Series: *The Julie Andrews Hour* (ABC)

Outstanding Continued Performance by an Actor in a Leading Role (Drama Series—Continuing): Richard Thomas, *The Waltons* (CBS)

Outstanding Continued Performance by an Actress in a Leading Role (Drama Series—Continuing): Michael Learned, *The Waltons* (CBS)

Outstanding Continued Performance by an Actor in a Leading Role in a Comedy Series: Jack Klugman, *The Odd Couple* (ABC)

Outstanding Continued Performance by an Actress in a Leading Role in a Comedy Series: Mary Tyler Moore, *The Mary Tyler Moore Show* (CBS)

1973–74

Outstanding Comedy Series: *M*A*S*H* (CBS)

Outstanding Drama Series: *Upstairs, Downstairs (Masterpiece Theatre)* (PBS)

Outstanding Music-Variety Series: *The Carol Burnett Show* (CBS)

Best Lead Actor in a Comedy Series: Alan Alda, *M*A*S*H* (CBS)

Best Lead Actor in a Drama Series: Telly Savalas, *Kojak* (CBS)

Best Lead Actress in a Comedy Series: Mary Tyler Moore, *The Mary Tyler Moore Show* (CBS)

Best Lead Actress in a Drama Series: Michael Learned, *The Waltons* (CBS)

1974–75

Outstanding Comedy Series: *The Mary Tyler Moore Show* (CBS)

Outstanding Drama Series: *Upstairs, Downstairs (Masterpiece Theatre)* (PBS)

Outstanding Comedy-Variety or Music Series: *The Carol Burnett Show* (CBS)

Outstanding Lead Actor in a Comedy Series:

Tony Randall, *The Odd Couple* (ABC)

Outstanding Lead Actor in a Drama Series: Robert Blake, *Baretta* (ABC)

Outstanding Lead Actress in a Comedy Series: Valerie Harper, *Rhoda* (CBS)

Outstanding Lead Actress in a Drama Series: Jean Marsh, *Upstairs, Downstairs (Masterpiece Theatre)* (PBS)

1975–76

Outstanding Comedy Series: *The Mary Tyler Moore Show* (CBS)

Outstanding Drama Series: *Police Story* (NBC)

Outstanding Comedy-Variety or Music Series: *NBC's Saturday Night Live* (NBC)

Outstanding Lead Actor in a Comedy Series: Jack Albertson, *Chico and the Man* (NBC)

Outstanding Lead Actor in a Drama Series: Peter Falk, *Columbo* (NBC)

Outstanding Lead Actress in a Comedy Series: Mary Tyler Moore, *The Mary Tyler Moore Show* (CBS)

Outstanding Lead Actress in a Drama Series: Michael Learned, *The Waltons* (CBS)

1976–77

Outstanding Comedy Series: *The Mary Tyler Moore Show* (CBS)

Outstanding Drama Series: *Upstairs, Downstairs (Masterpiece Theatre)* (PBS)

Outstanding Comedy-Variety or Music Series: *Van Dyke and Company* (NBC)

Outstanding Lead Actor in a Comedy Series: Carroll O'Connor, *All in the Family* (CBS)

Outstanding Lead Actor in a Drama Series: James Garner, *The Rockford Files* (NBC)

Outstanding Lead Actress in a Comedy Series: Beatrice Arthur, *Maude* (CBS)

Outstanding Lead Actress in a Drama Series: Lindsay Wagner, *The Bionic Woman* (ABC)

1977–78

Outstanding Comedy Series: *All in the Family* (CBS)

Outstanding Drama Series: *The Rockford Files* (NBC)

Outstanding Comedy-Variety or Music Series: *The Muppet Show* (syndicated)

Outstanding Lead Actor in a Comedy Series: Carroll O'Connor, *All in the Family* (CBS)

Outstanding Lead Actor in a Drama Series: Ed Asner, *Lou Grant* (CBS)

Outstanding Lead Actress in a Comedy Series: Jean Stapleton, *All in the Family* (CBS)

Outstanding Lead Actress in a Drama Series: Sada Thompson, *Family* (ABC)

1978–79

Outstanding Comedy Series: *Taxi* (ABC)

Outstanding Drama Series: *Lou Grant* (CBS)

Outstanding Comedy-Variety or Music Program (Special or Series): *Steve & Eydie Celebrate Irving Berlin* (NBC)

Outstanding Lead Actor in a Comedy Series (Continuing or Single Performance): Carroll O'Connor, *All in the Family* (CBS)

Outstanding Lead Actor in a Drama Series (Continuing or Single Performance): Ron Leibman, *Kaz* (CBS)

Outstanding Lead Actress in a Comedy Series (Continuing or Single Performance): Ruth Gordon, *Taxi* ("Sugar Mama") (ABC)

Outstanding Lead Actress in a Drama Series

(Continuing or Single Performance): Mariette Hartley, *The Incredible Hulk* ("Married") (CBS)

1979–80

Outstanding Comedy Series: *Taxi* (ABC)
Outstanding Drama Series: *Lou Grant* (CBS)
Outstanding Variety or Music Program (Special or Series): *IBM Presents Baryshnikov on Broadway* (ABC)
Outstanding Lead Actor in a Comedy Series (Continuing or Single Performance): Richard Mulligan, *Soap* (ABC)
Outstanding Lead Actor in a Drama Series (Continuing or Single Performance): Ed Asner, *Lou Grant* (CBS)
Outstanding Lead Actress in a Comedy Series (Continuing or Single Performance): Cathryn Damon, *Soap* (ABC)
Outstanding Lead Actress in a Drama Series (Continuing or Single Performance): Barbara Bel Geddes, *Dallas* (CBS)

1980–81

Outstanding Comedy Series: *Taxi* (ABC)
Outstanding Drama Series: *Hill Street Blues* (NBC)
Outstanding Variety, Music, or Comedy Program: *Lily: Sold Out* (CBS)
Outstanding Lead Actor in a Drama Series: Daniel J. Travanti, *Hill Street Blues* (NBC)
Outstanding Lead Actor in a Comedy Series: Judd Hirsch, *Taxi* (ABC)
Outstanding Lead Actress in a Drama Series: Barbara Babcock, *Hill Street Blues* (NBC)
Outstanding Lead Actress in a Comedy Series: Isabel Sanford, *The Jeffersons* (CBS)

1981–82

Outstanding Comedy Series: *Barney Miller* (ABC)
Outstanding Drama Series: *Hill Street Blues* (NBC)
Outstanding Variety, Music, or Comedy Program: *Night of 100 Stars* (ABC)
Outstanding Lead Actor in a Drama Series: Daniel J. Travanti, *Hill Street Blues* (NBC)
Outstanding Lead Actor in a Comedy Series: Alan Alda, *M*A*S*H* (CBS)
Outstanding Lead Actress in a Drama Series: Michael Learned, *Nurse* (CBS)
Outstanding Lead Actress in a Comedy Series: Carol Kane, *Taxi* ("Simka Returns") (ABC)

1982–83

Outstanding Comedy Series: *Cheers* (NBC)

Outstanding Drama Series: *Hill Street Blues* (NBC)
Outstanding Variety, Music, or Comedy Program: *Motown 25: Yesterday, Today, Forever* (NBC)
Outstanding Lead Actor in a Drama Series: Ed Flanders, *St. Elsewhere* (NBC)
Outstanding Lead Actor in a Comedy Series: Judd Hirsch, *Taxi* (ABC)
Outstanding Lead Actress in a Drama Series: Tyne Daly, *Cagney & Lacey* (CBS)
Outstanding Lead Actress in a Comedy Series: Shelley Long, *Cheers* (NBC)

1983–84

Outstanding Comedy Series: *Cheers* (NBC)
Outstanding Drama Series: *Hill Street Blues* (NBC)
Outstanding Variety, Music, or Comedy Program: "The 6th Annual Kennedy Center Honors: A Celebration of the Performing Arts" (CBS)
Outstanding Lead Actor in a Drama Series: Tom Selleck, *Magnum, P.I.* (CBS)
Outstanding Lead Actor in a Comedy Series: John Ritter, *Three's Company* (ABC)
Outstanding Lead Actress in a Drama Series: Tyne Daly, *Cagney & Lacey* (CBS)
Outstanding Lead Actress in a Comedy Series: Jane Curtin, *Kate & Allie* (CBS)

1984–85

Outstanding Comedy Series: *The Cosby Show* (NBC)
Outstanding Drama Series: *Cagney & Lacey* (CBS)
Outstanding Variety, Music, or Comedy Program: "Motown Returns to the Apollo" (NBC)
Outstanding Lead Actor in a Drama Series: William Daniels, *St. Elsewhere* (NBC)
Outstanding Lead Actor in a Comedy Series: Robert Guillaume, *Benson* (ABC)
Outstanding Lead Actress in a Drama Series: Tyne Daly, *Cagney & Lacey* (CBS)
Outstanding Lead Actress in a Comedy Series: Jane Curtin, *Kate & Allie* (CBS)

1985–86

Outstanding Comedy Series: *The Golden Girls* (NBC)
Outstanding Drama Series: *Cagney & Lacey* (CBS)
Outstanding Variety, Music, or Comedy Program: "The Kennedy Center Honors: A Cele-

bration of the Performing Arts" (CBS)
Outstanding Lead Actor in a Drama Series: William Daniels, *St. Elsewhere* (NBC)
Outstanding Lead Actor in a Comedy Series: Michael J. Fox, *Family Ties* (NBC)
Outstanding Lead Actress in a Drama Series: Sharon Gless, *Cagney & Lacey* (CBS)
Outstanding Lead Actress in a Comedy Series: Betty White, *The Golden Girls* (NBC)

1986–87

Outstanding Comedy Series: *The Golden Girls* (NBC)
Outstanding Drama Series: *L.A. Law* (NBC)
Outstanding Variety, Music, or Comedy Program: "The 1987 Tony Awards" (CBS)
Outstanding Lead Actor in a Drama Series: Bruce Willis, *Moonlighting* (ABC)
Outstanding Lead Actor in a Comedy Series: Michael J. Fox, *Family Ties* (NBC)
Outstanding Lead Actress in a Drama Series: Sharon Gless, *Cagney & Lacey* (CBS)
Outstanding Lead Actress in a Comedy Series: Rue McClanahan, *The Golden Girls* (NBC)

1987–88

Outstanding Comedy Series: *The Wonder Years* (ABC)
Outstanding Drama Series: *thirtysomething* (ABC)
Outstanding Variety, Music, or Comedy Program: "Irving Berlin's 100th Birthday Celebration" (CBS)
Outstanding Lead Actor in a Comedy Series: Michael J. Fox, *Family Ties* (NBC)
Outstanding Lead Actor in a Drama Series: Richard Kiley, *A Year in the Life* (NBC)
Outstanding Lead Actress in a Comedy Series: Beatrice Arthur, *The Golden Girls* (NBC)
Outstanding Lead Actress in a Drama Series: Tyne Daly, *Cagney & Lacey* (CBS)

1988–89

Outstanding Comedy Series: *Cheers* (NBC)
Outstanding Drama Series: *L.A. Law* (NBC)
Outstanding Variety, Music, or Comedy Program: *The Tracey Ullman Show* (Fox)
Outstanding Lead Actor in a Comedy Series: Richard Mulligan, *Empty Nest* (NBC)
Outstanding Lead Actor in a Drama Series: Carroll O'Connor, *In the Heat of the Night* (NBC)
Outstanding Lead Actress in a Comedy Series: Candice Bergen, *Murphy Brown* (CBS)
Outstanding Lead Actress in a Drama Series: Dana Delany, *China Beach* (ABC)

THE GRAMMYS

The "Grammys" are officially known as the National Academy of Recording Arts and Sciences Awards. Winners (in almost 70 categories) are selected yearly by the 6,000 or so voting members of the academy. The five award categories listed below have remained fairly constant over the years, although the overall "Best Vocal Performance" award was phased out in 1968; from that year on, our listing is for "Best Pop Vocal Performance" except where indicated.

Year	Record of the year	Album of the year	Song of the year[1]	Best vocal performance (male)	Best vocal performance (female)
1958	Domenico Modugno *Nel Blu Dipinto di Blu (Volare)*	Henry Mancini *The Music from Peter Gunn*	Domenico Modugno "Nel Blu Dipinto di Blu" ("Volare")	Perry Como *Catch a Falling Star*	Ella Fitzgerald *Ella Fitzgerald Sings the Irving Berlin Songbook*
1959	Bobby Darin *Mack the Knife*	Frank Sinatra *Come Dance with Me*	Jimmy Driftwood "The Battle of New Orleans"	Frank Sinatra *Come Dance with Me*	Ella Fitzgerald *But Not for Me*

Year	Record of the year	Album of the year	Song of the year[1]	Best vocal performance (male)	Best vocal performance (female)
1960	Percy Faith *Theme from a Summer Place*	Bob Newhart *Button-Down Mind*	Ernest Gold "Theme from Exodus"	Ray Charles *Georgia on My Mind*	Ella Fitzgerald *Mack the Knife*
1961	Henry Mancini *Moon River*	Judy Garland *Judy at Carnegie Hall*	Henry Mancini; Johnny Mercer "Moon River"	Jack Jones *Lollipops and Roses*	Judy Garland *Judy at Carnegie Hall*
1962	Tony Bennett *I Left My Heart in San Francisco*	Vaughn Meader *The First Family*	Leslie Bricusse; Anthony Newley "What Kind of Fool Am I?"	Tony Bennett *I Left My Heart in San Francisco*[2]	Ella Fitzgerald *Ella Swings Brightly with Nelson Riddle*[2]
1963	Henry Mancini *The Days of Wine and Roses*	Barbra Streisand *The Barbra Streisand Album*	Henry Mancini; Johnny Mercer "The Days of Wine and Roses"	Jack Jones *Wives and Lovers*	Barbra Streisand *The Barbra Streisand Album*[2]
1964	Stan Getz; Astrud Gilberto *The Girl from Ipanema*	Stan Getz; Astrud Gilberto *Getz/Gilberto*	Jerry Herman "Hello, Dolly!"	Louis Armstrong *Hello, Dolly!*	Barbra Streisand *People*
1965	Herb Alpert & the Tijuana Brass *A Taste of Honey*	Frank Sinatra *September of My Years*	Paul Francis Webster; Johnny Mandel "The Shadow of Your Smile"	Frank Sinatra *It Was a Very Good Year*	Barbra Streisand *My Name Is Barbra*[2]
1966	Frank Sinatra *Strangers in the Night*	Frank Sinatra *A Man and His Music*	John Lennon; Paul McCartney "Michelle"	Frank Sinatra *Strangers in the Night*	Eydie Gorme *If He Walked into My Life*
1967	5th Dimension *Up, Up and Away*	The Beatles *Sgt. Pepper's Lonely Hearts Club Band*	Jim Webb "Up, Up and Away"	Glen Campbell *By the Time I Get to Phoenix*	Bobbie Gentry *Ode to Billie Joe*
1968	Simon & Garfunkel *Mrs. Robinson*	Glen Campbell *By the Time I Get to Phoenix*	Bobby Russell "Little Green Apples"	Jose Feliciano[3] *Light My Fire*	Dionne Warwick[3] *Do You Know the Way to San Jose?*
1969	5th Dimension *Aquarius/Let the Sunshine In*	Blood, Sweat & Tears *Blood, Sweat & Tears*	Joe South "Games People Play"	Harry Nilsson[4] *Everybody's Talkin'*	Peggy Lee[4] *Is That All There Is?*
1970	Simon & Garfunkel *Bridge over Troubled Water*	Simon & Garfunkel *Bridge over Troubled Water*	Paul Simon "Bridge over Troubled Water"	Ray Stevens[4] *Everything Is Beautiful*	Dionne Warwick[4] *I'll Never Fall in Love Again*[2]
1971	Carole King *It's Too Late*	Carole King *Tapestry*	Carole King "You've Got a Friend"	James Taylor[5] *You've Got a Friend*	Carole King[5] *Tapestry*[2]
1972	Roberta Flack *The First Time Ever I Saw Your Face*	George Harrison; Ravi Shankar; Bob Dylan et al *Concert for Bangladesh*	Ewan McColl "The First Time Ever I Saw Your Face"	Harry Nilsson *Without You*	Helen Reddy *I Am Woman*
1973	Roberta Flack *Killing Me Softly with His Song*	Stevie Wonder *Innervisions*	Norman Gimbel; Charles Fox "Killing Me Softly with His Song"	Stevie Wonder *You Are the Sunshine of My Life*	Roberta Flack *Killing Me Softly with His Song*
1974	Olivia Newton-John *I Honestly Love You*	Stevie Wonder *Fulfillingness' First Finale*	Marilyn & Alan Bergman; Marvin Hamlisch "The Way We Were"	Stevie Wonder *Fulfillingness' First Finale*[2]	Olivia Newton-John *I Honestly Love You*
1975	Captain & Tennille *Love Will Keep Us Together*	Paul Simon *Still Crazy after All These Years*	Stephen Sondheim "Send in the Clowns"	Paul Simon *Still Crazy after All These Years*[2]	Janis Ian *At Seventeen*
1976	George Benson *This Masquerade*	Stevie Wonder *Songs in the Key of Life*	Bruce Johnston "I Write the Songs"	Stevie Wonder *Songs in the Key of Life*[2]	Linda Ronstadt *Hasten Down the Wind*[2]
1977	The Eagles *Hotel California*	Fleetwood Mac *Rumours*	Barbra Streisand; Paul Williams "Evergreen"	James Taylor *Handy Man*	Barbra Streisand *Evergreen*
1978	Billy Joel *Just the Way You Are*	Various Artists *Saturday Night Fever*	Billy Joel "Just the Way You Are"	Barry Manilow *Copacabana (At the Copa)*	Anne Murray *You Needed Me*

Year	Record of the year	Album of the year	Song of the year[1]	Best vocal performance (male)	Best vocal performance (female)
1979	The Doobie Brothers *What a Fool Believes*	Billy Joel *52nd Street*	Kenny Loggins; Michael McDonald "What a Fool Believes"	Billy Joel *52nd Street*[2]	Dionne Warwick *I'll Never Love This Way Again*
1980	Christopher Cross *Sailing*	Christopher Cross *Christopher Cross*	Christopher Cross "Sailing"	Kenny Loggins *This Is It*	Bette Midler *The Rose*
1981	Kim Carnes *Bette Davis Eyes*	John Lennon/Yoko Ono *Double Fantasy*	Donna Weiss; Jackie DeShannon "Bette Davis Eyes"	Al Jarreau *Breakin' Away*[2]	Lena Horne *Lena Horne: The Lady and Her Music Live on Broadway*
1982	Toto *Rosanna*	Toto *Toto IV*	Johnny Christopher; Mark James; Wayne Carson "Always on My Mind"	Lionel Richie *Truly*	Melissa Manchester *You Should Hear How She Talks about You*
1983	Michael Jackson *Beat It*	Michael Jackson *Thriller*	Sting "Every Breath You Take"	Michael Jackson *Thriller*[2]	Irene Cara *Flashdance . . . What a Feeling*
1984	Tina Turner *What's Love Got to Do with It?*	Lionel Richie *Can't Slow Down*	Graham Lyle; Terry Britten "What's Love Got to Do with It?"	Phil Collins *Against All Odds (Take a Look at Me Now)*	Tina Turner *What's Love Got to Do with It?*
1985	USA for Africa *We Are the World*	Phil Collins *No Jacket Required*	Michael Jackson; Lionel Richie "We Are the World"	Phil Collins *No Jacket Required*[2]	Whitney Houston *Saving All My Love for You*
1986	Steve Winwood *Higher Love*	Paul Simon *Graceland*	Various Artists "That's What Friends Are For"	Steve Winwood *Higher Love*	Barbra Streisand *The Broadway Album*[2]
1987	Paul Simon *Graceland*	U2 *The Joshua Tree*	Linda Ronstadt; James Ingram "Somewhere Out There"	Sting *Bring On the Night*[2]	Whitney Houston *I Wanna Dance with Somebody (Who Loves Me)*
1988	Bobby McFerrin *Don't Worry, Be Happy*	George Michael *Faith*	Bobby McFerrin "Don't Worry, Be Happy"	Bobby McFerrin *Don't Worry, Be Happy*	Tracy Chapman *Fast Car*

Notes: 1. Awarded to the composer, rather than the performer, of the song.   2. Awarded for an album, rather than an individual song.   3. Award given for "Best Contemporary—Pop Vocal Performance."   4. Award given for "Best Contemporary Vocal Performance."   5. From 1971 on, all awards in these columns are for "Best Pop Vocal Performance."

MTV VIDEO MUSIC AWARDS

Each year MTV Networks recognizes outstanding achievement in the field of video music with the MTV Video Music Awards. The professional categories include special effects, direction, editing, and choreography among others. Listed here are each of the winners in the general category since the inception of the awards in 1984.

1984
Best Video Cars, "You Might Think"
Best Male Video David Bowie, "China Girl"
Best Female Video Cyndi Lauper, "Girls Just Want to Have Fun"
Best Group Video ZZ Top, "Legs"
Best Concept Video Herbie Hancock, "Rockit"
Best Stage Performance in a Video Van Halen, "Jump"
Best New Artist in a Video Eurythmics, "Sweet Dreams (Are Made of This)"
Best Overall Performance in a Video Michael Jackson, "Thriller"

1985
Best Video Don Henley, "The Boys of Summer"
Best Male Video Bruce Springsteen, "I'm on Fire"
Best Female Video Tina Turner, "What's Love Got to Do With It"

Best Group Video USA for Africa, "We Are the World"
Best Concept Video Glenn Frey, "Smuggler's Blues"
Best Stage Performance in a Video Bruce Springsteen, "Dancing in the Dark"
Best New Artist in a Video til' tuesday, "Voices Carry"
Best Overall Performance in a Video Philip Bailey/Phil Collins, "Easy Lover"

1986
Best Video Dire Straits, "Money for Nothing"
Best Male Video Robert Palmer, "Addicted to Love"
Best Female Video Whitney Houston, "How Will I Know?"
Best Group Video Dire Straits, "Money for Nothing"
Best Concept Video a-Ha, "Take On Me"
Best Stage Performance in a Video Bryan Adams/Tina Turner, "It's Only Love"
Best New Artist in a Video a-Ha, "Take On Me"
Best Overall Performance in a Video David Bowie & Mick Jagger, "Dancing in the Streets"

1987
Best Video Peter Gabriel, "Sledgehammer"
Best Male Video Peter Gabriel, "Sledgehammer"

Best Female Video Madonna, "Papa Don't Preach"
Best Group Video Talking Heads, "Wild Wild Life"
Best Concept Video Peter Gabriel/Stephen Johnson, "Sledgehammer"
Best Stage Performance in a Video Bon Jovi, "Livin' on a Prayer"
Best New Artist in a Video Crowded House, "Don't Dream It's Over"
Best Overall Performance in a Video Peter Gabriel, "Sledgehammer"

1988
Best Video INXS, "Need You Tonight/Mediate"
Best Male Video Prince, "U Got the Look"
Best Female Video Suzanne Vega, "Luka"
Best Group Video INXS, "Need You Tonight/Mediate"
Best Concept Video Pink Floyd, "Learning to Fly"
Best Stage Performance in a Video Prince, "U Got the Look"
Best New Artist in a Video Guns N' Roses, "Welcome to the Jungle"
Best Video from a Film Los Lobos, "La Bamba" (*La Bamba*)

Source: MTV Networks.

THE TONY AWARDS, 1947–89

The Tony Awards are presented each year by the American Theatre Wing for distinguished achievement in the Broadway theater. Named for Antoinette Perry, an actress, producer, director, and chairman of the American Theatre Wing who died in 1946, the Tonys were first presented in 1947. Awards are given to performers, authors, producers, directors, composers, and choreographers, and scenic, costume, and lighting designers. Listed here is a selection of major awards for each year: best play (author), best performance by an actor in a play, best performance by an actress in a play, best musical (composer and lyricist), best performance by an actor in a musical, best performance by an actress in a musical.

PLAY

Year	Play	Actor	Actress
1947	no play	José Ferrer, *Cyrano de Bergerac*. Frederic March, *Year 1790*	Ingrid Bergman, *Joan of Lorraine*. Helen Hayes, *Happy Birthday*.
1948	*Mister Roberts*, Thomas Heggen and Joshua Logan	Henry Fonda, *Mister Roberts*. Paul Kelly, *Command Decision*. Basil Rathbone, *The Heiress*	Judith Anderson, *Medea*. Katharine Cornell, *Antony and Cleopatra*. Jessica Tandy, *A Streetcar Named Desire*
1949	*Death of a Salesman*, Arthur Miller	Rex Harrison, *Anne of a Thousand Days*	Martita Hunt, *The Mad Woman of Chaillot*
1950	*The Cocktail Party*, T.S. Eliot	Sidney Blackmer, *Come Back, Little Sheba*	Shirley Booth, *Come Back, Little Sheba*
1951	*The Rose Tattoo*, Tennessee Williams	Claude Rains, *Darkness at Noon*	Uta Hagen, *The Country Girl*
1952	*The Fourposter*, Jan de Hartog	José Ferrer, *The Shrike*	Julie Harris, *I Am a Camera*
1953	*The Crucible*, Arthur Miller	Tom Ewell, *The Seven Year Itch*	Shirley Booth, *Time of the Cuckoo*
1954	*The Teahouse of the August Moon*, John Patrick	David Wayne, *The Teahouse of the August Moon*	Audrey Hepburn, *Ondine*
1955	*The Desperate Hours*, Joseph Hayes	Alfred Lunt, *Quadrille*	Nancy Kelly, *The Bad Seed*
1956	*The Diary of Anne Frank*, Frances Goodrich and Albert Hackett	Paul Muni, *Inherit the Wind*	Julie Harris, *The Lark*
1957	*Long Day's Journey Into Night*, Eugene O'Neill	Frederic March, *Long Day's Journey Into Night*	Margaret Leighton, *Separate Tables*
1958	*Sunrise at Campobello*, Dore Schary	Ralph Bellamy, *Sunrise at Campobello*	Helen Hayes, *Time Remembered*
1959	*J.B.*, Archibald Macleish	Jason Robards, *The Disenchanted*	Gertrude Berg, *A Majority of One*
1960	*The Miracle Worker*, William Gibson	Melvyn Douglas, *The Best Man*	Anne Bancroft, *The Miracle Worker*
1961	*Becket*, Jean Anouilh	Zero Mostel, *Rhinoceros*	Joan Plowright, *A Taste of Honey*
1962	*A Man for All Seasons*, Robert Bolt	Paul Scofield, *A Man for All Seasons*	Margaret Leighton, *Night of The Iguana*
1963	*Who's Afraid of Virginia Woolf?*, Edward Albee	Arthur Hill, *Who's Afraid of Virginia Woolf?*	Uta Hagen, *Who's Afraid of Virginia Woolf?*
1964	*Luther*, John Osborne	Alec Guiness, *Dylan*	Sandy Dennis, *Any Wednesday*
1965	*The Subject was Roses*, Frank Gilroy	Walter Matthau, *The Odd Couple*	Irene Worth, *Tiny Alice*
1966	*Marat/Sade*, Peter Weiss	Hal Holbrook, *Mark Twain Tonight!*	Rosemary Harris, *The Lion in Winter*
1967	*The Homecoming*, Harold Pinter	Paul Rogers, *The Homecoming*	Beryl Reid, *The Killing of Sister George*
1968	*Rosencrantz and Guildenstern Are Dead*, Tom Stoppard	Martin Balsam, *You Know I Can't Hear You When the Water's Running*	Zoe Caldwell, *The Prime of Miss Jean Brodie*
1969	*The Great White Hope*, Howard Sackler	James Earl Jones, *The Great White Hope*	Julie Harris, *Forty Carats*
1970	*Borstal Boy*, Frank McMahon	Fritz Weaver, *Child's Play*	Tammy Grimes, *Private Lives* (R)
1971	*Sleuth*, Anthony Shaffer	Brian Bedford, *The School for Wives*	Maureen Stapleton, *Gingerbread Lady*
1972	*Sticks and Bones*, David Rabe	Cliff Gorman, *Lenny*	Sada Thompson, *Twigs*
1973	*That Championship Season*, Jason Miller	Alan Bates, *Butley*	Julie Harris, *The Last of Mrs. Lincoln*
1974	*The River Niger*, Joseph A. Walker	Michael Moriarty, *Find Your Way Home*	Colleen Dewhurst, *A Moon for the Misbegotten* (R)
1975	*Equus*, Peter Shaffer	John Kani and Winston Ntshona, *Sizwe Banzi Is Dead* and *The Island*	Ellen Burstyn, *Same Time, Next Year*
1976	*Travesties*, Tom Stoppard	John Wood, *Travesties*	Irene Worth, *Sweet Bird of Youth* (R)
1977	*The Shadow Box*, Michael Cristofer	Al Pacino, *The Basic Training of Pavlo Hummel*	Julie Harris, *The Belle of Amherst*
1978	*Da*, Hugh Leonard	Barnard Hughes, *Da*	Jessica Tandy, *The Gin Game*
1979	*The Elephant Man*, Bernard Pomerance	Tom Conti, *Whose Life Is It Anyway?*	Constance Cummings, *Wings*
1980	*Children of a Lesser God*, Mark Medoff	John Rubenstein, *Children of a Lesser God*	Phyllis Frelich, *Children of a Lesser God*
1981	*Amadeus*, Peter Shaffer	Ian McKellen, *Amadeus*	Jane Lapotaire, *Piaf*
1982	*Nicholas Nickleby*, David Edgar	Roger Rees, *Nicholas Nickleby*	Zoe Caldwell, *Medea*
1983	*Torch Song Trilogy*, Harvey Fierstein	Harvey Fierstein, *Torch Song Trilogy*	Jessica Tandy, *Foxfire*
1984	*The Real Thing*, Tom Stoppard	Jeremy Irons, *The Real Thing*	Glenn Close, *The Real Thing*
1985	*As Is*, William Hoffman	Derek Jacobi, *Much Ado About Nothing*	Stockard Channing, *Joe Egg* (R)
1986	*I'm Not Rappaport*, Herb Gardner	Judd Hirsch, *I'm Not Rappaport*	Lily Tomlin, *The Search for Intelligent Life in the Universe*
1987	*Fences*, August Wilson	James Earl Jones, *Fences*	Linda Lavin, *Broadway Bound*
1988	*M. Butterfly*, David Henry Hwang	Ron Silver, *Speed-The-Plow*	Joan Allen, *Burn This*
1989	*The Heidi Chronicles*, Wendy Wasserstein	Philip Bosco, *Lend Me a Tenor*	Pauline Collins, *Shirley Valentine*

MUSICAL

Year	Musical	Actor	Actress
1947	no award	no award	no award
1948	*Paul Hartman, Angel in the Wings*	Paul Hartman, *Angel in the Wings*	Grace Hartman, *Angel in the Wings*
1949	*Kiss Me Kate*, Cole Porter (M & L)	Ray Bolger, *Where's Charley?*	Nanette Fabray, *Love Life*
1950	*South Pacific*, Richard Rodgers (M), Oscar Hammerstein, (L)	Ezio Pinza, *South Pacific*	Mary Martin, *South Pacific*
1951	*Guys and Dolls*, Frank Loesser (M & L)	Robert Alda, *Guys and Dolls*	Ethel Merman, *Call Me Madam*
1952	*The King and I*, Richard Rodgers (M), Oscar Hammerstein (L)	Phil Silvers, *Top Banana*	Gertrude Lawrence, *The King and I*
1953	*Wonderful Town*, Leonard Bernstein (M), Betty Comden and Adolph Green (L)	Thomas Mitchell, *Hazel Flagg*	Rosalind Russell, *Wonderful Town*
1954	*Kismet*, Alexander Borodin (M), adapted by Robert Wright and George Forrest (L)	Alfred Drake, *Kismet*	Dolores Gray, *Carnival in Flanders*
1955	*The Pajama Game*, Richard Adler and Jerry Ross (M & L)	Walter Slezak, *Fanny*	Mary Martin, *Peter Pan*
1956	*Damn Yankees*, Richard Adler and Jerry Ross (M & L)	Ray Walston, *Damn Yankees*	Gwen Verdon, *Damn Yankees*
1957	*My Fair Lady*, Frederick Loewe (M), Alan Jay Lerner (L)	Rex Harrison, *My Fair Lady*	Judy Holliday, *Bells Are Ringing*
1958	*The Music Man*, Meredith Willson (M & L)	Robert Preston, *The Music Man*	Thelma Ritter, *New Girl in Town*
1959	*Redhead*, Albert Hague (M), Dorothy Fields (L)	Richard Kiley, *Redhead*	Gwen Verdon, *Redhead*
1960	(tie) *Fiorello*, Jerry Bock (M), Sheldon Harnick (L); *The Sound of Music*, Richard Rodgers (M), Oscar Hammerstein (L)	Jackie Gleason, *Take Me Along*	Mary Martin, *The Sound of Music*
1961	*Bye, Bye, Birdie*, Charles Strouse (M), Lee Adams (L)	Richard Burton, *Camelot*	Elizabeth Seal, *Irma la Douce*
1962	*How to Succeed in Business without Really Trying*, Frank Loesser (M & L)	Robert Morse, *How to Succeed in Business without Really Trying*	(tie) Anna Maria Alberghetti, *Carnival;* Diahann Carroll, *No Strings*
1963	*A Funny Thing Happened on the Way to the Forum*, Stephen Sondheim (M & L)	Zero Mostel, *A Funny Thing Happened on the Way to the Forum*	Vivien Leigh, *Tovarich*
1964	*Hello, Dolly!* Jerry Herman (M & L)	Bert Lahr, *Foxy*	Carol Channing, *Hello, Dolly!*
1965	*Fiddler on the Roof*, Jerry Bock (M), Sheldon Harnick (L)	Zero Mostel, *Fiddler on the Roof*	Liza Minnelli, *Flora, the Red Menace*
1966	*Man of La Mancha*, Mitch Leigh (M), Joe Darion (L)	Richard Kiley, *Man of La Mancha*	Angela Lansbury, *Mame*
1967	*Cabaret,* John Kander (M), Fred Ebb (L)	Robert Preston, *I Do! I Do!*	Barbara Harris, *The Apple Tree*
1968	*Hallelujah, Baby!* Jule Styne (M), Betty Comden and Adolph Green (L)	Robert Goulet, *The Happy Time*	Patricia Routledge, *Darling of the Day*
1969	*1776*, Sherman Edwards (M & L)	Jerry Orbach, *Promises, Promises*	Angela Lansbury, *Dear World*
1970	*Applause*, Charles Strouse (M), Lee Adams (L)	Cleavon Little, *Purlie*	Lauren Bacall, *Applause*
1971	*Company*, Stephen Sondheim (M & L)	Hal Linden, *The Rothchilds*	Helen Gallagher, *No, No, Nannette* (R)
1972	*Two Gentlemen of Verona* [best score: *Follies*, Stephen Sondheim (M & L)]	Phil Silvers, *A Funny Thing Happened on the Way to the Forum* (R)	Alexis Smith, *Follies*
1973	*A Little Night Music*, Stephen Sondheim (M & L)	Ben Vereen, *Pippin*	Glynis Johns, *A Little Night Music*
1974	*Raisin*, [best score: *Gigi*, Frederick Loewe (M), Alan Jay Lerner (L)]	Christopher Plummer, *Cyrano*	Virginia Capers, *Raisin*
1975	*The Wiz*, Charlie Smalls (M & L)	John Cullum, *Shenandoah*	Angela Lansbury, *Gypsy* (R)
1976	*A Chorus Line*, Marvin Hamlisch (M), Edward Kleban (L)	George Rose, *My Fair Lady* (R)	Donna McKenchie, *A Chorus Line*
1977	*Annie*, Charles Strouse (M), Martin Charnin (L)	Barry Bostwick, *The Robber Bridegroom*	Dorothy Loudon, *Annie*
1978	*Ain't Misbehavin'* [best score: *On the Twentieth Century,* Cy Coleman (M) Betty Comden and Adolph Green (L)]	John Cullum, *On the Twentieth Century*	Liza Minelli, *The Act*
1979	*Sweeney Todd*, Stephen Sondheim (M & L)	Len Cariou, *Sweeney Todd*	Angela Lansbury, *Sweeney Todd*
1980	*Evita*, Andrew Lloyd Webber (M), Tim Rice (L)	Jim Dale, *Barnum*	Patti LuPone, *Evita*
1981	*42nd Street*, [best score: *Woman of the Year,* John Kander (M), Fred Ebb (L)]	Kevin Kline, *The Pirates of Penzance*	Lauren Bacall, *Woman of the Year*
1982	*Nine*, Maury Yeston (M & L)	Ben Harney, *Dreamgirls*	Jennifer Holliday, *Dreamgirls*
1983	*Cats*, Andrew Lloyd Webber (M), T.S. Eliot (L)	Tommy Tune, *My One and Only*	Natalia Makarova, *On Your Toes* (R)
1984	*La Cage Aux Folles*, Jerry Herman (M & L)	George Hearn, *La Cage Aux Folles*	Chita Rivera, *The Rink*
1985	*Big River*, Roger Miller (M & L)	no award	no award
1986	*The Mystery of Edwin Drood*, Rupert Holmes (M & L)	George Rose, *The Mystery of Edwin Drood*	Bernadette Peters, *Song and Dance*
1987	*Les Misérables*, Claude-Michel Schönberg (M); Herbert Kretzmer & Alain Boublil (L)	Robert Lindsay, *Me and My Girl* (R)	Maryann Plunkett, *Me and My Girl* (R)
1988	*The Phantom of the Opera* [best score: *Into the Woods*, Stephen Sondheim (M & L)]	Michael Crawford, *The Phantom of the Opera*	Joanna Gleason, *Into the Woods*
1989	*Jerome Robbins' Broadway*	Jason Alexander, *Jerome Robbins' Broadway*	Ruth Brown, *Black and Blue*

M = music; L = lyrics; R = revival. **Note:** Since 1971 "Musical" and "Score" have been separate categories. See listing for 1972, 1974, 1978, 1981, and 1988.
Source: Isabelle Stevenson, *The Tony Award* (1987)—supplement, American Theatre Wing (1988), reprinted with permission.

PULITZER PRIZES IN LETTERS

THE PULITZER PRIZE FOR THE NOVEL/FICTION, 1918–89

Year	Author	Title	Year	Author	Title
1918	Ernest Poole	His Family	1954	No award	
1919	Booth Tarkington	The Magnificent Ambersons	1955	William Faulkner	A Fable
1920	No award		1956	MacKinlay Kantor	Andersonville
1921	Edith Wharton	The Age of Innocence	1957	No award	
1922	Booth Tarkington	Alice Adams	1958	James Agee	A Death in the Family[3]
1923	Willa Cather	One of Ours	1959	Robert Lewis Taylor	The Travels of Jaimie McPheeters
1924	Margaret Wilson	The Able McLaughlins	1960	Allen Drury	Advise and Consent
1925	Edna Ferber	So Big	1961	Harper Lee	To Kill a Mockingbird
1926	Sinclair Lewis	Arrowsmith	1962	Edwin O'Connor	The Edge of Sadness
1927	Louis Bromfield	Early Autumn	1963	William Faulkner	The Reivers
1928	Thornton Wilder	The Bridge of San Luis Rey	1964	No award	
1929	Julia Peterkin	Scarlet Sister Mary	1965	Shirley Ann Grau	The Keepers of the House
1930	Oliver LaFarge	Laughing Boy	1966	Katherine Anne Porter	Collected Stories
1931	Margaret Ayer Barnes	Years of Grace	1967	Bernard Malamud	The Fixer
1932	Pearl S. Buck	The Good Earth	1968	William Styron	The Confessions of Nat Turner
1933	T.S. Stribling	The Store	1969	N. Scott Momaday	House Made of Dawn
1934	Caroline Miller	Lamb in His Bosom	1970	Jean Stafford	Collected Stories
1935	Josephine Winslow Johnson	Now in November	1971	No award	
1936	Harold L. Davis	Honey in the Horn	1972	Wallace Stegner	Angle of Repose
1937	Margaret Mitchell	Gone with the Wind	1973	Eudora Welty	The Optimist's Daughter
1938	John Phillips Marquand	The Late George Apley	1974	No award	
1939	Marjorie Kinnan Rawlings	The Yearling	1975	Michael Shaara	The Killer Angels
1940	John Steinbeck	The Grapes of Wrath	1976	Saul Bellow	Humboldt's Gift
1941	No award		1977	No award	
1942	Ellen Glasgow	In This Our Life	1978	James Alan McPherson	Elbow Room
1943	Upton Sinclair	Dragon's Teeth	1979	John Cheever	The Stories of John Cheever
1944	Martin Flavin	Journey in the Dark	1980	Norman Mailer	The Executioner's Song
1945	John Hersey	A Bell for Adano	1981	John Kennedy Toole	A Confederacy of Dunces[2, 3]
1946	No award		1982	John Updike	Rabbit Is Rich
1947	Robert Penn Warren	All the King's Men	1983	Alice Walker	The Color Purple
1948[1]	James A. Michener	Tales of the South Pacific	1984	William Kennedy	Ironweed
1949	James Gould Cozzens	Guard of Honor	1985	Alison Lurie	Foreign Affairs
1950	A.B. Guthrie, Jr.	The Way West	1986	Larry McMurtry	Lonesome Dove
1951	Conrad Richter	The Town	1987	Peter Taylor	A Summons to Memphis
1952	Herman Wouk	The Caine Mutiny	1988	Toni Morrison	Beloved
1953	Ernest Hemingway	The Old Man and the Sea	1989	Anne Tyler	Breathing Lessons

THE PULITZER PRIZE FOR DRAMA, 1918–89

Year	Author	Title	Year	Author	Title
1918	Jesse Lynch Williams	Why Marry	1942	No award	
1919	No award		1943	Thornton Wilder	The Skin of Our Teeth
1920	Eugene O'Neill	Beyond the Horizon	1944	No award	
1921	Zona Gale	Miss Lulu Bett	1945	Mary Chase	Harvey
1922	Eugene O'Neill	Anna Christie	1946	Russel Crouse and Howard Lindsay	State of the Union
1923	Owen Davis	Icebound	1947	No award	
1924	Hatcher Hughes	Hell–Bent Fer Heaven	1948	Tennessee Williams	A Streetcar Named Desire
1925	Sidney Howard	They Knew What They Wanted	1949	Arthur Miller	Death of a Salesman
1926	George Kelly	Craig's Wife	1950	Richard Rodgers, Oscar Hammerstein II, and Joshua Logan	South Pacific
1927	Paul Green	In Abraham's Bosom			
1928	Eugene O'Neill	Strange Interlude	1951	No award	
1929	Elmer L. Rice	Street Scene	1952	Joseph Kramm	The Shrike
1930	Marc Connelly	The Green Pastures	1953	William Inge	Picnic
1931	Susan Glaspell	Alison's House	1954	John Patrick	The Teahouse of the August Moon
1932	George S. Kaufman, Morrie Ryskind, and Ira Gershwin	Of Thee I Sing	1955	Tennessee Williams	Cat on a Hot Tin Roof
			1956	Albert Hackett and Frances Goodrich	The Diary of Anne Frank
1933	Maxwell Anderson	Both Your Houses			
1934	Sidney Kingsley	Men in White	1957	Eugene O'Neill	Long Day's Journey Into Night
1935	Zoe Akins	The Old Maid	1958	Ketti Frings	Look Homeward, Angel
1936	Robert E. Sherwood	Idiot's Delight	1959	Archibald MacLeish	J.B.
1937	Moss Hart and George S. Kaufman	You Can't Take It with You	1960	Jerome Weidman and George Abbott (book); Jerry Bock (music); and Sheldon Harnick (lyrics)	Fiorello!
1938	Thornton Wilder	Our Town			
1939	Robert E. Sherwood	Abe Lincoln in Illinois			
1940	William Saroyan	The Time of Your Life			
1941	Robert E. Sherwood	There Shall Be No Night			

Year	Author	Title
1961	Tad Mosel	*All the Way Home*
1962	Frank Loesser and Abe Burrows	*How to Succeed in Business without Really Trying*
1963	No award	
1964	No award	
1965	Frank D. Gilroy	*The Subject Was Roses*
1966	No award	
1967	Edward Albee	*A Delicate Balance*
1968	No award	
1969	Howard Sackler	*The Great White Hope*
1970	Charles Gordone	*No Place to Be Somebody*
1971	Paul Zindel	*The Effect of Gamma Rays on Man-in-the-Moon Marigolds*
1972	No award	
1973	Jason Miller	*That Championship Season*
1974	No award	
1975	Edward Albee	*Seascape*
1976	Michael Bennett; Nicholas Dante &	*A Chorus Line*

Year	Author	Title
	James Kirkwood (book); Marvin Hamlisch (music); and Edward Kleban (lyrics)	
1977	Michael Cristofer	*The Shadow Box*
1978	Donald L. Coburn	*The Gin Game*
1979	Sam Shepard	*Buried Child*
1980	Lanford Wilson	*Talley's Folly*
1981	Beth Henley	*Crimes of the Heart*
1982	Charles Fuller	*A Soldier's Play*
1983	Marsha Norman	*'night Mother*
1984	David Mamet	*Glengarry Glen Ross*
1985	Stephen Sondheim (music and lyrics); James Lapine (book)	*Sunday in the Park with George*
1986	No award	
1987	August Wilson	*Fences*
1988	Alfred Uhry	*Driving Miss Daisy*
1989	Wendy Wasserstein	*The Heidi Chronicles*

THE PULITZER PRIZE FOR HISTORY, 1917–89

Year	Author	Title
1917	His Excellency J.J. Jusserand, French ambassador to the U.S.	*With Americans of Past and Present Days*
1918	James Ford Rhodes	*A History of the Civil War, 1861–1865*
1919	No award	
1920	Justin H. Smith	*The War with Mexico*
1921	William Sowden Sims, with Burton J. Hendrick	*The Victory at Sea*
1922	James Truslow Adams	*The Founding of New England*
1923	Charles Warren	*The Supreme Court in United States History*
1924	Charles Howard McIlwain	*The American Revolution— A Constitutional Interpretation*
1925	Frederic L. Paxson	*A History of the American Frontier*
1926	Edward Channing	*The History of the United States*
1927	Samuel Flagg Bemis	*Pinckney's Treaty*
1928	Vernon Louis Parrington	*Main Currents in American Thought*
1929	Fred Albert Shannon	*The Organization and Administration of the Union Army, 1861–1865*
1930	Claude H. Van Tyne	*The War of Independence*
1931	Bernadotte E. Schmitt	*The Coming of the War: 1914*
1932	John J. Pershing	*My Experiences in the World War*
1933	Frederick J. Turner	*The Significance of Sections in American History*
1934	Herbert Agar	*The People's Choice*
1935	Charles McLean Andrews	*The Colonial Period of American History*
1936	Andrew C. McLaughlin	*The Constitutional History of the United States*
1937	Van Wyck Brooks	*The Flowering of New England*
1938	Paul Herman Buck	*The Road to Reunion 1856–1900*
1939	Frank Luther Mott	*A History of American Magazines*
1940	Carl Sandburg	*Abraham Lincoln: The War Years*
1941	Marcus Lee Hansen	*The Atlantic Migration, 1607–1860*
1942	Margaret Leech	*Reveille in Washington*
1943	Esther Forbes	*Paul Revere and the World He Lived In*
1944	Merle Curti	*The Growth of American Thought*
1945	Stephen Bonsal	*Unfinished Business*
1946	Arthur Meier Schlesinger, Jr.	*The Age of Jackson*
1947	James Phinney Baxter III	*Scientists against Time*
1948	Bernard DeVoto	*Across the Wide Missouri*
1949	Roy Franklin Nichols	*The Disruption of American Democracy*
1950	Oliver W. Larkin	*Art and Life in America*
1951	R. Carlyle Buley	*The Old Northwest, Pioneer Period 1815–1840*
1952	Oscar Handlin	*The Uprooted*
1953	George Dangerfield	*The Era of Good Feelings*
1954	Bruce Catton	*A Stillness at Appomattox*

Year	Author	Title
1955	Paul Horgan	*Great River: The Rio Grande in North American History*
1956	Richard Hofstadter	*The Age of Reform*
1957	George F. Kennan	*Russia Leaves the War: Soviet American Relations, 1917–1920*
1958	Bray Hammond	*Banks and Politics in America*
1959	Leonard D. White, with Miss Jean Schneider	*The Republican Era: 1869–1901*
1960	Margaret Leech	*In the Days of McKinley*
1961	Herbert Feis	*Between War and Peace: The Potsdam Conference*
1962	Lawrence H. Gipson	*The Triumphant Empire, Thunder Clouds in the West*
1963	Constance McLaughlin Green	*Washington, Village and Capital, 1800–1878*
1964	Sumner Chilton Powell	*Puritan Village: The Formation of a New England Town*
1965	Irwin Unger	*The Greenback Era*
1966	Perry Miller[3]	*Life of the Mind in America*
1967	William H. Goetzmann	*Exploration and Empire: The Explorer and the Scientist in the Winning of the American West*
1968	Bernard Bailyn	*The Ideological Origins of the American Revolution*
1969	Leonard W. Levy	*Origins of the Fifth Amendment*
1970	Dean Acheson	*Present at the Creation: My Years in the State Department*
1971	James MacGregor Burns	*Roosevelt, The Soldier of Freedom*
1972	Carl N. Degler	*Neither Black Nor White*
1973	Michael Kammen	*People of Paradox: An Inquiry Concerning the Origins of American Civilization*
1974	Daniel J. Boorstin	*The Americans: The Democratic Experience*
1975	Dumas Malone	*Jefferson and His Time, Vols. I-V*
1976	Paul Horgan	*Larry of Santa Fe*
1977	David M. Potter (manuscript finished by Don E. Fehrenbacher	*The Impending Crisis[3]*
1978	Alfred D. Chandler, Jr.	*The Visible Hand: The Managerial Revolution in American Business*
1979	Don E. Fehrenbacher	*The Dred Scott Case*
1980	Leon F. Litwack	*Been in the Storm So Long*
1981	Lawrence A. Cremin	*American Education: The National Experience, 1783–1876*
1982	C. Vann Woodward (ed.)	*Mary Chesnut's Civil War*

Year	Author	Title
1983	Rhys L. Isaac	*The Transformation of Virginia, 1740–1790*
1984	No award	
1985	Thomas K. McCraw	*Prophets of Regulation*
1986	Walter A. McDougall	*...the Heavens and the Earth: A Political History of the Space Age*
1987	Bernard Bailyn	*Voyagers to the West: A Passage in the Peopling of America on the Eve of the Revolution*

Year	Author	Title
1988	Robert V. Bruce	*The Launching of Modern American Science 1846–1876*
1989	Taylor Branch	*Parting the Waters: America in the King Years, 1954–63*
	James M. McPherson	*Battle Cry of Freedom: The Civil War Era*

THE PULITZER PRIZE FOR BIOGRAPHY OR AUTOBIOGRAPHY, 1917–89

Year	Author	Title
1917	Laura E. Richards and Maude Howe Elliott, with Florence Howe Hall	*Julia Ward Howe*
1918	William Cabell Bruce	*Benjamin Franklin, Self-Revealed*
1919	Henry Adams	*The Education of Henry Adams*
1920	Albert J. Beveridge	*The Life of John Marshall*
1921	Edward Bok	*The Americanization of Edward Bok*
1922	Hamlin Garland	*A Daughter of the Middle Border*
1923	Burton J. Hendrick	*The Life and Letters of Walter H. Page*
1924	Michael Idvorsky Pupin	*From Immigrant to Inventor*
1925	M.A. DeWolfe Howe	*Barrett Wendell and His Letter*
1926	Harvey Cushing	*The Life of Sir William Osler*
1927	Emory Holloway	*Whitman*
1928	Charles Edward Russell	*The American Orchestra and Theodore Thomas*
1929	Burton J. Hendrick	*The Training of an American. The Earlier Life and Letters of Walter H. Page*
1930	Marquis James	*The Raven*
1931	Henry James	*Charles W. Eliot*
1932	Henry F. Pringle	*Theodore Roosevelt*
1933	Allan Nevins	*Grover Cleveland*
1934	Tyler Dennett	*John Hay*
1935	Douglas S. Freeman	*R.E. Lee*
1936	Ralph Barton Perry	*The Thought and Character of William James*
1937	Allan Nevins	*Hamilton Fish*
1938	Odell Shepard	*Pedlar's Progress*
	Marquis James	*Andrew Jackson*
1939	Carl Van Doren	*Benjamin Franklin*
1940	Ray Stannard Baker	*Woodrow Wilson, Life and Letters, vols. 7 & 8*
1941	Ola Elizabeth Winslow	*Jonathan Edwards*
1942	Forrest Wilson	*Crusader in Crinoline*
1943	Samuel Eliot Morison	*Admiral of the Ocean Sea*
1944	Carleton Mabee	*The American Leonardo: The Life of Samuel F.B. Morse*
1945	Russell Blaine Nye	*George Bancroft: Brahmin Rebel*
1946	Linnie Marsh Wolfe	*Son of the Wilderness*
1947	William Allen White	*The Autobiography of William Allen White*
1948	Margaret Clapp	*Forgotten First Citizen: John Bigelow*
1949	Robert E. Sherwood	*Roosevelt and Hopkins*
1950	Samuel Flagg Bemis	*John Quincy Adams and the Foundations of American Foreign Policy*
1951	Margaret Louise Coit	*John C. Calhoun: American Portrait*
1952	Merlo J. Pusey	*Charles Evan Hughes*
1953	David J. Mays	*Edmund Pendleton 1721–1803*
1954	Charles A. Lindbergh	*The Spirit of St. Louis*

Year	Author	Title
1955	William S. White	*The Taft Story*
1956	Talbot Faulkner Hamlin	*Benjamin Henry Latrobe*
1957	John F. Kennedy	*Profiles in Courage*
1958	Douglas Southall Freeman, John Alexander Carroll, Mary Wells Ashworth	*George Washington, vols. 1–4; and vol. 7, written after Dr. Freeman's death in 1953*
1959	Arthur Walworth	*Woodrow Wilson, American Prophet*
1960	Samuel Eliot Morison	*John Paul Jones*
1961	David Donald	*Charles Sumner and the Coming of the Civil War*
1962	No award	
1963	Leon Edel	*Henry James*
1964	Walter Jackson Bate	*John Keats*
1965	Ernest Samuels	*Henry Adams*
1966	Arthur M. Schlesinger, Jr.	*A Thousand Days: JFK in the White House*
1967	Justin Kaplan	*Mr. Clemens and Mark Twain*
1968	George F. Kennan	*Memoirs*
1969	Benjamin Lawrence Reid	*The Man From New York: John Quinn and His Friends*
1970	T. Harry Williams	*Huey Long*
1971	Lawrance Thompson	*Robert Frost: The Years of Triumph, 1915–1938*
1972	Joseph P. Lash	*Eleanor and Franklin*
1973	W.A. Swanberg	*Luce and His Empire*
1974	Louis Sheaffer	*O'Neill, Son and Artist*
1975	Robert A. Caro	*The Power Broker: Robert Moses and the Fall of New York*
1976	R.W.B. Lewis	*Edith Wharton: A Biography*
1977	John E. Mack	*A Prince of Our Disorder: The Life of T.E. Lawrence*
1978	Walter Jackson Bate	*Samuel Johnson*
1979	Leonard Baker	*Days of Sorrow and Pain: Leo Baeck and the Berlin Jews*
1980	Edmund Morris	*The Rise of Theodore Roosevelt*
1981	Robert K. Massie	*Peter the Great: His Life and World*
1982	William S. McFeely	*Grant: A Biography*
1983	Russell Baker	*Growing Up*
1984	Louis R. Harlan	*Booker T. Washington: The Wizard of Tuskegee, 1901–1915*
1985	Kenneth Silverman	*The Life and Times of Cotton Mather*
1986	Elizabeth Frank	*Louise Bogan: A Portrait*
1987	David J. Garrow	*Bearing the Cross: Martin Luther King, Jr. and the Southern Christian Leadership Conference*
1988	David Herbert Donald	*Look Homeward: A Life of Thomas Wolfe*
1989	Richard Ellmann	*Oscar Wilde*

THE PULITZER PRIZE FOR POETRY, 1922–89

Pulitzer Prizes in poetry were first awarded in 1922. The Poetry Society awarded prizes in 1918 to Sara Teasdale for *Love Songs,* and in 1919 to Margaret Widdemer for *Old Road to Paradise* and to Carl Sandburg for *Corn Huskers.*

Year	Author	Title
1922	Edward Arlington Robinson	*Collected Poems*
1923	Edna St. Vincent Millay	*The Ballad of the Harp–Weaver; A Few Figs from Thistles; Eight Sonnets in American Poetry, 1922, A Miscellany*

Year	Author	Title
1924	Robert Frost	*New Hampshire: A Poem with Notes and Grace Notes*
1925	Edward Arlington Robinson	*The Man Who Died Twice*
1926	Amy Lowell[2]	*What's O'Clock*

Year	Author	Title
1927	Leonora Speyer	*Fiddler's Farewell*
1928	Edward Arlington Robinson	*Tristram*
1929	Stephen Vincent Benét	*John Brown's Body*
1930	Conrad Aiken	*Selected Poems*
1931	Robert Frost	*Collected Poems*
1932	George Dillon	*The Flowering Stone*
1933	Archibald MacLeish	*Conquistador*
1934	Robert Hillyer	*Collected Verse*
1935	Audrey Wurdemann	*Bright Ambush*
1936	Robert P. Tristram Coffin	*Strange Holiness*
1937	Robert Frost	*A Further Range*
1938	Marya Zaturenska	*Cold Morning Sky*
1939	John Gould Fletcher	*Selected Poems*
1940	Mark Van Doren	*Collected Poems*
1941	Leonard Bacon	*Sunderland Capture*
1942	William Rose Benét	*The Dust Which Is God*
1943	Robert Frost	*A Witness Tree*
1944	Stephen Vincent Benét[2]	*Western Star*
1945	Karl Shapiro	*V–Letter and Other Poems*
1946	No award	
1947	Robert Lowell	*Lord Weary's Castle*
1948	W.H. Auden	*The Age of Anxiety*
1949	Peter Viereck	*Terror and Decorum*
1950	Gwendolyn Brooks	*Annie Allen*
1951	Carl Sandburg	*Complete Poems*
1952	Marianne Moore	*Collected Poems*
1953	Archibald MacLeish	*Collected Poems 1917–1952*
1954	Theodore Roethke	*The Waking*
1955	Wallace Stevens	*Collected Poems*
1956	Elizabeth Bishop	*Poems—North & South*
1957	Richard Wilbur	*Things of This World*
1958	Robert Penn Warren	*Promises: Poems 1954–1956*

Year	Author	Title
1959	Stanley Kunitz	*Selected Poems 1928–1958*
1960	W.D. Snodgrass	*Heart's Needle*
1961	Phyllis McGinley	*Times Three: Selected Verse from Three Decades*
1962	Alan Dugan	*Poems*
1963	William Carlos Williams[2]	*Pictures from Breughel*
1964	Louis Simpson	*At the End of the Open Road*
1965	John Berryman	*77 Dream Songs*
1966	Richard Eberhart	*Selected Poems*
1967	Anne Sexton	*Live or Die*
1968	Anthony Hecht	*The Hard Hours*
1969	George Oppen	*Of Being Numerous*
1970	Richard Howard	*Untitled Subjects*
1971	William S. Merwin	*The Carrier of Ladders*
1972	James Wright	*Collected Poems*
1973	Maxine Kumin	*Up Country*
1974	Robert Lowell	*The Dolphins*
1975	Gary Snyder	*Turtle Island*
1976	John Ashbery	*Self-Portrait in a Convex Mirror*
1977	James Merrill	*Divine Comedies*
1978	Howard Nemerov	*Collected Poems*
1979	Robert Penn Warren	*Now and Then*
1980	Donald Justice	*Selected Poems*
1981	James Schuyler	*The Morning of the Poem*
1982	Sylvia Plath	*The Collected Poems*[3]
1983	Galway Kinnell	*Selected Poems*
1984	Mary Oliver	*American Primitive*
1985	Carolyn Kizer	*Yin*
1986	Henry Taylor	*The Flying Change*
1987	Rita Dove	*Thomas and Beulah*
1988	William Meredith	*Partial Accounts: New and Selected Poems*
1989	Richard Wilbur	*New and Collected Poems*

THE PULITZER PRIZE FOR GENERAL NONFICTION, 1962–89

Year	Author	Title
1962	Theodore H. White	*The Making of the President 1960*
1963	Barbara W. Tuchman	*The Guns of August*
1964	Richard Hofstadter	*Anti-Intellectualism in American Life*
1965	Howard Mumford Jones	*O Strange New World*
1966	Edwin Way Teal	*Wandering Through Winter*
1967	David Brion Davis	*The Problem of Slavery in Western Culture*
1968	Will and Ariel Durant	*Rousseau and Revolution*, vol. 10 of the *Story of Civilization*
1969	René Jules Dubos	*So Human An Animal*
	Norman Mailer	*The Armies of the Night*
1970	Erik H. Erikson	*Gandhi's Truth*
1971	John Toland	*The Rising Sun*
1972	Barbara W. Tuchman	*Stilwell and the American Experience in China, 1911–1945*
1973	Robert Coles	*Children of Crisis*, vols. 2 & 3
	Frances Fitzgerald	*Fire in the Lake: The Vietnamese and the Americans in Vietnam*
1974	Ernest Becker[2]	*The Denial of Death*
1975	Annie Dillard	*Pilgrim at Tinker Creek*
1976	Robert N. Butler	*Why Survive? Being Old in America*
1977	William N. Warner	*Beautiful Swimmers*

Year	Author	Title
1978	Carl Sagan	*The Dragons of Eden*
1979	Edward O. Wilson	*On Human Nature*
1980	Douglas R. Hofstadter	*Gödel, Escher, Bach: An Eternal Golden Braid*
1981	Carl E. Schorske	*Fin-de-Siècle Vienna: Politics and Culture*
1982	Tracy Kidder	*The Soul of a New Machine*
1983	Susan Sheehan	*Is There No Place on Earth for Me?*
1984	Paul Starr	*The Social Transformation of American Medicine*
1985	Studs Terkel	*The Good War: An Oral History of World War Two*
1986	Joseph Lelyveld	*Move Your Shadow: South Africa, Black and White*
	J. Anthony Lukas	*Common Ground: A Turbulent Decade in the Lives of Three American Families*
1987	David K. Shipler	*Arab and Jew: Wounded Spirits in a Promised Land*
1988	Richard Rhodes	*The Making of the Atomic Bomb*
1989	Neil Sheehan	*A Bright Shining Lie: John Paul Vann and America in Vietnam*

SPECIAL CITATIONS IN LETTERS, 1944–84

Year	Author	Title
1944	Richard Rodgers and Oscar Hammerstein II	*Oklahoma!*
1957	Kenneth Roberts	For his historical novels
1960	Garret Mattingly	*The Armada*
1961	N.A.	*The American Heritage Picture History of the Civil War*

Year	Author	Title
1973	James Thomas Flexner	*George Washington*, vols. 1–4
1977	Alex Haley	*Roots*
1978	E.B. White	Lifetime achievement
1984	Theodore Seuss Geisel	Lifetime achievement (Dr. Seuss)

Notes: For the origins of the Pulitzer Prizes, see the Pulitzer Prizes for Journalism in the section called "The Media." N.A. = not applicable. 1. In 1948 the name of category was changed to "Fiction." 2. Awarded posthumously. 3. A posthumous publication. **Source:** Columbia University.

THE PULITZER PRIZE FOR MUSIC, 1943–89

Year	Composer	Title	Year	Composer	Title	Year	Composer	Title
1943	William Schuman	Secular Cantata No. 2, *A Free Song*			Orchestra	1977	Richard Wernick	*Visions of Terror and Wonder*
1944	Howard Hanson	Symphony No. 4, Opus 34	1960	Elliott Carter	Second String Quartet	1978	Michael Colgrass	*Déjà Vu* for Percussion Quartet and Orchestra
1945	Aaron Copland	*Appalachian Spring*	1961	Walter Piston	Symphony No. 7			
1946	Leo Sowerby	*The Canticle of the Sun*	1962	Robert Ward	*The Crucible* (opera)	1979	Joseph Schwantner	*Aftertones of Infinity*
1947	Charles Ives	Symphony No. 3	1963	Samuel Barber	Piano Concerto No. 1	1980	David Del Tredici	*In Memory of a Summer Day*
1948	Walter Piston	Symphony No. 3	1964	No award		1981	No award	
1949	Virgil Thomson	Music for the film *Louisiana Story*	1965	No award		1982	Roger Sessions	Concerto for Orchestra
			1966	Leslie Bassett	Variations for Orchestra	1983	Ellen Taaffe Zwilich	Symphony No. 1
1950	Gian Carlo Menotti	Music for *The Consul*	1967	Leon Kirchner	Quartet No. 3	1984	Bernard Rands	"Canti del Sole" for Tenor and Orchestra
1951	Douglas S. Moore	Music for the opera *Giants in the Earth*	1968	George Crumb	*Echoes of Time and the River* (orchestral suite)	1985	Stephen Albert	Symphony *RiverRun*
1952	Gail Kubik	*Symphony Concertante*	1969	Karel Husa	String Quartet No. 3	1986	George Perle	Wind Quintet IV
1953	No award		1970	Charles Wuorinen	*Time's Encomium*	1987	John Harbison	*The Flight into Egypt*
1954	Quincy Porter	Concerto for Two Pianos and Orchestra	1971	Mario Davidovsky	Synchronisms No. 6 for Piano and Electronic Sound	1988	William Bolcom	12 New Etudes for Piano
			1972	Jacob Druckman	*Windows*	1989	Roger Reynolds	*Whispers Out of Time*
1955	Gian Carlo Menotti	*The Saint of Bleecker Street* (opera)	1973	Elliott Carter	String Quartet No. 3	**SPECIAL CITATIONS IN MUSIC**		
1956	Ernest Toch	Symphony No. 3	1974	Donald Martino	*Notturno* (chamber music piece)	1974	Roger Sessions	Lifetime achievement
1957	Norman Dello Joio	*Meditations on Ecclesiastes*				1976	Scott Joplin[1]	Contributions to American music
1958	Samuel Barber	*Vanessa* (opera)	1975	Dominick Argento	From the *Diary of Virginia Woolf*			
1959	John LaMontaine	Concerto for Piano and	1976	Ned Rorem	*Air Music: Ten Etudes for Orchestra*	1982	Milton Babbitt	Lifetime achivement
						1985	William Schuman	Lifetime achivement

1. Awarded posthumously. **Source:** Columbia University.

NOBEL PRIZES FOR LITERATURE

1901 Sully Prudhomme (pen name of René F.A. Prudhomme) (France) "in special recognition of his poetic composition, which gives evidence of lofty idealism, artistic perfection and a rare combination of the qualities of both heart and intellect."

1902 Christian M.T. Mommsen (Germany) "the greatest living master of the art of historical writing, with special reference to his monumental work, *A History of Rome*."

1903 Bjørnstjerne M. Bjørnson (Norway) "as a tribute to his noble, magnificent and versatile poetry, which has always been distinguished by both the freshness of its inspiration and the rare purity of its spirit."

1904 Frederic Mistral (France) "in recognition of the fresh orginality and true inspiration of his poetic production, which faithfully reflects the natural scenery and native spirit of his people, and, in addition, his significant work as a Provencal philologist"; **José Echegaray y Eizaguirre** (Spain) "in recognition of the numerous and brilliant compositions which, in an individual and original manner, have revived the great traditions of the Spanish drama."

1905 Henryk Sienkiewicz (Poland) "because of his outstanding merits as an epic writer."

1906 Giosuè Carducci (Italy) "not only in consideration of his deep learning and critical research, but above all as a tribute to the creative energy, freshness of style, and lyrical force which characterize his poetic masterpieces."

1907 Rudyard Kipling (Great Britain) "in consideration of the power of observation, originality of imagination, virility of ideas and remarkable talent for narration which characterize the creations of this world-famous author."

1908 Rudolf C. Eucken (Germany) "in recognition of his earnest search for truth, his penetrating power of thought, his wide range of vision, and the warmth and strength in presentation with which in his numerous works he has vindicated and developed an idealistic philosophy of life."

1909 Selma O.L. Lagerlöf (Sweden) "in appreciation of the lofty idealism, vivid imagination and spiritual perception that characterize her writings."

1910 Paul J.L. Heyse (Germany) "as a tribute to the consummate artistry, permeated with idealism, which he has demonstrated during his long productive career as lyric poet, dramatist, novelist and writer of world-renowned short stories."

1911 Count Maurice (Mooris) P.M.B. Maeterlinck (Belgium) "in appreciation of his many-sided literary activities, and especially of his dramatic works, which are distinguished by a wealth of imagination and by a poetic fancy."

1912 Gerhart J.R. Hauptmann (Germany) "pri-marily in recognition of his fruitful, varied and outstanding production in the realm of dramatic art."

1913 Rabindranath Tagore (India) "because of his profoundly sensitive, fresh and beautiful verse, by which, with consummate skill, he has made his poetic thought, expressed in his own English words, a part of the literature of the West."

1914 No award.

1915 Romain Rolland (France) "as a tribute to the lofty idealism of his literary production and to the sympathy and love of truth with which he has described different types of human beings."

1916 Carl G.V. von Heidenstam (Sweden) "in recognition of his significance as the leading representative of a new era in our literature."

1917 Karl A. Gjellerup (Denmark) "for his varied and rich poetry, which is inspired by lofty ideals"; **Henrik Pontoppidan** (Denmark) "for his authentic descriptions of presentday life in Denmark."

1918 No award.

1919 Carl F.G. Spitteler (Switzerland) "in special appreciation of his epic, *Olympian Spring*."

1920 Knut P. Hamsun (Norway) "for his monumental work, *Growth of the Soil*."

1921 Anatole France (pen name of Jacques A. Thibault) (France) "in recognition of his brilliant literary achievements, characterized as they are by a nobility of style, a profound human sympathy, grace, and a true Gallic temperament."

1922 Jacinto Benavente (Spain) "for the happy

manner in which he has continued the illustrious traditions of the Spanish drama."

1923 William B. Yeats (Ireland) "for his always inspired poetry, which in a highly artistic form gives expression to the spirit of a whole nation."

1924 Wladyslaw S. Reymont (pen name of Reyment) (Poland) "for his great national epic, *The Peasants*."

1925 George B. Shaw (Great Britain) "for his work which is marked by both idealism and humanity, its stimulating satire often being infused with a singular poetic beauty."

1926 Grazia Deledda (pen name of Grazia Madesani) (Italy) "for her idealistically inspired writings which with plastic clarity picture the life on her native island and with depth and sympathy deal with human problems in general."

1927 Henri Bergson (France) "in recognition of his rich and vitalizing ideas and the brilliant skill with which they have been presented."

1928 Sigrid Undset (Norway) "principally for her powerful descriptions of Northern life during the Middle Ages."

1929 Thomas Mann (Germany) "principally for his great novel *Buddenbrooks*, which has won steadily increased recognition as one of the classic works of contemporary literature."

1930 Sinclair Lewis (U.S.) "for his vigorous and graphic art of description and his ability to create, with wit and humour, new types of characters."

1931 Erik A. Karlfeldt (Sweden) "the poetry of Erik Axel Karlfeldt."

1932 John Galsworthy (Great Britain) "for his distinguished art of narration which takes its highest form in *The Forsyte Saga*."

1933 Ivan A. Bunin (stateless domicile in France) "for the strict artistry with which he has carried on the classical Russian traditions in prose writing."

1934 Luigi Pirandello (Italy) "for his bold and ingenious revival of dramatic and scenic art."

1935 No award.

1936 Eugene G. O'Neill (U.S.) "for the power, honesty and deep-felt emotions of his dramatic works, which embody an original concept of tragedy."

1937 Roger Martin du Gard (France) "for the artistic power and truth with which he has depicted human conflict as well as some fundamental aspects of contemporary life in his novel-cycle *Les Thibault*."

1938 Pearl Buck (pen name of Pearl Walsh) (U.S.) "for her rich and truly epic descriptions of peasant life in China and for her biographical masterpieces."

1939 Frans E. Sillanpää (Finland) "for his deep understanding of his country's peasantry and the exquisite art with which he has portrayed their way of life and their relationship with Nature."

1940 No award.

1941 No award.

1942 No award.

1943 No award.

1944 Johannes V. Jensen (Denmark) "for the rare strength and fertility of his poetic imagination with which is combined an intellectual curiosity of wide scope and bold, freshly creative style."

1945 Gabriela Mistral (pen name of Lucila Godoy y Alcayaga) (Chile) "for her lyric poetry which, inspired by powerful emotions, has made her name a symbol of the idealistic aspirations of the entire Latin American world."

1946 Hermann Hesse (Switzerland) "for his inspired writings which, while growing in boldness and penetration, exemplify the classical humanitarian ideals and high qualities of style."

1947 André P.G. Gide (France) "for his comprehensive and artistically significant writings, in which human problems and conditions have been presented with a fearless love of truth and keen psychological insight."

1948 Thomas S. Eliot (Great Britain) "for his outstanding, pioneer contribution to presentday poetry."

1949 William Faulkner (U.S.) "for his powerful and artistically unique contribution to the modern American novel."

1950 Earl (Bertrand) Russell (Great Britain) "in recognition of his varied and significant writings in which he champions humanitarian ideals and freedom of thought."

1951 Pär F. Lägerkvist (Sweden) "for the artistic vigour and true independence of mind with which he endeavours in his poetry to find answers to the eternal questions confronting mankind."

1952 François Mauriac (France) "for the deep spiritual insight and the artistic intensity with which he has in his novels penetrated the drama of human life."

1953 Sir Winston L.P. Churchill (Great Britain) "for his mastery of historical and biographical description as well as for brilliant oratory in defending exalted human values."

1954 Ernest M. Hemingway (U.S.) "for his mastery of the art of narrative, most recently demonstrated in *The Old Man and the Sea*, and for the influence that he has exerted on contemporary style."

1955 Halldór K. Laxness (Iceland) "for his vivid epic power which has renewed the great narrative art of Iceland."

1956 Juan R. Jiménez (Spain [domicile in Puerto Rico]) "for his lyrical poetry, which in Spanish language constitutes an example of high spirit and artistical purity."

1957 Albert Camus (France) "for his important literary production, which with clear-sighted earnestness illuminates the problems of the human conscience in our times."

1958 Boris L. Pasternak (USSR) "for his important achievement both in contemporary lyrical poetry and in the field of the great Russian epic tradition." (Declined the

prize.)

1959 Salvatore Quasimodo (Italy) "for his lyrical poetry, which with classical fire expresses the tragic experience of life in our own times."

1960 Saint-John Perse (pen name of Alexis Léger) (France) "for the soaring flight and the evocative imagery of his poetry which in a visionary fashion reflects the conditions of our time."

1961 Ivo Andrić (Yugoslavia) "for the epic force with which he has traced themes and depicted human destinies drawn from the history of his country."

1962 John Steinbeck (U.S.) "for his realistic and imaginative writings, combining as they do sympathetic humour and keen social perception."

1963 Giorgos Seferis (pen name of Giorgos Seferiades) (Greece) "for his eminent lyrical writing, inspired by a deep feeling for the Hellenic world of culture."

1964 Jean-Paul Sartre (France) "for his work which, rich in ideas and filled with the spirit of freedom and the quest for truth, has exerted a far-reaching influence on our age." (Declined the prize.)

1965 Michail A. Solochov (USSR) "for the artistic power and integrity with which, in his epic of the Don, he has given expression to a historic phase in the life of the Russian people."

1966 Shmuel Y. Agnon (Israel) "for his profoundly characteristic narrative art with motifs from the life of the Jewish people; **Nelly Sachs** (Germany [domiciled in Sweden]) "for her outstanding lyrical and dramatic writing, which interprets Israel's destiny with touching strength."

1967 Miguel A. Asturias (Guatemala) "for his vivid literary achievement, deep-rooted in the national traits and traditions of Indian peoples of Latin America."

1968 Yasunari Kawabata (Japan) "for his narrative mastery, which with great sensibility expresses the essence of the Japanese mind."

1969 Samuel Beckett (Ireland) "for his writing, which—in new forms for the novel and drama—in the destitution of modern man acquires its elevation."

1970 Alexandr Solzjhenitsyn (USSR) "for the ethical force with which he has pursued the indispensable traditions of Russian literature."

1971 Pablo Neruda (Chile) "for a poetry that with the action of an elemental force brings alive a continent's destiny and dreams."

1972 Heinrich Böll (W. Germany) "for his writing which through its combination of a broad perspective on his time and a sensitive skill in characterization has contributed to a renewal of German literature."

1973 Patrick White (Australia) "for an epic and psychological narrative art which has introduced a new continent into literature."

1974 Eyvind Johnson (Sweden) "for a narrative art, far-seeing in lands and ages, in the service of freedom"; **Harry Martinson** (Sweden) "for writings that catch the dewdrop and reflect the cosmos."

1975 Eugenio Montale (Italy) "for his distinctive poetry which, with great artistic sensitivity, has interpreted human values under the sign of an outlook on life with no illusions."

1976 Saul Bellow (U.S.) "for the human understanding and subtle analysis of contemporary culture that are combined in his work."

1977 Vicente Aleixandre (Spain) "for a creative poetic writing which illuminates man's condition in the cosmos and in present-day society, at the same time representing the great renewal of the traditions of Spanish poetry between the wars."

1978 Isaac B. Singer (U.S.) "for his impassioned narrative art which, with roots in a Polish-Jewish cultural tradition, brings universal human conditions to life."

1979 Odysseus Elytis (pen name of Odysseus Alepoudhelis) (Greece) "for his poetry, which against the background of Greek tradition, depicts with sensuous strength and intellectual clearsightedness modern man's struggle for freedom and creativeness."

1980 Czeslaw Milosz (U.S. and Poland) "who with uncompromising clear-sightedness voices man's exposed condition in a world of severe conflicts."

1981 Elias Canetti (Great Britain) "for writings marked by a broad outlook, a wealth of ideas and artistic power."

1982 Gabriel García Marquez (Colombia) "for his novels and short stories, in which the fantastic and the realistic are combined in a richly composed world of imagination, reflecting a continent's life and conflicts."

1983 William Golding (Great Britain) "for his novels which, with the perspicuity of realistic narrative art and the diversity and universality of myth, illuminate the human condition in the world of today."

1984 Jaroslav Seifert (Czechoslovakia) "for his poetry which endowed with freshness, sensuality and rich inventiveness provides a liberating image of the indomitable spirit and versatility of man."

1985 Claude Simon (France) "who in his novel combines the poet's and the painter's creativeness with a deepened awareness of time in the depiction of the human condition."

1986 Wole Soyinka (Nigeria) "who in a wide cultural perspective and with poetic overtones fashions the drama of existence."

1987 Joseph Brodsky (U.S.) "for his all-embracing authorship imbued with clarity of thought and poetic intensity."

1988 Naguib Mahfouz (Egypt) "who, through works rich in nuance—now clear-sightedly realistic, now evocatively ambiguous—has formed an Arabian narrative art that applies to all mankind."

Sources: *Nobel Foundation Directory 1987–88*; Mission of Sweden.

AMERICAN INSTITUTE OF ARCHITECTS GOLD MEDALISTS

First awarded in 1907, the American Institute of Architects Gold Medal recognizes outstanding lifetime achievement by an architect.

Sir Aston Webb, London, 1907
Charles Follen McKim, New York, 1909
George B. Post, New York, 1911
Jean Louis Pascal, Paris, 1914
Victor Laloux, Paris, 1922
Henry Bacon, New York, 1923
Sir Edwin Landseer Lutyens, London, 1925
Bertram Grosvenor Goodhue, New York, 1925
Howard Van Doren Shaw, Chicago, 1927
Milton Bennett Medary, Philadelphia, 1929
Ragnar Ostberg, Stockholm, 1933
Paul Philippe Cret, Philadelphia, 1938
Louis Henri Sullivan, Chicago, 1944
Eliel Saarinen, Bloomfield Hills, Mich., 1947
Charles Donagh Maginnis, Boston, 1948
Frank Lloyd Wright, Spring Green, Wis., 1949
Sir Patrick Abercrombie, London, 1950
Bernard Ralph Maybeck, San Francisco, 1951
Auguste Perret, Paris, 1952
Williams Adams Delano, New York, 1953
Willem Marinus Dudock, Holland, 1955
Clarence S. Stein, New York, 1956
Ralph Walker, New York, 1957
Louis Skidmore, New York, 1957
John Wellborn Root, Chicago, 1958
Walter Gropius, Cambridge, Mass., 1959
Ludwig Mies van der Rohe, Chicago, 1960
Le Corbusier (Charles Edouard Jeanneret-Gris), Paris, 1961
Eero Saarinen, Bloomfield Hills, Mich., 1962[1]
Alvar Aalto, Helsinki, 1963
Pier Luigi Nervi, Rome, 1964
Kenzo Tange, Tokyo, 1966
Wallace K. Harrison, New York, 1967
Marcel Breuer, New York, 1968
William Wilson Wurster, San Francisco, 1969
Richard Buckminster Fuller, Carbondale, Ill., 1970
Louis I. Kahn, Philadelphia, 1971
Pietro Belluschi, Boston, 1972
Richard Joseph Neutra, Los Angeles, 1977[1]
Philip Johnson, New York, 1978
Ieoh Ming Pei, New York, 1979
Josep Lluis Sert, Cambridge, Mass., 1981
Romaldo Giurgola, New York, 1982
Nathaniel A. Owings, San Francisco, 1983
William Caudill, Houston, 1985[1]
Arthur Erickson, Canada, 1986
Joseph Esherick, San Francisco, 1989

1. Awarded posthumously. **Source:** American Institute of Architects.

THE MEDIA

NEWSPAPERS
U.S. Newspaper History

The mutual distrust between government and the media dates back to the very first American newspaper in 1690, when a three-page publication called *Publick Occurrences, Both Foreign and Domestick* was suppressed by the government after one issue. A number of newspapers sprang up during the pre-Revolutionary War period, and by 1775 the colonies, with a population of 2.5 million people, were served by 48 weekly newspapers, small in both size and circulation. The first daily, the *Pennsylvania Evening Post and Daily Advertiser*, was

MEDIA: A HALF-TRILLION-DOLLAR BUSINESS

As of Aug. 19, 1988, the media business had a private market value of approximately $480 billion, divided between sectors as follows:

Media segment	Private-market $ value (in billions)	% of all media
PUBLISHING		
Newspaper publishers	$175.5	
Magazine publishers	42.6	
Book publishers	31.1	
TOTAL Publishing	**$249.2**	**52%**
BROADCASTING		
TV stations	$79.6	
Radio stations	23.3	
Broadcast networks	9.5	
Radio networks	0.7	
TOTAL Broadcasting	**$113.1**	**24%**
CABLE		
Cable operators	$81.3	
Basic cable networks	1.4	
Video retailing networks	2.7	
Pay TV networks	2.3	
SMATV/MMDS/STV[1]	0.5	
TOTAL Cable	**$88.2**	**18%**
MOVIES/VIDEO		
Movie studios	$20.4	
Movie theaters	5.5	
Videocassette stores	4.0	
TOTAL Movie/video	**$29.9**	**6%**

1. Satellite Master Antenna TV is a satellite-fed cable system serving housing complexes or hotels; a Multichannel Multipoint Distribution Service delivers several TV channels via microwave; Subscription TV is broadcast as a "scrambled" system receivable only by viewers with special decoders.
Source: Paul Kagan Associates, Inc.

not published until 1783. By 1800 there were 20 daily newspapers and more than 1,000 small-town and frontier weeklies. Most of the dailies, filled with political and business news, were expensive and aimed at educated, affluent readers. The first of the mass-circulation dailies, known as the penny press, was the *New York Sun*, started in 1833 and sold for the bargain price of one cent. The *Sun*, with its crime stories and soft features, marked a dramatic change in newspaper coverage.

The next major change in newspapers came in the era during and after the Civil War. Dramatic technological improvements such as the transatlantic cable, the telephone, the electric light bulb, typewriters, web-fed presses, and the typesetting machine made possible cheap, mass-circulation newspapers. By 1900 the number of daily newspapers had jumped to 2,326. Over the next half-century, the number of newspapers steadily declined while readership increased owing in part to the popularity of Sunday editions.

Newspapers Today

In 1987, 1,645 daily newspapers were published in the United States—about 1,100 afternoon publications and 500 morning papers. The number of newspapers has been slowly declining for decades, in part because of radio and television, but also because, in the fight for readers and advertising, competing papers have battled until a single winner emerged. Only about 30 cities have competing newspapers today, a major change from the turn of the century when most major cities had more than two newspapers.

Between 1982 and 1987, total daily circulation actually increased slightly, to 62,826,273. The average paper sells 50,000 copies a day, and fewer than 100 have a daily circulation of more than 100,000. However, the 20 largest newspaper chains account for almost half the total daily circulation, reflecting a trend that started in the 1970s.

NEWSPAPERS—NUMBER AND CIRCULATION, 1900–87

	TOTAL		MORNING		EVENING		SUNDAY	
Year	No. of papers	Daily circulation (thousands)	No. of papers	Daily circulation (thousands)	No. of papers	Daily circulation (thousands)	No. of papers	Daily circulation (thousands)
1900	2,226	15,102	—	—	—	—	—	—
1915	2,580	28,777	—	—	—	—	571	16,480
1920	2,042	27,791	437	—	1,605	—	522	17,084
1925	2,008	33,739	427	—	1,581	—	548	23,355
1930	1,942	39,589	388	—	1,554	—	521	26,413
1935	1,950	38,156	390	—	1,560	—	518	28,147
1940	1,878	41,132	380	16,114	1,498	25,018	525	32,371
1945	1,749	48,384	330	19,240	1,419	29,144	485	39,680
1950	1,772	53,829	322	21,266	1,450	32,563	549	46,582
1955	1,760	56,147	316	22,183	1,454	33,964	541	46,448
1960	1,763	58,882	312	24,029	1,459	34,853	563	47,699
1965	1,751	60,358	320	24,107	1,444	36,251	562	48,600
1970	1,748	62,108	334	25,934	1,429	36,174	586	49,217
1975	1,756	60,655	339	25,490	1,436	36,165	639	51,096
1980	1,745	62,202	387	29,414	1,388	32,787	735	54,672
1985	1,676	62,766	482	36,362	1,220	26,405	798	58,826
1987	1,645	62,826	512	39,127	1,165	23,698	820	60,112

Sources: Editor and publisher, American Newspaper Publishers Assn.; *Historical Statistics of the U.S.*

50 LARGEST DAILY AND SUNDAY NEWSPAPERS, 1988

1988 rank (daily)	Newspaper	Average daily paid circulation	Average Sunday paid circulation
1.	Wall Street Journal	1,869,950	N.A.
2.	USA Today	1,338,734	N.A.
3.	New York News	1,281,706	1,568,862
4.	Los Angeles Times	1,116,334	1,394,910
5.	New York Times	1,038,829	1,601,085
6.	Washington Post	769,318	1,112,349
7.	Chicago Tribune	715,618	1,098,127
8.	Newsday	680,926	706,440
9.	Detroit News	677,385	828,166
10.	Detroit Free Press	629,065	710,112
11.	Chicago Sun-Times	579,272	600,257
12.	San Francisco Chronicle	559,312	712,400[1]
13.	New York Post	550,473	N.A.
14.	Boston Globe	509,060	786,829
15.	Philadelphia Inquirer	502,756	995,571
16.	Newark Star-Ledger	462,084	665,085
17.	Cleveland Plain Dealer	444,884	565,673
18.	Miami Herald	401,423	499,515
19.	Minneapolis Star & Tribune	400,914	644,946
20.	Houston Chronicle	400,320	561,664
21.	St. Louis Post-Dispatch	372,387	546,300
22.	Boston Herald	360,459	252,128
23.	Denver Rocky Mountain News	344,550	389,212
24.	Orange County Register	333,560	380,706
25.	Houston Post	318,218	359,046
26.	Portland Oregonian	317,711	409,562
27.	Phoenix Republic	314,829	507,081
28.	Buffalo News	311,384	378,458
29.	St. Petersburg Times	310,495	396,469
30.	Kansas City Times	281,886	N.A.
31.	New Orleans Times-Picayune	281,685	340,885
32.	Atlanta Constitution	275,183	650,542
33.	San Jose Mercury News	271,787	319,625
34.	Milwaukee Journal	269,155	509,795
35.	San Diego Union	261,558	421,943
36.	Columbus Dispatch	253,884	376,507
37.	Orlando Sentinel	253,740	349,250
38.	Sacramento Bee	243,838	297,095
39.	Tampa Tribune	242,805	330,382
40.	Seattle Times	237,245	502,940
41.	Los Angeles Herald Examiner	235,252	185,684
42.	Philadelphia News	235,177	151,445
43.	Louisville Courier-Journal	234,290	321,072
44.	Baltimore Sun (morning)	231,902	475,990
45.	Indianapolis Star	231,726	405,842
46.	Charlotte Observer	231,445	288,331
47.	Denver Post	231,020	409,257
48.	Pittsburgh Press	227,040	548,785
49.	Hartford Courant	223,448	303,272
50.	Memphis Commercial Appeal	215,245	289,127

Notes: For six months ending Sept. 30, 1988. N.A. indicates there is no Sunday edition. 1. Published in combination with the *San Francisco Examiner.* **Source:** American Newspaper Publishers Assn., 1989.

PULITZER PRIZES FOR JOURNALISM

MERITORIOUS PUBLIC SERVICE

Year	Winner	Distinction
1917	No award	
1918	New York Times	Reports, documents, and speeches relating to World War I.
1919	Milwaukee Journal	Campaign for Americanism.
1920	No award	
1921	Boston Post	Articles exposing operations and leading to arrest of Charles Ponzi.
1922	New York World	Articles exposing operations of Ku Klux Klan.
1923	Memphis Commercial Appeal	News and cartoons about Ku Klux Klan.
1924	New York World	Exposure of Florida peonage evil.
1925	No award	
1926	Columbus (Ga.) Enquirer Sun	Articles decrying Ku Klux Klan, dishonest public officials, lynching, and a law barring teaching of evolution.
1927	Canton (Ohio) Daily News	Articles about collusion between city government and organized crime, resulting in assassination of editor, Don R. Mellett.
1928	Indianapolis Times	Exposure of political corruption in Indiana.
1929	New York Evening World	Campaign to correct evil and corruption in administration of justice.
1930	No award	
1931	Atlanta Constitution	Municipal graft exposure leading to convictions.
1932	Indianapolis News	Campaign to eliminate waste in city management and reduce tax levy.
1933	New York World-Telegram	Series of articles on veterans' relief, real estate bond evil, campaign urging New York City voters to "write in" name of Joseph V. McKee, and articles exposing lottery schemes of various fraternal organizations.
1934	Medford (Ore.) Mail Tribune	Campaign against unscrupulous politicians in Jackson County, Ore.
1935	Sacramento (Calif.) Bee	Campaign against political machine influence in appointment of two federal judges in Nevada.
1936	Cedar Rapids (Iowa) Gazette	Crusade against corruption and misgovernment in state of Iowa.
1937	St. Louis Post-Dispatch	Exposure of registration fraud in St. Louis resulting in invalidation of more than 40,000 fraudulent ballots and appointment of new election board.
1938	Bismarck (N.D.) Tribune	News reports and editorials entitled "Self Help in the Dust Bowl."
1939	Miami Daily News	Campaign for recall of Miami City Commission.
1940	Waterbury (Conn.) Republican & American	Campaign exposing municipal graft.
1941	St. Louis Post-Dispatch	Campaign against city smoke nuisance.
1942	Los Angeles Times	Campaign resulting in clarification and confirmation of freedom of press rights for all American newspapers.
1943	Omaha (Neb.) World-Herald	Campaign for collection of scrap metal for war effort. Plan was adopted on national scale by daily newspapers.

Year	Winner	Distinction
1944	New York Times	Survey of teaching of American History.
1945	Detroit Free Press	Investigation of legislative graft and corruption at Lansing, Mich.
1946	Scranton (Pa.) Times	Fifteen-year investigation of judicial practices in U.S. District Court for middle district of Pennsylvania, resulting in removal of district judge and indictment of many others.
1947	Baltimore Sun	Series of articles by Howard M. Norton dealing with administration of unemployment compensation in Maryland, resulting in 93 criminal convictions and/or guilty pleas.
1948	St. Louis Post-Dispatch	Coverage of Centralia, Ill., mine disaster and follow-up articles resulting in reforms in mine safety laws and regulations.
1949	Nebraska State Journal	Campaign establishing "Nebraska All-Star Primary" that called attention to issues early in presidential campaign.
1950	Chicago Daily News and St. Louis Post-Dispatch	Work of George Thiem and Roy J. Harris, respectively, in exposing presence of 37 Illinois newspapermen on an Illinois state payroll.
1951	Miami Herald and Brooklyn Eagle	Crime reporting during year.
1952	St. Louis Post-Dispatch	Investigation and disclosures of corruption in Internal Revenue Bureau and other government departments.
1953	Whiteville (N.C.) News Reporter and Tabor City (N.C.) Tribune	Campaign against Ku Klux Klan by two weekly North Carolina newspapers.
1954	Newsday (Garden City, L.I., N.Y.)	Exposé of New York State's race track scandals and labor racketeering, leading to extortion indictment, guilty plea, and imprisonment of racketeer William C. DeKoonig, Sr.
1955	Columbus (Ga.) Ledger and Sunday Ledger-Enquirer	News coverage and editorial attack on corruption in neighboring Phenix City, leading to destruction of racket-ridden city government.
1956	Watsonville (Calif.) Register-Pajaronion	Exposure of corruption in public office leading to resignation of a district attorney and conviction of one of his associates.
1957	Chicago Daily News	Exposure of $2.5 million in office of Illinois state auditor, resulting in his indictment and reorganization of state procedures.
1958	Arkansas Gazette	Civic leadership, journalistic responsibility, and moral courage during school integration crisis of 1957.
1959	Utica (N.Y.) Observer-Dispatch and Utica Daily Press	Campaign against corruption, gambling, and vice and achievement of sweeping civic reforms.
1960	Los Angeles Times	Attack on narcotics traffic; reporting of Gene Sherman, which led to opening of negotiations between U.S. and Mexico to halt flow of illegal drugs into California and other border states.

Year	Winner	Distinction
1961	Amarillo (Tex.) Globe-Times	Exposure of lax law enforcement resulting in punitive action sweeping officials from their posts and creating election of reform slate.
1962	Panama City (Fla.) News-Herald	Three-year campaign against entrenched power and corruption, resulting in reforms in Panama City and Bay County.
1963	Chicago Daily News	Articles calling public attention to providing birth control services in public health programs.
1964	St. Petersburg (Fla.) Times	Investigation of illegal activity within Florida Turnpike Authority, resulting in major reorganization of state's road construction program.
1965	Hutchinson (Kans.) News	Campaign for more equitable reapportionment of Kansas legislature.
1966	Boston Globe	Campaign to prevent confirmation of Francis X. Morrissey as federal district judge in Massachusetts.
1967	Louisville Courier Journal and Milwaukee Journal	Campaign to control Kentucky strip-mining industry; campaign to stiffen water pollution laws in Wisconsin.
1968	Riverside (Calif.) Press-Enterprise	Exposure of corruption in courts in connection with handling of property and estates of an Indian tribe in California.
1969	Los Angeles Times	Exposure of wrongdoing within Los Angeles city government commissions, resulting in criminal convictions, resignations, and sweeping reforms.
1970	Newsday (Garden City, L.I., N.Y.)	Three-year investigation and exposure of secret land deals in eastern Long Island, leading to criminal convictions, resignations, and discharges among public and political officials.
1971	Winston-Salem (N.C.) Journal and Sentinel	Coverage of environmental problems, as exemplified by campaign to block a strip-mining operation that would have caused irreparable damage to northwest North Carolina hill country.
1972	New York Times	Publication of Pentagon Papers.
1973	Washington Post	Investigation of Watergate case.
1974	Newsday (Garden City, L.I., N.Y.)	Definitive report on illicit narcotics traffic in U.S. and abroad, entitled "The Heroin Trail."
1975	Boston Globe	Coverage of Boston school desegregation crisis.
1976	Anchorage Daily News	Disclosures of impact and influence of Teamsters Union on Alaska's economy and politics.
1977	Lufkin (Tex.) News	Obituary of local man who died in Marine training camp, which grew into investigation of that death and fundamental reform in Marine Corps' recruiting and training practices.
1978	Philadelphia Inquirer	Series of articles showing abuses of power by Philadelphia police.
1979	Point Reyes Light (Calif.)	Investigation of Synanon.
1980	Gannett News Service	Series on financial contributions to Pauline Fathers.
1981	Charlotte (N.C.) Observer	Series called "Brown Lung: A Case of Deadly Neglect."
1982	Detroit News	Series by Sydney P. Freedberg and David Ashenfelter exposing U.S. Navy's cover-up of circumstances

Year	Winner	Distinction
		surrounding deaths of seamen aboard ship and leading to significant reforms in naval procedures.
1983	Jackson (Miss.) Clarion-Ledger	Campaign supporting Gov. Winter in his legislative battle for reform of Mississippi's public education system.
1984	Los Angeles Times	In-depth examination of southern California's growing Ladino community.
1985	Fort Worth (Tex.) Star-Telegram	Reporting by Mark J. Thompson revealing that nearly 250 U.S. servicemen died because of a design problem in helicopters built by Bell Helicopter—causing the army to ground almost 600 Huey helicopters pending their modification.
1986	Denver Post	In-depth study of "missing children," revealing that most are involved in custody disputes or are runaways, and helping to mitigate national fears stirred by exaggerated statistics.
1987	Pittsburgh Press	Reporting by Andrew Schneider and Matthew Brelis, revealing inadequacy of FAA's medical screening of airline pilots, and leading to reform.
1988	Charlotte (N.C.) Observer	Revealing misuse of funds by the PTL television ministry, despite massive campaign by PTL to discredit the newspaper.
1989	Anchorage Daily News	For series revealing high incidence of alcoholism and suicide among Native Alaskans.

REPORTING

The Reporting category originally embraced all fields—local, national, and international. From 1929 through 1947, prizes were given for a category of reporting called Correspondence, which recognized Washington and foreign correspondence. In 1942 two new categories were added: Telegraphic Reporting (National) and Telegraphic Reporting (International). In 1948 the three newest categories were merged into two: National Reporting and International Reporting. In 1953 the original Reporting category was divided into Reporting on deadline and Reporting not on deadline. The names of these two categories were changed in 1964 to Local General or Spot News Reporting and Local Investigative or Specialized Reporting, respectively. In 1984 these names were changed to General Local Reporting and Special Local Reporting, respectively. In 1985 General Local Reporting was changed to General News Reporting; Special Local Reporting was subdivided into three categories: Investigative Reporting, Explanatory Journalism, and Specialized Reporting.

Year	Winner	Newspaper
1917	Herbert Bayard Swope	New York World
1918	Harold A. Littledale	New York Evening Post
1919	No award	
1920	John J. Leary, Jr.	New York World
1921	Louis Seibold	New York World
1922	Kirke L. Simpson	Associated Press
1923	Alva Johnston	New York Times
1924	Magner White	San Diego Sun
1925	James W. Mulroy Alvin H. Goldstein	Chicago Daily News
1926	William Burke Miller	Louisville Courier-Journal
1927	John T. Rogers	St. Louis Post-Dispatch

Year	Winner	Newspaper
1928	No award	
1929	Paul Y. Anderson	St. Louis Post-Dispatch
1930	Russell D. Owen	New York Times
1931	A.B. MacDonald	Kansas City Star
1932	W.C. Richards, D.D. Martin, J.S. Pooler, F.D. Webb, J.N.W. Sloan	Detroit Free Press
1933	Francis A. Jameson	Associated Press
1934	Royce Brier	San Francisco Chronicle
1935	William H. Taylor	New York Herald Tribune
1936	Lauren D. Lyman	New York Times
1937	John J. O'Neill	New York Herald Tribune
	William L. Laurence	New York Times
	Howard W. Blakeslee	Associated Press
	Gobind Behari Lal	Universal Service
	David Dietz	Scripps-Howard Newspaper Alliance
1938	Raymond Sprigle	Pittsburgh Post-Gazette
1939	Thomas Lunsford Stokes	Scripps-Howard Newspaper Alliance (articles published in New York World-Telegram)
1940	S. Burton Heath	New York World-Telegram
1941	Westbrook Pegler	New York World-Telegram
1942	Stanton Delaplane	San Francisco Chronicle
1943	George Weller	Chicago Daily News
1944	Paul Schoenstein and Associates	New York Journal American
1945	Jack S. McDowell	San Francisco Call-Bulletin
1946	William Leonard Laurence	New York Times
1947	Frederick Woltman	New York World-Telegram
1948	George E. Goodwin	Atlanta Journal
1949	Malcolm Johnson	New York Sun
1950	Meyer Berger	New York Times
1951	Edward S. Montgomery	San Francisco Examiner
1952	George de Carvalho	San Francisco Chronicle

REPORTING, EDITION TIME

Year	Winner	Newspaper
1953	Editorial Staff	Providence Journal and Evening Bulletin
1954	Staff	Vicksburg (Miss.) Sunday Post-Herald
1955	Caro Brown	Alice (Tex.) Daily Echo
1956	Lee Hills	Detroit Free Press
1957	Staff	Salt Lake (Utah) Tribune
1958	Staff	Fargo (N.D.) Forum
1959	Mary Lou Werner	Evening Star, Washington, D.C.
1960	Jack Nelson	Atlanta Constitution
1961	Sanche de Gramont	New York Herald-Tribune
1962	Robert D. Mullins	Deseret News, Salt Lake City
1963	Sylvan Fox, Anthony Shannon and William Longgood	New York World-Telegram and Sun

LOCAL GENERAL/SPOT NEWS REPORTING

Year	Winner	Newspaper
1964	Norman C. Miller, Jr.	Wall Street Journal
1965	Melvin H. Ruder	Hungry Horse News, Columbia Falls, Mont.
1966	Staff	Los Angeles Times
1967	Robert V. Cox	Chambersburg (Pa.) Public Opinion
1968	Staff	Detroit Free Press
1969	John Fetterman	Louisville Times and Courier-Journal
1970	Thomas Fitzpatrick	Chicago Sun-Times
1971	Staff	Akron (Ohio) Beacon Journal
1972	Richard Cooper and John Machacek	Rochester (N.Y.) Times-Union
1973	Staff	Chicago Tribune
1974	Arthur M. Petacque and Hugh F. Hough	Chicago Sun-Times
1975	Staff	Xenia (Ohio) Daily Gazette
1976	Gene Miller	Miami Herald
1977	Margo Huston	Milwaukee Journal

Year	Winner	Newspaper
1978	Richard Whitt	Louisville Courier-Journal
1979	Staff	San Diego Evening Tribune
1980	Staff	Philadelphia Inquirer
1981	Staff	Longview (Wash.) Daily News
1982	Staffs	Kansas City Star and Kansas City Times
1983	Editorial staff	Fort Wayne (Ind.) News-Sentinel

GENERAL LOCAL REPORTING

Year	Winner	Newspaper
1984	Team of reporters	Newsday (Garden City, L.I., N.Y.)

GENERAL NEWS REPORTING

Year	Winner	Newspaper
1985	Thomas Turcol	Virginian-Pilot and Ledger-Star
1986	Edna Buchanan	Miami Herald
1987	Staff	Akron (Ohio) Beacon Journal
1988	Staff	Alabama Journal
	Staff	Lawrence (Mass.) Eagle-Tribune
1989	Staff	Louisville (Ky.) Courier-Journal

Year	Winner	Newspaper

REPORTING, NO EDITION TIME

Year	Winner	Newspaper
1953	Edward J. Mowery	New York World-Telegram & Sun
1954	Alvin Scott McCoy	Kansas City Star
1955	Roland Kenneth Towery	Cuero (Tex.) Record
1956	Arthur Daley	New York Times
1957	Wallace Turner and William Lambert	Portland Oregonian
1958	George Beveridge	Evening Star, Washington, D.C.
1959	John Harold Brialin	Scranton (Pa.) Tribune and Scrantonian
1960	Miriam Ottenberg	Evening Star, Washington, D.C.
1961	Edgar May	Buffalo (N.Y.) Evening News
1962	George Bliss	Chicago Tribune
1963	Oscar Griffin, Jr.	Pecos (Tex.) Independent and Enterprise

LOCAL INVESTIGATIVE/SPECIALIZED REPORTING

Year	Winner	Newspaper
1964	James V. Magee, Albert V. Gaudiosi, Frederick A. Meyer	Philadelphia Bulletin
1965	Gene Goltz	Houston Post
1966	John Anthony Frasca	Tampa Tribune
1967	Gene Miller	Miami Herald
1968	J. Anthony Lukas	New York Times
1969	Albert L. Delugach and Denny Walsh	St. Louis Globe-Democrat
1970	Harold Eugene Martin	Montgomery Adviser and Alabama Journal
1971	William Jones	Chicago Tribune
1972	Timothy Leland, Gerard M. O'Neill, Stephen A. Kurkjian, Ann DeSantis	Boston Globe
1973	Staffs	Sun Newspapers of Omaha
1974	William Sherman	New York Daily News
1975	Staff	Indianapolis Star
1976	Staff	Chicago Tribune
1977	Acel Moore and Wendell Rawls, Jr.	Philadelphia Inquirer
1978	Anthony R. Dolan	Stamford (Conn.) Advocate
1979	Gilbert M. Gaul and Elliot G. Jaspin	Pottsville (Pa.) Republican
1980	Stephen A. Kurkjian, Nils Bruzelius, Alexander B. Hawes, Jr., Joan Vennochi, Robert M. Porterfield	Boston Globe Spotlight
1981	Clark Hallas and Robert B. Lowe	Arizona Daily Star
1982	Paul Henderson	Seattle Times
1983	Loretta Tofani	Washington Post

Year	Winner	Newspaper

SPECIAL LOCAL REPORTING

1984	Kenneth Cooper, Jonathan Kaufman, Joan Fitzgerald, Norman Lockman, Gary McMillan, Kirk Scharfenberg, David Wessel	Boston Globe

INVESTIGATIVE REPORTING

1985	William K. Marimow	Philadelphia Inquirer
	Lucy Morgan and Jack Reed	St. Petersburg Times
1986	Jeffrey A. Marx and Michael M. York	Lexington (Ky.) Herald Leader
1987	Daniel R. Biddle, H.G. Bissinger, Fredric N. Tulsky, John Woestendiek	Philadelphia Inquirer
1988	Dean Baquet, William Gaines, Ann Marie Lipinski	Chicago Tribune
1989	Bill Dedman	Atlanta Journal and Constitution

EXPLANATORY JOURNALISM

1985	Jon Franklin	Baltimore Evening Sun
1986	Staff	New York Times
1987	Jeff Lyon and Peter Gorner	Chicago Tribune
1988	Daniel Hertzberg and James B. Stewart	Wall Street Journal
1989	David Hanners, William Snyder, and Karen Blessen	Dallas Morning News

SPECIALIZED REPORTING

1985	Randall Savage and Jackie Crosby	Macon (Ga.) Telegraph News
1986	Andrew Schneider and Mary Pat Flaherty	Pittsburgh Press
1987	Alex S. Jones	New York Times
1988	Walt Bogdanich	Wall Street Journal
1989	Edward Humes	Orange County (Calif.) Register

CORRESPONDENCE

Year	Winner	Newspaper
1929	Paul Scott Mowrer	Chicago Daily News
1930	Leland Stowe	New York Herald Tribune
1931	H.R. Knickerbocker	Philadelphia Public Ledger and New York Evening Post
1932	Walter Duranty	New York Times
	Charles G. Ross	St. Louis Post-Dispatch
1933	Edgar Ansel Mowrer	Chicago Daily News
1934	Frederick T. Birchall	New York Times
1935	Arthur Krock	New York Times
1936	Wilfred C. Barber (posthumous)	Chicago Tribune
1937	Anne O'Hare McCormick	New York Times
1938	Arthur Krock	New York Times
1939	Louis P. Lochner	Associated Press
1940	Otto D. Tolischus	New York Times
1941	GROUP AWARD[1]	
1942	Carlos P. Romulo	Philippines Herald
1943	Hanson W. Baldwin	New York Times
1944	Ernest Taylor Pyle	Scripps-Howard Newspaper Alliance
1945	Harold V. (Hal) Boyle	Associated Press
1946	Arnaldo Cortesi	New York Times
1947	Brooks Atkinson	New York Times

TELEGRAPHIC REPORTING (NATIONAL)

1942	Louis Stark	New York Times
1943	No award	
1944	Dewey L. Fleming	Baltimore Sun
1945	James B. Reston	New York Times
1946	Edward A. Harris	St. Louis Post-Dispatch
1947	Edward T. Folliard	Washington Post

Year	Winner	Newspaper

NATIONAL REPORTING

1948	Bert Andrews	New York Herald Tribune
	Nat S. Finney	Minneapolis Tribune
1949	C.P. Trussell	New York Times
1950	Edwin O. Guthman	Seattle Times
1951	No award[2]	
1952	Anthony Leviero	New York Times
1953	Don Whitehead	Associated Press
1954	Richard Wilson	Des Moines Register and Tribune
1955	Anthony Lewis	Washington Daily News
1956	Charles L. Bartlett	Chattanooga Times
1957	James B. Reston	New York Times
1958	Relman Morin	Associated Press
	Clark Mollenhoff	Des Moines Register and Tribune
1959	Howard Van Smith	Miami News
1960	Vance Trimble	Scripps-Howard Newspaper Alliance
1961	Edward R. Cony	Wall Street Journal
1962	Nathan G. Caldwell and Gene S. Graham	Nashville Tennessean
1963	Anthony Lewis	New York Times
1964	Merriman Smith	United Press International
1965	Louis M. Kohlmeier	Wall Street Journal
1966	Haynes Johnson	Washington Evening Star
1967	Stanley Penn and Monroe Karmin	Wall Street Journal
1968	Howard James	Christian Science Monitor
	Nathan K. (Nick) Kotz	Des Moines Register and Minneapolis Tribune
1969	Robert Cahn	Christian Science Monitor
1970	William J. Eaton	Chicago Daily News
1971	Lucinda Franks and Thomas Powers	United Press International
1972	Jack Anderson	(Syndicated columnist)
1973	Robert Boyd and Clark Hoyt	Knight Newspapers
1974	James R. Polk	Washington Star-News
	Jack White	Providence Journal and Evening Bulletin
1975	Donald L. Barlett and James B. Steele	Philadelphia Inquirer
1976	James Risser	Des Moines Register
1977	Walter Mears	Associated Press
1978	Gaylord D. Shaw	Los Angeles Times
1979	James Risser	Des Moines Register
1980	Bette Swenson Orsini and Charles Stafford	St. Petersburg Times
1981	John M. Crewdson	New York Times
1982	Rick Atkinson	Kansas City Times
1983	Staff	Boston Globe
1984	John Noble Wilford	New York Times
1985	Thomas J. Knudson	Des Moines Register
1986	Arthur Howe	Philadelphia Inquirer
	Craig Flournoy and George Rodrigue	Dallas Morning News
1987	Staff	Miami Herald
	Staff	New York Times
1988	Tim Weiner	Philadelphia Inquirer
1989	Donald L. Barlett and James B. Steele	Philadelphia Inquirer

TELEGRAPHIC REPORTING (INTERNATIONAL)

1942	Lawrence Edmund Allen	Associated Press
1943	Ira Wolfert	North American Newspaper Alliance, Inc.
1944	Daniel DeLuce	Associated Press
1945	Mark S. Watson	Baltimore Sun
1946	Homer William Bigart	New York Herald Tribune
1947	Eddy Gilmore	Associated Press

INTERNATIONAL REPORTING

Year	Winner	Newspaper
1948	Paul W. Ward	Baltimore Sun
1949	Price Day	Baltimore Sun
1950	Edmund Stevens	Christian Science Monitor
1951	Keyes Beech	Chicago Daily News
	Homer William Bigart	New York Herald Tribune
	Marguerite Higgins	New York Herald Tribune
	Relman Morin	Associated Press
	Fred Sparks	Chicago Daily News
	Don Whitehead	Associated Press
1952	John M. Hightower	Associated Press
1953	Austin Wehrwein	Milwaukee Journal
1954	Jim G. Lucas	Scripps-Howard Newspaper Alliance
1955	Harrison E. Salisbury	New York Times
1956	William Randolph Hearst, Jr., Kingsbury Smith, Frank Conniff	International News Service
1957	Russell Jones	United Press
1958	Staff	New York Times
1959	Joseph Martin and Philip Santora	New York Daily News
1960	A.M. Rosenthal	New York Times
1961	Lynn Heinzerling	Associated Press
1962	Walter Lippmann	New York Herald Tribune Syndicate
1963	Hal Hendrix	Miami News
1964	Malcolm W. Browne	Associated Press
	David Halberstam	New York Times
1965	J.A. Livingston	Philadelphia Bulletin
1966	Peter Arnett	Associated Press
1967	R. John Hughes	Christian Science Monitor
1968	Alfred Friendly	Washington Post
1969	William Tuohy	Los Angeles Times
1970	Seymour M. Hersh	Dispatch News Service
1971	Jimmie Lee Hoagland	Washington Post
1972	Peter R. Kann	Wall Street Journal
1973	Max Frankel	New York Times
1974	Hedrick Smith	New York Times
1975	William Mullen (reporter)	Chicago Tribune
	Ovie Carter (photographer)	
1976	Sydney H. Schanberg	New York Times
1977	No award	
1978	Henry Kamm	New York Times
1979	Richard Ben Cramer	Philadelphia Inquirer
1980	Joel Brinkely (reporter)	Louisville Courier-Journal
	Jay Mather (photographer)	
1981	Shirley Christian	Miami Herald
1982	John Darnton	New York Times
1983	Thomas L. Friedman	New York Times
	Loren Jenkins	Washington Post
1984	Karen Elliott House	Wall Street Journal
1985	Josh Friedman and Dennis Bell (reporters) and Ozier Muhammad (photographer)	Newsday (Garden City, L.I., N.Y.)
1986	Lewis M. Simons, Pete Carey, Katherine Ellison	San Jose (Calif.) Mercury News
1987	Michael Parks	Los Angeles Times
1988	Thomas L. Friedman	New York Times
1989	Glenn Frankel	Washington Post
	Bill Keller	New York Times

1. Instead of an individual prize, the trustees commissioned the creation of a bronze plaque to symbolize the services and achievements of all American news reporters in the war zones of Europe, Asia, and Africa.
2. The board decided that Arthur Krock of the *New York Times* deserved the prize for National Reporting, but he could not accept the award because he was a board member. Therefore, no prize was awarded.

CARTOONS

Year	Winner	Newspaper	Year	Winner	Newspaper
1922	Rollin Kirby	New York World	1957	Tom Little	Nashville Tennesseean
1923	No award		1958	Bruce M. Shanks	Buffalo (N.Y.) Evening News
1924	Jay Norwood Darling	Des Moines Register and Tribune	1959	William H. ("Bill") Mauldin	St. Louis Post-Dispatch
1925	Rollin Kirby	New York World	1960	No award	
1926	Daniel R. Fitzpatrick	St. Louis Post-Dispatch	1961	Carey Orr	Chicago Tribune
1927	Nelson Harding	Brooklyn Daily Eagle	1962	Edmund S. Valtman	Hartford (Conn.) Times
1928	Nelson Harding	Brooklyn Daily Eagle	1963	Frank Miller	Des Moines Register
1929	Rollin Kirby	New York World	1964	Paul Conrad	Denver Post
1930	Charles R. Macauley	Brooklyn Daily Eagle	1965	No award	
1931	Edmund Duffy	Baltimore Sun	1966	Don Wright	Miami News
1932	John T. McCutcheon	Chicago Tribune	1967	Patrick Oliphant	Denver Post
1933	H.M. Talburt	Washington Daily News	1968	Eugene Gray Payne	Charlotte (N.C.) Observer
1934	Edmund Duffy	Baltimore Sun	1969	John Fischetti	Chicago Daily News
1935	Ross A. Lewis	Milwaukee Journal	1970	Thomas F. Darcy	Newsday (Garden City, L.I., N.Y.)
1936	No award		1971	Paul Conrad	Los Angeles Times
1937	C.D. Batchelor	New York Daily News	1972	Jeffrey K. MacNelly	Richmond News-Leader
1938	Vaughn Shoemaker	Chicago Daily News	1973	No award	
1939	Charles G. Werner	Daily Oklahoman	1974	Paul Szep	Boston Globe
1940	Edmund Duffy	Baltimore Sun	1975	Garry Trudeau	Universal Press Syndicate
1941	Jacob Burck	Chicago Times	1976	Tony Auth	Philadelphia Inquirer
1942	Herbert L. Block ("Herblock")	NEA Service	1977	Paul Szep	Boston Globe
1943	Jay Norwood Darling	Des Moines Register and Tribune	1978	Jeffrey K. MacNelly	Richmond News-Leader
1944	Clifford K. Berryman	Evening Star (D.C.)	1979	Herbert L. Block ("Herblock")	Washington Post
1945	Sgt. Bill Mauldin	United Feature Syndicate, Inc.	1980	Don Wright	Miami News
1946	Bruce Alexander Russell	Los Angeles Times	1981	Mike Peters	Dayton (Ohio) Daily News
1947	Vaughn Shoemaker	Chicago Daily News	1982	Ben Sargent	Austin (Tex.) American-Statesman
1948	Reuben L. Goldberg	New York Sun	1983	Richard Locher	Chicago Tribune
1949	Lute Pease	Newark Evening News	1984	Paul Conrad	Los Angeles Times
1950	James T. Berryman	Evening Star (D.C.)	1985	Jeffrey K. MacNelly	Chicago Tribune
1951	Reg Manning	Arizona Republic	1986	Jules Feiffer	Village Voice (New York City)
1952	Fred L. Packer	New York Mirror	1987	Berke Breathed	Washington Post Writers Group
1953	Edward D. Kuekes	Cleveland Plain Dealer	1988	Doug Marlette	Atlanta Constitution and Charlotte Observer
1954	Herbert L. Block ("Herblock")	Washington Post & Times Herald			
1955	Daniel R. Fitzpatrick	St. Louis Post-Dispatch	1989	Jack Higgins	Chicago Sun-Times
1956	Robert York	Louisville (Ky.) Times			

EDITORIALS

Year	Winner	Newspaper
1917	Luisitania editorial article	New York Tribune
1918	War editorials and articles	Lousiville Courier Journal
1919	No award	
1920	Harvey E. Newbranch	Evening World Herald
1921	No award	
1922	Frank M. O'Brien	New York Herald
1923	William Allen White	Emporia (Kans.) Gazette
1924[3]	Coolidge editorial	Boston Herald
1925	"Plight of the South" editorial	Charleston (S.C.) News and Courier
1926	Edward M. Kingsbury	New York Times
1927	F. Lauriston Bullard	Boston Herald
1928	Grover Cleveland Hall	Montgomery (Ala.) Advertiser
1929	Louis Isaac Jaffe	Norfolk Virginian-Pilot
1930	No award	
1931	Charles S. Ryckman	Fremont (Nebr.) Tribune
1932	No award	
1933	Series of editorials	Kansas City Star
1934	E.P. Chase	Atlantic (Iowa) News-Telegraph
1935	No award	
1936	Felix Morley	Washington Post
	George B. Parker	Scripps-Howard Newspapers
1937	John W. Owens	Baltimore Sun
1938	William Wesley Waymack	Des Moines Register and Tribune
1939	Ronald G. Callvert	Portland Oregonian
1940	Bart Howard	St. Louis Post-Dispatch
1941	Reuben Maury	New York Daily News
1942	Geoffrey Parsons	New York Herald Tribune
1943	Forrest W. Seymour	Des Moines Register and Tribune
1944	Henry J. Haskell	Kansas City Star
1945	George W. Potter	Providence Journal-Bulletin
1946	Hodding Carter	Delta Democrat-Times (Greenville, Miss.)
1947	William H. Grimes	Wall Street Journal
1948	Virginius Dabney	Richmond Times-Dispatch
1949	John H. Crider	Boston Herald
	Herbert Elliston	Washington Post
1950	Carl M. Saunders	Jackson (Mich.) Citizen Patriot
1951	William Harry Fitzpatrick	New Orleans States
1952	Louis LaCoss	St. Louis Globe Democrat
1953	Vermont Connecticut Royster	Wall Street Journal
1954	Don Murray	Boston Herald
1955	Royce Howes	Detroit Free Press
1956	Lauren K. Soth	Des Moines Register and Tribune
1957	Buford Boone	Tuscaloosa (Ala.) News
1958	Harry S. Ashmore	Arkansas Gazette
1959	Ralph McGill	Atlanta Constitution
1960	Lenoir Chambers	Norfolk Virginian-Pilot
1961	William J. Dorvillier	San Juan (Puerto Rico) Star
1962	Thomas M. Storke	Santa Barbara (Calif.) News-Press
1963	Ira B. Harkey, Jr.	Pascagoula (Miss.) Chronicle
1964	Hazel Brannon Smith	Lexington (Miss.) Advertiser
1965	John R. Harrison	Gainesville (Fla.) Daily Sun
1966	Robert Lasch	St. Louis Post-Dispatch
1967	Eugene Patterson	Atlanta Constitution
1968	John S. Knight	Knight Newspapers
1969	Paul Greenberg	Pine Bluff (Ark.) Commercial
1970	Philip L. Geyelin	Washington Post
1971	Horance G. Davis, Jr.	Gainesville (Fla.) Sun
1972	John Strohmeyer	Bethlehem (Pa.) Globe-Times
1973	Roger B. Linscott	Berkshire Eagle (Pittsfield, Mass.)
1974	F. Gilman Spencer	Trentonian (Trenton, N.J.)
1975	John Daniell Maurice	Charleston (W.Va.) Daily Mail
1976	Philip P. Kerby	Los Angeles Times
1977	Warren L. Lerude, Foster Church, Norman F. Cardoza	Reno (Nev.) Evening Gazette and Nevada State Journal
1978	Meg Greenfield	Washington Post
1979	Edwin M. Yoder, Jr.	Washington Star
1980	Robert L. Bartley	Wall Street Journal
1981	No award	
1982	Jack Rosenthal	New York Times
1983	Editorial board	Miami Herald
1984	Albert Scardino	Georgia Gazette
1985	Richard Aregood	Philadelphia Daily News
1986	Jack Fuller	Chicago Tribune
1987	Jonathan Freedman	San Diego Tribune
1988	Jane Healy	Orlando Sentinel
1989	Lois Wille	Chicago Tribune

3. A special prize was awarded to the widow of the late Frank I. Cobb of the *New York World* in recognition of his lifetime of editorial writing and service.

COMMENTARY

Year	Winner	Newspaper
1970	Marquis W. Childs	St. Louis Post-Dispatch
1971	William A. Caldwell	Record (Hackensack, N.J.)
1972	Mike Royko	Chicago Daily News
1973	David S. Broder	Washington Post
1974	Edwin A. Roberts, Jr.	National Observer
1975	Mary McGrory	Washington Star
1976	Walter ("Red") Smith	New York Times
1977	George F. Will	Washington Post Writers Group
1978	William Safire	New York Times
1979	Russell Baker	New York Times
1980	Ellen H. Goodman	Boston Globe
1981	Dave Anderson	New York Times
1982	Art Buchwald	Los Angeles Times Syndicate
1983	Claude Sitton	Raleigh (N.C.) News & Observer
1984	Vermont Royster	Wall Street Journal
1985	Murray Kempton	Newsday (Garden City, L.I., N.Y.)
1986	Jimmy Breslin	New York Daily News
1987	Charles Krauthammer	Washington Post
1988	Dave Barry	Miami Herald
1989	Clarence Page	Chicago Tribune

FEATURE WRITING

Year	Winner	Newspaper
1979	Jon D. Franklin	Baltimore Evening Sun
1980	Madeleine Blais	Miami Herald
1981	Teresa Carpenter	Village Voice (New York City)
1982	Saul Pett	Associated Press
1983	Nan Robertson	New York Times
1984	Peter Mark Rinearson	Seattle Times
1985	Alice Steinbach	Baltimore Sun
1986	John Camp	St. Paul Pioneer Press and Dispatch
1987	Steve Twomey	Philadelphia Inquirer
1988	Jacqui Banaszynski	St. Paul Pioneer Press and Dispatch
1989	David Zucchino	Philadelphia Inquirer

PHOTOGRAPHY

Year	Winner	Newspaper
1942	Milton Brooks	Detroit News
1943	Frank Noel	Associated Press
1944	Frank Filan	Associated Press
	Earle L. Bunker	World-Herald (Omaha, Nebr.)
1945	Joe Rosenthal	Associated Press
1946	No award	
1947	Arnold Hardy	Amateur; photo distributed by the Associated Press
1948	Frank Cushing	Boston Traveler
1949	Nathaniel Fein	New York Herald-Tribune
1950	Bill Crouch	Oakland (Calif.) Tribune
1951	Max Desfor	Associated Press
1952	John Robinson and Don Ultang	Des Moines Register and Tribune
1953	William M. Gallagher	Flint (Mich.) Journal
1954	Mrs. Walter M. Schau	Amateur; photo published by the Akron (Ohio) Beacon Journal
1955	John L. Gaunt, Jr.	Los Angeles Times
1956	Photography staff	New York Daily News
1957	Harry A. Trask	Boston Traveler
1958	William C. Beall	Washington Daily News
1959	William Seaman	Minneapolis Star
1960	Andrew Lopez	United Press International
1961	Yasushi Nagao	Mainichi (Tokyo); photo distributed by United Press International
1962	Paul Vathis	Associated Press
1963	Hector Rondon	La Republica (Caracas, Venezuela); photo distributed by the Associated Press
1964	Robert H. Jackson	Dallas Times-Herald
1965	Horst Faas	Associated Press
1966	Kyoichi Sawada	United Press International
1967	Jack R. Thornell	Associated Press

(In 1968 the Photography category was divided into two groups: Spot News Photography and Feature Photography.)

SPOT NEWS PHOTOGRAPHY

Year	Winner	Newspaper
1968	Rocco Morabito	Jacksonville Journal
1969	Edward T. Adams	Associated Press
1970	Steve Starr	Associated Press
1971	John Paul Filo	Valley Daily News and Daily Dispatch (New Kensington, Pa.)
1972	Horst Faas and Michel Laurent	Associated Press
1973	Huynh Cong Ut	Associated Press

Year	Winner	Newspaper
1974	Anthony K. Roberts	Freelance photographer, Beverly Hills, Calif.
1975	Gerald H. Gay	Seattle Times
1976	Stanley Forman	Boston Herald American
1977	Neal Ulevich	Associated Press
	Stanley Forman	Boston Herald American
1978	John H. Blair	United Press International
1979	Thomas J. Kelly III	Pottstown (Pa.) Mercury
1980	Unnamed photographer	United Press International
1981	Larry C. Price	Fort Worth (Tex.) Star-Telegram
1982	Ron Edmonds	Associated Press
1983	Bill Foley	Associated Press
1984	Stan Grossfeld	Boston Globe
1985	Photography staff	Register (Santa Ana, Calif.)
1986	Carol Guzy and Michel duCille	Miami Herald
1987	Kim Komenich	San Francisco Examiner
1988	Scott Shaw	Odessa (Tex.) American
1989	Ron Olshwanger	St. Louis Post-Dispatch

FEATURE PHOTOGRAPHY

Year	Winner	Newspaper
1968	Toshio Sakai	United Press International
1969	Moneta Sleet, Jr.	Ebony magazine
1970	Dallas Kinney	Palm Beach Post (West Palm Beach, Fla.)
1971	Jack Dykinga	Chicago Sun-Times
1972	Dave Kennerly	United Press International
1973	Brian Lanker	Topeka Capital-Journal
1974	Slava Veder	Associated Press
1975	Matthew Lewis	Washington Post
1976	Photography staff	Louisville Courier-Journal and Times
1977	Robin Hood	Chattanooga News-Free Press
1978	J. Ross Baughman	Associated Press
1979	Photography staff	Boston Herald American
1980	Erwin H. Hagler	Dallas Times Herald
1981	Taro M. Yamasaki	Detroit Free Press
1982	John H. White	Chicago Sun-Times
1983	James B. Dickman	Dallas Times Herald
1984	Anthony Suau	Denver Post
1985	Stan Grossfeld	Boston Globe
	Larry C. Price	Philadelphia Inquirer
1986	Tom Gralish	Philadelphia Inquirer
1987	David Peterson	Des Moines Register
1988	Michel duCille	Miami Herald
1989	Manny Crisostomo	Detroit Free Press

CRITICISM

Year	Winner	Newspaper
1970	Ada Louise Huxtable	New York Times
1971	Harold C. Schonberg	New York Times
1972	Frank Peters, Jr.	St. Louis Post-Dispatch
1973	Ronald Powers	Chicago Sun-Times
1974	Emily Genauer	Newsday syndicate
1975	Roger Ebert	Chicago Sun-Times
1976	Alan M. Kriegsman	Washington Post
1977	William McPherson	Washington Post
1978	Walter Kerr	New York Times
1979	Paul Gapp	Chicago Tribune

Year	Winner	Newspaper
1980	William A. Henry III	Boston Globe
1981	Jonathan Yardley	Washington Star
1982	Martin Bernheimer	Los Angeles Times
1983	Manuela Hoelterhoff	Wall Street Journal
1984	Paul Goldberger	New York Times
1985	Howard Rosenberg	Los Angeles Times
1986	Donal Henahan	New York Times
1987	Richard Eder	Los Angeles Times
1988	Tom Shales	Washington Post
1989	Michael Skube	Raleigh (N.C.) News and Observer

SPECIAL AWARDS AND CITATIONS

Year	Winner and/or paper	Citation
1930	William O. Dapping, Auburn (N.Y.) Citizen	Prison reporting
1938	Edmonton (Alberta) Journal	Freedom-of-the-press editorials
1941	New York Times	Foreign news reporting
1944	Byron Price, director of the Office of Censorship	Creation and administration of newspaper and radio codes
	Mrs. William Allen White	Services to Advisory Board, Graduate School of Journalism, Columbia University
1945	American press cartographers	Maps of war fronts
1947	Columbia University and Graduate School of Journalism	Governing Pulitzer prizes
	St. Louis Post-Dispatch	Adherence to ideals of journalism
1948	Dr. Frank Diehl Fackenthal	Interest and service

Year	Winner and/or paper	Citation
1951	Cyrus L. Sulzberger, New York Times	Interview with Archbishop Stepinac
1952	Max Kase, N.Y. Journal-American	Corruption in basketball
	Kansas City Star	Coverage of regional flood
1953	New York Times	Sunday "Review of the Week" section
1958	Walter Lippmann, New York Herald Tribune	Lifetime achievement
1964	Gannett Newspapers	"The Road to Integration" program
1976	Professor John Hohenberg	Administration of Pulitzer prizes
1978	Richard Lee Strout, Christian Science Monitor	Lifetime achievement
1987	Joseph Pulitzer, Jr.	Lifetime services to Pulitzer Board

MAGAZINES

In 1988, 11,566 consumer and trade magazines were published. Consumer magazines range from the very specialized (Fly Fisherman) to general interest (People) and are sold either by subscription or through retail outlets (supermarkets, newsstands, etc.). The Audit Bureau of Circulations (A.B.C.) monitors the sales of about 500 of the most popular consumer magazines. While single-copy sales of A.B.C. magazines have decreased steadily since 1978, subscriptions have increased about 50 percent during the same period, more than offsetting the single-copy decline.

Trade publications are magazines with a narrow focus in a particular area of business such as building (Remodeling), computers (PC Magazine), farming (Feed and Grain Times), industry (Adhesives Age), music (Billboard), restaurants (Restaurants & Institutions), and sewage disposal (Water and Wastes Digest). There are about 3,700 trade publications; they are sold either by subscription or distributed free.

Almost all magazines make money through revenues from both circulation and advertising. The most financially successful magazines are not necessarily the largest sellers, the difference being in the advertising fees they are able to obtain. The New Yorker, for example, is in the top 30 of all magazines in revenues but does not even make the top-100 list in circulation.

THE TOP 50 MAGAZINES BY PAID CIRCULATION, 1988

Rank	Magazines	Total paid circulation	% change
1.	Modern Maturity	17,924,783	12.1%
2.	NRTA/AARP news bulletins	17,623,715	13.5
3.	Readers Digest	16,964,226	0.7
4.	TV Guide	16,917,545	-2.1
5.	National Geographic	10,516,837	0.5
6.	Better Homes & Gardens	8,152,478	0.7
7.	Family Circle	5,900,794	-1.6
8.	McCall's	5,146,554	-2.8
9.	Woman's Day	5,138,280	-2.4
10.	Good Housekeeping	5,027,865	-2.2
11.	Ladies' Home Journal	5,013,761	-0.6
12.	Time	4,737,912	0.8
13.	Guideposts	4,371,861	0.8
14.	National Enquirer	4,303,631	-2.5
15.	Redbook	4,007,564	1.7
16.	Star	3,623,058	-2.2
17.	Sports Illustrated	3,438,998	9.2
18.	Playboy	3,405,786	-7.3
19.	Newsweek	3,315,369	4.2
20.	People Weekly	3,277,839	13.4
21.	Cosmopolitan	3,013,759	5.2
22.	American Legion	2,728,543	0.6
23.	U.S. News & World Report	2,365,930	0.6
24.	Southern Living	2,281,707	-0.1
25.	Smithsonian	2,280,808	-0.1
26.	Glamour	2,130,148	-5.2
27.	Penthouse	2,053,080	1.6
28.	Field & Stream	2,040,874	1.6
29.	Life	1,866,042	10.8
30.	Popular Science	1,831,538	-0.5
31.	Money	1,810,966	-3.6
32.	Seventeen	1,803,549	-3.0
33.	VFW Magazine	1,800,153	-0.5
34.	Motorland	1,784,497	3.5
35.	Parents	1,751,417	1.6
36.	Ebony	1,745,166	0.0
37.	Home & Away	1,719,690	1.5
38.	Country Living (N.Y.)	1,706,932	4.3
39.	Popular Mechanics	1,619,778	-0.8
40.	Workbasket	1,592,237	-10.8
41.	1001 Home Ideas	1,538,229	1.9
42.	Elks	1,523,658	-1.8
43.	Globe	1,516,823	-8.3

Rank	Magazines	Total paid circulation	% change
44.	Outdoor Life	1,512,533	-8.5
45.	Adventure Road	1,485,101	-2.3
46.	Boy's Life	1,464,108	1.5
47.	Sunset	1,431,303	-1.0
48.	Woman's World	1,401,689	0.3
49.	New Woman	1,393,027	9.6
50.	American Rifleman	1,364,933	-0.5

Note: Includes general-interest and farm magazines of the Audit Bureau of Circulations. Groups and comics are not included. The leading 100 A.B.C. magazines for the first six months of 1988 showed a 0.7% increase over the same period in 1987. **Source:** Audit Bureau of Circulations.

TOP 50 MAGAZINES RANKED BY REVENUES, 1988

Rank	Publication	Revenues	% change 1987–88
1.	Time	349,742,381	6.4%
2.	TV Guide	335,407,992	1.3
3.	Sports Illustrated	323,872,207	23.1
4.	People Weekly	305,341,523	14.7
5.	Newsweek	241,714,100	1.0
6.	Business Week	227,319,650	4.5
7.	Better Homes & Gardens	152,806,437	7.5
8.	Fortune	137,406,334	12.6
9.	Family Circle	134,358,209	8.4
10.	Good Housekeeping	129,288,336	-2.4
11.	Forbes	128,748,017	0.2
12.	U.S. News & World Report	128,140,585	20.8
13.	Woman's Day	115,649,901	0.2
14.	Cosmopolitan	114,573,684	2.7
15.	Reader's Digest	113,970,628	6.3
16.	Vogue	87,492,897	10.0
17.	Glamour	87,023,478	-0.7
18.	Ladies' Home Journal	83,771,579	9.2
19.	Money	79,767,127	1.5
20.	Redbook	68,558,081	5.7
21.	McCall's	62,592,194	-7.6
22.	Rolling Stone	62,073,163	12.5
23.	Southern Living	61,652,173	5.9
24.	Elle	55,416,648	42.1

Rank	Publication	Revenues	% change 1987–88
25.	Golf Digest	55,273,813	22.3
26.	Parents	53,099,992	6.1
27.	Life	48,727,894	39.8
28.	Mademoiselle	48,631,393	7.2
29.	New Yorker	47,812,021	−6.1
30.	Sunset	46,340,752	3.6
31.	Car and Driver	44,899,081	11.1
32.	Travel and Leisure	44,766,055	13.3
33.	New York Magazine	44,142,899	1.7
34.	Gentlemen's Quarterly	44,066,406	20.0
35.	Bride's	43,767,435	25.1
36.	Inc.	42,221,197	8.9
37.	Architectural Digest	42,157,775	24.4
38.	Smithsonian	41,390,380	6.3
39.	Playboy	40,654,466	8.2
40.	Modern Maturity	39,957,769	−5.2
41.	Seventeen	38,652,002	−1.8
42.	Ebony	37,954,324	2.4
43.	Country Living	37,290,403	18.2
44.	Field & Stream	36,886,240	−4.0
45.	National Geographic	35,734,461	24.2
46.	Self	34,760,967	14.5
47.	Road & Track	32,953,141	3.6
48.	Harper's Bazaar	32,582,747	0.1
49.	Town & Country	32,190,716	8.7
50.	Esquire	31,331,847	4.7

Note: Advertising and circulation combined.
Source: Publisher's Information Bureau.

TELEVISION, VIDEO, RADIO, AND FILM

THE ELECTRONIC HOME

% of American Homes	Facilities
98%	Have a TV set
98	Have a radio
94	Have a color TV set
90	Have an audio system
60	Have two or more TV sets
56	Have a VCR
53	Buy basic cable
42	Own prerecorded videocassettes
31	Receive 30 or more channels
28	Buy one or more pay channels
21	Have a home computer
20	Have a telephone answering device
18	Have a cordless telephone
12	Have color TV with MTS[1]
10	Have a compact disc player
10	Have a home alarm system
5	Have a camcorder
3	Have projection TV
2	Have LCD TV
2	Have satellite dishes

1. MTS—equipped for stereo sound. **Sources:** Television Information Office, 1988; Electronic Industries Association, 1988.

Television

TELEVISION FACTS, 1988

- TV is in **98.2%** of all U.S. households.
- Of households with TV, **96.6%** have color, while **62.6%** have two or more sets.
- Cable TV is in **52.8%** of all households; pay cable is at the **28.9%** level, and VCR penetration is up to **66%**.
- TV set sales continued to grow in 1987, topping the **23 million** mark for the first time.
- Commercial TV stations topped the **1,000 mark**. As of Jan. 1, 1988, there were **1,030 stations** on the air: 539 VHF, 491 UHF.
- At least one TV was on in each household an average of **7 hrs. and 3 min.** per day, in 1988 (up about one full hour since 1971, when the average was 6 hrs. and 2 min.).

Source: Television Advertising Bureau.

LONGEST-RUNNING NATIONAL NETWORK SERIES OF ALL TIME

Program	No. of Seasons	Years[1]
Walt Disney	32	1954–
The Ed Sullivan Show	24	1948–71
Gunsmoke	20	1955–75
The Red Skelton Show	20	1951–71
60 Minutes	20	1968–
Meet the Press	18	1947–65
What's My Line?	18	1950–67
I've Got a Secret	17	1952–76
Lassie	17	1954–71
The Lawrence Welk Show	17	1955–71

Note: Includes prime-time (6–11 p.m.) shows only; sports broadcasts and movie series are not included. 1. These dates reflect the first and last broadcasts of each show. Programs did not necessarily run continuously throughout this period.

SHORTEST-RUNNING NATIONAL NETWORK "SERIES"

The comedy show *Turn On* debuted at 8:30 p.m., Feb. 5, 1969, and closed one half-hour later. *Turn On* was summarily "turned off" when advertisers and senior ABC executives complained about double entendres and other sexually risqué material.

Source: BASELINE II, INC.

FIFTY TOP-RATED U.S. TV SHOWS (SINGLE EPISODE) OF ALL TIME

Program	Date	Network	Rating[1]
1. M*A*S*H Special	2/28/83	CBS	60.2
2. Dallas	11/21/80	CBS	53.3
3. Roots, part 8	1/30/77	ABC	51.1
4. Super Bowl XVI game	1/24/82	CBS	49.1
5. Super Bowl XVII game	1/30/83	NBC	48.6
6. Super Bowl XX game	1/26/86	NBC	48.3
7. Gone with the Wind, part 1	11/7/76	NBC	47.7
8. Gone with the Wind, part 2	11/8/76	NBC	47.4
9. Super Bowl XII game	1/15/78	CBS	47.2
10. Super Bowl XIII game	1/21/79	NBC	47.1
11. Bob Hope Christmas Show	1/15/70	NBC	46.6
12. Super Bowl XVIII game	1/22/84	CBS	46.4
13. Super Bowl XIX game	1/20/85	ABC	46.4
14. Super Bowl XIV game	1/20/80	CBS	46.3
15. ABC Theater "The Day After"	1/20/83	ABC	46.0
16. The Fugitive	8/29/67	ABC	45.9
17. Roots, part 6	1/28/77	ABC	45.9
18. Super Bowl XXI game	1/25/87	CBS	45.8
19. Roots, part 5	1/27/77	ABC	45.7
20. Ed Sullivan Show	2/9/64	CBS	45.3
21. Bob Hope Christmas Show	1/14/71	NBC	45.0
22. Roots, part 3	1/25/77	ABC	44.8
23. Super Bowl XI game	1/9/77	NBC	44.4
24. Super Bowl XV game	1/25/81	NBC	44.4
25. Super Bowl VI game	1/16/72	CBS	44.2
26. Roots, part 2	1/24/77	ABC	44.1
27. Beverley Hillbillies	1/8/64	CBS	44.0
28. Ed Sullivan Show	2/16/64	CBS	43.8
29. Roots, part 4	1/26/77	ABC	43.8
30. Academy Awards	4/7/70	ABC	43.4
31. Thorn Birds, part 3	3/29/83	ABC	43.2
32. Thorn Birds, part 4	3/30/83	ABC	43.1
33. NFC Championship game	1/10/82	CBS	42.9
34. Beverley Hillbillies	1/15/64	CBS	42.8
35. Super Bowl VII game	1/14/73	NBC	42.7
36. Thorn Birds, part 2	3/28/83	ABC	42.5
37. Beverley Hillbillies	2/26/64	CBS	42.4
38. Super Bowl IX game	1/12/75	NBC	42.4
39. Cinderella	2/22/65	CBS	42.3
40. Love Story (Sunday Night Movie)	10/1/72	ABC	42.3
41. Airport (Movie Special)	11/11/73	ABC	42.3
42. Super Bowl X game	1/18/76	CBS	42.3
43. Roots, part 7	1/29/77	ABC	42.3
44. Beverley Hillbillies	3/25/64	CBS	42.2
45. Beverley Hillbillies	2/5/64	CBS	42.0
46. Beverley Hillbillies	1/29/64	CBS	41.9
47. Super Bowl XXII game	1/31/88	ABC	41.9
48. Miss America Pageant	9/9/61	CBS	41.8
49. Beverley Hillbillies	1/1/64	CBS	41.8
50. Bonanza	3/8/64	NBC	41.6

Note: As of Jan. 1, 1989; does not include programs broadcast on more than one network, e.g., the Kennedy assassination or the Apollo moon landing. **Source:** A.C. Nielsen.

MOST SUCCESSFUL U.S. TV SHOWS OF THE FIFTIES, SIXTIES, AND SEVENTIES

These charts are based on a show's average rating throughout each decade, and are thus an indication of both popularity and longevity.

1950s

Program	Network	Avg. rating
1. A. Godfrey's Talent Scouts	CBS	32.9
2. I Love Lucy	CBS	31.6
3. You Bet Your Life	NBC	30.1
4. Dragnet	NBC	24.6
5. The Jack Benny Show	CBS	22.3
6. A. Godfrey and Friends	CBS	19.5
7. Gunsmoke	CBS	15.6
8. The Red Skelton Show	NBC	15.2
9. December Bride	CBS	13.8
10. I've Got a Secret	CBS	12.9
11. $64,000 Question	CBS	11.2
12. Disneyland	ABC	10.8
13. The Ed Sullivan Show	CBS	10.6
14. Have Gun—Will Travel	CBS	10.3
15. The Danny Thomas Show	CBS	9.9

1960s

Program	Network	Avg. rating
1. Bonanza	NBC	29.6
2. The Red Skelton Show	CBS	26.4
3. The Andy Griffith Show	CBS	22.4
4. The Beverly Hillbillies	CBS	21.9
5. The Ed Sullivan Show	CBS	21.7
6. The Lucy Show/Here's Lucy	CBS	21.3
7. The Jackie Gleason Show	CBS	16.5
8. Bewitched	ABC	14.8
9. Gomer Pyle	CBS	13.4
10. Candid Camera	CBS	11.2
11. The Dick Van Dyke Show	CBS	11.1
12. The Danny Thomas Show	CBS	10.7
13. Family Affair	CBS	9.8
14. Laugh-In	NBC	7.9
15. Rawhide	CBS	7.5

1970s

Program	Network	Avg. rating
1. All in the Family	CBS	23.1
2. M*A*S*H	CBS	17.6
3. Hawaii Five-O	CBS	16.5
4. Happy Days	ABC	15.9
5. The Waltons	CBS	14.0
6. The Mary Tyler Moore Show	CBS	13.7
7. Sanford & Son	NBC	13.4
8. One Day at a Time	CBS	11.4
9. Three's Company	ABC	10.8
10. 60 Minutes	CBS	10.0
11. Maude	CBS	9.8
12. Gunsmoke	CBS	9.7
13. Charlie's Angels	ABC	9.6
14. The Jeffersons	CBS	9.4
15. Laverne & Shirley	ABC	9.3

Source: BASELINE II, INC.; basic data—A.C. Nielsen.

PRODUCERS AND CONSUMERS: COMMERCIAL TV STATIONS ON THE AIR AND U.S. HOUSEHOLDS WITH TV, 1950–88

Year	Commerical TV stations on air	Households with TV (thousands)	% of all U.S. households
1950	98	3,800	9%
1955	411	32,000	67
1960	515	45,200	86
1965	569	53,800	95
1970	677	60,100	96
1975	706	71,500	97
1980	734	77,800	98
1981	756	79,900	98
1982	777	81,500	98
1983	813	83,300	98
1984	841	83,800	98
1985	883	84,900	98
1986	919	85,900	98
1987	968	87,400	98

Sources: A.C. Nielsen; *Television and Cable Factbook* (1988).

HIGHEST-RATED TV SHOWS OF 1987–88

A rating is the percentage of households with televisions tuned to a particular program. A share is the percentage of households with TV sets turned on and tuned to a particular program.

Program	Network	Rating	Share (%)
1. The Cosby Show	NBC	27.8	44
2. A Different World	NBC	25.0	39
3. Cheers	NBC	23.7	37
4. Growing Pains	ABC	22.8	34
5. Night Court	NBC	22.6	35
6. The Golden Girls	NBC	21.9	37
7. Who's the Boss?	ABC	21.2	33
8. 60 Minutes	CBS	20.6	34
9. Murder, She Wrote	CBS	20.2	30
10. The Wonder Years	ABC	19.0	30
11. Alf	NBC	18.8	29
12. Moonlighting	ABC	18.3	28
13. L.A. Law	NBC	18.3	28
14. NFL Monday Night Football	ABC	17.8	31
15. Matlock	NBC	17.7	27
16. Growing Pains	ABC	17.7	29
17. Amen	NBC	17.6	31
18. Family Ties	NBC	17.5	26
19. Hunter	NBC	17.4	34
20. CBS Sunday Movie	CBS	17.2	27

Note: Sept. 20, 1987–Apr. 17, 1988. **Source:** A.C. Nielsen.

Cable Television

Cable television was originally designed as a means of improving TV reception in some rural areas. In the 1960s operators realized that viewers were willing to pay for commercial-free programming, but their efforts to capitalize on the idea were hampered by stringent Federal Communications Commission restrictions. Not until 1975, when RCA put its first communications satellite into operation, did the industry really bloom. Under the name Home Box Office, the company started to transmit programming that could be received by independent operators around the country and then relayed to subscribers at minimal cost. With the dismissal of most of the FCC's regulations by a federal court in 1977, the door was opened for the development of what is now a multibillion-dollar industry.

BASIC CABLE TV SYSTEMS AND SUBSCRIBERS, 1952–88

Year	No. of systems	Subscribers (thousands)	% of U.S. households with TV
1952	70	14	0.1%
1955	400	150	0.5
1960	640	650	1.4
1965	1,325	1,275	2.4
1970	2,490	4,500	7.5
1975	3,506	9,800	13.2
1980	4,225	16,000	22.6
1981	4,375	18,300	28.3
1982	4,825	21,000	35.0
1983	5,600	25,000	40.5
1984	6,200	29,000	43.7
1985	6,600	32,000	46.2
1986	7,500	37,500	48.1
1987	7,900	41,000	50.5
1988	8,500	42,750	51.7

Sources: *Television and Cable Factbook* (1988); A.C. Nielsen.

TOP FIVE PAY-CABLE SERVICES, 1988

Network	Subscribers (thousands)	Content
Home Box Office (HBO)	16,500	Movies, variety, sports, documentaries, etc.
Showtime	6,100	Movies, variety, comedy specials, etc.
Cinemax	5,100	Movies, comedy, music specials.
The Disney Channel	4,000	Original and classic movies, cartoons, etc.
The Movie Channel	2,500	Movies, film festivals, etc.

Source: *Channels* magazine.

TOP 10 CABLE NETWORKS
(ranked by number of subscribers)

Network	Subscribers (thousands)	No. of systems	Launch date	Owner	Content
1. Entertainment and Sports Programming Network (ESPN)	48,800	19,000	9/1979	ABC/Capital Cities, Nabisco	Sports events, business news
2. Cable News Network (CNN)	47,900	8,200	6/1980	Turner Broadcasting System	24-hour news, special-interest reports
3. Superstation TBS	45,600	12,885	12/1976	Turner Broadcasting System	Movies, sports, original, and syndicated shows
4. USA Network	45,200	10,100	4/1980	Time, Inc., Paramount Pictures, MCA Inc.	Sports, family entertainment,
5. CBN Cable Network	42,700	8,225	4/1977	Christian Broadcasting Network	Movies, family entertainment, religious shows
6. Music Television (MTV)	42,600	5,050	8/1981	MTV Networks (Viacom)	Music videos, concerts, interviews
7. The Nashville Network (TNN)	42,000	7,510	3/1983	Opryland USA (Gaylord Broadcasting)	Country music, talk shows, sports
8. Nickelodeon	41,400	6,245	4/1979	MTV Networks (Viacom)	Children's programming
9. Lifetime	39,900	4,200	2/1984	Hearst, ABC, Viacom Entertainment Services	Women's programming
10. Cable Satellite Public Affairs Network (C-SPAN)	39,000	2,950	3/1979	Nonprofit	Public affairs

Source: National Cable Television Assn., *National Cable Network Directory* (1988).

Radio

U.S. RADIO STATIONS ON THE AIR, AND HOME RADIO SALES, 1946–88

Year	Radio stations on air[1]	Radio sales to dealers (thousands)[2]
1946	961	N.A.
1950	2,773	N.A.
1955	3,211	7,327
1960	4,133	18.031
1965	5,249	31,689
1970	6,760	34,049
1975	7,744	25,276
1980	8,566	28,104
1981	9,361	31,476
1982	9,461	31,782
1983	9,678	39,496
1984	10,021	46,453
1985	10,359	21,574
1986	9,824	25,363
1987	10,074	26,777
1988	10,244	26,000 (est.)

1. Includes AM and FM, commercial and noncommercial. 2. Includes table, clock, and portable—but not auto—radios. **Sources:** Federal Communications Commission; National Association of Broadcasters; Electronic Industries Assn.

U.S. COMMERCIAL RADIO STATIONS BY FORMAT, 1988

Format	Number of Stations[1]
Country/western	2,429
Adult contemporary	1,980
Contemporary hits/top 40	844
Nostalgia	637
Religious	546
Golden oldies	433
Easy listening	326
Album rock/progressive	295
News/talk	214
Urban contemporary	177
Spanish	150
Soft contemporary	121
Variety	100
Black/soul	82
Classic rock	79
Classical	44
Ethnic	29
New age	28
All news	23
Jazz	17
TOTAL	**8,763**

1. Includes AM and FM. **Source:** Radio Information Center, New York, N.Y.

Video

U.S. HOUSEHOLDS WITH VIDEOCASSETTE RECORDERS, 1978–88

Year	U.S. households with VCRs (thousands)	% of U.S. households with TVs
1978	200	0.3%
1979	400	0.5
1980	840	1.1
1981	1,440	1.8
1982	2,530	3.1
1983	4,580	5.5
1984	8,880	10.6
1985	17,600	20.8
1986	30,920	36.0
1987	42,560	48.7
1988	51,390	58.0

Source: A.C. Nielsen.

U.S. PRERECORDED VIDEOCASSETTE RENTALS, 1981–88

Year	rental units (thousands)	rental revenues (millions)	Average unit rental charge
1981	108,000	$ 351	$3.25
1982	201,240	604	3.00
1983	380,290	1,065	2.80
1984	705,780	1,835	2.60
1985	1,224,250	2,914	2.38
1986	1,795,700	4,094	2.28
1987	2,281,080	4,608	2.02
1988	2,512,800	5,123	2.04

VIDEOCASSETTE SALES, 1981–88

Year	Videocassette unit sales (thousands)	Videocassette sales revenue (millions)	Average purchase price
1981	720	$ 47	$65.28
1982	1,720	103	59.88
1983	3,760	218	57.98
1984	9,800	382	38.98
1985	21,940	658	29.99
1986	38,780	853	22.00
1987	64,900	1,103	17.00
1988	77,900	1,273	16.34

Source: Paul Kagan Associates, Inc.

RADIO FACTS, 1988

Radios in use:
527.4 million (up 16% since 1980)
342.0 million in homes
128.7 million in cars
36.2 million in trucks and vans
21.3 million at work

Households with radios: 99% of U.S. total

Who listens and how long:
95.3% of Americans over 12 listen 3 hours and 17 minutes each week

Source: Radio Advertising Bureau.

Film

U.S. MOVIE THEATERS/ SCREENS, 1945-87

Year	Indoor theaters	Drive-in theaters	Total
1945	20,355	102	20,457
1950	16,904	2,202	19,106
1955	14,613	4,587	19,200
1960	12,291	4,700	16,991
1965	10,150	4,150	14,300
1970	10,000	3,750	13,750
1971	10,335	3,720	14,055
1975	11,402	3,628	15,030
1980	14,029	3,561	17,590
1987	21,048	2,507	23,555

Note: Figures for 1945-70 represent theaters; from 1970 on, the accepted standard is movie screens. **Source:** Motion Picture Association of America.

MOST POPULAR FILMS DECADE BY DECADE

Title	Year	Director	Rental (millions)
Pre-1930			
The Birth of a Nation	1915	D.W. Griffith	$ 10.0
The Big Parade	1925	K. Vidor	5.5
The Singing Fool	1928	L. Bacon	4.0
1930s			
Gone with the Wind	1939	V. Fleming	77.6
Snow White and the Seven Dwarfs	1937	(Animated)	62.8
King Kong	1933	M. Cooper	5.0
The Wizard of Oz	1939	V. Fleming	4.5
San Francisco	1936	W.S. Van Dyke	4.0
1940s[1]			
Cinderella	1949	(Animated)	38.5
Pinocchio	1940	(Animated)	32.9
Song of the South	1946	H. Foster/ W. Jackson	29.2
Fantasia	1940	(Animated)	28.5
Bambi	1942	(Animated)	28.4
1950s			
The Ten Commandments	1956	C.B. DeMille	43.0
Lady and the Tramp	1955	(Animated)	40.2
Ben Hur	1959	W. Wyler	36.7
Around the World in 80 Days	1956	M. Anderson	23.1
Sleeping Beauty	1959	(Animated)	21.5
1960s			
The Sound of Music	1965	R. Wise	79.7
Doctor Zhivago	1965	D. Lean	47.1

Title	Year	Director	Rental (millions)
Butch Cassidy and the Sundance Kid	1969	G.R. Hill	46.0
Mary Poppins	1964	R. Stevenson	45.0
The Graduate	1968	M. Nichols	43.4
1970s			
Star Wars	1977	G. Lucas	193.50
Jaws	1975	S. Spielberg	129.50
Grease	1978	R. Kleiser	96.30
The Exorcist	1973	W. Friedkin	89.00
The Godfather	1972	F.F. Coppola	86.30
Superman	1978	R. Donner	82.80
Close Encounters of the Third Kind	1977	S. Spielberg	82.80
Saturday Night Fever	1977	J. Badham	74.10
The Sting	1973	G.R. Hill	71.40
American Graffiti	1973	G. Lucas	55.10
1980s[2]			
E.T.—The Extra-Terrestrial	1982	S. Spielberg	228.40
Return of the Jedi	1983	R. Marquand	168.00
The Empire Strikes Back	1980	J. Kershner	141.60
Ghostbusters	1984	I. Reitman	128.30
Raiders of the Lost Ark	1981	S. Spielberg	115.60
Indiana Jones and the Temple of Doom	1984	S. Spielberg	109.00
Beverly Hills Cop	1984	M. Brest	108.00
Back to the Future	1985	R. Zemeckis	104.20
Tootsie	1982	S. Pollack	95.30
Beverly Hills Cop II	1987	T. Scott	80.80

1. All films listed for this decade were made by Disney studios, and have been re-released on a regular basis ever since. Their dominance on this chart is partly due to the fact that they are "continually" generating revenue.   2. Through 1987.   **Source:** Variety.

U.S. FILM RELEASES, 1917-87

Year	New releases	Year	New releases
1917	687	1965	452
1920	796	1970	367
1925	579	1975	604
1930	595	1982	365
1935	766	1983	395
1940	673	1984	398
1945	377	1985	371
1950	622	1986	398
1955	392	1987	478
1960	387		

Note: Includes U.S.-produced and imported features; does not include re-releases. **Souces:** Motion Picture Association of America (1970-87); Film Daily Yearbook (1917-65).

U.S. FILM BOX-OFFICE RECEIPTS, ADMISSIONS, AND ADMISSION CHARGES, 1926-87

Despite headlines hailing 1987 as the best box-office year ever, the motion picture industry was healthier—in terms of both admissions and real-dollar earnings—in the 1930s, '40s, and '50s.

Year	Box office receipts (millions)	Receipts factored for inflation[1] (millions)	Admissions (thousands)	Average admission charge
1926	$720.0	$4,621.0	2,600,000	N.A.
1930	732.0	4,979.4	4,680,000	N.A.
1935	566.0	4,693.3	3,900,000	$0.24
1940	735.0	5,964.0	4,160,000	0.24
1945	1,450.0	9,151.1	4,680,000	0.35
1950	1,376.0	6,486.0	3,120,000	0.53
1955	1,326.0	5,620.7	3,392,000	0.50
1960	951.0	3,649.8	2,080,000	0.69
1965	927.0	3,343.1	2,288,000	1.01
1970	1,162.0	3,402.1	920,400	1.55
1975	2,115.0	4,465.9	988,000	2.05
1980	2,748.5	3,789.2	1,021,500	2.69
1981	2,965.6	3,706.2	1,060,000	2.78
1982	3,452.7	4,064.5	1,175,400	2.94
1983	3,766.0	4,925.4	1,196,900	3.15
1984	4,030.6	4,406.9	1,199,100	3.36
1985	3,749.4	3,958.5	1,056,100	3.55
1986	3,778.0	3,915.9	1,017,200	3.71
1987	4,252.9	4,252.9	1,088,500	3.91

1. Base year is 1987. **Sources:** BASELINE II, INC.; Motion Picture Association of America; U.S. Depart. of Commerce; Film Daily Yearbook.

TWENTY TOP-GROSSING FEATURE FILMS OF 1988

Title	Distributor	Box-office gross (millions)
1. Who Framed Roger Rabbit?	BV/Touchstone	$150.4
2. Coming to America	Paramount	128.1
3. Big	20th C. Fox	112.3
4. Crocodile Dundee II	Paramount	109.2
5. Die Hard	20th C. Fox	79.9
6. Cocktail	BV/Touchstone	77.0
7. Beetlejuice	Warner Bros.	73.3
8. A Fish Called Wanda	MGM/UA	60.0
9. Willow	MGM/UA	55.8
10. Twins	Universal	55.5
11. Scrooged	Paramount	54.9
12. Rambo III	Tri-Star	53.7
13. Bull Durham	Orion	50.3
14. Nightmare on Elm Street, Part IV	New Line	49.4
15. The Naked Gun	Paramount	47.9
16. Colors	Orion	46.1
17. Young Guns	20th C. Fox	43.4
18. Rain Man	MGM/UA	42.5
19. Biloxi Blues	Universal	41.5
20. Oliver & Company	BV/Disney	40.2

Note: As of Jan. 4, 1989. Box-office gross represents total receipts from all North American ticket sales. **Source:** BASELINE II, INC.

THE ECONOMY

Gross National Product

The goal of an economic system is to transform resources into final products, by way of business enterprises, for society's consumption. This includes the manufacture of goods such as cars, bread, furniture, and so on, and the provision of services such as health care, education, or motion pictures. The most commonly used measure associated with this goal is the Gross National Product (GNP). The GNP is the total value of all final goods and services (not including illegal transactions) currently produced in the economy measured at prices established in the market. The word *final* serves to exclude intermediate goods sold to producers and used to make finished products eventually sold to consumers in the market.

Auto parts such as batteries and tires sold to automakers are examples of intermediate goods and are included in the GNP only through the price of the car when it is sold. The GNP, in terms of expenditure categories, comprises purchases of goods and services by consumers and government, gross private domestic investment (or business purchases), and net exports.

Assessment of the GNP in current dollars is referred to as a nominal measure. Nominal measures may be misleading because the economy appears to grow as average prices rise with inflation. An alternative method is to evaluate the GNP by measuring the value of goods and services using constant prices for a given year; the government currently uses 1982 as the base year. Assessments based on constant prices are referred to as real measures because they indicate the change in quantity of output of the economy.

An important criticism of the GNP as an indicator of progress is that it may not be an accurate assessment of the standard of living an economy provides. Not all goods and services are equally important, for example, but all are counted equally in the GNP. Similarly, many of the characteristics that reflect the quality of life in an economy, such as education levels, the availability of health services, and leisure, may not be captured by GNP measures. For example, the fact that an economy generates high levels of pollution would not show up in a measure of the GNP. Two economies might be otherwise identical except for one being pollution free, while the other generates industrial wastes and poisons. Because the latter might demand many services to clean up the pollution and treat those exposed to it, the GNP would be higher in that economy. Yet most people would prefer to live in the pollution-free economy.

Income

Because the GNP is simply a measure of economic activity and not of general welfare, one might turn to income distribution statistics such as the change in the percentage of population below the poverty level to assess the quality of life in the economy.

Since 1979 the poor in the United States have gotten poorer and the rich richer. In 1987 the overall proportion of Americans living in poverty was 13.5%, or 32.5 million people.

GNP IN CURRENT AND CONSTANT (1982) DOLLARS, 1965–88 (in billions of dollars)

Item	1965	1970	1975	1980	1981	1982	1983
CURRENT DOLLARS							
Gross national product (GNP)	$705.1	$1,015.5	$1,598.4	$2,732.0	$3,052.6	$3,166.0	$3,405.7
Personal consumption expenditures	440.7	640.0	1,012.8	1,732.6	1,915.1	2,050.7	2,234.5
Durable goods	63.5	85.7	135.4	219.3	239.9	252.7	289.1
Nondurable goods	191.9	270.3	416.2	681.4	740.6	771.0	816.7
Services	185.4	284.0	461.2	831.9	934.7	1,027.0	1,128.7
Gross private domestic investment	116.2	148.8	219.6	437.0	515.5	447.3	502.3
Fixed investment	106.2	145.7	225.2	445.3	491.5	471.8	509.4
Nonresidential	73.1	105.2	162.9	322.8	369.2	366.7	356.9
Residential	33.1	40.5	62.3	122.5	122.3	105.1	152.5
Change in business inventories	9.9	3.1	-5.6	-8.3	24.0	-24.5	-7.1
Net exports of goods and services	9.7	8.5	31.1	32.1	33.9	26.3	-6.1
Exports	42.9	68.9	161.3	351.0	382.8	361.9	352.5
Imports	33.2	60.5	130.3	318.9	348.9	335.6	358.7
Government purchases[1]	138.6	218.2	335.0	530.3	588.1	641.7	675.0
Federal	68.7	98.8	129.2	208.1	242.2	272.7	283.5
National defense	51.0	76.8	89.6	142.7	167.5	193.8	214.4
State and local	69.9	119.4	205.9	322.2	345.9	369.0	391.5
CONSTANT (1982) DOLLARS							
Gross national product (GNP)	$2,087.6	$2,416.2	$2,695.0	$3,187.1	$3,248.8	$3,166.0	$3,279.1
Personal consumption expenditures	1,236.4	1,492.0	1,711.9	2,000.4	2,024.2	2,050.7	2,146.0
Durable goods	134.6	162.5	205.6	245.9	250.8	252.7	283.1
Nondurable goods	543.2	632.5	676.5	762.6	764.4	771.7	800.2
Services	558.5	697.0	829.8	991.9	1,009.0	1,027.0	1,062.7
Gross private domestic investment	367.0	381.5	383.3	509.3	545.5	447.3	504.0
Fixed investment	341.8	373.3	396.1	516.2	521.7	471.8	510.4
Nonresidential	227.6	264.0	281.2	379.2	395.2	366.7	361.2
Residential	114.2	109.3	114.9	137.0	126.5	105.1	149.3
Change in business inventories	25.2	8.2	-12.8	-6.9	23.9	-24.5	-6.4
Net exports of goods and services	-2.7	-30.0	18.9	57.0	49.4	26.3	-19.9
Exports	132.0	178.3	259.7	388.9	392.7	361.9	348.1
Imports	134.7	208.3	240.8	332.0	343.4	335.6	368.1
Government purchases[1]	487.0	572.6	580.9	620.5	629.7	641.7	649.0
Federal	244.4	268.3	226.3	246.9	259.6	272.7	275.1
National defense	N.A.	N.A.	161.1	171.2	180.3	193.8	206.9
State and local	242.5	304.3	354.6	373.6	370.1	369.0	373.9

Item	1984	1985	1986	1987	1988
CURRENT DOLLARS					
Gross national product (GNP)	$3,772.2	$4,014.9	$4,240.3	$4,526.7	$4,864.3
Personal consumption expenditures	2,430.5	2,629.0	2,807.5	3,012.1	3,227.5
Durable goods	335.5	372.2	406.5	421.9	451.1
Nondurable goods	867.3	911.2	943.6	997.9	1,046.9
Services	1,227.6	1,345.6	1,457.3	1,592.3	1,729.6
Gross private domestic investment	664.8	643.1	665.9	712.9	766.5
Fixed investment	597.1	631.8	650.4	673.7	718.1
Nonresidential	416.0	442.9	433.9	446.8	488.4
Residential	181.1	188.8	216.6	226.9	229.7
Change in business inventories	67.7	11.3	15.5	39.2	48.4
Net exports of goods and services	-58.9	-78.0	-104.4	-123.0	-94.6
Exports	383.5	370.9	378.4	428.0	519.7
Imports	442.4	448.9	482.8	551.1	614.4
Government purchases[1]	735.9	820.8	871.2	924.7	964.9
Federal	310.5	355.2	366.2	382.0	381.0
National defense	234.3	259.1	277.5	295.3	298.4
State and local	425.3	465.6	505.0	542.8	583.9
CONSTANT (1982) DOLLARS					
Gross national product (GNP)	$3,501.4	$3,618.7	$3,721.7	$3,847.0	$3,996.1
Personal consumption expenditures	2,249.3	2,354.8	2,455.2	2,521.0	2,592.2
Durable goods	323.1	355.1	385.0	390.9	409.7
Nondurable goods	825.9	847.4	879.5	890.5	899.6
Services	1,100.3	1,152.3	1,190.7	1,239.5	1,283.0
Gross private domestic investment	658.4	637.0	643.5	674.8	721.8
Fixed investment	596.1	627.9	628.1	640.4	679.3
Nonresidential	425.2	453.5	433.1	445.1	487.5
Residential	170.9	174.4	195.0	195.2	191.8
Change in business inventories	62.3	9.1	15.4	34.4	42.5
Net exports of goods and services	-84.0	-104.3	-137.5	-128.9	-100.2
Exports	371.8	367.2	378.4	427.8	504.8
Imports	455.8	471.4	515.9	556.7	605.0
Government purchases[1]	677.7	731.2	760.5	780.2	782.3
Federal	290.8	326.0	333.4	339.0	328.7
National defense	218.5	237.2	251.4	264.9	261.8
State and local	387.0	405.2	427.1	441.2	453.6

1. Purchases of goods and services. **Sources:** U.S. Bureau of Economic Analysis, *The National Income and Product Accounts of the United States, 1929–1982* and *Survey of Current Business* (July issues and Apr. 1989).

This is down from a peak of 15.2% in 1983 but higher than for all years between 1969 and 1980, a period when GNP growth was very slow. The proportion of families with incomes in excess of nine times the poverty line has more than doubled, from 3.1% in 1973 to 6.9% in 1987. As the income share of the highest fifth of all families increased from 41.1% in 1973 to 43.7% of all national income in 1987, the income share of the lowest fifth declined from 5.5% to 4.6%.

By race and Hispanic origin, there are wide disparities in income levels. In 1987 the percentage of whites below the poverty line was only 11%, as against 28% for Hispanics and 33% for blacks. These differences are even more pronounced when broken down by age groups. While the percentage of all children under 18 living in poverty was 20% in 1987—the highest child poverty rate of any industrialized nation in the world—for whites the rate was under 16%, for Hispanics it was 39%, and for blacks 45%.

Among the elderly, whose poverty rate is lower than the national average (12.1% v. 13.5%), there are also disparities by race and Hispanic origin. In the period 1979–87, the rate for whites decreased by more than 3%; among blacks the poverty rate decreased from 36% to 32% in 1986 but rose back to 34%; and among Hispanics there was a net increase of 0.6%, despite a low of 23% in 1986.

Definitions of Output, Income, and Expenditure Terms

Capital consumption adjustment Used for corporations, nonfarm sole proprietorships, and partnerships, this is the difference between capital consumption claimed on income tax returns and capital consumption allowances measured at straight-line depreciation, consistent-service lives, and replacement cost. The tax return data are valued at historical costs and reflect changes over time in service lives and depreciation patterns as permitted by tax regulations.

GNP, BY INDUSTRY, IN CONSTANT (1982) DOLLARS, 1980–87

Industry	1980	1985	1986	1987	1980–85	1985–86	1986–87
Gross national product (GNP)	**$3,187.1**	**$3,618.7**	**$3,721.7**	**$3,847.0**	**2.6%**	**2.8%**	**3.4%**
Domestic industries (GDP)	3,131.7	3,581.9	3,690.9	3,821.4	2.7	3.0	3.5
Private industries	2,739.5	3,183.1	3,281.6	3,408.5	3.0	3.1	3.9
Agriculture, forestry, fisheries	76.2	93.8	97.2	96.1	4.2	3.6	-1.1
Farms	64.2	79.4	83.7	82.5	4.3	5.4	-1.4
Mining	135.6	130.1	115.7	117.5	-0.8	-11.1	1.6
Construction	161.6	165.4	173.1	175.8	0.5	4.7	1.6
Manufacturing[1]	665.4	786.8	804.6	839.5	3.4	2.3	4.3
Durable goods[1]	401.5	493.7	505.0	525.2	4.2	2.3	4.0
Lumber and wood products	20.4	20.1	21.5	23.5	-0.3	7.0	9.3
Furniture and fixtures	10.2	12.2	11.9	12.5	3.6	-2.5	5.0
Stone, clay, and glass products	21.1	22.6	22.2	23.1	1.4	-1.8	4.1
Primary metal industries	46.4	34.2	34.3	34.3	-5.9	0.3	—
Fabricated metal products	52.5	56.8	56.7	58.5	1.6	-0.2	3.2
Machinery, except electrical	84.6	134.5	147.0	160.7	9.7	9.3	9.3
Electric and electronic equipment	62.7	79.7	80.3	82.5	4.9	0.8	2.7
Motor vehicles and equipment	33.7	50.9	44.9	40.3	8.6	-11.8	-10.2
Other transportation equipment	38.1	43.8	47.4	50.2	2.8	8.2	5.9
Instruments and related products	21.8	24.7	25.2	25.3	2.5	2.0	0.4
Nondurable goods[1]	263.9	293.0	299.7	314.3	2.1	2.3	4.9
Food and kindred products	56.7	63.1	61.6	63.7	2.2	-2.4	3.4
Tobacco manufactures	9.5	6.9	6.9	7.2	-6.2	—	4.3
Textile mill products	16.1	16.3	17.5	17.8	0.2	7.4	1.7
Apparel and other textile products	20.1	19.9	19.8	21.4	-0.2	-0.5	8.1
Paper and allied products	24.6	30.2	31.3	33.0	4.2	3.6	5.4
Printing and publishing	36.9	43.0	42.3	42.6	3.1	-1.6	0.7
Chemicals and allied products	50.1	59.1	64.1	68.8	3.4	8.5	7.3
Petroleum and coal products	26.7	24.9	26.3	26.6	-1.4	5.6	1.1
Rubber and misc. plastic products	18.9	26.2	26.8	29.8	6.8	2.3	11.2
Leather and leather products	4.3	3.4	3.0	3.3	-4.6	-11.8	10.0
Transportation and public utilities	293.4	326.0	331.6	349.5	2.1	1.7	5.4
Transportation	129.5	125.4	129.0	136.0	-0.6	2.9	5.4
Railroad transportation	27.2	19.3	18.2	16.9	-6.6	-5.7	-7.1
Local interurban passenger transit	7.0	6.3	6.4	6.6	-2.1	1.6	3.1
Trucking and warehousing	51.5	52.6	54.4	60.2	0.4	3.4	10.7
Water transportation	8.3	7.8	8.0	7.9	-1.2	2.6	-1.2
Transportation by air	23.1	24.4	26.6	28.4	1.1	9.0	6.8
Pipelines, except natural gas	5.1	4.9	5.0	5.1	-0.8	2.0	2.0
Transportation services	7.2	10.0	10.3	10.9	6.8	3.0	5.8

Industry	1980	1985	1986	1987	1980–85	1985–86	1986–87
Communications	78.4	95.2	99.2	107.6	4.0	4.2	8.5
Telephone and telegraph	71.1	85.8	89.3	97.6	3.8	4.1	9.3
Radio and television broadcasting	7.3	9.4	9.9	10.1	5.2	5.3	2.0
Electric, gas, and sanitary services	85.5	105.3	103.4	105.9	4.3	-1.8	2.4
Wholesale trade	213.5	268.5	282.7	291.7	4.7	5.3	3.2
Retail trade	286.9	341.8	360.2	368.3	3.6	5.4	2.2
Finance, insurance, and real estate	464.3	524.3	537.6	559.4	2.5	2.5	4.1
Banking	56.7	61.9	62.9	63.2	1.8	1.6	0.5
Credit agencies other than banks	5.2	7.0	7.8	8.3	6.1	11.4	6.4
Security and commodity brokers, and services	10.7	16.9	18.6	21.3	9.6	10.1	14.5
Insurance carriers	28.6	33.5	35.8	37.0	3.2	6.9	3.4
Insurance agents and brokers, and services	17.3	20.0	21.9	23.9	2.9	9.5	9.1
Real estate	339.6	376.0	380.8	394.8	2.1	1.3	3.7
Holding and other investment companies	6.3	9.0	9.8	10.9	7.4	8.9	11.2
Services[1]	442.6	546.4	578.9	610.8	4.3	5.9	5.5
Hotels and other lodging places	22.6	23.5	23.4	24.3	0.8	-0.4	3.8
Personal services	22.2	25.4	26.4	27.1	2.7	3.9	2.7
Business services	84.0	120.8	129.8	139.7	7.5	7.5	7.6
Auto repair, services, and garages	24.4	30.1	31.7	32.9	4.3	5.3	3.8
Motion pictures	5.7	7.5	7.7	7.6	5.6	2.7	-1.3
Amusement and recreation services	13.7	17.9	18.9	20.3	5.5	5.6	7.4
Health services	129.4	158.9	165.7	176.9	4.2	4.3	6.8
Legal services	28.9	35.0	36.3	37.9	3.9	3.7	4.4
Educational services	18.1	21.5	21.6	22.4	3.5	0.5	3.7
Social services and membership organizations	30.2	33.3	34.7	35.9	2.0	4.2	3.5
Misc. professional services	47.1	53.6	63.8	66.7	2.6	19.0	4.5
Private households	7.4	8.8	8.8	8.8	3.5	—	—
Government and government enterprises	382.7	400.8	407.9	415.7	0.9	1.8	1.9
Federal	138.3	146.5	147.1	148.8	1.2	0.4	1.2
State and local	244.4	254.4	260.8	266.9	0.8	2.5	2.3
Statistical discrepancy	5.9	-4.3	-12.1	-7.0	N.S.	N.S.	N.S.
Rest of the world[2]	55.5	36.9	30.9	25.6	-7.8	-16.3	-17.2

The column group header reads: AVERAGE ANNUAL PERCENT CHANGE *spanning the 1980–85, 1985–86, and 1986–87 columns.*

Note: N.S. = not significant. Dash (—) represents zero. 1. Includes items not shown separately. 2. Net property income from abroad, including profits, dividends, and interest on assets held overseas by domestic residents, minus profits, dividends, and interest paid to foreigners on assets held in the United States. **Sources:** U.S. Bureau of Economic Analysis, *The National Income and Product Accounts of the United States, 1929–82* and *Survey of Current Business* (July issues).

Consumer expenditure Consumer expenditure statistics presented in the accompanying tables are arrived at from the findings of the Consumer Expenditure Survey program, designed to provide a continuous flow of data on the buying habits of American consumers, necessary for future revisions of the Consumer Price Index. One group of 5,000 consumers in 85 urban areas around the country keep diaries of expenditures on small, frequently purchased items, such as food and beverages, tobacco, housekeeping supplies, nonprescription drugs, and personal care products and services. Another 5,000 consumers are interviewed quarterly for information about large expenditures, such as those for property, automobiles, and major appliances, or about expenditures occuring on a fairly regular basis, such as rent, utilities, and insurance premiums.

Discretionary income Households with spendable (after-tax) income at least 30% higher than that needed for average expenditures for their income group are considered to have discretionary income, allowing them to maintain a living standard comfortably higher than the average for similar households. According to the U.S. Census Bureau's March 1987 Current Population Survey, discretionary income totaled nearly $320 billion, or about 15% of total

NATIONAL INCOME, BY TYPE OF INCOME, 1970–88 (in billions of current dollars)

Type of income	1970	1975	1980	1985	1988
National Income	$832.6	$1,289.1	$2,203.5	$3,234.0	$3,968.4
Compensation of employees	618.3	948.7	1,638.2	2,367.5	2,904.7
Wages and salaries	551.5	814.7	1,372.0	1,975.2	2,436.9
Government and government enterprise	117.1	176.1	260.1	371.8	446.1
Other	434.3	638.6	1,111.8	1,603.4	1,990.7
Supplements to wages and salaries	66.8	134.0	266.3	392.4	467.8
Employer contributions for social insurance	34.3	68.0	127.9	204.8	249.6
Other labor income	32.5	65.9	138.4	187.6	218.3
Proprietors' income[1]	80.2	125.4	180.7	255.9	324.5
Farm	14.7	25.4	20.5	30.2	36.3
Nonfarm	65.4	100.0	160.1	225.6	288.2
Proprietors' income	66.0	102.2	164.3	194.6	254.0
Rental income of persons[2]	18.2	13.5	6.6	9.2	19.3
Corporate profits[1]	74.7	117.6	177.2	282.3	328.4
Corporate profits[3]	69.5	123.9	194.0	222.6	282.8
Profits before tax	76.0	134.8	237.1	224.3	306.6
Profits tax liability	34.4	50.9	84.8	96.4	142.7
Profits after tax	41.7	83.9	152.3	127.8	163.9
Dividends	22.5	29.6	54.7	83.3	104.5
Undistributed profits	19.2	54.3	97.6	44.6	59.4
Inventory valuation adjustment	-6.6	-11.0	-43.1	-1.7	-23.8
Capital consumption adjustment	5.2	-6.2	-16.8	59.7	45.6
Net interest	41.2	83.8	200.9	319.0	391.5

1. With inventory valuation and capital consumption adjustments.   2. With capital consumption adjustment.
3. With inventory valuation adjustment.   **Sources:** U.S. Bureau of Economic Analysis, *The National Income and Product Accounts of the United States, 1929–82* and *Survey of Current Business* (July issues).

PERCENT DISTRIBUTION AND AVERAGE ANNUAL PERCENT CHANGE OF SHARES OF NATIONAL INCOME, BY TYPE, 1970–87

Type of income	1970	1975	1980	1985	1987
National income, total	100.0%	100.0%	100.0%	100.0%	100.0%
Compensation of employees	74.3	73.6	74.3	73.2	72.9
Wages and salaries	66.2	63.2	62.3	61.1	61.1
Supplements to wages, salaries	8.0	10.4	12.1	12.1	11.8
Proprietors' income[1]	9.6	9.7	8.2	7.9	8.5
Farm	1.8	2.0	0.9	0.9	1.2
Nonfarm	7.9	7.8	7.3	7.0	7.3
Rental income of persons[2]	2.2	1.0	0.3	0.3	0.5
Corporate profits[1]	9.0	9.1	8.0	8.7	8.4
Profits before tax	9.1	10.5	10.8	6.9	7.5
Profits after tax	5.0	6.5	6.9	4.0	3.9
Inventory valuation adjustment	-0.8	-0.9	-2.0	-(Z)	-0.5
Capital consumption adjustment	0.6	-0.5	-0.8	1.8	1.4
Net interest	4.9	6.5	9.1	9.9	9.6

Note: Z = less than 0.05%.   1. With inventory valuation and capital consumption adjustments.
2. With capital consumption adjustment.   **Sources:** U.S. Bureau of the Census, based on data from U.S. Bureau of Economic Analysis, *The National Income and Product Accounts of the United States, 1929–82* and *Survey of Current Business* (July issues).

PERSONAL INCOME PER CAPITA IN CURRENT DOLLARS, BY STATE, 1970–87

State	1970	1980	1985	1987	Income rank 1980	Income rank 1987
Alabama	$2,945	$ 7,704	$10,705	$11,940	47	43
Alaska	5,073	13,835	18,726	18,230	1	4
Arizona	3,789	9,172	12,955	14,315	32	26
Arkansas	2,827	7,465	10,523	11,507	49	46
California	4,746	11,603	16,016	17,821	3	7
Colorado	4,025	10,598	14,678	15,584	13	17
Connecticut	5,037	12,112	18,217	21,266	2	1
Delaware	4,587	10,249	14,590	16,696	14	9
District of Columbia	5,250	12,322	17,756	20,457	—	—
Florida	3,943	9,764	13,921	15,584	24	16
Georgia	3,377	8,348	12,618	14,300	38	28
Hawaii	4,944	10,617	13,867	15,679	11	14
Idaho	3,467	8,569	10,823	11,868	36	45
Illinois	4,563	10,837	14,728	16,442	7	11
Indiana	3,771	9,245	12,433	13,914	31	32
Iowa	3,804	9,537	12,570	14,236	26	29
Kansas	3,770	9,941	13,826	15,126	17	21
Kentucky	3,141	8,022	10,775	12,059	43	41
Louisiana	3,071	8,682	11,291	11,473	34	47
Maine	3,405	8,218	11,876	13,954	39	31
Maryland	4,475	10,790	15,980	18,124	8	5
Massachusetts	4,514	10,612	16,305	19,142	12	3
Michigan	4,133	10,165	14,008	15,393	15	19
Minnesota	3,995	10,062	14,149	15,927	16	13
Mississippi	2,597	6,926	9,239	10,292	50	50
Missouri	3,809	9,298	13,256	14,687	29	23
Montana	3,528	8,924	11,021	12,347	33	40
Nebraska	3,759	9,274	12,982	14,328	30	25
Nevada	4,878	11,421	14,671	16,366	5	12
New Hampshire	3,890	9,788	15,373	17,529	23	8
New Jersey	4,805	11,573	17,626	20,352	4	2
New Mexico	3,145	8,169	11,203	11,875	41	44
New York	4,855	10,721	15,786	18,004	10	6
North Carolina	3,236	7,999	11,665	13,314	44	34
North Dakota	3,129	8,538	11,921	13,004	37	35
Ohio	4,033	9,723	13,219	14,612	25	24
Oklahoma	3,436	9,393	12,124	12,551	28	38
Oregon	3,889	9,866	12,628	14,041	19	30
Pennsylvania	4,042	9,891	13,573	15,212	18	20
Rhode Island	4,050	9,518	13,763	15,555	27	18
South Carolina	3,004	7,589	10,734	12,004	48	42
South Dakota	3,200	8,217	11,017	12,550	40	39
Tennessee	3,151	8,030	11,263	12,880	42	36
Texas	3,629	9,798	13,466	13,866	22	33
Utah	3,297	7,952	10,642	11,366	45	48
Vermont	3,604	8,577	12,383	14,302	35	27
Virginia	3,743	9,827	14,472	16,517	21	10
Washington	4,165	10,725	14,060	15,599	9	15
West Virginia	3,078	7,915	10,099	11,020	46	49
Wisconsin	3,889	9,845	13,174	14,742	20	22
Wyoming	3,797	11,339	12,827	12,709	6	37

Sources: U.S. Bureau of Economic Analysis, *Survey of Current Business* (August issues) and unpublished data.

after-tax income received by households. This is an increase of 22% over 1983. Some interesting statistics about discretionary income:

• Households with two or more people earning a paycheck account for 65% of all U.S. discretionary dollars.

• While only about 17% of households have pretax incomes of $50,000 or more, they control close to 80% of all discretionary income.

• While slightly more than one-fifth of all householders have a college degree, they account for more than half of all discretionary income.

• Both blacks and Hispanics are only half as likely as whites to have discretionary income.

• 34% of all homes in the New England states have discretionary income.

• Homes in the suburbs of major metropolitan areas are one-and-a-half times as likely to be in the discretionary income class as households in central cities.

Disposable personal income is that income after personal tax and nontax payments; this is the income available to persons for spending and saving. Personal tax and nontax payments are tax payments (except personal contributions for social insurance, net of refunds) by persons that are not chargeable to business expense, and also include certain personal payments to general government that are treated like taxes. Personal taxes include income, estate, gift, and personal property taxes

MONEY INCOME OF HOUSEHOLDS—PERCENT DISTRIBUTION BY MONEY INCOME LEVEL, BY SELECTED CHARACTERISTICS, 1987

Householder, type	Total households (thousands)	PERCENT DISTRIBUTION OF HOUSEHOLDS BY INCOME LEVEL (in dollars)								Median income
		Under $5,000	$5,000– $9,999	$10,000– 14,999	$15,000– 24,999	$25,000– 34,999	$35,000– 49,999	$50,000– 74,999	$75,000 & over	
Total[1]	91,066	6.9%	11.5%	10.6%	19.2%	16.1%	17.2%	12.2%	6.3%	$25,986
Age of householder:										
15–24	5,228	13.8%	16.6%	15.8%	25.6%	15.8%	8.1%	3.6%	0.9%	$16,204
25–34	20,583	5.7	7.8	9.6	22.2	20.3	20.4	10.9	3.0	26,923
35–44	19,323	4.3	6.1	6.6	15.7	17.5	23.5	17.5	8.9	34,929
45–54	13,630	4.9	5.6	6.6	14.0	15.3	20.5	20.0	13.1	37,250
55–64	12,846	7.5	9.9	9.5	18.8	15.2	17.0	13.7	8.3	27,538
65 +	19,456	9.9	24.5	17.8	22.1	11.5	7.9	4.1	2.3	14,334
White	78,469	5.4%	10.7%	10.2%	19.2%	16.7%	18.1%	13.0%	6.7%	$27,427
Black	10,186	17.9	17.7	13.3	20.7	12.2	10.8	5.5	2.0	15,475
Hispanic[2]	5,698	10.4	15.5	14.2	21.7	14.9	13.4	7.0	2.9	19,305
Northeast	19,137	6.0%	11.9%	9.0%	17.8%	15.9%	18.0%	13.5%	8.0%	$28,069
Midwest	22,402	6.7	11.9	10.7	19.3	17.1	17.5	11.8	5.0	25,722
South	31,047	9.0	11.7	11.6	20.0	15.3	16.3	10.9	5.3	23,719
West	18,480	4.6	10.2	10.6	19.5	16.3	17.7	13.5	7.7	27,914
Size of household:										
1 person	21,889	15.6%	25.2%	15.8%	20.9%	11.6%	7.3%	2.5%	1.2%	$12,544
2 persons	29,295	4.5	8.7	11.5	22.2	17.9	17.7	11.7	5.7	26,481
3 persons	16,163	4.8	6.1	7.7	17.8	17.6	21.4	16.6	8.0	32,348
4 persons	14,143	3.0	5.0	6.1	14.8	17.3	23.5	19.6	10.6	36,805
5 persons	6,081	2.9	6.6	6.7	14.9	17.2	23.1	17.9	10.7	35,825
6 persons	2,176	4.8	7.7	8.5	15.0	15.8	21.6	17.8	8.8	33,871
7 persons +	1,320	4.5	8.9	8.9	18.1	15.3	18.0	15.8	10.6	30,800
Marital status:										
Male householder	62,773	3.4%	6.7%	8.9%	18.9%	17.8%	20.7%	15.5%	8.1%	$31,534
Married, wife present	48,748	1.7	4.6	7.7	18.0	18.3	22.7	17.7	9.3	34,782
Married, wife absent	1,230	10.9	14.9	14.5	21.6	14.1	13.3	6.6	4.1	19,496
Widowed	1,920	10.8	26.7	17.3	18.7	11.3	7.3	6.2	1.8	13,424
Divorced	3,957	8.4	10.8	12.1	20.3	17.5	16.2	9.7	4.9	24,005
Single (never married)	6,477	8.9	11.9	12.5	24.4	16.4	14.4	7.7	3.7	21,493
Female householder	28,293	14.5	22.1	14.4	20.0	12.4	9.4	4.9	2.2	14,600
Married, husband present	3,061	2.7	6.6	7.3	16.4	17.4	22.8	16.7	10.2	34,847
Married, husband absent	2,156	24.7	23.4	15.5	19.9	9.0	5.8	1.2	0.6	10,517
Widowed	9,628	15.2	34.0	16.6	17.0	8.4	5.4	2.2	1.1	10,209
Divorced	6,527	12.1	16.2	15.2	23.8	14.7	11.2	5.0	1.7	17,597
Single (never married)	6,310	16.9	17.6	13.1	22.5	15.3	8.7	4.6	1.2	15,759
Educational attainment:[3]										
Elementary school	11,500	16.3%	26.7%	17.2%	19.7%	9.9%	6.4%	2.9%	0.8%	$11,730
Less than 8 yrs.	6,437	18.4	27.9	17.3	18.1	8.9	5.9	2.7	0.7	10,884
8 yrs.	5,063	13.7	25.2	17.1	21.7	11.0	7.0	3.1	1.0	12,999
High school	41,037	6.8	12.4	12.0	21.8	17.8	17.0	9.5	2.8	23,382
1–3 yrs.	10,476	10.9	19.4	14.9	22.2	14.2	11.2	5.6	1.6	16,727
4 yrs.	30,561	5.4	10.0	11.0	21.6	19.0	18.9	10.8	3.2	25,910
College	33,301	2.6	4.3	5.8	15.1	16.3	22.7	20.1	13.2	38,337
1–3	14,294	3.6	6.6	8.1	18.7	18.1	22.6	16.1	6.1	31,865
4 yrs. +	19,007	1.8	2.5	4.1	12.4	14.9	22.8	23.0	18.5	43,952

1. Includes other races not shown separately. 2. Hispanic persons may be of any race. 3. 25 years old and over. **Source:** U.S. Bureau of the Census, Current Population Reports (series).

and motor vehicle licenses. Nontax payments include passport fees, fines and penalties, donations, and tuitions and fees paid to schools and hospitals operated mainly by government.

Family income The term *family* refers to a group of two or more persons related by birth, marriage, or adoption who reside together; all such persons are considered members of one family. Family income refers to the sum of all income of the family members.

Gross domestic product (GDP) is the measure of the output of production attributable to all factors of production (labor and property) physically located in a country. The GDP therefore excludes net property income from abroad (such as the earnings of U.S. nationals working overseas), which is included in the GNP.

Gross national product (GNP) is the total national output of goods and services

valued at market prices. The GNP in this broad context, measures the output attributable to the factors of production—labor and property—supplied by U.S. residents. The GNP differs from "national income" mainly in that the GNP includes allowances for depreciation and for indirect business taxes (sales and property taxes).

Gross state product (GSP) is the gross market value of the goods and services attri-

MEDIAN MONEY INCOME OF YEAR-ROUND, FULL-TIME CIVILIAN WORKERS, BY SEX AND AGE, 1970–87

Age[1]	FEMALE				MALE			
	1970	1980	1985	1987	1970	1980	1985	1987
Total with income	$5,440[2]	$11,591	$16,252	$17,504	$ 9,184[2]	$19,173	$24,999	$26,722
15–19 yrs.	3,783[3]	6,779	8,372	9,417	3,950[3]	7,753	9,050	9,859
20–24 yrs.	4,928	9,407	11,757	12,905	6,655	12,109	13,827	14,665
25–34 yrs.	5,923	12,190	16,740	17,583	9,126	17,724	22,321	23,804
35–44 yrs.	5,531	12,239	18,032	19,897	10,258	21,777	28,966	30,655
45–54 yrs.	5,588	12,116	17,009	19,087	9,931	22,323	29,880	32,821
55–64 yrs.	5,468	11,931	16,761	17,831	9,071	21,053	28,387	30,946
65 and over	4,884	12,342	18,336	19,178	6,754	17,307	26,146	29,715

1. Age as of March of following year.   2. 14 years old and over.   3. 14–19 years old.   **Source:** U.S. Bureau of the Census, Current Population Reports (series).

MONEY INCOME OF FAMILIES—MEDIAN FAMILY INCOME, BY RACE AND HISPANIC ORIGIN, 1987

Characteristic	NUMBER (thousands)				MEDIAN FAMILY INCOME (dollars)			
	All families	White	Black	His-panic[1]	All families	White	Black	His-panic[1]
All families	**65,133**	**56,044**	**7,177**	**4,588**	**$30,853**	**$32,274**	**$18,098**	**$20,306**
Type of family:								
Married-couple families	51,809	46,644	3,682	3,204	34,700	35,295	27,182	24,677
Wife in paid labor force	29,112	25,800	2,424	1,655	40,422	41,023	33,333	31,354
Wife not in paid labor force	22,698	20,844	1,258	1,549	26,652	27,394	16,822	17,967
Male HHer, no wife present	2,715	2,165	421	312	24,804	26,230	17,455	19,411
Female HHer, no husband present	10,608	7,235	3,074	1,072	14,620	17,018	9,710	9,805
Number of earners:[2]								
TOTAL	**64,228**	**55,324**	**7,030**	**4,514**	**$30,951**	**$32,372**	**$17,990**	**$20,264**
No earners	9,440	7,803	1,396	648	12,849	14,924	5,528	6,262
One earner	18,009	15,064	2,396	1,458	23,192	25,369	13,774	15,148
Two earners	27,748	24,559	2,442	1,791	36,990	37,731	29,922	27,201
Three earners	6,329	5,545	569	419	46,961	47,860	37,458	34,183
Four or more earners	2,703	2,353	227	199	59,445	60,221	49,929	49,004

Notes: HH = household. HHer = householder. Families as of March 1988.   1. Hispanic persons may be of any race.   2. Excludes families with members who are in the armed forces.
Source: U.S. Bureau of the Census, Current Population Reports (series).

PER CAPITA MONEY INCOME IN CURRENT AND CONSTANT (1987) DOLLARS, BY RACE AND HISPANIC ORIGIN, 1970–87

Year	CURRENT DOLLARS				CONSTANT (1987) DOLLARS			
	All races	White	Black	Hispanic[1]	All races	White	Black	Hispanic[1]
1970	$ 3,177	$ 3,354	$1,869	N.A.	$ 9,299	$ 9,817	$5,470	N.A.
1975	4,818	5,072	2,972	$2,847	10,174	10,710	6,276	$6,012
1980	7,787	8,233	4,804	4,865	10,740	11,355	6,626	6,710
1985	11,013	11,671	6,840	6,613	11,635	12,330	7,226	6,987
1986	11,670	12,352	7,207	7,000	12,096	12,803	7,470	7,256
1987	12,287	13,031	7,499	7,611	12,287	13,031	7,499	7,611

1. Hispanic persons may be of any race.   **Source:** U.S. Bureau of the Census, Current Population Reports (series).

PERSONS BELOW POVERTY LEVEL, BY RACE, 1960–87 (millions of people)

	NUMBER BELOW POVERTY LEVEL				PERCENT BELOW POVERTY LEVEL				Average income cutoffs for family of four at poverty level[3]
Year	All races[1]	White	Black	Hispanic[2]	All races[1]	White	Black	Hispanic[2]	
1960	39.9	28.3	N.A.	N.A.	22.2%	17.8%	N.A.	N.A.	$ 3,022
1970	25.4	17.5	7.5	N.A.	12.6	9.9	33.5%	N.A.	3,968
1975	25.9	17.8	7.5	3.0	12.3	9.7	31.3	26.9%	5,500
1980	29.3	19.7	8.6	3.5	13.0	10.2	32.5	25.7	8,414
1985	33.1	22.9	8.9	5.2	14.0	11.4	31.3	29.0	10,989
1987	32.5	21.4	9.7	5.5	13.5	10.5	33.1	28.2	11,611

1. Includes other races not shown separately.   2. Hispanic persons may be of any race.   3. Prior to 1980, income cutoffs are for nonfarm families only.   **Source:** U.S. Bureau of the Census, Current Population Reports (series).

POVERTY LEVELS BASED ON MONEY INCOME FOR FAMILIES AND UNRELATED INDIVIDUALS, 1987

Size of unit	1987
1 person (unrelated individual)	$5,778
Under 65 years	5,909
65 years and over	5,447
2 persons	7,397
Householder under 65 years	7,641
Householder 65 years and over	6,872
3 persons	9,056
4 persons	11,611
5 persons	13,737
6 persons	15,509
7 persons	17,649
8 persons	19,515
9 persons	23,105

Note: Weighted averages.   **Source:** U.S. Bureau of the Census, Current Population Reports (series).

butable to labor and property located in a state. It is the state counterpart of the nation's GDP.

Household income A household includes related family members and all unrelated persons, if any—such as lodgers, foster children, wards, or employees—who share a house, an apartment, or a single room when it is occupied or intended for occupancy as separate living quarters by that household; that is, when the members of the household do not live and eat with any other persons in the structure and there is direct access from the outside or through a common hall. Household income, therefore, is the sum of all income of household members. The "householder" (which replaced the term *head of household* beginning with the 1980 Current Population Survey) is the person in whose name the home is owned or rented. In the case of joint ownership, one person in each household is designated as the householder for statistical purposes.

Inventory valuation adjustment This represents the difference between the book value of inventories used in production and the cost of replacing them.

Mean vs. median income Mean (or average) income refers to the sum of all incomes

of a group divided by the number of incomes in that group. Median income is the middle income when they are arranged in order of size—that is, there are the same number of incomes above and below the median. For example, consider incomes of $2,000, $3,000, $4,000 $15,000 and $95,000: the mean income is the sum of these divided by five, or $23,800; the median income is $4,000.

Money income This refers to income received (exclusive of certain money receipts such as capital gains) before payments for such things as personal income taxes, Social Security, union dues, and Medicare deductions. Money income does not include income in the form of noncash benefits such as food stamps, health benefits, and subsidized housing; rent-free housing and goods produced and consumed on farms; or the use of business transportation and facilities, full or partial payments by business for retirement programs, medical and educational expenses, and so on. These elements should be considered when comparing income levels. None of the aggregate income concepts (GNP, national income, or personal income) is exactly comparable with money income, although personal income is the closest.

National income, the aggregate of labor and property earnings derived from the current production of goods and services, is the sum of employee compensation, proprietors' income, rental income, corporate profits, and net interest. It measures the total factor costs of the goods and services produced by the economy. Income is measured before deduction of taxes.

Personal income is the current income received by persons from all sources minus their personal contributions for social insurance. *Persons* include individuals (including owners of unincorporated firms), nonprofit institutions serving individuals, private trust funds, and private noninsured welfare funds. Personal income includes transfers (payments not resulting from current production) from government and business, such as Social Security benefits and public assistance, but excludes transfers among persons. Also included are certain nonmonetary types of income: estimated net rental value to owner-occupants of their homes, the value of services furnished without payment by financial intermediaries, and food and fuel produced and consumed on farms.

Poverty level Families and unrelated individuals are classified as being above or below the poverty level according to their money income as a group and the number of people in the group (e.g., in 1987 a family of four with total money income below $11,611 lived below the poverty level). Classification is based on the poverty index originated by the Social Security Administration in 1964 and revised in 1969 and 1980. The poverty index is based solely on money income and does not reflect the fact that many low-income persons receive noncash benefits such as food stamps, medicaid, and public housing. The poverty thresholds are updated every year to reflect changes in the Consumer Price Index.

Private domestic investment This consists of (1) nonresidential fixed investment, i.e., firms' purchases of capital goods such as plants and equipment; (2) residential fixed investment (the building of single- and multi-family housing units); and (3) the change in business inventories, which are stocks on hand of raw materials and finished goods.

ECONOMIC INDICATORS

All market economies regularly go through cycles of recession—when output declines and unemployment rises—and expansion—when output and employment rise. These "business cycles" are one of the most important factors determining the socioeconomic conditions in any society. Although economists still have very little idea what actually causes recessions and what leads the economy to begin expanding again, they have had some success in predicting business cycles. Economic forecasting is the science of making these predictions. It is especially useful to be able to predict recessions sufficiently far in advance so that governments can take actions to stimulate the economy and reduce the severity of these downturns.

Economic indicators track developments in areas of the economy that are thought to be crucial to the future health of the economy, just as a barometer measures changes in air pressure that are crucial to changes in the weather. The development of economic indicators began around World War I but suffered a setback when the early forecasters failed to predict the Great Depression in 1929. During the depression the government asked a private research group, the National Bureau of Economic Research, to develop a set of measures that would help predict changes in business cycles. The group devised a list of measures based on analyses of previous business cycles. Since then, the list has been revised several times—most recently in March 1989--to reflect changes in the way the economy is structured.

Leading Indicators

There are currently 11 leading economic indicators, representing a broad spectrum of economic activity. These indicators are said to "lead" because their numbers change months in advance of a change in the general level of economic activity. They are as follows:

1. Average work week of production workers in manufacturing.

2. Average weekly state unemployment insurance claims.

3. New orders for consumers goods and materials in 1982 dollars.

4. Vendor performance (percent of companies receiving slower deliveries from suppliers).

5. Contracts and orders for plant and equipment in 1982 dollars.

6. Index of new private housing units authorized by local building permits.

7. Change in manufacturers' unfilled orders of durable goods in 1982 dollars. (See "Note" below.)

8. Change in sensitive materials prices.

9. Index of stock prices, i.e., of 500 common stocks (Standard and Poor's 500).

10. Money supply-M2 in 1982 dollars. (See "Money and Banking" section.)

11. Index of consumer expectations. [See "Note" below.]

(Note: Numbers 7 and 11 of the above list were added to the index in March 1989, while "change in business and consumer credit outstanding" and "change in manufacturing and trade inventories on hand and on order" were dropped, owing to untimely data availability. In addition the base year of the index was changed from 1972 to 1982.)

This composite of leading economic indicators is published by the U.S. Department of Commerce, Bureau of Economic Analysis. The composite has a noteworthy record: since 1948 it has accurately predicted every downturn and upswing in the economy. One major reason for this success is that many of the indicators represent commitments to economic activity in the coming months. The average lead for the index is 9.5 months at business cycle peaks (indicating the end of a business cycle expansion and the beginning of a recession) and 4.5 months at business cycle troughs (indicating the end of a business cycle recession and the beginning of an expansion).

Coincident and Lagging Economic Indicators

In addition to the leading economic indicators, two other sets of measures are used to track business cycles and the state of the economy. One set includes the coincident indicators, which measure how well the economy is doing at that moment (roughly, within 3 months of the business cycle turning points). These

COMPOSITE INDEX OF 11 LEADING, 4 COINCIDENT, AND 7 LAGGING INDICATORS, 1969–89 (1982 = 100)

Year	Leading indicators	Coincident indicators	Lagging indicators
1969	83.1	82.0	87.6
1970	79.0	83.5	93.2
1971	79.8	81.5	89.3
1972	88.1	85.4	85.4
1973	97.3	94.4	87.6
1974	95.5	96.3	97.7
1975	78.0	87.2	102.5
1976	93.0	89.8	88.0
1977	98.5	95.3	86.9
1978	101.9	101.1	92.5
1979	105.3	110.5	98.8
1980	101.2	111.0	108.3
1981	102.8	108.5	101.2
1982	97.2	102.1	104.9
1983	106.8	97.9	91.9
1984	123.5	109.1	94.1
1985	121.5	114.7	105.5
1986	127.9	117.8	111.0
1987	136.2	119.4	112.2
1988	138.7	125.6	114.0
1989	145.9	132.4	117.6

Note: Figures are for January of the year shown. See accompanying text for a description of specific indicators. **Source:** U.S. Dept. of Commerce, unpublished data, 1989.

include the number of employees on nonagricultural payrolls; manufacturing and trade sales in 1982 dollars; index of industrial production; and personal income less transfer payments in 1982 dollars. The second set includes lagging economic indicators. These are the ratio of consumer installment credit outstanding to personal income; commercial and industrial loans outstanding in 1982 dollars; the average prime interest rate charged by banks; the ratio of manufacturing and trade inventories to sales in 1982 dollars; the average duration of unemployment in weeks (inverted); the change in index of labor cost per unit of output in manufacturing; and the change in the Consumer Price Index for services per unit labor costs. At business cycle peaks, the average lag of the index is 4.5 months, and at business cycle troughs 8.5 months. It seems reasonable to wonder what use there is for an indicator that tells you where you have already been. But in fact that is exactly their use: they provide another way of measuring whether turning points in the business cycle truly have occurred.

The government produces a wide variety of economic indicators in addition to those discussed here for use in tracking more specific aspects of the economy, such as labor or capital markets.

PRICES

Consumer Price Index (CPI)

Often referred to as the "cost of living index," the Consumer Price Index is the most

commonly used measure of inflation. The index measures the average change in prices relative to an arbitrary base year of a common bundle of goods and services bought by the average consumer on a regular basis. The Bureau of Labor Statistics publishes two CPIs: (1) CPI-U for All Urban Consumers, which includes wage earners and clerical workers; professional, managerial, and technical workers; the self-employed; short-term workers; the unemployed; retirees and others not in the labor force—altogether covering 80% of the population—and (2) CPI-W for Urban Wage Earners and Clerical Workers, covering 32% of the population. Prices (including direct taxes) are collected from over 57,000 housing units and 19,000 establishments in 85 areas across the country. In calculating the index number, based on 100,000 price quotes a month, larger weights are assigned to goods that represent larger proportions of consumer expenditure. The index costs $26 million a year to produce and requires 40 economists and analysts tracking price changes in 365 categories.

Producer Price Index

The Producer Price Index measures average changes in prices received by producers of all commodities, at all stages of processing, produced in the United States. Prices used in constructing the index are collected from sellers and generally apply to the first significant large-volume commercial transaction for each commodity—i.e., the manufacturer's or other producer's selling price or the selling price on an organized exchange or at a central market. The weights used in the index represent the total net selling value of commodities produced or processed in the country. Values are f.o.b. (free on board) at the production point and are exclusive of excise taxes.

Implicit Price Deflator

The implicit price deflator (also called the GNP deflator) is derived from the ratio of current- to constant-dollar GNP (multiplied by 100) and

ANNUAL AVERAGE CONSUMER PRICE INDEX FOR ALL URBAN CONSUMERS (CPI-U), 1947–87 (1982 = 100)

Year	CPI
1947	23.1
1950	24.9
1955	27.7
1960	30.7
1965	32.7
1970	40.2
1975	55.8
1980	85.4
1981	94.2
1982	100.0
1983	103.2
1984	107.6
1985	111.4
1986	113.6
1987	117.7

Source: U.S. Bureau of Labor Statistics, 1988.

measures the value of current production in current prices relative to the value of the same goods and services in prices for the base year. For example, in 1987, GNP in current dollars was $4,526.7 billion, and GNP in constant (1982) dollars was $3,847.0 billion. Therefore, the GNP deflator for 1987 was (4,526.7/3,847.0) x 100, or 117.7, which is simply a comparison of 1982 and 1987 prices. It is a weighted average of the detailed price indexes used in the deflation of GNP, but the indexes are combined using weights that reflect the composition of GNP in each period. Thus, changes in the implicit price deflator reflect not only changes in prices but also changes in the composition of GNP.

PRODUCER PRICE INDEXES—MAJOR COMMODITY GROUPS, 1950–88 (1982 = 100)

Year	All commods.	Farm products[1]	Industrial commods.	Energy[2]	Metals and metal products
1950	27.3	37.7	25.0	12.6	22.0
1955	29.3	36.6	27.8	13.2	27.2
1960	31.7	37.7	30.5	13.9	30.6
1965	32.3	39.0	30.9	13.8	32.0
1970	38.1	44.9	35.2	15.3	38.7
1975	58.4	74.0	54.9	35.4	61.5
1980	89.8	98.3	88.0	82.8	95.0
1985	103.2	100.7	103.7	91.4	104.4
1988	106.9	110.0	106.3	66.8	118.7

1. Processed foods and feeds. 2. Fuels, related products, and power.
Source: U.S. Bureau of Labor Statistics, *Producer Price Indexes* (monthly and annual).

PURCHASING POWER OF THE DOLLAR, 1950–88
(PPI, 1982 = $1.00; CPI, 1982–84 = $1.00)

As indicated below, a 1982 dollar would have bought $4.15 worth of merchandise in 1950, while in 1988 only $0.85 worth of merchandise could be purchased with the same dollar.

Year	Annual average as measured by: Producer prices	Consumer prices
1950	$3.546	$4.151
1955	3.279	3.732
1960	2.994	3.373
1965	2.933	3.166
1970	2.545	2.574
1975	1.718	1.859
1980	1.136	1.215
1985	0.955	0.928
1988	0.926	0.846

Note: PPI = Producer Price Index; CPI = Consumer Price Index.
Source: U.S. Bureau of Labor Statistics and U.S. Bureau of Economic Analysis, *Survey of Current Business* (monthly data).

CONSUMER PRICE INDEXES, BY MAJOR GROUPS, 1960–87 (1982–84 = 100)

Note that for most groups the index rose evenly across the board, except during the oil crisis of the late 1970s and early 1980s. For the years 1975 through 1982, the Consumer Price Index for fuel oil rose from 34.9 to 105.0, tripling in seven years.

Year	All items	Energy	Food	Shelter	Apparel and upkeep	Transportation	Medical care	Fuel oil	Electricity	Utility (piped) gas)	Telephone services	All commodities
1960	29.6	22.4	30.0	25.2	45.7	29.8	22.3	13.5	29.9	17.6	58.3	33.6
1965	31.5	22.9	32.2	27.0	47.8	31.9	25.2	14.3	29.7	18.0	57.7	35.2
1970	38.8	25.5	39.2	35.5	59.2	37.5	34.0	16.5	31.8	19.6	58.7	41.7
1975	53.8	42.1	59.8	48.8	72.5	50.1	47.5	34.9	50.0	31.1	71.7	58.2
1980	82.4	86.0	86.8	81.0	90.9	83.1	74.9	87.7	75.8	65.7	77.7	86.0
1981	90.9	97.7	93.6	90.5	95.3	93.2	82.9	107.3	87.2	74.9	84.6	93.2
1982	96.5	99.2	97.4	96.9	97.8	97.0	92.5	105.0	95.8	89.9	93.2	97.0
1983	99.6	99.9	99.4	99.1	100.2	99.3	100.6	96.5	98.9	104.7	99.2	99.8
1984	103.9	100.9	103.2	104.0	102.1	103.7	106.8	98.5	105.3	105.5	107.5	103.2
1985	107.6	101.6	105.6	109.8	105.0	106.4	113.5	94.6	108.9	104.8	111.7	105.4
1986	109.6	88.2	109.0	115.8	105.9	102.3	122.0	74.1	110.4	99.7	117.2	104.4
1987	113.6	88.6	113.5	121.3	110.6	105.4	130.1	75.8	110.0	95.1	116.5	107.7

Sources: U.S. Bureau of Labor Statistics, *Monthly Labor Review* and *Handbook of Labor Statistics* (periodic).

CONSUMER PRICE INDEXES, BY SELECTED METROPOLITAN STATISTICAL AREAS, 1987 (1982–84 = 100)

Area	All items	Food and beverages	Food	Housing	Apparel and upkeep	Transportation	Medical care	Entertainment	Fuel and utilities
Index	**113.6**	**113.5**	**113.5**	**114.2**	**110.6**	**105.4**	**130.1**	**115.3**	**103.0**
Baltimore, Md.	114.2	116.8	117.1	112.6	119.7	106.9	127.9	118.9	94.0
Boston-Lawrence-Salem, Mass.-N.H.	117.1	119.4	119.2	116.8	115.8	103.3	139.2	119.4	88.9
Chicago-Gary-Lake County, Ill.-Ind.-Wis.	114.5	113.2	113.1	116.3	109.2	106.1	129.2	116.0	104.3
Cleveland-Akron-Lorain, Ohio	112.7	111.3	111.3	114.0	108.5	103.9	128.5	115.8	102.6
Dallas–Ft. Worth, Tex.	112.9	115.9	116.1	109.5	114.5	103.5	134.2	122.0	100.6
Detroit–Ann Arbor, Mich.	111.7	110.5	110.3	113.0	108.0	105.3	132.9	112.1	108.8
Houston-Galveston-Brazoria, Tex.	106.5	111.8	112.1	97.0	113.6	102.5	130.4	118.5	94.2
Los Angeles–Anaheim–Riverside, Calif.	116.7	113.2	112.9	121.0	112.5	108.9	129.5	111.2	112.6
Miami–Ft. Lauderdale, Fla.	111.8	113.0	113.5	108.7	115.6	106.6	126.6	113.7	109.8
New York–Northern New Jersey–Long Island, N.Y.-N.J.-Conn.	118.0	118.6	118.6	118.0	110.9	108.7	136.1	119.2	94.1
Philadelphia-Wilmington-Trenton, Pa.-N.J.-Del.-Md.	116.8	112.1	112.0	118.4	107.7	111.5	133.0	112.2	100.8
Pittsburgh–Beaver Valley, Pa.	111.4	109.4	109.3	113.4	107.0	100.5	130.2	121.4	108.4
St. Louis–East St. Louis, Mo.-Ill.	112.2	114.0	114.1	112.1	107.6	103.9	127.9	113.9	109.4
San Francisco–Oakland–San Jose, Calif.	115.4	113.7	114.0	121.5	104.6	102.4	128.7	121.6	105.4
Washington, D.C.–Md.–Va.	116.2	113.6	113.6	118.9	116.3	105.9	129.1	121.5	101.0

Sources: U.S. Bureau of Labor Statistics, *Monthly Labor Review* and *CPI Detailed Report* (Jan. issues).

PRODUCER PRICE INDEXES— SELECTED COMMODITIES, 1970–88 (1982 = 100)

Commodity group	1970	1975	1980	1985	1988
All commodities	38.1	58.4	89.8	103.2	106.9
FARM PRODUCTS AND PROCESSED FOODS AND FEEDS	44.9	74.0	98.3	100.7	110.0
Farm products	45.8	77.0	102.9	95.1	104.8
Processed foods and feeds	44.6	72.6	95.9	103.5	112.8
INDUSTRIAL COMMODITIES	35.2	54.9	88.0	103.7	106.3
Textile products and apparel	52.4	67.4	89.7	102.9	109.2
Hides, skins, leather, related products	42.0	56.5	94.7	108.9	131.5
Fuels, related products, power	15.3	35.4	82.8	91.4	66.8
Chemicals and allied products	35.0	62.0	89.0	103.7	116.4
Rubber and plastic-products	44.9	62.2	90.1	101.9	109.4
Lumber and wood products	39.9	62.1	101.5	106.6	118.9
Pulp, paper, and allied products	37.5	59.0	86.3	113.3	130.4
Metals and metal products	38.7	61.5	95.0	104.4	118.7
Machinery and equipment	40.0	57.9	86.0	107.2	113.2
Furniture and household durables	51.9	67.5	90.7	107.1	113.1
Nonmetallic mineral products	35.3	54.4	88.4	108.6	111.2
Transportation equipment	41.9	56.7	82.9	107.9	114.2

Source: U.S. Bureau of Labor Statistics, *Producer Price Indexes* (monthly and annual).

MONEY AND BANKING

The U.S. Banking System

Federal Reserve System The government's interest in monitoring and controlling the banking industry and managing the money supply led to the Federal Reserve Act of 1913. The act created the Federal Reserve System (or the "Fed," as it is popularly known), the nation's central bank. There are 12 regional Fed banks located in major cities throughout the country (Boston, New York, Philadelphia, Cleveland, Richmond, Atlanta, Chicago, St. Louis, Minneapolis, Kansas City, Dallas, and San Francisco). Commercial banks within each region select a majority of the directors who run each regional Fed bank. The president of the United States appoints a board of governors for the whole system, and the board is responsible for coordinating policies across the system. But the regional Feds play an important role in shaping those policies by representing regional interests and decentralizing the decision-making process.

The Fed has three main policy tools in managing the overall economy. First, it controls the reserve requirements at all depository institutions. These requirements determine what percentage of a bank's deposits must be held in reserve in the form of either deposits with Federal Reserve banks or vault cash—currently 3% (as of Dec. 31, 1988) for depository institutions with net transaction accounts of under $41.5 million and for nonpersonal time deposits that mature in less than 1.5 years. Raising the reserve requirements reduces the amount of loans available to borrowers and helps slow down the economy. The reserve ratios are rarely adjusted, however. A more frequently used instrument is *the discount rate*, the interest rate the Federal Reserve banks charge their commercial bank customers to borrow money. The Fed is known as the lender of last resort because of its responsibility to lend to banks in need, and it thus maintains the stability of the banking system. Raising the discount rate generally leads the commercial banks to raise the interest rates they charge their customers. This raises the costs of borrowing in the private sector and slows the economy. (Cutting the discount rate does the reverse and stimulates the economy.)

The Fed can also influence exchange rates by buying and selling foreign currency, referred to as *open market operations*; Selling British pounds and purchasing U.S. dollars, for example, will lower the price of the pound by increasing its supply to the foreign exchange market relative to dollars and by changing the exchange rate. More important, the Fed can control the money supply directly by selling and buying Treasury securities and other government debt instruments. When the Fed sells securities, it takes money from the buyer and holds it in its reserves, reducing the money supply; when it buys these instruments, it pays for them by taking money from its reserves, which then goes into circulation, increasing the money supply.

The Fed increased its holdings by $16 billion in 1988, for example, since it bought more securities than it sold by that amount, thereby increasing the money supply. This increase in money supply due to open market operations is nearly twice that of 1987, but only about half as much as that of 1986.

Controlling the money supply through open market operations is certainly the most common and, many would argue, the most important function of the Fed. The money supply shapes interest rates, through the supply and demand of money, and because the Fed is constantly involved in these open market operations (in order to keep the size of the money supply in proportion with a growing economy, for example), adjustments can be made subtly.

The Money Supply Money provides a medium of exchange as well as a way to store value, and traditionally, currency (paper money and coins) served that role exclusively. But over time, new financial instruments have developed that serve at least some of the functions of money; checking accounts serve exactly the same role as currency, and to an extent money market funds and other instruments can do so as well. In fact in 1986, 48% of household expenditures were paid for with checking accounts, and only 34% were paid for with cash.

The Fed uses four different measures of the money supply, which include different monetary instruments:

M1 is the original and most commonly reported measure of the money supply, which embraces currency and coins, demand deposits, traveler's checks, and other checkable deposits.

M2 is M1 plus overnight repurchasement agreements, overnight Eurodollars, money-market mutual-fund balances, money-market deposit accounts, and savings and small-time deposits.

M3 is M2 plus money-market mutual-fund balances held by financial institutions, term repurchase agreements and term Eurodollars, and large time-deposits.

L is M3 plus Treasury bills, commercial paper, and other very liquid assets such as savings bonds.

Commercial Banks are the largest financial institutions in the country and are the principal vehicles for exchanging money. The nation's first commercial bank was the Bank of America (now First Pennsylvania Bank), established in Philadelphia in 1782. Commercial banks hold about two-thirds of the nation's money deposits. Savings and Loans, the next-largest source of deposits, hold about half as much.

There are approximately 14,000 commercial banks in the country. They may be chartered either by the federal government or by individual states. While banks themselves may not operate across states, they may be owned by holding companies that can operate interstate, if state laws permit. Fifteen of the nation's largest 100 banks have foreign owners.

Commercial banks can make loans to individuals and to commercial operations, establish checking or demand deposits, maintain "trust" departments that make investments for customers, and perform a variety of other functions such as issuing credit cards. Until the deregulation of the 1980s, commercial banks were the only ones permitted to issue checking accounts. Regulations that developed after bank failures in the Great Depression still keep these banks out of the investment business—largely to protect depositors and the solvency of banks from potential effects of bad investments. But deregulation of the banking industry in the 1980s is blurring many of these distinctions. In particular, investment companies are now permitted to issue demand deposits and to compete with banks in other areas as well. (As a result these companies are sometimes referred to as nonbanks.)

Bank Failures The failure of a commercial bank is an especially serious problem because of the domino effect it may have on other financial institutions and businesses. Banks, and indeed all depository institutions, ultimately fail when many of their loans go bad and cannot be repaid. But even before that happens, depositors may get nervous about the security of their accounts and withdraw them all at once—a "run on the bank." Because banks loan out deposits and hold in reserve only a small percentage of the value of those deposits, banks experiencing a run would have to call in some of their loans (mainly those already due), putting sudden pressure on many commercial borrowers and causing some to fail. In addition the withdrawal of deposits and of loans reduces the money supply sharply. This process was an important cause of the Great Depression. Following the banking failures during the depression (2,293 banks failed in 1931, and 4,000 banks failed in 1933), the Federal Deposit Insurance

Corporation (FDIC) was created in 1933 to protect the accounts of depositors and, more important, to help prevent bank failures. The FDIC charges banks a premium to pay for this coverage. The corporation is designed to prevent runs on banks by insuring deposits and lending to banks to prevent the need to call in loans.

But banks still fail because of bad loans. Since 1945 U.S. banks have failed at the rate of about six per year. That number escalated rapidly in the 1980s, however—up to 200 failures in 1988. Most of these failures occurred in agricultural states where the failure of farms led to defaults on loans; more than half of all bank failures can be attributed to agriculture loans. Fraud also played an important role, especially in Tennessee, where more than 30 banks have failed since

1982. When a bank fails, the FDIC pays off each depositor (currently, up to $1000,000 in banks that are members of the Federal Reserve System and in such nonmember banks as join the insurance fund) and then sells the bank's assets. Sometimes the FDIC arranges for another bank's acquisition of the failed bank by subsidizing the sale.

Thrifts are depository institutions including savings and loans (S&Ls), savings banks, and credit unions. Of the 3,420 FDIC- and FSLIC- (Federal Savings and Loan Insurance Corporation-) insured thrifts in the country, the largest and most important are the S&Ls, which were created to provide home mortgages for borrowers and long-term savings deposits for individual investors. Until recently, thrifts were

FAILURES AT FDIC-INSURED BANKS, 1982–88

Year	Number
1982	42
1983	48
1984	79
1985	120
1986	138
1987	184
1988	200

Source: *American Banker.*

THE MONEY SUPPLY: MONEY STOCK AND LIQUID ASSETS, 1970–88
(in billions of dollars)

Item	1970	1975	1980	1985	1988
M1, TOTAL	**$215**	**$288**	**$412**	**$620**	**$763**
Currency[1]	47	73	115	168	201
Travelers checks[2]	1	2	4	6	7
Demand deposits[3]	165	212	261	267	288
Other checkable deposits[4]	(Z)	1	31	179	267
M2, TOTAL	**$628**	**$1,023**	**$1,633**	**$2,563**	**$2,968**
M1	215	288	412	620	763
Nontransaction components in M2[5]	414	736	1,221	1,943	2,205
Overnight repurchase (RP) agreements and Eurodollars[6]	1	6	28	70	75
Money market funds, general-purpose broker/dealer[6]	(Z)	3	62	177	235
Money market deposit accounts[6]	(Z)	(Z)	(Z)	514	525
Commercial banks	(Z)	(Z)	(Z)	333	361
Thrift institutions	(Z)	(Z)	(Z)	181	164
Savings deposits	327	389	400	301	420
Commercial banks	128	161	186	125	183
Thrift institutions	199	228	214	177	237
Small time-deposits[7]	266	338	728	880	954

Item	1970	1975	1980	1985	1988
Commercial banks	117	142	286	383	398
Thrift institutions	149	196	442	496	556
M3, TOTAL	**$677**	**$1,172**	**$1,991**	**$3,196**	**$3,745**
M2	628	1,023	1,633	2,563	2,968
Nontransaction components in M3[5]	49	149	358	633	777
Large time-deposits[8]	45	130	260	436	491
Commercial banks[9]	45	123	215	285	326
Thrift institutions	1	6	45	152	165
Term RPs and term Eurodollars[6,10]	4	18	84	142	197
Money market funds, institution only[6]	(Z)	(Z)	15	65	97
L, TOTAL	**$816**	**$1,367**	**$2,328**	**$3,825**	**$4,425**
M3	677	1,172	1,991	3,196	3,745
Savings bonds	52	67	72	79	104
Short-term Treasury securities[11]	49	68	134	301	256
Bankers acceptances	4	10	32	43	41
Commercial paper[12]	35	49	99	207	280

Notes: As of December of year shown, except March 1988. Z = less than $500 million. 1. Currency outside U.S. Treasury, Federal Reserve banks, and the vaults of depository institutions. 2. Outstanding amount of nonbank issuers. 3. At commercial banks and foreign-related institutions. 4. Consists of negotiable order of withdrawal (NOW) and automatic transfer service (ATS) accounts at all depository institutions, plus credit union share draft balances and demand deposits at thrift institutions. 5. This sum is seasonally adjusted as a whole. 6. Not seasonally adjusted. 7. Issued in amounts of less than $100,00. Includes retail repurchase agreements. Excludes individual retirement accounts (IRAs) and Keogh accounts. 8. Issued in amounts of $100,000 or more. Excludes those booked at international banking facilities. 9. Excludes those held by money market mutual funds, depository institutions, and foreign banks and official institutions. 10. Excludes those held by depository institutions and money market mutual funds. 11. U.S. Treasury bills and coupons with remaining maturities of less than 11 months held by other than depository institutions, Federal Reserve Banks, money market mutual funds, and foreign entities. 12. Excludes commercial paper held by money market mutual funds.
Sources: Board of Governors of the *Federal Reserve System*, Federal Reserve Bulletin (monthly) and *Money Stock, Liquid Assets, and Debt Measures, Federal Reserve Statistical Release H.6* (weekly).

FDIC-INSURED BANKS—NUMBER, BANKING OFFICES, AND DEPOSITS, BY CLASS OF BANK, 1987

				DEPOSITS (millions)			
				Individuals, partnerships, and corporations			
Class of bank	Banks (number)	Banking offices (number)	Total[1] deposits	Total	Transaction accounts[2]	Nontransaction accounts	Government
Total	**14,435**	**62,344**	**$2,137,284**	**$1,935,170**	**$544,879**	**$1,390,291**	**$112,083**
Commercial banks	13,955	58,806	1,935,940	1,734,036	527,073	1,206,963	112,073
National banks	4,747	28,339	1,110,273	992,380	307,365	685,015	62,752
State (Federal Reserve, member bank)	1,096	6,358	270,613	237,190	80,391	156,799	12,053
State (non-Federal Reserve member)	8,112	24,109	555,054	504,466	139,317	365,149	37,268
Savings banks	480	3,488	198,215	198,214	17,353	180,861	—
U.S. branches of foreign banks	—	50	3,129	2,920	453	2,467	10

Note: Dash (—) represents zero. 1. Includes other types of deposits, not shown separately. 2. Transaction account is a deposit or account on which the depositor or account holder is permitted to make withdrawals by negotiable or transferable instrument, payment orders of withdrawal, telephone transfers, or other similar devices for the purpose of making payments or transfers to others. **Source:** U.S. Federal Deposit Insurance Corp., *Data Book, Operating Banks and Branches, June 30, 1987* (1987).

prohibited from engaging in riskier loans—including most commercial loans—they could not issue checking deposits, and a ceiling was placed on the rate of interest they could pay depositors. Congress lifted the ceiling on interest payments to depositors in 1980 and in 1982 allowed the S&Ls to issue commercial loans and to invest directly in real estate developments.

The Federal Home Loan Bank System was established in 1932 to serve some of the same functions for S&Ls that the Federal Reserve provides for banks. All federally chartered S&Ls are regulated by the system (and must have the word *Federal* in their name). Less than half the thrifts are federally chartered, however; the rest are chartered by states, although most of these have joined the system as well. The FSLIC insures deposits at member S&Ls.

Credit Unions are employer-sponsored cooperative organizations that provide consumer and mortgage credit to their members. Employers often arrange for payroll-deduction savings plans through the credit union.

Mortgage Loans Mortgages are loans backed by buildings—either private dwellings or commercial buildings. In 1987 the value of mortgage loans outstanding in the country amounted to $1.5 billion. Traditionally, virtually all mortgages had fixed-interest payments and 30-year terms. With the escalation of interest rates beginning in the late 1970s, however, a range of alternative arrangements has been developed, including reducing the period of the loan, typically to 15 years—in order to reduce interest payments—and making the interest rate vary with market rates—*adjustable rate mortgages*. Some mortgages that hold payments in the first few years and then increase them rapidly for the remaining term of the mortgage are known as balloon mortgages.

The Savings and Loan Crisis The S&Ls came under enormous economic pressure in the 1970s, when interest rates paid by banks and other financial institutions rose well above the rate ceiling for thrifts, and they started losing depositors. Further, they were in a financial bind because their outstanding loans were all in mortgages—long-term, 30-year loans issued at low interest. In part because of

DEPOSIT-TAKING INSTITUTIONS, NUMBER AND PERCENTAGE SHARE OF DEPOSITS, 1987

Type of institution	Number of institutions	% share	Deposits[1] (in billions)	% share
Commercial banks	13,699	43.3%	$3,000.9	64.2%
Savings institutions[2]	3,631	11.5	1,513.5	32.4
Credit unions	14,335	45.3	162.2	3.4
Total	**31,665**	**100.0%**	**$4,676.6**	**100.0%**

1. Includes deposits gathered both domestically and internationally by U.S. institutions. 2. Savings institutions include savings banks and savings and loans. **Source:** *American Banker.*

TOP 25 U.S. THRIFTS RANKED BY ASSETS AND BY DEPOSITS, 1988

Rank by assets	Name/city	Assets (thousands)	Deposits (thousands)	Rank by dep's	Rank by assets	Name/city	Assets (thousands)	Deposits (thousands)	Rank by dep's
1.	Home Savings of America FA, Irwindale, Calif.	$40,917,353	$29,568,816	1	13.	Gibraltar Savings, Beverly Hills	$13,436,242	$7,573,847	19
2.	Great Western Bank, FSB, Beverly Hills	30,837,077	21,664,188	2	14.	Franklin Savings Assn., Ottawa, Kan.	13,266,390	3,309,257	53
3.	First Nationwide Bank, FSB, San Francisco	26,130,421	14,787,467	5	15.	Coast Savings & Loan Assn., Los Angeles	12,898,630	8,803,298	12
4.	California Federal Savings & Loan Assn., Los Angeles	25,857,500	18,787,200	3	16.	First Texas Bank FSB, Houston	12,497,352	8,484,642	15
					17.	Imperial Savings Assn., San Diego, Calif.	12,349,537	8,329,541	16
5.	Glendale Federal Savings & Loan Assn., Calif.	24,313,386	15,300,883	4	18.	Dime Savings Bank of New York FSB, Garden City	12,007,151	8,652,658	14
6.	Meritor Savings Bank, Philadelphia	17,172,011	12,209,344	7	19.	First Federal of Michigan, Detroit	11,941,525	4,911,701	28
7.	World Savings, FS&LA, Oakland, Calif.	16,352,299	10,141,780	11	20.	Columbia Savings & Loan Assn., Beverly Hills	11,752,238	8,089,177	18
8.	Home Federal Savings & Loan Assn. of San Diego, Calif.	16,261,058	11,558,328	8	21.	Empire of America Federal Savings Bank, Buffalo, N.Y.	11,281,412	8,325,671	17
9.	Great American First Savings Bank, San Diego, Calif.	16,084,341	10,799,471	9	22.	City Federal Savings Bank, Bedminster, N.J.	10,552,806	7,365,181	20
10.	American Savings Bank, Stockton, Calif.	15,409,744	13,401,466	6	23.	CenTrust Savings Bank, Miami	10,103,877	6,297,378	22
11.	CrossLand Savings FSB, Brooklyn, New York	15,143,802	8,791,305	13	24.	Standard Federal Bank, Troy, Mich.	9,803,376	5,272,603	24
12.	Goldome, Buffalo, N.Y.	14,962,534	10,529,276	10	25.	Sunbelt Savings FSB, Dallas	9,387,162	5,712,208	23

Note: Total deposits and savings accounts include noninterest- earning demand and NOW accounts; accounts earning in excess of regular rate in certificates with denominations of $100,000 or more and in other accounts; and accounts earning at or below regular rate in interest-earning NOW accounts, in passbook accounts, and all other accounts, except escrowed accounts. **Sources:** Compiled by *American Banker,* copyright 1989. American Banker questionnaire sent to the nation's 400 largest thrifts. For those thrifts not responding to American Banker, data from the Federal Home Loan Bank Board and the Federal Deposit Insurance Corp. were used.

TOP 25 U.S. COMMERCIAL BANKS RANKED BY ASSETS AND BY DEPOSITS, 1988

Rank by assets	Name/city	Assets (thousands)	Deposits (thousands)	Rank by dep's	Rank by assets	Name/city	Assets (thousands)	Deposits (thousands)	Rank by dep's
1.	Citibank NA, New York	$150,241,000	$104,996,000	1	14.	Bank of New York	$22,614,229	$16,665,898	14
2.	Bank of America NT&SA, San Francisco	82,912,000	69,640,000	2	15.	Mellon Bank NA, Pittsburgh	22,154,559	15,603,197	17
3.	Chase Manhattan Bank NA, New York	77,542,498	58,241,477	3	16.	Irving Trust Co., New York	21,627,800	14,154,588	19
4.	Morgan Guaranty Trust Co., New York	71,227,778	45,471,746	4	17.	Marine Midland Bank NA, Buffalo, N.Y.	20,987,400	16,659,085	15
5.	Bankers Trust Co., New York	55,349,881	33,261,373	9	18.	First Interstate Bank of California, Los Angeles	20,489,545	16,613,623	16
6.	Manufacturers Hanover Trust Co., New York	54,210,000	42,876,000	5	19.	Republic National Bank, New York	20,153,084	13,897,318	20
7.	Chemical Bank, New York	50,933,000	33,298,000	8	20.	Boston Safe Deposit & Trust Co.	17,517,376	15,464,313	18
8.	Security Pacific National Bank, Los Angeles	48,920,495	36,095,333	6	21.	Pittsburgh National Bank	16,793,779	10,045,593	29
9.	Wells Fargo Bank NA, San Francisco	43,732,080	35,109,059	7	22.	NCNB National Bank of North Carolina, Charlotte	16,741,026	11,054,684	24
10.	First National Bank, Chicago	35,172,664	27,372,439	10	23.	Bank of New England NA, Boston	15,564,083	10,904,043	25
11.	Continental Bank NA, Chicago	30,571,113	17,763,339	12	24.	National Bank of Detroit	15,459,413	11,989,495	21
12.	First National Bank, Boston	26,182,108	17,687,897	13	25.	First Union National Bank, Charlotte, N.C.	15,061,529	8,784,792	32
13.	NCNB Texas National Bank, Dallas[1]	25,573,596	20,474,765	11					

1. Bank was created by the FDIC on July 30, 1988, to merge the 40 bank affiliates of the insolvent First Republic Bank Corp. Compiled by *American Banker,* copyright 1989. **Sources:** *American Banker* questionnaire; Federal regulatory report of condition for Dec. 31, 1988; various state banking departments. With respect to mergers, American Banker follows the bank of charter in determining the surviving bank.

CONSUMER CREDIT OUTSTANDING, 1970–87 (billions of dollars)

Type of credit	1970	1975	1980	1985	1987
Credit outstanding	**$131.6**	**$204.9**	**$349.4**	**$592.4**	**$685.5**
Ratio to disposable personal income[1]	18.3%	17.9%	18.2%	20.8%	21.5%
INSTALLMENT	**$103.9**	**$167.0**	**$297.6**	**$517.8**	**$613.0**
By type of credit:					
Automobile paper	36.3	56.9	111.9	209.6	267.2
Revolving	4.9	14.5	54.8	122.0	159.3
Mobile-home paper	2.4	15.3	18.6	26.8	26.0
All other loans	60.2	80.1	112.1	159.2	160.6
By major holder:					
Commercial banks	48.6	82.9	145.5	241.6	281.6
Finance companies	27.2	32.7	61.9	111.0	140.1
Credit unions	12.8	25.4	43.6	71.9	81.1
Retailers[2]	12.9	16.6	26.1	39.1	42.7
Other[3]	2.3	9.2	20.3	53.9	67.5
NONINSTALLMENT	**27.7**	**37.9**	**51.8**	**74.7**	**72.5**
Single-payment loans	18.9	26.8	39.6	59.1	54.2
Charge accounts	8.7	11.0	12.1	15.6	18.2

Note: Data represent estimated amounts of credit outstanding as of end of year; seasonally adjusted. 1. Based on fourth-quarter seasonally adjusted disposable personal income at annual rates as published by the U.S. Bureau of Economic Analysis. 2. Excludes 30–day charge credit held by travel and entertainment companies. 3. Comprises savings institutions and gasoline companies. **Sources:** Board of Governors of the Federal Reserve System, *Federal Reserve Bulletin* (monthly), *Annual Statistical Digest,* and unpublished data.

FEDERAL RESERVE BANK OF NEW YORK— DISCOUNT RATES, 1976–88

Effective date	Rate per year[1]	Effective date	Rate per year[1]
Jan. 19, 1976	5.50%	May 5, 1981	14.00%
Nov. 22, 1976	5.25	Nov. 2, 1981	13.00
Aug. 31, 1977	5.75	Dec. 4, 1981	12.00
Oct. 26, 1977	6.00	July 20, 1982	11.50
Jan. 9, 1978	6.50	Aug. 2, 1982	11.00
May 11, 1978	7.00	Aug. 16, 1982	10.50
July 3, 1978	7.25	Aug. 27, 1982	10.00
Aug. 21, 1978	7.75	Oct. 12, 1982	9.50
Sept. 22, 1978	8.00	Nov. 22, 1982	9.00
Oct. 16, 1978	8.50	Dec. 15, 1982	8.50
Nov. 1, 1978	9.50	Apr. 9, 1984	9.00
July 20, 1979	10.00	Nov. 21, 1984	8.50
Aug. 17, 1979	10.50	Dec. 24, 1984	8.00
Sept. 19, 1979	11.00	May 20, 1985	7.50
Oct. 8, 1979	12.00	Mar. 7, 1986	7.00
Feb. 15, 1980[2]	13.00	Apr. 21, 1986	6.50
May 30, 1980	12.00	July 11, 1986	6.00
June 13, 1980	11.00	Aug. 21, 1986	5.50
July 28, 1980	10.00	Sept. 4, 1987	6.00
Sept. 26, 1980	11.00	Aug. 9, 1988	6.50
Nov. 17, 1980	12.00	Feb. 24, 1989[3]	7.00
Dec. 5, 1980	13.00		

1. Rates for short-term adjustment credit. 2. Discount rates for 1980 and 1981 do not include the surcharge applied to frequent borrowings by large institutions. The surcharge reached 3% in 1980 and 4% in 1981 and was eliminated in November 1981. 3. In effect as of Apr. 26, 1989. **Source:** Board of Governors of the Federal Reserve System, *Federal Reserve Bulletin* (monthly) and *Annual Statistical Digest.*

this, the thrifts were deregulated, released from many of the above restrictions on their activities, and allowed to pursue a more diverse market for loans. With this new freedom, however, many S&Ls took on loans that were at a higher level of risk in order to earn a higher rate of return. Some argue that the insurance on deposits provided by the Federal Home Loan Bank encouraged the S&Ls to make loans that were too risky.

Lending institutions fail mainly if a large percentage of their loans go bad and cannot be collected. And mortgage loans fail, not just because buyers cannot make their payments, but also because the collateral (the buildings) may decline in price so that it is less than the value of the loan. Especially in the Southwest, many of the loans for real estate development failed when the oil industry declined in the 1980s, taking local economies with it. By 1986 S&Ls started to collapse at an alarming rate, and the FSLIC ran out of money. The government dealt with 205 insolvent S&Ls in 1988 alone by subsidizing their sale to more secure institutions, but there are still more than 350 insolvent S&Ls, and government estimates suggest it will cost as much as $160 billion to bail them all out. Forty-seven of the nation's 100 largest insolvent S&Ls are in Texas. The largest single bailout was $1.7 billion to save the American Savings Bank of Stockton, California, the sixth-largest S&L in the country. Some estimates suggest that fraud contributed to more than one-third of these insolvent cases, suggesting that FSLIC monitoring and enforcement of regulations were hopelessly inadequate.

Financial Instruments
Money Instruments Treasury Bills are securities sold by the Treasury in denominations of $10,000 that mature at various dates, but all in less than one year. Treasury bills pay

an interest rate that is adjusted by the Treasury according to supply and demand. The Treasury bill rate is thought to be the highest risk-free rate of return among all investments.
Federal Funds or "Fed Funds" are the reserves the Fed requires depository institutions such as commercial banks to hold on deposit at their regional Federal Reserve Bank as protection against withdrawals. Banks and other depository institutions can loan reserves in excess of those required by the Fed to each other. These Fed Fund loans can provide institutions with large amounts of liquid assets on very short notice, and most loans are for no more than one day.
Commercial Paper consists of debt or promissory notes (similar to an I.O.U.) issued by corporations as a way to borrow money in the short-term, generally less than one year. Commercial paper provides an alternative, generally cheaper, way of raising money than taking a commercial bank loan. The rate of interest paid on commercial paper is higher than that on Treasury bills because of the greater risk; the risk that even large, secure companies such as IBM will default on their debts is still greater than the risk that the U.S. government will. Commercial paper is one of the most important investments made by money market accounts.
Certificates of Deposit, or "CDs" Customers who make these deposits at commercial banks or thrift institutions receive a certificate describing the maturity date of the deposit (e.g., a 5-year CD). CDs guarantee a rate of return for as long as 10 years into the future. In addition the fact that they can be purchased at local banks also makes them easy to secure. These factors make them appealing to the general public. The interest paid on CDs is set by the market and is generally the same across large institutions. However, some institutions that

are not as strong financially may have to pay a higher rate of return in order to compensate for the greater risk (although still perhaps negligible in an absolute sense) of default.
Money Market Accounts Customers pool their money into a fund that then purchases short-term debt such as Treasury bills and commercial paper in order to earn a high rate of return while maintaining liquidity (i.e., being able to convert assets quickly into cash). Customers typically can write checks on their money market accounts, which are processed through cooperating banks, but checks generally have to be in large denominations—greater than $250—to prevent customers from using them as demand deposit accounts with the high administrative costs associated with them.

Capital Instruments Stock, or Equity, the most important source of capital for firms, represents a claim on the assets or equity of a business as well as on its earnings. The owners of stock are literally the owners of the firm and vote on issues affecting it, most importantly voting to elect the directors who control the firm's management. The claims of stockholders are subordinate to the claims of bondholders. There is also a distinction between preferred stock and common stock; the claims of those holding the former must be paid first. The price of stock depends heavily on expectations about the firm's earnings. Stock prices vary with the state of the economy because the earnings prospects of firms vary depending on whether the economy is in an expansion or recession.

BOND AND STOCK YIELDS, 1970–88
(percent per year)

Type	1970	1975	1980	1985	1988
U.S. Treasury, constant maturities:[1, 2]					
3–year	7.29%	7.49%	11.55%	9.64%	8.26%
5–year	7.38	7.77	11.48	10.13	8.47
10–year	7.35	7.99	11.46	10.62	8.85
U.S. Govt., long-term bonds[2, 3]	6.58	6.98	10.81	10.75	8.98
State and local govt. bonds, Aaa[4]	6.12	6.42	7.86	8.60	7.36
State and local govt. bonds, Baa[4]	6.75	7.62	9.02	9.58	7.83
High-graded municipal bonds (Standard & Poor's)[5]	6.51	6.89	8.51	9.18	7.73[6]
Municipal (Bond Buyer, 20 bonds)	6.35	7.05	8.59	9.11	7.68
Corporate Aaa seasoned[4]	8.04	8.83	11.94	11.37	9.71
Corporate Baa seasoned[4]	9.11	10.61	13.67	12.72	10.83
Corporate Aaa utility bonds[7]	8.72	9.17	12.68	11.67	9.75
Corporate, by year to maturity:[8]					
5 years	8.10	7.70	12.80	10.40	6.80[6]
10 years	8.00	8.00	12.40	11.60	7.65[6]
20 years	7.60	8.35	12.30	12.50	8.00[6]
30 years	7.60	8.35	12.30	12.50	8.00[6]
Corporate (Moody's)[4]	8.51	9.57	12.75	12.05	10.18
Industrials (37 bonds)[9]	8.26	9.25	12.35	11.80	9.91
Railroads (13 bonds)[10]	8.77	9.39	11.48	11.94	10.03
Public utilities (40 bonds)	8.68	9.88	13.15	12.29	10.45
Stocks (Standard & Poor's):[5]					
Preferred (10 stocks)[11]	7.22	8.36	10.60	10.49	9.23
Common: Composite (500 stocks)	3.83	4.31	5.26	4.25	3.64
Industrials (400 stocks)	3.62	3.96	4.95	3.76	3.14

1. Yields on the more actively traded issues adjusted to constant maturities by the U.S. Treasury. 2. Yields are based on closing bid prices quoted by at least five dealers. 3. Averages (to maturity or call) for all outstanding bonds neither due nor callable in less than 10 years, including several very low yielding "flower" bonds. 4. **Source:** Moody's Investors Service, New York, N.Y. 5. **Source:** Standard & Poor's Corp., New York, N.Y., *Standard & Poor's Outlook* (weekly). 6. Data are for 1987. **Source:** Board of Governors of the Federal Reserve System, *Federal Reserve Bulletin* (monthly). 7. Based on first trading day of each month, deferred call, new issue estimate. **Source:** Salomon Brothers, Inc., New York, N.Y., *An Analytical Record of Yields and Yield Spreads.* 8. **Source:** Scudder, Stevens & Clark, New York, N.Y., unpublished data. 9. Covers 40 bonds for period 1970–83 and 38 bonds for 1984–86. 10. Covers 23 bonds for period 1970–81, 15 bonds for 1982, and 17 bonds for 1983. 11. Yields based on 10 stocks, 4 yields. Issues converted to a price equivalent to $100 par and a 7% annual dividend before averaging.

MONEY MARKET INTEREST RATES AND MORTGAGE RATES, 1970–88 (percent per year)

Type	1970	1975	1980	1985	1988
Federal funds, effective rate[1]	7.18%	5.82%	13.36%	8.10%	7.57%
Commercial paper, 3–month[1, 2]	N.A.	6.25	12.66	7.95	7.66
Prime rate charged by banks	7.91	7.86	15.27	9.93	9.32
Eurodollar deposits, 3–month	8.52	7.03	14.00	8.27	7.85
Finance paper, 3–month[2, 3]	7.18	6.15	11.49	7.77	7.38
Bankers acceptances, 90–day[2, 4]	7.31	6.29	12.72	7.92	7.56
Large negotiable certificates of deposit, 3–month, secondary market	7.56	6.44	13.07	8.05	7.73
Federal Reserve discount rate[5]	5.5–6.00	6.00–7.75	10.00–13.00	7.5–8.00	6.20
U.S. Government securities:[6]					
3–month Treasury bill	6.39	5.78	11.43	7.48	6.67
6–month Treasury bill	6.51	6.09	11.37	7.65	6.92
1–year Treasury bill	6.48	6.28	10.89	7.81	7.17
Prime 1–year municipals[7]	4.35	3.91	6.25	5.12	5.15
Home mortgages (HUD series):[8]					
FHA insured, secondary market[9]	9.03	9.19	13.44	12.24	10.49
Conventional, new-home[10, 11]	8.52	9.10	13.95	12.28	10.30
Conventional, existing-home[10]	8.56	9.14	13.95	12.29	10.14[12]

1. Based on daily offering rates of dealers. 2. Yields are quoted on a bank-discount basis, rather than an investment-yield basis (which would give a higher figure). 3. Placed directly; averages of daily offering rates quoted by finance companies. 4. Based on the most representative daily offering rates of dealers. Beginning Aug. 15, 1974, closing rates were used, and from Jan. 1, 1981, rates of top-rated banks only. 5. Federal Reserve Bank of New York, low and high. The discount rates for 1980 and 1981 do not include the surcharge applied to frequent borrowings by large institutions. The surcharge reached 3% in 1980 and 4% in 1981; it was eliminated in November 1981. 6. Averages based on daily closing bid yields in secondary market bank discount basis. 7. Averages based on quotation for one day each month. **Source:** Salomon Brothers, Inc., New York, *An Analytical Record of Yields and Yield Spreads.* 8. HUD = Housing and Urban Development. 9. Averages based on quotations for one day each month as compiled by the Federal Housing Administration. 10. Primary market. 11. Average contract rates on new commitments. 12. 1987 rate. **Sources:** Except as noted, Board of Directors of the Federal Reserve System, *Federal Reserve Bulletin* (monthly) and *Annual Statistical Digest.*

Unlike debt instruments that come due at a fixed point in the future, stock never comes due; it represents a permanent claim on future earnings, and that is why changes in even the most long-term prospects for a firm will affect the price of its stock.

Treasury Bonds, or notes, have longer-term dates of maturity, from one to 10 years, than do Treasury bills. They are sold by the Treasury in denominations of $1,000 and are the principal means of funding government borrowing and the national debt. The interest on these bonds is paid out regularly and is known as coupons. (Historically, owners of the bonds had to send in coupons that were then redeemed for interest payments, hence the phrase *clipping coupons*).

Other Government Securities Some agencies of the government that are involved in lending are permitted to sell securities in order to raise funds. The most important of these is the Federal National Mortgage Association—FNMA, or "Fanny Mae." It buys and sells mortgages insured by the federal government and stabilizes the market for those mortgages in the process.

Corporate Bonds are sold by corporations to dealers called underwriters and then to the public in order to raise long-term funds for investment. Corporate bonds are the alternative to issuing stock for raising funds. Bondholders are not the owners of the corporation the way stockholders are, and one advantage of issuing bonds therefore is that ownership and control over the corporation is not affected. So-called "junk bonds" are a type of corporate bond with very high risk, for example, where there is not enough collateral to back the value of the bonds.

Municipal Bonds are issued by state and local governments to raise funds generally to provide public works and other facilities. The federal government is prohibited by the Constitution from interfering in the ability of state and local governments to raise revenue, so income from municipal bonds is not subject to federal taxes. So-called revenue bonds are paid for by user fees—tolls collected on a parkway are used to pay for the bonds used to build it. General-obligation bonds are paid for through general taxes. Municipal bonds tend to be very safe, although there have been occasions on which some state and local governments have had to take extraordinary actions to avoid default—most notably, New York City in 1975, which received a federal loan and sold new bonds to its municipal employee unions in order to avoid default.

GOVERNMENT DEBT

One of the most debated economic issues in the 1980s has been the importance of the government's budget deficit, usually called the national debt. The national debt totaled over $2.7 trillion as of February 1989, with each family's proportionate share equal to $42,000, and increasing by approximately $480,000 every minute. The government raises most of its resources through taxes, but it can also raise money by borrowing or by selling bonds (e.g., treasury bonds and savings bonds)—which increasingly have been purchased by investors outside the country, who held 13% of the U.S. Treasury gross public debt in 1988. The bonds raise money now but must be repaid in the future through revenues from taxes. The budget deficit in any year indicates the difference between what the government takes in through taxes and other forms of revenues and what it expends. The deficit therefore suggests how much the government needs to borrow to fill that gap. The total amount of present and past borrowing, plus interest, constitutes the total government debt. In 1987, interest on the public debt amounted to $195.4 billion, or

19.5% of federal outlays. This is only partially offset by interest earnings received by trust funds such as the civil service retirement and disability fund, medicare, and Social Security, which brings the total of net interest paid by the federal government to $138.6 billion.

Governments routinely borrow to pay for long-term projects that will benefit the community both immediately and in the future. It can be argued that because much of the benefit from projects such as highways and other public works will be enjoyed by the next generation of taxpayers, the latter should also bear much of the cost. And they can do that by paying off the government debt (paying the premiums on government bonds) through taxes in the future. Controversy arises when the government borrows to pay for its more routine expenditures. One justification for such borrowing is that it can be used to manage business cycles in the economy; in other words, during recessions the government can borrow in order to increase expenditures and expand the economy without raising taxes, which would slow it down.

When the total amount of government debt becomes large, some economists believe that it damages the economy in the following ways. First, the fact that the government is selling large amounts of debt means that it is competing for limited investor dollars with private borrowers, driving up the cost of borrowing and making it harder for private-sector businesses to make investments for future growth. Second, the future taxes needed to pay off large amounts of government debt may place a serious drain on the future economy, again diverting resources from investment in the private sector. Politicians are concerned because debt payments must be funded from tax revenues, so they must either raise taxes or reduce government spending in other areas (e.g., in defense and entitlement programs).

The debate over debt really turns on how much is "too much." Between 1935 and 1981, the only two significant increases in the deficit occurred during World War II and certain years of the Vietnam War when deficits were about $25 billion; between 1981 and 1988, however, the Reagan administration consistently ran annual deficits of over $130 billion and increased the nation's total outstanding gross debt from just over $1 trillion to almost $2.4 trillion.

PUBLIC DEBT OF AND INTEREST PAID BY THE FEDERAL GOVERNMENT, 1940–87

	PUBLIC DEBT			INTEREST PAID	
Year	Total[1] (bils. of) dollars)	Average annual percent change[2]	Per capita[3] (dollars)	Total (bils. of) dollars)	Percent of federal outlays[4]
1940	$ 43.0	8.4%	$ 325	$ 1.0	10.5%
1945	258.7	43.0	1,849	3.8	4.1
1950	256.1	–0.1	1,688	5.7	13.4
1955	272.8	1.3	1,651	6.4	9.4
1960	284.1	0.9	1,572	9.2	10.0
1965	313.8	2.0	1,613	11.3	9.6
1970	370.1	3.3	1,814	19.3	9.9
1971	397.3	7.4	1,921	21.0	10.0
1972	426.4	7.3	2,037	21.8	9.4
1973	457.3	7.2	2,164	24.2	9.8
1974	474.2	3.7	2,223	29.3	10.9
1975	533.2	12.4	2,475	32.7	9.8
1976	620.4	16.4	2,852	37.1	10.0
1977	698.8	10.1	3,170	41.9	10.2
1978	771.5	10.4	3,463	48.7	10.6
1979	826.5	7.1	3,669	59.8	11.9
1980	907.7	9.8	3,985	74.9	12.7
1981	997.9	9.9	4,338	95.6	14.1
1982	1,142.0	14.4	4,913	117.4	15.7
1983	1,377.2	20.6	5,870	128.8	15.9
1984	1,572.3	14.2	6,640	153.8	18.1
1985	1,823.1	16.0	7,616	178.9	18.9
1986	2,125.3	16.6	8,793	187.1	18.9
1987	2,350.3	10.6	9,630	195.4	19.5

Notes: For fiscal years ending in year shown. Total public debt is restricted to borrowing by the Treasury and the value of savings bonds at current redemption value. 1. Adjusted to exclude nonmarketable issues to the International Monetary Fund and other international institutions for 1950, 1955, 1960, 1965, and 1970–74. 2. From preceding year shown; for 1940, change is from 1935. 3. For 1940–76, based on estimated July 1 population; thereafter, based on Oct. 1 resident population; prior to 1960, excludes Alaska and Hawaii. 4. Calculated on total expenditures not reduced by interfund transactions representing interest and certain other payments to Treasury through 1950. Beginning 1955, total budget outlays. **Sources:** Through U.S. fiscal 1980—U.S. Dept. of the Treasury, *Statistical Appendix to the Annual Report of the Secretary of the Treasury on the State of the Finances*; thereafter—U.S. Dept. of the Treasury, *Monthly Statement of the Public Debt of the United States* and *Final Monthly Treasury Statement of Receipts and Outlays of the U.S. Government.*

FEDERAL RECEIPTS, OUTLAYS, AND DEBT, 1977–89 (billions of dollars)

Fiscal year or period	Total receipts	Total outlays	Surplus or deficit (–)	GROSS FEDERAL DEBT (end of period) Total	Held by the public
1977	355.6	409.2	–53.6	709.1	551.8
1978	399.6	458.7	–59.2	780.4	610.9
1979	463.3	503.5	–40.2	833.8	644.6
1980	517.1	590.9	–73.8	914.3	715.1
1981	599.3	678.2	–78.9	1,003.9	794.4
1982	617.8	745.7	–127.9	1,147.0	929.4
1983	600.6	808.3	–207.8	1,381.9	1,141.8
1984	666.5	851.8	–185.3	1,576.7	1,312.6
1985	734.1	946.3	–212.3	1,827.5	1,509.9
1986	769.1	990.3	–221.2	2,120.1[1]	1,736.2[1]
1987	854.1	1,004.6	–150.4	2,345.6[1]	1,888.1[1]
1988[2]	909.2	1,064.1	–155.1	2,600.7	2,050.0
1989 (estimates)[1]	974.0	1,096.7	–122.7	2,818.2	2,138.6
Cumulative total, first 2 months:					
Fiscal year 1988	$119.3	$177.2	–$57.8	$2,404.8	$1,939.3
Fiscal year 1989	128.1	184.5	–56.5	2,658.4	2,092.1

1. Estimates from U.S. Office of Management and Budget, *Mid-Session Review of the 1989 Budget* (July 28, 1988). 2. Data from U.S. Dept. of the Treasury, *Monthly Treasury Statement*, for Sept. 1988, issued Oct. 29, 1988. **Source:** U.S. Office of Management and Budget, *Budget of the United States Government, Fiscal Year 1989* Feb. 1988, except as noted.

THE LABOR FORCE

Labor Force Participation Rate

The labor force (or Labor Force Participation Rate—LFPR) is that proportion of the population that is either employed or actively seeking employment. It represents the supply of labor available for the economy. The LFPR is lower for young people because many are in school, and also for older people because many have retired. It is highest for married men and for women who are heads of households.

Women in the Work Force One of the most important developments in the labor force has been the sharp increase in the LFPR of women, which has virtually doubled since the early 1960s. This increase can be attributed in part to changing attitudes toward appropriate roles for women as many have left traditional homemaking roles for careers in the labor force. Moreover, women are now attaining higher levels of education, are delaying childbearing, having fewer children, and returning to work sooner than ever before. Women are also branching out into occupations traditionally dominated by men (lawyers, physicians, and managers).

Women have joined the labor force at an astounding rate since 1960. A few highlights of this trend:

• In 1988, 54,742,000 women were in the U.S. civilian labor force (56.6% of all women). Of those, 29.8 million were married, 2.7 million separated, and 6.2 million divorced).

• In 1988 over half of all married women (56.5%) were either employed or actively seeking employment, compared to less than one-third (30.5%) in 1960.

• While there has been a smaller percentage increase among separated and divorced women, their LFPR in 1988 was 60.9% and 75.7%,respectively, compared with 52.1% and 71.5% in 1970 (statistics for 1960 are not available).

• Unemployment rates have dropped from 1960 to 1988 for married and divorced women. In other words, of the women who want to work, a greater percentage can successfully find employment, reflecting the increased acceptance of women's roles in the labor force.

• For married women with children under 6 years of age, the increase in labor participation during 1960-88 is even more dramatic—it more than tripled, from 18.6% to 57.1%.

• Of all married women, black women with children between the ages of 6 and 13 had the highest LFPR in 1988—81.4%.

• During the recession of 1982-83, when overall unemployment reached 9.7%, women who were separated and had children under the age of 6 were particularly hard hit, with an unemployment rate of 27.6%.

• Median weekly earnings for women working full-time (74% of all working women) was $320 per week in the fourth quarter of 1988, up 2.9% from one year earlier, but still only 70% of men's median weekly earning. Median weekly earnings for white women were $323, for black women $291, and $251 for Hispanic women.

Government Employment Of the 112.4 million people employed in 1987, civilian employees in all levels of government totaled 17.3 million, or 15.4% of the employed labor force in the nation, with a total civilian payroll of $32.4 billion. The inclusion of military personnel (1.4 million) raises total government employment to 18.7 million.

Unemployment Rate One of the most closely watched labor force statistics is the unemployment rate, which was 5.5% in 1988. Contrary to popular opinion, the unemployment rate is only an indirect measure of the people without jobs. In fact, the unemployment rate measures, as a proportion of the total labor force, those people without jobs who are actively seeking employment (within the last four weeks). So the unemployment rate may rise as new job seekers enter the labor force; every spring, for example, it rises slightly as school graduates enter the labor force and look for jobs. It may also fall as workers retire or otherwise leave the labor force. Further, when the economy is in a prolonged recession, the unemployment rate may actually drop slightly simply because some of the job seekers may give up trying to find a job and withdraw from the labor force.

The unemployment rate over time for the United States is a measure associated with identifying periods of expansion and recession. It reached a peak of 9.6% during the 1982–83 recession. The relatively high periods of unemployment beginning in the mid-1970s are in part due to the expansion of the labor force as the "baby boom" generation left school and began looking for work.

Hispanics One of the most interesting developments in the U.S. labor force is the rise of Hispanic workers. They are the fastest-growing population group in the labor force, in large part due to immigration, with Mexicans making up the largest share. By the year 2000, the number of Hispanic workers in the labor force will rise by 75%, and they will account for 10% of the total labor force. Most of this projected increase can be attributed to the rise in the proportion of Hispanic women working (historically, these women were more likely to stay at home). Overall, however, Hispanic workers earn only 75% as much as the average for all workers. They also have significantly higher unemployment rates: as of March 1988, it was 8.5%, which, while much lower than in recent years, was still higher than the 5.8% for the non-Hispanic population.

CIVILIAN EMPLOYMENT IN OCCUPATIONS WITH THE LARGEST JOB GROWTH AND IN THE FASTEST-GROWING AND FASTEST-DECLINING OCCUPATIONS, 1986 AND 2000

Occupation[1]	EMPLOYMENT (thousands) 1986	2000[2]	PERCENT CHANGE 1986–2000
Total[3]	111,623	137,533	19%
LARGEST JOB GROWTH[4]			
Salespersons, retail	3,579	4,780	34
Waiters and waitresses	1,702	2,454	44
Registered nurses	1,406	2,018	44
Janitors and cleaners[5]	2,676	3,280	23
General managers and top executives	2,383	2,965	24
Cashiers	2,165	2,740	27
Truck drivers, light and heavy	2,211	2,736	24
General office clerks	2,361	2,824	20
Food counter, fountain, and related workers	1,500	1,949	30
Nursing aides, orderlies, and attendants	1,224	1,658	35
Secretaries	3,234	3,658	13
Guards	794	1,177	48
Accountants and auditors	945	1,322	40
Computer programmers	479	813	70
Food preparation workers	949	1,273	34
Teachers, kindergarten and elementary	1,527	1,826	20
Receptionists and information clerks	682	964	41
Computer systems analysts, EDP	331	582	76
Cooks, restaurant	520	759	46
Licensed practical nurses	631	869	38
Gardeners and groundskeepers, except farm	767	1,005	31
Maintenance repairers, general utility	1,039	1,270	22
Stock clerks, sales floor	1,087	1,312	21
First-line supervisors and managers	956	1,161	21
Dining room and cafeteria attendants, bar-room helpers	433	631	46
Electrical and electronics engineers	401	592	48
Lawyers	527	718	36
Cooks, short order and fast food	591	775	31
Carpenters	1,010	1,192	18
Bartenders	396	553	40
Financial managers	638	792	24
Food service and lodging managers	509	663	30
Teachers, secondary schools	1,128	1,280	13
Electrical and electronic technicians, technologists	313	459	46
Real estate sales agents	313	451	44

Occupation[1]	EMPLOYMENT (thousands) 1986	2000[2]	PERCENT CHANGE 1986–2000
Computer operators, except peripheral equipment	263	387	47
Social workers	365	485	33
Medical assistants	132	251	90
Marketing, advertising, public relations managers	323	427	32
Legal assistants, tech., except clerical	170	272	60
FASTEST-GROWING			
Medical assistants	132	251	90%
Home health aides	138	249	80
Computer systems analysts, EDP	331	582	76
Computer programmers	479	813	70
Radiologic technologists and technicians	115	190	65
Legal assistants and technicians, except clerical	170	272	60
Dental assistants	155	244	57
Guards	794	1,177	48
Electrical and electronics engineers	401	592	48
Computer operators, except peripheral equipment	263	387	47
Restaurant cooks	520	759	46
Dining room and cafeteria attendants, bar-room helpers	433	631	46
FASTEST-DECLINING			
Electrical and electronic assemblers	249	116	–54%
Industrial truck and tractor operators	426	283	–34
Stenographers	178	128	–28
Farmers	1,182	850	–28
Textile draw-out and winding machine operators[6]	219	164	–25
Farm workers	940	750	–20
Data entry keyers, except composers	400	334	–16
Typists and word processors	1,002	862	–14
Sewing machine operators, garment	633	541	–14
Welding machine setters, operators, tenders	126	112	–12
Child care workers, private household	400	362	–10
TV and cable TV installers and repairers	119	108	–9

1. For occupations employing 100,000 or more in 1986. Includes wage and salary jobs, self-employed, and unpaid family members.   2. Based on moderate-trend assumptions.   3. Includes other occupations, not shown separately.   4. Based on absolute employment change 1986–2000.   5. Includes maids and housekeepers.   6. Includes tenders.   **Source:** U.S. Bureau of Labor Statistics, *Monthly Labor Review* (Sept. 1987).

Productivity measures how much output an economy or organization can generate from a given amount of inputs. Higher levels of productivity suggest greater efficiency—doing more with the same amount of resources, just as an efficient or economical car goes farther on a gallon of gasoline. Increases in productivity, as the result of better tools or improved methods, provide the main mechanism for increasing output in an economy and ultimately for raising standards of living. Productivity is usually measured in terms of labor—output per worker or per hour of labor—not only because labor is the most important resource but also because it is one of the easiest to measure.

Wages vary not only among the different professions but also between sexes and regions of the country. For example, women in year-round full-time executive, administrative, and managerial positions, have a median yearly income of only 61% of the median income for men in the same occupation group. This percentage is higher in the field of laborers, precision production, craft, and repair; but for all major occupation groups reported by the U.S. Bureau of the Census, women receive only a fraction of that received by their male counterparts. This may be due, in part, to the fact that women enter and leave the work force more times throughout their lives than do men and spend a smaller percentage of their lives economically active.

Another factor influencing the discrepancy between men's and women's wages is the concentration of women in occupations that pay less. In 1985, 70% of all women were employed in occupations in which 75% of employees were women. Five of the top 10 occupations employing women were in sales and clerical work and those of bookkeeper, cashier, and social worker. The next two most popular were those of registered nurse and elementary school teacher.

Minimum wage in the nation was first enacted by the state of Massachusetts in 1912, covered only women, and was designed to shorten hours and raise pay in the covered industries. Nationwide a minimum wage was established during the Great Depression, but the amount varied among industries, usually around $0.35 per hour. While it has risen steadily over the decades, in recent years inflation has made the $3.35 per hour currently in effect worth less than the previous minimum wage. Congress and the president continue to try to reach a compromise between $4.25 and $4.55 per hour.

Unions A labor union is an organization of workers who engage in collective bargaining with employers for higher wages, better working conditions, and increased benefits. In the United States, unions are organized at three levels: (1) labor federations or voluntary associations of national unions, which settle disputes between national unions, lobby for favorable labor legislation, and engage in public relations. There is only one labor foundation in the country—the American Federation of Labor and Congress of Industrial Organizations, or AFL-CIO—to which virtually all union members belong; (2) national unions, which coordinate agreements across local unions and conduct collective bargaining negotiations with industry employers; and (3) local unions, which administer labor contracts, serving individual members, employers, and in some cases, establishments directly. There are two kinds of unions in the country: (1) industrial unions, representing workers of a particular firm or industry, such as auto workers and steel workers, and (2) craft unions, representing employees with a specific skill, such as pilots and musicians.

Many workers choose not to unionize because of the potential costs involved in membership, such as dues, lost pay during strikes, and possible retribution by employers. Union membership in the nation declined between 1983 and 1987 by just under one million members (17.7 million to 16.9 million). In 1987, 17% of the total labor force and 36% of government employees belonged to unions. This is down from a peak of around 25.4% of the total labor force in 1954. Notable examples of membership decline are that of steelworkers, which fell by 53% during 1977–87, and that of musicians, which fell by 72% over the same period. Virtually all of these losses are due to the loss of jobs in unionized firms. A number of factors may have contributed to this decline, such as changes in technology that displace workers, as in the music industry, and increased factor costs and international competition that make production less economically feasible, as in the steel industry.

Working Hours Average weekly hours worked differ between industries, with the highest average in the petroleum and coal products and mining industries (44.4 hours and 43.6 hours, respectively) and the lowest average in the service-providing industries (32.6 hours). The Fair Labor Standards Act (FLSA) of 1938 specifies that nonsupervisory or "non-exempt" (i.e., not exempt from the FLSA) employees receive overtime pay at the rate of 1.5 times their hourly rate of pay for all hours over 40 worked. The overtime provisions of the FLSA were designed to make it costly for em-

AVERAGE HOURLY AND WEEKLY EARNINGS IN CURRENT AND CONSTANT (1977) DOLLARS, BY PRIVATE INDUSTRY GROUP, 1970–87

Although it is true that average hourly and weekly nominal wages (in current dollars) have risen over the past two decades—by 178% and 162%, respectively—when inflation is accounted for, real weekly earnings (in constant dollars) have actually fallen an average of 9.6% since 1970. Paychecks may be getting bigger, but a 1987 paycheck doesn't go as far as a 1970 paycheck in covering living expenses.

Private industry group	CURRENT DOLLARS					CONSTANT (1977) DOLLARS				
	1970	1975	1980	1985	1987	1970	1975	1980	1985	1987
Average hourly earnings	$3.23	$4.53	$6.66	$ 8.57	$ 8.98	$5.04	$5.10	$4.89	$4.88	$4.86
Manufacturing	3.35	4.83	7.27	9.54	9.91	5.23	5.44	5.34	5.44	5.37
Mining	3.85	5.95	9.17	11.98	12.52	6.01	6.70	6.74	6.83	6.78
Construction	5.24	7.31	9.94	12.32	12.69	8.17	8.23	7.30	7.02	6.87
Transportation, public utilities	3.85	5.88	8.87	11.40	12.03	6.01	6.62	6.52	6.50	6.52
Wholesale trade	3.44	4.73	6.96	9.16	9.59	5.37	5.33	5.11	5.22	5.20
Retail trade	2.44	3.36	4.88	5.94	6.11	3.81	3.78	3.59	3.38	3.31
Finance, insurance, real estate	3.07	4.06	5.79	7.94	8.73	4.79	4.57	4.25	4.52	4.73
Services	2.81	4.02	5.85	7.90	8.48	4.38	4.53	4.30	4.50	4.59
Average weekly earnings	$120	$164	$235	$299	$313	$187	$184	$173	$170	$169
Manufacturing	133	191	289	386	406	208	215	212	220	220
Mining	164	249	397	520	531	256	280	292	296	288
Construction	195	266	368	464	480	304	300	270	265	260
Transportation, public utilities	156	233	351	450	472	243	262	258	257	255
Wholesale trade	137	183	267	352	365	214	206	197	200	198
Retail trade	82	109	147	175	178	128	123	108	100	97
Finance, insurance, real estate	113	148	210	289	317	176	167	154	165	172
Services	97	135	191	257	276	151	152	140	146	149

Source: U.S. Bureau of Labor Statistics, *Employment and Earnings* (monthly).

EFFECTIVE FEDERAL MINIMUM HOURLY WAGE RATES, 1950–88

In effect	Minimum rates for nonfarm workers	Percent of avg. earnings[1]	Minimum rates for farm workers[2]
1950	$0.75	54%	N.A.
1956	1.00	52	N.A.
1961	1.15	50	N.A.
1963	1.25	51	N.A.
1967	1.40	50	$1.00
1968	1.60	54	1.15
1974	2.00	46	1.60
1975	2.10	45	1.80
1976	2.30	46	2.00
1978	2.65	44	2.65
1979	2.90	45	2.90
1980	3.10	44	3.10
1981	3.35	43	3.35
1988	3.35[3]	33	3.35[3]

Note: N.A. = not applicable.   1. Percent of gross average hourly earnings of production workers in manufacturing.   2. Not included until 1966.   3. In effect July 27, 1989.
Source: U.S. Dept. of Labor.

PROPORTION OF FEMALE WORKERS IN SELECTED OCCUPATIONS, 1975 AND 1985

Occupation	Women as % of total employed within an occupation 1975	1985
Airline pilot	–	2.6%
Auto mechanic	0.5%	11.3
Bartender	35.2	47.9
Bus driver	37.7	49.2
Cab driver, chauffeur	8.7	10.9
Carpenter	0.6	1.2
Child care worker	98.4	96.1
Computer programmer	25.6	34.3
Computer systems analyst	14.8	28.0
Data entry keyer	92.8	90.7
Data-processing equipment repairer	1.8	10.4
Dental assistant	100.0	99.0
Dentist	1.8	6.5
Economist	13.1	34.5
Editor, reporter	44.6	51.7
Garage gas station attendant	4.7	6.8
Lawyer, judge	7.1	18.2
Librarian	81.1	87.0
Mail carrier	8.7	17.2
Office machine repairer	1.7	5.7
Physician	13.0	17.2
Registered nurse	97.0	95.1
Social worker	60.8	66.7
Teacher, college/university	31.1	35.2
Teacher, elementary school	85.4	84.0
Telephone installer/repairer	4.8	12.8
Telephone operator	93.3	88.8
Waiter/waitress	91.1	84.0
Welder	4.4	4.8

Source: U.S. Dept. of Labor, Bureau of Labor Statistics, *Employment and Earnings* (monthly).

EMPLOYMENT STATUS OF THE POPULATION BY RACE AND HISPANIC ORIGIN, 1975–87 (numbers in thousands)

Year, race and Hispanic origin	Civilian noninstitutional population[1]	CIVILIAN LABOR FORCE Total	Percent of population	Number employed	Employment/ population ratio[2]	Percent unemployed
WHITE:						
1975	134,790	82,831	61.5%	76,411	56.7%	7.8%
1980	146,122	93,600	64.1	87,715	60.0	6.3
1983	150,805	97,021	64.3	88,893	58.9	8.4
1985	153,679	99,926	65.0	93,736	61.0	6.2
1987	156,958	103,290	65.8	97,789	62.3	5.3
BLACK:						
1975	15,751	9,263	58.8%	7,894	50.1%	14.8%
1980	17,824	10,865	61.0	9,313	52.2	14.3
1983	18,925	11,647	61.5	9,375	49.5	19.5
1985	19,664	12,364	62.9	10,501	53.4	15.1
1987	20,352	12,993	63.8	11,309	55.6	13.0
HISPANIC:[3]						
1975	N.A.	N.A.	N.A.	N.A.	N.A.	N.A.
1980	9,598	6,146	64.0%	5,527	57.6%	10.1%
1983	11,029	7,033	63.8	6,072	55.1	13.7
1985	11,915	7,698	64.6	6,888	57.8	10.5
1987	12,867	8,541	66.4	7,790	60.5	8.8

1. Age 16 and over.   2. Civilians employed as a percentage of the civilian noninstitutional population.   3. Hispanic persons may be of any race.
Source: U.S. Bureau of Labor Statistics, *Employment and Earnings* (monthly).

EMPLOYMENT STATUS OF THE POPULATION BY SEX, 1960–87 (numbers in thousands)

Year and sex	Civilian noninstitutional population[1]	CIVILIAN LABOR FORCE Total	Percent of population	Number employed	Employment/ population ratio[2]	Percent unemployed
TOTAL						
1960	117,245	69,628	59.4%	65,778	56.1%	5.5%
1965	126,513	74,455	58.9	71,088	56.2	4.5
1970	137,085	82,771	60.4	78,678	57.4	4.9
1975	153,153	93,775	61.2	85,846	56.1	8.5
1980	167,745	106,940	63.8	99,303	59.2	7.1
1985	178,206	115,461	64.8	107,150	60.1	7.2
1987	182,753	119,865	65.6	112,440	61.5	6.2
MALE						
1960	55,662	46,388	83.3%	43,904	78.9%	5.4%
1965	59,782	48,255	80.7	46,340	77.5	4.0
1970	64,304	51,228	79.7	48,990	76.2	4.4
1975	72,291	56,299	77.9	51,857	71.7	7.9
1980	79,398	61,453	77.4	57,186	72.0	6.9
1985	84,469	64,411	76.3	59,891	70.9	7.0
1987	86,899	66,207	76.2	62,107	71.5	6.2
FEMALE						
1960	61,582	23,240	37.7%	21,874	35.5%	5.9%
1965	66,731	26,200	39.3	24,748	37.1	5.5
1970	72,782	31,543	43.3	29,688	40.8	5.9
1975	80,860	37,475	46.3	33,989	42.0	9.3
1980	88,348	45,487	51.5	42,117	47.7	7.4
1985	93,736	51,050	54.5	47,259	50.4	7.4
1987	95,853	53,658	56.0	50,334	52.5	6.2

1. Age 16 and over.   2. Civilians employed as a percentage of the civilian noninstitutional population.
Source: U.S. Bureau of Labor Statistics, *Employment and Earnings* (monthly).

ployers to use overtime, not only to prevent a burdensome lengthening of the work week but also to encourage them to hire additional workers as opposed to working their current employees longer hours.

Of the current work force, 11.6% routinely work overtime hours, and the average amount of overtime hours per week is nine. Men work more overtime than women, perhaps because women have more commitments in the home, and middle-age workers work the most overtime, in part because they have the greatest family responsibilities, requiring more income.

Surveys of the work force suggest that 65% are happy with the amount of hours they work, while 27% would like to work additional hours in order to make more money. Younger workers tend to want more hours and money, while women tend to want less, possibly because of family, social, or other commitments. Among occupational groups, managers appear most content with the length of their work schedule.

Work Schedules Of all employees 25% work on Saturday, and 12.5% on Sunday; 12% have some flextime—some freedom in selecting the time to begin and to end the workday, subject to an overall weekly hours requirement. Contrary to popular belief, relatively few employees actually work 9 a.m.–5 p.m. schedules (8.4%). The most common workday is from 8–5 (22%), with roughly 10% working 7–4 or 8–4 shifts.

Absenteeism Of the full-time, nonagricultural workforce, 4.7% are absent from work at any given time, and a little more than half of absences (2.6%) is due to illness or injury. Absenteeism tends to be highest in service industries, especially education, and tends to be higher for women with children. Women with younger children have greater absenteeism, presumably because the children are sick more often. Women raising families by themselves have higher rates of absenteeism the more children they have, but additional children do not increase absenteeism where husbands are present; in fact, absenteeism actually falls somewhat with

more children. Perhaps by the time the second child arrives, parents have developed better arrangements for managing the problems of their children. There is some anecdotal evidence that absenteeism is rising for men with children as they are more likely than in the past to stay home with sick children.

Moonlighting More than 5% of all employees work more than one job, and this figure has been rising in recent years. It is highest for married men, who presumably have family commitments requiring additional income. Most

moonlighters are working to help pay their regular living expenses (32%), while only 13% do so to build up savings for the future.

Working at Home Eighteen million people report working in their homes for paid employment, but half of them work less than eight hours per week with the average being 11 hours. More than half of these workers are men, and one-fifth are over age 55 (a group rep-

WORK STOPPAGES, 1960–87

Year	No. of work stoppages[1]	Workers involved[2] (thousands)	DAYS IDLE No. [3] (thousands)	Percent estimated working time[4]
1960	222	896	13,260	0.09%
1965	268	999	15,140	0.10
1970	381	2,468	52,761	0.29
1975	235	965	17,563	0.09
1980	187	795	20,844	0.09
1985	54	324	7,079	0.03
1987	46	174	4,468	0.02

Note: Excludes work stoppages involving fewer than 1,000 workers and lasting less than one day. 1. Beginning in the year indicated. 2. Workers are counted more than once if involved in more than one stoppage during the year. 3. Resulting from all stoppages in effect in a year, including those that began in an earlier year. 4. Agricultural and government employees are included in the total working time; private household, forestry, and fishery employees are excluded. **Source:** U.S. Bureau of Labor Statistics, *Current Wage Developments* (monthly).

METROPOLITAN AREAS WITH HIGHEST JOB-GROWTH, 1985–2010
(in thousands)

Rank	Metropolitan statistical area	Number of jobs 1985	2010	Change in employment 1985–2010
1.	Los Angeles–Long Beach, Calif.	4,562	5,961	1,399
2.	Washington, D.C.-Md.-Va.	2,270	3,416	1,146
3.	Anaheim–Santa Ana, Calif.	1,231	2,209	978
4.	Houston, Tex.	1,743	2,700	957
5.	Atlanta, Ga.	1,505	2,367	862
6.	Philadelphia, Pa.	2,406	3,263	857
7.	Dallas, Tex.	1,533	2,383	850
8.	Boston-Lawrence-Salem-Lowell-Brockton, Mass.	2,357	3,171	814
9.	Chicago, Ill.	3,382	4,170	788
10.	New York, N.Y.	4,543	5,263	720
11.	Phoenix, Ariz.	991	1,672	681
12.	San Diego, Calif.	1,130	1,780	650
13.	Minneapolis–St. Paul, Minn.	1,394	1,969	575
14.	Denver, Colo.	1,000	1,566	566
15.	Nassau-Suffolk, N.Y.	1,293	1,845	552
16.	Tampa–St. Petersburg, Clearwater, Fla.	893	1,415	522
17.	San Jose, Calif.	928	1,430	502
18.	San Francisco, Calif.	1,131	1,597	466
19.	Baltimore, Md.	1,247	1,712	465
20.	Seattle, Wash.	1,014	1,479	465
21.	Oakland, Calif.	959	1,393	434
22.	Detroit, Mich.	1,963	2,397	434
23.	Miami-Hialeah, Fla.	957	1,369	413
24.	Fort Lauderdale, Hollywood, Pompano Beach, Fla.	535	948	412
25.	Orlando, Fla.	498	907	409
26.	St. Louis, Mo.-Ill.	1,292	1,672	380
27.	Sacramento, Calif.	629	1,005	376
28.	Riverside–San Bernadino, Calif.	707	1,065	358
29.	Columbus, Ohio	715	1,044	329
30.	West Palm Beach–Boca Raton–Delray Beach, Fla.	379	673	294
31.	Norfolk–Virginia Beach–Newport News, Va.	723	1,014	291
32.	Middlesex-Somerset-Hunterdon, N.J.	534	822	288
33.	San Antonio, Tex.	614	898	284
34.	Fort Worth–Arlington, Tex.	607	891	284
35.	Kansas City, Mo.	840	1,116	276
36.	Salt Lake City–Ogden, Utah	515	786	271
37.	Austin, Tex.	431	698	267
38.	Newark, N.J.	1,056	1,309	253
39.	Portland, Oreg.	638	889	251

Source: National Planning Association, 1987.

U.S. MEMBERSHIP IN AFL-CIO–AFFILIATED UNIONS, BY SELECTED UNION, 1975–87
(thousands of workers)

Labor organization	1975	1985	1987
Total[1]	14,070	11,250	12,692
Automobile, Aerospace and Agriculture (UAW)	N.A.	974	998
Bakery, Confectionery and Tobacco[2]	149	115	109
Boiler Makers, Iron Shipbuilders[2]	123	110	90
Bricklayers	143	95	84
Carpenters[2]	712	609	609
Clothing and Textile Workers (ACTWU)[2]	377	228	195
Communications Workers (CWA)	476	524	515
Electrical Workers (IBEW)	856	791	765
Electronic, Electrical, and Technical[2]	255	198	185
Operating Engineers	300	330	330
Firefighters	123	142	142
Food and Commercial Workers (UFCW)[2]	1,150	989	1,000
Garment Workers (ILGWU)	363	210	173
Government, American Federation (AFGE)	255	199	157
Graphic Communications[2]	198	141	136
Hotel Employees and Restaurant Employees	421	327	293
Ironworkers	160	140	122
Laborers	475	383	371
Letter Carriers (NALC)	151	186	200
Machinists and Aerospace (IAM)	780	520	509
Musicians	215	67	60
Oil, Chemical, Atomic Workers (OCAW)	145	108	96
Painters	160	133	128
Paperworkers International	275	232	221
Plumbing and Pipefitting	228	226	220
Postal Workers	249	232	230
Retail, Wholesale, Department Store[2]	120	106	140
Rubber, Cork, Linoleum, Plastic	173	106	97
Service Employees (SEIU)	490	688	762
State, County, Municipal (AFSCME)	647	997	1,032
Steelworkers	1,062	572	494
Teachers (AFT)	396	470	499
Transport Workers	95	85	85

Notes: N.A. = not applicable. Figures represent the labor organizations as constituted in 1987 and reflect past merger activity. Membership figures are based on average per capita paid membership to the AFL-CIO for the two-year period ending in June of the year shown and reflect only actively employed members. 1. Includes other AFL-CIO affiliated unions, not shown separately. 2. Figures reflect mergers with one or more unions since 1975. For details, see source. **Source:** American Federation of Labor and Congress of Industrial Organizations, *Report of the AFL-CIO Executive Council* (annual).

resenting only 12.5% of the population). It is no surprise that most of this work is in service occupations.

Temporary Workers Just under 700,000 people work for firms that provide temporary help to employers. Two-thirds of these are women, many are under age 24, and 40% work only part-time. Half of all the jobs are in technical, sales, and support positions.

Tenure We tend to think of occupations as being lifetime careers, but in fact most people change occupations several times in their working lifetime. The average tenure in occupations is only 6.6 years. Barbers have the highest tenure—most barbers have been in that field for almost 25 years—while waiters/food counter workers have the lowest tenure, averaging just 1.6 years. Surprisingly, occupational tenure is highest for workers with only elementary education, perhaps reflecting their limited alternatives, and for those with graduate education, no doubt associated with professional occupations such as medicine and law.

Benefits Employee benefits are the non-wage aspects of compensation. The cost of the benefit package for most employees is just under one-third of the value of their wages. The cost of benefits has risen substantially in recent decades largely because new benefits have been added to the compensation. One reason for the expansion of benefit packages is that employees have not paid income tax on the value of their benefits, creating an incentive to shift more of compensation to benefits.

Programs required by law such as worker's compensation insurance and unemployment insurance make up 30% of benefit costs. Another 25% is associated with vacations and other forms of paid leave. Medical insurance accounts for 20%, pensions for 13%, and various forms of pay supplements contribute 8% to the total benefit package.

THE NOBEL PRIZE IN ECONOMIC SCIENCES

1969 Ragnar Frisch (Norway) Oslo Univ., and **Jan Tinbergen** (Netherlands) The Netherlands School of Economics "for having developed and applied dynamic models for the analysis of economic processes."

1970 Paul A. Samuelson (U.S.) M.I.T. "for the scientific work through which he has developed static and dynamic economic theory and actively contributed to raising the level of analysis in economic science."

1971 Simon Kuznets (U.S.) Harvard Univ. "for his empirically founded interpretation of economic growth which has led to new and deepened insight into the economic and social structure and process of development."

1972 Sir John R. Hicks (Great Britain) All Souls College, and **Kenneth J. Arrow** (U.S.) Harvard Univ. "for their pioneering contributions to general economic equilibrium theory and welfare theory."

1973 Wassily Leontief (U.S.) Harvard Univ. "for the development of the input-output method and for its application to important economic problems."

1974 Gunnar Myrdal (Sweden), **Friedrich A. von Hayek** (Great Britain) (no univ. listed) "for their pioneering work in the theory of money and economic fluctuations and for their penetrating analysis of the interdependence of economic, social and institutional phenomena."

1975 Leonid Kantorovich (USSR) Academy of Sciences, and **Tjalling C. Koopmans** (U.S.) Yale Univ. "for their contributions to the theory of optimum allocation of resources."

1976 Milton Friedman (U.S.) Univ. of Chicago "for his achievements in the fields of consumption analysis, monetary history and theory and for his demonstration of the complexity of stabilization policy."

1977 Bertil Ohlin (Sweden) Stockholm School of Economics, and **James E. Meade** (Great Britain) Cambridge Univ. "for their pathbreaking contribution to the theory of international trade and international capital movements."

1978 Herbert A. Simon (U.S.) Carnegie-Mellon Univ. "for his pioneering research into the decision-making process within economic organizations."

1979 Theodore W. Schultz (U.S.) Univ. of Chicago, and **Sir Arthur Lewis** (Great Britain) (Princeton, N.J.) "for their pioneering research into economic development research with particular consideration of the problems of developing countries."

1980 Lawrence R. Klein (U.S.) Univ. of Pennsylvania "for the creation of economic models and their application to the analysis of economic fluctuations and economic policies."

1981 James Tobin (U.S.) Yale Univ. "for his analysis of financial markets and their relations to expenditure decisions, employment, production and prices."

1982 George J. Stigler (U.S.) Univ. of Chicago "for his seminal studies of industrial structures, functioning of markets and causes and effects of public regulation."

1983 Gerard Debreu (U.S.) University of California, Berkeley "for having incorporated new analytical methods into economic theory and for his rigorous reformulation of the theory of general equilibrium."

1984 Sir Richard Stone (Great Britain) Univ. of Cambridge "for having made fundamental contributions to the development of systems of national accounts and hence greatly improved [sic] the basis for empirical economic analysis."

1985 Franco Modigliani (U.S.) M.I.T. "for his pioneering analyses of saving and of financial markets."

1986 James M. Buchanan, Jr. (U.S.) Center for Study of Public Choice "for his development of the contractual and constitutional bases for the theory of economic and political decision-making."

1987 Robert M. Solow (U.S.) M.I.T. "for his contributions to the theory of economic growth."

1988 Maurice Allais (France) Centre d'analyse économique "for his pioneering contributions to the theory of markets and efficient utilization of resources."

Note: The Economic Sciences prize was instituted by the Sveriges Riksbank (Bank of Sweden) in 1968, when it placed an annual amount of money at the disposal of the Nobel Foundation for the economic science award. **Sources:** *Nobel Foundation Directory 1987–88*; Mission of Sweden.

U.S. BUSINESS

The Office of Management and Budget (OMB) classifies the entire national economy into industries, based on principal product or activity. There are nine industrial divisions, which are further classified into groups and subgroups. For example, under "manufacturing" would fall "Food and kindred products," and beneath that, "meat-packing plants." The nine industrial divisions listed in the OMB's Standard Industry Classification (SIC) are agriculture, forestry, and fishing; mining; construction; manufacturing; transportation and public utilities; finance, insurance, and real estate; wholesale trade; retail trade; and services. In 1986, 5.8 million companies employed 83.4 million workers, with payrolls totaling $1.6 trillion.

BIG BUSINESS: THE *FORTUNE* 500

The goal of almost all new companies is to one day make it onto *Fortune* magazine's annual list of the largest corporations in the United States.

Industrial America had its best year ever in 1988. Sales of *Fortune* 500 industrials rose 7.6%, breaking the $2 trillion level for the first time. Topping the list once again was General Motors, with sales of $121 billion. Profits of the Industrial 500 jumped 27% to a record $115 billion. Profits adjusted for inflation were also the highest ever, making 1988 the most prosperous year for the 500 since the list was first published in 1955. *Fortune* breaks down its list into 27 industry subgroups, and the earnings of nearly all of them grew in double digits in 1988. The metals industry led the way in 1988, posting a 110% increase in earnings thanks to large increases in the price of copper and the rebound of America's steel industry.

Companies on the Service 500 also had a record year in 1988; profits were $73.8 billion, up 55% over 1987. (This figure does not include life insurance companies, whose profits are not comparable with those of other companies.) The huge increase in profits by commercial banks led to most of this gain, however. In 1987, when huge debts to Third World nations had to be written off, 26 of the top 100 banks lost money, and the industry as a whole was $5.3 billion in the red. In 1988 profits were a record $17.5 billion, and only three banks lost money. Transportation companies also did very well in 1988, with profits up 50%.

The *Fortune* Service 500 is composed of eight different lists: the 100 largest diversified service companies; the 100 largest banks; the 50 largest savings institutions; the 50 largest financial services companies; the 50 largest retailers; the 50 largest insurers; the 50 largest utilities; and the 50 largest transporta-

tion companies. They are ranked according to sales or assets depending on the industry.

Heading the list of diversified service companies was AT&T with sales of $35.2 billion in 1988. Number 8 on the Industrial 500 in 1987, AT&T made more money in 1988 from its phone services than from manufacturing computers and telecommunications equipment and rejoined the Service 500 for the first time since its break-up in 1984. United Parcel Service led the way in transportation, packing up revenues of $11.0 billion.

Sears, Roebuck was the easy winner in the retailing business with sales of $50.2 billion. America's largest insurer in 1988 was Prudential of America, with assets of $116.2 billion. The largest savings institution in the U.S. in 1988 was H.F. Ahmanson of Los Angeles, which held assets of $40.3 billion. The largest American bank was New York's Citicorp with assets of $207.7 billion. American Express was the leading provider of financial services and held assets of $142.7 billion.

THE TOP *FORTUNE* 500, BY INDUSTRY AND SALES, 1988 (company overall *Fortune* 500 rank)

AEROSPACE
1. United Technologies (16)
2. Boeing (19)
3. McDonnell Douglas (25)
4. Rockwell International (28)
5. Allied Signal (29)
6. Lockheed (33)
7. General Dynamics (41)
8. Textron (61)
9. Northrop (75)
10. Martin Marietta (77)

APPAREL
1. VF (170)
2. Liz Claiborne (299)
3. Hartmarx (304)
4. Fruit of the Loom (333)
5. Kellwood (404)
6. Leslie Fay (409)
7. Warnaco (420)
8. Oxford Industries (456)
9. Phillips-Van Heusen (463)

BEVERAGES
1. Pepsico (26)
2. Anheuser-Busch (46)
3. Coca-Cola (49)
4. Coca-Cola Enterprises (121)
5. Seagram (191)
6. Coors (249)
7. Brown-Forman (320)
8. Dr. Pepper/Seven-Up (491)

BUILDING MATERIALS
1. American Standard (123)
2. Owens-Illinois (129)
3. Owens-Corning Fiber (151)
4. USG (152)
5. Hillsborough (171)
6. Manville (190)
7. Corning Glass Works (198)
8. Nortex (259)
9. Norton (264)
10. Lafarge (279)

CHEMICALS
1. Du Pont (9)
2. Dow Chemical (21)
3. Union Carbide (50)
4. Monsanto (51)
5. Hanson Ind. NA (67)
6. W.R. Grace (69)
7. Hoechst Celanese (78)
8. PPG Industries (79)
9. BASF (93)
10. Bayer USA (99)

COMPUTERS
(includes office equipment)
1. IBM (4)
2. Digital Equipment (30)
3. Unisys (38)
4. Hewlett-Packard (39)
5. NCR (72)
6. Apple Computer (114)
7. Control Data (125)
8. Wang Laboratories (145)
9. Zenith Electronics (159)
10. Pitney Bowes (162)

ELECTRONICS
1. General Electric (5)
2. Westinghouse Electric (27)
3. Motorola (52)
4. Raytheon (53)
5. Honeywell (60)
6. TRW (62)
7. Emerson Electric (66)
8. Texas Instruments (68)
9. North American Philips (84)
10. Whirlpool (104)

FOOD
1. Occidental Petroleum (14)
2. RJR Nabisco (20)
3. Sara Lee (36)
4. Conagra (44)
5. Beatrice (57)
6. Borden (59)
7. Archer Daniels (65)
8. Pillsbury (70)
9. Ralston Purina (71)
10. General Mills (76)

FOREST PRODUCTS
1. Weyerhaeuser (37)
2. International Paper (42)
3. Georgia-Pacific (43)
4. Kimberly-Clark (85)
5. Champion International (91)
6. James River (92)
7. Scott Paper (98)
8. Mead (103)
9. Boise Cascade (112)

FURNITURE
1. Interco (133)
2. Masco (175)
3. Leggett & Platt (371)
4. Mohasco (373)
5. Miller (Herman) (398)
6. Ohio Mattress (417)
7. Hon Industries (459)
8. Kimball International (481)

INDUSTRIAL AND FARM EQUIPMENT
1. Tenneco (24)
2. Caterpillar (35)
3. Deere (87)
4. Dresser Industries (118)
5. Cummins Engine (135)
6. Ingersoll-Rand (146)
7. Baker Hughes (184)
8. Black & Decker (187)
9. Parker Hannifin (189)
10. Dover (208)

JEWELRY, SILVERWARE
1. Jostens (450)

METAL PRODUCTS
1. Triangle Industries (111)
2. Gillette (128)
3. Combustion Engineering (131)
4. Emhart (155)
5. Illinois Tool Works (213)
6. Stanley Works (215)
7. Crown Cork & Seal (221)
8. Harsco (282)
9. Ball (318)
10. Tyler (334)

METALS
1. Aluminum Co. of America (40)
2. LTV (56)
3. Reynolds Metals (80)
4. Bethlehem Steel (82)
5. Inland Steel Ind. (116)
6. Amax (117)
7. Armco (140)
8. National Steel (165)
9. Phelps Dodge (182)
10. Asarco (207)

MINING, CRUDE-OIL PRODUCTION
1. Burlington Resources (194)
2. Cyprus Minerals (275)
3. Union Texas (310)
4. Vulcan Materials (326)
5. Louisiana Land & Exp. (395)
6. Nerco (416)
7. Westmoreland Coal (451)
8. Maxus Energy (460)
9. Mitchell Energy (466)

MOTOR VEHICLES AND PARTS
1. General Motors (1)
2. Ford Motor (2)
3. Chrysler (7)

4. Dana (90)
5. Eaton (108)
6. Navistar International (113)
7. Borg-Warner (142)
8. Paccar (143)
9. Fruehauf (196)
10. Mack Trucks (199)

PETROLEUM REFINING
1. Exxon (3)
2. Mobil (6)
3. Texaco (8)
4. Chevron (11)
5. Amoco (12)
6. Shell Oil (13)
7. Atlantic Richfield (17)
8. USX (23)
9. Phillips Petroleum (31)
10. Unocal (47)

PHARMACEUTICALS
1. Johnson & Johnson (45)
2. Bristol-Myers (73)
3. Merck (74)
4. American Home Products (81)
5. Pfizer (86)
6. Abbott Laboratories (94)
7. Smithkline Beckman (97)
8. Lilly (115)
9. Warner-Lambert (120)
10. Schering-Plough (147)

PUBLISHING, PRINTING
1. Time Inc. (102)
2. Gannett (134)
3. Times Mirror (138)
4. Donnelly (149)
5. Tribune (181)
6. Knight-Ridder (192)
7. Berkshire Hathaway (205)
8. McGraw-Hill (223)
9. New York Times (228)
10. Dow Jones (238)

RUBBER PRODUCTS
1. Goodyear Tire (32)
2. Johnson Controls (144)
3. Premark International (178)
4. Rubbermaid (297)
5. Armtek (301)
6. Ferro (332)
7. Cooper Tire & Rubber (391)
8. Millipore (433)
9. Carlisle (462)
10. Constar International (464)

SCIENTIFIC AND PHOTOGRAPHIC EQUIPMENT
1. Eastman Kodak (18)
2. Xerox (22)
3. Minnesota Mining (34)
4. Baxter International (64)
5. Litton Industries (96)
6. Henley Group (148)
7. Polaroid (218)
8. Becton Dickinson (220)
9. Perkin-Elmer (258)
10. Tektronix (261)

SOAPS, COSMETICS
1. Procter & Gamble (15)
2. Unilever U.S. (63)
3. Colgate-Palmolive (83)
4. Avon Products (132)
5. Revlon Group (172)
6. Clorox (286)
7. International Flavors (367)
8. Alberto Culver (443)
9. Fabergé (453)
10. Noxell (484)

TEXTILES
1. Armstrong World Ind. (160)
2. Burlington Holdings (174)
3. West Point Pepperell (195)
4. Springs Industries (222)
5. Fieldcrest Cannon (274)
6. DWG (306)
7. Shaw Industries (344)
8. United Merchants (393)
9. Dixie Yarns (441)
10. Guilford Mills (457)

TOBACCO
1. Philip Morris (10)
2. American Brands (58)
3. Universal (177)
4. Lorillard (263)
5. Standard Commercial (390)
6. UST (440)
7. Dibrell Brothers (470)

TOYS, SPORTING GOODS
1. Hasbro (273)
2. Mattel (337)

TRANSPORTATION EQUIPMENT
1. Brunswick (137)
2. Outboard Marine (237)
3. Fleetwood Enterprises (266)
4. Trinity Industries (431)
5. Avondale Industries (454)
6. Minstar (486)

Source: *Fortune* magazine (Apr. 24, 1989), reprinted by permission of Time-Life, Inc.

THE *FORTUNE* SERVICE 500

THE 20 LARGEST DIVERSIFIED SERVICE COMPANIES, BY SALES, 1988 (millions of dollars)

Company	Sales	Profits
1. American Telephone & Telegraph	$35,210.0	$1,669.0
2. Fleming Cos.	10,467.0	65.4
3. Super ValuStores	9,371.7	111.8
4. McKesson	7,297.7	95.0
5. American Financial	6,901.7	102.4
6. United Telecommunications	6,493.0	508.9
7. MCI Communications	5,137.0	346.0
8. Fluor	5,132.5	56.4
9. Ryder System	5,029.6	197.2
10. Halliburton	4,838.7	93.6
11. Capital Cities/ABC	4,773.5	387.1
12. Electronic Data Systems	4,744.6	384.1
13. Sysco	4,384.7	86.9
14. Dun & Bradstreet	4,267.4	499.0
15. Wetterau	4,155.9	38.6
16. Hospital Corp. of America	4,111.2	258.8
17. Ara Group	3,917.3	5.4
18. Alco Standard	3,809.6	110.0
19. Waste Management	3,565.6	464.2
20. Bergen Brunswig	3,486.4	34.7

THE 10 LARGEST UTILITIES, RANKED BY ASSETS (millions of dollars)

Company	Assets	Operating revenues
1. GTE	$31,103.9	$16,459.9
2. BellSouth	28,472.4	13,596.9
3. NYNEX	25,362.0	12,661.0
4. Bell Atlantic	24,729.2	10,880.1
5. US West	22,415.9	9,220.6
6. Pacific Telesis Group	21,191.0	9,483.0
7. Pacific Gas & Electric	21,067.7	7,645.7
8. Southwestern Bell	20,985.1	8,452.7
9. Southern	19,729.0	7,235.0
10. American Information Tech.	19,163.0	9,903.3

THE 10 LARGEST TRANSPORTATION COMPANIES, RANKED BY REVENUES (millions of dollars)

Company	Revenues	Profits
1. United Parcel Service	$11,032.1	$758.7
2. UAL	9,014.6	1,124.3
3. AMR	8,824.3	476.8
4. CSX	8,668.0	147.0
5. Texas Air	8,572.9	718.6
6. Delta Air Lines	6,915.4	306.8
7. Union Pacific	6,794.0	644.0
8. USAir Group	5,707.0	165.0
9. NWA	5,650.4	135.1
10. Santa Fe Southern Pacific	4,934.9	46.5

THE 10 LARGEST RETAILING COMPANIES, RANKED BY SALES (millions of dollars)

Company	Sales	Profits
1. Sears, Roebuck	$50,251.0	$1,453.7
2. K mart	27,301.0	803.0
3. Wal-Mart Stores	20,649.0	837.2
4. Kroger	19,053.0	34.5
5. American Stores	18,478.4	98.3
6. J.C. Penney	14,833.0	807.0
7. Safeway Stores	13,612.4	31.2
8. Dayton Hudson	12,204.0	287.0
9. May Department Stores	11,921.0	534.0
10. Great Atlantic & Pacific Tea	9,531.8	103.4

THE 10 LARGEST INSURANCE COMPANIES, RANKED BY ASSETS (millions of dollars)

Company	Assets	Premium and annuity income
1. Prudential of America	$116,197.0	$14,396.7
2. Metropolitan Life	94,232.0	15,487.1
3. Equitable Life Assurance	50,415.5	4,917.3
4. Aetna Life & Casualty	48,884.9	8,266.1
5. Teachers Insurance & Annuity	38,631.4	3,064.9
6. New York Life	35,153.8	6,929.3
7. Connecticut General Life	31,095.5	2,732.3
8. Travelers	30,672.2	4,200.9
9. John Hancock Mutual Life	28,315.2	4,865.9
10. Northwestern Mutual Life	25,349.0	3,542.1

THE 10 LARGEST FINANCIAL INSTITUTIONS, RANKED BY ASSETS (millions of dollars)

Company	Assets	Revenues
1. American Express	$142,704.0	$22,934.0
2. Federal Natl. Mortgage Assn.	112,258.0	10,635.0
3. Salomon	85,256.0	6,146.0
4. Aetna Life & Casualty	81,414.6	24,296.4
5. Merrill Lynch	64,402.7	10,547.2
6. Cigna	55,824.5	17,889.4
7. Travelers Corp.	53,332.0	18,986.0
8. ITT	41,941.0	19,355.0
9. Morgan Stanley Group	40,050.8	4,108.8
10. American International Group	37,408.7	13,613.2

SMALL BUSINESS

Small businesses account for 99% of the 19 million nonfarm businesses in the United States today. Sole proprietorships make up 13.2 million of these small businesses, while 1.8 million are partnerships and 4 million, corporations. Small businesses employ 55% of the private work force, make 44% of all sales in America, and produce 38% of the nation's gross national product. Since 1978 the number of small businesses has increased 56%.

Most Americans—nearly 67%—get their first employment experience through small firms. Small businesses lead the way in the creation of new jobs in the American economy. Between 1981 and 1986, small businesses with fewer than 500 employees created 62% of the 8.9 million new jobs in the country. Between September 1987 and September 1988 alone, 2.3 million new jobs were generated in small-business dominated industries. During the first six months of 1987, the most recent period for which statistics are available, small business income was $320.1 billion—up 12.9% from the same period in 1986.

Small businesses are twice as likely as large firms to produce innovations relative to the number of persons they employ, and they have created more than half of the new products and service innovations developed since World War II. Among the fastest-growing small businesses today are eating and drinking establishments, trucking firms, doctors' offices, computer and data servies, and amusements and recreation services.

The standards used by the U.S. Small Business Adminisistration to determine whether a business is small vary from industry to industry and are relative within an industry. In manufacturing, a firm with 500 to 1,500 employees is classified a small business. In construction, this classification applies to companies with gross annual receipts between $7 million and $14.7 million. A company in the services and retail industry with gross annual ·receipts between $2.5 million and $14 million is considered a small business. A wholesaler with as many as 100 employees also will be classified as a small business. Thus a steel mill with 1,200 employees is considered to be a small business right along with a mom-and-pop candy store.

Financing Business

When an individual or a group of individuals decides to start a new company, they need money to rent or buy office space and equipment and to pay workers. Since there is a time lag between the day a business opens and the day a business sells its first good or service, funds must be borrowed from a bank or other financial institution or from individual investors to meet costs before revenues are generated. Additional funds may be needed throughout the life of the business to finance research and development of a new product or service or for the construction of new factories. Financing can take many forms from short-term bank loans, commercial paper, or trade credit to long-term stocks and bonds.

Trade credit, the largest category of short-term financing, is an arrangement between a company and its suppliers whereby materials and supplies are delivered to the company with a promise to pay the invoice, plus interest, usually within a specified number of weeks. Commercial bank lending may take the form of a single loan with repayment in a lump sum or in installments over the life of the loan, or it may be a line of credit up to a maximum the bank will allow the company to overdraw on its account. Commercial paper is a promissory note of a well-established firm sold primarily to other business firms, with repayments made in two to six months. The only problem with commercial paper is that its resources are limited to the liquidity that corporations have at any given time for lending to other firms.

Intermediate-term financing (with a timeframe of 1–15 years) may take the form of lease financing, whereby a company rents, rather than buys, the assets it uses; conditional sales contracts, by which equipment is bought over a period of time (the seller continues to have title of ownership until payment is completed); or term loans or business credit supplied by commercial banks and life insurance companies, repaid by amortization payments over the life of the loan (1–15 years).

The issuance of stocks and bonds constitute the long-term source of finance for firms. Bonds are debt instruments (IOUs issued by a company to the bondholder) that obligate the firm to pay interest at specific times. Alternatively, firms can raise money by issuing preferred and common stocks. Unlike bonds, stocks entitle the holder to share in ownership and profits made by the firm through dividends paid out for the entire period the investor owns the stock. However, if the business has low profits or limited funds, bondholders are paid first, preferred stockholders next, and common stockholders last.

NUMBER OF BUSINESS ESTABLISHMENTS WITH EMPLOYEES AND PAYROLL, BY MAJOR GROUP, 1986

Major group	Number of establishments	Number of employees	Annual payroll (thousands)
Total	**5,806,973**	**83,380,465**	**$1,608,810,889**
AGRICULTURAL SERVICES, FORESTRY, AND FISHERIES	**68,076**	**412,010**	**$5,764,717**
Agricultural services	64,505	384,284	5,310,391
Forestry	1,690	17,174	234,768
Fishing, hunting, and trapping	1,809	8,340	156,169
Administrative and auxiliary	69	2,203	63,300
MINING	**34,973**	**847,143**	**$24,481,218**
Metal mining	937	37,830	1,121,533
Anthracite mining	129	2,363	47,571
Bituminous coal and lignite	3,773	173,483	5,574,272
Oil and gas extraction	23,322	407,314	9,994,225
Nonmetallic minerals[1]	5,367	101,075	2,644,672
Administrative and auxiliary	1,443	125,065	5,098,074
CONTRACT CONSTRUCTION	**492,132**	**4,658,669**	**$104,492,181**
General contractors and operative builders	146,378	1,224,577	26,590,615
Heavy construction contractors	30,321	693,078	18,486,848
Special trade contractors	315,055	2,721,543	58,654,398
Administrative and auxiliary	378	19,471	760,323
MANUFACTURING	**355,452**	**19,141,756**	**$467,835,988**
Food and kindred prods.	21,145	1,405,771	29,360,363
Tobacco manufacturers	153	48,080	1,369,634
Textile mill prods.	6,152	667,969	10,780,363
Apparel and other textile prods.	22,525	1,082,437	13,383,126
Lumber and wood prods.	31,263	657,853	11,855,005
Furniture and fixtures	10,888	492,802	8,557,683
Paper and allied prods.	6,374	620,234	16,578,812
Printing and publishing	57,299	1,451,383	31,608,371
Chemicals and allied prods.	12,069	832,862	24,451,630
Petroleum and coal prods.	2,327	126,243	4,348,285
Rubber and misc. plastics prods.	14,012	769,544	15,790,969
Leather and leather prods.	2,243	139,246	1,809,236
Stone, clay, and glass prods.	15,994	545,952	12,778,421
Primary metal industries	6,725	736,357	19,533,868
Fabricated metal prods.	35,020	1,476,672	34,168,222
Machinery, except electrical	50,168	1,980,031	51,985,085
Electric and electronic equipment	17,374	2,016,533	51,049,446
Transportation equipment	9,457	1,805,051	57,305,532
Instruments and related prods.	8,323	615,705	15,716,528
Miscellaneous manufacturing industries	15,830	375,153	6,764,581
Administrative and auxiliary	10,109	1,295,872	48,640,719
TRANSPORTATION AND OTHER PUBLIC UTILITIES	**209,920**	**4,884,297**	**$127,723,336**
Local and interurban passenger transit	14,236	272,495	3,210,810
Trucking and warehousing	91,767	1,308,879	28,331,709
Water transportation	7,440	170,127	4,471,782
Transportation by air	8,463	511,759	15,778,148
Pipe lines, except natural gas	600	17,695	678,213
Transportation services	35,888	302,980	5,450,478
Communication	30,570	1,265,531	35,893,647
Electric, gas, and sanitary services	18,094	837,949	26,977,468
Administrative and auxiliary	2,862	196,882	6,931,084
WHOLESALE TRADE	**439,960**	**5,724,864**	**$138,240,428**
Wholesale trade—durable goods	271,339	3,217,781	79,373,961
Wholesale trade—nondurable goods	162,833	2,216,759	48,097,579
Administrative and auxiliary	5,788	290,324	10,768,889
RETAIL TRADE	**1,441,236**	**17,549,841**	**$192,840,466**
Building materials and garden supplies	69,625	626,477	9,276,185
General merchandise stores	36,037	1,954,204	18,767,711
Food stores	187,430	2,722,802	29,437,539
Automotive dealers and service stations	201,631	1,930,359	34,196,919
Apparel and accessory stores	141,884	1,081,362	9,670,225
Furniture and home furnishings stores	101,445	668,194	9,601,967
Eating and drinking places	362,895	5,577,135	37,637,993
Miscellaneous retail	327,154	2,204,710	25,776,655
Administrative and auxiliary	13,135	784,598	18,475,333
FINANCE, INSURANCE, AND REAL ESTATE	**504,052**	**6,370,787**	**$150,513,495**
Banking	54,759	1,639,912	32,917,298
Credit agencies other than banks	62,347	813,318	17,914,303
Security, commodity brokers, and services	19,968	377,278	21,490,870
Insurance carriers	35,304	1,313,076	31,669,298
Insurance agents, brokers, and service	99,039	597,436	13,563,765
Real estate	205,597	1,220,293	21,828,327
Combined real estate, insurance, etc.	4,695	24,690	490,829
Holding and other investment offices	20,246	209,952	6,279,360
Administrative and auxiliary	2,097	174,832	4,359,445
SERVICES	**1,811,302**	**22,878,357**	**$380,409,435**
Hotels and other lodging places	49,006	1,331,632	13,938,358
Personal services	179,022	1,117,133	10,878,020
Business services	276,557	4,612,797	80,636,642
Auto repair, services, and garages	133,569	726,858	10,848,385
Miscellaneous repair services	58,399	338,723	6,162,074
Motion pictures	18,543	252,221	4,572,905
Amusement and recreation services	61,542	796,839	10,262,790
Health services	401,426	6,614,276	125,452,763
Legal services	128,714	745,566	22,065,712
Educational services	31,069	1,561,782	21,665,005
Social services	92,811	1,368,622	13,129,552
Museums, botanical, zoological gardens	2,018	37,060	530,565
Membership organizations	207,902	1,696,145	16,835,790
Miscellaneous services	164,969	1,409,941	36,162,106
Administrative and auxiliary	5,755	269,774	7,268,779
UNCLASSIFIED ESTABLISHMENTS	**449,870**	**912,741**	**$15,509,661**

Note: Excludes government employees, railroad employees, and self-employed persons.   1. Except fuels.   **Source:** U.S. Bureau of the Census, *Country Business Patterns, 1986* (1988).

Franchising: Nationally Known, Locally Owned

Franchising, a century-old tradition, has never been more popular in the United States than it is now. Franchises did more than $600 million in business in 1988; projections for the future are even greater.

Today franchised business represents nearly 40% of all U.S. retail sales. The Department of Commerce estimates that by the year 2000, franchising will account for more than half of all sales. Franchising has grown by more than 90% just since 1980, and more than 7.5 million people are employed in over a half-million American franchise outlets across the country and around the world.

The appeal of franchising is universal. The franchiser can expand a business without borrowing huge amounts of capital. He also receives an up-front fee from the franchisee and a steady flow of income from each franchised unit, usually 2–5% of the franchise's gross income. The franchisees get to own their own businesses with a national reputation already built in. Typically they also receive training, financial assistance, help in choosing sites, and other business expertise from the parent company. Franchisees also pay a portion of their income to nationwide advertising.

THE 100 LARGEST FRANCHISES, 1988

Rank/Name of company	Type of business	Franchise fees	Number of franchises	Rank/Name of company	Type of business	Franchise fees	Number of franchises
1. Century 21 Real Estate	Real estate brokers	$11–26,000	7,005	51. Computerland	Computer sales and service	15–35,000	800
2. McDonald's	Fast food restaurants	22,500	6,165	52. Carvel Corp.	Ice cream stores	NA.	775
3. Kentucky Fried Chicken	Fast food restaurants	20,000	5,782	53. The Medicine Shoppe	Drug stores	18,000	755
4. Dairy Queen	Ice cream stores	30,000	5,122	54. Decorating Den	Home decorating services	7–19,000	750
5. Servicemaster	Commercial cleaning services	12–26,000	4,500	55. AAMCO Transmission	Auto maintenance centers	30,000	741
6. Jazzercise	Dance fitness centers	500	4,000	56. Roto Rooter	Sewer and drain cleaning	N.A.	733
7. H&R Block	Tax preparation	600–1,200	3,886	57. Orange Julius	Fast food restaurants	30,000	709
8. Chem-Dry	Carpet and upholstery cleaning	7,100	3,500	58. West Coast Video	Video rental stores	40,000	700
9. Subway Sandwiches & Salads	Fast food restaurants	7,500	3,500	59. Popeye's Famous Fried Chicken	Fast food restaurants	25,000	675
10. Baskin-Robbins Ice Cream	Ice cream stores	N.A.	3,300	60. Little Caesars Pizza	Pizza takeout	15,000	655
11. 7-Eleven Store	Convenience stores	varies	3,190	61. Thrifty Rent-A-Car	Car and truck rental	7,500 +	655
12. Budget Rent A Car	Car rental	15,000	3,171	62. AM/PM Mini Markets	Convenience stores	N.A.	650
13. Wendy's	Fast food restaurants	25,000	2,597	63. Novus Windshield Repair	Windshield repair	2,900	650
14. Electronic Realty Associates	Real estate brokers	13,900	2,596	64. ServPro Industries	Commercial cleaning services	19–32,000	647
15. Diet Center	Weight loss centers	16–32,000	2,300	65. American Speedy Printing	Business printing	19,500	624
16. Radio Shack	Electronics retailers	15–40,000	2,200	66. Kampgrounds of America	Campgrounds	20,000	623
17. Fantastic Sam's	Discount hair cutters	25,000	2,120	67. Bonanza Restaurants	Family restaurants	30,000	615
18. Arby's	Fast food restaurants	25,000 +	2,000	68. Mr. Build	Home business remodeling	6–10,000	605
19. Dollar Rent A Car	Car rental	N.A.	1,800	69. Mister Donut	Donut shops	25,000	600
20. Realty World	Real estate brokers	9–13,000	1,767	70. Ramada Inns	Hotel/motel	30.000 +	600
21. Midas Muffler & Brake Shops	Auto maintenance centers	10,000	1,685	71. Ziebart Car Improvement	Auto maintenance	20,000	595
22. RE/MAX	Real estate brokers	10–20,000	1,500 +	72. General Business Services	Financial counseling	25,000	592
23. National Video	Video rental stores	12–29,900	1,500	73. Super 8 Motels Inc.	Hotel/motel	20,000	561
24. Holiday Inns	Hotel/motel	N.A.	1,490	74. Ice Cream Churn	Ice cream stores	7,500	550 +
25. Jani-King International	Janitorial services	6,500 +	1,412	75. Hertz	Car rental	varies	548
26. Domino's Pizza	Pizza delivery and takeout	1,320–3,250	1,369	76. Color-Tyme	TV/video equipment rental	6,000	534
27. Dunkin' Donuts	Donut shops	30–40,000	1,359	77. A&W Restaurants	Fast food restaurants	15,000	526
28. Coverall	Commercial cleaning services	3–25,000	1,242	78. Help-U-Sell	Real estate counselors	4,500 +	515
29. TCBY Yogurt	Frozen yogurt stores	20,000	1,240	79. Convenient Food Mart	Convenience stores	varies	513
30. Taco Bell	Mexican fast food restaurants	35,000	1,200	80. Supercuts	Discount hair cutters	10–25,000	508
31. PIP Printing	Business printing	40,000	1,178	81. Precision Tune	Auto maintenance	20,000	505
32. Systemax Network	Mailing & packaging services	995–1,295	1,150	82. Manpower	Employment agents	N.A.	504
33. Church's Fried Chicken	Fast food restaurants	15,000	1,100	83. United Package Mailing Svce.	Packaging and shipping	N.A.	490
34. Packy the Shipper	Packaging/shipping centers	N.A.	1,060	84. U-Save Auto Rental	Car rental	up to 17,000	489
35. Hardee's Food Systems	Fast food restaurants	15,000	1,038	85. Management Recruiters	Employment agents	20–30,000	481
36. One Hour Martinizing	Dry cleaners	20,000	1,030	86. Sizzler Restaurants	Family restaurants	30,000	478
37. Kwik-Kopy Printing Centers	Printing services	22,000	1,008	87. Econo-Lodges of America	Hotel/motel	20,000	477
38. Coast to Coast Total Hardware	Hardware retailers	5,000	1,000	88. Long John Silver's Seafood	Fast food restaurants	20,000	471
39. Jiffy Lube	Auto maintenance	35,000	1,000	89. Sylvan Learning Corp.	Supplemental education	19,000 +	472
40. Mail Boxes Etc.	Postal services	19,500	1,000	90. International House of Pancakes	Family restaurants	varies	461
41. Rainbow International	Carpet dying and cleaning	15,000	1,000	91. Miracle Ear	Hearing aid retailers	25,000	459
42. Sport It Inc.	Sporting goods retailers	N.A.	1,000	92. Pearle Vision Centers	Optical retailers	16,000	457
43. European Body Wrap	Body wrapping	1,000	911	93. Better Homes & Gardens	Real estate brokers	4,463	456
44. Meineke Discount Mufflers	Limited auto maintenance	22,500	900	94. The Athlete's Foot	Sporting goods retailers	15,000	450
45. Minuteman Press Intl.	Printing centers	27,500	900	95. Life Trends Tanning & Toning	Women's exercise programs	N.A.	450
46. Big Boy Family Restaurants	Family restaurants	25,000	874	96. Jitney Jungle/Jr. Food Mart	Convenience stores	7,500	440
47. Quality/Comfort Inns	Hotel/motel	30–50,000	865	97. Taco John's	Mexican fast food restaurants	16,500	438
48. Sir Speedy	Business printing centers	17,500	850	98. Maaco Auto Painting	Auto painting	25,000	435
49. Duraclean International	Carpet and upholstery cleaning	N.A.	812	99. Acoustic Clean	Ceiling cleaners	N.A.	425
50. Nutri-System	Weight Loss centers	N.A.	805	100. Merry Maids	Maid service systems	17,500	425

Source: Enterprise Magazines (Milwaukee, Wis.), *The Franchise Handbook* (Fall 1989), copyright © , reprinted by permission.

The American Stock Exchange (Amex)

The American Stock Exchange, located a few blocks from the New York Stock Exchange in New York's financial district, is known as the stock market for the small investor and small companies. The stock issues of organizations that do not meet the listing and size requirements of the NYSE typically are traded there. For years Amex was known as the "New York Curb Exchange" because its trading was conducted on the street outside the office building of many brokers. The exchange moved indoors in 1921.

Trading was down on Amex in 1988 following the October 1987 market crash. Average daily trading volume was 9.9 million shares, down from 13.9 million in 1987. There were 895 companies listed on Amex at the end of 1988, up from 866 the year before. The exchange added 114 new companies but lost 85 owing to corporate mergers. The value of the stocks traded on Amex rose 17.4% in 1988. The 2.5 billion shares that changed hands on Amex in 1988 accounted for 3.1% of the total U.S. market. Amex's dollar volume of $29.8 billion was 1.5% of the U.S. total for 1988.

Sources: *New York Times,* Apr. 12, 1989; NASDAQ, *Fact Book '89.*

SHARES TRADED: DAILY VOLUME, AVERAGE, HIGH, AND LOW, 1900–88 (in thousands)

Year	Average	High	Low
1900	505	1,627	89
1910	601	1,656	111
1920	828	2,008	227
1930	2,959	8,279	1,090
1940	751	3,940	130
1950	1,980	4,859	1,061
1955	2,578	7,717	1,230
1960	3,042	5,303	1,894
1965	6,176	11,434	3,028
1970	11,564	21,345	6,660
1975	18,551	35,158	8,670
1980	44,871	84,297	16,132
1985	109,169	181,027	62,055
1988	161,461	343,949	72,088

Source: New York Stock Exchange.

NYSE LISTED STOCKS
(figures in millions)

Year-end	Number	Market value	Average price[1]
1924	433	$ 27,072	$62.45
1945	1,592	73,765	46.33
1950	2,353	93,807	39.86
1960	6,458	306,967	47.53
1970	16,065	636,380	39.61
1975	22,478	85,110	30.48
1980	33,709	1,242,803	36.87
1985	52,427	1,950,332	37.20
1988	76,093	2,457,461	32.30

1. This average cannot be used as an index of price trend owing to changes in shares listed caused by new listings, suspensions, stock splits, and stock dividends. **Source:** New York Stock Exchange.

NYSE COMPANIES WITH LARGEST NUMBER OF COMMON STOCKHOLDERS-OF-RECORD, 1988 (in thousands)

Company	Stockholders	Company	Stockholders
AT&T	2,702	BCE Inc.[1]	372
General Motors	1,725	Sears, Roebuck	352
BellSouth Corp.	1,491	Pacific Gas & Electric	302
Bell Atlantic	1,280	Southern Co.	291
NYNEX Corp.	1,249	Philadelphia Electric	290
Southwestern Bell	1,169	Ford Motor	270
American Info. Tech.	1,164	Mobil Corp.	247
Pacific Telesis Group	1,027	Am. Electric Power	238
US WEST	1,007	Commonwealth Edison	237
IBM	834	Public Services	
Exxon Corp.	735	Enterprises	213
General Electric	531	Dominion Resources	208
GTE Corp.	440	Occidental Petroleum	207

1. Formerly Bell Canada Enterprises. **Source:** New York Exchange, Inc.

NYSE MEMBERSHIP PRICES

Year	High	Low	Year	High	Low
1875	$ 6,800	$ 4,300	1955	90,000	80,000
1895	20,000	17,000	1965	250,000	190,000
1905	85,000	72,000	1970	320,000	130,000
1915	74,000	38,000	1975	138,000	55,000
1925	150,000	99,000	1980	275,000	175,000
1935	140,000	65,000	1985	480,000	310,000
1945	95,000	49,000	1988	820,000	580,000

Source: New York Stock Exchange.

NASDAQ

The most heavily traded over-the-counter stocks are exchanged through the NASDAQ National Market system, the second-largest stock market in the United States and the third largest in the world in terms of the dollar value of shares. Founded in 1971, NASDAQ stands for the National Association of Securities Dealers Automated Quotations. It uses computers and high-technology telecommunications systems to trade—and to monitor the trading of—millions of securities daily.

More than 31 billion shares were traded through NASDAQ in 1988, down from 38 billion shares in 1987, the most active year in the market's history. The dollar volume of this trading was $347.1 billion. Only on the Tokyo exchange ($2.2 trillion) and the New York Stock Exchange ($1.3 trillion) was there a heavier dollar volume of trading.

The average number of shares traded daily on NASDAQ in 1988 was 122.8 million, more than a 10–fold increase over the 1978 average of 11 million. In 1978, when 11 billion shares were traded on the NASDAQ, NYSE, and Amex market combined, NASDAQ accounted for 26% of the total. Ten years later, with 74.4 billion shares traded on those same markets, NASDAQ's share of the total had risen to 42%. In 1988, 4,451 companies were listed with NASDAQ with a total share volume of 31.1 billion, a 79.8% increase in the number of companies traded on NASDAQ and a 99.2% jump in the number of issues offered since 1978. The total share volume of the 1,681 companies listed on the NYSE in 1988 was 40.8 billion. That of the 896 companies traded through Amex was 2.5 billion.

MERGERS AND ACQUISITIONS

A merger is a joint decision by two or more firms to combine their assets; an acquisition refers to the purchase of one company by another. There are several reasons for firms to merge or acquire each other. In merging their operations, two companies might make better use of their assets—a pool company busy in the summer might combine with a ski company busy in the winter to make year-round use of facilities and staff. In acquiring another firm, a company may believe that the business they are buying is worth more than its current price if, for example, they can manage it more efficiently.

Firms may also decide to use the acquisition process to purchase themselves. If management believes that the current price of their firm's stock is lower than it could be, they may purchase the firm's outstanding stock and "take the firm private," one advantage being that the government places fewer restrictions and regulations on privately held companies. Also, the firm is protected from unwanted ("hostile") takeovers because there are no outside shareholders from whom corporate raiders can purchase stock and thereby gain control.

Acquisitions and mergers receive attention because ownership of enormous productive assets changes hands very quickly. Despite the reasons offered for merging or acquiring companies, the generally poor showing of so many firms following mergers and acquisitions casts doubt on the efficiency arguments. The process often leads to reorganizations and profound changes—sharp reductions in some functions and employment, expansions in others—which influence people both inside and outside the firm. One such result is *divestiture*, the sale of a company's product line, division, or subsidiary because it no longer fits well with the expanded firm's overall goal or because the business may need a quick infusion of cash to pay off debt incurred in the merger or acquisition. Divestments can provide an opportunity for leveraged buyouts, in which a group of employees, typically upper-level management, purchases the division and operates it themselves, preserving their jobs in the process.

Another concern is the extent to which acquisitions, especially, have transferred ownership of U.S. industries to foreign interests. The pace of foreign acquisitions as measured by dollar value has increased sharply in recent years; the leading buyers of U.S. firms have been British concerns.

The rapid growth of mergers and acquisitions in the 1980s was due in part to the deregulation of banking (making consolida-

10 LARGEST MERGERS AND ACQUISITIONS

Buyer	Target	Price (billions)	Year
Standard Oil Co. of California[1]	Gulf Corp.	$13.300	1984
Philip Morris Cos.	Kraft Inc.	12.644	1988
Texaco Inc.	Getty Oil Co.	10.125	1984
Du Pont Co.	Conoco Inc.	6.924	1981
United States Steel Corp.[2]	Marathon Oil Co.	6.150	1982
General Electric Co.	RCA Corp.	6.142	1986
Mobil Corp.	Superior Oil Co.	5.700	1984
Philip Morris Cos.	General Foods Corp.	5.628	1985
Eastman Kodak Co.	Sterling Drug Inc.	5.093	1988
R.J. Reynolds Industries Inc.[3]	Nabisco Brands Inc.	4.904	1985

1. Now known as Chevron Corp.   2. Now known as USX Corp.   3. Now known as RJR Nabisco Inc.   **Source:** *Mergers & Acquisitions* (Philadelphia, Pa.), reprinted by permission.

10 LARGEST LEVERAGED BUYOUTS, 1979–89

Buyer	Target	Price (billions)	Year
Kohlberg Kravis Roberts & Co.	RJR Nabisco Inc.	$24,717	1989
Kohlberg Kravis Roberts & Co.	Beatrice Cos.	6,250	1986
Kohlberg Kravis Roberts & Co.	Safeway Stores Inc.	4,235	1986
Thompson Co.	Southland Corp.	4,004	1987
AV Holdings Corp.	Borg-Warner Corp.	3,764	1987
Kohlberg Kravis Robertss & Co.	Owens-Illinois Inc.	3,688	1987
TF Investments Inc.	Hospital Corp. of America	3,686	1989
FH Acquisitions Corp	Fort Howard Corp.	3,589	1988
Macy Acquiring Corp.	R.H. Macy & Co.	3,501	1986
Kiewit Murdock Investment Corp.	Continental Group Inc.	2,750	1984

Note: As of June 30.   **Source:** *Mergers & Acquisitions* (Philadelphia, Pa.), reprinted by permission.

10 LARGEST FOREIGN ACQUISITIONS IN THE U.S., 1979–89

Buyer	Target	Price (billions)	Year
British Petroleum Corp. (UK)	Standard Oil Co.	$7,565	1987
Campeau Corp. (Canada)	Federated Department Stores Inc.	6,506	1988
Grand Metropolitan PLC (UK)	Pillsbury Co.	5,758	1989
Royal Dutch/Shell Group (Netherlands-UK)	Shell Oil Co.	5,657	1985
B.A.T. Industries PLC (UK)	Farmers Group Inc.	5,169	1988
Campeau Corp. (Canada)	Allied Stores Corp.	3,597	1986
Unilever NV (Netherlands)	Chesebrough-Pond's Inc.	3,095	1987
News Corp. Ltd. (Australia)	Triangle Publications Inc.	3,000	1988
Nestle SA (Switzerland)	Carnation Co.	2,894	1985
Société Nationale Elf Aquitain (France)	Texasgulf Inc.	2,740	1981

Note: As of June 30.   **Source:** *Mergers and Acquisitions* (Philadelphia, Pa.), reprinted by permission.

tions in that industry easier); the government's more lenient antitrust policy and their allowing mergers even of direct competitors; and the 1982–83 recession, which left many firms weak and searching for stronger ownership. The trend peaked in 1986, and there were fewer mergers in 1987 than in any year since 1980.

WALL STREET

The U.S. stock market, commonly known as Wall Street, began in the late 18th century as a merchant-organized public auction in stocks and government bonds for the purpose of financing the government and expanding business and trade. At that time brokers handed over securities to auctioneers who sold securities to the highest bidder. Today, while the form of the stock exchange has changed dramatically, the purpose remains the same.

The most commonly cited index of Wall Street's performance is the Dow Jones average (see "Glossary of Financial Terms"). The Dow rose dramatically in the 1980s, passing the 2,000 mark in January 1987 and reaching over 2,700 by August, only to drop by over 500 points on "Black Monday," Oct. 19, 1987, losing over 22% of its value in one day (nearly 10 percentage points more than the day of the Great Crash of 1929) and closing around 1,700. Black Monday was precipitated by investors' fear of a falling dollar and increased interest rates in order to attract external funds to finance the enormous U.S. trade deficit ($15.7 billion for the month of Aug. 1987 alone). For corporations and consumers, this translates into increased borrowing costs, lower investment and spending, recession, and a decrease in corporate earnings, culminating in the heavy sales of equities on Oct. 19, 1987. Since then the Dow Jones Industrial Average has climbed back to 1987 levels, and on Aug. 24, 1989, closed at a new high of 2,734.64.

In 1987, 48.1 billion shares with a value of $1.9 trillion were traded on the New York Stock Exchange (NYSE), which was formally founded in 1817, when less than 100 shares were traded each day.

GLOSSARY OF FINANCIAL TERMS

Arbitrage Simultaneous purchase and sale of a commodity or currency in at least two markets where price discrepancies exist. The arbitrageur makes a profit by buying an asset with a low price in one market and selling it in another market where the asset carries a higher price.

Bear/bull A bear is a speculator who expects prices to fall and sells stocks or *bonds* in order to buy them later at a lower price. A bull expects prices to rise and therefore buys now for resale later. Thus, a bearish (bullish) market is one in which prices are generally falling (rising).

Blue chip stock A stock that is considered a safe investment, with a low *yield* and a high price per share, issued by companies that are well known and have a history of good management and increasing profit levels.

Bond A debt obligation requiring the issuer to pay a fixed sum of money annually until maturity (interest payments) and then, at maturity, a fixed sum of money to repay the initial amount borrowed (principal). (See "Corporate bonds").

Capital gain An increase in the market value of an asset above the price originally paid for it, realized when the asset is sold.

Capital loss A decrease in the market value of an asset below the price originally paid for it, realized when the asset is sold.

Common stock/equity A piece of paper that entitles the owner to a share of the *firm's* profits and a share of the voting power in shareholder elections. In other words, a shareholder is part owner of the firm. If he owns 50% of the issued shares of common stock (when no *preferred stock* is issued), he owns 50% of the company, and will receive 50% of profits paid out in *dividends*. Over 40 million Americans invest in common stocks.

Convertible bond A debt instrument that carries an option for the holder to convert it into a specified amount of company stock.

Corporate bond A debt obligation requiring the corporation to pay a fixed sum of money annually until maturity (interest payments) and then, at maturity, a fixed sum of money to repay the initial amount borrowed (principal). *Bonds* carry no claim to ownership and therefore pay no *dividends*, but payments to bondholders take priority over payments to stockholders.

Debenture A debt *security* that pays a fixed interest rate, issued by a company in order to raise finance for commercial or industrial operations.

Divestiture The sale by a company of a product line, subsidiary, or division. The number of divestitures sold peaked in 1986 with a total of 1,316, for a record total price of $65.2 billion.

Dividend A payment made to *common* and *preferred stock* holders out of a *firm's* profits either in the form of cash or additional shares.

Dow Jones Industrial Average Dating back to 1893, this index of 30 *blue chip stocks* in industry traded on the New York Stock Exchange (and determined by the editors of the *Wall Street Journal*) is the most widely cited indicator of how the stock market is doing.

Establishment A physical place of business activity such as a factory, assembly plant, retail store, or warehouse, where goods are made, stored, or processed or where services are performed.

Eurocurrency A currency deposited outside its country of origin for use as a medium of international credit. The Eurocurrency market developed in the late 1950s and constitutes a vast international pool of highly mobile money. Eurocurrencies are used to facilitate international trade and the payment of deficits and for currency speculation.

Firm A business organization that owns and/or operates one or more *establishments*. Also called a company, enterprise, or business venture. Firms can be of three types: (1) sole proprietorships—firms owned directly by one person; (2) partnerships—firms whose ownership is shared by a fixed number of proprietors; and (3) corporations—firms created by a government charter, which grants them greater accessibility to financial capital through the selling of *common* or *preferred stock*, greater accessibility to debt capital through the selling of *bonds*, and limited liability in the event of bankruptcy.

Futures market/forward market A market in which commodities or *securities* are bought and sold at prices fixed now, for delivery at specified future date. Futures are traded on the American Stock Exchange; the Chicago Board of Trade; Chicago Board Options Exchange; Chicago Mercantile Exchange; Chicago Rice and Cotton Exchange; Commodity Exchange, New York (COMEX); Kansas City Board of Trade; MidAmerica Commodity Exchange, Chicago; Minneapolis Grain Exchange; New York Coffee, Sugar, and Coca Exchange (including the Citrus Associates); New York Cotton Exchange; New York Futures Exchange; New York Mercantile Exchange; New York Stock Exchange; Pacific Stock Exchange, Los Angeles and San Francisco; and Philadelphia Stock Exchange.

Greenmail Analogous to blackmail, the practice of purchasing enough shares in a *firm* or trading company to threaten a takeover, thereby forcing the owners to buy them back at a higher rate in order to retain control of the business.

Insider trading Trading in the stock market based on information that has not been made public and that is intended to remain confidential—for example, information that a small company is about to become part of a national corporation. The penalties paid by individuals and corporations for such activities in recent years have reached into the hundreds of millions of dollars. Drexel Burnham Lambert, Inc., was fined $650 million to settle six charges of securities law violations, and investor Ivan Boesky was fined $100 million and imprisoned for his insider-trading activities.

Junk bond/high yield bond *Bonds* with a rating below investment grade—that is, at or below Ba1 (Moody's Investors Service), at or below BB+ (Standard & Poor's), or unrated. Issuers of junk bonds are usually small companies who in the past have been limited to borrowing from banks to raise capital for corporate growth. Despite the fact that the major ratings services consider junk bonds risky (hence their name), they have a historically low default rate—only 1.5% between the mid-1970s and mid-1980s. The junk market grew considerably in the 1980s, and by 1987 accounted for over 25% of the value of all *corporate bonds* outstanding.

Leveraged buyout The purchase of a company by one of its employee groups (usually upper management) or a large shareholder with borrowed funds, usually using the company's assets as security for the loans. Leveraged buyouts have been used to combat hostile takeover bids.

Mutual fund A pool of financial assets in which investors may buy shares and derive the benefits or share the losses, depending on the performance of the collective *securities*. Shares are sold publicly and can be redeemed at any time. Funds can consist of stocks, *bonds*, gold, government securities, or other assets, and their names are descriptive of their primary purpose; for example, bonds funds, equity-fund portfolios, income funds, money market–mutual funds, and municipal funds. (See "Money Market Accounts" under "Money and Banking" in the section "The Economy.")

Option A contract to buy or sell commodities or *securities* within a given time period at a fixed price. For stocks, this period is usually three months. A contract to sell is a *put option* (or put); to buy, a *call option* (or call); and one to buy or sell is a *double option*. A buyer (seller) will gain if the trading price rises (falls) by more than the cost of entering into the contract. Options are traded on the same exchanges as *futures* contracts (see "Futures market").

Over-the-counter (OTC) stock A *security* not listed on a *stock exchange* that is traded between two individuals. The name stems from the 18th century practice of merchants selling stocks directly to investors over the counter in their own shops, without the use of *stockbrokers* or auctioneers.

Pension fund A scheme whereby private- or public-sector employers, unions, and—as in the case of individual retirement accounts (IRAs) and Keogh plans—individuals contribute to a fund from which money is paid out to the employees, union members, or contributors (or their dependents) upon death, disability, or retirement. Contributions can be based on a percentage of salary or corporate profits; in some cases employees may make voluntary or mandatory contributions to the fund. Pension fund assets are usually held in the form of *securities* or property with a preference for long-term assets.

Preferred stock Similar to *common stock*, except that owners of preferred stock have no voting rights and are paid their *dividends* at a fixed rate, before common-stock holders receive any dividends.

Rating An agency evaluation of the quality of a debt instrument or a company issuing debt. Standard & Poor's and Moody's Investment Service are the two major credit ratings agencies in the United States. The ratings measure the safety of interest and principal payments of bonds. S&P bond ratings are, from most to least secure, AAA, AA, A, BBB, BB, B, CCC, CC, C. Moody's ratings are Aaa, Aa, A, Baa, Ba, B, Caa, Ca, C.

Securities Financial assets (usually long-term), such as equities or stocks and *debentures* or *bonds;* may also refer to shorter-term assets such as U.S. Treasury bills.

Securities and Exchange Commission (SEC) U.S. government agency that regulates the *securities* industry by requiring registration of *stockbrokers*, dealers, and *stock exchanges*. The SEC also reviews the financial position of companies issuing securities for public sale and investigates illegal activities such as *insider trading*.

Standard & Poor's 500 Composite Stock Price Index (S&P 500) A widely used measure of the movement of the U.S. stock market. The S&P 500 was introduced in 1957 and is one of 12 leading economic indicators used by the U.S. Commerce Department. The 500 issues include 400 industrial, 40 utility, 20 transportation, and 40 financial companies—primarily those listed on the New York Stock Exchange (NYSE). The index is considered to be value-weighted because each stock is weighted according to its market value. As of Dec. 31, 1987, the market value of issues tracked by the S&P 500 was equal to approximately 70% of the value of all publicly traded U.S. equities. Its value is calculated on a total return basis with *dividends* reinvested.

Stock exchange A market in which *securities* (other than bills and similar short-term instruments) issued by central and local government bodies and public companies are traded (e.g., the New York Stock Exchange, the American Stock Exchange, the London Stock Exchange). Only members of a stock exchange may deal on it, and membership and arrangements for trading are strictly regulated. Stock exchanges in the United States are the American Stock Exchange (New York); Boston Stock Exchange; Cincinnati Stock Exchange; Intermountain Stock Exchange (Salt Lake City); Midwest Stock Exchange (Chicago); New York Stock Exchange; Pacific Stock Exchange (Los Angeles, San Francisco); Philadelphia Stock Exchange; and Spokane Stock Exchange.

Stock market An institution in which stocks and shares are traded, existing in all advanced Western countries. Stock markets enable companies to raise equity or loan capital more easily from the public, since investors can quickly realize their holdings because of the stock exchange share quotation. The principal overseas stock markets are located in Amsterdam, Brussels, Frankfurt, Hong Kong, Johannesburg, London, Milan, Paris, Singapore, Stockholm, Sydney, Tokyo, Toronto, and Zurich.

Stockbroker An individual who acts as an adviser and an agent (working on commission) to buy and sell stocks on behalf of a client on a particular *stock exchange* of which the stockbroker is a member.

Wilshire 5000 Index The broadest measure of the U. S. stock market, containing some 5,000 issues, including all publicly traded U.S. stocks for which daily pricing is available (i.e., includes all Amex, NYSE, and *OTC stocks*).

Yield The annual return on a *security,* as a percentage of its current market price. A stock's *dividend* yield is the annual dividend divided by its current stock price.

double, and then almost double again by 1970. Between 1970 and 1988, as the Baby Boom generation entered the marketplace and the economy expanded, advertising expenditures grew at a spiraling rate, reaching $125 billion by 1989.

Over 60% of all advertising dollars are spent to place ads in newspapers or magazines or to run commercials on radio and television. Most of that money in turn is spent by the nation's largest manufacturers of automobiles, food, soft drinks, and beer.

In 1983 some 30 corporations spent over $100 million a year on advertising, but only four years later 87 did; moreover, three actually spent over $1 billion in that year (1987).

Most advertising dollars are filtered through about 6,000 advertising agencies, who create the ads and buy the space or time from the media. The agency business has undergone a dramatic restructuring recently as the corporate-raider mentality invaded Madison Avenue with a vengeance. Many of the largest agencies, most with worldwide connections, have merged with others to form enormous corporations, so the lists of the 25 largest found at the end of this section change rapidly from year to year.

ADVERTISING EXPENDITURES IN THE U. S., 1776–1980 (millions of dollars)

Year	Amount[1]	Year	Amount[1]
1776	$ 0.2	1955	$ 9,150.0
1800	1.0	1960	11,960.0
1820	3.0	1965	15,250.0
1840	7.0	1970	19,550.0
1850	12.0	1975	28,160.0
1860	22.0	1980	54,780.0
1867	40.0	1981	60,430.0
1876	150.0	1982	66,580.0
1880	175.0	1983	75,850.0
1890	300.0	1984	88,100.0
1900	450.0	1985	94,750.0
1909	1,000.0	1986	102,140.0
1915	1,100.0	1987	109,787.0
1940	2,110.0	1988	118,320.0[2]
1945	2,840.0	1989	125,550.0[2]
1950	5,700.0		

1. These are estimated figures of the monies spent on placing advertising in all media; the costs of producing the advertising are not included.   2. Preliminary estimates.   **Sources:** McCann-Erickson, N.Y.; figures through 1975 were compiled for *Advertising Age* and reprinted July 5, 1976.

ADVERTISING

If they wish to make a profit, both large and small purveyors of consumer products and services must find ways to let their potential customers know about their business. Since the U.S. media (newspapers, radio, television, magazines) also are run as profit-earning enterprises, it seems natural that the two forces would be joined by their common needs. This in fact happened about 150 years ago, when whole pages of newspapers were jammed with the unadorned but paid announcements of everything from patent medicines to clothing and hardware. By 1900 so many large businesses had sprung up (Procter & Gamble and Kellogg's, for example) that nationally distributed magazines (including *Ladies' Home Journal*) became enormously profitable ventures based on the advertising placed by these firms. By 1910 over $1 billion a year was being spent on advertising, which was itself now entrenched as a business of its own with established practices and with dozens of schools specially designed to teach the most persuasive selling techniques.

Throughout the 20th century, advertising expanded along with the economy, and it provided American business with a distinctly American voice that moved the merchandise in an unprecedented manner. Few facts reveal the extraordinary growth of the so-called mass-consumption society as vividly as those dealing with the advertising business. In 1950, as the postwar economy began to heat up, American business spent $5.7 billion to advertise its goods and services; by 1960 that figure would

TOP 25 U.S.-BASED ADVERTISING AGENCIES BY INCOME AND BILLINGS, 1988 (millions of dollars)

Rank/Agency, headquarters	Worldwide gross income 1988	Worldwide gross income 1987	Worldwide billings 1988	U.S. gross income 1988	U.S. billings 1988	Worldwide employees 1988
1. Young & Rubicam, N.Y.	$757.6	$735.5	$5,390.3	$372.8	$2,791.8	12,311
2. Saatchi & Saatchi Advertising Worldwide, N.Y.	740.5	685.3	5,053.9	326.3	2,209.6	7,750
3. Backer Spielvogel Bates Worldwide, N.Y.	689.8	600.7	4,677.9	282.7	1,964.2	6,739
4. McCann-Erickson Worldwide, N.Y.	656.8	512.5	4,381.0	197.0	1,314.0	8,606
5. FCB-Publicis, Chicago/Paris	653.3	518.5	4,357.6	273.7	1,825.8	7,661
6. Ogilvy & Mather Worldwide, N.Y.	635.2	563.9	4,110.1	281.1	1,874.9	7,671
7. BBDO Worldwide, N.Y.	585.9	549.7	4,051.2	340.5	2,414.3	5,497
8. J. Walter Thompson Co., N.Y.	559.3	487.6	3,857.5	257.5	1,787.9	6,738
9. Lintas: Worldwide, N.Y.	537.6	417.9	3,585.6	201.7	1,345.4	6,372
10. Grey Advertising, N.Y.	432.8	369.2	2,886.5	227.9	1,520.3	5,690
11. D'Arcy Masius Benton & Bowles, N.Y.	428.7	371.3	3,360.8	209.6	1,794.2	5,532
12. Leo Burnett Co., Chicago	428.4	369.2	2,865.1	263.4	1,765.0	5,211
13. DDB Needham Worldwide, N.Y.	399.9	368.5	3,020.3	244.4	1,929.3	4,697
14. HDM, N.Y.	279.0	204.0	1,937.7	28.6	228.9	2,528
15. N W Ayer, N.Y.	185.2	166.1	1,347.7	127.8	946.7	2,644
16. Bozell, Jacobs, Kenyon & Eckhardt, N.Y.	179.2	185.2	1,283.0	150.3	1,090.0	2,172
17. Wells, Rich, Greene, N.Y.	117.3	107.0	835.9	117.0	833.9	829
18. Scali McCabe Sloves, N.Y.	107.0	93.1	770.6	71.8	559.7	1,438
19. Ketchum Communications, Pittsburgh	105.9	88.1	776.0	102.1	726.0	1,410
20. Campbell-Mithun-Esty, Minneapolis	105.6	99.9	783.0	105.6	783.0	1,207
21. TBWA Advertising, N.Y.	97.4	74.6	671.9	23.1	154.1	816
22. Ogilvy & Mather Direct Response, N.Y.	97.0	84.0	647.0	41.0	272.0	1,212
23. Ross Roy Group, Bloomfield Hills, Mich.	85.2	71.3	568.1	85.2	568.1	955
24. Della Femina, McNamee WCRS, N.Y.	84.4	78.9	660.5	84.4	660.5	991
25. Wunderman Worldwide, N.Y.	68.6	62.1	457.5	39.9	266.1	622

Source: *Advertising Age* (Mar. 29, 1989), reprinted by permission of Crain Communications, Inc.

America's Leading Advertisers

In 1987 Philip Morris Co., which makes cigarettes (Marlboro), beer (Miller), and dozens of food products (Post cereals, Kool-Aid, Maxwell House coffee), overtook Procter & Gamble Co., also a producer of well-known household products (Tide, Bounty, and Crest, to name only a few) to win the number one spot in the ranks of national advertisers.

THE 100 LEADING NATIONAL ADVERTISERS, 1987
(thousands of dollars)

Rank/Company	Total spending
1. Philip Morris Co.	$1,557,846
2. Procter & Gamble Co.	1,386,710
3. General Motors Corp.	1,024,852
4. Sears, Roebuck & Co.	886,529
5. RJR Nabisco	839,589
6. PepsiCo Inc.	703,973
7. Eastman Kodak Co.	658,221
8. McDonald's Corp.	649,493
9. Ford Motor Co.	639,510
10. Anheuser-Busch Co.	635,067
11. K mart Corp.	631,845
12. Unilever NV/PLC	580,656
13. General Mills	572,233
14. Chrysler Corp.	568,722
15. Warner-Lambert Co.	558,115
16. AT&T	531,018
17. Kellogg Co.	524,865
18. J.C. Penney Co.	513,497
19. Pillsbury Co.	473,895
20. Johnson & Johnson	459,271
21. Ralston Purina Co.	436,606
22. Kraft Inc.	400,699
23. American Home Products Corp.	390,391
24. Mars Inc.	378,559
25. Coca-Cola Co.	364,737
26. Bristol-Myers Co.	358,934
27. Quaker Oats Co.	344,414
28. Nestle SA	340,825
29. U.S. Government	311,299
30. Colgate-Palmolive Co.	279,813
31. Sara Lee Corp.	278,141
32. General Electric Co.	272,607
33. Toyota Motor Corp.	257,738
34. American Cyanamid	250,376
35. Schering-Plough Corp.	250,184
36. Walt Disney Co.	249,823
37. Honda Motor Co.	245,365
38. H.J. Heinz Co.	245,264
39. IBM Corp.	240,846
40. Grand Metropolitan PLC	231,574
41. Campbell Soup Co.	230,708
42. Tandy Corp.	225,052
43. BCI Holdings Corp.	223,208
44. American Express Co.	212,479

45. Time Inc.	196,579
46. Pfizer Inc.	182,059
47. Nissan Motor Co.	181,438
48. IC Industries	169,309
49. Volkswagen AG	167,257
50. Mobil Corp.	166,285
51. Revlon Group	165,239
52. Hyundai Group	164,336
53. U.S. Dairy Associations	161,372
54. Beecham Group PLC	153,307
55. AMR Corp.	152,609
56. Mazda Motor Corp.	151,884
57. American Brands	151,371
58. ITT Corp.	151,321
59. E.I. Du Pont de Nemours & Co.	149,749
60. Bayer AG	145,392
61. Adolph Coors Co.	144,664
62. Nynex Corp.	142,798
63. Bell Atlantic Corp.	138,618
64. UAL Corp.	137,790
65. Dow Chemical Co.	135,689
66. Noxell Corp.	134,876
67. Hasbro Inc.	134,308
68. Texas Air Corp.	124,343
69. Hershey Foods Corp.	122,809
70. Seagram Co.	122,325
71. Cosmair Inc.	117,224
72. CPC International	115,329
73. Kroger Co.	115,263
74. Loews Corp.	115,200

75. Dr.Pepper/Seven-Up	114,117
76. Subaru of America	113,233
77. Wm. Wrigley, Jr. Co.	112,462
78. Prudential Insurance Co. of America	111,319
79. Warner Communications	110,428
80. Delta Air Lines	108,636
81. Wendy's International	107,599
82. Philips NV	107,226
83. B.A.T. Industries PLC	105,294
84. Daimler-Benz AG	105,018
85. Gillette Co.	103,831
86. Stroh Brewery Co.	102,878
87. Clorox Co.	102,132
88. BMW AG	99,456
89. S.C. Johnson & Son	96,397
90. Goodyear Tire & Rubber Co.	95,027
91. Hallmark Cards	93,913
92. E. & J. Gallo Winery	93,602
93. MCA Inc.	91,366
94. Marriott Corp.	88,523
95. Franklin Mint	86,620
96. Southland Corp.	86,134
97. United Biscuits (Holdings) PLC	84,758
98. Borden Inc.	84,743
99. Monsanto Co.	84,689
100. Ameritech	83,445

Source: *Advertising Age* (Sept. 28, 1988), reprinted by permission of Crain Communications, Inc.

U.S. ADVERTISING EXPENDITURES BY MEDIA, 1986–87
(millions of dollars)

Medium	1986 expenditures	Percent of total	1987 expenditures	Percent of total	Percent increase 1986–87
Daily newspapers	$ 26,990	26.4%	$ 29,412	26.8%	9.0%
National	3,376	3.3	3,494	3.2	3.5
Local	23,614	23.1	25,918	23.6	9.8
Magazines	5,317	5.2	5,530	5.0	4.0
Television	23,185	22.7	24,370	22.2	5.1
Network	8,570	8.4	8,830	8.0	3.0
Spot	13,084	12.8	13,730	12.5	4.9
Syndication	600	0.6	730	0.7	21.7
Cable	931	0.9	1,080	1.0	16.0
Radio	6,949	6.8	7,240	6.6	4.2
Farm publications	192	0.2	200	0.2	4.2
Direct mail	17,145	16.8	19,030	17.3	11.0
Business publications	2,382	2.3	2,480	2.3	4.1
Outdoor	985	1.0	1,030	0.9	4.6
Miscellaneous	18,995	18.6	20,495	18.7	7.9
National	9,575	9.4	10,250	9.3	7.0
Local	9,420	9.2	10,245	9.3	8.8
Grand total national	56,850	55.7	60,589	55.2	6.6
Grand total local	45,290	44.3	49,198	44.8	8.6
Total, all media	**$102,140**	**100.0%**	**$109,787**	**100.0%**	**7.5%**

Source: McCann-Erickson Inc., Newspaper Advertising Bureau Inc., reprinted with permission.

PART III SCIENCE AND TECHNOLOGY

SCIENCE

NATIONAL MEDALS OF SCIENCE

The National Medal of Science is the highest science award given by the U.S. government. Since 1962 it has been presented by the president for achievement in physical, biological, mathematical, engineering, behavioral, or social science.

The medal itself is intended to symbolize sci-ence. It shows a human being, surrounded by Earth, sea, and sky, contemplating and seek-ing to understand nature. The scientist holds a crystal in one hand, intended to symbolize the universal order and also the basic unit of living things. With the other hand, the scientist is sketching a formula in the sand.

The nominees are selected by a presidential committee of 12 members acting with the presi-dent's science adviser and the president of the National Academy of Sciences. The medals are not awarded every year.

NATIONAL MEDAL OF SCIENCE AWARDS

Year	Winner	Field	Affiliation
1962	Theodore von Karman	Aeronautics	Cal Tech
1963	Luis Walter Alvarez	Physics	Univ. of California, Berkeley
	Vannevar Bush	Electronics	Carnegie Institute
	John Robinson Pierce	Communications	Bell Labs
	Cornelius B. van Niel	Microbiology	Stanford Univ.
	Norbert Wiener	Mathematics	M.I.T.
1964	Roger Adams	Chemistry	Univ. of Illinois
	Othmar H. Ammann	Engineering	Ammann & Whitney
	Theodosius Dobzhansky	Medicine	Rockefeller Univ.
	Charles Stark Draper	Astronautics	M.I.T.
	Solomon Lefschetz	Mathematics	Princeton Univ.
	Neal Elgar Miller	Psychology	Yale Univ.
	Harold Marston Morse	Mathematics	Institute for Advanced Studies
	Marshall W. Nirenberg	Genetics	National Institutes of Health
	Julian Schwinger	Physics	Harvard Univ.
	Harold C. Urey	Chemistry	Univ. of California, Berkeley
	Robert B. Woodward	Chemistry	Harvard Univ.
1965	John Bardeen	Electronics	Univ. of Illinois
	Peter J.W. Debye	Chemistry	Cornell Univ.
	Hugh L. Dryden	Administration	NASA
	Clarence L. Johnson	Aeronautics	Lockheed
	Leon M. Lederman	Physics	Columbia Univ.
	Warren K. Lewis	Chemical eng.	M.I.T.
	Francis Peyton Rous	Medicine	Rockefeller Univ.
	William W. Rubey	Geophysics	UCLA
	George. G. Simpson	Paleontology	Harvard Univ.
	Donald Van Slyke	Chemistry	Brookhaven National Lab
	Oscar Zariski	Mathematics	Harvard Univ.
1966	Jacob Bjerknes	Meteorology	UCLA
	S. Chandrasekhar	Astrophysics	Univ. of Chicago
	Henry Eyring	Administration	Univ. of Utah
	E.F. Knipling	Entomology	U.S. Dept. of Agriculture
	Fritz A. Lipmann	Biochemistry	Rockefeller Univ.
	John W. Minor	Mathematics	Princeton Univ.
	William C. Rose	Chemistry	Univ. of Illinois
	Claude E. Shannon	Science history	M.I.T.
	J.H. Van Vleck	Physics	Harvard Univ.
	Sewall Wright	Genetics	Univ. of Wisconsin
	Vladimir Zworykin	Physics	RCA
1967	J.W. Beams	Physics	Univ. of Virginia
	A. Francis Birch	Geology	Harvard Univ.

Year	Winner	Field	Affiliation
	Gregory Breit	Physics	Yale Univ.
	Paul J. Cohen	Mathematics	Stanford Univ.
	Kenneth S. Cole	Biophysics	National Institutes of Health
	Louis P. Hammett	Chemistry	Columbia Univ.
	Harry F. Harlow	Psychology	Univ. of Wisconsin
	Michael Heidelberger	Immunology	New York Univ.
	G.S. Kistiakowsky	Chemistry	Harvard Univ.
	Edwin H. Land	Photography	Polaroid Corporation
	Igor I. Sikorsky	Aeronautics	United Aircraft
	Alfred H. Sturtevant	Biology	Cal Tech
1968	Horace A. Barker	Biochemistry	Univ. of California, Berkeley
	Paul D. Bartlett	Chemistry	Harvard Univ.
	Bernard B. Brodie	Pharmacology	National Institutes of Health
	Detlev W. Bronk	Medicine	Rockefeller Univ.
	J. Presper Eckert	Computer science	Sperry-Rand Corporation
	Herbert Friedman	Astrophysics	Naval Research Lab
	Jay L. Lush	Genetics	Iowa State Univ.
	N.M. Newmark	Civil eng.	Univ. of Illinois
	Jerzy Neyman	Mathematics	Univ. of California, Berkeley
	Lars Onsager	Chemistry	Yale Univ.
	B.F. Skinner	Psychology	Harvard Univ.
	Eugene P. Wigner	Physics	Princeton Univ.
1969	Herbert C. Brown	Chemistry	Purdue Univ.
	William Feller	Mathematics	Princeton Univ.
	Robert J. Huebner	Medicine	National Institutes of Health
	Jack S.C. Kilby	Computer science	Texas Instruments
	Ernst Mayr	Zoology	Harvard Univ.
	W.K.H. Panofsky	Physics	Stanford Univ.
1970	Richard D. Brauer	Mathematics	Harvard Univ.
	Robert H. Dicke	Physics	Princeton Univ.
	Barbara McClintock	Genetics	Carnegie Institute
	George E. Mueller	Administration	General Dynamics
	Albert B. Sabin	Medicine	Weizmann Institute
	Allan R. Sandage	Astronomy	Cal Tech
	John C. Slater	Physics	Univ. of Florida
	John A. Wheeler	Physics	Princeton Univ.
	Saul Winstein	Chemistry	UCLA
1971	No awards.		
1972	No awards.		
1973	Daniel I. Arnon	Biochemistry	Stanford Univ.

Year	Winner	Field	Affiliation
	Carl Djerassi	Chemistry	Stanford Univ.
	Harold E. Edgerton	Mathematics	M.I.T.
	William M. Ewing	Electrical eng.	Univ. of Texas
	Arie J. Haagen-Smit	Biochemistry	Cal Tech
	Vladimir Haensel	Geology	Universal Oil
	Frederick Seitz	Administration	Rockefeller Univ.
	Earl W. Sutherland	Biochemistry	Univ. of Miami
	John W. Tukey	Statistics	Princeton Univ.
	Richard T. Whitcomb	Aeronautics	Langley Center
	Robert P. Wilson	Administration	Fermilab
1974	Nicolaas Bloembergen	Physics	Harvard Univ.
	Britton Chance	Physics	Univ. of Pennsylvania
	Erwin Chargaff	Biochemistry	Columbia Univ.
	Paul J. Flory	Chemistry	Stanford Univ.
	William A. Fowler	Physics	Cal Tech
	Kurt Gödel	Mathematics	Institute for Advanced Study
	Rudolf Kompfner	Physics	Stanford Univ.
	James V. Neel	Genetics	Univ. of Michigan
	Linus Pauling	Chemistry	Stanford Univ.
	Ralph B. Peck	Engineering	Univ. of Illinois
	K.S. Pitzer	Chemistry	Univ. of California, Berkeley
	James A. Shannon	Medicine	Rockefeller Univ.
	Abel Wolman	Engineering	Johns Hopkins Univ.
1975	John Backus	Computer science	San Jose Laboratory
	Manson Benedict	Mathematics	M.I.T.
	Hans A. Bethe	Physics	Cornell Univ.
	Shiing-shen Chern	Mathematics	Univ. of California, Berkeley
	George B. Dantzig	Computer science	Stanford Univ.
	Hallowell Davis	Medicine	Washington Univ.
	Paul Gyorgy	Pediatrics	Univ. of Pennsylvania
	Sterling B. Hendricks	Chemistry	U.S. Dept. of Agriculture
	Joseph O. Hirschfelder	Chemistry	Univ. of Wisconsin
	William H. Pickering	Physics	Jet Propulsion Laboratory
	Lewis H. Sarett	Administration	Merck, Sharp, and Dohme
	Frederick E. Terman	Administration	Stanford Univ.
	Orville A. Vogel	Agronomy	Washington State Univ.
	Wernher von Braun	Administration	NASA
	E. Bright Wilson	Chemistry	Harvard Univ.
	Chien-Shiung Wu	Physics	Columbia Univ.
1976	Morris Cohen	Metallurgy	M.I.T.
	Kurt O. Friedrichs	Mathematics	New York Univ.
	Peter C. Goldmark	Communications	Goldmark Corporation
	Samuel A. Goudsmit	Physics	Univ. of Nevada
	Roger C. Guillemin	Neurology	Salk Institute
	Herbert S. Gutowsky	Chemistry	Univ. of Illinois
	Erwin W. Mueller	Physics	Pennsylvania State Univ.
	Keith R. Porter	Biology	Univ. of Colorado
	Efraim Racker	Biochemistry	Cornell Univ.
	Frederick D. Rossini	Chemistry	Rice Univ.
	Verner E. Suomi	Meteorology	Univ. of Wisconsin
	Henry Taube	Chemistry	Stanford Univ.
	George E. Uhlenbeck	Physics	Rockefeller Univ.
	Hassler Whitney	Physics	Princeton Univ.
	Edward O. Wilson	Zoology	Harvard Univ.
1977	No awards.		
1978	No awards.		
1979	Robert H. Burris	Biochemistry	Univ. of Wisconsin
	Elizabeth C. Crosby	Anatomy	Univ. of Michigan
	Joseph L. Doob	Mathematics	Univ. of Illinois
	Richard P. Feynman	Physics	Cal Tech
	Donald E. Knuth	Computer science	Stanford Univ.
	Arthur Kornberg	Biochemistry	Stanford Univ.
	Emmett N. Leith	Electrical eng.	Univ. of Michigan

Year	Winner	Field	Affiliation
	Herman F. Mark	Administration	Brooklyn Polytech
	Raymond D. Mindlin	Civil eng.	Columbia Univ.
	Robert N. Noyce	Computer science	Intel Corp.
	Severo Ochoa	Biochemistry	New York Univ.
	Earl R. Parker	Metallurgy	Univ. of California, Berkeley
	Edward M. Purcell	Physics	Harvard Univ.
	Simon Ramo	Administration	Thompson, Ramo, Wooldridge, Inc.
	John H. Sinfelt	Science adviser	Exxon
	Lyman Spitzer, Jr.	Astronomy	Princeton Univ.
	Earl R. Stadtman	Biochemistry	National Institutes of Health
	G. Ledyard Stebbins	Genetics	Univ. of California, Davis
	Paul A. Weiss	Biology	Rockefeller Univ.
	Victor F. Weisskopf	Physics	M.I.T.
1980	No awards.		
1981	Philip Handler	Biochemistry	National Academy of Sciences
1982	Philip W. Anderson	Physics	Bell Labs
	Seymour Benzer	Biology	Cal Tech
	Glenn W. Burton	Biology	U.S. Dept. of Agriculture
	Mildred Cohn	Chemistry	Univ. of Pennsylvania
	F. Albert Cotton	Chemistry	Texas A&M
	Edward H. Heinemann	Engineering	General Dynamics
	Donald Katz	Chemistry	Univ. of Michigan
	Yoichiro Nambu	Physics	Univ. of Chicago
	Marshall H. Stone	Mathematics	Univ. of Massachusetts
	Gilbert Stork	Chemistry	Columbia Univ.
	Edward Teller	Physics	Stanford Univ.
	Charles H. Townes	Physics	Univ. of California, Berkeley
1983	No awards.		
1984	No awards.		
1985	Howard L. Bachrach	Biochemistry	U.S. Dept. of Agriculture
	Paul Berg	Biology	Stanford Univ.
	Margaret Burbidge	Astronomy	Univ. of California, San Diego
	Maurice Goldhaber	Physics	Brookhaven National Lab
	Herman H. Goldstine	Computer science	American Philosophical Society
	William R. Hewlett	Electronics	Hewlett-Packard Company
	Roald Hoffmann	Chemistry	Cornell Univ.
	Helmut Landsberg	Climatology	Resources for the Future
	George M. Low	Space science	Rensselaer Polytechnic Inst.
	Walter Munk	Geophysics	Univ. of California, San Diego
	George C. Pimentel	Chemistry	Univ. of California, Berkeley
	Frederick Reines	Physics	Univ. of California, Irvine
	Wendell L. Roelofs	Biology	Cornell Univ.
	Bruno Rossi	Astronomy	M.I.T.
	Berta Scharrer	Medicine	Albert Einstein College of Medicine
	Robert Schrieffer	Physics	Univ. of Calif., Santa Barbara
	Isadore Singer	Mathematics	Univ. of California, Berkeley
	John G. Trump	Medicine	M.I.T.
	Richard N. Zare	Chemistry	Stanford Univ.
1986	Solomon J. Buchsbaum	Physics	Bell Labs
	Stanley Cohen	Biochemistry	Vanderbilt Univ.
	Horace R. Crane	Biophysics	Univ. of Michigan
	Herman Feshbach	Physics	M.I.T.
	Harry B. Gray	Chemistry	Cal Tech
	Donald A. Henderson	Medicine	Johns Hopkins Univ.
	Robert Hofstadter	Physics	Stanford Univ.
	Peter D. Lax	Mathematics	New York Univ.
	Yuan Tseh Lee	Chemistry	Univ. of California, Berkeley
	Hans W. Liepmann	Physics	Cal Tech
	Tung Yen Lin	Engineering	T.Y. Lin, International
	Carl S. Marvel	Chemistry	Univ. of Arizona
	Vernon B. Mountcastle	Medicine	Johns Hopkins Univ.

Year	Winner	Field	Affiliation
	Bernard M. Oliver	Electronics	NASA
	George E. Palade	Biology	Yale Univ.
	Herbert A. Simon	Psychology	Carnegie Mellon Univ.
	Joan A. Steitz	Biochemistry	Yale Univ.
	Frank H. Westheimer	Chemistry	Harvard Univ.
	Chen Ning Yang	Physics	State Univ. of N.Y., Stony Brook
	Antoni Zygmund	Mathematics	Univ. of Chicago
1987	Philip H. Abelson	Physics	American Association of Allied Sciences
	Anne Anastasi	Psychology	Fordham Univ.
	Robert Bird	Physics	Univ. of Wisconsin
	Raoul Bott	Mathematics	Harvard Univ.
	Michael E. DeBakey	Medicine	Baylor College of Medicine
	Theodor Diener	Biology	U.S. Dept. of Agriculture
	Harry Eagle	Biology	Albert Einstein College of Medicine
	Walter M. Elsasser	Physics	Johns Hopkins Univ.
	Michael Freedman	Mathematics	Univ. of California, San Diego
	William S. Johnson	Biochemistry	Stanford Univ.
	Har Gobind Khorana	Biology	M.I.T.
	Paul C. Lauterbur	Medicine	Univ. of Illinois
	Rita Levi-Montalcini	Medicine	Lab. of Cell Biology, Rome
	George E. Pake	Administration	Xerox Corporation
	H. Bolton Seed	Engineering	Univ. of California, Berkeley
	George J. Stigler	Economics	Univ. of Chicago
	Walter H. Stockmayer	Chemistry	Dartmouth College

Year	Winner	Field	Affiliation
	Max Tishler	Chemistry	Wesleyan Univ.
	James A. Van Allen	Astronomy	Univ. of Iowa
	Ernest Weber	Engineering	Polytechnic Inst. of N.Y.
1988	William O. Baker	Chemistry	Bell Labs
	Konrad E. Bloch	Medicine	Harvard Univ.
	D. Allan Bromley	Physics	Yale Univ.
	Michael S. Brown	Medicine	Univ. of Texas Medical Center
	Paul C.W. Chu	Physics	Univ. of Houston
	Stanley N. Cohen	Genetics	Stanford Univ.
	Elias J. Corey	Chemistry	Harvard Univ.
	Daniel C. Drucker	Engineering	Univ. of Florida
	Milton Friedman	Economics	Hoover Institution, Stanford
	Joseph L. Goldstein	Medicine	Univ. of Texas Medical Center
	Ralph E. Gomery	Mathematics	IBM Corporation
	Willis M. Hawkins	Aeronautics	Lockheed Corporation
	Maurice R. Hillerman	Medicine	Merck Institute
	George W. Housner	Earth science	Cal Tech
	Eric R. Kandel	Biochemistry	Columbia Univ.
	Joseph B. Keller	Physics	Stanford Univ.
	Walter Kohn	Physics	Univ. of Calif., Santa Barbara
	Norman F. Ramsey	Physics	Harvard Univ.
	Jack Steinberger	Physics	CERN (European Center for Nuclear Research), Geneva
	Rosalyn S. Yalow	Medicine	Mt. Sinai School of Medicine

Astronomy and Space

Astronomy is the oldest science, but it continues to be at the forefront of scientific thought. The ancients knew the skies, probably better than most of us do. They could recognize that most of the stars appeared to rise in the east at night and travel in circular paths across the sky and that a few were wanderers—planets—that moved among the other stars. They named the apparent groups of stars that we call constellations and recognized that constellations visible in winter were different from those visible in summer (although some were visible all year). They recognized that one star, Polaris, or the North Star, was always in the north, and other stars seemed to move around it. They learned how to find the extremities of the sunrise and probably built giant stone structures, such as Stonehenge, to locate certain of the positions of the Sun or other stars.

In 1609 Galileo introduced the first artificial device for exploring the universe—the telescope. Even in that first year, he saw wonders the ancients never knew. Since then, we have built larger and better telescopes, devices for detecting radio waves, microwaves, X rays, infrared waves, and gamma rays from space, and have even traveled to our own Moon. We have sent space probes to eight of the nine known planets. Astronomers have learned that the universe is vastly more complex than the ancients thought and that it contains many secrets of nature we hope to unlock.

MAJOR DISCOVERIES AND EVENTS IN ASTRONOMY AND SPACE

B.C.

2296 Chinese astronomers begin recording appearance of "hairy stars" (comets).

585 The scientist Thales (Greek: 624–546 B.C.) is reputed to have predicted solar eclipse appearing in 585 in Near East.

480 Astronomer Oenopides of Chios (Greek: n.d.) discovers that Earth is tilted with respect to Sun.

410 First horoscopes become available in Mesopotamia (now Iraq, Syria, and Turkey).

352 Chinese report first-known "guest star," or supernova, the earliest known sighting.

340 Astronomer Kiddinu (Mesopotamian: n.d.) discovers precession of equinoxes, the apparent change in position of stars caused by Earth's wobbling on its orbit.

300 Chinese astronomers compile accurate star maps.

240 Chinese astronomers observe Halley's comet.
Astronomer Eratosthenes (Hellenic: c. 276–196) correctly calculates Earth's size.

165 Chinese astronomers are first to notice sunspots.

130 Astronomer Hipparchus of Nicea (Hellenic: c. 190–120 B.C.) correctly determines distance to Moon.

A.D.

140 *Almagest* of Ptolemy (Hellenic: c. A.D. 100–170) develops astronomy of solar system in form based on Sun and planets rotating about Earth.

1543 *De Revolutionibus* by Nicholas Copernicus

(Polish: 1473–1543) presents convincing arguments that Earth and other planets orbit Sun.

1577 Tycho Brahe (Danish: 1546–1601) proves that comets are visitors from space, not weather phenomena as previously believed.

1592 David Fabricius (German: 1564–1617) discovers star, later named Mira, that gradually disappears; in studying it in 1638, Phocyclides Holawarda recognizes that it appears and reappears on regular basis—the first-known variable star.

1609 Galileo (Italian: 1564–1642) makes first astronomical telescope.
Johannes Kepler (German: 1571–1630) discovers that the planets move in elliptical orbits.

1610 Galileo observes Jupiter's moons, phases of Venus, and (although he does not recognize what they are) rings of Saturn.

1611 Several astronomers simultaneously discover sunspots for first time in West.

1633 Roman Catholic Church forces Galileo to recant his support of Copernicus's theory that Earth revolves about Sun.

1668 Isaac Newton (English: 1642–1727) constructs first reflecting telescope.

1671 Giovanni Domenico Cassini (Italian-French: 1625–1712) correctly determines distances of the planets from Sun.

1682 Edmond Halley (English: 1656–1742) describes comet now known by his name and correctly predicts its return in 1758.

1718 Halley discovers that stars move with respect to each other.

1755 Immanuel Kant (German: 1724–1804) proposes that many nebulas are actually composed of millions of stars and that solar system formed when giant cloud of dust condensed.

1758 Halley's comet returns as predicted by Halley.

1773 William Herschel (German-English: 1738–1822) shows that solar system is moving toward constellation Hercules.

1781 Herschel discovers planet Uranus.

1785 Herschel demonstrates that Milky Way is disk- or lens-shaped group of many stars, one of which is the Sun.

1801 Guiseppe Piazzi (Italian; 1746–1826) discovers first-known asteroid, Ceres.

1838 Friedrich Bessel (German: 1784–1846) is first to determine distance to star other than the Sun.

1846 Johann Galle (German: 1812–1910) discovers planet Neptune using predictions of Urbain Leverrier (French: 1811–77) and John Couch Adams (English: 1819–92).

1924 Edwin Hubble (American: 1889–1953) shows that galaxies are "island universes"—giant aggregations of stars as large as Milky Way.

1929 Hubble establishes that universe is expanding.

1930 Clyde Tombaugh (American: 1906–) discovers planet Pluto.

1931 Karl Jansky (American: 1905–50) discovers that radio waves are coming from space, leading to founding of radio astronomy.

1948 George Gamow (Russian-American: 1904–68), Ralph Alpher (American: 1921–), and Robert Herman (American: 1914–) develop Big Bang theory of origin of universe.

1957 USSR launches *Sputnik I,* the first man-made satellite.

1959 USSR launches rocket that hits the Moon.

1961 Soviet cosmonaut Yuri Gagarin (Russian: 1934–68) is first human to orbit Earth.

1962 U.S. space probe *Mariner 2* is first artificial object to reach vicinity of another planet.

1963 Maarten Schmidt (Dutch-American: 1929–) is first astronomer to recognize a quasar.

1965 Arno Penzias (German-American: 1933–) and Robert Wilson (American: 1936–) find radio waves caused by Big Bang, proving to most astronomers that Big Bang actually occurred.

1966 Soviet-launched space probe is first object produced by humans to land on Moon (Jan.), and another becomes first to orbit Moon.

1967 Joycelyn Bell (English: n.d.) discovers first-known pulsar while working for Anthony Hewish (English: 1924–); Hewish later gets Nobel Prize for discovery.

1969 U.S. lands two people, Neil Armstrong (American: 1930–) and Edwin ("Buzz") Aldrin (American: 1930–), on Moon.

1971 American spacecraft, *Mariner 9,* is first to orbit another planet, Mars.

1975 Soviet space probe transmits pictures from surface of Venus.

1976 Rings of Uranus are discovered.

U.S. Viking space probes begin transmitting pictures of surface of Mars—unsuccessful in detecting life on planet.

1979 U.S. space probe *Voyager 1* discovers that, like Saturn, Jupiter has rings.

1980 Alan Guth (American: 1947–) develops theory of inflationary universe, an explanation of how Big Bang occurred.

1981 U.S. introduces reusable spacecraft, the space shuttle.

1986 Space shuttle *Challenger* explodes, killing all seven aboard.

1987 Supernova 1987A, the nearest supernova that has been visible from Earth since 1604, explodes.

The Solar System

THE PLANETS

Earth is one of nine known planets. A planet is a large, fairly cool body traveling in a path, called its orbit, around a star. All of the bodies under the gravitational influence of our local star, the Sun, together with the Sun, form the solar system. All nine of the known planets are in the solar system, although there is some evidence for planets around other stars. Many stars are orbited by large, hot bodies—other stars—but these are not considered planets. Cool bodies smaller than planets that orbit a star are called asteroids if they have fairly regular orbits and are called comets if their orbits take them from the edge of the system to locations near the Sun (some actually hit the Sun and burn up). Very small objects in space are called meteoroids. A meteoroid that burns up in Earth's atmosphere is called a meteor. One that reaches Earth's surface without burning completely is a meteorite.

Planets often have smaller, cool bodies that orbit the planet. These are called satellites or moons.

It is currently believed that the solar system formed when a cloud of gas condensed to form the Sun. Parts of the cloud formed small bodies similar to today's asteroids, comets, and meteoroids. Collectively, these small bodies are called planetesimals or planetoids. Early in the history of the solar system, about 4.6 billion years ago or even before, the planetoids frequently crashed into one another. While this sometimes resulted in one or more of the planetoids breaking up, a small planetoid would often stick to a larger one, making it larger still. The end results of this process, it is proposed, are the nine known planets and their moons, along with the existing asteroids, comets, and meteoroids.

Although six of the nine planets were known to the ancients and astronomers found the remaining three by early in the 20th century, observation from Earth had not prepared us for what we learned when we began exploring the

solar system with space probes in 1962. Radar observations, both from Earth and from space probes, provided still more information. Satellite observation has also told us much we did not know about our own planet, Earth. While this age of exploration is far from over, here is an interim report.

The Terrestrial Planets

In terms of distance from the Sun, these are the first four planets of the solar system—Mercury, Venus, Earth, and Mars. Terrestrial planets all have a comparatively high density, a concentration of metallic elements, and hard, rocky surfaces. Earth is the largest of the terrestrial planets but is dwarfed by the enormous sizes of the outer, or "gas giant," planets (Jupiter, Saturn, Uranus, and Neptune). All the terrestrial planets have magnetic fields. Earth and Venus have thick atmospheres, Mars has a thin atmosphere, and Mercury's atmosphere is almost nonexistent.

Mercury is the planet closest to the Sun and in keeping with its namesake—Mercury, the winged messenger—moves the fastest in its orbit. Mercury orbits the Sun at a mean velocity of 29.7 miles (47.9 km) per second and completes one revolution every 88 days. Its period of rotation is 59 days. Usually obscured from view from Earth by the Sun's glare, it is sometimes visible on Earth's horizon just after sunset, when it is called the Evening Star, or just before dawn, when it is the Morning Star. About 14 times every 100 years, Mercury can also be seen crossing directly in front of the Sun's disk.

Mercury was long thought to be the smallest planet, but better measurements of Pluto's size have shown that Pluto is even smaller.

The U.S. *Mariner 10* space probe provided the first detailed pictures of Mercury's surface during flybys in 1974 and 1975. Mariner 10 mapped about 35% of the planet's heavily cratered, moonlike surface. No space probe has visited the planet since.

Mercury is a waterless, airless world that alternately bakes and freezes as it orbits the Sun. Its tenuous atmosphere is thought to be one-trillionth the density of Earth's atmosphere and largely composed of argon, neon, and helium. On Mercury's sunlit side temperatures reach 950°F (510°C) and plummet to –346°F (–210°C) on the dark side. These extremes are largely due to Mercury's slow rate of rotation; one Mercury "day" (or sol, as astronomers call a single rotation of a planet or satellite) is two-thirds of one Mercury year. Because it takes 59 Earth days to complete one sol, there is time for the surface to heat up or cool off.

Mercury's surface is scarred with hundreds of thousands of meteor craters. Many such craters were probably formed during the planetoid showers believed to have occurred soon after the formation of the solar system. Many areas have had the craters smoothed over by ancient lava flows, however. This indicates extensive volcanic activity on Mercury during and after the time of the asteroid showers. The surface is also crisscrossed by huge cliffs, or scarps.

These probably formed as Mercury's surface cooled and shrank. Some of the scarps are up to 1.2 miles (1.9 km) high and 932 miles (1,500 km) long.

Mercury is so dense for its size that astronomers think that its rocky outer crust is very thin and that the planet is mostly iron. It probably was once larger. During the early bombardment, it is conjectured that one of the larger planetoids (about a sixth of the size of the early planet) hit Mercury so hard that it blasted most of the rocky crust away.

> *So the sun sits as upon a royal throne, ruling his children the planets, which circle around him.*
> —NICHOLAS COPERNICUS (1543)

Because Mercury has a magnetic field, scientists believe the planet has a hot core of molten metal, perhaps iron with some nickel. The molten core is thought to make up about half the planet's volume.

Venus, as seen in the night sky from Earth, is second only to the Moon in brightness. Venus, named for the Roman goddess of love, is the planet that passes closest to Earth (26,000,000 mi., or 42,000,000 km). Since it is between Earth and the Sun, Venus, like Mercury, is seen either as the Morning Star or the Evening Star.

Because of its closer proximity to Earth and its position between Earth and the Sun, Venus became (in 1962) the first planet beyond Earth to be scanned by a space probe in its neighborhood (Mariner 2). The pull of the Sun's gravity makes Venus and Mercury "downhill," while one must travel against the Sun's gravity to reach other planets. Since 1962 Venus has been visited by numerous U.S. and Soviet spacecraft. Soviet space probes Venera 13 and Venera 14 were the first to make a soft landing and send back pictures from the Venusian surface.

The Venusian atmosphere is thick with clouds that have shrouded the planet's surface from view, making the planet somewhat mysterious. This dense atmosphere has been studied extensively by a series of U.S. and Soviet space probes. The atmospheric pressure at the surface is 90 times that of Earth, its atmosphere composed of 96% carbon dioxide (CO_2) and nitrogen, with small amounts of other substances. The Venusian clouds range from about 28 to 37 miles (45 to 60 km) above the planet's surface and are differentiated into three layers. Droplets of sulfuric acid and water have been identified in the clouds.

The clouds and high level of CO_2 in the atmosphere have combined to trap heat in the lower atmosphere of Venus. This is an extreme form of the greenhouse effect and is responsible for

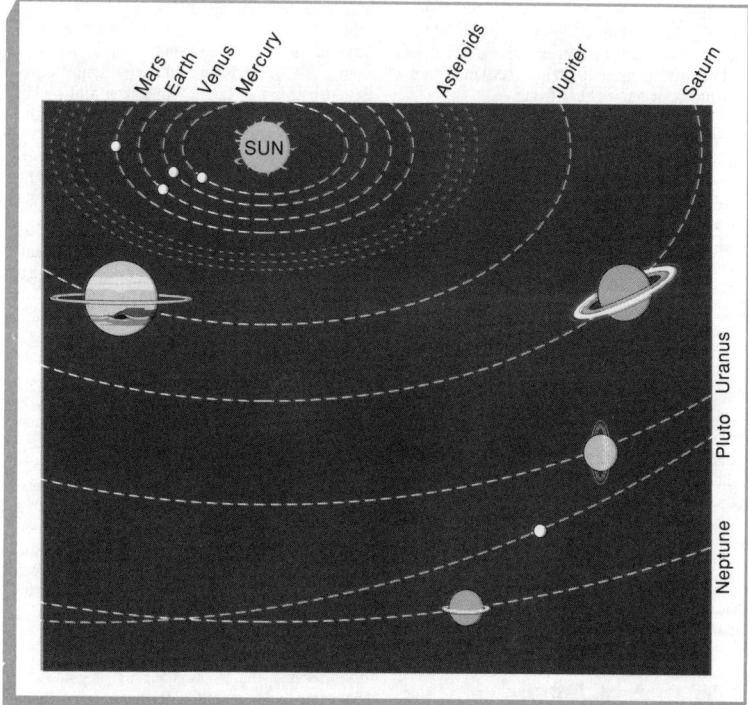

TERRESTRIAL PLANETS

	Mercury	Venus	Earth	Mars
Average distance from Sun	35,960,000 mi.	67,200,000 mi.	92,900,000 mi.	141,500,000 mi.
	57,700,000 km	108,150,000 km	150,000,000 km	227,700,000 km
Rotation period in Earth days	59	243.01	1	1.0004
		(retrograde)		
Period of revolution in Earth days	88	224.7	365.26	687
Average orbital velocity in miles per second	29.7	21.75	18.46	14.98
Inclination of axis	2°	3°	23°27'	25°12'
Inclination of orbit to the ecliptic	7°	3.39°	0°	1.9°
Eccentricity of orbit	0.206	0.007	0.0l7	0.093
Equatorial diameter	3,030 mi.	7,517 mi.	7,921 mi.	4,215 mi.
	4,880 km	12,104 km	12,756 km	6,787 km
Diameter relative to Earth	38.2%	94.9%	100%	53.2%
Mass	7.283×10^{23} lb.	10.7×10^{24} lb.	13.2×10^{24} lb.	14.2×10^{23} lb.
	3.303×10^{23} kg	4.87×10^{24} kg	5.98×10^{24} kg	6.42×10^{23} kg
Mass relative to Earth	5.58%	81.5%	100%	10.74%
Mass of Sun relative to planet mass (with atmosphere and satellites)	5,972,000	408,520	328,900	3,098,710
Average density	3.13 oz./in.³	3.03 oz./in.³	3.19 oz./in.³	2.27 oz./in.³
Gravity (at equator surface)	12.4 ft./sec.²	28.2 ft./sec.²	32.1 ft./sec.²	12.2 ft./sec.²
Gravity (relative to Earth)	38%	88%	100%	38%
Escape velocity at equator	2.7 mi./sec.	6.40 mi./sec.	6.96 mi./sec.	3.1 mi./sec.
	4.3 km/sec.	10.3 km/sec.	11.2 km/sec.	5 km/sec.
Average surface temperature	332°F	854°F	59°F	−67°F
	167°C	457°C	15°C	−55°C
Atmospheric pressure at surface	10^{-15} bar	90 bars	0.98 bar	0.007 bar
Atmosphere (main components)	Virtually none (of that present, 0.98 helium; 0.02 hydrogen)	Carbon dioxide 96%; nitrogen 3.5%	Nitrogen 77%; oxygen 21%; water 1%; argon 0.93%	Carbon dioxide 95% nitrogen 2.7%; argon 1.6%
Planetary satellites	None	None	1 moon	2 moons

high temperatures in the lower atmosphere, 900°F (482°C)—hot enough to melt lead. Radiation of heat from the lower atmosphere is so inefficient that there is little variation of temperature between night and day.

One feature of the Venusian upper atmosphere is markedly different from that of Earth. The atmosphere superrotates on Venus—that is, the atmosphere above the clouds moves 60 times faster than the planet rotates—whereas the Earth and its atmosphere rotate at the same speed. So, high winds are a dominant part of Venusian weather. Even at only 31 miles (50 km) above the surface, which is just under the cloud layer, the winds blow steadily at 109 miles (175 km) per hour.

Soviet space probes that soft-landed on Venus have provided photographs of the planet's surface; radar maps of 93% of the Venusian surface, completed by the U.S. Pioneer Venus spacecraft (from 1978), now give a detailed picture of the planet's surface. A new U.S. Venus orbiter, Magellan, is scheduled to complete the radar mapping and to provide higher resolution.

About 10% of the surface is highland terrain, 70% rolling uplands, and 20% lowland plains. There are two major highland areas: one about half the size of Africa and located in the equatorial region and the other, about the size of Australia, located to the north. The highest mountain on Venus—Maxwell Montes—is in the northern highlands and is higher than Earth's Mt. Everest. Two major areas of suspected volcanic activity have been found and make Venus only the third body in the solar system thought to be volcanically active (along with Earth and Io, a satellite of Jupiter).

Venus is thought to have an internal structure like that of Earth. The outer crust may be thicker than that of Earth, which averages 12.5 miles (20 km). Below that is a thick mantle. The core is believed to be composed of molten nickel-iron.

Earth is the third planet from the Sun and the only one in the solar system known to harbor life. From out in space, our planet appears as a bright, blue-and-white sphere—blue because some 70% of the surface is covered by water, and white because clouds cover about half the planet's surface.

Earth's atmosphere is composed of about 78% nitrogen, 21% oxygen, and traces of other gases. The tenuous outer layer of the atmosphere—the thermosphere—begins about 310 miles (500 km) above Earth's surface. Between about 62 miles down to about 31 miles (100 to 50 km) is the mesosphere; below this is the stratosphere (down to about 8 mi., or 13 km); finally, there is the troposphere, the bottom layer. The atmosphere, along with Earth's magnetic field, shields us from nearly all harmful radiation coming from the Sun and from outer space.

The interior consists of three main layers. The outer crust, largely made up of granite and basalt rock, varies from 55 miles (89 km) deep under the continents to 3 miles (5 km) deep under the oceans. The second main layer, the mantle, extends down to about 1,900 miles (3,060 km) below the surface and is composed of silicate rock rich in iron. The top part of the

mantle is semiliquid, down to about 150 miles (250 km). The rigid upper crust is broken into large plates that move slowly on this partially fluid layer, which is termed the asthenosphere. Beneath this lies the Earth's iron and nickel core. Scientists believe the temperature at the center of the core could be 7,200°F (4,000°C). The outer core is liquid due to the great heat, while an inner core is solid as a result of the great pressure at Earth's center.

The Moon is Earth's only natural satellite. Just over one-quarter the size of Earth in diameter, it is the brightest object in Earth's nighttime sky. The Moon regularly changes in appearance as seen from Earth. The main apparent changes are called phases; for example, the new moon, when the Moon is between Earth and the Sun, is the phase when the Moon cannot be seen; at full moon, when Earth is between the Moon and the Sun, the Moon is seen as completely round. Confusingly, when we see the moon as half a circle, the phase is called a quarter, with the first quarter appearing as the moon goes from a new moon toward a full moon, and the last quarter as the moon passes from a full moon toward a new moon. The full cycle, from new moon to new moon, takes about 28 days. It is believed that the lunar phases gave rise to both the week (7 days from one phase to the next) and the month.

The Moon rotates once during each revolution. Because the Moon is slightly egg-shaped, the same side of the satellite always faces Earth—this side being the elongated small end. The side we do not see is called the far side, not the dark side—all parts of the moon undergo 14 Earth days of light, followed by 14 Earth days of darkness.

Over a decade of exploration of the Moon by U.S. and Soviet space probes was capped by the landing of two U.S. astronauts on the Moon on July 20, 1969. A total of six two-man crews of

> *"The world, which took but six days to make, is likely to take us six thousand years to make out."*
> —Sir Thomas Browne

American astronauts eventually landed on the Moon between 1969 and 1972, and they brought back some 842 pounds (382 kg) of samples.

The world these astronauts found was airless, waterless, and devoid of life. Temperatures on the Moon range from up to 273°F (134°C) on the bright side to –274°F (–170°C) on the unlighted side.

The lunar surface is pockmarked with craters up to 56 miles (90 km) across and is broken by huge mountain ranges. The near side has large regions (called maria, or seas) of solidified lava, indicating that the Moon was once volcanically active. Lunar soil, a mixture of fine powder and broken rock, blankets the Moon's surface.

Mars is the outermost of the four terrestrial planets and has a distinctive reddish coloring, coming from iron oxide in the Martian soil. The Romans named the planet after their god of war, and the two irregularly shaped satellites of Mars have been named after the horses—Deimos (terror) and Phobos (fear)—that pulled the war god's chariot. Mars is visible in Earth's nighttime sky and is lined up with Earth between it and the Sun once every 780 days, though its closest approach to Earth (35,000,000 mi., or 56,000,000 km) comes at 15- or 17-year intervals.

The so-called canals on Mars—later found to be optical illusions—were first observed by 19th-century astronomers and led to the widespread belief that there was life on Mars. (In 1900 the French Academy offered a prize to the first person to find life on any planet *except* Mars, presumably because everyone knew that there was life on that planet.) The planet thus became the target of numerous space probes, both U.S. and Soviet, from the early years of interplanetary exploration.

The first successful flyby of Mars was achieved by the U.S. spacecraft Mariner 4 in 1965. The Soviets became the first to land a probe successfully on the surface of Mars in 1971, but the probe malfunctioned and stopped transmitting after only 20 seconds. It was not until 1976, when the U.S. Viking 1 and Viking 2 landers touched down on Mars, that extensive study of the planet from its surface became possible. In fact, the Viking 1 lander continued to function long after its mission had been completed and sent back information on Martian weather until 1982, when communications with Earth at last failed.

The big question of whether there is (or was) life on Mars has yet to be answered with certainty. The Viking landers conducted three experiments on Martian soil to check for biological processes. Some of the tests yielded positive results, but these could also be explained by the soil chemistry. The lack of other evidence of organic molecules adds to the case against life on Mars.

Orbiting satellites have mapped the entire planet down to a resolution of 492–984 feet (150–300 m).

The planet's surface is heavily cratered, and there is extensive evidence of once-active volcanoes. There are also such spectacular features as Olympus Mons (an extinct volcano 3 times as high as Earth's Mt. Everest); mammoth canyons, one of which is four times deeper than the Grand Canyon; and a gigantic basin (larger than Alaska) in the Southern Hemisphere that was probably created by a single, huge asteroid. The planet has ice caps at both poles (frozen carbon dioxide with some water), and the ice caps advance and recede with changes in the seasons.

But the most intriguing aspect of the Martian surface is an indication that water once flowed there in great quantities. Parts of the terrain apparently have sedimentary origins, and there are many long channels, complete with smaller tributary channels and islands, that extend for hundreds of kilometers. Scientists speculate that Mars once had a much thicker atmosphere, made up of gases vented during volcanic eruptions, which would have made it possible for water in its liquid state to exist on the surface. Martian atmospheric pressure is now so low, however, that surface water would immediately vaporize. It is conjectured that the water in the past flowed through the channels to lowland areas and then sank into the Martian regolith, or upper soil layer, since there is no geologic evidence that standing bodies of water ever existed. Astronomers believe that at least some of the primordial water may still be trapped as ice in the regolith.

Mars is too small to sustain continual volcanic activity. Its atmosphere apparently thinned out after volcanic activity ceased. Atmospheric pressure is now just two one-hundredths of that on Earth at sea level, and the predominant gas is carbon dioxide, which is relatively heavy. A small amount of water vapor in the atmosphere is enough to form some clouds, small patches of fog in some valleys, and occasionally even patches of frost. Surface temperatures vary from about 39°F (4°C) at the equator to about –189°F (–123°C) at the poles.

By far the most pronounced feature of Martian weather (apart from the bone-chilling cold) are the dust storms. Whipped by hurricane-force winds, these dust storms sometimes engulf the entire planet for weeks on end.

ASTEROIDS The asteroid belt—first crossed by the U.S. space probe Pioneer 10 on its way to Jupiter in 1973—lies between Mars and Jupiter. An asteroid is a body much smaller than a planet that orbits the Sun. The name *asteroid* means "starlike" and was given to asteroids because they are so small they appear as points of light (as do stars) even in powerful telescopes. Otherwise, asteroids are not like stars at all. Astronomers once thought the asteroid belt had been formed by the breakup of a planet between Mars and Jupiter, but they now think it is debris left over from the formation of the solar system. For some reason the asteroids did not accrete into a planet, perhaps because of Jupiter's strong gravitational pull.

Not all asteroids are found in the asteroid belt. Some cross Earth's orbit, for example.

The Outer Planets

Beyond Mars and the asteroid belt lie the five known outer planets of our solar system. Four of these planets—Jupiter, Saturn, Uranus, and Neptune—are the so-called gas giants. Many times larger than the terrestrial planets, these planets are huge, dense balls of hydrogen and other gases. Beyond them (most of the time) lies the solar system's outermost and smallest-known planet, Pluto, which may be nothing more than a tiny ball of frozen gases.

Jupiter is the largest planet in the solar system. It has 2.5 times more mass than all the other planets of the solar system together and is 11 times as large as Earth in diameter. Jupiter is so large that scientists believe it almost became a Sun: as the gases and dust contracted to form the planet, gravitational forces created tremendous pressure and temperature inside the core—perhaps as high as tens of thousands of degrees. But there was not enough mass

available to create the temperatures needed to start a fusion reaction such as that of the Sun (above 18,000,000°F or 10,000,000°C, at the sun's core); thus Jupiter has been slowly cooling down ever since. Even so, Jupiter still radiates about 2.5 times as much heat as it receives from the Sun.

The first object to reach Jupiter from Earth was Pioneer 10. It returned the first close-up pictures of the giant planet in 1973. Subsequently, the more sophisticated space probes Voyager 1 and Voyager 2 passed by Jupiter in 1979 and sent back images and more data on the planet. One of the most exciting discoveries by Voyager 1 was that Jupiter has a faint but extensive ring system that extends almost 186,000 miles (300,000 km) out from the planet's surface. And in 1983 a study of Voyager 2 readings indicated that Jupiter's magnetic field—stretched by solar wind into a long "tail" on the side away from the Sun—had actually reached Saturn when Jupiter and Saturn were aligned with the Sun (which occurs about once every 20 years).

Jupiter's thick atmosphere, which may extend downward by as much as 620 miles

(1,000 km), is primarily made up of hydrogen, some helium, and traces of methane, water, and ammonia. Because the planet spins so fast (one rotation in just under 10 hours), its clouds tend to form bands. They give the planet its red-, brownish-, and white-striped appearance. Bands of clouds at higher altitudes are carried eastward by jet streams, while those at lower levels are blown westward.

There are numerous eddies and swirls in Jupiter's atmosphere, but none can compare with the Great Red Spot, apparently a massive hurricane (rotating counterclockwise) located in the Southern Hemisphere near the equator. The Great Red Spot was first observed some 300 years ago, and this storm continues unabated today. Since 1938 three smaller white ovals have been observed to the south of the Great Red Spot.

Jupiter's cloud tops are extremely cold (about –202°F, or –130°C), but temperatures increase deeper inside the atmosphere. Pressure also increases, and at about 620 miles (1,000 km) below the outermost atmospheric layers, great oceans of liquid hydrogen form Jupiter's surface. These may be some 12,000 miles

GAS GIANTS

	Jupiter	Saturn	Uranus	Neptune
Position among planets	Fifth	Sixth	Seventh	Eighth
Average distance	483,300,000 mi.	914,000,000 mi.	1,782,000,000 mi.	2,793,000,000 mi.
from Sun	778,300,000 km	1,472,000,000 km	2,870,000,000 km	4,497,000,000 km
Rotation period	9 hrs. 55 min.	10 hrs. 39 min.	–23.9 hrs.	17 hrs.
	30 sec.	20 sec.	(retrograde)	
Period of revolution	4,332.6 Earth days	10,759.2 Earth days	30,685.4 Earth days	60,189 Earth days
	(11.86 yrs.)	(29.46 yrs.)	(84.01 yrs.)	(164.8 yrs.)
Average orbital velocity	8.1 mi./sec.	5.99 mi./sec.	4.2 mi./sec.	3.35 mi./sec.
	13.06 km/sec.	9.64 km/sec.	6.8 km/sec.	5.4 km/sec.
Inclination of axis	3°5'	26°44'	97°55'	28°41'
Inclination of orbit to the ecliptic	1.3°	2.5°	0.8°	1.8°
Eccentricity of orbit	0.048	0.056	0.047	0.009
Equatorial diameter	88,803 mi.	74,520 mi.	32,168 mi.	30,739 mi.
	143,000 km	120,000 km	51,800 km	49,500 km
Diameter relative to Earth	1,121%	941%	410%	388%
Mass	4.187×10^{27} lb.	12.538×10^{26} lb.	19.09×10^{25} lb.	2.271×10^{26} lb.
	1.899×10^{27} kg	5.686×10^{26} kg	8.66×10^{25} kg	1.030×10^{26} kg
Mass relative to Earth	31,790%	9,520%	1,460%	1,723%
Mass of Sun relative to planet mass (with atmosphere and satellites)	104,700%	349,800%	2,275,900%	1,933,200%
Average density	0.759 oz./in.^{3}	0.40 oz./in.^{3}	c. 0.7 oz./in.^{3}	1.0 oz/in.^{3}
Gravity (at equator surface)	75.06 ft./sec.^{2}	29.69 ft./sec.^{2}	25.5 ft./sec.^{2}	36 ft./sec.^{2}
Gravity (relative to Earth)	234%	92%	79%	112%
Escape velocity at equator	36.9 mi./sec.	22.1 mi./sec.	13.2 mi./sec.	14.66 mi./sec.
	59.5 km/sec	35.6 km/sec	21.2 km/sec	23.6 km/sec
Average temperature	(at surface)	(at surface)	(cloud tops)	(cloud tops)
in atmosphere	–162°F	–208°F	–355°F	–261°F
	–108°C	–133°C	–215°C	–177°C
Atmospheric pressure at surface	3,000,000 bars	8,000,000 bars	N.A.	N.A.
Atmosphere (main components)	(near cloud tops) hydrogen 90%; helium c. 10%	hydrogen 94%; helium c. 6%	hydrogen, helium, methane % N.A.	ethane, acetylene, hydrogen sulfide % N.A.
Other atmospheric gases	methane, water, ammonia, ethane, acetylene, phosphine, hydrogen cyanide, carbon monoxide	methane, ammonia	Unknown	Unknown
Planetary Satellites	16	15	5	8

(20,000 km) deep. Beneath them the hydrogen is so densely compacted it is in a metallic state. Within this is the core, thought to be an iron and silicate rock ball about the size of Earth.

Jupiter is now known to have 16 moons, the four largest being the Galilean moons, so called because they were first observed by Galileo. The Galilean moons are Ganymede, Callisto, Europa, and Io—after the Roman god Jupiter's cupbearer (Ganymede) and three of Jupiter's inamorata. Ganymede is the largest moon in the solar system—although previously this honor was accorded to Saturn's Titan—and is larger even than the planets Pluto and Mercury. It is a huge, cratered ball of ice and may have a core of solid silicate rock. Callisto, with an orbit outside that of Ganymede, is also covered with ice and is riddled with thousands of craters. Europa, which orbits inside Ganymede, is about the size of our Moon and has a smooth surface marked by networks of cracks. The most interesting of Jupiter's moons is Io, which of all four Galilean moon orbits is closest to Jupiter. Voyager 1 photographed volcanoes erupting on Io. Orange-red patches on Io's mottled surface are apparently molten sulfur beds, but most other parts of Io's surface are apparently very cold (about –229°F, or –145°C). The volcanic activity is caused by gravitational force from Jupiter, Europa, and Ganymede.

Saturn is the sixth planet of the solar system and the second largest, after Jupiter. The outermost of the planets that can be identified easily in Earth's nighttime sky with the unaided eye, Saturn has a pale yellowish color and is not nearly so bright as Mars. Saturn's spectacular ring system, which makes it one of the most interesting of the planets, is visible only through a telescope. Its rings are more extensive than those of any other planet.

Like Jupiter, Saturn is composed of densely compacted hydrogen, helium, and other gases. Liquid or metallic hydrogen probably exists underneath the planet's thick atmosphere, and scientists believe there is a solid core of rock about two times the size of Earth at its center. Saturn's high rotational speed (once every 10 hours 40 minutes) makes it the most oblate (flattened) of all the planets; it is almost 6,800 miles (11,000 km) wider at the equator than on a line through the poles.

Though exploration of Saturn began in 1979 with the first flyby (Pioneer 11), the Voyager 1 and Voyager 2 missions in 1980 and 1981, respectively, provided the first detailed look at the planet. Scientists will probably spend years sifting through the data and, though there were important new findings, many questions about Saturn remain unanswered.

The Voyagers found a huge storm thousands of miles across on Saturn, along with a wide band of extremely high winds—up to 994 miles (1,600 km) per hour—at the equator. Winds in this band all travel in the direction of the planet's rotation (unlike bands of wind on Jupiter). The Voyagers also discovered a vast hydrogen cloud circling the planet above the equator.

Voyager's most exciting discoveries concern the planetary rings. Previously, about six different rings had been identified within the ring system, but Voyager 1 pictures show as many as 1,000 separate rings. Narrow rings can even be seen within the Cassini Division, once thought to be an empty gap between the two major parts of the ring system. Some rings are not circular, and at least two rings are intertwined, or "braided." A strange new phenomenon was also discovered in the rings. Voyager 1 pictures clearly show dark, radial fingers—"spokes"—moving inside the rings in the direction of rotation. Scientists speculate that they are made of ice crystals.

Voyager 2 pictures show that Saturn has far more than 1,000 rings—perhaps as many as a hundred thousand or more. One of the brightest rings is shown to be under 152 meters (500 ft.) thick. The pictures do not show signs of moonlets that some scientists had thought were the cause of gaps between individual rings.

Saturn's 12 moons were known before the arrival of the Voyagers, and instruments aboard the space probe helped locate three new ones. Most of Saturn's moons are relatively small and composed of rock and ice. All but one of the small moons are pockmarked by meteor craters, and in some cases the moons appear to have been cracked by collisions with especially large meteors. But Voyager pictures show that one moon, Enceladus, is smooth in large regions apparently unmarked by collisions with meteors. Scientists believe that Enceladus is being pulled and stretched by the combined gravities of a nearby moon and Saturn itself. Tidal forces have apparently heated the core of Enceladus and made its surface soft enough to smooth over any craters formed by meteor impacts.

Titan, Saturn's largest moon (3,000 mi., or 4,800 km in diameter) is the only moon in the solar system known to have an atmosphere of any substance. Scientists suspect that at least some precursors of life may have formed there. For this reason Voyager 1 was guided to within about 2,500 miles (4,000 km) of Titan during the Saturn flyby. Though Titan's surface was obscured by dense clouds, Voyager's sensors nevertheless returned a considerable amount of information about the moon and its atmosphere. Titan's atmosphere is composed mostly of nitrogen, like that of Earth, with only a small percentage of methane and carbon monoxide. Atmospheric pressure is at least 1.5 times that on Earth and temperatures range around –294°F (–181°C). Titan in fact appears to be a frozen version of Earth before life evolved.

The possibility of oceans of liquid methane (or of nitrogen or methane rain) on Titan was a matter of considerable controversy for some time after Voyager 1 investigated the moon. But an analysis of Voyager data published in 1983 seems to indicate that Titan is "dry," at least in the regions investigated. Pools of liquid methane might still exist in other low-lying regions, but the study concludes that it is unlikely that either methane or nitrogen condenses to liquid form on Titan.

Voyager 2 also found seasonal differences between the planet's two hemispheres and photographed a storm some 4,000 miles (6,500 km) wide.

Uranus is the seventh planet in the solar system and the third of the gas giants. The planet is barely visible in Earth's nighttime sky (it looks like a faint star) and for that reason, it went undiscovered until 1781.

Nearly the same size as Neptune and only about 5% of Jupiter's mass, Uranus is a faintly greenish color, perhaps because its atmosphere contains methane. The planet's axis of rotation is tipped over on its side, and in 1977 a system of nine faint rings was discovered. There are five known moons of Uranus, which range between about 186 and 621 miles (300 and 1,000 km) in diameter.

The atmosphere of Uranus is composed of hydrogen, helium, and methane and is very clear and cold (–355°F, or –215°C). No clouds and little haze have been observed.

Scientists speculate that, as on Jupiter and Saturn, temperatures and pressures increase dramatically down through the outer layer of atmosphere. At some point the hydrogen and helium would be sufficiently compressed to form a liquid or slushy surface "crust." Underneath this crust they believe is a mantle of solidified methane, ammonia, and water; and inside this mantle, a rocky core of silicon and iron about 15 times as massive as Earth. The core is hot, probably about 12,000°F (7,000°C).

Neptune, the last of the gas giants, is the eighth planet in the solar system. It was discovered in 1846 after mathematical calculations based on irregularities in the orbit of Uranus provided astronomers with the correct location of the planet. Neptune, like Uranus, has been surrounded by considerable uncertainty because of its enormous distance from Earth. The 1989 visit by Voyager 2 contributed greatly to improved understanding of the planet.

Neptune is a pale bluish color, and its atmosphere is composed of hydrogen and helium. Unlike Uranus, Neptune's atmosphere is often hazy—perhaps because of ice or other particles formed from an unknown substance—and it is very cold at the cloud tops (about –261°F, or –177°C).

Scientists believe that Neptune has a three-layered structure similar to that of Uranus: a crust of solidified or liquid hydrogen and helium that gradually thins outward into an atmosphere; a mantle of solidified gases and water; and a hot, rocky core (about 12,000°F or 7,000°C) some 15 times as massive as Earth. But one aspect of Neptune remains a mystery. Despite similarities with Uranus, Neptune has been found to radiate more heat than it receives from the Sun (at a rate of 0.03 microwatts per ton of mass). Uranus, on the other hand, does not emit excess heat.

Neptune has eight known moons, Triton and Nereid, discovered from Earth, and six others discovered by Voyager 2, and a ring system containing three rings and two ringlike features. Triton is the largest moon and has an atmosphere. Triton is unusual in that it travels in a direction opposite that of Neptune's rotation, suggesting that it has a different origin from the planet.

Pluto, the ninth and outermost (most of the time) known planet of the solar system, is a ball of frozen gases probably only about the size of Earth's Moon. Because of its relatively small size and chaotic orbit (which at times crosses inside Neptune's orbit), some scientists think that Pluto is not really a planet at all. Instead, they theorize that Pluto is only a former moon of Neptune that has been pulled out of orbit by some other celestial body.

Pluto was discovered in 1930 as a result of an extensive search by Clyde Tombaugh. Although his search was based on mathematical calculations derived from deviations in the orbit of Neptune, most astronomers now think that Tombaugh found Pluto as a result of a lucky accident.

Frozen methane and a thin atmosphere of methane and some other gases have been detected on Pluto. Pluto has one known moon, Charon, discovered in 1978. Charon is about one-third the size of Pluto. Pluto and Charon rotate and revolve synchronously like a double planet system.

Basic Facts about the Planets

The inner, or terrestrial, planets are somewhat like Earth, and the outer, or gas giant, planets, except for Pluto, are similar to Jupiter. Pluto is not very much like the planets in either group as far as we know, but it is so far away that its exact nature is not known.

Some of the words and phrases used in the table are briefly defined below:

Bar A measure of pressure slightly less than Earth's air pressure at sea level under normal conditions, or about 29.53 (75 cm) inches of mercury, the measurement used in giving the weather report of barometric pressure; *bar* is derived from *barometer*. Earth's air pressure at sea level is 0.98 bar.

Eccentricity A number that measures the shape of a planet's orbit; all the planetary orbits are curves called ellipses, which are "squashed" circles; the smaller the eccentricity, the more an ellipse is like a circle, which has an eccentricity of 0.

Ecliptic The apparent path of the Sun through the stars as viewed from Earth, which is in a plane inclined 23.5° to Earth's equator. The planets are all roughly in the same plane, so like the Sun, they seem to move through the same groups of stars as the Sun does over the course of a year.

Escape velocity The speed needed for an object to be propelled from the surface of a planet and not fall back. Since the escape velocity for Earth is 6.96 miles per second (11.2 km), a rocket expected to reach the Moon or another planet must develop a speed of at least 7 miles (12 km) a second.

Inclination of axis The angle that the line about which a planet rotates makes with the plane defined by its path around the Sun.

Inclination of orbit to the ecliptic The angle that the plane defined by a planet's path around the Sun makes with the plane defined by the apparent path of the Sun among the stars as seen from Earth.

PLUTO

Position among planets	Ninth
Average distance from the sun	3,664,000,000 mi.
	5,900,000,000 km
Rotation period	6 days, 9 hrs.
	18 min.
	(retrograde)
Period of revolution	90,465 Earth days
	(247.7 yrs.)
Average orbital velocity	2.9 mi./sec.
	4.7 km/sec
Inclination of axis	60° (?)
Inclination of orbit to the ecliptic	17.2°
Eccentricity of orbit	0.25
Equatorial diameter	1,423 mi. 2,290 km
Diameter relative to Earth	18%
Mass	c. 14.5×10^{21} lb. c.
	6.6×10^{21} kg
Mass relative to Earth	c. 0.17%
Mass of sun relative to planet mass (with atmosphere and satellites)	300,000,000% (?)
Average density	c. 0.2 oz./in.^{3}
Gravity (at equator surface)	14.1 ft./sec.^{2}
Gravity (relative to Earth)	43%
Escape velocity at equator	3.29 mi./sec.
	5.3 km/sec
	(at surface)
Average temperature in atmosphere	c. −460°F
	c. −273°C
Atmospheric pressure at surface	0.1 millibar (?)
Atmosphere (main components)	Tenuous; methane and possibly neon
Other atmospheric gases	Unknown
Planetary satellites	1

Orbital velocity The speed of a planet in its path around the Sun.

Retrograde In the opposite direction of other planets.

Revolution The trip a planet makes about the Sun.

Rotation The turning of a planet about a line through its center.

The numbers used in tables are sometimes given in scientific notation because of their size. A large number, such as 1,840,000,000, might be written as 1.84×10^9. The exponent *9* signifies the number of places after the first digit. A small number such as 0.000000000000001 is written as 10^{-15}, where the exponent *−15* tells the number of zeroes—counting the one before the decimal place—before the numeral *1*.

THE SUN

The ancients may have been on to something when they worshiped the Sun. It is certainly the biggest and brightest thing in the immediate vicinity. Compared with other stars, however, the Sun is remarkably average, and is classed as a yellow dwarf.

Virtually all of the energy used by living things comes from the Sun. The Sun's light causes photosynthesis in green plants, and its heat causes winds. Fossil fuels, such as coal, oil, and natural gas, got their energy originally from photosynthesis, as did wood. Animals

CHARACTERISTICS OF THE SUN

Position in solar system	**Center**
Mean distance from Earth	**92,960,000 mi.**
	(149,600,000 km)
Distance from center of Milky Way galaxy	**27,710 light-yrs.**
Estimated velocity of revolution	**175 mi./sec.**
	(282 km/sec)
Period of rotation	**27 da. on average**
Inclination (relative to Earth's orbit)	**7°**
Equatorial diameter	**865,000 mi. (1,392,000 km)**
Diameter relative to Earth	**109 times**
Mass	**1,800,000,000,000,000,000,000,000,000 tons**
Gravity relative to Earth's	**27.8 times**
Temperature at core	**36,000,000°F (20,000°C)**
Temperature at surface	**10,260°F (5,700°C)**
Main components	**Hydrogen and helium**
Expected life of hydrogen fuel supply	**5,000,000,000 more years**

derive their energy from plants that photosynthesize, either directly or indirectly. The only natural nonsolar energy sources are nuclear reactions (which also produce geothermal energy) and the tides, which are produced largely by the Moon, but in part by the Sun.

Because the Sun is a ball of gases, it does not rotate as a whole. The equator rotates in about 25 days, while gas near the poles rotates in about 30 days. The period of rotation at each latitude can be found by observing sunspots, which are magnetic storms. Sunspots appear and disappear in a mysterious 22-year cycle that many think influences weather on Earth, although convincing proof is lacking. Sometimes sunspots disappear for tens of years at a time, as during the period from 1645 to 1715. It may or may not be a coincidence that those years coincided with the "Little Ice Age" in Europe, when temperatures were far below average.

Like Earth the Sun is composed of various layers. The part we see is called the photosphere. In the Sun's interior, energy is generated when hydrogen fuses to become helium in the core. Above the photosphere is a region of pinkish gases, the chromosphere. Above that is a large halo, visible only in eclipses, called the corona. Particles from the Sun, the solar wind, stream through the solar system, creating auroras on Earth. Strong increases in solar wind during solar flares can interfere with radio communication.

The Sun will eventually burn all its hydrogen fuel into helium. When that happens, the nature of the Sun will change from a yellow dwarf to a red giant. Such a star is typically larger in diameter than the orbit of Venus, and may be larger than Earth's orbit. In either case Earth would be burned to a cinder, and no life could survive on it. At the moment, however, it seems that other disasters are likely to happen first.

THE CONSTELLATIONS

Constellations are small groups of stars that from our vantage point on Earth, seem to form some particular shape. In actuality, however, the stars forming a constellation are usually at vastly different distances from the solar system. They only appear to form a particular figure from Earth.

Long ago, before recorded history, people began naming these groups. By Sumerian times (3000–2500 B.C.), stories were already being told about how particular constellations were formed. Most of our present knowledge of such stories comes from the Greeks, much of whose mythology were reflected in the stars and planets.

One group of constellations has exerted a special influence on human thought, at least since 1500 B.C. As the Sun, Moon, and planets move through the sky, they pass through a group of 12 constellations, called the constellations of the zodiac. Chaldean astronomers believed that the presence of the Sun, a planet, or even the Moon in one of these constellations at a person's birth (or at other significant times) influenced happenings on Earth. We call this belief astrology. Because of the precession of the equinoxes (see above), the traditional 12 constellations are no longer where they were 3,500 years ago. Modern astrologers have divided the year into 12 "houses," based on where the signs of the zodiac used to be. Thus, when an astronomer and an astrologer refer to the zodiac, they mean quite different things.

Today astronomers use constellations for their own purposes, such as for mapping the sky. Each part of the sky is named by a particular constellation. These constellations, especially in the Southern Hemisphere, may not be traditional ones, but rather, groups of stars astronomers have named so that for reference purposes all of the sky is labeled (such constellations are labeled "of modern origin" in the table below). The International Astronomical Union has decreed that each such constellation be bounded by straight north-south and east-west lines. As a result, many of the larger traditional constellations extend beyond the boundaries of modern astronomical constellations.

While astronomers often use the traditional names of stars, most of which come to us from Latin or Arabic sources, they also use another system for naming objects in the sky (galaxies, radio sources, quasars, etc.) that is based on constellations. Generally, the brightest star in a particular astronomical constellation is called alpha, the next brightest beta, and so on, through several letters of the Greek alphabet. Thus Sirius is also known as alpha Canis Majoris, usually abbreviated as α CMa, which means it is the brightest star in the constellation Big Dog (Sirius has long been known as the "dog star"). Since Sirius is a binary star (see "The Universe" below), the brighter main star is officially α CMa A. Bright radio sources were once designated by the name of a constellation followed by a letter of the Roman alphabet, such as Cassiopeia A (Cassiopeia is a character

CONSTELLATIONS AND BRIGHT STARS

The 25 brightest stars are listed in the constellation where they can be seen. The number following the official name is their rank. Thus Sirius is listed under Canis Major as "Contains Sirius (α CMa A) – 1," which means it is the brightest star, while Canopus, the second brightest, is followed by "– 2."

Name	Genitive	Abbreviation	Translation	Remarks
Andromeda	Andromedae	And	Andromeda	Character in Greek myth
Antlia	Antliae	Ant	Pump	Of modern origin
Apus	Apodis	Aps	Bird of Paradise	Of modern origin
Aquarius	Aquarii	Aqr	Water Bearer	In zodiac
Aquila	Aquilae	Aql	Eagle	Contains Altair (α Aql) – 12
Ara	Arae	Ara	Altar	—
Aries	Arietis	Ari	Ram	In zodiac
Auriga	Aurigae	Aur	Charioteer	Contains Capella (α Aur) – 6
Boötes	Boötis	Boo	Herdsman	Contains Arcturus (α Boo) – 3
Caelum	Caeli	Cae	Chisel	Of modern origin
Camelopardalis	Camelopardalis	Cam	Giraffe	Of modern origin
Cancer	Cancri	Cnc	Crab	In zodiac
Canes Venatici	Canum Venaticorum	CVn	Hunting Dogs	Of modern origin
Canis Major	Canis Majoris	CMa	Big Dog	Contains Sirius (α CMa A) – 1 and Adhara (ε CMa A) – 22
Canis Minor	Canis Minoris	CMi	Little Dog	Contains Procyon (α CMi A) – 8
Capricornus	Capricorni	Cap	Goat	In zodiac
Carina	Carinae	Car	Ship's Keel[1]	Of modern origin; contains Canopus (α Car) – 2
Cassiopeia	Cassiopeiae	Cas	Cassiopeia	Character in Greek myth
Centaurus	Centauri	Cen	Centaur	Character in Greek myth; Contains Rigil Kentaurus (α Cen A) – 4 and Hadar (β Cen AB) – 11
Cepheus	Cephei	Cep	Cepheus	Character in Greek myth
Cetus	Ceti	Cet	Whale	—
Chamaeleon	Chamaeleonis	Cha	Chameleon	Of modern origin
Circinus	Circini	Cir	Compass	Of modern origin
Columba	Columbae	Col	Dove	Of modern origin
Coma Berenices	Comae Berenices	Com	Berenice's Hair	Third-century B.C. Egyptian queen
Corona Australis	Coronae Australis	CrA	Southern Crown	Of modern origin
Corona Borealis	Coronae Borealis	CrB	Northern Crown	—
Corvus	Corvi	Crv	Crow	—
Crater	Crateris	Crt	Cup	—
Crux	Crucis	Cru	Southern Cross	Of modern origin; contains Beta Crucis (β Cru) – 19 and Acrux (α Cru A) – 21
Cygnus	Cygni	Cyg	Swan	(α Cyg) – 18
Delphinus	Delphini	Del	Dolphin	—
Dorado	Doradus	Dor	Goldfish	Of modern origin
Draco	Draconis	Dra	Dragon	—
Equuleus	Equulei	Equ	Little Horse	—
Eridanus	Eridani	Eri	River Eridanus	Contains Achernar (α Eri) – 10
Fornax	Fornacis	For	Furnace	Of modern origin
Gemini	Geminorum	Gem	Twins	In zodiac; contains Pollux (β Gem) – 17
Grus	Gruis	Gru	Crane	Of modern origin
Hercules	Herculis	Her	Hercules	Character from Greek myth
Horologium	Horologii	Hor	Clock	Of modern origin
Hydra	Hydrae	Hya	Hydra (water monster)	Monster from Greek myth
Hydrus	Hydri	Hyi	Sea Serpent	Of modern origin
Indus	Indi	Ind	Indian	Of modern origin
Lacerta	Lacertae	Lac	Lizard	Of modern origin
Leo	Leonis	Leo	Lion	In zodiac; contains Regulus (α Leo A) – 20
Leo Minor	Leonis Minoris	LMi	Little Lion	Of modern origin
Lepus	Leporis	Lep	Hare	—
Libra	Librae	Lib	Scales	In zodiac

Name	Genitive	Abbreviation	Translation	Remarks
Lupus	Lupi	Lup	Wolf	—
Lynx	Lyncis	Lyn	Lynx	Of modern origin
Lyra	Lyrae	Lyr	Harp	Contains Vega (α Lyr) – 5
Mensa	Mensae	Men	Table (mountain)	Of modern origin
Microscopium	Microscopii	Mic	Microscope	Of modern origin
Monoceros	Monocerotis	Mon	Unicorn	Of modern origin
Musca	Muscae	Mus	Fly	Of modern origin
Norma	Normae	Nor	Level (square)	Of modern origin
Octans	Octanis	Oct	Octant	Of modern origin
Ophiuchus	Ophiuchi	Oph	Ophiuchus (serpent bearer)	Character in Greek myth
Orion	Orionis	Ori	Orion	The hunter, character in Greek myth; contains Rigel (β Ori A) – 7, Betelgeuse (α Ori) – 9, and Bellatrix (γ Ori) – 24
Pavo	Pavonis	Pav	Peacock	—
Pegasus	Pegasi	Peg	Pegasus	Winged horse in Greek myth
Perseus	Persei	Per	Perseus	Character in Greek myth
Phoenix	Phoenicis	Phe	Phoenix	Of modern origin
Pictor	Pictoris	Pic	Easel	Of modern origin
Pisces	Piscium	Psc	Fish	In zodiac
Piscis Austrinus	Piscis Austrini	PsA	Southern Fish	Contains Fomalhaut (α PsA) – 16
Puppis	Puppis	Pup	Ship's Stern[1]	Of modern origin
Pyxis	Pyxidis	Pyx	Ship's Compass[1]	Of modern origin
Reticulum	Reticuli	Ret	Net	Of modern origin
Sagitta	Sagittae	Sge	Arrow	—
Sagittarius	Sagittarii	Sgr	Archer	In zodiac
Scorpius	Scorpii	Sco	Scorpion	In zodiac; contains Antares (α Sco A) – 15 and Shaula (λ Sco) – 23
Sculptor	Sculptoris	Scl	Sculptor	Of modern origin
Scutum	Scuti	Sct	Shield	Of modern origin
Serpens	Serpentis	Ser	Serpent	—
Sextans	Sextantis	Sex	Sextant	Of modern origin
Taurus	Tauri	Tau	Bull	In zodiac; contains Aldebran (α Tau A) – 13 and Elnath (β Tau) – 25
Telescopium	Telescopii	Tel	Telescope	Of modern origin
Triangulum	Trianguli	Tri	Triangle	—
Triangulum Australle	Trianguli Australis	TrA	Southern Triangle	Of modern origin
Tucana	Tucanae	Tuc	Toucan	Of modern origin
Ursa Major	Ursae Majoris	UMa	Big Bear	Big Dipper
Ursa Minor	Ursae Minoris	UMi	Little Bear	Little Dipper
Vela	Velorum	Vel	Ship's Sails[1]	Of modern origin
Virgo	Virginis	Vir	Virgin	In zodiac; contains Spica (α Vir) – 14
Volans	Volantis	Vol	Flying Fish	Of modern origin
Vulpecula	Vulpeculae	Vul	Little Fox	Of modern origin

1. Formerly formed the constellation Argo Navis, the Argonaut's Ship.

from Greek mythology) or Cygnus A (the Swan). Unfortunately, this system has been largely abandoned, so the same radio source may have several different names, depending on the astronomer. X-ray sources are still designated by the name of the constellation, followed by a hyphenated X and number. The number 1 is the brightest X-ray source in a given constellation, so Scorpius X-1 is the brightest X-ray source in the constellation Scorpio.

All the astronomer's constellations are named in Latin. When they use a constellation to locate a star, the grammatical form of the constellation's name that means "of the thing" (the genitive) is used. Thus the constellation

Big Dog is officially Canis Major, but Sirius is alpha Canis Majoris, or "alpha of Big Dog."

"Art is I; science is we."
—Claude Bernard (1813–78)

MAJOR TELESCOPES

Telescopes were first discovered in Holland about 400 years ago. The first telescopes used lenses, familiar at the time from lenses in spectacles, to gather light and focus it. Later in the 17th century, scientists realized that curved mirrors could also gather and focus light. Since the light did not need to pass through the mirror (as light passes through a lens), mirrors proved to be more efficient than lenses for large telescopes.

OPTICAL TELESCOPES

Year	Type	Importance
1608	Lens	Hans Lipperhey in Holland applies for first patent on a telescope
1609	Lens	Galileo builds first astronomical telescopes, eventually reaching 30 power
1611	Lens	Johannes Kepler introduces convex lens, producing greater power
1663	Mirror	James Gregory is first to think that reflecting telescope can be made
1668	Mirror	Isaac Newton builds first telescope to use mirror to collect light, rather than lens
1723	Mirror	John Hadley invents reflecting telescope based on parabola, which concentrates light at a point
1789	Lens	William Herschel builds telescope with 48-in. (122-cm) lens, the largest for many years
1897	Lens	Alvan Clark builds what is still world's largest telescope to use lens instead of mirror
1917	Mirror	Hooker Telescope at Mount Wilson in California is put into operation; it will be world's largest for about 30 years
1929	Combination	Bernard Schmidt's telescopes, combining lenses and mirrors, are the first made; Schmidt telescope becomes workhorse of astronomy
1948	Mirror	Hale Telescope (200 in., or 5 m), located on Mt. Palomar in California, becomes largest and best on Earth
1962	Mirror	Largest telescope devoted to observing the Sun is erected at Kitt Peak in Arizona
1976	Mirror	Soviet Zelenchukskaya becomes largest telescope, but various problems limit effectiveness
1979	Mirrors	MMT on Mt. Hopkins in Arizona uses six mirrors to obtain equivalent light-gathering power of 177-in. (4.5 m) reflector
1990	Mirror	Hubble Space Telescope (94 in., or 2.4 m) becomes first optical telescope in space

RADIO TELESCOPES

Before 1931 all telescopes were optical—i.e., they gathered and focused electromagnetic radiation in the range people can sense with their eyes. Stars, planets, and other objects in the universe also produce other wavelengths of radiation, however. A radio telescope gathers and focuses radiation at long wavelengths, the same kind of electromagnetic radiation used for for transmission of radio signals.

Year	Type	Importance
1931	Ordinary antenna	Karl Jansky accidentally discovers, in trying to track down sources of static, that radio waves are coming from space
1937	Parabolic dish	Grote Reber builds first intentional radio telescope in dish, Wheaton, Ill.
1957	Steerable dish	Parabolic dish (250 ft., or 75 m) at Jodrell Bank in England is first major radio telescope
1962	Steerable dish	Dish (300 ft., or 90 m) at Green Bank, W.Va., first used to search for extraterrestrial life; it collapses mysteriously on Nov. 15, 1988
1963	Fixed dish	Largest fixed-dish radio telescope, 1,000 ft. (305 m) across, is built in valley at Arecibo, Puerto Rico
1970	Steerable dish	World's largest steerable dish, at Effelsberg, W. Germany is 328 ft. (100 m) in diameter
1977	Several antennas	First Very Long Baseline Interferometry begins operating at Caltech's Owens Valley Radio Observatory
1980	27 antennas	Very Long Array (VLA) is built in 13 mi. (21 km) Y shape near Socorro, New Mex.

THE UNIVERSE

Most of the universe was greatly misunderstood until the 20th century. People saw planets, stars, and constellations but thought they were points of fire or light located on great spheres of crystal. The most common notion from the time of the ancient Greek philosophers until the end of the middle ages was that a number of crystal spheres revolved about Earth, and that each of the planets and Earth's Moon occupied one of these spheres. All the stars occupied the farthest sphere. There were only about 6,000 stars known, those visible to the naked eye (and about half of these were south of the equator, so few Europeans had ever seen them). That was it.

In 1609 Galileo of Italy turned the first astronomical telescope on the heavens. Galileo's early telescopes were good enough to show that the Milky Way was not merely a whitish band across the sky but consisted of a vast number of stars, far more than the few thousand visible with the naked eye in Italy. People soon began to speculate about astronomical entities beyond a simple sphere of stars, but it took a long time before telescopes were sufficiently powerful to

OTHER TYPES

Since both short wavelengths and long ones coming from space had been studied by optical and radio telescopes, it seemed likely that other wavelengths could also be detected. The problem was that Earth's atmosphere, relatively transparent to optical and radio waves, is almost opaque to other wavelengths of electromagnetic radiation. The solution to making telescopes that could detect other wavelengths was to put telescopes in satellites traveling above Earth's atmosphere.

Year	Type	Importance
1961	Gamma rays	First telescope in space observes gamma rays that do not penetrate Earth's atmosphere
1970	X rays	First telescope to detect X rays, known as Unuru ("Freedom" in Swahili) is launched into space
1972	Ultraviolet radiation	Copernicus spacecraft has a telescope designed to collect ultraviolet radiation
1978	X rays	Einstein Observatory, which detects X rays from space, becomes one of most productive satellite-based telescopes
1983	Infrared radiation	Infrared Astronomy Satellite (IRAS) becomes most successful satellite-based telescope, detecting possible new planetary systems and formation of stars

show that some cloudy patches in the sky consisted, as Galileo had discovered about the Milky Way, of millions of stars. This discovery eventually led to the recognition of much else about the universe.

Big Bang The accepted theory of how the universe began is known as the Big Bang theory, since it proposes that the universe began as something like an explosion, which has caused all parts of the universe to rush away from one another (the expansion of the universe). Such an expansion is observed. Other evidence for the Big Bang theory is the discovery of cosmic background radiation, a radiation that seems to come virtually equally from all directions. Cosmic background radiation has the characteristics expected if the universe resulted from a small, dense region exploding.

Binary Stars Almost half the stars in the visible universe are actually pairs of stars that orbit each other. Astronomers can sometimes see both stars, but more commonly they recognize that a star is part of a binary because of the influence of the dimmer star's gravitational pull on the other star.

Black Holes When a body becomes so mas-

sive for its size that not even light can escape the powerful gravitational pull it exerts, it is called a black hole. Black holes were predicted as early as 1784 (by John Michell) and invoked later by various astronomers and physicists to explain many strange astronomical phenomena. It is still not completely clear that any black holes have been found, but they are widely suspected of being at the center of many galaxies, including our own Milky Way.

Brown Dwarfs are bodies too small to be stars (since they emit no visible light and are not undergoing fusion) but too large to be planets (they give off a lot of energy in the infrared part of the electromagnetic spectrum as a result of gravitational contraction). No brown dwarfs have been positively identified, but some astronomers think there might be enough of them to account for the "missing mass" (see below).

Expanding Universe The farther away something is from us, the faster it is moving away from us. When Albert Einstein developed his general theory of relativity, he found it predicted that the universe would expand as if it were exploding. He tried to correct this prediction by inserting a factor in his equations to counteract the prediction, but in the 1920s, Carl Hubble discovered that the universe actually was expanding. It is easier to measure the speed of recession than the distance, so astronomers commonly use the speed something is moving away as the measure of its distance from us. Of course, it is not just moving away from *us*. In the expanding universe, everything is moving away from everything else.

Galaxies are systems of very many stars separated from one another by largely empty space (sometimes called island universes). In the 18th century, William Herschel concluded that many cloudy patches of light seen among the stars were actually giant systems of billions of stars, but so faraway from Earth as to look like clouds. Better telescopes proved him right in the early 20th century, and these far-off, great masses of stars became known as galaxies, after our own Milky Way, the galaxy that includes the Sun. Observation with large telescopes in the 20th century has revealed two main types of galaxy—spiral and elliptical—although some galaxies are neither (irregular).

Milky Way This is the galaxy to which the Sun and Earth belong. If you are in a place unafflicted with much light pollution, when you look at the night sky, you can see a faint band crossing it. The ancient Greeks named this the Milky Way (*galaxy* in Greek). Early in the 19th century, William Herschel determined that our Sun was a star in a vast lens-shaped star system, and that the Milky Way was the part of the star system we see from our vantage point inside it. Today, recognizing there are very many other such star systems, scientists often call it the Milky Way galaxy.

Missing Mass is matter that is apparently in the universe but that has not been observed. Astronomers note that galaxies are rotating as if they were embedded in larger, invisible bodies. Furthermore, there are theoretical reasons to believe there is even more matter in the universe than can be accounted for by the invisible matter surrounding galaxies. Ideas as to what this "missing mass" might be include everything from brown dwarfs to undiscovered subatomic particles.

Nebulae are patches of gas and dust observable in telescopes. Before Herschel discovered that some cloudy patches seen through telescopes were vast collections of stars, all such patches were called nebulae (meaning "clouds"). Some nebulae are galaxies, but many are not. The patches of gas emit light, often by the same mechanism that a fluorescent light does; energy ionizes the gas, which gives off visible light. Some patches of dust also glow, usually reflecting the light of nearby stars. Other patches of dust are opaque or nearly so, blocking out part of the sky. Some of the most striking nebulae consist of glowing gas surrounded by opaque dust or vice versa, which give the nebulae a definite shape, such as the North America Nebula (shaped like the continent of North America) or the Horsehead Nebula (which looks like a black horse's head against a glowing background). Herschel also studied a class of nebulae that looked to be giant spheres. He correctly concluded that these planetary nebulae were balls of gas produced when a star exploded.

Novae are stars that seem to appear in place of dim stars or out of nowhere. Early peoples were surprised from time to time by the appearance of a new (*nova*) star in the sky. Ancient Chinese astronomers called them guest stars. It is now clear that a truly new star does not appear; instead, a dim, existing star suddenly brightens. In early days, before the telescope, the dim stars could not be seen at all, so it looked as if a star came from nowhere. Today we know that there are two different types of "guest star," and we reserve the name nova for one type and call the other a supernova (see below). The type referred to today as novae are less bright than supernovae and may appear more than once. It is thought that they occur when material from one star in a binary pair falls on the other star, causing it to suddenly flare up.

Neutron Stars are those composed of neutrons instead of atoms. When a star's core collapses, it may collapse so much that the electrons and protons in the core are squeezed together to become neutrons. Such a star may be only a dozen miles in diameter but may have a mass twice that of the Sun.

Pulsars are neutron stars that emit radio signals from their poles in a direction that reaches Earth. All neutron stars emit radio signals from their poles and rotate very rapidly (at least when they are first formed; they gradually slow down). These signals form a tight beam. If the beam intersects Earth, a radio telescope observes a fast pulsing on and off of the signal. The pulses are so regular that when they were first discovered, they were thought to be the work of extraterrestrial beings.

Quasars are distant sources of great

ASTRONOMICAL RECORD-HOLDERS

Record	Record holder	Distinctive feature
Largest asteroid	Ceres	Diameter: 588 mi. (946 km)
Largest natural satellite	Ganymede (satellite of Jupiter)	Diameter: 3,276 mi. (5,271 km)
Largest-known planet	Jupiter	Size: 317.9 times Earth's mass
Largest star	R136A in Large Magellanic Cloud	Size: 400 to 1,000 times Sun's mass
Largest-known object	Combination of Lynx-Ursa Major supercluster with Pisces-Perseus supercluster of galaxies	Size: About 700,000,000 light-years long
Smallest-known natural satellite	Leda (satellite of Jupiter)	Diameter: 9.3 mi. (15 km)
Smallest-known planet	Pluto	Size: 0.0017 as big as Earth Diameter: about 1,400 mi.
Most distant supernova	In galaxy cluster AC118	Distance: About 5,000,000,000 light-years from Earth
Most distant galaxy	4C41.17	Distance: About 15,000,000,000 light-years from Earth
Most distant object	Quasar Q0000-26	Distance: About 18,000,000,000 light-years from Earth
Nearest star	Proxima Centauri	Distance: 4.22 light-years, or 24,800,000,000,000 mi.
Brightest-appearing star	Sirius A	Brightness: Apparent magnitude –1.47; absolute magnitude +1.45; about 26 times as bright as Sun; other stars are actually brighter but much farther away
Brightest star in reality	R136A in Large Magellanic Cloud	Brightness: Absolute magnitude –10.6; about 10,000,000 times as bright as Sun
Brightest object	Quasar S5 0014 +81	Brightness: Absolute magnitude of –33; about 1,000,000,000,000,000 times as bright as Sun
Fastest pulsar	Found in supernova 1987A	Speed of rotation: 1,968.429 revolutions per second
Oldest observatory	Tomb at Newgrange, Ireland, aligned with Sun at winter solstice	Age: About 5,150 years old

energy. The name *quasar* is short for Quasi-Stellar Object, and the objects are so called because they seem to be about the size and general appearance of stars, but produce far too much energy to be stars. No one knows for sure what they are, but there is some evidence that quasars are the central part of distant galaxies. The stars in the galaxies cannot be seen because of the great distance, so we see only the central part, which is the quasar.

Red Giants are stars that have used their hydrogen fuel and expanded as a result. Young stars "burn" hydrogen in a nuclear fusion process that leads to helium. When a star has consumed the hydrogen in its core, new fusion reactions that start with helium begin, leading to carbon. The new reactions are hotter than the fusion of hydrogen to helium. This added energy causes the hydrogen and helium outside the core to expand. When the Sun becomes a red giant in the distant future, it will expand almost to the orbit of Earth, completely engulfing Mercury and Venus, and charring Earth to a cinder. The star is red because the outer layers are relatively cool, but its large size makes it visible. Hotter stars are yellow, and still-hotter stars are blue-white, just as heated iron goes from red to blue-white with increased temperature. The hotter or larger a star is, the brighter it is.

Stars are bodies of gas large enough to undergo fusion reactions in their core. As a result of the energy produced by fusion, stars emit visible light, as well as electromagnetic radiation at other wavelengths. The Sun is a star.

Superclusters and Clusters of Galaxies are groups of galaxies associated in space. There may be just a few members of a cluster or as many as thousands. About two dozen galaxies near us form, with the Milky Way, our Local Group. The members of the Local Group also include the Andromeda galaxy and the Large and Small Magellanic Clouds. All are traveling through the universe together. The Local Group is a member of a supercluster of galaxies, called the Local Supercluster, that contains about 100 clusters. Clusters and superclusters are primarily recognized because the average distance within a cluster or a supercluster from one galaxy or cluster to another is much less than the distance to other galaxies or clusters.

Supernovae are large stars that explode. A supernova explosion is much more dramatic than the brightening of a nova. A supernova reported by Chinese astronomers from A.D. 1054 was visible in the daytime. The remnants of this explosion are known today as the Crab

Nebula. At its heart the Crab Nebula has a pulsar, all that is left of the star that exploded.

Variable Stars Any star that periodically changes brightness is called a variable (a nova changes brightness but not at regular intervals). The period varies with the cause of the change and the individual star. Some variables are part of a binary system in which one star periodically passes in front of the other. Other kinds of variables are called Mira variables and Cepheid variables, after the first stars known of each type. It is not clear what causes the brightness to vary.

White Dwarfs are stars whose cores have collapsed until all the atoms are pressed very close together. A single teaspoonful of the matter in a white dwarf weighs about 5 tons. The core collapses because a red giant has used all its helium for fuel, but the star is too small to start burning carbon.

Abundance of Elements in the Universe

Astronomers and physicists believe that the Big Bang produced a universe that contained 80% hydrogen, 20% helium, and probably no other elements at all. When clouds of hydrogen and helium began to collapse into small spaces as a result of gravitational forces, the nuclei of hydrogen atoms were pressed so close together that they fused into heavier hydrogen (deuterium and tritium), which in turn fused to form helium. The process released energy, and the balls of hydrogen and helium became stars. The energy released balanced the force of gravity, and the stars stabilized in size. This is the source of the Sun's energy, and the process continues today for other small stars. In larger stars the helium and hydrogen continue to fuse, producing nitrogen, carbon, neon, and some oxygen, as well as more helium. Still-larger stars go farther, and are able to produce magnesium, silicon, and iron, which have more protons and neutrons in their nuclei and are therefore heavier than the elements mentioned previously.

Iron is the end of the line for this process, because fusing iron nuclei takes more energy than the process produces. Gravitational energy, however, causes the star's core to contract with great speed when the fusion process begins to slacken. This contraction provides the necessary energy to fuse iron, but it provides so much energy that the star blows up, becoming a supernova. In the process of exploding, the elements heavier than iron are created. Furthermore, the explosion sends all the elements from the supernova into space, creating clouds that contain all elements. The solar system apparently formed from such a cloud, since silicon, oxygen, and iron are abundant, and elements as heavy as uranium occur in smaller amounts.

Since the Big Bang, some hydrogen and helium have remained as interstellar gases, and some have formed smaller stars in which the fusion process does not go beyond fusion of helium. As a result more hydrogen and helium are still present than any other elements. Carbon, nitrogen, and oxygen are the main components of the medium-size star's fusion cycle, so

ABUNDANCE OF ELEMENTS IN THE UNIVERSE

Atomic No.	Element	Abundance	Atomic No.	Element	Abundance
1	hydrogen	1,000,000,000,000	47	silver	6.61
2	helium	162,000,000,000	48	cadmium	28.2
3	lithium	3,160	49	indium	5.12
4	beryllium	631	50	tin	37.2
5	boron	758	51	antimony	8.92
6	carbon	398,000,000	52	tellurium	112
7	nitrogen	112,000,000	53	iodine	22.4
8	oxygen	891,000,000	54	xenon	115
9	fluorine	1,000,000	55	cesium	14.5
10	neon	551,000,000	56	barium	120
11	sodium	2,000,000	57	lanthanum	12.6
12	magnesium	25,100,000	58	cerium	19.5
13	aluminum	1,560,000	59	praseodymium	4.57
14	silicon	31,700,000	60	neodymium	22.9
15	phosphorus	251,000	61	promethium	trace
16	sulfur	22,400,000	62	samarium	7.76
17	chlorine	355,000	63	europium	3.02
18	argon	4,880,000	64	gadolinium	11.2
19	potassium	66,100	65	terbium	1.74
20	calcium	1,550,000	66	dysprosium	12.0
21	scandium	708	67	holmium	2.45
22	titanium	77,400	68	erbium	6.92
23	vanadium	6,610	69	thulium	0.120
24	chromium	240,000	70	ytterbium	6.03
25	manganese	132,000	71	lutetium	0.115
26	iron	3,710,000	72	hafnium	2.51
27	cobalt	56,200	73	tantalum	0.0562
28	nickel	891,000	74	tungsten	3.98
29	copper	10,000	75	rhenium	7.94
30	zinc	19,100	76	osmium	25.1
31	gallium	282	77	iridium	15.8
32	germanium	1,590	78	platinum	50.1
33	arsenic	129	79	gold	4.63
34	selenium	2,140	80	mercury	5.62
35	bromine	446	81	thallium	3.59
36	krypton	1,530	82	lead	31.6
37	rubidium	224	83	bismuth	3.16
38	strontium	501	84	polonium	0.0000000316
39	yttrium	56.2	85	astatine	trace
40	zirconium	316	86	radon	0.0000000001
41	niobium	31.6	87	francium	trace
42	molybdenum	75.8	88	radium	0.000126
43	technetium	trace	89	actinium	0.0000000631
44	ruthenium	27.5	90	thorium	1.00
45	rhodium	6.31	91	protactinium	0.00001
46	palladium	18.2	92	uranium	0.0501

they are the next most abundant elements. After iron is produced, the amount of heavier elements present through supernovae explosions goes down considerably, although nickel occurs in quantities near that of iron. With few exceptions fusion produces elements with even atomic numbers more easily than those with odd atomic numbers. Therefore, when arranged by atomic number, the abundance of the elements tends to seesaw back and forth. This effect becomes more pronounced for elements heavier than carbon.

In the following table, hydrogen is assumed to have an abundance of 1,000,000,000,000 (one trillion) units, a number arbitrarily chosen as a large number so that the numbers for the other elements will not all be very small; then the other elements can be assigned the follow-

ing amounts, based on data from astrophysical theories, astronomical measurements, elements found on Earth, and elements found in meteorites.

> *"Men love to wonder, and that is the seed of our science."*
> —**Ralph Waldo Emerson**

SPACEFLIGHTS CARRYING PEOPLE

The space programs of the Soviet Union and the United States both had dramatic flights by human pilots as an important component, although many scientists felt that most goals of the space program could be achieved without risking lives.

The *Vostok, Voskhod,* and *Soyuz* missions are part of the Soviet program; *Mercury, Gemini, Apollo,* and the shuttle are part of the U.S. program.

PROVING THAT PEOPLE CAN VENTURE INTO SPACE

Date	Craft	Duration	Crew	Remarks	Date	Craft	Duration	Crew	Remarks
4/12/61	Vostok 1	1 hr. 48 min.	Yuri A. Gagarin	First spaceflight by human	8/12/62	Vostok 4	70 hrs. 57 min.	Pavel R. Popovitch	Dual launch with Vostok 3; 48 orbits
5/5/61	Mercury 3	15 min.	Alan B. Shepard, Jr.	Freedom 7 (suborbital)	10/3/62	Mercury 8	9 hrs. 13 min.	Walter M. Schirra	Sigma 7; 6 orbits
7/21/61	Mercury 4	16 min.	Virgil I. Grissom	Liberty Bell 7 (suborbital)	5/15/63	Mercury 9	34 hrs. 20 min.	L. Gordon Cooper	Faith 7; 22 orbits
					6/14/63	Vostok 5	119 hrs. 6 min.	Valery F. Bikovsky	81 orbits
8/6/61	Vostok 2	25 hrs. 18 min.	Gherman S. Titov	First multiorbit flight; 17 orbits	6/16/63	Vostok 6	70 hrs. 50 min.	Valentina V. Tereshkova	First woman cosmonaut; 48 orbits; dual launch with Vostok 5
2/20/62	Mercury 6	4 hrs. 55 min.	John H. Glenn, Jr.	Friendship 7; first orbital flight by American; 3 orbits					
5/24/62	Mercury 7	4 hrs. 56 min.	M. Scott Carpenter	Aurora 7; 3 orbits	10/12/64	Voskhod 1	24 hrs. 17 min.	Vladimir M. Komarov, Konstantin P. Feoktistov, Boris B. Yegorov	First multihuman crew; 3 cosmonauts make 16 orbits
8/11/62	Vostok 3	94 hrs. 24 min.	Andrian G. Nikolayev	64 orbits; landing by parachute					

PLANNING FOR OPERATIONS IN SPACE

Date	Craft	Duration	Crew	Remarks	Date	Craft	Duration	Crew	Remarks
3/18/65	Voskhod 2	26 hrs.	Aleksei A. Leonov, Pavel I. Belyayev	First extravehicular activity (EVA) by Leonov (20 min.); 17 orbits	12/15/65	Gemini 6A	25 hrs. 51 min.	Walter M. Schirra, Thomas P. Stafford	15 orbits; accomplishes first rendezvous (with Gemini 7)
3/23/65	Gemini 3	4 hrs. 53 min.	Virgil I. Grissom, John W. Young	First American multiperson crew; 3 orbits	3/16/66	Gemini 8	10 hrs. 42 min.	Neil A. Armstrong, David R. Scott	6.5 orbits; first dual launch and docking; first Pacific landing
6/3/65	Gemini 4	97 hrs. 56 min.	James A. McDivitt, Edward H. White II	62 orbits; first American EVA; first use of personal propulsion unit	6/3/66	Gemini 9A	72 hrs. 21 min.	Thomas P. Stafford, Eugene A. Cernan	44 orbits; unable to dock with target vehicle; 2 hrs. 7 min. of EVA
8/21/65	Gemini 5	190 hrs. 56 min.	L. Gordon Cooper, Charles Conrad, Jr.	120 orbits; demonstrates feasibility of lunar mission; simulated rendezvous	7/18/66	Gemini 10	70 hrs. 47 min.	John W. Young, Michael Collins	43 orbits; first dual rendezvous, docked vehicle maneuvers; umbilical EVA
12/4/65	Gemini 7	330 hrs. 35 min.	Frank Borman, James A. Lovell, Jr.	206 orbits; extensions of testing and performance; target for first rendezvous	9/12/66	Gemini 11	71 hrs. 17 min.	Charles Conrad, Jr., Richard F. Gordon, Jr.	44 orbits; rendezvous and docking
					11/11/66	Gemini 12	94 hrs. 34 min.	James A. Lovell, Jr., Edwin A. Aldrin	59 orbits; final Gemini mission; 5 hrs. of EVA

TO THE MOON AND EXPERIMENTS IN SPACE

Date	Craft	Duration	Crew	Remarks	Date	Craft	Duration	Crew	Remarks
4/23/67	Soyuz 1	26 hrs. 48 min.	Vladimir M. Komarov	18 orbits; Komarov is killed when parachute fails, first fatality of space program	1/14/69	Soyuz 4	71 hrs. 14 min.	Vladimir A. Shatalov	48 orbits; docks with Soyuz 5 in first linkup of 2 space vehicles both carrying people
10/11/68	Apollo 7	260 hrs. 8 min.	Walter M. Schirra, Donn F. Eisele, R. Walter Cunningham	8 service propulsion firings; 7 live TV sessions with crew; rendezvous with S-IVB stage performed	1/15/69	Soyuz 5	72 hrs. 46 min.	Boris V. Volynov, Alexei S. Yeliseyev, Yevgeni V. Khrunov	3 cosmonauts perform EVA, transferred to Soyuz 4 in rescue rehearsal
					3/3/69	Apollo 9	241 hrs. 1 min.	James A. McDivitt, David R. Scott, Russell L. Schweickart	First flight of all lunar hardware in Earth orbit, incl. lunar module (LM)
10/26/68	Soyuz 3	94 hrs. 51 min.	Georgi T. Beregovoi	64 orbits; approaches unpiloted Soyuz 2 to distance of 650 ft. (198 m)	5/18/69	Apollo 10	192 hrs. 3 min.	Eugene A. Cernan, John W. Young, Thomas P. Stafford	Lunar mission development flight to evaluate LM performance in lunar environment; descent to within 50,000 ft. of Moon
12/21/68	Apollo 8	147 hrs.	Frank Borman, James A. Lovell, Jr., William A. Anders	First Saturn-V propelled flight; first lunar orbital mission (10 orbits); returns good lunar photography					

TO THE MOON AND EXPERIMENTS IN SPACE

Date	Craft	Duration	Crew	Remarks
7/16/69	Apollo 11	165 hrs. 18 min.	Neil A. Armstrong, Michael Collins, Edwin E. Aldrin, Jr.	First lunar landing; limited inspection, photography, evaluation, and sampling of lunar soil; touchdown: July 20
10/11/69	Soyuz 6	118 hrs. 42 min.	Georgi S. Shonin, Valery N. Kubasov	First triple launch (with Soyuz 7 and 8)
10/12/69	Soyuz 7	118 hrs. 41 min.	Anatoly V. Filipchenko, Vladislav N. Volkov, Viktor V. Gorbatko	With Soyuz 7 and 8, conducts experiments in navigation and photography 80 orbits
10/13/69	Soyuz 8	118 hrs. 59 min.	Vladimir A. Shatalov, Aleksei S. Yeliseyev	
11/14/69	Apollo 12	244 hrs. 36 min.	Charles Conrad, Jr., Richard F. Gordon, Jr., Alan L. Bean	Second lunar landing; demonstrates point landing capability; samples more area; total EVA time: 15 hrs. 32 min.
4/11/70	Apollo 13	142 hrs. 55 min.	James A. Lovell, Jr., Fred W. Haise, Jr., John L. Swigert, Jr.	Third lunar landing attempt aborted owing to loss of pressure in liquid oxygen in service module and fuel cell failure
6/2/70	Soyuz 9	424 hrs. 59 min. 17 da. 16 hrs.	Andrian G. Nikolayev, Vitaly I. Sevastianov	Longest spaceflight to this time
1/31/71	Apollo 14	216 hrs. 42 min.	Alan B. Shepard, Jr., Stuart A. Roosa, Edgar D. Mitchell	Third lunar landing, returned 98 lbs. of lunar material
4/23/71	Soyuz 10	47 hrs. 46 min.	Vladimir A. Shatalov, Alexei S. Yeleseyev, Nikolai N. Rukavishnikov	Docked with Salyut 1, the first space station
6/6/71	Soyuz 11	570 hrs. 22 min. (24 da.)	Georgi T. Dobrovolsky, Viktor I. Patsayev, Vladislav N. Volkov	All 3 cosmonauts killed during reentry
7/26/71	Apollo 15	295 hrs. 12 min.	David R. Scott, Alfred M. Worden, James B. Irwin	Fourth lunar landing; first to carry Lunar Roving Vehicle (LVR); total EVA time: 18 hrs. 46 min.; returns 173 lbs. of material
4/16/72	Apollo 16	265 hrs. 51 min.	John W. Young, Thomas K. Mattingly II, Charles M. Duke, Jr.	Fifth lunar landing; second to carry LRV; total EVA time: 20 hrs. 14 min.; returns 213 lbs. of material
12/7/72	Apollo 17	301 hrs. 52 min.	Eugene A. Cernan, Ronald E. Evans, Harrison H. Schmitt	Last manned lunar landing; third with LRV; total EVA time: 44 hrs. 8 min.; returned 243 lbs. of material

FIRST STATIONS IN SPACE

Date	Craft	Duration	Crew	Remarks
5/25/73	Skylab 2	28 da. 49 min.	Charles Conrad, Jr., Joseph P. Kerwin, Paul J. Weitz	First Skylab launch; establishes Skylab Orbital Assembly in earth orbit; conducts medical and other experiments
7/29/73	Skylab 3	1,427 hrs. 9 min. (59 da. 11 hrs)	Alan L. Bean, Owen K. Garriott, Jack R. Lousma	Second Skylab; Crew performs systems and operational tests, experiments, and thermal shield deployment
9/27/73	Soyuz 12	47 hrs. 16 min.	Vasily G. Lazarev, Oleg G. Makarov	First Soviet space flight to carry humans since the Soyuz 11 tragedy
11/16/73	Skylab 4	2,017 hr. 17 min. (84 da. 1 hr.)	Gerald P. Carr, Edward G. Gibson, William R. Pogue	Third Skylab; crew performs unmanned Saturn workshop operations; obtains medical data for extending space flights
12/18/73	Soyuz 13	188 hrs. 55 min.	Petr I. Klimuk, Valentin Lebedev	Performsd astrophysical and biological experiments
7/3/74	Soyuz 14	377 hrs. 30 min. (15 da. 17.5 hr.)	Pavel R. Popovich, Yuri P. Artyukhin	Crew occupies Salyut 3 space station; studies Earth resources
8/26/74	Soyuz 15	48 hrs. 12 min.	Gennady Sarafanov, Lev Demin	Makes unsuccessful attempt to dock with Salyut 3
12/2/74	Soyuz 16	142 hrs. 24 min.	Anatoly V. Filpchenko, Nikolai N. Rukavishnikov	Taken to check modifications in Saylut system
1/10/75	Soyuz 17	709 hrs. 20 min. (30 da.)	Alexei A. Gubarev, Georgi M. Grechko	Docks with Salyut 4; sets Soviet endurance record at this time
4/5/75	Soyuz 18A	22 min.	Vasily G. Lazarev, Oleg G. Makarov	Separation from booster fails, and craft fails to reach orbit, but crew successfully lands in western Siberia
5/24/75	Soyuz 18B	1,512 hrs. (63 da.)	Petr I. Klimuk, Vitaly I. Sevastyanov	Docks with Salyut 4
7/15/75	ASTP	217 hrs. 30 min.	Thomas P. Stafford, Vance D. Brand, Donald K. Slayton	Apollo-Soyuz Test Project, cooperative U.S.-Soviet mission
7/15/75	Soyuz 19	143 hrs. 31 min.	Alexei A. Leonov, Valery N. Kubasov	Docks with ASTP, the U.S. Apollo capsule

THE SOVIET STUDY OF HUMAN BIOLOGY IN SPACE

Date	Craft	Duration	Crew	Remarks
11/17/75	Soyuz 20	90 da.	No crew	Biological mission; docks with Salyut 4
7/6/76	Soyuz 21	49 da.	Boris V. Volynov, Vitaly Zholobov	Docks with Salyut 5 and performed Earth resource work
9/15/76	Soyuz 22	8 da.	Valery F. Bykovsky, Vladimir Aksenov	Takes Earth-resources photographs
10/14/76	Soyuz 23	2 da.	Vyacheslav Zudov, Valery Rozhdestvensky	Unsuccessful attempt to dock with Salyut 5; first landing in water for Soviet program (in Lake Tengiz; unplanned, but crew survives)

THE SOVIET STUDY OF HUMAN BIOLOGY IN SPACE

Date	Craft	Duration	Crew	Remarks
2/7/77	Soyuz 24	7 da.	Viktor G. Gorbatko / Yuri N. Glazov	Docks with Salyut 5 for 18 da. of experiments
10/9/77	Soyuz 25	2 da.	Vladimir Kovalyonok / Valery Ryumin	Unsuccessful attempt to dock with Salyut 6
12/10/77	Soyuz 26	96 da.	Yuri V. Romanenko / Georgi M. Grechko	Docks with Salyut 6; crew sets endurance record
1/10/78	Soyuz 27	6 da.	Valdimir Dzhanibekov / Oleg G. Makarov	Carries second crew to dock with Salyut 6 space station
3/2/78	Soyuz 28	8 da.	Vladimir Remek / Alexi A. Gubarev	Carries third crew to board Salyut 6; Remek first non-Russian, non-American in space (Czech)
6/15/78	Soyuz 29	140 da.	Vladimir Kovalyonok / Aleksander S. Ivanchenko	Docks with Salyut 6; crew sets new space endurance record
6/27/78	Soyuz 30	8 da.	Pyotr I. Klimuk / Miroslaw Hermaszewski	Carries second international crew to Salyut 6; first Polish cosmonaut, Hermaszewski
8/25/78	Soyuz 31	8 da.	Valery F. Bykovsky / Sigmund Jahn	Carries third international crew to Salyut 6; first East German, Jahn
2/25/79	Soyuz 32	175 da.	Vladimir Lyakhov / Valery Ryumin	Carries crew to Salyut 6; new endurance record set
4/10/79	Soyuz 33	2 da.	Nikolai N. Rukavishnikov / Georgi Ivanov	Engine failure prior to docking forces early termination; first Bulgarian, Ivanov
6/6/79	Soyuz 34	74 da.	No crew	Launches with no crew; returns with crew from Salyut 6
4/9/80	Soyuz 35	185 da.	Valery Ryumin / Leonid Popov	Carries 2 crew members to Salyut 6
5/26/80	Soyuz 36	8 da.	Valery N. Kubasov / Bertalan Farkas	Carries 2 crew members to Salyut 6; crew returns in Soyuz 35; first Hungarian, Farkas
6/5/80	Soyuz T-2	4 da.	Yuri Malyshev / Vladimir Aksenov	Test of modified Soyuz craft; docks with Salyut 6
7/23/80	Soyuz 37	8 da.	Viktor F. Gorbatko / Pham Tuan	Exchanges cosmonauts in Salyut 6; returns Soyuz 35 crew after 185 days in orbit; first Vietnamese in space, Tuan
9/18/80	Soyuz 38	8 da.	Yuri V. Romanenko / Tamayo-Mendez	Ferries to Salyut 6; first Cuban in space, Mendez
11/27/80	Soyuz T-3	13 da.	Leonard Kizim / Oleg G. Makarov / Genrodiy Strekalov	Ferries to Salyut 6; first 3-person crew since Soyuz 11
3/12/81	Soyuz T-4	75 da.	Vladimer Kovalyonok / Viktor Savinykh	Mission to Salyut 6
3/22/81	Soyuz 39	8 da.	Vladimir Dzhanibekov / Jugderdemuduyn Gurragcha	Docks with Salyut 6; first Mongolian, Gurragcha

THE SPACE SHUTTLE: U.S. REENTRY IN SPACE

Date	Craft	Duration	Crew	Remarks
4/12/81	Shuttle	2 da. 6 hrs.	John W. Young / Robert L. Crippen	First flight of reusable space shuttle Columbia; proves concept; first landing of U.S. spacecraft on land
5/14/81	Soyuz 40	8 da.	Leonid Popov / Dumitru Prunariu	First Romanian (Prunariu) in space
11/12/81	Shuttle	2 da. 6 hrs.	Joe H. Engle / Richard H. Truly	First reuse of spacecraft Columbia; ended early due to loss of fuel cell
3/22/82	Shuttle	8 da.	Jack R. Lousma / C. Gordon Fullerton	Third flight of orbiter Columbia; payload includes space science experiments
5/13/82	Soyuz T-5	211 da.	Anatoly Berezovoy / Valentin Lebedev	First flight to Salyut 7; space station equipped to measure body functions
6/24/82	Soyuz T-6	8 da.	Vladimir Dzhanibekov / Jean-Loup Chrétien / Aleksandr Ivanchenkov	Mission to Salyut 7; Soviet/French team; first French cosmonaut, Chrétien
6/27/82	Shuttle	7 da. 1 hr.	Thomas Mattingly II / Henry Hartsfield, Jr.	Fourth space Columbia shuttle mission; final development; first landing on hard surface
8/16/82	Soyuz T-7	8 da.	Leonid I. Popov / Svetlana Savitskaya / Alexander Serebrov	Mission to Salyut 7; second Soviet woman in space, Savitskaya
11/11/82	Shuttle	5 da. 2 hr.	Vance D. Brand / Robert F. Overmyer / Joseph P. Allen / William B. Lenoir	Fifth flight of Columbia; first operational mission; first 4-man crew; first deployment of satellites from shuttle
4/4/83	Shuttle	5 da.	Paul J. Weitz / Karol J. Bobko / Donald H. Peterson / Story Musgrave	First flight of space shuttle orbiter Challenger; deploys TDRS tracking satellite; first shuttle EVA
4/20/83	Soyuz T-8	48 hr.	Vladimir G. Titov / Gennadi M. Strekalov / Aleksandr A. Serebrov	3 cosmonauts fail in planned rendezvous with Salyut 7
6/18/83	Shuttle	6 da. 2 hr.	Robert L. Crippen / Frederick H. Hauck / John M. Fabian / Sally K. Ride / Norman E. Thagard	Second flight of Challenger; first 5-person crew; first American woman in space; first use of Remote Manipulator Structure to deploy and retrieve satellite

THE SPACE SHUTTLE: U.S. REENTRY IN SPACE

Date	Craft	Duration	Crew	Remarks
6/27/83	*Soyuz T-9*	150 da.	Vladimir Lyakhov, Aleksandr Aleksandrov	Crew spends 149 days in *Salyut 7* after *Soyuz 10* fails in relief mission
8/30/83	Shuttle	6 da.	Richard Truly, Daniel Brandenstein, William Thornton, Guion Bluford, Jr., Dale Gardner	Third *Challenger* flight; first night launch; first black American (Bluford); launches weather/communications satellite for India
11/28/83	Shuttle	10 da.	John Young, Brewster Shaw, Jr., Robert Parker, Owen Garriott, Byron Lichtenberg, Ulf Merbold	*Columbia* launches Spacelab; six-man crew performs numerous experiments in astronomy and medicine, including those on human ear
2/3/84	Shuttle	8 da.	Vance Brand, Bruce McCandless, Robert Stewart, Ronald McNair, Robert Gibson	Fourth *Challenger* flight; jet-propelled backpacks carry 2 astronauts on first untethered space walks; 2 satellites (Western Union and Indonesia) lost; first landing at Kennedy Space Center
2/8/84	*Soyuz T-10*	237 da.	Leonard Kizim, Oleg Atkov, Vladimir Solovyov	Mission to *Salyut 7* to repair propulsion system; sets new duration-in-space record for crew
4/2/84	*Soyuz T-11*	8 da.	Yuri Malyshev, Gennadi Strealov, Rakesh Sharma	Docked with *Salyut 7*; first Indian cosmonaut, Sharma
4/7/84	Shuttle	8 da.	Robert L. Crippen, Richard Scobee, Terry Hart, George Nelson, James van Hofte	Fifth *Challenger* flight; deploys Long Duration Exposure Facility for experiments in space durability; snares Solar Max satellite and repairs attitude-control system
7/18/84	*Soyuz T-12*	12 da.	Svetlana Savitskaya, Vladimir Djanibekov, Igor Volk	Savitskaya becomes first woman to walk in space
8/30/84	Shuttle	6 da.	Henry W. Hartsfield Jr., Michael L. Coates, Steven A. Hawley, Judith Resnik, Richard M. Mullane, Charles D. Walker	First *Discovery* launch; Deploys 3 satellites and tests a solar sail
10/5/84	Shuttle	7 da.	Robert L. Crippen, Jon A. McBride, Kathryn D. Sullivan, Sally K. Ride, Marc Gameau, David C. Leestma, Paul D. Scully-Power	Sixth *Challenger* flight; carries first Canadian, astronaut Gameau; deploys Earth Radiation Budget Satellite and monitors land formations, ocean currents, and wind patterns; uses Sir-B radar system to see beneath surface of sand
11/8/84	Shuttle	7 da.	Frederick H. Hauck, David M. Walker, Anna L. Fisher, Joseph P. Allen, Dale A. Gardner	Second *Discovery* mission; salvages 2 inoperative satellites and returns them to Earth for repair
1/24/85	Shuttle	2 da.	Thomas K. Mattingly, Loren J. Schriver, James F. Buchli, Ellison S. Onizuka, Gary E. Payton	Third *Discovery* mission; a "secret" military mission
4/12/85	Shuttle	6 da.	Karol J. Bobnko, Donald E. Williams, Jake Garn, Charles D. Walker, Jeffrey A. Hoffman, S. David Griggs, M. Rhea Seddon	Fourth *Discovery* mission; first U.S. senator in space, Garn
4/29/85	Shuttle	7 da.	Robert F. Overmeyer, Frederick D. Gregory, Don L. Lind, Taylor G. Wang, Lodewijk van den Berg, Norman Thagard, William Thornton	Seventh *Challenger* mission; carries European Spacelab module to conduct 15 experiments in space
6/6/85	*Soyuz T-13*	112 da.	Vladimir Dzhanibekov, Viktor Savinykh	Successful mission to repair damage to *Salyut 7*, which had suffered power failure
6/17/85	Shuttle	6 da.	John O. Creighton, Shannon W. Lucid, Steven R. Nagel, Daniel C. Brandenstein, John W. Fabian, Salman al-Saud, Patrick Baudry	Fifth *Discovery* mission; first Arab in space. Prince Sultan Salman al-Saud; successfully launches 4 satellites
7/29/85	Shuttle	7 da.	Roy D. Bridges, Jr., Anthony W. England, Karl G. Henize, F. Story Musgrave, C. Gordon Fullerton, Loren W. Acton, John-David F. Bartoe	Eighth *Challenger* mission; carries Spacelab 2, a group of scientific experiments
8/27/85	Shuttle	7 da.	John M. Lounge, James D. van Hoften, William F. Fisher, Joe H. Engle, Richard O. Covey	Sixth *Discovery* mission; repairs satellite Syncom 3
9/17/85	*Soyuz T-14*	65 da.	Vladimir Vasyutin, Aleksandr N. Volkov, Georgi M. Grechko	Takes supplies to *Salyut 7*; terminated early to return Vasyutin to Earth because he was ill
10/4/85	Shuttle	2 da.	Karol J. Bobco, Ronald J. Grabe, David C. Hilmers, William A. Pailes, Robert C. Stewart	First *Atlantis* mission
10/30/85	Shuttle	7 da.	Henry W. Hartsfield Jr., Steven R. Nagel, Bonnie J. Dunbar, Guion S. Bluford, Jr., Ernst Messerschmid, Reinhard Furrer, Wubbo J. Ockels	Ninth *Challenger* mission; carries Spacelab 1-D; scientific experiments conducted by West Germans

THE SPACE SHUTTLE: U.S. REENTRY IN SPACE

Date	Craft	Duration	Crew	Remarks	Date	Craft	Duration	Crew	Remarks
11/26/85	Shuttle	7 da.	Brewster H. Shaw, Jr. Bryan D. O'Conner Charles Walker Rudolfo Neri Vela Jerry L. Ross Sherwood C. Spring Mary L. Cleave	Second *Atlantis* mission; first Mexican in space, Vela; involved in assembling structures	1/28/86	Shuttle	73 sec.	Francis R. Scobee Michael J. Smith Robert E. McNair Ellison S. Onizuka Judith A. Resnik Gregory B. Jarvis Christa McAuliffe	*Challenger* disaster: O-rings in solid-fuel boosters wear through, and the entire fuel supply explodes, killing all 6 regular astronauts and elementary-school teacher McAuliffe
1/12/86	Shuttle	5 da.	Robert L. Gibson Charles F. Bolden, Jr. George D. Nelson Franklin R. Chang-Diaz Steven A. Hawley Robert J. Cenker	Seventh *Columbia* flight; first congressman in space, Nelson					

AFTER THE CHALLENGER DISASTER: THE FIRST SPACE STATION

Date	Craft	Duration	Crew	Remarks	Date	Craft	Duration	Crew	Remarks
2/20/86	*Mir*		Variable	Soviet space station, launches without crew	9/29/88	Shuttle	4 da.	Mike Lounge David Hilmers Rick Hauck Pinky Nelson Dick Covey	*Discovery*, redesigned in many ways, makes first shuttle flight since the *Challenger* disaster
5/5/86	*Soyuz T-15*	125 da.	Vladimir Solovyov Leonid Kizim	First cosmonauts to board *Mir* space station					
2/7/87	*Soyuz TM-2*	326 da.	Yuri Romanenko Aleksandr Laveykin	Romanenko and Laveykin begin marathon tours in space, thought to be leading toward a Mars expedition	11/26/88	*Soyuz TM-7*	152 da.	Aleksandr Volkov Sergei Krikalev Jean-Loup Chrétien	*Mir* is temporarily abandoned for first time after cosmonauts return to Earth
7/23/87	*Soyuz TM-3*	8 da.	Aleksandr Aleksanderov Aleksandr Viktorenko Muhammad Faris	First Syrian in space, Faris	12/2/88	Shuttle	4 da.	Robert L. Gibson Jerry L. Ross William M. Shepherd Guy S. Gardner Richard M. Mullane	"Secret" military mission of *Atlantis*; widely known to have deployed radar spy satellite
12/20/87	*Soyuz TM-4*	366 da.	Vladimir G. Titov Musa Manarov Anatoly Leuchenko	Cosmonauts set new record of a year in space, mostly in *Mir* space station—366 days	3/13/89	Shuttle	4 da.	Michael L. Coats John E. Blanha James F. Buchli James P. Bagian Robert C. Springer	*Discovery* deploys NASA's third relay satellite and tests thermal control system for proposed U.S. space station
6/7/88	*Soyuz TM-5*	10 da.	Aleksandr Aleksandrov Viktor P. Savinykh Anatoly Y. Solovyov	Aleksandrov becomes the first Bulgarian in space	5/4/89	Shuttle	4 da.	David M. Walker Ronald J. Grabe Mary L. Cleave Norman E. Thagard Mark C. Lee	*Atlantis* launches space probe Magellan on its way to Venus
8/29/88	*Soyuz TM-6*	9 da.	Vladimir Lyakhov Valery Polyakov (Abdul) Ahad (Mohmand)	Ahad (who usually uses only one name) is first Afghan in space; on 9/6/88 Lyakhov and Ahad are stranded in space for 24 hrs. as they attempt to return in *Soyuz TM-5,* but finally resolve problems and land safely on 9/7/88					

MAJOR ACCOMPLISHMENTS OF SATELLITES AND SPACE PROBES

While much attention is focused on human beings in space, most of the serious scientific progress has been made by satellites or probes—the general name for space vehicles that neither carry humans nor orbit Earth—that are directed internally or from Earth. Since 1957 there have been hundreds of such satellites and probes.

Launch date	Name	Accomplishment	Launch date	Name	Accomplishment
10/4/57	Sputnik 1	First satellite to orbit Earth (USSR)	10/4/59	Lunik III	First space probe to return photographs of far side of Moon (USSR)
1/31/58	Explorer 1	First satellite to detect Van Allen radiation belts; first U.S. satellite	4/1/60	Tiros I	First weather satellite (U.S.)
3/17/58	Vanguard	Demonstrates that Earth is pear shaped with slight bulge in Southern Hemisphere (U.S.)	6/22/60	Transit I-B	First navigational satellite (U.S.)
			8/12/60	Echo I	First communications satellite—actually a large balloon off which radio signals could be bounced (U.S.)
1/2/59	Mechta	First space probe to go into orbit around Sun, passing 5,000 mi. from Moon (at which it was aimed) (USSR)	12/12/61	Venera 1	First space probe intended to reach another planet—Venus (USSR)
3/3/59	Pioneer IV	First American probe aimed at Moon; like Mechta it misses and goes into orbit about Sun	3/7/62	OSO I	Orbiting Solar Observatory—first major astronomical satellite (U.S.)
9/12/59	Lunik II	First space probe to reach Moon, where it crash lands (USSR)			

Launch date	Name	Accomplishment
4/23/62	Ranger IV	First U.S. space probe to reach Moon
7/10/62	Telstar	First active communications satellite, allowing direct television between Europe and U.S. (U.S.)
8/27/62	Mariner II	First space probe to reach vicinity of another planet (Venus) and return scientific information (U.S.)
10/31/62	Anna I-B	First satellite intended for accurately measuring shape of Earth (U.S.)
11/1/62	Mars I	First space probe aimed at Mars; contact lost about 66 million mi. from Earth (USSR)
6/26/63	Syncom II	First communications satellite to go into synchronous orbit with Earth (U.S.)
7/28/64	Ranger VII	Returns close-up photographs of Moon before crashing into it (U.S.)
8/28/64	Nimbus I	First weather satellite to be stabilized so that its cameras always point toward Earth (U.S.)
11/28/64	Mariner IV	Flies by Mars and takes 21 pictures of its surface, successfully transmitting them back to Earth; its closest approach is 6,118 mi. (U.S.)
4/6/65	Early Bird	First commercial satellite (U.S.)
4/23/65	Molniya I	First Soviet communications satellite
7/16/65	Proton I	At 26,896 lbs., it is largest Earth satellite to this date (USSR)
11/16/65	Venera 3	Crash-lands on Venus; first space probe to make physical contact with another planet; radio contact lost before it reaches immediate vicinity of planet (USSR)
11/26/65	A-1	First satellite to be launched by nation other than the USSR or U.S. (France)
1/31/66	Luna 9	Although main vehicle crash-lands, ejected capsule lands non-destructively and transmits photographs to Earth (USSR)
5/30/66	Surveyor 1	First soft landing of complete vehicle on Moon (U.S.)
3/31/66	Luna 10	First space vehicle to go into orbit about Moon (USSR)
8/10/66	Lunar Orbiter 1	First American space vehicle to go into orbit about Moon (U.S.)
6/12/67	Venera 4	Ejects instrument package into atmosphere of Venus; package parachutes toward surface; contact lost before reaching surface (USSR)
6/14/67	Mariner 5	Second American satellite to reach vicinity of Venus (U.S.)
9/15/68	Zond 5	First Soviet satellite to return to Earth from vicinity of Moon
2/11/70	Ohsumi	First satellite to be launched by Japan
4/24/70	"The East Is Red"	First satellite to be launched by China; although satellite's name is not announced, it broadcasts song "The East Is Red" once a minute from orbit, pausing at the end for other signals
8/17/70	Venera 7	First Venus probe to return signals from planet's surface (USSR)
9/12/70	Luna 16	First space probe to land on Moon without humans aboard, scoop up samples, and return them to Earth (USSR)
11/10/70	Luna 17	Carries vehicle to Moon's surface; vehicle roams for 2 weeks at a time (during daylight), then "sleeps"; as it roams, it returns photos and other data to Earth (USSR)
12/12/70	Uhuru	First X-ray satellite telescope (U.S.)
5/28/71	Mars 3	First space probe to soft-land on Mars, although it quickly ceases functioning (USSR)
5/30/71	Mariner 9	First space probe to orbit another planet (Mars); returns 7,329 photographs of planet (U.S.)

Launch date	Name	Accomplishment
3/2/72	Pioneer 10	First space probe to study Jupiter and, on June 13, 1983, first to leave solar system (U.S.)
7/23/72	Landsat I	First Earth resources satellite (U.S.)
3/6/73	Pioneer 11	First space probe to reach vicinity of Saturn (U.S.)
11/3/73	Mariner 10	First space probe to observe 2 planets, Venus and Mercury, and only probe ever to observe Mercury (U.S.)
	Venera 9	Returns first photographs from surface of Venus (USSR)
12/10/74	Helios	First W. German space probe
8/20/75	Viking 1	First American space probe to soft-land on Mars; continues to return data until May 1983 (U.S.)
9/20/75	Viking 2	Successfully soft-lands on Mars (U.S.)
8/20/77	Voyager 2	After studying Jupiter and Saturn, it becomes first space probe to reach vicinities of Uranus and Neptune (U.S.)
9/5/77	Voyager 1	After studying Jupiter, it becomes first space probe to reach vicinity of Saturn (U.S.)
1/26/78	IUE	International Ultraviolet Explorer—the only astronomical satellite to be placed in geosynchronous orbit; it is still sending back data
5/20/78	Pioneer Venus 1	First space probe to go into orbit about Venus (U.S.)
6/26/78	Seasat	Analyzes ocean currents and ice flow (U.S.)
8/12/78	ISEE-3	Originally the third International Sun-Earth Explorer, space probe is renamed International Cometary Explorer (ICE) when it is redirected to study tail of comet Giacobini-Zinner in 1983 (U.S.)
12/13/78	HEAO-2	High-Energy Astronomy Observatory, also known as the Einstein Observatory—it makes high-resolution X-ray images of the universe (U.S.)
2/24/79	P78-1	Studies solar radiation until purposely shot down by U.S. Air Force 9/13/85; still working at time of its destruction, satellite is deemed by many scientists to be too valuable to be used as target (U.S.)
2/14/80	Solar Max	Studies solar radiation; after failure, it is repaired and relaunched from space shuttle (U.S.)
1/25/83	IRAS	Infrared Astronomical Satellite studies galactic and extragalactic infrared sources and discovers new stars forming as well as possible planet formation (U.S.)
12/15/84	Vega 1	First Soviet mission to study Halley's comet; along the way it drops balloon probe into atmosphere of Venus
12/21/84	Vega 2	Second Soviet mission to Halley's comet; it also releases a balloon probe at Venus
1/7/85	Sakigake	First Japanese mission to study Halley's comet (this one from far away)
7/2/85	Giotto	Joint European mission to Halley's comet; passes closest to the comet—375 mi.
8/18/85	Suisei	Japanese mission to Halley's comet
2/21/86	SPOT	French satellite designed to photograph surface details of Earth as small as 30 ft. across
5/4/89	Magellan	To orbit Venus and provide detailed map of its surface features
10/12/89 (sched.)	Galileo	To orbit Jupiter, report on Jovian moons, and drop probe into Jupiter's atmosphere
3/90 (sched.)	Hubble Space Telescope	Will carry first optical telescope on satellite orbiting Earth

The Voyager Mission

The most successful spaceflight in terms of scientific accomplishments since the space program started has been the flight of the twin space probes Voyagers 1 and 2. Some of the accomplishments so far:

• **1977** Voyager 1 and Voyager 2, each weighing about a ton, are successfully launched a few days apart.

• **1979** Voyagers 1 and 2 reach the neighborhood of the planet Jupiter in March and July, respectively, following a trail blazed in 1973 by the much more primitive Pioneers 10 and 11. Voyager 1 finds three new small satellites, each less than 25 miles in diameter (now named Thebe, Adrastea, and Metis). Both Pioneer and the two Voyagers report that Jupiter produces more heat than it absorbs from sunlight. The Voyagers are also able to confirm Earth-based observations of Jovian weather and considerably expand our knowledge. The Voyagers find that Jupiter has rings, which was largely unexpected. While Jupiter's rings are far less spectacular than the rings of Saturn, their presence (along with rings around Uranus discovered by airplane-based astronomers in 1977) suggests that all the gas-giant planets should have rings, including Neptune, where no rings had so far been detected. Both Voyagers detect strong belts of ionized particles and magnetism caused by Jupiter.

Voyager 1 makes the closest approach (170,000 mi.) on Mar. 5 and photographs spectacular volcanic eruptions on Io, Jupiter's third-largest moon, the first-known instance of an active volcano beyond Earth (scientists now think Venus also has active volcanoes).

Voyager 2 comes within 400,000 miles of the giant planet on July 9.

Both spacecraft return thousands of color images of Jupiter, its 16 moons, and its narrow rings.

• **1980** Voyager 1 in November becomes the second space probe to reach the neighborhood of Saturn, preceded by the more primitive Pioneer 11 in 1979. Voyager 1's most spectacular discoveries concern Saturn's famous rings. Spokelike material rotate along with the rings, some of the rings appear to be braided, and instead of the six rings visible from Earth, there are perhaps as many as a thousand. Voyager 1 passes within 2,500 miles of Saturn's largest moon, Titan, revealing much about its peculiar chemistry.

Because Voyager 1 passes so close to the planet, Saturn's gravitational force propels it toward deep space on a path that will take it out of the solar system.

• **1981** Voyager 2 in August becomes the third space probe to reach the neighborhood of Saturn. Mechanical problems limit Voyager 2's ability to record data, but the data successfully recorded include the discovery that there are even more rings than detected by Voyager 1, perhaps a hundred thousand.

Both Voyagers 1 and 2 contribute the best scientific picture of Saturn, its rings, and its moons to date.

Voyager 2 then uses Saturn's gravitational force to propel it toward Uranus and Neptune. (Scientists chose between this path and one that would have skipped Uranus and Neptune on its way to Pluto.)

• **1986** Voyager 2 arrives in the vicinity of Uranus in late January—the first space probe ever to approach the planet—and comes within 50,000 miles of the planet. It returns images of the Uranian moons and rings, as well as of the planet itself.

Among the scientific discoveries are a weak magnetic field tipped 55° away from the planet's axis; a mysterious "electro-glow," somewhat like an aurora; a peculiar atmosphere that is warmer on the side of the planet facing away from the Sun; 10 new moons to add to the five previously observed from Earth; strange markings on one moon, Miranda, unlike anything seen elsewhere in the solar system; and two previously undiscovered rings.

• **1989** On Aug. 25 Voyager 2 makes its closest approach to Neptune—about 18,000 miles—at midnight EDT. Because Uranus is so far away, the data won't reach Earth until 4:06 A.M. EST. See "The Chronology of the Year" for reports of what Voyager 2 finds there.

Earth Sciences

Earth science includes geology (the study of Earth's rocks and interior), oceanography (the study of ocean water, currents, and the ocean floor), paleontology (the study of fossils and ancient life-forms), parts of astronomy (see "Astronomy"), and meteorology (the study of the atmosphere, including weather). Except for astronomy and weather, which are covered in their own sections, this section deals with all of these studies.

MAJOR DISCOVERIES IN EARTH SCIENCE

B.C.

c. 300 Dicaearchus of Messina (Sicily) (Greek: 355–285 B.C.) develops map of Earth on a sphere using lines of latitude.

c. 100 Greek explorer Hippalus discovers regularity of monsoon in Arabian Sea and India.

A.D.

132 Chinese inventor Zhang Heng develops first crude seismograph.

1600 William Gilbert (English: 1544–1603) suggests that Earth is giant magnet, which is why magnetic compasses indicate north.

1669 Nicolaus Steno (Danish: 1638–86) correctly explains origin of fossils.

1777 Nicolas Desmarest (French: 1725–1815) proposes that the rock basalt is formed from lava.

1785 James Hutton (Scottish: 1726–97) explains features of Earth on basis of tiny changes taking place over very long periods of time.

1795 Georges Cuvier (French: 1769–1832) shows that giant bones found in Meuse River are remains of extinct giant reptile.

1797 James Hall (Scottish: 1761–1832) shows that melted rocks form crystals upon cooling.

1822 Gideon Mantell (English: 1790–1852) and his wife, Mary Ann, are first to discover and recognize dinosaur bones as those of a giant, extinct reptile.

1830 Charles Lyell (Scottish: 1797–1875) begins to publish *The Principles of Geology*, the work that convinced geologists that Earth is at least several hundred million years old.

1880 John Milne (English: 1850–1913) invents modern seismograph.

1896 Svante Arrhenius (Swedish: 1859–1927) discovers greenhouse effect of carbon dioxide in atmosphere; global temperatures rise with higher levels of carbon dioxide.

1902 Léon Teisserenc de Bort (French: 1855–1913) discovers the stratosphere.

1906 R.D. Oldham (English: 1858–1936) discovers Earth's core.

1907 Bertram B. Boltwood (American: 1870–1927) shows that age of rocks containing uranium can be determined by measuring ratio of uranium to lead.

1909 Andrija Mohorovicic (Croatian: 1857–1936) discovers boundary between Earth's crust and mantle, now known as Mohorovicic discontinuity, or "Moho."

1912 Alfred Wegener (German: 1880–1930) proposes his theory of continental drift, based on idea that at one time there was single continent, split since then into present-day continents, which have drifted away from each other.

1925 The German *Meteor* expedition discovers Mid-Atlantic Ridge, a giant mountain range in middle of the Atlantic Ocean.

1929 Motonori Matuyama (Japanese: 1884–1958) shows that Earth's magnetic field reverses every few hundred million years.

1943 Mexican farmer discovers that volcano is growing in his cornfield; volcano is later named Mount Parícutin.

1946 Vincent Schaefer (American: 1906–) discovers that dry ice can be used to cause clouds to release rain.

1953 Maurice Ewing (American: 1906–74) discovers rift that runs down middle of Mid-Atlantic Ridge.

1958 James Van Allen (American: 1914–) discovers belts of radiation that surround Earth in space, now known as Van Allen belts.

1960 Harry Hess (American: 1906–69) develops theory of seafloor spreading—oceans are getting wider as new seafloor is formed at midocean ridges.

1979 American oceanographers discover hot vents in oceans, surrounded by exotic forms of life based on sulfur, not oxygen.

1980 Walter Alvarez (American: 1911–88) and co-workers discover geologic layer of iridium in region identified with the demise of the dinosaurs; he attributes both iridium and extinction to impact of a large comet or meteorite on Earth.

1987 NASA determines that continents are moving in ways predicted by theory of plate tectonics, a theory based on idea that Earth's crust is broken into huge plates that are moving with respect to each other.

COMPOSITION OF EARTH

Earth is built of many layers. Following is a description from the inside out.

Core The innermost layers, called the core, are thought to be a mixture of iron and nickel. The core is actually two layers, a liquid outer core and a solid inner core. The inner core is more than 3,100 miles below the surface, and the other core is about 1,800 miles below the surface.

Mantle Outside the core is the bulk of the planet, which is called the mantle. It is not clear what the mantle is composed of. Nearly half of it is thought to be silicon dioxide, which is quartz when found in the crust but may have very different properties under the heat and pressure of the mantle. Another large part is thought to be magnesium oxide. After that, the mantle is probably composed of oxides of various metals in fairly small amounts, although iron oxides might account for about 8% of the total. The mantle extends to about 55 miles below the higher mountains and to as little as 3 miles below parts of the ocean. Part of the upper mantle is somewhat fluid and is known as the asthenosphere.

Crust Above the mantle, regions are accessible to accurate measurement. The solid part above the mantle is called the crust. It has been extensively sampled. The crust consists of light rocks in the relatively thick continents (from 15 to 55 mi.) and heavier rocks in the thin oceanic crust (3 to 5 mi.).

Hydrosphere Covering about 70% of the crust is a layer of water. While this can be divided into fresh water and ocean water, there is so much more water in the oceans only the latter will be described here.

Atmosphere Above the crust and the oceans is the atmosphere. It is also separated into layers. The lowest, extending upward 5 to 11 miles above the surface, is the troposphere. In this region, temperature falls with increasing height. Up to an altitude of about 30 miles, the next layer is the stratosphere, where temperature rises with increasing height. This pattern alternates: between 30 miles and 50 miles, in the mesosphere, temperatures fall again, whereas above 50 miles, in the thermosphere temperatures rise. The upper part of the mesosphere and all of the thermosphere contain many charged particles, or ions, so this region is also called the ionosphere. Above the mesophere, the gases that make up air begin to separate, with mostly oxygen out to 600 miles, followed by a layer of mostly helium that extends to about 1,500 miles above the Earth's surface. Above the helium a layer of hydrogen gradually thins out to become the vacuum of space.

COMPOSITION OF EARTH'S OCEANS

By weight pure water is 11% hydrogen and 89% oxygen. Ocean water varies in composition from place to place but on the average is 3.5% salts and other compounds by weight. The largest amount of salt in the ocean is sodium chloride, ordinary table salt, which is 2.7% of the total amount of water by weight If you evaporated some ocean water and tested the solids obtained, this would be a typical composition by weight:

Element	Compound Percent by weight
sodium chloride	77.8%
magnesium chloride	10.9
magnesium sulfide	4.7
calcium sulfate	3.6
potassium sulfate	2.5
calcium carbonate	0.3
magnesium bromide	0.2
other compounds	trace

PRINCIPAL ELEMENTS IN EARTH'S CRUST

Continental crust is very different from oceanic crust. Not only is the crust of the continent much thicker than the oceanic crust, but also the composition is different. Continental crust is mainly granite and other, relatively light rocks. The crust under the oceans is mainly basalt, a relatively heavy rock. In addition there is considerable variation from place to place in the composition of rock.

Element	Percent by weight[1]
oxygen	45.6%
silicon	27.3
aluminum	8.4
iron	6.2
calcium	4.7
magnesium	2.8
sodium	2.3
potassium	1.8
hydrogen	1.5
titanium	0.6

1. Greater than 100% due to rounding.

COMPOSITION OF EARTH'S AIR

Air is nearly the same all over Earth at the same altitude, but its composition changes at higher altitudes, where there is more of the lighter gases. There is, however, a variable amount of water vapor from place to place at the same altitude, which is generally reported in terms of relative humidity. The composition of air has changed slowly over time, although human activities have accelerated some of these changes. Carbon dioxide, for example, has gone from 0.0316% to 0.0340% in the last 25 years. Methane is also increasing at a rate that could cause it to double in the next 100 years. Both of these gases trap heat the way a greenhouse does, leading to fears that the "greenhouse" effect will change the climate. Another gas that causes concern is ozone (see p. 371). Ozone is formed from oxygen by sunlight, so there is more ozone at ground level in the summer than in the winter. There is also more ozone in cities than in rural regions because its formation is facilitated by auto-exhaust gases.

Constituent	Percent by volume[1]
nitrogen	78.084%
oxygen	20.946
argon	0.934
carbon dioxide	0.034
neon	0.00182
helium	0.00052
krypton	0.00011
hydrogen	0.00005
nitrous oxide	0.00005
xenon	0.0000087
ozone (summer)	0.000007
ozone (winter)	0.000002
methane	0.0000017

1. Based on dry air at sea level.

Geologic Disasters: Volcanoes and Landslides

In addition to earthquakes and the tsunamis they cause, the earth can be treacherous in other ways. Most spectacular are eruptions of volcanoes, which sometimes have worldwide effects. Landslides may ultimately be caused by the effects of weather—softening soil or opening cracks—but they sometimes occur for no apparent reason. A landslide into a lake or reservoir is often a deadly combination, as the water displaced causes an almost instantaneous flood.

Volcanoes kill in many different ways. An explosive eruption tosses rock and lava high in the air. Clouds of hot gases and dust may be swept down the side of the volcano. Heat from the volcano can melt glaciers or snowcaps, causing destructive, cold mudslides. Cold, poisonous gases may be emitted. Although it generally moves too slowly to be a menace to life, lava can sometimes flow too quickly for people to evade. Earthquakes associated with a volcanic eruption can be destructive and may cause landslides. Lakes of boiling water can be released as well.

VOLCANOES AND LANDSLIDES— THE HUMAN TOLL

Date	Disaster	Estimated deaths
1628 or 1645 B.C.	Mediterranean volcanic island of Thera (also known as Santorini) explodes.	N.A.
Aug. 24–26, A.D. 79	Mt. Vesuvius, near Naples, Italy, erupts, destroying towns of Pompeii and Herculaneum.	2,000+
260	Mt. Ilopango in El Salvador erupts, apparently destroying the early Maya civilization (replaced by later Maya civilization, after 200 years, in Yucatán).	N.A.
Sept. 4, 1618	Landslides hit Chiavenna Valley, Italy.	2,420
Dec. 16, 1631	Mt. Vesuvius again erupts.	4,000+
Mar. 25, 1669	Mt. Etna at Catania, Sicily erupts.	20,000
Jan. 11, 1683	Mt. Etna again erupts, accompanied by earthquakes.	60,000
Aug. 11–12, 1772	Mt. Papandayan on Java explodes.	3,000+
Jun. 1783– Feb. 1784	Laki fissure on Mt. Skaptar in Iceland erupts, producing poisonous gases that kill crops and livestock, as well as haze so thick that fishing in oceans is also interrupted.	9,800
Sept. 2, 1806	Rossberg Peak collapses, causing landslides to strike Goldau Valley in Switzerland.	500
Apr. 5, 1815	Mt. Tambora on Sumbawa in East Indies begins series of eruptions that results in immediate death of about 10,000 people; another 80,000 die of famine and disease locally; further problems affecting tens of thousands as eruptions alter weather around world.	162,000
Oct. 8 and 12, 1822	Mt. Galunggung on Java erupts, causing slides of mud and boiling water.	4,000

Date	Disaster	Estimated deaths
1845	Eruption of Nevada del Ruiz in northern Colombia causes mudslides from melting snow.	1,000
July 28, 1883	Epomeo volcano on Italian Isle of Ischia erupts, causing destructive earthquakes.	2,000+
Aug. 26, 1883	Krakatau volcano in East Indies erupts, producing giant waves that strike nearby islands.	37,000
July 15, 1888	Bandai volcano in Japan erupts, causing steaming mudslides.	500–
May 7, 1902	La Soufrière on St. Vincent in West Indies erupts.	1,500–2,000
May 8, 1902	Pelée volcano on neighboring Martinique erupts, pouring cloud of flaming gas on city of St. Pierre.	29,000
Aug. 30, 1902	Mt. Pelée erupts again.	2,000
Apr. 29, 1903	Landslide on Turtle Mt. strikes town of Frank, Alberta, Canada.	70
Apr. 18, 1906	Mt. Vesuvius near Naples erupts.	150+
1911	Taal volcano, near Manila, Philippines, erupts.	1,300
May, 1919	Crater lake of Mt. Kelud in Indonesia, boiling by volcanic activity, breaks through side of the mountain.	5,000
Jan. 15, 1951	Mt. Lamington on New Guinea produces cloud of hot gas and dust, similar to that at Mt. Pelée in 1902 and Mt. St. Helens in 1980.	3,000–5,000
Dec. 4, 1951	Mt. Catarman (Hibokhibok) in Philippines releases cloud of hot gas.	500
Sept. 24, 1952	Japanese research ship investigating undersea volcano is destroyed in eruptive event.	29
Dec. 25, 1953	Dam, created by 1945 eruption of Ruapehu volcano gives way, causing avalanche of mud and snow that strikes passenger train.	150
Mar. 20, 1956	Bezymianny volcano on Kamchatka Peninsula in Siberia explodes in most energetic eruption of 20th century.	–
Sept. 28, 1956	Taal volcano, near Manila, Philippines, erupts.	350
Jan 10, 1962	Landslide on Mt. Huascarán, Peru.	3,000
Mar. 14, 1962	Two landslides near Paucartambno Hydroelectric Station in Peru.	204
Mar. 17–21, 1963	Mt. Agung volcano in Bali, Indonesia, has second eruption of year.	1,584
Aug. 10, 1963	Landslide in Nepal sweeps villages into Trisuli River.	200
Oct. 9, 1963	Flood occurs when Valont Dam near Langarone, Italy, overflows as result of landslide into its reservoir.	2,200
Aug. 30, 1965	Avalanche near Saas-Fee, Switzerland, from Allalin glacier strikes workers building dam.	40–100
Jul. 22, 1970	Landslide diverts course of Alaknanda River in India, causing sudden flood.	600
Mar. 18, 1971	Landslide falls into Lake Yanahuani, creating 60-foot wave that sweeps over Chungar, Peru.	200
July 29, 1971	Landslide falls into high lake in Hindu Kush mountains of Afghanistan, causing instant flood.	1,000+

MEASURING EARTHQUAKES

The energy of an earthquake is generally reported using the Richter scale, a system developed by American geologist Charles Richter in 1935, based on measuring the heights of wave measurements on a seismograph. Each whole number on the Richter scale has 60 times as much energy as the number below it (often incorrectly stated as each step on the scale is ten times as strong as the one below). Consequently, very low numbers on the scale are not generally felt as earthquakes, but higher numbers measure very destructive earthquakes.

A different scale, the Mercalli scale, is based on the effects of the earthquake at a particular point. To understand the Richter Scale, it helps to compare it with the Mercalli, operating on the assumption that one is near the origin of the earthquake.

RICHTER AND MERCALLI SCALES COMPARED

Richter scale		Mercalli earthquake intensity scale
2.5	Generally not felt, but recorded on seismometers.	I. Not felt except by a very few under specially favorable circumstances.
		II. Felt only by a few persons at rest, especially on upper floors of buildings.
3.5	Felt by many people.	III. Felt quite noticeably indoors, especially on upper floors of buildings, but many people do not recognize as an earthquake.
		IV. During the day, felt indoors by many, outdoors by few. Sensation like heavy truck striking building.
		V. Felt by nearly everyone; many awakened. Disturbances of trees, poles, and other tall objects sometimes noticed.
4.5	Some local damage may occur.	VI. Felt by all; many frightened and run outdoors. Some heavy furniture moved; few instances of fallen plaster or damaged chimneys. Damage slight.
		VII. Everybody runs outdoors. Damage negligible in buildings of good design and construction; slight to moderate in well-built ordinary structures; considerable in poorly built or badly designed structures.
6.0	A destructive earthquake.	VIII. Damage slight in specially designed structures; considerable in ordinary substantial buildings with partial collapse; great in poorly built structures. (Collapse of chimneys, factory stacks, columns, monuments, walls.)
		IX. Damage considerable in specially designed structures. Buildings shifted off foundations. Ground cracked conspicuously.
7.0	A major earthquake. About 10 occur each year.	X. Some well-built wooden structures destroyed. Most masonry and frame structures destroyed with foundations. Ground badly cracked.
8.0 and above	Great earthquakes. These occur once every five to 10 years.	XI. Few, if any (masonry) structures remain standing. Bridges destroyed. Broad fissures in ground.
		XII. Damage total. Waves seen on ground surfaces. Objects thrown upward into air.

Date	Disaster	Estimated deaths	Date	Disaster	Estimated deaths
June 28, 1974	Landslides occur along Quebrada Blanca Canyon in Eastern Colombia.	200	Apr. 30, 1979	Landslide covers side of Merapi volcano in Sumatra, Indonesia.	82+
Jan. 10, 1977	Fast-moving stream of lava from volcano near Goma, Zaire, overtakes fleeing natives.	70	July 18, 1979	Landslide on Mt. Werung causes wave to strike beach areas on Lomblen island, Indonesia.	539
Feb. 21, 1979	Volcano in Java, Indonesia, erupts.	175+	May 18, 1980	Mt. St. Helens volcano in Washington State erupts.	61

Date	Disaster	Estimated deaths
Mar. 28, Apr. 3, Apr. 4, 1982	El Chichón in Chiapas State, Mexico, erupts, with major blast coming on Apr. 4, sending cloud of volcanic ash around world.	2,000
Aug. 16, 1984	Carbon dioxide emitted by Lake Monoun, Cameroon, spreads in region around lake.	37
Nov. 13, 1985	Eruption of Nevada del Ruiz in northern Colombia melts snow on its summit, causing massive mud slide that covers town of Armero.	25,000
Aug. 21, 1986	Carbon dioxide from Lake Nyos, Cameroon, caused either by underwater volcano or overturning of water layers, spreads through surrounding region.	1,700+

Major Active Volcanoes of the World

A volcano is an opening in the Earth's crust that emits melted rock (lava), various hot gases, and rocks of various sizes; it is also the mountain that forms as solidified lava and ejected rocks pile up around the opening, called a vent if it is like a crack, a crater if it is larger and fairly circular, or a caldera if it is very large. A caldera may have several vents or craters on its floor.

Although volcanoes have caused some of the world's worst disasters, they also have many positive effects. Minerals brought from deep in the earth help fertilize the land around many volcanoes. New land is built by volcanoes in the oceans. And the study of volcanoes has been a major factor in understanding the interior of the earth.

Volcanoes do not occur at random across the world. Almost all are found at plate boundaries, such as the famous "Ring of Fire" around the Pacific Ocean. A few, such as the volcanoes of Hawaii and the volcanic region (without a volcano) of Yellowstone Park appear to be over a "hot spot," a place where liquid rock flows upward with sufficient force to burn through Earth's crust.

Volcanoes seem to be born, be active, and die—or at least sleep, which is called being dormant. Technically, a volcano is considered active if it has shown signs of activity in historic times. Thus a volcano like Tambora, which has not erupted since 1815, is considered active. It is not usually clear whether or not a volcano is dormant (which suggests that it could be active in the future) or extinct. Some volcanoes once thought to be extinct have become active. About 600 volcanoes are now active. The following list contains about a third of all the known active volcanoes with special emphasis on volcanoes that have been active in recent years, volcanoes in the United States, and volcanoes that have had famous eruptions.

GEOLOGIC TIME SCALE

Geologists and other earth scientists divide the history of the planet into periods of varying length based on the fossils found in rock strata. Geologists often speak of the period before 570 million years ago as Precambrian Time. The eras after 570 million years ago are grouped into the Phanerozoic Eon.

Era or Eon	Period	Epoch	Organisms	Time before present (millions of years)
ARCHEAN EON			Monerans: bacteria and blue-green algae	4,600
PROTEROZOIC EON			Protists, algae, and soft-bodied creatures similar to jellyfish and worms	2,500
PHANEROZOIC EON PALEOZOIC ERA	Cambrian		Tiny fossils with skeletons followed by animals with shells, notably, trilobites	570
	Ordovician		Brachiopods (shellfish similar to clams), corals, starfish, and some organisms that have no modern counterparts, called sea scorpions, conodonts, and graptolites	500
	Silurian		Snails, clams and mussels, ammonoids (similar to the nautilus), jawless fish, sea scorpions, first land plants and animals (club mosses, land scorpions); modern groups of algae and fungi	425
	Devonian		Spiders, amphibians, jawed fish, lobe-finned fish, sharks, lungfish, and ferns	395
	Carboniferous		Insects, land snails, amphibians, early reptiles, sea lilies, giant club mosses, and seed ferns	350
	Permian		Mammal-like reptiles and fin-backed reptiles, cycads, ginkgoes, and conifers	290
MESOZOIC ERA	Triassic		Marine reptiles (plesiosaurs and ichthyosaurs), crocodiles, frogs, turtles, early mammals, and early dinosaurs	235
	Jurassic		Dinosaurs (such as stegosaurus), pterosaurs (such as pterodactyl), early birds, dinoflagellates, diatoms, early flowering plants	190
	Cretaceous		Dinosaurs (such as tyrannosaurus, triceratops, and brontosaurus), salamanders, modern bony fishes, mosasaurs (marine lizards), flowering plants, placental and marsupial mammals	130
CENOZOIC ERA	Tertiary	Paleocene	Early primates, early horses, rodents, sycamores	65
		Eocene	Whales, penguins, roses, bats, camels, early elephants, dogs, cats, weasels	55
		Oligocene	Deer, pigs, saber-toothed cats, monkeys	38
		Miocene	Seals, dolphins, grasses, daisies, asters, sunflowers, lettuce, giraffes, bears, hyenas, early apes	26
		Pliocene	Apes, australopithecines (early hominids), *Homo habilis* (first human species), mammoths, giant sloths, and armadillos	6
	Quaternary	Pleistocene	*Homo erectus* (ancestor of modern humans), modern humans, and Neanderthal humans; large mammals, such as giant bison and beavers; many kinds of hoofed animals	1.8
		Holocene	Modern humans and flora and fauna of today	0.01 (11,000 yrs)

WELL-KNOWN AND ACTIVE VOLCANOES OF THE WORLD

Volcano	Location	Height (ft. above sea level)	Last reported eruption
AFRICA AND THE INDIAN OCEAN			
Cameroon Mt.	Cameroon	13,354	1982
Erta-Ale	Ethiopia	1,650	1973
Karthala	Comoros	8,000	1977
Nyamulagira	Zaire	10,028	1988
Niragongo	Zaire	11,400	1977
Piton de la Fournaise	Réunion Island	5,981	1988
ANTARCTICA			
Big Ben	Heard Island	9,007	1986
Deception Island	South Shetland Islands	1,890	1970
Mount Erebus	Ross Island	12,450	1988
ASIA			
Agung	Bali, Indonesia	10,308	1964
Akita Komaga-take	Japan	5,449	1970
Alaid	Kuril Islands, Soviet Union	7,674	1972
Amburomrribu	Indonesia	7,051	1969
Asama	Honshu, Japan	8,300	1983
Aso	Kyushu, Japan	5,223	1988
Awu	Indonesia	4,350	1968
Azuma	Honshu, Japan	6,700	1978
Batur	Bali, Indonesia	5,636	1968
Bezymianny	Soviet Union	9,514	1986
Bulusan	Philippines	5,115	1988
Chokai	Honshu, Japan	7,300	1974
Dukono	Indonesia	3,566	1971
Gamalama	Indonesia	5,625	1980
Galunggug	Java, Indonesia	7,113	1982
Gamkonora	Indonesia	5,365	1981
Gerde	Indonesia	9,705	1949
Karymsky	Soviet Union	4,869	1985
Keli Mutu	Indonesia	5,460	1968
Kelud	Java, Indonesia	5,679	1967
Kerinci	Sumatra, Indonesia	12,467	1987
Kirishima	Japan	5,577	1982
Klyuchevskaya	Soviet Union	15,584	1985
Koraykskaya	Soviet Union	11,339	1957
Krakatau (or Anak Krakatau, since original volcano was destroyed in 1883)	Indonesia	330	1972
Lewotobi Laki-Laki	Indonesia	5,217	1968
Lokon-Empung	Indonesia	5,187	1988
Mayon	Philippines	9,991	1978
Me-akan	Japan	4,931	1966
Merapi	Sumatra, Indonesia	9,485	1988
Nasu	Japan	6,210	1977
Nigata Yakeyama	Japan	8,064	1987
On-Take	Kyushu, Japan	10,049	1980
Oshima	Japan	2,550	1988
Raung	Java, Indonesia	10,932	1982
Rindjani	Indonesia	12,224	1981
Sakurajima	Japan	2,640	1988
Sangeang Api	Indonesia	6,351	1988
Sarycheva	Kuril Islands, Soviet Union	5,115	1976
Semeru	Java, Indonesia	12,060	1988
Shiveluch	Soviet Union	10,771	1964
Siau	Indonesia	5,853	1976

RECORD BREAKERS FROM THE EARTH SCIENCES

Traditionally, the study of early life by way of its remains—which are called fossils—has been the province of earth scientists, rather than biologists. This is because fossils were the first known way to group rocks of the same age together, since it was assumed that at a given time in the past certain life-forms existed and later became extinct. Earth itself is thought to be about 4.5 billion years old.

BY AGE

Record	Record holder	Age in years
Oldest rocks	Zircons from Australia	4.4 billion
Oldest fossils	Single-celled algae or bacteria from Australia	3.5 billion
Oldest slime molds (bacteria)	Slime molds—also called slime bacteria—that gathered together to form multicellular bodies for reproduction	2.5 billion
Oldest petroleum	Oil from northern Australia	1.4 billion
Oldest land animal	Millipede? Known only from its burrows	488 million
Oldest fish	*Sacabambasis,* found in Bolivia	470 million
Oldest land plant	Moss or algae	425 million
Oldest insect	Bristletail (relative of modern silverfish)	390 million
Oldest reptile	"Lizzie the Lizard," found in Scotland	340 million
Oldest bird	*Protoavis,* fossils found near Post, Texas	225 million
Oldest dinosaur	Unnamed dinosaur the size of ostrich	225 million

BY SIZE

This group of record holders includes a couple of ancient life-forms but concentrates more on Earth's features that are studied by earth scientists.

Record	Record holder	Size or distance
Longest dinosaur	*Seismosaurus,* who lived about 150 million years ago in what is now New Mexico	100–120 ft. long
Tallest and heaviest dinosaur	*Ultrasaurus,* who lived in Utah	About as tall as 5-story building; weighed more than 80 tons
Largest exposed rock	Mt. Augustus in Western Australia	At 1,237 ft. high, 5 mi. long, and 2 mi. wide, it is twice size of more famous Ayers Rock
Largest island	Greenland, also known as Kalaallit Nunnaat	About 840,000 sq. mi.
Largest ocean	Pacific	64,186,300 sq. mi.
Deepest part of ocean	*Challenger* Deep in the Marianas Trench in Pacific Ocean	35,640 ft., or 6.85 mi.
Greatest tide	Bay of Fundy between Maine and New Brunswick	47.5 ft. between high and low tides
Largest geyser	Steamboat Geyser in Yellowstone Park	Shoots mud and rocks about 1,000 ft. in air
Longest glacier	Lambert Glacier in Antarctica (upper section known as Mellor Glacier)	At least 250 mi.
Longest known cave	Mammoth Cave, which is connected to Flint Ridge Cave system	Total mapped passageway of over 330 mi.
Largest single cave chamber	Sarawak Chaper, Lobang Nasip Bagus, on Sarawak, Indonesia	2,300 ft. long, 980 ft. wide on average, 230 ft. or more high
Largest canyon on land	Grand Canyon of the Colorado, in northern Arizona	Over 217 mi. long, from 4 to 13 mi. wide, as much as 5,300 ft. deep
Highest volcano	Cerro Aconagua in the Argentine Andes	22,834 ft. high
Most abundant mineral	Magnesium silicate perovskite	About ⅔ of planet, it forms Earth's mantle

Volcano	Location	Height (ft. above sea level)	Last reported eruption
Sinila	Indonesia	7,000	1979
Slamet	Java, Indonesia	11,247	1967
Soputan	Indonesia	5,994	1984
Suwanosezima	Japan	2,640	1987
Taal	Luzon, Philippines	4,752	1977
Tambora	Sumbawa, Indonesia	9,000	1815
Tangkuban Prahu	Java, Indonesia	6,637	1967
Ternate	Indonesia	5,627	1963
Tiatia	Kuril Islands, Soviet Union	6,013	1973
Tjarme	Indonesia	10,098	1938
Usu	Japan	2,390	1978
Yake Dake	Japan	8,064	1963
CENTRAL AMERICA AND THE CARIBBEAN			
Acatenango	Guatemala	12,992	1972
Arenal	Costa Rica	5,092	1988
Conchagua	El Salvador	4,100	1947
El Viejo (San Cristóbal)	Nicaragua	5,840	1987
Fuego	Guatemala	12,582	1988
Irazu	Costa Rica	11,260	1987
Izalco	El Salvador	7,749	1966
Kick-'em-Jenny	Subocean, off Grenada	–160	1988
Momotombo	Nicaragua	4,199	1982
Mount Pelée	Martinique	4,500	1930
Ometepe (Concepción)	Nicaragua	5,106	1986
Pacaya	Guatemala	8,346	1988
Póas	Costa Rica	8,930	1986
Rincon de la Vieja	Costa Rica	6,234	1987
San Miguel	El Salvador	6,994	1986
Santiaguito (Santa Maria)	Guatemala	12,362	1988
San Salvador	El Salvador	6,187	1923
Soufrière	St. Vincent and the Grenadines	4,048	1979
Tacana	Guatemala	12,400	1988
Telica	Nicaragua	3,409	1982
EUROPE AND THE ATLANTIC OCEAN			
Askja	Iceland	4,594	1961
Beerenberg	Jan Mayen Island, Norway	7,470	1985
Eldfell	Iceland	327	1973
Etna	Italy	11,053	1988
Fogo	Cape Verde Islands	9,300	1951
Hekla	Iceland	4,892	1981
Kafla	Iceland	2,145	1984
Leirhnukur	Iceland	2,145	1975

Volcano	Location	Height (ft. above sea level)	Last reported eruption
Stromboli	Italy	3,038	1986
Surtsey	Iceland	568	1967
Tristan de Cunha	St. Helena	6,760	1961
Vesuvius	Italy	4,203	1944
NORTH AMERICA			
Akutan	Alaska	4,265	1988
Amukta	Alaska	3,490	1963
Aniakchak	Alaska	4,450	1931
Augustine	Alaska	3,995	1986
Bogoslof	Alaska	150	1931
Carlisle	Alaska	5,315	1838
Cerberus	Alaska	2,560	1873
Chiginagak	Alaska	7,985	1929
Cinder Cone	California	6,907	1851
Cleveland	Alaska	5,710	1987
Colima	Mexico	14,003	1988
El Chichón	Mexico	7,300	1983
Fisher	Alaska	3,545	1826
Gareloi	Alaska	5,370	1982
Great Sitkin	Alaska	5,775	1974
Iliamna	Alaska	10,140	1978
Isanotski	Alaska	8,185	1845
Kagamil	Alaska	2,945	1929
Kanaga	Alaska	4,450	1933
Katmai	Alaska	7,540	1974
Keniuji	Alaska	885	1828
Kiska	Alaska	4,025	1969
Korovin	Alaska	4,885	1987
Lassen Peak	California	10,453	1914–21
Little Sitkin	Alaska	3,945	1828
Martin	Alaska	6,050	1960
Mageik	Alaska	7,295	1946
Makushin	Alaska	6,720	1987
Mt. Baker	Washington	10,778	1870
Mt. Hood	Oregon	11,245	1801
Mt. Rainier	Washington	14,410	1882
Mt. Shasta	California	14,161	1855
Mt. St. Helens	Washington	9,671	1986
Novarupta	Alaska	N.A.	1912
Okmok	Alaska	3,540	1988
Paricutin	Mexico	1,500	1952
Pavlof	Alaska	8,960	1988
Pavlof Sister	Alaska	7,050	1786
Peulik	Alaska	5,030	1852
Pogromni	Alaska	7,545	1964
Redoubt	Alaska	10,265	1966
Sarichef	Alaska	2,015	1812
Seguam	Alaska	3,465	1977
Shishaldin	Alaska	9,430	1987

Volcano	Location	Height (ft. above sea level)	Last reported eruption
Spurr	Alaska	11,070	1953
Tanaga	Alaska	7,015	1914
Trident	Alaska	6,830	1974
Tobert	Alaska	11,413	1953
Veniaminof	Alaska	8,450	1987
Vsevidof	Alaska	6,965	1880
Westdahl	Alaska	5,055	1964
Yunaska	Alaska	1,980	1937
OCEANIA—AUSTRALIA, NEW ZEALAND, AND THE PACIFIC ISLANDS			
Ambrym	Vanuatu	4,376	1979
Haleakala	Hawaii	10,025	1790
Hualalai	Hawaii	8,251	1801
Karkar	Papua New Guinea	4,920	1981
Kilauea	Hawaii	4,090	1988
Langila	New Britain, Papua New Guinea	3,586	1988
Lopevi	Vanuatu	4,755	1982
Manam	Papua New Guinea	6,000	1988
Mauna Loa	Hawaii	13,680	1987
Ngauruhoe	North Island, New Zealand	7,515	1975
Pagan	Mariana Islands	1,870	1985
Ruapehu	New Zealand	9,175	1988
Tarawera	North Island, New Zealand	3,645	1886
Ulawun	New Britain, Papua New Guinea	7,532	1988
White Island	New Zealand	1,075	1988
SOUTH AMERICA			
Alcedo	Galapagos Islands, Ecuador	3,599	1970
Cotacachi	Ecuador	16,204	1955
Cotopaxi	Ecuador	19,347	1975
Guagua Pichincha	Ecuador	15,696	1982
Guallatiri	Chile	19,882	1987
Hudson	Chile	8,580	1973
Lascar	Chile	19,652	1986
Llaima	Chile	10,239	1988
Lonquimay	Chile	9,400	1989
Nevado del Ruiz	Colombia	17,720	1988
Puracé	Colombia	15,604	1977
Reventador	Ecuador	11,434	1973
Sangay	Ecuador	17,159	1976
Shoshuenco	Chile	7,743	1960
Tupungatito	Chile	18,504	1986
Villarica	Chile	9,318	1984

Life Sciences

While the scientific study of living creatures seems to have begun with Aristotle, there was much practical experimentation with living things much earlier, going back to the domestication of a species, the dog, around 10,000 B.C. In the years that followed the Scientific Revolution of the 17th century, the science of biology came to include most of the then-known life sciences: zoology (the study of animals), botany (the study of plants), and taxonomy (the study of classification of living things). In the 19th century, biology began to fragment into other studies: microbiology (the study of creatures visible only through the microscope), genetics (the study of how traits are inherited), biochemistry (the study of molecules created by living things), and so forth. At the same time, different ways of studying living organisms were developed, among them anthropology (the study of human beings), ecology (the study of interactions between different living things and their environment), and ethology (the study of animal behavior).

MAJOR DISCOVERIES IN LIFE SCIENCE

B.C.

c. 9000 Agricultural Revolution starts in Near East with domestication of sheep and goats in Persia (Iran) and Afghanistan and cultivation of wheat in Canaan (Israel).

c. 8000 Agricultural Revolution starts independently in what are now Peru, Central America, and Indochina.

c. 350 Aristotle (Greek: 384–322 B.C.) classifies known animals in system that will continue to be used until 1735.

A.D.

1648 Jan Baptista van Helmont (Flemish: 1580–1635 or –1644) shows that plants do not obtain large amounts of material for their growth from soil.

1665 Robert Hooke (English: 1635–1703) describes and names the cell.

1668 Francesco Redi (Italian: 1626–1697) shows that maggots in meat do not arise spontaneously but are hatched from flies' eggs.

1669 Anton van Leeuwenhoek (Dutch: 1632–1723) discovers microorganisms—creatures too small to see with naked eye—and recognizes that sperm are part of reproduction.

1683 Anton van Leeuwenhoek is first to observe bacteria.

1735 Carolus Linnaeus (Swedish: 1707–78) introduces system in use today for classifying plants and animals.

1779 Jan Ingenhousz (Dutch: 1730–99) discovers that plants release oxygen when exposed to sunlight and that they consume carbon dioxide; this is first step in our understanding of photosynthesis.

1827 John James Audubon (American: 1785–1851) starts publication of *Birds of America,* a collection of engravings of 435 detailed paintings Audubon had made of American birds.

1839 Theodor Schwann (German: 1810–82), building on work of Matthias Schleiden (German: 1804–81) in 1838, develops cell theory of life.

1856 First skeleton of what we now call Neanderthals is found in cave in Neander valley, near Düsseldorf (W. Germany). Louis Pasteur (French: 1822–95) discovers that fermentation is caused by microorganisms.

1858 Charles Darwin (English: 1809–82) and Alfred Wallace (English: 1823–1913) announce their theory of evolution by natural selection to the Linnean Society.

1859 Darwin's *On the Origin of Species* is published.

1865 Gregor Mendel's (Austrian: 1822–84) theory of dominant and recessive genes is published in obscure local journal.

1868 Workers building road in France discover skeletons of first-known Cro-Magnons in cave.

1894 Marie-Eugène Dubois (Dutch: 1858–1940) announces discovery of "Java ape-man," now known to be first-discovered specimen of *Homo erectus.*

1898 Mosaic disease of tobacco plants is recognized as being caused by virus, the first identification of a virus (viruses cannot be seen at this time, being known only from their effects).

1900 Three different biologists rediscover laws of genetics originally found by Gregor Mendel.

1901 The okapi is discovered, the last large land animal to have been unknown to science.

LIFE-SCIENCE RECORD HOLDERS

Record	Record holder	Distinctive feature
BY SIZE		
Largest structure made by living organisms	Great Barrier Reef off coast of Australia, made by tiny animals called corals	Length: 1,260 mi. Area: 80,000 sq. mi.
Largest living organism	"General Sherman," a sequoia in Sequoia National Park	Height: 274.9 ft. Circumference: 114.6 ft.
Largest living animal	Blue whale	Length: 110 ft. Weight: 136 tons
Largest living land animal	African elephant	Height: 13 ft. Weight: 13 tons
Longest animal	Bootlace worm, a sea worm	180 ft.
Smallest free-living organism	Pleuro-pneumonia-like organisms of genus *Mycoplasma*	Diameter: 0.000004 in.
Smallest organism of any kind	Viroids, viruslike plant pathogens without coats	Diameter: 0.00000000007 in.
Largest invertebrate	Giant squid	Length: up to 55 ft. Weight: over a ton
Most teeth in mammal	Toothed whales	260 teeth
Longest trip by shore bird	Semipalmated sandpiper	28,000 mi. in four days
Largest egg ever	Extinct elephant bird of Madagascar	Capacity: 2.35 gal. Weight: 27 lb.
Largest nest	Bald eagle	Weight: 6,700 lbs.
TIME		
Oldest living organism	King Clone, a creosote plant in California desert	11,700 years
Longest recorded age of an animal	Ocean quahog (clam)	220 years
Longest gestation	Alpine black salamander	Up to 38 months
SPEED		
Fastest flight	Peregrine falcon	While diving, 212 mph
Fastest swimmer	Cosmopolitan sailfish	68 mph
Slowest mammal	Three-toed sloth	4 mi. a day on ground

1919 Karl von Frisch (Austrian–German: 1886–1982) discovers that bees have language that can be used to communicate where to find good source of flower nectar.

1924 Raymond Dart (Australian–South African: 1893–1988) identifies first fossil of an australopithecine, a close relative of early humans.

1938 First-known live coelacanth, a lobe-finned fish, is captured in waters off Comoro Islands; scientists had believed species had been extinct for 60 million years.

1952 Eugene Aserinsky (American: 1921–) discovers that sleep with rapid eye movements (REMs) is different stage of sleep, later found to be associated with dreams.

1953 James Watson (American: 1928–) and Francis Crick (English: 1916–) determine structure of DNA, the basis of heredity.

1961 Louis Leakey (English: 1903–72) and Mary Leakey (English: 1913–) discover a previously unknown ancestor of humans, *Homo habilis,* in the Olduvai Gorge of northern Tanzania.

1961 Marshall Nirenberg (American: 1927–) learns to read one of "letters" of genetic code.

1962 Rachel Carson's (American: 1907–64) *Silent Spring* is attack on pesticides that launches the environmental movement.

1968 Werner Arber (Swiss: 1929–) discovers restriction enzymes, a class of proteins that will make genetic engineering possible.

1969 Jonathan Beckwith (American: 1935–) and co-workers are first to isolate a single gene.

1970 Har Gobind Khorana (Indian-American: 1922–) and co-workers produce first artificial gene. Howard Temin (American: 1934–) and David Baltimore (American: 1938–) discover enzyme that causes RNA to be transcribed to DNA, a key step in development of genetic engineering.

1973 Stanley Cohen (American: 1917–) and Herbert Boyer (American: 1936–) succeed in putting specific gene into bacterium, the first instance of true genetic engineering.

1974 Donald C. Johanson (American: 1943–) and co-workers discover Lucy in Afar region of Ethiopia, the nearly complete skeleton of *Australopithecus afarensis*, an early relative of humans (more than 3 million years old).

1975 César Milstein (English: 1927–) announces discovery of how to produce monoclonal antibodies, highly specific chemicals that can be made to react with particular proteins or other chemicals in the body.

1980 Martin Cline (American: 1934–) and co-workers succeed in transferring functioning gene from one mouse to another.

1981 Chinese scientists succeed in cloning a fish.

MAJOR GROUPS OF LIVING ORGANISMS

Biologists classify all living things (organisms) according to a system first introduced by Carolus Linnaeus in 1735. At that time Linnaeus and other scientists divided all life forms into two kingdoms—plants and animals. Since then, biologists have learned that there are fundamental differences among organisms that go beyond the differences between plants and animals and have added three kingdoms.

Monerans: Bacteria and certain one-celled algae

Protists: More complex one-celled organisms

Fungi: Mushrooms, molds, and yeasts

Plants: Mosses, ferns, and higher plants

Animals: Jellyfish to humans

Scientists believe that organisms in a given kingdom are more closely related to one another than they are to organisms from a different kingdom.

Following Linnaeus, all classification terms are usually given in Latin. In the following list, English terms are substituted when they are exactly equivalent—for example, *animals* instead of *animalia* and *birds* instead of *aves*. If no exact English equivalent is known, the Latin form is kept.

Each kingdom is divided into two or more phyla (singular: phylum). Organisms within one phylum are more closely related to one another than they are to members of other phyla.

The phyla are also divided into parts, which are then further divided, each time on the basis of closer and closer relationships. In descending order of size, the main divisions are as follows:

Kingdom
  Phylum
    Class
      Order
        Family
          Genus
            Species

Many biologists add to this list by classifying groups of species with *sub-* or *super-*, as in subphylum or superfamily.

By convention, Latin names except for genus and species are given in Roman type, while genus and species are in italics.

Kingdom: Monerans One-celled organisms with simple cells that lack a membrane around the genetic material. Bacteria do not produce their own food; blue-green algae do.

Phylum: Bacteria

Phylum: Blue-green algae, also called blue-green bacteria or cyano bacteria

Kingdom: Protists One-celled or colonial; complex cells that have a membrane around their genetic material; protozoans and slime molds do not produce their own food; all other phyla in this kingdom can.

Phylum: Protozoans

  Class: Ciliophora (ciliated protozoans such as Paramecium)

  Class: Mastigophora (protozoans with flagella such as trypanosomes; the cause of sleeping sickness)

  Class: Sarcodina (protozoans that move by flowing, such as amoebas)

  Class: Sporozoa (parasitic protozoans with no means of motion during most of their lives, such as Plasmodium, the cause of malaria)

Phylum: Euglenas

Phylum: Golden algae and diatoms

Phylum: Fire or golden brown algae

Phylum: Green algae

Phylum: Brown algae

Phylum: Red algae

Phylum: Slime molds

Kingdom: Fungi One-celled or multicelled; cells have nuclei, which stream between cells, giving the appearance that cells have many nuclei; fungi do not produce their own food.

Phylum: Zygomycetes (e.g., black bread-mold)

Phylum: Ascomycetes (includes Penicillium, truffles, yeasts)

Phylum: Basidiomycetes (includes mushrooms)

Phylum: Fungi imperfecti (includes fungus that causes athlete's foot, ringworm, and molds used in cheese production)

Kingdom: Plants Multicellular land-living organisms that carry out photosynthesis; cells have nuclei.

Phylum: Mosses and liverworts

Phylum: Horsetails

Phylum: Ferns

Phylum: Conifers

Phylum: Cone-bearing desert plants

Phylum: Cycads

Phylum: Ginkgoes

Phylum: Flowering plants

  Subphylum: dicots (plants with two seed leaves—e.g., most fruits and vegetables, common flowers, and trees)

  Subphylum: monocots (plants with a single seed leaf—e.g., onions, lilies, and grasses)

Kingdom: Animals Multicellular organisms that get their food by ingestion; most are able to move from place to place; cells have nuclei.

Phylum: Porifera (sponges)

Phylum: Coelenterates (jellyfish)

Phylum: Platyhelminthes (flatworms)

Phylum: Nematodes (roundworms)

Phylum: Rotifers (microscopic wormlike or spherical animals)

Phylum: Bryozoa (moss animals)

Phylum: Brachiopods (lampshells)

Phylum: Phoronidea (tube worms)

Phylum: Annelids (segmented worms, such as earthworms)

Phylum: Mollusks (soft-bodied animals with a mantle and foot)

  Class: Chitons

  Class: Bivalves (clams, oysters, mussels)

  Class: Scaphopoda (tooth or tusk shells)

  Class: Gastropods (slugs and snails)

  Class: Cephalopods (octopus, squid)

Phylum: Arthropods (segmented animals with an external skeleton)

  Class: Horseshoe crabs

  Class: Crustaceans (lobsters, crabs, shrimp)

  Class: Arachnids (spiders, mites, ticks)

  Class: Insects

  Class: Centipedes

  Class: Millipedes

Phylum: Echinoderms (starfish, brittle stars)

Phylum: Hemichordata (acorn worms)

Phylum: Chordates

Subphylum: Tunicates

Subphylum: Lancets

Subphylum: Vertebrates (animals with backbones)

  Class: Agnatha (lampreys, hagfish)

  Class: Sharks and rays

  Class: Bony fish

  Class: Amphibians

  Class: Reptiles

  Class: Birds

  Class: Mammals

    Subclass: Monotremes (egg-laying mammals)

    Subclass: Marsupials

    Subclass: Placentals

      Order: Insectivores (shrews)

      Order: Flying lemurs

      Order: Bats

      Order: Primates (lemurs, monkeys, apes, humans)

      Order: Edentates (anteaters)

      Order: Pangolins

      Order: Lagomorphs (rabbits, hares)

      Order: Rodents (squirrels, rats, mice, porcupines)

      Order: Cetaceans (whales, dolphins)

      Order: Carnivores (wolves, cats, bears, raccoons, weasels, badgers, skunks, otters, hyenas)

      Order: Seals

      Order: Aardvark

      Order: Elephants

      Order: Hyraxes

      Order: Sirenians (dugongs, manatees)

      Order: Odd-toed ungulates (horses, tapirs, rhinoceroses)

      Order: Even-toed ungulates (pigs, hippopotamuses, camels, deer, giraffes, pronghorns, cattle, goats, sheep)

A human being in this scheme could be classified as follows:

Kingdom   Animals: Organisms that use other organisms for food and that often move rapidly.

Phylum   Chordates: Animals that are partially supported by a rod of cartilage or bone vertebrae and an internal skeleton.

Subphylum   Vertebrates: Chordates that have vertebrae, such as fish, amphibians, reptiles, birds, and mammals.

Class   Mammals: Vertebrates that have hair and suckle their young.

Order   Primates: Mammals that use sight more than scent, have nails instead of claws on grasping hands and feet, are mostly active in daylight, and have relatively large brains.

Superfamily   Hominoids: Primates that are tailless, generally large in size, can climb trees, and have relatively flat faces; specifically, the great apes, australopithecines, and human beings.

Family   Hominids: Hominoids that walk upright, have small canines, and large brains; specifically, the australopithecines and human beings.

Genus   *Homo:* Hominids with especially large brains that make tools and show other signs of culture; specifically, *Homo habilis, Homo erectus,* and *Homo sapiens.*

Species   *Homo sapiens:* Modern human beings.

THE HUMAN BODY

Systems The human body consists of nine main systems: the skeleton, the muscles, the nervous system, the hormonal system, the circulatory system, the digestive system, the respiratory system, the immune system, and the reproductive system.

Organs Each system is made up of a number of organs. An organ is a part of the body with a specific purpose. Some organs, such as the liver or the skin, have more than one function. A few organs, such as the eyes and ears, are not really part of a major system.

Tissues Organs are made from tissues. A tissue is a part of the organ made from similar cells and, in some cases, extracellular material (for example, bone tissue consists of bone cells and extracellular minerals).

Cells are the fundamental components of all organisms. Even they are composed of several different parts—the nucleus, the cytoplasm, the cell membrane, and various smaller parts—that have different functions.

Skeleton

Bones There are 206 bones in the human body, or one or two more or less, depending on how they are counted. Their main function is to provide a structural support for everything else, but they also have other vital functions. Bones might be classified as part of the circulatory system, for example, since they produce all of the body's blood cells within their mar-

row. Bones are also part of the hormonal system in that they are an important reservoir for calcium, an element necessary for life. If the body's intake of calcium is too low, the bones make up the deficit. This weakens their role as structural support and can result in the condition osteoporosis, or fragile bone structure.

Cartilage is a flexible substance that precedes bone development in children and that is found in adults at joints, places where bones meet, as well as in the nose and ears.

Ligaments Bones are attached to each other by flexible tissues called ligaments. A few bones, such as those in the skull, grow together, forming rigid attachments.

Muscles

There are over 600 muscles in the body that have been named. They occur in three different systems.

Skeletal Muscles are used to move various parts of the body. They are what one normally thinks of when one thinks of muscles, and nearly all of them are attached to bones by tendons, long or flat sheets of tough tissue. They are made from fibers that are striped (or striated) in appearance under a microscope. Each fiber can contract or lengthen when the muscle receives a message from the brain. Because the individual controls the use of these muscles, they are also called voluntary muscles.

Smooth Muscles are found in the walls of the stomach and intestines, in the walls of veins and arteries, and in various other internal organs. They are for the most part not controlled by the will, so they also are known as the involuntary muscles. People do have partial control over some of the "involuntary" muscle, however; for example, you can stop the smooth muscle of the diaphragm from causing you to breathe for a time.

Cardiac Muscle The muscles of the heart resemble both skeletal muscle in being striped and smooth muscle in its involuntary nature.

Nervous System and Senses

Brain The organ that controls the rest of the body and undertakes thought is composed of three main parts. Located in the head, it is protected by the bones of the skull. The cerebrum is the folded, outer part of each half of the brain; it governs thought, the senses, and movement. The cerebellum controls balance and muscle coordination. Deep in the brain is the brain stem, which governs involuntary muscles. A small, but important, part of the human brain is the hypothalamus, which controls the hormonal system (see below).

Spinal Cord Extending from the brain to the base of the torso, protected by the vertebrae, the spinal cord is the main highway for messages to and from the brain. The spinal cord can initiate actions on its own, which are known as reflexes.

Nerves Twelve pairs of cranial nerves connect directly to the brain. Ten of these pairs are connected to parts of the head concerned with sight, sound, smell, and taste, such as the optic nerves to the eyes and the auditory nerves to the ears. The vagus nerves extend to various

organs of the torso, where they control involuntary muscles. The twelfth pair of cranial nerves are connected to the shoulder, where they are mostly involved in the sense of position (e.g., knowing what position your arms are).

Thirty-one pairs of spinal nerves connect to the spinal cord and are the nerves involved in touch and other sensations, in control of skeletal muscles, and in partial control over internal organs. For example, the median nerve connects from the spinal cord to the finger muscles. Some nerves connected to the cranial and spinal nerves form the autonomic nervous system, one set of nerves that handles stress and another set of nerves that directly controls most of the organs of the body.

Hormonal System

Hormones are chemicals produced in the body that control various body processes. The important chemicals used to regulate activity of the nervous system (such as dopamine and serotonin) and various other chemical messengers are not considered hormones, however. See the chart on pages 342–43 for the main hormones and their purposes.

Many hormones are produced by organs called glands. Some hormones are produced by organs that have other purposes as well and are not considered glands. For example, the stomach, the heart, and the small intestine all produce important hormones. For the most part, glands come in two varieties—those that release hormones into the blood and those that release chemicals through tubes called ducts. The former are called endocrine glands, and the latter are known as exocrine glands. Some glands, such as the pancreas, have both endocrine and exocrine functions. The exocrine glands are all part of the digestive system, and, with the exception of the pancreas, are included under that heading.

Major Endocrine Glands are the following:

Pineal Responds to light and helps regulate reproduction. Located in the forehead.

Pituitary Under control of the brain, this "master gland" produces hormones that control many other glands and also produces growth hormone. Located in the head, below the center of the brain.

Thyroid Regulates metabolism, growth, and calcium uptake by bones. Located in the neck or just below it.

Parathyroids Regulates the release of stored calcium from bones. Located on the thyroid gland.

Adrenal Helps regulate blood pressure, blood sugar, and the sex drive and also partially controls metabolism. Located in the abdomen.

Pancreas Controls blood sugar. The pancreas, located in the abdomen, is also a part of the digestive system; acting as an exocrine gland, it releases chemicals that break down fats, carbohydrates, and proteins in the small intestine.

Ovary Produces hormones that regulate pregnancy, produces female secondary sexual characteristics, and also helps control calcium uptake into bones. Located in the pelvis in women.

Testis Produces secondary sexual characteristics in males and is involved in sperm production. Located in a sack suspended below the penis in men.

Circulatory System

Blood is the main messenger that carries chemicals around the body, although its white cells are essentially part of the immune system and are treated under that heading. If blood flow is cut off from any organ, it cannot obtain oxygen, it has no nutrients, and it cannot get rid of wastes. After a short time, the cells of the organ die.

Blood is a complex substance that contains a number of different kinds of cells and extracellular substances. It can be described as the body's only liquid organ. Its red color comes from erythrocytes, commonly known as red blood cells. Unlike true cells, erythrocytes lack nuclei and internal structure. They are produced by true cells in the bone marrow (called stem cells) for just one purpose, to carry oxygen needed by cells for metabolism and to remove carbon dioxide, produced when cells metabolize. Another component of blood is also made by the bone's stem cells—the platelets, which are even less like cells than erythrocytes. Their function is to keep blood from flowing out of the body when there is a break in the circulatory system—to cause clotting. About half of blood is an extracellular mix of water and chemicals that is called plasma or (when separated from proteins that, with the platelets, are involved in clotting) serum.

Blood Vessels are a closed system of tubes that carry blood throughout the body. Vessels carrying blood away from the heart are called arteries. Arteries have strong, four-layered walls to maintain blood under pressure. Arteries connect to very tiny tubes with quite thin walls called capillaries. The walls are so thin that oxygen and nutrients pass through them to reach the cells, while carbon dioxide and wastes from the cells enter through the walls into the blood. The waste-carrying blood then passes into vessels that lead back to the heart, the veins. Most of the blood pressure has been lost by this point, so veins do not need the strong walls of arteries. Instead, veins need and have valves that ensure the blood does not travel in the wrong direction.

Heart Primarily a pump that pushes the blood through blood vessels, it consists of four chambers. Blood from the body enters the chamber known as the right atrium and is pumped through a valve to a larger chamber below the atrium called the right ventricle, which pumps the blood into an artery leading to the lungs. After picking up oxygen and leaving carbon dioxide behind, the blood returns to the heart, entering the left atrium. The blood is pumped through a valve to the left ventricle, which is the largest chamber (and therefore the most powerful pump). The left ventricle sends the blood into the arteries that lead to the body. The heart is also an endocrine gland, secreting a hormone that helps regulate blood pressure.

Spleen This organ is a cleaner and storehouse for blood. Chiefly, it removes damaged red blood cells or platelets. It also stores excess blood and red blood cells until they are needed. Some now believe it may have a role in the immune system. A person can live without a spleen.

Kidneys and the bladder and associated tubes, are often considered the urinary system. Technically, however, kidneys are part of the circulatory system in that they remove chemical wastes from blood. They also act as an endocrine gland by secreting hormones that aid in regulating blood pressure. Additionally, they regulate the composition of blood, keeping it from becoming too acid or alkaline. The wastes removed by the kidneys are dissolved in water as urine, which is stored in the bladder before passing through the urethra to leave the body.

Digestive System

The digestive system consists largely of a pathway for food from the mouth to the anus with several ducted or exocrine glands that empty into it (the pancreas, one of these, is treated as part of the hormonal system).

Teeth Thirty-two permanent teeth (if none have been lost) in an adult are used to chop food into small bits.

Salivary Glands release saliva, the first of many enzymes (proteins that promote particular chemical reactions) that are used to break down large molecules, such as carbohydrates, proteins, and fats, into smaller molecules that the body can then reassemble to meet its needs. Saliva breaks down some starches into sugars, as you can tell by noticing how much sweeter a cracker becomes if you chew it and then keep it in your mouth for a short while.

Tongue While an important organ of speech in humans, the tongue is basically the part of the digestive system that moves food around and pushes it down the throat.

Esophagus This is a tube through which food moves on its way to the stomach. The pyloric valve at its base prevents food from traveling back up again.

Stomach This organ produces enzymes (and therefore acts as a gland) and hydrochloric acid. These are mixed with the food by churning motions of the stomach, which also tend to further break food into smaller particles, even as the stomach enzymes and acid are chemically changing food. From this point forward, one can no longer call this soup of nutrients food.

Liver The main chemical factory of the body and, after the skin, the largest organ in the body is the liver. As part of the digestive system, it acts as a ducted, or exocrine, gland that produces bile, a substance that helps reduce the acidity of the nutrient mixture and also helps break down fats. The liver is also part of the circulatory system, since it cleans poisons out of the blood and regulates blood's composition in various other ways. In many cases the liver scavenges unwanted chemicals from the blood, takes them apart, and reassembles the parts into needed chemicals.

Gall Bladder This organ simply stores bile from the liver until food is consumed, at which time it releases the bile into the small intestine.

Small Intestine Like the stomach, the 21–foot-long small intestine produces enzymes that further break down the nutrients that pass through it. The upper portion of the small intestine is called the duodenum. As nutrients become broken into small enough molecules, they are able to pass through projections, or villi, in the wall of the small intestine into the blood.

Large Intestine With most of the nutrients gone, the remains of the food pass into the 5-foot-long large intestine as a kind of soup. Water is transferred to the blood from the soup through the walls of the capillaries that line the large intestine.

Rectum A short tube collects the partially dehydrated waste in preparation for evacuation, which is through a valve called the anus.

Respiratory System

The main purpose of the respiratory system is to get oxygen to the blood and to remove carbon dioxide. Along the way, the air is sampled for chemicals (smelled), partly cleaned, and frequently used to make sounds.

Nose In addition to being an organ of smell, the nose is the place best designed to admit air into the body, for it can warm and moisten it, and hairs in the nose can filter out dust. Often there is a need for more air than can pass through the nose, however, and the mouth is used as a supplemental way to take in air. From either the nose or the mouth, air then passes through the throat (also called the pharynx). The sinuses are air-filled cavities in the skull that are connected to the nose.

Trachea After passing through your throat, air goes into a tube called the trachea. A flap called the epiglottis closes the top of the trachea when food or water is being swallowed and opens to permit air to enter the trachea. The trachea branches into two tubes called bronchi (singular, *bronchus*) that carry the air into the lungs.

Larynx Near the top of the trachea is the larynx, or voice box. The main feature of the larynx is a pair of membranes that stretch across the air passageway. As air is exhaled, these membranes can be tightened across the passage to produce sound.

Lungs, the principal organs of respiration, are two large spongy masses located in the chest that are protected by the ribs. Air enters a lung through a bronchus. The bronchus is divided into smaller bronchial tubes, which continue to divide until they become very fine tubes called bronchioles. Each bronchiole ends in a cluster of tiny round bodies called an air sac. As small as air sacs are, each of these contains even smaller cavities called alveoli. It is in the thin-walled alveoli that the exchange of oxygen to and carbon dioxide from the blood actually takes place. The lungs contain about 300 million aveoli, and although each alveolus is tiny, the total surface area they present is about 40 times the surface area of the skin.

Diaphragm The reason air moves in and out of the body is that the volume of the lungs is continually being changed. The principal agent of change is the diaphragm, a muscle stretched across the abdomen just below the lungs. When the diaphragm is pulled down, the volume of the chest cavity is increased, causing air to enter the lungs. Similarly, when the diaphragm is pulled up, it reduces the volume of the chest cavity and expels air. This process is aided by the muscles of the rib case, which also expand and contract the size of the chest cavity.

Immune System

The immune system was not recognized as a separate system until recently. Although evidence of immune protection was known in ancient times, the first inkling of how the body develops immunity was in 1884, when macrophages (see "Phagocytes" below) were first observed. Since then, many different components of the system have been found. Much still remains to be learned about this system, however.

Skin Although a part of the immune system, skin is often viewed as simply a barrier between the body and the outside world. The largest organ in the body, the skin is far more complex. Its immune functions include not only the barrier against invaders but also production of oil and sweat, both of which kill or retard many bacteria and fungi. On the other hand, the skin harbors millions of helpful bacteria that resist invasion by other bacteria. The skin even has a role in the development of some lymphocytes (white blood cells—see below).

Skin also helps regulate body temperature, helps produce cholesterol (a necessary body chemical, even though it is inadvisable to have too much of it in our blood), and is the location of sensors for heat, cold, and pressure.

Thymus The thymus is a medium-size organ in the upper chest that looks as if it could be an endocrine gland (and was often identified as one in the past). It becomes smaller as a person ages. In some as-yet-unknown way, the thymus "trains" certain lymphocytes to be part of the immune system. If the thymus is removed from a very young animal, the animal does not develop the immune response that causes transplant rejection, for example.

Lymphatic System When blood passes through capillaries, it loses some of its plasma, which becomes part of a liquid between the cells. This liquid is known as lymph. Lymph needs to be returned to the circulatory system to keep the blood volume fairly constant, so a system of tubes called the lymphatic system drains the lymph back into the blood. Along the way it passes through masses of spongy tissue called lymph nodes that filter out any debris, including bacteria, from the lymph. Lymph nodes are made of lymphoid tissue, but they are not the only organs where lymphoid tissue is found; it is found everywhere that bacteria or other germs can easily invade the body, specifically in the linings of the parts of the body exposed to the outside, such as the respiratory system and parts of the digestive system. Most of the action of the immune system takes place in lymphoid tissue.

Lymphocytes Although lymphocytes are known as white blood cells, they are found in the lymph as well as in the blood. Draining all the lymph from an animal's body would remove all the lymphocytes, which would suppress immune reactions. Like red blood cells, lymphocytes are produced in bone marrow, a very well-protected place, suggesting their importance to the body. Scientists have found and continue to find many distinct types of lymphocytes, but there seem to be two main varieties.

The T lymphocytes are those that must mature in the thymus before they can be involved in the immune response. The *T* is for thymus. They are the principal cells involved in graft rejection, but they also play a role in fighting bacteria and other invaders. A deficiency of one type of T cell is a major symptom of the disease AIDS, although AIDS seems to affect the immune system in many other ways as well.

The B lymphocytes mature directly in the bone, but the *B* does not stand for *bone*. In birds, B lymphocytes mature in an organ that humans do not have, the bursa of Fabricius, and the *B* stands for *bursa*. B cells react to invaders by releasing chemicals called antibodies. An antibody is a chemical that is specific to a particular protein, sugar, nucleic acid, or fat, but the strongest reaction is with proteins. If, for example, a measles virus is in the blood or lymph, a B lymphocyte will release an antibody that attaches to a protein on the surface of the virus. In some unknown way, one kind of T cell then stimulates the production of many B cells that release the same antibody. The next measles virus that comes along is met with great amounts of the antibody, causing immunity to measles.

Phagocytes There are many other cells produced as part of the immune system by the bone marrow that were formerly grouped under the general heading "white blood cell," including neutrophils, mast cells, and macrophages. When an antibody binds to a protein, it attracts a macrophage, which proceeds to "eat" it, thus removing it. The ability to ingest cells indicates that macrophages are phagocytes, or "eaters of cells." The macrophage also pushes the original protein that triggered the antibody to its surface, where it projects from the cell membrane and causes more B lymphocytes to make the antibody against it. Neutrophils are smaller phagocytes than macrophages, or "big eaters." Mast cells collect near a source of infection and release the chemical histamine, which causes phagocytes to gather and quell the infection.

Reproductive System

The male and female reproductive systems differ in fundamental ways.

Male Reproductive System Sperm are formed in the two testes, which hang below the groin, so situated because human body temperature is too high for proper sperm formation. Sperm are stored in the epididymis, just above the testes. During sex the sperm move through tubes and are mixed with secretions from the prostate and Cowper's gland, both ducted glands. The result is called semen. Semen exits the body through a tube in the penis called the urethra, which is otherwise used for excretion of urine.

Female Reproductive System Corresponding to the testes in males, the ovaries produce eggs (also known as ova). Unlike sperm, eggs can be produced at human body temperature, allowing for the ovaries and related organs to be located inside the pelvis. Eggs pass through the Fallopian tubes to the uterus, or womb, which is sealed at the other end by the cervix. On the other side of the cervix is a muscular tube called the vagina, or birth canal.

Pregnancy and Birth Female physiology changes considerably during pregnancy, although the organs remain the same, with one exception.

Sperm that have been implanted in the vagina swim to the uterus, where they fertilize an egg. The egg gradually develops into an embryo attached to a new organ, which consists of the placenta and cord. The placenta has many functions, including the production of hormones, making it an endocrine gland. It is formed from tissue both from the embryo and from the uterus. When the baby is fully formed, the cervix opens and the baby passes through the vagina, still attached to its mother by the cord, which is cut at the navel. The placenta also passes through the vagina and is discarded.

Elements of the Human Body

The normal human body contains almost all of the chemical elements, mostly in small amounts. Not all are used by the body, and some elements found in tiny quantities in the body are poisonous, such as lead.

The elements that the body uses are necessary for health. For the body to grow, it needs large amounts of elements found in four major nutrients—proteins, carbohydrates, fats, and water—as well as smaller amounts of other elements, known as minerals. When very small amounts are needed, the minerals are called trace elements. (Vitamins, the remaining nutrient, are needed compounds that the body cannot make itself in sufficient quantity.)

THE ELEMENTS IN A 150-POUND INDIVIDUAL

Element	Weight (lbs.)	Use by the body
Oxygen	97.5	Part of all major nutrients, which make up tissues of the body, but also vital to production of energy in form of elemental oxygen obtained from air.
Carbon	27.0	Essential element for life—most compounds based on carbon are called organic, meaning "from life." An essential part of proteins, carbohydrates, and fats, the building blocks of human cells.
Hydrogen	15.0	Part of each of major nutrients, and thus a building block of every cell. Unlike oxygen, has no part in respiration.
Nitrogen	4.5	Essential part of proteins, DNA, and RNA, the compounds most active in controlling cells; most of the body's functions depend on nitrogen compounds at one stage or another.
Calcium	3.0	Mostly locked into hard compounds that form nonliving parts of bone. Another of calcium's roles is even more important—as one of principal messengers between cells, telling them when to act and when to stay quiet.

Element	Weight (lbs.)	Use by the body
Phosphorus	1.8	Important element in bone building, but, like calcium, has another role: it is essential in producing energy in cell.
Potassium	0.3	Regulates contraction of muscle cells (and some other cell functions) along with sodium. In general, potassium is involved with muscle contractions and general maintenance of pressure a cell exerts on its covering membrane.
Sulfur	0.3	Essential to almost all forms of life, just as are all of elements listed above it. An important constituent of proteins.
Chlorine	0.3	Used in form of chloride ions to transport messages from the body to cells; helps regulate electrical activity.
Sodium	0.165	Not required by all living creatures, but required by vertebrates (including humans) which use it (along with potassium) to control fluid pressure in cells.

Element	Weight (lbs.)	Use by the body
Magnesium	0.06	Required by both plants (it is in chlorophyll) and animals. In humans, works with enzymes to speed chemical reactions, is involved in transmission of messages between nerves, and has a role in bone structure.
Iron	0.006	Essential for carrying oxygen to cells and carbon dioxide waste away, although present only in small amount; lack of iron causes anemia.
Cobalt	0.00024	Part of vitamin B_{12}, found in meats and dairy products; its exact role in the body is not well understood.
Copper	0.00023	Helps form red blood cells, maintain nervous system, and regulate cholesterol levels.
Manganese	0.00020	Aids in bone formation, helps regulate nervous system, and is part of sex hormones.
Iodine	0.00006	Part of thyroid hormone that controls rate at which food is burned for energy.

Element	Weight (lbs.)	Use by the body
Zinc	trace	Needed for some enzymes, for proper sex development, in healing wounds, for sense of taste, and for normal sperm count.
Boron	trace	Low levels required by plants, and hence, element appears in human body, but its role, if any, is not known.
Aluminum	trace	Its role in the body is not clear, but too much aluminum may have role in Alzheimer's disease or other neurological disorders.
Vanadium	trace	Its role, if any, in the body is poorly understood.
Molybdenum	trace	Contained in various enyzmes.
Silicon	trace	Among most abundant elements on Earth, so is not surprising to find silicon in the body, but its necessity to any essential function is unclear.
Fluorine	trace	Strengthens teeth and bones.
Chromium	trace	Used in metabolism of sugar and the regulation of fats.
Selenium	trace	In small amounts, may reduce cell damage and promote growth.

Human Hormones

Hormones are chemicals made in the body that regulate body functions or achieve specific tasks. Some are fairly familiar, such as insulin and estrogen. Others, though less familiar, are clear from their description or name, for example, growth hormone. Increasingly, hormones are available either as products of genetic engineering (human insulin and human growth hormone, for example) or as synthetics. The notorious steroids used for body building are synthetic testosterone. (See "Health and Medicine.") Such manufactured hormones offer both the promise of relief from hormone-deficiency diseases and the possibility of hormone abuse.

EVOLUTION OF THE HUMAN FAMILY

The understanding of the various relatives of modern human beings and just how they are related is undergoing great changes. Often what seems to be true one year is overturned the next. Currently there is little consensus among paleoanthropologists, the people who study early humans and their relatives, about the details of who is related to whom.

All of the relatives of human beings are mammals called primates; that classification includes everything from small tarsiers and tree lemurs to us. Primates more closely related to humans are called hominoids, a classification that includes the great apes (gibbons, orangu-

HUMAN HORMONES—THEIR FUNCTION AND GLAND(S) OF ORIGIN

Hormone	Associated gland(s)	Function
Adrenalin (epinephrine)	Adrenal medulla	Increases blood sugar, pulse, and blood pressure
Adrenocorticotropic hormone (ACTH)	Anterior pituitary	Stimulates adrenal cortex
Aldosterone	Adrenal cortex	Controls reabsorption of sodium and potassium by kidneys
Calcitonin (Thyrocalcitonin)	Thyroid gland	Lowers level of calcium in blood by inhibiting calcium release from bones
Cholecystokinin (CCK)	Glands in small intestine	Stimulates pancreatic secretions and contraction of gall bladder
Chorionic gonadotropin	Placenta	Stimulates ovaries to continue producing estrogens and progesterone during early stages of pregnancy; hormone detected in pregnancy test
Cortisol and related hormones	Adrenal cortex	Affect metabolism of proteins, carbohydrates, and lipids; reduce inflammation
Estrogens	Ovaries and placenta	Stimulate development of secondary sexual characteristics in females; help regulate ovaries and uterus during menstrual cycle and pregnancy
Follicle-stimulating hormone (FSH)	Anterior pituitary	Stimulates follicle development in females and sperm production in males

Hormone	Associated gland(s)	Function
Gastrin	Glands in stomach	Stimulates secretion of gastric juice
Glucagon	Pancreas (Islet cells)	Increases blood sugar level by stimulating breakdown of glycogen
Growth hormone (somatotropin or somatotrophic hormone or STP)	Anterior pituitary	Stimulates bone and muscle growth
Insulin	Pancreas (Islet cells)	Lowers blood sugar level and increases storage of glycogen
Luteinizing hormone (LH)	Anterior pituitary	Stimulates ovulation and formation of corpus luteum in females and testosterone production in males
Norepinephrine	Adrenal medulla	Increases metabolic rate and constricts blood vessels
Oxytocin	Produced in hypothalamus, stored in posterior pituitary	Stimulates uterine contractions during childbirth and milk release
Parathormone (Parathyroid hormone or PTH)	Parathyroid glands	Increases level of calcium in blood by increasing calcium release from bones; decreases blood phosphate level
Progesterone	Ovaries and placenta	Helps regulate uterus during menstrual cycle and pregnancy
Prolactin (lactogenic hormone or LTH)	Anterior pituitary	Stimulates milk production (lactation)
Secretin	Glands in small intestine	Stimulates secretion of pancreatic digestive juices
Testosterone (androgens)	Testes	Stimulate development of male sex organs and secondary sexual characteristics; supports sperm production
Thyroid-stimulating hormone (TSH)	Anterior pituitary	Stimulate thyroid gland to produce and secrete thyroxin
Thyroxin (Thyroxine)	Thyroid gland	Controls rate of metabolism and growth
Vasopressin	Produced in hypothalamus, stored in posterior pituitary	Controls reabsorption of water by kidneys; increases blood pressure

tans, gorillas, and chimpanzees), humans, and their closest ancestors. Our relatives that are not great apes are classed along with us as hominids. Hominids have two main branches, the australopithecines and humans. Although there is only a single species of human alive today, in the past there were at least two others.

The first column below gives scientific and common names (with *man* used only because of traditional terminology; modern paleoanthropologists shun the use of *man* to mean "human") along with the time and place in which the animal is known to have flourished.

THE HUMAN FAMILY TREE

Aegyptopithecus
c. 30 million years ago
Egypt

Proconsul; three known species
c. 20 million years ago
East Africa

Monkeylike creature; may be earliest-known ancestor of hominoids.

Oddly named after popular chimpanzee, Consul, in London Zoo (hence, *Proconsul*— "before Consul"); generally recognized as an ancestor of all hominoids.

Sivepithecus
c. 10 million years ago
Asia and Turkey

Pan troglodytes
Pan paniscus
Chimpanzee
c. 7 million years ago to present
Sub-Saharan African forests

Australopithecus afarensis
c. 4 million years ago
Ethiopia and East Africa

Australopithecus africanus
"The Taung Child"
c. 2.5 million years ago
South Africa

Once believed to be directly on the line to humans, today *Sivepithecus* is thought to be ancestor of orangutan.

Several studies of proteins and DNA suggest chimpanzee is our closest living relative; some evidence indicates we are more closely related to pygmy chimpanzee, *P. paniscus*, than to common chimp.

Many believe *A. afarensis* is ultimate ancestor of humans, but it is not all that clear who ultimate ancestor of *A. afarensis* is. Famous fossil known as "Lucy" is member of this species, as well as group known as "The First Family."

First nonhuman hominid to be discovered (1924) and widely doubted at first. Like all australopithecines, walked upright and had brain much smaller than members of *Homo* of same size.

Homo habilis
"Handy Man"
c. 2 million years ago
East Africa

Australopithecus boisei
"Zinj"
"Nutcracker man"
c. 2 million years ago
East Africa

Homo erectus
"Java Ape Man"
"Peking Man"
c. 2 million–90,000 years ago
Africa, Asia, and Europe

Australopithecus robustus
c. 1.5 million years ago
South Africa

"Neanderthal Man"
100,000–35,000 years ago
Mostly European, but some fossils from Africa and Near East

Archaic Homo Sapiens
c. 90,000–? years ago
Africa and possibly Europe

Homo sapiens
"Cro Magnon Man"
Since 35,000 years ago
Worldwide

First-known member of our own genus, and—if classified correctly—probably direct ancestor; widely believed that stone tools found that date from the same time were made by *H. habilis*. Not clear whether *H. habilis* was hunter or scavenger or both.

A still controversial classification that some would label merely East African subspecies of *A. robustus*. When first specimen was found by L.S.B. Leakey (1959), he thought it was new genus, *Zinjanthropus*—hence, nickname.

Depending on how one classes Neanderthals, this is first non-human hominid discovered (1890, by Eugene Dubois). It was successful creature who could make fire and was probably good hunter. That it did not change its basic tool kit for 1.5 million years suggests limited intelligence. Generally thought to be immediate ancestor of *Homo sapiens*. Other hominids became extinct, and by at least million years ago, *H. erectus* was only hominid on Earth, with possible exception of very early archaic *H. sapiens*.

Despite name, not especially "robust" by modern human standards; however, compared with "gracile" *A. afarensis* and *A. africanus*, this is larger and stronger species.

While general sentiment among paleoanthropologists since World War II has classified this well-known group as subspecies of modern humans—*Homo sapiens neandertalis*—current thinking is that this "cave man" of ice age may be separate species. They share certain traits with modern human, e.g., large brain and customs such as burial of dead. Anatomical differences between Neanderthals and modern humans not pronounced but are clear.

Today many anthropologists recognize that our species evolved about 90,000 years ago from *Homo erectus* but that first humans were not fully evolved. This is us! We may have started with Archaic *H. sapiens* (see above), and we may—although most think it is not likely—have evolved from Neanderthals around 35,000 years ago. In any case, we replaced all other hominids about 35,000 years ago.

Physical Sciences

Traditionally, the physical sciences are chemistry and physics, but these have both merged with each other (and other sciences) to form such sciences as physical chemistry, biochemistry, astrophysics, and biophysics and fractured to form such fields as particle physics and condensed-matter physics.

Chemistry is concerned with the way one substance interacts with another. It is now known that these interactions are chiefly the result of outer electrons of an atom interacting with the outer electrons of another atom. In that sense, chemistry becomes a part of physics. However, it has increasingly become clear that the shapes of the various combinations of atoms joined by electron interactions (called molecules) also affect chemical reactions. The study of the shapes of molecules and how they cause behavior is one of the most vital parts of chemistry today. Another vital branch is biochemistry, the study of the chemistry of molecules in living organisms. Organic chemistry generally deals with chemicals formed by living organisms and other chemicals containing carbon, but it treats them as chemicals outside the organism. Inorganic chemistry is concerned with chemicals that do not contain carbon, an element found in all proteins, carbohydrates, and fats.

Physics is a vast field that is the basis of the other sciences because it is concerned with the fundamental interactions of matter and energy. The first physicists studied how ordinary objects and very large objects (moon, planets, and stars) moved in response to forces. Their study was extremely successful. Near the end of the 19th century, physicists began to investigate various forms of radiation in detail, leading to the discovery of various forms of electromagnetic radiation (of which only ordinary light was known previously) and particles smaller than the atom (subatomic particles, such as the electron and proton). In the 20th century, the study of subatomic particles, called particle physics, has become a major branch of the science. Enough particle physicists limit their work to the particles in the nucleus of atoms and to the behavior of nuclei, that the field of nuclear physics is generally considered to be separate from that of particle physics. Another major branch, condensed-matter physics, is concerned with the physical behavior of materials—for example, their electrical and magnetic properties. Major successes in condensed-matter physics include development of the transistor and related devices (chips) and developments in superconductivity, a state in which electric currents can be transmitted with no resistance. Today many physicists are also cosmologists, who study how the universe began and is constructed, or astrophysicists, who study processes in stars.

MAJOR DISCOVERIES IN CHEMISTRY

B.C.
450 Greek philosopher Leucippus (b. 490 B.C.) of Miletus introduces concept of atom, later expanded upon c. 430 B.C. by his pupil Democritus (Greek: 470–380? B.C.).

A.D.
1662 Robert Boyle (Anglo-Irish: 1627–91) announces what becomes known as Boyle's law: For gas kept at constant temperature, pressure and volume vary inversely.
1670 Robert Boyle discovers hydrogen.
1755 Joseph Black (Scottish: 1728–99) discovers carbon dioxide.
1772 Joseph Priestley (English-American: 1733–1804) notes that burning hydrogen produces water.
Daniel Rutherford (Scottish: 1794–1819) and several other chemists discover nitrogen.
Karl Wilhelm Scheele (Swedish: 1742–86) discovers oxygen but does not announce discovery until after independent discovery by Joseph Priestly in 1774.
1778 Antoine-Laurent Lavoisier (French: 1743–94) discovers that air is mostly mixture of nitrogen and oxygen.
1781 Lavoisier states law of conservation of matter: In chemical change, matter is neither created nor destroyed.
1784 Henry Cavendish (English: 1731–1810) announces that water is compound of hydrogen and oxygen.
1791 Jeremias Richter (German: 1762–1807) shows that acids and bases always neutralize each other in same proportion.
1803 John Dalton (English: 1766–1844) develops atomic theory of matter.
1807 Amedeo Avogadro (Italian: 1776–1856) proposes that equal volumes of gas at same temperature and pressure contain same number of molecules (Avogadro's law).
1824 Joseph-Louis Gay-Lussac (French: 1778–1850) discovers chemical isomers, chemicals with same formula but different structures.
1828 Friedrich Wöhler (German: 1800–82) prepares organic compound from inorganic chemicals, showing that life is basically same as other matter.
1859 Gustav Kirchhoff (German: 1824–87) and Robert Bunsen (German: 1811–1899) introduce use of spectroscope to identify elements from light they give off when heated or burned.
1868 Pierre-Jules-César Janssen (French: 1824–1907) and Sir Joseph Lockyer (English: 1836–1920) discover helium by observing sun's spectrum.
1869 Dimitri Mendeléev (Russian: 1834–1907) publishes his first version of periodic table of elements.
1875 Paul-Emile Lecoq de Boisbaudran (French: 1838–1912) discovers gallium, the first discovery of a predicted element (predicted by Mendeléev on basis of his periodic table).

1906 Mikhail Tsvett (Russian: 1872–1919) develops paper chromotography, the beginning of modern methods of chemical analysis.
1908 Fritz Haber (German: 1868–1934) develops cheap process for making ammonia from nitrogen in the air.
1943 Albert Hofmann (Swiss: 1906–) discovers that LSD is hallucinogenic.
1962 Neil Bartlett (English: 1932–) shows, by creating compound of xenon, that the noble gases can form compounds.
1974 Chemists warn that chlorofluorocarbons (Freons) are destroying ozone layer in atmosphere that protects life on Earth from harmful ultraviolet radiation.
1987 Scientists confirm that hole in ozone layer of atmosphere that forms above Antarctica in August and September is caused by chlorofluorocarbons.

NOBEL PRIZES IN CHEMISTRY

1901 Jacobus H. Van't Hoff (Netherlands) Berlin Univ. (Germany) "in recognition of the extraordinary services he has rendered by the discovery of the laws of chemical dynamics and osmotic pressure in solutions."
1902 Hermann E. Fischer (Germany) Berlin Univ. "in recognition of the extraordinary services he has rendered by his work on sugar and purine syntheses."
1903 Svante A. Arrhenius (Sweden) Stockholm Univ. "in recognition of the extraordinary services he has rendered to the advancement of chemistry by his electrolytic theory of dissociation."
1904 Sir William Ramsay (Great Britain) London Univ. "in recognition of his services in the discovery of the inert gaseous elements in air, and his determination of their place in the periodic system."
1905 Johann F.W.A. von Baeyer (Germany) Munich Univ. "in recognition of his services in the advancement of organic chemistry and the chemical industry, through his work on organic dyes and hydroaromatic compounds."
1906 Henri Moissan (France) Sorbonne Univ. "in recognition of the great services rendered by him in his investigation and isolation of the element fluorine, and for the adoption in the service of science of the electric furnace called after him."
1907 Eduard Buchner (Germany) Agricultural College "for his biochemical researches and his discovery of cellfree fermentation."
1908 Lord Ernest Rutherford (Great Britain) Victoria Univ. "for his investigations into the disintegration of the elements, and the chemistry of radioactive substances."
1909 Wilhelm Ostwald (Germany) Leipzig Univ. "in recognition of his work on catalysis, and for his investigations into the fundamental principles governing chemical equilibria and rates of reaction."

(continued on page 348)

PROPERTIES, ABUNDANCE, AND DISCOVERY OF THE ELEMENTS

All ordinary matter is made from one or more substances called elements (because they cannot be changed by chemical means). Ninety elements are found in nature, and people have created others, for a current total of 109. In this table each of the elements are listed in alphabetic order along with several of their important properties. The chemical symbol and the atomic number can be used to locate other information about the elements in the periodic table on page 351. The relative abundance of the elements is given as parts per million in the Earth's crust—83,600 parts per million for aluminum means that of a million atoms chosen at random from the crust, 83,600 atoms, on average, would be aluminum atoms. Some elements have so few parts per million that they are simply listed as rare, whereas others are "synthetic,"—artificial elements not found in the crust at all. Many elements, known from ancient times, are labeled "prehistoric." Others are given with their first discovery—many elements having been independently rediscovered by others.

Element	Symbol/ atomic no.	Type[1]	Melting point[1]	Boiling point[1]	Parts per million in crust	Year discovered & by whom	Derivation of name
Actinium	Ac 89	Radioactive metal	1920°F 1050°C	5790°F 3200°C	Rare	1899 André-Louis Debierne	Greek *aktis,* a ray
Aluminum	Al 13	Metal	1220°F 660°C	4473°F 2467°C	83,600	1825 Hans Christian Oersted	Latin *alumen,* a substance having astringent taste
Americium	Am 95	Radioactive metal	1821°F 994°C	4725°F 2607°C	Synthetic	1944 Glenn T. Seaborg & co-workers	For America
Antimony	Sb 51	Metal	1167°F 631°C	3180°F 1750°C	0.2	c. 900 Rhazes	Greek *antimonos,* opposed to solitude; symbol Sb from Greek *stibi*
Argon	A 18	Gas	−308.6°F −189.2°C	−302.3°F −185.7°C	Rare	1892 Sir William Ramsey	Greek *argus,* neutral inactive
Arsenic	As 33	Nonmetal	1502°F[2] 817°C	1135°F[1] 613°C	1.8	1649 J. Schroder & N. Lémery	Greek *arsenicos,* valiant or bold; from its action on other metals
Astatine	At 85	Radioactive nonmetal	576°F 302°C	639°F 337°C	Synthetic	1940 Emilio Segrè & co-workers	Greek *astatos,* unstable
Barium	Ba 56	Metal	1337°F 725°C	2980°F 1640°C	390	1774 Karl Wilhelm Scheele	Greek *baros,* heavy; because its compounds are dense
Berkelium	Bk 97	Radioactive metal	N.A.	N.A.	Synthetic	1949 Glenn T. Seaborg & co-workers	First made at Univ. of California at Berkeley
Beryllium	Be 4	Metal	2332°F 1278°C	5380°F 2970°C	2	1798 Louis-Nicolas Vauquelin	Latin *beryllus,* Greek *beryllos,* gem
Bismuth	Bi 83	Metal	520°F 271°C	2840°F 1560°C	0.008	1450 Basil Valentine	German *weisse masse,* white mass; changed to *bismat*
Boron	B 5	Nonmetal	4170°F 2300°C	4620°F 2550°C	9	1808 Joseph-Louis Gay-Lussac & Louis-Jacques Thénard	Aryan *borak,* white
Bromine	Br 35	Liquid nonmetal	19°F −7.2°C	137.8°F 58.8°C	2.5	1825 Carl Löwig	Greek *bromos,* a stench; because of odor of its vapors
Cadmium	Cd 48	Metal	609.6°F 320.9°C	1409°F 765°C	0.16	1817 Friedrich Strohmeyer	Greek *cadmia,* earthy
Calcium	Ca 20	Metal	1542°F 839°C	2703°F 1484°C	46,600	1808 Humphry Davy	Latin *calx, calcis,* lime
Californium	Cf 98	Radioactive metal	N.A.	N.A.	Synthetic	1950 Glenn T. Seaborg	First made at Univ. of California
Carbon	C 6	Nonmetal	6420°F 3550°C	8721°F 4827°C	180	Prehistoric	Latin *carbo,* coal
Cerium	Ce 58	Rare earth	1468°F 798°C	5895°F 3257°C	66.4	1803 Martin Klaproth	For asteroid Ceres, discovered in 1801
Cesium	Cs 55	Metal	83.1°F 28.4°C	1253.1°F 678.4°C	2.6	1860 Gustav Kirchhoff & Robert Bunsen	Latin *caesius,* bluish grey
Chlorine	Cl 17	Gas	−150°F −101°C	−30.3°F −34.6°C	126	1774 Karl Wilhelm Scheele	Greek *chloros,* grass-green; from color of gas
Chromium	Cr 24	Metal	3375°F 1857°C	4842°F 2672°C	122	1797 Louis-Nicolas Vauquelin	Greek *chroma,* color; because many of its compounds are colored
Cobalt	Co 27	Metal	2723°F 1495°C	5200°F 2870°C	29	1735 George Brandt	Greek *kobolis,* a goblin
Copper	Cu 29	Metal	1981°F 1083°C	4653°F 2567°C	68	Prehistoric	Latin *cuprum;* for island of Cyprus
Curium	Cm 96	Radioactive metal	2444°F 1340°C	N.A.	Synthetic	1944 Glenn T. Seaborg	After Pierre and Marie Curie
Dysprosium	Dy 66	Rare earth	2568°F 1409°C	4235°F 2335°C	Rare	1886 Paul-Emile Lecoq de Boisbaudran	Greek *dysprositos,* difficult of access
Einsteinium	Es 99	Radioactive	N.A.	N.A.	Synthetic	1952 Albert Ghiorso & co-workers	After Albert Einstein
Element 106	N.A. 106	Radioactive metal	N.A.	N.A.	Synthetic	1974 N.A.	Claimed by Russia and U.S.
Element 107	N.A. 107	Radioactive metal	N.A.	N.A.	Synthetic	1981 N.A.	Identified in W. Germany following earlier disputed claim by Dubna

Element	Symbol/ atomic no.	Type[1]	Melting point[1]	Boiling point[1]	Parts per million in crust	Year discovered & by whom	Derivation of name
Element 108	N.A. 108	Radioactive metal	N.A.	N.A.	Synthetic	1984 N.A.	Created in W. Germany by bombarding lead with iron ions
Element 109	N.A. 109	Radioactive metal	N.A.	N.A.	Synthetic	1982 N.A.	Created in W. Germany by bombarding bismuth with iron ions
Erbium	Er 68	Rare earth	2772°F 1522°C	4550°F 2510°C	3.46	1843 Carl Gustav Mosander	For Ytterby, village in Sweden
Europium	Eu 63	Rare earth	1512°F 822°C	2907°F 1597°C	2.1	1896 Eugène-Anatole Demarçay	For Europe
Fermium	Fm 100	Radioactive metal	N.A.	N.A.	Synthetic	1953 Albert Ghioroso & co-workers	After Enrico Fermi, Italian physicist
Fluorine	F 9	Gas	−363.3°F −219.6°C	−306.7°F −188.1°C	544	1886 Ferdinand-Frédéric-Henri Moissan	Latin fluere, to flow
Francium	Fr 87	Radioactive metal	80.6°F 27°C	1256°F 677°C	Rare	1939 Marguerite Perey	For France
Gadolinium	Gd 64	Rare earth	2392°F 1311°C	5851°F 3233°C	6.1	1886 Jean-Charles Marignac	After Johan Gadolin, Finnish chemist
Gallium	Ga 31	Metal	86.6°F 29.8°C	4357°F 2403°C	19	1875 Paul-Emile Lecoq de Boisbaudran	Latin Gallia, France; also latin gallus, a cock—pun on Lecoq de Boisbaudran
Germanium	Ge 32	Metal	1719°F 937°C	5126°F 2830°C	1.5	1886 Clemens Winkler	For Germany
Gold	Au 79	Metal	1947°F 1064°C	5085°F 2807°C	0.002	Prehistoric	Anglo-Saxon gold; Sanskrit juel, to shine; symbol from Latin aurum, shining down
Hafnium	Hf 72	Metal	4041°F 2227°C	8316°F 4602°C	2.8	1923 Dirk Coster & György Hevesy	From Hafnia, ancient name of Copenhagen
Hahnium (nielsbohrium)	Ha 105	Radioactive metal	N.A.	N.A.	Synthetic	1970 Albert Ghiorso & co-workers	Hahnium, the name used in U.S.; after German physicist Otto Hahn; nielsbohrium, name used in USSR, after the Danish physicist Niels Bohr
Helium	He 2	Gas	−458°F −272°C	−452°F −269°C	Rare	1868 Pierre-Jules-César Janssen & Sir Joseph Norman Lockyer	Greek helios, the sun; first observed in sun's atmosphere
Holmium	Ho 67	Rare earth	2678°F 1470°C	4928°F 2720°C	1.26	1879 Per Teodor Cleve	From Holmia, Latinized form of Stockholm
Hydrogen	H 1	Gas	−434.6°F −259.1°C	−423.2°F −252.9°C	1520	1766 Henry Cavendish	Greek hydor, water, plus gen, forming
Indium	In 49	Metal	313.9°F 156.6°C	3776°F 2080°C	0.24	1863 Ferdinand Reich & Hieronymus Theodor Richter	Latin indicum, indigo
Iodine	I 53	Nonmetal	236.3°F[3] 113.5°C[3]	363.9°F 184.4°C	0.46	1811 Bernard Courtois	Greek iodes, violet; from color of its vapor
Iridium	Ir 77	Metal	4370°F 2410°C	7466°F 4130°C	0.001	1803 Smithson Tennant	Greek iris, a rainbow, from changing color of its salts
Iron	Fe 26	Metal	2795°F 1535°C	4982°F 2750°C	62,200	Prehistoric	Anglo-Saxon iren; symbol from Latin ferrum
Krypton	Kr 36	Gas	−249.9°F −156.6°C	−242.1°F −153.3°C	Rare	1898 Alexander Ramsay & Morris William Travers	Greek kryptos, hidden
Lanthanum	La 57	Rare earth	1688°F 920°C	6249°F 3454°C	34.6	1839 Carl Mosander	Greek lanthanein, to be concealed
Lawrencium	Lr 103	Radioactive metal	N.A.	N.A.	Synthetic	1961 Albert Ghioroso & co-workers	After Ernest Lawrence, American physicist
Lead	Pb 82	Metal	621.5°F 327.5°C	3164°F 1740°C	13	Prehistoric	Anglo-Saxon lead; symbol from Latin plumbum
Lithium	Li 3	Metal	356.9°F 180.5°C	2457°F 1347°C	18	1817	Greek lithos, stony
Lutetium	Lu 71	Rare earth	3013°F 1656°C	5999°F 3315°C	Rare	1907 Georges Urbain	Latin Lutetia, ancient name for Paris
Magnesium	Mg 12	Metal	1200°F 649°C	1994°F 1090°C	27,640	1808 Humphry Davy	Latin Magnesia, a district in Asia Minor
Manganese	Mn 25	Metal	2271°F 1244°C	3564°F 1962°C	1060	1774 Karl Wilhelm Scheele	Latin magnes, magnet; because of confusion with magnetic iron ores
Mendelevium	Md 101	Radioactive metal	N.A.	N.A.	Synthetic	1955 Albert Ghiorso & co-workers	After Dmitri Mendeléev, Russian chemist
Mercury	Hg 80	Liquid metal	−38.0°F −38.9°C	673.9°F 356.6°C	0.08	Prehistoric	For Roman god Mercurius; symbol from Latin hydrogyrum
Molybdenum	Mo 42	Metal	4743°F 2617°C	8334°F 4612°C	1.2	1778 Karl Wilhelm Scheele	Greek molybdaina, galena (lead ore)

Element	Symbol/atomic no.	Type[1]	Melting point[1]	Boiling point[1]	Parts per million in crust	Year discovered & by whom	Derivation of name
Neodymium	Nd 60	Rare earth	1850°F 1010°C	5661°F 3127°C	39.6	1885 Karl Auer	Greek *neo*, new, plus *didymon*, twin (with the element praseodymium)
Neon	Ne 10	Gas	−416.7°F −248.7°C	−411°F −246°C	Rare	1898 Alexander Ramsay & Morris William Travers	Greek *neo*, new
Neptunium	Np 93	Radioactive metal	1184°F 640°C	7056°F 3902°C	Synthetic	1940 Edwin McMillan & Philip Abelson	For planet Neptune
Nickel	Ni 28	Metal	2647°F 1453°C	4950°F 2732°C	99	1751 Axel Cronstedt	German *Nickel*, Satan (Old Nick)
Niobium	Nb 41	Metal	4474°F 2468°C	8568°F 4742°C	20	1801 Charles Hachett	Latin *Niobe*, daughter of Tantalus
Nitrogen	N 7	Gas	−345.8°F −209.9°C	−320.4°F −195.8°C	19	1772 Daniel Rutherford	Latin, forming *niter*, a compound of nitrogen
Nobelium	No 102	Radioactive metal	N.A.	N.A.	Synthetic	1957 P.R. Fields & co-workers	After Alfred Nobel; made at Nobel Institute
Osmium	Os 76	Metal	5513°F 3045°C	9081°F 5027°C	0.005	1803 Smithson Tennant	Greek *osme*, smell; for malodorousness
Oxygen	O 8	Gas	−361°F −218.4°C	−297°F −183°C	456,000	1774 Joseph Priestley	Greek *oxyx*, sharp, plus *gen*, forming; from incorrect belief that oxygen forms acids
Palladium	Pd 46	Metal	2826°F 1552°C	5684°F 3140°C	0.015	1803 William Hyde Wollaston	For Greek goddess Pallas; from asteroid Pallas
Phosphorus	P 15	Nonmetal	111.4°F 44.1°C	536°F 280°C	1120	1669 Hennig Brand	Greek *phosphoros*, light-bringer; glows because of rapid oxidation
Platinum	Pt 78	Metal	3222°F 1772°C	6921°F 3827°C	0.01	1735 Antonio de Ulloa	Spanish *plata*, silver; from color of the metal
Plutonium	Pu 94	Radioactive metal	1186°F 641°C	5850°F 3232°C	Synthetic	1940 Glenn T. Seaborg & co-workers	For planet Pluto
Polonium	Po 84	Radioactive metal	489°F 254°C	1764°F 962°C	Rare	1898 Marie Curie & Pierre Curie	Named by Marie Curie for her native Poland
Potassium	K 19	Metal	146.7°F 63.7°C	1425°F 774°C	18,400	1807 Humphry Davy	For potash, a compound of potassium; symbol from Latin *kalium*
Praseodymium	Pr 59	Rare earth	1708°F 931°C	5814°F 3212°C	9.1	1885 Karl Auer (later Baron von Welsbach)	Greek *prasios*, green, plus *didymos*, twin (with the element Neodymium)
Promethium	Pm 61	Radioactive rare earth	1976°F 1080°C	4460°F 2460°C	Rare	1947 J.A. Marinsky, L.E. Glendenin, & C.D. Coryell	For Greek god Prometheus, who stole fire from heaven
Protactinium	Pa 91	Radioactive metal	2912°F 1600°C	N.A. N.A.	Rare	1917 Otto Hahn & Lise Meitner	Latin *proto*, first, plus actinium, one of the elements
Radium	Ra 88	Radioactive metal	1292°F 700°C	2084°F 1140°C	Rare	1898 Marie Curie & Pierre Curie	Latin *radius*, ray
Radon	Rn 86	Radioactive gas	−96°F −71°C	−79°F −61.8°C	Rare	1900 Friedrich Ernst Dorn	*Radium* plus *on*, as in *neon*
Rhenium	Re 75	Metal	5756°F 3180°C	10,161°F 5627°C	0.0007	1925 Walter Noddack, Ida Tacke, & Otto Berg	Latin *Rhenus*, Rhine
Rhodium	Rh 45	Metal	3571°F 1966°C	6741°F 3727°C	Rare	1803 William Hyde Wollaston	Greek *rhodios*, roselike; for red color of its salts
Rubidium	Rb 37	Metal	102°F 38.9°C	1270°F 688°C	78	1861 Gustav Kirchhoff & Robert Bunsen	Latin *rubidus*, red; from red lines in its spectrum
Ruthenium	Ru 44	Metal	4190°F 2310°C	7052°F 3900°C	Rare	1844 Carl Claus	For Ruthenia in Urals, where ore was first found
Rutherfordium	Rf 104	Radioactive metal	N.A.	N.A.	Synthetic	1969 Albert Ghiorso & co-workers	After Ernest Rutherford, British physicist
Samarium	Sm 62	Rare earth	1962°F 1072°C	3232°F 1778°C	7	1879 Paul-Emile Lecoq de Boisbaudran	For Scandinavian mineral samarskite
Scandium	Sc 21	Metal	2802°F 1539°C	5130°F 2832°C	25	1879 Lars Fredrik Nilson	For Scandinavia
Selenium	Se 34	Nonmetal	423°F 217°C	1265°F 685°C	0.05	1817 Jöns Jakob Berzelius	Greek *selene*, the moon
Silicon	Si 14	Nonmetal	2570°F 1410°C	4271°F 2355°C	273,000	1823 Jöns Jakob Berzelius	Latin *silex*, flint
Silver	Ag 47	Metal	1763.4°F 961.9°C	4014°F 2212°C	0.08	Prehistoric	Assyrian *sarpu*; Anglo-Saxon *soelfor*; symbol is from Latin *argentum*
Sodium	Na 11	Metal	208.0°F 97.8°C	1621.2°F 882.9°C	22,700	1807 Humphry Davy	English soda, compound of sodium; symbol from Latin *natrium*
Strontium	Sr	Metal	1416°F	2523°F	384	1808	For Strontian, a town in Scotland

Element	Symbol/ atomic no.	Type[1]	Melting point[1]	Boiling point[1]	Parts per million in crust	Year discovered & by whom	Derivation of name
Sulfur	S 16	Nonmetal	235.0°F 112.8°C	832.5°F 444.7°C	340	Prehistoric	Sanskrit *solvere*
Tantalum	Ta 73	Metal	5425°F 2996°C	9797°F 5425°C	1.7	1802 Anders Ekeberg	For mythical king Tantalus, condemned to thirst; because of its insolubility
Technetium	Tc 43	Radioactive metal	3942°F 2172°C	8811°F 4877°C	Synthetic	1937 Emilio Segrè	Greek *technetos* artificial; first artificial element
Tellurium	Te 52	Metal	841.1°F 449.5°C	1814°F 990°C	Rare	1782 Franz Joseph Müller	Latin *tellus*, the earth
Terbium	Tb 65	Rare earth	2480°F 1360°C	5506°F 3041°C	1.18	1843 Carl Gustav Mosander	For Ytterby, village in Sweden
Thallium	Tl 81	Metal	578.3°F 303.5°C	2655°F 1457°C	0.7	1861 William Crookes	Greek *thallos*, a young, or green, twig (after color of its spectrum)
Thorium	Th 90	Radioactive metal	3182°F 1750°C	8654°F 4790°C	8.1	1829 Jöns Jakob Berzelius	For Norse god Thor
Thulium	Tm 69	Rare earth	2813°F 1545°C	3141°F 1727°C	0.5	1879 Per Teodor Cleve	Greek *Thoule*, northernmost region of world
Tin	Sn 50	Metal	450°F 232°C	4118°F 2270°C	2.1	Prehistoric	Anglo-Saxon *tin*; symbol from Latin *stannum*
Titanium	Ti 22	Metal	3020°F 1660°C	5949°F 3287°C	6,320	1791 William Gregor	For Titans of classical mythology
Tungsten	W 74	Metal	6170°F 3410°C	10,220°F 5660°C	1.2	1783 Don Fausto d'Elhuyar	Swedish *tung sten*, heavy stone; symbol from German *Wolfram*
Uranium	U 92	Radioactive metal	2070°F 1132°C	6904°F 3818°C	2.3	1789 Martin Klaproth	For planet Uranus
Vanadium	V 23	Metal	3434°F 1890°C	6116°F 3380°C	136	1801 Andrès del Rio	For Scandinavian goddess Vanadin
Xenon	Xe 54	Gas	−169.4°F −111.9°C	−161°C −107°C	Rare	1898 Alexander Ramsay & Morris William Travers	Greek *xenon*, stranger
Ytterbium	Yb 70	Rare earth	1516.1°F 824.5°C	2179°F 1193°C	3.1	1907 George Urbain	For Ytterby, a village in Sweden
Yttrium	Y 39	Rare earth	2773°F 1523°C	6039°F 3337°C	31	1794 Johan Gadolin	For Ytterby, a village in Sweden
Zinc	Zn 30	Metal	787.3°F 419.6°C	1665°F 907°C	76	Prehistoric	German *zink*
Zirconium	Zr 40	Metal	3366°F 1852°C	7911°F 4377°C	162	1789 Martin Klaproth	Arabic *zargun*, gold color

1. At a pressure of one atmosphere and, for type, at room temperature. 2. At a pressure of 28 atmospheres. 3. Instead of melting, this element turns into a gas at this temperature (sublimes).

1910 Otto Wallach (Germany) Goettingen Univ. "in recognition of his services to organic chemistry and the chemical industry by his pioneer work in the field of alicyclic compounds."

1911 Marie Curie (France) Sorbonne Univ. "in recognition of her services to the advancement of chemistry by the discovery of the elements radium and polonium, by the isolation of radium and the study of the nature and compounds of this remarkable element."

1912 Victor Grignard (France) Nancy Univ. "for the discovery of the so-called Grignard reagent, which in recent years has greatly advanced the progress of organic chemistry"; **Paul Sabatier** (France) Toulouse Univ. "for his method of hydrogenating organic compounds in the presence of finely disintegrated metals whereby the progress of organic chemistry has been greatly advanced in recent years."

1913 Alfred Werner (Switzerland) Zurich Univ. "in recognition of his work on the linkage of atoms in molecules by which he has thrown new light on earlier investigations and opened up new fields of research especially in inorganic chemistry."

1914 Theodore W. Richards (U.S.) Harvard Univ. "in recognition of his accurate determinations of the atomic weight of a large number of chemical elements."

1915 Richard M. Willstätter (Germany) Munich Univ. "for his researches on plant pigments, especially chlorophyll."

1916 No award.

1917 No award.

1918 Fritz Haber (Germany) Kaiser-Wilhelm-Institut (now Fritz-Haber-Institut) "for the synthesis of ammonia from its elements."

1919 No award.

1920 Walther H. Nernst (Germany) Berlin Univ. "in recognition of his work in thermochemistry."

1921 Frederick Soddy (Great Britain) Oxford Univ. "for his contributions to our knowledge of the chemistry of radioactive substances, and his investigations into the origin and nature of isotopes."

1922 Francis W. Aston (Great Britain) Cambridge Univ. "for his discovery, by means of his mass spectrograph, of isotopes in a large number of nonradioactive elements, and for his enunciation of the whole-number rule."

1923 Fritz Pregl (Austria) Graz Univ. "for his invention of the method of microanalysis of organic substances."

1924 No award.

1925 Richard A. Zsigmondy (Germany) Goettingen Univ. "for his demonstration of the heterogeneous nature of colloid solutions and for the methods he used, which have since become fundamental in modern colloid chemistry."

1926 The (Theodor) Svedberg (Sweden) Uppsala Univ. "for his work on disperse systems."

1927 Heinrich O. Wieland (Germany) Munich Univ. "for his investigations of the constitution of the bile acids and related substances."

1928 Adolf O.R. Windaus (Germany) Goettingen Univ. "for the services rendered through his research into the constitution of the sterols and their connection with the vitamins."

1929 Sir Arthur Harden (Great Britain) London Univ., **Hans K.A. von Euler-Chel-**

pin (Sweden) Stockholm Univ. "for their investigations on the fermentation of sugar and fermentative enzymes."

1930 Hans Fischer (Germany) Institute of Technology "for his researches into the constitution of haemin and chlorophyll, and especially for his synthesis of haemin."

1931 Carl Bosch (Germany) Heidelberg Univ. and I.G. Farbenindustrie A.G., and Friedrich Bergius (Germany) Heidelberg Univ. and I.G. Farbenindustrie A.G. "in recognition of their contributions to the invention and development of chemical high pressure methods."

1932 Irving Langmuir (U.S.) General Electric Co. "for his discoveries and investigations in surface chemistry."

1933 No award.

1934 Harold C. Urey (U.S.) Columbia Univ. "for his discovery of heavy hydrogen."

1935 Frédéric Joliot (France) Institut du Radium, and his wife Irène Joliot-Curie (France) Institut du Radium "in recognition of their synthesis of new radioactive elements."

1936 Petrus (Peter) J.W. Debye (Netherlands) Berlin Univ. and Kaiser-Wilhelm-Institut (now Max-Planck-Institut) für Physik (Berlin-Dahlem) "for his contributions to our knowledge of molecular structure through his investigations on dipole moments and on the diffraction of X-rays and electrons in gases."

1937 Sir Walter N. Haworth (Great Britain) Birmingham Univ. "for his investigations on carbohydrates and vitamin C"; Paul Karrer (Switzerland) Zurich Univ. "for his investigations on carotenoids, flavins and vitamins A and B-2."

1938 Richard Kuhn (Germany) Heidelberg Univ. and Kaiser-Wilhelm-Institut (now Max-Planck-Institut) für Medizinische Forschung "for his work on carotenoids and vitamins." (Compelled by the authorities of his country to decline the award, but later received the diploma and the medal.)

1939 Adolf F.J. Butenandt (Germany) Berlin Univ. and Kaiser-Wilhelm-Institut (now Max-Planck-Institut) für Biochemie "for his work on sex hormones." (Compelled by the authorities, but later received the diploma and the medal); Leopold Ruzicka (Switzerland) Federal Institute of Technology "for his work on polymethylenes and higher terpenes."

1940 No award.

1941 No award.

1942 No award.

1943 George de Hevesy (Hungary) Stockholm Univ. (Sweden) "for his work on the use of isotopes as tracers in the study of chemical processes."

1944 Otto Hahn (Germany) Kaiser-Wilhelm-Institut (now Max-Planck-Institut) für Chemie "for his discovery of the fission of heavy nuclei."

1945 Artturi I. Virtanen (Finland) Helsinki Univ. "for his research and inventions in agricultural and nutrition chemistry, espe-

cially for his fodder preservation method."

1946 James B. Sumner (U.S.) Cornell Univ. "for his discovery that enzymes can be crystallized"; John H. Northrop (U.S.) Rockefeller Institute for Medical Research, and Wendell M. Stanley (U.S.) Rockefeller Institute for Medical Research "for their preparation of enzymes and virus proteins in a pure form."

1947 Sir Robert Robinson (Great Britain) Oxford Univ. "for his investigations on plant products of biological importance, especially the alkaloids."

1948 Arne W.K. Tiselius (Sweden) Uppsala Univ. "for his research on electrophoresis and adsorption analysis, especially for his discoveries concerning the complex nature of the serum proteins."

1949 William F. Giauque (U.S.) Univ. of California, Berkeley "for his contributions in the field of chemical thermodynamics, particularly concerning the behavior of substances at extremely low temperatures."

1950 Otto P.H. Diels (Germany) Kiel Univ., and Kurt Alder (Germany) Cologne Univ. "for their discovery and development of the diene synthesis."

1951 Edwin M. McMillan (U.S.) Univ. of California, Berkeley, and Glenn T. Seaborg (U.S.) Univ. of California, Berkeley "for their discoveries in the chemistry of the transuranium elements."

1952 Archer J.P. Martin (Great Britain) National Institute for Medical Research, and Richard L.M. Synge (Great Britain) Rowett Research Institute (Scotland) "for their invention of partition chromatography."

1953 Hermann Staudinger (Germany) State Research Institute for Macromolecular Chemistry "for his discoveries in the field of macromolecular chemistry."

1954 Linus C. Pauling (U.S.) California Institute of Technology "for his research into the nature of the chemical bond and its application to the elucidation of the structure of complex substances."

1955 Vincent du Vigneaud (U.S.) Cornell Univ. "for his work on biochemically important sulphur compounds, especially for the first synthesis of a polypeptide hormone."

1956 Sir Cyril N. Hinshelwood (Great Britain) Oxford Univ., and Nikolaj N. Semenov (USSR) Institute for Chemical Physics of the Academy of Sciences of the USSR "for their researches into the mechanism of chemical reactions."

1957 Lord Alexander R. Todd (Great Britain) Cambridge Univ. "for his work on nucleotides and nucleotide co-enzymes."

1958 Frederick Sanger (Great Britain) Cambridge Univ. "for his work on the structure of proteins, especially that of insulin."

1959 Jaroslav Heyrovsky (Czechoslovakia) Polarographic Institute of the Czechoslovak Academy of Science "for his discovery and development of the polarographic methods of analysis."

1960 Willard F. Libby (U.S.) Univ. of California, Los Angeles "for his method to use carbon-14 for age determination in archaeology, geology, geophysics and other branches of science."

1961 Melvin Calvin (U.S.) Univ. of California, Berkeley "for his research on the carbon dioxide assimilation in plants."

1962 Max F. Perutz (Great Britain) Laboratory of Molecular Biology, and Sir John C. Kendrew (Great Britain) Laboratory of Molecular Biology "for their studies of the structures of globular proteins."

1963 Karl Ziegler (Germany) Max-Planck-Institut for Carbon Research, and Giulio Natta (Italy) Institute of Technology "for their discoveries in the field of chemistry and technology of high polymers."

1964 Dorothy C. Hodgkin (Great Britain) Royal Society, Oxford Univ. "for her determinations by X-ray techniques of the structures of important biochemical substances."

1965 Robert B. Woodward (U.S.) Harvard Univ. "for his outstanding achievements in the art of organic synthesis."

1966 Robert S. Mulliken (U.S.) Univ. of Chicago "for his fundamental work concerning chemical bonds and the electronic structure of molecules by the molecular orbital method."

1967 Manfred Eigen (W. Germany) Max-Planck-Institut für Physikalische Chemie, Ronald G.W. Norrish (Great Britain) Institute of Physical Chemistry, and Sir George Porter (Great Britain) The Royal Institution "for their studies of extremely fast chemical reactions, effected by disturbing the equilibrium by means of very short pulses of energy."

1968 Lars Onsager (U.S.) Yale Univ. "for the discovery of the reciprocal relations bearing his name, which are fundamental for the thermodynamics of irreversible processes."

1969 Sir Derek H.R. Barton (Great Britain) Imperial College of Science and Technology, and Odd Hassel (Norway) Kjemisk Institut "for their contributions to the development of the concept of conformation and its application in chemistry."

1970 Luis F. Leloir (Argentina) Institute for Biochemical Research "for his discovery of sugar nucleotides and their role in the biosynthesis of carbohydrates."

1971 Gerhard Herzberg (Canada) National Research Council of Canada "for his contributions to the knowledge of electronic structure and geometry of molecules, particularly free radicals."

1972 Christian B. Anfinsen (U.S.) National Institutes of Health "for his work on ribonuclease, especially concerning the connection between the amino acid sequence and the biologically active conformation"; Stanford Moore (U.S.) Rockefeller Univ., and William H. Stein (U.S.) Rockefeller Univ. "for their contribution to the understanding of the connection between chemical structure and catalytic activity of the active center of the ribonuclease molecule."

1973 Ernst O. Fischer (W. Germany) Technical Univ. of Munich, and **Sir Geoffrey Wilkinson** (Great Britain) Imperial College "for their pioneering work, performed independently, on the chemistry of the organometallic, so-called sandwich compounds."

1974 Paul J. Flory (U.S.) Stanford Univ. "for his fundamental achievements, both theoretical and experimental, in the physical chemistry of the macromolecules."

1975 Sir John W. Cornforth (Australia and Great Britain) Univ. of Sussex "for his work on the stereochemistry of enzyme-catalyzed reactions"; **Vladimir Prelog** (Switzerland) Eidgenossische Technische Hochschule "for his research into the stereochemistry of organic molecules and reactions."

1976 William N. Lipscomb (U.S.) Harvard Univ. "for his studies on the structure of boranes illuminating problems of chemical bonding."

1977 Ilya Prigogine (Belgium) Université Libre de Bruxelles, Brussels (Univ. of Texas, U.S.) "for his contributions to nonequilibrium thermodynamics, particularly the theory of dissipative structures."

1978 Peter D. Mitchell (Great Britain) Glynn Research Laboratories "for his contribution to the understanding of biological energy transfer through the formulation of the chemiosmotic theory."

1979 Herbert C. Brown (U.S.) Purdue Univ., and **Georg Wittig** (Germany) Univ. of Heidelberg "for their development of the use of boron- and phosphorus-containing compounds, respectively, into important reagents in organic synthesis."

1980 Paul Berg (U.S.) Stanford Univ. "for his fundamental studies of the biochemistry of nucleic acids, with particular regard to recombinant-DNA"; **Walter Gilbert** (U.S.) Biological Laboratories, and **Frederick Sanger** (Great Britain) MRC Laboratory of Molecular Biology "for their contributions concerning the determination of base sequences in nucleic acids."

1981 Kenichi Fukui (Japan) Kyoto Univ., and **Roald Hoffmann** (U.S.) Cornell Univ. "for their theories, developed independently, concerning the course of chemical reactions."

1982 Aaron Klug (Great Britain) MRC Laboratory of Molecular Biology "for his development of crystallographic electron microscopy and his structural elucidation of biologically important nucleic acid–protein complexes."

1983 Henry Taube (U.S.) Stanford Univ. "for his work on the mechanisms of electron transfer reactions, especially in metal complexes."

1984 Robert B. Merrifield (U.S.) Rockefeller Univ. "for his development of methodology for chemical synthesis on a solid matrix."

1985 Herbert A. Hauptman (U.S.) The Medical Foundation of Buffalo, and **Jerome Karle** (U.S.) U.S. Naval Research Laboratory "for their outstanding achievements in the development of direct methods for the determination of crystal structures."

1986 Dudley R. Herschbach (U.S.) Harvard Univ., **Yuan T. Lee** (U.S.) Univ. of California, Berkeley, and **John C. Polanyi** (Canada) Univ. of Toronto "for their contributions concerning the dynamics of chemical elementary processes."

1987 Donald J. Cram (U.S.) Univ. of California, Los Angeles, **Jean-Marie Lehn** (France) Université Louis Pasteur, and **Charles J. Pedersen** (U.S.) Du Pont Laboratory "for their development and use of molecules with structure specific interactions of high selectivity."

1988 Johann Deisenhofer (U.S.) Howard Hughes Medical Institute, **Robert Huber** (W. Germany) Max-Planck-Institut für Biochemie, and **Hartmut Michel** (W. Germany) Max-Planck-Institut für Biophysik "for the determination of the three-dimensional structure of a photosynthetic reaction centre."

Source: *Nobel Foundation Directory* (1987–88); Mission of Sweden.

THE PERIODIC TABLE

In the 19th century, chemists began to determine how much one atom of an element weighed with respect to another—the atomic weight (now known as the atomic mass and measured in atomic mass units, or amu, a mass equal to one-twelfth the mass of the most common form of carbon atom). The first really good list was prepared by Jöns Jakob Berzelius in 1828. When chemists made lists of elements in the order of atomic weights, they noticed that every seven or eight elements in the list had similar properties. In 1869 Dmitri Mendeléev went further and boldly interchanged some elements in the list and left blanks for others to make sure the properties matched for every "period" of eight elements. This was the first periodic table. Mendeléev had only 63 elements to work with, but he correctly predicted three more that would make his list more complete. Today there are 109 elements in the periodic table.

Early in the 20th century, atoms were discovered to consist of protons and electrons (in 1932 it was discovered that neutrons also are found in atoms). Normally, the number of protons and electrons are equal. This number is the atomic number, which is a different counting number for every element from hydrogen (atomic number 1) to the unnamed element numbered 109. When the concept of atomic number was discovered, it was possible to improve the periodic table by arranging the elements in order of atomic number instead of atomic weight. This did not require the rearrangements Mendeléev had to make, and it clearly showed where the blanks were—all of which have been filled in since 1940. Any other newly discovered or created elements must go at the end of the table.

What It Reveals

Each column of the periodic table includes elements with similar properties, although hydrogen in the first column is less typical in this respect. But the other elements in the first column are all soft metals that react strongly. Similarly, the last column of the table contains only the gases that react only minimally. In general, elements are metals on the left side of the table (except for hydrogen), becoming mostly nonmetals in the last six columns. These last columns include some elements that are metals, such as aluminum. (A broken, heavy line separates the metals from the nonmetals.)

The row of rare-earth elements beginning with lanthanum and the row of actinide elements beginning with actinium do not fit neatly into the rest of the table. Elements from atomic number 57 to 71 are all similar to lanthanum, while elements from atomic number 89 to 103 are similar to actinium. The rare earths are not generally rare, nor do they resemble soil. They are moderately common metals that, because of atomic structure, are very similar chemically. The actinide elements are radioactive metals.

The periodic table also includes the atomic mass as well as the atomic number. The atomic mass is essentially the sum of the protons and neutrons in an atom of an element, although different standards have been used at various times to measure this. As protons and neutrons join to form an atomic nucleus, a little of their energy becomes mass, the amount of which depends on how many protons and neutrons there are (this effect is exploited in nuclear fission, in which the reverse process—splitting the nucleus—releases the energy). Consequently, a particular atom is chosen upon which to base the amu. Today the atomic mass is adjusted to make the most common form of carbon have an atomic mass of exactly 12 (6 protons and 6 neutrons). Most elements occur with several different atomic masses (in addition to carbon-12, for example, there are both carbon-13 and carbon-14; carbon-14 has 6 protons and 8 neutrons and is radioactive). These different forms are called isotopes. Therefore, in the periodic table, the atomic mass given for most elements is the one that would be found by averaging the different isotopes in the amounts they naturally occur. Carbon is given an atomic mass of 12.01 because there is so much more carbon-12 than there is carbon-13 or carbon-14 in an ordinary sample of carbon. For some radioactive elements, natural abundance is meaningless, since there is no stable form. For these, the atomic mass of the most stable form is given, indicated by putting the atomic mass in parentheses.

THE PERIODIC TABLE OF THE ELEMENTS

Legend:
6 — atomic number
C — chemical symbol
12.01 — atomic mass
Carbon — name of element

alkali metals — IA
alkaline earth metals — II A
transition metals
nonmetals
noble gases — O
other metals
rare earth elements — Lanthanide series
Actinide series

	IA	II A	III B	IV B	V B	VI B	VII B		VIII		IB	II B	III A	IV A	V A	VI A	VII A	O
Period 1	1 **H** 1.01 Hydrogen																	2 **He** 4.00 Helium
Period 2	3 **Li** 6.94 Lithium	4 **Be** 9.01 Beryllium											5 **B** 10.81 Boron	6 **C** 12.01 Carbon	7 **N** 14.01 Nitrogen	8 **O** 16.00 Oxygen	9 **F** 19.00 Fluorine	10 **Ne** 20.18 Neon
Period 3	11 **Na** 23.00 Sodium	12 **Mg** 24.31 Magnesium											13 **Al** 26.98 Aluminum	14 **Si** 28.09 Silicon	15 **P** 30.97 Phosphorus	16 **S** 32.06 Sulfur	17 **Cl** 35.45 Chlorine	18 **Ar** 39.95 Argon
Period 4	19 **K** 39.10 Potassium	20 **Ca** 40.08 Calcium	21 **Sc** 44.96 Scandium	22 **Ti** 47.90 Titanium	23 **V** 50.94 Vanadium	24 **Cr** 52.00 Chromium	25 **Mn** 54.94 Manganese	26 **Fe** 55.85 Iron	27 **Co** 58.93 Cobalt	28 **Ni** 58.71 Nickel	29 **Cu** 63.55 Copper	30 **Zn** 65.37 Zinc	31 **Ga** 69.72 Gallium	32 **Ge** 72.59 Germanium	33 **As** 74.92 Arsenic	34 **Se** 78.96 Selenium	35 **Br** 79.90 Bromine	36 **Kr** 83.80 Krypton
Period 5	37 **Rb** 85.47 Rubidium	38 **Sr** 87.62 Strontium	39 **Y** 88.91 Yttrium	40 **Zr** 91.22 Zirconium	41 **Nb** 92.91 Niobium	42 **Mo** 95.94 Molybdenum	43 **Tc** 98.91 Technetium	44 **Ru** 101.07 Ruthenium	45 **Rh** 102.91 Rhodium	46 **Pd** 106.4 Palladium	47 **Ag** 107.87 Silver	48 **Cd** 112.40 Cadmium	49 **In** 114.82 Indium	50 **Sn** 118.69 Tin	51 **Sb** 121.75 Antimony	52 **Te** 127.60 Tellurium	53 **I** 126.90 Iodine	54 **Xe** 131.30 Xenon
Period 6	55 **Cs** 132.91 Cesium	56 **Ba** 137.34 Barium	57 **La** 138.91 Lanthanum	72 **Hf** 178.49 Hafnium	73 **Ta** 180.95 Tantalum	74 **W** 183.85 Tungsten	75 **Re** 186.2 Rhenium	76 **Os** 190.2 Osmium	77 **Ir** 192.22 Iridium	78 **Pt** 195.09 Platinum	79 **Au** 196.97 Gold	80 **Hg** 200.59 Mercury	81 **Tl** 204.37 Thallium	82 **Pb** 207.2 Lead	83 **Bi** 208.98 Bismuth	84 **Po** (209) Polonium	85 **At** (210) Astatine	86 **Rn** (222) Radon
Period 7	87 **Fr** (223) Francium	88 **Ra** (226) Radium	89 **Ac** (227) Actinium	104 **Rf** (261) Rutherfordium	105 **Ha** (262) Hahnium	106 (263)	107 (262)	108 (265)	109 (266)									

Lanthanide series

58 **Ce** 140.12 Cerium	59 **Pr** 140.91 Praseodymium	60 **Nd** 144.24 Neodymium	61 **Pm** (145) Promethium	62 **Sm** 150.4 Samarium	63 **Eu** 151.96 Europium	64 **Gd** 157.25 Gadolinium	65 **Tb** 158.93 Terbium	66 **Dy** 162.50 Dysprosium	67 **Ho** 164.93 Holmium	68 **Er** 167.26 Erbium	69 **Tm** 168.93 Thulium	70 **Yb** 173.04 Ytterbium	71 **Lu** 174.97 Lutetium

Actinide series

90 **Th** 232.04 Thorium	91 **Pa** 231.04 Protactinium	92 **U** 238.03 Uranium	93 **Np** 237.05 Neptunium	94 **Pu** (244) Plutonium	95 **Am** (243) Americium	96 **Cm** (247) Curium	97 **Bk** (247) Berkelium	98 **Cf** (251) Californium	99 **Es** (254) Einsteinium	100 **Fm** (257) Fermium	101 **Md** (258) Mendelevium	102 **No** (255) Nobelium	103 **Lw** (256) Lawrencium

MAJOR DISCOVERIES IN PHYSICS

1586 Simon Stevinus (Belgian-Dutch: 1548–1620) shows that two different weights dropped at same time from same height will reach ground at same time.

1604 Galileo (Italian: 1564–1642) discovers that a body falling freely will increase its distance as square of time.

Johannes Kepler (German: 1571–1630) shows that light diminishes as square of distance from source.

1663 Blaise Pascal (French: 1623–62) proposes what becomes known as Pascal's Law: pressure in fluid is transmitted equally in all directions. (Published year after his death.)

1675 Ole Römer (Danish: 1644–1710) becomes first to measure speed of light, although his value is somewhat too slow by today's standards.

1676 Robert Hooke (English: 1635–1703) discovers what becomes known as Hooke's Law: The amount a spring stretches varies directly with its tension.

1678 Christiaan Huygens (Dutch: 1629–95) develops wave theory of light.

1687 Isaac Newton's (English: 1642–1727) *Principia* is published, containing his laws of motion and theory of gravity.

1746 At least two experimenters in Leiden (sometimes spelled *Leyden*), Holland, invent method for storing static electricity, which becomes known as Leyden jar.

1752 Benjamin Franklin (American: 1706–90) performs kite experiment, demonstrating that lightning is form of electricity.

1787 Jacques Charles (French: 1746–1823) discovers what is later known as Charles' law: All gases expand same amount with given rise in temperature; e.g., same rise in temperature that will cause hydrogen to double in volume will also cause air to double in volume.

1791 Luigi Galvani (Italian: 1737–98) announces his discovery that when two different metals touch in frog's muscle, they produce electric current.

1798 Count Rumford (American-British-German-French: 1753–1814) shows that heat is form of motion.

Henry Cavendish (English: 1731–1810) determines gravitational constant and mass of Earth.

1800 Alessandro Volta (Italian: 1745–1827) announces his invention, made the previous year, of electric battery, a combination of chemicals and metals producing electric current.

1801 Johann Ritter (German: 1776–1810) discovers ultraviolet light.

1802 Thomas Young (English: 1773–1829) develops his wave theory of light—more detailed than ideas of Christiaan Huygens and based on convincing experiments.

1819 Hans Christian Oersted (Danish: 1777–1851) discovers that magnetism and electricity are two different manifestations of same force (not published until 1820).

1820 André-Marie Ampère (French: 1775–1836) formulates first laws of electromagnetism.

1830 Michael Faraday (English: 1791–1867) in England and Joseph Henry (American: 1797–1878) in U.S. independently discover principle of electrical dynamo.

1842 Julius Robert Mayer (German: 1814–78) is first scientist to state law of conservation of energy: In chemical reactions energy is neither created nor destroyed.

1850 Rudolf Clausius (German: 1822–88) makes first clear statement of second law of thermodynamics: Energy in closed system tends to degrade into heat.

1851 William Thompson, later Lord Kelvin (Scottish: 1824–1907), proposes concept of absolute zero, the lowest theoretically possible temperature ($-460°$F, or $-273°$C).

1873 James Clerk Maxwell (Scottish: 1831–79) publishes complete theory of electromagnetism, which includes his prediction that radio waves must exist.

1887 Albert Michelson (German-American: 1852–1931) and Edward Morley (American: 1838–1923) attempt to measure changes in velocity of light produced by motion of Earth through space; inability to find such changes is later interpreted as helping to establish Einstein's special theory of relativity.

1888 Heinrich Hertz (German: 1857–94) produces and detects radio waves.

1895 Wilhelm Konrad Roentgen (German: 1845–1923) discovers X rays.

1896 Antoine-Henri Becquerel (French: 1852–1908) discovers natural radioactivity.

1897 Joseph John Thomson (English: 1856–1940) discovers electron.

1900 Max Planck (German: 1858–1947) explains behavior of light by proposing that there is smallest step a physical process can take, which he names quantum.

1905 Albert Einstein (German-Swiss-American: 1879–1955) shows that photoelectric effect —ejection of electrons from metal by action of light—can be explained if light has particle nature as well as wave nature.

Einstein shows that motion of small particles in liquid ("Brownian motion") can be explained by assuming that the liquid is made of molecules.

Einstein develops his theory of relativity and the law $E = mc^2$ (energy equals mass times square of speed of light).

1911 Heike Kamerlingh Onnes (Dutch: 1853–1926) discovers superconductivity in metals cooled near to absolute zero.

1914 Ernest Rutherford (British: 1871–1937) discovers the proton.

1915 Albert Einstein completes his general theory of relativity, a theory of gravity more accurate than that of Sir Isaac Newton.

1919 An expedition to observe bending of starlight by sun's gravity during eclipse led by Arthur Eddington (English: 1882–1944) confirms that Einstein's theory of gravity is more accurate than Newton's in predicting effect of gravity on light.

1923 Louis-Victor de Broglie (French: 1892–1987) theorizes that particles, such as

electron, also have wave nature.

1925 Wolfgang Pauli (Austrian-American: 1900–58) discovers exclusion principal: Two electrons or protons described by same numbers (called quantum numbers) cannot exist in same atom.

Werner Heisenberg (German: 1901–76) develops matrix version of quantum mechanics, a mathematical treatment that explains behavior of electrons and protons.

1926 Erwin Schrödinger (Austrian: 1887–1961) develops wave version of quantum mechanics, a different mathematical treatment of behavior of electrons and protons producing same results as Heisenberg's matrix mechanics.

1927 Werner Heisenberg develops his uncertainty principle: It is impossible to measure accurately position and momentum of electron or proton at same time.

1932 James Chadwick (British: 1891–1974) discovers neutron, a neutral particle about same size as proton.

Carl Anderson (American: 1905–) discovers positron, a positively charged analog of electron.

John Cockcroft (English: 1897–1967) and Ernest Walton (Irish: 1903–) develop first particle accelerator, a device for speeding subatomic particles, which causes them to react more intensely with atoms or other particles (often still known as "atom smasher").

1937 Carl Anderson discovers muon, which we now know is subatomic particle just like electron, but with more mass.

1938 Otto Hahn (German: 1879–1968) splits uranium atom, opening way for nuclear bombs and nuclear power.

1945 Scientists funded by U.S. government and led by J. Robert Oppenheimer detonate first nuclear-fission explosion (atomic bomb).

1947 Quantum electrodynamics (QED) is born, with many parents: notably, Richard Feynman (American: 1918–88), Julian Schwinger (American: 1918–), Schin'ichiro Tomonaga (Japanese: 1906–1949), Willis Lamb, Jr. (American: 1913–) (all of whom received Nobel Prizes for this concept), and Hans Bethe (German-American: 1906–). Cecil Powell (English: 1903–69) and coworkers discover pion, first-known meson, a subatomic particle involved in holding nucleus of atom together.

1952 Group of scientists in U.S. led by Edward Teller (Hungarian-American: 1908–) develops first artificial nuclear-fusion device (hydrogen bomb).

1955 Owen Chamberlain (American: 1920–) and Emilio Segrè (Italian-American: 1905–) produce first-known antiprotons, negatively charged analogs of proton.

Clyde Cowan, Jr. (American: 1919–) and Frederick Reines (American: 1918–) are first to observe neutrino, a subatomic particle with no mass or charge produced in certain forms of radioactive decay (technically, they observe antineutrinos, which have opposite spin of neutrinos).

1957 Experiments by group led by Chien-Shiung Wu (Chinese-American: 1912–)

and quickly confirmed by others show that Law of Conservation of Parity does not hold for weak interaction; broadly speaking, right and left are distinguished by behavior of electrons emitted in certain forms of radioactivity.

John Bardeen (American: 1908–), Leon Cooper (American: 1930–), and John Schrieffer (American: 1931–) develop a theory explaining superconductivity.

1961 Murray Gell-Mann (American: 1929–) and, independently, Yu'val Ne'eman (Israeli: 1925–) and others develop method of classifying heavy subatomic particles that comes to be known as "eight-fold way."

1964 Murray Gell-Mann introduces concept of quarks as components of heavy subatomic particles, such as protons and neutrons.

1967 Steven Weinberg (American: 1933–), Abdus Salam (Pakistani-British: 1926–), and Sheldon Glashow (American: 1932–) independently develop theory that combines electromagnetic force with weak force.

1986 Alex Müller (Swiss: 1927–) and Georg Bednorz (German: 1950–) discover first warm-temperature superconductor.

THE BASIC LAWS OF PHYSICS

Key Terms *Mass* is a measure of the amount of matter. Near the surface of Earth it is roughly equivalent to weight.

Velocity measures how an object changes position with time.

Acceleration is how an object changes velocity with time.

Momentum is the product of mass and velocity.

Energy is the ability to do work.

Law of Gravity

The gravitational force between any two objects is proportional to the product of their masses and inversely proportional to the square of the distance between them. If F is the force, G is the number that represents the ratio (the gravitational constant), m and M are the two masses, and r is the distance between the objects:

$$F = \frac{GmM}{r^2} .$$

In metric measure, the gravitational constant is 0.0000000667 (6.67 $\times$ 10^{-8}) dyne cm^2/g^2, so another way of writing the basic law of gravity is

$$F = \frac{0.0000000667mM}{r^2} .$$

This law implies that objects falling near the surface of Earth will fall with the same rate of acceleration (ignoring drag caused by air). This rate is 32.174 feet per second per second (ft./ sec^2), or 980.665 cm/sec^2, and is conventionally labeled g. Applying this rate to falling objects gives the velocity, v, and distance, d, after any amount of time, t, in seconds. If the object starts at rest and 32 ft./sec^2 is used as an approximation for g,

$$v = 32t$$
$$d = 16t^2.$$

For example, after 3 seconds, a dropped object that is still falling will have a velocity of 32 $\times$ 3 = 96 feet per second and will have fallen a distance of 16 $\times$ 3^2 = 144 feet.

If the object has an initial velocity v_0 and an initial height above the ground of a, the equations describing the velocity and the distance, d, above the ground (a positive velocity is *up* and a negative velocity is *down*) become

$$v = v_0 - 32t$$
and
$$d = -16t^2 + v_0 t + a.$$

After 3 seconds, an object tossed in the air from a height of 6 feet with a velocity of 88 feet per second will reach a speed of 88 – 96 = –8 feet per second, meaning that it has begun to descend, and will have a height of (–16 $\times$ 9) + (88 $\times$ 3) + 6 = –144 + 264 + 6 = 126 feet above the ground.

The maximum height, H, reached by the object with an initial velocity v_0 and initial height a is

$$H = \frac{a + v_0^2}{64} .$$

For the object tossed upward at 88 feet per second from a height of 6 feet, the maximum height reached would be 6 + 88^2/64 = 6 + 121 = 127 feet. Therefore, after 3 seconds, the object has just reached its peak and has fallen back only 1 foot.

Albert Einstein's general theory of relativity introduced laws of gravity more accurate than those just given, which were discovered by Sir Isaac Newton. Newton's gravitational theory is extremely accurate for most practical situations, however. For example, Newton's theory is used to determine how to launch satellites into proper orbits.

Newton's Laws of Motion

Newton's Laws of Motion apply to objects in a vacuum and are not easily observed in the real world, where forces such as friction tend to overwhelm the natural motion of objects. To obtain realistic solutions to problems, however, physicists and engineers begin with Newton's laws and then add in the various forces that also affect motion.

1. *Any object at rest tends to stay at rest. A body in motion moves at the same velocity in a straight line unless acted upon by a force.* This is also known as the law of inertia. Note that this law implies that an object will travel in a curved path only so long as a force is acting on it. When the force is released, the object will travel in a straight line. A weight on a string swung in a circle will travel in a straight line when the string is released, for the string was supplying the force that caused circular motion.

2. *The acceleration of an object is directly proportional to the force acting on it and inversely proportional to the mass of the object.* This law, for an acceleration a, a force F, and a mass m, is more commonly expressed in terms of finding the force when you know the mass and the acceleration. In this form it is written as

$$F = ma.$$

The implication of this law is that a constant force will produce acceleration, which is an increase in velocity. Thus, a rocket, which is propelled by a constant force as long as its fuel is burning, constantly increases in velocity. If there were enough fuel, the rocket would eventually cease to increase in velocity, however, because Einstein's other relativity theory, the special theory of relativity, states that no object can exceed the speed of light in a vacuum (see "Conservation of Mass-Energy" below). Nevertheless, even a small force, constantly applied, can cause a large mass to reach velocities near the speed of light if enough time is allowed.

3. *For every action there is an equal and opposite reaction.*

Conservation Laws

Many results in physics come from various conservation laws. A conservation law is a rule that a certain entity must not change in amount during a certain class of operations. All such conservation laws have to treat closed systems. Anything added from outside the system could affect the amount of the entity being consumed.

Conservation of Momentum *In a closed system, momentum stays the same.* This law is equivalent to Newton's third law. Since momentum is the product of mass and velocity, if the mass of a system changes, then the velocity must change. For example, consider a person holding a heavy weight, such as an anchor, in a stationary canoe in the water. The momentum of the system is 0, since the masses have no velocity. Now the person in the canoe tosses the anchor toward the shore. The momentum of the anchor is now a positive number if velocity toward the shore is measured as positive. To conserve momentum, the canoe has to be accelerated in the opposite direction, away from the shore. The positive momentum of the anchor is balanced by the negative momentum of the canoe and its cargo. In terms of two masses, m and M, and matching velocities v and V,

$$mv = MV.$$

Conservation of Angular Momentum An object moving in a circle has a special kind of momentum, called angular momentum. As noted above, motion in a circle requires some force. Angular momentum combines mass, velocity, and acceleration (produced by the force). For a body moving in a circle, the acceleration depends on both the speed of the body in its path and the square of the radius of the circle. The product of this speed, the mass, and the square of the radius are the angular momentum of the mass.

In a closed system, angular momentum is conserved. This effect is used by skaters to change their velocity of spinning. Angular momentum is partly determined by the masses of a skater's arms combined with the rate of rotation and the square of the radius to the center of mass of each arm (the point that can represent the total mass of the arm). When skaters bring their arms close to their body, this would tend to reduce the angular momentum, because the center of mass is closer to the body. But, since angular momentum is conserved, the rate of rotation has to increase to compensate for the decreased radius. Because the rate depends on the square of the rotation, the rate increases dramatically.

Conservation of Mass *In a closed system, the total amount of mass appears to be conserved in all but nuclear reactions and other extreme conditions.*

Conservation of Energy *In a closed system, energy appears to be conserved in all but nuclear reactions and other extreme conditions.* Energy comes in very many forms: mechanical, chemical, electrical, heat, and so forth. As one form is changed into another (excepting nuclear reactions and extreme conditions), this law guarantees that the total amount remains the same. Thus, when you change the chemical energy of a dry cell into electrical energy and use that to turn a motor, the total amount does not change (although some becomes heat energy—see "Laws of Thermodynamics" below).

Conservation of Mass-Energy Einstein discovered that his special theory of relativity implied that energy and mass are related. Consequently, mass and energy by themselves are not conserved, since one can be converted into the other. Mass and energy appear to be conserved in ordinary situations because the effect of Einstein's discovery is very small most of the time. The more general law, then, is the law of conservation of mass-energy: *The total amount of mass and energy must be conserved.* Einstein found the following equation that links mass and energy.

$$E = mc^2$$

In this equation, E is the amount of energy, m is the mass, and c is the speed of light in a vacuum.

One instance of energy changing to mass occurs in Einstein's equation for how the mass increases with velocity. If m_0 is the mass of the object when it is not moving, v is the velocity of the object in relation to an observer who is considered to be at rest, and c is the speed of light in a vacuum, then the mass, m, is given by the equation

$$m = \frac{m^o}{1 - \frac{v^2}{c^2}}.$$

This accounts for the rule that no object can exceed the speed of light in a vacuum. As the object approaches this speed, so much of the energy is converted to mass that it cannot continue to accelerate.

In both nuclear fission (splitting of the atomic nucleus) and nuclear fusion (the joining of atomic nuclei, producing the energy of a hydrogen bomb), mass is converted into energy.

Conservation for Particles Many properties associated with atoms and subatomic particles are also conserved. Among them are charge, spin, isospin, and a combination known as CPT for *charge conjugation, parity,* and *time.*

First and Second Laws of Thermodynamics

First Law This is the same as the law of conservation of energy. It is a law of thermodynamics, or the movement of heat, because heat must be treated as a form of energy to keep the total amount of energy constant. All bodies contain heat as energy no matter how cold they are, although there is not much heat at temperatures close to absolute zero.

Second Law *Heat in a closed system can never travel from a low temperature region to one of higher temperature in a self-sustaining process.* *Self-sustaining* in this case means a process that does not need energy from outside the system to keep it going. In a refrigerator, heat from the cold inside of the refrigerator is transferred to a warmer room, but energy from outside is required to make the transfer happen, so the process is not self-sustaining.

The second law has many implications. One of them is that no perpetual motion machine can be constructed. Another is that all energy in a closed system eventually becomes heat that is diffused equally throughout the system, so that one can no longer obtain work from the system.

The equations that describe the behavior of heat also can be applied to order and therefore to information. The word *entropy* refers to diffused heat, disorder, or lack of information. Another form of the second law of thermodynamics is that in a closed system, entropy always increases.

Laws of Current Electricity

Key Terms When electrons flow in a conductor, the result is electric *current.* The amount of current is based on an amount of electric charge called the *coulomb,* which is the charge of about 6,250,000,000,000,000,000 (6.25×10^{18}) electrons. When 1 coulomb of charge moves past a point in 1 second, it creates a current of 1 ampere. Just as a stream can carry the same amount of water swiftly through a narrow channel or slowly through a broad channel, the energy of an electric current varies depending on the difference in charge between places along the conductor. This is called *potential difference* and is measured in *volts.* The voltage is affected by the nature of the conductors. Some substances conduct an electric current much more easily than others. This *resistance* to the current is also measured in volts. Electric *power* is the rate at which electricity is used.

Ohm's Law *Electric current is directly proportional to the potential difference and inversely proportional to resistance.* If you measure current, I, in amperes, potential difference, V, in volts, and resistance, R, in volts, then the current is equal to the potential difference divided by the resistance.

$$I = \frac{V}{R}$$

Law of Electric Power *If electric power, P, is measured in watts, then the power is equal to the current measured in amperes and the potential difference measured in volts.*

$$P = IV$$

Laws of Waves, Light, and Electromagnetic Radiation

Key Terms Light is a part of a general form of radiation known as *electromagnetic waves,* or, when thought of as particles, *photons.* Here, electromagnetic radiation is considered as a wave phenomenon for the most part. The *velocity* of a wave is how fast the wave travels as a whole. The *wavelength* is the distance between one crest of the wave and the next crest. The *frequency* is how many crests pass a particular location in a unit of time.

Law of Wave Motion All waves (including water waves and sound waves) obey the wave equation that relates the velocity of the wave to its frequency and wavelength. *For all waves, the velocity is equal to the product of the frequency and wavelength.* The letters traditionally used in this equation have already been used in the equations above to mean something else, so here, W will be used for the velocity of the wave, f for the frequency, and l for the wavelength.

$$W = fl$$

Law of Electromagnetic Energy The energy of an electromagnetic wave depends on a small number known as Planck's constant. Measured in ergs (a unit of energy) per second, Planck's constant is 6.6×10^{-27}, a number with 26 0s after the decimal point before you get to a nonzero digit. *The energy is equal to the product of Planck's constant and the frequency.* Using E for energy, h for Planck's constant, and f for frequency,

$$E = hf.$$

When thought of in terms of the particles called photons, the energy of a photon obeys the same law. The law of wave motion and the law of electromagnetic energy can be combined with the speed of light in a vacuum (c) to give

$$E = \frac{hc}{l}.$$

The energy of a photon is the product of Planck's constant and the speed of light, divided by the wavelength of the photon.

Inverse-Square Law All radiation obeys an inverse-square law, which is similar to the law of gravity. *The intensity of the radiation decreases as the inverse of the square of the distance from the source of the radiation.*

Two Basic Laws of Quantum Physics

When one considers effects on very small masses and at very small distances, different forces begin to affect how objects behave than occur at the sizes and distances one can observe directly. Since these effects occur in discrete steps, as with Planck's quantum—which is the size by which energy changes in steps (instead of continuously)—the science of such effects is called quantum physics. Small masses act sometimes like particles and sometimes like waves and sometimes like nothing we know about at the scale we live. Two laws that describe their behavior in particular are basic and easily stated.

Heisenberg's Uncertainty Principle *It is impossible to specify completely the position and momentum of a particle, such as an electron.*

Pauli's Exclusion Principle *Two particles of a certain class that are essentially the same cannot be in the same exact state.* This class, the fermions, includes such particles as the electron, neutron, and proton. Particles of a different class, the bosons, do not obey Pauli's exclusion principle. (See "Subatomic Particles" below.)

SUBATOMIC PARTICLES

During the 19th century, most scientists came to believe that everything was made from atoms, even though they had no way then to observe atoms. It is now known they were right, and there are even "photographs" of individual atoms available, images made with the scanning tunneling microscope. At the turn of the 20th century, physicists discovered that atoms themselves were made from smaller pieces—subatomic particles. These smaller pieces seemed at first to be the ultimate limit of matter, but in the 1960s, physicists proposed that many subatomic particles were themselves made from smaller particles that could not be detected. Like the unobserved atoms of the 19th century, the undetectable smaller particles, called quarks, have come to be accepted. Perhaps in the next century, there will be "photographs" of quarks.

Quarks are considered to be "fundamental" in that scientists believe they are not made up of still smaller pieces. Beside the quarks, various other groups of particles are thought to be fundamental. Among these are the leptons. Together, quarks and leptons form what we think of as matter. They are characterized by a spin of ½, as are the particles made from three quarks, the baryons. *Spin* is a number for each particle that has a behavior similar to angular momentum (see "Basic Laws," above). Other apparently fundamental subatomic particles are similar to the photon, the particle that makes up light. Particles such as the photon and other particles with a spin of either 0 or 1 are called bosons, and they act as "glue" that holds matter together. Bosons produce the four known forces: gravity, electromagnetism, the strong force, and the weak force. (Under certain conditions electromagnetism and the weak force become a single force, the electroweak force.)

Many subatomic particles carry a charge, which is a unit of electromagnetism. Nearly all charges are counted as either –1 or +1 or 0 (no charge), based on the charge of the electron, which is –1. Quarks, however, have charges in multiples of ⅓. No one knows why charges come only in these particular amounts and do not occur in other amounts. No known law, for example, predicts that the charge of the large proton will be exactly the same amount (but opposite: +1) as the charge of the small electron.

The masses of subatomic particles are measured in terms of the particle's energy, for energy, E, is related to mass, m, and the speed of light, c, by Albert Einstein's famous equation $E = mc^2$. Since c is a very large number, the energy of a particle is much larger than its mass. Even so, the energy is expressed in a very small unit, the MeV, which is a million electron volts. An electron volt is 0.00000000000000000001602 (1.602 × 10⁻¹⁹) joule.

Recently, many physicists have proposed various other still undetected particles, called WIMPs (for Weakly Interacting Massive Particles); these are far from being fully accepted at this time and are omitted from the following list. Every particle mentioned has an antiparticle whose charge is the opposite (negative particles have positive antiparticles) and whose spin is in the opposite direction. Unless there is something special about the antiparticle, it will not be mentioned.

Principal Subatomic Particles
Fermions—all spin ½
Fundamental Particles of Matter

THE ELECTRON (A LEPTON) Movement of electrons is the source of current electricity, while an excessive deficit of electrons causes static electricity. The properties of the electron form the basis of electronic devices, such as computer chips. Electrons are found in all atoms, where they occupy several shells around the outside of the atom. Interactions between electrons account for all chemical reactions. The electron is stable and very light. Its mass is 0.511 MeV. Its charge is –1. Like all subatomic particles, it has a related particle, the antiparticle, known as the positron. The positron is a mirror-image of the electron with a charge of +1. The positron was the first antiparticle to be discovered. It was proposed in 1931 by Paul Adrien Maurice Dirac and discovered (accidentally) in 1932 by Carl David Anderson.

MUONS AND TAUONS (LEPTONS) The muon is often described as a "fat electron," since it has all the properties of an electron except that its mass is 200 times as great—105.7 MeV. Similarly, the tauon is a "fat muon," with a mass of 1,750 MeV. No one predicted these particles, and no one knows what their role in the universe is.

THE NEUTRINO FAMILY (LEPTONS) is a group of leptons associated with electrons, muons, and tauons, with which they form three "families." A family consists of a charged particle, such as an electron, its antiparticle, such as a positron, and an associated neutrino and an antineutrino. Aside from their separate associations, there would seem to be no differences among the three types of neutrino. All have no charge and probably no mass and a spin of ½. (Some evidence suggests that neutrinos have a very small mass.) They do not interact strongly with anything. Neutrinos are passing through your body all the time, and most go on to pass through the earth and out the other side.

QUARKS were first proposed by Murray Gell-Mann in 1964 to account for the relationships

between various kinds of baryons (see below). Each baryon is composed of three quarks, and each meson (see below) of two quarks. Common baryons and mesons are composed of quarks known as *up* (charge +⅔ and mass 1.0 MeV) and *down* (charge –⅓ and mass 3.0 MeV). Even though their individual masses are small, the binding energy between them in a baryon produces most of the mass in the universe. Other baryons or mesons have a quality known as "strangeness," which is conferred by the *strange quark* (charge –⅓ and mass 102.2 MeV), or a quality known as "charm," conferred by the *charm quark* (charge –⅔ and mass 1,530 MeV). Two other quarks, variously known as *top* and *bottom* or as *truth* and *beauty* complete the list of six "flavors." Each quark also comes in one of three "colors," although physicists disagree on what to call the colors (red, blue, and green are one of the popular choices.) In a meson or a baryon, the colors are always combined so as to produce absence of color; thus color cannot be detected directly. Furthermore, quarks are confined within the particles they make up, making direct detection impossible; but various experiments have established that all, except possibly top or truth, actually exist.

Baryons

THE PROTON is found in the nucleus of the atom. For about 20 years, it was assumed that atoms consisted of a core of protons surrounded by electrons, although the true situation is somewhat more complex. The proton appears to be stable, although recently some theorists have proposed that protons may decay into pure energy after about 10,000,000,000,000,-000,000,000,000,000,000 (10³¹) years. So far, although much watched, no one has seen a proton decay. Protons are heavy particles with a mass of 938.3 MeV, and they have a charge of +1. Every atom contains an equal number of +1 protons and –1 electrons, giving a total charge to the atom of 0. (An atom that has lost or gained an electron—and therefore a charge—is called an ion.)

THE NEUTRON is almost exactly like a proton but with no charge and therefore much harder to detect. Neutrons in the nuclei of atoms are stable, but outside the nucleus, each neutron soon decays into a proton, an electron, and an electron antineutrino. All atoms except hydrogen must have neutrons in their nuclei to be stable. Neutrons have a mass of 939.6 MeV.

OTHER BARYONS These include two hyperons, three sigmas, two xis, and an omega. Except for the omega, none were predicted. Instead they were found in cosmic-ray and particle-accelerator experiments in the late 1940s and in the 1950s. In 1961 Murray Gell-Mann predicted the omega on the basis of a theory preliminary to the quark theory. The omega was discovered in 1964. None of these particles are stable, decaying after much less than a second into other particles. They are not constituents of ordinary matter; i.e., they do not exist at ordinary energies on Earth.

Bosons (spin 0 or 1)
Mesons

PIONS are the bosons that hold the nucleus of atoms together, producing the strong force. Pions come in positive, negative, and neutral forms. In 1935 Hideki Yukawa predicted the pion in his theory of the strong force. When a pion is exchanged between a proton and a neutron, it can change each into the other particle. In the process, it produces the strong force, which is needed to keep the positively charged protons from rushing apart because of the electromagnetic force (positive charges repel each other). When the muon was first discovered in 1937, scientists thought it was the particle Yukawa predicted, but by 1945 it was known that the muon's properties were wrong for that role. In 1947 Cecil Frank Powell and co-workers located the pion in cosmic rays. Each form of the pion has a slightly different mass (positive 139.6 MeV, negative 189.6 MeV, and neutral 135 MeV), and all decay in much less than a second. Pions, like all mesons, are composite particles made from two quarks. Other bosons are thought to be elementary particles, not made up of other particles.

OTHER MESONS Various short-lived mesons heavier than the pion incorporate such quarks as strange, top, and bottom. None of them are constituents of ordinary matter, but the neutral K mesons, or kaons, have been very important in experiments extending basic physical theories.

Other Bosons

THE PHOTON is the agent of electromagnetic radiation, including ordinary light, radio waves, microwaves, X rays, and gamma rays. In the 19th century, Thomas Young demonstrated the wave nature of electromagnetic radiation, but in 1905 Albert Einstein showed that it also had a particle nature. The particle, a vector boson (see "Vector Bosons" below) came to be called the photon. It has no mass and a spin of 1. Exchanging photons causes charged particles to be attracted (if the charges are unlike) or repelled (if the charges are alike). When an electron absorbs or emits a photon of sufficient energy, it can change into a positron. If a positron and an electron meet, they disappear, leaving an energetic photon. Electrons can emit and absorb photons in other ways as well. The photon has no mass and a spin of 1.

GLUONS Although the Yukawa theory of the pion seemed to explain the strong force, the quark theory soon led to the understanding that pions and the strong force are side effects of a more essential strong force, one carried by eight neutral particles called gluons. Exchanging gluons between quarks usually causes quarks to change from one color to another, keeping the quarks attracted to each other. Gluons have no mass and a spin of 1.

VECTOR BOSONS These include the photon, but there are also others. The *positive and negative W particles* and the *neutral Z particle* were predicted by the electroweak theory and produced and detected by Carlo Rubbia and co-workers in 1983. They are quite massive (W particles 81,000 MeV and Z particle 93,800 MeV) and have a spin of 1. Two other particles of this class have been predicted but not detected: the *Higgs particle*, a massive particle that helps give mass to the W and Z particles, and the massless *graviton*, which should have the same relation to gravity as the photon does to electromagnetism. Both have a spin of 0.

FERMI AWARDS

The Enrico Fermi Award is given by the U.S. Department of Energy for exceptional scientific and technical achievement in atomic energy. The award is named for Enrico Fermi, the first recipient and the scientist who constructed the first nuclear reactor (called an atomic pile at the time). Since the award is for a lifetime achievement, a specific work is not cited. The Fermi Award includes a prize of $25,000.

Year	Winners	Year	Winners
1954	Enrico Fermi	1974	No award
1955	No award	1975	No award
1956	John von Neumann	1976	William L. Russell
1957	Ernest O. Lawrence	1977	No award
1958	Eugene P. Wigner	1978	Harold M. Agnew and
1959	Glenn T. Seaborg		Wolfgang Panofsky
1960	No award	1979	No award
1961	Hans Bethe	1980	Alvin M. Weinberg and
1962	Edward Teller		Rudolf E. Peiris
1963	J. Robert Oppenheimer	1981	No award
1964	Hyman G. Rickover	1982	W. Bennett Lewis
1965	No award	1983	Herbert Anderson and
1966	Otto Hahn, Lise Meitner, and		Seth Neddermeyer
	Fritz Strassman	1984	Alexander Hollaender and
1967	No award		John Lawrence
1968	John A. Wheeler	1985	Robert R. Wilson and
1969	Walter H. Zinn		Georges Vendryès
1970	Norris E. Bradbury	1986	Norman C. Rasmussen and
1971	Shields Warren and		Marshall N. Rosenbluth
	Stafford L. Warren	1987	Ernest D. Courant and
1972	Manson Benedict		M. Stanley Livingstone
1973	No award	1988	Richard Setlow and
			Victor Weisskopf

NOBEL PRIZES

Physics

1901 Wilhelm C. Rüntgen (Germany) Munich Univ. "in recognition of the extraordinary services he has rendered by the discovery of the remarkable rays subsequently named after him."

1902 Hendrik A. Lorentz (Netherlands) Leyden Univ., and **Pieter Zeeman** (Netherlands) Amsterdam Univ. "in recognition of the extraordinary service they rendered by their researches into the influence of magnetism upon radiation phenomena."

1903 Antoine H. Becquerel (France) Ecole Polytechnique "in recognition of the extraordinary services he has rendered by his discovery of spontaneous radioactivity"; **Pierre Curie** (French) Municipal School of Industrial Physics and Chemistry, and his wife **Marie Curie** (France [born in Poland]) "in recognition of the extraordinary services they have rendered by their joint researches on the radiation phenomena discovered by Professor Henri Becquerel."

1904 Lord Rayleigh (John W. Strutt) (Great Britain) Royal Institution of Great Britain" for his investigations of the densities of the most important gases and for his discovery of argon in connection with these studies."

1905 Philipp E.A. Lenard (Germany) Kiel Univ. "for his work on cathode rays."

1906 Sir Joseph J. Thomson (Great Britain) Cambridge Univ. "in recognition of the great merits of his theoretical and experimental investigations on the conduction of electricity by gases."

1907 Albert A. Michelson (U.S.) Univ. of Chicago "for his optical precision instruments and the spectroscopic and metrological investigations carried out with their aid."

1908 Gabriel Lippmann (France) Sorbonne Univ. "for his method of reproducing colours photographically based on the phenomenon of interference."

1909 Guglielmo Marconi (Italy) Marconi Wireless Telegraph Co., Ltd., and **Carl F. Braun** (Germany) Strasbourg Univ. "in recognition of their contributions to the development of wireless telegraphy."

1910 Johannes D. van der Waals (Netherlands) Amsterdam Univ. "for his work on the equation of state for gases and liquids."

1911 Wilhelm Wien (Germany) Würzburg Univ. "for his discoveries regarding the laws governing the radiation of heat."

1912 Nils G. Dalén (Swedish) Swedish Gas-Accumulator Co. "for his invention of automatic regulators for use in conjunction with gas accumulators for illuminating lighthouses and buoys."

1913 Heike Kamerlingh-Onnes (Netherlands) Leyden Univ. "for his investigations on the properties of matter at low temperatures which led, inter alia, to the production of liquid helium."

1914 Max von Laue (Germany) Frankfurt-am-Main Univ. "for his discovery of the

diffraction of X-rays by crystals."
1915 Sir William Henry Bragg (Great Britain) London Univ., and his son **Sir William Lawrence Bragg** (Great Britain) Victoria Univ. "for their services in the analysis of crystal structure by means of X-rays."
1916 No award.
1917 Charles G. Barkla (Great Britain) Edinburgh Univ. "for his discovery of the characteristic Röntgen radiation of the elements."
1918 Max K.E.L. Planck (Germany) Berlin Univ. "in recognition of the services he rendered to the advancement of Physics by his discovery of energy quanta."
1919 Johannes Stark (Germany) Greifswald Univ. "for his discovery of the Doppler effect in canal rays and the splitting of spectral lines in electric fields."
1920 Charles E. Guillaume (Switzerland) International Bureau of Weights and Measures "in recognition of the service he has rendered to precision measurements in Physics by his discovery of anomalies in nickel steel alloys."
1921 Albert Einstein (Germany) Kaiser-Wilhelm-Institut für Physik (now Max-Planck-Institut) "for his services to Theoretical Physics, and especially for his discovery of the law of the photoelectric effect."
1922 Niels Bohr (Denmark) Copenhagen Univ. "for his services in the investigation of the structure of atoms and the radiation emanating from them."
1923 Robert A. Millikan (U.S.) California Institute of Technology "for his work on the elementary charge of electricity and on the photoelectric effect."
1924 Karl M.G. Siegbahn (Sweden) Uppsala Univ. "for his discoveries and research in the field of X-ray spectroscopy."
1925 James Franck (Germany) Goettingen Univ., and **Gustav Hertz** (Germany) Halle Univ. "for their discovery of the laws of governing the impact of an electron upon an atom."
1926 Jean B. Perrin (France) Sorbonne Univ. "for his work on the discontinuous structure of matter, and especially for his discovery of sedimentation equilibrium."
1927 Arthur H. Compton (U.S.) Univ. of Chicago "for his discovery of the effect named after him"; **Charles T.R. Wilson** (Great Britain) Cambridge Univ. "for his method of making the paths of electrically charged particles visible by condensation of vapour."
1928 Sir Owen W. Richardson (Great Britain) London Univ. "for his work on the thermionic phenomenon and especially for the discovery of the law named after him."
1929 Prince Louis-Victor de Broglie (France) Sorbonne Univ. "for his discovery of the wave nature of electrons."
1930 Sir Chandrasekhara V. Raman (India) Calcutta Univ. "for his work on the scattering of light and for the discovery of the effect named after him."
1931 No award.
1932 Werner Heisenberg (Germany) Leipzig

Univ. "for the creation of quantum mechanics, the application of which, has, inter alia, led to the discovery of the allotropic forms of hydrogen."
1933 Erwin Schrödinger (Austria) Berlin Univ., and **Paul A.M. Dirac** (Great Britain) Cambridge Univ. "for the discovery of new productive forms of atomic theory."
1934 No award.
1935 Sir James Chadwick (Great Britain) Liverpool Univ. "for his discovery of the neutron."
1936 Victor F. Hess (Austria) Innsbruck Univ. "for his discovery of cosmic radiation"; **Carl D. Anderson** (U.S.) California Institute of Technology "for his discovery of the positron."
1937 Clinton J. Davisson (U.S.) Bell Telephone Laboratories, and **Sir George P. Thomson** (Great Britain) London Univ. "for their experimental discovery of the diffraction of electrons by crystals."
1938 Enrico Fermi (Italy) Rome Univ. "for his demonstrations of the existence of new radioactive elements produced by neutron irradiation, and for his related discovery of nuclear reactions brought about by slow neutrons."
1939 Ernest O. Lawrence (U.S.) Univ. of California, Berkeley "for the invention and development of the cyclotron and for results obtained with it, especially with regard to artificial radioactive elements."
1940 No award.
1941 No award.
1942 No award.
1943 Otto Stern (U.S.) Carnegie Institute of Technology (now Carnegie Mellon Univ.) "for his contribution to the development of the molecular ray method and his discovery of the magnetic moment of the proton."
1944 Isidor I. Rabi (U.S.) Columbia Univ. "for his resonance method for recording the magnetic properties of atomic nuclei."
1945 Wolfgang Pauli (Austria) Princeton Univ. "for the discovery of the Exclusion Principle, also called the Pauli Principle."
1946 Percy W. Bridgman (U.S.) Harvard Univ. "for the invention of an apparatus to produce extremely high pressures, and for the discoveries he made therewith in the field of high pressure physics."
1947 Sir Edward V. Appleton (Great Britain) Dept. of Scientific and Industrial Research "for his investigations of the physics of the upper atmosphere, especially for the discovery of the so-called Appleton layer."
1948 Lord Patrick M.S. Blackett (Great Britain) Victoria Univ. "for his development of the Wilson cloud chamber method, and his discoveries therewith in the fields of nuclear physics and cosmic radiation."
1949 Hideki Yukawa (Japan) Kyoto Imperial Univ. and Columbia Univ. "for his prediction of the existence of mesons on the basis of theoretical work on nuclear forces."
1950 Cecil F. Powell (Great Britain) Bristol

Univ. "for his development of the photographic method of studying nuclear processes and his discoveries regarding mesons made with this method."
1951 Sir John D. Cockcroft (Great Britain) Atomic Energy Research Establishment, and **Ernest T.S. Walton** (Ireland) Dublin Univ. "for their pioneer work on the transmutation of atomic nuclei by artificially accelerated atomic particles."
1952 Felix Block (U.S.) Stanford Univ., and **Edward M. Purcell** (U.S.) Harvard Univ. "for their development of new methods for nuclear magnetic precision measurements and discoveries in connection therewith."
1953 Frits (Frederik) Zernike (Netherlands) Groningen Univ. "for his demonstration of the phase contrast method, especially for his invention of the phase contrast microscope."
1954 Max Born (Great Britain) Edinburgh Univ. "for his fundamental research in quantum mechanics, especially for his statistical interpretation of the wavefunction"; **Walther Bothe** (Germany) Heidelberg Univ., Max-Planck-Institut "for the coincidence method and his discoveries made therewith."
1955 Willis E. Lamb (U.S.) Stanford Univ. "for his discoveries concerning the fine structure of the hydrogen spectrum"; **Polykarp Kusch** (U.S.) Columbia Univ. "for his precision determination of the magnetic moment of the electron."
1956 William Shockley (U.S.) Semiconductor Laboratory of Beckman Instruments, Inc., **John Bardeen** (U.S.) Univ. of Illinois, and **Walter H. Brattain** (U.S.) Bell Telephone Laboratories "for their researches on semiconductors and their discovery of the transistor effect."
1957 Chen N. Yang (China) Institute for Advanced Study (Princeton, N.J.), and **Tsung-Dao Lee** (China) Columbia Univ. "for their penetrating investigation of the so-called parity laws which has led to important discoveries regarding the elementary particles."
1958 Pavel A. Cerenkov (USSR) Physics Institute of USSR Academy of Sciences, **Il'ja M. Frank** (USSR) Univ. of Moscow and Physics Institute of USSR Academy of Sciences, and **Igor J. Tamm** (USSR) Univ. of Moscow and Physics Institute of USSR Academy of Sciences "for the discovery and the interpretation of the Cerenkov effect."
1959 Emilio G. Segrè (U.S.) Univ. of California, Berkeley, and **Owen Chamberlain** (U.S.) Univ. of California, Berkeley "for their discovery of the antiproton."
1960 Donald A. Glaser (U.S.) Univ. of California, Berkeley "for the invention of the bubble chamber."
1961 Robert Hofstadter (U.S.) Stanford Univ. "for his pioneering studies of electron scattering in atomic nuclei and for his thereby achieved discoveries concerning the structure of the nucleons"; **Rudolf L. Mössbauer** (Germany) Technische Hoch-

schule (Munich), and California Institute of Technology "for his researches concerning the resonance absorption of gamma radiation and his discovery in this connection of the effect which bears his name."

1962 Lev D. Landau (USSR) Academy of Sciences "for his pioneering theories for condensed matter, especially liquid helium."

1963 Eugene P. Wigner (U.S.) Princeton Univ. "for his contributions to the theory of the atomic nucleus and the elementary particles, particularly through the discovery and application of fundamental symmetry principles"; **Maria Goeppert-Mayer** (U.S.) Univ. of California, La Jolla, and **J. Hans D. Jensen** (Germany) Univ. of Heidelberg "for their discoveries concerning nuclear shell structure."

1964 Charles H. Townes (U.S.) M.I.T., **Nikolai G. Basov** (USSR) Lebedev Institute for Physics, and **Aleksandre M. Prochorov** (USSR) Lebedev Institute for Physics "for fundamental work in the field of quantum electronics, which has led to the construction of oscillators and amplifiers based on the maser-laser-principle."

1965 Sin-Itiro Tomonaga (Japan) Tokyo Univ. of Education, **Julian Schwinger** (U.S.) Harvard Univ., and **Richard Feynman** (U.S.) California Institute of Technology "for their fundamental work in quantum electrodynamics, with deep-ploughing consequences for the physics of elementary particles."

1966 Alfred Kastler (France) Ecole Normale Supérieure, Université de Paris "for the discovery and development of optical methods for studying hertzian resonances in atoms."

1967 Hans A. Bethe (U.S.) Cornell Univ. "for his contributions to the theory of nuclear reactions, especially his discoveries concerning the energy production in stars."

1968 Luis W. Alvarez (U.S.) Univ. of California, Berkeley "for his decisive contributions to elementary particle physics, in particular the discovery of a large number of resonance states, made possible through his development of the technique of using hydrogen bubble chamber and data analysis."

1969 Murray Gell-Mann (U.S.) California Institute of Technology "for his contributions and discoveries concerning the classification of elementary particles and their interactions."

1970 Hannes Alfvén (Sweden) Royal Institute of Technology "for fundamental work and discoveries in magneto-hydrodynamics with fruitful applications in different parts of plasma physics"; **Louis Neel** (France) Univ. of Grenoble "for fundamental work and discoveries concerning antiferromagnetism and ferrimagnetism which have led to important applications in solid state physics."

1971 Dennis Gabor (Great Britain) Imperial College of Science and Technology "for his invention and development of the holographic method."

1972 John Bardeen (U.S.) Univ. of Illinois, **Leon N. Cooper** (U.S.) Brown Univ., and **Robert J. Schrieffer** (U.S.) Univ. of Pennsylvania "for their jointly developed theory of superconductivity, usually called the BCS-theory."

1973 Leo Esaki (Japan) IBM Thomas J. Watson Research Center (Yorktown Heights, N.Y.), and **Ivar Giaever** (U.S.) General Electric Co. "for their experimental discoveries regarding tunneling phenomena in semiconductors and superconductors, respectively"; **Brian D. Josephson** (Great Britain) Cambridge Univ. "for his theoretical predictions of the properties of a supercurrent through a tunnel barrier, in particular those phenomena which are generally known as the Josephson effects."

1974 Sir Martin Ryle (Great Britain) Cambridge Univ., and **Antony Hewish** (Great Britain) Cambridge Univ. "for their pioneering research in radio astrophysics: Ryle for his observations and inventions, in particular of the aperture synthesis technique, and Hewish for his decisive role in the discovery of pulsars."

> *"The most incomprehensible thing about the world is that it is comprehensible."*
> —Albert Einstein

1975 Aage Bohr (Denmark) Niels Bohr Institute, **Ben Mottelson** (Denmark) Nordita, and **James Rainwater** (U.S.) Columbia Univ. "for the discovery of the connection between collective motion and particle motion in atomic nuclei and the development of the theory of the structure of the atomic nucleus based on this connection."

1976 Burton Richter (U.S.) Stanford Linear Accelerator Center, and **Samuel C.C. Ting** (U.S.) M.I.T. "for their pioneering work in the discovery of a heavy elementary particle of a new kind."

1977 Philip W. Anderson (U.S.) Bell Laboratories, **Sir Nevill F. Mott** (Great Britain) Cambridge Univ., and **John H. van Vleck** (U.S.) Harvard Univ. "for their fundamental theoretical investigations of the electronic structure of magnetic and disordered systems."

1978 Peter L. Kapitsa (USSR) Academy of Sciences "for his basic inventions and discoveries in the area of low-temperature physics; **Arno A. Penzias** (U.S.) Bell Laboratories, and **Robert W. Wilson**(U.S.) Bell Laboratories "for their discovery of cosmic microwave background radiation."

1979 Sheldon L. Glashow (U.S.) Lyman Lab-

oratory, Harvard Univ., **Abdus Salam** (Pakistan) International Centre for Theoretical Physics (Trieste), and Imperial College of Science and Technology, (London), and **Steven Weinberg** (U.S.) Harvard Univ. "for their contributions to the theory of the unified weak and electromagnetic interaction between elementary particles, including, inter alia, the prediction of the weak neutral current."

1980 James W. Cronin (U.S.) Univ. of Chicago, and **Val L. Fitch** (U.S.) Princeton Univ. "for the discovery of violations of fundamental symmetry principles in the decay of neutral K-mesons."

1981 Nicolaas Bloembergen (U.S.) Harvard Univ., and **Arthur L. Schawlow** (U.S.) Stanford Univ. "for their contributions to the development of laser spectroscopy"; **Kai M. Siegbahn** (Sweden) Uppsala Univ. "for his contribution to the development of high-resolution electron spectroscopy."

1982 Kenneth G. Wilson (U.S.) Cornell Univ. "for his theory for critical phenomena in connection with phase transitions."

1983 Subrahmanyan Chandrasekhar (U.S.) Univ. of Chicago "for his theoretical studies of the physical processes of importance to the structure and evolution of the stars"; **William A. Fowler** (U.S.) California Institute of Technology "for his theoretical and experimental studies of the nuclear reactions of importance in the formation of the chemical elements in the universe."

1984 Carlo Rubbia (Italy) CERN, Geneva, and **Simon van der Meer** (Netherlands) CERN, Geneva "for their decisive contributions to the large project, which led to the discovery of the field particles W and Z, communicators of weak interaction."

1985 Klaus von Klitzing (W. Germany) Max-Planck-Institut for Solid State Research "for the discovery of the quantized Hall effect."

1986 Ernst Ruska (W. Germany) Fritz-Haber-Institut der Max-Planck-Gesellschaft "for his fundamental work in electron optics, and for the design of the first electron microscope"; **Gerd Binnig** (W. Germany) IBM Zurich Research Laboratory, and **Heinrich Rohrer** (Switzerland) IBM Zurich Research Laboratory "for their design of the scanning tunneling microscope."

1987 Georg J. Bednorz (Switzerland) IBM Zurich Research Laboratory, and **Dr. K. Alex Müller** (Switzerland) IBM Zurich Research Laboratory "for the discovery of new superconducting materials."

1988 Leon M. Lederman (U.S.) Fermi National Accelerator Laboratory, **Melvin Schwartz** (U.S.) Digital Pathways, Inc., and **Jack Steinberger** (Switzerland) CERN "for the neutrino beam method and the demonstration of the doublet structure of the leptons through the discovery of the muon neutrino."

Source: *Nobel Foundation Directory* (1987–88); Mission of Sweden.

TECHNOLOGY

In our modern world, most technological advances are closely related to and driven by science. The inventors of better ways to chip flint or forge iron were not scientists. Even Thomas Alva Edison, perhaps the greatest single contributor to modern technology, made only one scientific discovery (the Edison effect, an electric current produced when a hot wire is near a conductor in a vacuum). Instead, Edison was an inventor. The list of major discoveries in technology is essentially a list of inventions.

Since the Industrial Revolution in the late 18th century, the pace of invention has increased. This is shown dramatically by the rise in the number of U.S. patents issued. At the same time, there are fewer lone inventors—in fact, Edison himself was only a lone inventor in the beginning, for he pioneered the idea of a large group of people working together on new inventions. The creations of the lone inventor gradually have been overtaken by inventions patented by corporations. As technology has become a worldwide mainstay of business, the number of foreign patents issued to corporations has surpassed those obtained by U.S. corporations.

Although the lone inventor is to some degree gone, he or she is not forgotten by the U.S. Patent Office, which maintains the Inventor's Hall of Fame.

MAJOR DISCOVERIES IN THE HISTORY OF TECHNOLOGY

(See also "Chronology of Information Processing" in "The Computer.")

B.C.

2,400,000 Ancestors of human beings begin to manufacture stone tools.

750,000 Ancestors of human beings learn to control fire.

23,000 Bow and arrow developed in Mediterranean regions of Europe and Africa.

7000 People in Asia Minor begin to make pottery and cloth.

5000 Egyptians start mining and smelting copper ore.

3500 Potter's wheel and (shortly after) wheeled vehicles appear in Mesopotamia.

2900 Great Pyramid of Giza and first form of Stonehenge (having only three stones) are built.

2000 Interior bathrooms are built in palaces in Crete.

522 Eupalinus of Megara constructs 3,600-ft. tunnel on Greek isle of Samos to supply water from one side of Mt. Castro to other.

290 Pharos lighthouse at Alexandria is built.

260 Archimedes (Greek: c. 287–212 B.C.) develops mathematical descriptions of the lever and other simple machines.

200 Romans develop concrete.

140 Chinese start making paper but do not use it for writing.

100 In Ilyria (now Yugoslavia and Albania), water-powered mills are introduced.

A.D.

1 Approximately when Chinese invent the ship's rudder.

190 Chinese develop porcelain.

600 First windmills are built in what is now Iran.

704 Between 704 and 751, Chinese start printing with woodblocks.

1040 Chinese develop gunpowder.

1041 Between 1041 and 1048, Chinese inventor Pi Sheng invents movable type.

1070 Chinese begin to use the magnetic compass for navigation.

1190 First-known reference to a compass, in Europe.

1267 Book written by Roger Bacon (English, c. 1220–92) in 1267 mentions eyeglasses to correct farsightedness.

1288 First-known gun, a small cannon, is made in China.

1310 Mechanical clocks driven by weights begin to appear in Europe.

1440 Johannes Gutenberg (German, c. 1398–1468) reinvents printing with movable type about this time.

1450 Nicholas Krebs (Nicholas of Cusa; German, 1401–64) develops eyeglasses for the nearsighted.

1555 Georg Bauer (Georgius Agricola; German, 1494–1555) writes *De re metallica*, a handbook of mining techniques.

1590 Approximatly when the compound microscope (using two lenses) is invented in Holland, probably by Zacharias Janssen (Dutch, 1580–c. 1638).

1608 Telescope developed in Holland, probably by Hans Lippershey (German-Dutch, c. 1570–1619).

1620 Cornelius Drebbel (Dutch, 1572–1633) builds first navigable submarine.

1642 Blaise Pascal (French, 1623–62) invents first adding machine.

1643 Evangelista Torricelli (Italian, 1608–47) makes first barometer, producing in the process first vacuum known to science.

1654 Christiaan Huygens (Dutch: 1629–95) develops pendulum clock.

1658 Robert Hooke (English: 1635–1703) invents balance spring for watches.

1671 Gottfried Wilhelm Leibniz (German: 1646–1716) builds a calculating machine that can multiply and divide as well as add and subtract.

1698 Thomas Savery (English: c. 1650–1715) patents the "Miner's Friend," the first practical steam engine.

1701 Jethro Tull (English: 1674–1741), possibly inspired by Chinese devices, invents device for planting seeds called a seed drill.

1709 Daniel Gabriel Fahrenheit (German-Dutch: 1686–1736) develops first accurate thermometer.

1733 John Kay (English: 1704–64) invents flying-shuttle loom, which, along with the steam engine and improvements in making iron, is a key to the start of Industrial Revolution.

1751 Benjamin Huntsman (English: 1704–76) invents crucible process for casting steel.

1761 A clock (called marine chronometer) built by John Harrison (English: 1693–1776) is shown to be accurate within seconds over long sea voyage, making modern navigation possible.

1764 James Hargreaves (English, 1720–78) introduces spinning jenny, a machine that spins from 8 to 120 threads at once.

1765 James Watt (Scottish: 1736–1818) builds model of his improved steam engine.

1769 Richard Arkwright (English: 1732–92) patents the water frame, a spinning machine that complements spinning jenny.

1783 Joseph-Michel Montgolfier (French: 1740–1810) and his brother Jacques-Etienne (1745–99) develop first hot-air balloon. Jacques Charles (French, 1746–1823) builds first hydrogen balloon.

1785 Edmund Cartwright (English: 1743–1823) invents first form of the power loom.

1792 William Murdock (Scottish: 1754–1839) is first to use coal gas for lighting.

1793 Eli Whitney (American: 1765–1825) invents cotton gin, a machine for separating cotton fibers from seeds.

1800 Alessandro Volta (Italian: 1745–1827) invents first form of the chemical battery for producing electric current.

1804 Nicolas Appert (French: c. 1750–1841) develops canning as means of preserving food.

1807 Robert Fulton (American: 1765–1815) introduces first commercially successful steamboat.

1816 David Brewster (Scottish: 1781–1868) invents kaleidoscope.

1822 Joseph Niepce (French: 1765–1833) produces earliest form of the photograph.

1823 Charles Macintosh (Scottish: 1766–1843) patents a waterproof fabric.

1825 George Stephenson (English: 1781–1848) develops first steam-powered locomotive to carry both passengers and freight.

1835 William Henry Fox Talbot (English: 1800–77) invents photographic negative using silver chloride, essentially how black-and-white pictures are made today.

1837 Samuel Finley Breese Morse (American: 1791–1872) patents first commercially successful version of the telegraph.

1839 Louis-Jacques Daguerre (French: 1789–1851) announces his process for making photographs, which come to be called daguerreotypes.

Charles Goodyear (American: 1800–60) discovers how to make rubber resistant to heat and cold, a process called vulcanization.

1842 John Bennet Lawes (English: 1814–99) patents manufacture of superphosphate, the first manufactured fertilizer.

1846 Elias Howe (American: 1819–67) patents lock-stitch sewing machine.

Richard March Hoe (American: 1812–96) invents rotary printing press.

1851 Isaac Merritt Singer (American: 1811–75) patents continuous-stitch sewing machine.

1852 Elisha Graves Otis (American: 1811–61) installs first modern elevator, incorporating his safety device that automatically prevents cage from falling if the cable breaks.

1856 Henry Bessemer (English: 1813–98) develops way of making inexpensive steel, now known as Bessemer process.

1859 Edwin Drake (American: 1819–80) drills first oil well, in Titusville, Pa.

1862 Richard Jordan Gatling (American: 1818–1903) invents first form of machine gun.

1865 Joseph Lister (English: 1827–1912) discovers use of antiseptics in surgery.

1866 Robert Whitehead (English: 1823–1905) invents naval torpedo.

Georges Leclanché (French: 1839–82) develops first form of dry cell for producing electricity.

1867 Christopher L. Sholes (American: 1819–90), Carlos Glidden, and Samuel W. Soulé (Americans) invent first practical typewriter.

1869 Hippolyte Mège Mouriés (French: 1817–80) patents margarine.

1874 Joseph Farwell Glidden (American: 1813–1906) invents the kind of barbed wire used today.

1876 Alexander Graham Bell (Scottish-American, 1847–1922) invents telephone.

Karl von Linde (German: 1842–1934) invents first practical refrigerator.

1877 Nikolaus Otto (German, 1832–91) invents type of internal combustion engine still used in most automobiles.

Thomas Alva Edison (American: 1847–1931) invents phonograph, which uses a wax cylinder.

1878 Louis-Marie-Hilaire Bernigaud (French: 1839–1924) develops rayon.

Carl Gustav Patrik de Laval (Swedish: 1845–1913) invents turbine-operated centrifugal cream separator.

1879 Thomas Alva Edison and Joseph Swan (English: 1828–1914) independently discover how to make practical electric lights.

1885 Karl Benz (German: 1844–1929) builds precursor of modern automobile.

Rover Safety Bicycle, built in England, is first bicycle with essentially modern features.

1886 George Westinghouse (American: 1846–1914) invents airbrake for railroad cars.

1888 Emile Berliner (German: 1851–1929) invents phonograph disk.

John Dunlop (Scottish: 1840–1921) patents air-filled tire.

George Eastman (American: 1854–1932) develops first camera using roll film.

1889 Gustave Eiffel (French: 1832–1923) builds his famous tower in Paris; at 993 ft. it is tallest freestanding structure of the time.

1893 Rudolf Diesel (German: 1858–1913) describes diesel engine.

1895 First public showing of a motion picture, in Paris (Edison's *Great Train Robbery* was not produced until 1903).

Guglielmo Marconi (Italian: 1874–1937) transmits signals for a mile with his wireless telegraph (a precursor of radio) near Bologna, Italy.

1897 Karl Ferdinand Braun (German: 1850–1918) invents cathode-ray tube oscilloscope.

1898 Valdemar Poulsen (Danish: 1869–1942) invents magnetic wire recorder, the precursor to the modern tape recorder.

1902 Willis H. Carrier (American: 1876–1950) invents air conditioning.

1903 Orville Wright (American: 1871–1948) and his brother Wilbur (1867–1912) fly the first successful airplane at Kitty Hawk, N.C.

1904 John Fleming (English: 1849–1945) develops first vacuum tube, a device for changing alternating current to direct.

1907 Lee De Forest (American: 1873–1961) patents Audion vacuum tube, a device for magnifying weak electronic signals.

1908 Henry Ford (American: 1863–1947) introduces Model T, the first affordable automobile.

1909 Leo Baekeland (Belgian-American: 1863–1944) patents Bakelite, the first truly successful plastic.

1912 Reginald Aubrey Fessenden (Canadian-American: 1866–1932) develops heterodyne circuit, an important improvement in radio reception.

1917 Clarence Birdseye (American: 1886–1956) develops freezing as a means of preserving food.

1924 Vladimir Kosma Zworykin (Russian-American: 1889–1982) develops iconoscope, the beginning of modern television.

1928 Alexander Fleming (Scottish: 1881–1955) discovers penicillin.

1929 Robert Goddard (American: 1882–1945) launches first instrumented, liquid-fueled rocket.

1930 Frank Whittle (British: 1907–) patents jet engine.

1931 Ernst Ruska (German: 1906–) builds first electron microscope.

1934 Wallace Hume Carothers (American: 1896–1937) invents nylon, first marketed in 1938.

1935 Robert Alexander Watson-Watt (Scottish, 1892–1973) has idea that, over next three years, he develops into radar.

1937 Chester Carlson (American: 1906–68) invents xerography, the first method of photocopying.

1939 Paul Müller (Swiss: 1899–1965) discovers that DDT is potent and long-lasting insecticide.

Igor Sikorsky (Russian-American: 1889–1972) designs and flies first helicopter developed for mass production.

1940 Peter Carl Goldmark (Hungarian-American: 1906–77) develops and demonstrates first successful color television system.

1941 John Rex Whinfield (English: 1901–66) invents Dacron.

1942 Enrico Fermi (Italian-American: 1901–54) builds first nuclear reactor.

1947 Dennis Gabor (Hungarian-British: 1900–79) develops holography, which becomes much more important after the invention of the laser in 1960.

1948 William Shockley (English-American: 1910–), Walter Brattain (American: 1902–87), and John Bardeen (American: 1908–) invent transistor.

Peter Carl Goldmark develops the 33⅓ rpm long-playing phonograph record.

1957 Gordon Gould (American: 1920–) develops basic idea for the laser, which he succeeds in patenting in 1986 after long struggle.

THE NATIONAL INVENTORS HALL OF FAME

In 1973 the U.S. Patent Office began the practice of naming certain American and foreign inventors with U.S. patents to the National Inventors Hall of Fame. Although many of those honored have many patents, the committee selects one for each inventor as the occasion for the award, which they identify by the title of the original patent application. The date at the end of each of the following entries denotes the year of induction.

Ernst Alexanderson

(Swedish-American: 1881?–1975)

HIGH FREQUENCY ALTERNATOR This is the basic device that makes it possible for radio (and television) to transmit voices and music, not just dots and dashes. Alexanderson was also a pioneer in television and many other kinds of electrical equipment, receiving 322 patents. (1983)

Andrew Alford
(Russian-American, 1904-)
LOCALIZER ANTENNA SYSTEM With this and other inventions, Alford developed the radio system for navigation as well as instrument landing systems for airplanes. (1983)

Luis Walter Alvarez
(American: 1911-88)
RADIO DISTANCE AND DIRECTION INDICATOR Despite his citation, Alvarez is far better known as the developer of specialized equipment for studying subatomic particles (which led to his 1968 Nobel Prize) and as the proponent—along with his son—of the theory that the dinosaurs became extinct as the result of the impact of a massive body on Earth 65 million years ago. (1978)

Edwin Howard Armstrong
(American: 1890-1954)
METHOD OF RECEIVING HIGH FREQUENCY OS-CILLATIONS Armstrong's several inventions connected with radio broadcasting and reception made him rich and created the "radio days" of the 1920s through the 1940s. In 1939 he invented FM broadcasting and reception, which helped lead to another revolution in radio. (1980)

Leo Hendrik Baekeland
(Belgian-American: 1863-1944)
SYNTHETIC RESINS Baekeland's plastic (synthetic resin) that he named Bakelite was not the first plastic to be manufactured (that was celluloid), but it was the first to make people realize the potential of plastics in general. Baekeland also developed the first commercially successful photographic paper. (1978)

John Bardeen
(American: 1908-)
TRANSISTOR Invented by Bardeen, William Shockley, and Walter Brattain (all of whom are in the Hall of Fame), the transistor is the essential semiconductor device used on microprocessors and other chips. (1974)

Arnold O. Beckman
(American: 1900-)
APPARATUS FOR TESTING ACIDITY Although there are many simple ways to tell how acid a substance is, a precise measuring instrument developed by Beckman became the foundation of a leading company in the scientific instrument field today. Beckman's other inventions of precision instruments also contributed to the company's growth. (1987)

Alexander Graham Bell
(Scottish-American, 1874-1922)
TELEGRAPHY Despite the title of this patent, the invention here was the telephone. Another important Bell invention was the disk phonograph. (1974)

Harold Stephen Black
(American: 1898-)
NEGATIVE FEEDBACK AMPLIFIER The basic principle of the negative feedback amplifier, the feedback of information to control a process, has become fundamental to many other devices since Black's first use of it to control distortion.

Black also invented pulse-code modulation, which remains an important concept in communications. (1981)

Walter H. Brattain
(American: 1902-87)
TRANSISTOR (see John Bardeen.)

Luther Burbank
(American: 1849-1926)
PEACH Burbank holds 16 plant patents, all of which were issued posthumously. His work in developing more than 800 new varieties of plants was in part responsible for the development of the Plant Patent program, which began in 1930. (1986)

William Seward Burroughs
(American: 1857-98)
CALCULATING MACHINE Although a calculating machine had been built as early as 1623 (and others, such as Pascal's significant advance in 1642, had followed), Burroughs was the first to develop a practical device that could be mass produced and easily used. (1987)

William Meriam Burton
(American: 1865-1954)
MANUFACTURE OF GASOLINE The highlight of Burton's years in the oil business came when he developed the first commercially successful cracking process, a method that yields twice the amount of gasoline from crude oil that previous methods had. (1984)

Marvin Camras
(American: 1916-)
METHOD AND MEANS OF MAGNETIC RECORDING Before the tapes currently used to record sound and pictures, sound was recorded on the wire recorder that Camras invented in the 1930s. He went on to develop over 500 inventions, most connected with improvements in recording methods. (1985)

Chester F. Carlson
(American: 1906-68)
ELECTROPHOTOGRAPHY Carlson invented the dry copying method used in most offices today, which he named xerography. Although first patented in 1940, the dry copier did not reach the market until 1958, by which time Carlson had many patents on improvements in the process. (1981)

Wallace Hume Carothers
(American: 1896-1937)
DIAMINE-DICARBOXYLIC ACID SALTS AND PROCESS OF PREPARING SAME AND SYNTHETIC FIBER Despite the formidable title of his patent, Carothers's invention of nylon contributed an important fiber to the world; he also developed the first commercially successful synthetic rubber. (1984)

Willis Haviland Carrier
(American: 1876-1950)
APPARATUS FOR TREATING AIR Not only did Carrier invent the first really workable air-conditioning system, but he also invented many of the techniques used in modern refrigerators. (1985)

Frank B. Colton
(Polish-American: 1923-)
ORAL CONTRACEPTIVES Colton not only developed the first "pill" in 1960, but he also pioneered the development of anabolic steroids. (1988)

NUMBER OF PATENTS ISSUED FOR INVENTIONS BY DECADE, 1790-1980

Period	Patents issued
1790–1800	309
1801–10	1,093
1811–20	1,930
1821–30	3,086
1831–40	5,519
1841–50	5,933
1851–60	23,065
1861–70	79,459
1871–80	125,438
1881–90	207,514
1891–1900	220,608
1901–10	315,193
1911–20	383,117
1921–30	423,089
1931–40	439,863
1941–50	308,436
1951–60	430,120
1961–70	585,115
1971–80	687,800[1]
1981–88	551,300[1]

Note: Excludes patents granted for designs and botanical plants. 1. Numbers rounded in source. **Sources:** U.S. Bureau of the Census, *The Statistical History of the United States* (1976) and *Statistical Abstract of the United States 1989* (1989).

William D. Coolidge
(American: 1873-1974)
VACUUM TUBE The "Coolidge tube" is actually an X-ray generator. Among his many other inventions was the modern tungsten-filament electric light. (1975)

Raymond V. Damadian
(American: 1936-)
APPARATUS AND METHOD FOR DETECTING CANCER IN TISSUE Damadian was the first to realize that the nuclear magnetic resonance technique could be used on living creatures (it was already a success as a laboratory tool used by chemists) and that it could detect cancer cells. (1989)

John Deere
(1804-86)
PLOW Anyone who grew up near a farm knows the name John Deere. His vastly improved plow was the start of his commercial success, and the company he founded still makes farm tools. (1989)

Lee De Forest
(American: 1873-1961)
AUDION AMPLIFIER Although he eventually acquired more than 300 patents related to radio, De Forest's invention of the triode was the key to modern radio and later developments in the amplification of signals. (1977)

Rudolf Diesel
(German: 1858-1913)
INTERNAL COMBUSTION ENGINE The pressure-ignited heat engine is still called the diesel engine. (1976)

Carl Djerassi
(Austrian-American: 1923-)
ORAL CONTRACEPTIVES Djerassi has been a major influence on modern organic chemistry; his work on the chemistry of steroids and his

NUMBER OF PATENTS GRANTED FOR INVENTIONS BY PATENTEE, SELECTED YEARS, 1901–88

Year	Total number granted	Indi- viduals	Corporations U.S.	Corporations Foreign	U.S. Gov- ernment[1]
1901	25,546	20,896	4,370	280	N.A.
1921	37,798	27,098	9,860	840	N.A.
1930	45,226	23,726	19,700	1,800	N.A.
1940	42,238	17,627	22,165	2,406	40
1950	43,040	18,960	21,782	1,660	622
1960	47,170	13,069	28,187	4,670	1,244
1965	62,857	16,063	37,158	8,096	1,540
1970	64,427	13,511	36,896	12,294	1,726
1980[2]	61,800	13,300	29,400	18,200	1,232
1985[2]	71,700	12,900	31,300	26,400	1,125
1987[2]	83,000	15,300	33,800	32,900	975
1988	77,900	14,300	31,400	31,450	728

1. Excludes patents issued to Alien Property Custodian until 1942.
2. Figures rounded in source. **Sources:** U.S. Bureau of the Census, *The Statistical History of the United States* (1976) and *Statistical Abstract of the United States 1989* (1989).

synthesis of antihistamines are only two of his many contributions. (1978)

Herbert Henry Dow
(Canadian-American: 1866–1930)
BROMINE Besides new methods of extracting bromine and chlorine from naturally occurring salt deposits, Dow patented over 90 inventions and founded the Dow Chemical Company. (1983)

Charles Stark Draper
(American: 1901–87)
GYROSCOPIC EQUIPMENT Draper's gyroscopic stabilizer helped both antiaircraft guns and falling bombs hit their targets during World War II. Later he developed gyroscopic systems for air and marine navigation and for guided missiles. (1983)

George Eastman
(American: 1854–1932)
METHOD AND APPARATUS FOR COATING PLATES FOR USE IN PHOTOGRAPHY Eastman developed the dry plate negative, as well as the means of preparing these plates commercially. He also invented the transparent roll film that was the basis of the first Kodak box camera and a stronger motion picture film for use in the newly invented cinema. (1977)

Harold E. Edgerton
(American: 1903–)
STROBOSCOPE Edgerton created the special device called the stroboscope to produce flashes that would stop action in a photograph at regular intervals. (His classic photograph of the crown produced by a drop of milk falling into a bowl of milk dates from the 1930s.) Edgerton also contributed inventions to underwater photography. (1986)

Thomas Alva Edison
(American: 1847–1931)
ELECTRIC LAMP In addition to the carbon-filament electric lamp, Edison patented a phonograph, the mimeograph, the fluoroscope, and motion picture cameras and projectors. (1973)

Philo Taylor Farnsworth
(American: 1906–71)
TELEVISION SYSTEM Farnsworth patented many of the components of all-electronic television. Crude pictures had been transmitted previously, but the most common system relied on spinning mirrors. He also was a pioneer with regard to the electronic microscope, radar, the use of ultraviolet light for seeing in the dark, and nuclear fusion. (1984)

Enrico Fermi
(Italian-American: 1901–54)
NEUTRONIC REACTOR Fermi's nuclear reactor is the basis of nuclear power today. His many contributions to modern physics include basic theoretical work as well as experimental physics. (1976)

Henry Ford
(American: 1863–1947)
TRANSMISSION MECHANISM Many of Ford's "inventions" that revolutionized society, such as the automobile assembly line, the vertical integration of manufacturing, inexpensive automobiles, and the $5–a–day wage (in 1914), were not patentable. Ford did, however, invent and patent numerous mechanisms used in automobiles. (1982)

Jay W. Forrester
(American: 1918–)
MULTICOORDINATED DIGITAL INFORMATION STORAGE DEVICE A pioneer in the development of electronic computers after World War II, Forrester's main invention was the magnetic storage of information. Most computers today, from giant mainframes to lightweight laptops, still use magnetic storage to store data even when the computer has been shut off. (1979)

Robert Hutchings Goddard
(American: 1882–1945)
CONTROL MECHANISM FOR ROCKET APPARATUS The father of American rocketry, Goddard's experiments with liquid-fueled rockets between the two world wars were often derided. During both wars, however, the military accepted his help, and he devised successful rocket weapons and rocket-assisted take-off mechanisms for carrier-based airplanes. He obtained 214 patents on various aspects of rocketry. (1979)

Charles Goodyear
(American: 1800–60)
IMPROVEMENT IN INDIA-RUBBER FABRICS In 1844 Goodyear was working on ways of making rubber resistant to heat and cold, when he accidentally dropped rubber mixed with sulfur on a hot stove. The result, which Goodyear named vulcanized rubber, was what he had been seeking. Although Goodyear patented vulcanization and other ways to improve rubber, his patents were constantly infringed upon and he died poor. (1976)

Wilson Greatbatch
(American: 1919–)
MEDICAL CARDIAC PACEMAKER Greatbatch's pacemaker has helped millions of people with heart disease. He is also the inventor and manufacturer of batteries that can be implanted along with the pacemaker to keep the machinery running without adverse physical effects from the battery chemicals. (1986)

Charles Martin Hall
(American: 1863–1914)
MANUFACTURE OF ALUMINUM After a college chemistry teacher remarked that discovering a way to make cheap aluminum (then selling at 5 dollars a pound) would make a person rich and famous, Hall set himself to the task. In only eight months, he found the method and indeed became rich and famous. That same year, French metallurgist Paul-Louis-Toussaint Héroult discovered the same process. Patent litigation between the two independent discoverers was eventually resolved amicably. (1976)

René Alphonse Higonnet
(French: 1902–83)
PHOTO COMPOSING MACHINE Along with Louis Marius Moyroud, Higonnet developed (in 1946) the first machine to set type by recording the images of letters on film. Film composition became the standard way of setting type, replacing type set from metal, for the next 40 years, after which it was replaced by electronic composition. (1985)

James Hillier
(Canadian-American: 1915–)
ELECTRON LENS CORRECTION DEVICE Although Hillier was not the first to make a microscope using electrons, his microscopes became the standard in the field. Electron microscopes can enlarge much smaller details than light microscopes because the wavelength of an electron is much smaller than the wavelength of a photon of visible light. (1980)

Charles Franklin Kettering
(American: 1875–1958)
ENGINE STARTING DEVICES AND IGNITION SYSTEM Kettering's first invention was the electric cash register while he was with National Cash Register. Later, his Delco company produced the self-starter for automobiles and the first small generator for use in isolated farms before rural electrification. After he sold Delco to General Motors, Kettering continued to run a research laboratory. In addition to automobile-related inventions, Kettering's laboratory developed diesel locomotive engines. (1980)

Jack S. Kilby
(American: 1923–)
MINIATURIZED ELECTRONIC CIRCUITS A number of people worked on putting many transistors and other solid-state electronic devices on a single chip, but the monolithic integrated circuit that Kilby developed for Texas Instruments in 1959 was the beginning of the modern integrated circuit. (1982)

Willem J. Kolff
(Dutch-American: 1911–)
SOFT SHELL MUSHROOM SHAPED HEART Although the patent cited is for an early version of an artificial heart, Kolff's most important work was the development of the artificial-kidney dialysis machine. (1985)

Edwin Herbert Land
(American: 1909–)
PHOTOGRAPHIC PRODUCT COMPRISING A RUPTURABLE CONTAINER CARRYING A PHOTOGRAPHIC PROCESSING LIQUID Land's first success was not the instant camera for which he became world famous, but the development and application of substances that polarize light. He also

made important contributions to the theory of color vision. (1977)

Irving Langmuir
(American: 1881–1957)
INCANDESCENT ELECTRIC LAMP The original Edison-Swan light bulbs relied on a vacuum to keep the filament from burning too fast, but Langmuir realized in 1913 that filling the bulb with a nonburning gas would result in a longer-lasting light. He also made many basic scientific discoveries, including work with the chemistry of surfaces that won him a Nobel Prize in 1932. (1989)

Ernest Orlando Lawrence
(American: 1901–58)
METHOD AND APPARATUS FOR THE ACCELERATION OF IONS Although Lawrence did not develop the very first particle accelerator (popularly known as an "atom smasher"), his 1930 cyclotron has been the basic pattern for the most successful and powerful machines of its kind ever since. (1982)

Theodore Harold Maiman
(American: 1927–)
RUBY LASER SYSTEMS Although there has been much dispute about the invention of the laser, Maiman's ruby laser was the first to be recognized worldwide and to be commercially successful. (1984)

Guglielmo Marconi
(Italian: 1874–1937)
TRANSMITTING ELECTRICAL SIGNALS Marconi's patent was for using radio waves to carry coded messages—also known as wireless telegraphy. (1975)

Cyrus McCormick
(American: 1809–84)
REAPER McCormick developed his machine for harvesting grain in 1831 and patented it in 1834. By 1847 his factory was turning out the machines that would help revolutionize American agriculture. (1976)

Ottmar Mergenthaler
(German-American: 1854–99)
MACHINE FOR PRODUCING PRINTING BARS Mergenthaler's invention, known as the Linotype, was the first major improvement in setting type since Gutenberg began using movable type about 1440. This typesetting machine, which is controlled by a keyboard, casts individual lines of type from melted lead. Versions of the Linotype are still in use, though most typesetting today is done by photographic or electronic processes. (1982)

Samuel F.B. Morse
(American: 1791–1872)
TELEGRAPH SIGNALS Morse developed the first commercially successful telegraph. Joseph Henry was the genius behind the electronics, but Morse and his dot-dash code made instantaneous long-distance communications possible. (1975)

Andrew J. Moyer
(American: 1899–1959)
METHOD FOR PRODUCTION OF PENICILLIN Moyer, a microbiologist at the U.S. Department of Agriculture's Northern Regional Research Laboratory in Peoria, Illinois, developed a way of producing penicillin in bulk during World War II. The basic method is still used today in the manufacture of many antibiotics and other substances produced by microorganisms. (1987)

Louis Marius Moyroud
(French: 1914–)
PHOTO COMPOSING MACHINE (See "René Alphonse Higonnet.")

Robert N. Noyce
(American: 1927–)
SEMICONDUCTOR DEVICE-AND-LEAD STRUCTURE Noyce has been at the center of development for two important semiconductor producers, the Fairchild and Intel Corporations, both of which he helped found. Intel today makes the most widely used microprocessor chips for personal computers, those at the heart of various IBM models and their clones. (1983)

Elisha Graves Otis
(American: 1811–61)
IMPROVEMENT IN HOISTING APPARATUS Modern skyscrapers would have been impossible without the safety elevator that Otis devised in 1853, when his employer asked him to build a hoist to lift heavy equipment. Eight years later the first Otis passenger elevators were being installed. (1988)

Nikolaus August Otto
(German: 1832–91)
GAS MOTOR ENGINE While Otto's four-stroke engine of 1876 is the basis of the modern internal combustion engine, it ran on compressed natural gas instead of gasoline (a development pioneered by Gottlieb Daimler and Wilhelm Maybach in 1889). (1981)

Louis W. Parker
(Hungarian-American: 1906–)
TELEVISION RECEIVER Parker not only invented the basic type of television receiver in common use today, but also the type of color television transmission and reception that is most commonly used. (1988)

Louis Pasteur
(French: 1822–95)
BREWING OF BEER AND ALE Pasteur is not usually thought of as an inventor (and his work on beer and ale is generally considered unsuccessful). But he did invent several vaccines, and he developed pasteurization, the heating process that protects beverages and food from microbe contamination. (1978)

Charles J. Plank
(American: 1915–)
CATALYTIC CRACKING OF HYDROCARBONS WITH A CRYSTALLINE ZEOLITE CATALYST COMPOSITE Along with Edward J. Rosinski, Plank discovered in the early 1960s that zeolites (various aluminum silicates, a fairly common kind of mineral) could be used to improve the production of gasoline and other petroleum products. (1979)

Roy J. Plunkett
(American, 1910–)
TETRAFLUOROETHYLENE POLYMERS In 1938 Plunkett discovered the tetrafluoroethylene polymer known as Teflon. He later developed many of the hydrofluorocarbons (Freons) that have since been found to be eroding the atmosphere's protective layer of ozone. (1985)

Edward J. Rosinski
(American: 1921–)
CATALYTIC CRACKING OF HYDROCARBONS WITH A CRYSTALLINE ZEOLITE CATALYST COMPOSITE (See "Charles J. Plank.")

Lewis Hastings Sarett
(American: 1917–)
THE PROCESS OF TREATING PREGNENE COMPOUNDS In 1944 Sarett found a way to produce cortisone as an artificial steroid from its predecessor chemicals, known as pregnene compounds. By 1949 he and his collaborators had learned to make cortisone from simple inorganic chemicals. Cortisone and related steroids are widely used for the medical treatment of conditions ranging from psoriasis to arthritis. (1980)

William Bradford Shockley
(English-American: 1910–89)
TRANSISTOR (See "John Bardeen.")

Igor I. Sikorsky
(Russian-American, 1889–1972)
HELICOPTER CONTROLS Sikorsky designed and built many successful airplanes, but in 1931, he made a critical breakthrough in helicopter design that he had worked on for years. His continued developments essentially produced the helicopter of today. (1987)

Charles Proteus Steinmetz
(German-American: 1865–1923)
SYSTEM OF ELECTRICAL DISTRIBUTION Steinmetz was an important theoretician and inventor whose most significant work was in developing the theory of alternating current that made power grids possible. Among his inventions was a machine that produced "lightning in the laboratory." (1977)

George R. Stibitz
(American: 1904–)
COMPLEX COMPUTER Stibitz was one of several scientists who developed electromechanical computers in the late 1930s and during World War II. His innovations at Bell Telephone Laboratories and in the U.S. Office of Scientific Research and Development include floating decimal arithmetic and taped computer programs. (1983)

Donalee L. Tabern
(American: 1900–74)
THIO-BARBITURIC ACID DERIVATIVES Along with Ernest H. Volwiler, Tabern in 1936 discovered Pentothal, the anesthetic of choice for short surgical procedures and for preceding the administration of general anesthesia. Tabern later introduced the therapeutic use of radioactive chemicals. (1986)

Nikola Tesla
(Croatian-American: 1857–1943)
ELECTRO-MAGNETIC MOTOR Tesla's induction motor was simpler than previous electric motors and was powered by alternating current (AC), which can be distributed more easily over a long distance than direct current (DC). (1975)

Max Tishler
(American: 1906–)
RIBOFLAVIN AND SULFAQUINOXALINE In the late 1930s, Tishler developed an economical method for synthesizing riboflavin, also known as vitamin B[2]. Later he and his coworkers developed a way to produce sulfaquinoxaline (an antibiotic that prevents and cures a disease common in poultry) commercially. (1982)

Charles Hard Townes
(American: 1915–)
MASERS The maser, which preceded the better-known laser, is essentially a laser that

works at microwave wavelengths instead of at the shorter wavelength of visible light. Masers are used in many applications. Townes, who was solely responsible for the maser, also contributed to the development of the laser. (1976)

Ernest H. Volwiler
(American: 1893–)
THIO-BARBITURIC ACID DERIVATIVES (See "Donalee L. Tabern.")

An Wang
(Chinese-American: 1920–)
MAGNETIC PULSE CONTROLLING DEVICE Although best known for his state-of-the-art word processor of the 1960s and 1970s, Wang contributed many fundamental ideas to the development of electronic computers, including the principle on which magnetic core memory is built. (1988)

George Westinghouse
(American: 1846–1914)
STEAM-POWERED BRAKE DEVICES Westinghouse specialized in improving rail transportation at the time of its greatest expansion. In 1869 he patented an air brake for locomotives, his most important contribution to railroad safety. His later work on signals and switches led him to form the Westinghouse Electric Co. in 1884, chiefly to implement the possibilities of alternating current. (1989)

Eli Whitney
(American: 1765–1825)
COTTON GIN By making it possible to remove seeds from cotton mechanically, the gin made large-scale cotton farming possible. Whitney also introduced interchangeable parts, the beginning of mass production. (1974)

Orville Wright
(American: 1871–1948) &
Wilbur Wright
(American: 1867–1912)
FLYING MACHINE Not only did the Wright brothers invent the first airplane, but they also popularized, manufactured, and sold the new machines. For the first few years after their 1903 flight, people took little notice of their work. In 1908, however, Orville demonstrated a one-hour flight. By World War I, airplanes were used regularly by the world's major armed services. (1975)

Vladimir Kosma Zworykin
(Russian-American: 1889–1982)
CATHODE RAY TUBE The cathode ray tube that Zworykin invented in 1928 is the kinescope, the basic picture tube used in modern television. Ten years later he developed the iconoscope, the first practical television camera. His later work on electron microscopes created the type that has been used the most, although it was not the first electron microscope to be developed. (1977)

The Computer

Introduction

A computer is a machine for storing and processing information. It converts any information that it receives into a binary code—a string of signals, in which each signal is either *1* or *0*. The basic working component of a computer is a series of electronic switches, each of which can be set either "off" or "on" and thus represent 1 or 0 in the binary system. The history of computers is, to some extent, a history of the electronic switching devices that have been used to represent 1 and 0. These fall into three main categories: vacuum tubes, transistors, and integrated circuits.

The relative size and power of these three items are so disparate that it is almost impossi-

RECORDS IN TECHNOLOGY

Record	Record holders	Duration, speed, or height
SPACE		
Longest single mission	Vladimir G. Titov Sergei Krikalev Valery Polyakov	365 days, from Dec. 20, 1987, to Dec. 19, 1988, most spent aboard the *Mir* space station
Fastest speed	Thomas Patton Stafford Eugene Andrew Cernan John Watts Young	24,791 mph, on May 26, 1969, in *Apollo 10* command module
Highest flight	Frank Borman James A. Lovell, Jr. William Anders	234,672.5 mi., on Dec. 21–27, 1968, in *Apollo 8* command module
AIR		
Speed in fixed-wing aircraft	William J. Knight	4,520 mph, on Oct. 3, 1967, in X-15A-2 rocket plane
Speed over straight course	Elden W. Joerez George T. Morgan, Jr.	2,193.16 mph, on July 28, 1976, in Lockheed SR-71A
Speed over closed circuit	Adolphus H. Bledsoe, Jr.	2,092.294 mph, on July 27, 1976, in Lockheed SR-71A
Highest flight (airplane)	Alexander Fedotov	123,523.58 ft., on Aug. 31, 1977, in MG-25
Highest flight (balloon)	Malcolm D. Ross	113,739.9 ft., on May 4, 1961, in the Lee Lewis Memorial Winzen Research Balloon
Longest flight	Robert Timm John Cook	64 days, 22 hrs., 19 min., 5 sec., on Dec. 4, 1958, through Feb. 7, 1959, in Cessna 172 (refueled in air)
LAND		
Highest land speed in wheeled vehicle	Stan Barrett	739.666 mph (faster than speed of sound), on Dec. 17, 1979, in *Budweiser Rocket*
Official land speed record for a two-run of 1 mi.	Richard Noble	633.468 mph, on Oct. 4, 1983, in jet-powered *Thrust 2*
Highest speed in stock car	Bill Elliot	212 mph, on Apr. 30, 1987, in Ford Thunderbird
Highest speed in human-powered vehicle	Fred Markham	65.484 mph over 200 mi., on May 12, 1986, on bicycle designed by Gardner Martin
WATER		
Highest speed	Kenneth Peter Warby	319.627 mph, on Nov. 20, 1977, in *Spirit of Australia* hydroplane
Highest speed in propeller-powered craft	Eddie Hill	229.00 mph, on Sep. 5, 1982, in *Texan* hydrodrag boat
Deepest dive	Jacques Piccard Donald Walsh	35,820 ft., on Jan. 23, 1960, in *Trieste* bathyscaphe

ble to compare them; there is no single scale against which they can be measured. In 1946 the ENIAC (Electronic Numerical Integrator and Computer)—which occupied 2,000 square feet, weighed 50 tons, and used 18,000 vacuum tubes—could perform about 3,000 multiplications per second and had an internal memory capacity of 200 decimal digits, or about 20 words. In 1989 a silicon chip measuring a quarter of an inch across can outperform ENIAC by a factor of about one million and has a memory capable of storing 50,000 words.

A GLOSSARY OF COMPUTER TERMS

ASCII (American Standard Code for Information Exchange) Computers work with numbers, not letters. ASCII is the numerical code used by personal computers (*microcomputers*). While many programs also use special codes of their own, data from one computer to another are best transmitted in "pure ASCII."

Baud rate A transmission rate used in sending data from one computer to another, with a baud approximately equal to one *bit* per second. Most *modems* use either 1,200 baud or 2,400 baud. Rates must be the same between modems for data to be transmitted.

Bit In the binary system, a bit is either of the digits *0* or *1*. The bit (for *binary digit*) is the basic unit for storing data, with "off" representing 0 and "on" representing 1.

Buffer Any memory location where data can be stored temporarily while the computer is doing something else; specifically, a memory location in the computer, in a printer, or in a separate storage device (*peripheral*) that stores a file being printed so that the computer is not tied up waiting for the printing to finish.

Bug An error in a *software* program or in the *hardware*.

Byte A group of 8 *bits* that together represent one character, whether alphabetic, numeric, or otherwise. A byte is the smallest accessible unit in a computer's memory.

Cathode ray tube (CRT) The display device, or *monitor*, similar to a television screen, used with most desktop computers (usually referred to by the acronym).

Central processing unit (CPU) The group of circuits that directs the entire computer system by (1) interpreting and executing *program* instruction and (2) coordinating the interaction of input, output, and storage devices.

Chip See "Silicon chip."

CPU See "Central processing unit."

CRT See "Cathode ray tube."

Cursor A marker on the computer display that shows which region of the screen is active.

Database Either a *program* for arranging facts in the computer and retrieving them (the computer equivalent of a filing system) or a *file* set up by such a system. Often databases are central files that can be accessed by a *modem* for a fee.

Desktop publishing The electronic, rather than mechanical, production of books and documents. A combination of *hardware* (laser printers capable of printing a range of type sizes and styles) and *software* (programs such as Aldus's PageMaker and Xerox's Ventura) enables the writer to design, typeset, and print his or her own work.

Disk drive A mechanism for retrieving information stored on a magnetic disk. The drive rotates the disk at high speed and "reads" the data with a magnetic head similar to those used in tape recorders.

Documentation The manual that explains the use of *hardware* or *software*.

File Any group of data treated as a single entity by the computer, such as a word processor document, a *program*, or a *database*.

Floppy disk A thin, flexible magnetic disk encased in a protective jacket. On the surface of the disk are a number of "tracks" on which data may be recorded in the form of magnetic spots.

Hard disk A sealed cartridge containing magnetic storage disk(s) that holds much more memory—typically 20 to 90 *megabytes*—than *floppy disks*. Usually a hard disk is built into the computer, but it can be a *peripheral*.

Hardware The physical equipment, as opposed to the *programs* and procedures, used in data processing. The term covers not only computers themselves but also *peripherals* (see "Software").

Integrated circuit An entire electronic circuit contained on one piece of material. Originally, electronic components (transistors, capacitors, etc.) were placed on a metal chassis and then wired together. The first integrated circuit began with a single board (originally plastic), onto which strips of conducting material were sprayed. Electronic components could then be inserted directly onto the board (see "Silicon chip").

Kilobyte (K) A unit of measurement for storage capacity; equivalent to 1,024 *bytes*, but often rounded to 1,000 (see "Megabyte").

Laptop A portable *microcomputer* small enough to operate in one's lap (for example, on a commuter train or an airplane). Generally a laptop weighs less than 15 pounds and uses a liquid-crystal display rather than a *cathode ray tube*.

Mainframe computer Generally the largest, fastest, and most expensive kind of computer, usually costing millions of dollars and requiring special cooling. Mainframe computers can accommodate hundreds of simultaneous users and normally are run around the clock; typically they are owned by large companies (see "Microcomputer"; "Minicomputer"; "Supercomputer").

Megabyte (M) A unit of measurement for storage capacity equivalent to one million *BYTES*.

Menu-driven A *program* that uses a number of "menus," or lists of possible activities from which the operator chooses in order to activate the appropriate commands. This is the alternative to a command-driven program, for which the operator must remember a number of commands in order to tell the computer what to do.

Microcomputer Generally the smallest and least expensive kind of computer, usually costing hundreds or thousands of dollars and small enough to fit on a desk top. The heart of the microcomputer is the *microprocessor* (see "Mainframe computer"; "Minicomputer").

Microprocessor A complete *Central processing unit* assembled on one, single *silicon chip*.

Minicomputer A small computer, usually used by medium-size or smaller businesses. Minicomputers often perform scientific or industrial tasks, cost tens or hundreds of thousands of dollars, and are housed in large cabinets (see "Mainframe computer"; "Microcomputer").

MIPS (million instructions per second) A measure of computer processing speed.

Modem (*modulator-demodulator*) A device capable of converting a digital (computer-compatible) signal to an analog signal, which can be transmitted via a telephone line, reconverted, and then "read" by another computer.

Monitor The display device on a computer, similar to a television screen.

Mouse A small box connected by cable to a computer and featuring one or more button-style switches. When moved around a desk, the mouse causes a symbol on the computer screen to make corresponding movements. By selecting items on the screen and pressing a button on the mouse, the user can perform certain functions much more quickly than by typing commands on the keyboard.

Operating system A set of *programs* that allows a computer to manage and coordinate its component elements.

Network An interconnected group of computers that can exchange information or work together on different parts of the same problem.

Peripheral A device connected to the computer that provides communication or auxiliary functions. There are three types of peripherals: input devices, such as keyboards; output devices, such as *monitors* and printers; and storage devices, such as magnetic disks.

Personal computer A *microcomputer* used by an individual at home or in the office.

Program As a noun, a prepared set of instructions for the computer, often with provisions for the operator to choose among various options. As a verb, to create such a set of instructions.

Random access memory (RAM) A temporary storage space in which data may be held on a *chip* rather than being stored on disk or tape. The contents of RAM may be accessed or altered at any time during a session, but will be lost when the computer is turned off (see "ROM").

Read-only memory (ROM) A type of *chip* memory, the contents of which have been permanently recorded in a computer by the manufacturer and cannot be altered by the user (see "RAM").

Silicon chip A special kind of *integrated circuit* in which traditional electronic components have been replaced by chemicals. Tiny wafers (chips) of silicon are covered with layers of chemicals, each of which acts as an electrical component (a *transistor*, capacitor, etc.). The first chips, made in the early 1960s, contained two transistors. By 1989 chips existed that contained 10 million transistors. The industry standard is one million transistors per chip.

Software The *programs* and procedures, as opposed to the physical equipment, used in data processing (see "Hardware").

Spreadsheet A *program*, such as Lotus 1-2-3,

that performs mathematical operations on numbers arranged in large arrays; used mainly for accounting and other record keeping.

Supercomputer The fastest of the *mainframe* class of computers, usually used for complex scientific calculations.

Transistor A small piece of semiconducting material (material that conducts electricity better than, say, wood but not as well as metal). Flows of electrons within the transistor can be controlled, enabling it to act as an electronic "switching" device. In other words, it can record information in the form of an "on" or an "off" signal. Early transistors were about one-hundredth the size of *vacuum tubes*, required very little energy, and generated no heat.

Vacuum tube A glass tube, shaped like a light bulb, that contains a heating element that pumps electrons through a vacuum. In the earliest computers, the status of the electrical current—"on" or "off"—was used as a means of storing information. Two major drawbacks of the vacuum tube were that it generated excessive heat and used large amounts of energy.

Window A portion of the screen display used to view simultaneously a different part of the file in use or a part of a different file than the one in use.

Workstation A powerful *microcomputer* designed for use by scientists and engineers.

CHRONOLOGY OF INFORMATION PROCESSING

B.C.
500 Bead-and-wire abacus in use in Egypt.
A.D.
200 Computing trays in use in China and Japan.
1340 Double-entry bookkeeping originates in Lombardy.
1612 Scottish inventor John Napier develops logarithms, a means of performing multiplication and division by addition and subtraction.
1622 English mathematician William Oughtred invents slide rule. He later introduces symbol x for multiplication and terms *sine*, *cosine*, and *tangent* to express trigonometric ratios.
1642 Blaise Pascal invents "pascaline"—the first calculating machine, capable of addition and subtraction.
1666 G.W. Leibniz argues that all reasoning reducible to an ordered combination of elements—the first principle of computer theory.
1679 Leibniz perfects binary system of notation that eventually will be used by all computers; also develops improved version of pascaline, capable of multiplication and division.
1801 Joseph-Marie Jacquard uses punched cards to control operation of his mechanical loom—precursor of cards used in modern data-storage systems.
1822 Charles Babbage designs and builds prototype of "Difference Engine" for calculating logarithms.
1833 Babbage designs "Analytical Engine," a

computing machine featuring printed-card input, memory, and printed output, and capable of being programmed to perform different tasks. Forerunner of modern computer, it never goes beyond design stage.
1847 George Boole publishes *Mathematical Analysis of Logic*, which shows logic to be a branch of mathematics.
1855 George and Edvard Scheutz build and market simplified version of Babbage's Difference Engine. One client is British government, which uses Scheutz engine to calculate life expectancy tables.
1886 William Burroughs develops first commercially successful mechanical adding machine.
1887 U.S. Census Bureau holds competition to find device to speed up computation of census information; won by Herman Hollerith's tabulating machine.
1890 Hollerith's electromechanical machine, using perforated cards, processes U.S. census results in six weeks—one-third the time taken in 1880.
1894 Otto Steiger develops "Millionaire," the first commercially successful machine capable of direct multiplication, as opposed to multiplication by repeated addition. Nearly 5,000 sold between 1894 and 1935.
1896 Hollerith develops mechanical sorting machine.
1911 Hollerith's Tabulating Machine Co. merges with Computing Scale Co. and International Time Recording Co. to form Computer-Tabulating-Recording Co.
1924 Computer-Tabulating-Recording Co. changes name to International Business Machines (IBM).
1930 Vanneval Bush, at M.I.T., builds "differential analyser," first computing machine to use electronic components (vacuum tubes in which values could be stored as voltages).
1936 English mathematician Alan Turing publishes *On Computable Numbers*, in which he describes hypothetical computer with infinite storage capacity, capable of performing any conceivable calculation.
1937 John V. Atansoff starts work on first electronic computer.
1938 Konrad Zuse builds "Z1," the first computing machine to use binary, instead of decimal, method of operation. Other features include keyboard to input information and system of electric bulbs to signal results of calculations. Hewlett-Packard founded.
1940 Zuse's Z2 machine introduces electromagnetic relays (as used in telephone switching gear) to store numbers. (Relays were capable of switching, i.e., calculating, 5 times per second.)

The First Generation: Vacuum Tubes

1943 British government uses first successful, fully electronic computer—"Colossus"—to crack German military codes during World War II. Designed by mathemati-

cian Alan Turing, Colossus uses 2,000 vacuum tubes to perform calculations and digest information at rate of 5,000 characters per second.
1944 Completion of "Harvard Mark I," designed by Howard Aiken and built by IBM. Vast, over 50 ft. long, it was obsolete almost immediately because it used electromagnetic relays rather than vacuum tubes.
1946 At press conference at University of Pennsylvania, the ENIAC (Electronic Numerical Integrator and Calculator) multiplies five-digit number by itself 5,000 times in half a second. Designed by Eckert and Mauchley to calculate ballistic trajectories, ENIAC occupies 2,000 sq. ft., weighs 50 tons, uses 18,000 vacuum tubes, and can store about 20 words in its memory.
Johann Von Neumann publishes paper suggesting that instructions given to computer—"programs"—can themselves be stored by computer in numerical form. First use of term *bit* to mean binary digit.
1948 "Mark I," designed by Kilburn and Williams at Manchester University, England, is first computer to utilize Von Neumann's concept of series of instructions stored in machine's memory. It can thus be "programmed" to perform infinite variety of functions.
Bardeen, Brattain, and Shockley invent the transistor; it will eventually replace vacuum tube and make computers faster and more reliable.
IBM, Bell Telephone, and Sperry-Rand each begin production of commercial computers.
First chess-playing computer built at M.I.T.
1950 Eckert and Mauchley's EDVAC (Electronic Discrete Variable Automatic Computer) is first to use magnetic disks for storage.
1951 Lyons Tea Shop Co. in England uses specially designed computer ("LEO") to perform routine administrative functions.
Eckert and Mauchley's UNIVAC (*Universal Automatic Computer*) is installed at U.S. Bureau of Census. UNIVAC uses magnetic tape for input and becomes first commercially successful machine, selling over 50 models.
Wang Laboratories founded in Boston.
1952 One hour after polls close, CBS television network uses UNIVAC to predict Eisenhower's landslide victory in U.S. presidential election. Prediction was based on less than 10% of the votes.
1953 First high-speed printer linked to a computer.
IBM introduces its first stored-program computer, the vacuum-tube based "701."
1954 IBM develops FORTRAN (*Formula Translator*), a programming language designed to handle complex economic and scientific formulas.
1956 First use of term *artificial intelligence*.
1957 Development of LISP (*List Processing*),

first computer language designed to process nonnumeric data.

The Second Generation: Transistors

1958 Control Data Corp. introduces first fully transistorized computer, the CDC 1604. Working independently, Jack Kilby of Texas Instruments and Robert Noyce of Intel Corp. produce first integrated circuits.

Conference of Data System Languages (composed of U.S. government and industry representatives) introduces COBOL (*Common Business-Oriented Language*); becomes standard language for business programs.

1959 First commercially marketed program. IBM markets its first transistorized computers, the 1620 and 1790.

1960 First minicomputer, the PDP-1, developed by Digital Equipment Corp. ALGOL (*Algorithmic Language*) introduced in Zurich; designed primarily for scientific functions.

Introduction of removable magnetic disks for data storage.

1965 John Kemeny and Thomas Kurtz at Dartmouth develop BASIC (*Beginner's All-purpose Symbolic Instructions Code*); designed for student use, it soon gains widespread popularity due to its simplicity and versatility.

The Third Generation: Integrated Circuits

1965 IBM markets its first integrated-circuit based computer, the 360.

1968 Stanley Kubrick's *2001: A Space Odyssey* stars supercomputer called "Hal," which critics complain is the most "human" character in film.

1969 Graduate student Alan Kay, later to become top designer with Apple Computer Co., writes doctoral thesis describing hypothetical "personal computer."

First international conference on artificial intelligence.

1970 Lexitron introduces first word processor, a computer designed specifically to handle written text. It features a cathode ray tube (CRT) terminal, as used in television sets, to display information.

Floppy disk is introduced for data storage.

1971 Intel Corp. announces first microprocessor, several integrated circuits contained on one silicon chip.

First electronic pocket calculator produced by Texas Instruments; it weighs about 2½ lbs. and costs about $150.

1973 IBM introduces "Winchester" disk drive, a sealed storage module containing several rotating magnetic disks.

Introduction of "bit-mapped" monitor capable of high-resolution graphics display.

Xerox markets first hand-held "mouse," a time-saving device for giving commands to computer.

Intel introduces 8080 microprocessor,

which will become the central processing unit (CPU) of several microcomputers.

1975 First personal computer, the MITS Altair 8800, is marketed in kit form, with memory capacity of 256 bytes.

1976 Apple Computer Co. founded by Stephen Wozniak and Steven Jobs in the Wozniak family garage; first Apple "boards" (self-assembly personal computer kits) go on sale.

1977 Apple moves to new premises, markets Apple II—the first widely accepted personal computer. Commodore and Tandy also begin to sell personal computers.

Microsoft Corp. is founded to produce microcomputer operating systems—programs allowing a central processing-unit to control and coordinate the different elements of computer's hardware. Microsoft systems used for Radio Shack TRS-80 and Altair PC.

1978 Hayes introduces Micromodem 100, the first microcomputer-compatible modem.

1979 Micropro International releases Word-Star, popular word-processing program for personal computers.

WordPerfect Corp., producers of rival WordPerfect program, begins operation.

1980 Microsoft adapts UNIX (an operating system for mainframe and minicomputers) for use with microcomputers; paves way for personal computers to begin performing tasks associated with larger machines.

1981 IBM introduces its first personal computer, the IBM PC. Using operating system called PC-DOS, developed by Microsoft, it almost immediately becomes the industry standard.

First fully portable computer, the Osborne 1, is introduced.

Xerox markets the Star, a mouse-driven computer that prefigures many features of Apple Macintosh.

Ashton-Tate introduces dBASE II, the first popular database program for microcomputers.

1982 Microsoft introduces MS-DOS, a version of the PC-DOS operating system designed for IBM PC; allows other manufacturers to produce copies ("clones") of the IBM machine.

Compaq announces its first portable computer (IBM compatible).

1983 Apple introduces Apple IIe (last of Apple II family) and "Lisa," an important step toward development of the Macintosh.

IBM announces PC Junior, which is commercially unsuccessful.

Radio Shack markets Model 100 portable, weighing just 4 lbs.

First IBM-compatible "laptop" computer introduced by Gavilan Corp.

Lotus Development Corp. introduces 1-2-3, a best-selling program for managing business spreadsheets.

Introduction of optical (laser-readable) storage disks.

1984 Apple introduces "Macintosh," named for designer's favorite apple. With list price of $2,495, it includes Apple's first

"Mac" software programs, MacWrite (for text) and MacPaint (for graphics). Fifty thousand are sold within three months, but sales are in decline by year's end.

IBM markets the PC AT (Advanced Technology) model; features include Enhanced Graphics Adapter (EGA) for improved screen resolution.

1985 Apple's LaserWriter printer and Aldus Corp.'s PageMaker program usher in age of desktop publishing—electronic, rather than mechanical, production of documents and books.

Introduction of erasable optical storage disks.

Voice data entry becomes feasible.

Toshiba markets its first laptop, the T1100.

1986 IBM announces OS/2, a new operating system that allows personal computers to run several programs simultaneously (called multitasking).

Apple markets Macintosh Plus and LaserWriter Plus.

1987 Apple introduces Macintosh SE and Macintosh II. IBM introduces Personal System/2 (PS/2), features of which include high-resolution VGA (Video Graphics Array) display.

Aldus releases IBM-compatible version of its PageMaker program.

1988 Computer security becomes an urgent issue when a "worm" program penetrates thousands of systems on Internet information network.

Steven Jobs, now with Next, Inc., unveils "computer workstation," featuring an optical disk drive capable of storing 250 times as much data as floppy disks used by IBM and Apple.

Motorola announces new microprocessor, the 88000.

First IBM PS/2 "clones" announced by rival manufacturers.

Compaq markets SLT/286, the first laptop with VGA display.

1989 Intel announces the 80860 chip, which will contain one million transistors; designed to give a microcomputer the power and speed normally associated with supercomputers.

IBM announces production of commercial quantities of 4–megabyte chips.

COMPUTER LANGUAGES

Name	Source of name	Introduced	Creators	Uses
Ada	For Lady Ada Lovelace, the first computer programmer	1979	Team headed by Jean Ichbiah of Honeywell	Based on Pascal; devised to manage complex computing activities needed by U.S. Army, Navy, and Air Force.
Algol	*Algorithmic Language*	1960	International committee	Designed for solving math problems; both readable and practical, forerunner of many other languages, including Pascal.
APL	*A Programming Language*	1961	Kenneth Iverson of IBM	First used for expressing problems in applied mathematics because it can handle large numbers easily; now useful to airlines for complex routing and scheduling.
BASIC	*Beginners All-purpose Symbolic Instruction Code*	1965	John Kemeny and Thomas Kurtz of Dartmouth College	Most popular and versatile of all computer languages; most often used as introduction to computing.
C	Successor to B language (Bell Computer programming Language/BCPL)	early 1970s	Dennis Ritchie at Bell Laboratories	Unusually flexible language; coming into wide use because programs are easily transferable between types of computers.
COBOL	*Common Business Oriented Language*	1959	Grace Murray Hopper and committee of computer manufacturers	Principal language for large-scale data processing in government, banking, and insurance.
Forth	*Fourth* generation language	1970	Charles Moore of National Radio Astronomy Observatory	Originally invented to control telescope at Kitts Peak Observatory, Ariz.; has been adapted for many mini- and microcomputer uses, including robotics and arcade games.
FORTRAN	*Formula Translator*	1954	John Backus and team at IBM	Standard computer language for scientists and mathematicians; first designed for large computers, now used by microcomputers for many business calculations.
LISP	*List Processing*	1956	John McCarthy at M.I.T.	Used primarily for research in artificial intelligence; not mathematical, but composed of words.
Logo	From Greek *logos*, meaning "word"	late 1960s	Seymour Papert and others at M.I.T.	A learning language, simple enough for a child to program, but complex enough to use in higher education.
Pascal	For Blaise Pascal, French mathematician and inventor of first computing device	1971	Niklaus Wirth of the Swiss Federal Institute of Technology	Noted for its simplicity, was devised as a tool for teaching but later adapted to many other uses; is becoming most popular language for application software.
PILOT	*Programmed Inquiry, Learning or Teaching*	1969	University of California at San Francisco	First language for computer-aided instruction; can be used by teachers with little computer experience to devise learning programs.
PL/1	*Programming Language One*	1964	Team at IBM	Designed by IBM to run its mainframe computer, now becoming popular with users of minicomputers; rich in useful features, but more difficult to master than other languages.

TOP 10 COMPUTER COMPANIES BY REVENUES, 1987

Company	Country	Millions
MAINFRAME COMPUTERS:		
1. IBM	U.S.	$11,193.0
2. Fujitsu Ltd.	Japan	3,318.2
3. NEC Corp.	Japan	3,082.0
4. Hitachi Ltd.	Japan	1,850.4
5. Unisys Corp.	U.S.	1,427.0
6. Groupe Bull	France	962.8
7. Amdahl Corp.	U.S.	926.2
8. Siemens AG	Germany	695.5
9. STC plc	England	596.8
10. Cray Research Inc.	U.S.	588.0
MINICOMPUTERS:		
1. IBM	U.S.	$4,300.0
2. Digital Equipment Corp.	U.S.	3,248.4
3. Hewlett-Packard	U.S.	1,221.0
4. Toshiba Corp.	Japan	919.6
5. Wang Laboratories	U.S.	909.3
6. Fujitsu Ltd.	Japan	804.3
7. Mitsubishi Electric Corp.	Japan	644.3
8. Olivetti SpA	Italy	603.9
9. Nixdorf Computer AG	Germany	566.6
10. NCR Corp.	U.S.	483.4
MICROCOMPUTERS:		
1. IBM	U.S.	$7,007.7
2. Apple Computer Inc.	U.S.	2,069.0
3. Compaq Computer Corp.	U.S.	1,224.0
4. Olivetti SpA	Italy	1,176.0
5. Tandy Corp.	U.S.	1,132.2
6. Unisys Corp.	U.S.	1,075.0
7. Zenith Corp.	U.S.	1,040.0
8. NEC Corp.	Japan	933.2
9. Toshiba Corp.	Japan	800.0
10. AT&T	U.S.	540.0

Source: *Datamation* magazine.

Computer Equipment and Software

With orders up 19% over mid-1987 levels, the U.S. computer industry enjoyed a vigorous recovery in 1988. Total employment grew an estimated 6% by the end of 1988. Although the weak dollar was largely responsible for a 34% rise in exports, imports continued to flood the U.S. market. Japan and Singapore were main importers of computer parts (floppy disk drives, printers, RAM chips, etc.) accounting for more than $10 billion in sales.

The U.S. software industry continued to grow during this period, with domestic revenues increasing 20% and worldwide revenues up 23%. Artificial intelligence technology—computer systems that function at or near the level of human expert knowledge—is making inroads in the service area, banks, insurance companies, and manufacturing. The U.S. government increased its artificial intelligence research and development funding from $48.5 million in 1984 to $172.5 million in 1988. The total U.S. artificial intelligence market for both hardware and software in 1988 was $2 billion, representing a 50% increase over the 1987 level. During the 1980s a host of applications for supercomputers were developed, such as aerodynamics, computational chemistry, nuclear reactors, and weapons design. The United States represents about two-thirds of the world market for minisupercomputers, which perform many of the same functions as supercomputers and sell at a fraction of the cost.

In 1988 U.S. companies shipped a record 220,000 computer workstations, capturing 90% of the European market. Japanese attempts to penetrate the workstation market suffered from a lack of applications software and few distribution channels. U.S. factory shipments of computers priced less than $15,000 exceeded $11 billion in 1988, rising 25% from 1987. Although representing only 10% of the personal computer market, portables are steadily gaining market share, led by the popularity of the improved laptops.

Shipments of computer equipment are projected to increase by 10% in 1989. Demand for advanced scientific and engineering systems, workstations, and personal computers should remain at a fairly high level and offset the sluggishness in mainframes and minicomputers. Domestic software should grow by 25% in 1989. PC-based expert systems will broaden the uses of artificial intelligence technology. U.S. supercomputers and minicomputers will continue to dominate the market due to their superior applications software. U.S. shipments of PCs should increase by 20%. In the future the industry is expected to shift its emphasis away from manufacturing and toward system design and integration, software development, and after-scale maintenance.

The United States exports 16% of the computers it produces and imports 11% of those that it uses, for a trade surplus in computers of $1,187.3 million in 1986 and $1,438.9 in 1987.

THE ENVIRONMENT

Recently, it has become common to announce that the major issues confronting the world no longer concern war or politics but the environment. Many European nations, notably West Germany, have active and increasingly successful political parties, called Greens, whose main agenda consists of environmental issues. Elementary school children in the United States frequently study the environment in science or social studies courses, and may even take whole courses of environmental studies.

Such concern with the environment is not new. Plato noted that Greece had been deforested. Tudor rulers tried to control coal smoke in London. The U.S. environmental movement of the 19th century led to creation of the national park system. Many other examples could be cited, but all these previous responses to environmental damage and destruction were limited to a single issue. What is different today?

Two changes have taken place. One concerns our perceptions only. The other concerns both a new reality and our perception of it.

In the United States, our perception of environmental problems began in 1962 when Rachel Carson tackled a brand-new environmental problem in her book *Silent Spring*. The new problem was pesticides. Although the first modern insecticide, DDT, was discovered as early as 1874, it was not until 1939 that it was recognized as an agent that killed insects. During World War II and the immediate postwar period, DDT successfully routed the lice that carry typhus, saving a great many lives. After the war it was used on insect pests everywhere. Farmers, especially, took to DDT and to other new insecticides inspired by its success. Scientists found a new class of pesticides, chemicals that would kill weeds and leave crops alone. The nature of farming in the United States was completely changed. Previously, farmers had a few inorganic or natural chemicals that could be used to kill insects and used mechanical means to eliminate weeds. Now they had potent artificial organic insecticides. Around the same time, artificial fertilizers became popular.

What Rachel Carson and a few other scientists soon perceived was that the new pesticides were reducing the number of birds (hence, the "silent spring" of the title). Furthermore, some of the pesticides, notably DDT, tended to accumulate in the food chain, so that meat- or fish-eating animals, including humans, were accumulating more and more DDT in their body fat. Ten years after *Silent Spring*, enough people in America were convinced that DDT was dangerous to the environment that use of the

pesticide in this country was severely restricted.

The recognition of the problems caused by pesticides led many people to think more seriously about the human ability to cause large-scale changes in the environment. Smog in Los Angeles was no longer just something you heard comedians joke about. Water pollution was so bad in some rivers that there was a persistent tale—not quite true, but almost—that one of them caught fire. Pesticides in the water supply led to massive fish kills. Lake Erie was declared "dead," as fish populations dropped dramatically. By Apr. 22, 1970, it was possible for the new environmentalists to organize the first "Earth Day," an educational event in schools, offices, and parks across America. It was now perceived that the environment as a whole was the issue, not just some individual problems.

Although the environmental movement was at first frequently derided (bumper stickers read "Save Your Job; Eat an Environmentalist"), it became more and more respectable. Unfortunately, the main reason for taking the environmental movement more seriously was that problems were getting worse. The 1973 OPEC oil crisis alerted people to the finite and dwindling nature of some natural resources. Municipal taxes began to be affected by increasingly complex problems of solid-waste disposal. People learned that acid rain was killing fish in lakes and dissolving marble statues—and wondered what it might be doing to humans. Various chemicals that caused cancer in animals had to be banned, and asbestos insulation was definitely causing cancer in people who had installed it 30 years earlier. Industrial chemicals, such as polychlorobyphenyls (PCBs), were found to have properties similar to DDT, to which they are related, and had to be banned in the 1970s—although they are still present in some rivers many years later. It also became clear that many animal and plant species were becoming extinct or nearly so at a much faster rate than in the recent past. A general impression developed that something was seriously wrong.

This perception was amplified when new threats arose that affected the entire Earth, not just the neighborhood. Of course, acid rain was known to travel hundreds of miles to do its damage, but one could always move somewhere that was not downwind of the cause, the cause being, for the most part smelters and coal-burning power plants. As early as 1967, scientists began to warn against a threat from which you could not move away—the greenhouse effect, the global warming caused by carbon dioxide and other gases that accumulate in the atmosphere as a result of human activity. Such a warming, which is still not accepted as fact by all scientists, would result in great environmental changes everywhere on Earth.

In 1974 another global threat was discovered. The ozone layer in the atmosphere protecting us from harmful ultraviolet radiation was being eroded by chemicals called chlorofluorocarbons, which are commonly used as spray propellants and in refrigeration. Acceptance of this threat was much swifter than

acceptance of the greenhouse effect. By 1978 the United States had banned use of chlorofluorocarbons in sprays. Today most of the nations of the world have banded together to eliminate their use altogether.

Because threats to the environment are so many and varied, and because they touch upon important aspects of most of our lives, the *Universal Almanac* includes a special section detailing where we are on environmental issues.

THE GREENHOUSE EFFECT

Recently, whenever there is a hot summer or a warmer-than-usual winter, people have tended to blame the greenhouse effect. The greenhouse effect is a real phenomenon, but its effect on current weather is not clear to most scientists. Here are the causes of the effect and what is known about how it is changing climate now, as well as expectations for future change.

Causes Gases tend to be transparent, or pervious, to electromagnetic radiation at visible wavelengths because light does not react easily with electrons in isolated molecules. At different wavelengths, however, gases generally are not transparent. One example is ozone, which is less transparent to ultraviolet radiation than other gases in the atmosphere. Another example is carbon dioxide, which is less transparent to infrared radiation, or heat, than it is to light. Both of these reactions between a gas and electromagnetic radiation have proved to be involved in worldwide environmental problems (see "Ozone" below).

Carbon dioxide (and several other gases) in the atmosphere permits solar radiation in the form of light to reach the Earth's surface. There it is absorbed by solids or liquids, although some is reflected in all directions. The light absorbed heats the solid or the liquid. This heat is emitted from the surface as infrared radiation. The gases that are not transparent to infrared radiation, such as carbon dioxide, collect this heat and keep it in the atmosphere. If all gases in the atmosphere were transparent to infrared radiation, the heat would escape. Mars, although its atmosphere is 95% carbon dioxide, has a total amount of carbon dioxide that is insufficient to trap very much heat (its air pressure is about seven-thousandths that of Earth's air pressure). Thus, its surface temperature is –67°F. Venus also has a 96% carbon dioxide atmosphere, but its air pressure at the surface is 90 times that of Earth. Consequently, it retains much more heat, resulting in a surface temperature of about 854°F. Earth has been comfortably in between these extremes. Our atmosphere is only 0.035% carbon dioxide, but that, combined with other gases, traps 88% of the sun's energy, some of which is reradiated toward Earth's surface, while the rest is radiated into space. This process then repeats, with some reradiated heat collected by the gases and some escaping into space. Eventually, 70% of the infrared radiation is emitted toward space, while the remaining 30% stays in the vicinity of Earth's surface and atmosphere, giving Earth an average surface temperature of 59°F.

Because a similar process traps infrared radiation in a greenhouse, this is known as the greenhouse effect, and gases that are less transparent to infrared radiation are called greenhouse gases. Besides carbon dioxide, the principal greenhouse gases in the atmosphere are methane, chlorofluorocarbons, nitrogen oxides, and low-level ozone. Methane is produced primarily by natural sources, such as the digestive processes of cattle and termites; chlorofluorocarbons are synthetics; and the other two are forms of air pollution caused mainly by automobile exhausts and the burning of wood or fossil fuels (coal, oil, and natural gas).

The greenhouse effect is an environmental problem because the greenhouse gases are increasing in the atmosphere. Carbon dioxide has increased by roughly 25% since about 1850. It is generally assumed that much of this increase is due to the burning of fossil fuels, but it is also clear from the geologic record that carbon dioxide levels have varied from time to time in the past, resulting in periods when most of Earth was tropical and in periods in which ice ages occurred. A major source of carbon dioxide is deforestation, by both the burning and rotting of cut wood. Dr. Paul Crutzen, an atmospheric scientist at the Max-Planck-Institut in Mainz, West Germany, estimates that two-thirds of the carbon dioxide being added to the atmosphere comes from burning fossil fuels, with the remaining third from deforestation. Other greenhouse gases are also increasing, in most cases clearly as a result of human activity, although it is less clear what is causing the rise in methane levels.

The Greenhouse Effect and Climate

Climate does change in response to the greenhouse effect. Recent evidence suggests that such dramatic changes as the end of the most recent ice age some 11,000 years ago were precipitated by a rise in carbon dioxide and methane, which resulted in a global warming of 9°F. This was enough to change drastically the climate and environment of North America.

Scientists have fairly good data for global temperatures in the past 100 years, during which time carbon dioxide increased from about 0.028% of the air to 0.035%, and other greenhouse gases also increased. Although the trend has not been constantly in the direction of increase, overall the increase in temperature during this period has been about 0.9°F. Some scientists think this accounts for the 1980s being the warmest decade of that 100-year period, with 1981, 1987, and 1988 the warmest years.

If trends in the use of fossil fuels are not changed, scientists expect the amount of carbon dioxide in the air to reach 0.06% in the 21st century. The would produce a global warming variously estimated from 1.8°F to 9°F. Even the lowest projection of 1.8°F would result in considerable climactic change, while anything over a 3°F increase would drastically change the climate. This is because a global temperature rise is not evenly distributed and because changes in temperature affect weather patterns around the world.

At this time, different projections of regional effects arise from different scientific studies. Most predict that more of the global warming will occur in the temperate and arctic zones than in the tropics. They also predict changes in rainfall; for example, in some projections the American Midwest becomes a semidesert. Different studies give different projections because it is not clear how the many variables will interact. These interactions have to be assumed, and different assumptions lead to different projections.

Other Complications Carbon dioxide is not a bystander in the ecology of Earth; it is an active player in many ways. Since it is used by green plants in photosynthesis, the size of the world's population of green plants affects the amount of carbon dioxide in the air. Trees, especially, tie up large amounts of carbon in their woody parts for years—as long as thousands of years in the case of a few species. They take the carbon dioxide from the air, use it to collect energy from the sun, release much of the oxygen, and keep the carbon. The carbon returns to circulation when the wood rots or is burned.

Sometimes carbon locked up by green plants does not return to the atmosphere for much longer. If it is buried or formed into peat in bogs, it can become fossilized as coal, oil, or natural gas. Certainly, in the past this process removed vast amounts of carbon from the atmosphere. It seems less likely that creation of fossil fuels is a major factor today.

The ocean also collects carbon dioxide. Some is merely dissolved in ocean water (where it ceases to contribute to the greenhouse effect), and some is incorporated with calcium carbonate, the principal component of most seashells. After the organism that made the shell dies, the shell either becomes buried, where it may later be converted to limestone or chalk, or is dissolved in ocean water. In the latter case, the calcium carbonate becomes available for other organisms to use in their cells. Mechanisms such as these remove large amounts of carbon dioxide from the air and keep it out of the air for long periods of time. Eventually, limestone or chalk may be thrust up from the ocean floor by geological processes. Only then does some of the carbon return to the atmosphere.

It is believed that changes in oceans and ocean currents caused by movements of tectonic plates have caused variations in carbon dioxide resulting in pronounced climate changes in the past. Also, locking up carbon in vast forests or as fossil fuels created changes. The biological storage of carbon may also have been caused in part by movements of tectonic plates: when all the continents were joined in the tropics, a warm climate developed—caused by large amounts of greenhouse gases—the polar regions were all sea, and forests became vast. The forests gradually removed carbon and cooled the climate. In contrast, when a continent is directly over a pole, as Antarctica is today, it can develop an ice cap and essentially store no carbon, which would gradually tend to warm the climate.

These factors make it difficult to predict the amount of carbon dioxide over long periods of time. Furthermore, cloud cover and the presence of snow change the climate in ways that are hard to predict. Thick clouds screen out solar radiation, but if the radiation is coming from the earth, they trap it. Snow is cold, and it also is white, which means that it reflects most light back into space.

Possible Consequences of the Greenhouse Effect With the difficulties of making accurate projections in mind, it is still useful to list some of the possible consequences of the greenhouse effect.

Climate Climates will change, though it is not absolutely clear how they will change. In the United States, one of the concerns is how much water will fall in various regions. One study suggests that a local temperature increase in the neighborhood of 5°F might reduce runoff in the Colorado River basin by as much as 10%. This would affect water use over much of the West. Reduction of rainfall or increased heat could change crop patterns all over the country. Some fruits, such as apples, need a certain amount of winter cooling to flower and fruit, for example. Corn needs a lot of rain at the right time. Winter wheat needs the groundwater that comes with snowmelt. Furthermore, rising temperatures would permit insect and fungal pests from the south to migrate into northern farming regions.

Sea Level Rise Ice caps will melt faster than they are now. This, combined with water's increase in volume with increasing temperature, will cause sea levels to rise around the world. Predictions are that this rise will be from 1½ feet to 5 feet over the next 50 to 100 years. Such a rise would affect coastal regions, wetlands, and fishing. The U.S. Environmental Protection Agency (EPA) estimates that if the sea level rises 3 feet, the country might spend as much as $111 billion to protect critical shorelines, but would still lose an area the size of Massachusetts. Worldwide, most coastal cities would have to build dikes, and low-lying countries, such as Bangladesh, might lose a large portion of their land.

The EPA also is concerned about the effects on crucial coastal wetlands (see "U.S. Wetlands and Surface Waters," below). Their pro-

CHANGING COASTAL WETLANDS WITH SEA LEVEL RISE

Region	Total wetlands (acres)	Net loss/gain by A.D. 2100 (acres)
Northeast	120,900	−4,000
Mid–Atlantic	733,300	−92,200
South Atlantic	1,376,600	+61,800
Florida	736,300	+211,700
Alabama, Mississippi	401,400	+36,000
Louisiana	2,874,600	−2,306,900
Texas	609,400	−85,500
Pacific Coast	89,100	−36,300
TOTAL	**6,941,600**	**−2,213,400**

jections by region are as follows. The projection assumes a 5-foot rise in sea level and reveals that the nation would lose 30% of its coastal wetlands.

Vegetation Plants that spread easily can adapt to new climates, but trees do not migrate—as scientists call it—very fast. If climates change faster than southern forests can migrate north, much of the temperate forest might be lost. In this scenario, as in many others, the speed of climate change is important. Most scientists think the climate will change faster than it has in the past 5,000 years, so civilization has no experience to judge how well it can react.

Possible Responses The EPA has proposed the following ways to mitigate the greenhouse effect: raise prices on fossil fuels; increase use of alternative energy sources, especially those such as solar and nuclear power that do not produce greenhouse gases; grow new forests around the planet; stop use of chlorofluorocarbons (an action already agreed to because of the effect of these chemicals on the ozone layer); capture gases now released by landfills (primarily methane); and change ways of raising rice and cattle to reduce production of methane.

The bad news is that the EPA says that if all this were to be done worldwide, starting in 1990, it would result in the rate of gas buildup leveling off sometime in the 22d century. Still, by the year 2100, greenhouse warming might be reduced to as little as 1°F to 2.5°F.

Ozone: Too Much and Too Little at the Same Time

What Is Ozone? Ozone is a gas like oxygen. In fact, ozone is oxygen—but oxygen with a difference. Ordinary oxygen always contains two atoms combined into a single molecule. This is the oxygen we breathe. With a slight energy boost, however, three atoms of oxygen can combine to form an ozone molecule. Ozone has different properties from oxygen. For example, oxygen is odorless, but ozone has a distinct odor, which can often be noticed near electric sparks or powerful ultraviolet lights. Oxygen is transparent, but ozone is blue. Ozone is to oxygen rather like hydrogen peroxide is to water. Ozone is much more reactive than oxygen. Also, just as hydrogen peroxide gradually turns into water, ozone gradually turns into ordinary oxygen. The action of light speeds up these processes.

Too Much Ozone Burning fuels at high temperature can result in some unstable molecules containing oxygen. When exposed to sunlight, these break down, and some of their oxygen becomes ozone. Also, some chemicals in auto exhausts can catalyze oxygen in the air to become ozone; the exhaust gases produce ozone. Other sources of ground-level ozone include fumes from gasoline, other volatile liquids such as dry-cleaning fluids, emissions from bakeries, gases released by hazardous wastes, and fires set to clear forests in South America or savannas in Africa. This ozone, especially if it is trapped near the ground, becomes an important component of air pollution. Because the chemical reactions that produce ozone make the air hazy or even brown, this form of air pollution is called photochemical smog, or just smog (although, it is not the combination of *smoke* and *fog* that is the origin of the name *smog*). Increasingly, it has become clear that the most damaging part of smog and the hardest to control is ozone.

Ozone by itself is harmful to plants and animals—so harmful that ozone can be used to sterilize, since it kills microorganisms. Ozone, at levels found in many cities, damages trees. Ozone can also damage food crops, especially grains. The EPA estimates that the United States loses about $2.5-3 billion each year in ozone damage to crops, while the World Resources Institute thinks the losses to U.S. crops caused by ozone annually reach $5 billion. When animals breathe ozone, it causes immediate inflammation in the lungs, followed by a long-term abnormal stiffening, reducing the lungs' ability to take in air.

This last property is the main reason that some cities declare a "smog alert" when ozone levels get too high. People are discouraged from exercising; the ill, the elderly, and the very young are even told to stay indoors. The EPA has set 0.12 parts per million of ozone in the air as the maximum safe limit, but 100 cities, counties, or other regions in the United States fail to meet that standard, including virtually all of the Atlantic Coast and southern California. In 1988 the ozone situation was especially bad, reaching levels not seen since 1978, before major efforts were undertaken to curb it. Also in 1988, excessive levels were recorded in places where excess ozone had not been previously found, including rural Maine and northern New York State.

Too Little Ozone Although ozone is damaging when it interacts with life directly, ozone high in the atmosphere is important in protecting life. In the upper atmosphere, ozone is both formed and broken down by ultraviolet light. When ozone is broken down by light, one atom of oxygen quickly replaces the ozone molecule that was broken. In the process the energy of the ultraviolet light is trapped as energy by the electrons in the ozone. As a result the ozone keeps some ultraviolet light from reaching Earth's surface, especially the light with higher energy levels. The amount of ultraviolet light that does reach the surface is blamed for most skin cancers. Furthermore, high-energy ultraviolet light kills microorganisms.

Scientists believe that if more ultraviolet light reached the surface, the number of skin cancers, some of them fatal, would drastically increase. It is also thought that small ocean algae, which produce much of the oxygen in the air and break down much of the carbon dioxide, and bacteria important to crop production would be greatly reduced.

Chlorofluorocarbons (Freon is the most familiar type) are gases that have been used as spray propellants, in refrigeration, as cleaning agents, and in plastic foams, such as Styrofoam. Since 1974 it has been known that chlorine can be produced when chlorofluorocarbons break down in the upper atmosphere. The chlorine can then destroy ozone, turning it into ordinary oxygen. Each chlorine molecule destroys only one ozone molecule, but it does so in a process that leaves the original chlorine molecule intact, so it can then proceed to destroy many, many ozone molecules.

Ozone levels in the atmosphere are difficult to measure. The current best guess is that in the temperate zone of the Northern Hemisphere, ozone has declined between 1.7% and 3% in the period 1968–86. These changes are about double in winter, however, so the winter decline might be as high as 6.3%.

Since the discovery that chlorofluorocarbons can destroy high-atmosphere ozone, evidence has gradually accumulated that the amount of ozone in the upper atmosphere is decreasing. This process is especially noticeable in the Antarctic, where tiny ice particles increase the rate of breakdown, producing an ozone "hole" during the Antarctic summer, when there is nearly continuous sunlight. Increasing evidence shows that the same forces are also at work in the Arctic, where such a "hole" would be more dangerous because of the greater amount of life in that region—including humans—than in the Antarctic.

Furthermore, chlorofluorocarbons are contributing to another problem. Although about half the greenhouse effect (see above) is caused by carbon dioxide, the other half is caused by other gases. Carbon dioxide affects the temperature because there is so much of it, but chlorofluorocarbons are a thousand times more effective as "greenhouse gases" than carbon dioxide is. Consequently, even though there is not much chlorofluorocarbon in the atmosphere, the contribution of chlorofluorocarbons to the greenhouse effect is great.

For both ozone destruction and the greenhouse effect, it does not take many chlorofluorocarbon molecules to make a difference.

What Is Being Done Near ground level, the EPA is monitoring ozone levels much more than it used to, but monitoring does not stop production. On June 12, 1989, President George Bush called for a program to reduce ozone further.

A reduction in automobile traffic in central U.S. cities and elimination of industrial or other plants that burn coal or oil for fuel would help but are very difficult to achieve. Ways to reduce ozone by "scrubbing" the gases, as catalytic converters and other devices do for automobiles and smokestacks, are not very effective. Indeed, street-level ozone caused by automotive smog doubled between the summers of 1987 and 1988 in many U.S. cities, and the average ozone level in 1988 was 5% higher than it had been in 1983. President Bush called for stricter controls on automobile and smokestack emissions. New gasoline pumps at service stations that prevent vapors from reaching the atmosphere are expected to help. The president called for extending the use of such devices and also for gasoline manufacturers to reduce the volatility of their product. In the most seriously polluted regions, automobiles and trucks that run on natural gas or alcohol would be required. The president also called for tighter control of emissions from small industries and their wastes. All cities except Los Angeles, New York, and Houston—which have the worst problems—would be required by the president's plan to comply with existing ozone standards by the year 2000, the other three cities by 2010. The 20 cities furthest from compliance would be required to reduce ozone levels by 3% each year.

Steps are being taken to protect ozone in the upper atmosphere. Chlorofluorocarbons have not been used as spray propellants in the United States for years, although they continue to be used in other ways. An international treaty in 1987, signed by the United States, calls for limiting production of chlorofluorocarbons and related gases; however in 1989 the European Economic Community agreed to completely eliminate chlorofluorocarbon production in its 12 nations by the turn of the century. It called on other nations to join in sharper reductions more immediately than the 1987 treaty requires and to work toward a complete ban, a call the United States joined the following day. Steps to find acceptable substitutes for chlorofluorocarbons have been undertaken in the United States and the United Kingdom. So far the substitutes found are less effective in use and more expensive to manufacture than chlorofluorocarbons, but nearly everyone agrees that anything is better than permanently damaging the worldwide environment.

OCEAN POLLUTION

The years 1988 and 1989 marked the turning point in public perception of ocean pollution. In 1988 beaches were closed all along the U.S. northeastern coast owing to various forms of ocean pollution washing up on shore, including medical wastes that cause particular concern among the public (a concern professionals say was greatly exaggerated). The following spring the grounding of the *Exxon Valdez* resulted in the release of 35,000 tons of toxic petroleum into an environmentally sensitive region in Alaska. Missteps that caused and then followed the spill outraged much of the American public against Exxon in particular and against environmental pollution in general. Not since the early 1970s had there been so much concern about the environment.

While the unexpected beach pollution in the Northeast and the *Exxon Valdez* captured the largest headlines, the worst problems of ocean pollution were elsewhere. In the United States, various forms of ocean pollution were outlawed or restricted in the 1970s and early 1980s, but lack of compliance has rendered the laws almost useless. One example is pollution by municipal sewage systems, restricted by a 1972 law that set 1977 as a date for compliance. Gradually, that date was extended to July 1, 1988, but on that date, 34 cities on the U.S. East Coast still were not treating their sewage except to screen out large, floating objects.

Another example concerns New York City, its suburbs, and parts of New Jersey, which dump sewage sludge in the oceans. Currently,

they dump about 5.5 million gallons a day into a site on the edge of the continental shelf, having had to abandon a previous site closer to the New Jersey shore when it became completely unable to support life. The dumping was outlawed in 1981, but New York State has been able to get a reprieve from the courts. New Jersey now has a law on the books calling for its dumping to end in 1991. The U.S. Congress has once again outlawed all ocean dumping, this time by 1992. It is not clear how New York City will solve its sludge problem if the 1992 ban is enforced, although the city and nearby Westchester County have agreed to comply with the deadline.

Yet another problem afflicting the oceans has been an increase in algae, some of it toxic to fish or shellfish. The famous bay scallops of Long Island disappeared from the market completely in 1987 and 1988 as a result of an algal bloom, and millions of fish in various parts of the ocean were killed in the summer of 1988 by other algal blooms. Although part of the problem is caused by untreated sewage, other factors are thought to be agricultural runoff carried to the ocean by rivers and streams and the nitric-acid component of acid rain.

Plastic, which generally does not break down in the ocean, is another hazard. Although the U.S. Senate has ratified an international treaty to prohibit disposal of plastic wastes that can kill or maim marine creatures becoming entangled in them, the new treaty is difficult to enforce.

Toxic wastes have affected ocean wildlife. Striped bass along the East Coast, which breed in rivers, are polluted with PCBs, potentially cancer-causing chemicals, and the commercial fishery industry has had to be closed. Nearly a third of Louisiana's oyster beds and half of Texas's shellfish beds were closed in 1988 because of toxic pollution of one form or another.

Oil spills have come somewhat under control since 1979, when they reached a worldwide amount from all causes on both land and sea estimated at 1,116,000 tons. Since 1983, total oil spills have stayed in a range between 82,000 and 187,000 tons. Although ship accidents and oil-well blowouts command the public's main attention, most oil pollution in the ocean actually comes from municipal and industrial runoff, cleaning of ships' bilges or tanks, and other routine events.

LEADING OIL SPILLS

Date	Cause	Location	Tons spilled
12/15/76	*Argo Merchant* grounded	Off southeastern Massachusetts	26,000
3/16/78	*Amoco Cadiz* grounded	Off northwest France	223,000
7/1/79	*Atlantic Empress* collides with *Aegean Captain*	Off Trinidad and Tobago	300,000
11/1/79	*Burmah Agate* burns after collision	In Galveston Bay, Texas	36,000
8/6/83	Fire aboard *Castillo de Beliver*	Off Cape Town, South Africa	250,000
3/24/89	*Exxon Valdez* grounded	Prince William Sound, Alaska	35,000

U.S. WETLANDS AND SURFACE WATERS

Wetlands are swamps, marshes, tidal flats, tidal portions of rivers (estuaries), and other watery areas. Once considered worthless, they are now recognized as having several very important roles in the environment. Not only are they the home of many unique species but also the breeding grounds for many species that range far from the wetlands, especially fish such as the striped bass. Wetlands are also feeding grounds for many species of migratory birds on their annual migrations. Destruction of wetlands has been particularly hard on migratory waterfowl, with the midwestern drought year of 1988 recording the second-lowest duck migration ever.

In addition to their significance to plant and animal life, wetlands are an essential part of the water cycle. In many cases they control floods or prevent erosion. They help maintain underground water supplies both in quantity and quality.

Wetlands are thought to have occupied 215 million acres of what are now the contiguous 48 states when Europeans first arrived in North America. Today they occupy an estimated 99 million acres. For the extent of U.S. coastal wetlands, see "The Greenhouse Effect," above. U.S. wetlands have recently been lost at a rate estimated in 1989 by the National Wildlife Federation of 300,000 to 500,000 acres a year.

In campaigning for president, George Bush announced that his administration would permit no further net loss of wetlands in America. Anticipating that policy, the EPA announced on Jan. 18, 1989, that it would maintain the total amount of wetlands in the country at its present level, either by preventing destruction of existing wetlands or by creating new ones of the size of any that are destroyed.

Furthering that goal will be the National Wetlands Inventory by the U.S. Fish and Wildlife Service, expected to be completed in 1990. The service is using high-altitude photographs to identify the various wetlands.

Before then, in 1989, the EPA completed its massive survey of water pollution in lakes, rivers and streams, estuaries, and coastal wetlands. They identified 17,365 segments of polluted surface water in 49 states and six territories that are contaminated by one or more of 126 toxic chemicals or by sewage or both, about 10% of all U.S. surface water. (Arizona did not report, but it is assumed to have polluted waters as well.) Of the reported segments, 595 segments, averaging 6 to 10 miles each, contain the toxic chemicals. Pollution may be worse than reported, however, since chemicals not included in the 126 may contaminate other waters.

The toxic chemicals are produced or released by 240 local governments, 627 industrial plants, and 12 federal installations, including military bases and Department of Energy nuclear facilities. All those identified have until June 4, 1992, to stop polluting the water. If they do not succeed, they will be subject to fines and other penalties.

ACID RAIN

Acid rain caused by industrial pollution has been known since 1872, when Robert Angus Smith discussed its appearance in England in the wake of the Industrial Revolution, then roughly at its centennial. It was not until 1961, however, that acid rain reached public consciousness. The Swedish scientist Svante Odén rediscovered the phenomenon in Scandinavia and took his findings to the press instead of to obscure scientific journals. In 1976 Odén showed that acid rain was a regional phenomenon. By 1980 acid rain was understood as a major environmental issue in the United States, Canada, and Western Europe, and the U.S. Acid Precipitation Act of that year initiated a 10-year study program. That year also marked the start of negotiations between the United States and Canada on halting acid precipitation that crossed over from one country into the other. More recently still, scientists have recognized that acid rain is found in nonindustrial parts of the world. Reports in June 1989 showed that acid rain falls almost continuously on the African rain forest and seasonally on the South American rain forest.

Effect of Acid Rain *Acid rain* is the commonly used term to denote acidic precipitation of all kinds, as well as acidic dust particles, which may contribute as much as actual wet precipitation in the form of rain, snow, and fog. Although rainwater is normally slightly acid, precipitation is noticeably higher in acidity in certain regions than in others. One result of the higher acidity is that small lakes also become more acid than they were in the past—technically, they lose the ability to buffer the acidity with alkaline chemicals from rocks and soil. As these lakes become more acid, they progressively lose populations of various types of organisms. Many small invertebrates are the first to go. This reduces the food supply for fish, frogs, and other vertebrates. Different species of fish stop breeding at different levels of acidity, and soon only a few adult fish are left, with little for them to eat. Eventually, all forms of animal life are lost. This particular effect of acid rain was the first to call widespread attention to acid rain. It has affected lakes in Scandinavia, the U.S. Appalachian mountains, and southeastern Canada. One study in 1988 estimated that more than 25% of the lakes in New York's Adirondack mountains had become too

acidic to support life.

Another clear effect of acid rain has been increased weathering of marble, limestone, and sandstone. Bronze is also attacked. Statues have lost their features, and tombstones have become unreadable. This is particularly evident in Gettysburg National Military Park, which contains 1,600 monuments and is in the highest acid-rain state (Pennsylvania) in the nation.

More controversial is the effect of acid rain on forests, crops, and human beings. Forests at high altitudes in the United States and even at lower levels in Europe are severely stressed, and many trees are dying. Many take this as evidence of acid rain, but the situation seems to be much more complex. Acid rain may be one of the factors involved, but not even that is clear. Some tests have shown that acid rain injures leaves on some food crops, such as beans, broccoli, and spinach. This damage does not seem to be very severe; furthermore, few major food crops are grown in regions of highly acid precipitation. As for human beings, it is clear that breathing sulfuric acid, the main component of acid rain, is not a good idea—but it is much less clear how much sulfuric acid actually reaches the lungs. There is no definite indication that humans are directly injured by acid rain.

> *"Nature is trying very hard to make us succeed, but Nature does not depend on us. We are not the only experiment."*
> —R. Buckminster Fuller

Causes of Acid Rain Although sulfuric acid, a product of reactions of sulfur dioxide, is the main component of acid rain, nitric acid, produced from nitrogen oxides, also contributes to the acidity. Sulfur dioxide is released primarily by industrial or other plants that use coal or oil for fuel. Sulfur is commonly found in both coal and oil, but high—and expensive—grades of coal and oil contain much less sulfur than lower grades. Nitrogen oxides are produced largely by reactions, occuring at high temperatures, of nitrogen in air with oxygen in air. Thus nitrogen oxides occur in automobile exhausts as well as in emissions from industrial or other plants that burn almost any kind of fuel at sufficiently high temperatures. Burning vegetation causes acid rain by a different mechanism, producing formic acid and acetic acid, as well as nitric acid.

A surprising effect of nitric-acid rain is that it can promote plant growth, since availability of nitrogen compounds is one of the factors that limit plant growth. A study released by the Environmental Defense Fund in 1988 revealed that about 25% of the excess nitrogen in Chesapeake Bay came from acid rain. (The remaining 75% came from crop fertilizer runoff and sewage.) This nitrogen is resulting in excessive growth of algae, which is choking out

fish and shellfish production in the bay.

Acid rain can travel great distances from its source, with as much as 10–80% increases in acidity noted as far as 2,500 miles from the source. In North America that source is principally the northern United States east of the Mississippi River and the southeastern part of Canada. Because of prevailing winds, however, the eastern Midwest, especially the Ohio Valley and Great Lakes region, produces emissions causing the most damage. Acid rain from these regions is most likely to fall on lakes with little buffering capacity. Most of the acid rain is thought to be caused by emissions from electrical power plants, especially those that burn high-sulfur coal or oil. In Europe acid rain is produced in various industrial regions, including West Germany, northern England, and parts of the Soviet Union. In China some of the worst acid rain falls on the Xishuangbanna National Nature Reserve in southwestern China. The reserve is home to several rare mammals, 35% of all of China's bird species, half of its butterfly species, and 4,000 types of flowering plants. In sub-saharan Africa, acid rain falls on the tropical rain forest as a result of year-round burning of the savanna to make land suitable for agriculture. The Amazonian rain forest also receives acid rain from land clearing, although burning the rain forest in the Amazon region is seasonal, not year-round.

At present, power plants in the United States release about 20 million tons of sulfur dioxide into the atmosphere each year. On June 12, 1989, President Bush called for a reduction of 10 million tons by the year 2000, with half the reduction to take place by 1995. Nitrogen oxides from all sources are produced in amounts only a million tons or so less than sulfur dioxide, but are harder to control than sulfur dioxide. The president proposed cutting emissions of nitrogen oxides by about 2 million tons a year by the year 2000.

Methods of prevention Reduction in sulfur dioxide can be accomplished in many ways. Among these are switching to low-sulfur coal or oil as a fuel, a change that does not require capital investment but raises annual expenses. Switching to natural gas as fuel is even more effective, since natural gas contains almost no sulfur, but it does require new furnaces. Devices called scrubbers can be added to smokestacks to remove sulfur dioxide, but these are expensive to install and maintain. Encouraging conservation of electric power is one of the least expensive ways to reduce the need for fuel and therefore reduce emissions. The trick is to reduce power production without reducing profits. Finally, various new technologies, based mainly on getting sulfur out of coal before it is burned, can be used. Also, alternative energy sources (see below) can replace part of the generating capacity. In the case of use of new technologies, the president's plan would provide an extension to the year 2003 for compliance.

As noted, reduction in nitrogen oxides is more difficult. Automobile emissions can be partly controlled by various means, including catalytic converters and use of alternate fuels. Converters can also be added to smokestacks.

OUTDOOR AIR POLLUTION

In 1989 the EPA released the first nation-wide survey of air pollution, following a congressional mandate. Covering the year 1987, the survey showed that 1,350,000 tons of 308 different toxic chemicals were released into the atmosphere. Ten of these chemicals were especially important because the amounts exceeded 50,000 tons for the year.

Outdoor air pollution has several causes nationwide, as well as strong individual sources particular to a given locality. For example, copper smelting occurs in only a few places in the United States but contributes greatly to air pollution in those localities. Nationwide the principal causes of air pollution are automobiles, power-generating plants, and factories of all types. Recent research has shown that ex-president Ronald Reagan was right when he proposed that trees also contribute to air pollution, emitting hydrocarbons that catalyze the formation of ozone.

Although total air pollution has been reduced in America, it remains a major problem in many localities, especially in cities. In 1989 California adopted a radical plan for reducing air pollution in that state that would require vast changes in the way Californians live.

OUTDOOR AIR POLLUTION IN THE U.S., 1978–87

Type of pollution	Change during 1978–87	Estimated tons emitted in 1987	Comments
Total suspended particulates	–23%	6,300,000	Essentially, dust; starting in 1987 a new measure will be used by EPA that will concentrate on tiny particles thought to cause most respiratory ailments.
Sulfur dioxide	–17%	18,500,000	Considered to be principal cause of acid rain.
Carbon monoxide	–25%	55,700,000	Similar to the familiar carbon dioxide except that only a single oxygen atom is bonded to a single carbon atom; carbon atom would "prefer" two oxygen atoms, and in bloodstream is able to bind to oxygen, making carbon monoxide an effective poison. One measure that can help prevent carbon monoxide forming is to add extra oxygen to gasoline.
Nitrogen dioxide	–8%	17,700,000	Contributes to acid rain and is one of principal catalysts that causes ozone formation near ground level.
Ozone	–17%	19,600,000[1]	Near ground level, ozone is toxic to plants and animals for reasons similar to toxicity of carbon monoxide; see "Ozone: Too Much and Too Little" above.
Lead	–94%	7,300,000	Lead tends to accumulate in tissues, where it interferes with various biochemical reactions, leading to mental retardation and various physical ailments. Most lead in air comes from burning leaded gasoline in automobiles. Reductions in use of leaded gasoline have resulted in substantial declines of lead in air.

1. Volatile organic compounds that produce ozone, rather than ozone itself.

Source: U.S. Environmental Protection Agency, *National Air Quality and Emissions Trends Report,* 1987.

MAJOR INDOOR AIR POLLUTANTS IN THE HOME

Until recently, most air pollution was viewed as something that occurred outside the house and was in the house only when it drifted in through open windows. Today, with better sealed houses, it has become clear that the house itself, chemicals or activities within it, and even the ground the house is built upon may contribute to air pollution indoors. Some of the pollutants found indoors are more dangerous to individuals than any outdoor air pollution. One estimate is that one-fifth to one-third of office buildings in America have polluted indoor air.

Pollutant	Sources	Effects	Levels in homes	Steps to reduce exposure
Asbestos	Old or damaged insulation, fireproofing, or acoustical tiles.	Many years later, chest and abdominal cancers and lung diseases.	Elevated levels can occur where asbestos-containing materials are damaged or disturbed.	Seek professional help from trained contractors; follow proper procedures for replacing wood stove gaskets that may contain asbestos.
Biological pollutants	Bacteria, mold and mildew, viruses, animal dander and cat saliva, mites, cockroaches, and pollen.	Eye, nose, and throat irritation; shortness of breath; dizziness; lethargy; fever; digestive problems; asthma; influenza and other infectious diseases.	Higher levels occur in homes with wet or moist walls, ceilings, poorly maintained humidifiers, dehumidifiers, or air conditioners; and household pets.	Use fans vented to outdoors in kitchens and bathrooms; vent clothes dryers outdoors; clean humidifiers daily; empty water trays in appliances frequently; clean and dry or remove water-damaged carpets; use basement living areas only if they are leakproof and have adequate ventilation, keeping humidity at 30–50%.
Carbon monoxide	Unvented kerosene and gas heaters; leaking chimneys and furnaces; wood stoves and fireplaces; gas stoves; automobile exhaust from attached garages; tobacco smoke.	At low levels, fatigue in healthy people and chest pain in people with heart disease. At higher levels, impaired vision and coordination; headaches; dizziness; confusion; nausea. Fatal at very high concentrations.	Homes without gas stoves vary from 0.5 to 5 ppm. Levels near properly adjusted gas stoves are often 5–15 ppm; near poorly adjusted gas stoves, can be 30 ppm.	Keep gas appliances properly adjusted; use vented gas space heaters and furnaces; use proper fuel in kerosene space heaters; install exhaust fan vented to outside over gas stoves, open flues when gas fireplaces are used; choose wood stoves that meet EPA emission standards; have annual inspection of home heating system; do not idle car inside garage.
Formaldehyde	Plywood, wall paneling, particleboard, fiberboard; foam insulation; fire and tobacco smoke; durable press drapes, textiles, and glues.	Eye, nose, and throat irritation; wheezing and coughing; fatigue; skin rash; severe allergic reactions; may cause cancer.	Average concentration in older homes without urea-formaldehyde foam insulation generally below 0.1 ppm, but may be greater that 0.3 ppm in newer homes using pressed-wood products.	Use exterior-grade wood products; use air conditioners and dehumidifiers to maintain moderate temperatures and reduce humidity levels; increase ventilation after bringing new formaldehyde sources into home.

Pollutant	Sources	Effects	Levels in homes	Steps to reduce exposure
Lead	Automobile exhaust; sanding or burning of lead paint; soldering.	Impaired mental and physical development in fetus and children; decreased coordination and mental abilities; damage to kidneys, nervous system, and red blood cells; may raise blood pressure.	Lead dust levels are 10–100 times greater in homes where sanding or burning of lead paint has occurred.	Have paint tested before removing it in older homes; if it is lead based, cover it with wallpaper or other building material and replace moldings and woodwork; use no-lead solder; have drinking water tested for lead; if exposure is suspected, consult your health department.
Nitrogen dioxide	Kerosene heaters, unvented gas stoves and heaters; tobacco smoke.	Eye, nose, and throat irritation; may impair lung function and increase repiratory infections in young children.	Average levels in homes without heaters is about half that of outdoors; homes with gas stoves or unvented gas or kerosene heaters often exceed outdoor levels.	Same steps that prevent carbon monoxide should be taken to prevent build-up of nitrogen dioxide.
Organic gases	Paints, paint strippers, solvents, wood preservatives; aerosol sprays; cleansers and disinfectants; moth repellents; air fresheners; stored fuels; hobby supplies; dry-cleaned clothing.	Eye, nose, and throat irritation; headaches; loss of coordination; nausea; damage to liver, kidney, and nervous system; some organics cause cancer in animals and are suspected of causing cancer in humans.	May average 2–5 times higher indoors than outside; activities such as paint stripping can raise levels to 1,000 times outdoor levels.	Follow manufacturers instructions when using household products; use volatile products outdoors or in well-ventilated places; dispose of unused or little-used products safely; buy volatiles in quantities you will use soon.
Particles (soot)	Fireplaces, wood stoves, kerosene heaters, and tobacco smoke.	Eye, nose, and throat irritation; respiratory infections and bronchitis; lung cancer.	Unless the home contains smokers or other strong particle sources, levels are same as or lower than outdoors	Vent all furnaces outdoors; keep doors to rest of house open when using unvented heaters; choose wood stoves that meet EPA standards; have annual tune-up of heating system; change filters on central-heating and cooling systems and air cleaners according to manufacturer's directions.
Pesticides	Products used to kill household pests and products used on lawns or gardens that drift or are tracked inside the house.	Irritation to eye, nose, and throat; damage to nervous system and kidneys; cancer.	Preliminary research shows widespread presence of pesticide residues in homes.	Use strictly according to manufacturer's instructions; mix or dilute outdoors; take plants or pets outside when possible; increase ventilation when using indoors; use other methods of pest control when possible; do not store pesticides indoors; dispose of unwanted containers safely.
Radon	Earth and rock beneath home; well water; building materials.	No immediate symptoms; estimated to cause about 10% of lung cancer deaths; smokers at higher risk.	Estimated national average is 1.5 picocuries per liter, but levels in homes have been found as high as 200 picocuries per liter. EPA believes levels in homes should be less than 4 picocuries per liter.	Test your home for radon; get professional advice if radon reduction is indicated; seal cracks and other openings in basement floor; ventilate crawl space; install subslab ventilation or air-to-air heat exchangers; treat wellwater by aerating or filtering through granulated activated charcoal.
Tobacco smoke	Cigarette, pipe, and cigar smoking.	Eye, nose, and throat irritation; headaches; bronchitis; pneumonia; increased risk of respiratory and ear infections in children; causes lung cancer; contributes to heart disease.	Homes with one or more smokers may have level several times higher than outdoor levels.	Stop smoking and discourage others from smoking; if you do smoke, smoke outdoors.

Note: ppm = parts per million.   **Source:** U.S. Environmental Protection Agency, adapted from *The Inside Story: A Guide to Indoor Air Quality.*

SOLID WASTE: THE GARBAGE CRISIS

The solid waste problem is not litter; it is household and industrial wastes, often called garbage (technically, garbage consists of food wastes, which are not by themselves a serious problem). Each year cities and towns pick up well over 100 million tons of trash and garbage. This does not include many other forms of solid waste—tailings from mines, wastes produced by factories, construction and demolition waste, sludge from sewage treatment, and junked machinery, such as automobiles. In brief, there is more solid waste per person, there are more people, and there are fewer options available on how to get rid of wastes.

More specifically, the amount of solid wastes has grown by 80% since 1960 and is currently expected to grow by another 20% over the next 10 years. Each year Americans produce about 1,300 pounds of solid waste per person. Some of this is industrial waste, but much of it is more personal. For example, 1.6 billion disposable pens are thrown into the garbage each year, along with 2 billion disposable razors and 16 billion disposable diapers.

Here is a breakdown by category:

SOLID WASTE IN AMERICA, 1984

Type	% of total
Paper and paperboard	37.1%
Yard wastes	17.9
Glass	9.7
Metals	9.6
Food	8.1
Plastics	7.2
Wood	3.8
Rubber and leather	2.5
Textiles	2.1
Other	1.9

Note: Figures do not add, owing to rounding.

Over time the types of solid wastes disposed of as municipal garbage have changed, with much more plastic and somewhat more paper and paperboard being the main change—clearly a result of new packaging techniques. Partly this is also a result of changes in the style of purchases; for example, people buy more fresh and frozen food today than they used to and less canned food. One result is that plastic and paper tend to increasingly replace metal in the municipal garbage pail. It is less clear what accounts for the percentage reduction in food wastes, although a probable explanation is that the *amount* of food waste per person is not changing. With everything else increasing—from 82,300,000 million tons of municipal waste in 1960 to 148,100,000 million tons in 1984—the percentage that is food wastes is decreasing.

Methods of Disposal

There are essentially three methods of disposing of solid wastes. They can be stored somewhere until most of the wastes have gone away by some form of decay or seepage into the groundwater, or at least until they are covered with layers of soil (landfills). They can be burned and the ashes stored somewhere until they decay, seep away, or are covered (incineration). Or they can be collected and used again (recycling). None of these methods seems to solve the problems solid wastes create, but there is a pattern of change emerging in how solid wastes are handled.

Landfills Until recently, the best-known way to dispose of solid wastes was to take them to a site where people did not live and throw them on the ground. This method is still used today, generally illegally. An improved method was to designate a spot for leaving your garbage that would be legal—the town dump, for instance—with everywhere else being illegal. Such dumps attracted rats and other pests, so the next step was to separate places for ordinary household garbage from places for disposing of old tires, refrigerators, couches, and the like. The town dump was used for the latter sort of trash (and picked over by people who wanted to recycle it), while household garbage was shipped elsewhere, where it could be professionally managed (soil was placed over it from time to time). Gradually, these makeshift

arrangements evolved into landfills—sites that accepted all forms of solid waste until they were full, after which they were covered with soil and reclaimed for other uses, such as residential housing.

Modern landfills are vast improvements over the town dumps that preceded them. They are lined with clay so that potentially toxic wastes do not seep into the water system. Even so, hazardous wastes are separated from those that are not hazardous and handled separately. Given a reasonable site, there is nothing especially wrong with a landfill that contains no hazardous wastes. However, the site has become the problem, in that the United States is running out of suitable sites for landfills. A survey by the Long Island, New York, newspaper *Newsday* in 1988 revealed that although there were still 8,801 landfills in the nation, 2,991 landfills had closed in the past five years, either for environmental or space reasons. People do not want landfills near their residence. Landfill sites need to meet strict environmental standards (e.g., they cannot be located where there is a noticeable slope to the site). These conditions combined to make it difficult to develop new landfills. And new landfills—or some other solution—are required, for the old ones invariably get full.

Incineration Although many communities today resort to paying to use another community's landfill—often hundreds of miles from where the garbage originated—no one thinks that this is a long-term solution. One alternative is to burn the garbage. Like the town dump, burning garbage has a long history, but one that has changed drastically. Today garbage is burned in special plants, usually equipped with machinery to separate the garbage into different types, with scrubbers to reduce air pollution from the burning, and often with electrical generators powered by heat from the garbage fire.

There are two major ways to produce energy by burning solid wastes. In the mass-burning system, developed in Europe but recently popular in the United States, the garbage is separated slightly by human operators for an optimal burning mix, tossed on a moving grate, and burned at about 2,000°F. All the garbage is burned. As it burns, forced air is used above the fire to cause the most harmful products of burning to burn further. The heat is used to boil water for a steam generator; the ashes fall

PROFILE OF U.S. WASTE GENERATION, DISPOSAL, AND REUSE

Year	Pounds of waste generated per person per day	Pounds of waste recycled per person per day	Pounds of waste recovered for energy production	Net Pounds of waste disposed of per day
1965	2.77	0.17	0.01	2.59
1970	3.16	0.21	0.01	2.94
1975	3.11	0.23	0.02	2.86
1980	3.35	0.32	0.06	2.96
1981	3.36	0.31	0.05	2.99
1982	3.25	0.30	0.08	2.86
1983	3.37	0.32	0.12	2.92
1984	3.43	0.35	0.15	2.93

through the grate. The ashes are about 20% of the original volume of garbage and 35% of its weight. Any iron residues are removed with magnets, and the remainder is taken to a landfill for burial.

In the refuse-derived fuel process, which is most common at present in the United States, garbage is put through a shredder to promote more even burning, iron is separated out by magnets, and the garbage is passed over screens that separate it further. At this point about half the garbage has been removed and will be recycled (i.e., the iron and perhaps other metals) or hauled to a landfill. It is shredded still further, into what is called fluff, or perhaps compressed into pellets or briquets. This material is then burned, usually at another site and perhaps together with coal, to produce electricity. The ash is handled by the public utility as it would handle any other ash, which often means selling it to towns to use on roads.

One problem with these methods is that the ash is often toxic. In New York State, tests showed that more than half the ash from incinerators in the state exceeded federal standards for toxic wastes. The main known problems are two heavy metals, cadmium and lead, both of which are serious poisons. It is unknown, however, what all the compounds found in ash are. Dioxins, for example, are likely. These are considered to be extremely dangerous, although their exact effects on humans are in dispute.

Another problem are the substances going out the chimney of the incinerator or the utility

PERCENTAGE OF WASTES REMAINING AFTER RECYCLING

Year	Paper and paperboard	Glass	Metals	Plastics	Rubber and leather	Textiles	Wood	Food wastes	Yard wastes	Other
1960	32.1%	8.4%	13.7%	0.5%	2.2%	2.6%	3.9%	14.6%	20.3%	1.7%
1965	35.0	9.2	11.6	1.5	2.4	2.4	3.8	13.1	19.2	1.7
1970	33.1	11.3	12.2	2.7	2.7	2.0	3.6	11.5	19.0	1.7
1975	30.4	11.6	11.8	3.9	3.3	2.2	3.8	11.8	19.5	1.9
1980	33.6	11.3	10.3	6.0	3.3	2.3	3.9	9.2	18.2	1.9
1981	34.5	11.3	10.0	6.1	3.2	2.4	3.5	8.9	18.2	1.9
1982	33.2	11.0	10.1	6.7	3.0	2.4	4.0	8.8	18.7	2.0
1983	35.3	10.4	9.9	7.0	2.6	2.3	4.0	8.5	18.1	1.9
1984	37.1	9.7	9.6	7.2	2.5	2.1	3.8	8.1	17.9	1.9

that is burning the garbage. A mass-burn incinerator, where sorting of solid wastes is minimal and all wastes are burned, may emit the following wastes: soot or smoke, sulfur dioxide, nitrogen oxides, hydrogen chloride, hydrogen fluoride, carbon monoxide, arsenic, cadmium, chromium, lead, mercury, dioxins, and furans. Some of these cause acid rain, while the others are directly toxic.

Finally, since the ash still has to be disposed of, unless it can be used in concrete or in some other way (recycled), the problem of diminishing landfill sites is only reduced, not eliminated.

Recycling The method of reducing the amount of solid waste that most recently has increasing support is recycling. Recycling is the conversion of wastes into useful products. Most of the time, waste cannot be recycled into the same product it was originally, but rather, into some other form. Most newspapers are recycled into cardboard, insulation, animal bedding, and cat litter, but, in an exception to the general rule, some is recycled into newsprint. About 10% of the fibers used in newsprint in America has been recycled.

In 1988 Americans bought 13.2 million tons of newspapers and set out 4.7 million tons, or about 35%, for recycling. Roughly 3.3 million tons were actually recycled, the remainder either piled up as excess inventory in paper mills or dumped or burned. There is at present more paper available for recycling than existing plants have capacity to use.

Despite problems of supply and demand, newspaper recycling is more successful than many other recycling programs. Although newspapers account for only 10% of noncommercial solid waste, they are 25% of recycled waste. This eases pressure on landfills, reduces gases produced by incineration, eases water pollution caused by paper mills, and saves trees.

Nuclear Wastes

Nuclear wastes are a special problem. These are the wastes from nuclear fission reactors. Although such reactors have been in existence only since World War II, they have generated a lot of waste, and because the waste is radioactive and some of it stays radioactive for thousands of years, it has proven very difficult to dispose of. Current plans to store some wastes in an underground site have run into various difficulties. Most nuclear waste in the United States is stored at the site that generated it, pending some long-term plan for handling it.

Nuclear wastes can explode. While a chain reaction resulting in an explosion caused by nuclear fission is unlikely except with relatively pure plutonium or enriched uranium, chemical reactions caused a major explosion of nuclear wastes in the Soviet Union in 1957. The explosion spread radioactive chemicals over thousands of square miles, resulting in the evacuation of thousands of people. Some thirty towns and villages disappeared from the map. After 15 years 20% of the region was still too radioactive for any use and has been set aside as a permanent "preserve." Although Soviet officials claim there were no casualties, outside

50 WORST TOXIC-WASTE SITES, 1988

Not all the problems with solid wastes have to do with those being generated today. Solid wastes from the past are often hazardous and need to be incinerated or moved to more secure landfills. Otherwise, they can affect the health of people living near the waste site, often by seeping into the water supply. The U.S. Environmental Protection Agency is committed to cleaning up such sites under the Superfund laws of 1980 and 1986. As a first step, they have developed a National Priorities List of sites that need attention, ranking them on a hazard ranking system. The following table lists the most hazardous 50 such sites in alphabetical order by state.

State	Site	Location	Rank	Listed since
Alabama	Triana/Tennessee River	Limestone/Morgan	31	Oct. 1981
Arkansas	Vertac, Inc.	Jacksonville	18	Oct. 1981
California	Stringfellow	Glen Avon Heights	32	Oct. 1981
Colorado	Sand Creek Industrial	Commerce City	36	Dec. 1982
Delaware	Army Creek Landfill	New Castle County	9	Oct. 1981
Delaware	Tybouts Corner Landfill	Mantua Township	2	Oct. 1981
Florida	American Creosote (Pensacola Plant)	Pensacola	50	Oct. 1981
Florida	Reeves Southeast Galvanizing Corp.	Tampa	45	Oct. 1981
Florida	Schuylkill Metals Corp.	Plant City	41	Dec. 1982
Iowa	LaBounty Site	Charles City	8	Dec. 1982
Maine	McKin Co.	Gray	33	Dec. 1982
Massachusetts	Baird & McGuire	Holbrook	14	Dec. 1982
Massachusetts	Industri-Plex	Woburn	5	Oct. 1981
Massachusetts	Nyanza Chemical Waste Dump	Ashland	11	Oct. 1981
Massachusetts	W.R. Grace & Co. Inc. (Acton Plant)	Acton	38	Dec. 1982
Michigan	Berlin & Farro	Swartz Creek	13	July 1982
Michigan	Liquid Disposal, Inc.	Utica	24	July 1982
Minnesota	FMC Corp. (Fridley Plant)	Fridley	17	July 1982
Minnesota	New Brighton/Arden Hills	New Brighton	43	July 1982
Minnesota	Reilly Tar (St. Louis Park Plant)	St. Louis Park	42	Oct. 1981
Montana	Anaconda Co. Smelter	Anaconda	47	Dec. 1982
Montana	East Helena Site	East Helena	29	Sept. 1983
Montana	Silver Bow Creek/Butte Area	Sil Bow/Deer Lodge	20	Dec. 1982
New Hampshire	Keefe Environmental Services	Epping	19	Oct. 1981
New Hampshire	Somersworth Sanitary Landfill	Somersworth	16	Dec. 1982
New Hampshire	Sylvester	Nashua	23	Oct. 1981
New Jersey	Bridgeport Rental & Oil Services	Bridgeport	35	Sept. 1983
New Jersey	Burnt Fly Bog	Marlboro Township	39	Oct. 1981
New Jersey	CPS/Madison Industries	Old Bridge Township	10	Dec. 1982
New Jersey	GEMS Landfill	Gloucester Township	12	July 1982
New Jersey	Helen Kramer Landfill	Mantua Township	4	July 1982
New Jersey	Lipari Landfill	Pitman	1	Oct. 1981
New Jersey	Lone Pine Landfill	Freehold Township	15	Sept. 1983
New Jersey	Price Landfill	Pleasantville	6	Sept. 1983
New Jersey	Shieldalloy Corp.	Newfield Borough	46	Sept. 1983
New Jersey	Vineland Chemical Co. Inc.	Vineland	40	Sept. 1983
New York	Old Bethpage Landfill	Oyster Bay	44	Oct. 1981
New York	Pollution Abatement Services	Oswego	7	Oct. 1981
Ohio	Arcanum Iron & Metal	Darke County	28	Dec. 1982
Pennsylvania	Bruin Lagoon	Bruin Borough	3	Oct. 1981
Pennsylvania	McAdoo Associates	McAdoo Borough	26	Oct. 1981
Pennsylvania	Tysons Dump	Upper Merion Twp.	25	Sept. 1983
South Dakota	Whitewood Creek	Whitewood	21	Oct. 1981
Texas	Crystal Chemical Co.	Houston	34	July 1982
Texas	French, Ltd.	Crosby	22	Oct. 1981
Texas	Geneva Industries/Fuhrmann Energy	Houston	37	Sept. 1983
Texas	Motco, Inc.	La Marque	27	Oct. 1981
Texas	Sikes Disposal Pits	Crosby	30	Oct. 1981
Washington	Western Processing Co., Inc.	Kent	48	July 1982
Wisconsin	Omega Hills North Landfill	Germantown	49	Sept. 1983

scientists estimate that hundreds of people were fatally contaminated.

Medical Wastes

Another special problem concerns medical wastes. This problem goes beyond the medical wastes that have washed up in small amounts on the beaches of the U.S. Northeast. Many landfills refuse to accept medical wastes, and little in the way of medical wastes can be recycled. Therefore, incineration is the disposal method of choice, usually at a hospital incinerator. But most hospital incinerators are less efficient than municipal incinerators, and most hospitals are located in regions of high population density. As a result hospital incineration contributes a disproportionate amount of air pollution.

Increasingly, moreover, medical wastes come from sources other than hospitals—walk-in clinics, nursing homes, specialized treatment centers, blood banks, doctors' or dentists' offices, or the home. About a billion disposable hypodermic needles used by diabetics are simply thrown into the household garbage. Doctors' and dentists' offices are much more of a source of medical waste than they were in the past because of an increase in disposables and because of tests and other procedures designed for office use that were once restricted to hospitals or outside laboratories.

Medical waste is different from other types of solid waste. Not only is about 10 to 15% of it infectious or potentially infectious, but about 20% is environmentally troublesome plastic—contributing about three times as much discarded plastic as that in the average municipal-waste site. Some medical waste is radioactive. Improperly disposed-of medical equipment has been known to cause radiation deaths in Mexico and Brazil, although not in the United States.

In 1988 new federal regulations went into effect, requiring closer tracking of medical wastes. Critics of the new rules suggest it will encourage hospitals to burn more wastes in their own already inadequate incinerators.

Hazardous Chemicals

The EPA by law must determine which substances used in the United States that might be released into the environment are hazardous. Hundreds of substances are classified as hazardous, and releases of more than a specified amount must be reported to the National Response Center—the toll-free number is (800) 424-8802. Substances are considered hazardous if they easily catch fire, are corrosive, react easily with other chemicals, or are poisonous (toxic). Some substances are hazardous because they cause cancer, such as asbestos.

Toxic chemicals must also be reported annually, and extremely hazardous substances require emergency planning if you possess over a certain amount, called the Threshold Planning Quantity (TPQ). If you exceed the TPQ, you must have a plan for emergencies.

Since 1963 there have been 17 U.S. industrial accidents in which the amounts and toxicity of chemicals released exceeded that of the accident in Bhopal, India, which killed about 3,000 people and seriously injured many more. Luck, planning, and other circumstances, however, resulted in fatalities in only a single accident, a release of vinyl chloride in Maine in 1964 that took five lives. It is disturbing, however, to note that 15 of the 17 accidents of this magnitude took place in the 1980s.

Smaller toxic releases have also caused death and injury. From 1982 to 1988, for example, 11,048 toxic spills caused a total of 309 deaths, as well as 11,341 injuries.

Following are some of the most commonly used substances in the United States, general information about them, and the amount that must be reported to the National Response Center if any are released into the environment.

COMMON HAZARDOUS CHEMICALS IN THE U.S. REQUIRING NRC NOTIFICATION (partial list)

Substance	Remarks	Amount that must be reported
Acetic acid	Vinegar is generally 2% acetic acid, but acetic acid is used in many manufacturing processes and is toxic as vapor at 10 parts per million in air.	5,000 lbs. (2,270 kg)
Acetone	Toxic chemical (1,000 parts per million in air) used in large amounts as solvent for resins and fats.	5,000 lbs. (2,270 kg)
Aluminum sulfate	Used sometimes in dyeing or in foam fire extinguishers.	5,000 lbs. (2,270 kg)
Ammonia	Use as fertilizer does not need to be reported; however, it is toxic and extremely hazardous; emergency planning required if 500 lbs. possessed.	100 lbs. (45.4 kg)
Benzene	Used in drugs, dyes, explosives, plastics, detergents, and paint remover; can cause cancer; toxic.	1,000 lbs. (454 kg)
Butadiene (1–3)	Used in synthetic rubber; toxic at concentration of 1,000 parts per million in air; toxic.	1 lb. (0.454 kg)
Chlorine	Widely used to disinfect water, the gas is toxic at concentration of one part per million in air; extremely hazardous; requires emergency planning if 100 lbs. is possessed.	10 lbs. (4.54 kg)
Cumene	Additive for high-octane fuels; toxic to skin at 50 parts per million in air.	1,000 lbs. (454 kg)
Cyclohexane	Petroleum derivative.	1,000 lbs. (454 kg)
Ethylbenzene	Toxic at 100 parts per million in air.	1,000 lbs. (454 kg)
Ethylene dichloride	Additive to gasoline that combines with lead to make "Ethyl" gasoline; also used in making plastics.	1,000 lbs. (454 kg)
Ethylene oxide	Widely used in making plastics; toxic at 50 parts per million in air; extremely hazardous; requires emergency planning if 1,000 lbs. possessed.	1 lb. (0.454 kg)
Formaldehyde	Used in wood substitutes and plastics; toxic and may cause cancer; extremely hazardous; requires emergency planning if 500 lbs. possessed.	1,000 lbs. (454 kg)
Methanol	Commonly called wood alcohol; used as antifreeze, solvent, and starting material for other compounds; toxic.	5,000 lbs. (2,270 kg)
Hydrochloric acid	Used in petroleum, manufacturing, and metals industries; toxic; as the gas hydrogen chloride, it is extremely hazardous and requires emergency planning if 500 lbs. possessed.	5,000 lbs. (2,270 kg)
Nitric acid	Used in preparing fertilizers and explosives; toxic and extremely hazardous; requires emergency planning if 1,000 lbs. possessed.	1,000 lbs. (454 kg)
Phenol	Used in making plastics; vapor is toxic to skin at 5 parts per million in air; extremely hazardous; requires emergency planning if 500 pounds possessed and further planning if 10,000 pounds possessed.	1,000 lbs. (454 kg)
Phosphoric acid	Used as flavoring agent, in pharmaceuticals, and in manufacturing fertilizers; toxic.	5,000 lbs. (2,270 kg)
Sodium hydroxide	Commonly known as lye or as caustic soda; toxic.	1,000 lbs. (454 kg)
Styrene	Used in manufacture of styrene plastics and artificial rubber; toxic.	1,000 lbs. (454 kg)
Sulfuric acid	Most common chemical used in U.S.; toxic and extremely hazardous; emergency planning required if 1,000 lbs. possessed.	1,000 lbs. (454 kg)
Toulene	Used in making explosives, drugs, and dyes; toxic.	1,000 lbs. (454 kg)
Vinyl chloride	Used to make plastics and aerosols; causes cancer; toxic.	1 lb. (0.454 kg)
Xylene	Used to make other compounds; toxic.	1,000 lbs. (454 kg)

Endangered Species

A species is one specific kind of organism, such as the common earthworm, the daffodil, the American opossum, or the human. Since life developed more than 600 million years ago, many different species have appeared and disappeared, or become extinct. Mostly this occurred before the modern human species existed, which has been only in the past 100,000 years or so. Today a vast wave of extinctions is taking place, and the human species is the ultimate or at least proximate cause. To reverse this trend, governments around the world are designating some species as endangered and trying to preserve them. Species are classified as endangered when they are thought likely to become extinct.

In the United States, species are classified as threatened or endangered by the U.S. Fish and Wildlife service in accordance with the 1973 Endangered Species Act, renewed and extended in 1988. The list of endangered species maintained by the Department of the Interior goes back to the original Endangered Species Act of 1966. The first list of endangered species, in March 1967, included 78 species. The current list runs 32 pages and contains more than 1,200 species. Species listed are protected in various ways, most specifically by a prohibition against killing them. Also, a critical habitat can be protected against change if the change would contribute to species extinction.

It is possible to have a large population and still be threatened with extinction. The African elephant probably has a population today of about 625,000, but this is less than half of what it was in 1979. A report commissioned by the International Union for the Conservation of Nature predicted that if conditions did not change, the African elephant would be extinct in 50 years.

The reason is ivory poaching. About 80% of the world's supply of ivory is thought to be a result of poaching. Decades of war on the African continent have left as one legacy a large number of high-powered weapons. Poachers use these to kill the elephants for their tusks and to intimidate (and often kill) the rangers or wardens whose job it is to protect the elephants. Thus, even in national parks, poaching proceeds at a terrifying pace. In Kenya 70% of the elephant population in its national parks has disappeared. It is thought that if poaching were to become 10% worse, the African elephant would become extinct in as little as 15 years.

Although the United States has not declared the African elephant an endangered species, it has halted imports of ivory, as has the European Economic Community. Previously, Japan imported about 40% of the world's ivory. Starting June 19, 1989, Japan limited imports of ivory to that sold directly by African governments from regions where the elephant is not viewed as endangered. This would cut Japan's imports from about 110 to about 16 tons a year. It was expected that the October meeting of the Convention on International Trade in Endangered Species would lead to a complete ban on ivory trading (although some nations may reserve for themselves the right to trade legal ivory).

Japan is usually not as concerned about endangered species as other nations. Although a signer of the 1980 Convention on International Trade in Endangered Species, Japan has more formal reservations (that permit trade in specified endangered species) than any other nation. Also, despite efforts by the International Whaling Commission to ban all whaling—since most commercially valuable whales are endangered—Japan plans to take at least 400 minke whales in 1990. Japan says that this whaling is research, but it sells the meat and oil to finance the "research."

SELECTED ENDANGERED SPECIES OF THE WORLD
Mammals

Cheetah (*Acinonyx jubatus*) It is believed the the cheetah almost became extinct at some time in the recent past, causing a "genetic bottleneck" when the population contained only a few closely related individuals. One cause of the fragility of the present cheetah population, which ranges from Africa to India, is this lack of genetic variability—although all the big cats are under pressure from changes in the environment and from hunters.

Chimpanzee, African (*Pan troglodytes*) Endangered status applies to chimpanzees in Africa only; the 600 or so chimpanzees in the United States are classified as threatened and may continue to be used in research.

Dugong (*Dugong dugon*), **or sea cow** An inoffensive sea mammal living in shallow waters around the coasts of the Western Pacific, the dugong is easy to capture and desirable as food. Its hide makes excellent leather. It is so vulnerable, however, that any organized hunting soon leads to local extinction. Although the dugong is protected by law in large parts of its range, controlling hunting at sea is difficult.

Gibbon (*Hylobates*, all species) As recently as 1969, a major list of endangered species failed to include any gibbon species. Today this most primitive of apes has all species endangered, primarily because of habitat destruction, a result of population growth.

Gorilla (*Gorilla gorilla beringei*) Unlike the gibbon the gorilla was recognized early as endangered, especially the mountain gorilla, which is sometimes treated as the subspecies *Gorilla gorilla beringei* and which was thought to have been endangered since 1933, only 31 years after its discovery. In the United States, however, both mountain and lowland gorillas are considered endangered. Part of the problem is habitat destruction, another is the use of gorillas as a food source, and the most disturbing part of the problem is the sale of baby gorillas to people outside Africa.

Jaguar (*Panthera onca*) It is surprising that an animal with a historic range extending from the U.S. Southwest to practically the southern tip of South America could become endangered. Habitat destruction and hunting for its pelt are the most likely causes.

Leopard (*Panthera pardus, P. unica,* and *Neofelis nebulosa*) Three species of leopard are endangered, although the common leopard, *P. pardus,* is considered threatened only in the southern part of its African range. The other two are commonly called the clouded leopard (*N. nebulosa*), found in Southeast and south central Asia, and the snow leopard (*P. unica*), found in the Himalaya mountains.

Monkey Many species of monkey, especially those from Latin America, such as the howler monkey (*Alouatta palliata*) and the spider monkey (*Ateles geoffroyi*), are endangered. A few African species, such as some colobus monkeys (e.g., *Colobus kirki*) are also endangered. The colobus monkeys are hunted for their fur, while habitat destruction and collecting for pets have been problems for Latin American monkeys. Another group of endangered Latin American monkeys are the tamarins (*Leontopithecus* spp.).

Orangutan (*Pongo pygmaeus*) This great ape has seen its range shrink from much of southern Asia to parts of the islands of Sumatra and Borneo. Habitat destruction and the capture of animals for pets or zoos have been factors, but also, young orangutans are likely to catch human diseases. Orangutans also have a very low reproductive rate.

Panda, giant (*Ailuropada melanoleuca*) One of the last large mammals to become known to Western science (brought to its attention in 1869), the giant panda has become one of the favorite creatures of all who have seen it. Entire books have been devoted to this rare species from a part of Asia that few visit. Its restricted habitat in China's western mountains and restricted diet of bamboo shoots contribute greatly to its endangered status. There are so few individual pandas that collecting them for zoos probably is a factor as well. Some attempts to breed pandas in zoos have been successful, but it is not easy to accomplish.

Rhinoceros All species of rhinoceros are endangered, with the black rhinoceros (*Dicedros bicornis*) and the white rhinoceros (*Ceratotherium simum*) the principal foci of concern. Several other rhinoceros species in Asia have been close to extinction for many years, but the black and the white of Africa were once very common. The southern range of the white rhinoceros was depleted in the same way and at the same time (and for somewhat similar reasons) that Americans caused the near extinction of the American bison, commonly called the buffalo. Today the problem is poaching for the horns, which are valued by Chinese in traditional medicine and for knife or sword handles by Arabs. Both of these demands probably contributed to the near demise of the Asian rhinoceroses.

Tiger (*Panthera tigris*) Habitat destruction and excessive hunting have nearly done in the species.

Whales The blue whale (*Balaenoptera physalus*), bowhead whale (*Balaena mysticetus*), gray whale (*Eschrichtius robustus*), humpback whale (*Megaptera novaeangliae*), right whale (*Balaena glacialis*), sei whale (*Balaenoptera borealis*), and sperm whale (Physeter catadon) are all listed as endangered by the United States. Since 1896 the International Whaling Commission has prohibited essentially all whaling, although a few whales are allowed to be taken by traditional whalers such as the Inuit (or Eskimo) or for research purposes (often disputed). The most serious situation is that of the blue whale, the largest animal of any kind that has ever lived. A survey in 1989 resulted in an estimate of 1,200 to 1,500 blue whales left from a population estimated to have been as high as 225,000 before commercial whale hunting started and the development in 1865 of the harpoon gun and steam-powered catcher. Estimates of whale populations are not very trustworthy, however. In 1967 a "Committee of Three Scientists" of the International Whaling Commission estimated that there were only 600 blue whales left. The 1989 survey suggested that the total number of humpback whales was 10,000, sei whales 54,000, and sperm whales 2,000,000. Good figures on other species of whales are not available, but the species known as the right whale has been nearly extinct since the 19th century.

Reptiles

Many species or subspecies of alligators, crocodiles, iguanas, and sea turtles are endangered. In the United States, protection of alligators has produced a resurgence in the species. Probably the greatest problem is the sea turtles, hunted from the egg to the adult for their food value or their shells. Beaches where they lay their eggs are raided, and another problem contributing to their endangered status is plastic debris in the ocean, which they often ingest, with fatal consequences.

Birds

There are about 9,000 species of birds currently identified around the world. According to the International Council on Bird Preservation, more than 1,000 of these species are threatened or endangered, three times the number at risk in 1978. Dramatic changes in their population have occurred especially in the tropics, where the number of threatened parrot species has almost doubled since 1978. In Indonesia, for example, the number of threatened species rose from 14 to 126 in the period 1978–88.

Birds have been particularly vulnerable to human-caused extinctions. The first extinctions definitely known to be caused by humans were the extinctions of some 20 species of flightless moas in New Zealand by the Maori, who probably arrived around A.D. 800. The last moa of any species was killed about the time of Capt. James Cook's voyage around the islands in 1769–70. Together with the Europeans who colonized the islands, the Maoris caused the extinction of about a third of the 150 bird species.

Some bird extinctions are well known, such as the dodo (late 17th century), the passenger pigeon (1914), and the Carolina parakeet (1914). But these are only the tip of the iceberg, since about 100 species of birds have become extinct since A.D. 1600 (about the time that good world-wide records of species first became available).

Fish

Most ocean fish are thought to be so numerous that they are not endangered, but overfishing has drastically reduced stocks of commercial fish in many specific grounds. Many Pacific salmon runs have been cut in half as a result of fishing in the ocean, mainly by Japanese and

Korean vessels, with plastic mesh nets 40 miles long. These nets not only catch salmon but also trap marine mammals, sea birds, and any other fish in the area. Much of this fishing is conducted illegally, as well, in waters where it is supposed to be banned by international agreements. The productive Georges Bank region off the coast of Massachusetts has seen takes of cod, flounder, and haddock drop to a quarter of what they were in the 1960s as a result of overfishing, first by foreign factory ships and later, when the region was restricted to U.S. fishing, by a modernized fishing fleet from New England.

Pressures on freshwater fish can also be heavy, but there are no significant species in danger of extinction. Most endangered species are fish with a limited habitat, which can be altered by dam building or introduction of foreign species.

Plants

Worldwide the most concern for plant extinctions is in the tropical rain forest. Tropical rain forests have the greatest number of species per unit of area than that of any other type of environment. This is true for all kinds of organisms in tropical rain forests, not just plants, but plant extinctions are of particular concern because of the possibility of extracting useful products, such as medicines, from the plants.

In the U.S., a survey by the Center for Plant Conservation claims that about 8% of all plant species are endangered, for a total of 3,000 species. (This is much higher than the approximately 200 U.S. plant species listed as threatened or endangered by the U.S. Fish and Wildlife Service.) The CPC projects that more than 250 species may vanish within the next five years and that up to 700 may become extinct by the year 2000.

ENDANGERED ANIMALS IN THE UNITED STATES

Although the world's attention is often on large endangered mammals from Africa or the oceans, the U.S. contains many endangered species or subspecies. A subspecies, sometimes called a race, is a local population of a given animal that has some distinctive trait, such as a different size or color, setting it off from the

main species but that is still classed as part of the species because the two populations can and sometimes do breed with each other. If breeds of dogs had occurred naturally in different regions, they would be classed as subspecies.

Note in the table below that many endangered species and subspecies, especially endangered birds, live on islands. Of the 95 known species of birds that have become extinct since 1600, 85 lived on islands. Because islands have small populations and limited habitats and allow the introduction of new species easily, they are especially dangerous environments.

In 1989 the General Accounting Office, an investigative arm of the U.S. Congress, reported that only 16% of endangered or threatened species were improving their status, while a third were deteriorating. Two percent of the species placed on the list since the 1973 law requiring classification of species as endangered or threatened have become extinct. Only five species have been removed from the list because their populations recovered: the American alligator, the Palau dove, the Palau fantail, the Palau owl, and southeastern U.S. populations of the brown pelican.

ANIMALS IN THE U.S. OFFICIALLY LISTED AS ENDANGERED, 1988

Common name	Scientific name	Remarks	Common name	Scientific name	Remarks
MAMMALS					
Bat, Hawaiian hoary	*Lasiurus cinereus semotus*	Related to hairy-tailed bats found on mainland of the Americas.	Bat, Sanborn's long-nosed	*Leptonycteris sanborni* (= *yerbabyebae*)	Found in New Mexico, Texas, and Central America, as well as Mexico.
Bat, Indiana	*Myolis sodalis*	Found in both East and Midwest.	Bat, Virginia big-eared	*Plecotus townsendii virginianus*	Subspecies of big-eared bat found in Kentucky, North Carolina, West Virginia, and Virginia.
Bat, Mexican long-nosed	*Leptonycteris nivalis*	Found in New Mexico, Texas, and Central America, as well as Mexico.			
Bat, Ozark big-eared	*Plecotus townsendii ingens*	Lives in caves in Missouri, Oklahoma, and Arkansas.	Deer, Columbian white-tailed	*Odocoileus virginianus leucunus*	Subspecies of white-tailed deer found in Washington and Oregon.

Common name	Scientific name	Remarks
Deer, key	*Odocoileus virginianus clavium*	Subspecies of white-tailed deer found in Florida.
Fox, San Joaquin kit	*Vulpes macrotis mutica*	California subspecies of kit fox, a smaller fox than the well-known red fox.
Jaguarundi	*Felis uagouaroundi cacomitli*	Found in Texas and Mexico, this is northern subspecies of small, dark gray or reddish brown wildcat—not a form of jaguar.
Manatee, Florida	*Trichechus manatus*	Large plant-eating water mammal believed to have been inspiration for mermaid legend.
Mouse, Alabama beach	*Peromyscus polionotus ammobates*	Subspecies of white-footed beach mouse found only in Alabama.
Mouse, Florida beach	*Peromyscus polionotus allophrys*	Subspecies of white-footed beach mouse found only in Florida.
Mouse, Key Largo cotton	*Peromyscus gossypinus allapaticola*	Subspecies of white-footed mouse found only in Florida.
Mouse, Perdido Key beach	*Peromyscus polionotus trissyllepis*	Subspecies of white-footed beach mouse found only in Florida and Alabama.
Mouse, salt marsh harvest	*Reithrodontomys raviventris*	Species of American harvest mouse found only in California.
Ocelot	*Felis pardalis*	Small spotted cat found in Arizona and Texas but is endangered throughout Central and South America as well.
Panther, Florida	*Felis concolor coryi*	Formerly found in much of American Southeast, now confined to Florida; it is estimated that only 30–50 are still alive.
Pronghorn, Sonoran	*Antilocapra americana sonoriensis*	Desert subspecies of pronghorn found in Arizona and Mexico.
Rat, Fresno kangaroo	*Dipodomys nitratoides exilis*	California subspecies of kangaroo rat, a desert rodent not closely related to true rats.
Rat, giant kangaroo	*Dipodomys ingens*	California species of kangaroo rat.
Rat, Morro Bay kangaroo	*Dipodomys heermanni morroensis*	Another subspecies of kangaroo rat found in California.
Rat, Tipton kangaroo	*Dipdodomys nitratoides nitratpoides*	Another subspecies of kangaroo rat found in California.
Seal, Hawaiian monk	*Monachus schauinslandi*	Other monk seals, found in Caribbean and Mediterranean, are also endangered.
Squirrel, Carolina northern flying	*Glaucomys sabrinus coloratus*	Subspecies of northern flying squirrel found in North Carolina and Tennessee.
Squirrel, Delmarva peninsula fox	*Sciurus niger cinereus*	Subspecies of fox squirrel, a tree squirrel larger than more common gray squirrel, found on Delmarva peninsula and eastern Pennsylvania.
Squirrel, Mt. Graham red	*Tamiasciurus hudsonicus grahamensis*	Subspecies of American red squirrel found in Arizona.
Squirrel, Virginia northern flying	*Glaucomys sabrinus fuscus*	Subspecies of northern flying squirrel found in Virginia and West Virginia.

Common name	Scientific name	Remarks
Vole, Amargosa	*Microtus californicus scirpensis*	California subspecies of vole, a small mouselike creature that lives in meadows.
Vole, Hualapai Mexican	*Microtus mexicanus hualpaiensis*	Arizona subspecies of the Mexican vole.
Wolf, gray	*Canis lupis*	The most common wolf, endangered only in lower 48 states of U.S., except for Minnesota, where it is classified as "threatened."
Wolf, red	*Canis rufus*	Found only in southeastern U.S., considered endangered except for an experimental population in North Carolina.

BIRDS

Common name	Scientific name	Remarks
Akepa, Hawaii, or honeycreeper	*Loxops coccineus coccineus*	Subspecies of one of 22 known species of Hawaiian honeycreepers, 8 of which have already become extinct, with another 8 threatened or endangered.
Akepa, Maui	*Loxops coccineus ochraceus*	Subspecies of Akepa that lives on island of Maui.
Akialoa, Kauai, or honeycreeper	*Hemignathus procerus*	Species of Hawaiian honeycreeper.
Akiapolaau, or honeycreeper	*Hemignathus munroi (= wilsoni)*	Species of Hawaiian honeycreeper.
Blackbird, yellow-shouldered	*Agelaius zanthomus*	Relative of common red-winged blackbird.
Bobwhite, masked (quail)	*Colinus virginianus ridgwayi*	Subspecies of common bobwhite found in Sonora desert of Arizona and Mexico.
Condor, California	*Gymnogyps californiaus*	At present this species continues only in captivity, but there are hopes of reintroducing it to wild.
Coot, Hawaiian (= alae keo keo)	*Fulica americana alai*	Hawaiian subspecies of common American coot.
Crane, Mississippi sandhill	*Grus canadensis pulla*	Subspecies of sandhill crane found only in Mississippi.
Crane, whooping	*Grus americana*	Among most famous of endangered species, whooping crane has been making a comeback, in part owing to program in which sandhill cranes hatch and rear whooping cranes.
Creeper, Hawaii	*Oreomystis (= Loxops) mana*	Either finch or honeycreeper subspecies found only in Hawaii.
Creeper, Molokai (= kakawehie)	*Paroreomyza (= Oreomystis, = Loxops) flammea*	Either finch or honeycreeper subspecies found only in Hawaii.
Creeper, Oahu (= alauwahio)	*Paroreomyza (= Oreomystis, = Loxops) flammea*	Either finch or honeycreeper subspecies found only in Hawaii.
Crow, Hawaiian (= 'alala)	*Corvus hawaiiensis (= tropicus)*	Species of crow found only in Hawaiian Islands.
Curlew, Eskimo	*Numenius borealis*	Until near end of 19th century, large flocks were seen and hunted extensively in eastern U.S. as curlew migrated from Alaska and Canada to Argentina; one of rarest birds on Earth today.
Duck, Hawaiian (= koloa)	*Anas wyvilliana*	Closely related to common mallard.

Common name	Scientific name	Remarks	Common name	Scientific name	Remarks
Eagle, Bald	*Haliaeetus leucocephalus*	Endangered in all states except Alaska, Washington, Oregon, Minnesota, Wisconsin, and Michigan.	Palila (honeycreeper)	*Loxiodes* (= *Psittirostra*) *bailleiu*	Found only on "big island" of Hawaii, palila was once common there.
Falcon, peregrine (incl. subspecies)	*Falco peregrinus*	Although population declined severely as result of DDT, which interfered with breeding, they have been making comeback; continued concern about use of DDT in their winter range in Latin America.	Parrot, Puerto Rican	*Amazona vittata*	Once common on Puerto Rico and nearby islands; sole remaining population is in Luquillo National Forest.
			Parrotbill, Maui (honeycreeper)	*Pseudonestor xanthophrys*	Extremely rare Hawaiian honeycreeper occasionally sighted on Maui.
Finch, Laysan (honeycreeper)	*Telespyza* (= *Psittirostra*) *cantans*	Found on small island of Laysan, west of main Hawaiian islands.	Pelican, brown	*Pelecanus occidentalis*	Endangered along Pacific coast and in Central and South America, but has made comeback along coast of southeastern U.S. since ban of DDT.
Finch, Nihoa (honeycreeper)	*Telespyza* (= *Psittirostra*) *yktima*	Found on small island of Nihoa, west of main Hawaiian islands.			
Goose, Aleutian Canada	*Branta canadensis leucopareia*	One of 10 subspecies of common Canada goose.	Petrel, Hawaiian dark-rumped	*Pterodroma phaeopygia sandwichensis*	This subspecies of gadfly petrel has become endangered because of predation by rats introduced onto Hawaiian islands, where it breeds.
Goose, Hawaiian (= nene)	*Nesochen* (= *Branta*) *sandvicensis*	Once almost extinct; captive breeding program has been successful in preserving species and reintroducing it to the wild.			
			Pigeon, Puerto Rican plain	*Columba inomata Wernorei*	Subspecies of pigeon related to common pigeons.
Hawk, Hawaiian (= io)	*Buteo solitarius*	Found only in upland forests on island of Hawaii.	Po'ouli (honeycreeper)	*Melanprosops phaeosoma*	One of 28 species of Hawaiian finches, of which 20 are either endangered or threatened.
Honeycreeper, crested (= 'akohekohe)	*Palmeria dolei*	Formerly found both on Molokai and Maui in Hawaii; now confined to high forest on Maui, where it is rarely sighted or heard.	Prairie chicken, Atwater's greater	*Tympanuchus cupido attwateri*	Of 4 subspecies of prairie chicken, easternmost one became extinct on Martha's Vineyard, Mass., in 1830, after wide distribution in eastern U.S.; endangered Atwater's subspecies is limited to Texas.
Kite, Everglades snail	*Rostrhamus sociabilis plumbeus*	Loss of habitat in Florida has confined bird to one small nesting population there; also found in Cuba, where it is not endangered.			
Millerbird, Nihoa (Old World warbler)	*Acrocephalus familaris kingi*	Found only on tiny Hawaiian island of Nihoa and only in limited habitat there; one of rarest birds on Earth.	Rail, Yuma clapper	*Rallus longirostris yumanensis*	One of pair of clapper rail subspecies that is endangered; unlike California clapper rail, however, Yuma subspecies is endangered over its entire range.
Moorhen (= gallinule), Hawaiian common	*Gallinula chloropus sandvicensis*	Revered by Hawaiians as bird that brought fire to the islands' people; Moorhen, or alae, is now extinct on Hawaii and Maui and endangered on the other islands.	Shrike, San Clemente loggerhead	*Lanius ludovicianus mearnsi*	California subspecies of loggerhead shrike, one limited to North America.
			Sparrow, Cape Sable seaside	*Ammodramus* (= *Ammospiza*) *martimus mirabilis*	Subspecies closely related to dusky seaside sparrow, which became extinct in 1988.
Nightjar (= whippoorwill)	*Caprimulgus noctitherus*	At first this Puerto-Rican relative of American whippoorwill was thought extinct; then it was sighted alive in early 1900s; with no sightings for next 50 years, it was thought extinct; currently classed as alive and endangered.	Sparrow, Florida grasshopper	*Ammodramus savannarum floridanus*	This subspecies, like Cape Sable seaside sparrow, is actually a New World bunting.
			Stilt, Hawaiian (= Ae'o)	*Himantopus mexicanus* (= *himantopus*) *knudseni*	Subspecies of black-winged stilt, a wading bird.
Nukupu'u (honeycreeper)	*Hemignathus lucidus*	Originally found on Hawaiian islands of Maui, Oahu, and Kauai; now known only from occasional sightings on Kauai.	Thrush, large Kauai	*Myadestes* (= *Phaeornis*) *myadestinus*	Formerly, there were subspecies of this "Hawaiian thrush" on several other islands besides Kauai, but three subspecies became extinct, in 1825 (Oahu), 1931 (Lanai), and 1936 (Molokai); there is subspecies on Hawaii.
'O'o Kauai (= 'O'o 'A'a) (honeyeater)	*Moho braccatus*	Of 5 species of honeyeater in Hawaii, 4 have become extinct since 1859, leaving only 'O'o, rarely seen on Kauai.			
			Thrush, Molokai (= oloma'o)	*Myadestes* (= *Phaeornis*) *lanaiensis* (= *obsurus*) *rutha*	Once believed to have become extinct in 1936, this is the other species of "Hawaiian thrush."
'O'u (honeycreeper)	*Psittiostra psittacea*	Once common on all Hawaiian islands, 'O'u is now rare and extinct on Oahu, Lanai, and Molokai.			

Common name	Scientific name	Remarks
Thrush, small Kauai (= puaiohi)	*Myadestes* (= *Phaeornis*) *palmeri*	Found only in forests on Kauai; probably rarest of surviving Hawaiian thrushes.
Vireo, black-capped	*Vireo atricapillus*	Found in Kansas, Oklahoma, Texas, and Mexico.
Vireo, least Bell's	*Vireo bellii pusillus*	Subspecies of Bell's vireo found in California and Mexico.
Warbler (wood), Bachman's	*Vermivora bachmanii*	Considered rarest North American native songbird; may already have been near extinction when first noticed by science in 1833.
Warbler (wood), Kirtland's	*Dendroica kirtlandii*	Nesting only in Michigan and wintering in Bahamas, about 1,000 of these birds seem to be surviving, with human help.
Woodpecker, ivory-billed	*Campephilus principalis*	This large American woodpecker is close to extinction, due to destruction of forests with populations of old trees in southeastern U.S. and Cuba.
Woodpecker, red-cockaded	*Picoides* (= *Dendrocopos*) *borealis*	Another woodpecker of forests of southeastern U.S.; related to more common downy and hairy woodpeckers.

REPTILES

Common name	Scientific name	Remarks
Anole, Culebra Island giant	*Anolis roosevelti*	Lizard endangered in Puerto Rico as well as on Culebra Island.
Crocodile, American	*Crocodylus acutus*	Found only in Florida, in U.S., but endangered throughout its range in tropical North, Central, and South America.
Gecko, Monito	*Sphaerodactylus micropithecus*	Puerto-Rican lizard.
Lizard, blunt-nosed leopard	*Gambelia* (= *Crotaphytus*) *silus*	California lizard.
Snake, San Francisco garter	*Thamnophis sirtalis tetrataenia*	California subspecies of garter snake.
Turtle, Alabama red-bellied	*Pseudemys alabamensis*	Alabama fresh-water turtle.
Turtle, Kemp's (= Atlantic) Ridley sea	*Lepidochelys kempii*	One of its few remaining breeding grounds is on Padre Island, Tex.
Turtle, leatherback sea	*Dermochelys coriacea*	Although it no longer breeds in U.S., it can sometimes be found in U.S. waters.
Turtle, Plymouth red-bellied	*Pseudemys* (= *Chrysemys*) *rubiventris bangsi*	Subspecies of freshwater turtle found only in Massachusetts.

AMPHIBIANS

Common name	Scientific name	Remarks
Salamander, desert slender	*Batrachoseps aridus*	Lungless salamander found only in California.
Salamander, Santa Cruz long-toed	*Ambystoma macrodactylum croceum*	Mole salamander subspecies found only in California.
Salamander, Texas blind	*Typhlomolge rathbuni*	Living in caves, this salamander has external gills, vestigial eyes, and white body.
Toad, Huston	*Bufo houstonensis*	True toad found only in Texas.
Toad, Wyoming	*Bufo hemiophrys baxteri*	Subspecies of true toad found only in Wyoming.

FISH

Common name	Scientific name	Remarks
Chub, bonytail	*Gila elegans*	Historic range: Arizona, California, Colorado, Nevada, Utah, and Wyoming.

Common name	Scientific name	Remarks
Chub, bicolor	*Gila Bicolor* ssp.	Historic range: Oregon.
Chub, Borax Lake	*Gila boraxobius*	Historic range: Oregon.
Chub, humpback	*Gila cypha*	Historic range: Arizona, Colorado, Utah, and Wyoming.
Chub, Mohave tui	*Gila bicolor mohavensis*	Historic range: California.
Chub, Owens tui	*Gila bicolor snyderi*	Historic range: California.
Chub, Pahranagat roundtail	*Gila robusta jordani*	Historic range: Nevada.
Chub, Yaqui	*Gila purpurea*	Historic range: Arizona, Mexico.
Cui-ui	*Chasmistes cujus*	Historic range: Nevada.
Dace, Ash Meadows speckled	*Rhinicthys osculus nevadensis*	Historic range: Nevada.
Dace, Kendall Warm Springs	*Rhinichthys occulus thermalis*	Historic range: Wyoming.
Dace, Moapa	*Moapa coriacea*	Historic range: Warm Springs in southern Nevada.
Darter, amber	*Percina antesella*	Historic range: Georgia, Tennessee.
Darter, boulder	*Etheostoma* sp.	Historic range: Alabama, Tennessee.
Darter, fountain	*Etheostoma fonticola*	Historic range: Texas.
Darter, Maryland	*Etheostoma sellare*	Historic range: one or two streams, Maryland.
Darter, Okaloosa	*Etheostoma okaloosae*	Historic range: Florida.
Darter, snail	*Percini tanasi*	Famous for its role in delaying construction of dam, although new populations have since been found, changing its classification from endangered to threatened.
Darter, watercress	*Etheostoma nuchale*	Historic range: Alabama.
Gambusia, Amistad	*Gambusia amistadensis*	Historic range: Texas.
Gambusia, Big Bend	*Gambusia gaigei*	Historic range: Two springs near Big Bend National Park in Texas; in 1957 it reached low point of two males and one female but has since recovered somewhat.
Gambusia, Clear Creek	*Gambusia heterochir*	Historic range: headwaters of one creek in Texas; threatened by competition and interbreeding with introduced mosquito fish.
Gambusia, Pecos	*Gambusia nobilis*	Historic range: New Mexico, Texas; now extinct in New Mexico and confined to region around Toyahvale, Tex.
Gambusia, San Marcos	*Gambusia georgei*	Historic range: Texas.
Killifish, Pahrump	*Empetrichthys latos*	Historic range: three springs in western Nevada, but one went dry and another was filled in by the owner.
Logperch, Conasauga	*Percina jenkinsi*	Historic range: Georgia, Tennessee.
Madtom, Scioto	*Noturus trautmani*	Historic range: Ohio.
Madtom, Smoky	*Noturus baileyi*	Historic range: Tennessee.
Pupfish, Ash Meadows Amargosa	*Cyprinodon nevadensis mionectes*	Historic range: Nevada.
Pupfish, Comanche Springs	*Cyprinodon elegans*	Historic range: Large springs in Pecos County, Tex.; these have gone dry, and now pupfish survives only in irrigation ditches.
Pupfish, desert	*Cyprinodon macularius*	Historic range: Arizona, California, Mexico.

Common name	Scientific name	Remarks
Pupfish, Devils Hole	Cyprinodon diabolis	Historic range: one spring hole in Nevada; perhaps most restricted range of any vertebrate.
Pupfish, Leon Springs	Cyprinodon bovinus	Historic range: Leon Springs, near Fort Stockton, Tex.
Pupfish, Owens	Cyprinodon radiosus	Historic range: California.
Pupfish, Warm Springs	Cyprinodon negadensis pectoralis	Historic range: Nevada.
Spinedace, White River	Lepidomeda albivallis	Historic range: Nevada.
Springfish, Hiko White River	Crenichthys baileyi grandis	Historic range: Nevada.
Squawfish, Colorado	Ptychochelius lucius	Historic range: southwestern U.S. and Mexico.
Stickleback, unarmoured three-spine	Gasterosteus aculeatus williamsoni	Historic range: California.
Sturgeon, shortnose	Acipenser brevirostrum	Historic range: U.S. Atlantic coast and Canada.
Sucker, June	Chasmistes liorus	Historic range: Utah Lake in Utah and spawning run up Provo River in Utah; nearly became extinct during droughts of 1930s.
Sucker, Lost River	Deltistes luxatus	Historic range: California, Oregon.
Sucker, Modoc	Catostomus microps	Historic range: California.
Sucker, shortnose	Chasmistes brevirostris	Historic range: California, Oregon.
Topminnow, Gila	Poeciliopsis occidentalis	Historic range: Lower Gila River basin of Arizona and New Mexico, and northern Mexico; competition from introduced mosquito fish is main problem.
Trout, Gila	Salmo gilae	Historic range: Gila River basin of Arizona and New Mexico; suffers from competition with introduced trout and from habitat destruction.
Woundfin	Plagopterus argentissimus	Historic range: Arizona, Nevada, and New Mexico.

SHELLFISH (clams, crustaceans, and snails)

Common name	Scientific name	Remarks
Amphipod, Hay's Spring	Stgobromus hayi	Historic range: District of Columbia.
Crayfish (no common name)	Cambarus zophonastes	Historic range: Arkansas.
Crayfish, Nashville	Orconectes shoupi	Historic range: Tennessee.
Isopod, Socorro	Thermosphaeroma (= Exosphaeroma) thermophilis	Historic range: New Mexico.
Mussel, Curtis'	Pleurobema curtum	Historic range: Alabama, Mississippi.
Mussel, Judge Tait's	Pleurobema taitianum	Historic range: Alabama, Mississippi.
Mussel, Marshall's	Pleurobema marshalli	Historic range: Alabama, Mississippi.
Mussel, penitent	Epioblasma (= Dysnomia) penita	Historic range: Alabama, Mississippi.
Pearlshell, Louisiana	Margaritifera hembeli	Historic range: Louisiana.
Pearly mussel, Alabama lamp	Lampsilis virescens	Historic range: Alabama, Tennessee.
Pearly mussel, Appalachian monkeyface	Quadrula sparsa	Historic range: Tennessee, Virginia.
Pearly mussel, birdwing	Conradilla caelata	Historic range: Tennessee, Virginia.
Pearly mussel, Cumberland bean	Vilosa (= Micromya) trabalis	Historic range: Tennessee, Virginia.
Pearly mussel, Cumberland monkeyface	Quadrula intermedia	Historic range: Alabama, Tennessee, Virginia.

Common name	Scientific name	Remarks
Pearly mussel, Curtis'	Epioblasma (= Dysnomia) florentina curtsi	Historic range: Missouri.
Pearly mussel, dromedary	Dromus dromas	Historic range: Tennessee, Virginia.
Pearly mussel, green-blossom	Epioblasma (= Dysnomia) torulosa gubermaculum	Historic range: Tennessee, Virginia.
Pearly mussel, Higgins' eye	Lampsilis higgini	Historic range: midwestern U.S.
Pearly mussel, orange-footed	Plethobasus cooperianus	Historic range: midwestern U.S.
Pearly mussel, pale lilliput	Topxolasma (= Carunculina) cylindrelius	Historic range: Alabama, Tennessee.
Pearly mussel, pink mucket	Lampsilis orbiculata	Historic range: midwestern U.S.
Pearly mussel, tubercled-blossom	Epioblasma (= Dysnomia) torulosa torulosa	Historic range: midwestern U.S.
Pearly mussel, turgid-blossom	Epioblasma (= Dysnomia) turgidula	Historic range: Alabama, Tennessee.
Pearly mussel, white cat's paw	Epioblasma (= Dysnomia) sulcata delicata	Historic range: Indiana, Michigan, Ohio.
Pearly mussel, white wartyback	Plethobasus cicatricosus	Historic range: Alabama, Indiana, Tennessee.
Pearly mussel, yellow-blossom	Epioblasma (= Dysnomia) florentina florentina	Historic range: Alabama, Tennessee.
Pigtoe, fine-rayed	Fusconaia cuneolus	Clam-like mollusk found in Alabama, Tennessee, and Virginia.
Pigtoe, rough	Pleurobema plenum	Historic range: Indiana, Kentucky, Tennessee, Virginia.
Pigtoe, shiny	Fusconaia edgariana	Historic range: Alabama, Tennessee, Virginia.
Pocketbook, fat	Potamilus (= Proptera) capax	Clam-like mollusk found in Arkansas, Indiana, Missouri, and Ohio.
Riffle-shell, tan	Epioblasma walkeri	Pearly mussel found in Kentucky, Tennessee, and Virginia.
Shrimp, Alabama cave	Palaemonias alabamae	Historic range: Alabama.
Snail, Iowa Pleistocene	Discus macclintocki	Historic range: Iowa.
Snail, Oahu tree	Achatinella (all species)	Historic range: Hawaii.
Snail, Virginia fringed mountain	Polygyriscus virginianus	Historic range: Virginia.
Spiny mussel, James (= James River)	Pleurobema (= Canthryria) collina	Historic Range: Virginia, West Virginia.
Spiny mussel, Tar River	Elliptio (= Canthyria) steinstansana	Historic range: North Carolina.
Stirrup shell	Quadrula stapes	Pearly mussel found in Alabama and Mississippi.

INSECTS AND ARACHNIDS

Common name	Scientific name	Remarks
Beetle, Kretschmarr cave mold	Texamaurops reddelli	Historic range: Texas.
Beetle, Tooth Cave ground	Rhadine persephone	Historic range: Texas.
Butterfly, El Segundo blue	Euphilotes (= Shijimiaeoides) battoides allyni	Historic range: California.
Butterfly, Lange's metalmark	Apodemia mormo langei	Historic range: California.
Butterfly, lotis blue	Lycaeides argyrognomon lotis	Historic range: California.
Butterfly, mission blue	Icaricia icarioides missionensis	Historic range: California.
Butterfly, Palos Verdes blue	Glaucopsyche lygdamus paloverdesensis	Historic range: California.
Butterfly, San Bruno elfin	Callophrys mossii bayensis	Historic range: California.
Butterfly, Schaus swallowtail	Heraclides (= Papilio) aristodemus ponceanus	Historic range: Florida.
Butterfly, Smith's blue	Euphilotes (= Shijimiaeoides) enoptes smithi	Historic range: California.
Harvestman, Bee Creek Cave	Texella reddelli	"Daddy longlegs" found in Texas.
Pseudoscorpion, Tooth Cave	Microcreagris texana	Historic range: Texas.
Spider, Tooth Cave	Leptoneta myopica	Historic range: Texas.

PART IV THE WORLD

THE NATIONS OF THE WORLD

Afghanistan
Democratic Republic of Afghanistan
Geography Location: landlocked country in southwestern Asia. **Boundaries:** USSR to N, China to NE, Pakistan to E and S, Iran to W. **Total land area:** 251,773 sq. mi. (652,225 sq km). **Coastline:** none. **Comparative area:** slightly smaller than Texas. **Land use:** 12% arable land; negl. % permanent crops; 46% meadows and pastures; 3% forest and woodland; 39% other; includes negl. % irrigated. **Major cities:** (1982 est.) Kabul (capital) 1,036,407; Qandahar 191,345; Herat 150,497; Mazar-i-Sharif 110,367; Jalalabad 57,824.

People Population: 14,480,863 (1988). **Nationality:** noun—Afghan(s); adjective—Afghan. **Ethnic groups:** 50% Pashtun, 25% Tajik, 9% Uzbek, 9% Hazara. **Languages:** 50% Pashtu, 35% Afghan Persian (Dari), 11% Turkic langs. (primarily Uzbek and Turkmen), 4% minor langs. (30, primarily Baluchi and Pashai); much bilingualism. **Religions:** 74% Sunni Muslim, 15% Shi'a Muslim, 11% other.

Government Type: communist regime backed by multidivisional Soviet force. **Independence:** Aug. 1919 (from UK). **Constitution:** adopted Nov. 30, 1987. **National holiday:** Apr. 27. **Heads of government:** Mohammad Najibullah, president (since Nov. 1987). **Structure:** president elected by legislature; cabinet and judiciary responsible to president; Council of Ministers has full authority when legislature is not in session; Revolutionary Council acting as legislature and final court of appeal to be replaced eventually by bicameral legislature.

Economy Monetary unit: afghani. **Budget:** (1987 est.) *income:* N.A.; *expend.:* current expend. Af42.1 bil., capital expend. Af24.1 bil. **GNP:** $3.08 bil., $220 per capita (1986). **Chief crops:** subsistence farming and animal husbandry; wheat, fruits, nuts, karakul pelts,

wool; illegal producer of opium poppy and cannabis for international drug trade. **Livestock:** sheep, cattle, goats, asses, horses. **Natural resources:** natural gas, crude oil, coal, copper, talc. **Major industries:** small-scale production of textiles, soap, furniture, shoes, fertilizer, and cement for domestic use; handwoven carpets for export; extractive industries (oil and copper). **Labor force:** 4.98 mil. (1980 est.); 67.8% agriculture and animal husbandry, 10.7% services and other, 10.2% industry; current figures unavailable because of fighting (1986). **Exports:** $565 mil. (f.o.b., 1986); fruits, nuts, natural gas, carpets. **Imports:** $848 mil. (c.i.f., 1986); food supplies, petroleum products, machinery. **Major trading partners:** *exports:* USSR, Czechoslovakia, W. Germany; *imports:* USSR, Japan, China, Czechoslovakia.

Intl. Orgs. Colombo Plan, FAO, G-77, IAEA, IBRD, ICAO, IDA, IFAD, IFC, ILO, IMF, INTELSAT, ITU, NAM, UN, UNESCO, UPU, WHO, WMO.

Remote and landlocked, Afghanistan has been a crossroads of trans-Asian trade and conquest since antiquity. Alexander the Great's invasion gave rise to the kingdom of Bactria. In the seventh century, a flourishing Buddhist civilization there fell to Islamic conquests. Genghis Khan overthrew the 11th-century empire of Mahmud of Gazni in the early 13th century, and Afghanistan was the center of Tamerlane's empire in the late 14th century. Thereafter, the region was divided among various tribes and petty kingdoms.

Modern Afghan history began with the establishment of a united emirate by Ahmed Shah Durrani in 1747. In the 19th century, Russia and Great Britain contested domination of Afghanistan. The British Afghan Wars of 1838–42 and 1878–80 left Afghanistan unconquered but within Britain's sphere of influence, confirmed by the Anglo-Russian agreement of 1907. The emirate became an independent monarchy in 1926, and modern reforms were instituted by King Amanullah and his successors Mohammed Nadir Shah (1929) and Mohammed Zahir Shah (1933).

The monarchy fell to a military coup in 1973, and Mohammed Daud Khan established a republic. In 1978 pro-Soviet leftists took power in a coup, and, ostensibly at the government's invitation, Soviet troops invaded Afghanistan in December 1979 to put down widespread popular revolts against Communist rule. In the ensuing civil war, the government's forces and their Soviet allies (with an eventual troop strength of more than 100,000) controlled the cities and main transportation routes, but guerrilla forces contested the countryside. After years of stalemate, in May 1988 the Soviet Union pledged to withdraw its troops. Half of the Soviet forces had left by

November 1988, and the rest by February 1989, leaving the Afghan Communist government to face an uncertain future confronting continued popular rebellion on its own.

Albania
People's Socialist Republic of Albania
Geography Location: southeastern Europe. **Boundaries:** Yugoslavia to N and E, Greece to S, and Adriatic and Ionian seas (parts of Mediterranean Sea) to W. **Total land area:** 11,100 sq. mi. (28,748 sq km). **Coastline:** 225 mi. (362 km). **Comparative area:** slightly larger than Maryland. **Land use:** 21% arable land; 4% permanent crops; 15% meadows and pastures; 38% forest and woodland; 22% other; includes 1% irrigated. **Major cities:** (1983) Tiranë (Tirana; capital) 206,100; Durrës (Durazzo) 72,400; Shkodër (Scutari) 71,200; Elbasan 69,900; Vlorë (Vlonë or Valona) 61,100.

People Population: 3,147,352 (1988). **Nationality:** noun—Albanian(s); adjective—Albanian. **Ethnic groups:** 96% Albanian, 4% Greek, Vlach, Gypsy, Serb, and Bulgarian. **Languages:** Albanian (Tosk is official dialect), Greek. **Religions:** Albania claims to be world's first atheist state; all churches and mosques were closed in 1967 and religious observances prohibited; pre-1967 estimates of religious affiliation—70% Muslim, 20% Albanian Orthodox, 10% Roman Catholic.

Government Type: communist state (Stalinist). **Independence:** Nov. 28, 1912 (from Turkey). **Constitution:** Dec. 27, 1976. **National holiday:** Liberation Day, Nov. 29. **Heads of government:** Ramiz Alia, chairman, Presidium of the People's Assembly (since Nov. 1982); Adil Çarçani, chairman, Council of Ministers (since Nov. 1982). **Structure:** Council of Ministers; legislature (People's Assembly); judiciary.

Economy Monetary unit: lek. **Budget:** (1986) *income:* $2.24 bil.; *expend.:* $2.23 bil. **GNP:** $2.7–2.9 bil., about $930 per capita (1986). **Chief crops:** vegetables, wheat, potatoes, tobacco, sugar beets, cotton, corn. **Livestock:** sheep, goats, cattle, pigs, asses. **Natural resources:** crude oil, natural gas, coal, chromium, copper. **Major industries:** food processing, textiles and clothing, lumber; shortages of spare parts, machinery and equipment, some food products and consumer goods. **Labor force:** 1.5 mil. (1987); about 60% agriculture, 40% industry and commerce (1986). **Exports:** $427 mil. (1986 est.); asphalt, bitumen, petroleum products, metals and metallic ores, electricity, oil, vegetables, fruits, tobacco. **Imports:** $363 mil. (1986 est.); machinery, machine tools, iron and steel products, textiles, chemicals. **Major trading partners:** (1986) *exports:* Greece, Czechoslovakia, Yugoslavia, Poland, Romania; *imports:* Czechoslovakia, Yugoslavia, Romania Poland, Hungary.

Note: Every recognized nation of the world is represented in this section; territories and possessions of these countries are in the following section. Each entry contains geographic, demographic, and economic facts and statistics for the present followed by a brief summary of the nation's political history.

The sources consulted include standard histories of the world, of various regions and time periods, as well as of individual countries. All the contemporary and demographic data are from publications of the United Nations, the U.S. Bureau of the Census, and the U.S. Central Intelligence Agency.

Intl. Orgs. CMEA, FAO, IAEA, ITU, UN, UNESCO, UPU, WHO, WMO; has not participated in CMEA since rift with USSR in 1961; officially withdrew from Warsaw Pact Sept. 13, 1968.

Anciently the Roman province of Illyricum, Albania became a much-contested area after the fall of Rome, being ruled at various times by Byzantines, Normans, Venetians, Slavs, and the kings of Naples. Albania was conquered by the Ottoman Empire in 1478 and ruled as an Ottoman province until 1912. Ottoman rule succeeded in converting most of the populace to Islam (with Catholic minorities in the north and Greek Orthodox in the south) but did not destroy the Albanian sense of national identity, based on ties of tribe, clan, and family.

Independence came in 1912 as a result of the First Balkan War, when Austria-Hungary and Italy fostered the creation of an Albanian state (under a titular monarch, the German prince Vilhelm von Wied) as a means of blocking Serbian access to the Adriatic. Occupied by its sponsors during World War I, Albania emerged from the war as a nominal republic but in fact was in a state of near-anarchy. With Yugoslav support, a tribal chief, Ahmed Zogu, became president of the republic in 1924. With Italian backing he proclaimed himself King Zog I in 1928.

In 1939 Italy invaded and annexed Albania. During World War II, partisan resistance to Italy was dominated by a leftist force under the leadership of Enver Hoxa. Allied forces landed in Albania in 1944, and Hoxa seized control of the liberated country's government. A socialist republic was established in 1946: foreigners were expelled and their assets nationalized; churches were closed; agriculture and industry were collectivized. Albania under Hoxa became one of the world's most thoroughly totalitarian states with close ties to the Soviet Union.

A doctrinaire Stalinist, Hoxa broke with Nikita Khruschev's Soviet Union in 1961 and became a client state of China. But with liberalization in China after 1977, Hoxa broke that link as well. Albania became almost totally isolated from world affairs.

In 1981 Hoxa's heir apparent, Mehmet Shehu, was reported to have committed suicide; it was later admitted that he had been liquidated. Hoxa died in April 1985 and was succeeded as president and first secretary of the Albanian Communist party by Ramiz Alia. Under Alia, Albania has relaxed its policies somewhat, seeking trade links with Greece, Turkey, and Yugoslavia (while continuing to support an ethnic Albanian separatist movement in Yugoslavia's Kosovo province).

With Chinese aid, the Albanian economy developed some basic industry and an export trade in chromium and processed foodstuffs. Despite industrialization, more than half the population remains in the agricultural sector.

Algeria
Democratic and Popular Republic of Algeria
Geography **Location:** northern coast of Africa. **Boundaries:** Mediterranean Sea to N, Tunisia and Libya to E, Mali and Niger to S,

Morocco, Western Sahara, Mauritania to W. **Total land area:** 919,595 sq. mi. (2,381,741 sq km). **Coastline:** 620 mi. (998 km). **Comparative area:** slightly less than 3.5 times size of Texas. **Land use:** 3% arable land; negl. % permanent crops; 13% meadows and pastures; 2% forest and woodland; 82% other; includes negl. % irrigated. **Major cities:** (1983 est.) Algiers (capital) 1,721,607; Oran 663,504; Constantine 448,-578; Annaba 348,322; Blida 191,314.

People **Population:** 24,194,777 (1988). **Nationality:** noun—Algerian(s); adjective—Algerian. **Ethnic groups:** 99% Arab-Berber, less than 1% European. **Languages:** Arabic (official), French, Berber dialects. **Religions:** 99% Sunni Muslim (state religion), 1% Christian and Jewish.

Government **Type:** republic. **Independence:** July 5, 1962 (from France). **Constitution:** Nov. 19, 1976, effective Nov. 22, 1976. **National holiday:** Anniversary of the Revolution, Nov. 1. **Heads of government:** Col. Chadli Bendjedid, president (since Feb. 1979); Kasdi Merbah, prime minister (since Jan. 1984). **Structure:** executive; unicameral legislature (National People's Assembly); judiciary.

Economy **Monetary unit:** Algerian dinar. **Budget:** (1987 est.) *income:* $23.0 bil.; *expend.:* $23.1 bil. **GDP:** $59 bil., $2,600 per capita (1986 est.). **Chief crops:** wheat, barley, oats, grapes, olives. **Livestock:** chickens, sheep, goats, cattle, horses. **Natural resources:** crude oil, natural gas, iron ore, phosphates, uranium. **Major industries:** petroleum, light industries, natural gas; automotive plants under construction. **Labor force:** 3.7 mil. (1984); 40% industry and commerce, 30% agriculture, 17% government, 10% services; 16% unemployment rate. **Exports:** $8.5 bil. (f.o.b., 1987 est.); petroleum and gas account for 98% of exports; 23% France, 19% U.S. (1984). **Imports:** $7.2 bil. (f.o.b., 1987 est.); 35% capital goods, 25% semi-finished goods, 18% foodstuffs; 25.7% France, 6.0% U.S. **Major trading partners:** U.S., W. Germany, France, Italy, Belgium, Netherlands, Canada.

Intl. Orgs. Arab League, FAO, G-77, GATT (de facto), IAEA, IBRD, ICAO, IDA, IFAD, ILO, IMF, IMO, INTELSAT, INTERPOL, ITU, NAM, OAU, OPEC, UN, UNESCO, UPU, WHO, WIPO, WMO.

From around 3000 B.C. nomadic ancestors of the Berbers inhabited Algeria, as the expanding Sahara desert displaced prehistoric grasslands and forests. The Phoenicians established trading centers in the Mediterranean coastal plain around 1200 B.C. Those centers were taken over by the Romans beginning around 200 B.C. With Roman support the Berber chief Massinissa formed the kingdom of Numida in what is now northern Algeria. From 46 B.C. to about A.D. 640, the area was controlled successively by the Romans, Germanic Vandal tribes, and the Byzantine Empire.

In the seventh century A.D., the Islamic conquests swept across North Africa, spreading Arab culture to Numida (Algeria) and ultimately as far as Spain. Most of the Berbers converted to Islam. The blend of Berber and Arab

culture in Algeria gave rise to a flourishing and rich Islamic civilization in the coastal plain, while Tuareg and other nomadic peoples controlled the sparsely inhabited interior.

Around 1500 the Christian kingdom of Spain captured Algiers and other coastal cities. In 1518 Barbarossa, a Turkish sea captain, captured Algiers and drove the Spanish out. In so doing, he joined Algeria to the expanding Turkish Ottoman Empire. Piracy became a key source of income for the Ottoman cities of Algeria. In the early 1800s, France, along with England and the United States, began military operations to suppress piracy in the Mediterranean. In 1830 France invaded Algeria, putting an end to Ottoman rule and establishing their own administration. Algeria was ruled as part of France itself. Many French settlers (*colons*) migrated to Algeria. Both they and the native Algerians were considered citizens of France, but the colons were granted substantial political and economic advantages over the indigenous population.

In 1847 a rebellion led by Abd-al-Qadir, a powerful Muslim leader, was suppressed by the French, but the spirit of Algerian nationalism remained alive. In 1848, in the wake of the rebellion, all of Algeria was conquered by the French and legally confirmed as an integral part of France. During World War II, many Algerians joined the Free French, hoping that their display of loyalty would be rewarded with greater self-rule after the war. Those hopes were disappointed, as French administration was resumed in 1945.

In 1954 the Front de Liberation Nationale (FLN) began a guerrilla war against the French in Algeria. They were opposed by French police and military forces and by the Secret Army Organization (OAS), an underground movement of colons who favored continued French rule. As the FLN gained strength, by 1958 French Premier Charles de Gaulle established a policy designed to prepare Algeria for self-rule.

Algerian independence was proclaimed on July 3, 1962; a million colons fled to France. A power struggle within the new Algerian government was resolved when Ahmed Ben Bella became the country's first premier in 1963. In 1965 Ben Bella was deposed by Col. Houari Boumidienne, who ruled as the head of a military government. In 1967 Algeria declared war on Israel, broke with the West, and established close relations with the USSR. Since the early 1970s, relations with the West, and particularly with France, have improved, but Algeria remains a member of the hard-line anti-Israel block of the Arab League.

Algeria's economic mainstay is petroleum. Agriculture (grain, wine grapes, dates, vegetables) is the principal economic activity in coastal areas, while pastoralism and mining dominate in the interior. Despite attempts at industrialization (steel, textiles, fertilizer, plastics, light manufacturing), the economy is plagued by instability and high unemployment.

Andorra
Principality of Andorra
Geography **Location:** landlocked country in eastern Pyrenees Mountains, in south-

western Europe. **Boundaries:** France to N and E, Spain to S and W. **Total land area:** 180 sq. mi. (467 sq km). **Coastline:** none. **Comparative area:** slightly more than 2.5 times size of Washington, D.C. **Land use:** 2% arable land; 0% permanent crops; 56% meadows and pastures; 22% forest and woodland; 20% other. **Major cities:** Andorra la Vella (capital).

People **Population:** 49,422 (1988). **Nationality:** noun—Andorran(s); adjective—Andorran. **Ethnic groups:** Catalan stock; 61% Spanish, 30% Andorran, 6% French, 3% other. **Languages:** Catalan (official); many also speak some French and Castilian. **Religions:** virtually all Roman Catholic.

Government **Type:** unique co-principality under formal sovereignty of president of France and Spanish bishop of Seo de Urgel, who are represented locally by officials called verguers. **Independence:** N.A. **Constitution:** none; some decrees, mostly custom and usage. **National holiday:** N.A. **Heads of government:** French co-prince François Mitterrand, president of France (since 1981) and Spanish Episcopal co-prince Msgr. Juan Marti y Alanís, bishop of Seo de Urgel, Spain (since 1971). **Structure:** legislative—General Council of the Valleys (28 members); executive—syndic (manager) and deputy subsyndic chosen by General Council; judiciary—chosen by co-princes, who appoint two civil judges, judge of appeals, and two battles (court prosecutors); final appeal to Supreme Court of Andorra at Perpignan, France, or to Ecclesiastical Court of Bishop of Seo de Urgel, Spain.

Economy **Monetary unit:** French franc and Spanish peseta. **Budget:** N.A. **GNP:** N.A. **Chief crops:** sheep raising; small quantities of tobacco, rye, wheat, barley, oats, and some vegetables. **Livestock:** N.A. **Natural resources:** hydropower, mineral water, timber, iron ore, lead. **Major industries:** tourism (particularly skiing), sheep, timber, tobacco, smuggling. **Labor force:** largely shepherds and farmers. **Exports:** N.A. **Imports:** N.A. **Major trading partners:** France, Spain.

Intl. Orgs. UNESCO.

Set high in the Pyrenees, the tiny state of Andorra is both a medieval relic and a modern capitalist land. Since 1278 Andorra has owed feudal allegiance to two co-rulers: the count of Foix in France and the bishop of Seo de Urgel in Spain, with claims of the former now exercised by the president of the French Republic. Andorra has no constitution, so the exact rights of the co-rulers remain vague. Foreign affairs are handled by France. Each of the seven Catholic parishes elects four members to the legislature, which in turn elects the syndic general, who is the chief magistrate and de facto head of government.

Andorra has no customs department, no registration or regulation of businesses, and no penal code. Since ancient times, and currently, its economic mainstay has been the "transshipment of goods" (a polite term for smuggling) between France and Spain. More recently, Andorra has become a center for tourists drawn by bargain shopping, and a banking center for the transshipment of money to other tax havens. These activities have fueled a seemingly endless economic boom in the postwar period.

Three problems cloud the horizon. First, Spain's entry into the EEC threatens Andorra's advantages as a duty-free haven. Second, unrestrained currency movements invite intervention by the country's co-rulers. Third, the tourist boom poses a danger of overdevelopment and environmental destruction.

Angola
People's Republic of Angola

Geography **Location:** western coast of Africa. **Boundaries:** Zaire to N and NE, Zambia to E, Namibia to S, South Atlantic Ocean to W; Cabinda district separated from rest of country by Congo to N, Zaire to S. **Total land area:** 481,354 sq. mi. (1,246,700 sq km). **Coastline:** 994 mi. (1,600 km). **Comparative area:** slightly less than twice size of Texas. **Land use:** 2% arable land; negl. % permanent crops; 23% meadows and pastures; 43% forest and woodland; 32% other. **Major cities:** Luanda (capital) 1,200,000 (1982 est.); Huambo (Nova Lisboa) 61,885; Lobito 59,258; Benguela 40,996; Lubango (Sá de Bandeira) 31,674 (1970 census).

People **Population:** 8,236,461 (1988). **Nationality:** noun—Angolan(s); adjective—Angolan. **Ethnic groups:** 37% Ovimbundu, 25% Kimbundu, 13% Bakongo, 2% Mestiço, 1% European, 22% other. **Languages:** Portuguese (official), various Bantu dialects. **Religions:** 68% Roman Catholic, 20% Protestant, 12% indigenous beliefs.

Government **Type:** Marxist people's republic. **Independence:** Nov. 11, 1975 (from Portugal). **Constitution:** Nov. 11, 1975. **National holiday:** Independence Day, Nov. 11. **Heads of government:** José Eduardo dos Santos, president (since Sept. 1979). **Structure:** legislative—National People's Assembly; official party is supreme political institution.

Economy **Monetary unit:** kwanza. **Budget:** (1986 est.) *income:* N.A.; *expend.:* $2.7 bil. **GDP:** $4.7 bil., $600 per capita (1986 est.). **Chief crops:** cash crops—coffee, sisal, corn, cotton, sugar; food crops—cassava, corn, vegetables, plantains, bananas and other local foodstuffs; disruptions caused by civil war require food imports. **Livestock:** cattle, goats, pigs, sheep. **Natural resources:** petroleum, diamonds, iron ore, phosphates, copper. **Major industries:** petroleum, mining (phosphate rock, diamonds), fish processing. **Labor force:** 2.8 mil. (1985 est.); 85% agriculture, 15% industry. **Exports:** $1.1 bil. (f.o.b., 1986 est.); oil, coffee, diamonds, sisal, fish and fish products. **Imports:** $1.4 bil. (f.o.b., 1986 est.); capital equipment (machinery, electrical equipment), food, vehicles and spare parts, textiles and clothing, medicines; substantial military deliveries. **Major trading partners:** U.S., USSR, Cuba, Portugal, Brazil.

Intl. Orgs. FAO, G-77, GATT (de facto), ICAO, IFAD, ILO, IMO, INTELSAT, ITU, NAM, OAU, UN, UNESCO, UPU, WHO, WMO.

Bantu peoples have occupied Angola for at least 2,000 years. Portuguese explorers arrived in the 15th century, and Portugal established control of the coast in 1583, interrupted by a brief Dutch invasion, 1641–48. Portugal, in alliance with the north Angolan kingdom of Bakongo, engaged in an extensive trade of slaves to Brazil.

In the late 19th century, Angola was organized as a Portuguese colony, sometimes called Portuguese West Africa. Nearly half a million Portuguese settlers immigrated to Angola and dominated local government, trade, and small-scale industry in addition to organizing plantation-style cultivation of cotton, palm oil, bananas, and coffee. A railroad was built across Angola to transport exports of metal from the Katanga region of the Belgian Congo (now Zaire) to the West African coast.

By the 1950s the native peoples of Angola began to agitate for independence from Portugal. The National Front was organized and spearheaded the liberation movement. Guerrilla warfare began in 1961, with several feuding factions all fighting the Portuguese. Following the Portuguese revolution of 1974, independence was promised to Angola, and factional warfare intensified. Most Portuguese settlers fled the country, leaving it seriously lacking in trained administrative and commercial personnel. Independence came on Nov. 11, 1975.

Civil war between the National Front, the Popular Movement for the Liberation of Angola (MPLA), and the National Union for the Total Independence of Angola (UNITA) led, in 1976, to the victory of the MPLA. A Marxist state was organized, with Soviet backing and the use of Cuban support troops as well as Cuban teachers, doctors, and other professionals and administrators. But large portions of the country remained in the hands of UNITA, which continued the civil war with Chinese and American support. In 1979, José Eduardo dos Santos became president of Angola at the head of the MPLA government.

As many as 37,000 Cuban troops continued to operate in support of the Angolan government. Direct clashes between Angolan and South African troops occurred during the 1980s, as Angola gave shelter to the guerrilla forces of the South-West African People's Organization seeking independence for Namibia. UNITA forces, operating from bases in northern Angola and across the border in Zaire, were granted increased aid by the U.S. government in 1987.

In 1988, talks between South Africa, Cuba, and Angola, mediated by the United States, convened in London to discuss the withdrawal of Cuban troops from Angola and the related issue of Namibian independence. On Dec. 13, 1988, a tentative agreement was announced in Brazzaville, Congo, calling for Namibian independence and a phased withdrawal of Cuban troops from Angola by July 1, 1991. The first phase of the withdrawal began in January 1989.

In the spring of 1989, direct talks between Angola's Pres. dos Santos and UNITA's Jonas Savimbi led to a tentative agreement for power-sharing between the two factions once the Cuban withdrawal has been completed. Details have yet to be worked out, however, and the situation in Angola remains tense. Both the United States and the USSR have declared themselves in favor of a peaceful political solution in Angola.

Much of Angola consists of an arid plateau. The densely forested northeastern region yields hardwoods and also produces diamonds. Most agriculture, including grains and plantation crops, is confined to a narrow coastal strip. Angola is rich in mineral resources, including copper, manganese, sulphur, phosphates, and petroleum. There is some industrial development, including food processing, paper, textiles, shoes, and other light manufacturing. Despite the damage of civil war and economic mismanagement, which has led to widespread poverty, Angola's long-term economic prospects are promising. An immediate benefit of an end to the civil war will be the reopening of the country's major transportation artery, the Angola-Zaire railway.

Antigua and Barbuda

Geography Location: three islands in eastern Caribbean Sea lying approximately 300 mi. (480 km) SE of Puerto Rico. **Boundaries:** Atlantic Ocean to N and E, Caribbean Sea to S and W. **Total land area:** 171 sq. mi. (441.6 sq km). **Coastline:** 95 mi. (153 km). **Comparative area:** slightly less than 2.5 times size of Washington, D.C. **Land use:** 18% arable land; 0% permanent crops; 7% meadows and pastures; 16% forest and woodland; 59% other; includes N.A. % irrigated. **Major cities:** St. John's (capital) 36,000.

People Population: 70,925 (1988). **Nationality:** noun—Antiguan(s); adjective—Antiguan. **Ethnic groups:** almost entirely of black African origin; some of British, Portuguese, Lebanese, and Syrian origin. **Languages:** English (official), local dialects. **Religions:** Anglican (predominant), other Protestant sects, some Roman Catholic.

Government Type: independent state recognizing Elizabeth II as chief of state. **Independence:** Nov. 1, 1981 (from UK). **Constitution:** Nov. 1, 1981. **National holiday:** Nov. 1. **Heads of government:** Sir Wilfred Ebenezer Jacobs, governor-general (since 1967); Vere C. Bird, prime minister (since 1976). **Structure:** executive—prime minister and cabinet; bicameral legislature—17-member popularly elected House of Representatives and 17-member Senate; judiciary—court of appeals.

Economy Monetary unit: East Caribbean (EC) dollar. **Budget:** (1986) *income:* $70 mil.; *expend.:* $144 mil. GDP: $173 mil., $2,200 per capita (1985). **Chief crops:** cotton (main crop), sugar. **Livestock:** cattle, sheep, goats, pigs. **Natural resources:** negl.; pleasant climate fosters tourism. **Major industries:** tourism, construction, light manufacturing (clothing, alcohol, household appliances). **Labor force:** 30,000 (1983); 82% commerce and services, 11% agriculture, 7% industry; 20% unemployment (1983). **Exports:** $25 mil. (f.o.b., 1986); clothing, rum, lobsters. **Imports:** $181 mil. (f.o.b., 1986); fuel, machinery, food. **Major trad-**

ing partners: *exports:* (1984) 24% Trinidad and Tobago, 11% Barbados, 3% Jamaica; *imports:* (1985) 56% U.S., 11% UK, 7% Jamaica, 2% Trinidad and Tobago.

Intl. Orgs. Commonwealth, FAO, G-77, IBRD, ICAO, ILO, IMF, OAS, UN, UNESCO, WHO, WMO.

English settlers colonized Antigua and Barbuda in 1632, and it remained a British possession for most of its history until gaining independence in 1981. The current Antigua Labour party government of Prime Minister Vere Cornwall Bird has held power since that time. The residents of Barbuda have been intent on severing political relations between the two islands as a result of cultural and political differences with Antiguans. Tourism is the main contributor to the national income.

Argentina
Argentine Republic

Geography Location: southern part of South America. **Boundaries:** Bolivia, Paraguay, and Brazil to N.; Uruguay and South Atlantic Ocean to E.; Chile to W. **Total land area:** 1,068,302 sq. mi. (2,766,889 sq km) (figures exclude Falkland Islands and Antarctic territory claimed by Argentina). **Coastline:** 3,099 mi. (4,986 km). **Comparative area:** slightly more than four times size of Texas. **Land use:** 9% arable land; 4% permanent crops; 52% meadows and pastures; 22% forest and woodland; 13% other; includes 1% irrigated. **Major cities:** (1980 census) Buenos Aires (capital) 2,922,829; Córdoba 983,969; Rosario 957,301; Mendoza 605,623; La Plata 564,750.

People Population: 31,532,538 (1988). **Nationality:** noun—Argentine(s); adjective—Argentine. **Ethnic groups:** 85% white, 15% mestizo, Indian, and other nonwhite groups. **Languages:** Spanish (official), English, Italian, German, French. **Religions:** 90% nominally Roman Catholic (less than 20% practicing), 2% Protestant, 2% Jewish, 6% other.

Government Type: republic. **Independence:** July 9, 1816 (from Spain). **Constitution:** May 1, 1853. **National holiday:** Independence Day, May 25. **Head of government:** Carlos Saúl Menem, president (since May 1989). **Structure:** executive (president, vice president, cabinet); legislative (National Congress—Senate, Chamber of Deputies); national judiciary.

Economy Monetary unit: austral. **Budget:** *income:* N.A.; *expend.:* $13.3 bil. (1987). GDP: $77.2 bil., $2,510 per capita (1986). **Chief crops:** cereals, oilseed, livestock products; major world exporter of temperate-zone foodstuffs. **Livestock:** cattle, sheep, pigs, horses, goats. **Natural resources:** fertile plains of the pampas, lead, zinc, copper. **Major industries:** food processing (especially meat packing), motor vehicles, consumer durables. **Labor force:** 10.9 mil. (1985 est.); 57% services, 31% industry, 12% agriculture, 5.4% unemployment (1987). **Exports:** $6.8 bil. (f.o.b., 1986) wheat, corn, oilseed, hides, wool. **Imports:** $4.7 bil. (c.i.f., 1986) chemical products, machinery, metallurgical products, fuel, lubricants. **Major**

trading partners: (1986) *exports:* 9% U.S., 8% Netherlands, 8% Brazil, 7% W. Germany, 7% Japan; *imports:* 18% U.S., 14% Brazil, 12% W. Germany, 7% Bolivia, 7% Japan.

Intl. Orgs. FAO, G-77, GATT, IAEA, IBRD, ICAO, IDA, IFAD, IFC, ILO, IMF, IMO, INTELSAT, INTERPOL, ITU, NAM, OAS, UN, UNESCO, UPU, WHO, WMO.

The indigenous hunter-gatherer populations of the Argentine pampas put up fierce resistance to the Europeans and provided little in the way of cultural or agricultural infrastructure needed to support Spanish colonization. After initial Spanish discovery in 1516, the first attempt at Spanish settlement in the Plata region took place under the leadership of Pedro de Mendoza in 1535–36. Trade between Buenos Aires and Potosí was important during the early colonial period. Buenos Aires's Portuguese population used the city to carry on trade with Peru.

The reforms of the Bourbon dynasty led to further development of the region when the viceroyalty of La Plata was created in 1776. Two years later, trade within the empire for the port of Buenos Aires was legalized, leading to the growth of the settlement from a small town to a city of 50,000 by 1800. A provisional junta of the Provinces of Río de la Plata was established in 1810 in response to the Napoleonic occupation of Spain, and in 1816 the United Provinces of the Río de la Plata declared their independence.

After independence the question of political relations among the United Provinces was settled by a federalist solution in which the provinces dissolved into a number of practically independent republics, each of which was ruled by its own caudillo, or leader, and his followers. In an attempt to establish a national government, a constituent assembly met in December 1824, created the office of president, and named Bernardino Rivadavia to the position. However, dissatisfaction with Pres. Rivadavia's handling of the war with Brazil (1825–28) led to the failure to ratify a workable constitution and caused Rivadavia to resign.

Juan Manuel de Rosas became governor of Buenos Aires in 1829 and presided over the construction of a federal agreement between the provinces in 1831. Rosas governed Buenos Aires with an iron hand until his expulsion in 1852. The other provinces formed the Argentine Federation, based on a constitution of 1853, but Buenos Aires refused to join. Buenos Aires and the Argentine Federation entered into war between 1859 and 1861; they reached an agreement on the inclusion of Buenos Aires in the Argentine Republic in 1862.

Argentina allied itself with Brazil in a war (1865–70) that resulted in the defeat of Paraguay. During the latter part of the 1870s, the Argentines took the initiative against the indigenous population in the unsubdued territories of Argentina. Then a period of stepped-up immigration from Italy and Spain from the mid-19th century until 1930 resulted in a huge demographic shift in the country's population. By the early part of the 20th century, a full 30 percent of the population was made up of these immigrants.

The Argentine military, led by Lt. Gen. José F. Uriburu, ousted the civilian government of the Radical party in 1930 with the intention of following the European model of politics. In 1946 Juan Domingo Perón won the presidential election and constructed a populist political alliance that included workers, industrialists, and the armed forces. The Perón-inspired populist ideology of *justicialismo* included extension of the franchise to women and redistribution of income to workers and the poor. The activities of Perón's charismatic wife, Eva, bolstered justicialismo through her effort to distribute goods to the poor through the Social Aid Foundation.

Tied in with Perón's populist strategy was his policy of nationalist economic development, whereby state-led development was financed through extraction of capital from the old export-agricultural elite and politically supported through populism. The Perón government incurred great expense to gain control over foreign-owned economic infrastructure. A number of events led to Perón's downfall in 1955. The market for Argentine goods deteriorated after World War II. As Perón shifted his strategy to encourage foreign investment and impose economic austerity, repression against the political opposition grew. The death of Eva Perón in 1952 robbed Perón of an important political resource, and when the government challenged the Catholic church on a number of issues, the military ousted Perón.

After a brief period of military rule, in which an attempt was made to roll back "Perónismo," Arturo Frondizi of the "Intransigent" faction of the Radical party won the presidency and assumed office in 1958. In the following years, the military repeatedly attempted to keep the Perónistas from returning to power on the basis of their electoral support. When Frondizi refused to annul a Perónist victory in 1962, the armed forces withdrew their support and removed him from office. Pres. Arturo Illia was ousted from office in 1966 for the same reason: his failure to tame Perón's followers.

A military bureaucratic authoritarian regime led by a series of Argentine officers was established during 1966-73. The political arena was undergoing polarization, and extreme violence by factions on the left and right led the military to accept Perón's return to the presidency in 1973. Perón died the following year, and his second wife, Isabel, replaced him in office; she was unable to retain power, and the military removed her in 1976.

Determined to deal with what they saw as a leftist threat, the military again opted for a bureaucratic authoritarian solution. As part of this "solution," the armed forces launched what was later called the "dirty war" against leftists, during which up to 20,000 people lost their lives. The authoritarian government lasted until 1983, when it collapsed as a result of the ill-starred 1982 Falkland Islands War against Britain. Instead of achieving its goals of garnering support through nationalistic symbolism, defeat at the hands of the British completely undermined the military government and led to the resignation of the junta and the holding of elections. Raúl Alfonsín, of the Radical Union party, was elected president in the wake of these events in 1983. In May 1989, he was succeeded by Carlos Saúl Menem, a man widely proclaimed as the political heir of Juan Perón.

Australia
Commonwealth of Australia

Geography Location: occupies whole of island continent of Australia, lying between Indian and Pacific oceans, and its offshore islands, principally Tasmania to SE. **Boundaries:** nearest neighbor is Papua New Guinea, to N. **Total land area:** 2,966,151 sq. mi. (7,682,300 sq km). **Coastline:** 16,010 mi. (25,760 km). **Comparative area:** slightly smaller than U.S. **Land use:** 6% arable land; negl. % permanent crops; 58% meadows and pastures; 14% forest and woodland; 22% other; includes negl. % irrigated. **Major cities:** (1985 est.) Canberra (capital) 273,600; Sydney 3,391,600; Melbourne 2,916,600; Brisbane 1,157,200; Perth 1,001,000.

People Population: 16,260,436 (1988). **Nationality:** noun—Australian(s); adjective—Australian. **Ethnic groups:** 95% Caucasian, 4% Asian, 1% aboriginal and other. **Languages:** English, native langs. **Religions:** 26.1% Anglican, 26.0% Roman Catholic, 24.3% other Christian.

Government Type: federal parliamentary state recognizing Elizabeth II as sovereign or head of state. **Independence:** Jan. 1, 1901 (from federation of UK colonies). **Constitution:** July 9, 1900; effective Jan. 1, 1901. **National holiday:** Australia Day, Jan. 26. **Heads of government:** Sir Ninian Stephen, governor general (since July 1982); Robert Hawke, prime minister (since Mar. 1983). **Structure:** prime minister and cabinet responsible to House; bicameral legislature (Federal Parliament—Senate and House of Representatives); independent judiciary.

Economy Monetary unit: Australian dollar. **Budget:** (1987 est.) *income:* $47.0 bil; *expend.:* $49.3 bil. **GDP:** $196.0 bil., $12,190 per capita (1987 est.). **Chief crops:** large areas devoted to grazing; 60% of area used for crops is planted in wheat; major products—wool, lamb, beef, wheat, fruits; self-sufficient in food. **Livestock:** sheep, cattle, pigs. **Natural resources:** bauxite, coal, iron ore, copper, tin. **Major industries:** mining, industrial and transportation equipment, food processing. **Labor force:** 7.7 mil. (1987); 33.8% finance and services, 22.3% public and community services, 20.1% wholesale and retail trade, 16.2% manufacturing and industry, 7.8% unemployment rate. **Exports:** $22.6 bil. (f.o.b., 1986); wheat, barley, beef, lamb, dairy products. **Imports:** $26.1 bil. (c.i.f., 1986); manufactured raw materials, capital equipment, consumer goods. **Major trading partners:** (1984) *exports:* 26% Japan, 11% U.S., 6% New Zealand, 4% N. Korea, 4% Singapore; *imports:* 22% U.S., 22% Japan, 7% UK, 6% W. Germany, 4% New Zealand.

Intl. Orgs. Colombo Plan, Commonwealth, FAO, GATT, IAEA, IBRD, ICAO, IDA, IFAD, IFC, ILO, IMF, IMO, INTELSAT, INTERPOL, ITU, OECD, UN, UNESCO, UPU, WHO, WIPO, WMO.

Geologically, Australia has been isolated for millions of years, accounting for its unusual fauna dominated by marsupial mammals and corvid birds. Australia was first populated by two waves of migrants, the ancestors of today's aborigines, from Southeast Asia as much as 40,000 years ago. Thereafter, aborigine culture evolved in isolation except for some contact between the peoples of the northern coast and New Guinea. Australia was first sighted by Europeans at the beginning of the 17th century. In the 18th century, it was visited by the Dutch, who named it New Holland. The eastern coast was systematically explored in 1770 by Capt. James Cook, who claimed it for Great Britain.

British settlement began in 1788, with the landing of a party of transported convicts. Australia remained a penal colony during the first half of the 19th century, during which time the continent was explored and separate colonies were established in the various states. Aboriginal populations were displaced and decimated; in some areas (e.g., Tasmania), they were totally exterminated. Discovery of gold in Victoria in 1851 created a gold rush that greatly accelerated immigration. By the end of the 19th century, the three mainstays of the Australian economy—livestock (beef and sheep) raising, mining, and wheat growing—were firmly established.

A constitution, drafted in 1891 and passed by Parliament in 1901, created a commonwealth consisting of a confederation of the various states except for the Northern Territories, which were added in 1911. The British Crown is represented by an appointed governor-general; the national government is a parliamentary system, but much local authority resides in the separate states. Comprehensive social welfare legislation was passed by the state and national governments soon after the commonwealth's formation. The population is highly educated and enjoys a generally high standard of living, but most aboriginals are detribalized and live in considerable poverty.

Australian troops fought with distinction in both world wars. A Japanese threat to Australia in 1942 was averted by Allied victory in the Battle of the Coral Sea. The aftermath of both wars gave Australia trusteeship powers over numerous island territories in the South Pacific and the Indian Ocean. Most trusteeship territories have since achieved independence, but Australia still administers several external island groups and claims territory in Antarctica.

In 1951 Australia joined New Zealand and the United States in the ANZUS mutual-defense treaty. The treaty was dissolved by New Zealand's withdrawal in 1986, but the agreement between Australia and the United States remains in force.

Until 1973 Australia's immigration laws were designed to restrict immigration primarily to the English-speaking countries of the world. The abandonment of discriminatory immigration practices has led to a new wave of immigration since 1973, particularly from Asia. In the process Australian economic ties to Asia and the Pacific Rim have expanded considerably. New exploitation of mineral and hydrocarbon resources has in many cases been accomplished with Japanese investment or with long-term export contracts to Japan. Australia has also undergone considerable industrial development in the post–World War II period, and especially in the past two decades. Nevertheless, a depressed international market for agricultural products has created balance-of-payments difficulties and has contributed to a long-term decline in the value of the Australian dollar.

Austria
Republic of Austria
Geography Location: landlocked country in central Europe. **Boundaries:** West Germany and Czechoslovakia to N, Hungary to E, Yugoslavia and Italy to S, Switzerland and Liechtenstein to W. **Total land area:** 32,377 sq. mi. (83,855 sq km). **Coastline:** none. **Comparative area:** slightly smaller than Maine. **Land use:** 17% arable land; 1% permanent crops; 24% meadows and pastures; 39% forest and woodland; 19% other; includes negl. % irrigated. **Major cities:** (1981 census) Vienna (capital) 1,531,346; Graz 243,166; Linz 199,910; Salzburg 139,426; Innsbruck 117,287.

People Population: 7,577,072 (1988). **Nationality:** noun—Austrian(s); adjective—Austrian. **Ethnic groups:** 99.4% German, 0.3% Croatian, 0.2% Slovene, 0.1% other. **Languages:** German. **Religions:** 85% Roman Catholic, 6% Protestant, 9% none or other.

Government Type: federal republic. **Constitution:** 1920; revised 1929; reinstated Dec. 1945. **National holiday:** Oct. 26. **Heads of government:** Kurt Waldheim, president (since July 1986); Franz Vranitzky, chancellor (since June 1986). **Structure:** bicameral legislature (Federal Assembly—Federal Council, National Council); directly elected president whose functions are largely representational; independent federal judiciary.

Economy Monetary unit: schilling. **Budget:** (1987) **income:** $27.6 bil.; **expend.:** $36.8 bil. **GDP:** $66.26 bil., $8,750 per capita (1985). **Chief crops:** forest products, cereals, potatoes, sugar beets; 84% self-sufficient. **Livestock:** chickens, pigs, cattle, turkeys, sheep. **Natural resources:** iron ore, crude oil, timber, magnesite, aluminum. **Major industries:** foods, iron and steel, machinery. **Labor force:** 3.2 mil. (1987 est.); 56.4% services, 35.4% industry and crafts; 5.4% unemployment rate; estimated 200,000 Austrians are employed in other European countries; foreign laborers in Austria number 138,700, about 5.4% of labor force (1984). **Exports:** $22.5 bil. (f.o.b., 1986); iron and steel products, machinery and equipment, lumber, textiles, paper products. **Imports:** $26.8 bil. (c.i.f., 1986); machinery and equipment, chemicals, textiles and clothing, petroleum, foodstuffs. **Major trading partners:** (1986) **exports:** 32.9% W. Germany, 9.3% Italy, 8.9% Eastern Europe (excluding USSR), 7.8% Switzerland, 4.8% U.S., 3.8% OPEC;

imports: 44.2% W. Germany, 9.0% Italy, 6.2% Eastern Europe (excluding USSR), 4.8% Switzerland, 3.2% U.S., 3.0% USSR.

Intl. Orgs. EFTA, FAO, GATT, IAEA, IBRD, ICAO, IDA, IFAD, IFC, ILO, IMF, IMO, INTELSAT, INTERPOL, ITU, OECD, UN, UNESCO, UPU, WHO, WIPO, WMO; Austria is neutral and is not a member of NATO or EEC.

The Celtic tribes in what is now Austria were conquered by Rome under Emperor Augustus. After the fall of Rome, it was overrun by Huns, Lombards, Ostrogoths, and Bavarians. In 788 it was incorporated into the empire of Charlemagne. From the ninth to the 13th century, its territory was divided among a variety of feudal domains. In the late 13th century, Austria was reunited under Rudolph I of Habsburg, whose dynasty became synonymous with Austrian history for the next seven centuries. Rudolph's successors steadily enlarged their domain by conquest and marital diplomacy until, by the reign of Charles V (1500–58), they ruled not only the Holy Roman Empire, encompassing most of central Europe, but also Spain, the Netherlands, and all of Spain's colonial possessions.

After the reign of Charles V, the Habsburg empire was split into two branches, one governing Spain, the other the Holy Roman Empire. Habsburg power in Germany ended after the Thirty Years' War (1618–48) but was affirmed in the Danube Valley after the defeat of the Turkish siege of Vienna in 1683. Further adjustments to the Habsburg domains ensued as a result of warfare and diplomacy under Maria Theresa (1717–80). In 1804 the Austrian empire was founded, and two years later, the defunct Holy Roman Empire was abolished. In 1867 the empire became known as the Dual Monarchy of Austria-Hungary.

In 1914 the assassination of Archduke Franz Ferdinand, the heir to the Austrian throne, led to the outbreak of World War I, which resulted in a wholesale redrawing of national boundaries in Central Europe. Austria emerged as a small Alpine republic, with about 12 percent of the territory of the old Dual Monarchy. The new republic faced a severe postwar economic crisis, as well as a political stalemate between the Christian Social party and the Social Democratic party, each with the support of about half of the electorate, and each with its own paramilitary organization.

In 1933, as Hitler's National Socialists rose to power in Germany, Austrian Chancellor Engelbert Dollfuss, leader of the Christian Social party, instituted rule by decree and began building a corporate state modeled on Italian fascism. His attempt to disarm the Social Democratic militia in 1934 led to civil war. The government triumphed, but Dollfuss was assassinated by Nazi thugs in July 1934. The 1936 alliance between Adolf Hitler and Benito Mussolini doomed further Austrian attempts to stave off domination by the National Socialists. Austria was occupied by German troops in March 1938 and incorporated into Hitler's Third Reich.

Conquered by American and Soviet troops early in 1945, Austria, after World War II, was

divided into French, British, American, and Russian zones of occupation, but the occupying powers permitted the formation of a unified national government. A coalition government was formed in November 1945 and recognized by the Western powers in 1946. The occupation ended in 1955 with the signing of the Austrian State Treaty. The four powers withdrew their forces, and Austria pledged itself to a policy of permanent neutrality, with no foreign military alliances or military bases on Austrian territory.

A coalition government continued to 1966, when the People's party under Josef Klaus gained a parliamentary majority. In 1970 the Socialist party under Bruno Kreisky came to power. Socialist dominance continued until 1983, when the Socialists had to form a coalition with the right-wing Freedom party in order to stay in power. Kreisky resigned and was succeeded by Fred Sinowatz.

The titular post of president of Austria became the focus of controversy when Kurt Waldheim, former UN secretary general, was elected to that post. Campaign revelations that Waldheim had been a German army officer in the Balkans at a time when Nazi atrocities were committed brought soul-searching at home and a storm of protest from abroad.

The Austrian economy, decimated after World War I, has flourished in the post–World War II period under a mild form of socialism and with a boost from the American Marshall Plan. Tourism, a highly developed manufacturing sector, and substantial petroleum reserves have contributed to the country's prosperity; economic agreements with the EEC have made Austria a well-integrated participant in the Western European economy.

Bahamas
Commonwealth of the Bahamas
Geography Location: nearly 700 islands forming archipelago that extends 590 mi. (950 km) SE–NW between southwest Florida and island of Hispaniola. **Boundaries:** western Atlantic Ocean to N, E, S, and W. **Total land area:** 5,382 sq. mi. (13,939 sq km). **Coastline:** 2,200 mi. (3,542 km). **Comparative area:** slightly larger than Connecticut. **Land use:** 1% arable land; negl. % permanent crops; negl. % meadows and pastures; 32% forest and woodland; 67% other; includes N.A. % irrigated. **Major cities:** (1980 est.) Nassau (capital) 110,000.

People Population: 242,983 (1988). **Nationality:** noun—Bahamian(s); adjective—Bahamian. **Ethnic groups:** 85% black, 15% white. **Languages:** English, some Creole among Haitian immigrants. **Religions:** 29% Baptist, 23% Anglican, 22% Roman Catholic; smaller groups of other Protestants, of Greek Orthodox and Jews.

Government Type: independent commonwealth recognizing Elizabeth II as chief of state. **Independence:** July 10, 1973 (from UK). **Constitution:** July 10, 1973. **National holiday:** Independence Day, July 10. **Heads of government:** Sir Henry Milton Taylor, governor-general (since June 1988); Lynden O. Pindling,

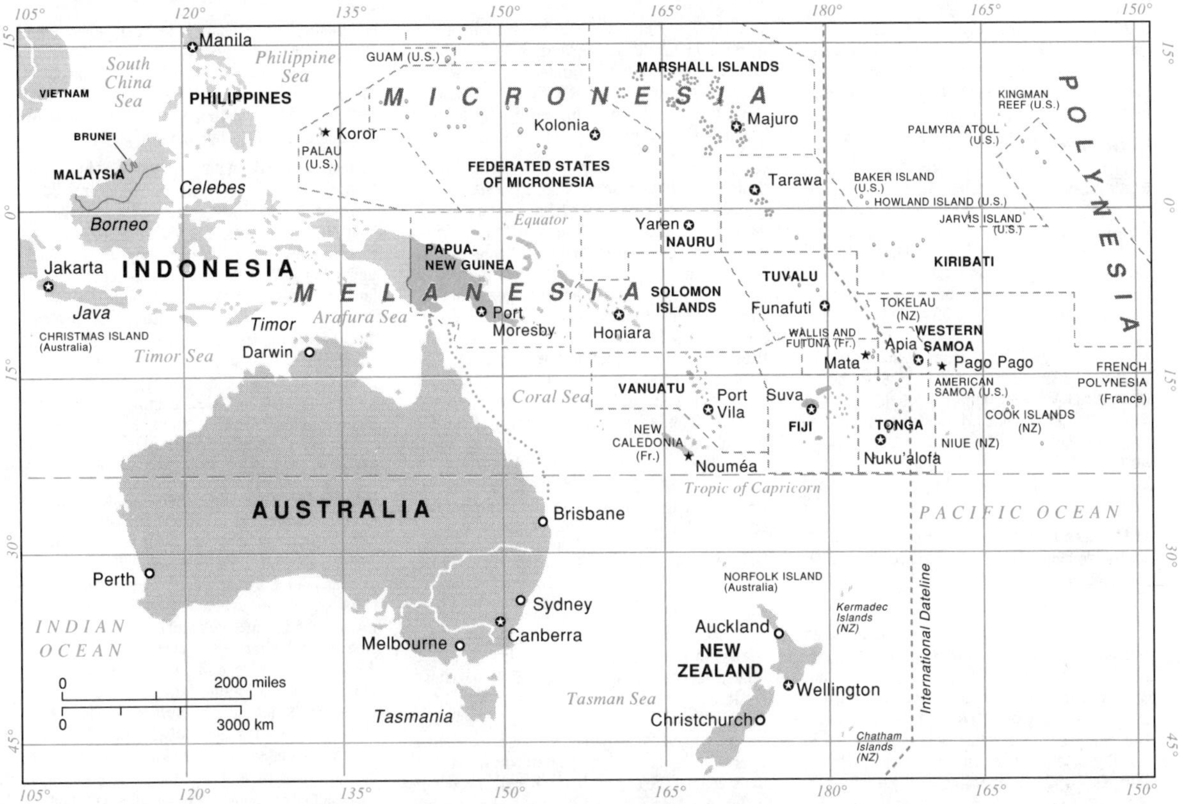

Manila
South China Sea
Philippine Sea
VIETNAM
PHILIPPINES
GUAM (U.S.)
MARSHALL ISLANDS
M I C R O N E S I A
Koror
PALAU (U.S.)
Kolonia
Majuro
BRUNEI
MALAYSIA
FEDERATED STATES OF MICRONESIA
Celebes
Tarawa
Borneo
Equator
Yaren
NAURU
Jakarta
INDONESIA
PAPUA-NEW GUINEA
M E L A N E S I A
SOLOMON ISLANDS
TUVALU
Java
Port Moresby
Honiara
Funafuti
CHRISTMAS ISLAND (Australia)
Timor
Arafura Sea
Timor Sea
Darwin
WALLIS AND FUTUNA (Fr.)
Mata
Coral Sea
VANUATU
Port Vila
Suva
FIJI
NEW CALEDONIA (Fr.)
Nouméa
TONGA
Nuku'alofa
Tropic of Capricorn
AUSTRALIA
Brisbane
Perth
NORFOLK ISLAND (Australia)
Sydney
Kermadec Islands (NZ)
INDIAN OCEAN
Auckland
Canberra
Melbourne
NEW ZEALAND
Wellington
Tasman Sea
Tasmania
Christchurch
Chatham Islands (NZ)
International Dateline
2000 miles
3000 km
KINGMAN REEF (U.S.)
PALMYRA ATOLL (U.S.)
P O L Y N E S I A
BAKER ISLAND (U.S.)
HOWLAND ISLAND (U.S.)
JARVIS ISLAND (U.S.)
KIRIBATI
TOKELAU (NZ)
Apia
WESTERN SAMOA
Pago Pago
AMERICAN SAMOA (U.S.)
FRENCH POLYNESIA (France)
COOK ISLANDS (NZ)
NIUE (NZ)
PACIFIC OCEAN
105° 120° 135° 150° 165° 180° 165° 150°
15° 0° 15° 30° 45°

Arafura Sea
INDONESIA
Darwin
Gulf of Carpentaria
Coral Sea
Great Barrier Reef
Timor Sea
NORTHERN TERRITORY
AUSTRALIA
Great Sandy Desert
Hamersley Range
Gibson Desert
Alice Springs
QUEENSLAND
Great Dividing Range
Great Artesian Basin
WESTERN AUSTRALIA
SOUTH AUSTRALIA
Lake Eyre
Great Victoria Desert
Nullarbor Plain
Lake Gairdner
Lake Torrens
Darling R.
Brisbane
Perth
Great Australian Bight
Adelaide
NEW SOUTH WALES
Sydney
Canberra
INDIAN OCEAN
VICTORIA
Melbourne
Bass Strait
Tasman Sea
TASMANIA
Hobart
400 miles
600 km

PACIFIC OCEAN
NORTH ISLAND
Auckland
Hamilton
Tasman Sea
Palmerston North
Nelson
Wellington
SOUTH ISLAND
SOUTHERN ALPS
Christchurch
NEW ZEALAND
Dunedin
Invercargill
200 miles
300 km

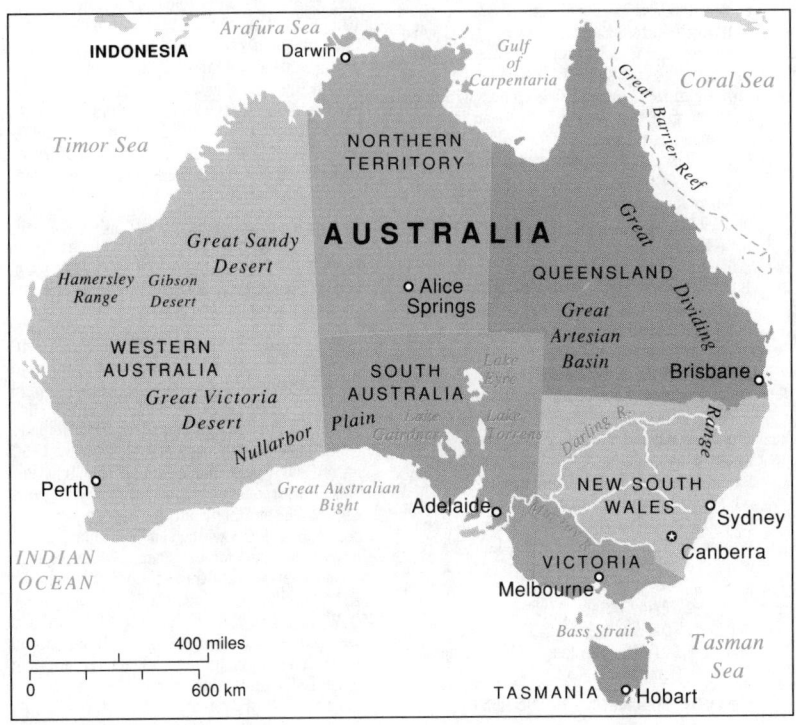

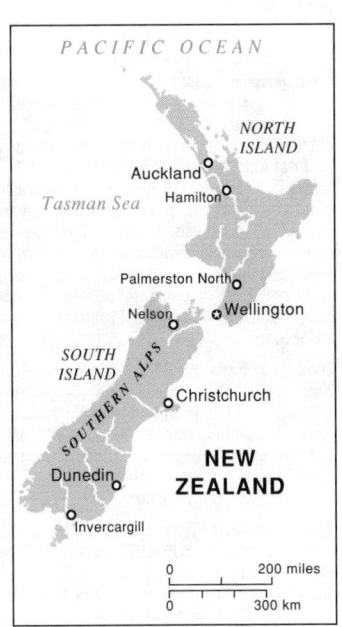

prime minister (since 1967). **Structure:** executive (prime minister and cabinet); bicameral legislature (Parliament—16-member appointed Senate, 49-member elected House of Assembly); judiciary.

Economy **Monetary unit:** Bahamian dollar. **Budget:** (1986 est.) *income:* $458.2 mil.; *expend.:* $359.8 mil. **GDP:** $2.1 bil., $8,950 per capita (1986 est.) **Chief crops:** vegetables, tomatoes, pineapples, bananas, citrus fruits; food importer. **Livestock:** sheep, pigs, goats, cattle. **Natural resources:** salt, argonite, timber. **Major industries:** banking, tourism, cement. **Labor force:** 132,600 (1986); 30% government, 25% hotels and restaurants, 10% business services; 30% unemployment (1986). **Exports:** $825 mil. (f.o.b., 1986); pharmaceuticals, cement, rum, crawfish. **Imports:** $1.6 bil. (f.o.b., 1986); foodstuffs, manufactured goods, mineral fuels. **Major trading partners:** (1981); *exports:* 90% U.S., 10% UK; *imports:* 30% Iran, 20% Nigeria, 10% U.S., 10% EC, 10% Gabon.

Intl. Orgs. Commonwealth, FAO, G-77, GATT (de facto), IBRD, ICAO, ILO, IMF, IMO, INTERPOL, ITU, NAM, OAS, UN, UNESCO, UPU, WHO, WIPO, WMO.

Though Christopher Columbus claimed the Bahamas for Spain in 1493, the Spanish made no efforts toward settling the area. British colonization of the Bahamas began in 1629 and continued slowly over the next two centuries. Independent from Great Britain since 1973, the Bahamas have been governed by Prime Minister Lynden O. Pindling's Progressive Liberal party, supported by the country's 85-percent black majority. Implications of narcotics trafficking have plagued Pindling's government. A high rate of Bahamian unemployment also continues to be a problem for the current government.

Bahrain
State of Bahrain
Geography **Location:** group of 35 islands situated in western part of Persian (Arabian) Gulf. **Boundaries:** Saudi Arabia about 15 mi. (24 km) to W and Qatar about 17 mi. (28 km) to E. **Total land area:** 267 sq. mi. (691 sq km). **Coastline:** 161 mi. (259 km). **Comparative area:** slightly less than 3.5 times size of Washington, D.C. **Land use:** 2% arable land; 2% permanent crops; 6% meadows and pastures; 0% forest and woodland; 90% other; includes negl. % irrigated. **Major cities:** (1981 census) Manama (capital) 121,986; Muharraq Town 61,853.

People **Population:** 480,383 (1988). **Nationality:** noun—Bahraini(s); adjective—Bahraini. **Ethnic groups:** 63% Bahraini, 13% Asian, 10% other Arab, 8% Iranian, 6% other. **Languages:** Arabic (official), Farsi, Urdu; English widely spoken. **Religions:** 70% Shi'a Muslim, 30% Sunni Muslim.

Government **Type:** traditional monarchy. **Independence:** Aug.15,1973 (from UK). **Constitution:** May 26, 1973 (effective Dec. 1973). **National holiday:** Dec. 16. **Heads of government:** Isa bin Sulman al-Khalifa, amir (since

Nov. 1961); Khalifa bin Sulman al-Khalifa, prime minister. **Structure:** amir rules with help of cabinet led by prime minister; amir dissolved National Assembly (Aug. 1975) and suspended constitutional provision for election of assembly; independent judiciary.

Economy **Monetary unit:** Bahrain dinar. **Budget:** (1987) *income:* N.A.; *expend.:* $880 mil. **GDP:** $3.77 bil., $8,110 per capita (1987 est.) **Chief crops:** not self-sufficient in food production; produces some fruits and vegetables; engages in dairy and poultry farming and in shrimping and fishing. **Livestock:** goats, sheep, cattle. **Natural resources:** oil, associated and nonassociated natural gas, fish. **Major industries:** petroleum processing and refining, aluminum smelting and fabrication. **Labor force:** 140,000 (1982); 85% industry and commerce (note: 42% of labor force is Bahraini). **Exports:** $2.6 bil. (f.o.b., 1987); nonoil exports $340 mil.; oil exports $2.2 bil. (1985). **Imports:** $2.4 bil. (f.o.b., 1987); nonoil imports $1.4 bil.; oil imports $1.0 bil. (1985). **Major trading partners:** UK, Japan, U.S., Saudi Arabia.

Intl. Orgs. Arab League, FAO, G-77, GATT (de facto), IBRD, ICAO, ILO, IMF, IMO, INTERPOL, NAM, UN, UNESCO, UPU, WHO.

Bahrain and the about 30 adjacent small islands in the Persian Gulf were from ancient times centers of pearl fishing and of maritime trade between Arabia and India. The Portuguese fortified Bahrain in the 16th century but were driven out by the Iranian Shah Abbas I early in the 17th century. Bahrain was ruled by Iran until the end of the 18th century, when it became an Arab sheikhdom. Bahrain controlled the Qatar peninsula until 1872.

Bahrain entered into treaty relations with Great Britain in 1820 and became a British Protectorate in 1861. Oil was discovered on Bahrain in 1932. After British forces withdrew from the gulf, the nation became an independent emirate, in August 1971, under Amir Isa bin Sulman al-Khalifa, who came to the throne in 1961.

Oil reserves were largely depleted by the mid-1970s. The economy now has diversified to include oil refining, aluminum smelting, international banking, and shipping services. Bahrain has close relations with Saudi Arabia; a causeway permits direct-road communication between the two countries.

Bangladesh
People's Republic of Bangladesh
(PREVIOUS NAME: EAST PAKISTAN)
Geography **Location:** southern Asia. **Boundaries:** India to N, E, and W; Burma to E, Bay of Bengal to S. **Total land area:** 55,598 sq. mi. (143,998 sq km). **Coastline:** 360 mi. (580 km). **Comparative area:** slightly smaller than Wisconsin. **Land use:** 67% arable land; 2% permanent crops; 4% meadows and pastures; 16% forest and woodland; 11% other; includes 14% irrigated. **Major cities:** (1981 census) Dhaka (formerly Dacca) (capital) 3,430,312; Chittagong 1,391,877; Khulna 646,359; Rajshahi 253,740; Comilla 184,132.

People **Population:** 109,963,551 (1988).

Nationality: noun—Bangladeshi(s); adjective—Bangladesh. **Ethnic groups:** 98% Bengali, 250,000 Biharis, less than 1 mil. tribals. **Languages:** Bangla (official); English widely used. **Religions:** 83% Muslim, 16% Hindu, less than 1% Buddhist, Christian and other.

Government **Type:** republic. **Independence:** Dec. 16, 1971 (from Pakistan). **Constitution:** Nov. 4, 1972, effective Dec. 16, 1972, suspended following coup of Mar. 24, 1982, restored Nov. 10, 1986; civil liberties curtailed under Nov. 27, 1987, State of Emergency Declaration. **National holiday:** National Day, Mar. 26; Victory Day, Dec. 16. **Heads of government:** Hussain Muhammad Ershad, president (since Dec. 1983); Moudud Ahmed, prime minister (since 1988). **Structure:** presidential system of government, 330-member unicameral legislature (parliament), and independent judiciary; president has substantial control over judiciary; parliament dissolved on Dec. 6, 1987.

Economy **Monetary unit:** taka. Budget: (1988) *income:* N.A.; *expend.:* current, $1.45 bil.; capital expenditures, $1.63 bil. **GNP:** $15.6 bil., $150 per capita (1986, current prices). **Chief crops:** large-scale subsistence farming, heavily dependent on Monsoon rain; main crops are jute, tea, and rice; grain, cotton, and oilseed shortages. **Livestock:** chickens, ducks, cattle, goats, buffalo. **Natural resources:** natural gas, uranium, arable land, timber. **Major industries:** jute manufactures, food processing, cotton textiles. **Labor force:** 35.1 mil. (1986); extensive export of labor to Saudi Arabia, UAE, Oman, and Kuwait; 74% agriculture, 15% services, 11% industry and commerce, unemployment and underemployment rate 40% (est.). **Exports:** $820 mil. (f.o.b., 1986); raw and manufactured jute, frozen shrimp, garments, leather. **Imports:** $2.3 bil. (c.i.f., 1986); food grains, fuels, raw cotton, fertilizer, manufactured products. **Major trading partners:** *exports:* 24% U.S., 22% Western Europe, 9% Middle East, 8% Japan, 7% Eastern Europe; *imports:* 18% Western Europe, 14% Japan, 9% Middle East, 8% U.S.

Intl. Orgs. Colombo Plan, Commonwealth, FAO, G-77, GATT, IAEA, IBRD, ICAO, IDA, IFAD, IFC, ILO, IMF, IMO, INTELSAT, INTERPOL, ITU, NAM, UN, UNCTAD, UNESCO, UPU, WHO, WMO.

Bengal, in northeastern India, was conquered by Turkic invaders around 1200, and many inhabitants converted to Islam. Bengal became part of the Mughal empire in the 16th century. The British East India Company established a settlement in 1642, and by 1750 all of Bengal was under British rule. The formerly diverse agricultural economy became dominated by monoculture export crops of opium and jute, while rice continued to be grown in the fertile Ganges-Brahmaputra delta. The region's trade flowed through the British-built city of Calcutta.

With Indian independence in 1947, Bengal was partitioned along religious lines, Hindu West Bengal (including Calcutta) remaining with India and Islamic East Bengal becoming the eastern province of Pakistan, with its capital at Dacca. In the elections of 1971, the Bengali Awami League gained control of Pakistan's National Assembly. Seating of the new National Assembly was postponed, and riots broke out in East Pakistan. Troops from West Pakistan were sent to quell the riots on May 25, 1971; the following day East Pakistan declared its independence as Bangladesh. Civil war followed; 10 million refugees fled to India. India intervened in the civil war on Dec. 3, and on Dec. 15, Pakistan surrendered and acknowledged Bangladesh's independence.

The first prime minister, Sheik Mujibur Rahman, was assassinated in 1974. Politics in Bangladesh since then have been dominated by coups and a series of military governments. Lt. Gen. Hossain Mohammad Ershad, who seized power in a coup in March 1982, was elected president for a five-year term on Oct. 15, 1986. The election was boycotted by opposition parties.

Plagued by overpopulation, a decline in the world market for jute, persistent grain shortages, and frequent catastrophic floods, Bangladesh remains one of the world's poorest countries.

Barbados

Geography Location: most eastern of the Caribbean islands, situated about 200 mi. (320 km) NE of Trinidad and about 100 mi. (160 km) SE of St. Lucia. **Boundaries:** Atlantic Ocean to N, E, S, and W. **Total land area:** 166 sq. mi. (430 sq km). **Coastline:** 60 mi. (97 km). **Comparative area:** slightly less than 2.5 times size of Washington, D.C. **Land use:** 77% arable land; 0% permanent crops; 9% meadows and pastures; 0% forest and woodland; 14% other; includes N.A. % irrigated. **Major cities:** (1980 census) Bridgetown (capital) 7,517.

People Population: 256,784 (1988). **Nationality:** noun—Barbadian(s); adjective—Barbadian. **Ethnic groups:** 80% African, 16% mixed, 4% European. **Languages:** English. **Religions:** 70% Anglican, 9% Methodist, 4% Roman Catholic, 17% other, including Moravian.

Government Type: independent sovereign state within commonwealth recognizing Elizabeth II as chief of state. **Independence:** Nov. 30, 1966 (from UK). **Constitution:** Nov. 30, 1966. **National holiday:** Independence Day, Nov. 30. **Heads of government:** Sir Hugh Springer, governor-general (since Jan. 1984); Erskine Sandiford, prime minister (since June 1987). **Structure:** cabinet headed by prime minister; bicameral legislature (Parliament—21-member appointed Senate and 27-member elected House of Assembly).

Economy Monetary unit: Barbados dollar. **Budget:** (1986) *income:* $390 mil.; *expend.:* $430 mil. **GDP:** $1.231 mil., $4,870 per capita (1985). **Chief crops:** sugarcane, subsistence foods. **Livestock:** sheep, pigs, goats, cattle. **Natural resources:** crude oil, fishing, natural gas. **Major industries:** tourism, sugar, light manufacturing. **Labor force:** 112,300 (1985 est.); 37% services and government, 22% commerce, 22% manufacturing and construction. **Exports:**

$300 mil. (f.o.b., 1985); sugar and sugarcane by-products, electrical parts, clothing. **Imports:** $559 mil. (f.o.b., 1985); foodstuffs, consumer durables, machinery, fuels. **Major trading partners:** (1984) *exports:* 42% U.S., 22% CARICOM, 7% UK; *imports:* 48% U.S., 12% CARICOM, 8% UK, 6% Canada.

Intl. Orgs. Commonwealth, FAO, G-77, GATT, IBRD, ICAO, IFAD, IFC, ILO, IMF, IMO, INELSAT, INTERPOL, ITU, NAM, OAS, UN, UNESCO, UPU, WHO, WMO.

Barbados remained under continuous British rule from the first British settlement in the early 17th century until 1966, when it achieved independence. The country is fairly prosperous relative to other Caribbean states, and Prime Minister Erskine Sandiford (Democratic Labour party) seeks to play a leading role in Caribbean politics. The 1966 Constitution mandates government effort toward the promotion of economic equality among Barbadians.

Belgium
Kingdom of Belgium

Geography Location: northwestern Europe. **Boundaries:** Netherlands to N, Luxembourg and W. Germany to E, France to S, and North Sea to W. **Total land area:** 11,783 sq. mi. (30,519 sq km). **Coastline:** 40 mi. (64 km). **Comparative area:** slightly larger than Maryland. **Land use:** 24% arable land; 1% permanent crops; 20% meadows and pastures; 21% forest and woodland; 34% other; includes negl. % irrigated. **Major cities:** (1986) Bruxelles (Brussels—capital) 973,499; Antwerpen (Anvers, Antwerp) 479,748; Gent (Gand, Ghent) 233,856; Charleroi 209,395; Liège (Luik) 200,891.

People Population: 9,880,522 (1988). **Nationality:** noun—Belgian(s); adjective—Belgian. **Ethnic groups:** 55% Fleming, 33% Walloon, 12% mixed or other. **Languages:** 56% Flemish (Dutch), 32% French, 1% German; 11% legally bilingual; divided along ethnic lines. **Religions:** 75% Roman Catholic; remainder Protestant or other.

Government Type: constitutional monarchy. **Independence:** Oct. 4, 1830 (from Netherlands). **Constitution:** Feb. 7, 1831; last revised Aug. 8–9, 1980. **National holiday:** National Day, July 21. **Heads of government:** Baudouin I, king (since Aug. 1950); Wilfried Martens, prime minister (since Apr. 1979, with 10-month interruption in 1981). **Structure:** executive branch consists of king and cabinet; cabinet responsible to bicameral parliament (Senate and Chamber of Representatives); independent judiciary; coalition governments are usual.

Economy Monetary unit: Belgian franc. **Budget:** (1986) *income:* $31.6 bil.; *expend.:* $39.6 bil. **GNP:** $114.9 bil., $11,650 per capita (1986). **Chief crops:** grains, sugar beets, flax, potatoes, other vegetables; livestock production predominates. **Livestock:** pigs, cattle, sheep, horses, goats. **Natural resources:** coal, natural gas. **Major industries:** engineering and metal products, processed food and beverages, chemicals. **Labor force:** 4 mil. (1987); 58% ser-

vices, 37% industry; 12.1% unemployment. **Exports:** (Belgium-Luxembourg Economic Union) $68.6 bil. (f.o.b., 1986); iron and steel products (cars), petroleum products, chemicals. **Imports:** (Belgium-Luxembourg Economic Union) $68.0 bil. (c.i.f., 1986); fuels, foodstuffs, chemicals. **Major trading partners:** (Belgium-Luxembourg Economic Union, 1986) *exports:* 73.3% EC (20% France, 19.7% W. Germany, 15.8% Netherlands, 8.7% UK), 5.2% U.S., 3.8% oil-exporting developing countries, 2.3% communist countries; *imports:* 72.8% EC (23.3% W. Germany, 18.0 Netherlands, 15.9% France, 8.4% UK), 5.1% U.S., 4.4% oil-exporting developing countries, 2.7% communist countries.

Intl. Orgs. EC, FAO, GATT, IAEA, IBRD, ICAO, IDA, IFAD, IFC, ILO, IMF, IMO, INTELSAT, INTERPOL, ITU, NATO, OAS (observer), OECD, UN, UNESCO, UPU, WHO, WIPO, WMO.

The country now known as Belgium was, during the Middle Ages, part of the powerful duchy of Burgundy. By marriage and diplomacy, the "Low Countries" became part of the Habsburg empire in 1482 (see "Austria"). In a struggle lasting from the late 16th century to the Treaty of Westphalia in 1648, the northern part of that region (Netherlands) became independent, but the southern portion remained part of the Habsburg empire—under the Spanish branch until 1715, and then under the Austrian branch until the Napoleonic Wars. After the defeat of Napoleon in 1815, the Congress of Vienna attached the lands to an enlarged Kingdom of the Netherlands.

In 1830 the Belgians revolted against the Dutch, and in 1831 the Treaty of London recognized an independent Kingdom of Belgium. Throughout the 19th century, its unity was precarious, as the country was bitterly divided politically between Catholic and Liberal parties, and ethnically between Dutch-speaking Flemings and French-speaking Walloons.

In 1885 Belgium became a major colonial power in Africa with Leopold II's establishment of the Congo Free State (after 1908, called the Belgian Congo), a colony of the Belgian monarchy rather than of the Belgian state.

Belgium was the site of major battles during World War I. Its boundaries were reestablished in 1919 by the Treaty of Versailles. When German troops of Hitler's Third Reich overran Belgium in May 1940, King Leopold III quickly signed an armistice, hoping to placate Hitler and avert further fighting. But the Belgian government fled to England, repudiated the armistice, and joined the Allies. The Germans established a military government of occupation that controlled Belgium until the liberation of Brussels in September 1944.

Belgium suffered little economic damage during World War II and made a swift postwar recovery. But the political atmosphere was poisoned by the issue of what to do about wartime collaborators up to and including the king. A referendum in 1950 narrowly approved Leopold III's return to the throne, but he was persuaded to abdicate in 1951 in favor of his son,

Baudouin I.

Belgium's prewar neutrality was abandoned after World War II with Belgium becoming a founding member of the United Nations, the Benelux Pact, NATO, and the EEC (of which Brussels is in effect the capital, as the seat of the European Parliament). In 1960, after a bitter struggle, Belgium gave up control of the Congo.

Postwar Belgium has emerged with a flourishing economy and a highly modernized industrial sector complemented by tourism and agriculture. Politically, the postwar period has been one of shifting and complex coalition governments among three major parties (Christian Socialists, Socialists, and Liberals) and numerous minor ones. The issue of language dominates politics; since the 1960s, Belgium has devolved into a de facto confederation of Flemish-, French-, and German-speaking regions, with Brussels a multilingual region unto itself.

Belize
(PREVIOUS NAME: BRITISH HONDURAS)

Geography **Location:** northeastern coast of Central America. **Boundaries:** Mexico to N, Caribbean Sea to E, Guatemala to S and W. **Total land area:** 8,867 sq. mi. (22,965 sq km). **Coastline:** 240 mi. (386 km). **Comparative area:** slightly larger than Massachusetts. **Land use:** 2% arable land; negl. % permanent crops; 2% meadows and pastures; 44% forest and woodland; 52% other; includes negl. % irrigated. **Major cities:** (1985 est.) Belmopan (capital) 4,500; Belize City 47,000; Corozal 10,000; Orange Walk 9,600; Dangriga 7,700.

People **Population:** 171,735 (1988). **Nationality:** noun—Belizean(s); adjective—Belizean. **Ethnic groups:** 39.7% Creole, 33.1% mestizo, 9.5% Maya, 7.6% Garifuna. **Languages:** English (official), Spanish, Maya, Garifuna (Carib). **Religions:** 60% Roman Catholic, 40% Protestant (Anglican, Seventh-Day Adventist, Methodist, Baptist, Jehovah's Witnesses, Mennonite).

Government **Type:** parliamentary. **Independence:** Sept, 21, 1981 (from UK). **Constitution:** Sept. 21, 1981. **National holiday:** N.A. **Heads of government:** Dr. Elmira Minita Gordon, governor-general (since Dec. 1981); Manuel Esquivel, prime minister (since Dec. 1984). **Structure:** cabinet; bicameral legislature (National Assembly—electoral redistricting in Oct. 1984 expanded House of Representatives from 18 to 28 seats; eight-member appointed Senate; either house may choose its speaker or president, respectively, from outside its membership); judiciary.

Economy **Monetary unit:** Belizean dollar. **Budget:** (1986) **income:** $58 mil.; **expend.:** $70 mil. **GDP:** $193 mil., $1,190 per capita (since 1985). **Chief crops:** sugarcane, citrus fruits, corn, molasses, rice, beans, bananas; net importer of food; illegal producer of cannabis for international drug trade. **Livestock:** cattle, pigs, horses, mules, sheep, goats. **Natural resources:** arable land potential, timber, fish. **Major industries:** sugar refining, clothing, timber, and forest products. **Labor force:** 51,500

(1985); 30% agriculture, 16% services, 15.4% government, 11.2% commerce; shortage of skilled labor and all types of technical personnel; over 14% unemployment. **Exports:** $75 mil. (1986); sugar, garments, seafood, molasses, citrus. **Imports:** $110 mil. (1986); machinery and transportation equipment, food, manufactured goods, fuels, chemicals. **Major trading partners:** (1983) **exports:** 36% U.S., 22% UK, 11% Trinidad and Tobago, 10% Canada; **imports:** 55% U.S., 17% UK, 8% Netherlands Antilles, 7% Mexico.

Intl. Orgs. Commonwealth, FAO, G-77, GATT, IBRD, IDA, IFAD, IFC, ILO, IMF, ITU, UN, UNESCO, UPU, WHO, WMO.

During the 1700s, Spain held sovereignty over Belize but never attempted to settle it. The British gradually did settle there, however, and in 1862, British Honduras, as it was called, became a Crown colony. Although Britain granted Belize independence in 1981, Guatemala claims sovereignty over the area. Due to the threat of hostilities between the two countries, Belize's government, headed by Prime Minister Manuel Esquivel, is currently backed by British troops. High unemployment rates continue to be a problem for Belize.

Benin
People's Republic of Benin
(PREVIOUS NAME: DAHOMEY)

Geography **Location:** western coast of Africa. **Boundaries:** Burkina Faso and Niger to N, Nigeria to E, Gulf of Guinea to S, Togo to W. **Total land area:** 43,484 sq. mi. (112,622 sq km). **Coastline:** 75 mi. (121 km). **Comparative area:** slightly smaller than Pennsylvania. **Land use:** 12% arable land; 4% permanent crops; 4% meadows and pastures; 35% forest and woodland; 45% other; includes negl. % irrigated. **Major cities:** (1981 est.) Porto-Novo (capital) 144,000; Cotonou 383,250.

People **Population:** 4,497,150 (1988). **Nationality:** noun—Beninese (sing., pl.); adjective—Beninese. **Ethnic groups:** 99% African (Fon, Adja, Yoruba, Bariba); 5,500 Europeans. **Languages:** French (official); Fon and Yoruba in south; six major tribal languages in north. **Religions:** 70% indigenous beliefs, 15% Muslim, 15% Christian.

Government **Type:** Soviet-modeled civilian government. **Independence:** Aug. 1, 1960 (from France). **Constitution:** May 23, 1977. **National holiday:** Nov. 30. **Heads of government:** Brig. Gen. Mathieu Kerekou, president (since Oct. 1972). **Structure:** National Executive Council; Revolutionary National Assembly.

Economy **Monetary unit:** Communauté Financière Africaine (CFA) franc. **Budget:** (1987) **income:** $168 mil.; **expend.:** $313 mil. **GNP:** $1.4 bil., $340 per capita (1986 est.). **Chief crops:** cash crops—palm oil, peanuts, cotton, coffee, shea nuts, tobacco; food crops—corn, cassava, yams, rice, sorghum, millet. **Livestock:** sheep, goats, cattle, pigs, horses. **Natural resources:** small offshore oil deposits, limestone, marble, timber. **Major industries:**

palm oil and palm kernel oil processing, textiles, beverages. **Labor force:** 1.9 mil. (1987); 60% agriculture, 2% industrial sector, remainder employed in transport, commerce, and public services; 49% of population of working age. **Exports:** $131 mil. (f.o.b., 1986); palm products, cotton, other agricultural products. **Imports:** $329 mil. (f.o.b., 1986); thread, cloth, clothing and other consumer goods, construction materials, iron. **Major trading partners:** France, other EC countries, franc zone countries.

Intl. Orgs. FAO, G-77, GATT, IBRD, ICAO, IDA, IFAD, ILO, IMF, IMO, INTERPOL, ITU, NAM, UN, UNESCO, UPU, WHO, WIPO, WMO.

Benin, located on Africa's west coast, was originally a collection of kingdoms that achieved wealth and power through the slave trade. The most powerful of these kingdoms was Dahomey, whose trading posts at Porto Novo and Ouidah attracted traders from all of Europe. The French colonized Dahomey in 1892, and it remained a colony until it achieved independence as the Republic of Dahomey in 1960.

Numerous coups plagued the nation from its birth until 1972, when a military coup led by Mathieu Kerekou, who is still in power today, took over and established a Marxist regime. The name of the country was changed in 1975 to the People's Republic of Benin. The Kerekou government established close ties with the Soviet Union, nationalized large private businesses, and abolished opposition parties. The United States withdrew its ambassador from Benin in 1976. Relations with the United States were strained further in 1988 when the American government accused Benin of allowing Libyan terrorists to use Beninese territory as a base for their operations.

Bhutan
Kingdom of Bhutan

Geography **Location:** landlocked country in Himalayan mountain range in southern Asia. **Boundaries:** China to N and W, India to S and E. **Total land area:** 17,954 sq. mi. (46,500 sq km). **Coastline:** none. **Comparative area:** slightly more than half the size of Indiana. **Land use:** 2% arable land; negl. % permanent crops; 5% meadows and pastures; 70% forest and woodland; 23% other. **Major cities:** (1985 est.) Timphu (capital) 30,000; Phuntsholing 30,000.

People **Population:** 1,503,180 (1988). **Nationality:** noun—Bhutanese (sing., pl.); adjective—Bhutanese. **Ethnic groups:** 60% Bhote, 25% ethnic Nepalese, 15% indigenous or migrant tribes. **Languages:** Dzongkha (official), various Tibetan dialects, various Nepalese dialects. **Religions:** 75% Lamaistic Buddhism, 25% Indian- and Nepalese-influenced Hinduism.

Government **Type:** monarchy; special treaty relationship with India. **Independence:** Aug. 8, 1949 (from India). **Constitution:** no written constitution or bill of rights. **National holiday:** Dec. 17. **Heads of government:** Jigme Singye Wangchuck, king (since 1974). **Struc-**

ture: appointed ministers; 150-member indirectly elected National Assembly consisting of 110 village elders or heads of family, 10 monastic representatives, and 30 senior government administrators.

Economy **Monetary unit:** ngultrums and rupees are legal tender. **Budget:** (1986 est.) **income:** $59.2 mil.; **expend.:** $66.9 mil. **GDP:** $300 mil., $210 per capita (1986). **Chief crops:** rice, corn, barley, wheat, potatoes. **Livestock:** cattle, poultry, pigs, sheep, yaks. **Natural resources:** timber, hydropower, gypsum, calcium carbide. **Major industries:** cement, chemical products, mining. Labor force: (1983) 95% agriculture, 1% industry and commerce, massive lack of skilled labor. **Exports:** $15.1 mil. (1985); agricultural and forestry products, coal. **Imports:** $69.4 mil. (1985); imports from India $61.0 mil.; textiles, cereals, vehicles, fuels, machinery. **Major trading partner:** India.

Intl. Orgs. Colombo Plan, FAO, G-77, IBRD, IDA, IFAD, IMF, NAM, UN, UNESCO, UPU, WHO.

A Tibetan-style Lamaistic Buddhist theocracy was established in this Himalayan enclave in the 16th century. The region came under the domination of the British raj in India in 1865. The present monarchy dates from 1907; Britain established a protectorate in 1910. A 1949 treaty with India granted independence to Bhutan but essentially transferred the kingdom's foreign affairs from British to Indian control. Foreign access to Bhutan remains strictly controlled, and the kingdom plays little role in world trade and international affairs.

Bolivia
Republic of Bolivia
Geography **Location:** landlocked country in central South America. **Boundaries:** Brazil to N and E, Paraguay and Argentina to S, Chile and Peru to W. **Total land area:** 424,164 sq. mi. (1,098,581 sq km). **Coastline:** none. **Comparative area:** slightly less than three times size of Montana. **Land use:** 3% arable land; negl. % permanent crops; 25% meadows and pastures; 52% forest and woodland; 20% other; includes negl. % irrigated. **Major cities:** (1986 est.) La Paz (administrative capital) 1,033,288; Sucre (legal capital and seat of judiciary) 88,774; Santa Cruz de la Sierra 457,619; Cochabamba 329,941; Oruro 184,101; Potosí 117,010.

People **Population:** 6,448,297 (1988). **Nationality:** noun—Bolivian(s); adjective—Bolivian. **Ethnic groups:** 30% Quechua, 25% Aymara, 25–30% mixed, 5–15% European. **Languages:** Spanish, Quechua, and Aymara (all official). **Religions:** 95% Roman Catholic; active Protestant minority, especially Methodist.

Government **Type:** republic. **Independence:** Aug, 6, 1825 (from Spain). **Constitution:** Feb. 2, 1967. **National holiday:** Independence Day, Aug. 6. **Heads of government:** Jaime Paz Zamora, president (since Aug. 1989); since 1985 election, two parties rule in tactical alliance. **Structure:** executive; bicameral legislature (National Congress—Senate and Chamber of Deputies); congress began meeting again in Oct. 1982; judiciary.

Economy **Monetary unit:** boliviano. **Budget:** (1987 est.) **income:** $731.4 mil.; **expend.:** $967.5 mil. **GDP:** $3.87 bil., $610 per capita (1987 est.). **Chief crops:** potatoes, corn, rice, sugarcane, yucca, bananas, coffee; imports significant quantities of wheat; illegal producer of coca for international drug trade. **Livestock:** sheep, cattle, goats, pigs, asses. **Natural resources:** tin, natural gas, crude oil, zinc, tungsten. **Major industries:** mining, smelting, petroleum refining. **Labor force:** 1.7 mil. (1983); 50% agriculture, 26% services and utilities, 10% manufacturing, 10% other. **Exports:** $495 mil. (f.o.b., 1987 est.); tin, natural gas, silver, tungsten, zinc. **Imports:** $750 mil. (c.i.f., 1987 est.); foodstuffs, chemicals, capital goods, pharmaceuticals, transportation. **Major trading partners:** (1984) **exports:** 44% Argentina, 24% U.S., 19% EC, 6% W. Germany, 4% UK. **imports:** 22% Brazil, 16% U.S., 16% EC, 14% Argentina, 13% Japan.

Intl. Orgs. FAO, G-77, IAEA, IBRD, ICAO, IDA, IFAD, IFC, ILO, IMF, INTELSAT, INTERPOL, ITU, NAM, OAS, UN, UNESCO, UPU, WHO, WMO.

Until the arrival of the Spanish, the people living in the area that is now Bolivia were a part of the Inca empire. The Spanish discovered the fabulous silver deposits of the region in 1545 and established their presence in the area in the cities of Potosí and Sucre (founded as Chuquisaca in 1538). From the early colonial period on, Bolivia—or as it was then called, Upper Peru—depended heavily on the export of minerals. The exploitation of tin, oil, and natural gas has always had an important economic and political impact on the country's development.

In the early 1800s, revolutionary leader Símon Bolívar envisioned a political confederation of Upper Peru (Bolivia), Peru, and Gran Colombia (Ecuador, Colombia, and Venezuela), but he soon abandoned the plan as being politically unworkable due to conflict among the elite in the region. During 1836–39, Peru did form a brief union with Bolivia, until Chile intervened to break up the confederation.

Because Bolivia shares its borders with Peru, Brazil, Paraguay, Argentina, and Chile, the country has lost much of its original territory. The dictator Mariano Melgarejo sold large chunks of Bolivian territory to her neighbors during his rule, from 1865 to 1871. As a result of its defeat by Chile in the War of the Pacific (1879–83), Bolivia became a landlocked country. And in the 1932–35 Chaco War with Paraguay, Bolivian defeat led to a further loss of territory in the east.

In addition to its topographical and economic fragmentation, Bolivia has suffered from Indian/non-Indian racial and cultural divisions, resulting in a lack of political cohesion. Elites from the Potosí region vied with those from La Paz and Santa Cruz for political control. The Conservatives of the silver-mining southern region of Potosí controlled the government until their ouster in 1898 by the Liberal tin interests of the La Paz region. The La Paz interests then proceeded to preside over a period of stable republican politics, which lasted until the Great Depression and the Chaco War.

One of the results of the Chaco War was the fragmentation of the Bolivian military into competing factions as the factions took sides in the struggle for power between conservative landowners and middle-class reformers; this caused extreme instability of the political order right up until the Bolivian National Revolution in 1952. In 1941 the National Revolutionary Movement (MNR) was formed with the aim of transferring control of the country from conservative landowning elites to the middle sectors. The leadership of the movement found itself outpaced by revolts sponsored by workers and peasants; the MNR therefore incorporated these elements into its program. When the 1952 revolution brought the MNR to power, its leadership, which included the future four-time president Victor Paz Estenssoro, embarked on a reformist political program. The military overthrew the MNR in 1964, and it has since fragmented, but Paz Estenssoro was again elected to the presidency in 1985.

Botswana
Republic of Botswana
(PREVIOUS NAME: BECHUANALAND)
Geography **Location:** landlocked country in southern Africa. **Boundaries:** Namibia to N and W, Zimbabwe to NE, South Africa to SE and S. **Total land area:** 224,711 sq. mi. (582,000 sq km). **Coastline:** none. **Comparative area:** slightly smaller than Texas. **Land use:** 2% arable land; 0% permanent crops; 75% meadows and pastures; 2% forest and woodland; 21% other; includes negl. % irrigated. **Major cities:** (1981 census) Gaborone (capital) 59,657; Francistown 31,065; Selebi-Pikwe 29,469; Serowe 23,661; Mahalapye 20,712.

People **Population:** 1,189,900 (1988). **Nationality:** noun and adjective—Motswana (sing.), Batswana (pl.). **Ethnic groups:** 95% Batswana; 4% Kalanga, Basarwa, and Kgalagadi; 1% white. **Languages:** English (official), Setswana. **Religions:** 50% Christian, 50% indigenous beliefs.

Government **Type:** parliamentary republic. **Independence:** Sept. 30, 1966 (from UK). **Constitution:** Mar. 1965, effective Sept. 30, 1966. **National holiday:** Botswana Day, Sept. 30. **Heads of government:** Quett K.J. Masire, president (since July 1980). **Structure:** executive—president appoints and presides over cabinet; legislative—bicameral legislature (National Assembly with 34 popularly elected members and four members elected by the 34 representatives; House of Chiefs with deliberative powers only); judiciary—local courts administer customary law; high court and subordinate courts have criminal jurisdiction; court of appeal.

Economy **Monetary unit:** pula. **Budget:** (1988 est.) **income:** $738.0 mil.; **expend.:** $675.6 mil. **GDP:** $905 mil., $880 per capita (1985). **Chief crops:** corn, sorghum, millet, cowpeas; heavy dependence on imported food. **Livestock:** cattle, goats, sheep, donkeys, horses. **Natural**

resources: diamonds, copper, nickel, salt, soda ash. **Major industries:** livestock processing; mining of diamonds, copper, nickel, coal, salt, soda ash, potash; tourism. **Labor force:** about 400,000 total; 110,000 formal-sector employees (1984); most others engaged in cattle raising and subsistence agriculture; 40,000 formal-sector employees spend at least six to nine months per year as wage earners in South Africa (1980); 17% unemployment (1983). **Exports:** $653 mil. (f.o.b., 1985); diamonds, cattle, animal products, copper, nickel. **Imports:** $535 mil. (c.i.f., 1985); foodstuffs, vehicles, textiles, petroleum products. **Major trading partners:** Switzerland, U.S., UK, other EC-associated members of Southern African Customs Union.

Intl. Orgs. Commonwealth, FAO, G-77, GATT (de facto), IBRD, ICAO, IDA, IFAD, IFC, ILO, IMF, INTERPOL, ITU, NAM, UN, UNESCO, UPU, WHO, WMO.

Botswana, occupying a high and relatively arid tableland in southern Africa, was traditionally occupied by diverse groups of farmers, pastoralists, and hunter-gatherers. European missionaries arrived from South Africa in the early 19th century. In the late 19th century, native peoples resisted the encroachment of Afrikaners from the Transvaal; in response the British government established a protectorate in what was then called Bechuanaland in 1886. The southern part of the protectorate was organized as a Crown Colony and ultimately passed under the control of South Africa. During the 20th century, the territory remaining in the protectorate saw a steady evolution of local rule.

In 1920 two advisory councils were established to represent the interests of native and European inhabitants. In 1934 British authorities promulgated regulations establishing the powers and jurisdictions of native chiefs and the functions of native councils and courts. Local fiscal powers were established soon thereafter. In 1951 a joint (native-European) advisory council was set up, and 10 years later an elected legislature met under the provisions of a constitution promulgated on May 2, 1961.

In 1963–64 the British government accepted Botswanan proposals for self-government. A new capital was established at Gaborone in February 1965; a new constitution came into effect in the following month, and Botswana became fully independent on Sept. 30, 1966. Since independence, Botswana has been a multiparty, multiracial democracy that has remained untouched by the political turmoil affecting most of its neighbors.

Botswana is also one of the most prosperous countries in Africa. It is the world's largest producer of diamonds; revenues from diamond exports have been wisely managed, leading to significant budgetary surpluses in recent years. Gold and soda ash are also mined. Tourism, bolstered by Botswana's large herds of big game, is the country's major nonmining industry. About 75 percent of the population is engaged in agriculture and herding; Botswana is one of Africa's largest exporters of meat and animal products.

Brazil
Federative Republic of Brazil

Geography Location: central and north-eastern South America. **Boundaries:** Colombia, Venezuela, Guyana, Suriname, and French Guiana to N.; North Atlantic Ocean to NE.; South Atlantic Ocean to SE.; Uruguay, Argentina, and Paraguay to S.; Peru and Bolivia to W. **Total land area:** 3,286,488 sq. mi. (8,511,965 sq km). **Coastline:** 4,652 mi. (7,491 km). **Comparative area:** slightly smaller than U.S. **Land use:** 7% arable land; 1% permanent crops; 19% meadows and pastures; 67% forest and woodland; 6% other; includes negl. % irrigated. **Major cities:** (1985 est.) Brasília (capital) 1,576,657; São Paulo 10,099,086; Rio de Janeiro 5,615,149; Belo Horizonte 2,122,073; Salvador 1,811,367.

People Population: 150,685,145 (1988). **Nationality:** noun—Brazilian(s); adjective—Brazilian. **Ethnic groups:** Portuguese, Italian, German, Japanese, black, Amerindian; 55% white, 38% mixed, 6% black, 1% other. **Languages:** Portuguese (official), Spanish, English, French. **Religions:** 90% Roman Catholic (nominal).

Government Type: federal republic; democratically elected president since 1985. **Independence:** Sept. 7, 1822 (from Portugal). **Constitution:** Jan. 24, 1967, extensively amended in 1969; Senate and Chamber of Deputies combined to form Constituent Assembly in 1987 to draft new constitution. **National holiday:** Independence Day, Sept. 7. **Heads of government:** José Sarney, president (since Apr. 1985). **Structure:** strong executive with broad powers; bicameral legislature (National Congress) with growing powers, composed of Senate and Chamber of Deputies; 11-member Supreme Court.

Economy Monetary unit: cruzado. **Budget:** (1986) *income:* 380 bil. cruzados (public sector); *expend.:* 548 bil. cruzados **GNP:** $270 bil., $1,880 per capita (1986). **Chief crops:** coffee, rice, corn, sugarcane, cocoa, soybeans; nearly self-sufficient except for wheat; illegal producer of coca and cannabis for international drug trade. **Livestock:** cattle, pigs, sheep, goats, horses, mules, asses. **Natural resources:** iron ore, manganese, bauxite, nickel, uranium. **Major industries:** textiles and other consumer goods, chemicals, cement. **Labor force:** 50 mil. (1984); 40% services, 35% agriculture, 25% industry. **Exports:** $22.4 bil. (f.o.b., 1986); soybeans, coffee, transport equipment, iron ore, steel products. **Imports:** $15.6 bil. (f.o.b., 1986); petroleum, machinery, chemicals, fertilizers, wheat. **Major trading partners:** (1986) *exports:* 28% U.S., 26% EC, 12% Latin America, 7% Japan, 27% other; *imports:* 23% U.S., 23% EC, 17% Middle East, 13% Latin America, 6% Japan.

Intl. Orgs. FAO, G-77, GATT, IAEA, IBRD, ICAO, IDA, IFAD, IFC, ILO, IMF, IMO, INTELSAT, ITU, OAS, UN, UNESCO, UPU, WHO, WIPO, WMO.

The Portuguese arrived on the coast of what would become Brazil with the expedition of Pedro Alvares Cabral in 1500. The European explorers found an indigenous population of semisedentary and nonsedentary cultures. Many of the semisedentary Indian groups encountered by the Portuguese spoke the Tupian language and shared similar cultural features. The Tupians quickly formed economic relationships with the first Europeans, who were interested in the valuable dyewood that was so abundant in Brazil.

The transition of Indian-European economic relations from barter to slavery was given momentum by the introduction of sugar export agriculture, a trend that began in the region in the 1540s. The 1560s saw epidemics of smallpox and measles in the coastal areas, which greatly reduced the indigenous population. Although the European sugar growers initially favored the use of indigenous peoples over imported African slave labor (owing to the lower price of Indian slaves), the shortage of labor resulting from the epidemics led to increasing use of African slave labor by the Portuguese.

The Portuguese vied with other European powers for control of Brazilian territory, and in 1624 the Dutch briefly seized the northeastern sugar-growing area. Brazil's southern regions were underpopulated during the early colonial period, and Portuguese activity was largely limited to cattle raising. With the discovery of gold (1690s) and diamonds (1729), European interest in and settlement of the Minas Gerais area quickened.

The beginnings of Brazilian independence can be traced to the Napoleonic wars of Europe. The Portuguese royal court was able to escape Napoleon's armies with the help of the British fleet, and the prince regent, Dom João VI, sought refuge in Brazil in 1808, making it the seat of the Portuguese empire. Dom João returned to a Portugal liberated from Napoleonic occupation in 1821, leaving his son Dom Pedro behind as prince regent. In 1822, defying orders to return to Portugal and opposed to the imminent reversion of Brazil to colonial status, Dom Pedro declared Brazil's independence and was crowned emperor. By 1823 Brazil's independence had been achieved in fact, and in 1825 an agreement mediated by the British between Portugal and Brazil led to Portuguese recognition of Brazil as a separate kingdom.

The early years of independence were rocky. Dom Pedro became increasingly estranged from his people and began losing control of the Brazilian political situation owing to a continuing series of landowner revolts and to the loss of a war with the United Provinces of Rio de la Plata over what would become Uruguay. In 1831 Dom Pedro abdicated in favor of his 5-year-old son, Dom Pedro II; a regency governed Brazil until his accession to the throne in 1840.

The Brazilian empire found itself continually involved in the wars and internal politics of Uruguay, Argentina, and Paraguay in the 1850s and 1860s. The bloody five-year war with Paraguay that began in 1865 resulted in Paraguay's eventual defeat, but the process of the war had important consequences for the future of Brazil: the expansion of the military in numbers and power, the fragmentation of the political party system, and the undermining of the legitimacy of slavery. Slavery was abolished in 1888, and the following year, a military coup overthrew the emperor.

The "Old Republic," which lasted between 1889 and 1930, was a federal system in which much of the political control in Brazilian society was relegated to state-based political networks with local bosses. The presidency was assigned in a de facto rotation system called the politics of the governors, in which the president's office was controlled in turn by the most important state power networks. The world depression of 1929 hit the Brazilian agricultural export economy hard, and in 1930 the military overthrew the elected president; Getulio Vargas, a politician from the state of Rio Grande do Sul, took over the office.

Vargas proceeded to centralize power in the presidency, diminishing states' rights dramatically. Civil unrest allowed Vargas to declare a state of siege with military backing, and in 1937 he declared the establishment of the Estado Novo, a state wherein Vargas had absolute power, in imitation of Portuguese and Italian regimes of the period. The military ousted Vargas in 1945, ushering in the period of the "Second Republic." Vargas again won reelection in 1950 but committed suicide in 1954. Juscelino Kubitschek was elected to the presidency in 1955 and took office the following year. As part of his vision of developing the country, he led the way for construction of the new capital of Brasília in the previously undeveloped interior of the country.

After only seven months in office, newly elected Pres. Jânio Quadros resigned in 1961, and the presidency passed to populist Vice Pres. João Goulart. The populist mobilization of peasants and workers endorsed by the Goulart government led to his overthrow by the military in 1964.

The Brazilian military governed the country from 1964 until 1985. Military rule was not maintained in the form of a dictatorship during this period; rather, the military ruled as a more or less cohesive institution. The succession of generals and their technocratic allies attempted to develop the country through a pattern of state-led growth in which civilian politics were excluded. The tendency for the military to become institutionally divided through its involvement in political governance combined with social groups' increasing demand to be included in the political process led to the transition toward civilian leadership in Brazil.

In 1985 a civilian president was selected, and the process of writing a new constitution began the following year. Although Tancredo Neves was supposed to assume the presidency, he died before taking office. Thus, José Sarney, the vice presidential candidate, became Brazil's first civilian president since 1964. Presidential elections under the new constitutional structure were to be held in 1989, with the handling of Brazil's massive foreign debt to be a key political issue.

Brunei
Brunei Darussalam
Geography Location: Southeast Asia, on NW coast of island of Kalimantan (Borneo).

Boundaries: surrounded and bisected on landward side by Sarawak, one of two eastern states of Malaysia; South China Sea to N. **Total land area:** 2,226 sq. mi. (5,765 sq km). **Coastline:** 100 mi. (161 km). **Comparative area:** slightly larger than Delaware. **Land use:** 1% arable land; 1% permanent crops; 1% meadows and pastures; 79% forest and woodland; 18% other; includes negl. % irrigated. **Major cities:** Bandar Seri Begawan (formerly Brunei Town) (capital) 55,070 (1985 est.); Seria, Kuala Belait, Tutong.

People Population: 316,565 (1988). **Nationality:** noun—Bruneian(s); adjective—Bruneian. **Ethnic groups:** 64% Malay, 20% Chinese, 16% other. **Languages:** Malay (official), English, Chinese. **Religions:** 60% Muslim (official), 32% Buddhist and indigenous beliefs, 8% Christian.

Government Type: constitutional sultanate. **Independence:** Jan. 1, 1984 (from UK). **Constitution:** Sept. 29, 1959 (some provisions suspended since Dec. 1962, others since independence). **National holiday:** National Day, Feb. 23. **Heads of government:** Sir Hassanal Bolkiah, sultan and prime minister (since Aug. 1968). **Structure:** chief of state is sultan (advised by appointed privy council), who appoints executive council and legislative council.

Economy Monetary unit: brunei dollar. **Budget:** (1985) *income:* $2,109 mil. *expend.* $1,219 mil. **GDP:** $2.94 bil., $10,970 per capita (1986). **Chief crops:** rice, pepper. **Livestock:** pigs, buffalo, cattle, goats. **Natural resources:** crude oil, natural oil, natural gas, timber. **Major industries:** crude petroleum, liquefied natural gas, construction. **Labor force:** 68,128 (1984; includes members of army); 50.4% production of oil and natural gas, construction; 47.6% trade, services, and other; 2.0% agriculture, forestry, and fishing. **Exports:** $2.2 bil. (1986); 98–99% crude oil, liquefied natural gas, petroleum products. **Imports:** $625 mil. (1986); includes machinery and transport equipment, manufactured goods, beverages, tobacco; most consumer goods and food imported. **Major trading partners:** (1985) *exports:* (crude petroleum and liquefied natural gas) roughly two-thirds to Japan; *imports:* 24% Singapore, 20% Japan, 16% U.S.

Intl. Orgs. ASEAN, ICAO, IMO, INTERPOL, ITU, UN, UPU, WHO, WMO.

The Islamic sultanate of Brunei became dominant in northern Borneo in the 16th century but declined in power after the 17th century under pressure from the Dutch and other foreign powers. An Anglo-Dutch agreement of 1824 assigned North Borneo to Great Britain's sphere of influence in Asia. In 1841 a British adventurer, James Brooke, aided the sultan of Brunei in putting down a rebellion and was rewarded by being given the province of Sarawak, comprising more than half of the sultanate's area. Britain established a protectorate over Sabah, the eastern portion of Brunei, in 1881. That left the sultan with a tiny realm on the Brunei River, which also ultimately was placed under British protection in 1888. The

discovery of Southeast Asia's richest oilfield in Brunei and its offshore waters made the sultanate an enclave of tremendous wealth from the late 19th century onward.

Following Japanese occupation during World War II, British rule resumed in North Borneo. Sarawak and Sabah became part of Malaysia in 1963. Brunei was granted independence from Great Britain on Dec. 1, 1984. The sultan of Brunei, an absolute monarch, rules from the world's largest royal palace in Bandar Seri Begawan, the nation's capital. The economy is centered almost entirely on petroleum and international banking and investments.

Bulgaria
People's Republic of Bulgaria
Geography Location: southeastern Europe, in eastern Balkan Mountains. **Boundaries:** Romania to N, Black Sea to E, Turkey and Greece to S, Yugoslavia to W. **Total land area:** 42,823 sq. mi. (110,912 sq km). **Coastline:** 220 mi. (354 km). **Comparative area:** slightly larger than Tennessee. **Land use:** 34% arable land; 3% permanent crops; 18% meadows and pastures; 35% forest and woodland; 10% other; includes 11% irrigated. **Major cities:** (1983) Sofia (capital) 1,093,752; Plovdiv 373,235; Varna 295,218; Burgas (Bourgas) 183,477; Ruse (Roussé) 181,185.

People Population: 8,966,927 (1988). **Nationality:** noun—Bulgarian(s); adjective—Bulgarian. **Ethnic groups:** 85.3% Bulgarian, 8.5% Turk, 2.6% Gypsy, 2.5% Macedonian, 0.3% Armenian, 0.2% Russian, 0.6% other. **Languages:** Bulgarian; secondary languages closely correspond to ethnic breakdown. **Religions:** regime promotes atheism; religious background of population is 85% Bulgarian Orthodox, 13% Muslim, 0.8% Jewish, 0.7% Roman Catholic, 0.5% Protestant, Gregorian-Armenian, and other.

Government Type: communist state. **Independence:** Sept. 22, 1908 (from Ottoman Empire). **Constitution:** May 16, 1971, effective May 18, 1971. **National holiday:** National Liberation Day, Sept. 9. **Heads of government:** Todor Khristov Zhivkov, chairman, State Council (since July 1971); Georgi Ivanov Atanasov, chairman, Council of Ministers (since Mar. 1986). **Structure:** legislative—National Assembly; judiciary—Supreme Court.

Economy Monetary unit: leva. **Budget:** N.A. **GNP:** $61.2 bil., $6,800 per capita (1986). **Chief crops:** grain, tobacco, fruits, vegetables, cheese, sunflower seeds; mainly self-sufficient. **Livestock:** poultry, sheep, pigs, goats, horses. **Natural resources:** bauxite, copper, lead, zinc, coal. **Major industries:** food processing, machine and metal building, electronics. **Labor force:** 5.16 mil. (1986); 27% industry, 17% agriculture, 56% other. **Exports:** $14.5 bil. (f.o.b., 1986); 53.5% machinery and equipment; 18.4% agricultural products; 10.0% fuels, mineral raw materials, and metals; 9.7% manufactured consumer goods; 8.4% other. **Imports:** $15.3 bil. (f.o.b., 1986); 47.0% fuels and minerals, 33.2% machinery and equipment, 9.5% agricultural and forestry products, 3.8% manufactured consumer goods, 6.6% other. **Major trading partners:** (1986 est.) 60% USSR, 18% Eastern Europe, 11% developed countries, 8% developing countries.

Intl. Orgs. CMEA, FAO, IAEA, ICAO, ILO, IMO, ITU, UN, UNESCO, UPU, Warsaw Pact, WHO, WIPO, WMO.

Turkic Bulgars arrived at the west shore of the Black Sea in the seventh century, mingling with the indigenous Slavic population. The Bulgars accepted Eastern Orthodox Christianity in the ninth century and were conquered and incorporated into the Byzantine Empire by Basil II in the late 10th century. With the decline of Byzantium, Bulgaria became an independent kingdom, but it was conquered by the Ottoman Turks in 1396 and remained part of the Ottoman Empire for the next 500 years.

In the Treaty of San Stefano, ending the Russo-Turkish War in 1878, a Bulgarian state was promised that was to stretch from the Adriatic to the Black Sea. But the Great Powers would not permit so large a Russian client state, and instead the Berlin Conference of 1878 sanctioned the creation of a much smaller Bulgarian state, under a German dynasty with the Ottoman sultan as nominal overlord. Bulgaria gained full independence in 1908.

The Balkan Wars of 1912 and 1913 led to an expansion of Bulgarian territory, but after World War I, Bulgaria, which had been allied with the Central Powers, lost its Aegean coastline to Greece. A series of weak parliamentary governments under King Boris III (r. 1918–43) ended when the king established a personal dictatorship in 1935. Bulgaria joined the Axis powers in 1941 and declared war against the Western powers but not against Russia. Under occupation by its German allies, Bulgaria once again expanded to the Aegean during the war.

Russian troops entered Bulgaria in 1944 and organized a communist government on the basis of the leftist anti-Nazi resistance. The boy-king Simeon II remained on the throne until 1946, when the monarchy was abolished by a popular referendum. The People's Republic of Bulgaria was established in 1946.

Until the end of World War II, Bulgaria was a peasant society, with 80 percent of the population engaged in agriculture; industrial development was rudimentary. The People's Republic established a planned economy on the Soviet model; Russian credits and trade agreements permitted a rapid industrialization focused on machinery and equipment for export. Russia became and remained Bulgaria's principal export market.

In 1954 Todor Zhivkov became first secretary of the Bulgarian Communist party. He served as premier in the 1960s and has been president since 1971. The death of his daughter Lyudmila in 1981 averted the likelihood of the establishment of "dynastic" government.

In the 1960s Zhivkov promoted a certain amount of decentralization and responsiveness to market forces, but with the 1968 Russian invasion of Czechoslovakia, he returned the economy to central planning, collective farming, and giant state-industrial enterprises.

Since 1979, policy has reverted to decentralization on the Hungarian model. In October 1985 Zhivkov met with Mikhail Gorbachev in Belgrade and soon afterward announced the appointment of a new premier, Georgi Atanasov, and the appointment of a group of younger ministers. Reforms based on Gorbachev's "self-management" policies were instituted in 1986 and met with rapid success; in 1987 Gorbachev met with Zhivkov in Moscow and asked him to slow the pace of reform. By 1988 central planning decisions had become advisory rather than mandatory for state enterprises.

Bulgaria's mixed industrial and agricultural economy remains closely tied to the Soviet economy; its future rests in part on the fate of economic reform in the USSR.

Burkina Faso
(PREVIOUS NAME: UPPER VOLTA)
Geography   Location: landlocked country in western Africa. **Boundaries:** Mali to N and W, Niger to E, Benin, Togo, Ghana and Ivory Coast to S. **Total land area:** 105,870 sq. mi. (274,200 sq km). **Coastline:** none. **Comparative area:** slightly larger than Colorado. **Land use:** 10% arable land; negl. % permanent crops; 37% meadows and pastures; 26% forest and woodland; 27% other; includes negl. % irrigated. **Major cities:** (1985 census) Ouagoudougou (capital) 442,233; Bobo-Diolasso 231,162; Koudougou 51,670; Ouahigouya 38,604; Banfora 35,204.

People   Population: 8,485,737 (1988). **Nationality:** noun—Burkinabe; adjective—Burkinabe. **Ethnic groups:** Mossi (about 2.5 mil.), Gurunsi, Senufo, Lobi, Bobo, Mande, Fulani. **Languages:** French (official); tribal languages spoken by 90% of population. **Religions:** 65% indigenous beliefs, 25% Muslim, 10% Christian (mainly Roman Catholic).

Government   Type: military; established by coup on Aug. 4, 1983. **Independence:** Aug. 5, 1960 (from France). **Constitution:** none; Constitution of Nov. 1977 was abolished following coup of Nov. 25, 1980. **National holiday:** Independence Day, Aug. 4. **Heads of government:** Capt. Blaise Compaore, president (since Oct. 1987). **Structure:** executive—president; military council of unknown number; 21-member military and civilian cabinet; judiciary.

Economy   Monetary unit: Communauté Financiè Africaine (CFA) franc. **Budget:** (1986) *income:* $259 mil.; *expend.:* $280 mil. **GDP:** $1.2 bil., $170 per capita (1985). **Chief crops:** cash crops—peanuts, shea nuts, seasame, cotton; food crops—sorghum, millet, corn, rice; food shortages. **Livestock:** cattle, goats, sheep, pigs, asses. **Natural resources:** manganese, limestone, marble; small deposits of gold, antimony, copper, nickel, bauxite. **Major industries:** agricultural processing plants; brewery, cement, and brick plants. **Labor force:** 3.3 mil. (1984); 82% agriculture, 13% industry, 5% other; 20% of male labor force migrates annually to neighboring countries for seasonal employment; 30,000 are wage earners; 44% of population of working age. **Exports:** $82 mil. (f.o.b., 1985); livestock, peanuts, shea nut

products, cotton, sesame. **Imports:** $324 mil. (f.o.b., 1985); textiles, food and other consumer goods, transport equipment, machinery, fuels. **Major trading partners:** Ivory Coast, Ghana, France, other EC countries.

Intl. Orgs. FAO, G-77, GATT, IBRD, ICAO, IDA, IFAD, IFC, ILO, IMF, INTELSAT, INTERPOL, ITU, NAM, UN, UNESCO, UPU, WHO, WIPO, WMO.

The Mossi empire dominated the area of what is now Burkina Faso, a landlocked nation in western Africa with few natural resources and poor agricultural conditions, from as early as the 11th century. They ruled the region, often resisting Moselm invaders, until modern times.

The French arrived in 1896, capturing the Mossi capital city of Ouagoudougou and establishing a protectorate over the area. The French created Upper Volta in 1919, naming it for the upper basin of the Volta River that takes up most of the country. Upper Volta became a self-governing state with the French Overseas Community in 1958 and an independent republic outside of the French Community on Aug. 5, 1960. In September 1960 Upper Volta became a member of the United Nations.

After a brief period of military rule, the nation ratified a new constitution on June 14, 1970, and made a peaceful transition to civilian rule based on the French model. In 1980 the Constitution was overthrown and a military government was set up. There was another coup on Aug. 4, 1983, and a government was established patterned after the Libyan government of Muammar al-Qaddafi. On Aug. 14, 1984, Upper Volta officially changed its name to Burkina Faso.

Burma
Socialist Republic of the Union of Burma
Geography   Location: NW region of Southeast Asia. **Boundaries:** China and Laos to NE, Bangladesh and India to NW, Thailand to SE, Andaman Sea to S, and Bay of Bengal to SW. **Total land area:** 261,218 sq. mi. (676,552 sq km). **Coastline:** 1,902 mi. (3,060 km). **Comparative area:** slightly smaller than Texas. **Land use:** 15% arable land; 1% permanent crops; 1% meadows and pastures; 49% forest and woodland; 34% other; includes 2% irrigated. **Major cities:** (1983 est.) Rangoon (capital) 2,458,712; Mandalay 532,895; Bassein 335,000; Moulmein 219,991; Akyab 143,000.

People   Population: 39,632,183 (1988). **Nationality:** noun—Burmese (sing., pl.); adjective—Burmese. **Ethnic groups:** 68% Burman, 9% Shan, 7% Karen, 4% Raljome, 3% Chinese, 2% Indian, 7% other. **Languages:** Burmese, minority ethnic langs. **Religions:** 85% Buddhist, 15% indigenous beliefs, Muslim, Christian, and other.

Government   Type: republic. **Independence:** Jan. 4, 1948 (from UK). **Constitution:** Jan. 3, 1974. **National holiday:** Independence Day, Jan. 4. **Heads of government:** Gen. Saw Maung, prime minister (since Sept. 1988). **Structure:** Council of State rules through Council of Ministers; National Assembly (Pyithu

Hluttaw, or People's Congress) has legislative power.

Economy **Monetary unit:** kyat. **Budget:** (1986 est.) *income:* $3,754 mil.; *expend.:* $4,381 mil. **GDP:** $7.97 bil., $210 per capita (1986). **Chief crops:** paddy, beans, pulses, maize, oilseeds; most rice grown in deltaic land; illegal producer of opium poppy and cannabis for international drug trade. **Livestock:** cattle, pigs, buffalo, goats, sheep. **Natural resources:** crude oil, timber, tin, copper, tungsten. **Major industries:** agricultural processing, textiles and footwear, wood and wood products. **Labor force:** 14.8 mil. (1985/86 est.); 66.1% agriculture, 12.0% industry, 10.6% government. **Exports:** $407 mil. (1987 est.); teak and hardwoods, rice, pulses and beans, base metals, ores. **Imports:** $627 mil. (1987 est.); machinery and transportation equipment, building materials, oil industry equipment. **Major trading partners:** *exports:* Singapore, Western Europe, China, UK, Japan; *imports:* Japan, Western Europe, Singapore, UK.

Intl. Orgs. Colombo Plan, FAO, G-77, GATT, IAEA, IBRD, ICAO, IDA, IFC, ILO, IMF, IMO, INTERPOL, ITU, UN, UNESCO, UPU, WHO, WMO.

Burma, an independent Buddhist monarchy from the 11th century, fell to the Mongol empire in the 13th century and after the 14th century, was a satellite state of China. Anglo-French rivalry over trade left Burma under French influence in the early 19th century, but in a series of three wars (1824-26, 1852, 1885), Great Britain succeeded in bringing all of Burma into the British raj of India. The country became self-governing under a British protectorate in 1937.

Japanese occupation of Burma in early 1942 made the country a major theater of fighting during World War II. The Burma Road, built by the Allies to connect northeastern India with southwestern China, was a key link in bringing supplies to the Chinese Nationalist army during the war.

Burma achieved independence as the Union of Burma on Jan. 4, 1948. Promises of autonomy to ethnic minority regions such as the Shan and Karen States have not been fulfilled, leading to armed separatist movements in those areas ever since. In 1962 a coup led by Gen. Ne Win overthrew the democratic government and established a one-party state under the Burmese Socialist Program party. The party's "Burmese Path to Socialism" resulted in self-imposed international isolation and economic stagnation at home despite the country's potential wealth in agriculture, timber, minerals, and gems. Many commodities became available only through the black market.

In July 1988 Ne Win resigned from office in the face of mounting popular demonstrations. A series of short-lived successor governments were unable to restore public order and normal governmental functions; direct military rule was announced in September 1988 as demonstrations continued.

Burundi
Republic of Burundi

Geography **Location:** landlocked country on northeastern shore of Lake Tanganyika in central Africa. **Boundaries:** Rwanda to N, Tanzania to E and S, Zaire to W. **Total land area:** 10,747 sq. mi. (27,834 sq km). **Coastline:** none. **Comparative area:** slightly larger than Maryland. **Land use:** 43% arable land; 8% permanent crops; 35% meadows and pastures; 2% forest and woodland; 12% other; includes negl. % irrigated. **Major cities:** Bujumbura (capital) 172,201 (1979 census); Gitega 15,943 (1978).

People **Population:** 5,155,665 (1988). **Nationality:** noun—Burundian(s); adjective—Burundi. **Ethnic groups:** 85% Hutu (Bantu), 14% Tutsi (Hamitic), 1% Twa (Pygmy); 70,000 refugees, mostly Rwandans and Zairians; 3,000 Europeans and 2,000 South Asians. **Languages:** Kirundi and French (both official), Swahili (along Lake Tanganyika and in Bujumbura area). **Religions:** 67% Christian (62% Roman Catholic, 5% Protestant), 32% indigenous beliefs, 1% Muslim.

Government **Type:** republic. **Independence:** July 1, 1962 (from UN trusteeship under Belgian administration). **Constitution:** Nov. 20, 1981; on taking power Maj. Pierre Buyoya suspended Constitution and formed Military Council for National Redemption. **National holiday:** Independence Day, July 1. **Heads of government:** Maj. Pierre Buyoya, leader of bloodless coup on Sept. 3, 1987; Adrien Sibomana, prime minister. **Structure:** executive—president and cabinet; legislature—National Assembly reestablished in 1982; judiciary.

Economy **Monetary unit:** Burundi franc. **Budget:** (1985) *income:* $159.8 mil.; *expend.:* $202.7 mil. **GDP:** $1.33 bil., $240 per capita (1986). **Chief crops:** cash crops—coffee, cotton, tea; food crops—manioc, yams, peas, corn, sorghum. **Livestock:** goats, cattle, sheep, pigs. **Natural resources:** nickel, uranium, rare earth oxide, peat, cobalt. **Major industries:** light consumer goods such as blankets, shoes, soap; assembly of imports; public works construction. **Labor force:** 1.9 mil. (1983); 93% agriculture, 7% other. **Exports:** $169.1 mil. (1986); 87% coffee; tea, cotton, hides, skins. **Imports:** $207.2 mil. (1986); textiles, foodstuffs, transport equipment, petroleum products. **Major trading partners:** U.S., EC, Finland.

Intl. Orgs. FAO, G-77, GATT, IBRD, ICAO, IDA, IFAD, IFC, ILO, IMF, INTERPOL, ITU, NAM, UN, UNESCO, UPU, WHO, WIPO, WMO.

Burundi's population is divided between two ethnic groups, the majority Hutu and the minority, but politically powerful, Tutsi. The Hutu were the original settlers of the country and practiced agriculture; the cattle-herding Tutsi arrived several hundred years ago and established a form of feudal overlordship over the Hutu. The traditional government was monarchical, with a king (*mwami*) chosen from among a group of aristocratic families (*ganwa*). European exploration of Burundi began in

1858, and the territory was incorporated into German East Africa in 1899. It was occupied by Belgian troops in 1916. Following World War I, the League of Nations in 1923 awarded Burundi, along with neighboring Rwanda, to Belgium as a mandated territory. Belgian rule over the Territory of Ruanda-Urundi, as it was then called, continued under a UN trusteeship after World War II.

Burundi became independent on July 1, 1962, as a constitutional monarchy under the traditional mwami. The country rapidly lapsed into political chaos. In 1966, with the backing of the army, Capt. Michel Micombero overthrew the monarchy and proclaimed a republic. A Hutu rebellion in 1972 against Tutsi political domination left 10,000 Tutsi dead; Tutsi reprisals in 1972-73 resulted in the slaughter of 150,000 Hutu. The Micombero government was overthrown in a bloodless coup, and on Nov. 1, 1976, Lt. Col. Jean-Baptiste Bagaza took control of the government.

Bagaza was overthrown in September, 1987, while attending a conference of French-speaking African nations in Quebec. His successor is Maj. Pierre Buyoya. The Buyoya government has proclaimed a policy of nonalignment in foreign affairs, seeking closer links with the West, while maintaining relations with Libya and the Eastern bloc. Domestically, the government has pledged to eradicate Bagaza's record of persecution of the Catholic church (65% of Burundians are Catholic) and to seek ethnic reconciliation between Hutus and Tutsis. The latter policy was threatened, however, by renewed outbreaks of ethnic violence in 1988.

Burundi's economy is based primarily on agriculture; the country's dense population is distributed throughout the land on small farms. Overpopulation and soil impoverishment have overwhelmed the country's once-prosperous rural economy, and Burundi is now one of the world's poorest countries. The principal export crop is coffee; tea and cotton are also exported. The recent discovery of substantial nickel deposits promises to enhance Burundi's export sector.

Cambodia
(PREVIOUS NAME: KAMPUCHEA)

Geography **Location:** occupies part of Indochinese Peninsula in Southeast Asia. **Boundaries:** Thailand to W and N, Laos to N, Gulf of Thailand to S, Vietnam to E. **Total land area:** 69,898 sq. mi. (181,035 sq km). **Coastline:** 275 mi. (443 km). **Comparative area:** slightly smaller than Oklahoma. **Land use:** 16% arable land; 1% permanent crops; 3% meadows and pastures; 76% forest and woodland; 4% other; includes 1% irrigated. **Major cities:** (1986 est.) Phnom Penh (capital) 700,000.

People **Population:** 6,685,592 (1988). **Nationality:** noun—Kampuchean(s); adjective—Kampuchean. **Ethnic groups:** 90% Khmer (Cambodian), 5% Chinese, 5% other minorities. **Languages:** Khmer (official), French. **Religions:** 95% Theravada Buddhism, 5% other.

Government **Type:** disputed. **Independence:** Nov. 9, 1953 (from France). **Constitu-**

tion: June 27, 1981. **National holiday:** Apr. 17. **Heads of government:** Prince Norodom Sihanouk, president (since July 1982); Son Sann, prime minister (since July 1982). **Structure:** Council of Ministers, comprising an inner cabinet and a number of coordination committees.

Economy Monetary unit: riel. **Budget:** N.A. **GDP:** N.A. **Chief crops:** mainly subsistence except for rubber plantations; main crops—rice, rubber, corn; food shortages—rice, meat, vegetables, dairy products, sugar, flour. **Livestock:** cattle, pigs, buffalo, horses. **Natural resources:** timber, gemstones, some iron ore, manganese, phosphates, hydropower potential. **Major industries:** rice milling, fishing, wood and wood products. **Labor force:** N.A. **Exports:** $3.2 mil. (1985); natural rubber, rice, pepper, wood. **Imports:** $27.6 mil. (1985); international food aid, fuels, consumer goods. **Major trading partners:** Vietnam, USSR, Eastern Europe, Japan, India.

Intl. Orgs. Colombo Plan, FAO, G-77, GATT (de facto), IAEA, IBRD, ICAO, IDA, ILO, IMF, IMO, INTERPOL, ITU, NAM, UN, UNESCO, UPU, WHO, WMO.

The dominant power in Indochina from the eighth through the 13th centuries, the Khmer empire encompassed present-day Kampuchea and much of western Thailand, southern Laos, and central and southern Vietnam. It built magnificent Buddhist temple cities at Angkor Wat and Angkor Thon. From the 14th century onward, the Khmer empire came under increasing pressure from the expansionist Vietnamese state of Annam, which absorbed the territories east of the Mekong River. In the 18th century, the kingdom of Siam (Thailand) annexed three western provinces of the Khmer empire. The remaining Khmer territory became the French protectorate of Cambodia in 1863, and a French colony as part of the Union of Indochina in 1887. In 1907 France forced Siam to return some territory to Cambodia.

During World War II, Cambodia was occupied by Japan from 1942 to 1945, when French control was restored. After the French defeat in Indochina, Cambodia became independent in 1953 under Prince Norodom Sihanouk, who had ascended the throne in 1941. In 1960 Sihanouk was named head of state under a constitutional monarchy. Shaken by the Vietnam War in the 1960s, Cambodia broke relations with the United States in 1965 because of South Vietnamese incursions across the border. In 1969 relations were restored when Sihanouk charged North Vietnam with arming the Khmer Rouge Cambodian Communist rebels. In the same year, American planes began secret bombing raids in Cambodia. In 1970 Sihanouk was ousted by a coup led by pro-U.S. Gen. Lon Nol; the monarchy was abolished, and Prince Sihanouk went into exile. In April 1975 the Khmer Rouge, led by Pol Pot, captured the capital, Phnom Penh, and established a new government, the Kampuchean People's Republic. In an ensuing reign of terror, several hundred thousand people were killed and tens of thousands more fled to refugee camps in Thailand. In 1978, Vietnamese

troops invaded, capturing Phnom Penh on Jan. 7, 1979, and installing a new government led by Heng Samrin. The Kampuchean People's Republic continued to be recognized as the legal government of Cambodia in the United Nations and by most non-Soviet-bloc nations. A coalition dominated by the Khmer Rouge resisted the Vietnamese takeover, but by 1985 almost all of the country was under Vietnamese control.

At the end of 1988, with international pressure mounting to force a Vietnamese withdrawal from Cambodia, Prince Sihanouk (the one generally acknowledged national leader) was engaged in maneuvers to keep any successor government from being entirely dominated by Pol Pot's Khmer Rouge forces. In support of this policy, China has offered political asylum to Pol Pot and several other top Khmer Rouge leaders.

Cameroon
Republic of Cameroon
(PREVIOUS NAME: FRENCH CAMEROON)

Geography Location: western coast of central Africa. **Boundaries:** Nigeria to NW, Chad to NE, Central African Republic to E, Congo to SE, Gabon and Equatorial Guinea to S, Gulf of Guinea to W. **Total land area:** 183,569 sq. mi. (475,442 sq km). **Coastline:** 250 mi. (402 km). **Comparative area:** slightly larger than California. **Land use:** 13% arable land; 2% permanent crops; 18% meadows and pastures; 54% forest and woodland; 13% other; includes negl. % irrigated. **Major cities:** Yaoundé (capital) 583,470; Douala 852,705 (1985 est.); Nkongsamba 71,298; Maroua 67,187; Garoua 63,900 (1973 census).

People Population: 10,531,954 (1988). **Nationality:** noun—Cameroonian(s); adjective—Cameroonian. **Ethnic groups:** 31% Cameroon Highlanders, 19% Equatorial Bantu, 11% Kirdi, 10% Fulani, 8% Northwestern Bantu, 7% Eastern Nigritic, 13% other African; less than 1% non-African; over 200 ethnic groups of widely differing background. **Languages:** English and French (both official); 24 major African language groups. **Religions:** 51% indigenous beliefs, 33% Christian, 16% Muslim.

Government Type: unitary republic; one-party presidential regime. **Independence:** Jan. 1, 1960 (from UN trusteeship under French administration). **Constitution:** May 20, 1972. **National holiday:** National Day, May 20. **Heads of government:** Paul Biya, president (since Nov. 1982). **Structure:** executive—president; legislative—National Assembly; judiciary—Supreme Court has power of judicial review when questions of constitutionality are referred to it by president.

Economy Monetary unit: Communauté Financière Africaine (CFA) franc. **Budget:** (1987) *income:* $1.6 bil.; *expend.:* $2.3 bil. **GDP:** $12.6 bil., $1,230 per capita (1987 est.). **Chief crops:** coffee, cocoa, timber, cotton, rubber. **Livestock:** poultry, cattle, goats, sheep, pigs. **Natural resources:** crude oil, bauxite, iron ore, timber, hydropower potential. **Major industries:** crude oil production, small aluminum

plant, food processing. **Labor force:** (1983) 74.4% agriculture, 11.4% industry and transport, 14.2% other services; 50% of population of working age (1985). **Exports:** $2.2 bil. (f.o.b., 1987 est.); crude oil, cocoa, coffee, timber, aluminum. **Imports:** $1.7 bil. (c.i.f., 1987 est.); consumer goods, machinery, transport equipment, alumina for refining, petroleum products. **Major trading partners:** France, other EC countries, U.S.

Intl. Orgs. FAO, G-77, GATT, IAEA, IBRD, ICAO, IDA, IFAD, IFC, ILO, IMF, IMO, INTELSAT, INTERPOL, ITU, NAM, UN, UNESCO, UPU, WHO, WIPO, WMO.

Cameroon was settled by the Sao people about 1,000 years ago. In later times others, including the Bamileke, Bassa, Douala, and Fulani, migrated into the region. Portuguese trading stations were established along the coast beginning in the 15th century, and between 1500 and the early 19th century, the population was severely depleted by the slave trade in the hands of various European nations. European rivalries for domination in Cameroon were settled temporarily in 1884 when Germany established a protectorate.

British and French troops invaded German Cameroon during World War I, and following the war the League of Nations divided the protectorate into two mandated territories—French in the eastern sector and British in the west. French Cameroon rejected the Vichy government in World War II and became an important African base for Charles de Gaulle's Free French. In 1946 British and French rule in western and eastern Cameroon was reaffirmed under UN trusteeships.

In 1958 the French trusteeship was abolished, and the Republic of Cameroon became independent on Jan. 1, 1960. In February 1961 a UN-supervised plebiscite was held in British Cameroon, allowing the people of that region to choose between union with Nigeria and union with the Republic of Cameroon. The northern two-thirds of the British territory elected union with Nigeria; the southern portion joined the Republic of Cameroon on Oct. 1, 1961, to form the Federal Republic of Cameroon. In 1972 the federal structure was abolished by a national referendum, and the United Republic of Cameroon was established. In 1984 the nation's name reverted to the Republic of Cameroon.

During the federal period, Cameroon had a multiparty political system, with party divisions coinciding with the old distinctions between west and east Cameroon. In 1966 all political parties were amalgamated to form the Cameroon National Union, which, with various changes in name, has dominated the political life of Cameroon ever since. In 1980 Pres. Ahidjo, the long-time political leader of Cameroon, was elected without opposition to a fifth five-year term in office. He resigned in 1982 and was replaced by Prime Minister Paul Biya. Pres. Biya was reelected in his own right in 1984; he retained the backing of the military in putting down an attempted coup in April of that year. He abolished the office of prime minister, thus strengthening presidential government, and has instituted political reforms whereby multiple candidates stand for office within the structure of the country's single-party system.

The economy of Cameroon is based primarily on agriculture. The country is self-sufficient in food and exports coffee, cocoa, rubber, cotton, palm oil, and other agricultural commodities, as well as timber from substantial forest reserves. Oil is the principal export, however, accounting for 60 percent of export earnings. Overreliance on oil export earnings in the 1970s led to the growth of government bureaucracy, corruption, and excessive spending; the fall in oil prices in the 1980s thus led to economic turmoil and dislocation. These negative effects were cushioned to some extent by the health of the agricultural sector of the economy; austerity measures in the 1980s have allowed the government to begin to adjust to an era of shrinking petroleum revenues.

Canada

Geography Location: northern part of North America (excluding Alaska and Greenland); second-largest country in the world, after USSR. **Boundaries:** Arctic Ocean to N, Greenland to NE across Baffin Bay, Atlantic Ocean to E, United States to S, Pacific Ocean and Alaska to W. **Total land area:** 3,553,303 sq. mi. (9,203,054 sq km). **Coastline:** 151,492 mi. (243,791 km). **Comparative area:** slightly larger than U.S. **Land use:** 5% arable land; negl. % permanent crops; 3% meadows and pastures; 35% forest and woodland; 57% other; includes negl. % irrigated. **Major cities:** (1986 census) Ottawa (capital) 819,263; Toronto 3,427,168; Montréal 2,921,357; Vancouver 1,380,729; Edmonton 785,465.

People Population: 26,087,536 (1988). **Nationality:** noun—Canadian(s); adjective—Canadian. **Ethnic groups:** 40% British Isles origin, 27% French origin, 20% other European, 1.5% indigenous Indian or Eskimo. **Languages:** English, French. **Religions:** 46% Roman Catholic, 16% United Church, 10% Anglican.

Government Type: federal state recognizing Elizabeth II as sovereign. **Independence:** July 1, 1867 (from UK). **Constitution:** amended British North America Act of 1867 transferred power and rights to Canada, Apr. 17, 1982; charter of rights and unwritten customs. **National holiday:** Canada Day, July 1. **Heads of government:** Brian Mulroney, prime minister (since Sept. 1984); Jeanne Suave, governor-general (since May 1984). **Structure:** executive—cabinet collectively responsible to House of Commons and headed by prime minister; legislative—282-seat Parliament with queen represented by governor-general, Senate, and House of Commons; judiciary—judges appointed by governor-general with Supreme Court as highest tribunal.

Economy Monetary unit: Canadian dollar. **Budget:** (1987) *income:* $70.51 bil.; *expend.:* $85.10 bil. **GDP:** $412.8 bil., $15,910 per capita (1987). **Chief crops:** grain (principally wheat), feedgrains, oilseeds, tobacco. **Livestock:** cattle, pigs, sheep. **Natural resources:** nickel, zinc, copper, gold, lead. **Major indus-**

tries: processed and unprocessed minerals, food products, wood and paper products. **Labor force:** 13.12 mil. (1987); 69% services, 17% manufacturing; 8.9% unemployment. **Exports:** $90.1 bil. (f.o.b., 1986); transportation equipment, wood and wood products, including paper, ferrous and nonferrous ores, crude oil, natural gas; major food exporter, especially wheat. **Imports:** $85.1 bil. (c.i.f., 1986); transportation equipment, machinery, crude oil, communication equipment, textiles. **Major trading partners:** (1986) *exports:* 77.5% U.S., 5.1% Japan, 2.2% UK; *imports:* 74.0% U.S., 5.8% Japan, 3.5% UK.

Intl. Orgs. Colombo Plan, Commonwealth, FAO, GATT, IAEA, IBRD, ICAO, IDA, IFAD, IFC, ILO, IMF, IMO, INTELSAT, INTERPOL, ITU, NATO, OAS (observer), OECD, UNESCO, UPU, WHO, WIPO, WMO.

Canada is geographically the second-largest country in the world, but most of its territory is very sparsely settled. The vast majority of the country's 26 million people live in a narrow band along the border with the United States. Despite a long tradition of national independence, Canada's history has been dominated by relations with Great Britain, the United States, and, to a lesser extent, France.

Canada's earliest inhabitants arrived via the Bering land bridge from Asia around 15,000 years ago and diversified to form the various Inuit (Eskimo), Northwest Indian, Plains Indian, and forest Indian cultures that still contribute significantly to Canada's national identity. The earliest-known European settlers of Canada were Vikings, who established a short-lived colony in Newfoundland around A.D. 1000. British, French, and other European explorers made numerous voyages to Canada during the 16th century, stimulated by Canada's rich resources of fish, forest products, and furs.

The first permanent European settlement in Canada was the French trading station at Quebec, founded by Samuel de Champlain in 1608. Fur traders rapidly spread into the interior along the St. Lawrence River and the Great Lakes; European diseases, particularly smallpox, decimated Native American populations as the explorers advanced. In 1663 New France was organized as a French Crown Colony, and royal governors replaced private commercial interests in governing Quebec.

The Hudson Bay Company was chartered by the British Crown in 1670, inaugurating a long period of commercial and territorial rivalry in Canada between Britain and France. In general, France sought to expand New France northward and westward, while Britain sought to expand its domination southward and westward from Hudson Bay. French and British interests clashed directly along the Atlantic coast, where both British and French settlements were established. Local and regional wars between the French and the British were endemic in Canada throughout the 17th and 18th centuries; each side enlisted Native American allies. These wars were often inconclusive, but in Queen Anne's War (1702–13), Britain gained a significant advantage by winning

control of Acadia and Newfoundland, and by driving the French from Hudson Bay.

The French and Indian Wars of 1756–63, a North American extension of Europe's Seven Years' War, proved to be the decisive turning point in the Anglo-French rivalry in Canada. Prior to the outbreak of full-scale war, in 1755 the British deported some 7,000–10,000 French settlers from Acadia, in Nova Scotia, to the West Indies; many later settled in Louisiana. When war broke out in Europe in 1756, Britain employed its superior sea power to cut New France off from Europe and captured Quebec in the Battle of the Plains of Abraham in 1759. Montreal capitulated in 1760, leaving Britain in control of New France.

Faced with the difficult problem of governing New France's large and rapidly growing French population (which far outnumbered the English-speaking population of Canada), the British in 1774 passed the Quebec Act, which recognized the territory's legal code and manorial system of land tenure, and granted legal status to the Roman Catholic church. The act also extended Canadian territory south to the Ohio river, which enraged the inhabitants of the 13 American colonies and helped fuel the American Revolution.

During the American Revolution, nearly 40,000 loyalists fled to Canada from the rebellious colonies, establishing English-speaking settlements in New Brunswick and in western Quebec. Friction between English- and French-speaking Canadians led the British in 1791 to divide Canada (west of the Atlantic maritime provinces) into two provinces, Upper Canada and Lower Canada. Each was granted a legislature; that of Upper Canada was based on British institutions, while that of Lower Canada retained the French forms established by the Quebec Act of 1774.

During the War of 1812 between Great Britain and the United States, Canada became a battleground; Toronto was captured and pillaged by the Americans in 1813. Many Americans hoped to expand the territory of the United States at the expense of Canada, or even to entice Canada into a continental American union, but Canadians, whether English- or French-speaking, showed no enthusiasm for joining the United States. A small British garrison, with the support of Native American irregular forces, kept the Americans at bay. The Convention of 1818 established the border between Canada and the United States at latitude 49° north, as far west as the Rocky Mountains, and provided for joint U.S.-British control of Oregon (i.e., the entire Columbia River basin).

Following the War of 1812, British authorities actively encouraged British immigration to Canada, and between 1815 and 1855, one million Britons answered the call. This immigration radically altered the ethnic balance of Canada, making French-speaking Canadians a minority population for the first time. The Francophones of Lower Canada, hemmed in on all sides by English speakers, rose in rebellion under the leadership of the Parti Patriote in 1837–38. In response, Lord Durham recommended in 1839 that Canada be united under a single government, and the Union of Canada was enacted in 1841. This move did not, however, quell the growing nationalism of French Canadians.

Oregon became an issue in the American presidential election of 1844, with the United States claiming the entire Columbia River basin north to 54°40' ("fifty-four forty or fight"). War threatened but diplomacy triumphed; in 1846 the boundary at 49° was extended westward to the Pacific Ocean. Gold was discovered in British Columbia in 1856, leading to a gold rush and a substantial increase in the population of western Canada.

Growing trade between Canada and the United States from the 1840s onward, and the development of a continental system of railroads in both Canada and the United States in the 1850s, led to a relative decline in British influence in Canada. The American Civil War had the indirect effect of prompting Canadians to seek self-government in a federal union. Previously, there had been little contact between the Canadas (Upper and Lower) and the maritime provinces, while the vast territories of the west were still privately administered by the Hudson Bay Company. A federal union was forged in a series of conferences beginning in 1864, and the federation of Quebec, Ontario, Nova Scotia, and New Brunswick was recognized by the British North America Act of July 1, 1867.

The Dominion of Canada thus established in 1867 became a self-governing entity within the British Empire; Sir J.A. Macdonald became Canada's first prime minister (1867–73). The dominion rapidly expanded. In 1869 it purchased the western territories of the Hudson Bay Company, and in 1870, in response to a rebellion of French-speaking Métis in Manitoba, Manitoba was granted provincial status within the federation. In 1871 the union of British Columbia with Canada was secured with the promise of a transcontinental railway within 10 years; the Canadian Pacific Railway was completed in 1885. Prince Edward Island joined the federation in 1873, but neighboring Newfoundland remained a British colony outside the Canadian federation until 1949.

A second Francophone rebellion broke out in Manitoba in 1885. Its leader, Louis Riel, was executed and became a symbol of French Canadian grievances against the English-speaking majority. Wilfred Laurier became Canada's first Francophone prime minister in 1896, but he was unable to achieve a solution to the problem of the rights of Catholics and French-speakers outside Quebec. Legislation restricting those rights had already been enacted in Manitoba in 1890.

The Klondike Gold Rush of 1897–98 brought Canada to worldwide attention and indirectly helped promote the settlement of rich agricultural lands in the Canadian west. Immigrants to the prairie region came not only from eastern Canada, but also from Europe, notably Germany, Scandinavia, and the Ukraine. Japanese farmers and Chinese railroad and mining workers settled west of the Rockies, further increasing Canada's ethnic diversity, though Asian immigrants were denied citizenship through discriminatory legislation. Alberta and Saskatchewan were granted provincial status in 1905; the Yukon Territory and the Northwest Territories continued to be governed by controllers appointed by the federal government and patrolled by the famous Royal Canadian Mounted Police.

Urbanization and industrialization were stimulated in the early 20th century by the exploitation of extensive mineral resources in western Canada and in northern Quebec, and by the development of hydroelectric projects and transportation facilities throughout the country. The long-lived Laurier government fell in 1911, when his proposal for free trade with the United States evoked widespread fears that Canada's nascent industries would suffer without protective tariffs.

Laurier's Conservative successor, Robert Borden, sent Canadian volunteer troops to fight in World War I in 1914 and, over the objections of most French Canadian leaders, bolstered Canada's war efforts in Europe through national conscription in 1917. The distinguished performance of Canada's armed forces in the war bought the country renewed international respect and appreciation.

Borden's wartime English-speaking Conservative-Liberal coalition collapsed in 1921. He was succeeded by the Liberal leader William L. Mackenzie King, who was to be Canada's prime minister for over 20 years (1921–30, 1935–48). Mackenzie King faced a challenge from the Progressive party, based in the agricultural plains provinces, but he managed to outwit and neutralize the Progressive leadership; the party disappeared as a political force after the mid-1920s. Mackenzie King skillfully managed the economic prosperity of the 1920s, which saw the establishment in Canada of branch plants of many American industrial firms.

The Statute of Westminster, which created the British Commonwealth in 1931, had the effect of granting full self-government to Canada within the Commonwealth.

Canada's federal structure was ill-equipped to manage the economic collapse of the 1930s, which brought both industrial depression and a drought-induced agricultural crisis. Efforts to deal with unemployment, land foreclosures, and other economic ills fell almost entirely to the provincial governments, which were not up to the task. The growth of private cooperative movements brought some relief to the maritime provinces and the plains provinces, while interest grew in constitutional reform to strengthen the federal government.

Canada's recovery from the Great Depression was stimulated primarily by the advent of World War II, which Canada entered in 1939. Although the war years brought price controls, rationing, and other emergency measures, the overall effect of the war was to strengthen all sectors of Canada's economy and to enhance Canada's international status as a leading military and industrial power. Canada's overseas troops during the war were almost entirely volunteers; conscription for overseas service was not imposed until late in 1944. This policy proved highly popular in both English- and French-speaking Canada and contributed to the Liberal electoral victory of 1945 that gave Mackenzie King a renewed mandate for the postwar era.

The two decades following the war saw the gradual expansion of federal financial responsibility for national welfare measures, including pensions, unemployment insurance, and comprehensive medical care, though the administration of such programs remained a provincial matter. These developments coincided with an increase in urbanization and industrialization in the major centers of Vancouver, Toronto, and Montreal. Formal "equalization payments" were enacted in the 1950s to reduce economic disparities between rich and poor provinces. The early stages of these developments played a part in persuading Newfoundland to join the federation as Canada's 10th province in 1949.

A landslide Conservative victory in 1958 brought John Diefenbaker to the prime ministership, but the Conservatives proved unable to offer a coherent political program for the nation and were ousted in the elections of 1963, which returned the Liberals to power. Canadian politics since the 1960s have been marked by increasing regionalization; the Liberal Party is based largely in the east, while the New Democratic party, organized in 1961, has little support east of Ontario. The Conservatives offer a broad but insecure national alternative. Regional politics revolve in part around the different responses of agricultural and industrial provinces to the political and economic impact of the American colossus to the south.

The language issue has continued to divide Canada politically and ideologically in the postwar period. The rise of an aggressive Quebecois nationalism in the 1960s led directly to the Liberal prime ministership of Pierre Trudeau, a Quebecois who was known as a supporter of a strong federal constitution. Trudeau's efforts toward conciliation and for constitutional guarantees for Quebec within a strong federal structure proved unavailing, however. In 1970 he invoked the War Measures Act to send troops to Quebec to put down a wave of separatist terrorism, leaving the province subdued but sullen.

The 1976 electoral victory in Quebec of the Parti Québécois under René Lévesque provoked fears that Quebec would secede from Canada. Lévesque's plan for a separate "sovereignty-association" status for Quebec was rejected by a popular referendum in 1980, but only because of Trudeau's pledge to seek full autonomy for Canada in order to secure constitutional protection for Quebec's special interests.

In November 1981, despite Lévesque's protests that the measures did not go far enough, Canada's provincial governments reached agreement on proposals for constitutional change. The result was the passage by the British Parliament of the Canada Act, which came into effect on Apr. 17, 1982, granting full independence and constitutional autonomy to Canada and severing its last colonial ties to the British government. Canada's new 1982 Constitution more clearly delineated the powers of

ARCTIC OCEAN
Ellesmere
ICELAND
GREENLAND (Den.)
Prince Patrick
NORTH MAGNETIC POLE (c.1980)
Beaufort Sea
Melville
Bathurst
Devon
Banks
Parry Channel
Somerset
Prince of Wales
Baffin Bay
ALASKA (U.S.)
Inuvik
Victoria
Boothia Pen.
Baffin
Davis Strait
Dawson
YUKON
Port Radium
Great Bear L.
Prince Charles
Foxe Basin
L. Amadjuak
Whitehorse
NORTHWEST TERRITORIES
DISTRICT OF MACKENZIE
Mackenzie
Juneau
Yellowknife
Great Slave L.
Dubawnt L.
Thelon
DISTRICT OF KEEWATIN
Southampton
Hudson Strait
Ivujivik
Cape Chidley
Labrador Sea
ROCKY MOUNTAINS
BRITISH COLUMBIA
Athabasca
L. Athabasca
Uranium City
L. Nueltin
Ungava Bay
Nain
Fort Chimo
NEWFOUNDLAND
Queen Charlotte Islands
Prince Rupert
Churchill
Hudson Bay
LABRADOR
Schefferville
Goose Bay
Prince George
Reindeer L.
Churchill
Nelson
SASKATCHEWAN
ALBERTA
Fort Severn
MANITOBA
James Bay
QUEBEC
Newfoundland
St. John's
Edmonton
Kamloops
Vancouver
Banff
Saskatchewan
L. Winnipeg
L. Mistassini
Anticosti Is.
Gulf of St. Lawrence
Gaspé Pen.
PRINCE EDWARD ISLAND
ST. PIERRE AND MIQUELON (France)
Vancouver
Calgary
Saskatoon
ONTARIO
Victoria
Regina
L. Manitoba
NEW BRUNSWICK
Charlottetown
WASH.
Winnipeg
L. Nipigon
Quebec
Fredericton
NOVA SCOTIA
Lake of the Woods
Thunder Bay
Trois-Rivières
ME.
Halifax
MONT.
N.D.
L. Superior
Montreal
Sault Ste.Marie
Bay of Fundy
PACIFIC OCEAN
ORE.
MINN.
Ottawa
VT.
N.H.
IDAHO
S.D.
MICH.
L. Huron
Toronto
MASS.
ATLANTIC OCEAN
UNITED STATES
WIS.
L. Michigan
Ontario
N.Y.
R.I.
CONN.
CALIF.
NEV.
COLO.
L. Erie
0
500 miles
NEB.
IOWA
PA.
UTAH
N.J.
ILL.
IND.
OHIO
0
750 km

L. Superior
ONTARIO
Anticosti Is.
Gouin Res.
L. St. Jean
Chicoutimi
Gaspé Peninsula
Sault Ste.Marie
Rimouski
Gulf of St. Lawrence
Saguenay
QUEBEC
Sudbury
Magdalen
Quebec
North Bay
NEW BRUNSWICK
PRINCE EDWARD ISLAND
Georgian Bay
Ottawa
Trois-Rivières
St. Lawrence
L. Huron
Montreal
Moncton
Sydney
Charlottetown
Ottawa
Sherbrooke
Fredericton
Cape Breton Island
MICH.
ME.
Toronto
St. John
NOVA SCOTIA
Kingston
Kitchener
Sarnia
Hamilton
VT.
Bay of Fundy
L. Ontario
London
Windsor
Niagara Falls
Halifax
L. Erie
N.H.
N.Y.
Yarmouth
ATLANTIC OCEAN
OHIO
PA.
MASS.

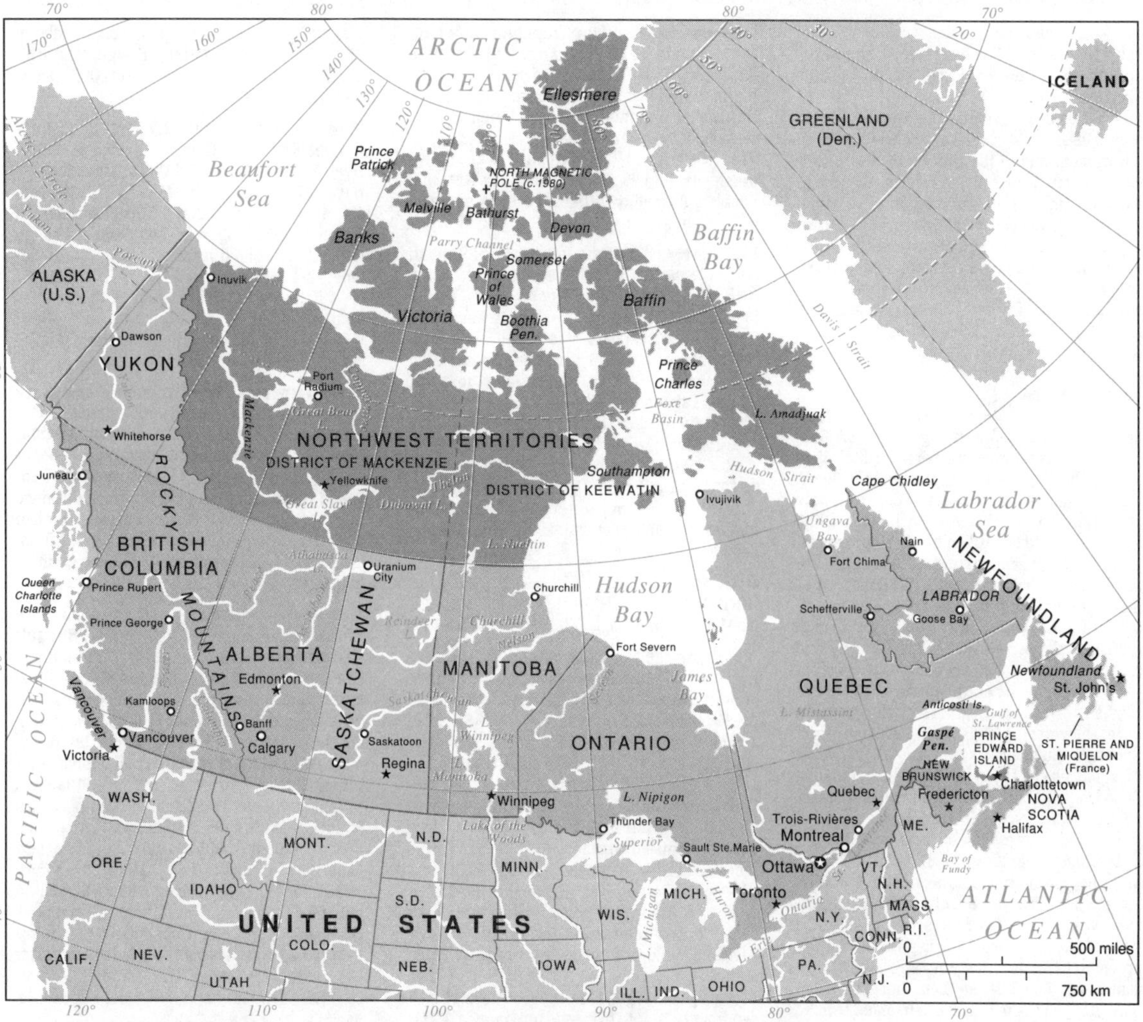

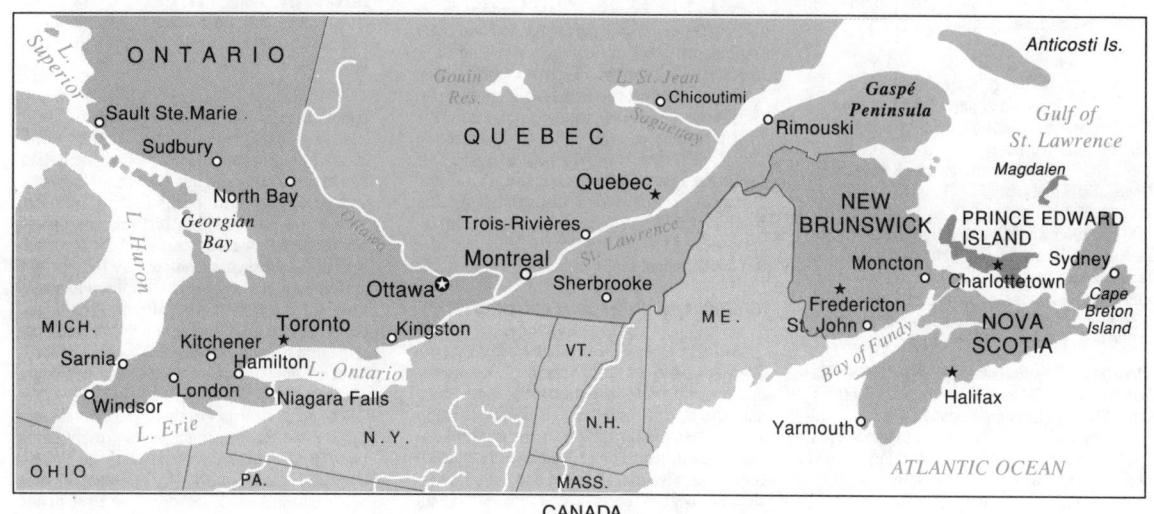

CANADA

the federal and provincial governments, provided for Supreme Court review of legislation, and included a Charter of Rights to protect civil liberties.

A national recession in the late 1970s and early 1980s led to the fall of Trudeau's Liberal government and to the election of the Conservative party leader Brian Mulroney (also a native of Quebec) as prime minister in 1984. The Mulroney government has encouraged foreign investment and privatization as a means of revitalizing Canada's economy, with considerable success. A notable development has been an influx of wealthy Chinese immigrants from Hong Kong, over 10,000 of whom have become Canadian citizens since 1984, bringing with them an estimated $10 billion in new investment funds.

The Meech Lake Agreement, containing a number of articles clarifying the 1982 Constitution, was worked out between Mulroney and Quebec's Liberal Premier Robert Bourassa, along with the leaders of Canada's nine other provinces, and signed on June 3, 1987, but it has yet to be ratified by all 10 provincial legislatures. In general, its provisions enhance the power of the provinces as against that of the federal government; a key provision grants constitutional protection to Quebec's efforts to remain a "distinct society," linguistically and culturally French. The aggressive measures of the Quebec government to eradicate the use of English in the public affairs of the province have, however, provoked a backlash from Quebec's English-speaking minority, while bilingualism continues to be widely resented in Canada's English-speaking provinces. The language question remains for Canada an unresolved, and perhaps unresolvable, problem.

The most significant achievement of the Mulroney government has been the negotiation and passage, in 1988–89, of a free-trade agreement with the United States, scheduled to be implemented in stages during the 1990s. It promises to create a North American free-trade zone that should strengthen Canada's economy, but at the cost, some Canadians fear, of further erosion of Canada's sovereignty and distinctive national identity.

Cape Verde
Republic of Cape Verde
Geography   Location: an archipelago of 10 islands and five islets in Atlantic Ocean, off west coast of northern Africa. **Boundaries:** Senegal about 300 mi. (500 km) to E. **Total land area:** 1,557 sq. mi. (4,033 sq km). **Coastline:** 600 mi. (965 km). **Comparative area:** slightly larger than Rhode Island. **Land use:** 9% arable land; negl. % permanent crops; 6% meadows and pastures; negl. % forest and woodland; 85% other; includes 1% irrigated. **Major cities:** (1980 census) Cidade de Praia (capital) 57,748.

People   Population: 353,885 (1988). **Nationality:** noun—Cape Verdean(s); adjective—Cape Verdean. **Ethnic groups:** 71% Creole (mulatto), 28% African, 1% European. **Languages:** Portuguese and Crioulo (blend of Portuguese and West African). **Religions:** Roman Catholicism fused with indigenous beliefs.

Government   Type: republic. **Independence:** July 5, 1975 (from Portugal). **Constitution:** Sept. 7, 1980, amended Feb. 12, 1981. **National holiday:** Independence Day, July 5. **Heads of government:** Aristides Pereira, president (since July 1975); Pedro Pires, prime minister (since July 1975). **Structure:** executive—president; legislative—56-member National People's Assembly; official party is supreme political organization.

Economy   Monetary unit: escudo. **Budget:** (1984) *income:* $20.4 mil.; *expend.:* $26.7 mil. **GNP:** $135.1 mil., $390 per capita (1983). **Chief crops:** bananas, coffee, sugarcane, corn, beans. **Livestock:** goats, pigs, cattle, asses. **Natural resources:** salt, basalt rock, pozzolana, limestone, kaolin, fish. **Major industries:** salt mining. **Labor force:** 57% agriculture, 29% services, 14% industry (1981); 50% of population of working age (1983). **Exports:** $3.0 mil. (f.o.b., 1985); fish, bananas, salt, flour. **Imports:** $59.1 mil. (c.i.f., 1985); petroleum products, corn, rice, machinery, textiles. **Major trading partners:** Portugal, UK, Japan, Angola, Zaire.

Intl. Orgs. FAO, G-77, GATT (de facto), IBRD, ICAO, IDA, IFAD, ILO, IMF, IMO, ITU, NAM, UN, UNESCO, UPU, WHO, WMO.

In 1462 the Portuguese founded the first European city in the tropics at Ribeira Grande on Santiago, one of the 15 islands that compose the Republic of Cape Verde. Located 385 miles off the west coast of Africa, the Cape Verde Islands prospered during the slave trade in the 16th century and later served as supply stations on sea routes and trading lanes. The rise of whaling in the 19th century led to contact with the United States, as American ships recruited crews from the islands. Relations between Cape Verde and the United States resulted in the establishment of an American consulate, headquarters for the U.S. Navy African Squadron, and a transatlantic cable station.

Portugal changed the status of the archipelago from colony to overseas province in 1951; five years later, citizens of Cape Verde and Portuguese Guinea organized the African Party for the Independence of Guinea-Bissau and Cape Verde (PAIGC) for the purpose of petitioning Portugal to improve their living conditions. Beginning as a clandestine organization, the PAIGC became an overt political movement on the islands after the 1974 revolution in Portugal. An agreement between the PAIGC and Portugal, providing for a transitional government in Cape Verde, paved the way for full independence in 1975 with the election of a national assembly.

Central African Republic
(PREVIOUS NAME: CENTRAL AFRICAN EMPIRE)
Geography   Location: landlocked country in central Africa. **Boundaries:** Chad to N, Sudan to E, Zaire and Congo to S, Cameroon to W. **Total land area:** 240,535 sq. mi. (622,984 sq km). **Coastline:** none. **Comparative area:** slightly smaller than Texas. **Land use:** 3% arable land; negl. % permanent crops; 5% meadows and pastures; 64% forest and woodland; 28% other. **Major cities:** Bangui (capital) 473,817 (1984 est.); Berbérati 100,000; Bouar 55,000 (1982 est.).

People   Population: 2,736,478 (1988). **Nationality:** noun—Central African(s); adjective—Central African. **Ethnic groups:** 34% Baya, 27% Banda, 21% Mandija, 10% Sara, 4% Mboum, 4% M'Baka; 6,500 Europeans, of which 3,600 are French. **Languages:** French (official), Sangho (lingua franca and national language), Arabic, Hunsa, Swahili. **Religions:** 25% Protestant, 25% Roman Catholic, 24% indigenous beliefs, 15% Muslim, 11% other; indigenous beliefs and practices strongly influence Christian majority.

Government   Type: republic; one-party presidential regime since 1986. **Independence:** Aug. 13, 1960 (from France). **Constitution:** Nov. 21, 1986. **National holiday:** Independence Day, Aug. 13. **Heads of government:** Gen. André-Dieudonné Kolingba, chief of state (since Sept. 1985). **Structure:** executive—chief of state; legislative—parliament, includes National Assembly and Social and Economic Council; judiciary.

Economy   Monetary unit: Communauté Financière Africaine (CFA) franc. **Budget:** (1984) *income:* $93.3 mil.; *expend.:* $90.8 mil. **GDP:** $764 mil., $290 per capita (1984). **Chief crops:** cash crops—cotton, coffee, peanuts, sesame, tobacco; food crops—manioc, corn, millet, sorghum, peanuts. **Livestock:** cattle, goats, pigs, sheep. **Natural resources:** diamonds, uranium, timber, gold, oil. **Major industries:** sawmills, breweries, diamond mining. **Labor force:** 775,413 (1986 est.); 85.0% agriculture, 8.9% commerce and services, 6.1% other. **Exports:** $145.2 mil. (f.o.b., 1984); diamonds, cotton, coffee, timber, tobacco. **Imports:** $139.6 mil. (f.o.b., 1984 est.); textiles, petroleum products, machinery, electrical equipment, motor vehicles. **Major trading partners:** *exports:* France, Belgium, Japan, U.S.; *imports:* France, other EC countries, Japan, Algeria, Yugoslavia.

Intl. Orgs. FAO, G-77, GATT, IBRD, ICAO, IDA, IFAD, ILO, IMF, INTELSAT, INTERPOL, ITU, NAM, UN, UNESCO, UPU, WHO, WIPO, WMO.

A landlocked country in Africa's central region, the Central African Republic is one of the least-developed countries in the world. Most of its people are farmers, and the nation has little manufacturing, few reliable roads, and no railroad. Europeans first came to the area in the early 1800s in their search for slaves, but it was not until 1889 that the French established an outpost as the current capital city of Bangui. The region was organized as the territory of Ubangi-Shari five years later. In 1910 Ubangi-Shari was incorporated into French Equitorial Africa along with what are now the countries of Chad, the Congo, and Gabon.

The country was granted internal self-government by the French under its present name in 1958 and became a member of the French Overseas Community. Independence was achieved on Aug. 13, 1960. The first prime minister, Barthelemy Boganda, was killed in an airplane crash in 1959 and was succeeded by his nephew, David Dacko. Dacko was elected to a seven-year term in January 1964, but an army coup in 1966 overthrew his government. The head of the army, Jean-Bedel Bokassa, was installed as the new president. Bokassa was named president for life in 1972, and in 1976 he declared himself emperor and changed the name of the country to the Central African Empire.

Dacko returned to power in 1979, however, and Bokassa went into exile in France. The name of the country was changed back to the Central African Republic. A multiparty political system was reinstated in March 1981, but army officers threw Dacko out of office once again six months later and banned all political parties. Though the military was again in control, the government put Bokassa on trial for a variety of crimes, including murder and torture, after he attempted to return in 1986. He was convicted and sentenced to death in 1987, but his sentence was later reduced to life in prison.

Chad
Republic of Chad

Geography Location: landlocked country in north central Africa. **Boundaries:** Libya to N, Sudan to E, Central African Republic to S, Cameroon and Nigeria to SE, Niger to W. **Total land area:** 486,180 sq. mi. (1,259,200 sq km). **Coastline:** none. **Comparative area:** slightly more than three times size of California. **Land use:** 2% arable land; negl. % permanent crops; 36% meadows and pastures; 11% forest and woodland; 51% other; includes negl. % irrigated. **Major cities:** (1979 est.) N'Djamena (capital) 402,000; Sarh 124,000; Moundou 87,000; Bongor 69,000; Doba 64,000.

People Population: 4,777,963 (1988). **Nationality:** noun—Chadian(s); adjective—Chadian. **Ethnic groups:** 200 distinct ethnic groups, most of whom are Muslims (Arabs, Toubou, Fulbe, Kotoko, Hausa, Kanembou, Baguirmi, Boulala, and Maba) in north and center and non-Muslims (Sara, Ngambaye, Mbake, Goulaye, Moudang, Moussei, Massa) in south; some 15,000 nonindigenous, of whom 1,000 are French. **Languages:** French and Arabic (both official); Sara and Sango in south; more than 100 different languages and dialects. **Religions:** 44% Muslim, 33% Christian, 23% indigenous beliefs.

Government Type: republic. **Independence:** Aug. 11, 1960 (from France). **Constitution:** Apr. 14, 1962 (currently suspended); Fundamental Act of the Republic proclaimed Oct. 18, 1982, currently serves as basis for government with decrees promulgated by president. **National holiday:** Independence Day, Aug. 11. **Heads of government:** Hissein Habre, president (since Oct. 1982). **Structure:** executive—president; Council of Ministers; National Consultative Council; judiciary—court of appeal.

Economy Monetary unit: Communauté Financière Africaine (CFA) franc. **Budget:**

(1987 est.) **income:** $59.3 mil.; **expend.:** $84.7 mil. **GDP:** $817 mil., $160 per capita (1986 est.). **Chief crops:** cash crops—cotton, gum arabic, peanuts, fish; food crops—millet, sorghum, rice, sweet potatoes, yams, cassava, dates. **Livestock:** goats, sheep, cattle, asses, camels. **Natural resources:** small quantities of crude oil (unexploited but exploitation beginning), uranium, natron (sodium carbonate), kaolin, fish (Lake Chad). **Major industries:** cotton textile mills, slaughterhouses, brewery, natron. **Labor force:** 85% agriculture—unpaid subsistence farming, herding and fishing, 15% other. **Exports:** $98.6 mil. (f.o.b., 1986); 80% cotton; meat, fish, animal products. **Imports:** $206.1 mil. (f.o.b., 1986); cement, petroleum, flour, sugar, tea. **Major trading partners:** France, Central African Customs and Economic Union countries.

Intl. Orgs. EC (associate), FAO, G-77, GATT, IBRD, ICAO, IDA, IFAD, IFC, ILO, IMF, INTELSAT, INTERPOL, ITU, NAM, UN, UNESCO, UPU, WHO, WIPO, WMO.

The Sao and other ancient peoples built centers of civilization near Lake Chad that flourished for many centuries until they were displaced by the medieval kingdoms of Kanem-Bornu, Baguirmi, and Ouaddai. From about 1400 onward, Chad became a meeting-ground between the Moslem cultures of the Sahara and the Sahel and the black African societies of the tropics. Between 1500 and 1800, Arab slave raiders were active around Lake Chad, supplying slaves for European traders on Africa's west coast.

French military forces reached Chad from West Africa in 1891 and fought a series of battles over the next two decades with the Arab rulers of the region. A French governorship of Chad was established in 1905 (based in Brazzaville, the Congo), but the country was not brought entirely under French control until 1914. Chad was incorporated into the federation of French Equatorial Africa in 1910 and was organized as a colony within the federation in 1920.

French Equatorial Africa was dissolved in 1959, and Chad (along with Gabon, The Central African Republic, and the Congo) became an autonomous member of the French Community. Full independence followed on Aug. 11, 1960; François Tombalbage became Chad's first president. In 1965 the Moslem northern and eastern parts of the country rebelled against the southern-led government; despite the aid of French troops, the government was unable to suppress the rebellion, and civil war became endemic.

Tombalbage was overthrown in 1975 in a military coup led by another southerner, Gen. Felix Malloum. Efforts to broaden the composition of the national government broke down, and in 1979 Prime Minister Hissein Habre broke with the government and led northern forces against the national army. A cease-fire was negotiated under international auspices, and a National Unity Transitional Government (GUNT) was installed in November 1979, but civil war broke out again in March 1980. Pres. Goukouni Oueddei sought Libyan aid in restor-

ing order; a contingent of 7,000 Libyan troops occupied the country until 1981. They were replaced by an international peacekeeping force organized by the Organization of African Unity.

Civil war broke out yet again in February 1982, and in June of that year, northern forces occupied the capital, N'Djamena. A new republican government, under the presidency of Hissein Habre, was proclaimed on June 7. OAU forces withdrew, and Habre's government soon controlled all of the country except for a few northern areas, where GUNT, under now ex-president Goukouni Oueddei, held out with Libyan assistance. In 1983 GUNT launched a counterattack and after initial defeats regained some territory with the aid of Libyan forces, which carried out bombing raids and ground attacks against government positions. French and Zairian troops were sent to aid Habre's forces. In September 1984 France and Libya agreed to the withdrawal of all foreign forces from Chad. French and Zairian troops were withdrawn in November 1984, but Libyan forces remained, in violation of the agreement. GUNT forces, with Libyan backing, controlled all of the country north of the 16th parallel; Libyan forces occupied the Aozou Strip, along the Libyan border, with the apparent intention of annexing it to Libya.

Between 1984 and 1986 Habre, aided by the good offices of Gabon's Pres. Bongo, succeeded in persuading most Chadean dissident forces (with the notable exception of GUNT) to rejoin the national government. In November 1986 the Habre government launched a campaign to recapture the north. The lightly armed but highly mobile Chadean forces won a series of victories against the Libyans in 1987, culminating with the capture of Aozou Town in August. Libyan forces recaptured Aozou a month later and continue to occupy the Aozou Strip, now dominated by a Libyan airbase built just inside Chadean territory. In May 1988 Libya's Col. Qaddafi declared an end to the 20-year war with Chad, recognized the Habre government, and offered aid in rebuilding the northern part of the country. He did not, however, relinquish Libya's claim to the Aozou Strip, which remains in dispute between the two countries.

Chad, largely arid and lacking natural resources, is overwhelmingly an agricultural and pastoral country; the national economy remains at the subsistence level with only rudimentary industrial development. The country is precariously self-sufficient in food; principal exports are cotton and livestock.

Chile
Republic of Chile

Geography Location: South Pacific coast of South America. **Boundaries:** Peru and Bolivia to N, Argentina to E, South Pacific Ocean to W. **Total land area:** 292,132 sq. mi. (756,626 sq km). **Coastline:** 3,999 mi. (6,435 km). **Comparative area:** slightly smaller than twice size of Montana. **Land use:** 7% arable land; negl. % permanent crops; 16% meadows and pastures; 21% forest and woodland; 56% other; includes 2% irrigated. **Major cities:**

(1985) Gran Santiago (capital) 4,318,305; Viña del Mar 315,947; Valparaíso 267,025; Talcahuano 220,910; Concepción 217,756.

People Population: 12,638,046 (1988). **Nationality:** noun—Chilean(s); adjective—Chilean. **Ethnic groups:** 95% European and European-Indian, 3% Indian, 2% other. **Languages:** Spanish. **Religions:** 89% Roman Catholic, 11% Protestant, small Jewish population.

Government Type: republic. **Independence:** Sept. 18, 1810 (from Spain). **Constitution:** Sept. 11, 1980, effective Mar. 11, 1981; provides for continued direct rule for Pres. Pinochet for term ending in Mar. 1997. **National holiday:** Independence Day, Sept. 18. **Heads of government:** Gen. Augusto Pinochet Ugarte, president (since Sept. 1973). **Structure:** four-man military junta exercises constituent and legislative powers and has delegated executive powers to president; state of siege lifted Jan. 1986, but state of emergency remains in effect; civilian judiciary remains.

Economy Monetary unit: peso. **Budget:** (1986) *income:* $5 bil.; *expend.:* $5.2 bil. **GDP:** $16.4 bil., $1,300 per capita (1986). **Chief crops:** wheat, potatoes, corn, sugar beets, onions, beans, fruit; net agricultural importer. **Livestock:** sheep, cattle, pigs, goats, horses. **Natural resources:** copper, timber, iron ore, nitrates, precious metals. **Major industries:** copper, other minerals, foodstuffs, fish processing. **Labor force:** 3.84 mil. (1985); 38.6% services (including government—12%), 31.3% industry and commerce, 15.9% agriculture, forestry and fishing; 13.9% unemployed (1984). **Exports:** $2.9 bil. (f.o.b., 1986); copper, molybdenum, iron ore, paper products, steel products. **Imports:** $3 bil. (c.i.f., 1986); petroleum, sugar, wheat, capital goods, vehicles. **Major trading partners:** (1985) *exports:* 22.4% U.S., 10.2% W. Germany, 9.3% Japan, 6.7% Brazil, 5.4% UK; *imports:* 20.5% U.S., 9.8% Japan, 7.9% W. Germany, 7.5% Brazil, 4.8% Venezuela.

Intl. Orgs. FAO, G-77, GATT, IAEA, IBRD, ICAO, IDA, IFAD, IFC, ILO, IMF, IMO, INTELSAT, INTERPOL, ITU, OAS, UN, UNESCO, UPU, WHO, WIPO, WMO.

Before the arrival of Europeans in the mid-1530s, indigenous habitation of the territory that would become Chile included the Araucanian population in the south and peoples under the influence of the Inca empire in the north.

The Spanish founded the cities of Valparaiso in 1536, Santiago in 1541, and Concepción in 1550. Chile was under the authority of the viceroyalty of Peru, established in 1544. Between 1810 and 1818, fortunes of the Chilean independence movement ebbed and flowed, culminating in the victory of Bernardo O'Higgins and the separatist forces in 1817. They declared an independent Chile in 1818.

From 1818 to 1833, Chile underwent a period of political instability, the roots of which can be traced to power struggles among elite Chilean families. In 1833 a strong presidential-dominant constitution was written under the influence of leading political figure Diego Por-

tales that set the form of government in Chile until 1891. Chile expanded its territory at the expense of Peru and Bolivia, first in a war with the Peruvian-Bolivian Confederation (1836–39) and later as a result of the War of the Pacific (1879–83).

A civil war was fought in 1890–91 between forces of the president, José Balmaceda, and the Chilean Congress over the issue of the limits of presidential authority. The defeat of the presidential forces led to the establishment of a congressional-dominant parliamentary system. The checks on policy initiative resulting from the parliamentary system left government deadlocked in the face of mounting social and political problems arising at the turn of the century. The occurrence of a number of bloody strike actions crystallized political debate around social issues such as better wages and working conditions. The immobilized parliamentary system was unable to respond to these problems. In 1925, when Congress failed to allocate funds for military pay, the armed forces overthrew the parliamentary government.

A new constitution was drawn up that same year that moved governmental structure toward presidential dominance. Nevertheless, political instability continued until 1933, when the new constitution was implemented. The Chilean balance of political power from 1958 until 1973 remained almost equally divided among parties representing the right, the center, and the left of the political spectrum. In order to prevent an electoral victory for the leftist parties, forces on the right allied themselves with the centrist Christian Democrats in the 1964 election, and this resulted in the victory of Christian Democratic presidential candidate Eduardo Frei Montalva.

The program of the Christian Democrats, based on ideology and political strategy, included an ambitious agrarian reform and attempts to organize Chile's urban poor. It was believed that these stances would benefit the Christian Democrats at the polls in the 1970 presidential election. As in 1958, the 1970 election fielded three presidential candidates who represented the political right, center, and left. The candidate of the leftist Popular Unity coalition, Dr. Salvador Allende Gossens, won with 36.3 percent of the vote, and the Congress recognized Dr. Allende's victory after a bitter debate.

The Allende government nationalized the foreign-owned copper industry, but the resulting international boycott of Chilean copper imposed in retaliation for this action left Chile unable to market her copper. Other nationalizations by the government included the coal and steel industries and 60 percent of private banking. The Popular Unity government found itself unable to control peasant seizures of land and factory takeovers by workers. The copper embargo, land and factory seizures, government subsidies to the poor for basic goods, and runaway inflation resulted in a deterioration of the national economy that particularly affected the middle classes. Members of Congress from the center and right had hoped to gain enough seats in the 1973 congressional elections to

impeach Allende, but instead the Popular Unity made impressive electoral gains, just as it had in the municipal elections of 1971. As political struggle intensified, the president resorted to inclusion of military officers in the government in order to bolster the legitimacy of the Popular Unity administration in the eyes of political opponents.

On Sept. 11, 1973, segments of the military led by commanders of three of Chile's four armed forces took control of the government, killing Allende in the process. Gen. Augusto Pinochet Ugarte emerged from the junta as the new president. The junta announced the arrest of some 13,000 persons, many of whom then lost their lives in a wave of brutal repression. In March 1974 the dictatorship published its Declaration of Principles, elaborating the values and policy direction of the new political order. The essential elements of the Principles included a laissez-faire economic orientation, anti-Marxism, and nationalism.

A new constitution was approved by plebiscite in 1978 and was to be implemented by 1980. The new constitutional order envisioned a two-phase evolution of Chile's political structure, including an authoritarian "transitional period" between 1980 and 1989 and full implementation of a new political structure thereafter. The new constitution created a presidential system with very extensive powers for the executive and a "guardian" role for the military.

A plebiscite was held in 1988 on the question of continuation of Pinochet rule. A coalition of disparate opposition political groups formed to effect a victory for the "no" vote, signaling a desire among a majority of Chilean voters for an end to the dictatorship.

China
People's Republic of China

Geography Location: covers vast area of eastern Asia. **Boundaries:** USSR to N and W; Mongolia to N; N. Korea to NE; Pacific Ocean to E; India, Nepal, Bhutan, Burma, Laos, and Vietnam to S; Afghanistan and Pakistan to W. **Total land area:** 3,695,500 sq. mi. (9,571,300 sq km). **Coastline:** 9,112 mi. (14,500 km). **Comparative area:** slightly larger than U.S.. **Land use:** 10% arable land; negl. % permanent crops; 31% meadows and pastures; 14% forest and woodland; 45% other; includes 5% irrigated. **Major cities:** (1985 est.) Beijing (capital) 5,860,000; Shanghai 6,980,000; Tianjin 5,380,000; Shenyang 4,200,000; Wuhan 3,400,000.

People Population: 1,088,169,192 (1988). **Nationality:** noun—Chinese (sing., pl.); adjective—Chinese. **Ethnic groups:** 93.3% Han Chinese, 6.7% Zhuang, Uygur, Hui, Yi, Tibetan, Miao, Manchu, Mongol, Buyi, Korean, and numerous lesser nationalities. **Languages:** Standard Chinese (Putonghua) or Mandarin (based on the Beijing dialect); also Yue (Cantonese), Wu (Shanghainese), Minbei (Fuzhou), Minnan (Hokkien-Taiwanese), Xiang, Gan, Hakka dialects, and minority langs. (see "Ethnic groups" above). **Religions:** officially atheist, but traditionally pragmatic and eclectic; most important elements of religion are Confucianism, Taoism, and Buddhism; about 2–3% Muslim, 1% Christian.

Government Type: communist state; real authority lies with Communist party's politburo; National People's Congress, in theory the highest organ of government, usually ratifies party's programs; State Council actually directs government. **Constitution:** Dec. 4, 1982. **National holiday:** National Day, Oct. 1. **Heads of government:** Gen. Yang Shangkun, president (since Apr. 1988); Li Peng, premier (since Apr. 1988). **Structure:** control is exercised by Chinese Communist party, through State Council, which supervises ministries, commissions, and bureaus; all are technically under Standing Committee of National People's Congress.

Economy Monetary unit: renminbi yuan. **Budget:** *income:* N.A.; *expend.:* N.A. **GNP:** $286 bil., $280 per capita (1987). **Chief crops:** rice, wheat, corn, other grains, oilseed; mainly subsistence agriculture. **Livestock:** pigs, sheep, cattle and buffalo, goats, horses. **Natural resources:** coal, iron ore, crude oil, mercury, tin; world's largest hydropower potential. **Major industries:** iron, steel, coal. **Labor force:** 513 mil. (1986 est.); 61.1% agriculture and forestry, 25.2% industry and commerce. **Exports:** $31.1 bil. (f.o.b., 1986); manufactured goods, agricultural products, grain (mostly corn), oil, minerals. **Imports:** $43.2 bil. (c.i.f., 1986); grain (mostly wheat), chemical fertilizer, steel, industrial raw materials, machinery. **Major trading partners:** (1987) Hong Kong, Japan, U.S., W. Germany, USSR.

Intl. Orgs. FAO, IAEA, IBRD, ICAO, IDA, IFAD, IFC, ILO, IMF, IMO, INTELSAT, ITU, UN, UNESCO, UPU, WHO, WIPO, WMO.

China is one of the world's oldest civilizations. Dynastic rule in the North China Plain began around 2000 B.C. The unifying Qin (221 B.C.) and Han (206 B.C.) dynasties greatly expanded the territory of the empire and established the basic pattern of imperial bureaucratic government that would endure until the beginning of the 20th century. Major dynasties during that period include the Han (206 B.C.–A.D. 220), Tang (618–907), Song (960–1279), Yuan or Mongol (1279–1368), Ming (1368–1644), and Qing (1644–1911).

By the late 18th century, the Qing dynasty faced increasingly dangerous problems of explosive population growth, bureaucratic stagnation, and trade pressure from the West. Opium—introduced by Great Britain to balance its trade in tea, silk, porcelain, and other goods—created severe social problems. Western demands for free trade resulted in the Opium War (1839–42), in which China was humiliatingly defeated by the British. The treaties of Nanjing (1842) and Tianjin (1858) opened China to Western merchants and missionaries and created foreign-ruled enclaves on Chinese soil. At the same time, the Taiping Rebellion and other popular uprisings led to the deaths of at least 20 million Chinese between 1850 and 1870.

Such reform efforts as the Self-Strengthening Movement (1870s) and the 1898 Reform Movement proved inadequate to the task of strengthening and modernizing China's dynastic government. Japan, modernizing rapidly after the Meiji Restoration of 1868, joined the race for commercial access to China, decisively winning the Sino-Japanese War of 1894–95. The antiforeign Boxer Uprising of 1900 was put down by a joint foreign military force, dealing a mortal blow to Qing rule. On Oct. 10, 1911, the dynasty fell to a coalition of forces led by the veteran revolutionary nationalist Sun Yat-sen.

China's first attempt at republican government, under Pres. Yuan Shikai and subsequent presidents, quickly degenerated into factionalism and warlord control in the provinces. In 1915 Japan successfully demanded further concessions, provoking public outcries. When news reached China on May 4, 1919, that the Treaty of Versailles granted Japan all of Germany's former concessions in China, students rioted throughout the country, demanding reforms and modernization (the May Fourth Movement). Sun Yat-sen's Nationalist party (Kuomintang, or KMT) and the Chinese Communist party (CCP, founded in 1921 by Mao Zedong and others) joined forces in 1922 in an attempt to create a second republican revolution.

Sun Yat-sen died in 1925. His successor, Chiang Kai-shek, consolidated KMT forces in Guangzhou and mounted the Northern Expedition (1927–29) to defeat or co-opt the various provincial warlords and reunify the country. In the course of this successful effort, Chiang turned on his Communist allies. A series of failed Communist uprisings and KMT anti-Communist extermination campaigns between 1927 and 1934 nearly wiped out the CCP. Remnants of the party broke out of encirclement in Jiangxi Province in 1934 and undertook the 6,000-mile Long March to a secure base in Yan'an, Shanxi Province. There, under Mao, Zhou Enlai, and Zhu De, the CCP recovered its strength. In the Xi'an Incident of December 1936, Chiang was kidnapped by mutinous KMT allies and forced at gunpoint to agree to forming a United Front with the CCP against Japan.

Meanwhile Japan continued its penetration of China, with the assassination of Manchurian warlord and KMT ally Jiang Zuolin in 1928, the invasion of Manchuria on Sept. 18, 1931, and the establishment of the puppet state of Manchuguo in 1934. On July 7, 1937, fighting erupted between Japanese and Chinese troops near Beijing. The Japanese rapidly moved south to the Yangtse Valley, bombing and capturing Shanghai. The Nationalist capital at Nanjing fell in November 1937, amid widespread atrocities against civilians. The KMT army and government retreated to a wartime capital at Chongqing. The remainder of World War II in China was largely a stalemate, with Japan occupying most of the country. KMT-held areas opposed the Japanese with conventional forces (supported, after 1941, by the Americans), while the Communists harassed the Japanese with guerrilla tactics.

At the end of World War II, American forces ensured that the KMT would receive Japan's surrender throughout most of China, giving the Nationalists a commanding position while U.S. Gen. George Marshall attempted to mediate the creation of a KMT-CCP coalition government. That effort failed, and civil war broke out. The KMT advantage was dissipated by ruinous inflation, corruption, mismanagement, and military ineffectiveness. At the end of 1947, with the Communist forces making continual advances, the United States pulled out of China. After losing several major battles throughout 1948–49, KMT forces retreated to Taiwan; in Beijing, Mao Zedong proclaimed the establishment of the People's Republic of China (PRC) on Oct. 1, 1949.

With American backing, the Republic of China established a temporary capital at Taipei (see "Taiwan") and continued to claim sovereignty over all of China, retaining China's seat in the United Nations. The PRC quickly granted diplomatic recognition by Soviet bloc nations and some Western nations, notably Great Britain, but was effectively isolated in most international affairs by American support for Nationalist China. Chinese troops entered the Korean War in November 1950, as UN forces approached the Sino-Korean border at the Yalu River. This direct confrontation between China and the United States forestalled any possibility of normal contacts for more than two decades thereafter, as U.S.-Chinese relations were held in the grip of the Cold War.

Within China the CCP rapidly consolidated its control of the country and began the task of rebuilding the nation after decades of internal and external warfare. Priority was given to land reform. Land was confiscated from landlords and returned to peasant ownership; landlords and other "class enemies" set up under tried and condemned by People's Courts set up under party auspices. Under the first five-year plan, announced in 1953, peasants were urged to set up rural cooperatives, while industrial recovery began with Soviet assistance. Artists, writers, and intellectuals were ordered to devote themselves to the service of the party and the nation. In 1956 Mao announced a policy of "let a hundred flowers bloom, let a hundred schools of thought contend," inviting criticism of the party and government. He was shocked by the vigor of the criticism thus produced; many critics were sent to labor camps in the ensuing Anti-Rightist Campaign of 1957.

Angered by the arrogance of Soviet advisers and by Soviet refusal to share nuclear weapons technology with China, Mao broke with the Soviet Union and expelled all Soviet personnel in 1958. At the same time, he announced the policy of the Great Leap Forward, under which China was to make rapid progress on all fronts without outside aid. Huge rural communes took the place of peasant smallholdings and cooperatives, and agriculture was placed under the direction of centralized planning. In industry, labor and enthusiasm were expected to make up for a shortage of capital and technical expertise. The Great Leap was a catastrophic failure, causing widespread famine and social dislocation, as Mao admitted in a forced self-criticism in 1960. Mao temporarily withdrew into the background as a group of party pragmatists led by Liu Shaoqi assumed power in the early 1960s.

In foreign affairs Chinese shelling of the Nationalist-held offshore islands of Quemoy and Matsu in 1958 led to a crisis in the Taiwan Straits, patrolled by the U.S. Seventh Fleet to prevent a recurrence of China's civil war. A rebellion in Tibet in 1959 was suppressed with much bloodshed, and the dalai lama fled to India. Chinese troop movements into Tibet contributed to the outbreak in 1960 of a border war with India. Throughout the 1960s China worried about being drawn into the escalating war in Vietnam.

In late 1965 Mao made a bid to return to full power. His vehicle was the Great Proletarian Cultural Revolution, formally launched in 1966. Shock troops of teenage Red Guards were used to attack the entrenched party bureaucracy; Liu Shaoqi was placed under house arrest, and other prominent officials, including Deng Xiaoping, were exiled to rural areas. By 1968 internal disorder was so great that the military intervened to restore control in many areas. Most established organs of power were replaced under the Cultural Revolution by Revolutionary Committees; intellectuals, technical workers, and bureaucrats were severely persecuted. In 1971 Mao's second-in-command, Marshal Lin Biao, staged an abortive coup and died while attempting to flee the country. With Mao increasingly old and ill, most of his power was exercised by his wife, Jiang Qing, and her associates. Her rival, Premier Zhou Enlai, attempted to maintain orderly government functions in the face of this turmoil.

The 1968 Soviet invasion of Czechoslovakia convinced Mao that the USSR was potentially a greater threat to China than America, and he quietly encouraged the growth of better relations with the U.S. With tacit American approval, the PRC replaced the Republic of China (Taiwan) in the UN on Oct. 25, 1971. During Feb. 21-28, 1972, U.S. Pres. Richard Nixon visited China. The Shanghai Communiqué, issued at the end of that visit, clarified the positions of both sides and paved the way for the resumption of U.S.-China relations short of formal diplomatic recognition.

Zhou Enlai died in January 1976, and Deng Xiaoping became acting premier. In April 1976 a rally in Beijing commemorating Zhou's birthday was dispersed by police on orders from Jiang Qing, and a riot ensued (the Tiananmen Square Incident). Deng was dismissed from office. But when Mao died on Sept. 9, 1976, Deng reemerged as China's paramount leader, behind the new acting premier and acting party chairman, figurehead Hua Guofeng. Jiang Qing and three associates were arrested along with many of their allies. Labeled the Gang of Four, Jiang Qing's clique was blamed for all the ills of the Cultural Revolution; they were tried and convicted for crimes against the state in 1981.

China's post-Mao transformation took a decisive turn in 1978, with the announcement of the policy of the Four Modernizations (agriculture, industry, science and technology, and

defense). Foreign investment and technology transfer were encouraged, and thousands of students were sent to study abroad. For a few months in the winter of 1978-79, the authorities tolerated the public posting of written critiques of the government ("Democracy Wall"). Deng consolidated power in his own hands, still acting behind the scenes; Hua Guofeng was dismissed from office, while Deng's allies Hu Yaobang and Zhao Ziyang were promoted to leadership of the party and government in 1982.

On Jan. 1, 1979, China and the United States entered into formal diplomatic relations; the United States rescinded its recognition of the Republic of China as China's legal government but maintained separate nongovernmental relations with the ROC under the Taiwan Relations Act. China's relations with Vietnam deteriorated in 1978 following Vietnam's invasion of Cambodia. In February 1979, China attempted, with little success, to "teach Vietnam a lesson" in a brief but violent border war. A conflict with Great Britain was resolved in 1984 as both sides agreed that Hong Kong would be returned to Chinese sovereignty, but with considerable local autonomy, in 1997. Relations with the Soviet Union remained strained, China insisting that no improvement could come before the USSR reduced its troop concentrations on the Sino-Soviet border, withdrew from Afghanistan, and pressured Vietnam into withdrawing from Cambodia. China's overall foreign-policy stance in the post-Mao era has been low-key and nonconfrontational.

In the 1980s, China has achieved spectacular improvements in agricultural production through dismantling rural communes and returning land to individual peasant holdings under long-term leases. Small-scale private enterprise has been encouraged in both rural and urban areas. Reform in industry and in the centrally controlled price structure has been harder to achieve and has led to such side-effects as inflation and increased corruption. Within the overall context of reform, factions of relatively more conservative and reformist leaders have coexisted uneasily. A conservative drive against "spiritual pollution" in 1986 was quickly blunted by Deng, but in January 1987, the reformist party-secretary Hu Yaobang was ousted after student demonstrations calling for more democracy. The CCP 12th Party Congress in October 1987 forced the retirement of some older conservatives, named the reformist Zhao Ziyang as party secretary, and elevated the conservative pragmatist Li Peng as premier.

Colombia
Republic of Colombia

Geography **Location:** northwestern coast of South America. **Boundaries:** Caribbean Sea to N, Venezuela and Brazil to E, Peru and Ecuador to S, Panama and Pacific Ocean to W. **Total land area:** 440,831 sq. mi. (1,141,748 sq km). **Coastline:** 1,992 mi. (3,208 km). **Comparative area:** slightly less than three times size of Montana. **Land use:** 4% arable land; 2% permanent crops; 29% meadows and pastures; 49% forest and woodland; 16% other; includes negl. % irrigated. **Major cities:** (1985) Bogotá

(capital) 3,982,941; Medellín 1,468,089; Cali 1,350,565; Barranquilla 899,781; Cartagena 531,426.

People **Population:** 31,298,803 (1988). **Nationality:** noun—Colombian(s); adjective—Colombian. **Ethnic groups:** 58% mestizo, 20% white, 14% mulatto, 4% black, 4% other. **Languages:** Spanish. **Religions:** 95% Roman Catholic.

Government **Type:** republic; executive branch dominates government structure. **Independence:** July 20, 1810 (from Spain). **Constitution:** Aug. 4, 1886, with amendments codified in 1946 and 1968. **National holiday:** Independence Day, July 20. **Heads of government:** Virgilio Barco Vargas, president (since Aug. 1986; term ends 1990). **Structure:** president; bicameral legislature (Congress—Senate, House of Representatives); judiciary.

Economy **Monetary unit:** peso. **Budget:** (1988 est.) *income:* $4.6 bil.; *expend.:* $4.7 bil. **GNP:** $34 bil., $1,110 per capita (1987 est.). **Chief crops:** coffee, rice, corn, sugarcane, plantains, cotton, tobacco, bananas; illegal producer of coca and cannabis for international drug trade. **Livestock:** cattle, sheep, pigs, horses, goats. **Natural resources:** crude oil, natural gas, coal, iron ore, nickel. **Major industries:** textiles, food processing, oil. **Labor force:** 11 mil. (1986); 53% services, 26% agriculture, 21% industry (1981); 12% unemployment (1987). **Exports:** $5.4 bil. (f.o.b., 1986): coffee, coal, fuel oil, cotton, tobacco. **Imports:** $3.9 bil. (c.i.f., 1986): transportation equipment, machinery, industrial metals, and raw materials, chemicals and pharmaceuticals, fuels. **Major trading partners:** (1986) *exports:* 36% U.S., 18% W. Germany, 5% Japan, 4% Netherlands, 3% France, 3% Sweden; *imports:* 38% U.S., 11% Japan, 8% W. Germany, 4.4% France, 4.3% Spain.

Intl. Orgs. FAO, G-77, GATT, IAEA, IBRD, ICAO, IDA, IFAD, IFC, ILO, IMF, IMO, INTELSAT, INTERPOL, ITU, NAM, OAS, UN, UNESCO, UPU, WHO, WIPO, WMO.

The territory that is now Colombia was home to various sedentary and semisedentary cultures prior to the arrival of Europeans. The Chibcha population of the Andean region might have numbered about one million prior to European contact. Portions of the area that make up modern Colombia fell under the authority of the Inca empire.

In 1538 the colony of New Granada, with its capital at Bogotá, was established, and for most of the period up until 1740, the area was within the jurisdiction of the viceroyalty of Peru. It was in that year that a new viceroyalty was established at Bogotá that included the areas of modern-day Colombia, Ecuador, Panama, and Venezuela. During the wars of independence against Spain, forces under Simón Bolívar were victorious over the royalists at the Battle of Boyacá in 1819, and the region gained its independence in 1821.

Colombian territory was a part of the federation of Gran Colombia until the collapse of the federal arrangement in 1830. Thereafter, the country—called New Granada—remained a separate political entity (which included the area of Panama). By the 1850s a federal system had been adopted for the country. But this arrangement rapidly disintegrated, and the practically semisovereign states were involved in a constant struggle with the central government for autonomy. The effort to define the political structure was largely resolved with the Constitution of 1886, which ended federalist regional autonomy and made Colombia a unitary republic.

Colombian political struggle since the 1850s had been characterized by a rivalry between two groups that coalesced into the Liberal and Conservative parties. During much of the 19th century, the Liberal-Conservative ideological battle was influenced to a great extent by the definition of the role of the Roman Catholic church in the country's political and social life. The 1887–88 Concordat represented a settlement on the role of the church in which the church was to have "official protection," while the state was to have authority over public education. The settlement left a central position for the church in Colombian society that was not substantially altered by the Concordat of 1942.

The Liberal-Conservative struggle led to at least six civil wars, which often ended in interparty compromise. A struggle in 1854 involved the issue of the future direction of the country's economic development and was followed by a settlement among elites. The Liberal-Conservative war of 1860–63 led to a Liberal victory and a period of Liberal political hegemony that lasted until 1886. The period of Conservative rule from 1886 until 1930 was punctuated by the "War of a Thousand Days" (1899–1902), in which the Conservatives defeated the Liberals. In 1903 the Colombian government rejected a U.S. offer for construction of a canal in Panama. As a result Panama (backed by the U.S.) revolted against the Colombian government, ending in the separation of Panama from Colombia.

As was the case with so many other Latin American countries, the world depression of 1929 seriously disrupted both the economy and the politics of Colombia. The loss of popularity of the ruling Conservatives due to both the overall economic collapse and their increasingly brutal repression of the labor movement led to a Liberal victory in 1930. A new civil war between peasants loyal to the two parties also broke out that year. It seemed that some form of socioeconomic reform was on the political agenda, and by 1934 Liberal Pres. Alfonso López Pumarejo had inaugurated his reformist "Revolution on the March" program.

During the 1946 presidential election, Conservatives won the presidency with a minority of the overall vote, defeating a split Liberal party. Armed conflict originally instigated by the two party elites erupted. The political violence, however, soon took on a momentum of its own, expanding in scope. This marked the beginning of the period of Colombian history known as La Violencia, 1948–57. The violence of the period was to claim the lives of more than 200,000 people. In the summer of 1957, leaders of the Liberal and Conservative parties

reached an agreement on constitutional reform in an attempt to end the violence. The agreement, known as the National Front, was to be in force for 16 years and included provisions for regular alternation of the presidency between the parties, as well as an accord on equal staffing of all political positions by both parties. The Liberal and Conservative parties agreed they alone would monopolize the arena of legitimate political competition for the 16-year period. The agreement held up until 1968 constitutional revisions allowed for other organized political groups to be officially recognized.

Several problems developed in the 1960s and 1970s that reduced the ability of either of the major parties to govern the country effectively. The first of these problems was the emergence of guerrilla and paramilitary groups on both the right and the left. The leftist National Liberation Army (ELN) emerged in the 1960s, the Maoist "People's Liberation Army" (EPL) formed in 1968, and in 1966 the Communist party founded the Revolutionary Armed Forces of Colombia (FARC). Both the April 19 movement (M-19) and the Trotskyist Worker's Self-Defense movement (MAO) took form in 1970. On the right, the Death to Kidnappers (MAS) death squad, which was tied to the drug trade and to the armed forces, emerged in 1981.

The other major problem of governance in Colombia has been the burgeoning narcotics trade. By the 1980s, ties with drug money had been established with many of the country's leading politicians as well as with officials of the police and the armed forces. By the end of the decade, violence and political assassination once again wracked Colombia.

In the midst of these continuing problems, Liberal party candidate Virgilio Barco Vargas was elected to the presidency in 1986.

Comoros
Federal Islamic Republic of the Comoros

Geography Location: an archipelago in Mozambique Channel comprising three main islands (Njazidja, Nzwami and Mwali, formerly Grande-Comore, Anjouan and Mohéli, respectively) and numerous islets and coral reefs. **Boundaries:** between island of Madagascar and Mozambique on southeast coast of African mainland. **Total land area:** 719 sq. mi. (1,862 sq km). **Coastline:** 211 mi. (340 km). **Comparative area:** slightly more than 12 times size of Washington, DC. **Land use:** 35% arable land; 8% permanent crops; 7% meadows and pastures; 16% forest and woodland; 34% other. **Major cities:** (1980 census) Moroni (capital) 17,267; Mutsamudu 13,000; Fomboni 5,400.

People Population: 429,479 (1988). **Nationality:** noun—Comoran(s); adjective—Comoran. **Ethnic groups:** Antalote, Cafre, Makoa, Oimatsaha, Sakalava. **Languages:** Shaafi Islam (Swahili dialect), Malagasy, French. **Religions:** 86% Sunni Muslim, 14% Roman Catholic.

Government Type: republic. **Independence:** July 6, 1975 (from France). **Constitution:** Oct. 1, 1978, amended Oct. 1982 and Jan. 1985. **National holiday:** N.A. **Heads of govern-**

ment: Ahmed Abdallah Abderemane, president (since Oct. 1978). **Structure:** executive—president; legislative—38-member Federal Assembly.

Economy Monetary unit: Comoran franc. **Budget:** (1987) *income:* $67 mil.; *expend.:* $70 mil. **GNP:** $163 mil., $390 per capita (1986 est.). **Chief crops:** cash crops—essential oils for perfumes (mainly ylang-ylang), vanilla, copra, cloves; food crops—rice, manioc, maize, fruits, vegetables. **Livestock:** poultry, cattle, sheep. **Natural resources:** negligible. **Major industries:** perfume distillation. **Labor force:** 140,000 (1982); 80% agriculture, 3% government, 17% other; significant unemployment; 51% of population of working age (1985). **Exports:** $22.8 mil. (f.o.b., 1986 est.); perfume oils, vanilla, copra, cloves. **Imports:** $42 mil. (c.i.f., 1986 est.); rice and other foodstuffs, cement, fuels, chemicals, textiles. **Major trading partners:** *exports:* France, W. Germany, U.S.; *imports:* France, other EC countries, Kenya, Réunion, China.

Intl. Orgs. FAO, G-77, IBRD, IDA, IFAD, ILO, IMF, ITU, NAM, UN, UNESCO, UPU, WHO, WMO.

Stretching across the northern end of the Mozambique Channel in the Indian Ocean, the Comoros Federal Islamic Republic is an archipelago composed of four prominent islands and several smaller islands. Numerous groups from Africa, Europe, and Asia invaded the islands over the centuries, including the Shirazi Arabs, who introduced Islam to Comoros around the turn of the 16th century. The French established colonial rule over the archipelago between 1841 and 1912 and developed a plantation-based economy. The islands served as a French territory from the end of World War II until 1961 when political autonomy was granted. Comoros gained independence in 1975, but the parliamentary government only retains control over three of the four major islands; representatives from the island of Mayotte abstained on the vote for unilateral independence, and it remains under French administration. Although overthrown by foreign mercenaries in 1975, Pres. Ahmed Abdallah Abderemane returned to power in 1978 and helped establish the country's first Constitution.

Much of the nation's soil is laden with lava, making it unsuitable for farming, especially on the island of Grand Comore, which is dominated by Mount Kartala, an active volcano. This obstacle to agriculture hinders the growth of Comoros, one of the poorest and least developed nations in the world. A poor road system and harsh cyclone season add further to the country's problems.

Congo
People's Republic of the Congo
(PREVIOUS NAME: CONGO/ BRAZZAVILLE)

Geography Location: equatorial country on western coast of Africa. **Boundaries:** Cameroon to NW, Central African Republic to NE, Zaire to E and S, Angolan district of Cabinda to S, Gulf of Guinea to SW, Gabon to W. **Total land**

area: 132,047 sq. mi. (342,000 sq km). **Coastline:** 105 mi. (169 km). **Comparative area:** slightly smaller than Montana. **Land use:** 2% arable land; negl. % permanent crops; 29% meadows and pastures; 62% forest and woodland; 7% other. **Major cities:** (1974 census) Brazzaville (capital) 456,383; Pool 219,329; Pointe-Noire 214,466; Bouenza 135,999; Cuvette 127,558.

People Population: 2,153,685 (1988). **Nationality:** noun—Congolese (sing., pl.); adjective—Congolese or Congo. **Ethnic groups:** 75 groups, almost all Bantu—48% Kongo, 20% Sangha, 17% Teke, 12% M'Bochi; about 8,500 Europeans, mostly French. **Languages:** French (official); many African languages with Lingala and Kikongo most widely used. **Religions:** 50% Christian, 42% indigenous beliefs, 2% Muslim.

Government Type: people's republic. **Independence:** Aug. 15, 1960 (from France). **Constitution:** July 8, 1979. **National holiday:** National Day, Aug. 15. **Heads of government:** Col. Denis Sassou-Nguesso, president (since Feb. 1979); Ange-Edouard Poungui, prime minister (since Aug. 1984). **Structure:** executive—president; Council of State; judiciary; all policy made by Congolese Labor Party and Central Committee and Politburo.

Economy Monetary unit: Communauté Financière Africaine (CFA) franc. **Budget:** (1984) **income:** $721 mil.; **expend.:** $508 mil. **GDP:** about $1.8 bil., $1,140 per capita (1984). **Chief crops:** cash crops—sugarcane, wood, coffee, cocoa beans, palm kernels; food crops—root crops, rice, corn, bananas, manioc. **Livestock:** goats, cattle, sheep, pigs. **Natural resources:** petroleum, timber, potash, lead, zinc. **Major industries:** crude oil, cement, sawmills. **Labor force:** 79,100 (1985); 75% agriculture, 25% commerce, industry, government; 51% of population of working age with 40% economically active; 40,000–60,000 unemployed. **Exports:** $1.3 bil. (f.o.b., 1984); 90% oil; lumber, tobacco, veneer, plywood. **Imports:** $618.0 mil. (f.o.b., 1984); machinery, transport equipment, manufactured consumer goods, iron and steel, foodstuffs. **Major trading partners:** France, Italy, W. Germany, U.S.

Intl. Orgs. FAO, G-77, GATT, IBRD, ICAO, IDA, IFAD, IFC, ILO, IMF, IMO, INTELSAT, INTERPOL, ITU, NAM, UN, UNESCO, UPU, WHO, WIPO, WMO.

Beginning around 1,500 years ago, the lower reaches of the Congo River formed the focus of a number of well-organized states. The Kongo and Ndonga flourished south of the river, in what is now Zaire; north of the river, the Loango, Teke, and Bobangi were dominant. These states were weakened beginning in the 16th century by the slave trade, primarily in the hands of the Portuguese who dominated the West African coast.

The Congo River was explored by David Livingstone in 1858. With the weakening of Portuguese power, the French became dominant in western Africa. In 1883 they established a protectorate over the Teke kingdom, which they renamed Middle Congo. The treaty with the Teke king was concluded by Pierre

Savorgnan de Brazza, whose name was honored in the territory's capital, Brazzaville.

In 1910 the French authorities confederated their protectorates of Gabon, Middle Congo, Ubangi-Shari (later the Central African Republic), and Chad to form French Equatorial Africa. That territory became an important base of Free French activity during World War II.

In 1944 Gen. Charles de Gaulle rewarded the territory with a pledge of political reforms. In 1946 French citizenship was granted to the territory's inhabitants, and local power was devolved upon advisory assemblies. A 1958 constitutional referendum granted full autonomy to the Republic of the Congo upon the dissolution of the confederation of French Equatorial Africa in 1959. The nation gained full independence on Apr. 15, 1960.

In August 1963 Pres. Fulbert Youlou was driven from office by violent labor unrest; the military took control and then installed a provisional civilian government led by Alphonse Massamba-Debat. He was subsequently elected president for a five-year term.

In 1968 Massamba-Debat was overthrown in a military coup and replaced by Capt. Marien Ngouabi. In 1969 Ngouabi reorganized the Congo as a People's Republic and changed the name of the ruling party from the National Revolutionary Movement party to the Congolese Labor party. Both China and the USSR vied for influence in the new People's Republic which, despite its Marxist-Leninist stance, remained strongly linked to France—its main source of trade, aid, and foreign investment.

Ngouabi was assassinated on Mar. 18, 1977. He was replaced by an 11-man military committee of the Congolese Labor party, led by Gen. Joachim Yhomby-Opango. Yhomby-Opango resigned and was arrested for treason in 1979; he was replaced as president by Denis Sassou-Nguesso. The Sassou-Nguesso government signed a 20-year treaty of friendship with the USSR in 1981 but has also sought closer ties with the West.

The topography of the Congo consists of fertile plains and thick forests. The country is primarily agricultural; palm oil, coffee, cocoa, and tobacco are cultivated for export. The country is rich in minerals, including oil, natural gas, potash, lead, copper, and zinc. Much of the nation's mineral and petroleum earnings has been spent on ill-conceived and unproductive state projects. Corruption and economic mismanagement are rampant, and the country remains poor and underdeveloped.

Costa Rica
Republic of Costa Rica

Geography Location: Central American isthmus. **Boundaries:** Nicaragua to N, Caribbean Sea to E, Panama to S, and Pacific Ocean to W. **Total land area:** 19,730 sq. mi. (51,100 sq km). **Coastline:** 801 mi. (1,290 km). **Comparative area:** slightly smaller than West Virginia. **Land use:** 6% arable land; 7% permanent crops; 45% meadows and pastures; 34% forest and woodland; 8% other; includes 1% irrigated. **Major cities:** (1984 census) San José (capital) 245,370; Puntarenas 47,851; Limón 43,158; Alajuela 33,929; Cartago 23,884.

People Population: 2,888,227 (1988). **Nationality:** noun—Costa Rican(s); adjective—Costa Rican. **Ethnic groups:** 96% white, 3% black, 1% Indian. **Languages:** Spanish (official), Jamaican dialect of English spoken around Puerto Limón. **Religions:** 95% Roman Catholic.

Government Type: democratic republic. **Independence:** Sept. 15, 1821 (from Spain). **Constitution:** Nov. 9, 1949. **National holiday:** Independence Day, Sept. 18. **Heads of government:** Oscar Arias Sánchez, president (since May 1986). **Structure :** executive—president (head of government and chief of state), elected for single four-year term; two vice presidents; legislative—57-delegate unicameral Legislative Assembly elected at four-year intervals (legislator may not serve consecutive terms); judiciary—Supreme Court of Justice (17 magistrates elected by Legislative Assembly at eight-year intervals).

Economy Monetary Unit: colón. **Budget:** (1987) **income:** $673 mil.; **expend.:** $819 mil. **GDP:** $4.2 bil., $1,530 per capita (1986 est.). **Chief crops:** coffee, bananas, sugarcane, rice, corn, cocoa; illegal producer of cannabis for international drug trade. **Livestock:** cattle, pigs, horses. **Natural resources:** hydropower potential. **Major industries:** food processing, textiles and clothing, construction materials. **Labor force:** 868,300 (1985 est.); 35.1% industry and commerce, 27% agriculture, 26.1% government and services, 11.8% other; 24% total unemployment, 6.5% official unemployment (1987 est.). **Exports:** $1,077 mil. (f.o.b., 1986); coffee, bananas, beef, sugar, cocoa. **Imports:** $1,163 mil. (c.i.f., 1986); manufactured products, machinery, transportation equipment, chemicals, fuels. **Major trading partners:** (1983) **exports:** 47% U.S., 18% CACM, 9% W. Germany; **imports:** 40% U.S., 12% Japan, 11% CACM, 4% W. Germany.

Intl. Orgs. FAO, G-77, IAEA, IBRD, ICAO, IDA, IFAD, IFC, ILO, IMF, IMO, INTELSAT, INTERPOL, ITU, UN, UNESCO, UPU, WHO, WMO.

Costa Rica was under the jurisdiction of the Spanish colonial kingdom of Guatemala until it broke with Spain in 1821, along with other parts of Central America. With the collapse of the United Provinces of Central America in 1838, Costa Rica became an independent republic. The country experienced an early economic shift as part of the Central American coffee boom in the mid-19th century.

An attempt at electoral fraud in 1948 led to a brief civil war, which was won by the National Liberation forces under "Don Pepé" Jose Figueres Ferrer. The Costa Rican army was subsequently abolished. The country has experienced competitive multiparty electoral democracy since 1949.

Cuba
Republic of Cuba

Geography Location: one large island and several small ones in northern Caribbean Sea, about 100 mi. (160 km) S of Florida. **Boundaries:** North Atlantic Ocean to N, Windward

Passage to E, Caribbean Sea to S, Yucatan Channel to W. **Total land area:** 42,803 sq. mi. (110,860 sq km). **Coastline:** 2,319 mi. (3,735 km). **Comparative area:** slightly smaller than Pennsylvania. **Land use:** 23% arable land; 6% permanent crops; 23% meadows and pastures; 17% forest and woodland; 31% other; includes 10% irrigated. **Major cities:** (1986 est.) La Habana (Havana—capital) 2,036,799; Santiago de Cuba 364,554; Camagüey 265,588; Holguín 199,861; Santa Clara 182,349.

People Population: 10,353,932 (1988). **Nationality:** noun—Cuban(s); adjective—Cuban. **Ethnic groups:** 51% mulatto, 37% white, 11% black, 1% Chinese. **Languages:** Spanish. **Religions:** at least 85% nominally Roman Catholic before Castro assumed power.

Government Type: Communist state. **Independence:** May 20, 1902 (from Spain). **Constitution:** Feb. 24, 1976. **National holiday:** Anniversary of the Revolution, Jan. 1. **Heads of government:** Fidel Castro Ruz, president (since Jan. 1959). **Structure:** executive; legislative (National Assembly of the People's Power); controlled judiciary.

Economy Monetary unit: peso. **Budget:** (1986 est.) *income:* $15.1 bil.; *expend.:* N.A. **GNP:** $18.7 bil., $1,800 per capita in 1974 dollars (1987 est.). **Chief crops:** sugar, tobacco, rice, potatoes, tubers, citrus, coffee. **Livestock:** cattle, pigs, horses, sheep. **Natural resources:** cobalt, nickel, iron ore, copper, manganese. **Major industries:** sugar milling, petroleum refining, food and tobacco processing. **Labor force:** 3.2 mil. (1985); 52% industry and commerce, 31% services and government, 17% agriculture. **Exports:** $6.4 bil. (f.o.b., 1986); sugar, nickel, shellfish, tobacco, coffee. **Imports:** $9.2 bil. (c.i.f., 1986); capital goods, industrial raw materials, food, petroleum. **Major trading partners:** (1986) *exports:* 74% USSR, 14% other Communist countries; *imports:* 70% USSR, 15% other Communist countries.

Intl. Orgs. FAO, G-77, GATT, IAEA, ICAO, IFAD, ILO, IMO, ITU, NAM, OAS (nonparticipant), UN, UNESCO, UNIDO, UPU, WHO, WIPO, WMO.

At the time of Christopher Columbus's arrival in 1492, Cuba was home to Arawak, Ciboney, and Guanahatabey Indian people. Cuba served as a launching point for Spanish imperial conquests in the Americas, and the early 19th century wars of independence that swept the rest of Spanish America did not overthrow the imposing Spanish garrison there. Slavery was abolished in 1886, but Spanish colonialism lingered in Cuba until the 1890s.

Spanish control of the island began to deteriorate in the late 1860s with the beginning of the "Ten Years War" (1868-78), and Cuba finally separated from Spain as a result of the Cuban-U.S.-Spanish war, which ended with the signing of the Treaty of Paris in 1898. Cuba became a U.S. protectorate by virtue of the U.S.-sponsored Platt Amendment (1901) to the new Cuban constitution. The Platt Amendment gave the United States the right to intervene in Cuban affairs, and after the initial occupation

of the island, U.S. troops repeatedly invaded and occupied the former Spanish colony.

Corruption and political repression plagued Cuban politics during the first half of the 20th century. Gerardo Machado won election to the presidency in 1925, but he quickly turned his administration of the island into a dictatorship that lasted until his ouster by a progressive coalition of students and labor in 1933. The "revolution" of 1933 installed Ramón Grau San Martín as the new head of the government, but the United States supported Grau's ouster, and army Sgt. Fulgencio Batista replaced him. Batista ruled the country either directly or indirectly from 1934 until Jan. 1, 1959, when he fled in the wake of the Cuban revolution.

Fidel Castro Ruz and 165 others staged an attack on the Moncada army barracks in Santiago, Cuba, in 1953, but the action was a failure. In 1956 Fidel and Raúl Castro, Argentine physician Ernesto "Che" Guevara, and 79 other revolutionaries returned to Cuba aboard the yacht *Granma*. Upon reaching the island, the revolutionaries fled into Cuba's eastern Sierra Maestra, which they used as their base of operations. Batista's military failed to defeat the guerrillas in 1958, and in the wake of increasing demonstrations of public antipathy for his government, the dictator fled the country. The Fidelistas took control Jan. 1, 1959.

By mid-1959, revolutionary tribunals had tried and executed more than 500 political "enemies." The leaders announced an agrarian reform, and by 1960 the nationalization of the economy was in full swing. In 1961 U.S.-Cuban diplomatic relations were severed, and the U.S.-sponsored Bay of Pigs invasion attempt failed. Later that year Castro declared himself a Marxist-Leninist. Cuba was at the center of a world crisis in 1962 when U.S. spy planes uncovered Soviet intentions to place nuclear weapons on the island. The Soviets agreed to the withdrawal of missiles in exchange for a U.S. pledge not to invade Cuba.

A 1976 constitution established an institutional political structure for the country, providing a formal role for the Communist party and amounting to a small step away from Fidel Castro's personal dominance of Cuban politics.

Cyprus
Republic of Cyprus

Geography Location: island in eastern Mediterranean Sea. **Boundaries:** 62 mi. (100 km) S of Turkey, Syria to E. **Total land area:** 3,572 sq. mi. (9,521 sq km). **Coastline:** 403 mi. (648 km). **Comparative area:** slightly smaller than three times size of Rhode Island. **Land use:** 40% arable land; 7% permanent crops; 10% meadows and pastures; 18% forest and woodland; 25% other; includes 10% irrigated. **Major cities:** Nicosia (capital) 149,100 (excludes Turkish-occupied portion); Limassol 107,200; Larnaca 48,300 (1982); Famagusta (Gazi Magusa) 39,500 (mid-1974); Phaphos 20,800 (1982).

People Population: 691,966 (1988). **Nationality:** noun—Cypriot(s); adjective—Cypriot. **Ethnic groups:** 78% Greek, 18% Turkish, 4% other. **Languages:** Greek, Turkish, English.

Religions: 78% Greek Orthodox, 18% Muslim, 4% Maronite, Armenian, Apostolic, and other.

Government Type: republic. **Independence:** Aug. 16, 1960 (from UK). **Constitution:** Aug. 16, 1960; negotiations have been held intermittently to create basis for new or revised constitution to govern the island and relations between Greek and Turkish Cypriots. **National holiday:** Independence Day, Oct. 1. **Heads of government:** George Vassiliou, president (since Feb. 1988); Turkish sector—Rauf Denktash, president (since 1975). **Structure:** currently, government of Cyprus has effective authority over only Greek Cypriot community; headed by president of republic and comprising Council of Ministers, House of Representatives, and Supreme Court; Turkish Cypriots declared their own Constitution and governing bodies within Turkish Federated State of Cyprus in 1975; state renamed Turkish Republic of Northern Cyprus in 1983.

Economy Monetary unit: Cyprus pound. **Budget:** (1984) *income:* $663.2 mil.; *expend.:* $804.9 mil.; Turkish area—(1986) *income:* $46.3 mil.; *expend.:* $110.9 mil. **GDP:** $2.4 bil., $3,610 per capita (1984); Turkish area—$205.9 mil., $1,340 per capita (1983). **Chief crops:** potatoes and other vegetables, grapes, citrus, wheat, carob beans. **Livestock:** chickens, sheep, goats, pigs, cattle. **Natural resources:** copper, pyrites, asbestos, gypsum, timber. **Major industries:** mining (iron pyrites, gypsum, asbestos), manufactures principally for local consumption (beverages, footwear, clothing, cement). **Labor force:** Greek area—251,406 (1986); 42% services, 33% industry, 22% agriculture; 3.4% unemployed; Turkish area—undetermined. **Exports:** $561.2 mil. (f.o.b., 1985); principal items—food and beverages, including citrus, raisins, potatoes, wine; also, cement, clothing; Turkish area—$48.8 mil. (f.o.b., 1984); principal items—citrus, potatoes, metal pipes, pyrites. **Imports:** $1,469.7 mil. (c.i.f., 1985); principal items—manufactured goods, machinery and transport equipment, fuels, food; Turkish area—$170 mil. (c.i.f., 1984); principal items—foodstuffs, raw materials, fuels, machinery. **Major trading partners:** (1984) *exports:* 17% UK, 14.1% Lebanon, 11.4% Libya, 7.5% Saudi Arabia, 3.4% USSR; Turkish area—61% EC, 22% Turkey, 16% Arab countries; *imports:* 12.1% UK, 12% Japan, 10.5% Italy, 8.3% W. Germany, 5.2% Iraq; Turkish area—46% Turkey, 36% EC, 17% Arab countries.

Intl. Orgs. Commonwealth, FAO, G-77, GATT, IAEA, IBRD, ICAO, IDA, IFAD, IFC, ILO, IMF, IMO, INTELSAT, INTERPOL, ITU, NAM, UN, UNESCO, UPU, WHO, WMO.

The early civilization of Cyprus was greatly influenced by Greece. In antiquity the island was ruled at various times by Assyria, Persia, and Egypt before being annexed by the Roman Empire in 58 B.C. Following the division of the Roman Empire, Cyprus was part of the Eastern (later Byzantine) Empire until a crusader state, established by Richard the Lion-Hearted of England, was established in A.D. 1191. The Lusignan dynasty ruled until 1489, when

Cyprus was annexed by Venice. It was subsequently conquered by the Ottoman Empire in 1571.

In 1878 the Congress of Berlin placed Cyprus under British administration. In 1914 it was annexed outright by Great Britain and was made a British colony in 1925. From 1945 to 1948, the British used Cyprus as a detention area for "illegal" Jewish immigrants to Palestine.

After 1947 the Greek Cypriot community continued its long-standing agitation for union (enosis) with Greece; that policy was strongly opposed by the Turkish Cypriot community. Communal violence broke out in 1954–55. In 1960 Cyprus was granted full independence as a republic; Archbishop Makarios, leader of the enosis movement, was elected president.

The independence agreement forbade both enosis and partition and included guarantees of the rights of both Greeks (80% of the population) and Turks. Attempts by Pres. Makarios to alter the Constitution to favor the Greek majority provoked further communal clashes in 1964, when a UN peacekeeping force was sent to the island. On July 15, 1974, a military coup by officers who favored union with Greece deposed the Makarios government. On July 20 Turkey invaded Cyprus and, after the collapse of cease-fire talks in August, occupied the northern two-fifths of the island. In 1975 the Turkish government announced a de facto partition of Cyprus; the northern territory was proclaimed the Turkish Federated State of Cyprus, under Pres. Rauf Denktash.

Makarios returned as president of the Republic of Cyprus, which was thus reduced in size, and remained in office until his death in 1977. He was succeeded by Spyros Kyprianou. Some 200,000 Greek Cypriots were expelled from the Turkish sector to the Republic; many Turks fled from the Republic to the Turkish sector. With a return of political stability, renewed foreign investment, and a customs union negotiated with the EEC, the Republic's economy has prospered, led by agriculture, light manufacturing, and tourism.

In the Turkish sector, the economy remained stagnant, hampered by the loss of population, wartime damage, and stringent economic controls. The Turkish sector proclaimed its independence as the Turkish Republic of Northern Cyprus in 1983, but the new Republic has not gained international recognition.

In 1988 George Vassiliou was elected president of the Republic of Cyprus. Talks aimed at achieving a federation of Cyprus's two republics remain stalemated.

Czechoslovakia
Czechoslovak Socialist Republic
Geography Location: landlocked country in central Europe. **Boundaries:** Poland to N, USSR to E, Hungary to SE, Austria to SW, W. Germany to W, E. Germany to NW. **Total land area:** 49,384 sq. mi. (127,905 sq km). **Coastline:** none. **Comparative area:** slightly larger than New York State. **Land use:** 40% arable land; 1% permanent crops; 13% meadows and pastures; 37% forest and woodland; 9% other; includes 1% irrigated. **Major cities:** (1986)

Praha (Prague, capital) 1,193,513; Bratislava 417,103; Brno 385,684; Ostrava 327,791; Košice 175,244.

People Population: 15,620,722 (1988). **Nationality:** noun—Czechoslovak(s); adjective—Czechoslovak. **Ethnic groups:** 64.3% Czech, 30.5% Slovak, 3.8% Hungarian, 0.4% German, 0.4% Polish, 0.3% Ukrainian, 0.1% Russian, 0.2% other (Jewish, Gypsy). **Languages:** Czech and Slovak (both official), Hungarian. **Religions:** 77% Roman Catholic, 20% Protestant, 2% Orthodox, 1% other.

Government Type: communist state. **Independence:** Oct. 18, 1918 (from Austro-Hungarian empire). **Constitution:** July 11, 1960; amended in 1968 and 1970. **National holiday:** Liberation Day, May 9. **Heads of government:** Gustáv Husak, president (since May 1975); Lavislav Admec, premier (since Mar. 1988). **Structure:** president elected by Federal Assembly, cabinet appointed by president; legislative (Federal Assembly, elected directly—Chamber of Nations, Chamber of the People); Czech and Slovak national councils (also elected directly) legislate on limited area of regional matters; judiciary, Supreme Court (elected by Federal Assembly); entire governmental structure dominated by Communist party.

Economy Monetary unit: kčs or koruna. **Budget:** N.A. **GNP:** $143.9 bil., $9,280 per capita (1986 est.). **Chief crops:** diversified agriculture; main crops—wheat, rye, oats, corn, barley; net food importer—meat, wheat, vegetable oils, fresh fruits and vegetables. **Livestock:** pigs, cattle, sheep, goats, horses. **Natural resources:** coal, coke, timber, lignite, uranium. **Major industries:** iron and steel, machinery and equipment, cement. **Labor force:** 8.14 mil. (1986); 50.8% construction and communications, 36.9% industry, 12.3% agriculture (1982). **Exports:** $21.9 bil. (f.o.b., 1986); 57.1% machinery and equipment, 15.5% manufactured consumer goods, 13.2% fuels, minerals, and metals; 6.4% agricultural and forestry products, 8.2% other products (1984 est.). **Imports:** $21.97 bil. (f.o.b., 1986); 40.5% fuels, minerals, and metals; 34.5% machinery and equipment; 12.3% agricultural and forestry products, 7.3% other products (1984). **Major trading partners:** (1986) USSR, E. Germany, Poland, Hungary, W. Germany, Yugoslavia, Austria, Bulgaria, Romania; 80% with communist countries, 20% with noncommunist countries.

Intl. Orgs. CMEA, FAO, GATT, IAEA, ICAO, ILO, IMO, ITU, UN, UNESCO, UPU, Warsaw Pact, WHO, WIPO, WMO.

Bohemia, Moravia, and Slovakia—"lands of the Crown of St. Vaclav"—were formed into the Moravian empire in the ninth century. Slovakia was later conquered by the Magyars, while Bohemia and Moravia remained an independent kingdom under the Přemyslid dynasty, within the Holy Roman Empire. Prague became a great university city in the 14th century. After the Battle of Mohacs in 1526, Bohemia came under Habsburg control. An unsuccessful Bohemian revolt in 1618 initiated the Thirty Years' War; renewed Habsburg control lasted until World War I.

Bohemia and Moravia were among the richest lands in the Austro-Hungarian Empire. Agriculture prospered in the lowlands and plains, while the hills and mountains, settled by ethnic Germans in the 13th century, were rich in minerals. The nobility was largely Czech, the burgher class in the cities German and Jewish. The growth of industry in the 19th century led to great prosperity for the urban elite, whereas the nobility, dedicated to landholding, military careers, and administration, became relatively stagnant.

The Habsburg monarchy crumbled during World War I, and a new state of Czechoslovakia emerged in 1918. It was a multinational state formed by the complete restructuring of the borders of Europe under the Treaty of Versailles; it included not only Czechs but also Germans, Slovaks, Magyars, Poles, and Ukrainians. Under its founders, Eduard Beneš and Thomas Masaryk, it managed to forge a national identity and became the most democratic state in Central Europe in the period between the two world wars.

Czechoslovakia was doomed by the 1938 takeover of Austria by Nazi Germany. Following the Munich Pact of September 1938, Hitler annexed the German-speaking regions of the "Sudetenland" and in 1939 absorbed the Czech lands, establishing a "protectorate" over Slovakia. Under Nazi rule Czechoslovakia was governed with great severity, but the economy boomed with wartime production for the German army. Prague was occupied by Russian troops in 1945.

After World War II, Beneš returned as president. Czechoslovakia ceded its easternmost lands, Carpatho-Ruthenia, to the USSR and expelled or executed over 3 million Germans, along with all German-speaking Jews who had survived the Hitler era. In 1948 a Communist coup forced Beneš to resign; he was replaced by the Communist leader Klement Gottwald. Jan Masaryk, the foreign minister, committed suicide or was murdered. Purges and persecutions followed.

With Stalin's death in 1953, Gottwald was replaced as party first secretary by Antonin Novotny, who also became president in 1957. Novotny was a hard-liner who permitted no de-Stalinization or liberalization. In 1968 Novotny was replaced as first secretary by a liberal, Alexander Dubcek; Ludvik Svoboda became president. Czechoslovakia suddenly was in the vanguard of communist reform. The new regime abolished censorship, denounced Stalin, decentralized economic decision-making, and granted real power to the national assembly.

The brief "Prague Spring" ended in August 1968, when Warsaw Pact troops invaded. The "Brezhnev doctrine" was proclaimed, under which no independence was to be permitted to satellites of the USSR. In 1969 Dubcek was replaced by Gustáv Husak, who became president in 1975. The party was purged, censorship restored, dissent repressed, and the centralized economy restored.

The 1970s brought inflation and economic stagnation but produced no change in policy. The rise of the Solidarity movement in Poland in the early 1980s provoked a backlash of preventive repression in Czechoslovakia, aimed especially at Charter 77, a human-rights organization, and at the Catholic church.

In 1987 Husak resigned as party chief and was replaced by Milos Jakes, a compromise candidate between hard-line and reformist factions. Czechoslovakia has resisted Gorbachev-style economic reform despite persistent economic stagnation, and its government remains one of Eastern Europe's most repressive regimes.

Denmark
Kingdom of Denmark

Geography Location: northern Europe. **Boundaries:** Skagerrak channel to N, Baltic Sea to E, W. Germany to S, North Sea to W. **Total land area:** 16,638 sq. mi. (43,092 sq km). **Coastline:** 2,100 mi. (3,379 km). **Comparative area:** slightly more than twice size of Massachusetts. **Land use:** 61% arable land; negl. % permanent crops; 6% meadows and pastures; 12% forest and woodland; 21% other; includes 9% irrigated. **Major cities:** (1985) Køenhavn (Copenhagen—capital) 1,358,540; Århus (Aarhus) 194,348; Odense 136,803; Alborg (Aalborg) 113,865; Esbjerg 70,975.

People Population: 5,125,676 (1988). **Nationality:** noun—Dane(s); adjective—Danish. **Ethnic groups:** Scandinavian, Eskimo, Faeroese, German. **Languages:** Danish, Faeroese, Greenlandic (Eskimo dialect); small German-speaking minority. **Religions:** 97% Evangelical Lutheran, 2% other Protestant and Roman Catholic, 1% other.

Government Type: constitutional monarchy. **Constitution:** June 5, 1953. **National holiday:** Birthday of the Queen, Apr. 16. **Heads of government:** Margrethe II, queen (since Jan. 1972); Poul Schlüter, prime minister (since Sept. 1982). **Structure:** executive power vested in Crown but exercised by cabinet responsible to parliament; legislative authority rests jointly with Crown and parliament (Folketing); Supreme Court, two superior courts, 106 lower courts.

Economy Monetary unit: krone. **Budget:** (1987) *income:* $33.04 bil.; *expend.:* $33.06 bil. **GNP:** $78.7 bil., $15,370 per capita (1986). **Chief crops:** highly intensive specialties in dairying and animal husbandry; main crops—cereals, root crops; food imports—oilseed, grain, animal foodstuffs. **Livestock:** chickens, pigs, cattle, ducks, turkeys. **Natural resources:** crude oil, natural gas, fish, salt, limestone. **Major industries:** food processing, machinery and equipment, textiles, clothing. **Labor force:** 2.86 mil. (1987); 31.3% services, 26.4% government, 18.4% manufacturing; 8.0% unemployment. **Exports:** $21.3 bil. (f.o.b., 1986); principal items—meat, dairy products, industrial machinery and equipment, textiles, clothing, chemical products, transport equipment, fish, furs, furniture. **Imports:** $22.9 bil. (c.i.f., 1986); principal items—industrial machinery, transport equipment, petroleum, textile fibers and yarns, iron and steel products, chemicals, grain and feedstuffs, wood, paper. **Major trading partners:** (1986) *exports:* 45.3% EC (16.2%

W. Germany, 11.4% UK), 11.4% Sweden, 8.4% U.S., 7.7% Norway; *imports:* 21% W. Germany, 13% Sweden, 9% UK, 6% U.S., 4% France, 4% Norway.

Intl. Orgs. EC, FAO, GATT, IAEA, IBRD, ICAO, IDA, IFAD, IFC, ILO, IMF, IMO, INTELSAT, INTERPOL, ITU, NATO, OECD, UN, UNESCO, UPU, WHO, WIPO, WMO.

The obscure Norse kingdom of Denmark made its debut in world history in the eighth century, when Viking raiders began to plunder northwestern Europe. The Danish overseas possessions of the Faeroe Islands and Greenland are a modern reminder of the high point of Viking exploration and conquest. King Harold Bluetooth (d. 985) was Denmark's first Christian monarch; his son, King Canute, ruled an empire that included Denmark, England, Norway, and southern Sweden. Danish royal power reached its high point in the late 14th century but began to wane with the establishment of an independent Swedish monarchy in 1523. In the 16th century, Copenhagen was an important center of European intellectual life.

Further losses of territory were imposed by the Treaty of Copenhagen (1660). Denmark lost control of Norway at the Congress of Vienna (1815) and of Schleswig-Holstein after a civil war in 1864. Iceland, part of Denmark since the 14th century, was granted home rule in 1874, becoming independent in 1944.

In the 19th century, Denmark was transformed from a poor peasant society to one of Europe's richest agricultural nations by means of reforms that established agricultural cooperatives and emphasized intensive specialization in the production of dairy products and pork. These products remain a mainstay of the Danish economy.

Denmark remained neutral during World War I. In 1939 Denmark signed a 10-year nonaggression pact with Germany, but Germany nevertheless invaded Denmark in April 1940; the country surrendered without a fight. In 1941 Denmark's ambassador in Washington transferred defense of Greenland to the United States, and much of Denmark's merchant fleet joined the Allied war effort. Denmark was placed under German martial law in August 1943 and treated as an enemy nation. Danish resistance succeeded in evacuating 7,000 Jews to neutral Sweden. Denmark was liberated by British troops in May 1945.

Although Denmark was not technically a participant on the Allied side in World War II, it received favorable treatment in the postwar period, becoming a UN member in 1946 and a founding member of NATO in 1949. By the latter year, the postwar recovery was complete, with industrial levels exceeding those of the prewar period. High taxes, unemployment, and inflation remained problems, but the economy was aided by the growth of trade with West Germany, which was just beginning its "economic miracle."

In 1953 the king assented to a constitutional reform that abolished the upper house of the legislature, leaving the Folketing as the sole legislative body. Proportional representation meant that it was virtually impossible for any

political party to gain a parliamentary majority; Denmark is always governed by coalition regimes. In the postwar period, these normally have been led by the Social Democrats.

In the 1950s Denmark adopted a characteristically Scandinavian program of free enterprise, high taxes, and extensive social welfare systems. A high rate of economic growth, spurred by agricultural exports, continued throughout the 1960s. Denmark joined the EEC in 1972. The 1970s brought economic difficulties, as Danish oil exploration in the North Sea yielded disappointing results, and inflation reached double digits annually.

The elections of 1982 installed Denmark's first Conservative government since 1905. A Conservative four-party coalition formed in 1984 has remained in office to the present. The general revival of the world economy in the 1980s coupled with government austerity measures have led to renewed growth and lowered inflation, with both figures now averaging 3 percent annually.

The Faeroe Islands were granted self-rule in 1948; the economy is based on fishing and sheep-raising. Greenland was granted self-rule in 1979. Geographically huge but with a population of under 60,000, the island bases its economy on fishing, tourism, and revenues from military bases.

Djibouti
Republic of Djibouti
(PREVIOUS NAME: FRENCH SOMALIA)

Geography Location: northeastern Africa. **Boundaries:** Red Sea to N, Gulf of Aden to E, Somalia to SE, Ethiopia to S, W, and NW. **Total land area:** 8,958 sq. mi. (23,200 sq km). **Coastline:** 195 mi. (314 km). **Comparative area:** slightly larger than Massachusetts. **Land use:** 0% arable land; 0% permanent crops; 9% meadows and pastures; negl. % forest and woodland; 91% other. **Major cities:** Djibouti (capital) 200,000 (1981); Dikhil, Ali-Sabieh, Tadjourah, Obock.

People Population: 320,444 (1988). **Nationality:** noun—Djiboutian(s); adjective—Djiboutian. **Ethnic groups:** 60% Somali (Issa), 35% Afar, 5% French, Arab, Ethiopian, and Italian. **Languages:** French (official); Arabic, Somali, and Afar widely used. **Religions:** 94% Muslim, 6% Christian.

Government Type: republic. **Independence:** June 27, 1977 (from France). **Constitution:** partial Constitution ratified Jan. 1981 by National Assembly. **National holiday:** June 27. **Heads of government:** Hassan Gouled Aptidon, president (since June 1977). **Structure:** executive; legislative—65-member parliament (National Assembly); judiciary.

Economy Monetary unit: Djibouti franc. **Budget:** (1986 est. in percent of GDP) *income:* 33%; *expend.:* 46%. **GDP:** $333 mil., $1,067 per capita (1986). **Chief crops:** livestock; limited commercial crops, including fruits and vegetables. **Livestock:** goats, sheep, camels, cattle, asses. **Natural resources:** geothermal areas. **Major industries:** limited to a few small-scale enterprises, such as dairy products and mineral-water boiling. **Labor force:** small number of semiskilled workers at port; 3,000 railway workers; 52% of population of working age (1983). **Exports:** $96 mil. (f.o.b., 1985 est.); hides and skins and transit of coffee; a large portion consists of reexports to foreign residents of Djibouti. **Imports:** $205 mil. (f.o.b., 1985 est.); foods, machinery, transport equipment, chemicals, petroleum. **Major trading partners:** N.A.

Intl. Orgs. Arab League, FAO, G-77, IBRD, ICAO, IDA, IFAD, IFC, ILO, IMF, IMO, INTERPOL, ITU, NAM, OAU, UN, UPU, WHO, WMO.

This small, arid region on the Horn of Africa near the southern mouth of the Red Sea became the object of British-French rivalry with the opening of the Suez Canal in 1869. The French sphere of influence, called French Somaliland, was affirmed by agreements with Ethiopia in 1897, 1945, and 1954. In the early 20th century, the French constructed a railroad from Addis Ababa to Djibouti, adding to the colony's strategic value.

French and Italian forces clashed at the border of Ethiopia and French Somaliland with the Italian invasion of Ethiopia in the 1930s. During World War II, the territorial administration at first sided with the Vichy government but in December 1942 established ties with the Free French and the Allies.

The colony was reorganized in 1957 and in 1958 became, by referendum, a French Overseas Territory. In July 1967 its name was changed to the Territory of the Afars and Issas. Growing nationalist sentiment led to a referendum in favor of complete independence. The Republic of Djibouti became independent on June 27, 1977.

Djibouti's only significant natural resource is its geothermal areas. Shipping provides some income in the port city of Djibouti, but overall the economy depends heavily on French aid and on income derived from the French garrisons that remain stationed there.

Dominica
Commonwealth of Dominica
Geography Location: island in eastern Caribbean Sea, between French overseas department of Guadeloupe to N and Martinique to S. **Boundaries:** Dominica Passage to N, Atlantic Ocean to E, Martinique Passage to S, Caribbean Sea to W. **Total land area:** 290 sq. mi. (751 sq km). **Coastline:** 92 mi. (148 km). **Comparative area:** slightly more than four times size of Washington, D.C. **Land use:** 9% arable land; 13% permanent crops; 3% meadows and pastures; 41% forest and woodland; 34% other; includes N.A. % irrigated. **Major cities:** (1981 census) Roseau (capital) 8,279; Portsmouth 2,200.

People Population: 97,763 (1988). **Nationality:** noun—Dominican(s); adjective—Dominican. **Ethnic groups:** mostly black, some Carib-Indians. **Languages:** English (official), French patois widely spoken. **Religions:** 80% Roman Catholic, some Anglican and Methodist.

Government Type: independent state within commonwealth. **Independence:** Nov. 3,

1978 (from UK). **Constitution:** Nov. 3, 1978. **National holiday:** Nov. 3. **Heads of government:** Sir Clarence Seignoret, president (since Dec. 1983); Mary Eugenia Charles, prime minister (since July 1980). **Structure:** executive—cabinet headed by prime minister; legislative—31-member bicameral House of Assembly (1 ex-officio member, 9 appointed members, and 21 popularly elected members); judicial—magistrate's courts and regional court appeals.

Economy Monetary unit: East Caribbean (EC) dollar. **Budget:** (1986) *income:* $49.5 mil.; *expend.:* $48.7 mil. **GDP:** $91 mil., $1,090 per capita (1985). **Chief crops:** bananas, citrus, coconuts, cocoa, yams, essential oils. **Livestock:** pigs, goats, cattle, sheep. **Natural resources:** timber. **Major industries:** agricultural processing, tourism, soap and other coconut-based products. **Labor force:** 25,000 (1984); 40% agriculture, 32% industry and commerce, 28% services; 15–20% unemployment. **Exports:** $28.4 mil. (f.o.b., 1985); bananas, coconuts, lime juice and oil, cocoa, re-exports. **Imports:** $57 mil. (f.o.b., 1985); machinery and equipment, foodstuffs, manufactured articles, cement. **Major trading partners:** (1985) *exports:* 50% UK, 15% Jamaica, 11% OECS, 4% Trinidad and Tobago, 8% rest of CARICOM; *imports:* 25% U.S., 17% UK, 10% OECS, 9% Trinidad and Tobago.

Intl. Orgs. Commonwealth, FAO, G-77, GATT (de facto), IBRD, IDA, IFAD, IFC, ILO, IMF, IMO, INTERPOL, OAS, UN, UNESCO, UPU, WHO, WMO.

From 1632 until 1805, the French and British fought for control over Dominica. Administratively joined to the Leeward and then the Windward Islands, and then part of the West Indies Federation, Dominica entered into political association with the United Kingdom in 1967. In 1978 Dominica gained independence from Britain. Prime Minister Mary Eugenia Charles's Freedom party has held power since 1980 on a program of economic reconstruction. Hurricanes in 1979–80 largely destroyed the banana crops of Dominica, already a poor country. The government has attempted to effect economic diversification policies since the disaster.

Dominican Republic
Geography Location: eastern part of island of Hispaniola, which lies between Cuba and Puerto Rico in Caribbean Sea. **Boundaries:** North Atlantic to N, Mona Passage to E, Caribbean Sea to S, Haiti to W. **Total land area:** 18,680 sq. mi. (48,380 sq km). **Coastline:** 800 mi. (1,288 km). **Comparative area:** slightly more than four times size of Washington, D.C. **Land use:** 23% arable land; 7% permanent crops; 43% meadows and pastures; 13% forest and woodland; 14% other; includes 4% irrigated. **Major cities:** (1981) Santo Domingo (capital) 1,313,172; Santiago de los Caballeros 278,638; La Romana 91,571; San Pedro de Macorís 78,562; San Francisco de Macorís 64,906.

People Population: 7,136,748 (1988). **Nationality:** noun—Dominican(s); adjective—Do-

minican. **Ethnic groups:** 73% mixed, 16% white, 11% black. **Languages:** Spanish. **Religions:** 95% Roman Catholic.

Government Type: republic. **Independence:** Feb. 27, 1844 (from Haiti). **Constitution:** Nov. 28, 1966. **National holiday:** Independence Day, Feb. 27. **Heads of government:** Joaquín Balaguer Ricardo, president (since Aug. 1986). **Structure:** president popularly elected for four-year term; bicameral legislature (National Congress—30-seat Senate and 120-seat Chamber of Deputies elected for four-year terms); Supreme Court.

Economy Monetary unit: peso. **Budget:** (1985 est.) *income:* $828 mil.; *expend.:* $750 mil. **GDP:** $5.6 bil., $800 per capita (1986 est.). **Chief crops:** sugarcane, coffee, rice, cocoa, tobacco, corn. **Livestock:** cattle, pigs, goats, horses, asses, mules, sheep. **Natural resources:** nickel, bauxite, gold, silver. **Major industries:** tourism, sugar processing, ferro-nickel and gold mining. **Labor force:** 2.3–2.6 mil. (1986); 49% agriculture, 33% services, 18% industry. **Exports:** $718 mil. (f.o.b., 1986); sugar, nickel, coffee, tobacco, cocoa. **Imports:** $1.4 bil. (c.i.f., 1986); foodstuffs, petroleum, cotton and manufactures, chemicals and pharmaceuticals. **Major trading partners:** (1984) *exports:* 77% U.S., including Puerto Rico; *imports:* 34% U.S., including Puerto Rico.

Intl. Orgs. FAO, G-77, GATT, IAEA, IBRD, ICAO, IDA, IFAD, IFC, ILO, IMF, IMO, INTELSAT, INTERPOL, ITU, UN, UNESCO, UPU, WHO, WMO.

Both the Dominican Republic and Haiti share the island of Hispaniola, which was "discovered" by Christopher Columbus in 1492. In 1795 the French took control of the entire island. The Dominicans declared independence from Haiti in 1844 only to be reclaimed by Spain in 1861. The country regained its independence in 1865. The United States occupied the Dominican Republic between 1916 and 1924. In 1930 Rafael Trujillo set up a dictatorship lasting 31 years. Dominican political strife triggered a U.S. invasion of the country from 1965 to 1966 to end the revolution. Reformist party candidate Joaquín Balaguer Ricardo, president from 1966 to 1978, again won the presidency in 1986.

Ecuador
Republic of Ecuador
Geography Location: northwestern coast of South America. **Boundaries:** Colombia to N, Peru to E and S, Pacific Ocean to W. **Total land area:** 106,860 sq. mi. (276,840 sq km); includes Galapagos Islands. **Coastline:** 1,389 mi. (2,237 km). **Comparative area:** slightly smaller than Nevada. **Land use:** 6% arable land; 3% permanent crops; 17% meadows and pastures; 51% forest and woodland; 23% other; includes 2% irrigated. **Major cities:** (1986 est.) Quito (capital) 1,093,278; Guayaquil 1,509,108; Cuenca 193,012; Machala 137,321; Portoviejo 134,393.

People Population: 10,231,630 (1988). **Nationality:** noun—Ecuadorian(s); adjective—Ecuadorian. **Ethnic groups:** 55% mestizo, 25%

Indian, 10% Spanish, 10% black. **Languages:** Spanish (official), Indian languages, especially Quechua. **Religions:** 95% Roman Catholic.

Government Type: republic. **Independence:** May 24, 1822 (from Spain). **Constitution:** Aug. 10, 1979. **National holiday:** Independence Day, Aug. 10. **Heads of government:** Rodrigo Borja-Cevallos, president (since Aug. 10, 1988). **Structure:** executive; unicameral legislature (Chamber of Representatives); independent judiciary.

Economy Monetary unit: sucre. **Budget:** (1986) *income:* $1,633 mil.; *expend.:* $1,878 mil. **GNP:** $13.1 bil., $1,310 per capita (1986). **Chief crops:** bananas, coffee, cocoa, sugarcane, corn, potatoes, rice; illegal producer of coca for international drug trade. **Livestock:** pigs, cattle, sheep. **Natural resources:** petroleum, fish, timber. **Major industries:** food processing, textiles, chemicals. **Labor force:** 2.8 mil. (1983); 52% agriculture, 20% services, 13% manufacturing. **Exports:** $2.0 bil. (f.o.b., 1987); petroleum, shrimp, fish products, coffee, bananas. **Imports:** $2.1 bil. (c.i.f., 1987); agricultural and industrial machinery, industrial raw materials, building supplies, chemical products, transportation and communication equipment. **Major trading partners:** (1985); *exports:* 54% U.S., 10% Latin America and Caribbean, 4% EC, 2% Japan; *imports:* 33% U.S., 23% EC, 16% Latin America and Caribbean, 12% Japan.

Intl. Orgs. FAO, G-77, IAEA, IBRD, ICAO, IDA, IFAD, IFC, ILO, IMF, IMO, INTELSAT, INTERPOL, ITU, NAM, OAS, OPEC, UN, UNESCO, UPU, WHO, WMO.

The Inca empire maintained control over the territory that is now Ecuador until the arrival of Spanish conqueror Francisco Pizarro in 1532. The Spanish conquistadores quickly dismantled the indigenous political structure, which had been weakened by a series of wars between the Inca chief Atahualpa and his half brother Huáscar. The Spaniards arrived in the Quito region in 1533 and established the city of Guayaquil shortly thereafter. The administrative center of Spanish rule was originally established through the viceroyalty of Peru in 1544, and an *audiencia* (a regional high court under the nominal authority of the viceroy) was established at Quito in 1563. Administrative control of the region was transferred to Bogotá and the viceroyalty of New Grenada in 1718.

The local junta of Quito ousted the audiencia in 1809, but they did not achieve independence for the region until after the military victory of the rebel forces over the royalists at the battle of Pichincha in 1822. Ecuador formed a part of the Confederation of Gran Colombia until the confederation's collapse in 1830. The leader of the forces for independence, Gen. Juan José Flores, removed the country from the Gran Colombian confederation and ruled as dictator until his ouster in 1845. A political rivalry existed between the Liberals of Guayaquil and the Conservatives of Quito, but Conservative dominance of the government lasted until 1895.

During the rule of Conservative Pres. Gabriel García Moreno (1861-75), the Roman Catholic church gained a central place in the political and cultural life of the country. García Moreno tied citizenship requirements to Catholic religious affiliation and brought in the Jesuits to "purify" the country through a new educational program. In 1873 García Moreno dedicated his country to a popular image of Christ, the Sacred Heart of Jesus. The conservative dictator was assassinated in 1875.

In 1895 the Radical Liberal party seized power and held it until 1944. José María Velasco Ibarra, who was in and out of power until 1972, dominated the political scene. Political stability within the country had much to do with the state of the economy. The traditional reliance on cacao production was superseded in the 1950s by a "banana boom," and the discovery of large oil deposits by U.S. corporations in the 1960s led to a shift toward reliance on oil revenues by the following decade. An invasion by Peruvian troops in 1941 led to the loss of almost half of Ecuador's national territory; a simmering hostility has remained between the two countries ever since. Earthquakes in 1987 caused the destruction of the oil pipeline infrastructure and had serious economic consequences for the country.

Military factions kidnapped Pres. León Febres Cordero in 1987, making his release contingent on the granting of amnesty for Lt. Gen. Frank Vargas Pazos, held responsible for two attempted coups against the government. Having secured Gen. Vargas's amnesty, the military released the president. In 1988 Rodrigo Borja, of the Democratic Left party (ID), was elected to the presidency. The new government faces the grave challenge of dealing with Ecuador's $9.4-billion debt.

Egypt
Arab Republic of Egypt
(PREVIOUS NAME: UNITED ARAB REPUBLIC)

Geography Location: northeastern coast of Africa, with an extension across Gulf of Suez into Sinai peninsula, sometimes regarded as lying within Asia. **Boundaries:** Mediterranean Sea to N, Israel to NE, Red Sea to E, Sudan to S, and Libya to W. **Total land area:** 385,229 sq. mi. (997,739 sq km)—inhabited and cultivated territory accounts for 13,587 sq. mi. (35,189 sq km). **Coastline:** 1,523 mi. (2,450 km). **Comparative area:** slightly more than three times size of New Mexico. **Land use:** 3% arable land; 2% permanent crops; 0% meadows and pastures; negl. % forest and woodland; 95% other; includes 2% irrigated. **Major cities:** (1976 census) El-Qahira (Cairo) (capital) 5,074,016; El-Iskandriyah (Alexandria) 2,317,705; El-Giza 1,230,446; Shoubra El-Khiema 394,223; El-Mahalla El-Koubra 292,114.

People Population: 53,347,679 (1988). **Nationality:** noun—Egyptian(s); adjective—Egyptian. **Ethnic groups:** 90% Eastern Hamitic stock, 10% Greek, Italian, Syro-Lebanese. **Languages:** Arabic (official), English and French widely understood by educated classes. **Religions:** (official estimate) 94% Muslim (mostly Sunni), 6% Coptic Christian and other.

Government Type: republic. **Independence:** Feb. 28, 1922 (from UK). **Constitution:** Sept. 11, 1971. **National holiday:** National Day, July 23. **Heads of government:** Mohammed Hosni Mubarak, president (since 1981); Dr. Atef Sidky, prime minister (since Nov. 1986). **Structure:** executive power vested in president, who appoints cabinet; People's Assembly is principal legislative body, with Shura Council having consultative role; independent judiciary administered by minister of justice.

Economy Monetary unit: Egyptian pound. **Budget:** (1987) *income:* $10 bil. *expend.:* $14 bil. (including capital expenditures of $5.2 bil.). **GDP:** $34 bil., $655 per capita (in 1980 dollars). **Chief crops:** fodder, maize, wheat, cotton, rice; not self-sufficient in food. **Livestock:** chickens, ducks, buffalo, cattle, goats. **Natural resources:** crude oil, natural gas, iron ore, phosphates, manganese. **Major industries:** textiles, food processing, tourism. **Labor force:** about 13 mil. (1985); 40-45% agriculture, 36% government (local and national), public sector enterprises and armed forces, 20% privately owned service and manufacturing enterprises (1984); shortage of skilled labor; unemployment about 7% (official est.); about 2 million Egyptians work abroad, mostly in Iraq and Gulf Arab states (1986). **Exports:** $2.9 bil. (f.o.b., 1986); crude petroleum, refined petroleum, raw cotton, cotton yarn, fabric. **Imports:** $11.5 bil. (c.i.f., 1986); foodstuffs, machinery and equipment, fertilizers, wood products, durable consumer goods. **Major trading partners:** U.S., EC, Japan, Eastern Europe.

Intl. Orgs. FAO, G-77, GATT, IAEA, IBRD, ICAO, IDA, IFAD, IFC, ILO, IMF, IMO, INTELSAT, INTERPOL, ITU, NAM, OAU, UN, UNESCO, UPU, WHO, WIPO, WMO; Egypt suspended from Arab League in Apr. 1979.

Civilization began in the fertile valley of the Nile River around 5000 B.C. In about 3200 B.C., King Menes established the first of many dynasties of pharaohs that unified the country from the Nile Delta to Upper Egypt, creating a distinctive ancient civilization of great wealth and cultural brilliance.

The last pharaonic dynasty was overthrown by the Persians in 341 B.C. The Persians in turn were replaced by the Alexandrian and Ptolemaic Greek dynasties and then by the rule of the Roman Empire. Egypt was part of the Byzantine Empire from the third to the seventh centuries A.D., when it was conquered by the Arab Islamic expansion. Arab rule was ended around 1250 when the Mameluke dynasty, of Caucasian origin, established control. The Mamelukes were defeated by the Turks in 1517, and Egypt was incorporated into the Ottoman Empire.

The Suez Canal was built by a French corporation during 1859-69 but was taken over by the British in 1875. This, together with the expansion of the British Empire in East Africa and the Sudan, led to the establishment of de facto British rule in Egypt in 1882, although Egypt remained nominally part of the Ottoman Empire until 1914. A British protectorate was established in Egypt in that year, replaced by a League of Nations Mandate in 1922. The autonomy of the Egyptian monarchy was strengthened in an Anglo-Egyptian treaty of 1936, but Great Britain continued to maintain military forces in Egypt and controlled the Sudan as an Anglo-Egyptian condominium.

Egypt saw heavy fighting between British and Italian and German forces during World War II. After the war, a nationalist movement gained strength. The 1936 treaty was abrogated by Egypt in 1951. An uprising of the Society of Free Officers on July 23, 1952, forced King Farouk to abdicate. A republic was proclaimed on June 18, 1953. Lt. Col. Gamal Abdel Nasser became premier in 1954 and president in 1956.

British troops were withdrawn from the Suez Canal zone in June 1956. On July 26, 1956, Egypt announced the nationalization of the canal. Israel invaded the Sinai Peninsula at the end of October 1956. France and Great Britain landed forces and bombed Egyptian positions; a cease-fire went into effect under U.N. supervision on Nov. 17. A UN peacekeeping force patrolled the border between Egypt and Israel from 1957 to 1967.

Increasing Soviet involvement in Egypt was confirmed in 1956 with the announcement that the USSR would aid Egypt in the construction of the Aswan Dam. The dam, completed in 1971, has provided both irrigation and hydropower but at the cost of extensive environmental damage.

Egypt and Syria joined together as the United Arab Republic in 1958; the union was dissolved in 1961.

Egyptian incursions into the Gaza Strip and the Sharm el Sheikh in early June 1967 led to the outbreak of full-scale war with Israel on June 5. The war ended on June 10 with Israel in full control of Gaza and the Sinai peninsula to the banks of the Suez Canal. Sporadic fighting between Egyptian and Israeli forces continued throughout 1969–70. The Suez Canal remained closed to shipping until 1975.

Nasser died in 1970 and was succeeded by Vice Pres. Anwar Sadat. Sadat concluded a new treaty of friendship with the USSR, but subsequently expelled all Soviet troops and advisers in July 1972.

On Oct. 6, 1973, Egyptian forces crossed the Suez Canal and attacked Israeli positions in the Sinai; simultaneously, Syrian forces attacked Israeli positions in the Golan Heights. Israel drove back the attackers, and the war ended in a cease-fire on Oct. 24.

In 1974 Sadat's government became increasingly friendly to the West, welcoming foreign investment and American aid. In 1974 and 1975 disengagement accords were signed with Israel, providing for the return of the Sinai to Egypt in stages. In November 1977 Sadat visited Jerusalem as a gesture of peace, and a peace treaty between Israel and Egypt was signed (after a series of American-mediated talks at Camp David, Md.) on Mar. 26, 1979. Formal diplomatic relations were established in 1982. As a result of the peace treaty with Israel, Egypt was ostracized by the other nations of the Arab League and attacked by Libyan forces on several occasions along the Egyptian-Libyan border.

Popular unrest fomented by the Moslem Brotherhood in September 1981 led to a military crackdown. Pres. Sadat was assassinated by members of a military conspiracy on Oct. 6, 1981, and was succeeded by Vice Pres. Mohammed Hosni Mubarak. Despite occasional strains, Mubarak's government has remained on friendly terms with both Israel and the United States and has gradually improved relations with the rest of the Arab world.

Egypt has a mixed and rapidly developing economy. The industrial sector is dominated by textiles, petrochemicals, cement, fertilizer, chemicals, mining, and light manufacturing. Egypt is one of the world's largest producers of cotton, and the agricultural sector also includes grain, dates, sugar, citrus fruits, and vegetables. The economy has been hampered by unrestrained population growth, especially in the Cairo megalopolis.

El Salvador
Republic of El Salvador

Geography Location: Pacific coast of Central America. **Boundaries:** Honduras to N and E, North Pacific Ocean to S, Guatemala to W. **Total land area:** 8,260 sq. mi. (21,393 sq km). **Coastline:** 191 mi. (307 km). **Comparative area:** slightly smaller than Massachusetts. **Land use:** 27% arable land; 8% permanent crops; 29% meadows and pastures; 6% forest and woodland; 30% other; includes 5% irrigated. **Major cities:** (1985 est.) San Salvador (capital) 462,652.

People Population: 5,388,644 (1988). **Nationality:** noun—Salvadoran(s); adjective—Salvadoran. **Ethnic groups:** 89% mestizo, 10% Indian, 1% white. **Languages:** Spanish, Nahua (among some Indians). **Religions:** 97% Roman Catholic; activity by Protestant groups throughout country.

Government Type: republic. **Independence:** Sept. 15, 1821 (from Spain). **Constitution:** Dec. 20, 1983. **National holiday:** Independence Day, Sept. 15. **Heads of government:** Alfredo Cristiani, president (since June 1989). **Structure:** executive; Legislative Assembly (60 seats); Supreme Court.

Economy Monetary unit: colón. **Budget:** (1986) *income:* $650 mil.; *expend.:* $790 mil. **GDP:** $4.36 bil., $870 per capita (1985 est.). **Chief crops:** coffee, cotton, corn, sugar, beans, rice, sorghum, wheat. **Livestock:** cattle, pigs, horses, mules, goats, sheep. **Natural resources:** hydropower and geothermal power, crude oil. **Major industries:** food processing, textiles, clothing. **Labor force:** 1.7 mil. (1982 est.); 40% agriculture, 16% manufacturing, 16% commerce, 13% government; shortage of skilled labor and large pool of unskilled labor, but manpower-training programs improving situation; 45% unemployment and underemployment (1987 est.). **Exports:** $755 mil. (f.o.b., 1986); coffee, cotton, sugar, shrimp. **Imports:** $884 mil. (c.i.f., 1986); machinery, intermediate goods, petroleum, construction materials, fertilizers. **Major trading partners:** *exports:* 33% U.S., 15% W. Germany, 12% Guatemala; *imports:* 39% U.S., 18% Guatemala, 9% Mexico.

Intl. Orgs. FAO, G-77, IAEA, IBRD, ICAO, IDA, IFAD, IFC, ILO, IMF, IMO, INTELSAT, INTERPOL, ITU, OAS, UN, UNESCO, UPU, WIPO, WMO.

A number of Indian tribes, of which the Pipil were dominant, originally inhabited the area now called El Salvador. The native population resisted the first attempt at Spanish colonization, begun in 1524, for almost 15 years. In 1821 El Salvador gained its independence from Spain, first as a jurisdiction under the Mexican empire and two years later as a member of the United Provinces of Central America. The Central American Federation collapsed in 1838, and in 1840 El Salvador emerged from a bloody two-year struggle as an independent republic.

The Salvadoran economy came to be dominated by coffee production from the 1860s onward, and a series of laws in the 1880s allowed for concentration of both land ownership and political power in the hands of a coffee oligarchy. In 1931 a reformist president won election, but the military subsequently dismissed him. A revolt ensued (1932) in which 10,000 to 20,000 Salvadorans—mostly peasants—were killed. The apparent result of the massacre, which was called La Matanza, was a period of relative political stability that lasted until the 1970s.

In 1979 a political coup led by a group of junior military officers overthrew Pres. Gen. Carlos Humberto Romero. Owing to the polarization between conservative and reformist political groups, the first two civilian-military juntas resigned as a result of their failure to have their programs implemented by the military. A third government, which included Christian Democrat José Napoleón Duarte, took over on Mar. 5, 1980, on the basis of an armed forces' pledge to carry out an agrarian reform program. In 1980 the coalition of opposition political organizations became the Democratic Revolutionary Front (FDR), and five revolutionary military organizations consolidated under the banner of the Farabundo Marti Front for National Liberation (FMLN). Six social-democratic political leaders were assassinated in November 1980, further cementing the political opposition around the FMLN-FDR coalition. Although the revolutionary opposition called for a "final offensive" to overthrow the political-military structure of rule, this action ultimately failed.

A three-part agrarian reform program was initiated in 1980 in El Salvador. Land redistribution has always been a central political issue in the country, which has a high population density and a majority of the population involved in agriculture. The central part of the agrarian reform, called Phase II, was dropped in 1982 as a result of opposition from the agricultural elite. Phase II was to redistribute most of the land involved in production for export agriculture, including coffee production.

Elections for a constituent assembly took place in March 1982; a majority of seats went to the rightist ARENA coalition. In December 1983 a new constitution went into effect, and in 1984 Christian Democrat José Napoleón Duarte assumed the presidency, which he held until 1989. Christian Democrats achieved another victory in congressional and municipal elections in 1985. Although attempts at negotiation between the warring factions in the Salvadoran civil war began in 1986 and still continue, the fighting has not ceased as of early 1989, and the political stalemate between Left and Right continues.

Equatorial Guinea
Republic of Equatorial Guinea
(PREVIOUS NAME: SPANISH GUINEA)

Geography Location: mainland territory of Río Muni on western coast of Africa and five inhabited islands: Bioko, Corsico, Great Elobey, Small Elobey, and Pagalu. **Boundaries:** Cameroon to N, Gabon to E and S, Gulf of Guinea to W. **Total land area:** 10,831 sq. mi. (28,051 sq km). **Coastline:** 184 mi. (296 km). **Comparative area:** slightly larger than Maryland. **Land use:** 5% arable land; 4% permanent crops; 4% meadows and pastures; 61% forest and woodland; 26% other. **Major cities:** (1983 census) Malabo (capital) 15,323; Bata 24,100.

People Population: 346,839 (1988). **Nationality:** noun—Equatorial Guinean(s); adjective—Equatorial Guinean. **Ethnic groups:** indigenous population of Bioko, primarily Bubi, some Fernandinos; Río Muni, primarily Fang; less than 1,000 Europeans, mostly Spanish. **Languages:** Spanish (official), pidgin English, Fang. **Religions:** nominally Christian, predominantly Roman Catholic, indigenous practices.

Government Type: republic. **Independence:** Oct. 12, 1968 (from Spain). **Constitution:** Aug. 15, 1982. **National holiday:** Oct. 12. **Heads of government:** Col. Teodoro Obiang Nguema Mbasogo, president (since Aug. 1979); Don Cristino Seriche Bioco Malabo, prime minister (since 1989). **Structure:** executive—president with broad powers, prime minister; unicameral legislature—House of Representatives of the People; free judiciary.

Economy Monetary unit: Communauté Financière Africaine (CFA) franc. **Budget:** (1985) *income:* $17.7 mil.; *expend.:* $17.0 mil. **GNP:** $75 mil., $300 per capita (1986); economy destroyed during regime of former Pres. Masie Nguema. **Chief crops:** cash crops—timber and coffee from Río Muni, cocoa from Bioko; food crops—rice, yams, cassava, bananas, oil palm nuts. **Livestock:** sheep, goats, pigs, cattle. **Natural resources:** timber, crude oil, small unexploited deposits of gold, manganese, uranium. **Major industries:** fishing, sawmilling. **Labor force:** (1981) 76% agriculture, 16% services, 8% other; labor shortages on plantations; 58% of population of working age. **Exports:** $16.9 mil. (1982 est.); cocoa, coffee, wood. **Imports:** $41.5 mil. (1982 est.); foodstuffs, chemicals and chemical products. **Major trading partner:** Spain.

Intl. Orgs. FAO, G-77, GATT (de facto), IBRD, ICAO, IDA, IFAD, ILO, IMF, IMO, INTERPOL, ITU, NAM, UN, UNESCO, UPU, WHO.

Equatorial Guinea consists of the Mbini River basin on the West African coast, plus the offshore islands of Bioko and Annobon. Indige-nous Pygmies were displaced beginning in the 17th century by migrations of various peoples that now inhabit the coastal region and by the Fang, who comprise 80 percent of the present population. Bioko is inhabited by Bubis and a Creole population.

Bioko was discovered in 1473 by the Portuguese explorer Fernando Po, and until modern times the island bore his name. Portugal controlled the islands and adjacent mainland, exploiting them for the slave trade, until 1778 when the territory was ceded to Spain. Great Britain established a naval base on Fernando Po island from 1827 to 1843 to combat the slave trade.

Throughout the 19th and early 20th centuries, Equatorial Guinea remained underdeveloped because of conflicting territorial claims and a lack of Spanish investment in the territory. Eventually, however, a plantation system was developed for the cultivation of cocoa, particularly on Bioko, using workers imported from Nigeria.

In 1959 the Spanish territories in the Gulf of Guinea were given status equivalent to a province of Spain. Investment in education, health care facilities, and other social infrastructure, combined with the flourishing plantation economy, made the territory one of the most prosperous and best educated in West Africa. In 1963 the territory's name was changed to Equatorial Guinea, and local autonomy was granted. Full independence came after a UN-supervised referendum in 1968. Riots in the mainland Río Muni Province, protesting the dominance of the economically more advanced Bioko Province, resulted in the promise, but not the delivery of reforms.

Francisco Macias Nguema was elected Equatorial Guinea's first president in 1968. In 1970 he dissolved all opposition parties and declared a one-party state, and in 1971 he abrogated key provisions of the constitution. In 1972, Macias Nguema proclaimed himself president for life and commenced rule by decree. During the next seven years, a reign of terror resulted in the death or exile of one-third of the country's people; through pillage and neglect, industry, roads, hospitals, schools, and other facilities collapsed. Nigerian workers, along with other foreigners, were expelled from the country in 1976; without their labor and technical skills, the economy was quickly ruined.

Macias Nguema was overthrown in August 1979 in a military coup led by his nephew, Lt. Col. Teodoro Obiang Nguema Mbasogo. Macias Nguema was tried and executed a month later. The Spanish-educated Nguema Mbasogo moved to reduce Soviet influence in the country and to improve relations with Spain. A new constitution was approved in a referendum in August 1982; it provided for Nguema Mbasogo to remain in power until the holding of elections, promised for 1989.

As a result of the depredations of the Macias Nguema regime and despite improvements under his successor, Equatorial Guinea is a desperately poor nation. Ninety-five percent of the population is engaged in agriculture; exports of cocoa, coffee, bananas, and timber have recovered somewhat, but the country has yet to regain its preindependence prosperity. The government has sought aid from Spain and other foreign countries to help rebuild the economy.

Ethiopia
(PREVIOUS NAME: ABYSSINIA)

Geography Location: extends inland from eastern coast of Africa. **Boundaries:** Red Sea and Djibouti to NE, Somalia to E and SE, Kenya to S, Sudan to W and NW. **Total land area:** 483,123 sq. mi. (1,251,282 sq km). **Coastline:** 680 mi. (1,094 km). **Comparative area:** slightly less than twice size of Texas. **Land use:** 12% arable land; 1% permanent crops; 41% meadows and pastures; 24% forest and woodland; 22% other; includes negl. % irrigated. **Major cities:** (1984 census) Addis Ababa (capital) 1,412,577; Asmara 275,385; Dire Dawa 98,104; Gondar (including Azeso) 80,886; Nazret 76,284.

People Population: 48,264,570 (1988). **Nationality:** noun—Ethiopian(s); adjective—Ethiopian. **Ethnic groups:** 40% Oromo, 32% Amhara and Tigrean, 9% Sidamo, 6% Shankella. **Languages:** Amharic (official), Tigrinya, Orominga, Arabic; English is major foreign language taught in schools. **Religions:** 40–45% Muslim, 35–40% Ethiopian Orthodox, 15–20% Animist, 5% other.

Government Type: communist state. **Constitution:** Sept. 1987. **National holiday:** Popular Revolution Commemoration Day, Sept. 12. **Heads of government:** Mengistu Haile-Mariam, president (chairman from Sept. 1977 until becoming president Sept. 10, 1987). **Structure:** executive power exercised by president, elected for five-year term by National Assembly (Shengo); 835-member legislature has nominal powers, elected every five years; cabinet selected by prime minister, appointed by president; judiciary at higher levels based on Western pattern, at lower levels on traditional pattern.

Economy Monetary unit: Ethiopian birr. **Budget:** as shares of GDP (1987) *income:* 26%; *expend.:* 36%. **GDP:** $5.4 bil., $110 per capita (1987 est.). **Chief crops:** main crop—coffee; also cereals, pulses, oilseed, meat, hides and skins. **Livestock:** cattle, sheep, goats, asses, horses. **Natural resources:** small reserves of gold, platinum, copper, potash. **Major industries:** cement, textiles, food processing. **Labor force:** 90% agriculture and animal husbandry, 10% government, military, and quasigovernment; 51% of population of working age (1985). **Exports:** $390 mil. (f.o.b., 1987 est.); 60% coffee. **Imports:** $900 mil. (c.i.f., 1987); food. **Major trading partners:** (1985) *exports:* U.S., W. Germany, Djibouti, Japan, S. Yemen. *imports:* USSR, Italy, W. Germany, Japan, UK.

Intl. Orgs. FAO, G-77, IAEA, IBRD, ICAO, IDA, IFAD, IFC, ILO, IMF, IMO, INTELSAT, INTERPOL, ITU, NAM, OAU, UN, UNESCO, UPU, WHO, WMO.

Ethiopia played an important role in the Red Sea trade of the classical world and was mentioned by the Greek historian Herodotus in the fifth century B.C. According to legend, the Ethiopian monarchy was founded by Melelik I, son of Israel's King Solomon and the Queen of Sheba (Sab'a, i.e. North Yemen). Coptic Christianity became Ethiopia's dominant religion in the fourth century A.D. Ethiopia successfully resisted Islamic invasions in the seventh century except in areas along the Red Sea coast but was cut off from the rest of the Christian world by the Islamic states of North Africa and the Middle East.

Portugal established forts and trading stations on the Red Sea coast beginning in 1493, strengthening their domination of trade in the Indian Ocean. The Portuguese also sponsored Roman Catholic missionaries but with little success. A century of religious strife ended with the expulsion of all foreign missionaries in the 1630s. Ethiopia successfully resisted an attempted Italian invasion in 1880.

Ethiopia began to emerge into the modern world under Melelik II (r. 1889–1913). A period of instability after his death ended with the accession in 1930 of Haile Selassie. Italy invaded again in 1936 and soon conquered the entire country. Protests by the League of Nations had no effect; Haile Selassie fled to exile in England. The Italians were driven out during World War II by British and Ethiopian forces, and Haile Selassie returned to his throne.

Civil unrest broke out in February 1974, and Haile Selassie was deposed on Sept. 13, 1974. A coalition of urban elites and the armed forces took over, abolishing the monarchy in 1975 and curbing the power of the Coptic church. Land reform was instituted, and a socialist state proclaimed. In 1977–78 a period of "red terror" resulted in the arrest and execution of thousands of the new regime's opponents. A provisional military council, the Dergue, was confirmed in power under the leadership of Col. Mengistu Haile-Mariam.

A military assistance agreement in 1976 between Ethiopia and the USSR ended an earlier military relationship with the United States; American military advisers were expelled. In 1977 Somalia, taking advantage of Ethiopia's shifting military situation, attacked across the Ogaden desert, aiming to restore certain disputed areas of Ethiopia to Somalia. A massive infusion of Soviet arms and Cuban troops expelled the Somalis in March 1978, but border clashes continued thereafter.

After the expulsion of the Italians during World War II, the province of Eritrea, under a UN plan, was to have become autonomous in a federation with Ethiopia. Instead, Eritrea was made a province of the Ethiopian Empire in 1962. A coalition of Marxist and non-Marxist Eritrean liberation movements has battled ever since for Eritrean independence. Throughout the 1980s Eritrean liberation forces have controlled the province's countryside, while Ethiopian garrisons hold Asmara and other cities. The stalemate in Eritrea has led to continued political instability within Ethiopia, including several unsuccessful coup attempts against the government of the Dergue. Ethiopia has supported insurgent movements in the southern Sudan in an attempt to stop the flow of arms

and aid to the Eritrean rebels through the Sudan.

A Marxist liberation movement, the Tigre People's Liberation Front, has also fought the Ethiopian government to a stalemate in Tigre Province, adjacent to Eritrea.

A series of famines in Ethiopia beginning in 1984 led to widespread suffering and death in many parts of the country despite extensive international aid efforts.

Ethiopia is one of the world's poorest countries. The economy has been extensively disrupted by famine, warfare, and political turmoil. The economy is a mixture of agriculture, small industry, and pastoralism; coffee exports are the country's principal source of foreign exchange.

Fiji

Geography **Location:** more than 300 islands of which 100 are inhabited, situated about 1,300 mi. (2,100 km) N of Auckland, New Zealand, in South Pacific Ocean. **Boundaries:** South Pacific Ocean to N, S, and W; Koro Sea to E; nearest neighbor is Vanuatu, about 600 mi. (1,000 km) to W. **Total land area:** 7,095 sq. mi. (18,376 sq km). **Coastline:** 702 mi. (1,129 km). **Comparative area:** slightly smaller than New Jersey. **Land use:** 8% arable land; 5% permanent crops; 3% meadows and pastures; 65% forest and woodland; 19% other; includes negl. % irrigated. **Major cities:** (1986) Suva (capital) 69,481.

People **Population:** 740,761 (1988). **Nationality:** noun—Fijian(s); adjective—Fijian. **Ethnic groups:** 49% Indian; 46% Fijian, 5% European, other Pacific Islanders, overseas Chinese, and others. **Languages:** English (official), Fijian, Hindustani. **Religions:** Fijians are mainly Christian, Indians are Hindu with Muslim minority.

Government **Type:** military coup leader Col. Sitiveni Rabuka formally declared Fiji a republic Oct. 6, 1987. **Independence:** Oct. 10, 1970 (from UK). **Constitution:** Oct. 10, 1970 (suspended Oct. 1987). **National holiday:** Fiji Day, Oct. 10. **Heads of government:** Ratu Sir Penaia Ganilau, president; Ratu Sir Kamisese Mara, prime minister; both appointed by coup leader Gen. Sitiveni Rabuka in Dec. 1987. **Structure:** executive—prime minister and cabinet; judicial—Supreme Court, court of appeal, magistrate's courts.

Economy **Monetary unit:** Fiji dollar. **Budget:** (1986) *income:* $317 mil.; *expend.:* $326 mil. **GDP:** $1.18 bil., $1,660 per capita (1986). Chief crops: sugar, copra, ginger, rice; major deficiency, grains. **Livestock:** cattle, goats, horses, pigs. **Natural resources:** timber, fish, gold, copper, offshore oil potential. **Major industries:** sugar, copra, tourism. **Labor force:** 176,000 (1979); 40% paid employees; remainder involved in subsistence agriculture. **Exports:** $246 mil. (1986); 55% sugar, 16% gold, 7% fish, 3% molasses, 2% coconut oil. **Imports:** $368 mil. (1986); 23% machinery, 21% manufactured goods, 16% foodstuffs, 16% fuels. **Major trading partners:** (1986) 45% UK, 21% Australia, 8% Malaysia, 6% New Zealand, 5% U.S.

Intl. Orgs. Colombo Plan, EC (associate), FAO, G-77, GATT (de facto), IBRD, ICAO, IDA, IFAD, IFC, ILO, IMF, IMO, INTELSAT, INTERPOL, ITU, UN, UNESCO, UPU, WHO, WIPO, WMO (resigned from Commonwealth Oct. 1986).

First reported to the West by the Dutch navigator A.J. Tasman in 1643, the Fiji Islands were annexed as a British Crown Colony in 1874. Between 1879 and 1916, large numbers of Indian indentured laborers were imported to work on sugar plantations; eventually the original Melanesian inhabitants were outnumbered by persons of Indian descent. Fiji became an independent parliamentary democracy on Oct. 10, 1970, with most land ownership and political power vested in the Fijian minority. A parliamentary election in 1987 brought the Indian party to power; the elected government was ousted in a military coup, and Lt. Col. Sitiveni Rabuka assumed control of the government on May 21, 1987. The coup and its aftermath provoked a constitutional crisis that remains unresolved.

Fiji's economy is based largely on agriculture. Rice, vegetables, and livestock are produced for local consumption; sugar, copra, and ginger are important export crops. Gold and silver mining and limestone quarrying are economically important, as is tourism. There is some light industry. Fuel and most manufactured goods are imported, leading to a persistent balance-of-payments deficit.

Finland
Republic of Finland

Geography **Location:** northern Europe. **Boundaries:** Norway to N, USSR to E, Baltic Sea to S, Gulf of Bothnia and Sweden to W. **Total land area:** 130,559 sq. mi. (338,145 sq km). **Coastline:** 700 mi. (1,126 km) excluding islands and coastal indentations. **Comparative area:** slightly smaller than Montana. **Land use:** 8% arable land; 0% permanent crops; negl. % meadows and pastures; 76% forest and woodland; 16% other; includes negl. % irrigated. **Major cities:** (1986) Helsingfors (Helsinki—capital) 487,521; Tammerfors (Tampere) 169,994; Turku (Åbo) 161,188; Espoo (Esbo) 160,406.

People **Population:** 4,949,716 (1988). **Nationality:** noun—Finn(s); adjective—Finnish. **Ethnic groups:** Finn, Swede, Lapp, Gypsy, Tatar. **Languages:** 93.5% Finnish, 6.3% Swedish (both official); small Lapp- and Russian-speaking minorities. **Religions:** 97% Evangelical Lutheran, 1.2% Eastern Orthodox, 1.8% other.

Government **Type:** republic. **Independence:** Dec. 6, 1917 (from USSR). **Constitution:** July 17, 1919. **National holiday:** Independence Day, Dec. 6. **Heads of government:** Dr. Mauno Koivisto, president (since Jan. 1982); Harri Holkeri, prime minister (since Apr. 1987). **Structure:** executive power is vested in president and coalition cabinet responsible to parliament; legislative authority rests jointly with president and unicameral legislature (Eduskunta); Supreme Court, four superior courts, 193 lower courts.

Economy **Monetary unit:** Finn-mark. **Budget:** (1986) *income:* $21.4 bil.; *expend.:* $20.8 bil. **GNP:** $70.35 bil., $14,290 per capita (1986). **Chief crops:** cereals, sugar beets, potatoes; 85% self-sufficient, but short of food and fodder grains. **Livestock:** poultry, cattle, pigs, reindeer, sheep. **Natural resources:** timber, copper, zinc, iron ore, silver. **Major industries:** metal manufacturing and shipbuilding, forestry and wood processing (pulp, paper), copper refining; shortages—fossil fuels; industrial raw materials (except wood, iron ore); food and fodder grains. **Labor force:** 2.57 mil. (1986); 33.1% services; 22.9% mining and manufacturing; 13.8% commerce; 10.3% agriculture, forestry, and fishing; 5.4% unemployment. **Exports:** $16.36 bil. (f.o.b., 1986); timber, paper and pulp, ships, machinery, clothing, footwear. **Imports:** $15.33 bil. (c.i.f., 1986); foodstuffs, petroleum and petroleum products, chemicals, transport equipment, iron and steel. **Major trading partners:** (1986) *exports:* 37.7% EC (10.3% UK, 9.5% W. Germany), 20.2% USSR, 14.7% Sweden, 5.4% U.S.; *imports:* 42.9% EC (16.9% W. Germany, 6.5% UK), 15.2% USSR, 13.4% Sweden, 4.8% U.S.

Intl. Orgs. CMEA (special cooperation agreement), EC (free trade agreement), EFTA (associate), FAO, GATT, IAEA, IBRD, ICAO, IDA, IFAD, IFC, ILO, IMF, IMO, INTERPOL, ITU, OECD, UN, UNESCO, UPU, WHO, WIPO, WMO.

The Finns are a Uralic-Altaic Asian people, whose language is akin to Mongolian, Turkish, and Hungarian, and closely similar to Estonian. Migrating from western Siberia to what is now Finland in the eighth century, they drove the indigenous Lapps to northernmost Scandinavia. Finland was conquered and Christianized by the Swedes in the 12th century and in the 16th century, became a Swedish grand duchy. Ethnic Swedes make up about 7 percent of the present population. Finland was frequently a battleground in wars between Sweden and Russia; about one-third of the population perished in a war-induced famine in 1696. In 1721 Sweden ceded the province of Viborg to Russia, and all of Finland was taken over by Russia in 1809.

Under the Russians the czars became simultaneously grand dukes of Finland and ruled it as a semiautonomous province. Attempts to "russify" Finland in the later 19th century provoked great popular resistance. When the Russian empire and then the Russian Republic fell in the 1917 Revolution, Finland lapsed into a fierce civil war between Communists and non-Communists. The "whites" under Baron Gustaf Mannerheim were the victors, and Finland became an independent country for the first time in its history.

In 1939 the USSR attacked the Finnish Republic; Finland's resistance in the "Winter War" was heroic but unavailing. Defeated, it was forced to cede Western Keralia to the USSR. After the German invasion of Russia in 1941, fighting between Finland and Russia resumed; England, but not America, declared war on Finland as a cocombatant with Germany. Russia again defeated Finland in 1944 and obliged the Finns to wage war against the German occupying army in northern Finland; much of the country was devastated.

The terms of the 1944 armistice between Finland and the USSR were very harsh: Finland ceded the Petsamo region to the Soviet Union, and thus was cut off from the Barents Sea; the Porkkala peninsula was leased to the Soviets for 50 years, and reparations amounting to 80 percent of Finland's exports were paid in kind. Soviet pressure forced Finland to reject Marshall Plan aid after World War II, but Finland benefited indirectly from the rapid postwar recovery of the Scandinavian region. The gross national product returned to prewar levels by 1947.

Finland's economy had traditionally been centered on timber and other forest products, including pulp and paper, and on small-scale, highly productive agriculture. In the postwar period, industrial development was emphasized; the production of heavy machinery is now the country's leading industry.

In foreign affairs Finland has been a semi-satellite of the Soviet Union. In 1948 the Finns signed a mutual defense pact with the USSR; it was renewed in 1955, 1970, and 1983. Finland's presidents, Juho Paasikivi (1946–56) and Urho Kekkonen (1956–81), although conservative and nationalistic, realized that the country's independence required the avoidance of any appearance of anti-Soviet moves in foreign policy. Economically, Finland is also tied to the USSR, accounting for one-seventh of Finland's exports, and 15 percent of its imports. Finland became a member of Comecon in 1973.

With the establishment of good Soviet-Finnish relations, the Porkkala peninsula was returned to Finland in 1956. Russia has not opposed Finland's gradual development of economic ties with the West. Finland joined the Nordic Council and the United Nations in 1955. It became an associate member of the European Free Trade Association in 1961 and a full member in 1985, and negotiated a free-trade agreement with the EEC in 1973.

With a strong presidency providing stability despite revolving-door coalition governments in the Eduskunta (parliament), and a prudent foreign policy in the shadow of the USSR, Finland has preserved its free economy and civil liberties and has attained a modest prosperity sufficient to support a typically Scandinavian social welfare state.

France
French Republic

Geography **Location:** western Europe. **Boundaries:** English Channel to N, Belgium, Luxembourg, W. Germany, Switzerland, and Italy to E, Mediterranean Sea and Spain to S, Atlantic Ocean to W. **Total land area:** 210,026 sq. mi. (543,965 sq km). **Coastline:** 2,130 mi. (3,427 km). **Comparative area:** slightly more than twice size of Colorado. **Land use:** 32% arable land; 2% permanent crops; 23% meadows and pastures; 27% forest and woodland; 16% other; includes 2% irrigated. **Major cities:** (1982 census) Paris (capital) 2,188,918; Mar-seille (Marseilles) 878,689; Lyon (Lyons) 418,476; Toulouse 354,289; Nice 338,486.

People **Population:** 55,798,282 (1988). **Nationality:** noun—Frenchman (men), Frenchwoman (women); adjective—French. **Ethnic groups:** Celtic and Latin with Teutonic, Slavic, North African, Indochinese, and Basque minorities. **Languages:** French (100% of population); rapidly declining regional dialects (Provençal, Breton, Alsacian, Corsican, Catalan, Basque, Flemish). **Religions:** 90% Roman Catholic, 2% Protestant, 1% Jewish, 1% Muslim (North African workers), 6% unaffiliated.

Government **Type:** republic, with president whose previously wide powers have been somewhat curtailed by current power-sharing arrangement with prime minister. **Constitution:** Sept. 28, 1958, amended concerning election of president in 1962. **National holiday:** National Day, July 14. **Heads of government:** François Mitterrand, president (since May 1981); Jacques Chirac, prime minister (since March 1986). **Structure:** presidentially appointed prime minister heads Council of Ministers, which is formally responsible to National Assembly; bicameral legislature—National Assembly (577 members), Senate (317 members)—restricted by a delaying action; judiciary independent in principle.

Economy **Monetary unit:** French franc. **Budget:** (1988) *income:* $197.4 bil.; *expend.:* $217.5 bil. **GDP:** $724.1 bil., $13,020 per capita (1986). **Chief crops:** cereals, sugar beets, potatoes, wine grapes (western Europe's foremost producer); self-sufficient for most temperate foodstuffs; agricultural shortages include fats and oils, tropical produce. **Livestock:** cattle, pigs, sheep, goats, horses, asses. **Natural resources:** coal, iron ore, bauxite, fish, timber. **Major industries:** steel, machinery and equipment, textiles and clothing. **Labor force:** 24.04 mil. (1987); 39.9% services, 14.7% industry, 6.7% agriculture; 10.2% unemployment; 28.5% other. **Exports:** $124.9 bil. (f.o.b., 1986); machinery and transport equipment, chemicals, foodstuffs, agricultural products, iron and steel products. **Imports:** $129.4 bil. (c.i.f., 1986); crude petroleum, machinery and equipment, agricultural products, chemicals, iron and steel products. **Major trading partners:** (1986) *exports:* 16.1% W. Germany, 11.8% Italy, 9.1% Belgium-Luxembourg, 8.8% UK, 7.4% U.S., 4.9% Netherlands, 4.1% Spain, 1.4% Japan, 1.3% USSR; *imports:* 19.3% W. Germany, 11.6% Italy, 9.4% Belgium-Luxembourg, 7.5% U.S., 6.5% UK, 5.7% Netherlands, 4.1% Spain, 3.6% Japan, 2.1% USSR.

Intl. Orgs. EC, FAO, GATT, IAEA, IBRD, ICAO, IDA, IFAD, IFC, ILO, IMF, IMO, INTELSAT, INTERPOL, ITU, NATO (signatory), OAS (observer), OECD, UN, UNESCO, UPU, WHO, WIPO, WMO.

Pre-Roman France, known as Gaul, was populated by Celtic and Germanic tribes that had displaced earlier populations, probably including the Basques. Its Mediterranean coast had been colonized by Phoenician and Greek traders and was conquered by Rome in the second century B.C. The Roman conquest of all of

Gaul was carried out by Julius Caesar between 58 and 51 B.C. Gaul thereafter became a prosperous and thoroughly Latinized province of the Roman Empire. Christianity was introduced in the first century A.D.

The barbarian invaders of Rome—the Visigoths, Franks, Burgundii, and others—swept through France in the fifth century. In 486 Clovis, chief of the Franks, unified the country and accepted Christianity, but his dynasty, the Merovingians, became fragmented soon after his death. France was invaded by Muslim Saracens in the 7th century, but in 732 Charles Martel defeated the Saracens, making way for a new dynasty. His son, Pepin the Short, overthrew the last Merovingian ruler in 751 and proclaimed himself king. Pepin's son, Charlemagne, greatly expanded his kingdom and was crowned emperor of the West by the Pope in 800.

The rise of feudalism greatly weakened the power of the Carolingian dynasty, as France broke up into estates, some of them effectively independent countries, ruled by great aristocrats. Among the most important were the dukedoms of Aquitaine and Burgundy and the counties of Flanders, Blois, and Anjou. In 911 the Vikings, who had repeatedly raided the Atlantic coast of France, established the duchy of Normandy.

In 987 the Carolingian line died out in France (although it survived in the Holy Roman Empire), and was replaced by a new line, the Capetians, founded by Hugh Capet. Steadily expanding in both territory and power from their base in Paris, the Capetians solidified the foundations of the French monarchy. Paris became a great monastic and university city as well as a center of trade and manufacturing. Under the crusader-king Louis IX (St. Louis), France also became a great international power.

During the 14th century, dynastic struggles led to the Hundred Years' War (1337–1453). The Black Death, peasant rebellions, and war with England further weakened the French monarchy. The Norman conquest of England in 1066 had entwined the fortunes of the French and English monarchies, and with the Capetian line in decline, England pursued its claims in France. Henry V of England defeated the French at Agincourt in 1415, and in 1420 Charles IV made Henry V heir to the throne of France and allied himself with the duchy of Burgundy, under Philip the Good. Henry's forces subsequently were defeated by French armies inspired by Joan of Arc, and in 1429 Henry's claim to the French throne was overturned. In 1435 Burgundy allied itself with France, and in 1453 the English were driven out of France, except for an enclave at Calais.

After the death in 1477 of Charles the Bold of Burgundy, Louis XI completed the consolidation, under the Frence monarchy, of almost all the territory of France. France prospered as a center of commerce, industry, agriculture, learning, and culture throughout the 16th century but was disrupted by religious disputes stemming from the Reformation. The Protestant Henry of Navarre, heir to the throne, was obliged to accept Catholicism before being

crowned in 1594; he became founder of the Bourbon monarchy.

The consolidation of power under a highly centralized monarchy advanced during the reigns of Henry IV's son and grandson, Louis XIII and Louis XIV. France considerably enhanced its power in Europe by defeating the Habsburgs in the Thirty Years' War, 1618–48. Louis XIII and Louis XIV were aided by powerful advisers, Cardinal de Richelieu and Jules Mazarin—both cardinals—and the minister of finance for Louis XIV, Jean Baptiste Colbert. Louis XIV moved the court from Paris to his new palace at Versailles and presided over the wealthiest and most powerful monarchy in Europe.

Louis XIV's persecution of the Huguenots resulted in a great emigration of Protestants from France. A grand alliance of European states thwarted France's expansionist aims on the continent, but under Louis XIV, France became a major colonial power in North America, controlling Canada and Louisiana (which included most of the Mississippi-Missouri valley) and pursued overseas ventures in Africa and Asia as well.

Louis XV inherited a united and powerful France, but one still encumbered by aristocratic, clerical, and guild privileges; both politically and economically, it was far from being a modern state. In the mid-18th century, France was weakened internationally by the expensive and fruitless Wars of the Austrian Succession and the Seven Years' War. Under the Treaty of Paris (1763), France ceded control of Canada to Great Britain. The Enlightenment made France a world center of intellectual activity but also led to the questioning of the political and social bases of the French monarchy. An increasingly wealthy and politically active bourgeoisie chafed under the restrictions of an archaic socioeconomic order.

France under Louis XVI supported the American colonies in the Revolutionary War, incurring a large public debt in the process. Combined with unrestrained extravagance on the part of the court and the aristocracy, poverty increased among the rural peasantry and the urban working class, while the bourgeoisie demanded a greater voice in government. These trends came to a head with the storming of the Bastille on July 14, 1789; soon thereafter, the Estates-General took control of the country, and France was in the throes of revolution.

Revolutionary leaders at first allowed Louis XVI to remain on the throne in a limited monarchy, but the king and Marie Antoinette were subsequently tried for treason and executed in 1793. The Reign of Terror held sway throughout 1793–94, resulting finally in the execution of the revolutionary leaders Augustin Robespierre, Georges Danton, and many others. The Directory, with five heads of each division of government (1795–99), failed to maintain public order and suffered military reverses in foreign wars in which successive revolutionary governments had been embroiled since 1792. On Nov. 9, 1799, the Directory was overthrown by the Consulate, with Napoleon Bonaparte named first consul.

Napoleon proclaimed himself emperor of France in 1804. He transformed French law through the Code Napoleon and initially expanded the French empire in Europe and the Middle East. Suffering repeated reverses against British naval forces and disastrous losses in his 1812 invasion of Russia, Napoleon was defeated by the British under Wellington at Waterloo in 1815, and the French empire collapsed.

Emerging from the revolution as a modern, bureaucratized state dominated by the bourgeoisie, France restored its monarchy in 1815 but not its monarchical absolutism. Charles X, successor to Louis XVIII, was ousted in a coup d'état in 1830 and replaced by the moderate Louis Philippe. The monarchy came to an end in the wave of popular revolt that swept France, along with most of Europe, in 1848; Louis Napoleon became president of the Second Republic. In 1852 he created the Second Empire, ruling as Napoleon III and presiding over a court that set the standards of fashion for the wealthy bourgeois society of 19th-century Europe.

During the 19th century, France again became a major colonial power, acquiring important possessions in North and West Africa and Indochina. It also became a world leader in art, science, and literature and was transformed into a major industrial power. Politically, however, France suffered from endemic weakness. The Second Empire ended disastrously with defeat in the Franco-Prussian War of 1870–71; the Paris Commune, formed during that war, was overthrown with great bloodshed. The Third Republic (1871–1914), despite the glittering pleasures of the Belle Epoque and France's considerable prestige as a world power, was shaken by the Dreyfus Affair of 1894–1906 and ill-served by both its political and military leaders.

France joined with Great Britain and Russia in forming the Triple Entente of 1907, a defensive agreement against the Triple Alliance of Germany, Italy, and the Austro-Hungarian empire. World War I was in effect a war between these two sets of allied powers; in the four years 1914–18, France suffered millions of casualties and severe war damage in the north. Although its role as a leader of the victorious alliance was confirmed at the Versailles Conference of 1919, France was seriously weakened by the war and played a diminished role as a world power in the postwar era.

France suffered badly in the world depression of the 1930s and could muster neither political nor military energy to offer effective opposition to the rise of Nazi Germany and fascist Italy. France was a participant in the Munich Agreement of 1938, which sealed the fate of central Europe. When World War II broke out in 1939, Hitler initially held off his attack on France, but when it came in May-June 1940, France was swiftly and ignominiously defeated.

During World War II, northern France was under German occupation, while in the south a collaborationist, semifascistic state was organized, with its capital at Vichy. Meanwhile, in London, Gen. Charles de Gaulle rallied the Free

French forces, which fought on the allied side in various campaigns. During the war de Gaulle's followers drew up a Constitution for a Fourth Republic; following France's liberation and the war's end, the Free French forces assumed power, and the Constitution was ratified in 1946.

Although it suffered from inherent political weaknesses and often failed to provide stable cabinets, the Fourth Republic presided over postwar recovery, aided by the Marshall Plan; it promoted a mixed socialist–free enterprise economy and instituted social reforms such as women's suffrage and social security. It also led the way toward a united Europe, playing a leading role in the organization of the EEC in 1957. Despite a 20–year alliance with the Soviet Union concluded in 1944, France became a founding member of NATO in 1949.

The Fourth Republic was unable, however, to withstand the strains of the dismantling of France's empire during the postwar wave of decolonization. France's recovery of Indochina in 1945 set off a war of national liberation there that lasted until France withdrew from the colony in 1954. Rebellions in Morocco and Tunisia led to their independence in 1956; in Algeria, regarded as part of France itself, the rebels fought on.

The Algerian war seriously polarized French public opinion, and, threatened with an army coup, the National Assembly voted in 1958 to grant Pres. Charles de Gaulle emergency powers for six months. De Gaulle outmaneuvered his army backers and negotiated to turn Algeria over to the Algerians, a process completed in 1962. Meanwhile he also restored order at home and presided over the drafting of a new constitution that created the Fifth Republic in 1958.

The new Constitution created a strong presidency, with powers to name the premier and the Council of Ministers and to preside over their meetings. The legislature was required to give priority to government initiatives and lacked authority over national defense, education, labor, and local government. Under the governments of Premiers Michel Debré and Georges Pompidou, the Gaullist regime further advanced modernization of French industry and greatly benefited French agriculture by expanding the Common Market to include agricultural as well as industrial goods.

De Gaulle followed an independent foreign policy, pursuing European integration as well as closer relations with the Communist bloc and the Third World without American interference. He blocked British entry into the Common Market; developed an independent nuclear force, refusing to sign nuclear test-ban and nonproliferation treaties; pursued a historic rapprochement with Germany; recognized the People's Republic of China; established a leading French role in the former French colonies of Africa; and withdrew French forces from the NATO military command.

Reelected president in 1965, after a runoff election against the Socialist-Communist alliance candidate François Mitterrand, de Gaulle continued his independent policy until student riots in early 1968 provoked police repression, which led to further popular support for the students, especially in Paris. De Gaulle dissolved the National Assembly and, in an emotional campaign on behalf of national stability, won a new electoral majority. In 1969, however, following political reverses, de Gaulle resigned as president.

The elections of June 1969 gave the presidency to former premier Georges Pompidou, who died in office in April 1974. He was succeeded by the Independent Republican Valery Giscard d'Estaing, who served until May 1981. During these years the Gaullist heritage was developed and consolidated. In foreign policy the movement toward European unity continued with the development of the European Parliament and, in a reversal of policy in 1973, French support for British membership in the EEC. The economic shock of the OPEC price rises of 1973–74 led to a decision to stress new industrial ventures in high-technology fields, symbolized by the Anglo-French Concorde supersonic transport.

An aging population and the expansion of welfare provisions put a strain on the economy. The 1970s were years of social ferment, with a relaxation of divorce laws and the legalization of contraception and abortion, and a decline in church membership and attendance. In 1978 disillusionment stemming from inflation and social difficulties under Giscard d'Estaing brought about a leftist electoral victory for the first time under the Fifth Republic.

The Gaullist era came to an end in 1981, when Socialist François Mitterrand defeated Giscard in a presidential election. Giscard immediately dissolved the National Assembly, and in the ensuing election, the Gaullists won a popular majority and formed a coalition cabinet with the Communists. Mitterrand's government pursued an aggressive program of nationalization of banks and major industries and reform of local government. Continued economic difficulties led to a loss of popular support for Mitterrand's policies; and in the elections of 1986, Jacques Chirac's coalition of Gaullists and Giscardists won an absolute majority in the National Assembly, and Chirac became premier—the first time since 1958 that the president and the premier were of opposing parties. An accommodation was worked out in which Mitterrand concentrated on foreign affairs, and Chirac on domestic matters. Mitterrand oversaw a restoration of French military cooperation with NATO and a continuation of Franco-German cooperation, supported Chad in its war with Libya, and attempted to find a settlement in the mineral-rich French Overseas Territory of New Caledonia, where an armed separatist movement of native Kanaks has been bitterly opposed by French settlers, who form a majority of the island's population.

At home Chirac and his party reversed Mitterrand's policy of nationalization of banking and industry, cut taxes, and brought about a significant reduction in the inflation rate. Chirac ran for president against Mitterrand in 1988 but was defeated, leading to a continuation of the leftist-rightist "cohabitation government."

Despite postwar decolonization, France continues to control a far-flung, though geographically small, empire around the world. It has five "overseas departments," politically an integral part of France: French Guiana, on the northeastern coast of South America; the Caribbean islands of Guadaloupe and Martinique; St. Pierre and Miquelon, off the coast of Newfoundland; and Mayotte, part of the Comoros group in the Indian Ocean. France also controls a number of "overseas territories," including New Caledonia, French Polynesia, the Wallis and Fortuna Islands—all in the Pacific—and the French Southern and Antarctic Lands, comprising territories in Antarctica and adjacent waters of the Indian Ocean.

Gabon
Gabonese Republic

Geography Location: equatorial country on western coast of Africa. **Boundaries:** Equatorial Guinea to NW, Cameroon to N, Congo to E and S, Atlantic Ocean to W. **Total land area:** 103,347 sq. mi. (267,667 sq km). **Coastline:** 550 mi. (885 km). **Comparative area:** slightly smaller than Colorado. **Land use:** 1% arable land; 1% permanent crops; 18% meadows and pastures; 78% forest and woodland; 2% other. **Major cities:** (1975) Libreville (capital) 251,400; Port-Gentil 77,611; Lambaréné 22,682.

People Population: 1,051,937 (1988). **Nationality:** noun—Gabonese (sing., pl.); adjective—Gabonese. **Ethnic groups:** about 40 Bantu groups, including four major tribal groupings (Fang, Eshira, Bapounou, Bateke); about 100,000 expatriate Africans and Europeans, including 27,000 French. **Languages:** French (official), Fang, Myene, Bateke, Bapounou/Eshira, Bandjabi. **Religions:** 55–75% Christian, less than 1% Muslim, remainder indigenous beliefs.

Government Type: republic; one-party presidential regime since 1964. **Independence:** Aug. 17, 1960 (from France). **Constitution:** Feb. 21, 1961, revised Apr. 15, 1975. **National holiday:** Renovation Day, Mar. 12; Independence Day, Aug. 17. **Heads of government:** El Hadj Omar Bongo, president (since Dec. 1967); Léon Mebiame, prime minister (since Apr. 1975). **Structure:** power centralized in president, elected by universal suffrage for seven-year term; unicameral legislature—93-member National Assembly, including nine members chosen by Omar Bongo, has limited powers; constitution amended in 1979 so that assembly deputies will serve five year terms; independent judiciary.

Economy Monetary unit: Communauté Financière Africaine (CFA) franc. **Budget:** (1984) *income:* $1.25 bil.; *expend.:* $1.31 bil. **GNP:** $3.3 bil., $3,300 per capita (1986). **Chief crops:** cash crops—cocoa, coffee, wood, palm oil, rice; food crops—pineapples, bananas, manioc, peanuts, root crops; imports food. **Livestock:** pigs, sheep, goats, cattle. **Natural resources:** crude oil, manganese, uranium, gold, timber, iron ore. **Major industries:** sawmills, petroleum, food, beverages; mining of increasing importance, especially for manganese and uranium. **Labor force:** 120,000 (1983); 65%

agriculture, 30% industry and commerce; 58% of population of working age. **Exports:** $1.5 bil. (f.o.b., 1986 est.); crude petroleum, wood and wood products, minerals (manganese, uranium concentrates, gold). **Imports:** $0.8 bil. (c.i.f., 1986 est.); mining, road-building machinery, electrical equipment, transport vehicles, foodstuffs, textiles. **Major trading partners:** France, U.S., W. Germany.

Intl. Orgs. FAO, G-77, GATT, IAEA, IBRD, ICAO, IDA, IFAD, IFC, ILO, IMF, IMO, INTELSAT, INTERPOL, ITU, NAM, OPEC, UN, UNESCO, UPU, WHO, WIPO, WMO.

Gabon, an equatorial nation largely covered by dense rain forest, is inhabited by a highly diverse mixture of people who migrated into the region over the course of the past 700 years; the now dominant Fang arrived during the 19th century. The first Europeans to reach the area were the Portuguese in the 15th century; they were followed by Dutch, French, and British traders in the 16th century. All engaged in the slave trade.

France established an informal protectorate in 1839–41 and set about suppressing the slave trade. In 1849 a group of freed slaves settled near the American mission station at Baraka and renamed the town Libreville. Various French explorers, including Pierre Savorgnan de Brazza, explored Gabon during the later 19th century. France occupied Gabon in 1885 and established a colonial administration in 1903.

In 1910 the French authorities confederated the territories of Gabon, Middle Congo, Ubangi-Shari (later the Central African Republic), and Chad to form French Equatorial Africa. The territory became an important base of Free French activity during World War II.

In 1944 Gen. Charles de Gaulle rewarded the territory with a pledge of political reforms. In 1946 French citizenship was granted to the territory's inhabitants, and local power was devolved upon advisory assemblies. In 1959 French Equatorial Africa was dissolved; Gabon became fully independent on Aug. 17, 1960.

Gabon has remained politically stable under its 1961 constitution. Gabon's first president, Leon M'Ba, was briefly deposed by a military coup in 1964 but quickly reinstated with the aid of French troops. He died in 1967 and was succeeded by the vice president, Omar Bongo. Bongo combined all political parties into the Gabonese Democratic party in 1968, was elected president in his own right in 1975, and was reelected in 1979 (to a seven-year term) and in 1986.

Gabon is rich in natural resources, including petroleum, manganese, uranium, and timber. Petroleum exports account for 60 percent of foreign earnings. The country was badly hit by the fall in petroleum prices in the early 1980s, but the economy remained fundamentally sound, and in 1988 foreign creditors agreed to a restructuring of the country's external debt. Prospects for increased petroleum production, as well as expanded exploitation of other resources, seem bright. The country is underdeveloped agriculturally, however, and imports 90 percent of its food.

Unlike many African countries, Gabon is relatively underpopulated. It has a large corps of well educated people, including 18,000 French residents (up from 5,000 in 1959). Plans for future economic development revolve around expanding the country's infrastructure, notably the TransGabon Railway (the third stage of which was completed in 1986) and a national highway network, as well as attracting increased foreign investment.

The Gambia
Republic of The Gambia
Geography Location: narrow territory around Gambia River on northwestern coast of Africa. **Boundaries:** Senegal to N, E, and S, Atlantic Ocean to W. **Total land area:** 4,361 sq. mi. (11,295 sq km). **Coastline:** 50 mi. (80 km). **Comparative area:** slightly more than twice size of Delaware. **Land use:** 16% arable land; 0% permanent crops; 9% meadows and pastures; 20% forest and woodland; 55% other; includes 3% irrigated. **Major cities:** (1983 census) Banjul (capital) 44,188; Serrekunda 68,433; Brikama 19,584; Bakau 19,309; Farafenni 10,168.

People Population: 779,488 (1988). **Nationality:** noun—Gambian(s); adjective—Gambian. **Ethnic groups:** 42% Mandinka, 18% Fula, 16% Wolof, 10% Jola, 9% Serahuli, 1% non-Gambian, 4% other. **Languages:** English (official), Mandinka, Wolof, Fula, other indigenous vernaculars. **Religions:** 90% Muslim, 9% Christian, 1% indigenous beliefs.

Government Type: republic; on Feb. 1, 1982, The Gambia and Senegal formed a loose confederation named Senegambia that calls for eventual integration of their armed forces and economic cooperation. **Independence:** Feb. 18, 1965 (from UK). **Constitution:** Apr. 24, 1970; formally signed agreement of confederation with Senegal Dec. 12, 1981 (effective Feb. 1, 1982) named Senegambia. **National holiday:** Independence Day, Feb. 18. **Heads of government:** Alhaji Sir Dawda Kairaba Jawara, president (since Feb. 1970). **Structure:** unicameral legislature—43-member parliament in which four seats are reserved for tribal chiefs, four are government-appointed, 35 are elected for five-year terms; judiciary.

Economy Monetary unit: dalasi. **Budget:** (1983 est.) *income:* $44.2 mil.; *expend.:* $34.9 mil. **GDP:** $125 mil., $260 per capita (1985). **Chief crops:** peanuts, millet, sorghum, rice, maize. **Livestock:** cattle, goats, sheep, pigs, asses. **Natural resources:** fish. **Major industries:** peanut processing, tourism, beverages. **Labor force:** 165,000 (1983 est.); 75.0% agriculture, 18.9% industry, commerce, and services; 55% of population of working age. **Exports:** $59 mil. (f.o.b., 1985 est.); peanuts and peanut products, fish, palm kernels. **Imports:** $73 mil. (f.o.b., 1985 est.); textiles, foodstuffs, tobacco, machinery, petroleum products, chemicals. **Major trading partners:** EC countries, African countries.

Intl. Orgs. Commonwealth, FAO, G-77, GATT, IBRD, ICAO, IDA, IFAD, IFC, IMF, IMO, ITU, NAM, UN, UNESCO, UPU, WHO, WMO.

Portuguese explorers first made contact with The Gambia in the 15th century when it was part of the Kingdom of Mali. Gold-seekers and slave traders did not settle the area, however, until the 16th century. In 1588 exclusive rights to the Gambia River were sold to English merchants, and in 1618 King James I granted a land charter to a British company to trade and settle there. England and France struggled for 200 years to gain political and economic control over the territory, but in 1783 the French ceded Great Britain possession of The Gambia. The British abolished the slave trade in 1807. The Gambia's present boundaries were established in 1889 when it became a British Crown Colony. Between 1901 and 1906, legislative councils were established to encourage self-government, and slavery within the country was abolished.

During World War II, Gambian troops fought with the British in Burma, and The Gambia was a stop for British and American aircraft. After World War II the country moved quickly toward constitutional government. Elections were held in 1962, and in 1963 full self-government was granted. On Feb. 18, 1965, The Gambia achieved complete independence as a constitutional monarchy in the British Commonwealth of Nations. In November of that year, a proposal to change the nation to a republic was defeated. The proposal was voted on again in 1970 and passed; The Gambia became a republic on Apr. 24, 1970.

Germany, East
German Democratic Republic
(ABBREV.: GDR OR GERMANY, DR)
(PREVIOUS NAME: GERMANY)
Geography Location: eastern Europe. **Boundaries:** Baltic Sea to N, Poland to E, Czechoslovakia to SE, W. Germany to SW and W. **Total land area:** 41,828 sq. mi. (108,333 sq km). **Coastline:** 560 mi. (901 km). **Comparative area:** slightly smaller than Tennessee. **Land use:** 45% arable land; 3% permanent crops; 12% meadows and pastures; 28% forest and woodland; 12% other; includes 2% irrigated. **Major cities:** (1985 est.) E. Berlin (capital) 1,215,600; Leipzig 553,700; Dresden 519,800; Karl-Marx-Stadt (Chemnitz) 315,500; Magdeburg 285,000.

People Population: 16,596,875 (1988). **Nationality:** noun—German(s); adjective—German. **Ethnic groups:** 99.7% German, 0.3% Slavic and other. **Languages:** German, Sorbian. **Religions:** 47% Protestant, 7% Roman Catholic, 46% unaffiliated or other; less than 5% of Protestants and 25% of Roman Catholics are active participants.

Government Type: communist state. **Constitution:** Apr. 9, 1968, amended Oct. 7, 1974. **National holiday:** Foundation of German Democratic Republic, Oct. 7. **Heads of government:** Erich Honecker, chairman, Council of State (since Oct. 1976); Willi Stoph, chairman, Council of Ministers (premier, since Oct. 1976). **Structure:** executive—Council of State, Council of Ministers; unicameral legislature—Volkskammer (People's Chamber, elected directly); judiciary—Supreme Court; entire structure dominated by Socialist Unity (Communist) party.

Economy Monetary unit: mark. **Budget:** N.A. **GNP:** $187.5 bil., $11,300 per capita (1986). **Chief crops:** potatoes, rye, wheat, barley, oats; shortages—grain, vegetables, vegetable oil. **Livestock:** poultry, pigs, cattle, sheep, beehives. **Natural resources:** brown coal, potash, uranium, copper, natural gas. **Major industries:** metal fabrication, chemicals, brown coal; shortages—coking coal, coke, crude oil, rolled-steel products, nonferrous metals. **Labor force:** 8.96 mil. (1986); 37.7% industry, 21.0% services, 10.8% agriculture and forestry, 10.3% commerce. **Exports:** $27.9 bil. (f.o.b., 1986 est.). **Imports:** $27.6 bil. (f.o.b., 1986 est.). **Major trading partners:** (1985) 65.9% socialist countries, 30.7% developed West, 3.4% developing countries.

Intl. Orgs. CMEA, IAEA, ILO, IMO, ITU, UN, UNESCO, UPU, Warsaw Pact, WHO, WIPO, WMO.

(For pre–World War II background, see "Germany, West.")

Even before the fighting in Germany subsided in 1945, the Soviet Air Force brought Walter Ulbricht, the exiled leader of the German Communist party, back to the USSR's zone of occupation in Germany. Backed by 20 Soviet divisions, Ulbricht and the party commenced the communization of the eastern zone. Other parties were abolished, and the Communist party itself was purged of non-Stalinists in preparation for elections, eventually held in 1950; the Communist vote was a reported 99.7 percent.

While Ulbricht attempted to collectivize agriculture and plan industrial development in the eastern zone, the Soviet Union extracted heavy reparations payments from Germany, bringing on an acute economic crisis. In June 1953, three months after Joseph Stalin's death, strikes and riots erupted; order was quickly restored. Soon afterward, the USSR renounced further reparation payments and declared East Germany a sovereign state.

By 1963 East Germany had become the second-largest industrial power in Eastern Europe, and in 1968 it surpassed Czechoslovakia in output. A significant shift of labor to industry reduced the farm population to under 20 percent of total population by 1960. Farming became mechanized and, with more use of fertilizer and irrigation, more productive, though still relatively inefficient; East Germany remains a net importer of grain, meat, and vegetables.

Although East Germany enjoyed prestige within the Eastern bloc as an industrial power, the steady stream of emigrants to West Germany told a different story. When, after a renewed collectivization policy was implemented in 1960, the stream became a flood, East Germany responded by building the Berlin Wall. The wall was a visible sign of political failure, but it did slow the stream of emigration to a trickle.

As Ulbricht grew old and ill, he was replaced in May 1971 as party first secretary by Erich Honecker, who also became head of state in 1976. Honecker built on the Ulbricht legacy by completing state ownership of all industry in 1972 and grouping industries into 133 giant monopolies known as Kombinate, each covering one industrial sector and vertically integrated from research to sales. In recent years industrial planning has shifted away from heavy industry and toward high technology, such as computers and machine tools.

East Germany has resisted Mikhail Gorbachev's reform policies in the 1980s, trying to establish itself as a model of old-style communism in Eastern Europe. Plainly, the regime also fears the political consequences of economic reform.

Since the "opening to the east" (*Ostpolitik*) of Willi Brandt (see "Germany, West"), the two Germanies have grown closer, at least economically. East Germany's trade with West Germany, regarded as "intranational" by Bonn, gives it access to the EEC. In 1987 Honecker became the first East German head of state to visit West Germany, where he was cordially received by Chancellor Helmut Kohl.

Germany, West
Federal Republic of Germany
(ABBREV.: FRG OR GERMANY, FR)
(PREVIOUS NAME: GERMANY)
Geography Location: central Europe. **Boundaries:** Denmark to N., E. Germany and Czechoslovakia to E., Austria and Switzerland to S., France, Luxembourg, Belgium, and Netherlands to W., and North Sea to NW. **Total land area:** 96,027 sq. mi. (248,708 sq km). **Coastline:** 925 mi. (1,488 km). **Comparative area:** slightly smaller than Oregon. **Land use:** 30% arable land; 1% permanent crops; 19% meadows and pastures; 30% forest and woodland; 20% other; includes 1% irrigated. **Major cities:** (1986 est.) Bonn (capital) 290,800; W. Berlin 1,868,700; Hamburg 1,575,700; München (Munich) 1,269,400; Köln (Cologne) 914,000.

People Population: 60,980,202 (1988). **Nationality:** noun—German(s); adjective—German. **Ethnic groups:** primarily German; Danish minority. **Languages:** German. **Religions:** 45% Roman Catholic, 44% Protestant, 11% other.

Government Type: federal republic. **Constitution:** May 23, 1949; provisional constitution known as Basic Law. **National holiday:** N.A. **Heads of government:** Richard von Weizsäcker, president (since July 1984); Dr. Helmut Kohl, chancellor (since Oct. 1982). **Structure:** executive—president (titular head of state), chancellor (executive head of government); bicameral parliament—Bundesrat (Federal Council, upper house), Bundestag (National Assembly, lower house); judiciary—independent.

Economy Monetary unit: mark. **Budget:** (1986) *income:* $110.6 bil.; *expend.:* $121.3 bil. **GNP:** $908.3 bil., $14,890 per capita (1986). **Chief crops:** grains, potatoes, sugar beets; 75% self-sufficient. **Livestock:** chickens, pigs, cattle, ducks, sheep. **Natural resources:** iron ore, coal, potash, timber. **Major industries:** among world's largest producers of iron, steel, coal, cement, chemicals, machinery, ships, vehicles, machine tools, electronics, food and beverages; shortages—fats and oils, pulses, tropical products, sugar, cotton, wool, rubber, petroleum, iron ore, bauxite, nonferrous metals, sulfur. **Labor force:** 27.83 mil. (1986 est.); 41.6% industry, 34.7% services and other, 18.2% trade and transport; 8.9% unemployment (1987). **Exports:** $243 bil. (f.o.b., 1986); 86.1% manufactures (includes machines and machine tools, chemicals, motor vehicles, iron and steel products), 5.1% agricultural products, 2.3% raw materials, 1.3% fuels, 4.9% other. **Imports:** $191.0 bil. (f.o.b., 1986); 65.6% manufactures, 12.7% agricultural products, 11.5% fuels, 7.6% raw materials, 2.7% other. **Major trading partners:** (1986) 50.9% EC (11.6% France, 9.9% Netherlands, 8.6% Italy, 7.9% UK, 7.1% Belgium-Luxembourg), 11.1% non-OPEC developing countries, 8.7% U.S., 6.2% communist countries, 3.3% OPEC.

Intl. Orgs. EC, FAO, GATT, IAEA, IBRD, ICAO, IDA, IFAD, IFC, ILO, IMF, IMO, INTELSAT, INTERPOL, ITU, NATO, OAS (observer), OECD, UN, UNESCO, UPU, WHO, WIPO, WMO.

The ancient tribes of Germany resisted Roman conquest with mixed success. German mercenaries served in the Roman legions, and Germanic invasions contributed to the fall of Rome. Most of Germany was united within the empire of Charlemagne. Divided among his three sons in 843, the empire's eastern regions became the heart of the Germanies. The Holy Roman Empire, founded in 962, gave some unity to the politically fragmented German territories, but its boundaries included more than Germany, and some Germans remained outside it. But that unity was fragile; the Holy Roman emperor was a feudal overlord rather than a ruler, and hundreds of separate political bodies coexisted within the imperial domain. Along the North Sea and Baltic coasts, the Hanseatic League controlled much of the commerce of northern Europe.

With the Reformation in the 16th century, religious divisions added to Germany's existing political fragmentation and local allegiances. The Thirty Years' War (1618–48) resulted in the virtual extinction of the Holy Roman Empire and left Germany without even a shadow of unity.

After the Napoleonic Wars, in which much of Germany was conquered by France, the Congress of Vienna (1814–15) sanctioned the creation of a German League to succeed the Holy Roman Empire. The league consisted of 39 states, including five substantial kingdoms and the Austro-Hungarian empire. Prussia, one of the five kingdoms, had already risen to prominence under Frederick the Great in the 18th century. In a series of wars in the mid-19th century, Prussia conquered the other German states; after defeating France in the Franco-Prussian War of 1870–71, Prussia declared the establishment of the German empire. Under its chancellor, Otto von Bismarck, Germany became a major European power in the late 19th century, with a booming industrial economy, flourishing agriculture, an expanding colonial empire, and growing military might.

The German empire reached its height under Kaiser Wilhelm II on the eve of World War I. Germany's disastrous defeat in that war was compounded by the harsh terms of the Treaty of Versailles (1919), which stripped Germany of its colonial empire, awarded part of Schleswig to Denmark, Alsace-Lorraine to France, and part of Prussia to Poland, and abolished the German monarchy.

The Weimar Republic, established in 1919, gradually overcame economic difficulties, including ruinous inflation, to achieve a measure of postwar recovery in the 1920s. The republic was, however, disrupted by labor strife, political fragmentation, and the rise of armed extremist political movements on both Left and Right. After the onset of the world economic depression in 1929, Adolf Hitler's National Socialist movement gained increasing power, both at the polls and through open thuggery against its opponents. Hitler's appointment as chancellor in 1933 effectively put an end to the Weimar Republic as a functioning democracy.

The onset of World War II in Europe was presaged by Hitler's annexation of Austria and Czechoslovakia in 1938 and precipitated by the German invasion of Poland in 1939. Early military successes gave Germany control of most of Europe, but the eventual victory of the Allied powers in 1945 left the country exhausted and in ruins. Much of the Jewish population of Germany, and of other territories under German control, had been killed during the Holocaust of World War II. German cities were reduced to rubble, and a quarter of the country's homes were uninhabitable. Famine and fuel shortages added to the general misery.

Politically, Germany had essentially ceased to exist in 1945. The Allies divided the country into four zones of occupation, with a similar four-part division of Berlin. As the Cold War rift between the Western powers and the USSR intensified during the late 1940s, so too the division of Germany hardened. In 1948 the USSR imposed a blockade on West Berlin; the city was supplied by a massive airlift from the West for several months. In 1949 two Germanies were created: the German Democratic Republic in the Russian zone in the east, and the Federal Republic of Germany in the Allied zone in the west.

The Federal Republic was largely the creation of one man, Konrad Adenauer. A veteran pre-Hitler politician, he founded the Federation of Christian Democratic Parties (CDU-CSU) in 1945, and as president of the Parliamentary Council formed during the occupation, he virtually wrote the new constitution for West Germany. In the first elections held in the Federal Republic (August 1949), the CDU-CSU won a parliamentary majority in the Bundestag, and Adenauer became chancellor, a post he held for 14 years. In 1951 the Western powers formally concluded a peace treaty with West Germany.

In foreign affairs Adenauer relied heavily on friendship with the United States and reconciliation with France. He also supported European integration: In 1951 West Germany joined both the Council of Europe and the Coal and Steel Community. West Germany was admitted to NATO in 1955 and in 1957 became one of the six founding members of the EEC.

In domestic affairs the political alliance between Adenauer and Ludwig Erhard led to political stability and the creation of a market-driven economy. With a currency reform program and Marshall Plan aid in place by 1948 under occupation administration, the stage was set for Germany's "economic miracle" of the 1950s. Between 1949 and 1964, industrial production increased by 60 percent and gross national product tripled, while unemployment fell to 1 percent, even as millions of refugees from East Germany were integrated into the West Germany economy. In the same period, over 8 million houses and apartments were constructed.

In the early 1960s, tensions between West and East Germany increased, as East Germany constructed the Berlin Wall (1961) to stem the flow of refugees to the West. In 1963 Erhard succeeded Adenauer as chancellor. Economic growth slowed to an annual 3 percent rate, but West Germany had already become one of Europe's strongest economic powers, with not only full employment but also jobs for hundreds of thousands of "guest workers" from southern Europe and Turkey.

Erhard resigned in 1966 when his coalition fell apart over the issue of a planned tax increase. He was succeeded by Kurt Kiesinger, who as chancellor presided over a historic "great coalition" of Christian Democrats and Social Democrats. The latter party, under its leader Willi Brandt (who served as deputy chancellor and foreign minister), had by then shifted its orientation from a Marxist party to a reformist, market-oriented stance.

Elections in 1966 produced a Social Democratic majority, which endured until 1982; Brandt succeeded Kiesinger as chancellor. Brandt pursued an "opening to the East," regularizing relations with East Germany, signing a nonaggression pact with the USSR, and recognizing the border between East Germany and Poland. But domestically, West Germany suffered serious dislocations from the OPEC oil price increases of the early 1970s; inflation reached almost 8 percent. Revelations that a Brandt aide was an East German spy led to his replacement as chancellor by Helmut Schmidt in 1974.

Schmidt continued Brandt's eastern policy but also pursued improved relations with the West. Economic difficulties persisted, however, and Schmidt's government fell in 1982. The Christian Democrats returned to power under chancellor Helmut Kohl. The general improvement of the world economy in the 1980s led to economic recovery in Germany, boosting Kohl's popularity; however, his agreement to allow the United States to deploy cruise missiles and Pershing-2 ballistic missiles provoked a political outcry. The 1980s saw the rise to political prominence (though not to power) of the pacifist-environmentalist Green party.

Throughout the 1970s and 1980s, Germany has been disrupted by terrorism, both homegrown (the Baader-Meinhoff Gang) and foreign, most notably the massacre of Israeli athletes by PLO terrorists at the 1972 Munich Olympics. In 1989 relations between the United States and West Germany were shaken by revelations that West German firms had supplied equipment for an alleged chemical warfare plant in Muammar al-Qaddafi's Libya.

Ghana
Republic of Ghana
(PREVIOUS NAME: GOLD COAST)

Geography Location: western coast of Africa. **Boundaries:** Burkina Faso to N, Togo to E, Gulf of Guinea to S, Ivory Coast to W. **Total land area:** 92,100 sq. mi. (238,537 sq km). **Coastline:** 335 mi. (539 km). Comparative area: slightly smaller than Oregon. **Land use:** 5% arable land; 7% permanent crops; 15% meadows and pastures; 37% forest and woodland; 36% other; includes negl. % irrigated. **Major cities:** (1984 census) Accra (capital) 964,879; Kumasi 348,880; Tamale 136,828; Tema 99,608; Takoradi 61,527.

People Population: 14,360,121 (1988). **Nationality:** noun—Ghanaian(s); adjective—Ghanaian. **Ethnic groups:** 99.8% black African (major groups—44% Akan, 16% Moshi-Dagomba, 13% Ewe, 8% Ga), 0.2% European and other. **Languages:** English (official); Akan, Moshi-Dagomba, Ewe, Ga. **Religions:** 38% indigenous beliefs, 30% Muslim, 24% Christian, 8% other.

Government Type: military. **Independence:** Mar. 6, 1957 (from UK). **Constitution:** Sept. 24, 1979; suspended Dec. 31, 1981. **National holiday:** Independence Day, Mar. 6. **Heads of government:** Flt. Lt. (Ret.) Jerry John Rawlings, chairman of PNDC (since Jan. 1982). **Structure:** executive—seven-member Provisional National Defense Council (PNDC); on Jan. 21, 1982, PNDC appointed secretaries to head most ministries.

Economy Monetary unit: cedi. **Budget:** (1986 est.) **income:** $611 mil.; **expend.:** $604 mil. **GNP:** $5.7 bil. (1986 est.). **Chief crops:** cocoa, coffee, root crops, corn, sorghum, millet, peanuts; not self-sufficient in food production but has that potential; an illegal producer of cannabis for international drug trade. **Livestock:** goats, sheep, cattle, pigs, asses. **Natural resources:** gold, timber, industrial diamonds, bauxite, manganese. **Major industries:** mining, lumbering, light manufacturing. **Labor force:** 3.7 mil. (1983); 54.7% agriculture and fishing, 18.7% industry, 15.2% sales and clerical; 400,000 unemployed; 48% of population of working age. **Exports:** $863 mil. (f.o.b., 1986); 60% cocoa; wood, gold, diamonds, manganese, bauxite, aluminum (aluminum regularly excluded from balance-of-payments data). **Imports:** $783 mil. (c.i.f., 1986); textiles and other manufactured goods, food, fuels, transport equipment. **Major trading partners:** UK, EC countries, U.S., Nigeria.

Intl. Orgs. Commonwealth, FAO, G-77, GATT, IAEA, IBRD, ICAO, IDA, IFAD, IFC, ILO, IMF, IMO, INTELSAT, INTERPOL, ITU, NAM, UN, UNESCO, UPU, WHO, WIPO, WMO.

The great Ghana empire covered the area of what is now the Republic of Ghana between the fourth and 13th centuries, when it was destroyed in clashes with neighboring kingdoms. The Portuguese first explored the area, on Africa's west coast, in 1471, naming it the Gold Coast because of its gold deposits and its reserves of "black gold"—slaves. In the 16th and 17th centuries, the British, Danes, and Dutch established slave trading posts there, which is where most American slaves came from. The slave trade ended in the 1850s, and the British gained control of the Gold Coast, making it a protectorate in 1871 and a colony in 1886.

Great Britain gave the colony a new constitution in 1946 under which Africans held a majority of seats in the legislature. Kwame Nkrumah became prime minister of the colony in 1952 and the first prime minister of the nation when it became independent, but still a member of the British Commonwealth, in 1957. The nation declared itself an independent republic on July 1, 1960, and Nkrumah was elected its first president. Nkrumah began to limit the freedom of opposition parties, court Communist bloc nations, and exert absolute authority. In January 1964 all opposition parties were outlawed. A military council seized power in February 1966 and ousted Nkrumah.

Though democratic elections were promised, he was followed by a succession of military leaders until a civilian government took control in September 1979. But the military returned to power in 1981. As a result of this instability, Ghana suffered severe economic problems throughout the 1970s and 1980s, and many of Ghana's people left for Nigeria to find work. In 1983 Nigeria ousted more than one million of these migrant workers, returning them to their homeland and increasing Ghana's economic woes.

Greece
Hellenic Republic

Geography Location: southeastern Europe. **Boundaries:** Yugoslavia and Bulgaria to N, Turkey to NE, Aegean Sea to E, Mediterranean Sea to S, Ionian Sea to W, Albania to NW; numerous Greek Islands to E, S, and W of mainland. **Total land area:** 50,949 sq. mi. (131,957 sq km). **Coastline:** 8,500 mi. (13,676 km). **Comparative area:** slightly smaller than Alabama. **Land use:** 23% arable land; 8% permanent crops; 40% meadows and pastures; 20% forest and woodland; 9% other; includes 7% irrigated. **Major cities:** (1981 census) Athinai (Athens, capital) 885,737; Thessaloniki (Salonika) 406,413; Piraeus 196,389; Patras 142,163; Larissa 102,426.

People Population: 10,015,041 (1988). **Nationality:** noun—Greek(s); adjective—Greek. **Ethnic groups:** 97.7% Greek, 1.3% Turkish, 1.0% Vlach, Slav, Albanian, Pomach (note: Greek government states there are no ethnic divisions in Greece). **Languages:** Greek (official); English and French widely understood. **Religions:** 98% Greek Orthodox, 1.3% Muslim, 0.7% other.

Government Type: presidential parliamentary government; monarchy rejected by referendum Dec. 8, 1974. **Constitution:** June 11, 1975. **National holiday:** Independence Day, Mar. 25. **Heads of government:** Dr. Andreas Papandreou, prime minister (since Oct. 1981); Christos Sartzetakis, president (since Mar. 1985). **Structure:** executive—president elected by Vouli (Parliament), prime minister, and cabinet; legislative—unicameral legislature (300-member Vouli); judiciary—independent.

Economy Monetary unit: Greek drachma. **Budget:** (1986) *income:* $12.1 bil.; *expend.:* $15.0 bil. **GNP:** $39.5 bil., $3,950 per capita (1986). **Chief crops:** wheat, olives, tobacco, cotton, raisins, fruit; nearly self-sufficient. **Livestock:** chickens, sheep, goats, pigs, cattle. **Natural resources:** bauxite, lignite, magnesite, crude oil, marble. **Major industries:** food and tobacco processing, textiles, chemicals. **Labor force:** 3.86 mil. (1985); 43% services, 27% agriculture, 20% manufacturing and mining; 8.3% unemployment. **Exports:** $5.6 bil. (f.o.b., 1986); textiles, fruits, minerals. **Imports:** $10.1 bil. (c.i.f., 1986); petroleum and petroleum products, manufactured goods, chemicals, meat, live animals. **Major trading partners:** (1985 est.) *exports:* 23.7% W. Germany, 13.5% Italy, 9.5% France, 7.1% U.S., 6.8% UK; *imports:* 21.1% W. Germany, 11.5% Italy, 8.1% France, 6.7% Netherlands, 6.5% Saudi Arabia.

Intl. Orgs. EC, FAO, GATT, IAEA, IBRD, ICAO, IDA, IFAD, IFC, ILO, IMF, IMO, INTELSAT, INTERPOL, ITU, NATO, OECD, UN, UNESCO, UPU, WHO, WIPO, WMO.

The Bronze Age and Iron Age cultures of Greece evolved to create the most glorious civilization of the ancient world. During their high point, from the fifth to the third century B.C., the city-states of Greece led the world in art, philosophy, political culture, and science. Greece vied with the Persian empire for control of Asia Minor and competed with the Phoenicians in maritime commerce in the Mediterranean. Alexander the Great, king of Macedonia, spread Greek civilization widely by conquering much of the Middle East and western Asia, but his empire did not long outlast his death in 323 B.C.

Greece was absorbed into the Roman Empire during the second and first centuries B.C. In the fourth century A.D., with the division of the Roman Empire, Greece became part of the Byzantine (Eastern Roman) Empire. Seven years after the Ottoman Turks captured Constantinople in 1453, they overran Greece and ruled it as part of the Ottoman Empire for 350 years.

Under Ottoman rule, much of the administration of Greece was left in local hands, keeping alive a sense of Greek nationhood and a tradition of Greek leadership, particularly through the clergy of the Greek Orthodox church. In 1821 Greece rebelled against Turkish rule, inspired by the French Revolution, a romanticized ideal of the classical past, and religious nationalism. With the support of England, France, and Russia, Greek independence was won in 1827, although the country included only about half of its present territory.

The Western powers sponsored a monarchical government in Greece, ruled by a German prince. When he was deposed in a revolt, a second monarchy, under a Danish prince, was established. King George I ruled from 1863 until his assassination in 1913. In the three Balkan Wars of 1912, 1913, and 1914, Greece expanded its borders to reach approximately its present size.

In 1923 a Greek Republic was established, but in 1935 King George II returned to his throne, placing government control in the hands of the patriotic but semifascistic Gen. Ioannis Metaxas. In 1940 Metaxas resisted Italy's attempt to conquer Greece, defeating Mussolini's armies so badly that Hitler sent crack troops to his ally's assistance. The German occupation of Greece was complete by June 1941. The Germans pillaged the country and massacred Jews; their Bulgarian allies colonized Macedonia.

During World War II, resistance grew among both Communist and anti-Communist groups, both beyond the reach of the government-in-exile in London. With the German withdrawal in October 1944, resistance groups battled each other; this led to full-scale civil war by 1946. British, and then American assistance (under the Truman Doctrine), enabled the Greek government to defeat the Communist forces when Stalin, as previously agreed, refused to intervene.

King George II died in 1947, succeeded by his brother, King Paul I. Political instability—16 governments during 1946–52—prevailed until, under American pressure, the Greeks adopted a new constitution designed to ensure stable government.

Until the postwar period, Greece's economy had been dominated by agriculture (food crops, wine grapes, olives, and tobacco) and livestock raising (primarily sheep and goats). Industry was limited largely to textiles and food processing; shipping was the major service industry. Under new policies instituted in 1952 by the government of Marshall Alexandros Papagos, and continued after his death in 1955 by Constantine Karamanlis, the industrial sector led a period of vigorous economic growth lasting into the 1960s. A market-oriented economy, tariff protection for Greek industry, tight internal security, and close ties with the West formed the mainstays of Greek policy.

Greece joined NATO in 1951, as did Turkey. Conflict over Cyprus divided the two nominal allies, however; and the failure of the Karamanlis government to resolve the Cyprus situation eroded its popularity. Karamanlis was replaced in 1964 by George Papandreou, who governed at the head of a Left-Center coalition. King Constantine, who succeeded his father in 1963, forced Papandreou to resign in 1964, after he and members of his government had been accused of various improprieties. A military coup, led by Col. George Papadopoulos, toppled the government in 1967. A countercoup by the king on Dec. 13, 1967, failed, and the king fled the country.

A military dictatorship ruled from 1967 to 1974. Its failed attempt to intervene in Cyprus in 1974 provoked a Turkish invasion of the island and led to the military regime's collapse. Government was turned over to Karamanlis once again; his party won a large majority in parliamentary elections in November 1974, and a republic was formally established with the promulgation of a new constitution in 1975. Karamanlis's New Democracy party received a renewed but smaller majority in parliamentary elections in 1977.

Greece, an associate member of the EEC since 1961, successfully negotiated in 1979 for full membership, effective as of Jan. 1, 1981. Full military membership in NATO was restored in 1980. In 1981 the Panhellenic Socialist Movement under Andreas Papandreou won a parliamentary majority, renewed in 1984. The left-wing Papandreou government has been outspokenly anti-NATO, anti-EEC, and anti-American, but its policy has been more moderate than its rhetoric, extending even to modest cooperation with Turkey in the Aegean. The Papandreou government has been badly shaken by several pro-Palestinian terrorist incidents on Greek soil.

The Greek economy, now more industrial than agricultural, has been hurt by persistent inflation, severe environmental problems, and the fluctuating fortunes of the shipping industry.

Grenada

Geography Location: several islands in southeastern Caribbean Sea, located about 100 mi. (160 km) N of Trinidad and 65 mi. (109 km) SW of St. Vincent. **Boundaries:** Atlantic Ocean to NE, E, and SE.; Caribbean Sea to SW, W, and NW. **Total land area:** 133 sq. mi. (344 sq km). **Coastline:** 75 mi. (121 km). **Comparative area:** slightly less than twice size of Washington, D.C. **Land use:** 15% arable land; 26% permanent crops; 3% meadows and pastures; 9% forest and woodland; 47% other; includes N.A. irrigated. **Major cities:** (1980 est.) St. George's (capital) 7,500.

People Population: 84,455 (1988). **Nationality:** noun—Grenadian(s); adjective—Grenadian. **Ethnic groups:** mainly of black African descent. **Languages:** English (official), some French patois. **Religions:** largely Roman Catholic, some Anglican and other Protestant sects.

Government Type: independent state; recognizes Elizabeth II as chief of state. **Independence:** Feb. 7, 1974 (from UK). **Constitution:** Dec. 19, 1973. **National holiday:** Independence Day, Feb. 7. **Heads of government:** Sir Paul Scoon, governor-general (since Sept. 1978); Herbert Blaize, prime minister (since Dec. 1984). **Structure:** executive (cabinet led by prime minister); bicameral legislature (15-member elected House of Representatives and 13-member appointed Senate); judiciary (Grenada Supreme Court, composed of High Court of Justice and two-tier court of appeals).

Economy Monetary unit: East Caribbean (EC) dollar. **Budget:** (1986 est.) *income:* $66 mil.; *expend.:* $70 mil. **GDP:** $129 mil., $1,520 per capita (1986). **Chief crops:** cocoa, nutmeg, mace, bananas. **Livestock:** sheep, goats, pigs, cattle, asses. **Natural resources:** none. **Major industries:** tourism, fish, beverages. **Labor force:** 36,000 (1985); 31% services, 24% agriculture, 45% other. **Exports:** $28 mil. (f.o.b.,

1986); cocoa beans, nutmeg, bananas, mace. **Imports:** $83 mil. (c.i.f., 1986); food, machinery and transport equipment, oil, building materials. **Major trading partners:** (1985) *exports:* 27% UK, 18% Netherlands, 10% W. Germany, 3% U.S.; *imports:* 24% U.S., 18% UK, 13% Trinidad and Tobago.

Intl. Orgs. FAO, G-77, GATT (de facto), IBRD, ICAO, IDA, IFAD, IFC, ILO, IMF, ITU, NAM, OAS, UN, UNESCO, UPU, WHO.

Dominated in the early 1600s by the warlike Carib Indians, Grenada alternated between French and British possession between 1650 and 1783, at which time British rule took over until Grenada's independence in 1974. The leftist New Jewel Movement seized power in a 1979 coup, but its leader, Maurice Bishop, was assassinated during a military coup in 1983. Shortly thereafter, the United States invaded the island, removed the leaders of the coup, and returned power to the governor-general until a general election in 1984. Political centrist Herbert Blaize is currently prime minister.

Guatemala
Republic of Guatemala

Geography Location: northern part of Central American isthmus. **Boundaries:** Mexico to N and W, Honduras and Belize to E, El Salvador to S. **Total land area:** 42,042 sq. mi. (108,889 sq km). **Coastline:** 248 mi. (400 km). **Comparative area:** slightly smaller than Tennessee. **Land use:** 12% arable land; 4% permanent crops; 12% meadows and pastures; 40% forest and woodland; 32% other; includes 1% irrigated. **Major cities:** (1981 census) Guatemala City (capital) 754,243; Escuintla 75,442; Quezaltenango 72,922; Puerto Barrios 46,882; Retalhuleu 46,652.

People Population: 8,831,148 (1988). **Nationality:** noun—Guatemalan(s); adjective—Guatemalan. **Ethnic groups:** 56% Ladino (mestizo and westernized Indian), 44% Indian. **Languages:** Spanish, but over 40% of population speaks an Indian language as primary tongue (18 Indian dialects, including Quiche, Cakchiquel, Kekchi). **Religions:** predominantly Roman Catholic, some Protestant and traditional Mayan.

Government Type: republic. **Independence:** Sept. 15, 1821 (from Spain). **Constitution:** May 31, 1985, effective Jan. 1986. **National holiday:** Independence Day, Sept. 15. **Heads of government:** Marco Vinicio Cerezo Arévalo, president (since Jan. 1986). **Structure:** traditionally dominant executive; new 100-member congress installed Jan. 14, 1986; power vested in office of president; seven-member (minimum) Supreme Court.

Economy Monetary unit: quetzal. **Budget:** (1986 est.) *income:* $975 mil.; *expend.:* $1.71 bil. **GDP:** $9.2 bil., $1,120 per capita (1986). **Chief crops:** coffee, cotton, corn, beans, sugarcane, bananas; illegal producer of opium poppy and cannabis for international drug trade. **Livestock:** cattle, pigs, sheep, horses, goats. **Natural resources:** crude oil, nickel, rare woods, fish, chicle. **Major industries:** sugar, textiles and clothing, furniture. **Labor force:** 2.5 mil.

(1985); 57% agriculture, 14% manufacturing, 13% services, 7% commerce; 50% unemployment and underemployment (1987 est.). **Exports:** $0.65 bil. (f.o.b., 1986); coffee, cotton, sugar, bananas, meat. **Imports:** $0.61 bil. (c.i.f., 1986); manufactured products, machinery, transportation equipment, chemicals, fuels. **Major trading partners:** *exports:* (1983) 35% U.S., 17% El Salvador, 6% Honduras, 5% Costa Rica; *imports:* (1985) 33% U.S., 10% El Salvador, 8% Netherlands Antilles, 7% Mexico, 7% Venezuela.

Intl. Orgs. FAO, G-77, IAEA, IBRD, ICAO, IDA, IFAD, IFC, ILO, IMF, IMO, INTELSAT, INTERPOL, ITU, UN, UNESCO, UPU, WHO, WMO.

Guatemala is located in the territorial heartland of the former Mayan civilization (A.D. 300–900). Having left the Spanish empire in 1821 as part of Agustín de Iturbide's Mexican empire, Guatemala seceded from Mexico with the rest of Central America in 1823 and became an independent republic after dissolution of the United Provinces of Central America in 1838.

A period of democratic reformist government (1944-54) ended with the reestablishment of direct military rule until the election of civilian Pres. Marco Vinicio Cerezo Arévalo in 1986. In the 1980s, guerrilla war and military violence have been directed against the indigenous Indian population.

Guinea
Republic of Guinea
(PREVIOUS NAME: FRENCH GUINEA)

Geography Location: northwestern coast of Africa. **Boundaries:** Guinea-Bissau to NW, Senegal to N, Mali to NE, Ivory Coast to SE, Liberia and Sierra Leone to S, Atlantic Ocean to W. **Total land area:** 94,926 sq. mi. (245,857 sq km). **Coastline:** 199 mi. (320 km). **Comparative area:** slightly smaller than Oregon. **Land use:** 6% arable land; negl. % permanent crops; 12% meadows and pastures; 42% forest and woodland; 40% other; includes negl. % irrigated. **Major cities:** (1972) Conakry (capital) 525,671; Kankan 60,000.

People Population: 6,909,298 (1988). **Nationality:** noun—Guinean(s); adjective—Guinean. **Ethnic groups:** Fulani, Malinke, Sousou, 15 smaller groups. **Languages:** French (official); tribal languages. **Religions:** 85% Muslim, 10% Christian, 5% indigenous beliefs.

Government Type: republic. **Independence:** Oct. 2, 1958 (from France). **Constitution:** May 14, 1982, suspended after coup of Apr. 3, 1984. **National holiday:** Independence Day, Oct. 2. **Heads of government:** Gen. Lansana Conte, president (since Apr. 1984). **Structure:** coup on Apr. 3, 1984, established 17-member Military Committee for National Redressment (CMRN) to determine government policy; highest ranking CMRN member became president, with other CMRN members assuming most cabinet portfolios.

Economy Monetary unit: Guinean franc. **Budget:** (1986) *income:* $226 mil.; *expend.:* $342 mil. **GNP:** $1.7 bil., $250 per capita

(1987 est.). **Chief crops:** cash crops—coffee, bananas, palm products, peanuts, citrus fruits, pineapples; food crops—cassava, rice, millet, corn, sweet potatoes. **Livestock:** cattle, sheep, goats, pigs, asses. **Natural resources:** bauxite, iron ore, diamonds, gold, uranium. **Major industries:** bauxite mining, alumina, diamond mining. **Labor force:** 2.4 mil. (1983); 82% agriculture, 11% industry and commerce; 88,112 civil servants (1987); 52% of population of working age (1985). **Exports:** $538 mil. (f.o.b., 1986 est.); bauxite, alumina, diamonds, coffee, pineapples. **Imports:** $511 mil. (c.i.f., 1986 est.); petroleum products, metals, machinery and transport equipment, foodstuffs, textiles. **Major trading partners:** *exports:* France, U.S., USSR, W. Germany, Spain; *imports:* France, USSR, U.S., Italy.

Intl. Orgs. FAO, G-77, IBRD, ICAO, IDA, IFAD, ILO, IMF, IMO, INTELSAT, INTERPOL, ITU, NAM, UN, UNESCO, UPU, WHO, WMO.

Guinea was formed out of the remains of a series of empires that flourished in West Africa between the 10th and 15th centuries. Situated at the southern end of the Sahara desert on the west coast of Africa, Guinea provides access to the Atlantic Ocean and was a commercial focal point for the peoples of Africa long before Europeans arrived.

French merchants began trading in what is now Guinea in the early 17th century. France began acquiring land in the area in the mid-19th century, and in 1845 the territories were organized as a separate colony. The colony received the name French Guinea in 1893.

Most high political posts were held by Europeans until after World War II. In 1946 French Guinea became a territory in the federation of French West Africa. Colonial reforms gradually allowed Guineans greater autonomy. In September 1958 Guinea became the only French colony to reject membership in the Fifth French Republic, resulting in the severance of political ties with France. The territorial assembly proclaimed Guinean independence on Oct. 2, 1958, and a new government headed by Sekou Toure was formed on the same day.

Though he claimed that an independent Guinea would like to remain associated with France, Toure led Guinea into the Communist bloc. By 1962 most of Guinea's trade was with communist countries. Toure remained in power until his death in April 1984. A military government gained power a week after his death. By the end of 1987, relations with France improved, and free market mechanisms were implemented.

Guinea-Bissau
Republic of Guinea-Bissau
(PREVIOUS NAME: PORTUGUESE GUINEA)

Geography Location: northwestern coast of Africa. **Boundaries:** Senegal to N, Guinea to E and S, Atlantic Ocean to W. **Total land area:** 10,811 sq. mi. (28,000 sq km). **Coastline:** 217 mi. (350 km). **Comparative area:** slightly less than three times size of Connecticut. **Land use:** 9% arable land; 1% permanent crops; 46% meadows and pastures; 38% forest and woodland; 6% other. **Major cities:** (1979 census) Bissau (capital) 109,214; Bafatá 13,429; Gabú 7,803; Mansoa 5,390; Catió 5,170.

People Population: 950,742 (1988). **Nationality:** noun—Guinea-Bissauan(s); adjective—Guinea-Bissauan. **Ethnic groups:** about 99% African (30% Balanta, 20% Fula, 14% Manjaca, 13% Mandinga, 7% Papel); less than 1% European and mulatto. **Languages:** Portuguese (official), Criolo, numerous African languages. **Religions:** 65% indigenous beliefs, 30% Muslim, 5% Christian.

Government Type: republic; highly centralized one-party regime since Sept. 1974. **Independence:** Sept. 24, 1973 (from Portugal). **Constitution:** May 16, 1984. **National holiday:** Independence Day, Sept. 24. **Heads of government:** Brig. Gen. João Bernardo Vieira, president (since Nov. 1980). **Structure:** executive—president and cabinet; legislature—50-member National Popular Assembly, overseen by 15–member Council of State.

Economy Monetary unit: Guinea Bissauan pesos. **Budget:** (1983 est.) *income:* $12.2 mil.; *expend.:* $27.4 mil. **GDP:** $190 mil., $180 per capita (1984). **Chief crops:** rice, palm products, root crops, coconuts, peanuts. **Livestock:** cattle, goats, pigs, sheep. **Natural resources:** unexploited deposits of petroleum, bauxite, phosphates; fish, timber. **Major industries:** agricultural processing, beer, soft drinks. **Labor force:** (1983) 90% agriculture; 53% of population of working age. **Exports:** $8.6 mil. (1983); principally peanuts; also palm kernels, shrimp, fish, lumber. **Imports:** $57.1 mil. (1983); foodstuffs, manufactured goods, fuels, transport equipment. **Major trading partners:** Portugal, Spain, other European countries.

Intl. Orgs. FAO, G-77, GATT (de facto), IBRD, ICAO, IDA, IFAD, IFC, ILO, IMF, IMO, ITU, NAM, UN, UNESCO, UPU, WHO, WMO.

The Portuguese began exploring and trading in what is now Guinea-Bissau in the 15th century and in 1630 began to exert administrative control over the territory. The area, on the west coast of Africa, soon became the center of the Portuguese slave trade. When the slave trade declined in the 19th century, the coastal port of Bissau became a major commercial center. Later in the 19th century, the Portuguese began to conquer the interior of the territory and in 1879 consolidated the region into a territory called Portuguese Guinea. In 1952 Portuguese Guinea became an overseas province of Portugal.

A nationalist movement began in 1956 under the leadership of Amilcar Cabral and the African Party for the Independence of Guinea and Cape Verde (PAIGC). Armed insurrection broke out in 1961. By 1972 the PAIGC exerted influence over much of the country. Civilian rule was established in the territory that it controlled, and elections were held for a national assembly. Cabral was assassinated in 1973 but soon after, the PAIGC National Assembly declared the independence of Guinea-Bissau from Portugal. Portugal acknowledged the country's new status on Sept. 24, 1973, after it received U.S. recognition.

The civilian government was overthrown by a military coup in 1980, and the country was run by a Revolutionary Council headed by Brig. Gen. João Bernardo Vieira until a new constitution was adopted in May 1984. Under the new Constitution, a new national assembly was selected, and Vieira was elected to a five-year term as president. A coup attempt was thwarted in November 1985, and since then Guinea-Bissau has been tranquil.

Guyana
Co-operative Republic of Guyana
(PREVIOUS NAME: BRITISH GUIANA)

Geography Location: northern coast of South America. **Boundaries:** North Atlantic Ocean to N, Suriname to E, Brazil to S, Venezuela to W. **Total land area:** 83,000 sq. mi. (214,969 sq km). **Coastline:** 285 mi. (459 km). **Comparative area:** slightly smaller than Idaho. **Land use:** 3% arable land; negl. % permanent crops; 6% meadows and pastures; 83% forest and woodland; 8% other; includes 1% irrigated. **Major cities:** (1976 est.) Georgetown (capital) 72,049.

People Population: 765,796 (1988). **Nationality:** noun—Guyanese (sing., pl.); adjective—Guyanese. **Ethnic groups:** 51% East Indian, 43% black and mixed, 4% Amerindian, 2% European and Chinese. **Languages:** English, Amerindian dialects. **Religions:** 57% Christian, 33% Hindu, 9% Muslim, 1% other.

Government Type: republic within Commonwealth. **Independence:** May 26, 1966 (from UK). **Constitution:** Oct. 6, 1980. **National holiday:** Republic Day, Feb. 23. **Heads of government:** Hugh Desmond Hoyte, president (since Aug. 1985); Hamilton Green, prime minister (since Aug. 1985). **Structure:** executive—president, who appoints and heads cabinet; unicameral legislature (53-member National Assembly) elected by proportional representation every five years.

Economy Monetary unit: Guyanese dollar. **Budget:** (1986 est.) *income:* $220.3 mil.; *expend.:* $465.3 mil. **GDP:** $519 mil., $680 per capita (1986). **Chief crops:** sugarcane, rice, other food crops; food shortages—wheat flour, cooking oil, processed meat, dairy products. **Livestock:** pigs, cattle, sheep, goats. **Natural resources:** bauxite, gold, diamonds, hardwood timber, shrimp, fish. **Major industries:** bauxite mining, sugar, rice milling. **Labor force:** 268,000 (1985); public-sector employment amounts to 60–80% of total labor force; 44.5% industry and commerce, 33.8% agriculture, 21.7% services; unemployment and underemployment 30% (1985 est.). **Exports:** $214 mil. (f.o.b., 1985); bauxite, sugar, rice, shrimp, molasses. **Imports:** $209.1 mil. (f.o.b., 1985); manufactures, machinery, food, petroleum. **Major trading partners:** (1983); *exports:* 29% UK, 17% U.S., 17% CARICOM, 6% Canada; *imports:* 33% CARICOM, 21% U.S., 11% UK, 3% Canada.

Intl. Orgs. FAO, G-77, GATT, IBRD, ICAO, IDA, IFAD, IFC, ILO, IMF, IMO, INTERPOL, ITU, NAM, OAS (observer), UN, UNESCO,

UPU, WHO, WMO.

Originally settled by the Dutch in the early 17th century, Guyana was under the rule of either the French or the British between 1780 and 1815. British colonization took hold in the 19th century and remained, except for Venezuela's claims to the territory, until Guyana's independence in 1966. Guyana drifted toward authoritarianism under the leadership of former president Forbes Burnham, who held power until 1985. Although current president Desmond Hoyte has pledged a greater openness and a socialist direction for the country, the government still controls the flow of public information in the society.

Haiti
Republic of Haiti
Geography Location: western past of island of Hispaniola and several small islands in northern Caribbean Sea. **Boundaries:** North Atlantic Ocean to N, Dominican Republic to E, Caribbean Sea to S, Windward Passage to W. **Total land area:** 10,714 sq. mi. (27,750 sq km). **Coastline:** 1,100 mi. (1,771 km). **Comparative area:** slightly larger than Maryland. **Land use:** 20% arable land; 13% permanent crops; 18% meadows and pastures; 4% forest and woodland; 45% other; includes 3% irrigated. **Major cities:** (1984 est.) Port-au-Prince (capital) 738,342.

People Population: 6,295,570 (1988). **Nationality:** noun—Haitian(s); adjective—Haitian. **Ethnic groups:** 95% black, 5% mulatto and European. **Languages:** French (official, but spoken by only 10% of population); all speak Creole. **Religions:** 75–80% Roman Catholic—of which majority also practice voodoo (called vodun)—10% Protestant.

Government Type: republic. **Independence:** Jan. 1, 1804 (from France). **Constitution:** Aug. 27, 1983, suspended Feb. 1986; draft constitution approved Mar. 1987. **Heads of government:** Lt. Gen. Prosper Avril, president (since Sept. 1988). **Structure:** military-dominated government following end of 29 years of Duvalier family rule; Consultative Council (45-member civilian advisory body) is moribund; judiciary appointed by president.

Economy Monetary unit: gourde. **Budget:** (1986) *income:* $484 mil.; *expend.:* $511 mil. **GDP:** $2.1 bil., $350 per capita (1986). **Chief crops:** coffee, sugarcane, rice, corn, sorghum. **Livestock:** cattle, goats, pigs, horses, asses, sheep, mules. **Natural resources:** bauxite. **Major industries:** sugar refining, textiles, flour milling. **Labor force:** 2.3 mil. (1982); 66% agriculture, 25% services, 9% industry; shortage of skilled labor, unskilled labor abundant; significant unemployment. **Exports:** $191 mil. (1986); coffee, light industrial products, essential oils, sisal, sugar. **Imports:** $326 mil. (f.o.b., 1986); consumer durables, foodstuffs, industrial equipment, petroleum products, construction materials. **Major trading partners:** (1985) *exports:* 81% U.S.; *imports:* 63% U.S.

Intl. Orgs. FAO, G-77, GATT, IAEA, IBRD, ICAO, IDA, IFAD, IFC, ILO, IMF, IMO, INTEL-

SAT, INTERPOL, ITU, UN, UNESCO, UPU, WHO, WMO.

The Western Hemisphere's poorest country, Haiti achieved its independence from France in 1804. Authoritarian rule has characterized much of the political history of the country. From 1915 until 1934, the United States occupied Haiti, and in 1957 François Duvalier took power. His son, Jean-Claude, inherited the presidency in 1971, ruling until his ouster by the military in 1986. Haiti has experienced a succession of rulers since that time. Attempts at elections in 1987 and 1988 have failed to resolve the question of power in the country, and short-lived governments remain unable to address Haiti's severe economic problems.

Honduras
Republic of Honduras
Geography Location: middle of Central American isthmus. **Boundaries:** Caribbean Sea to N, Nicaragua to E, El Salvador and Nicaragua to S, Guatemala and El Salvador to W. **Total land area:** 43,277 sq. mi. (112,088 sq km). **Coastline:** 509 mi. (820 km). **Comparative area:** slightly larger than Tennessee. **Land use:** 14% arable land; 2% permanent crops; 30% meadows and pastures; 34% forest and woodland; 20% other; includes 1% irrigated. **Major cities:** (1986 est.) Tegucigalpa (capital) 604,600; San Pedro Sula 399,700; La Ceiba 63,800; Choluteca 58,300; El Progreso 40,900.

People Population: 4,972,287 (1988). **Nationality:** noun—Honduran(s); adjective—Honduran. **Ethnic groups:** 90% mestizo, 7% Indian, 2% black, 1% white. **Languages:** Spanish, Indian dialects. **Religions:** 97% Roman Catholic, small Protestant minority.

Government Type: republic. **Independence:** Sept. 15, 1821 (from Spain). **Constitution:** Jan. 11, 1982 (effective Jan. 20, 1982). **National holiday:** Independence Day, Sept. 15. **Head of government:** José Azcona Hoyo, president (since Jan. 1986). **Structure:** constitution provides for elected president, unicameral legislature (134-member National Congress), and national judicial branch.

Economy Monetary unit: lempira. **Budget:** (1986 est.) *income:* $589 mil.; *expend.:* $861 mil. **GDP:** $2.6 bil., $560 per capita (1986). **Chief crops:** bananas, coffee, corn, beans, sugarcane, rice, tobacco. **Livestock:** cattle, pigs, horses, mules. **Natural resources:** timber, gold, silver, copper, lead. **Major industries:** agricultural processing (sugar and coffee), textiles, clothing. **Labor force:** 1.3 mil. (1985); 62% agriculture, 20% services, 9% manufacturing, 3% construction; 12% unemployment, much underemployment (1987 est.). **Exports:** $875 mil. (f.o.b., 1986); bananas, coffee, lumber, meat, minerals. **Imports:** $957 mil. (f.o.b., 1986); manufactured products, machinery, transportation equipment, chemicals, petroleum. **Major trading partners:** (1984) *exports:* 50% U.S., 32% Europe, 10% Japan, 7% Latin America; *imports:* 37% U.S., 17% Europe, 15% CACM, 11% Venezuela, 10% Japan.

Intl. Orgs. FAO, G-77, IBRD, ICAO, IDA, IFAD, IFC, ILO, IMF, IMO, INTELSAT,

INTERPOL, ITU, UN, UNESCO, UPU, WHO, WMO.

The Mayan civilization extended south to the pre-Columbian city of Copán in what is now northwestern Honduras. The territory was also home to the Lenca Indians and the indigenous people of the Moskitia area. Honduras was a province of the Spanish kingdom of Guatemala, a member of the United Provinces of Central America after independence from Spain and Mexico, and an independent republic after the 1838 collapse of the Central American Federation.

A major exporter of bananas between 1900 and 1930, Honduras alternated between civilian and military rule for many years. Since 1982 the country has had civilian elected leadership. Nicaraguan Contra rebels have been using Honduran territory, thus creating problems for current Pres. José Azcona Hoyo.

Hungary
Hungarian People's Republic
Geography Location: landlocked country in eastern Europe. **Boundaries:** Czechoslovakia to N, USSR to NE, Romania to E, Yugoslavia to S, Austria to W. **Total land area:** 35,920 sq. mi. (93,033 sq km). **Coastline:** none. **Comparative area:** slightly smaller than Indiana. **Land use:** 54% arable land; 3% permanent crops; 14% meadows and pastures; 18% forest and woodland; 11% other; includes 2% irrigated. **Major cities:** (1987) Budapest (capital) 2,093,487; Debrecen 214,836; Miskolc 211,156; Szeged 185,559; Pécs 179,051.

People Population: 10,588,271 (1988). **Nationality:** noun—Hungarian(s); adjective—Hungarian. **Ethnic groups:** 96.6% Hungarian, 1.6% German, 1.1% Slovak, 0.3% Southern Slav, 0.2% Romanian. **Languages:** 98.2% Hungarian, 1.8% other. **Religions:** 67.5% Roman Catholic, 20.0% Calvinist, 5.0% Lutheran, 7.5% atheist and other.

Government Type: communist state. **Constitution:** Aug. 18, 1949; effective Aug. 20, 1949; revised Apr. 19, 1972. **National holiday:** Liberation Day, Apr. 4. **Heads of government:** Bruno Straub, president, Presidential Council (since July 1988); Karoly Grosz, premier, Council of Ministers (since June 1987). **Structure:** executive—Presidential Council (elected by parliament); unicameral legislature—National Assembly (elected by direct suffrage); judicial—Supreme Court (elected by parliament).

Economy Monetary unit: forint. **Budget:** N.A. **GNP:** $84 bil., $7,910 per capita (1986). **Chief crops:** corn, wheat, potatoes, sugar beets, barley; normally, self-sufficient. **Livestock:** chickens, pigs, sheep, ducks, cattle. **Natural resources:** bauxite, coal, natural gas, fertile soils. **Major industries:** mining, metallurgy, engineering industries. **Labor force:** 4.89 mil. (1986); 42.6% services, trade, government, and other; 31.4% industry, 18.9% agriculture. **Exports:** $15.4 bil. (f.o.b., 1986); 34.7% machinery and equipment; 26.5% fuels, raw materials, and semifinished products; 22% agricultural and forestry products, 16.8% manufactured consumer goods. **Imports:** $15.8 bil.

(c.i.f., 1986); 46% fuels, raw materials, and semifinished products; 28.6% machinery and equipment; 15.2% agricultural and forestry products; 10.2% manufactured consumer goods. **Major trading partners:** (1986) 32.4% USSR, 10.4% W. Germany.

Intl. Orgs. CMEA, FAO, GATT, IAEA, IBRD, ICAO, ILO, IMF, IMO, ITU, UN, UNESCO, UPU, Warsaw Pact, WHO, WIPO, WMO.

The Magyars, a tribe of Central Asian horsemen, invaded Europe in the ninth century A.D. and settled in the Hungarian Plain where, under their chieftain Arpad, they displaced earlier Germanic and Slavic settlers and organized a kingdom in 896. The Hungarians converted to Christianity during the 10th century, and King Stephen (later St. Stephen) received a royal crown from Pope Sylvester II in 1001.

After the Battle of Mohacs in 1526, most of Hungary fell under Ottoman rule. The Turks were driven out in a series of battles with the Habsburg Holy Roman emperors at the end of the 17th century. Thereafter Hungary was part of the Habsburg empire until 1867, when the Dual Monarchy of Austria-Hungary was organized, making Hungary independent of Austria in all but finance, the military, and foreign affairs.

During the late 19th century, Hungary experienced extensive immigration of Romanians from the east and Slovaks from the north; by 1900 Magyars formed only a bare majority of the population. The pre–World War I economy was largely agricultural, with most of the population living in rural poverty. Agriculture-related industry (beet sugar factories, breweries, tanneries, textile mills) developed in the late 19th century, along with some heavy industry.

In the dismemberment of Austria-Hungary following the defeat of the Central Powers in World War I, Hungary surrendered extensive territories to Romania, Yugoslavia, and Czechoslovakia. The country lost 70 percent of its territory and 60 percent of its population; one-third of the Magyar people lived on foreign soil.

Short-lived governments—a republic under Michael Karolyi, and a Bolshevist state under Bela Kun—were replaced in 1920 by a new monarchy, with Adm. Miklós Horthy serving as regent. The Horthy regime was authoritarian but not fascist; its main objective was the recovery of Hungary's lost territories. Hungary established common cause with Germany in 1938, recovering some territory from Czechoslovakia and Romania in the bargain, but at the price of participating in Hitler's war with the Soviet Union. Germany occupied Hungary in 1944 and set up a Hungarian Nazi regime. Late in 1944 the Russian army drove out the Germans and set up their own occupation.

The establishment of a full-scale Soviet-satellite regime was relatively slow. A republic was declared in February 1946, and the non-Communist Zoltan Tildy was elected president. Tildy was forced out in 1947, however, and replaced by the Stalinist dictator, Matias Rakosi. After the death of Stalin in 1953, the moderate Imre Nagy became premier and introduced some economic reforms. Nagy was forced out of office in 1955.

Nikita Khrushchev's denunciation of Stalin in 1956, combined with an atmosphere of rising expectations for further reforms in Hungary, led to a popular uprising in October 1956. Nagy, backed by the army, formed a coalition government on Oct. 23, proclaimed Hungary's neutrality, ended censorship, opened the country's borders, and withdrew from the Warsaw Pact. The ousted Communist party secretary, Erno Gero, called for Soviet support; on Nov. 4, Soviet troops launched a massive invasion that soon crushed the rebellion. The Soviet army then installed János Kadar as premier; Nagy was executed. About 200,000 Hungarians fled the country, and many more were imprisoned.

After several years of repressive rule, the Kadar regime announced, in 1963, amnesty for participants in the 1956 rebellion. Stalinists were gradually removed from the government, economic reforms emphasizing profit and productivity were introduced, and trade with the West was expanded. Hungary reluctantly took part in the suppression of Czechoslovakia's "Prague Spring" in 1968. In the same year, it announced the New Economic Mechanism (NEM) policy, ending central economic planning and introducing semifree enterprise under bureaucratic control.

After a brief return to central planning in the 1970s, the NEM was reintroduced in 1979 and expanded in 1982, when Hungary joined the World Bank and the IMF. Private ownership of subsidiaries of state-owned enterprises was permitted. In 1987 a pro-Gorbachev premier, Karoly Grosz, took office and in 1988 became head of the Communist party as well.

Hungary, often regarded as a model of *perestroika*, remains a society troubled by its socialist/free enterprise and authoritarian/democratic dualities. Economic growth has become less robust in the late 1980s; social problems such as suicide, alcoholism, and divorce are on the rise. About 50,000 Russian troops remain in Hungary, and relations with Romania have become tense as a result of Romanian social planners obliterating scores of ethnic Hungarian villages in that country.

Iceland
Republic of Iceland
Geography **Location:** one large island and numerous smaller ones near Arctic Circle in North Atlantic Ocean. **Boundaries:** Greenland about 190 mi. (300 km) to NW, Norway about 620 mi. (1,000 km) to E, UK 500 mi. (800 km) to S. **Total land area:** 39,679 sq. mi. (103,000 sq km). **Coastline:** 3,100 mi. (4,988 km). **Comparative area:** slightly smaller than Kentucky. **Land use:** negl. % arable land; 0% permanent crops; 23% meadows and pastures; 1% forest and woodland; 76% other. **Major cities:** (1980) Reykjavík (capital) 83,766.

People **Population:** 246,526 (1988). **Nationality:** noun—Icelander(s); adjective—Icelandic. **Ethnic groups:** homogeneous mixture of descendants of Norwegians and Celts. **Languages:** Icelandic (official). **Religions:** 95% Evangelical Lutheran, 3% other Protestant and Roman Catholic, 2% no affiliation.

Government **Type:** republic. **Independence:** June 7, 1944, (from Denmark). **Constitution:** June 16, 1944; effective June 17, 1944. **National holiday:** Anniversary of the Establishment of the Republic, June 17. **Heads of government:** Vigdís Finnbogadottir, president (since Aug. 1980); Steingrímur Hermannsson, prime minister (since Sept. 1988). **Structure:** executive power vested in president but exercised by cabinet responsible to parliament; legislative authority rests jointly with president and parliament (Althing); Supreme Court and 29 lower courts.

Economy **Monetary unit:** krona. **Budget:** (1986) *income:* $930.2 mil.; *expend.:* $978.8 mil. **GDP:** $3.9 bil., $16,200 per capita (1986). **Chief crops:** dairying, hay, potatoes, turnips. **Livestock:** cattle, sheep, horses, pigs, poultry. **Natural resources:** fish, hydroelectric and geothermal power, diatomite. **Major industries:** fish processing, aluminum smelting, ferrosilicon production. **Labor force:** 122,800 (1985); 55.4% commerce, finance, and services; 11.3% agriculture; 20.3% other manufacturing; 13.0% fishing and fish processing; 0.7% unemployment. **Exports:** $1.1 bil. (f.o.b., 1986); fish and fish products, animal products, aluminum, diatomite. **Imports:** $1.12 bil. (c.i.f., 1986); machinery and transportation equipment, petroleum, foodstuffs, textiles. **Major trading partners:** (1986) *exports:* 54.2% EC (20.4% UK, 9.1% W. Germany, 3.8% Denmark), 21.7% U.S., 4.2% USSR, 2.6% developing countries; *imports:* 52.9% EC (15.2% W. Germany, 10.8% Denmark, 8.2% UK), 7.0% U.S., 5.6% USSR, 3.1% developing countries.

Intl. Orgs. EC (free-trade agreement pending resolution of fishing limits issue), EFTA, FAO, GATT, IAEA, IBRD, ICAO, IDA, IFC, ILO, IMF, IMO, INTELSAT, INTERPOL, ITU, NATO, OECD, UN, UNESCO, UPU, WHO, WMO.

The volcanic island of Iceland was settled in the ninth century A.D. by Vikings, who established Europe's oldest body of representative government, the Althing, in 930. Christianity was introduced around 1000. In the 13th century, Iceland acknowledged Norwegian rule. In 1380 Denmark, by then in control of all of Scandinavia, conquered Iceland as well. Iceland gained its independence in 1918 but shared a common king, Christian X, with the Danes. During World War II, first British, and then American, troops garrisoned the island; in 1944, with Denmark occupied by the Nazis, Iceland deposed their king and proclaimed itself a republic.

Iceland became a UN member in 1946 and a member of NATO in 1949. Lacking its own armed forces, it grudgingly tolerated the presence of an American air base at Keflavik. The republic developed a Scandinavian-style welfare state, with comprehensive social benefits that have produced one of the world's healthiest and best-educated peoples.

Less than 1 percent of Iceland's territory is arable; the island imports grain and vegetables but is self-sufficient in meat and dairy products. Fishing is the principal industry, accounting for 75 percent of exports and engaging one-seventh of the work force. Between 1958 and 1976, Iceland carried on "cod wars" with the United Kingdom, Norway, and Denmark, involving disputes over Iceland's claim to extensive territorial waters.

Multiparty representation in the Althing has created a trend of government by coalitions or minority cabinets. Politically stable, the republic faces economic problems brought on by high taxes, chronic inflation, and a huge national debt. Iceland maintains close ties with Scandinavia and actively participates in the Nordic Council.

India
Republic of India

Geography Location: forms natural subcontinent in Asia, with Himalayan mountain range to N. **Boundaries:** Pakistan to NW; China, Bhutan, and Nepal to N; and Burma to NE; Bangladesh is surrounded by Indian territory except for short frontier with Burma in E; Bay of Bengal to E; Sri Lanka near India's southern tip across Palk Strait; and Arabian Sea to W. **Total land area:** 1,269,219 sq. mi. (3,287,263 sq km). **Coastline:** 4,350 mi. (7,000 km). **Comparative area:** slightly more than one-third the size of U.S. **Land use:** 55% arable land; 1% permanent crops; 4% meadows and pastures; 23% forest and woodland; 17% other; includes 13% irrigated. **Major cities:** (1981 census) New Delhi (capital) 273,036; Greater Bombay 8,243,405; Delhi 4,884,234; Calcutta 3,305,006; Madras 3,276,622.

People Population: 816,828,360 (1988). **Nationality:** noun—Indian(s); adjective—Indian. **Ethnic groups:** 72% Indo-Aryan, 25% Dravidian, 3% Mongoloid and other. **Languages:** Hindi, English, and 14 other official languages; 24 langs. spoken by million or more persons each; numerous other langs. and dialects, for the most part mutually unintelligible; Hindi is national language and primary tongue of 30% of people; English enjoys associate status but is the most important language for national, political, and commercial communication; Hindustani, a popular variant of Hindi/Urdu, is spoken widely throughout northern India. **Religions:** 82.6% Hindu, 11.4% Muslim, 2.4% Christian, 2.0% Sikh.

Government Type: federal republic. **Independence:** Aug. 15, 1947 (from UK). **Constitution:** Jan. 26, 1950. **National holiday:** Republic Day, Jan. 26. **Heads of government:** Ramaswamy Venkataraman, president (since July 1987); Rajiv Gandhi, prime minister (since Oct. 1984). **Structure:** bicameral parliament—Government Assembly (Rajya Sabha) and People's Assembly (Lok Sabha); relatively independent judiciary.

Economy Monetary unit: rupee. **Budget:** (1986) *income:* $43.2 bil.; *expend.:* $48 bil. **GNP:** $200 bil., $250 per capita (1987). **Chief crops:** rice, other cereals, pulses, oilseed, cotton; legal producer of opium poppy for pharmaceutical trade but also illegal producer of opium poppy and cannabis for international drug trade. **Livestock:** cattle, goats, buffalo, sheep, pigs. **Natural resources:** coal (4th

largest reserves in world), iron ore, manganese, mica, bauxite. **Major industries:** textiles, food processing, steel. **Labor force:** 284.4 mil. (1985); 67% agriculture, more than 10% unemployed and underemployed (1987). **Exports:** $11.7 bil. (f.o.b., 1987); engineering goods, textiles and clothing, tea. **Imports:** $17.1 bil. (c.i.f., 1987); machinery and transport equipment, petroleum, edible oils, fertilizers. **Major trading partners:** U.S., UK, USSR, Japan.

Intl. Orgs. Colombo Plan, Commonwealth, FAO, G-77, GATT, IAEA, IBRD, ICAO, IDA, IFAD, IFC, ILO, IMF, IMO, INTELSAT, INTERPOL, ITU, NAM, UN, UNESCO, UPU, WHO, WIPO, WMO.

Indian civilization is one of the oldest in the world. Neolithic agricultural communities appeared in the Indus River valley no later than 3000 B.C.; the great cities at Harappa and Mohenjo-Daro were founded around 2500 B.C. Around 1500 B.C. Indo-European (Aryan) invaders from Central Asia overthrew the ancient civilization and imposed their own religion, culture, and political system on the indigenous population. The invasion also set in motion waves of population movements toward southern India.

The new Indo-European civilization was characterized by the institution of caste, under which every person was a member of one of four fundamental divisions of society: Brahmins, hereditary priests responsible for higher learning and for rituals as set forth in the *Vedas* and other sacred texts written in the Sanskrit language; Ksatrias, warriors and administrators; Vaisas, merchants; and Sudras, farmers and subjugated peoples. There was also, at the bottom of the social scale, a group of casteless people, known in much later times as untouchables. Over the course of time, the caste system was elaborated to create numerous subcastes within the basic fourfold division.

By the mid-first millennium B.C., Brahminism had declined into a state of religious formalism. That situation prompted two reformations around 600 B.C., the first of which produced the Jain religion; the second, Buddhism. Thereafter, Jainism remained confined largely to India, while Buddhism spread widely, eventually influencing most of the cultures of Asia but gradually dying out in India itself. Buddhism was adopted as a state religion by Asoka, third and greatest emperor of the Mauryan empire, which ruled most of India from 325 to 184 B.C. In the five centuries of disorder that followed the collapse of the Mauryan empire, Buddhism merged with the remnants of Brahminism and with various local cults to form Hinduism, which became the dominant religion of India. During the same period, the *Mahabharata*, the great Hindu epic, was composed, along with the devotional hymns called Upanishads.

South India in the post-Mauryan period was divided into numerous states, the most prominent of which was Chola, a Tamil kingdom in the southeast that had extensive trade connections throughout the Indian Ocean.

The Gupta dynasty (c. A.D. 320–544), based in the Ganges River valley, established its rule over

most of northern India and created what is generally regarded as a golden age of north Indian culture, with flourishing cities and significant achievements in art, literature, and science.

In the seventh century, King Sri Harsha, ruling from Kanauj in the upper Ganges valley, created a short-lived feudal empire that united most of the petty states from Gujarat to Bengal. At the same time, the Chalyuka dynasty dominated much of southern India. In the early eighth century, the Indus River valley was invaded by Moslem Arabs and thereafter became permanent part of the world of Islam (see "Pakistan"). The empire of Sri Harsha fell apart, to be replaced by the numerous petty kingdoms of the Rajputs, while political power became fragmented in the south as well.

The 11th century saw the ascendency of Islam throughout northern India, which came under the shadow of the empire of Mamud of Ghazni, based in Afghanistan. In 1192 the Ghaznavid general Kutb ud-din Aibak defeated a coalition of Rajput states; in 1206 he founded the Sultanate of Delhi, which in the course of the 13th century, held off the Mongol invasions in northwestern India and brought all of the subcontinent, except for the southernmost states, under its control. While the rulers of the sultanate were Muslims, most of the population under their control remained Hindu.

Internal rebellions combined with the sacking of Delhi by Timur Leng (Tamerlane) in 1398 greatly weakened the Sultanate of Delhi and led to the rise of numerous successor states in most of its former domains. In 1526 Babur, a fifth-generation descendent of Timur Leng, conquered all of northern India and established the Moghul empire. Under the third Moghul ruler, Akbar the Great, ruling from his newly built capital at Fatehpur Sikri, the empire flourished; Moghul culture gave rise to new styles of architecture, painting, and music.

In the 17th century, the Moghul emperors began to be threatened by the Hindu Marathas, whose kingdom on the west-central coast rapidly expanded to encompass most of south India. By the late 18th century, Maratha power had spread to the north, and most of the petty kingdoms that had made up the Moghul empire became part of a Maratha confederacy, owing only nominal allegiance to Delhi. By that time all of India was threatened by the expansion of the European powers.

Vasco Da Gama had landed at Calicut in 1498, and in 1510 the Portuguese founded a colony at Goa. Dutch traders competed with the Portuguese during the 16th century, and British and French merchants were attracted by the expanding trade with India in the early 17th century. British trading stations were established at Surat in 1612, Bombay in 1661, and Calcutta in 1690, by which time Great Britain had become the dominant, but by no means the sole, European power along the coasts of India. In the mid-18th century, open warfare broke out between British and French forces in India; the result was to reduce the French presence to a few insignificant enclaves. The growing instability of the Moghul empire in the face of Marathan and Rajput revolts and the expansion of the southern kingdom of Mysore encouraged the British to seek further control of Indian territory. Robert Clive's victory at Plassey, near Calcutta, in 1757 brought Orissa, Bihar, and Bengal under British control; British rule was extended to the upper Ganges in 1775. Victory over Tipu, the maharaja of Mysore, in 1792 paved the way for British control over much of the south.

British parliamentary acts of 1773 and 1784 placed these new acquisitions of the East India Company firmly under government control. Under Richard Wellesley, the turn of the 19th century saw consolidation of the various British conquests in India and beginnings of unified imperial control. In 1803 the Moghul emperor accepted Wellesley's offer of a protectorate, and British suzerainty in India was assured. After a protracted war, 1812–23, Marathan resistance to British control was broken. The first Anglo-Afghan War, 1838–42, led to a stalemate in Afghanistan but also to consolidation of British control of the Punjab.

The East India Company's monopoly on trade with India was withdrawn in 1833; Parliament assumed political control of British interests in South Asia, while private merchants had unrestricted access to the economy. Plantation crops, such as opium and cotton, began to displace subsistence agriculture in some areas. This made India more dependent on imported goods under British control, tying India's economy more closely to that of Great Britain.

In 1857 Indian troops in the British colonial armed forces, angered by reports that cartridges were greased with pork fat and beef tallow (taboo to Muslims and Hindus, respectively), staged a mutiny in north-central India. The military uprising was joined by segments of the local population, and the rebellion was put down only after 14 months of fighting. In 1858, in the wake of the mutiny, the Moghul empire was dissolved, as was the East India Company. The government of India was made directly subject to the British Crown, which exercised control through a viceroy and through the British Colonial Office. Queen Victoria was crowned empress of India in 1877.

The British raj in India developed into a patchwork quilt of direct and indirect rule. In general, coastal areas, major river valleys, and strategic frontier regions were ruled directly by the British authorities, while in the interior, native states, large and small, continued to exist as British protectorates controlled by British advisers to the native princes. In 1861, in a concession to early Indian nationalists who looked forward to eventual dominion status for India, Indians were appointed to advisory councils of the viceroy and provincial governors.

The Indian National Congress was organized in 1885, and became the principal vehicle for the expression of Indian political aspirations. The colonial government tended to repress or ignore nationalist sentiments but gradually made some concessions in deference to popular opinion. In the wake of popular demonstrations in 1905, elections were instituted to choose Indian members of the viceroy's legislative council. Separate electorates were created for the Muslim and Hindu communities, formaliz-

ing a divisive force in Indian politics and thus weakening opposition to British rule.

In 1914, with Chinese loss of control in Tibet following China's 1911 revolution, the northern boundary of India was pushed forward to the McMahon Line, following the highest peaks in the Himalayas. This frontier set the stage for numerous later boundary disputes between China and India, Pakistan, and Burma.

The Government of India Act of 1919 transferred some political power to elected provincial officials but left the appointed British governors firmly in control. In that year Mohandas K. Gandhi organized the first of many passive-resistance campaigns and was imprisoned as an agitator. In the face of rising nationalist sentiments and a growing non-cooperation movement, further reforms were discussed by the colonial authorities, but no concrete changes resulted until enactment in 1935 of the Government of India Act, which created elected provincial legislatures. In the first elections held under the act, in 1937, the Congress party under the leadership of Jawaharlal Nehru won control of seven of the 11 provinces. Nehru's goal of a united Indian opposition to British rule was thwarted, however, by a break with Mohammed Ali Jinnah's Moslem League, which demanded the creation of a separate Muslim state (see "Pakistan").

During World War II, the British military position in South Asia was greatly complicated by the rising demand for Indian independence. An offer of local autonomy, with independence to follow after the end of the war, was spurned by Nehru and the Congress party. An Indian National army under Subhas Bose fought with the Japanese against the British. Jinnah's position as the advocate of an independent Pakistan was greatly enhanced by his wholehearted support of the British during the war.

In 1946 the British government offered independence to India on terms that left the Congress party with little choice but to agree to the creation of a Muslim Pakistan. British withdrawal in August 1947 was accompanied by the formal creation of the dominions of India and Pakistan. The states of Bengal and the Punjab were divided between the two dominions. Agreement could not be reached on the status of Kashmir; border hostilities there continued until Jan. 1, 1949, when a cease-fire line negotiated under under UN auspices was accepted by both sides. That "temporary" line has never been ratified as a formal national boundary.

With the division of British India into India and Pakistan, and the rather abrupt withdrawal of British forces, pockets of Hindu populations in Pakistan and Muslim populations in India became targets of violence and atrocities by the majority populations. At least 12 million refugees fled in both directions to join their co-religionists; attacks on refugees created a death toll in the hundreds of thousands and created a legacy of bitterness that continues to dominate relations between India and Pakistan. On Jan. 30, 1948, Gandhi was assassinated by a Hindu extremist who blamed him for the partitioning of India.

Following India's independence in 1947,

hundreds of princely states were brought under control of the central government.

The British legacy in India included a sizable national elite, well educated and committed to principles of parliamentary democracy. The English language served as a vehicle to link the elites of India's linguistically diverse regions, easing fears by Bengalis, Tamils, and others of domination by a Hindi-speaking majority. India's economy had seen some industrial development under the British, but its infrastructure was geared to integration in a colonial empire rather than to independence as a developing nation. Port cities, heavy industry, and plantation agriculture coexisted with widespread rural poverty in subsistence-level villages; the early years following independence saw a massive migration of the rural poor into overburdened cities.

Under Prime Minister Jawaharlal Nehru, India assumed a leadership role in the world movement of nonaligned nations and followed a policy of neutrality in international affairs. The gradual development of good relations between the United States and Pakistan led to correspondingly difficult U.S.-India relations. In August 1971 India signed a 20-year friendship treaty with the Soviet Union.

Nehru died on May 27, 1964, and was succeeded by Lal Bahadur Shastri. Nehru's daughter, Mrs. Indira Gandhi, was named prime minister on Jan. 19, 1966. In 1967 the dominant Congress Party faced electoral setbacks; in 1969 it split into "Old" and "New" wings. Mrs. Gandhi's New Congress party won control of the legislature.

Within South Asia, India's foreign affairs since independence were dominated by conflicts over border issues. In the early 1950s, France peacefully ceded its five small coastal colonies to India. The Portuguese colony of Goa was annexed in 1961. In 1962 India fought a border war with China in northeastern Kashmir and in Assam; a 1963 cease-fire left the borders still unsettled. India and Pakistan went to war in April 1965 over the Rann of Kutch, a swampy delta area on the border between Gujarat and Sind. In 1968 an international arbitration commission awarded 90 percent of the area to India, 10 percent to Pakistan. In 1971 Bhutan was granted independence by India, with Bhutan's foreign policy and defense remaining under Indian control. The independent princely state of Sikkim was annexed by India in 1974, and its monarchy abolished in 1975.

After East Pakistan attempted to secede from Pakistan in April 1971, 10 million Bengali and Bihari refugees fled to India. India intervened in the war on Dec. 3, 1971, on both the eastern and western fronts. Pakistani soldiers in East Pakistan surrendered on Dec. 16, and Pakistan agreed to a cease-fire the following day, assuring the independence of Bangladesh. India and Pakistan agreed in July 1972 to seek a peaceful solution to their conflict and mutually withdraw troops. In August 1973 India agreed to free more than 90,000 Pakistani prisoners of war, who were released by the following April. The two countries resumed full diplomatic relations in 1976.

Faced with public protests and strikes after the New Congress party was convicted of voting irregularities in 1975, Mrs. Gandhi declared a state of emergency in June. Under emergency rule, censorship was imposed, thousands were arrested for political offences, and various economic-control measures were adopted. Mrs. Gandhi's son, Sanjay Gandhi, assumed significant informal power within his mother's government and was accused of corruption and of promoting a coercive program of population control in some areas. An opposition coalition led by the Jananta party won a massive victory in parliamentary elections in 1977. Mrs. Gandhi was driven from office, and the state of emergency was annulled.

Mrs. Gandhi's party was returned to power in 1980, and she resumed the prime ministership. Throughout the postindependence period, India had been plagued by separatist and nationalist movements, in Assam, Tamil Nadu, and other areas. In the early 1980s, a powerful Sikh separatist movement arose in the Punjab. Mrs. Gandhi's attempts to co-opt moderate Sikh leadership failed, and extremists took control of the Golden Temple in Amritsar, leading to open warfare between government troops and Sikh separatists. Mrs. Gandhi was assassinated by Sikh extremists on Oct. 31, 1984; more than 1,000 Sikhs were killed in the subsequent anti-Sikh rioting in Delhi. Mrs. Gandhi was succeeded in office by her son, Rajiv. In the face of rising violence in 1986–87, the Punjab was placed under the direct control of the federal government. Sikh terrorists continue to be active in the Punjab, and the situation remains unresolved.

In June 1980 over 700 Bengali residents in the village of Mandai, Tripura State, were massacred by local native extremists. In Tripura and Assam, protesters continue to demand the repatriation to Bangladesh of Bengali refugees who have become a majority of the population in some districts.

On Dec. 3, 1984, methyl isocyanate gas leaked from a Union Carbide plant in Bhopal, killing over 2,500 people. The accident prompted a broad inquiry into industrial safety standards in India.

Indian troops, in July 1987, intervened in the growing civil war in Sri Lanka between the government and Tamil separatists. A negotiated truce under Indian auspices broke down, and Indian troops continue to be involved in the conflict.

India has enjoyed significant domestic and international achievements in the 40 years since independence. The nation's territory has been consolidated, and separatist movements in various provinces have been successfully resisted. The federal parliamentary system has proved workable, and the federal government has established its constitutional right to intervene in state affairs under some conditions. India's armed forces are large, well trained, and well equipped, with a very small nuclear capability. India has maintained firm and watchful, but generally peaceful, relations with two unfriendly neighbors, Pakistan and China, and continues to play a leading role in the non-aligned movement. The Green Revolution of the 1970s, with improved hybrid crops and increased irrigation and fertilization, has made the country self-sufficient in food for the first time since the 19th century. The country has a large, well-educated middle class and a growing industrial economy.

Nevertheless, the government of Prime Minister Rajiv Gandhi faces ongoing problems. Separatist movements, regional grievances, and communal conflicts are a constant threat to national unity. Much of the population (65%) consists of illiterate people living in rural and urban poverty or near-poverty; the benefits of modernization have been unevenly distributed. Corruption is rife in politics and business. The national economy continues to be hampered by government intervention and severe controls on international trade and finance. Measures to control population growth have been generally unsuccessful. India's historical legacy of diversity and disunity under both native and colonial rule continues to make difficult the country's transformation into a modern nation-state.

Indonesia
Republic of Indonesia
(PREVIOUS NAME: NETHERLANDS OR DUTCH ANTILLES)

Geography Location: archipelago of about 13,700 islands, lying between mainland of Southeast Asia and Australia, stretching from Malay peninsula to New Guinea. **Boundaries:** only land frontiers with Papua New Guinea, to E of Irian Jaya, and with Malaysian states of Sarawak and Sabah, which occupy northern Borneo. **Total land area:** 735,538 sq. mi. (1,904,569 sq km). **Coastline:** 34,006 mi. (54,716 km). **Comparative area:** slightly less than three times the size of Texas. **Land use:** 8% arable land; 3% permanent crops; 7% meadows and pastures; 67% forest and woodland; 15% other; includes 3% irrigated. **Major cities:** (1983 est.) Jakarta (capital) 7,347,800; Surabaya 2,223,600; Medan 1,805,500; Bandung 1,566,700; Semarang 1,205,800.

People Population: 184,015,906 (1988). **Nationality:** noun—Indonesian(s); adjective—Indonesian. **Ethnic groups:** majority of Malay stock comprising 45% Javanese, 14% Sudanese, 7.5% Madurese, 7.5% coastal Malays. **Languages:** Indonesian (modified form of Malay; official); English and Dutch, leading foreign languages; local dialects, most widely spoken of which is Javanese. **Religions:** 88% Muslim, 6% Protestant, 3% Roman Catholic, 2% Hindu.

Government Type: republic. **Independence: Aug. 17, 1945 (from Netherlands). Constitution:** Aug. 1945, abrogated by Federal Constitution of 1949 and Provisional Constitution of 1950, restored July 5, 1959. **National holiday:** Independence Day, Aug. 17. **Heads of government:** Gen. (ret.) Suharto, president (since Mar. 1968). **Structure:** executive—headed by president who is chief of state and head of cabinet; cabinet selected by president; unicameral legislature (DPR, or House of Representatives) of 500 members (100 appointed, 400 elected); second body (MPR, or People's Consultative Assembly) of 1,000 members includes legisla-ture and 500 other members (chosen by several processes but not directly elected); MPR elects president and vice president and theoretically determines national policy; judicial—Supreme Court is highest court.

Economy Monetary unit: rupiah. **Budget:** (1988) *income:* $10.5 bil.; *expend.:* $13.9 bil. **GNP:** $59 bil., $330 per capita (1987 est.). **Chief crops:** subsistence food production, and smallholder and plantation production for export; rice, cassava, peanuts, rubber, cocoa; illegal producer of cannabis for international drug trade. **Livestock:** goats, cattle, sheep, pigs, buffalo. **Natural resources:** crude oil, tin, natural gas, nickel, timber. **Major industries:** petroleum, textiles, mining. **Labor force:** 67 mil. (1985 est.); 55% agriculture, 10% manufacturing, 4% construction, 3% transport and communication. **Exports:** $15 bil. (1987 est.); 55% petroleum and liquefied natural gas, 10% timber, 6% coffee, 5% rubber (1986). **Imports:** $11.1 bil. (1987 est.); 25% machinery, 23% chemical products, 12% base metals, 12% transport equipment, 9% food, beverages, and tobacco (1986). **Major trading partners:** (1985) *exports:* 46% Japan, 22% U.S., 9% Singapore, 2% Netherlands; *imports:* 26% Japan, 17% U.S., 9% Saudi Arabia, 8% Singapore, 7% W. Germany.

Intl. Orgs. ASEAN, FAO, G-77, GATT, IAEA, IBRD, ICAO, IDA, IFAD, IFC, ILO, IMF, IMO, INTELSAT, INTERPOL, ITU, NAM, OPEC, UN, UNESCO, UPU, WHO, WIPO, WMO.

The precolonial East Indies consisted of several Islamic and Hindu kingdoms in the western islands and tribal societies in the easterly ones. The Portuguese established trading posts in the 16th century; by the 17th century, control had largely passed to the Dutch East India Company. With the company's bankruptcy in 1799, the Dutch established direct colonial rule. Several 19th-century anticolonial uprisings, though costly to the Dutch, failed to dislodge them. Nationalist sentiment grew in the early 20th century, organized around Islamic groups, the Indonesian Communist party (PKI, founded 1920), and the Indonesian Nationalist party (PNI, founded 1927). Sukarno, founder of the PNI, achieved prominence as a nationalist leader and was jailed by the Dutch.

The Dutch East Indies fell quickly to the Japanese early in 1942. Some nationalists at first hailed the Japanese as liberators but quickly turned against their harsh occupation. On Aug. 17, 1945, Sukarno proclaimed Indonesia's independence. With British aid, the Dutch returned and tried to reestablish colonial rule; in 1949, threatened with a cutoff of American Marshall Plan aid, they withdrew and acknowledged Indonesia's independent status. With the Bogor Conference of Non-Aligned Nations in 1953, Indonesia under Sukarno took a leading role in Third World international affairs.

In 1963 Indonesia gained control of the last Dutch outpost in the Indies, Irian Jaya (western New Guinea). Sukarno then launched a disastrous policy of "confrontation" with Malaysia in North Borneo. Sukarno's politics moved steadily to the left, and Indonesia became hostile to the West and friendly with China. The influence of the PKI grew steadily. On Sept. 30, 1965, the army crushed an attempted coup by the PKI, setting off a popular reaction in which several hundred thousand people were killed as suspected Communists. Sukarno was shunted aside, and power devolved to Gen. Suharto, who became president in 1968. Indonesia played an instrumental role in founding the Association of Southeast Asian Nations (ASEAN) in 1967. The PKI was banned, and Indonesian policy swung sharply in favor of the West and the non-Communist states of Southeast Asia.

The economy grew rapidly, aided by oil revenue, timber exports to Japan, and the Green Revolution in rice agriculture. Foreign investment aided industrial development, which was hampered, however, by domestic content-laws and other trade restrictions. A policy of "transmigration" attempted, with mixed success, to move farmers from overcrowded Java and Bali to underdeveloped areas in Sumatra, Borneo, Sulawesi, and Irian Jaya. In 1975 Indonesia invaded the Portuguese colony of East Timor, which was annexed in 1976 amid persistent reports of human-rights violations.

In recent years declining oil revenues have been partly offset by the growth of industry and tourism. Pres. Suharto remains in power, at the head of the Golkar united-front party, which has been routinely returned to office in elections held every five years.

Iran
Islamic Republic of Iran

Geography Location: western Asia. **Boundaries:** USSR and Caspian Sea to N, Pakistan and Afghanistan to E, Persian (Arabian) Gulf and Gulf of Oman to S, and Turkey and Iraq to W. **Total land area:** 636,296 sq. mi. (1,648,000 sq km). **Coastline:** 1,976 mi. (3,180 km). **Comparative area:** slightly larger than Alaska. **Land use:** 8% arable land; negl. % permanent crops; 27% meadows and pastures; 11% forest and woodland; 54% other; includes 2% irrigated. **Major cities:** Tehran (Teheran) (capital) 6,022,029; Mashad (Meshed) 1,500,000; Isfahan 1,000,000 (1986 census); Tabriz 852,296; Shiraz 800,416 (1982 est.).

People Population: 51,923,689. **Nationality:** noun—Iranian(s); adjective—Iranian. **Ethnic groups:** 63% ethnic Persian, 18% Turkic, 13% other Iranian, 3% Kurdish. **Languages:** Farsi, Turki, Kurdish, Arabic, English, French. **Religions:** 93% Shi'a Muslim; 5% Sunni Muslim; 2% Zoroastrian, Jewish, Christian, and Baha'i.

Government Type: theocratic republic. **Constitution:** Dec. 2–3, 1979. **National holidays:** Shi'a Islam religious holidays observed nationwide; Victory of the Islamic Revolution, Feb. 11; Islamic Republic Day, April 1. **Heads of government:** Hujjat-ul-Islam Ali Khamenei, president (since Oct. 1981); Mir Hossein Mousavi, prime minister (since Sept. 1981). **Structure:** Ayatollah ol-Ozma Ruhollah Khomeini, leader of revolution, provides general guidance

for government, which is divided into executive, unicameral legislature (Islamic Consultative Assembly), and judicial branches.

Economy Monetary unit: rial. **Budget: income:** N.A.; **expend.:** proposed, $50 bil.; domestic lending provided about $13 bil. for expenditures. **GNP:** $86.4 bil., $1,756 per capita (1987). **Chief crops:** wheat, barley, rice, sugar beets; illegal producer of opium poppy for international drug trade. **Livestock:** sheep, goats, cattle, asses, horses. **Natural resources:** petroleum, natural gas, coal, chromium. **Major industries:** petroleum, petrochemicals, textiles. **Labor force:** 15.4 mil. (1988 est.); 33% agriculture, 21% manufacturing; shortage of skilled labor; unemployment may be as high as 35%. **Exports:** $12.3 bil. (1987 est.); 90% petroleum; carpets, fruits, nuts, hides. **Imports:** $10.0 bil. (1987 est.); machinery, military supplies, metal works, foodstuffs, pharmaceuticals. **Major trading partners: exports:** Japan, Turkey, Italy, Netherlands, Spain; **imports:** W. Germany, Japan, Turkey, UK, Italy.

Intl. Orgs. FAO, G-77, IAEA, IBRD, IDA, IFC, ILO, IMO, INTELSAT, OPEC, UN, UNESCO, UNIDO, WHO.

The Persian empire was established in 549 B.C. by Cyrus the Great, who united Persia and conquered Babylonia. His successors Darius and Xerxes tried unsuccessfully to conquer Greece. Alexander the Great conquered Persia in 333 B.C., but the Persians regained their independence after his death. The Persian Sassanian empire, established in A.D. 226, was the principal eastern rival of the Roman Empire. In 641 the Sassanians were defeated by invading Arabs, and Islam replaced the indigenous Zoroastrian religion. Persia reasserted its national identity—though not its political independence—under Islam and became a major center of Islamic culture, as well as the center of the Shi'a sect of Islam, which, in contrast to "orthodox" Sunni Islam, developed an organized clerical hierarchy and emphasized personal religious fervor and the ideal of martyrdom for the faith. In the early 13th century, Persia was conquered by the Mongols, who ruled the country until 1502.

The brilliant Safavid dynasty (1499–1736) was followed by two centuries of decline. During the 19th century, Persia lost control over Afghanistan and the Caucasus, while internal affairs came increasingly under British and Russian control. In 1907 an Anglo-Russian agreement formally divided Persia into spheres of influence. Following World War I, Persia was recognized as an independent nation, but was virtually a British protectorate. The Soviet Union renounced all claims to Persia in 1921.

In 1921 Reza Khan established a military dictatorship and had himself declared a hereditary monarch, Reza Shah Pahlavi, in 1925. In March 1935, the country's name was formally changed to Iran. In 1941 Great Britain, charging Iran with pro-Axis activity, occupied Iran and forced the abdication of Reza Shah in favor of his son, Mohammad Reza Shah Pahlavi. In 1945 Iran became a charter member of the United Nations, but Anglo-Soviet rivalry over

access to Iran's rich oil fields continued.

Under Mohammed Mossadegh the National Front gained power in 1951. With Mossadegh as premier, parliament nationalized the oil industry; Britain responded with an economic blockade. The shah was briefly driven from power, but in August 1953, monarchist elements with clandestine British and American support ousted Mossadegh and restored the shah to the throne. The shah pursued a pro-Western policy of modernization and anticommunism and was rewarded with massive military and economic aid. His combination of secular, authoritarian rule and economic and social modernization was popular with the urban business sector but deeply resented by the rural population and the urban poor. Unrestrained use of the secret police to suppress any sign of dissent led to widespread popular disaffection.

Religiously inspired protests resulted in widespread violence in late 1978. A military government was installed by the shah on Nov. 6, with Prime Minister Shahpur Bakhtiar given sweeping powers. The shah went into exile on Jan. 16, 1979. On Jan. 31 Iran's dominant religious leader, Ayatollah Ruhollah Khomeini, returned to Iran from his exile in France. Government forces were routed by Khomeini's supporters, and Bakhtiar's government fell on Feb. 11. Throughout 1979 clashes took place between rival religious factions, between religious parties and secular leftists, and between the urban middle class and the disenfranchised poor. Thousands of people were arrested and executed by the religious militia forces.

On Nov. 4, 1979, militants seized the U.S. embassy in Tehran and held 62 Americans hostage, provoking a long international crisis. An American military raid in April 1980 failed in an attempt to free the hostages. The hostages were finally freed on Jan. 21, 1981, minutes after Ronald Reagan was inaugurated as president of the United States. The following day Iran's president, Abolhassan Bani-Sadr, was dismissed from office, and the Ayatollah Khomeini took over direct executive powers. This was followed by a new wave of executions, with political moderates and non-Islamic religious believers among the principal victims.

On Sept. 22, 1980, a dispute between Iran and Iraq over the Shatt al-Arab waterway flared into open warfare. Fighting continued thereafter with no significant permanent gains for either side; casualties on the battlefield and from air raids have been extremely heavy. The war has hampered Iran's oil production and absorbed nearly all the revenue from oil exports, leaving the country nearly bankrupt.

In November 1986 American officials traveled secretly to Tehran in an attempt to trade U.S. arms to secure the release of hostages held by pro-Iranian elements in Lebanon, despite an official embargo on U.S. trade with Iran. Reports of this policy initiative provoked a major scandal in the United States and strengthened the hand of anti-American elements in Iran. In early 1988 American warships began patrolling the Persian Gulf to protect shipping from Iranian attacks. This led to a tragedy on July 3, 1988, when the USS *Vincennes* mistakenly shot down an Iranian civil jetliner, killing all on board.

In September 1988 a UN initiative led to a cease-fire between Iran and Iraq and to the opening of negotiations to find a permanent settlement to the war. Largely isolated from the world community, Iran's domestic priorities in the wake of the war are the rebuilding of the nation's economy and the planning of an orderly eventual transfer of power from the aged and infirm ayatollah to whoever will be his successor.

Iraq
Republic of Iraq
(PREVIOUS NAME: MESOPOTAMIA)

Geography **Location:** western Asia with narrow outlet to Persian (Arabian) Gulf. **Boundaries:** Turkey to N, Iran to E, Saudi Arabia and Kuwait to S, Syria and Jordan to W. **Total land area:** 169,190 sq. mi. (438,317 sq km). **Coastline:** 36 mi. (58 km). **Comparative area:** slightly more than twice size of Idaho. **Land use:** 12% arable land; 1% permanent crops; 9% meadows and pastures; 3% forest and woodland; 75% other; includes 4% irrigated. **Major cities:** Baghdad (capital) 3,236,000 (1987 census); Basrah (Basia) 1,540,000; Mosul 1,220,000; Kirkuk 535,000 (1977 census).

People **Population:** 17,583,467 (1988). **Nationality:** noun—Iraqi(s); adjective—Iraqi. **Ethnic groups:** 75–80% Arab, 15-20% Kurdish, 5% Turkoman, Assyrian, and other. **Languages:** Arabic (official), Kurdish (official in Kurdish areas), Assyrian, Armenian. **Religions:** 97% Muslim (60–65% Shi'a, 32–37% Sunni), 3% Christian and other.

Government **Type:** republic. **Independence:** Oct. 3, 1932 (from League of Nations mandate under British administration). **Constitution:** Sept. 22, 1968, effective July 16, 1970 (interim constitution). **National holidays:** anniversaries of 1958 and 1968 revolutions celebrated July 14 and 17; various religious holidays. **Heads of government:** Saddam Hussein, president and prime minister (since July 1979). **Structure:** Ba'ath party of Iraq has been in power since 1968 coup; unicameral legislature (National Assembly).

Economy **Monetary unit:** Iraqi dinar. **Budget:** *income:* $20.0 bil. (1987); *expend.:* $18.6 bil. (1984 est.). **GNP:** $40 bil., $2,400 per capita (1987 est.). **Chief crops:** dates, wheat, barley, rice, cotton. **Livestock:** sheep, goats, asses, camels. **Natural resources:** crude oil, natural gas, phosphates, sulphur. **Major industries:** petroleum, textiles, shoes. **Labor force:** 3.5 mil. (1980); 44% agriculture, 26% industry, 31% services; severe labor shortage due to war; about 900,000 Iraqis work abroad. **Exports:** $12.1 bil. (f.o.b., 1987 est.); nonoil receipts $600.0 mil. **Imports:** $10.5 bil. (f.o.b., 1987 est.); 5% from communist countries (1986). **Major trading partners:** (1986) *exports:* France, Italy, Brazil, Japan, Turkey, UK, Spain, USSR, other communist countries; *imports:* W. Germany, Japan, France, Italy, U.S., UK, Turkey, USSR, other communist countries.

Intl. Orgs. Arab League, FAO, G-77, IAEA, IBRD, ICAO, IDA, IFAD, IFC, ILO, IMF, IMO, INTELSAT, INTERPOL, ITU, NAM, OPEC, UN, UNESCO, UPU, WHO, WIPO, WMO.

The fertile lands of Mesopotamia, between the Tigris and Euphrates rivers, were the site of one of the world's oldest civilizations. The city-states of Sumer were founded before 3000 B.C. and later became the heart of the Babylonian empire. Babylon became subject to the Assyrian empire after 1350 B.C. and was conquered by the Persians under Cyrus and Darius in the mid-sixth century B.C. Mesopotamia remained under the control of various Persian dynasties for the next 1,000 years.

In the seventh century A.D., the region was rapidly incorporated into the expanding Islamic world. The battle of Basra in 656 decisively established Arab control. In 762 the Caliphate, the center of Islamic rule, was moved from Damascus to the newly founded city of Baghdad, near the ruins of ancient Babylon. Mongol invaders sacked Baghdad in 1258 and destroyed its irrigation works; thereafter the region entered a period of long-term decline. Baghdad fell to the Ottoman Turks in 1534, and Iraq remained a province of the Ottoman Empire until the 20th century.

British troops occupied Iraq in 1915, and Great Britain governed the country under a League of Nations Mandate after World War I. A Hashemite monarchy was organized under British protection in 1921. The kingdom of Iraq was granted independence in 1932 but remained closely tied to Great Britain by treaties guaranteeing British interests in petroleum and regional defense. Iraqi oil flowed through British-controlled pipelines traversing Jordan to Haifa (in Israel) and through a French-controlled pipeline traversing Syria to Latakia (in Lebanon).

After 1932 several attempted coups by anti-British factions were put down with the aid of British troops. One such coup in April 1941, sought aid from Italy and Germany; British troops landed at Basra in May and restored the pro-British monarchy. Iraq declared war against the Axis powers in 1943 and became a member of the United Nations in 1945.

In 1948 a proposed revision of the Iraqi-British treaty was defeated by the Iraqi parliament, which demanded that a date be set for the withdrawal of British forces. In 1948 Iraq joined the Arab League and participated in the first Arab-Israeli War. Most of Iraq's 85,000 Jews emigrated to Israel after the war ended.

In 1952 a new agreement with Great Britain gave the Iraq Petroleum Company greater control over the country's oil, and a greater share of oil revenues. While remaining part of the Arab League, Iraq in 1955 broke ties with Egypt and also expelled the Soviet ambassador. Iraq signed a mutual defense treaty with Turkey and became part of the Middle East Treaty Organization.

A leftist pan-Arab revolutionary coup overthrew the monarchy in 1958 and established a republic, reversing Iraq's former pro-Western stance in international affairs. Oil resources and other industries were nationalized, and large landholdings were broken up. In 1968 a

local branch of the international Ba'ath Socialist party came to power and established rule by decree within the republican framework of government. In 1972 the Soviet Union sent arms and advisors to Iraq. In the 1973 Arab-Israeli War, Iraq sent troops to aid Syrian forces on the front lines.

Iranian aid to a long-standing Kurdish rebellion in Iraq's northern mountains strained relations between the two countries. The Kurds were decisively defeated in a bloody campaign in 1975, following the withdrawal of Iranian support. The Kurdish rebellion continued, however, leading to Iraq's bombing of Kurdish villages in 1979 and other subsequent incidents.

The execution of 21 alleged Communist conspirators in 1978 disrupted relations between Iraq and the USSR. Trade relations with the West were resumed. On July 16, 1979, Gen. Saddam Hussein at-Takriti assumed control of the government and immediately purged leftist elements in the Baath movement.

Several months of intermittent fighting in 1980 between Iraq and Iran for control of the Shatt al-Arab waterway in southern Iraq led to the outbreak of open warfare on Sept. 22, when each country launched bombing attacks on the other's cities. Warfare quickly spread along the entire Iraq-Iran border. Iraqi troops occupied territory around the Iranian city of Abadan but were driven back across the border in May 1982. The Iran-Iraq War produced eight years of fierce but generally stalemated fighting, with reports of the use of poison gas by both sides. The war spread to the gulf in 1984, as both Iran and Iraq attacked tankers using each other's ports. On June 7, 1981, Israeli warplanes destroyed a nuclear reactor near Baghdad, claiming it was capable of producing nuclear weapons.

On May 17, 1987, the U.S.S. *Stark*, an American frigate on station in the gulf, was struck by missiles fired by an Iraqi fighter; 37 American sailors were killed. Iraq claimed that the attack was inadvertent and apologized to the U.S. government.

In September 1988, a UN conference led to a cease-fire in the Iran-Iraq War; fighting halted except for sporadic incidents as details of a peace settlement were being worked out. In the autumn of 1988, refugees in Turkey reported that poison gas had been used against Kurdish villages in northeastern Iraq as the Kurdish rebellion there continued.

Iraq's economy is dominated by production of oil in the Mosul and Kirkuk oil fields in the northern part of the country, carried by pipelines to the gulf terminals at Basra and Fao. Agriculture also remains important. Cotton and dates are produced in the hot, sandy south, while wheat and vegetables are important crops in the fertile lands between the Tigris and Euphrates near Baghdad.

Ireland

Geography **Location:** 26 of 32 counties comprising Island of Ireland, an island in Atlantic Ocean; remaining six counties, in NE, form Northern Ireland, which is part of United Kingdom. **Boundaries:** about 50 mi. (80 km) W of Great Britain. **Total land area:** 26,593 sq. mi. (68,895 sq km). **Coastline:** 900 mi. (1,448 km). **Comparative area:** slightly larger than W. Virginia. **Land use:** 14% arable land; negl. % permanent crops; 71% meadows and pastures; 5% forest and woodland; 10% other. **Major cities:** (1986 census) Dublin (capital) 920,956; Cork 173,694; Limerick 76,557; Galway 47,104; Waterford 41,054.

People Population: 3,531,502 (1988). **Nationality:** noun—Irishman (men), Irishwoman (women), Irish (collective pl.); adjective—Irish. **Ethnic groups:** Celtic, with English minority. **Languages:** Irish (Gaelic) and English (official); English widely spoken. **Religions:** 94% Roman Catholic, 4% Anglican, 2% other.

Government Type: republic. **Independence:** Dec. 6, 1921 (from UK). **Constitution:** Dec. 29, 1937. **National holiday:** St. Patrick's Day, Mar. 17. **Heads of government:** Dr. Patrick Hillery, president (since Nov. 1976); Charles J. Haughey, prime minister (since Mar. 1987). **Structure:** elected president; bicameral parliament (Seanad, Dail) reflecting proportional and vocational representation; judiciary appointed by president on advice of government.

Economy Monetary unit: Irish pound. **Budget:** (1987 est.) *income:* $8.17 bil.; *expend.:* $9.97 bil. **GNP:** $21.7 bil., $6,130 per capita (1986). **Chief crops:** livestock and dairy products, turnips, barley, potatoes, sugar beets, wheat; food shortages—grains, fruits, vegetables. **Livestock:** cattle, sheep, pigs. **Natural resources:** zinc, lead, natural gas, crude oil, barite. **Major industries:** food products, brewing, textiles, clothing. **Labor force:** 1.3 mil. (1986); 46.5% services, 21.4% manufacturing and construction, 12.9% agriculture, forestry, and fishing; 18.5% unemployment (1987). **Exports:** $12.6 bil. (f.o.b., 1986); foodstuffs (primarily dairy and meat products), data-processing equipment, live animals, machinery, chemicals, pharmaceuticals, clothing, glass, crystal. **Imports:** $11.6 bil. (c.i.f., 1986); machinery, petroleum and petroleum products, semifinished goods, cereals. **Major trading partners:** (1986) *exports:* 72.0% EC (34.1% UK, 10.9% W. Germany, 9.5% France), 8.7% U.S., 1.0% communist countries; *imports:* 67.3% EC (41.6% UK, 8.9% W. Germany, 5.1% France), 15.8% U.S., 1.9% communist countries.

Intl. Orgs. EC, FAO, GATT, IAEA, IBRD, ICAO, IDA, IFAD, IFC, ILO, IMF, IMO, INTELSAT, INTERPOL, ITU, OECD, UN, UNESCO, UPU, WIPO, WMO.

Ireland, a collection of warring Celtic chieftainships, was converted to Christianity by St. Patrick in the fifth century. Over the next two centuries, Ireland became a great center of monastic Christianity, sending missionaries to Scotland, England, and the continent. While the Roman Empire decayed, Ireland was a center of peace, culture, and learning. Viking invasions in the ninth and 10th centuries caused substantial damage and overturned the rule of the great monasteries and their secular allies.

By the time an Irish monarchy was reestablished by Brian Boru in 1014 and the surviving invaders were integrated into Irish society, Ireland had become an isolated, poor backwater on the periphery of Europe.

Trade gave rise to English commercial interests in Ireland and to Henry II's claim to overlordship of Ireland in the 12th century. Henry VIII declared himself king of Ireland and introduced the Reformation there. Large-scale Scottish immigration to Ulster began during the reign of Elizabeth I. Penal laws were applied, banning Catholics from public life and making the Mass an act of treason. A rebellion in 1641 was crushed by Oliver Cromwell over the course of a decade, ending with a massacre of thousands of Irish at Drogheda. After William of Orange's "Glorious Revolution" of 1688, the Irish supported James II, who was defeated at the Battle of the Boyne in 1690.

Following these events, British economic sanctions destroyed Ireland's flourishing export trade in wool. "Plantations" were established by British and Scottish Presbyterian landlords and farmers on lands seized from Irish Catholics. Much of the native aristocracy fled into exile, and the Gaelic language declined to near extinction.

A separate Irish Parliament, dominated by the Anglo-Irish establishment, was instituted in 1782, but it had little power. In 1798 a popular uprising led by Wolf Tone, with inspiration and aid from revolutionary France, was put down with great loss of life.

In 1800 Ireland and England were joined by the Act of Union, whereby Ireland was ineffectively represented in the British Parliament. After popular agitation led by Daniel O'Connell, the Catholic Emancipation Act was enacted by Parliament in 1829, though mandatory tithes continued to support the established Anglican church until 1869.

Under absentee landlords, the Irish population had been reduced to a subsistence diet based largely on potatoes. When a potato blight struck the country in the 1840s, disaster ensued. Between 1846 and 1851, one million people starved to death, and 1.6 million emigrated, most of them to America.

In the late 19th century, a home-rule movement under Thomas Parnell won wide popular support. A Home Rule Act finally was passed by Parliament in 1914, but its effect was postponed for the duration of World War I. Meanwhile the separatist Sinn Fein movement gained momentum, aided by an Irish literary and cultural renaissance in the early 20th century. The Land Purchase Acts of the early 20th century enabled dispossessed peasants to buy land from absentee landlords, creating a rural economic basis for an independent Ireland. The country's economy, based largely on agriculture and pasturage, began to recover. (Industry, principally shipbuilding and textiles, was largely confined to Northern Ireland.)

The postponement of home rule led to the Easter Rebellion of 1916; brutally suppressed, it was followed by the "Troubles," a period of guerrilla warfare lasting to 1920. In that year the Government of Ireland Act established six of Ulster's nine counties as Northern Ireland,

an integral part of the United Kingdom but with its own home-rule Parliament. The south's refusal of similar status led to the passage on Dec. 11, 1922, of the Irish Free State Act, by which Ireland became an independent dominion within the British Commonwealth.

The Fine Gael (People of Ireland) party governed until 1932, when Eamon De Valera, as the head of the Fianna Fail (Soldiers of Destiny) party, was elected president, holding that office until 1948. In 1938 the Constitution was revised to sever all connections with the British government except for an "external association" with the British monarchy. The outlawed Irish Republican Army (IRA) pressed for forcible reunification of Ireland and carried out attacks on British interests in both Ireland and Northern Ireland.

Ireland remained neutral during World War II, and its government objected to British military activities in Northern Ireland. But it was generally sympathetic to the Allied war effort, especially after the United States entered the war in 1941. Ireland's wartime neutrality, and its refusal to recognize the USSR, led to its being denied UN membership after the war; Ireland was admitted to the UN in 1955.

In 1949 Ireland severed all ties to the British Crown, becoming a fully independent republic. The Fianna Fail, normally the majority party since 1932, won a majority in the republic's first elections, and De Valera became prime minister. In 1954 a coalition government under John Costello took power. De Valera was elected president of the republic in 1959, as a new generation of parliamentary leadership arose.

During the 1950s, Ireland developed a moderate welfare state with the support of both the Fianna Fail and Fine Gael. In the 1960s attention turned to industrial development: zinc and lead mining, and export-oriented production of textiles, ceramics, and machinery. Ireland was admitted to the EEC in 1973. Ireland also became more active in international affairs; as a small nonaligned state, it frequently contributed troops to UN peacekeeping forces.

Beginning in the late 1960s, civil rights demonstrations led frequently to civil disorders and an increase in IRA guerrilla activity in the north. While the 1970s were a boom period for the Irish Republic, sectarian violence and terrorism in the north left over 2,500 dead. The 1980s saw the establishment of an Anglo-Irish Intergovernmental Council (1981) and the Hillsborough accords (1985) between the Thatcher government and the Fine Gael-Labour coalition, which gave Ireland a consultative role in Northern Irish disputes.

The government of Charles Haughey, elected in 1987, faces severe economic problems, including high tax rates, high inflation and unemployment, and a high level of public debt. The government is also preoccupied with events in the north, where sectarian problems remain unresolved and where a formula for the withdrawal of British troops continues to elude all parties. As a result, in the spring of 1989, Haughey's party lost ground in a hastily called general election, and he was forced to form a coalition government.

Israel
State of Israel

Geography Location: western Asia occupying narrow strip of territory on eastern shore of Mediterranean Sea; also has narrow outlet to Red Sea at northern tip of Gulf of Aqaba. **Boundaries:** Lebanon to N, Syria to NE, Jordan to E, Egypt to SW, Mediterranean Sea to W. **Total land area:** 8,302 sq. mi. (21,501 sq km). **Coastline:** 170 mi. (273 km). **Comparative area:** slightly larger than New Jersey. **Land use:** 17% arable land; 5% permanent crops; 40% meadows and pastures; 6% forest and woodland; 32% other; includes 11% irrigated. **Major cities:** (1983) Jerusalem (capital) 428,668; Tel Aviv-Jaffa 327,625; Haifa 235,775; Holon 133,460; Petach-Tikva 123,868.

People Population: 4,297,379 (1988). **Nationality:** noun—Israeli(s); adjective—Israeli. **Ethnic groups:** 83% Jewish, 17% non-Jewish (mostly Arab). **Languages:** Hebrew (official), Arab (official for Arab minority); English most widely used foreign language. **Religions:** 83% Judaism, 13.1% Islam (mostly Sunni Muslim), 2.3% Christian, 1.6% Druze.

Government Type: republic. **Independence:** May 14, 1948 (from League of Nations Mandate under British administration). **Constitution:** no formal constitution; some functions of constitution are filled by Declaration of Establishment (1948), the basic laws of the Knesset (legislature)—relating to the Knesset, Israeli lands, the president, government—and Israeli citizenship law. **National holidays:** Israel declared independence on May 14, 1948; because Jewish calendar is lunar, holiday varies from year to year; all major Jewish religious holidays are also observed as national holidays. **Heads of government:** Chaim Herzog, president (since May 1983); Yitzhak Shamir, prime minister (since Oct. 1986). **Structure:** president has largely ceremonial functions, except for authority to decide which political leader should try to form ruling coalition following election or fall of previous government; executive power vested in cabinet; unicameral parliament (Knesset) of 120 members elected under system of proportional representation; legislation provides fundamental laws in absence of written constitution; two distinct court systems (secular and religious).

Economy Monetary unit: new shekel. **Budget:** (1987) *income:* $23.5 bil.; *expend.:* $23.3 bil. **GNP:** $21.0 bil., $5,070 per capita (1986 est.). **Chief crops:** citrus and other fruits, vegetables, cotton, beef, and dairy products. **Livestock:** poultry, cattle, sheep, goats. **Natural resources:** copper, phosphates, bromide, potash, clay. **Major industries:** food processing, diamond cutting and polishing, textiles and clothing. **Labor force:** 1,400,000 (1984 est.); 29.5% public services; 22.8% industry, mining, and manufacturing; 12.8% commerce; unemployment about 6.7% (1985). **Exports:** $7.1 bil. (1986); polished diamonds, citrus and other fruits, textiles and clothing, processed foods, fertilizer and chemical products. **Imports:** $10.4 bil. (c.i.f., 1986); military equipment, rough diamonds, oil, chemicals,

machinery. **Major trading partners:** *exports:* U.S., UK, W. Germany, France, Belgium; *imports:* U.S., W. Germany, UK, Switzerland, Italy.

Intl. Orgs. FAO, GATT, IAEA, IBRD, ICAO, IDA, IFAD, IFC, ILO, IMF, IMO, INTELSAT, INTERPOL, ITU, OAS (observer), UN, UNESCO, UPU, WHO, WIPO, WMO.

In ancient times called the Land of Canaan, the region between the Jordan River and the Mediterranean Sea was one of the earliest sites of agricultural civilization in the Middle East. Hebrew exiles from Egypt arrived c. 1200 B.C.; their kingdom, Eretz Israel, was well established by 1000 B.C., with its capital at Jerusalem. The kingdom expanded under Kings Saul and David, who extended domination over the Philistines, a local seafaring people, and established the norms of Jewish religious worship at the great temple of Jerusalem.

After the reign of King Solomon, the kingdom split into two parts, Israel and Judah. Israel was conquered by the Assyrians in 722 B.C., and Judah by the Babylonians in 586 B.C. A locally autonomous state was reestablished under the Persian empire in the fifth century B.C. And in the fourth century B.C., Alexander the Great conquered the region, beginning a period of Hellenizing influence.

A new Jewish state was established in 141 B.C. after the revolt of the Maccabees against Hellenic rule, the state falling to the Roman Empire around 70 B.C. Roman rule was exerted through the puppet kings of the Herodian dynasty. Christianity, a messianic religion centering on the teachings of Jesus of Nazareth, was suppressed in Israel by both the Herodian kings and the Jewish priesthood but spread widely in the eastern Mediterranean in the early first century A.D.

A Jewish rebellion against Rome in A.D. 66 was forcibly suppressed, and the temple at Jerusalem was destroyed by the Romans in A.D. 70. Large numbers of Jews were expelled from Judea, beginning the Jewish Diaspora throughout the Roman world and beyond. A second rebellion of Jews in Israel was quelled in A.D. 132. The territory of the former kingdoms of Israel and Judah became generally known as Palestine, after the name of its ancient inhabitants, the Philistines.

With the official toleration of Christianity in the Roman Empire under Constantine I (early 4th century), Palestine became a major center of Christian pilgrimage. Politically, Palestine was administered as part of the Byzantine Empire.

Expansion of Islam from Arabia brought Palestine under Islamic rule in 636. Thereafter the region was ruled by the Caliphates of Damascus (661–750) and Baghdad (762–1258). Part of Palestine was captured in 1099 by European Crusaders, who established the short-lived Latin Kingdom of Jerusalem. The region was briefly conquered by the Mongols in 1258; defeat of the Mongols in 1260 at the battle of Ain Jalyut, near Nazareth, prevented a Mongol invasion of Egypt.

Palestine next became part of the Mamluk empire and in turn was incorporated into the

Ottoman Empire in 1516. The later Ottoman period was one of administrative decline, although the holy places of Judaism, Christianity, and Islam were maintained by local religious authorities.

The emigration of Jews from Europe to the homeland of Israel began around 1870, under the influence of the Zionist movement. Zionism, traceable in part to the thought of Moses Mendelssohn (1729–86), originally emphasized the need to maintain Jewish identity and religious consciousness as well as to promote Jewish assimilation into European culture. By the time of the First World Zionist Congress, convened in Basel by Theodor Herzl in 1897, emphasis had shifted to the need for a specific Jewish homeland. After 1905, under the leadership of Chaim Weizmann, Jewish emigration to Palestine increased as Weizmann attempted to win Turkish approval for a new state of Israel.

With the collapse of the Ottoman Empire during World War I, Palestine came under British rule in 1917. In that year the British government issued the Balfour Declaration, committing Britain to aiding the establishment of a Jewish homeland in Palestine. After Britain received a League of Nations Mandate to govern Palestine (as well as Transjordan) in 1923, Jewish immigration into Palestine increased significantly. Faced with rising Palestinian Arab opposition to a further increase in Jewish immigration, Britain reinterpreted the Balfour Declaration in greatly restricted terms and attempted to limit the number of Jewish arrivals.

The crisis thus provoked lasted until the outbreak of World War II. During the war the Palestinian Jewish community (then about 500,000) generally supported the British war effort, while some Palestinian Arab leaders translated anti-Zionist sentiments into sympathy for the Axis. In 1946 British authorities refused a recommendation of the Anglo-American Committee of Inquiry that they permit resettlement of 100,000 European Jews in Palestine and that limited further immigration to 2,000 per month. Jewish leaders pressed their cause at the United Nations, while in Palestine, Zionist terrorist organizations waged covert war against the British authorities.

In 1947 a UN Special Committee on Palestine, boycotted by Palestinian Arabs, recommended the partition of Palestine into Jewish and Arab sectors, with Jerusalem to be administered under international control. The United Nations adopted the recommendations on Nov. 29, 1947, and the British began to withdraw their forces, while Palestinian Jews and Arabs prepared for war.

On May 14, 1948, the independent state of Israel was established, with its capital at Tel Aviv. On the same day, troops from the Arab League nations attacked Israel. Fighting and cease-fires alternated throughout 1948; Israel lost control of the Old City of Jerusalem but retained the New City, and elsewhere consolidated its territorial control. Separate armistices between Israel and the Arab nations were concluded in 1949; Jordan retained control of the West Bank, and Egypt occupied

Gaza. Large numbers of Palestinian Arab refugees departed for camps in Jordan, Lebanon, and Syria, while equally large numbers of Jews from Arab countries resettled in Israel.

Elections to the Knesset (parliament) were held in January 1949 and resulted in a coalition government. Chaim Weizmann was elected president, and David Ben-Gurion became prime minister. Laws were enacted to ensure religious control of education and civil law and to affirm the "Right of Return" of all Jews to Israel. The role of labor (organized in the Histadrut) was protected by law, as was the establishment of agricultural collectives (kibbutzim).

Taking advantage of the Suez Crisis between Great Britain, France, and Egypt, Israel invaded Egypt's Sinai Peninsula on Oct. 29, 1956. Israeli forces withdrew under the terms of a UN cease-fire on Nov. 6 but retained control of Gaza. Thereafter an uneasy peace prevailed for 11 years under UN supervision.

Throughout this period Israel's population continued to swell with immigrants from Europe, the United States, and other Western countries, and also from the dwindling Jewish communities of the Arab world. Israel's economy, aided by foreign aid and private remittances, grew rapidly, while foreign military aid and the growth of a substantial domestic armaments industry increased its military preparedness.

On May 19, 1967, UN peacekeeping forces withdrew from the Egypt-Israel border on the insistence of Egypt's Pres. Gamal Abdel Nasser. Egyptian forces then reoccupied Gaza and closed the Gulf of Aqaba to Israeli shipping. In the Six-Day War, June 5–10, Israel recaptured Gaza, occupied the Sinai Peninsula to the Suez Canal, and captured the West Bank and the Old City of Jerusalem from Jordan and the Golan Heights from Syria. Another UN-supervised cease-fire went into effect.

Egypt and Syria, backed by Soviet airlifts, invaded Israel on Yom Kippur, Oct. 6, 1973. Israel, with strong U.S. support, counterattacked, driving back the Syrian forces and crossing the Suez Canal from the Sinai into Egypt. Fighting ceased on Oct. 24, and a disengagement agreement was signed on Jan. 18, 1974. Israeli forces withdrew from the west bank of the Suez Canal and, following further agreements, withdrew in stages from the Sinai Peninsula, completing the withdrawal in 1982.

The government of Prime Minister Golda Meir fell after the Yom Kippur War, and a new coalition took power. A period of domestic and international difficulties followed, with severe inflation in the economy and a marked rise in Palestinian and other terrorist attacks against Israeli targets. Israeli forces repeatedly attacked Palestinian bases in southern Lebanon and aided the Christian militia forces in the Lebanese civil war of 1975–76. On July 3, 1976, Israeli commandos raided the airport at Entebbe, Uganda, to rescue 103 hostages held by Arab and German hijackers.

The 1977 parliamentary elections brought a conservative coalition to power, with Menachem Begin elected prime minister. Egypt's president Anwar Sadat visited Jerusalem in

November 1977, and Begin and Sadat met at a conference with U.S. Pres. Jimmy Carter at Camp David in 1979. On Mar. 26, 1979, Egypt and Israel signed a formal peace treaty ending 30 years of war and establishing diplomatic relations between the two nations.

In July 1980 Israel affirmed the transfer of its national capital from Tel Aviv to Jerusalem and the incorporation of the (formerly Jordanian) Old City into Israeli territory. The Israeli government decided in 1980 to promote increased Jewish settlement in the West Bank, provoking protest from Palestinian leaders.

Israeli forces invaded southern Lebanon in March 1978. After a brief occupation, most Israeli forces withdrew and were replaced by a UN peacekeeping force, but Israel continued to cooperate with Lebanese Christian militia forces in anti-Palestinian operations. Israeli forces again reoccupied southern Lebanon for five days in April 1980.

Israeli and Syrian forces clashed briefly in April 1981. On June 7, 1981, Israeli jets destroyed a nuclear reactor near Baghdad, Iraq, that Israel claimed could have been used to manufacture materials for nuclear weapons. Prime Minister Begin was returned to office in a close election on June 30, 1981, and he retired in 1983.

Attacking Palestine Liberation Organization strongholds in Lebanon in May, 1982, Israel mounted a full-scale invasion of Lebanon on June 6. Israeli and Syrian forces fought in Lebanon's Bekaa Valley on June 9 but disengaged after a few days. On June 14 Israeli forces surrounded and shelled Beirut, forcing the PLO to evacuate the city. On Sept. 14 Israeli forces occupied West Beirut, following the assassination of the newly elected Lebanese president, Bashir Gemayel. Lebanese Christian militia, with tacit Israeli permission, entered two Palestinian refugee camps at Sabra and Shatila on Sept. 16 and massacred hundreds of civilians, provoking an international outcry against Israel's occupation of Lebanon. Israeli forces withdrew from Lebanon in June 1985.

Parliamentary elections in 1984 resulted in a stalemate between the conservative Likud party and the Labor party, and increased the strength of several splinter right-wing religious parties. A grand-coalition government was formed, with power shared by Likud leader Yitzhak Shamir and Labor leader Shimon Peres. The coalition proved unable to undertake any serious initiatives in foreign or domestic policy. Shamir vetoed an agreement negotiated by Peres with Jordan's King Hussein I to attend a UN-sponsored peace conference in April 1987. Domestically, serious inflation continued to damage the economy, while social stresses caused by the rising power of ultraconservative religious factions grew more severe.

In December 1987, Palestinian residents of Gaza and the West Bank launched a series of violent demonstrations against Israeli authorities. The *intifada*, or uprising, continued into 1989 in a cycle of protest and police reaction that has led to the deaths of hundreds of demonstrators and a crisis of Israeli control in the occupied territories.

Parliamentary elections in November 1988 continued the Likud-Labor stalemate and brought increased power to the minor religious parties. A planned conservative coalition between Likud and some religious parties, involving a Likud pledge to enact into law a set of Orthodox restrictions on the Right of Return, was abandoned after an outcry from the international Jewish community. In January 1989 a new grand-coalition government was announced, with Yitzhak Shamir as prime minister and Shimon Peres as minister of finance.

Despite a near-constant condition of war or threat of war since 1948, Israel's economy is thriving in comparison with the other nations of the Middle East. Advanced irrigation techniques have led to abundant production of cotton, vegetables, dates, olives, and fruit. Israel has few mineral or petroleum resources, but the industrial sector is diverse, including textiles, diamond cutting, electronics, plastics, machinery, and pharmaceuticals. There is a large and sophisticated armaments industry. Nevertheless, the economy is hampered by chronic inflation and is heavily dependent on foreign (mostly U.S.) aid from both the public and private sectors.

Italy
Italian Republic

Geography Location: peninsula, extending from southern Europe into Mediterranean Sea, with a number of adjacent islands, principally Sicily to SW, and Sardinia to W. **Boundaries:** Switzerland and Austria to N, Yugoslavia to NE, Adriatic Sea to E, Ionian Sea to SE, Mediterranean Sea to W, France to NW. **Total land area:** 116,324 sq. mi. (301,277 sq km). **Coastline:** 3,105 mi. (4,996 km). **Comparative area:** slightly larger than Arizona. **Land use:** 32% arable land; 10% permanent crops; 17% meadows and pastures; 22% forest and woodland; 19% other; includes 10% irrigated. **Major cities:** (1986) Roma (Rome; capital) 2,815,457; Milano (Milan) 1,495,260; Napoli (Naples) 1,204,211; Torino (Turin) 1,035,565.

People Population: 57,455,362 (1988). **Nationality:** noun—Italian(s); adjective—Italian. **Ethnic groups:** primarily Italian, but includes small clusters of German-, French-, and Slovene-Italians in north and Albanian-Italians in south; Sicilians. **Languages:** Italian; parts of Trentino-Alto Adige region (e.g., Bolzano) are predominantly German-speaking; significant French-speaking minority in Valle d'Aosta region; Slovene-speaking minority in Trieste-Gorizia area. **Religions:** almost 100% nominally Roman Catholic.

Government Type: republic. **Independence:** N.A. **Constitution:** Jan. 1, 1948. **National holiday:** Anniversary of the Republic, June 2. **Heads of government:** Francesco Cossita, president (since June 1985); Guilio Andreotti, prime minister (since 1989). **Structure:** executive—president empowered to dissolve parliament and call national election; commander of armed forces presides over Supreme Defense Council; otherwise, authority to govern invested in Council of Ministers; bicameral legislature—popularly elected parliament (315-member Senate, 630-member Chamber of Deputies); judiciary—independent.

Economy Monetary unit: lire. **Budget:** N.A. **GNP:** $743.0 bil., $12,955 per capita (1987). **Chief crops:** fruits, wine, vegetables, cereals, potatoes, olives; 95% self-sufficient; food shortages—fats, meat, fish, eggs. **Livestock:** sheep, pigs, cattle, goats, horses. **Natural resources:** mercury, potash, marble, sulphur, dwindling natural gas and crude oil reserves. **Major industries:** machinery transportation equipment, iron and steel, chemicals. **Labor force:** 22.37 mil. (1986); 48.6% services (1984), 30.5% industry, 10.5% agriculture; 12% unemployment (1987). **Exports:** $97.8 billion (f.o.b., 1986); transportation equipment (rail and auto), textiles, chemicals, footwear, foodstuffs (wine, olive oil, pasta). **Imports:** $99.4 billion (c.i.f., 1986); petroleum, machinery, transport equipment; foodstuffs; ferrous and nonferrous metals; wool, cotton. **Major trading partners:** (1986) 54.5% EC (19.3% W. Germany, 15.0% France, 6.0% UK, 4.4% Switzerland), 8.2% U.S., 5.5% Middle East (1.4% Libya), 2.9% Eastern Europe, 2.0% USSR.

Intl. Orgs. EC, FAO, GATT, IAEA, IBRD, ICAO, IDA, IFAD, IFC, ILO, IMF, IMO, INTELSAT, INTERPOL, ITU, NATO, OAS (observer), OECD, UN, UNESCO, UPU, WHO, WIPO, WMO.

Rome became the major power in Italy around 500 B.C., dominating the Etruscans in the north and Greek settlements in the south. The Roman Republic already dominated most of the Mediterranean and western Europe by the time imperial rule was established under Julius Caesar. The empire was divided between Rome and Byzantium in the fourth century A.D. The Roman Empire in the west was severely weakened by Germanic invasions in the fifth century and thereafter gradually dissolved, so that Italy became a disunited collection of aristocratic holdings and independent cities.

By the 10th century, the city-states, especially in the north, emerged as major powers, rivaling the Papal States of the central peninsula. Venice and Genoa emerged as major maritime powers during the medieval period, while Florence, Siena, and other cities developed into centers of agricultural and commercial wealth, impelling the successive renaissances of the 12th and 15th centuries. With the rise of the Habsburg empire, the monarchical powers of northern Europe vied for power in Italy, and the peninsula's small states became pawns of France, Spain, and Austria.

At the turn of the 19th century, Napoleon created the short-lived Kingdom of Italy as a French satellite, but after his fall, there was a general return to the old pattern, with Austria dominating the north. Metternich in 1815 called Italy a "geographic expression."

The 19th century saw the spread in Italy of French revolutionary ideals, accompanied by a growing sense of nationalism in both politics and culture. The revolutionary military leader, Giuseppe Garibaldi, and the statesman, Conte Camillo di Cavour, brought about, by war and diplomacy, the establishment of the Kingdom of Italy in 1861. The kingdom wrested Venice away from Austria and absorbed the Papal States in 1870.

Although united territorially, the kingdom was divided by conflict between church and state, north and south, modern urban industry versus semifeudal rural poverty. Parliamentary politics under the constitutional monarchy created a regime that was weak and venal, inspiring little popular support.

Italy joined the Allied powers in World War I, but its minor gains from the Treaty of Versailles scarcely seemed to justify its wartime suffering and one million dead. Postwar economic dislocation and fear of communism combined with political disillusionment to create fertile ground for the rise of fascism. Benito Mussolini took over the Italian government at the invitation of the king in 1922 and soon acquired dictatorial powers. Papal secular authority in Vatican City was reestablished by the Lateran Agreement of 1929. In the late 1920s and early 1930s, Italy appeared to be a major power, defending Austria from Germany, colonizing Ethiopia, supporting Francisco Franco in the Spanish civil war, and joining in an "axis" with Hitler's Germany.

Mussolini, the senior partner in the fascist axis, soon was eclipsed by Hitler, and Italy was drawn into the disaster of World War II in 1939. Italy annexed Albania and invaded Greece, but that campaign turned into a fiasco from which German troops had to save the Italian army. In 1943 Allied attacks on Italy began; the fascist Grand Council restored to power the king, Victor Emmanuel III, who then had Mussolini arrested. Hitler intervened in September 1943 and began the war in Italy anew, rescuing Mussolini who established another fascist regime in northern Italy, while the legal Italian government in the south switched sides and welcomed Italy's liberation.

As the Allies moved north, liberated territory was placed into the hands of opponents of the fascist regime. The head of the first postwar government was a Christian Democrat, Alcide de Gasperi. The monarchy was abolished by plebiscite in 1946, and the Republic of Italy was established. The north supported the republic, while monarchism retained significant support in the south.

This division reflected a roughly accurate generalization that sees Italy as comprising a progressive commercial and industrial north and a backward agricultural/pastoral south. Despite such industrial giants of the north as Fiat and Pirelli, however, Italy's manufacturing is primarily carried on by medium-size and small firms, while agriculture has been characteristic of the whole of the country. As late as 1956, there were more Italian workers in agriculture than in industry. Agriculture in the north is generally more prosperous than in the south, with its more arid climate and impoverished soil. Italy is a net food importer.

In the first elections under the republic, in 1948, the Christian Democrats benefited from obvious American patronage and a split in the ranks of the Left to win a clear parliamentary majority. Italy accepted Marshall Plan aid and membership in NATO; reintegration into the European mainstream found expression in membership in the Council of Europe and the Coal and Steel Community.

Domestically, reconstruction was the major task, with both industrial and agricultural output severely hampered by social and physical damage from the war; inflation was rampant and basic social services impaired. The Christian Democrats, normally in Center-Right coalitions in the 1950s and Center-Left coalitions in the 1960s, adopted a policy rather like that of West Germany, with efforts directed at creating a stable currency, a free market, comprehensive social welfare programs, and occasional state intervention in the economy. This created an Italian "economic miracle," with industrial production doubling between 1953 and 1961 and increasing an additional 40 percent by 1966, led by steel, automobiles, machinery, and electrical equipment.

State holding companies have been dominant in banking and energy production and have had a leading role in other large enterprises. An important goal has been to direct investment to the south, including the islands of Sardinia and Sicily. That program has had only marginal success, with the south remaining relatively poor, and increasingly depopulated by migration from rural to urban areas.

In the 1970s and 1980s, the Christian Democrats have gradually declined in political influence, normally gaining less than 40 percent of the popular vote while continuing to provide premiers in often short-lived coalition cabinets. Left-wing terrorism became a major national problem, provoking crises when the Christian Democratic leader and former prime minister Aldo Moro was kidnapped and murdered in 1978, and U.S. Brig. Gen./NATO officer James Dozier was kidnapped (and subsequently rescued) in 1981. The government of Bettino Craxi, Italy's first Socialist premier, was severely shaken in the aftermath of the 1985 *Achille Lauro* hijacking, when it refused to cooperate with the United States in apprehending and trying the hijackers. Craxi resigned in 1987 and was replaced by Giovanni Goria.

Throughout the 1980s, Italy, like the rest of Europe, contended with slowed economic growth, higher inflation, and increased unemployment. Lacking effective political unity, Italy's coalition governments have tended to muddle along in the face of these problems.

Ivory Coast
Republic of Cote D'Ivoire
Geography Location: western coast of Africa. **Boundaries:** Mali and Burkina Faso to N, Ghana to E, Gulf of Guinea to S, Liberia and Guinea to W. **Total land area:** 122,780 sq. mi. (318,000 sq km). **Coastline:** 320 mi. (515 km). **Comparative area:** slightly larger than New Mexico. **Land use:** 9% arable land; 4% permanent crops; 9% meadows and pastures; 26% forest and woodland; 52% other; includes negl. % irrigated. **Major cities:** (1979) Yamoussoukro (capital—not recognized by U.S., which recognizes Abidjan; population N.A.); Abidjan 1,423,323; Bouaké 272,640.

People **Population:** 11,184,847 (1988). **Nationality:** noun—Ivorian(s); adjective—Ivorian. **Ethnic groups:** 23% Baoule, 18% Bete, 15% Senoufou, 11% Malinke and Agni; over 60 ethnic groups; 2 million foreign Africans, mostly Burkinabe; about 130,000–330,000 non-Africans (100,000–300,000 Lebanese, 30,000 French). **Languages:** French (official); over 60 dialects with Dioula most widely spoken. **Religions:** 63% indigenous beliefs, 25% Muslim, 12% Christian.

Government **Type:** republic; one-party presidential regime established 1960. **Independence:** Aug. 7, 1960 (from France). **Constitution:** Nov. 3, 1960. **National holiday:** Dec. 7. **Heads of government:** Félix Houphouet-Boigny, president (since 1960). **Structure:** executive—president has broad powers; unicameral legislature—175-member National Assembly; judiciary.

Economy **Monetary unit:** Communauté Financière Africaine (CFA) franc. **Budget:** (1986) *income:* $1.6 bil.; *expend.:* $1.6 bil. **GDP:** $10.4 bil., $970 per capita (1987). **Chief crops:** cash crops—coffee, cocoa, wood, bananas, pineapples, palm oil; food crops—corn, millet, yams, rice; other commodities—cotton, rubber, tobacco. **Livestock:** goats, sheep, cattle, pigs. **Natural resources:** crude oil, diamonds, manganese, iron ore, cobalt. **Major industries:** foodstuffs, wood processing, oil refinery. **Labor force:** (1985) over 85% agriculture, forestry, livestock raising; 11% wage earners, nearly half in agriculture and remainder in government, industry, commerce, and professions; 54% of working age. **Exports:** $3.4 bil. (f.o.b., 1986 est.); 30% cocoa, 20% coffee, 11% tropical woods; cotton, bananas. **Imports:** $1.6 bil. (c.i.f., 1986 est.); 50% manufactured goods and semifinished products, 40% consumer goods, 10% raw materials and fuels. **Major trading partners:** (1984) France, Nigeria, W. Germany, Netherlands, U.S.

Intl. Orgs. FAO, G-77, GATT, IAEA, IBRD, ICAO, IDA, IFAD, IFC, ILO, IMF, IMO, INTELSAT, INTERPOL, ITU, NAM, UN, UNESCO, UPU, WHO, WIPO, WMO.

The peoples of the Ivory Coast belong to various tribes that had established small and mutually hostile kingdoms prior to the 18th century. The dominant Baule migrated to the Ivory Coast from Ghana about 200 years ago. European contact began with the Portuguese, who established coastal trading stations in the 15th century. They were followed in rapid succession by the Dutch, British, and French, who landed at Assinie in 1637. The region's dense tropical forests, along with a lack of good harbors on its surf-pounded coast, retarded European exploration.

France established a protectorate over the coastal zone in 1842 and during the remainder of the 19th century expanded their control, by conquest and diplomacy, into the interior. In 1893 the Ivory Coast was organized as a French colony, and in 1904 it was confederated with the other nations of French West Africa. Upper Volta was administratively joined with the Ivory Coast in 1932 but separated again in 1947.

France's Vichy government controlled French West Africa during World War II and harshly suppressed the region's growing nationalist movements. In 1946 a group of West African leaders, inspired by Félix Houphouet-Boigny, formed the African Democratic Assembly, which initially opposed French rule but later cooperated with the French authorities in the implementation of reforms. These included, by 1956, universal suffrage and the formation of locally autonomous assemblies.

In 1958 a referendum in the Ivory Coast approved the French Community of Nations, which provided the basic structure for French decolonization. On May 29, 1959, the Ivory Coast joined with Upper Volta, Dahomey, and Niger in a loose union called the Council of the Entente, which was later joined by Togo. Complete independence for the Ivory Coast came on Aug. 4, 1960, and the country was admitted to the United Nations in the following month.

Félix Houphouet-Boigny was unanimously elected the first president of the Ivory Coast and has been repeatedly reelected since. He has emerged as one of Africa's strongest and most enlightened leaders, and he played a key role in forming the Organization of African Unity in 1963. Under his presidency, the Ivory Coast has enjoyed both political stability and economic prosperity. The Ivory Coast maintains strong commercial and cultural ties to France and is on good terms with other Western-bloc nations.

The country's diversified economy includes agriculture, with coffee and cocoa as leading exports; forest products, including timber and rubber; diamond and manganese mining; and fishing. Despite the government's efforts to restrain immigration of short-term foreign workers, about one-third of the country's population is made up of migrants from neighboring West African nations.

Jamaica

Geography **Location:** 145 km south of Cuba in Caribbean Sea. **Boundaries:** Caribbean Sea to N, E, S, and W. **Total land area:** 4,244 sq. mi. (10,991 sq km). **Coastline:** 635 mi. (1,022 km). **Comparative area:** slightly smaller than Connecticut. **Land use:** 19% arable land; 6% permanent crops; 18% meadows and pastures; 28% forest and woodland; 29% other; includes 3% irrigated. **Major cities:** Kingston (capital) 104,000 (1980 census); Montego Bay 42,800 (1970 census); Spanish Town 41,600 (1970 census).

People **Population:** 2,458,102 (1988). **Nationality:** noun—Jamaican(s); adjective—Jamaican. **Ethnic groups:** 76.3% African, 15.1% Afro-European, 3.4% East Indian and Afro-East Indian, 3.2% white, 2% other. **Languages:** English, Creole. **Religions:** predominantly Protestant (including Anglican and Baptist), some Roman Catholic, some spiritualist cults.

Government **Type:** independent state within Commonwealth, recognizing Elizabeth II as head of state. **Independence:** Aug. 6, 1962 (from UK). **Constitution:** Aug. 6, 1962.

National holiday: Independence Day, first Monday in August. **Heads of government:** Michael Manley, prime minister (since Feb. 1989); Sir Florizel Glasspole, governor-general (since 1973). **Structure:** cabinet headed by prime minister; bicameral legislature—21-member Senate (13 nominated by prime minister, 8 by opposition leader, if any; currently no official opposition because of People's National party boycott of Dec. 1983 election; eight non-Jamaican Labor party members appointed to current Senate by Prime Minister Seaga), 60-member elected House of Representatives; judiciary follows British tradition under chief justice.

Economy **Monetary unit:** Jamaican dollar. **Budget:** (FY 1987 est.) *income:* $788 mil.; *expend.:* $878 mil. **GDP:** $2.4 bil., $1,000 per capita (1986). **Chief crops:** sugarcane, citrus fruits, bananas, pimento, coconuts, coffee, cocoa, tobacco; illegal producer of cannabis for international drug trade. **Livestock:** goats, cattle, pigs, asses, mules, horses, sheep. **Natural resources:** bauxite, gypsum, limestone. **Major industries:** tourism, bauxite mining, textiles. **Labor force:** 728,700 (1984); 32% agriculture, 28% industry and commerce, 27% services, 13% government; shortage of technical and managerial personnel; 22% unemployment. **Exports:** $596 mil. (f.o.b., 1986); alumina, bauxite, sugar, bananas, citrus fruits and fruit products. **Imports:** $964 mil. (c.i.f., 1986); fuels, machinery, transportation and electrical equipment, food, fertilizer. **Major trading partners:** (1985) *exports:* 48% U.S., 15% EC, 12% UK, 3% Norway; *imports:* 42% U.S., 14% Netherlands Antilles, 11% Venezuela, 5% UK.

Intl. Orgs. Commonwealth, FAO, GATT, G-77, IAEA, IBRD, ICAO, IFAD, IFC, ILO, IMF, IMO, INTERPOL, ITU, NAM, OAS, UN, UNESCO, UPU, WHO, WIPO, WMO.

"Discovered" by Christopher Columbus in 1494, Jamaica remained under Spanish rule until it fell to British control in 1655. Because of its sugar crop, Jamaica had become an extremely valuable colonial possession by the 18th century, as well as one of the busiest slave markets in the world. Emancipation of the slaves in 1833 and abolition of tariff protection in 1846 contributed strongly to the subsequent downfall of the plantation economy.

In 1962 the island gained its independence. The country has been plagued by racial and class division set within the context of an underdeveloped economy. People's National party candidate Michael Manley became prime minister and governed during most of the 1970s. His administration steered the country in a socialist direction, and his government established close ties with Cuba. Edward Seaga's Jamaica Labor party came to power in 1980, but Manley was reelected to office in 1988. That same year a powerful hurricane caused extensive death and destruction on the island.

Japan

Geography **Location:** chain of more than 3,000 islands extending some 1,300 mi. (2,200 km) NE to SW between Sea of Japan and Pacific

Ocean in eastern Asia; southern Japan is about 93 mi. (150 km) E of S. Korea; four large islands—(from N to S) Hokkaido, Honshu, Shikoku, and Kyushu—account for 98% of land area. Boundaries: Sea of Okhotsk to N, Pacific Ocean to E, East China Sea to SW, and Sea of Japan to W. **Total land area:** 145,870 sq. mi. (377,657 sq km). **Coastline:** 8,505 mi. (13,685 km). **Comparative area:** slightly smaller than California. **Land use:** 11% arable land; 2% permanent crops; 2% meadows and pastures; 68% forest and woodland; 17% other; includes 9% irrigated. **Major cities:** (1986) Tokyo (capital) 8,354,615; Yokohama 2,992,926; Osaka 2,636,249; Nagoya 2,116,381; Sapporo 1,542,979.

People Population: 122,626,038 (1988). **Nationality:** noun—Japanese (sing., pl.); adjective—Japanese. **Ethnic groups:** 99.4% Japanese, 0.6% other (mostly Korean). **Languages:** Japanese. **Religions:** most Japanese observe both Shinto and Buddhist rites; about 16% belong to other faiths, including 0.8% Christian.

Government Type: constitutional monarchy. **Constitution:** May 3, 1947. **National holiday:** Foundation Day, Feb. 11. **Heads of government:** Akihito, emperor (since 1989); Noboru Takeshita, prime minister (since Nov. 1987). **Structure:** Emperor is symbol of state; executive power is vested in cabinet appointed by prime minister, chosen by lower house of bicameral, elective legislature—diet (House of Councillors, House of Representatives); judiciary is independent.

Economy Monetary unit: yen. **Budget:** (1988) *income:* $341 bil.; *expend.:* $423 bil. **GNP:** $2,664 bil., $21,820 per capita (1986). **Chief crops:** land intensively cultivated; rice, sugar, vegetables, fruits; 71% self-sufficient in food (1985); food shortages—wheat, corn, beans. **Livestock:** chickens, pigs, cattle, goats, sheep. **Natural resources:** negl. mineral resources, fish. **Major industries:** metallurgical and engineering industries, electrical and electronic industries, textiles. **Labor force:** 60.2 mil. (1987); 53% trade and services, 33% manufacturing, mining, and construction. **Exports:** $210.8 bil. (f.o.b., 1986); 97% manufactures (including 33% machinery, 26% motor vehicles, 8% consumer electronics). **Imports:** $127.5 bil. (c.i.f., 1986); 34% manufactures, 31% fossil fuels, 18% foodstuffs, 16% nonfuel raw materials. **Major trading partners:** *exports:* 38% U.S., 20% Southeast Asia, 18% Western Europe, 7% communist countries, 5% Middle East; *imports:* 23% Southeast Asia, 23% U.S., 15% Middle East, 14% Western Europe, 7% communist countries.

Intl. Orgs. Colombo Plan, FAO, GATT, IAEA, IBRD, ICAO, IDA, IFAD, IFC, ILO, IMF, IMO, INTELSAT, INTERPOL, ITU, UN, UNESCO, UPU, WHO, WIPO, WMO.

Japan's ancient Jomon civilization was displaced by proto-Japanese Yayoi migrants from mainland northeast Asia beginning in the fourth century B.C. In the early Yayoi period, a mounted military aristocracy dominated rice-growing commoners. The shamanic religion of the time was ancestral to Japan's later indigenous religion, Shinto. Yayoi society evolved into the Yamato protostate, c. A.D. 250–500. The Yamato kings were buried in large, elaborate tomb mounds together with haniwa clay sculptures. From the third century A.D., contact with the mainland increased. Korean missionaries introduced Buddhism and Chinese writing in the mid-sixth century. A centralized monarchy developed in the Yamato Plain, central Honshu Island; Prince Shotoku, a great patron of Buddhism, founded the Horyuji and other great temples in the early seventh century.

In 710 the Yamato kings established a permanent capital for the first time, at Nara; the city was modeled on the contemporary Chinese capital. In 785 the court, split by factionalism and dominated by Nara's large and wealthy Buddhist temples, abandoned the capital; in 794 the new capital at Heian (Kyoto) was completed. The ensuing Heian period was one of the most brilliant in Japanese history. A small civil aristocracy, dominated by the Fujiwara family, drew great wealth from provincial estates and created a metropolitan culture of extreme refinement. From the ninth through the 11th centuries, strong Chinese influences were incorporated into Japanese culture.

In the 12th century the power of the Heian court waned as the influence of the provincial military aristocracy (samurai) grew stronger. In 1156 the capital was seized by the Taira family; in 1185 the Taira were overthrown by their rivals, the Minamoto. The Minamoto established a military government under a shogun (generalissimo) at Kamakura; the emperor remained at Kyoto, stripped of all governmental authority. In Kamakura the Minamoto were soon displaced by their former vassals, the Hojo. During the Kamakura period, the Japanese drew away from Chinese influence in art, architecture, literature, and religion in the process of creating a more distinctively Japanese culture. In 1274 and again in 1281, attempted Mongol invasions were repulsed with the aid of timely typhoons (*kamikaze*, "divine winds").

In the course of a failed attempt at imperial restoration, the Kamakura shogunate was overthrown, in the 1330s, by the Ashikaga family, which in 1338 established a new shogunal government at Muromachi, a precinct of Kyoto. The Muromachi period saw the flowering of a new warrior culture, marked by such military virtues as bravery, loyalty, personal honor, and skill with weapons and by adherence to Zen Buddhism and its associated arts (tea ceremony, flower arranging, calligraphy, etc.). With the Onin Wars of the mid-15th century, the Muromachi shogunate lost most of its power, and the country fell into a century of civil war.

The civil wars were brought to an end during the second half of the 16th century by three successive unifiers, Oda Nobunaga, Hideyoshi, and Tokugawa Ieyasu. At the same time, the Jesuit Francis Xavier and his successors established a short-lived Japanese Christian community. Hideyoshi made several attempts (1592–98) to conquer and annex Korea. In 1601 Tokugawa Ieyasu defeated his rivals in the Battle of Sekigahara. He established a shogunal government at Edo (later Tokyo) in 1603; he and his successors formalized the structure of Japanese feudalism, created a rigid class structure, suppressed Christianity, and enforced the isolation of Japan from virtually all outside influence. Some trade with the mainland and a small Dutch trading station at Nagasaki provided Japan's only windows to the outside world for the next 250 years. The Edo period was marked by urbanization and the development of urban culture (Kabuki theater, wood-block prints, etc.) as the merchant class prospered from internal trade.

The Tokugawa shogun's inability to repel the 1854 visit of American Commodore Matthew Perry and subsequently to avoid establishing commercial and diplomatic relations with Western nations deeply shocked the samurai class. Patriotic young samurai from Choshu, Satsuma, and other outlying feudal domains began to call for the abolition of the shogunate and the restoration of imperial rule in order to confront the threat of contact with the West. Quickly realizing that isolationism was doomed, the young radicals' program changed from "respect the emperor, expel the barbarians" to "enrich the state, strengthen the military." With the accession of the Meiji emperor in 1868, shogunal government ended.

Under direct imperial rule, feudalism was abolished and a wide-ranging program of military, industrial, commercial, and social modernization was implemented. The Meiji Constitution of 1889 created a constitutional monarchy and a parliamentary system of government. Having avoided domination by Western nations, Japan itself became an imperialist power. Defeating China in the Sino-Japanese War of 1894–95 and Russia in the Russo-Japanese War of 1904–05, Japan gained a dominant position in Manchuria and in Korea, which became a Japanese colony in 1910.

Under the ineffectual Taisho emperor (reigned 1912–26), parliamentary government flourished. Japan sided with the Allied Powers in World War I, and the Treaty of Versailles advanced Japan's international interests, particularly in China. The general prosperity of the 1920s was threatened by the Tokyo earthquake of 1923, by labor strife, and by a stagnant agricultural economy. Militant right-wing nationalism began to play an important role in domestic politics.

During the international economic depression of the early 1930s, right-wing militants gained the upper hand; they assassinated many moderate political figures. Japan invaded Manchuria in 1931 and established the puppet state of Manchuguo in 1934. An attempted military coup in 1936 failed in its immediate objectives but led to the establishment of martial law, under which the Showa emperor (Hirohito; reigned 1926–89) became a pawn of the ultranationalists. An invasion and military takeover of eastern China in 1937 was seen as the first step in the creation of a "Greater East Asian Co-prosperity Sphere," designed to unite Asia under Japanese control.

In 1940 Japan entered the Tripartite Alliance with Italy and Nazi Germany. Japan occupied French Indochina in June 1941, provoking increased Allied resistance to Japanese imperial ambitions. Gen. Hideki Tojo became prime minister in October 1941 and ordered simultaneous preemptive strikes against Pearl Harbor, the Philippines, and Malaya on Dec. 7–8. By mid-1942, Japan controlled most of Southeast Asia and the western Pacific, but American victories at the Battle of the Coral Sea in May 1942 and the Battle of Midway in June 1942 halted further Japanese expansion. Thereafter, Japanese forces were steadily pushed back in "island-hopping" campaigns in the central Pacific and along the western Pacific rim, and by Allied counterattacks in Burma. Air attacks on Japan itself culminated in the nuclear bombing of Hiroshima and Nagasaki in August 1945.

Following Japan's formal surrender on Sept. 2, 1945, an American army in Japan under Gen. Douglas MacArthur took control of the country. A new constitution was promulgated, relegating the emperor to purely symbolic status, renouncing the use of military force, and guaranteeing the civil rights of citizens. The industrial combines that had lent strength to Japan's empire were partially dismantled. An international tribunal tried many wartime leaders as war criminals in 1948. In 1949 considerable authority was returned to the conservative government of Premier Shigeru Yoshida. Japan served as a base for American forces during the Korean War, 1950–53, greatly accelerating Japan's postwar economic recovery. On Apr. 28, 1952, a peace treaty between Japan and the United States went into effect, ending the Occupation. On Mar. 8, 1954, the two nations signed a mutual defense assistance pact. Protests over an extension of that treaty, under which substantial U.S. forces were based in Japan, led to the cancellation of a planned visit to Japan by Pres. Dwight Eisenhower in 1960.

Japan was admitted to the United Nations in 1956. The success of Japan's postwar recovery was symbolized by the Tokyo Olympic Games of 1964 and Expo '70 at Osaka. Violent student-protest movements in 1968–69 had no clear political goals and no lasting effect. Politically stable under an unbroken succession of Liberal Democratic party governments, Japan emerged as a major and steadily expanding world industrial power.

The United States returned the Bonin and Marcus Islands to Japanese sovereignty in 1968, and Okinawa in 1972. Also in 1972, diplomatic relations were restored between Japan and China. The USSR continues to occupy the southern Kuril Islands north of Hokkaido, an issue that has impeded relations between Japan and the Soviet Union.

In general, Japan has shown reluctance to play an international political role consistent with its vast economic power. From the mid-1970s onward, the balance of trade between Japan and the United States has weighed heavily in Japan's favor, leading to strains in U.S.-Japan relations and American charges that Japan engages in unfair trade practices. In a series of conferences of the noncommunist world's seven leading economic powers in the 1980s, Japan has pledged to take various measures to improve foreign access to Japan's domestic economy. In 1986–87 the Japanese yen appreciated markedly against the U.S. dollar. This has had relatively little effect on the balance of trade but has led to a marked increase in Japanese economic investment in the United States.

Domestically, Japan in the 1980s enjoyed a very high standard of living, marred by the extremely high cost and relatively low quality of housing, and by underinvestment in the public infrastructure. A real estate boom that led prices of commercial property in downtown Tokyo to increase as much as 200-fold in the span of a decade showed signs of softening in 1988.

Japan has been essentially a one-party state in the postwar period. National politics centers on factions within the ruling Liberal Democratic party. The government is run by political professionals operating according to a system of consensus; despite occasional scandals, there has been little public enthusiasm for political change. A resurgence of nationalism, seen in recent official revisions of school textbooks justifying Japan's role in World War II and in visits of government leaders to the Yasukuni Shrine to pay respects to Japan's war dead, has provoked protests from other Asian nations but little comment at home.

Emperor Hirohito died on Jan. 7, 1989, and was immediately succeeded by his son, Akihito.

Jordan
Hashemite Kingdom of Jordan
(PREVIOUS NAME: TRANSJORDAN)

Geography Location: western Asia. **Boundaries:** Syria to N, Iraq to NE, Saudi Arabia to E and S, Israel to W. **Total land area:** 37,738 sq. mi. (97,740 sq km). **Coastline:** 16 mi. (26 km). **Comparative area:** slightly smaller than Indiana. **Land use:** 4% arable land; 0.5% permanent crops; 1% meadows and pastures; 0.5% forest and woodland; 94% other; includes 0.5% irrigated. **Major cities:** (1986) Amman (capital) 972,000; Zagra 392,220; Irbid 271,000; Salt 134,100.

People Population: 2,850,482 (1988). **Nationality:** noun—Jordanian(s); adjective—Jordanian. **Ethnic groups:** 98% Arab, 1% Circassian, 1% Armenian. **Languages:** Arabic (official); English widely understood among upper and middle classes. **Religions:** 95% Sunni Muslim, 5% Christian.

Government Type: constitutional monarchy. **Independence:** May 25, 1946 (from League of Nations Mandate under British administration). **Constitution:** Jan. 8, 1952. **National holiday:** Independence Day, May 25. **Heads of government:** Hussein ibn Talal, king (since Aug. 1952); Zeid al-Rifa'i, prime minister (since Apr. 1985). **Structure:** king holds balance of power; prime minister exercises executive authority in name of king; cabinet appointed by king and responsible to parliament; bicameral parliament with House of Representatives, dissolved by king in Feb. 1976 and reconvened Jan. 1984, following national elections; Senate last appointed by king in Jan. 1984; secular court system based on differing legal systems of former Transjordan and Palestine; law western in concept and structure; Sharia (religious) courts for Muslims, and religious community council courts for non-Muslim communities; desert police carry out quasi-judicial functions in desert areas.

Economy Monetary unit: Jordanian dinar. **Budget:** (1988) *income:* $3,026 bil.; *expend.:* $3,225 bil. **GNP:** $5.5 bil., $2,070 per capita (1986). **Chief crops:** vegetables, fruits, olive oil, wheat; self-sufficient in only a few foodstuffs. **Livestock:** poultry, goats, sheep, cattle, camels. **Natural resources:** phosphates, potash, shale oil. **Major industries:** phosphate mining, petroleum refining, cement. **Labor force:** 550,000 (1987 est.); 20% agriculture, 20% mining and manufacturing. **Exports:** $733 mil. (f.o.b., 1986); fruits and vegetables, phosphates, fertilizers. **Imports:** $2.4 bil. (c.i.f., 1986); crude oil, textiles, capital goods, motor vehicles, foodstuffs. **Major trading partners:** N.A.

Intl. Orgs. Arab League, FAO, G-77, IAEA, IBRD, ICAO, IDA, IFAD, IFC, ILO, IMF, IMO, INTELSAT, INTERPOL, ITU, NAM, UN, UNESCO, UPU, WHO, WIPO, WMO.

The present territory of the Kingdom of Jordan corresponds to the biblical lands of Edom, Gilead, and Moab. The ancient rock city of Petra was the capital of the Edomite and Nabataean kingdoms. The region was incorporated into the Roman Empire, and later the Latin Kingdom of Jerusalem; it was an important early center of Christianity.

In the 630s Jordan became one of the first areas outside Arabia to fall to the expansion of Islam. It became subject to the Caliphate, located at Damascus and later at Baghdad, and in the 11th century became part of the empire of the Seljuk Turks. The Crusades brought European invaders, but with little lasting impact. The Mongols conquered Jordan in the mid-13th century, and it later passed into the control of the Mamluk sultanate. In 1517 Jordan was incorporated into the Ottoman Empire.

Following the post–World War I breakup of the Ottoman Empire, Jordan came under British control as part of a League of Nations Mandate of Palestine. By agreement with France, Palestine's borders included a corridor in northeastern Jordan extending to the border with Iraq, thereby keeping the Iraq-Haifa pipeline entirely under British control. In 1921 Great Britain sponsored the establishment of a monarchy by Abdullah, son of Hussein ibn Ali, ruler of the Hejaz in Arabia (see "Saudi Arabia"). Britain recognized the independence of the Hashemite Kingdom of Transjordan in 1923; a 1928 treaty gave Britain the unrestricted right to station troops in the kingdom.

Transjordan supported the Allies in World War II and was rewarded with full independence in 1946, though, by treaty, strong military ties to Great Britain were maintained. In 1948 the kingdom joined the Arab League, changed its name to Jordan, and joined other Arab states in the first Arab-Israeli War. The war resulted in the occupation by Jordanian troops of the West Bank and the Old City of

Jerusalem, which were formally annexed in 1950.

The present ruler, King Hussein I, came to the throne on Aug. 11, 1952. All British military forces were withdrawn from the kingdom in 1957.

Israel recaptured the West Bank and the Old City of Jerusalem in the Six-Day War of 1967, and large numbers of Palestinian refugees fled to Jordan. Jordan played no substantial role in the October 1974 Arab-Israeli War. In 1974 Jordan accepted the decision of an Arab summit conference designating the Palestine Liberation Organization the sole representative of Palestinians in the West Bank. Jordan's role as a front-line opponent of Israel has won it a large annual subvention from Arab oil states; King Hussein's reputation as an Arab moderate has led to significant American economic and military support.

King Hussein strongly opposed the 1979 Camp David Accords and the Egypt-Israeli peace treaty; Jordan broke off diplomatic relations with Egypt in March 1979 but resumed full relations in 1984.

In July 1971 King Hussein, charging the Palestine Liberation Organization with subversion, had forced withdrawal of PLO troops and political headquarters from Jordan. Consequently, throughout the Reagan administration, American proposals for a settlement of the Palestinian question rested on the hope that Hussein would represent the Palestinians in talks with Israel. In 1988 the king flatly rejected any such role, implied that the PLO should declare an independent state on the West Bank and in the Gaza Strip, and declared that any future settlement would require direct talks between Israel and the PLO.

Most of Jordan's territory is arid, and the kingdom has no petroleum reserves. The economy depends in part on subsidies from Arab oil states. Grain, olives, dates, fruit, and vegetables are grown in the fertile western region of the country; potassium and potash are mined, and cement is produced. Other industries include textiles, food processing, and light manufacturing.

Kenya
Republic of Kenya
(PREVIOUS NAME: BRITISH EAST AFRICA)

Geography Location: equatorial country on eastern coast of Africa. **Boundaries:** Sudan to NW, Ethiopia to N, Somalia to E, Indian Ocean to SE, Tanzania to SW, Lake Victoria and Uganda to W. **Total land area:** 219,788 sq. mi. (569,250 sq km). **Coastline:** 333 mi. (536 km). **Comparative area:** slightly more than twice size of Nevada. **Land use:** 3% arable land; 1% permanent crops; 7% meadows and pastures; 4% forest and woodland; 85% other; includes negl. % irrigated. **Major cities:** Nairobi (capital) 1,103,554; Mombasa 247,073 (1984 est.); Nakuru 47,151; Kisumu 32,431; Thika 18,387 (1969 census).

People Population: 23,341,638 (1988). **Nationality:** noun—Kenyan(s); adjective—Kenyan. **Ethnic groups:** 21% Kikuyu, 14% Luhya, 13% Luo, 11% Kalenjin, 11% Kamba, 6% Kisii,

6% Meru, 1% Asian, European, Arab; 17% other. **Languages:** English and Swahili (both official), indigenous languages. **Religions:** 38% Protestant, 28% Catholic, 26% indigenous beliefs, 6% Muslim, 2% other.

Government Type: republic within Commonwealth. **Independence:** Dec. 12, 1963 (from UK). **Constitution:** Dec. 12, 1963. **National holiday:** Jamhuri Day, Dec. 12. **Heads of government:** Daniel T. arap Moi, president (since Oct. 1978). **Structure:** executive—president and cabinet; legislative—unicameral National Assembly of 200 seats, 188 elected by constituencies and 12 appointed by president; judiciary—high court, with chief justice and at least 11 justices, has unlimited original jurisdiction to hear and determine any civil or criminal proceeding; provision for courts of appeal.

Economy Monetary unit: Kenyan shilling. **Budget:** as percent of GDP (1986 est.)—*income:* 24%; *expend.:* 28%. **GDP:** $5 bil., $230 per capita (1986 est.). **Chief crops:** cash crops—coffee, tea, sisal, pyrethrum, cotton; food crops—corn, wheat, sugarcane, rice, cassava; largely self-sufficient in food; an illegal producer of cannabis for international drug trade. **Livestock:** cattle, goats, sheep, camels, pigs. **Natural resources:** gold, limestone, diotomite, salt barytes, magnesite. **Major industries:** small-scale consumer goods (plastic, furniture, batteries, textiles, soap, cigarettes, flour), agricultural processing, oil refining. **Labor force:** 7.4 mil. (1985); 50% public sector, 18% industry and commerce, 17% agriculture, 13% services; 1.1 mil. wage earners; 45% of population of working age. **Exports:** $1.17 bil. (f.o.b., 1986); reexporting of petroleum products, coffee, tea, sisal, livestock products. **Imports:** $1.46 bil. (f.o.b., 1986); machinery, transport equipment, crude oil, paper and paper products, iron and steel products, textiles. **Major trading partners:** EC, Japan, Middle East, U.S., Rwanda, Uganda.

Intl. Orgs. Commonwealth, FAO, G-77, GATT, IAEA, IBRD, ICAO, IDA, IFAD, IFC, ILO, IMF, IMO, INTELSAT, INTERPOL, ITU, NAM, UN, UNESCO, UPU, WHO, WIPO, WMO.

Kenya formed part of an ancient network of trade between the Red Sea and the coast of East Africa at the time of the Roman Empire. Persian and Arab trading posts were established on the coast by the eighth century A.D. At about the same time, the indigenous Cushitic people of Kenya had been joined by Bantu and Nilotic immigrants. Swahili, a mixture of Bantu and Arabic, developed as a language of trade throughout the region.

Portuguese explorers reached Kenya in 1498. Portuguese control of the coastal area ended in 1729, when the region came under the control of the sultans of Oman. British adventurers explored Kenya in the late 19th century. In 1885 the Berlin Conference divided East Africa into European spheres of influence. The British East Africa Company, chartered in 1888, established a protectorate over the coastal region in 1890 and extended its control

into the interior in 1895.

British settlers soon began to establish farms, mission stations, and towns in Kenya, dominating the country's affairs even before Kenya was given colonial status in 1920.

During World War II, parts of northern Kenya were briefly occupied by troops from the Italian colony of Ethiopia. After the British reasserted control over the entire country, Africans were granted the right to participate in local government in 1944.

From 1952 to 1959, a state of emergency was declared in Kenya because of the "Mau Mau" rebellion against British colonial rule. In response to local unrest, British authorities widened African participation in government. The first elections of Africans to the Legislative Council took place in 1957.

Kenya became independent on Dec. 12, 1963, and in 1964 assumed the status of a republic within the British Commonwealth. Jomo Kenyatta, a member of the dominant Kikuyu population and leader of the main political party, the Kenya African National Union (KANU), was elected Kenya's first president. The minority Kenya African Democratic Union (KADU) voluntarily amalgamated itself with KANU in 1964. A leftist party, the Kenya People's Union (KPU) was organized in 1966, led by Oginga Odinga. In 1969 it was implicated in the assassination of Tom Mboya, a prominent political leader; its leaders were imprisoned and the party dissolved. Since 1969 KANU has been Kenya's sole political party; multiple KANU candidates compete for each seat in the legislature.

Kenyatta died on Aug. 22, 1978, and Vice Pres. Daniel arap Moi succeeded as provisional president. Moi was elected president in his own right in October 1978. In 1982 the Constitution was amended to give KANU legal status as Kenya's only political party. Moi was reelected president in 1983 and again in 1988. The latter election was controversial because, for the first time since independence, it was conducted without the use of secret ballots. In recent years foreign observers have accused the Moi government of widespread abuses of human rights.

Despite numerous changes in the form of government (federation to republic, parliamentary to presidential, multiparty to single-party, bicameral to unicameral legislature), Kenya has enjoyed political stability throughout its period of independence. That political stability has not been matched by economic stability. Kenya enjoyed a high rate of economic growth in the 1960s, but the growth rate slowed in the 1970s, while the population increased at the highest rate in the world. Most of Kenya's people are engaged in agriculture and animal husbandry. Unemployment is estimated at 30 percent, higher in urban areas.

Kenya's economy began to recover somewhat in the mid-1980s, bolstered by high international prices for its chief export, coffee, by excellent grain harvests, and by a burgeoning tourist industry. Industrial development remains slow and plagued by inefficiencies, while the country's basic infrastructure remains underdeveloped.

Kiribati
Republic of Kiribati
(PREVIOUS NAME: GILBERT ISLANDS)

Geography **Location:** 33 atolls, in three principal groups, scattered within area of about 2,000 sq. mi. (5,000 sq km) in mid-Pacific Ocean; extends about 2,400 mi. (3,870 km) from E to W and about 1,275 mi. (2,050 km) from N to S. **Boundaries:** surrounded by Pacific Ocean; nearest neighbors are Nauru to W, and Tuvalu and Tokelau to S. **Total land area:** 332 sq. mi. (861 sq km). **Coastline:** 710 mi. (1,143 km). **Comparative area:** slightly more than four times size of Washington, D.C. **Land use:** 0% arable land; 51% permanent crops; 0% meadows and pastures; 3% forest and woodland; 46% other. **Major cities:** Tarawa (capital).

People **Population:** 67,638 (1988). **Nationality:** noun—Kiribatian(s); adjective—Kiribati. **Ethnic groups:** Micronesian. **Languages:** English (official), Gilbertese. **Religions:** 48% Roman Catholic, 45% Protestant (Congregational), some Seventh-Day Adventist and Baha'i.

Government **Type:** republic. **Independence:** July 12, 1979 (from UK). **Constitution:** July 12, 1979. **National holiday:** none. **Heads of government:** Ieremia T. Tabai, president (since July 1979). **Structure:** nationally elected president; unicameral legislature—National Assembly (composed of 39 elected members and one nominated representative of Banaban community).

Economy **Monetary unit:** Australian dollar. **Budget:** (1986 est.) *income:* revenues and grants $20 mil.; *expend.:* $20 mil. **GDP:** $20 mil., $310 per capita (1985). **Chief crops:** coconuts, copra; subsistence crops of roots and tubers, vegetables, melons, bananas; pigs and chickens; domestic fishing. **Livestock:** chickens, pigs. **Natural resources:** phosphate (production discontinued in 1979). **Major industries:** fishing and handicrafts. **Labor force:** 7,870 economically active (1985 est.). **Exports:** $1.4 mil. (1986); 42% copra, 55% fish. **Imports:** $11.7 mil. (1986); foodstuffs, fuel, transportation equipment. **Major trading partners:** (1984) *exports:* 52% Western Europe, 23% American Samoa, 19% Marshall Islands, 3% U.S.; *imports:* 45% Australia, 17% Japan, 11% New Zealand, 4% UK, 4% U.S.

Intl. Orgs. Commonwealth, GATT (de facto), ICAO, IMF, WHO.

In 1892 the British established a protectorate over the Gilbert Islands, inhabited principally by Micronesians. In 1915 Britain joined the islands administratively with the Polynesian-speaking Ellice Islands to the south to form a British colony, the Gilbert and Ellice Islands. The colony later was expanded to include, by 1937, other territories: Ocean Island, Christmas Island and the rest of the Line Islands, part of the Phoenix Islands, and other nearby islands. The Japanese occupied the Gilbert Islands in 1942; in 1943 the Allied forces recaptured them. The principal island, Tarawa, was the scene of some of the fiercest combat in the American "island-hopping" campaign in the Pacific.

In 1971 Britain granted the Gilbert and Ellice Islands colony self-rule. The Ellice Islands broke away in 1975, becoming the independent nation of Tuvalu in 1978. On July 12, 1979, the Gilbert Islands, along with the remainder of the former colony, became independent as Kiribati. After World War II, the United States had laid claim to portions of the Line and Phoenix islands; those claims were settled by a U.S.-Kiribati friendship treaty in 1979, under which the United States relinquished all but three of the northern Line Islands.

Kiribati's economy is based on subsistence farming and on fishing; the latter provides the principal source of cash income. Copra exports and the sale of fishing rights (principally to Japan) are the main earners of hard currency. Formerly important phosphate deposits on Banaba Island have been depleted, and mining was discontinued in 1979. The islands remain heavily dependent on foreign aid, principally from the United Kingdom.

Korea, North
Democratic People's Republic of Korea
(ABBREV: DPRK)
(PREVIOUS NAME: KOREA)

Geography **Location:** northern part of Korean peninsula in eastern Asia. **Boundaries:** China to NW, Sea of Japan to E, Republic of Korea to S, Yellow Sea to SW. **Total land area:** 46,540 sq. mi. (120,538 sq km). **Coastline:** 1,551 mi. (2,495 km). **Comparative area:** slightly smaller than Mississippi. **Land use:** 18% arable land; 1% permanent crops; negl. % meadows and pastures; 74% forest and woodland; 7% other; includes 9% irrigated. **Major cities:** (1976 est.) Pyongyang (capital) 1,500,000; Chongjin 300,000; Hungnam 260,000; Kaesong 240,000.

People **Population:** 21,983,795 (1988). **Nationality:** noun—Korean(s); adjective—Korean. **Ethnic groups:** racially homogeneous. **Languages:** Korean. **Religions:** Buddhism and Confucianism; religious activities now almost nonexistent.

Government **Type:** communist state; one-man rule. **Constitution:** adopted 1948, revised Dec. 27, 1972. **National holiday:** Sept. 9. **Heads of government:** Kim Il Sung, president (since Dec. 1972); Yon Hyong Muk, prime minister (since Dec. 1988). **Structure:** Supreme People's Assembly theoretically supervises legislative and judicial functions; State Administration Council (cabinet) oversees ministerial operations.

Economy **Monetary unit:** won. **Budget:** N.A. **GNP:** $19 bil., $910 per capita (1986). **Chief crops:** corn, rice, vegetables; food shortages—meat, fish, cooking oils; production of foodstuffs adequate for domestic needs. **Livestock:** pigs, cattle, sheep, goats, horses. **Natural resources:** coal, lead, tungsten, zinc, graphite. **Major industries:** machine building, electric power, chemicals. **Labor force:** 6.1 mil. (1980); 48% agricultural, 52% nonagricultural; shortage of skilled and unskilled labor. **Exports:** $1.7 bil. (1986); minerals, metallurgical products, agricultural products, manu-

factures. **Imports:** $2.0 bil. (1986); petroleum, machinery and equipment, coking coal, grain. **Major trading partners:** total trade turnover $3.7 bil. (1986); 75% with communist countries, 25% with noncommunist countries.

Intl. Orgs. FAO, G-77, IAEA, ICAO, ITU, NAM, UNCTAD, UNESCO, UPU, WHO, WIPO, WMO; official observer status at UN.

(For pre-1945 history, see "Republic of Korea.")

The Soviet Union's declaration of war against Japan in the waning days of World War II accomplished its intended effect of strengthening the Soviet position in northeast Asia, and particularly in Korea. After Japan's surrender, Korea was arbitrarily divided into zones of Soviet and American occupation, north and south of latitude 38° north. The Korean Communist party (KCP), founded in 1922, had functioned in exile in the USSR during the Japanese colonial period in Korea; KCP workers were quickly moved into the Soviet occupation zone in 1945.

U.S.-Soviet talks aimed at Korean reunification broke down, and in 1948 the establishment of separate regimes in North and South Korea formalized the postwar occupation zones. The Korean Democratic People's Republic was proclaimed on May 1, 1948, and its government was organized in September of that year. It inherited most of the industrial and hydroelectric power infrastructure built during the Japanese colonial period and enjoyed strong Soviet backing.

On June 25, 1950, North Korean troops crossed the 38th parallel in an effort to force the reunification of Korea under a communist regime. UN troops under American leadership came to the defense of the South. (For the Korean War, see "South Korea.") The war was fought to a stalemate, and a truce was signed on July 27, 1953.

North Korea has had a single leader throughout its national history: Kim Il Sung, chairman of the KCP since 1945 and president of the DPRK since 1972. Under Kim Il Sung, North Korea has been a typically Stalinist soviet nation, concentrating its economic energies on heavy industry and imposing a strictly regimented political and social life on its citizens. Economic development has been strongly supported by aid from the Soviet Union and, to a lesser degree, China. After an impressive program of postwar reconstruction in the 1950s and 1960s, the country has fallen into economic stagnation.

Relations between North and South Korea have been implacably hostile; the North has made numerous attempts to infiltrate and sabotage the South. On Oct. 9, 1983, 17 people, including four South Korean cabinet ministers, were killed in Rangoon, Burma, by a bomb planted by North Korean agents. Since 1985, occasional North-South discussions on such matters as permitting contacts between families divided by the war have produced little result. North Korea originally agreed to co-sponsor the 1988 Summer Olympics with South Korea but later boycotted the games. Current concerns revolve around coming to terms with the Soviet policy of *perestroika*—a concept alien to the DPRK's conservative communist regime—and preparing for a transition of leadership from the aging Kim Il Sung to his son and political heir presumptive, Kim Jong-Il.

Korea, South
Republic of Korea
(PREVIOUS NAME: KOREA)

Geography **Location:** southern part of Korean peninsula in eastern Asia. **Boundaries:** North Korea to N, separated by frontier roughly following 38th parallel; Sea of Japan to E, East China Sea to S, and Yellow Sea to W. **Total land area:** 38,291 sq. mi. (99,173 sq km). **Coastline:** 1,500 mi. (2,413 km). **Comparative area:** slightly larger than Indiana. **Land use:** 21% arable land; 1% permanent crops; 1% meadows and pastures; 67% forest and woodland; 10% other; includes 12% irrigated. **Major cities:** (1985 census) Seoul (capital) 9,639,110; Pusan 3,514,798; Taegu 2,029,853; Inchon 1,386,911; Kwangju 905,896.

People **Population:** 42,772,956 (1988). **Nationality:** noun—Korean(s); adjective—Korean. **Ethnic groups:** homogeneous; small Chinese minority (about 20,000). **Languages:** Korean; English widely taught in high school. **Religions:** strong Confucian tradition; vigorous Christian minority (28% of total population); Buddhism; pervasive folk religion (shamanism); Chondokyo (religion of the heavenly way), eclectic religion with nationalist overtones founded in 19th century, claiming about 1.5 mil. adherents.

Government **Type:** republic; power centralized in strong executive. **Constitution:** approved by voters on Oct. 27, 1987, effective Feb. 25, 1988; requires direct presidential elections and protects human rights. **National holiday:** Independence Day, Aug. 15. **Heads of government:** Roh Tae Woo, president (since Feb. 1988); Young Hoon Kang, prime minister (since Dec. 1988). **Structure:** unicameral legislature (National Assembly), judiciary.

Economy **Monetary unit:** won. **Budget:** (1988) *income:* N.A.; *expend.:* planned, $21.8 bil. **GNP:** $118 bil., $2,800 per capita (1987 in 1987 dollars). **Chief crops:** 9 mil. people (22% of population) live in farm households, but agriculture, forestry, and fishing constitute 15% of GNP; main crops—rice, barley, vegetables, legumes. **Livestock:** chickens, pigs, cattle, ducks, rabbits. **Natural resources:** coal (limited), tungsten, graphite, molybdenum. **Major industries:** textiles and clothing, footwear, food processing. **Labor force:** 17.6 mil. (1987 est.); 49% services and other, 27% mining and manufacturing, 24% agriculture, fishing, and forestry; 3% average unemployment. **Exports:** $46.9 bil. (f.o.b., 1987); textiles and clothing, electrical machinery, footwear, steel, automobiles. **Imports:** $40.5 bil. (c.i.f., 1987); machinery, oil, steel, transport equipment, textiles. **Major trading partners:** (1987) *exports:* 39% U.S., 18% Japan; *imports:* 34% Japan, 21% U.S.

Intl. Orgs. Colombo Plan, FAO, G-77, GATT, IAEA, IBRD, ICAO, IDA, IFAD, IFC, IMF, IMO, INTELSAT, INTERPOL, ITU, UNCTAD, UNDP, UNESCO, UNICEF, UNIDO, UPU, WHO, WIPO, WMO; official observer status at UN.

From ancient times Korea has struggled successfully to preserve its national independence. To the native culture—marked by a warrior aristocracy, shamanic religion, and a subject class of rice cultivators—was added, under continuous Chinese influence, a strong adherence to Buddhism and a system of government modeled on Chinese Confucian bureaucratism. The three rival kingdoms of Silla, Paekche, and Koguryo were united, through Chinese intervention, in the seventh century A.D.; unified dynastic rule was maintained thereafter.

The Yi dynasty (1392–1910), under which Korea was known as the Kingdom of Choson, was a staunch tributary ally of China under both the Ming (1368–1644) and Qing (1644–1911) dynasties. A Japanese invasion of Korea in 1592 conquered most of the country but was finally repelled by combined Chinese and Korean forces. From the late 17th century to the 1870s, all non-Chinese foreign influence was rigorously excluded from the country.

Korea's isolation, and its status as a Chinese tributary, ended in 1874, when Japan imposed on it the Treaty of Kwanghwa, guaranteeing Japanese commercial access and other interests. The Sino-Japanese War of 1894–95 was fought primarily over the status of Korea; following Japan's victory in that war, Korea was made a Japanese protectorate and was annexed as a Japanese colony in 1910. A harsh colonial regime was established with the aim of eradicating Korean culture and incorporating Korea entirely into the Japanese empire.

During the colonial period, Korean resistance to the Japanese regime was violently suppressed, but resistance movements survived in exile—notably the Korean Communist party in the Soviet Union and a republican movement in China. During World War II, tens of thousands of Koreans were conscripted as forced laborers to work in Japan and in Japanese-occupied territories.

Following Japan's surrender, Korea was arbitrarily divided into zones of Soviet and American occupation, north and south of 38° north latitude. The dividing line split Korea economically as well as geographically and politically; Korea's industry and hydroelectric power was concentrated in the north, while the south was primarily agricultural. In contrast to well-laid Soviet plans for installing a communist government in the north (see "North Korea"), American attempts to reunify the country under a republican regime were inept. By 1948 it had become clear that plans for reunification were hopeless. In May of that year, the Republic of Korea was organized in the south, with Dr. Syngman Rhee as president. The United States withdrew its occupation forces in June 1949.

On June 25, 1950, North Korean troops invaded the south in an apparent attempt to unify the country forcibly under the communist regime. An emergency session of the UN Security Council voted to send troops to Korea; the USSR, having boycotted the session, was unable to exercise its veto on North Korea's behalf. UN troops, dominated by American forces and commanded by Gen. Douglas MacArthur, launched a counterattack in September with a landing at Inchon and swept north, reaching the Chinese border by Nov. 20. On Nov. 26 the tide turned again when Chinese troops entered the war, ostensibly to defend the Chinese border but also to aid their North Korean allies in driving the UN forces south again. Seoul fell once more on Jan. 4, 1951. In February and March another UN counteroffensive drove the combined Chinese and North Korean forces back to the 38th parallel again. Thereafter, the battle lines remained generally stable, although fierce fighting continued at intervals for another two years. On Apr. 11, 1951, Gen. MacArthur was relieved of the Korean command for making unauthorized policy statements and was replaced by Gen. Matthew Ridgway.

Armistice talks began in July 1951 but broke down repeatedly. A truce was signed on July 27, 1953, creating a demilitarized zone along the 38th parallel and establishing a framework for talks on a permanent settlement of the war. Negotiations have continued fruitlessly at the Panmunjom armistice conference headquarters ever since.

Postwar reconstruction, with significant U.S. aid, was overseen by the government of Syngman Rhee. Pres. Rhee resigned in 1960 after a wave of student demonstrations charging him with corruption and undemocratic practices. On May 16, 1961, Gen. Park Chung Hee seized power in a military coup. The military government was given democratic trappings when in 1972 a referendum was passed allowing Gen. Park to run for an unlimited series of six-year presidential terms. Gen. Park was assassinated on Oct. 26, 1979, by the chief of intelligence of the Korean government. In the aftermath of this event, Gen. Chun Doo Hwan rose to power, continuing the military-rule policies of Gen. Park. Gen. Chun's regime was marked by widespread and violent political protest demonstrations.

Despite political repression, South Korea's economy made great strides under Gen. Chun's regime. The traditionally agrarian country was transformed into a modernized, urban, industrial nation. The industrial economy developed a dual structure, dominated by a few conglomerates but also with a very large number of small-scale firms. In 1986 South Korea for the first time achieved a favorable balance-of-payments ratio in foreign trade, and since then the favorable balance has increased rapidly, led by exports of automobiles, textiles and clothing, and consumer electronic goods.

After weeks of widespread demonstrations in mid-1987, Gen. Chun agreed to allow direct presidential elections to choose his successor. The elections, held in November 1987, were generally regarded as fair; the government candidate, Roh Tae Woo, achieved a plurality over the sharply divided opposition parties. Under Pres. Roh, the political situation has calmed, although student demonstrations have continued, calling for greater efforts for Korean reunification and protesting the presence of large numbers of American troops in the country.

The 1988 summer Olympics were held in South Korea, bringing widespread, favorable international attention.

Kuwait
State of Kuwait

Geography Location: eastern coast of Arabian peninsula. **Boundaries:** Iraq to NW, Saudi Arabia to S, Persian Gulf to E. **Total land area:** 6,880 sq. mi. (17,818 sq km). **Coastline:** 310 mi. (499 km). **Comparative area:** slightly smaller than New Jersey. **Land use:** negl. % arable land; 0% permanent crops; 8% meadows and pastures; negl. % forest and woodland; 92% other; includes negl. % irrigated. **Major cities:** (1985 census); Kuwait City (capital) 44,335; Salmiya 153,369; Hawalli 145,126; Faranawiya 68,701; Abraq Kheetan 45,120.

People Population: 1,938,075 (1988). **Nationality:** noun—Kuwaiti(s); adjective—Kuwaiti. **Ethnic groups:** 39% Kuwaiti, 39% other Arab, 9% South Asian, 4% Iranian, 9% other. **Languages:** Arabic (official), English widely spoken. **Religions:** 85% Muslim (30% Shi'a, 45% Sunni, 10% other), 15% Christian, Hindu, Parsi, and other.

Government Type: nominal constitutional monarchy. **Independence:** June 19, 1961 (from UK). **Constitution:** Nov. 16, 1962 (some provisions suspended since Aug. 29, 1962). **National holiday:** National Day, Feb. 25. **Head of government:** Jaber al-Ahmad al-Jaber al Sabah, amir (since Dec. 1977); Saad al-Abdullah al-Salem al-Sabah, prime minister. **Structure:** executive—Council of Ministers; legislature—National Assembly.

Economy Monetary unit: Kuwaiti dinar. **Budget:** (1987) *income:* $9.9 bil.; *expend.:* $10.0 bil. **GDP:** $16.9 bil., $9,040 per capita (1987). **Chief crops:** virtually none; dependent on imports for food; about 75% of potable water must be distilled or imported. **Livestock:** goats, sheep, cattle, camels. **Natural resources:** petroleum, fish, shrimp, natural gas. **Major industries:** petroleum, petrochemicals, desalination. **Labor force:** 566,000 (1986); 45% services, 20% construction, 12% trade; 70% of labor force is non-Kuwaiti. **Exports:** $7.4 bil. (f.o.b., 1987); 81% crude petroleum. **Imports:** $5.8 bil. (c.i.f., 1987). **Major trading partners:** *exports:* Japan, Italy, Netherlands, U.S.; *imports:* Japan, U.S., W. Germany, UK.

Intl. Orgs. Arab League, FAO, G-77, GATT, IAEA, IBRD, ICAO, IDA, IFAD, IFC, ILO, IMF, IMO, INTELSAT, INTERPOL, ITU, NAM, OPEC, UN, UNESCO, UPU, WHO, WMO.

Kuwait, at the head of the Persian Gulf, was part of the Abbasid empire from the eighth century and was absorbed into the Ottoman Empire in the late 16th century. It was organized as a principality under the al-Sabah dynasty in 1756, but the Ottomans continued to assert sovereignty. Increasing British influence during the 19th century was formalized in 1899, when Kuwait became a British Protectorate.

The discovery of oil, first exported from Kuwait after World War II, rapidly made the principality one of the wealthiest in the Middle East. The British Protectorate ended in 1961, when Kuwait gained full independence. The great majority of oil field workers in Kuwait are non-Kuwaiti Arabs, including many Palestinians. Oil revenues have made possible a total welfare state for Kuwaiti citizens, who pay no taxes and enjoy a wide range of free social services.

Kuwait allied itself with Iraq in the Iran-Iraq War of 1980–88; Kuwaiti tankers came under heavy attack from Iranian warships in the gulf. In July 1987, Kuwaiti tankers were reflagged with the U.S. flag and placed under escort of American warships in an operation that continued into 1989. Most of Kuwait's territory is barren and sparsely inhabited. The economy depends almost entirely on the petroleum industry.

Laos
Lao People's Democratic Republic

Geography Location: landlocked country in Southeast Asia. **Boundaries:** Burma to NW, China to N, Vietnam to E, Kampuchea to S, and Thailand to W. **Total land area:** 91,400 sq. mi. (236,800 sq km). **Coastline:** none. **Comparative area:** slightly larger than Utah. **Land use:** 4% arable land; negl. % permanent crops; 3% meadows and pastures; 58% forest and woodland; 35% other; includes 1% irrigated. **Major cities:** (1973) Vientiane (capital) 176,637; Savannaket 50,690; Pakse 44,860; Luang Prabang 44,244; Saya Bury 13,775.

People Population: 3,849,752 (1988). **Nationality:** noun—Lao (sing. and pl.); adjective—Lao or Laotian. **Ethnic groups:** 50% Lao, 20% ethnic Thai; 15% Phouteung (Kha); 15% Meo, Hmong, Yao, and other. **Languages:** Lao (official), French, English. **Religions:** 85% Buddhist, 15% animist and other.

Government Type: communist state. **Independence:** July 19, 1949 (from France). **Constitution:** draft constitution under discussion since 1976. **National holiday:** Dec. 2. **Heads of government:** Souphanouvong, president (since 1975); Phoumi Vongvichit, acting president (since Oct. 1986); Kaysone Phomvihane, chairman (since Dec. 1975). **Structure:** president; Supreme People's Assembly; cabinet; cabinet is totally Communist but council contains a few nominal neutralists and non-Communists; National Congress of People's Representatives established current government structure in Dec. 1975.

Economy Monetary unit: kip. **Budget:** (1986) *income:* $93 mil.; *expend.:* $175 mil. **GNP:** $660 mil.; $180 per capita (1986 est.). **Chief crops:** rice (overwhelmingly dominant), corn, vegetables, tobacco, coffee; formerly self-sufficient; food shortages (due in part to distribution deficiencies) include rice; illegal producer of opium poppy and cannabis for international drug trade. **Livestock:** pigs, buffalo, cattle, goats, horses. **Natural resources:** tin, timber, gypsum, hydropower potential. **Major industries:** tin mining, timber, electric power. **Labor force:** about 1–1.5 mil.; 85–90% in agriculture. **Exports:** $58.5 mil. (f.o.b., 1986 est.); electric power, forest products, tin con-centrates, coffee. **Imports:** $205 mil. (c.i.f., 1986 est.); rice and other foodstuffs, petroleum products, machinery, transportation equipment. **Major trading partners:** *exports:* Thailand, Malaysia, Vietnam; *imports:* Thailand, USSR, Japan, France, Vietnam.

Intl. Orgs. Colombo Plan, FAO, G-77, IBRD, ICAO, IDA, IFAD, ILO, IMF, INTERPOL, ITU, NAM, UN, UNCTAD, UNESCO, UPU, WHO, WMO.

Inhabited by the Thai-speaking Lao people in the river valleys and by Hmong and other tribal people in the highlands, Laos historically had little national cohesion and was dominated by its more powerful neighbors, Siam (Thailand) to the west and Vietnam to the east. In 1893 France forced Siam to recognize Laos as a French protectorate; the country was thereafter incorporated into the French Union of Indochina. Laos was occupied by Japan during World War II but saw little major fighting.

In 1946 Laos was united under the Luang Prabang dynasty and was granted local autonomy as a constitutional monarchy in 1949. During the final phases of the Indochina War against French colonialism in 1953–54, Vietnamese Communist (Vietminh) incursions reinforced the position of the Laotian Communist party (Pathet Lao) in Laotian politics. Following the French withdrawal in December 1954, Lao became an independent nation and was admitted to the United Nations in 1955.

The creation of a coalition government under Prince Souvana Phouma in 1962 temporarily resolved a turbulent political situation; an international agreement signed in Geneva in that year guaranteed Laos's neutrality. The Pathet Lao withdrew from the coalition in 1964 and renewed its armed uprising against the government, with North Vietnamese support. American planes bombed Vietnamese supply lines along the Ho Chi Minh trail, and American agents recruited Hmong tribesmen as irregular troops to attack Pathet Lao positions. The Pathet Lao nevertheless made steady gains, especially after 1970. In 1973, Prince Souvana Phouma ordered a cease-fire, and in 1975 the Pathet Lao took control of the capital, Vientiane. The Lao People's Democratic Republic was proclaimed on Dec. 3, 1975. Large numbers of Hmong and other tribal people fled to Thailand.

Subsequently, Laos has been strongly dominated by Vietnam, which has stationed significant numbers of troops in the country. Attempts to collectivize the economy have had only partial success. Economic activity continues to be limited mainly to small-scale agriculture and some tin mining and small industry.

Lebanon
Republic of Lebanon

Geography Location: western Asia. **Boundaries:** Syria to N and E, Israel to S, Mediterranean Sea to W. **Total land area:** 4,036 sq. mi. (10,452 sq km). **Coastline:** 140 mi. (225 km). **Comparative area:** slightly more than 3 times size of Rhode Island. **Land use:** 21% arable land; 9% permanent crops; 1% meadows and pastures; 8% forest and woodland; 61% other; includes 7% irrigated. **Major cities:** (1975 est.) Beirut (capital) 1,500,000; Tarabulus (Tripoli) 160,000; Zahleh 45,000; Saida (Sidon) 38,000; Sur (Tyre) 14,000.

People Population: 2,674,385 (1988). **Nationality:** noun—Lebanese (sing., pl.); adjective—Lebanese. **Ethnic groups:** 93% Arab, 6% Armenian, 1% other. **Languages:** Arabic and French (both official), Armenian, English. **Religions:** 75% Islam, 25% Christian, negl. Judaism.

Government Type: republic. **Independence:** Nov. 22, 1943 (from League of Nations Mandate under French administration). **Constitution:** May 26, 1926 (amended). **National holiday:** Independence Day, Nov. 22. **Heads of government:** no president or prime minister due to internal strife. **Structure:** power lies with president, who is elected by unicameral legislature (National Assembly); cabinet appointed by president, approved by legislature; independent secular courts on French pattern; religious courts for matters of marriage, divorce, inheritance, etc.; by custom, president is Maronite Christian, prime minister is Sunni Muslim, and president of legislature is Shi'a Muslim; each of nine religious communities are represented in legislature in proportion to their national numerical strength derived from (outdated) census.

Economy Monetary unit: Lebanese pound. **Budget:** (1987 est.) *income:* $44 mil.; *expend.:* $712 mil. **GDP:** $1.8 bil. (1985). **Chief crops:** fruits, wheat, corn, barley, potatoes; not self-sufficient in food; illegal producer of opium poppy and cannabis for international drug trade. **Livestock:** goats, sheep, cattle, asses, pigs. **Natural resources:** limestone, iron ore, salt; water-surplus state in water-deficit region. **Major industries:** banking, food processing, textiles. **Labor force:** 650,000 (1985); 79% industry, commerce and services; 11% agriculture, 10% government; high unemployment. **Exports:** $500 mil. (f.o.b., 1986). **Imports:** $2.2 bil. (f.o.b., 1986). **Major trading partners:** N.A.

Intl. Orgs. Arab League, FAO, G-77, IAEA, IBRD, ICAO, IDA, IFAD, IFC, ILO, IMF, IMO, INTELSAT, INTERPOL, ITU, NAM, UN, UNESCO, UPU, WHO, WMO.

The ancient history of Lebanon is essentially identical to that of Syria, of which it was long a part. The port cities of Tripoli, Tyre, and Sidon were important centers of the Phoenician empire. The parallel ranges of the Lebanon and Anti-Lebanon mountains, crowned with the country's famous cedar trees, enclose the fertile Bekaa Valley. The coastal cities became strongholds of early Christianity, later fragmented into numerous sects, including Maronites (Syrian Catholic), Roman Catholic, Greek Orthodox, Syrian Orthodox, and others. The mountains of the south became the center of the Druze sect of Islam, while orthodox Sunni Islam dominated in the Bekaa Valley.

Lebanon came under French influence in the late 18th century, as France claimed the role of protector of Syria's Christian community.

France intervened in Lebanon in 1841 and again in 1860 when fighting between Maronite and Druze communities led to the massacre of many Christians. Under pressure from France, the Ottoman Empire granted some local autonomy to the Maronites of greater Lebanon.

In the dismemberment of the Ottoman Empire after World War I, France was granted a League of Nations Mandate over the Levant States (Lebanon and Syria), ensuring French control of the Iraq Petroleum Company pipeline from Iraq to Tripoli. In 1926 Lebanon became a self-governing republic under the mandate, but internal unrest and anti-French sentiment continued. In 1936 France promised to grant full independence to Lebanon in three years, but the agreement was not implemented.

In June 1940 the French administration in Lebanon declared its allegiance to the Vichy government. British and Free French forces occupied Lebanon in June 1941 and declared it an independent republic; but the French retained control, and full independence did not come until Jan. 1, 1944.

Under a National Covenant declared in 1943, political power in the Lebanese parliament was apportioned among the nation's various communities. The president was always to be a Maronite Christian, the prime minister a Sunni Muslim. This provided a workable formula for power sharing but also ensured that the national government would always be hostage to the considerable political, economic, and even military power of separate communities and clans.

The years from the end of World War II to the early 1970s were a brief golden age for Lebanon. Beirut developed into a wealthy, cosmopolitan city, the center of Middle Eastern banking and trade. A Syrian-backed Muslim uprising in 1958 had no significant impact; U.S. Marines landed in May 1958 to protect American interests and remained until October. By the late 1960s, however, Lebanon's stability was threatened by PLO attacks on Israel from Palestinian refugee camps in southern Lebanon and by a shift in the country's demographic balance. Muslims had become a majority in Lebanon by the late 1960s and demanded a revision of the National Covenant, while Maronite Christians continued to cling to their position of political dominance.

Throughout the 1970s, Palestinian raids from Lebanon into Israel brought Israeli retaliatory strikes in southern Lebanon. Israeli troops occupied southern Lebanon in March 1978 and again in April 1980. The Palestinian-Israeli conflict polarized opinion within Lebanon, inflaming nationalist and anti-Western feelings among Lebanon's Sunni Muslims.

Civil war broke out in 1975 and lasted throughout 1976, with Palestinian and leftist Muslim militias battling militias of the Maronite community, the Christian Phalange party, and other groups. More than 60,000 persons died, and damage ranged into the billions of dollars. Syrian troops intervened in the war in 1976, battling Palestinian forces in an attempt to restore the status quo. Arab League efforts to negotiate a cease-fire produced an

unstable peace at the end of 1976; Syrian troops remained in Lebanon.

Fighting broke out between Syrian forces and Christian militiamen near Zahle on Apr. 1, 1981. Other groups joined the fighting in a general war of each against all. Israel staged commando raids against Palestinian positions in Tyre and Tulin. Israeli air raids on Beirut caused extensive loss of life and property damage. A Palestinian-Israeli cease-fire went into effect on July 24, but hostilities continued within Lebanon.

Israel invaded Lebanon in a full-scale air and sea assault on June 6, 1982, in an attempt to drive out the PLO. Israeli and Syrian forces came into direct conflict in the Bekaa Valley. Israeli forces surrounded Beirut and began a heavy bombardment of the city. On Aug. 1, Palestinian forces withdrew from Beirut under international supervision. On Sept. 14 newly elected Pres. Bashir Gemayel, a Maronite Christian, was assassinated; Israeli troops occupied the Muslim quarters of West Beirut in response. With tacit Israeli approval, Christian militiamen invaded two refugee camps on Sept. 16 and slaughtered hundreds of Palestinian civilians.

Beirut remained a battle zone in 1983, divided by the "Green Line" into Christian and Muslim sectors. Terrorist bombings were common. The United States, France, Italy, and other Western nations stationed troops in Beirut in an attempt to enforce a cease-fire. Fifty people were killed when a bomb partly destroyed the U.S. embassy on Apr. 18; separate attacks on military installations on Oct. 23 killed 241 U.S. Marines and 58 French soldiers.

Syrian-backed PLO leftist factions fought for six weeks against the main force of the PLO under Yasir Arafat in Tripoli in late 1983. After a cease-fire was negotiated, Arafat and some 4,000 PLO troops were evacuated from the city.

Rashid Karami became premier with Syrian support on Apr. 26, 1984. Meanwhile, the civil war continued, with fighting among various groups of Christian, Druze, Sunni, Shiite, and Palestinian militias. Full-scale war between Shiite and Palestinian forces broke out in May 1985. In June 1985, Shiite terrorists held a group of U.S. citizens hostage at Beirut airport for 17 days.

Israeli forces withdrew from most of Lebanon in June 1985 but continued to defend strategic positions in the southern part of the country.

Kidnappings of foreign nationals at the hands of various terrorist factions became commonplace in the late 1980s. Premier Karami was assassinated on June 1, 1987, when a bomb destroyed his helicopter.

Prior to the civil war, Lebanon's economy was based on a mixture of international trade and banking, centered in Beirut, and agriculture, pastoralism, and small-scale industry in the rest of the country. The civil war has severely disrupted the national economy, virtually wiping out the international sector and causing significant damage to the domestic sector.

Lesotho
Kingdom of Lesotho
(PREVIOUS NAME: BASUTOLAND)

Geography Location: landlocked country in southern Africa. **Boundaries:** entirely surrounded by South African territory. **Total land area:** 11,720 sq. mi. (30,355 sq km). **Coastline:** none. **Comparative area:** slightly larger than Maryland. **Land use:** 10% arable land; 0% permanent crops; 66% meadows and pastures; 0% forest and woodland; 24% other. **Major cities:** (1976) Maseru (capital) 45,000.

People Population: 1,666,012 (1988). **Nationality:** noun—Mosotho (sing.), Basotho (pl.); adjective—Basotho. **Ethnic groups:** 99.7% Sotho; 1,600 Europeans, 800 Asians. **Languages:** Sesotho and English (official); Zulu, Xhosa. **Religions:** 80% Christian, 20% indigenous beliefs.

Government Type: constitutional monarchy; independent member of Commonwealth. **Independence:** Oct. 4, 1966 (from UK). **Constitution:** Oct. 4, 1966, suspended Jan. 1970. **National holiday:** Oct. 4. **Heads of government:** Moshoeshoe II, king (since 1966); Maj. Gen. Justinus Metsing Lekhanya, chairman of Military Council and minister of defense and internal security (since Jan. 1986). **Structure:** executive and legislative authority nominally vested in king; real power rests with Military Council, established after Jan. 1986 coup; 20-member Council of Ministers responsible for administrative duties; judiciary—63 Lesotho courts administer customary law, high court and subordinate courts have criminal jurisdiction, court of appeal at Maseru has appellate jurisdiction.

Economy Monetary unit: maloti. **Budget:** (1985) *income:* $160 mil.; *expend.:* $130 mil. GDP: $247 mil., $163 per capita (1985). **Chief crops:** corn, wheat, pulses, sorghum, barley; mostly subsistence farming and livestock. **Livestock:** sheep, goats, cattle, horses, asses. **Natural resources:** some diamonds and other minerals, water, agricultural and grazing land. **Major industries:** tourism. **Labor force:** 662,000 economically active (1985 est.); 86.2% subsistence agriculture; 150,000–250,000 spend from six months to many years as wage earners in South Africa. **Exports:** labor to South Africa (remittances $300 mil. est. in 1985); $25 mil. (f.o.b., 1986); wool, mohair, wheat, cattle, peas. **Imports:** $343 mil. (f.o.b., 1986); mainly corn, building materials, clothing, vehicles, machinery. **Major trading partner:** South Africa.

Intl. Orgs. Commonwealth, FAO, G-77, GATT (de facto), IBRD, ICAO, IDA, IFAD, IFC, ILO, IMF, INTERPOL, ITU, NAM, UN, UNESCO, UPU, WHO, WMO.

Lesotho, located within east-central South Africa, was originally called Basutoland. It was sparsely populated by Bushmen until the 16th century when refugees from tribal wars in surrounding areas began to move in, an influx that continued through the 19th century. These immigrants eventually coalesced into a fairly homogenous cultural group, the Basothos.

Under King Moshoeshoe, who ruled from 1823 to 1870, several Basotho groups were consolidated. But during his reign much land was lost in a series of wars with South Africa, and Moshoeshoe appealed to Queen Victoria for aid. In 1868 the nation became a British protectorate. Between 1884 and 1959 all executive and legislative authority was in the hands of a British high commissioner. In 1903 a Basotho consultative body was established, and in 1959 a new constitution gave the council power to legislate on internal affairs.

The British began to move the country toward full independence, and in 1964 elections with universal adult suffrage were held and won by the Basutoland National party (BNP). On Oct. 4, 1966, Basutoland achieved full independence as the Kingdom of Lesotho (pronounced le-SOO-too). The first elections after independence, held in January 1970, were nullified by the leader of the ruling BNP when early returns indicated that the party might lose. A national state of emergency was declared, the Constitution was suspended, and the Parliament dissolved.

Elections in 1985 were boycotted by opposition parties, and in 1986 the BNP government was ousted in a coup. The nation is now run by a military council in conjunction with King Moshoeshoe II and a civilian cabinet. Although critical of apartheid, Lesotho has long had close economic ties with South Africa. In late 1982 South African troops entered Lesotho, claiming that the African National Congress was launching raids from inside Lesotho. But the new military regime worked to improve relations with South Africa, lessening the criticism of apartheid and increasing economic links.

Liberia
Republic of Liberia

Geography Location: western coast of Africa. **Boundaries:** Sierra Leone and Guinea to N, Ivory Coast to E, Atlantic Ocean to S and W. **Total land area:** 37,743 sq. mi. (97,754 sq km). **Coastline:** 360 mi. (579 km). **Comparative area:** size of Oregon. **Land use:** 1% arable land; 3% permanent crops; 2% meadows and pastures; 39% forest and woodland; 55% other; includes negl. % irrigated. **Major cities:** (1978) Monrovia (capital, including Congotown) 208,629.

People Population: 2,463,190 (1988). **Nationality:** noun—Liberian(s); adjective—Liberian. **Ethnic groups:** 95% indigenous peoples, including Kpelle, Bassa, Gio, Kru, Grebo, Mano, Krahn, Gola, Gbandi, Loma, Kissi, Vai, Bella; 5% descendants of repatriated slaves known as Americo-Liberians. **Languages:** 20% English (official); more than 20 local languages of Niger-Congo language group. **Religions:** 70% indigenous beliefs, 20% Muslim, 10% Christian.

Government Type: republic. **Independence:** July 26, 1847. **Constitution:** Jan. 6, 1986. **National holiday:** Independence Day, July 26. **Heads of government:** Gen. Samuel Kanyon Doe, president (since Jan. 1986). **Structure:** executive—president, assisted by appointed cabinet; legislative—bicameral legislature; judiciary.

Economy Monetary unit: uses U.S. dollar and Liberian dollar. **Budget:** (1987) *income:* $210 mil.; *expend.:* $367 mil. GDP: $711 mil., $310 per capita (1986). **Chief crops:** rubber, rice, oil palm, cassava, coffee, cocoa; imports rice and wheat. **Livestock:** sheep, goats, pigs, cattle; imports livestock. **Natural resources:** iron ore, timber, diamonds, gold. **Major industries:** rubber processing, food processing, construction materials. **Labor force:** 510,000; 70.5% agriculture, 10.8% services, 4.5% industry and commerce, 14.2% other; 220,000 wage earners; non-Africans hold about 95% of top-level management and engineering jobs; 52% of population of working age. **Exports:** $408 mil. (f.o.b., 1986); iron ore, rubber, diamonds, lumber and logs, coffee, cocoa. **Imports:** $259 mil. (c.i.f., 1986); machinery, transportation equipment, petroleum products, manufactured goods, foodstuffs. **Major trading partners:** 25% U.S.; W. Germany, Netherlands, Italy, Belgium.

Intl. Orgs. FAO, G-77, IAEA, IBRD, ICAO, IDA, IFAD, IFC, ILO, IMF, IMO, INTERPOL, ITU, NAM, UN, UNESCO, UPU, WHO, WMO.

Liberia was populated by migrants from the north and east beginning in the 12th century, but it remained relatively isolated from the remainder of West Africa and was not incorporated into any of the region's premodern kingdoms and empires. Portuguese explorers first reached the Liberian coast in 1461 to be followed by other European traders. Until the 19th century, Liberia was largely ignored by the world except for a small-scale coastal trade in slaves and forest products.

In 1816 the U.S. Congress granted a charter to the American Colonization Society, ACS, a private organization dedicated to the African repatriation of freed slaves. The first settlers landed in 1822 at the town that was later to become Monrovia. In 1838 the settlers organized the Commonwealth of Liberia under a governor appointed by the ACS. The commonwealth declared its independence as the Republic of Liberia in 1847 and adopted a constitution modeled after that of the United States. The new government, Africa's first independent republic, was granted diplomatic recognition by Great Britain in 1848, France in 1852, and the United States in 1862.

Bolstered by the moral backing of the United States, Liberia in its first 100 years of independence succeeded, with difficulty, in fending off British and French attempts to encroach on its territory from their neighboring colonies. Although descendents of freed American slaves are a minority in Liberia's ethnically diverse population, they have consistently dominated the country's political (and to a lesser extent, economic) life.

William V.S. Tubman was elected president in 1944 and served until his death in 1971, successfully steering Liberia through the post-World War II age of African nationalism and decolonization. He was succeeded by William R. Tolbert, Jr. On Apr. 12, 1980, Tolbert was deposed in a military coup led by Master Sgt. Samuel K. Doe. Doe suspended the Constitution and imposed martial law but pledged a new constitution and the resumption of civilian rule by 1985.

Presidential elections were held on Oct. 15, 1985, under the terms of a provisional constitution that for the first time enacted universal suffrage. Samuel Doe was elected president, and his party won 80 percent of the seats in the national legislature. Despite allegations of fraud that led to a violent but unsuccessful coup attempt in November 1985, the Second Republic, under the new constitution, was inaugurated on Jan. 6, 1986, and the Doe government assumed office. Pres. Doe has since moved to restore harmony with opposition party leaders.

The majority of Liberia's people are engaged in agriculture, but the country is not self-sufficient in food production. The national economy is based primarily on rubber, iron ore, and timber, which form the country's major exports; other important resources include gold, diamonds, coffee, cocoa, and palm oil. Imports include food (especially rice), machinery, and other manufactured goods. Liberia also derives substantial revenue from flag-of-convenience shipping registration.

Liberia maintains close ties to the United States and is a major recipient of American economic and military aid, as well as of private American investment. The Peace Corps and the African operations of the Voice of America maintain a conspicuous presence in Liberia. Liberia is also an active participant in African multinational organizations, including the Organization of African Unity and the Economic Community of West African States.

Libya
Socialist People's Libyan Arab Jamahiriya

Geography Location: along Mediterranean coast of North Africa. **Boundaries:** Mediterranean Sea to N, Egypt to E, Sudan to SE, Niger and Chad to S, Tunisia and Algeria to W. **Total land area:** 685,524 sq. mi. (1,775,500 sq km). **Coastline:** 1,100 mi. (1,770 km). **Comparative area:** slightly larger than Alaska. **Land use:** 1% arable land; 0% permanent crops; 8% meadows and pastures; 0% forest and woodland; 91% other; includes negl. % irrigated. **Major cities:** in Jan. 1987, Col. Qaddafi designated Hun, a town 404 mi. (650 km) SE of Tripoli, as administrative capital of country (population N.A.); (1973 census) Tripoli 481,295; Benghazi 219,317; Misurata 42,815; Al-Zania (Azzawiya) 39,382; Al-Beida 31,796.

People Population: 3,956,211 (1988). **Nationality:** noun—Libyan(s); adjective—Libyan. **Ethnic groups:** 97% Berber and Arab; some Greeks, Maltese, Italians, Egyptians, Pakistanis, Turks, Indians, Tunisians. **Languages:** Arabic, Italian, and English widely understood in major cities. **Religions:** 97% Sunni Muslim.

Government Type: Jamahiriya, or a state of the masses; in theory, governed by populace. **Independence:** Dec. 24, 1951 (from Italy). **Constitution:** Dec. 11, 1969, amended Mar. 2, 1977. **National holidays:** Revolution Day, Sept. 1; British Evacuation Day, Mar. 28; U.S. Evac-

uation Day, June 16; Declaration of People's Power, Mar. 2. **Heads of government:** Col. Muammar al-Qaddafi (no official title; runs country and is treated as chief of state). **Structure:** officially, paramount political power and authority rests with General People's Congress, which theoretically functions as a parliament with a cabinet called General People's Committee.

Economy Monetary unit: dinar. **Budget:** (1985 est.) *income:* $10.0 bil.; *expend.:* $9.9 bil., including development expend. of $5.7 bil. **GNP:** roughly $20 bil., $5,410 per capita (1986). **Chief crops:** wheat, barley, olives, dates, citrus fruits; 65% of food is imported. **Livestock:** chickens, sheep, goats, cattle, camels. **Natural resources:** crude oil, natural gas, gypsum. **Major industries:** petroleum, food processing, textiles. **Labor force:** 1 mil., of which about 280,000 are resident foreigners; 31% industry, 27% services, 24% government, 18% agriculture. **Exports:** $5.0 bil. (f.o.b., 1986); petroleum. **Imports:** $4.5 bil. (f.o.b., 1986); manufactures, food. **Major trading partners:** *exports:* Italy, W. Germany, Spain, France, Japan; *imports:* Italy, W. Germany.

Intl. Orgs. Arab League, FAO, G-77, IAEA, IBRD, ICAO, IDA, IFAD, IFC, ILO, IMF, IMO, INTELSAT, INTERPOL, ITU, NAM, OAU, OPEC, UN, UNESCO, UPU, WHO, WIPO, WMO.

The coastal cities of Libya played an important cultural and commercial role in the Mediterranean in antiquity and were prized possessions of numerous empires. The Libyan coast was successively ruled by Phoenicians, Carthaginians, Greeks, Romans, and Vandals before being incorporated into the Byzantine Empire in the fourth century A.D.; nomadic tribes in the interior were beyond the reach of any government. The Islamic conquests of the seventh century brought Libya into the Arab world.

Libya was incorporated into the Ottoman Empire shortly after the Ottoman conquest of Egypt in 1517 and was ruled by local Ottoman vassals until 1835 when direct Ottoman government was established. In 1911 Libya was invaded and conquered by Italy. After World War I, local resistance to Italian colonial rule was led by King Idris I, Emir of Cyrenaica. British troops drove Italian and German forces from Libya in 1943. King Idris returned from exile in 1944. Following World War II, most of Libya was ruled as a British protectorate with a smaller portion under French administration.

A UN resolution of 1949 calling for the end of foreign control was implemented on Dec. 24, 1951, when Libya became an independent constitutional monarchy. In 1959 significant oil reserves were discovered; oil production rapidly transformed Libya from one of the poorest states in North Africa to one of the wealthiest.

A military coup on Sept. 1, 1969, led by Col. Muammar al-Qaddafi, deposed the monarchy and declared the establishment of the Libyan Arab Republic. The republic, with Col. Qaddafi as chief of state, moved rapidly to nationalize foreign assets, expel foreign troops, and close foreign libraries, cultural centers, and so on.

Col. Qaddafi assumed full dictatorial powers under a political system that gives equal weight to Islamic law and his own political philosophy. Popular participation in elections is mandatory, although no government organization outside Qaddafi and his circle of advisers exerts any real authority.

Libya has given strong political and financial aid to various radical Palestinian groups and other enemies of Israel and its supporters, sponsoring terrorist activities throughout Europe and the Middle East in real or putative support of the Palestinian cause. Numerous anti-Qaddafi Libyan exiles have been assassinated in Europe. Libya has also engaged in sporadic military campaigns against Egypt and the Sudan and supports a rebel movement in Chad.

Relations between Libya and the United States have been very hostile in the 1980s. On May 6, 1981, the United States closed the Libyan "People's Bureau" (embassy) in Washington, D.C. On Aug. 2, 1981, American jets shot down two attacking Libyan warplanes as U.S. naval forces conducted exercises in the Gulf of Sidra, which Libya claims as national waters. In 1986 the United States imposed economic sanctions on Libya, ordered all Americans to leave the country, and froze Libyan assets in the United States. Another clash in the Gulf of Sidra in March 1986 ended with American forces sinking two Libyan ships. On Apr. 5, 1986, Libyan-sponsored terrorists bombed a nightclub in West Berlin, killing two U.S. soldiers; in response, American bombers attacked Tripoli and Benghazi on Apr. 14 in an apparent attempt to kill Col. Qaddafi himself.

Great Britain broke off diplomatic relations with Libya in April 1984 after machine-gun fire from the Libyan "People's Bureau" in London killed a policeman and wounded 10 Libyan exiles demonstrating against Qaddafi's government. In May 1984 an attempted coup against Qaddafi was foiled; this was followed by a purge in which thousands of people were imprisoned or executed.

The Libyan economy depends heavily on petroleum and natural gas. Other industrial activities include gypsum mining and light manufacturing, including textiles and carpets. A narrow strip of fertile land along the coast supports mixed agriculture, and sheep, goats, and camels are raised in the desert interior.

Liechtenstein
Principality of Liechtenstein

Geography Location: landlocked country in central Europe. **Boundaries:** Austria to N and E, Switzerland to S and W. **Total land area:** 61.8 sq. mi. (160 sq km). **Coastline:** none. **Comparative area:** about 9/10 size of Washington, D.C. **Land use:** 25% arable land; 0% permanent crops; 38% meadows and pastures; 19% forest and woodland; 18% other. **Major cities:** (1986 est.) Vaduz (capital) 4,920; Schaan 4,757; Balzers 3,477; Triesen 3,180; Eschen 2,844.

People Population: 27,825 (1988). **Nationality:** noun—Liechtensteiner(s); adjective—Liechtenstein. **Ethnic groups:** 95% Alemannic, 5% Italian and other. **Languages:** German (official), Alemannic dialect. **Religions:** 82.7% Roman Catholic, 7.1% Protestant, 10.2% other.

Government Type: hereditary constitutional monarchy. **Independence:** N.A. **Constitution:** Oct. 5, 1921. **National holiday:** N.A. **Heads of government:** Franz Josef II, prince (since July 1938); Hans Brunhart, prime minister (since May 1978); prince transferred most of his executive powers to his son, Prince Hans Adam, in Aug. 1984. **Structure:** executive—hereditary prince; legislative—unicameral legislature (diet; 15 deputies elected to four-year terms); judiciary—independent.

Economy Monetary unit: Swiss franc. **Budget:** (1983); *income:* $108 mil.; *expend.:* $86 mil. **GNP:** about $15,000 per capita (1984). Note: Liechtenstein has prosperous economy based primarily on small-scale light industry and some farming; sale of postage stamps to collectors, estimated at $10 mil. annually, provides 10% of state budget; companies incorporated in Liechtenstein solely for tax purposes provide additional 30% of state budget; low business taxes (maximum tax rate 20%) and easy incorporation rules have induced about 25,000 holding, or so-called letter box, companies to establish nominal offices there; economy is tied closely to that of Switzerland in customs union; no national accounts data available. **Chief crops:** vegetables, corn, wheat, potatoes, grapes. **Livestock:** cattle, pigs, horses, sheep, goats. **Natural resources:** hydroelectric potential. **Major industries:** electronics, metal manufacturing, textiles. **Labor force:** 12,258; 5,078 foreign workers (mostly from Switzerland and Austria); 54.4% industry, trade, and building; 41.6% services; 4.0% agriculture, fishing, forestry, and horticulture; no unemployment. **Exports:** $440 mil. (1984); 39% EC, 32% EFTA (24% Switzerland), 29% other. **Imports:** N.A. **Major trading partners:** N.A.

Intl. Orgs. EFTA, IAEA, INTELSAT, INTERPOL, ITU, UNCTAD, UNICEF, UNIDO, UPU, WIPO; considering UN membership; has consultative status in EC; under several post–World War I treaties, Switzerland handles Liechtenstein's customs and represents principality abroad on diplomatic and consular level whenever requested to do so by Liechtenstein government.

The alpine principality of Liechtenstein, bordered by Austria and Switzerland, is a remnant of the Holy Roman Empire, an ancient constitutional monarchy with a modern industrial economy. The current dynasty was established in 1699; Prince Franz Josef II came to the throne in 1938, yielding his executive powers to his heir apparent, Hans Adam, in 1984.

Liechtenstein was tied to the Austro-Hungarian monarchy until 1918. Since then it has remained in a customs union with Switzerland, which also handles its foreign affairs. The single-chamber diet, the Landtag is elected by universal suffrage, women having won the right to vote in 1984. The relatively conservative Progressive Citizen's party ruled continuously during 1928–70. From 1970 to 1974, and

again from 1978 to the present, the relatively liberal Fatherland Union has controlled the government.

The economy, dominated by dairy farming before 1945, has since been radically transformed by industrialization and the development of service industries. National expenditures, and hence taxes, are low, and the dynasty is wealthy. Liechtenstein has thus become a corporate haven, with some 25,000 corporations maintaining nominal headquarters there. Foreign workers constitute about 40 percent of the work force.

The country's only significant problem is industrial and automotive pollution. A policy of free public transportation, introduced in 1988, has met with some success in curbing the proliferation of automobiles.

Luxembourg
Grand Duchy of Luxembourg

Geography Location: landlocked country in western Europe. **Boundaries:** Belgium to N and W, W. Germany to E, France to S. **Total land area:** 999 sq. mi. (2,586 sq km). **Coastline:** none. **Comparative area:** slightly smaller than Rhode Island. **Land use:** 24% arable land; 1% permanent crops; 20% meadows and pastures; 21% forest and woodland; 34% other. **Major cities:** (1981 census) Luxembourg-Ville (capital) 78,900; Esch-sur-Alzette 25,100; Differdange 14,100; Petange 12,100.

People Population: 366,232 (1988). **Nationality:** noun—Luxembourger(s); adjective—Luxembourg. **Ethnic groups:** Celtic base, with French and German blend; also, guest and worker residents from Portugal, Italy, and European countries. **Languages:** Luxembourgish, German, French; many also speak English. **Religions:** 97% Roman Catholic, 3% Protestant and Jewish.

Government Type: constitutional monarchy. **Independence:** N.A. **Constitution:** Oct. 17, 1868, occasional revisions. **National holiday:** Grand Duke's birthday, June 23. **Heads of government:** Jean, grand duke (since Nov. 1964); Jacques Santer, prime minister (since July 1984). **Structure:** parliamentary democracy; seven ministers compose Council of Government, headed by president, which constitutes executive; it is responsible to unicameral legislature (Chamber of Deputies); Council of State, appointed for indefinite term, exercises some powers of an upper house; judicial power exercised by independent courts; coalition governments are usual.

Economy Monetary unit: Luxembourg franc. **Budget:** (1986) *income*: $1.76 bil.; *expend.:* $1.75 bil. **GNP:** $4.6 bil., $12,570 per capita (1986). **Chief crops:** mixed farming, wine. **Livestock:** cattle, horses, pigs, sheep, poultry. **Natural resources:** iron ore (no longer exploited). **Major industries:** banking, iron and steel, food processing. **Labor force:** 161,000 (1984); 48.9% services, 24.7% industry, 13.2% government; one-third of work force is foreign, comprising mostly workers from Portugal, Italy, France, Belgium, and W. Germany; 1.6% unemployment (1987). **Exports:** $2.81 bil. (f.o.b., 1985); iron and steel products,

chemicals, rubber products, glass, aluminum. **Imports:** $3.1 bil. (c.i.f., 1985); minerals, metals, foodstuffs, machinery, quality consumer goods. **Major trading partners:** Luxembourg has customs union with Belgium, under which foreign trade is recorded jointly for the two countries; most foreign trade is with W. Germany, Belgium, France, and other EC countries (for totals, see "Belgium").

Intl. Orgs. EC, FAO, GATT, IAEA, IBRD, ICAO, IDA, IFAD, IFC, ILO, IMF, INTELSAT, INTERPOL, ITU, NATO, UN, UNESCO, UPU, WHO, WIPO, WMO.

One of hundreds of small principalities in the Holy Roman Empire, Luxembourg joined the German league when the empire was abolished in 1806. It shared a monarchy with the Netherlands, but the two countries remained distinct under a single sovereign. In 1831 Luxembourg lost its French-speaking territory to Belgium. The Treaty of London granted sovereignty to Luxembourg in 1867. When King William III died in 1890, different rules of succession severed the dual monarchy; Queen Wilhelmina succeeded him in the Netherlands, while Adolf of Nassau became grand duke of Luxembourg. The nation's full independence dates from that event.

During the 19th century, Luxembourg developed a balanced modern economy, with prosperous small farms being complemented by industry, particularly mining and steel production. As late as 1970, steel accounted for over 25 percent of the nation's GDP and five-eighths of export earnings.

Luxembourg was overrun by Germany during World War I and again in May 1940, in the early stages of World War II. Archduchess Charlotte fled to London and returned with the Allied armed forces in 1944. The constitutional monarchy has enjoyed political stability since the war, with the Christian Social party normally the senior partner in a three-way coalition. Pierre Warner was prime minister from 1959 to 1979, and again from 1979 to 1984, when he was succeeded by the current prime minister, Jacques Santer.

Luxembourg formed a customs union with Belgium in 1921 and joined the Benelux union even before World War II had ended. A founding member of the United Nations in 1945, Luxembourg abandoned its traditional neutrality in 1948 and joined NATO in 1949. It was a founding member of the EEC under the 1954 Treaty of Rome and is now home to numerous Common Market institutions, including the Secretariat of the European Parliament and the European Investment Bank.

The depletion of Luxembourg's iron ore and rising international competition led to a decline in the mining and steel industries in the 1970s. The economy turned increasingly to the service sector, and Luxembourg is now a center of international banking, which accounts for over half of its gross national product. Tax cuts stimulated the economy and aided recovery from a recession of 1981–85. The country's chief problem is a shrinking and aging citizenry, leading to strains on social services and dependence on foreign workers.

Madagascar
Democratic Republic of Madagascar
(PREVIOUS NAME: MALAGASY REPUBLIC)

Geography **Location:** one large island and several smaller ones in western Indian Ocean. **Boundaries:** about 300 mi. (500 km) E of Mozambique. **Total land area:** 224,532 sq. mi. (581,540 sq km). **Coastline:** 3,000 mi. (4,828 km). **Comparative area:** slightly less than twice size of Arizona. **Land use:** 4% arable land; 1% permanent crops; 58% meadows and pastures; 26% forest and woodland; 11% other; includes 1% irrigated. **Major cities:** Antananarivo (capital) 662,585 (1985 est.); Antsirabé 78,941; Toamasina (Tamatave) 77,395; Fianarantsoa 68,054; Mahajanga (Majunga) 65,864 (1975 census).

People **Population:** 11,073,361 (1988). **Nationality:** noun—Malagasy (sing., pl.); adjective—Malagasy. **Ethnic groups:** highlanders of predominantly Malayo-Indonesian origin (Merina 1,643,000 and related Betsileo 760,000); coastal peoples collectively termed Cotiers, with mixed African, Malayo-Indonesian, and Arab ancestry (Betsimisaraka 941,000; Tsimihety 442,000; Antaisaka 415,000; Sakalava 375,000); 11,000 European French, 5,000 Indians of French nationality, 5,000 Creoles. **Languages:** French and Malagasy (both official). **Religions:** 52% indigenous beliefs, 41% Christian, 7% Muslim.

Government **Type:** real authority in hands of president, although Supreme Revolutionary Council is theoretically ultimate executive authority. **Independence:** June 26, 1960 (from France). **Constitution:** Dec. 21, 1975. **National holiday:** Independence Day, June 26. **Heads of government:** Adm. Didier Ratsiraka, president (since Dec. 1975); Lt. Col. Victor Ramahatra, prime minister (since Feb. 1988). **Structure:** executive—president, Supreme Revolutionary Council (made up of military and political leaders) assisted by cabinet (Council of Ministers); unicameral legislature—Popular National Assembly; judiciary—courts patterned after French system, High Council of Institutions has power of constitutional review.

Economy **Monetary unit:** Malagasy franc. **Budget:** (measured as share of GDP, 1986 est.) *income:* 15%; *expend.:* 25%. **GDP:** $2.7 bil., $267 per capita (1986). **Chief crops:** cash crops—coffee, vanilla, cloves, sugar, tobacco; food crops—rice, cassava, cereals, potatoes, corn. **Livestock:** cattle, pigs, goats, sheep. **Natural resources:** graphite, chromite, coal, bauxite, salt. **Major industries:** agricultural processing (meat canneries, soap factories, brewery, tanneries, sugar refining), light consumer goods industries (textiles, glassware), cement. **Labor force:** 4.9 mil. (1985); 95% nonsalaried family workers engaged in subsistence agriculture; 175,000 wage and salary earners (26% agriculture, 17% domestic service, 15% industry, 14% commerce, 11% construction); 51% of population of working age. **Exports:** $350 mil. (f.o.b., 1986 est.); coffee, vanilla, sugar, cloves; agricultural and livestock products account for about 85% of export earnings.

Imports: $453 mil. (c.i.f., 1986 est.); 35.9% raw materials, 26.8% equipment, 13.2% food, 12.7% energy, 11.4% consumer goods. **Major trading partners:** (1985) *exports:* 34.0% France, 13.1% U.S., 10.4% Japan, 7.6% Indonesia, 5.5% Italy; *imports:* 32.5% France, 8.6% USSR, 6.1% West Germany, 5.7% Qatar, 5.6% U.S.

Intl. Orgs. FAO, G-77, GATT, IAEA, IBRD, ICAO, IDA, IFAD, IFC, ILO, IMF, IMO, INTELSAT, INTERPOL, ITU, NAM, UN, UNESCO, UPU, WHO, WMO.

Lying near the east coast of Africa, Madagascar was settled by Malayo-Indonesian migrants some 2,000 years ago. Although later waves of African and Arab migrants were absorbed into the population, to a large extent it is still ethnically and culturally Asian. A Portuguese attempt to colonize the island in the 16th century failed, and during the 18th and 19th centuries, a unified kingdom backed by the British ruled the country. Foreign interests—largely British and French—developed extensive coffee plantations, and the French made Madagascar a protectorate in 1885 and a colony in 1896.

During World War II Madagascar sided with the Free French, and French colonial rule was reestablished after the war. The Malagasy Republic was founded as an independent nation on June 26, 1960. A coup in 1972 brought an anti-French and generally anti-Western government to power. Repression and economic stagnation characterized the 1970s, and in recent years the Malagasy government has become more moderate. Madagascar's unique wildlife—a mixture of African species and others of domestic evolution—makes it of unique scientific interest.

Malawi
Republic of Malawi
(PREVIOUS NAME: NYASALAND)

Geography **Location:** landlocked country in southern central Africa. **Boundaries:** Tanzania to N, Mozambique to E, S, and SW, Zambia to W; Lake Malawi forms much of eastern boundary. **Total land area:** 45,747 sq. mi. (118,484 sq km). **Coastline:** none. **Comparative area:** slightly larger than Pennsylvania. **Land use:** 25% arable land; negl. % permanent crops; 20% meadows and pastures; 50% forest and woodland; 5% other; includes negl. % irrigated. **Major cities:** Lilongwe (capital) 75,000 (1976 est.); Blantyre 219,011 (1977 census).

People **Population:** 7,679,368 (1988). **Nationality:** noun—Malawian(s); adjective—Malawian. **Ethnic groups:** Chewa, Nyanja, Tumbuko, Yao, Lomwe, Sena, Tonga, Ngoni, Asian, European. **Languages:** English and Chichewa (both official); Tombuka. **Religions:** 55% Protestant, 20% Roman Catholic, 20% Muslim, indigenous beliefs.

Government **Type:** one-party state. **Independence:** July 6, 1964 (from UK). **Constitution:** July 6, 1964. **National holiday:** Republic Day, July 6. **Heads of government:** Dr. Hastings Kamuzu Banda (since 1966). **Structure:** executive—strong presidential system with cabinet appointed by president; legislative—

unicameral National Assembly of 87 elected and up to 15 nominated members; judiciary—high court with chief justice and at least two justices.

Economy **Monetary unit:** Malawi kwacha. **Budget:** (measured as share of GDP, 1985) *income:* 23%; *expend.:* 34%. **GDP:** $1.23 bil., $170 per capita (1986). **Chief crops:** cash crops—tobacco, tea, sugar, peanuts, cotton; subsistence crops—corn, sorghum, millet, pulses, root crops; self-sufficient in food production. **Livestock:** cattle, goats, pigs, sheep. **Natural resources:** limestone; unexploited deposits of uranium, coal, bauxite. **Major industries:** agricultural processing (tea, tobacco, sugar), sawmilling, cement. **Labor force:** 344,052 (1982); 52% agriculture, 16% personal services, 9% manufacturing. **Exports:** $240 mil. (f.o.b., 1986); tobacco, tea, sugar, peanuts, cotton. **Imports:** $260 mil. (c.i.f., 1986); manufactured (c.i.f., 1986); manufactured goods, machinery and transport equipment, building and construction materials, fuel, fertilizer. **Major trading partners:** *exports:* UK, W. Germany, U.S., Netherlands, South Africa; *imports:* South Africa, UK, Japan, W. Germany.

Intl. Orgs. Commonwealth, EC (associated member), FAO, G-77, GATT, IBRD, ICAO, IDA, IFAD, IFC, ILO, IMF, INTELSAT, INTERPOL, ITU, NAM, UN, UNESCO, UPU, WHO, WIPO, WMO.

Malawi derives its name from the Maravi, a Bantu people that settled in the region in the 13th century and whose descendants, the Chewas, comprise a significant segment of the current population. The arrival of the Scottish missionary David Livingstone in 1859 led to the establishment of the British-controlled Nyasaland Protectorate in 1891. Despite attempts to obtain independence, the British continued to rule Malawi through the first half of the 20th century. Nyasaland formed a federation with Northern and Southern Rhodesia and began to organize an independence movement. The fight for independence was led by Dr. H. Kamuzu Banda, an expatriate who assumed the presidency of the Nyasaland African Congress, later the Malawi Congress party, upon his return in 1958. The British granted Nyasaland self-governing status in 1962, and Banda was elected prime minister the following year. Malawi achieved full independence under its present name in 1964 and later became a republic with Banda as its president for life.

Malawi currently hosts one of the largest refugee populations in Africa due to political and social strife in neighboring Mozambique. The influx of nearly 500,000 refugees has placed a great strain on the Malawian economy.

Malaysia

Geography **Location:** 13 states in Southeast Asia; 11 are in Peninsular Malaysia and two, Sabah and Sarawak, lie about 400 mi. (640 km) across South China Sea on northern coast of island of Borneo (Kalimantan). **Boundaries:** Peninsular Malaysia—Thailand to N, South China Sea to E, Island of Singapore to S across Johor Strait, and Indonesian island of

Sumatra to W across Strait of Malacca; Sabah and Sarawak—South China Sea to NW, Sulu Sea to NE, Celebes Sea to E, Indonesia to S; Brunei is enclosed withing Sarawak on coast of South China Sea. **Total land area:** 127,320 sq. mi. (329,757 sq km). **Coastline:** 2,905 mi. (4,675 km). **Comparative area:** slightly larger than New Mexico. **Land use:** 3% arable land; 10% permanent crops; negl.% meadows and pastures; 63% forest and woodland; 24% other; includes 1% irrigated. **Major cities:** (1980 census) Kuala Lumpur (capital) 919,610; Ipoh 293,849; George Town (Penang) 248,241; Johore Bahru 246,395; Petaling Jaya 207,805.

People **Population:** 16,398,306 (1988). **Nationality:** noun—Malaysian(s); adjective—Malaysian. **Ethnic groups:** 59% Malay and other indigenous, 32% Chinese, 9% Indian. **Languages:** Peninsular Malaysia—Malay (official); English, Chinese dialects, Tamil; Sabah—English, Malay, numerous tribal dialects, Mandarin and Hakka dialects predominate among Chinese; Sarawak—English, Malay, Mandarin, numerous tribal langs. **Religions:** Peninsular Malaysia—Malays nearly all Muslim, Chinese predominantly Buddhist, Indians predominantly Hindu; Sabah—38% Muslim, 17% Christian, 45% other; Sarawak—35% tribal religion, 24% Buddhist and Confucianist, 20% Muslim, 16% Christian, 5% other.

Government **Type:** Federation of Malaysia formed July 9, 1963; constitutional monarchy nominally headed by paramount ruler (king); bicameral Parliament; Peninsular Malaysian states—hereditary rulers in all but Penang and Melaka, where governors are appointed by Malaysian government, with powers of state governments limited by federal constitution; Sabah—self-governing state, holding 20 seats in House of Representatives, with foreign affairs, defense, internal security, and other powers delegated to federal government; Sarawak—self-governing state, which holds 24 seats in House of Representatives, with foreign affairs, defense, internal security, and other powers delegated to federal government. **Independence:** Aug. 31, 1957 (from UK). **Constitution:** Aug. 31, 1957, amended Sept. 6, 1963, when Federation of Malaya became Federation of Malaysia. **National holiday:** Independence Day, Aug. 31. **Heads of government:** Azlan Shah, king (since Apr. 1989); Dr. Mahathir Mohamad, prime minister (since July 1981). **Structure:** nine state rulers alternate as paramount ruler for five-year terms; locus of executive power vested in prime minister and cabinet, who are responsible to bicameral Parliament (58-member Senate, 177-member House of Representatives); Peninsular Malaysia—executive branches of 11 states vary in detail but are similar in design, with chief minister, appointed by hereditary ruler or governor, heading an executive council (cabinet), which is responsible to elected, unicameral legislature; Sarawak—executive branch headed by governor, appointed by central government, having largely ceremonial role; executive power exercised by chief minister who heads parliamentary cabinet responsible to unicameral legislature; judiciary is part of Malaysian judicial system.

Economy **Monetary unit:** Malaysian ringgit. **Budget:** (1986) *income:* N.A. *expend.:* operating, $7.4 bil.; development expend., $2.9 bil. **GDP:** $25.8 bil., $1,600 per capita (1986 est.). **Chief crops:** Peninsular Malaysia—natural rubber, palm oil, rice; 10–15% of rice requirements imported; Sabah—mainly subsistence, main crops are rubber, timber, coconut, rice (rice is also food deficit); Sarawak—main crops are rubber, timber, pepper (rice is food deficit). **Livestock:** pigs, cattle, goats, buffalo, sheep. **Natural resources:** tin, crude oil, timber, copper, iron ore. **Major industries:** Peninsular Malaysia—rubber and oil-palm processing and manufacturing, light manufacturing industry, electronics; Sabah—logging, petroleum production; Sarawak—agriculture processing, petroleum production and refining, logging. **Labor force:** 5.95 mil. (1985); 34.5% agriculture; trade, hotels, and restaurants; 15.6% manufacturing, 14.9% government. **Exports:** $13.9 bil. (f.o.b., 1986); natural rubber, palm oil, tin, timber, petroleum. **Imports:** $10.8 bil. (c.i.f., 1986). **Major trading partners:** (1985) *exports:* 23% Japan, 17% Singapore, 16% U.S., 15% EC; *imports:* 21% Japan, 19% U.S., 15% EC, 15% Singapore.

Intl. Orgs. ASEAN, Colombo Plan, Commonwealth, FAO, G-77, GATT, IAEA, IBRD, ICAO, IDA, IFC, ILO, IMF, IMO, INTELSAT, INTERPOL, ITU, NAM, UN, UNESCO, UPU, WHO, WMO.

From ancient times a group of petty principalities in the southern part of the Malay Peninsula, bordering the Strait of Malacca, maintained extensive ties of maritime commerce throughout Southeast Asia. The early Malay states were Hindu, under Indian influence; with the rise of the Kingdom of Malacca in the 15th century, conversion to Islam was widespread. European influence began in the 16th century; the Portuguese, initially dominant, gave way to the Dutch, who seized Malacca in 1641.

British influence grew during the 18th century, with the founding of a trading settlement at Penang in 1789. Singapore was founded in 1819, and the Dutch ceded Malacca to Great Britain in 1824. By a series of treaties in the late 19th century, the various Malay states became British protectorates; Britain controlled the entire southern peninsula after 1909. Under British rule, commercial tin mining and the establishment of extensive rubber plantations led to the importation of many Indian and Chinese laborers; eventually ethnic Chinese dominated most of Malaya's domestic economy.

In the 19th century, Great Britain also gained a dominant position in northern Borneo, portions of which eventually became incorporated into Malaysia (see "Brunei").

Japan overran Malaya in December 1941–February 1942 and held the country until August 1945. Following World War II, the various Malay states (excluding Singapore) organized into a federation, which replaced the confusing prewar regime of federated and unfederated protectorates. A Communist rebellion disrupted the country throughout the early 1950s. Following the suppression of the Communist movement, elections were held in mid-1955 for a home-rule government. The elections brought the Alliance party of Tungku Abdul Rahman to power, and the Federation of Malaya became self-governing in domestic affairs in 1957.

Full independence came on Sept. 16, 1963, with the creation of Malaysia, incorporating the Federation of Malaya as well as Singapore and the former British colonies of North Borneo (thereafter called Sabah) and Sarawak. Singapore seceded from Malaysia in 1965 and became an independent nation. Malaysia is a constitutional monarchy with a parliamentary system; monarchs are chosen for five-year terms from among the hereditary rulers of the old Malay states. In March 1989 the sultan of Perak, Azlan Muhibuddin Shah, was elected king, succeeding Mahmood Iskandar, sultan of Johore.

Ethnic concerns have dominated Malaysian politics, as the Islamic Malays have enacted various laws to restrict the economic power and ethnic cohesion of the non-Islamic Chinese and Indian minorities. In 1987 the federal government provoked a constitutional crisis when it tried unsuccessfully to prevent the seating of an elected opposition provincial government in Sabah.

Malaysia's economy continues to be dominated by rubber, tin, and other natural-resource-based commodities (palm oil, timber, spices); modernization has created an export-oriented industrial sector producing textiles, electronic equipment, and other manufactured goods.

Maldives
Republic of Maldives

Geography **Location:** chain of more than 1,200 small coral islands of which about 220 are inhabited, extending over 475 mi. (764 km) from N to S and 80 mi. (207 km) from W to E in Indian Ocean; northernmost atoll about 370 mi. (960 km) southwest of India. **Boundaries:** Laccadive Sea to NE, Arabian Sea to N, Indian Ocean to S and W. **Total land area:** 115 sq. mi. (298 sq km). **Coastline:** 400 mi. (644 km). **Comparative area:** slightly more than 1.5 times size of Washington, D.C. **Land use:** 10% arable land; 0% permanent crops; 3% meadows and pastures; 3% forest and woodland; 84% other. **Major cities:** (1985) Male (capital) 46,334.

People **Population:** 203,187 (1988). **Nationality:** noun—Maldivian(s); adjective—Maldivian. **Ethnic groups:** admixtures of Sinhalese, Dravidian, Arab, and black. **Languages:** Divehi (dialect of Sinhala; script derived from Arabic); English spoken by most government officials. **Religions:** Sunni Muslim.

Government **Type:** republic. **Independence:** July 26, 1965 (from UK). **Constitution:** June 4, 1964. **National holidays:** Independence Day, July 26; Republic Day, Nov. 11. **Heads of government:** Maumoon Abdul Gayoom, president (since 1978). **Structure:** elected president, chief executive; popularly elected unicameral national legislature, People's Council (members elected for five-year terms); appointed chief justice responsible for administration of Islamic law.

Economy **Monetary unit:** Maldivian rufiya. **Budget:** (1985) *income:* $25.0 mil.; *expend.:* $43.0 mil. **GDP:** $68.3 mil., $440 per capita (1985 est.). **Chief crops:** coconut, limited production of millet, corn, pumpkins, sweet potatoes; shortages—rice, sugar, flour. **Livestock:** N.A. **Natural resources:** fish. **Major industries:** fishing, tourism, some coconut processing. **Labor force:** about 66,000; fishing industry employs about 80% of labor force. **Exports:** $22.5 mil. (1986). **Imports:** $52.0 mil. (1986). **Major trading partners:** Japan, Sri Lanka, Thailand.

Intl. Orgs. Colombo Plan, Commonwealth (special member), FAO, G-77, GATT (de facto), IBRD, ICAO, IDA, IFAD, IFC, IMF, IMO, ITU, NAM, UN, UNESCO, UPU, WHO, WMO.

The small sultanate of the Maldive Islands, with an Islamic population of Sinhalese descent, was made a British protectorate in 1887. The islands' tiny area and poor soil limited development; fishing and fish processing are the main industries, and copra is the only significant crop. The Maldives became an independent nation on July 26, 1965. In 1968 the sultanate was abolished and replaced by a republic. Since independence, tourism has become economically important and now accounts for 10 percent of the gross national product. Protests over the concentration of development on the island of Malé in recent years have led to political unrest in the other islands, while attempts to address the basic needs of those islands have strained the nation's tiny economic base.

The current president, Maumoon Abdul Gayoom, was elected to office in 1978 and subsequently reelected twice. The elections of September 1988 were marked by considerable unrest and demonstrations. An attempted coup against the Gayoom government on Nov. 4, 1988, was put down with the intervention of Indian troops.

Mali
Republic of Mali
(PREVIOUS NAME: FRENCH SUDAN)
Geography **Location:** landlocked country in northwestern Africa. **Boundaries:** Algeria to N, Niger to E, Burkina Faso, Ivory Coast and Guinea to S, Senegal and Mauritania to W. **Total land area:** 471,042 sq. mi. (1,220,000 sq km). **Coastline:** none. **Comparative area:** slightly less than twice size of Texas. **Land use:** 2% arable land; negl. % permanent crops; 25% meadows and pastures; 7% forest and woodland; 66% other; includes negl. % irrigated. **Major cities:** (1976 census) Bamako (capital) 404,000; Ségou 65,000; Mopti 54,000; Sikasso 47,000; Kayes 45,000.

People **Population:** 8,665,548 (1988). **Nationality:** noun—Malian(s); adjective—Malian. **Ethnic groups:** 50% Mande (Bambara, Malinke, Sarakole), 17% Peul, 12% Voltaic, 6% Songhai, 5% Tuareg and Moor. **Languages:** French (official); Bambara spoken by 80% of population. **Religions:** 90% Muslim, 9% indige-

nous beliefs, 1% Christian.

Government **Type:** republic; single-party constitutional government. **Independence:** Sept. 22, 1960 (from France). **Constitution:** June 2, 1974, effective June 19, 1979. **National holiday:** Independence Day, Sept. 22. **Heads of government:** Gen. Moussa Traore, president (since June 1979). **Structure:** executive—cabinet composed of civilians and army officers; unicameral legislature—National Council; judiciary.

Economy **Monetary unit:** Communauté Financière Africaine (CFA) franc. **Budget:** (1982) *income:* $154 mil.; *expend.:* $169 mil. **GDP:** $1.1 bil., $150 per capita (1985). **Chief crops:** millet, sorghum, rice, corn, peanuts; cash crops—peanuts, cotton. **Livestock:** goats, sheep, cattle, asses, camels. **Natural resources:** gold, phosphates, kaolin, salt, limestone, uranium; bauxite, iron ore, manganese, tin, and copper deposits are known but not exploited. **Major industries:** small local consumer goods and processing, construction, phosphate, gold, fishing. **Labor force:** 3.1 mil. (1981); 80% agriculture, 19% services; 50% of population of working age (1985). **Exports:** $174.5 mil. (f.o.b., 1985); livestock, peanuts, dried fish, cotton, skins. **Imports:** $294.6 mil. (f.o.b., 1985); textiles, vehicles, petroleum products, machinery, sugar, cereals. **Major trading partners:** mostly franc zone and Western Europe; also USSR, China.

Intl. Orgs. FAO, G-77, GATT (de facto), IAEA, IBRD, ICAO, IDA, IFAD, IFC, ILO, IMF, INTELSAT, INTERPOL, ITU, NAM, UN, UNESCO, UPU, WHO, WMO.

Mali has been a center of North African civilization for over 4,000 years. Iron Age civilizations flourished on the middle reaches of the Niger River since about 200 B.C. Kingdoms based in Mali dominated the Niger river basin between the 10th and 12th centuries A.D. and expanded their reach to the north and east from about 1200 to 1400 at which time Islam became the dominant religious and cultural influence in the region. In 1460 the Songhai empire, based in Timbuktu, became the dominant power in the region. Timbuktu was an important center of Moslem scholarship and art and the key commercial link between the Sahara and southern and western Africa.

The Songhai empire collapsed after Timbuktu was sacked by Moroccans in 1591. It fragmented into a series of smaller states, and power shifted from the desert fringe back to the Niger valley, bringing with it a further spread of Islam.

French exploration of Mali led to conquest in 1896 and the creation of the colony of French Sudan in 1898, governed from Dakar, Senegal. Timbuktu continued to decline in importance, and Bamako became the country's principal urban center.

Malians were granted French citizenship and limited self-rule in 1946. In 1958 the territory became autonomous within the French Overseas Community. In 1959, with French support, the French Sudan and Senegal formed the Federation of Mali, which became indepen-

dent on June 20, 1960. Senegal seceded from the federation almost immediately, and Mali became an independent republic on Sept. 22, 1960. Modibo Keita was elected the country's first president.

Keita's program of radical control of society and the economy by the central government provoked discontent, and he was overthrown in 1968 by military officers led by Lt. Moussa Traore. Traore's Military Committee of National Liberation ruled until 1979 when it was reorganized under a new constitution as the Malian People's Democratic Union. Traore remains president; his military-backed government has made little progress in bringing political unity to the country or in solving its pressing economic problems.

Mali is primarily agricultural in the south and west, pastoral in the north and east. Principal crops are millet, rice, peanuts, and cotton. The livestock sector has been repeatedly devastated by drought and spreading desertification. The country has some mineral resources, including bauxite, iron, and gold. Mali maintains close ties with France, and the economy remains heavily dependent on foreign assistance.

Malta
Republic of Malta
Geography **Location:** an archipelago (largest and only inhabited islands are Malta, Gozo, and Comino) in central Mediterranean Sea. **Boundaries:** Sicily 58 mi. (93 km) to N, Libya 180 mi. (290 km) to S, Tunisia to W. **Total land area:** 122 sq. mi. (316 sq km). **Coastline:** 87 mi. (140 km). **Comparative area:** slightly less than twice size of Washington, D.C. **Land use:** 38% arable land; 3% permanent crops; 0% meadows and pastures; 0% forest and woodland; 59% other; includes 3% irrigated. **Major cities:** (1984 est.) Valletta (capital) 14,013; Sliema 20,071; Birkirkara 18,041; Qormi 17,130.

People **Population:** 369,240 (1988). **Nationality:** noun—Maltese (sing., pl.); adjective—Maltese. **Ethnic groups:** mixture of Arab, Sicilian, Norman, Spanish, Italian, English. **Languages:** Maltese and English. **Religions:** 98% Roman Catholic.

Government **Type:** parliamentary democracy, independent republic within Commonwealth. **Independence:** Sept. 21, 1964 (from UK). **Constitution:** Apr. 26, 1974; effective June 2, 1974. **National holiday:** Freedom Day, Mar. 31. **Heads of government:** Paul Xureb, acting president (since Feb. 1987); Eddie Fenech Adami, prime minister (since May 1987). **Structure:** executive—prime minister and cabinet; legislature—65-member House of Representatives; judiciary—independent.

Economy **Monetary unit:** Maltese lire. **Budget:** (1986) *income:* $651.4 mil.; *expend.:* $611.8 mil. **GDP:** $1.5 bil., $4,110 per capita (1986). **Chief crops:** potatoes, cauliflower, grapes, wheat, barley; adequate supplies of vegetables, milk, and pork products; seasonal or periodic shortages in grain, animal fodder, fruits, other basic foodstuffs; 20% self-sufficient overall. **Livestock:** pigs, cattle, goats, sheep. **Natural resources:** limestone, salt.

Major industries: tourism, ship repair yard, clothing. **Labor force:** 125,674 (1987); 30% services (except government), 24% manufacturing, 21% government (except job corps); 4.6% registered unemployment. **Exports:** $527.3 mil. (f.o.b., 1986); clothing, textiles, ships, printed matter. **Imports:** $943.0 mil. (c.i.f., 1986). **Major trading partners:** 74% EC (23.5% W. Germany, 18.8% Italy, 16.2% UK), 6% U.S.

Intl. Orgs. Commonwealth, FAO, G-77, GATT, IBRD, ICAO, IFAD, ILO, IMF, IMO, INTERPOL, ITU, NAM, UN, UPU, WHO, WIPO, WMO.

Malta, an ancient crossroads of Mediterranean trade, was ruled successively by Phoenicians, Greeks, Carthaginians, and the Roman Empire before being conquered by Islamic Saracens from North Africa in the ninth century. In 1090 the Norman kings of Sicily conquered it and made it into a way station for the First Crusade. In 1530 Charles V gave the island to the Knights Hospitalers (thereafter sometimes known as the Knights of Malta). The island withstood a siege by the Ottoman Turks in 1565; it fell to Napoleon in 1798.

Malta came under British rule in 1800 and was annexed in 1814. Limited self-rule was granted under the constitutions of 1921 and 1939. During World War II, Malta suffered heavy air raids by German and Italian forces; the entire population was awarded the George Cross for bravery.

In 1964 Malta was granted independence within the British Commonwealth, with Elizabeth II as its sovereign. Abrogating its mutual defense treaty with Great Britian in 1971, the Maltese government severed all ties to the British Crown, becoming a fully independent republic. British forces withdrew from the island in 1979.

Malta was governed by the leftist, anticlerical, and neutralist Labour party from 1971 to 1987. Its leader, the ardent nationalist Dominic Mintoff, was prime minister from 1971 until his retirement in 1984, when he was succeeded by Mifsud Bonnici. In 1987 the Cathodic and pro-Western Nationalist party won a popular electoral majority but not a majority in the parliament. Under the terms of a 1987 constitutional amendment, it was granted sufficient extra seats in the parliament to allow it to organize a government, under Prime Minister Eddie Fenech Adami.

In 1983 the Labour party government passed a law confiscating 75 percent of the wealth of the Catholic church and attempted to ban religiously sponsored schools. Resolution of the church-state issue is the key problem facing the Nationalist government. In foreign affairs it is faced with the need both to maintain good relations with its close neighbor Libya and to pursue improved relations with the West.

Dry and infertile, the five islands of the Republic of Malta nevertheless support some agriculture. Following the 1979 closing of the British naval base, which had been a principal source of revenue, the government pursued a policy of industrialization, led by textiles, fur-

niture, and paper products. Malta's major port, Marsaxlokk, is an important transshipment point for Mediterranean trade.

Marshall Islands
Republic of the Marshall Islands

Geography Location: two groups of islands, the Ratak and Ralik chains, comprising 31 atolls in western Pacific Ocean. **Boundaries:** Guam about 1,300 mi. (2,100 km) to NW, Hawaii about 2,000 mi. (3,200 km) to NE, Kiribati to S, Federated States of Micronesia to W. **Total land area:** 70 sq. mi. (180 sq km). **Coastline:** undetermined. **Comparative area:** slightly larger than Washington, D.C. **Land use:** 0% arable land; 60% permanent crops; 0% meadows and pastures; 0% forest and woodland; 40% other. **Major cities:** Majuro (capital—pop. N.A.).

People Population: 40,609 (1988). **Nationality:** noun—Marshallese; adjective—Marshallese. **Ethnic groups:** almost entirely Micronesian. **Languages:** English (official), two major dialects from Malayo-Polynesian family, Japanese. **Religions:** predominantly Christian, mostly Protestant.

Government Type: constitutional government in free association with U.S.; Compact of Free Association entered into force Oct. 21, 1986. **Independence:** Oct. 21, 1986 (from U.S.-administered UN trusteeship). **Constitution:** May 1, 1979. **National holiday:** May 1. **Heads of government:** Amata Kabua, president (since 1979). **Structure:** parliamentary-type government with legislative authority vested in 33-member parliament (Nitijela) and Council of Chiefs (Iroj), a consultative body; supreme court, high court.

Economy Monetary unit: U.S. dollar. **Budget:** (1987 est.) $55 mil. **GDP:** $31.9 mil., $1,000 per capita (1981). **Chief crops:** coconuts, cacao, taro, breadfruit, fruits, copra. **Livestock:** pigs, cattle, goats. **Natural resources:** phosphate deposits, marine products, deep seabed minerals. **Major industries:** copra, fish, tourism. **Labor force:** 4,800 (1986); 22% males and 27% females unemployed (1980). **Exports:** $2.5 mil. (f.o.b., 1985); copra, copra oil, agricultural products, handicrafts. **Imports:** $29.2 mil. (c.i.f., 1985); foodstuffs, beverages, building materials. **Major trading partners:** U.S., Japan.

The Marshall Islands, part of the geographic region known as Micronesia, are made up of 31 atolls of the Ratak (Sunrise) and Ralik (Sunset) chains located between 4° and 14°N and 160° and 173°E. The capital, Majuro, lies about 2,300 miles west-southwest of Honolulu and 1,300 miles southeast of Guam. Claimed by Spain in 1592, they were left undisturbed by the Spanish empire for 300 years. In 1885, Germany took over the administration on the islands of Jaluit and Ebon. At that time copra (dried coconut meat) trade was the primary industry. Japan assumed control of the Marshalls at the beginning of World War I and held them until 1944, when Allied forces occupied the islands. In 1947 the islands were included in the UN Trust Territory of the Pacific and

placed under U.S. administration. In 1946 the U.S. government resettled the inhabitants of Bikini and Enewetak in order to begin nuclear tests, which continued through 1958. Residents began returning to Enewetak in 1980; but the estimated cost of a complete clean-up of Bikini is put at $100 million.

Mauritania
Islamic Republic of Mauritania

Geography Location: northwestern coast of Africa. **Boundaries:** territory of Western Sahara to N, Algeria to NE, Mali to E and S, Senegal to S, North Atlantic Ocean to W. **Total land area:** 397,840 sq. mi. (1,030,400 sq km). **Coastline:** 469 mi. (754 km). **Comparative area:** slightly larger than three times size of New Mexico. **Land use:** negl. % arable land; negl. % permanent crops; 38% meadows and pastures; 15% forest and woodland; 47% other; includes negl. % irrigated. **Major cities:** Nouakchott (capital) 350,000 (1984 est.); Nouadhibou (Port Etienne) 21,961; Kaédi 20,848; Zouérate 17,474; Rosso 16,466 (1977 census).

People Population: 1,919,106 (1988). **Nationality:** noun—Mauritanian(s); adjective—Mauritanian. **Ethnic groups:** 40% mixed Moor/black, 30% Moor, 30% black. **Languages:** French (official), Hasaniya Arabic (national), Toucouleur, Fula, Sarakole. **Religions:** nearly 100% Muslim.

Government Type: republic; military first seized power in bloodless coup July 10, 1978; palace coup on Dec. 24, 1984, brought president to power. **Independence:** Nov. 28, 1960 (from France). **Constitution:** May 20, 1961, abrogated after coup of July 10, 1978; provisional constitution published Dec. 17, 1980 but abandoned in 1981; new constitutional charter published Feb. 27, 1985. **National holiday:** Independence Day, Nov. 28. **Heads of government:** Col. Maaouiya Ould Sid Ahmed Ould Taya, president (since Dec. 1984). **Structure:** executive—Military Committee for National Salvation rules by decree; national assembly and judiciary suspended pending restoration of civilian rule.

Economy Monetary unit: ouguiya. **Budget:** (1984 est.) *income:* N.A.; *expend.:* $184 mil. **GNP:** $971 mil., $540 per capita (1985 est.). **Chief crops:** most Mauritanians were nomads or subsistence farmers until drought forced them into cities; cash crop—gum arabic; cereals, vegetables, dates. **Livestock:** sheep, goats, cattle, camels, asses. **Natural resources:** iron ore, gypsum, fish, copper, phosphate. **Major industries:** fishing, fish processing, mining of iron ore and gypsum. **Labor force:** 465,000 (1981 est.); 47% agriculture, 29% services, 14% industry and commerce, 10% government; 45,000 wage earners (1980); considerable unemployment; 53% of population of working age. **Exports:** $400 mil. (f.o.b., 1986); iron ore, processed fish, small amounts of gum arabic and gypsum; also unrecorded but numerically significant cattle exports to Senegal. **Imports:** $494 mil. (c.i.f., 1986); foodstuffs and other consumer goods, petroleum products, capital goods. **Major trading partners:** France and other EC countries, Senegal, U.S.

Intl. Orgs. FAO, G-77, GATT, IBRD, ICAO, IDA, IFAD, IFC, ILO, IMF, IMO, INTELSAT, INTERPOL, ITU, NAM, UN, UNESCO, UPU, WHO, WIPO, WMO.

The population of Mauritania is divided between an Arab and Berber majority in the north and various black African peoples in the south and southwest. Anciently, parts of Mauritania were under the control of empires in Ghana and Mali.

Portuguese trade on the Mauritania coast began in the early 15th century; the Portuguese remained dominant until about 1600 when their control was contested by the British, French, and Dutch. France established a protectorate in 1903, and the area was made a French colony in 1920.

In 1946 Mauritania was granted partial local autonomy within the French Union. In 1958 it became a self-governing republic within the French Overseas Community. In 1959 Mokhtar Ould Daddah was elected prime minister, and the country became fully independent on Nov. 28, 1960. A new constitution was adopted in 1961, establishing a presidential form of government. The four major political parties were combined into a single party in 1965.

Morocco claimed Mauritania as part of its sphere of influence; after talks about unifying the two countries broke down, Morocco recognized Mauritanian independence in 1970.

Spain relinquished its claim to the Spanish Sahara in 1976. The southern part of that territory was annexed by Mauritania, while the larger northern section was annexed by Morocco. Rebels of the Polisario Front, proclaiming the independent state of Western Sahara, fought against Mauritanian control in 1977; they were resisted by joint Mauritanian/Moroccan military operations. In 1980 Mauritania relinquished its claims to its portion of the Western Sahara, signed a treaty with Polisario, and resumed relations with Algeria, Polisario's chief backer. Morocco then annexed the former Mauritanian portion of the Western Sahara.

In 1978 Ould Daddah was removed from office in a military coup and was replaced as president by Lt. Col. Haidalla. He in turn was overthrown on Dec. 12, 1984, by Chief of Staff Maaouiya Ould Sid Ahmed Ould Taya. Taya normalized relations with Morocco, adopted a neutral position on the question of Western Sahara, and held regional and local elections in 1986 and 1987 in a first step toward the restoration of democracy.

Mauritania maintains close ties to France and is heavily dependent on French aid. The country has little arable land; some grain is produced, and dates are grown in oases. Most of the economy depends on livestock, which has been severely depleted in droughts during the past decade. Mineral resources include iron ore and gypsum.

Mauritius

Geography Location: one large and seven small islands about 500 mi. (800 km) E of Madagascar in southwestern Indian Ocean. **Boundaries:** surrounded by Indian Ocean; nearest neighbor is Réunion to SW. **Total land area:** 788 sq. mi. (2,040 sq km). **Coastline:** 110 mi (177 km). **Comparative area:** slightly less than 10.5 times the size of Washington, D.C. **Land use:** 54% arable land; 4% permanent crops; 4% meadows and pastures; 31% forest and woodland; 7% other; includes 9% irrigated. **Major cities:** (1985) Port Louis (capital) 136,323; Beau Bassin/Rose Hill 91,786; Quatre Bornes 64,506; Curepipe 63,181; Vacoas-Phoenix 54,430.

People Population: 1,099,983 (1988). **Nationality:** noun—Mauritian(s); adjective—Mauritian. **Ethnic groups:** 68% Indo-Mauritian, 27% Creole, 3% Sino-Mauritian, 2% Franco-Mauritian. **Languages:** English (official), Creole, French, Hindi, Urdu, Hakka, Bojpoori. **Religions:** 51% Hindu, 30% Christian (mostly Roman Catholic with a few Anglicans), 17% Muslim.

Government Type: independent state, recognizing Elizabeth II as chief of state. **Independence:** Mar. 12, 1968 (from UK). **Constitution:** Mar. 12, 1968. **National holiday:** Independence Day, Mar. 12 **Heads of government:** Veerasamy Ringadoo, governor-general (since Jan. 1986); Anerood Jugnauth, prime minister (since June 1982). **Structure:** executive power exercised by prime minister and 19-member Council of Ministers; unicameral legislature (Legislative Assembly) with 62 members elected by direct suffrage, eight specially elected by the so-called "best loser" system.

Economy Monetary unit: Mauritian rupee. **Budget:** as percent of GDP (1987 est.) *income:* 21.3% *expend.:* 27.7% **GDP:** $1.5 bil., $1,390 per capita (1987 est.). **Chief crops:** about 90% of cultivated land area is planted in sugar; also sugar derivatives, tea, tobacco; most food imported. **Livestock:** cattle, goats, pigs, sheep. **Natural resources:** cultivated land, fish. **Major industries:** food processing (largely sugar milling), textiles and wearing apparel. **Labor force:** 335,000 (1985); 29% government services, 27% agriculture and fishing, 22% manufacturing, 22% other; 15–20% unemployed; 43% of working age. **Exports:** $676 mil. (f.o.b., 1986); about 40% sugar; Export Processing Zone handles about 50% of total. **Imports:** $685 mil. (c.i.f., 1986); food, petroleum products, manufactured goods, capital equipment, chemicals. **Major trading partners:** UK, France, U.S.; all EC countries and U.S. have preferential treatment; UK buys almost all of Mauritius's sugar export at subsidized prices; small amount of sugar exported to Canada, U.S., and Italy; non-oil imports from UK and EC primarily, also from South Africa, Australia, U.S., and Japan; some minor trade with China.

Intl. Orgs. Commonwealth, FAO, G-77, GATT, IAEA, IBRD, ICAO, IDA, IFAD, IFC, ILO, IMF, IMO, INTERPOL, ITU, NAM, OAU, UN, UNESCO, UPU, WHO, WIPO, WMO.

The Dutch named this small island nation, which lies off the African coast about 500 miles east of Madagascar, after their Prince of Nassau, Maurice, when they claimed it in 1598. They brought in slaves to obtain the priceless ebony from the island's forests but later abandoned Mauritius. When the French took possession of the island in 1715, they renamed it Ile de France and began colonization. They built plantations and used the island as a base to raid British trading ships. The British retaliated by capturing the island; they made it part of their colonial system and restored its original name. Abolishing slavery in 1833, the British began bringing in Indian laborers to work on the flourishing plantations.

Mauritius began moving toward independence in the 1940s on the increasing strength of the Mauritius Labor party, which consisted mainly of Hindus, the island's dominant population. Led by Labor party leader Sir Seewoosagur Ramgoolan, Mauritius gained independence in 1968. Discord between political parties led to a period of instability in the early 1980s, until a 1983 election gave Anerood Jugnauth of the Militant Socialist Movement a clear mandate as prime minister.

Mauritius remains a culturally vigorous nation with a booming economy based on trade, tourism, and investment ties with South Africa. Although the government opposes apartheid, the nation's economic dependency must dictate its policies.

Mexico
United Mexican States

Geography Location: largest state in Central America. **Boundaries:** U.S. to N, Gulf of Mexico to E, Belize and Guatemala to S, Pacific Ocean to W. **Total land area:** 756,066 sq. mi. (1,958,201 sq km). **Coastline:** 5,798 mi. (9,329 km). **Comparative area:** slightly less than three times size of Texas. **Land use:** 12% arable land; 1% permanent crops; 39% meadows and pastures; 24% forest and woodland; 24% other; includes 3% irrigated. **Major cities:** (1979 est.) Ciudad de México (Mexico City—capital) 9,191,295; Netzahualcóyotl 2,331,351; Guadalajara 1,906,145; Monterrey 1,064,629; Heróica Puebla de Zaragoza (Puebla) 710,833.

People Population: 83,527,567 (1988). **Nationality:** noun—Mexican(s); adjective—Mexican. **Ethnic groups:** 60% mestizo, 30% Amerindian or predominantly Amerindian, 9% white or predominantly white, 1% other. **Languages:** Spanish. **Religions:** 97% nominally Roman Catholic, 3% Protestant.

Government Type: federal republic operating under centralized government. **Independence:** Sept. 16, 1910 (from Spain). **Constitution:** Feb. 5, 1917. **National holiday:** Independence Day, Sept. 16. **Heads of government:** Miguel de la Madrid Hurtado, president (since Dec. 1982). **Structure:** dominant executive; bicameral legislature (National Congress—Senate, Federal Chamber of Deputies); Supreme Court.

Economy Monetary unit: peso. **Budget:** (1986) *income:* $39.4 bil.; *expend.:* $68.3 bil. **GDP:** $127.22 bil., $1,580 per capita (1986). **Chief crops:** corn, cotton, wheat, coffee, sugarcane. **Livestock:** cattle, pigs, goats, sheep, horses. **Natural resources:** crude oil, silver, copper, gold, lead. **Major industries:** food and beverages, tobacco, chemicals. **Labor force:** 24.7 mil. (1986); 31.4% services; 26% agriculture, forestry, hunting, fishing; 13.9% commerce; 12.8% manufacturing; 9.5% construction. **Exports:** $16.2 bil. (f.o.b., 1986); cotton, coffee, nonferrous minerals (including lead and zinc), shrimp, petroleum. **Imports:** $12.0 bil. (f.o.b., 1986); machinery, equipment, industrial vehicles, intermediate goods. **Major trading partners:** *exports:* 73% U.S., 13.5% EC, 7% Japan; *imports:* 71.1% U.S., 15.1% EC, 6.6% Japan.

Intl. Orgs. FAO, G-77, GATT, IAEA, IBRD, ICAO, IDA, IFAD, IFC, ILO, IMF, IMO, INTELSAT, INTERPOL, ITU, NAM, OAS, UN, UNESCO, UPU, WHO, WIPO, WMO.

The pre-Columbian history of indigenous Mexican cultures is very rich and includes the high civilizations of the Olmecs, Mayas, Toltecs, and Aztecs, in addition to numerous nomadic cultures. In 1519 Hernán Cortés and his entourage of several hundred Spanish soldiers entered Tenochtitlán; a two-year campaign ensued, with the Spaniards finally capturing the city in 1521. The viceroyalty of New Spain, with its political center at Mexico City, was founded in 1535.

As was the case with the rest of Spanish America, the movement for independence in New Spain coincided with the weakening of the authority of the Spanish Crown as a result of the Napoleonic takeover of Spain in 1808. In 1810 Miguel Hidalgo led a failed uprising and was executed. Following in Hidalgo's footsteps, José María Morelos led another uprising in the south, and he in turn was captured and put to death. Agustín de Iturbide, leader of the royalist forces, defected to the side of those struggling for independence in 1821. Envisioning independent Mexico as a monarchy, military groups proclaimed Iturbide emperor of Mexico in 1822. The Mexican empire did not last long, and the Central American states seceded from Mexico with the downfall of Iturbide in 1823.

Mexico lost the northern half of its territory to the United States over the period 1835–48 as a result of the Texas rebellion and war with the United States. The hostilities that existed between the Mexican and U.S. governments over the 1845 annexation of Texas flared into war between the two countries in 1846, and by September of the following year, U.S. forces entered Mexico City. The settlement with the United States—the 1848 Treaty of Guadalupe Hidalgo—called for Mexico to cede California, New Mexico, and Texas to the United States.

A liberal constitution was proclaimed in 1857, but Conservative oppositionists declared it void. A "Three Years War" (1857–60) ensued between the Liberals and Conservatives in which the Liberals had the victory. France, Britain, and Spain, who had become involved in the civil war, claimed compensation from the new government for debts owed in connection with the destruction of property owned by their citizens, and in 1862 landed their forces at Veracruz. Britain and Spain withdrew after a settlement, but Napoleon III had intended to establish a dependent empire in Mexico. After a successful occupation of major Mexican cities,

the French and their Conservative Mexican allies asked Habsburg Archduke Ferdinand Maximilian of Austria to take the Mexican throne, which he did in 1864. As a result of Mexican Liberal resistance and U.S. military threats, France decided to end the Mexican adventure, and in 1867 Liberal forces captured and shot Maximilian.

Benito Juárez was a major force behind the liberal movement called La Reforma, which stressed the promotion of capitalism and the destruction of what were seen as vestiges of feudalism (abolition of *fueros*, traditional corporatist privileges) in Mexico. Juárez won a third presidential term in 1871 but died shortly thereafter of a heart attack. He was succeeded in office by Sebastián Lerdo de Tejada, who was in turn overthrown by Gen. Porfirio Díaz. Thus began the period of stable dictatorship known as the Porfiriato (1876–1910).

The Mexican Revolution began in 1910 after Porfirio Díaz had his electoral opponent, Francisco I. Madero, jailed, and it was obvious that free elections were not going to take place. In response, Madero formulated his Plan of San Luis Potosí, calling for armed resistance to the dictatorship. Rebellions broke out in the northern state of Chihuahua under the leadership of Pancho Villa and in the southern state of Morelos led by Emiliano Zapata. The two states soon came under rebel control, and in 1911 Díaz left Mexico. Madero was elected president that same year, but his failure to carry through promised reforms resulted in the continuation of the rebellion.

Gen. Victoriano Huerta overthrew Madero (with the backing of the U.S. ambassador Henry Lane Wilson) in 1913. As the fighting continued, Huerta lost the support of the United States and resigned in 1914. During 1914-15 Zapata and Villa fought against the governor of Coahuila, Venustiano Carranza, and his ally Alvaro Obregón. By 1916 Obregón had driven Villa back to Chihuahua, and Zapata's armies had been contained. Carranza called for the election of delegates to a constitutional convention in 1916, and by the following year, the progressive Mexican Constitution of 1917 was in place.

Lázaro Cárdenas won the presidency in 1934, sending Plutarco Elías Calles, the ex-president and power behind the scene, into exile. This, coupled with Cárdenas's decision to remove himself from politics at the end of his term, greatly stabilized the institutional structure created by the Mexican Revolution. Cárdenas was the last of the "revolutionary" Mexican leaders in that he to some extent made good on the revolutionary promises to labor and the peasantry. He presided over extensive redistribution of land to the peasants and in 1938 reorganized the ruling party into four functional constituencies: peasants, labor, the military, and the popular sector (middle class, professionals). Cárdenas also enforced Article 27 of the Mexican Constitution (national ownership of subsoil rights) against U.S. oil companies, thus assuring his credentials as a hero of Mexican nationalism.

The political movement of Mexican presidents since Cárdenas has been away from its

peasant and labor constituencies toward business and the popular sector, beginning with Miguel Alemán's election in 1946.

The stability of the dominant political order of the official party (Partido Revolucionario Institucional, PRI) has been seriously challenged in the 1980s as a result of the economic crisis stemming from the severe decline in the price of oil. Mexico borrowed heavily from foreign creditors during the 1970s on the expectation that oil prices would remain high. The debt problem led to cutbacks in government spending, a catastrophic drop in the value of the currency, and capital and human flight out of the country. The political repercussions of this could be seen in the elections of 1988, in which the ruling PRI had its worst showing ever. Although the PRI presidential candidate Carlos Salinas de Gortari apparently won the election, his opponents from the socialist political coalition and the opposition Partido Acción Nacional (PAN) party challenged the result.

Micronesia
Federated States of Micronesia

Geography **Location:** forms (with Palau) archipelago of Caroline Islands, consisting of states of Yap, Truk, Pohnpei (Ponape), and Kosrae, in western central Pacific Ocean. **Boundaries:** Guam to NW, Marshall Islands to E, Papua New Guinea to S., Philippines about 497 mi. (800 km) to W. **Total land area:** 271 sq. mi. (702 sq km). **Coastline:** undetermined. **Comparative area:** slightly less than four times size of Washington, D.C. **Land use:** N.A. **Major cities:** Kolonia (capital—population N.A.).

People **Population:** 86,094 (1988). **Nationality:** noun—Micronesian(s); adjective—Micronesian. **Ethnic groups:** nine ethnic Micronesian and Polynesian groups. **Languages:** English (official), Trukese, Pohnpeian, Yapese, Kosrean. **Religions:** predominantly Christian, divided between Roman Catholic and Protestant; also, Assembly of God, Jehovah's Witnesses, Seventh-Day Adventists, Latter-day Saints, and Baha'i.

Government **Type:** constitutional government in free association with U.S.; Compact of Free Association entered into force Nov. 3, 1986. **Independence:** Nov. 3, 1986 (from U.S.-administered UN Trusteeship). **Constitution:** May 10, 1979. **National holiday:** May 10. **Heads of government:** John R. Haglelgam, president (since 1986). **Structure:** executive—national president and vice president elected from ranks of popularly elected senators; legislative—National Congress (unicameral); judicial—national Supreme Court headed by chief justice.

Economy **Monetary unit:** U.S. dollar. **Budget:** (1983) $110.8 mil. **GNP:** $111 mil., $1,300 per capita (1983). **Chief crops:** copra, black pepper, tropical fruits and vegetables, coconuts, cassava, sweet potatoes; mainly subsistence economy. **Livestock:** pigs, chickens. **Natural resources:** forests, marine products, deep seabed minerals. **Major industries:** tourism, craft items from shell, wood, pearl. **Labor force:** undetermined. **Exports:** $1.6 mil. (f.o.b., 1983); copra. **Imports:** $48.9 mil. (c.i.f., 1983).

Major trading partners: U.S., Japan.

The Federated States of Micronesia extend 1,800 miles across an archipelago of the Caroline Islands in the larger island group of Micronesia. Kolonia lies 3,100 miles southwest of Honolulu and 1,000 miles southeast of Guam. The islands are located between the equator and latitude 9° north, and longitude 138° and 168° east. Ethnically diverse (there are eight primary languages, not including dialects), the islands are thought to be the first in the Pacific settled by argonauts from the Philippines and Indonesia, about 1500 B.C. Ferdinand Magellan landed in the Marianas in 1521, and Spain claimed sovereignty from 1565 to 1899, when the Carolines were sold to Germany. After World War I, the League of Nations mandated the islands to Japan, which developed agriculture (especially sugarcane), mining, and fishing. In 1947 the islands were included in the UN Trust Territory of the Pacific and placed under U.S. administration. They achieved independence in 1979, and a compact of free association between Micronesia and the United States was signed in 1986.

Monaco
Principality of Monaco
Geography Location: small enclave in southeastern France. **Boundaries:** France to N, E, and W; Mediterranean Sea to S. **Total land area:** 1.21 sq. mi. (1.95 sq km). **Coastline:** 2.6 mi. (4.1 km). **Comparative area:** about three times size of the Mall in Washington, D.C. **Land use:** 0% arable land; 0% permanent crops; 0% meadows and pastures; 0% forest and woodland; 0% other. **Major cities:** Monaco (capital).

People Population: 28,917 (1988). **Nationality:** noun—Monacan(s) or Monegasque(s); adjective—Monacan or Monegasque. **Ethnic groups:** 47% French, 16% Monegasque, 16% Italian, 21% other. **Languages:** French (official), English, Italian, Monegasque. **Religions:** 95% Roman Catholic.

Government Type: constitutional monarchy. **Constitution:** Dec. 17, 1962. **National holiday:** Nov. 19. **Heads of government:** Prince Ranier III, chief of state (since Nov. 1949). **Structure:** executive—prince, minister of state (senior French civil servant appointed by prince), and Council of Government as cabinet; legislative—prince and National Council of 18 members; judicial—authority delegated by prince to Supreme Tribunal.

Economy Monetary unit: French franc. **Budget:** N.A. **GNP:** N.A. **Chief crops:** N.A. **Livestock:** N.A. **Natural resources:** none. **Major industries:** pharmaceuticals, food processing, precision instruments. **Labor force:** N.A. **Exports:** N.A. **Imports:** N.A. **Major trading partners:** full customs integration with France, which collects and rebates Monacan trade duties; also participates in EC market system through customs union with France.

Intl. Orgs. IAEA, ICAO, INTELSAT, INTERPOL, ITU, UN (permanent observer), UPU, WHO, WIPO.

Founded on the site of an ancient Phoenician

port, as a western colony of the great trading city-state of Genoa, in the 13th century, Monaco in 1368 became an independent principality under the rule of the Grimaldi family. At various times a protectorate of Spain, France, and Sardinia, it was restored to independence in 1861 by the Franco-Monegasque treaty.

In 1911 Monaco became a constitutional monarchy under the Matignon-Grimaldi dynasty; the 18 seats of its National Council have normally been controlled by the National and Democratic Union. In 1918 France required the principality to conform to its national interests in all respects; by an agreement of 1919, should the dynasty fail to produce a male heir, Monaco would be absorbed into France. However, the family is allowed to adopt an heir if they so choose. The marriage of Prince Ranier III (who came to the throne in 1949) to the American film star Grace Kelly produced an heir apparent for this generation.

Despite the fame of the Monte Carlo casino, gambling accounts for only 4 percent of the principality's revenues. The principal industry is tourism, followed by light manufacturing (including plastics, glass, and cosmetics). Monaco also supports a well-known institute of oceanography. Land reclamation projects, impelled by a real estate boom, have added about 20 percent to the nation's territory since World War II.

Mongolia
Mongolian People's Republic
(PREVIOUS NAME: OUTER MONGOLIA)
Geography Location: landlocked country in central Asia. **Boundaries:** USSR to N, China to E, S, and W. **Total land area:** 604,250 sq. mi. (1,565,000 sq km). **Coastline:** none. **Comparative area:** slightly larger than Alaska. **Land use:** 1% arable land; 0% permanent crops; 79% meadows and pastures; 10% forest and woodland; 10% other; includes negl. % irrigated. **Major cities:** Ulan Bator (capital) 515,000 (1987); Darhan 74,000 (1986); Erdenet 45,400 (1986); Baga Nuur 25,000 (1984).

People Population: 2,067,624 (1988). **Nationality:** noun—Mongolian(s) adjective—Mongolian. **Ethnic groups:** 90% Mongol, 4% Kazakh, 2% Chinese; 2% Russian, 2% other. **Languages:** Khalkha Mongol used by over 90% of population; Turkic, Russian, Chinese. **Religions:** predominantly Tibetan Buddhist, about 4% Muslim; limited religious activities because of communist regime.

Government Type: communist state. **Independence:** Mar. 13, 1921 (from China). **Constitution:** July 6, 1960. **National holiday:** People's Revolution Day, July 11. **Heads of government:** Jambyn Batmunkh, secretary-general (since Dec. 1984); Dumaagiin Sodnom, prime minister (since Dec. 1984). **Structure:** executive—Council of Ministers; legislative—unicameral Great People's Hural; judicial—court system; Supreme Court elected by Great People's Hural.

Economy Monetary unit: tugrik. **Budget:** N.A. **GDP:** $1.67 bil., $880 per capita (1985 est.). **Chief crops:** livestock raising predomi-

nates; wheat, oats, barley. **Livestock:** sheep, goats, cattle, horses, camels. **Natural resources:** coal, copper, molybdenum, tungsten, phosphates. **Major industries:** processing of animal products, building materials, foods and beverages. **Labor force:** primarily agricultural; over half adult population is in labor force, including large percentage of women; shortage of skilled labor. **Exports:** livestock, animal products, wool, hides, fluorospar. **Imports:** machinery and equipment, petroleum, clothing, building materials, sugar. **Major trading partners:** nearly all trade with communist countries (about 80% with USSR); total turnover about $1.0 bil.

Intl. Orgs. CMEA, FAO, IAEA, IBRD, ICAO, IDA, IFAD, IFC, ILO, IMF, IMO, ITU, UN, UNESCO, UNIDO, UPU, WHO, WIPO, WMO.

Mongols under Genghis Khan conquered most of Eurasia in the early 13th century. The Mongol empire broke up in the mid-14th century, and Mongolia lapsed into tribal disunion and political insignificance. Chinese rule was established thereafter in Inner Mongolia (ruled directly) and, in 1691, in Outer Mongolia (a province under local rule). With the 1911 Chinese Revolution, Outer Mongolia unsuccessfully proclaimed its independence from China. The nationalist religious leader the Bogdo Lama sought Russian support in 1920. Under the revolutionary leaders Sukhe Bataar and Khorloin Choibalsan, a "provisional people's government" again declared independence in 1921. Sukhe Bataar died in 1923; on Nov. 26, 1924, the Mongolian People's Republic (MPR) was established with Soviet sponsorship. The early years of the republic were marked by repeated Stalinist purges of Mongol revolutionary leaders and by disastrous attempts at centralized planning.

Choibalsan emerged as party leader in the late 1930s and was confirmed as premier in 1940. In 1939 combined Soviet and Mongolian armies prevented a Japanese conquest of Mongolia. In 1945 the Republic of China recognized the MPR; recognition was reaffirmed by the People's Republic of China in 1949 but abrogated by the Republic of China (on Taiwan) in 1953. In 1948 the first of a new series of five-year plans began to bring industrial and agricultural development to Mongolia, with extensive Soviet aid and support. Choibalsan died in 1952 and was succeeded as premier by Yumjaagiyn Tsedenbal. Following the Sino-Soviet split of 1958, heavy concentrations of Soviet troops and missiles were stationed along the Chinese-Mongolian border. On Oct. 27, 1961, the MPR was admitted to the United Nations; diplomatic relations with various other non-Soviet bloc nations developed gradually thereafter. Tsedenbal was ousted as party chairman and premier in 1984; he was replaced by Jambyn Batmunkh as party chairman and by Dumaagiin Sodnom as premier. The United States and the MPR established diplomatic relations on Jan. 27, 1987.

Mongolia's economy remains concentrated on livestock raising and animal-product processing, with some agriculture, mining, and heavy industry. One-fourth of the country's 2 million people live in the capital, Ulan Bator (UlaanbataaR), another 10 percent in mining and industrial cities such as Erdenet and Darsan. Half of the population is under 25 years of age.

Morocco
Kingdom of Morocco

Geography Location: northwestern coast of Africa. **Boundaries:** long coastline on North Atlantic Ocean to W and NW, Strait of Gibraltar to N, Mediterranean Sea to NE, Algeria to E and SE, Western Sahara to SW. **Total land area:** 274,461 sq. mi. (710,850 sq km). **Coastline:** 1,140 mi. (1,835 km). **Comparative area:** slightly larger than California. **Land use:** 18% arable land; 1% permanent crops; 28% meadows and pastures; 12% forest and woodland; 41% other; includes 1% irrigated. **Major cities:** (1981 est.) Rabat (including Sale; capital) 841,800; Casablanca 2,408,600; Fes (Fez) 562,000; Marrakech (Marrakesh) 548,700; Meknes 486,600.

People Population: 24,976,168 (1988). **Nationality:** noun—Moroccan(s); adjective—Moroccan. **Ethnic groups:** 99.1% Arab-Berber, 0.7% non-Moroccan, 0.2% Jewish. **Languages:** Arabic (official), several Berber dialects; French is language of business, government, diplomacy, and postprimary education. **Religions:** 98.7% Muslim, 1.1% Christian, 0.2% Jewish.

Government Type: constitutional monarchy. **Independence:** Mar. 2, 1956 (from France). **Constitution:** Mar. 10, 1972. **National holiday:** Independence Day, Nov. 18. **Heads of government:** Hassan II, king (since Mar. 1961); Azedine Laraki, prime minister (since Sept. 1986). **Structure:** king has paramount executive powers; Constitution provides for prime minister and ministers named by and responsible to king; unicameral legislature (Chamber of Representatives) of which two-thirds of members are directly elected and one-third are indirectly elected; judiciary independent of other branches.

Economy Monetary unit: dirham. **Budget:** (1984 est.) *income:* $4.5 bil.; *expend.:* $3.6 bil. **GDP:** $11.9 bil., $510 per capita (1985). **Chief crops:** not self-sufficient in food; cereal farming and livestock raising predominant; barley, wheat, citrus fruit, wine, vegetables; illegal producer of cannabis for international drug trade. **Livestock:** sheep, goats, cattle, asses, mules. **Natural resources:** phosphates, iron ore, manganese, lead, zinc, fish, salt. **Major industries:** phosphate rock mining and processing, food processing, leather goods. **Labor force:** 7.4 mil. (1985); 50% agriculture, 26% services, 15% industry; at least 12% unemployment. **Exports:** $2.45 bil. (f.o.b., 1986); 24% phosphates, 76% other. **Imports:** $3.80 bil. (c.i.f., 1986); 25% petroleum products, 75% other. **Major trading partners:** France, W. Germany, Italy, Saudi Arabia, Benelux, Iraq.

Intl. Orgs. Arab League, EC (associate), FAO, G-77, GATT, IAEA, IBRD, ICAO, IDA, IFAD, IFC, ILO, IMF, IMO, INTELSAT, INTERPOL, ITU, NAM, UN, UNESCO, UPU, WHO, WIPO, WMO.

Neolithic inhabitants of Morocco were displaced by Berbers around 1000 B.C. Phoenician and Carthaginian settlements were established along the Mediterranean coast. Morocco came under Roman rule around 40 A.D. and was invaded via Spain by Germanic Vandals in the fifth century. The Islamic invasions of the mid-seventh century established Arab rule in Morocco, and most of the indigenous Berbers converted to Islam. Ethnic tension between Berbers and Arabs has been a basic element of Moroccan politics and society ever since.

In the late eighth century, King Idris ibn Adballah united Berbers and Arabs in a monarchy that lasted for 200 years and made the capital city of Fez one of the major religious and cultural centers of the Islamic world. The Idrisid dynasty and its successors ruled a territory that expanded to include much of North Africa and southern Spain and Portugal. After about 1200 the tide of Moorish expansion in the Iberian Peninsula turned; in 1492 Ferdinand and Isabella expelled the last Moors from Grenada.

Naval conflict between Morocco, Spain, and Portugal continued in the western Mediterranean and along the Atlantic coast of northwestern Africa for several centuries more. In the mid-17th century, Morocco was reunited under the present Alawid dynasty. In the early 19th century, American and British forces combatted Moroccan piracy in the Mediterranean, and Spain established colonies in Tangier in the north and along the Atlantic coast between Morocco and Mauritania.

The attempts of Sultan Hassan I (r. 1873–94) to implement reforms to strengthen Morocco's independence were thwarted by European interests. By the early 20th century, France, securely established in Algeria, began exerting increasing control in Morocco. A multipower conference at Algeciras in 1906 affirmed Moroccan independence but upheld the special rights claimed by Spain and France. The Treaty of Fez, signed in 1912 between France and Sultan Abd-al-Hafidn, ended Moroccan independence by granting the country to France and reaffirming a Spanish sphere of influence in the southwest.

Nationalist unrest and tribal uprisings disrupted French administration in Morocco throughout the 1920s and 1930s. Morocco became a battleground during World War II between the Axis-supported Vichy French government and the Free French and their Allied backers. In 1943 Churchill and Roosevelt met at Casablanca to discuss wartime strategy; in the same year, the Istiqlal (Independence) Party was founded to fight for independence from the French in the postwar era.

In 1947 an autonomy program proposed by Sultan Mohammad V was rejected by France, and the sultan was sent into exile. In response, Moroccan liberation forces began open warfare against the French. Sultan Mohammad V was allowed to return, and France promised to make Morocco independent by 1955.

With the withdrawal of French forces, Morocco became independent on Mar. 2, 1956. Tangier (under international administration since 1923) was incorporated into the newly independent state in October 1956, and the

Spanish enclave of Ifni was ceded to Morocco in 1969.

A period of instability ensued after 1957 as newly formed political parties vied for power. King Mohammad I died in 1961 and was succeeded by his son, Hassan II. In 1962 an elected parliamentary government took power under the constitutional monarchy. Political unrest and economic difficulties led to the declaration of states of emergency in 1965 and 1970 and a new constitution in 1977.

Spain withdrew from its former territory of Spanish Sahara, a phosphate-rich desert territory on Morocco's southern border, in February 1976. On Apr. 14, 1976, Morocco annexed the northern two-thirds of the territory, while Mauritania claimed the remainder. The Polisario Spanish Saharan liberation movement, backed by Algeria and Libya, conducted guerrilla operations against Moroccan and Mauritanian forces. In 1979 Mauritania gave up its claims, and Morocco claimed the entire region.

In April 1987, Morocco completed construction of a 2000-mile sand wall completely enclosing the former Spanish Sahara, now known as Western Sahara. The Polisario forces, partly cut off from Algerian aid, nevertheless control much of the Western Saharan countryside, while Morocco holds the cities and towns. In May 1987 a Moroccan-Algerian summit was held under the sponsorship of Saudi Arabia, which offered King Hassan $260 million to rebuild Morocco's war-torn economy in return for allowing a self-determination referendum in the Western Sahara. The king refused, contending that the problem is purely an internal matter for Morocco to resolve. Fighting continues, widely supported by the Moroccan people but at considerable economic cost.

The Moroccan economy nevertheless has shown rapid development, led by mining, mixed light industry, tourism, and the export of fresh winter fruit and vegetables to Europe.

Mozambique
People's Republic of Mozambique

Geography Location: eastern coast of Africa. **Boundaries:** Zambia and Malawi to NW, Tanzania to N, Indian Ocean to E and SE, South Africa and Swaziland to SW, Zimbabwe to W. **Total land area:** 302,739 sq. mi. (784,090 sq km). **Coastline:** 1,535 mi. (2,470 km). **Comparative area:** slightly less than twice size of California. **Land use:** 4% arable land; negl. % permanent crops; 56% meadows and pastures; 20% forest and woodland; 20% other; includes negl. % irrigated. **Major cities:** (1987 est.) Maputo (capital) 1,006,765.

People Population: 14,947,554 (1988). **Nationality:** noun—Mozambican(s); adjective—Mozambican. **Ethnic groups:** Majority from indigenous tribal groups; about 35,000 Euro-Africans, 15,000 Indians, 10,000 Europeans. **Languages:** Portuguese (official), indigenous dialects. **Religions:** 60% indigenous beliefs, 30% Christian, 10% Muslim.

Government Type: people's republic. **Independence:** June 25, 1975 (from Portugal). **Constitution:** June 25, 1975. **National holiday:**

Independence Day, June 25. **Heads of government:** Joachím Alberto Chissano, president (since Nov. 1986); Mario de Graca Machungo, prime minister (since July 1986). **Structure:** unicameral legislature (People's Assembly; last convened Dec. 1985).

Economy Monetary unit: meticai. **Budget:** N.A. **GNP:** $1.3 bil., $90 per capita (1987 est.). **Chief crops:** cash crops—cotton, cashew nuts, sugar, tea, copra; other crops—corn, wheat, peanuts, potatoes, beans; imports—corn. **Livestock:** cattle, goats, pigs, sheep, asses. **Natural resources:** coal, natural gas, copper, bauxite, titanium. **Major industries:** food and beverages, chemicals (fertilizer, soap, paints), petroleum. **Labor force:** 95% agriculture, 5% other. **Exports:** $80 mil. (1986 est.); cashews, shrimp, sugar, tea, cotton. **Imports:** $480 mil. (1986 est.); refined petroleum products, machinery, transportation goods, spare parts, consumer goods. **Major trading partners:** *exports:* U.S., Western Europe, *imports:* Western Europe, Eastern Europe, USSR.

Intl. Orgs. FAO, G-77, GATT (de facto), IBRD, ICAO, IFAD, ILO, IMF, IMO, ITU, NAM, UN, UNESCO, UPU, WHO, WMO.

Mozambique has been inhabited since prehistoric times by a variety of Bantu peoples. Portuguese trading stations were established in 1505, and Portugal controlled an extensive coastal trade in slaves and ivory. Mozambique also served as a way station for Portuguese trade to East Asia.

Despite competition from other European nations, Portugal maintained control of the Mozambique coast. Settlement by sizable numbers of Portuguese immigrants began in the late 19th century. Mozambique was organized as a colony, sometimes called Portuguese East Africa, in 1885; boundaries in the interior were defined in 1891.

Economic development of Mozambique in the 20th century remained almost entirely in Portuguese hands. By the 1950s native peoples began to protest Portuguese rule; a rebellion of the Frelimo (Front for the Liberation of Mozambique) guerrilla movement began in 1961. Rebels controlled most of the northern part of the country by 1964. Fighting continued for another decade.

Following the Portuguese revolution of 1974, Portugal agreed to independence for Mozambique, and many Portuguese settlers returned to Portugal, leaving the country bereft of administrative personnel and infrastructure support. Mozambique became fully independent on June 25, 1975. A Marxist Frelimo government took office, with Samora Michel as the country's first president. The new government formed agricultural collectives and nationalized most private land and industry as well as all social services.

In the late 1970s, fighting broke out between Mozambique and Rhodesia. With the independence of Rhodesia as Zimbabwe in 1980, relations between the two governments improved. Mozambique has become to some extent politically and economically dependent on the goodwill of South Africa, despite the ideological differences between the two coun-

tries. At the same time, Mozambique has accused South Africa of aiding a rebel movement, Renamo (Mozambique National Resistance), dedicated to overthrowing the Frelimo government.

Severe drought, compounded by mismanagement of the economy, led to extensive malnutrition and suffering throughout the country in the 1980s.

In 1986, following the death of Samora Michel, Joachím Chissano became president. The Chissano government has reintroduced some private small-scale agriculture, loosened ties to the Eastern bloc, and appealed to the West for economic assistance. In 1987 a UN-led relief effort began. In 1988 the government offered amnesty to any Renamo guerrillas who surrendered within the year but without much success.

Mozambique is rich in agricultural land and mineral resources. Chief crops include cotton, sugar, copra, tea, and cashews. Coal and bauxite are mined; there has also been some industrialization, including production of cement, textiles, and light manufactured goods. Nevertheless, 15 years of communism, drought, and civil war have left the country poor and dependent on foreign aid.

Namibia
(PREVIOUS NAME: SOUTHWEST AFRICA)

Geography Location: southwest Africa. **Boundaries:** Angola to N, Botswana to E, South Africa to S, Atlantic Ocean to W. **Total land area:** 317,873 sq. mi. (823,290 sq km). **Coastline:** 925 mi. (1,489 km). **Comparative area:** slightly more than half size of Alaska. **Land use:** 1% arable land; negl. % permanent crops; 64% meadows and pastures; 22% forest and woodland; 13% other; includes negl. % irrigated. **Major cities:** (1986 est.) Windhoek (capital) 110,000.

People Population: 1,301,598 (1988). **Nationality:** noun—Namibian(s); adjective—Namibian. **Ethnic groups:** 85.6% black (half of whom are Ovambos), 7.5% white, 6.9% mixed. **Languages:** white population—60% speak Afrikaans, 33% German, and 7% English (all official); several indigenous languages. **Religions:** whites predominantly Christian, non-whites either Christian or indigenous beliefs.

Government Type: former German colony of South-West Africa mandated to South Africa by League of Nations in 1920; UN formally ended South Africa's mandate Oct. 27, 1966, but South Africa has retained administrative control. **Independence:** N.A. **Constitution:** N.A. **National holiday:** N.A. **Heads of government:** Louis A. Pienaar, administrator-general (since July 1985). **Structure:** since Sept. 1977 administrator-general, appointed by South Africa, has coordinated zone of white settlement and tribal homelands, where traditional chiefs and representative bodies exercise limited autonomy; administrator can also veto legislation proposed by National Assembly; interim government established June 1985 with eight-member cabinet, 16-member Constitutional Council and 62-member National Assembly.

Economy Monetary unit: South African rand. **Budget:** N.A. **GDP:** N.A. **Chief crops:** subsistence crops (millet, sorghum, corn, and some wheat) are raised, but most food must be imported. **Livestock:** sheep, cattle, goats, poultry, horses. **Natural resources:** diamonds, copper, uranium, lead, tin. **Major industries:** meat packing, fish processing, dairy products, mining (copper, lead, zinc, diamonds, and uranium). **Labor force:** about 500,000 (1981); 60% agriculture, 19% industry and commerce; 15–17% unemployment. **Exports:** $878 mil. (f.o.b., 1986). **Imports:** $652 mil. (f.o.b., 1986). **Major trading partners:** N.A.

Intl. Orgs. FAO, ILO, UNESCO, WHO.

The Kalahari desert, on the Namibian plateau, has been inhabited since ancient times by San hunter-gatherers. Various Nama and Bantu peoples migrated into the area more recently. British and Dutch explorers and traders began to penetrate Namibia in the 18th century.

In 1872 Great Britain occupied the area around Walvis Bay and in 1884 annexed it to the Cape Colony. Also in 1884 Germany claimed most of South-West Africa; negotiations between the two powers resulted in German acceptance of Britain's claim of Walvis Bay and British acceptance of Germany's claim to the rest of the coastal region with a sphere of influence in the interior.

During World War I, South African troops occupied South-West Africa in 1915. In 1920 South Africa received a League of Nations mandate to administer the area. In 1946 when the United Nations succeeded the League, the United Nations proposed that South Africa continue its administration under a UN trusteeship. South Africa refused and annexed South-West Africa.

The proposed UN trusteeship was revoked by the United Nations in 1966. At the same time, the South-West Africa People's Organization (SWAPO), operating from bases in Zambia and Angola, began guerrilla actions against South African troops in the region. In 1968 the United Nations formally renamed the territory Namibia and appointed an 11-nation council to supervise its affairs and devise a plan leading to independence.

In 1971 the International Court of Justice upheld the UN's authority over Namibia and ruled that South Africa's continued occupation of the territory was illegal. In 1975 South Africa convened the Turnhalle Conference, which proposed a plan for Namibian independence based on the racial-separation principles of apartheid. This plan was rejected by the United Nations. In 1978 the UN Security Council approved Resolution 435, which had been worked out through consultations with South Africa, Angola, Botswana, Mozambique, Tanzania, Zambia, and Zimbabwe. The resolution called for a general cease-fire to be followed by UN-supervised elections.

In response to Resolution 435, in 1978 South Africa unilaterally held elections in Namibia, which were boycotted by SWAPO and other African organizations and rejected by the United Nations. In 1982 South Africa declared that it would enter into talks about the future of Namibia only after Cuban troops were withdrawn from Angola. In 1983 South Africa launched a major military operation against SWAPO forces in Angola. In 1984 South Africa offered to withdraw its troops from southern Namibia on condition that the area not then be occupied by Namibian rebels and their Cuban allies. That condition was rejected and fighting continued.

In October 1984 Angolan Pres. dos Santos agreed to work out a plan for withdrawal of Cuban troops as part of a settlement in Namibia. In June 1985 South Africa granted limited local authority to a Namibian government made up of a coalition of parties, which excluded SWAPO, however. In 1987 South African troops occupied southern Angola to aid the rebel National Union for Total Independence of Angola (UNITA). In early 1988, fighting between South African troops and Namibian rebels in northern Namibia and southern Angola intensified.

In May 1988, talks on the future of Namibia (and the related issue of Cuban troops in Angola) between South Africa, Cuba, and Angola, mediated by the United States, convened in London. Further rounds of negotiations were held during the next six months in Cairo, New York, Geneva, and Brazzaville. In Brazzaville on Dec. 13, 1988, the three parties agreed on a plan for Namibian independence and a pullout of Cuban troops from Angola.

In January 1989 the Cuban withdrawal from Angola began. On Apr. 1 UN Resolution 435 went into effect in Namibia, and a UN peacekeeping force arrived to supervise the steps leading to independence. Progress was briefly halted when SWAPO troops under arms entered Namibia from Angola in violation of the accord and fighting broke out with South African forces. The SWAPO leadership agreed to adhere to the terms of the agreement, and a withdrawal of South African troops from Namibia continued, with the aim of reducing forces to 1,500 by July 1.

Cuban forces in Angola are to be reduced to half of their 1988 levels by Nov. 1, 1989, with all forces withdrawn from the southern region. The Cuban withdrawal of all forces from Angola is to be completed by July 1, 1991.

UN-supervised elections in Namibia are scheduled for Nov. 1, 1989. The National Assembly elected at that time is to approve a constitution, after which Namibia will become fully independent.

Most of Namibia consists of a high, semiarid to desert plateau. The country is sparsely inhabited and supports little agriculture; most of the rural population is engaged in raising livestock. Namibia is rich in minerals, including diamonds, copper, lead, and zinc.

Nauru
Republic of Nauru
(PREVIOUS NAME: PLEASANT ISLAND)

Geography **Location:** small island in central Pacific Ocean, lying about 25 mi. (40 km) S of equator and about 2,500 mi. (4,000 km) N of Sydney, Australia. **Boundaries:** nearest neighbor is Banaba (Ocean Island), in Kiribati, about

185 mi. (300 km) to E. **Total land area:** 8.2 sq. mi. (21.3 sq km). **Coastline:** 15 mi. (24 km). **Comparative area:** about ¹⁄₁₀ size of Washington, D.C. **Land use:** 0% arable land; 0% permanent crops; 0% meadows and pastures; 0% forest and woodland; 100% other. **Major cities:** none as such; government offices in Yaren district.

People **Population:** 8,902 (1988). **Nationality:** noun—Nauruan(s) adjective—Nauruan. **Ethnic groups:** 58% Nauruan, 26% other Pacific Islander, 8% Chinese, 8% European. **Languages:** Nauruan, a distinct Pacific Island language (official); English widely understood and spoken for most government and commercial purposes. **Religions:** Christian (two-thirds Protestant, one-third Catholic).

Government **Type:** republic. **Independence:** Jan. 31, 1968 (from UN trusteeship under Australia, New Zealand, and UK). **Constitution:** Jan. 29, 1968. **National Holidays:** Independence Day, Jan. 31; Constitution Day, May 17; Angram Day, Oct. 26. **Heads of Government:** Hammer DeRoburt, president (since May 1968). **Structure:** president elected from and by Parliament for unfixed term; popularly elected 18-member unicameral legislature (Parliament); four-member cabinet to assist president, appointed by him from Parliament members.

Economy **Monetary unit:** Australian dollar. **Budget:** (1987 est.) *income:* A$59.5 mil.; *expend.:* N.A. **GNP:** over $160 mil., $20,000 per capita (1985). **Chief crops:** negl.; almost completely dependent on imports for food and water. **Livestock:** pigs. **Natural resources:** phosphates. **Major industries:** phosphate mining (about 2 mil. tons per year), financial services, coconuts. **Labor force:** N.A. **Exports:** $93 mil. (1984); phosphates. **Imports:** $73 mil. (1984); food, fuel, manufactures, machinery. **Major trading partners:** *exports:* Australia, New Zealand; *imports:* Australia, UK, New Zealand, Japan.

Intl. Orgs. Commonwealth (special member), ICAO, INTERPOL, ITU, UPU.

Nauru, formerly known as Pleasant Island, is an isolated island lying west of the Gilbert Islands. It became a German protectorate in 1888. After World War I, Nauru was administered by Australia under a League of Nations mandate. It was occupied by Japan throughout World War II. In 1947 it became a UN Trust Territory administered by Australia, and on Jan 31, 1968, an independent republic. Nauru has a parliament of 18 members, who elect a prime minister and a cabinet. Most of the island's assets are owned by the state-controlled Nauru Phosphate Corporation and by the Nauru Cooperative Society.

Much of the island is covered by phosphate deposits. Phosphate mining and exports, under leases largely controlled by Australian interests, have given Nauru one of the world's highest per-capita incomes. Currently, national attention is focused on attempts to renegotiate the terms of long-term phosphate export contracts, and on the administration of a national

trust fund in preparation for a new era, in the relatively near future, when phosphate deposits will have been exhausted.

Nepal
Kingdom of Nepal

Geography **Location:** landlocked Asian country in Himalayan mountain range. **Boundaries:** China to N, India to E, S, and W. **Total land area:** 56,827 sq. mi. (147,181 sq km). **Coastline:** none. **Comparative area:** slightly larger than Arkansas. **Land use:** 17% arable land; negl. % permanent crops; 13% meadows and pastures; 33% forest and woodland; 37% other; includes 2% irrigated. **Major cities:** (1981 census) Kathmandu (capital) 235,160.

People **Population:** 18,252,001 (1988). **Nationality:** noun—Nepalese (sing. and pl.); adjective—Nepalese. **Ethnic groups:** Newars, Indians, Tibetans, Gurungs, Magars, Tamangs, Bhotias, Rais, Limbus, Sherpas, as well as many smaller groups. **Languages:** Nepali (official); 20 langs. divided into numerous dialects. **Religions:** only official Hindu kingdom in world, although no sharp distinction between many Hindu (about 88%) and Buddhist groups; small groups of Muslims and Christians.

Government **Type:** nominally, constitutional monarchy; king exercises autocratic control over multitiered system of government. **Constitution:** Dec. 16, 1962. **National holiday:** Birthday of the king and National Day, Dec. 28. **Heads of government:** Birendra Bir Bikram Shah Dev, king (since 1973); Marich Man Singh Shrestha, prime minister (since 1986). **Structure:** Council of Ministers, appointed by king; Rastriya Panchayat, or National Assembly, (140 members including 112 directly elected and 28 appointed by king, who serve five-year terms).

Economy **Monetary unit:** Nepalese rupee. **Budget:** (1986 est.) *income:* $305 mil.; *expend.:* $512 mil. **GDP:** $2.4 bil., $130 per capita (1987). **Chief crops:** over 90% of population engaged in agriculture; rice, corn, wheat, sugarcane, oilseeds; illegal producer of cannabis for international drug trade. **Livestock:** cattle, goats, buffalo, sheep, pigs. **Natural resources:** quartz, water, timber, hydroelectric potential, scenic beauty. **Major industries:** small rice, jute, sugar, and oilseed mills; cigarette and brick factories; tourism. **Labor force:** 4.1 mil.; 93% agriculture, 5% services, 2% industry; great lack of skilled labor. **Exports:** $130 mil. (1987); rice and other food products, jute, timber, manufactures. **Imports:** $365 mil. (1987); manufactured consumer goods, fuel, construction materials, fertilizers, food products. **Major trading partner:** India.

Intl. Orgs. Colombo Plan, FAO, G-77, IBRD, ICAO, IDA, IFAD, IFC, ILO, IMF, IMO, INTERPOL, ITU, NAM, UN, UNESCO, UPU, WHO, WMO.

The birthplace of Gautama Buddha (c. 600 B.C.), Nepal was for many centuries a collection of petty principalities, inhabited by various Tibeto-Burman peoples who mostly practiced Lamaistic Buddhism. In 1769 the country's three geographical zones—floodplain, foothills, and high mountains—were united under an ascendant group, the Gurkhas, who made Hinduism the country's official religion. Nepal established treaty relations with Great Britain in 1792 and fought a border war with British India in 1814–16, but it was never incorporated into the British Empire.

In 1951 King Tribhubana Bir Bikram abolished the system of rule through hereditary prime ministers and established a cabinet form of government under a constitutional monarchy. Road and air links to India, Pakistan, and Tibet were improved, and Nepal began to emerge from its customary isolation. The successful climb of Mt. Everest by Sir Edmund Hillary and Tenzing Norgay in 1953 focused international attention on Nepal.

In recent years tourism, especially mountaineering and trekking, have increased the country's prosperity but also have created new ecological problems. Additionally, a rapidly increasing population and drastic deforestation have had severe impacts on the country. Reform policies under the present king, Birendra Bir Bikram Shah Dev, have led to somewhat greater popular participation in the political process. Apart from tourism, the economy remains largely in the stage of small-scale agriculture and craft industries.

Netherlands
Kingdom of the Netherlands
(PREVIOUS NAME: HOLLAND)

Geography Location: western Europe. **Boundaries:** North Sea to N and W, W. Germany to E, Belgium to S. **Total land area:** 13,103 sq. mi. (33,937 sq km). **Coastline:** 280 mi. (451 km). **Comparative area:** slightly less than half size of New Jersey. **Land use:** 25% arable land; 1% permanent crops; 34% meadows and pastures; 9% forest and woodland; 31% other; includes 15% irrigated. **Major cities:** (1987 est.) Amsterdam (capital) 682,702; Rotterdam 572,642; 's-Gravenhage (The Hague) 445,127; Utrecht 229,326; Eindhoven 190,962; Amsterdam is capital, while The Hague is seat of government.

People Population: 14,716,100 (1988). **Nationality:** noun—Dutchman (men), Dutchwoman (women); adjective—Dutch. **Ethnic groups:** 99% Dutch, 1% Indonesian and other. **Languages:** Dutch (official). **Religions:** 40% Roman Catholic, 31% Protestant, 24% unaffiliated, 5% none.

Government Type: constitutional monarchy. **Independence:** N.A. **Constitution:** Feb. 17, 1983. **National holiday:** Queen's Day, Apr. 30. **Heads of government:** Beatrix Wilhelmina Armgard, queen (since Apr. 1980); Ruud Lubbers, prime minister (since Nov. 1982). **Structure:** executive (queen and Cabinet of Ministers), which is responsible to bicameral parliament (States General) consisting of First Chamber (75 indirectly elected members) and Second Chamber (150 directly elected members); independent judiciary; coalition governments are usual.

Economy Monetary unit: guilder. **Budget:** (1985) *income:* $65.0 bil.; *expend.:* $70.9 bil.

GDP: $175.3 bil., $12,050 per capita (1986) **Chief crops:** horticultural crops, grains, potatoes, sugar beets; food shortages—grains, fats, oils. **Livestock:** chickens, pigs, cattle, sheep, horses, ponies. **Natural recources:** natural gas, crude oil, fertile soil. **Major industries:** agro-industries, metal and engineering products, electrical machinery and equipment. **Labor force:** 5.3 mil. (1986); 50.1% services, 28.2% manufacturing and construction, 15.9% government; 13.3% unemployment (1986). **Exports:** $80.5 bil. (f.o.b., 1986); foodstuffs, machinery, chemicals, petroleum products, natural gas. **Imports:** $75.6 bil. (f.o.b., 1986); machinery, transportation equipment, crude petroleum, foodstuffs, chemicals. **Major trading partners:** (1986) *exports:* 74.9% EC (28.3% W. Germany, 14.2% Belgium-Luxembourg, 10.7% France, 10.2% UK), 4.7% U.S., 0.9% communist countries; *imports:* 63.8% EC (26.5% W. Germany, 23.1% Belgium-Luxembourg, 8.1% UK), 7.9% U.S., 1.9% communist countries.

Intl. Orgs. EC, FAO, GATT, IAEA, IBRD, ICAO, IDA, IFAD, IFC, ILO, IMF, IMO, INTELSAT, INTERPOL, ITU, NATO, OAS (observer), OECD, UN, UNESCO, UPU, WHO, WIPO, WMO.

Historically, the name Netherlands referred to the low-lying areas of the Holy Roman Empire near the mouths of the Rhine, Meuse, and Scheldt rivers. The Habsburg emperor Charles V willed these territories to his son Philip II of Spain in 1555, but by the end of the 16th century, the northern provinces—the Union of Utrecht, formed in 1579 by William the Silent, of the House of Orange—won their independence in a war that was both religious (Calvinist vs. Catholic) and constitutional (aristocratic/patrician vs. foreign monarchy). The independence of the Netherlands was recognized in the Treaty of Westphalia, which ended the Thirty Years' War in 1648.

Dutch prosperity, founded on the woolen trade with England, grew tremendously through trade and seafaring under the 17th-century republic. The Netherlands amassed a world empire, including the Indonesian archipelago, the island of Ceylon, South Africa, Surinam (Suriname), parts of the West Indies, and the Hudson valley in New Amsterdam (later New York); in addition it monopolized Western trade with Japan after 1637.

The Netherlands were incorporated into the Napoleonic empire. At the Congress of Vienna in 1815, a Dutch monarchy was established, which included Belgium until 1830. Land drainage and reclamation programs maintained the prosperity of the country's small-scale agriculture, while trade and colonial revenues were increasingly supplemented by industrial development in the 19th century. Dutch prosperity and the country's strategic position gave the Netherlands extraordinary influence and prestige in European affairs into the 20th century, despite the country's small size. It remained neutral in World War I.

Germany invaded the Netherlands in May 1940, taking control of the country after five days of fighting. Preparing to incorporate Hol-

land into the Third Reich, Hitler installed a Nazi civilian government that ruled through totalitarian exploitation and cooperated in the persecution of Jews. But Queen Wilhelmina and the Dutch government escaped to England and maintained a government-in-exile throughout the war.

The final stages of fighting on the western front inflicted severe damage on the country, while in Asia the recovery of Indonesia from Japan led immediately to a declaration of independence under Sukarno. Marshall Plan aid was intended to support a domestic postwar recovery; an equal amount was spent by the Dutch government in an attempt to recapture control of Indonesia before that country's independence was recognized in 1949.

Devastated by World War II and the loss of its empire, the country faced a bleak future in the postwar years. Forced to turn its attention to recovery at home, the Netherlands worked through the Benelux union (founded in 1944) and the Common Market to create another European "economic miracle" between the early 1950s and the 1970s. The older bases of the economy—commerce, maritime industry, dairy farming, and flower farming—were expanded and modernized; Rotterdam was rebuilt to become Europe's most important port. Newer industries, such as chemicals and oil refining, electronics, and steel, relied on the country's highly skilled and productive labor force to turn imported raw materials into finished high-value exports. A huge impoundment project turned the Zuider Zee into a new province, increasing the country's land area by 10 percent.

This postwar prosperity has been based in large part on political stability. Queen Wilhelmina retired in 1948 after a 50-year reign and was succeeded by her daughter, Queen Juliana. At the same time, a grand coalition between the Catholic State party and the Labor (formerly Social Democratic) party was formed and governed for 10 years under Premier Willem Drees. After 1958 a pattern emerged whereby cabinets normally were formed from coalitions headed by three Christian parties (merged in 1980 to form the United Christian Appeal) or by the Liberal party; all pursued essentially the same policies of free enterprise, comprehensive social welfare programs, high taxation, and social liberalism.

Queen Juliana was succeeded in 1980 by Queen Beatrix. Since 1982 a coalition of Christian Democrats and Liberals has provided a cabinet headed by Prime Minister Ruud Lubbers. Despite tax increases and cuts in government spending, the government was returned to office in elections in 1986. Government support for the deployment in Holland of NATO cruise missiles has provoked a popular backlash and the growth of the Green party; an antimissile petition was signed by 4 million Dutch citizens.

The Netherlands retains a remnant of its colonial empire in the Netherlands Antilles. The islands, largely self-governing under the Dutch monarchy, derive most of their revenue from tourism, an industry that also contributes substantially to the country's prosperity.

New Zealand

Geography Location: South Pacific Ocean about 1,100 mi. (1,750 km) SE of Australia. **Boundaries:** South Pacific Ocean to N, E, and S; Tasman Sea to W. **Total land area:** 103,883 sq. mi. (269,057 sq km). **Coastline:** 9,406 mi. (15,134 km). **Comparative area:** about size of Colorado. **Land use:** 2% arable land; 0% permanent crops; 53% meadows and pastures; 38% forest and woodland; 7% other; includes 1% irrigated. **Major cities:** (1986 census) Wellington (capital) 352,035; Auckland 889,225; Christchurch 333,191; Hamilton 167,711; Dunedin 113,592.

People Population: 3,343,339 (1988). **Nationality:** noun—New Zealander(s); adjective—New Zealand. **Ethnic groups:** 88% European, 8.9% Maori, 2.9% Pacific Islander, 0.2% other. **Languages:** English (official), Maori. **Religions:** 81% Christian; 18% none or unspecified; 1% Hindu, Confucian, and other.

Government Type: independent state within Commonwealth, recognizing Elizabeth II as head of state. **Independence:** Sept. 26, 1907 (from UK). **Constitution:** no formal, written constitution; consists of various documents, including certain acts of UK and New Zealand parliaments; Constitution Act 1986 was to have come into effect Jan. 1, 1987, but has not been enacted. **National holiday:** Waitangi Day, Feb. 6. **Heads of government:** Paul Reeves, governor-general (since Nov. 1985); David Lange, prime minister (since July 1984). **Structure:** unicameral legislature (97-member House of Representatives, commonly called Parliament); three-level court system (magistrates and courts, Supreme Court, and court of appeal).

Economy Monetary unit: New Zealand dollar. **Budget:** (1988 est.) *income:* $13.2 billion; *expend.:* $15.6 bil. **GDP:** $23.5 bil., $7,153 per capita (1986). **Chief crops:** fodder and silage crops, wool, meat, dairy products; food-surplus country. **Livestock:** sheep, cattle, goats, pigs, horses. **Natural resources:** natural gas, iron ore, sand, coal, timber. **Major industries:** food processing, wood and paper products, textiles. **Labor force:** 1,591,900 (1987); 67.4% services, 19.8% manufacturing, 9.3% primary production, 6.8% unemployment rate. **Exports:** $5.88 bil. (f.o.b., 1987); beef, wool, dairy products. **Imports:** $6.1 bil. (c.i.f., 1987); petroleum, cars, trucks, machinery and electrical equipment, iron and steel. **Major trading partners:** (1987) *exports:* 16.3% U.S., 15.1% Japan, 14.9% Australia, 9.3% UK, 3.5% China; *imports:* 20.7% Japan, 18.1% Australia, 16.1% U.S., 9.8% UK.

Intl. Orgs. Colombo Plan, Commonwealth of Nations, FAO, GATT, IAEA, IBRD, ICAO, IDA, IFAD, IFC, ILO, IMF, IMO, INTELSAT, INTERPOL, ITU, UN, UNESCO, UPU, WHO, WMO.

Settled by Maori migrants from Polynesia around the 14th century A.D., New Zealand was first brought to Europe's attention by the Dutch explorer A.J. Tasman in 1642. In 1769 it was visited and claimed for Great Britain by Capt. James Cook. The first British missionaries arrived in 1814. By the Treaty of Waitangi in 1840, the Maoris were guaranteed possession of their ancestral lands in return for permission to admit British settlers. New Zealand was organized as a full-fledged British colony in 1841. In a series of bloody wars lasting until 1870, the Maoris were defeated and displaced from lands devoted to the expanding British settlements.

In 1907 New Zealand was elevated to the status of a British Dominion. It is an independent member of the British Commonwealth; the crown is represented by a governor-general, while government is vested in a parliament headed by a prime minister. The nation's 250,000 Maoris remain a cohesive culture and directly elect four members of Parliament.

New Zealand is remarkable for having been one of the world's first nations to create a comprehensive welfare state; a legislative history dating back to 1898 has regulated labor practices and mandated universal old-age pensions, public-sector medical care, and other social services. Most mines, forests, transportation facilities, power plants, and communications facilities are publicly owned.

New Zealand troops fought on the side of the allies in both world wars and with UN forces in the Korean War. In 1951 New Zealand joined with Australia and the United States in the ANZUS mutual-defense treaty. New Zealand's denial in 1985 of port facilities to U.S. ships carrying nuclear weapons put strains on the ANZUS alliance, which was dissolved in 1986. New Zealand has also objected strenuously to French testing of nuclear weapons in the South Pacific. In July 1985 the *Rainbow Warrior*, ship owned by the Greenpeace organization that had engaged in antinuclear protests, was bombed and sunk in Auckland harbor by French secret service agents.

New Zealand's economy is dominated by livestock raising; principal exports are dairy products, meat, and wool. Timber and minerals are also exported, along with some manufactured goods. Fisheries and tourism are also economically important.

In addition to the four islands of New Zealand proper, the country also administers the foreign affairs and defense of the otherwise self-governing Cook Islands, Niue Island, and Tokelau Island. Since 1923 New Zealand has also administered the Ross Dependency in Antarctica.

Nicaragua
Republic of Nicaragua

Geography Location: Central American isthmus. **Boundaries:** Honduras to N, Caribbean Sea to E, Costa Rica to S, Pacific Ocean to W. **Total land area:** 46,430 sq. mi. (120,254 sq km). **Coastline:** 565 mi. (910 km). **Comparative area:** slightly larger than New York State. **Land use:** 9% arable land; 1% permanent crops; 43% meadows and pastures; 35% forest and woodland; 12% other; includes 1% irrigated. **Major cities:** (1979 est.) Managua (capital) 608,020.

People Population: 3,407,183 (1988). **Nationality:** noun—Nicaraguan(s); adjective—Nicaraguan. **Ethnic groups:** 69% mestizo, 17% white, 9% black, 5% Indian. **Languages:** Spanish (official); English- and Indian-speaking minorities on Atlantic coast. **Religions:** 95% Roman Catholic.

Government Type: republic. **Independence:** Sept. 28, 1821 (from Spain). **Constitution:** Jan. 1987. **National holidays:** Independence Day, Sept. 15; Anniversary of the Revolution, July 19. **Head of government:** Commandante José Daniel Ortega Saavedra, president (since Jan. 1985). **Structure:** executive and administrative responsibility formally reside with president, vice president, and cabinet; in reality, nine-member National Directorate of Sandinista National Liberation Front shares power with and dominates executive; National Assembly elected in Nov. 1984 and inaugurated in Jan. 1985; country's highest judicial authority is Sandinista-appointed Supreme Court, composed of seven members.

Economy Monetary unit: córdoba. **Budget:** (1986) *income:* $0.64 bil.; *expend.:* $1 bil. **GDP:** $2 bil., $600 per capita (1987). **Chief crops:** cotton, coffee, sugarcane, rice, corn, beans. **Livestock:** cattle, pigs, horses, mules, sheep, goats. **Natural resources:** gold, silver, copper, tungsten, lead. **Major industries:** food processing, chemicals, metal products. **Labor force:** 1,086,000 (1986); 44% agriculture, 43% service, 13% industry; 22% unemployment. **Exports:** $251 mil. (f.o.b., 1987); coffee, cotton, seafood, bananas. **Imports:** $775 mil. (c.i.f., 1987); food and nonfood agricultural products, petroleum, chemicals and pharmaceuticals, transportation equipment, machinery. **Major trading partners:** (1986) *exports:* 40% CMEA, 39% EC, 6% CACM, 7% other; *imports:* 52% CMEA, 12% EC, 10% Mexico, 6% CACM, 20% other.

Intl. Orgs. FAO, G-77, GATT, IAEA, IBRD, ICAO, IDA, IFAD, IFC, ILO, IMF, IMO, INTELSAT, INTERPOL, ITU, NAM, OAS, UN, UNESCO, UPU, WHO, WMO.

As was the case with the other Central American countries, Nicaragua gained its independence from Spain in 1821 and formed a constituent part of the United Provinces of Central America in 1823. With the dissolution of the federation in 1838, Nicaragua became an independent republic. Throughout the territory of the United Provinces, an intra-elite struggle between Liberal and Conservative factions defined the political arena during the early part of the 19th century. Nicaraguan Liberals invited the adventurer William Walker of Tennessee to take their part against their Conservative rivals in 1855. Walker took control of the country in 1856 but was driven out by a combined Central American force the following year.

As a result of Liberal complicity in this affair, the Conservatives held power in Nicaragua until 1893, when a planters' revolt brought Liberal José Santos Zelaya to the presidency. Because of Zelaya's intention to pursue an isthmian canal project, the U.S. government intervened in support of a Conservative uprising. The United States sent marines to Nicaragua in 1909, and Zelaya resigned in 1910.

The Marines occupied the country during 1909–25 and 1926–33.

Refusing to abide by a political settlement between the U.S. government and Nicaraguan Liberal forces in 1927, a Liberal officer, Augusto César Sandino, led a guerrilla war against U.S. occupation forces until 1933. Anastasio Somoza García, head of the Nicaraguan National Guard, had Sandino assassinated in 1934 and took over the presidency in 1937. Somoza and his sons Luis and Anastasio Somoza Debayle controlled Nicaragua until 1979.

A broad coalition of groups led by the Sandinista National Liberation Front (FSLN) overthrew the Somoza dictatorship. The FSLN comprised three groups, or "tendencies": the Prolonged Popular War (GPP), the Proletarian Tendency (TP), and the Insurrectional Tendency (TI), or "Terceristas." Each of these three groups is represented equally on a Sandinista governing board called the National Directorate. Elections were held in 1984 for the presidency, vice presidency, and a constituent assembly, and a new constitution was promulgated for the country in 1987. The Sandinistas won the 1984 election for the presidency and vice presidency as well as receiving a working majority in the National Assembly. The current president, Daniel Ortega Saavedra, belongs to the Tercerista tendency of the FSLN and is a member of the Sandinista National Directorate.

Nicaragua has experienced a civil war since 1981 between the Sandinista government and a group of U.S.-backed, antigovernment forces known collectively as the Contras.

Niger
Republic of Niger

Geography Location: landlocked country in western Africa. **Boundaries:** Algeria and Libya to N, Chad to E, Nigeria to S, Benin and Burkina Faso to SW, Mali to W. **Total land area:** 489,076 sq. mi. (1,266,700 sq km). **Coastline:** none. **Comparative area:** slightly more than three times size of California. **Land use:** 3% arable land; 0% permanent crops; 7% meadows and pastures; 2% forest and woodland; 88% other; includes negl. % irrigated. **Major cities:** Niamey (capital) 225,314; Zinder 75,000 (1981 est.); Marodi 45,852; Tahoua 31,265; Agadez 20,475 (1977).

People Population: 7,213,945 (1988). **Nationality:** noun—Nigerien(s); adjective—Nigerien. **Ethnic groups:** 56.0% Hausa, 22.0% Djerma, 8.5% Fula, 8.0% Tuareg, 4.3% Beri Beri (Kanouri); 1.2% Arab, Toubou, and Gourmantche; about 4,000 French expatriates. **Languages:** French (official), Hausa, Djerma. **Religions:** 80% Muslim, 20% indigenous beliefs and Christians.

Government Type: republic; military regimes in power since Apr. 1974. **Independence:** Aug. 3, 1960 (from France). **Constitution:** Nov. 8, 1960, suspended after coup of Apr. 15, 1974. **National holiday:** Independence Day, Aug. 3. **Heads of government:** Col. Ali Saibou, president (since Nov. 1987); Mamane Oumarou, prime minister (since 1987). **Structure:** executive—president in name of Supreme Military Council (SMC), which is composed of army officers; prime minister.

Economy Monetary unit: Communauté Financière Africaine (CFA) franc. **Budget:** (1986 est.) **income:** $173.0 mil.; **expend.:** $364.6 mil. **GDP:** $1.2 bil., $180 per capita (1985 est.). **Chief crops:** cash crops—cowpeas, groundnuts, cotton; food crops—millet, sorghum, rice. **Livestock:** goats, sheep, cattle, asses, camels. **Natural resources:** uranium, coal, iron ore, tin, phosphates. **Major industries:** cement, brick, rice mill. **Labor force:** 2.5 mil. (1982); 90% agriculture; 51% of population of working age. **Exports:** $250.6 mil. (f.o.b., 1985); uranium, livestock, cowpeas, onions, hides, skins; exports understated because much regional trade not recorded. **Imports:** $309.4 mil. (f.o.b., 1985); petroleum products, primary materials, machinery, vehicles and parts, electronic equipment. **Major trading partners:** France (about half), other EC countries, Nigeria, UDEAC countries, U.S. (3.8% 1981); preferential tariff to EC and franc zone countries.

Intl. Orgs. FAO, G-77, GATT, IAEA, IBRD, ICAO, IDA, IFAD, IFC, ILO, IMF, INTELSAT, INTERPOL, ITU, NAM, UN, UNESCO, UPU, WHO, WIPO, WMO.

Most of Niger's territory is dominated by the Sahara and the Sahel, which have spread southward since prehistoric times. Much of the population lives in the narrow fertile belt south of the Niger River. Much of Niger was incorporated during medieval times in large empires centered in neighboring Mali, Chad, and Nigeria.

In the 18th century, Tuaregs migrating from the northern desert began to form tribal confederations in Niger. They united with local Hausa peoples to wage war against the Fulani Empire.

In the 19th century, British and German explorers seeking the source of the Niger River explored the region. In the European rivalry that followed, the French, from bases in Mali and Chad, began to dominate Niger by 1900; Niger became a French colony in 1922, administered from Dakar, Senegal.

In 1946 the people of Niger, in common with other peoples in French Africa, were granted French citizenship, and limited self-rule began. This local autonomy was expanded in 1956, and in 1958 Niger became an autonomous state within the French Overseas Community. Full independence followed on Aug. 3, 1960; Niger maintained close ties to France.

Hamani Diori was elected Niger's first president in 1960 and was reelected in 1965 and 1970. He was overthrown in 1974 in a military coup led by Lt. Col. Seyni Kountche, who became Niger's next president. In 1987, Pres. Kountche died of natural causes and was succeeded by Col. Ali Saibou, who was elected president by the Supreme Military Council.

Since 1988 the United States and France have pursued closer relations with Niger; an increase in aid is designed in part to offset Libyan influence.

In its limited arable lands Niger grows some peanuts and cotton and uranium is mined, but livestock-raising remains the mainstay of the economy. In recent years the country has been devastated by drought, which has killed off much of the country's cattle, sheep, and goats and led to widespread famine.

Nigeria
Federal Republic of Nigeria

Geography Location: western coast of Africa. **Boundaries:** Niger to N, Cameroon to E, Gulf of Guinea to S, Benin to W. **Total land area:** 351,649 sq. mi. (910,770 sq km). **Coastline:** 530 mi. (853 km). **Comparative area:** slightly more than twice size of California. **Land use:** 31% arable land; 3% permanent crops; 23% meadows and pastures; 15% forest and woodland; 28% other; includes negl. % irrigated. **Major cities:** (1975 est.) Lagos (capital) 1,060,848; Ibadan 847,000; Ogbomosho 432,000; Kano 399,000; Oshogbo 282,000.

People Population: 111,903,502 (1988). **Nationality:** noun—Nigerian(s); adjective—Nigerian. **Ethnic groups:** 250 tribal groups; Hausa and Fulani in north, Yoruba in southwest, and Ibos in southeast make up 65% of population; 27,000 non-Africans. **Languages:** English (official); Hausa, Yoruba, Ibo, Fulani, and several other languages also widely used. **Religions:** 50% Muslim, 40% Christian, 10% indigenous beliefs.

Government Type: military government since Dec. 31, 1983. **Independence:** Oct. 1, 1960 (from UK). **Constitution:** Oct. 1, 1979, amended Feb. 9, 1984. **National holiday:** Independence Day, Oct. 1. **Heads of government:** Ibrahim Babangida, president (since Aug. 1985). **Structure:** Armed Forces Ruling Council; National Council of Ministers and National Council of States; judiciary headed by Supreme Court.

Economy Monetary unit: niara. **Budget:** (1985) **income:** $15 bil.; **expend:** $12 bil. **GDP:** $53.4 bil., $520 per capita (1985). **Chief crops:** peanuts, cotton, cocoa, rubber, yams; illegal producer of cannabis for international drug trade. **Livestock:** goats, sheep, cattle, pigs, asses. **Natural resources:** crude oil, tin, columbite, iron ore, coal. **Major industries:** mining—crude oil, natural gas, coal, tin, columbite; processing industries—palm oil, peanut, cotton, rubber, petroleum; manufacturing industries—textiles, cement, building materials, food products, footwear. **Labor force:** 45–50 mil. (1984 est.); 54% agriculture, 19% industry, commerce and services, 15% government; 49% of population of working age. **Exports:** $6.97 bil. (f.o.b., 1986 est.); 95% oil; cocoa, palm products, rubber, timber, tin. **Imports:** $5.50 bil. (c.i.f., 1986 est.); machinery and transport equipment, manufactured goods, chemicals, wheat, nonprocessed and processed fish. **Major trading partners:** UK, EC countries, U.S.

Intl. Orgs. Commonwealth, FAO, G-77, GATT, IAEA, IBRD, ICAO, IDA, IFAD, IFC, ILO, IMF, IMO, INTELSAT, INTERPOL, ITU, NAM, OPEC, UN, UNESCO, UPU, WHO, WMO.

The Nok culture of central Nigeria (500–200 B.C.) was one of the richest and most advanced ancient civilizations in western Africa. Around A.D. 1000, the Moslem Kanem civilization expanded into northern Nigeria; by the 14th century, the amalgamated kingdom of Kanem-Bornu took northern Nigeria as its political center, from which it dominated the Sahel and developed trade routes stretching throughout northern Africa and as far as Europe and the Middle East.

During the 15th and 16th centuries, the Hausa Songhai empire rose to power. It was overthrown by the Fulani Moslem leader Uthman Dan Fodio, who created the Sokoto caliphate.

Southern Nigeria is dominated by the Yoruba, whose Oyo kingdom, centered at Ife, became a major power by A.D. 1000. Oyo gave rise to the Benin civilization, which flourished from the 15th to the 18th centuries and is famous for its brass, bronze, and ivory sculpture.

The Portuguese established trading stations on the Benin coast in the 15th century; initially, trade relations were cordial, and Benin became well-known in Europe as a powerful and advanced kingdom. With the rise of the slave trade (which began with the cooperation of the Benin kings, who brought slaves from the interior), relations became hostile, and Benin declined under European pressure. The Dutch, British, and other Europeans competed strenuously with Portugal for control of the slave trade, and by the 18th century, most of the coastal region of Nigeria was under British control. By the turn of the 19th century, Britain suppressed the slave trade; slaves captured aboard European ships were transported by the British to Freetown in Sierra Leone.

With the slave trade ended, the British traded with Nigerians for agricultural and forest products and commenced exploration of the Niger River. Lagos came under British control in 1851, and in 1861 Nigeria was made a British colony. Despite native resistance the colony was expanded in 1906 to include territory east of the Niger River, which was called the Protectorate of Southern Nigeria, The two areas were administratively joined in 1914.

During the 1920s Britain began to respond to Nigerian demands for local self-rule. In 1946 the colony was divided into three regions, each with an advisory assembly. In 1954 the colony was reorganized as the Nigerian Federation, and the assemblies were given more authority. Sir Akubar Tafawa Balewa became Nigeria's first prime minister.

In 1961 a UN-supervised referendum in British Cameroon led to the joining with Nigeria of the northern part of that territory, while the southern part joined the new nation of Cameroon.

The 1960s were marked by a struggle for political dominance among the major ethnic groups of Nigeria, including the Ibo (or Igbo), Yoruba, Hausa, and Fulani. Attempts to partition the country on tribal lines for administrative purposes provoked controversy, and charges of corruption and fraud in elections held in 1964 and 1965 led to violence and rioting.

In January 1966 civil war broke out when a group of Ibo army officers overthrew the central government and several of the regional governments. Prime Minister Balewa was killed, along with many other political leaders in the northern and western parts of the country. Gen. Johnson Aguiyi-Ironsi, leader of the Ibo forces, took control of the government.

Aguiyi-Ironsi abolished the country's federal structure and set up a strong central government, dominated by the Ibo. Anti-Ibo riots broke out in the north, and many Ibo were massacred. In July 1966 Aguiyi-Ironsi was assassinated by a group of northern army officers. Army Chief of Staff Yakubu Gowon became head of a new military government. The Eastern Region refused to acknowledge Gowon's government.

In 1967 Gowon reapportioned Nigeria into 12 states. The Eastern Region, led by Ojukwu, rejected this plan and seceded from Nigeria to form the independent state of Biafra. The civil war provoked by Biafra's secession lasted until January 1970, when Biafra surrendered and was rejoined with Nigeria. During the war an estimated one million Biafrans, mostly Ibos, died from military action or starvation.

In the early 1970s the Gowon government tried, with limited success, to aid in the reconstruction of the Eastern Region and to create a harmonious multitribal government. Gowon was overthrown in a coup in 1975, and Gen. Murtala Ramal Mohammad became head of the new government. He was assassinated in 1976 and succeeded by Lt. Gen. Olusegun Obasanjo. The Obasanjo government increased the number of states from 12 to 19 and promised a return to civilian rule.

Elections were held in October 1979, and Shehu Shagari was elected president. He was reelected in 1983, but in December 1983 the military again intervened; the civilian government was overthrown and replaced by military rule under Maj. Gen. Mohammed Buhari. Buhari was replaced on Aug. 30, 1985, by Maj. Gen. Ibrahim Gbadamosi Babangida.

Despite political difficulties Nigeria's recovery from the Biafran War was greatly aided in the 1970s by revenues from petroleum exports. Corruption, mismanagement, and overspending of projected petroleum revenues led to a major economic crisis in the early 1980s with the collapse of world crude oil prices. Petroleum export earnings declined from $26 billion in 1980 to $5 billion in 1986. With a high foreign debt, high inflation rate, unemployment, and shortages of basic goods, riots broke out in major population centers. Industrial and infrastructure development stagnated.

In addition, in March 1987 religious violence broke out between the Christian south and the Moslem north; numerous churches and mosques were destroyed or vandalized.

The Babangida government in 1987 announced various economic austerity measures and promoted a campaign to lower the birth rate and control the population—the largest in Africa and the eighth largest in the world. The government also announced plans to restore civilian rule by 1992. A new constituent assembly was elected, under close government control, in April 1988. Elections for a bicameral legislature are scheduled for 1990, and a new constitution is to come into force two years later.

The Nigerian economy, now dominated by petroleum (which makes up 95% of exports by value), is potentially one of the richest in Africa. The country's mineral resources include coal, iron, columbium, tin, and limestone. Export crops include cocoa, tobacco, palm oil, peanuts, cotton, and soybeans. Nigeria also has substantial resources of livestock and forest products and a productive offshore fishing industry. Industrial development, while crippled by the depression of the 1980s, had previously progressed to a high level relative to other West African nations.

Norway
Kingdom of Norway

Geography Location: northwestern part of Scandinavian peninsula in northern Europe. **Boundaries:** Norwegian Sea to N and W, short frontier with USSR at northwestern tip, North Sea to S and SE, Sweden to W, Finland to NW. **Total land area:** 125,050 sq. mi. (323,878 sq km). **Coastline:** 13,626 mi. (21,925 km)— 2,125 mi. (3,419 km) mainland; 1,500 mi. (2,413 km) large islands; 10,002 mi. (16,093 km) long fjords, numerous small islands, and minor indentations. **Comparative area:** slightly larger than New Mexico. **Land use:** 3% arable land; 0% permanent crops; negl. % meadows and pastures; 27% forest and woodland; 70% other; includes negl. % irrigated. **Major cities:** (1987) Oslo (capital) 451,099; Bergen 208,809; Trondheim 134,496; Stavanger 95,437; Kristiansand 63,293.

People Population: 4,190,758 (1988). **Nationality:** noun—Norwegian(s); adjective—Norwegian. **Ethnic groups:** Germanic (Nordic, Alpine, Baltic) and racial-cultural minority of 20,000 Lapps. **Languages:** Norwegian (official), small Lapp- and Finnish-speaking minorities. **Religions:** 94% Evangelical Lutheran (state church), 4% other Protestant and Roman Catholic, 2% other.

Government Type: constitutional monarchy. **Independence:** Oct. 26, 1905 (from Sweden). **Constitution:** May 17, 1814 and modified in 1884. **National holiday:** Constitution Day, May 17. **Heads of government:** Olav V, king (since Sept. 1957); Gro Harlem Brundtland, prime minister (since May 1986). **Structure:** executive power vested in Crown but exercised by cabinet responsible to parliament; legislative authority rests jointly with Crown and parliament (Storting-Lagting, upper house; Odelsting, lower house); Supreme Court, five superior courts, 104 lower courts.

Economy (1986) **Monetary unit:** Norwegian krone. **Budget: income:** $33.2 bil.; **expend.:** $30.4 bil. **GDP:** $60.1 bil., $14,650 per capita. **Chief crops:** feed grains, potatoes, fruits, vegetables; 40% self-sufficient; food shortages—food grains, sugar. **Livestock:** sheep, cattle, pigs, goats, horses. **Natural resources:** crude oil, copper, natural gas, pyrites, nickel. **Major industries:** petroleum and gas, food processing, shipbuilding. **Short-**

ages: most raw materials except timber, petroleum, iron, copper, and ilmenite ore. **Labor force:** 2.13 mil.; 33.0% services, 17.4% commerce, 17.2% mining and manufacturing; 2.0% unemployment. **Exports:** $18.2 bil. (f.o.b.); oil, natural gas, metals, chemicals, machinery. **Imports:** $20.3 bil. (c.i.f.); machinery, fuels and lubricants, transport equipment, chemicals, foodstuffs. **Major trading partners:** *exports:* 65% EC (27.7% UK, 19.1% W. Germany), 11% developing countries, 9.8% Sweden, 5.4% U.S., 0.5% USSR; *imports:* 49.2% EC (16.9% W. Germany, 8.0% UK), 17.7% Sweden, 6.8% U.S., 5.9% developing countries, 0.5% USSR.

Intl. Orgs. EC (free-trade agreement), EFTA, FAO, GATT, IAEA, IBRD, ICAO, IDA, IFAD, IFC, ILO, IMF, IMO, INTELSAT, INTERPOL, ITU, NATO, OECD, UN, UNESCO, UPU, WHO, WIPO, WMO.

At the beginning of the 10th century, the Viking king Harold I conquered and united the petty kingdoms of western Scandinavia to form Norway and extended his realm as far as the Orkney and Shetland islands. Viking nobles fleeing from his conquests settled in Iceland and Greenland, consolidating the Norse duchy of Normandy in France. Over the next several centuries, kings of Harold's dynasty occasionally succeeded in uniting the kingdom again and in fending off predatory claims of England and Denmark. Christianity was established under Olaf II at the beginning of the 11th century.

Under Magnus VI (1263–80), medieval Norway reached the height of its power and prosperity. Norwegian independence ended with the accession in 1319 of Magnus VII, who was king of Sweden as well. Under the Kalmar Union of 1397, the three kingdoms of Scandinavia were merged under Danish control; Norway ceased to exist as a nation-state and was governed by the Danes for the following four centuries.

In 1814 Denmark, which had sided with France in the Napoleonic wars, was forced by the victorious powers to cede Norway to Sweden. Under Sweden's military control, but with a growing sense of nationalism, Norway attempted to establish its own monarchy. The attempt failed, but in 1815 Sweden acknowledged the independence of Norway in perpetual union with the Swedish Crown.

Relations between Norway and Sweden remained strained throughout the 19th century. In 1905 the Norwegian legislature, the Storting, declared the union void and deposed Swedish King Oscar II as king of Norway. Sweden acquiesced, and Prince Charles of Denmark was enthroned as king of Norway, ruling as Haakon VII.

During the 19th century, large numbers of Norwegians emigrated to North America. A rising tide of cultural nationalism was expressed in the flourishing Norwegian literature and art, as well as in a tradition of Arctic exploration. In the 20th century, industrialization, aided by the development of hydroelectric power, began to supplement Norway's traditional economic mainstays of fishing and seafaring.

Norway remained neutral during World War I and was relatively unaffected by the postwar upheavals. Industrialization led to the rise of the Labor party in 1927.

Norway attempted to remain neutral in World War II as well but was invaded by German troops in April 1940; the country fell after a brief resistance aided by a Franco-British expeditionary force. The king and government fled to London and established a government-in-exile there. The Norwegian merchant marine fleet was also largely transferred to Great Britain and contributed to the Allied cause in the North Atlantic. At home, resistance grew to the collaborationist government of the Fascist leader Vidkun Quisling. As the Nazis retreated in 1945, King Haakon and his government returned home in triumph. Within three years the Norwegian economy had returned to prewar levels.

Elections in 1945 returned a majority Labor government in the Storting, a position the party retained until 1961. With the return of prosperity, Labor set about establishing a characteristic Scandinavian welfare state, emphasizing privately owned, free-market industry, publicly owned utilities, state planning to ensure ample housing as well as full employment through export-oriented industries, a comprehensive social welfare system, and—to pay for the latter—high taxes.

As a member of the Allied cause during World War II, Norway was a founding member of the United Nations, providing that body with its first secretary-general, Trygve Lie. With the hardening of the Cold War, especially after the Communist coup in Czechoslovakia and the USSR's Mutual Assistance Pact with Finland, both in 1948, Norway's foreign policy took on a clear pro-Western stance; Norway joined the NATO alliance in 1949. In 1959 Norway became one of the original members of the European Free Trade Association.

Labor lost its majority in 1961 but remained in office at the head of a minority government until 1965. In that year it yielded to a non-Socialist coalition that remained in office until 1971. Through the 1960s industrial development and exports continued to fuel an economic boom that led to great national prosperity and stability.

The 1970s were, for Norway, the decade of oil and gas. As development of North Sea oil and gas fields proceeded at the beginning of the decade, Labor returned to government power in 1971, ruling after 1976 in a coalition with the Socialist Left party. With energy prices rising throughout the decade, the government's petroleum monopoly, Statoil, established in 1976, seemed to provide an endless source of funds. Because Norway's hydroelectric plants made the country self-sufficient in electric power, almost all of the oil and gas was available for export; by 1981 energy exports amounted to one-third, and by 1985 one-half, of Norway's total exports.

The government proved unable to resist the temptation to use its wealth to expand the welfare state and encourage large wage increases. Public spending swelled, inflation outpaced wages, and government debt mounted; meanwhile Norway became an economic hostage to OPEC oil prices.

In the 1981 elections, the Conservative party formed a government for the first time since 1928; it remained in power at the head of a non-Socialist coalition in the 1985 elections. The new government's austerity policy of holding down government spending while increasing taxes on consumer goods aroused popular opposition, and the government fell in 1986. The new Socialist coalition government faced even greater drops in oil revenues, combined with labor unrest and continued inflation. But in 1987 Norway negotiated the sale of gas to EEC countries, and the recovery of energy prices in that year brought a partial return to economic stability and prosperity, as well as solidification of the position of the Labor party going into the 1989 elections.

Oman
Sultanate of Oman
(PREVIOUS NAME: MUSCAT)

Geography Location: extreme eastern part of Arabian peninsula. **Boundaries:** Gulf of Oman to N, Arabian Sea to E and S, S. Yemen to SW, Saudi Arabia to W, United Arab Emirates to NW; detached portion of Oman lies at tip of Musandam peninsula, on southern shore of Strait of Hormuz, N of United Arab Emirates. **Total land area:** 120,000 sq. mi. (300,000 sq km). **Coastline:** 1,299 mi. (2,092 km). **Comparative area:** slightly smaller than Kansas. **Land use:** negl. % arable land; negl. % permanent crops; 5% meadows and pastures; 0% forest and woodland; 95% other; includes negl. % irrigated. **Major cities:** (1981 est.) Muscat (capital) 50,000.

People Population: 1,265,382 (1988). **Nationality:** noun—Omani(s); adjective—Omani. **Ethnic groups:** almost entirely Arab, with small Baluchi, Zanzibari, and Indian groups. **Languages:** Arabic (official), English, Baluchi, Urdu, Indian dialects. **Religions:** 75% Ibadhi Muslim, remainder Sunni Muslim, Shi'a Muslim, some Hindu.

Government Type: absolute monarchy; independent, with residual UK influence. **Constitution:** none. **National holiday:** National Days, Nov. 18–19. **Head of government:** Qaboos bin Said, sultan and prime minister (since July 1970). **Structure:** executive—sultan appoints 45-member State Consultative Assembly to advise him; judicial—traditional Islamic judges and nascent civil court system.

Economy Monetary unit: rial. **Budget:** (1986) *income:* $3.2 bil.; *expend.:* $4.9 bil. **GDP:** $7.5 bil., $5,900 per capita (1986 est.). **Chief crops:** based on subsistence farming—fruits, dates, cereals. **Livestock:** cattle, camels. **Natural resources:** crude oil, copper, asbestos, some marble, limestone. **Major industries:** crude oil production and refining, natural gas production, construction. **Labor force:** 430,000; 58% are non-Omani; est. 60% agriculture. **Exports:** $2.8 bil. (f.o.b.); mostly petroleum; nonoil consist mostly of reexports, processed copper, and some agricultural goods. **Imports:** $2.6 bil. (c.i.f.); machinery, transportation equipment, manufactured goods, food, livestock. **Major trading partners:** *exports:* 54% Japan, 17% Korea, 5% Thailand; *imports:* 17%

UK, 20% Japan, 20% UAE, 8% W. Germany, 6% U.S.

Intl. Orgs. Arab League, FAO, G-77, IBRD, ICAO, IDA, IFAD, IFC, IMF, IMO, INTELSAT, INTERPOL, ITU, NAM, UN, UNESCO, UPU, WHO, WMO.

Oman, until 1970 Muscat and Oman, occupies the southeastern corner of Arabia, including, discontinuously, the tip of the Ruus-al-Jebal peninsula on the southern shore of the Strait of Hormuz. From ancient times an important center of trade in the Persian Gulf and the Indian Ocean, Oman was frequently dominated by Persia prior to the mid-18th century. The principal port, Masqat (Muscat), was captured by the Portuguese in 1508 and held by them until 1659, when the Ottoman Turks took possession. They were driven out in 1741 by Ahmed ibn Said of Yemen, who consolidated the sultanate of Oman in 1744, founding the present royal line.

In the early 19th century, Oman was the most powerful state in Arabia, controlling Zanzibar, the southern coast of Iran, and much of Baluchistan. Zanzibar was separated from Oman in 1856, confirmed by an agreement with Great Britain in 1861; the Persian coast and much of Baluchistan was detached from Oman during the latter half of the 19th century. In 1958 Oman's sole remaining Baluchi possession, the city-state of Gwadar, was ceded to Pakistan in return for a monetary settlement.

Growing British influence was consolidated by the formation of a British Protectorate in Muscat and Oman in 1891; that arrangement was reconfirmed in 1951. In the 1950s Britain aided the sultanate in putting down rebellions in the desert interior. The British Protectorate ended with Britain's withdrawal from the gulf in 1971.

On July 23, 1970, Sultan Said ibn Taimur was overthrown by his son, Sultan Qabus ibn Said. The latter instituted a national development program and in 1975 defeated a leftist uprising in the western desert that had been aided by South Yemen.

The economy of Oman is dominated by petroleum, which makes up 95% of exports, and by banking and shipping services. The country is generally barren, with scattered flocks of sheep and camels. A narrow coastal strip supports some agriculture, chiefly groves of dates and other fruits. Fishing is also commercially important.

Pakistan
Islamic Republic of Pakistan
(PREVIOUS NAME: WEST PAKISTAN)

Geography **Location:** southern Asia. **Boundaries:** Afghanistan to N, short frontier with China in far NE, India to E, Arabian Sea to S, and Iran to W. **Total land area:** 310,403 sq. mi. (803,943 sq km). **Coastline:** 650 mi. (1,046 km). **Comparative area:** slightly less than twice size of California. **Land use:** 26% arable land; negl. % permanent crops; 6% meadows and pastures; 4% forest and woodland; 64% other; includes 19% irrigated. **Major cities:** (1981 census) Islamabad (capital) 204,364; Karachi 5,180,562; Lahore 2,952,689; Faisalabad

(Lyallpur) 1,104,209; Rawalpindi 794,843.

People **Population:** 107,467,457 (1988). **Nationality:** noun—Pakistani(s); adjective—Pakistani. **Ethnic groups:** Punjabi, Sindhi, Pashtun (Pathan), Baluch, Muhajir (immigrants from India and their descendants). **Languages:** Urdu and English (official); total spoken languages—64% Punjabi, 12% Sindhi, 8% Pashtu, 7% Urdu, 9% Baluchi and other; English is lingua franca of Pakistani elite and most government ministries, however, official policies are promoting its gradual replacement by Urdu. **Religions:** 97% Muslim (77% Sunni, 20% Shi'a); 3% Christian, Hindu, and other.

Government **Type:** parliamentary with strong executive; federal republic. **Independence:** Aug. 15, 1947 (from UK). **Constitution:** Apr. 10, 1973; suspended July 5, 1977; restored Dec. 30, 1985. **National holiday:** Pakistan Day, Mar. 23. **Heads of government:** Ghulam Isheq Khan, president (since Dec. 1988); Benazir Bhutto, prime minister (since Dec. 1988). **Structure:** based on English common law but gradually being transformed to correspond to Koranic injunction; former president Mohammad Zia's government established Islamic sharia courts paralleling secular courts and introduced Koranic punishments for some criminal offenses; martial law courts abolished Dec. 30, 1985, and all cases, including those concerning national security, now tried by civilian judiciary under due process safeguards.

Economy (1987) **Monetary unit:** rupee. **Budget:** (est.) *income:* $5.8 bil.; *expend.:* current, $6.6 bil.; development expend., $2.5 bil. **GNP:** $33 bil., $330 per capita. **Chief crops:** wheat, rice, sugarcane, cotton; illegal producer of opium poppy and cannabis for international drug trade. **Livestock:** goats, sheep, cattle, buffalo, asses. **Natural resources:** land, extensive natural gas reserves, limited crude oil, poor quality coal, iron ore. **Major industries:** cotton textiles, steel, food processing. **Labor force:** 28.9 mil. (est.); extensive export of labor; 54% agriculture, 33% services, 13% mining and manufacturing. **Exports:** $3.7 bil. (c.i.f.); rice, cotton, textiles. **Imports:** $5.4 bil. (f.o.b.); petroleum (crude and products), cooking oil, machinery. **Major trading partners:** (1986) *exports:* 10% U.S., 10% Japan, 8% UK; *imports:* 15% Japan, 12% U.S., 9% W. Germany.

Intl. Orgs. Colombo Plan, FAO, G-77, GATT, IAEA, IBRD, ICAO, IDA, IFAD, IFC, ILO, IMF, IMO, INTELSAT, INTERPOL, ITU, NAM, UN, UNESCO, UPU, WHO, WIPO, WMO.

Pakistan occupies the heartland of ancient South Asian civilization, in the Indus River Valley. Agricultural settlements in that area arose by 3000 B.C., and the great cities at Harappa and Mohenjo-Daro were founded some 500 years later. Indo-European (Aryan) invaders from Central Asia overthrew the ancient civilization around 1500 B.C. and established a new culture that spread throughout what is now Pakistan and northern India. Brahmanism, the religious culture of the early Indo-European invaders, gave rise to Buddhism and Jainism around the sixth century B.C., and

evolved into Hinduism in the early centuries A.D. The Indus Valley was incorporated into the empire of Alexander the Great, c. 350 B.C., and then into the Mauryan empire of Asoka, which by the third century B.C. controlled all of South Asia except for the southernmost portion of India.

Under various rulers the Indus Valley and the areas to its northwest were a great center of Buddhist culture until the beginning of the eighth century, when the area fell to Muslim Arab invaders. Thereafter, Islam was firmly established throughout the region, but Baluchistan and the Northwest Frontier region became culturally allied to the Persian civilization of Iran and Afghanistan, while Sind and the Punjab were more closely akin to the culture of northern India.

Northern Pakistan was incorporated into the empire of Mahmud of Gazni in the 11th century, and fell to the Mongols in the 13th century. The Indus River became the boundary between the Mongol Inkhanate of Persia and the Sultanate of Delhi. The region was conquered by Timur Leng at the end of the 14th century and after the fall of the Timurid empire, was divided between the Kingdoms of Sind and Multan, in southern and central Pakistan, and the Sultanate of Delhi, in the Punjab. All of Pakistan and northern India was reunited after 1526, when the conquests of Babur established the Mogul empire.

The expansion of British power in India during the 18th century left Pakistan largely untouched; the area was divided among various states, including Sind, the Punjab, Kashmir, and the western reaches of Rajputana. In the first half of the 19th century, British rule extended to the northwest; after the defeat of the Mutiny of 1857, the entire Indus Valley, along with the rest of India, was under British rule. Sind and the Punjab were ruled directly by the British, while Baluchistan and Kalat, the Northwest Territories, Jammu and Kashmir, and Rajputana were native states ruled as British protectorates.

From the beginning of the 20th century, various nationalist movements arose throughout British India. The Moslem League, under the leadership of Mohammad Ali Jinnah after 1916, advocated greater popular political participation, dominion status for India, and a strong Muslim voice in Indian administration. Muslims and Hindus were allied in the Non-Cooperation movement of the 1920s, but the alliance soon broke down and degenerated into communal frictions. With growing power of the Congress Party in Hindu areas and Gandhi's civil disobedience movement in the 1930s, Jinnah's Moslem League charted an increasingly separate course and called for the creation of a separate Muslim state in 1940.

With the British withdrawal from India in 1947, Hindus in the Muslim majority areas of the Indus Valley and in East Bengal fled to Hindu northern India, while Muslims in Hindu areas fled in the opposite direction. These massive population movements were accompanied by widespread violence leading to the loss of hundreds of thousands of lives. Jinnah, the father of modern Pakistan, died in 1948. Pakistan, encompassing Sind, the Punjab, Baluchistan, the Northwest Frontier Territories, part of Jammu and Kashmir, and adjacent areas in the west and East Bengal in the east, was granted dominion status within the British Commonwealth in 1947, becoming an independent republic in 1956.

Pakistan joined the Central Treaty Organization and became allied with the West, in contrast to the Soviet-leaning nonalignment of India. In 1958 Gen. Mohammad Ayub Khan seized power in a coup; he was elected president in 1960 and reelected in 1965. Following border clashes with India in 1962, Pakistan entered into friendly relations with China, which also had engaged in border warfare with India. Ayub Khan resigned as president in early 1969 after failing to put down widespread demonstrations in East Pakistan. A new government was formed under Gen. Yahya Khan, and martial law was declared. A parliamentary victory by the East Pakistani Awami League in December 1970 led to civil war and the secession of East Pakistan in 1971 (see "Bangladesh").

India's intervention on behalf of East Bengal had led to war on a western front with Pakistan as well. Following the surrender of Pakistani troops in the east on Dec. 16, 1971, a cease-fire went into effect on the western front. On July 3, 1972, India and Pakistan agreed to a mutual withdrawal of troops and entered into negotiations designed to settle border disputes and other outstanding problems. Diplomatic relations between India and Pakistan were resumed in 1976.

The elections of 1970 that had precipitated the secession of East Pakistan also brought Zulfikar Ali Bhutto to the presidency of Pakistan. He remained in office until July 1977, when he was overthrown in a military coup led by Gen. Mohammad Zia ul-Haq. Subsequently, Bhutto was convicted of complicity in a 1974 political murder and was hanged in April 1979. Under Pres. Zia, Pakistan moved toward the implementation of Islamic law in parallel with the constitutional law of Pakistan's parliamentary system. In 1986 Bhutto's daughter, Benazir Bhutto, returned to Pakistan from exile in Europe to organize opposition parties against Pres. Zia; this movement led to widespread rioting in the months that followed.

On Aug. 17, 1988, Pres. Zia along with several senior government officials and the American ambassador was killed in an airplane crash, the cause of which remains under investigation. Zia's death left the government of Pakistan severely weakened, at least temporarily.

Following the invasion of Afghanistan by Soviet troops in 1979, areas of Pakistan bordering on Afghanistan were flooded with Afghan refugees, eventually numbering more than two million. Pakistan, with American and Chinese support, gave shelter and substantial assistance to the various Afghan anti-Soviet resistance movements.

Pakistan's economy is largely agricultural; wheat, rice, and tobacco are grown in the Indus Valley, while pastoralism predominates in the drier areas of the north and west. Urban areas support considerable industry, including tex-

tiles, food processing, and manufacturing. Pakistan remains a major recipient of American foreign aid.

Panama
Republic of Panama
Geography Location: southern end of Central American isthmus. **Boundaries:** Caribbean Sea to N, Colombia to E, Pacific Ocean to S, Costa Rica to W. **Total land area:** 29,762 sq. mi. (77,082 sq km). **Coastline:** 1,546 mi. (2,490 km). **Comparative area:** slightly smaller than South Carolina. **Land use:** 6% arable land; 2% permanent crops; 15% meadows and pastures; 54% forest and woodland; 23% other; includes negl. % irrigated. **Major cities:** (1980 census) Panamá (Panama City—capital) 389,172; Colón 59,840; David 50,016.

People Population: 2,323,622 (1988). **Nationality:** noun—Panamanian(s); adjective—Panamanian. **Ethnic groups:** 70% mestizo, 14% West Indian, 10% white, 6% Indian. **Languages:** Spanish (official), 14% speak English as native tongue; many Panamanians bilingual. **Religions:** over 90% Roman Catholic, 6% Protestant.

Government Type: centralized republic. **Independence:** Nov. 3, 1903 (from Colombia); became independent from Spain Nov. 28, 1821. **Constitution:** Oct. 11, 1972, with major reforms adopted in Apr. 1983. **National holiday:** Independence Day, Nov. 3. **Head of government:** Manuel Solis Palma, president (since Feb. 1988). **Structure:** under Apr. 1983 reforms, president, two vice presidents, and 67-member Legislative Assembly are elected by popular vote for five-year terms; nine Supreme Court justices and nine alternates serve 10-year terms; two justices and their alternates are replaced every other December by presidential nomination and legislative confirmation.

Economy Monetary unit: balboa. **Budget:** (1986) **income:** $1,034 mil.; **expend.:** $1,510 mil. **GDP:** $5.1 bil., $2,290 per capita (1986). **Chief crops:** bananas, rice, sugarcane, coffee, corn; self-sufficient in basic foods; illegal producer of cannabis for international drug trade. **Livestock:** cattle, pigs. **Natural resources:** copper, mahogany forests, shrimp. **Major industries:** food processing, beverages, petroleum products. **Labor force:** 719,000 (1986); 29% agriculture, hunting, and fishing; 28% government and community services; 15% commerce, restaurants and hotels; 10% manufacturing and mining; shortage of skilled labor, but oversupply of unskilled labor; 20% unemployed (1986 est.). **Exports:** $326.6 mil. (f.o.b., 1986); bananas, shrimp, sugar, coffee, clothing. **Imports:** $1.25 bil. (c.i.f., 1986); petroleum products, manufactured goods, machinery and transportation equipment, chemicals, foodstuffs. **Major trading partners:** (1984) **exports:** 59% U.S., 17% Central America and Caribbean, 16% EC, 8% other; **imports:** 30% U.S., 19% Central America and Caribbean, 10% Mexico, 8% Japan, 8% Venezuela.

Intl. Orgs. FAO, G-77, IAEA, IBRD, ICAO, IDA, IFAD, IFC, ILO, IMF, INTELSAT, INTERPOL, ITU, NAM, OAS, UN, UNESCO,

UPU, WHO, WMO.

The Spanish first arrived in what is now Panama in 1501. Vasco Nuñez de Balboa returned in 1510, and Pedro Arias Dávila founded the City of Panama in 1519. Panama became attached to the viceroyalty of New Granada after 1739 and left the Spanish empire with the rest of New Granada in 1821, becoming a part of Gran Colombia. The first canal company proposing the construction of a transisthmian passageway was formed in 1825–26. The completion of a U.S.-financed railway from Colón to Panama City by 1855 enhanced Panama's importance as a transoceanic passage.

Panamanian nationalists waged a "War of a Thousand Days" against the Bogotá government between 1899 and 1902. In 1903 Panama gained independence from Colombia with U.S. complicity. Within a month Panamanian officials accepted an agreement with the United States that created a canal zone under the control of the U.S. government "in perpetuity," and the Panama Canal was completed and opened in 1914.

Panama experienced protectorate status under U.S. control after independence insofar as the United States "guaranteed the independence" of Panama. The United States explicitly upheld its right of unilateral military intervention in Panama when in 1918 it sent troops there without the permission of the Panamanian government. The 1936 Hull-Alvaro Treaty eliminated protectorate status, and the United States dropped its claim to a right of intervention in the cities of Panama and Colón.

In 1968 a power struggle between Pres. Arnulfo Arias and the Panamanian National Guard led to the ouster of the president. A National Guard junta took control of the government, and Col. (later Gen.) Omar Torrijos Herrera became the ruler of the country the following year. In 1972 a new Assembly under Torrijos's control offered him the title of Jefe Maximo (chief executive) in addition to drafting a new constitution for the country. Torrijos constructed a populist following through the creation of housing projects, a new labor code, an agrarian reform and an increase in tax rates imposed on foreign banana-interests.

The Panamanian government and the United States concluded a new canal treaty in 1977 the key provisions of which included integration of the Canal Zone with the rest of Panamanian territory and full Panamanian control of the canal in the year 2000. In 1981 Omar Torrijos died in an air accident.

A crisis in Panamanian-U.S. relations occurred in 1988 when the head of the Panamanian military and de facto ruler of the country, Gen. Manuel Noriega, was indicted in the United States on narcotics charges. Gen. Noriega refused to succumb to U.S. demands for his resignation. When Panama's Pres. Eric Arturo Delvalle ordered Noriega to resign, the general refused. Pres. Delvalle was forced to go into hiding, and Manuel Solis Palma replaced him in the presidency. The United States responded by freezing Panamanian assets in the United States, thus creating a severe currency shortage (Panama uses the U.S. dollar as currency) and associated economic hardship.

Papua New Guinea

Geography **Location:** eastern section of island of New Guinea and about 600 smaller islands, including Bismarck Archipelago (mainly New Britain, New Ireland, and Manus) and northern part of Solomon Islands (mainly Bougainville and Buka). **Boundaries:** Bismarck Sea to N, Solomon Sea to E, NE extremity of Australia to S, and Indonesia to W. **Total land area:** 178,704 sq. mi. (462,840 sq km). **Coastline:** 3,202 mi. (5,152 km). **Comparative area:** slightly larger than California. **Land use:** negl. % arable land; 1% permanent crops; negl. % meadows and pastures; 71% forest and woodland; 28% other. **Major cities:** (1987 est.) Port Moresby (administrative capital) 145,300.

People **Population:** 3,649,503 (1988). **Nationality:** noun—Papua New Guinean(s); adjective—Papua New Guinean. **Ethnic groups:** predominantly Melanesian and Papuan; some Negrito, Micronesian, and Polynesian. **Languages:** 715 indigenous languages; English spoken by 1–2%, pidgin English widespread, Motu spoken in Papua region. **Religions:** over half of population nominally Christian (490,000 Catholic, 320,000 Lutheran and other Protestant sects); remainder indigenous beliefs.

Government **Type:** independent parliamentary state within Commonwealth recognizing Elizabeth II as head of state. **Independence:** Sept. 16, 1975 (from UN trusteeship under Australian administration). **Constitution:** Sept. 16, 1975. **National holiday:** Independence Day, Sept. 16. **Heads of government:** Sir Ignatius Kilage, governor-general (since Mar. 1989); Rabbie Namaliu, prime minister (since July 1988). **Structure:** executive—National Executive Council; legislature—House of Assembly (109 members); judiciary—court system consists of Supreme Court of Papua New Guinea and various inferior courts (district courts, local courts, children's courts, wardens' courts).

Economy **Monetary unit:** kina. **Budget:** (1987) **income:** $870 mil.; **expend.:** $892 mil. **GDP:** $2.4 bil., $700 per capita (1985). **Chief crops:** copra, cocoa, coffee, rubber, oil palm. **Livestock:** pigs, cattle, goats, chickens, sheep. **Natural resources:** gold, copper, silver, natural gas, timber. **Major industries:** copra crushing, oil-palm processing, plywood processing. **Labor force:** 1.66 mil.; 732,806 in salaried employment (1980); 54% agriculture, 25% government. **Exports:** $1,033 mil. (f.o.b., 1986); 39% gold, 23% coffee, 16% copper, 7% forest products, 6% cocoa. **Imports:** $978 mil. (1986); 30% machinery and equipment, 19% food and live animals, 16% fuels and lubricants, 7% chemicals, 9% other manufactured goods. **Major trading partners:** (1985) **exports:** 39% W. Germany, 23% Japan, 10% Australia, 8% UK, 5% Spain; **imports:** 41% Australia, 15% Singapore, 14% Japan, 9% U.S., 5% New Zealand.

Intl. Orgs. Commonwealth, FAO, G-77, GATT (de facto), IBRD, ICAO, IDA, IFAD, IFC, ILO, IMF, IMO, INTELSAT, INTERPOL, ITU, UN, UNESCO, UPU, WHO, WMO.

New Guinea, the world's second-largest island (after Greenland), was settled many thousands of years ago by waves of Papuan and Melanesian migrants. In isolation a society developed characterized by large numbers of linguistically diverse and mutually hostile tribes of hunters and small cultivators. In the 19th century, the island was divided by European powers into three colonial areas: Dutch New Guinea, the western half of the island (now the Indonesian province of Irian Jaya); the German Territory of New Guinea, including the northeastern quadrant and also the Bismarck Archipelago (New Britain, New Ireland, and smaller islands) and part of the North Solomon Islands, notably Bougainville Island; and British New Guinea in the southeast. The German sector was occupied by Australia in 1914 and administered under a League of Nations Mandate after World War I.

Japanese attempts to occupy New Guinea in 1942 met with only partial success. In a series of counteroffensives, the Allies regained control over the entire island by mid-1944.

Beginning in 1949 the former German and British colonies were administered jointly by Australia under a UN mandate. The territories were made self-governing in 1973 and achieved full independence as Papua New Guinea on Sept. 16, 1975. The nation maintains close ties with Australia. Relations are strained with Indonesia, which accuses Papua New Guinea of giving shelter to an Irian Jaya liberation movement.

Papua New Guinea's economy remains largely in the stage of small-scale agriculture. Coffee, copra, and cocoa are exported, along with timber and some minerals.

The government of Prime Minister Paias Wingti, elected in 1985, has been shaken by a severe crime wave in Port Moresby, attributed largely to alcoholism and urban detribalization.

Paraguay
Republic of Paraguay

Geography **Location:** landlocked country in central South America. **Boundaries:** Bolivia to N, Brazil to E, Argentina to S and W. **Total land area:** 157,048 sq. mi. (406,752 sq km). **Coastline:** none. **Comparative area:** slightly smaller than California. **Land use:** 20% arable land; 1% permanent crops; 39% meadows and pastures; 35% forest and woodland; 5% other; includes negl. % irrigated. **Major cities:** (1982 census) Asunción (capital) 455,517; Pedro Juan Caballero 37,331; Puerto Presidente Stroessner 36,676; Encarnación 27,632; Villarrica 21,203.

People **Population:** 4,386,024 (1988). **Nationality:** noun—Paraguayan(s); adjective—Paraguayan. **Ethnic groups:** 95% mestizo, 5% white and Indian. **Languages:** Spanish (official), Guaraní. **Religions:** 97% Roman Catholic, Mennonite and other Protestant denominations.

Government **Type:** republic under authoritarian rule. **Independence:** May 14, 1811 (from Spain). **Constitution:** Aug. 25, 1967. **National holiday:** Independence Days, May 14-15. **Heads of government:** Gen. Andrés

Rodriguez, president (since May 1989). **Structure:** president heads executive; bicameral legislature (Senate, Chamber of Deputies); judiciary headed by Supreme Court.

Economy **Monetary unit:** guaraní. **Budget:** (1986 est.) **income:** $620 mil.; **expend.:** $762 mil. **GDP:** $3.8 bil., $920 per capita (1986). **Chief crops:** oilseed, soybeans, cotton, wheat, manioc, sweet potatoes, tobacco, corn, rice, sugarcane; self-sufficient in most foods; illegal producer of cannabis for international drug trade. **Livestock:** cattle, pigs, sheep, horses, goats. **Natural resources:** iron ore, manganese, limestone, hydropower, timber. **Major industries:** meat packing, oilseed crushing, milling. **Labor force:** 1.3 mil. (1986); 44% agriculture, 34% industry and commerce, 18% services. **Exports:** $316 mil. (f.o.b., 1986); cotton, oilseeds, meat products, tobacco, timber. **Imports:** $578 mil. (c.i.f., 1986); fuels and lubricants, machinery and motors, motor vehicles, beverages and tobacco, foodstuffs. **Major trading partners:** (1986) **exports:** 26% Brazil, 13% Netherlands, 11% Argentina, 11% Switzerland, 7% U.S.; **imports:** 33% Brazil, 16% Argentina, 13% U.S., 7% Algeria, 6% Japan.

Intl. Orgs. FAO, G-77, IAEA, IBRD, ICAO, IDA, IFAD, IFC, ILO, IMF, INTELSAT, INTERPOL, ITU, OAS, UN, UNESCO, UPU, WHO, WMO.

When Europeans arrived in what is now Paraguay in the early 16th century, they encountered various groups of semisedentary and nonsedentary indigenous peoples. As was always the case, the Spanish found it easier to establish relations with agriculturally based Indians. They therefore entered into alliances with the Tupian semisedentary Guaraní against the nomadic Guaycuru Indians in the west of the region. Asunción, founded in 1537, soon became little more than a Spanish defense outpost against the Portuguese and a trading stopover between the silver mines of Potosí and Buenos Aires.

From early in the 17th century, the Jesuits established an extensive network of missions in the southern portion of the colony, and a rivalry grew between the Jesuits and the elites of Asunción over who would determine the colony's social and economic structure. The isolation of the settlers from the mainstream of Spanish colonial society combined with the lack of valuable resources led to the evolution of a relatively egalitarian social structure in Spanish imperial terms. The political elite of Asunción deposed Spanish authority in 1811, and Paraguayan independence was declared in 1813.

Stable authoritarian rule marked the period from independence until 1870. José Gaspar Rodríguez de Francia was declared ruler for life in 1816 and remained in power until his death in 1840. A period of political turmoil followed the death of Francia but was resolved in the election of Carlos Antonio López in 1844; in 1857 he was named president for life. López chose his son Francisco Solano López to succeed him in office in 1862. Francisco Solano intervened in a Brazilian attempt to control the fate of Uruguay, beginning the Paraguayan War, or the War of the Triple Alliance, in 1865. Paraguay found itself fighting Brazil, Argentina, and Uruguay in a bloody conflict that lasted until Paraguay's defeat and occupation in 1870. The war was catastrophic for Paraguay, reducing the population from 450,000 in 1865 to 220,000 by 1870. Almost the entire male population of the country was wiped out, and Paraguay lost 60,000 square miles of territory while being saddled with a war debt of 19 million gold pesos ($200,000,000). The Brazilian government later dropped the unrealistic payment demand.

The victorious powers imposed a constitutional structure in 1870 that was alien to the country's political tradition, resulting in extreme political instability in which the Constitution was virtually ignored. After the war the Colorado and Liberal parties developed, although the real political distinctions were not so much party-based as dependent on individuals and families. Colorado-party Gen. Bernardino Caballero, backed by Brazil, was the power behind the scenes of frequent changes in government personnel between 1874 and 1904. The Liberals, with the backing of Argentina, captured power in 1904 and held on to it until 1936.

After 18 years of authoritarian rule by a number of military officers, Gen. Alfredo Stroessner, with the backing of Colorado-party factions, began his rule in 1954. Stroessner held power until 1989, when Gen. Andrés Rodríguez overthrew him.

Peru
Republic of Peru

Geography Location: western coast of South America. **Boundaries:** Ecuador and Colombia to N, Brazil and Bolivia to E, Chile to S, South Pacific Ocean to W. **Total land area:** 496,225 sq. mi. (1,285,216 sq. km). **Coastline:** 1,546 mi. (2,414 km). **Comparative area:** slightly smaller than Alaska. **Land use:** 3% arable land; negl. % permanent crops; 21% meadows and pastures; 55% forest and woodland; 21% other; includes 1% irrigated. **Major cities:** (1985 est.) Lima (capital) 5,330,800; Arequipa 531,829; Callao 515,200; Trujillo 438,709; Chiclayo 347,702.

People Population: 21,269,074 (1988). **Nationality:** noun—Peruvian(s); adjective—Peruvian. **Ethnic groups:** 45% Indian, 37% mestizo, 15% white, 3% black, Japanese, Chinese, and other. **Languages:** Spanish and Quechua (official), Aymara. **Religions:** predominantly Roman Catholic.

Government Type: republic. **Independence:** July 28, 1821 (from Spain). **Constitution:** July 28, 1980; often referred to as 1979 Constitution because constituent assembly met in 1979, but Constitution actually took effect following year; reestablished civilian government with popularly elected president and bicameral legislature. **National holiday:** Independence Day, July 28. **Heads of government:** Alan Garcia Pérez, president (since July 1985); Armando Villanueva-del-Campo, prime minister (since 1988). **Structure:** executive;

bicameral legislature (Senate, Chamber of Deputies); judicial.

Economy Monetary unit: inti. **Budget:** (1986) **income:** $3.0 bil.; **expend.:** $3.4 bil. **GDP:** $19.8 bil., $980 per capita. **Chief crops:** wheat, potatoes, beans, rice, barley, coffee, cotton, sugarcane; imports wheat, meat, lard and oils, rice, corn; illegal producer of coca for international drug trade. **Livestock:** sheep, cattle, pigs, goats, horses. **Natural resources:** copper, silver, gold, petroleum, timber. **Major industries:** mining of metals, petroleum, fishing. **Labor force:** 6.8 mil. (1986); 44% government and other services, 37% agriculture, 19% industry; 8.2% unemployment; 51.4% underemployment (1984). **Exports:** $2.5 bil. (f.o.b., 1986); fish meal, cotton, sugar, coffee, copper. **Imports:** $2.8 bil. (f.o.b., 1986); foodstuffs, machinery, transport equipment, iron and steel semimanufactures, chemicals. **Major trading partners:** (1986) **exports:** 28% U.S., 23% EC, 11% Latin America, 11% Japan, 5% UK; **imports:** 20% U.S., 17% Latin America, 14% EC, 7% Japan, 7% W. Germany.

Intl. Orgs. FAO, G-77, GATT, IAEA, IBRD, ICAO, IDA, IFAD, IFC, ILO, IMF, IMO, INTELSAT, INTERPOL, ITU, NAM, OAS, UN, UNESCO, UPU, WHO, WMO.

Peru was the site of the civilization of the Inca empire before the arrival of Europeans. The Incas had extended their control over most of the Andean region by the late 15th century. The civilization was advanced in terms of its ability to provide for the welfare of its subjects and was in possession of sophisticated knowledge in a number of fields, including medicine. By the time of the arrival of the Spanish conqueror Francisco Pizarro in 1532, the empire seems already to have been in decline, and a combination of plague and civil war in the decade prior to the appearance of Europeans no doubt made the empire more vulnerable to Spanish conquest. Despite Spanish victories, Inca resistance to Spanish domination was not effectively quelled until the execution of Tupac Amarú in 1571. As was the case in general with European contact with indigenous populations in the Americas, European-borne diseases such as smallpox and measles devastated the Indian population of the region.

Because of the great wealth of precious metals discovered by the Spanish and the adaptability of a sedentary indigenous civilization to the imposition of Spanish imperial control, Peru quickly became a major focal point of Spanish colonialism in the Indies. The Spaniards considered Cuzco unsuitable as a central administrative city because of its high elevation; thus they founded Lima in 1535, along the Peruvian coastal lowlands. The viceroyalty of Peru, established in 1544, originally served as the political and administrative nerve center of Spanish colonization of South America. For nearly two centuries, Lima was the seat of power and wealth for the whole region. It is understandable that a political center of such importance would become the focal point of entrenched imperial interests; it was partially this development that accounted for the lack of a successful local independence group in Lima.

Peru was "liberated" by Simón Bolívar and José de San Martín in 1821. Bolívar's army—the majority not Peruvians—finally defeated the royalist forces at the battles of Junín and Ayacucho, thus achieving definitive separation of Peru from the Spanish empire.

Peru failed to establish a stable political order for 40 years after its independence. During this period the presidency changed hands 35 times, and the country generated at least 15 different constitutions. Only four of the presidents of the period were constitutionally chosen, and the vast majority of the chief executives were military figures. In 1829 Peru tried and failed to annex Ecuador; in the 1830s an attempt at political federation between Peru and Bolivia collapsed with the Chilean invasion of 1839.

A political movement in favor of civilian rule, the Civilistas, began to organize by the 1860s. Chile defeated Peru in the War of the Pacific (1879–83), and Chileans occupied Lima and its port city of Callao for two years. The Peruvian government was deeply in debt after the war, resulting in the loss of ownership of much of Peru's infrastructure and natural resources to foreigners.

Peru experienced a period of civilian leadership between 1895 and 1930. Pres. Augusto B. Leguía (1908–12, 1919–30) extended his rule in an extraconstitutional manner until 1930. Col. Luis Sánchez Cerro seized power in 1930 and ruled until his assassination in 1933. Gen. Oscar Benavides succeeded Cerro and managed to restore confidence in the economy. In 1939 civilian banker Manuel Prado was elected to the presidency, and the military allowed him to complete his term in office, which expired in 1945. During Prado's administration, Peru went to war with Ecuador and was victorious, seizing a great deal of its neighbor's territory.

Víctor Raúl Haya de la Torre founded Peru's most prominent political party, the American Popular Revolutionary Alliance (APRA), in 1924. As initiated, the party put forward an "antiimperialist" platform aiming at nationalization of land and reconstruction of society in favor of oppressed people. Haya de la Torre was apparently fraudulently deprived of a presidential electoral victory in 1931. The following year members of his movement seized Trujillo and killed some military personnel in the process. By way of revenge, the army massacred 6,000 Apristas (APRA supporters) when it retook the city. The result was a continuing enmity between the Peruvian armed forces and the APRA party lasting until the 1980s. Although APRA clearly had majority support from the Peruvian electorate in the intervening period, the party was not allowed to take power directly until the election of incumbent Pres. Alan García Peréz in 1985.

The Peruvian military, led by Gen. Juan Velasco Alvarado, seized power in 1968 and proceeded to embark upon a nationalist course of reform that included the nationalization of Standard Oil's International Petroleum Company holdings. The Peruvian military took steps to restructure economic and political power in the country by joining the Andean Pact and undermining the power of the traditional agricultural elite in the country. This last initiative led to a permanent shift in power relations among Peru's contending social groups. By the late 1970s, however, the military government began to move toward the Right, but only after it had successfully sponsored an agrarian reform that mobilized peasant sectors of the population and changed the relations between landlord and peasant in Peru.

The presidency of Peru returned to civilian leadership under the administration of Fernando Belaúnde Terry (1980–85). In 1985, for the first time since its founding, the military allowed the APRA presidential candidate, Alan García Pérez, to take office. García Pérez made it clear that Peru would devote no more than 10 percent of the country's export earnings toward payment of Peru's huge outstanding foreign debt. The new president was enormously popular during his first years in office, but the nagging problems plaguing the country soon undermined his public support. These problems included a growing insurgency sponsored by the Sendero Luminoso ("Shining Path") Maoist guerrillas and runaway inflation that has yet to be brought under control.

Philippines
Republic of the Philippines

Geography Location: archipelago of some 7,100 islands and islets lying about 500 mi. (800 km) off southeastern coast of Asia; spans about 1,100 mi. (2,800 km) from N to S at longest extent and about 650 mi. (1,684 km) from W to E at widest point; main islands are Luzon in N and Mindanao in S, accounting for 66% of country's land area. **Boundaries:** Luzon Strait to N, Phillipine Sea to E, Celebes Sea to S, Sulu Sea to SW, and South China Sea to W. **Total land area:** 115,831 sq. mi. (300,000 sq km). **Coastline:** 22,554 mi. (36,289 km). **Comparative area:** slightly larger than Arizona. **Land use:** 26% arable land; 11% permanent crops; 4% meadows and pastures; 40% forest and woodland; 19% other; includes 5% irrigated. **Major cities:** (1980 census) Manila (capital) 1,630,485; Quezon City 1,165,865; Davao City 610,375; Cebu City 490,281; Caloocan City 467,816.

People Population: 63,199,307 (1988). **Nationality:** noun—Filipino(s); adjective—Philippine. **Ethnic groups:** 91.5% Christian Malay, 4% Muslim Malay, 1.5% Chinese, 3% other. **Languages:** Pilipino (based on Tagalog) and English (both official). **Religions:** 83% Roman Catholic, 9% Protestant, 5% Muslim, 3% Buddhist and other.

Government Type: republic. **Independence:** July 4, 1946 (from U.S.). **Constitution:** Feb. 2, 1987, effective Feb. 11, 1987. **National holiday:** Independence Day, June 12. **Heads of government:** Corazon Aquino, president (since Feb. 1986). **Structure:** constitution provides for presidential form of government with directly elected president and vice president and U.S.-style bicameral legislature (24-seat Senate and 200-member House of Representatives); judicial branch headed by Supreme Court with

descending authority in three-tiered system of local, regional trial, and intermediate appellate courts.

Economy Monetary unit: peso. **Budget:** (1987 est.) *income:* $4.9 bil.; *expend.:* $5.9 bil. **GDP:** $33.1 bil., $540 per capita (1986). **Chief crops:** rice, corn, coconut, sugarcane, bananas; illegal producer of cannabis for international drug trade. **Livestock:** pigs, buffalo, goats, cattle, horses. **Natural resources:** timber, crude oil, nickel, cobalt, silver. **Major industries:** textiles, pharmaceuticals, chemicals. **Labor force:** 22.9 mil. (1987); 47.0% agriculture, 20% industry and commerce, 13.5% services, 10% government; 11% official unemployment rate, much underemployment. **Exports:** $5.2 bil. (f.o.b., 1987); coconut products, sugar, logs and lumber, copper concentrates, bananas. **Imports:** $6.2 bil. (f.o.b., 1987 est.); petroleum, industrial equipment, wheat. **Major trading partners:** (1986) *exports:* 36% U.S., 18% Japan; *imports:* 25% U.S., 17% Japan.

Intl. Orgs. ASEAN, Colombo Plan, FAO, G-77, GATT, IAEA, IBRD, ICAO, IDA, IFAD, IFC, ILO, IMF, IMO, INTELSAT, INTERPOL, ITU, UN, UNESCO, UPU, WHO, WIPO, WMO.

The Philippines were anciently settled by various Malayan peoples in several waves of migration from Southeast Asia. Tribal societies coexisted with petty principalities that had trade links to China, the East Indies, and countries in the Indian Ocean. The Philippines were visited by Magellan in 1521 and by other Spanish expeditions thereafter; Spanish conquest of the islands began in 1564. The Spanish colonial capital at Manila was founded in 1571 and became a key transit point for trade between Mexico and the Far East. Under Spanish rule a majority of Filipinos became Christian except in the southwestern islands, which remained Muslim. The Spanish period as a whole was marked by a torpid colonial administration and a gradual rise in the power and wealth of the Catholic church.

In the late 19th century, a nationalist movement led by José Rizal gained a wide following. In 1896 an armed uprising began, led by Emilio Aguinaldo. The 1898 victory of Adm. George Dewey at the Battle of Manila Bay during the Spanish-American War led Spain to cede the Philippines to the United States in return for a payment of $20 million. Expecting immediate independence with U.S. support, Aguinaldo declared the islands a republic. When this was not recognized by the United States, Aguinaldo led a new war for independence, which was bloodily suppressed by American troops in a six-year campaign, 1899–1905.

American policy in the Philippines combined military control with an expressed desire to encourage home rule leading to eventual independence. In 1935 the Commonwealth of the Philippines was established, with Manuel Quezon as its first president, beginning what was conceived of as a 10-year period of controlled autonomy leading to full independence on July 4, 1946. In November 1941, Quezon was reelected to the presidency. On Dec. 8,

1941, Japan attacked Manila and destroyed the American bases there. American and Filipino troops, after weeks of fierce fighting, evacuated the islands in March 1942. Quezon went into exile in America. The battle to recapture the Philippines began with the Battle of Leyte Gulf in October 1944 and was completed by July 1945.

In April 1946, Manuel Roxas was elected president of the Commonwealth. Independence came as scheduled on July 4 of that year, with the United States retaining military bases by treaty and establishing a special economic relationship with the Philippines. The leftist Hukbalahap Rebellion, originally a partisan campaign against the Japanese, caused severe difficulties for the new nation until it was finally defeated in military campaigns led by Ramon Magsaysay. Magsaysay was elected to the presidency in November 1953; the last Huk leaders surrendered in 1954.

The early years of independence were marked by some economic development, but also great economic inequality. Most land was held by huge estates, and the economy depended primarily on plantation crops (sugar, copra), mining, and timber. Villagers fleeing the rural subsistence economy poured into the cities, leading to huge slums and a climate of urban poverty and violence. Many Filipinos emigrated to America.

In 1966 Ferdinand Marcos was elected president on a reform platform. Overwhelmed in the early 1970s by demonstrations, a new leftist guerrilla movement, and a separatist rebellion by Islamic Moros in Mindanao, Marcos declared martial law on Sept. 21, 1972. On Jan. 17, 1973, Marcos promulgated a new constitution giving unprecedented power to the presidency. His wife, Imelda, began to wield considerable influence, and the climate of unrest, poverty, and corruption worsened throughout the 1970s. Martial law was lifted, however, on Jan. 17, 1981, and Marcos was reelected to a new six-year term as president.

The airport assassination of opposition leader Benigno Aquino on his return to the Philippines on Aug. 21, 1983, led to a new phase in opposition to Marcos's rule. Marcos retained a majority in elections to the National Assembly in 1984, amid widespread reports of electoral fraud. In a bitterly contested presidential election in February 1986, Marcos was officially declared the winner over Corazon Aquino, widow of Benigno Aquino. Mrs. Aquino also declared herself the winner, and her supporters took to the streets in massive anti-Marcos demonstrations. Deserted by key supporters in the military, church, and middle class, Marcos fled the country on Feb. 25, 1986. Mrs. Aquino took office pledging land reform, a new constitution, and a commission to recover the corruptly gained wealth of the Marcos family.

Under Pres. Aquino the situation in the Philippines has remained unsettled. Her former ally, Vice Pres. Salvadore Laurel, has formed an opposition party. A key military supporter from February 1986, Juan Ponce Enrile, has been implicated in several pro-Marcos coup attempts. Military and political measures aimed at putting down the Communist insurrection have yielded mixed results. Corruption remains widespread in politics and the economy. Progress in drawing up a new constitution and in instituting land reform has been slow. The economy of the Philippines continues to be dependent on U.S. and international assistance. In October 1988 an agreement was reached with the United States that clarified terms of American leases on military bases in the Philippines through 1991. Negotiations on the post-1991 renewal of the leases for those bases have created significant tensions in U.S.-Philippine relations.

Poland
Polish People's Republic

Geography Location: eastern Europe. **Boundaries:** Baltic Sea to N, USSR to E, Czechoslovakia to S, E. Germany to W. **Total land area:** 120,727 sq. mi. (312,683 sq km). **Coastline:** 305 mi. (491 km). **Comparative area:** slightly smaller than New Mexico. **Land use:** 48% arable land; 1% permanent crops; 13% meadows and pastures; 29% forest and woodland; 9% other; includes negl. % irrigated. **Major cities:** (1986) Warszawa (Warsaw; capital) 1,664,700; Lodz 847,400; Krakow (Cracow) 744,000; Wroclaw 640,000; Poznan 578,100.

People Population: 37,958,420 (1988). **Nationality:** noun—Pole(s); adjective—Polish. **Ethnic groups:** 98.7% Polish, 0.6% Ukrainian, 0.5% Byelorussian, less than 0.05% Jewish. **Languages:** Polish. **Religions:** 95% Roman Catholic (about 75% practicing), 5% Uniate, Russian Orthodox, Protestant, and other.

Government Type: communist state. **Independence:** N.A. **Constitution:** July 22, 1952. **National holiday:** National Liberation Day, July 22. **Heads of government:** Tadeusz Mazowiecki, prime minister (since Sept. 1989; noncommunist); Army Gen. Wojciech Jaruzelski, president (since 1988). **Structure:** executive, unicameral legislature (Sejm), judicial systems dominated by parallel Communist party apparatus.

Economy Monetary unit: zloti. **Budget:** N.A. **GNP:** $259.8 bil., $6,903 per capita (1986). **Chief crops:** grain, sugar beets, oilseed, potatoes; exporter of livestock products and sugar; importer of grains; self-sufficient for minimum requirements. **Livestock:** chickens, pigs, cattle, sheep, ducks. **Natural resources:** coal, sulfur, copper, natural gas, silver. **Major industries:** machine building, iron and steel, extractive industries. **Labor force:** 18.6 mil. (1986); 44% industry and commerce, 30% agriculture, 11% services (1985). **Exports:** $21.7 bil. (f.o.b., 1986); 49.3% machinery and equipment; 23.3% fuels, minerals, and metals; 13.0% manufactured consumer goods; 9.7% agricultural and forestry products; 4.7% other. **Imports:** $21.2 bil. (f.o.b., 1986); 37.5% fuels, minerals, and metals; 32.9% machinery and equipment; 13.1% agricultural and forestry products; 9.2% manufactured consumer goods; 7.3% other. **Major trading partners:** $34.6 bil. (1985); 61% communist countries, 32% developed countries, 7% developing countries.

Intl. Orgs. CMEA, FAO, GATT, IAEA, ICAO, ILO, IMO, ITU, UN, UNESCO, UPU, Warsaw Pact, WHO, WIPO, WMO.

The Slavic people known as Polonians accepted Christianity in the second half of the 10th century, during the reign of Duke Mieszko, whose close relationship with the papacy prevented the Byzantine Empire from absorbing Poland. A strong and united Polish kingdom existed under the Piast dynasty until 1370. With that dynasty's extinction, the Anjou king of Hungary succeeded to the throne, followed by his daughter Jadwiga, who in 1386 married the grand duke of Lithuania. Thus was formed the great Commonwealth of Poland-Lithuania. Cracow became one of the great cities of late medieval Europe.

With the extinction of the Jagiellonian line in 1572, the monarchy became elective. With a large nobility, equaling about 10 percent of the population, the monarchy grew weak, and Poland increasingly was subject to foreign intervention. The rise of the expansionist powers of Sweden, Prussia, Russia, and Austria came in part at the expense of the Poles. Jan Sobieski (1624–96), who ruled Poland as John III, saved Vienna from the Turks and briefly revived the Polish monarchy, but Polish royal power ended with his death. In a series of partitions in 1772, 1793, and 1795, Poland was dismembered and finally obliterated as a state.

Napoleon revived a Polish national entity with the Grand Duchy of Warsaw; with Napoleon's fall, the Congress of Vienna re-created a Kingdom of Poland in 1815, under the rule of the czar of Russia. After 1830 Poland was subjected to systematic Russification.

The fall of Russia in World War I led to Poland's revival. The Lithuanian Socialist Jósef Pilsudski led Poland in war against the new Bolshevik government of Russia until, in the 1921 Treaty of Riga, Poland emerged with its boundaries restored to approximately those after the partition of 1793. It was ethnically about 70 percent Polish, a triumph for Polish nationalism but the end of Pilsudski's dream of a federation of northeastern Europe. Poland also had the largest Jewish population of any country in Europe.

With a strong legislature and a weak president, the new state seemed to Pilsudski too weak for its own defense. He assumed dictatorial powers in 1926 and ruled by fiat until his death in 1935. After his death a weak parliamentary government was controlled by military officers; the tentative revival of republicanism was halted by Hitler's aggression in 1939.

Like other countries of east-central Europe, Poland was primarily an agricultural country, with grains, sugar beets, and potatoes its principal crops. The postwar republic attempted land reform with some success; about 750,000 new private farm holdings were created by 1938. Mining—of coal and copper—was the principal traditional industrial activity in the 20th century, supplemented by extraction of natural gas. In the mid-1930s shipbuilding and railroad construction led the way toward a modern economy.

World War II commenced in September 1939, with attacks on Poland by Germany and Russia. The war brought severe destruction to Poland and the extermination of virtually its entire Jewish population. A government-in-exile was established in London, but it was prevented by the Russians from returning to the war-ravaged country in 1945, because in 1943 Russia had broken relations with it (when it dared to request a Red Cross investigation into the murder of 14,000 Polish officers whose bodies were discovered in Katyn Forest), establishing a puppet government in Lublin in 1944. In August 1944 the Red Army paused in its western advance on the outskirts of Warsaw, permitting the Nazis to obliterate the Polish Home Army, which had risen in revolt in anticipation of its liberation. On Jan. 1, 1945, the USSR recognized the Lublin regime as Poland's provisional government.

By the time of the Allied Powers Conference in Yalta in February 1945, the Red Army was only 40 miles from Berlin and had total control of Poland. The Allies agreed to Stalin's proposal concerning the eastern boundary of Poland (allowing Russia to incorporate the eastern half of the country) and agreed that the government should be constituted from an enlargement of the Lublin regime. At Potsdam in August 1945, it was further agreed that Poland should absorb the eastern portion of Germany. Poland's borders were shifted approximately 200 miles westward from the prewar configuration, becoming once again those of the 10th century.

The free elections promised in the Yalta Agreement were postponed until 1947, by which time a Communist victory could be assured. In 1948 the Socialists were forcibly merged into the Communist party; in 1949 Premier Boleslaw Bierut requested that Soviet Gen. Konstantin Rokossovski be appointed minister of defense and commander in chief of the Polish army. In the same year, all cultural periodicals and all writers' and artists' associations were taken over by the Communist party.

But there was little collectivization of Polish agriculture or forced industrialization on the Stalinist model. Intellectuals, bolstered by the Catholic church (which deeply resented a 1953 law requiring government approval for appointment of bishops), questioned the regime with some boldness. In 1956 both Bierut and Party Secretary Minc died, and the party refused to reelect Rokossovski to the politburo. Wladislaw Gomulka was elected party chairman in October 1956. As Soviet warships sailed through the Baltic toward Poland, Nikita Khrushchev flew to Poland with a delegation of Soviet generals, where Gomulka assured them that Poland would follow the Soviet lead in foreign policy. Distracted by the crisis in Hungary, the Russians left Gomulka in power and even canceled Poland's debt and allowed the dismantling of agricultural collectives.

For a short time Gomulka permitted cultural and educational freedom, gaining the support of intellectuals and artists. But by 1958 he had reverted to Stalinist form, imposing controls and pursuing a somewhat anti-Semitic Polish nationalism. Gomulka ruled until 1970, when he was replaced as party secretary by Edward Gierek. But moral leadership within Poland had clearly passed to Stefan Cardinal Wyszynski, leader of the increasingly vocal Catholic church; Gierek was forced to improve relations with the church in order to maintain his own credibility as a national leader.

Gierek presided over a decade of increasing unrest, with rising prices and growing discontent. Polish exports of ham and furniture to the West under liberalized terms earned some hard currency but were insufficient to curb the rising national debt. The most significant event in Poland in the 1970s was the election of Karol Wojtyla, bishop of Krakow, as Pope John Paul II in October 1978. His visit to Poland in 1979 set the stage for the extraordinary events of the 1980s.

Gierek's austerity program of February 1980 sent meat prices soaring—60 percent in July alone. Strikes for wage adjustments, especially at the Lenin Shipyards in Gdansk, thrust into a position of national leadership the greatest statesman of postwar Poland, the shipyard worker Lech Walesa. Walesa was elected chairman of the national coordinating committee of independent labor unions, Solidarity. Solidarity demands went far beyond lower prices and higher wages; they included independent labor unions with the right to strike, freedom for political prisoners, and an end to censorship. In September 1980 Gierek resigned as party Secretary and was replaced by Stanislaw Kania.

By December, 40 independent trade unions had been formed, and a "rural Solidarity" movement was growing. In February 1981 Soviet Army Gen. Wojciech Jaruzelski was named prime minister, and in October he replaced Kania as party secretary. When in December Solidarity announced plans to hold a referendum on the Jaruzelski regime, martial law was declared; Solidarity leaders were arrested, all its activities were banned, and the right to strike was abolished. Solidarity's funds were impounded and turned over to the regime's National Trade Union Accord. The United States temporarily rescinded Poland's preferential trade status in protest.

The government was confident enough to release Walesa in 1982 and ended martial law in July 1983. Jaruzelski gave up the prime ministership in 1985 but remained party chairman and head of state. Still the movement continued. In July 1987 Pope John Paul II returned to Poland, met privately with Walesa, and, referring to Solidarity as a "model in the struggle for human rights," called for its legalization and criticized the Jaruzelski regime. When Jaruzelski called for a referendum on his austerity program of wage freezes and price hikes, Solidarity announced an electoral boycott, and the referendum was canceled.

In 1989 Poland again legalized Solidarity, agreeing to its participation as a political party in parliamentary elections. The elections of May 1989 gave an overwhelming popular majority to Solidarity, giving it control of the upper house; by prior arrangement the Communist party retained control of the lower house despite the popular vote. Jaruzelski recognized the legitimacy of the election and agreed to govern as head of a minority party. His call to Solidarity to join him in a coalition government was rejected, and by the middle of August, he felt it necessary to have a noncommunist-led government for the first time in 50 years.

Portugal
Portuguese Republic

Geography **Location:** western Europe, on Atlantic side of Iberian Peninsula; also includes two archipelagos in Atlantic Ocean, Azores and Madeira Islands. **Boundaries:** Spain to N and E, Atlantic Ocean to S and W. **Total land area:** 33,549 sq. mi. (92,072 sq km). **Coastline:** 1,114 mi. (1,793 km). **Comparative area:** slightly smaller than Indiana. **Land use:** 32% arable land; 6% permanent crops; 6% meadows and pastures; 40% forest and woodland; 16% other; includes 7% irrigated. **Major cities:** (1981 census) Lisboa (Lisbon, capital) 807,937; Porto (Oporto) 327,368; Amadora 95,518; Setubal 77,885; Coimbra 74,616.

People **Population:** 10,388,421 (1988). **Nationality:** noun—Portuguese (sing., pl.); adjective—Portuguese. **Ethnic groups:** homogeneous Mediterranean stock on mainland, in Azores, and on Madeira Islands; citizens of black African descent who immigrated during decolonization number less than 100,000. **Languages:** Portuguese. **Religions:** 97% Roman Catholic, 1% Protestant, 2% other.

Government **Type:** republic. **Independence:** N.A. **Constitution:** Apr. 25, 1976, revised Oct. 1982; new discussions on constitutional revisions began Oct. 1987. **National holiday:** Apr. 25. **Heads of government:** Mario Soàres, president (since Feb. 1986);. Anibal Cavaco Silva, prime minister (since Oct. 1985). **Structure:** executive—president and prime minister; legislative—unicameral legislature (popularly elected 250-seat Assembly of the Republic); judiciary—independent.

Economy **Monetary unit:** escudo. **Budget:** (1986) *income:* $11.2 bil.; *expend.:* $13.6 bil. **GNP:** $35.0 bil., $3,393 per capita (1987). **Chief crops:** generally underdeveloped; grains, potatoes, olives, grapes for wine; deficit foods—sugar, grain, meat, fish, oilseed. **Livestock:** sheep, pigs, cattle, goats, asses. **Natural resources:** fish, forests (cork), tungsten, iron ore, uranium ore, marble. **Major industries:** textiles, footwear, wood pulp, paper, cork. **Labor force:** 4.58 mil. (1987); 44% services, 34% industry, 22% agriculture; 8% unemployment. **Exports:** $7.2 bil. (f.o.b., 1986); cotton textiles, cork and cork products, canned fish, wine, timber and timber products. **Imports:** $9.6 bil. (c.i.f., 1986); petroleum, cotton, foodgrains, industrial machinery, iron and steel. **Major trading partners:** 63% EC, 7% U.S., 1% communist countries, 15% other developed countries, 14% developing countries.

Intl. Orgs. EC, EFTA, FAO, GATT, IAEA, IBRD, ICAO, IFAD, IFC, ILO, IMF, IMO, INTELSAT, INTERPOL, ITU, NATO, OECD, UN, UNESCO, UPU, WHO, WIPO, WMO.

Portugal traces its origins back to the warlike Lusitanian tribes of Roman times. The nation-state originated as a county of the Kingdom of Castile, reconquered from the Moors in the 11th century. Portugal won recognition as an independent kingdom in 1143, and conquered Lisbon four years later. In 1250 the Algarve was conquered, and by then Portugal had expanded to its modern boundaries. Except for the period 1580–1640, when it was ruled by the Spanish Habsburgs, the Portuguese dynasty maintained its independence into the 20th century.

Portuguese fisherman had probably frequented the Grand Banks from before the time of Columbus, and the nation's tradition of seafaring gave rise to a world empire in the 15th and 16th centuries. Prince Henry the Navigator (1394–1460) colonized the Azores and the Madeiras and sponsored voyages of exploration along the west coast of Africa. Under his successors, Portugal controlled the west African coast, the shores of the Indian Ocean, and large stretches of southern Asia, as well as, in the Western Hemisphere, Brazil. Yet the rise of the empires of Spain and the Netherlands quickly reduced the Portuguese to second-rank status, leaving only Macao, Goa, and Timor in Asia; Portuguese Guinea (Guinea Bissau), Mozambique, and Angola in Africa; and the great territory of Brazil in Latin America.

In the 19th century, a series of dynastic civil wars weakened the monarchy, allowing Britain to gain control of the country's foreign policy (in addition to the wine trade of Oporto, long in British hands). Brazil declared its independence in 1822.

In 1910 Portugal became the first kingdom in Europe to be transformed into a republic. But in the next 15 years, chaos ensued: eight presidents, 44 governments, and a near-collapse of the economy. Finally, the military stepped in and established a dictatorship, lasting until recent times. In 1928 the military installed a civilian dictator, a professor of economics, Antonio Salazar. A firm believer in law and order, he managed to control the turbulence of political life and made the escudo one of Europe's most stable currencies, yet he could do nothing to alter Portugal's fundamental poverty. Although he ruled through civilian governments, his essential power always came from the army.

Portugal has long been Western Europe's poorest country. As late as 1960, almost half of the country's work force was engaged in agriculture, forestry, and fishing. In the north, agriculture was traditionally carried on in smallholdings; the south was characterized by large estates, remnants of feudal fiefs. Even today half of the country's food is imported. Exports were traditionally based on agricultural products (cork, olive oil, port wine) and fish. Industrialization came late to Portugal, and today manufacturing is mostly carried on by small firms engaged in textile and clothing production and other labor-intensive production.

World War II affected Portugal very little. Salazar deftly managed to remain Britain's ally while keeping his country out of the war as a neutral state. In the postwar period, Portugal accepted Marshall Plan aid and became a member of NATO in 1949. Portugal was a founding member of the European Free Trade Association in 1959 and negotiated a special relationship with the EEC in 1972 (when its trading partner and ally, Great Britain, joined that body).

Portugal joined the United Nations in 1955 (having been vetoed until then by the Soviet Union), just in time to become embroiled in the worldwide movement for decolonization. Protesting that Portugal had, not colonies, but "overseas provinces," Salazar refused to bow to the pressure of world opinion. In 1961 India forcibly annexed Goa and other Portuguese enclaves on the subcontinent. In the same year, nationalist revolts broke out in Angola, with Guinea and Mozambique following soon after.

The colonial wars of the 1960s placed a terrible strain on Portugal's economy, resulting in severe military losses, and had the unintended effect of spreading Marxist ideas in the armed forces and the universities. And in the end, the colonies gained their independence. Salazar, gravely ill, retired in 1968 and was replaced by Marcelo Caetano. In 1974 Caetano was deposed in a bloodless coup staged by the secret Armed Forces Movement. The coup's leader, Antonio de Spinola, after reaching agreements on the independence of most of Portugal's old colonies, resigned as head of government in September 1974. Costa Gomez replaced Spinola, as a Revolutionary Council was instituted. The council survived two coup attempts, one by right-wing soldiers, the other by Communists, and it promulgated a socialist Constitution in 1976. Through a series of unstable governments (16 between 1974 and 1987), the old agrarian estates were expropriated, and banking, insurance, and large industrial concerns were nationalized. The shock of this economic transformation, along with the OPEC price rises, created an economic recession in the 1970s. In addition Portugal had to absorb about a million ethnic Portuguese refugees from the former colonies.

Attempts by Center-Right coalitions in the 1980s to undo the nationalizations of the 1970s have been thwarted by vetoes of the Constitutional Tribunal (successor to the Revolutionary Council), even when, as currently, the free-market Social Democratic party holds an absolute majority in the assembly. But the world economic expansion of the 1980s, the revival of trade, and cheaper oil prices have produced a growth in foreign investment in Portugal and a decline in both inflation and unemployment. Portugal entered the EEC on Jan. 1, 1986, pledging to reduce tariffs and end agricultural subsidies over a 10–year transitional period.

Qatar
State of Qatar
Geography Location: occupies a peninsula, projecting northward from Arabian mainland, into western part of Persian (Arabian) Gulf. **Boundaries:** Persian Gulf to N, E, and W; Saudi Arabia and United Arab Emirates to S. **Total land area:** 4,416 sq. mi. (11,437 sq km). **Coastline:** 350 mi. (563 km). **Comparative area:** slightly smaller than Connecticut. **Land use:** negl. % arable land; 0% permanent crops;

5% meadows and pastures; 0% forest and woodland; 95% other. **Major cities:** (1986 est.) Doha (capital) 217,294.

People Population: 328,044 (1988). **Nationality:** noun—Qatari(s); adjective—Qatari. **Ethnic groups:** 40% Arab, 18% Pakistani, 18% Indian, 10% Iranian, 14% other. **Languages:** Arabic (official), English commonly used as second language. **Religions:** 95% Muslim.

Government Type: traditional monarchy. **Independence:** Sept. 3, 1971 (from UK). **Constitution:** provisional constitution enacted Apr. 2, 1970. **National holiday:** Independence Day, Sept. 3. **Head of government:** Khalifa bin Hamad al-Thani, amir and prime minister (since Feb. 1972). **Structure:** executive—amir and Council of Ministers; legislature—State Advisory Council.

Economy Monetary unit: Qatar riyal. **Budget:** (1986) *income:* $2.6 bil.; *expend.:* $4.2 bil. **GDP:** $5.4 bil., $17,070 per capita (1987). **Chief crops:** farming and grazing on small scale; commercial fishing increasing in importance; most food imported; rice and dates are staple diet. **Livestock:** sheep, goats, camels, cattle, horses. **Natural resources:** crude oil, natural gas, fish. **Major industries:** crude oil production and refining, fertilizers, petrochemicals. **Labor force:** 104,000 (1983); 85% non-Qatari in private sector. **Exports:** $1.9 bil. (f.o.b., 1987); of which petroleum accounted for $1.6 bil. **Imports:** $0.89 bil. (f.o.b., 1987). **Major trading partners:** N.A.

Intl. Orgs. Arab League, FAO, G-77, GATT (de facto), IBRD, ICAO, IFAD, ILO, IMF, IMO, INTELSAT, INTERPOL, ITU, NAM, OPEC, UN, UNESCO, UPU, WHO, WIPO, WMO.

The Qatar peninsula was ruled as part of the sheikhdom of Bahrain from the late 18th century until the mid-19th century. An informal British protectorate was established in 1868; the Ottoman Empire also asserted authority over the sheikhs of Qatar from 1872 to 1916. The Ottomans ceded authority to the British in that year, and a formal British Protectorate was organized. When British forces withdrew from the gulf in 1971, Qatar entered into negotiations with the emirates of the Trucial Coast to join the federation of the United Arab Emirates. When those negotiations broke down, Qatar declared its independence on Sept. 3, 1971. Amir Khalifah bin Hamad al-Thani came to the throne on Feb. 22, 1972.

Qatar's economy, formerly limited to fishing, maritime trade, and pastoralism, is now almost entirely dominated by oil, banking, and shipping services in the port of Doha.

Romania
Socialist Republic of Romania
Geography Location: southeastern Europe. **Boundaries:** USSR to N and NE, Black Sea to E, Bulgaria to S, Yugoslavia to SW, Hungary to NW. **Total land area:** 91,699 sq. mi. (237,500 sq km). **Coastline:** 140 mi. (225 km). **Comparative area:** slightly smaller than Oregon. **Land use:** 43% arable land; 3% permanent crops; 19% meadows and pastures; 28% forest and woodland; 7% other; includes 11%

irrigated. **Major cities:** (1986) Bucuresti (Bucharest, capital) 1,989,823; Braşov 351,493; Constanta 327,676; Timisoara 325,272; Iasi 313,060.

People Population: 23,040,883 (1988). **Nationality:** noun—Romanian(s); adjective—Romanian. **Ethnic groups:** 89% Romanian, 7.8% Hungarian, 1.5% German, 1.6% Ukrainian, Serb, Croat, Russian, Turk, and Gypsy. **Languages:** Romanian, Hungarian, German. **Religions:** 80% Romanian Orthodox, 6% Roman Catholic, 4% Calvinist, Lutheran, Jewish, Baptist.

Government Type: communist state. **Independence:** N.A. **Constitution:** Aug. 21, 1965. **National holiday:** Liberation Day, Aug. 23. **Heads of government:** Nicolae Ceauşescu, president of the Socialist Republic (since Mar. 1974); Constantin Dăscălescu, prime minister (since May 1982). **Structure:** presidency; Council of Ministers; Grand National Assembly, under which is office of prosecutor general and Supreme Court; Council of State.

Economy (1986) **Monetary unit:** lei. **Budget:** N.A. **GNP:** $138 bil., $6,030 per capita. **Chief crops:** corn, wheat, oilseed; consumer and food supplies weak; net exporter. **Livestock:** poultry, sheep, pigs, cattle, horses. **Natural resources:** crude oil, timber, construction materials. **Major industries:** mining, timber, construction materials. **Labor force:** 10.6 mil.; 34% industry, 28% agriculture, 38% other. **Exports:** $12.5 bil. (f.o.b.); 34.7% machinery and equipment; 24.7% fuels, minerals, and metals; 16.9% manufactured consumer goods; 11.9% agricultural materials and forestry products; 11.6% other. **Imports:** $10.6 bil. (f.o.b.); 51.0% fuels, minerals, and metals, 26.7% machinery and equipment; 11.0% agricultural and forestry products; 4.2% manufactured consumer goods; 7.1% other. **Major trading partners:** $22.6 bil. (1984); 60% communist countries, 40% noncommunist countries.

Intl. Orgs. CMEA, FAO, G-77, GATT, IAEA, IBRD, ICAO, IFAD, ILO, IMF, IMO, INTERPOL, ITU, UN, UNESCO, UPU, Warsaw Pact, WHO, WIPO, WMO.

The Roman province of Dacia was sufficiently Latinized to retain the name of Rome long after the empire collapsed in A.D. 286. Overrun by invading Bulgars in the eighth century, the Romanians retained their Latinate language and orthodox Christianity; Romania remained beyond the borders of the Byzantine Empire but was in close contact with it. The country was conquered by the Mongols in the 13th century and formed the independent principalities of Moldavia and Walachia after the Mongols withdrew at the end of that century.

By the 15th century, Moldavia and Walachia had become vassal states of the Ottoman Empire, though with some local autonomy that permitted retention of orthodox Christianity and the creation of a rich local culture. Attempts at national unity against Ottoman rule in 1601 and 1711 failed; in 1861 the provinces united as an autonomous state under the name Romania, within the Ottoman Empire, under

Greek administration.

Romania was for centuries the poorest country in Europe. Thoroughly agricultural, it was a land of unfree peasants working the great estates of landowners who were generally wealthy, usually absentee, and often Greek. The peasants not only paid taxes but also were required to perform feudal labor services for the estate owners. Neither industry nor a middle class existed before the 20th century.

After enlarging itself at Bulgaria's expense in the Second Balkan War (1913) on the eve of World War I, Romania switched sides three times, joining the Allies just before the war's end. Its reward was a huge expansion in size, doubling its territory with lands taken from Austria, Hungary, Russia, and Bulgaria.

The interwar period was one of political turbulence, marked by violence and assassinations. Twice King Carol II went into exile, leaving his throne to his son Prince Michael; the second time was in 1940, when Russia (in accordance with the Hitler-Stalin pact) reclaimed the territories of Bessarabia and northern Bukovina that it had lost to Romania in 1920, while Hitler required Romania to return about half of Transylvania to Hungary.

During World War II, the pro-Hitler dictator Marshall Ion Antonescu took power, supported by a semifascist "Iron Guard," but when the latter attempted a coup, the military crushed the uprising. Romanian troops participated in Hitler's invasion of Russia in 1941, and the country paid the price in 1944 when Russian troops "liberated" the country, with devastating results. King Michael arrested Antonescu and switched to the Allied side, but to no avail. The country was quickly transformed into a Soviet satellite through rigged elections in which the communist National Democratic Front replaced the Peasant Alliance in power; a People's Republic was proclaimed on Dec. 30, 1947, and King Michael was forced to abdicate. A peace treaty in 1947 confirmed the loss of Bessarabia to Russia but returned Transylvania to Romania.

Under Russian occupation Romania was a virtual Soviet colony. The occupying armies did not leave until after reparation payments were completed in 1958, leaving the dictator Gheorghe Gheorghiu-Dej in power. Despite COMECON plans for Romania to become a major food supplier for the Soviet bloc, Gheorghiu-Dej pursued industrialization on the Stalinist model, in the process ruining Romanian agriculture while creating large, labor-intensive, and highly inefficient factories. The result was an economic depression; politically, however, it produced a de facto independence for Romania within the Soviet bloc. Russian troops were forbidden on Romanian soil, and Romania declined to participate in COMECON policies.

With the death of Gheorghiu-Dej in 1965, power passed to the current leader, Nicolae Ceauşescu. He promulgated a new Constitution and instituted a series of purges, lasting to 1968; he became successively party leader in 1965, prime minister in 1967, and president of the republic in 1974. Ceauşescu continued his predecessor's economic policy, deepening the country's misery; he also pursued a policy of "independence" from the USSR, refusing to go along with Soviet policies of de-Stalinization and liberalization.

Romania's "national communism" is expressed in intense and militant nationalism, coupled with severe repression of ethnic minorities, especially Germans and Magyars in Transylvania. Hundreds of ethnically Hungarian villages have been bulldozed into oblivion in the name of agricultural collectivization, leading to increased tensions with Hungary. The damage was compounded by a major earthquake in 1977 that caused extensive damage to Bucharest and surrounding areas. Ceauşescu has announced plans to raze an additional 7,000 to 8,000 farms and villages over the next decade in order to complete agricultural collectivization on his own eccentric model, as well as to demolish the historic central districts of Romania's cities to make way for urban development.

Ceauşescu's ambitions extend to the creation of an un-Marxist family dynasty in the Romanian leadership. In 1979 his wife Elena was named first deputy premier and elevated to the Council of Ministers, from which position she dominates scientific and cultural policy. Her brothers have been given important government positions, in part replacing the Communist party with the Ceauşescu-Petrescu clan. Ceauşescu's son, despite his reputation as a decadent playboy, is being groomed to replace his father as the country's supreme leader.

Chronic shortages, extreme nepotism, inefficiency, and bureaucratic stifling of initiative at all levels combine with increasing hostility between Hungary and Romania to make the status of Romania one of the most volatile and potentially dangerous issues in the Eastern bloc today.

Rwanda
Republic of Rwanda

Geography **Location:** landlocked country in central Africa. **Boundaries:** Uganda to N, Tanzania to E, Burundi to S, Zaire to W. **Total land area:** 10,169 sq. mi. (26,338 sq km). **Coastline:** none. **Comparative area:** slightly smaller than Maryland. **Land use:** 29% arable land; 11% permanent crops; 18% meadows and pastures; 10% forest and woodland; 32% other; includes negl. % irrigated. **Major cities:** (1978 census) Kigali (capital) 117,749; Butare 21,691; Ruhengeri 16,025; Gisenyi 12,436.

People **Population:** 7,058,350 (1988). **Nationality:** noun—Rwandan(s); adjective—Rwandan. **Ethnic groups:** 90% Hutu, 9% Tutsi, 1% Twa (Pygmy). **Languages:** Kinyarwanda, French (both official); Kiswahili used in commercial centers. **Religions:** 65% Catholic, 9% Protestant, 9% Muslim; indigenous beliefs.

Government **Type:** republic; presidential system in which military leaders hold key offices. **Independence:** July 1, 1962 (from UN trusteeship under Belgian administration). **Constitution:** Dec. 17, 1978. **National holiday:** National Day, July 1. **Heads of government:** Maj. Gen. Juvénal Habyarimana, president (since July 1978). **Structure:** executive—president, 16-member cabinet; unicameral legislature—National Development Council; judiciary—four senior courts, magistrates.

Economy **Monetary unit:** Rwanda franc. **Budget:** (1984) *income:* $148.3 mil.; *expend.:* $198.5 mil. **GDP:** $1.84 bil., $290 per capita (1985 est.). **Chief crops:** cash crops—coffee, tea, pyrethrum; food crops—bananas, cassava; self-sufficiency declining; country imports foodstuffs. **Livestock:** goats, cattle, sheep, pigs. **Natural resources:** gold, cassiterite (tin ore), wolframite (tungsten ore), natural gas, hydropower. **Major industries:** mining of cassiterite and wolframite, tin, cement. **Labor force:** 3.6 mil. (1985); 93% agriculture, 7% other. **Exports:** $162.4 mil. (f.o.b., 1986 est.); coffee, tea, tin, cassiterite, wolframite, pyrethrum (insecticide made from chrysanthemums). **Imports:** $379.0 mil. (c.i.f., 1986 est.); textiles, foodstuffs, machines, equipment, capital goods. **Major trading partners:** U.S., Belgium, W. Germany, Kenya.

Intl. Orgs. FAO, G-77, GATT, IBRD, ICAO, IDA, IFAD, IFC, ILO, IMF, INTERPOL, ITU, NAM, UN, UNESCO, UPU, WHO, WMO.

Tutsi cattle-breeders came to Rwanda, on Africa's east coast, in the late 15th century and slowly conquered the native Hutu farmers. The Tutsi established a monarchy, forcing the Hutus into serfdom. Germans were the first Europeans to arrive in Rwanda and declared it a protectorate in 1899. Belgian troops occupied Rwanda during World War I and were given a League of Nations mandate over the territory after the war.

Tutsi traditionalists resisted Belgian attempts in the 1950s to institute democratic political institutions. In 1959 the Hutus revolted against the monarchy in a bloody conflict which led to a mass exodus of Tutsis. Two years later the Hutus won a UN-supervised referendum and were granted internal autonomy by Belgium on Jan. 1, 1962. Full independence came on July 1, 1962. Political unrest led to the overthrow of the government by the military, led by Maj. Gen. Juvénal Habyarimana, in 1973. Habyarimana dissolved the national assembly and banned all political activity. He has served as president since 1978.

Saint Kitts and Nevis
Federation of Saint Kitts and Nevis
(PREVIOUS NAME: SAINT CHRISTOPHER AND NEVIS)

Geography **Location:** two islands in eastern Caribbean Sea; Nevis is 2 mi. (3.2 km) SE of St. Kitts; St. Kitts is located about 45 mi. (72 km) NW of Antigua. **Boundaries:** Caribbean Sea to N, E, S, and W. **Total land area:** 101 sq. mi. (261 sq km). **Coastline:** 84 mi. (135 km). **Comparative area:** slightly more than twice size of Washington, D.C. **Land use:** 22% arable land; 17% permanent crops; 3% meadows and pastures; 17% forest and woodland; 41% other; includes N.A. % irrigated. **Major cities:** (1980 est.) Basseterre (capital) 14,161.

People **Population:** 36,738 (1988). **Nationality:** noun—Kittsian(s), Nevisian(s); adjective—Kittsian, Nevisian. **Ethnic groups:** mainly of black African descent. **Languages:** English.

Religions: Anglican, other Protestant sects, Roman Catholic.

Government Type: independent state within Commonwealth, recognizing Elizabeth II as chief of state. **Independence:** Sept.19, 1983 (from UK). **Constitution:** Sept. 19, 1983. **National holiday:** Independence Day, Sept 19. **Heads of government:** Sir Clement Arrindell, governor-general (since Nov. 1981); Dr. Kennedy Alphonse Simmonds, prime minister (since Feb. 1980). **Structure:** executive (cabinet headed by prime minister); legislative (11-member popularly elected House of Assembly; separate Nevis Island Legislature and Nevis Island Assembly headed by premier).

Economy Monetary unit: East Caribbean (EC) dollar. **Budget:** (1986) *income:* $26 mil.; *expend.:* $30 mil. **GDP:** $70 mil., $1,870 per capita (1986 est.). **Chief crops:** sugar on St. Kitts, cotton on Nevis. **Livestock:** sheep, pigs, goats, cattle. **Natural resources:** negl. **Major industries:** sugar processing, tourism, cotton. **Labor force:** 20,000 (1981). **Exports:** $33.5 mil. (1986); sugar. **Imports:** $63.4 mil. (1986); foodstuffs, manufactures, fuel. **Major trading partners:** *exports:* U.S., UK; *imports:* UK, Japan, U.S.

Intl. Orgs. Commonwealth, FAO, IBRD, IMF, OAS, UN.

The French settled St. Kitts in 1627; the English settled Nevis in 1628. In 1783 both became British possessions, and the two islands were united in 1882. Britain granted them independence in 1983, and Prime Minister Kennedy Alphonse Simmonds, who pledges national economic diversification, currently heads the government of this twin-island state. Ninety percent of the country's economy is based on sugar exports, thus leaving the welfare of the citizenry dependent on the fluctuating international sugar market.

Saint Lucia

Geography Location: island in southeastern Caribbean Sea, lying between French overseas department of Martinique to N and St. Vincent to SW. **Boundaries:** St. Lucia Channel to N, Atlantic Ocean to E, St. Vincent Passage to S, Caribbean Sea to W. **Total land area:** 238 sq. mi. (616 sq km). **Coastline:** 98 mi. (158 km). **Comparative area:** slightly less than 3.5 times size of Washington, D.C. **Land use:** 8% arable land; 20% permanent crops; 5% meadows and pastures; 13% forest and woodland; 54% other; includes 2% irrigated. **Major cities:** (1986 est.) Castries (capital) 52,868; Vieux Fort; Soufrière; Gros Islet.

People Population: 136,564 (1988). **Nationality:** noun—St. Lucian(s); adjective—St. Lucian. **Ethnic groups:** 90.3% African descent, 5.5% mixed, 3.2% East Indian, 0.8% Caucasian. **Languages:** English (official), French patois. **Religions:** 90% Roman Catholic, 7% Protestant, 3% Church of England.

Government Type: independent state within Commonwealth, recognizing Elizabeth II as chief of state. **Independence:** Feb. 22, 1979 (from UK). **Constitution:** Feb. 22, 1979.

National holiday: Independence Day, Feb. 22. **Heads of government:** Vincent Floissac, acting governor-general (since Apr. 1987); John Compton, prime minister (since May 1982). **Structure:** executive (cabinet headed by prime minister); bicameral legislature (Senate, House of Representatives).

Economy Monetary unit: East Caribbean (EC) dollar. **Budget:** (1986 est.) *income:* $65 mil.; *expend.:* $70 mil. **GDP:** $158 mil., $1,180 per capita (1986). **Chief crops:** bananas, coconuts, sugar, cocoa, spices. **Livestock:** sheep, cattle, goats, pigs. **Natural resources:** forests, sandy beaches, minerals (pumice), mineral springs, geothermal potential. **Major industries:** clothing, assembly of electronic components, beverages. **Labor force:** 43,800 (1983 est.); 43.4% agriculture, 38.9% services, 17.7% industry and commerce; 30% unemployment (1984). **Exports:** $24.3 mil. (f.o.b., 1986); bananas, cocoa. **Imports:** $141 mil. (f.o.b., 1986); foodstuffs, machinery and equipment, fertilizers, petroleum products. **Major trading partners:** (1986 est.) *exports:* 66% UK, 18% CARICOM, 11% U.S.; *imports:* 34% U.S., 16% UK, 16% CARICOM.

Intl. Orgs. FAO, G-77, GATT (de facto), IBRD, ICAO, IDA, IFAD, IFC, ILO, IMF, IMO, NAM, OAS, UN, UNESCO, UPU, WHO, WMO.

In 1650 the French settled St. Lucia, which was ceded to Britain in 1814. A member of the Federation of the West Indies from 1958 to 1962, St. Lucia became internally self-governing in 1967 but was still under Great Britain's protection. In 1979 St. Lucia gained full independence and now enjoys stable competitive politics. Hurricane Allen destroyed many of the country's banana plantations in 1980, and the economy is still recovering from the disaster. The current government of Prime Minister John Compton of the United Workers party has pledged an agrarian reform.

Saint Vincent and the Grenadines

Geography Location: large island of St. Vincent and about 50 smaller islands situated in southeastern Caribbean Sea about 21 mi. (34 km) SW of St. Lucia and 100 mi. (160 km) W of Barbados. **Boundaries:** St. Vincent Passage to N, Atlantic Ocean to E and SE, Caribbean Sea to SW and W. **Total land area:** 150 sq. mi. (389 sq km). **Coastline:** 52 mi. (84 km). **Comparative area:** slightly less than twice size of Washington, D.C. **Land use:** 38% arable land; 12% permanent crops; 6% meadows and pastures; 41% forest and woodland; 3% other; includes 3% irrigated. **Major cities:** (1986 est.) Kingstown (capital) 18,830.

People Population: 107,425 (1988). **Nationality:** noun—St. Vincentian(s) or Vincentian(s); adjective—St. Vincentian or Vincentian. **Ethnic groups:** mainly of black African descent, remainder mixed, with some white, East Indian, and Carib Indian. **Languages:** English, French patois. **Religions:** Anglican, Methodist, Roman Catholic, Seventh-Day Adventist.

Government Type: independent state within Commonwealth, recognizing Elizabeth II as chief of state. **Independence:** Oct. 27, 1979 (from UK). **Constitution:** Oct. 27, 1979. **National holiday:** Independence Day, Oct. 27. **Heads of government:** Henry Williams, acting governor-general (since Feb. 1989); James Mitchell, prime minister (since July 1984). **Structure:** bicameral legislature (13-member elected House of Representatives and 6-member appointed Senate); judiciary (Supreme Court).

Economy Monetary unit: East Caribbean (EC) dollar. **Budget:** (1986) *income:* $43 mil.; *expend.:* $43 mil. **GDP:** $95 mil., $900 per capita (1986 est.). **Chief crops:** bananas, arrowroot. **Livestock:** sheep, cattle, pigs, goats. **Natural resources:** negl. **Major industries:** food processing (sugar, flour), cement, furniture. **Labor force:** 67,000 (1984 est.); 35% unemployed (1986). **Exports:** $68 mil. (f.o.b., 1986); bananas, arrowroot, copra. **Imports:** $87 mil. (c.i.f., 1986); foodstuffs, machinery and equipment, chemicals and fertilizers, minerals and fuels. **Major trading partners:** (1985) *exports:* 60% CARICOM, 27% UK, 11% U.S.; *imports:* 37% U.S., 18% CARICOM, 13% UK, 5% Canada.

Intl. Orgs. FAO, G-77, GATT (de facto), IBRD, ICAO, IDA, IFAD, IMF, IMO, OAS, UN, UNESCO, UPU, WHO.

Although ceded to Britain in 1763, St. Vincent was inhabited by the fierce Carib Indians, who continued fighting for control of the island until 1796, when they had all been either killed or deported. Just prior to its independence in 1979, St. Vincent and the Grenadines was a self-governing state in association with Great Britain. It is one of the poorest countries in the West Indies. Several natural disasters have plagued the economy, including a 1979 volcanic eruption and two destructive hurricanes in 1980 and 1986. Prime Minister James Mitchell of the New Democratic party currently governs the country.

San Marino
Republic of San Marino

Geography Location: on slopes of Mt. Titano, in the Apennines, within central Italian region of Emilia-Romagna. **Boundaries:** surrounded by Italian territory. **Total land area:** 23.4 sq. mi. (60.5 sq km). **Coastline:** none. **Comparative area:** about 3/10 size of Washington, D.C. **Land use:** 17% arable land; 0% permanent crops; 0% meadows and pastures; 0% forest and woodland; 83% other. **Major cities:** San Marino (capital).

People Population: 22,986 (1988). **Nationality:** noun—Sanmarinese (sing., pl.); adjective—Sanmarinese. **Ethnic groups:** N.A. **Languages:** Italian. **Religions:** Roman Catholic.

Government Type: republic. **Independence:** N.A. **Constitution:** Oct. 8, 1600; electoral law of 1926 serves some of functions of constitution. **National holiday:** Anniversary of the Liberation of the Republic, Feb. 5. **Heads of government:** Gabriele Gatti, secretary of state for foreign and political affairs and for information (since July 1986); Alvaro Selva, secretary of state for internal affairs and justice (since July 1978). **Structure:** executive—two captain-regents with six-month terms; actual power wielded by secretary of state for foreign affairs and secretary of state for internal affairs; legislative—Grand and General Council elected by popular vote for five-year terms; Congress of State whose members head administrative departments; judicial—Council of Twelve is supreme judicial body.

Economy Monetary unit: Italian lire. **Budget:** N.A. **GNP:** N.A. **Chief crops:** wheat, grapes, other grains, fruits, vegetables. **Livestock:** N.A. **Natural resources:** building stones. **Major industries:** wine, olive oil, cement. **Labor force:** about 4,300. **Exports:** trade data included with Italian statistics; commodity trade consisting primarily of exchanging building stone, lime, wood, chestnuts, wheat, and wine for a wide variety of consumer manufactures. **Imports:** see exports. **Major trading partners:** N.A.

Intl. Orgs. ITU, NAM (observer status), UNESCO, UPU, WHO.

The "Most Serene Republic" of San Marino, entirely surrounded by Italy near the city of Rimini, is the oldest republic in the world, with communitarian roots dating to the fourth century A.D. While Piedmont-Sardinia was conquering all of the rest of the Italian peninsula during the period 1860–70, it left San Marino independent; the new Kingdom of Italy signed a treaty of friendship and cooperation with the republic in 1862, and Italy has adhered to it ever since.

Four major parties contend for seats in the Grand and General Council, which elects the republic's two chief magistrates, the capitani reggenti. The Christian Democrats are the largest party. Leftist coalitions governed from 1978 through 1986, giving San Marino the only communist government west of the Soviet bloc. Since 1986 the government has been controlled by a coalition of Communists and Christian Democrats.

The economy is balanced between small-scale agriculture (primarily wine grapes and livestock) and industry, including textiles, ceramics, and furniture. Philatelic sales and tourism are important sources of revenue. Lacking extremes of wealth and poverty and with low unemployment, the republic enjoys general prosperity.

Abraham Lincoln accepted honorary citizenship of San Marino in 1861 and has been a culture hero ever since.

São Tomé and Príncipe
Democratic Republic of São Tomé and Príncipe

Geography Location: two main islands, São Tomé and Príncipe, and the rocky islets of Caroço, Pedras, Tinhosas (off Príncipe) and Rolas (off São Tomé), off west coast of Africa. **Boundaries:** west of Gabon in Gulf of Guinea. **Total land area:** 372 sq. mi. (964 sq km). **Coastline:** 130 mi. (209 km). **Comparative area:** slightly less than 5.5 times size of Washington,

D.C. **Land use:** 1% arable land; 36% permanent crops; 1% meadows and pastures; 0% forest and woodland; 62% other. **Major cities:** São Tomé (capital).

People Population: 117,430 (1988). **Nationality:** noun—São Toméan(s); adjective—São Toméan. **Ethnic groups:** Mestiço, Angolares (descendants of Angolan slaves), Servicais (contract laborers from Angola, Mozambique, and Cape Verde), Tongas (children of Servicais born on the islands), and Europeans (primarily Portuguese). **Languages:** Portuguese (official). **Religions:** Roman Catholic, Evangelical, Protestant, Seventh-Day Adventist.

Government Type: republic. **Independence:** July 12, 1975 (from Portugal). **Constitution:** Nov. 5, 1975, approved Dec. 15, 1982. **National holiday:** Independence Day, July 12. **Heads of government:** Dr. Manuel Pinto da Costa, president (since 1975); Celestino Rocha da Costa, prime minister (since 1988). **Structure:** executive—president assisted by cabinet of ministers; unicameral legislature—40-member National People's Assembly, elected for five years.

Economy Monetary unit: dobra. **Budget:** (1981 est.) $22.0 mil. **GDP:** $37.7 mil., $340 per capita (1986 est.). **Chief crops:** cash crops—cocoa, copra, coconuts, coffee, palm oil, bananas. **Livestock:** goats, pigs, cattle, sheep. **Natural resources:** fish. **Major industries:** small processing factories producing shirts, soap, beer; fish and shrimp processing. **Labor force:** 21,096 (1981); subsistence agriculture and fishing; some unemployment; labor shortages on plantations and for skilled workers; 56% of population of working age (1983). **Exports:** $9.8 mil. (f.o.b., 1986 est.); 90% cocoa, 7% copra, coffee, palm oil. **Imports:** $2.6 mil. (c.i.f., 1986 est.); food products, machinery and electrical equipment, fuels. **Major trading partners:** Netherlands, Portugal, U.S., W. Germany, E. Germany.

Intl. Orgs. FAO, G-77, GATT (de facto), IBRD, ICAO, IDA, IFAD, IFC, ILO, IMF, ITU, NAM, UN, UNESCO, UPU, WHO, WMO.

The islands of São Tomé and Príncipe, located in the Atlantic Ocean 275 and 125 miles, respectively, off the northern coast of Gabon, make up one of Africa's tiniest nations. They were uninhabited when first discovered by the Portuguese in 1470 but by the mid-1500s became Africa's foremost exporter of sugar. As the sugar market declined, the islands became a major slave-trading center and producer of coffee and cocoa. By 1908 São Tomé was the world's largest cocoa producer.

Portugal did not abolish slavery until 1876, and abusive labor practices continued until well into the 20th century. In 1953 hundreds of workers were killed in clashes with the Portuguese. Soon after, a small number of São Toméans formed the Movement for the Liberation of São Tomé and Príncipe (MLSTP) with its base in Gabon. But the islands did not gain independence until July 12, 1975, one year after the dictatorship in Portugal was overthrown.

The MLSTP took over after independence and still is the only official party in the country. By 1986 the country relied on foreign aid for approximately 41 percent of its gross national product. Although in the past it received military advisers from the Soviet Union and economic advisers from Cuba, São Tomé and Príncipe has announced a foreign policy based upon nonalignment and expressed a willingness to cooperate with any country willing to offer economic development aid.

Saudi Arabia
Kingdom of Saudi Arabia
(PREVIOUS NAME: ARABIA)

Geography Location: occupies $^4/_5$ of Arabian peninsula in southwestern Asia. **Boundaries:** Jordan, Iraq, and Kuwait to N; Persian Gulf, Qatar, and United Arab Emirates to E, Oman and S. Yemen to SE; N. Yemen to S; Red Sea to W. **Total land area:** 864,869 sq. mi. (2,240,000 sq km). **Coastline:** 1,559 mi. (2,510 km). **Comparative area:** slightly less than $^1/_4$ size of U.S. **Land use:** 1% arable land; negl. % permanent crops; 39% meadows and pastures; 1% forest and woodland; 59% other; includes negl. % irrigated. **Major cities:** (1974 census) Riyadh (capital) 666,840; Jeddah 561,104; Makkah (Mecca) 366,801; Ta'If 204,857; Al-Madinah (Medina) 198,186.

People Population: 15,452,123 (1988). **Nationality:** noun—Saudi(s); adjective—Saudi or Saudi Arabian. **Ethnic groups:** 90% Arab, 10% Afro-Asian. **Languages:** Arabic. **Religions:** 100% Muslim.

Government Type: monarchy. **Constitution:** none; governed according to Sharia or Islamic law. **National holiday:** Sept. 23. **Head of government:** Fahd ibn Abdul-Aziz al-Saud, king and prime minister (since 1982). **Structure:** king rules in consultation with royal family and Council of Ministers.

Economy Monetary unit: Saudi riyal. **Budget:** (1988 est.) *income:* $28.0 bil.; *expend.:* $37.7 bil. **GDP:** $85.0 bil., $6,030 per capita (1987). **Chief crops:** dates, grains, livestock; not self-sufficient in food except for wheat. **Livestock:** sheep, goats, cattle, asses, camels. **Natural resources:** crude oil, natural gas, iron ore, gold, copper. **Major industries:** crude oil production, petroleum refining, basic petrochemicals. **Labor force:** about one-third ($^1/_2$ foreign) of population; 45% commerce, services, and government; 30% agriculture, 15% construction. **Exports:** $25 bil. (f.o.b., 1987); 92% petroleum and petroleum products. **Imports:** $19 bil. (c.i.f., 1987) manufactured goods, transportation equipment, construction materials, processed food products. **Major trading partners:** (1987) *exports and reexports:* 22% Japan, 17% U.S., 9% France, 6% Bahrain; *imports:* 16% U.S., 13% Japan, 10% UK, 7% W. Germany.

Intl. Orgs. Arab League, FAO, G-77, IAEA, IBRD, ICAO, IDA, IFAD, IFC, ILO, IMF, IMO, INTELSAT, INTERPOL, ITU, NAM, OPEC, UN, UNESCO, UPU, WHO, WMO.

In ancient times various cultures flourished in parts of the Arabian peninsula, particularly along the western rim, in cities devoted to trade between the Gulf of Aden and the eastern Mediterranean, and in such agricultural and trading centers as Yemen and Oman. Cultural and political unity was lacking, however, until the rise of Mohammed, the prophet of Islam. In A.D. 622 Mohammed fled from Mecca, the holy city of Arabian paganism, to the nearby city of Medina; the Islamic era dates from that year. Preaching from Medina, Mohammed soon gained converts to Islam throughout Arabia. His army captured Mecca in 630, converting its sacred shrine, the Kaaba, to an Islamic place of worship. By 632, when Mohammed died, all of Arabia was unified under Islamic rule.

In 661 the Caliphate, the ruling body of early Islam, moved from Medina to Damascus. Thereafter Arabia was nominally unified under Islamic rule—but in practice was usually divided among various principalities in the arable areas and trading centers—and under tribal rule in the arid interior. Mecca fell to the Ottoman Empire in 1517, but Ottoman control of Arabia was never complete. The rise of the Wahabi sect of Islam in the 18th century posed a challenge to Ottoman rule. In the 19th century, the Saud family rose to leadership in the Wahabi movement and established a kingdom in Nejd, the central region of Arabia, with a capital at Riyadh.

In 1902 ibn Saud (1880–1953) consolidated his family's control at Riyadh and in 1912–13 led a new Wahabi revolt against the Ottoman Turks. During World War I, the British aided Ibn Saud's rebellion in the Nejd, along with that of Ibn Saud's rival Husein ibn Ali in the Hejaz, in the mountains of western Arabia along the coast of the Red Sea. A British protectorate was established in both regions in 1915, and Great Britain maintained a dominant position in Arabia immediately after World War I.

In 1924 ibn Saud captured Husein ibn Ali's capital at Mecca, and he proclaimed himself king of Hejaz in 1926 and of Nejd in 1927. Ibn Saud consolidated his control over the following two years, and his kingdom was formally recognized by Great Britain in 1927. The country was renamed Saudi Arabia in 1932.

Saudi Arabia is an absolute monarchy based on Islamic law; it has no written constitution and no parliament. The king exercises sole authority and rules in consultation with a Council of Ministers. Islamic law is enforced; alcohol is prohibited and the public activities of women severely restricted. The Saudi kings have great power within the Islamic world through their control over the holy cities of Mecca and Medina and their administration of the annual Muslim pilgrimages to those cities.

The discovery of oil in eastern Arabia in the early 1930s rapidly transformed Saudi Arabia from an impoverished nation to a center of great wealth. In 1933 an exclusive concession for the exploitation of Saudi Arabian oil was granted to an American-chartered corporation, the Arabian-American Oil Company (Aramco). For many years wealth remained concentrated in the hands of the Saudi clan, and little change was felt in the desert interior, where Bedouin nomads continued to raise sheep and camels, little affected by modernization. Large num-

bers of Yemenis, Palestinians, Pakistanis, and other foreign workers are employed in the oil fields.

Saudi Arabia remained neutral during most of World War II but declared war on the Axis powers in March 1945; in the same year, it became a founding member of both the United Nations and the Arab League.

Ibn Saud became a leader of Arab anti-Zionism and contributed a small contingent of troops to the 1948 Arab-Israeli War. That policy was maintained by ibn Saud's second son and successor, King Faisal, who instituted a policy of providing large annual subsidies to Egypt and other Arab League states following the 1967 Arab-Israeli War. In 1973 King Faisal sent Saudi units to fight in the Arab-Israeli War of that year. He played a leading role in organizing the 1973–74 Arab oil embargo in an effort to force the United States and its allies to take a harder line with Israel.

King Faisal was assassinated by his nephew, Prince Faisal, on Mar. 25, 1975, and was succeeded by King Khalid. Little change in policy resulted. In 1979 Saudi Arabia denounced the Camp David talks and the Egyptian-Israeli peace treaty and led the Arab League effort to ostracize Egypt within the Arab world.

At the same time, Saudi Arabia has consistently opposed leftist and radical movements in the Arab world, sending troops to help put down leftist rebellions in North Yemen and Oman in the 1970s. The Saudi kings have also taken a generally cautious and moderate approach toward Arab relations with the West. Following the transfer of Aramco assets to full Saudi Arabian ownership during 1973–76, Saudi Arabia has used its leading position within the Organization of Petroleum Exporting Countries (OPEC) to argue for a policy of stable production and prices.

This anti-leftist and moderate policy has been rewarded by the willingness of the United States, Great Britain, France, and other Western nations to sell arms—including jet fighters, tanks, and other sophisticated weapons—to Saudi Arabia despite Israeli protests. A trade in arms valued in the many billions of dollars has helped to offset the Western oil trade deficit with Saudi Arabia. In 1981, over Israeli objections and following a major congressional debate, the United States sold five Airborne Warning and Control System (AWACS) aircraft to Saudi Arabia. In 1984, after Saudi Arabian tankers were attacked by Iranian aircraft during the Iran-Iraq War, the United States sold Saudia Arabia 400 Stinger antiaircraft missiles.

Saudi Arabia has experienced repeated disturbances in the 1980s. Muslim fundamentalist terrorists seized the Grand Mosque at Mecca on Nov. 20, 1979, provoking a crisis for the Saudi monarchy; the mosque was retaken by security forces. On July 31, 1987, Iranian pilgrims rioted in Mecca and were fired upon by Saudi security forces; 402 persons died, including 275 Iranians. On Aug.1 a mob in Tehran sacked the Saudi embassy, and on Aug. 3 Iran's Ayatollah Khomeini denounced the Saudi government and said it was unworthy of being the guardian of Islam's sacred shrines. In 1988

Iranians' participation in the annual haj pilgrimage to Mecca was severely limited by the Saudi government.

The Saudi economy remains heavily based on oil. Dates, fruit, and grain are grown in the few arable regions and oases. Sheep, goats, and camels are raised in the desert interior. Many formerly nomadic Bedouins now live in permanent houses and enjoy a wide range of social services.

Senegal
Republic of Senegal

Geography Location: northwestern coast of Africa. **Boundaries:** Mauritania to N, Mali to E, Guinea and Guinea-Bissau to S, Atlantic Ocean to W; The Gambia forms narrow enclave extending 200 mi. (320 km) inland from Atlantic coast. **Total land area:** 74,206 sq. mi. (192,192 sq km). **Coastline:** 330 mi. (531 km). **Comparative area:** slightly smaller than South Dakota. **Land use:** 27% arable land; 0% permanent crops; 30% meadows and pastures; 31% forest and woodland; 12% other; includes 1% irrigated. **Major cities:** (1979 est.) Dakar (capital) 850,000; Thiès 120,000; Kaolack 110,000.

People Population: 7,281,022 (1988). **Nationality:** noun—Senegalese (sing., pl.); adjective—Senegalese. **Ethnic groups:** 36% Wolof, 17% Fulani, 17% Serer, 9% Toucouleur, 9% Diola, 9% Mandingo, 1% European and Lebanese. **Languages:** French (official), Wolof, Pulaar, Diola, Mandingo. **Religions:** 92% Muslim, 6% indigenous beliefs, 2% Christian (mostly Roman Catholic).

Government Type: republic under multiparty democratic rule; on Feb. 1, 1982, Senegal and The Gambia formed loose confederation named Senegambia that calls for eventual integration of their armed forces and economic cooperation. **Independence:** Apr. 4, 1960 (from France). **Constitution:** Mar. 3, 1963 (formally signed agreement of confederation with The Gambia Dec. 12, 1981, effective Feb. 1, 1982 as Senegambia). **National holiday:** Independence Day, Apr. 4. **Heads of government:** Abdou Diouf, president (since Jan. 1981). **Structure:** executive—president; legislative—unicameral 120-member National Assembly, elected for five-year term by universal suffrage; judiciary—Supreme Court, members appointed by president.

Economy Monetary unit: Communauté Financière Africaine (CFA) franc. **Budget:** (1985) *income:* $467 mil.; *expend.:* $489 mil. **GDP:** $2.3 bil., $380 per capita (1984). **Chief crops:** peanuts (primary cash crop), millet, sorghum, manioc, maize, rice; deficit production of food. **Livestock:** sheep, cattle, goats, asses, horses. **Natural resources:** fish, phosphates, iron ore. **Major industries:** fishing, agricultural processing, phosphate mining. **Labor force:** 2.5 mil. (1985); 77% subsistence agricultural workers; 175,000 wage earners—60% government and parapublic, 40% private sector; 52% of working age. **Exports:** $525 mil. (f.o.b., 1984); peanuts and peanut products, phosphate rock, fish, petroleum products (reexport). **Imports:** $805 mil. (f.o.b., 1984); food, consumer goods, machinery, transport equipment, petroleum. **Major trading partners:** France, other EC countries, and franc zone.

Intl. Orgs. FAO, G-77, GATT, IAEA, IBRD, ICAO, IDA, IFAD, IFC, ILO, IMF, IMO, INTELSAT, INTERPOL, ITU, NAM, UN, UNESCO, UPU, WHO, WIPO, WMO.

Inhabited since ancient times, Senegal was dominated in the 13th and 14th centuries by the Mandingo and Jolof empires. Portuguese traders and explorers arrived in Senegal in the early 15th century and later competed with the British, Dutch, and French for domination in Senegal. The French established a trading station at Saint-Louis in 1659 and maintained possession thereafter, except for the British enclave along the Gambia River.

In the early 19th century, the French began a series of campaigns to bring the entire country under their control; the last independent sultanate surrendered in 1893. Senegal became a French colony in 1920, and Dakar became the capital of French West Africa. Senegal became a major contributor of African troops to the French armed forces.

In 1946 a territorial assembly was established, with a limited electorate and advisory powers, which were gradually expanded in subsequent years. With the creation of the French Community of Nations in 1958, Senegal achieved local self-rule within the community.

In 1959, with the encouragement of France, Senegal and French Sudan (now Mali) formed the Federation of Mali, which became fully independent on June 20, 1960. Senegal seceded from the federation on Aug. 20 and declared itself the Republic of Senegal. Leopold Sedar Senghor, who had already become famous as one of Africa's leading statesmen, became Senegal's first president.

In 1962 Prime Minister Mamdou Dia attempted a coup against the Senghor government; it failed, and Dia was imprisoned. A new constitution was subsequently adopted, strengthening the power of the presidency. Senghor retired from office in 1981 and was succeeded by Adbou Diouf. He encouraged political pluralism and has presided over a generally stable and democratic government. Diouf was elected in his own right in 1983 and reelected in 1988. Following the 1988 elections, riots broke out over charges of electoral fraud, and a state of emergency was declared.

In 1981 Senegal and Gambia announced plans to merge their monetary and defense systems in a confederation of the two states and to seek further integration of the two nations.

Senegal remains closely tied to France commercially, culturally, and in foreign affairs. Beginning in the mid-1980s, there has been a surge in illegal immigration of Senegalese to the United States.

Senegal's economy is primarily agricultural; peanuts are the principal crop. Industries include fishing and fish processing (the principal source of export earnings), food processing, light manufacturing, and phosphate mining. Senegalese merchants are active in commercial networks throughout West Africa. The economy has been hampered by a high foreign debt and by depressed world prices for peanuts.

Seychelles
Republic of Seychelles

Geography Location: more than 90 islands, widely scattered over western Indian Ocean about 1,000 mi. (1,600 km) E of Kenya. **Boundaries:** surrounded by Indian Ocean; nearest neighbor is Madagascar about 130 mi. (210 km) S of southernmost island group. **Total land area:** 175 sq. mi. (454 sq km). **Coastline:** 305 mi. (491 km). **Comparative area:** slightly more than 2.5 times the size of Washington, D.C. **Land use:** 4% arable land; 18% permanent crops; 0% meadows and pastures; 18% forest and woodland; 60% other. **Major cities:** (1977 census) Victoria (capital) 23,334 (includes suburbs).

People Population: 68,615 (1988). **Nationality:** noun—Seychellois (sing., pl.); adjective—Seychelles. **Ethnic groups:** Seychellois (mixture of Asians, Africans, Europeans). **Languages:** English, French (official); Creole. **Religions:** 90% Roman Catholic, 8% Anglican, 2% other.

Government Type: republic; member of Commonwealth. **Independence:** June 29, 1976 (from UK). **Constitution:** June 5, 1979. **National holiday:** June 5 and 29. **Head of government:** France Albert René, president (since June 1979). **Structure:** president; Council of Ministers; People's Assembly (25 members—23 elected and two appointed by president for four-year terms).

Economy Monetary unit: Seychelles rupee. **Budget:** measured as share of GDP (1985 est.) **income:** 43.4%; **expend.:** 63.8% **GDP:** $175 mil., $2,670 per capita (1985). **Chief crops:** islands depend largely on coconut production and export of copra; cinnamon, vanilla, green leaf tea, and patchouli (used for perfumes) are other cash crops; food crops—small quantities of sweet potatoes, cassava, sugarcane, and bananas; islands not self-sufficient in foodstuffs and bulk of supply must be imported. **Livestock:** pigs, goats, cattle. **Natural resources:** fish, copra, cinnamon trees. **Major industries:** tourism is largest industry; processing of coconut and vanilla, fishing. **Labor force:** formal employment (all sectors)—38.4% government, 30.7% parastatal, 30.8% private; formal employment (by sector)—49.0% industry and commerce, 39.0% services, 11.5% agriculture, forestry, and fishing (1984 est.); 57% of population of working age (1983). **Exports:** $4.5 mil. (f.o.b., 1985); fish, copra, cinnamon bark; reexports—petroleum products. **Imports:** $90 mil. (f.o.b., 1985); manufactured goods, food, tobacco, beverages, machinery and transport equipment. **Major trading partners:** exports: Pakistan, France, Réunion, UK, Mauritius; imports: Bahrain, UK, South Africa, Singapore, Japan.

Intl. Orgs. FAO, G-77, GATT (de facto), IBRD, ICAO, IFAD, IFC, ILO, IMF, IMO, INTERPOL, NAM, UN, UNESCO, UPU, WHO, WMO.

The Seychelles Islands were occupied by France in the 18th century and seized by Great Britain in 1794. They were administered along with Mauritius until 1903, when the Seychelles became a separate British colony. African and Indian workers were brought in to work in coconut and spice plantations and in guano mining. The present population is of mixed African, Indian, and European descent.

In the post-World War II period, a home-rule government rejected independence as impracticable. At the urging of the Organization of African Unity and the United Nations, the Seychelles declared independence on June 29, 1976. Its first president was ousted in a socialist coup in 1977 led by Prime Minister France Albert René. A new constitution, promulgated in March 1979, formalized one-party rule.

Sierra Leone
Republic of Sierra Leone

Geography Location: northwestern coast of Africa. **Boundaries:** Guinea to N and E, Liberia to S, Atlantic Ocean to W. **Total land area:** 27,653 sq. mi. (71,620 sq km). **Coastline:** 250 mi. (402 km). **Comparative area:** slightly smaller than South Carolina. **Land use:** 23% arable land; 2% permanent crops; 31% meadows and pastures; 29% forest and woodland; 15% other; includes negl. % irrigated. **Major cities:** Freetown (capital) 469,776 (1985 census); Koidu 80,000; Bo 26,000; Kenema 13,000; Makeni 12,000.

People Population: 3,963,289 (1988). **Nationality:** noun—Sierra Leonean(s); adjective—Sierra Leonean. **Ethnic groups:** over 99% African (30% Temne, 30% Mende, 2% Creole), rest European and Asian. **Languages:** English (official); regular use limited to literate minority; principal languages are Mende in south and Temne in north; Krio is language of resettled ex-slave population of Freetown area and is lingua franca. **Religions:** 30% Muslim, 30% indigenous beliefs, 10% Christian, 30% other or none.

Government Type: republic under presidential regime since Apr. 1971. **Independence:** Apr. 27, 1961 (from UK). **Constitution:** June 14, 1978. **National holiday:** Republic Day, Apr. 19. **Heads of government:** Gen. Joseph S. Momoh, president (since Nov. 1985). **Structure:** executive—president; legislature—unicameral parliament consists of 104 authorized seats, 85 of which are filled by elected representatives of constituencies and 12 by Paramount Chiefs elected by fellow Paramount Chiefs in each district; president authorized to appoint up to seven members; judiciary.

Economy Monetary unit: leone. **Budget:** (1984) **income:** $109 mil.; **expend.:** $146 mil. **GDP:** $965 mil., $247 per capita (1987). **Chief crops:** palm kernels, coffee, cocoa, rice, yams; much of cultivated land devoted to subsistence farming; food crops insufficient for domestic consumption. **Livestock:** N.A. **Natural resources:** diamonds, titanium ore, bauxite, iron ore, gold, chromite. **Major industries:** mining (diamonds, iron ore, bauxite, rutile), small-scale manufacturing (beverages, textiles, cigarettes, footwear), petroleum refinery. **Labor**

force: about 1.5 mil. (1981); 65% agriculture, 19% industry, 16% services; only small minority, some 65,000, earn wages; 55% of population of working age (1985). **Exports:** $137 mil. (f.o.b., 1986); diamonds, iron ore, palm kernels, cocoa, coffee. **Imports:** $155 mil. (c.i.f., 1986); machinery and transportation equipment, manufactured goods, foodstuffs, petroleum products. **Major trading partners:** UK, other EC (Netherlands, W. Germany), U.S., Japan, Communist countries.

Intl. Orgs. Commonwealth, FAO, G-77, GATT, IAEA, IBRD, ICAO, IDA, IFAD, IFC, ILO, IMF, IMO, INTERPOL, ITU, NAM, UN, UNESCO, UPU, WHO, WMO.

Portuguese domination of the Sierra Leone coast began in 1462. English explorers, including Francis Drake, arrived in the late 16th century. Europeans traded for slaves in Sierra Leone, but in 1787 Freetown was founded by the British Sierra Leone Co. as a haven for freed slaves. The settlement was populated by former slaves from Great Britain, North America, and the Caribbean, and later by slaves liberated from slave trading ships by the British navy.

Sierra Leone was reorganized as a British colony in 1808. The ex-slave population, from diverse tribal and national backgrounds, developed an English-speaking Creole culture unique in Africa. Freetown became the center of British colonial administration and trade in West Africa and was the focus of missionary-supported projects in education, health care, and economic development.

The native peoples of Sierra Leone staged numerous rebellions against the British and the Creole elite; resentment focused on the tax system and on the privileges of the English-speaking descendents of ex-slaves.

During the 20th century, home rule developed through an elected advisory legislature. In 1951 a constitutional framework had been developed as the basis of decolonization. Sir Milton Margei became chief minister in 1953, and prime minister in 1961. Full independence came on Apr. 27, 1971. The last ties with the British Crown were cut in 1971, when Sierra Leone became a republic. A referendum in 1978, implemented in 1979, created a one-party state.

Sierra Leone has a mixed economy. Cocoa, coffee, palm oil, ginger, and other crops are grown for export; rice is the dietary staple. Mining, particularly for diamonds, bauxite, chrome, and gold, is the most important industry. Tourism is a major foreign exchange earner. Despite political stability and relatively abundant resources, the Sierra Leone economy has been burdened by inflation, corruption, and mismanagement, leading to heavy dependence on foreign borrowing.

Singapore
Republic of Singapore
Geography Location: Singapore Island and some 57 islets situated off southern extremity of Malay peninsula to which Singapore Island is linked by a causeway; on passageway between Indian and Pacific oceans about 77 mi.

(124 km) N of Equator. **Boundaries:** Johor Strait to N; Pacific Ocean to E; Strait of Malacca to SW, separating Singapore from Indonesian island of Sumatra; and Indian Ocean to W. **Total land area:** 240 sq. mi. (622 sq km). **Coastline:** 120 mi. (193 km). **Comparative area:** slightly less than 3.5 times size of Washington, D.C. **Land use:** 4% arable land; 7% permanent crops; 0% meadows and pastures; 5% forest and woodland; 84% other. **Major cities:** Singapore (capital).

People Population: 2,645,443 (1988). **Nationality:** noun—Singaporean(s); adjective—Singapore. **Ethnic groups:** 76.4% Chinese, 14.9% Malay, 6.4% Indian, 2.3% other. **Languages:** Chinese, Malay, Tamil, and English (official); Malay (national). **Religions:** majority of Chinese are Buddhists or atheists; Malays nearly all Muslim; minorities include Christians, Hindus, Sikhs, Taoists, Confucianists.

Government Type: republic within Commonwealth. **Independence:** Aug. 9, 1965 (from Malaysia). **Constitution:** June 3, 1959, amended 1965; based on preindependence State of Singapore constitution. **National holiday:** Aug. 9. **Heads of government:** Wee Kim Wee, president (since Sept. 1965); Lee Kuan Yew, prime minister (since June 1959). **Structure:** ceremonial president; executive power exercised by prime minister and cabinet responsible to unicameral legislature (Parliament).

Economy (1986) **Monetary unit:** Singapore dollar. **Budget:** *income:* $3.91 bil.; *expend.:* $2.89 bil. **GDP:** $18.6 bil., $ 6,700 per capita. **Chief crops:** agriculture occupies position of minor importance in economy; self-sufficient in pork, poultry, and eggs; must import much of its other food requirements; major crops—rubber, copra, fruits, vegetables. **Livestock:** N.A. **Natural resources:** negl. **Major industries:** petroleum refining, electronics, oil drilling equipment. **Labor force:** 1,149,022; 31.3% services, 25.2% manufacturing, 23.1% trade; 6.5% unemployment. **Exports:** $22.5 bil. (f.o.b.); manufactured products, petroleum, rubber, electronics. **Imports:** $25.5 bil. (c.i.f.); major retained imports—capital equipment, manufactured goods, petroleum. **Major trading partners:** *exports:* 23% U.S., 15% Malaysia, 9% Japan, 7% Hong Kong, 4% Thailand; *imports:* 20% Japan, 15% U.S., 13% Malaysia, 6% China.

Intl. Orgs. ASEAN, Colombo Plan, Commonwealth, G-77, GATT, IAEA, IBRD, ICAO, IFC, ILO, IMF, IMO, INTELSAT, INTERPOL, ITU, NAM, UN, UNESCO, UPU, WHO, WMO.

Singapore was founded in 1819 by Sir Thomas Stamford Raffles on land ceded to the East India Company by the sultanate of Johore. An Anglo-Dutch treaty turned Singapore over to the British Crown in 1824, and eventually it was administered as part of the Straits Settlements. With its excellent harbor, Singapore quickly eclipsed Penang and Malacca as the dominant port for trade through the Straits of Malacca.

Fortified as a bastion of British defense in Southeast Asia, Singapore was overrun from

the rear by Japanese troops in February 1942. The British reoccupied the city of Singapore in September 1945 and reorganized Singapore as a British colony in 1946. On June 5, 1959, Singapore became a self-governing parliamentary democracy within the British Commonwealth. Its first prime minister, Lee Kwan Yew, has been in office ever since as head of the People's Action party. On Sept. 16, 1963, Singapore, along with Malaya, Sarawak, and Sabah, formed the Malaysian Federation. Singapore, ethnically Chinese, was uncomfortable within the Malay-dominated federation and seceded after two years, becoming an independent nation on Aug. 9, 1965.

Independent Singapore has enjoyed orderly, if authoritarian, government, steady economic growth, and a high standard of living. Still a major port, its economy now also encompasses international banking, finance, communications, high-technology manufacturing, and tourism. The 1985 financial collapse of Pan-Electric Industries, a major conglomerate, contributed to a recession in 1986. Several financial and political scandals in the wake of these events were widely reported in the international press, leading Singapore to restrict the domestic circulation of some foreign periodicals.

Solomon Islands
(PREVIOUS NAME: BRITISH SOLOMON ISLANDS)
Geography Location: scattered archipelago in South Pacific Ocean E of Papua New Guinea and about 1,000 mi. (1,600 km) NE of Australia. **Boundaries:** South Pacific Ocean to N, E, and S, Solomon Sea to W; nearest neighbor is Santa Cruz Islands to SE. **Total land area:** 10,639 sq. mi. (27,556 sq km). **Coastline:** 3,302 mi. (5,313 km). **Comparative area:** slightly larger than Maryland. **Land use:** 1% arable land; 1% permanent crops; 1% meadows and pastures; 93% forest and woodland; 4% other. **Major cities:** (1986 census) Honiara (capital) 30,499.

People Population: 312,196 (1988). **Nationality:** noun—Solomon Islander(s); adjective—Solomon Islander. **Ethnic groups:** 93% Melanesian, 4% Polynesian, 1.5% Micronesian, 0.8% European. **Languages:** 120 indigenous languages; Melanesian pidgin in much of country is lingua franca; English spoken by 1–2% of population. **Religions:** almost all at least nominally Christian; Anglican, Seventh-Day Adventist, and Roman Catholic churches dominant.

Government Type: independent parliamentary state within Commonwealth. **Independence:** July 7, 1978 (from UK). **Constitution:** July 7, 1978. **National holiday:** Independence Day, July 7. **Heads of government:** George G. D. Lepping, governor-general (since Feb. 1989); Soloman Mamaloni, prime minister (since Apr. 1989). **Structure:** executive authority in governor-general; unicameral legislature (38-member National Parliament).

Economy Monetary unit: Solomon Island dollar. **Budget:** (1986) **income:** revenues and grants $50 mil.; *expend.:* $60 mil. **GDP:** $115 mil., $380 per capita (1986). **Chief crops:** copra, cocoa, palm oil, rice, fruits, vegetables. **Livestock:** pigs and cattle. **Natural resources:** fish, forests, gold, bauxite, phosphates. **Major industries:** copra, fish (tuna). **Labor force:** 23,448 economically active (1984); 32.4% agriculture, forestry, and fishing. **Exports:** $65 mil. (1986); 46% fish, 31% timber, 5% copra, 5% palm oil. **Imports:** $59 mil. (1986); 30% plant and machinery, 19% fuel, 16% food. **Major trading partners:** (1985) *exports:* 51% Japan, 12% UK, 9% Thailand, 8% Netherlands, 2% Australia; *imports:* 36% Japan, 23% U.S., 9% Singapore, 9% UK, 9% New Zealand.

Intl. Orgs. Commonwealth, G-77, GATT (de facto), IBRD, IDA, IFAD, IFC, ILO, IMF, UN, UPU, WHO.

In 1893 Great Britain established a protectorate over the South Solomon Islands, including the large islands of Guadalcanal, San Cristobal, and Malata; the protectorate was extended to the smaller easterly islands of the chain in 1898. In 1900 Germany relinquished to Great Britain its claim to the North Solomons, including Choiseul and Santa Isabel; Bougainville Island was retained by Germany (see "Papua New Guinea"). The major islands were occupied by Japan in 1942 and retaken by the Allies in a series of bloody battles in 1943.

The Solomon Islands were made self-governing in January 1976 and became an independent nation on July 7, 1978. The domestic economy is based on subsistence agriculture and fishing. A number of light manufacturing and craft industries have been established in recent years. Copra, cacao, palm oil, and lumber are the principal exports. The sale of tuna fishing rights in the waters surrounding the Solomon Islands has given the nation a favorable balance of payments.

Somalia
Somali Democratic Republic
Geography Location: eastern coast of Africa. **Boundaries:** short frontier with Djibouti to NW, Gulf of Aden to N, long coastline on Indian Ocean to E, Kenya to SW, Ethiopia to W. **Total land area:** 246,201 sq. mi. (637,657 sq km). **Coastline:** 1,880 mi. (3,025 km). **Comparative area:** slightly smaller than Texas. **Land use:** 2% arable land; negl. % permanent crops; 46% meadows and pastures; 14% forest and woodland; 38% other; includes 3% irrigated. **Major cities:** (1981 est.) Mogadishu (capital) 500,000; Hargeish 70,000; Kismayu 70,000; Berbera 65,000; Merca 60,000.

People Population: 7,990,085 (1988) **Nationality:** noun—Somali(s); adjective—Somali. **Ethnic groups:** 85% Somali, rest mainly Bantu; 30,000 Arabs, 3,000 Europeans, 800 Asians. **Languages:** Somali (official), Arabic, Italian, English. **Religions:** almost entirely Sunni Muslim.

Government Type: republic. **Independence:** July 1, 1960 (from a merger of British Somaliland, which became independent from UK June 26, 1960, and Italian Somaliland, which became independent from Italian-administered UN trusteeship July 1, 1960, to form

Somali Republic). **Constitution:** Aug. 25, 1979, presidential approval Sept. 23, 1979. **National holiday:** Oct. 21. **Heads of government:** Maj. Gen. Mohamed Siad Barre, president and commander in chief of army (since Oct. 1969). **Structure:** president dominates political system; cabinet carries out day-to-day government functions; unicameral legislature (National People's Assembly) exists but has little power.

Economy Monetary unit: Somali shilling. **Budget:** (1986 est. in percent of GDP) *income:* 5.3%; *expend.:* 17.3%. **GDP:** $1.4 bil., about $200 per capita (1982 est.); no reliable figures of national income data. **Chief crops:** mainly a pastoral country, raising livestock; crops—bananas, sugarcane, cotton, cereals. **Livestock:** goats, sheep, camels, cattle, asses. **Natural resources:** uranium, largely unexploited reserves of iron ore, tin, gypsum, bauxite. **Major industries:** a few small industries, including sugar refining, textiles, petroleum refining. **Labor force:** about 2.2 mil. (1985); very few are skilled laborers; 70% pastoral nomads, 30% agricultural, government, traders, fishermen, handicraftsman, other; 53% of population of working age. **Exports:** $99 mil. (f.o.b., 1986); livestock, hides, skins, bananas. **Imports:** $363 mil. (c.i.f.,1986); textiles, cereals, transport equipment, machinery, construction materials and equipment. **Major trading partners:** (1985) *exports:* 34.6% Saudi Arabia, 19.6% Italy; *imports:* 26% Italy, 17% U.S., 12% Saudi Arabia.

Intl. Org. Arab League, FAO, G-77, IBRD, ICAO, IDA, IFAD, IFC, ILO, IMF, IMO, INTELSAT, INTERPOL, ITU, NAM, OAU, UN, UNESCO, UPU, WHO, WMO.

Arab trading settlements in Somalia were established in the seventh century and gradually evolved into independent sultanates. Portuguese traders established settlements and forts along the coast during the 15th and 16th centuries.

In the early 19th century, Great Britain arranged through local treaties to use harbors along the Somali coast and gained control over the northern part of the country by 1840. The border between Somalia and Ethiopia was demarcated by a treaty between Great Britain and Ethiopia in 1897. In 1885 the sultan of Zanzibar granted commercial advantages to Italy, and by further agreements in 1897 and 1908 Italy gained control over southern Somalia.

During the early 20th century, an uprising against British rule was led by Mohamed Abdullah. Abdullah was defeated by the British with help from his local rivals but is now regarded as the father of Somali nationalism.

The Italian invasion of Ethiopia in 1936 gave Italy a dominant position in the Horn of Africa. In the early phases of World War II, Italian troops drove the British from British Somaliland, but a 1940 counterattack led to British occupation of all of Somalia by 1941. After World War II, as discussions of Somalia's future continued, Britain handed over the Ogaden and neighboring territories to Ethiopia.

A United Nations pact of 1949 created an Italian trusteeship in the former Italian Somalia. Italy terminated its trusteeship and withdrew its forces in 1960. British Somali-

land was granted its own independence on June 26, 1960, and on July 1 joined with the former Italian territory to form the Somali Republic. The new country was plagued by regional rivalries, with the Somali Youth League emerging as a unifying national force. In 1969 Maj. Gen. Mohamed Siad Barre took control in a bloodless coup, abolished the national assembly, established a ruling Supreme Revolutionary Council, instituted a socialist regime, and established friendly relations with the USSR.

Beginning in 1972 Somali forces began border raids into Ethiopia's Ogaden region, peopled largely by Somalis. The Somali army mounted a full-scale invasion of the Ogaden in 1977. The Soviet Union switched its support to Ethiopia; in response, Somalia expelled all Soviet advisors. With Soviet aid and Cuban troops, Ethiopia drove back the Somali invasion in 1978. Over a million refugees fled from Ethiopia into Somalia, placing a severe burden on the country's fragile economy. The United States has been Somalia's principal source of military and economic aid since 1978. Sporadic conflict continues in the Ogaden between Somalia and Ethiopia, and the refugee situation remains critical.

Somalia's economy consists primarily of subsistence-level agriculture and pastoralism, with some mining. Chief exports are minerals and aromatic gums.

South Africa
Republic of South Africa
Geography Location: southern extremity of African mainland. **Boundaries:** Namibia to NW, Botswana and Zimbabwe to N, Mozambique to NE, Swaziland and Indian Ocean to E, Atlantic Ocean to W; Lesotho entirely surrounded by South African territory. **Total land area:** 471,445 sq. mi. (1,221,037 sq km). **Coastline:** 1,791 mi. (2,881 km). **Comparative area:** slightly less than twice size of Texas. **Land use:** 10% arable land; 1% permanent crops; 65% meadows and pastures; 3% forest and woodland; 21% other; includes 1% irrigated. **Major cities:** (1985 census) Cape Town (legislative capital) 1,911,521; Pretoria (administrative capital) 822,925; Johannesburg 1,609,408; Durban 982,075; Port Elizabeth 651,993.

People Population: 35,093,971 (1988). **Nationality:** noun—South African(s); adjective—South African. **Ethnic groups:** 69.9% black, 17.8% white, 2.9% Indian; 9.4% other. **Languages:** Afrikaans, English (official); Zulu, Xhosa, North and South Sotho, Tswana. **Religions:** most whites and about 60% of blacks are Christian; roughly 60% of Indians are Hindu, 20% Muslim.

Government Type: republic. **Independence:** May 31, 1910 (from UK). **Constitution:** Sept. 3, 1984. **National holiday:** Republic Day, May 31. **Heads of government:** Frederik W. de Klerk, president (since Aug. 1989). **Structure:** executive—president is head of government and chairman of cabinet; tricameral legislature—House of Assembly (whites), House of Representatives, and House of Delegates (Indians) elected directly by respective racial electorates; judiciary—courts maintain substantial independence from government influence.

Economy **Monetary unit:** South African rand. **Budget:** (1988) *income:* $24.3 bil.; *expend.:* $29.0 bil. **GDP:** $60 bil., $1,700 per capita (1987). **Chief crops:** corn, wheat, sugarcane, tobacco, citrus fruits; self-sufficient in foodstuffs. **Livestock:** sheep, cattle, goats, pigs, horses. **Natural resources:** gold, chromium, antimony, coal, iron ore. **Major industries:** mining (world's largest producer of diamonds, gold, chrome), automobile assembly, metalworking. **Labor force:** 11 mil. economically active (1985); 34% services, 30% agriculture, 29% industry and commerce, 7% mining. **Exports:** $21 bil. (f.o.b., 1987); gold, coal, diamonds, corn, uranium, other mineral and agricultural products; net gold output $7.0 bil. (1985). **Imports:** $14 bil. (c.i.f.,1987); machinery, motor vehicle parts, petroleum products, textiles, chemicals. **Major trading partners:** Japan, U.S., W. Germany, UK, Italy, Southern African Customs Union.

Intl. Orgs. GATT, IAEA, IBRD, ICAO, IDA, IFC, IMF, INTELSAT, ITU, UN, UPU, WHO, WIPO, WMO (membership rights in IAEA, ICAO, ITU, WHO, and WIPO suspended or restricted).

South Africa was originally inhabited by San and related peoples. Bantu peoples, including the Zulu and Xhosa, migrated to the region beginning around the 15th century and established large native kingdoms.

The Portuguese explorer Bartholomew Diaz discovered and named the Cape of Good Hope in 1488. The Dutch East India Company established a permanent settlement at Cape Town in 1652, which served as a supply and transshipment point for Dutch trade to the East Indies and which attracted Protestant settlers from throughout Western Europe. In a series of wars, the Xhosa people were expelled from the area under Dutch rule.

Great Britain began to dispute Dutch control of the Cape of Good Hope region in the late 18th century. To escape increasing British hegemony, in 1836 many Dutch farmers undertook a great overland migration to the north to lands not under the control of any European power. These Afrikaner pioneers later became known as Boers (farmers). They came into conflict with the Zulu kingdom that, under King Shaka, had recently widened its dominion in the South African interior. The Zulus were defeated at the Battle of Blood River in 1838, but they retained substantial power and territory for another 40 years.

Great Britain formally took control of the Cape Colony in 1841 and annexed Natal in 1843. The other two Afrikaner provinces, the Orange Free State and the Transvaal, remained temporarily free of British control. But when diamonds were discovered in the Orange Free State in 1867 and gold in the Transvaal in 1886, an influx of British miners and entrepreneurs provoked Boer rebellions.

In 1878 the Zulu Kingdom under its last great king, Cetewayo, rebelled against British rule in Natal. British troops attacked Zululand in 1878 and crushed the rebellion in 1879.

The first Anglo-Boer War of 1881–82 led to an inconclusive British victory. A renewed uprising led to the Boer War of 1899–1902,

which was fought with great ferocity between British regular troops and Afrikaner guerrilla forces. The eventual British victory led to the establishment of British rule in all of South Africa and to the formation of the Union of South Africa in 1910. The Union became a self-governing state within the British Empire in 1934.

South African politics became dominated by friction between British and Afrikaner whites; no effective black participation in government was permitted. The United South African party, led by Jan C. Smuts, advocated cooperation between the two groups and led South Africa to join World War II on the Allied side, over the opposition of the pro-Afrikaner Nationalist party.

After the war the Nationalists prevailed and won control of the government in 1948. Racial politics became the country's paramount concern, and the Nationalists introduced the policy of "apartheid" (separateness), under which racial groups were rigidly defined as white, black, Asian (primarily Indian), and colored (mixed ancestry). Each group was to be kept physically separate and develop its own political institutions within defined areas of residence; mixed neighborhoods, intermarriage, and other relations were prohibited. Blacks, in particular, were restricted by "pass laws" that allowed them only temporary access to white areas for employment.

International condemnation of these policies began almost immediately, as India broke relations with South Africa in 1946 over discrimination against Asians, and South Africa became the focus of mounting protest, UN resolutions, and international sanctions beginning in the 1960s. On May 31, 1961, South Africa gave up its dominion status and became a republic; its application for membership in the British Commonwealth was withdrawn in the face of opposition from the Commonwealth community. The African National Congress (ANC), organized in 1912, was banned by South African authorities. The imprisonment of its leader, Nelson Mandela, provided a focus for black political protest and nationalist aspirations. An uprising in Soweto in 1976 was put down by South African police and armed forces with the loss of hundreds of lives, providing a further focus of black protest. Pieter Willem Botha was elected president in 1978, pledging to uphold apartheid while seeking solutions to racial problems. In 1983 a majority of white voters approved the adoption of a new constitution that provided for limited power sharing by coloreds and Asians; blacks continued to be excluded (see "South African Homelands," below).

In the early 1980s, South African troops intervened in civil wars in Angola and Mozambique and were deployed to counteract growing proindependence rebellions in Namibia. Within South Africa terrorism and uprisings led by the African National Union grew in intensity in 1983–84. A state of emergency was declared in 1985 accompanied by renewed political and economic pressure from abroad. In 1986, Bishop Desmond Tutu, a leading black nationalist, addressed the United Nations and called for renewed sanctions. The Botha government announced an end to the pass laws and prom-

ised limited black participation in government. Fighting between black groups in 1986–87 further increased domestic tension.

On May 19, 1987, South African troops conducted raids against ANC bases in Zambia, Zimbabwe, and Botswana. A new national state of emergency was declared in June, as strikes and riots marked the 10th anniversary of the Soweto uprising. The United States announced measures designed to end American investment in South Africa.

The Brazzaville accords of Dec. 13, 1988, designed to bring about political settlements in Angola and Namibia, have given the South African government some breathing space in settling the domestic political situation. In early 1989, in anticipation of elections to be held in September, various proposals were put forward for constitutional reform. Most called for expanded power sharing but still within the context of defined racial groups.

South Africa has the continent's most highly developed economy; it is a fully-developed, capitalist industrial-commercial society with manufacturing, mining, agricultural, service, and other sectors. International sanctions have hampered the economy to a limited extent, but their impact has been lessened by South Africa's status as the world's largest producer of gold, a key source of chromium and other strategic metals, and of gem-quality diamonds. There remains a wide economic gap between the white minority and the black majority.

In July 1989 Pres. Botha had an unprecedented meeting with Nelson Mandela, and there are strong suggestions that the white government is seeking an accommodation with the antiapartheid leadership.

South African Homelands The so-called homelands of South Africa were established in implementation of the policy of apartheid to create separate states for South African blacks. Residents of the homelands are not citizens of South Africa but rather of the homelands, which are governed by a chief minister and a legislature. The homelands are intended by the South African government to be regarded as separate nations, but they have not been internationally recognized.

The territory of the homelands comprises only a small portion of the total area of South Africa, although blacks make up nearly 70 percent of the South African population. They tend to include relatively poor and underdeveloped lands on the ground that economic development in South Africa has so far been accomplished by white settlers. The homeland policy has been criticized for perpetuating racial segregation and giving homeland citizens working in South Africa the status of temporary migrant workers, and also for tending to set off an alliance of whites, colored, and Asians against the black majority.

Homelands were established under the Promotion of Bantu Self-Government Act of 1959; their form of government was set up in the Black Constitution Act of 1971. The first homeland to be established was Transkei, established in 1963 and granted "independence" in 1976. Of the 10 homelands established to date, the four major ones are Transkei, Bophut-swana, Venda, and Ciskei. A dispute has broken out between South Africa and Swaziland over attempts, resisted by Swaziland, to cede some homeland territories to that nation.

Soviet Union
Union of Soviet Socialist Republics
(ABBREV.: USSR)

Geography Location: central Asia; largest country in world. **Boundaries:** Arctic Ocean to N; Pacific Ocean to E; China, Mongolia, Afghanistan, Iran, and Black Sea to S; Turkey, Bulgaria, Romania, Hungary, Czechoslovakia, Poland, and Baltic Sea to W; Finland and short frontier with Norway to NW. **Total land area:** 8,599,228 sq. mi. (22,272,000 sq km). **Coast-line:** 26,582 mi. (42,777 km). **Comparative area:** slightly less than 2.5 times size of U.S. **Land use:** 10% arable land; negl. % permanent crops; 17% meadows and pastures; 41% forest and woodland; 32% other; includes 1% irrigated. **Major cities:** (1986 est.) Moskva (Moscow—capital) 8,703,000; Leningrad 4,901,000; Kiyev (Kiev) 2,495,000; Tashkent 2,073,000; Baku 1,722,000.

People Population: 286,434,844 (1988). **Nationality:** noun—Soviet(s); adjective—Soviet. **Ethnic groups:** 52% Russian, 16% Ukrainian, 32% other; 100 ethnic groups. **Languages:** Russian (official); more than 200 languages and dialects (at least 18 with more than one million speakers); 75% Slavic group, 12% Altaic, 8% other Indo-European, 3% Uralian, 2% Caucasian. **Religions:** 70% atheist, 18% Russian Orthodox, 9% Muslim, 3% Jewish, Protestant, Georgian Orthodox, or Roman Catholic.

Government Type: communist state. **Independence:** N.A. **Constitution:** Oct. 7, 1977. **National holiday:** October Revolution Day, Nov. 7. **Heads of government:** Mikhail Sergeyevich Gorbachev, general secretary of Central Committee of the Communist party (since Mar. 1985); Nikolay Ivanovich Ryzhkov, chairman of USSR Council of Ministers (since Sept. 1985); **Structure:** executive—USSR Council of Ministers; legislative—USSR Supreme Soviet; judicial—Supreme Court of USSR.

Economy Monetary unit: ruble. **Budget:** N.A. **GNP:** $2,356.7 bil., $8,375 per capita (1986). **Chief crops:** grain (especially wheat), potatoes, sugar beets, cotton, sunflowers, flax; degree of self-sufficiency depends on fluctuations in crop yields, particularly grain; large grain importer over past decade. **Livestock:** sheep, cattle, pigs, goats, horses. **Natural resources:** self-sufficient in oil, natural gas, coal, and strategic minerals, except bauxite, alumina, tantalum, tin, tungsten, fluorspar, and molybdenum; timber, gold, manganese, lead, zinc, nickel, mercury, potash, phosphates. **Major industries:** diversified, highly developed capital goods industries; consumer goods industries comparatively less developed. **Labor force:** civilian 150 mil. (1986); 77% industry and other nonagricultural fields; 23% agriculture; shortage of skilled labor. **Exports:** $97,053 mil. (f.o.b.,1986); petroleum and petroleum products, natural gas, metals, wood,

agricultural products, wide variety of manufactured goods (primarily capital goods and arms). **Imports:** $88,874 mil. (f.o.b.,1986); grain and other agricultural products, machinery and equipment, steel products (including large-diameter pipe), consumer manufactures. **Major trading partners:** $185.9 bil. (1986) 67% communist countries, 22% industrialized West, 11% developing countries.

Intl. Orgs. CMEA, IAEA, ICAO, ILO, IMO, ITU, UN, UPU, Warsaw Pact, WHO, WIPO, WMO.

In the ninth century A.D., Viking traders organized a state, which they called Rus, in the river valleys between the Baltic and the Black seas, centered on the cities of Kiev and Novgorod. In time the Vikings were absorbed into the native Slavic population; in 998 a Ruthenian prince of Kiev accepted Christianity from Constantinople. In the 13th century, Mongols under Genghis Khan and his descendants conquered most of Russia, and the Mongol Golden Horde maintained its power through the 14th century, exercising loose control over Novgorod and Moscow.

From the mid-14th century, Moscow grew to become the center of a new state that gathered in other cities and territories as Mongol power waned. Ivan III (Ivan the Great, 1440–1505) consolidated the power of Moscow; his marriage to a Byzantine princess led him to regard his empire as a third Rome, heir to the religious tradition of Constantinople. His grandson, Ivan IV (Ivan the Terrible, 1530–84), adopted the title czar (from the Latin *caesar*) when he came to power. He broke the power of the aristocratic Boyar class and greatly extended the power of Moscow through military conquest.

Over the next two centuries, Russia carried out a steady program of expansion eastward into Siberia and across the Bering Strait to Alaska, until the empire covered one-sixth of the land surface of the globe. Peter the Great (1672–1725) made Russia a Baltic and Black sea naval-power, brought Russia into the European state system, and instituted a sweeping, if superficial, Westernization of his realm. His new capital at St. Petersburg (now Leningrad) became one of the most splendid cities in Europe. At the end of the 18th century, Catherine the Great (1729–96) participated with Prussia and Austria in the partitions of Poland that temporarily caused that state to disappear from the map; Russia thereby became a major power in central Europe. Catherine's grandson Alexander I (1777–1825), member of the grand coalition that defeated Napoleon, became not only czar of Russia but also king of Poland and grand duke of Finland. His troops occupied Paris in 1815. The Russian aristocracy became ardent Francophiles in the 19th century, ignoring growing problems at home. After losing the Crimean War in 1856, Russia turned away from foreign ventures to develop Siberia and the southern territories near the border of Persia. In a major reform of the agricultural system, serfdom was abolished under Alexander II in 1861, though the newly independent peasantry, organized into agricultural cooperatives, only slowly

derived benefits from its freedom. The late 19th century also marked the beginning of modern industrialization in Russia and of extensive development in Siberia, aided by state investment in railroads and mining.

Under the last czar, Nicholas II (1868–1918), Russia was defeated by Japan in a war over Manchuria in 1905. The defeat sparked a naval mutiny and an abortive revolution, which led to the establishment of a constitutional monarchy and other limited political reforms. Further military losses in World War I set the stage for the monarchy's downfall in the Revolution of 1917.

The initial revolution of March 1917 brought a relatively moderate socialist (Menshevik) group to power. Its principal leader, Aleksandr Kerensky, organized a republican government and tried to maintain the Russian war effort but failed to gain control of the many contending revolutionary factions of the time. The Germans allowed the radical Bolshevik leader, V.I. Lenin, to return to Russia, where he and his followers organized workers' soviets hostile to the Menshevik republic. Bolshevik forces occupied Leningrad on Nov. 7, 1917 (October in the old Byzantine calendar, hence the name October Revolution), arrested the cabinet, and put in place a Council of People's Commissars, under Lenin's chairmanship. There followed four years of civil war between Bolshevik, Menshevik, and czarist forces, in the course of which Nicholas II and his family were executed in 1918.

Decreeing land to the peasants, worker management in industry, and repudiation of czarist debts, the Bolsheviks won the survival of their regime by withdrawing from World War I. The 1918 Treaty of Brest-Litovsk, which gained peace with Germany, granted freedom to Finland, the Baltic republics, Poland, the Ukraine, and Bessarabia. At the conclusion of the civil war (complicated by a war with Poland) in 1921, the Soviet state was established, with the Ukraine reabsorbed into the Soviet Union. The Bolshevik victory also resulted in the creation in 1921 of the Mongolian People's Republic as a close Soviet ally.

The early 1920s are now remembered as a "golden age" of Soviet history. Lenin's "New Economic Policies" allowed some role for market forces and private ownership and led to a brief burst of economic growth. Art, literature, and science flourished in an atmosphere of revolutionary enthusiasm and little censorship.

Lenin died on Jan. 21, 1924, and after a power struggle, was succeeded by Josef Stalin. Stalin supported communist revolutions in China and elsewhere through the Communist International (Comintern) but generally withdrew from foreign engagements in order to concentrate on domestic affairs. Under Lenin, and even more under Stalin, the Communist party established a police state, condemning millions of people to internal exile in the 1920s and consolidating all power in the hands of the state. In 1929 agriculture was forcibly collectivized, leading to the starvation or execution of an estimated 10 million peasants, while forced industrialization was carried out under a series of five-year plans.

Stalin's chief rival, Leon Trotsky, was expelled from the USSR in 1929 (and assassinated by Stalinist agents in Mexico in 1940). Stalin's obsession with eliminating all possible rivals for power led to a series of purges which, at their height in 1934–39, saw the summary execution of hundreds of thousands of presumed "enemies of the state" and the imprisonment in concentration camps of millions more.

Russia's reemergence as a world power was signaled by the signing in August 1939 of the Hitler-Stalin Pact, a nonaggression treaty through which Stalin aimed to recover territories lost to Russia in 1918. Poland was again partitioned, Bessarabia annexed (as the Moldavian Republic), Finland conquered and partitioned, and the Baltic republics absorbed.

When, in June 1941, Hitler turned against his ally and invaded Russia, unprepared and ill-equipped Russian armies retreated on a broad front. But Stalin emerged as a national leader in the "Great Patriotic War," restructuring the army and enlisting the support of the Orthodox church in rallying the population. In the early winter of 1942, the war changed course as Russia broke the German siege of Stalingrad, and Russian armies began their westward push that would carry them to the Elbe River by April 1945. As the war progressed, Stalin rose to the status of a world leader, treated as an equal by his allies Churchill and Roosevelt.

By the end of World War II, Stalin had reestablished the old czarist boundaries of Russia and more; he had a ring of occupied states all along his western boundary and a divided Germany beyond. Over the years 1945–48, he engineered a thorough communization of those occupied states, turning them into Russian satellites. Only Yugoslavia escaped total Russian domination.

Stalin lived until March 1953, becoming increasingly paranoid and unstable in his old age, apparently planning another purge even on his deathbed. He was succeeded by a collegial form of party and government leadership, from which Nikita Khrushchev, the party chairman, gradually emerged as the paramount figure. In a secret speech to the party leadership in 1956, Krushchev denounced Stalin for crimes against the party. He announced a set of new policies designed to bring about rapid modernization and consolidated his power when he became premier in 1958. The Khrushchev years brought a small but steady rise in living standards and a "thaw" in police state methods, the KGB (state security police) being brought under party control.

In foreign policy there was a thaw as well. In 1953 the Soviets agreed to an armistice in Korea, and tolerated the formation of a more liberal government in Hungary. In 1955 Russia returned the Porkkala peninsula to Finland and agreed to the Austrian State Treaty, whereby all foreign troops were withdrawn from Austria, which became independent and neutral. But the limits of disengagement became clear in 1956 with the ruthless Soviet suppression of the Hungarian uprising. A summit conference between Khrushchev and Eisenhower in 1960 led to a propaganda victory for Russia when an American U-2 spy plane was shot down over Russian territory on May 1. And in 1962 Khrushchev engaged in the reckless adventure of trying to install Soviet missiles in Cuba, an attempt from which he had to back down during the "Cuban Missile Crisis."

While on vacation in 1964, Khrushchev was informed that he had been removed from office and replaced as party secretary by Leonid Brezhnev and as premier by Aleksei Kosygin. His failure to deliver on extravagant promises for domestic economic growth and his recklessness in foreign affairs seem to have been responsible for his downfall. The new leaders embarked on an ambitious program of military (and especially naval) expansion, with military spending rising about 3 percent per year. The Soviet Union also pressed ahead vigorously with a space program that had begun with the triumphant launching of Sputnik I in 1957.

Under Brezhnev and Kosygin (with Brezhnev as senior partner), the USSR became more aggressive in foreign policy. The severe suppression of Czechoslovakia's "Prague Spring" in 1968 occasioned development of the Brezhnev Doctrine, whereby Russia claimed the right to intervene militarily in any socialist state. Soviet involvement in the Third World grew, with Russia supporting Vietnam against China in Southeast Asia; Syria and the PLO against Israel in the Middle East; leftist regimes in Angola, Ethiopia, and elsewhere in Africa; and the Sandanistas in Nicaragua. Cuba emerged as the principal Soviet proxy in supplying troops for leftist causes in the Third World. In 1979 Soviet troops moved into Afghanistan, allegedly at the invitation of its Marxist government, and remained bogged down there for a decade. Under American pressure, Brezhnev permitted the emigration of about 130,000 Jews and 40,000 ethnic Germans in the 1970s.

Domestically, the regime grew more oppressive; censorship was tightened and dissidents sentenced to terms in penal mental institutions. Elitism and nepotism created a self-perpetuating and interlocking network of power at the top, while the nation as a whole stagnated.

Brezhnev's death in 1982 brought about a rapid series of leadership transfers. Yuri Andropov, for 15 years head of the KGB, succeeded Brezhnev as party secretary but died after only 15 months in office. The downing by Soviet fighters of a Korean Airlines 747 on Sept. 1, 1983, brought a chill to Soviet-U.S. relations. Andropov was succeeded by Konstantin Chernenko, who died 13 months later. In March 1985 Mikhail Gorbachev became party secretary, ushering in a new era in Soviet history.

Gorbachev first instituted a cautious shakeup of state and party bureaucrats, promoting younger men who were technocrats rather than party professionals. Under the slogan *glasnost* (openness, candor), censorship was relaxed; by 1988 criticism of not only Stalin but also Brezhnev was permitted, and policy was openly debated in the press. Jamming of broadcasts from the West was ended.

Gorbachev's other motto, *perestroika* (restructuring), addresses his aim to boost morale and increase economic efficiency by devolving responsibility for economic decisions away from the party and government and toward industrial and agricultural managers. Borrowing from the Chinese experience in agricultural reform and the Hungarian model of decentralized industrial management, perestroika has so far raised expectations but not output; the system remains sluggish, inefficient, and burdened with the vested interests of state planners. The nuclear power plant disaster at Chernobyl in April 1986 and a gas pipeline fire that killed hundreds of passengers in passing railroad trains in June 1989 exemplify the industrial mismanagement against which Gorbachev's policies are aimed.

In foreign policy Gorbachev has pursued arms reduction agreements with the United States and has disentangled Soviet forces from Afghanistan, with complete withdrawal of troops beginning in early 1989. His international stature exceeds that of any previous Soviet leader; but his principal problems remain at home.

Foremost among those problems is the nationalities question. The Muslim southern regions of the USSR have been the scene of turmoil since the anti-Russian riots in Kazakhstan in 1986; in 1988 riots broke out in the Christian republic of Armenia over the status of ethnic Armenians in the neighboring Muslim republic of Azerbaijan; in 1989 ethnic warfare broke out between Uzbeks and Turks in Uzbekistan. The Soviet defeat in Afghanistan and inflammatory Shiite fundamentalist broadcasts from Iran further raised Muslim consciousness in the USSR, while the disastrous Armenian earthquake of 1988 and the ineptness of disaster relief efforts added fuel to Armenian grievances against the central government.

In the northwest, the Baltic republics of Estonia, Latvia, and Lithuania have raised their old national flags over their parliaments, enacted laws giving their native languages priority over Russian, and proclaimed the superiority of local republican law over the laws of the Soviet Union; all three republics seem to be heading for unilateral declarations of political autonomy. Meanwhile, in Eastern Europe, the Soviet hold grows weaker. East Germany has made clear its opposition to both glasnost and perestroika, while in Poland the noncommunist Solidarity party won an overwhelming victory in parliamentary elections in May 1989.

The Soviet Union in 1989 had clearly reached a historic turning point, with the future of its multinational empire at stake.

Spain
Spanish State
Geography Location: more than four-fifths of Iberian Peninsula in southwestern Europe. **Boundaries:** Bay of Biscay and France to N; Mediterranean Sea to E; Morocco 19 mi. (30 km) to S, across Strait of Gibraltar; Portugal to W. **Total land area:** 194,897 sq. mi. (504,782 sq km). **Coastline:** 3,085 mi. (4,964 km). **Comparative area:** slightly more than

twice size of Oregon. **Land use:** 31% arable land; 10% permanent crops; 21% meadows and pastures; 31% forest and woodland; 7% other; includes 6% irrigated. **Major cities:** (1981 census) Madrid (capital) 3,188,297; Barcelona 1,754,900; Valencia 751,734; Sevilla (Seville) 653,833; Zaragoza (Saragossa) 590,750.

People Population: 39,209,765 (1988). **Nationality:** noun—Spaniard(s); adjective— Spanish. **Ethnic groups:** composite of Mediterranean and Nordic types. **Languages:** Castilian Spanish; second langs. include 17% Catalán, 7% Galician, 2% Basque. **Religions:** 99% Roman Catholic, 1% other.

Government Type: parliamentary monarchy. **Independence:** N.A. **Constitution:** Dec. 6, 1978, effective Dec. 29, 1978. **National holiday:** June 24. **Heads of government:** Juan Carlos, king (since Nov. 1975); Felipe Gonzalez Márquez, prime minister (since Dec. 1982). **Structure:** executive—with acts of king subject to countersignature—prime minister and his ministers responsible to lower house; bicameral legislature—Cortes Generales, consisting of more powerful Congress of Deputies (350 members) and Senate (208 members) with possible addition of one to six members from each new autonomous region; judiciary—independent.

Economy Monetary unit: peseta. **Budget:** (1986) *income:* $79 bil.; *expend.:* $90 bil. **GNP:** $282.2 bil., $7,240 per capita (1987 est.). **Chief crops:** grains, citrus, fruits, vegetables, wine grapes; virtually self-sufficient in good crop years. **Livestock:** sheep, pigs, cattle, horses, mules. **Natural resources:** coal, lignite, iron ore, uranium, mercury. **Major industries:** textiles, apparel (including footwear), food and beverages, metals and metal manufacturing. **Labor force:** 14.2 mil. (1987 est.); 44.8% services, 30.9% industry, 15.6% agriculture, 9.1% construction; 20.2% unemployment; other 8.7% (1987). **Exports:** $27.2 bil. (f.o.b., 1986); iron and steel products, machinery, automobiles, citrus, fruits, vegetables, wine. **Imports:** $35.1 bil. (c.i.f., 1986); fuels (38%), machinery, chemicals, iron and steel, automobiles. **Major trading partners:** (1986) 55% EC, 21% developing countries, 11% other developed countries, 10% U.S., 3% communist countries.

Intl. Orgs. EC, FAO, GATT, IAEA, IBRD, ICAO, IDA, IFAD, IFC, ILO, IMF, IMO, INTELSAT, INTERPOL, ITU, NATO, OAS (observer), OECD, UN, UNESCO, UPU, WHO, WIPO, WMO.

Prehistoric Spain was populated by Iberians, Basques, and Celts. Its Mediterranean ports were frequented by Phoenician traders, and part of the country was incorporated into the empire of Carthage. Spain fell under the Roman Empire around 200 B.C.; Roman rule ended when the Visigoths invaded and took control of the Iberian Peninsula in the fifth century. The Visigoths adopted Christianity but were in turn conquered by Moors from northwest Africa in A.D. 711. The Berber/Arab civilization of the Moors produced the most elegant and cultivated culture in medieval Europe, and was an important conduit for the reintroduc-

tion of Greek science into Europe in the 12th century.

The Christian reconquest of the Iberian Peninsula began almost immediately after the Moors had established themselves and proceeded slowly but steadily over a period of 750 years. The consolidation of the region's small, contentious Christian kingdoms came with the marital alliance of Ferdinand of Aragon and Isabella of Castile in 1469. Grenada, the last Moorish outpost in Spain, fell to the forces of Ferdinand and Isabella in 1492, just as Columbus, with their sponsorship, was discovering the lands that were to become Spain's New World empire.

Under the Habsburg dynasty (1516–1700), Spain reached the zenith of its power and prestige around the year 1600 (despite the 1588 defeat of the Spanish Armada by England), controlling an empire that embraced nearly all of South America (except Brazil), Central America, Mexico, western North America, the Philippines, and smaller territories in Africa and Asia. But Spain's loss of the Netherlands, endless struggles with the French in Europe and the Turks in the Mediterranean, and relentless inflation caused by imports of New World silver—all took their toll. During the 18th century, the Bourbons ruled a declining but still powerful Spain, until Napoleon installed his brother as king in 1808.

After Napoleon's defeat, the Bourbons returned in 1814, but in the 19th century, the loss of the South American colonies, three dynastic wars, and a brief republican interlude after 1868 were all signs of progressive weakness. The crowning blow to Spanish power and prestige was the loss of the Spanish-American War to the United States in 1898, leading to the independence of Cuba and the American takeover of Puerto Rico and the Philippines.

Spain remained neutral in World War I. In 1923 Primo de Rivera established a dictatorship; he was forced out of office by King Alfonso XIII in 1930, but in 1931 the king himself was forced to abdicate. A republic replaced the monarchy. Its volatile mixture of socialism, anticlericalism, and decentralization provoked a right-wing reaction and exacerbated regional separatist tendencies. The government moved to the Right, and in 1934 a miner's strike in Asturia was put down with great bloodshed. A left-wing government was elected in 1936 and deposed in a coup, which led to the terrible Civil War of 1936–39, in which Spain became a battleground for competing world ideologies. The Nationalists, aided by Hitler and Mussolini, defeated the Republicans, aided by Stalin and by leftist volunteers from many countries. Out of the wreckage emerged the dictatorship of the apolitical and intensely patriotic and Catholic Gen. Francisco Franco.

At the time of the Civil War, Spain was still largely an agricultural country, with smallholdings in the north and great estates in the south. Traditional crops included grains, grapes and wine, citrus fruits, olives, and olive oil. In the Basque country, the mining of iron, copper, and lead provided the basis for both exports and a domestic iron and steel industry, which had been the case since the 19th cen-

tury. In the 20th century, shipbuilding and chemicals were added to the traditional textile industries of the Mediterranean coastal cities. The civil war largely destroyed this industrial base, which was not rebuilt until the 1950s.

Except for a contingent of troops sent to fight with the German invaders of the Soviet Union, Spain remained precariously neutral during World War II; Franco declined to repay Hitler for his support in the Civil War. But wartime Spain, despite its neutrality, could not muster the resources to undertake national reconstruction.

In postwar Europe, the Franco regime seemed like a remnant of the fascism of the 1930s; Stalin's active hostility led the United Nations to treat Spain as an international pariah. Despite foreign disapproval, however, at home Franco represented peace and stability; few Spaniards were willing to risk a return to civil strife by opposing him. Over time the military and Catholic aspects of the regime grew more pronounced, while fascist elements were downplayed. In 1947 the Law of Succession made Spain a monarchy without a king, awaiting the restoration of the throne in the post-Franco era.

In the 1950s the Cold War led to friendlier American relations with Spain and the establishment of American military bases there in 1953. UN membership followed in 1955. Despite some resultant growth in international trade, Spain's economy lagged, with industrialization barely beginning.

In 1958 Franco turned the direction of the economy over to a group of technocrats, mostly neoliberal members of the Opus Dei lay Catholic order. With U.S. economic and military aid, a growing tourist industry, increased foreign investment, and, especially, freer markets, the economy revived. Older industries like iron, steel, and textiles were rejuvenated, while newer ones, such as chemicals, plastics, automobile assembly, and power plants, were created. Agriculture was increasingly mechanized, and it shifted to export-oriented ranching and horticulture.

In 1967 Franco proclaimed the Organic Law, which, while confirming him as head of state, granted some independence to the Cortes (legislature) and permitted heads of families to vote for some of its delegates. This, along with a relaxation of censorship, softened the growing opposition to the regime among students, labor unions, and regional separatists. In 1969 Prince Juan Carlos was named heir apparent to the Spanish throne.

Franco died in 1975 and was duly succeeded by Juan Carlos. With the new prime minister, Adolfo Suarez, the king worked to liberalize the Franco inheritance: Political parties were legalized; the Cortes was transformed into a bicameral legislature, with both houses elected by universal suffrage; the first elections since 1936 were held; and a new constitution was promulgated—all by 1978.

In 1980 Catalonia and the Basque country were granted home rule, following overwhelming victories in home-rule plebiscites. In the Basque lands, however, violent terrorist agitation for complete independence continues.

In February 1981 a right-wing coup attempted to depose the government; armed conspirators entered the Cortes and held the legislators hostage. The coup collapsed in a day when the armed forces declared their loyalty to the king.

Since 1982 the Socialist Workers' party has controlled both houses of the Cortes. Although socialist, the party has abandoned both Marxism and the traditional labor radicalism of prewar Spain; it now resembles, under Prime Minister Filipe Gonzalez Márquez, the mainstream Social Democratic parties of the rest of Western Europe.

Under the new monarchy, Spain joined the Council of Europe in 1977, NATO in 1982, and the EEC in 1986. Spain is now a full participant in the affairs of Western Europe.

Sri Lanka
Democratic Socialist Republic of Sri Lanka
(PREVIOUS NAME: CEYLON)

Geography Location: one large island and several smaller islands in Indian Ocean about 50 mi. (80 km) SE of peninsular India. **Boundaries:** Palk Strait to N, Bay of Bengal to E, Indian Ocean to S and SW, and Gulf of Mannar to NW. **Total land area:** 24,886 sq. mi. (64,454 sq km). **Coastline:** 833 mi. (1,340 km). **Comparative area:** slightly larger than West Virginia. **Land use:** 16% arable land; 17% permanent crops; 7% meadows and pastures; 37% forest and woodland; 23% other; includes 8% irrigated. **Major cities:** (1986 est.) Colombo (capital) 683,000; Dehiwala-Mount Lavinia 191,000; Jaffna 143,000; Moratuwa 138,000; Kandy 130,000.

People Population: 16,639,695 (1988). **Nationality:** noun—Sri Lankan(s); adjective—Sri Lankan. **Ethnic groups:** 74% Sinhalese; 18% Tamil; 7% Moor; 1% Burgher, Malay, and Veddha. **Languages:** Sinhala (official); Sinhala and Tamil listed as national langs.; Sinhala spoken by about 74% of population, Tamil spoken by about 18%; English commonly used in government and spoken by about 10% of population. **Religions:** 69% Buddhist, 15% Hindu, 8% Christian, 8% Muslim.

Government Type: republic. **Independence:** Feb. 4, 1948 (from UK). **Constitution:** Aug. 31, 1978. **National holiday:** Independence Day, May 22. **Heads of government:** Ranasinghe Premadasa, president (since Dec. 1988); Dingiri Banda Wijetunga, prime minister (since Mar. 1989). **Structure:** 1978 Constitution established strong presidential form of government.

Economy Monetary unit: rupee. **Budget:** (1985) **income:** $1.5 bil.; **expend.:** $2.1 bil. **GDP:** $6.3 bil., $390 per capita (1986). **Chief crops:** paddy, coconuts, tea, rubber; agriculture accounts for about 26% of GDP. **Livestock:** cattle, buffalo, goats, pigs, sheep. **Natural resources:** limestone, graphite, mineral sands, gems, phosphates. **Major industries:** processing of rubber, tea, coconuts, and other agricultural commodities; cement, petroleum refinery. **Labor force:** 6.6 mil. (1985 est.); 45.9% agriculture, 13.3% mining and

manufacturing, 12.4% trade and transport, 28.4% services and other; extensive underemployment; 19% unemployment (1986 est.). **Exports:** $1.2 bil. (f.o.b., 1986); tea, textiles and garments, petroleum products, coconut, rubber. **Imports:** $1.95 bil. (c.i.f., 1986); petroleum, machinery and equipment, textiles and textile materials, wheat, transport equipment. **Major trading partners:** (1985) **exports:** U.S. (22%), Egypt, Iraq, UK, W. Germany; **imports:** Japan, Saudi Arabia, U.S., India, Singapore.

Intl. Orgs. Colombo Plan, Commonwealth, FAO, G-77, GATT, IAEA, IBRD, ICAO, IDA, IFAD, IFC, ILO, IMF, IMO, INTELSAT, INTERPOL, ITU, NAM, UN, UNESCO, UPU, WHO, WIPO, WMO.

The ancient Veddah inhabitants of Sri Lanka were conquered by Sinhalese migrants from northern India in the sixth century B.C. The island's spices and precious stones and its position on the trans-Indian Ocean trade routes made it well known in ancient times. Sri Lanka was known to the Greeks as Tabrobane and to the Arabs as Serendip. From the third century A.D., Sri Lanka became a major center of Buddhist culture. Despite numerous invasions from India, the island was usually ruled by native kingdoms, but the invasions added a Tamil community to the premodern population.

The Portuguese conquered the coastal areas after 1505 and also introduced Roman Catholicism. The Dutch displaced the Portugese in 1648; the British expelled the Dutch in 1795. Great Britain was the first foreign power to extend its rule over the entire island, with the defeat of the central kingdom of Kandy in 1833. In that year all of Sri Lanka was incorporated into the British Crown colony of Ceylon. Under British rule, tea and rubber plantations were established in the island's interior, and coconut plantations in coastal areas were consolidated under foreign control.

During the 20th century, there were increasing demands for self-rule and dominion status. Ceylon became an independent member of the British Commonwealth on Feb. 4, 1948; the Republic of Sri Lanka was proclaimed on May 22, 1972.

Prime Minister W.R.D. Bandaranaike was assassinated on Sept. 25, 1959. His widow, Sirimavo Bandaranaike, leader of the Freedom party, was elected as his successor. In 1962 her government expropriated the property of foreign oil companies. The conservative United National party won a majority in parliament in March 1965 and agreed to pay compensation for the expropriated assets. In May 1970 Mrs. Bandaranaike was again elected prime minister. Violent demonstrations by leftist elements were put down with great severity in 1971, but some of the leftist demands were subsequently met through the nationalization of foreign plantations in the mid-1970s. Mrs. Bandaranaike's party was ousted again by the United National party in 1977. In 1978 a constitutional reform aimed at increasing stability by establishing a presidential form of government. Pres. J.R. Jayawardene was elected to office on Feb. 4, 1978.

Sri Lanka's economy continues to be domi-

nated by plantation agriculture; tea, rubber, copra, spices, and forest products (timber, plywood, paper pulp) are major exports. Rice is the principal food crop. Gemstones, particularly sapphires, are an important mineral resource, along with graphite, phosphate, and limestone. Industrial development has centered on textiles and light manufacturing. Tourism was an important industry before the outbreak of separatist violence in 1986.

Further migrations of Tamils from southern India in modern times resulted in Tamil majority populations in Sri Lanka's northern and northeastern coastal provinces. In the 1980s Tamil separatist movements developed in those areas, and widespread communal violence erupted between Sinhalese and Tamils in those areas and in major cities. (The older Tamil populations of the central highlands were not involved.) The most extreme separatist organization, the Tigers of Tamil Eelam, carried out a program of systematic terrorism that claimed hundreds of lives in 1987; retaliatory attacks by Sinhalese on Tamil communities claimed many additional victims.

In June 1987 government troops besieged the rebel forces in the Jaffna peninsula. In July Pres. Jayawardene accepted an offer from India's Prime Minister Rajiv Gandhi to supervise a truce in the Jaffna region. Tamil forces were to surrender their arms in a negotiated cease-fire, while the government pledged to hold a referendum aimed at granting self-rule to Tamil majority areas in the north and northeast. The plan failed, however; Indian troops became bogged down in battling the rebels, while the planned referendum was disrupted in 1988 by terrorism by the separatists (who demanded total independence for Tamil areas) against more moderate Tamil groups willing to accept self-rule. Instability continues, and the situation has already inflicted severe damage on the nation. The important tourist industry has collapsed, other sectors of the economy have declined, and communal mistrust reigns throughout the island.

Sudan
Republic of the Sudan
(PREVIOUS NAME: SOUDAN)

Geography Location: northeastern Africa. **Boundaries:** Egypt to N, Red Sea and Ethiopia to E, Kenya, Uganda, and Zaire to S, Central African Republic, Chad and Libya to W. **Total land area:** 967,500 sq. mi. (2,505,813 sq km). **Coastline:** 530 mi. (853 km). **Comparative area:** slightly more than ¼ size of U.S. **Land use:** 5% arable land; negl. % permanent crops; 24% meadows and pastures; 20% forest and woodland; 51% other; includes 1% irrigated. **Major cities:** (1983 census) Khartoum (capital) 476,218; Omdurman 526,287; Khartoum North 341,146; Port Sudan 206,727; Wadi Medani 141,065.

People Population: 24,014,495 (1988). **Nationality:** noun—Sudanese (sing., pl.); adjective—Sudanese. **Ethnic groups:** 52% black, 39% Arab, 6% Beja, 2% foreigners. **Languages:** Arabic (official), Nubian, Ta Bedawie, diverse dialects of Nilotic, Nilo-Hamitic, and Sudanic languages, English; program of Arabization in progress. **Religions:** 70% Sunni Muslim in north, 20% indigenous beliefs, 5% Christian (mostly in south).

Government Type: republic. **Independence:** Jan. 1, 1956 (from Egypt and UK). **Constitution:** Apr. 12, 1973, suspended following coup of Apr. 6, 1985; interim constitution Oct. 10, 1985. **National holiday:** Independence Day, Jan. 1. **Heads of government:** Sadiq al-Mahdi, prime minister (since May 1986). **Structure:** Supreme Council and Civilian Cabinet; regional military governors.

Economy Monetary unit: Sudanese pound. **Budget:** (1986) *income:* $630 mil.; *expend.:* $1.023 bil., including development expenditure of $255 mil. **GDP:** $4.55 bil., $200 per capita (1985). **Chief crops:** cotton, sorghum, millet, wheat, sesame; not self-sufficient in food production; main cash crops—cotton, sesame, gum arabic, peanuts, sorghum. **Livestock:** cattle, sheep, goats, chickens, camels. **Natural resources:** modest reserves of crude oil, iron ore, copper, chromium ore, zinc. **Major industries:** cotton ginning, textiles, cement. **Labor force:** 6.5 mil. (1983); 80% agriculture, 10% industry and commerce; labor shortages for almost all categories of skilled employment; 52% of population of working age (1985). **Exports:** $369 mil. (f.o.b., 1985); cotton (44%), sesame, gum arabic, groundnuts. **Imports:** $760 mil. (c.i.f., 1985); petroleum products, manufactured goods, machinery and equipment, medicines and chemicals. **Major trading partners:** Saudi Arabia, UK, U.S., W. Germany, Netherlands, France.

Intl. Orgs. Arab League, FAO, G-77, IAEA, IBRD, ICAO, IDA, IFAD, IFC, ILO, IMF, IMO, INTELSAT, INTERPOL, ITU, NAM, OAU, UN, UNESCO, UPU, WHO, WIPO, WMO.

The northern Sudan, the ancient land of Nubia, was loosely controlled by Egypt in antiquity and incorporated into the Arab world by the Islamic expansion of the seventh century. The southern Sudan was part of tribal black Africa, under no external control but subject to continual raids by slave traders from the north.

Ottoman Egypt conquered the northern Sudan in 1820–21; British influence in Egypt in the 19th century extended into the Sudan as well. In 1881 Muhammed Ahmed ibn Abdalla, a religious leader known as the Mahdi, united northern and north-central Sudan and led a resistance movement against Anglo-Egyptian control. Khartoum, defended by British Gen. Charles George Gordon, fell in 1885, but the Mahdi died soon thereafter, and his revolt came to an end. An Anglo-Egyptian force under Kitchener regained control in 1898; Anglo-Egyptian joint rule was established in the Sudan in 1899.

Great Britain and Egypt granted self-government and self-determination to the Sudan in 1953. A Sudanese parliament was seated in 1954, and full independence was achieved in 1956. Gen. Ibrahim Abboud took power in a bloodless coup in 1958 but was forced to resign after riots in 1964. In 1969 a new military coup installed a ruling Revolutionary Command Council and instituted a socialist regime. The council's leader, Gen. Muhammed Nimeiri, became prime minister. Disputes between Marxists and non-Marxists, and between arabized northerners and black southerners, led to continual difficulties. An attempted coup was foiled in 1971. In 1972 the Sudan's three black southern provinces were granted local autonomy. Another attempted coup in 1976 was put down by the Nimeiri government, and hundreds of prominent citizens were arrested and executed. The government accused Libya of sponsoring the coup.

In 1983 attempts by the Nimeiri government to institute Islamic law throughout the Sudan led to riots in the south and the imposition of a nationwide state of emergency in 1984. Popular unrest was exacerbated by drought and famine in 1985, leading to severe price increases for food and fuel. On Apr. 6, 1985, Nimeiri was overthrown in a coup led by Gen. Suwar El Dahab. After a brief period of rule by a transitional military council, a civilian cabinet was installed, and free parliamentary elections were held in 1986.

Refugees from war zones in Chad and Ethiopia have placed additional burdens on the Sudanese government, already hard-pressed by drought and internal refugees from famine areas. The Sudanese economy is a mixed developing economy featuring light industry including textiles and food processing; mineral resources include chrome, gold, copper, mica, and asbestos. The agricultural sector remains dominant; chief exports are cotton, gum arabic, and coffee.

Suriname
Republic of Suriname
(PREVIOUS NAME: DUTCH GUIANA)

Geography Location: northeastern coast of South America. **Boundaries:** North Atlantic Ocean to N, French Guiana to E, Brazil to S, Guyana to W. **Total land area:** 63,037 sq. mi. (163,265 sq km). **Coastline:** 240 mi. (386 km). **Comparative area:** slightly larger than Georgia. **Land use:** negl. % arable land; negl. % permanent crops; negl. % meadows and pastures; 97% forest and woodland; includes negl. % irrigated. **Major cities:** (1980 census) Paramaribo (capital) 67,718.

People Population: 394,999 (1988). **Nationality:** noun—Surinamer(s); adjective—Surinamese. **Ethnic groups:** 37% Hindustani (East Indian), 31% Creole (black and mixed), 15.3% Javanese, 10.3% Bush black. **Languages:** Dutch (official), English widely spoken, Sranan Tongo (sometimes called Taki-Taki, the native language of Creoles and much of younger population and lingua franca among others), Hindi Suriname Hindustani, Javanese. **Religions:** 27.4% Hindu, 25.2% Protestant (predominantly Moravian), 22.8% Roman Catholic, 19.6% Muslim.

Government Type: in transition from military to civilian rule as of Jan. 1988. **Independence:** Nov. 25, 1975 (from Netherlands). **National holiday:** Independence Day, Nov. 25. **Heads of government:** Ramsewak Shankar, president (since Jan. 1988). **Structure:** civilian government moving away from military control.

Economy Monetary unit: Suriname guilder. **Budget:** (1986) *income:* $280 mil.; *expend.:* $558 mil. **GDP:** $904 mil., $2,290 per capita (1986). **Chief crops:** rice, bananas, palm oil, timber. **Livestock:** cattle, pigs, goats, sheep, horses, mules, asses. **Natural resources:** timber, hydropower potential, fish, shrimp, bauxite. **Major industries:** bauxite mining, alumina and aluminum production, lumbering. **Labor force:** 104,000 (1984); 11% agriculture, animal husbandry, fishing; 25–30% unemployment (1987). **Exports:** $332 mil. (f.o.b., 1986); alumina, bauxite, aluminum, agricultural products, wood and wood products. **Imports:** $320 mil. (c.i.f., 1986); capital equipment, petroleum, iron and steel, cotton, flour. **Major trading partners:** (1986) *exports:* 22% Netherlands, 16% U.S., 16% Norway; *imports:* 32% U.S., 19% Netherlands, 11% Trinidad and Tobago.

Intl. Orgs. FAO, GATT, G-77, IBRD, ICAO, IFAD, ILO, IMF, IMO, INTERPOL, ITU, NAM, OAS, UN, UNESCO, UPU, WHO, WIPO, WMO.

In the early 17th century, the Dutch and English settled Suriname, which became a Dutch colony in 1667. Except for brief episodes of British rule, Suriname remained under Dutch control until its independence in 1975, shifting toward authoritarian military rule in 1980. The military created its own political party (the February 25 movement) and banned opposition organizations. The 1988 National Assembly election of Pres. Ramsewak Shankar marked an end to direct military rule, but the government still largely restricts civil liberties.

Swaziland
Kingdom of Swaziland

Geography Location: landlocked country in southern Africa. **Boundaries:** South Africa to N, SE, S, and W; Mozambique to E. **Total land area:** 6,704 sq. mi. (17,363 sq km). **Coastline:** none. **Comparative area:** slightly smaller than New Jersey. **Land use:** 8% arable land; negl. % permanent crops; 67% meadows and pastures; 6% forest and woodland; 19% other; includes 2% irrigated. **Major cities:** Mbabane (capital).

People Population: 735,302 (1988). **Nationality:** noun—Swazi(s); adjective—Swazi. **Ethnic groups:** 97% African, 3% European. **Languages:** English and siSwati (both official); government business conducted in English. **Religions:** 57% Christian, 43% indigenous beliefs.

Government Type: monarchy; independent member of Commonwealth. **Independence:** Sept. 6, 1968 (from UK). **Constitution:** suspended Apr. 12, 1973; new constitution promulgated Oct. 13, 1978 but not yet formally presented to people. **National holiday:** Somhlolo (Independence) Day, Sept. 6. **Heads of government:** Mswati III, king (since Apr. 1986); Sotsha Ernest Dlamini, prime minister (since Oct. 1986). **Structure:** executive—king or queen (with advice of Supreme Council of State), whose assent is required before parliamentary acts become law; king's authority exercised through prime minister and cabinet; legislative—bicameral parliament (Senate, House of Assembly) formally opened Jan. 1979;

80-member electoral college chose 40 members of lower house and 10 members of upper house; additional 10 members of each house chosen by king; judiciary—part of Ministry of Justice but otherwise independent of executive and legislative branches; cases can be appealed to high court and court of appeal.

Economy **Monetary unit:** Swazi lilangeni. **Budget:** (1988 est.) *income:* $285 mil.; *expend.:* $347 mil. **GNP:** $478 mil., $690 per capita (1986 est.). **Chief crops:** maize, cotton, rice, sugar, citrus fruits. **Livestock:** goats, cattle, sheep, pigs, asses. **Natural resources:** asbestos, coal, clay, tin, hydroelectric power. **Major industries:** mining (coal and asbestos), wood pulp, sugar. **Labor force:** 195,000 (1987); about 92,000 wage earners (many whose employment is off-and-on); with 36% agriculture and forestry, 20% community and social services, 14% manufacturing, 9% construction, 21% other; over 60,000 in subsistence agriculture; 24,000–29,000 employed in South Africa. **Exports:** $311 mil. (f.o.b., 1986); sugar, asbestos, wood and forest products, citrus, canned fruits. **Imports:** $353 mil. (f.o.b., 1986); motor vehicles, chemicals, petroleum products, foodstuffs. **Major trading partners:** South Africa, UK, U.S.

Intl. Orgs. FAO, G-77, GATT (de facto), IBRD, ICAO, IDA, IFAD, IFC, ILO, IMF, INTERPOL, ITU, NAM, UN, UNESCO, UPU, WHO.

The Kingdom of Swaziland, a landlocked African country, is surrounded on three sides by South Africa and on the fourth by Mozambique. The Swazi are of Bantu origin. They are believed to have migrated in the late 1700s, under their chief Ngwane II, into what is now southeastern Swaziland, finding several different peoples there. Ngwane II and his successors united these tribal clans by the beginning of the 19th century.

Although British and Boer traders began exploring the area in the 1830s, it was not until gold was discovered in the 1880s that settlers began coming in large numbers. They hoodwinked the illiterate Swazi leadership into signing away their rights to the land. The British and Boer governments agreed in 1894 that the Boers would control Swaziland, but power reverted to Great Britain after they defeated the Boers in the Boer War, which ended in 1902. Not until the 1967 did they give Swaziland authority over its internal affairs. Under the British-authored Constitution, Swaziland gained its independence in September 1968 as a constitutional monarchy led by King Sobhuza II. He set aside the Constitution in 1973 and disbanded the legislature. He ruled the country with the aid of a council of conservative ministers and named a committee to write a new constitution that was supposed to be more in keeping with Swazi traditions. A new legislature was created in 1979. The king died in 1982 and was replaced by his 18–year-old son, who took the name King Mswati III, in 1986.

Sweden
Kingdom of Sweden

Geography **Location:** about two-thirds of Scandinavian peninsula in northwestern Europe. **Boundaries:** Norway to NE and W, Finland to NE, Gulf of Bothnia to E, Baltic Sea to E and S, Skagerrak channel to SW. **Total land area:** 170,250 sq. mi. (440,945 sq km). **Coastline:** 2,000 mi. (3,218 km). **Comparative area:** slightly larger than California. **Land use:** 7% arable land; 0% permanent crops; 2% meadows and pastures; 64% forest and woodland; 27% other; includes negl. % irrigated. **Major cities:** (1987 est.) Stockholm (capital) 666,810; Göteburg (Gothenburg) 431,521; Malmö 230,838; Uppsala 159,962; Orebro 119,066.

People **Population:** 8,393,071 (1988). **Nationality:** noun—Swede(s); adjective—Swedish. **Ethnic groups:** homogeneous white population; small Lappish minority; about 12% foreign-born or first-generation immigrants (Finns, Yugoslavs, Danes, Norwegians, Greeks, Turks). **Languages:** Swedish, small Lapp- and Finnish-speaking minorities; immigrants speak native languages. **Religions:** 93.5% Evangelical Lutheran, 1.0% Roman Catholic, 5.5% other.

Government **Type:** constitutional monarchy. **Independence:** N.A. **Constitution:** Jan. 1, 1975. **National holiday:** Sweden Day, June 6; King's Birthday, Apr. 30. **Heads of government:** Carl XVI Gustaf, king (since Sept. 1973); Ingvar Carlsson, prime minister (since Mar. 1986). **Structure:** executive power vested in cabinet, responsible to parliament; legislative authority rests with unicameral parliament (Riksdag); Supreme Court, six superior courts, 108 lower courts.

Economy **Monetary unit:** Swedish krone. **Budget:** (1987) *income:* $42.13 bil.; *expend.:* $47.75 bil. **GNP:** $105.5 bil., $12,590 per capita (1986). **Chief crops:** grain, sugar beets, potatoes; 100% self-sufficient in grains and potatoes, 85% self-sufficient in sugar beets; milk and dairy products account for 37% of farm income;. **Livestock:** poultry, pigs, cattle, sheep, goats. **Natural resources:** zinc, iron ore, lead, copper, silver. **Major industries:** iron and steel, precision equipment (bearings, radio and telephone parts, armaments), wood pulp. **Labor force:** 4.39 mil. (1986); 32.8% private services, 30.0% government services, 22.0% mining and manufacturing. **Exports:** $37.3 bil. (f.o.b., 1986); machinery, motor vehicles, paper products, pulp and wood, iron and steel products. **Imports:** $32.7 bil. (c.i.f., 1986); machinery, petroleum and petroleum products, chemicals, motor vehicles, foodstuffs. **Major trading partners:** *exports:* 50.0% EC (11.5% W. Germany, 10.4% UK, 8.0% Denmark), 11.2% Norway, 11.2% U.S., 9.3% developing countries; *imports:* 57.2% EC (20.5% W. Germany, 10.4% UK, 6.8% Denmark), 7.8% U.S., 7.3% developing countries, 5.6% Norway.

Intl. Orgs. EC (Free Trade Agreement), EFTA, FAO, GATT, IAEA, IBRD, ICAO, IDA, IFAD, IFC, ILO, IMO, INTELSAT, INTERPOL, ITU, OECD, UN, UNESCO, UPU, WHO, WIPO, WMO.

The earliest Swedes, the Svear, conquered and merged with their southern neighbors, the Gotar, by the sixth century. Organized into petty kingdoms, Swedes joined with other Norsemen in the Viking raids of the seventh through 11th centuries; in the 10th century, they began to dominate a trading empire that stretched through Russia to the Black Sea. Christianity was introduced by St. Ansgar in 829 but became fully established only in the 12th century, during the reign of Eric IX, who also conquered Finland. For centuries Sweden warred with its neighbors, Norway and Denmark, for control in the north, and it competed with the German Hanseatic League for control of the Baltic trade.

The Swedish and Norwegian monarchies were merged in 1319 by Magnus VII, and in 1397 Queen Margaret effected the Kalmar Union, which united Sweden, Denmark, and Norway under a single monarch. Sweden resisted Danish rule, and in 1520 King Christian II responded with the massacre of the Swedish nobility at Stockholm. Sweden then rose against the Danish throne and in 1523 enthroned Gustavus Wasa as Gustavus I, founder of the Swedish monarchy. The Wasa dynasty slowly introduced Lutheran Christianity and in 1604 banned Catholicism.

Sweden became a European champion of Protestantism in the 17th century, intervening against the Habsburgs in the Thirty Years' War. Emerging among the victors after 1648, Sweden successfully waged wars with Denmark and Poland, built a great northern empire, and made the Baltic Sea virtually a Swedish lake. But in the late 17th century and into the 18th, the Russians deprived Sweden of the Baltic's eastern shore and, in 1808, of Finland, while the Prussians drove Sweden from the southern Baltic coast.

The kings of Sweden during the 18th century pursued a pointless despotism that weakened the country politically and socially. Sweden joined the European powers against Napoleon in 1813 and was rewarded with Norway in 1814. In 1905 Norway gained its independence, and Sweden took on its modern boundaries.

Sweden's greatest natural resources are timber, iron ore, and hydroelectric power. The first two were exploited by traditional industries, which supplemented other long-term economic activities such as fishing, maritime trade, and agriculture. All three provided the basis for industrialization in the 19th and 20th centuries, leading to an economic prosperity that was enhanced and protected by political neutrality.

Sweden's neutality was largely respected by Hitler during World War II, though Sweden was forced to accede to transportation of German troops to Norway over Swedish rails. Through the war Sweden continued to be ruled, under King Gustavus V, by a national coalition government lasting until 1945. Sweden's gross national product (GNP) rose by 20 percent during the war years.

Alone or in coalitions, the Social Democratic party had dominated the Swedish government since 1936, and after 1945 its governance was reestablished, lasting until 1976 under the leadership of Tage Erlander. Sweden, like its Scandinavian neighbors, constructed an economy based on free enterprise, public ownership of utilities, exports, social welfare, and high taxes.

A UN charter member, Sweden accepted Marshall Plan aid and joined the Council of Europe in 1948. Sweden's plan for a Nordic Defense Alliance failed when Norway and Denmark joined NATO (Sweden, remaining neutral, refused to join the North Atlantic pact), but the political and economic Nordic Council was formed with strong Swedish backing in 1952–53. This consultative body of parliamentarians for member states (Sweden, Norway, Denmark, Iceland, and, after 1956, Finland) led to the establishment of the SAS as the joint national airline of the first three members, to coordination of the welfare programs of member states, and to abolition of passport controls and controls on the migration of labor within Scandinavia.

Sweden maintains its neutrality by means of one of the highest rates of defense spending in Western Europe—13 percent of GNP in 1970, declining to 8 percent by 1985. Swedish armed forces have mobilized on a number of occasions to defend Sweden's airspace from Soviet aircraft and its territorial waters from intrusions by Soviet submarines.

Erlander retired as prime minister in 1969 and was succeeded by Olaf Palme, who pursued a more rigid socialist program than his predecessor. He advocated legislation to make incomes more equal, provoking some labor unrest. When King Gustav VI Adolf died in 1953—to be succeeded by King Carl XVI Gustaf—the Palme government passed the 1974 Instrument of Government Act, divesting the king of his role as commander in chief of the armed forces and of his right to appoint prime ministers.

Economic growth came to a virtual halt in the 1970s; lacking petroleum and gas resources, Sweden's oil import costs rose 700 percent between 1972 and 1979. Consumer prices rose sharply, and labor unrest grew. The Social Democrats were turned out of office by a conservative coalition in 1976 but were returned to office with a minority cabinet in 1982.

Palme was assassinated in 1986, a still-unsolved crime that shocked the nation. He was succeeded by Ingvar Carlsson, whose Social Democratic program has focused on a scheme whereby business profits are taxed to fund labor union purchases of sufficient stock to gain labor ownership of private enterprise; thus Sweden continues to be the most strongly socialist of the Scandinavian countries.

Switzerland
Swiss Confederation
Geography Location: landlocked country in central Europe. **Boundaries:** W. Germany to N, Austria to E, Italy to S, and France to W. **Total land area:** 15,943 sq. mi. (41,293 sq km). **Coastline:** none. **Comparative area:** slightly more than twice size of New Jersey. **Land use:** 10% arable land; 1% permanent crops; 40%

meadows and pastures; 26% forest and woodland; 23% other; includes 1% irrigated. **Major cities:** (1987) Berne (Bern, capital) 137,134; Zürich 349,549; Basel (Bâe) 173,160; Genève (Genf or Geneva) 160,645; Lausanne 124,206.

People Population: 6,592,558 (1988). **Nationality:** noun—Swiss (sing., pl.); adjective—Swiss. **Ethnic groups:** total population—65% German, 18% French, 10% Italian, 1% Romansh, 5% other; Swiss nationals—74% German, 20% French, 4% Italian, 1% Romansh, 1% other. **Languages:** total population—65% German, 18% French, 12% Italian, 1% Romansh, 4% other; Swiss nationals—74% German, 20% French, 4% Italian, 1% Romansh, 1% other. **Religions:** 49% Catholic, 48% Protestant.

Government Type: federal republic. **Independence:** N.A. **Constitution:** May 29, 1874. **National holiday:** National Day, Aug. 1. **Heads of government:** Jean-Pascal Delamuraz, president (since 1988; president rotates annually); Arnold Koller, vice president (since 1988; term runs concurrently with that of president). **Structure:** federal council (Bundesrat) has executive authority; bicameral parliament (National Council, Council of States) has legislative authority; judiciary left chiefly to cantons.

Economy Monetary unit: Swiss franc. **Budget:** (1985) *income:* $8.5 bil.; *expend.:* $8.7 bil. **GNP:** $126.2 bil., $19,250 per capita (1986). **Chief crops:** less than 50% self-sufficient; food shortages—fish, refined sugar, fats and oils (other than butter), grains, eggs, fruits, vegetables, meat; dairy farming predominates. **Livestock:** pigs, cattle, sheep, goats, horses. **Natural resources:** hydropower potential, timber, salt. **Major industries:** machinery, chemicals, watches. **Labor force:** 3.05 mil.; 822,746 foreign workers, mostly Italian (1987); 42% services, 39% industry and crafts, 11% government; 0.7% unemployment. **Exports:** $37.5 bil. (f.o.b., 1986); machinery and equipment, chemicals, precision instruments, metal products, textiles. **Imports:** $41.0 bil. (c.i.f., 1986); machinery and transportation equipment, metals and metal products, foodstuffs, chemicals, textile fibers and yarns. **Major trading partners:** 59% EC, 21% other developed countries, 17% developing countries, 3% communist countries.

Intl. Orgs. EFTA, FAO, GATT, IAEA, ICAO, IFAD, ILO, IMO, INTELSAT, INTERPOL, ITU, OECD, UNESCO, UPU, WHO, WIPO, WMO; permanent observer status at UN.

Switzerland, the Roman province of Helvetia, began to assume its modern form in A.D. 1291, when three independent cantons formed a defensive league against the expansion of Habsburg power. The Swiss League grew to eight cantons in 1353, 13 in 1513, 22 in 1815. The league continues to evolve; it reached its present size of 20 cantons and six half-cantons with the creation of the Canton of Jura in 1979.

The Treaty of Westphalia, which ended the Thirty Years' War in 1648, gave international recognition to the independence of Switzerland from the Holy Roman Empire. Switzerland

became a client state of France in the Napoleonic period; the European powers recognized and guaranteed Swiss independence and neutrality at the Congress of Vienna in 1815. Constitutional changes in 1848 and 1874 somewhat increased the power of the central government, but the individual cantons cling stubbornly to their independence within the confederation. This policy has helped ensure stability within a multilingual nation.

The Swiss government consists of an upper house, representing the cantons, and a lower house that is directly elected. No executive can veto, nor court disallow, a bill of the Swiss legislature. Executive power is vested in a seven-member committee chosen by the legislature, with a rotating presidency.

Swiss neutrality is defended by more than simply international guarantees. Switzerland is a highly militarized society; every male is required to serve in the citizen's militia until age 47, keeping an assault rifle and other equipment ready at home. The armed forces are equipped with sophisticated modern weapons, and military spending amounts to 30 percent of the Swiss federal budget.

Landlocked, with little fertile farmland and limited Alpine pastures, lacking both natural resources and a colonial empire, Switzerland was traditionally one of Europe's poorest countries. Until the 19th century, its principal export was soldiers, mercenaries who supplied military services to any European sovereign who could pay for them. (The pope's Swiss Guard is a remnant of this tradition.) With the spread in the late 18th century of the Romantic movement, Europeans learned to appreciate the glamour of Alpine scenery, and a tourist industry was born. It was much expanded in the 20th century with the development of Alpine skiing. Tourism remains a conspicuous, though relatively minor, part of the Swiss economy.

Swiss prosperity came in the 20th century with specialized manufacturing and free trade within the world economy. By 1940 half of the population was engaged in manufacturing, producing specialty products requiring high degrees of skill: processed foods, watches, electrical machinery, engines, fine textiles, and the like.

Neutral in both world wars, Switzerland required no postwar recovery in the 1940s. It capitalized on the restructuring of European politics and economics to expand into the service sector, which now employs half of the work force (while manufacturing has declined to 40%). Tourism, banking, insurance, and clerical/bureaucratic services to the many international organizations with headquarters in Switzerland help give the nation one of Europe's highest standards of living.

In the postwar period, Switzerland has enjoyed both political and economic stability. Government is normally controlled by a three- or four-party coalition, representing about 70–80 percent of the total vote. A cautious approach to economic development led to annual growth rates of over 6 percent in the 1950s and early 1960s, declining to 2 percent in the 1970s; the world economic boom of the 1980s produced higher growth rates again in Switzerland. In general the economy has avoided inflation, and the stability of the Swiss franc has been maintained.

Switzerland is a member of the European Free Trade Association and has ties to the EEC, although it is not a member. Recent referenda brought overwhelming rejection of UN membership (it currently has observer status), and support for restrictive immigration legislation. The most significant political change in the postwar period has been the gradual extension, canton by canton, of women's right to vote.

Syria
Syrian Arab Republic
(PREVIOUS NAME:
UNITED ARAB REPUBLIC)

Geography Location: western Asia. **Boundaries:** Turkey to N, Iraq to E, Jordan to S, Lebanon and Israel to SW, Mediterranean Sea to W. **Total land area:** 71,043 sq. mi. (184,050 sq km). **Coastline:** 120 mi. (193 km). **Comparative area:** slightly larger than North Dakota. **Land use:** 28% arable land; 3% permanent crops; 46% meadows and pastures; 3% forest and woodland; 20% other; includes 3% irrigated. **Major cities:** (1981 census) Damascus (capital) 1,112,214; Aleppo 985,413; Homs 346,871; Latakia 196,791; Hama 177,208.

People Population: 11,569,659 (1988). **Nationality:** noun—Syrian(s); adjective—Syrian. **Ethnic groups:** 90.3% Arab, 9.7% Kurds, Armenians, and other. **Languages:** Arabic (official), Kurdish, Armenian, Aramaic, Circassian; French and English widely understood. **Religions:** 74% Sunni Muslim; 16% Alawite, Druze, and other Muslim sects; 10% Christian.

Government Type: republic; under leftwing military regime since Mar. 1963. **Independence:** Apr. 17, 1946 (from League of Nations Mandate under French administration). **Constitution:** Mar. 12, 1973. **National holiday:** Independence Day, Apr. 17. **Heads of government:** Lt. Gen. Hafez al-Assad, president (since Feb. 1971); Mahmoud Zoubi, prime minister (since Nov. 1987). **Structure:** executive powers vested in president and Council of Ministers; power rests in unicameral legislature (People's Council); seat of power is Baath party's Regional (Syrian) Command.

Economy Monetary unit: Syrian pound. **Budget:** (1987) *income:* $2.6 bil.; *expend.:* $3.7 bil. **GDP:** $20.3 bil., $1,970 per capita (1985). **Chief crops:** cotton, wheat, barley, tobacco. **Livestock:** sheep, goats, cattle, asses, horses. **Natural resources:** crude oil, phosphates, chrome and manganese ores, asphalt, iron ore. **Major industries:** textiles, food processing, beverages. **Labor force:** 2.4 mil. (1984); 36% miscellaneous services, 32% agriculture, 32% industry (including construction); majority unskilled; shortage of skilled labor. **Exports:** $1.3 bil. (f.o.b., 1986); petroleum, cotton, and textile products; tobacco; light industrial products. **Imports:** $2.7 bil. (f.o.b., 1986); petroleum, machinery, and metal products; foodstuffs; consumer items. **Major trading partners: exports:** Romania, Italy, France, USSR;

imports: Iran, W. Germany, Italy, Libya.

Intl. Orgs. Arab League, FAO, G-77, IAEA, IBRD, ICAO, IDA, IFAD, IFC, ILO, IMF, IMO, INTELSAT, INTERPOL, ITU, NAM, UN, UNESCO, UPU, WHO, WMO.

The home of some of the world's most ancient centers of civilization, Syria was successively part of the Hittite, Assyrian, and Persian empires. At various times it was conquered by the Babylonians and the Egyptians. From about 1250 B.C., the coastal cities came under Phoenician rule. Alexander the Great brought Syria into the Hellenic world with his conquests in 332 B.C. After the fall of the Alexandrian empire, Syria came under the domain of the Seleucid empire but was constantly threatened by the Hellenic kingdom of Egypt, based in Alexandria.

In the classical period, Syria embraced a much larger territory than that of the present Syrian nation; it included the entire Levant and parts of present-day Turkey, Iraq, Iran, and Jordan. Greater Syria was conquered by Rome in 63 B.C. Under Roman rule the oasis region of Palmyra grew into a powerful semiautonomous kingdom. With the division of the Roman Empire in the fourth century A.D., Syria became part of the Eastern Roman (Byzantine) Empire. Throughout the Roman and Byzantine periods, the country was an important center of Christianity.

Syria was one of the first areas conquered when Islam began expansion from Arabia; Islamic rule was established by 636. From 661 to 751, Damascus was the center of the Caliphate, the ruling body of the Islamic world. By the late 11th century, the Seljuk Turks had conquered Syria. The large Syrian Christian population welcomed the European Crusaders as liberators from the Turks, but both Christians and Turks were defeated by the Arab general Saladin in the late 12th century. Saladin's rule was followed by that of the Mamluk empire of Egypt. During the Mamluk period, Mongol armies twice invaded Syria, in the mid-13th century and at the turn of the 15th century.

An Ottoman army defeated the Mamluks in Syria in 1516, making Syria part of the Ottoman Empire. In the 18th century, France declared itself the protector of Syria's Christian community against Ottoman abuses. Napoleon invaded Syria in 1799 but withdrew after a brief occupation. In the 1830s Egyptian troops occupied Syria but were forced to withdraw under pressure from the European powers.

Syrian nationalist aspirations emerged as the Ottoman Empire began to crumble before World War I. During the war the British encouraged Syrians to rebel against Turkish rule. After World War I, France governed both Syria and Lebanon (the Levant States) under a League of Nations Mandate. Under French rule, the region was divided into small territorial states along communal lines; Lebanon became independent in 1926. After prolonged negotiations much of Syria was organized into a semiautonomous state, in 1930–32.

In June 1940 the French administration in Syria declared its loyalty to the Vichy government. British and Free French forces invaded

in June 1941, and an independent Syrian republic was established in September 1941. Separately administered territories were consolidated with the republic over the next two years, and full independence was declared on Jan. 1, 1944; foreign troops did not withdraw, however, until April 1946.

Syria became a founding member of the Arab League and participated in the first Arab-Israeli War in 1948. An armistice with Israel was signed in July 1949. Severe political instability marked the early years of Syrian independence; the government was overthrown by military coups three times in 1949 alone.

Most of Syria's Jews emigrated to Israel before or during 1948, and much of its once-substantial Christian population has emigrated also. Syrian politics remain dominated by communal concerns, however; the Arab majority is divided into Sunni, Shiite, Alawite, and Druze communities.

Syria and Egypt merged as the United Arab Republic in February 1958; Syria seceded from the federation on Sept. 30, 1961. In Mar. 1963 a military coup established the pan-Arab Socialist Baath party in power; all other political parties were abolished. The Baath party leadership is dominated by the minority Alawite community.

In the 1967 Arab-Israeli War, Israel seized and held the Golan Heights region of Syria, from which Syria had long shelled Israeli communities and military installations. The Golan Heights have since been incorporated into Israeli territory.

Syrian troops aided Palestinian forces fighting government troops in Jordan in September 1970. After the expulsion of Palestinian forces from Jordan in July 1971, Syria broke off relations with Jordan; relations were restored in 1975.

Pres. Hafez al-Assad took power on Feb. 22, 1971.

On Oct. 6, 1973, Syrian and Egyptian forces attacked Israel, touching off the third Arab-Israeli War, the Yom Kippur War. A cease-fire took effect on Oct. 24; Syria failed to regain territory lost to Israel in 1967. Following the 1973 war, Syria became a major recipient of economic aid from the Arab oil states and of military equipment and supplies from the Soviet Union.

In 1976 Syrian troops entered Lebanon in an attempt to mediate in that nation's civil war and became enmeshed in that conflict. Major fighting between Syrian troops and Lebanese Christian militiamen broke out in April 1981. On June 6, 1982, Israeli troops invaded Lebanon and engaged Syrian troops in a five-day war in the Bekaa Valley. Following serious losses of aircraft and troops, Syria agreed to a cease-fire with Israel on June 11. Syrian troops continue to occupy parts of Lebanon.

An attempted coup, in February 1982, by the Moslem Brotherhood led to serious fighting within Syria, but the rebellion was put down; casualties on both sides were estimated at more than 5,000.

Since the 1973 Arab-Israeli War, Syria has consistently adopted a radical stance in Middle Eastern politics, rejecting the 1979 Egyptian-

Israeli accord and all other attempts at Arab-Israeli reconciliation. Supporting radical movements within the Palestine Liberation Organization, Syria aided Palestinian militants in driving Yasir Arafat's centrist faction of the PLO from its headquarters in Tripoli in 1983. The country is closely aligned with Libya and the USSR and supported Iran in the Iran-Iraq war. The Syrian government has been accused of aiding various acts of international terrorism in support of Palestinian, Libyan, and Iranian causes.

Syria possesses modest oil reserves; its economy is based on a mixture of oil, agriculture, pastoralism, mining, and light manufacturing. Principal crops are cotton, tobacco, grain, olives, and vegetables, along with meat products and wool. Mining and industrial goods include phosphates, gypsum, cement, textiles, glass, and brass ware.

Taiwan
Also Called Nationalist China
(PREVIOUS NAME: FORMOSA)

Geography **Location:** one large island and several smaller islands about 100 mi. (160 km) off SE coast of mainland China. **Boundaries:** East China Sea to N, Pacific Ocean to E, Bashi Channel to S, and Formosa Strait to W; separated from mainland by Formosa Strait, which is about 90 mi. (145 km) wide at its narrowest point. **Total land area:** 13,900 sq. mi. (36,000 sq km). **Coastline:** 900 mi. (1,448 km). **Comparative area:** slightly less than three times size of Connecticut. **Land use:** 24% arable land; 1% permanent crops; 5% meadows and pastures; 55% forest and woodland; 15% other; includes 14% irrigated. **Major cities:** (1986 est.) Taipei (capital) 2,575,180; Kaohsiung 1,320,552; Taichung 695,562; Tainan 646,298; Panchiao 491,721.

People **Population:** 20,004,391 (1988). **Nationality:** noun—Chinese (sing., pl.); adjective—Chinese. **Ethnic groups:** 84% Taiwanese, 14% mainland Chinese, 2% aborigine. **Languages:** Mandarin Chinese (official); Taiwanese and Hakka dialects also used. **Religions:** 93% mixture of Buddhist, Confucian, and Taoist; 4.5% Christian, 2.5% other.

Government **Type:** one-party presidential regime; 1988 political organizations bill permits legal formation of new political parties. **Constitution:** Dec. 25, 1947. **National holiday:** Oct. 10. **Heads of government:** Li Teng-hui, president (since Jan. 1988); Yu Kuo-Hwa, premier (since Dec. 1987). **Structure:** five independent branches (executive, legislative, judicial, plus traditional Chinese functions of examination and control), dominated by executive branch; president and vice president elected by National Assembly.

Economy **Monetary unit:** New Taiwan dollar. **Budget:** (1983) *income:* N.A.; *expend.:* $42.5 bil. **GNP:** $71 bil., $3,640 per capita (in 1985 U.S. dollars). **Chief crops:** rice, sweet potatoes, sugarcane, bananas, pineapples. **Livestock:** chickens, ducks, pigs, geese, turkeys. **Natural resources:** small deposits of coal, natural gas, limestone, marble, and asbestos.

Major industries: textiles, clothing, chemicals. **Labor force:** 7,880,000 (1986); 41% industry and commerce, 32% services, 20% agriculture; 2.5% unemployment. **Exports:** $39.8 bil. (f.o.b., 1986 est.); 20.5% textiles, 18.8% electrical machinery, 9% general machinery and equipment, 7.4% basic metals and metal products. **Imports:** $24.2 bil. (c.i.f., 1986 est.); 25% machinery and equipment, 17.7% crude oil, 11.9% chemical and chemical products, 6.7% basic metals, 6.3% foodstuffs. **Major trading partners:** (1983) *exports:* 49% U.S., 10% Japan; *imports:* 29% Japan, 23% U.S., 8.6% Saudi Arabia.

Intl. Orgs. expelled from UN General Assembly and Security Council on Oct. 25, 1971, and withdrew on same date from other charter-designated subsidiary organs; expelled from IMF/World Bank group Apr./May 1980; seeking to join GATT and/or MFA; attempting to regain membership in INTELSAT and INTERPOL; suspended from IAEA in 1972 but still allows IAEA controls over extensive atomic development.

Nominally part of the Chinese empire since the Song dynasty (960–1279), Taiwan was inhabited only by non-Chinese aboriginals before the 17th century. Around 1600 the Portuguese established a trading station on Taiwan; they named the island Ilha Formosa. In 1620 the Dutch built Fort Zeelandia near present-day Tainan, controlling the island until they were driven out by the Chinese pirate-patriot Koxinga (Zheng Chenggong). Remnants of the overthrown Ming dynasty (1368–1644) held out on the island until 1683, when it came under the sway of the Qing dynasty (1644–1911). Thereafter, substantial numbers of farmers from Fujian Province migrated to the fertile western lowlands of the island, driving the aboriginals into the central mountains. The Qing dynasty administered Taiwan as a semiautonomous subprovince of Fujian Province.

Following China's defeat by Japan in the Sino-Japanese War of 1894–95, Taiwan was ceded to Japan as a colony. The Japanese built roads and railroads to exploit Taiwan's resources of rice, timber, and minerals. In 1945, after Japan's defeat in World War II, Taiwan was returned to Chinese sovereignty.

As the Chinese civil war turned against the Nationalist party of Chiang Kai-shek (see "China"), Nationalist troops began to prepare Taiwan as a base for a retreat from the mainland. In 1947 Nationalist agents executed several thousand students and others suspected of favoring Taiwan's independence from China. In 1949 approximately two million Nationalist soldiers, government officials, and civilian sympathizers retreated to Taiwan. The relocated Republic of China (ROC) continued to claim to be the legitimate government of all of China, now under Communist control. In addition to Taiwan proper, the Nationalists occupied the P'eng-hu islands in the Taiwan Straits and the small islands of Quemoy and Matsu just off the coast of Fujian. Recovery of the mainland became a cornerstone of ROC pol-

icy, but no serious attempt was made to do so. U.S. policy in the Taiwan Straits was to defend Taiwan against Communist attack but also to keep the two rival governments of China well separated from each other.

A successful program of land reform in the early 1950s led to the creation of surplus capital, which fueled the development of an industrial base on the island. Foreign investment from Japan and the United States, and American military and economic aid, also enhanced economic development. By the early 1970s, the island had developed an export-oriented economy, producing textiles, cement, plastics, assembled electronic appliances, and other manufactured goods.

Chiang Kai-shek, president of the Republic of China since 1928, died in 1975 and was succeeded by his son, Chiang Ching-kuo. Under both father and son, the Nationalist party (Kuomintang, or KMT) controlled both the ROC and the Taiwan Provincial governments; mainland refugees and their descendants (15% of the population) dominated senior government posts and the military officer corps. Native Taiwanese played the leading role in agriculture, industry, and, increasingly, in local and county governments.

In foreign affairs the Republic of China became more and more isolated from the world community. In 1971 China's seat in the United Nations was taken away from the ROC and awarded to the People's Republic of China; international diplomatic recognition of the ROC dwindled steadily thereafter. On Jan. 1, 1979, the United States withdrew its recognition of the ROC and inaugurated mutual diplomatic relations with the People's Republic. Under the Taiwan Relations Act of 1979, nominally nongovernmental relations were maintained between the United States and Taiwan through the American Institute in Taipei and Taiwan's Coordination Council for North American Affairs in Washington, D.C. Similar arrangements elsewhere ensured that Taiwan's trade and other interests would be secured throughout the noncommunist world. Taiwan's economy has continued to be one of the world's most vigorous; Taiwan enjoys a substantial favorable balance of trade with the United States and has foreign-exchange holdings in excess of $75 billion.

In 1986 Pres. Chiang Ching-kuo began a policy of liberalization; in the fall of 1987, he abolished martial law and allowed non-KMT political parties to function legally. Some barriers to travel and to communication with the mainland by ROC citizens were eased, but Taiwan's government continued to rebuff all calls from the mainland for direct contacts and discussions of reunification. Chiang Ching-kuo died in January 1988 and was succeeded in office by his vice president, Lee Teng-hui, a native Taiwanese long active in KMT affairs. Under Pres. Lee, Taiwan continues to be a de facto nation with a regime that claims to be the *de jure* government of China. This anomalous situation, with the political voice of the Taiwanese majority growing steadily stronger, has uncertain implications for the future of Taiwan and the Republic of China.

Tanzania
United Republic of Tanzania
(PREVIOUS NAME: UNITED REPUBLIC
OF TANGANYIKA AND ZANZIBAR)
Geography Location: Tanganyika, on
eastern coast of Africa, and islands of Zanzibar
and Pemba, about 25 mi. (40 km) off Tanganyika coast in Indian Ocean. **Boundaries:**
Burundi and Rwanda to NW, Uganda and
Kenya to N, Indian Ocean to E, Mozambique
and Malawi to S, Zambia to SW, Zaire to W.
Total land area: 342,102 sq. mi. (886,040 sq
km). **Coastline:** 885 mi. (1,424 km). **Comparative area:** slightly larger than twice size of
California. **Land use:** 5% arable land; 1% permanent crops; 40% meadows and pastures;
47% forest and woodland; 7% other; includes
negl. % irrigated. **Major cities:** (1978 census)
Dar es Salaam (capital) 757,346; Zanzibar
110,669; Mwanza 110,611; Tanga 103,409.

People Population: 24,295,250 (1988).
Nationality: noun—Tanzanian(s); adjective—
Tanzanian. **Ethnic groups:** mainland—99%
native Africans of over 100 groups; 1% Asian,
European, and Arab; Zanzibar—almost all
Arab. **Languages:** Swahili and English (both
official); English primary language of commerce, administration, and higher education;
Swahili widely understood and generally used
for communication between ethnic groups; first
language of most people is one of local languages; primary education generally in Swahili. **Religions:** mainland—33% Christian, 33%
Muslim, 33% indigenous beliefs; Zanzibar—
almost all Muslim.

Government Type: republic. **Independence:** Tanganyika became independent Dec.
9, 1961 (from UN trusteeship under British
administration); Zanzibar became independent
Dec. 19, 1963 (from UK); Tanganyika united
with Zanzibar Apr. 26, 1964. **Constitution:**
Apr. 25, 1977 (Zanzibar has own Constitution
but remains subject to provisions of union Constitution). **National holiday:** Union Day, Apr.
26; Independence Day, Dec. 9. **Heads of government:** Ali Hassan Mwinyi, president (since
Nov. 1985); Joseph Sinde Warioba, prime minister (since Nov. 1985). **Structure:** executive-
president has authority on mainland, with government policies subject to validation by party,
which is technically superior to government;
legislative—National Assembly with 233 members, 72 from Zanzibar, 65 appointed from
mainland, and 96 directly elected from mainland; National Assembly dominated by Chama
Cha Mapinduzi (Revolutionary Party).

Economy Monetary unit: Tanzanian shilling. **Budget:** (1985) *income:* $891.8 mil.;
expend.: $1.017 bil. **GDP:** $4.9 bil., $240 per
capita (1987). **Chief crops:** cotton, coffee, sisal,
vegetables, fruits, grain on mainland; cloves
and coconuts on Zanzibar. **Livestock:** N.A. **Natural resources:** hydropower potential, tin,
phosphates, large unexploited deposits of iron
ore and coal, gemstones. **Major industries:**
agricultural processing (sugar, beer, cigarettes, sisal twine), diamond mine, oil refinery.
Labor force: 208,680 wage earners (1983);
90% agriculture, 10% industry and commerce.
Exports: $411 mil. (f.o.b., 1987); coffee, cotton,

sisal, cashew nuts, meat, cloves. **Imports:**
$1.15 bil. (f.o.b., 1987); manufactured goods,
machinery and transport equipment, cotton
piece goods, crude oil, foodstuffs. **Major trading
partners:** *exports:* W. Germany, UK, U.S; *imports:* W. Germany, UK, U.S., Iran.

Intl. Orgs. Commonwealth, FAO, G-77,
GATT, IAEA, IBRD, ICAO, IDA, IFAD, IFC,
ILO, IMF, IMO, INTELSAT, INTERPOL, ITU,
NAM, UN, UNESCO, UPU, WHO, WMO.

Tanzania was formed from the union of Tanganyika and Zanzibar on April 26, 1964. The
united republic's constitution was revised in
1983; Zanzibar maintains domestic self-rule.

Tanganyika's indigenous population includes people of diverse ethnic background,
including San, Bantu, and Nilotic peoples. It
was the site of a number of relatively advanced
and well-organized societies.

Zanzibar and the neighboring island of
Pemba were a crossroads of trade in East
Africa since ancient times. Trade via Zanzibar
between the Tanganyika coast and the Middle
East dates back to the late Roman Empire with
ivory, gold, and iron the main items of trade.
The coast was dominated by various Arab and
Persian powers, usually based in Zanzibar,
from about the eighth century. Zanzibar and
Tanganyika were visited by the Portuguese
explorer Vasco da Gama in 1498, and Portugal
claimed Zanzibar in 1503 and the entire Tanganyika coast in 1506. The Portuguese established coastal trading stations but did not
colonize the interior.

The Portuguese were driven from Zanzibar
in 1652 by the sultanate of Oman, which soon
expelled them from the mainland as well.
Under Omani rule, trade in gold, ivory, and
gems was supplemented by a sizable slave
trade, and the clove plantations of Zanzibar
became commercially important. Under Sultan
Seyyid Said, the capital of the sultanate of
Oman was transferred to Zanzibar in 1824, and
Zanzibar became independent of Oman upon
his death in 1856.

Both Germany and Great Britain became
active in the region in the 19th century, motivated by trade and, in the British case, by the
antislavery movement. Tanganyika was organized as the colony of German East Africa in
1884, while Zanzibar became a British protectorate in 1890. Tanganyika became a secondary battlefield of World War I, with frequent
clashes between German and British troops.

Britain assumed control of Tanganyika in
1920 under a League of Nations Mandate and
maintained control under a UN trusteeship
after 1946. The temperate southern highlands
were extensively colonized by British immigrants, and railroads and mines were developed
by the British administration.

Under British administration, elections for a
local legislature were held in Zanzibar in July
1957. The island's politics were dominated by a
split between Arab and African residents.
Zanzibar became independent on Dec. 19,
1963. In January 1964 an African revolt overthrew the sultan of Zanzibar and resulted in the
deaths of thousands of Arab residents and the
emigration of many more. Political control

shifted to the African party and Abeid Karume
became president.

Tanganyika became independent on Dec. 9,
1961, and became a republic within the British
Commonwealth in the following year. Julius K.
Nyerere was, from the beginning, Tanganyika's dominant political figure. The political
union of Tanganyika and Zanzibar took place
in April 1964, with Zanzibar retaining local
autonomy. In Zanzibar Abeid Karume was
assassinated in 1972 and was followed in office
by Aboud Jumbe.

The United Republic of Tanzania, under
Nyerere's leadership, advocated an "African
socialist" form of development and formed close
ties with China. Some British settlers left the
country, but despite tensions, relations with
Great Britain remained important. The Tan-
Zan Railroad between Dar es Salaam and
Lusaka, Zambia, was built with Chinese aid
between 1970 and 1975. The ruling parties of
Tanganyika and Zanzibar were united in 1977
under Nyerere's leadership. Elections were
held in 1981 and 1985, as political tensions
eased and Tanzania adopted a more open and
democratic political structure. Since 1985
Pres. Ali Hassan Mwinyi has pressed for free-
market economic policies.

In 1979 Tanzanian troops invaded Uganda
to drive Idi Amin from power there. In May
1987 ministers from Kenya, Uganda, and Tanzania met to plan closer economic and political
ties in East Africa.

Despite some stagnation during the socialist
period of 1967–85, Tanzania's economy remains fundamentally strong because of the
country's extensive natural resources. Diamonds, gold, nickel, and mica are mined, while
important export crops include sisal, coffee,
tea, cotton, and tobacco. Zanzibar remains one
of the world's most important sources of cloves
and clove oil. Light industry, including clothing, textiles, and food processing, has been
developed. The country has one of Africa's best
educational systems, and literacy, in both English and Swahili, is high.

The Olduvai Gorge, part of East Africa's
Great Rift Valley, has yielded extensive fossil
remains of early hominids.

Thailand
Kingdom of Thailand
Geography Location: extends southward,
along Isthmus of Kra, to Malay peninsula, in
Southeast Asia. **Boundaries:** Burma to W and
N, Laos to NE, Kampuchea and Gulf of Thailand to E, Malaysia to S, Andaman Sea to SW.
Total land area: 198,115 sq. mi. (513,115 sq
km). **Coastline:** 2,001 mi. (3,219 km). **Comparative area:** slightly more than twice size of
Wyoming. **Land use:** 34% arable land; 4% permanent crops; 1% meadows and pastures; 30%
forest and woodland; 31% other; includes
7% irrigated. **Major cities:** Bangkok Metropolis (capital) 5,468,915 (1986 est.); Songkla
172,604; Chonburi 115,350; Nakhon Si Tham-
marat 102,123; Chiang Mai 101,594 (1980
census).

People Population: 54,588,731 (1988).
Nationality: noun—Thai (sing., pl.); adjective—
Thai. **Ethnic groups:** 75% Thai, 14% Chinese,

11% other. **Languages:** Thai; English is secondary language of elite; ethnic and regional dialects. **Religions:** 95.5% Buddhist, 4% Muslim, 0.5% other.

Government Type: constitutional monarchy. **Constitution:** Dec. 22, 1978. **National holiday:** King's Birthday, Dec. 5. **Heads of government:** Bhumibol Adulyadej, king (since June 1946); Gen. (ret.) Chatichai Choonhavan, prime minister (since Aug. 1988). **Structure:** king is head of state with nominal powers; bicameral legislature (National Assembly—Senate appointed by king, elected House of Representatives); judiciary relatively independent except in important political subversion cases. **Economy** (1986) **Monetary unit:** baht. **Budget:** *income:* $6.4 bil. *expend.:* $8.0 bil. **GDP:** $41.8 bil., $790 per capita. **Chief crops:** rice, sugar, corn, rubber, manioc; illegal producer of opium poppy and cannabis for international drug trade. **Livestock:** buffalo, cattle, pigs, goats, sheep. **Natural resources:** tin, rubber, natural gas, tungsten, tantalum. **Major industries:** textiles and garments, agricultural processing, beverages; world's second-largest tungsten producer and third-largest tin producer; tourism—largest source of foreign exchange. **Labor force:** 26 mil. (1984); 73% agriculture, 11% industry and commerce, 10% services; 8% unemployment rate. **Exports:** $8.8 bil. (f.o.b.); textiles and garments, rice, tapioca, rubber, integrated circuits. **Imports:** $9.2 bil. (c.i.f.); machinery and transport equipment, fuels and lubricants, base metals, chemicals, fertilizer. **Major trading partners:** *exports:* U.S., Japan, Netherlands, Singapore, Malaysia; *imports:* Japan, U.S., Saudi Arabia, Singapore, Malaysia.

Intl. Orgs. ASEAN, Colombo Plan, FAO, G-77, GATT, IAEA, IBRD, ICAO, IDA, IFAD, IFC, ILO, IMF, IMO, INTELSAT, INTERPOL, ITU, UN, UNESCO, UPU, WHO, WMO.

Ethnic Thai migrating south from China after about A.D. 1000 created a number of petty states in the region, most notably the kingdom of Sukhothai. These came under the influence of Indian civilization from the adjacent states of Burma and the Khmer empire, and Buddhism became established as the dominant religion of the Thai. A unified kingdom of Siam was established c. 1350, with its capital at Ayutthaya. Portuguese and other European traders and missionaries were active in Siam after 1511.

In 1767 Ayutthaya was destroyed in a war with Burma. In 1782 the Chakkri dynasty was established at Bangkok and restored the power of the Thai monarchy. By skillfully playing off the European powers against one another, Kings Mongkut (reigned 1851–68) and Chulalongkorn (reigned 1868–1910) enabled Siam to be the only Southeast Asian nation to escape European colonization or political domination. In a series of treaties with Great Britain and France, however, King Chulalongkorn was forced to renounce Siam's claims to portions of Malaya, Laos, and Cambodia.

Absolute monarchy ended in 1932, when a military coup forced the granting of a constitution. Japanese troops occupied Siam in December 1941. Siam concluded a nominal alliance with Japan in 1942 and declared war on Great Britain and the United States, while at the same time the monarchy secretly supported a strong anti-Japanese resistance movement. A period of postwar political turmoil ended with the accession in 1950 of King Phumiphon, who instituted a reformist and pro-Western policy. Thai politics since World War II have been democratic but dominated by an oligarchy of military officers and civilians with strong military ties. The current prime minister, Prem Tinsulanond, came to power in the elections of 1980 and has subsequently been reelected twice.

During the Vietnam War, Thailand served as an important staging area for American forces. U.S. and other foreign investment has contributed to significant industrialization and economic growth since 1975 and especially in the mid-1980s. Tourism, service industries, and manufacturing have joined agriculture, forestry, mining, and fisheries as the principal sectors of the Thai economy. Large numbers of Lao, Vietnamese, and Cambodian refugees have created a significant foreign-policy problem for Thailand; Vietnamese troops have crossed into Thailand on several occasions to attack refugee camps along the border with Kampuchea.

Togo
Republic of Togo
(PREVIOUS NAME: FRENCH TOGO)

Geography Location: western coast of Africa. **Boundaries:** Burkina Faso to N, Benin to E, Gulf of Guinea to S, Ghana to W. **Total land area:** 21,925 sq. mi. (56,785 sq km). **Coastline:** 35 mi. (56 km). **Comparative area:** slightly smaller than West Virginia. **Land use:** 25% arable land; 1% permanent crops; 4% meadows and pastures; 28% forest and woodland; 42% other; includes negl. % irrigated. **Major cities:** (1977 est.) Lomé (capital) 229,400; Sokodé 33,500; Palimé 25,500; Atakpamé 21,800; Bassari 17,500.

People Population: 3,336,433 (1988). **Nationality:** noun—Togolese (sing., pl.); adjective—Togolese. **Ethnic groups:** 37 groups; largest are Ewe, Mina, and Kabyè; under 1% European and Syrian-Lebanese. **Languages:** French (both official and language of commerce); Ewe and Mina in south, Dagomba and Kabyè in north. **Religions:** about 70% indigenous beliefs, 20% Christian, 10% Muslim.

Government Type: republic; one-party presidential regime. **Independence:** Apr. 27, 1960 (from UN trusteeship under French administration). **Constitution:** Dec. 30, 1979. **National holiday:** Independence Day, Apr. 27. **Heads of government:** Gen. Gnassingbé Eyadema, president (since 1967). **Structure:** executive—president; unicameral legislature—National Assembly; judiciary, including State Security Court, established 1970; Constitution provides for elective presidential system and 67-member National Assembly.

Economy Monetary unit: Communauté Financière Africaine (CFA) franc. **Budget:** (1984 est.) *income:* $184.4 mil.; *expend.:* $219.0 mil. **GNP:** $696 mil., $240 per capita (1985). **Chief crops:** cash crops—coffee, cocoa, cotton; food crops—yams, cassava, corn, beans, rice. **Livestock:** sheep, goats, pigs, cattle. **Natural resources:** phosphates, limestone, marble. **Major industries:** phosphate mining, agricultural processing, cement, handicrafts, textiles, beverages. **Labor force:** 78% agriculture, 22% industry; about 88,600 wage earners, evenly divided between public and private sectors (1985); 50% of population of working age. **Exports:** $191 mil. (f.o.b., 1984); phosphates, cocoa, coffee, palm kernels. **Imports:** $233 mil. (f.o.b., 1984); consumer goods, fuels, machinery, tobacco, foodstuffs. **Major trading partners:** mostly France and other EC countries.

Intl. Orgs. FAO, G-77, GATT, IBRD, ICAO, IDA, IFAD, IFC, ILO, IMF, IMO, INTERPOL, ITU, NAM, UN, UNESCO, UPU, WHO, WIPO, WMO.

Ewe-speaking peoples began to emigrate into what is now Togo, located on Africa's west coast, early in the 14th century. Portuguese explorers arrived in the late 15th century, turning the coast into a point of departure for slaves captured from nearby villages, and between the 1600s and 1800s, the coast became known as the "coast of slaves." Germans started to explore and trade in the region in the mid-19th century and declared a protectorate over the area in 1884. After World War I, however, Britain and France divided the nation between them, Britain receiving the western third, France the eastern two-thirds. The League of Nations confirmed this arrangement in 1923, giving mandates to British Togoland and French Togoland.

In 1956 British Togoland voted to join the Gold Coast, which later became Ghana. That same year France made French Togo an autonomous republic within the French Union but retained control of its foreign affairs, defense, and currency. But the United Nations rejected this plan and supervised elections in 1958 in which advocates of complete independence from France won control of the legislature. On Apr. 27, 1960, French Togo cut its ties with France and became the fully independent Republic of Togo. Sylvanus Olympio became the new nation's first prime minister. His foe Nicholas Grunitzsky, who favored remaining in the French Union, went into exile but returned when Olympio was assassinated in January 1963. He led the new government and oversaw the writing of a new constitution allowing more political freedoms. In 1967 army officers led by Lt. Col. Gnassingbé Eyadema overthrew Grunitzsky, suspended the Constitution, and named Eyadema president. Eyadema's presidency was confirmed by a referendum in which he ran unopposed, and he was reelected in uncontested elections in 1979.

Tonga
Kingdom of Tonga
(PREVIOUS NAME: FRIENDLY ISLANDS)

Geography Location: 172 islands in South Pacific Ocean, 36 of which are permanently inhabited. **Boundaries:** surrounded by South Pacific Ocean; Fiji is about 400 mi. (650 km.) to NW and Western Samoa lies N. **Total land**

area: 289 sq. mi. (748 sq km). **Coastline:** 260 mi. (419 km). **Comparative area:** slightly less than four times size of Washington, D.C. **Land use:** 25% arable land; 55% permanent crops; 6% meadows and pastures; 12% forest and woodland; 2% other. **Major cities:** (1986 census) Nuku'alofa (capital) 28,899; Tongatapu 63,614; Vava'u 15,170; Ha'apai 8,979; 'Eua 4,393.

People Population: 99,620 (1988). **Nationality:** noun—Tongan(s); adjective—Tongan. **Ethnic groups:** Polynesian; about 300 Europeans. **Languages:** Tongan, English. **Religions:** Christian: Free Wesleyan Church claims over 30,000 adherents.

Government Type: constitutional monarchy within Commonwealth. **Independence:** June 4, 1970 (from UK). **Constitution:** Nov. 4, 1875; revised Jan. 1, 1967. **National holiday:** King's Birthday, July 4; Constitution Day, Nov. 4. **Heads of government:** Taufa'ahau Tupou IV, king (since Dec. 1965); Prince Fatafehi Tu'ipelehake, premier (since Dec. 1965). **Structure:** executive—king, cabinet, and privy council; unicameral legislature—28-seat Legislative Assembly consists of king, privy council (composed of eight ministers and governors of Vava'u and Ha'apai), nine representatives of nobles elected by their peers, nine elected representatives of the people elected by the people; king appoints one noble as speaker; judiciary—Supreme Court, magistrate's court, land court.

Economy Monetary unit: Tonga dollar. **Budget:** (1985) *income:* $16 mil.; *expend.:* $14 mil. **GDP:** $47 mil., $630 per capita (1983). **Chief crops:** dominated by coconut, copra, and banana production; vanilla beans, cocoa, coffee, ginger, black pepper. **Livestock:** poultry, pigs, goats, horses, cattle. **Natural resources:** fish, fertile soil. **Major industries:** tourism, fishing. **Labor force:** 70% engaged in agriculture; 600 engaged in mining. **Exports:** $5 mil. (1985); coconut oil, desiccated coconut, vanilla, copra, bananas. **Imports:** $41 mil. (1985); textiles, food, consumer products, machinery, petroleum. **Major trading partners:** (1985) *exports:* 54% New Zealand, 35% Australia, 5% Fiji; *imports:* 41% New Zealand, 23% Fiji, 14% Australia, 5% Japan, 3% UK.

Intl. Orgs. Commonwealth, FAO, GATT (de facto), IFAD, ITU, UNESCO, UPU, WHO.

The Polynesian islands that now compose Tonga were settled some 3,000 years ago. A highly stratified society evolved; the kings of Tonga dominated much of Polynesia by the 13th century. The islands were visited in 1643 by A.J. Tasman, and in 1773 by Capt. James Cook, who named them the Friendly Islands. English missionaries arrived in 1797, and the islands came under British political influence. A code of laws was promulgated in 1862, and a constitutional monarchy established in 1875. A series of treaties with Western powers recognized Tonga's independence, but the kingdom became a British protectorate in 1900.

The islands were outside the Japanese perimeter in the Pacific theater of World War II. On June 4, 1970, the British dissolved their protectorate and the Kingdom of Tonga became independent as a member of the British Commonwealth. The present king, Taufa'ahau Tupou IV, came to the throne in 1965.

The Tongan economy is based on subsistence farming and fishing, with some handicraft industries and light manufacturing. Exports include copra, bananas, and vanilla. The tourist industry is developing rapidly. Remittances from Tongans temporarily working abroad (especially in New Zealand) are an important source of income.

Trinidad and Tobago
Republic of Trinidad and Tobago
Geography Location: two islands in southeastern Caribbean Sea, just off northern coast of South America. **Boundaries:** Caribbean Sea to N and W, Atlantic Ocean to E and S. **Total land area:** 1,980 sq. mi. (5,128 sq km). **Coastline:** 225 mi. (362 km). **Land use:** 14% arable land; 17% permanent crops; 2% meadows and pastures; 44% forest and woodland; 23% other; includes 4% irrigated. **Major cities:** (1980) Port of Spain (capital) 58,400; San Fernando 34,200; Arima 24,600.

People Population: 1,279,920 (July 1988). **Nationality:** noun—Trinidadian(s), Tobagonian(s); adjective—Trinidadian, Tobagonian. **Ethnic groups:** 43% black, 40% East Indian, 14% mixed, 1% white. **Languages:** English (official), Hindi, French, Spanish. **Religions:** 36.2% Roman Catholic, 23% Hindu, 13.1% Protestant, 6% Muslim, 21.7% unknown.

Government Type: parliamentary democracy. **Independence:** Aug. 31, 1962 (from UK). **Constitution:** Aug. 31, 1976. **National holiday:** Independence Day, Aug. 31. **Heads of government:** Noor Mohammed Hassanali, president (since Mar. 1987); Arthur Robinson, prime minister (since Dec. 1976). **Structure:** executive is cabinet led by prime minister; bicameral legislature (36-member elected House of Representatives and 31-member appointed Senate); judiciary headed by chief justice and includes court of appeal, high court, and lower courts.

Economy Monetary unit: Trinidad and Tobago dollar. **Budget:** (1986 est.) *income:* $1.5 bil.; *expend.:* $1.8 bil. **GDP:** $5 bil., $4,160 per capita (1986). **Chief crops:** sugar, cocoa, coffee, rice, citrus, bananas; largely dependent on food imports. **Livestock:** pigs, cattle, goats, sheep, buffalos. **Natural resources:** crude oil, natural gas, asphalt. **Major industries:** petroleum, chemicals, tourism. **Labor force:** 463,900 (1986); 47.9% services (1985 est.), 18.1% construction and utilities, 14.8% manufacturing, mining, and quarrying, 10.9% agriculture; 17% unemployment (1986). **Exports:** $1.4 bil. (f.o.b., 1986); petroleum and petroleum products, ammonia, fertilizer, chemicals, sugar. **Imports:** $1.2 bil. (f.o.b., 1985); 33% crude petroleum, machinery, fabricated metals, transportation equipment, manufactured goods. **Major trading partners:** (1984 est.) *exports:* 56% U.S., 10% CARICOM, 8% UK; *imports:* 37% U.S., 10% UK, 7% CARICOM.

Intl. Orgs. Commonwealth, FAO, G-77, GATT, IBRD, ICAO, IDA, IFC, ILO, IMF, IMO,

INTELSAT, INTERPOL, ITU, NAM, OAS, UN, UNESCO, UPU, WHO, WMO.

Trinidad was a possession of Spain from 1498 to 1797, when it was surrendered to the British. England took control of Tobago in 1802. Together the two islands achieved independence from the UK in 1962. Prime Minister Arthur Robinson's National Alliance for Reconstruction currently governs the country. Civil and political rights are well respected, and political party competition tends to divide along ethnic (black, East Indian) lines. Agrarian reform designed to create tenable landholdings is a central political issue.

Tunisia
Republic of Tunisia
Geography Location: northern coast of Africa. **Boundaries:** Mediterranean to N and E, Libya to SE, Algeria to W. **Total land area:** 63,170 sq. mi. (163,610 sq km); includes land and inland waters. **Coastline:** 714 mi. (1,148 km). **Comparative area:** slightly more than twice size of South Carolina. **Land use:** 20% arable land; 10% permanent crops; 19% meadows and pastures; 4% forest and woodland; 47% other; includes 1% irrigated. **Major cities:** (1984 census) Tunis (capital) 596,654; Sfax (Safaqis) 231,911; Ariana 98,655; Bizeria (Bizerie) 94,509; Djerba 92,269.

People Population: 7,738,026 (1988). **Nationality:** noun—Tunisian(s); adjective—Tunisian. **Ethnic groups:** 98% Arab, 1% European, less than 1% Jewish. **Languages:** Arabic (official), Arabic and French (commerce). **Religions:** 98% Muslim, 1% Christian, less than 1% Jewish.

Government Type: republic. **Independence:** Mar. 20, 1956 (from France). **Constitution:** June 1, 1959. **National holiday:** Independence Day, June 1. **Heads of government:** Zine el-Abidine Ben Ali, president (since Nov. 1987). **Structure:** executive dominant; unicameral legislative (National Assembly) largely advisory; judiciary patterned on French and Koranic systems.

Economy Monetary unit: Tunisian dinar. **Budget:** (1985 est.) *income:* $3.04 bil.; *expend.:* operating budget $2.50 bil., capital budget $1.20 bil. **GDP:** $9.3 bil., $1,230 per capita (1987 est.). **Chief crops:** cereals (barley and wheat), olives, grapes, citrus fruits, vegetables; not self-sufficient in food. **Livestock:** sheep, goats, cattle, asses, camels. **Natural resources:** crude oil, phosphates, iron ore, lead, zinc, salt. **Major industries:** petroleum, mining (particularly phosphates and iron ore), textiles. **Labor force:** 2.25 mil.; 32% agriculture; 15–25% unemployed; shortage of skilled labor. **Exports:** $2.9 bil. (f.o.b., 1987 est.); 40% hydrocarbons, 18% agricultural, 18% phosphates and chemicals. **Imports:** $3.5 bil. (c.i.f., 1987 est.); 57% industrial goods, 13% hydrocarbons, 12% food, 18% other. **Major trading partners:** France, Italy, W. Germany, U.S.

Intl. Orgs. Arab League, FAO, G-77, GATT (de facto), IAEA, IBRD, ICAO, IDA, IFAD, IFC, ILO, IMF, IMO, INTELSAT, INTERPOL, ITU, NAM, OAU, UN, UNESCO, UPU, WHO, WIPO, WMO.

The Phoenicians, an ancient seafaring people from the eastern Mediterranean, founded settlements in Tunisia dating back to 1000 B.C. The most important of these was Carthage, which dominated trade in the central Mediterranean until it was conquered and destroyed by Rome in 146 B.C. Tunisia remained part of the Roman Empire until it was conquered by the Vandals in the mid-fifth century A.D. The Byzantine Empire reconquered Tunisia in the sixth century.

Tunisia became part of the Arab world with the expansion of Islam in the seventh century and soon emerged as a principal center of Islamic culture in North Africa. Tunisia was incorporated into the Ottoman Empire in 1574 and was ruled from Constantinople by Turkish governors, or beys.

With the waning of Ottoman power in the 19th century, Tunisia became a French protectorate in 1881. Nationalist movements began in the early 20th century. During World War II Tunisia was under Vichy French rule and was the scene of fighting between the Axis and Allies in 1942–43. Nationalist unrest resumed when France reestablished its rule in the postwar period. Widespread popular unrest in the early 1950s led to a French grant of self-rule in 1954. Full independence was proclaimed on March 20, 1956; large numbers of French settlers returned to France. The French-sponsored monarchy was abolished in 1957, and the Neo-Destour (New Constitution) party under the leadership of Habib Bourguiba took power. Bourguiba was elected president in 1959 without opposition and was later named president for life. Under Bourguiba's rule, political parties ranging from Communist to monarchist have flourished, leading to both democratic politics and political confusion.

Relations with France were strained in 1964 when Tunisia nationalized foreign assets but have since improved. The basic thrust of Tunisian government has been socialist, with state ownership of principal industries and heavy subsidies of basic commodities. In foreign affairs Tunisia has been closely tied to France and has been a moderate voice within the Arab League. The southern Tunisian mining town of Gafsa was invaded by Libya in 1980, but the invasion was repulsed.

Popular unrest and labor strife have characterized Tunisia's internal situation in the 1980s, as political maneuvering began in anticipation of the end of the Bourguiba era, which came in 1987 when the aged leader was overthrown by Ben Ali.

Tunisia's economy, though plagued by labor difficulties, has developed rapidly, led by textiles, food processing and other light industry, tourism, phosphate mining, and other mineral processing. The large agricultural sector includes grain, olives, dates, and winter fruit and vegetables for export to Europe.

Turkey
Republic of Turkey

Geography **Location:** partly in southeastern Europe and partly in western Asia. **Boundaries:** Black Sea to N; USSR to NE; Iran to E; Iraq, Syria, and Mediterranean Sea to S;

Aegean Sea and Greece to W; and Bulgaria to NW. **Total land area:** 300,948 sq. mi. (779,452 sq km). **Coastline:** 4,471 mi. (7,200 km). **Comparative area:** slightly less than twice size of California. **Land use:** 30% arable land; 4% permanent crops; 12% meadows and pastures; 26% forest and woodland; 28% other; includes 3% irrigated. **Major cities:** (1985 census) Ankara (capital) 2,235,035; Istanbul 5,475,982; Izmir 1,489,772; Adana 777,554; Bursa 612,510.

People **Population:** 54,167,857 (1988). **Nationality:** noun—Turk(s); adjective—Turkish. **Ethnic groups:** 85% Turkish, 12% Kurd, 3% other. **Languages:** Turkish (official), Kurdish, Arabic. **Religions:** 98% Muslim (mostly Sunni), 2% other (mostly Christian and Jewish).

Government **Type:** republican parliamentary democracy. **Independence:** Oct. 29, 1923 (from Ottoman Empire). **Constitution:** Nov. 7, 1982. **National holiday:** Republic Day, Oct. 29. **Heads of government:** Gen. Kenan Evren, president (since 1982); Turgut Özal, prime minister (since 1983). **Structure:** executive—president empowered to call new elections, promulgate laws (elected for 7-year term); unicameral legislature (450-member Grand National Assembly); independent judiciary.

Economy **Monetary unit:** Turkish lira. **Budget:** (1986) *income:* $10.16 bil.; *expend.:* $12.01 bil. **GNP:** $58.1 bil., $1,120 per capita. **Chief crops:** cotton, tobacco, cereals, sugar beets, fruits; self-sufficient in food in average years; legal producer of opium poppy for pharmaceutical trade. **Livestock:** sheep, cattle, goats, asses, horses. **Natural resources:** antimony, coal, chromium, mercury, copper. **Major industries:** textiles, food processing, mining (coal, chromite, copper, boron minerals). **Labor force:** 18.8 mil.; 56% agriculture, 30% services, 14% industry; about one million Turks work abroad (1987); unemployment rate 15.5%. **Exports:** $8 bil. (f.o.b.); cotton, fruits, nuts, metals. **Imports:** $11 bil. (c.i.f.); crude oil, machinery, transport equipment, metals, pharmaceuticals. **Major trading partners:** *exports:* 19.4% W. Germany, 7.8% Italy, 7.6% Iran, 7.4% Iraq, 7.4% U.S.; *imports:* 15.9% W. Germany, 10.6% U.S., 7.8% Italy, 6.9% Iraq, 6.2% Japan.

Intl. Orgs. EC (associate member), FAO, GATT, IAEA, IBRD, ICAO, IDA, IFAD, IFC, ILO, IMF, IMO, INTELSAT, INTERPOL, ITU, NATO, UN, UNESCO, UPU, WHO, WIPO, WMO.

The Hittites, an Indo-European people, created an empire in Anatolia before 2000 B.C. and controlled most of what is modern-day Turkey for nearly 1,000 years. The rise of Troy and other Hellenic city-states on the coast of Asia Minor and the expansion of the Assyrian empire led to the collapse of Hittite power by around 900 B.C. Except for some Hellenic enclaves, all of Turkey was incorporated into the Persian empire of Cyrus and Darius in the sixth century B.C. Alexander the Great conquered Turkey, but it returned to Persian rule following the collapse of his empire, c. 300 B.C.

All of Turkey, comprising Thracia, Asia, Galatia, Cappadocia, Cilicia, and other provinces, was incorporated into the Roman Empire by the end of the first century A.D. Constantine the Great founded the city of Constantinople on the site of ancient Byzantium in 330 as the empire's eastern capital. Following the decline of the western Roman Empire in the seventh century, Constantinople became the capital of the independent Eastern Roman (Byzantine) Empire. The Byzantine Empire fought off repeated attacks by Arab Islamic forces in the seventh and eighth centuries but lost control of central Anatolia to the Seljuk Turkish rulers of Persia after 1038.

The 13th-century Mongol invasions left Turkey largely untouched but weakened both Byzantine and Seljuk power. At the end of the 13th century, the Ottomans, a small Turkish tribe, expanded from their stronghold in western Anatolia and within a century captured most of Turkey, Bulgaria, and Serbia. Constantinople fell to the Ottomans in 1453. By the middle of the 16th century, the Ottoman Empire extended from southeastern Europe into the Crimea and Iran and included most of the Middle East, Egypt, and Arabia.

At its height the Ottoman Empire was a great world power and a substantial participant in European international relations. But beginning in the 18th century, the empire lost much of its autonomy through unequal treaties with European powers, and throughout the 19th century, parts of the empire were detached and either granted independence or placed under European protection. The Ottoman Empire became the "Sick Man of Europe." A liberal constitution was adopted in 1876 but largely ignored until the Young Turk Rebellion of 1908 forced the sultan to accept its provisions.

Siding with the Central Powers in World War I, the Ottoman Empire lost most of its non-Turkish possessions to the Allies. The Treaty of Sovres (1920) reduced the Ottoman state to a small part of northern Anatolia. Before the treaty was ratified, however, Kemal Ataturk seized power and regained much territory in a series of campaigns with Soviet assistance. The Treaty of Lausanne (1923) established the present boundaries of Turkey, and Turkey was proclaimed a republic in October 1923. The Caliphate was renounced in 1924, ending the Ottoman claim of spiritual leadership in the Islamic world.

The Turkish Republic became officially a secular and multiethnic state. Large numbers of Armenians had been killed or driven from the country in widespread campaigns of persecution in the late 19th and early 20th centuries; after 1923 most Greek and Bulgarian residents were forcibly repatriated. The large minority of Kurds in southeastern Turkey were pressured to abandon their ethnic identity. Today more than 85 percent of the population is Turkish, ultimately of Central Asian origin. Islam is widely practiced, but the veil and other Islamic dress are prohibited, as are religious political parties. In 1928 the Latin alphabet was adopted in place of Arabic script for writing Turkish. In 1930 Constantinople was officially renamed Istanbul.

Turkey joined the League of Nations in 1932. A series of treaties in the 1930s made small adjustments to Turkey's borders and confirmed Turkey's status as a European nation. Under Ismet Inonu, who became president upon Ataturk's death in 1938, Turkey remained neutral throughout most of World War II but was on friendly terms with the Allied powers. Turkey declared war against Germany in January 1945 and became a founding member of the United Nations at the end of the war.

Following World War II, Turkish relations with the Soviet Union cooled; Turkey became a major recipient of American aid under the Truman Doctrine. Turkish troops joined UN forces in the Korean War. Continuing the Europe-oriented policy instituted by Ataturk, Turkey has joined both NATO and the OECD. Soviet warships are allowed passage through the Bosporus between the Black Sea and the Mediterranean.

In 1974, long-standing discord with Greece erupted over the status of Cyprus, an independent nation with strong ties to Greece. On July 20, 1974, Turkish troops invaded Cyprus, occupying the northeastern 40 percent of the island. The United States cut off military aid to Turkey in 1975. Turkey forced resettlement of Greek and Turkish Cypriot residents; the Turkish sector seceded from Cyprus and became a Turkish federated state on July 8, 1975. American aid was restored in 1978. Despite many attempts at reconciliation, relations between Turkey and Greece remain strained.

Politically, postwar Turkey has alternated between civil and military governments. In the wake of mounting violence, martial law was imposed in 1978, and a military takeover of the government occurred on Sept. 12, 1980. Civil government was restored in 1983, and martial law lifted in 1984. Communism and other leftist political movements are strongly suppressed. Turkey has tried to remain aloof from the political turmoil of the Middle East but has suffered occasional terrorist violence from leftist elements linked to the Palestinian movement. Turkish diplomatic missions abroad have been frequent targets of Armenian nationalist terrorists.

Lacking substantial petroleum reserves, Turkey has a mixed economy. The traditional agricultural and pastoral sectors remain important, producing animal products, grain, cotton, tobacco, and various vegetable crops. Turkey has extensive coal reserves and is one of the world's major exporters of chromium; antimony, mercury, and copper are also mined. With strong government encouragement and a recent rise in foreign investment, the industrial sector has developed rapidly, particularly in the Istanbul-Izmir region; iron, steel, machinery, automobiles, electric and electronic goods, and other products are made for both domestic use and exportation. Turkey has applied for admission to the European Common Market.

Tuvalu
(PREVIOUS NAME: ELLICE ISLANDS)

Geography Location: scattered group of nine small atolls, extending about 350 mi. (560 km) from N to S, in South Pacific Ocean. **Boundaries:** surrounded by South Pacific Ocean; Kiribati to N, Fiji to S, Solomon Islands to W. **Total land area:** 10 sq. mi. (26 sq km). **Coastline:** 15 mi. (24 km). **Comparative area:** about ¹⁄₁₀ size of Washington, D.C. **Land use:** 0% arable land; 0% permanent crops; 0% meadows and pastures; 0% forest and woodland; 100% other. **Major cities:** (by atoll; 1985 census) Funafuti (capital) 2,810; Vaitupu 1,231; Niutao 904; Nanumea 879; Nukufetau 694.

People Population: 8,475 (1988). **Nationality:** noun—Tuvaluan(s); adjective—Tuvaluan. **Ethnic groups:** 96% Polynesian. **Languages:** Tuvaluan, English. **Religions:** Christian, predominantly Protestant.

Government Type: independent state, special member of Commonwealth. **Independence:** Oct. 1, 1978 (from UK). **Constitution:** Oct. 1, 1978. **National holiday:** N.A. **Heads of government:** Tupua Leupena, governor-general (since Mar. 1986); Dr. Tomasi Puapua, prime minister (since Sept. 1981). **Structure:** executive—prime minister and cabinet; unicameral legislature—12-member House of Parliament; judicial—high court, 8 island courts with limited jurisdiction.

Economy (1983) **Monetary unit:** Australian dollar. **Budget:** *income:* $2.59 mil. *expend.:* $3.6 mil. **GNP:** $4 mil., $450 per capita (1984 est.). **Chief crops:** coconuts, copra. **Livestock:** pigs. **Natural resources:** none. **Major industries:** fishing, tourism, copra. **Labor force:** N.A. **Exports:** (est.) $1.0 mil.; copra. **Imports:** $2.8 mil.; food, animals, mineral fuels, machinery, manufactured goods. **Major trading partners:** Fiji, Australia, New Zealand.

Intl. Orgs. Commonwealth (special member), GATT (de facto), UPU.

A British protectorate was established in 1892, and the islands were incorporated into the British colony of the Gilbert and Ellice Islands in 1915. The nine principal islands that make up the Ellice group escaped Japanese occupation in World War II and were used as Allied bases in the campaign to recapture the Pacific.

The Gilbert and Ellice Islands colony was granted self-rule in 1971. In 1975 the Ellice Islands, inhabited mainly by Polynesians, seceded from the other (mainly Micronesian) islands of the colony and became independent as Tuvalu on Oct. 1, 1978. (See also "Kiribati.") In a 1979 U.S.-Tuvalu friendship treaty, the United States relinquished claims, based on 19th-century guano mining, to the four southernmost islands, in return for access to World War II military airfields and veto power over other nations' use of the islands for military purposes.

The economy of the islands was badly disrupted by a typhoon in 1972. The economy is based on subsistence farming and fishing. Exports include copra and woven palm-leaf

products. With foreign assistance, hydroponic agriculture and offshore fisheries are being developed. Tuvalu remains heavily dependent on foreign aid, principally from Australia, New Zealand, and the United Kingdom.

Uganda
Republic of Uganda

Geography Location: landlocked equatorial country in eastern Africa. **Boundaries:** Sudan to N, Kenya to E, Tanzania to S, Rwanda to SW, Zaire to W. **Total land area:** 76,084 sq. mi. (197,058 sq km). **Coastline:** none. **Comparative area:** slightly smaller than Oregon. **Land use:** 23% arable land; 9% permanent crops; 25% meadows and pastures; 30% forest and woodland; 13% other; includes negl. % irrigated. **Major cities:** (1980 est.) Kampala (capital) 458,423; Jinja 45,060; Masaka 29,123; Mbale 28,039; Mbarara 23,155.

People Population: 16,446,906 (1988). **Nationality:** noun—Ugandan(s); adjective—Ugandan. **Ethnic groups:** 99% African, 1% European, Asian, Arab. **Languages:** English (official), Luganda, Swahili, other Bantu and Nilotic languages. **Religions:** 33% Roman Catholic, 33% Protestant, 16% Muslim, 18% indigenous beliefs.

Government Type: republic. **Independence:** Oct. 9, 1962 (from UK). **Constitution:** Sept. 8, 1967, suspended following coup of July 27, 1985. **National holiday:** Independence Day, Oct. 9. **Heads of government:** Yoweri Kaguta Museveni, president (since Jan. 1986); Samson B.M. Kisekka, prime minister (since Jan. 1986). **Structure:** president heads National Resistance Council.

Economy Monetary unit: Uganda shilling. **Budget:** in percent of GDP (1986) *income:* 13.2%; *expend.:* 15.5%. **GDP:** $5.9 bil., $220 per capita (1983 est.). **Chief crops:** coffee, cotton, tobacco, tea, sugar. **Livestock:** cattle, goats, sheep, pigs, asses. **Natural resources:** copper, cobalt, limestone, salt. **Major industries:** sugar, brewing, tobacco. **Labor force:** 4.5 mil. (1983 est.); about 250,000 in paid labor; remainder in subsistence activities; 50% of population of working age. **Exports:** $352 mil. (f.o.b., 1986 est.); over 90% coffee; cotton, tea. **Imports:** $325 mil. (c.i.f., 1986 est.); petroleum products, machinery, cotton piece goods, metals, transport equipment, food. **Major trading partners:** (1985) *exports:* 27% U.S., 14% UK, 9% Spain; *imports:* 39% Kenya, 17% UK, 7% Japan.

Intl. Orgs. Commonwealth, FAO, G-77, GATT, IAEA, IBRD, ICAO, IDA, IFAD, IFC, ILO, IMF, INTELSAT, INTERPOL, ITU, NAM, UN, UNESCO, UPU, WHO, WIPO, WMO.

Prior to 1800 Uganda was the site of several important kingdoms, notably Buganda, centered on Kampala on the northern shore of Lake Victoria. After 1830 Arabs from the sultanate of Oman, based in Zanzibar, asserted loose control over the region and dominated its trade. British explorers, seeking the source of the Nile, reached the Lake Victoria region in the mid-19th century. Mission stations were established in 1877; a Moslem rebellion destroyed the missions and occupied Kampala in 1888.

Buganda was brought under the control of the British East Africa Company in 1890, and Britain established a protectorate in 1894 that was expanded to include neighboring territories in 1896. In 1902 some of the protectorate's territory was transferred to Kenya. British immigrants extensively developed the agricultural potential of Uganda's fertile and temperate highlands, establishing large and prosperous farms. Lake Victoria was the scene of naval battles between Great Britain and Germany (established in neighboring Tanganyika) during World War I.

In 1955 the British administration created a local parliamentary government in which both whites and Africans held ministerial office. Talks on the terms for independence began in 1961 and after some difficulty arrived at a formula for a national structure in which Buganda and other traditional kingdoms would retain local autonomy. Several political parties competed for power; the Uganda People's Congress led by Milton Obote gradually became dominant. Uganda became independent within the British Commonwealth on Oct. 9, 1962.

Several constitutional changes in the early 1960s led to an end to the autonomy of the kingdoms and the effective concentration of all power in Obote's presidency. In 1967 a new constitution proclaimed Uganda an independent republic.

Obote was overthrown on Jan. 25, 1971, by Idi Amin Dada, commander of Uganda's armed forces. Amin declared himself president, dissolved the parliament, and assumed absolute powers. In 1972 he expelled nearly all of Uganda's Asians (primarily people of Indian and Pakistani descent), who controlled most of the country's small-scale commerce. The United States broke off diplomatic relations in 1973. In 1976 Amin declared himself president for life. His eight-year reign was marked by extreme violence and persecution of political and tribal opponents; as many as 300,000 Ugandans may have been killed between 1971 and 1979. The country's prosperous agricultural, mining, and commercial economy was devastated, and its infrastructure, including a good road and rail network and Makerere University, one of Africa's preeminent educational institutions, fell into ruins.

On July 3, 1976, Israeli airborne troops landed at Entebbe and rescued 103 hostages who had been captured in a skyjacking carried out by Palestinian and German terrorists.

In 1978 Amin, with the aid of Libyan troops, invaded Tanzania. In the following year, Tanzanian troops countered by invading Uganda; they captured Kampala on Apr. 11, 1979, and drove Amin into exile. Diplomatic relations with the United States resumed. After a series of interim governments, elections in 1981 returned Obote to power. Obote's new regime was marked by fierce repression of opponents and by the outbreak of rebellion in the northern part of the country by the National Resistance Army (NRA) under Yoweri Museveni.

Obote fled into exile in 1985 and was suc-

ceeded by Lt. Gen. Basilio Olara-Okello, but the NRA rebellion continued. Kenyan president Daniel arap Moi mediated peace talks between Olara-Okello and the NRA in late 1985; in January 1986 Olara-Okello fled into exile, and Museveni organized a new government. Despite continued insurgencies by rival military factions and by a rebellion led by the charismatic religious leader Alice Lakwena, the Museveni government has generally restored order and, with aid from the World Bank and the IMF, has begun to rebuild Uganda's shattered society. In 1987 Uganda joined in talks with Kenya and Tanzania designed to promote closer political and economic relations in East Africa.

Nearly three decades of misrule have left Uganda in desperate economic straits. The country, despite its resources, is one of the poorest in Africa; inflation, corruption, and public disorder are continuing problems. In addition, the southern part of the country is threatened by an extensive epidemic of AIDS.

United Arab Emirates
(ABBREV.: UAE)
(PREVIOUS NAME: TRUCIAL STATES)

Geography **Location:** eastern part of Arabian peninsula. **Boundaries:** Persian Gulf to N, Gulf of Oman to NE, Oman to E, Saudi Arabia to S and W, short frontier with Qatar to NW. **Total land area:** 30,000 sq. mi. (77,700 sq km). **Coastline:** 899 mi. (1,448 km). **Comparative area:** slightly smaller than Maine. **Land use:** negl. % arable land; negl. % permanent crops; 2% meadows and pastures; negl. % forest and woodland; 98% other; includes negl. % irrigated. **Major cities:** (1985 census) Abu Dhabi (capital) 670,125; Dubai 419,104; Sharjah 268,722; Ras al-Khaimah 116,470; Ajman 64,318.

People **Population:** 1,980,354 (1988). **Nationality:** noun—Emirian(s); adjective—Emirian. **Ethnic groups:** 19% Emirian, 23% other Arab, 50% South Asian (fluctuating), 8% other expatriates (includes Westerners and East Asians); less than 20% of population are UAE citizens (1982). **Languages:** Arabic (official), Hindi, Urdu; Farsi and English widely spoken in major cities. **Religions:** 96% Muslim (16% Shi'a), 4% Christian, Hindu, and other.

Government **Type:** federation with specified powers delegated to UAE central government and other powers reserved to member sheikhdoms. **Independence:** Dec. 2, 1971 (from UK). **Constitution::** Dec. 2, 1971 (provisional). **National holiday:** Dec. 2. **Head of government:** Sheikh Zayed bin Sultan al-Nahyan of Abu Dhabi, president (since Dec. 1971); Sheikh Rashid ibn Sa'id al-Maktoun of Dubai, vice president (since 1971) and prime minister (since Apr. 1979). **Structure:** executive—Supreme Council of Rulers (seven members), from which president and vice president are elected; prime minister and Council of Ministers; unicameral legislature—Federal National Council; judicial—Union Supreme Court.

Economy **Monetary unit:** UAE dirham. **Budget:** (1986) *income:* $3.4 bil.; *expend.:* $3.5 bil. **GNP:** $22.0 bil., $11,900 per capita

(1987 est.). **Chief crops:** food imported; some dates, alfalfa, vegetables, fruit, tobacco. **Livestock:** goats, sheep, camels, cattle. **Natural resources:** crude oil, natural gas. **Major industries:** petroleum, fishing, petrochemicals. **Labor force:** 580,000 (1986 est.); 85% industry and commerce; 80% of labor force is foreign. **Exports:** $8.3 bil. (f.o.b., 1987); $6.8 bil. in crude oil, $1.45 bil. consisting mostly of gas, reexports, dried fish, dates. **Imports:** $6.5 bil. (f.o.b., 1987); food, consumer, and capital goods. **Major trading partners:** Japan, EC, U.S.

Intl. Orgs. Arab League, FAO, G-77, GATT (de facto), IAEA, IBRD, ICAO, IDA, IFAD, IFC, ILO, IMF, IMO, INTELSAT, INTERPOL, ITU, NAM, OPEC, UN, UNESCO, UPU, WHO, WIPO.

In the 1820s Great Britain established protectorates over seven small sheikhdoms along the gulf coast between Qatar and Oman—Abu Dhabi, Dubai, Sharjah, Ajmar, Fujairah, and Umm al-Qaiwain. The region, which had been known as the Pirate Coast, then was generally referred to as the Trucial Coast or Trucial Oman. Under terms of a supplementary treaty in 1892, the sheikhdoms agreed not to enter into relations with any other country.

After Great Britain announced that it would withdraw its forces from the gulf in 1971, the seven sheikhdoms formed a federation and became independent as the United Arab Emirates on Dec. 2, 1971. The Emir of Abu Dhabi, Zayed bin Sultan al-Nahyan, became the federation's first president.

The economy, formerly limited to herding of nomadic sheep and camels, oasis agriculture, coastal shipping, and pearl diving, is now almost entirely dominated by petroleum. Large numbers of foreign workers are employed in the oil fields; citizens of the UAE receive extensive social services and enjoy one of the world's highest per capita incomes.

United Kingdom
United Kingdom of Great Britain and Northern Ireland
(ABBREV.: UK)

Geography **Location:** northwestern Europe, occupying major portion of British Isles. **Boundaries:** Atlantic Ocean to NW and W, North Sea to E; separated from France by English Channel to S; Republic of Ireland to W. **Total land area:** 94,249 sq. mi. (244,103 sq km). **Coastline:** 7,723 mi. (12,429 km). **Comparative area:** slightly smaller than Oregon. **Land use:** 29% arable land; negl. % permanent crops; 48% meadows and pastures; 9% forest and woodland; 14% other; includes 1% irrigated. **Major cities:** (1986 est.) Greater London (capital) 6,775,200; Birmingham 1,004,100; Glasgow 725,100; Leeds 710,900; Sheffield 534,300.

People **Population:** 56,935,845 (1988). **Nationality:** noun—Briton(s), British (collective pl.); adjective—British. **Ethnic groups:** 81.5% English, 9.6% Scottish, 2.4% Irish, 1.9% Welsh, 1.8% Ulster, 2.8% West Indian, Indian, Pakistani, and other. **Languages:** English, Welsh (about 26% of population of Wales), Scottish form of Gaelic (about 60,000 in Scotland).

Religions: 27 mil. Anglican, 5.3 mil. Roman Catholic, 2.0 mil. Presbyterian, 760,000 Methodist, 450,000 Jewish (registered).

Government **Type:** constitutional monarchy. **Independence:** N.A. **Constitution:** unwritten; partly statutes, partly common law and practice. **National holiday:** Birthday of queen, June 16. **Heads of government:** Elizabeth II, queen (since Feb. 1952); Margaret Thatcher, prime minister (since May 1979). **Structure:** executive authority lies with collectively responsible cabinet led by prime minister; legislative authority rests with Parliament (House of Lords, House of Commons); House of Lords is supreme judicial authority and highest court of appeals.

Economy **Monetary unit:** pound sterling. **Budget:** (1987) *income:* $312.7 bil.; *expend.:* $314.5 bil. **GNP:** $556.8 bil., $9,800 per capita (1986). **Chief crops:** wheat, barley, potatoes, sugar beets, dairy products; 62.1% self-sufficient (1983); dependent on imports for more than half of consumption of refined sugar, butter, oils and fats, bacon, ham. **Livestock:** chickens, sheep and lambs, cattle, pigs, ducks, geese. **Natural resources:** coal, crude oil, natural gas, tin, limestone. **Major industries:** machinery and transportation equipment, metals, food processing. **Labor force:** 27.9 mil. (1987); 51.9% services, 23.7% manufacturing and construction, 9.8% self-employed; 10.3% unemployment. **Exports:** $107 bil. (f.o.b., 1986); manufactured goods, machinery, fuels, chemicals, semifinished goods, transportation equipment. **Imports:** $126 bil. (c.i.f., 1986); manufactured goods, machinery, semifinished goods, foodstuffs, consumer goods. **Major trading partners:** (1986) *exports:* 48.1% EC (11.7% W. Germany, 8.5% France, 7.5% Netherlands), 14.2% U.S., 2.7% communist countries; *imports:* 52.0% EC (16.5% W. Germany, 8.6% France, 7.7% Netherlands), 10.0% U.S., 2.3% communist countries.

Intl. Orgs. Colombo Plan, EC, FAO, GATT, IAEA, IBRD, ICAO, IDA, IFAD, IFC, ILO, IMF, IMO, INTELSAT, INTERPOL, ITU, NATO, OECD, UN, UPU, WHO, WIPO, WMO.

Early megalithic and Iron Age peoples of Britain, primarily Celtic, developed tribal petty states that were conquered by Roman invaders in A.D. 43. After Roman legions withdrew from Britain in 410, invasions of Jutes, Angles, and Saxons conquered much of England, while Celtic peoples flourished in Wales, Scotland, and especially Ireland. Viking invaders established settlements in the eighth century. A united Saxon kingdom fell to the Norman invasion of William the Conquerer in 1066.

An aristocratic rebellion against the royal absolutism of King John in 1215 led to the royal acceptance of the Magna Carta, guaranteeing legal rights and laying the foundations of parliamentary government. From the 12th to the 15th century, the Plantagenet dynasty ruled England and claimed overlordship over Ireland; Wales was conquered in 1283; beginning in 1301—and continuing since then—the heir apparent to the British throne has was given the title Prince of Wales. The Plantagenet monarchs also controlled sizable territories in France.

The Hundred Years' War (1337–1453) cost England its French possessions; the War of the Roses, (1455–85) ended the Plantagenet dynasty and brought Henry Tudor to the throne. The Tudors gradually centralized royal control by bringing pressure against both the church and the nobility; Henry VIII broke with Rome in 1534 and established the Church of England. Under Elizabeth I, the last of the Tudors, England defeated Spain at sea and laid the foundations of later worldwide English sea power. The English Renaissance began under Elizabeth I (1533–1603) with the works of Shakespeare and continued into the 17th century with Milton and Newton.

The Stuart dynasty was founded by James I (1566–1625), uniting the crowns of England and Scotland. James's son Charles I (1600–1649) was executed by act of Parliament in the Puritan Revolution. British colonization of North America was fueled by both royal policy and religious dissent. Following the fall of Cromwell's dictatorship in 1660 the Stuart monarchy was restored. It was overthrown in the Glorious Revolution of 1688, which brought William and Mary of Orange to the throne, confirmed the supremacy of Parliament, and established a bill of rights.

In the last gasp of the Stuart claimants to the throne, Irish supporters of James II were defeated at the Battle of the Boyne (1690), which temporarily crushed Irish resistance to annexation by England. Scotland was joined with England in a common Parliament by the Act of Union in 1707; this created the United Kingdom, comprising England, Scotland, Wales, and Ireland. A Scottish uprising led by the Young Pretender, Charles Edward Stuart, was crushed at Culloden Moor in 1745.

After the Glorious Revolution, the United Kingdom was widely viewed as a model of constitutional monarchy. It became the greatest sea power in the world, controlling an empire that included both eastern North America and India by the mid-18th century. Agrarian "enclosures" of the 18th century ruined the British peasantry but created an entrepreneurial revolution in agriculture that ultimately led to greatly increased agricultural productivity. The capital created in that process made England the home of the Industrial Revolution, which over the next century, made England the wealthiest land on earth.

Despite the loss of most of its American empire after the American Revolution of 1775–83, England in the 19th century expanded its empire to include not only the Indian subcontinent but also Malaya and Hong Kong (as well as a dominant but not strictly colonial position in trade with China), eastern Africa from Egypt to the Cape of Good Hope, and a worldwide network of other outposts. Britain's control of the Suez Canal after 1875 confirmed its position as the dominant world power.

The repeal of the protectionist Corn Laws in 1846 led to an agricultural depression and hastened the migration of labor from the countryside to the industrial cities. The rise of labor activism led in 1906 to laws granting privileged status to trade unions, which organized the Labour party to promote their interests.

Britain's alliance with France and Russia in the Triple Entente created a confrontation with Germany, Italy, and Austria-Hungary in 1914, sparked by events in the Balkans and Central Europe. Victory in World War I came at the cost of an entire generation of British youth, but Britain emerged from the war with its empire at a high point, adding Tanganyika, Jordan, Palestine, and Iraq as part of the postwar division of spoils. Most of Ireland became independent in 1921, however, leaving only Northern Ireland as part of the United Kingdom.

Between the two world wars, Britain's navy and air force were the largest in the world, its army the third largest. Yet its industry was aging, the Great Depression hit especially hard in the British Isles, strikes and labor unrest weakened the social fabric, and colonial ties began to weaken in the 1930s. The abdication of Edward VIII in 1936, and the scandal surrounding his love affair with a divorced woman provoked a crisis in a country where the monarchy normally enjoyed broad support. Economic retrenchment led to a failure to rearm in the face of the rising threat of Hitler's Germany and Mussolini's Italy.

The Munich Pact of 1938 gave Hitler a license for war; his invasion of Poland in 1939 forced Britain into the conflict. When Winston Churchill became prime minister in 1940, Britain was under daily air attack and in danger of invasion; the country was isolated and embattled, dependent on American friendship and lend-lease war materials. But 1941 brought alliance with the United States and the Soviet Union, and a slowly turning tide of war leading to victory in 1945. Still, postwar Britain quickly dropped to the second rank of superpowers.

The coalition between the Conservative and Labour parties that had governed Great Britain during the war seemed no longer necessary in 1945 as the war wound down. Labour won a landslide victory in the 1945 elections; Churchill was recalled in the midst of the Potsdam Conference, and Clement Atlee became prime minister. A brief Labour flirtation with the USSR quickly ended in the postwar 1940s; England became a founding member of the United Nations and also, in 1949, of NATO. As the Cold War took shape, Britain developed its own nuclear arsenal.

Decolonization was a cornerstone of British postwar foreign policy. India was granted its independence in 1947, and Palestine, Burma, and Ceylon in 1948; others would follow later.

But domestic policy was Labour's principal focus. The party moved rapidly in the late 1940s to nationalize the Bank of England along with railroads, public utilities, and heavy industry. A comprehensive welfare state apparatus was created, including a national health service, unemployment and retirement benefits, and free education at all levels. But postwar Britain was in many respects too poor to afford such changes; in order to cut expenditures, the government hastened the process of withdrawal from colonies and military bases around the world.

The elections of 1951 brought Churchill

back to the prime ministership at the head of a Conservative majority that would last for 13 years. The Conservatives returned steel and trucking to the private sector but in general refrained from undoing the social policies of their Labour predecessors. Economic growth began in the 1950s and held steady at about 2.5 percent per year, a significantly lower rate than in contemporary continental Europe; obsolescence, excessive wage and benefit settlements with labor, and a low savings rate all took their toll. The coronation of Elizabeth II in 1953 added a much-needed element of national celebration.

Churchill retired in 1955 and was succeeded by Anthony Eden. Eden's government fell in 1956 over the failed and bungled Anglo-French invasion of Suez (see "Egypt"). Eden's fall brought Harold Macmillan to power in 1957. Macmillan pursued close relations with the United States and attempted, with shrinking armed forces, to uphold Britain's role in Europe. Most important, he presided over the transformation of an empire to a Commonwealth; in the early 1960s, Ghana, Nigeria, Malaya, Singapore, and numerous other colonies were granted independence and Commonwealth status. Immigrants from the Commonwealth promptly flocked to England, straining housing, social services, and the labor market and creating problems of assimilation that remain unsolved.

Britain under Macmillan was the moving force behind the European Free Trade Association in 1960. In 1961 Britain applied for membership in the EEC, but that application was humiliatingly vetoed by France's Charles de Gaulle in 1963. Macmillan's government fell with the Profumo Scandal of 1963, and Douglas Home became a caretaker prime minister pending new elections.

The 1964 elections brought the Labour party to power under Harold Wilson. Under Wilson, Britain applied again for EEC membership in 1967 but was again denied. The continuing devolution of the empire brought the Rhodesian question to public prominence; Wilson's moderate position made him unpopular with his own party, even more so when he sponsored legislation to ban wildcat strikes. Strikes, wage inflation, the steady growth of the public sector (including renationalization of the steel industry), and the rise of turmoil in Northern Ireland in 1968–69 combined to make public support for Labour evaporate.

The Conservative victory in the 1970 elections brought Edward Heath to the office of prime minister. Promising to cut expenditures and taxes, reward initiative, and curb union power, the Conservatives were able to accomplish none of those aims. Heath's government imposed ineffective wage controls in an attempt to slow inflation and passed the 1971 Industrial Relations Act to regulate unions. When unions defied that act, the government fell. Heath's major achievement was the United Kingdom's admission to the EEC in 1973. Continued turmoil in Northern Ireland was met with the abolition of the Ulster Parliament in 1972 and the imposition of direct British rule— a policy that did nothing to stem the growing sectarian violence.

Wilson returned to the prime ministership in 1974 and retired in 1976, passing on the office to James Callaghan, who governed until 1979 at the head of a Labour-Liberal coalition. The continued power of trade unions was seen in the repeal of the Industrial Relations Act and the extension of union privileges. The left wing of the Labour party brought increasing pressure against defense spending, membership in NATO, and the policy of moderation in Rhodesia, and also loudly criticized American foreign policy.

The OPEC oil price rises of 1972–74 hurt Great Britain in the short run but also encouraged development of oil and gas fields in the North Sea, which made the nation a major petroleum exporter and helped revitalize the economy. Oil exploration in the North Sea also encouraged Scottish nationalism, with some damage to national unity, although in both Scotland and Wales, proposals in 1979 for separate parliaments were soundly defeated by plebiscites. The end of the 1970s brought another upsurge in violence in Northern Ireland.

The 1979 elections brought the Conservatives to power again, behind Margaret Thatcher, Great Britain's (and Europe's) first female prime minister. She proved to be the only British prime minister in modern times to lead her party successfully in three elections, the Thatcher era continuing to this day. Thatcher took office with an agenda that involved undoing much of the course of postwar British history.

The first target was inflation, attacked through a freeze on expenditures and reduction of government borrowing. The policy was a success; inflation fell from 18 percent in 1980 to 3 percent in 1989. But the austerity program had a high cost in unemployment, which remained at 14 percent in the mid-1980s, higher in older industrial areas.

In 1982 national attention turned abruptly from domestic to overseas concerns, as Argentina invaded the Falkland ("Malvinas") Islands, which it claimed as Argentine national territory, on April 2. On May 21 British forces launched a counteroffensive, and the invading Argentine forces surrendered on June 14. The war was a costly one in both lives and materiel, but it provoked an upsurge of British patriotism at home that swept Thatcher's party into a second term of office in 1983.

After the election the government turned to denationalization, or privatization, of industry. Over $30 billion in state property—from industrial giants, such as Britoil and British Gas, to individual apartments in municipal housing projects—was sold to private interests. This program was followed in 1986 by tax cuts, in which the top income-tax rate dropped from 98 percent to 60 percent. In foreign affairs, Britain agreed in 1985 to return Hong Kong to Chinese sovereignty in 1997.

The 1987 elections pitted the Conservatives against a Labour Party that had moved sharply to the Left, opposing NATO missile deployment in Great Britain, advocating unilateral disarmament, and calling for renationalization of industry and a return to higher taxes for the wealthy. The weak Liberal-Social Democratic Alliance played little role in the election, which the Conservatives won resoundingly. By 1989 the "Thatcher Revolution" had produced a decisive long-term economic recovery, but one that was unevenly distributed: the southern part of the country enjoyed an economic boom, while the older industrial cities of the north remained stagnant. Nationalism remained a live issue in Scotland and Wales, but in the 1980s, Northern Ireland returned to a state of relative calm, with the governments of Britain and Ireland actively cooperating to seek a peaceful solution to the perennial "Irish Question."

Future policy questions for the Thatcher government include rebuilding university education, which was severely constrained by the spending cuts of the early 1980s, and imposing the central government's discipline on quasi-independent local government authorities. In foreign affairs the key question is Britain's role in the united Europe, which is scheduled to become a reality in 1992.

The British Empire, now a shadow of its former grandeur, remains a global responsibility for the British government, one that can flare up unexpectedly, as the Falklands War showed. The turmoil in China in the spring of 1989 raised questions about the security of the 1985 Sino-British Agreement on Hong Kong; Spain continues to call for a referendum aimed at returning Gibralter to Spanish control. Other island possessions of long standing, such as the Isle of Man, the Channel Islands, and Bermuda, remain serene, enjoying their status as tourist economies and tax havens.

Uruguay
Oriental Republic of Uruguay

Geography Location: southeastern coast of South America. **Boundaries:** Brazil to N, South Atlantic Ocean to E and S, Argentina to W. **Total land area:** 68,037 sq. mi. (176,215 sq km). **Coastline:** 410 mi. (660 km). **Comparative area:** slightly smaller than Washington State. **Land use:** 8% arable land, negl. % permanent crops; 78% meadows and pastures; 4% forest and woodland; 10% other; includes 1% irrigated. **Major cities:** (1985 census) Montevideo (capital) 1,246,500; Salto 77,400; Paysandú 75,200; Las Piedras 61,300; Rivera 55,400.

People Population: 2,976,138 (1988). **Nationality:** noun—Uruguayan(s); adjective—Uruguayan. **Ethnic groups:** 88% white, 8% mestizo, 4% black. **Languages:** Spanish. **Religions:** 66% Roman Catholic, 2% Protestant, 2% Jewish, 30% nonprofessing or other (less than half adult population attends church regularly).

Government Type: republic. **Independence:** Aug. 25, 1828 (from Brazil). **Constitution:** Nov. 27, 1966; effective Feb. 1967; suspended June 27, 1972; new constitution rejected by referendum, Nov. 30, 1980. **National holiday:** Independence Day, Aug. 25. **Heads of government:** Julio M. Sanguinetti, president (since Mar. 1985). **Structure:** executive, headed by president; bicameral legislature (Senate and House of Deputies); national judiciary headed by Court of Justice.

Economy Monetary unit: new peso. **Budget:** (1986) *income:* $968 mil.; *expend.:* $995 mil. **GDP:** $6.9 bil., $2,330 per capita (1987 est.). **Chief crops:** wheat, rice, corn, sorghum; large areas devoted to extensive livestock grazing; self-sufficient in most basic foodstuffs. **Livestock:** sheep, cattle, horses, pigs. **Natural resources:** soil, hydropower potential, minor minerals. **Major industries:** meat processing, wool and hides, sugar. **Labor force:** 1.2 mil. (1986); 25% government; 19% manufacturing; 12% commerce; 12% utilities, construction, transport, and communications; 11% agriculture; 9% unemployment (1987 est.). **Exports:** $1.14 bil. (f.o.b., 1987 est.); meat, textiles, wool, hides, leather products. **Imports:** $910 mil. (f.o.b., 1987 est.); fuels and lubricants (37%), metals, machinery, transportation equipment, industrial chemicals. **Major trading partners:** (1986) *exports:* 20% Brazil, 15% U.S.; *imports:* 39% LAIA (13% Brazil, 11% Argentina), 15% EC, 7% U.S.

Intl. Orgs. FAO, G-77, GATT, IAEA, IBRD, ICAO, IFAD, IFC, ILO, IMF, IMO, INTELSAT, INTERPOL, ITU, OAS, UN, UNESCO, UPU, WHO, WIPO, WMO.

Uruguay was known as the Banda Oriental del Uruguay (Eastern Shore of the Uruguay River) during the colonial period. Although the Spanish first explored the area in 1516, they did not immediately settle there. Instead, the Portuguese founded the Colonia de Sacramento, near Buenos Aires, in 1680. They did not permanently establish the settlement of Montevideo until 1726. Under the leadership of José Gervasio Artigas, Uruguayans fought against both the Portuguese and the junta of Buenos Aires between 1811 and 1814 in an effort to establish their independence; in 1815 they proclaimed the Autonomous Government of the Eastern Provinces.

In 1817 the Portuguese again took control of the region, but Uruguayan nationals ousted them in 1828. A new constitution for the country was promulgated in 1830; however, domestic rivalry among elites soon led to civil war. The two contending factions, Liberals and Conservatives, wore white and red armbands, respectively, thus generating their lasting party labels: Blancos (Conservatives) and Colorados (Liberals). Civil war continued through the 1840s and 1850s, until the victory of the Colorados in 1865. In the War of the Triple Alliance (1865-70), Uruguay allied itself with Argentina and Brazil against Paraguay. The consequence of the war for Uruguay was the definitive establishment of its independence from the other regional powers.

The Colorado party dominated Uruguayan government from 1865 until 1958. Waves of European immigrants transformed Uruguayan society during the latter half of the 19th century, and by 1880 immigrants made up almost half of the population. The last civil war between the Blancos and the Colorados took place in 1904; the Colorados won a definitive victory under the leadership of Pres. José Batlle y Ordóñez, who was to become one of the major political figures of Uruguay.

Batlle inaugurated a labor and social-welfare reform program that created Latin America's first eight-hour working day as well as progressive legislation on women's rights. A proposal for the extension of the franchise to women was put forward in 1917. Impressed with the Swiss plural executive Federal Council during his stay in Switzerland, Batlle believed such a structure could help Uruguay avoid the Latin American hazard of *caudillismo* (authoritarian rule). Batlle proposed the idea of a plural executive, but it was not immediately implemented in the 1910 electoral reform law. Instead, a version of the idea became part of the 1917 Constitution, which went into effect in 1919. The new constitution provided for both a president and a collegial National Council, both of which would make up the executive structure of the government.

In 1933 Uruguay experienced a military coup sponsored by the president, Gabriel Terra. Terra used troops to dissolve both the legislature and the National Council. It had been Terra's wish to reestablish the single executive presidential system, and he managed this by sponsoring a constituent assembly that drew up a new constitution in 1934. In a 1951 plebiscite, Uruguayan voters approved a return to the plural executive system, and a new constitutional order reflecting this went into effect the following year. The debate over the form of the executive was not over, however; in 1966 the public voted for yet another constitution, which once again established the single president as the executive power.

Uruguay's economy began to experience problems during the 1950s as world market prices for its exports began to slump. This, combined with the constant expansion of governmental bureaucracy tied to the country's social welfare programs, led to increasing popular discontent and decreasing room for maneuvering on the part of political elites. One sign of the growing public disenchantment with the political elite could be seen beginning in 1958 with two successive victories of the Blancos at the polls (for the first time in nearly a century). A candidate from the conservative wing of the Colorado party, Jorge Pacheco Areco, regained the presidency for the traditional ruling party in 1967, but neither the Blancos nor the Colorados were able to effectively deal with Uruguay's deteriorating economy or with its growing political unrest.

Uruguay's politics became increasingly polarized during the 1960s and into the 1970s. The leftist National Liberation Movement (MLN), also known as the Tupamaros, formed in 1967 and began urban guerrilla activity that included robbery and kidnapping. The Tupamaros, many of whom were young and middle class, embarked on a series of actions designed to embarrass government officials and police and were largely successful in eroding the public image of the civilian government. Tupamaro activity generated violence from the military and police, and as the political situation deteriorated in the early seventies, the government granted the military ever-expanding authority to deal with the situation.

By 1973 the military was in control of the country, and they dissolved the Congress. The military allowed Pres. Juan María Bordaberry to remain in office until 1976, at which time they imposed their man, Aparicio Méndez, in the presidency. It was Bordaberry, however, who proposed the dismantling of the political parties in 1976. By all accounts, the period of Uruguayan military rule was brutally repressive, and the armed forces perpetrated many human rights abuses (kidnapping, torture, murder). Some have estimated that during this period, the Uruguayan military regime had the world's largest number of political prisoners in proportion to the population.

The military government held a plebiscite in 1980 on a new constitution that would have amounted to continued de facto military control. The popular vote went against the military, and a slow process of political transition began, in which the military tried to bargain with civilian political elites. In 1984 the civilian Colorado candidate Julio María Sanguinetti was elected to the presidency. He took office the following year as the military withdrew from governance, restoring civilian rule.

Vanuatu
Republic of Vanuatu
(PREVIOUS NAME: NEW HEBRIDES)

Geography Location: chain of 12 principal and some 60 smaller islands in South Pacific Ocean, about 500 mi. (800 km) W of Fiji and about 1,100 mi. (2,800 km) E of Australia. **Boundaries:** surrounded by South Pacific Ocean; nearest neighbor is Santa Cruz Islands to N. **Total land area:** 4,707 sq. mi. (12,190 sq km). **Coastline:** 1,571 mi. (2,528 km). **Comparative area:** slightly larger than Connecticut. **Land use:** 1% arable land; 5% permanent crops; 2% meadows and pastures; 1% forest and woodland; 91% other. **Major cities:** (1986 est.) Port Vila (capital) 14,184.

People Population: 154,691 (1988). **Nationality:** noun—Vanuatuan(s); adjective—Vanuatuan. **Ethnic groups:** 94% indigenous Melanesian, 4% French; remainder Vietnamese, Chinese, and various Pacific Islanders. **Languages:** English and French (official); pidgin (known as Bislama or Bichelam). **Religions:** most at least nominally Christian.

Government Type: republic. **Independence:** July 30, 1980 (from France and UK). **Constitution:** July 30, 1980. **National holiday:** July 30. **Heads of government:** Fred Karlomoana Timakata, president (since Jan. 1989); Father Walter Hadye Lini, prime minister (since July 1980). **Structure:** unicameral legislature (46-member Parliament).

Economy (1986) **Monetary unit:** vatu **Budget:** *income:* revenues and grants $53 mil.; *expend.:* $58 mil. **GDP:** $84 mil., $580 per capita. **Chief crops:** export crops of copra, cocoa, coffee, and fish; subsistence crops of copra, taro, yams, coconuts, fruits, vegetables. **Livestock:** poultry, cattle, pigs, goats, horses. **Natural resources:** manganese, hardwood forests, fish. **Major industries:** food and fish-freezing, forestry processing, meat cannning. **Labor**

force: N.A. **Exports:** $14.3 mil., including reexports of $5.5 mil.; 29% copra, 13% cocoa, 9% meat, 8% fish, 4% timber. **Imports:** $58.0 mil., including $2.0 mil. for reexport; 25% machines and vehicles, 23% food and beverages, 18% basic manufactures, 11% raw materials and fuels, 6% chemicals. **Major trading partners:** *exports:* 34% Netherlands, 27% France, 17% Japan, 4% Belgium, 3% New Caledonia; *imports:* 36% Australia, 13% Japan, 10% New Zealand, 8% France, 5% Fiji.

Intl. Orgs. Commonwealth, FAO, G-77, IBRD, ICAO, IDA, IFC, IMF, ITU, NAM, UN, WHO, WMO.

Formerly New Hebrides, Vanuatu is a rugged, volcanic island chain with heavily forested mountains; peaks rise to over 6,000 feet (on Espiritu Santo, the largest island). The people are Melanesians. In 1887 the islands were placed under the administration of an Anglo-French naval commission, becoming a joint Anglo-French colony (condominium) in 1906. The islands escaped Japanese occupation during World War II; they sided with the Free French and were used as bases for Allied campaigns in the Pacific. The New Hebrides were granted independence as Vanuatu on July 30, 1980, with membership in the British Commonwealth. The government is a parliamentary system, complemented by a National Council of Chiefs to decide matters of tradition and customary law.

The economy is based on subsistence agriculture, cattle raising, and fishing. Exports consist primarily of copra, beef, and fish. Tourism is developing rapidly, along with light industry, particularly food processing. The sale of long-term tuna-fishing rights, principally to Japan, Australia, and the United States, is an important earner of foreign exchange; in the 1980s Vanuatu came into conflict with the United States through the sale of fishing rights to the Soviet Union.

Vatican City
State of the Vatican City
Geography Location: entirely within city of Rome, Italy. **Boundaries:** surrounded by Italian territory. **Total land area:** 0.17 sq. mi. (0.44 sq km). **Coastline:** none. **Comparative area:** about 7/10 size of the Mall in Washington, D.C. **Land use:** 0% arable land; 0% permanent crops; 0% meadows and pastures; 0% forest and woodland; 100% other. **Major cities:** Vatican City (capital).

People Population: 752 (1988). **Nationality:** N.A. **Ethnic groups:** primarily Italians, but also many other nationalities. **Languages:** Italian, Latin, various other languages. **Religions:** Roman Catholic.

Government Type: monarchical-sacerdotal state, seat of Holy See. **Independence:** Feb. 11, 1929 (from Italy). **Constitution:** N.A. **National holiday:** installation day of Pope John Paul II, Oct. 22. **Heads of government:** John Paul II, supreme pontiff (Karol Wojtyla, elected pope Oct. 16, 1978). **Structure:** pope possesses full executive, legislative, and judicial powers; he delegates these powers to presi-

dent of Pontifical Commission, who is subject to pontifical appointment and recall; Secretariat of State and Council of Public Affairs (which handles Vatican diplomacy) and Prefecture of Economic Affairs; College of Cardinals acts as chief papal adviser.

Economy Monetary unit: Vatican issues its own coinage, which is interchangeable with Italian lira. **Budget:** supported financially by contributions (known as Peter's Pence) from Roman Catholics throughout world; some income derived from sale of Vatican postage stamps and tourist mementos, fees for admission to museums, and sale of publications. **GDP:** N.A. **Chief crops:** N.A. **Livestock:** N.A. **Natural resources:** N.A. **Major industries:** consists of printing and production of small amount of mosaics and staff uniforms; worldwide banking and financial activities. **Labor force:** about 1,500; Vatican City employees are divided into three categories—executives, office workers, and salaried employees. **Exports:** N.A. **Imports:** N.A. **Major trading partners:** N.A.

Intl. Orgs. IAEA, INTELSAT, ITU, UPU, WIPO; permanent observer status at FAO, OAS, UN, UNESCO.

Vatican City is the smallest sovereign state in the world both in size and in population. It is a remnant of the "Patrimony of St. Peter," the secular state donated to the popes in the eighth century by Pepin the Short, father of Charlemagne. One of the major political powers on the Italian peninsula throughout the Middle Ages and into modern times, the States of the Church were conquered in 1870 by the new Kingdom of Italy, which made Rome its capital. In 1929 Mussolini's government made peace with the papacy in the Lateran Treaty, which recognized Vatican City as an independent state. The treaty was incorporated into the Italian Constitution of 1947. Under the terms of the treaty, the pope is pledged to perpetual neutrality and may intervene in international affairs as a mediator only upon request.

The pope is the sovereign of Vatican City in his capacity as bishop of Rome, and in that capacity, he accepts the credentials of the 113 foreign ambassadors assigned to the Holy See. The United States opened diplomatic relations with the Holy See in 1984, following the repeal of an 1867 law forbidding such relations.

As sovereign of Vatican City, the pope is an elected absolute monarch who appoints a Pontifical Council to govern the city on his behalf. The council meets only a few times each year. The economy is based on service industries, including printing; its revenues come from museum fees, philatelic sales, and sales of publications.

Venezuela
Republic of Venezuela
Geography Location: northern coast of South America. **Boundaries:** Caribbean Sea to N, Guyana to E, Brazil to S, Colombia to W. **Total land area:** 352,144 sq. mi. (912,050 sq km). **Coastline:** 1,739 mi. (2,800 km). **Comparative area:** slightly more than twice size of California. **Land use:** 3% arable land; 1% permanent crops; 20% meadows and pastures;

39% forest and woodland; 37% other; includes negl. % irrigated. **Major cities:** (1987 est.) Caracas (capital) 3,247,698; Maracaibo 1,295,421; Valencia 1,134,623; Maracay 857,982; Barquisimeto 718,197.

People Population: 18,775,780 (1988). **Nationality:** noun—Venezuelan(s); adjective—Venezuelan. **Ethnic groups:** 67% mestizo, 21% white, 10% black, 2% Indian. **Languages:** Spanish (official), Indian dialects (spoken by about 200,000 Amerindians in remote interior). **Religions:** 96% nominally Roman Catholic, 2% Protestant.

Government Type: republic. **Independence:** July 5, 1821 (from Spain). **Constitution:** Jan. 23, 1961. **National holiday:** Independence Day, July 5. **Head of government:** Carlos Andrés Pérez, president (since Feb. 2, 1988). **Structure:** executive (president); bicameral legislature (National Congress—Senate, Chamber of Deputies); judiciary.

Economy Monetary unit: bolívar. **Budget:** (1987) *income:* $12.2 bil.; *expend.:* $16.6 bil. **GDP:** $53.9 bil., $3,030 per capita. **Chief crops:** cereals, fruits, sugar, coffee, rice; illegal producer of cannabis for international drug trade. **Livestock:** cattle, pigs, goats, horses, asses, sheep. **Natural resources:** crude oil, natural gas, iron ore, gold, bauxite. **Major industries:** petroleum, iron ore mining, construction materials. **Labor force:** 5.8 mil. (1985); 56% services, 28% industry, 16% agriculture; 10.5% unemployment (Dec. 1986). **Exports:** $10.4 bil. (f.o.b., 1987); 84% petroleum. **Imports:** $8.1 bil. (c.i.f., 1987). **Major trading partners:** (1985) *exports:* 41% U.S., 17% Netherlands Antilles, 7% W. Germany, 5% Canada, 4% Italy; *imports:* 50% U.S., 6% Italy, 5% Japan, 5% W. Germany, 4.5% France.

Intl. Orgs. FAO, G-77, IAEA, IBRD, ICAO, IFAD, IFC, ILO, IMF, IMO, INTELSAT, INTERPOL, ITU, OAS, OPEC, UN, UNESCO, UPU, WHO, WMO.

At the time of European contact in the early 16th century, coastal Venezuela was home to nearly 50,000 semisedentary Indians. Although the region was "discovered" by Christopher Columbus in 1498, European settlement of the area was slow in comparison with the neighboring region of New Granada. The Spaniards explored and exploited Venezuela in the 1520s, their activity originally characterized by gold and pearl expeditions.

Early attempts at agriculture by the Spaniards failed until they discovered that the area around Caracas (founded in 1567) could sustain the production of both wheat and cacao. African slave labor was an important part of the economic structure of the area, and as markets for cacao expanded, Caracas grew in importance. Venezuela became a captaincy general (an administrative region below the level of viceroyalty) with an *audiencia* (high court) established at Caracas in 1777–78.

As early as 1797, Venezuelan society was in rebellion against the Spanish empire. One characteristic of the independence movement in the region was the underlying class war, which took the form of a white elite against lower classes of mixed African-European descent (*pardos*). The independence movement leadership vacillated in its position between these two groups. The leaders of the war against the empire needed the support of conservative landowners, but at the same time, the participation of the pardos was necessary for military victory. This dilemma left revolutionary leader Simón Bolívar trying to weld together a coherent force from antagonistic elements.

The wars of independence were particularly destructive in Venezuela, but by 1821 the region had achieved its independence and had become part of the federation of Gran Colombia, which also included Colombia and Ecuador. By 1830 Gran Colombia was in a state of political collapse, and Venezuela became an independent republic.

The militarization of Venezuela that resulted from the protracted independence struggle was to have profound consequences for the country's future politics. Domination of political life by military caudillos (leaders) became a prominent feature, as can be seen in the early dominance of José Antonio Páez, whose control over the country lasted for three decades. With the demise of Antonio Páez and his conservative allies in the 1860s, the forces of liberalism under the control of Guzmán Blanco took over. The Guzmán Blanco era ended during a brief civil war in 1889. The victor of the struggle, Gen. Cipriano Castro, then proceeded to establish his own rule. In 1909 Gen. Juan Vicente Gómez occupied the presidency, and he controlled the politics of Venezuela until his death, in 1935.

The beginning of the shift in Venezuelan politics from dictatorship to democracy can be traced back to the formation of a university student movement called the Generation of 1928. This group set out to organize urban workers and peasants into a viable base of support necessary to constitute a political opposition. The Generation of 1928 later became the modern Democratic Action party. In 1945 a group of young military officers, the Patriotic Military Union, overthrew the conservative dictatorship and supported the Democratic Action group in writing a new democratic constitution. Democratic Action won the elections of 1947, but conservative military elements overthrew the new government the following year. Apparently, reform programs of the Democratic Action party were too wide in scope and too rapid in pace to be acceptable to conservative elements in the country.

The conservative coup brought Col. Marcos Pérez Jiménez to power. The Pérez Jiménez dictatorship lasted until 1958, when it in turn was ousted. The following year Democratic Action candidate Romulo Betancourt became president. From that time to the present, Venezuela has experienced stable multiparty democratic politics. The stability of the system owes much to political possibilities provided by the country's petroleum revenues. Just as important to the political stability of the country has been an agreement, or pact, between the major political parties and their respective elites. The pact assures that no one group will lose its political standing completely as a result of an electoral loss. This helps ensure adherence of all major players in the Venezuelan political arena to the forms of democratic competition.

Despite the nationalization of foreign-owned oil and iron firms in 1976, Venezuela's dependence on petroleum revenues has precipitated economic and political problems for the country in the 1980s. The downturn of the global oil market has caused Venezuela's economic base to shrink, and the country's massive foreign debt has introduced substantial constraints in terms of possibilities for the continuance of populist political strategies.

The Christian Democrats defeated Democratic Action in 1968 and again in 1978. Pres. Luis Herrera Campíns's administration took the country in a more conservative direction for a short time. The Christian Democrat government was a vociferous supporter of Argentina's claim to the Falkland Islands in Argentina's war against Great Britain. Democratic Action regained the presidency in 1983 under the leadership of Jaime Lusinchi. Venezuela, as an original member of the multinational Latin American diplomatic organization, the Contadora group, made an early contribution to the international effort to bring about a diplomatic solution to conflicts in Central America.

The problem of managing Venezuela's foreign debt has been a major issue for both the Lusinchi government and the Democratic Action successor administration of Carlos Andrés Pérez, who took office in 1989. The Lusinchi administration successfully renegotiated a debt package in 1985, but the resulting constraints on Democratic Action governments in terms of restrictions on populist programs has amounted to a serious problem for the peaceful governance of the country. Riots protesting government policy followed the inauguration of the new president in 1989.

Vietnam
Socialist Republic of Viet Nam

Geography Location: E coast of Southeast Asia. **Boundaries:** China to N, Gulf of Tonkin to NE, South China Sea to E, Laos and Kampuchea to W. **Total land area:** 127,246 sq. mi. (329,566 sq km). **Coastline:** 2,140 mi. (3,444 km) excluding islands. **Comparative area:** slightly larger than New Mexico. **Land use:** 22% arable land; 2% permanent crops; 1% meadows and pastures; 40% forest and woodland; 35% other; includes 5% irrigated. **Major cities:** Hanoi (capital) 2,674,400 (1983); Ho Chi Minh City (formerly Saigon) 3,419,978 (1979 census); Haiphong 1,279,067 (1979 census); Da Nang 492,194 (1973 est.); Nha Trang 216,227 (1973 est.).

People Population: 65,185,278 (1988). **Nationality:** noun—Vietnamese (sing., pl.); adjective—Vietnamese. **Ethnic groups:** 85–90% Vietnamese, 3% Chinese; ethnic minorities include Muong, Thai, Meo, Khmer, Man, Cham; other mountain groups. **Languages:** Vietnamese (official); French, Chinese, English, Khmer, ethnic langs. (Mon-Khmer and Malayo-Polynesian). **Religions:** Buddhist, Confucian, Taoist, Roman Catholic.

Government Type: communist state.

Independence: Sept. 2, 1945 (from France). **Constitution:** Dec. 18, 1980. **National holiday:** Sept. 2. **Heads of government:** Vo Chi Cong, chairman, (since June 1988); Du Muoi, prime minister (since June 1988). **Structure:** highest authority of land is technically Council of State, whose chairman serves as country's president; Council of Ministers oversees implementation of party policies—chairman is equivalent of premier; unicameral legislature (National Assembly).

Economy (1986) **Monetary unit:** dong. **Budget:** N.A. **GNP:** $12.4 bil.; $200 per capita. **Chief crops:** rice, rubber, fruits, vegetables; some corn, manioc, sugarcane; major food imports—wheat, corn, dairy products. **Livestock:** pigs, buffalo, cattle, goats, horses. **Natural resources:** phosphates, coal, manganese, bauxite, apatite. **Major industries:** food processing, textiles, machine building. **Labor force:** 31.9 mil., not including military (shortages—foodgrains, petroleum, capital goods and machinery, fertilizer, insecticides, spare parts, raw materials). **Exports:** $785 mil.; agricultural and handicraft products, coal, minerals, ores. **Imports:** $1,590 mil.; petroleum, steel products, railroad equipment, chemicals, medicines. **Major trading partners:** USSR, Eastern Europe, Japan, Singapore.

Intl. Orgs. CMEA, Colombo Plan, FAO, G-77, IAEA, IBRD, ICAO, IDA, IFAD, IFC, ILO, IMF, INTELSAT, ITU, NAM, UN, UNDP, UNESCO, UNICEF, UPU, WHO, WIPO, WMO.

The southward expansion of the Chinese empire in the first millennium B.C. drove the Vietnamese peoples southward into northern Vietnam (Tonkin). The area came under direct Chinese rule in 111 B.C. Chinese rule endured, with some interruptions, until A.D. 948; thereafter, Vietnam was independent under strong Chinese influence.

The Hindu-Buddhist kingdom of Annam, in central Vietnam, gradually increased in size and power at the expense of Tonkin, to the north, and the Khmer empire and Champa, to the west and south. In 1558 the Kingdom of Annam split, with independent courts established at Hanoi, controlling Tonkin and the Red River valley, and Hue, in central Vietnam. A remnant of the old Champa state remained independent in the Mekong delta in the south. In 1802 the monarchy was reunited, with the court at Hue controlling all of Vietnam and exercising hegemony over Cambodia.

European penetration of the region began in the 16th century; by the early 19th century, France was the dominant foreign power in Indochina. Efforts to establish French military control began in 1858–59 with the establishment of a colony in Cochin China, in southern Vietnam. Campaigns in the Red River valley in 1873 and 1882 were complicated by Chinese intervention and the determined resistance of the Vietnamese court. In 1884 separate protectorates were established in Tonkin and Annam; in 1887 those, along with Cochin China and Cambodia, were combined into the Union of Indochina under French colonial rule. Rubber plantations were established, and rice and timber exports were under French control. A nationalist rebellion under Phan Boi Chau was suppressed in the early 20th century.

Nationalist resistance to French colonialism continued, resulting in the creation in 1939 of the Vietminh, or Independence League. In 1940 Japanese troops occupied French Indochina, with the collaboration of colonial administrators loyal to the Vichy regime. The Vietminh spearheaded anti-Japanese guerrilla resistance and in 1945 forced the abdication of King Bao Dai, head of a pro-Japanese puppet state. In 1945 France reoccupied Indochina; in 1946 the leader of the Vietminh, Ho Chi Minh, became president of a separatist government at Hanoi. France ceded local autonomy to Tonkin and Annam but sought to retain Cochin China as a colony. Fighting between the French and the Vietminh resumed. On July 1, 1949, the French reinstalled Bao Dai as king of Vietnam, and in February 1950 recognized the independence of Vietnam within the French Union. Ho Chi Minh's republican government also claimed control of all of Vietnam.

Fighting between the two rivals culminated in the French defeat at Dienbienphu on May 7, 1954. An armistice was concluded according to which the country was partitioned at a demilitarized zone at latitude 17° north, the northern part going to the communist-controlled Vietminh government, the southern to Bao Dai. Nearly one million refugees, including many ethnic Chinese, fled from the north to the south. An international conference in Geneva agreed that elections would be held throughout Vietnam in 1956. In June 1954 Ngo Dinh Diem became premier of South Vietnam; full sovereignty in the south was transferred by France to the Vietnamese government in December 1954. In October 1955 Diem held elections in the south that resulted in the dismissal of Bao Dai as king and the proclamation of an independent Republic of Vietnam.

The scheduled elections of 1956 were never held. French troops completed withdrawal from South Vietnam in that year. Fighting continued in the south, as the Vietminh-backed National Liberation Front (Vietcong) sought to overthrow the Diem government. On Dec. 31, 1959, the Democratic Republic of Vietnam in the north adopted a new constitution calling for the reunification of the country; northern aid to the Vietcong increased significantly, as did American aid to the south. After 1962 American military advisers steadily increased in number and combat exposure.

In 1963 widespread public demonstrations, under Buddhist leadership, led to a coup on Nov. 1-2 in which Diem was deposed and assassinated. A series of short-lived military regimes followed until September 1967, when Nguyen Van Thieu was elected president. U.S. air strikes against North Vietnam began in 1964. In the same year, the flow of troops and supplies from north to south increased markedly. American combat troops entered the war in 1965. Despite U.S.–South Vietnamese superiority in arms and troops, and total control of the air, Vietcong control over the countryside increased. Both Operation Phoenix, in which antigovernment rural leaders were assassi-

nated, and the establishment of fortified strategic hamlets to control the rural population, failed to reverse the tide.

The combined Vietcong-North Vietnamese Tet Offensive in early 1968 resulted in serious losses for South Vietnamese and American forces. The war spread to Laos and to Cambodia, the latter bombed in 1969. American air strikes in North Vietnam were stepped up, and U.S. troop strength reached a maximum of 543,000 in 1969. In July 1969 a series of U.S. troop withdrawals began, and secret talks were initiated in search of a negotiated settlement of the war. Following heavy U.S. bombardment of the north in 1972, a cease-fire agreement was signed in Paris by South Vietnam, North Vietnam, the Vietcong, and the United States on Jan. 27, 1973. It was never implemented, but the American withdrawal continued. In early 1975 South Vietnamese forces collapsed in the face of a series of North Vietnamese-Vietcong offensives. Remaining U.S. personnel were evacuated, and Saigon fell on Apr. 30, 1975. Over the next few years, hundreds of thousands of refugees ("boat people") fled the country.

Following the fall of Saigon, the country was occupied by northern troops and administrators. Businesses were nationalized, agriculture collectivized, and tens of thousands of people sent to labor camps for "reeducation." A unified National Assembly met in 1976, and the country was officially reunified on July 2, 1976, under the existing government of the north. Saigon was renamed Ho Chi Minh City. A Soviet naval base was established at the former U.S. base at Cam Ranh Bay.

In 1978 Vietnamese troops occupied Kampuchea, ousting the government of Pol Pot and installing Heng Samrin as premier. In February 1979 China launched an unsuccessful punitive attack over its border with Vietnam to display displeasure with the invasion of Kampuchea and with the treatment of ethnic Chinese in Vietnam. In 1988 Vietnam pledged to withdraw its troops from Kampuchea.

Vietnam's communist government rules through the party's powerful Central Committee; no strong personalities have emerged to replace the leaders of the wartime generation. The economy functions only at a basic level, with the infrastructure in disrepair and agriculture and small business hampered by excessive collectivization and central planning. The economy is heavily dependent on Soviet aid. Resumption of contacts with the U.S. has been precluded by American insistence that Vietnam account more fully for American prisoners of war and troops missing in action.

Western Sahara

Geography **Location:** northwestern coast of Africa. **Boundaries:** Morocco to N, Algeria and Mauritania to E, North Atlantic Ocean to W. **Total land area:** 102,703 sq. mi. (266,000 sq km). **Coastline:** 690 mi. (1,110 km). **Comparative area:** slightly smaller than Colorado. **Land use:** negl. % arable land; 0% permanent crops; 19% meadows and pastures; 0% forest and woodland; 81% other. **Major cities:** (1982) El Aaiun (capital) 93,785.

People **Population:** 181,411 (1988). **Nationality:** noun—Saharan(s), Moroccan(s); adjective—Saharan, Moroccan. **Ethnic groups:** Arab, Berber. **Languages:** Hassaniya Arabic, Moroccan Arabic. **Religions:** Muslim.

Government **Type:** legal status of territory and question of sovereignty still unresolved. **Independence:** N.A. **Constitution:** N.A. **National holiday:** N.A. **Heads of government:** Mohamed Abdelaziz, president (since Oct. 1982). **Structure:** N.A.

Economy **Monetary unit:** Moroccan dirham. **Budget:** N.A. **GDP:** N.A. **Chief crops:** practically none; some barley grown in nondrought years; fruit and vegetables in the few oases; food imports; water shortage. **Livestock:** N.A. **Natural resources:** phosphates, iron ore. **Major industries:** phosphate, fishing, handicrafts. **Labor force:** 12,000; 50% animal husbandry and subsistence farming. **Exports:** up to $5 mil. in phosphates, all other exports valued at under $3 mil. (1982). **Imports:** up to $30 mil. (1982); fuel for fishing fleet, foodstuffs. **Major trading partners:** Morocco claims administrative control over Western Sahara and controls all trade with country; trade figures are included in overall Moroccan accounts.

Intl. Orgs. N.A.

Western Sahara, a small area on the northwest coast of Africa peopled mostly by nomads, was originally named Spanish Sahara. Spain controlled the territory in the early 1500s and again between 1860 and 1976. In the interim years, Morocco held the Western Sahara. Spain made the Western Sahara a province in 1958 but ceded it to Morocco and Mauritania in 1976 when it became known as Western Sahara. Morocco claimed the northern region while Mauritania claimed the south. Algeria joined a group of Western Saharans organized as the Polisario Front in demanding independence for the country, and fighting broke out. The Polisario Front was aided by Algeria and Libya in the fighting. Mauritania withdrew its claim in 1979 and left the fighting, but Morocco proceeded to claim the Mauritanian portion of the Western Sahara and fighting continued into the mid-1980s. A treaty between Libya and Morocco signed in 1984 fell apart in 1986, and fighting resumed.

Western Samoa
Independent State of Western Samoa
Geography **Location:** two large and seven small islands, five of which are inhabited, in South Pacific Ocean, about 1,500 mi. (2,400 km) NE of New Zealand. **Boundaries:** surrounded by South Pacific Ocean; nearest neighbor is American Samoa to E. **Total land area:** 1,093 sq. mi. (2,831 sq km). **Coastline:** 250 mi. (403 km). **Comparative area:** slightly smaller than Rhode Island. **Land use:** 19% arable land; 24% permanent crops; negl. % meadows and pastures; 47% forest and woodland; 10% other. **Major cities:** (1981 census) Apia (capital) 33,170.

People **Population:** 178,045 (1988). **Nationality:** noun—Western Samoan(s); ad jective—Western Samoan. **Ethnic groups:** Samoan; about 7% Euronesians (persons of European and Polynesian blood), 0.4% Europeans. **Languages:** Samoan (Polynesian), English. **Religions:** 99.7% Christian (about half of population associated with London Missionary Society; includes Congregational, Roman Catholic, Methodist, Latter-day Saints, Seventh-Day Adventist).

Government Type: constitutional monarchy under native chief. **Independence:** Jan. 1, 1962 (from UN trusteeship administered by New Zealand). **Constitution:** Jan. 1, 1962. **National holiday:** Independence Day, Jan. 1. **Heads of government:** Malietoa Tanumafili II, head of state (since 1962); Tofilau Eti, prime minister (since Feb. 1988). **Structure:** Head of state and executive council; unicameral legislature (47-member Legislative Assembly); Supreme Court, court of appeal, land and titles court, village courts.

Economy Monetary unit: WS tala. **Budget:** (1985) **income:** $40 mil.; **expend.:** $41 mil. (including development expend. of $20 mil.). **GDP:** $102 mil., $520 per capita (1986 est.). **Chief crops:** coconuts, fruit (including bananas, taro, yams). **Livestock:** poultry, pigs, cattle, horses. **Natural resources:** hardwood forests, fish. **Major industries:** timber, tourism, food processing. **Labor force:** about 37,000 (1983); about 22,000 employed in agriculture. **Exports:** $10.5 mil. (1986); 43% coconut oil, 10% copra, 6% cocoa, 3% timber (1985 est.). **Imports:** $43 mil. (1986); 58% intermediate goods, 17% food, 12% capital goods. **Major trading partners:** **exports:** (1985) 35% New Zealand, 25% U.S., 24% Australia, 4% W. Germany; **imports:** (1983) 29% New Zealand, 28% Australia, 11% U.S., 11% Japan, 6% Singapore.

Intl. Orgs. Commonwealth, FAO, G-77, IBRD, IDA, IFAD, IFC, IMF, UN, UNESCO, WHO.

The Polynesian island group of Samoa (Navigator's Islands) was partitioned in 1899 between the United States, which had established a naval base at Pago Pago on Tutuila in 1878, and Germany, which organized the westerly islands into a colony in 1894. In 1914 New Zealand troops occupied the German-held islands. New Zealand administered Western Samoa under a League of Nations mandate beginning in 1920 and continued to control the islands as a UN Trust Territory after 1945. In 1959 home rule was established under an elected local government. Western Samoa became an independent nation on Jan. 1, 1962. The constitution blends Western parliamentary government and traditional Samoan forms of rule. The parliamentary electorate is limited to the malai, heads of extended families; the malai are wholly responsible for local affairs. The local culture is similarly a blend of Samoan tradition with Christianity.

The economy is based on subsistence agriculture, forestry, fishing, and tourism. Nearly 50 percent of the land area is forested; lumber and wood products (plywood, veneer) are important exports. Offshore fisheries are being developed, along with light industry, particularly food processing.

Yemen Arab Republic
(ABBREV.: YEMEN AR OR YAR)
(COMMON NAME: YEMEN [SANAA] OR NORTH YEMEN)

Geography Location: southwest corner of Arabian peninsula. **Boundaries:** Saudi Arabia to N and E, S. Yemen to S and E, Red Sea to W. **Total land area:** 77,220 sq. mi. (200,000 sq km). **Coastline:** 325 mi. (523 km). **Comparative area:** slightly smaller than South Dakota. **Land use:** 14% arable land; negl. % permanent crops; 36% meadows and pastures; 8% forest and woodland; 42% other; includes 1% irrigated. **Major cities:** (1981 census) San'a (capital) 277,818; Hodeia 126,386; Taiz 119,576.

People Population: 6,732,420 (1988). **Nationality:** noun—Yemeni(s); adjective—Yemeni. **Ethnic groups:** 90% Arab, 10% Afro-Arab (mixed). **Languages:** Arabic. **Religions:** 100% Muslim (Sunni and Shi'a).

Government Type: republic; military regime assumed power June 1974. **Independence:** Nov. 1918 (from Ottoman Empire). **Constitution:** Dec. 28, 1970; suspended June 19, 1974. **National holiday:** Proclamation of the Republic, Sept. 26. **Heads of government:** Ali Abdullah Saleh, president (since 1978); Abdulaziz Abdul-Ghani, prime minister (since 1983). **Structure:** executive—president, prime minister, cabinet; legislature—People's Constituent Assembly.

Economy Monetary unit: rial. **Budget:** (1986 est.) **income:** $1.18 bil.; **expend.:** $1.68 bil. **GDP:** $3.2 bil., $505 per capita (1986). **Chief crops:** sorghum, millet, qat (a mild narcotic), cotton, coffee. **Livestock:** goats, sheep, cattle, asses, camels. **Natural resources:** crude oil; rock salt; marble; small deposits of coal, nickel, and copper; fertile soil. **Major industries:** crude oil production, small-scale production of cotton textiles and leather goods; food processing. **Labor force:** about 30% expatriate laborers; remainder almost entirely agriculture and herding. **Exports:** $11.0 mil. (f.o.b.; 1987); qat, cotton, coffee, hides, vegetables. **Imports:** $1.3 bil. (f.o.b.; 1987); textiles, petroleum products, sugar, grain, flour. Major trading partners: (1985) **exports:** 41% U.S., 14% S. Yemen, 12% Japan; **imports:** 10% Italy, 9% Japan, 9% Saudi Arabia, 8% UK.

Intl. Orgs. Arab League, FAO, G-77, IBRD, ICAO, IDA, IFAD, IFC, ILO, IMF, IMO, INTELSAT, INTERPOL, ITU, NAM, UN, UNESCO, UPU, WHO, WIPO, WMO.

Yemen—in ancient times Sheba or Saba—is strategically located in the southwestern corner of the Arabian peninsula, near the southern end of the Red Sea. In biblical times and for many centuries thereafter, Yemen dominated the caravan trade in spices, gold, and other luxury goods from India and Africa to the Middle East.

The Islamic unification of Arabia in 628 resulted in the incorporation of Yemen into Arabia as a whole, but many local uprisings broke out over the course of the following three centuries. In the 10th century, control passed to a line of Yemeni kings who were concurrently imams of the Zaidi sect of Islam; the

Zaidi imams ruled until 1962. The southern portion of Yemen, around the port of Aden, was under partial Portuguese control from the mid-16th century and became part of the British Protectorate of Aden in 1839 (see "South Yemen").

Yemen came under control of the Ottoman Empire from the mid-16th to the mid-17th century, and again from 1849 to 1918. The Turks were expelled at the end of World War I, and Yemen became an independent kingdom in 1918. The kingdom's independence was threatened by a short-lived Saudi invasion in 1934 and by a dispute with Great Britain over the status of Aden in 1954.

Imam Ahmed came to the throne in 1948, following the assassination of his predecessor. Most of Yemen's large Jewish population was evacuated to Israel in 1949–50. A palace coup against the imam in 1955 failed, but after he died on Sept. 19, 1962, his successor was quickly driven from the throne, and a republic was proclaimed under the leadership of Brig. Gen. Abdullah al-Salal. Civil war between royalist and republican factions lasted until April 1970, when a coalition republican government was formed with the aid of Saudi mediation.

Col. Ibrahim al-Hamidi came to power in a military coup on June 13, 1974; he was assassinated on Oct. 11, 1977. Pres. Ali Abdullah Saleh assumed office on July 17, 1978, following the assassination of the previously elected president, Ahmad ibn Hussein al-Ghashmi.

Border skirmishes between North and South Yemen broke out during 1972–73. After several years of uneasy peace, South Yemen launched a full-scale war against the north on Feb. 24, 1979. Arab League pressure quickly led to a mutual disengagement on Mar. 19. A cease-fire agreement between the two Yemeni nations was signed on Mar. 29, 1979.

North Yemen's economy has remained largely agricultural in recent years. The chewing of qat, a mildly stimulant leaf, is widespread; cultivation of qat bushes has replaced traditional coffee plantations in many areas. Oil was discovered in North Yemen in 1984, and commercial deliveries of crude oil commenced in 1987. Remittances from the more than 400,000 Yemenis working in other Arab nations provide the bulk of the country's nonpetroleum foreign earnings.

Yemen, People's Democratic Republic of
(ABBREV.: YEMEN, PDR, OR PDRY)
(COMMON NAME: YEMEN [ADEN] OR SOUTH YEMEN)

Geography Location: southern shore of Arabian peninsula. **Boundaries:** N. Yemen to NW, Saudi Arabia to N, Oman to NE, Arabian Sea to E, Gulf of Aden to S. **Total land area:** 130,066 sq. mi. (336,869 sq km). **Coastline:** 859 mi. (1,383 km). **Comparative area:** slightly larger than New Mexico. **Land use:** 1% arable land; negl. % permanent crops; 27% meadows and pastures; 7% forest and woodland; 65% other; includes negl. % irrigated. **Major cities:** (1973 census) Aden (capital) 291,000; Hadhramaut 451,000; Abyan 311,000; Lahej 273,000; Shabwah 162,000.

People Population: 2,425,620 (1988). **Nationality:** noun—Yemeni(s); adjective—Yemeni. **Ethnic groups:** mostly Arab; a few Indians, Somalis, and Europeans. **Languages:** Arabic. **Religions:** Sunni Muslim; some Christian and Hindu.

Government Type: republic. **Independence:** Nov. 30, 1967 (from UK). **Constitution:** Oct. 31, 1978. **National holiday:** Oct. 14. **Heads of government:** Haider Abubaker al-Attas, chairman, Presidium, Supreme People's Council (since Feb. 1986); Yasin Said Numan, prime minister (since 1986). **Structure:** executive—Supreme Cabinet; legislature—unicameral legislature (People's Assembly).

Economy Monetary unit: dinar. **Budget:** (1985 est.) *income:* $433 mil.; *expend.:* $495 mil. **GDP:** $1.1 bil., $500 per capita (est.). **Chief crops:** cotton is main cash crop; cereals, dates, qat (a mild narcotic), coffee, livestock; large amount of food must be imported (particularly for Aden). **Livestock:** goats, sheep, asses, cattle, camels. **Natural resources:** fish, oil, minerals (gold, copper, lead). **Major industries:** petroleum refinery at Little Aden operates on imported crude; fish. **Labor force:** N.A. **Exports:** $316 mil. (f.o.b., est.); cotton, hides, skins, dried and salted fish. **Imports:** $762 mil. (f.o.b., est.). **Major trading partners:** *exports:* 36% Japan, 23% N. Yemen, 10% Singapore; *imports:* 14% USSR, 9% Australia, 7% UK.

Intl. Orgs. Arab League, FAO, G-77, GATT (de facto), IBRD, ICAO, IDA, IFAD, ILO, IMF, IMO, ITU, NAM, UN, UNESCO, UPU, WHO, WMO.

Aden was the most important port of the ancient kingdom of Sheba (or Saba) and retained that status under the Islamic imams of Yemen (see "North Yemen"). Portuguese activity around Aden began in the 15th century; from the mid-16th century, control of the port was disputed by the Portuguese, the Yemeni kings, the Ottoman Turks, and, from the 18th century, the British.

In 1839 Aden was made a British Crown Colony; the Hadhramaut region of southern Arabia, extending north and east of Aden, became the British Protectorate of Aden. Both the colony and the protectorate were administered as part of British India. After India gained independence in 1947, Aden became the key stronghold of British military power in the western Indian Ocean and the Gulf of Aden.

A struggle for independence began in Aden and the Protectorate in 1963, with two rival groups competing for power. The National Liberation Front (NLF) gained the upper hand over the Egyptian-backed Front for the Liberation of Occupied South Yemen (FLOSY), as both groups waged guerrilla war against the British. Most of the country's Jewish population fled to Israel. British forces withdrew in 1967, and South Yemen became independent on Nov. 30 of that year. The nation's territory included Socotra and adjacent islands off the Horn of Africa, which had been British possessions since 1876.

In 1969 a leftist faction of the NLF seized power, nationalized key industries, and

instituted a socialist regime. In 1972–73 South Yemen fought several border skirmishes with North Yemen. South Yemeni troops aided leftist guerrillas in Oman in the mid-1970s, and fought in Ethiopia against Eritrean rebels. Subsequently Pres. Salem Robaye Ali took a more moderate stance and improved relations with Oman and Saudi Arabia. He was overthrown in a coup in June 1978 and executed.

South Yemen launched a full-scale war against North Yemen on Feb. 24, 1979. Arab League pressure quickly led to a mutual disengagement on Mar. 19, with cease-fire agreement between the two Yemeni nations being signed on Mar. 29, 1979. The government was overthrown in another coup on Jan. 13, 1986; on Feb. 8, Yasin Said Numan became prime minister of the new government.

South Yemen's economy is largely agricultural. Cotton is the principal export; sheep and goats are raised in the arid countryside. Shipping services in the port of Aden form the main basis of the country's commercial economy. Oil was discovered on Apr. 15, 1987; by October of that year, production reached 10,000 barrels a day.

Yugoslavia
Socialist Federal Republic of Yugoslavia
Geography Location: southeastern Europe. **Boundaries:** Austria and Hungary to N, Romania and Bulgaria to E, Greece and Albania to S, Adriatic Sea to W; short frontier with Italy to NW. **Total land area:** 98,766 sq. mi. (255,804 sq km). **Coastline:** 2,446 mi. (3,935 km). **Comparative area:** slightly larger than Wyoming. **Land use:** 28% arable land; 3% permanent crops; 25% meadows and pastures; 36% forest and woodland; 8% other; includes 1% irrigated. **Major cities:** (1981 census) Beo Grad (Belgrade, capital) 1,470,073; Osijek 867,646; Zagreb 768,700; Nis 643,470; Skoplje (Skopje) 506,547.

People Population: 23,580,148 (1988). **Nationality:** noun—Yugoslav(s); adjective—Yugoslav. **Ethnic groups:** (1981 census) 19.7% Croat, 8.9% Muslim, 7.8% Slovene, 7.7% Albanian, 6.3% Serb, 5.9% Macedonian, 5.4% Yugoslav, 2.5% Montenegrin, 1.9% Hungarian, 3.9% other. **Languages:** Serbo-Croatian, Slovene, Macedonian (all official), Albanian, Hungarian. **Religions:** 50% Eastern Orthodox, 30% Roman Catholic, 10% Muslim, 1% Protestant, 9% other.

Government Type: communist state; federal republic in form. **Independence:** N.A. **Constitution:** Feb. 21, 1974. **National holiday:** Day of the Republic, Nov. 29. **Heads of government:** Rais Dizdarević, president (since May 1988); Branko Mikulic, prime minister (since Jan. 1986). **Structure:** executive includes cabinet (Federal Executive Council) and federal administration; bicameral legislature (Federal Assembly—Federal Chamber, Chamber of Republics and Provinces); judiciary; State Presidency is collective, rotating, policy-making body composed of representatives from each republic and province.

Economy Monetary unit: dinar. **Budget:** N.A. **GNP:** $145.0 bil., $6,220 per capita

(1986). **Chief crops:** corn, wheat, tobacco, sugar beets, sunflowers; diversified agriculture with many small private holdings and large agricultural combines; occasionally net exporter of corn, tobacco, foodstuffs, live animals. **Livestock:** poultry, sheep, cattle, pigs, horses. **Natural resources:** coal, copper, bauxite, timber, iron ore. **Major industries:** metallurgy, machinery and equipment, petroleum. **Labor force:** 9.6 mil. (1986); 27% mining and manufacturing, 22% agriculture; about 5% of labor force are guest workers in Western Europe; unemployment about 10% of domestic labor force, including private agriculture (1987). **Exports:** $10.4 bil. (f.o.b., 1986); 49% raw materials and semimanufactures, 31% consumer goods, 20% equipment. **Imports:** $11.8 bil. (c.i.f., 1986); 81% raw materials and semimanufactures, 14% equipment, 4% consumer goods. **Major trading partners:** (1985) 59% noncommunist countries, 41% communist countries, of which 24% USSR.

Intl. Orgs. CMEA (observer but participates in certain commissions), FAO, G-77, GATT, IAEA, IBRD, ICAO, IDA, IFAD, IFC, ILO, IMF, IMO, INTELSAT, INTERPOL, ITU, NAM, OECD (participant in some activities), UN, UNESCO, UPU, WHO, WIPO, WMO.

The lands that now compose Yugoslavia were incorporated into the Roman Empire as the province of Illyricum in the first century A.D. Christianity became dominant by A.D. 600. With the fall of Rome, most of the territory was conquered by the Bulgars before being incorporated into the Byzantine Empire. Bulgarians were largely displaced by Slavic immigrants in the ninth century. Dalmatia and Serbia were detached from the Byzantine Empire at the time of the First Crusade in the 11th century; Serbia was conquered by the Ottoman Empire at the Battle of Kosovo in 1389, gaining its independence from the Ottoman Empire at the Congress of Berlin in 1878.

The complexities of Balkan politics occupied European statesmen throughout the late 19th century, and the Balkan Wars of 1912 and 1913 led directly to the outbreak of World War I. After the collapse of the Austro-Hungarian empire during the war, the multiethnic and multinational state of Yugoslavia was patched together in 1918–19. To Serbia were annexed the old Austro-Hungarian lands of Slovenia and Croatia, as well as the ethnically Croatian and Serbian lands of Bosnia and Herzegovina in the northwest, and, in the south and southwest, Montenegro, Macedonia, and Kosovo.

The nationalities coexisted in a state of mutual hostility, provoking a royal dictatorship instituted by King Alexander in 1929 and enduring after his assassination in 1934. Hitler invaded Yugoslavia in 1941; German troops were welcomed in Croatia as liberators from the Serbs. Resistance began almost immediately, split into two mutually hostile groups: Draža Mihajlović's Serbian royalist Chetniks, and Tito's leftist Partisans, composed of pan-Yugoslav Communists and non-Serbian anti-German forces. By the end of the war, over 2 million Yugoslavs had died and 3½ million were homeless. Marshall Tito (whose real name was

Josip Broz), backed by both Churchill and Stalin, ruled over a ruined land, the newly created Federal People's Republic of Yugoslavia.

Until World War II, Yugoslavia was primarily agricultural and pastoral, with peasants who were virtual serfs living on a subsistence level in a largely infertile land. Agriculture was more prosperous in the northern river valleys that formerly had been under Austro-Hungarian control, and there was some industrialization in those areas as well. Virtually all these areas had to be rebuilt after the war.

Tito imposed agricultural collectivization on the Stalinist model and pushed for the development of industry under state ownership. Politically, harsh repression fell on members of the Chetnik resistance as well as on wartime collaborators. But the postwar period of tyranny was short-lived.

Tito, who had achieved power as an independent Communist leader rather than as a beneficiary of the Red Army, refused to permit Yugoslavia to become a Soviet satellite. In March 1948 he expelled Russian military advisers and was himself expelled from the Cominform. Despite economic pressure and military threats, Tito turned westward.

Stalinism yielded to decentralized communism. The 1953 Agrarian Reform laws permitted private agricultural smallholdings, and over 80 percent of the land returned to private ownership; in the rest, "self-management" rather than central control was encouraged. Self-management was instituted in the industrial sector as well, with emphasis varying between capital goods and consumer goods. Economic growth averaged over 7 percent per year for three decades, lifting Yugoslavia into the ranks of the semideveloped countries.

Despite a reconciliation with Nikita Khrushchev's Soviet Union in 1955-56, Tito continued to chart an independent course, taking a leading role in the Third World Non-Aligned Movement and providing a political and economic alternative model for Eastern Europe. But Yugoslavian nationalism in foreign affairs masked the development of separate nationalisms within the Yugoslavian federation. By the time Tito died in 1980, there was a real question as to whether the nation could survive without his leadership.

In addition to resurgent national antagonisms, the country was plagued by an economic slowdown. Inflation and chronic trade deficits led to soaring national debt, bringing austerity measures and a decline in the standard of living. On the one hand, the post-Tito "collegial rule," whereby the presidency of the country and the chairmanship of the Party Presidium rotate annually among the six republics and two autonomous regions, has worked well, bringing a measure of calm and stability to national politics. On the other hand, since the summer of 1988, ethnic protests and riots have broken out in Serbia's autonomous regions of Kosovo and Vojvodina, in Slovenia, in Serbia, and in Montenegro. Montenegrin demonstrations in 1989 provoked mass resignations at all levels of political and party leadership.

Zaire
Republic of Zaire
(PREVIOUS NAMES: BELGIAN CONGO, CONGO/LEOPOLDVILLE, CONGO/ KINSHASA)

Geography Location: equatorial country in central Africa. **Boundaries:** Central African Republic and Sudan to N, Uganda, Rwanda, Burundi, and Tanzania to E, Zambia to S, Angola to SW, Atlantic Ocean, Cabinda district of Angola, and Congo to W. **Total land area:** 875,525 sq. mi. (2,267,600 sq km). **Coastline:** 23 mi. (37 km). **Comparative area:** slightly more than ¼ size of U.S. **Land use:** 3% arable land; negl. % permanent crops; 4% meadows and pastures; 78% forest and woodland; 15% other; includes negl. % irrigated. **Major cities:** (1976 est.) Kinshasa (capital) 2,443,876; Kananga (formerly Luluabourg) 704,211; Lubumbashi (Elizabethville) 451,332; Mbuji-Mayi 382,632; Kisangani (Stanleyville) 339,210.

People Population: 33,293,946 (1988). **Nationality:** noun—Zairian(s); adjective—Zairian. **Ethnic groups:** 45% of the people belong to one of four largest groups—Mongo, Luba, Kongo (all Bantu), and Mangbetu-Azande; over 200 other ethnic groups. **Languages:** French (official), English, Lingala, Swahili, Kingwana, Kikongo, Tshiluba. **Religions:** 50% Roman Catholic, 20% Protestant, 10% Kimbanguist, 10% Muslim, 10% other syncretic sects and traditional beliefs.

Government Type: republic with strong presidential system. **Independence:** June 30, 1960 (from Belgium). **Constitution:** June 24, 1967, amended Aug. 1974, revised Feb. 15, 1978. **National holiday:** Independence Day, June 30. **Heads of government:** Marshal Mobutu Sese Seko, president (since 1965). **Structure:** executive—president elected originally for seven-year term; Marshal Mobutu reelected July 1984 and limits on reelection removed by new constitution; legislative—unicameral National Legislative Council with 310 members elected for five-year terms; official party is supreme political institution.

Economy Monetary unit: zaire. **Budget:** (1985) *income:* $827 mil.; *expend.:* $1.096 bil. **GDP:** $4.5 bil., $140 per capita (1986). **Chief crops:** cash crops—coffee, palm oil, rubber, quinine; food crops—manioc, bananas, root crops, corn; some provinces self-sufficient; illegal producer of cannabis for international drug trade. **Livestock:** goats, cattle, pigs, sheep. **Natural resources:** cobalt, copper, cadmium, crude oil, industrial and gem diamonds. **Major industries:** mining, mineral processing, consumer products (including textiles, footwear, cigarettes). **Labor force:** about 15 mil., but only 13% wage earners (1985); 75% agriculture, 13% industry, 12% services; 51% of population of working age (1981). **Exports:** $1.8 bil. (f.o.b., 1986 est.); 37% copper; cobalt, diamonds, petroleum, coffee. **Imports:** $1.4 bil. (f.o.b., 1986 est.); consumer goods, foodstuffs, mining and other machinery, transport equipment, fuels. **Major trading partners:** Belgium, U.S., France, W. Germany.

Intl. Orgs. FAO, G-77, GATT, IAEA, IBRD, ICAO, IDA, IFAD, IFC, ILO, IMF, IMO, INTELSAT, INTERPOL, ITU, NAM, UN, UNESCO, UPU, WHO, WIPO, WMO.

Pygmies were probably the earliest inhabitants of the Congo region, followed much later by Bantu and Nilotic peoples. By the eighth century A.D., a number of well-established kingdoms and empires occupied the lower reaches of the Congo (now Zaire) River and the coastal plain; these included Kongo (Bakongo), Kuba, Luba, and Lunda.

Portuguese explorers and merchants arrived along the coast in the 1480s and initially traded with these kingdoms on a basis of relative equality; an indigenous Catholic church became established. Soon, however, the Portuguese established a slave trade that brought turmoil and decline to the native states. Europeans did not penetrate the interior of Zaire until the 19th century, but the slave trade (partly in Arab hands, in inland regions) had repercussions everywhere.

Henry Stanley descended the Congo River from east to west in 1876, opening the area for further exploration. In 1878 Stanley was engaged by King Leopold II of Belgium to establish Belgian trading stations along the river. King Leopold established the Congo Free State in 1885, not as a Belgian colony but as a personal possession of which he was king as well as chief stockholder.

The management corporation that ran the Free State abolished slavery but instituted a harsh and exploitative regime that reduced native peoples to a condition of involuntary servitude. Forced labor and harsh suppression of rebellion resulted in the deaths of unnumbered thousands of people. Protests against these conditions, led by Great Britain and the United States, led to the transformation of the Free State into the colony of the Belgian Congo in 1908 with promises of reforms.

By the 1920s the Belgian Congo had become a major world producer of copper, diamonds, gold, rubber, palm oil, and other commodities. Railroads were developed to bring these goods to market, notably the line from Elizabethville (now Lubumbashi) in the Katanga region through Angola to the Atlantic coast. River navigation on the Congo was also developed. All mining, plantation agriculture, industry, and administration was in Belgian hands with no native participation in government except at the most local level.

The depression of the 1930s led to reduced commodity prices worldwide and hurt the Belgian Congo badly. The colony recovered swiftly after World War II, as demand increased sharply.

In the 1950s agitation for increased native participation in government led, in 1957, to elections for local councils. In 1959 rioting against Belgian rule broke out. Elections were held on May 31 in anticipation of independence; Joseph Kasavubu became president, and Patrice Lumumba, head of the Congolese National Movement, became prime minister. On June 30, 1960, Belgium granted independence to the Congo; many Europeans fled the country. On July 4 the army mutinied, and on

July 11, Katanga Province, under the leadership of Moise Tshombe, seceded from the Congo and declared its independence. Belgium sent troops to quell the disorder.

On Aug. 9 the United Nations called on Belgium to withdraw its troops. Kasavubu removed Lumumba as prime minister. Lumumba, with the backing of Ghana, fought for control. He fled to Stanleyville (now Kisangani) but was kidnapped in January 1961 and taken to Katanga, where he was murdered, apparently with American and Belgian complicity. Fighting continued in Katanga, where Tshombe's regime was supported by European mercenaries and opposed by UN peacekeeping forces. The Katangan rebellion ended in late 1963; rebels fled to Angola, and UN forces were withdrawn in June 1964. In a surprising political settlement, Tshombe became president of the Congo on June 30. On Sept. 7 leftist rebels attempted to establish a "people's republic" based in Stanleyville. Tshombe again resorted to the use of mercenaries to put down the rebellion. Many white settlers, as well as Congolese, were killed in fierce fighting and terrorist atrocities. The rebellion ended in July 1965. In November 1965 Tshombe was deposed in a military coup led by Joseph Mobutu. The Mobutu government took immediate steps to consolidate its control over the country and reduce European influence and struggled to rebuild the country's shattered economic infrastructure.

In 1971 Mobutu changed the country's name to Zaire and renamed Leopoldville Kinshasa. In 1972 he ordered all Zairians with European names to change them to African names; he became Mobutu Sese Seko. Attempts in 1974 to force foreign investors to sell their holdings to Zairians brought economic disruption, and foreign investors were invited back into the country in 1977.

In 1977 another rebellion broke out in Katanga (now Shaba) Province; the government put down the rebellion with the aid of France, Egypt, and Morocco. The rebels fled to Angola, but the province's rich mining economy was again disrupted; many European technical workers fled, and production plummeted.

Despite Zaire's rich natural resources in minerals, forest products, hydroelectric potential, and agriculture, the country has been impoverished by the nearly unprecedented corruption of the Mobutu regime. The president personally is estimated to have amassed a fortune of $3 billion during his term in office. Rival political leaders attempted to organize opposition to the Mobutu government in late 1987 and 1988, but most were arrested or driven into exile.

In June 1989 Mobutu won international acclaim for his role in bringing together the leaders of rival factions in Angola in an attempt to end that country's long-standing civil war.

Zambia
Republic of Zambia
(PREVIOUS NAME: NORTHERN RHODESIA)

Geography Location: landlocked country in southern central Africa. **Boundaries:** Zaire to N, Tanzania to NE, Malawi to E, Mozambique to SE, Zimbabwe to S, Namibia to SW, Angola to W. **Total land area:** 285,994 sq. mi. (740,720 sq km). **Coastline:** none. **Comparative area:** slightly larger than Texas. **Land use:** 7% arable land; negl. % permanent crops; 47% meadows and pastures; 27% forest and woodland; 19% other; includes negl. % irrigated. **Major cities:** (1987 est.) Lusaka (capital) 818,994; Kitwe 449,442; Ndola 418,142; Mufulira 192,333; Kabwe (Broken Hill) 190,752.

People Population: 7,546,177 (1988). **Nationality:** noun—Zambian(s); adjective—Zambian. **Ethnic groups:** 98.7% African, 1.1% European, 0.2% other. **Languages:** English (official), about 70 indigenous languages. **Religions:** 50–75% Christian, 1% Muslim and Hindu, indigenous beliefs.

Government Type: one-party state. **Independence:** Oct. 24, 1964 (from UK). **Constitution:** Aug. 25, 1973. **National holiday:** Independence Day, Oct. 24. **Heads of government:** Kenneth David Kaunda, president (since Oct. 1964); Kebby Musokotwane, prime minister (since Apr. 1985). **Structure:** executive-modified presidential system; legislative—unicameral National Assembly; judiciary.

Economy Monetary unit: kwacha. **Budget:** (1984 est.) **income:** $610 mil.; **expend.:** $733 mil. **GDP:** $2.1 bil. $300 per capita (1986 est.). **Chief crops:** corn, tobacco, cotton; net importer of most major agricultural products. **Livestock:** cattle, goats, pigs, sheep. **Natural resources:** copper, cobalt, zinc, lead, coal. **Major industries:** copper mining and processing, transport, construction. **Labor force:** 2.5 mil.; 85% agriculture, 9% transport and services, 6% mining, manufacturing, and construction. **Exports:** $689 mil. (f.o.b., 1986); copper, zinc, cobalt, lead, tobacco. **Imports:** $517 mil. (c.i.f., 1986); machinery, transport equipment, foodstuffs, fuels, manufactures. **Major trading partners:** EC, Japan, South Africa, U.S.

Intl. Orgs. Commonwealth, FAO, G-77, GATT (de facto), IAEA, IBRD, ICAO, IDA, IFAD, IFC, ILO, IMF, INTELSAT, INTERPOL, ITU, NAM, UN, UNESCO, UPU, WHO, WIPO, WMO.

Bantu peoples—including Luba, Lunda, Ngoni, and others—moved into what is now Zambia between the 15th and the 19th centuries, displacing or absorbing aboriginal populations. Occasional Portuguese explorers from Angola and Mozambique entered the region, and Angolan slave-raiders were active in the late 18th and early 19th centuries, but serious European influence did not begin until the mid-19th century. At that time British missionaries and merchants arrived, most notably David Livingstone and Cecil Rhodes.

Local rulers granted mineral concessions to Rhodes in both Northern and Southern Rhodesia (now Zambia and Zimbabwe). Rhodesia was declared a British sphere of influence in 1888; a British protectorate was established in 1891 and enlarged in 1894–95. The borders of Northern Rhodesia were established in 1911. The country was administered by the British South Africa Co. until 1924, when direct colonial rule began. Large numbers of British settlers arrived and developed extensive farms and ranches and mined the region's substantial copper deposits. A railroad was built linking Northern Rhodesia with Elizabethville in the Belgian Congo (now Zaire).

In 1953 Northern and Southern Rhodesia were joined with Nyasaland (now Malawi) to form the Federation of Rhodesia and Nyasaland. In the 1950s the country entered a period of unrest with native peoples demanding greater participation in government, while white settlers clung to their privileged positions.

As the result of an election in 1962, the federation was dissolved in 1963. A national assembly was created on the basis of a broader, multiracial electorate. Northern Rhodesia became independent as the Republic of Zambia on Oct. 24, 1964. Relations between Zambia and Rhodesia (formerly Southern Rhodesia) became strained in 1965 in a dispute over ownership and administration of the railway that spanned both countries. A new constitution was promulgated in 1973, creating a stronger presidency and a unicameral legislature; the United National Independence party was declared the sole legal political party.

Pres. Kenneth Kaunda, in office since Zambia's independence, has led a generally moderate government that has won the support of both whites and blacks, despite some early white emigration from the country. Although the country has only one legal political party, elections are freely contested, and there is substantial freedom of the press.

Zambia's economy, however, has not fared well under independence. The nation's wildlife supports a small tourist industry, and ivory is exported (both legally and illegally). The agricultural sector, which produces corn, tobacco, peanuts, cotton, rubber, sugar, and livestock, was hurt by the departure of some white settlers and subsequent land redistribution. Although the country's mineral resources include cobalt, zinc, lead, vanadium, and manganese in addition to copper, copper is overwhelmingly the nation's main earner of foreign exchange. A steep decline in the world price of copper since the mid-1970s has led to massive foreign debt and labor unrest at home. In 1987 Pres. Kaunda announced a program of economic restructuring to deal with these problems; the IMF has demanded reforms as a condition for future aid.

In April 1987 South African troops raided Zambian bases of the African National Congress in an action that led to heavy casualties and was condemned by the United Nations. Zambia, under Pres. Kaunda, has played an active role in pan-African affairs and actively supports anticommunist and anti–South African movements in neighboring countries.

Zimbabwe
Republic of Zimbabwe
(PREVIOUS NAME: SOUTHERN RHODESIA)

Geography Location: landlocked country in southern Africa. **Boundaries:** Zambia to NW, Mozambique to NE and E, South Africa to S, Botswana to SW. **Total land area:** 149,293 sq. mi. (386,670 sq km). **Coastline:** none. **Comparative area:** slightly larger than Montana. **Land use:** 7% arable land; negl. % permanent crops; 12% meadows and pastures; 62% forest and woodland; 19% other; includes negl. % irrigated. **Major cities:** (1982 census) Harare (Salisbury, capital) 656,000; Bulawayo 413,800; Chitungwiza 172,600; Gweru (Gwelo) 78,900; Mutare (Umtali) 69,600.

People Population: 9,728,547 (1988). **Nationality:** noun—Zimbabwean(s); adjective—Zimbabwean. **Ethnic groups:** 98% African (71% Shona, 16% Ndebele, 11% other), 1% white, 1% mixed and Asian. **Languages:** English (official), ChiShona, Si Ndebele. **Religions:** 50% syncretic (part Christian, part indigenous beliefs), 25% Christian, 24% indigenous beliefs, 1% Muslim.

Government Type: presidential system with bicameral legislature. **Independence:** Apr. 18, 1980 (from UK). **Constitution:** Dec. 21, 1979. **National holiday:** Apr. 18. **Heads of government:** Robert Gabriel Mugabe, president (since Dec. 1987). **Structure:** executive—cabinet led by president; legislative—parliament consisting of 100-member House of Assembly and 40-member Senate; judiciary—high court is supreme judicial authority.

Economy Monetary unit: Zimbabwean dollar. **Budget:** (1987) *income:* $1.76 bil.; *expend.:* $2.35 bil. **GDP:** $4.9 bil., $540 per capita (1986). **Chief crops:** tobacco, corn, tea, sugar, cotton. **Livestock:** cattle, goats, sheep, pigs, asses. **Natural resources:** coal, chromium ore, asbestos, gold, nickel. **Major industries:** mining, steel, clothing and footwear. **Labor force:** 3.1 mil. (1987); 74% agriculture, 16% transport and services, 10% mining, manufacturing, construction. **Exports:** $1.3 bil. (f.o.b., 1986), including net gold sales and reexports; tobacco, asbestos, cotton, copper, tin. **Imports:** $1.0 bil. (f.o.b., 1986); machinery, petroleum products, wheat, transport equipment. **Major trading partners:** South Africa, UK.

Intl. Orgs. Commonwealth, FAO, G-77, GATT, IBRD, ICAO, IDA, IFAD, IFC, ILO, IMF, INTERPOL, NAM, UN, UNESCO, UPU, WHO, WMO.

Massive stone structures at Great Zimbabwe give evidence of a sizable urban society that flourished from the ninth to the 13th centuries and dominated iron-age trade in southeastern Africa. Bantu peoples migrated into the region beginning in the 15th century; the Mashona dominated until the early 19th century, when they were displaced by the Matebele.

Portuguese slave raiders from Mozambique were active in Zimbabwe from the 16th to the mid-19th centuries. Mineral concessions were granted to Cecil Rhodes by local rulers in the late 19th century, and the region became a British protectorate in 1888. Salisbury (now Harare) was founded in 1890, and the territory comprising Zimbabwe and Zambia was named Rhodesia in 1895. Rhodesia was governed by the British South Africa Co. until 1923, when it was partitioned into Northern and Southern Rhodesia. Northern Rhodesia became a British colony, whereas Southern Rhodesia, rejecting union with South Africa, became a self-governing (and white-ruled) state within the British Empire.

Southern Rhodesia had been heavily settled by whites from Great Britain, South Africa, and elsewhere, who developed extensive farms and ranches, forest products industries, and the country's rich mines. The country prospered but with little native participation in government except at the most local level.

In 1953 Northern Rhodesia, Southern Rhodesia, and Nyasaland were joined in the Federation of Rhodesia and Nyasaland. Increasing agitation for black participation in government, especially in the north and in Nyasaland, led to the dissolution of the federation in 1963; Northern Rhodesia subsequently became independent as Zambia, Nyasaland as Malawi. In 1961 Southern Rhodesia had adopted a constitution that guaranteed the continuation of white rule. White resistance to black political demands led to the rise of the Rhodesian Front party, whose leader, Ian D. Smith, became prime minister of Rhodesia (formerly Southern Rhodesia). After British-led negotiations for a biracial political compromise broke down, the Smith government on Nov. 11, 1965, issued a unilateral declaration of independence, which was declared illegal and invalid by the British government.

The United Nations condemned the Smith government and imposed economic sanctions, which were ineffective, however, because of support for the Rhodesian government from South Africa and from Mozambique (before that country's independence in 1975). In May 1968 the United Nations voted to impose a trade embargo on Rhodesia.

A new constitution was adopted in 1970, again effectively barring black participation in national politics. A British-initiated political settlement of 1972 was dropped because of black opposition. By 1974 mounting pressure from other African countries led the Smith government to enter into more serious negotiations. Guerrilla warfare between black nationalist groups and white settlers backed by mercenaries raged sporadically throughout the country, and many white settlers emigrated. A conference in Geneva in 1976 broke down, but a 1977 British-American proposal for majority rule, supervised elections to precede independence, a new constitution, and an integrated army provided the basis for a settlement of the crisis. An "internal settlement" was announced in April 1978 by Smith and three major nationalist leaders: Bishop Abel Muzorewa, leader of the United African National Congress (UANC), the Rev. Ndabaningi Sithole, former leader of the Zimbabwe African National Union (ZANU), and Chief Jeremiah Chirau. The settlement was, however, rejected by the guerrilla Patriotic Front that united Robert Mugabe's Zimbabwe African National Union (ZANU) and Joshua Nkomo's Zimbabwe African People's Union (ZAPU).

Elections were held in April 1979 and were won by UANC. Bishop Muzorewa assumed office on June 1 as prime minister of "Zimbabwe-Rhodesia," but the Patriotic Front continued to oppose the government. On Dec. 10 the "Zimbabwe-Rhodesia" parliament dissolved itself, and the country reverted briefly to British colonial rule. On Dec. 21 all parties agreed to a cease-fire and to a period of transitional British rule pending the drafting of a new constitution that would grant majority rule and guarantee minority rights, leading to independence. International economic sanctions were lifted.

Elections were held on Feb. 27–29, 1980, and resulted in a clear majority for Mugabe's ZANU party. Zimbabwe became independent, with Mugabe as prime minister, on April 18 and joined the United Nations on Aug. 25. As Mugabe embarked on an ambitious program of national reconstruction, Nkomo became leader of the opposition. Guerrillas linked to ZAPU, with Nkomo's tacit (or perhaps active) leadership and with alleged support from South Africa, continued to engage in sporadic warfare against Mugabe's government, and banditry and sabotage disrupted the countryside.

The elections of 1985 increased ZANU's majority in parliament. In 1987 the Constitution was amended to strengthen the presidency and to end the separate role of blacks and whites in government; new elections were held for black members of parliament to fill seats formerly reserved for whites. Guerrillas renewed attacks on white-owned farms.

In December 1987 Mugabe and Nkomo agreed to merge ZANU and ZAPU, creating a one-party state under Mugabe's leadership. This fragile political settlement remains in force, though scattered political and tribal armed unrest persists, and Nkomo's commitment to Mugabe's government remains in doubt.

Remarkably, despite decades of political turmoil, Zimbabwe's economy remains relatively strong. Agriculture is the major employer; principal crops are corn, wheat, cotton, tobacco, and sugar. Mineral resources are the country's major source of foreign earnings; Zimbabwe is an important world supplier of chromium, as well as having extensive deposits of coal, asbestos, copper, nickel, gold, and iron. An excellent transportation network and ample electric power (both hydroelectric and coal-fired) support a strong industrial base; major industries include steel, heavy equipment, ore processing, motor vehicle assembly, textiles, and food processing. Drought in the 1980s has led to some food shortages, however, and political difficulties have prevented other sectors of the economy from performing up to their potential.

TERRITORIES OF THE WORLD

DEBRIS OF EMPIRE

One of the most significant developments in international affairs since World War II has been the breakup of the great empires of the European states and the creation of myriad independent states. Yet the empires have not vanished utterly; fragments remain in a bewildering variety of arrangements. What the U.S. Tariff Commission said in 1922 remains, in diminished form, true today: "The subtle and constantly changing political relations of the world's territorial divisions defy simple or hard-and-fast definition and classification."

In general, a dependency (or dependent state) has a relationship with another state, normally defined by a treaty that limits in some measure (sometimes great, sometimes small) the dependency's freedom of action. If the relationship is established not by treaty but by conquest, the territory is better called a possession. In either case, if the territory is settled by citizens of the sovereign state, it is called a colony.

A once-common form of dependency is the protectorate, a dependent state that is autonomous in internal affairs but not in foreign affairs. Under varying names, many such remain. According to the United Nations, the term *associated state* is preferred to protectorate, first because it sounds less pejorative, and second because it implies that the governed (and not just the rulers) have consented to the relationship.

Another term favored at the United Nations is nonself-governing territory. This is generally equivalent to dependency, but in practice its use describes only European dependencies outside Europe—not, for instance, the Isle of Man nor Azad Kashmir. Two further, all-but-obsolete terms should be mentioned. Mandates are former dependencies of Germany or Turkey, administered in the name of the League of Nations by one of the victorious allies after World War I. Trust territories are similar creations of the United Nations in the post–World War II period. Only one of each remains. South-West Africa (the mandate) is on its way to independence from South Africa and will be known as Namibia. The Trust Territory of the Pacific Islands has been divided into four states, three of which have achieved associated state status with the United States, and one of which, the Republic of Palau, remains a trust territory (see "States, Territories, and Possessions").

Australia

Christmas Island
Territory of Christmas Island

Geography Location: island in eastern Indian Ocean. **Boundaries:** Java Head, Indonesia, 224 mi. (360 km) to N, North West Cape, Australia, 875 mi. (1,408 km) to SE. **Total land area:** 52 sq. mi. (135 sq km). **Coastline:** 34 mi. (54 km). **Comparative area:** about 7/10 size of Washington, D.C. **Land use:** 0% arable land; 0% permanent crops; 0% meadows and pastures; 0% forest and woodland; 100% other. **Major cities:** The Settlement (capital).

People Population: 2,278 (1988). **Nationality:** noun—Christmas Islander(s); adjective—Christmas Island. **Ethnic groups:** 61% Chinese, 25% Malay, 11% European, 3% other; no indigenous population. **Languages:** English.

Government Type: territory of Australia. **Heads of government:** T.F. Paterson, administrator. **Structure:** Advisory Council advises appointed administrator.

Economy Monetary unit: Australian dollar. **Natural resources:** phosphates. **Major industries:** phosphate extraction (near depletion). **Labor force:** all workers are employees of Phosphate Mining Co. of Christmas Island, Ltd. **Exports:** about 1.2 million metric tons of phosphate exported to Australia, New Zealand, and some Asian nations. **Major trading partners:** Australia, New Zealand.

Cocos (Keeling) Islands
Territory of Cocos (Keeling) Islands

Geography Location: 27 islands in eastern Indian Ocean. **Boundaries:** island of Sumatra (part of Indonesia) about 932 mi. (1,500 km) to NE; Perth, Australia 1,720 mi. (2,768 km) to SE. **Total land area:** 5.4 sq. mi. (14.0 sq km). **Coastline:** undetermined. **Comparative area:** about 24 times size of the Mall in Washington, D.C. **Land use:** 0% arable land; 0% permanent crops; 0% meadows and pastures; 0% forest and woodland; 100% other. **Major cities:** West Island (capital).

People Population: 600 (1988). **Nationality:** noun—Cocos Islander(s); adjective—Cocos Islander. **Ethnic groups:** mostly Europeans on West Island and Cocos Malays on Home Island. **Languages:** English.

Government Type: territory of Australia. **Heads of government:** Carolyn Stuart, administrator; Parson bin Yapat, chairman of Islands Council. **Structure:** administrator, appointed by governor-general of Australia; Cocos Malay community is represented by Cocos (Keeling) Islands Council; supreme court.

Economy Monetary unit: Australian dollar. **Chief crops:** vegetables, bananas, pawpaws, coconuts. **Natural resources:** fish. **Major industries:** copra products. **Exports:** (1984) 202 metric tons of copra. **Imports:** foodstuffs from Australia, fuel, consumer items. **Major trading partners:** Australia.

Norfolk Island
Territory of Norfolk Island

Geography Location: island in western South Pacific Ocean. **Boundaries:** Vanuatu to N, New Zealand to SE, Brisbane, Australia 870 mi. (1,400 km) to W. **Total land area:** 13.3 sq. mi. (34.5 sq km). **Coastline:** 20 mi. (32 km). **Comparative area:** about 1/5 size of Washington, D.C. **Land use:** 0% arable land; 0% permanent crops; 25% meadows and pastures; 0% forest and woodland; 75% other. **Major cities:** Kingston (capital).

People Population: 2,448 (1988). **Nationality:** noun—Norfolk Islander(s); adjective—Norfolk Islander. **Ethnic groups:** descendants of *Bounty* mutiny; more recently, Australian and New Zealand settlers. **Languages:** English (official), Norfolk (a mixture of 18th century English and ancient Tahitian). **Religions:** Church of England, Roman Catholic, Uniting Church in Australia, Seventh-Day Adventist.

Government Type: territory of Australia. **National holiday:** Pitcairners Arrival Day Anniversary, June 8. **Heads of government:** David E. Buffett, chief minister (since 1983). **Structure:** nine-member elected Legislative Assembly; chief executive is Australian administrator named by governor-general.

Economy Monetary unit: Australian dollar. **Budget:** (1985) *income:* $3.2 mil.; *expend.:* $3.2 mil. **Chief crops:** Kentia palm seed, cereals, vegetables, fruit. **Natural resources:** fish. **Major industries:** tourism. **Exports:** $1.9 mil. (1984); seeds of Norfolk Island pine and Kentia Palm, small quantities of avocados. **Imports:** $14.4 mil. (1984). **Major trading partners:** Australia, Pacific Islands, New Zealand, Asia, Europe.

Uninhabited Territories

Ashmore Island, Cartier Island, Coral Sea Islands, Heard Island and McDonald Islands.

Denmark
Faeroe Islands

Geography Location: group of 18 islands (17 inhabited) in North Atlantic Ocean due N of Scotland. **Boundaries:** Iceland to NW, Norwegian Sea to N, Norway to E, Shetland Islands to SE, UK to S. **Total land area:** 540 sq. mi. (1,399 sq km). **Coastline:** 475 mi. (764 km). **Comparative area:** slightly less than eight times size of Washington, D.C. **Land use:** 2% arable land; 0% permanent crops; 0% meadows and pastures; 0% forest and woodland; 98% other. **Major cities:** (1984 est.) Tórshavn (capital) 13,408.

People Population: 46,853 (1988). **Nationality:** noun—Faeroese (sing., pl.); adjective—Faeroese. **Ethnic groups:** homogeneous Scandinavian population. **Languages:** Faeroese (derived from Old Norse), Danish. **Religions:** Evangelical Lutheran.

Government Type: self-governing overseas administrative division of Denmark. **Heads of government:** Margrethe II, queen (since Jan. 1972); Atli Dam, home-rule chairman (since Dec. 1984). **Structure:** legislative authority lies jointly with Crown, acting through appointed high commissioner, and 32-member provincial parliament (Lagting) in matters of strictly Faeroese concern; executive power vested in Crown, acting through high commissioner, but exercised by provincial cabinet responsible to provincial parliament.

Economy Monetary unit: Danish krone. **Budget:** (1981) *income:* $98.8 mil.; *expend.:* $98.8 mil. **GDP:** $369.3 mil., $8,800 per capita (1980). **Chief crops:** sheep and cattle grazing. **Natural resources:** fish. **Major industries:** fishing. **Labor force:** 17,585; fishing, manufacturing, transportation, commerce. **Exports:** $178.7 mil. (f.o.b., 1980); mostly fish and fish products. **Imports:** $222.1 mil. (c.i.f., 1980); machinery and transport equipment, petroleum and petroleum products, food products. **Major trading partners:** (1981) *exports:* 21.3% Denmark, 13.4% UK, 12.4% W. Germany, 11.7% U.S.; *imports:* N.A.

Greenland

Geography Location: world's largest island, in Arctic Circle in North Atlantic Ocean. **Boundaries:** Iceland about 190 mi. (300 km) to E across Denmark Strait, Canada to SW and W across Baffin Bay and Davis Strait. **Total land area:** 840,000 sq. mi. (2,175,600 sq km); land area 131,931 sq. mi. (341,700 sq km) ice free. **Coastline:** 27,400 mi. (44,087 km). **Comparative area:** slightly more than three times size of Texas. **Land use:** 0% arable land; 0% permanent crops; 1% meadows and pastures; negl. % forest and woodland; 99% other. **Major cities:** Godthab (Nuuk, capital).

People Population: 54,790 (1988). **Nationality:** noun—Greenlander(s); adjective–Greenlandic. **Ethnic groups:** 86% Greenlander (Eskimos and Greenland-born whites), 14% Danish. **Languages:** Danish, Eskimo dialects. **Religions:** Evangelical Lutheran.

Government Type: self-governing overseas administrative division of Denmark. **National holiday:** Apr. 16. **Heads of government:** Margrethe II, queen (since Jan. 1972); Jonathan Motzfeldt, home-rule chairman (since May 1979). **Structure:** executive—home-rule chairman and four-person council; legislative—elected 27-seat Landsting and Danish parliament.

Economy Monetary unit: Danish krone. **GNP:** included in that of Denmark. **Chief crops:** arable land largely in hay; sheep grazing, garden produce. **Natural resources:** zinc, lead, iron ore, coal, molybdenum. **Major industries:** mining, fishing, sealing. **Labor force:** 22,800; largely engaged in fishing, hunting, sheep breeding. **Exports:** $256.9 mil. (f.o.b., 1986); fish and fish products, metallic ores and concentrates. **Imports:** $359.9 mil. (c.i.f., 1986); petroleum and petroleum products, machinery and transport equipment, food products. **Major trading partners:** (1980) 49.4% Denmark, 9.5% Finland, 8.1% W. Germany, 6.3% U.S., 2.9% UK.

France
French Guiana
Department of Guiana

Geography Location: NE coast of South America. **Boundaries:** North Atlantic Ocean to N, Brazil to E and S across Oyapock River, Suriname to W across Maroni River. **Total land area:** 34,750 sq. mi. (90,000 sq km). **Coastline:** 235 mi. (378 km). **Comparative area:** slightly smaller than Indiana. **Land use:** negl. % arable land; negl. % permanent crops; negl. % meadows and pastures; 82% forest and woodland; 18% other. **Major cities:** (1985) Cayenne (capital) 38,091.

People Population: 91,641 (1988). **Nationality:** noun—French Guianese (sing., pl.); adjective—French Guiana. **Ethnic groups:** 66% black or mulatto, 12% Caucasian, 12% East Indian, Chinese or Amerindian, 10% other. **Languages:** French. **Religions:** predominantly Roman Catholic.

Government Type: overseas department of France. **Heads of government:** Jacques Dewatre, commissioner of the republic. **Structure:** executive—prefect appointed by Paris; legislative—popularly elected 16-member General Council and Regional Council composed of members of the local General Council and of the locally elected deputy and senator to the French parliament; judicial—under jurisdiction of French judicial system.

Economy Monetary unit: French franc. **Budget:** (1985) *income:* $268 mil. *expend.:* $268 mil. **GDP:** $2 bil., $3,240 per capita (1981). **Chief crops:** limited vegetables for local consumption; rice, corn, manioc, cocoa, bananas, sugar. **Livestock:** cattle, pigs, goats. **Natural resources:** bauxite, timber, gold, cinnabar, kaolin, fish. **Major industries:** construction, shrimp processing, forestry products. **Labor force:** 23,265 (1980); 60.6% services, government and commerce, 21.2% industry, 18.2% agriculture; 10% unemployment. **Exports:** $37.5 mil. (1985); shrimp, timber, rum, rosewood essence. **Imports:** $257.0 mil. (1985); food (grains, processed meat), other consumer goods, producer goods, petroleum. **Major trading partners:** (1984) *exports:* 41% U.S., 18% Japan, 9% France; *imports:* 55% France, 13% Trinidad and Tobago, 3% U.S.

French Polynesia
Territory of French Polynesia

Geography Location: several scattered groups of islands in South Pacific Ocean, about two-thirds of way between Panama Canal and New Zealand. **Boundaries:** Kiribati to NE, Cook Islands to E. **Total land area:** 1,622 sq. mi. (4,200 sq km). **Coastline:** 1,569 mi. (2,525 km). **Comparative area:** slightly less than ⅓ size of Connecticut. **Land use:** 1% arable land; 19% permanent crops; 5% meadows and pastures; 31% forest and woodland; 44% other. **Major cities:** (1983) Papeete (capital) 23,496.

People Population: 190,939 (1988). **Nationality:** noun—French Polynesian(s); adjective—French Polynesian. **Ethnic groups:** 78% Polynesian, 12% Chinese, 6% local French, 4% metropolitan French. **Religions:** 55% Protestant, 32% Roman Catholic, 13% other.

Government Type: overseas territory of France. **Heads of government:** Pierre Angeli, high commissioner of republic (since Apr. 1986); Alexandre Leontieff, president of territorial government (since Dec. 1987). **Structure:** 30-member Territorial Assembly, popularly elected; five-member Council of Government, elected by assembly; popular election of two deputies to National Assembly and one senator to Senate in Paris.

Economy Monetary unit: Colonial Francs Pacifique (CFP). **Budget:** (1979) US$180 mil. **GDP:** A$931.3 mil., US$6,400 per capita (1980). **Chief crops:** coconuts. **Livestock:** pigs, cattle, goats, sheep, horses. **Natural resources:** timber, fish, cobalt. **Major industries:** tourism. **Labor force:** N.A. **Exports:** $21 mil. (1977); 79% coconut products, 14% mother-of-pearl, vanilla. **Imports:** $419 mil. (1977); fuels, foodstuffs, equipment. **Major trading partners:** *exports:* 86% France; *imports:* 59% France, 14% U.S.

French Southern and Antarctic Lands
Territory of the French Southern and Antarctic Lands

Geography Location: Adélie Land, a narrow segment of mainland Antarctica, and several islands in southern Indian Ocean. **Total land area:** 195,973 sq. mi. (507,567 sq km). **Coastline:** undetermined. **Comparative area:** slightly less than 1.5 times size of Delaware. **Land use:** 0% arable land; 0% permanent crops; 0% meadows and pastures; 0% forest and woodland; 100% other. **Major cities:** none.

People Population: 210 (1988).

Government Type: overseas territory of France. **Heads of government:** Vice Adm. Claude Pieri, high administrator.

Economy Monetary unit: French franc. **Budget:** (1986) 160 mil. francs. **Natural resources:** fish, crayfish. **Major industries:** N.A. **Exports:** fish, crayfish. **Major trading partners:** France, Réunion.

Guadeloupe
Department of Guadeloupe

Geography Location: island in eastern Caribbean Sea. **Boundaries:** St. Barthélemy 75 mi. (120 km) to NW, St. Martin about 110 mi. (175 km) to NW, Dominica to S. **Total land area:** 687 sq. mi. (1,780 sq km). **Coastline:** 190 mi. (306 km). **Comparative area:** 10 times size of Washington, D.C. **Land use:** 18% arable land; 5% permanent crops; 13% meadows and pastures; 40% forest and woodland; 24% other; includes 1% irrigated. **Major cities:** (1981 est.) Basse-Terre (capital) 13,656; Pointe á Pitre 25,310.

People Population: 338,730 (1988). **Nationality:** noun—Guadeloupian(s); adjective—Guadeloupe. **Ethnic groups:** 90% black or mulatto, 5% white, 5% East Indian, Lebanese, Chinese. **Languages:** French, Creole patois. **Religions:** 95% Roman Catholic, 5% Hindu and African.

Government Type: overseas department of France. **Heads of government:** Bernard Sarazin, prefect (since Dec. 1987). **Structure:** executive—prefect appointed by Paris; legislative—popularly elected General Council of 36 members and Regional Council composed of members of local General Council and locally elected deputies and senators to French parliament; judicial—under jurisdiction of French judicial system.

Economy Monetary unit: French franc. **Budget:** (1985) $380.5 mil. **GNP:** $998 mil., $3,630 per capita (1984). **Chief crops:** sugarcane, bananas, pineapples, vegetables. **Livestock:** cattle, pigs, goats. **Natural resources:** cultivable land, beaches and climate that foster tourism. **Major industries:** construction, cement, rum. **Labor force:** 120,000; 53.0% services, government, and commerce, 25.8% industry, 21.2% agriculture; insignificant unemployment. **Exports:** $75 mil. (1985); bananas, sugar, rum. **Imports:** $647 mil. (1985); vehicles, foodstuffs, clothing and other consumer goods, construction materials, petroleum products. **Major trading partners:** (1984) exports: 72% France, 16% Martinique; imports: 59% France.

Martinique
Department of Martinique
Geography Location: island in eastern Caribbean Sea. **Boundaries:** Dominica to N, St. Lucia to S. **Total land area:** 425 sq. mi. (1,100 sq km). **Coastline:** 180 mi. (290 km). **Comparative area:** slightly more than six times size of Washington, D.C. **Land use:** 10% arable land; 8% permanent crops; 30% meadows and pastures; 26% forest and woodland; 26% other; includes 5% irrigated. **Major cities:** (1982) Fort-de-France (capital) 97,814.

People Population: 351,105 (1988). **Nationality:** noun—Martiniquais (sing., pl.); adjective—Martiniquais. **Ethnic groups:** 90% African and African-Caucasian-Indian mixture, 5% Caucasian, 5% East Indian, Lebanese, Chinese. **Languages:** French, Creole patois. **Religions:** 95% Roman Catholic, 5% Hindu and African.

Government Type: overseas department of France. **Heads of government:** Edouard Lacroix, commissioner of the republic (since 1985). **Structure:** executive—prefect appointed by Paris; legislative—popularly elected council of 36 members and Regional Council, including all members of local General Council and locally elected deputies and senators to French parliament; judicial—under jurisdiction of French judicial system.

Economy Monetary unit: French franc. **Budget:** (1981) income: N.A.; expend.: $215 mil. **GDP:** $1.3 bil., $3,650 per capita (1984). **Chief crops:** bananas, pineapples, vegetables, flowers, sugarcane for rum. **Livestock:** sheep, cattle, pigs, goats. **Natural resources:** coastal scenery and beaches, cultivable land. **Major industries:** construction, rum, cement. **Labor force:** 100,000; 31.7% service industry, 29.4% construction and public works, 13.1% agriculture; 14% unemployed. **Exports:** $145 mil. (1985); refined petroleum products, bananas, rum, pineapples. **Imports:** $683 mil. (1985);

petroleum products, foodstuffs, construction materials, vehicles, clothing and other consumer goods. **Major trading partners:** (1984) exports: 54% France, 36% Guadeloupe; imports: 54% France.

Mayotte
Territorial Collectivity of Mayotte
Geography Location: southernmost of four main islands of Comoros archipelago in northern part of Mozambique Channel. **Boundaries:** Indian Ocean to N, Madagascar 300 mi. (480 km) to SE, Mozambique Channel to S, Mozambique to W. **Total land area:** 145 sq. mi. (376 sq km). **Coastline:** 5,798 mi. (9,330 km). **Comparative area:** slightly more than twice size of Washington, D.C. **Land use:** N.A. **Major cities:** (1985 census) Dzaoudzi (capital) 5,865; Mamoudzou 12,026; Pamanzi-Labattoir 4,106.

People Population: 66,882 (1988). **Nationality:** noun—Mahorais (sing., pl.); adjective—Mahoran. **Languages:** Mahorian (a Swahili dialect), French. **Religions:** 99% Muslim, 1% Christian (mostly Roman Catholic).

Government Type: territorial collectivity of France. **Heads of government:** Akli Khider, representative of government (since 1983); Younoussa Bamana, president of General Council (since 1976). **Structure:** elected 17-member General Council; appointed representative.

Economy Monetary unit: French franc. **Budget:** (1985) 313 mil. francs. **Chief crops:** vanilla, ylang-ylang, coffee, copra. **Natural resources:** none. **Major industries:** newly created lobster and shrimp industry. **Exports:** 34 mil. francs (1984); ylang-ylang, vanilla. **Imports:** 183 mil. francs (1984); building materials, transport equipment, rice, clothing, flour. **Major trading partners:** exports: 79% France, 19% Réunion, 10% Comoros; imports: 57% France, 16% Kenya, 11% South Africa, 8% Pakistan.

New Caledonia
Territory of New Caledonia and Dependencies
Geography Location: one large island and several smaller ones in western South Pacific Ocean. **Boundaries:** Vanuatu to N, Australia about 930 mi. (1,500 km) to W. **Total land area:** 7,376 sq. mi. (19,103 sq km). **Coastline:** 1,401 mi. (2,254 km). **Comparative area:** slightly smaller than Massachusetts. **Land use:** negl. % arable land; negl. % permanent crops; 14% meadows and pastures; 51% forest and woodland; 35% other. **Major cities:** (1983 census) Nouméa (capital) 60,112.

People Population: 150,981 (1988). **Nationality:** noun—New Caledonian(s); adjective—New Caledonian. **Ethnic groups:** 42.5% Melanesian, 37.1% European, 8.4% Wallisian, 3.8% Polynesian, 3.6% Indonesian, 1.6% Vietnamese, 3.0% other. **Languages:** French, Melanesian-Polynesian dialect. **Religions:** 60% Roman Catholic, 30% Protestant, 10% other.

Government Type: overseas territory of France. **Heads of government:** Jean Montpezat, high commissioner and president of Council of Government (since 1986); Kanak Provisional Government—Jean-Marie Tjibaou, president

(since Dec. 1984). **Structure:** administered by high commissioner, responsible to French Ministry for Overseas France and Council of Government; 46-seat Territorial Assembly.

Economy Monetary unit: Colonial Francs Pacifique (CFP). **Budget:** (1981) income: $187.1 mil.; expend.: $168.3 mil. **GNP:** $1.21 bil., $8,050 per capita (1983). **Chief crops:** coffee, maize, wheat, vegetables. **Livestock:** cattle, goats, pigs, horses. **Natural resources:** nickel, chrome, iron, cobalt, manganese, silver. **Major industries:** nickel mining. **Labor force:** 50,469 (1980 est.); immigrant labor now coming from Wallis and Futuna, Vanuatu, and French Polynesia; 8% unemployment (est.). **Exports:** $217.8 mil. (1983); 95% nickel metal, nickel ore. **Imports:** $350 mil. (1983); fuels and minerals, machines and electrical equipment. **Major trading partners:** (1980) exports: 54.9% France; imports: 32.5% France.

Intl. Orgs. WMO.

Réunion
Department of Réunion
Geography Location: island in southwestern Indian Ocean. **Boundaries:** 500 mi. (800 km) E of Madagascar. **Total land area:** 970 sq. mi. (2,512 sq km). **Coastline:** 125 mi. (201 km). **Comparative area:** slightly smaller than Rhode Island. **Land use:** 20% arable land; 2% permanent crops; 4% meadows and pastures; 35% forest and woodland; 39% other; includes 2% irrigated. **Major cities:** (1982 census) Saint-Denis (capital) 109,068; Saint-Paul 58,410; Saint-Pierre 50,061.

People Population: 557,441 (1988). **Nationality:** noun—Réunionese (sing., pl.); adjective—Réunionese. **Ethnic groups:** mostly intermixed French, African, Malagasy, Chinese, Pakistani, Indian ancestry. **Languages:** French (official), Creole. **Religions:** 94% Roman Catholic.

Government Type: overseas department of France. **Heads of government:** Jean Anciaux, commissioner of republic. **Structure:** administered by prefect appointed by French minister of interior, assisted by secretary general and elected 36-man General Council; in 1974 France created an elected 45-member Regional Assembly to coordinate economic and social development policies; in 1981 both General Council and Regional Assembly received greater authority for fiscal policy.

Economy Monetary unit: French franc. **GNP:** $1.76 bil. (1983). **Chief crops:** cash crops—almost entirely sugarcane, small amounts of vanilla and perfume plants; food crops—tropical fruit and vegetables, manioc, bananas, corn, market garden produce; most food imported. **Livestock:** pigs, goats, cattle, sheep. **Natural resources:** negl. **Major industries:** sugar, rum, cigarettes, handicraft items. **Labor force:** (1981) 49% services, 30% agriculture, 21% industry; 37% unemployment (high seasonal unemployment); 63% of population of working age (1983). **Exports:** $93 mil. (f.o.b., 1984); 75% sugar, 4% rum and molasses, 4% perfume essences, 1% vanilla and tea. **Imports:** $788 mil. (c.i.f., 1984); manufactured goods, food, beverages, tobacco, machinery and transportation equipment, raw materials, petroleum products. **Major trading partners:** France, Mauritius.

St. Pierre and Miquelon
Department of St. Pierre and Miquelon
Geography Location: group of small islands in North Atlantic Ocean off east coast of Canada. **Boundaries:** Newfoundland, Canada 16 mi. (25 km) to N, North Atlantic Ocean to E and S. **Total land area:** 93 sq. mi. (242 sq km). **Coastline:** 75 mi. (120 km). **Comparative area:** slightly less than 1.5 times size of Washington, D.C. **Land use:** 13% arable land; 0% permanent crops; 0% meadows and pastures; 4% forest and woodland; 83% other. **Major cities:** (1982 census) St. Pierre (capital) 5,415; Miquelon 626.

People Population: 6,274 (1988). **Nationality:** noun—Frenchmen; adjective—French. **Ethnic groups:** originally Basques and Bretons (French fishermen). **Languages:** French. **Religions:** 98% Roman Catholic.

Government Type: territorial collectivity of France. **National holiday:** National Day, July 14. **Heads of government:** Bernard Leurquin, commissioner of republic; Marc Plantegenest, president of General Council. **Structure:** executive—government commissioner appointed by Paris; legislative—popularly elected 14-member General Council elected for six-year terms; judiciary—under jurisdiction of French judicial system.

Economy Monetary unit: French franc. **Budget:** (1985) 50 mil. francs. **Chief crops:** vegetables. **Livestock:** cattle, sheep, pigs. **Natural resources:** N.A. **Major industries:** fishing, supply base for fishing fleets, tourism. **Labor force:** 2,510 (1982); 11% unemployment (1983). **Exports:** fish and fish products, fox and mink pelts. **Imports:** meat, clothing, fuel, electrical equipment, machinery, building materials. **Major trading partners:** (1983) *exports:* U.S., France, UK, Canada, Portugal; *imports:* Canada, France, U.S., Netherlands, UK.

Wallis and Futuna
Territory of the Wallis and Futuna Islands
Geography Location: two groups of islands in southern Pacific Ocean. **Boundaries:** Western Samoa to E, Fiji to SW. **Total land area:** 106 sq. mi. (274 sq km). **Coastline:** 80 mi. (129 km). **Comparative area:** slightly larger than Washington, D.C. **Land use:** 5% arable land; 20% permanent crops; 0% meadows and pastures; 0% forest and woodland; 75% other. **Major cities:** Mata-Utu (capital).

People Population: 14,254 (1988). **Nationality:** noun—Wallisian(s), Futunan(s), or Wallis and Futuna Islander(s); adjective—Wallisian, Futunan, or Wallis and Futuna Islander. **Ethnic groups:** almost entirely Polynesian. **Languages:**)French (official). **Languages:** French (official). **Religions:** largely Roman Catholic.

Government Type: overseas territory of France. **Heads of government:** Jacques le Henaff, high administrator. **Structure:** Territorial Assembly of 20 members; popular election of one deputy to National Assembly in Paris and one senator.

Economy Monetary unit: Colonial Francs Pacifique (CFP). **Budget:** N.A. **Chief crops:** dominated by coconuts, subsistence crops of yams, taro, bananas. **Livestock:** pigs, goats. **Natural resources:** none. **Major industries:** copra, handicrafts. **Exports:** negl. **Imports:** $3.4 mil. (1977); largely foodstuffs and some equipment associated with development programs.

Uninhabited Territories
Bassas da India, Clipperton Island, Europa Island, Glorioso Island, Juan de Nova Island, Tromelin Islands.

Netherlands
Aruba
Geography Location: island in southern Caribbean Sea off northern coast of Venezuela. **Boundaries:** Curaçao, Netherlands Antilles 42 mi. (68 km) to E, Venezuela 16 mi. (25 km) to S. **Total land area:** 74.5 sq. mi. (193.0 sq km). **Coastline:** about 45 mi. (about 72 km). **Comparative area:** slightly larger than Washington, D.C. **Land use:** 0% arable land; 0% permanent crops; 0% meadows and pastures; 0% forest and woodland; 100% other. **Major cities:** Oranjestad (capital).

People Population: 62,322 (1988). **Nationality:** noun—Aruban(s); adjective—Aruban. **Ethnic groups:** 80% mixed European/Caribbean Indian. **Languages:** Dutch (official), Papiamento (a Spanish-Portuguese-Dutch-English dialect), English widely spoken. **Religions:** 82% Roman Catholic, 8% Protestant; also small Hindu, Muslim, Confucian, Jewish minorities.

Government Type: self-governing until complete independence from Netherlands is granted in 1996. **Heads of government:** Maximo Croes, acting governor; Henny Eman, prime minister (since Jan. 1986).

Economy Monetary unit: Aruban florin. **Budget:** (1985) *income:* $100 mil.; *expend.:* $150 mil. **GNP:** $378 mil., $6,100 per capita (1986). **Chief crops:** negl. **Livestock:** N.A. **Natural resources:** negl.; white sandy beaches. **Major industries:** tourism, light manufacturing (tobacco, beverages, consumer goods). **Labor force:** (1986) mostly tourism; 23% unemployment.

Netherlands Antilles
Geography Location: two groups of islands in Caribbean Sea, about 500 mi. (800 km) apart. **Boundaries:** southern group (Curaçao and Bonaire)—Caribbean Sea to N, Venezuela to S; northern group (St. Eustatius, Saba, and St. Maarten)—North Atlantic Ocean to N, Antigua to E, Caribbean Sea to S, Virgin Islands to W. **Total land area:** 309 sq. mi. (800 sq km). **Coastline:** 226 mi. (364 km). **Comparative area:** slightly less than 5.5 times size of Washington, D.C. **Land use:** 8% arable land; 0% permanent crops; 0% meadows and pastures; 0% forest and woodland; 92% other. **Major cities:** Willemstad (capital).

People Population: 182,676 (1988). **Nationality:** noun—Netherlands Antillean(s); adjective—Netherlands Antillean. **Ethnic groups:** 85% mixed African; remainder Carib Indian, European, Latin, Oriental. **Languages:** Dutch (official), Papiamento (a Spanish-Portuguese-Dutch-English dialect) predominates; English widely spoken; Spanish. **Religions:** predominantly Roman Catholic; Protestant, Jewish, Seventh-Day Adventist.

Government Type: autonomous part of Netherlands. **Constitution:** Dec. 29, 1954. **Heads of government:** Domenico Felip Martina, prime minister (since Jan. 1986); Dr. Rene Romer, governor-general (since 1983). **Structure:** executive—governor (appointed by Crown); actual power exercised by eight-member Council of Ministers or cabinet presided over by minister-president; legislative—22-member Legislative Council; judicial—independent court system under control of chief justice of Supreme Court of Justice; each island territory has island council headed by lieutenant governor.

Economy Monetary unit: Netherlands Antillean guilder or florin. **Budget:** (1984) *income:* $616 mil.; *expend.:* $656 mil. **GDP:** $1.36 bil., $9,140 per capita (1984). **Chief crops:** corn, pulses. **Livestock:** goats, sheep, cattle, pigs. **Natural resources:** phosphates (Curaçao only), salt (Bonaire only). **Major industries:** tourism on Curaçao and St. Maarten; petroleum refining on Curaçao; petroleum transshipment facilities on Curaçao and Bonaire; light manufacturing on Curaçao. **Labor force:** 89,000 (1983); 65% government, 28% industry and commerce; 30% unemployment (1987 est.). **Exports:** $3.7 bil. (f.o.b., 1984); 98% petroleum products, phosphate. **Imports:** $4.0 bil. (c.i.f., 1984); 64% crude petroleum, food, manufactures. **Major trading partners:** (1984) *exports:* 55% U.S., 7% UK, 5% Jamaica; *imports:* 52% Venezuela, 15% Nigeria, 12% U.S.

New Zealand
Cook Islands
Geography Location: 13 inhabited and two uninhabited islands in South Pacific Ocean. **Boundaries:** French Polynesia to E, American Samoa to W. **Total land area:** 91.5 sq. mi. (237.0 sq km). **Coastline:** 75 mi. (120 km). **Comparative area:** slightly less than 1.5 times size of Washington, D.C. **Land use:** 4% arable land; 22% permanent crops; 0% meadows and pastures; 0% forest and woodland; 74% other. **Major cities:** Avarua (capital).

People Population: 17,995 (1988). **Nationality:** noun—Cook Islander(s); adjective—Cook Islander. **Ethnic groups:** 81.3% Polynesian (full blood), 7.7% Polynesian and European, 7.7% Polynesian and other, 2.4% European, 0.9% other. **Languages:** English. **Religions:** Christian; majority of populace members of Cook Islands Christian Church.

Government Type: self-governing in free association with New Zealand; Cook Islands government fully responsible for internal affairs and has right at any time to move to full independence by unilateral action; New Zealand responsible for external affairs, in consultation with Cook Islands government. **Heads of government:** Dr. Pupuke Robati, prime minister (since 1987). **Structure:** New Zealand governor-general appoints representative to Cook Islands, who represents Queen of England and New Zealand government; representative appoints prime minister; popularly elected 24-member parliament; 15-member House of Arikis (chiefs), appointed by representative, is advisory body only.

Economy **Monetary unit:** New Zealand dollar. **Budget:** (1977) $121 mil. **GDP:** $21 mil., $1,170 per capita (1983). **Chief crops:** cash crops—copra, citrus fruits, pineapples, tomatoes, bananas; food crops—yams, taro. **Livestock:** poultry, pigs, horses, goats. **Natural resources:** negl. **Major industries:** fruit processing, tourism. **Exports:** $4.2 mil. (1983); copra, fresh and canned fruit. **Imports:** $24.3 mil. (1983); foodstuffs, textiles, fuels. **Major trading partners:** (1983) **exports:** 98% New Zealand; **imports:** 76% New Zealand, 7% Japan.

Intl. Orgs. IFC, IMF.

Niue

Geography **Location:** coral island in western South Pacific Ocean. **Boundaries:** Tonga 300 mi. (480 km) to W, southern Cook Islands 580 mi. (930 km) to E. **Total land area:** 100 sq. mi. (259 sq km). **Coastline:** 40 mi. (64 km). **Comparative area:** slightly less than 1.5 times size of Washington, D.C. **Land use:** 61% arable land; 4% permanent crops; 4% meadows and pastures; 19% forest and woodland; 12% other. **Major cities:** Alofi (capital).

People **Population:** 2,520 (1988). **Nationality:** noun—Niuean(s); adjective—Niuean. **Ethnic groups:** Polynesian, with about 200 Europeans, Samoans, Tongans. **Languages:** Polynesian dialect closely related to Tongan and Samoan; English. **Religions:** 75% Ekalesia Nieue (Niuean Church)—a Christian Protestant church closely related to London Missionary Society, 10% Mormon, 5% Roman Catholic, Jehovah's Witnesses, Seventh-Day Adventist.

Government **Type:** self-governing territory in free association with New Zealand. **Heads of government:** Sir Robert R. Rex, premier (since early 1950s); John Springford, New Zealand representative (since 1974). **Structure:** executive—cabinet of four members—premier (elected by assembly) and three ministers (chosen by premier from among assembly members); Legislative Assembly consists of 20 members (14 village representatives and six elected on a common roll); if requested by assembly, New Zealand will also legislate for island.

Economy **Monetary unit:** New Zealand dollar. **Budget:** (1985 est.) **income:** $4.4 mil.; **expend.:** $4.8 mil. **GNP:** $3 mil., $1,080 per capita (1984). **Chief crops:** cash crops—copra, coconuts, passion fruit, honey, limes; food crops—taro, yams, cassava (tapioca). **Livestock:** chickens, pigs, cattle. **Natural resources:** negl. **Major industries:** tourism, handicrafts. **Labor force:** about 1,000 (1981);

most Niueans work on family plantations; paid work exists only in government service, small industry, and Niue Development Board. **Exports:** $301,224 (f.o.b., 1983); canned coconut cream, copra, honey, passion fruit products, pawpaw. **Imports:** $1,504,180 (c.i.f., 1983); food, live animals, manufactured goods, machinery, fuels, lubricants, chemicals, drugs. **Major trading partners:** **exports:** New Zealand, Fiji, Cook Islands, Australia; **imports:** New Zealand, Fiji, Japan, Western Samoa, Australia, U.S.

Tokelau

Geography **Location:** three atolls (Atafu, Nukunonu, Fakaofo) in South Pacific Ocean. **Boundaries:** northern Cook Islands to E, Western Samoa 300 mi. (480 km) to S, Tuvalu to W. **Total land area:** 3.9 sq. mi. (10.1 sq km). **Coastline:** 62 mi. (101 km). **Comparative area:** about 17 times size of the Mall in Washington, D.C. **Land use:** 0% arable land; 0% permanent crops; 0% meadows and pastures; 0% forest and woodland; 100% other. **Major cities:** none; each atoll has own administrative center.

People **Population:** 1,745 (1988). **Nationality:** noun—Tokelauan(s); adjective—Tokelauan. **Ethnic groups:** all Polynesian, with cultural ties to Western Samoa. **Languages:** Tokelauan (a Polynesian language), English. **Religions:** 70% Congregational Christian Church, 30% Roman Catholic—on Atafu, all Congregational Christian Church of Samoa; on Nukunonu, all Roman Catholic; on Fakaofo, both denominations.

Government **Type:** territory of New Zealand. **National holiday:** Waitangi Day, Feb. 6. **Heads of government:** H.H. Francis, administrator (since Feb. 1985). **Structure:** minister of foreign affairs of New Zealand is empowered to appoint administrator to region; powers of administrator are delegated to official secretary at Office of Tokelau Affairs, Apia, Western Samoa.

Economy **Monetary unit:** New Zealand dollar and Tokelau souvenir coin; Western Samoan tala also used. **Budget:** (1984) **income:** $1,358,105; **expend.:** $1,358,105; New Zealand subsidy, $1.2 mil. **GDP:** $1 mil., $670 per capita (1983). **Chief crops:** cash crops—coconuts, copra; food crops—pulaka, breadfruit, pawpaw, bananas. **Livestock:** pigs. **Natural resources:** negl. **Major industries:** small-scale enterprises for copra production, woodwork, plaited craft goods, stamps, coins. **Labor force:** N.A. **Exports:** $98,000 (1983); stamps, handicrafts. **Imports:** $323,400 (1983); foodstuffs, machinery, fuel. **Major trading partners:** New Zealand.

Norway

Svalbard

Geography **Location:** nine large and numerous smaller islands in Arctic Ocean. **Boundaries:** Arctic Ocean to N, Barents Sea to E, Norway to S across Norwegian Sea, Greenland to W across Greenland Sea. **Total land area:** 24,000 sq. mi. (62,000 sq km). **Coastline:** undetermined. **Comparative area:** slightly

smaller than West Virginia. **Land use:** 0% arable land; 0% permanent crops; 0% meadows and pastures; 0% forest and woodland; 100% other; no trees; only bushes are crowberry and cloudberry. **Major cities:** Longyearbyen (capital).

People **Population:** 3,403 (1988). **Ethnic groups:** 64% Russian, 35% Norwegian, 1% other. **Languages:** Russian, Norwegian.

Government **Type:** territory of Norway. **Heads of government:** Leif Eldring, governor.

Economy **Monetary unit:** Norwegian krone. **Budget:** (1986) $73 mil. kroner. **Natural resources:** coal, copper, iron ore, phosphate, zinc, wildlife, fish. **Major industries:** coal mining; trapping of seal, polar bear, fox, walrus. **Exports:** 507,000 metric tons of coal from Norwegian mines, 500,000 tons of coal from Soviet mines (1987).

Uninhabited Territories
Boovet Island, Jan Mayen Island.

Portugal

Macau

Geography **Location:** peninsula of Macau, an enclave on mainland of southern China, and three nearby islands. **Boundaries:** China to N, Hong Kong to NE, South China Sea to S. **Total land area:** 6.5 sq. mi. (16.9 sq km). **Coastline:** 25 mi. (40 km). **Comparative area:** about 1/10 size of Washington, D.C. **Land use:** 0% arable land; 0% permanent crops; 0% meadows and pastures; 0% forest and woodland; 100% other. **Major cities:** Macau (capital).

People **Population:** 432,232 (1988). **Nationality:** noun—Macanese (sing., pl.); adjective—Macau. **Ethnic groups:** 95% Chinese, 3% Portuguese, 2% other. **Languages:** Portuguese (official); Cantonese is language of commerce. **Religions:** mainly Buddhist; 17,000 Catholics, of whom half are Chinese.

Government **Type:** Chinese territory under Portuguese administration. **Heads of government:** Carlos Melancia, governor (since July 1987). **Structure:** governor assisted by five secretaries-adjunct (all appointed by president of Portugal), 17-member Legislative Assembly (five appointed by governor, six elected by direct and universal suffrage, six elected indirectly by various groups and associations).

Economy **Monetary unit:** pataca. **Budget:** (1985) **income:** N.A.; **expend.:** $300 mil. **GDP:** $2 bil., $4,350 per capita (1987 est.). **Chief crops:** rice, vegetables; food shortages—rice, vegetables; not self-sufficient in food production. **Livestock:** pigs, buffalo, cattle. **Natural resources:** none. **Major industries:** clothing, textiles, toys, plastic products, furniture, tourism. **Labor force:** 180,000 (1986); 2% unemployment. **Exports:** $1.08 bil. (1986); textiles, clothing. **Imports:** $913.0 mil. (1986); raw materials, foodstuffs. **Major trading partners:** (1986) **exports:** 33% U.S., 16% Hong Kong, 12% France, 11% W. Germany; **imports:** 46% Hong Kong, 20% China.

United Kingdom

Anguilla

Geography **Location:** island in northeastern Caribbean Sea. **Boundaries:** St. Martin 5 mi. (8 km) to S, St. Kitts 70 mi. (113 km) to SE. **Total land area:** 36 sq. mi. (96 sq km). **Coastline:** 38 mi. (61 km). **Comparative area:** about ½ size of Washington, D.C. **Land use:** N.A.; mostly rock with sparse scrub oak, few trees, some commercial salt ponds. **Major cities:** The Valley (capital).

People **Population:** 6,875 (1988). **Nationality:** noun—Anguillan(s); adjective—Anguillan. **Ethnic groups:** mainly of black African descent. **Languages:** English. **Religions:** Anglican, Methodist, Roman Catholic.

Government **Type:** dependent territory of UK. **Constitution:** Apr. 1, 1982. **Heads of government:** Geoffrey O. Whittaker, governor and president of Executive Council (since 1987). **Structure:** 11-member House of Assembly, seven-member Executive Council.

Economy **Monetary unit:** East Caribbean dollar. **Budget:** (1985) *income:* $5.6 mil.; *expend.:* $5.8 mil. **GDP:** $6 mil., $880 per capita (1983 est.). **Chief crops:** pigeon peas, corn, sweet potatoes. **Natural resources:** negl.; salt, fish, lobsters. **Major industries:** tourism, boat building, salt, fishing. **Labor force:** 2,780 (1984); 26.4% unemployment. **Exports:** lobsters.

Intl. Orgs. Commonwealth.

Bermuda

Geography **Location:** isolated archipelago, comprising about 150 islands, in southern North Atlantic Ocean. **Boundaries:** Cape Hatteras 580 mi. (933 km) to W. **Total land area:** 21 sq. mi. (53 sq km). **Coastline:** 64 mi. (103 km). **Comparative area:** about 3/10 times size of Washington, D.C. **Land use:** 0% arable land; 0% permanent crops; 0% meadows and pastures; 20% forest and woodland; 80% other. **Major cities:** (1980) Hamilton (capital) 1,617; St. George's 1,647.

People **Population:** 58,137 (1988). **Nationality:** noun—Bermudian(s); adjective—Bermudian. **Ethnic groups:** 61% black, 39% white and other. **Languages:** English. **Religions:** 37% Anglican, 14% Roman Catholic, 10% African Methodist Episcopal (Zion), 6% Methodist, 5% Seventh-Day Adventist, 28% other.

Government **Type:** British dependent territory. **Constitution:** June 8, 1968. **Heads of government:** Viscount Dunrossil, governor (since 1983); John William David Swan, premier (since 1982). **Structure:** cabinet (Executive Council) appointed by governor, led by government leader; bicameral legislature with appointed Senate and 40-member directly elected House of Assembly; supreme court.

Economy **Monetary unit:** Bermuda dollar. **Budget:** (1986 est.) *income:* $208 mil.; *expend.:* $218 mil. **GDP:** $1,148.1 mil., $19,800 per capita (1986). **Chief crops:** bananas, vegetables, Easter lilies, dairy products, citrus fruits. **Livestock:** poultry, pigs, cat-

tle. **Natural resources:** limestone, pleasant climate fostering tourism. **Major industries:** tourism, finance, structural concrete products. **Labor force:** 32,000 (1984); 25% clerical, 22% services, 21% laborers, 13% professional and technical, 10% administrative and managerial. **Exports:** $38 mil. (1984); semitropical produce, light manufactures. **Imports:** $404 mil. (1984); fuel, foodstuffs, machinery. **Major trading partners:** 56% U.S., 11% Caribbean countries, 8% UK, 6% Canada, 19% other; tourists, 90% U.S.

Intl. Orgs. INTERPOL, WHO.

British Virgin Islands

Geography **Location:** more than 40 mountainous islands, of which 15 are inhabited, in northeastern Caribbean Sea. **Boundaries:** Puerto Rico about 100 mi. (161 km) to W. **Total land area:** 59 sq. mi. (153 sq km). **Coastline:** 50 mi. (80 km). **Comparative area:** about 4/5 size of Washington, D.C. **Land use:** 20% arable land; 7% permanent crops; 33% meadows and pastures; 7% forest and woodland; 33% other. **Major cities:** Road Town (capital).

People **Population:** 12,075 (1988). **Nationality:** noun—Virgin Islander(s); adjective—Virgin Islander. **Ethnic groups:** over 90% black, remainder of white and Asian origin. **Languages:** English. **Religions:** majority Methodist; others include Anglican, Church of God, Seventh-Day Adventist, Baptist, Roman Catholic.

Government **Type:** dependent territory of UK. **Constitution:** June 1, 1977. **National holiday:** Territory Day, July 1. **Heads of government:** Mark Herdman, governor and chairman of Executive Council (since 1986); H. Lavitty Stout, chief minister (since 1986). **Structure:** cabinet (Executive Council) consists of governor as chairman, four ministers of legislature, and ex officio member, who is attorney general; Legislative Council consists of Speaker (elected from outside council), nine elected members, and ex officio member, who is attorney general.

Economy **Monetary unit:** U.S. dollar. **Budget:** (1985) *income:* $18.9 mil.; *expend.:* $24.5 mil. **GDP:** $84.5 mil., $7,260 per capita (1985). **Chief crops:** limited—fruit, vegetables. **Natural resources:** negl. **Major industries:** tourism, construction, rum. **Labor force:** 4,911 (1980). **Exports:** $2.5 mil. (1985); fresh fish, gravel, sand, fruits, vegetables. **Imports:** $91.4 mil. (1985); building materials, automobiles, foodstuffs, machinery. **Major trading partners:** Virgin Islands (U.S.), Puerto Rico, U.S.

Intl. Orgs. Commonwealth.

Cayman Islands

Geography **Location:** three main and numerous smaller islands in western Caribbean Sea. **Boundaries:** Cuba to N, Jamaica 180 mi. (290 km) to SE. **Total land area:** 100 sq. mi. (259 sq km). **Coastline:** 100 mi. (160 km). **Comparative area:** slightly less than 1.5 times size of Washington, D.C. **Land use:** 0% arable land; 0% permanent crops; 8% meadows and pastures; 23% forest and woodland; 69% other. **Major cities:** (1987 est.) Georgetown (capital) 9,500.

People **Population:** 23,037 (1988). **Nationality:** noun—Caymanian(s); adjective—Caymanian. **Ethnic groups:** 40% mixed, 20% white, 20% black, 20% expatriates of various ethnic groups. **Languages:** English. **Religions:** United Church (Presbyterian and Congregational), Anglican, Baptist, Roman Catholic, Church of God, other Protestant denominations.

Government **Type:** British dependent territory. **National holiday:** Constitution Day, July 8. **Heads of government:** George Peter Lloyd, governor and president of Executive Council (since 1982). **Structure:** executive—governor and Executive Council; legislative—unicameral Legislative Assembly; judicial—Summary Court, Supreme Court, Cayman Islands Court of Appeals, Her Majesty's Privy Council.

Economy **Monetary unit:** Cayman dollar. **Budget:** (1985) *income:* $44.8 mil.; *expend.:* $38.0 mil. **GDP:** $254.5 mil., $12,100 per capita (1985). **Chief crops:** minor production of vegetables; turtle farming. **Natural resources:** fish, climate and beaches that foster tourism. **Major industries:** tourism, banking, insurance, finance. **Labor force:** 8,061 (1979); 18.7% service workers, 18.6% clerical, 12.5% construction. **Exports:** $2.4 mil. (1983); turtle products. **Imports:** $140.4 mil. (1983). **Major trading partners:** *exports:* mostly U.S.; *imports:* U.S., Trinidad and Tobago, UK, Netherlands Antilles, Japan.

Intl. Orgs. Commonwealth.

Falkland Islands
Colony of the Falkland Islands

Geography **Location:** two large islands and about 2,000 smaller ones in southwestern Atlantic Ocean. **Boundaries:** Cape Horn, South America, about 480 mi. (770 km) to SW. **Total land area:** 4,700 sq. mi. (12,173 sq km). **Coastline:** 800 mi. (1,288 km). **Comparative area:** slightly smaller than Connecticut. **Land use:** 0% arable land; 0% permanent crops; 99% meadows and pastures; 0% forest and woodland; 1% other. **Major cities:** (1986) Stanley (capital) 1,239.

People **Population:** 1,821 (1988). **Nationality:** noun—Falkland Islander(s); adjective—Falkland Island. **Ethnic groups:** mostly British. **Languages:** English. **Religions:** predominantly Anglican.

Government **Type:** colony of UK. **Constitution:** Oct. 3, 1985. **Heads of government:** Gordon W. Jewkes, governor (since 1985). **Structure:** governor advised by Executive Council; Legislative Council.

Economy **Monetary unit:** Falkland Island pound. **Budget:** (1982) *income:* $5.0 mil.; *expend.:* $4.8 mil. **Livestock:** sheep, cattle, horses. **Natural resources:** fish, wildlife. **Major industries:** wool processing. **Labor force:** 1,100 (est.); 95% agriculture, mostly sheepherding. **Exports:** to UK, $14.7 mil. (1987 est.); wool, hides, skins, other. **Imports:** from UK, $13.9 mil. (1987 est.); food, clothing, fuels, machinery. **Major trading partners:** *exports:* nearly all to UK, some to Netherlands and Japan; *imports:* Netherlands Antilles (Curaçao), Japan, UK.

Gibraltar
Colony of Gibraltar

Geography Location: narrow peninsula running southward from southwest coast of Spain, to which it is connected by an isthmus. **Boundaries:** Spain to W and N, Mediterranean Sea to E, Morocco to S across Strait of Gibraltar. **Total land area:** 2.125 sq. mi. (5.5 sq km). **Coastline:** 7.5 mi. (12 km). **Comparative area:** about 11 times size of the Mall in Washington, D.C. **Land use:** 0% arable land; 0% permanent crops; 0% meadows and pastures; 0% forest and woodland; 100% other. **Major cities:** Gibraltar (capital).

People Population: 29,141 (1988). **Nationality:** noun—Gibraltarian(s); adjective—Gibraltar. **Ethnic groups:** Italian, English, Maltese, Portuguese, and Spanish descent. **Languages:** English and Spanish are primary languages; Italian, Portuguese, Russian also spoken; English used in schools and for official purposes. **Religions:** 75% Roman Catholic, 8% Church of England, 2% Jewish.

Government Type: colony of UK. **Constitution:** May 30, 1969. **Heads of government:** Air Chief Marshal Sir Peter Terry, governor and commander in chief (since 1985); Joe Bossano, chief minister (since Mar. 1988). **Structure:** parliamentary system comprising Gibraltar House of Assembly, Council of Ministers headed by chief minister, and Gibraltar Council; governor appointed by Crown.

Economy Monetary unit: Gibraltar pound. **Budget:** (1987) *income:* $105 mil.; *expend.:* $104 mil. **GNP:** $129 mil. (1985 est.). **Chief crops:** N.A. **Livestock:** N.A. **Natural resources:** none. **Major industries:** tourism, banking and finance, construction; support to large UK naval and air bases. **Labor force:** about 14,800 (including non-Gibraltar laborers); UK military establishments and civil government employ nearly 50% of insured labor force. **Exports:** $62.2 mil. (1985); principally re-exports—75% petroleum, 12% beverages and tobacco, 8% manufactured goods. **Imports:** $147.0 mil. (1985); manufactured goods, fuels, foodstuffs. **Major trading partners:** UK, Morocco, Portugal, Netherlands, Spain, U.S., W. Germany.

Hong Kong

Geography Location: in East Asia, off southern coast of China; consists of island of Hong Kong, Stonecutters Island, Kowloon peninsula, and New Territories, which are partly on mainland. **Boundaries:** China to N, China Sea to E, S, and W. **Total land area:** 413 sq. mi. (1,069 sq km). **Coastline:** 456 mi. (733 km). **Comparative area:** slightly less than six times size of Washington, D.C. **Land use:** 7% arable land; 1% permanent crops; 1% meadows and pastures; 12% forest and woodland; 79% other; includes 3% irrigated. **Major cities:** Victoria (capital).

People Population: 5,651,193 (1988). **Nationality:** adjective—Hong Kong. **Ethnic groups:** 98% Chinese, 2% other. **Languages:** Chinese (Cantonese), English. **Religions:** 90% eclectic mixture of local religions, 10% Christian.

Government Type: colony of UK; scheduled to revert to China in 1997. **Heads of government:** David Cline Wilson, governor (since Apr. 1987). **Structure:** governor, assisted by advisory Executive Council, legislates with advice and consent of Legislative Council; Executive Council composed of governor, four ex officio senior officials, and 12 nominated members; Legislative Council composed of governor, three ex officio members, seven official members, 22 appointed unofficial members, and 24 unofficial members elected indirectly by functional constituencies and by an electoral college; Urban Council, consisting of 15 elected members and 15 appointed by governor, responsible for health, recreation, and resettlement in urban areas; Regional Council (established Apr. 1, 1986)—composed of 12 directly elected members, nine indirectly elected, 12 appointed, and three ex officio—has similar responsibilities in nonurban areas; independent judiciary.

Economy Monetary unit: Hong Kong dollar. **Budget:** (1988) $5.7 bil. **GDP:** $41.8 bil., $7,550 per capita (1986). **Chief crops:** rice, vegetables, dairy products; minor part of economy. **Livestock:** chickens, pigeons, quail, ducks. **Natural resources:** none. **Major industries:** textiles, clothing, tourism, electronics, plastics, toys, watches, clocks. **Labor force:** 2.64 mil. (1986); 35.8% manufacturing, 22.7% wholesale and retail trade, restaurants and hotel, 17.1% services; 2.8% unemployment. **Exports:** $47.6 bil. (1987 est.), including $22.9 bil. re-exports; clothing, plastic articles, textiles, electrical goods. **Imports:** $47.4 bil. (1987 est.). **Major trading partners:** (1987) *exports:* 38% U.S., 14% China, 8% W. Germany, 6% UK, 5% Japan; *imports:* 31% China, 9% Taiwan, 8% U.S.

Intl. Orgs. GATT, IMO, INTERPOL, WMO.

Montserrat

Geography Location: island in eastern Caribbean Sea. **Boundaries:** Guadeloupe 35 mi. (55 km) to S, Antigua 27 mi. (47 km) to NE. **Total land area:** 102 sq. mi. (264 sq km). **Coastline:** 25 mi. (40 km). **Comparative area:** about ⅗ size of Washington, D.C. **Land use:** 20% arable land; 0% permanent crops; 10% meadows and pastures; 40% forest and woodland; 30% other. **Major cities:** (1980) Plymouth (capital) 3,500.

People Population: 12,078 (1988). **Nationality:** noun—Montserratian(s); adjective—Montserratian. **Ethnic groups:** mostly black, with a few Europeans. **Languages:** English. **Religions:** Anglican, Methodist, Roman Catholic, Pentecostal, Seventh-Day Adventist, other Christian denominations.

Government Type: colony of UK. **Heads of government:** Arthur C. Watson, governor (since 1985); J.A. Osborne, chief minister (since 1978). **Structure:** Executive Council presided over by governor, consisting of two ex officio members (attorney general and financial officer) and four unofficial members (chief minister and three other ministers); Legislative Council presided over by speaker chosen by council, seven elected, two official, and two nominated members.

Economy Monetary unit: East Caribbean dollar. **Budget:** (1985) *income:* $8.3 mil.; *expend.:* $10.3 mil. **GDP:** $37.1 mil., $3,130 per capita (1986). **Chief crops:** cotton, limes, potatoes, tomatoes, hot peppers. **Livestock:** sheep, goats, cattle, pigs. **Natural resources:** negl. **Major industries:** tourism, light manufacturing—rum, textiles, electronic appliances. **Labor force:** 5,100 (1983 est.); 40.5% community, social and personal services, 13.5% construction, 12.3% trade, restaurants and hotels, 10.5% manufacturing. **Exports:** $2.8 mil. (1985); plastic bags, electronic parts, textiles, hot peppers, live plants, cattle. **Imports:** $18.3 mil. (1985); machinery and transport equipment, foodstuffs, manufactured goods, fuels, lubricants, related materials. **Major trading partners:** UK.

Pitcairn Islands
Pitcairn, Henderson, Ducie, and Oeno Islands

Geography Location: Pitcairn Island and three uninhabited islands in South Pacific Ocean. **Boundaries:** about halfway between Panama and New Zealand; French Polynesia to NW. **Total land area:** 1.75 sq. mi. (4.5 sq km). **Coastline:** 32 mi. (51 km). **Comparative area:** ³/₁₀ size of Washington, D.C. **Major cities:** Adamstown (capital).

People Population: 55 (1988). **Nationality:** noun—Pitcairn Islander(s); adjective—Pitcairn Islander. **Ethnic groups:** descendants of *Bounty* mutineers. **Languages:** English (official), also a Tahitian/English dialect. **Religions:** 100% Seventh-Day Adventist.

Government Type: colony of UK. **Heads of government:** Terence D. O'Leary, governor and UK high commissioner to New Zealand (since 1982). **Structure:** administered locally by Island Council consisting of four elected island officers, a secretary, and five nominated members.

Economy Monetary unit: New Zealand dollar. **Budget:** (1984 est.) *income:* NZ $812,639 mil.; *expend.:* NZ$1,119,882 mil. **GNP:** NZ $1,911,000 (1982). **Chief crops:** citrus, sugarcane, watermelons, bananas, yams. **Natural resources:** miro trees (used for handicrafts), fish. **Major industries:** postage stamp sales. **Labor force:** no business community in usual sense; some public works; subsistence farming and fishing. **Exports:** fruits, vegetables, curios. **Imports:** fuel oil, machinery, building materials, flour, sugar, other foodstuffs.

St. Helena

Geography Location: in eastern South Atlantic Ocean. Ascension Island is 700 mi. to NE, and the Tristan da Cunha Islands 1,500 to SSW; both are dependencies. **Boundaries:** Angola about 1,200 mi. (1,930 km) to E. **Total land area:** 47 sq. mi. (122 sq km). **Coastline:** 37 mi. (60 km). **Comparative area:** slightly more than 1.5 times size of Washington, D.C. **Land use:** 7% arable land; 0% permanent crops; 7% meadows and pastures; 3% forest and woodland; 83% other. **Major cities:** (1976) Jamestown (capital) 1,516.

People Population: 8,624 (1988). **Nationality:** noun—St. Helenian(s); adjective—St. Helenian. **Languages:** English. **Religions:** Anglican majority; also Baptist, Seventh-Day Adventist, Roman Catholic.

Government Type: colony of UK. **Constitution:** Jan. 1, 1967. **Heads of government:** Francis E. Baker, governor and commander in chief (since 1984). **Structure:** Executive Council, 12-member elected Legislative Council.

Economy Monetary unit: British pound. **Budget:** (1984) *income:* 4.3 mil. pounds sterling; *expend.:* 3.9 mil. pounds sterling. **Chief crops:** maize, potatoes, vegetables; timber production being developed; crawfishing on Tristan de Cunha. **Livestock:** poultry, goats, sheep, cattle. **Natural resources:** fish; Ascension is sea turtle and sooty tern breeding ground; no minerals. **Major industries:** crafts (furniture, lacework, fancy woodwork), fish. **Labor force:** large proportion employed overseas. **Exports:** fish (frozen skipjack, tuna, salt-dried skipjack), handicrafts. **Imports:** food, drink, tobacco, fuel oils, animal feed, building materials. **Major trading partners:** UK, South Africa.

Turks and Caicos Islands

Geography Location: more than 30 islands forming southeastern end of Bahamas Islands in Caribbean Sea. **Boundaries:** Haiti 90 mi (145 km) to S. **Total land area:** 166 sq. mi. (430 sq km). **Coastline:** about 186 mi. (about 300 km). **Comparative area:** slightly less than 2.5 times size of Washington, D.C. **Land use:** 2% arable land; 0% permanent crops; 0% meadows and pastures; 0% forest and woodland; 98% other. **Major cities:** Jamestown (capital).

People Population: 9,295 (1988). **Ethnic groups:** mostly African descent. **Languages:** English. **Religions:** Anglican, Roman Catholic, Baptist, Methodist, Church of God, Seventh-Day Adventist.

Government Type: colony of UK. **Constitution:** introduced on Aug. 30, 1976, suspended in 1986, and at present a constitutional commission is reviewing its contents. **National holiday:** Commonwealth Day, May 31. **Heads of government:** Christopher J. Turner, governor. **Structure:** executive, bicameral legislature (Executive Council, 14-member Legislative Council), judicial (Supreme Court).

Economy Monetary unit: U.S. dollar. **Budget:** (1986) *income:* $12.4 mil.; *expend.:* $13.0 mil. **GDP:** $15 mil., $2,020 per capita (1980). **Chief crops:** corn, beans. **Natural resources:** spiny lobster, conch. **Major industries:** fishing, tourism, offshore financial services. **Labor force:** some subsistence agriculture; majority engaged in fishing and tourist industries. **Exports:** $2.9 mil. (1984); crawfish, dried and fresh conch, conch shells. **Imports:** $26.3 mil. (1984); foodstuffs, drink, tobacco, clothing. **Major trading partners:** U.S. (lobster, conch, tourism), UK; considering trade agreement with Canada.

Uninhabited Territories

British Antarctic Territory, British Indian Ocean Territory, South Georgia and South Sandwich Islands.

THE UNITED NATIONS

Establishment President Franklin D. Roosevelt coined the name United Nations, which was first used in the "Declaration by United Nations," Jan. 1, 1942, during World War II, when representatives of 26 countries pledged their governments to continue fighting together against the Axis Powers. From August to October 1944, representatives of China, the Soviet Union, the United Kingdom, and the United States met at Dumbarton Oaks, a mansion in Washington, D.C., to discuss creating an international peacekeeping organization. Out of these meetings came a general outline for the UN.

At the UN Conference on International Organization, which met at San Francisco from Apr. 25 to June 26, 1945, representatives from 50 countries drew up the UN Charter and signed it on June 26, 1945. Poland, not present at the conference, signed on Oct. 15, 1945, and is considered one of the five founding member states.

The UN officially came into existence on Oct. 24, 1945, when the charter was ratified by China, France, the Soviet Union, the United Kingdom, the United States and by a majority of the other signatories.

UN Charter Full text of the charter may be purchased for $1 from the United Nations, Sales Section, New York, NY 10017 U.S. The preamble to the charter set forth the hopes for the UN:

WE THE PEOPLES OF THE UNITED NATIONS DETERMINED
- to save succeeding generations from the scourge of war . . .
- to reaffirm faith in fundamental human rights, in the dignity and worth of the human person, in the equal rights of men and women and of nations large and small . . .
- to establish conditions under which justice and respect for the obligations arising from treaties and other sources of international law can be maintained . . .
- to promote social progress and better standards of life in larger freedom.
AND FOR THESE ENDS
- to practice tolerance and live together in peace with one another as good neighbors, and
- to unite our strength to maintain international peace and security, and
- to ensure, by the acceptance of principles and the institution of methods, that armed force shall not be used, save in the common interest, and
- to employ international machinery for the promotion of the economic and social advancement of all peoples.
HAVE RESOLVED TO COMBINE OUR EFFORTS TO ACCOMPLISH THESE

AIMS. Accordingly, our respective Governments, through representatives assembled in the city of San Francisco, who have exhibited their full powers found to be in good and due form, have agreed to the present Charter of the United Nations and do hereby establish an international organization to be known as the United Nations.

Purposes The purposes of the United Nations are set forth in Article 1 of the Charter. They are:

1. To maintain international peace and security.

2. To develop friendly relations among nations based on respect for the principle of equal rights and self-determination of peoples.

3. To cooperate in solving international problems of an economic, social, cultural or humanitarian character, and in promoting respect for human rights and fundamental freedoms for all.

4. To be a center for harmonizing the actions of nations in the attainment of these common ends.

Six Official Languages Originally, there were five official languages of the UN: Chinese, English, French, Russian and Spanish. Arabic was added to the General Assembly in 1973, to the Security Council in 1982, and to the Economic and Social Council in 1983. All major UN documents and all meetings of the General Assembly, the Security Council, and the Economic and Social Council are translated into the six working languages.

United Nations Headquarters United Nations, New York, NY 10017 U.S. The UN Headquarters covers a 16-acre site in New York City along the East River from 42d to 48th streets. It consists of the interconnected General Assembly, Secretariat, and Dag Hammarskjold Library buildings. Across the street are other UN office buildings: One, Two, and Three UN Plaza. Acquisition of the site was made possible by a gift of $8.5 million from John D. Rockefeller, Jr., and one-third of that amount from New York City. The Board of Design who drew the architectural plans consisted of an international team of architects from 10 countries. In the spring of 1951, the 39-story Secretariat building was complete and began functioning as the official UN home. The interiors of the buildings have been decorated by many gifts from governments and peoples from all over the world.

Geneva Office United Nations, Palais des Nations, 1211 Geneva 10, Switzerland. The Palais des Nations houses the European offices of the UN. Located in Geneva, Switzerland, and built in 1936, the complex was the headquarters for the League of Nations.

Vienna Office United Nations International Centre, A-1400 Vienna, Austria. The Austrian government built the Vienna International Centre at a cost of $700 million and offers the space rent-free to the UN and its agencies.

UNITED NATIONS MEMBER STATES

(159 member states as of June 15, 1989)

Country	Joined U.N.
Afghanistan	1946
Albania	1955
Algeria	1962
Angola	1976
Antigua and Barbuda	1981
Argentina	1945
Australia	1945
Austria	1955
Bahamas	1973
Bahrain	1971
Bangladesh	1974
Barbados	1966
Belgium	1945
Belize	1981
Benin[1]	1960
Bhutan	1971
Bolivia	1945
Botswana	1966
Brazil	1945
Brunei Darussalam	1984
Bulgaria	1955
Burkina Faso[2]	1960
Burma	1948
Burundi	1962
Byelorussian Soviet Socialist Republic	1945
Cameroon	1960
Canada	1945
Cape Verde	1975
Central African Republic	1960
Chad	1960
Chile	1945
China[3]	1945
Colombia	1945
Comoros	1975
Congo	1960
Costa Rica	1945
Cuba	1945
Cyprus	1960
Czechoslovakia	1945
Democratic Yemen	1967
Denmark	1945
Djibouti	1977
Dominica	1978
Dominican Republic	1945
E. Ger. (German Democratic Repub.)	1973
Ecuador	1945
Egypt[5]	1945
El Salvador	1945
Equatorial Guinea	1968
Ethiopia	1945
Fiji	1970
Finland	1955
France	1945
Gabon	1960
Gambia	1965
Ghana	1957
Greece	1945
Grenada	1974
Guatemala	1945
Guinea	1958
Guinea-Bissau	1974
Guyana	1966
Haiti	1945

Country	Joined U.N.
Honduras	1945
Hungary	1955
Iceland	1946
India	1945
Indonesia	1950
Iran (Islamic Republic of)	1945
Iraq	1945
Ireland	1955
Israel	1949
Italy	1955
Ivory Coast (Côte d' Ivoire)	1960
Jamaica	1962
Japan	1956
Jordan	1955
Kampuchia (Democratic Kampuchea)[4]	1955
Kenya	1963
Kuwait	1963
Lao People's Democratic Repub.	1955
Lebanon	1945
Lesotho	1966
Liberia	1945
Libyan Arab Jamahiriya	1955
Luxembourg	1945
Madagascar	1960
Malawi	1964
Malaysia[6]	1957
Maldives	1965
Mali	1960
Malta	1964
Mauritania	1961
Mauritius	1968
Mexico	1945
Mongolia	1961
Morocco	1956
Mozambique	1975
Nepal	1955
Netherlands	1945
New Zealand	1945
Nicaragua	1945
Niger	1960
Nigeria	1960
Norway	1945
Oman	1971
Pakistan	1947
Panama	1945
Papua New Guinea	1975
Paraguay	1945
Peru	1945
Philippines	1945
Poland	1945
Portugal	1955
Qatar	1971
Romania	1955
Rwanda	1962
Saint Kitts and Nevis	1983
Saint Lucia	1979
Saint Vincent and the Grenadines	1980
Samoa	1976
São Tomé and Principe	1975
Saudi Arabia	1945
Senegal	1960
Seychelles	1976
Sierra Leone	1961
Singapore[6]	1965
Solomon Islands	1978
Somalia	1960
South Africa	1945
Spain	1955
Sri Lanka	1955

Country	Joined U.N.
Sudan	1956
Suriname	1975
Swaziland	1968
Sweden	1946
Syrian Arab Republic	1945
Thailand	1946
Togo	1960
Trinidad and Tobago	1962
Tunisia	1956
Turkey	1945
Uganda	1962
UK of Great Britain and Northern Ireland	1945
Ukrainian Soviet Socialist Republic	1945
Union of Soviet Socialist Republics	1945
United Arab Emirates	1971
United Republic of Tanzania[7]	1961
United States	1945
Uruguay	1945
Vanuatu	1981
Venezuela	1945
Vietnam (Viet Nam)	1977
W. Ger. (Fed. Repub. of Germany)	1973
Yemen	1947
Yugoslavia	1945
Zaire	1960
Zambia	1964
Zimbabwe	1980

1. Formerly Dahomey. 2. Formerly the Upper Volta. 3. By resolution 2758 (XXVI) of Oct. 25, 1971, the General Assembly decided "to restore all its rights to the People's Republic of China and to recognize the representatives of its Government as the only legitimate representatives of China to the United Nations, and to expel forthwith the representatives of Chiang Kai-shek from the place they unlawfully occupy at the United Nations and in all the organizations related to it." 4. Formerly Cambodia. 5. Egypt and Syria were original UN Members from Oct. 24, 1945. Following a plebiscite on Jan. 21, 1958, the United Arab Republic was established by a union of Egypt and Syria and continued as a single member. On Oct. 13, 1961, Syria resumed its status as an independent state and simultaneously its UN membership. On Sept. 2, 1971, the United Arab Republic changed its name to Arab Republic of Egypt. 6. The Federation of Malaya joined the UN on Sept. 17, 1957. On Sept. 16, 1963, its name was changed to Malaysia, following the admission to the new federation of Singapore, Sabah (North Borneo), and Sarawak. Singapore became an independent state on Aug. 9, 1965 and a UN member on Sept. 21, 1965. 7. Tanganyika was a UN member from Dec. 14, 1961, and Zanzibar was a member from Dec. 16, 1963. Following the ratification on Apr. 26, 1964, of Articles of Union between Tanganyika and Zanzibar, the United Republic of Tanganyika and Zanzibar continued as a single member, changing its name to the United Republic of Tanzania on Nov. 1, 1964.

Permanent Observers to the UN at the New York Headquarters cannot vote and do not have diplomatic privileges or immunities. They do have free access to the public meetings and distribution of relevant documentation.

Nonmember Observer States are the Holy See, Monaco, North Korea, San Marino, South Korea, and Switzerland.

Intergovernmental and Other Observer Organizations are the following: African, Caribbean, and Pacific Group of States; Agency for Cultural and Technical Cooperation; Asian-African Legal Consultative Committee; Commonwealth Secretariat; Council for Mutual Economic Assistance (CMEA); European Economic Community (EEC); Latin American Economic System; League of Arab States; Organization of African Unity (OAU); Organization of American States (OAS); Organization of the Islamic Conference; Palestine Liberation Organization (PLO); South West Africa People's Organization (SWAPO).

PRINCIPAL ORGANS

The charter established six principal organs of the UN.

General Assembly

The Assembly is the world's forum for discussing major issues facing the world community, including world peace and security, human rights, global environment, disarmament, health issues including AIDS, and the rights of women and children.

The Assembly consists of all 159 member states, each having one vote. On important issues a two-thirds majority of those present and voting is required; other questions require a simple majority vote. It usually holds annual sessions from September to December and may call for extra sessions when needed. Its agenda of more than 140 matters for discussion is first dealt with in seven main committees: First Committee—disarmament and related security issues; Second Committee—economic and financial matters; Third Committee—social, humanitarian, and cultural areas; Fourth Committee—decolonization; Fifth Committee—administrative and budgetary issues; Sixth Committee—legal matters; and the Special Political Committee. The Assembly discusses reports from each committee as well as reports from each UN program, other UN bodies, and the secretary-general. It conducts studies and makes recommendations (called resolutions) but has no power to enforce its decisions (resolutions), except the power of world opinion.

The Assembly considers and approves the UN budget and assesses member states according to their ability to pay.

The General Assembly designated 1990 as International Literacy Year and called upon governments, nongovernmental organizations, and individuals to intensify literacy programs worldwide.

Security Council

The Council may investigate any dispute or situation that might lead to international friction, and may recommend methods for adjusting such disputes or terms for their settlement. While other UN organs make recommendations to governments, the Council alone has the power to make decisions that member states are obligated under the charter to carry out.

The Security Council has 15 members. The charter designated five permanent members, and the General Assembly elects 10 other members for two-year terms. They are not eligible for immediate reelection. The presidency rotates monthly among each of the members in turn, according to English alphabetical order. The Council may be called into session at any time, and a representative of each member state must be present at UN Headquarters at all times.

The five permanent members are China, France, the Soviet Union, the United Kingdom, and the United States.

The terms of office of each current (1989) nonpermanent member end on Dec. 31 of the year indicated in parentheses: Algeria (1989),

Brazil (1989), Canada (1990), Colombia (1990), Ethiopia (1990), Finland (1990), Malaysia (1990), Nepal (1989), Senegal (1989), Yugoslavia (1989).

Decisions on matters of procedure require the approval of at least nine of the 15 members. Decisions on all other matters also require nine votes, including the concurring votes of all five permanent members. A negative vote by any permanent member on a nonprocedural matter is often referred to as the veto, which results in the rejection of the proposal.

Economic and Social Council (ECOSOC)

The ECOSOC is the principal organ that coordinates the economic and social work of the UN and its specialized agencies. It makes recommendations and initiates activities relating to world trade, industrialization, natural resources, human rights, the status of women, population, social welfare, education, health and related matters, science and technology, and many other economic and social questions.

The ECOSOC has 54 members elected for three-year terms by the General Assembly. The term of office of current (1989) members expires on Dec. 31 of the year indicated in parentheses below:

Bahamas (1991); Belize (1989); Bolivia (1989); Brazil (1991); Bulgaria (1989); Cameroon (1991); Canada (1989); China (1989); Colombia (1990); Cuba (1990); Czechoslovakia (1991); Denmark (1989); France (1990); Ghana (1990); Greece (1990); Guinea (1990); India (1990); Indonesia (1991); Iran (1989); Iraq (1991); Ireland (1990); Italy (1991); Japan (1990); Jordan (1991); Kenya (1991); Lesotho (1990); Liberia (1990); Libya (1990); Netherlands (1991); New Zealand (1991); Nicaragua (1991); Niger (1991); Norway (1989); Oman (1989); Poland (1989); Portugal (1990); Rwanda (1989); Saudi Arabia (1990); Somalia (1989); Sri Lanka (1989); Sudan (1989); Thailand (1991); Trinidad and Tobago (1990); Tunisia (1991); UK (1989); Ukraine (1991); United States (1991); Uruguay (1989); USSR (1989); Venezuela (1990); West Germany (1990); Yugoslavia (1990); Zaire (1989); Zambia (1991).

The Council generally holds two monthlong sessions each year, one in New York and the other in Geneva. Its subsidiary bodies carry out year-round work. They consist of six Functional Commissions: Statistical Commission, Population Commission, Commission for Social Development, Commission on Human Rights, Commission on the Status of Women, Commission on Narcotic Drugs; and five Regional Commissions: Economic Commission for Africa (ECA), in Addis Ababa, Ethiopia; Economic and Social Commission for Asia and the Pacific (ESCAP) in Bangkok, Thailand; Economic Commission for Europe (ECE) in Geneva, Switzerland; Economic Commission for Latin America and the Caribbean (ECLAC) in Santiago, Chile; Economic and Social Commission for Western Asia (ESCWA) in Baghdad, Iraq.

Relations with Nongovernmental Organizations (NGOs) Under the charter the ECOSOC Council may consult with non-

governmental organizations (NGOs) that are concerned with matters within the Council's competence. Over 750 nongovernmental organizations have consultative status with the Council and may send observers to public meetings of the Council and its subsidiary bodies and may submit written statements relevant to the Council's work. Examples of nongovernmental organizations affiliated with ECOSOC include Amnesty International, Catholic Relief Services, Greenpeace International Council, Jaycees International, The Hunger Project, the Sierra Club, and the Salvation Army.

Trusteeship Council

Supervising the administration of trust territories, the Council's goal is to promote the development of a territory toward self-government or independence.

As of July 1, 1989, only one Trust Territory of the original 11 trusteeships remained—the Trust Territory of the Pacific Islands (Micronesia) administered by the United States. The Council has five members: the United States (administering state) and the other permanent members of the Security Council—China, France, the Soviet Union, and the United Kingdom.

International Court of Justice (World Court)

Created under the UN Charter as the UN's official judicial organ, it has its seat at The Hague, Netherlands. All UN member states are automatically members of the Court. Three countries that are not UN members are parties to the Court—Switzerland (1948), Liechtenstein (1950), and San Marino (1954).

The Court is not open to individuals. It issues judgments on all questions that states refer to it and all matters provided for in the UN Charter or in treaties or conventions in force. Both the General Assembly and the Security Council can ask the Court for an advisory opinion on any legal question, as can other organs of the UN or its specialized agencies when authorized to do so by the Assembly.

The Court has dealt with a wide variety of subjects, including territorial rights, the delimitation of territorial waters and continental shelves, fishing jurisdiction, questions of nationality and the right of individuals to asylum, territorial sovereignty, and the right of passage through foreign territory.

The judgment of the Court is final and without appeal. However, a revision may be applied for within 10 years from the date of the judgment on the ground of a new decisive factor. If a party rejects the judgment, the other party may take the issue to the Security Council.

Judges The International Court of Justice has 15 independent judges, of different nationalities, elected by both the General Assembly and the Security Council. Judges hold nine-year terms and may be reelected. The Court itself elects its president and vice president for three-year terms and is in permanent session, except during vacations. All questions are decided by a majority of the judges present; the president votes only in case of a tie.

The judges, listed in their official order of precedence, are the following (terms end on Feb. 5 of the year indicated in parentheses): *president:* Jose Maria Ruda of Argentina (1991); *vice president:* Keba Mbaye of Senegal (1991); *judges:* Manfred Lachs of Poland (1994); Taslim Olawale Elias of Nigeria (1994); Shigeru Oda of Japan (1994); Roberto Ago of Italy (1997); Raghunanden S. Pathak of India (1991); Mohamed Shahabuddeen of Guyana (1997), Stephen Schwebel of the United States (1997); Sir. Robert Y. Jennings of the United Kingdom (1991); Mohammed Bedjaoui of Algeria (1997); Ni Zhengyu of China (1994); Jens Evensen of Norway (1994); Nikolai K. Tarassov of the Soviet Union (1997); Gilbert Guillaume of France (1991).

Secretariat

Servicing the other UN organs and administering the programs and policies they develop, it is headed by the secretary-general. It consists of an international staff of more than 25,000 men and women from over 150 countries. Its work includes administering peacekeeping operations; organizing international conferences on problems of worldwide concern; surveying world economic and social trends and problems; preparing studies on such subjects as human rights, disarmament, and development; interpreting speeches, translating documents, and supplying the world's communications media with information about the UN.

Secretary-General The General Assembly elects the secretary-general who may be reelected to terms of office of five years. The secretary-general cannot be from one of the permanent member states of the Security Council. Those who have served in this post are the following:

Trygve Lie, Norway, Feb. 1, 1946, to Nov. 10, 1952; Dag Hammarskjold, Sweden, Apr. 11, 1953, to Sept. 17, 1961; U Thant, Burma, Nov. 3, 1961, to Dec. 31, 1971; Kurt Waldheim, Austria, Jan. 1, 1972, to Dec. 31, 1981; Javier Pérez de Cuéllar, Peru, Jan. 1, 1982, to present.

UNITED NATIONS PROGRAMS

Each UN program was created by the General Assembly and reports to it through the Economic and Social Council.

UN programs, agencies, and commissions are headquartered around the world.

United Nations Centre for Human Settlements (Habitat) Estab.: 1978; **HQ:** P.O. Box 30030, Nairobi, Kenya. Works to provide models and tools so people can improve their housing. Major concerns are planning, financing, and management of human settlements—especially in developing countries.

International Research and Training Institute for the Advancement of Women (INSTRAW) Estab.: 1979 (made UN program in 1985); **HQ:** Calle César

Nicolas Penson, 102-A, Santo Domingo, Dominican Republic. Carries out research, training, and information activities worldwide to show and increase women's key role in development.

United Nations Conference on Trade and Development (UNCTAD) Estab.: 1964; **HQ:** Place des Nations, 1211 Geneva 10, Switzerland. Formulates international trade policies, mediates multilateral trade agreements, and coordinates trade and development policies of governments and regional economic groups. Seeks to make international financial and monetary system more responsive to needs of developing countries.

United Nations Development Programme (UNDP) Estab.: 1965; **HQ:** One UN Plaza, New York, NY 10017, U.S. Coordinates all development activities within UN system. Operates over 5,000 projects in 150 countries and territories to facilitate development in economic and social sectors, including farming, fishing, forestry, mining, manufacturing, power, transport, communications, housing, trade, health and environmental sanitation, economic planning and public administration.

United Nations Environment Programme (UNEP) Estab.: 1972; **HQ:** P.O. Box 30552, Nairobi, Kenya. Monitors significant changes in environment and encourages and coordinates sound environmental practices. Programs include Earthwatch, an international surveillance network with three main components: (1) Global Environmental Monitoring System, which monitors selected environmental factors and reports them to governments; (2) INFOTERRA, a computerized referral service to 20,000 sources in some 100 countries for environmental information; and (3) International Register of Potentially Toxic Chemicals, which works to provide scientific and regulatory information on chemicals.

United Nations Population Fund Activities (UNPF) Estab.: 1969; **HQ:** 220 E. 42d St., New York, NY 10017, U.S. Provides assistance to population programs in developing countries; promotes understanding of key population factors—population growth, fertility, mortality, spatial distribution, and migration.

Office of the United Nations High Commissioner for Refugees (UNHCR) Estab.: 1950; **HQ:** Place des Nations, 1211 Geneva 10, Switzerland. Provides food, clothing, and shelter for refugees and works with governments to establish safe conditions whereby refugees may return home, and when that is not possible, seeks to ensure that refugees receive asylum. In 1988 UNHCR provided services for more than 12 million refugees worldwide.

United Nations Children's Fund (UNICEF) Estab.: 1946; **HQ:** UNICEF House, Three UN Plaza, New York, NY 10017, U.S. Provides care for children in developing countries by working in both rural and urban settings to provide low-cost, community-based

services in interrelated fields of maternal and child health, applied nutrition, clean water and sanitation, formal and nonformal education, and supporting services for women and girls. UNICEF has brought about a virtual revolution in child survival at low cost and in relatively short time, by emphasizing immunization, breast-feeding, growth monitoring, and a simple oral rehydration method.

United Nations Institute for Training and Research (UNITAR) Estab.: 1965; **HQ:** 801 UN Plaza, New York, NY 10017, U.S. Provides training for members of UN's permanent missions, including courses on international economics, workshops in drafting and negotiating international legal instruments and in dispute settlement, and training in peace, security, human rights, and humanitarian assistance issues.

United Nations University (UNU) Estab.: 1973; **HQ:** Toho Seimei Building, 15-1, Shibuya 2-chome, Shibuya-ku, Tokyo 150, Japan. Has no students of its own, no campus, and no faculty. It is an international community of scholars engaged in research operating through worldwide networks of academic research institutions and is concerned with nine program areas, including peace and conflict resolution; global economy; energy systems and policy; resource policy and management; food-energy nexus; food, nutrition, biotechnology, and poverty; human and social development; and regional perspectives. Operates two research and training centers, one for development economics research, in Finland, and one for natural resources, on the Ivory Coast.

World Food Council (WFC) Estab.: 1974; **HQ:** Via delle Terme di Caracalla, 00100 Rome, Italy. Encourages developing countries to adopt national food strategy whereby they assess their food situation—needs, supply, potential for increasing production, storage, processing, transportation, and distribution; not engaged in field operations.

World Food Programme (WFP) Estab.: 1963; **HQ:** Via Cristoforo Colombo, 426, 00145 Rome, Italy. (Joint program operated by United Nations and Food and Agriculture Organization [FAO]). Provides food to support development activities and in times of emergencies. Operates projects in forestry, soil erosion control, irrigation, land rehabilitation, and rural settlements.

Office of the United Nations Disaster Relief Co-ordinator (UNDRO) Estab.: 1972; **HQ:** Place des Nations, 1211 Geneva 10, Switzerland. Acts as focal point and clearinghouse for information on relief needs and on supplies sent by donors to meet those needs. Promotes study, prevention, control, and prediction of natural disasters and provides governments requesting it with assistance in predisaster planning.

SPECIALIZED AGENCIES

The specialized agencies associated with the United Nations are self-governing, independent organizations that work with the UN system and each other through the coordination machinery of the Economic and Social Council (ECOSOC). Each country affiliates with each agency on an individual basis. Membership in an agency is separate from UN membership.

International Atomic Energy Agency (IAEA)
113 member states; Estab.: July 29, 1957; HQ: Vienna International Centre, P.O. Box 100, A-1400 Vienna, Austria. (Not regular specialized agency in that it does not report through ECOSOC but directly to General Assembly.) To foster and guide development of peaceful uses of atomic energy, it establishes standards for nuclear safety and environmental protection, aids member countries through technical cooperation, and fosters exchange of scientific and technical information on nuclear energy.

International Labour Organisation (ILO)
150 member states; Estab.: 1919, under Treaty of Versailles, became UN specialized agency Dec. 14, 1946; HQ: 4, route des Morillons, CH-1211 Geneva 22, Switzerland. Promotes social justice for working people everywhere by formulating international policies and programs to help improve working and living conditions; creates international labor standards to serve as guidelines for governments and assists in vocational training, management techniques, occupational safety and health.

Food and Agriculture Organization of the United Nations (FAO)
158 member states; Estab.: Oct. 16, 1945; HQ: Via delle Terme di Caracalla, 00100 Rome, Italy. Works to increase output of farmlands, forests, and fisheries and to raise nutritional levels. Cosponsors World Food Programme, which uses food, cash, and services donated by member states for programs of social and economic development and for emergency situations.

United Nations Educational, Scientific and Cultural Organization (UNESCO)
158 member states; Estab.: Nov. 4, 1946; HQ: 7, Place de Fontenoy, 75007 Paris, France. Promotes literacy through programs in teacher training, building schools, and developing textbooks. Natural-science programs include Man and the Biosphere; Intergovernmental Oceanographic Commission; and International Hydrological and International Geological Correlation programs. Other activities include study and development of cultures, and conservation of world's inheritance of books, art, and monuments.

World Health Organization (WHO)
166 member states; Estab.: Apr. 7, 1948; HQ: 20, avenue Appia, 1211 Geneva 27, Switzerland. Coordinates programs aimed at solving health problems by working with governments, other UN agencies, and nongovernmental organizations. In 1977 WHO set "Health for All by the Year 2000" as overriding priority and developed eight-point strategy for implementation, including education on current health issues; proper food supply and nutrition; safe water and sanitation; maternal and child health; immunization against major infectious diseases; and prevention and control of local diseases. WHO is coordinating global strategy to control and prevent AIDS (acquired immune deficiency syndrome).

The World Bank
Group of three institutions sharing one address. HQ: 1818 H St., N.W., Washington, D.C. 20433 *International Bank for Reconstruction and Development (IBRD)* 151 member states; Estab.: Dec. 27, 1945, to provide loans and technical assistance to developing countries to assist in their reconstruction and development. *International Finance Corporation (IFC)* 131 member states (membership open only to World Bank members); Estab.: July 20, 1956, to stimulate flow of private capital into productive investment in member countries. While closely associated with Bank, IFC is separate legal entity and its funds are distinct from those of Bank. *International Development Association (IDA)* 135 member states; Estab.: Sept. 24, 1960. (Affiliate of Bank, IDA has same directors and staff as Bank.) Lends money to poor countries on easier terms than Bank alone could give.

International Monetary Fund (IMF)
151 member states; Estab.: Dec. 27, 1945; HQ: 700 19th St., N.W., Washington, D.C. 20431. Makes financing available to members in balance-of-payments difficulties and provides technical assistance to improve their economic management.

International Civil Aviation Organization (ICAO)
156 member states; Estab.: Apr. 4, 1947; HQ: 1000 Sherbrooke St. West, Suite 400, Montreal, Quebec H3A 2R2, Canada. Works for safer air travel conditions worldwide. Establishes visual and instrument flight rules for pilots and crews; develops aeronautical charts for navigation; coordinates aircraft radio frequencies and works with customs procedures.

Universal Postal Union (UPU)
168 member states; Estab.: July 1, 1875 (became UN specialized agency July 1, 1948); HQ: Weltpoststrasse 4, Berne, Switzerland. Establishes regulations for smooth exchange of mail worldwide.

International Telecommunication Union (ITU)
160 member states; Estab.: 1865 (became UN specialized agency Jan. 1949); HQ: Place des Nations, 1211 Geneva 20, Switzerland. Coordinates use of radio frequencies, tracks positions assigned by countries to geostationary satellites, creates telecommunication equipment, promotes safety measures, and conducts studies.

World Meteorological Organization (WMO)
158 member states; Estab.: 1873 (became UN specialized agency Mar. 23, 1950); HQ: 41, avenue Giuseppe-Motta, 1211 Geneva 20, Switzerland. Facilitates exchange of weather reports among countries; established World Weather Watch to track global weather conditions.

International Maritime Organization (IMO)
127 member states; Estab.: Mar. 17, 1958; HQ: 4 Albert Embankment, London SE1 SR, England. Works to improve international shipping procedures and encourages highest standards in maritime safety; seeks to prevent and control marine pollution from ships and sets standards for training and certification of seafarers.

World Intellectual Property Organization (WIPO)
112 member states; Estab.: 1883 (became a UN specialized agency Dec. 17, 1974); HQ: 34, chemin des Colombettes, 121 Geneva 20, Switzerland. Promotes protection of intellectual property and cooperation in enforcement of agreements on matters such as copyrights, trademarks, industrial designs, and patents.

International Fund for Agricultural Development (IFAD)
139 member states; Estab.: Nov. 30, 1977; HQ: Via del Serafico 10, 00142 Rome, Italy. Lends money to peoples in developing countries for agricultural development projects, including livestock, fisheries, processing and storage, irrigation, research, and training.

United Nations Industrial Development Organization (UNIDO)
118 member states; Estab.: 1966 (became UN specialized agency Jan. 1, 1986); HQ: Wagramerstrasse 5, Vienna XXII, Austria. Promotes and accelerates industrialization of developing countries by providing technical assistance, training programs, and advisory services. Serves as clearinghouse for industrial information; collects, analyzes, publishes, standardizes, and improves industrial statistics.

General Agreement on Tariffs and Trade (GATT)
member states —94 are contracting parties; 30 apply Agreement on de facto basis, and one acceded provisionally; Estab.: Jan. 1, 1948; HQ: Centre William Rappard, 154 rue de Lausanne, 1211 Geneva 21, Switzerland. (Not UN specialized agency in formal sense.) Principal international body concerned with reduction of trade barriers and other measures that distort competition, and with conciliation of trade disputes. Contracting parties account for four-fifths of world trade. Major negotiating conferences, called Rounds, last for several years. In September 1986 GATT trade ministers launched the Uruguay Round in Uruguay.

PEACEKEEPING OPERATIONS

UN peacekeeping is the use of multinational forces, under UN command, to keep disputing countries or communities from fighting while efforts are made to help them negotiate a solution. It is undertaken only with the agreement of both hostile parties. UN Peacekeeping Forces received the Nobel Peace Prize in 1988. Size of each UN peacekeeping is as of Mar. 1, 1989.

United Nations Truce Supervision Organization (UNTSO) Estab.: 1948. Mandate has evolved. Currently UN observers (299) assist peacekeeping operations in Middle East and small detachments are in Beirut and Amman.

United Nations Military Observer Group in India and Pakistan (UNMOGIP) Estab.: 1948. UN observers (38) are stationed on both sides of Line of Control agreed on by India and Pakistan under Simla agreement of July 1972.

United Nations Peacekeeping Force in Cyprus (UNFICYP) Estab.: 1964. UN troops (2,150) and civilian police (34) control 111.9-mi.- (180-km-) long buffer zone on Cyprus between cease-fire lines agreed on by Cyprus National Guard and Turkish forces, and ensure that status quo along the lines is maintained.

United Nations Disengagement Observer Force (UNDOF) Estab.: 1974. UN troops and observers (1,330) maintain "area of separation" on Golan Heights between Israel and Syria.

United Nations Interim Force in Lebanon (UNIFIL) Estab.: 1978. UN troops (5,800) are in southern Lebanon to confirm withdrawal of Israeli forces, restore international peace and security, and assist Lebanese government in ensuring return of its authority in area.

United Nations Iran-Iraq Military Observer Group (UNIIMOG) Estab.: 1988. UN troops (347) monitor two sides' compliance with ceasefire and supervise troop withdrawal.

KEY EVENTS IN UN HISTORY

1946 (Jan. 10) First session of General Assembly begins at London with delegates of 51 member states.

1947 (Nov. 29) General Assembly passes Plan of Partition with Economic Union concerning the future government of Palestine, thereby paving way for government of Tel Aviv to declare State of Israel on May 14, 1948.

1948 (Dec. 10) Universal Declaration of Human Rights adopted by General Assembly.
UN pioneers concept of peacekeeping observer missions and peacekeeping forces (1956).
UN technical assistance to developing countries begins with appropriation of $350,000. Today UN Development Program alone helps finance development activities valued at over $2 billion a year.

1949 Mediates cease-fire between India and Pakistan, ending two years of fighting over control of Kashmir.

United Nations Angola Verification Mission (UNAVEM) Estab.: 1989. Observer mission of 27 observers verify withdrawal of Cuban troops from Angola.

United Nations Transition Assistance Group (UNTAG) Estab.: 1989. Peacekeeping troops (4,650) in Namibia (formerly known as South West Africa) to monitor free elections and process of installing Namibian government.

U.S. REPRESENTATIVES TO THE UNITED NATIONS

The U.S. representative to the UN holds the title Ambassador Extraordinary and Plenipotentiary and heads the U.S. Mission to the UN.

Year	Ambassador
1946	Edward R. Stetinius, Jr.
1946	Herschel V. Johnson (acting)
1947	Warren R. Austin
1953	Henry Cabot Lodge, Jr.
1960	James J. Wadsworth
1961	Adlai E. Stevenson
1965	Arthur J. Goldberg
1968	George W. Ball
1968	James Russell Wiggins
1969	Charles W. Yost
1971	George Bush
1973	John A. Scali
1975	Daniel P. Moynihan
1976	William W. Scranton
1977	Andrew Young
1979	Donald McHenry
1981	Jeane J. Kirkpatrick
1985	Vernon A. Walters
1989	Thomas R. Pickering

Mediates cease-fire between Israel and Arab states.

1950 Security Council calls member states to help South Korea repel invasion from North Korea. (USSR absent from Council, protesting exclusion of People's Republic of China from UN.)
Economic and Social Council adopts Standard International Trade Classification as basis for gathering world trade statistics.

1953 UN coordinates first global-census effort and establishes earth's population for first time in history—2.4 billion people.
Signs truce with North Korea ending conflict with South Korea.

1955 First of ongoing congresses of criminologists and police officials draws up international principles and standards of criminal justice.

1959 UN General Assembly adopts Declaration on the Rights of the Child.

1960 Under decolonization program seventeen territories become newly independent States, 16 in Africa, and join UN.

UN Educational, Scientific and Cultural Organization coordinates aid from 50 nations to move Egyptian temples at Abu Simbel to higher ground while Aswan High Dam being built.

1962 Secretary-general plays key role in resolving U.S.-Soviet confrontation over issue of nuclear missiles in Cuba.

1963 Security Council calls for voluntary arms embargo against South Africa. (Made mandatory in 1977.)

1964 Having restored law and order, peacekeeping troops withdraw from Congo (now Zaire).

1967 After war erupts in Middle East, Security Council adopts Resolution 242, calling for withdrawal of forces from occupied territories, and recognizes right of all states in area to security.
UN begins international standardization of geographical names and publishes international geographical dictionaries.
Mediates settlement of Six-Day Arab-Israeli War.

1970 General Assembly adopts first internationally agreed-on set of principles on seabed and ocean floor beyond national jurisdiction. Declares area "common heritage" of humanity.
Commission on Human Rights establishes procedure whereby citizens may bring human rights violations by governments to commission; accused governments notified and invited to respond.

1972 UN Environment Conference meets at Stockholm; adopts declaration to coordinate environmental issues internationally.

1973 Security Council orders cease-fire in 17-day-old Middle East War and sends peacekeeping force to prevent further fighting between Israel and Arab states.

1975 UN conference at Mexico City launches Decade for Women to begin major effort toward women's equality worldwide.

1979 World Health Organization announces smallpox eradicated from all peoples on earth.

1982 Convention on Law of the Sea covers navigational rights, definition of territorial jurisdiction in coastal regions, economic exploitation of continental shelf and deep seabed, and protection of marine environment.

1983 Commission on Status of Women establishes procedure to receive and respond to citizens' complaints of sex discrimination by governments.

1985 General Assembly establishes Program of Action for African Recovery and Development, 1986–90.
UN Decade for Women culminates in conference at Nairobi that launches Forward-looking Strategies for the Advancement of Women to the Year 2000.

1987 First International Conference on Drug Abuse and Illicit Trafficking (at Vienna) develops program on international coordination of illicit-drug issues.
General Assembly receives Report of World Commission on Environment and

Development ("Our Common Future")—describes environmental threats and plan for "sustainable development."

1988 All UN programs and specialized agencies incorporate environmental factors into their programs.

UN mediates ending of Iran and Iraq war. UN mediates Soviet withdrawal from Afghanistan and establishes Operation Salam to rebuild country.

1989 UN mediates withdrawal of Cuban troops from Angola and South African troops from Namibia.

UN sends peacekeeping troops and advisers to Namibia to supervise free elections aimed at setting up independent self-government.

MODEL UNITED NATIONS

The Model United Nations (MUN) is a simulation of the activities of the UN conducted by high school and college students worldwide. The MUN introduces students to important concepts in international relations and global diplomacy by having them assume the roles of nations' delegates in simulated sessions of the General Assembly, the Security Council, and various UN committees. Current situations are simulated, and the participants must use accurate documentation.

In the United States, more than 60,000 students in approximately 2,000 high schools and colleges participate in MUN simulations, and approximately 100 major annual conferences are held at colleges and universities.

While teachers and students can conduct their simulations informally, the United Nations Association-USA provides coordinating services to those who chose to affiliate. UNA-USA provides a calendar of conferences, teacher and student guides, and training sessions. UNA-USA, 485 Fifth Avenue, New York, NY 10017; (212) 697-3232.

UN documents are provided by the Public Inquiries Unit. Cost is $15 for postage.

FURTHER UN INFORMATION

General Information UN Information Center, 1889 F St., N.W., Washington, D.C. 20006; (202) 289-8670—free materials, loans UN films, interlibrary loan program, library. Public Inquiries Unit, UN, Room GA-57, New York, N.Y. 10017; (212) 963-4475—general information, free charts, booklets, and study kits on work of the UN.

Sales Publications UN Sales, UN, Room DC2-853, New York, N.Y. 10017; (212) 963-8302—free publications catalog describing materials for sale.

Computer Database United Nations Information Service (UNISER), Global Education Motivators, Inc., Chestnut Hill College, Chestnut Hill, Pa. 19118-2695; (215) 248-1150—includes daily UN press releases, news highlights, and Spanish language news. Access is by paid subscription plus on-line time.

International Political, Economic, and Military Organizations

Only those states having full official membership are listed as members; states having special relations and observer status to an organization are not included. Membership is as of May 1989. Contact headquarters to obtain publications produced by the organization.

Association of South East Asian Nations (ASEAN) HQ: Jalan Sisingamangaraja, POB 2072, Jakarta, Indonesia. **Estab.:** Aug. 9, 1967, in Bangkok, to promote political and economic cooperation among non-Communist states of region by coordinating policies in trade, transportation, communications, agriculture, science, finance, and culture. **Members** (6): Brunei, Indonesia, Malaysia, Philippines, Singapore, Thailand.

Colombo Plan for Co-operative Economic and Social Development in Asia and the Pacific (the Colombo Plan) HQ: 12 Melbourne Ave, POB 596, Colombo 4, Sri Lanka. **Estab.:** 1950, by seven Commonwealth nations to promote development by newly independent Asian members. Plan has expanded to fostering international effort to aid economic and social development of Asian members. Developed member states provide assistance to developing nations, and countries within region promote economic and technical cooperation among themselves. **Members** (26): Afghanistan, Australia, Bangladesh, Bhutan, Burma, Canada, Fiji, India, Indonesia, Iran, Japan, Kampuchea, Laos, Malaysia, Maldives, Nepal, New Zealand, Pakistan, Papua New Guinea, Philippines, South Korea, Singapore, Sri Lanka, Thailand, UK, U.S.

Commonwealth HQ: Marlborough House, Pall Mall, London, SW1Y 5HX, England. **Estab.:** By some members of British Empire through evolutionary process formalized by Statute of Westminster on Dec. 31, 1931. Modern Commonwealth was born in 1949, when member countries accepted India's intention of becoming republic while continuing "her full membership of the Commonwealth of Nations." Created to promote cooperation among countries presently or formerly part of British Empire, Commonwealth is voluntary association of independent states and has no written constitution and no rigid contractual obligations. Emphasis is on consultation and exchange of views for cooperation, especially in economic affairs, drug trafficking, international terrorism, and technical assistance to less developed states. Some countries that were part of British Empire are not part of Commonwealth. Observer at the UN. **Members** (46) (years of entry): Antigua and Barbuda (1981), Australia (1931), Bahamas (1973), Bangladesh (1972), Barbados (1966), Belize (1981), Botswana (1966), Brunei (1984), Canada (1931), Cyprus (1961), Dominica (1978), Gambia (1965), Ghana (1957), Grenada (1974), Guyana (1966), India (1947), Jamaica (1962), Kenya (1963), Kiribati (1979), Lesotho (1966), Malawi (1964), Malaysia (1957), Maldives (1982), Malta (1964), Mauritius (1968), New Zealand (1931), Nigeria (1960), Papua New Guinea (1975), Seychelles (1976), Sierra Leone (1961), Singapore (1965), Solomon Islands (1978), Sri Lanka (1948), St. Christopher and Nevis (1983), St. Lucia (1979), St. Vincent and the Grenadines (1979), Swaziland (1968), Tanzania (1961), Tonga (1970), Trinidad and Tobago (1962), Uganda (1962), UK (1931), Vanuatu (1980), Western Samoa (1970), Zambia (1964), Zimbabwe (1980).

Council for Mutual Economic Assistance (CMEA/COMECON) HQ: Prospekt Kalinina 56, Moscow 121205, USSR. **Estab.:** Apr. 1949, to assist each member in economic and technological development through sharing of resources and coordinated efforts with focus on intergroup trade. In 1985 60% of their foreign trade was with member states. Projects include cooperation in production, standardization of equipment and components, introduction of robots in industry, and joint power-engineering projects and supply networks with emphasis on development of nuclear and solar power and reduction of petroleum use. **Members** (10): Bulgaria, Cuba, Czechoslovakia, East Germany, Hungary, Mongolia, Poland, Romania, USSR, Vietnam.

European Communities (EC, the Common Market) HQ: None. Meetings of principal organs in Brussels, Luxembourg, and Strasbourg. (Publications available from Office for the Official Publications of the EC, 5 rue du Commerce, 2985 Luxembourg.) **Estab.:** By treaty signed at Brussels, effective July 1, 1967. EC is composed of European Coal and Steel Community (ECSC), established Apr. 8, 1965; European Economic Community (EEC), also known as Common Market, created by Treaty of Rome, effective Jan. 1, 1958; and European Atomic Energy Community (Euratom), created in 1957. The three organizations are united under one secretariat and work to integrate their economies and coordinate social development. **Members** (12): Belgium, Denmark, France, Greece, Ireland, Italy, Luxembourg, Netherlands, Portugal, Spain, West Germany, UK. Approximately 60 nations in Africa, Caribbean, and Pacific are affiliated under Lome Convention.

European Free Trade Association (EFTA) HQ: 9–11 rue de Varenbe, 1211 Geneva 20, Switzerland. **Estab.:** May 3, 1960, to achieve free trade in industrial products between members, to assist in creation of single market of Western European countries and to contribute to expansion of world trade in general. First goal achieved in 1966, three years ahead of schedule. EFTA created as response to six-state European Economic Community (EEC) when attempts to establish one all-European, free-trade organization encompassing both groups broke down. EFTA entered into free-trade agreements with EC Jan. 1, 1973, and trade barriers were removed July 1, 1976. **Members** (6): Austria, Finland, Ireland, Norway, Sweden, Switzerland. Liechtenstein is participant because of its customs union with Switzerland.

Group of 77 (G-77) Correspondence: c/o Permanent Representative UN, UN Plaza, Box 20, New York, NY 10017. **Estab.**: Oct. 1967, in Algiers following first session of UN Conference on Trade and Development (UNCTAD) in 1964. Orginally ad hoc group of 77 developing countries that coordinated their negotiating positions on matters of trade and development within UNCTAD sessions, Group now functions as negotiating Third World block in international community. Group aims to promote mutual cooperation in trade, technology, food, agriculture, energy, raw materials, finance, industrialization, and technical development and works cooperatively for establishment of "New Economic Order"—briefly, the position that developing countries should have negotiating power in dialogues with industrialized nations. **Members** (125): (asterisk indicates original 77 members): Afghanistan,* Algeria,* Angola, Antigua and Barbuda, Argentina,* Bahamas, Bahrain, Bangladesh, Barbados, Belize, Benin,* Bhutan, Bolivia,* Botswana, Brazil,* Burkina Faso,* Burma,* Burundi,* Cameroon,* Cape Verde, Central African Republic,* Chad,* Chile,* Colombia,* Comoros, Congo.* Costa Rica,* Cuba, Cyprus,* Djibouti, Dominica, Dominican Republic,* Egypt,* El Salvador,* Equador,* Equatorial Guinea, Ethiopia,* Fiji, Gabon,* Gambia, Ghana,* Grenada, Guatemala,* Guinea,* Guinea-Bissau, Guyana, Haiti,* Honduras,* India,* Indonesia,* Iran,* Iraq,* Ivory Coast, Jamaica,* Jordan,* Kampuchea,* Kenya,* Kuwait,* Laos,* Lebanon, Lesotho,* Liberia, Libya,* Madagascar,* Malawi, Malaysia,* Maldives,* Mali,* Malta, Mauritania,* Mauritius, Mexico,* Morocco,* Mozambique, Nepal,* Nicaragua,* North Korea, Oman, Pakistan,* Palestine (PLO), Panama,* Papua New Guinea, Paraguay,* People's Democratic Republic of Yemen, Peru,* Philippines,* Niger, Nigeria,* Qatar, Romania, Rwanda,* Samoa, São Tomé and Principe, Saudia Arabia,* Senegal,* Seychelles, Sierra Leone,* Singapore, Solomon Islands, Somalia,* South Korea,* Sri Lanka,* St. Lucia, St. Vincent and the Grenadines, Sudan,* Suriname, Swaziland, Syria,* Tanzania,* Thailand,* Togo,* Tonga, Trinidad and Tobago,* Tunisia,* Uganda,* United Arab Emirates, Uruguay,* Vanuatu, Venezuela,* Vietnam,* Yemen Arab Repub.,* Yugoslavia,* Zaire,* Zambia, Zimbabwe.

International Criminal Police Organization (ICPO/INTERPOL) HQ: 26

rue Armengaud, 92210 Saint-Cloud, France. **Estab.**: By Second International Criminal Police Congress at Vienna in 1923, "to ensure and promote the widest possible mutual assistance between all criminal police authorities within the limits of the law existing in the different countries and in the spirit of the Universal Declaration of Human Rights." **Members** (146): Algeria, Angola, Andorra, Antigua and Barbuda, Argentina, Aruba, Australia, Austria, Bahamas, Bahrain, Bangladesh, Barbados, Belgium, Belize, Benin, Bolivia, Botswana, Brazil, Brunei, Burkina Faso, Burma, Burundi, Cameroon, Canada, Central African Republic, Chad, Chile, China, Colombia, Congo, Costa Rica, Cuba, Cyprus, Denmark, Djibouti, Dominica, Dominican Republic, Ecuador, Egypt, Equatorial Guinea, Ethiopia, Fiji, Finland, France, Gabon, Gambia, Ghana, Greece, Grenada, Guatemala, Guinea, Guyana, Haiti, Honduras, Hungary, Iceland, India, Indonesia, Iran, Iraq, Ireland, Israel, Ivory Coast, Italy, Jamaica, Japan, Jordan, Kampuchea, Kenya, Kiribati, Kuwait, Laos, Lebanon, Lesotho, Liberia, Libya, Liechtenstein, Luxembourg, Madagascar, Malawi, Malaysia, Maldives, Mali, Malta, Mauritania, Mauritius, Mexico, Monaco, Morocco, Nauru, Nepal, Netherlands, Netherlands Antilles, New Zealand, Nicaragua, Niger, Nigeria, Norway, Oman, Pakistan, Panama, Papua New Guinea, Paraguay, Peru, Philippines, Portugal, Qatar, Romania, Rwanda. Saudi Arabia, Senegal, Seychelles, Sierra Leone, Singapore, Somalia, South Korea, Spain, Sri Lanka, St. Christopher and Nevis, St. Lucia, St. Vincent, Sudan, Suriname, Swaziland, Sweden, Switzerland, Syria, Tanzania, Thailand, Togo, Tonga, Trinidad and Tobago, Tunisia, Turkey, Uganda, United Arab Emirates, UK, Uruguay, U.S., Venezuela, West Germany, Yemen Arab Repub., Yugoslavia, Zaire, Zambia, Zimbabwe.

International Telecommunication Satellite Organization (INTELSAT) HQ: 3400 Internal Drive, N.W., Washington, D.C. 20008. **Estab.**: Feb. 12, 1973, by two international agreements to maintain and operate the global satellite system used by public international telecommunication services. Operates space equipment and earth stations owned by telecommunication entities in each country. INTELSAT's 13-satellite system provides about two-thirds of world's international telecommunication services to more than 140 countries. Services include telephone, television, facsimile, data, and telex transmissions. **Members** (144): Afghanistan, Algeria, Angola, Argentina, Australia, Austria, Bangladesh, Bahamas, Barbados, Belgium, Benin, Bolivia, Burkina Faso, Brazil, Cameroon, Canada, Central African Republic, Chad, Chile, China, Colombia, Congo, Costa Rica, Cyprus, Denmark, Dominican Republic, Ecuador, Egypt, El Salvador, Ethiopia, Fiji, Finland, France, Gabon, Ghana, Greece, Guatemala, Guinea, Haiti, Honduras, Iceland, India, Indonesia, Iran, Iraq, Ireland, Israel, Italy, Ivory Coast, Jamaica, Japan, Jordan, Kenya, Kuwait, Lebanon, Libya, Liechtenstein, Luxembourg, Madagascar, Malawi, Malaysia, Mali, Mau-

rihhtania, Mauritius, Mexico, Monaco, Morocco, Netherlands, New Zealand, Nicaragua, Niger, Nigeria, Norway, Oman, Pakistan, Panama, Papua New Guinea, Paraguay, Peru, Philippines, Portugal, Qatar, Rwanda, Saudi Arabia, Senegal, Singapore, Somalia, South Africa, South Korea, Spain, Sri Lanka, Sudan, Sweden, Switzerland, Syria, Tanzania, Thailand, Togo, Trinidad and Tobago, Tunisia, Turkey, Uganda, United Arab Emirates, United Kingdom, Uruguay, U.S., Vatican City, Venezuela, Vietnam, Yemen Arab Repub., Yugoslavia, West Germany, Zaire, Zambia.

League of Arab States (Arab League) HQ: 37 avenue Khereddine Pacha, Tunis, Tunisia. **Estab.**: By treaty signed on Mar. 22, 1945, at Cairo, Egypt, to promote cultural, economic, and communication ties among members and to mediate internal disputes. Because Egypt signed peace treaty with Israel, its membership was suspended in Mar. 1979, and league's headquarters moved from Cairo to Tunis. Egypt was readmitted to league on May 23, 1989. Observer at UN. **Members** (21): Algeria, Bahrain, Djibouti, Iraq, Jordan, Kuwait, Lebanon, Libya, Mauritania, Morocco, Oman, Palestine (PLO), People's Democratic Republic of Yemen, Qatar, Saudi Arabia, Somalia, Sudan, Syria, Tunisia, United Arab Emirates, Yemen Arab Repub.

Nonaligned Movement (NAM) HQ: None. Chairship on three-year rotating basis. Yougoslavia is 1989–92 chair. Mission of Yugoslavia to the United Nations, 854 Fifth Ave., New York, NY 10021. **Estab.**: Through series of conferences, first of which met in Belgrade, Yugoslavia, Sept. 1–6, 1961, to ensure national independence and security of nonaligned countries in their "struggle against imperialism, colonialism, neocolonialism, apartheid, racism, including Zionism, and all forms of foreign aggression, occupation, domination, interference or hegemony, as well as against great power and bloc politics." In mid-1970s NAM called for "New International Economic Order"—briefly, the position that developing countries should have negotiating power in dialogues with industrialized nations. **Members** (101): Afghanistan, Algeria, Angola, Argentina, Bahamas, Bahrain, Bangladesh, Barbados, Belize, Benin, Bhutan, Bolivia, Botswana, Burkina Faso, Burundi, Cameroon, Cape Verde Islands, Central African Republic, Chad, Colombia, Comoros, Congo, Cuba, Cyprus, Djibouti, Ecuador, Egypt, Equatorial Guinea, Ethiopia, Gabon, Gambia, Ghana, Grenada, Guinea, Guinea-Bissau, Guyana, India, Indonesia, Iran, Iraq, Ivory Coast, Jamaica, Jordan, Kampuchea, Kenya, Kuwait, Laos, Lebanon, Lesotho, Liberia, Libya, Madagascar, Malawi, Malaysia, Maldives, Mali, Malta, Mauritania, Mauritius, Morocco, Mozambique, Nepal, Nicaragua, Niger, Nigeria, North Korea, Oman, Pakistan, Palestine (PLO), Panama, People's Democratic Republic of Yemen, Peru, Qatar, Rwanda, São Tomé and Principe, Saudi Arabia, Senegal, Seychelles, Sierra Leone, Singapore, Somalia, South West African People's Organization (SWAPO), Sri Lanka, St. Lucia, Sudan, Suriname, Swaziland, Syria,

Tanzania, Togo, Trinidad and Tobago, Tunisia, Uganda, United Arab Emirates, Vanuatu, Vietnam, Yemen Arab Repub., Yugoslavia, Zaire, Zambia, Zimbabwe.

North Atlantic Treaty Organization (NATO) HQ: 1110 Brussels, Belgium. Estab.: By North Atlantic Treaty on Aug. 24, 1949, as international defense organization composed of European countries, Canada, and U.S. Members agree to settle disputes among each other by peaceful means and regard attack on one as attack on all. Members develop joint defense plans, consult on political problems, share science and technology, and organize joint training. NATO attempts to maintain military balance with countries of Warsaw Pact. NATO forces comprise three elements: conventional forces, intermediate and short-range nuclear forces, and strategic nuclear forces of UK and U.S. NATO consists of three commands: European Command, HQ in Casteau, Belgium; Atlantic Ocean Command, HQ in Norfolk, Virginia, U.S.; and Channel Command, HQ in Northwood, UK. Members (16): Belgium, Canada, Denmark, France, Greece, Iceland, Italy, Luxembourg, Netherlands, Norway, Portugal, Spain, Turkey, UK, U.S., West Germany.

Organization of African Unity (OAU) HQ: POB 3243, Addis Ababa, Ethiopia. Estab.: By charter on May 25, 1963 at Addis Ababa, to promote unity and solidarity among African states. OAU works to eradicate all forms of colonialism from Africa and to defend their sovereignty, territorial integrity, and independence. Observer at UN. Members (50): Algeria, Angola, Benin, Botswana, Burkina Faso, Burundi, Cameroon, Cape Verde Islands, Central African Republic, Chad, Comoros, Congo, Djibouti, Egypt, Equatorial Guinea, Ethiopia, Gabon, Gambia, Ghana, Guinea, Guinea-Bissau, Ivory Coast, Kenya, Lesotho, Liberia, Libya, Madagascar, Niger, Nigeria, Rwanda, Sahrawi Arab Democratic Republic, São Tomé and Principe, Senegal, Seychelles, Sierra Leone, Somalia, Sudan, Swaziland, Tanzania, Togo, Tunisia, Uganda, Zaire, Zambia, Zimbabwe.

Organization of American States (OAS) HQ: 1889 F St., N.W., Washington, D.C. 20006, U.S. Estab.: By charter signed at Bogota, Colombia, effective Dec. 13, 1951, to work for "order of peace and justice, promoting solidarity among the American states," and to establish "new objectives and standards for the promotion of the economic, social and cultural development of the peoples of the Hemisphere, and to speed the process of economic integration." Programs include promotion of human rights, education, economic and social development, and scientific exchanges. Observer at UN. Members (32): Antigua and Barbuda, Argentina, Bahamas, Barbados, Bolivia, Brazil, Chile, Colombia, Costa Rica, Cuba (was suspended from OAS activities but not membership in 1962), Dominica, Dominican Republic, Ecuador, El Salvador, Grenada, Guatemala, Haiti, Honduras, Jamaica, Mexico, Nicaragua, Panama, Paraguay, Peru, St. Kitts and Nevis, St. Lucia, St. Vincent and the Grena-

dines, Suriname, Trinidad and Tobago, Uruguay, U.S., Venezuela.

Organization of Economic Cooperation and Development (OECD) HQ: 2 rue Andre pascal, 75775 Paris Cedex 16, France. Estab.: By convention signed at Paris, effective Sept. 30, 1961, to help "member countries promote economic growth, employment, and improved standards of living through the coordination of policy [and] to help promote the sound and harmonious development of the world economy and improve the lot of the developing countries, particularly the poorest." Members (24): Australia, Austria, Belgium, Canada, Denmark, Finland, France, Greece, Iceland, Ireland, Italy, Japan, Luxembourg, Netherlands, New Zealand, Norway, Portugal, Spain, Sweden, Switzerland, Turkey, UK, U.S., West Germany.

Organization of the Petroleum Exporting Countries (OPEC) HQ: Obere Donaustrasse 93, 1020 Vienna, Austria. Estab.: Nov. 14, 1960, by resolution adopted at Baghdad, Iraq, to attempt to set world oil prices by coordinating their oil production. OPEC countries conduct research on all areas affecting oil, from uses and development to economic and financial issues. In 1985 it was estimated that OPEC members possessed 67.3% of world's known reserves of crude petroleum and 34.7% of known reserves of natural gas. Observer at UN. Members (13): Algeria, Ecuador, Gabon, Indonesia, Iran, Iraq, Kuwait, Libya, Nigeria, Qatar, Saudia Arabia, United Arab Emirates, Venezuela. (See also "World Energy.")

Warsaw Treaty Organization (WTO, the Warsaw Pact) HQ: Moscow, USSR. Estab.: By treaty signed at Warsaw, Poland, on May 14, 1955, to work cooperatively on all important international issues relating to security and political cooperation. As mutual military defense alliance among Communist countries, Pact maintains three types of forces: conventional, intermediate, and short-range and strategic nuclear forces. Attack against one is considered attack against all. Aims to balance military forces with those of countries in NATO. Members (7): Bulgaria, Czechoslovakia, East Germany, Hungary, Poland, Romania, USSR.

NOBEL PEACE PRIZE RECIPIENTS

1901 Jean-Henri Dunant (Switzerland) Founder of International Committee of the Red Cross; **Frédéric Passy** (France) Founder of first French peace society.
1902 Elie Ducommun (Switzerland) Director of Permanent International Peace Bureau;

Charles A. Gobat (Switzerland) Secretary-general of Inter-Parliamentary Union.
1903 Sir William R. Cremer (Great Britain) Founder of International Arbitration League.
1904 Institute of International Law Founded in 1873.
1905 Baroness Bertha S.F. von Suttner (Austria) Author of antiwar novel *Lay Down Your Arms*.
1906 Theodore Roosevelt (U.S.) President; mediated Russo-Japanese War.
1907 Ernesto T. Moneta (Italy) Founder of Lombard League of Peace; **Louis Renault** (France) Leading jurist at Hague Peace conferences.
1908 Klas P. Arnoldson (Sweden) Founder of Swedish Peace and Arbitration League; **Fredrik Bajer** (Denmark) Writer and peace activist.
1909 Auguste M.F. Beernaert (Belgium) Prime minister and peace activist; **Paul H.B.B. D'Estournelles de Constant (Baron de Constant de Rebecque)** (France) Founder of French parliamentary group for voluntary arbitration.
1910 Permanent International Peace Bureau Founded 1891.
1911 Tobias M.C. Asser (Netherlands) A founder of Institute of International Law; **Alfred H. Fried** (Austria) Journalist and founder of many peace publications.
1912 Elihu Root (U.S.) Secretary of State and originator of several arbitration treaties.
1913 Henri Lafontaine (Belgium) President of Permanent International Peace Bureau in Bern.
1914–16 No award.
1917 International Committee of the Red Cross Founded 1863.
1918 No award.
1919 Thomas Woodrow Wilson (U.S.) President; instrumental in establishing League of Nations.
1920 Léon Victor A. Bourgeois (France) Drafted framework for League of Nations.
1921 Karl H. Branting (Sweden) Prime minister and pacifist; **Christian L. Lange** (Norway) A founder of Inter-Parliamentary Union.
1922 Fridtjof Nansen (Norway) Scientist, explorer, originator of "Nansen passports" for refugees.
1923–24 No award.
1925 Sir Austen Chamberlain (Great Britain) Foreign secretary; worked for Locarno Pact; **Charles G. Dawes** (U.S.) Vice president; drafted Dawes Plan settling German reparations issue.
1926 Aristide Briand (France) and **Gustav Stresemann** (Germany) Creators of Locarno Pact.
1927 Ferdinand Buisson (France) Human rights advocate; **Ludwig Quidde** (Germany) Lifelong peace activist.
1928 No award.
1929 Frank B. Kellogg (U.S.) Secretary of state; a creator of Kellogg-Briand Pact.
1930 L.O. Nathan Söderblom (Sweden) Archbishop; leader in the ecumenical movement.
1931 Jane Addams (U.S.) President of Women's International League for Peace and Freedom; **Nicholas M. Butler** (U.S.) Promoter of Kellogg-Briand Pact.
1932 No award.
1933 Sir Norman Angell (Ralph Lane) (Great Britain) Author of antiwar book *The Great Illusion*.
1934 Arthur Henderson (Great Britain) Presi-

dent of League of Nations World Disarmament Conference 1932.

1935 Carl von Ossietzky (Germany) Journalist and pacifist.

1936 Carlos Saavedra Lamas (Argentina) Secretary of state; president of League of Nations and mediator in a conflict between Paraguay and Bolivia.

1937 Lord Edgar Algernon R.G. Cecil (Great Britain) An architect of League of Nations.

1938 Nansen International Office for Refugees Founded 1921.

1939–43 No award.

1944 International Committee of the Red Cross Founded 1863.

1945 Cordell Hull (U.S.) Secretary of state; instrumental in creating UN.

1946 Emily G. Balch (U.S.) Leader of international women's movement for peace; **John R. Mott** (U.S.) Leader of Christian ecumenical movement.

1947 The Friends Service Council and **The American Friends Service Committee (The Quakers)**.

1948 No award.

1949 Lord John Boyd Orr (Great Britain) Nutritionist; worked to eliminate world hunger.

1950 Ralph Bunche (U.S.) Mediator in Middle East war.

1951 Léon Jouhaux (France) Advocate of improved working-class conditions.

1952 Albert Schweitzer (France) Missionary surgeon and founder of Lambarene Hospital in Africa.

1953 George C. Marshall (U.S.) General; originator of Marshall Plan, which provided recovery loans and technical aid to European nations after World War II.

1954 Office of the United Nations High Commissioner for Refugees .

1955–56 No award.

1957 Lester B. Pearson (Canada) Secretary of state; worked to resolve Suez Canal Crisis of 1956.

1958 Georges Pire (Belgium) Dominican priest and leader of relief organization for refugees, l'Europe du Coeur au Service du Monde.

1959 Philip J. Noel-Baker (Great Britain) Lifelong worker for international peace through disarmament.

1960 Albert J. Luthuli (South Africa) President of the African National Congress; led peaceful resistance to apartheid.

1961 Dag Hammarskjöld (Sweden) Secretary-general of UN; worked for peace in the Congo.

1962 Linus C. Pauling (U.S.) Chemist; warned against dangers of radioactive fallout in nuclear weapons testing and war.

1963 International Committee of the Red Cross and **League of Red Cross Societies**.

1964 Martin Luther King, Jr. (U.S.) Leader of American civil rights movement.

1965 United Nations Children's Fund (UNICEF).

1966–67 No award.

1968 René Cassin (France) President of European Court for Human Rights.

1969 International Labour Organization UN agency involved in improving worldwide working and social conditions.

1970 Norman Borlaug (U.S.) Agricultural scientist and developer of high-yield grains credited with helping to alleviate world hunger.

1971 Willy Brandt (Federal Republic of Germany) Chancellor; champion of East-West détente.

1972 No award.

1973 Henry A. Kissinger (U.S.) Secretary of state and **Le Duc Tho** (Democratic Republic of Viet Nam) Foreign minister; negotiated Vietnam cease-fire agreement. Mr. Tho declined the prize.

1974 Seán MacBride (Ireland) President of International Peace Bureau and UN commissioner for Namibia; **Eisaku Sato** (Japan) Prime minister of Japan and campaigner against nuclear weapons.

1975 Andrei Sakharov (USSR) Nuclear physicist and human rights campaigner.

1976 Betty Williams and **Mairead Corrigan** (Northern Ireland) Founders of Northern Ireland Peace Movement.

1977 Amnesty International A human rights organization.

1978 Anwar el-Sadat (Egypt) President and **Menachem Begin** (Israel) Prime minister; negotiated Israeli-Egyptian peace accord.

1979 Mother Teresa (India) Worker for the poor in Calcutta.

1980 Adolfo Pérez Esquivel (Argentina) Architect, sculptor and human rights leader.

1981 Office of the United Nations High Commissioner for Refugees .

1982 Alva Myrdal (Sweden) and **Alfonso García Robles** (Mexico) Campaigners for disarmament.

1983 Lech Walesa (Poland) Leader of the Solidarity trade union federation.

1984 Desmond M. Tutu (South Africa) Bishop of Johannesburg; a leader of the antiapartheid movement.

1985 International Physicians for the Prevention of Nuclear War Organization jointly headed by a Soviet and an American doctor.

1986 Elie Wiesel (U.S.) Writer on the Holocaust and Nazi death camp survivor.

1987 Oscar Arias Sánchez (Costa Rica) President of Costa Rica; creator of a peace plan for Central America.

1988 United Nations Peacekeeping Forces (see "The United Nations").

MAJOR PEACE GROUPS IN THE U.S.

American Friends Service Committee 1501 Cherry St., Philadelphia, PA 19102; (215) 241–7000. Provides humanitarian work alternatives for conscientious objectors to war; promotes nuclear disarmament. Founded 1917 by Religious Society of Friends (Quakers); not a membership organization. Won 1947 Nobel Peace Prize.

Clergy and Laity Concerned 198 Broadway, Room 302, New York, NY 10038; (212) 964–6730. Interfaith organization advocating citizen action on issues of militarism, economic and racial justice, and human rights. Founded 1965; membership 16,000.

Common Cause 2030 M St., N.W., Washington, D.C. 20036; (202) 833–1200. Lobbies for nuclear arms control, and for public accountability in government. Founded 1970; membership 280,000.

Council for a Liveable World 20 Park Plaza, Boston, MA 02116; (617) 542–2282. Promotes arms control treaties and other measures to stop proliferation of nuclear weapons. Founded 1962 by physicists who had developed first atomic bomb; membership 100,000.

Fellowship of Reconciliation P.O. Box 271, Nyack, NY 10960; (914) 358–4601. Promotes resolution of conflicts through active nonviolence. Founded 1915; membership 15,000. Affiliation: **International Fellowship of Reconciliation,** Hof van Sonoy 17, 1811 LD Alkmaar, The Netherlands. Founded 1914 by English Quaker and German Lutheran who pledged to work together for peace although their countries were at war. Branches in 27 countries; membership 125,000.

Freeze Voter 733 15th St., Suite 526, Washington, D.C. 20005; (202) 783–8747. Works to elect congressional and presidential candidates who support nuclear weapons freeze. Founded 1983; membership 50,000.

Greenpeace USA 1436 U St. N.W., Washington, D.C. 20009; (202) 466–1177. Fights threats to natural environment through nonviolent direct action; monitors radioactive and toxic waste dumping, acid rain, and comprehensive test ban for nuclear weapons. Founded 1970; membership 550,000. Affiliation: **Greenpeace International,** 25–26 High St., Lewes, East Sussex BN7 2LU, England. Founded 1971; membership 1,200,000.

Pax Christi 348 E. 10th St., Erie, PA 16503; (814) 453–4955. Works for disarmament and a just world order. Founded 1973; membership 10,000. Affiliation: **Pax Christi International,** Plantijn Moretuslei 174, B-2018 Antwerp, Belgium. Founded 1945; membership 85,000 in 18 countries.

Physicians for Social Responsibility 1601 Connecticut Ave., N.W., Suite 800, Washington, D.C. 20009; (202) 939–5750. Promotes education about medical dangers of nuclear weapons and nuclear war. Founded 1961; membership 40,000. Affiliation: **International Physicians for the Prevention of Nuclear War,** 126 Rogers St., Cambridge, MA 02142. Founded 1980 by Soviet and American physician; federation of groups in 34 nations. Won 1985 Nobel Peace Prize.

SANE/FREEZE 711 G St., S.E., Washington, D.C. 20003; (202) 546–7100. Seeks U.S./USSR agreement to stop production, testing, and deployment of nuclear weapons. Committee for Sane Nuclear Policy founded 1957; Nuclear Weapons Freeze Campaign. Founded 1981; merged 1987. Not membership organization.

Union of Concerned Scientists 26 Church St., Cambridge MA 02238; (617) 547–5552. Studies hazards of U.S. nuclear policy; promotes education through publications. Founded 1969; not a membership group.

War Resisters League 339 Lafayette St., New York, NY 10012; (212) 228–0450. Engages in pacifist war resistance; supports conscientious objectors. Founded 1923; membership 16,000. Affiliation: **War Resisters International,** 55 Dawes St., London SE17 1EL, England. Founded 1921; membership 150,000.

WORLD RELIGIONS

In 1985, of an estimated 4.8 billion people on earth, about four out of five were identified as adherents of a religion. The remainder were either nonreligious (agnostic) or atheistic (actively opposed to theistic religion). The following table identifies the major groups in order of estimated number of adherents (all figures in this section are derived from *The World Christian Encyclopedia*).

CHRISTIANITY

Founder Jesus Christ, who is seen by most Christians as the Son of God. The Western calendar is dated from the supposed year of his birth. Scholars today believe he was actually born about 3 B.C. and died about A.D. 30. Jesus was born and raised a Jew, and became a rabbi, or teacher. According to Christian scripture, he was the Messiah awaited by the Jewish people. He took up preaching and healing at the age of 30. Three years later he was sentenced to death in Jerusalem and was executed by crucifixion. The scriptures further report that he soon rose from the dead.

Scripture The Bible, which consists of the Old Testament, a collection of books originally written in Hebrew (which are also the holy books of Judaism), and the New Testament, writings in Greek about the life and teachings of Jesus and his early followers.

Beliefs Orthodox belief is in one God as revealed in three persons—God the Father (the Creator), God the Son (Jesus Christ, the Redeemer), and God the Holy Spirit (the Sanctifier). Christians believe that Jesus restored a right relationship between God and human beings through his death by crucifixion and his resurrection from the dead.

Practice Most Christian denominations observe the rite of baptism, administered to children and to newly converted members, and the Eucharist, or Communion, in which members partake of bread and wine in commemoration of Jesus Christ.

Christians are organized into congregations and gather for worship in churches. Most denominations have designated Sunday (the day Jesus rose from the dead) as the day for special observance and worship. A few have designated Saturday, the Jewish Sabbath, instead.

In most Christian denominations, men and women observe monogamy, and divorce is forbidden or discouraged. There are many different standards of personal conduct, ranging from the ascetic to the celebratory.

Schools and Sects There are two historic divisions in Christianity. In A.D. 1054 the Eastern (or Orthodox) church and Western (or Roman) church separated. Then, in the 1500s, reformers including Martin Luther and John Calvin broke from the Roman church to form a number of separate denominations that together are called Protestant. The Orthodox churches remain dominant in Greece, the Soviet Union, and in parts of eastern Europe. The Roman church (known today as the Roman Catholic or simply the Catholic church) dominates in southern Europe and Latin America. Protestant churches predominate in northern Europe (including Great Britain), North America, and Australia. Both Catholic and Protestant churches have conducted industrious mission programs in Africa and Asia and share influence in those regions. In addition to the three main groups are many small denominations and sects that do not fit comfortably into any of the three main groups.

History At the time of his death, Jesus had only a small handful of followers. Within a century, however, they had spread the new teaching to much of the Roman Empire. There were small communities of worshipers in the cities of Greece, Asia Minor, and Palestine and in Rome itself. Christians were persecuted cruelly by the Roman state and in many places were driven underground. By A.D. 300, however, Christians had attained some influence. In 313 the emperor Constantine decreed toleration for Christianity and reportedly was baptized on his deathbed. By the end of the century, Christianity was the official religion of the empire.

This marked the beginning of a newly militant phase. Missionaries were sent to the far reaches of Europe to establish churches. Christianity gradually triumphed from the isles of Ireland to the plains of Poland. In the 900s Christianity reached Russia through envoys from the Eastern church.

During the Middle Ages, the Eastern and Western churches divided. The Western church was a major preserver and extender of learning at home. Abroad it sought to dislodge, in a series of Crusades, the Muslim Turks who had control of the Holy Land.

A long period of religious strife began with the Reformation after 1517. Brutal religious wars convulsed Europe, causing untold suffering. At the same time, European exploration and conquests were spreading Christianity to the Americas and to Asia. Roman Catholics and Protestants proselytized wherever they predominated.

From the mid-1800s to the mid-1900s, the Western churches (Catholic and Protestant) carried out energetic missionary programs to Africa and East Asia. Although they failed in their aim to Christianize the world, they did contribute to the growth of vigorous and independent churches in Africa and Asia. Today there are more Christians in Africa than in North America.

WORLD RELIGIONS

Group	Adherents	% of World pop.
MAJOR WORLD RELIGIONS		
Christianity	1,548,500,000	32.4%
Islam	817,000,000	17.1
Hinduism	647,500,000	13.5
Buddhism	295,600,000	6.2
Judaism	17,800,000	0.4
TOTAL		69.6%
OTHER BROAD RELIGIOUS GROUPINGS		
Chinese folk religions	188,000,000	3.9%
New Asian religions	106,400,000	2.2
Tribal religions	91,200,000	1.9
TOTAL		8.0%
REGIONAL AND SMALLER RELIGIOUS GROUPS		
Sikhism	16,100,000	0.34%
Shamanism	12,200,000	0.26
Spiritism	6,700,000	0.14
Confucianism	5,200,000	0.11
Bahaism	4,400,000	0.09
Jainism	3,300,000	0.07
Shintoism	3,200,000	0.07
Parsiism (Zoroastrianism)	500,000	0.01
TOTAL		1.1%
UNAFFILIATED		
Nonreligious	805,900,000	16.9%
Atheist	210,500,000	4.4
TOTAL		21.3%
TOTAL	**4,781,200,000**	**100.0%**

CHRISTIANS

Region	Roman Catholic	Orthodox	Protestants & others[1]	Crypto-Christians[2]	Total	% of all Christians & total
Europe	251,100,000	35,800,000	115,700,000	18,300,000	420,900,000	27.2%
Latin America	369,100,000	400,000	21,500,000	1,200,000	392,200,000	25.3
Africa	89,700,000	22,000,000	118,100,000	6,500,000	236,300,000	15.3
North America	86,500,000	5,800,000	134,900,000	0	227,200,000	14.7
South Asia	72,800,000	3,200,000	30,800,000	19,100,000	125,900,000	8.1
USSR	3,900,000	63,000,000	4,500,000	30,800,000	102,200,000	6.6
East Asia	3,600,000	100,000	16,400,000	2,200,000	22,300,000	1.4
Oceania	7,400,000	500,000	13,600,000	0	21,500,000	1.4
TOTAL	884,100,000	130,800,000	455,500,000	78,100,000	1,548,500,000	100.0%

1. Includes some Christian groups not traditionally classified as Protestant.   2. People who identify themselves as Christian but who (often for reasons of personal safety or prudence) are not included in membership lists of any Christian organization.

Geography and Numbers Although Christianity began in the Middle East, the lands of its origin are now dominated by Judaism and Islam. Yet it has spread quite literally to every continent of the world and claims more than 1.5 billion adherents—about one person in every three in the world population. The following table shows adherents by world region.

Christianity is the predominant religion in Europe, North and South America, and Oceania (Australia, New Zealand, and the Pacific Islands). It is also a major force in sub-Saharan Africa and in parts of South Asia. It is least significant in the Middle East and East Asia.

ISLAM

Founder Muhammad, who is seen as a special prophet of the one God. Muhammad was born about A.D. 570 at Mecca (now in Saudi Arabia) and died in 632 in the nearby city of Medina.

Scripture The Koran (original language: Arabic). Muslims believe the Koran to be the word of the one God, spoken to Muhammad by angels.

Beliefs Muhammad began preaching about A.D. 610 and established Islam as a powerful new force before his death in 632. His teachings were based in part on those of Judaism and Christianity. In agreement with these, Muhammad recognized one God. He acknowledged Hebrew history and its religious teachers and recognized Jesus as a prophet. However, Muhammad's was a distinct new revelation. His teachings are contained in the Islamic holy book, the Koran.

Practice A Muslim has five main religious duties:

1. To profess faith in a statement that may be translated, "There is only one God and Muhammad is his prophet."
2. To pray five times each day, facing Mecca. In Islamic countries criers in tall minarets call the times of prayer.
3. To give alms for the support of the faith and of the poor.
4. To observe a solemn fast during Ramadan, the ninth month in the Islamic calendar.
5. To make, at least once in a lifetime, a pilgrimage to Mecca.

Devout Muslims maintain strict rules of conduct. Women are expected to dress modestly,

even to cover their faces in public. Sale and consumption of alcohol is forbidden. As in orthodox Judaism, eating pork is forbidden. Muslim places of worship are called mosques. The principal weekly worship is on Friday at midday.

Schools and Sects The largest division in Islam is between the Sunnites (often called orthodox Muslims), and the Shiites, who have about 20 million members (less than 3% of all Muslims). Most Shiites live in Iran and Iraq, ironically, the two Muslim countries recently involved in a bitter and protracted war against each other. The original cause of the break between Sunnites and Shiites was disagreement about the transferal of power from Muhammad to his descendants. Today Shiites follow somewhat different rituals than those of the Sunnites and recognize additional holy days and holy places (mainly in Iraq and Iran).

History From its earliest days, Islam was a militant faith. During the first 100 years, the leaders established an empire that stretched from Spain to India. In 732 a Muslim army aiming to conquer Europe was defeated at Tours, in southern France. Otherwise, southern Europe might also have become Muslim.

Muslim leaders often allowed practice of other religions in their territories, but eventually many people in the conquered lands became Muslims. The empire broke into smaller units as leaders fought against each other. During the Middle Ages, Christian Europe mounted several attacks on Islamic states, seeking to free the Christian holy lands. These were known as the Crusades. The Europeans had brief successes, but the Middle East remained predominantly Muslim.

In 1453 the Ottoman Turks conquered the important Christian capital of Constantinople. Eventually the city's name was changed to Istanbul. The Turks pushed westward into Europe but were finally defeated near Vienna, Austria, in 1683.

From 1700 to the mid-1900s, many Islamic nations fell under the control of European powers. Europeans brought modern technology and business and, for the most part, a strong prejudice against Islamic laws and ways.

In Muslim countries after World War II, modernist politicians (with strong support from the West) fought many battles against Muslim traditionalists. Beginning in the 1970s, traditionalists, often appealing to the national pride of their people, began a powerful counteroffensive. Muslim traditionalists overthrew the shah of Iran, a major ally of the United States. In 1979 the new government took scores of Americans hostage and held them for more than 500 days.

Geography and Numbers With an estimated 800 million adherents, Islam is the second largest of the major world religions after Christianity. The center of Islam is the Arabian peninsula, where the new faith was established. Mecca and Medina in Saudi Arabia are its holiest places. Predominantly Islamic countries stretch from Morocco in the west to Indonesia in the Far East; these include Egypt, Iran, Pakistan, Bangladesh, and Indonesia.

Saudi Arabia and other oil-producing states of the Arabian peninsula are also influential. Muslims are an important minority in sub-Saharan Africa and the Soviet Union.

HINDUISM

Founder No single teacher founded Hinduism. Its origins are lost in the mists of time. Some elements date to 3000 B.C. Other elements may have been brought by Aryan peoples who invaded India about 1500 B.C. Hinduism has gone through many stages and changed its form many times.

Scripture Many writings are considered part of Hindu scriptures. They include four Vedas, among the oldest religious writings known to humankind; two long epic poems, the *Ramayana* and the *Mahabharata;* and the *Bhagavadgita*, a philosophical part of the *Mahabharata*. Indian holy books include ancient prayers and hymns, instructions for religious rituals, philosophy, and elaborate stories about gods and humans. They were first written down in Sanskrit, an ancient language still learned by devoted Hindus.

Beliefs Hinduism is polytheistic, recognizing not just a handful of gods, but thousands of gods. Among the more important are Brahma, the creator; Vishnu, who preserves the world and may appear as the Hindu hero Krishna; and Siva, the god of destruction. Many Hindus are devoted to Siva's wife, who is known by several names. As Uma, she is a protector and goddess of motherhood. As Kali or Durga, she is a destroyer. Many Hindu deities have mixed powers—they are both good and bad, creative and destructive.

Hindus have a deep respect for all living things—even insects. The holiest animal is the cow. In India cattle roam freely, and killing them for their meat is considered a grave offense. From this respect for life grew the philosophy of Mahatma Gandhi, the hero of Indian independence in the mid-1900s. Gandhi's life and writings inspired people in many parts of the world.

Hindus believe in reincarnation. They believe that when a person dies, his or her soul lives on and appears in a new body. If the person has done good things, the soul may appear in an individual at a higher level of existence. An evil person's soul might reappear in the body of a lowly animal.

MUSLIMS

Region	Adherents	%
South Asia	534,900,000	65.5%
Africa	215,800,000	26.4
USSR	31,500,000	3.9
East Asia	22,300,000	2.7
Europe	9,200,000	1.1
North America	2,600,000	0.3
Latin America	600,000	0.1
Oceania	100,000	0.0
TOTAL	817,000,000	100.0%

HINDUS

Region	Adherents	%
South Asia	644,000,000	99.5%
Africa	1,300,000	0.2
North America	700,000	0.1
Latin America	600,000	0.1
Europe	600,000	0.1
Oceania	300,000	0.0
TOTAL	647,500,000	100.0%

One of the schools of Hindu philosophy is called yoga. A student of yoga learns bodily and mental exercises to help create readiness for meditation. Yoga has become popular in Western countries, often as a nonreligious discipline to enhance physical and emotional health.

Practice Hindu devotion is largely an individual and family matter. Hindus do not form congregations that meet regularly for worship. Many homes have a shrine to honor particularly important gods.

Hindu temples are buildings devoted to a particular god or group of gods. Many Hindus believe that a statue in a temple is the god himself. Priests at a temple may bathe and dress the statue each day and bring it food. A Hindu priest may serve at a particular temple and be devoted to a particular god. Once or twice a year, a temple may celebrate a holy day in honor of its god. Thousands or even millions may come to see or participate in the festival and to give honor to the god. Some of the most famous temples are on the banks of the Ganges and other rivers in India.

Traditional Hinduism observed caste, the division of people into rigid groups by occupation and social standing. The four traditional castes are (1) Brahmans—priestly leaders and their families, (2) Kshatriyas—princes and soldiers, (3) Vaisyas—merchants and landowners, and (4) Sudras—farmers and workers. In addition there was a large group of outcasts—people with no caste and no standing. Known as untouchables, they were ignored and mistreated until modern times. In 1950 the government of India outlawed the caste system. Still, many Hindus prefer to mix primarily with members of their own caste.

Schools and Sects Through its long history, Hinduism has seen many sects. Tantrism, which grew up after A.D. 600, emphasized special rituals as a means of enlightenment. They used mystical diagrams (mandalas) and chants (mantras) in their search. Bhakti, a sect begun after A.D. 1300, emphasized the primacy of love for a deity and used love between humans as an illustration. This sect rejected caste, ritual, and creeds, emphasizing the need for sincerity. Today sects that have melded elements of Hinduism, Christianity, and Islam are seeking converts in India. One of these so-called new religions may develop into a new and distinct world religion.

History From its prehistoric beginnings, Hinduism developed into the first great world religion, extending its influence through the Indian subcontinent and many surrounding regions—especially Sri Lanka, Burma, and parts of Indonesia.

With the rise of Buddhism after 600 B.C., however, Hinduism sank gradually into eclipse. Buddhism dominated India and soon spread through most of the rest of Asia, where it remained a dominant force until recent times. In India, Hinduism gradually regained its primary position. Similarly, after A.D. 650 Islam swept into India from the west. It, too, gained many converts at the expense of Hinduism. Again Hinduism gradually regained its earlier dominance. (Islam remained dominant in the northwestern and northeastern extremities of the subcontinent—now Pakistan and Bangladesh.)

Hinduism has had great influence on distant parts of the world. The founders of Buddhism, Jainism, and Sikhism were all Hindus. The influence of Hinduism in modern times has been mostly indirect. Traditional Hinduism is not a proselytizing religion, and its deep ties to India make it difficult to transport. Still, Hindu doctrines and disciplines promoting meditation have become well known by many in Western countries.

Geography and Numbers Hinduism is the traditional religion of India. Its almost 650 million adherents make it the third-largest religious group in the world after Christianity and Islam. Nearly all practicing Hindus in the world live in India itself or in neighboring South Asia. Outside Asia, Hinduism flourishes mainly in expatriate communities of Indians.

BUDDHISM

Founder Siddhartha Gautama (c. 563–483 B.C.), who came to be known as Buddha. According to Buddhist scriptures, Siddhartha Gautama was born into a princely family on the Indian subcontinent (in the present-day country of Nepal). At the age of 29, he had a series of visions that persuaded him to leave his wife and young son. He wandered for some years seeking enlightenment. One day, while sitting under a bo tree in a village, he gained enlightenment. Soon his followers called him Enlightened One, or Buddha. For the rest of his life (he lived to be perhaps 80 years old), Buddha wandered through northern India teaching.

Scripture The Tripitika, or "three baskets," is a collection of sayings and rules for conduct collected by Buddha's early followers. Nearly all Buddhists reverence the Tripitika, although many treasure other works as well.

Beliefs Buddhists share with Hinduism a belief in the cycle of reincarnation. When a person's body dies, the soul is reborn in another person or animal. Buddha believed there was a way to end this cycle of death and rebirth. He taught that a person should seek a state of detachment from worldly things and desires. Achieving this state, called nirvana, could bring contentment and would be the end of the reincarnation cycle for the soul.

Buddha rejected extreme asceticism and extreme self-indulgence. He recommended a Middle Way. The Buddhist discipline is summarized in the Eightfold Path, which consists of right knowledge, right thought, right action, right livelihood, right effort, right mindfulness, right concentration, and right speech.

Practice From early times Buddhists established orders of monks. The monks withdraw from the everyday world and live austere lives of meditation. They live on alms contributed by lay Buddhists. Although many monks devote their lives to their orders, others may spend a year or two as monks before taking up responsibility as laymen. Early monks served as missionaries, carrying the tenets of Buddhism through all of Asia.

Collective rituals play a smaller part in the life of a Buddhist than in the lives of Jews, Christians, or Moslems. Buddhist temples are primarily for individual meditation.

Schools and Sects The most significant division in Buddhism is between the Therevada and Mahayana schools. Therevada Buddhism, which remains most influential in Sri Lanka, Burma, Thailand, and Cambodia is most traditional in seeking to concentrate on the life and teachings of Gautama. Mahayana Buddhism, which became predominant in China and Japan, offers a more liberal interpretation of Buddhist teachings. It reveres other enlightened teachers, or Buddhas, and emphasizes the importance of each person's seeking to become a bodhisattva, one who seeks Buddhahood through compassion and action as well as contemplation.

A more recent school, Zen, has received particular attention in the Western world. This "meditation" school began in the A.D. 700s. One branch emphasizes mental meditation, finding wisdom in the paradoxical statements (koans) of earlier Zen masters. A second branch emphasizes physical discipline as an aid to true meditation.

History The original teachings of Buddhism were spoken and written in Pali, a language of India. Therevada Buddhists still study Buddhist writings in this language. Therevada missionaries carried Buddhism eastward to the rest of South Asia.

Between 200 B.C. and A.D. 200, Mahayana Buddhism spread widely in China. Chinese missionaries carried the teachings to Korea and Japan. The flowering of Buddhism in China provided a second center for the religion, one in which language and practice differed.

After A.D. 700, in a remarkable shift, Buddhism began to lose its influence in India. Islamic conquests claimed many converts, and Hinduism (having absorbed some Buddhist thinking) reawakened. By 1000, Buddhism was virtually nonexistent in India, but it continued to prosper among India's neighbors to the east.

Geography and Numbers Although Buddhism originated in India, today the vast majority of Buddhists are outside India in neighboring countries to the east and in East

BUDDHISTS

Region	Adherents	%
South Asia	150,900,000	51.0%
East Asia	143,400,000	48.5
Latin America	500,000	0.2
USSR	400,000	0.1
Europe	200,000	0.1
North America	200,000	0.1
TOTAL	295,600,000	100.0%

Asia. Recent estimates are that 300 million people adhere to Buddhist beliefs and practices. Many of these may also observe rituals in other religions, such as folk religion (in China) or Shinto (in Japan).

JUDAISM

Founder Judaism was not founded by a single religious leader. It developed among wandering Semitic tribes who came to be known variously as Hebrews, Israelites, and eventually, Jews. The traditional patriarch of the Jewish people is Abraham, to whom God promised a land of plenty. The lawgiver, some centuries later, was Moses, who received God's commandments at Mount Sinai. The Jewish nation reached its height of power under the kings David and Solomon. The latter built an elaborate and beautiful temple at Jerusalem.

Scripture The Jewish scriptures, originally written and still often read and studied in Hebrew, are the same books Christians call the Old Testament. The first five books, known to Jews as the Torah, have special significance. These books tell of the Covenant God made with the Jewish people and outline the laws (including the Ten Commandments) by which they were to live. The remaining books provide additional history, the exhortations of the prophets, hymns and songs for worship (especially the Psalms), and other poetry and wisdom writings.

Beliefs The early Jews, in contrast to neighboring peoples, worshiped one God, whom they recognized as the Creator of all things and the God of all. Among God's characteristics were both judgment and mercy. His Covenant with the Jews promised them his care and protection; they were to follow his laws. During the time of the prophets, when the Jewish states had declined, the prophets told of the coming of a leader anointed by God—the Messiah. Jews still await the coming of the Messiah.

Practice Jews worship in synagogues, often modest places of worship for a small congregation. Saturday, the seventh day of the week, is the Sabbath, a special day of rest and worship. Worship consists of readings from the scriptures, the chanting or singing of psalms or other songs of praise, and prayer.

JEWS

Region	Adherents	%
North America	7,900,000	44.4%
South Asia	3,900,000	21.9
USSR	3,100,000	17.4
Europe	1,500,000	8.4
Latin America	1,000,000	5.6
Africa	300,000	1.7
Oceania	100,000	0.6
TOTAL	17,800,000	100.0%

Schools and Sects There are three main branches of modern Judaism. Orthodox Judaism is the most conservative branch, observing laws concerning clean and unclean foods, purification, and other ancient rituals. One part of orthodoxy is the Hasidim, fundamentalist sects that grew up in eastern Europe in the 1700s and 1800s.

Reform Judaism, strong in the United States, is the most liberal of the three main branches. Reform Jews seek to follow the spirit of Judaism and are free to disregard part of the ancient rules of conduct and ritual. Reform places of worship are called temples. Some temples resemble Christian churches in their design and in their observances, which may include, for example, music from a pipe organ and choir.

Conservative Judaism seeks a middle road between Orthodox and Reform. It is the most recent of the three branches and is strong in the United States.

History After wealth and influence during the reigns of David and Solomon (c. 1000 B.C.), the Jewish state was divided by dynastic feuds into a northern and a southern kingdom. Both kingdoms eventually fell victim to neighboring peoples. In 587 the southern kingdom (Judah) was overrun by the Babylonians, and many Jews were taken as slaves to Babylon. Solomon's Temple at Jerusalem was destroyed. Fifty years later the Jews were freed, and they rebuilt the temple. In the 100s B.C., the whole region was conquered by Rome. The Jews mounted a revolt against Rome in A.D. 66. This resulted in Roman reprisals, including the destruction of the second temple in A.D. 70. Jews were dispersed in all directions and were to have no land of their own for nearly 1,900 years.

Judaism and the Jewish people survived in many parts of the world. Some lived in Palestine, some in Babylon. Many moved to Europe—especially to Spain, France, Germany, Poland, and western Russia.

Christians of Europe often persecuted the Jews. They passed laws against Jews owning land or engaging in certain businesses. Sometimes mobs of angry people destroyed Jewish settlements and killed the inhabitants. In the 1930s Adolf Hitler and his Nazi party blamed Jews for Germany's defeats and sufferings. He planned to exterminate all the Jews in Europe and succeeded in killing an estimated 6 million. This event is known as the Holocaust.

Even before the Holocaust, Jewish leaders had begun a campaign for the establishment of a Jewish state in the Middle East. After World War II, they received the support of Britain and the United States, and a new country called Israel was carved from Palestine. Since Israel's beginning in 1948, it has often been attacked and harassed by its neighbors, who are Muslim and never agreed to the new state.

Geography and Numbers The largest number of Jews live in North America, to which they emigrated in large numbers between 1880 and 1920. They are concentrated in and near large cities, especially New York. The Jews in South Asia are nearly all residents of Israel. Jews in the USSR have been harassed in recent

years, and many are seeking to emigrate to Israel or the United States.

OTHER RELIGIONS

According to scholars who helped assemble *The World Christian Encyclopedia*, three types of religion (in addition to those listed above) claim tens of millions of adherents in the world. These they call Chinese Folk Religion, New Religions, Tribal Religions. In addition there are many smaller religious groups, some of which have had influence far beyond their present numbers.

Chinese Folk Religion, estimated to be a primary faith for about 180 million people (about 20% of China's population), consists of a blend of ancient ancestor worship with some elements of Buddhism, Confucianism, and Taoism. Confucius, a great Chinese philosopher and teacher, lived in the sixth century B.C. He taught respect for family and ruler. Taoism is a philosophy or religion based on the teachings of Lao Tse, another great teacher of Confucian times. Chinese folk religion is also followed by many in scattered Chinese settlements in other parts of the world.

New Religions are those that have grown up in the past century, principally in Asia. A new religion typically blends elements of (a) local religious tradition and practice; (b) Hinduism, Buddhism, or Islam; and (c) modern Western thought. Whether any of these new religions will develop a truly international following remains to be seen. But together they account for an estimated 100 million adherents, mainly in such Asian countries as Indonesia, the Philippines, and Japan.

Tribal Religions are animistic religions practiced by isolated peoples, primarily in Africa and South Asia.

The more important smaller groups are the following:

Sikhism and **Jainism** are developments from certain strands of Hinduism. There are an estimated 16 million Sikhs and more than 3 million Jains, predominantly in India.

Confucianism is based on the teachings of Confucius, a Chinese teacher of the 500s B.C. Confucianism has had a powerful influence on Chinese history and philosophy. An estimated 5 million people in East Asia consider themselves Confucianists.

Baha'i is a faith recognizing one God and seeking to harmonize the teaching of all major religions. It originated in the 1800s in the Middle East. Its main leader called himself Baha'Ullah, meaning "glory of God." The Baha'i faith has an estimated 4 million adherents worldwide. Its headquarters are in Haifa, Israel. A major U.S. temple in Wilmette, Illinois, attracts many visitors.

Parsees, a people who emigrated centuries ago from Persia (Iran) to India, follow the teachings of the Persian prophet Zoroaster, who lived in the 500s B.C. They are a prosperous sect centered on Bombay, marrying only among themselves and seeking no converts. Estimates of their number range from 200,000 to 500,000.

NONRELIGIOUS AND ATHEISTS

According to *The World Christian Encyclopedia,* more than a billion of the world's people consider themselves nonreligious (agnostic about religious claims) or atheistic (actively opposed to religion). Nearly three-quarters of these people live in East Asia, where they are a majority of the population of China. Nonreligious persons and atheists also make up a majority of people in the Soviet Union.

If the estimates of non- and antireligious peoples are correct, these peoples make up the largest religious bloc in the world after Christianity.

WORLD RELIGIONS: A Brief Chronology

B.C.

c. 3000 Earliest elements of Hinduism develop in India.

c. 2500 Egyptian pyramids at Giza completed.

c. 1500 Aryan peoples invade India; bring additional elements of Hinduism.

c. 1290 Moses leads Jewish people out of Egypt.

1010– Reigns of Jewish kings David and Solo-
922 mon. A great temple built at Jerusalem.

740 Jewish prophet Isaiah flourishes.

628 Traditional birth date of Zoroaster, religious teacher in Persia. Followers today are Parsees in India.

604 Traditional birth date of Chinese teacher Lao-Tzu, a founder of Taoism.

587 Babylonians destroy Jewish temple at Jerusalem and take many Jews as slaves. Fifty years later, Jews are freed; begin to rebuild temple.

560 Birth of Siddhartha Gautama in northern India; later known as Buddha. Dies c. 480. His teachings, on which Buddhism is based, gain many followers in India; later spread to Southeast Asia.

551 Birth of Chinese teacher Confucius. Dies c. 479.

469 Birth of Greek teacher-philosopher Socrates in Athens. His sayings preserved and elaborated on by his student Plato. In 399 Socrates put to death for offenses against the state.

200– Mahayana Buddhism spreads widely
200 in China and Japan.

100s Jewish lands conquered by Roman Empire.

3 Birth of Jesus Christ; Western calendar dated from supposed year of his birth.

A.D.

30 Death and resurrection of Jesus Christ. By 100, Christians are in many parts of present-day Greece, Turkey, Syria, Lebanon, Israel, Egypt, despite active persecution by Romans.

66– Jewish revolt against Romans ends in
70 destruction of second temple and scattering of Jews in all directions.

175 Apostles' Creed, a brief statement of Christian beliefs, formulated.

303– In final organized program of persecu-
12 tion, Romans kill estimated 500,000 Christians.

313 The emperor Constantine decrees toleration for Christianity in Roman Empire. In 325 he calls synod of Nicaea, which formulates Nicene Creed. By end of 300s, Christianity is official religion of empire.

354 Birth of St. Augustine, influential Christian teacher, in North Africa. Dies 430.

570 Muhammad, founder of Islam, born at Mecca (now in Saudi Arabia). Dies in 632 in nearby city of Medina.

600 + Tantrism, a Hindu school, grows up, emphasizing special rituals as means of enlightenment; uses mystical diagrams (mandalas) and chants (mantras).

650 + Islam sweeps into India; gains many converts.

700 + Development in China of Zen, a school of Buddhism, which has received particular attention in the modern Western world.

732 A Muslim army aiming to conquer Europe defeated by Franks at Tours in southern France.

988 Christianity reaches Russia through missionaries from eastern churches.

1054 Eastern (or Orthodox) and Western (or Roman) churches go separate ways after disputes about doctrine and authority.

1096 Christians in Europe go on first Crusade to take Holy Land from Muslims. Seven other major Crusades pursued between 1100 and 1300. Christian warriors temporarily occupy Jerusalem and other cities but soon lose them again to Muslims.

1227 Birth of Thomas Aquinas, great Christian theologian, in Italy.

1300 + Bhakti, a Hindu sect, develops, emphasizing primacy of love for a deity and using love between humans as illustration; rejects caste, ritual, and creeds and emphasizes need for sincerity.

1452 Ottoman Turks (Muslims) conquer capital of Eastern Christian church, Constantinople. Eventually, city's name changed to Istanbul. Turks push westward into Europe.

1469 Birth of Nanak, founder of Sikhism, in Punjab region of India.

1517 Martin Luther, a German priest, posts 95 theses on cathedral door, questioning church teachings. Luther refuses to recant; is excommunicated from Catholic church. With cooperation of north German princes, he forms new Protestant churches. This begins Reformation, which ultimately divides European Christianity into two warring camps.

1534 King Henry VIII of England denies power of pope over church in England and establishes Church of England responsible to monarch. New church gradually adopts Protestant beliefs but maintains many practices of earlier Catholic era.

1536 John Calvin, a young French scholar, publishes *Institutes of the Christian Religion,* and becomes second major leader of Protestant Christianity, helping to create Presbyterian and other Reformed churches.

1540 Ignatius Loyola, a Spaniard, establishes the Jesuits (Society of Jesus) with papal approval. This order becomes powerful instrument of Catholic church, both in disputes with Protestants, in missionary efforts around world, and in education.

1545– Council of Trent makes major reforms
63 in Catholic church and defines disagreements with Protestants. Its work begins Catholic Reformation, or Counter-Reformation.

1618– Thirty Years War, caused in part by
48 Protestant-Catholic hatreds, decimates central Europe. Calvinist leaders in England overthrow monarchy and execute king in civil war (1642–49). Monarchy is restored in 1660.

1620 Pilgrims, a small group of English Calvinists, establish colony at Plymouth in North America to escape persecution in England. They are first of thou-

NONRELIGIOUS AND ATHEISTS

	Nonreligious	Atheist	Total	%
East Asia	618,900,000	123,400,000	742,300,000	73.0%
USSR	83,100,000	60,600,000	143,700,000	14.1
Europe	49,400,000	17,400,000	66,800,000	6.6
South Asia	18,400,000	5,100,000	23,500,000	2.3
North America	19,000,000	1,000,000	20,000,000	2.0
Latin America	12,900,000	2,400,000	15,300,000	1.5
Oceania	2,900,000	500,000	3,400,000	0.3
Africa	1,300,000	100,000	1,400,000	0.1
TOTAL	805,900,000	210,500,000	1,016,400,000	100.0%

sands of Calvinists to settle in present-day New England.

1683 Muslim Turks defeated near Vienna, Austria, in their last attempt to establish foothold in western Europe.

1734 The Great Awakening, a religious revival, sweeps New England, begun by prominent Massachusetts preacher Jonathan Edwards. English evangelist George Whitefield tours American colonies beginning in 1738, preaching to outdoor gatherings.

1738 Christian conversion experienced by brothers John and Charles Wesley in England. They begin evangelical activities, leading to development of independent Methodist church.

1792 Second Awakening sweeps new United States, lasting more than 20 years. Revivals in Kentucky in 1800 result in formation of new denominations, ancestors of Disciples of Christ, Churches of Christ, and Christian churches.

1830 American Joseph Smith has religious visions that lead him to organize the Church of Jesus Christ of the Latter-Day Saints (Mormons). Movement grows rapidly but generates intense opposition. Smith murdered by anti-Mormons in 1844.

1844 Faith of Baha'i established in Iran as offshoot of Islam. It seeks to harmonize teachings of all major religions.

1869–79 Vatican Council I, convened by Pope Pius IX, declares that teachings of pope in matters of faith and morals are infallible.

1875 Mary Baker Eddy publishes *Science and Health with Key to the Scriptures*, in Boston; it becomes basis of Church of Christ, Scientist.

1900 First documented modern Pentecostal experience—worshipers speak in unknown tongues during prayer meeting in Kansas. Within 20 years, Pentecostal churches form major new Christian denomination.

1938–45 German government carries out destruction of estimated 6 million European Jews. This event known as the Holocaust.

1948 Allied powers guarantee new state of Israel in Middle East for settlement by Jews.

1948 World Council of Churches established at huge assembly in Amsterdam. This ecumenical organization supported by many Protestant, Anglican, and Orthodox denominations. Headquarters are in Geneva, Switzerland.

1962–65 Vatican Council II, convened by Pope John XXIII, announces many liberalizing changes in Roman Catholic liturgy and practice; supports cautious involvement in ecumenical discussions with other Christians.

1966 Six-Day War between Israel and its Muslim neighbors. Israel occupies West Bank and Gaza strip.

1979 Fundamentalist Muslims take control of Iran; take U.S. nationals hostage.

WORLD POPULATION

World population has now surpassed 5 billion and continues to increase, with striking differences in population growth rates, fertility rates, and life expectancy among countries and regions. A child born this year in Switzerland, Hong Kong, and Japan, for example, may expect to live about 78 years, but one born in The Gambia, Western Sahara, or Chad may expect to live only about 40 years. In Afghanistan, one of each six children born will die before its first birthday, but in Japan only one in 172 will die (in the United States, one in 94).

The countries and areas listed here are classified by development categories according to the UN format. While the United Nations does not issue a precise definition, "developed" countries and regions are considered to be the industrialized nations, those with a high gross national product (GNP) and a high per capita GNP, and those with high levels of science and technology. The developed countries and areas include all of North America and Europe, as well as the Soviet Union, Japan, Australia, and New Zealand.

"Developing" countries are also not defined, but are generally understood to be nations whose populations are poorer, whose economy is based on agricultural production, whose GNP and per capita GNP is low, and who lack advanced technologies. In general, developing countries are members of the Group of 77 (G-77), currently 125 countries (see "International Political, Economic, and Military Organizations," "Group of 77"). Developing countries and areas include all of sub-Saharan Africa, the Near East and North Africa, Latin America and the Caribbean, Asia (except Japan), and Oceania (except Australia and New Zealand).

In 1950 two-thirds of the world's population lived in developing countries; by 1987 the rate had increased to three-fourths. Asia has the world's largest landmass and holds just over half of the world's people. The other half are about evenly distributed between the developed nations and the remaining developing regions.

WORLD BIRTHS, DEATHS, AND POPULATION GROWTH, 1989

Births	142,527,300
Deaths	49,966,900
Natural increase	92,561,000
Births per 1,000 population	27.0
Deaths per 1,000 population	10.0
Growth rate (percent)	1.8

AVERAGE ANNUAL GROWTH RATE, BY REGION AND DEVELOPMENT CATEGORY, 1950–2025 (by percent)

Region	1950–1960	1960–1970	1970–1980	1980–1990	1990–2000	2000–2025
World	1.7%	2.0%	1.8%	1.7%	1.6%	1.3%
Developed	1.3	1.0	0.8	0.6	0.5	0.3
Developing	1.9	2.4	2.2	2.0	1.9	1.5
Sub-Saharan Africa	2.1	2.5	2.7	3.0	3.1	2.7
Near East and North Africa	2.6	2.6	2.8	2.8	2.7	2.2
Asia	1.7	2.2	2.0	1.7	1.5	1.1
Developed	1.2	1.0	1.1	0.5	0.4	-0.1
Developing	1.8	2.3	2.1	1.7	1.6	1.2
Latin America and the Caribbean	2.7	2.7	2.4	2.2	1.9	1.4
North America	1.8	1.3	1.1	0.9	0.7	0.4
Europe	0.8	0.8	0.5	0.3	0.2	Z
Soviet Union	1.7	1.2	0.9	0.8	0.7	0.6
Oceania	2.3	2.1	1.6	1.4	1.3	0.9
Developed	2.2	1.9	1.4	1.2	1.0	0.6
Developing	2.3	2.7	2.5	2.3	2.2	1.7
Excluding China						
World	1.8	1.9	1.9	1.8	1.7	1.5
Developing	2.2	2.4	2.4	2.3	2.2	1.8
Asia	1.9	2.2	2.1	2.0	1.8	1.3
Developing	2.0	2.3	2.2	2.1	1.9	1.4

Note: Z = between 0.5 and –0.5%. **Source:** U.S. Bureau of the Census, *World Population Profile: 1987* (1987).

WORLD POPULATION TRENDS

Currently, about 90 million people are added each year to the world's total population, more than the present population of Mexico. During the period 2015–20, the annual increment is projected to be nearly 100 million. In 1987 the world's population reached over 5 billion for the first time. Latest population projections indicate that it will take just over 50 years for the second 5 billion to be added. For although the population growth rate is projected to decline from 1.7% in 1987 to 1.3% in the period 2015–20, the average net number of people will continue to rise because the percentage increase of the population is larger than the percentage decline of the growth rate.

During the next half-century, all regions of Europe and Japan are anticipated to have declining populations. In fact, the process has already begun. Between 1980 and 1985 the populations of Denmark, East Germany, West Germany, and Hungary declined and that trend is expected to continue into the next century.

But in other areas, Africa specifically, the trend is quite different. Africa's infant mortality rate is 42% higher than the world average, its overall death rate 58% higher, its birth rate 68% higher, and its population growth rate 82% higher. According to the most recent projections, from 1950 to 2050, the population of Africa south of the Sahara will have grown from just 7% to nearly 21% of the world total.

During this period the world population will have experienced a fourfold increase, from 2.56 billion to 10.81 billion, while that of sub-Saharan Africa will have experienced a twelvefold increase, from 186 million to 2.26 billion.

WORLD POPULATION PROJECTIONS

1990	5,319,719,000
2000	6,240,748,000
2025	8,675,128,000
2050	10,805,207,000

NUMBER OF YEARS BETWEEN EACH BILLION ADDED TO WORLD POPULATION

Year	World Population	Number of years for next billion
1801	1 billion	N.A.
1925	2 billion	124
1959	3 billion	34
1974	4 billion	15
1986	5 billion	12
1997	6 billion	11
2008	7 billion	11
2018	8 billion	10
2028	9 billion	10
2040	10 billion	12

Source: U.S. Bureau of the Census, *World Population Profile: 1987* (1987).

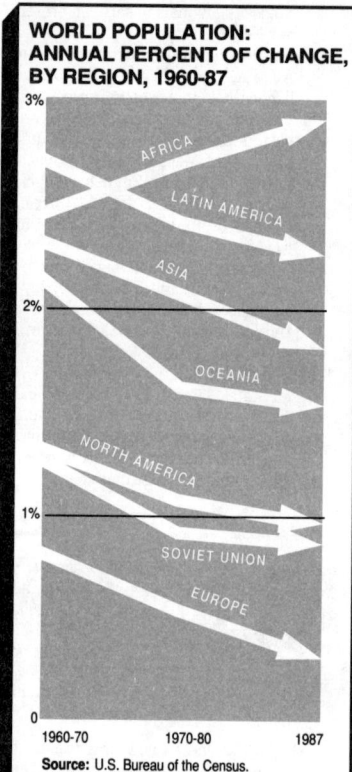

WORLD POPULATION: ANNUAL PERCENT OF CHANGE, BY REGION, 1960-87

AFRICA
LATIN AMERICA
ASIA
OCEANIA
NORTH AMERICA
SOVIET UNION
EUROPE

1960-70   1970-80   1987

Source: U.S. Bureau of the Census.

WORLD POPULATION BY REGION AND DEVELOPMENT CATEGORY, 1950–2025
(in millions)

Region	1950	1960	1970	1980	1990	2000	2025
WORLD	**2,565**	**3,050**	**3,721**	**4,476**	**5,320**	**6,241**	**8,675**
Developed	832	945	1,049	1,137	1,211	1,269	1,351
Developing	1,733	2,105	2,672	3,339	4,109	4,971	7,324
Sub-Saharan Africa	186	228	292	383	514	699	1,385
Near East and North Africa	120	154	199	264	351	461	803
Asia	1,343	1,596	1,996	2,440	2,906	3,381	4,462
Developed	84	94	104	117	124	129	127
Developing	1,260	1,502	1,892	2,323	2,783	3,252	4,335
Latin America and the Caribbean	166	218	286	365	455	551	789
North America	166	199	226	252	277	296	328
Europe	392	425	460	484	499	510	506
Soviet Union	180	214	243	266	291	312	364
Oceania	12	16	19	23	26	30	38
Developed	10	13	15	18	20	22	26
Developing	2	3	4	5	6	8	12
Excluding China							
World	2,002	2,399	2,901	3,493	4,205	4,998	7,193
Developing	1,170	1,454	1,852	2,356	2,994	3,729	5,842
Asia	781	945	1,176	1,457	1,792	2,138	2,980
Developing	697	851	1,071	1,340	1,668	2,010	2,853

Note: Figures may not add to totals owing to rounding. **Source:** U.S. Bureau of the Census, *World Population Profile: 1987* (1987).

VITAL EVENTS AND RATES BY REGION AND DEVELOPMENT CATEGORY, 1987

Region	Births (thousands)	Deaths (thousands)	Natural increase	Births per 1,000	Deaths per 1,000	Rate of natural increase
WORLD	137,273	49,796	87,477	27	10	1.7%
Developed	17,899	11,566	6,333	15	10	0.5
Developing	119,374	38,230	81,145	31	10	2.1
Sub-Saharan Africa	21,416	7,288	14,128	46	16	3.0
Near East and North Africa	12,606	3,449	9,157	39	11	2.8
Asia	73,995	25,226	48,769	27	9	1.8
Developed	1,457	851	607	12	7	0.5
Developing	72,538	24,376	48,162	27	9	1.8
Latin America and the Caribbean	12,615	3,060	9,555	30	7	2.2
North America	4,129	2,316	1,813	15	9	0.7
Europe	6,503	5,229	1,275	13	11	0.3
Soviet Union	5,507	3,022	2,485	19	11	0.9
Oceania	501	204	297	20	8	1.2
Developed	302	148	154	16	8	0.8
Developing	199	56	143	34	10	2.5
Excluding China						
World	115,686	42,450	73,236	29	11	1.8
Developing	97,787	30,884	66,903	35	11	2.4
Asia	52,407	17,880	34,527	31	11	2.0
Developing	50,950	17,030	33,921	33	11	2.2

Source: U.S. Bureau of the Census, *World Population Profile: 1987* (1987).

THE WORLD'S MOST POPULOUS NATIONS RANKED BY POPULATION SIZE, 1950–2050

Shifting population size in developed and developing nations is causing dramatic changes in the ranking of countries by population. In 1950 Iran was 28th in size, moved to 21st in 1987 and is projected to be the 10th-largest country by 2025. Nigeria and Pakistan, ranked 13th and 14th in 1950, are expected to become the 3rd- and 4th-largest countries by 2050. As populations in developing countries continue to increase, populations in developed regions have already begun to decline and are projected to continue decreasing. The United Kingdom was eighth in size in 1950, dropped to 16th in 1987, and is projected to be 27th by 2025, and not on the list of top 30 countries by 2050. Similarly, West Germany dropped from ninth position in 1950 to 14th in 1987 and is projected to be 29th by 2025 and not on the list by 2050.

1950	1987	2025	2050
1. China	1. China	1. China	1. India
2. India	2. India	2. India	2. China
3. Soviet Union	3. Soviet Union	3. Soviet Union	3. Nigeria
4. United States	4. United States	4. Indonesia	4. Pakistan
5. Japan	5. Indonesia	5. Nigeria	5. Soviet Union
6. Indonesia	6. Brazil	6. United States	6. Brazil
7. Brazil	7. Japan	7. Indonesia	7. Indonesia
8. United Kingdom	8. Nigeria	8. Pakistan	8. United States
9. West Germany	9. Bangladesh	9. Bangladesh	9. Bangladesh
10. Italy	10. Pakistan	10. Iran	10. Iran
11. Bangladesh	11. Mexico	11. Ethiopia	11. Ethiopia
12. France	12. Vietnam	12. Mexico	12. Philippines
13. Nigeria	13. Philippines	13. Philippines	13. Mexico
14. Pakistan	14. West Germany	14. Vietnam	14. Vietnam
15. Mexico	15. Italy	15. Japan	15. Kenya
16. Spain	16. United Kingdom	16. Egypt	16. Zaire
17. Vietnam	17. France	17. Turkey	17. Egypt
18. Poland	18. Thailand	18. Zaire	18. Tanzania
19. Egypt	19. Turkey	19. Kenya	19. Turkey
20. Philippines	20. Egypt	20. Thailand	20. Japan
21. Turkey	21. Iran	21. Tanzania	21. Saudi Arabia
22. South Korea	22. Ethiopia	22. Burma	22. Thailand
23. Ethiopia	23. South Korea	23. South Africa	23. Uganda
24. Thailand	24. Spain	24. Sudan	24. Sudan
25. Burma	25. Burma	25. South Korea	25. Burma
26. East Germany	26. Poland	26. France	26. South Africa
27. Argentina	27. South Africa	27. United Kingdom	27. Syria
28. Iran	28. Zaire	28. Italy	28. Morocco
29. Yugoslavia	29. Argentina	29. West Germany	29. Algeria
30. Romania	30. Colombia	30. Uganda	30. Iraq

Note: Developing countries are shown in **bold**.   **Source:** U.S. Bureau of the Census, *World Population Profile: 1987* (1987).

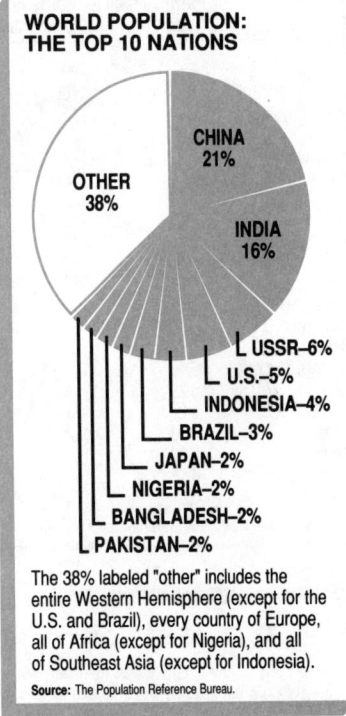

WORLD POPULATION: THE TOP 10 NATIONS

OTHER 38%

CHINA 21%

INDIA 16%

USSR–6%
U.S.–5%
INDONESIA–4%
BRAZIL–3%
JAPAN–2%
NIGERIA–2%
BANGLADESH–2%
PAKISTAN–2%

The 38% labeled "other" includes the entire Western Hemisphere (except for the U.S. and Brazil), every country of Europe, all of Africa (except for Nigeria), and all of Southeast Asia (except for Indonesia).

Source: The Population Reference Bureau.

COUNTRIES WITH LOWEST BIRTH RATES AND INFANT MORTALITY RATES, 1987

Country	Birth rate	Infant mortality rate (per 1,000 live births)	Country	Birth rate	Infant mortality rate (per 1,000 live births)
Monaco	1.12	11	Sweden	1.73	6
San Marino	1.30	11	Spain	1.74	12
West Germany	1.34	8	East Germany	1.76	11
Hong Kong	1.38	7	Cuba	1.78	17
Italy	1.44	8	United Kingdom	1.78	9
Luxembourg	1.46	9	Japan	1.79	6
Denmark	1.49	7	France	1.81	9
Austria	1.50	9	Taiwan	1.81	19
Netherlands	1.53	8	Malta	1.82	9
Switzerland	1.54	6	Hungary	1.84	20
Belgium	1.57	8	United States	1.84	11
Liechtenstein	1.60	10	Portugal	1.85	16
Singapore	1.62	9	Iceland	1.90	7
Finland	1.66	7	New Zealand	1.91	10
Canada	1.68	8	Australia	1.92	8
Norway	1.68	8	Bulgaria	1.93	18
Antigua and Barbuda	1.69	10			
Greece	1.69	12			

Source: U.S. Bureau of the Census, *World Population Profile: 1987* (1987).

COUNTRIES WITH HIGHEST BIRTH RATES AND INFANT MORTALITY RATES, 1987

Country	Birth rate	Infant mortality rate (per 1,000 live births)
Rwanda	8.49	122
Kenya	7.94	94
Benin	7.87	167
North Yemen	7.75	137
Malawi	7.68	137
Somalia	7.29	133
Mauritania	7.25	100
South Yemen	7.25	118
Western Sahara	7.25	176
Iraq	7.23	86
Tanzania	7.09	113
Maldives	7.07	87
Comoros	7.05	96
Ethiopia	7.03	118
Uganda	7.02	103
Zambia	7.00	87
Madagascar	6.94	103
Saudi Arabia	6.94	79
Syria	6.92	43
Congo	6.85	112
Niger	6.80	140
Botswana	6.75	66
Jordan	6.75	57
Angola	6.72	115
Cape Verde	6.69	70
Ivory Coast	6.69	107
Oman	6.69	112

Country	Birth rate	Infant mortality rate (per 1,000 live births)
Senegal	6.65	99
Namibia	6.64	76
Solomon Islands	6.64	43
Togo	6.64	117
Pakistan	6.62	122
Afghanistan	6.60	178
Mali	6.59	155
Zimbabwe	6.59	72
Burkina Faso	6.56	143
Burundi	6.55	117
Nigeria	6.55	124
Sudan (North)	6.52	103
Mozambique	6.49	147
Djibouti	6.44	126
Gambia, The	6.40	177
Iran	6.29	113
Liberia	6.27	124
Swaziland	6.23	132
Zaire	6.22	112
Sierra Leone	6.18	163
Guinea	6.07	154

Source: U.S. Bureau of the Census, *World Population Profile: 1987* (1987).

URBANIZATION

According to the U.S. Census Bureau, 29% of the world's population lived in urban areas in 1950; by 1970, 37% did. The movement of millions of people from rural areas to urban complexes then continued with even greater intensity, so that by 1985, 45% of the world's population were urban dwellers.

In 1950, 54% of the people in developed regions lived in urban areas; in developing regions, 17% were urban dwellers. By 1985 urbanization had reached 72% in the developed areas and 36% in developing countries. In other words, from 1950 to 1985, nearly 1.5 billion people were added to urban areas in developing regions, while the developed urban areas added 400 million people.

The U.S. Census Bureau projects that from 1985 to 2000, the urban areas in developing regions will add one billion inhabitants, while those in the developed urban areas will add 200 million. At that point, 52% of the world's total population will be living in urban centers; the developed regions will be 75% urbanized and the developing areas 47%. Demographers estimate that by 2000, half the world's people will be living in urban areas; almost eight out of 10 people in developed regions, and almost five out of 10 in developing countries will be urban residents.

Trends in World Urbanization In 1970 there were 62 urban areas of 2 million or more inhabitants; by 1985 there were 99, 12 with 10 million or more inhabitants, and eight of these were in less-developed regions. The nine countries containing the world's 12 largest urban areas constitute 52% of the world's population. Among the 99 urban areas, 35 were in developed countries in 1985.

By 2000, 23 urban areas are expected to have more than 10 million people, 17 of these areas in less-developed countries and six in more-developed regions.

Africa has six urban areas with more than 2 million residents: Alexandria, Egypt; Algiers, Algeria; Cairo/Giza, Egypt; Casablanca, Morocco; Kinshasa, Zaire; and Lagos, Nigeria. They are expected to increase at an annual growth rate of 3.8% during 1985–2000.

Asia contains 44 of the 99 large urban areas, including 14 in China, nine in India, and four in Japan. The projected annual growth rate of urban areas in Asia, excluding China and Japan, is 3.3% between 1985 and 2000, implying a population increase of 64% of the urban areas in the 15-year period.

Latin America is the most urbanized region among the less-developed areas; 69% of the population lived in urban areas in 1985, and experts project this will rise to 77% by 2000. Of its 14 large urban areas, four are among the 12 largest in the world, each with a population of over 10 million in 1985: Mexico City, Mexico; São Paulo, Brazil; Buenos Aires, Argentina; and Rio de Janeiro, Brazil.

Some urban areas in the United States and Europe have experienced declines in population in recent years. Five urban areas are projected to remain at the same level during 1985–2000: Hamburg, West Germany; London and Manchester, United Kingdom; Detroit and New York, United States. Only three of the 12 most populous cities in 1985, New York, London, and Los Angeles, are from these regions. Projections indicate that by 2000, only New York will rank among the 12 most populous cities of the world.

Over 85% of the population in Australia and New Zealand lives in urban areas, and very little increase in the level of urbanization can be foreseen.

Urban areas in more developed regions are growing more slowly than those in less-developed countries. By the end of this century, the Tokyo-Yokohama complex will reach 20 million people, and the New York, London, Los Angeles, Osaka-Kobe, and Moscow metropolitan areas will grow to more than 10 million residents each.

In less-developed regions, urban areas are growing rapidly in both number and size, and the United Nations estimates that by the year 2000 more than 20 of the 30 largest cities in the world will be in developing countries. Mexico City is projected to reach 26 million and São Paulo about 24 million. Bombay and Calcutta are each expected to exceed 16 million, and Seoul, Rio de Janeiro, Jakarta, Tehran, Delhi, and Shanghai are each forecast to reach 13 million.

Rural Population

Rural population growth has been relatively modest. In fact, most developed countries have been losing rural population since around 1950 and will continue to do so in the future. However, in developing countries, especially in Africa and Asia, the growth in rural population is still quite significant. According to the U.S. Census Bureau, the world's rural population doubled from 1950 to 1985, from approximately

WORLD'S LARGEST URBAN AREAS PROJECTED FOR 2000 (population in millions)

The following 23 urban areas are projected to contain over 10 million inhabitants each in 2000. Only six are in developed regions: Tokyo/Yokohama, New York, London, Los Angeles, Osaka/Kobe, and Moscow.

City, country	Projected population
1. Mexico City, Mexico	25.82
2. São Paulo, Brazil	23.97
3. Tokyo/Yokohama, Japan	20.22
4. Calcutta, India	16.53
5. Bombay, India	16.00
6. New York, United States	15.78
7. Shanghai, China	14.30
8. Seoul, South Korea	13.77
9. Tehran, Iran	13.58
10. Rio de Janeiro, Brazil	13.26
11. Jakarta, Indonesia	13.25
12. Delhi, India	13.24
13. Buenos Aires, Argentina	13.18
14. Karachi, Pakistan	12.00
15. Beijing, China	11.17
16. Dhaka, Bangladesh	11.16
17. Cairo/Giza, Egypt	11.13
18. Manila/Quezon City, Philippines	11.07
19. Los Angeles, United States	10.99
20. Osaka/Kobe, Japan	10.49
21. Bangkok, Thailand	10.71
22. London, United Kingdom	10.51
23. Moscow, USSR	10.40

Source: United Nations, Department for International Economic and Social Affairs, *The Prospects of World Urbanization: Revised as of 1984–85* (1987).

WORLD CITIES WITH GREATEST POPULATION DENSITY, 1989

Urban area, country	Pop. density per sq. mi.
1. Hong Kong, Hong Kong	247,004
2. Lagos, Nigeria	129,705
3. Dhaka, Bangladesh	125,511
4. Jakarta, Indonesia	122,033
5. Bombay, India	120,299
6. Ho Chi Minh City, Vietnam	114,914
7. Ahmadabad, India	108,618
8. Shenyang, China	108,080
9. Tianjin, China	97,291
10. Chengdu, China	93,242
11. Cairo, Egypt	92,168

Source: U.S. Bureau of the Census, International Data Base (1989).

1.8 billion to 2.7 billion, and is expected to reach 3 billion by 2000. While rural population in the developed regions decreased from 385 million to 335 million, in developing regions it nearly doubled, from 1.4 billion to 2.4 billion.

In the same time frame, the population in Latin America and the Caribbean had modest growth, from 98 million to 127 million. Asia's total rural population increased from 1.1 to 1.8

billion, with most growth in its developing regions. Developed regions in Asia had a net loss of rural population from 42 million in 1950 to 28 million in 1985.

North America, Europe, and the Soviet Union experienced rural population decreases also, from 341 million to 304 million in the same period.

Just as the rural areas are losing people, they also are losing land. As people move into urban areas, those areas are expanding their boundaries to claim more and more once-rural land. For example, New Delhi appropriated more than 14,000 hectares between 1941 to 1971. The Food and Agricultural Organization (FAO) estimates that about 1.4 billion hectares of arable land will be claimed by urban development worldwide between 1980 and 2000. Urban areas in developing countries are expected to double in area from about 8 million hectares to more than 17 million. The FAO projects that more than 476,000 hectares of land a year will be built up in developing countries over the 20-year period. Population projections indicate that only after 2020 will there be a significant decline in rural population growth in these regions.

POPULATION OF THE WORLD'S LARGEST URBAN AREAS, 1960–2000, RANKED BY 1985 POPULATION (population in millions)

The following urban areas had populations of 2 million or more in 1985. An urban area is a central city, or several cities, and the surrounding urbanized areas; also called a metropolitan area.

Urban area	1960	1970	1985	1990[1]	2000[1]	Urban area	1960	1970	1985	1990[1]	2000[1]
1. Tokyo/Yokohama, Japan	10.69	14.91	18.82	19.28	20.22	51. Belo Horizonte, Brazil	0.89	1.63	3.25	3.89	5.11
2. Mexico City, Mexico	5.22	9.12	17.30	20.25	25.82	52. Barcelona, Spain	1.94	2.66	3.20	3.24	3.35
3. São Paulo, Brazil	4.84	8.22	15.88	18.77	23.97	53. Toronto, Canada	1.76	2.55	3.16	3.33	3.58
4. New York, United States	14.23	16.29	15.64	15.69	15.78	54. Melbourne, Australia	1.88	2.34	3.15	3.23	3.41
5. Shanghai, China	10.67	11.41	11.96	12.35	14.30	55. Ahmadabad, India	1.21	1.74	3.14	3.76	5.28
6. Calcutta, India	5.62	7.12	10.95	12.54	16.53	56. Hyderabad, India	1.27	1.80	3.12	3.70	5.13
7. Buenos Aires, Argentina	6.93	8.55	10.88	11.71	13.18	57. Istanbul, Turkey	1.45	2.78	2.94	2.98	3.29
8. Rio de Janeiro, Brazil	5.07	7.17	10.37	11.37	13.26	58. Alexandria, Egypt	1.51	2.02	2.93	3.35	4.40
9. London, United Kingdom	10.73	10.59	10.36	10.40	10.51	59. Washington, D.C., United States	1.83	2.50	2.91	3.03	3.22
10. Seoul, South Korea	2.39	5.42	10.28	11.66	13.77	60. Ankara, Turkey	0.64	1.27	2.90	3.63	5.20
11. Bombay, India	4.15	5.98	10.07	11.79	16.00	61. Birmingham, United Kingdom	2.67	2.81	2.87	2.89	2.93
12. Los Angeles, United States	6.56	8.43	10.05	10.48	10.99	62. Montreal, Canada	2.04	2.70	2.84	2.86	2.90
13. Osaka/Kobe, Japan	5.75	7.61	9.45	9.82	10.49	63. Houston, United States	1.16	1.70	2.83	3.19	3.65
14. Beijing, China	7.31	8.29	9.25	9.59	11.17	64. Guadalajara, Mexico	0.93	1.58	2.77	3.20	4.11
15. Moscow, USSR	6.29	7.07	8.97	9.54	10.40	65. Pôrto Alegre, Brazil	1.04	1.55	2.74	3.18	4.02
16. Paris, France	7.23	8.34	8.68	8.68	8.72	66. Recife, Brazil	1.24	1.82	2.74	3.04	3.65
17. Jakarta, Indonesia	2.81	4.48	7.94	9.48	13.25	67. Rangoon, Burma	0.96	1.42	2.73	3.17	4.32
18. Tianjin, China	5.98	6.87	7.89	8.25	9.70	68. Boston, United States	2.43	2.67	2.71	2.74	2.83
19. Cairo/Giza, Egypt	4.46	5.69	7.69	8.64	11.13	69. Chongqing, China	2.15	2.46	2.70	2.81	3.33
20. Tehran, Iran	1.79	3.29	7.52	9.38	13.58	70. Casablanca, Morocco	1.10	1.54	2.69	3.24	4.49
21. Delhi, India	2.33	3.64	7.40	9.13	13.24	71. Kinshasa, Zaire	0.50	1.23	2.69	3.30	5.04
22. Milan, Italy	4.51	5.52	7.22	7.53	8.15	72. Dallas, United States	1.16	2.04	2.68	2.87	3.13
23. Manila/Quezon City, Philippines	2.32	3.60	7.03	8.26	11.07	73. Athens, Greece	1.81	2.10	2.68	2.80	3.04
24. Chicago, United States	6.00	6.76	6.84	6.90	7.03	74. Chengdu, China	1.12	1.58	2.67	3.02	3.87
25. Karachi, Pakistan	1.82	3.14	6.70	8.16	12.00	75. Algiers, Algeria	0.87	1.19	2.66	3.38	5.09
26. Bangkok, Thailand	2.19	3.27	6.07	7.38	10.71	76. Ho Chi Minh City, Vietnam	1.53	2.30	2.62	2.85	3.75
27. Lima/Callao, Peru	1.75	2.92	5.68	6.78	9.14	77. Kiev, USSR	1.19	1.65	2.61	2.92	3.44
28. Madras, India	1.74	3.12	5.19	6.03	8.15	78. Harbin, China	1.55	2.00	2.61	2.82	3.46
29. Hong Kong, Hong Kong	2.74	3.53	5.13	5.62	6.37	79. Singapore, Singapore	1.27	1.58	2.56	2.70	2.95
30. Leningrad, USSR	3.46	3.96	5.11	5.43	5.93	80. Monterrey, Mexico	0.93	1.28	2.53	3.01	3.97
31. Dhaka, Bangladesh	0.66	1.54	4.89	6.53	11.16	81. Manchester, United Kingdom	2.53	2.53	2.50	2.51	2.53
32. Madrid, Spain	2.22	3.37	4.71	4.95	5.36	82. Taibai, China	0.97	1.50	2.50	2.84	3.68
33. Bogotá, Colombia	1.32	2.37	4.49	5.27	6.53	83. Zibo, China	0.80	1.30	2.39	2.78	3.66
34. Baghdad, Iraq	1.02	2.10	4.42	5.34	7.42	84. Surabaja, Indonesia	0.98	1.53	2.37	2.73	3.68
35. Philadelphia, United States	3.66	4.05	4.18	4.24	4.36	85. Turin, Italy	1.25	1.62	2.26	2.40	2.61
36. Santiago, Chile	2.12	3.01	4.16	4.55	5.26	86. Xi'an, China	1.34	1.73	2.26	2.44	3.00
37. Naples, Italy	3.20	3.59	4.11	4.15	4.30	87. Salvador, Brazil	0.73	1.16	2.24	2.65	3.45
38. Pusan, South Korea	1.17	1.85	4.11	4.90	6.20	88. Bucharest, Romania	1.40	1.69	2.23	2.37	2.64
39. Shenyang, China	2.47	3.14	4.08	4.39	5.35	89. Liupanshui, China	1.19	1.66	2.19	2.37	2.92
40. Bangalore, India	1.20	1.66	3.97	5.14	7.96	90. Hamburg, West Germany	2.09	2.20	2.19	2.19	2.19
41. Detroit, United States	3.56	3.99	3.83	3.86	3.96	91. Nanjing, China	1.45	1.78	2.14	2.28	2.75
42. Sydney, Australia	2.14	2.68	3.78	3.93	4.23	92. Poona, India	0.74	1.13	2.13	2.58	3.69
43. Caracas, Venezuela	1.31	2.12	3.74	4.18	5.03	93. Tashkent, USSR	1.00	1.40	2.13	2.36	2.74
44. Lahore, Pakistan	1.24	1.97	3.70	4.35	6.16	94. Munich, West Germany	1.33	1.71	2.11	2.18	2.22
45. Rome, Italy	2.33	3.07	3.69	3.75	3.87	95. Medan, Indonesia	0.47	0.64	2.09	3.01	5.36
46. Lagos, Nigeria	0.70	1.44	3.65	4.79	8.34	96. Kitakyushu, Japan	1.31	1.60	2.06	2.13	2.22
47. Wuhan, China	2.17	2.73	3.38	3.60	4.35	97. Budapest, Hungary	1.81	1.95	2.06	2.06	2.09
48. Guangzhou (Canton), China	1.93	2.50	3.30	3.57	4.37	98. Kanpur, India	0.97	1.29	2.03	2.35	3.17
49. San Francisco, United States	2.45	3.01	3.30	3.40	3.55	99. Nagoya, Japan	1.50	1.85	2.03	2.03	2.03
50. Katowice, Poland	2.44	2.77	3.27	3.46	3.77						

1. Projected figures.　**Source:** United Nations, Department for International Economic and Social Affairs, *The Prospects of World Urbanization: Revised as of 1984–85* (1987).

GLOBAL TOPICS

Military Spending

Although world military spending exceeded $1 trillion for the first time in 1987, in constant dollars growth in world military spending began to slow after 1985, and appeared to have virtually stopped growing in 1987, for the first time since 1971.

The slowdown is attributed mainly to the decline in military spending by developing countries. In 1985, spending was down 2% over the year before; it declined 5.8% in 1986, and 9.1% in 1987.

Military spending by developed countries—which accounted for $844 billion, or 83% of the world total in 1987—continued to grow in the same period, though the average annual growth rate dropped from 2.9% in the period 1980-85, to 1.9% in the period 1985-87.

Nuclear Weapons

Five countries have developed nuclear forces: the United States, the Soviet Union, Great Britain, France, and China. (Coincidentally, these countries are also the five permanent members of the UN Security Council.) Although figures vary depending on the source consulted, according to the National Resources Defense Council, as of 1987, the United States had 13,002 nuclear warheads and the USSR 10,442. While the United States and the USSR are attempting to scale down their huge arsenals, the spread of

MILITARY EXPENDITURES: SHARES AND GROWTH, 1977–87

	WORLD SHARE 1977	WORLD SHARE 1987	REAL GROWTH RATE 1977–87	REAL GROWTH RATE 1982–87
WORLD	100.0%	100.0%	2.8%	1.8%
Developed	78.4	83.0	3.3	2.9
Developing	21.6	17.0	0.9	-2.8
REGION				
Africa	1.6	1.4	0.7	-1.3
East Asia	6.9	6.9	2.4	1.9
Europe, all	55.2	51.7	1.8	1.4
NATO Europe	14.7	13.9	1.9	1.1
Warsaw Pact	38.3	35.9	1.8	1.6
Other Europe	2.2	2.0	1.7	0.5
Latin America	1.5	1.5	4.5	-1.3
Middle East	10.5	6.6	-0.7	-6.9
North America	22.8	30.0	6.1	5.3
Oceania	0.5	0.6	4.5	3.8
South Asia	0.9	1.3	6.0	6.9
ORGANIZATION				
NATO, all	37.5	43.9	4.5	3.9
Warsaw Pact	38.3	35.9	1.8	1.6
OPEC	8.9	5.6	-1.1	-7.6
OECD	41.6	48.7	4.5	3.8

Source: Arms Control and Disarmament Agency, *World Military Expenditures and Arms Transfers 1988* (1989).

NUCLEAR WEAPONS IN EUROPE, 1987

Type	U.S.	U.K.	France	NATO total	USSR
Land-based missiles	1,224	—	62	1,286	2,418
Aircraft bombs	1,400	261	129	1,790	2,150
Artillery	1,665	—	—	1,665	1,400
Other (ASW, SAM, etc.)[1]	290	264	240	794	N.A.
Total	**4,579**	**525**	**431**	**5,535**	**5,968**

Note: Numbers for INF (Intermediate-range nuclear forces) missiles are official, others represent best estimates. Soviet allies have no nuclear weapons. The INF Treaty eliminates 1,836 Soviet land-based missiles (1,418 in Europe) and 867 U.S. missiles (529 in Europe).   1. Antisubmarine warfare, surface-to-air-missile.   **Source:** U.S. Dept. of Defense; Center for Defense Information, *The Defense Monitor*, 17:3 (1988).

THE ARMS RACE: GROWTH OF U.S. AND USSR NUCLEAR WEAPONS ARSENALS, 1946–87

Year		ICBMs[1] L.[3]	W.[4]	SLBMs[2] L.[3]	W.[4]	BOMBERS L.[3]	W.[4]	TOTALS L.[3]	W.[4]
1946	U.S.	—	—	—	—	125	9	125	9
	USSR	—	—	—	—	—	—	—	—
1950	U.S.	—	—	—	—	462	400	462	400
	USSR	—	—	—	—	—	—	—	—
1956	U.S.	—	—	—	—	1,470	2,123	1,470	2,123
	USSR	—	—	—	—	22	84	22	84
1960	U.S.	12	12	32	32	1,515	3,083	1,559	3,117
	USSR	4	4	30	30	104	320	138	354
1965	U.S.	854	854	384	384	650	3,013	1,888	4,251
	USSR	225	225	75	72	163	532	463	829
1970	U.S.	1,054	1,244	656	656	390	3,060	2,100	4,960
	USSR	1,361	1,361	317	287	157	568	1,835	2,216
1975	U.S.	1,054	2,144	656	3,968	396	3,716	2,106	9,828
	USSR	1,587	1,917	771	732	157	568	2,515	3,217
1980	U.S.	1,054	2,144	592	4,896	376	3,568	2,022	10,608
	USSR	1,398	5,002	990	1,910	157	568	2,545	7,480
1985	U.S.	1,020	2,110	648	5,760	297	4,104	1,965	11,974
	USSR	1,398	6,420	980	2,872	160	720	2,538	10,012
1987	U.S.	1,000	2,300	640	5,632	361	5,070	2,001	13,002
	USSR	1,418	6,542	962	3,130	165	860	2,535	10,442

1. Intercontinental ballistic missiles.   2. Submarine-launched ballistic missiles.   3. Launchers, that is, the rockets or aircraft carrying the nuclear weapon.   4. Warheads, that is, the specific nuclear weapon. The fact that from 1970 on the number of warheads grows larger than the number of launchers results from the introduction of multiple warheads (MRVs and MIRVs), so that one missile can carry several warheads, each capable of being aimed at a different target.   **Source:** Natural Resources Defense Council, *Nuclear Weapons Databook* (1988).

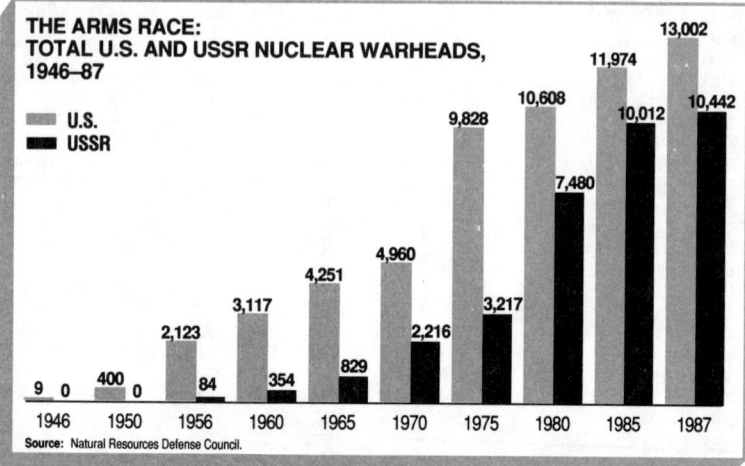

THE ARMS RACE: TOTAL U.S. AND USSR NUCLEAR WARHEADS, 1946–87

■ U.S.
■ USSR

1946	1950	1956	1960	1965	1970	1975	1980	1985	1987
9 / 0	400 / 0	2,123 / 84	3,117 / 354	4,251 / 829	4,960 / 2,216	9,828 / 3,217	10,608 / 7,480	11,974 / 10,012	13,002 / 10,442

Source: Natural Resources Defense Council.

nuclear weapons technology throughout other countries is a growing threat to world security. It is widely believed that Israel and South Africa have already developed nuclear weapons, and that India and Pakistan have the capacity to do so on short notice.

Nuclear weapons can be deployed in the same manner as conventional weapons—on land (intercontinental ballistic missiles, or ICBMs, and short-range artillery), in ships and submarines (submarine-launched ballistic missiles, or SLBMs), and in aircraft (both land- and carrier-based). Launchers can carry either single warheads or more than one, as in MRVs (multiple reentry vehicles) or MIRVs (multiple independently retargetable vehicles).

A nuclear weapon's explosive force is measured in terms of its equivalent in tons of TNT, commonly given in the metric form of kilotons (Kt) or megatons (Mt). The smallest weapons in the U.S. nuclear arsenal are about 0.01 Kt (10 tons of TNT), while the largest are 15 Mt (15 million tons of TNT). The average yield of U.S. and Soviet nuclear weapons is about 400 Kt, those in the United States being slightly less powerful, those in the USSR slightly more.

While Soviet and American nuclear arsenals are roughly comparable, their deployment differs significantly. ICBMs make up more than half of both arsenals (52% U.S., 56% USSR), and SLBMs roughly a third (32% U.S., 37% USSR); but the less vulnerable nuclear bombers make up 16% of the U.S. arsenal against only 9% of the Soviet. The distribution of total warheads is more uneven still. The United States has 19% of all warheads in ICBMs, 41% in SLBMs, and 40% in bombers. Soviet warheads are overwhelmingly concentrated in land-based ICBMs—60%—while 31% are in SLBMs, and only 10% in bombers.

Ballistic Missiles

In December 1987, the United States and the Soviet Union ratified the Intermediate-range Nuclear Forces (INF) Treaty, theoretically eliminating all nuclear weapons delivery systems with ranges of between 500 and 5,000 kilometers. This means a reduction of 867 U.S. missiles (529 of which are based in Europe) and 1,836 Soviet missiles (1,418 based in Europe). Despite that, the proliferation of ballistic mis-

siles throughout the rest of the world poses an increasingly significant threat to international security.

In all, 16 countries in the developing world have or are developing short- and intermediate-range missiles. In the Middle East, nine countries have deployed missiles with ranges of from 40 to 600 miles. In the Far East and southwest Asia, both Koreas have deployed missiles with ranges of up to 190 miles, while Pakistan and India are either testing or developing them. Taiwan has suspended development of two missile systems. Argentina and Brazil are both developing a variety of missiles with ranges of from 60 to 740 miles. While many of the ballistic missile systems have been provided by either the United States or the Soviet Union and their allies, many countries are developing weapons systems by themselves, as in the case of Israel, India, North Korea, Pakistan, and Brazil, or in cooperation with others, most notably Argentina, Egypt, Iraq, Iran, and North Korea.

MARKET SHARES OF MAJOR ARMS EXPORTERS AND IMPORTERS, 1987

Importers	Percent share	Exporters	Percent share
India	14.8%	Soviet Union	35.0%
Iraq	10.0	United States	32.8
Egypt	6.3	France	10.3
Saudi Arabia	4.8	Britain	5.1
Israel	4.6	West Germany	4.0
Japan	3.7	China	2.9
Syria	3.7	Netherlands	1.4
Turkey	3.4	Sweden	1.1
Czechoslovakia	3.4	Brazil	1.1
Angola	3.1	Czechoslovakia	0.9
Spain	3.1	Others	5.5
Canada	1.9		
Australia	1.9		
Taiwan	1.7		
South Korea	1.6		
Others	31.9		

Note: Percentages are based on trade in 1987, figured in 1985 dollars. Totals may not add to 100% because of rounding. **Source:** Stockholm International Peace Research Institute.

NUCLEAR POWER REACTORS AROUND THE WORLD, 1989

Twenty-six nations now generate electricity from nuclear power plants. In 11 nations nuclear power produces over 30 percent of all electricity, and in three nations over 50 percent.

Nation	Reactors in operation	Units under construction	Percent of electricity supplied[1]
Argentina	2	1	13.4%
Belgium	7	—	66.0
Brazil	1	1	0.5
Bulgaria	5	2	28.6
Canada	18	4	15.1
China	—	3	0.0
Cuba	—	2	0.0
Czechoslovakia	8	8	25.9
Finland	4	—	36.6
France	55	9	69.8
Germany, East	5	6	9.7
Germany, West	23	2	31.3
Hungary	4	—	39.2
India	6	8	2.6
Iran	—	2	0.0
Italy	2	3	0.1
Japan	36	14	29.1
Korea, South	8	1	53.3
Mexico	—	2	0.0
Netherlands	2	—	5.2
Pakistan	1	—	1.0
Poland	—	2	0.0
Romania	—	5	0.0
South Africa	2	—	4.5
Spain	10	—	31.2
Sweden	12	—	45.3
Switzerland	5	—	38.3
Taiwan	6	—	48.5
UK	40	2	17.5
U.S.	108	7	17.7
USSR	57	25	11.2
Yugoslavia	1	—	5.6
World total	**428**	**109**	**N.A.**

1. Figures are for 1987. **Source:** International Atomic Energy Agency.

PRINCIPAL SOURCE COUNTRIES OF WORLD'S REFUGEES IN 1988

Counts may understate the total number of refugees from a given country because asylum nations do not always specify the origin of their refugees.

Afghanistan	5,937,180[1]
Area formerly known as Palestine	3,373,090
Mozambique	1,147,000[1]
Ethiopia	1,101,300[1]
Iraq	508,300[1]
Angola	395,700
Sudan	355,000
Cambodia	354,190[1]
Somalia	350,000[1]
Iran	348,800[1]

1. Sources vary significantly in numbers reported. **Source:** The U.S. Committee for Refugees, *World Refugee Survey—1988 in Review* (1989).

INTERNATIONAL TERRORIST INCIDENTS, 1968–88

Type of event	1968	1970	1975	1980	1985	1986	1987	1988
Armed attack	21	34	52	169	141	158	131	129
Arson	12	56	43	46	102	135	150	239
Assault	—	—	—	—	17	16	10	16
Bombing	83	125	195	225	399	559	473	413[1]
Extortion	—	—	—	—	8	6	—	4
Terrorist skyjacking	3	18	4	8	6	2	1	2
Kidnapping	1	43	56	16	87	58	53	32
Sabotage-vandalism	1	—	1	1	11	5	6	8
Nonair hijacking	—	—	—	—	1	1	2	3
Theft	3	22	7	15	2	2	1	1
Other	—	3	8	19	44	2	1	1
TOTAL	**125**	**309**	**382**	**532**	**824**	**944**	**832**	**855[1]**

Note: Incident figures may exceed event totals due to overlapping. 1. This number includes the bombing of Pan Am flight 103 (Dec. 2, 1988). **Source:** U.S. Dept. of State, *Patterns of Global Terrorism: 1988* (1989).

WORLD GEOGRAPHY

THE CONTINENTS: AREA AND POPULATION

Continent	AREA Square miles	Square kilometers	Percent of world's total land area	Population (1988 est.)	Percent of world population
Asia	17,240,000	44,651,600	29.9%	3,031,100,000	60.0%
Africa	11,700,000	30,303,000	20.3	615,300,000	12.2
North America	9,410,000	24,371,900	16.3	413,100,000	8.2
South America	6,860,000	17,767,400	11.9	282,200,000	5.6
Antarctica	5,405,000	13,998,950	9.4	—	0.0
Europe	3,840,000	9,945,600	6.6	684,800,000	13.5
Australia and Oceania	3,290,000	8,521,100	5.7	25,500,000	0.5

Source: Rand McNally, *Cosmopolitan World Atlas* (1985).

THE CONTINENTS: HIGHEST AND LOWEST ELEVATIONS

Continent	Highest point	Location	Feet above sea level	Meters above sea level	Lowest point	Location	Feet below sea level	Meters below sea level
Asia	Mt. Everest	Nepal-China	29,028	8,848	Dead Sea	Israel-Jordan	1,312	400
S. America	Mt. Aconcagua	Argentina	22,834	6,960	Valdes Peninsula	Argentina	131	40
N. America	Mt. McKinley	U.S. (Alaska)	20,320	6,194	Death Valley	U.S. (California)	282	86
Africa	Mt. Kilimanjaro	Tanzania	19,340	5,895	Lake Assal	Djibouti	512	156
Europe	Mt. Elbrus	USSR	18,510	5,642	Caspian Sea	USSR	92	28
Antarctica	Vinson Massif	Ellsworth Mts.	16,864	5,140	Unknown			
Australia	Mt. Kosciusko	New South Wales	7,310	2,228	Lake Eyre	South Australia	52	16

Source: *National Geographic Atlas of the World* (1981).

THE WORLD'S LARGEST ISLANDS

Island	Location	Flags	AREA Sq. mi.	Sq km	Island	Location	Flags	AREA Sq. mi.	Sq km
Greenland	N. Atlantic Ocean	Denmark	840,000	2,175,600	Cuba	Caribbean Sea	Cuba	44,218	114,525
New Guinea	S. Pacific Ocean	Indonesia, Papua New Guinea	306,000	792,540	North Island	S. Pacific Ocean	New Zealand	44,035	114,051
Borneo	Pacific Ocean	Indonesia, Malaysia, Brunei	280,100	725,459	Newfoundland	N. Atlantic Ocean	Canada	42,030	108,858
					Luzon	N. Pacific Ocean	Philippines	40,880	105,879
Madagascar	Indian Ocean	Madagascar	226,658	587,044	Iceland	N. Atlantic Ocean	Iceland	39,769	103,002
Baffin	Arctic Ocean	Canada	195,928	507,454	Mindanao	N. Pacific Ocean	Philippines	36,775	95,247
Sumatra	Indian Ocean, S. Pacific Ocean	Indonesia	165,000	427,350	Novaya Zemlya	Arctic Ocean	USSR	35,000	90,650
Honshu	N. Pacific Ocean	Japan	87,805	227,415	Ireland	N. Atlantic Ocean	Ireland, UK	32,599	84,431
Great Britain	N. Atlantic Ocean	United Kingdom	84,200	218,078	Hokkaido	S. Pacific Ocean	Japan	30,144	78,073
Victoria	Arctic Ocean	Canada	83,896	217,291	Hispaniola	Caribbean Sea	Haiti, Dominican Republic	29,530	76,483
Ellesmere	Arctic Ocean	Canada	75,767	196,237	Sakhalin	N. Pacific Ocean	USSR	29,500	76,405
Celebes	Pacific Ocean	Indonesia	69,000	178,710	Banks	Arctic Ocean	Canada	27,033	70,015
South Island	S. Pacific Ocean	New Zealand	58,305	151,010	Tasmania	S. Pacific Ocean	Australia	26,178	67,801
Java	Indian Ocean, S. Pacific Ocean	Indonesia	48,900	126,651	Sri Lanka	Indian Ocean	Sri Lanka	25,332	65,610
					Devon	Arctic Ocean	Canada	21,331	55,247

Source: National Geographic Society.

MAJOR RIVERS OF THE WORLD, BY LENGTH

River	LENGTH Miles	km	Source	Outflow	River	LENGTH Miles	km	Source	Outflow
Nile	4,145	6,673	Tributaries of Lake Victoria, Africa	Mediterranean Sea	Ob-Irtysh	3,360[2]	5,410[2]	Altai Mts., China	Gulf of Ob (Arctic Ocean)
Amazon	4,000	6,440	Andes Mts., Peru	Atlantic Ocean	Plata-Parana	3,030[2]	4,878[2]	Confluence of the Paranaiba and Grande rivers, Brazil	Atlantic Ocean
Mississippi-Missouri	3,740[1]	6,021[1]	Lake Itasca, north-western Minnesota	Gulf of Mexico					
Changjiang (Yangtze)	3,720	5,989	Kunlun Mts., China	China Sea	Huang He (Yellow)	2,903	4,674	Kunlun Mts., China	Gulf of Chihli (Yellow Sea)
Yenisei-Angara	3,650[2]	5,877[2]	Lake Baikal, USSR	Kara Sea (Arctic Ocean)	Congo (Zaire)	2,900	4,669	Confluence of the Luapula and Lualaba rivers, Zaire	Atlantic Ocean
Amur-Argun	3,590[2]	5,780[2]	Khingan Mts., China	Tatar Strait					

River	LENGTH Miles	km	Source	Outflow
Lena	2,730	4,395	Baikal Mts., USSR	Laptev Sea (Arctic Ocean)
MacKenzie	2,635[2]	4,242[2]	Headwaters of the Finlay River, British Columbia, Canada	Beaufort Sea (Arctic Ocean)
Mekong	2,600	4,186	T'ang-ku-la Mts., Tibet (China)	South China Sea
Niger	2,600	4,186	Guinea	Gulf of Guinea
Missouri	2,533	4,078	Confluence of the Jefferson, Madison, and Galatin rivers, southern Montana	Mississippi River
Mississippi	2,348[3]	3,780[3]	Lake Itasca, north-western Minnesota	Gulf of Mexico
Murray-Darling	2,330	3,751	Great Dividing Range, Australia	Indian Ocean
Volga	2,290	3,687	Valdai Hills, USSR	Caspian Sea
Madeira	2,013	3,241	Confluence of the Mamore and Beni rivers, Bolivia/Brazil	Amazon River
Sao Francisco	1,988	3,201	Minas Gerais State, Brazil	Atlantic Ocean
Yukon	1,979	3,186	Confluence of the Lewes and Pelly rivers, Yukon Territory, Canada	Bering Sea
Rio Grande	1,885	3,035	San Juan Mts., southwestern Colorado	Gulf of Mexico
Purus	1,860	2,995	Andes Mts., Peru	Amazon River
Tunguska, Lower	1,860	2,995	North of Lake Baikal, USSR	Yenesei River
Indus	1,800	2,898	Himalayas, Tibet (China)	Arabian Sea
Danube	1,776	2,859	Confluence of the Breg and Brigach rivers, West Germany	Black Sea
Brahmaputra	1,770	2,850	Himalayas, Tibet (China)	Ganges River

River	LENGTH Miles	km	Source	Outflow
Salween	1,750	2,818	Tibetan Plateau, Tibet (China)	Gulf of Martaban (Bay of Bengal)
Para-Tocantins	1,710[2]	2,753[2]	Goias State, Brazil	Atlantic Ocean
Zambezi	1,700	2,737	Northwestern Zambia	Mozambique Channel
Paraguay	1,610	2,592	Mato Grosso State, Brazil	Parana River
Kolyma	1,600	2,576	Kolyma Mts., north-eastern USSR	Arctic Ocean
Nelson-Saskatchewan	1,600	2,576	Rocky Mts., Canada	Hudson Bay
Orinoco	1,600	2,576	Sierra Parima Mts., Venezuela	Atlantic Ocean
Amu Darya	1,578	2,541	Pamir Mts., USSR	Aral Sea
Ural	1,575	2,536	Ural Mts., USSR	Caspian Sea
Ganges	1,560	2,512	Himalayas, India	Bay of Bengal
Euphrates	1,510	2,431	Confluence of the Murat Nehri and Kara Su rivers, Turkey	Shatt-al-Arab
Arkansas	1,450	2,335	Central Colorado	Mississippi River
Colorado	1,450	2,335	Northern Colorado	Gulf of California
Dneiper	1,420	2,286	Valdai Hills, USSR	Black Sea
Atchafalaya-Red	1,400	2,254	Eastern New Mexico	Atchafalaya Bay (Gulf of Mexico)
Syr Darya	1,370	2,206	Tien Shan, China/USSR	Aral Sea
Kasai	1,338	2,154	Central Angola	Congo (Zaire) River
Irrawaddy	1,300	2,093	Confluence of the Mali and Nmai rivers, Burma	Bay of Bengal
Ohio-Allegheny	1,300	2,093	North-central Pennsylvania	Mississippi River
Orange	1,300	2,093	Lesotho	Atlantic Ocean
Columbia	1,243	2,001	Columbia Lake, British Columbia, Canada	Pacific Ocean
Tigris	1,180	1,900	Eastern Turkey	Shatt-al-Arab
Rhine	820	1,320	Confluence of the Hinterrhein and Vorderrhein rivers, southeastern Switzerland	North Sea
St. Lawrence	800	1,288	Lake Ontario	Gulf of St. Lawrence

1. From the mouth of the Mississippi up to its source in Minnesota.   2. Includes the length of tributaries that are part of the main trunk stream.   3. From the mouth of the Mississippi up the Missouri to the Red Rock River in Montana.   **Source:** U.S. Dept. of Commerce, National Oceanic and Atmospheric Admin., *Principal Rivers and Lakes of the World* (1982).

THE WORLD'S LARGEST DAMS, BY VOLUME

Dam	VOLUME (thousands of cu. yds.)	(thousands of cu m)	River or basin, and location	Year completed (or completion expected)
Syncrude Tailings	707,400	540,000	Alberta[1]	(1992)
Chapeton	388,022	296,200	Parana, Argentina	(1996)
Pati	301,536	230,180	Parana, Argentina	(1990)
New Cornelia Tailings	274,445	209,500	Ten Mile Wash, Arizona	1973
Tarbela	138,297	105,570	Indus, Pakistan	1976
Fort Peck	125,825	96,050	Missouri, Montana	1937
Lower Usuma	121,830	93,000	Usuma, Nigeria	(1990)
Cipasang	117,900	90,000	Cimanuk, Indonesia	(1)
Ataturk	111,350	85,000	Euphrates, Turkey	(1990)
Guri (Raul Leoni—final stage)	102,142	77,971	Caroni, Venezuela	1986
Rogun	98,905	75,500	Vakhsh, USSR	1987
Oahe Tailings	92,144	70,339	Missouri, South Dakota	1960
Gardiner	85,726	65,440	South Saskatchewan, Saskatchewan	1968

Dam	VOLUME (thousands of cu. yds.)	(thousands of cu m)	River or basin, and location	Year completed (or completion expected)
Mangla	85,646	65,379	Jhelum, Pakistan	1967
Tucurui	84,233	64,300	Tocantins, Brazil	1984
Afsluitdijk	83,093	63,430	Zuider Zee, Netherlands	1932
Yacyreta-Apipe	80,172	61,200	Parana, Paraguay/Argentina	(1991)
Oroville	78,122	59,635	Feather, California	1968
San Luis	78,022	59,559	San Luis, California	1967
Nurek	75,980	58,000	Vakhsh, USSR	1980
Garrison	66,607	50,845	Missouri, North Dakota	1956
Cochiti	65,801	50,230	Grande, New Mexico	1975
Oosterschelde	65,500	50,000	Vense Gat Oosterschelde, Netherlands	1986
Tabqua (Thawra)	60,260	46,000	Euphrates, Syria	1976
Aswan (High)	58,033	44,300	Nile, Egypt	1970

1. No information available.   **Source:** *International Water Power & Dam Construction Handbook 1987.*

THE WORLD'S HIGHEST MOUNTAIN PEAKS

Mountain peak	Range	Location	Feet	Meters
Everest	Himalayas	Nepal-China	29,028	8,848
K2 (Godwin Austen)	Karakoram	Kashmir	28,250	8,611
Kanchenjunga	Himalayas	Nepal-India	28,208	8,598
Lhotse I	Himalayas	Nepal-China	27,923	8,511
Makalu I	Himalayas	Nepal-China	27,824	8,481
Lhotse II	Himalayas	Nepal-China	27,560	8,400
Dhaulagiri	Himalayas	Nepal	26,810	8,172
Manaslu I	Himalayas	Nepal	26,760	8,156
Cho Oyu	Himalayas	Nepal-China	26,750	8,153
Nanga Parbat	Himalayas	Kashmir	26,660	8,126
Annapurna	Himalayas	Nepal	26,504	8,078
Gasherbrum	Karakoram	Kashmir	26,470	8,068
Broad	Karakoram	Kashmir	26,400	8,047
Gosainthan	Himalayas	China	26,287	8,012
Annapurna II	Himalayas	Nepal	26,041	7,937
Gyachung Kang	Himalayas	Nepal-China	25,910	7,897
Disteghil Sar	Himalayas	Kashmir	25,858	7,882
Himalchuli	Himalayas	Nepal	25,801	7,864
Nuptse	Himalayas	Nepal-China	25,726	7,841
Masherbrum	Karakoram	Kashmir	25,660	7,821
Nanda Devi	Himalayas	India	25,645	7,817
Rakaposhi	Karakoram	Kashmir	25,550	7,788
Kanjut Sar	Karakoram	Kashmir	25,461	7,761
Kamet	Himalayas	India-China	25,447	7,756
Namcha Barwa	Himalayas	China	25,445	7,756
Kua-la-man-ta-t'a (Gurla Mandhata)	Himalayas	China	25,355	7,728
Wu-lu-k'o-mu-shih (Ulugh Muztagh)	Kunlun	China	25,340	7,724
Kung-ko-erh (Kungur)	Mu-ssu-t'a-ko-a-t'e (Muztagh Ata)	China	25,325	7,719
Tirich Mir	Hindu Kush	Pakistan	25,230	7,690
Saser Kangri	Karakoram	Kashmir	25,172	7,672
Makalu II	Himalayas	Nepal-China	25,120	7,657
Minya Konka (Gonggashan)	Daxue Shan	China	24,900	7,590
Kula Kangri	Himalayas	Bhutan-China	24,784	7,554
Chang-tzu	Himalayas	Nepal-China	24,780	7,553
Mu-ssu-t'a-ko-a-t'e (Muztagh Ata)	Mu-ssu-t'a-ko-a-t'e (Muztagh Ata)	China	24,757	7,546
Skyang Kangri	Himalayas	Kashmir	24,750	7,544
Communism Peak	Pamirs	USSR	24,590	7,495
Jongsong Peak	Himalayas	Nepal-India	24,472	7,459
Pobeda Peak	Tian Shan	USSR-China	24,406	7,439
Sia Kangri	Himalayas	Kashmir	24,350	7,422
Haramosh Peak	Karakoram	Kashmir	24,270	7,397
Istoro Nal	Hindu Kush	Pakistan	24,240	7,388
Tent Peak	Himalayas	Nepal-India	24,165	7,365
Chomo Lhari	Himalayas	Bhutan-China	24,040	7,327
Chamlang	Himalayas	Nepal	24,012	7,319
Kabru	Himalayas	Nepal-India	24,002	7,316
Alung Gangri	Himalayas	China	24,000	7,315
Baltoro Kangri	Himalayas	Kashmir	23,990	7,312
Muztag	Kunlun	China	23,890	7,282
Mana	Himalayas	India	23,860	7,273
Baruntse	Himalayas	Nepal	23,688	7,220
Nepal Peak	Himalayas	Nepal-India	23,500	7,163
Amne Machin	Kunlun	China	23,490	7,160
Gauri Sankar	Himalayas	Nepal-China	23,440	7,145
Badrinath	Himalayas	India	23,420	7,138
Nunkun	Himalayas	Kashmir	23,410	7,135
Lenin Peak	Pamirs	USSR	23,405	7,134
Pyramid	Himalayas	Nepal-India	23,400	7,132
Api	Himalayas	Nepal	23,399	7,132
Pauhunri	Himalayas	India-China	23,385	7,128
Trisul	Himalayas	India	23,360	7,120
Korzhenevski Peak	Pamirs	USSR	23,310	7,105
Kangto	Himalayas	India-China	23,260	7,090
Nyainqentanglha	Nyainqentanglha Shan	China	23,255	7,088
Trisuli	Himalayas	India	23,210	7,074
Dunagiri	Himalayas	India	23,184	7,066
Revolution Peak	Pamirs	USSR	22,880	6,974
Aconcagua	Andes	Argentina	22,834	6,960
Ojos del Salado	Andes	Argentina-Chile	22,572	6,880
Bonete	Andes	Argentina	22,546	6,872
Tupungato	Andes	Argentina-Chile	22,310	6,800
Moscow Peak	Pamirs	USSR	22,260	6,785
Pissis	Andes	Argentina	22,241	6,779
Mercedario	Andes	Argentina	22,211	6,770
Huascaran	Andes	Peru	22,205	6,768
Llullaillaco	Andes	Argentina-Chile	22,057	6,723
El Libertador	Andes	Argentina	22,047	6,720
Cachi	Andes	Argentina	22,047	6,720
Kailas	Himalayas	China	22,027	6,714
Incahuasi	Andes	Argentina-Chile	21,720	6,620
Yerupaja	Andes	Peru	21,709	6,617
Kurumda	Pamirs	USSR	21,686	6,610
Galan	Andes	Argentina	21,654	6,600
El Muerto	Andes	Argentina-Chile	21,457	6,540
Sajama	Andes	Bolivia	21,391	6,520
Nacimiento	Andes	Argentina	21,302	6,493
Illimani	Andes	Bolivia	21,201	6,462
Coropuna	Andes	Peru	21,083	6,426
Laudo	Andes	Argentina	20,997	6,400
Ancohuma	Andes	Bolivia	20,958	6,388
Ausangate	Andes	Peru	20,945	6,384
Toro	Andes	Argentina-Chile	20,932	6,380
Illampu	Andes	Bolivia	20,873	6,362
Tres Cruces	Andes	Argentina-Chile	20,853	6,356
Huandoy	Andes	Peru	20,852	6,356
Parinacota	Andes	Bolivia-Chile	20,768	6,330
Tortolas	Andes	Argentina-Chile	20,745	6,323
Ampato	Andes	Peru	20,702	6,310
El Condor	Andes	Argentina	20,669	6,300
Salcantay	Andes	Peru	20,574	6,271
Chimborazo	Andes	Ecuador	20,561	6,267
Huancarhuas	Andes	Peru	20,531	6,258
General Manuel Belgrano	Andes	Argentina	20,505	6,250
Pumasillo	Andes	Peru	20,492	6,246
Solo	Andes	Argentina	20,492	6,246
Polleras	Andes	Argentina	20,456	6,235
Pular	Andes	Chile	20,423	6,225
Chani	Andes	Argentina	20,341	6,200
McKinley	Alaska	U.S. (Alaska)	20,320	6,194
Aucanquilcha	Andes	Chile	20,295	6,186
Juncal	Andes	Argentina-Chile	20,276	6,180
Negro	Andes	Argentina	20,184	6,152
Quela	Andes	Argentina	20,128	6,135
Condoriri	Andes	Bolivia	20,095	6,125
Palermo	Andes	Argentina	20,079	6,120
Solimana	Andes	Peru	20,068	6,117
San Juan	Andes	Argentina-Chile	20,049	6,111
Nevada	Andes	Argentina-Chile	20,023	6,103
Antofalla	Andes	Argentina	20,013	6,100
Marmolejo	Andes	Argentina-Chile	20,013	6,100

Note: Mountains over 20,000 feet.   **Source:** National Geographic Society.

THE WORLD'S LARGEST MAN-MADE LAKES (RESERVOIRS)

Reservoir	CAPACITY (millions) (cu. yds.)	(cu m)	River or basin, and location	Year completed (or completion expected)	Reservoir	CAPACITY (millions) (cu. yds.)	(cu m)	River or basin, and location	Year completed (or completion expected)
Owen Falls	3,537,000[1]	2,700,000[1]	Lake Victoria/Nile, Uganda	1954	La Grande 3	78,626	60,020	La Grande, Quebec	1981
Bratsk	221,744	169,270	Angara, USSR	1964	Ust-Ilim	77,683	59,300	Angara, USSR	1977
Aswan (High)	221,259	168,900	Nile, Egypt	1970	Volga—V.I. Lenin				
Kariba	210,082	160,368	Zambezi, Zimbabwe/Zambia	1959	(Kuibyshev)	75,980	58,000	Volga, USSR	1955
Akosombo	193,880	148,000	Volta, Ghana	1965	Sao Felix	72,312	55,200	Tocantins, Brazil	(1989)
Daniel Johnson	185,826	141,852	Manicouagan, Quebec	1968	Caniapiscau (KA-3,				
Guri (Raul Leoni—					KA-4, and KA-5)	70,478	53,800	Caniapiscau, Quebec	1981
final stage)	180,780	138,000	Caroni, Venezuela	1986	Bukhtarma	65,238	49,800	Irtysh, USSR	1960
Krasnoyarsk	96,023	73,300	Yenesei, USSR	1967	Ataturk	63,797	48,700	Euphrates, Turkey	(1990)
Bennett W.A.C.					Irkutsk	60,260	46,000	Angara, USSR	1956
(Portage Mt.)	92,105	70,309	Peace, British Columbia	1967	Lower Tunguska	58,950	45,000	Lower Tunguska, USSR	(1994)
Zeya	89,604	68,400	Zeya, USSR	1978	Bakun	57,378	43,800	Rajang, Malaysia	(1995)
Cabora Bassa	82,530	63,000	Zambezi, Mozambique	1974	Cerros Colorados	56,330	43,000	Neuquen, Argentina	1972
La Grande 2	80,847	61,715	La Grande, Quebec	1978	Tucurui	56,330	43,000	Tocantins, Brazil	1984
Chapeton	79,386	60,600	Parana, Argentina	(1996)					

1. Includes a natural lake.   **Source:** *International Water Power & Dam Construction Handbook 1987.*

MAJOR NATURAL LAKES OF THE WORLD

Lake	SURFACE AREA Sq. mi.	Sq km	Location	MAXIMUM DEPTH Feet	Meters	ELEVATION Feet	Meters	Lake	SURFACE AREA Sq. mi.	Sq km	Location	MAXIMUM DEPTH Feet	Meters	ELEVATION Feet	Meters
Caspian Sea[1]	143,240	370,992	Asia: USSR, Iran	3,363	1,025	-92	-28	Onega	3,720	9,635	Europe: USSR	394	120	108	33
Superior	31,700	82,103	N. America: Ontario, Can.; Mich., Wis., Minn.	1,333	406	600	183	Titicaca	3,200	8,288	S. America: Bolivia, Peru	990	302	12,500	3,810
Victoria	26,820	69,464	Africa: Uganda, Kenya, Tanzania	279	85	3,720	1,134	Nicaragua	3,150	8,159	N. America: Nicaragua	230	70	102	31
Aral Sea[1]	24,904	64,501	Asia: USSR	220	67	174	53	Mai-Ndombe	3,100[2]	8,029[2]	Africa: Zaire	36	11	(4)	(4)
Huron	23,000	59,570	N. America: Ontario, Can.; Mich.	750	229	576	176	Athabasca	3,064	7,936	N. America: Saskatchewan, Alberta, Can.	407	124	700	213
Michigan	22,300	57,757	N. America: Mich., Ind., Ill., Wis.	923	281	579	176	Eyre[1]	2,970[2]	7,692[2]	Australia	4	1	-52	-16
Tanganyika	12,350	31,987	Africa: Burundi, Tanzania, Zambia, Zaire	4,800	1,463	2,543	775	Reindeer	2,568	6,651	N. America: Manitoba, Saskatchewan, Can.	720	219	1,106	337
Baikal	12,160	31,494	Asia: USSR	5,315	1,620	1,493	455	Tonle Sap	2,500[2]	6,475[2]	Asia: Cambodia	39	12	(4)	(4)
Great Bear	12,028	31,153	N. America: Northwest Terr., Can.	1,356	413	512	156	Rudolf[1]	2,473	6,405	Africa: Kenya, Ethiopia	720	219	1,230	375
Nyasa (Malawi)	11,150	28,879	Africa: Tanzania, Mozambique, Malawi	2,280	695	1,550	472	Issyk-Kul[1]	2,355	6,099	Asia: USSR	2,303	702	5,279	1,609
Great Slave	11,030	28,568	N. America: Northwest Terr., Can.	2,015	614	513	156	Torrens[1]	2,230[2]	5,776[2]	Australia	0.5	0.2	92	28
Erie	9,910	25,667	N. America: Ontario, Can.; N.Y., Pa., Ohio, Mich.	210	64	570	174	Albert	2,160	5,594	Africa: Uganda, Zaire	168	51	2,030	619
Winnipeg	9,417	24,390	N. America: Manitoba, Can.	92	28	713	217	Vanern	2,156	5,581	Europe: Sweden	325	99	144	44
Ontario	7,540	19,529	N. America: Ontario, Can.; N.Y.	802	244	245	75	Winnipegosis	2,075	5,374	N. America: Manitoba, Can.	39	12	830	253
Balkhash[1]	7,115[2]	18,428[2]	Asia: USSR	87	27	1,115	340	Bangweulu	1,930	4,999	Africa: Zambia	5	2	3,500	1,067
Ladoga	6,835	17,703	Europe: USSR	755	230	13	4	Nipigon	1,872	4,848	N. America: Ontario, Can.	541	165	1,050	320
Chad	6,300	16,317	Africa: Chad, Nigeria, Niger	24	7	787	240	Nettilling	1,870	4,843	N. America: Baffin Is., Northwest Terr., Can.	(4)	(4)	95	29
Maracaibo[3]	5,200	13,468	S. America: Venezuela	197	60	sea level (4)	sea level (4)	Gairdner[1]	1,840[2]	4,763	Australia	0.5	0.2	112	34
Patos[3]	3,920	10,153	S. America: Brazil	15	5	(4)	(4)	Urmia[1]	1,815[2]	4,701[2]	Asia: Iran	49	15	4,180	1,274
								Manitoba	1,800	4,662	N. America: Manitoba, Can.	92	28	813	248
								Kyoga	1,710	4,429	Africa: Uganda	26	8	(4)	(4)
								Khanka	1,700	4,403	Asia: China, USSR	33	10	(4)	(4)
								Lake of the Woods	1,695	4,390	N. America: Minn.; Ontario, Manitoba, Can.	55	17	1,060	323

Lake	SURFACE AREA Sq. mi.	Sq km	Location	MAXIMUM DEPTH Feet	Meters	ELEVATION Feet	Meters	Lake	SURFACE AREA Sq. mi.	Sq km	Location	MAXIMUM DEPTH Feet	Meters	ELEVATION Feet	Meters
Great Salt[1]	1,680	4,351	N. America: Utah	48	15	4,200	1,280	Dubawnt	1,600	4,144	N. America: Northwest Terr.,				
Mweru	1,680	4,351	Africa: Zambia, Zaire	10	3	3,008	917				Can.	[4]	[4]	[4]	[4]
Peipus	1,660	4,299	Europe: USSR	41	12	98	30	Tung-t'ing Hu	1,430[2]	3,704[2]	Asia: China	[4]	[4]	[4]	[4]
Koko Nor (Tsing Hai)	1,650	4,274	Asia: China	125	38	10,515	3,205	Van Golu[1]	1,420	3,678	Asia: Turkey	82	25	5,643	1,720
								Tana	1,390	3,600	Africa: Ethiopia	30	9	6,003	1,830

1. Saltwater. A lake is a body of water surrounded by land; the Caspian Sea is thus a lake. It was called a sea by the Romans because of its salty water.   2. Subject to large seasonal variation in surface area.   3. Lagoon.
4. No information available.   **Source:** U.S. Dept. of Commerce, National Oceanic and Atmospheric Admin., *Principal Rivers and Lakes of the World* (1982).

OCEANS OF THE WORLD
(area in thousands)

Name	AREA Sq. mi.	Sq km	MAXIMUM DEPTH Feet	Meters	Name	AREA Sq. mi.	Sq km	MAXIMUM DEPTH Feet	Meters
Pacific Ocean:	63,800	165,250	36,200	11,034	**Atlantic Ocean:**	31,830	82,440	30,246	9,219
with marginal seas	69,370	179,680	—	—	with marginal seas	41,100	106,460	—	—
South China Sea	1,331	3,447	18,241	5,560	Arctic Ocean	5,400	14,090	17,881	5,450
Sea of Okhotsk	610	1,580	11,063	3,372	Caribbean Sea	1,063	2,754	25,197	7,680
Bering Sea	876	2,270	13,750	4,191	Mediterranean Sea	967	2,505	16,470	5,020
East China Sea	482	1,248	29,910	9,840	Norwegian Sea	597	1,547	13,189	4,020
Yellow Sea	480	1,243	300	91	Gulf of Mexico	596	1,544	14,370	4,380
Sea of Japan	389	1,007	12,280	3,733	Hudson Bay	475	1,230	850	259
					Greenland Sea	465	1,205	15,899	4,846
Indian Ocean:	28,360	73,440	24,442	7,450	North Sea	222	575	2,170	659
with marginal seas	28,930	74,920	—	—	Black Sea	178	461	7,360	2,237
Arabian Sea	1,492	3,863	19,029	5,800	Baltic Sea	163	422	1,440	437
Bay of Bengal	839	2,172	17,251	5,258					
Red Sea	169	438	7,370	2,240					

Source: International Hydrographic Organization.

GREAT DESERTS OF THE WORLD

Desert	Location	Approximate size	Desert	Location	Approximate size
An Nafud (part of Great Arabian desert)	Northern Saudi Arabia	40,000 sq. mi. (103,600 sq km)	Libyan (part of Sahara desert)	Libya, southwestern Egypt, and Sudan	450,000 sq. mi. (1,165,500 sq km)
Atacama	Northern Chile	600 mi. (1,000 km) long	Mojave	Southern California and western Arizona	15,000 sq. mi. (38,900 sq km)
Black Rock	Northwestern Nevada	1,000 sq. mi. (2,600 sq km)	Namib	Namibia	800 mi. (1,290 km) long; 30 to 100 mi. (48 to 160 km) wide
Chihuahuan	Texas, New Mexico, Arizona, and Mexico	140,000 sq. mi. (362,600 sq km)	Negev	Southern Israel	4,700 sq. mi. (12,200 sq km)
Dasht-e-Kavir	Central Iran	300 mi. (485 km) long; 100 mi. (160 km) wide	Nubian (part of Sahara desert)	Northeastern Sudan	100,000 sq. mi. (259,000 sq km)
Dasht-e-Lut	Eastern Iran	20,000 sq. mi. (51,800 sq km)	Painted desert	Northern Arizona	200 mi. (320 km) long; 15 to 30 mi. (24 to 48 km) wide
Death Valley	Eastern California and southwestern Nevada	3,000 sq. mi. (7,800 sq km)	Rub al-Khali ("Empty Quarter"; part of Great Arabian desert)	Southern Saudi Arabia	250,000 sq. mi. (647,500 sq km)
Gibson (part of Great Australian desert)	Western Australia	120,000 sq. mi. (310,800 sq km)	Sahara	Northern Africa	3,500,000 sq. mi. (9,065,000 sq km)
Gobi	Mongolia and China	500,000 sq. mi. (1,295,000 sq km)	Simpson (part of Great Australian desert)	Central Australia	40,000 sq. mi. (103,600 sq km)
Great Sandy (part of Great Australian desert)	Northwestern Australia	150,000 sq. mi. (388,500 sq km)	Sonoran	Southwestern Arizona, southeastern California, and northwestern Mexico	70,000 sq. mi. (181,300 sq km)
Great Victoria (part of Great Australian desert)	Southwestern Australia	150,000 sq. mi. (388,500 sq km)	Syrian (part of Great Arabian desert)	Northern Saudi Arabia, eastern Jordan, southern Syria, and western Iraq	100,000 sq. mi. (259,000 sq km)
Kalahari	Southern Africa	225,000 sq. mi. (582,800 sq km)	Taklimakan	Xinjiang Uygur Autonomous Region, China	40,000 sq. mi. (362,600 sq km)
Kara Kum (Turkestan)	Turkmen SSR (Asiatic USSR)	120,000 sq. mi. 310,800 sq km	Thar (Great Indian desert)	Northwestern India and Pakistan	100,000 sq. mi. (259,000 sq km)
Kyzyl Kum	Kazakh SSR and Uzbek SSR (Asiatic USSR)	100,000 sq. mi. (259,000 sq km)			

THE OCEANS OF THE WORLD

The water of the world's oceans covers more than 70 percent of the world's surface. While for many years the so-called World Ocean was divided into five parts—the Pacific, Atlantic, Indian, Arctic, and Antarctic—scientists today commonly recognize only the first three as separate and distinct oceans. The Arctic and Antarctic, as well as other large bodies of water such as the Caribbean Sea, the Gulf of Mexico, Hudson Bay, the Mediterranean and Black seas, and the South China Sea are termed marginal seas. The International Hydrographic Organization identifies 66 seas, gulfs, bays, bights, straits, channels, and passages, many of which are further subdivided. For instance, the Mediterranean Sea is divided into western and eastern basins, and the western basin is subdivided into the Strait of Gibralter, the Balearic Sea, Ligurian Sea, Tyrrhenian Sea, Ionian Sea, Adriatic Sea, and Aegean Sea. The facing table gives the area and maximum depths of the world's three major oceans and selected marginal seas.

GREAT DESERTS OF THE WORLD

To many people, the word *desert* brings to mind images of shifting sand dunes, scorching sun, and occasional lush oases. But there are actually many kinds of deserts, because a desert is simply an area that receives little precipitation and has little plant cover. Thus polar areas can be considered deserts, for their precipitation is locked into ice and snow. So are places such as the Taklimakan, which lies in a rain shadow on the leeward side of mountain ranges, and the Atacama, which is near cold ocean currents that cool the air and prevent the formation of rain clouds. But most deserts are found in the tropics, where giant high-pressure cells keep rain from forming. Some deserts are indeed flat and sandy, but others are solid rock, loose pebbles, or even mountain plateaus. One of the many fascinating characteristics of deserts is their strangely shaped rock formations, created by wind-whipped sand.

Desert statistics Altogether, arid lands cover about a fifth of the earth's total land surface—a third, if semiarid areas are also included. About a billion people live in arid and semiarid areas, and more than 100 countries are facing problems associated with expanding deserts.

Deserts account for some of the world's extremes.
- The Sahara is the largest desert, with an area greater than the continental United States.
- The driest place on earth is in the Atacama desert of Chile, where no rainfall at all was recorded between 1570 and 1971.
- The highest temperature ever recorded—136°F (58°C)—was at Al-Aziziya, in the Libyan desert.

- The lowest point in the world—1,302 feet (397 m) below sea level—is on the shores of the Dead Sea in the Negev desert.
- The lowest point in the Western Hemisphere—282 feet (86 m) below sea level—is in Death Valley, California.

Uses of the Desert Even the hot, sandy, tropical deserts are not necessarily, as their name implies, deserted. Traders, herders, and farmers have called the desert home for thousands of years. Settlements have grown up around oases or in irrigated areas, from ancient times to the present. Deserts are important to historians, archaeologists, paleontologists, and other scientists for the relics of the past that are preserved there. Dinosaur eggs have been found in the Gobi desert, for instance, and whole cities are said to lie buried beneath the Taklimakan desert.

Deserts are also important for extractive industries. The Negev was the site of the fabled King Solomon's Mines. In the 19th century, borax was mined in Death Valley. Petroleum is found in the Sahara and in the deserts of the Arabian peninsula. The Atacama is famed for its deposits of nitrate and copper. The Rub al-Khali, or "Empty Quarter," of Saudi Arabia is thought to contain deposits of limestone and gravel, but no one is certain because it never has been fully explored.

CLIMATES OF THE WORLD

Knowing the similarities and differences between climates in various parts of the world helps us understand many things about our planet: why people live where they do; how they make their living; the problems and potentials of their land. Climates are very complex, however, and no climatic classification is ideal. The most commonly used classification was developed more than 50 years ago by a German climatologist, Wladimir Koppen. The Koppen system uses temperature and precipitation as the major criteria for grouping climates. Boundaries between climatic zones are determined by the limits of where certain plants grow. The five major climatic zones are known by the capital letters **A**, **B**, **C**, **D**, and **E**; each major zone has subzones. High-altitude areas are sometimes shown with the letter **H** because their climates are so complex that small maps cannot show all the detail.

(Note: In the following chart, R stands for the annual rainfall in centimeters; T is the average annual temperature in degrees Celsius.)

A Humid tropical climates The average temperature of every month is 64°F (18°C) or higher. There is no winter.

Af Rain forest. The driest month has at least 2.4 inches (6 cm) of rain. The Amazon basin is an example of an **Af** climate.

Am Monsoon. Similar to **Af**, but with a short dry season. The amount of rainfall in the driest month is less than 2.4 inches (6 cm), but equal to or greater than $10 - (R/25)$. The southwestern coast of India is an example of an **Am** climate.

Aw Savanna. There is a well-defined dry season in the winter. The amount of rainfall in the driest month is less than $10- (R/25)$. The Brazilian highlands are a large area with an **Aw** climate.

As (Rare) There is a well-defined dry season in the summer.

B Dry climates Annual rainfall is less than annual potential evaporation. The boundary between dry areas and humid areas is $R < 2T + 28$ when at least 70% of the rainfall occurs in the warmer six months; $R < 2T$ when at least 70% of the rainfall occurs in the cooler six months; or $R < 2T + 14$ when neither half of the year receives at least 70% of the total annual rainfall.

BS Steppe. The boundary between steppe and desert is half of the dry/humid boundary. Steppes border many of the world's large deserts.

BSh Low-latitude steppe. The average annual temperature is at least 64°F (18°C).

BSk Mid-latitude steppe. The average annual temperature is less than 64°F (18°C).

BW Desert. The boundary between desert and steppe is half of the dry/humid boundary. The Sahara desert is the largest area with a **BW** climate.

BWh Low-latitude desert. The average annual temperature is at least 64°F (18°C).

BWk Mid-latitude desert. The average annual temperature is less than 64°F (18°C).

C Subtropical Climates The average temperature of the coldest month is between 64°F (18°C) and 27°F (–3°C). These are mainly humid mid-latitude areas with mild winters. The principal natural vegetation is broad-leaved forest.

Cw (Rare) The wettest month occurs in summer and has at least 10 times as much rainfall as the driest month in winter. **Cw** zones are mainly areas of evergreen forest in mountainous **Aw** zones.

Cs Dry summer. The wettest month occurs in winter and has at least three times as much rainfall as the driest month in summer. Less than 1.5 inches (4 cm) of rain falls during the driest summer month.

Csa Warm, dry summer. The average temperature of the warmest month is more than 72°F (22°C), and for at least four months the average temperature is more than 50°F (10°C). Italy and other Mediterranean countries have a **Csa** climate.

Csb Cool, dry summer. In no month is the average temperature more than 72°F (22°C), but for at least four months the average temperature is more than 50°F (10°C). **Csb** climates are found near San Francisco, California; on the coast near Santiago, Chile; and in Portugal.

Cf Humid summer. Areas that cannot meet the criteria for **Cw** and **Cs**.

Cfa Humid, warm summer. The average temperature of the warmest month is more than 72°F (22°C), and for at least four months the average temperature is more than 50°F (10°C). Much of the eastern United States is in a **Cfa** zone.

Cfb Marine west coast. In no month is the

average temperature more than 72°F (22°C), but for at least four months the average temperature is more than 50°F (10°C). Great Britain, New Zealand, and the west coast of Alaska are all examples of **Cfb** climates.

D Continental Climates The average temperature of the warmest month is more than 50°F (10°C), and the average temperature of the coldest month is 27°F (–3°C) or below. Forests are the principal natural vegetation.

Dfa Humid, warm summer. All seasons have some precipitation. The average temperature of the warmest month is more than 72°F (22°C), and for at least four months the average temperature is more than 50°F (10°C). The northern Great Plains of the United States have a **Dfa** climate.

Dwa Humid, warm summer. The wettest month occurs in summer and has at least 10 times as much rainfall as the driest month in winter. The average temperature of the warmest month is more than 72°F (22°C), and for at least four months the average temperature is more than 50°F (10°C). The land around the northern part of the Yellow Sea has a **Dwa** climate.

Dfb Humid, cool summer. All seasons have some precipitation. In no month is the average temperature more than 72°F (22°C), but for at least four months the average temperature is more than 50°F (10°C). A large **Dfb** area stretches from eastern Europe into Asia.

Dwb Humid, cool summer. The wettest month occurs in summer and has at least 10 times as much rainfall as the driest month in winter. In no month is the average temperature more than 72°F (22°C), but for at least four months the average temperature is more than 50°F (10°C). Much of the area between Manchuria and the Sea of Okhotsk has a **Dwb** climate.

Dfc Subpolar. All seasons have some precipitation. For one to three months, the average temperature is 50°F (10°C) or more. A huge **Dfc** area is in Siberia and adjacent parts of the Soviet Union.

E Polar climates The average temperature of the warmest month is less than 50°F (10°C). There is no summer, and no trees grow.

ET Tundra. The average temperature of the warmest month is less than 50°F (10°C) but more than 32°F (0°C). Vast areas of northern North America, Europe, and Asia lie in the **ET** climate zone.

EF Ice cap. The average temperature of the warmest eight months is 32°F (0°C) or less. The **EF** climate is found at the North and South poles and in interior Greenland.

GLOSSARY OF COMMON GEOGRAPHICAL WORDS AND TERMS

Altitude How high a place or a thing is, usually measured from sea level or from the surface of the land.

Archipelago A cluster of islands.

Arctic Circle An imaginary line drawn along approximately latitude 66½° N. The climate north of the Arctic Circle is very cold, and relatively few people live there.

Atmosphere The mass of air that extends outward from the surface of the earth into space. The atmosphere is divided into four layers: the troposphere, in which temperature decreases as altitude increases; the stratosphere, in which temperature is constant, then increases; the mesosphere, in which it decreases; and the thermosphere, in which it increases again.

Atoll A coral reef that partially or completely surrounds a lagoon.

Basin A portion of land that is lower than the surrounding area. Basins are created when vertical movement causes the earth's crust to warp. Also, the area drained by a river and its tributaries.

Bay Part of an ocean, sea, or other body of water that extends inland. Bays are generally smaller than gulfs.

Bight A bay formed by a bend in the coastline.

Caldera A huge crater formed when the top of a volcano collapses or is exploded away.

Canyon A narrow, deep valley with steep sides. Many canyons have a river on their floor.

Climate General weather conditions over a long period of time. (See "Climates of the World.")

Continent A large unbroken land mass, distinguished from an island or peninsula. The seven continents are North America, South America, Europe, Asia, Africa, Australia, and Antarctica, though Europe and Asia are a continuous land mass divided along the spine of the Ural mountains running south from the Arctic Ocean.

Continental drift theory The theory, proposed in 1915 by Alfred Wegener, that all of the continents used to be joined in one supercontinent, Pangaea. Some 200 million years ago, Pangaea began to break up, and the continents "drifted" through the oceans to their present locations. The continental drift theory has now largely been replaced by the plate tectonics theory. (See the section "Earth Sciences.")

Continental shelf The edge of a continent covered by shallow ocean water, up to about 100 fathoms (600 feet), beyond which is the continental slope, which descends to the deep-sea plain, about 13,000–20,000 feet (4,000–6,000 m).

Core The innermost part of the earth. The outer core, which is liquid, is approximately 1,400 miles (2,250 km) thick. The inner core, which is solid (mostly iron), is approximately 750 miles (1,200 km) thick. (See *Crust; Mantle.*)

Cove A small and sheltered bay or inlet. Also, a small valley in a mountain.

Crater The bowl-shaped depression at the top of a volcano. Also, the depression made when a meteorite hits the earth. (See *Caldera.*)

Crust The outermost part of the earth. Under the continents the crust is approximately 19–25 miles (30–40 km) thick; under the oceans, only approximately 6 miles (10 km) thick. (See *Core; Mantle.*)

Cyclone A hurricane formed in the Indian Ocean.

Delta A triangular-shaped piece of land formed by sediment at the mouth of a river.

Desert (See "Great Deserts of the World" in this section.)

Dune A hill or ridge of sand that has been deposited by wind.

Equator An imaginary line that circles the earth halfway between the Poles. The equator is at latitude 0°.

Equinox The two times during the year (on or about Mar. 21 and Sept. 23) when the sun's rays strike the equator vertically. At equinox, day and night are the same length everywhere in the world. (See *Solstice.*)

Erosion The gradual wearing away of the surface of the land. For example, soil is eroded by wind and water; rock is eroded by freezing and thawing.

Estuary A valley at the mouth of a river where fresh water and sea water mix. Estuaries are created either when the land sinks or when the sea level rises and are generally shaped like a funnel.

Fjord A long, narrow inlet of the ocean with steeply sloping sides.

Floodplain Flat, low-lying land along either side of a river that is subject to flooding.

Geyser A jet of hot water or steam periodically thrown up by a hot spring.

Glacier A large mass of slowly moving ice. Glaciers are formed on land when snow is compacted and recrystallizes.

Gorge An especially narrow and steep-walled canyon.

Gulf Part of an ocean or sea that extends inland. Gulfs are generally larger than bays.

Hemisphere One-half of the earth's surface, whether divided latitudinally or longitudinally. For example, the Northern Hemisphere lies north of the equator, the Southern Hemisphere south of the equator. By convention, the Eastern Hemisphere consists of the continents of Europe, Asia, and Africa; the Western Hemisphere, of North America and South America.

Hurricane A huge tropical rainstorm with winds that swirl rapidly around a calm, dry, central "eye." To be classified a hurricane, a tropical storm must have wind speeds of more than 74 miles (119 km) an hour. The average hurricane is 375 miles (600 km) in diameter and extends up 40,000 feet (12,000 m) above the surface of the ocean. The eye averages 12.5 miles (20 km) in diameter. When a hurricane hits land, its fierce winds and floods can do great damage. On average five hurricanes each year threaten the eastern and southern United States.

Inlet An indentation in the shore of a sea, an ocean, or the bank of a river. Also, a narrow waterway that connects a lagoon to a larger body of water or that passes between two peninsulas.

Island A landmass completely surrounded by water.

Isthmus A narrow strip of land that connects two larger land masses.

Jet stream A "river" of high-altitude wind that travels from west to east at between 75 and 150 miles (120–240 km) an hour.

Lagoon A shallow pool or pond completely, or almost completely, separated from the sea.

Lake A body of water, often of considerable size, surrounded by land.

Latitude and longitude Latitude is the angle (measured in degrees, minutes, and seconds) between a point on the earth's surface north or south of the equator, the center of the earth, and the equator (0°0'0" latitude). Longitude is the angle between a point on the earth's surface, the center of the earth, and the prime meridian (0°0'0" longitude). There are 90 degrees of latitude between the equator and each of the poles (shown on a globe as parallel horizontal lines). There are 360 degrees of longitude (shown as vertical lines) divided into 180° east and west of the prime meridian (180°E and 180°W are thus the same). Since 1884 Greenwich, England (near London), has been universally recognized as the point through which the prime meridian passes. A degree (°) is 1/360 of a circle, a minute (') 1/60 of a degree, and a second (") 1/60 of a minute.

Lava Magma that reaches the surface of the earth and from which most of the gases have escaped. (See *Volcano.)*

Leeward The direction or side sheltered from the wind. (See *Windward.)*

Magma Molten rock that lies deep within the earth. In a volcanic eruption, magma bursts through the outer surface of the earth's crust. (See *Lava, Volcano.)*

Mantle The layer of rocky material that lies between the crust and the core of the earth. The mantle is approximately 1,800 miles (2,900 km) thick.

Monsoon A wind system in which the prevailing direction of the wind reverses itself from season to season. Southeast Asia is the most typical monsoon region. The summer (southwest) monsoon, characterized by hot, moist air and heavy rains, lasts from April to September. The winter (northeast) monsoon lasts from October to March and is characterized by cool, dry air.

Mountain Land that rises above its surroundings. Mountains are higher than hills. Older mountain ranges, like the Appalachians, are rounded because they are old and worn down; younger ranges, like the Andes or the Himalayas, have jagged peaks because they are still rising.

North Pole The northernmost point on the earth, or the northern axis on which the earth spins. The North Pole, at latitude 0°N, lies in the middle of the Arctic Circle.

Ocean The body of salt water that covers more than two-thirds of the earth's surface. Also, a part of that body (the Pacific Ocean, the Atlantic Ocean, the Indian Ocean, and the Arctic Ocean).

Peninsula A portion of land almost entirely surrounded by water.

Plain A large portion of level or rolling land that is treeless.

Plate tectonics theory The theory, first proposed in 1968, that the lithosphere is made up of some 20 sections, each of which consists of continental and ocean crust. The plates shift, moving continents, changing the size and shape of oceans, causing earthquakes, and creating volcanos and mountains. The plate tectonics theory has largely replaced the continental drift theory.

Plateau A portion of land, generally large and with a level surface, that is sharply elevated above the surrounding land. Plateaus are created when vertical movement causes the earth's crust to warp.

Pond A small body of water surrounded by land.

Prairie Level or rolling land generally covered with grasses, with few trees.

Rain shadow An area on the leeward side of a mountain range that receives little rainfall.

River A large stream.

Savanna A portion of land in the tropics or subtropics with only scattered trees but whose grasses can survive with scant rainfall.

Sea A large body of salt water, generally considered smaller than an ocean.

Solstice The time when the sun's rays strike vertically the Tropic of Cancer or the Tropic of Capricorn. At solstice the daylight hours reach their maximum or minimum. In the Northern Hemisphere, for example, summer solstice occurs on or about June 22; that is the "longest day of the year" and signals the beginning of summer. The winter solstice occurs on or about Dec. 22; that is the "shortest day of the year" and signals the beginning of winter. In the Southern Hemisphere, the longest and shortest days of the year occur on Dec. 22 and June 22, respectively. (See *Equinox.)*

Sound A body of water that separates an island from the mainland, or that connects two oceans, seas, or other bodies of water. Sounds are generally long and narrow.

South Pole The southernmost point on the earth, or the southern axis on which the earth spins. The South Pole, at latitude 0°S, lies in the middle of the Antarctic Ocean.

Steppe A portion of land with little rainfall, extreme temperature variations, and drought-resistant vegetation.

Strait A narrow body of water that connects two large bodies of water.

Stream Any body of running water that flows on or under the surface of the earth. Brooks and creeks are small streams; rivers are large streams.

Swamp A portion of wet, waterlogged, or flooded land.

Tide The rise and fall of the surface of the ocean and of bays, gulfs, and other bodies of water connected to the ocean. Tides are caused by the gravitational pull of the moon, which passes over the same meridian of the earth about once every 24 hours and 50 minutes. The length of time between successive high (or low) tides is about 12 hours and 25 minutes.

Tornado A small and short-lived but very severe windstorm. Tornadoes are whirling columns of air that reach down from a cloud, and they often accompany thunderstorms, rain, and hail. With wind speeds up to 300 miles (480 km) an hour tornadoes can do tremendous damage. The diameter of the average tornado is between 500 and 2,000 feet (150–600 m). The average tornado moves along the ground at 28 miles (45 km) an hour and has a "path" that is 16 miles (26 km) long. In the United States, some 750 tornadoes are reported every year, most frequently between April and June.

Tributary A stream or river that flows into a larger stream or river.

Tropic of Cancer Latitude 23½°N, which marks the northernmost limit of the sun's vertical rays. The area between the Tropic of Cancer and the Tropic of Capricorn is known as the "tropics." (See *Equinox.)*

Tropic of Capricorn Latitude 23½°S, which marks the southernmost limit of the sun's vertical rays.

Tundra An area of treeless plain near or above the Arctic Circle. Tundra subsoil is permanently frozen, but the soil thaws enough to support the growth of mosses, lichens, and some small flowering shrubs.

Typhoon A hurricane formed in the western Pacific Ocean.

Valley A long and sometimes narrow depression on the surface of the earth, usually between two mountain ridges or ranges.

Volcano A mountain formed by lava and/or other materials that have burst forth from deep within the earth. (See *Caldera, Crust, Lava, Magma.)*

Weather The condition of the atmosphere—temperature, rain, and wind, for example—in a particular place. A climate is defined by weather conditions over a long period of time.

Wind Any current of air, measured on land in miles per hour and at sea in knots. The direction of a given wind is determined from the point of the compass from which it blows (e.g., northeast, south). In various regions of the world, names are given to seasonal winds of particular quality. Among these are the *bora, a cold, usually dry north/northeast wind along the eastern Adriatic; brickfielder,* a hot north wind of southeastern Australia; *buran, a cold, violent north/northeast wind of Siberia and central Asia, common in winter; chinook,* a dry winter or spring wind that blows down the eastern slopes of the Rocky mountains, often warm enough to melt the snow; *harmattan,* a hot, dry north wind in West Africa that cools as it evaporates the moist air of the coast; *mistral,* a cold, strong north/northwest wind of the western Mediterranean, with a surface strength of 60 km/hour, frequent in winter; *pampero,* a sudden, cold south or west wind in Argentina and Uruguay, frequent in summer; *Santa Ana,* a hot, dry wind that blows from the north or east in Southern California; *sirocco,* a hot south wind of North Africa and southern Italy; *southerly burster,* a cold, violent south wind of southeastern Australia; *williwaw,* a violent squall that blows in the Strait of Magellan (South America); and *zonda,* a hot, dry north wind of Argentina and Uruguay.

Windward The direction or side facing the wind.

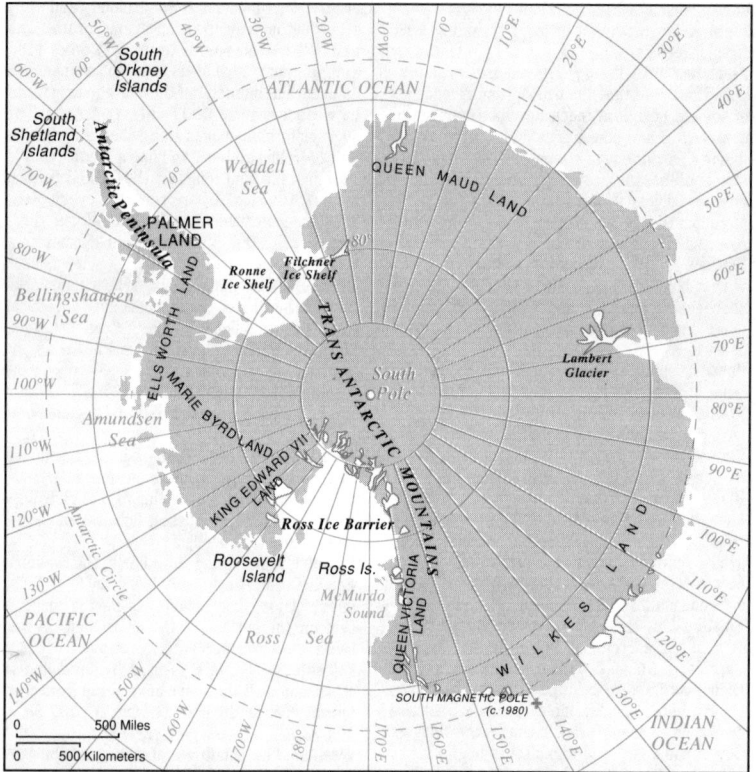

Antarctica

Geography **Location:** centered on the South Pole and situated almost entirely within the Antarctic Circle at 66½°S. **Land:** total area: about 5,404,000 sq. mi. (14,000,000 sq km). **Land boundary:** none; bordered by South Atlantic, Indian, and South Pacific oceans. **Temperature:** varies with location and altitude. East Antarctica is coldest; Antarctic peninsula in the west is mildest; mean annual temperature of the interior regions is –57°C (–71°F); mean temperatures at the coastal McMurdo station range from –28°C (–18°F) in August to –3°C (27°F) in January. **Daylight/darkness:** six months of continuous daylight from mid-September to mid-March; six months of continuous darkness from mid-March to mid-September. **Coastline:** undetermined. **Comparative area:** slightly less than 1.5 times size of U.S.; second smallest continent, after Australia. **Land use:** 0% cultivated, 0% forests, 0% lakes. **Major cities:** none.

People **Population:** no indigenous inhabitants; staffing of research stations varies seasonally; summer (January) pop.: approx. 3,300; winter (July) pop.: approx. 11,503.

Government **Type:** Antarctic Treaty (see below). **Natural Resources:** estimates are imprecise. May contain some 900 major mineral deposits, but only about 20 are in ice-free areas. Quantities of iron ore, coal, and offshore deposits of oil and natural gas are basically inaccessible. Small amounts of copper, chromium, platinum, nickel, gold, and hydrocarbons.

The Land: Some 200 million years ago, Antarctica was joined to South America, Africa, India, and Australia as one large continent. Geological changes caused the breakup into separate continents. Studies indicate that Antarctica once had a tropical environment, but that its present ice form is at least 20 million years old. Approximately 98% of the continent is covered by ice; it contains about 90% of the world's ice and 70% of the fresh water.

Elevations average from 6,600–13,200 ft. (2,000–4,000 m); mountain ranges, up to 16,500 ft. (5,000 m) high. Ice-free coastal areas include parts of southern Victoria Land, Wilks Land, and Ross Island. The Antarctic ice sheet averages 7,090 ft. (2,160 m) in depth and is 15,670 ft. deep at its thickest point. Altitude at the South Pole is about 9,800 ft. (3,000 m).

Land/sea life: Land life includes bacteria, lichens, mosses, two kinds of flowering plants in the ice-free areas, penguins, and some flying birds. Sea life includes several types of seals and whales, many of which were hunted to near extinction, but are now protected by international conventions.

Exploration: In 1772–75 British Capt. James Cook circumnavigated the continent without sighting land. U.S. Capt. John Davis made the first-known landing on the continent on Feb. 7, 1821. In 1908 the United Kingdom became the first nation to claim a "slice" of the continent, subsequently followed by claims from New Zealand (1923), France (1924), Australia (1933), Norway (1939), Chile (1940), and Argentina (1943). The United States and the USSR have never claimed any Antarctica territory. Claims made by other nations are not recognized by other countries or the United Nations.

In 1911 Capt. Robert F. Scott and Roald Amundsen of Norway began a "race to the pole." Amundsen's party arrived at the South Pole on Dec. 14, 1911, while Scott located the pole on Jan. 18, 1912.

Scientific research: The greatest scientific study ever conducted in Antarctica occurred in 1957–58, when 67 nations participated in the International Geophysical Year (IGY). Twelve countries established more than 50 stations to study the effects of the continent's huge ice mass on global weather, the oceans, the aurora australis, and the ionosphere. During the late 1980s, research was focused on the study of the ozone depletion in the stratosphere—called the ozone hole—which allows high levels of potentially harmful ultraviolet radiation to reach the earth's surface.

In 1987 the following countries maintained research stations year-round: USSR (7), Argentina (6), UK (4), Chile (3), Australia (3), United States (3), Japan (2), and one each by Brazil, China, West Germany, France, India, Italy, New Zealand, Poland, and South Africa.

Antarctica Treaty: Signed in 1959 by the 12 IGY nations (in force as of June 23, 1961), it establishes a legal framework for exploration and research until 1991. The treaty states that the area is to be used for peaceful purposes only, and military activity such as weapons testing is prohibited; calls for freedom of scientific investigation and cooperation, and a free exchange of information and personnel; nuclear explosions or disposal of radioactive wastes is forbidden; and, treaty-state observers have free access, including aerial observation, to any area and may inspect all stations, installations, and equipment.

Two types of members: consultative (voting) members conduct research programs and acceding (nonvoting) members agree to the terms of the treaty. The original 12 signatories: Argentina, Australia, Belgium, Chile, France, Japan, New Zealand, Norway, South Africa, United Kingdom, United States, and the USSR. Other consultative members that conduct Antarctic research: Poland (1977), West Germany (1981), Brazil (1983), India (1983), China (1985), Uruguay (1985), Italy (1987), and East Germany (1987). As of May 1989, there were also 24 acceding (nonvoting) members.

MAJOR LANGUAGES OF THE WORLD

The world's linguistic geography is extremely complex, for almost 10,000 languages and dialects (regional variations of a language) have been identified. Mapping languages is very complex, too, for many reasons. Opinions vary as to the definition of a language and the relationship between languages. Languages are always changing, with new words being created or adopted from other languages. As ethnic groups die out or are absorbed into the mainstream of society, some languages become extinct. Languages also travel. In ancient times they were carried from their place of origin by explorers, traders, and missionaries. In colonial times the language of the motherland was imposed on conquered territories. Today, languages are carried to the farthest corners of the earth and out into space by radio, television, and computers.

Reliable, current data on language use are notoriously difficult to obtain. Not all nations include language questions in their census, and not all nations conduct a census frequently. Data are gathered sometimes on mother tongue (the language a person speaks first and usually best), sometimes on the language a person uses most, sometimes on all of the languages a person speaks (bilingualism or multilingualism). For political or social reasons, some people may not admit that they speak a certain language. And, of course, language use involves more than speech: the full geography of a language must include reading and writing as well as speaking.

Language Families Languages are usually grouped into families. Most groupings assume that all the languages in the family developed from the same ancient language. Similarities in the structure of language can also be used to classify languages into families, particularly when a language has no written form.

The largest language family is **Sino-Tibetan**, which includes Chinese, Burmese, Tibetan, and the other languages of the countries in Southeast Asia.

The most intricate language family is **Indo-European**. Just where and among whom the Indo-European languages originated is not known, but the family includes languages throughout Europe and eastward all the way to the Indian subcontinent. English, for example, developed from Anglo-Frisian, a member of the prehistoric Germanic branch of Indo-European. Another member of the same branch is Modern German, which evolved from High German. The prehistoric Italic branch of Indo-European gave rise to the so-called Romance languages, including, among others, Spanish, Portuguese, and French. Hindi, Urdu, and Bengali are among the languages that derived from Sanskrit, a member of the Indo-Iranian branch of Indo-European. Yet another branch, the Balto-Slavic, led to Russian through Old Church Slavonic.

The **Afro-Asiatic** (or Hamito-Semitic) language family, also large and intricate, includes Arabic, Hebrew, and many other languages in Africa, the Middle East, and southwest Asia.

Japanese belongs to yet another language family, **Japanese**. Some scholars believe that the family also includes Korean and some minor dialects spoken in the Ryukyu Islands.

The 12 Principal Languages of the World

Even without uniform and precise data, the general geography of the most widely used languages is clear, for only about a dozen languages make up the mother tongue of about half of the world's more than 5 billion people.

Chinese is by far the most widely used language on earth. It is the mother tongue of more than one billion people. Chinese consists of many dialects, not all the spoken forms of which can be mutually understood. But all written Chinese can be understood by anyone who reads the language, because all of the dialects share the same writing system, *kanji*, in which symbols represent objects or ideas, not sounds. Written Chinese dates back at least 4,000 years.

Mandarin is the principal dialect of Chinese, and it is the official language of China, Taiwan, and Singapore. Mandarin is based on the dialect spoken around Beijing, in northern China. It is the mother tongue of some 500–825 million people, and its use is expected to increase rapidly, because it is now being taught in all Chinese schools. The other principal Chinese dialects are Cantonese, or Yue, used in southern China and Hong Kong (of which it is an official language); Wu, spoken in Shanghai and nearby provinces in eastern China; Min, found in southeastern China, Taiwan, and Malaysia; Xiang, spoken in central and southern Hunan Province, in southeastern China; Gan; and Hakka, also used in southeastern China and Taiwan.

English, although it is not the mother tongue of as many people as Chinese (some 300–450 million), is more widely spoken: perhaps as many as a third of the people in the world speak English. From the small island kingdom of England, it spread throughout the British Empire to North America, Africa, India, and beyond. Now English is an official language in 87 nations and territories, far more than any other language. The main concentrations of English speakers are found in the United States, Great Britain, India, Nigeria, Canada, and Australia.

Spanish is spoken by 125–320 million people around the world, especially in Mexico, Argentina, Colombia, and other former Spanish colonies in Central and South America. It is an official language in Spain and in 19 other nations, colonies, and territories.

Portuguese, like Spanish, was spread by 16th-century explorers and conquerors. Today it is spoken by 100–170 million people, the overwhelming majority of whom live in Brazil. Portuguese is the official language of Portugal, Brazil, and six other nations and territories.

French is not the mother tongue of as many people as Spanish and Portuguese are, but it is widely used as a lingua franca (a common language used by people who do not understand each other's mother tongues) and has an unusually long and noble history in the arts and the sciences. All told, 100–150 million people speak French, chiefly in France, Canada, Belgium, Switzerland, Haiti, and the former French colonies in Africa. It is an official language in 37 nations and territories.

German, like French, may be more widely read than spoken. Even so, it is an official language in West Germany, East Germany, Austria, Switzerland, Belgium, Liechtenstein, and Luxembourg. It is the mother tongue of large numbers of people in the United States, France, the Soviet Union, Brazil, Canada, Rwanda, Italy, Hungary, and Australia. Altogether, some 90–150 million people speak German.

Hindi is used by 140–325 million people, most of whom are in India. It is one of India's two official languages (English is the other). Significant numbers of Hindi speakers are also found in Fiji, Nepal, Mauritius, and Jamaica.

Urdu is the official language of Pakistan. It is spoken by 40–90 million people, chiefly in Pakistan but also in India and Mauritius. In their spoken form, Hindi and Urdu are very much the same, a language called Hindustani. However, written Hindi uses a script called Devanagari, whereas Urdu uses a modified Arabic script.

Bengali is spoken by some 100–180 million people. It is the dominant—and official—language of Bangladesh. Large numbers of Indians also speak Bengali, because Bangladesh used to be part of India; and it is found in Oman as well.

Russian, though spoken by a vast number of people (some 130–300 million), is overwhelmingly concentrated within the Soviet Union, of which it is the official language.

Arabic is the official language of 17 nations in North Africa and the Middle East. It is thought to be the mother tongue of 100–190 million people, chiefly in Egypt, Algeria, Morocco, Sudan, Iraq, Saudi Arabia, and Syria.

Japanese, like Russian, is highly concentrated. The vast majority of the 100–125 million people whose mother tongue is Japanese live in Japan, although there are substantial numbers in Brazil and the United States. Interestingly, no written form of Japanese existed until the Chinese system, kanji, was adopted about 2,000 years ago.

NORTH POLE · ARCTIC OCEAN

80° · 80° · 70° · 70° · 60° · 60° · 50° · 50° · 40° · 40° · 30° · 30° · 20° · 20° · 10° · 10° · 0° · 0° · 10° · 10° · 20° · 20° · 30° · 30° · 40° · 40° · 50° · 50° · 60° · 60° · 70° · 70° · 80° · 80°

GREENLAND (Den.)
W. GERMANY
ICELAND
NETH.
LUX.
BELG.
DEN.
E. GER.
POLAND
U.K.
CZECH
IRELAND
FRANCE
AUST.
HUNG.
SWITZ.
ROM.
SPAIN
ITALY
YUGO.
ALB.
BULG.
PORTUGAL
GREECE
TURKEY
MADEIRA (Port.)
CYPRUS
SYRIA
MOROCCO
MALTA
LEBANON
ISRAEL
CANARY IS. (Spain)
TUNISIA
AFGHAN-ISTAN
JORDAN
W. SAHARA
ALGERIA
LIBYA
EGYPT
KUWAIT
BAHRAIN
QATAR
MAURITANIA
MALI
NIGER
CHAD
SUDAN
SAUDI ARABIA
OMAN
C.A.R.

NORWAY
SWEDEN
FINLAND

SIBERIA

SOVIET UNION

EUROPE

ASIA

MONGOLIA

N. KOREA
S. KOREA
JAPAN

CHINA

PACIFIC OCEAN

IRAQ
IRAN
PAKISTAN
NEPAL
BHUTAN
INDIA
TAIWAN
HONG KONG (UK)
BURMA
BANGLA-DESH
LAOS
THAI-LAND
VIET NAM
CAM.
MARIANA ISLANDS
MARSHALL ISLANDS

AFRICA

NIGERIA
GUINEA
BURKINA FASO
IVORY COAST
LIBERIA
SIERRA LEONE
GUINEA-BISSAU
GAMBIA
SENEGAL
EQUAT. GUINEA
SÃO TOMÉ AND PRINCIPE
GABON
CAMEROON
CONGO
ZAIRE
RWANDA
BURUNDI
UGANDA
ETHIOPIA
SOMALIA
KENYA
TANZANIA
MALDIVES
SRI LANKA
YEMEN A.R.
PDR YEMEN
DJIBOUTI
SEYCHELLES
COMOROS
MALAWI

PHILIPPINES

FEDERATED STATES OF MICRONESIA

SINGAPORE
MALAYSIA
BRUNEI
INDONESIA
PAPUA-NEW GUINEA
SOLOMON ISLANDS
NAURU
KIRIBATI
TUVALU

ATLANTIC OCEAN

ANGOLA
ZAMBIA
ZIMB.
NAMIBIA
BOTSWANA
MOZAMBIQUE
MADAGASCAR
MAURITIUS

INDIAN OCEAN

SWAZILAND
SOUTH AFRICA
LESOTHO

VANUATU
FIJI

AUSTRALIA

TRISTAN DE CUNHA (UK)

KERGUÉLEN (France)

NEW ZEALAND

ANTARCTICA

SOUTH POLE

ANTARCTICA

SOUTH POLE

15° · 0° · 15° · 30° · 45° · 60° · 75° · 90° · 105° · 120° · 135° · 150° · 165° · 180°

547

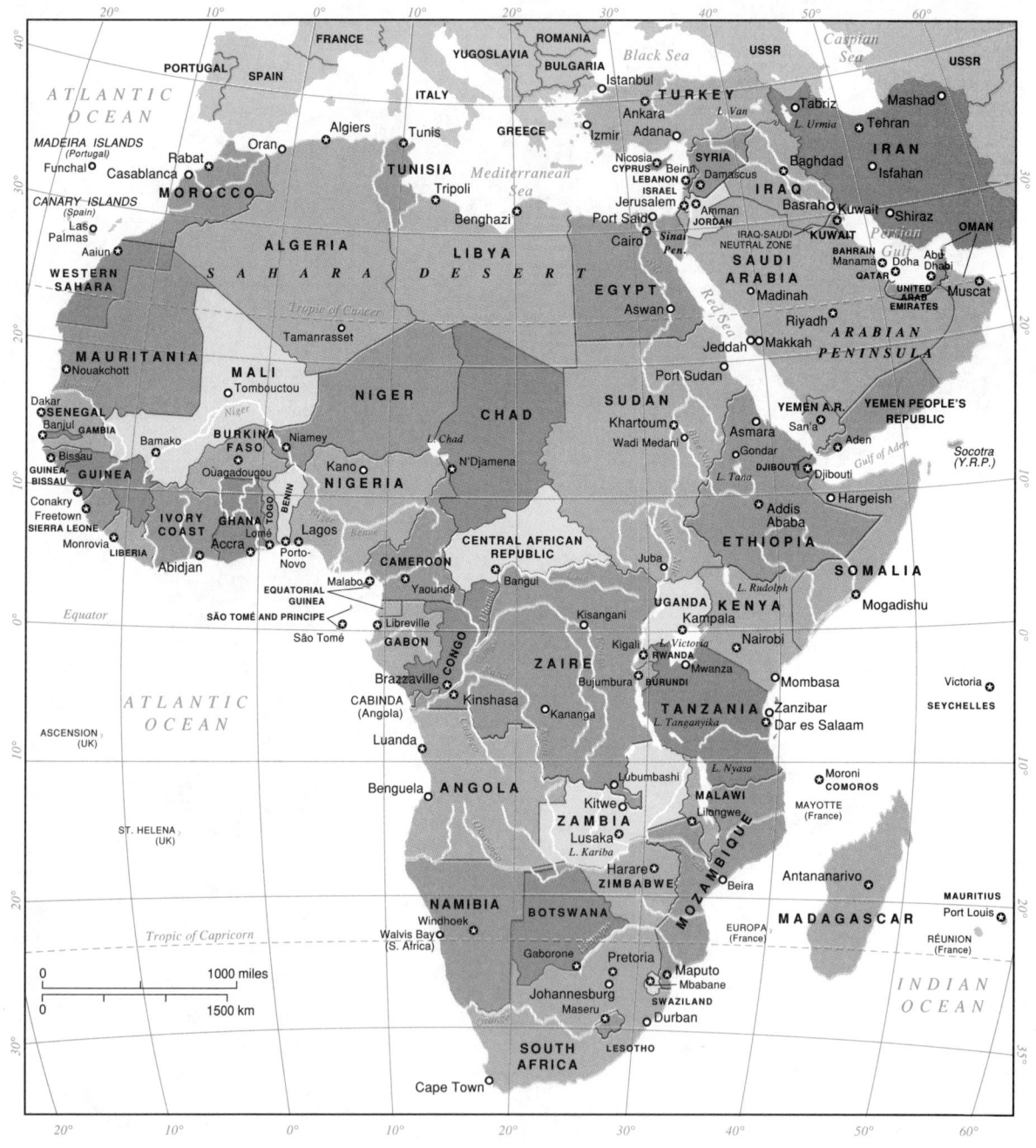

ATLANTIC
OCEAN

PORTUGAL
SPAIN
FRANCE
YUGOSLAVIA
ROMANIA
BULGARIA
Black Sea
USSR
Caspian Sea
USSR

ITALY
GREECE
Istanbul
TURKEY
Ankara
Izmir
Adana
Tabriz
L. Van
L. Urmia
Tehran
Mashad

MADEIRA ISLANDS
(Portugal)
Funchal
Algiers
Tunis
Nicosia
CYPRUS
Beirut
SYRIA
Damascus
Baghdad
IRAN
Isfahan

Oran
Rabat
Casablanca
TUNISIA
Tripoli
LEBANON
ISRAEL
Jerusalem
Amman
JORDAN
IRAQ
Basrah
Kuwait
Shiraz

CANARY ISLANDS
(Spain)
Las
Palmas
MOROCCO
Benghazi
Port Said
Cairo
Sinai
Pen.
KUWAIT
IRAQ-SAUDI
NEUTRAL ZONE
BAHRAIN
Manama
QATAR
Doha
Abu
Dhabi
OMAN

WESTERN
SAHARA
Aaiun
ALGERIA
LIBYA
EGYPT
Aswan
SAUDI
ARABIA
Madinah
UNITED
ARAB
EMIRATES
Muscat

SAHARA   DESERT
Tropic of Cancer
Tamanrasset
Riyadh
Jeddah
Makkah
ARABIAN
PENINSULA

MAURITANIA
Nouakchott
MALI
Tombouctou
NIGER
CHAD
Port Sudan
SUDAN
Khartoum
Wadi Medani
YEMEN A.R.
Asmara
San'a
YEMEN PEOPLE'S
REPUBLIC
Aden
Socotra
(Y.R.P.)

Dakar
SENEGAL
Banjul
GAMBIA
Bissau
GUINEA-
BISSAU
Bamako
BURKINA
FASO
Niamey
L. Chad
N'Djamena
Gondar
DJIBOUTI
Djibouti
Gulf of Aden
Hargeish

Conakry
Freetown
SIERRA LEONE
GUINEA
Ouagadougou
Kano
NIGERIA
Addis
Ababa
ETHIOPIA

Monrovia
LIBERIA
IVORY
COAST
GHANA
Accra
Lomé
Porto-
Novo
Lagos
CENTRAL AFRICAN
REPUBLIC
Juba
SOMALIA
Mogadishu

Abidjan
CAMEROON
Bangui
UGANDA
KENYA

EQUATORIAL
GUINEA
SÃO TOMÉ AND PRINCIPE
Malabo
Yaoundé
Libreville
Kisangani
Kampala
L. Rudolph
Nairobi

Equator
São Tomé
GABON
CONGO
ZAIRE
Kigali
RWANDA
L. Victoria
Mwanza
Mombasa
Victoria
SEYCHELLES

ATLANTIC
OCEAN
Brazzaville
CABINDA
(Angola)
Kinshasa
Kananga
Bujumbura
BURUNDI
TANZANIA
Zanzibar
Dar es Salaam

ASCENSION
(UK)
Luanda
Lubumbashi
L. Tanganyika
Moroni
COMOROS

Benguela
ANGOLA
Kitwe
ZAMBIA
Lusaka
L. Nyasa
MALAWI
Lilongwe
MAYOTTE
(France)

ST. HELENA
(UK)
L. Kariba
Harare
ZIMBABWE
Beira
Antananarivo
MAURITIUS
Port Louis

NAMIBIA
Windhoek
BOTSWANA
MOZAMBIQUE
EUROPA
(France)
MADAGASCAR
RÉUNION
(France)

Tropic of Capricorn
Walvis Bay
(S. Africa)
Gaborone
Pretoria
Maputo
Mbabane
SWAZILAND
INDIAN
OCEAN

0   1000 miles
0   1500 km
Johannesburg
Maseru
Durban

SOUTH
AFRICA
LESOTHO

Cape Town

548

AFRICA

EUROPE

Caribbean Sea

NICARAGUA

NETHERLANDS ANTILLES
(Neth.)

GRENADA

ST. VINCENT

TRINIDAD
AND TOBAGO

COSTA
RICA

Panama
Canal

PANAMA

Barranquilla

Maracaibo

Caracas

ATLANTIC
OCEAN

VENEZUELA

Georgetown

Medellín

GUYANA

Paramaribo

Bogotá

SURINAME

Cayenne

COLOMBIA

Cali

FRENCH
GUIANA
(France)

Orinoco

Quito

Equator

ECUADOR

Manaus

Belém

Guayaquil

Amazon

Amazon

Fortaleza

Iquitos

P
E
R
U

B R A Z I L

Recife

Callao

Lima

San Francisco

Cuzco

PACIFIC
OCEAN

Lake
Titicaca

Arequipa

La Paz

Salvador

Brasília

B O L I V I A

Iquique

Sucre

Tropic of Capricorn

C
H
I
L
E

P
A
R
A
G
U
A
Y

Concepción

Rio de Janeiro

SAN FÉLIX
(Chile)

A
R
G
E
N
T
I
N
A

Asunción

São Paulo

Paraná

Uruguay

ISLAS DE JUAN
FERNANDEZ
(Chile)

Valparaíso

Rosario

Salto

URUGUAY

Santiago

Buenos
Aires

Montevideo

ATLANTIC
OCEAN

Río de
la Plata

Mar del Plata

0   500 miles

0   750 km

FALKLAND
ISLANDS
(UK)

Stanley

SOUTH GEORGIA
ISLANDS
(UK)

Punta Arenas

Cape Horn

SOUTH AMERICA

Top Map

ATLANTIC OCEAN

UNITED STATES

San Diego
Mexicali
Tijuana
Nogales
El Paso
Ciudad Juárez
Chihuahua
San Antonio
New Orleans
La Paz
Durango
Monterrey
Gulf of Mexico
Miami
Nassau
BAHAMAS
Tropic of Cancer
San Luis Potosí
Tampico
Guadalajara
Mérida
Havana
CUBA
BRITISH VIRGIN ISLANDS (UK)
TURKS AND CAICOS (UK)
DOMINICAN REPUBLIC
Leeward Islands
Mexico City
Campeche
Yucatan
CAYMAN ISLANDS (UK)
JAMAICA
HAITI
Port-au-Prince
Santo Domingo
PUERTO RICO (U.S.)
Puebla
Veracruz
Kingston
VIRGIN ISLANDS (U.S.)
Acapulco
MEXICO
BELIZE
Belmopan
Caribbean Sea
NETHERLANDS ANTILLES (Neth.)
Windward Islands
GUATEMALA
HONDURAS
TRINIDAD & TOBAGO
Guatemala City
Tegucigalpa
San Salvador
EL SALVADOR
NICARAGUA
PACIFIC OCEAN
Managua
COSTA RICA
Panama Canal
VENEZUELA
San José
Caracas
Panama City
PANAMA
COLOMBIA

SIERRA MADRE OCCIDENTAL
BAJA CALIFORNIA
Gulf of California

0 ____ 500 miles
0 ____ 750 km

Bottom Map

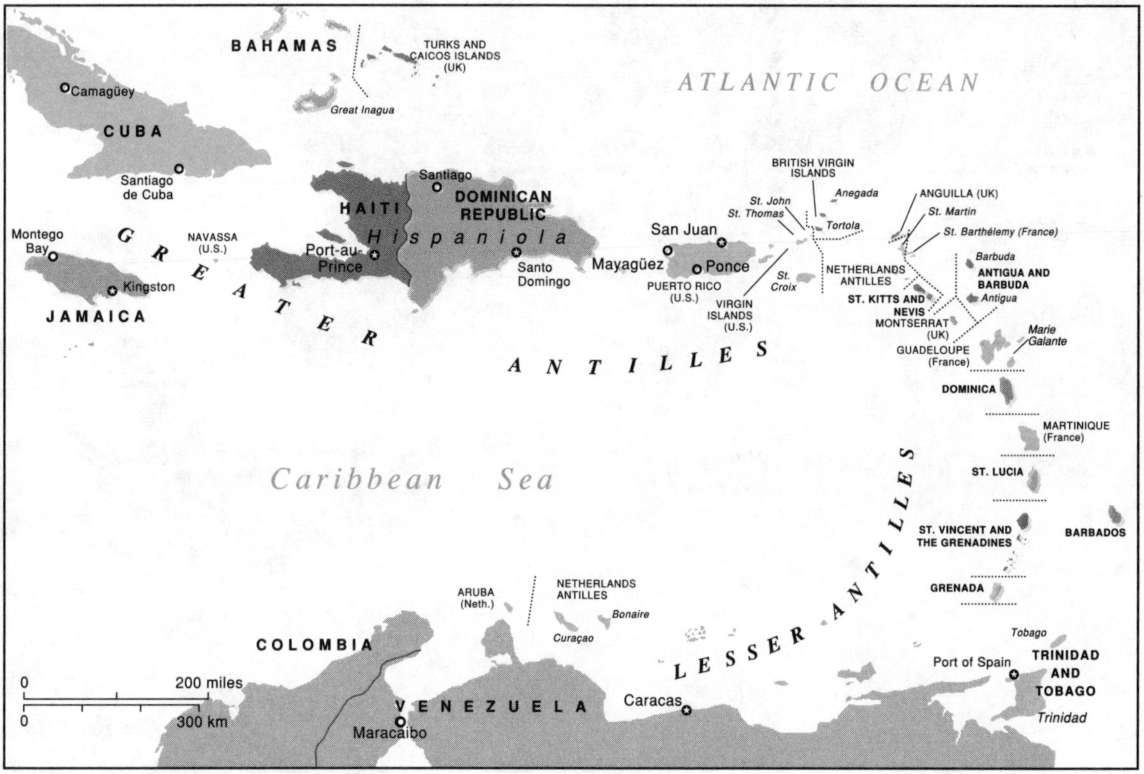

BAHAMAS
TURKS AND CAICOS ISLANDS (UK)
ATLANTIC OCEAN
Camagüey
Great Inagua
CUBA
Santiago
Santiago de Cuba
DOMINICAN REPUBLIC
BRITISH VIRGIN ISLANDS
ANGUILLA (UK)
St. John
St. Thomas
Anegada
St. Martin
St. Barthélemy (France)
Montego Bay
NAVASSA (U.S.)
HAITI
Hispaniola
Tortola
Barbuda
ANTIGUA AND BARBUDA
Port-au-Prince
San Juan
Antigua
Kingston
Santo Domingo
Mayagüez
Ponce
NETHERLANDS ANTILLES
ST. KITTS AND NEVIS
JAMAICA
GREATER
PUERTO RICO (U.S.)
St. Croix
MONTSERRAT (UK)
Marie Galante
VIRGIN ISLANDS (U.S.)
GUADELOUPE (France)
ANTILLES
DOMINICA
MARTINIQUE (France)
Caribbean Sea
ST. LUCIA
LESSER ANTILLES
ST. VINCENT AND THE GRENADINES
BARBADOS
COLOMBIA
ARUBA (Neth.)
NETHERLANDS ANTILLES
GRENADA
Bonaire
Curaçao
Tobago
TRINIDAD AND TOBAGO
VENEZUELA
Caracas
Port of Spain
Maracaibo
Trinidad

0 ____ 200 miles
0 ____ 300 km

CENTRAL AMERICA

ATLANTIC
OCEAN

ARCTIC OCEAN

North Pole

Chukchi Sea

Barents Sea

Kara Sea

Laptev Sea

Bering Sea

Sea of Okhotsk

Kamchatka Peninsula

Yakutsk

SOVIET UNION (U.S.S.R.)

Sakhalin

Moscow

Sverdlovsk
Chelyabinsk
Omsk
Novosibirsk
Krasnoyarsk
Irkutsk

Arctic Circle

Black Sea

TURKEY
CYPRUS
LEBANON
SYRIA
ISRAEL
JORDAN
IRAQ

Caspian Sea

Aral Sea

Lake Balkhash

Tashkent
Alma-Ata
Samarkand

Ulan Bator

Harbin

Vladivostok

MONGOLIA

JAPAN
Tokyo
Yokohama
Kyoto
Osaka

Sea Of Japan

NORTH KOREA
Pyongyang
Seoul
SOUTH KOREA

Beijing

KUWAIT
BAHRAIN

IRAN

AFGHANISTAN
Kabul
Islamabad
Lahore

Persian Gulf

Tropic of Cancer

QATAR
UNITED ARAB EMIRATES
OMAN

SAUDI ARABIA

Red Sea

YEMEN A.R.
P.D.R. YEMEN

Gulf of Aden

SOMALIA

Arabian Sea

PAKISTAN
Karachi

Delhi
New Delhi

Tibet

TAKLIMAKAN DESERT

CHINA

Chungking

Wuhan

Shanghai

Yellow Sea

East China Sea

Shanghai

Taipei
TAIWAN

Guangzhou (Canton)
HONG KONG (UK)
MACAU (Port.)

NEPAL
Kathmandu
BHUTAN
Timphu
Dhaka

INDIA

Bombay

Madras

Laccadive Islands (India)

Colombo
Male

MALDIVES

Equator

SEYCHELLES

COMOROS

MADAGASCAR

RÉUNION (France)
MAURITIUS

Calcutta
BANGLA-DESH

Mandalay

BURMA

Rangoon

Bangkok

THAILAND

Hanoi
LAOS
Vientiane

VIETNAM

CAMBODIA
Phnom Penh
Ho Chi Minh City (Saigon)

Bay of Bengal

Andaman Islands (India)

Nicobar Islands (India)

SRI LANKA

BRITISH INDIAN OCEAN TERRITORY (UK)

Manila

PHILIPPINES

Davao

South China Sea

Bandar Seri Bagawan
BRUNEI

Medan

MALAYSIA
Kuala Lumpur
SINGAPORE

Borneo

Celebes

I N D O N E S I A

Sumatra

Jakarta
Surabaya
Java
Bali

PACIFIC OCEAN

INDIAN OCEAN

CHRISTMAS ISLAND (Australia)

COCOS ISLANDS (Australia)

0   1000 miles
0   1500 km

AUSTRALIA

PROFESSIONAL SPORTS

Baseball

FINAL STANDINGS—1989

NATIONAL LEAGUE EAST

Team	W	L	Pct.	GB
Chicago	93	69	.574	—
N.Y. Mets	87	75	.537	6
St. Louis	86	76	.531	7
Montreal	81	81	.500	12
Pittsburgh	74	88	.457	19
Philadelphia	67	95	.414	26

NATIONAL LEAGUE WEST

San Francisco	92	70	.568	—
San Diego	89	73	.549	3
Houston	86	76	.531	6
Los Angeles	77	83	.481	14
Cincinnati	75	87	.463	17
Atlanta	63	97	.394	28

AMERICAN LEAGUE EAST

Toronto	89	73	.549	—
Baltimore	87	75	.537	2
Boston	83	79	.512	6
Milwaukee	81	81	.500	8
N.Y. Yankees	74	87	.460	14½
Cleveland	73	89	.451	16
Detroit	59	103	.364	30

AMERICAN LEAGUE WEST

Oakland	99	63	.611	—
Kansas City	92	70	.568	7
California	91	71	.562	8
Texas	83	79	.512	16
Minnesota	80	82	.494	19
Seattle	73	89	.451	26
Chicago	69	92	.429	29

THE WORLD SERIES

A championship series between the winners of two leagues was held in 1882 between the National League and the American Association and was played at the end of each season until the AA folded in 1890. Following this, the top two NL clubs played each other for the "Temple Cup," but the idea never really caught on with the public. When the American League began operations in 1901, there was great animosity between the two circuits due to bidding wars for the services of star players. Peace was established before the 1903 season, and when it became clear that Pittsburgh would win the NL and Boston the AL, the owners of each club reached a private agreement to hold a "World Series" in October. Many were surprised when the newer American League won the title.

There was no agreement to play such a series every year, however, and in 1904 the New York Giants refused to meet the Boston club, probably because of John McGraw's dislike of American League President Ban Johnson. But the baseball public wanted a championship series, and by 1905 Giants' owner John Brush proposed rules governing a mandatory series to be played every year. With minute changes, those rules stand to this day.

1903. Boston (A) over Pittsburgh (N), 5–3. The upstart American League emerged victorious in the first World Series, a best-of-nine affair. The "Pilgrims" (Red Sox) staged one of the greatest comebacks in history by sweeping the final four games. Bill Dineen and Cy Young each won two for Boston, and held Pirate immortal Honus Wagner to one harmless single in those four contests.

1904. No series. New York Giants owner John T. Brush and manager John McGraw refused to play the American League Boston club, dismissing them as representative of an "inferior league."

1905. New York (N) over Philadelphia (A), 4–1. Every game was won by a shutout, with Christy Mathewson throwing three for the Giants. In 27 innings, he allowed 14 hits, striking out 18 and walking one. The Athletics committed five errors in Game Three, the pivotal contest.

1906. Chicago (A) over Chicago (N), 4–2. The first "subway series" was a stunning upset. The "Hitless Wonders" White Sox had batted .230 with 7 home runs during the season, while the Cubs were winning 116 games, still the all-time record. Utilityman George Rohe hit two game-winning triples for the Sox and Ed Walsh pitched two of their wins.

1907. Chicago (N) over Detroit (A), 4–0. Avenging the past year, the Cubs shut down Ty Cobb, Sam Crawford et al, behind a superb four-man pitching performance, and the hitting of Harry Steinfeldt (.471) and Johnny Evers (.350).

1908. Chicago (N) over Detroit (A), 4–1. Only a little closer this year. Johnny Evers repeated his .350 average of 1907, joining player-manager Frank Chance (.421) and outfielder Wildfire Schulte (.389) in the Cub attack. Ty Cobb led Detroit (.368), to no avail.

1909. Pittsburgh (N) over Detroit (A), 4–3. The Tigers lost their third straight series, as Honus Wagner won the "Battle of the Titans" with Ty Cobb. The Pirate shortstop hit .333 with six RBIs and six stolen bases, and Babe Adams pitched in with three complete game victories.

1910. Philadelphia (A) over Chicago (N), 4–1. Connie Mack's infielders combined to bat .364 as the A's rolled to an easy title. Jack Coombs pitched three wins and tossed in a .385 batting average. The great Cubs pitching staff was growing old.

1911. Philadelphia (A) over New York (N), 4–2. Regarded by some as the greatest team ever, the A's wrestled down a strong New York club featuring Mathewson and Rube Marquard. Frank "Home Run" Baker got his nickname from game-winning blasts in Games Two and Three.

1912. Boston (A) over New York (N), 4–3. This thrill-a-minute series featured an 11–inning tie in Game Two, and an extra-inning final game. Two Giant errors, by Fred Merkle and, Snodgrass, enabled Boston to score two runs in the bottom of the 10th inning of the final contest.

1913. Philadelphia (A) over New York (N), 4–1. Home Run Baker again hammered Giant pitching, batting .450 with seven RBIs. Eddie Collins also starred for the As, hitting .421 with three stolen bases.

1914. Boston (N) over Philadelphia (A), 4–0. The red-hot "Miracle Braves" swept the heavily favored Athletics, who scored only six runs in the four games. Catcher Hank Gowdy (.545) and second baseman Johnny Evers (.438) led the Boston offense.

1915. Boston (A) over Philadelphia (N), 4–1. The famous Red Sox outfield of Speaker, Lewis, and Hooper combined to bat .364 while Rube Foster pitched two complete game wins. Foster also batted .500, driving in the winning run in Game Two.

1916. Boston (A) over Brooklyn (N), 4–1. After three one-run games, Boston took charge with 6–2 and 4–1 victories. A young lefthander named Babe Ruth twirled a 14–inning six hitter in Game Two.

1917. Chicago (A) over New York (N), 4–2. The pitching of Red Faber (3–1, 2.33) and the hitting of Eddie Collins, Buck Weaver, and Joe Jackson were too much for the Giants in a sloppy (23 errors) series.

1918. Boston (A) over Chicago (N), 4–2. Every game a pitchers duel, the losing Cubs posted a 1.04 ERA over the six games. The Boston staff allowed but nine runs in the series, led by Babe Ruth who extended his consecutive scoreless inning streak to 29⅔.

1919. Cincinnati (N) over Chicago (A), 5–3. Results declared invalid after eight Chicago "Black Sox" were found to have acted to lose games intentionally. All eight, plus 14 other major leaguers, were barred from baseball for life in the ensuing scandal.

1989 INDIVIDUAL LEADERS

AMERICAN LEAGUE

BATTING AVERAGE		HOME RUNS		RUNS BATTED IN		PITCHING—WINS		PITCHING—ERA	
Puckett, Minnesota	.339	McGriff, Toronto	36	Sierra, Texas	119	Saberhagen, Kansas City	23-6	Saberhagen, Kansas City	2.16
Lansford, Oakland	.336	Carter, Cleveland	35	Mattingly, N.Y. Yankees	113	Stewart, Oakland	21-9	Finley, California	2.57
Boggs, Boston	.330	McGwire, Oakland	33	Esasky, Boston	108	Davis, Oakland	19-7	Moore, Oakland	2.61
Yount, Milwaukee	.318	Jackson, Kansas City	32	Carter, Cleveland	105	Moore, Oakland	19-11	Blyleven, California	2.73
Franco, Texas	.316	Esasky, Boston	30	Jackson, Kansas City	105	Ballard, Baltimore	18-8	McCaskill, California	2.93
Molitor, Milwaukee	.315	Sierra, Texas	29	Bell, Toronto	104			Bosio, Milwaukee	2.95
Sax, N.Y. Yankees	.315	Whitaker, Detroit	28	Yount, Milwaukee	103				
Baines, Texas	.309	Deer, Milwaukee	26	Evans, Boston	100				
Greenwell, Boston	.308	Tettleton, Baltimore	26	Parker, Oakland	97				
Sierra, Texas	.306								

NATIONAL LEAGUE

BATTING AVERAGE		HOME RUNS		RUN BATTED IN		PITCHING—WINS		PITCHING—ERA	
Gwynn, San Diego	.336	Mitchell, San Francisco	47	Mitchell, San Francisco	125	Scott, Houston	20-10	Garrelts, San Francisco	2.28
Clark, San Francisco	.333	Johnson, N.Y. Mets	36	Guerrero, St. Louis	117	Maddux, Chicago	19-12	Hershiser, Los Angeles	2.31
L. Smith, Atlanta	.315	Davis, Cincinnati	34	Will Clark, San Francisco	111	Bielecki, Chicago	18-7	Langston, Montreal	2.39
Grace, Chicago	.314	Davis, Houston	34	Davis, Cincinnati	101	Magrane, St. Louis	18-9	Whitson, San Diego	2.66
Guerrero, St. Louis	.311	Sandberg, Chicago	30	Johnson, N.Y. Mets	101	Reuschel, San Francisco	17-8	Hurst, San Diego	2.69
R. Alomar, San Diego	.295	Strawberry, N.Y. Mets	29	Jack Clark, San Diego	94			Drabek, Pittsburgh	2.80
Walton, Chicago	.293	Jack Clark, San Diego	26	Davis, Houston	89				
Oquendo, St. Louis	.291	V. Hayes, Philadelphia	26	Murray, Los Angeles	88				
Mitchell, San Francisco	.291			Bonilla, Pittsburgh	86				
Sandberg, Chicago	.290								

1920. Cleveland (A) over Brooklyn (N), 5–2. Game Five was surely the most freakish in series history. It featured a) the first World Series grand slam home run (Indians right-fielder Elmer Smith), b) the first World Series home run by a pitcher (Indians Jim Bagby), and c) the first and only unassisted triple play in series action (Indians second baseman Billy Wambsganss).

1921. New York (N) over New York (A), 5–3. Six Giants batted over .300, and their pitchers held Babe Ruth to a .500 slugging average. Giant hurler Jesse Barnes won two games and batted .444.

1922. New York (N) over New York (A), 4–0. The result was said to be final proof that "brains beat brawn." Giant pitching shut down Ruth & Co., allowing only 11 runs in the five contests (one tie).

1923. New York (A) over New York (N), 4–2. The Yankees took the last three to break the spell of their cross-river rivals, behind Babe Ruth's three homers and eight RBIs. Casey Stengel hit two home runs for the losers.

1924. Washington (A) over New York (N), 4–3. A 12-innning seventh game won by Walter Johnson in relief capped an exciting affair. Twenty-seven-year-old player-manager Bucky Harris starred for the Senators (.333, 7 RBIs), as did outfielder Goose Goslin (.344, 7 RBIs).

1925. Pittsburgh (N) over Washington (A), 4–3. Pirate centerfielder Max Carey had 11 hits and three stolen bases, as Pittsburgh became the first team since 1903 to come back from a three games to one deficit.

1926. St. Louis (N) over New York (A), 4–3. Babe Ruth hit three homers in Game Four, but in the seventh inning of the seventh contest Grover Cleveland Alexander struck out Tony Lazzeri with the bases loaded, saving the game and the series for the Cardinals.

1927. New York (A) over Pittsburgh (N), 4–0. Generally regarded as the greatest team of all time, the "Murderers' Row" Yankees disposed of the Pirates behind two more Babe Ruth homers, plus the pitching of Wilcy Moore, Herb Pennock, and George Pipgrass.

1928. New York (A) over St. Louis (N), 4–0. Another Yankee sweep. Ruth and Lou Gehrig combined to bat .593, with seven home runs and 13 RBIs. Waite Hoyt pitched two complete game victories.

1929. Philadelphia (A) over Chicago (N), 4–1. Trailing 8–0 in Game Four, the A's roared back to score 10 runs in the seventh inning, a series record. In the next contest, the Mackmen took the series with a three-run ninth inning.

1930. Philadelphia (A) over St. Louis (N), 4–2. Lefty Grove and George Earnshaw pitched well, while Al Simmons, Jimmie Foxx, and Mickey Cochrane combined for 11 extra-base hits. Cardinal regulars batted only .185 in the six games.

1931. St. Louis (N) over Philadelphia (A), 4–3. Cardinal centerfielder Pepper Martin set a record that stood for 33 years with his 12 hits. Martin also stole five bases and hit a home run. Bill Hallahan and Burleigh Grimes handled the pitching, combining for a 4–0, 1.25 ERA.

1932. New York (A) over Chicago (N), 4–0. The Yankees completed a streak of 12 straight World Series victories in sweeping the Cubs. This time Ruth and Gehrig combined to bat .438, with five homers and 14 RBIs.

1933. New York (N) over Washington (A), 4–1. Same teams as 1924, different result. Bill Terry's Giants defeated Joe Cronin's Senators in a battle of player-managers. Carl Hubbell won two for New York and did not allow an earned run.

1934. St. Louis (N) over Detroit (A), 4–3. Dizzy and Paul Dean hurled the Cardinals to the title, winning all four Redbird victories. A bad defensive series, with 27 errors and 13 unearned runs.

1935. Detroit (A) over Chicago (N), 4–2. The Cubs won 21 straight games in September, but came up short when faced with Mickey Cochrane's Tigers. Charlie Gehringer and Tommy Bridges starred for Detroit, while Lou Warneke (2–0, 0.54) was superb for the losers.

1936. New York (A) over New York (N), 4–2. The Yankees hammered Giant pitching in Games Two and Six, ending with 43 runs for the series. Tony Lazzeri and Bill Dickey each drove in five runs in the second contest, when Joe McCarthy's "Windowbreakers" scored 18 times to set a record.

1937. New York (A) over New York (N), 4–1. Lefty Gomez pitched two of the Yankee wins and drove in the winning run with a single in the final game. The Yanks scored seven runs in the sixth inning of Game One, then coasted to an easy championship.

1938. New York (A) over Chicago (N), 4–0. In a replay of 1932, the Bronx Bombers blew out an overmatched Cub squad. Cub fans are still waiting for their team's first series victory over the Yankees.

1939. New York (A) over Cincinnati (N), 4–0. New York won its fourth straight World Championship the same way they won the first three—easily. Charlie Keller batted .438 with three homers, and scored as many runs as the entire Reds team, eight.

1940. Cincinnati (N) over Detroit (A), 4–3. The Reds repeated as NL champs, then prevailed over the Tigers when Paul Derringer beat Bobo Newsome 2–1 in the seventh game. Derringer and Bucky Walters each won two games.

1941. New York (A) over Brooklyn (N), 4–1. With two outs in the ninth inning of Game

MAJOR LEAGUE BASEBALL LEAGUE CHAMPIONSHIP SERIES RESULTS
(Divisional play began in 1969.)

AMERICAN LEAGUE

Year	Winner	Loser	MVP
1969	Baltimore Orioles-3	Minnesota Twins-0	
1970	Baltimore Orioles-3	Minnesota Twins-0	
1971	Baltimore Orioles-3	Oakland A's-0	
1972	Oakland A's-3	Detroit Tigers-2	
1973	Oakland A's-3	Baltimore Orioles-2	
1974	Oakland A's-3	Baltimore Orioles-1	
1975	Boston Red Sox-3	Oakland A's-0	
1976	N.Y. Yankees-3	Kansas City Royals-2	
1977	N.Y. Yankees-3	Kansas City Royals-2	
1978	N.Y. Yankees-3	Kansas City Royals-1	
1979	Baltimore Orioles-3	California Angels-1	
1980	Kansas City Royals-3	N.Y. Yankees-0	Frank White, Kansas City
1981	N.Y. Yankees-3	Oakland A's-0	Graig Nettles, N.Y.
1982	Milwaukee Brewers-3	California Angels-2	Fred Lynn, California
1983	Baltimore Orioles-3	Chicago White Sox-1	Mike Boddicker, Baltimore
1984	Detroit Tigers-3	Kansas City Royals-0	Kirk Gibson, Detroit
1985[1]	Kansas City Royals-4	Toronto Blue Jays-3	George Brett, Kansas City
1986	Boston Red Sox-4	California Angels-3	Marty Barrett, Boston
1987	Minnesota Twins-4	Detroit Tigers-1	Gary Gaetti, Minnesota
1988	Oakland A's-4	Boston Red Sox-0	Dennis Eckersley, Oakland
1989	Oakland A's-4	Toronto Blue Jays-1	Rickey Henderson, Oakland

NATIONAL LEAGUE

Year	Winner	Loser	MVP
1969	N.Y. Mets-3	Atlanta Braves-0	
1970	Cincinnati Reds-3	Pittsburgh Pirates-0	
1971	Pittsburgh Pirates-3	S.F. Giants-1	
1972	Cincinnati Reds-3	Pittsburgh Pirates-2	
1973	N.Y. Mets-3	Cincinnati Reds-2	
1974	L.A. Dodgers-3	Pittsburgh Pirates-1	
1975	Cincinnati Reds-3	Pittsburgh Pirates-0	
1976	Cincinnati Reds-3	Philadelphia Phillies-0	
1977	L.A. Dodgers-3	Philadelphia Phillies-1	Dusty Baker, L.A.
1978	L.A. Dodgers-3	Philadelphia Phillies-1	Steve Garvey, L.A.
1979	Pittsburgh Pirates-3	Cincinnati Reds-0	Willie Stargell, Pittsburgh
1980	Philadelphia Phillies-3	Houston Astros-2	Manny Trillo, Philadelphia
1981	L.A. Dodgers-3	Montreal Expos-2	Burt Hooton, L.A.
1982	St. Louis Cardinals-3	Atlanta Braves-0	Darrell Porter, St. Louis
1983	Philadelphia Phillies-3	L.A. Dodgers-1	Gary Matthews, Philadelphia
1984	San Diego Padres-3	Chicago Cubs-2	Steve Garvey, San Diego
1985[1]	St. Louis Cardinals-4	L.A. Dodgers-2	Ozzie Smith, St. Louis
1986	N.Y. Mets-4	Houston Astros-2	Mike Scott, Houston
1987	St. Louis Cardinals-4	S.F. Giants-3	Jeff Leonard, S.F.
1988	L.A. Dodgers-4	N.Y. Mets-3	Orel Hershiser, L.A.
1989	S.F. Giants-4	Chicago Cubs-1	Will Clark, S.F.

1. In 1985 the League Championship Series was switched to a best-of-seven format.

Four, Dodger catcher Mickey Owen dropped a third strike on Tommy Henrich, allowing him to reach first base. The Yankees then scored four times to win the ballgame, and finished Brooklyn off the next day.

1942. St. Louis (N) over New York (A), 4–1. The Cardinals, winners of 106 games during the regular season, lost Game One with the tying run at bat. They then swept four in a row, behind the pitching of Johnny Beazley (2–0, 2.50) and Ernie White's shutout in Game Three.

1943. New York (A) over St. Louis (N), 4–1. In a turnaround from 1942, the Yanks held St. Louis to nine runs in the five games. Joe Gordon and Bill Dickey homered, while third baseman Billy Johnson drove in three runs for New York.

1944. St. Louis (N) over St. Louis (A), 4–2. The Browns struggled valiantly in their only World Series appearance, but fell short against a strong Cardinal club left relatively intact by World War II. Ten Brown errors gave the Redbirds their third title in five years.

1945. Detroit (A) over Chicago (N), 4–3. Tiger Ace Hal Newhouser was hit hard in Game One, but he bounced back to win Games Five and Seven. Doc Cramer (.379) and Hank Greenberg (2 HRs, 7 RBIs) led the Detroit offense.

1946. St. Louis (N) over Boston (A), 4–3. Enos Slaughter scored from first on a base-hit by Harry Walker in the eighth inning of the seventh game, giving St. Louis its third title in five years. Harry Brecheen won three games for the Cardinals, allowing but one run.

1947. New York (A) over Brooklyn (N), 4–3. Yankee pitcher Bill Bevens had a no-hitter for 8 ⅔ innings in Game Four, but lost the game on a double by Cookie Lavagetto. Tommy Henrich (.323) had the game winning RBIs in Games One, Two, and Seven.

1948. Cleveland (A) over Boston (N), 4–2. The series featured fine pitching on both sides, including the first game, when Boston's Johnny Sain beat Bob Feller 1–0. Cleveland's Gene Beardon did not allow a run in 10⅔ innings.

1949. New York (A) over Brooklyn (N), 4–1. Game One was 0–0 until Tommy Henrich led off the bottom of the ninth with a home run off Don Newcombe. Bobby Brown (currently president of the American League) batted .500 with five RBIs.

1950. New York (A) over Philadelphia (N), 4–0. New York struggled to win the first three contests by scores of 1–0, 2–1, and 3–2, in a series that was closer than it looks. The "Whiz Kid" Phillies held the Yanks to a .222 batting average but managed to hit only .203 themselves.

1951. New York (A) over New York (N), 4–2. A tired Giant pitching staff held the Yankees in check for three games, but the AL champs broke out to score 23 runs in the final three. Eddie Lopat (2–0, 0.50) starred for the winners.

1952. New York (A) over Brooklyn (N), 4–3. Allie Reynolds and Vic Raschi each won two games, combining for a 1.69 ERA. Johnny Mize hit three homers, and Mickey Mantle and Yogi Berra each hit two. Duke Snider batted .345 with four roundtrippers in a losing cause.

1953. New York (A) over Brooklyn (N), 4–2. The Yankees won their fifth straight World Championship as second baseman Billy Martin tied a record with 12 hits. Martin slugged .958 and drove in eight runs.

1954. New York (N) over Cleveland (A), 4–0. The Indians won 111 games during the season still an AL record. The Giants, sparked by a spectacular Willie Mays catch in the first game, went on to defeat Cleveland easily. Pinch hitter-outfielder Dusty Rhodes drove in seven runs on two homers and two singles in six at bats.

1955. Brooklyn (N) over New York (A), 4–3. The Dodgers finally won a World Series in their eighth try, behind the pitching of series MVP Johnny Podres (2–0, 1.00). Duke Snider hit four homers in a series for the second time, and Dodger leftfielder Sandy Amoros made a game-saving catch in the seventh game.

1956. New York (A) over Brooklyn (N), 4–3. Yankee righthander and series MVP Don Larsen pitched a perfect game in the fifth contest, while Mickey Mantle and Yogi Berra each hit three homers for the winners.

1957. Milwaukee (N) over New York (A), 4–3. Lew Burdette won three times for the Braves, allowing but two runs in 27 innings and won the MVP. Milwaukee's hitting was led by Hank Aaron (.393, 3 HRs, 7 RBIs).

1958. New York (A) over Milwaukee (N), 4–3. Yankees Hank Bauer and Moose Skowron combined for six homers and 15 RBIs as the Bronx Bombers came back from a 3–1 deficit to sweep the last three games. Yankee pitcher "Bullet" Bob Turley earned MVP honors.

1959. Los Angeles (N) over Chicago (A), 4–2. Los Angeles enjoyed its first World Championship as the transplanted Dodgers prevailed, aided by the relief pitching of MVP Larry Sherry (2 wins, 2 saves). Ted Kluszewski of the "Go-Go" White Sox hit .391, with three homers and 10 RBIs.

1960. Pittsburgh (N) over New York (A), 4–3. Pirate second baseman Bill Mazeroski's home run in the bottom of the ninth in the seventh game capped one of the most exciting contests in history. In the 10–9 ballgame, 10 of the runs were scored in the last two innings. Yankee second baseman Bobby Richardson, a hitting star throughout the series, was named MVP.

1961. New York (A) over Cincinnati (N), 4–1. Whitey Ford tossed two shutouts in winning the MVP, and the Yankee offense pounded out 16 extra-base hits in the five games. Bobby Richardson (.391) and John Blanchard (.400, 2 HRs) starred for New York.

1962. New York (A) over San Francisco (N), 4–3. Ralph Terry's four-hit shutout won the seesaw affair for the Yanks, and earned him the MVP. Whitey Ford completed his series record 33 consecutive scoreless innings in the first game, and for the Giants, Chuck Hiller hit the first National League series grand slam home run in Game Four.

1963. Los Angeles (N) over New York (A), 4–0. Dodger pitchers held New York to four runs, led by Sandy Koufax's two wins and 23 strikeouts, including a record-breaking 15 in the first game. Koufax was the runaway choice for MVP.

1964. St. Louis (N) over New York (A), 4–3. Ten Yankee home runs were not enough to beat the Cardinals. Bob Gibson was the series MVP, and Tim McCarver (.478) also starred. Highlights included Ken Boyer's game-winning grand slam in Game Four, and Bobby Richardson's record 13 hits.

1965. Los Angeles (N) over Minnesota (A), 4–3. As in 1963, MVP Sandy Koufax again excelled for the Dodgers, allowing only two runs in 24 innings, striking out 29. Jim "Mudcat" Grant won two games and hit a three-run homer for the Twins.

1966. Baltimore (A) over Los Angeles (N), 4–0. The Orioles made the most of their first World Series appearance, as their young pitchers did not allow a run after the third inning of the first game. Slugger Frank Robinson capped a great year with the series MVP award.

1967. St. Louis (N) over Boston (A), 4–3. Bob Gibson pitched three complete game victories, added a home run in Game Seven, and was named MVP. Lou Brock batted .414 and stole seven bases, tying Eddie Collins' record and pacing the Cards.

1968. Detroit (A) over St. Louis (N), 4–3. The Cardinals were rolling behind Bob Gibson's record 17 strikeouts in Game One and his record seventh straight series win in Game Four. Again Lou Brock joined him in the record books with 13 hits and seven stolen bases. But their feats couldn't stop the Tigers, led by the MVP pitching of Mickey Lolich (3–0, 1.67).

1969. New York (N) over Baltimore (A), 4–1. The Mets stunned the baseball world by winning four in a row after dropping the opener. Their young pitchers held the Orioles to only nine runs, aided by the great outfield catches of Ron Swoboda and Tommie Agee. Series MVP Donn Clendenon (.357, 3 HRs) and Al Weis (.455, 1 HR) led the Met attack.

1970. Baltimore (A) over Cincinnati (N), 4–1. Brooks Robinson almost singlehandedly beat the Reds with spectacular defense at third base and a .429 average with two homers and two doubles. His dominance of the series earned the MVP. Also chipping in for the O's were Paul Blair (.474), Frank Robinson, and Boog Powell (two homers each).

1971. Pittsburgh (N) over Baltimore (A), 4–3.

Roberto Clemente played in 14 World Series games and hit safely in every one. Here he batted .414, slugged .759, and won MVP honors. Steve Blass, Nelson Briles, and Bruce Kison won all the Pirate victories with a combined ERA of 0.54.

1972. Oakland (A) over Cincinnati (N), 4–3. A's backup catcher Gene Tenace hit home runs in his first two series at bats, then went on to hit two more, becoming the surprise star and MVP selection. Rollie Fingers relieved in six of the contests, winning one and saving two.

1973. Oakland (A) over New York (N), 4–3. The Mets had the worst record of any pennant winner ever (82–79), but they lasted till the seventh game in a sloppily played (19 errors) affair. Darold Knowles pitched in all seven games for the A's, saving two. Reggie Jackson slugged his way to the first of his two series MVP awards.

1974. Oakland (A) over Los Angeles (N), 4–1. The A's won their third straight World Championship behind the three saves and one win of MVP Rollie Fingers. Joe Rudi (.333) and Bert Campaneris (.353) starred with the bats.

1975. Cincinnati (N) over Boston (A), 4–3. Five of the seven games were decided by one run, including the famous 12 inning sixth contest won on a Carlton Fisk home run. Cincinnati used 23 relief pitchers to set a record. Pete Rose, the heart and soul of the Big Red Machine, hustled his way to MVP honors.

1976. Cincinnati (N) over New York (A), 4–0. The Big Red Machine drove over the Yankees, slugging .522 as a team. Seven of nine Reds hitters batted over .300, led by MVP Johnny Bench's .533 (1.133 slugging average).

1977. New York (A) over Los Angeles (N), 4–2. Reggie Jackson hit five homers, including three in the final game, to equal records set by Babe Ruth, and win the MVP for the second time. Mike Torrez won two for the Yankees.

1978. New York (A) over Los Angeles (N), 4–2. Shortstop Bucky Dent and backup infielder Brian Doyle batted .417 and .438 respectively, pacing New York in its second straight six-game triumph. Dent was named MVP. In the last four contests, the Yankees outscored L.A. 28–8.

1979. Pittsburgh (N) over Baltimore (A), 4–3. The Pirates overcame a three games to one deficit as Earl Weaver's Orioles waited for the three-run homer that never came. Led by Willie Stargell (.400, 3 HRs) and Phil Garner (.500), Pittsburgh batted .323 as a team. "Pops" Stargell's on-field performance and team leadership of the Pirates' "family" was honored with the MVP.

1980. Philadelphia (N) over Kansas City (A), 4–2. The two teams batted .292 in a series decided largely by the relief pitching of Tug McGraw (1–1, 2 saves) vs. Dan Quisenberry (1–2, 1 save). Mike Schmidt took MVP honors with a .381 average and seven RBIs.

1981. Los Angeles (N) over New York (A), 4–2. Many observers called this sloppy series a fitting end to this strike-stricken 1981 season. Even the MVP award proved impossible to settle, as Pedro Guerrero, Steve Yeager, and Ron Cey shared the honor.

1982. St. Louis (N) over Milwaukee (A), 4–3.

Joaquin Andujar won two games for the Cardinals, and Willie McGee had perhaps the greatest single series game by a rookie, with two homers and two great catches in Game Four. American League MVP Robin Yount batted .414 for the losers.

1983. Baltimore (A) over Philadelphia (N), 4–1. The Phillies couldn't hit Orioles' pitching, scoring but nine runs in the five games. Catcher Rick Dempsey hit four doubles and a home run, held the Phils to one stolen base, and was named MVP.

1984. Detroit (A) over San Diego (N), 4–1. The Tigers belted seven homers and backed them up with the pitching of Jack Morris (2–0, 2.00). Sparky Anderson become the first manager to win World Championships in both leagues. The Tigers' sure-handed shortstop, Alan Trammell, fielded flawlessly and hit with power to earn MVP honors.

1985. Kansas City (A) over St. Louis (N), 4–3. The Cards were one inning away from the title, but a disputed call at first base opened the door for the Royals in Game Six. They won that contest, then blew St. Louis away 11–0 in the finale. Bret Saberhagen won three for Kansas City, and the MVP.

1986. New York (N) over Boston (A), 4–3. As in 1985, misplays in the final inning of Game Six caused the series to turn around, as the Red Sox lost their fourth straight seven game series. Mets third baseman Ray Knight capped a comeback year with clutch hitting and the series MVP.

1987. Minnesota (A) over St. Louis (N), 4–3. The Twins won their first championship by taking all four games in their exotic home park, the Metrodome. Cardinal pitching held them to five runs in the three games in St. Louis, but in Minnesota the Twins could not be contained, scoring 33 times. Frank Viola (2–1, ERA 3.72) was the MVP.

1988. Los Angeles (N) over Oakland (A), 4–1. Series MVP Orel Hershiser (2–0, 17 Ks) dazzled the powerful A's. Injured Dodger Kirk Gibson's dramatic two-out home run in the bottom of the ninth in Game One set the tone for the unexpected Los Angeles triumph.

1989. Series delayed by earthquake. In the first all-Bay Area series, the Oakland A's took a commanding two-games to none lead over the S.F. Giants on the strength of Dave Stewart's and Mike Moore's pitching; the powerful S.F. bats produced only one run in two games. As the third game was about to begin in Candlestick Park a devastating earthquake rocked the entire area causing hundreds of deaths and enormous damage (see p. viii). As this book went to press, the Series had been postponed for at least one week, and talk centered on finding a neutral site if the Bay Area parks proved unusable. Officials stated that the games would definitely be played since nothing, not even two world wars, has prevented play since 1904.

A MOST VALUABLE TEAM

Only nine players have won the Most Valuable Player Award in consecutive seasons; oddly enough there is only one from each fielding position.

Position	Player	Team	Years
First Base	Jimmie Foxx	Philadelphia A's	1932–33
Second Base	Joe Morgan	Cincinnati Reds	1975–76
Third Base	Mike Schmidt	Philadelphia Phillies	1980–81
Shortstop	Ernie Banks	Chicago Cubs	1958–59
Outfield	Mickey Mantle	N.Y. Yankees	1956–57
Outfield	Roger Maris	N.Y. Yankees	1960–61
Outfield	Dale Murphy	Atlanta Braves	1982–83
Catcher	Yogi Berra	N.Y. Yankees	1954–55
Pitcher	Hal Newhouser	Detroit Tigers	1944–45

MOST VALUABLE PLAYER AWARD WINNERS

Betwen 1911 and 1914 the Chalmers Award was given to the player judged to be the most valuable in each league. It was not until 1922 that the American League began to select a league MVP. The National League began to do so as well two years later. By the end of the decade, though, both leagues failed to select an MVP. In 1931 the Baseball Writers Association of America began to select the league MVPs, and has continued to do so through today.

NATIONAL LEAGUE

Year	Name	Team	HRs	RBIs	Avg.
1911	Frank Schulte	Chicago Cubs	21	121	.300
1912	Larry Doyle	N.Y. Giants	10	90	.330
1913	Jake Daubert	Brooklyn Dodgers	2	52	.350
1914	Johnny Evers	Chicago Cubs	1	40	.279
1924	Dazzy Vance (P)	Brooklyn Dodgers	28W	6L	2.16 ERA
1925	Rogers Hornsby	St. Louis Cardinals	29	143	.403
1926	Bob O'Farrell	St. Louis Cardinals	7	68	.293
1927	Paul Waner	Pittsburgh Pirates	9	131	.380
1928	Jim Bottomley	St. Louis Cardinals	31	136	.325
1929	Rogers Horsby	St. Louis Cardinals	39	149	.380
1931	Frankie Frisch	St. Louis Cardinals	4	82	.311
1932	Chuck Klein	Philadelphia Phillies	38	137	.348
1933	Carl Hubbell (P)	N.Y. Giants	23W	12L	1.66 ERA
1934	Dizzy Dean (P)	St. Louis Cardinals	30W	7L	2.66 ERA
1935	Gabby Hartnett	Chicago Cubs	13	91	.344
1936	Carl Hubbell (P)	N.Y. Giants	26W	6L	2.31 ERA
1937	Joe Medwick	St. Louis Cardinals	31	154	.374
1938	Ernie Lombardi	Cincinnati Reds	19	95	.342
1939	Bucky Walters (P)	Cinncinati Reds	27W	11L	2.29 ERA
1940	Frank McCormick	Cinncinati Reds	19	127	.309
1941	Dolph Camilli	Brooklyn Dodgers	34	120	.285
1942	Mort Cooper (P)	St. Louis Cardinals	22W	7L	1.78 ERA
1943	Stan Musial	St. Louis Cardinals	13	81	.357
1944	Marty Marion	St. Louis Cardinals	6	63	.267
1945	Phil Cavarretta	Chicago Cubs	6	97	.355
1946	Stan Musial	St. Louis Cardinals	16	103	.365
1947	Bob Elliott	Boston Braves	22	113	.317
1948	Stan Musial	St. Louis Cardinals	39	131	.376
1949	Jackie Robinson	Brooklyn Dodgers	16	124	.342
1950	Jim Konstanty (P)[1]	Philadelphia Phillies	16W	7L	2.66 ERA
1951	Roy Campanella	Brooklyn Dodgers	33	108	.325
1952	Hank Sauer	Chicago Cubs	37	121	.270
1953	Roy Campanella	Brooklyn Dodgers	41	142	.312
1954	Willie Mays	N.Y. Giants	41	110	.345
1955	Roy Campanella	Brooklyn Dodgers	32	107	.318
1956	Don Newcombe (P)	Brooklyn Dodgers	27W	7L	3.06 ERA
1957	Hank Aaron	Milwaukee Braves	44	132	.322
1958	Ernie Banks	Chicago Cubs	47	129	.313
1959	Ernie Banks	Chicago Cubs	45	143	.304

Year	Name	Team	HRs	RBIs	Avg.
1960	Dick Groat	Pittsburgh Pirates	2	50	.325
1961	Frank Robinson	Cincinnati Reds	37	124	.323
1962	Maury Wills	L.A. Dodgers	6	48	.299
1963	Sandy Koufax (P)	L.A. Dodgers	25W	5L	1.88 ERA
1964	Ken Boyer	St. Louis Cardinals	24	119	.295
1965	Willie Mays	San Francisco Giants	52	112	.317
1966	Roberto Clemente	Pittsburgh Pirates	29	119	.317
1967	Orlando Cepeda	San Francisco Giants	25	111	.325
1968	Bob Gibson (P)	St. Louis Cardinals	22W	9L	1.12 ERA
1969	Willie McCovey	San Francisco Giants	45	126	.320
1970	Johnny Bench	Cincinnati Reds	45	148	.293
1971	Joe Torre	St. Louis Cardinals	45	137	.363
1972	Johnny Bench	Cincinnati Reds	40	125	.270
1973	Pete Rose	Cincinnati Reds	5	64	.338
1974	Steve Garvey	L.A. Dodgers	21	111	.312
1975	Joe Morgan	Cincinnati Reds	17	94	.327
1976	Joe Morgan	Cincinnati Reds	27	111	.320
1977	George Foster	Cincinnati Reds	52	149	.320
1978	Dave Parker	Pittsburgh Pirates	30	117	.334
1979	Keith Hernandez	St. Louis Cardinals	11	105	.344
	Willie Stargell	Pittsburgh Pirates	32	82	.281
1980	Mike Schmidt	Philadelphia Phillies	48	121	.286
1981	Mike Schmidt	Philadelphia Phillies	31	91	.316
1982	Dale Murphy	Atlanta Braves	36	109	.281
1983	Dale Murphy	Atlanta Braves	36	121	.302
1984	Ryne Sandberg	Chicago Cubs	19	84	.314
1985	Willie McGee	St. Louis Cardinals	10	82	.353
1986	Mike Schmidt	Philadelphia Phillies	37	119	.290
1987	Andre Dawson	Chicago Cubs	49	137	.287
1988	Kirk Gibson	L.A. Dodgers	25	76	.290

1. Twenty-two saves in 1950.   **Source:** Baseball Writers' Assn.

AMERICAN LEAGUE

Year	Player	Team	HRs	RBIs	Avg.
1911	Ty Cobb	Detroit Tigers	8	144	.420
1912	Tris Speaker	Boston Red Sox	10	98	.383
1913	Walter Johnson (P)	Washington Senators	36W	7L	1.09 ERA
1914	Eddie Collins	Philadelphia A's	2	85	.344
1922	George Sisler	St. Louis Browns	8	105	.420
1923	Babe Ruth	N.Y. Yankees	41	131	.393
1924	Walter Johnson (P)	Washington Senators	23W	7L	2.72 ERA
1925	Roger Peckinpaugh	Washington Senators	4	64	.294
1926	George Burns	Cleveland Indians	4	114	.358
1927	Lou Gehrig	N.Y. Yankees	47	175	.373
1928	Mickey Cochrane	Philadelphia A's	10	57	.293
1931	Lefty Grove (P)	Philadelphia A's	31W	4L	2.06 ERA
1932	Jimmie Foxx	Philadelphia A's	58	169	.364
1933	Jimmie Foxx	Philadelphia A's	48	163	.356
1934	Mickey Cochrane	Detroit Tigers	2	76	.320
1935	Hank Greenberg	Detroit Tigers	36	170	.328
1936	Lou Gehrig	N.Y. Yankees	49	152	.354
1937	Charley Gehringer	Detroit Tigers	14	96	.371
1938	Jimmie Foxx	Boston Red Sox	50	175	.349
1939	Joe DiMaggio	N.Y. Yankees	30	126	.381
1940	Hank Greenberg	Detroit Tigers	41	150	.340
1941	Joe DiMaggio	N.Y. Yankees	30	125	.357
1942	Joe Gordon	N.Y. Yankees	18	103	.322
1943	Spud Chandler (P)	N.Y. Yankees	20W	4L	1.64 ERA
1944	Hal Newhouser (P)	Detroit Tigers	29W	9L	2.22 ERA
1945	Hal Newhouser (P)	Detroit Tigers	25W	9L	1.81 ERA
1946	Ted Williams	Boston Red Sox	38	123	.342
1947	Joe DiMaggio	N.Y. Yankees	20	97	.315
1948	Lou Boudreau	Cleveland Indians	18	106	.355
1949	Ted Williams	Boston Red Sox	43	159	.343
1950	Phil Rizzuto	N.Y. Yankees	7	66	.324
1951	Yogi Berra	N.Y. Yankees	27	88	.294
1952	Bobby Shantz (P)	Philadelphia A's	24W	7L	2.48 ERA
1953	Al Rosen	Cleveland Indians	43	145	.336
1954	Yogi Berra	N.Y. Yankees	22	125	.307

Year	Player	Team	HRs	RBIs	Avg.
1955	Yogi Berra	N.Y. Yankees	27	108	.272
1956	Mickey Mantle	N.Y. Yankees	52	130	.353
1957	Mickey Mantle	N.Y Yankees	34	94	.365
1958	Jackie Jensen	Boston Red Sox	35	122	.286
1959	Nelson Fox	Chicago White Sox	2	70	.306
1960	Roger Maris	N.Y. Yankees	39	112	.283
1961	Roger Maris	N.Y. Yankees	61	142	.269
1962	Mickey Mantle	N.Y. Yankees	30	89	.321
1963	Elston Howard	N.Y. Yankees	28	85	.287
1964	Brooks Robinson	Baltimore Orioles	28	118	.317
1965	Zoilo Versalles	Minnesota Twins	19	77	.273
1966	Frank Robinson	Baltimore Orioles	49	122	.316
1967	Carl Yastrzemski	Boston Red Sox	44	121	.326
1968	Denny McLain (P)	Detroit Tigers	31W	6L	1.96 ERA
1969	Harmon Killebrew	Minnesota Twins	49	140	.276
1970	Boog Powell	Baltimore Orioles	35	114	.297
1971	Vida Blue (P)	Oakland A's	24W	8L	1.82 ERA
1972	Dick Allen	Chicago White Sox	37	113	.308
1973	Reggie Jackson	Oakland A's	32	117	.293
1974	Jeff Burroughs	Texas Rangers	25	118	.301
1975	Fred Lynn	Boston Red Sox	21	105	.331
1976	Thurman Munson	N.Y. Yankees	17	105	.302
1977	Rod Carew	Minnesota Twins	14	100	.388
1978	Jim Rice	Boston Red Sox	46	139	.315
1979	Don Baylor	California Angels	36	139	.296
1980	George Brett	Kansas City Royals	24	118	.390
1981	Rollie Fingers (P)[1]	Milwaukee Brewers	6W	3L	1.04 ERA
1982	Robin Yount	Milwaukee Brewers	29	114	.331
1983	Cal Ripken, Jr.	Baltimore Orioles	27	102	.318
1984	Willie Hernandez (P)[2]	Detroit Tigers	9W	3L	2.48 ERA
1985	Don Mattingly	N.Y. Yankees	35	145	.324
1986	Roger Clemens (P)	Boston Red Sox	24W	4L	2.48 ERA
1987	George Bell	Toronto Blue Jays	47	134	.308
1988	Jose Canseco	Oakland A's	42	124	.307

1. Had 28 saves in 1981.   2. Had 32 saves in 1984.   **Source:** Baseball Writers' Assn.

MAJOR LEAGUE PLAYERS WITH 400 OR MORE HOME RUNS

Player	HRs	Player	HRs
Hank Aaron	755	Ernie Banks	512
Babe Ruth	714	Eddie Mathews	512
Willie Mays	660	Mel Ott	511
Frank Robinson	586	Lou Gehrig	493
Harmon Killebrew	573	Stan Musial	475
Reggie Jackson	563	Willie Stargell	475
Mike Schmidt[1]	548	Carl Yastrzemski	452
Mickey Mantle	536	Dave Kingman	442
Jimmie Foxx	534	Billy Williams	426
Willie McCovey	521	Darrell Evans[1]	414
Ted Williams	521	Duke Snider	407

1. Active during the 1989 season.

MAJOR LEAGUE PITCHERS WITH 300 OR MORE VICTORIES

Name	Years	Won	Lost	Name	Years	Won	Lost
Denton T. "Cy" Young	22	511	315	John Clarkson	12	327	175
Walter Johnson	21	416	279	Don Sutton	23	324	256
Grover Alexander	20	373	208	Phil Niekro	24	318	274
Christy Mathewson	17	373	188	Gaylord Perry	22	314	265
Warren Spahn	21	363	245	Tom Seaver	20	311	205
James F. "Pud" Galvin	15	361	309	Charles "Old Hoss" Radbourne	11	308	191
Charles "Kid" Nichols	15	361	202	Mickey Welch	13	307	214
Tim Keefe	14	342	225	Eddie Plank	17	305	190
Steve Carlton	24	329	244	"Lefty" Grove	17	300	141
				Early Wynn	23	300	244

Source: Major League Baseball

CY YOUNG AWARD WINNERS

Year	Name	Team	Won	Lost	ERA
1956	Don Newcombe	Brooklyn Dodgers	27	7	3.06
1957	Warren Spahn	Milwaukee Braves	21	11	2.69
1958	Bob Turley	N.Y. Yankees	21	7	2.97
1959	Early Wynn	Chicago White Sox	22	10	3.17
1960	Vernon Law	Pittsburgh Pirates	20	9	3.08
1961	Whitey Ford	N.Y. Yankees	25	4	3.21
1962	Don Drysdale	L.A. Dodgers	25	9	2.83
1963	Sandy Koufax	L.A. Dodgers	25	5	1.88
1964	Dean Chance	L.A. Angels	20	9	1.65
1965	Sandy Koufax	L.A. Dodgers	26	8	2.04
1966	Sandy Koufax	L.A. Dodgers	27	9	1.73

NATIONAL LEAGUE

Year	Name	Team	Won	Lost	ERA
1967	Mike McCormick	S.F. Giants	22	10	2.85
1968	Bob Gibson	St. Louis Cardinals	22	9	1.12
1969	Tom Seaver	N.Y. Mets	25	7	2.21
1970	Bob Gibson	St. Louis Cardinals	23	7	3.12
1971	Ferguson Jenkins	Chicago Cubs	24	13	2.77
1972	Steve Carlton	Philadelphia Phillies	27	10	1.97
1973	Tom Seaver	N.Y. Mets	19	10	2.08
1974	Mike Marshall[1]	L.A. Dodgers	15	12	2.42
1975	Tom Seaver	N.Y. Mets	22	9	2.38
1976	Randy Jones	San Diego Padres	22	14	2.74
1977	Steve Carlton	Philadelphia Phillies	23	10	2.64
1978	Gaylord Perry	San Diego Padres	21	6	2.72
1979	Bruce Sutter[2]	Chicago Cubs	6	6	2.23
1980	Steve Carlton	Philadelphia Phillies	24	9	2.34
1981	Fernando Valenzuela	L.A. Dodgers	13	7	2.48
1982	Steve Carlton	Philadelphia Phillies	23	11	3.10
1983	John Denny	Philadelphia Phillies	19	6	2.37
1984	Rick Sutcliffe	Chicago Cubs	20	6	3.64
1985	Dwight Gooden	N.Y. Mets	24	4	1.53
1986	Mike Scott	Houston Astros	18	10	2.22
1987	Steve Bedrosian[3]	Philadelphia Phillies	5	3	2.83
1988	Orel Hershiser	L.A. Dodgers	23	8	2.26

AMERICAN LEAGUE

Year	Name	Team	Won	Lost	ERA
1967	Jim Lonborg	Boston Red Sox	22	9	3.16
1968	Denny McLain	Detroit Tigers	31	6	1.96
1969	Mike Cuellar	Baltimore Orioles	23	11	2.38
1970	Jim Perry	Minnesota Twins	24	12	3.03
1971	Vida Blue	Oakland A's	24	8	1.82
1972	Gaylord Perry	Cleveland Indians	24	16	1.92
1973	Jim Palmer	Baltimore Orioles	22	9	2.40
1974	Catfish Hunter	Oakland A's	25	12	2.49
1975	Jim Palmer	Baltimore Orioles	23	11	2.09
1976	Jim Palmer	Baltimore Orioles	22	13	2.51
1977	Sparky Lyle[4]	N.Y. Yankees	13	5	2.17
1978	Ron Guidry	N.Y. Yankees	25	3	1.74
1979	Mike Flanagan	Baltimore Orioles	23	9	3.08
1980	Steve Stone	Baltimore Orioles	25	7	3.23
1981	Rollie Fingers[5]	Milwaukee Brewers	6	3	1.04
1982	Peter Vuckovich	Milwaukee Brewers	18	6	3.34
1983	LaMarr Hoyt	Chicago White Sox	24	10	3.66
1984	Willie Henandez[6]	Detroit Tigers	9	3	1.92
1985	Bret Saberhagen	K.C. Royals	20	6	2.87
1986	Roger Clemens	Boston Red Sox	24	4	2.48
1987	Roger Clemens	Boston Red Sox	20	9	2.97
1988	Frank Viola	Minnesota Twins	24	7	2.64

1. In 1974, 21 saves.   2. In 1979, 37 saves.   3. In 1987, 40 saves.   4. In 1977, 26 saves.
5. In 1981, 28 saves.   6. In 1984, 32 saves.

MAJOR LEAGUE BASEBALL ALL-TIME CAREER LEADERS

BATTING AVERAGE
1.	Ty Cobb	.367
2.	Rogers Hornsby	.358
3.	Joe Jackson	.356
4.	Pete Browning	.354
5.	Dan Brouthers	.349
6.	Ed Delahanty	.346
7.	Willie Keeler	.345
8.	Tris Speaker	.345
9.	Ted Williams	.344
10.	Billy Hamilton	.344

TOTAL BASES
1.	Hank Aaron	6,856
2.	Stan Musial	6,134
3.	Willie Mays	6,066
4.	Ty Cobb	5,863
5.	Babe Ruth	5,793
6.	Pete Rose	5,752
7.	Carl Yastrzemski	5,539
8.	Frank Robinson	5,373
9.	Tris Speaker	5,105
10.	Lou Gehrig	5,059

SLUGGING AVERAGE
1.	Babe Ruth	.690
2.	Ted Williams	.634
3.	Lou Gehrig	.632
4.	Jimmie Foxx	.609
5.	Hank Greenberg	.605
6.	Joe DiMaggio	.579
7.	Rogers Hornsby	.577
8.	Johnny Mize	.562
9.	Stan Musial	.559
10.	Willie Mays	.557

RUNS BATTED IN
1.	Hank Aaron	2,297
2.	Babe Ruth	2,204
3.	Lou Gehrig	1,991
4.	Ty Cobb	1,959
5.	Stan Musial	1,951
6.	Jimmie Foxx	1,922
7.	Willie Mays	1,903
8.	Mel Ott	1,860
9.	Carl Yastrzemski	1,844
10.	Ted Williams	1,839

RUNS
1.	Ty Cobb	2,245
2.	Babe Ruth	2,174
3.	Hank Aaron	2,174
4.	Pete Rose	2,165
5.	Willie Mays	2,062
6.	Stan Musial	1,949
7.	Lou Gehrig	1,888
8.	Tris Speaker	1,881
9.	Mel Ott	1,849
10.	Frank Robinson	1,829

HITS
1.	Pete Rose	4,256
2.	Ty Cobb	4,191
3.	Hank Aaron	3,771
4.	Stan Musial	3,630
5.	Tris Speaker	3,515
6.	Honus Wagner	3,430
7.	Carl Yastrzemski	3,419
8.	Eddie Collins	3,309
9.	Willie Mays	3,283
10.	Nap Lajoie	3,252

EXTRA BASE HITS
1.	Hank Aaron	1,477
2.	Stan Musial	1,377
3.	Babe Ruth	1,356
4.	Willie Mays	1,323
5.	Lou Gehrig	1,190
6.	Frank Robinson	1,186
7.	Carl Yastrzemski	1,157
8.	Ty Cobb	1,139
9.	Tris Speaker	1,133
10.	Jimmie Foxx	1,117
	Ted Williams	1,117

GAMES PLAYED
1.	Pete Rose	3,562
2.	Carl Yastrzemski	3,308
3.	Hank Aaron	3,298
4.	Ty Cobb	3,093
5.	Stan Musial	3,026
6.	Willie Mays	2,992
7.	Rusty Staub	2,951
8.	Brooks Robinson	2,896
9.	Al Kaline	2,834
10.	Eddie Collins	2,826

STOLEN BASES
1.	Lou Brock	938
2.	Ty Cobb	892
3.	Rickey Henderson	871
4.	Eddie Collins	742
5.	Max Carey	738
6.	Honus Wagner	703
7.	Joe Morgan	689
8.	Bert Campaneris	649
9.	Maury Wills	586
10.	Willie Wilson	564

LIFETIME PITCHING LEADERS

WINS
1.	Cy Young	511
2.	Walter Johnson	416
3.	Christy Mathewson	373
4.	Grover Alexander	373
5.	Warren Spahn	363
6.	Steve Carlton	329
7.	Eddie Plank	327
8.	Don Sutton	324
9.	Phil Niekro	318
10.	Gaylord Perry	314

INNINGS PITCHED
1.	Cy Young	7,356
2.	Pud Galvin	5,941
3.	Walter Johnson	5,924
4.	Phil Niekro	5,404
5.	Gaylord Perry	5,362
6.	Don Sutton	5,281
7.	Warren Spahn	5,244
8.	Steve Carlton	5,216
9.	Grover Alexander	5,189
10.	Kid Nichols	5,089

EARNED RUN AVERAGE (ERA)
1.	Ed Walsh	1.82
2.	Addie Joss	1.88
3.	Mordecai "Three Finger" Brown	2.06
4.	Christy Mathewson	2.13
5.	Rube Waddell	2.16
6.	Walter Johnson	2.17
7.	Orval Overall	2.24
8.	Ed Reulbach	2.28
9.	Jim Scott	2.32
10.	Eddie Plank	2.34

STRIKEOUTS
1.	Nolan Ryan	5,076
2.	Steve Carlton	4,136
3.	Tom Seaver	3,640
4.	Don Sutton	3,574
5.	Bert Blyleven	3,562
6.	Gaylord Perry	3,534
7.	Walter Johnson	3,508
8.	Phil Niekro	3,342
9.	Ferguson Jenkins	3,192
10.	Bob Gibson	3,117

SHUTOUTS
1.	Walter Johnson	113
2.	Grover Alexander	90
3.	Christy Mathewson	83
4.	Cy Young	77
5.	Eddie Plank	70
6.	Warren Spahn	63
	Mordecai "Three Finger" Brown	63
7.	Tom Seaver	61
8.	Don Sutton	58
	Ed Walsh	58
9.	Pud Galvin	57
10.	Bob Gibson	56

Note: As of the end of the 1989 season. Source: Major League Baseball.

ROOKIE OF THE YEAR

NATIONAL LEAGUE

Year	Name	Team
1947[1]	Jackie Robinson	Brooklyn Dodgers
1948[1]	Alvin Dark	Boston Braves
1949	Don Newcombe (P)	Brooklyn Dodgers
1950	Sam Jethroe	Boston Braves
1951	Willie Mays	N.Y. Giants
1952	Joe Black (P)	Brooklyn Dodgers
1953	Junior Gilliam	Brooklyn Dodgers
1954	Wally Moon	St. Louis Cardinals
1955	Bill Virdon	St. Louis Cardinals
1956	Frank Robinson	Cincinnati Reds
1957	Jack Sanford (P)	Philadelphia Phillies
1958	Orlando Cepeda	S.F. Giants
1959	Willie McCovey	S.F. Giants
1960	Frank Howard	L.A. Dodgers
1961	Billy Williams	Chicago Cubs
1962	Ken Hubbs	Chicago Cubs
1963	Pete Rose	Cincinnati Reds
1964	Richie Allen	Philadelphia Phillies
1965	Jim Lefebvre	L.A. Dodgers
1966	Tommy Helms	Cincinnati Reds
1967	Tom Seaver (P)	N.Y. Mets
1968	Johnny Bench	Cincinnati Reds
1969	Ted Sizemore	L.A. Dodgers
1970	Carl Morton (P)	Montreal Expos
1971	Earl Williams	Atlanta Braves
1972	Jon Matlack (P)	N.Y. Mets
1973	Gary Matthews	S.F. Giants
1974	Bake McBride	St. Louis Cardinals
1975	John Montefusco (P)	S.F. Giants
1976	Pat Zachry (P)	Cincinnati Reds
	Butch Metzger (P)	San Diego Padres
1977	Andre Dawson	Montreal Expos
1978	Bob Horner	Atlanta Braves
1979	Rick Sutcliffe (P)	L.A. Dodgers
1980	Steve Howe[2] (P)	L.A. Dodgers
1981	Fernando Valenzuela (P)	L.A. Dodgers
1982	Steve Sax	L.A. Dodgers
1983	Darryl Strawberry	N.Y. Mets
1984	Dwight Gooden (P)	N.Y. Mets
1985	Vince Coleman	St. Louis Cardinals
1986	Todd Worrell[3] (P)	St. Louis Cardinals
1987	Benito Santiago	San Diego Padres
1988	Chris Sabo	Cincinnati Reds

AMERICAN LEAGUE

Year	Player	Team
1949	Roy Sievers	St. Louis Browns
1950	Walt Dropo	Boston Red Sox
1951	Gil McDougald	N.Y. Yankees
1952	Harry Byrd (P)	Philadelphia A's
1953	Harvey Kuenn	Detroit Tigers
1954	Bob Grim (P)	N.Y. Yankees
1955	Herb Score (P)	Cleveland Indians
1956	Luis Aparicio	Chicago White Sox
1957	Tony Kubek	N.Y. Yankees
1958	Albie Pearson	Washington Senators
1959	Bob Allison	Washington Senators
1960	Ron Hansen	Baltimore Orioles

1961	Don Schwall (P)	Boston Red Sox
1962	Tom Tresh	N.Y. Yankees
1963	Gary Peters (P)	Chicago White Sox
1964	Tony Oliva	Minnesota Twins
1965	Curt Blefary	Baltimore Orioles
1966	Tommie Agee	Chicago White Sox
1967	Rod Carew	Minnesota Twins
1968	Stan Bahnsen (P)	N.Y. Yankees
1969	Lou Piniella	K. C. Royals
1970	Thurman Munson	N.Y. Yankees
1971	Chris Chambliss	Cleveland Indians
1972	Carlton Fisk	Boston Red Sox
1973	Al Bumbry	Baltimore Orioles
1974	Make Hargrove	Texas Rangers
1975	Fred Lynn	Boston Red Sox
1976	Mark Fidrych (P)	Detroit Tigers
1977	Eddie Murray	Baltimore Orioles
1978	Lou Whitaker	Detroit Tigers
1979	John Castino	Minnesota Twins
	Alfredo Griffin	Toronto Blue Jays
1980	Joe Charboneau	Cleveland Indians
1981	Dave Righetti (P)	N.Y. Yankees
1982	Cal Ripken, Jr.	Baltimore Orioles
1983	Ron Kittle	Chicago White Sox
1984	Alvin Davis	Seattle Mariners
1985	Ozzie Guillen	Chicago White Sox
1986	Jose Canseco	Oakland A's
1987	Mark McGwire	Oakland A's
1988	Walt Weiss	Oakland A's

1. One player selected as Major League Rookie of the Year. Policy of naming a player from each league was inaugurated in 1949.   2. 17 saves in 1980.   3. 36 saves in 1986.   **Source:** Baseball Writers' Assn.

BATTING CHAMPIONS

NATIONAL LEAGUE

Year	Name	Team	Avg.
1876	Roscoe Barnes	Chicago Cubs	.403
1877	James White	Boston Braves	.385
1878	Abner Dalrymple	Milwaukee Brewers	.356
1879	Cap Anson	Chicago Cubs	.407
1880	George Gore	Chicago Cubs	.365
1881	Cap Anson	Chicago Cubs	.399
1882	Dan Brouthers	Buffalo Bisons	.367
1883	Dan Brouthers	Buffalo Bisons	.371
1884	Jim O'Rourke	Buffalo Bisons	.350
1885	Roger Connor	N.Y. Giants	.371
1886	Mike Kelly	Chicago Cubs	.388
1887	Cap Anson	Chicago Cubs	.421
1888	Cap Anson	Chicago Cubs	.343
1889	Dan Brouthers	Boston Braves	.373
1890	Jack Glasscock	N.Y. Giants	.336
1891	Billy Hamilton	Philadelphia Phillies	.338
1892	"Cupid" Childs	Cleveland Spiders	.335
	Dan Brouthers	Brooklyn Dodgers	.335
1893	Hugh Duffy	Boston Braves	.378
1894	Hugh Duffy	Boston Braves	.438
1895	Jesse Burkett	Cleveland Spiders	.423
1896	Jesse Burkett	Cleveland Spiders	.410
1897	Willie Keeler	Baltimore Orioles	.432
1898	Willie Keeler	Baltimore Orioles	.379
1899	Ed Delahanty	Philadelphia Phillies	.408
1900	Honus Wagner	Pittsburgh Pirates	.380
1901	Jesse Burkett	St. Louis Cardinals	.382
1902	C.H. Beaumont	Pittsburgh Pirates	.357
1903	Honus Wagner	Pittsburgh Pirates	.355
1904	Honus Wagner	Pittsburgh Pirates	.349
1905	J. Bentley Seymour	Cincinnati Reds	.377
1906	Honus Wagner	Pittsburgh Pirates	.339
1907	Honus Wagner	Pittsburgh Pirates	.350
1908	Honus Wagner	Pittsburgh Pirates	.354
1909	Honus Wagner	Pittsburgh Pirates	.339
1910	Sherwood Magee	Philadelphia Phillies	.331
1911	Honus Wagner	Pittsburgh Pirates	.334
1912	Heinie Zimmerman	Chicago Cubs	.372
1913	Jake Daubert	Brooklyn Dodgers	.350
1914	Jake Daubert	Brooklyn Dodgers	.329
1915	Larry Doyle	N.Y. Giants	.320
1916	Hal Chase	Cincinnati Reds	.339
1917	Edd Roush	Cincinnati Reds	.341
1918	Zack Wheat	Brooklyn Dodgers	.335
1919	Edd Roush	Cincinnati Reds	.321
1920	Rogers Hornsby	St. Louis Cardinals	.370
1921	Rogers Hornsby	St. Louis Cardinals	.397
1922	Rogers Hornsby	St. Louis Cardinals	.401
1923	Rogers Hornsby	St. Louis Cardinals	.384
1924	Rogers Hornsby	St. Louis Cardinals	.424
1925	Rogers Hornsby	St. Louis Cardinals	.403
1926	Bubbles Hargrave	Cincinnati Reds	.353
1927	Paul Waner	Pittsburgh Pirates	.380
1928	Rogers Hornsby	Boston Braves	.387
1929	Lefty O'Doul	Philadelphia Phillies	.398
1930	Bill Terry	N.Y. Giants	.401
1931	Chick Hafey	St. Louis Cardinals[1]	.349
1932	Lefty O'Doul	Brooklyn Dodgers	.368
1933	Chuck Klein	Philadelphia Phillies	.368
1934	Paul Waner	Pittsburgh Pirates	.362
1935	Arky Vaughan	Pittsburgh Pirates	.385
1936	Paul Waner	Pittsburgh Pirates	.373
1937	Joe Medwick	St. Louis Cardinals	.374
1938	Ernie Lombardi	Cincinnati Reds	.342
1939	Johnny Mize	St. Louis Cardinals	.349
1940	Debs Garms	Pittsburgh Pirates	.355
1941	Pete Reiser	Brooklyn Dodgers	.343
1942	Ernie Lombardi	Boston Braves	.330
1943	Stan Musial	St. Louis Cardinals	.357
1944	Dixie Walker	Brooklyn Dodgers	.357
1945	Phil Cavarretta	Chicago Cubs	.355
1946	Stan Musial	St. Louis Cardinals	.365
1947	Harry Walker	St. Louis-Philadelphia	.363
1948	Stan Musial	St. Louis Cardinals	.376
1949	Jackie Robinson	Brooklyn Dodgers	.342
1950	Stan Musial	St. Louis Cardinals	.346
1951	Stan Musial	St. Louis Cardinals	.355
1952	Stan Musial	St. Louis Cardinals	.336
1953	Carl Furillo	Brooklyn Dodgers	.344
1954	Willie Mays	N.Y. Giants	.345
1955	Richie Ashburn	Philadelphia Phillies	.338
1956	Hank Aaron	Milwaukee Braves	.328
1957	Stan Musial	St. Louis Cardinals	.351
1958	Richie Ashburn	Philadelphia Phillies	.350
1959	Hank Aaron	Milwaukee Braves	.355
1960	Dick Groat	Pittsburgh Pirates	.325
1961	Roberto Clemente	Pittsburgh Pirates	.351
1962	Tommy Davis	L.A. Dodgers	.346
1963	Tommy Davis	L.A. Dodgers	.326
1964	Roberto Clemente	Pittsburgh Pirates	.339
1965	Roberto Clemente	Pittsburgh Pirates	.329
1966	Matty Alou	Pittsburgh Pirates	.342
1967	Roberto Clemente	Pittsburgh Pirates	.357
1968	Pete Rose	Cincinnati Reds	.335
1969	Pete Rose	Cincinnati Reds	.348
1970	Rico Carty	Atlanta Braves	.366
1971	Joe Torre	St. Louis Cardinals	.363
1972	Billy Williams	Chicago Cubs	.333
1973	Pete Rose	Cincinnati Reds	.338
1974	Ralph Garr	Atlanta Braves	.353
1975	Bill Madlock	Chicago Cubs	.354
1976	Bill Madlock	Chicago Cubs	.339
1977	Dave Parker	Pittsburgh Pirates	.338
1978	Dave Parker	Pittsburgh Pirates	.334
1979	Keith Hernandez	St. Louis Cardinals	.344
1980	Bill Buckner	Chicago Cubs	.324
1981	Bill Madlock	Pittsburgh Pirates	.341
1982	Al Oliver	Montreal Expos	.331
1983	Bill Madlock	Pittsburgh Pirates	.323
1984	Tony Gwynn	San Diego Padres	.351
1985	Willie McGee	St. Louis Cardinals	.353
1986	Tim Raines	Montreal Expos	.334
1987	Tony Gwynn	San Diego Padres	.370
1988	Tony Gwynn	San Diego Padres	.313

AMERICAN LEAGUE

Year	Player	Team	Avg.
1901	Nap Lajoie	Philadelphia A's	.422
1902	Ed Delahanty	Washington Senators	.376
1903	Nap Lajoie	Cleveland Indians	.355
1904	Nap Lajoie	Cleveland Indians	.381
1905	Elmer Flick	Cleveland Indians	.306
1906	George Stone	St. Louis Browns	.358
1907	Ty Cobb	Detroit Tigers	.350
1908	Ty Cobb	Detroit Tigers	.324
1909	Ty Cobb	Detroit Tigers	.377
1910	Ty Cobb	Detroit Tigers	.385
1911	Ty Cobb	Detroit Tigers	.420
1912	Ty Cobb	Detroit Tigers	.410
1913	Ty Cobb	Detroit Tigers	.390
1914	Ty Cobb	Detroit Tigers	.368
1915	Ty Cobb	Detroit Tigers	.370
1916	Tris Speaker	Cleveland Indians	.386
1917	Ty Cobb	Detroit Tigers	.383
1918	Ty Cobb	Detroit Tigers	.382
1919	Ty Cobb	Detroit Tigers	.407
1920	George Sisler	St. Louis Browns	.407
1921	Harry Heilmann	Detroit Tigers	.394
1922	George Sisler	St. Louis Browns	.420
1923	Harry Heilmann	Detroit Tigers	.403
1924	Babe Ruth	N.Y. Yankees	.378
1925	Harry Heilmann	Detroit Tigers	.393
1926	Heinie Manush	Detroit Tigers	.377
1927	Harry Heilmann	Detroit Tigers	.398
1928	Goose Goslin	Washington Senators	.379
1929	Lew Fonseca	Cleveland Indians	.369
1930	Al Simmons	Philadelphia A's	.381
1931	Al Simmons	Philadelphia A's	.390
1932	Dale Alexander	Detroit-Boston	.367
1933	Jimmie Foxx	Philadelphia A's	.356
1934	Lou Gehrig	N.Y. Yankees	.363
1935	Buddy Myer	Washington Senators	.349
1936	Luke Appling	Chicago White Sox	.388
1937	Charlie Gehringer	Detroit Tigers	.371
1938	Jimmie Foxx	Boston Red Sox	.349
1939	Joe DiMaggio	N.Y. Yankees	.381
1940	Joe DiMaggio	N.Y. Yankees	.352
1941	Ted Williams	Boston Red Sox	.406
1942	Ted Williams	Boston Red Sox	.356
1943	Luke Appling	Chicago White Sox	.328
1944	Lou Boudreau	Cleveland Indians	.327
1945	Snuffy Stirnweiss	N.Y. Yankees	.309
1946	Mickey Vernon	Washington Senators	.352
1947	Ted Williams	Boston Red Sox	.343
1948	Ted Williams	Boston Red Sox	.369
1949	George Kell	Detroit Tigers	.343
1950	Billy Goodman	Boston Red Sox	.354
1951	Ferris Fain	Philadelphia A's	.344
1952	Ferris Fain	Philadelphia A's	.327
1953	Mickey Vernon	Washington Senators	.337
1954	Bobby Avila	Cleveland Indians	.341
1955	Al Kaline	Detroit Tigers	.340
1956	Mickey Mantle	N.Y. Yankees	.353
1957	Ted Williams	Boston Red Sox	.388
1958	Ted Williams	Boston Red Sox	.328

1959	Harvey Kuenn	Detroit Tigers	.353	1969	Rod Carew	Minnesota Twins	.332	1979	Fred Lynn	Boston Red Sox	.333
1960	Pete Runnels	Boston Red Sox	.320	1970	Alex Johnson	California Angels	.329	1980	George Brett	K. C. Royals	.390
1961	Norm Cash	Detroit Tigers	.361	1971	Tony Oliva	Minnesota Twins	.337	1981	Carney Lansford	Boston Red Sox	.336
1962	Pete Runnels	Boston Red Sox	.326	1972	Rod Carew	Minnesota Twins	.318	1982	Willie Wilson	K. C. Royals	.332
1963	Carl Yastrzemski	Boston Red Sox	.321	1973	Rod Carew	Minnesota Twins	.350	1983	Wade Boggs	Boston Red Sox	.361
1964	Tony Oliva	Minnesota Twins	.323	1974	Rod Carew	Minnesota Twins	.364	1984	Don Mattingly	N.Y. Yankees	.343
1965	Tony Oliva	Minnesota Twins	.321	1975	Rod Carew	Minnesota Twins	.359	1985	Wade Boggs	Boston Red Sox	.368
1966	Frank Robinson	Baltimore Orioles	.316	1976	George Brett	K. C. Royals	.333	1986	Wade Boggs	Boston Red Sox	.357
1967	Carl Yastrzemski	Boston Red Sox	.326	1977	Rod Carew	Minnesota Twins	.388	1987	Wade Boggs	Boston Red Sox	.363
1968	Carl Yastrzemski	Boston Red Sox	.301	1978	Rod Carew	Minnesota Twins	.333	1988	Wade Boggs	Boston Red Sox	.366

1. Hafey led with .3489, Bill Terry, N.Y., second with .3486, Jim Bottomley, St. Louis, third with .3482.

ALL STAR GAME RESULTS, 1933–89

Year	Winner	Score	Year	Winner	Score
1933	American	4-2	1961(1)	National	5-4
1934	American	9-7	1961(2)	Tie[2]	1-1
1935	American	4-1	1962(1)	National	3-1
1936	National	4-3	1962(2)	American	9-4
1937	American	8-3	1963	National	5-3
1938	National	4-1	1964	National	7-4
1939	American	3-1	1965	National	6-5
1940	National	4-0	1966	National	2-1
1941	American	7-5	1967	National	2-1
1942	American	3-1	1968	National	1-0
1943	American	5-3	1970	National	5-4
1944	National	7-1	1971	American	6-4
1945	No game due to wartime		1972	National	4-3
1946	American	12-0	1973	National	7-1
1947	American	2-1	1974	National	7-2
1948	American	5-2	1975	National	6-3
1949	American	11-7	1976	National	7-1
1950	National	4-3	1977	National	7-5
1951	National	8-3	1978	National	7-3
1952	National	3-2	1979	National	7-6
1953	National	5-1	1980	National	4-2
1954	American	11-9	1981	National	5-4
1955	National	6-5	1982	National	4-1
1956	National	7-3	1983	American	13-3
1957	American	6-5	1984	National	3-1
1958	American	4-3	1985	National	6-1
1959(1)[1]	National	5-4	1986	American	3-2
1959(2)	American	5-3	1987	National	2-0
1960(1)	National	5-3	1988	American	2-1
1960(2)	National	6-0	1989	American	5-3

1. Two All Star games were played 1959–62. 2. Game was called after nine innings because of rain.

TRIPLE CROWN WINNERS

Only 11 players have led their league in home runs, runs batted in, and batting average in one season.

Player	Team	Year	HRs	RBIs	Avg.
Ty Cobb	Detroit Tigers	1909	9	115	.377
Henry Zimmerman	Chicago Cubs	1912	14	98	.372
Rogers Hornsby	St. Louis Cardinals	1922	42	152	.401
Rogers Hornsby	St. Louis Cardinals	1925	39	143	.403
Chuck Klein	Philadelphia Phillies	1933	28	120	.368
Jimmie Foxx	Philadelphia A's	1933	48	163	.356
Lou Gehrig	N.Y. Yankees	1934	49	165	.363
Joe Medwick	St. Louis Cardinals	1937	31	154	.374
Ted Williams	Boston Red Sox	1942	36	137	.356
Ted Williams	Boston Red Sox	1947	32	114	.343
Mickey Mantle	N.Y. Yankees	1956	52	130	.353
Frank Robinson	Baltimore Orioles	1966	49	122	.316
Carl Yastrzemski	Boston Red Sox	1967	44	121	.326

THE BASEBALL HALL OF FAME

National Baseball Hall of Fame and Museum
Main Street, Cooperstown, NY 13326
(607) 547-9988

Hours: From May 1 to Oct. 31—9:00 a.m. to 9:00 p.m.
From Nov. 1 to Apr. 30—9:00 a.m. to 5:00 p.m.
(Every day of the year except Thanksgiving, Christmas,
and New Year's.)

The Hall of Fame was established in 1936 and opened in Cooperstown, N.Y., in 1939. From the start there were two ways to be elected: by receiving 75 percent of the votes cast by the Baseball Writers Association of America or 75 percent of the votes cast by a Committee on Old Timers. In the first year, the writers picked the top five players of the post-1900 era: Ty Cobb, Walter Johnson, Christy Mathewson, Babe Ruth, and Honus Wagner. To be elected, a player must have played at least 10 years in the major leagues and been retired for at least five years. The Committee on Old Timers, originally created to consider 19th century players, was replaced by a Special Veterans Committee whose scope includes all players retired for a minimum of 25 years who may have been overlooked when they were first eligible. In 1971 a Special Committee on the Negro Leagues was set up to consider ballplayers who played in the old Negro Leagues.

BASEBALL HALL OF FAME

Player/Position/Year Inducted	Games	At bats	HRs	BA	Hits	RBIs
Aaron, Henry (Hank) OF 1982	3,298	12,364	755	.305	3,771	2,297
All-time leader in home runs and RBIs						
Anson, Adrian (Cap) 1B 1939	2,276	9,108	96	.334	3,041	1,715
Managed 20 years, 1879–98, winning five pennants						
Aparicio, Luis SS 1984	2,599	10,230	83	.262	2,677	791
2,581 games at shortstop, most all-time						
Appling, Luke SS 1964	2,422	8,857	45	.310	2,749	1,116
Batted .388 in 1936						
Averill, Earl OF 1975	1,669	6,358	238	.318	2,020	1,165
232 hits in 1936						
Baker, Frank (Home Run) 3B 1955	1,575	5,985	96	.307	1,838	1,013
Batted .363 in six World Series						
Bancroft, Dave SS 1971	1,913	7,182	32	.279	2,004	591
Modern leader in total chances per game among shortstops						
Banks, Ernie SS, 1B 1977	2,528	9,421	512	.274	2,583	1,636
Consecutive MVP awards, 1958–59						
Beckley, Jake 1B 1971	2,386	9,527	88	.308	2,931	1,575
244 career triples, mostly in 19th century						
Bench, Johnny C 1989	2,158	7,658	389	.267	2,048	1,376
All-time HR leader for catchers; MVP 1970, 1972						
Berra, Lawrence (Yogi) C, OF 1972	2,120	7,555	358	.285	2,150	1,430
Three MVP awards, 1951, 1954, 1955						
Bottomley, Jim 1B 1974	1,991	7,471	219	.310	2,313	1,422
Twelve RBIs in one game, 1924						
Boudreau, Lou SS 1970	1,646	6,030	68	.295	1,779	789
MVP in 1948; managed 16 years						

Player/Position/Year Inducted	Games	At bats	HRs	BA	Hits	RBIs
Bresnahan, Roger C, OF 1945	1,430	4,478	26	.279	1,251	530
212 stolen bases, most ever by a catcher						
Brock, Lou OF 1985	2,616	10,332	149	.293	3,023	900
All-time stolen base leader with 938; batted .391 in three World Series						
Brouthers, Dan 1B 1945	1,673	6,716	106	.343	2,304	1,056
Seven slugging and five batting titles during 19th century						
Burkett, Jesse OF 1946	2,072	8,430	75	.341	2,873	952
Led NL in batting three times and in hits four times						
Campanella, Roy C 1969	1,215	4,205	242	.276	1,161	856
Three MVP awards, 1951, 1953, 1955						
Carey, Max OF 1961	2,476	9,363	69	.285	2,665	800
738 stolen bases						
Chance, Frank 1B 1946	1,286	4,295	20	.297	1,274	596
Managed Chicago (NL) to four pennants in five years, 1906–10						
Clarke, Fred OF 1945	2,245	8,588	67	.315	2,708	1,015
223 career triples, sixth-best ever						
Clemente, Roberto OF 1973	2,433	9,454	240	.317	3,000	1,305
Career average of over 18 outfield assists per season						
Cobb, Ty OF 1936	3,034	11,429	118	.367	4,191	1,961
Batted .320 or better in 23 straight years						
Cochrane, Mickey C 1947	1,482	5,169	119	.320	1,652	832
Two MVP awards, 1928 and 1934						
Collins, Eddie 2B 1939	2,826	9,949	47	.333	3,311	1,299
All-time leader in games, putouts, and assists at second base						
Collins, Jimmy 3B 1945	1,728	6,796	64	.294	1,997	982
Led NL in home runs, 1898						
Combs, Earle OF 1970	1,454	5,748	58	.325	1,866	629
Averaged 127 runs scored per season						
Comiskey, Charles 1B 1939	1,390	5,796	29	.264	1,531	467
Manager and owner of Chicago White Sox						
Connor, Roger 1B 1976	1,998	7,798	136	.318	2,480	1,078
233 career triples in 19th century, fifth-best all-time						
Crawford, Sam OF 1957	2,517	9,580	97	.309	2,964	1,525
312 triples, best ever						
Cronin, Joe SS 1956	2,124	7,579	170	.301	2,285	1,424
MVP in 1930; managed 1933–47						
Cuyler, Hazen (Kiki) OF 1968	1,879	7,161	127	.321	2,299	1,065
Led NL in runs scored twice, stolen bases four times						
Delahanty, Ed IF, OF 1945	1,834	7,502	100	.345	2,591	1,464
Batted .408 in 1899						
Dickey, Bill C 1954	1,789	6,300	202	.313	1,969	1,209
Catcher on eight AL pennant winning teams						
DiMaggio, Joe OF 1955	1,736	6,821	361	.325	2,214	1,537
56-game hitting streak in 1941						
Doerr, Bobby 2B 1986	1,865	7,093	223	.288	2,042	1,247
Led AL in slugging 1944						
Duffy, Hugh OF 1945	1,736	7,062	103	.328	2,314	1,299
Batted .438 in 1894, highest ever						
Evers, Johnny 2B 1946	1,783	6,134	12	.270	1,658	538
NL MVP in 1914						
Ewing, Buck C, IF, OF 1939	1,315	5,363	70	.303	1,625	733
Regarded as greatest player of 19th century						
Ferrell, Rick C 1984	1,884	6,028	28	.281	1,692	734
Led AL catchers at times in putouts, assists, fielding average, and double plays						
Flick, Elmer OF 1963	1,484	5,603	47	.315	1,767	756
Led AL in triples 1905, 1906, 1907						
Foxx, Jimmie 1B, 3B 1951	2,317	8,134	534	.325	2,646	1,921
Slugged over .700 three seasons						
Frisch, Frank 2B, 3B 1947	2,311	9,112	105	.316	2,880	1,244
Highest career batting average ever for a switch hitter						
Gehrig, Lou 1B 1939	2,164	8,001	493	.340	2,721	1,990
2,130 consecutive games played						
Gehringer, Charlie 2B 1949	2,323	8,860	184	.320	2,839	1,427
60 doubles in 1936						
Goslin, Leon (Goose) OF 1968	2,287	8,655	248	.316	2,735	1,609
100 + RBIs 11 years						
Greenberg, Hank 1B 1956	1,394	5,193	331	.313	1,628	1,276
58 home runs in 1938; 183 RBIs in 1937						
Hafey, Charles (Chick) OF 1971	1,283	4,625	164	.317	1,466	833
NL batting title (.349) in 1931						
Hamilton, Billy OF 1961	1,593	6,284	40	.344	2,163	736
Scored 196 runs in 1894, with a .509 on-base average and 99 stolen bases						
Hartnett, Charles (Gabby) C 1955	1,990	6,432	236	.297	1,912	1,179
Played on four NL pennant winners, managed one						
Heilmann, Harry OF, 1B 1952	2,146	7,787	183	.342	2,660	1,551
Batted .403 in 1923						
Herman, Billy 2B 1975	1,922	7,707	47	.304	2,345	839
57 doubles in 1935						
Hooper, Harry OF 1971	2,308	8,785	75	.281	2,466	817
375 career stolen bases						
Hornsby, Rogers 2B, IF 1942	2,259	8,173	301	.358	2,930	1,584
Batted .402 in years 1921–25; nine slugging titles						
Huggins, Miller 2B 1964	1,585	5,557	9	.265	1,474	318
Managed N.Y. Yankees 1913–29; 1,002 career walks						
Jackson, Travis SS 1982	1,656	6,086	135	.291	1,768	929
Batted over .300 six times in 1920s and 1930s						
Jennings, Hugh SS 1945	1,285	4,905	18	.312	1,531	840
Managed Detroit 1907–20; batted .398 in 1896						
Kaline, Al OF 1980	2,834	10,116	399	.297	3,007	1,583
3,007 career hits						
Keeler, Willie OF 1939	2,124	8,591	34	.345	2,962	810
Batted .432 in 1897; 495 career stolen bases						
Kell, George 3B 1983	1,795	6,702	78	.306	2,054	870
AL batting champ (.343) in 1949						
Kelley, Joe OF 1971	1,845	7,018	65	.319	2,242	1,193
Averaged 151 runs scored, 1894–96						
Kelly, George 1B 1973	1,622	5,993	148	.297	1,778	1,020
Led NL in RBIs, 1920 and 1925						
Kelly, Mike (King) OF, C 1945	1,463	5,923	69	.307	1,820	794
Two batting titles, 1884 and 1886; 315 career stolen bases						
Killebrew, Harmon 1B, 3B 1984	2,435	8,147	573	.256	2,086	1,584
40 + home runs eight years						
Kiner, Ralph OF 1975	1,472	5,205	369	.279	1,451	1,015
Second-highest home run per at bat ratio of all-time						
Klein, Chuck OF 1980	1,753	6,486	300	.320	2,076	1,201
44 outfield assists in 1930						
Lajoie, Napoleon (Larry) 2B 1937	2,475	9,589	82	.339	3,251	1,599
Batted .422 in 1901						
Lindstrom, Fred 3B, OF 1976	1,438	5,611	103	.311	1,747	779
231 hits in 1928						
Lombardi, Ernie C 1986	1,853	5,855	190	.306	1,792	990
Two NL batting titles, 1938 and 1942						
Lopez, Al C 1977	1,950	5,916	52	.261	1,547	652
Managed 17 years; 1,918 games caught is second-highest all-time						
Mantle, Mickey OF 1974	2,401	8,102	536	.298	2,415	1,509
52 home runs in 1956, 54 in 1961						
Manush, Heinie OF 1964	2,009	7,653	110	.330	2,524	1,173
Hit .378 in 1926						
Maranville, Walter (Rabbit) SS, 2B 1954	2,670	10,078	28	.258	2,605	884
23-year career; hit .308 in two World Series						
Mathews, Eddie 3B 1978	2,388	8,537	512	.271	2,315	1,453
1,444 career walks						
Mays, Willie OF 1979	2,992	10,881	660	.302	3,283	1,903
Slugged over .600 six seasons						
McCarthy, Tommy OF 1946	1,275	5,128	44	.292	1,496	666
Averaged 122 runs scored, 1888–94						
McCovey, Willie 1B, OF 1986	2,588	8,197	521	.270	2,211	1,555
45 intentional walks in 1969, an NL record						
McGraw, John 3B, SS 1937	1,009	3,922	13	.334	1,308	462
.549 on-base average in 1899						
Medwick, Joe OF 1968	1,984	7,635	205	.324	2,471	1,383
Won NL triple crown in 1937						
Mize, Johnny 1B 1981	1,884	6,443	359	.312	2,011	1,337
Four-time NL home run champ						
Musial, Stan OF, 1B 1969	3,026	10,972	475	.331	3,630	1,951
725 doubles and 177 triples						
O'Rourke, Jim OF 1945	1,774	7,435	51	.310	2,304	830
Batted .300 + 11 times in the 19th century						
Ott, Mel OF 1951	2,732	9,456	511	.304	2,876	1,860
Averaged 121 RBIs 1929–38						

Player/Position/Year Inducted	Games	At bats	HRs	BA	Hits	RBIs
Reese, Harold (Pee Wee) SS 1984	2,166	8,058	126	.269	2,170	885
Finished in top 10 MVP ballotting nine times						
Rice, Sam OF 1963	2,404	9,269	34	.322	2,987	1,078
Only 18 strikeouts per 154 games						
Robinson, Brooks 3B 1983	2,896	10,654	268	.267	2,848	1,357
16 consecutive Gold Gloves, 1960–75						
Robinson, Frank OF 1982	2,808	10,006	586	.294	2,943	1,812
MVP in both leagues; AL Triple Crown in 1966						
Robinson, Jackie 2B 1972	1,382	4,877	137	.311	1,518	734
First black player in MLB; Rookie of the Year 1947; MVP and batting champ 1949						
Robinson, Wilbert C 1945	1,347	5,077	18	.273	1,399	740
Managed Brooklyn 1914–31, winning two pennants						
Roush, Edd OF 1962	1,967	7,363	68	.323	2,376	981
Two NL batting titles, 1917 and 1919						
Ruth, George (Babe) OF, P 1936	2,503	8,399	714	.342	2,873	2,211
Slugged .847 1920–21						
Schalk, Ray C 1955	1,760	5,306	12	.253	1,345	594
176 stolen bases						
Schoendienst, Albert (Red) 1989	2,216	8,479	84	.289	2,449	773
Managed Cards to two pennants and 1967 World Series crown						
Sewell, Joe SS, 3B 1977	1,902	7,132	49	.312	2,226	1,051
Only 22 strikeouts in his last 2,500 at bats, 1929–33						
Simmons, Al OF 1953	2,215	8,761	307	.334	2,927	1,827
Drove in over 100 runs his first 11 years, 1924–34						
Sisler, George 1B 1939	2,055	8,267	100	.340	2,812	1,175
Batted .400 1920–22						
Slaughter, Enos OF 1985	2,380	7,946	169	.300	2,383	1,304
52 doubles in 1939						
Snider, Edwin (Duke) OF 1980	2,143	7,161	407	.295	2,116	1,333
Averaged 41 home runs, 1953–57						
Speaker, Tris OF 1937	2,789	10,208	117	.344	3,515	1,559
793 doubles, best all-time						
Stargell, Willie OF, 1B 1988	2,360	7,927	475	.282	2,232	1,540
MVP in 1979						
Terry, Bill 1B 1954	1,721	6,428	154	.341	2,193	1,078
Last NL .400 hitter, .401 in 1930						
Thompson, Sam OF 1974	1,410	6,005	128	.331	1,986	1,299
166 RBIs in 1887, 165 in 1895						
Tinker, Joe SS 1946	1,805	6,441	31	.263	1,695	782
Played in four World Series with Chicago Cubs						
Traynor, Pie 3B 1948	1,941	7,559	58	.320	2,416	1,273
100+ RBIs seven years						
Vaughan, Joseph (Arky) SS 1985	1,817	6,622	96	.318	2,103	926
.385 in 1935						
Wagner, Honus SS 1936	2,786	10,427	101	.329	3,430	1,732
Eight batting titles, four in a row 1906–1909						
Wallace, Bobby SS 1953	2,386	8,652	35	.267	2,314	1,121
6.1 chances per game at shortstop, fifth-best all-time						
Waner, Lloyd OF 1967	1,992	7,772	28	.316	2,459	598
234 hits in 1929						
Waner, Paul OF 1952	2,549	9,459	112	.333	3,152	1,309
62 doubles in 1932						
Wheat, Zack OF 1959	2,410	9,106	132	.317	2,884	1,261
Batted .375 at age 36 in 1924						
Williams, Billy OF 1987	2,488	9,350	426	.290	2,711	1,475
30+ home runs in five seasons						
Williams, Ted OF 1966	2,292	7,706	521	.344	2,654	1,839
Last .400 hitter in majors, .406 in 1941						
Wilson, Lewis (Hack) OF 1979	1,348	4,760	244	.307	1,461	1,062
56 home runs and 190 RBIs in 1930, both NL records						
Wright, George SS 1937	329	1,494	2	.256	N/A	N/A
Pioneer of professional baseball						
Yastrzemski, Carl (Yaz) OF, 1B 1989	3,308	11,988	452	.285	3,419	1,844
Won triple crown in 1967, three batting titles, most GP in AL history						
Youngs, Ross OF 1972	1,211	4,627	42	.322	1,491	592
Killed at age 30; .398 on-base average in four World Series, 1921–24						

HALL OF FAME—PITCHERS

Player/Year Inducted	Wins	Losses	ERA	Games	Innings pitched	Strike-outs
Alexander, Grover 1938	373	208	2.56	696	5,189	2,199
Won 30 games three years; led NL in ERA five times						
Bender, Charles (Chief) 1953	210	127	2.46	459	3,017	1,711
Led AL in winning percentage three seasons						
Brown, Mordecai (Three-Finger) 1949	239	129	2.06	481	3,172	1,375
1.04 ERA in 1906						
Chesbro, Jack 1946	198	132	2.68	392	2,897	1,265
41 wins in 1904						
Clarkson, John 1963	326	177	2.81	531	4,536	2,015
53 wins in 1885, with 623 innings pitched						
Coveleski, Stan 1969	215	142	2.88	450	3,093	981
Led AL in ERA in 1925, 2.84						
Cummings, Williams (Candy) 1939	21	22	2.78	43	372	37
Inventor of the curveball						
Dean, Jay (Dizzy) 1953	150	83	3.03	317	1,966	1,155
30 wins in 1934						
Drysdale, Don 1984	209	166	2.95	518	3,432	2,486
56⅔ consecutive scoreless innings, 1968						
Faber, Urban (Red) 1964	254	212	3.15	669	4,088	1,471
Led AL in ERA in 1921 and 1922						
Feller, Bob 1962	266	162	3.25	570	3,827	2,581
Led AL in wins six times, in shutouts seven						
Ford, Edward (Whitey) 1974	236	106	2.75	498	3,170	1,956
25–4 in 1961, 24–7 in 1963						
Galvin, James (Pud) 1965	361	310	2.87	697	5,941	1,799
46 wins in 1883 and 1884						
Gibson, Bob 1981	251	174	2.91	528	3,885	3,117
1.12 ERA in 1968, seven straight wins in World Series play						
Gomez, Vernon (Lefty) 1972	189	102	3.34	368	2,503	1,468
Led AL in shutouts three years						
Grimes, Burleigh 1964	270	212	3.53	617	4,180	1,512
Last legal spitball pitcher, he won 20+ five times						
Grove, Robert (Lefty) 1947	300	141	3.06	616	3,941	2,266
Led AL in ERA nine times, in strikeouts seven						
Haines, Jesse 1970	210	158	3.64	555	3,209	981
Twice led NL in shutouts, 1921 and 1927						
Hoyt, Waite 1969	237	182	3.59	674	3,763	1,206
1.83 in 84 World Series innings						
Hubbell, Carl 1947	253	154	2.97	535	3,589	1,678
26–6 in 1936; 1.66 ERA in 1933						
Hunter, Jim (Catfish) 1987	224	166	3.26	500	3,448	2,012
21 or more wins, 1971–75						
Johnson, Walter 1936	416	279	2.17	802	5,924	3,508
36–7, 1.09 ERA in 1913						
Joss, Addie 1978	160	97	1.88	286	2,336	926
Averaged 21–11, 1.66 ERA in years 1904–08						
Keefe, Tim 1964	344	225	2.62	601	5,072	2,533
Averaged 37 wins 1883–85						
Koufax, Sandy 1972	165	87	2.76	397	2,324	2,396
95–27, 1.85 ERA for seasons 1963–66						
Lemon, Bob 1976	207	128	3.23	460	2,850	1,277
Won 20 or more seven times						
Lyons, Ted 1955	260	230	3.67	594	4,161	1,073
Pitched 27 shutouts						
Marichal, Juan 1983	243	142	2.89	471	3,509	2,303
Only 1.8 walks per nine innings over career						
Marquard, Richard (Rube) 1971	201	177	3.08	536	3,307	1,593
73–23 in years 1911–13						
Mathewson, Christy 1936	373	188	2.13	636	4,782	2,502
80 career shutouts						
McGinnity, Joe 1946	247	144	2.64	466	3,459	1,068
35–8 in 1904, with an ERA of 1.61						

Nichols, Charles (Kid) 1949 360 203 2.94 621 5,084 1,885
Won 30 or more games seven straight seasons, 1891–97
Pennock, Herb 1948 240 162 3.61 617 3,558 1,227
162–90 as a New York Yankee, 1923–33
Plank, Eddie 1946 327 193 2.34 622 4,505 2,246
1.32 ERA in seven World Series games
Radbourn, Charles (Hoss) 1939 308 191 2.67 528 4,535 1,830
60–12 in 1884, with 679 innings pitched
Rixey, Eppa 1963 266 251 3.15 692 4,495 1,350
Won 25 games in 1922
Roberts, Robin 1976 286 245 3.41 676 4,689 2,357
28–7 in 1952; five-time NL leader in complete games
Ruffing, Charles (Red) 1967 273 225 3.80 624 4,344 1,987
.645 winning percentage as a New York Yankee
Rusie, Amos 1977 243 160 3.07 462 3,770 1,957
Won 30+ games three years
Spahn, Warren 1973 363 245 3.09 750 5,244 2,583
Won 20 or more games 13 times, including 23 at age 42
Spalding, Al 1939 48 13 1.78 65 540 41
First 200-game winner, 207–56 from 1871–75
Vance, Clarence (Dazzy) 1955 197 140 3.24 442 2,697 2,045
60–15 over two years, 1924–25
Waddell, George (Rube) 1946 191 145 2.16 407 2,961 2,316
349 strikeouts in 1904
Walsh, Ed 1946 195 126 1.82 430 2,964 1,736
40–15 in 1908 with 11 shutouts; all-time ERA leader
Ward, Montgomery 1964 161 101 2.10 291 2,462 920
87 wins 1879, 1880
Welch, Mickey 1973 311 207 2.71 564 4,802 1,850
44–11 in 1885
Wilhelm, Hoyt 1985 143 122 2.52 1,070 2,254 1,610
All-time leader in games pitched; 227 career saves
Wynn, Early 1972 300 244 3.54 691 4,564 2,334
Led AL in shutouts at age 40 in 1960
Young, Cy 1937 511 313 2.63 906 7,359 2,799
All-time leader in wins, losses, complete games, and innings pitched

ELECTED FOR MANAGING

Alston, Walter 1983
Comiskey, Charles 1939
Griffith, Clark 1946
Harris, Bucky 1975
Huggins, Miller 1964
Lopez, Al 1977
Mack, Connie 1937

McCarthy, Joe 1957
McGraw, John 1937
McKechnie, Bill 1962
Robinson, Wilbert 1945
Stengel, Casey 1966
Wright, George 1937
Wright, Harry 1953

ELECTED FOR MERITORIOUS SERVICE

Barlick, Al
Barrow, Edward
Bulkeley, Morgan
Cartwright, Alexander
Chadwick, Henry
Chandler, Happy
Conlan, John (Jocko)
Connolly, Thomas
Evans, William
Foster, Andrew (Rube)
Frick, Ford

Giles, Warren
Harridge, William
Hubbard, Cal
Johnson, B. Bancroft
Klem, William
Landis, Kenesaw
  Mountain
MacPhail, Larry
Rickey, W. Branch
Weiss, George
Yawkey, Tom

In 1971 Satchel Paige became the first player admitted to Cooperstown based on achievement in the old Negro Leagues. Since then, the following men have been granted the same honor.

Gibson, Josh 1972
Leonard, William "Buck" 1972
Irvin, Monte 1973
Bell, James "Cool Papa" 1974
Johnson, Judy 1975

Charleston, Oscar 1976
DiHigo, Martin 1977
Lloyd, John Henry 1977
Dandridge, Ray 1987

Basketball

NBA PLAYOFF RESULTS, 1989
FIRST ROUND

EASTERN CONFERENCE

NEW YORK vs. PHILADELPHIA
(New York wins series, 3–0)
Phil. 96 at N.Y. 102
Phil. 106 at N.Y. 107
N.Y. 116 at Phil. 115 (ot)
DETROIT vs. BOSTON
(Detroit wins series, 3–0)
Bos. 91 at Det. 101
Bos. 95 at Det. 102
Det. 100 at Bos. 85
CLEVELAND vs. CHICAGO
(Chicago wins series, 3–2)
Chi. 95 at Clev. 88
Chi. 88 at Clev. 96
Clev. 94 at Chi. 101
Clev. 108 at Chi. 105 (ot)
Chi. 101 at Clev. 100
ATLANTA vs. MILWAUKEE
(Milwaukee wins series, 3–2)
Mil. 92 at Atl. 100
Mil. 108 at Atl. 98
Atl. 113 at Mil. 117 (ot)
Atl. 113 at Mil. 106 (ot)
Mil. 96 at Atl. 92

WESTERN CONFERENCE

L.A. LAKERS vs. PORTLAND
(L.A. wins series, 3–0)
Port. 108 at L.A. 128
Port. 105 at L.A. 113
L.A. 116 at Port. 108
UTAH vs. GOLDEN STATE
(Golden State wins series, 3–0)
G.S. 123 at Utah 119
G.S. 99 at Utah 91
Utah 106 at G.S. 120
PHOENIX vs. DENVER
(Phoenix wins series, 3–0)
Den. 103 at Phoe. 104
Den. 114 at Phoe. 132
Phoe. 130 at Den. 121

SEATTLE vs. HOUSTON
(Seattle wins series, 3–1)
Hou. 107 at Sea. 111
Hou. 97 at Sea. 109
Sea. 107 at Hou. 126
Sea. 98 at Hou. 96

CONFERENCE SEMIFINALS

CHICAGO vs. NEW YORK
(Chicago wins series, 4–2)
Chi. 120 at N.Y. 109 (ot)
Chi. 97 at N.Y. 114
N.Y. 88 at Chi. 111
N.Y. 93 at Chi. 106
Chi. 114 at N.Y. 121
N.Y. 111 at Chi. 113
MILWAUKEE vs. DETROIT
(Detroit wins series, 4–0)
Mil. 80 at Det. 85
Mil. 92 at Det. 112
Det. 110 at Mil. 90
Det. 96 at Mil. 94

GOLDEN STATE vs. PHOENIX
(Phoenix wins series, 4–1)
G.S. 103 at Phoe. 130
G.S. 127 at Phoe. 122
Phoe. 113 at G.S. 104
Phoe. 135 at G.S. 99
G.S. 104 at Phoe. 116

L.A. LAKERS vs. SEATTLE
(L.A. wins series, 4–0)
Sea. 102 at L.A. 113
Sea. 108 at L.A. 130
L.A. 91 at Sea. 86
L.A. 97 at Sea. 95

CONFERENCE FINALS

DETROIT vs. CHICAGO
(Detroit wins series, 4–2)
Chi. 94 at Det. 88
Chi. 91 at Det. 100
Det. 97 at Chi. 99
Det. 86 at Chi. 80
Chi. 85 at Det. 94
Det. 103 at Chi. 94

L.A. LAKERS vs. PHOENIX
(L.A. wins series, 4–0)
Phoe. 119 at L.A. 127
Phoe. 95 at L.A. 101
L.A. 110 at Phoe. 107
L.A. 122 at Phoe. 117

NBA CHAMPIONSHIP SERIES

L.A. LAKERS vs. DETROIT
(Detroit wins series, 4–0)
L.A. 97 at Det. 109
L.A. 105 at Det. 108
Det. 114 at L.A. 110
Det. 105 at L.A. 97

NBA FINAL STANDINGS, 1988–89

EASTERN CONFERENCE

Team	W	L	Pct.	Home	Away	Conf.	1987–88
1. Detroit Pistons	63	19	.768	37–4	26–15	41–15	54–28
2. Cleveland Cavaliers	57	25	.695	37–4	20–21	38–18	42–40
3. Atlanta Hawks	52	30	.634	33–8	19–22	38–18	50–32
N.Y. Knicks (tie)	52	30	.634	35–6	17–24	36–20	38–44
5. Milwaukee Bucks	49	33	.598	31–10	18–23	29–27	42–40
6. Chicago Bulls	47	35	.573	30–11	17–24	28–28	50–32
7. Philadelphia 76ers	46	36	.561	30–11	16–25	31–25	36–46
8. Boston Celtics	42	40	.512	32–9	10–31	27–29	57–25
9. Washington Bullets	40	42	.488	30–11	10–31	25–31	38–44
10. Indiana Pacers	28	54	.341	20–21	8–33	15–41	38–44
11. New Jersey Nets	26	56	.317	17–24	9–32	16–40	19–63
12. Charlotte Hornets	20	62	.244	12–29	8–33	12–44	N.A.

WESTERN CONFERENCE

Team	W	L	Pct.	Home	Away	Conf.	1987–88
1. L.A. Lakers	57	25	.695	35–6	22–19	43–15	62–20
2. Phoenix Suns	55	27	.671	35–6	20–21	41–17	28–54
3. Utah Jazz	51	31	.622	34–7	17–24	37–21	47–35
4. Seattle SuperSonics	47	35	.573	31–10	16–25	37–21	44–38
5. Houston Rockets	45	37	.549	31–10	14–27	33–25	46–36
6. Denver Nuggets	44	38	.537	35–6	9–32	32–26	54–28
7. Golden State Warriors	43	39	.524	29–12	14–27	29–29	20–62
8. Portland Trail Blazers	39	43	.476	28–13	11–30	30–28	53–29
9. Dallas Mavericks	38	44	.463	24–17	14–27	30–28	53–29
10. Sacramento Kings	27	55	.329	21–20	6–35	23–35	24–58
11. L.A. Clippers	21	61	.256	17–24	4–37	17–41	17–65
San Antonio Spurs (tie)	21	61	.256	18–23	3–38	15–43	31–51
13. Miami Heat	15	67	.183	12–29	3–38	10–48	N.A.

Note: The top eight teams from each conference qualified for the playoffs.   **Source:** The NBA.

1989 NBA CHAMPIONSHIP
Composite Box Score

LOS ANGELES LAKERS (0–4)

	G.	Min.	FG M-A	Pct.	FT M-A	Pct.	Reb. O-T	A	Pts.	Avg.
Worthy	4	170	39–81	.481	22–31	.710	7–17	14	102	25.5
Abdul-Jabbar	4	104	20–46	.435	10–12	.833	5–20	7	50	12.5
Cooper	4	163	17–45	.378	5–6	.833	1–6	27	48	12.0
E. Johnson	3	75	12–26	.462	10–11	.909	3–11	24	35	11.7
Campbell	4	83	15–24	.625	13–17	.765	3–10	4	44	11.0
Thompson	4	103	13–30	.433	14–22	.636	12–19	3	40	10.0
Woolridge	4	87	11–18	.611	16–19	.842	5–21	6	38	9.5
Green	4	134	11–25	.440	13–19	.684	11–37	2	35	8.8
Rivers	3	26	4–12	.333	4–5	.800	0–3	5	12	4.0
Lamp	4	11	2–3	.667	1–2	.500	0–1	0	5	1.3
McNamara	2	4	0–0		0–0		0–0	0	0	0.0
Totals	**4**	**960**	**144–310**	**.465**	**108–144**	**.750**	**47–145**	**92**	**409**	**102.3**

DETROIT PISTONS (4–0)

	G.	Min.	FG M-A	Pct.	FT M-A	Pct.	Reb. O-T	A	Pts.	Avg.
Dumars	4	147	38–66	.576	33–38	.868	1–7	24	109	27.3
Thomas	4	141	32–66	.485	19–25	.760	2–10	29	85	21.3
V. Johnson	4	95	30–50	.600	7–11	.636	3–13	11	68	17.0
Edwards	4	97	12–27	.444	12–16	.750	6–14	1	36	9.0
Laimbeer	4	94	12–22	.545	6–7	.857	3–21	9	32	8.0
Salley	4	81	13–19	.684	4–7	.571	2–10	5	30	7.5
Aguirre	4	107	12–33	.364	6–8	.750	9–24	6	30	7.5
Mahorn	4	98	10–18	.556	4–6	.667	6–21	6	24	6.0
Rodman	4	94	7–15	.467	6–7	.857	13–40	5	20	5.0
Long	1	2	1–1	1.000	0–0		0–0	0	2	2.0
Dembo	1	2	0–0		0–0		0–0	0	0	0.0
Williams	1	2	0–0		0–0		0–0	1	0	0.0
Totals	**4**	**960**	**167–317**	**.527**	**97–125**	**.776**	**45–160**	**97**	**436**	**109.0**

Scoring by quarters

L.A. Lakers	111	109	104	85	—	409
Detroit	104	113	108	111	—	436

NBA LEADERS, 1988–89

SCORING

	G	Pts.	Avg.
Michael Jordan, Chicago	81	2,633	32.5
Karl Malone, Utah	80	2,326	29.1
Dale Ellis, Seattle	82	2,253	27.5
Clyde Drexler, Portland	78	2,123	27.2
Chris Mullin, Golden State	82	2,176	26.5
Alex English, Denver	82	2,175	26.5
Dominique Wilkins, Atlanta	80	2,099	26.2
Charles Barkley, Philadelphia	79	2,037	25.8
Tom Chambers, Phoenix	81	2,085	25.7
Akeem Olajuwon, Houston	82	2,034	24.8
Terry Cummings, Milwaukee	80	1,829	22.9
Patrick Ewing, N.Y.	80	1,815	22.7
Kelly Tripucka, Charlotte	71	1,606	22.6
Kevin McHale, Boston	78	1,758	22.5
Magic Johnson, L.A. Lakers	77	1,730	22.5
Mitch Richmond, Golden State	79	1,741	22.0
Jeff Malone, Washington	76	1,651	21.7
Chuck Person, Indiana	80	1,728	21.6
Eddie Johnson, Phoenix	70	1,504	21.5
Bernard King, Washington	81	1,674	20.7

REBOUNDS

	G	Tot.	Avg.
Akeem Olajuwon, Houston	82	1,105	13.5
Charles Barkley, Philadelphia	79	986	12.5
Robert Parish, Boston	80	996	12.5
Moses Malone, Atlanta	81	956	11.8
Karl Malone, Utah	80	853	10.7
Charles Oakley, N.Y.	82	861	10.5
Mark Eaton, Utah	82	843	10.3
Otis Thorpe, Houston	82	787	9.6
Bill Laimbeer, Detroit	81	776	9.6
Michael Cage, Seattle	80	765	9.6

FIELD GOAL PERCENTAGE

	FGM	FGA	Pct.
Dennis Rodman, Detroit	316	531	.595
Charles Barkley, Philadelphia	700	1,208	.579
Robert Parish, Boston	596	1,045	.570
Patrick Ewing, N.Y.	727	1,282	.567
James Worthy, L.A. Lakers	702	1,282	.548
Kevin McHale, Boston	661	1,211	.546
Otis Thorpe, Houston	521	961	.542
Benoit Benjamin, L.A. Clippers	491	907	.541
Larry Nance, Cleveland	496	920	.539
John Stockton, Utah	497	923	.538

FREE THROW PERCENTAGE

	FTM	FTA	Pct.
Magic Johnson, L.A. Lakers	513	563	.911
Jack Sikma, Milwaukee	266	294	.905
Scott Skiles, Indiana	130	144	.903
Mark Price, Cleveland	263	292	.901
Chris Mullin, Golden State	493	553	.892
Kevin Johnson, Phoenix	508	576	.882
Joe Kleine, Boston	134	152	.882
Walter Davis, Denver	175	199	.879
Mike Gminski, Philadelphia	297	341	.871
Jeff Malone, Washington	296	340	.871

3–PT. FIELD GOALS

	FGM	FGA	Pct.
Jon Sundvold, Miami	48	92	.522
Dale Ellis, Seattle	162	339	.478
Mark Price, Cleveland	93	211	.441
Hersey Hawkins, Philadelphia	71	166	.428
Craig Hodges, Chicago	75	180	.417
Eddie Johnson, Phoenix	71	172	.413
Walter Berry, Sacramento	65	160	.406
Harold Pressley, Sacramento	119	295	.403
Reggie Miller, Indiana	98	244	.402
Byron Scott, L.A. Lakers	77	193	.399

BLOCKED SHOTS	G	No.	Avg.
Manute Bol, Golden State	80	345	4.31
Mark Eaton, Utah	82	315	3.84
Patrick Ewing, N.Y.	80	281	3.51
Akeem Olajuwon, Houston	82	282	3.44
Larry Nance, Cleveland	73	206	2.82
Benoit Benjamin, L.A. Clippers	79	221	2.80
Wayne Cooper, Denver	79	211	2.67
Mark West, Phoenix	82	187	2.28
Alton Lister, Seattle	82	180	2.20
Rik Smits, Indiana	82	151	1.84

Source: NBA.

ASSISTS	G	No.	Avg.
John Stockton, Utah	82	1,118	13.6
Magic Johnson, L.A. Lakers	77	988	12.8
Kevin Johnson, Phoenix	81	991	12.2
Kevin Porter, Portland	81	770	9.5
Nate McMillan, Seattle	75	696	9.3
Sleepy Floyd, Houston	82	709	8.6
Mark Jackson, N.Y.	72	619	8.6
Mark Price, Cleveland	75	631	8.4
Isiah Thomas, Detroit	80	663	8.3
Michael Jordan, Chicago	81	650	8.0

STEALS	G	No.	Avg.
John Stockton, Utah	82	263	3.21
Alvin Robertson, San Antonio	65	197	3.03
Michael Jordan, Chicago	81	234	2.89
Lafayette Lever, Denver	71	195	2.75
Clyde Drexler, Portland	78	213	2.73
Akeem Olajuwon, Houston	82	213	2.60
Glenn Rivers, Atlanta	76	181	2.38
Ron Harper, Cleveland	82	185	2.26
Winston Garland, Golden State	79	175	2.22
Lester Conner, New Jersey	82	181	2.21

NBA WORLD CHAMPIONSHIP SERIES

Year	Winner	Loser	Games
1947	Philadelphia Warriors	Chicago Stags	4–1
1948	Baltimore Bullets	Philadelphia Warriors	4–2
1949	Minneapolis Lakers	Washington Capitols	4–2
1950	Minneapolis Lakers	Syracuse Nationals	4–2
1951	Rochester Royals	N.Y. Knicks	4–3
1952	Minneapolis Lakers	N.Y. Knicks	4–3
1953	Minneapolis Lakers	N.Y. Knicks	4–1
1954	Minneapolis Lakers	Syracuse Nationals	4–3
1955	Syracuse Nationals	Ft. Wayne Pistons	4–3
1956	Philadelphia Warriors	Ft. Wayne Pistons	4–1
1957	Boston Celtics	St. Louis Hawks	4–3
1958	St. Louis Hawks	Boston Celtics	4–2
1959	Boston Celtics	Minneapolis Lakers	4–0
1960	Boston Celtics	St. Louis Hawks	4–3
1961	Boston Celtics	St. Louis Hawks	4–1
1962	Boston Celtics	L.A. Lakers	4–3
1963	Boston Celtics	L.A. Lakers	4–2
1964	Boston Celtics	San Francisco Warriors	4–1
1965	Boston Celtics	L.A. Lakers	4–1
1966	Boston Celtics	L.A. Lakers	4–3
1967	Philadelphia 76ers	San Francisco Warriors	4–2
1968	Boston Celtics	L.A. Lakers	4–2
1969	Boston Celtics	L.A. Lakers	4–3
1970	N.Y. Knicks	L.A. Lakers	4–3
1971	Milwaukee Bucks	Baltimore Bullets	4–0
1972	L.A. Lakers	N.Y. Knicks	4–1
1973	N.Y. Knicks	L.A. Lakers	4–1
1974	Boston Celtics	Milwaukee Bucks	4–3
1975	Golden State Warriors	Washington Bullets	4–0
1976	Boston Celtics	Phoenix Suns	4–2
1977	Portland Trail Blazers	Philadelphia 76ers	4–2
1978	Washington Bullets	Seattle SuperSonics	4–3
1979	Seattle Super Sonics	Washington Bullets	4–1
1980	L.A. Lakers	Philadelphia 76ers	4–2
1981	Boston Celtics	Houston Rockets	4–2
1982	L.A. Lakers	Philadelphia 76ers	4–2
1983	Philadelphia 76ers	L.A. Lakers	4–0
1984	Boston Celtics	L.A. Lakers	4–3
1985	L.A. Lakers	Boston Celtics	4–2
1986	Boston Celtics	Houston Rockets	4–2
1987	L.A. Lakers	Boston Celtics	4–2
1988	L.A. Lakers	Detroit Pistons	4–3
1989	Detroit Pistons	L.A. Lakers	4–0

NBA MOST VALUABLE PLAYERS

Year	Name	Team	Pts.	Avg.	Reb.
1955–56	Bob Pettit	St. Louis Hawks	1,849	25.7	1,164
1956–57	Bob Cousy	Boston Celtics	1,319	20.6	309
1957–58	Bill Russell	Boston Celtics	1,142	16.6	1,564
1958–59	Bob Pettit	St. Louis Hawks	2,105	29.2	1,182
1959–60	Wilt Chamberlain	Philadelphia Warriors	2,207	37.6	1,941
1960–61	Bill Russell	Boston Celtics	1,322	16.9	1,868
1961–62	Bill Russell	Boston Celtics	1,436	18.9	1,790
1962–63	Bill Russell	Boston Celtics	1,309	16.8	1,843
1963–64	Oscar Robertson	Cincinnati Royals	2,480	31.4	783
1964–65	Bill Russell	Boston Celtics	1,102	14.1	1,878
1965–66	Wilt Chamberlain	Philadelphia 76ers	2,649	33.5	1,943
1966–67	Wilt Chamberlain	Philadelphia 76ers	1,956	24.1	1,957
1967–68	Wilt Chamberlain	Philadelphia 76ers	1,992	24.3	1,952
1968–69	Wes Unseld	Baltimore Bullets	1,131	13.8	1,491
1969–70	Willis Reed	N.Y. Knicks	1,755	21.7	1,126
1970–71	Kareem Abdul-Jabbar	Milwaukee Bucks	2,596	31.7	1,311
1971–72	Kareem Abdul-Jabbar	Milwaukee Bucks	2,822	34.8	1,346
1972–73	Dave Cowens	Boston Celtics	1,684	20.5	1,329
1973–74	Kareem Abdul-Jabbar	Milwaukee Bucks	2,191	27.0	1,178
1974–75	Bob McAdoo	Buffalo Braves	2,831	34.5	1,155
1975–76	Kareem Abdul-Jabbar	L.A. Lakers	2,275	27.7	1,383
1976–77	Kareem Abdul-Jabbar	L.A. Lakers	2,152	26.2	1,090
1977–78	Bill Walton	Portland Trail Blazers	1,097	18.9	766
1978–79	Moses Malone	Houston Rockets	2,031	24.8	1,444
1979–80	Kareem Abdul-Jabbar	L.A. Lakers	2,034	24.8	886
1980–81	Julius Erving	Philadelphia 76ers	2,014	24.6	657
1981–82	Moses Malone	Houston Rockets	2,520	31.1	1,188
1982–83	Moses Malone	Philadelphia 76ers	1,908	24.5	1,194
1983–84	Larry Bird	Boston Celtics	1,908	24.2	796
1984–85	Larry Bird	Boston Celtics	2,295	28.7	842
1985–86	Larry Bird	Boston Celtics	2,115	25.8	805
1986–87	Magic Johnson	L.A. Lakers	1,909	23.9	504
1987–88	Michael Jordan	Chicago Bulls	2,868	35.0	449
1988–89	Magic Johnson	L.A. Lakers	1,730	22.5	607

NBA FIRST-ROUND DRAFT PICKS, 1989

Team	Player	College	Pos.
1. Sacramento	Pervis Ellison	Louisville	F
2. L.A. Clippers	Danny Ferry	Duke	F
3. San Antonio	Sean Elliott	Arizona	F
4. Miami	Glen Rice	Michigan	F
5. Charlotte	J.R. Reid	UNC	F
6. Chicago from New Jersey	Stacey King	Oklahoma	F
7. Indiana	George McCloud	Florida State	F
8. Dallas	Randy White	Louisiana Tech	F
9. Washington	Tom Hammonds	Georgia Tech	F
10. Minnesota	Pooh Richardson	UCLA	G
11. Orlando	Nick Anderson	Illinois	G
12. New Jersey from Portland	Mookie Blaylock	Oklahoma	G
13. Boston	Michael Smith	Brigham Young	F

NBA CAREER LEADERS

GAMES		SCORING		REBOUNDING		ASSISTS		FIELD GOALS MADE	
Kareem Abdul-Jabbar	1,560	**Name**	**Points**	Wilt Chamberlain	23,924	Oscar Robertson	9,887	Kareem Abdul-Jabbar	15,837
Elvin Hayes	1,303	Kareem Abdul-Jabbar	38,387	Bill Russell	21,620	Magic Johnson	8,025	Wilt Chamberlain	12,681
John Havlicek	1,270	Wilt Chamberlain	31,419	Kareem Abdul-Jabbar	17,440	Len Wilkens	7,211	Elvin Hayes	10,976
Paul Silas	1,254	Elvin Hayes	27,313	Elvin Hayes	16,279	Bob Cousy	6,955	John Havlicek	10,513
Hal Greer	1,122	Oscar Robertson	26,710	Nate Thurmond	14,464	Guy Rodgers	6,917	Alex English	9,702
Len Wilkens	1,077	John Havlicek	26,375	Walt Bellamy	14,241	Nate Archibald	6,476	Oscar Robertson	9,508
Dolph Schayes	1,059	Jerry West	25,192	Wes Unseld	13,769	Norm Nixon	6,386	Jerry West	9,016
Johnny Green	1,057	Adrian Dantley	23,782	Moses Malone	13,371	Jerry West	6,238	Elgin Baylor	8,693
Don Nelson	1,053	Alex English	23,417	Jerry Lucas	12,942	Isiah Thomas	6,220	Hal Greer	8,504
Leroy Ellis	1,048	Moses Malone	23,340	Bob Pettit	12,849	John Lucas	6,216	Moses Malone	8,070
		Elgin Baylor	23,149						
		Hal Greer	21,586						

Source: NBA. **Note:** As of June, 1989.

Team	Player	College	Pos.
14. Golden State	Tim Hardaway	UTEP	G
15. Denver	Todd Lichti	Stanford	G
16. Seattle from Golden State	Dana Barros	Boston College	G
17. Seattle from Philadelphia	Shawn Kemp	Trinity Vall. CC	C
18. Chicago	B.J. Armstrong	Iowa	G
19. Philadelphia from Seattle	Kenny Payne	Louisville	F
20. Chicago	Jeff Sanders	Ga. Southern	F
21. Utah	Blue Edwards	East Carolina	G
22. Portland from New York	Byron Irvin	Missouri	G
23. Atlanta	Roy Marble	Iowa	G
24. Phoenix[1]	Anthony Cook	Arizona	F
25. Cleveland	John Morton	Seton Hall	G
26. L.A. Lakers	Vlade Divac	Yugoslavia	C
27. Detroit[1]	Kenny Battle	Illinois	F

1. Pistons traded Battle and Michael Williams to Suns for Cook.

OVERALL NUMBER-ONE DRAFT PICK IN THE NBA DRAFT, 1966–89

Year	Player	Team drafted by	College
1966	Cazzie Russell	N.Y. Knicks	Michigan
1967	Jimmy Walker	Detroit Pistons	Providence
1968	Elvin Hayes	San Diego Rockets	Houston
1969	Lew Alcindor	Milwaukee Bucks	UCLA
1970	Bob Lanier	Detroit Pistons	St. Bonaventure
1971	Austin Carr	Cleveland Cavaliers	Notre Dame
1972	Larue Martin	Portland Trail Blazers	Loyola
1973	Doug Collins	Philadelphia 76ers	Illinois State
1974	Bill Walton	Portland Trail Blazers	UCLA
1975	David Thompson	Atlanta Hawks	N.C. State
1976	John Lucas	Houston Rockets	Maryland
1977	Kent Benson	Milwaukee Bucks	Indiana
1978	Mychal Thompson	Portland Trail Blazers	Minnesota
1979	Earvin Johnson	L.A. Lakers	Michigan State
1980	Joe Barry Carroll	Golden State Warriors	Purdue
1981	Mark Aguirre	Dallas Mavericks	DePaul
1982	James Worthy	L.A. Lakers	North Carolina
1983	Ralph Sampson	Houston Rockets	Virginia
1984	Akeem Olajuwon	Houston Rockets	Houston
1985	Patrick Ewing	N.Y. Knicks	Georgetown
1986	Brad Daugherty	Cleveland Cavaliers	North Carolina
1987	David Robinson	San Antonio Spurs	Navy
1988	Danny Manning	L.A. Clippers	Kansas
1989	Pervis Ellison	Sacramento Kings	Louisville

NBA NAISMITH MEMORIAL HALL OF FAME

MODERN PLAYERS

Player (year elected)	Games	Points	FG%	FT%	Rebs.	Assts.
Arizin, Paul J. (1977)	713	16,266	.421	.810	6,129	1,665
NBA scoring leader in 1952 (25.4 ppg) and 1957 (25.6 ppg)						
Barry, Rick (1986–87)	794	18,395	.449	.900	5,168	4,017
(ABA)	226	6,884	.477	.880	1,695	935
NBA all-time free-throw percentage leader						
Baylor, Elgin (1976)	846	23,149	.431	.780	11,463	3,650
Named to NBA All-Star First Team 10 times						
Bradley, Bill (1982)	742	9,217	.448	.840	2,533	2,363
Averaged 30.2 ppg in 83 games at Princeton University						
Chamberlain, Wilt (1978)	1,045	31,419	.540	.511	23,924	4,643
Holds NBA single-game records for points (100) and rebounds (55); all-time rebound leader						
Cousy, Bob (1970)	924	16,960	.375	.803	4,786	6,955
Led NBA in assists eight consecutive seasons (1953–60)						
Cunningham, Billy (1985–86)	654	13,626	.446	.720	6,638	2,625
(ABA)	116	2,684	.483	.791	1,343	680
Coached Philadelphia 76ers to 454–196 record in eight years						
Davies, Bob (1969)	462	6,594	.378	.759	980[1]	2,050
(NBL)[2]	107	1,177		.747		
NBL MVP, 1947						
DeBusschere, Dave (1982)	875	14,053	.432	.699	2,497	2,801
NBA All-Defensive team six consecutive seasons (1969–74)						
Frazier, Walt (Clyde) (1986–87)	825	15,581	.490	.786	4,830	5,040
NBA All-Defensive team seven consecutive seasons (1969–75)						
Fulks, Joe (1977)	489	8,003	.302	.766	1,382[1]	587
NBA scoring leader in 1947 (23.2 ppg)						
Gola, Tom (1975)	698	7,871	.431	.760	5,605	2,953
One of only two major-college players with more than 2,000 points and 2,000 rebounds in career						
Greer, Harold (Hal) (1981)	1,122	21,586	.452	.801	5,665	4,540
Scored 19 points in one quarter of 1968 All-Star game						
Hagan, Cliff (1977)	746	13,447	.450	.798	5,019	2,236
(ABA)	94	1,423	.496	.807	436	398
Helped St. Louis to 1958 championship with 27.7 ppg in playoffs						
Havlicek, John J. (Hondo) (1983)	1,270	26,395	.439	.815	8,007	6,114
Fifth among NBA career scoring leaders						
Heinsohn, Tom (1985–86)	654	12,194	.405	.790	5,749	1,318
Played for eight NBA championship teams and coached two others						
Houbregs, Robert J. (1986–87)	281	2,611	.404	.721	1,552	500
NCAA Player of the Year, 1953						
Jones, K.C. (1988–89)	676	5,011	.387	.647	2,399	2,908
High scorer in 1955 NCAA finals (24 points), while holding Tom Gola scoreless for 21 min.						
Jones, Sam (1983)	871	15,411	.456	.803	4,305	2,209
Member of 10 NBA championship teams						

Player (year elected)	Games	Points	FG%	FT%	Rebs.	Assts.
Lovellette, Clyde (1987–88)	704	11,947	.443	.756	6,663	1,165
Three-time All-American at University of Kansas (1950–52)						
Lucas, Jerry Ray (Luke) (1979)	829	14,053	.499	.783	12,942	2,730
NBA Rookie of the Year and field-goal percentage leader (.527) in 1964						
Macauley, Edward (Easy Ed) (1960)	641	11,234	.436	.761	2,079	1,667
NBA All-Star Game MVP, 1951						
Maravich, Pete (Pistol) (1986–87)	658	15,948	.441	.820	2,747	3,563
NCAA career record holder for points scored (3,667) and scoring average (44.2 ppg)						
Martin, Slater (1981)	745	7,337	.364	.762	2,302[1]	3,160
Played in seven straight All-Star Games, 1953–59						
Mikan, George L. (1959)	439	10,156	.404	.782	4,167[1]	1,245
(NBL)[2]	81	1,608		.756		
Three-time NBA scoring leader (1949, 1950, 1952)						
Pettit, Robert L. (1970)	792	20,880	.436	.761	12,849	2,369
Led NBA in scoring (25.7 ppg) and rebounds (1,164) in 1956						
Phillip, Andy (1961)	701	6,384	.368	.695	2,395[1]	3,759
Led NBA in assists, 1951 and 1952						
Pollard, Jim (1977)	438	5,762	.360	.750	2,487[1]	1,417
(NBL)[2]	59	760		.676		
Started in four NBA All-Star Games						
Ramsey, Frank (1981)	623	8,378	.402	.804	3,410	1,136
Member of seven NBA championship teams						
Reed, Willis (1981)	650	12,183	.476	.747	8,414	1,186
In 1970 was named NBA MVP, All-Star Game MVP, and Playoff MVP						

Player (year elected)	Games	Points	FG%	FT%	Rebs.	Assts.
Robertson, Oscar (1979)	1,040	26,710	.485	.838	7,804	9,887
NBA all-time leader in rebounds by a guard, assists and free throws made (7,694)						
Russell, Bill (1974)	963	14,522	.440	.561	21,620	4,100
Five-time NBA MVP; 32 rebounds in one half vs. Philadelphia, 1957						
Schayes, Adolph (Dolph) (1972)	996	18,438	.380	.849	11,256[1]	3,072
(NBL)[2]	63	811		.724		
NBA Coach of the Year (1966)						
Sharman, Bill (1974)	711	12,665	.426	.883	2,779	2,101
Led NBA in free-throw percentage for seven seasons						
Thurmond, Nate (1984)	964	14,437	.421	.667	14,464	2,575
Holds NCAA tournament record for most rebounds in one game (31)						
Twyman, Jack (1982)	823	15,840	.450	.778	5,421	1,969
Led NBA in field-goal percentage, 1958 (.452)						
Unseld, Wes (1987–88)	984	10,624	.509	.633	13,769	3,822
Named NBA MVP and Rookie of the Year in same year (1969)						
Wazner, Robert (1986–87)	502	5,891	.388	.800	1,652[1]	1,575
Free-throw percentage leader, 1952 (.904)						
West, Jerry Alan (1979)	932	25,192	.474	.814	5,376	6,238
All-time playoff scoring average leader (29.1 ppg)						
Wilkens, Lenny (1988–89)	1,077	17,772	.432	.774	5,030	7,211
Ranks third in the NBA in career assists						

Notes: Named after Dr. James Naismith, the game's founder. All statistics for NBA career unless otherwise noted. NBL = National Basketball League; ABA = American Basketball Association. 1. Does not include seasons played prior to 1950–51, when the NBA first began keeping statistics for rebounds. 2. The National Basketball League did not keep statistics for field-goal percentage, rebounds, or assists.

Football

1988 POSTSEASON AT A GLANCE

AFC First Round	Houston 24, CLEVELAND 23
AFC Divisional Playoffs	BUFFALO 17, Houston 10
	CINCINNATI 21, Seattle 13
AFC Championship Game	CINCINNATI 21, Buffalo 10
NFC First Round	MINNESOTA 28, Los Angeles Rams 17
NFC Divisional Playoffs	SAN FRANCISCO 34, Minnesota 9
	CHICAGO 20, Philadelphia 12
NFC Championship Game	San Francisco 28, CHICAGO 3
Super Bowl XXIII at Joe Robbie Stadium, Miami, Florida	
	SAN FRANCISCO (NFC) 20, Cincinnati (AFC) 16
AFC-NFC Pro Bowl at Honolulu, Hawaii	NFC 34, AFC 3

Note: Home team in capital letters.

NFL LEADERS, 1988

RUSHING

AFC	No.	Yds.	Avg.	Long	TD
Eric Dickerson, Indianapolis	388	1,659	4.3	41	14
John Stephens, New England	297	1,168	3.9	52	4
Gary Anderson, San Diego	225	1,119	5.0	36	3
Ickey Woods, Cincinnati	203	1,066	5.3	56	15
Curt Warner, Seattle	266	1,025	3.9	29	10
Mike Rozier, Houston	251	1,002	4.0	28	10
Freeman McNeil, N.Y. Jets	219	944	4.3	28	6
NFC					
Herschel Walker, Dallas	361	1,514	4.2	38	5
Roger Craig, San Francisco	310	1,502	4.8	46	9
Greg Bell, L.A. Rams	288	1,212	4.2	44	16
Neal Anderson, Chicago	249	1,106	4.4	80	12
Joe Morris, N.Y. Giants	307	1,083	3.5	27	5
John Settle, Atlanta	232	1,024	4.4	62	7
Earl Ferrell, Phoenix	202	924	4.6	47	7

PASSING

AFC	Att.	Comp.	Yds.	TD	Int.	Rating
Boomer Esiason, Cincinnati	388	223	3,572	28	14	97.4
Dave Krieg, Seattle	228	134	1,741	18	8	94.6
Warren Moon, Houston	294	160	2,327	17	8	88.4
Bernie Kosar, Cleveland	259	156	1,890	10	7	84.3
Dan Marino, Miami	606	354	4,434	28	23	80.8
Ken O'Brien, N.Y. Jets	424	236	2,567	15	7	78.6
Jim Kelly, Buffalo	452	269	3,380	15	17	78.2
NFC						
Wade Wilson, Minnesota	332	204	2,746	15	9	91.5
Jim Everett, L.A. Rams	517	308	3,964	31	18	89.2
Joe Montana, San Francisco	397	238	2,981	18	10	87.9
Neil Lomax, Phoenix	443	255	3,395	20	11	86.7
Phil Simms, N.Y. Giants	479	263	3,359	21	11	82.1
Bobby Hebert, New Orleans	478	280	3,156	20	15	79.3
R. Cunningham, Philadelphia	560	301	3,808	24	16	77.6
D. Williams, Washington	380	213	2,609	15	12	77.4

Note: Standing based on percentage of completions, percentage of touchdowns, percentage of interceptions, and average gain per attempt.

RECEIVING

AFC	No.	Yds.	Avg. gain	TD
Al Toon, N.Y. Jets	93	1,067	11.5	5
Mark Clayton, Miami	86	1,129	13.1	14
Drew Hill, Houston	72	1,141	15.8	10
Jerry Reed, Buffalo	71	968	13.6	6
Mickey Shuler, N.Y. Jets	70	805	11.5	5
Vance Johnson, Denver	68	896	13.2	5
Stephone Paige, Kansas City	61	902	14.8	7
NFC				
Henry Ellard, L.A. Rams	86	1,414	16.4	10
Eric Martin, New Orleans	85	1,083	12.7	7
J.T. Smith, Phoenix	83	986	11.9	5
Keith Jackson, Philadelphia	81	869	10.7	6
Roger Craig, San Francisco	76	534	7.0	1
Barry Sanders, Washington	73	1,148	15.7	12
Anthony Carter, Minnesota	72	1,225	17.0	6

NFL NUMBER-ONE DRAFT PICKS, 1936–89

Year	Player	Team	Pos.	College
1936	Jay Berwanger	Philadelphia Eagles	RB	Chicago
1937	Sam Francis	Philadelphia Eagles	RB	Nebraska
1938	Corbett Davis	Cleveland Rams	RB	Indiana
1939	Charles Aldrich	Chicago Cardinals	OL	Texas Christian
1940	George Cafego	Chicago Cardinals	QB	Tennessee
1941	Tom Harmon	Chicago Bears	RB	Michigan
1942	Bill Dudley	Pittsburgh Steelers	RB	Virginia
1943	Frank Sinkwich	Detroit Lions	RB	Georgia
1944	Angelo Bertelli	Boston Yanks	QB	Notre Dame
1945	Charley Trippi	Chicago Cardinals	RB	Georgia
1946	Frank Dancewicz	Boston Yanks	QB	Notre Dame
1947	Bob Fenimore	Chicago Bears	RB	Oklahoma A&M
1948	Harry Gilmer	Washington Redskins	QB	Alabama
1949	Chuck Bednarik	Philadelphia Eagles	OL	Pennsylvania
1950	Leon Hart	Detroit Lions	RB	Notre Dame
1951	Kyle Rote	New York Giants	E/K	Southern Methodist
1952	Bill Wade	Los Angeles Rams	QB	Vanderbilt
1953	Harry Babcock	San Francisco 49ers	E	Georgia
1954	Bobby Garrett	Cleveland Browns	QB	Stanford
1955	George Shaw	Baltimore Colts	QB	Oregon
1956	Gary Glick	Pittsburgh Steelers	QB	Colorado State
1957	Paul Hornung	Green Bay Packers	RB	Notre Dame
1958	King Hill	St. Louis Cardinals	QB	Rice
1959	Randy Duncan	Green Bay Packers	QB	Iowa
1960	Billy Cannon	Los Angeles Rams	RB	Louisiana State
1961	Tommy Mason	Minnesota Vikings	RB	Tulane
1962	Ernie Davis	Washington Redskins	RB	Syracuse
1963	Terry Baker	Los Angeles Rams	QB	Oregon State
1964	Dave Parks	San Francisco 49ers	E	Texas Tech
1965	Tucker Frederickson	New York Giants	RB	Auburn
1966	Tommy Nobis	Atlanta Falcons	LB	Texas
1967	Bubba Smith	Baltimore Colts	DL	Michigan State
1968	Ron Yary	Minnesota Vikings	OL	USC
1969	O.J. Simpson	Buffalo Bills	RB	USC
1970	Terry Bradshaw	Pittsburgh Steelers	QB	Louisiana Tech
1971	Jim Plunkett	Boston Patriots	QB	Stanford
1972	Walt Patulski	Buffalo Bills	DL	Notre Dame
1973	John Matuszak	Houston Oilers	DL	Tampa
1974	Ed Jones	Dallas Cowboys	DL	Tennessee State
1975	Steve Bartkowski	Atlanta Falcons	QB	California
1976	Lee Roy Selmon	Tampa Bay Buccaneers	DL	Oklahoma
1977	Ricky Bell	Tampa Bay Buccaneers	RB	USC
1978	Earl Campbell	Houston Oilers	RB	Texas
1979	Tom Cousineau	Buffalo Bills	LB	Ohio State
1980	Billy Sims	Detroit Lions	RB	Oklahoma
1981	George Rogers	New Orleans Saints	RB	South Carolina
1982	Kenneth Sims	New England Patriots	DL	Texas
1983	John Elway	Baltimore Colts	QB	Stanford
1984	Irving Fryar	New England Patriots	WR	Nebraska
1985	Bruce Smith	Buffalo Bills	DL	Virginia Tech
1986	Bo Jackson	Tampa Bay Buccaneers	RB	Auburn
1987	Vinny Testaverde	Tampa Bay Buccaneers	QB	Miami
1988	Aundray Bruce	Atlanta Falcons	LB	Auburn
1989	Troy Aikman	Dallas Cowboys	QB	UCLA

NATIONAL FOOTBALL LEAGUE 1989 FIRST-ROUND DRAFT CHOICES

Team	Choice	Pos.	College
Dallas	Troy Aikman	QB	UCLA
Green Bay	Tony Mandarich	T	Michigan State
Detroit	Barry Sanders	RB	Oklahoma State
Kansas City	Derrick Thomas	LB	Alabama
Atlanta	Deion Sanders	DB	Florida State
Tampa Bay	Broderick Thomas	LB	Nebraska

Team	Choice	Pos.	College
Pittsburgh	Tim Worley	RB	Georgia
San Diego	Burt Grossman	DE	Pittsburgh
Miami	Sammie Smith	RB	Florida State
Phoenix	Eric Hill	LB	Louisiana State
Chicago from L.A. Raiders	Donnell Woolford	DB	Clemson
Chicago from Washington	Trace Armstrong	DE	Florida
Cleveland from Denver	Eric Metcalf	RB	Texas
New York Jets	Jeff Lageman	LB	Virginia
Seattle from Indianapolis	Andy Heck	T	Notre Dame
New England	Hart Lee Dykes	WR	Oklahoma State
Phoenix from Seattle	Joe Wolf	G	Boston College
New York Giants	Brian Williams	G	Minnesota
New Orleans	Wayne Martin	DE	Arkansas
Denver from Cleveland	Steve Atwater	DB	Arkansas
Los Angeles Rams	Bill Hawkins	DE	Miami
Indianapolis from Philadelphia	Andre Rison	WR	Michigan State
Houston	David Williams	T	Florida
Pittsburgh from Minnesota	Tom Ricketts	T	Pittsburgh
Miami from Chicago	Louis Oliver	DB	Florida
Los Angeles Rams from Buffalo	Cleveland Gary	RB	Miami
Atlanta from Cincinnati	Shawn Collins	WR	Northern Arizona
San Francisco	Keith DeLong	LB	Tennessee

NFL PLAYER OF THE YEAR

Year		Player	Pos.	Team
1957		Jim Brown	RB	Cleveland Browns
1958		Jim Brown	RB	Cleveland Browns
1959		Johnny Unitas	QB	Baltimore Colts
1960		Norm Van Brocklin	QB	Philadelphia Eagles
1961		Paul Hornung	HB	Green Bay Packers
1962		Y.A. Tittle	QB	New York Giants
1963		Y.A. Tittle	QB	New York Giants
1964		Johnny Unitas	QB	Baltimore Colts
1965		Jim Brown	RB	Cleveland Browns
1966		Bart Starr	QB	Green Bay Packers
1967		Johnny Unitas	QB	Baltimore Colts
1968		Earl Morrall	QB	Baltimore Colts
1969		Roman Gabriel	QB	Los Angeles Rams
1970	NFC:	John Brodie	QB	San Francisco 49ers
	AFC:	George Blanda	QB-PK	Oakland Raiders
1971	NFC:	Roger Staubach	QB	Dallas Cowboys
	AFC:	Bob Griese	QB	Miami Dolphins
1972	NFC:	Larry Brown	RB	Washington Redskins
	AFC:	Earl Morrall	QB	Miami Dolphins
1973	NFC:	John Hadl	QB	Los Angeles Rams
	AFC:	O.J. Simpson	RB	Buffalo Bills
1974	NFC:	Chuck Foreman	RB	Minnesota Vikings
	AFC:	Ken Stabler	QB	Oakland Raiders
1975	NFC:	Fran Tarkenton	QB	Minnesota Vikings
	AFC:	O.J. Simpson	RB	Buffalo Bills
1976	NFC:	Walter Payton	RB	Chicago Bears
	AFC:	Ken Stabler	QB	Oakland Raiders
1977	NFC:	Walter Payton	RB	Chicago Bears
	AFC:	Craig Morton	QB	Denver Broncos
1978	NFC:	Archie Manning	QB	New Orleans Saints
	AFC:	Earl Campbell	RB	Houston Oilers
1979	NFC:	Ottis Anderson	RB	St. Louis Cardinals
	AFC:	Dan Fouts	QB	San Diego Chargers
1980		Brian Sipe	QB	Cleveland Browns
1981		Ken Anderson	QB	Cincinnati Bengals
1982		Mark Moseley	PK	Washington Redskins
1983		Eric Dickerson	RB	Los Angeles Rams
1984		Dan Marino	QB	Miami Dolphins
1985		Marcus Allen	RB	Los Angeles Raiders
1986		Lawrence Taylor	LB	New York Giants
1987		Jerry Rice	WR	San Francisco 49ers
1988		Boomer Esiason	QB	Cincinnati Bengals

Note: In 1970–79 a player was selected as Player of the Year for both the NFC and AFC. In 1980 *The Sporting News* reinstated the selection of one player as Player of the Year for the entire NFL. **Source:** *The Sporting News.*

ALL-TIME PRO FOOTBALL RECORDS

RUSHING

Player	League	Yrs.	Yds.	Att.	Avg.
1. Walter Payton	NFL	13	16,726	3,838	4.4
2. Tony Dorsett[1]	NFL	12	12,739	2,936	4.3
3. Jim Brown	NFL	9	12,312	2,359	5.2
4. Franco Harris	NFL	13	12,120	2,949	4.1
5. John Riggins	NFL	14	11,352	2,916	3.9
6. O.J. Simpson	AFL–NFL	11	11,236	2,404	4.7
7. Eric Dickerson[1]	NFL	6	9,915	2,166	4.6
8. Joe Perry	AAFC–NFL	16	9,723	1,929	5.0
9. Earl Campbell	NFL	8	9,407	2,187	4.3
10. Jim Taylor	NFL	10	8,597	1,941	4.4

RECEIVING

Player	League	Yrs.	No.	Yds.	Avg.
1. Steve Largent[1]	NFL	13	791	12,686	16.0
2. Charlie Joiner	AFL–NFL	18	750	12,146	16.2
3. Charley Taylor	NFL	13	649	9,110	14.0
4. Don Maynard	NFL–AFL	15	633	11,834	18.7
5. Raymond Berry	NFL	13	631	9,275	14.7
6. Ozzie Newsome[1]	NFL	11	610	7,416	12.2
7. James Lofton[1]	NFL	11	599	11,085	18.5
8. Harold Carmichael	NFL	14	590	8,985	15.2
9. Fred Biletnikoff	AFL–NFL	14	589	8,974	15.2
10. Harold Jackson	NFL	16	579	10,372	17.9

SCORING

Player	League	Yrs.	Total	TD	PAT	FG
1. George Blanda	NFL–AFL	26	2,002	9	943	335
2. Jan Stenerud	AFL–NFL	19	1,699	—	580	373
3. Lou Groza	AAFC–NFL	21	1,608	1	810	264
4. Jim Turner	AFL–NFL	16	1,439	1	521	304
5. Mark Moseley	NFL	16	1,382	—	482	300
6. Jim Bakken	NFL	17	1,380	—	534	282
7. Fred Cox	NFL	15	1,365	—	519	282
8. Pat Leahy[1]	NFL	15	1,190	—	467	241
9. Chris Bahr[1]	NFL	13	1,133	—	461	224
10. Gino Cappelletti	AFL	11	1,130	42	350	176

1. Active player.

NFL ROOKIE OF THE YEAR, 1975–88

Year		Player	Pos.	Team
1975	NFC:	Steve Bartkowski	QB	Atlanta Falcons
	AFC:	Robert Brazile	LB	Houston Oilers
1976	NFC:	Sammy White	WR	Minnesota Vikings
	AFC:	Mike Haynes	CB	New England Patriots
1977	NFC:	Tony Dorsett	RB	Dallas Cowboys
	AFC:	A.J. Duhe	DT	Miami Dolphins
1978	NFC:	Al Baker	DE	Detroit Lions
	AFC:	Earl Campbell	RB	Houston Oilers
1979	NFC:	Ottis Anderson	RB	St. Louis Cardinals
	AFC:	Jerry Butler	WR	Buffalo Bills
1980		Billy Sims	RB	Detroit Lions
1981		George Rogers	RB	New England Patriots
1982		Marcus Allen	RB	Los Angeles Raiders
1983		Dan Marino	QB	Miami Dolphins
1984		Louis Lipps	WR	Pittsburgh Steelers
1985		Eddie Brown	WR	Cincinnati Bengals
1986		Rueben Mayes	RB	New Orleans Saints
1987		Robert Awalt	TE	St. Louis Cardinals
1988		Keith Jackson	TE	Philadephia Eagles

Note: In 1980 *The Sporting News* began selecting one rookie as Rookie of the Year for the entire NFL.

ALL-TIME PASSING LEADERS

PASSING

Rank	Player	League	Yrs.	Att.	Comp.	Yds.	TD	Int.	Rating pts.
1. (2)	Joe Montana[1]	NFL	10	3,673	2,322	27,533	190	99	92.0
2. (1)	Dan Marino[1]	NFL	6	3,100	1,866	23,856	196	103	91.5
3. (4)	OTTO GRAHAM	AAFC–NFL	10	2,626	1,464	23,584	174	135	86.6
4. (—)	Boomer Esiason[1]	NFL	5	1,830	1,038	14,825	98	65	86.2
5. (5)	Dave Krieg[1]	NFL	9	2,344	1,358	17,549	148	96	85.5
6. (3)	Ken O'Brien[1]	NFL	5	1,990	1,183	14,243	84	50	85.0
7. (6)	ROGER STAUBACH	NFL	11	2,958	1,685	22,700	153	109	83.4
8. (9)	Neil Lomax[1]	NFL	8	3,153	1,817	22,771	136	90	82.7
9. (7)	SONNY JURGENSEN	NFL	18	4,262	2,433	32,224	255	189	82.62
10. (8)	LEN DAWSON	NFL–AFL	19	3,741	2,136	28,711	239	183	82.55

Notes: Bernie Kosar (1,427 attempts, 84.5) would rank as number seven if he had the required 1,500 attempts. Number in parenthesis indicates rank at the start of the 1988 season. Rating points based on a combination of performances in the following four categories: percentage of completions, percentage of touchdown passes, percentage of interceptions and average gain per pass attempts. Pro Football Hall of Fame members in capital letters. AAFC = All-America Football Conference; AFL = American Football League; NFL = National Football League. 1. Active in 1988 season.

TOTAL PASSES ATTEMPTED

1.	Fran Tarkenton	6,467
2.	Dan Fouts	5,604
3.	Johnny Unitas	5,186
4.	Jim Hart	5,076
5.	John Hadl	4,687
6.	Roman Gabriel	4,498
7.	John Brodie	4,491
8.	Ken Anderson	4,475
9.	Joe Ferguson[1]	4,421
10.	Y.A. Tittle	4,395
11.	Norm Snead	4,353
12.	Sonny Jurgensen	4,262
13.	Ron Jaworski[1]	4,056
14.	George Blanda	4,007
15.	Terry Bradshaw	3,901
16.	Ken Stabler	3,793
17.	Craig Morton	3,786
18.	Joe Namath	3,762
19.	Len Dawson	3,741
20.	Jim Plunkett	3,701

TOTAL TOUCHDOWN PASSES

1.	Fran Tarkenton	342
2.	Johnny Unitas	290
3.	Sonny Jurgensen	255
4.	Dan Fouts	254
5.	John Hadl	244
6.	Y.A. Tittle	242
7.	Len Dawson	239
8.	George Blanda	236
9.	John Brodie	214
10.	Terry Bradshaw	212
11.	Jim Hart	209
12.	Roman Gabriel	201
13.	Ken Anderson	197
14.T	Norm Snead	196
14.T	Bobby Layne	196
14.T	Dan Marino[1]	196
17.	Ken Stabler	194
18.	Joe Ferguson[1]	193
19.	Bob Griese	192
20.	Joe Montana[1]	190

TOTAL PASSES COMPLETED

1.	Fran Tarkenton	3,686
2.	Dan Fouts	3,297
3.	Johnny Unitas	2,830
4.	Ken Anderson	2,654
5.	Jim Hart	2,593
6.	John Brodie	2,469
7.	Sonny Jurgensen	2,433
8.	Y.A. Tittle	2,427
9.	Roman Gabriel	2,366
10.	John Hadl	2,363
11.	Joe Ferguson[1]	2,323
12.	Joe Montana[1]	2,322
13.	Norm Snead	2,276
14.	Ken Stabler	2,270
15.	Ron Jaworski[1]	2,151
16.	Len Dawson	2,136
17.	Craig Morton	2,053
18.	Joe Theismann	2,044
19.	Terry Bradshaw	2,025
20.	Archie Manning	2,011

TOTAL YARDS PASSING

1.	Fran Tarkenton	47,003
2.	Dan Fouts	43,040
3.	Johnny Unitas	40,239
4.	Jim Hart	34,665
5.	John Hadl	33,513
6.	Y.A. Tittle	33,070
7.	Ken Anderson	32,838
8.	Sonny Jurgensen	32,224
9.	John Brodie	31,548
10.	Norm Snead	30,797
11.	Roman Gabriel	29,444
12.	Joe Ferguson[1]	29,263
13.	Len Dawson	28,711
14.	Terry Bradshaw	27,989
15.	Ken Stabler	27,938
16.	Craig Morton	27,908
17.	Ron Jaworski[1]	27,805
18.	Joe Namath	27,663
19.	Joe Montana[1]	27,533
20.	George Blanda	26,920

Note: Through the end of 1988 season. 1. Active in 1988 season. **Source:** The National Football League.

NFL CHAMPIONS, 1921–66

Year	Team
1921	Chicago Staleys (10–1–1)[1]
1922	Canton Bulldogs (10–0–2)
1923	Canton Bulldogs (11–0–1)
1924	Cleveland Bulldogs (7–1–1)[2]
1925	Chicago Cardinals (11–2–1)
1926	Frankford Yellowjackets (14–1–1)
1927	New York Giants (11–1–1)
1928	Providence Steamrollers (8–1–2)
1929	Green Bay Packers (12–0–1)
1930	Green Bay Packers (10–3–1)
1931	Green Bay Packers (12–2–0)
1932	Chicago Bears (7–1–6)
1933	Chicago Bears (10–2–1)
1934	New York Giants (8–5–0)
1935	Detroit Lions (7–3–2)
1936	Green Bay Packers (10–1–1)
1937	Washington Redskins (8–3–0)
1938	New York Giants (8–2–1)
1939	Green Bay Packers (9–2–0)
1940	Chicago Bears (8–3–0)
1941	Chicago Bears (10–1–1)
1942	Washington Redskins (10–1–1)
1943	Chicago Bears (8–1–1)
1944	Green Bay Packers (8–2–0)
1945	Cleveland Rams (9–1–0)
1946	Chicago Bears (8–2–1)
1947	Chicago Cardinals (9–3–0)
1948	Philadelphia Eagles (9–2–1)
1949	Philadelphia Eagles (11–1–0)
1950	Cleveland Browns (10–2–0)
1951	Los Angeles Rams (8–4–0)
1952	Detroit Lions (9–3–0)
1953	Detroit Lions (10–2–0)
1954	Cleveland Browns (9–3–0)
1955	Cleveland Browns (9–2–1)
1956	New York Giants (8–3–1)
1957	Detroit Lions (8–4–0)
1958	Baltimore Colts (9–3–0)
1959	Baltimore Colts (9–3–0)
1960	Philadelphia Eagles (10–2–0)
1961	Green Bay Packers (11–3–0)
1962	Green Bay Packers (13–1–0)
1963	Chicago Bears (11–1–2)
1964	Cleveland Browns (10–3–1)
1965	Green Bay Packers (10–3–1)
1966	Green Bay Packers (12–2–0)

1. Later called the Chicago Bears. 2. Franchise moved from Canton.

SUPER BOWL RESULTS

Super Bowl I
Jan. 15, 1967, Memorial Coliseum
Los Angeles, California
Green Bay Packers 35
Kansas City Chiefs 10

Green Bay's Max McGee was a surprise star, as he filled in for ailing Boyd Dowler. McGee had caught only three passes all year, but in Super Bowl I he caught seven from quarterback Bart Starr for 138 yards and two touchdowns. Starr himself was the game's MVP, as he completed 16 of 23 passes for 250 yards and two touchdowns. Green Bay broke up the game with three second-half touchdowns, the first of which was set up by all-pro safety Willie Wood's 40-yard return of an interception to the Chiefs' five-yard line.

Super Bowl II
Jan. 14, 1968, Orange Bowl
Miami, Florida
Green Bay Packers 22
Oakland Raiders 14

Bart Starr again dominated proceedings with 13 completions in 24 passing attempts, totaling 202 yards and a touchdown, winning his second straight MVP award. The Pack attack was in control all the way after building a 16–7 halftime lead. Don Chandler kicked four field goals and all-pro cornerback Herb Adderley capped the Green Bay scoring with a 60-yard run on an interception.

Super Bowl III
Jan. 12, 1969, Orange Bowl
Miami, Florida
New York Jets 16
Baltimore Colts 7

Joe Namath became a prophet with honor—on the Thursday before the game, he "guaranteed" victory for New York. He did just that, earning MVP honors by completing 17 of 28 passes for 206 yards and directing a steady attack that racked up 337 total yards. Three times in the first half, the Jet defense intercepted Colts quarterback Earl Morrall, who was playing for an injured Johnny Unitas. With the Jets ahead 16–0 in the fourth quarter, Unitas came off the bench and orchestrated Baltimore's sole touchdown.

Super Bowl IV
Jan. 11, 1970, Tulane Stadium
New Orleans, Louisiana
Kansas City Chiefs 23
Minnesota Vikings 7

Superb quarterbacking continued to be the key to Super Bowl victory as MVP Len Dawson called a nearly flawless game for Kansas City, completing 12 of 17 passes and hitting Otis Taylor on a 46-yard pass for the final Chiefs touchdown. The Kansas City defense limited Minnesota's strong rushing game to 67 yards and had three interceptions and two fumble recoveries. The Chiefs rolled up a 16–0 halftime lead and stood off the Vikings after that.

Super Bowl V
Jan. 17, 1971, Orange Bowl
Miami, Florida
Baltimore Colts 16
Dallas Cowboys 13

First-year kicker Jim O'Brien booted a 32-yard field goal to give the Colts a victory over the Cowboys in the final seconds of the Super Bowl. Dallas led 13–6 at halftime, but two Colt interceptions set up a Baltimore touchdown and O'Brien's crucial kick. Earl Morrall relieved an injured Johnny Unitas in the first half. Unitas's lone scoring pass was dramatic—the ball caromed off receiver Eddie Hinton's fingertips, off Dallas defensive back Mel Renfro, and finally settled into the grasp of tight end John Mackey, who went 45 yards to score on a 75-yard play. Dallas linebacker Chuck Howley was the MVP.

Super Bowl VI
Jan. 16, 1972, Tulane Stadium
New Orleans, Louisiana
Dallas Cowboys 24
Miami Dolphins 3

The Cowboys rushed for a record 252 yards, and their defense limited the Dolphins to a record low 185 while not permitting a touchdown. Dallas converted Chuck Howley's recovery of Larry Csonka's first fumble of the season into a 3–0 advantage. At halftime Dallas led 10–3. An eight-play, 71-yard march made it a 17–3 game. Cowboys' quarterback Roger Staubach was voted MVP for his 12 completions in 19 attempts, 119 yards passing, and two touchdowns.

Super Bowl VII
Jan. 14, 1973, Memorial Coliseum
Los Angeles, California
Miami Dolphins 14
Washington Redskins 7

The Dolphins dominated the first half. On its third possession, Miami opened its first scoring drive from the Dolphins' 37-yard line. An 18-yard pass from Bob Griese to Paul Warfield was quickly followed by a Griese 28-yard touchdown pass to Howard Twilley. Miami scored their second touchdown in the first half with 18 seconds to go, after Nick Buoniconti's interception of Billy Kilmer's pass at the Miami 41 started the scoring drive. Safety Jake Scott was the MVP. Washington's sole touchdown came with 7:07 left in the game and resulted from a misplayed field goal attempt and a fumble.

Super Bowl VIII
Jan. 13, 1974, Rice Stadium
Houston, Texas
Miami Dolphins 24
Minnesota Vikings 7

On their first two possessions, Miami scored, on 62- and 56-yard marches. The initial 10-play drive was climaxed by a Larry Csonka touchdown bolt through right guard after 5:27 had elapsed. Four plays later, Miami's second assault sent Jim Kiick bursting one yard through the middle for the second touchdown. By halftime Miami led 17–0. Minnesota came back from its 20 to a second-and-two situation on the Miami seven-yard line with 1:18 left in the half, but Miami limited Minnesota's Oscar Reed to one yard. On the fourth-and-one from the six, Reed went over right tackle, but Dolphin middle linebacker Nick Buoniconti jarred the ball loose and Jake Scott recovered for Miami to end the Minnesota threat. Csonka rushed 33 times for a Super Bowl record 145 yards, winning the MVP.

Super Bowl IX
Jan. 12, 1975, Tulane Stadium
New Orleans, Louisiana
Pittsburgh Steelers 16
Minnesota Vikings 6

Steeler Dwight White downed Fran Tarkenton's fumbled pass attempt in the end zone for a safety to put the Steelers on the board in the second quarter. They took advantage of another break in the second half, when Minnesota's Bill Brown fumbled on the kickoff and Marv Kellum recovered for Pittsburgh on the Vikings' 30. Franco Harris carried three straight times for 27 yards and a touchdown, putting the Steelers in front 9-0. Minnesota was able to block Bobby Walden's punt attempt, and Terry Brown recovered the ball for a touchdown. But the Steelers roared back with a 66-yard march, climaxed by Terry Bradshaw's four-yard scoring pass to Larry Brown. Pittsburgh's defense controlled the game by permitting Minnesota only 119 yards total offense and a record low 17 yards rushing. Franco Harris's record 158 yards rushing on 34 carries won him MVP honors, and paced the Steelers' 333-yard rushing attack.

Super Bowl X
Jan. 18, 1976, Orange Bowl
Miami Florida
Pittsburgh Steelers 21
Dallas Cowboys 17

Steeler quarterback Terry Bradshaw hurled a 64-yard touchdown pass to Lynn Swann to win the game, while his aggressive defense stopped the Cowboys' last rally with an end-zone interception in the game's final play. It was a battle of quarterbacks with Cowboy Roger Staubach and Bradshaw both hurling two touchdowns. Lynn Swann earned his MVP award with a record 161 yards gained on his four receptions. The Steelers blasted out in front with a 14-point fourth quarter.

Super Bowl XI
Jan. 9, 1977, Rose Bowl
Pasadena, California
Oakland Raiders 32
Minnesota Vikings 14

A record 81 million TV viewers watched the Raiders gain a record breaking 429 yards, including running back Clarence Davis's 137 yards rushing. Wide receiver Fred Biletnikoff made four key receptions, which earned him the game's MVP trophy. Oakland scored on three successive possessions in the second quarter to build a 16-0 halftime lead. Minnesota's Fran Tarkenton passed for a touchdown in the third to cut the deficit, but two fourth-quarter interceptions clinched the title for the Raiders. One set up Pete Banaszak's second touchdown run, the other resulted in cornerback Willie Brown's Super Bowl record 75-yard interception return.

Super Bowl XII
Jan. 15, 1978, Louisiana Superdome
New Orleans, Louisiana
Dallas Cowboys 27
Denver Broncos 10

The TV audience climbed to 102 million, a new record, as Dallas converted two interceptions into 10 points and Efren Herrera added a 35-yard field goal for a 12-0 Dallas halftime lead. Butch Johnston made a spectacular diving catch in the end zone of a Roger Staubach pass to make it 20-3. Dallas clinched the victory when running back Robert Newhouse threw a 29-yard touchdown pass to Golden Richards with 7:04 remaining in the game. It was the first pass thrown by Newhouse since 1975. Co-

MVPs Harvey Martin and Randy White led the Cowboys' defense, which recovered four fumbles and intercepted four passes.

Super Bowl XIII
Jan. 21, 1979, Orange Bowl
Miami, Florida
Pittsburgh Steelers 35
Dallas Cowboys 31

Terry Bradshaw hurled a record four touchdown passes to lead the Steelers to victory, making them the first team to win three Super Bowls. His accurate arm enabled the Steelers to outlast the Cowboys in a mean-fought contest. Bradshaw completed 17 of 30 passes for 318 yards, a personal high. Cowboy quarterback Roger Staubach threw two touchdown passes himself. In the fourth quarter, the Steelers broke open the contest with two touchdowns in 19 seconds. Franco Harris rambled 22 yards up the middle to put Pittsburgh in front 28-17. The Steelers got the ball right back when Randy White fumbled the kickoff and Dennis Winston recovered for the Steelers. On first down Bradshaw hit Lynn Swann with an 18-yard scoring pass to boost the Steelers to 35-17. The Cowboys came back with a Staubach touchdown pass to Billy Joe DuPree and by recovering an onside kick. But Rocky Bleier recovered another onside kick with 17 seconds remaining to seal the victory for Pittsburgh—and the MVP award for Bradshaw.

Super Bowl XIV
Jan. 20, 1980, Rose Bowl
Pasadena, California
Pittsburgh Steelers 31
Los Angeles Rams 19

It was all Terry Bradshaw again as he completed 14 of 21 passes for 309 yards and set two passing records as the Steelers became the first team to win four Super Bowls. Despite three interceptions by the Rams, Bradshaw brought the Steelers back from behind twice in the second half. On Pittsburgh's first possession of the final period, Bradshaw lofted a 73-yard scoring pass to John Stallworth to put the Steelers in front to stay, 24-19. Franco Harris scored on a one-yard run later to seal the verdict. A 45-yard pass from Bradshaw to Stallworth was the key play in the drive to Harris's score. Bradshaw was the MVP for the second straight Super Bowl and set career Super Bowl records for most touchdown passes (nine) and most passing yards (932). Vince Ferragamo passed for 212 yards, completing 15 of 25.

Super Bowl XV
Jan. 25, 1981, Louisiana Superdome
New Orleans, Louisiana
Oakland Raiders 27
Philadelphia Eagles 10

Jim Plunkett threw three touchdown passes, including an 80-yarder to Kenny King—the longest play in Super Bowl history—to give Oakland a decisive 14-0 advantage nine seconds before halftime. Oakland linebacker Rod Martin intercepted three passes for a Super Bowl record, as the Raiders completely stifled Eagle quarterback Ron Jaworski's offense. Jaworski managed an eight-yard touchdown

pass in the fouth quarter, but the issue had been decided by Plunkett, who completed 13 of the 21 pass attempts for 261 yards and was named MVP. The Raiders dedicated their win to the newly freed 52 American hostages, who had been held in Tehran by Iranian militants. Many of the former hostages watched the game on a wide-screen television at West Point while resting from their ordeal.

Super Bowl XVI
Jan. 24, 1982, Pontiac Silverdome
Pontiac, Michigan
San Francisco 49ers 26
Cincinnati Bengals 21

This was a game of a failed comeback, as the 49ers led 20-0 at halftime, and barely hung on to their lead. Ray Wersching kicked a record tying four field goals for San Francisco. Quarterback Joe Montana capped a San Francisco 11-play, 68-yard drive with a one-yard run. Another key play was a record 92-yard drive, which ended in a touchdown pass by Montana. The Bengals rebounded in the second half as quarterback Ken Anderson ran in a touchdown and passed for another. He set Super Bowl records for completions, 25, and completion percentage, 73.5% on 25 of 34. With 16 seconds remaining, the Bengals managed to score on an Anderson-to-Dan Ross three-yard pass, but the odds were too great. Ross set a Super Bowl record with 11 receptions for 104 yards. Montana, the MVP, completed 14 of 22 passes for 157 yards. Cincinnati compiled 345 yards to San Francisco's 275, which marked the first time in Super Bowl history that the team that gained the most yards from scrimmage lost the game.

Super Bowl XVII
Jan. 30, 1983, Rose Bowl
Pasadena, California
Washington Redskins 27
Miami Dolphins 17

Washington fullback John Riggins carried the ball for a record 166 yards on 38 carries to lead Washington to victory, their first NFL title since 1942. Their 400 total yards offense, a Super Bowl record 276 yards rushing and 124 yards passing, was paced by Riggins, the MVP, and quarterback Joe Theismann, who passed 23 times for 15 completions, 143 yards, and two touchdowns. He also notched two interceptions. Miami tied the score with help from a 76-yard touchdown pass from quarterback David Woodley to wide receiver Jimmy Cefalo. But the game's main force was Riggins, who took the ball on fourth-and-one and ran 43 yards off left tackle for a touchdown to put Washington in front.

Super Bowl XVIII
Jan. 22, 1984, Tampa Stadium
Tampa, Florida
Los Angeles Raiders 38
Washington Redskins 9

This hopelessly lopsided victory set records. Raider reserve linebacker Jack Squirek intercepted a Joe Theismann pass at the Redskins' five-yard line and ran the ball in for a touchdown with seven seconds left in the first half.

Raiders' Marcus Allen rushed for a record 191 yards on 20 carries, including two touchdowns, one of which was on a record 74-yard run. Allen was voted game MVP. The 38 points was the highest total scored by a Super Bowl team.

Super Bowl XIX
Jan. 20, 1985, Stanford Stadium
Stanford, California
San Francisco 28
Miami Dolphins 16

The Dolphins led 10–7 at the end of the first period, but 49er running back Roger Craig set a Super Bowl record by scoring three touchdowns. Joe Montana dominated the game with an MVP performance—24 of 35 passes for a record 331 yards and three touchdowns. He also rushed five times for 59 yards and a touchdown. Craig had 56 yards on 15 carries and caught seven passes for 77 yards. Wendell Tyler rushed 13 times for 65 yards, as San Francisco's running game racked up mileage. As a team San Francisco gained 537 yards, setting a new record, while holding the ball for 37:11 as opposed to Miami's 22:49.

Super Bowl XX
Jan 26, 1986, Louisiana Superdome
New Orleans, Louisiana
Chicago Bears 46
New England Patriots 10

The Patriots took the quickest lead in Super Bowl history when Tony Franklin kicked a 36-yard field goal with 1:19 elapsed in the first period. But the Bears rebounded by mauling the Pats. Chicago tied the record for sacks (seven) and limited the Pats to a record-low seven yards rushing. Total yardage on the day told the story: Chicago 236, New England minus 19. The 46 points scored by the Bears was also a record. The Bears ran up a fat 23–3 lead by halftime. In the second half, the Bears marched 96 yards in nine plays, and capped it as quarterback Jim McMahon rushed one yard for a touchdown. He became the first quarterback in Super Bowl history to rush for two touchdowns. Bears defensive end Richard Dent won the MVP after contributing one-and-a-half sacks and leading the ferocious Chicago defense. McMahon completed 12 of 20 passes for 256 yards before leaving the game with an injury. NFL all-time rushing leader Walter Payton carried 22 times for 61 yards.

Super Bowl XXI
Jan. 25, 1987, Rose Bowl
Pasadena, California
New York Giants 39
Denver Broncos 20

The Broncos got off to a 10–9 lead at halftime, the narrowest such margin in Super Bowl history, backed by the passing of John Elway. He capped a 58-yard scoring drive on six plays with a four-yard touchdown run. But in the second half, the Giants' defense took over, sacking Elway in his end zone for a safety. The Broncos had a first-and-goal but failed to score on three plays and a field goal attempt. After that the Giants took over, scoring 30 points in the second half, a record, one a nine-play, 63-yard touchdown drive that began on a fourth-and-

one situation on the Giants' 46-yard line and ended with Mark Bavaro's 13-yard touchdown catch, MVP Giants' quarterback Phil Simms set Super Bowl records for most consecutive completions (10) and highest completion percentage (88% on 22 completions in 25 attempts). He passed for 268 yards and three touchdowns. The Giants' top rusher was Joe Morris with 20 carries for 67 yards.

Super Bowl XXII
Jan 31, 1988, Jack Murphy Stadium
San Diego, California
Washington Redskins 42
Denver Broncos 10

A 35-point record second quarter was the key to Washington's convincing Super Bowl triumph. The Broncos jumped in front early as John Elway hurled a 56-yard touchdown pass to wide receiver Ricky Nattiel on the Broncos' first play from scrimmage. But the Redskins erupted for 35 points on five straight possessions. Redskins' quarterback Doug Williams led the assault, hurling a record-tying four touchdown passes, including 80- and 50-yarders to wide receiver Gary Clark and an 8-yarder to tight end Clint Didier. Washington scored five touchdowns in 18 plays in 5:47 of possession. MVP Williams completed 18 of 29 passes for 340 yards, a new Super Bowl record. Rookie running back Timmy Smith ran 22 times for a record 204 yards. Washington's six touchdowns and 602 total yards gained also set Super Bowl records, as the Redskins coasted after the decisive second quarter.

Super Bowl XXIII
Jan. 22, 1989, Joe Robbie Stadium
Miami, Florida
San Francisco 49ers 20
Cincinnati Bengals 16

San Francisco captured its third Super Bowl of the 1980s by defeating the Bengals in a rematch of Super Bowl XVI. The 49ers thus became the first NFC team to capture three Super Bowl trophies. Even though San Francisco held an advantage in total yards (454 vs. 229), they found themselves trailing late in the game. With the score tied at 13 points each, Cincinnati took a 16–13 lead on Jim Breech's 40-yard field goal with 3:20 remaining. Breech's kick capped a one-play, 46-yard ball control effort, which had consumed 5:27. The 49ers started their winning drive at their own 8-yard line. Over the next 11 plays, they drove 92 yards to the winning score, a 10-yard touchdown pass from Joe Montana to wide receiver John Taylor with only 34 seconds remaining. San Francisco's swift wide receiver Jerry Rice won the MVP after catching 11 passes for a Super Bowl record 215 yards. Montana completed 23 of 36 passes for a record 357 yards and two touchdowns.

NFL HALL OF FAME MEMBERS

Alphabetical listing of the members of the Professional Football Hall of Fame. Listing includes enshrinee's name, and year of enshrinement, and his pro team(s).

Herb Adderley (1980) CB, Packers, Cowboys.
Lance Alworth (1978) WR, Chargers, Cowboys.
Doug Atkins (1982) DE, Browns, Bears, Saints.
Morris (Red) Badgro (1981) E, Yankees, Giants, Dodgers.
Cliff Battles (1968) HB, QB, Braves, Redskins. Coach, Dodgers.
Sammy Baugh (1963 Charter) QB, Redskins. Coach, Titans, Oilers, Lions.
Chuck Bednarik (1967) C, LB, Eagles.
Bert Bell (1963 Charter) Commissioner, NFL, Founder, Eagles, 1933. Coach Eagles, Steelers. Club president, Eagles, Steelers.
Bobby Bell (1983) LB, DE, Chiefs.
Raymond Berry (1973) E, Colts. Coach, Patriots.
Charles W. Bidwill, Sr. (1967) Owner and president, Chicago Cardinals.
Fred Biletnikoff (1988) WR, Raiders.
George Blanda (1981) QB, PK, Bears, Colts, Bears, Oilers, Raiders.
Mel Blount (1988) CB, Steelers.
Terry Bradshaw (1988) QB, Steelers.
Jim Brown (1971) RB, Browns.
Paul E. Brown (1967) Coach and GM, Browns, Bengals.
Roosevelt Brown (1975) OT, Giants.
Willie Brown (1984) CB, Broncos, Raiders.
Dick Butkus (1979) LB, Bears.
Tony Canadeo (1974) HB, Packers.
Joe Carr NFL President.
Guy Chamberlin (1965) E, Bulldogs, Staleys, Bulldogs, Yellowjackets, Cardinals. Coach, Bulldogs, Yellowjackets, Cardinals.
Jack Christiansen (1970) DB, Spartans, Lions. Coach, 49ers.
Earl (Dutch) Clark (1963) DB, Spartans, Lions, Rams.
George Connor (1975) OT, DT, LB, Bears.
Jimmy Conzelman (1964) QB, Staleys, Independents, Badgers, Panthers. Owner, Steamrollers, Cardinals, Panthers.
Larry Csonka (1987) RB, Dolphins, Giants, Dolphins.
Willie Davis (1981) DE, Browns, Packers.
Len Dawson (1987) QB, Steelers, Browns, Texans, Chiefs.
Mike Ditka (1988) TE, Bears, Eagles, Cowboys. Coach, Bears.
Art Donovan (1968) DT, Colts, Yankees, Texans, Colts.
John (Paddy) Driscoll (1965) QB, Pros, Staleys, Cardinals, Bears. Coach, Cardinals, Bears.
Bill Dudley (1966) RB, Steelers, Lions, Redskins.
Albert Glen (Turk) Edwards (1969) OT, Braves, Redskins. Coach, Redskins.
Weeb Ewbank (1978) Coach, Colts, Jets.
Tom Fears (1970) E, Rams. Coach, Saints.
Ray Flaherty (1976) E, Wildcats, Yankees, Giants. Coach, Redskins, Yankees.
Leonard (Len) Ford (1976) DE, OE, Dons. Browns, Packers.
Daniel J. Fortmann, M.D. (1965) G, Bears.
Frank Gatski (1985) C, Browns, Lions.
Bill George (1974) LB, Bears, Rams.
Frank Gifford (1977) RB, Giants.
Sid Gillman (1983) Head coach, Rams, Chargers, Oilers. Browns, Bengals, Packers. Head coach.
Otto Graham (1965) QB, Browns. Head coach, Redskins.
Harold (Red) Grange (1963 Charter) RB, Bears, Yankees, Bears.
(Mean) Joe Greene (1987) DT, Steelers.
Forrest Gregg (1977) OL, Packers, Cowboys. Head coach, Browns, Bengals, Packers.
Lou Groza (1974) OT, PK, Browns.
Joe Guyon (1966) RB, Bulldogs, Indians, Independents, Cowboys, Giants.
George Halas (1963) Founder, head coach, player, Staleys. President, head coach, player, Bears.
Jack Ham (1988) LB, Steelers.
Ed Healey (1964) OT, Independents, Bears.
Mel Hein (1963) C, Giants. Head coach, Dons.
Wilbur (Pete) Henry (1963) OT, Bulldogs, Giants, Maroons.
Arnie Herber (1966) QB, Packers, Giants.
Bill Hewitt (1971) E, Bears, Eagles, Phil-Pitt.
Clarke Hinkle (1964) RB, Packers.

Elroy (Crazy Legs) Hirsch (1968) RB, E, Rockets, Rams.
Paul Hornung (1986) RB, Packers.
Ken Houston (1986) DB, Oilers, Redskins.
Robert (Cal) Hubbard (1963) OT, Giants, Packers, Pirates.
Sam Huff (1982) LB, Giants, Redskins.
Lamar Hunt (1972) Founder, AFL, Owner, Texans, Chiefs.
Don Hutson (1963) E, Packers.
John Henry Johnson (1987) RB, 49ers, Lions, Steelers, Oilers.
David (Deacon) Jones (1980) DE, Rams, Chargers, Redskins.
Sonny Jurgensen (1983) QB, Eagles, Redskins.
Walt Kiesling (1966) G, Eskimos, Maroons, Chicago Cardinals, Bears, Packers, Pirates. Head coach, Pirates, Steelers.
Frank (Bruiser) Kinard (1971) OT, Dodgers, Yankees.
Early (Curly) Lambeau (1963) HB, Packers. Founder, Packers. Head coach, Packers, Cardinals, Washington Redskins.
Dick (Night Train) Lane (1974) DB, Rams, Cardinals, Lions.
Jim Langer (1987) C, Dolphins, Vikings.
Willie Lanier (1986) LB, Chiefs.
Yale Lary (1979) DB, Lions.
Dante Lavelli (1975) E, Browns.
Bobby Layne (1967) QB, Bears, Bulldogs, Lions, Steelers.
Alphonse (Tuffy) Leemans (1978) RB, Giants.
Bob Lilly (1980) DT, Cowboys.
Vince Lombardi (1971) Head coach, Packers, Redskins.
Sid Luckman (1965) QB, Bears.
William Roy (Link) Lyman (1964) OT, Bulldogs, Yellowjackets, Bears.
Tim Mara (1963) Founder, president, Giants.
Gino Marchetti (1972) DE, Texans, Colts.
George Preston Marshall (1963) Founder, president, Braves, (Redskins).
Ollie Matson (1972) RB, Cardinals, Rams, Lions, Eagles.
Don Maynard (1987) WR, Giants, Titans, Jets, Cardinals.
George McAfee (1966) RB, Bears.
Mike McCormack (1984) OT, Yankees, Browns. Head coach, Eagles, Colts, Seahawks.
Hugh McElhenny (1970) RB, 49ers, Vikings, Giants, Lions.
John (Blood) McNally (1963) RB, Badgers, Eskimos, Maroons, Packers, Pirates. Head coach and player, Pirates.
August (Mike) Michalske (1964) G, Yankees, Packers.
Wayne Millner (1968) E, Redskins. Head coach, Eagles.
Bobby Mitchell (1983) WR, RB, Browns, Redskins.
Ron Mix (1979) OT, Chargers, Raiders.
Leonard (Lenny) Moore (1975) WR, RB, Colts.
Marion Motley (1968) RB, Browns, Steelers.
George Musso (1982) OT, G, Bears.
Bronko Nagurski (1963) RB, Bears.
Joe Namath (1985) QB, Jets, Rams.
Earle (Greasy) Neale (1969) E, Bulldogs. Head coach, Eagles.
Ernie Nevers (1963) RB, Eskimos, Cardinals. Head coach and player, Eskimos, Cardinals.
Ray Nitschke (1978) LB, Packers.
Leo Nomellini (1969) DT, 49ers.
Merlin Olson (1982) DT, Rams.
Jim Otto (1980) C, Raiders.
Steven Owen (1966) OT, Cowboys, Giants. Head coach, Giants.
Alan Page (1988) DT, Vikings, Bears.
Clarence (Ace) Parker (1972) QB, Dodgers, Yankees.
Jim Parker (1973) G, OT, Colts.
Fletcher (Joe) Perry (1969) RB, 49ers, Colts.
Pete Pihos (1970) E, Eagles.
Hugh (Shorty) Ray (1966) Supervisor of officials.
Dan Reeves (1967) Owner, Rams.
Jim Ringo (1981) C, Packers, Eagles. Head coach, Bills.
Andy Robustelli (1971) DE, Rams, Giants.
Art Rooney (1964) Founder, president, Pirates, Steelers.
Pete Rozelle (1985) Commissioner, NFL.
Gale Sayers (1977) RB, Bears.
Joe Schmidt (1973) LB, Lions. Head coach, Lions.
Art Shell (1988) OT, Raiders. Head coach, Raiders.
O.J. Simpson (1985) RB, Bills, 49ers.
Bart Starr (1977) QB, Packers. Head coach, Packers.
Roger Staubach (1985) QB, Cowboys.
Ernie Stautner (1969) DT, Steelers.
Ken Strong (1967) RB, Stapletons, Giants, Yankees.
Joe Stydahar (1967) OT, Bears. Head coach, Rams, Cardinals.
Fran Tarkenton (1986) QB, Vikings, Giants.
Charley Taylor (1984) WR, RB, Redskins.
Jim Taylor (1976) RB, Packers, Saints.
Jim Thorpe (1963) RB, Bulldogs, Indians, Maroons, Independents, Giants, Cardinals. Head coach, Bulldogs.

Y.A. Tittle (1971) QB, Colts, 49ers, Giants.
George Trafton (1964) C, Staleys, Bears.
Charley Trippi (1968) RB QB, Cardinals.
Emlen Tunnell (1967) DB, Giants, Packers.
Clyde (Bulldog) Turner (1966) C, LB, Bears. Head coach, Titans.
Johnny Unitas (1979) QB, Colts, Chargers.
Gene Upshaw (1987) G, Raiders.
Norm Van Brocklin (1971) QB, Rams, Eagles. Head coach, Vikings, Falcons.
Steve Van Buren (1965) RB, Eagles.
Doak Walker (1986) RB, Lions.
Paul Warfield (1983) WR, Browns, Dolphins.
Bob Waterfield (1965) QB, Rams. Head coach, Rams.
Arnie Weinmeister (1984) DT, Yankees, Giants.
Bill Willis (1977) G, MG, Browns.
Larry Wilson (1978) DB, Cardinals.
Alex Wojciechowicz (1968) C, LB, Lions, Eagles.
Willie Wood (1988) DB, Packers.

Ice Hockey

NHL TEAM STANDINGS 1988–89

CLARENCE CAMPBELL CONFERENCE
NORRIS DIVISION

	GP	W	L	T	GF	GA	Pts.
Detroit	80	34	34	12	313	316	80
St. Louis	80	33	35	12	275	285	78
Minnesota	80	27	37	16	258	278	70
Chicago	80	27	41	12	297	335	66
Toronto	80	28	46	6	259	342	62

SMYTHE DIVISION

	GP	W	L	T	GF	GA	Pts.
Calgary	80	54	17	9	354	226	117
Los Angeles	80	42	31	7	376	335	91
Edmonton	80	38	34	8	325	306	84
Vancouver	80	33	39	8	251	253	74
Winnipeg	80	26	42	12	300	355	64

PRINCE OF WALES CONFERENCE
ADAMS DIVISION

	GP	W	L	T	GF	GA	Pts.
Montreal	80	53	18	9	315	218	115
Boston	80	37	29	14	289	256	88
Buffalo	80	38	35	7	291	299	83
Hartford	80	37	38	5	299	290	79
Quebec	80	27	46	7	269	342	61

PATRICK DIVISION

	GP	W	L	T	GF	GA	Pts.
Washington	80	41	29	10	305	259	92
Pittsburgh	80	40	33	7	347	349	87
N.Y. Rangers	80	37	35	8	310	307	82
Philadelphia	80	36	36	8	307	285	80
New Jersey	80	27	41	12	281	325	66
N.Y. Islanders	80	28	47	5	265	325	61

STANLEY CUP PLAYOFFS 1989
(All rounds are seven-game series.)

ROUND 1

PRINCE OF WALES CONFERENCE

Pittsburgh Penguins	4	New York Rangers	0
Philadelphia Flyers	4	Washington Capitols	2
Boston Bruins	4	Buffalo Sabres	1
Montreal Canadiens	4	Hartford Whalers	0

CAMPBELL CONFERENCE

Chicago Black Hawks	4	Detroit Red Wings	2
St. Louis Blues	4	Minnesota North Stars	1
Calgary Flames	4	Vancouver Canucks	3
Los Angeles Kings	4	Edmonton Oilers	3

ROUND 2

PRINCE OF WALES CONFERENCE

Montreal Canadiens	4	Boston Bruins	1
Philadelphia Flyers	4	Pittsburgh Penguins	3

CAMPBELL CONFERENCE

Chicago Black Hawks	4	St. Louis Blues	1
Calgary Flames	4	Los Angeles Kings	0

CONFERENCE CHAMPIONSHIPS

Montreal Canadiens	4	Philadelphia Flyers	2
Calgary Flames	4	Chicago Black Hawks	1

STANLEY CUP CHAMPIONSHIP

Calgary Flames	4	Montreal Canadiens	2

TOP 10 SCORERS 1988–89

Player, team	GP	G	A	Pts.
Mario Lemieux, Pittsburgh Penguins	76	85	114	199
Wayne Gretzky, Los Angeles Kings	78	54	114	168
Steve Yzerman, Detroit Red Wings	80	65	90	155
Bernie Nichols, Los Angeles Kings	79	70	80	150
Rob Brown, Pittsburgh Penguins	68	49	66	115
Paul Coffey, Pittsburgh Penguins	75	30	83	113
Joe Mullen, Calgary Flames	76	44	58	102
Jari Kurri, Edmonton Oilers	76	44	58	102
Jimmy Carson, Edmonton Oilers	80	49	51	100
Luc Robitaille, Los Angeles Kings	78	46	52	98

THE STANLEY CUP

Awarded annually to the team winning the National Hockey League's best-of-seven final playoff round, it is symbolic of the World's Professional Hockey Championship.

The first four teams in each division at the end of the regular schedule advance to the playoffs. In each division, the first-place team opposes the fourth-place club while the second- and third-place teams meet, all in best-of-five Division Semifinals. The winners oppose the other winners in each division in best-of-seven Division Final Series. The division winners then play the opposite winners in each of the two conferences in best-of-seven Conference Championships. The Prince of Wales Conference champions then meet the Clarence Campbell Conference champions in the best-of-seven Stanley Cup Championship Series.

NHL AWARD WINNERS

HART TROPHY (MVP)	CONN-SMYTHE TROPHY (Playoff MVP)	ART ROSS TROPHY (Leading Point Scorer)	JAMES NORRIS TROPHY (Top Defenseman)	VEZINA TROPHY (Top Goalie)
1976 Bobby Clarke, Philadelphia	1976 Reggie Leach, Philadelphia	1976 Guy Lafleur, Montreal	1976 Denis Potvin, N.Y. Islanders	1980 Bob Sauvé, Buffalo
1977 Guy Lafleur, Montreal	1977 Guy Lafleur, Montreal	1977 Guy Lafleur, Montreal	1977 Larry Robinson, Montreal	Don Edwards
1978 Guy Lafleur, Montreal	1978 Larry Robinson, Montreal	1978 Guy Lafleur, Montreal	1978 Denis Potvin, N.Y. Islanders	1981 Richard Sevigny, Montreal
1979 Bryan Trottier, N.Y. Islanders	1979 Bob Gainey, Montreal	1979 Bryan Trottier, N.Y. Islanders	1979 Denis Potvin, N.Y. Islanders	Denis Herron
1980 Wayne Gretzky, Edmonton	1980 Bryan Trottier, N.Y. Islanders	1980 Marcel Dionne, Los Angeles	1980 Larry Robinson, Montreal	Michel Larocque
1981 Wayne Gretzky, Edmonton	1981 Butch Goring, N.Y. Islanders	1981 Wayne Gretzky, Edmonton	1981 Randy Carlyle, Pittsburgh	1982 Bill Smith, N.Y. Islanders
1982 Wayne Gretzky, Edmonton	1982 Mike Bossy, N.Y. Islanders	1982 Wayne Gretzky, Edmonton	1982 Doug Wilson, Chicago	1983 Pete Peeters, Boston
1983 Wayne Gretzky, Edmonton	1983 Bill Smith, N.Y. Islanders	1983 Wayne Gretzky, Edmonton	1983 Rod Langway, Washington	1984 Tom Barrasso, Buffalo
1984 Wayne Gretzky, Edmonton	1984 Mark Messier, Edmonton	1984 Wayne Gretzky, Edmonton	1984 Rod Langway, Washington	1985 Pelle Lindbergh, Philadelphia
1985 Wayne Gretzky, Edmonton	1985 Wayne Gretzky, Edmonton	1985 Wayne Gretzky, Edmonton	1985 Paul Coffey, Edmonton	1986 John Vanbiesbrouck, N.Y. Rangers
1986 Wayne Gretzky, Edmonton	1986 Patrick Roy, Montreal	1986 Wayne Gretzky, Edmonton	1986 Paul Coffey, Edmonton	1987 Ron Hextall, Philadelphia
1987 Wayne Gretzky, Edmonton	1987 Ron Hextall, Philadelphia	1987 Wayne Gretzky, Edmonton	1987 Ray Bourque, Boston	1988 Grant Fuhr, Edmonton
1988 Mario Lemieux, Pittsburgh	1988 Wayne Gretzky, Edmonton	1988 Mario Lemieux, Pittsburgh	1988 Ray Bourque, Boston	1989 Patrick Roy, Montreal
1989 Wayne Gretzky, Los Angeles	1989 Al MacInnis Calgary	1989 Mario Lemieux, Pittsburgh	1989 Chris Chelios, Montreal	

History: The Stanley Cup, the oldest trophy competed for by professional athletes in North America, was donated by Frederick Arthur, Lord Stanley of Preston and son of the Earl of Derby, in 1893. Lord Stanley purchased the trophy for 10 guineas ($50 at that time) for presentation to the amateur hockey champions of Canada. Since 1910, when the National Hockey Association took possession of the Stanley Cup, the trophy has been the symbol of professional hockey supremacy. Since 1926 only NHL teams have competed for the Stanley Cup. It has been under the exclusive control of the NHL since 1946.

STANLEY CUP CHAMPIONS 1917-18—1988-89

Season	Champion	Finalist	GP in final
1917-18	Toronto Arenas	Vancouver Millionaires	5
1918-19	No decision[1]	No decision	5
1919-20	Ottawa Senators	Seattle Metropolitans	5
1920-21	Ottawa Senators	Vancouver Millionaires	5
1921-22	Toronto St. Pats	Vancouver Millionaires	5
1922-23	Ottawa Senators	Edmonton Eskimos	2
1923-24	Montreal Canadiens	Calgary Tigers	2
1924-25	Victoria Cougars	Montreal Canadiens	4
1925-26	Montreal Maroons	Victoria Cougars	4
1926-27	Ottawa Senators	Boston Bruins	2
1927-28	New York Rangers	Montreal Maroons	5
1928-29	Boston Bruins	New York Rangers	2
1929-30	Montreal Canadiens	Boston Bruins	2
1930-31	Montreal Canadiens	Chicago Black Hawks	5
1931-32	Toronto Maple Leafs	New York Rangers	3
1932-33	New York Rangers	New York Rangers	4
1933-34	Chicago Black Hawks	Detroit Red Wings	4
1934-35	Montreal Maroons	Toronto Maple Leafs	3
1935-36	Detroit Red Wings	Toronto Maple Leafs	4
1936-37	Detroit Red Wings	New York Rangers	5
1937-38	Chicago Black Hawks	Toronto Maple Leafs	4
1938-39	Boston Bruins	Toronto Maple Leafs	5
1939-40	New York Rangers	Toronto Maple Leafs	6
1940-41	Boston Bruins	Detroit Red Wings	4
1941-42	Toronto Maple Leafs	Detroit Red Wings	7
1942-43	Detroit Red Wings	Boston Bruins	4
1943-44	Montreal Canadiens	Chicago Black Hawks	4
1944-45	Toronto Maple Leafs	Detroit Red Wings	7
1945-46	Montreal Canadiens	Boston Bruins	5
1946-47	Toronto Maple Leafs	Montreal Canadiens	6
1947-48	Toronto Maple Leafs	Detroit Red Wings	4
1948-49	Toronto Maple Leafs	Detroit Red Wings	4
1949-50	Detroit Red Wings	New York Rangers	7
1950-51	Toronto Maple Leafs	Montreal Canadiens	5
1951-52	Detroit Red Wings	Montreal Canadiens	4
1952-53	Montreal Canadiens	Boston Bruins	5
1953-54	Detroit Red Wings	Montreal Canadiens	7
1954-55	Detroit Red Wings	Montreal Canadiens	7
1955-56	Montreal Canadiens	Detroit Red Wings	5
1956-57	Montreal Canadiens	Boston Bruins	5
1957-58	Montreal Canadiens	Boston Bruins	6
1958-59	Montreal Canadiens	Toronto Maple Leafs	5
1959-60	Montreal Canadiens	Toronto Maple Leafs	4
1960-61	Chicago Black Hawks	Detroit Red Wings	6
1961-62	Toronto Maple Leafs	Chicago Black Hawks	6
1962-63	Toronto Maple Leafs	Detroit Red Wings	5
1963-64	Toronto Maple Leafs	Detroit Red Wings	7
1964-65	Montreal Canadiens	Chicago Black Hawks	7
1965-66	Montreal Canadiens	Detroit Red Wings	6
1966-67	Toronto Maple Leafs	Montreal Canadiens	6
1967-68	Montreal Canadiens	St. Louis Blues	4
1968-69	Montreal Canadiens	St. Louis Blues	4
1969-70	Boston Bruins	St. Louis Blues	4
1970-71	Montreal Canadiens	Chicago Black Hawks	7
1971-72	Boston Bruins	New York Rangers	6
1972-73	Montreal Canadiens	Chicago Black Hawks	6
1973-74	Philadelphia Flyers	Boston Bruins	6
1974-75	Philadelphia Flyers	Buffalo Sabres	6
1975-76	Montreal Canadiens	Philadelphia Flyers	4
1976-77	Montreal Canadiens	Boston Bruins	4
1977-78	Montreal Canadiens	Boston Bruins	6
1978-79	Montreal Canadiens	New York Rangers	5
1979-80	New York Islanders	Philadelphia Flyers	6
1980-81	New York Islanders	Minnesota North Stars	5
1981-82	New York Islanders	Vancouver Canucks	4
1982-83	New York Islanders	Edmonton Oilers	4
1983-84	Edmonton Oilers	New York Islanders	5
1984-85	Edmonton Oilers	Philadelphia Flyers	5
1985-86	Montreal Canadiens	Calgary Flames	5
1986-87	Edmonton Oilers	Philadelphia Flyers	7
1987-88	Edmonton Oilers	Boston Bruins	4
1988-89	Calgary Flames	Montreal Canadiens	6

1. In the spring of 1919 the Montreal Canadiens traveled to Seattle to meet Seattle, champs of the Pacific Coast Hockey League. After five games had been played—teams were tied at 2 wins and 1 tie—the series was called off by the local Department of Health because of the influenza epidemic; and the death of Joe Hall from influenza.

TOP 10 ALL-TIME NHL SCORING LEADERS

	GOALS			Goals/
Player	Seasons	Games	Goals	game
Gordie Howe	26	1,767	801	.453
Marcel Dionne	18	1,348	731	.542
Phil Esposito	18	1,282	717	.572
Wayne Gretzky	10	774	637	.836
Bobby Hull	16	1,063	610	.574
Mike Bossy	10	752	573	.762
John Bucyk	23	1,540	556	.361
Maurice Richard	18	978	544	.556
Stan Mikita	22	1,394	541	.388
Guy Lafleur	15	1,028	536	.521

	ASSISTS			Assts./
Player	Seasons	Games	Assists	game
Wayne Gretzky	10	774	1,200	1.550
Gordie Howe	26	1,767	1,049	.593
Marcel Dionne	18	1,348	1,040	.771
Stan Mikita	22	1,394	926	.664
Phil Esposito	18	1,282	873	.681
Bobby Clarke	15	1,144	852	.745
Bryan Trottier	14	1,064	842	.784
Alex Delvecchio	23	1,549	825	.533
Gilbert Perreault	17	1,191	814	.683
John Bucyk	23	1,540	813	.528

	POINTS				
Player	Seasons	Games	Goals	Assists	Points
Gordie Howe	26	1,767	801	1,049	1,850
Wayne Gretzky	10	774	637	1,200	1,837
Marcel Dionne	18	1,348	731	1,040	1,771
Phil Esposito	18	1,282	717	873	1,590
Stan Mikita	22	1,394	541	926	1,467
John Bucyk	23	1,540	556	813	1,369
Bryan Trottier	14	1,064	487	842	1,329
Gilbert Perreault	17	1,191	512	814	1,326
Guy Lafleur	15	1,028	536	755	1,291
Alex Delvecchio	23	1,549	456	825	1,281

Source: The National Hockey League.

Other Sports

GOLF—MEN

MAJOR CHAMPIONSHIPS

U.S. OPEN

Year	Winner	Year	Winner
1966	Billy Casper	1978	Andy North
1967	Jack Nicklaus	1979	Hale Irwin
1968	Lee Trevino	1980	Jack Nicklaus
1969	Orville Moody	1981	David Graham
1970	Tony Jacklin	1982	Tom Watson
1971	Lee Trevino	1983	Larry Nelson
1972	Jack Nicklaus	1984	Fuzzy Zoeller
1973	Johnny Miller	1985	Andy North
1974	Hale Irwin	1986	Ray Floyd
1975	Lou Graham	1987	Scott Simpson
1976	Jerry Pate	1988	Curtis Strange
1977	Hubert Green	1989	Curtis Strange

PGA

Year	Winner	Year	Winner
1966	Al Geiberger	1978	John Mahaffey
1967	Don January	1979	David Graham
1968	Julius Boros	1980	Jack Nicklaus
1969	Ray Floyd	1981	Larry Nelson
1970	Dave Stockton	1982	Raymond Floyd
1971	Jack Nicklaus	1983	Hal Sutton
1972	Gary Player	1984	Lee Trevino
1973	Jack Nicklaus	1985	Hubert Green
1974	Lee Trevino	1986	Bob Tway
1975	Jack Nicklaus	1987	Larry Nelson
1976	Dave Stockton	1988	Jeff Sluman
1977	Lanny Wadkins	1989	Payne Stewart

MASTERS

Year	Winner	Year	Winner
1966	Jack Nicklaus	1978	Gary Player
1967	Gay Brewer, Jr.	1979	Fuzzy Zoeller
1968	Bob Goalby	1980	Seve Ballesteros
1969	George Archer	1981	Tom Watson
1970	Billy Casper	1982	Craig Stadler
1971	Charles Coody	1983	Seve Ballesteros
1972	Jack Nicklaus	1984	Ben Crenshaw
1973	Tommy Aaron	1985	Bernhard Langer
1974	Gary Player	1986	Jack Nicklaus
1975	Jack Nicklaus	1987	Larry Mize
1976	Ray Floyd	1988	Sandy Lyle
1977	Tom Watson	1989	Nick Faldo

Note: All Masters Tournaments are held on the same course at the Augusta National Golf Club, Augusta, Ga.

BRITISH OPEN

Year	Winner	Year	Winner
1966	Jack Nicklaus	1978	Jack Nicklaus
1967	Roberto DeVicenzo	1979	Seve Ballesteros
1968	Gary Player	1980	Tom Watson
1969	Tony Jacklin	1981	Bill Rogers
1970	Jack Nicklaus	1982	Tom Watson
1971	Lee Trevino	1983	Tom Watson
1972	Lee Trevino	1984	Seve Ballesteros
1973	Tom Weiskopf	1985	Sandy Lyle
1974	Gary Player	1986	Greg Norman
1975	Tom Watson	1987	Nick Faldo
1976	Johnny Miller	1988	Seve Ballesteros
1977	Tom Watson	1989	Mark Calcavecchia

LEADING MONEY WINNERS, 1965–88

MEN

Year	Name	Winnings	Year	Name	Winnings
1965	Jack Nicklaus	$140,752	1977	Tom Watson	$ 310,653
1966	Billy Casper	121,944	1978	Tom Watson	362,428
1967	Jack Nicklaus	188,998	1979	Tom Watson	462,636
1968	Billy Casper	205,168	1980	Tom Watson	530,808
1969	Frank Beard	164,707	1981	Tom Kite	375,698
1970	Lee Trevino	157,037	1982	Craig Stadler	446,462
1971	Jack Nicklaus	244,490	1983	Hal Sutton	426,668
1972	Jack Nicklaus	320,542	1984	Tom Watson	476,260
1973	Jack Nicklaus	308,362	1985	Curtis Strange	542,321
1974	Johnny Miller	353,021	1986	Greg Norman	653,296
1975	Jack Nicklaus	298,149	1987	Curtis Strange	925,941
1976	Jack Nicklaus	266,438	1988	Curtis Strange	1,147,644

WOMEN

Year	Name	Winnings	Year	Name	Winnings
1965	Kathy Whitworth	$ 28,658	1977	Judy T. Rankin	$122,890
1966	Kathy Whitworth	33,517	1978	Nancy Lopez	189,813
1967	Kathy Whitworth	32,937	1979	Nancy Lopez	197,488
1968	Kathy Whitworth	48,379	1980	Beth Daniel	231,000
1969	Carol Mann	49,152	1981	Beth Daniel	206,977
1970	Kathy Whitworth	30,235	1982	JoAnne Carner	310,399
1971	Kathy Whitworth	41,181	1983	JoAnne Carner	291,404
1972	Kathy Whitworth	65,063	1984	Betsy King	266,771
1973	Kathy Whitworth	82,864	1985	Nancy Lopez	416,472
1974	JoAnne Carner	87,094	1986	Pat Bradley	492,021
1975	Sandra Palmer	76,374	1987	Ayako Okamoto	466,034
1976	Judy T. Rankin	150,734	1988	Sherri Turner	350,851

Source: Professional Golfer's Assn.

GOLF—WOMEN

MAJOR WOMEN'S CHAMPIONSHIPS

U.S. WOMEN'S OPEN

Year	Winner	Year	Winner
1966	Sandra Spuzich	1978	Hollis Stacy
1967	Catherine LaCoste	1979	Jerilyn Britz
1968	Susie Berning	1980	Amy Alcott
1969	Donna Caponi	1981	Pat Bradley
1970	Donna Caponi	1982	Janet Anderson
1971	JoAnne Carner	1983	Jan Stephenson
1972	Susie Berning	1984	Hollis Stacy
1973	Susie Berning	1985	Kathy Baker
1974	Sandra Haynie	1986	Jane Geddes
1975	Sandra Palmer	1987	Laura Davies
1976	JoAnne Carner	1988	Liselotte Neumann
1977	Hollis Stacy	1989	Betsy King

LPGA

Year	Winner	Year	Winner
1966	Gloria Ehret	1978	Nancy Lopez
1967	Kathy Whitworth	1979	Donna Caponi
1968	Sandra Post	1980	Sally Little
1969	Betsy Rawls	1981	Donna Caponi
1970	Shirley Englehorn	1982	Jan Stephenson
1971	Kathy Whitworth	1983	Patty Sheehan
1972	Kathy Ahern	1984	Patty Sheehan
1973	Mary Mills	1985	Nancy Lopez
1974	Sandra Haynie	1986	Pat Bradley
1975	Kathy Whitworth	1987	Jane Geddes
1976	Betty Burfeindt	1988	Sherri Turner
1977	Chako Higuchi	1989	Nancy Lopez

TENNIS—MEN

THE GRAND SLAM OF TENNIS

Only six players have won the French Open, the Australian Open, the U.S. Open, and Wimbledon in the same year. Don Budge became the first "grand slammer" in 1938. Maureen Connolly became the first woman winner in 1953 when she won straight-set victories in all four final round matches. Australian Rod Laver won the Grand Slam in 1962 and 1969, making him the only repeat winner. Margaret Court swept through the tournaments in 1970. Steffi Graf became the youngest to accomplish the feat in 1988. Martina Navratilova won the four tournaments consecutively but not in the same calendar year; she won the French Open in 1984, following 1983 victories in the other three.

Eleven players have won each of the four tournaments but never in the same year. Several others have dominated tennis without winning all the events. Sweden's Bjorn Borg won five consecutive Wimbledon titles but failed to win the U.S. Open in nine attempts.

THE GRAND SLAM CHAMPIONSHIPS—MEN

FRENCH

Year	Winner	Year	Winner
1966	Tony Roche	1978	Bjorn Borg
1967	Roy Emerson	1979	Bjorn Borg
1968	Ken Rosewall	1980	Bjorn Borg
1969	Rod Laver	1981	Bjorn Borg
1970	Jan Kodes	1982	Mats Wilander
1971	Jan Kodes	1983	Yannick Noah
1972	Andres Gimeno	1984	Ivan Lendl
1973	Ilie Nastase	1985	Mats Wilander
1974	Bjorn Borg	1986	Ivan Lendl
1975	Bjorn Borg	1987	Ivan Lendl
1976	Adriano Panatta	1988	Mats Wilander
1977	Guillermo Vilas	1989	Michael Chang

AUSTRALIAN

Year	Winner	Year	Winner
1966	Roy Emerson	1977	Vitas Gerulaitis
1967	Roy Emerson	1978	Guillermo Vilas
1968	Bill Bowrey	1979	Guillermo Vilas
OPEN CHAMPIONSHIPS		1980	Brian Teacher
1969	Rod Laver	1981	Johan Kriek
1970	Arthur Ashe	1982	Johan Kriek
1971	Ken Rosewall	1983	Mats Wilander
1972	Ken Rosewall	1984	Mats Wilander
1973	John Newcombe	1985	Stefan Edberg
1974	Jimmy Connors	1986	Not held; moved to Jan. 1987
1975	John Newcombe	1987	Stefan Edberg
1976	Mark Edmondson	1988	Mats Wilander
1977	Roscoe Tanner	1989	Ivan Lendl

U.S.

Year	Winner	Year	Winner
1966	Fred Stolle	1977	Guillermo Vilas
1967	John Newcombe	1978	Jimmy Connors
1968	Arthur Ashe	1979	John McEnroe
1969	Rod Laver	1980	John McEnroe
OPEN CHAMPIONSHIPS		1981	John McEnroe
1968	Arthur Ashe	1982	Jimmy Connors
1969	Rod Laver	1983	Jimmy Connors
1970	Ken Rosewall	1984	John McEnroe
1971	Stan Smith	1985	Ivan Lendl
1972	Ilie Nastase	1986	Ivan Lendl
1973	John Newcombe	1987	Ivan Lendl
1974	Jimmy Connors	1988	Mats Wilander
1975	Manuel Orantes	1989	Boris Becker
1976	Jimmy Connors		

WIMBLEDON

Year	Winner	Year	Winner
1966	Manuel Santana	1978	Bjorn Borg
1967	John Newcombe	1979	Bjorn Borg
1968	Rod Laver	1980	Bjorn Borg
1969	Rod Laver	1981	John McEnroe
1970	John Newcombe	1982	Jimmy Connors
1971	John Newcombe	1983	John McEnroe
1972	Stan Smith	1984	John McEnroe
1973	Jan Kodes	1985	Boris Becker
1974	Jimmy Connors	1986	Boris Becker
1975	Arthur Ashe	1987	Pat Cash
1976	Bjorn Borg	1988	Stefan Edberg
1977	Bjorn Borg	1989	Boris Becker

Source: Men's International Professional Tennis Council.

LEADING MONEY WINNERS, 1968–88

Year	Player	Official earnings	Year	Player	Official earnings
1968	Tony Roche	$ 63,504	1979	Bjorn Borg	$1,008,742
1969	Rod Laver	124,000	1980	John McEnroe	972,369
1970	Rod Laver	201,453	1981	John McEnroe	991,000
1971	Rod Laver	292,717	1982	Ivan Lendl	2,028,850
1972	Ilie Nastase	176,000	1983	Ivan Lendl	1,747,128
1973	Ilie Nastase	228,750	1984	John McEnroe	2,026,109
1974	Jimmy Connors	285,490	1985	Ivan Lendl	1,971,074
1975	Arthur Ashe	326,750	1986	Ivan Lendl	1,987,537
1976	Raul Ramirez	484,343	1987	Ivan Lendl	2,003,656
1977	Guillermo Vilas	766,065	1988	Mats Wilander	1,726,731
1978	Eddie Dibbs	575,273			

TENNIS—WOMEN

THE GRAND SLAM CHAMPIONSHIPS—WOMEN

FRENCH

Year	Winner	Year	Winner
1966	Ann Jones	1978	Virginia Ruzici
1967	Francoise Durr	1979	Chris Evert Lloyd
1968	Nancy Richey	1980	Chris Evert Lloyd
1969	Margaret Smith Court	1981	Hana Mandlikova
1970	Margaret Smith Court	1982	Martina Navratilova
1971	Evonne Goolagong	1983	Chris Evert Lloyd
1972	Billie Jean King	1984	Martina Navratilova
1973	Margaret Smith Court	1985	Chris Evert Lloyd
1974	Chris Evert	1986	Chris Evert Lloyd
1975	Chris Evert	1987	Steffi Graf
1976	Sue Barker	1988	Steffi Graf
1977	Mima Jausovec	1989	Arantxa Sanchez

AUSTRALIAN

Year	Winner	Year	Winner
1966	Margaret Smith	1978	Chris O'Neil
1967	Nancy Richey	1979	Barbara Jordan
1968	Billie Jean King	1980	Hana Mandlikova
1969	Margaret Smith Court	1981	Martina Navratilova
1970	Margaret Smith Court	1982	Chris Evert Lloyd
1971	Margaret Smith Court	1983	Martina Navratilova
1972	Virginia Wade	1984	Chris Evert Lloyd
1973	Margaret Smith Court	1985	Martina Navratilova
1974	Evonne Goolagong	1986	Not held;
1975	Evonne Goolagong		moved to Jan. 1987
1976	Evonne Goolagong Cawley	1987	Hana Mandlikova
1977	Kerry Melville Reid	1988	Steffi Graf
1977	Evonne Goolagong Cawley	1989	Steffi Graf

U.S.

Year	Winner	Year	Winner
1966	Maria Bueno	1978	Chris Evert
1967	Billie Jean King	1979	Tracy Austin
1968	Virginia Wade	1980	Chris Evert Lloyd
1969	Margaret Smith Court	1981	Tracy Austin
1970	Margaret Smith Court	1982	Chris Evert Lloyd
1971	Billie Jean King	1983	Martina Navratilova
1972	Billie Jean King	1984	Martina Navratilova
1973	Margaret Smith Court	1985	Hanna Mandlikova
1974	Billie Jean King	1986	Martina Navratilova
1975	Chris Evert	1987	Martina Navratilova
1976	Chris Evert	1988	Steffi Graf
1977	Chris Evert	1989	Steffi Graf

WIMBLEDON

Year	Winner	Year	Winner
1966	Billie Jean King	1978	Martina Navratilova
1967	Billie Jean King	1979	Martina Navratilova
1968	Billie Jean King	1980	Evonne Goolagong Cawley
1969	Ann Jones	1981	Chris Evert Lloyd
1970	Margaret Smith Court	1982	Martina Navratilova
1971	Evonne Goolagong	1983	Martina Navratilova
1972	Billie Jean King	1984	Martina Navratilova
1973	Billie Jean King	1985	Martina Navratilova
1974	Chris Evert	1986	Martina Navratilova
1975	Billie Jean King	1987	Martina Navratilova
1976	Chris Evert	1988	Steffi Graf
1977	Virginia Wade	1989	Steffi Graf

LEADING MONEY WINNERS, 1988

Players	Singles	Doubles	Total
Steffi Graf	$1,285,842	$ 92,286	$1,378,128
Martina Navratilova	1,133,699	200,083	1,333,782
Gabriela Sabatini	889,601	105,798	995,399
Chris Evert	668,473	30,176	698,649
Pam Shriver	464,808	156,519	621,327
Zina Garrison	270,454	148,581	419,035
Helena Sukova	290,887	97,430	388,317
Natalia Zvereva	294,405	66,949	361,354
Lori McNeil	250,597	107,446	358,043
Manuela Maleeva	242,864	13,310	256,174
Claudia Kohde-Kilsch	178,142	57,430	235,572
Patty Fendick	128,995	76,862	205,857
Barbara Potter	172,792	13,613	185,405
Gigi Fernandez	56,301	125,121	181,422
Stephanie Rehe	162,026	18,138	180,164
Larisa Savchenko	117,692	61,115	178,807
Katerina Maleeva	158,438	19,923	178,361
Robin White	59,549	103,887	163,436
Helen Kelesi	133,417	16,301	149,718
Jana Novotna	63,964	76,080	140,044
Nicole Provis	108,812	30,527	139,339
Sylvia Hanika	131,415	4,425	135,840
Nathalie Tauziat	93,607	41,536	135,143
Rosalyn Fairbank	89,205	44,972	134,177
Katrina Adams	39,219	88,599	127,818

BOXING CHAMPIONS

Although many governing bodies now issue and certify their own boxing championships, the two most widely accepted are the World Boxing Association (WBA) and World Boxing Council (WBC). Recently, the International Boxing Federation (IBF) has risen to a position of near parity with the WBA and WBC.

CURRENT BOXING CHAMPIONS (8/15/89)

Class	WBA	WBC	IBF
Heavyweight	Mike Tyson United States	Mike Tyson United States	Mike Tyson United States
Cruiserweight	Taoufik Balbouli France	Carlos DeLeon Puerto Rico	Glenn McCrory Great Britain
Light Heavyweight	Virgil Hill United States	Jeff Harding Australia	Charles Williams United States
Middleweight	Mike McCallum Jamaica	Sugar Ray Leonard United States	Michael Nunn United States
Jr. Middleweight	Julian Jackson Virgin Islands	Rene Jacquot France	Gianfranco Rosi Italy
Welterweight	Mark Breland United States	Marlon Starling United States	Simon Brown United States
Jr. Welterweight	Juan Coggi Argentina	Julio Chavez Mexico	Meldrick Taylor United States
Lightweight	Edwin Rosario Puerto Rico	Pernell Whitaker United States	Pernell Whitaker United States
Jr. Lightweight	Brian Mitchell South Africa	Azumah Nelson Ghana	Tony Lopez United States
Featherweight	Antonio Esparragoza Venezuela	Jeff Fenech Australia	Jorge Paez Mexico
Jr. Featherweight	Juan Jose Estrada Mexico	Daniel Zaragoza Mexico	Fabrice Benichou France
Bantamweight	Khaokor Galaxy Thailand	Raoul Perez Mexico	Orlanda Canizales United States
Flyweight	Fidel Bassa Colombia	Sot Chitalada Thailand	Dave McAuley Ireland

Note: The WBC recognizes a supermiddleweight title, held since 1987 by Sugar Ray Leonard. **Source:** *KO Magazine.*

PROFESSIONAL BOWLERS ASSOCIATION

The PBA was founded by 33 charter members who competed in three 1959 tournaments for prizes worth a total of $49,500. The traditional Winter Tour, which has been augmented and expanded into four separate seasonal tours, now pays more than $3,000,000 in prize money.

Source: Professional Bowlers Assn.

1988 PBA LEADING MONEY WINNERS

1.	Brian Voss	$225,485	6.	Marshall Holman	$138,179
2.	Bob Benoit	171,695	7.	Walter Ray Williams, Jr.	131,565
3.	Peter Weber	160,102	8.	Dave Husted	126,580
4.	Dave Ferraro	150,395	9.	Tony Westlake	120,555
5.	Mark Williams	140,999	10.	Joe Berardi	115,910

LADIES PRO BOWLING TOUR (LPBT) LEADING MONEY WINNERS, 1988

Bowler	Money	Bowler	Money
Lisa Wagner	$105,500	Leanne Barrette	$42,625
Jeanne Maiden	54,670	Wendy Macpherson	38,540
Robin Romeo	49,320	Cindy Coburn	35,815
Donna Adamek	46,735	Tish Johnson	30,635
Lorrie Nichols	45,590	Nikki Gianulias	27,962

AUTO RACING

INDY 500

UNDER AAA SANCTION

Year	Winner	Time	MPH
1911	Ray Harroun	6:42:08	74.602
1912	Joe Dawson	6:21:06	78.719
1913	Juses Goux	6:35:05	75.933
1914	Rene Thomas	6:03:45	82.474
1915	Ralph DePalma	5:33:55	89.840
1916	Dario Resta	3:34:17[1]	84.001
1919	Howard Wilcox	5:40:42	88.050
1920	Gaston Chevrolet	5:38:32	88.618
1921	Tommy Milton	5:34:34	89.621
1922	Jimmy Murphy	5:17:30	94.484
1923	Tommy Milton	5:29:50	90.954
1924	L.L. Corum and Joe Boyer	5:05:23	98.234
1925	Peter DePaolo	4:56:39	101.127
1926	Frank Lockhart	4:10:14[2]	95.904
1927	George Souders	5:07:33	97.545
1928	Louis Meyer	5:01:33	99.482
1929	Ray Keech	5:07:25	97.585
1930	Billy Arnold	4:58:39	100.448
1931	Louis Schneider	5:10:27	96.629
1932	Fred Frame	4:48:03	104.144
1933	Louis Meyer	4:48:00	104.162
1934	William Cummings	4:46:05	104.863
1935	Kelly Petillo	4:42:22	106.240
1936	Louis Meyer	4:35:03	109.069
1937	Wilbur Shaw	4:24:07	113.580
1938	Floyd Roberts	4:15:58	117.200
1939	Wilbur Shaw	4:20:47	115.035
1940	Wilbur Shaw	4:22:31	114.277
1941	Floyd Davis and Mauri Rose	4:20:36	115.117
1946	George Robson	4:21:16	114.820
1947	Mauri Rose	4:17:52	116.338
1948	Mauri Rose	4:10:23	119.814
1949	Bill Holland	4:07:15	121.327
1950	Johnnie Parsons	2:46:55[3]	124.002
1951	Lee Wallard	3:57:38	126.244
1952	Troy Ruttman	3:52:41	128.922
1953	Bill Vukovich	3:53:01	128.740
1954	Bill Vukovich	3:49:17	130.840
1955	Bob Sweikert	3:53:59	128.209

UNDER USAC SANCTION

Year	Winner	Time	MPH
1956	Pat Flaherty	3:53:28	128.490
1957	Sam Hanks	3:41:14	135.601
1958	Jim Bryan	3:44:13	133.791
1959	Rodger Ward	3:40:49	135.857
1960	Jim Rathmann	3:36:11	138.767
1961	A.J. Foyt, Jr.	3:35:37	139.131
1962	Rodger Ward	3:33:50	140.293
1963	Parnelli Jones	3:29:35	143.137
1964	A.J. Foyt, Jr.	3:23:35	147.350
1965	Jim Clark	3:19:05	150.686
1966	Graham Hill	3:27:52	144.317
1967	A.J. Foyt, Jr.	3:18:24	151.207
1968	Bobby Unser	3:16:13	152.882
1969	Mario Andretti	3:11:14	156.867
1970	Al Unser	3:12:37	155.749
1971	Al Unser	3:10:11	157.735
1972	Mark Donohue	3:04:05	162.962
1973	Gordon Johncock	2:05:26[4]	159.036
1974	Johnny Rutherford	3:09:10	158.589
1975	Bobby Unser	2:54:55[5]	149.213
1976	Johnny Rutherford	1:42:52[6]	148.725
1977	A.J. Foyt, Jr.	3:05:57	161.331
1978	Al Unser	3:05:54	161.363
1979	Rick Mears	3:08:47	158.899
1980	Johnny Rutherford	3:29:59	142.862
1981	Bobby Unser	3:35:41	139.084
1982	Gordon Johncock	3:05:09	162.029
1983	Tom Sneva	3:05:03	162.117
1984	Rick Mears	3:30:21	163.612
1985	Danny Sullivan	3:16:06	152.982
1986	Bobby Rahal	2:55:43	170.722[7]
1987	Al Unser	3:04:59	162.175
1988	Rick Mears	3:27:10	144.809
1989	Emerson Fittipaldi	2:59:01	167.581

1. 300 miles (scheduled).   2. 400 miles (rain).   3. 345 miles (rain).   4. 332½ miles (rain).   5. 435 miles (rain).   6. 255 miles (rain).   7. Track record.
Source: Indianapolis Motor Speedway Hall of Fame and Museum.

INDY 500 TOTAL PRIZE MONEY, SELECTED YEARS

Year	Total	Year	Total
1911	$ 27,550	1982	2,067,475
1920	93,550	1983	2,411,450
1930	96,250	1984	2,795,899
1940	85,525	1985	3,271,025
1950	201,035	1986	4,001,450
1960	369,150	1987	4,490,375
1970	1,000,002	1988	5,025,400
1980	1,503,225	1989	5,723,725
1981	1,605,375		

DAYTONA 500 WINNERS, 1959–89

Year	Driver	Avg. speed (mph)
1959	Lee Petty	135.521
1960	Junior Johnson	124.740
1961	Marvin Panch	149.601
1962	Fireball Roberts	152.529
1963	Tiny Lund	151.566
1964	Richard Petty	154.334
1965	Fred Lorenzen	141.539
1966	Richard Petty	160.627
1967	Mario Andretti	146.926
1968	Cale Yarborough	143.251
1969	LeeRoy Yarbrough	157.950
1970	Pete Hamilton	149.601
1971	Richard Petty	144.462
1972	A.J. Foyt, Jr.	161.550
1973	Richard Petty	157.205
1974	Richard Petty	140.894
1975	Benny Parsons	153.649
1976	David Pearson	152.181
1977	Cale Yarborough	153.218
1978	Bobby Allison	159.730
1979	Richard Petty	143.977
1980	Buddy Baker	177.602
1981	Richard Petty	169.651
1982	Bobby Allison	153.991
1983	Cale Yarborough	155.979
1984	Cale Yarborough	150.994
1985	Bill Elliott	172.265
1986	Geoff Bondine	148.124
1987	Bill Elliott	176.263
1988	Bobby Allison	137.531
1989	Darrell Waltrip	148.466

Source: NASCAR.

THE WORLD CUP

From its origins in various "football" games dating back to ancient Greece and China, soccer (as it is called in the United States) has become the world's most popular sport, with over 20 million participants in over 140 nations. The World Cup championship, modern soccer's most spectacular event, is staged by the Federation Internationale de Football Association (FIFA). Formally known as the Jules Rimet Trophy, the World Cup is awarded every four years to the victor in a 24-nation, 52-game final tournament. Players must represent their home country, regardless of where they regularly play. Millions attend the Cup's many contests and in recent years the televised final has been viewed by over a billion people worldwide. In 1986 12.8 billion viewers saw at least some live coverage. The host country for the 1990 tournament is Spain.

Year	Host	Winner	Leading scorer, goals	PN[1]
1930	Uruguay	Uruguay	Stabile, Argentina (8)	13
1934	Italy	Italy	Conen, Germany (9)	29
			Nejedly, Czechoslovakia (9)	
			Schiavo, Italy (4)	
1938	France	Italy	Leonidas, Brazil (8)	26
1942	No tournament—World War II			
1946	No tournament—World War II			
1950	Brazil	Uruguay	Ademir, Brazil (7)	28
1954	Switzerland	West Germany	Kocsis, Hungary (11)	36
1958	Sweden	Brazil	Fontaine, France (13)	53
1962	Chile	Brazil	Jerkovic, Yugoslavia (5)	57
1966	England	England	Eusebio, Portugal (9)	71
1970	Mexico	Brazil	Muller, West Germany (10)	73
1974	West Germany	West Germany	Lato, Poland (7)	95
1978	Argentina	Argentina	Kempes, Argentina (6)	105
1982	Spain	Italy	Rossi, Italy (6)	109
1986	Mexico	Argentina	Lineker, England (6)	112

1. PN: Participating Nations.   **Source:** FIFA.

MAJOR COLLEGE SPORTS

NCAA DIVISION I MEN'S BASKETBALL FINAL FOUR RESULTS

The first NCAA men's basketball tournament was held in 1939, when eight teams, selected by committee, from eight geographical regions gathered in Evanston, Ill. In the past 50 years, the tournament has grown tremendously, and 64 teams now compete for the title of national champion. The tournament field, consisting of 30 conference champions and 34 "at-large" bids, is divided into four regions, each one sending a team to the Final Four through a single-game elimination process.

Year	Champion	Score	Runner-up	Third place	Fourth place	Champion coach	Outstanding player award
1939	Oregon	46–33	Ohio State	Oklahoma[1]	Villanova[1]	Howard Hobson	None selected
1940	Indiana	60–42	Kansas	Duquesne[1]	Southern California[1]	Branch McCracken	Marvin Huffman	Indiana
1941	Wisconsin	39–34	Washington State	Pittsburgh[1]	Arkansas[1]	Harold Foster	John Kotz	Wisconsin
1942	Stanford	53–38	Dartmouth	Colorado[1]	Kentucky[1]	Everett Dean	Howard Dallmar	Stanford
1943	Wyoming	46–34	Georgetown	Texas[1]	DePaul[1]	Everett Shelton	Ken Sailors	Wyoming
1944	Utah	42–40[3]	Dartmouth	Iowa State[1]	Ohio State[1]	Vadal Peterson	Arnold Ferrin	Utah
1945	Oklahoma State	49–45	New York Univ.	Arkansas[1]	Ohio State[1]	Henry Iba	Bob Kurland	Oklahoma State
1946	Oklahoma State	43–40	North Carolina	Ohio State	California	Henry Iba	Bob Kurland	Oklahoma State
1947	Holy Cross	58–47	Oklahoma	Texas	CCNY	Alvin Julian	George Kaftan	Holy Cross
1948	Kentucky	58–42	Baylor	Holy Cross	Kansas State	Aldolph Rupp	Alex Groza	Kentucky
1949	Kentucky	46–36	Oklahoma State	Illinois	Oregon State	Aldolph Rupp	Alex Groza	Kentucky
1950	CCNY	71–68	Bradley	North Carolina State	Baylor	Nat Holman	Irwin Dambrot	CCNY
1951	Kentucky	68–58	Kansas State	Illinois	Oklahoma State	Aldolph Rupp	None selected
1952	Kansas	80–63	St. John's	Illinois	Santa Clara	Forrest Allen	Clyde Lovellette	Kansas
1953	Indiana	69–68	Kansas	Washington	Louisiana State	Branch McCracken	B.H. Born	Kansas
1954	La Salle	92–76	Bradley	Penn State	Southern California	Kenneth Loeffler	Tom Gola	La Salle
1955	San Francisco	77–63	La Salle	Colorado	Iowa	Phil Woolpert	Bill Russell	San Francisco
1956	San Francisco	83–71	Iowa	Temple	Southern Methodist	Phil Woolpert	Hal Lear	Temple
1957	North Carolina	54–53[3]	Kansas	San Francisco	Michigan State	Frank McGuire	Wilt Chamberlain	Kansas
1958	Kentucky	84–72	Seattle	Temple	Kansas State	Adolph Rupp	Elgin Baylor	Seattle
1959	California	71–70	West Virginia	Cincinnati	Louisville	Pete Newell	Jerry West	West Virginia
1960	Ohio State	75–55	California	Cincinnati	New York Univ.	Fred Taylor	Jerry Lucas	Ohio State
1961	Cincinnati	70–65[2]	Ohio State	St. Joseph's (Pa.)[4]	Utah	Edwin Jucker	Jerry Lucas	Ohio State
1962	Cincinnati	71–59	Ohio State	Wake Forest	UCLA	Edwin Jucker	Paul Hogue	Cincinnati
1963	Loyola (Ill.)	60–58[2]	Cincinnati	Duke	Utah	George Ireland	Art Heyman	Duke
1964	UCLA	98–83	Duke	Michigan	Kansas State	John Wooden	Walt Hazzard	UCLA
1965	UCLA	91–80	Michigan	Princeton	Wichita State	John Wooden	Bill Bradley	Princeton
1966	UTEP	72–65	Kentucky	Duke	Utah	Don Haskins	Jerry Chambers	Utah
1967	UCLA	79–64	Dayton	Houston	North Carolina	John Wooden	Lew Alcindor	UCLA
1968	UCLA	78–55	North Carolina	Ohio State	Houston	John Wooden	Lew Alcindor	UCLA
1969	UCLA	92–72	Purdue	Drake	North Carolina	John Wooden	Lew Alcindor	UCLA
1970	UCLA	80–69	Jacksonville	New Mexico State	St. Bonaventure	John Wooden	Sidney Wicks	UCLA
1971	UCLA	68–62	Villanova[2]	Western Kentucky[2]	Kansas	John Wooden	Howard Porter	Villanova
1972	UCLA	81–76	Florida State	North Carolina	Louisville	John Wooden	Bill Walton	UCLA
1973	UCLA	87–66	Memphis State	Indiana	Providence	John Wooden	Bill Walton	UCLA
1974	North Carolina State	76–64	Marquette	UCLA	Kansas	Norm Sloan	David Thompson	North Carolina State
1975	UCLA	92–85	Kentucky	Louisville	Syracuse	John Wooden	Richard Washington	UCLA
1976	Indiana	86–68	Michigan	UCLA	Rutgers	Bob Knight	Kent Benson	Indiana
1977	Marquette	67–59	North Carolina	UNLV	North Carolina at Charlotte	Al McGuire	Butch Lee	Marquette
1978	Kentucky	94–88	Duke	Arkansas	Notre Dame	Joe Hall	Jack Givens	Kentucky
1979	Michigan State	75–64	Indiana State	DePaul	Penn	Jud Heathcote	Earvin Johnson	Mighigan State
1980	Louisville	59–54	UCLA[4]	Purdue	Iowa	Denny Crum	Darrell Griffith	Louisville
1981	Indiana	63–50	North Carolina	Virginia	Louisiana State	Bob Knight	Isiah Thomas	Indiana
1982	North Carolina	63–62	Georgetown	Houston[1]	Louisville[1]	Dean Smith	James Worthy	North Carolina
1983	North Carolina State	54–52	Houston	Georgia[1]	Louisville[1]	Jim Valvano	Akeem Olajuwon	Houston
1984	Georgetown	84–75	Houston	Kentucky[1]	Virginia[1]	John Thompson	Patrick Ewing	Georgetown
1985	Villanova	66–64	Georgetown	St. John's[1]	Memphis State[1, 4]	Rollie Massemino	Ed Pinckney	Villanova
1986	Louisville	72–69	Duke	Kansas[1]	Louisiana State[1]	Denny Crum	Pervis Ellison	Louisville
1987	Indiana	74–73	Syracuse	UNLV[1]	Providence[1]	Bob Knight	Keith Smart	Indiana
1988	Kansas	83–79	Oklahoma	Arizona[1]	Duke[1]	Larry Brown	Danny Manning	Kansas
1989	Michigan	80–79[2]	Seton Hall	Illinois[1]	Duke[1]	Steve Fisher	Glen Rice	Michigan

1. Tied for third place.   2. Overtime.   3. Triple overtime.   4. Later declared ineligible.

NCAA FOOTBALL—MAJOR BOWL GAMES, 1975–89

ROSE BOWL (Pasadena, Calif.)

1975 Southern California 18, Ohio State 17
1976 UCLA 23, Ohio State 10
1977 Southern California 14, Michigan 6
1978 Washington 27, Michigan 20
1979 Southern California 17, Michigan 10
1980 Southern California 17, Ohio State 16
1981 Michigan 23, Washington 6
1982 Washington 28, Iowa 0
1983 UCLA 24, Michigan 14
1984 UCLA 45, Illinois 9
1985 Southern California 20, Ohio State 17
1986 UCLA 45, Iowa 28
1987 Arizona State 22, Michigan 15
1988 Michigan State 20, Southern California 17
1989 Michigan State 22, Southern California 14

ORANGE BOWL (Miami, Fla.)

1975 Notre Dame 13, Alabama 11
1976 Oklahoma 14, Michigan 6
1977 Ohio State 27, Colorado 10
1978 Arkansas 31, Oklahoma 6
1979 Oklahoma 31, Nebraska 21
1980 Oklahoma 24, Florida State 7
1981 Oklahoma 18, Florida State 17
1982 Clemson 22, Nebraska 15
1983 Nebraska 21, Louisiana State 20
1984 Miami (Fla.) 31, Nebraska 30
1985 Washington 28, Oklahoma 17
1986 Oklahoma 25, Penn State 10
1987 Oklahoma 42, Arkansas 8
1988 Miami (Fla.) 20, Oklahoma 14
1989 Miami (Fla.) 23, Nebraska 3

SUGAR BOWL (New Orleans, La.)

1975 Nebraska 13, Florida 10
1976 Alabama 13, Penn State 6
1977 Pittsburgh 27, Georgia 3
1978 Alabama 35, Ohio State 6
1979 Alabama 14, Penn State 7
1980 Alabama 24, Arkansas 9
1981 Georgia 17, Notre Dame 10
1982 Pittsburgh 24, Georgia 20
1983 Penn State 27, Georgia 23
1984 Auburn 9, Michigan 7
1985 Nebraska 28, Louisiana State 10
1986 Tennessee 35, Miami (Fla.) 7
1987 Nebraska 30, Louisiana State 15
1988 Syracuse 16, Auburn 16
1989 Florida State 13, Auburn 7

COTTON BOWL (Dallas, Tex.)

1975 Penn State 41, Baylor 20
1976 Arkansas 31, Georgia 10
1977 Houston 30, Maryland 21
1978 Notre Dame 38, Texas 10
1979 Notre Dame 35, Houston 34
1980 Houston 17, Nebraska 14
1981 Alabama 30, Baylor 2
1982 Texas 14, Alabama 12
1983 Southern Methodist 7, Pittsburgh 3
1984 Georgia 10, Texas 9
1985 Boston College 45, Houston 28
1986 Texas A&M 36, Auburn 16
1987 Ohio State 28, Texas A&M 12
1988 Texas A&M 35, Notre Dame 10
1989 UCLA 17, Arkansas 3

HEISMAN MEMORIAL TROPHY

Honoring the outstanding college football player in the United States, and presented by the Downtown Athletic Club of New York, this award is named for John Heisman, former player, coach, and club director.

Year	Player	College	Pos.
1935	Jay Berwanger	Chicago	HB
1936	Larry Kelley	Yale	E
1937	Clint Frank	Yale	HB
1938	Davey O'Brien	Texas Christian	QB
1939	Nile Kinnick	Iowa	HB
1940	Tom Harmon	Michigan	HB
1941	Bruce Smith	Minnesota	HB
1942	Frank Sinkwich	Georgia	HB
1943	Angelo Bertelli	Notre Dame	QB
1944	Les Horvath	Ohio State	QB
1945	Doc Blanchard[1]	Army	FB
1946	Glenn Davis	Army	HB
1947	John Lujack	Notre Dame	QB
1948	Doak Walker[1]	Southern Methodist	HB
1949	Leon Hart	Notre Dame	E
1950	Vic Janowicz[1]	Ohio State	HB
1951	Dick Kazmaier	Princeton	HB
1952	Billy Vessels	Oklahoma	HB
1953	John Lattner	Notre Dame	HB
1954	Alan Ameche	Wisconsin	FB
1955	Howard Cassady	Ohio State	HB
1956	Paul Hornung	Notre Dame	QB
1957	John Crow	Texas A&M	HB
1958	Pete Dawkins	Army	HB
1959	Billy Cannon	Louisiana State	HB
1960	Joe Bellino	Navy	HB
1961	Ernie Davis	Syracuse	HB
1962	Terry Baker	Oregon State	QB
1963	Roger Staubach[1]	Navy	QB
1964	John Huarte	Notre Dame	QB
1965	Mike Garrett	Southern California	HB
1966	Steve Spurrier	Florida	QB
1967	Gary Beban	UCLA	QB
1968	O.J. Simpson	Southern California	HB
1969	Steve Owens	Oklahoma	HB
1970	Jim Plunkett	Stanford	QB
1971	Pat Sullivan	Auburn	QB
1972	Johnny Rodgers	Nebraska	FL
1973	John Cappelletti	Penn State	HB
1974	Archie Griffin[1]	Ohio State	HB
1975	Archie Griffin	Ohio State	HB
1976	Tony Dorsett	Pittsburgh	HB
1977	Earl Campbell	Texas	HB
1978	Billy Sims[1]	Oklahoma	HB
1979	Charles White	Southern California	HB
1980	George Rogers	South Carolina	HB
1981	Marcus Allen	Southern California	HB
1982	Herschel Walker[1]	Georgia	HB
1983	Mike Rozier	Nebraska	HB
1984	Doug Flutie	Boston College	QB
1985	Bo Jackson	Auburn	HB
1986	Vinny Testaverde	Miami (Fla.)	QB
1987	Tim Brown	Notre Dame	WR
1988	Barry Sanders[1]	Oklahoma State	RB

1. Junior.

NCAA NATIONAL FOOTBALL CHAMPIONS

The NCAA Football Guide recognizes as unofficial national champion the team selected each year by press association polls. Where the Associated Press poll (of writers) does not agree with the United Press International poll (of coaches), the guide lists both teams selected.

Year	Team	Year	Team
1936	Minnesota	1963	Texas
1937	Pittsburgh	1964	Alabama
1938	Texas Christian	1965	Alabama and Michigan State
1939	Texas A&M	1966	Notre Dame
1940	Minnesota	1967	Southern California
1941	Minnesota	1968	Ohio State
1942	Ohio State	1969	Texas
1943	Notre Dame	1970	Nebraska and Texas
1944	Army	1971	Nebraska
1945	Army	1972	Southern California
1946	Notre Dame	1973	Notre Dame
1947	Notre Dame	1974	Oklahoma and Southern California
1948	Michigan		
1949	Notre Dame	1975	Oklahoma
1950	Oklahoma	1976	Pittsburgh
1951	Tennessee	1977	Notre Dame
1952	Michigan State	1978	Alabama and Southern California
1953	Maryland		
1954	Ohio State and UCLA	1979	Alabama
1955	Oklahoma	1980	Georgia
1956	Oklahoma	1981	Clemson
1957	Auburn and Ohio State	1982	Penn State
1958	Louisiana State	1983	Miami (Fla.)
1959	Syracuse	1984	Brigham Young
1960	Minnesota	1985	Oklahoma
1961	Alabama	1986	Penn State
1962	Southern California	1987	Miami (Fla.)
		1988	Notre Dame

Source: NCAA.

TRACK AND FIELD

TRACK AND FIELD WORLD RECORDS (as of Aug. 1, 1989)

MEN

Event	Record (min./sec.)	Record holder (country)	Date
100 m	9.92	Carl Lewis (U.S.)	9/24/88
200 m	19.72	Pietro Mennea (Italy)	9/17/79
400 m	43.29	Butch Reynolds (U.S.)	8/17/88
800 m	1:41.73	Sebastian Coe (G. Brit.)	6/10/81
1,500 m	3:29.46	Said Aouita (Morocco)	8/23/85
Mile	3:46.32	Steve Cram (G. Brit.)	7/27/85
Steeplechase	8:05.35	Peter Koech (Kenya)	7/3/89
5,000 m	12:58.39	Said Aouita (Morocco)	7/22/87
10,000 m	27:08.23	Arturo Barrios (Mexico)	8/18/89
Marathon	2:06:50	Belayneh Densimo (Ethiopia)	4/17/88
110-m hurdles	12.92	Roger Kingdom (U.S.)	7/16/89
400-m hurdles	47.02	Edwin Moses (U.S.)	8/31/83
20-km walk	1:18:40.00	Ernesto Canto (Mexico)	5/5/84
50-km walk	3:41:38.40	Raul Gonzales (Mexico)	5/25/79
4 x 100 m	37.83	United States	8/11/84
(Sam Graddy, Ron Brown, Calvin Smith, Carl Lewis)			
4 x 400 m	2:56.16	United States	10/20/68
(Vince Matthews 45.0, Ron Freeman 43.2, Larry James 43.8, Lee Evans 44.1)			
	2:56.16	United States	10/1/88
(Danny Everett 43.79, Steve Lewis 43.69, Kevin Robinzine 44.74, Butch Reynolds 43.94)			

Event	Record Meters	Ft./in.	Record holder (country)	Date
High jump	2.44	8-0	Javier Sotomayor (Cuba)	7/29/89
Pole vault	6.06	19-10½	Sergey Bubka (USSR)	7/9/88
Long jump	8.90	29-2½	Bob Beamon (U.S.)	10/18/68
Triple jump	17.97	58-11½	Willie Banks (U.S.)	6/16/85
Shot put	23.06	75-8	Ulf Timmermann (E. Ger.)	5/22/88
Discus	74.08	243-0	Jurgen Schult (E. Ger.)	6/6/86
Hammer	86.74	284-7	Yuriy Syedikh (USSR)	8/30/86
Javelin	87.66	287-7	Jan Zelezny (Czech.)	5/31/87
Decathlon	8,847 points		Daley Thompson (G. Brit.)	8/9/84
(10.44, 26-3½, 51-7, 6-8, 46.97, 14.33, 152-9, 16-4¾, 214-0, 4:35.00)				

WOMEN

Event	Record (min./sec.)	Record holder (country)	Date
100	10.49	Florence Griffith Joyner (U.S.)	7/16/88
200 m	21.34	Florence Griffith Joyner (U.S.)	9/29/88
400 m	47.60	Marita Koch (E. Ger.)	10/6/85
800 m	1:53.28	Jarmila Kratochvilova (Czech.)	7/26/83
1,500 m	3:52.47	Tatyana Kazankina (USSR)	8/13/80
Mile	4:15.61	Paula Ivan (Romania)	7/10/89
3,000 m	8:22.62	Tatyana Kazankina (USSR)	8/26/84
5,000 m	14:37.33	Ingrid Kristiansen (Norway)	8/5/86
10,000 m	30:13.74	Ingrid Kristiansen (Norway)	7/5/86
Marathon	2:21:06	Ingrid Kristiansen (Norway)	4/21/85
100-m hurdles	12.25	Ginka Zagorcheva (Bulgaria)	8/8/87
	12.21P	Yordanka Donkova (Bulgaria)	8/20/88
400-m hurdles	52.94	Marina Stepanova (USSR)	9/17/86
4 x 100 m	41.37	East Germany	10/6/85
(Silke Moller, Sabine Rieger, Ingrid Auerswald, Marlies Gohr)			
4 x 400 m	3:15.18	Soviet Union	10/1/88
(Tatyana Ledovskaya 50.12, Olga Nazarova 47.82, Maria Pinigina 49.43, Olga Bryzgina 47.78)			
10-km walk	43:36.41	Elena Nikolayeva (USSR)	7/30/88
	43:26.12P	Kerry Saxby (Austria)	1/26/89

Event	Record Meters	Ft./in.	Record holder (country)	Date
High jump	2.09	6-10¼	Stefka Kostadinova (Bulgaria)	8/30/87
Long jump	7.52	24-8¼	Galina Chistyakova (USSR)	6/11/88
Shot put	22.63	74-3	Natalya Lisovskaya (USSR)	6/7/87
Discus	76.80	252-0	Gabriele Reinsch (E. Ger.)	7/9/88
Javelin	80.00	262-5	Petra Felke (E. Ger.)	9/9/88
Heptathalon	7,291		Jackie Joyner-Kersee (U.S.)	9/24/88
(12.69, 6-1¼, 51-10, 22.56, 23-10¼, 149-10, 2:08.51)				
Triple jump	14.52	47-7¾	Galina Chistyakova (USSR)	2/19/89

Source: International Amateur Athletic Federation/The Athletics Congress/USA
Marks pending approval by the IAFF are denoted by P.

INDOOR WORLD RECORDS

MEN

Event	Record (min./sec.)	Record holder	Date
50 yds.	5.22	Stanley Floyd (U.S.)[1]	2/1/82
	5.00	Kirk Clayton (U.S.)[2]	10/1/70
		Herb Washington[2]	
440 yds.	46.40	Sunder Nix (U.S.)	3/3/84
500 yds.	54.40	Lee Evans (U.S.)	1/8/71
		Lee Evans (U.S.)	1/30/71
500 m	1:00.17	Ken Lowery (U.S.)	1/16/87
600 yds.	1:07.60	Martin McGrady (U.S.)	2/27/70
600 m	1:15.77	Donato Sabia (Italy)	2/4/84
800 m	1:44.91	Sebastian Coe (G. Brit.)	3/12/83
880 yds.	1:46.80	Johnny Gray (U.S.)	1/17/86
1,000 yds.	2:04.39	Johnny Gray (U.S.)	2/23/86
1,000 m	2:16.40	Rob Druppers (Holland)	2/20/88
1,500 m	3:35.60	Eamonn Coughlan (Ireland)	2/20/81
Mile	3:49.78	Eamonn Coghlan (Ireland)	2/27/83
2,000 m	4:54.07	Eamonn Coghlan (Ireland)	2/21/87
3,000 m	7:39.20	Emiel Puttemans (Belgium)	2/18/73
2 mi.	8:13.20	Emiel Puttemans (Belgium)	2/18/73
3 mi.	12:54.60	Emiel Puttemans (Belgium)	1/10/76
5,000 m	13:20.40	Suleiman Nyambi (Tanzania)	2/6/81
50-yd. hurdles	5.88	Greg Foster (U.S.)	1/17/86
50-m hurdles	6.25	Mark McKoy (Canada)	3/5/86
60-yd. hurdles	6.82	Renaldo Nehemiah (U.S.)	1/30/82
60-m hurdles	7.36	Greg Foster (U.S.)	1/16/87
110-m hurdles	13.58	Arto Bryggare (Finland)	12/30/82
1,500-m walk	5:13.53	Tim Lewis (U.S.)	2/13/88
Mile walk	5:33.53	Tim Lewis (U.S.)	2/5/88
3,000-m walk	10:54.61	Carlo Mattioli (Italy)	2/6/80
2-mi. walk	12:05.94	Jim Heiring (U.S.)	2/28/86
3-mi. walk	18:44.30	Anatoly Solomin (USSR)	3/4/77
5,000-m walk	18:27.79	Mikhail Shchennikov (USSR)	3/7/87
10-km walk	38:31.40	Werner Heyer (E. Ger.)	2/12/80
15-km walk	1:00:09	Ronald Weigel (E. Ger.)	1/27/80
20-km walk	1:20:40	Ronald Weigel (E. Ger.)	1/27/80
4 x 200 m	1:22.32	Italian National Team	2/11/84
4 x 220 yds.	1:26.90	Idaho State (U.S.)	3/6/71
4 x 400 m	3:05.90	Russian National Team	3/14/70
4 x 440 yds.	3:09.40	Pacific Coast Club (U.S.)	2/27/71
4 x 800 m	7:17.80	Russian National Team	3/14/71
4 x 880 yds.	7:20.80	Univ. of Chicago Track Club (U.S.)	2/9/74
4 x mile	16:19.00	Villanova (U.S.)	1/16/76
Sprint medley	3:18.70	Eastern Michigan (U.S.)	1/28/84
Distance medley	9:36.90	Michigan (U.S.)	2/18/83
4 x 60-yd. hurdles	27.60	Air Force Academy (U.S.)	2/22/75

Event	Record Ft./in.	Record holder (country)	Date
High jump	7-10¾	Patrik Sjoberg (Sweden)	2/1/87
	7-11¼	Carlo Thranhardt (W. Ger.)	2/26/88
Pole vault	19-7	Sergey Bubka (USSR)	3/17/87
Long jump	28-10-1/4	Carl Lewis (U.S.)	1/27/84
Triple jump	58-3-1/4	Mike Conley (U.S.)	2/27/87
Shot put	73-½	Wernew Gunthor (Switz.)	2/8/87
Weight throw	78-6-1/2	Tore Johnson (Norway)	2/25/84

WOMEN

Event	Record (min./sec.)	Record holder (country)	Date
50 yds.	5.74	Evelyn Ashford (U.S.)[1]	2/18/83
		Angella Issajenko (Canada)[1]	1/29/88
	5.50	Iris Davis (U.S.)[2]	2/2/73
		Alice Annum (Ghana)[2]	1/5/75
50 m	6.06	Angella Issajenko (Canada)[1]	1/31/87
	6.00	Barbara Ferrell (U.S.)[2]	2/17/68
		Barbara Ferrell (U.S.)[2]	2/21/69
		Renate Stecher (E. Ger.)[2]	2/14/71
		Renate Stecher (E. Ger.)[2]	2/20/71
		Renate Stecher (E. Ger.)[2]	2/28/71
		Annie Alize (France)[2]	1/15/77
		Annegret Richter (W. Ger.)[2]	3/6/77
60 yds.	6.54	Evelyn Ashford (U.S.)	2/26/82
		Jeanette Bolden (U.S.)	2/21/86
60 m	7.00	Nellie Cooman (Holland)[1]	2/23/86
	6.90	Alice Annum (Ghana)[2]	6/17/75
		Marlies Gohr (E. Ger.)[2]	2/10/79
100 yds.	10.15	Heike Drechsler (E. Ger.)	2/8/87
100 m	11.15	Marita Koch (E. Ger.)	1/12/80
200 m	22.27	Heike Drechsler (E. Ger.)	3/7/87
220 yds.	22.89	Marita Koch (E. Ger.)	2/28/86
300 yds.	32.63	Merlene Ottey (Jamaica)	3/13/82
300 m	35.83	Merlene Ottey (Jamaica)[1]	3/14/81
	35.50	Jarmila Kratochvilova (Czech.)[2]	3/7/82
400 m	49.59	Jarmila Kratochvilova (Czech.)	3/7/82
440 yds.	52.20	Diane Dixon (U.S.)	2/22/85
500 yds.	1:02.09	Diane Dixon (U.S.)	2/21/86
500 m	1:07.67	Olga Nazarova (USSR)	1/10/88
600 yds.	1:17.38	Delisa Walton (U.S.)	3/13/82
600 m	1:25.46	Lyubov Kiryukhina (USSR)	2/15/87
800 m	1:56.40	Christine Wachtel (E. Ger.)	2/13/88
880 yds.	1:59.70	Mary Decker (U.S.)	2/22/80
1,000 yds.	2:23.50	Joetta Clark (U.S.)	3/9/86
1,000 m	2:34.80	Brigitte Kraus (E. Ger.)	2/19/78
1,500 m	4:00.80	Mary Decker (U.S.)	2/8/80
Mile	4:18.86	Doina Melinte (Romania)	2/13/88
2,000 m	5:34.52	Mary Decker (U.S.)	1/18/85
3,000 m	8:39.79	Zola Budd (G. Brit.)	2/8/86
2 mi.	9:28.15	Lynn Jennings (U.S.)	2/28/86
3 mi.	14:53.80	Christine McMiken (New Zeal.)	2/22/86
5,000 m	15:34.50	Margaret Groos (U.S.)	2/20/81
50-yd. hurdles	6.20	Johanna Klier (E. Ger.)	2/10/78
50-m hurdles	6.58	Cornelia Oschkenat (E. Ger.)	2/20/88
60-yd. hurdles	7.36	Stephanie Hightower (U.S.)	2/25/83
60-m hurdles	7.74	Yordanka Donkova (Bulgaria)	2/14/87
100-m hurdles	13.12	Anneliese Ehrhardt (E. Ger.)[1]	1/14/76
	12.60	Svetlana Gusova (USSR)[2]	3/2/85
1,500-m walk	6:01.16	Maryanne Torrellas (U.S.)	2/14/87
Mile walk	6:28.46	Giuliana Salce (Italy)	2/16/85
3,000-m walk	12:05.49	Olga Krishtop (USSR)	3/6/87
5,000-m walk	21:44.52	Giuliana Salce (Italy)	2/20/85
4 x 200 m	1:32.55	SC Eintracht Hamm (W. Ger.)	2/20/88
4 x 220 yds.	1:36.50	Tennessee State (U.S.)	2/10/79
880 medley	1:41.90	The Colorado Gold (U.S.)	3/19/72
4 x 400 m	3:34.38	West German National Team	1/30/81
4 x 440 yds.	3:39.58	Morgan State (U.S.)	3/12/83
4 x 800 m	8:29.35	Florida (U.S.)	3/9/86
4 x 880 yds.	8:41.60	Russian National Team	3/17/72
Sprint medley	3:58.50	Michigan State (U.S.)	2/6/81
Distance medley	10:54.34	Villanova (U.S.)	1/30/88

Event	Record Ft./in.	Record holder (country)	Date
High jump	6-9	Stefka Kostadinova (Bulgaria)	2/20/88
Long jump	24-2¼	Heike Drechsler (E. Ger.)	2/13/88
Triple jump	45-10½	Galina Chistyakova (USSR)	1/3/87
Shot put	73-10	Helena Fibingerova (Czech.)	2/19/77

1. Timed by electronic device. 2. Timed by hand.
Source: The Athletics Congress/USA.

THOROUGHBRED RACING

KENTUCKY DERBY, 1960–89

Site: Churchill Downs, Lexington, Kentucky
Distance: 1¼ miles[1]

Year	Horse	Jockey	Time
1960	Venetian Way	W. Hartack	2:02.2
1961	Carry Back	J. Sellers	2:04.0
1962	Decidedly	W. Hartack	2:00.2
1963	Chateaugay	B. Baeza	2:01.4
1964	Northern Dancer	W. Hartack	2:00.0
1965	Lucky Debonair	W. Shoemaker	2:01.1
1966	Kauai King	D. Brumfield	2:02.0
1967	Proud Clarion	R. Ussery	2:00.3
1968	Forward Pass[2]	R. Ussery	2:02.1
1969	Majestic Prince	W. Hartack	2:01.4
1970	Dust Commander	M. Manganello	2:03.2
1971	Canonero II	G. Avila	2:03.1
1972	Riva Ridge	R. Turcotte	2:01.4
1973	Secretariat	R. Turcotte	1:59.23
1974	Cannonade	A. Cordero	2:04.0
1975	Foolish Pleasure	J. Vasquez	2:02.0
1976	Bold Forbes	A. Cordero	2:01.3
1977	Seattle Slew	J. Cruquet	2:02.1
1978	Affirmed	S. Cauthen	2:01.1
1979	Spectacular Bid	R. Franklin	2:02.2
1980	Genuine Risk	J. Vasquez	2:02.0
1981	Pleasant Colony	J. Velasquez	2:02.0
1982	Gato Del Sol	E. Delahoussaye	2:02.2
1983	Sunny's Halo	E. Delahoussaye	2:02.1
1984	Swale	L. Pincay	2:02.2
1985	Spend A Buck	A. Cordero	2:00.1
1986	Ferdinand	W. Shoemaker	2:02.4
1987	Alysheba	C. McCarron	2:03.2
1988	Winning Colors	G. Stevens	2.02.2
1989	Sunday Silence	P. Valenzuela	2:05.0

1. Prior to 1896 the distance was 1½ miles. 2. In 1968 Dancer's Image finished first but was later disqualified from the purse money, and Forward Pass was declared winner. 3. Record.
Source: *Daily Racing Form.*

PREAKNESS STAKES, 1960–89

Site: Pimlico Racetrack, Baltimore, Maryland
Distance: 1³/₁₆ miles

Year	Horse	Jockey	Time
1960	Bally Ache	R. Ussery	1:57.3
1961	Carry Back	J. Sellers	1:57.3
1962	Greek Money	J. L. Rotz	1:56.1
1963	Candy Spots	W. Shoemaker	1:56.1
1964	Northern Dancer	W. Hartack	1:56.4
1965	Tom Rolfe	R. Turcotte	1:56.1
1966	Kauai King	D. Brumfield	1:55.2
1967	Damascus	W. Shoemaker	1:55.1
1968	Forward Pass	I. Valenzuela	1:56.4
1969	Majestic Prince	W. Hartack	1:55.3
1970	Personality	E. Belmonte	1:56.1
1971	Canonero II	G. Avila	1:54.0
1972	Bee Bee Bee	E. Nelson	1:55.3
1973	Secretariat	R. Turcotte	1:54.2
1974	Little Current	M. Rivera	1:54.3
1975	Master Derby	D. McHargue	1:56.2
1976	Elocutionist	J. Lively	1:55.0
1977	Seattle Slew	J. Cruguet	1:54.2
1978	Affirmed	S. Cauthen	1:54.2
1979	Spectacular Bid	R. Franklin	1:54.1
1980	Codex	A. Cordero	1:54.1
1981	Pleasant Colony	J. Velasquez	1:54.3
1982	Aloma's Ruler	J. Kaenel	1:55.2
1983	Deputed Testamony	D. Miller	1:55.2
1984	Gate Dancer	A. Cordero	1:53.3
1985	Tank's Prospect	P. Day	1:53.2
1986	Snow Chief	A. Solis	1:54.4
1987	Alysheba	C. McCarron	1:55.4
1988	Risen Star	E. Delahoussaye	1:56.1
1989	Sunday Silence	P. Valenzuela	1:53.4

Source: *Daily Racing Form.*

BELMONT STAKES, 1960–89

Site: Belmont Park, New York
Distance: 1½ miles

Year	Horse	Jockey	Time
1960	Celtic Ash	W. Hartack	2:29.3
1961	Sherluck	B. Baeza	2:29.1
1962	Jaipur	W. Shoemaker	2:28.4
1963	Chateaugay	B. Baeza	2:30.1
1964	Quadrangle	M. Ycaza	2:28.2
1965	Hail to All	J. Sellers	2:28.2
1966	Amberoid	W. Boland	2:29.3
1967	Damascus	W. Shoemaker	2:28.4
1968	Stage Door Johnny	H. Gustines	2:27.1
1969	Arts and Letters	B. Baeza	2:28.4
1970	High Echelon	J.L. Rotz	2:34.0
1971	Pass Catcher	W. Blum	2:30.2
1972	Riva Ridge	R. Turcotte	2:28.0
1973	Secretariat	R. Turcotte	2:24.0
1974	Little Current	M. Rivera	2:29.1
1975	Avatar	W. Shoemaker	2:28.1
1976	Bold Forbes	A. Cordero	2:29.0
1977	Seattle Slew	J. Cruguet	2:29.3
1978	Affirmed	S. Cauthen	2:26.4
1979	Coastal	R. Hernandez	2:28.3
1980	Temperance Hill	E. Maple	2:29.4
1981	Summing	G. Martens	2:29.0
1982	Conquistador Cielo	L. Pincay	2:28.1
1983	Caveat	L. Pincay	2:27.4
1984	Swale	L. Pincay	2:27.1
1985	Creme Fraiche	E. Maple	2:27.0
1986	Danzig Connection	C. McCarron	2:29.4
1987	Bet Twice	C. Perret	2:28.1
1988	Risen Star	E. Delahoussaye	2:26.1
1989	Easy Goer	P. Day	2:26.0

Source: *Daily Racing Form.*

THE OLYMPIC GAMES

WINTER OLYMPICS CHAMPIONS

ALPINE SKIING—MEN

		Time
DOWNHILL		
1948	Henri Oreiller, France	2:55.00
1952	Zeno Colo, Italy	2:30.80
1956	Anton Sailer, Austria	2:52.20
1960	Jean Vuarnet, France	2:06.00
1964	Egon Zimmerman, Austria	2:18.16
1968	Jean-Claude Killy, France	1:59.85
1972	Bernhard Russi, Switzerland	1:51.43
1976	Franz Klammer, Austria	1:45.73
1980	Leonhard Stock, Austria	1:45.50
1984	William Johnson, U.S.	1:45.59
1988	Pirmin Zurbriggen, Switzerland	1:59.63
GIANT SLALOM		
1952	Stein Eriksen, Norway	2:25.00
1956	Anton Sailer, Austria	3:00.10
1960	Roger Staub, Switzerland	1:48.30
1964	François Bonlieu, France	1:46.71
1968	Jean-Claude Killy, France	3:29.28
1972	Gustavo Thöni, Italy	3:09.62
1976	Heini Hemmi, Switzerland	3:26.97
1980	Ingemar Stenmark, Sweden	2:40.74
1984	Max Julen, Switzerland	2:41.18
1988	Alberto Tomba, Italy	2:06.37
SUPER GIANT SLALOM		
1988	Frank Piccard, France	1:39.66
SLALOM		
1948	Edi Reinalter, Switzerland	2:10.30
1952	Othmar Schneider, Austria	2:00.00
1956	Anton Sailer, Austria	3:14.70
1960	Ernst Hinterseer, Austria	2:08.90
1964	Josef Stiegler, Austria	2:11.13
1968	Jean-Claude Killy, France	1:39.73
1972	Francisco Fernandez Ochoa, Spain	1:39.73
1976	Piero Gros, Italy	2:03.29
1980	Ingemar Stenmark, Sweden	1:44.26
1984	Philip Mahre, U.S.	1:39.41
1988	Alberto Tomba, Italy	1:39.47

ALPINE SKIING—WOMEN

		Time
DOWNHILL		
1948	Hedi Schlunegger, Switzerland	2:28.30
1952	Trude Jochum-Beiser, Austria	1:47.10
1956	Madeleine Berthod, Switzerland	1:40.70
1960	Heidi Biebl, Germany	1:37.60
1964	Christl Haas, Austria	1:55.39
1968	Olga Pall, Austria	1:40.87
1972	Marie-Theres Nadig, Switzerland	1:36.68
1976	Rosi Mittermaier, West Germany	1:46.16
1980	Annemarie Moser-Pröll, Austria	1:37.52
1984	Michela Figini, Switzerland	1:13.361
1988	Marina Kiehl, West Germany	1:25.86
1. Race shortened by weather conditions.		

GIANT SLALOM

1952	Andrea Mead Lawrence, U.S.	2:06.80
1956	Ossi Reichert, Germany	1:56.50
1960	Yvonne Rüegg, Switzerland	1:39.90
1964	Marielle Goitschel, France	1:52.24
1968	Nancy Greene, Canada	1:51.97
1972	Marie-Theres Nadig, Switzerland	1:29.90
1976	Kathy Kreiner, Canada	1:29.13
1980	Hanni Wenzel, Liechtenstein	2:41.66
1984	Debbie Armstrong, U.S.	2:20.98
1988	Vreni Schneider, Switzerland	2:06.49

SUPER GIANT SLALOM

1988	Sigrid Wolf, Austria	1:19.03

SLALOM

1948	Gretchen Fraser, U.S.	1:57.20
1952	Andrea Mead Lawrence, U.S.	2:10.60
1956	Renée Colliard, Switzerland	1:52.30
1960	Anne Heggtveigt, Canada	1:49.60
1964	Christine Goitschel, France	1:29.86
1968	Marielle Goitschel, France	1:25.86
1972	Barbara Cochran, U.S.	1:31.24
1976	Rosi Mittermaier, West Germany	1:30.54
1980	Hanni Wenzel, Liechtenstein	1:25.09
1984	Paoletta Magoni, Italy	1:36.47
1988	Vreni Schneider, Switzerland	1:36.69

NORDIC SKIING AND JUMPING—MEN

		Time
15-KILOMETER (9.3-MI.) CROSS-COUNTRY		
1968	Harald Grönningen, Norway	47:54.20
1972	Sven-Ake Lundbäck, Sweden	45:28.24
1976	Nikolai Bazhukov, USSR	43:58.47
1980	Thomas Wassberg, Sweden	41:57.63
1984	Gunde Svan	41:25.60
1988	Mikhail Deviatiarov, USSR	41:18.90

30-KILOMETER (18.6-MI.) CROSS-COUNTRY

1956	Veikko Hakulinen, Finland	1:44:06.00
1960	Sixten Jernberg, Sweden	1:51:03.90
1964	Eero Mäntyranta, Finland	1:30:50.70
1968	Franco Nones, Italy	1:35:39.20
1972	Vyacheslav Vedenin, USSR	1:36:31.15
1976	Sergei Saveliev, USSR	1:30:29.38
1980	Nikolai Zimyatov, USSR	1:27:02.80
1984	Nikolai Zimyatov, USSR	1:28:56.30
1988	Aleksei Prokourorov, USSR	1:24:26.30

SKI JUMP

		Points
70-METER (229.7 FT.)		
1964	Veikko Kankkonen, Finland	229.90
1968	Jiri Raska, Czechoslovakia	216.50
1972	Yukio Kasaya, Japan	244.20
1976	Hans-Georg Aschenbach, East Germany	252.00
1980	Anton Innauer, Austria	266.30
1984	Jens Weissflog, East Germany	215.20
1988	Matti Nykänen, Finland	229.10
90-METER (295.3 FT.) JUMP		
1924	Jacob Tullin Thambs, Norway	18.960
1928	Alf Andersen, Norway	19.208
1932	Birger Ruud, Norway	228.10
1936	Birger Ruud, Norway	232.00
1948	Petter Hugsted, Norway	228.10
1952	Arnfinn Bergmann, Norway	226.00
1956	Antti Hyvarinen, Finland	227.00
1960	Hulmut Recknagel, Germany	227.20
1964	Toralf Engan, Norway	230.70
1968	Vladimir Beloussov, USSR	231.30
1972	Wojiech Fortuna, Poland	219.90
1976	Karl Schnabl, Austria	234.80
1980	Jouko Tormanen, Finland	271.00
1984	Matti Nykänen, Finland	231.20
1988	Matti Nykänen, Finland	224.00

THE WINTER GAMES

Olympics/year		Place	COMPETITORS		NATIONS REPRESENTED
			Men	Women	
I	1924	Chamonix, France	281	13	16
II	1928	St. Moritz, Switzerland	468	27	25
III	1932	Lake Placid, U.S.	274	32	17
IV	1936	Garmisch-Partenkirchen, Germany	675	80	28
V	1948	St. Moritz, Switzerland	636	77	28
VI	1952	Oslo, Norway	623	109	30
VII	1956	Cortina D'Ampezzo, Italy	686	132	32
VIII	1960	Squaw Valley, U.S.	521	144	30
IX	1964	Innsbruck, Austria	986	200	36
X	1968	Grenoble, France	1,081	212	37
XI	1972	Sapporo, Japan	1,015	217	35
XII	1976	Innsbruck, Austria	900	228	37
XIII	1980	Lake Placid, U.S.	833	234	37
XIV	1984	Sarajevo, Yugoslavia	1,002	276	49
XV	1988	Calgary, Canada	1,445 (total)		57

Sources: David Wallechinsky, *The Complete Book of the Olympics* (1988), reprinted by permission; U.S. Olympic Committee.

NORDIC SKIING—WOMEN

10-KILOMETER (6.2-MI.) CROSS-COUNTRY

	Time
1952 Lydia Wideman, Finland	41:40.00
1956 Lyubov Kosyreva, USSR	38:11.00
1960 Maria Gusakova, USSR	39:46.60
1964 Claudia Boyarskikh, USSR	40:24.30
1968 Toini Gustafsson, Sweden	36:46.50
1972 Galina Kolakova, USSR	34:17.82
1976 Raisa Smetanina, USSR	30:31.54
1980 Barbara Petzold, East Germany	30:31.54
1984 Marja-Liisa Hämäläinen, Finland	31:44.20
1988 Vida Ventsene, USSR	30:08.20

20-KILOMETER (12.4 MI.) CROSS-COUNTRY

1984 Marja-Liisa Hämäläinen, Finland	1:01:45.00
1988 Tamara Tikhonova, USSR	55:53.60

ICE HOCKEY

1920 Canada, U.S., Czechoslovakia
1924 Canada, U.S., Great Britain
1928 Canada, Sweden, Switzerland
1932 Canada, U.S., Germany
1936 Great Britain, Canada, U.S.
1948 Canada, Czechoslovakia, Switzerland
1952 Canada, U.S., Sweden
1956 USSR, U.S., Canada
1960 U.S., Canada, USSR
1964 USSR, Sweden, Czechoslovakia
1968 USSR, Czechoslovakia, Canada
1972 USSR, U.S., Czechoslovakia
1976 USSR, Czechoslovakia
1980 U.S., USSR, Sweden
1984 USSR, Czechoslovakia, Sweden
1988 USSR, Finland, Sweden

LUGE

SINGLES (men)

	Time
1964 Thomas Köhler, East Germany	3:26.77
1968 Manfred Schmid, Austria	2:52.48
1972 Wolfgang Scheidel, East Germany	3:27.58
1976 Dettlef Günther, East Germany	3:27.68
1980 Bernhard Glass, East Germany	2:54.79
1984 Paul Hildgartner, Italy	3:04.25
1988 Jens Mueller, East Germany	3:05.54

TWO-SEATER (men)

	Time
1964 Austria	1:41.62
1968 East Germany	1:35.85
1972 Italy, East Germany (tie)	1:28.35
1976 East Germany	1:25.60
1980 East Germany	1:19.33
1984 West Germany	1:23.62
1988 East Germany	1:31.94

SINGLES (women)

	Time
1964 Ortrun Enderlein, East Germany	3:24.67
1968 Erica Lechner, Italy	2:28.66
1972 Anna M. Müller, East Germany	2:59.18
1976 Margit Schumann, East Germany	2:50.62
1980 Vera Zozulya, USSR	2:36.53
1984 Steffi Martin, East Germany	2:46.57
1988 Steffi Walter, East Germany	3:03.97

BOBSLEDDING

TWO-MAN

	Time		Time
1932 U.S.	8:14.74	1968 Italy	4:41.54
1936 U.S.	5:29.29	1972 West Germany	4:57.07
1948 Switzerland	5:29.20	1976 East Germany	3:44.42
1952 Germany	5:24.54	1980 Switzerland	4:09.36
1956 Italy	5:30.14	1984 East Germany	3:25.56
1964 Great Britain	4:21.90	1988 USSR	3:54.19

FOUR-MAN

1924 Switzerland	5:45.54	1964 Canada	4:14.46
1928 U.S. (5-Man)	3:20.50	1968 Italy (2 races)	2:17.39
1932 U.S.	7:53.68	1972 Switzerland	4:43.07
1936 Switzerland	5:19.85	1976 East Germany	3:40.43
1948 U.S.	5:20.10	1980 East Germany	3:59.42
1952 Germany	5:07.84	1984 East Germany	3:20.22
1956 Switzerland	5:10.44	1988 Switzerland	3:47.51

FIGURE SKATING

MEN

1908 Ulrich Salchow, Sweden
1920 Gillis Grafstrom, Sweden
1924 Gillis Grafstrom Sweden
1928 Gillis Grafstrom, Sweden
1932 Karl Schafer, Austria
1936 Karl Schafer, Austria
1948 Richard Button, U.S.
1952 Richard Button, U.S.
1956 Hayes Alan Jenkins, U.S.
1960 David W. Jenkins, U.S.
1964 Manfred Schnelldorfer, Germany
1968 Wolfgang Schwartz, Austria
1972 Ondrej Nepela, Czechoslovakia
1976 John Curry, Great Britain
1980 Robin Cousins, Great Britain
1984 Scott Hamilton, U.S.
1988 Brian Boitano, U.S.

WOMEN

1908 Madge Syers, Great Britain
1920 Magda Julin-Mauroy, Sweden
1924 Heima von Szabo-Planck, Austria
1928 Sonja Henie, Norway
1932 Sonja Henie, Norway
1936 Sonja Henie, Norway
1948 Barbara Ann Scott, Canada
1952 Jeanette Altwegg, Great Britain
1956 Tenley Albright, U.S.
1960 Carol Heiss, U.S.
1964 Sjoukje Dijkstra, Netherlands
1968 Peggy Fleming, U.S.
1972 Beatrix Schuba, Austria
1976 Dorothy Hamill, U.S.
1980 Annett Pötzsch, East Germany
1984 Katarina Witt, East Germany
1988 Katarina Witt, East Germany

PAIRS

1908 Germany—Anna Hubler, Heinrich Burger
1920 Finland—Ludovika & Walter Jakobsson
1924 Austria—Helene Engelman, Alfred Berger
1928 France—Andrée Joly, Pierre Brunet
1932 France—Andrée Joly, Pierre Brunet
1936 Germany—Maxie Herber, Ernst Baier
1948 Belgium—Micheline Lannoy, Pierre Baugniet
1952 Germany—Ria & Paul Falk
1956 Austria—Elisabeth Schwartz, Kurt Oppelt
1960 Canada—Barbara Wagner, Robert Paul
1964 USSR—Ludmila Beloussova, Oleg Protopopov
1968 USSR—Ludmila Beloussova, Oleg Protopopov
1972 USSR—Irina Rodnina, Alexei Ulanov
1976 USSR—Irina Rodnina, Aleksandr Zaitsev
1980 USSR—Irina Rodnina, Aleksandr Zaitsev
1984 USSR—Elena Valova, Oleg Vassiliev
1988 USSR—Ekaterina Gordeeva, Sergei Grinko

SPEED SKATING—MEN

500 METERS (1,641 FT.)

	Time
1924 Charles Jewtraw, U.S.	0:44.00
1928 Clas Thunberg, Finland, and Bernst Evensen, Norway (tie)	0:43.40
1932 John A. Shea, U.S.	0:43.40
1936 Ivar Ballangrud, Norway	0:43.40
1948 Finn Helgesen, Norway	0:43.10
1952 Ken Henry, U.S.	0:43.20
1956 Yevgeny Grishin, USSR	0:40.20
1960 Yevgeny Grishin, USSR	0:40.20
1964 Terry McDermott, U.S.	0:40.10
1968 Erhard Keller, West Germany	0.40.30
1972 Erhard Keller, West Germany	0.39.40
1976 Yergeny Kulikov, USSR	0:39.17
1980 Eric Heiden, U.S.	0:38.03
1984 Sergei Fokichev, USSR	0:38.19
1988 Jens-Uwe Mey, East Germany	0:36.45

1,000 METERS (3,281 FT.)

1976 Peter Mueller, U.S.	1:19.32
1980 Eric Heiden, U.S.	1:15.18
1984 Gaétan Boucher, Canada	1:15.80
1988 Nikolai Guiliaev, USSR	1:13.03

1,500 METERS (4,922 FT.)

1924 Clas Thunberg, Finland	2:20.80
1928 Clas Thunberg, Finland	2:21.10
1932 John A. Shea, U.S.	2:57.50
1936 Charles Mathisen, Norway	2:19.20
1948 Sverre Farstad, Norway	2:17.60
1952 Hjalmar Andersen, Norway	2:20.40
1956 Yevgeni Grishin and Yuri Mikhailov, USSR (tie)	2:08.60
1960 Roald Aas, Norway, and Yevgeni Grishin, USSR (tie)	2:10.40
1964 Ants Anston, USSR	2:10.30
1968 Cornelis Verkerk, Netherlands	2:03.40
1972 Ard Schenk, Netherlands	2:02.90
1976 Jan Egil Storholt, Norway	1:59.38
1980 Eric Heiden, U.S.	1:55.40
1984 Gaétan Boucher, Canada	1:58.36
1988 Andre Hoffmann, East Germany	1:52.06

5,000 METERS (16,405 FT.)

1924 Clas Thunberg, Finland	8:39.00
1928 Ivar Ballangrud, Norway	8:50.50
1932 Irving Jaffee, U.S.	9:40.80
1936 Ivar Ballangrud, Norway	8:19.60
1948 Reidar Liaklev, Norway	8:29.40
1952 Hjalmar Andersen, Norway	8:10.60
1956 Boris Shilkov, USSR	7:48.70
1960 Viktor Kosichkin, USSR	7:51.30
1964 Knut Johannesen, Norway	7:38.40
1968 F. Anton Maier, Norway	7:22.40
1972 Ard Schenk, Netherlands	7:23.61
1976 Sten Stensen, Norway	7:24.48
1980 Eric Heiden, U.S.	7:02.29
1984 Sven Tomas Gustafson, Sweden	7:12.28
1988 Tomas Gustafson, Sweden	6:44:63

10,000 METERS (32,810 FT.)

1924 Julien Skutnabb, Finland	18:04.80
1928 (ice thawed, so event canceled)	
1932 Irving Jaffee, U.S.	19:13.60
1936 Ivar Ballangrud, Norway	17:24.30
1948 Ake Seyffarth, Sweden	17:26.30
1952 Hjalmar Andersen, Norway	16:45.80
1956 Sigvard Ericsson, Sweden	16:35.90
1960 Knut Johannessen, Norway	15:46.60
1964 Jonny Nilsson, Sweden	15:50.10
1968 Johnny Hoeglin, Sweden	15:23.60
1972 Ard Schenk, Netherlands	15:01.30
1976 Piet Kleine, Netherlands	14:50.59
1980 Eric Heiden, U.S.	14:28.13
1984 Igor Malikov, USSR	14:39.90
1988 Tomas Gustafson, Sweden	13:48.20

SPEED SKATING—WOMEN

500 Meters (1,641 ft.)

	Time
1960 Helga Haase, Germany	0:45.90
1964 Lydia Skoblikova, USSR	0:45.00
1968 Ludmila Titova, USSR	0:46.10
1972 Anne Henning, U.S.	0:43.30
1976 Sheila Young, U.S.	0:42.76
1980 Karin Enke, East Germany	0:41.78
1984 Christa Rothenburger, East Germany	0:41.02
1988 Bonnie Blair, U.S.	0:39.10

1,000 METERS (3,281 FT.)

1960 Klara Guseva, USSR	1:34.10
1964 Lydia Skoblikova, USSR	1:33.20
1968 Carolina Geiissen, Netherlands	1:32.60
1972 Monika Pflug, West Germany	1:31.40
1976 Tatiana Averina, USSR	1:28.43
1980 Natalia Petruseva, USSR	1:24.10
1984 Karin Enke, East Germany	1:21.61
1988 Christa Rothenburger, East Germany	1:17.65

1,500 METERS (4,922 FT.)

1960 Lydia Skoblikova, USSR	2:25.20
1964 Lydia Skoblikova, USSR	2:22.60
1968 Kaija Mustonen, Finland	2:22.40
1972 Dianne Holum, U.S.	2:20.80
1976 Galina Stepanskaya, USSR	2:16.58
1980 Annie Borchink, Netherlands	2:10.95
1984 Karin Enke, East Germany	2:03.42
1988 Yvonne Van Gennip, Netherlands	2:00.68

3,000 METERS (9,843 FT.)

1960 Lydia Skoblikova, USSR	5:14.30
1964 Lydia Skoblikova, USSR	5:14.90
1968 Johanna Schut, Netherlands	4:56.20
1972 Stien Kaiser-Baas, Netherlands	4:52.10
1976 Tatiana Averina, USSR	4:45.19
1980 Bjoerg Eva Jensen, Norway	4:32.13
1984 Andrea Schöne, East Germany	4:24.79
1988 Yvonne Van Gennip, Netherlands	4:11.94

Summer Olympics Champions

SWIMMING AND DIVING—MEN

Year Champion, country	Time
50-METER FREESTYLE	**Min./sec.**
1988 Matt Biondi, U.S.	22.14
100-METER FREESTYLE	
1896 Alfred Hajos, Hungary	1:22.20
1904 Zoltan de Halmay, Hungary (100 yds.)	1:02.80
1908 Charles Daniels, U.S.	1:05.60
1912 Duke Kahanamoku, U.S.	1:03.40
1920 Duke Kahanamoku, U.S.	1:01.40
1924 John Weissmuller, U.S.	0:59.00
1928 John Weissmuller, U.S.	0:58.60
1932 Yasuji Miyazaki, Japan	0:58.20
1936 Ferenc Csik, Hungary	0:57.60
1948 Walter Ris, U.S.	0:57.30
1952 Clarke Scholes, U.S.	0:57.40
1956 Jon Hendricks, Australia	0:55.40
1960 John Devitt, Australia	0:55.20
1964 Donald A. Schollandler, U.S.	0:53.40
1968 Michael Wenden, Australia	0:52.20
1972 Mark Spitz, U.S.	0:51.20
1976 Jim Montgomery, U.S.	0:49.99
1980 Jorg Woithe, East Germany	0:50.40
1984 Ambrose ("Rowdy") Gaines, U.S.	0:49.80
1988 Matt Biondi, U.S.	0:48.63
200-METER FREESTYLE	
1968 Michael Wenden, Australia	1:55.20
1972 Mark Spitz, U.S.	1:52.80
1976 Bruce Furniss, U.S.	1:50.29
1980 Sergei Kopliakov, USSR	1:49.81
1984 Michael Gross, West Germany	1:47.44
1988 Duncan Armstrong, Australia	1:47.25
400-METER FREESTYLE	
1896 Paul Neumann, Austria (500 m)	8:12.60
1904 Charles Daniels, U.S. (440 yds.)	6:16.20
1908 Henry Taylor, Great Britain	5:36.80
1912 George Hodgson, Canada	5:24.40
1920 Norman Ross, U.S.	5:26.80
1924 John Weissmuller, U.S.	5:04.20
1928 Albert Zorilla, Argentina	5:01.60
1932 Clarence "Buster" Crabbe, U.S.	4:48.40
1936 Jack Medica, U.S.	4:44.50
1948 William Smith, U.S.	4:41.00
1952 Jean Boiteux, France	4:30.70
1956 Murray Rose, Australia	4:27.30
1960 Murray Rose, Australia	4:18.30
1964 Donald A. Schollander, U.S.	4:12.20
1968 Michael Burton, U.S.	4:09.00
1972 Bradford Cooper, Australia	4:00.30
1976 Brian Goodell, U.S.	3:51.93
1980 Vladimir Salnikov, USSR	3:51.31
1984 George DiCarlo, U.S.	3:51.23
1988 Ewe Dassler, East Germany	3:46.95
1,500-METER FREESTYLE	
1896 Alfred Hajos, Hungary (1,200 m)	18:22.20
1900 John Jarvis, Great Britain (1,000 m)	13:40.20
1904 Emil Rausch, Germany (1,609 m)	27:18.20
1908 Henry Taylor, Great Britain	22:48.40
1912 George Hodgson, Canada	22:00.00
1920 Norman Ross, U.S.	22:23.20
1924 Andrew Charlton, Australia	20:06.60
1928 Arne Borg, Sweden	19:51.80
1932 Kusuo Kitamura, Japan	19:12.40
1936 Noboru Terada, Japan	19:13.70
1948 James P. McLane, U.S.	19:18.50
1952 Ford Konno, U.S.	18:30.00
1956 Murray Rose, Australia	17:58.90
1960 John Konrads, Australia	17:19.60
1964 Robert Windle, Australia	17:01.70
1968 Michael Burton, U.S.	16:38.90
1972 Michael Burton, U.S.	15:52.60
1976 Brian Goodell, U.S.	15:02.40
1980 Vladimir Salnikov, USSR	14:58.27
1984 Michael O'Brien, U.S.	15:05.20
1988 Vladimir Salnikov, USSR	15:00.40
200-METER BREASTSTROKE	
1908 Frederick Holman, Great Britain	3:09.20
1912 Walter Bathe, Germany	3:01.80

THE SUMMER GAMES

			Competitors Men	Competitors Women	Nations represented
I	1896	Athens, Greece	311	—	13
II	1900	Paris, France	1,319	11	22
III	1904	St. Louis, U.S.	681	6	12
—	1906	Athens, Greece	877	7	20
IV	1908	London, UK	1,999	36	23
V	1912	Stockholm, Sweden	2,490	57	28
VI	1916	Berlin, Germany	—	—	—
VII	1920	Antwerp, Belgium	2,543	64	29
VIII	1924	Paris, France	2,956	136	44
IX	1928	Amsterdam, Holland	2,724	290	46
X	1932	Los Angeles, U.S.	1,281	127	37
XI	1936	Berlin, Germany	3,738	328	49
XII	1948	London, UK	3,714	385	59
XIII	1952	Helsinki, Finland	4,407	518	69
XIV	1960	Rome, Italy	4,738	610	83
XV	1964	Tokyo, Japan	4,457	683	93
XVI	1968	Mexico City, Mexico	4,750	781	112
XVII	1972	Munich, Germany	5,848	1,299	122
XVIII	1976	Montreal, Canada	4,834	1,251	92
XIX	1980	Moscow, USSR	4,265	1,088	81
XX	1984	Los Angeles, U.S.	5,458	1,620	141
XXI	1988	Seoul, South Korea	9,593 (total)[1]		160

1. Gender breakdown not available. **Source:** David Wallechinsky, *The Complete Book of the Olympics* (1988), reprinted by permission.

1920	Haken Malmroth, Sweden	3:04.40
1924	Robert Skelton, U.S.	2:56.60
1928	Yoshiyuki Tsuruta, Japan	2:48.80
1932	Yoshiyuki Tsuruta, Japan	2:45.40
1936	Tetsuo Hamuro, Japan	2:41.50
1948	Joseph Verdeur, U.S.	2:39.30
1952	John Davies, Australia	2:34.40
1956	Masura Furukawa, Japan	2:34.70
1960	William Mulliken, U.S.	2:37.40
1964	Ian O'Brien, Australia	2:27.80
1968	Felipe Muñoz, Mexico	2:28.70
1972	John Hencken, U.S.	2:21.50
1976	David Wilkie, Great Britain	2:15.11
1980	Robertas Zhulpa, USSR	2:15.85
1984	Victor Davis, Canada	2:13.34
1988	Jozsef Szabo, Hungary	2:13.52

100-METER BUTTERFLY

1968	Douglas Russell, U.S.	0:55.90
1972	Mark Spitz, U.S.	0:54.30
1976	Matt Vogel, U.S.	0:54.35
1980	Par Arvidsson, Sweden	0:54.92
1984	Michael Gross, West Germany	0:53.08
1988	Anthony Nesty, Suriname	0:53.00

200-METER BUTTERFLY

1956	William Yorzyk, U.S.	2:19.30
1960	Michael Troy, U.S.	2:12.80
1964	Kevin Berry, Australia	2:06.60
1968	Carl Robie, U.S.	2:08.70
1972	Mark Spitz, U.S.	2:00.70
1976	Michael Bruner, U.S.	1:59.23
1980	Sergei Fesenko, USSR	1:59.76
1984	Jon Sieben, Australia	1:57.04
1988	Michael Gross, West Germany	1:56.94

200-METER INDIVIDUAL MEDLEY

1968	Charles Hickcox, U.S.	2:12.00
1972	Gunnar Larsson, Sweden	2:07.20
1984	Alex Baumann, Canada	2:01.42
1988	Tamas Darnyi, Hungary	2:00.17

100-METER BACKSTROKE

1904	Walter Brack, Germany (100 yds.)	1:16.80
1908	Arno Bieberstein, Germany	1:24.60
1912	Harry Hebner, U.S.	1:21.20
1920	Warren Kealoha, U.S.	1:15.20
1924	Warren Kealoha, U.S.	1:13.20
1928	George Kojac, U.S.	1:08.20
1932	Masaji Kiyokawa, Japan	1:08.60
1936	Adolph Kiefer, U.S.	1:05.90
1948	Allen Stack, U.S.	1:06.40
1952	Yoshinobu Oyakawa, U.S.	1:05.40
1956	David Thiele, Australia	1:02.20
1960	David Thiele, Australia	1:01.90
1964	Not on program	
1968	Roland Matthes, East Germany	0:58.70
1972	Roland Matthes, East Germany	0:56.60
1976	John Naber, U.S.	0:55.49
1980	Bengt Baron, Sweden	0:56.33
1984	Richard Carey, U.S.	0:55.79
1988	Daichi Suzuki, Japan	0:55.05

200-METER BACKSTROKE

1900	Ernest Hoppenberg, Germany	2:47.00
1964	Jed R. Graef, U.S.	2:10.30
1968	Roland Matthes, East Germany	2:09.60
1972	Roland Matthes, East Germany	2:02.80
1976	John Naber, U.S.	1:59.19
1980	Sandor Wladar, Hungary	2:01.93
1984	Richard Carey, U.S.	2:00.23
1988	Igor Polianski, USSR	1:59.37

100-METER BREASTSTROKE

1968	Donald McKenzie, U.S.	1:07.70
1972	Nobutaka Taguchi, Japan	1:04.90
1976	John Hencken, U.S.	1:03.11
1980	Duncan Goodhen, Great Britain	1:03.44
1984	Steve Lundquist, U.S.	1:01.99
1988	Adrian Moorhouse, Great Britain	1:02.04

400-METER INDIVIDUAL MEDLEY

1964	Richard W. Roth, U.S.	4:45.40
1968	Charles Hickcox, U.S.	4:48.40
1972	Gunnar Larsson, Sweden	4:32.00
1976	Rod Strachan, U.S.	4:23.68
1980	Aleksandr Sidorenko, USSR	4:22.89
1984	Alex Baumann, Canada	4:17.41
1988	Tamas Darnyi, Hungary	4:14.75

400-METER FREESTYLE RELAY

1964	U.S.	3:33.20	1984	U.S.	3:19.03
1968	U.S.	3:31.70	1988	U.S.	3:16.53
1972	U.S.	3:26.40			

400-METER MEDLEY RELAY

1960	U.S.	4:05.40	1976	U.S.	3:42.22
1964	U.S.	3:58.40	1980	Australia	3:45.70
1968	U.S.	3:54.90	1984	U.S.	3:39.30
1972	U.S.	3:48.20	1988	U.S.	3:36.93

800-METER FREESTYLE RELAY

1908	Great Britain	10:55.60	1956	Australia	8:23.60
1912	Australia	10:11.20	1960	U.S.	8:10.20
1920	U.S.	10:04.40	1964	U.S.	7:52.10
1924	U.S.	9:53.40	1968	U.S.	7:52.30
1928	U.S.	9:36.20	1972	U.S.	7:38.80
1932	Japan	8:58.20	1976	U.S.	7:23.22
1936	Japan	8:51.50	1980	USSR	7:23.50
1948	U.S.	8:31.10	1984	U.S.	7:15.69
1952	U.S.	8:31.10	1988	U.S.	7:12.51

SPRINGBOARD DIVING		**Points**
1908	Albert Zurner, Germany	85.50
1912	Paul Guenther, Germany	79.23
1920	Louis Kuehn, U.S.	675.00
1924	Albert C. White, U.S.	696.40
1928	Pete Desjardins, U.S.	185.04
1932	Michael Galitzen, U.S.	161.38
1936	Richard Degener, U.S.	163.57
1948	Bruce Harlan, U.S.	163.64
1952	David Browning, U.S.	205.29
1956	Robert L. Clotworthy, U.S.	159.56
1960	Gary Tobian, U.S.	170.00
1964	Kenneth R. Sitzberger, U.S.	159.90
1968	Bernard Wrightson, U.S.	170.15
1972	Vladimir Vasin, USSR	594.09
1976	Phil Boggs, U.S.	619.52
1980	Aleksandr Portnov, USSR	905.02
1984	Gregory Louganis, U.S.	754.41
1988	Gregory Louganis, U.S.	730.80

PLATFORM DIVING

1904	Dr. G. E. Sheldon, U.S.	12.75
1908	Hjalmar Johansson, Sweden	83.75
1912	Erik Adlerz, Sweden	73.94
1920	Clarence Pinkston, U.S.	100.67
1924	Albert C. White, U.S.	97.46
1928	Pete Desjardins, U.S.	98.74
1932	Harold Smith, U.S.	124.80
1936	Marshall Wayne, U.S.	113.58
1948	Dr. Samuel Lee, U.S.	130.05
1952	Dr. Samuel Lee, U.S.	156.28
1956	Joaquin Capilla, Mexico	152.44
1960	Robert Webster, U.S.	165.56
1964	Robert Webster, U.S.	148.58
1968	Klaus DiBiasi, Italy	164.18
1972	Klaus DiBiasi, Italy	504.12
1976	Klaus DiBiasi, Italy	600.51
1980	Falk Hoffmann, East Germany	835.65
1984	Gregory Louganis, U.S.	710.91
1988	Gregory Louganis, U.S.	638.61

SWIMMING AND DIVING—WOMEN

50-METER FREESTYLE

1988	Kristin Otto, East Germany	25.49

100-METER FREESTYLE

1912	Fanny Durack, Australia	1:22.20
1920	Ethelda Bleibtrey, U.S.	1:13.60
1924	Ethel Lackie, U.S.	1:12.40
1928	Albina Osipowich, U.S.	1:11.00
1932	Helene Madison, U.S.	1:06.80
1936	Hendrika Mastenbroek, Netherlands	1:05.90
1948	Greta Andersen, Denmark	1:06.30
1952	Katalin Szoke, Hungary	1:06.80
1956	Dawn Fraser, Australia	1:02.00
1960	Dawn Fraser, Australia	1:01.20
1964	Dawn Fraser, Australia	0:59.50
1968	Margo Jan Henne, U.S.	1:00.00
1972	Sandra Neilson, U.S.	0:58.60
1976	Kornelia Ender, East Germany	0:55.65
1980	Barbara Krause, East Germany	0:54.79
1984	Nancy Hogshead, U.S.	0:55.92
1988	Kristin Otto, East Germany	0:54.93

200-METER FREESTYLE

1968	Deborah Meyer, U.S.	2:10.50
1972	Shane Gould, Australia	2:03.60
1976	Kornelia Ender, East Germany	1:59.26
1980	Barbara Krause, East Germany	1:58.33
1984	Mary Wayte, U.S.	1:59.23
1988	Heike Friederich, East Germany	1:57.65

400-METER FREESTYLE

1920	Ethelda Bleibtrey, U.S. (300 m)	4:34.00
1924	Martha Norelius, U.S.	6:02.20
1928	Martha Norelius, U.S.	5:42.40
1932	Helene Madison, U.S.	5:28.50
1936	Hendrika Mastenbroek, Netherlands	5:26.40
1948	Ann Curtis, U.S.	5:17.80
1952	Valeria Gyenge, Hungary	5:12.10
1956	Lorraine Crapp, Australia	4:54.60
1960	S. Chris Von Saltza, U.S.	4:50.60
1964	Virginia Duenkel, U.S.	4:43.30
1968	Deborah Meyer, U.S.	4:31.80
1972	Shane Gould, Australia	4:19.00
1976	Petra Thuemer, East Germany	4:09.89
1980	Ines Diers, East Germany	4:08.76
1984	Tiffany Cohen, U.S.	4:07.10
1988	Janet Evans, U.S.	4:03.85

800-METER FREESTYLE

1968	Deborah Meyer, U.S.	9:24.00
1972	Keena Rothhammer, U.S.	8:53.70
1976	Petra Thuemer, East Germany	8:37.14
1980	Michelle Ford, Australia	8:28.90
1984	Tiffany Cohen, U.S.	8:24.95
1988	Janet Evans, U.S.	8:20.20

100-METER BACKSTROKE

1924	Sybil Bauer, U.S.	1:23.20
1928	Marie Braun, Netherlands	1:22.00
1932	Eleanor Holm, U.S.	1:19.40
1936	Dina Senff, Netherlands	1:18.90
1948	Karen Harup, Denmark	1:14.40
1952	Joan Harrison, South Africa	1:14.30
1956	Judy Grinham, Great Britain	1:12.90
1960	Lynn Burke, U.S.	1:09.30
1964	Cathy Ferguson, U.S.	1:07.70
1968	Kaye Hall, U.S.	1:06.20
1972	Melissa Belote, U.S.	1:05.80
1976	Ulrike Richter, East Germany	1:01.83
1980	Rica Reinisch, East Germany	1:00.86
1984	Theresa Andrews, U.S.	1:02.55
1988	Kristin Otto, East Germany	1:00.89

200-METER BACKSTROKE

1968	Lillian "Pokey" Watson, U.S.	2:24.80
1972	Melissa Belote, U.S.	2:19.20
1976	Ulrike Richter, East Germany	2:13.43
1980	Rica Reinisch, East Germany	2:11.77
1984	Jolanda de Rover, Netherlands	2:12.38
1988	Krisztina Egerszegi, Hungary	2:09.29

100-METER BUTTERFLY

1956	Shelley Mann, U.S.	1:11.00
1960	Carolyn Schuler, U.S.	1:09.50
1964	Sharon Stouder, U.S.	1:04.70
1968	Lynn McClements, Australia	1:05.50
1972	Mayumi Aoki, Japan	1:03.30
1976	Kornelia Ender, East Germany	1:00.13
1980	Caren Metschuck, East Germany	1:00.42
1984	Mary T. Meagher, U.S.	0:59.26
1988	Kristin Otto, East Germany	0:59.00

200-METER BUTTERFLY

1968	Ada Kok, Netherlands	2:24.70
1972	Karen Moe, U.S.	2:15.60
1976	Andrea Pollack, East Germany	2:11.41
1980	Ines Geissler, East Germany	2:10.44
1984	Mary T. Meagher, U.S.	2:06.90
1988	Kathleen Nord, East Germany	2:09.51

100-METER BREASTSTROKE

1968	Djurdjica Bjedov, Yugoslavia	1:15.80
1972	Cathy Carr, U.S.	1:13.60
1976	Hannelore Anke, East Germany	1:11.16
1980	Ute Geweniger, East Germany	1:10.22
1984	Petra Van Staveren, Netherlands	1:09.69
1988	Tania Dangalakova, Bulgaria	1:07.95

200-METER BREASTSTROKE

1924	Lucy Morton, Great Britain	3:33.20
1928	Hilde Schrader, Germany	3:12.60
1932	Clare Dennis, Australia	3:06.30
1936	Hideko Maehata, Japan	3:03.60
1948	Nelly Van Vliet, Netherlands	2:57.20
1952	Eva Szekely, Hungary	2:51.70
1956	Ursula Happe, Germany	2:53.10
1960	Anita Lonsbrough, Great Britain	2:49.50
1964	Galina Prozumenshikova, USSR	2:46.40
1968	Sharon Wichman, U.S.	2:44.40

1972 Beverly Whitfield, Australia 2:41.70
1976 Marina Koshevaya, USSR 2:33.35
1980 Lina Kaciusyte, USSR 2:29.54
1984 Anne Ottenbrite, Canada 2:30.38
1988 Silke Hoerner, East Germany 2:26.71

400-METER FREESTYLE RELAY

1912	Great Britain	5:52.80	1960	U.S.	4:08.90
1920	U.S.	5:11.60	1964	U.S.	4:03.80
1924	U.S.	4:58.80	1968	U.S.	4:02.50
1928	U.S.	4:47.60	1972	U.S.	3:55.20
1932	U.S.	4:38.00	1976	U.S.	3:44.82
1936	Netherlands	4:36.00	1980	East Germany	3:42.71
1948	U.S.	4:29.20	1984	U.S.	3:43.43
1952	Hungary	4:24.40	1988	East Germany	3:40.63
1956	Australia	4:17.10			

400-METER MEDLEY RELAY

1960	U.S.	4:41.10	1980	East Germany	4:06.67
1964	U.S.	4:33.90	1984	U.S.	4:08.34
1968	U.S.	4:28.30	1988	East Germany	4:03.74
1972	U.S.	4:20.70			
1976	East Germany	4:07.95			

200-METER INDIVIDUAL MEDLEY

1968 Claudia Kolb, U.S. 2:24.70
1972 Shane Gould, Australia 2:23.10
1984 Tracy Caulkins, U.S. 2:12.64
1988 Daniela Hunger, East Germany 2:12.59

400-METER INDIVIDUAL MEDLEY

1964 Donna de Varona, U.S. 5:18.70
1968 Claudia Kolb, U.S. 5:08.50
1972 Gail Neall, Australia 5:03.00
1976 Ulrike Tauber, East Germany 4:42.77
1980 Petra Schneider, East Germany 4:36.29
1984 Tracy Caulkins, U.S. 4:39.24
1988 Janet Evans, U.S. 4:37.76

SPRINGBOARD DIVING — Points

1920 Aileen Riggin, U.S. 539.90
1924 Elizabeth Becker, U.S. 474.50
1928 Helen Meany, U.S. 78.62
1932 Georgia Coleman, U.S. 87.52
1936 Marjorie Gestring, U.S. 89.27
1948 Victoria Draves, U.S. 108.74
1952 Patricia McCormick, U.S. 147.30
1956 Patricia McCormick, U.S. 142.36
1960 Ingrid Kramer, Germany 155.81
1964 Ingrid Engle-Kramer, Germany 145.00
1968 Sue Gossick, U.S. 150.77
1972 Micki King, U.S. 450.03
1976 Jennifer Chandler, U.S. 506.19
1980 Irina Kalinina, USSR 725.91
1984 Sylvie Bernier, Canada 530.70
1988 Gao Min, China 580.23

TRACK AND FIELD—MEN

Time

100-METER DASH

1896 Thomas E. Burke, U.S. 12.00
1900 Francis W. Jarvis, U.S. 10.80
1904 Archie Hahn, U.S. 11.00
1908 Reginald E. Walker, South Africa 10.80
1912 Ralph C. Craig, U.S. 10.80
1920 Charles W. Paddock, U.S. 10.80
1924 Harold M. Abrahams, Great Britain 10.60
1928 Percy Williams, Canada 10.80
1932 Eddie Tolan, U.S. 10.30
1936 Jesse Owens, U.S. 10.30
1948 Harrison Dillard, U.S. 10.30
1952 Lindy J. Remigino, U.S. 10.40
1956 Bobby J. Morrow, U.S. 10.50
1960 Armin Hary, Germany 10.20
1964 Robert L. Hayes, U.S. 10.00
1968 James Hines, U.S. 9.90
1972 Valery Borzov, USSR 10.10
1976 Hasely Crawford, Trinidad and Tobago 10.06
1980 Allan Wells, Great Britain 10.25
1984 Carl Lewis, U.S. 9.99
1988 Carl Lewis, U.S. 9.92

200 METERS

1900 John W.B. Tewksbury, U.S. 22.20
1904 Archie Hahn, U.S. 21.60
1908 Robert Kerr, Canada 22.60
1912 Ralph C. Craig, U.S. 21.70
1920 Allan Woodring, U.S. 22.00
1924 Jackson V. Scholz, U.S. 21.60
1928 Percy Williams, Canada 21.80
1932 Eddie Tolan, U.S. 21.20
1936 Jesse Owens, U.S. 20.70
1948 Melvin Patton, U.S. 21.10
1952 Andrew W. Stanfield, U.S. 20.70
1956 Bobby J. Morrow, U.S. 20.60
1960 Livio Berruti, Italy 20.50
1964 Henry Carr, U.S. 20.30
1968 Tommie Smith, U.S. 19.80
1972 Valery Borzov, USSR 20.00
1976 Donald Quarrie, Jamaica 20.23
1980 Pietro Mennea, Italy 20.19
1984 Carl Lewis, U.S. 19.80
1988 Joe DeLoach, U.S. 19.75

400 METERS

1896 Thomas E. Burke, U.S. 54.20
1900 Maxwell W. Long, U.S. 49.40
1904 Harry I. Hillman, U.S. 49.20
1908 Wyndham Halswelle, Great Britain 50.00
1912 Charles D. Reidpath, U.S. 48.20
1920 Bevil G.D. Rudd, South Africa 49.60
1924 Eric H. Liddel, Great Britain 47.60
1928 Ray Barbuti, U.S. 47.80
1932 William A. Carr, U.S. 46.20
1936 Archie Williams, U.S. 46.50
1948 Arthur Wint, Jamaica 46.20
1952 George Rhoden, Jamaica 45.90
1956 Charles L. Jenkins, U.S. 46.70
1960 Otis Davis, U.S. 44.90
1964 Michael D. Larrabee, U.S. 45.10
1968 Lee Evans, U.S. 43.80
1972 Vince Matthews, U.S. 44.70
1976 Alberto Juantorena, Cuba 44.26
1980 Viktor Markin, USSR 44.60
1984 Alonzo Babers, U.S. 44.27
1988 Steven Lewis, U.S. 43.87

800 METERS

1896 Edwin H. Flack, Australia 2:11.00
1900 Alfred E. Tysoe, Great Britain 2:01.40
1904 James D. Lightbody, U.S. 1:56.00
1908 Melvin W. Sheppard, U.S. 1:52.80
1912 James E. Meredith, U.S. 1:51.90
1920 Albert G. Hill, Great Britain 1:53.40
1924 Douglas G.A. Lowe, Great Britain 1:52.40
1928 Douglas G.A. Lowe, Great Britain 1:51.80
1932 Thomas Hampson, Great Britain 1:49.80
1936 John Woodruff, U.S. 1:52.90
1948 Malvin Whitfield, U.S. 1:49.20
1952 Malvin Whitfield, U.S. 1:49.20
1956 Thomas W. Courtney, U.S. 1:47.70
1960 Peter Snell, New Zealand 1:46.30
1964 Peter Snell, New Zealand 1:45.10
1968 Ralph Doubell, Australia 1:44.30
1972 Dave Wottle, U.S. 1:45.90
1976 Alberto Juantorena, Cuba 1:43.50
1980 Steven Ovett, Great Britain 1:45.40
1984 Joaquim Cruz, Brazil 1:43.00
1988 Paul Ereng, Kenya 1:43.45

1,500-METER RUN

1896 Edwin H. Flack, Great Britain 4:33.20
1900 Charles Bennett, Great Britain 4:06.20
1904 James D. Lightbody, U.S. 4:05.40
1908 Melvin W. Sheppard, U.S. 4:03.40
1912 Arnold N.S. Jackson, Great Britain 3:56.80
1920 Albert G. Hill, Great Britain 4:01.80
1924 Paavo Nurmi, Finland 3:53.60
1928 Harry E. Larva, Finland 3:53.20
1932 Luigi Beccali, Italy 3:51.20
1936 Jack E. Lovelock, New Zealand 3:47.80
1948 Henry Eriksson, Sweden 3:49.80
1952 Joseph Barthel, Luxembourg 3:45.20
1956 Ronald Delany, Ireland 3:41.20
1960 Herbert Elliott, Australia 3:35.60
1964 Peter Snell, New Zealand 3:38.10
1968 Kipchoge Keino, Kenya 3:34.90
1972 Pekka Vasala, Finland 3:36.30
1976 John Walker, New Zealand 3:39.17
1980 Sebastian Coe, Great Britain 3:38.40
1984 Sebastian Coe, Great Britain 3:32.53
1988 Peter Rono, Kenya 3.35.96

5,000 METERS

1912 Hannes Kolehmainen, Finland 14:36.60
1920 Joseph Guillemot, France 14:55.60
1924 Paavo Nurmi, Finland 14:31.20
1928 Willie Ritola, Finland 14:38.00
1932 Lauri Lehtinen, Finland 14:30.00
1936 Gunnar Hocket, Finland 14:22.20
1948 Gaston Reiff, Belgium 14:17.60
1952 Emil Zatopek, Czechoslovakia 14:06.60
1956 Vladimir Kuts, USSR 13:39.60
1960 Murray Halberg, New Zealand 13:43.40
1964 Robert K. Schul, U.S. 13:48.80
1968 Mohamed Gammoudi, Tunisia 14:05.10
1972 Lasse Viren, Finland 13:26.40
1976 Lasse Viren, Finland 13:24.76
1980 Miruts Yifter, Ethiopia 13:21.00
1984 Said Aouita, Morocco 13:05.59
1988 John Ngugi, Kenya 13:11.70

10,000 METERS

1912 Hannes Kolehmainen, Finland 31:20.80
1920 Paavo Nurmi, Finland 31:45.80
1924 Willie Ritola, Finland 30:23.20
1928 Paavo Nurmi, Finland 30:18.80
1932 Janusz Kusocinski, Poland 30:11.40
1936 Ilmari Salminen, Finland 30:15.40
1948 Emil Zatopek, Czechoslovakia 29:59.60
1952 Emil Zatopek, Czechoslovakia 29:17.00
1956 Vladimir Kuts, USSR 28:45.60
1960 Petr Bolotnikov, USSR 28:32.20
1964 William Mills, U.S. 28:24.40
1968 Naftali Temu, Kenya 29:27.40
1972 Lasse Viren, Finland 27:38.40
1976 Lasse Viren, Finland 27:40.38
1980 Miruts Yifter, Ethiopia 27:42.70
1984 Alberto Cova, Italy 27:47.54
1988 Brahim Boutaib, Morocco 27:21.46

MARATHON

1896 Spyros Loues, Greece 2:58:50.00
1900 Michel Theato, France 2:59:45.00
1904 Thomas J. Hicks, U.S. 3:28:53.00
1908 John J. Hayes, U.S. 2:55:18.40
1912 Kenneth McArthur, South Africa 2:36:54.80
1920 Hannes Kolehmainen, Finland 2:32:35.80
1924 Albin Stenroos, Finland 2:41:22.60
1928 A.B. El Quafi, France 2:32:57.00
1932 Juan Zabala, Argentina 2:31:36.00
1936 Kitei Son, Japan 2:29:19.20
1948 Delfo Cabrera, Argentina 2:34:51.60
1952 Emil Zatopek, Czechoslovakia 2:23:03.20
1956 Alain Mimoun, France 2:25:00.00
1960 Abebe Bikila, Ethiopia 2:15:16.20
1964 Abebe Bikila, Ethiopia 2:12:11.20
1968 Mamo Wolde, Ethiopia 2:20:26.40
1972 Frank Shorter, U.S. 2:12:19.70
1976 Waldemar Cierpinski, East Germany 2:09:55.00
1980 Waldemar Cierpinski, East Germany 2:11.03.00
1984 Carlos Lopes, Portugal 2:09.21.00
1988 Gelindo Bordin, Italy 2:10.32.00

110-METER HURDLES

1896 Thomas P. Curtis, U.S. 17.60
1900 Alvin E. Kraenzlein, U.S. 15.40
1904 Frederick W. Schule, U.S. 16.00
1908 Forrest Smithson, U.S. 15.00
1912 Frederick W. Kelley, U.S. 15.10
1920 Earl J. Thomson, Canada 14.80
1924 Daniel C. Kinsey, U.S. 15.00
1928 Sydney Atkinson, South Africa 14.80
1932 George Saling, U.S. 14.60
1936 Forrest Towns, U.S. 14.20
1948 William Porter, U.S. 13.90
1952 Harrison Dillard, U.S. 13.70
1956 Lee Q. Calhoun, U.S. 13.50
1960 Lee Q. Calhoun, U.S. 13.80
1964 Hayes W. Jones, U.S. 13.60
1968 Willie Davenport, U.S. 13.30
1972 Rod Milburn, U.S. 13.20
1976 Guy Drut, France 13.30
1980 Thomas Munkelt, East Germany 13.39
1984 Roger Kingdom, U.S. 13.20
1988 Roger Kingdom, U.S. 12.98

400-METER HURDLES

1900 John W.B. Tewksbury, U.S. 57.60
1904 Harry L. Hillman, U.S. 53.00
1908 Charles J. Bacon, U.S. 55.00
1920 Frank F. Loomis, U.S. 54.00
1924 F. Morgan Taylor, U.S. 52.60
1928 Lord David Burghley, Great Britain 53.40
1932 Robert Tisdall, Ireland 51.80
1936 Glenn Hardin, U.S. 52.40
1948 Roy Cochran, U.S. 51.10
1952 Charles Moore, U.S. 50.80
1956 Glenn A. Davis, U.S. 50.10
1960 Glenn A. Davis, U.S. 49.30
1964 Warren "Rex" Cawley, U.S. 49.60
1968 David Hemery, Great Britain 48.10
1972 John Akii-Bau, Uganda 47.80
1976 Edwin Moses, U.S. 47.64
1980 Volker Beck, East Germany 48.70
1984 Edwin Moses, U.S. 47.75
1988 Andre Phillips, U.S. 47.19

3,000-METER STEEPLECHASE

1920 Percy Hodge, Great Britain 10:00.40
1924 Willie Ritola, Finland 9:33.60
1928 Toivo A. Loukola, Finland 9:21.80
1932 Volmari Iso-Hollo, Finland 10:33.40
(3,460 m—extra lap by official error)
1936 Volmari Iso-Hollo, Finland 9:03.80
1948 Thore Sjostrand, Sweden 9:04.60
1952 Horace Ashenfelter, U.S. 8:45.40
1956 Chris Brasher, Great Britain 8:41.20
1960 Zdzislaw Krzyszkowiak, Poland 8:34.20
1964 Gaston Roelants, Belgium 8:30.80
1968 Amos Biwott, Kenya 8:51.00
1972 Kipchoge Keino, Kenya 8:23.60
1976 Anders Gärderud, Sweden 8:08.20
1980 Bronislaw Malinowski, Poland 8:09.70
1984 Julius Korir, Kenya 8:11.80
1988 Julius Karuiki, Kenya 8:05.51

400-METER RELAY

1912	Great Britain	42.40	1960	West Germany	39.50
1920	U.S.	42.20			
1924	U.S.	41.00	1964	U.S.	39.00
1928	U.S.	41.00	1968	U.S.	38.20
1932	U.S.	40.00	1972	U.S.	38.19
1936	U.S.	40.00	1976	U.S.	38.33
1948	U.S.	40.30	1980	USSR	38.26
1952	U.S.	40.10	1984	U.S.	37.83
1956	U.S.	39.50	1988	USSR	38.19

1,600-METER RELAY

1908	U.S.	3:29.40	1956	U.S.	3:04.80
1912	U.S.	3:16.60	1960	U.S.	3:02.20
1920	Great Britain	3:22.20	1964	U.S.	3:00.70
1924	U.S.	3:16.00	1968	U.S.	2:56.10
1928	U.S.	3:14.20	1972	Kenya	2:59.80
1932	U.S.	3:08.20	1976	U.S.	2:58.65
1936	Great Britain	3:09.00	1980	USSR	3:01.10
1948	U.S.	3:10.40	1984	U.S.	2:57.91
1952	Jamaica	3:03.90	1988	U.S.	2:56.16

POLE VAULT — Height

1896 William W. Hoyt, U.S. 10′9 3/4″
1900 Irving K. Baxter, U.S. 10′9 9/10″
1904 Charles E. Dvorak, U.S. 11′6″
1908 Albert C. Gilbert, U.S.
Edward T. Cook, Jr., U.S. 12′2″
1912 Harry S. Babcock, U.S. 12′11 1/2″
1920 Frank K. Foss, U.S. 12′5 9/16″
1924 Lee S. Barnes, U.S. 12′11 1/2″
1928 Sabin W. Carr, U.S. 13′9 3/8″
1932 William Miller, U.S. 14′1 7/8″
1936 Earle Meadows, U.S. 14′3 1/4″
1948 O. Guinn Smith, U.S. 14′1 1/4″
1952 Robert Richards, U.S. 14′11 1/4″
1956 Robert Richards, U.S. 14′11 1/2″
1960 Donald Bragg, U.S. 15′5 1/8″
1964 Fred M. Hansen, U.S. 16′8 3/4″
1968 Robert Seagren, U.S. 17′8 1/2″
1972 Wolfgang Nordwig, East Germany 18′1/2″
1976 Tadeusz Slusarki, Poland 18′1/2″
1980 Wladyslaw Kozakiewicz, Poland 18′11 1/2″
1984 Pierre Quinon, France 18′10 1/4″
1988 Sergei Bubka, USSR 19′9 1/4″

HIGH JUMP

1896 Ellery Clark, U.S. 5′11 1/4″
1900 Irving K. Baxter, U.S. 6′2 4/5″
1904 Samuel Jones, U.S. 5′11″
1908 Harry Porter, U.S. 6′3″
1912 Almer Richards, U.S. 6′4″
1920 Richmond Landon, U.S. 6′4 1/4″
1924 Harold Osborn, U.S. 6′5 15/16″
1928 Robert W. King, U.S. 6′4 3/8″
1932 Duncan McNaughton, Canada 6′5 5/8″
1936 Cornelius Johnson, U.S. 6′7 15/16″
1948 John Winter, Australia 6′6″
1952 Walter Davis, U.S. 6′8 1/4″
1956 Charles E. Dumas, U.S. 6′11 1/4″
1960 Robert Shavlakadze, USSR 7′1″
1964 Valery Brumel, USSR 7′1 3/4″
1968 Richard Fosbury, U.S. 7′4 1/4″
1972 Juri Tarmak, USSR 7′3 3/4″
1976 Jacek Wszola, Poland 7′4 1/2″
1980 Gerd Wessig, East Germany 7′8 3/4″
1984 Dietmar Mogenburg, West Germany 7′8 1/2″
1988 Guennadi Avdeenko, USSR 7′9 1/2″

LONG JUMP

		Distance
1896	Ellery Clark, U.S.	20'10"
1900	Alvin Kraenzlein, U.S.	23'6 7/8"
1904	Meyer Prinstein, U.S.	24'1"
1908	Francis Irons, U.S.	24'6 1/2"
1912	Albert Gutterson, U.S.	24'11 1/4"
1920	William Pettersson, Sweden	23'5 1/2"
1924	DeHart Hubbard, U.S.	24'5 1/8"
1928	Edward Hamm, U.S.	25'4 3/4"
1932	Edward Gordon, U.S.	25'3/4"
1936	Jesse Owens, U.S.	26'5 3/8"
1948	Willie Steel, U.S.	25'8"
1952	Jerome Biffle, U.S.	24'10"
1956	Gregory C. Bell, U.S.	25'8 1/4"
1960	Ralph H. Boston, U.S.	26'7 3/4"
1964	Lynn Davies, Great Britain	26'5 3/4"
1968	Robert Beamon, U.S.	29'2 1/2"
1972	Randy Williams, U.S.	27'1/2"
1976	Arnie Robinson, U.S.	27'4 3/4"
1980	Lutz Dombrowski, East Germany	28'1/4"
1984	Carl Lewis, U.S.	28'1/4"
1988	Carl Lewis, U.S.	28'7 1/4"

TRIPLE JUMP

1896	James B. Connolly, U.S.	45'0"
1900	Myer Prinstein, U.S.	47'4 1/4"
1904	Myer Prinstein, U.S.	47'0"
1908	Timothy Ahearne, Great Britain	48'11 1/4"
1912	Gustaf Lindblom, Sweden	48'5 1/8"
1920	Vilho Tuulos, Finland	47'6 7/8"
1924	Archibald Winter, Australia	50'11 1/8"
1928	Mikio Oda, Japan	49'10 13/16"
1932	Chuhei Nambu, Japan	51'7"
1936	Naoto Tajima, Japan	52'5 7/8"
1948	Arne Ahman, Sweden	50'6 1/4"
1952	Adhemar Ferreira da Silva, Brazil	53'2 1/2"
1956	Adhemar Ferreira da Silva, Brazil	53'7 1/2"
1960	Jozef Schmidt, Poland	55'1 3/4"
1964	Jozef Schmidt, Poland	55'3 1/4"
1968	Viktor Saneyev, USSR	57'3/4"
1972	Viktor Saneyev, USSR	56'11"
1976	Viktor Saneyev, USSR	56'8 3/4"
1980	Jaak Uudmae, USSR	56'11 1/4"
1984	Al Joyner, U.S.	56'7 1/2"
1988	Hristo Markov, Bulgaria	57'9 1/4"

16-POUND SHOT PUT

1896	Robert Garrett, U.S.	36'9 3/4"
1900	Richard Sheldon, U.S.	46'3 1/8"
1904	Ralph Rose, U.S.	48'7"
1908	Ralph Rose, U.S.	46'7 1/2"
1912	Patrick McDonald, U.S.	50'4"
1920	Ville Porhola, Finland	48'7 1/8"
1924	Clarence Houser, U.S.	49'2 1/2"
1928	John Kuck, U.S.	52'13/16"
1932	Leo Sexton, U.S.	52'6 3/16"
1936	Hans Woellke, Germany	53'1 3/4"
1948	Wilbur Thompson, U.S.	56'2"
1952	William Parry O'Brien, Jr., U.S.	57'1 1/2"
1956	William Parry O'Brien, Jr., U.S.	60'11"
1960	William Nieder, U.S.	64'6 3/4"
1964	Dallas C. Long, U.S.	66'8 1/2"
1968	James Randel Matson, U.S.	67'4 3/4"
1972	Wladyslaw Komar, Poland	69'6"
1976	Udo Beyer, East Germany	69'6 7/10"
1980	Vladimir Kiselyov, USSR	70'1/2"
1984	Allesandro Andrei, Italy	69'9"
1988	Ulf Timmermann, East Germany	73'8 3/4"

DISCUS THROW

1896	Robert Garrett, U.S.	95'7 1/2"
1900	Rudolf Bauer, Hungary	118'2 9/10"
1904	Martin Sheridan, U.S.	128'10 1/2"
1908	Martin Sheridan, U.S.	134'2"
1912	Armas Taipale, Finland	145'9/16"
1920	Elmer Niklander, Finland	146'7"
1924	Clarence Houser, U.S.	151'5 1/4"
1928	Clarence Houser, U.S.	155'2 4/5"
1932	John Anderson, U.S.	162'4 7/8"
1936	Kenneth Carpenter, U.S.	165'7 1/2"
1948	Adolfo Consolini, Italy	173'2"
1952	Sim Iness, U.S.	180'6 1/2"
1956	Alfred A. Oerter, U.S.	184'10 1/2"
1960	Alfred A. Oerter, U.S.	194'2"
1964	Alfred A. Oerter, U.S.	200'1 1/2"
1968	Alfred A. Oerter, U.S.	212'6 1/2"
1972	Ludwick Danek, Czechoslovakia	211'3 1/2"
1976	Mac Wilkins, U.S	221'5 2/5"
1980	Viktor Raschupkin, USSR	218'8"
1984	Rolf Danneberg, West Germany	218'6"
1988	Jurgen Schult, East Germany	225'9 1/4"

16-POUND HAMMER THROW

1900	John Flanagan, U.S.	167'4"
1904	John Flanagan, U.S.	168'1"
1908	John Flanagan, U.S.	170'4 1/4"
1912	Matthew McGrath, U.S.	179'7 1/8"
1920	Patrick Ryan, U.S.	173'5 5/8"
1924	Frederick Tootell, U.S.	174'10 1/4"
1928	Patrick O'Callaghan, Ireland	168'7 1/2"
1932	Patrick O'Callaghan, Ireland	176'11 1/8"
1936	Karl Hein, Germany	185'4 1/4"
1948	Imre Nemeth, Hungary	183'11 1/2"
1952	Jozsef Csermak, Hungary	197'11 3/4"
1956	Harold V. Connolly, U.S.	207'3 1/2"
1960	Vasiliy Rudenkov, USSR	220'1 5/8"
1964	Romuald Klim, USSR	229'9 1/2"
1968	Gyula Zsivotzky, Hungary	240'8"
1972	Anatol Bondarchuk, USSR	247'8"
1976	Yuri Sedykh, USSR	254'4"
1980	Yuri Sedykh, USSR	268'4"
1984	Juha Tiainen, Finland	256'2"
1988	Sergei Litinov, USSR	278'2 1/2"

JAVELIN THROW

1908	Erik Lemming, Sweden	179'10 1/2"
1912	Erik Lemming, Sweden	198'11 1/4"
1920	Jonni Myyra, Finland	215'9 3/4"
1924	Jonni Myyra, Finland	206'6 3/4"
1928	Erik Lundquist, Sweden	218'6 1/8"
1932	Matti Jarvinen, Finland	238'7"
1936	Gerhard Stock, Germany	235'8 5/16"
1948	Tapio Rautavaara, Finland	228'10 1/2"
1952	Cyrus Young, U.S.	242'3/4"
1956	Egil Danielson, Norway	281'2 1/4"
1960	Viktor Tsibulenko, USSR	277'8 3/8"
1964	Pauli Nevala, Finland	271'2 1/4"
1968	Janis Lusis, USSR	295'7 1/4"
1972	Klaus Wolfermann, West Germany	296'10"
1976	Miklos Nemeth, Hungary	310'4 1/2"
1980	Dainis Kula, USSR	299'2"
1984	Arto Harkonen, Finland	284'8"
1988	Tapio Korjus, Finland	276'6"

DECATHLON

		Points
(Old point system, 1912–32)		
1912	Hugo Wieslander, Sweden	7,724.49
1920	Helge Lovland, Norway	6,804.35
1924	Harold Osborn, U.S.	7,710.77
1928	Paavo Yrjola, Finland	8,053.29
1932	James Bausch, U.S.	8,462.23
(Revised point system, 1936–60)		
1936	Glenn Morris, U.S.	7,900.00
1948	Robert Mathias, U.S.	7,139.00
1952	Robert Mathias, U.S.	7,887.00
1956	Milton G. Campbell, U.S.	7,937.00
1960	Rafer Johnson, U.S.	8,392.00
(New scoring system)		
1964	Willi Holdorf, Germany	7,887.00
1968	William Toomey, U.S.	8,193.00
1972	Nikolai Avilov, USSR	8,454.00
1976	Bruce Jenner, U.S.	8,618.00
1980	Francis Thompson, Great Britain	8,495.00
1984	Francis Thompson, Great Britain	8,798.00
1988	Christian Schenk, East Germany	8,488.00

TRACK AND FIELD—WOMEN

100-METER DASH

		Time
1928	Elizabeth Robinson, U.S.	12.20
1932	Stanislawa Walasiewicz, Poland	11.90
1936	Helen Stephens, U.S.	11.50
1948	Francina Blankers-Koen, Netherlands	11.90
1952	Marjorie Jackson, Australia	11.50
1956	Betty Cuthbert, Australia	11.50
1960	Wilma Rudolph, U.S	11.00
1964	Wyomia Tyus, U.S.	11.40
1968	Wyomia Tyus, U.S.	11.00
1972	Renate Stecher, East Germany	11.10
1976	Annegret Richter, West Germany	11.01
1980	Lyudmila Kondratyeva, USSR	11.06
1984	Evelyn Ashford, U.S.	10.97
1988	Florence Griffith-Joyner, U.S.	10.54

200 METERS

1948	Francina Blankers-Koen, Netherlands	24.40
1952	Marjorie Jackson, Australia	23.70
1956	Betty Cuthbert, Australia	23.40
1960	Wilma Rudolph, U.S.	24.00
1964	Edith McGuire, U.S.	23.00
1968	Irena Kirszenstein Szewinska, Poland	22.50
1972	Renate Stecher, East Germany	22.40
1976	Bärbel Eckert, East Germany	22.37
1980	Bärbel Wöckel (Eckert), East Germany	22.03
1984	Valerie Brisco-Hooks, U.S.	21.81
1988	Florence Griffith-Joyner, U.S.	21.34

400 METERS

1964	Betty Cuthbert, Australia	52.00
1968	Colette Besson, France	52.00
1972	Monika Zehrt, East Germany	51.10
1976	Irena Szewinska, Poland	49.29
1980	Marita Koch, East Germany	48.88
1984	Valerie Brisco-Hooks, U.S.	48.83
1988	Olga Bryzgina, USSR	48.65

800 METERS

1928	Linda Radke-Batschauer, Germany	2:16.80
1960	Lyudmila Shevcova-Lysenko, USSR	2:04.30
1964	Ann Packer, Great Britain	2:01.10
1968	Madeline Manning, U.S.	2:00.90
1972	Hildegard Falck, West Germany	1:58.60
1976	Tatyana Kazankina, USSR	1:54.94
1980	Nadezhda Olizarenko, USSR	1:53.42
1984	Doina Melinte, Romania	1:57.[illegible]0
1988	Sigrun Wodars, East Germany	1:56.10

1,500 METERS

1972	Lyudmila Bragina, USSR	4:01.40
1976	Tatyana Kazankina, USSR	4:05.48
1980	Tatyana Kazankina, USSR	3:56.60
1984	Gabrielle Dorio, Italy	4:03.25
1988	Paula Ivan, Romania	3:53.96

3,000 METERS

1984	Maricica Puica, Romania	8:35.96
1988	Tatyana Samolenko, USSR	8:26.53

10,000 METERS

1988	Olga Boldarenko, USSR	31:44.69

MARATHON

1984	Joan Benoit, U.S.	2:24.52
1988	Rosa Mota, Portugal	2:25.40

400-METER RELAY

1928	Canada	48.40
1932	U.S.	47.00
1936	U.S.	46.90
1948	Netherlands	47.50
1952	U.S.	45.90
1956	Australia	44.50
1960	U.S.	44.50
1964	Poland	43.60
1968	U.S.	42.80
1972	West Germany	42.80
1976	East Germany	42.55
1980	East Germany	41.60
1984	U.S.	41.65
1988	U.S.	41.98

1,600-METER RELAY

1972	East Germany	3:23.00
1976	East Germany	3:19.23
1980	USSR	3:20.02
1984	U.S.	3:18.29
1988	USSR	3:15.18

8-LB. 13-OZ. SHOT PUT

1948	Micheline Ostermeyer, France	45'1 1/2"
1952	Galina Zybina, USSR	50'1 1/2"
1956	Tamara Tishkyevich, USSR	54'5"
1960	Tamara Press, USSR	56'9 3/4"
1964	Tamara Press, USSR	59'6"
1968	Margitta Gummel, East Germany	64'4"
1972	Nadezhda Chizhova, USSR	69'0"
1976	Ivanka Khristova, Bulgaria	69'5"
1980	Ilona Slupianek, East Germany	73'6 1/4"
1984	Claudia Losch, West Germany	67'2 1/4"
1988	Natalya Lisovskaya, USSR	72'11 1/2"

JAVELIN THROW

1932	Mildred Didrikson, U.S.	143'4"
1936	Tilly Fleischer, Germany	148'2 3/4"
1948	Herma Bauma, Austria	149'6"
1952	Dana Zatopekova, Czechoslovakia	165'7"
1956	Inessa Janzeme, USSR	176'8"
1960	Elvira Ozolina, USSR	183'8"
1964	Mihaela Penes, Romania	198'7 1/2"
1968	Angela Nemeth, Hungary	198'1/2"
1972	Ruth Fuchs, East Germany	209'7"
1976	Ruth Fuchs, East Germany	216'4"
1980	Maria Colon Ruenes, Cuba	224'5"
1984	Theresa Sanderson, Great Britain	228'2"
1988	Petra Felke, East Germany	245'0"

PENTATHLON

		Points
1964	Irina Press, USSR	5,246
1968	Ingrid Becker, West Germany	5,098
1972	Mary Peters, Great Britain	4,801
1976	Siegrun Siegl, East Germany	4,745
1980	Nadezhda Tkachenko, USSR	5,083

HEPTATHLON

1984	Glynis Nunn, Australia	6,390
1988	Jackie Joyner-Kersee, U.S.	7,215

100-METER HURDLES

1972	Annelie Erhardt, East Germany	12.60
1976	Johanna Schaller, East Germany	12.77
1980	Vera Komisova, USSR	12.56
1984	Benita Brown-Fitzgerald	12.84
1988	Jordanka Donkova, Bulgaria	12.38

HIGH JUMP

		Height
1928	Ethel Catherwood, Canada	5'3"
1932	Jean Shiley, U.S.	5'5 1/4"
1936	Ibolya Csak, Hungary	5'3"
1948	Alice Coachman, U.S.	5'6 1/8"
1952	Esther Brand, South Africa	5'5 3/4"
1956	Mildred McDaniel, U.S.	5'9 1/4"
1960	Iolanda Balas, Romania	6'1/4"
1964	Iolanda Balas, Romania	6'2 3/4"
1968	Miloslava Rezkova, Czechoslovakia	5'11 3/4"
1972	Ulrika Meyfarth, West Germany	6'3 1/2"
1976	Rosemarie Ackermann, East Germany	6'4"
1980	Sara Simeoni, Italy	6'5 1/2"
1984	Ulrike Meyfarth, West Germany	6'7 1/2"
1988	Louise Ritter, U.S.	6'8"

LONG JUMP

		Distance
1948	Olga Gyarmati, Hungary	18'8 1/4"
1952	Yvette Williams, New Zealand	20'5 3/4"
1956	Elzibieta Krzeskinska, Poland	20'9 3/4"
1960	Vyera Krepkina, USSR	20'10 3/4"
1964	Mary Rand, Great Britain	22'2"
1968	Viorica Viscopoleanu, Romania	22'4 1/2"
1972	Heidemarie Rosendahl, West Germany	22'3"
1976	Angela Voigt, East Germany	22'2 1/2"
1980	Tatiana Kolpakova, USSR	23'2"
1984	Anisoara Cusmir-Stanciu, Romania	22'10"
1988	Jackie Joyner-Kersee, U.S.	24'3 1/2"

TEAM SPORTS (since 1948)

BASKETBALL—MEN

1948	U.S.
1952	U.S.
1956	U.S.
1960	U.S.
1964	U.S.
1968	U.S.
1972	USSR
1976	U.S.
1980	Yugoslavia
1984	U.S.
1988	USSR, Yugoslavia, U.S.

BASKETBALL—WOMEN

1976	USSR
1980	USSR
1984	U.S.
1988	U.S., Yugoslavia, USSR

SOCCER (FOOTBALL)

1948	Sweden
1952	Hungary
1956	USSR
1960	Yugoslavia
1964	Hungary
1968	Hungary
1972	Poland
1976	East Germany
1980	Czechoslovakia
1984	France
1988	USSR, Brazil, West Germany

VOLLEYBALL—MEN

1964	USSR
1968	USSR
1972	Japan
1976	Poland
1980	USSR
1984	U.S.
1988	U.S., USSR, Argentina

VOLLEYBALL—WOMEN

1964	Japan
1968	USSR
1972	USSR
1976	Japan
1980	USSR
1984	China
1988	USSR, Peru, China

WATER POLO

1948	Italy
1952	Hungary
1956	Hungary
1960	Italy
1964	Hungary
1968	Yugoslavia
1972	USSR
1976	Hungary
1980	USSR
1984	Yugoslavia
1988	Yugoslavia, U.S., USSR

594